THE ROUGH GUIDE TO

Rock

ROUGH GUIDES

Rough Guides online

www.roughguides.com

Acknowledgments

Thanks go foremost to the contributors and fans who wrote the articles in this book, and helped keep them up-to-date. This is your book – thanks and congratulations.

This book has benefited enormously from emails sent in response to its online counterpart. To all the fans, and also the musicians, thanks for taking the trouble to correct us on points large and small. It goes without saying that we'd like further feedback, both on articles in this book and on the continuously updated pages at www.roughguides.com/music

The editor would like to thank Al, Blue and Michelle for their invaluable help with the words and pictures; Katie Pringle for her brilliant typesetting and never-ending patience; Mark and Jonathan for keeping his metaphors in check; David Price for proofreading way beyond the call of duty; all of the contributing photographers and agencies; everyone at Selectadisc; and the too-many-to-mention record labels who have supplied discs, biographies and answers to strange queries about bands they had forgotten were once on their roster.

Credits

Picture research: Peter Buckley, Blue MacAskill and Michelle Bhatia
Proofreading: David Price
Design and picture origination: Katie Pringle and Henry Iles
Layout: Katie Pringle
Production: John McKay

Publishing Information

This third edition published October 2003 by Rough Guides Ltd,
80 Strand, London WC2R 0RL.

Distributed by the Penguin Group
Penguin Books Ltd, 80 Strand, London WC2R 0RL
Penguin Putnam, Inc. 375 Hudson Street, NY 10014, USA
Penguin Books Australia Ltd, 487 Maroondah Highway, PO Box 257, Ringwood, Victoria 3134, Australia
Penguin Books Canada Ltd, 10 Alcorn Avenue, Toronto, Ontario,
Canada M4V 1E4
Penguin Books (NZ) Ltd,182–190 Wairau Road, Auckland 10, New Zealand

Printed in Italy by LegoPrint S.p.A

1232pp includes index
A catalogue record for this book is available from the British Library
ISBN 1-85828-457-0

THE ROUGH GUIDE TO

Rock

Edited by
Peter Buckley

Photographs by
Ben Browton, Jill Furmanovsky, Charlie Gillett Collection,
Steve Gillett, Steve Gullick, Jak Kilby,
Angela Lubrano, Redferns, SIN,

ROUGH GUIDES

Rough Guides online
www.roughguides.com

CONTRIBUTORS

Candy Absorption
William Alberque
Richard Allan
Michael Andrews
Benn Barr
Andi Bebb
Will Bedard
Darling Bell
Jonathan Bell
Essi Berelian
Michelle Bhatia
Bibi L
James Bickers
Neil Blackmore
Michael Booth
Charles Bottomley
Jonathan Bousfield
Stephen Boyd
Andrew Bradley
Eran Breiman
Chris Brook
Patrick Broomfield
Peter Buckley
Huw Bucknell
Ryan Burger
Richard Butterworth
Ian Canadine
David Castle
Liv Cecilia
Chas B
Alan Clayson
Piers Clifton
Chris Coe
Paul Collins
John Collis
Susan Compo
Brian Connolly
Duncan Cooper
Robert Coyne
Nick Dale
Sarah Dallas
Guy Davies
Sean Diamond
Nick Dillon
Steve Dinsdale
Michael Dixon
Richard Dodd
Tony Drayton
Jim Dress
Nick Duerden
East Bay Ray
Roy Edroso
Nick Edwards
Mark Ellingham

Marc Elliot
Tom Ewing
T. Frances Farmer
Justin Farrington
David Fenigsohn
Matt Fink
Richard Fontenoy
Shaun Goater
Glenn Gossling
Matthew Grant
Louise Gray
Gerard Grech
Hugh Gregory
Jason Gross
Pavel Gurevich
Hugh Hackett
Martin Haggerty
Link Hall
Duncan Harris
Phil Harrison
Christoph Heise
Brian Hinton
Nig Hodgkins
Jonathan Holden
Gareth Holder
Ross Holloway
Jane Holly
Michael Hood
Mark Hooper
Neil Horner
Mark Hughes
Ken Hunt
Ben Hunter
Simon Ives
Daniel Jacobs
Owen James
Andrew Jeffries
Chris Jenkins
Mark Jones
Robert Jones
Craig Joyce
Jeffrey S. Kaye
Jonathan Kennaugh
Penny Kiley
Lara Kilner
Adam Kimmel
Veronica Kofman
Jane La Dolce
Bruce Laidlaw
Kirk Lake
Maria Lamle
Chris Lark
Len Lauk
Glenn Law

Andy Lewis
Justin Lewis
Jenny Lind
Andy Lowe
Ian Lowey
Richard Luck
George Luke
Philip G. Lynch
Bruno MacDonald
Nomi Malone
Rhodri Marsden
Mike Martin
André Mayer
Hisham Mayet
Maxine McCaghy
Terry McGaughey
Conrad Mendez
Mike C
Almo Miles
David A. Mills
Peter Mills
Steven Mirkin
David Moreton
David Morgan
Pierce Morgan
Robin Morley
Paul Morris
Andrew Mosley
Pete Moyse
Robert E. Murray
Joe Nahmad
Patrick Neylan-
   Francis
Neil Nixon
Paul O'Brien
Alex Ogg
Nicholas Oliver
James Owen
Ryan Michael Painter
Valerie Palmer
Neil Partrick
Ian Peel
Lance Phillips
Annebella Pollen
Keith Prewer
Paul Reilly
James Robert
Anna D. Robinson
Charlotte Robinson
Andrew Rosenberg
Clifton Ross
Martin Rowsell
Malcolm Russell
Roger Sabin

Matt Saldana
Rolf Semprebon
Joanna Severs
Dave Sewell
Peter Shapiro
Andy Shields
Jeremy Simmonds
Andy Smith
Ben Smith
Iain Smith
Pip Southall
Al Spicer
Gavin Stoker
Andrew Stone
Ian Stonehouse
Derryck Strachan
Michael Sumsion
Matthew Surridge
James Sutherland
Jonathan Swift
Julie Taraska
Daniella Taylor
Graham Taylor
Tony Thewlis
Tyrone Thomas
Steve Thompson
Patrick Thorne
Gerard F. Tierney
Tom Tierney
Chris Tighe
John Treffeisen
Alwyn W. Turner
Phil Udell
Robin Underwood
Richie Unterberger
Mauro Venegas
Vinad Vijayakumar
Helen Waddell
John Webber
Melvin Welters
Simon Whittaker
Jason, Omz and
   Mark Williamson
Ada Wilson
Hugh Wilson
James Wirth
Erica Wissolik
Kurt Wolff
David Wren
Chris Wright
Jonathan Wright
David W. Zingg

ABOUT THIS BOOK

The **Rough Guide to Rock** is an unusual book: it is written by the people who know the music best – fans, rather than professional critics – and its huge number of contributors (see page opposite) means that it is based upon mutiple lifetimes of interest, experience and enthusiasm. Which is not to say that you'll find articles of slavish devotion in the pages following. When the music turns to dust, our writers say so as fervently as they champion the triumphs.

The book is unusual, too, in its relation to the Internet. The first edition was commissioned partly from adverts in the press and partly through the Net, where we posted entries as a work-in-progress. The second edition and this new edition have been developed almost entirely on and through the Net and, as the project has grown more interactive, fans, and often the artists themselves, have contributed updates and corrections, and fought their corners for the inclusion of neglected or forgotten bands.

Like everyone else who's ever done a rock book, or a rock magazine, we found ourselves locked right from square one in the 'But Is It Rock?' debate. Sure, we all had the same basic idea of what constitutes the term (noisy, guitar-based stuff, in the main, from America and Britain), but, as the decades have rolled on, the edges have become ever more blurred. We wanted a book with its feet firmly in the present, that gave at least as much space to indie/alternative groups as to the MTV/radio establishment. But we also wanted a book that reflected rock's history and inheritance, and might introduce new audiences to enduring or seminal figures from both decades past and music's current, ever-broadening horizons. So we made decisions to include key rock'n'roll, country, and dance musicians – people with a continuing influence in the rock world. Given the constraints of space, however, we opted to minimize inclusions of 'world music', reggae, hip-hop and soul because of other current and forthcoming Rough Guides music titles.

It's for that reason that you'll find surprising choices in this book. There are not too many other rock tomes that include pieces on Half Japanese or Slapp Happy alongside Slade, The Rolling Stones, The White Stripes and Neil Young. Still, their proponents made them sound interesting enough for us to feature, and we hope some of you will feel moved to check them out. We hope, too, that readers of the previous editions will enjoy discovering the 150 or so completely new entries in this book. We've re-evaluated a whole bunch of stuff – we're still wondering how we managed to print two editions without Kyuss or Lee Hazlewood – and, driven by a barrage of email, have welcomed into the fold a stew of 'stoner' rockers, several long-overlooked luminaries of the 1960s, and even a few more bleep-mongers from the electronica stage.

Our roster of bands now nudges the 1400 mark – even more if you include the 'before and after' bands covered in many of the articles. There's always room for more online but, to keep the book a manageable size and weight and price, and to cram all this juicy new material into the guide, we've had to make a few cuts and harsh editorial decisions – so, gosh darn it, there's still no room for the Electric Light Orchestra or Moody Blues, and Michael Jackson's out as we feel his current musical direction should in no way be encouraged (Oasis came very close to sharing his fate). And though the temptation was there to include such up-and-coming troupes as The Darkness and Kings Of Leon, they are gonna have to earn their stripes before they make it into our guide. If you are outraged by these omissions, or any of our exclusions, don't scowl at the book: write to us. We've set up this project with a democratic brief, so get writing, and we hope to see you on the Net at www.roughguides .com/music

A note on the structure and icons

The **individual entries** in the guide are arranged alphabetically by band or artist, while further bands and artists (especially solo careers of key personnel) are discussed at the end of the main accounts. For an index of all bands and artists discussed at any length, turn to the Directory of Bands and Artists that begins on page 1218. Within the entries, you'll notice groups and individuals in **THIS FONT**, which means there's an individual entry on them which can be referred to for more detail.

The discographies at the end of each entry are listed in order of their recording dates, and the title of each disc is followed, in brackets, by the date of the original recording and the current label. Each disc is preceded by a symbol: c for an album on CD, r for one that's still only issued on vinyl. To make sense of the quantity of discs, we've been selective: the number of album recommendations are to some extent a reflection of status, though with younger bands and artists we've often included reviews of everything to date.

A CERTAIN RATIO

Formed Manchester, England, 1977.

Starting out as a punk/thrash outfit, **A Certain Ratio** have become elder statesmen of Manchester dance music, on the strength of fifteen years of merging an eclectic and colourful mix of sounds and styles. Combining the 'do-it-yourself' attitudes of punk with music of a more industrial nature, **Jeremy Kerr** (bass), **Martin Moscrop** (guitar), **Peter Terrell** (keyboards/tape loops) and **Simon Topping** (vocals) quickly came to the attention of two of the senior figures of the Manchester music industry. **Anthony Wilson** (founder of Factory Records) became the band's manager after **Rob Gretton** – his business partner and original manager of New Order – tipped him off. Factory released ACR's debut single, "All Night Party", pressing 5000 copies in May 1979, which soon sold out.

The band quickly fixed on dance music as the direction they would take, and released the legendary single "Shack Up", which made the Billboard R&B chart in America. Years ahead of the Manchester dance explosion, ACR built a catalogue of experimental dance releases that in the early 80s stood at odds with the dominant goth and new wave scenes. Joined by drummer **Donald Johnson**, the band released the well-reviewed THE GRAVEYARD AND THE BALLROOM, put out their first 12" single, "Flight", and embarked on a US tour that led to another experimental album, TO EACH. Inspired by the sound of Nu Yorican street percussion music the band's sound was evolving into an almost South American blend of jazz-funk, aided in part by the addition of trumpet and the move of Simon Topping from vocals to percussion. Typified by the 1982 album SEXTET, this style continued to win good press though almost all ACR releases were overlooked by the public.

Late 1982 saw the exit of two founder members, Peter Terrell and Simon Topping – who left to study congas in New York – and a transitional third album I'D LIKE TO SEE YOU AGAIN, featuring new recruit **Carol McKenzie** on vocals. Another new addition, saxophonist **Tony Quigley**, made 1985's farewell Factory single, "Wild Party", their biggest underground hit yet. Leaving on the high note of the FORCE album, the band then signed to A&M records and set up their own SoundStation studio in their home town.

ACR's short dalliance with A&M produced just two criminally ignored albums, GOOD TOGETHER and ACR:MCR. Including the dance hit "Won't Stop Loving You" (aka "The Big E"), ACR:MCR was released as the Manchester dance explosion of 1989 was in full swing and was in part an attempt to stake a claim on the genre they had pioneered. This paved the way for a move to robsrecords, the label set up by Rob Gretton after he left Factory. By the end of 1992 ACR had built a new following through five single releases and the album UP IN DOWNSVILLE (which contained vocals from Primal Scream's **Denise Johnson**). The band went into another period of hiatus, only surfacing for LOOKING FOR A CERTAIN RATIO, a remix album from Creation Records that accompanied the label's reissues of the ACR back catalogue. LOOKING FOR... featuring mixes by the likes of Electronic, Sub Sub and The Other Two, created a certain amount of interest, but was sadly lost in a sea of similar remix projects emerging at the time. In 1997, however, CHANGE THE STATION (robsrecords) brought the elder statesmen of gritty northern English dance music back into the public eye with a fine blend of silken vocals courtesy of Denise Johnson and **Lorna Bailey**, ambient pieces and clean-cut hard-edged rhythm.

The band have been lying low ever since, though Moscrop now DJs under the ACR banner and Soul Jazz Records have done their bit for the band's cause with their 2002 release EARLY.

- ⦿ **Sextet** (1982; Factory).
  The epitome of their 80s output, this album mixes jazz with ambient influences. Sleeve design by Ben Kelly, who went on to design Factory's renowned Hacienda nightclub in Manchester.

- ⦿ **Acr:Mcr** (1989; A&M).
  ACR live, featuring the dance-floor classic "Won't Stop Loving You".

- ⦿ **Up In Downsville** (1992; robsrecords).
  ACR's only album for Rob Gretton includes a brace of dance-floor singles.

- ⦿ **Early** (2002; Soul Jazz Records).
  This definitive two-disc collection showcases the best of the band's early recordings, featuring both classic cuts and a selection of B-sides, alternate mixes and Peel session recordings. Listening to these tracks now, it's easy to trace the trajectory of ACR's influence through the sound of electronic 80s pop, through techno, through house, electronica, and beyond.

Ian Peel

A HOUSE

Formed Dublin, Ireland, 1985; disbanded 1997.

The core of **A House** was the trio of **Dave Couse**, who wrote all the lyrics and sometimes played acoustic guitar, **Fergal Bunbury** (lead guitar) and **Martin Healy** (bass). Three other members – **Dave Dawson** (drums), **David Morrissey** (keyboards) and **Susan Kavanagh** (backing vocals) – recorded and toured with the band but were less involved in the group's writing and development.

The often bitter or irony-laden lyrics of Dave Couse on A House's early releases were bolstered by the seemingly effortless musicality of the band's traditional, guitar-based rock. After self-releasing their first two singles, A House signed a major deal with Blanco y Negro and brought out their first album, ON OUR BIG FAT MERRY GO ROUND (1988). Having earned a reputation as a live act in Dublin's pubs, the band then went out on the road on their first major US tour, with The Go-Betweens.

After some success in the US, the group's main members went off to Inishboffin, a small island off the west coast of Ireland, to develop new material and a strategy for mainstream success. The result was I WANT TOO MUCH (1990), which achieved a good critical response but poor sales. Soon after, the band were without a contract.

By the end of the year they had switched to indie label Setanta and brought out two EPs – DOODLE and BINGO, which included "Endless Art", a song recorded with former Orange Juice singer **Edwyn Collins**. Sticking to their early stripped-down rock sound, the song listed artists, writers and musicians who were 'all dead, but still alive, in endless times, in endless art', set to a gritty guitar rhythm and extracts from Beethoven's *Fifth*. The fact that only men were listed attracted the wrath of many, and an all-female revision was issued after the original version had featured on I AM THE GREATEST (1991), the album that finally broke through with the music press and the record-buying public.

"Take It Easy On Me" (1992), the next single, dipped into the lower end of the charts and led to a reissue of I AM THE GREATEST to even wider acclaim. Another Setanta album, WIDE EYED AND IGNORANT (1994), met with less enthusiasm, but the band persevered and completed a new album, entitled NO MORE APOLOGIES, which they released in 1996. Another collection of twisted beauties, their fifth set revealed them to be masters of disturbing melodies reflecting the world as seen through their own, strangely coloured spectacles. It proved to be their swansong, however, as the group performed their final concert at Dublin's Olympia Theatre in February 1997. After a three-year silence, Couse and Bunbury re-emerged in the form of **Lokomotiv**, whose "Next Time Round" single was issued on the Shifty Disco label.

⊙ **On Our Big Fat Merry Go Round** (1988; Blanco y Negro).
A House were clearly enjoying themselves even if no one else was paying much attention. Harder and less clearly defined than their later releases, but one of their most enjoyable.

⊙ **I Am The Greatest** (1991; Setanta/Parlophone).
Lock yourself into a room with copious supplies of whisky, jump around to the early songs, then get depressed by the lyrics about blind faith and not being strong enough for two.

Matthew Grant

ABC

Formed Sheffield, England, 1980.

ABC rose from the ashes of post-punk group Vice Versa, deciding that Earth, Wind & Fire were just as important and exciting as the Sex Pistols. They crossed the former's tight disco-funk arrangements with witty incisive lyrics more usually associated with new wave bands. **Martin Fry** (vocals) was ABC's lyricist, while the remainder of the original line-up comprised **Mark White** (guitar), **Mark Lickley** (bass), **Steve Singleton** (saxophone) and **David Palmer** (drums).

Their first single, "Tears Are Not Enough", was released in the autumn of 1981, and before long was in the British Top 20. In one interview, Fry proclaimed not only that his favourite group was The Clash, but that his favourite current single was Dollar's "Hand Held In Black And White". This contradictory enthusiasm for credible punk and kitsch disco-pop was something he shared with Phil Oakey of The Human League, who announced at roughly the same time how much he'd always loved Abba.

Fry's championing of Dollar led him to contact the producer of "Hand Held". **Trevor Horn**, formerly one half of Buggles, would later produce Frankie Goes To Hollywood, Malcolm McLaren and Art of Noise, but ABC's debut album, THE LEXICON OF LOVE (1982), remains his finest overall production. Lush, cinematic and danceable, it divided the critics. Some sneered at the way this symbol of 'new pop' had transformed 1977's punk ethics into some tacky joke; others enjoyed its embracing of pop's glamour. Whatever, record buyers loved it, and it hit the #1 spot in the UK album charts during the summer of 1982, and reached #24 in the US, too. Its songs even inspired a spin-off film, *Mantrap* (1982), directed by Julien Temple, whose previous work had included the Sex Pistols' *Great Rock'n'Roll Swindle* (1979).

It was always going to be a problem following up THE LEXICON OF LOVE - ABC's subsequent records, however varied, were inevitably compared unfavourably with their debut. In fact, for a while, it seemed as if the group itself wouldn't survive. Mark Lickley had left the band in early 1982 after the completion of their second single "Poison Arrow". David Palmer jumped ship while they were on the Japanese leg of their 1982–83 world tour. He decided he 'wanted to audition for the Yellow Magic Orchestra', Fry later rued, although Palmer ended up playing for the most part with **THE THE**. Then, shortly after finishing ABC's second album, Steve Singleton announced that he too was leaving.

Fry and White chose to soldier on, and found that in trying to move on musically they had been left behind by critics and public alike. BEAUTY STAB (1983; reissued 1998; Mercury) was a lunge into rock, complete with guitar solos and 'socially-aware lyrics'. In 1983, it was almost universally loathed, but in retrospect it was one of the more daring career moves of the time, and it pre-empted a trend of political pop that would follow two or three years later. Nevertheless, while the motives were admirable, the album itself was clumsy and misplaced – both for ABC and for the 1983 pop scene in general.

How To Be A Zillionaire (1985) was a better record, but showed that, once again, Fry and White were in the right place at the wrong time. The set sported the influence of New York disco and the emerging electro and hip-hop sounds that were not yet mainstream genres in Britain. The album sold well in America, and one single, "Be Near Me", reached #9 in the Billboard Hot 100. Britain was less certain about the album – it was difficult to know which market the group was aiming for any more. There was a tongue-in-cheek attempt at a new image – the band as cartoon characters – with new members Eden (aka style journalist Fiona Russell Powell) and David Yarritu – but this didn't help the album's sales or the band's overall profile.

ABC nearly split up after How To Be A Zillionaire, not least because Fry had fallen seriously ill during 1985–86. Thankfully he recovered and, inspired by the American success of "Be Near Me" (Zillionaire's closest relative to the much-missed sound of Lexicon), the next album was very much a back-to-basics affair. A contemporary pop-dance LP, Alphabet City (1987) was their most successful since their first. It also contained their tribute to Smokey Robinson, "When Smokey Sings", a big hit on both sides of the Atlantic.

Fry and White's enthusiasm for the burgeoning house trend led to the spirited but ultimately forgettable UP (1989), while Abracadabra (1991) seemed a half-hearted attempt to reheat the tried and tested formula created and perfected a decade earlier. With no official announcement of a split, it was something of a surprise to find ABC (now essentially a Fry solo project) returning in 1997 with a brand new LP, Skyscraping. Unfortunately, sporadic glimmers of pop excellence failed to propel it into the public consciousness, and sadly, judging by their inclusion on numerous 80s revival package tours, it would seem that for now, ABC/Fry can only survive within a nostalgic bubble.

⊙ The Lexicon Of Love (1982; Phonogram/Mercury). The album by which all ABC's subsequent work has been judged. It's dated slightly, but if you want a demonstration of early 80s pop at its best, this is right up there with The Human League's DARE. The 1996 reissue includes an additional six tracks of remixes, B-sides and live versions – none of which are particularly essential, but a good-value package all the same.

⊙ The Look Of Love: The Very Best Of ABC (2001; Phonogram/Mercury).
The obligatory greatest hits collection, where we discover that even in the lumpiest of ABC's albums lurked sparkling four-minute gems.

Justin Lewis

AC/DC

Formed Sydney, Australia, 1973.

One of the longest-running, most theatrical hard-rock bands of the last three decades was formed by **Malcolm Young** (guitar) when his previous outfit, uncannily named the Velvet Underground, hit the rocks. Young's brother George, already an Australian star following a career with the Easybeats, persuaded him to enlist younger brother **Angus** (lead guitar). Making the formation a truly family affair, their sister suggested Angus should wear his school uniform on stage, a gimmick that would still be in use more than twenty years into the band's career.

The two Young brothers made their debut at the Chequers club in Sydney with **Dave Evans** on vocals, **Larry Van Knedt** on bass and **Colin Burgess** on drums. Another early incarnation saw **Rob Bailey** and **Peter Clark** form the rhythm section and it was this line-up that recorded the rather glammy version of "Can I Sit Next To You Girl", which became their first single in July 1974. A move to Melbourne brought yet another change as **Mark Evans** (bass) and **Phil Rudd** (drums) were brought in. One night, when Dave Evans refused to go on stage, the band's chauffeur, **Bon Scott**, was asked to take over. In Scott they had the perfect combination of rasping, sleazy vocals, a knack for smutty lyrics and a magnetic frontman able to hold his own against Angus's bad-schoolboy image.

Having signed to Albert Productions, the next couple of years brought the release of High Voltage (1974, reissued 1998) and TNT (1975). The pop-glam that had influenced their first single had been stripped away and in its place a love of blues-based rock'n'roll gave them a raucous and raw studio sound. All you had to do was listen to their pumped-up cover version of Chuck Berry's "School Daze" to know exactly where they were coming from. Neither record was officially released outside of Australia, but upon signing to Atlantic and moving base to the UK a selection of the material was released as High Voltage (1976).

Once the band began touring beyond the shores of Australia, notoriety and a cult following seemed a foregone conclusion. The stage show was a furious mixture of hard-rocking, bad-boy boogie conducted with salacious glee by the twin focus of Bon and Angus. Their first UK headlining tour was dubbed *Lock Up Your Daughters*, whilst the summer of 1976 brought an appearance at the Reading Festival and the winter, the release of Dirty Deeds Done Dirt Cheap (1976; reissued 1998) – yet another collection of tracks from the Australian albums and not to be confused with the Antipodean version bearing the same name.

By now the band were alternating their touring and recording schedules at a hectic pace. Unable to take the pressure Mark Evans was replaced by **Cliff Williams**. Up to this point the band's ideas were

Angus Young – the best-known knees in rock

bad-boy image coupled with their risqué lyrics made them obvious targets for moral extremists and also ensured that the US finally took notice; the album became their first million-seller and peaked in the US at #17. This first highly successful collaboration with Lange also proved to be the last with Bon Scott. Following a heavy drinking binge in Camden Town, on 20 February 1980, Scott was found dead, having choked on his own vomit. The coroner stated that he had 'drunk himself to death'.

Scott had been one of the group's main attractions and it seemed inconceivable that any replacement could hope to emulate his easy charisma or vulgar turn of lyrical phrase. Incredibly the band found **Brian Johnson** (former lead singer with UK band Geordie), and were recording a new album within two months. With Lange guiding the production, BACK IN BLACK (1980) was a storming return to form with the band giving the collective finger to their detractors on the closing anthem, "Rock And Roll Ain't Noise Pollution". The album went on to sell over ten million copies over the next decade in the US alone.

It was business as usual with FOR THOSE ABOUT TO ROCK (1981; reissued 1998) although it was clear to some that the band could do better. Nevertheless, the headlining slot at the UK Monsters Of Rock Festival in 1981 merely added to their list of effortless conquests; they would headline again in 1984 and 1991. After FLICK OF THE SWITCH (1983; reissued 1998) Rudd left due to exhaustion and **Simon Wright** took his place. But it wasn't just Rudd who was tired: the songwriting for FLICK OF THE SWITCH was disappointing, with the exception, perhaps, of "Bedlam In Belgium" and the heavy riffing of "Nervous Shakedown".

Despite signs that they were running out of ideas, the fact that they had entered the rarified world of rock's superleague meant that the insipid FLY ON THE WALL (1985; reissued 1998) sold millions worldwide. The following year brought WHO MADE WHO (1986), essentially a compilation album with a handful of tracks recorded especially for the Stephen King movie *Maximum Overdrive*. Following a lengthy silence the band returned with the dull BLOW YOUR VIDEO (1988), eclipsed only by the monumental tedium of THE RAZOR'S EDGE (1990) – by now with veteran **Chris Slade** taking over from Wright. Although they managed to knock out hit singles with relative ease, they were clearly becoming self-

often stretched to the point of tedium – witness the Status Quo-like monstrosity that is "Ain't No Fun Waiting Round To Be A Millionaire" – but with LET THERE BE ROCK (1977) the band at last began to produce classic material. From the opening fumbled bars of "Overdose" – one of their finest, least-acknowledged compositions – to the ballsy brilliance of "Whole Lotta Rosie", it was clear that they were well into their creative stride. The album hit the UK charts – some feat considering much of the rock world was gripped by punk at the time – and the mighty POWERAGE (1978; reissued 1998), featuring hit single "Rock And Roll Damnation", proved the addictive power of simple heartfelt rock-'n'roll. As a live attraction, their appeal was simply staggering; widely acknowledged as one of the all-time great live rock albums, IF YOU WANT BLOOD – YOU'VE GOT IT (1978) peaked at #13 in the UK charts and remains a definitive statement to this day.

But it wasn't until producer **Mutt Lange** was brought in for HIGHWAY TO HELL (1979; reissued 1998) that they became true international stars. The

parodies; it was as though they were their own covers band, recycling their finest moments into faded carbon copies of the originals, and 1992's LIVE album failed to capture the sweaty intensity of IF YOU WANT BLOOD – YOU'VE GOT IT.

The next few years saw the band sticking to an increasingly relaxed schedule with bouts of touring carefully planned to support each unchanging release. A collaboration with producer Rick Rubin on the track "Big Gun", used on the soundtrack of the Arnold Schwarzenegger movie *The Last Action Hero*, was a return to form of sorts and BALLBREAKER (1995) was a vast improvement on the stale material of the mid-80s.

Christmas 1997 brought the band's first foray into box set territory with BONFIRE. Put together as a tribute to Bon Scott it included some classic concert recordings as well as a disc of unreleased demos and live rarities. It also served as a useful stopgap exercise whilst the band started work on a new studio album.

When the new album – cheekily dubbed STIFF UPPER LIP (2000) – finally emerged, a full five years after their last studio effort, it was hailed by some as a return to form. Whether it could ever hope to capture the imagination in the same fashion as albums from their 70s and early-80s heyday was debatable, but it certainly recaptured the raw blues flavour lacking from some of their more recent works. And if the album was sonically more successful then the live shows were nothing short of spectacular; the towering bronze statue of Angus glowering from the stage will no doubt take its place next to the giant bell (for "Hells Bells") and cannons (for "For Those About To Rock We Salute You") in the line-up of classic AC/DC stage props. The whole gloriously over-the-top extravaganza was captured for posterity on the STIFF UPPER LIP LIVE DVD (2001).

⦿ **If You Want Blood – You've Got It** (1978; Atlantic; reissued 1998; EMI).
The last word in live hard rock albums. If the amplifier hum and opening notes of "Riff Raff" don't hook, then you must be dead. This album takes the studio tracks and transforms them into timeless classics. Definitive and indispensable.

⦿ **Highway To Hell** (1979; Atlantic).
One of their finest studio albums. Mutt Lange's production is crisp and powerful, fully harnessing their filthy Gibson guitar sound. "Touch Too Much" and "Shot Down In Flames" are two of the best tracks on an album groaning under the weight of potential hit singles.

⦿ **Back In Black** (1980; Atlantic).
Brian Johnson's voice bears a passing similarity to Bon Scott's but altogether it's the quality of the writing that makes this a remarkable album. They were at their peak here and it shows.

⦿ **Bonfire** (1997; EMI).
One for the collectors out there. A stonking box set including the famed Atlantic Studios radio session from 1977 on CD for the first time; a double CD album of the soundtrack to the concert movie *Let There Be Rock*; a CD called Volts featuring a whole host of Bon Scott demo rarities and live cuts. Cool, and an excellent investment.

Essi Berelian

Formed Kentish Town, 1963; disbanded 1972.

The **Action** were the ultimate mod band, who translated themselves into **Mighty Baby**, the closest England came to a counterpart for the Grateful Dead (with better songs!). And yet neither incarnation gained acceptance outside a cult audience until quite recently.

The front man of The Action was singer **Reg King**, a natural lunatic in the Keith Moon mould. He and rhythm section **Alan 'Bam!' King** (guitar), **Mike Evans** (bass) and **Roger Powell** (drums) – cockneys all – had come together as the 'Boys' (which they virtually were at the time) to back singer **Sandra Barry**. With **Peter Watson** on lead guitar, The Action sought out the best of American soul music, and played their discoveries to hip audiences everywhere. At Portsmouth, a phalanx of mods on scooters would meet their van outside the city limits, and escort them to the gig as if they were royalty.

No less a figure than George Martin spotted them and he recorded a string of near hit singles with them, in which underground soul covers – "Land Of A Thousand Dances", "I'll Keep On Holding On" – gave way to band compositions, "Never Ever" and "Shadows And Reflections". The latter was particularly gorgeous, paying homage to the softer harmony sound of the likes of The Association, percolating through from the West Coast.

Although an LP was planned, and readers of *Rave* magazine were even invited to design its cover, the band imploded at this point and Watson jumped ship. It was not until 1981 that The Action finally released an album – rediscovered by such proto-mods as Paul Weller, who wrote the liner notes. But this merely collected together the singles and other stray tracks. Finally in 1995, Brain Records issued a CD, THE LOST RECORDINGS 1967/68. Demos for the never-released album ROLLED GOLD, they captured perfectly the point when mod was becoming hippie, a mix of the tuneful and the other-worldly when all was fresh and hopeful.

The recordings showed the added musical dimension given by new arrivals **Martin Stone** and **Ian Whiteman**. Whiteman brought a jazz sensibility on keyboards and flute and saxophone, while Stone was already a blues legend from his guitar work on the first Savoy Brown LP, and with his own band, Stone's Masonry. He also brought a huge knowledge of the occult and arcane philosophies to the band, which in the spirit of the times renamed itself Mighty Baby.

A bemused Reg King had already left and Mighty Baby signed with Blackhill. Demos from late 1968 eventually emerged on the 1985 ACTIONS SPEAK LOUDER THAN LP, mistakenly attributed to The Action, and with a picture of that band on the cover. Some are embryonic versions of the songs that emerged on the band's long-awaited MIGHTY BABY (1969) – an archetypal product of the London underground on the independent Head label, produced by DJ and scene-maker Guy Stevens.

In the pages of *International Times*, Mark Williams (perhaps Britain's finest ever rock critic) gave the debut album a rave review, and the band became a fixture at open-air festivals. Live, their music stretched out into infinity on set-piece jams like "India", based on the John Coltrane tune. "India" was intended to appear as the centrepiece of their projected LP THE DAY OF THE SOUP, and certainly exists in rough demo form. The band performed it as part of a Peel session, and part of a three-hour improvisation around its weird rhythms appears as "A Blanket In My Muesli" on the GLASTONBURY FAYRE triple LP (1996).

Mighty Baby re-emerged in 1971 with a quieter second album A JUG OF LOVE. Although released on the Blue Horizon label, this was gentle, almost acoustic music, in which a hard, wan mysticism blended with quiet resignation. A year later the band had split.

A long way from Tamla Motown covers, Martin Stone went on to form CHILLI WILLI and **Almost Presley**; Alan King founded **Ace** and actually had a hit single after all the years of struggle. The rest of the band recorded an acoustic LP of Sufi devotions under the name **The Habbibya**, and toured with fellow English Muslim Richard Thompson. All reconvened for Reg King's long-delayed solo LP, featuring songs from the 1968 demos. Martin Stone eventually released a new CD after far too long an absence from the rock world.

The original line-up of The Action reunited on August Bank Holiday 1998 at Ryde Town Hall on the Isle of Wight as the highlight of a mod rally. Though somewhat rusty, and balder and broader than thirty-odd years before, the band swung with a passion and played much the same set that they would have done in 1966. Reg King – who time did not seem to have much altered – proved himself again to be one of the great English voices. Hopefully, more is to follow...

⊙ **Mighty Baby** (1994; Big Beat).
The original 1969 Head album, with startling cover art from Martin Sharpe and an excellent history of the band written by John Reed. Added to the CD are six earlier tracks recorded when the band was still called The Action. There is a quintessentially English charm to Ian Whiteman's songs. Real soul music, translated into psychedelia.

⊙ **Glastonbury Fayre** (1996; Fest).
Limited repro of dubious status, but historically fascinating. Mighty Baby's sixteen-minute instrumental "A Blanket In My Muesli", loosely based on John Coltrane's "India", is gently insistent, with wonderful drumming and Martin Stone's guitar piercing the dawn.

Brian Hinton

ADAM AND THE ANTS

Formed London, 1977; Adam still going strong.

There was always a touch of art-school posing linked with punk. **Adam And The Ants** had a touch too much for many tastes, and Adam's career is probably better defined by his changing image than by his music. There's some great fun to be had in his music though, ranging from the sleazy S&M humour of "Whip In My Valise" to the camp bravado of "Stand And Deliver".

The band started off in early 1977, one of a dozen groups trying to keep up in the wake of the Sex Pistols. An original line-up of **Adam** (**Stuart Goddard**), **Andy Warren** (bass), **Lester Square** (guitar) and **Paul Flanagan** (drums) boasted a fairly standard black-leather, sour-puss punk image, with songs that had a habit of building slowly towards a full-volume 'Sturm-und-Drang' climax. What turned them into a top-of-the-bill band was the bondage routines – the sadomasochist set pieces between Adam and the band's manager **Jordan**, a punk ex-crony of Malcolm McLaren.

Although the music was not exceptional, the stage act kept the crowd away from the bar and landed Adam (and Jordan) parts in Derek Jarman's film, *Jubilee*. In it, Adam played Kid, who sang a couple of songs, pouted a bit and eventually got killed; all good promotion for the first LP, DIRK WEARS WHITE SOX, released in 1979. By now, the original line-up had been replaced by guitarist **Mark Gaumont** (himself replaced soon after by **Matthew Ashman**), drummer **Dave Barbe** and bass player **Leigh Gorman**. However, soon after the album's release, this new line-up was rustled by Malcolm McLaren, who reinvented them as BOW WOW WOW. The fickle music press was delighted, cheerfully writing Adam off as one more whose career was over.

Undeterred, Adam recruited a new band, comprising **Marco Pirroni** (guitar), **Terry Lee Miall** (drums), **Merrick** (drums) and **Kevin Mooney** (bass), who was replaced in the spring of 1981 by **Gary Tibbs**, formerly of **Roxy Music** and **The Vibrators**. Adam also found himself a new image, appearing in a bizarre mix of pirate costume and Red Indian makeup, and fronting a rhythm-heavy pop band, inspired by the African drummers of Burundi.

Fuelled by these rhythms, Adam's second LP, KINGS OF THE WILD FRONTIER (1980), was a major success, with the singer, drop-dead gorgeous to behold, cheerfully warbling defiant new-wave corkers. He even had an anthem to rally under – "Antmusic", which, along with "Dog Eat Dog", gave him his first mainstream chart successes. 'Antmania' was briefly newsworthy and, with the help of flamboyant promotional videos, sold a lot of records, especially in the UK. Between 1980 and 1982 Adam released eight singles – all hits in Britain, including three that reached the #1 spot.

But teenybopper fame is a brief thing, alas, and Adam's came to an end after the poorly received PRINCE CHARMING LP in late 1981. 'Ridicule is nothing to be scared of', declared our hero in the title track; but it was if you dressed up like that – just ask the other Prince. This wasn't rock'n'roll, it was haberdashery.

Adam bit the bullet and terminated the band in the spring of 1982, though he continued to collaborate with Ant guitarist Pirroni, notably on his last UK #1 single "Goody Two Shoes". They plodded on

Leather trousers, pained expression? That'll be Adam and the Ants, then – before the dressing-up box arrived

together through the early 1980s, putting out LPs only to have them shot down in flames, both critically and increasingly commercially. In 1985, after a brief Live Aid appearance, Adam hung up his frills to concentrate on his acting career, while Marco joined **SPEAR OF DESTINY**, and recorded with **Sinéad O'Connor**.

In 1990, the duo reunited temporarily for the Top 20 album, MANNERS & PHYSIQUE, but the thrill had gone, and it all went quiet until early 1995 when Adam brought his sexpot looks and downright dirty voice back with WONDERFUL, aiming to warm another generation of underwear.

⊙ **Kings Of The Wild Frontier** (1980; CBS).
Adam's first hit album, recorded with a different band and a new image. Half the tracks are leftovers from the first Ants (like the ghastly "Los Rancheros" and "Jolly Roger") cater for his new audience. Not an essential purchase really but fun if you want fun in your music.

⊙ **Hits 1980–85** (1986; CBS).
Thirteen tracks, all winners. Buy this and "Dirk" and you'd have the essential Ant oeuvre.

Al Spicer

RYAN ADAMS

Born Jacksonville, North Carolina, 1974.

If Gram Parsons is the 'holy ghost' of alternative country, then **Ryan Adams** is surely its messiah, both in his alleged on-the-road, Parsons–esque excesses and in the emotional depth and genre reinventions of his music. Yet throughout his musical career Adams has seemed uncomfortable with the whole alternative country tag, and through numerous stylistic shifts has simultaneously shrugged off lazy categorizations while preparing the way for something approaching mainstream stardom.

The soul of Adams's music is country, but he formed his first band, The Patty Duke Syndrome, when he was fifteen, citing early influences as Black Flag, Hüsker Dü and Dead Kennedys. The group spent the next four years creating a significant local following but its canvas clearly wasn't broad enough for Adams's tastes. In 1994, shortly after relocating to nearby Raleigh, he left Patty Duke Syndrome and began to assemble a new band with guitarist **Phil Wandscher** and violinist/vocalist **Caitlin Cary**. Adding **Steve Grothman** and **Eric 'Skillet' Gilmore** to the line-up they became **Whiskeytown**.

This new group proved to be a perfect outlet for Adams, taking in the full scope of country, punk, pop and rock. They were well supported by the ~~~~ piece of the emerging alternative count ~~~~ *Depression* magazine, especially in the w~~~~ debut album FAITHLESS ST (1996). Re~~~~ haze of alcohol with the dBs' **Chris Sta**~~~~ controls, FAITHLESS ST was a sparse, alm~~~~ melancholic collection.

NO'

It was a genre-defining moment; part-Replacements, part-Parsons. Yet Adams wasn't content to stay still. 1997's STRANGERS ALMANAC bore the sheen of higher production values, no doubt a consequence of signing to a major label. The album's high points showed just how well developed and mature Adams's writing craft had become, his sentimentality cut through with an authentic world-weariness that belied his years. By this time major things were expected of Whiskeytown, but internal strife was threatening to tear the group asunder: touring had always been volatile, the recording of STRANGERS ALMANAC had been difficult, and there was clear animosity between Adams and Wandscher.

On their return to the studio only Cary, Adams and (new recruit) multi-instrumentalist **Mike Daly** were left. Produced by Ethan Johns, PNEUMONIA (2001) managed to balance the rawness of their indie debut with the glossiness demanded by major labels. With guest appearances by Smashing Pumpkins' **James Iha** and Replacements drummer **Tommy Stinson**, their third album was, like Wilco's BEING THERE, a largely successful attempt to break free of *No Depression* associations, but by the time the album was released – after a three-year delay due to record label 'restructuring' – Cary had released an album of his own, Adams was beginning to assert his solo credentials, and Whiskeytown were finished.

Adams's first venture as a solo artist was to hit the road for a series of acoustic dates before convening in a studio in Nashville (where else?) with songwriters **Gillian Welch** and **David Rawlings**. Released on the magnificent Bloodshot Records, HEARTBREAKER (2000) was received with open arms by a press waiting expectantly for something big to emerge from this much-lauded talent. Welch and Rawlings brought an earnest rootsiness to Adams's raw, heart-on-sleeve delivery while **Emmylou Harris** was guest on "Oh My Sweet Carolina", providing additional country kudos.

Major labels once again crowded round for a piece of the action and Adams was signed to Universal's Lost Highway imprint, which released his second album GOLD (2001) – the same year that PNEUMONIA eventually appeared. GOLD jettisoned much of the twang in favour of 70s rock: the album's sound took in everyone from Neil Young to the Rolling Stones, even stopping off at Hotel California on the way. Always incredibly prolific, Adams had apparently recorded four albums' worth of material in the year prior to GOLD's release. Thirteen of these tracks were issued as DEMOLITION in 2002; outwardly it was a stop-gap collection to keep enthusiastic punters happy while they waited for an official follow-up, but of course there were some real gems such as the dreamy "Tennessee Sucks" and the tear-jerking "Cry On Demand".

Adams's punk credentials remain – he's a member of the **Fucking Virgins** along with James Iha, Evan Dando and Melissa Auf Der Maur; he is also (allegedly) involved in hardcore punk outfit, **The Finger**. He began 2003 on tour with the Rolling Stones, along with his newly formed band **The Pink Hearts**.

Parsons would certainly have been proud of his musical scion.

Whiskeytown

Faithless St (1996; Outpost).
Adams enters the world of country in a baptism by booze. Raucous in places, sometimes ropy but ultimately rewarding – especially in emotionally raw tracks like "Excuse Me While I Break My Own Heart Tonight".

Ryan Adams

Heartbreaker (1996; Cooking Vinyl).
After several years of upheaval, Adams goes back to source with this bittersweet offering and emerges as a more rounded performer and writer.

Gold (1996; Lost Highway).
In parts overindulgent and excessive, in others a timely reworking of the country-rock model. Nobody has translated the ideas of alt-country to a bigger stage as successfully as Adams.

Derryck Strachan

BARRY ADAMSON

Born England, 1958.

The unique musical pastiche of **Barry Adamson** first began to take shape during his stint as the bassist for the too-smart-for-their-own-good art-punkers **MAGAZINE**. Adamson's passion for what he would later develop into a kind of cinematic funk showed up in Magazine covers of John Barry's theme for *Goldfinger* and Sly And The Family Stone's "Thank You (Falettinme Be Mice Elf Agin)". After the dissolution of Magazine in 1981, Adamson worked briefly with another ex-Buzzcock, **Pete Shelley**, before joining **NICK CAVE**'s Bad Seeds. Adamson stayed with the Bad Seeds for four albums, including THE FIRSTBORN IS DEAD and KICKING AGAINST THE PRICKS, before leaving in 1987 to pursue a career as a solo artist and soundtrack composer.

Adamson's debut album, MOSS SIDE STORY (1989), was conceived as the soundtrack to an imaginary film noir set in the shady underworld of the Moss Side area of Manchester. It was a brooding masterpiece that blended the conventions of soundtrack music with industrial detritus, Jack McDuff-style lounge-jazz Hammond organs, the ghoulish howling of Diamanda Galas, and the cut'n'paste techniques of collagists such as Steinski & The Mass Media and Coldcut. With its use of hip-hop's sound manipulation techniques amidst a setting of abstract melancholia, MOSS SIDE STORY was an unacknowledged ancestor of the soon-to-rule trip-hop of bands such as Portishead, DJ Food, and Kruder & Dorfmeister.

The success of MOSS SIDE STORY led to Adamson providing real soundtracks for films like *Delusion* and *Gas Food Lodging*. His next proper album was SOUL MURDER (1992), which reprised MOSS SIDE's scope with its ska influences, bleak electronica and orchestral sweeps. 1993's THE NEGRO INSIDE ME was a brilliant cut-up of rare groove jazz-funk, hip-hop and French schlock-pop. Although it was less oblique and less shrouded in dope fog and sexual psychosis, THE NEGRO INSIDE ME presaged Tricky's games with the idea of a single black identity.

The musical style, if not the ideology, of THE NEGRO INSIDE was replayed on A PRAYER MAT OF FLESH (1995). "Something Wicked This Way Comes" nicked the title from a Ray Bradbury novel in an attempt to make the MOR keyboard riff from Atlanta Rhythm Section's "Spooky" live up to its title. The album was enjoyable but, devoid of a clever context, it failed to transcend the muckiness of its source material.

1996 saw Adamson product once more in the record stores. His third solo outing, OEDIPUS SCMOEDIPUS, featured ex-Associates' frontman **Billy Mackenzie** on guest vocals in a set of swirling, atmospheric, mood music for the late 90s. 1998's AS ABOVE, SO BELOW found Adamson exploring slightly darker, more aggressive territory, though still

working within the same parameters. THE MURKY WORLD OF BARRY ADAMSON (1999) collected some of the choicest tracks from his previous albums, but the 'best-of' format didn't suit a musician whose work depends so much on context. In 2001 Adamson collaborated with Finnish avant-gardists **Pan Sonic** on MOTORLAB 3, an EP for the Icelandic Kitchen Motors label. "The Hymn of the 7th Illusion" combined Adamson's arrangement for an Icelandic choir with Pan Sonics brutally minimal electronics, while "The Illusion of the 7th Hymn" was an equally uncompromising remix of the track from Germany's **The Hafler Trio**.

In 2002 Adamson delivered THE KING OF NOTHING HILL, which pulled his gravelly vocal style to the fore, complementing the cinematic themes that were still, obviously, his primary concern.

⦿ **Moss Side Story** (1989; Mute).
Well ahead of its time, Adamson's first album remains his best. Tetchy, funny, ugly and clever, this replays the dynamic of a first-class film noir.

⦿ **Oedipus Scmoedipus** (1996; Mute).
Effortlessly combining jazz, R&B and soundtrack atmospherics, this set was for many an album of the year.

Peter Shapiro

ADD N TO (X)

Formed London, 1994

"There is no past and no future, it's just what happens when you turn the machine on." Barry Smith

Since their inception, **Add N To (X)** have not only pulled off the remarkable feat of making ancient technology sound good, loud and modern, but they've also managed to attract a broad audience for their unique brand of banging electronic pop-rock, widening the appeal of analogue equipment abuse in the process.

Initially meeting at the We Are Electric club, **Barry Smith** and **Ann Shenton** formed Add N To (X) when Smith found a discarded MS20 synth in a waste bin. With the addition of further scavenged keyboards, theremins and oscillators, they played a series of pretty standard electronic gigs in London and Paris before taking a new direction, which coincided with new arrival **Steve Claydon** in 1997. Taking a line they like to term 'Avant-hard', the reconfigured Add N To (X) released the VERO ELECRONIC mini-album for Blow Up records before signing to Satellite records and recording two 12" singles. "The Black Regent" and "King Wasp" (the latter included stunning artwork and 3D glasses) were both *NME Singles Of The Week*. A further track, "Demon Seed", appeared on a single split with **Fridge** on the Piao! label and the group became favourites of John Peel, recording a session for him in 1998.

Their debut album ON THE WIRES OF OUR NERVES (1998) sparked extensive interest from the

BARRY ADAMSON
The King of Nothing Hill

Add N To (X)'s daring Moog heist!

stab at electro-poppery, aided by the phenomenally catchy "Plug Me In" single and its floor-filling disco remix. 2002's LOUD LIKE NATURE built strongly on previous efforts, its standout cut being the furious techno stomp mouthful "Lick A Battery (Tongues Across The Terminals)".

⊙ **On The Wires Of Our Nerves** (1998; Satellite).
Somewhere between the Electro of Giorgio Moroder and The Beastie Boys and the nihilist spasms of Throbbing Gristle, this album has done more to popularize buzzing and bleeping oscillator workouts than any group since Suicide. Even the touches of The Human League or Gary Numan-style synth-pop are mixed with vocoders and a combination of Kosmische and Junglist drumming to queasy effect, though moments of calm seep through.

⊙ **Add Insult To Injury** (2000; Mute).
A groovy blend of the oldest synth sounds around, mellow grooves and noisy charges – a vocoded journey through the denser reaches of electro-noise pop. Add N To (X) like their electronics perverted, and this album gives them plenty of opportunity to thrust some unhealthy computer S & M deviance into the mix.

Richard Fontenoy

music press and radio; there was even a local TV documentary on the band, which featured both their music and some of their abstract films. The album's combination of old music technology, in the tradition of Throbbing Gristle and Cabaret Voltaire, with the sub-Junglist drumming of **Rob Alum** (The High Llamas) received glowing reviews and led to live appearances – with the addition of live drumming by **Andy Ramsay** (Stereolab) and **John Russell** – at John Peel's eclectic Meltdown Festival and with Pulp in London's Finsbury Park. Add N To (X) even played live at the Megadog club, where ravers were baffled by an energetic set of the group's customary blend of aggression and hypnotic analogue electronica. Fronted by Smith in a full-length leather coat, wielding his keyboard like a guitar, they were a formidable live act, considerably harsher than their records indicated.

A deal with Mute in mid-1998 produced the epic LITTLE BLACK ROCKS IN THE SUN EP (1998) and the mechano-pornographic video for the single "Metal Fingers In My Body" (1999), while the group's second album, AVANT HARD (1999), provided further bouts of genre-bending electronic fun. Sell-out tours, the addition of **Ross Orton** on drums, a name change to **Barry 7** for Smith and side-project **Shenton Engine** preceded ADD INSULT TO INJURY (2000). This set offered a more accessible

THE ADVERTS

Formed London, 1976; split late 1979.

"The Adverts know one chord, the Damned know three. See all four..." Tour Poster, 1977

TV **Smith** (guitar/vocals) and **Gaye Advert** (bass) met, put together a band, and played their first gigs at the Roxy – a sweaty, sleazy cauldron of a nightclub in London's pre-gentrified Covent Garden. Recruiting **Howard Pickup** (guitar) and **Laurie Driver** (drums), they supported The Damned, and signed to Stiff Records. After a swift session in the studio, their debut 45, "One Chord Wonders", hit the record stores – a great early punk single, making a defiant virtue of inexperience.

A second single in summer 1977 managed to attract more than a cult following. "Gary Gilmore's Eyes" was a nasty little fantasy based on the executed murderer's request that his body be given for medical research. The subject matter generated interest in the tabloid press, boosted by exploitative publicity shots of Gaye put out by the band's new record company, while a TV appearance on *Top Of The Pops* suddenly created thousands of new punks, mainly adolescent males strangely moved by Gaye's amphetamine-waif looks. They had a ready-made anthem in the single's B-side, "Bored Teenagers".

Two follow-up singles failed to capitalize on this mainstream success, although the LP CROSSING THE RED SEA WITH THE ADVERTS (1978) crawled to the lower end of the UK Top 40. This featured the singles, plus rather tepid renditions of the rest of their set – and while they were intense, vital and compelling in concert, on record they could be as dull and listless as TV Smith's hair.

In the wake of Laurie Driver's departure from the band, TV and Gaye recruited a few temporary drummers. They even switched record labels, but found it difficult to find a producer able to capture the energy and excitement of the band's live sound. By the time the second LP, CAST OF THOUSANDS (1998; reissued Anagram), came out, they'd lost all trace of punk credibility, even drafting in a synthesizer player who'd previously worked for Mike Oldfield. After seeing the record either ignored or seriously assaulted in the reviews, Gaye and TV reverted back to their original names and rode off into the sunset. Style to the last.

⊙ **Crossing The Red Sea With The Adverts** (1978; CBS).
All the decent singles, plus a muddy mix of the rest of their set.

Al Spicer

AEROSMITH

Formed Sunapee, New Hampshire, 1970.

"We weren't too ambitious when we started out. We just wanted to be the biggest thing that ever walked the planet." Steven Tyler

Stadium rockers par excellence, **Aerosmith** have proved remarkably adaptable, emerging from a late 70s decline to regain megastar status in the age of video and MTV. Formed by singer **Steven Tyler** (born Steven Talarico) and rhythm guitarist **Brad Whitford**, the band was completed by drummer **Joey Kramer**, bassist **Tom Hamilton** and gifted lead guitarist **Joe Perry**, who with Tyler came to be the band's fulcrum.

An eponymous debut LP for Columbia in 1972 featured the rocking call-and-response of "Mama Kin" and the forlorn ballad "Dream On", but GET YOUR WINGS (1974), produced by **Jack Douglas**, was a less derivative effort, showcasing the band's hallmark tight rock rhythms and Tyler's hoarse, blues-drenched vocal acrobatics. The multimillion-selling TOYS IN THE ATTIC (1975), featuring the seminal funk strut of "Walk This Way" and the characteristically broad innuendo of "Big Ten Inch", established the band as stadium-fillers, while dis-

pelling early suggestions that the band were simply Rolling Stones clones – a view prompted by Tyler's Jaggeresque looks and Perry's lazy guitar style.

For ROCKS (1976), Aerosmith built on a now-distinct blend of Beatles harmonies and sleazy heavy-metal riffs on tracks such as the opener, "Back In The Saddle". The Beatles element of their sound was a possible explanation for being selected to appear in the 1978 movie, *Sgt. Pepper's Lonely Hearts Club Band*, where they performed "Come Together".

On stage Aerosmith had become highly skilled performers, with the provocatively androgynous Tyler prowling the stage twirling his mike-stand like a bandleader's baton, whilst the band provided a pumping background for Perry's flashy guitar excesses. Such was the band's appeal (Tyler was regularly groped by his audience) that for a time members were protected by a purpose-built cage. Unfortunately, the excesses of the rock'n'roll lifestyle began to take their toll – Tyler has since boasted to have spent in excess of a million dollars on drugs. Another source of stress was the band's failure to achieve similar success across the Atlantic: 1977 witnessed a disastrous European tour that drowned in the wake of punk.

The flat and formulaic DRAW THE LINE (1978) was, ironically, only saved by the blistering punk of the title track, and though LIVE BOOTLEG (1979) was an outstanding album, drug-induced mutual intolerance marred the tired NIGHT IN THE RUTS (1980). Brad Whitford quit the band, as did Perry, who went on to release three albums with **The Joe Perry Project**. Tyler persevered on ROCK IN A HARD PLACE (1982), recruiting guitarists **Jim Crespo** and **Rick Dufay**, but aside from Crespo's commendable licks on "Lightning Strikes" and "Bolivian Ragamuffin", the album was a poor product.

The original line-up – now detoxicated – reformed in 1985, and signed to the Geffen label, releasing DONE WITH MIRRORS (1985). The album signalled a return to form, its highlight being a reworking of the title track from a Perry solo outing titled "Let The Music Do The Talking". The following year saw platinum-selling rappers **Run-D.M.C.** invite the band to appear on the hit cover version of "Walk This Way".

PERMANENT VACATION (1987), a collaboration with Bon Jovi producer **Bruce Fairbairn**, was eagerly anticipated by a rock press excited by the emergence of the Aerosmith-influenced Guns N' Roses. This broad, ambitious work featured the brassy hit "Dude (Looks Like A Lady)", the bluesy stomp "Rag Doll", the calypso-tinged title track and an energetic cover of the Beatles' "I'm Down". The band embarked on lengthy tours and re-established themselves – this time on both sides of the Atlantic. The Grammy-award-winning PUMP (1989) included the hits "Janie's Got A Gun" and "Love In An Elevator", the latter affording much play on the phrase 'going down'.

GET A GRIP (1993) was another huge sales success and one indicative of the band's ability to survive the

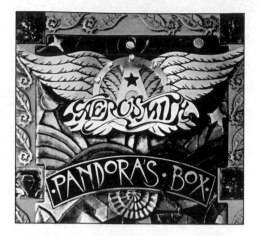

'grunge boom' that had left other glamorous rock acts without an audience. Four years of struggle with drugs, egos and difficult chord progressions intervened before 1997's NINE LIVES (Columbia) eventually fell into the record stores. Despite its difficult birth, the album was big and strong: seventy minutes of guitar solos, histrionic vocals, terrible lyrics and steamy innuendo. Whilst GEMS (1998) showcases the best of their career prior to their resurrection at the hands of Run-D.M.C., these days, the adage 'life begins at forty' has become appropriate to a band who have proved fitter with age, revelling in old-fashioned formulas while others grapple with rock's new sensibility. One simply has to cop a healthy earful of the solid live album A LITTLE SOUTH OF SANITY (1998) or JUSY PUSH PLAY (2001) to understand that little changes in the Aerosmith performance and songwriting vocabulary. And just to underline their now legendary status the band were inducted into the Rock And Roll Hall Of Fame in March 2001.

⊙ **Rocks** (1976; Columbia).
Guns N' Roses guitarist Slash cites this seminal sleaze classic as 'the album that changed my life'. Including "Last Child" and "Slick As A Dog", this is the definitive Aerosmith album.

⊙ **Permanent Vacation** (1987; Geffen).
A masterly set, bringing years of rocking experience to a daring range of tunes. It's loud, fresh and funky with a neat commercial sheen.

⊙ **Pandora's Box** (1991; Sony).
The ultimate Aerosmith collection, lodged in a handsome 3-CD box, and featuring key cuts from 1966 (Steven Tyler's pre-Aerosmith band, Chain Reaction) through to ROCK IN A HARD PLACE.

Michael Andrews

AFGHAN WHIGS

Formed Hamilton, Ohio, 1987; disbanded 2001.

The **Afghan Whigs** are fronted by one **Greg Dulli** (guitar/vocals), a man possessed of a voice that reflects to perfection the small-town alienation of his songs. The band is essentially his own, its inception inspired by a Hüsker Dü gig that struck him so deeply that he quit film studies for the lure of the music circuit. He forged the initial line-up out of a spell in a Cincinnati jail, earned for urinating in front of a police officer. There he met **John Curley** (bass; detained for drug offences). Back in Hamilton, a steel town thirty miles from Cincinnati, the duo fleshed out a group with **Rick McCollum** (guitar) and **Steve Earle** (drums).

The Whigs made their debut in 1988 with BIG TOP HALLOWEEN, a surly, guttural exposition of 70s rock chords played with gusto and surprising sophistication. Dulli's alcohol-baked lyrics were a revelation, half flight of fancy, half pained realism, and with a strong movie influence. The band were the first non-Seattle signings to the legendary Sub Pop label, and two years later they enlisted the services of production supremo **Jack Endino** for UP IN IT. Though this album never quite hit its targets with the same accuracy as their debut, it served as a calling card to the burgeoning audience for what was soon to be called 'grunge'.

Beneath the bluster the Afghan Whigs were managing to balance volume with subtlety – the country-rock bastardization "Son Of The South" was a signpost to their UPTOWN AVONDALE EP of soul covers. 1992's CONGREGATION offered a broody, inconclusive performance, evocative but too often morose. The Afghan Whigs were heading into new territories, but were still seemingly far from their destination.

With the world going grunge crazy, the Whigs became the latest in a long line of Sub Pop bands to be poached by a major. They made their new home with Elektra, though not before Dulli had insisted upon the right to manage, produce and direct all videos for the band without interference. There was also press talk of a movie project.

If GENTLEMEN (1993) didn't send the Afghan Whigs into quite the same league as Nirvana, there were enough critical plaudits flying around to ensure the band's longevity. Its music was the group's most cultured to date, the lyrics maintaining their abrasive edge: Dulli described the album as 'a song-cycle going for an Astral Weeks kind of thing, about when people stay in relationships too long for the wrong reasons'. The following year Dulli was enlisted as part of the 'grunge supergroup' that provided the backing music for the Stuart Sutcliffe biopic, *Backbeat*. He got to play John Lennon, which must have come as some compensation after missing out on the social misfit role in John Hughes' *The Breakfast Club* a decade earlier.

Dulli contributed a cover of Barry White's "Can't Get Enough Of Your Love, Babe" to the soundtrack of *Beautiful Girls*, a move towards soul music which was further refined on the next Afghan Whigs set, BLACK LOVE (1996). This collection saw the band in good shape, retaining their traditions of twisted passions and bleak emotional narratives.

A new album, 1965, was released on Columbia in

1999 but failed to set the charts alight. The following year, however, Dulli resurfaced with **The Twilight Singers** and an album, TWILIGHT AS PLAYED BY THE TWILIGHT SINGERS. The tracks had been conceived back in 1997 and widely bootlegged, though, thanks to several additional guest musicians and the production hands of down-tempo stalwarts **Fila Brazillia**, the completed, official set was a rich and imaginative masterpiece that offered some of Dulli's most soulful, and surprisingly optimistic, material to date.

But the The Afghan Whigs were finding it harder and harder to exist with the various members living so far apart, and in 2001, despite reports of new studio material emerging, the group announced that they were to split on good terms.

⊙ **Big Top Halloween** (1988; Ultrasuede).
A hell of a debut, boasting exemplary pace and timing, with lyrics that most of Seattle's musical population would swap their Jack Daniels'-clutching right arms for.

⊙ **Gentlemen** (1993; Elektra).
The major-label debut wrestles with all the old Afghan faithfuls – religion, isolation and sex (or lack of). The musical mood, though, is much more seductive, and closest yet to a rocking take on the Motown sound so beloved of Dulli – as black a record as the white world of grunge has yet produced.

Alex Ogg

AIR

Formed Paris, France, 1996.

In 1992 the French newspaper *Le Figaro* ran a headline that read: 'Thirty Years of French Rock'n'Roll And Still Not One Good Song'. Since the article's appearance, however, a host of Gallic musicians have emerged to make the bad taste of Johnny Hallyday, Magma and Indochine distant memories. While the French may still be incapable of making a decent rock record, the influx of dance music and hip-hop into France in recent years has meant that French music is no longer simply a parade of jailbait nymphets singing Eurovision cannon fodder or kitsch hymns to the latest tropical dance craze. Positioned in a long line of post-hip-hop artists, **Air** mix the traditional Gallic virtues of Françoise Hardy-style breathiness, Serge Gainsbourg-style seediness and Jacques Brel-style melancholia with an almost-British religious devotion to pure pop and a deep affection for ancient American analogue electronics.

Jean-Benoit Dunckel and **Nicolas Godin** were high-school friends from Versailles who, after a few years of teaching mathematics and architecture, decided to rekindle the spirit of their old high-school band, **Orange**. Instead of picking up their old guitars and David Bowie records, they picked up a cheap vocoder and dusted off some Nina Simone and Debussy records. Their first single, "Modular" (1996), was originally released on the Source label and then licensed to Mo' Wax in the UK where the slow and low emotionalism of its Gainsbourgian groove was welcomed with open arms by a down-tempo scene bored with its own pot-fuelled anesthesia. "Casanova 70" (1996) and "Le Soleil Est Près De Moi" (1997) followed suit with retooled easy listening floating on top of dreamy atmospheres and gossamer textures.

After contributing the Nina Simone-sampling "Soldissimo" to the excellent SUPER DISCOUNT (1997) compilation, Dunckel and Godin quickly became the darlings of the British music press with their debut album, MOON SAFARI (1998). Capitalizing on the vogue for both lounge music ("All I Need" and "Ce Matin La") and retro-electronics ("Sexy Boy" and "Kelly Watch The Stars"), MOON SAFARI perfectly encapsulated the underground's urges for a semi-remembered time when technology was fun and not leading humanity down an Orwellian path to enslavement. In other words, it was retrograde pop fluff with a suntan and continental flair that seemed positively revolutionary compared to the cheap and nasty products of the clumsy oafs churned out by the British star machine.

2000 found the duo soundtracking Sophia Coppola's film version of Jeffrey Eugenides' novel *The Virgin Suicides*. Aside from an almost total absence of vocals and a moodier, more low-key take on the same territory, THE VIRGIN SUICIDES featured the same shimmering electronic pop as their debut, only in sketchier form. 10,000 HZ LEGEND (2001) was darker still, a not entirely successful combination of suave pop and alienated textures. Those damned vocoders were still there, even though everyone bar Bon Jovi had used them in the previous couple of years, and their pastiches were no longer clever, just tired and passé. The problems were further confounded by 2002's pointless remix album EVERYBODY HURTZ and 2003's **Alessandro Baricco** spoken-word collaboration CITY READING PROJECT.

Like too many other hipster icons of the millennium, they seem to have no idea what they want to be and try to be all things to all people, even Radiohead fans. Maybe *Le Figaro* is still right after all.

- **Premiers Symptomes** (1999; Virgin).
  Collecting the duo's earlier singles, this mini-album is a great introduction to Air, though avoid the Gordini mix at the end of the set at all costs.
- **Moon Safari** (1998; Virgin).
  Not as awesome as a jaded music press would have you believe, but an enjoyable record that doesn't take itself too seriously.
- **The Virgin Suicides** (2000; Virgin).
  A set of cool and slightly melancholic tunes, arguably their finest moment.

Peter Shapiro

ALABAMA 3

Formed London, 1989.

Wild, whimsical and scary, to say **Alabama 3** are unpredictable would be an understatement. It was at a party sometime in 1988 that Welshman **Rob Spragg** (aka **Larry Love** – smooth vocals and production) met the swaggering Glaswegian **Jake Black** (**Dr. D Wayne Love** – preaching vocals) who was toasting the lyrics of Hank Williams' "Lost Highway" over a banging house tune. The two Celts hit it off immediately and their melting pot of country and house was first put on to stew. The results were two 12" singles, **Shed's**' "In That Morning" and the extremely-hard-to-come-by Alabama 3 debut "I Shall Be Released", both on the DIY label.

In 1994, the guys enlisted **Piers Marsh** (Mountain of Love – programmer and engineer), **Simon Edwards** (**Sir Real Congaman Love** – percussionist), **Orlando Harrison** (Holy Ghost Of Love – aka The Spirit – keyboards), **Rob Bailey** (Mississippi Guitar Man Love – aka Fuzzbox Guitar Man Love – guitar) and **Johnny Delafons** (Little Boy Dope The Human 808 – drums). They spent most of 1995 in Italy developing their sound and stage show.

"Ain't Going To Goa" (1996), independently released in Europe and England, was their first stab at the singles chart. With heady beats, tasteful samples and moments of mind-altering acid squidge, this was a swipe at the dance scene's more sheep-like followers and incorporated elements of gospel, country and blues. An instant mainstream radio hit, it led to wider coverage in the music press (the band dreamt up a juicy and plausible story of having met at a drug rehab clinic in Brixton) and sold well.

There was more to Alabama 3 than the mere dreaming up of legendary origins, however. Their original intentions were to break up the monotony of the London dance scene and inject a little humour and imagination. Mixing technology with wholesome, down-home musical styles they created a different sound to other dance/trance acts. Matched only by Beck in their skilled merging of past sounds and future pop, Alabama 3 even dragged old-time religious revival techniques into the show.

Disciples **Chris Mckay** (Luce De La Amour), **Stuart Green** (Irvine BB Love III), **Madde Ross** (Mandi Warhol), **Scott** and **Emma Lush** added their skills to the team and, following the Reverend's twelve-step plan, *The First Presleyterian Church of Elvis the Divine* was formed. Worshippers would gather for all-night rituals and they were soon able to consecrate their own church in the band's backyard in Brixton.

Signing with Geffen Records in 1996, their next release was "Woke Up This Morning" (1997), complete with a stunning Howlin' Wolf sample – 'You woke this morning and got yourself a gun, Mama always said you'd be the Chosen one'. They followed up with the full-length recording EXILE ON COLDHARBOUR LANE (1997). Produced by the talented **Bob Clearmountain** (who'd worked with such acts as Roxy Music and Elton John) the result was a new hybrid – country-acid-house – a mix of Appalachian craziness and pirate-radio breakbeats.

On stage Alabama 3 swelled to include **Tattoo Man**, a reincarnated Lenin and a chorus of soul/gospel-singing sweethearts, evolving into left-wing love cowboys with a new agenda. Out with the old drugs and in with the new was the slogan, and A.C.C. (Accelerated Class Consciousness) – a serum made from the bone marrow of Vladimir Ilyich Lenin – was the promise.

The Holy Roller Revival '97 Roadshow established their almost lunatic live performances as unmissable events and for many they were the ecstatic highlight of 1998's wet Glastonbury and sunnier Reading festivals. Their next single, however, showed the band at their most sincere – a faithful rendition of John Prine's bluesy "Speed Of The Sound Of Loneliness". Performed live it would prove to be a techno roadhouse stormer. Having, of course, sworn off most of the sins of the flesh, they were able to keep some of their income long enough to set up the Steam Rooms studios in London's East End.

With accolades from the likes of Bobby Gillespie (Primal Scream), and the album track "Peace In The Valley" finding its way onto the soundtrack of the movie *A Life Less Ordinary* it seemed as though A3 were well on track to fulfil their ambition to rave it up at the Grand Ol' Opry – especially when they were introduced to American audiences via a chaotic US tour and the fitting honour of supplying the theme ("Woke Up This Morning") to the award-winning TV gangster series *The Sopranos*.

However, the release of their second LP, LA PESTE (2000), was greeted by mixed reviews and public indifference. Equally, while 2002's POWER IN THE BLOOD was by far the group's most accomplished dance release, it was just in the wrong place at the wrong time, and did nothing for the band's status. Despite their continued success as an inflammatory and entertaining live act (the band have even been joined on stage by one of the Birmingham Six) their undeniably good ideas seem to be hampered by the very factors – comedy accents, drugs references etc – that make them so unique.

- **Exile On Coldharbour Lane** (1997; Geffen).
  The big revival sound from Brixton town.

Tyrone Thomas

THE ALARM

Formed Rhyl, Wales, 1981; disbanded 1991.

Though they were one of the most inspirational live bands of the 80s, **The Alarm** never reached the commercial heights for which they seemed destined. Changing their name from **Seventeen** (formed when all the members were – yes – aged 17), **Mike Peters** (vocals/guitar), **Dave Sharp** (guitar), **Eddie MacDonald** (bass) and **Nigel Twist** (drums) took their new ID from one of their first compositions, "Alarm, Alarm".

Following extensive touring outside of their native Wales and the release of a self-financed debut single, "Unsafe Building", The Alarm began to build up what was to become a massive underground following. After a period with Police manager Miles Copeland's Illegal label, the band signed with IRS and released their first album, the aptly named DECLARATION, in 1984. The record drew immediate comparisons with The Clash: Peters' vocal style was similar, and the instrumental section of the single "Sixty Eight Guns" (a UK #17) would appear to have been borrowed wholesale from The Clash's "London Calling". Nevertheless, the band had enough talent to forge their own identity, as their potent mix of acoustic and electric on anthemic songs such as "Blaze Of Glory" (the high point of any Alarm concert) and "Where Were You Hiding When The Storm Broke?" powerfully demonstrated.

The choice of the band as support act for U2 in the early 80s was a natural pairing – besides their Celtic origins, both bands were profoundly affected both by the energy of punk and by religion; Alarm lyrics strongly reflected Peters' Christian beliefs. After the release of "The Chant Has Just Begun"/"The Bells Of Rhymey", the latter an acoustic treatment of a Welsh poem, the band followed up with the patchy album STRENGTH (1985). While leaning more towards stadium rock (the following year they would support Queen and Status Quo at Wembley), it had its share of fine moments, notably the title track, "Spirit Of '76" and the contemplative "Walk Forever By My Side". There was less to redeem 1987's EYE OF THE HURRICANE, which was distinguished only by its Top 20 single, "Rain In The Summertime", and the live track, "One Step Closer To Home".

By 1989's CHANGE, the band had abandoned their mix of folk and punk in favour of a much more bluesy approach, as demonstrated by the likes of "Sold Me Down The River" and "Devolution Workin' Man Blues". The highlight of the album for many, however, was the heartfelt "A New South Wales", which featured a Welsh male-voice choir and the Welsh Symphony Orchestra. Ever keen to display their roots, the band also released a version of the album with Peters singing in Welsh.

Following a US tour where they opened for Bob Dylan, the band released a live mini-album, ELECTRIC FOLKLORE (1988). While containing extended versions of their most famous songs, it failed to capture the almost evangelical excitement of a packed Alarm concert.

What would turn out to be The Alarm's final studio album, RAW (1991), was their most satisfying outing since DECLARATION. The thrilling mix of acoustic and electric, so apparent on their debut, was once again evident on songs such as the title track and "Save Your Crying". Sometime vocalist Dave Sharp had come into his own, too, managing his best Keith Richards drawl on numbers like "God Save Somebody".

After a packed gig at London's Brixton Academy in 1991, Mike Peters shocked his colleagues and fans alike by announcing his departure, effectively ending the band. He has since forsaken stadium superstardom in favour of a solo career playing smaller clubs with his new band **The Poets Of Justice**, and released a debut solo album, BREATH, in 1994, well worth the wait, as was an acoustic version of the album.

Dave Sharp also released a solo LP, HARD TRAVELLIN', and played numerous venues around the UK before seeking quieter glories as a backing musician, guesting with Stiff Little Fingers for a while. He is currently believed to be attempting to crack that famed bastion of rock'n'roll, New Orleans.

A subsequent solo album, DOWNTOWN AMERICA, was released on Dinosaur Records in 1996, and Sharp is currently working with a new band, **Sugarland**.

Declaration (1984; IRS).
Once you've fought past the Tina Turner fright-wig hairdos on the cover, you'll discover one of the most fiery, passionate and powerful debuts of the post-punk generation. Their finest moment.

Standards (1990; IRS).
Apart from the heinous omission of the likes of "The Bells Of Rhymey" and "The Chant Has Just Begun", this generally cuts the mustard as greatest hits packages go and features gems such as "Unsafe Building" and "Absolute Reality", which were never included on any album.

Raw (1991; IRS).
More rock-orientated and less original than their early stuff maybe, but this swansong contains some great material in the form of the title track, Dave Sharp's contributions and that great Neil Young cover, "Rockin' In The Free World". Pity about the bloody awful barbershop quartet sentimentality of "These Moments In Time", though.

The Best Of The Alarm And Mike Peters (1998; EMI).
In retrospect, probably the only Alarm album anyone really needs.

Paul Morris

ALBERTO Y LOST TRIOS PARANOIAS

Formed Manchester, England, 1973; disbanded 1981.

The great British parody band of the 70s, **Alberto Y Lost Trios Paranoias** established a cult following but failed to break through in any major way.

Nonetheless their skill, vision and attention to the detail of 70s rock gives them a lingering appeal, and they are a fond memory for those who were there at the time.

With songs like "Anadin" – which sounded like a drawling comedy song about a well-known medicine, unless you were familiar with the Velvet Underground's "Heroin" – the band found its greatest champions in the music press, which was developing a self-conscious and arty division, and on the college and university gig circuit, where performances were more like social events. The stage performances were triumphs of cheap props, ridiculous overacting and stunts with instant crowd appeal – like the power-chord solo through an underpowered amp that would be reduced to a smoking ruin in seconds. Basically this lot could prat around, play some good music and leave everyone feeling better.

Their first album, ALBERTO Y LOST TRIOS PARANOIAS (1976), hit some big targets – "Jesus Wept" was a savage attack on right-wing evangelicalism – but elsewhere ran the risk of dating quickly, a constant danger with rock humour. ITALIANS FROM OUTER SPACE (1977) again featured some hilarious stuff – "Brrrr!" was a phone call in which Barry White rings up an unsuspecting female and gives her some of his sex growl – but as fast as the Albertos caught on, the world changed around them.

Punk rock threatened to destroy their favourite targets with a fury that mere satirists could never manage and the rock world was plunged into a period of uncertainty. The Albertos took punk on directly and presented the play *Sleak* at the Royal Court Theatre. Written by **C. P. Lee** (vocals/guitar), the story followed Norman Sleak as his quest for fame led to his agreement to provide the ultimate rock performance – suicide on stage. The highly collectable SNUFF ROCK EP (1977) that came out of this work, released appropriately enough on Stiff Records, included accurate parodies of the emerging punk stars. The Sex Pistols take-off "Gobbing On Life" captured Johnny Rotten's phrasing to good effect.

Sleak and its spin-off were a watershed in a number of ways, showing that the band was appealing to an older audience, to whom the new wave was a threat. A double single briefly dented the charts in 1978 when their Status Quo send-up "Heads Down No Nonsense Mindless Boogie" reached the Top 50. Despite this success, producing parody records in a rapidly changing rock climate was a precarious balancing act and by the start of the 80s the Albertos were taking *Sleak* to Broadway and working on a follow-up, *Never Mind The Bullocks*.

By this point the band were in decline as leukaemia took its toll on vocalist **Les Pryor**. The loss of his comic genius seriously limited future potential, and later projects, such as a send-up of the mod revival and a re-formation as **The Mothmen,** failed to make much headway.

By the early 80s, in any case, members of the large and often unwieldy line-up had ventured into other areas. **Chas Jankel** (keyboards) became sidekick to Ian Dury, **Jimmy Hibbert** (vocals/bass) made a heavy metal album and went on to mastermind the sound and voice of children's cartoon character Count Duckula. C. P. Lee went on to an eclectic career that included the stage persona of **Lord Buckley**, a hipster, poet and drinker who had made a living as a raconteur in the days of the Beat poets.

In the end the Albertos are a colourful footnote to the sometimes self-conscious rock culture of the 70s. Musically they are closest to the Bonzo Dog Doo Dah Band, although their concentration on rock as the source of most of their humour gave them an identity of their own. In recent years only the reggae parody of Led Zeppelin, **Dread Zeppelin**, has matched the style, musical ability and comic vision of the Albertos. With MR LOVE PANTS (1998), the late, great, Ian Dury maintained the combination of music hall, observation and madness that made up the Albertos' most sublime moments. But then, his greatest moments came with former Alberto Jankel in his band.

Snuff Rock (1991; Mau Mau).
With an identical title to their 1977 EP, just to top the chaos, this carefully chosen collection of the best moments is recommended for any connoisseur of the weird and inspired in rock lunacy.

Neil Nixon

ALICE IN CHAINS

Formed Seattle, 1987; disbanded 2002.

Guitars and "God Smack" paved the path to stardom for **Alice In Chains**: Nirvana-crazed journos fell over themselves to cover more Seattlites who not only played neck-snapping metal but also permanently verged on junk-fuelled collapse. Alice In Chains had, however, participated in that quaint practice of paying their dues. Like Pantera, they were conceived as glam-rockers, before transforming into more manly metallers, shedding their original moniker (**Diamond Lie**) and singer **Nick Pollock** (whose own next project, **My Sister's Machine**, had a distinctly Alice-ish flavour).

Settling on a line-up of **Jerry Cantrell** (guitar), **Layne Staley** (vocals), **Mike Starr** (bass) and **Sean Kinney** (drums), the band issued their 1990 debut, FACELIFT, to critical cheers and public antipathy. Relentless touring contributed to its eventual success, but more important was the adoption of the single "Man In The Box" as a *Beavis And Butthead* MTV anthem and Alice's appearance in Cameron Crowe's movie *Singles*. From the latter came "Would?", an international hit in the summer of 1992, by which time the band had completed arena tours with Slayer and Van Halen and, contrarily, released a low-key acoustic EP, SAP (1991).

'Low-key' and 'acoustic' were terms rarely applied to their next album, DIRT (1992), which wrapped choirboy harmonies around sledgehammer guitars, peddling an ambiguous line about the merits of heroin.

Appropriately, Alice then began to fall apart. Founder member Starr quit, to be replaced by mild-mannered **Mike Inez** (ex-Ozzy Osbourne, whom Alice had supported); then, after an acclaimed European tour, they cancelled a high-profile support slot with Metallica, and recorded the icily beautiful JAR OF FLIES (1994), a mini-album that made Slayer sound chirpy. *Kerrang* magazine subsequently gave away 'Cheer up Layne, it might never happen' stickers.

Opting not to tour in support of JAR OF FLIES, the group prompted speculation about Staley, who was variously rumoured to be: a) clean; b) reacquainted with the business end of needles; or c) dead. He instead emerged as frontman of **Mad Season**, in the company of Pearl Jam's **Mike McReady**. This ongoing project yielded the fine ABOVE album (1995), a handful of gigs and a spot-on John Lennon tribute album WORKING CLASS HERO. Mike Inez, meanwhile, toured with Slash's **Snakepit**.

These extracurricular activities meant no one was very surprised when Alice's next album, ALICE IN CHAINS (1995), was announced – by the press – as their last. But, the lead-off single "Grind" warned, 'You'd be well advised not to plan my funeral before the body dies'. Defiant, unlovely, yet compelling as ever, the album debuted at #1 in the US. The following year brought UNPLUGGED and a sense that, despite Staley's dubious health, Alice would eventually produce another noteworthy studio album or two. Indeed, they recorded the songs "Died" and "Get Born Again" which both appeared on MUSIC BANK (1999), a box set of hits and rarities. ALICE IN CHAINS LIVE (2000), however, seemed to be just a stopgap release designed to keep the flame alive, as did GREATEST HITS (2001). And then in 2002, the news all Alice fans feared hit the headlines: on April 19, Layne Staley was found dead in his Seattle home. The irony of the situation lay in the fact that guitarist Jerry Cantrell was on the verge of releasing his second solo album, DEGRADATION TRIP (2002) – his first, the low-key BOGGY DEPOT, was released in 1997 – an album that lay very close in spirit to Alice's finest recording, DIRT. The story of a band that had hit so many obstacles but lived to play on was finally to come to an end.

⦿ **Dirt** (1992; Columbia).
Alice's Wonderland.

⦿ **Jar Of Flies/Sap** (1994; Columbia).
Hard to imagine anything owing so much to The Eagles could be any good, but this gloom-fest is as powerful as Dirt.

Bruno MacDonald

ALIEN ANT FARM

Formed: Riverside, California 1995.

L et's face it, there aren't many metal bands who can claim to have come to prominence through an off-kilter cover version of a Michael Jackson tune. Nevertheless, that's precisely what **Alien Ant Farm**

achieved when they issued "Smooth Criminal" as a single in 2001 and almost instantly found themselves catapulted towards the top of the nu-metal heap over the heads of their peers and detractors.

Things had started at a more modest pace, however, when **Dryden Mitchell** (vocals), **Terence Corso** (guitar), **Tye Zamora** (bass) and **Mike Cosgrove** (drums) first got together, jamming on the usual apprenticeship diet of cover versions while moonlighting from various other bands. Their name was apparently conjured up by Corso during a day-dream reverie when he was struck by the notion of aliens cultivating human civilization on earth in much the same way as a kid would nurture an ant farm for a science project.

Mitchell was inspired by his father, a guitarist, who originally got the youngster interested in six-string finger flinging before he decided to hone his vocal skills; Mitchell often namechecks the likes of Edie Brickell and Tracy Chapman as sources of inspiration. Corso's budding brilliance was encouraged by his mother and more formal training in a band workshop; Zamora started out on the guitar before bands such as Primus promoted the joys of the four-string rumble; and Cosgrove was a self-taught skin pounder. The resulting amalgam of metal, funk, pop and hard rock – topped off with a deliberately odd-ball stage presence, that featured Zamora's weird gurning and Mitchell's geeky dancing – gradually won them a loyal fan base in southern California. If their undoubted tightness as a unit made them stand out from the crowd and turn more than a few heads on the local punk and metal scene, then their association with fellow scenesters Papa Roach didn't do any harm either. The two outfits would promote each other whenever the opportunity arose.

The band's first independently released album, the ironically titled GREATEST HITS (1999), landed them a gong at the LA Music Awards for *Best Independent Rock Album* of the year and proved to be just a taster of the plaudits they would eventually earn. The motherlode was struck with ANTHOLOGY (2001), which was released on Papa Roach's New Noize imprint giving them the benefit of major label distribution via Dreamworks. Nestling within the polished nu-metal grooves was hit single "Movies" and their blistering, heavied-up take on Jacko's "Smooth Criminal". The former featured lyrics penned by Mitchell exploring relationships and their demise and underlined the care taken to craft songs with a little more poetic bite than your average angst-ridden chart fodder. However, it was the aggressive and jokey pop-metal of "Smooth Criminal" that really kick-started the Ant Farm phenomenon. As big fans of Jackson's output, great care was taken to create a classic cover version and so, complete with all the requisite yells and whoops, the single made its home in the pop charts and sent the band stratospheric.

Success was halted somewhat abruptly in May 2002, however, when the band's tour bus collided with a truck in Spain. The bus driver was killed and the band and their entourage came away with a variety of serious injuries – not least Mitchell, who damaged his spine. At the time of writing the band are hoping to be in the studio soon to record a new album.

⊙ **Anthology** (2001; Dreamworks).
Polished and commercial, this is chart-friendly nu-metal at its most professional. Worth checking out, if only for "Movies" and "Smooth Criminal".

Essi Berelian

ALIEN SEX FIEND

Formed London, 1982.

Emerging from a squat in north London via such smoke-machine-infested clubs as The Batcave, **Alien Sex Fiend** were the brainchild of **Nik Wade**, aka Nik **Fiend** (vocals) and **Chrissie Wade**, aka **Mrs Fiend** (synths/programming), with **David James**, aka **Yaxi Highrizer** (guitars) and **John Freshwater**, aka **Johnny Ha-Ha** (drums). Part of the burgeoning goth scene, ASF mixed Cramps-style post-punk guitar with electro synths in the Suicide vein and the macabre theatrics of Alice Cooper. White face make-up, enough hairspray to constitute a fire hazard and speed-friendly electronic body music were the order of the day, and ASF were arch exponents of the genre.

Their debut single, "Ignore The Machine" (produced by Killing Joke bassist **Youth**), became a goth club classic, and the follow-up album, WHO'S BEEN SLEEPING IN MY BRAIN? (1983), was a psychedelic cocktail of retro-acid guitars and pulsating synth basslines, topped off with Nik Fiend's inimitably depraved vocals. Live, they were a dazzling show of lights, smoke and Nik's demented, twisting performance as the freshly revivified horror-show icon, backed up by the omnipresent synth manipulations of Mrs Fiend.

Following on with a series of club and indie chart hits with singles such as "R.I.P.", "Dead And Buried" and "E.S.T. (Trip To The Moon)" (all 1984), the next LP was the deep-fried ACID BATH. ASF's hectic global touring schedule resulted in the live LP LIQUID HEAD IN TOKYO, succeeded by MAXIMUM SECURITY in October 1985, by which time Johnny Ha-Ha had

departed. The band were the opening act on Alice Cooper's 1986 *Nightmare Returns* tour.

With IT – THE ALBUM (1986) and the HERE CUM GERMS mini-LP (1987), Alien Sex Fiend found themselves experimenting in search of new ideas, broadening their scope beyond the embers of a fast-dissipating subculture, and the compilation ALL OUR YESTERDAYS (1987) marked the end of phase one of the band's existence.

1988 brought the more synth- and sample-based ANOTHER PLANET, an electronic slant continued on 1990's epic CURSE, featuring the chemically crazed "Now I'm Feeling Zombified" single, which was a hit not only in the remaining goth clubs but also on MTV. By this point the band's line-up had changed to the Fiends plus **'Doc' Milton** (keyboards) and **Rat Fink Jr** (guitars), an outfit that recorded OPEN HEAD SURGERY in 1992. ALTERED STATES OF AMERICA (a live album) and THE LEGENDARY BATCAVE TAPES (early live recordings) appeared in 1993, before the release of a CD-ROM game, *Inferno*, in late 1994, with music provided by ASF, subsequently released as the first ever soundtrack album from a computer game. Various remixes were put out, and THE SINGLES 1983–1995 was their last for Anagram Records, their label for twelve years.

The third phase of ASF's development occurred in late 1995, when Nik and Mrs Fiend set up 13th Moon Records. The change of direction was confirmed with the release of the trancey EVOLUTION EP (1996), and the follow-up album NOCTURNAL EMISSIONS (1997), which took them yet further from their goth roots and found them at home in the hybridized multimedia landscape of millennial electronica. A new album, INFORMATION OVERLOAD, is expected sometime in 2003.

⊙ **Curse** (1990; Plague/Anagram).
Starts with the extended psychedelic quartet "Katch 22" and proceeds via "Ain't Got Time To Bleed" and the surreal "Dali-isms" to the slightly redundant throwback of "Burger Bar Baby". "Now I'm Feeling Zombified", however, is the highlight of the album. The CD includes several peculiar sound collages, and the slowed-down Cramps cover, "Mad Daddy Drives A UFO".

⊙ **The Singles 1983–1995** (1995; Plague/Anagram).
Essential double-CD compilation, which includes the A-sides of all the Fiend's singles, including the very silly "Stuff The Turkey" and the "Bootiful Dub" mix.

⊙ **Nocturnal Emissions** (1997; 13th Moon).
ASF fully embrace trance techno, aided by Pod's Mat Rowlands. Nik Fiend's vocal style is still as demented as ever, and Mrs Fiend keeps the use of samples and sound sources nicely weird. Breakbeats, bleeps and psychedelic guitars add to the *Zeitgeist*-surfing, fiendishly warping out to a new dimension.

Richard Fontenoy

ALL ABOUT EVE

Formed London, 1985; disbanded 1992; reformed 1999.

Julianne Regan (vocals, keyboards, guitar) took her first tentative step to pop stardom when she

played bass guitar on **Gene Loves Jezebel**'s debut single. She didn't last long but caught the bug, moving on to form **All About Eve**, named after a 1950 Bette Davis film, with guitarist **Tim Bricheno**.

The duo recruited **Andy Cousin** to pump the bass but chose a drum machine for their well-received first single, "D For Desire", a mix of Cocteau Twins and Banshees which struck a chord at the time. Its follow-up, "In The Clouds", led The Mission's **Wayne Hussey** to invite Regan to sing backing vocals on their debut album, a compliment Regan returned by asking Hussey to co-produce the storming "Our Summer" single, with his fellow band member **Mick Brown** on drums. By the end of 1987, the two bands had cemented their relationship, sharing both management and label (Phonogram).

Midway through the sessions for their self-titled debut album, All About Eve finally found a permanent drummer in **Mark Price**, who featured on the re-recorded version of "In The Clouds", their first major-label single. It charted, briefly, in the UK, as did their tribute to Janis Joplin, "Wild Hearted Woman". With support tours to The Shamen and The Mission, the band's profile was never higher, and ALL ABOUT EVE finally hit the British album charts in the spring of 1988.

At around this point Phonogram began to see the band's potential, and switched on the marketing. "Martha's Harbour", a plaintive, windswept acoustic lament, unexpectedly went Top 10 in the UK, and even a disastrous live *Top Of The Pops* appearance – when the backing tape wasn't fed through to the band so they had no idea what they were miming to – didn't deter record buyers.

Sessions for the second album were strained, partly because of the increasing record company pressure, but also because Regan and Bricheno had begun a relationship that effectively blocked out the rest of the band. With SCARLET (AND OTHER STORIES) (1989) they seemed to have lost the innocence and subtlety of old, replacing it with dour guitar chords. Bricheno left in 1990, joining the **Sisters Of Mercy**

and later forming industrial noise band **CNN** (later **XC-NN** after litigation threats from the Cable News Network). After brief collaborations with Wayne Hussey and The Cure's **Robert Smith**, the band found a permanent replacement in **Marty Willson-Piper** (already holding down a dual role as solo artist and member of Australian band The Church). Anxious to put the past behind them, they began work on their third album, TOUCHED BY JESUS (1991), with **Warne Livesey**, noted left-field producer, replacing old stalwart **Paul Samwell-Smith**. The result was dramatic, ditching all hint of previous tweeness and dourness. Yet the album failed to give Phonogram the hit they were looking for and both sides were relieved when the label opted out of a fourth album.

All About Eve promptly signed to MCA Records, who gave them carte blanche to produce ULTRAVIOLET (1992), a serious statement of intent, but, alas, a short-lived one. Phonogram spoiled its release with a greatest hits package, the singles charted briefly and, after one further swansong single, "Some Finer Day", the band split.

Subsequently, Cousin joined **THE MISSION**, Price went into session work and Willson-Piper returned to his dual career. Regan has appeared at Fairport Convention's annual reunion festival, and in 1995 formed a band called **Mice**, who released their debut album, BECAUSE I CAN in 1996. Featuring ex-Eve members Andy Cousin and Mark Price plus guitarist **Bic** (ex-Cardiacs), it took ULTRAVIOLET into a more extreme, indie direction and was eventually reissued in 2001 as BECAUSE I CAN – NEW & IMPROVED.

All About Eve reformed in late 1999 to the surprise and delight of press and fans alike. They played several critically acclaimed live shows, later documented on disc. Regan and Cousin were joined by keyboardist **Rik Carter** (The Mission), drummer **Del Hood**, and a new guitarist **Toni Haimi**, who joined from the band **Malluka**. More recently, Del departed to be replaced by **Robin Guy** of the band **Rachel Stamp**. An enchanting new studio collection, ICELAND, appeared in 2002.

All About Eve (1988; Mercury).
This debut album is a folk/goth barnstormer, ranging from lilting ballads to the riff-monster crunch of "In The Meadow" – a live highlight. Every other All About Eve album has points for and against. There are no againsts here.

Duncan Harris

THE ALLMAN BROTHERS BAND

Formed Macon, Georgia, 1969; disbanded 1976; re-formed 1978; disbanded 1982; re-formed 1991.

This is a story of sex, drugs and Cher. **The Allman Brothers Band** are a barely walking concordance of rock lore, open to heroin and hatred, murdered tunes and murdered people. The brainchild of whizzkid guitarist **Duane Allman**, the band initiated the 70s Southern rock boom that would result in R.E.M.'s world domination. They paid the price, but made some classic rock along the way.

Duane was born in Nashville on November 20, 1946, and soaked up the music of the South as his military family moved from state to state. When not tearing around Daytona Beach on his motorcycle, he studied B. B. King and Coltrane. The blond brothers Duane and **Gregg** (vocals/organ) hung with black musicians – a no-no in the segregated South – and formed the **Allman Joys**, Brit-invasion blues boomers with a Florida drawl. Gregg shot himself in the foot to avoid the draft and the band toured the garbage circuit before landing a deal with West Coast label Liberty.

As **Hourglass** they recorded two hopeless albums in 1968, and split. Gregg's whiskey-soaked vocals gave him continued employment at Liberty, while Duane worked as a sideman at the Muscle Shoals studio in Alabama, coaxing from his bottleneck a battery of tones for anyone from Wilson Pickett to Delaney and Bonnie. When asked how he'd become so shit hot, he replied, 'Man, I took speed every night for three years and practiced.' Otis Redding's manager Phil Walden came out of retirement to snap him up.

Duane preferred working off others to composing. He was searching for a new music in a wilderness of jamming. The Allman Brothers Band became his knights: Gregg, **Dickey Betts** (guitar/vocals), **Berry Oakley** (bass), **Butch Trucks** (drums) and Otis Redding's old drummer **Jaimoe Johanson** – Duane wanted two drummers to provide the muscle of James Brown's band. He got a spiritual brotherhood whose bond was such that each tattooed a mushroom to his ankle to reflect their taste for psychedelics. These good ole boys could turn the blues into a rainbow.

The pot of gold was at the end of every two-bit dive with a stage, and they played them all. Opportunity knocked when Bill Graham made them fixtures at his two Fillmore venues. They adopted Macon, Georgia, as their home, composing in the local graveyard. The Allmans' gumbo of jazzy improvisation and apocalyptic ballads respected their Delta roots, explored the hallucinogenic future, and made more sense the more you inhaled. They walked a razor edge, with Duane as an unhinged Aguirre, bullying and cajoling Gregg to greater songwriting heights.

THE ALLMAN BROTHERS BAND (1969) and IDLEWILD SOUTH (named after the Macon mansion the group shared) were as smooth as a cotton gin. Their real heart lay between the grooves of THE ALLMAN BROTHERS AT FILLMORE EAST (1971), a double LP dominated by the sweaty side-long mantra "Whipping Post". By 1970 they were *the* American band – a Dead unafraid to boogie. Duane sat in on Eric Clapton's LAYLA (1970) sessions, too, and dominated the whole album. The great "Layla" riff and

closing slide symphony were his, a tribute to Charlie Parker.

A motorcycle crash unplugged his amp in 1971, and a shattered Berry Oakley died in a similar accident a year later. The bereaved band remained on the road and attached to a drip-feed of drugs and nymphets, relying on an unruly Mafia of roadies (pictured on the back of the FILLMORE EAST album) to keep them alive.

Gregg went from Duane's whipping post to a drug-filled punching bag, getting it together to record EAT A PEACH (1973) – a grab bag of new and live tunes featuring Duane. "Mountain Jam", his variations on a theme by Donovan, took up an entire disc. The Allmans still had the courage to make a sterling album like BROTHERS AND SISTERS (1973), but they also made do with slop like WIN, LOSE OR DRAW (1975). Live, they still smoked – with **Chuck Leavell** (piano) replacing Duane – and played to 600,000 people at the 1973 Watkins Glen Summer Jam.

Betts took over the songwriting. His "Rambling Man" reached #2 in the US that year and kept the band afloat and poppy. Manager Walden also ran their Capricorn record company, and screwed them out of royalties. Endless touring paid the bills. But Jaimoe's jazz leanings pissed off the conservative Betts. Ructions formed.

Tired of the view from a Greyhound bus, Gregg fled to LA and married Cher in 1975. The marriage broke up pretty well instantly when he started demanding she call him 'Mr Allman' – when he was around, that is, because Gregg could disappear for days, searching out his next fix. Fans got their kicks from the smelly hillbillyisms of Lynyrd Skynyrd, while lame solo projects like Gregg's PLAYIN' UP A STORM, DICKEY BETTS AND GREAT SOUTHERN, and Leavell and Jaimoe's SEA LEVEL filled the bargain bins.

The final straw came in 1976 when Gregg testified against his personal pusher Scooter Herring, in return for amnesty. The band now barely spoke to each other, but let Gregg know that he might as well have loosened the screws on Duane's Harley. The fans were similarly disgusted, although they still turn out in their Stars and Bars-bedecked droves for the frequent cash-register-ringing 'reunions' that end with one or more members storming off stage midset.

Record sales, if not fraternity, got them inducted into the Rock And Roll Hall Of Fame. It was recognition that, in 1970, the Allmans handed the South their pride and musical heritage, while reaching heights many other bands only dreamt of (stand up, Black Oak Arkansas). Losing their most inspiring members was their Gettysburg, and they have toured with the looks of ghosts and the grudge of the defeated ever since.

Beginnings (1974; Capricorn).
The first two albums – ALLMAN BROTHERS BAND and IDLEWILD SOUTH – on one CD. Standout track is "Whipping Post", Gregg's acute analysis of his relationship with Duane, who responds with lashings of guitar.

The Allman Brothers At Fillmore East (1971; Capricorn).
On the nights of March 12 and 13, 1971, Duane could have turned water into Old Thunderbird. The voodoo atmosphere is as heavy as swamp gas, and the Allmans play like the future of the Confederacy depended on it. Tobacco juice in the eye for those who say all live albums are crap.

Eat A Peach (1973; Capricorn).
A version of a Donovan song longer than his entire career? Fans swear by it. On "Ain't Wastin' Time No More" the band acknowledged their loss while making felt their intentions to storm heaven in search of their muse.

Brothers And Sisters (1973; Capricorn).
The post-Duane Allman Brothers delivered only once. "Rambling Man" is deft and evocative and, if "Jessica" didn't exist, car manufacturers would have had to create it. Take the top down!

Charles Bottomley

MARC ALMOND

Born Southport, England, 1961.

In 1982, looking for a less commercial outlet for his ideas than **SOFT CELL**, vocalist **Marc Almond** released the UNTITLED LP (reissued 1998), credited to **Marc & The Mambas**. Featuring **Billy McGee** and the classically trained **Annie Hogan** (both of whom stayed with Almond throughout the 80s), The Mambas were a mainly acoustic line-up, and gave Almond the freedom to explore a variety of styles –

the LP included covers of songs by Jacques Brel, Scott Walker and Lou Reed.

By the release of the final Soft Cell record in 1984, Marc & The Mambas had released a second LP, the passionate, sprawling TORMENTS AND TOREROS (1983; reissued 1998). The album provoked extremely mixed reactions, and soon afterwards Almond announced the dissolution of The Mambas and his retirement from the music business. This retirement was very short-lived, as late 1984 brought the appropriately titled single "The Boy Who Came Back", and an album, VERMIN IN ERMINE, (reissued 1998) recorded with new band **The Willing Sinners**. Titles such as "Hell Was A City" and "Gutter Hearts" showed Almond's interests still lay in the seedier side of life, but the theatricality of the album's sleeve suggested that Almond was willing to have a joke at his own expense, and the expense of anyone opposed to any whiff of showmanship.

Never happy with Phonogram, Almond switched to Virgin in mid-1985, and rewarded them with a fair-sized hit in "Stories of Johnny", the title track of a new and poppier LP. The hits were becoming rarer, but the press were starting to pay attention to Almond's improving voice and his interpretative powers – always happy with other artists' songs, Almond was now more a traditional torch singer than a conventional rock/pop performer.

Marc and friend – who's a pretty boy then?

This was confirmed by his next release, the mini-LP A WOMAN'S STORY (1986), which consisted entirely of obscure cover versions. Almond's bisexuality and his fascination with drag and transvestism gave him licence to tackle songs written specifically for women, without changing the gender. Major chart action continued to elude him, though, and 1987's downbeat, controversial MOTHER FIST AND HER FIVE DAUGHTERS (reissued 1998) proved to be a step too far for Virgin.

Almond's debut LP for Parlophone, THE STARS WE ARE (1988), turned out to be his most commercial solo offering to date, and this latest comeback was completed when his duet with **Gene Pitney** on a remake of "Something's Gotten Hold Of My Heart" topped the British charts for a month in early 1989, and was a considerable success worldwide.

Typically, Almond followed this with a profoundly uncommercial set, JACQUES (1990), a venture endorsed by Brel's widow but unloved by most. Another LP for Parlophone, ENCHANTED (1990), despite boasting some of Almond's finest songs to date, was neither a commercial nor artistic success, and the singer and label parted company. However, chart success came in 1991 with another contemporary-sounding effort, TENEMENT SYMPHONY, released on WEA, and produced by arch pop stylist **Trevor Horn**, with contributions from **Dave Ball**, formerly the other half of Soft Cell, and now with **THE GRID**. Preceded by a heavily dance-orientated version of Brel's "Jacky" (which made the UK Top 20), the album also featured another 60s cover, David McWilliams' "The Days Of Pearly Spencer", which returned Almond to the UK Top 5 in 1992.

In the autumn of 1992, Almond bade farewell to his high-profile career in spectacular fashion with *Twelve Years Of Tears*, two grand retrospective concerts, the latter at London's Royal Albert Hall, with an album, TWELVE YEARS OF TEARS (1993), to put the icing on the cake. Soon afterwards he released the single "What Makes A Man A Man", his most openly gay statement on record so far, which duly fell foul of the self-appointed censors who have dogged Almond's unconventional career. He followed this with a distinctly low-key release, ABSINTHE (1993), an album of old French songs plus arrangements of poems by Baudelaire and Rimbaud.

In 1995, Almond released TREASURE BOX and returned to the live stage with a new band featuring ex-Sigue Sigue Sputnik man, **Neil X**, and a much tougher sound, epitomized by the pseudo glam-rock single "The Idol". This presaged FANTASTIC STAR (1996), an album recorded in New York with a big cast and a lush sound.

In 1998 Almond collaborated with **Jim Thirlwell** (aka **FOETUS**) for FLESH VOLCANO/SLUT – an unconventional and disturbing blend of the camp and industrial schools of modern pop. OPEN ALL NIGHT (1999) returned to the more familiar sound of synths and strings via the West End stage and Montmartre with two standout duets on "Theatre Of Love" (with Siouxsie Sioux & The Creatures) and "Almost Diamonds" (with **Kelly Dayton** formerly of the Sneaker Pimps).

After seventeen years away Almond reconvened Soft Cell for a warmly received solo tour. Far from entering nostalgia circuit drudgery Almond et al sounded wonderfully fresh and, revitalized, the duo recorded a new album, CRUELTY WITHOUT BEAUTY (2002). But before that came Almond's thirteenth solo album, STRANGER THINGS (2001). There's a furtive whiff still lingering around his brassy, theatrical campery; Almond's persona takes its lead from Joel Grey's knowing emcee in *Cabaret*, a nudging, winking star brave enough to wear his heart on his sleeve and revel in the glorious seediness of life.

⊙ **A Virgin's Tale Vols. 1 & 2** (1992; Virgin).
The nearest to a definitive compilation and the easiest way to track down neglected gems like "Blond Boy", Scott Walker's "The Plague", Brecht's "Surabaya Johnny" and the inimitable "I'm Sick Of You Tasting Of Somebody Else".

Joe Nahmad

ALTERNATIVE TV (ATV)

Formed London, 1976; disbanded 1978; re-formed 1981 and 1995.

Short-lived but enormously influential, **Alternative TV** (usually abbreviated to **ATV**) was formed by punk's most experienced observer, **Mark Perry** (vocals/guitar), who, as **Mark P**, was the founder, editor and main writer on London's seminal punk rock fanzine, *Sniffin Glue*. His aggressive, belligerent writing style indicated that when he formed ATV, with guitarist **Alex Ferguson**, bassist and sometime guitarist **Tyrone Thomas** and drummer **Chris Bennett**, it would be a similarly defiant venture.

ATV had ideas and a musical confidence that other punks found hard to understand, much less emulate. Stumbling, delirious and intense, like a street-ranting drunk, ATV had a vision to deliver. Early songs such as "Alternatives To NATO", "Love Lies Limp" and "These Are The Good Times" dealt with isolation, fear, violence and impotence. When the young punks were still trying to find an image, queuing up to buy overpriced shock-tactic clothes from Malcolm McLaren, ATV were already asking, 'How much longer will people wear/Nazi armbands and dye their hair?'.

The music, too, went a little further, especially live. Influenced by The Velvet Underground, Zappa and The Stooges, it boomed around the hall, colliding with tape cut-ups and other sound effects. There was a William Burroughs feel to performances; songs blended one into another, and a concise three-minute statement at one gig could easily turn into a twenty-minute improvised harangue the following evening.

Apart from the flexi-disc of "Love Lies Limp", given away with *Sniffin Glue*, the band preferred to spread the word by playing live. It wasn't until the end of 1977 that the first single, "How Much Longer?"/"You Bastard", was released. Its raw power was pretty much of its time but it had a bit more anger, a bit more sincerity, than the rest. Subsequent releases lost that initial edge, as the band looked to more complex expressions of their art.

Before they got to the studio to record their first LP, THE IMAGE HAS CRACKED, produced by **John Cale**, Ferguson had left to form **The Cash Pussies**, while Thomas had moved elsewhere, owing to 'musical differences'. Their replacements – **Mark Linehan** (guitar), **Dennis Burns** (bass) and ex-Chelsea and Generation X drummer **John Towe** – were more malleable, and ATV increasingly became an outlet for Perry's angst alone.

By refusing to compromise, Perry had little chance of stardom, so he settled on becoming a minor legend instead. By the end of 1978, with only the faithful Burns remaining from the line-up, he strode boldly into the undergrowth of hippiedom and the avant-garde. For a time, he teamed up with **Genesis P. Orridge**, toured with **Here & Now** (a gaggle of well-meaning but overtly stoned hippies – see **GONG**, and changed his band name to **The Good Missionaries** and **The Door And The Window**. He returned with the original ATV line-up, however, at the end of 1981 for STRANGE KICKS, a power-packed wedge of personal venom.

Everything Perry has produced since then has veered towards the experimental. His voice – capable of more venom than Johnny Rotten ever managed – is always worth a listen and his lyrics can be compelling, but the music provides a challenging evening's entertainment. If you're curious, take a listen to MY LIFE AS A CHILD STAR, which provides an interesting sidelight on the 70s mayhem. Alternatively, try and catch Perry live. He re-formed ATV again in 1995 with his old partners and has gigged sporadically in London ever since. APOLLO (1999), saw him working alongside the **Ugly Brothers** (with whom Perry has also worked in **The Long Decline**), magicking up a distinctive south London meets Latin America sound. It was followed in 2001 by the reinitiated punk sound of REVOLUTION.

⊙ **The Image Has Cracked** (1978; Deptford Fun City). Track down this vinyl-only first LP: Perry's sour-eyed vision was at its most acute, while Jools Holland (of southeast London neighbours Squeeze) feeds in over-the-top overdubs. The first track is a collage of live sets where the audience has been invited to use the stage as their 'own personal soapbox'.

⊙ **Splitting In Two – Selected Viewing** (1989; Anagram). All the early singles plus an introduction to Perry's early wanderings in hippieland with "The Good Missionaries" and the eerie "Force Is Blind".

Al Spicer

THE AMBOY DUKES

Formed Detroit, Michigan, 1968; disbanded 1975.

There are two reasons why **The Amboy Dukes** matter. Firstly their 1968 US hit "Journey To The Centre Of The Mind" remains one of the defining cuts of the psychedelic era, combining psychedelia, garage band grunt and classic pop hooks. Secondly, the band launched heavy metal hard man **Ted Nugent**, one of rock's more notable characters. Their history also contains a few entertaining events.

Nugent formed the Dukes in 1966 and like many garage bands of the era the line-up soon mastered a set drawn from US rock'n'roll and the R&B-inspired bands from the first wave of the British invasion. A spirited reworking of "I'm Not A Juvenile Delinquent" was an early cut and the band's first real success came when their version of Them's "Baby Please Don't Go" became a local radio hit.

Blooded on live work and hungry for success, the latter mainly on the strength of Nugent's fierce ambition, The Amboy Dukes embraced the self-conscious self-realization of hippie-era pop and by August 1968 had themselves a big hit single. "Journey To The Centre Of The Mind" hit #16 in the US and dragged the album of the same title to #74. Developing an overblown style similar to burgeoning UK 'progressive' outfits of the time, the Dukes earned underground US success on the back of the cringingly pretentious lyrics of **Steve Farmer** (guitar/vocals) and Nugent's increasingly showy displays.

Musical divisions were never far from the surface, and when subsequent releases failed to match the success of "Journey", Nugent's irrepressible ambition began to forge a new direction for the band. The early 70s were marked by line-up changes, ceaseless gigging and a musical style that gradually returned to the hard garage rock of Detroit contemporaries like the MC5 and Stooges before mutating again into full-blown heavy metal. The billing went from Amboy Dukes, via Ted Nugent And The Amboy Dukes to Ted Nugent's Amboy Dukes, as Nugent moved the Dukes from the centre of the mind to the female reproductive organs, and threw in a few songs about his beloved blood sports to vary things.

It is testament to Nugent's drive that a terminally unfashionable band managed to lodge albums between #150 and #200 in the US charts. This was achieved on the back of 150 to 200 gigs a year in the first half of the 70s. Nugent staged ridiculously hyped guitar 'duels' in which he would trade licks with other emerging metal heroes such as **Frank Marino**. Meanwhile he became famous for firing personnel who had any involvement with drugs, and by 1974 his blood-sports skills had won him a national squirrel-shooting contest. Nugent took out a helpless animal on a tree from a distance of 150 yards to win the title. Some two dozen other bushy-tailed creatures bit the dust along the way to this grande finale.

By early 1975 Nugent's efforts had gained him what he wanted: a contract with Aerosmith's management and a solo deal with the potential for serious money. Poaching bassist **Rob Grange** from the final Dukes line-up, who were little more than Nugent's backing band anyway, he embarked on a howling heavy metal career that would see him headlining massive festival bills within five years and touring behind the slogan 'If it's too loud you're too old'. Nugent would mark the crowning moment of his career, a headlining slot to 250,000 at California Jam II, by announcing that he couldn't wait to finish his set and sample some 'sweet Californian pussy'. America's wildlife doubtless breathed a sigh of relief every time Ted headed out on another marathon tour, but Nugent got his own back by sinking some of his massive rock earnings into a restaurant called – appropriately enough – *Red Meat*.

○ **Journeys And Migrations** (1973; Mainstream – vinyl only).
Currently out of print, with luck you'll find a secondhand copy of this double compilation, which is such a solid period piece that it's worth the (normally) extortionate asking price.

⊙ **Journey Through The Underground Volume II** (1994; Disky Communications).
The Dukes rub shoulders with tracks by the likes of Moby Grape and Commander Cody And His Lost Planet Airmen in a compilation that gives a real feel of the underground scene that produced The Amboy Dukes.

Neil Nixon

AMERICA

Formed London, 1970.

America's founding fathers – **Dan Peek** (guitar/vocals), **Gerry Beckley** (guitar/keyboards/bass/vocals) and **Dewey Bunnell** (guitar/vocals) – came together in Britain, where their folks were stationed in US military bases. It was an ironic twist for a band steeped in American country-rock and named after their homeland.

After a low-key start, performing in folk clubs, they auditioned at the offices of Warner Brothers, where the trio carried guitars into the office and played their entire first album, plus a song called "Horse With No Name". Warners promptly released this as a single and it became a worldwide chart-topper in 1972 – and remains today a staple track of classic rock radio.

America's accessible folk-rock style, criticized by some as a pale imitation of Crosby, Stills, Nash And Young, sent their debut album, AMERICA (1972), to #1 in the States. This was closely followed by a second Top 10 album, HOMECOMING (1972) and the ambitious HAT TRICK (1973), a commercial failure but arguably one of country-rock's great lost albums. The band's response to this lack of sales was a characteristically pragmatic decision – they brought in **George Martin** as producer.

Martin echoed his work with The Beatles, wrapping inventive arrangements around direct songs on HOLIDAY (1974), HEARTS (1975), HIDEAWAY (1976) and HARBOUR (1977), and giving them a second US chart-topper in 1975 with "Sister Golden Hair". Meanwhile the arrivals of **David Dickey** (bass) and **Willie Leacox** (drums) allowed the band to reproduce the studio sound in a live setting. The band's style, simpler and poppier than other country-rock

giants, found acclaim almost everywhere except the UK, where they gave up gigging in 1974.

In 1977, Peek's born-again Christianity led to his departure for more spiritual musical pastures. Electing to continue as a duo, Beckley and Bunnell signed to Capitol Records, and targeted a more MOR audience. As the 70s petered out, America could console themselves with the thought that they had outgigged and out-recorded most of the country-rock competition and outsold them all apart from The Eagles.

1982 saw America's return to the US Top 10 with the single "You Can Do Magic", which even dented the bottom end of the UK charts. In 1985, unable to secure a high-profile record deal, they parted company from Capitol Records and since then the duo's CV has ranged from songwriting for Wild Man Fischer to session work on a *Simpsons* TV tie-in album. Their own material has been dominated by reissues, though 1994 saw a return to the studio with HOURGLASS, which did well commercially and with the critics.

Although America have tended to be seen as bland, they have maintained a huge international fan base, and in a few surprising quarters, too – British indie-dance act Ultramarine dedicated their brilliant 1992 album, EVERY MAN AND WOMAN IS A STAR, to Dewey. A measure of the faith the band had managed to rekindle by the mid-90s was the long-term contract they signed with Oxygen Records, HUMAN NATURE (1998) being the first result. *Billboard* magazine called it 'Vintage America', a good description for a sound that now combined the classic AOR angle with a hint of the folky roots of the 70s.

Since then the group have issued a Christmas album, HOLIDAY HARMONY (2002), and an acoustic live collection, THE GRAND CAYMAN CONCERT (2002).

⊙ **America** (1972; Warner Brothers).
Fine acoustic guitar work and close harmonies from a band just into their twenties. The CD reissue includes "Horse With No Name".

⊙ **Hat Trick** (1973; Warner Brothers).
A subtle and at times spine-tingling collection featuring an eight-minute title track built from three separate songs, and multi-layered production.

⊙ **America Live** (1978; Warner Brothers).
Currently out of print, this is arguably a better representation of their 70s work than the platinum-selling greatest hits collection, HISTORY.

⊙ **Hourglass** (1994; American Gramophone).
A quality example of vintage adult country-rock.

⊙ **Live On The King Biscuit Flower Hour** (1998; Strange Fruit).
America are inveterate giggers, still playing note-perfect renditions of the old favourites. The attraction here is the chance to hear the stuff live and to marvel at the harmonies and pristine sound. Good gig, too.

⊙ **Human Nature** (1998; Oxygen).
Beckley has the lion's share of composing on an album that rekindles some of the spirit of HOURGLASS but lacks the songs to appeal to those outside the die-hard audience. "Hidden Talent" features some of the last vocals ever recorded by Beach Boy Carl Wilson.

Neil Nixon

AMERICAN MUSIC CLUB

Formed San Francisco, 1986; disbanded 1995.

Any evaluation of **American Music Club** inevitably focuses on its frontman, **Mark Eitzel** (guitar/vocals), considered by many to be one of the greatest songwriters of recent times. Though on first hearing Eitzel and his colleagues – **Dan Pearson** (bass), **Tom Mallon** (guitar) and **Vudi** (guitar) – would appear to be playing a fairly traditional strain of country-rock, American Music Club at their best utterly transcended the conservatism of the genre through Eitzel's unflinching view of existential desperation, and a musical hard edge which was the legacy of a background in the early-80s San Francisco punk scene.

The raw exposure of Eitzel's songs would be unbearable were it not for the world-weary humour and compassion that tempers them. Set in the doomed romantic's milieu of late-night rainy streets, shadowy bars and shabby bedsits, they relate the bruised life of the emotional outsider, trampled by life but never quite ready to give up. In these songs love is both a beacon of redemption and a ritual of subjugation, while alcohol assumes the mantle of salvation. Unsurprisingly, AMC's music has been adopted by a generation of bedsit dreamers, who have hailed Mark Eitzel as a genius, much to his own embarrassment.

The group's first release was THE RESTLESS STRANGER (1986; reissued by WEA 1998), a not particularly impressive debut, which was followed up by the far more successful ENGINE the next year. Although more straightforwardly a rock record than their later material, this album already indicated American Music Club's urge to strip their music to its bare bones, as well as highlighting Eitzel's central lyrical concerns in songs such as "Electric Light" and "Outside This Bar".

ENGINE was succeeded by the band's two unequivocal masterpieces, CALIFORNIA (1988) and UNITED KINGDOM (1989), which included some of Eitzel's most haunting writing. The stark expression of the lyrics was matched in the skeletal minimalism of the music, with its use of space and silence, eerie washes of feedback, and mournful pedal steel. These two records were complemented by a live solo album from Eitzel, SONGS OF LOVE (1991), which featured many of the songs from this period effectively stripped down even further.

A more polished radio-friendly sound was in evidence on the group's next studio album, EVERCLEAR (1991), which was named after a particularly potent malt liquor brew. Despite its tendency towards overproduction, the record still found Eitzel's intensity undimmed, still drinking deep of life's bitterest dregs, but laughing as he choked. Perhaps in reaction against the musically more commercial direction of this record, Eitzel took time off from American Music Club to work with **Toiling Midgets**, a grungier side-project which produced the patchy SON album in 1992.

By now Eitzel was beginning to weary of his image as patron saint of lost souls, claiming in interviews that he was, as he had once sung, 'tired of being a spokesman for every tired thing'. As a result American Music Club's next LP, MERCURY (1993), saw him upping his tone of self-deprecation virtually to the point of self-parody; it constituted something of a disappointment. It also increased the overproduction, which EVERCLEAR had managed to survive, to the extent that much of the band's subtlety had been lost. SAN FRANCISCO (1994), their final album, unfortunately continued this tendency.

Although Eitzel and his colleagues had long been favourites with the critics, they never achieved a great

American Music Club's Mark Eitzel

deal of popular success, and it was perhaps in the face of this that they finally disbanded in 1995. Eitzel returned the following year with a more jazz-tinged solo album, 60 WATT SILVER LINING, which was well received by the critics, as well as by fans of one of rock's great lost causes.

He returned to the record stores with WEST (1997; Warner Brothers) having changed direction significantly and moved towards a feeling of optimism. Helped out, no doubt, by the companionship of R.E.M.'s **Peter Buck** on guitar and other rock-'n'roll therapists, the album at times verges on jollity. Longer-standing enthusiasts will be relieved by the gloom evident in "Old Photographs" and "Helium" but there's an infectious catchiness to "Move Myself Ahead" that they should be warned of in advance.

After the release of the 1998 album CAUGHT IN A TRAP AND I CAN'T BACK OUT 'CAUSE I LOVE YOU TOO MUCH BABY, Eitzel took a three year sabbatical, resurfacing with the sparse, electronically backed THE INVISIBLE MAN (2001). The following year, he returned with an admirably eclectic collection of covers, MUSIC FOR COURAGE AND CONFIDENCE (2002). Few would attempt to release an album encompassing compositions by Phil Ochs, Culture Club, Bill Withers, Anne Murray and Curtis Mayfield, but Eitzel confirmed his interpretative strengths.

American Music Club

⊙ **California** (1988; Frontier/Demon).
Minimalist songs of life on the edge between hope and defeat, laughter and despair. Absolutely essential.

⊙ **United Kingdom** (1989; Frontier/Demon).
AMC's most austere recording, UNITED KINGDOM yields more on every hearing. Returning again and again to the theme of dreams and disillusionment, in "Kathleen" it boasts Eitzel's single most poignant evocation of dispossession.

Mark Eitzel

⊙ **Songs Of Love** (1991; Demon).
A live set capturing Eitzel's performance in all its brilliant awkwardness, this album brings out the humour as well as the visceral truth in his scenarios of brutality.

Ian Canadine

AMON DÜÜL II

Formed Munich, Germany, 1968; disbanded 1980; sporadically active from 1981; 'officially' re-formed 1992.

Krautrock – that late-60s phenomenon so beloved of Julian Cope and specialist record stores – emerged in large part from the German political and musical underground. It was from these murky waters that the eleven-strong **Amon Düül** commune came into being in 1967, and swiftly split into two. Both offshoots encompassed bands and performed at the 1968 Essen Festival. It was the branch known as **Amon Düül II**, however, that caught the ear. While Amon Düül, their erstwhile colleagues,

brought forth ('produced' would be too generous) almost unlistenable studio jams, based around excessive chanting and percussion, Düül II began a journey that was to produce some of the most haunting and disturbing music of the period.

The band's stalwarts were guitarists **Chris Karrer** and **John Weinzierl**, singer **Renate** and drummer **Peter Leopold**. The original bassist, **Dave Anderson**, soon departed for **HAWKWIND**, to be replaced by **Lothar Meid**, an inventive player whose work rivalled American heroes like Phil Lesh and Jack Casady. Early Düül II recordings also featured a variety of guest artists, many associated with the jazz-rock group **Embryo**.

Amon Düül II's debut album, PHALLUS DEI (1969), had a feeling of controlled experimentation, notably on the side-long title track – a far more radical piece than anything being put out by, say, Pink Floyd during the same period. The band moved to the United Artists label – home of their archrivals, Can – for YETI (1970) and DANCE OF THE LEMMINGS (1971), which consolidated their reputation in prog-rock circles. Each featured short, driving acid-rock songs ("Archangel's Thunderbird" on YETI boasts one of the great bone-shaking guitar riffs) plus lengthy improvisations: YETI was adorned by "Sandoz In The Rain" (featuring two members of the 'other' Amon Düül), while the first record of LEMMINGS was devoted to side-long suites by each of the guitarists.

Two LPs followed in 1972 – CARNIVAL IN BABYLON and WOLF CITY – but the patchy LIVE IN LONDON (1973) suggested all was not well, and members started to drift away, some to temporary sojourns in other bands (Embryo, **Popol Vuh**), some permanently. Amon Düül II released several more albums but officially broke up in 1980, by which time Karrer or Weinzierl was often the only original member present. After a brief re-formation for VORTEX (1981), there was a further split.

Yet, towards the end of the decade, recordings started to emerge from Wales, where Dave Anderson had a studio. Most of these were credited to Amon Düül (UK), and were disowned by the original members – even by Weinzierl, who'd been involved in their production. Meanwhile, in 1989, some of the original band re-formed at a memorial concert for ex-Hawkwind lyricist Robert Calvert (who, confusingly, had himself appeared on some of the Welsh recordings). It was a temporary gig, for at this time Weinzierl was working in Austria a great deal, while Karrer was collaborating with Italian, Asian and African musicians, as well as with Embryo.

In 1992, however, the main protagonists reunited, after a bracing courtroom tussle over rights to the band name, and a more permanent arrangement was announced. A CD release, BBC IN CONCERT PLUS (1992), containing archive recordings, was a striking testimony to the old Amon Düül II, and SURROUNDED BY BARS, a 1993 release, comprised ten re-recordings of earlier work. The re-formed band produced a trio of new songs for NADA MOONSHINE (1996) and brought out a fairly uninspiring LIVE IN TOKYO album in 1997. A more promising release, FLAWLESS (1997; Mystic), featuring new material, re-recordings and remixes of older material, was published to celebrate the band's 30th anniversary. New chapters in the Amon Düül saga may yet be written.

⊙ **Yeti** (1970; Repertoire).
Awesome and essential, veering from deranged hard rock to gentle improvisation.

⊙ **Dance Of The Lemmings** (1971; Repertoire).
Another classic from the fertile early years.

Gerard F. Tierney

Thanks to Paul O'Brien for updates

TORI AMOS

Born North Carolina, 1963.

"If your work is any more than one dimension, you believe in faeries... alternate realities make you a good writer."

OK, first thing about **Tori Amos** is that she is well out-there. This is a woman who talks of Jesus and Lucifer like college friends, believes in faeries as a matter of course, and views anyone who lacks her sense of 'alternate realities' with great suspicion. This is a woman, and a lyricist, who based the fourteen songs of one album around the myth of the Egyptian gods Osiris and Isis, and named the disc – BOYS FOR PELE – in honour not of the great Brazilian footballer but of a Hawaiian goddess. This is a woman who makes Kate Bush – with whom, throughout her career, she has been compared – appear positively grounded. And she is loved for it all by legions of fans, selling out tours without need of a hit single, and dominating cyberspace with perhaps the most Net traffic of any musicians bar The Grateful Dead.

Amos, ... and part-C... and raised in ... playing piano in t... viewed as a prodigy, w... sical piano at Baltimore ... There, in her early teens, sh... especially Led Zeppelin. By 13, s... her studies and was performing he... Washington DC clubs.

Amos recorded a single, "Baltimore", for a... label in that city, but in 1984 moved to Los Ang... where, renaming herself Tori, she fronted a band called **Y Kant Tori Read**. This was also the title of her first album, for Atlantic, in 1988: it was pop-metal fare, with a corseted Tori waving a sabre on the cover, and perhaps deservedly ignored by press and public alike. The group soon folded – drummer **Matt Sorrum** going on to better things with **Guns N' Roses**) and Amos went back to the piano to write a new set of songs.

The experiences of this frustrating period were to emerge on Amos's first solo album, LITTLE EARTHQUAKES (1992), a sparse set of songs, introducing her distinctive piano sound – which she plays like a rock'n'roll instrument – alongside lyrics as personal as any singer-songwriter of the decade. These included, most famously, "Me And A Gun", an account of the singer's rape by an acquaintance, which Amos performed on stage in a husky, 'come on' whisper, legs astride the piano stool. The album broke first in London, where Amos moved to play club gigs, going gold there in 1992, and in the US a year later. It was compared, inevitably, with Kate Bush: the cover image alone invited such reviews, and Amos actually sounded (and still, at times, sounds) uncannily like Bush on some of the songs. However, its originality and strength, both in lyrics and melodies, and the complexity of its piano playing and orchestration, suggested far more than a Kate Bush clone; indeed a talent that stood in line with the likes of Joni Mitchell.

Charged by this success, Amos recorded an EP of intriguing covers, CRUCIFY (1992), paying homage to Led Zeppelin ("Thank You"), The Rolling Stones ("Angie") and Nirvana ("Smells Like Teen Spirit") in versions absolutely her own. She then turned back to her own songs, producing the million-selling UNDER THE PINK (1994) album. The Kate Bush comparisons returned to haunt the reviews, and seemed justified with the vocal approach of the lead-off single "Cornflake Girl", a Top 10 hit in both the US and UK (the album itself again hit #1 in the UK and reached #12 in the US). It was an adventurous record, nonetheless, exploring her fundamentalist background on "God" and delving deeper into the personal psyche than most singer-songwriters allowed themselves.

A 250-date world tour revealed Amos's strength as a performer and the size and commitment of her

engineer since 1994 – the following March and recorded a new album, FROM THE CHOIRGIRL HOTEL (1998), which reached the upper levels of the chart both in the UK and in the US. A deeply personal album with triumph and tragedy woven throughout the lyrics, this was also Amos's most mature and reflective work musically. Standout track "Raspberry Swirl" (as in the saucy lyrical advice 'Boy, you'd better make her raspberry swirl') blended her best sardonic attitude with elegant electronics, taking the edge off the kookiness and leaving a pleasant aftertaste.

To VENUS AND BACK (1999) began as a live album project but, with Amos suddenly delivering a clutch of new compositions, it expanded into a 2-CD set, divided into studio (Venus Orbiting) and live discs (Still Orbiting). It maintained her ethereal style, but her 2001 album STRANGE LITTLE GIRLS, was more of a curiosity. A compilation of covers, it offered Amos's take on songs composed by male writers from Neil Young and Joe Jackson to Depeche Mode's Martin Gore and Eminem.

After such an intriguing compendium of covers, 2002's SCARLET'S WALK was distinctly disappointing and offered little more than a tired retread of old paths paved with plodding piano and brow-furrowing lyrics.

⊙ **Little Earthquakes** (1992; Atlantic/East West).
As fine an example of the modern singer-songwriter trade as can be found: tightly written melodies and moodily simple production lend plenty of space to Amos's voice.

⊙ **Boys For Pele** (1996; Atlantic/EastWest).
Four years on, this wild, off-the-wall allbum suggests Amos is an enduring talent, prepared to experiment without regard for hits – and all the more appreciated for it.

⊙ **To Venus And Back** (1999; EastWest).
The complexity of previous outings is here replaced with a restrained concentration on piano, vocals, and a welcome dusting of dislocated beats and breaks.

⊙ **Strange Little Girls** (2001; EastWest).
Though a set of covers, Amos has created an original, intense experience that is totally her own, daring to approach sacred classics like "Happiness Is A Warm Gun" and "Heart Of Gold". Tori Amos loves to give her all, but unfortunately this is sometimes too much: the sinister overtones of "I'm Not In Love" are chillingly histrionic.

Almo Miles

LAURIE ANDERSON

Born Chicago, 1948.

Growing up in the American midwest, New York seemed like a promised land to **Laurie Anderson**: 'it was always an hour later, darker, and somehow more alive ... things were always coming to you Live from New York.' She reached the city at the end of the 60s to study at Columbia University,

Tori, well out there at her piano

fan base (which draws equally on the sexes). She then broke up with her long-term partner, and co-producer on her two albums, **Eric Rosse**, and headed off to rural Ireland and to New Orleans to record a third solo album, BOYS FOR PELE (1996). Q magazine described this as Amos's counterpart to Joni's BLUE – high and deserved praise for a record that stripped away the orchestration to a stark mix of virtuoso piano, harmonium and 'thrash' harpsichord, albeit backed at times by a brass band, bagpipes, gospel choirs and church bells. Lyrically, some of the songs were as off the wall as the cover image (Tori cradling a pig), but the songs reflected more self-awareness than the pain of earlier releases and had some startling images ('And I shaved every place where you been, boy'). There was certainly enough here, lyrically and musically, to confirm a unique spirit.

Amos became the world's least likely dance-music artist in 1997 with the various remixes of "Professional Widow" topping club charts all over the globe. She married Mark Hawley – her sound

graduating in 1972 with an MFA in sculpture, and an involvement in the so-called Downtown scene in SoHo, where she numbered Philip Glass among her associates.

Anderson had been engaged in various performance artworks while at college, and, remaining in New York, embarked on a new series of creations: a self-playing violin, a pillow which sang to the sleeper, music for dance groups, a musical book, a concerto for automobiles, and several short film and video works. One notable piece involved her playing violin on street corners, accompanying a tape of herself concealed inside the instrument, while wearing ice skates embedded in a block of ice, playing until the ice melted. She took these events, and many others, on a near-constant tour of the alternative art spaces of America and Europe throughout the early 70s, making a name for herself on the flourishing avant-garde scene.

Having worked with a number of electronic musicians, and designed the tape-bow violin (an instrument with magnetic tape instead of a bow, and a playback head instead of strings), Laurie Anderson began to perform and record as a musician with her 'United States I–IV' series of works. From these, a single, "O Superman", was issued on the small New York label, One Ten Records, in 1981. Only a thousand copies were pressed, to be sold via mail order, but the record, with its beguiling but accessible electronic minimalism, was picked up for radio play in the UK, where a distributor ordered 40,000 copies, and, before long, it reached #2 in the charts. Its surprise success secured Anderson a distribution deal with Warners, who released her 1982 album, BIG SCIENCE.

BIG SCIENCE featured an extended version of the single, together with pieces such as "Born, Never Asked" and "From The Air" from the 'United States' set (also available as a live recording somewhere), along with newer songs, all on the general theme of alienation in the post-industrial, technology-dominated world. This was a relatively fresh area for popular culture, and Laurie Anderson became one of the most prominent investigators of the junction of culture and technology. With backing from Warners,

and grants from various foundations, her stage-shows increased in size, eventually allowing eight-hour performances of 'United States' in New York, London and Zurich during 1983.

Her next album, MISTER HEARTBREAK, followed a year later, featuring contributions from **William S. Burroughs**, **Peter Gabriel** and **Bill Laswell**, and accompanied by a large-scale tour. It had its moments – especially from Burroughs – but suffered from the early-80s mainstream art-pop syndrome: too much production, too much gloss and a lack of real innovation.

Maybe this wasn't surprising. Anderson had become heavily committed to the production of her concert film, *Home Of The Brave*. She had originally asked Talking Heads movie collaborator **Jonathan Demme** (*Stop Making Sense*) to direct, but ended up doing the job herself, to keep as much control as possible. Both the film and accompanying soundtrack album flopped – though the movie won subsequent critical acclaim at the 1987 Cannes Festival.

Disappointed, Anderson returned to small-scale videos and the recording studio, releasing STRANGE ANGELS in 1989. This signalled a more overtly political content, and was performed in a style which allowed her to sing rather than talk through most of the songs. Following its release, she embarked on a six-month tour of America and Europe, and then branched out into lecture tours, documentary work, and conceptual plans for an as-yet-unrealized Barcelona theme park in conjunction with **Brian Eno** and **Peter Gabriel**.

A career shift followed with publication of a book, *Stories From The Nerve Bible* (1992), a retrospective collage of material from her first twenty years of work, promoted by a small-scale theatrical tour. One show, at London's Sadler's Wells, was recorded and released as THE UGLY ONE WITH THE JEWELS (1995), a valuable record of her ironic (though oft-repeated) stories and previews of material from her 1994 CD, BRIGHT RED.

In 2000 Anderson turned her attention to Herman Melville with her staged work *Songs And Stories From Moby Dick*. More a homage than direct rendering of the literary classic, *Moby Dick* saw her extend the use of electronics on stage through her 'talking stick'. This instrument, designed with Interval Research in California, can be used variously like a harpoon or staff to control a bank of computers, and marks yet another advance Anderson has made in multimedia technology.

Having curated the 1997 Meltdown festival at London's South Bank Arts Centre, and compiled the entry for New York City in the *Encyclopaedia Britannica*, it seems that Anderson has transcended the superficial postmodern life for which she became known, to become one of the most important and wry commentators in mainstream American culture.

BIG SCIENCE LAURIE ANDERSON

● **Big Science** (1982; WEA).
Laurie Anderson's impressive pop debut combines minimalism, vocoders and violins with ironic commentaries on American life. "O Superman" stands out as an aural symbol of postmodernism, adapted for video works and car adverts alike.

● **Strange Angels** (1989; WEA).
  Anderson seems to have learned how to sing for this album (not necessarily a good thing…), but "Coolsville" is America, Prozac and malls, all condensed into a few minutes, while "Strange Angels" and "Hiawatha" positively soar.

Richard Fontenoy

ANDREW WK

Born Los Angeles, California, 1979.

From time to time an artist emerges fully formed and seemingly from nowhere – meet **Andrew WK**, (born Andrew Wilkes-Krier) who exploded onto the rock scene in a shower of sweat and a blur of manic head banging. With his **W** representing eternal mental strength and resilience, and **K** standing for the mystical power of the universe, it was apparent from the start that there was more to this musician than simply the ability to pen a catchy tune.

It should come as no surprise to find that an artist exuding such self-confidence started playing at a very early age, and indeed Andrew was tickling the ivories from around the age of four. His family moved to Michigan, and in his teens the young Andrew was to be heard playing in punk and metal bands in the Detroit area, developing his skills on drums, keyboards and guitar. Deciding he really needed a band for his material to shine, he moved to New York to begin circulating demos, and by the age of 20 had earned a reputation for extremely hard-rocking solo shows.

GIRLS OWN JUICE, an EP assembled from early recordings, was released on Bulb records, an indie label which was soon pushing his PARTY TIL YOU PUKE EP; no prizes for guessing that he was promoting a party-hard manifesto as some sort of path to spiritual enlightenment, the focus being on the purity of purpose and hedonistic happiness as the ultimate goal.

At age 22 Andrew had a band, a record deal and an album in the bag. I GET WET (2001) said everything it needed to say in the title. If you're going to commit yourself one hundred per cent to any course of action, to really go for your goals in life, then you're going to get wet; according to the man himself it could be 'blood, sweat, urine, semen or girls' lubricant'. Not surprisingly such an attitude gave the album a manic and uplifting quality; it sounded something like Kiss playing thrash, spouting positivist lyrics cobbled together from any of the myriad self-help books available at your local mystic bookshop. Everything was recorded with the amps set at 'eleven'; the drums didn't just provide a spine to the tunes, they propelled them forward at breakneck speed; the guitars never left the red zone; the keyboards sounded incredibly bright and happy; and over the top Andrew WK yelled at everyone that "It's Time To Party", to "Party Hard", that you've "Got To Do It" and "Don't Stop Living In The Red", all with perfect harmonies and killer choruses guaranteed to work their way into your memory with the insistence of a nursery rhyme.

The happy metal formula came with a live show featuring mucho head banging, frantic jumping around, and the man himself – in his uniform of sweat-drenched, filthy T-shirt and jeans – exhorting the crowds to go nuts. With such an extreme and unsubtle formula to his rock it's hard to know quite where Andrew WK is going to take things next.

Andrew WK doing the hokey-cokey

Wherever it may be you can rest assured that it'll be very, very loud indeed.

⊙ **I Get Wet** (2001; Mercury).
The maddest party soundtrack you could hope to find. This doesn't just encourage a good time; it commands it with crunching guitars and some irritatingly catchy tunes. It's basic, good time rock from a bloke who believes in the liberating power of never changing your underwear.

Essi Berelian

ANGELIC UPSTARTS

Formed South Shields, England, 1977; disbanded 1986; re-formed 1992.

The Angelic Upstarts have tended to attract one of two reactions. One school of thought castigates them as banal, inarticulate rabble-rousers who represented a pale reflection of punk rock, while another sees their work as a meeting of working-class ideology and musical aspiration. **Mensi** (aka **Thomas Mensforth**; vocals) was always liable to provoke such polarization. His lyrics made much of his impoverished upbringing, and lashed out at London's middle-class intelligentsia, as well as standard punk targets like the police and politicians.

With **Mond** (guitar), **Ronnie Wooden** (bass) and **Sticks** (drums) on board, the Angelic Upstarts launched their three-chord crusade with the independently released single "Murder Of Liddle Towers" (1978). Its attack on police brutality earned them an early patron in Sham 69's **Jimmy Pursey**, who chased a similar constituency of disaffected working-class fans.

Pursey produced the minimalist TEENAGE WARNING (1979), a cul-de-sac of single-idea songs made palatable by the band's wholehearted delivery and their denunciation of racism – a particularly admirable stance at a time when other 'skinhead' bands, such as Skrewdriver, were flirting with right-wing elements.

With the UK hit singles, "I'm An Upstart" and "Teenage Warning" (both 1979), they focused on the plight of the 'working man' (at this stage, it was generally gender-specific stuff), though their identification of the cause of that oppression was simplistic. ANGEL DUST (THE COLLECTED HIGHS) (1983) was a useful compilation of their best early work, and paved the way for REASON WHY? (1983), an album on which the Angelic Upstarts came closest to the intensity and diversity of The Clash. Now with **Tony Feedback** (bass), **Bryan Hayes** (rhythm guitar) and ex-Roxy Music drummer **Paul Thompson**, they had also broadened their sound with the introduction of saxophones and keyboards. Mensi was at his most affecting when reciting an unaccompanied poem, "Geordie's Wife" – a brave step for a musician closely identified with working-class machismo.

THE POWER OF THE PRESS (1986) incorporated working-class folk ballads such as Eric Bogle's "Green Fields Of France", while the controversial single release "Brighton Bomb" celebrated the IRA's attempt to assassinate the Conservative cabinet. However, there was limited evidence that Angelic Upstarts fans were growing with the band, and this was confirmed by their break-up in late 1986.

Following a slew of avoidable live albums and compilations, they reunited in 1992 for the lacklustre BOMBED OUT – a return to their hard-hitting punk roots. The career low point here was another poem, the profoundly embarrassing "Proud And Loud".

⊙ **Angel Dust** (The Collected Highs) (1983; Anagram).
Streamlined adrenaline rushes alongside Mensi's more thoughtful moments, such as "England", an attempt to liberate the Union Jack from those who would use it as a badge for race hatred. The CD version also appends the group's best studio album, REASON WHY?

Alex Ogg

THE ANIMALS

Formed Newcastle, England, 1960; disbanded 1968; re-formed sporadically in 70s and 80s.

Alan Price (keyboards) started out as a northern British bluesman, playing with a combo that was making a name for itself on the Newcastle club circuit. Price played a mean set of keyboards and had a soul-tinged voice that was sexy but standard, lacking the ferocity to cover the grubbier end of rock. In 1962 they recruited a suitably mean lead singer to fill out the sound and beef up the image: **Eric Burdon** had one of the grimiest voices in the business; he would throw himself into the songs, whip the band into overdrive and slaughter the audience. The group solidified when **John Steel** (drums) hooked up with Price, Burdon, **Hilton Valentine** (guitar) and **Chas Chandler** (bass); their original name, **The Alan Price Combo**, had to go and **The Animals** came into being.

As they toured the UK, the band grew into a professional unit, with Eric perfecting his skills as a rabble-rouser. They shared bills with older, black musical legends like Sonny Boy Williamson and, after their first hit, John Lee Hooker. The only dark cloud on the horizon was the rivalry between Alan and new frontman Eric, and the first signs of resentment soon began to show. In 1964 they moved to London, where they teamed up with then-unknown producer **Mickie Most**, and signed to Columbia. They released an exquisite Price-credited (much to the rest of the band's enduring fury) arrangement of the traditional "House Of The Rising Sun", which went to #1 in the UK, the US and around the world.

For the rest of the 60s, The Animals hit the charts regularly, most famously with "Please Don't Let Me Be Misunderstood" and "We've Gotta Get Out Of This Place". However, it wasn't long before ego problems resurfaced. After only two LPs – THE ANIMALS (1964; reissued 1998; EMI) and ANIMAL TRACKS (1965) – were recorded the conflicts came to a head and Price left to pursue a more mainstream solo career. He was quickly replaced by Newcastle's **Dave**

The Animals circa 1965, left to right:
A Bassist (not Chas), Eric Burdon, John Steel, Alan Price, Hilton Valentine

Rowberry. Steel had also left the band by the release of its third album, ANIMALISMS (1966), the new drummer being the ex-Nashville Teen **Barry Jenkins**.

In the limbo of these personnel changes, Burdon recorded a solo single and an LP (ERIC IS HERE) and moved his base to California. There he formed a second incarnation of the band, **Eric Burdon & The Animals**, comprising Burdon, Jenkins, ex-Steampacket guitarist **Vic Briggs**, **John Weider** (guitar/violin) and **Danny McCulloch** (bass). This line-up produced two LPs with a different style from the R&B stompers they'd kicked around in the clubs of London and the north of England. 1967's WIND OF CHANGE featured tracks with titles such as "Poem By The Sea", "It's All Meat", and "Yes, I Am Experienced", Burdon's reply to the title of Jimi Hendrix's just-released debut.

The new, 'psychedelic' Animals did fairly well, with chart successes at home and in the US. The line-up expanded with the appearance of bassist **Zoot Money**, but then contracted again when, fuelled by antagonism from Burdon, McCulloch and Briggs left to be replaced by guitarist **Andy Summers**.

This final line-up was packed full of skilled musicians, each of whom had his own musical statement to make, though after only two minor LP releases, The Animals folded when a tour of Japan, marred by mafia threats, led Burden to quit.

Alan Price was by now an 'all-round entertainer' having done TV, novelty songs, and worked briefly with fellow British bluesman **Georgie Fame** in a kind of R&B supergroup. Chas Chandler had hung up his bass to reinvent himself as a producer, working with Hendrix and British glam-popsters Slade. Weider went on to become part of **Family**, Zoot

Money went solo, and Andy Summers worked with **Kevin Ayers** and **Kevin Coyne**, before joining **THE POLICE**. Eric Burdon kept on rocking, digging back down into the dirt for his next venture, **WAR**.

After War's urban, Latin-tinged funk disintegrated the original Animals re-formed in early 1976, releasing an album, BEFORE WE WERE SO RUDELY INTERRUPTED, which generated some interest on the nostalgia circuit. However, Price left almost immediately to continue his solo career and nothing more was heard from The Animals until they re-formed again in 1983, recording a studio LP, ARK (reissued 1997; Castle), undertaking a lengthy world tour, and issuing RIP IT TO SHREDS, a live hits compilation (reissued by Castle as GREATEST HITS – LIVE). They then, once again, returned to their solo projects.

⊙ **Rip It To Shreds: Greatest Hits – Live** (1984; IRS).
A whole bunch of early singles tracks, performed with gusto in front of a worshipping crowd. Highly recommended.

⊙ **Singles Plus** (1987; EMI).
This fine compilation puts together the first ten single A-sides (easily the best of their recordings) with their original flip sides.

⊙ **The Very Best Of** (1998; EMI).
Taken from Eric's time amongst the flower people in California. Innocent to the point of sickliness in parts, there's a naive charm here, missing from so much of the home-grown crop of 1967.

Al Spicer/Sean Egan

ANTHRAX

Formed New York, 1981.

E merging from the thrash explosion of the 1980s, **Anthrax** are one of the few bands that have

THE ANIMALS ▪ ANTHRAX

managed to endure and adapt to the wild fashion changes in the rock scene of the last two decades.

The band's early line-up consisted of key songwriter **Scott 'Not' Ian** (guitars), the diminutive **Danny Spitz** (guitars), **Dan Lilker** (bass), **Neil Turbin** (vocals) and **Charlie Benante** (drums). They were brought together by a mutual love of skateboarding, comics and the New York hardcore punk scene, and their early material bore all the hallmarks of their influences – heavy metal given a vicious shot of hardcore speed and attitude.

After a bout of hectic small-town touring in 1982, the band met thrash guru **Johnny Z**, who signed them to his Megaforce label and released "Soldiers Of Metal" on a rock audience hungry for the adrenaline rush that thrash metal could provide. Under his guidance, the band undertook support slots with macho metalmen Manowar, and the fledgling Metallica, and in 1984 released their debut album, FISTFUL OF METAL (1984), a record of little note except for the savage speed of the guitar work, unless you count the appalling title and dubious cover art. During this early period Anthrax coexisted with Ian, Lilker and Benante's side-project, the **Stormtroopers Of Death** (SOD), whose distinctly hardcore stance was caught on a single album, SPEAK ENGLISH OR DIE (1984). Lilker left Anthrax to form **Nuclear Assault** soon afterwards and roadie **Frank Bello** stepped in as a permanent replacement in Anthrax. The stability was short-lived, however, as Turbin was fired, to be replaced first by **Matt Fallon** and then by ex-Bible Black member, **Joey Belladonna**.

Belladonna's power and operatic style gave Anthrax's subsequent work a depth and polish they had lacked. The five-track mini-LP, ARMED AND DANGEROUS (1985), their first release with the revamped line-up, featured a muscular reworking of the Sex Pistols' classic "God Save The Queen", which was to become a live favourite. Having attracted the attention of some major companies, they recorded their next album for Island Records. SPREADING THE DISEASE (1986) catapulted them into the mainstream and effectively set the tone for the next five years. There were songs about all the usual metal faves such as nuclear war ("Aftershock") and mythic monsters ("Medusa"), but a fun quotient was maintained by the hit single "Madhouse" and the spaghetti western-inspired "Lone Justice".

The band's image at this time also contributed to their popularity as they single-handedly made surfing shorts, baseball caps and skateboarding the latest rock fashion trends. Later years would see them trying hard to shake the goofball image. At the time, however, they were too busy giving bands like Metallica a run for their money as they supported them on tour in late 1986.

With the release of AMONG THE LIVING (1987), the Anthrax style finally crystallized. Under the guidance of legendary producer **Eddie Kramer**, they produced standout material in the shape of hit single "Indians" and the epic "ADI"/"Horror Of It All". And the fun factor was still present in full force: both the title track and "Skeleton In The Closet" were based on Stephen King stories, while the band endeared themselves to British heavy metal fans with "I Am The Law", based on 2000 AD's legendary lawman, Judge Dredd. With the album going gold in America and a UK chart place of #18, the band then had a singles hit with "I'm The Man", a spoof rap crossover that reached #20 in the UK charts. The rap connection would prove to be significant some way down the line.

The following year brought a consolidation of the band's commercial success with an appearance at the Donington Monsters of Rock Festival and a gold album in STATE OF EUPHORIA (1988). The single from the album, "Make Me Laugh", reached #26 in the UK, but the fact that a cover version of Trust's "Anti-Social" was one of the standout cuts on STATE OF EUPHORIA showed in reality how patchy their latest LP was.

Yet the band seemed to have an unstoppable momentum – not even a fire at their Yonkers rehearsal studio, which destroyed $100,000 worth of equipment, could slow them down. PERSISTENCE OF TIME (1990) punched effortlessly into the charts and peaked at #13, though once again the most memorable cut was a cover – a melodic, super-swift version of Joe Jackson's "Got The Time", which charted as a single. It was an odd choice, and contrasted with the band's ensuing experiment with rap – one that would have made more traditional rock acts pale at the thought – in which they teamed up with Public Enemy's **Chuck D** on "Bring The Noise" and released ATTACK OF THE KILLER BS (1991), a mixture of rap, rerecorded old SOD material and B-sides.

By this point it was becoming apparent that the band were no longer functioning as a group, despite their commercial success. In the grunge climate of the early 90s, rock music underwent a groundshift and heavy metal dipped in popularity. Coupled with this general trend, Belladonna's feather-headed approach to the music began to grate with the other members. He was eventually jettisoned and replaced by the less polished but tougher-sounding **John Bush**.

By the time THE SOUND OF WHITE NOISE (1993) emerged on Warners, the band had done its utmost to give a more contemporary flavour to their guitar barrage. But it was still hard to ditch the frivolous cartoon image that had dogged them for so many years, and although the album entered the *Billboard* chart at #7 it did not attain the heights scaled by their previous efforts.

The dissatisfaction with Belladonna had resulted in change, but things were still not running smoothly, as Dan Spitz's lead style and less-than-enthusiastic stage attitude was holding the others back. His minimal songwriting input and self-exclusion from band activities led to his leaving in 1995.

Notwithstanding Anthrax's second album for Warners, STOMP 442 (1995), recorded with guitar duties split between Benante, Ian, **Dimebag Darrell** (of Pantera) and **Paul Crook** (who had played guitar in Belladonna's old band), was one of their strongest albums to date. It stiffed, but more through the US heavy metal scene's plunge, amid grunge fallout, than through any fault of their own.

When STOMP 442 failed to set the world alight, the band retreated to rethink their approach as a four-piece. The time away resulted in one of their most accomplished releases in VOLUME 8: THE THREAT IS REAL (1998). Though still recognizably Anthrax, the songwriting took the sound they had experimented with over the preceding five years and guided it to its logical conclusion. The heaviness of the new material compared more than favourably with fresh-faced nu-metal bands hungry for success, but the band were powerless to halt what seemed to be a tortuously slow slide into obscurity. And then the truly bizarre happened – a new horror gripped the US following the September 11 attacks on New York: biological terrorism, namely anthrax. Suddenly the band's name was synonymous with real death and destruction. In the face of this blow the band characteristically chose to fight on with more touring and recording; a gloriously melodic new album, WE'VE COME FOR YOU ALL, appeared in 2003.

Clearly, Anthrax remain one of the most uncompromising groups on the scene and will doubtless continue to spread their disease regardless.

(•) Spreading The Disease (1986; Island).
A brash second outing, bursting with energy and speedy riffing: the dumb, manic blur of "Gung Ho" is awesome, and the general preoccupation with war, fantasy and heavy metal makes for an entertaining blitz.

(•) Among The Living (1987; Island).
Another colourful trawl through popular culture, but in amongst the ephemera there are stabs at more serious subjects such as world peace ("One World") and the plight of Native Americans ("Indians").

(•) The Sound Of White Noise (1993; Elektra/Warners).
Having ditched Belladonna, they produced an album brimming with an intensity and fury rarely paralleled. Admirable stuff.

(•) Stomp 442 (1995; Elektra/Warners).
Possibly their heaviest, most angry album to date. Without Spitz's tuneless lead solos the songs have greater cohesion, and the guest guitarists add an extra dimension to the brutal sonic attack.

(•) Volume 8: The Threat Is Real (1998; Ignition Records).
Taut, economical songwriting is the key to this album's success. There are even a couple of humorous "Noo Yoik" hardcore tunes in the shape of "604" and "Cupajoe".

Essi Berelian

ANTI-NOWHERE LEAGUE

Formed Tunbridge Wells, England, 1980.

I n good punk tradition, the **Anti-Nowhere League** formed out of boredom. **Animal** (vocals), **Magoo** (guitar), **Winston** (bass) and **P. J.** (drums) were old friends, congenital trouble-makers and occasional bikers who discovered the potential irritancy of ineptly played guitars. In a time when any self-respecting punk band had to be called 'Anti-something', they became the Anti-Nowhere League – a 'Nowhere' being defined as someone happy to live a drab, nine-to-five existence. Their first gig saw them playing uninvited during a local fair on a Tunbridge Wells common (Tunbridge Wells, for those happily ignorant, is a very genteel town in the south of England), where, if nothing else, they proved they could get arrested by... getting arrested.

By the autumn of 1981 the boys had secured a deal with WXYZ Records and were touring as support to The Damned. Their first single, released in January 1982, was a cover of buskers' fave, "Streets Of London", recorded, the band said, because they 'wanted to fuck up something nice'. The accompanying video portrayed the League doing their utmost to look menacing, while Animal, clad in leather, chains, studs and wraparound shades, swung an axe around for no apparent reason.

However, it was the single's B-side, "So What", that gained the band notoriety, as Animal detailed graphic experiences with sex, drugs, alcohol, bestiality, paedophilia and VD. Animal's philosophical musings were lost on the Obscene Publications Squad, who, as the record appeared in the lower reaches of the chart, raided WXYZ's offices, seized all the copies they could find and destroyed them. The record was promptly banned, greatly enhancing the League's following amongst the hardcore punk fraternity.

Over the next year another three singles – "I Hate... People", "Woman" and "For You" – were unleashed. The latter was supposedly an attempt at commerciality and, ironically, the only one not to chart. There was an album, too, WE ARE... THE LEAGUE (1982; reissued 1998), which contained all the singles bar "For You" and "So What". The band went quiet after that, when the punk scene lost momentum. The dreadful LIVE IN YUGOSLAVIA (1983), featuring a truly painful cover of The Stones' "Paint It Black", and a version of "So What" with the lyrics buried deep in the mix, did little to demand attention. Then in 1985, the boys re-emerged as an 'epic-rock' band, renamed **The League**. They had, it seemed, grown up, and wanted to be taken seriously. To this end, P. J. was replaced on drums by **Michael Bettell**, and the band set off on tour, even supporting Big Country at one point. This would have been very embarrassing for their original audience but few people seemed to notice, and a single, "Out On The Wasteland", and album, THE PERFECT CRIME (1987), slipped into the void. The band reverted to their original name, and persist today on the punk cabaret circuit, having long ago fallen into the rut they always professed to despise.

(•) We Are... The League (1982; WXYZ Records; reissued 1998; Recall).
Contains pretty much everything you could possibly want to hear – including "So What" on the current CD reissue.

Glenn Law

APHEX TWIN

Born Cornwall, England, 1971.

Richard James – aka **Aphex Twin** – was a bit of an electronics prodigy, building and customizing his own machines from an early age. He began recording experiments in the mid-80s and has since developed a sound in geographical isolation from the specialist record shops and pirate radio stations that have shaped and styled dance music. The result is a truly experimental and innovative body of post-acid electronic music, ranging from full-on industrial noise through to slow groovy breakbeats and ambient drones.

Aphex's first release, ANALOGUE BUBBLEBATH #1 (1991) featured **Schizophrenia** (aka **Tom Middleton**, half of ambient/techno duo, Global Communications/Reload) on one side – the only release on which the two worked together. Played regularly by Colin Dale of London dance-music station Kiss FM, it created an early cult following. Aphex followed this with a second 12" release, ANALOGUE BUBBLEBATH #2 (1991). Its A-side, at 160bpm, was faster than anything else around at the time, while the two tracks on the flip sounded so weird that nobody could even work out what their correct speed was.

Both "Analogue Bubblebath" records were white-label releases, but a track from each, along with a couple of new tracks, were reissued by R&S as a single, "Didgeridoo" (1992). This was followed by another 12", "Xylem Tube", before the release of the SELECTED AMBIENT WORKS 85–92 album, a compilation that included material he had recorded when he was 14 years old. On signing to Sheffield-based dance label Warp Records, Aphex released SURFING ON SINE WAVES (1993), under the alias of **Polygon Window**, and "Quoth", a clear-vinyl single that was deleted the same day.

Aphex's indefinable musical genre was now attracting a considerable following in the British press, and people ranging from Japanese artists to the likes of Jesus Jones and Saint Etienne queued up to be remixed by him. A minor commercial breakthrough occurred in late 1993 with the UK Top 40 hit single "On", with its highly impressive, though conceptually simple, video featuring an English seaside bay and plenty of stop frame animation.

The third Aphex album, SELECTED AMBIENT WORKS VOL 2 (1994), was not well received – critics did not take to its long moody drones and distant melodies – but his next album, I CARE BECAUSE YOU DO (1995), more along trip-hop lines, met with a far better reception. In the meantime, he released the undercover single, "Gak" (1994), supposedly sent to Warp by a mystery musician in 1989.

Aphex has continued to put out releases on Warp, has provided soundtracks for TV advertisements, and has even been sought after for film soundtracks. As a result, his own Rephlex label has been able to release more challenging and experimental works, such as ANALOGUE BUBBLEBATH #3 (1994). Nicely packaged in a brown paper bag, it contained an information sheet of places of interest to visit in Cornwall, with an Aphex perspective on each. One cut, entitled "0180871", has a different track on each channel of the stereo – you choose with the balance control, and a horrible clashing noise results if both channels are played together. To this day he remains eager to test sound boundaries: when DJing, he has spun discs of sandpaper and other textures, and on his 1995 single "Ventolin" he incorporated the sound of asthmatic inhalers.

THE HANGABLE AUTO BULB EP later in the year reinforced Aphex Twin's position as master of the merciless, while the DONKEY RHUBARB EP (also 1995) featured "Icct Hedral" reorchestrated by **Phillip Glass** to create a surprisingly pastoral gem. EXPERT KNOB TWIDDLERS (1996) was a lightweight, easy-to-digest collaboration between James and **Michael Paradinas** (µ-Ziq) with the album credited to **Mike & Rich**, the duo appearing on the cover in the guise of two kiddies playing MB Games' 'Downfall'. RICHARD D. JAMES (1996), and the accompanying BOY/GIRL EP, took him back to the experimental once again, and was followed by 1998's COME TO DADDY EP (boosted by the scariest video of all time) and 1999's "Windowlicker" single (boosted by one of the foulest-mouthed intros in video history).

2001 brought the double CD set DRUKQS, a sprawling collection of hit or miss experiments and genius piano compositions that seemed to pay homage to experimental composer John Cage. James's most recent release was 2003's 26 MIXES FOR CASH, a mammoth document of the Twin's remixing duties to date, with many of the cuts sounding so unlike their source material that they add weight to the rumours that James has been known to palm record labels off with random tapes from his studio floor when faced with a remix deadline.

Aphex releases are more than just albums or singles: they are commandments that shape electronica's

progress until James once again descends from his mountain with more stone tablets.

- **Selected Ambient Works 85–92** (1992; R&S). Creating moods for the listener, sometimes with a funky breakbeat but often with no beats at all, this is an accessible introduction to Aphex's world.

- **Surfing On Sine Waves** (1993; Warp). Aphex's best non-ambient album – up-tempo, and not as heavy as he can sometimes be, it demonstrates a more sophisticated sound than his earlier industrial works.

- **Selected Ambient Works Vol 2** (1994; Warp). Aphex's biggest bomb with critics and consumers alike, but in fact his most experimental album, containing dark, moody pieces with no drumbeat to hold them together. Densely layered sounds create textures akin to a sinister film score.

- **Classics** (1995; R&S). A roundup of Aphex material from "Analogue Bubblebath" through to most of the R&S output plus a few remixes of other acts such as Seefeel. This is as good a compilation of Aphex material as you'll get.

- **Richard D. James** (1996; Warp). Prime cuts of West Country weirdness. May we suggest you try the Cornish Acid?

- **Drukqs** (2001; Warp). This set makes you feel like you've tipped the pieces of a jigsaw out onto the floor only to realize that there's no picture on the box. Before long however, familiarity leads to clarity and Drukqs starts to make sense. The explosive beats and bursts of percussive cutlery perfectly contrast the suffocating pillows of hush; mania and control effortlessly nestle alongside each other.

David Wren, Daniel Jacobs and Scott Moyse

FIONA APPLE

Born New York City 1977.

Singer-songwriters have often been accused of taking themselves too seriously; **Fiona Apple** is undeniably guilty as charged, but she can just about be forgiven, seeing as her work is so extraordinarily rich and rewarding. At a time when the likes of Sheryl Crow and Alanis Morrisette ruled the charts and the radio airwaves, this 18-year-old New Yorker's first album was to take the American scene by surprise. That record was TIDAL.

Following the separation of her mother and actor father when she was four, and a traumatic childhood and adolescence, she exorcized her demons through therapy and sought solace in the piano: 'The piano is percussive, you hit it. It was a huge release for me just banging on it'. After improvising music to accompany *National Geographic* TV documentaries for her own amusement, she began songwriting at fourteen with "Sleep To Dream", which would be a suitably self-assured opening cut for her debut album, 1996's TIDAL. Her talent was fully recognized when she sent a demo, through a friend, to the producer and manager **Andrew Slater** – in the blink of an eye she was signed to the giant major label Sony.

Apple was completely unprepared for the success of TIDAL – at the time she did not want to be a star. She tried to deal with this at the MTV Awards in 1997 when, accepting an award for *Best New Artist*,

she declared 'This world is bullshit'. Ultimately, she dealt with success by disappearing to make a second album, and by leaving street magician David Blaine (for Paul Thomas Anderson, the director of the films *Boogie Nights* and *Magnolia*).

Not even an unwieldy ninety-word album title could stop Fiona Apple's second release, WHEN THE PAWN HITS THE CONFLICTS HE THINKS LIKE A KING WHAT HE KNOWS THROWS THE BLOWS WHEN HE GOES TO THE FIGHT AND HE'LL WIN THE WHOLE THING' FORE HE ENTERS THE RING THERE'S NO BODY TO BATTER WHEN YOUR MIND IS YOUR MIGHT SO WHEN YOU GO SOLO, YOU HOLD YOUR OWN HAND AND REMEMBER THAT DEPTH IS THE GREATEST OF HEIGHTS AND IF YOU KNOW WHERE YOU STAND, THEN YOU KNOW WHERE TO LAND AND IF YOU FALL IT WON'T MATTER, CUZ YOU'LL KNOW THAT YOU'RE RIGHT (Sony; 2000), from being another commercial success in the US, and a critical favourite on both sides of the Atlantic. Its first single, the jazzy, frantic "Fast As You Can" became a radio hit, although the exposure did not translate into sales; the song only managed to scrape the margins of the Top 30. The set did, however, garner her a *Grammy* nomination for *Best Female Artist*. Since then, nothing – perhaps Apple is having trouble coming up with a title to top her previous mouthful.

- **Tidal** (Columbia; 1996). Fiona Apple's debut found itself in four million American homes. "Sullen Girl" is quietly furious, "Slow Like Honey" is simply sensuous, and the Latin-flavoured "The First Taste" adds Sade to a list of reference points that includes Nina Simone and Carole King.

- **When The Pawn...** (Columbia; 2000). A dreadful title, even cut from ninety words to three, but in just about every other way, this is a considerable advancement on its predecessor. The up-tempo tracks (and obvious singles) like "Paper Bag" and "Fast As You Can" stand-out, while the slow-burning and downbeat "I Know" and "Get Gone" give this collection its edge.

Justin Lewis

ARAB STRAP

Formed Falkirk, 1995.

Few bands polarize opinion amongst rock fans as much as **Arab Strap**: they seem to invite either obsessive fandom or showers of derision. Arab Strap was originally a one-man band, **Aidan Moffat** (vocals/drums/kazoo), who recorded demos filled with 'self-indulgent wank' (as he put it) in his bedroom. Meanwhile, guitarist **Malcolm Middleton**, a vague acquaintance (they were allegedly arrested together once), was doing similar things under the moniker of the Laughing Stock. The two joined forces in 1995, lifting their name from a sex toy, and adding **Gary Miller** (bass) and **David Gow** (drums) to the line up. Initially the band spurned gigs in favour of recording demos. One such tape was passed on to Glasgow band The Delgados, whose Chemikal Underground label signed Arab Strap and released their debut single "The First Big Weekend" in 1996.

Post-Britpop, the track gained notice for its originality, with heavy airplay on BBC Radio 1's specialist shows and much attention mirrored in the music press. The track itself was remarkably simple, consisting of a drum machine, guitar and a (mostly) spoken vocal from Moffat, detailing the weekend of the England vs. Scotland game in the Euro 96 soccer tournament. Although somewhat at odds with the nascent post-rock scene that dominated the fringes of indie, they did fit in well with their diverse Scottish lo-fi contemporaries, such as Belle & Sebastian, Mogwai and Uresei Yatsura.

The band made their live debut late in 1996 at Glasgow's urban festival, The Ten Day Weekend, where they started their habit of changing the lyrics of "The First Big Weekend" for each and every gig. THE WEEK NEVER STARTS ROUND HERE (1996) continued the minimalist mood laid down by the single. As well as "The First Big Weekend", there were many alternative music gems, notably the follow-up single "The Clearing".

After a break, Aidan worked with Mogwai on their album MOGWAI YOUNG TEAM (1997), guesting on "R U Still Down". The band then released THE GIRLS OF SUMMER EP (1997) to critical acclaim. Although marking an interesting departure (featuring a gospel-influenced outro that recycled the lyrics to "The First Big Weekend"), it was a disappointing record musically, though it did provide a minor hit. The band then reworked David Holmes's "Don't Die Just Yet" as the lush, string-laden "The Holiday Girl", complete with (surprisingly) innocent lyrics about Aidan's adolescent romance. It was Arab Strap's version that got the radio play and provided a top 40 hit single.

PHILOPHOBIA (1998) covered similar downbeat lyrical and musical territory to the debut, yielding two lesser hits with the double A-side "Here We Go"/"Trippy" and "(Afternoon) Soaps". Other highlights included "Not Quite A Yes" and the sublime "New Birds", neither of which quite captured the intensity of the group's debut single. The band signed to Go! Beat (making them label mates with David Holmes and Portishead) and began work on new material.

In 1999 they returned with a limited live collection, MAD FOR SADNESS, and the marvellous ELEPHANT SHOE. Then in 2001, another full-length studio collection hit the streets: THE RED THREAD. Having returned to Chemikal Underground the set found the boys in a playful, reflective, but as ever, sordid mood. These feelings were again represented in 2003 by MONDAY AT THE HUG & PINT, a beer-stained collection of bar stool observations and romantic rantings. Though they continue to charm and irritate in equal measures, Arab Strap are sure to be around for a while.

⊙ **The Week Never Starts Round Here** (1996; Chemikal Underground).
Contains their finest moment "The First Big Weekend" and other lo-fi gems.

⊙ **Elephant Shoe** (1999; Go!Beat).
Arab Strap's most accomplished and satisfying recording to date. Snapshots of dissolute living and boozed-up regret are immaculately framed, from the opening track "Cherubs" to the closing cut "Hello Daylight".

⊙ **The Red Thread** (2001; Chemikal Underground).
With THE RED THREAD, Arab Strap assemble ten different ways of looking at the post-coital, post-pub comedown, using lyrics that sound as if they were transcribed from yellowed ceilings above soiled single beds in rented flats.

Naeem Yar

ARCHERS OF LOAF

Formed Chapel Hill, North Carolina, 1992, disbanded 1999.

The core **Archers Of Loaf** duo – **Eric Bachman** (guitar/vocals) and **Eric Johnson** (guitar) – grew up in the sleepy retirement town of Asheville, before being offered places at the University of Carolina in Chapel Hill. It was there in January 1992 that they met **Mark Price** (drums)

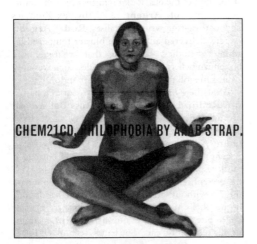

CHEM21CD, PHILOPHOBIA BY ARAB STRAP.

and **Matt Gentling** (bass), and the Archers were born. The band name is an enigma which they have chosen not to explain.

Whilst Bachman was waiting for Archers Of Loaf to take off he played with fellow Chapel Hill punksters **Small**, who released a couple of singles on Matt Records. Despite Small's reasonable success, Archers Of Loaf remained Bachman's primary concern, and when a local fanzine offered them the chance to record a single, he pledged allegiance solidly to Loaf. The result of the early sessions was "Wrong"/"South Carolina", two slabs of wrought, angst-ridden punk that attracted the attention of San Francisco label Alias.

The first release on their new label was "Web In Front", recorded in February 1993. The music press drew comparisons with art-school rockers Pavement, although the Loaf were less overtly quirky, and nor were they as straightforwardly punky as fellow Chapel Hill residents Superchunk, the other obvious comparison. Still, as the Archers came to prominence, the music industry began talking up Chapel Hill as a fertile breeding ground for alternative rock stars, like a latterday Seattle.

At the annual C.M.J. Festival in New York, the group headlined an Alias showcase before releasing their debut album, ICKY METTLE (1993), which was both articulate and challenging at a time when much of the alternative American music scene was 'grunge-by-numbers'. Acclaimed by the music press, the Archers hit the road for some nonstop touring, winning over all who saw them. Their live shows were not to be missed: the intensity of Eric Bachman, the dreaminess of Eric Johnson, and the muppet-like qualities of Matt Gentling combined to make one of the most solid live bands of the day.

The following year saw the release of VS. THE GREATEST OF ALL TIMES, an EP that packed more of a punch than anything prior, and stayed with the listener longer, especially the songs "Audiowhore" and "Freezing Point". Robert Christgau of the *Village Voice* picked it as the #1 EP of the year; the record industry had pricked up its ears, too, with just about every major label coming a-courting. The Archers turned them all down, including Madonna, who turned up at a show in NYC to try and get them to sign to her Maverick label.

The second Archers Of Loaf album, VEE VEE (1995), thus emerged on Alias, and to much critical acclaim, powered along by a single, "Harnessed In Slums," that got huge airplay on college and alternative radio stations. Almost three years after the release of the Archers' debut, it was clear how much the band's songwriting ability had improved. Cuts such as "Nostalgia" and "Fabricoh" show the angst-ridden, harder side of Archers, while "Step Into The Light" brought out their more melodic sensitive side.

Constant touring also proved fruitful for Archers. They were asked to open for Weezer on their tour of the United States, which brought them into an untapped market – teenagers. It was time to make a

serious bid for fame, and the Archers, prior to moving to a major label, set about fulfilling their contract with SPEED OF CATTLE (1996), a compilation of all the hard-to-find (but well worth having) B-sides, Peel sessions and unreleased tracks. It was the Peel session songs, however, that made the album worth having, recorded just prior to the VS. EP, and featuring a particularly energetic version of "Revenge". In 1995 Alias also released a solo effort by Eric Bachman, BARRY BLACK; it was mainly instrumental but possessed a defiantly Archers groove. A second solo effort followed in 1997 titled TRAGIC ANIMAL STORIES.

1996 had Alias signed up for distribution purposes with Elektra and saw the release of ALL THE NATION'S AIRPORTS. The album built on the solid foundations laid in their previous outings and featured more piano than before but otherwise contained nothing to frighten the horses. Similarly, 1998's WHITE TRASH HEROES failed to clarify the Loaf's position in the ever-fluid alternative scene, and proved to be their last album.

After the split, Bachmann resurfaced with a new band, **Crooked Fingers**, releasing a self-titled debut in 1999, the overly indulgent BRING ON THE SNAKES in 2001, a grueling collection of covers – RESERVOIR SONGS – in 2002, and RED DEVIL DAWN the following year. He has also dabbled with soundtrack work, witnessed by 2002's SHORT CAREERS, released on Merge.

⊙ **Icky Mettle** (1993; Alias).
Featuring the band's first two singles, "Wrong" and "Web In Front", this debut owes an obvious debt to alternative bands such as Fugazi and the Pixies. The influences are not too overbearing, though – the Archers consistently offer an identity of their own.

Jonathan Swift and Jeffrey S. Kaye

ARGENT

Formed London, 1969; disbanded 1976.

If you ever wondered what happened to the naive idealism of the 60s, look no further than the semi-pop pomp of **Argent**. Led by ex-Zombies keyboardist-songwriter-vocalist **Rod Argent**, Argent delivered an art-rock bluster tempered by simple melodies, signifying that whatever the bohemian beliefs of the hippie hordes, rock was now a full-time job to be taken very, very seriously.

After the Zombies broke up, Argent and bassist **Jim Rodford** recruited guitarist **Russ Ballard** and drummer **Bob Henrit** and released ARGENT, their debut album, in 1970. Featuring Ballard's "Liar" (a future American hit for Three Dog Night) and Argent's "Dance In The Smoke", the band managed to successfully bridge 60s youth-ritual mysticism with the pretentious professionalism that would dominate the 70s without sounding like it was the handiwork of the label's marketing department.

Despite the obvious popsmanship, the album largely fell on deaf ears. The band's second set, RING

OF HANDS (1971), didn't help matters any and sounded as if they were haunted by the ghosts of Tolkien and **YES**. Despite the wretched suite that closed out ALL TOGETHER NOW (1972), the album featured Argent's one truly transcendent moment – the eternal "Hold Your Head Up" (1971). With its union of riff and screaming title hook, "Hold Your Head Up" was an undeniable anthem, particularly when it blared out of a tinny car speaker.

A wannabe anthem, "God Gave Rock And Roll To You", featured on IN DEEP (1973) (which also included the truly loathsome "Christmas For The Free"); its chant-along chorus was so cheap that it would have embarrassed even Slade or Roy Wood. By the time of NEXUS (1974), Argent were such consummate pros that all they wanted to do was make classical records. They started calling their 'compositions' such things as "The Coming Of Kohoutec" and "Music From The Spheres".

After NEXUS Ballard left to produce Leo Sayer and write songs for the mighty Rainbow. He was replaced by guitarists **John Verity** and **John Grimaldi**, who joined in time to record the abysmal concept album CIRCUS (1975) (with song titles "Circus", "Highwire", "Clown", "Trapeze", "The Ring", "The Jester"). The ludicrous soloing and grandstanding continued on COUNTERPOINT (1975), which turned out to be the band's final opus. The group split in 1976 when Grimaldi quit, Argent began a career as a producer and the rest of the musicians started art-rock nightmare, **Phoenix**.

(•) **An Anthology – The Best of Argent** (1976; Epic).
It's got "Hold Your Head Up" and, really, what more do you need?

Peter Shapiro

A. R. KANE

Formed London, 1986; vanished 1995.

There is nothing on earth like **A. R. Kane**. They use funk but remove the groove, they use dub but remove the ruff-edged righteousness, they draped their music in swathes of feedback, sculpting it rather than letting it stand, they evoked a sense of bliss that decayed into morbidity. And all this within the framework of a pop sensibility.

Initially hailed as 'the black Jesus And Mary Chain', this duo of **Alex Ayuli** and **Rudi Tambala** originally claimed to be replicating the 70s works of Miles Davis on guitars. It's hard to see this in their debut single, "When You're Sad" (1987), a pleasant piece of soppy-boys' power pop that showed their command of the idiom but not too much else. "Lolita" (1987), the follow-up, was something else again: a song so dreamy it made you feel queasy, as Alex's languorous voice enticed you into a honeycombed trap. Its B-sides, "Sado-Masochism Is A Must" and "Butterfly Collector", detailed wonderful-turned-hellish sexual situations by imprisoning perfect pop within nightmarish swirls of feedback.

While "Pump Up The Volume"/"Antina" (1987), their single collaboration with Colourbox under the name **M/A/R/R/S**, hit #1 in the UK singles charts, A. R. Kane continued their quest for fresh entry points into the pop song. The debut album, 69 (1988), one of the best of the decade, charted extremities with bewildering subtlety, twisting into ecstatic, melancholic, disturbing, spaced-out modes – sometimes all at the same time. They went on to embrace an unfeasibly wide array of genres on their sprawling double album, i (1990). From ten-second shards of feedback noise to six-minute dub panoramas, from deceptively breezy tunes to jagged-edged rock; from cod acid house to weird semi-tribal clatter – it sounded like part of an immense concept kept in reserve by Alex and Rudi.

And that was more or less it. Their eventual return with NEW CLEAR CHILD (1995) was a disappointing combination of trite New Age lyrics and polite retreads of past glories; the group disintegrated soon after. Alex became a museum curator in the US and then released Soul Surging in 1999, while Rudi became a shadowy Svengali figure to a number of arcane bands in London and has occasionally popped his head up to release under the name **Sufi**.

(•) **69** (1988; Rough Trade).
An amazing perversion of late 80s dream-pop, ranging from the blissful alcoves of "Crazy Blue" to the echoing death chambers of "The Madonna Is With Child".

(•) **i** (1990; Rough Trade).
Although some found this self-consciously eclectic, it remains an unprecedented combination of twisted soul music and showman's sleight-of-hand.

Ben Smith

JOAN ARMATRADING

Born St. Kitts, West Indies, December 1950.

The first black female singer–songwriter to come to prominence in the UK, **Joan Armatrading** has had a career of steady rather than spectacular success, and tends to be thought of principally as an influence on younger artists such as Tasmin Archer and Tracy Chapman. However, in an era that has not proved too hospitable for singer-songwriters in the traditional mould, she has outlasted all those who pretended to her throne, proving that more is needed for a career in music than good looks and good sales.

Born on the island of St. Kitts, she and her family moved to Birmingham when she was still young. A shy and self-reliant child, she spent a lot of time listening to the radio and teaching herself to play the guitar and piano. At the instigation of friends and relatives she began to play sets in local clubs as a teenager, despite a shyness that made live performances daunting.

At this stage she thought of herself primarily as a songwriter. However, her voice secured her a part in the long-running musical *Hair* in 1970. There she met **Pam Nestor**, another West Indian immigrant, who was to be an important musical and personal influence. They started to write songs together and Joan was persuaded to record some demo tapes. The circulation of these resulted in the duo being signed as a songwriting team to the Cube label, based in London. The first result of this collaboration was WHATEVER'S FOR US, which was released in 1972, but credited solely to Armatrading.

Produced by Gus Dudgeon, who had been working with Elton John, it had a rather Elton-esque sound to it, particularly in the piano role, but also because Dudgeon had recruited percussionist **Ray Cooper** and guitarist **Davey Johnstone** from Elton's band. Yet all that is best in her later work was also here: a warm and rich vocal presence, fluent and rhythmic guitar work, and the lyrics of an unsentimental observer who nevertheless possesses a romantic streak.

The record received a favourable reception, but Armatrading and Nestor parted ways soon after, and a restrictive contract meant a second album was delayed until 1975, when A&M released BACK TO THE NIGHT. This was followed the following year by her first commercial success, JOAN ARMATRADING. These, and the albums that quickly followed – SHOW SOME EMOTION (1977) and TO THE LIMIT (1978) – saw her refining her musical identity, finding the confidence to give tender songs such as "Love And Affection", "Willow" and "Down To Zero" room to breathe. Rootsy influences also came to light on tracks such as "Bottom To The Top" and "Rosie". All these albums were produced by Glyn Johns, who managed to strike a balance between Armatrading's natural energy and the melancholy often present in her lyrics.

A loyal fan base was accumulating, sufficient to ride out the minor controversy engendered by her writing the soundtrack to *The Wild Geese* (1980), a film about mercenaries in Southern Africa. The early 80s saw her move to a rockier sound on ME, MYSELF, I (1980), which featured **Sly Dunbar** and **Robbie Shakespeare**, WALK UNDER LADDERS (1981) and THE KEY (1983). Armatrading proved she could carry off this harder sound whilst retaining her skill with dark but gentler things, notably "The Weakness In Me" and "All The Way From America".

Always a prolific writer, she has continued to release albums at regular intervals, including HEARTS AND FLOWERS (1990) and SQUARE THE CIRCLE (1992). These were pleasant enough, but, aside from the occasional track ("Wrapped Around Her", for instance), they tended towards a rather weighty blandness, lacking the stark edge and immediacy of her earlier work. A career retrospective LOVE AND AFFECTION (1997; A&M), comprising 39 tracks, gives a good overview of her career but only emphasizes the strength of her late-70s work when compared to the frankly insipid remainder.

⦿ **Joan Armatrading** (1976; A&M).
A cracking album that sees her stride into top form. It contains two intense songs that are as good as anything she's done - "Water In The Wine" and "Down To Zero". It also includes her most famous song, "Love And Affection".

⦿ **Track Record** (1983; A&M).
Despite the weak pun of the title, this is slightly the better of the two greatest hits albums, principally because it focuses on the first half of her career.

James Owen

ART OF NOISE

Formed London, 1983; disbanded 1990.

The formation of **Art Of Noise** coincided with the launch of ABC producer Trevor Horn's new record label ZTT (Zang Tumb Tuum), a subsidiary of Chris Blackwell's Island label. It was rumoured that Horn was offered the distribution deal because, as co-creator of Buggles' "Video Killed The Radio Star" (1979), he had provided Island Records with its only British #1 single to date.

The sessions for ABC's debut album, THE LEXICON OF LOVE (1982), were to bring together string arranger and Royal College of Music graduate **Anne Dudley** (keyboards), engineer **Gary Langan** and **JJ Jeczalik**, who had brought to the album's sound a novel new piece of keyboard hardware: the Fairlight, which could musicalize and reproduce any sound or sample. During a stressful period working on Yes's 1983 album 90125, the foursome embarked on a series of experimental sessions, in which Jeczalik's new toy and Dudley's ear for melody collided with the influence of the emerging New York hip-hop scene.

Taking their name from an Italian futurist manifesto from the 1920s, Art Of Noise were born in the autumn of 1983. Horn's co-founder at ZTT, former music journalist **Paul Morley**, became its fifth member, responsible for publicity, the (very) occasional lyric, and increasingly eccentric sleeve notes. Enigmatic to the full, this new part-time quintet refused to be photographed, preferring the representation of masks. Or even, as Morley evasively said, 'A spanner in the works. Because a spanner is intrinsically more interesting than the lead singer of Tears For Fears.'

Yet, if all of this sounds too whimsical by half, there was a period when Art Of Noise had serious credibility. A six-track EP, INTO BATTLE WITH THE ART OF NOISE (ZTT's first release in 1983), became a cult dance-floor favourite, especially the embryonic version of "Beatbox". Enormous success in the American dance charts followed in 1984, leading to stateside assumptions that Art Of Noise were a black group.

After arranging and remixing tracks for **FRANKIE GOES TO HOLLYWOOD**, the group eventually hit the British charts in their own right, with the album WHO'S AFRAID OF THE ART OF NOISE (1984). It contained the Top 10 single, "Close (To The Edit)", with its memorable 'Fairlighting' of a car engine set to another thunderous hip-hop rhythm. The album was much more diverse, presenting an unholy alliance of the eccentric and the beautiful, which reached its pinnacle on the ten-minute "Moments In Love".

But it didn't last long. In the summer of 1985, Dudley, Jeczalik and Langan left ZTT and signed to

Chrysalis subsidiary China Records. Horn and Morley reportedly threatened to form a rival group called **Act And Art**, although this never actually materialized. Horn went on to produce the Pet Shop Boys, Grace Jones, Rod Stewart and Seal, while Morley returned to journalism and TV.

Art Of Noise mark 2 retained a sense of novelty, largely through their collaborative work on singles with **Duane Eddy** (on a 1986 revival of his own "Peter Gunn"), computerized animated cult hero **Max Headroom** ("Paranoimia", 1986), **Tom Jones** (on a stunning cover of Prince's "Kiss" in 1988), and South African singers **Mahlathini And The Mahotella Queens** (on "Yebo!", 1989). However, their three late-80s albums – IN VISIBLE SILENCE (1986), IN NO SENSE? NONSENSE! (1987) and BELOW THE WASTE (1989) – were patchy affairs, finding the trio locked somewhere between the film soundtrack and the dance floor, and were compared unfavourably with their debut. Better results came out of their film and TV work, notably for the movie *Dragnet* (1988).

Gary Langan had become a part-time member of Art Of Noise by the release of THE AMBIENT COLLECTION (1990), their final album. It was packed with languid but lively instrumentals and, as ever, quirks – like a reworking of the theme music from the 60s TV series *Robinson Crusoe*. It didn't chart.

Post-Art Of Noise, Jeczalik and Langan continued with session and production work, but Dudley appears to have been the most successful: not only has she collaborated with the likes of Pulp and Pet Shop Boys, she provided the soundtrack for TV's *Jeeves And Wooster* (1990) and Neil Jordan's Oscar-winning movie *The Crying Game* (1992). Her profile was raised still further when her original music for the 1997 movie *The Full Monty* won her an Oscar. In the meantime, she had worked with Killing Joke's **Jaz Coleman** on SONGS FROM THE VICTORIOUS CITY (1991), an intriguing exploration of Egyptian and Oriental music and sounds, and branched into the classical crossover market with an electro-updating of the Christian hymnbook, entitled ANCIENT AND MODERN (1995).

Yet Art Of Noise's dance-floor origins were never quite forgotten: several rave and techno innovators acknowledged their influence with a compilation of specially remixed tracks called THE FON MIXES (1992) and THE DRUM AND BASS COLLECTION (1996). Also in 1996, an inimitable vocal sample from "Close (To The Edit)" could clearly be heard on The Prodigy's UK #1, "Firestarter".

● **Daft** (1987; ZTT/Island).
An hour-long reissue of the WHO'S AFRAID OF THE ART OF NOISE album, with tracks from the INTO BATTLE EP and two superb remixes of the hypnotic favourite, "Moments In Love".

● **The Best Of The Art Of Noise** (1988; China/Chrysalis).
A double album of greatest hits and misses, which concentrates on their later years. It also featured a few intriguing album tracks, including the curiosity "Opus 4" from IN VISIBLE SILENCE.

Justin Lewis

ASH

Formed Downpatrick, Northern Ireland, 1992.

Ash belong in the same camp as Oasis, crunching out guitar riffs and tuneful songs that hark back to the 70s. Stalwarts of the Britrock scene, the band had an inauspicious start. 'Geeky' **Rick McMurray** was only recruited because he was the only drummer known to **Mark Hamilton** (bass) and **Tim Wheeler** (guitar/vocals). With his peroxide locks and all-round cool demeanour, he is now arguably the band's most fully fledged rock star. But then things have moved fast for Ash since 1995 when Wheeler left school and the band went full-time professional, having already turned down prestigious slots supporting Pearl Jam and Soul Asylum.

They celebrated their precociousness on the cover of their debut mini-album, TRAILER (1994), with a picture of a howling baby in a highchair and a woman on a phone saying, 'They're still kids – too young to marry, vote or drink in a pub. But tragically, they're not too young to sell themselves for sex.' This grunge/pop/punk hybrid took up residence in the UK indie charts in October 1994, supported by an increasingly effective line of singles: "Petrol" and "Uncle Pat", which were lifted from the album, and "Kung Fu" (1995), which stormed the indie singles list and brushed the UK Top 60.

In Britain's long hot summer of 1995, Ash released "Girl From Mars", arguably the catchiest pop workout of the year. The B-sides were the surreal "Astral Conversations With Toulouse Lautrec" and an equally offbeat cover of "Cantina Band", a track first heard in *Star Wars*, where it was played by aliens in an eatery peopled by some of the galaxy's weirdest life forms.

By now the band had signed a five-album deal with Warner Reprise in the US, and the serious work had started. This included festival dates at Glastonbury and Reading, European tours, and the small matter of recording the first album for a major label.

Punk-influenced thrash pop was big business in the wake of the likes of Green Day, and Ash clearly had the vision and ability to capitalize. Their second album, 1977 (1996), mixed grinding riffs, killer hooks and bags of attitude and went straight to #1 in the UK charts. It featured "Girl From Mars", of course, and did a good job of matching it with the likes of "Goldfinger" (masses of melody and power chords) and "Gone The Dream" (which had echoes of early Pink Floyd).

In the wake of 1977's success, Ash toured widely, landing high-profile support and festival slots, such as Glastonbury. Touring took precedence over studio work and, to satisfy demand for new product, the UK independent label Death Star released the rough-and-ragged LIVE AT THE WIRELESS (1996), an 'official bootleg' of ten tracks assembled 'live in the studio' during their 1996 tour of Australia. In August

Ash's Tim Wheeler practising his enunciation

1997, the band announced the addition of guitarist **Charlotte Hatherley**. Hatherley was sharing composing credits by the spring of 1998, when Ash contributed the title song to the film *A Life Less Ordinary*. Their second full-length studio set, Nu Clear Sounds, was released in 1998 and was followed by a full-scale UK tour. Produced by Chris Kimsey, it attempted a wider-ranging rock sound, the hard edges and solid hooks joined by extended intros and production effects. Sales of the album were respectable but reviews were mixed. By the time "Wildsurf" was released as the second single, McMurray had joined the writing crew, contributing "Stormy Waters" as a B-side. After the patchy reception accorded to Nu Clear Sounds, Ash's next release would be pivotal. 2002's Free All Angels showed a band keen to revisit its roots. The album's more effective moments saw a return to the punk–pop thrash with which they made their name. It showed the band playing to their strengths and developing in a way that felt unforced and natural. Time is still on their side and their work rate remains impressive, which suggests they still have the potential to build an international reputation.

Trailer (1994; Infectious).
An insistent blend of noise, riffs and catchy melodies. As strong a debut album as, for example, Nirvana's Bleach and all the better for running a mere 25 minutes or so.

1977 (1996; Infectious).
The title says a lot – we're back to the era of punk energy, channelled on this fab follow-up into some of the most melodic power pop committed to record, with Tim Wheeler on top vocal form. The title, though, refers back to the year they were born more than to rock'n'roll's year zero.

Neil Nixon

ASH RA TEMPEL

Formed Berlin, 1970.

Manuel Gottsching (guitar) and **Hartmut Enke** (bass) had played together in various psychedelic blues and pop combos for a few years before they formed **Ash Ra Tempel** in August 1970 with drummer/keyboardist **Klaus Schulze**, who had just left **TANGERINE DREAM**. The most cosmic of the Krautrock bands, Ash Ra Tempel became legendary for their wild improvisational free-form live jams, influenced by Pink Floyd but eschewing songs to take the concept of space-rock much further, enhanced by both Schulze's and Gottsching's interest in experimental electronic music.

Their debut, Ash Ra Tempel (1971), contained just two long instrumental pieces, although Gottsching does provide some wordless vocal trills. "Amboss" starts off with quiet electronic drones before building into furious guitar riffs and pounding drums, whereas "Traummaschine" was more ethereal. This was the blueprint for several albums to follow, acid-frenzied freakouts on the first side, chill-out on the second.

Schulze soon left for a solo career but several other musicians passed through the group's revolving door, and with some of them Gottsching and Enke recorded the amazing SCHWINGUNGEN (1972). With the idea of recording the ultimate psychedelic trip, Ohr label-head Rolf Kaiser next took Ash Ra Tempel to Switzerland to party endlessly and to record the album SEVEN UP (1973) with LSD guru **Timothy Leary**, who was living there in exile. The results were a more song-orientated first section, with Leary singing, followed by several conventional rock songs melded into a single track divided by spacey electronic segues.

In 1973 Schulze rejoined briefly for JOIN INN (1973), recorded while the three musicians, plus Gottsching's girlfriend **Rosi** on vocals, waited for other musicians to show up during the WALTER WEGMULLER TAROT SESSIONS. Around this time all three musicians contributed to the music that was later to be released on several albums under the moniker of the **Cosmic Jokers**. Not long after, acid-fried Enke flipped out in the middle of a concert, stopped playing and just stood on stage, and afterwards Ash Ra Tempel became more a Gottsching solo project, either with guest musicians, or simply solo – as on his fascinating INVENTIONS FOR ELECTRIC GUITAR (1975). The results were far less intense.

By 1977 he'd shortened the name to **Ashra**, and the music had become more synth-orientated and often less interesting, coming off like so much New Age aural wallpaper. The experimental WALKIN' THE DESERT (1989) is, however, a noteworthy exception. Gottsching has also released a couple albums under his own name, most notably E2–E4 (1984) which features one sixty-minute rhythm machine and guitar piece.

⊙ **Schwingungen** (1972; Ohr).
Mind-warping sounds, from Gottsching's frenzied guitar riffing to (non)-vocalist John L.'s screams and rants on side one to the weird electronic effects that at moments turn the music inside out.

⊙ **Join Inn** (1973; Ohr).
Side one contains some of Ash Ra Tempel's most intense jamming, while the cosmic flip side features Schulze's shimmering electronics, Rosi's intoned vocals, and an occasional deep throb of Enke's bass.

⊙ **Inventions For Electric Guitar** (1975; Kosmische Musik).
Long mellow spacey pieces that are created from guitars through tape and delay effects. Not mind-blowing like the first four 'classic' albums, but this one does have its charm.

Rolf Semprebon

ASIAN DUB FOUNDATION

Formed London, 1993.

The Community Music House in Farringdon, near the City of London, can best be described as a music laboratory for established and aspiring musicians to experiment and create in. It was here in the summer of 1993 that the Arts Council filmed *Identical Beat*, a documentary following the progress of a series of workshops held to teach Asian youths the basics of music technology.

Aniruddha Das, aka **Dr. Das** (bass), was the tutor in charge of the workshops. Helping him out was youth worker and DJ **John Pandit** (**Pandit G**). Amongst the kids who attended was a 15-year-old Bengali rapper called **Deedar Zaman** (**Master D**). The three formed **Asian Dub Foundation** a few months later as a sound system, before evolving into a band with the arrival of Birmingham-born guitarist **Steve Chandra Savale** in 1994. Savale's habit of tuning all his guitar strings to one note (like those of a sitar), cranking up his distortion and playing the instrument with a knife earned him the nickname '**Chandrasonic**'.

All the ADF's members were raised on both Asian and Western music. Chandrasonic had been a member of **Headspace**, a dub/noise outfit, before co-founding **The Higher Intelligence Agency**. His style of guitar playing was inspired by years of listening to the classical sitar music his father would play at home, before later punk leanings diversified into dub, P-funk, techno and ambient music. Tabla player Das had been taught Bengali folk songs by an aunt, Pandit G's first major musical influence was The Fall, and Master D had been rapping since the age of 9, joining the more socially aware **State Of Bengal**, and becoming one of the Asian community's most popular junglist DJs.

The ADF found a welcoming fan base among the anti-fascist movement, addressing the issue of racism as it affected Britain's ethnic minorities in general. 'Massive not passive' became their catchphrase, a reaction to the stereotypical image of Asian people as doormats. Their emergence on the rock scene could not have been better timed: the extreme right-wing British National Party (BNP) had very narrowly won its first election victory in East London, and violent incidents against Asians across Britain were on the increase.

In the summer of 1994, an ADF demo caught the attention of Nation Records, who commissioned the critically acclaimed EP, CONSCIOUS (1994). At the end of that year, having played several benefit gigs, they supported Trans-Global Underground at several London dates. Their punk influences really came to the fore in their stage act, which incorporated a slide show and a chance to showcase their newest members: dancer **Bubble-E** and another DJ, **Sun-J**. Their second release, "Rebel Warrior" (1995), wowed the critics: *DJ* magazine described it as 'multi-cultural tribal dub hop', while *Melody Maker* called it 'a mixture of phat beats embellished with syncopated trickles, squeaks and squelches'. FACTS AND FICTIONS, their debut album, was released in October 1995, featuring "Rebel Warrior" and re-recorded tracks from CONSCIOUS.

RAFI'S REVENGE (1998) was, surprisingly, even more confident and bubbled over with gleeful vitriol. A mess of tight, frantic breakbeats backdropped the urgent rap; evil, dirty samples and twisted guitar noise added to the chaos in one of the most exciting albums of the year. Live, they were getting even better. RAFI'S REVENGE was shortlisted for the 1998 *Mercury Music Prize*, but lost out to Gomez.

COMMUNITY MUSIC followed in 2000 to even more critical acclaim, and saw the group widening their sonic palette even further, while 2003's darker ENEMY OF THE ENEMY was a brooding amalgam of heavy sounds and political bluster.

George Luke

THE ASSOCIATES

Formed Edinburgh, 1979; disbanded 1990.

Often presenting themselves more as a corporation than as a band, **The Associates** have been belatedly acknowledged as one of the 80s' most inspired pop groups. Dundee-born vocalist **Billy Mackenzie** and multi-instrumentalist **Alan Rankine** used their shared love of Bowie, disco and 70s art-rock to create a unique hybrid, which bloomed into ever stranger forms in isolation from much of the Scottish music scene.

The Associates' recorded debut was an unhinged cover of "Boys Keep Swinging" (1979), released in the slipstream of Bowie's original. Many heads were turned, but it was Fiction Records who held out the chequebook and released 1980's THE AFFECTIONATE PUNCH album. Stark, scratchy and guitar-dominated, it nevertheless held a brace of epic ballads, showing the duo had an innate grasp of musical drama. Mackenzie was heralded as a major new vocalist, his operatic swoops and yelps eliciting comparisons with Scott Walker and Russell Mael of Sparks.

A series of quick-fire singles followed, on Beggars Banquet subsidiary Situation Two. On these Rankine took the initiative, creating astonishing soundscapes that seemed to owe no allegiance to any music on earth. Often veering close to chaos, pulsing synths and distorted guitars gave the effect of soundtracks for a travelogue of unknown countries, with dialogue provided by Mackenzie's playfully opaque verbosity. Still too left-field for the Top 40, The Associates jumped at an offer from Warners as a chance to aim themselves at the charts.

Their debut Warners single was "Party Fears Two" (1982), named after a pair of scary habitual gatecrashers Mackenzie remembered from college parties. This was a major change in style, built around an instantly memorable piano riff, and even the paranoid lyrics couldn't stop it barging into the UK Top 10, followed by further hits, "Club Country" and "18 Carat Love Affair". The attendant album, SULK (1982), featured original Cure bassist **Michael Dempsey** and scored with both the critics and the

buyers. Slipping into the glamour revival pioneered by the likes of ABC, the album's lush and dense sound seesawed between oblique funky pop and dark cabaret moments, with Mackenzie's unsettling and surreal lyrics adding a veil of otherworldliness.

Relations became strained, though, and after working on a successful overhaul of THE AFFECTIONATE PUNCH the introverted Rankine jumped ship; since his disappointing solo album, SHE LOVES ME NOT, he has been lying low. Undaunted, Mackenzie took on **Howard Hughes** (keyboards) and **Steve Reid** (guitar) for PERHAPS (1985). Moving still further towards pop, the album was more romantic and direct than earlier work, but idiosyncrasy had by then long since departed from the charts, and the album was an unexpected flop. A planned follow-up, "The Glamour Chase", was axed by Warners after a rather desperate cover of Blondie's "Heart Of Glass" also bombed.

The group then moved to Virgin subsidiary Circa, who were happy to release 1990's WILD AND LONELY, but the original Associates magic had faded and the album made no impression. Despite frequent rumours of an epic orchestral solo album, and one-off collaborations with Yello and Heaven 17's offshoot project, the **British Electric Foundation**, Billy Mackenzie seemed to have put The Associates to bed. He took his own life, overcome by the death of his mother, on January 1, 1997. Later the same year his solo collection, BEYOND THE SUN, was posthumously released, receiving rave reviews but failing to capture the public's imagination. It remains an overlooked classic.

The Associates

Popera: The Singles Collection (1990; Warner Bros).
Only the singles from the AFFECTIONATE PUNCH and WILD AND LONELY eras are missing from this excellent compilation. Explore the sumptuous SULK singles, the Situation Two oddities, and post-Rankine treats such as "Those First Impressions" and the near hit, "Breakfast".

Billy Mackenzie

Beyond The Sun (1997; Nude).
This is a moody collection of torch songs, with sparse piano accompaniment. Several of the best cuts received Simon Raymonde's Midas touch, who imbued them with a similar polished beauty to This Mortal Coil releases.

Chris Tighe

AT THE DRIVE-IN

Formed El Paso, Texas, 1994; disbanded, 2001.

The desert town of El Paso isn't perhaps the most obvious place from which to start a musical revolution, but it had to start somewhere. **At The Drive-In**'s success at fusing styles ranging from balls-out punk rock to soul-quaking emo – encompassing all points in between – was the result of an uncompromising spirit and a truly astonishing work ethic.

The best known line-up consisted of **Cedric** (vocals), **Jim** (guitar/keyboards/backing vocals),

Cedric performing his famous microphone levitation

Omar (guitar), **Paul** (bass) and **Tony** (drums) – a bunch of passionate individuals who believed whole-heartedly in the power of great rock'n'roll and the genuine value of the indie scene; they also dispensed with surnames, going for that personal touch common to 'emo' bands, not to mention instigating a no crowd-surfing rule at gigs in case anyone got hurt. Their most accomplished album, RELATIONSHIP OF COMMAND (2000), was a land-mark release for the burgeoning post-hardcore scene and a superb example of art triumphing over com-mercial enterprise. It was a blueprint for many of the emo/post-hardcore bands plying their 'emotional-hardcore' trade today.

Any revolution has to start small and it was with the fondly remembered "Hell Paso" 7" single, released on their own label, that they started their rise to recognition as celebrated alternative pioneers. Their music showed a passion for punk and the single was a raw expression of emotion that resonated with kids growing up in the middle of nowhere. The band's almost endless touring career began soon after its release with a jaunt across their native state. This was consolidated with the release of another single, "Alfaro Vive, Carajo" in 1995.

These two records are now highly sought after, but it took a great deal more touring before the band showed up in Los Angeles to record their full-length debut, ACROBATIC TENEMENT (1996). Cedric was already developing his own oblique and personal way with words (anyone who has scanned through ATDI lyrics will appreciate the impenetrable nature of the lead singer's thought processes), the album cost a mere $600 to record and buzzed with nascent energy.

A line-up jiggle resulted in EL GRAN ORGO (1997), a more melodic but no less heartfelt out-pouring of intense emotion. At this point, however, a problem arose with the band's label, Flipside, which meant the band had to find another company – only no one was willing to give them a chance. Fearless (true to their name) came to the rescue, and any fans worried that a label more at home with pop punk might destroy the unique creativity that ATDI were nurturing were soon able to relax when IN/CASINO/OUT (1998), recorded by Alex Newport, appeared. The band's first attempt at cap-turing their frenetic live sound on tape, it was recorded as though the band were playing a gig, with only a minor overdub or two added prior to release. Bigger shows, playing alongside heroes such as Fugazi, Jimmy Eat World and Archers Of Loaf, ensued and the band seemed doomed to live forever on the road, honing their explosive performance skills.

The pathway to RELATIONSHIP OF COMMAND began with VAYA (1999), a seven-song mini-LP that eventually led to their collaboration with producer Ross Robinson, the man best known for launching

AT THE DRIVE-IN

45

the bass-heavy nu-metal sound of bands such as Korn and Slipknot. They met him while on tour and became convinced that he was the man to really do them justice on CD. At the same time, rap-metallers Rage Against The Machine decided that the dynamic Texans would be an ideal support act; the resulting massive hike in profile did the band absolutely no harm.

When RELATIONSHIP OF COMMAND eventually hit the shelves, released through Grand Royal, the Beastie Boys' label, fans who had been in on the ground floor were heard to mutter 'sell-out' in light of the set's international distribution. The quality of the music was undiminished, however, with Cedric's lyrics at their abstract best and the music veering from electronic wibbling and eerily theatrical spoken-word passages to charging punk rock; they even harnessed **Iggy Pop**'s help on "Rolodex Propaganda".

Success and recognition was to get the better of them, however, and ATDI dissolved in 2001 to pursue other musical goals in various splinter factions **The Mars Volta**, **Sparta** and **De Facto**. Whether any of these bands will have the same impact as ATDI remains to be seen.

⊙ **Acrobatic Tenement** (1996; Flipside).
Their first album and a bristling statement of intent. Their arty hardcore punk roots are very much in evidence, though there's a lot more to their sound than sheer brute power.

⊙ **Vaya** (1999; Fearless).
The bridge to their groundbreaking final record. This is beautiful, raw, sonically diverse and intense, displaying all the flamboyance and power of their live shows.

⊙ **Relationship Of Command** (2000; Grand Royal).
Proper international distribution brought the band to the world at last. Ironically, it also instigated their split. A classic.

Essi Berelian

ATOMIC ROOSTER

Formed England, 1969; disbanded 1974; re-formed 1980; disbanded 1983; re-formed 1998.

Atomic Rooster were the band who put the word 'heavy' into heavy rock. Despite a huge following and two hit singles (and one near miss) in the early 70s, however, they generally fill no more than a paragraph in the majority of music guides. Except this one.

In 1969, the Crazy World of Arthur Brown imploded during an American tour. **Vincent Crane**, the band's distinctive organist and co-writer of Brown's #1 hit "Fire", bailed out of the rapidly sinking ship mid-tour and, curiously enough, bumped into **Carl Palmer**, who had also jumped ship, on the same plane home. They decided to stay together, and having recruited **Nick Graham** on bass and vocals, Atomic Rooster were born. A deal was signed with Chris Blackwell's nascent B&C label and the first album, ATOMIC ROOSTER, appeared. Unfortunately, Graham's vocals seemed a little

unsuited to the music and he soon left to form **Skin Alley**, a fine band much more suited to his style.

John Cann, ex-member of ultra-heavy rock band **Andromeda**, was asked to join and the band threw themselves into a frenetic round of gigs and radio sessions (BBC sessions appear from this line-up but no records were released). Just as things were taking off, Carl Palmer left to join Keith Emerson and Greg Lake (see **EMERSON, LAKE AND PALMER**) in their new venture. It might seem odd in retrospect that Palmer was reluctant to leave Atomic Rooster, but Rooster were tipped for the top at that point and were a highly respected live act.

Ric Parnell briefly filled the vacant drum stool but was quickly ousted by **Paul Hammond**, whose heavy, but controlled, style fitted perfectly with Crane's organ assaults and Cann's sinister, spitting vocals and staccato guitar.

The second album, DEATH WALKS BEHIND YOU (1970), showcased the band brilliantly and chart success was achieved with "Tomorrow Night" and "Devil's Answer". A new deal was signed with Pegasus Records and the band were augmented by **Pete French** on vocals. One of the greatest, though mostly ignored, voices in British rock, French – best known in collectors' circles for his work with **Black Cat Bones** and **Leafhound** – only stayed long enough to record the album IN HEARING OF, which successfully complemented the previous set.

All was not well in the Rooster camp and French's departure was followed by those of Cann and Hammond, who formed heavy rock band **Hard Stuff** with Johnny Gustavson (ex-Big Three and Jesus Christ Superstar) on bass. Crane was left with an album to promote and no band.

Ric Parnell was hurriedly re-recruited, **Steve Bolton** was added on guitar and **Chris Farlowe** was drafted in following the demise of **Colosseum**. An appearance on Belgian TV playing a selection of songs from the IN HEARING OF album (1971) showed the band to be stunningly good live but the next two albums, on Pye's Dawn label, MADE IN ENGLAND (1972, complete with novelty denim sleeve) and NICE AND GREASY (1973, with **Johnny Mandala** replacing Bolton), were patchy affairs to say the least, although "Stand By Me" from the former was a hit all over Europe whilst narrowly missing the charts in the UK.

Rooster finally ground to a halt after a one-off single for Decca, "Tell Your Story, Sing Your Song", backed by the sadly prophetic "OD". The rest of the 70s and early 80s saw Crane recording with **Klaus Schulze** and **Arthur Brown** as well as an appearance in **Mick Green**'s band.

Suddenly, in the early 80s, Rooster were back on the scene and another eponymous album appeared on EMI. Crane and Cann (now du Cann) were augmented by **Preston Heyman** for the album. This time Rooster were back and were taking no prisoners – the album was more heavy metal than heavy rock but still sounded like a Rooster album. Live, the band were given a boost by the presence of **Ginger Baker**, but soon found themselves being advertised as "Ginger Baker's Atomic Rooster". He had to go, and when the gun smoke cleared, Paul Hammond was back – the classic line-up had returned again. What a shame that the audience hadn't – the band played a stunning set to often half-empty clubs and a couple of fine singles for Polydor came and went. Even the presence of **Dave Gilmour** on the final album, HEADLINE NEWS (1983), couldn't conceal the fact that Rooster were 'out of time'. HEADLINE NEWS, on the Towerbell label, was head and shoulders above the majority of rock albums of the time but as an Atomic Rooster album it was frankly disappointing.

John du Cann had bailed out before HEADLINE NEWS and prior to rejoining Rooster had had success when his solo single "Don't Be A Dummy", on Vertigo, was used on a Lee Cooper jeans advertisement – remember the sinister blue-faced punks with the luminous eyes? Vincent Crane ended up playing pub piano in a late **Dexy's Midnight Runners** line-up and shortly after came the sad news that he had committed suicide, overdosing on sleeping tablets. Not long after came the news of Paul Hammond's death.

Rooster were, at best, a stunning band who, unfortunately, were never able to break out of the mould they made for themselves with DEATH WALKS BEHIND YOU.

⊙ **Death Walks Behind You** (1970; B&C).
The album that defined the Rooster image as dark, satanic, leather-clad, moody and magnificent. From the opening freaky piano solo and scrunchy guitar to the final crashing chord, this album is the epitome of heavy rock (as distinct from heavy metal). Buy it now.

⊙ **Atomic Rooster** (1980; EMI).
The second ATOMIC ROOSTER-titled album sees them reborn and spitting venom at an unsuspecting audience. This is the album you suspect most metal bands wish they'd recorded, but with enough tell-tale Roosterisms to please the old fans too. "Watch Out", "Lost In Space" and "In the Shadows" stand out, quiter moments in a maelstrom of noise – not that these are that quiet!

⊙ **Devil's Answer – BBC Sessions** (1998; Hux).
This has it all, BBC sessions covering 1970–1972 and 1981. Played live, even the dodgier songs sound fresh. And the good songs sound even better.

Mark Jones

THE AU PAIRS

Formed Birmingham, England, 1979; disbanded 1983.

Equally at home at a 'Rock Against Racism' benefit or a CND rally as in a sweaty club or the back room of the pub, **The Au Pairs** formed part of the second wave of punk, a group of bands who carried a more focused political brief than the original anarchic crew.

The group – **Lesley Woods** (vocals/guitar), **Paul Foad** (guitar/vocals), **Jane Munro** (bass) and **Pete Hammond** (drums) – formed in Birmingham in 1979, and absorbed all the post-punk influences of that time and place. Reggae, ska, blue-beat and riff-heavy garage thrash were adapted through Munro's heavy basslines and twin guitars, which eschewed riffing and histrionics for the chopping rhythms of Jamaica. This had the effect of making the group compulsively danceable while not detracting attention from the lyrics, which were projected by Woods' powerful and controlled blues voice – the band's biggest asset.

Two albums – PLAYING WITH A DIFFERENT SEX (1981) and SENSE AND SENSUALITY (1982) – and nonstop touring built a following without threatening to catapult the band to major status. The latter featured guest spots from some of **The Pop Group**, which of course did little to add catchiness or promote mainstream success. The group disbanded after Woods failed to turn up for a date in Belgium, in 1983.

Often spoken of in the same breath as the all-female bands The Slits and The Raincoats, The Au Pairs actually had more in common with Leeds band the Gang of Four, both in their raw sound and in their conviction that political issues were appropriate subjects for rock songs. Both bands concentrated on the exercise of power, in particular the power relations between the sexes, with The Au Pairs using their mixed line-up to highlight the gender clash in songs that were incisive and funny. Their legacy of overtly political independent pop may not have been widely followed, although its influence can be seen in the work of bands such as Stereolab.

⊙ **Playing With A Different Sex** (1981; RPM).
Songs covering everything from equal pay to faking orgasm, via patriarchy and British imperialism, mixing humour and righteous anger. They don't make them like this any more.

Owen James

THE AUTEURS/BLACK BOX RECORDER

Luke Haines born Surrey, England, 1967.

"Your music's alright, but it's a bit Steely Dan. We fought wars to get rid of that stuff." Mark E. Smith to long-term Fall fan Luke Haines

Luke Haines (vocal/piano/guitar), a classically trained pianist and guitarist, had seen pop stardom pass him by during a stretch as guitarist in 80s also-rans **The Servants**. Deciding to form his own band, he recruited girlfriend **Alice Readman** (bass), plus **Glenn Collins** (drums), and gigged around London in summer 1992 as **The Auteurs**.

The band started out producing classic guitar pop, written and sung by Haines in the manner of a stroppy, latter-day Ray Davies. A demo impressed the *NME* and in November 1992 The Auteurs were signed to Hut records, who released their debut single, "Showgirl", a song of aching melody and off-beat lyrics. It found favour with the critics and helped ensure the band a place on the *NME*-sponsored *On Into 93* gig in January 1993.

The Auteurs' eagerly awaited debut album, NEW WAVE, arrived a month later, with a po-faced Haines masquerading as Rudolph Valentino on the sleeve. It offered a glimpse into a world of stardust and greasepaint, with barbed lyrics of revenge and mistrust: in "Valet Parking", Haines cast himself as a malevolent chauffeur; "Idiot Brother" related to his adversaries at a former record company; "American Guitars" railed against British bands who modelled themselves on Americans. Gaining rave reviews, the album cracked the UK Top 40 and went Top 10 in the indie chart. More importantly, perhaps, it was nominated for the prestigious *Mercury Music Prize*.

The band headed off on a UK tour, and a brief trip to the US, with cellist **James Banbury** added to the line-up. They played Glastonbury in the summer and toured with The The towards the end of the year. Life on the road was never The Auteurs' strong point, though. They were thrown off The The's last dates after Haines rowed with Matt Johnson, and his taciturn nature was not the stuff of frontmen of the year.

Still, the band nearly made it big, as a trio of singles – "How Could I Be Wrong", "Lenny Valentino" (both 1993) and "Chinese Bakery" (1994) – each just missed the UK Top 40. "Valentino", in particular, deserved a higher place – a song continuing Haines' fascination with Rudolph Valentino (and Lenny Bruce), with sneering vocals and menacing strings reminiscent of those in the film *Psycho*.

The band's second album, NOW I'M A COWBOY (1994), signalled a new line-up – **Barney Crockford** replaced Glenn Collins on drums, and cellist Banbury was promoted to a full-time member, adding his talents on Hammond organ. The record featured the last two singles, though its linchpin was the epic "The Upper Classes" – increasingly Haines'

favourite subject. It reached #27 in the UK chart, and a further tour, with Barney and James sporting bleached skinheads and Haines as unkempt and unruly as ever, culminated in an appearance at the Reading Festival.

The band largely disappeared from the public eye in 1995, spending time recording that difficult third album, which eventually emerged as AFTER MURDER PARK (1996). Produced by master of menace **Steve Albini**, it was a quantum leap from previous efforts, mixing understated strings and spiky vocal assaults to craft a Raymond Carver-esque collection of songs telling of missing children and the like. Despite critical acclaim, however, it sold a lot less than its predecessors.

Between 1996 and 1998, Haines decided to concentrate his efforts on two distinct side projects. The first – **Baader Meinhof** – produced a bizarrely compelling, self-titled, concept album (1996) with a lean, minimalist sound and a strong set of songs that unsurprisingly dealt with death, mayhem, and general political unrest. Haines also mixed in Eastern instrumentation and orchestration to provide exotic backdrops. Art terrorism, indeed.

Haines then changed direction with the first **Black Box Recorder** album, ENGLAND MADE ME (1998), by welding easy listening and 70s-styled theme music to disturbing and bitter lyrics, all sung with breathless faux-innocence by **Sarah Nixey**.

Neither efforts sold particularly well but they retained a strong cult following. The same fate awaited HOW I LEARNED TO LOVE THE BOOT BOYS (1999), Haines' attempt to resurrect the Auteurs' name in 1999. It was a brutal, scathing album that seemed to mock both the dull predictability of Britpop and the flabby, hedonistic laziness of dance culture. This mini-masterpiece deliberately sought to kick some life into a moribund indie rock scene. The result? More cultish adoration but weak sales. However, fortune favours the brave, and Black Box Recorder's second album, THE FACTS OF LIFE (2000), was well received, its title track providing Haines with copious radio play and a surprise Top 20 hit.

It took until 2001 for Haines to issue his first solo recordings. CHRISTIE MALRY'S OWN DOUBLE-ENTRY was the soundtrack to the movie version of B.S. Johnson's cult comic novel of the early 70s, while THE OLIVER TWIST MANIFESTO utilized hip-hop influences to great effect. Both found Haines addressing a select audience once more, but continuing to innovate and challenge listeners and the marketplace alike. The latter also saw its release coincide with Haines' idealistic call for a week-long 'National Pop Strike', when he had hoped their would be no new releases, charts, or pop music on the airwaves. As you might expect, Haines failed to bring the music industry to its knees.

Having returned to his post in the music business's global factory, Haines re-emerged in early 2003 with a new Black Box Recorder album, PASSIONOIA.

Black Box Recorder — England Made Me

Anna Robinson

THE AVENGERS

Formed San Francisco, 1977; broke up 1979; reunited briefly in 1999.

The **Avengers** were one of the greatest American punk bands ever. They were one of the first on the West Coast. And they were one of the first to release their music independently. It all started when lead singer **Penelope Houston** met up with guitarist **Greg Ingraham** at a San Fran art school. They quickly decided to form a band with bassist **Jimmy Wilsey** and drummer **Danny Furious**. They called themselves The Avengers – not borrowing from the brilliant Marvel comic or equally fab 60s TV show of the same name, but from a local artistic collective called The Art Avengers who they were to tour with and open for their 'art' happenings.

They soon fell out with the Art Avengers and started touring California on their own. Their sound was ferocious to say the least. Ingraham's speedy, heavy cannonball riffing, along with Furious and Wilsey's bulldozer rhythm section and Penelope's intelligent, searing lyrics were quite a sound and site to behold. Later in 1977 they became the first West Coast punk act to release their own music on a independent label when "We Are The One"/"Car Crash"/"I Believe In Me" was issued by the Dangerhouse label. All three cuts were defiant anthems of self-realization. They recorded more vinyl sides whilst touring, and without help from any US or UK Punk labels. Soon they'd attracted the attention of the biggest punk act of the time – **The Sex Pistols**.

The Pistols offered them the opening slot on what was to be their final gig ever in San Francisco. Rumour has it that The Avengers blew The Pistols off the stage. After The Pistols broke up **Steve Jones** stayed behind and offered to produce The Avengers. He worked on a four-song self-titled EP for them; before long Penelope and co. had returned to touring.

In late 1979, however, they stopped touring and disbanded completely. After that The Avengers myth only got bigger. In 1983 a label called CD Presents collected all the group's singles and released them as a disc simply called THE AVENGERS. It became a huge hit on American college radio. Yet this was also problematic: the label soon folded taking the Avengers masters with them. Penelope was obviously pissed, and vowed never to do any Avengers material again. She instead embarked upon a solo career making sharp folk pop/rock, which continues to this day.

But The Avengers would not go away. A whole new legion of female artists had grown up with their music and started bands claiming The Avengers as an influence. Finally, a Swedish indie label called Really Fast pressed two previously unreleased Avengers songs culled from Danny's private collection. This led to Penelope taking a new interest in her previous work and checking around for local collectors' bootlegs of Avengers shows. She found many and decided to release them and reunite with Ingraham and a new rhythm section (both big Avengers fans) to re-record some other Avengers gems. DIED FOR YOUR SINS was released by Lookout! Records in 1999 and was a brilliant document of the group (and the only one available publicly). They even toured briefly and still sounded as ragged and righteous as ever.

The Avengers' presence is still a mighty one. They've influenced many a US punk band. Jello Biafra claimed to have started The Dead Kennedys directly because of their work. Many bands in the Riot Grrl movement also cited them as an influence. Jimmy Wilsey now plays bass for another San Fran star, Chris Isaak. Penelope still records dazzling folk pop and tours constantly.

- **Died For Your Sins** (1999 Lookout!).
  An incredible 'band-approved' document. Raw concert footage blends well with re-recorded classics painting an impressive picture.

Chris Lark

KEVIN AYERS

Born Herne Bay, Kent, England, August 16, 1944.

Back in the hazy, hippie early 70s, **Kevin Ayers** was forever being touted for stardom. With his **SOFT MACHINE** background, his deadpan baritone, his witty lyrics and catchy tunes, how could he fail? He was Bryan Ferry with cool; Noël Coward on acid. Yet for the best part of a decade, Ayers kept blowing it, making an album, then drifting off to the Mediterranean for a spell of wine-soaked hedonism. His cult following never translated to mainstream success, and then came punk and it was all too late.

Ayers grew up in Malaysia, where his father was a District Officer, returning to his Kent birthplace as a teenager. He soon fell in with the Canterbury avant-garde, forming **The Wilde Flowers** (the final 'e' being a homage to Oscar) with **ROBERT WYATT**, **Daevid Allen** (**GONG**) and various future members of **CARAVAN**. Later, with Wyatt and Allen, and keyboard player **Mike Ratledge**, Ayers founded **Soft Machine**, court musicians to the London underground. His songs and cyclical bass playing formed the central core of the band's first LP.

After a gruelling six-month American tour with Jimi Hendrix in 1968, Ayers left the Softs, taking much of the band's melody and mystery. He retreated to Ibiza and began working on a series of songs. Released the following year on EMI's new progressive label, Harvest, as an Ayers solo album, JOY OF A TOY (1969) was a sumptuous affair, with arrangements by **David Bedford** and backing by the Soft Machine. It seemed to represent an image of the direction that the parent band never took.

Ayers next recorded the first of many singles which should have been hits, but weren't – "Singing A Song In The Morning" with Caravan and, so it was rumoured, his friend **Syd Barrett**. He then assembled a deeply eccentric touring band, the ambitiously named **Whole World**. Classical composer Bedford – who played his organ with a brick – joined busker and free-form saxophonist **Lol Coxhill**, and shy boy-genius **Mike Oldfield** on bass and guitar. The band soon fell apart, but left as its legacy the wildly experimental SHOOTING AT THE MOON.

Rarely has an LP filed under rock been so varied, from the sensuous crooning of "May I" to the edginess of "Lunatics Lament" to the cut-up musical techniques of "Rheinhart And Geraldine" and avant-garde nonsense of "Pisser Dans Un Violin". On the road, the Whole World would perform old music-hall songs, short radio plays and acoustic ballads, before suddenly launching into free-form freakouts.

The same band recorded, more conventionally, a 1971 BBC Radio 1 session (released as a CD twenty years later), with a full orchestra. As Ayers writes in the sleeve notes, 'there was a sense of family within that group that I have not found since. We were exploring together as opposed to just marking time which is what most of my generation do these days, myself, of course, included.'

Ayers toured briefly with Gong and released a killer single, "Stranger In Blue Suede Shoes", before retreating at the first sign of success. Its languid charm characterized the ensuing album, WHATEVERSHEBRINGSWESING (1972), which was recorded with members of the now-disbanded Whole World. Joined by veteran bassist **Archie Leggett** and drummer **Eddie Sparrow**, Ayers turned his attention to a kind of cabaret, *Banana Follies*, from which various odd ditties were later to surface. 'When things get too serious', he proclaimed, 'throw in a banana.'

In 1973, however, a chart hit looked assured with the single "Caribbean Moon", which matched Ayers' voice to a reggae-calypso backdrop. It didn't work out (though EMI kept re-releasing it throughout the decade), and nor did rock stardom beckon with the next album, BANANAMOUR (1973).

Ayers subsequently left the Harvest label for Island, and signed up with Elton John's manager, **John Reid**, in an apparently serious bid for fame. THE CONFESSIONS OF DR DREAM AND OTHER STORIES (1974) was a smooth, almost conventional affair which revisited old Softs terrain. "Why Are We Sleeping", inspired by Ayers' longtime fixation with Gurdjieff, had some cracking soul-girl backing from the **Soporifics**, and introduced guitarist **Ollie Halsall**. However, commercial success remained elusive despite a concert at the London Rainbow in which Ayers was joined by former Velvets **Nico** and **John Cale**, recent Roxy exile **Brian Eno**, and Mike Oldfield (then basking in TUBULAR BELLS fame).

The gig was rush-released as the album JUNE 1ST 1974, but Ayers' contribution was undistinguished. Indeed, he seemed to be running out of creative puff, and his next effort, SWEET DECEIVER (1975), which featured Elton John, received less critical response than a Harvesting of odds and ends released as ODD DITTIES.

As a final bid for rock stardom, Ayers recorded the lukewarm YES WE HAVE NO MAÑANAS (1976), and set off on tour with a band featuring **Andy Summers** and **Zoot Money**. The following year's RAINBOW TAKEAWAY had a whiff of LP-as-product and, in any case, coincided inappropriately with the advent of punk rock. Summers formed **THE POLICE** and Ayers loped off to Mallorca, where he has lived ever since.

Subsequently, he periodically and half-heartedly attempted to relaunch his career but an awareness of his own decline had begun to surface. In 1988 he reviewed his life and career to good effect on the ironically titled FALLING UP, which he backed with a short English tour. It was like a return from the living dead, and to mark it Harvest released a long-overdue 'best of', BANANA PRODUCTIONS.

Ayers has since released STILL LIFE WITH GUITAR (1992), a largely acoustic affair, nothing very new, but carried off with some grace and wit. In 1995, he also re-emerged as a performer, gigging around Britain with Liverpool band, The Wizards Of Twiddly. The following year, SINGING THE BRUISE (1996) – a compilation taken mainly from Ayers' sessions at the BBC in the early 1970s – appeared in the shops to little fanfare, with further releases from the period promised for the future.

Though he has maintained a low profile in terms of gigs or new songs, Ayers' presence continues to haunt rock culture. The likes of Gorky's Zygotic Mynci have namechecked him as an influence and Richard Branson's autobiography told an odd tale of a love triangle which involved both himself and Ayers. FIRST SHOW IN THE APPEARANCE BUSINESS (1996) featured sessions from 1973, 1974 and 1976. The last of these featured Zoot Money and Andy Summers, just prior to his joining The Police, and looking back to the early days of the Soft Machine.

Yet more has followed: GARDEN OF LOVE, a twenty-minute piece with the Whole World and a choir, and a CD issue on HUX of a radio broadcast by *Banana Follies* – under that title – with 'a host of gorgeous guests', alongside the late, great bassist Archie Leggett. TOO OLD TO DIE YOUNG (1998) was a double CD from the *In Concert* series. Captured alongside live tracks from 1975/76 is a whole disc of the Whole World in 1972 augmented by a small orchestra playing arrangements by David Bedford. Remember Kevin this way.

⊙ **Bananamour** (1973; BGO).
Ayers at his most consistent, with support from Wyatt, Hillage and Ratledge. It's been said he only ever wrote three kinds of songs: while drunk, while drinking and when hung over – well, they're all here.

⊙ **Banana Productions: The Best Of Kevin Ayers** (1989; Harvest).
A good overview of a quirky career, including some of the rarities first collected on ODD DITTIES.

Brian Hinton

AZTEC CAMERA

Formed East Kilbride, Scotland, 1980; put to bed, 1998.

"I think by now everyone realizes that I'm the boss of the thing."
Roddy Frame

Aband in name only, **Aztec Camera** began with singer, songwriter and guitarist **Roddy Frame**. A precocious talent, at 13 Frame was giving vent to an obsession with The Clash by covering Strummer/Jones compositions in an otherwise inconsequential combo called **Neutral Blue**. By the time he was 15, however, he was penning wistful ballads such as the early B-side, "We Could Send Letters", which demonstrated a lyrical and musical maturity far in advance of his age.

Barely out of school, Frame was snapped up by Alan Horne's Postcard label, a signing which did much to strengthen the imprint's claim to represent 'the sound of young Scotland'. Indeed, Aztec Camera embodied perfectly the idiosyncratic ethos of a label run by a man who reportedly saw his enterprise as a cross between Berry Gordy's Motown and Andy Warhol's Factory. For, in transcending the strictures of his punk apprenticeship, Frame had crafted a fragile songwriting style that owed much to the American West Coast bands of the late 60s, such as Love, Buffalo Springfield and The Byrds.

Sadly, Aztec Camera's second single, "Mattress Of Wire", was to be Postcard's final offering before it ceased operations in 1981 following the departure of prime movers, Orange Juice, to Polydor. Despite critical acclaim and attendant indie success, major-label interest was not yet forthcoming and Frame was forced into a sideways move to Rough Trade. Early in 1983 the band scored a minor hit with "Oblivious", a piece of sunny optimism quite at odds with the gloomy existentialism of the early 80s alternative scene. Reissued by WEA later in the year, after the success of the debut album, it deservedly became the band's first UK Top 20 success.

HIGH LAND HARD RAIN (1983) was a remarkable first album: gone was the cool detachment of the Postcard singles in favour of a lighter, airier, more uplifting style, melding elements of jazz, Latin and gospel into a sound which remained distinctly focused via Frame's characteristic semi-acoustic arrangements. The second album, KNIFE (1984), was a commercial success but failed to break new ground – unless you count the sheen of sophistication brought to the project by producer **Mark Knopfler**. Fortunately, Roddy could still surprise and delight – notably with his gloriously languid interpretation of Van Halen's "Jump", which graced the flip side of "All I Need Is Everything", the first single from the album.

Despite rumours that he would replace the departing Johnny Marr in the soon-to-split Smiths, the never-prolific Frame eventually returned with Aztec Camera's third LP in 1987. LOVE represented a significant shift in direction, its departure into the realm of blue-eyed soul alienating some fans reared on the eloquent pop-rock of his previous work. Aptly titled, the album positively embraced the pop mainstream both in its lyrical concerns and its smoothly seductive rhythms, but it took the belated and hitherto unprecedented success of the single "Somewhere In My Heart" to generate wider interest in the album, which finally went Top 10 in the UK in June 1988, some eight months after its release.

Perversely, STRAY (1990), characterized by noodling, jazz-tinged melancholia and foot-stomping rockers, seemed designed to throw any recent converts off the trail. However, the fact that Frame attained respectable chart entries for both "Stray" and the less challenging DREAMLAND (1993) indicated that he retained a core following for his thoughtful pop.

Nonetheless, Frame was under pressure to deliver a better commercial return with FRESTONIA (1995). And so he did, re-creating old form on his best release since LOVE. The key, as ever, lay in Frame's melodies, which rolled out in apparently effortless fashion on "Rainy Season", "Sun" and a great, aching ballad, "Crazy". Sadly, it failed to become a huge success and was his swansong for WEA, who finally lost patience with their former boy wonder, although they certainly had a plethora of highlights for THE BEST OF AZTEC CAMERA, a 1999 compilation which collected singles, classic album tracks and oddities such as the aforementioned cover of "Jump".

Frame had signed to Independiente in 1998, laying the Aztec Camera name to rest, but unleashing the exemplary solo album THE NORTH STAR (1998). Recent releases of his own have been scarce, but his guitar-playing cameos on **Playgroup**'s eponymously-titled reclamation of early–80s funk, dub and disco styles, released in 2001, were a delight.

High Land Hard Rain (1983; WEA).
A brash and confident debut, marred only slightly by ex-Ruts drummer Dave Ruffy's incongruous use of electronic percussion.

Love (1987; WEA).
Gloriously slick and overproduced arrangements bring to the fore synthesizers, soulful harmonies and programmed percussion, to invest Frame's compositions with a far more rounded commercial appeal.

Stray (1990; WEA).
An album where diverse musical moods are underpinned by a previously uncharacteristic cynicism. Features guest appearances from Edwyn Collins, Micky Gallagher, and a stirring duet with Mick Jones on the hit single, "Good Morning Britain".

Frestonia (1995; WEA).
A marvellous album, proving that Frame could still do it in the 90s, both in his songwriting and voice, which is at his most soulful.

Ian Lowey

B

BABES IN TOYLAND

Formed Minneapolis, Minnesota, 1989; split 1998.

Like L7, Hole and Bikini Kill, **Babes In Toyland** exerted a female twist on the macho world of loud guitars and squealing vocals, launching a visual assault of baby-doll dresses, smeared lipstick and manic eyes. Core members were **Kat Bjelland** (guitar/vocals) – on/off friend of Courtney Love – and **Lori Barbero** (drums/vocals); the trio's bassist was **Maureen Herman**, who replaced **Michelle Leon** in 1992.

The debut album was SPANKING MACHINE (1990), a loud and sometimes painful experience, with songs such as "Vomit Heart" and "Fork Down Throat" screaming of betrayal and survival. To MOTHER (1991) showed an (inevitable) development, with songs such as "Catatonic" and "Primus" being less in your face, though live they still lacked quality control. The band could be angrily dynamic and ragingly ordinary, sometimes on the same night.

After a change of label and bass player came FONTANELLE (1992), a slicker production, but there was a shortage of memorable songs and Kat's voice was no longer an instrument but merely something lost in the mush of sound. As Babes In Toyland lost direction they watched the likes of Courtney Love's Hole gain enormous crossover success. But with NEMESISTERS (1995), their time in the wilderness seemed to be over. Rather than raucous, tuneless grunge songs they concentrated on rhythmically and technically controlled numbers that expressed anger

through insinuation rather than direct threat. The shift in Babes In Toyland's music-making found them triumphantly embracing a place in rock where punk meets feminism.

Maureen Herman left the band in mid-1996, planning a return to college and to writing. Her place was filled by **Dana Cochrane** (ex-Mickey Finn).

For all their passion, however, Babes In Toyland eventually seemed to drift apart towards the end of the 90s and Bjelland put all her creative energy into **Katastrophy Wife**, a band that included her husband, drummer **Glen Mattson**. In 2001 Katasptrophy Wife issued AMUSIA, which featured many of Bjelland's trademark songwriting twists, not least her fearsome scream. Meanwhile, a series of Babes In Toyland retrospectives titled DEVIL, LIVED and VILED emerged in 2000 and 2001, pulling together live tracks and rarities. Most recently Bjelland has reunited the band in order to play a series of gigs both in the US and UK, but whether this results in a new album remains to be seen.

⊙ **Spanking Machine** (1990; Twin Tone).
Naive but passionate, these raw guitar squalls set the tone for a generation.

⊙ **Nemesisters** (1995; Reprise).
Their major-label debut is the band's most focused offering – and the cover version of "We Are Family" is life-affirming brilliance.

Duncan Harris

BABY BIRD

Formed Sheffield, England, 1994.

There are two incarnations of **Baby Bird**. The first is **Stephen Jones**, former performer with experimental theatre group **Dogs In Honey**, who, after writing some four hundred songs in his spare time, reinvented himself, somewhere towards the end of 1994, and hit upon the idea of releasing five albums within the space of a year.

The first, I WAS BORN A MAN (1995), released on Jones's own label, was, in his own words, 'an elaborate demo to gauge response'. Its thirteen songs were resolutely lo-fi: like the subsequent albums it was recorded at home on a four-track paid for by an Arts Council grant. Jones, a non-musician, played all instruments and patently revelled in the cheesy sound made by cheap samplers and guitars. As an introduction to the world of Baby Bird, the album epitomized the difficulties critics would have pinning the Bird down. Some heard early Lou Reed or Dan Harper others, early Pulp; or, in Jones's studiedly strange

babes in toyland

lyrics, mid-70s Eno. Whatever Jones's musical points of contact, songs such as the grunged-out "Cornershop" or the wistful "C.F.C." and "Man's Tight Vest" (containing the much-quoted lines, 'I feel like a woman/Yet I was born a man/I wish I was christened Valerie/Instead of Stan'), were a clear indication that this maverick sensibility did little to disguise an important talent.

The critics barely had enough time to enthuse, however. Further limited-edition albums – BAD SHAVE, FATHERHOOD, THE HAPPIEST MAN ALIVE – followed (the fifth and last, the lo-fi DYING HAPPY, was released in 1997). Though these releases generally reinforced Jones's growing status as a solo artist, they also contributed to the second Baby Bird incarnation. With the addition of **Luke Scott**, **Huw Chadbourn**, **Robert Gregory** and **John Pedder** for much-lauded live dates, Baby Bird became a five-piece band.

Quickly signed by Echo Records, the first full band album, UGLY BEAUTIFUL (1996), shot into the Top 10. Comprising rerecordings of Jones's lo-fi songs, the set's pop edges were accentuated, a process that managed to enhance the unreality of the songs' thematic concerns. Four singles – "Candy Girl", "Goodnight", "You're Gorgeous" and "Cornershop" – made stars of the band. ("You're Gorgeous", in particular, becoming an anthem in 1996; it peaked at #3 and stayed in the UK Top 30 for months.)

After a swift cash-in US-only album, GREATEST HITS (1997), Baby Bird released their first band-written collection, THERE'S SOMETHING GOING ON (1998). The pop influences of their recent past were audible, but so too was the return to Jones's original lo-fi days in singles "Bad Old Man" and "If You'll Be Mine". They both did creditably well, although without the stellar success of "You're Gorgeous": it was a level of success that Jones found acceptable.

Decamping to a studio in southern Spain with just Scott and instrumentalist/engineer **Matt Hay**, the 17 songs that made up the next album, BUGGED (2000), marked Jones's return to solo writing. Not as lo-fi as Jones may say it is, BUGGED was, in its own odd way, a rock album that stopped well short of the darker nuances of earlier work. The same year Jones also published his debut novel, THE BAD BOOK (IMP Fiction), a dystopian tale set in the near-future. With BUGGED out of his system Jones then decided to lay low, only emerging in 2002 to record "We All Make The Little Flowers Grow", again with Scott, as a contribution to TOTAL LEE, a tribute album to legendary songsmith Lee Hazlewood.

By 2003 he had produced a new album from his home studio. Released under his own name, ALMOST CURED OF SADNESS saw Jones come full circle, returning to the lo-fi, homespun sound of his earliest sets.

⊙ **I Was Born A Man** (1995; Baby Bird Recordings).
With only 1000 copies made of Jones's debut CD-only album, and about as rare as a dodo's egg, this is the perfect introduction to Bird's land. Grunge, pappy pop and slightly

off-kilter ballads feature, all stitched together with even-further-off-kilter lyrics and a voice that reveals surprising range and richness.

⊙ **Bugged** (2000; Echo).
Though lacking the impending menace of the older material, increased experience and better studio conditions mean that *Bugged* isn't as lo-fi as the first few sets, and its songs – more complex in both mood and purpose – indicate a maturing talent.

⊙ **The Original Lo-Fi** (Boxset) (2002; Castle).
This tasty little package pulls together Jones's first five albums along with the previously unheard BLACK ALBUM, a collection of demos and oddities from his 4-track days. Essential.

Louise Gray

BACHMAN-TURNER OVERDRIVE

Formed Winnipeg, Canada, 1972; disbanded 1979; re-formed 1984.

"So I took what I could get. And then she looked at me with those big brown eyes – and said, 'You ain't seen nothing yet...'"

Staples of the AOR airwaves, **Bachman-Turner Overdrive**'s origins can be traced back to the substantial commercial achievements of **GUESS WHO** in the late 60s. **Randy Bachman** (guitar/vocals) was a prominent member of that band but left in 1970 when his Mormon beliefs began to conflict with the excesses of a touring rock'n'roll band. After recording an unsuccessful solo album, he teamed up with his drumming brother **Robbie Bachman**, **C. F. Turner** (bass) and another former Guess Who colleague, **Chad Allan**, to form **Brave Belt**. Two non-charting albums for Reprise followed before the group changed name to Bachman-Turner Overdrive and replaced Allan with guitarist (and brother) **Tim Bachman**. The suffix was taken from a trucking magazine, *Overdrive*, and typified the group's straightforward bar-room rock'n'roll.

An eponymous debut album followed in 1973 for Mercury, after which the group embarked on the sort of strenuous touring schedule that would become their trademark. While the album contained nothing revolutionary in terms of songwriting or execution, few denied the energy or authenticity of the performances. However, a casualty of the first tour was Tim Bachman, later replaced by **Blair Thornton** on guitar.

In December 1973 they enjoyed their first US chart hit with the agenda-setting "Blue Collar". Subsequent singles and albums would all fare well in the US charts, as well as domestic listings. Taken from BACHMAN-TURNER OVERDRIVE 2 (1974), "Takin' Care Of Business" provided a substantial US hit, before the November release of "You Ain't Seen Nothing Yet". The group's signature tune, it was originally written for Bachman's brother and manager Gary, who suffered from a stammer – hence the song's stuttering hook. The single became a US #1 and peaked at #2 in the UK charts.

None of the group's subsequent releases had the same impact, though further chart action came with "Roll On Down The Highway", "Take It Like A Man" and "Looking Out For No. 1" – the clichéd titles giving fair warning of the hackneyed blues-rock style they had evolved. Randy Bachman was clearly losing interest and left the group in 1977. **Jim Clench** replaced him in the wake of the Randy-dominated FREEWAYS (1977), after which the group shortened its name to **BTO**. Their achievements in this form were minimal, and Bachman's subsequent work with **Ironhorse** and **Union** proved similarly undistinguished.

He re-formed Bachman-Turner Overdrive in 1984, and they continued to tour throughout the decade while Bachman himself would split his time between the band and Guess Who re-formations. In 1993 he recorded a further solo album, ANY ROAD, with contributions from, among others, **Neil Young** and **Margo Timmins** of The Cowboy Junkies.

⊙ **Not Fragile** (1974; reissued 2002; Phonogram).
Despite the excellence of the debut, this was BTO's defining moment. Yes, you're sick of "You Ain't Seen Nothing Yet", and the lyrics seldom stray from the favourite themes (being a rock star and/or driving powerful trucks/cars). But bar-room rock was never heavier, or better, than on tracks such as "Not Fragile", "Rock Is My Life" or "Givin' It All Away".

⊙ **The Anthology** (1995; Phonogram).
A two-CD set which contains everything you need to hear by Bachman-Turner Overdrive and a great deal more that you don't. Excellent sleeve notes, though.

Alex Ogg

BAD BRAINS

Formed Washington DC, 1978.

Though sharing the Washington hardcore patch with the likes of Black Flag and Minor Threat, **Bad Brains** were unique in that their sound owed a lot to the influence of dub and reggae. The original line-up, consisting of **H. R.** (vocals), **Darryl Jennifer** (bass), **Earl Hudson** (drums) and **Dr. Know** (guitar), played tiny venues around Washington before moving to New York. They were supposed to support The Damned on a UK tour of 1979 but were denied work permits. Probably the first exposure most Europeans had to Bad Brains was through the Alternative Tentacles compilation LET THEM EAT JELLYBEANS (1981), which included their first single, "Pay To Cum". To get signed to an independent label, Bad Brains had to overcome the politically correct straitjacket of the anarcho-punk scene. After making some homophobic remarks in an interview there was a veritable witch-hunt against them, which the band turned to their own ends on a re-recording of "Pay To Cum".

BAD BRAINS (1981), a primitive cassette-only release on ROIR Records, was the only studio recording of their early, ferocious material. A 12" single, "I And I Survive"/"Destroy Babylon" (1982), boasted an improved production, and ROCK FOR LIGHT (1983) was a landmark set. Bad Brains applied the technical skills of jazz to the framework of punk/metal, using multiple registers to create a polyphony of different melodies. ROCK FOR LIGHT seesawed between barely believable speedcore and deft reggae riffs: the quality and speed of their playing was not to be matched until the likes of The Stupids or Adrenaline O. D. several years later.

By 1986, Bad Brains had moved on to the seminal independent label SST, where they released perhaps the best of their albums, I AGAINST I. Rather than sticking to the formula that had won them their audience, this album slowed the pace a little and introduced new elements to their melting pot. H. R.'s vocals carried much of the tune and the complex rhythmic structures gave Dr. Know the space necessary to deliver the kind of blitzkrieging guitar solos that could outshine most of the competition. The funk/punk style favoured by the Red Hot Chili Peppers and Living Colour was more or less invented here.

A live album, simply entitled LIVE (1988), was an effective summary of their performance at the time, but by then H. R. had surprised everyone by quitting the band. He proceeded to release two solo LPs, HUMAN RIGHTS (1987) and IT'S ABOUT LUV (1988), which failed to achieve much popular acclaim though many fans rated them amongst his best work. Meanwhile, in 1988, Dr. Know and Darryl Jennifer teamed up with ex-Faith No More vocalist **Chuck Mosely** and Cromags drummer **Mackie** to take Bad Brains back on tour. This was a disastrous move: Mosely was no replacement for H. R., and by 1989 the original band line-up was back in place for QUICKNESS, which lacked the polish and invention of earlier releases. Still, a world tour re-established the faith of the fans, and some astounding performances were captured on the album YOUTH ARE GETTING RESTLESS (1990), before H. R. and Earl once again departed. Again, Mackie was drafted as drummer, while **Israel Joseph I** took over on vocals.

In 1993, Bad Brains signed to Epic and released RISE, which possessed a spark of brilliance sorely missing from QUICKNESS. Joseph's vocals were particularly impressive, while the sharper snare sound of Mackie's drums made the band's sound even more clean and precise. The following year, H. R. and Earl once again returned to the fold and restored the original line-up. Offered a contract with Madonna's Maverick label, they reunited with ROCK FOR LIGHT's producer Ric Ocasek to record GOD OF LOVE (1995). The first few tracks revealed that the band had matured but not mellowed: everything was precise and concise, while Dr. Know's guitar work was controlled but dazzling. The musical balance also shifted more towards reggae – "Long Time" was outstanding, combining a rampant ragga beat and a classic melody.

While the album demonstrated that Bad Brains' uncompromising inventiveness was undimmed after nearly two decades on the alternative music scene, the record suffered poor sales and H. R. and Hudson dropped out again. Unsurprisingly, the band was then dropped by Maverick. Despite this less than auspicious episode the group decided to rekindle the magic in 1998 by reforming under the more positive moniker of **Soul Brains** for a series of tours. Several live albums have since emerged that document this stage incarnation.

The group popped up again, minus H. R., in 2002 for the dub reggae set I & I SURVIVED, which featured some impressive reworks of old favourites as well as a bunch of new jams.

⊙ **Rock For Light** (1983; Abstract).
A white-hot launch of thrash and speedcore, streets ahead of most of the competition.

⊙ **I Against I** (1986; SST).
This is the best studio album that the original line-up ever produced. It loses the extremes of thrash and dub that were the mainstays of their live performances, but incorporates such a range of styles and sounds that it ranks alongside the most influential rock albums of its time.

Glenn Gossling

BAD COMPANY

Formed London, 1973; disbanded 1983;
re-formed 1986.

Comprising ex-members of **FREE**, **MOTT THE HOOPLE** and **KING CRIMSON**, **Bad Company** were an instant supergroup when they formed in late 1973, and virtually created the genre of stadium rock. Bands such as Foreigner, Bon Jovi and Def Leppard have all taken their cue, to some extent, from Bad Company: super-clean production values, tight hard-rock songs with formulaic guitar solos, the occasional ballad, gravelly vocals, and lots of macho posturing.

The main attraction of the band was the voice of **Paul Rodgers**, who had established himself in Free as hard rock's premier vocalist. Completed by ex-Free cohort **Simon Kirke** (drums), Mott's guitarist **Mick Ralphs**, and bassist **Boz Burrell** from King Crimson, Bad Company promoted the image of outlaw drifters, leaving a trail of broken hearts and empty bottles – an image orchestrated by manager **Peter Grant**, the *éminence grise* behind Led Zeppelin.

Simplicity was the key to their debut album, BAD COMPANY (1974), with its black-and-white cover and unpretentious arrangements. More soulful than later efforts, with Beatles and Otis Redding references alongside the power chords, it was an instant success, topping the charts on both sides of the Atlantic. "Can't Get Enough" was the obvious single and sold by the truckload, establishing the band as that rare phenomenon – a rock band you could dance to.

Excellent hit singles "Good Lovin' Gone Bad" and "Feel Like Makin' Love" followed from the second album, STRAIGHT SHOOTER (1975), but the rest of the set was patchy and the band had begun to lose a grip on quality control, partly due to the testosterone overkill of the lyrics. If Rodgers' singing was Bad Company's strongest point, his lyrics were often their weakest. Lines such as, 'The first time that I met you, you were only seventeen/But I had to put you down 'cos I didn't know where you'd been', were both laughable and offensive.

Despite being one of the most popular bands in the world, it was clear that Bad Company were always going to be compared unfavourably with Free. As the 70s progressed, their albums became less inspired and, although 1979's DESOLATION ANGELS would still reach the charts (and include a fine ballad in "She Brings Me Love" and the American hit single "Rock'n'Roll Fantasy"), they seemed to be a band out of time and ideas. They finally threw in the towel after 1982's ROUGH DIAMONDS.

Rodgers went on to release a fine solo album, CUT LOOSE (1983), on which he played all instruments, but which disappeared without trace. The two albums he subsequently made with **Jimmy Page** in **The Firm** were unexciting but moderately successful, while the outfit he formed with The Who's **Kenny Jones**, **The Law**, made one disastrously overproduced offering before splitting. His 1993 blues CD, MUDDY WATERS BLUES, however, re-established Rodgers as a contender, and attracted contributions from the likes of **Dave Gilmour**, **Slash** and **Buddy Guy**. In 1997 he released a double CD containing a new studio album and a live set; however, this merely served to highlight the dullness of the new material, including, as it did, electrifying performances of old Free and Bad Company songs.

Unbelievably, in the mid-80s, Kirke, Ralphs and Burrell re-formed Bad Company without Rodgers. Ralphs was clearly still capable of some serious riffing (notably on 1988's DANGEROUS AGE) and new singer **Brian Howe** had the throaty roar to attract a reasonable stateside following and notch up several chart albums in the US – notably HERE COMES TROUBLE (1992) with its hook-filled standout track "How 'Bout That".

In 1995 new vocalist **Robert Hart**, second guitarist **Dave Colwell** and bassist **Rick Wills** were drafted in to beef up their sound, and the album COMPANY OF STRANGERS was a considerable return to form, although the success of their mid-70s glory days was clearly gone.

Album releases and personnel changes continued into the 90s, but without Rodgers the reality was that only a hard-core following were interested. And then the unexpected happened: Rodgers rejoined the band and a live album, modestly titled MERCHANTS OF COOL (2002), was released through Sanctuary Records and followed by a world tour, which included the group's first British dates in 26 years. Whether Rodgers elects to remain part of the Bad Company setup remains to be seen, but for a while at least some of the old magic was flowing again.

Bad Company (1974; Atlantic).
A mighty, riff-heavy, stadium-rocking album that provided much fodder for American 'classic rock' radio.

Straight Shooter (1975; Atlantic).
A powerful hard rock album including the all-time classic, "Feel Like Makin' Love".

10 From 6 (1986; Atlantic).
A retrospective that includes all their classic rockers but sadly none of the ballads.

Chris Coe

BAD RELIGION

Formed Los Angeles, 1980.

There are two success stories behind **Bad Religion**: that of the band, and that of Epitaph, the now-legendary label they formed out of frustration at their failure to secure a record deal. Not bad for something that grew from the vision of 17-year-old guitar hopeful **Brett Gurewitz**, and 15-year-olds **Jay Bentley** (bass) and **Gregg Graffin** (vocals).

The band's first album, HOW COULD HELL BE ANY WORSE (1982), can be considered the genesis of the US punk revival that culminated with the stellar success of the likes of Green Day and Offspring. At the time, however, everything was less than rosy for Bad Religion, and just one more EP sneaked out before the band disappeared for a period that still remains somewhat shrouded in mystery. (A second LP, INTO THE UNKNOWN, was almost instantly disowned and deleted.)

In 1987 Bad Religion reunion shows started happening in California with a line-up of Graffin, Gurewitz and Bentley, plus drummer **Peter Finestone** and guitarist **Gregg Hetson** (who still does shows with his previous band, **The Circle Jerks**). The album that followed, SUFFER (1988), firmly established the archetypal BR sound, marrying breakneck speedbursts to unerringly infectious melodies carried by Graffin's excellent vocals, backed by Bentley and Gurewitz with what the album sleeves have always called 'oozin' aahs'. The winner of several *Album Of The Year* awards, it remains a genre classic.

Capitalizing on the resurgence in sales, especially in Europe, NO CONTROL (1989) followed to equally justified praise, and on its back Bad Religion headed to Europe, where they were welcomed as conquering heroes. AGAINST THE GRAIN (1990) and GENERATOR (1992) were, however, seen as inconsistent and disappointing efforts – certainly true in the latter's case, despite the added impetus of new drummer **Bobby Schayer**. Nevertheless, Bad Religion's reputation continued to grow, as another two London shows sold out without even being advertised, and near-superstardom was achieved in Germany. During this period Epitaph satisfied the needs of completist fans with the release of 80–85 (1991), a compilation featuring HOW COULD HELL along with the EPs and an assortment of unreleased material.

What made their achievements more impressive was the fact that the band tied their career in with regular jobs, Graffin studying for a PhD in palaeontology and lecturing at New York's Cornell University, and Gurewitz busying himself in LA running Epitaph, where Bentley was also employed. This double life seemed to do no harm, however, and RECIPE FOR HATE (1993) found them back in top form. But it became clear that Epitaph was having difficulty distributing the records, and so the decision to sign with Columbia/Dragnet was taken. Another new factor was the employment of **Andy Wallace** for STRANGER THAN FICTION (1994), the first time the band had used an outside producer. But trouble was at hand. Gurewitz, having played on the album, quit the band, allegedly unable to reconcile his punk ethics with running a label – the crisis might have had something to do with the fact that Offspring's SMASH, an Epitaph release, was well on its way to shifting over eight million copies. Initially the split was supposed to be temporary, but it eventually became clear that the rift was bitter and that Brett's replacement, **Brian Baker**, was permanent. Significantly, Jay Bentley claimed going on tour with Baker was "the most pleasant experience of the last three years", and STRANGER THAN FICTION proceeded to comfortably outsell previous releases.

Gurewitz meanwhile issued ALL AGES (1995), a compilation culled from the band's Epitaph LPs, emphasizing Bad Religion's impeccable pedigree and providing a welcome stopgap until the release of THE GRAY RACE (1996). Produced by The Cars' **Ric Ocasek**, it provided clear evidence, with the likes of "Punk Rock Song" and "10 In 2010", that immense quality was still there to be had. However, too many fillers left the album as one of the weaker efforts in the Bad Religion collection. TESTED (1997) was better – a live set compiled from various shows the previous year and featuring many well-loved classics. Rather worrying, though, was the lacklustre nature of the three new songs included.

It was a major relief when No Substance (1998) proved a towering return to form, sitting comfortably with the late-80s highpoints. The Process Of Belief (2002), found Gurewitz reunited with the band. However, the album's positive aspects were slightly clouded by the permanent replacement of Bobby Schayer with veteran punk drummer **Brooks Wackerman** after the former was forced to retire from music due to illness. Despite the setbacks, Bad Religion show no sign of abandoning their commitment to truth, justice and the punk rock way.

- **Suffer** (1988; Epitaph).
  The rebirth of Bad Religion and springboard to greater things. "Do What You Want" and "Best For You" are brief, bruising and brilliant Californian punk, though it is the astounding "What Can You Do?" that takes the greatest honours. Essential.

- **No Control** (1989; Epitaph).
  Bad Religion's greatest album, says Jay Bentley, and he's right.

- **Stranger Than Fiction** (1994; Dragnet/Columbia).
  A new label but the same quality. "The Handshake" cheerfully rips off the Buzzcocks' "Ever Fallen In Love", and there's a triumphant rerecording of "21st Century Digital Boy" (originally on Against The Grain).

- **No Substance** (1998; Dragnet).
  Sixteen songs, no duffers, and minor classics in "Shades of Truth", "Mediocre Minds", "All Fantastic Images", and, oh, maybe ten others. Lyrically, Bad Religion have never been better, either.

Hugh Hackett

BADFINGER

Formed Swansea, Wales, 1966.

One of the first acts signed to The Beatles' Apple label, **Badfinger** had their first major success with a Paul McCartney composition, "Come And Get It". But their best-known song was in fact a hit for someone else – Harry Nilsson's chart-topping cover of "Without You", a hit again for Mariah Carey in 1994. Badfinger's back catalogue reveals a wealth of highly melodic and well-crafted guitar-pop songs, which makes the deaths of songwriters **Pete Ham** and **Tom Evans** all the more tragic.

The group's original line-up of Ham (vocals/guitar/piano), **Mike Gibbins** (drums), **Ron Griffiths** (bass) and **David Jenkins** (guitar) first recorded together in 1968, as a backing group to singer **David Garrick**. Following the replacement of Jenkins by Tom Evans, the group signed to the infant Apple label, adopting the name of **The Iveys**. Their first single, "Maybe Tomorrow", a sugary pop ballad written by Evans, became a minor hit in the US. After Evans replaced Griffiths on bass and **Joey Molland** joined on guitar, the group's definitive line-up was together, and they settled with the name Badfinger in 1969.

"Come And Get It" reached #4 in the UK charts in January 1970, also becoming a hit in the US later that year. The song was used in the Apple-produced film, *The Magic Christian*, starring Ringo Starr, and appeared on the group's own debut album, Magic

Christian Music (1970). This was followed by No Dice (1970), which included the group's next single, the Pete Ham composition "No Matter What", a cracking piece of power pop. Another hit on both sides of the Atlantic, its success was in turn echoed in 1972 by the dreamy ballad, "Day After Day", produced by George Harrison. In the meantime, "Without You", from No Dice, had been recorded by Nilsson, and subsequently topped the British charts for five weeks.

Unfortunately, in the progressive-rock era, UK audiences were seemingly unprepared to accept Badfinger as a credible albums band. Straight Up (1972) fared poorly in the UK and the group were unable to capitalize upon the critical and commercial success the record achieved in the States. There were no more UK hits, and after "Baby Blue", another Pete Ham power-pop foot-tapper, the hits also dried up in America.

Ironically, given that The Beatles' stated purpose in setting up the Apple label had been to ensure artists were dealt with fairly, Badfinger felt they had been poorly treated by Apple. In 1974, prior to the release of their final Apple album, Ass (rereleased in 1996), they joined Warner Brothers, subsequently releasing a further two collections, Badfinger and Wish You Were Here. Both revealed a continuing Beatles-like attachment to melody and harmony, with harder-edged guitar work – indeed several of the tracks oddly anticipated mid-90s Britpop frontrunners, and professed Beatle fans, Oasis.

The departure from Apple had not marked the end of Badfinger's problems. The group's finances became the subject of a legal dispute between the label and their management and Wish You Were Here was withdrawn shortly after its release. Disillusioned, Joey Molland quit at the end of 1974, to be replaced by keyboardist **Bob Jackson**; the new lineup recorded a middling album at the very end of the year, Head First, that remained unissued until 2000. The following April, Pete Ham hanged himself at his London home.

Joey Molland and Tom Evans re-formed Badfinger in 1978, and temporarily recruited various other musicians. Two albums were released on Elektra, Airwaves (1979) and Say No More (1981), but commercial success was still elusive. This, coupled with royalty disputes, culminated in Evans' suicide in 1983.

Molland, now resident in the US, later recorded the solo albums, After The Pearl (1985) and The Pilgrim (1992) and continues to perform as Joey Molland's Badfinger. Perhaps because of the Britpop parallels, the mid 90s saw a rekindling of interest in Badfinger, with the release of archive material in the form of BBC Live In Concert (1997) and a collection of Pete Ham home demos 7 Park Avenue (1997) and Golders Green (1999), plus the reissue on CD of all the Apple albums.

- **The Best Of Badfinger** (1995; Apple).
  Excellent compilation taken from the four Apple albums.

⊙ **The Best Of Badfinger Vol II** (1990; Rhino).
A valuable collection of material from BADFINGER and
WISH YOU WERE HERE, with added cuts from a never-released
third Warners album. Complete with a couple of tracks from
AIRWAVES, this is the best way to find any of their post-Apple
output.

Keith Prewer

BADLY DRAWN BOY

Damon Gough, born Bolton, 1969.

Woolly-hatted northerner **Damon Gough** is the man behind the fumbling, fragile inventiveness of **Badly Drawn Boy**. In the days before the emergence of his alter ego, while he was still known by his proper name, Gough dreamed of becoming Bruce Springsteen. Such ambition demanded a more substantial arena, however, and it was with his move to Manchester in 1997 that the wheels of his fortune were set in motion.

Having hooked up with DJ **Andy Votel** in a local nightclub, these two like-minds conspired to create the Twisted Nerve record label, through which Gough channelled a prolific outpouring of four Badly Drawn Boy EPs between 1997 and 1999. A&R bidding wars, six-figure sums and inclusion in a celebrity-brimming **U.N.K.L.E.** compilation helped consolidate the hype that announced the arrival of 2000's debut album, THE HOUR OF THE BEWILDERBEAST (XL). Gough crafted an eighteen-track, hourlong song-cycle full of surprises; from French horn to theremin, the lush sound rounded out sorrowful, shape-shifting tones and belied the shambolic live shows for which Badly Drawn Boy then became known. In turns twinkly and funky, cynical and sweet, the quality of BEWILDERBEAST was consistent, as was the experimentation. Summing up the mood of the summer of 2000 with the anthemic "Spitting In The Wind" single, and subsequently bagging the *Mercury Music Prize* that year, Gough's debut album was widely applauded and promptly hailed as a contemporary classic. But Gough knew that acquiring that 'classic' status was something that only time could award. Confident in person, even if self-doubting in persona, he declared: 'I don't mind if it takes 20 years for people to realize how good an album this is'.

Though his work is at times reminiscent of The Beta Band's and then at others of Nick Drake's, the clearest comparisons must come from Elliot Smith and Beck, both of whom have worked with Badly Drawn Boy's producer **Tim Rothrock**. Taking a circuitous route through styles and effects, Damon Gough's musical journey is always listenable and breezy, quietly clever and ultimately charming. These qualities did not go unnoticed by novelist Nick Hornby, who

STEVE GULLICK

Damon Gough reveals why he is more frequently to be seen with a hat

enlisted Badly Drawn Boy to compose the soundtrack to the film version of *About A Boy*, released in 2002. The set focused on orchestral fragments and rich emotional pop songs, while the discipline of the soundtrack structure found Gough even easier on the ear, but of no less value. The same natural lightness that Badly Drawn Boy showed on BEWILDERBEAST carried through into the lilting strings of the instrumentals and the lyric-driven sing-a-longs. Perhaps more of a diversionary exercise than a follow-up to the debut, ABOUT A BOY was a glossy trailer for the promise of more messy, honest and complex work to come.

When the next album, HAVE YOU FED THE FISH (2002), did appear, it proved to be even more spectacular than had been hoped. The set had a big sound, and in many ways found Gough, at last, embracing the Springsteen-stylings that had once been his inspiration.

⊙ **The Hour Of The Bewilderbeast** (XL; 2000).
Scatty instrumental doodles sit comfortably alongside pop classics, while the textural and imaginative accompaniment (courtesy of the band Alfie, members of the Doves, and label-mates Mum & Dad) is consistently stunning. Gough's debut is an uplifting and endearing work of genius.

⊙ **Have You Fed The Fish** (XL; 2002).
This second album proper finds Gough leaving the lo-fi bedroom setting and riding out of town on a stallion of big-production. Once again, a work of genius.

Annebella Pollen

THE BAND

Formed: Toronto, Canada, 1967; disbanded 1976;
reformed 80s and 90s.

The Band were one of the most influential yet insular rock groups to emerge from the late-60s music scene. These four Canadians, **ROBBIE ROBERTSON** (guitar), **Richard Manuel** (piano/drums/vocals), **Rick Danko** (bass/fiddle/vocals) and **Garth Hudson** (keyboards/saxophones), and Arkansas native **Levon Helm** (drums/mandolin/vocals) came to embody the new-found musical maturity that followed the flower-power era, welding songcraft with passion in songs that reintroduced a sense of perspective and tradition into American music.

As **The Hawks**, they backed wild rockabilly singer **Ronnie Hawkins**, moulding into a tight and cohesive unit, dominated by Robertson's feral guitar work. Having broken away from Hawkins' limited range, their growing palette of musical styles attracted the attentions of **BOB DYLAN**, who invited Helm and Robertson to back him at his controversial Forest Hills 'electric' concert. Helm left, disenchanted at the level of hostility at these concerts, but the rest of the group joined up to back Dylan on his 1965 world tour.

As Helm rejoined, the group followed Dylan to Woodstock to record a rootsier set of informal sessions, later issued as THE BASEMENT TAPES (1975), a mixed bag of traditional and new material, both serious and playful in turn. The distinctive voices of the three lead singers now began to emerge, with Manuel's soulful Ray Charles voice offset by Helm's solid, gritty Southern twang, and Danko's edgy, quavering tone.

More significantly, both Robertson and Manuel began to develop as songwriters in the presence of Dylan. This was evident on the release of the group's debut album, MUSIC FROM BIG PINK (1968), which came across as a calming and restrained voice in a world of feedback-drenched guitar solos. With the three singers trading call-and-response vocals, and players switching instruments according to the needs of the particular song, the group were about the sheer joy of playing music stripped of gimmick and artifice. Robertson's guitar moved sparely in and out of the songs, with Danko's Motown-influenced bass filling the gaps, whilst Helm's drums gave a rock-solid backbeat over which Hudson's whirling, inventive organ let loose an imaginative array of sounds to match the oddball small-town characters that peopled the richly metaphorical songs. There was a powerful sense of mystery in Robertson songs such as "The Weight" and "Caledonia Mission", whereas Manuel was more direct on the plaintive ballads "In A Station" and "Lonesome Suzie" and the magical "We Can Talk", which more than any other song showcased the breadth of the group's abilities. Add to this the transformation worked on Dylan's "Tears Of Rage" by Manuel's vocal, and the result was an album that caused the rock community suddenly to sit up and pay very close attention to this unassuming group.

The Band did not tour the album, instead recording THE BAND (1969; reissued, remastered on vinyl 1998; EMI). Rooted heavily in a sense of rural tradition, the set came across like a folk history of an America that was in danger of being lost in the chaotic swirl of postwar life. Musically and lyrically more direct than its predecessor, it reached deeper into the storytelling tradition. Robertson, in particular, reached a creative peak with compelling narratives such as "The Night They Drove Old Dixie

Down", "The Unfaithful Servant" and "King Harvest (Has Surely Come)".

Despite a terrible initial live appearance (where Robertson was unsuccessfully hypnotized to overcome stage fright), they were able to provide controlled and often compelling concert performances. All the same, their multi-instrumental prowess could not save a gradual descent into rockstar bad habits. Manuel's songwriting talent suffered, in particular, leaving Robertson to take over such duties, notably on STAGE FRIGHT (1970). Here, he cast his gaze over early-70s unease and paranoia on "The Rumor", while slices of narrative Americana like "Just Another Whistle Stop" made the album a worthy, if inconsistent and unsettling, listen. But CAHOOTS (1971) revealed that such negative moods had invaded the group, to the detriment of the songs. They took stock with a live album, ROCK OF AGES (1972), which showcased **Allen Toussaint**'s horn arrangements and Garth Hudson's astonishing organ work – a reminder of his importance in filling out the group's sound.

The covers album, MOONDOG MATINEE (1973), reproduced a club setting The Hawks would have played ten years earlier, but, after further collaborations with Dylan, their 1975 album, NORTHERN LIGHTS, SOUTHERN CROSS, highlighted by Hudson's intricately layered keyboards, did not resolve their growing personal problems.

With Robertson announcing enough was enough, The Band organized THE LAST WALTZ farewell concert for Thanksgiving Day, 1976. A supporting cast ranging from **Muddy Waters** and **Van Morrison**, to Dylan, **Neil Young** and **Joni Mitchell**, joined the group on stage for a stylish (if overblown) celebration. Nevertheless, the event was a success, especially **Martin Scorsese**'s accompanying, revealing film – one of rock's finer moments on celluloid. After the dismal, contract-filling ISLANDS (1977), Helm, Danko and Robertson embarked on solo careers.

The Band re-formed in the mid-80s, without Robertson, but were knocked back when Richard Manuel took his own life in 1986. A second comeback, in the 90s, produced JERICHO (1994), HIGH ON THE HOG (1996) and JUBILATION (1998). For these outings, three new members replaced Robertson and Manuel, while the material relied on blues and R&B covers. Nonetheless, occasional moments of magic did rise to the surface, notably HIGH ON THE HOG's "The Caves Of Jericho".

⦿ **Music From Big Pink** (1968; Capitol).
Demonstrates just how closely five bearded white men could get to the feel of gospel and soul music, whilst still being unmistakably a rock group. It also highlights Richard Manuel's much-missed songwriting capabilities.

⦿ **The Band** (1969; Capitol; reissued, remastered on vinyl 1998; EMI).
An album as brilliant today as when it was released. The Band at their most essential.

⦿ **Stage Fright** (1970; Capitol).
Another strong set of songs, despite the bad vibes seeping from them. "The Rumor" is one of the best songs ever written about gossip and intrigue.

⦿ **Rock Of Ages** (1972; Capitol).
Cheaper than THE LAST WALTZ, and more focused than LIVE AT WATKINS GLEN, this remains their best available live album. Manuel's voice had started to deteriorate, but the cracking horns cover any gaps and reinvigorate the songs. This also serves as a useful greatest hits package.

Nicholas Oliver

BAND OF SUSANS

Formed New York, 1986; disbanded 1995.

In the 1980s, when New York's art-noise scene was at its apex, British imprint Blast First willingly signed its innovators. In a quick swoop, the label became the home of Sonic Youth, Big Black, Dinosaur Jr. and **Band Of Susans**. The group was the latest in New York's lineage of bands melding rock with the avant-garde – a pedigree that began in the late 60s with The Velvet Underground.

Formed by avant-garde flautist **Susan Stenger** and guitarist **Robert Poss**, Band Of Susans was a rock group without the rock clichés: no guitar histrionics, no standard time signatures and no vocals at the front of the mix. Each instrument was given its own part, and they fitted together like building blocks to create droning, dense textures.

The band's name came from the trio of Susans in the group's original line-up: Stenger on bass and Susans **Tallman** and **Lyall** on guitars. With Poss serving as the third guitarist and **Ron Spitzer** on drums, the quintet released the BLESSING AND CURSE EP in 1987. The poppy single "Hope Against Hope" was chosen by *Melody Maker* as a *Single Of The Week*.

Waves of distortion blew across the Susans' 1988 debut LP, HOPE AGAINST HOPE. Unusual tunings, and staccato drums and melody lines that proceeded vertically rather than horizontally, made the listener feel caught in an electrical storm. Tallman and Lyall departed prior to 1989's LOVE AGENDA; the vacancies were filled by **Karen Haglof**, who had played in Rhys Chatham's guitar ensembles with Poss and Stenger, and **Page Hamilton**, who later formed **Helmet**. The new line-up's songs were grinding and angular, as melodies stopped, started and shifted to expose underlying layers. The blues – as well as The Rolling Stones' version of them – threaded through the music. The Stones' influence eventually culminated in the 1992 Susans' EP NOW, which featured instrumental and vocal versions of "Paint It Black".

By the time the Susans' 1991 tribute to the E chord – entitled THE WORD AND THE FLESH – was released, guitarists **Mark Lonergan** and **Anne Husick** had replaced Haglof and Hamilton. The subsequent LP, VEIL (1993), supplanted R&B rhythms with crunched sonic shards. 1995's HERE COMES SUCCESS – a title meant as both a sarcastic barb and a nod to Iggy Pop – used rock beats to aerate melodic, prolonged compositions. Also released in 1995 was the greatest hits compilation WIRED FOR SOUND, which devoted one disc to songs with vocals and another to instrumentals, an often overlooked component of the Susans' work.

The group split shortly after the release of HERE COMES SUCCESS; Stenger and Poss are now working on various new projects – Poss's DISTORTION IS TRUTH (2002) and CROSSING CASCO BAY (2002) are both worth a dabble – and occasionally talk about working together again. Indeed, the duo were seen on stage as part of a trio with Wire's **Bruce Gilbert** in the late 90s. Continuing this theme, the final Susans cuts to make it to wax were contributions to the WHORE (1996) and DUGGA DUGGA DUGGA (1998) Wire tribute albums.

⦿ **Hope Against Hope** (1988; Blast First).
The marriage of minimalism and caustic punk. Brutal and brilliant.

⦿ **Love Agenda** (1989; Blast First/Restless).
Rough riffs pick and pick at the scab of rock'n'roll. Relentless.

⦿ **Here Comes Success** (1995; Restless/Rough).
Shorter songs and sharper lyrics give this the perfect rock/experimental balance. You'll wonder why Sonic Youth received all the attention.

⦿ **Wired For Sound - Band Of Susans 1986-1993** (1995; Blast First/Rough Trade).
A thorough overview; good for patient beginners and true fans.

Julie Taraska

THE BANGLES

Formed in Los Angeles, California in 1980; disbanded October 1989; reformed 1999.

An all-girl quartet, **The Bangles** spawned eighties pop anthems such as "Manic Monday", "Walk Like An Egyptian" and "Eternal Flame". Lumped in with the Paisley Underground of the LA music scene, alongside bands such as the **Rain Parade** and the **Dream Syndicate**, their love for the music of the sixties and their desire to create a small revival brought them to the attention of others.

They were originally known as **the (Supersonic) Bangs** and played a strict set of bouncy, 60s-style tunes. Their debut, eponymous EP of 1982 went with a bang to match the name, selling 40,000 copies. Their line-up was **Susanna Hoffs**, **Vicki Peterson**, **Debbi Peterson** and **Annette Zilinskas** who was later replaced by **Michael Steele** (ex-RUNAWAYS) on bass. CBS cleaned up their image and signed the group to a four-album deal: their first full-length set, ALL OVER THE PLACE (1984), proved to be 60s-influenced and somewhat feminist in style.

An intensive first round of touring and marketing made the girls grow up fast. With their new CBS-tailored look, the introduction of synthesizers and with the most memorable songs penned by outside songwriters, including Liam Sternberg and **Prince**, they released the heavily commercial DIFFERENT LIGHT (1985), which went multi-platinum. They spent the next two years vigorously touring and promoting the album, pausing to record a rock version of the Simon & Garfunkel hit "Hazy Shade Of Winter" for the *Less Than Zero* soundtrack in 1987: an attempt to rid themselves of the 'Go-go' image and establish themselves as an independent rock band.

EVERYTHING (1988) was a departure from their original material of the early 80s and was more romantic, rich in ethereal ballads written by Hoffs and balanced by the somewhat harder sound of the other members. It spawned a few minor hits and the #1 "Eternal Flame", written by Hoffs and Madonna's songwriters, Steinberg and Kelly.

The four band members had grown into four songwriters, each with her own musical styles. The original union of the band worked under a strong 60s influence which had slowly faded with age and due to various commercial pressures. Their initial decade-long union ended with a GREATEST HITS (1990) compilation album.

Nearly ten years later, after numerous rumours of reunification, Susanna and Debbi found themselves back in the studio together, and by 1999 The Bangles had fully reunited. They officially announced their second coming in 2000 and started to tour; an album produced by **Brad Wood**, DOLL REVOLUTION, followed in 2003.

⦿ **Different light** (1986).
Featuring "Manic Monday" and "Walk Like An Egyptian", this is the band's greatest artistic achievement. Chart-topping stuff.

⦿ **Everything** (1988).
More orchestral, more complicated material and an excess of production. Still with traces of magic though.

Jenny Lind

BARK PSYCHOSIS

Formed Woodford, England, 1986; disbanded 1997.

Inspired by a bizarre mixture of Joy Division, Swans, Sonic Youth, Big Black, Cocteau Twins, Dead Can Dance, Talk Talk and others, **Graham Sutton** (vocals/samples, etc) and **John Ling** (bass/samples, etc) formed **Bark Psychosis** in 1986 while still at school, where they performed Napalm Death covers in front of bemused classmates and teachers. The band's line-up, after at least four different membership configurations, only took shape in 1988, when Sutton and Ling left school and were joined by **Mark Simnett** (drums) and **Daniel Gish** (keyboards). They were already known to the small independent label, Cheree, which snapped them up for a single with Spacemen 3, released in 1990.

Bark Psychosis's first 'proper' gig was at the George Robey pub in London, supporting Extreme Noise Terror. Tours with The Telescopes, Cranes and Spiritualized quickly followed. By now, the group had established a reputation as one of the most unpredictable and innovative live bands in the country, although their recorded output was more studied.

By the end of 1991, the band were picking up musical influences from a number of different sources, including techno, and were increasingly fascinated by the infinite possibilities of synthesizers, sampling, programming and breakbeats. The following year, Bark Psychosis signed to Virgin and finally began to fulfil the promise of their live shows. A single, "Manman", appeared in 1992, followed by another, "Scum", which received impressive reviews, particularly in *Melody Maker*, where it was awarded *Single Of The Week* status. Clocking in at over 21 minutes, "Scum" was an eerie, understated masterpiece, which revolved around a single jarring bass line. Recorded live in a church in Stratford, it mapped out the musical direction for Bark Psychosis's debut album, which would prove to be a gruelling project.

The band began recording HEX in November 1992, and the process took over twelve months to complete, after which time the band was penniless and exhausted. Daniel Gish was first to jump ship – he walked out in the summer of 1993, giving 'lack of record company support' as his motive, and spent the next six months travelling. The album's centrepiece, "Big Shot", was finished without him. In January 1994, the three-piece began rehearsals for a five-date tour in support of the single, "A Street Scene", which would precede the album's release. But now John Ling couldn't bring himself to play; burned out, he departed. Soon after Ling left, Gish was invited to return, though only to play gigs. Effectively, Bark Psychosis had split during the making of HEX.

Still, it was a great album – sprawling, emotionally charged, and infinitely rewarding. One more single was recorded after the initial split. It was an upbeat track (at least by Bark Psychosis standards), designed to break from the intensity of HEX and to help Sutton purge himself of a stormy personal relationship that had recently ended. "Blue", written with Mark Simnett, was Bark Psychosis's finest single to date, multi-themed and memorable for the whispered vocal refrain, 'You're only as good as your last goddamn mistake', and for the astonishing closing minute, which featured a gorgeous, meandering bassline and lush synth arrangements straight out of New Order's book of pure pop. Perversely, for a track designed to introduce Bark Psychosis to the pop world, it was backed by more heavy-duty listening, a remix of "Big Shot" (courtesy of **Rudi Tambala** from A. R. Kane), and a track called "Hex", which consisted of three and a half minutes of deafening machine noise, eventually giving way to drifting keyboards and a distant, lonely trumpet.

In April 1994 the band played an electronic music festival in Russia, alongside Seefeel, Autechre, Ultramarine and Aphex Twin, following up with a series of dates in the UK aimed at promoting "Blue". But, by the time these concerts ended, Bark Psychosis was no more. Graham Sutton and Daniel Gish had begun working on jungle projects and putting together a new sound based almost entirely on hyperspeed breakbeats, samples and synthesizer. They played the UK Phoenix Festival (and other concerts) that year with help from trumpet player, **Del Crabtree**, eventually re-emerging as avant-jungle supremos **Boymerang** and releasing the Phoenix tracks, "Theme From Boymerang", "Rules" and "The Don" in early 1995 (on the Leaf label).

Since then, Gish has taken a different route, venturing into the realms of 'dark garage', 'dreamhouse' and the intriguingly named 'night music'. Bark Psychosis's second compilation album, GAME OVER was released early in 1997; an essential purchase for the dedicated collector, it includes new and previously unreleased material. The official debut Boymerang outing, BALANCE OF THE FORCE (1997), roped in Talk Talk's drummer **Lee Harris** to produce one of the finest drum'n'bass albums of the time.

⊙ **Hex** (1994; Virgin).
Featuring long periods in which a single blissful piano note seems to resound endlessly, punctuated by moments during which the instruments build to a ferocious howling noise – easy listening it ain't.

Andy Shields

SYD BARRETT

Born Cambridge, England, 1946; founder member of Pink Floyd 1965; started solo career in 1968.

Three decades after he last released a record, **Syd Barrett** remains one of rock's great cult figures. As the James Dean of British psychedelia, he had a brief but dazzling flash of brilliance in the 60s, only to have his career cut short by drug-induced mental problems. He has inspired many of the most creative people in rock, from Marc Bolan and David Bowie to the Sex Pistols, and you can still hear his influence in the work of blossoming artists today such as The Coral.

Having founded **PINK FLOYD** in 1965, Barrett soon became a key player in London's psychedelic underground scene of 1966–67. During his time with the Floyd, he pioneered the art of free-form electronic improvisation in rock and was closely involved in the band's innovative integration of sound and lights. Most importantly, he was a highly talented songwriter, penning their two hit singles, "Arnold Layne" and "See Emily Play", and most of their magical first album, THE PIPER AT THE GATES OF DAWN (1967), with its cast of gnomes, scarecrows and a mouse called Gerald. As a guitarist, he made up for lack of technique with the sheer originality of his playing, once described as 'a revolutionary source of electronic racket'. His unique style combined elements of lead and rhythm playing, often at the same time, with an almost punk aggression and disregard for convention.

However, the pressures of fame, which forced Syd's anarchic style into a more commercial mould, coupled with a punishing regime of daily LSD trips, pushed him right over the edge. Although feigning madness was part of the fun in those heady drug-cul

ture days, Syd wasn't pretending. Throughout the second half of 1967, his behaviour became so erratic that the others had little choice but to bring in Dave Gilmour as a second guitarist and vocalist. This arrangement lasted only a few weeks before Barrett was booted out of the band he had named and created. Floyd manager Pete Jenner left with him and they immediately went into the studio to launch his solo career. Unfortunately, Syd's condition rendered the sessions a disaster. Shortly afterwards, he split with long-term girlfriend, Lyndsey Korner, and, after a manic drive around the country in his Mini, ended up back in Cambridge undergoing treatment in a mental hospital.

Seemingly recovered, Syd returned to London in December 1968, rented a flat with artist Duggie Fields and approached EMI with the intention of launching a solo career. His first album, THE MADCAP LAUGHS (1970), appeared after more than a year of delays and shambolic studio sessions – its chaotic mix of finished, unfinished and muffed takes giving a most accurate impression of Barrett's state of mind. Gems such as "Octopus" were balanced on the borderline of genius and madness, whereas "Dark Globe" and "If It's In You" were almost too harrowing to listen to.

Although Barrett's mental health had been declining, the album was well received, with few reviewers realizing the tragedy hidden within the grooves. After a rare live appearance at London's Olympia, he began recording a much tighter second set, BARRETT (1970; reissued 1998; EMI), with the help of Floyd's **Dave Gilmour** and **Richard Wright**, plus Humble Pie drummer **Jerry Shirley**. The songs were perhaps not as strong as before, but overall it was a much more pleasant listen. On "Baby Lemonade" and "Gigolo Aunt", Syd was as lyrically opaque as ever, while "Wined & Dined" and "Dominoes" were attractive, straightforward love songs, with a strong undercurrent of English melancholy.

Tiring of London, Syd then returned to Cambridge, forming a short-lived band called **Stars**, before retiring from the music business. He still lives in Cambridge on an invalidity pension, enjoying the life of a recluse, having rejected music for his first love, painting.

In the absence of the hero, the legend of the mad genius behind Pink Floyd developed, fuelled by fanzines, reissues, books, cover versions and, most importantly of all, the Floyd themselves. If the band had split up back in 1968, Barrett would be seen as just another acid casualty. But Pink Floyd have gone on to global megastardom and much of their best work – WISH YOU WERE HERE, DARK SIDE OF THE MOON and THE WALL – has either been directly inspired by Syd (most famously "Shine On You Crazy Diamond") or shot through with references to his madness, alienation and withdrawal.

It could easily be argued that Pink Floyd have made a career out of mythologizing Syd Barrett, with the final irony that, while they have gone on to conquer the world, Barrett is a recluse in his Cambridge semi. While it seems unlikely that he will emerge from his self-imposed exile, Roger Barrett (as he is now known) might one day use his fame to launch a new career as an artist. Then again, he might just prefer to stay at home and watch TV.

⦿ **The Madcap Laughs** (1970; Harvest; reissued 1998; EMI).
A curious sense of inertia and distance hangs over this brilliant and occasionally disturbing kaleidoscope of unrelated mood fragments.

⦿ **Barrett** (1970; Harvest).
Syd's most consistent solo work, though many prefer the barely controlled chaos of the first album.

⦿ **The Peel Sessions** (1988; Strange Fruit).
Excellent five-track session, showcasing a relaxed Syd strumming some of his best tunes to a hippie backing of bongos.

Iain Smith

BAUHAUS

Formed Northampton, England, 1978; disbanded 1983.

Bauhaus were formed at art college by **Peter Murphy** (vocals), **Daniel Ash** (guitar/sax), **David Jay** (bass) and Jay's younger brother **Kevin Haskins** (drums). Their debut single, "Bela Lugosi's Dead" (1978) was released on the same Small Wonder label responsible for the first Cure single. Its dub-informed bass and lyrics of gleeful morbid fascination made the band an instant hit in Britain, and set them apart as a more esoteric outfit than many of their punk contemporaries.

The band's androgynous appearance and camp theatrics owed much to The New York Dolls and more to David Bowie; apart from having their biggest UK hit single with a cover of his "Ziggy Stardust" (1982), they also made a brief appearance playing their debut single in the film *The Hunger*, in which Bowie starred. Their persona also owed a lot to grainy monochromatic late-night horror movies, a trait manifested in their live renditions of the song

"In Heaven (Everything Is Fine)" from David Lynch's cult flick, *Eraserhead*.

The music relied heavily on a machine-tight rhythm section, leaving the pouting Murphy and Ash to flaunt their anarchic flash. Ash's idiosyncratic guitar playing provided splashes of sounds and textural noise rather than actual tunes, and at times almost competed with the warped sexuality that Murphy's vocals evoked. Not surprisingly, given their striking visual appearance, Bauhaus made some excellent promo videos right up to the feigned decadence of "She's In Parties" (1983). All their promo clips are available on the video ARCHIVE, while a live video, SHADOW OF LIGHT, amply captured their undoubted showmanship.

Bauhaus released four studio LPs, beginning with IN THE FLAT FIELD (1979), issued on 4AD, and moving to Beggars Banquet for MASK (1981), THE SKY'S GONE OUT (1982) and BURNING FROM THE INSIDE (1983). (All four CD reissues also feature singles and B-sides as extra tracks.) They also made a live album, PRESS THE EJECT AND GIVE ME THE TAPE (1982), while a double-LP compilation was released in 1988, followed by SWING THE HEARTACHE (1989), a collection of BBC radio sessions.

Bauhaus consistently managed to create music of genuine substance and invention – The Velvet Underground's John Cale rated them enough to write a song about them, and Nico actually guested with the band. In their time they had a huge cult following, and when they split up, still in their early twenties, they left behind a little magic that would remain absent from their subsequent projects. Three-quarters of the band later became **LOVE AND ROCKETS**, while Peter Murphy went solo via **DALI'S CAR**.

⊙ **Mask** (1981; Beggars Banquet).
The quintessential Bauhaus album, featuring the singles "Passion Of Lovers" and "Kick In The Eye".

⊙ **Press The Eject And Give Me The Tape** (1982; Beggars Banquet).
Live recordings of earlier material; the back cover's recommendation to 'play very loud' should be heeded.

⊙ **Burning From The Inside** (1983; Beggars Banquet).
Haunting and verging on psychedelic, this LP contains "She's In Parties" and the wonderful "Who Killed Mr. Moonlight".

Ross Holloway

BE-BOP DELUXE

Formed Wakefield, England, 1971;
disbanded 1978.

"Be Bop took elements from rock'n'roll, deconstructed them and reconstructed them. I'd not have used the term post-modernist then, but would now."
Bill Nelson

Born in that fallow post-glam and pre-punk period, when dinosaurs still stalked the sta-diums, **Be-Bop Deluxe** were essentially a vehicle for **BILL NELSON**, a man who can lay claim to being the last of the great guitar heroes. Bill had a breathtakingly fluid guitar style which, while echoing the flash and feedbackery of Hendrix, usually eschewed the blues notes in favour of lightning jazz-tinged major-scale workouts. Enhancing the image were his cadaverous cheekbones, Alice Cooper eye shadow and a line in dense lyrical symbolism that more than sufficed to pull in the Bowie clones.

The live performances which earned Nelson, **Ian Parkin**, **Rob Bryan** and **Nicholas Chatterton-Dew** a strong grassroots following and a contract with Harvest were documented on the first album, AXE VICTIM (1974). A patchy if lovable affair, its moments of great pastoral beauty were marred in places by some plodding backing and badly concealed reference points. At the time of its release Nelson declared himself unhappy with much of it, and committed himself to change.

Change he did. Out went Parkin, Bryan and Chatterton-Dew, to be replaced by a leaner and more capable outfit comprising ebullient Maori bassist **Charlie Tummahai**, seasoned session drummer **Simon Fox** and, later, **Andrew Clarke**, whose keyboards would go on to grace Bowie's SCARY MONSTERS. The result was the astonishing FUTURAMA (1975), on which Nelson's personal vision was given full kitchen-sink realization by Queen producer **Roy Thomas Baker**. Top-heavy with massed guitars and melodic ideas pursued on a whim and just as quickly abandoned, it nevertheless contained two of the most perfect pop singles never to make the charts – "Maid In Heaven" and "Sister Seagull".

Be-Bop toured with Cockney Rebel and then in their own right, finally enjoying chart success in 1976 with the throwaway "Ships In The Night" from the SUNBURST FINISH album. Dodgy cover aside (nude holding flaming guitar), SUNBURST was much more accessible than FUTURAMA and received wide critical acclaim. Die-hard fans, however, were disappointed by Nelson's reluctance to keep on playing the guitar hero.

At the height of their powers in the UK, the group inevitably turned their attention to America, where, despite a reception which would have ensured them stadium-capacity success for the rest of their days, Nelson became disillusioned fairly quickly. This was much in evidence on the US-tailored MODERN MUSIC (1976), in titles such as "Dance Of The Uncle Sam Humanoids", "Honeymoon On Mars" and "Lost In The Neon World".

Nelson's restlessness and yearning for experimentation saw him at loggerheads with the industry moguls intent on milking the cash cow he'd reared and, after treading water with DRASTIC PLASTIC (1977), the group split up. Nelson has subsequently resisted lucrative offers to re-form the outfit, but has opted instead to mine an individual seam of ambient and conceptual works in quiet Yorkshire isolation.

The influence of Be-Bop Deluxe, however, should not be underestimated. Big Country frontman Stuart Adamson became the proud owner of the guitar that Nelson brandished on the cover of AXE VICTIM, and today there is even a group dedicated to re-creating, to the last dramatic flourish, the group's *Sunburst Finish Tour* set.

⦿ **Futurama** (1975; Harvest).
Brimming over with melodic and rhythmic ideas, this is Nelson at his most romantic and bombastic. Heavily recommended to guitar nuts, too.

⦿ **Sunburst Finish** (1976; Harvest).
The band at their slick and polished peak.

⦿ **Air Age Anthology** (1997; EMI).
The perfect introduction to the magnificent Mr Nelson, this two-CD compilation scoops the cream off the band's six studio albums.

⦿ **Tramcar To Tomorrow** (1998; Hux).
An intriguing collection of previously unreleased John Peel sessions from 1974 to 1978.

⦿ **Tremulous Antenna** (2002; Hux).
This set witnesses the very welcome reappearance of the BBC's *In Concert* recordings of 1976 and 1978, previously available as the RADIOLAND album.

Ada Wilson

THE BEACH BOYS

Formed Hawthorne, near Los Angeles, 1961; a line-up is still in existence.

There's some TV comedy footage from the mid 70s where an obese ex-rock star is dragged out of his mansion by two cops, taken to a frozen beach and forced to surf. He's in on the 'joke', but behind his eyes you can register humiliation and fear at the crashing waves. The ex-rock star is **Brian Wilson**, whose band, **The Beach Boys**, provided some of the most poignant and euphoric moments of their era, both in their music and in their lives. It's ironic that Wilson hated surfing, as by the mid 70s The Beach Boys had become forever associated with the sun and surf motifs of their early hits; despite outgrowing those times, they could never escape them.

From the outset it was a family affair, with the tyrannical and manipulative father **Murray Wilson** encouraging his three boys to record. Brian, **Carl** and **Dennis Wilson** joined forces with their cousin **Mike Love**, and **David Marks**, in the summer of 1961, releasing the first single, "Surfin'". A minor hit, it was overshadowed the following year by the breakthrough single, "Surfin' Safari", the epitome of The Beach Boys' early teen-dream confections, reflecting an age of confidence in white middle America. In late 1963 Marks was eventually pressurized out of the group by Murray Wilson, and his place was filled by erstwhile folk singer **Al Jardine**. (It is a testament to the commercial durability of early Beach Boys material that Marks has managed to live off his royalties since his dismissal, despite being in the band for less than two years.) The classic Beach Boys line-up – Brian, Carl and Dennis, plus Love and Jardine – was augmented on tour by session men (including **Glen**

Campbell), and one of these – **Bruce Johnston** – joined in April 1965.

The 45rpm single was still the prime currency of pop music in the early 60s. As such, early Beach Boys albums tend to be collections of great singles and so-so filler material. ALL SUMMER LONG (1964) was the first album to edge away from this formula, and represented a quantum leap in terms of production. Brian Wilson, a disciple of Phil Spector's 'Wall of Sound' technique, was becoming more of a competitor than a follower. TODAY (1965) and SUMMER DAYS (AND SUMMER NIGHTS) (1965) consolidated the band's progress with a number of sublime tracks distilling the essence of the California dream – "Help Me Rhonda" and "California Girls" to name but two. The increasing complexity of the material highlighted Brian's obsession with studio technique and sonic perfectionism, a development paralleled by his move away from surfing and driving towards deeper, more reflective topics.

The new maturity was crystallized on the masterpiece PET SOUNDS (1966), where Wilson collaborated with lyricist **Tony Asher**. "God Only Knows" – reportedly Paul McCartney's favourite song – still deserves a place on God's own jukebox, and the entire LP remains a gorgeous mood piece, possessed of a dreamy, ethereal quality. But its intimacy sometimes gave way to melancholia and a sense of loss, such as on "Caroline No", a track which Bruce Johnston commented was 'about Brian himself, and the death of a quality within him that was so vital ... his innocence.'

PET SOUNDS was voted the greatest album of all time by *Mojo* magazine in the UK. It would be a mistake, however, to think that the band's new direction was universally welcomed at the time. The conservatism of the group's fans even spread to the band members themselves. Mike Love described PET SOUNDS as 'Brian's ego music', feeling that the self-obsessed tone and complex sonic craftsmanship had their origins within Wilson's increasing use of LSD. Brian, meanwhile, sensed that things were changing in the music industry, and felt eclipsed by the releases of Dylan's BLONDE ON BLONDE and The Beatles' REVOLVER in August 1966. The result was a spiralling use of marijuana, pills and LSD, and the onset of behaviour that was eccentric, reclusive and ultimately self-destructive.

The marketing of the group by Capitol Records was also not without controversy. Even as PET SOUNDS was selling respectably in the US, Capitol redirected efforts towards the first of a series of 'best of' albums. This recycling of the past – even as the band strived to develop – would return to haunt Brian over the years, constantly emphasizing the continuing appeal of his earlier work. Capitol also forced the band to compromise, insisting on the inclusion of "Sloop John B" on PET SOUNDS, despite the fact that it clashed with the overall mood of the set.

Amidst this atmosphere of frustration and tension, Brian resolved to produce a studio masterpiece with

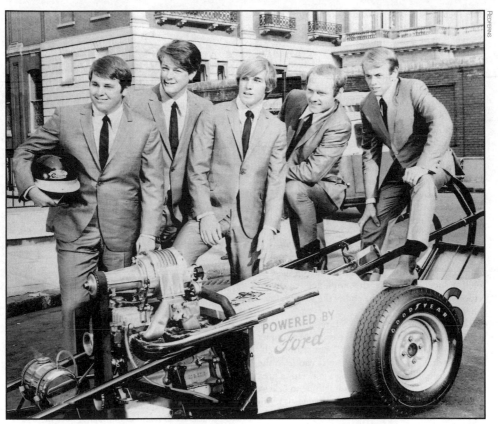

Spot the genius. Left to right: Carl, Brian and Dennis Wilson, Mike Love and Al Jardine

his next effort, provisionally entitled "Dumb Angel", but later dubbed SMILE. However, he collapsed under the pressure of expectation, compounded by an excessive drug habit. SMILE, as Brian conceived it, has never been released, although tantalizing glimpses of what might have been have surfaced through tracks from the sessions appearing (often haphazardly) on subsequent Beach Boys collections.

Yet, as Brian's situation deteriorated largely out of sight of the public, resurrection was at hand with a single recorded prior to the SMILE sessions. "Good Vibrations", released in the autumn of 1966, was a metaphor for the heartbroken dreams of the 60s and, like SGT PEPPER, it neatly divided the decade between innocence and experience. The product of six months' work, it was co-written by Mike Love, who would soon become a key figure in the songwriting axis of the group.

"Good Vibrations" cost £50,000 to record, reached #1 on both sides of the Atlantic, and represented a career peak. Although there would be further strong singles, such as "Heroes And Villains", which Wilson co-wrote with **Van Dyke Parks**, the momentum was waning. They seemed hopelessly unhip to the Haight-Astbury counterculture, and after they cancelled a scheduled appearance at the Monterey Festival in the summer of 1967, Jimi Hendrix introduced one of his songs with the dismissive phrase, 'this ain't no surf music.' Their image was dented by their unwillingness to embrace music as a political tool, while their manufactured studio-based recording techniques were out of fashion, as bands were becoming increasingly assessed by their live performances.

Some of the SMILE sessions were eventually cobbled together and released as the indulgent SMILEY SMILE in late 1967. The LP fared badly in the States, but the band released a surprisingly fresh and cohesive set in early 1968 – the organ-led, white-soul classic WILD HONEY. It was the sound of a group trying hard to please an audience that was no longer there, but it outsold SMILEY SMILE. Love co-wrote the whole album, apart from a spirited cover of Stevie Wonder's "I Was Made To Love Her".

The curious follow-up LP – FRIENDS (1968) – was a gentle, restrained and unremarkable set, and was a favourite of the group's more obsessive fans, who were presumably attracted to the band's dalliance with Eastern mysticism, "Transcendental Meditation". 1969 brought 20/20, a mish-mash of recent hit-and-miss singles and SMILE sessions (most notably "Cabin Essence"), which also featured a bizarre oddity. At this time Dennis Wilson was hanging out with a young unknown musician named **Charles Manson** and "Never Learn Not To Love" (originally entitled "Cease To Exist") was apparently co-written with the soon-to-be mass murderer, whom Dennis referred to as 'The Wizard'. As Brian began to lose control, the other band members started to form their own battle lines: Mike Love and Al Jardine – the drug-free transcendental meditators – versus Dennis and Carl Wilson, the increasingly wild bohemians.

By the release of 20/20, the market was saturated with products that no one wanted to buy. After twenty albums in less than seven years, they left Capitol for Warner Brothers, but SUNFLOWER (1970) was no improvement. Their subsequent revival and belated acceptance into the rock fold was one of the period's more surprising reversals. The reappraisal was set in motion in April 1971 with an impromptu and unlikely jam session with **The Grateful Dead** at New York's Fillmore East. After the Dead's three-hour set, The Beach Boys timidly hit the stage to total silence. Gradually the audience began to respond, though, and by the end of the set the atmosphere was euphoric.

The impressive SURF'S UP (1971; reissued on vinyl 1998; EMI) glanced back to the passing of a simpler era in songs such as "Disney Girls", but with its self-mocking title and downbeat cover it captured the waning spirit of the age, addressing a generation tired of 'revolution' and searching for something to believe in. Brian's contributions – collaborations with Van Dyke Parks such as the title track, which Brian wanted to exclude because it reminded him of his former peaks – were old songs, but they meshed seamlessly into a strong, moving album. For a while, the time seemed right for The Beach Boys.

However, they failed to capitalize upon the momentum. Brian was lost in booze and drugs, compounded by paranoia and a deep sense of failure. Dennis was developing as a songwriter, but the other band members were struggling to deliver quality material. The 1972 album, CARL AND THE PASSIONS (an early working name for the band) was a wretched album, and The Beach Boys saga took another strange turn when they decamped to Amsterdam to record HOLLAND (1973). The LP cost a fortune to make and is either 'a veritable shit-load of meditative drivel' (*Rolling Stone*), or a strong, overlooked gem. Brian managed to deliver a song for the album – "Sail On Sailor", sung by **Blondie Chaplin**, on his only album with The Beach Boys. It was arguably the last great Beach Boys track, as the band increasingly became a vehicle for nostalgia.

Despite "Sail On Sailor", Brian's condition was worsening. He ballooned to 300lbs on a diet of fast food, cocaine and heroin, and in the late 70s attempted suicide by drowning, but was saved by brother Dennis. Business and financial difficulties also beset the band, probably a consequence of Murray Wilson's selling the publishing rights to Brian's songs in a 1969 deal.

By the early 80s, The Beach Boys' music, in seemingly terminal decline, seemed tailor-made for the Reagan nation – a country increasingly cocksure and bullish, with a craving for patriotic nostalgia. For the curious, the BEACH BOYS LOVE YOU album (from 1977) is probably the only post-HOLLAND LP worthy of inspection, with Brian producing all new songs for the first time since SMILEY SMILE.

In December 1983, tragedy of a personal kind darkened the saga of The Beach Boys. Dennis Wilson – a haggard and bloated booze and cocaine binger, drowned in California. He did leave behind a solo legacy, the excellent PACIFIC OCEAN BLUE, released to modest acclaim and encouraging sales in 1977.

The story of The Beach Boys took on the dimensions of a horribly engrossing soap opera, incorporating tawdry business squabbles, mental illness, creative inertia, death and, in Brian Wilson especially, a descent into the dark corners of Californian mythology. Brian quit the band to concentrate on his psychiatric treatment with Dr Eugene Landy, whom he had first met in the mid-70s. Some Beach Boys obsessives consider Landy a cruel and manipulative opportunist who brainwashed Brian in order to share his glory. Many cite the fawning psychobabble of Wilson's autobiography, *Wouldn't It Be Nice*, as ample evidence of an unhealthy reverence towards Landy. More objective onlookers would reflect that Landy forced Wilson to work again and to get a solo deal with Sire Records in 1987, which resulted in his best new music for twenty years – 1988's BRIAN WILSON. Yet Sire refused to release a second solo effort, SWEET INSANITY, even though it contained a duet with Bob Dylan on "The Spirit Of Rock And Roll".

Subsequently, Wilson has survived lawsuits to claim the rights to his songs, counterclaims from Mike Love, and a restraining order preventing Landy from contacting him. Meanwhile, he has experienced a degree, at least, of creative renaissance. In 1995, Brian was seen on film reworking old classics under the direction of **Don Was** – material released, with some harrowing 'lost years' tapes, as the album I JUST

WASN'T MADE FOR THESE TIMES. The same year also saw fresh sessions with Van Dyke Parks for a duo album, ORANGE CRATE ART; the songs were all by Parks, and somewhat overwrought, but Brian at least was back and singing in the studio. And, despite all the animosity, there was even a return to work with his old band.

The Beach Boys certainly need a shot in the arm from their errant genius. They may have returned to the charts in 1988 with "Kokomo", featured in the Tom Cruise movie *Cocktail*, but it is widely felt that they exist in a sad, albeit lucrative, twilight of self-parody. They haven't moved with the times, and nor, perhaps, could they. Mike Love's decision to work with the British cabaret-rock outfit **Status Quo**, sleepwalking through "Fun, Fun, Fun" in early 1996, was a nadir ruthlessly exceeded when the whole band, including Brian, decamped to Nashville to play as backing band to a depressing set of tired old country-music hacks such as **Willie Nelson**. The resulting album STARS AND STRIPES VOL 1 (1996) is an awful legacy.

Carl Wilson's death from cancer in February 1998 left the group bereft of its leader and cast their permanently touring career into doubt. Wilson's involvement (as performer and co-producer) made the proceedings appear even more ominous as The Beach Boys dredged through a selection of their songs in a 'country' setting.

Overweight, and seemingly even more malleable post-Landy, one would still have expected Brian Wilson to see through this glib facade. The Stones may have become a mere pantomime of their glory years, but at least they know their formula and can restyle it with panache. The Beach Boys seem to have forgotten what made them so special in the first place.

As their present paled, so the past gleamed ever brighter. The Beach Boys were credited with producing the greatest single of all time – "Good Vibrations" in August 1997's *Mojo* magazine. "Don't Worry Baby" and "God Only Knows" were listed at 11 and 28 respectively. The band has spawned an industry of biographers keen to pore over every piece of minutiae about the group, in the process swamping the reality with myth. For a scholarly, exhaustive overview, Timothy White's *The Nearest Faraway Place* (1996; Macmillan) comes recommended. For the only real eyewitness account of disintegrating genius, Brian Wilson's own autobiography, *Wouldn't It Be Nice* (Bloomsbury) is hard to beat.

Wilson himself played some solo shows with the **Wondermints** in 95/96, and is quoted as saying, "If I'd had the Wondermints back in 67 I would have taken SMILE on the road", a veiled snub to his fellow Beach Boys.

A new Brian Wilson album, IMAGINATION, emerged in 1998, but was a sterile and vapid slab of tired LA pop. It was glossy; it was jaunty and brisk; but, like an ageing hostess with a fixed smile and tired eyes that try too hard to be happy, the cracks in the makeup and the memories of better days were all too obvious. BRIAN WILSON, released ten years before, got by with a certain kooky charm and sweet warmth to disguise the thin songwriting on display – IMAGINATION couldn't even muster that level of quality.

Wilson had more than his fair share of defenders, obsessives, oddballs and plain fans ready to hang on his every word and talk up IMAGINATION. But they were wrong, of course, and fundamentally so. They were in love with the idea of Brian Wilson. Worse than that, they were in love with their own past and the music that shaped it oh so perfectly. It's the worst kind of nostalgia and they are the worst kind of rock fans. The process rolled on in 2002 with Wilson playing at the Royal Festival Hall, the set captured as the occasionally magical PET SOUNDS LIVE (2002); meanwhile, Al Jardine quit The Beach Boys and Mike Love has re-recruited David Marks (who was ousted in 1963!) to add 'authenticity'.

Surf's still up... but the fire is out. Stop meddling with the ashes.

The Beach Boys

Pet Sounds (1966; Capitol).
A tender, soulful map of the heart, PET SOUNDS creates a dreamy world of love, devotion and obsession. Music to retreat into.

Wild Honey (1968; Capitol).
The Beach Boys' party album, shooting desperately from the hip with a mixture of pop, soul and R&B. Infectious, innocent and joyous. (It was reissued on CD with its predecessor, SMILEY SMILE.)

Surf's Up (1971; Warners; reissued on vinyl 1998; EMI).
The band resurrect themselves. Strong songs address current issues, and explore personal themes. Airy, lush and textured, SURF'S UP has aged better than much of the weightier competition of the time.

The Best Of The Beach Boys (1995; Capitol).
This digitally remastered two-CD release is the essential compilation of early material, while also acknowledging the later 'semi-hits'. "Little Deuce Coupe", "Surfin' USA", "California Girls" and the rest distil the essence of the California Dream into delicious moments that still sound fresh.

Good Vibration: Thirty Years Of The Beach Boys (1993; Capitol).
A four-CD box set, as uneven as you'd expect. Chiefly of interest because it included several otherwise unavailable fragments from the SMILE sessions that took anally retentive obsessive behaviour to previously unknown heights. Some may consider wading through two versions of the album plus several hours of outtakes to be a joy – many of us will feel that tampering with perfection somehow dilutes its charm and/or that life is simply too short.

Beach Boys Christmas Album (1998; Capitol).
A generally sweet and touching reminder of happier times, with well-worn favourites nestling next to strangely affecting oddities, some from an abortive Christmas project which never saw the light of day in the mid-70s. Hardly essential, but not without charm.

Brian Wilson Productions

Pet Projects: The Brian Wilson Productions (2003; Ace).
This is a must have artifact for any Wilson fan, featuring a plethora of long-lost gems that all boast Brian behind the mixing desk. The Sharon Marie, American Spring and The Honeys cuts stand out.

Nig Hodgkins

THE BEASTIE BOYS

Formed New York, 1979.

The Beastie Boys first appeared on the scene as talentless, sniggering, bratty punks. Helped out, no doubt, by the fact that they had parents 'in the bizz', they played Max's Kansas City, CBGBs and the like with bands such as **Bad Brains** and **Influence**. In the beginning, there was POLLYWOG STEW; an indie EP release on the not terribly well-known Ratcage label (reissued in 1993) – its eight tracks caused only minor ripples in and around New York. Then came "Cookie Puss", a pre-Jerky Boys crank call (the Cookie Puss of the title is a heavily advertised ice-cream novelty) heard over amateurish hardcore bashing. In the ensuing years, they remained sniggering and bratty (you could also add sophomoric, moronic and tasteless to the list), before mutating into the global musical power that they are today – it is impossible to deny their talent.

By the time they had released their debut album, LICENSED TO ILL (1986; Def Jam), the Beasties – **Adam 'King Ad-Rock' Horowitz** (vocals/guitar), **Michael 'Mike-D' Diamond** (vocals/drums) and **Adam 'MCA' Yauch** (vocals/bass) – had made the move from hardcore to rap, a move that has to be at least partially attributed to their association with producer **Rick Rubin**, who signed the band to his Def Jam label. The genius of LICENSED (which was a surprise #1 US hit) was in re-creating the attitudes, poses and ideas of rap while transferring them to a suburban milieu. They could brag and do the dozens with the best of them, but instead of righteous inner-city rage and exhortations to fight the power, The Beasties fought for their right to party. The samples also reflected The Beasties' upbringing, replacing funk with metal: Aerosmith, Zeppelin, AC/DC and War were in the mix, along with the theme song from the *Mr. Ed* television show. For all its self-conscious goofiness ("Brass Monkey" and "No Sleep 'Til Brooklyn"), LICENSED was an exhilarating album that opened new avenues for rap music.

But it seemed that they might miss out on their own trailblazing. A fight with Rubin led to a court battle, forcing The Beasties to wait three years to follow up LICENSED TO ILL. When it came out, PAUL'S BOUTIQUE (1989) angered and confused a lot of people. Ambitious and dense, if muddled and sometimes one-dimensional, the album heralded a new, more serious Beasties. The samplescapes, created in large part with the aid of **The Dust Brothers**, had moved beyond simple grooves into sound collages, at times the equal (in density, if not in power) of Public Enemy's Bomb Squad. PAUL'S BOUTIQUE stands as the ultimate statement of hopelessly hip city kids grooving to their own world of made-for-TV movies, urban radio, 70s kitsch, The Eagles, secondhand clothes, Mountain, locker-room humour, Johnny Cash, beer, Funky Four Plus One, and too much grass.

Unsurprisingly, PAUL'S BOUTIQUE was commercially dead on arrival.

CHECK YOUR HEAD (1992) was a radical reinterpretation of The Beastie Boys' formula and image. Picking up their instruments again, the band added hardcore and Meters-styled funk to the brew. Adding **Money Mark Nishita** (keyboards) to the band, The Beasties stripped their sound down to funk rudiments; even the trash culture aesthetic was kept to a minimum of samples of a Cheap Trick song intro and comedian Jimmy Walker's catchphrase, 'Dyno-mite'. ILL COMMUNICATION (1994) took those experiments even further. From the thrash of "Sabotage" to the old-school boasting of "Root Down" and the spacey collage of "Flute Loop", The Beasties managed to forge their seemingly disparate influences into a satisfying whole.

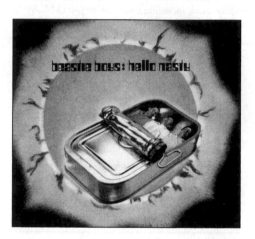

The next Beastie Boys outing on record was THE IN SOUND FROM WAY OUT (1996), a funky but laid-back time-filler of instrumental reworkings from the previous two albums. The Boys, however, kept themselves busy, expanding their Grand Royal label – signing among others **Luscious Jackson** (who featured original Beastie Girl **Kate Schellenbach** on drums) – developing the X-Large and X-Girl lines of skate-chic clothing, and publishing the brilliant *Grand Royal* magazine. Adam Yauch developed an interest in Tibet and turned Buddhist, launching the Milarepa Fund and offshoot *Tibetan Freedom Concerts*.

This delayed, but didn't stop, the B-Boy train and the album HELLO NASTY (1998). While no great leap forward stylistically, it had enough chewy bits to surprise listeners and keep them entertained through repeated listenings. The single "Intergalactic" – a UK number one and *Grammy Award* winner to boot – was enough to keep the faithful happy and draw a fair number of new recruits. A world tour followed, conducted on a giant turntable to give audiences a better view; at time of writing a new Beasties album was taking shape, but until its release fans will have to make do with the hits and rarities collection, SOUNDS OF SCIENCE (1999).

● **Paul's Boutique** (1989; Capitol).
The Beasties' masterpiece. Although they already more or less relocated to LA, this is the ultimate New York album. Full of unbelievably dense sampladelic collages, in-jokes, and ludicrous, namechecking raps, this perfectly captures the compressed, hyperactive energy of the Big Apple.

● **Check Your Head** (1992; Capitol).
Where The Beasties re-imagine themselves as the punked-up Meters, immersing themselves in the new school of old-school beat fetishization.

● **Ill Communication** (1994; Capitol).
Another stunning, sprawling collection that well and truly reacquainted The Beastie Boys with the mainstream, while still remaining true to the group's roots.

● **Sounds Of Science** (1999; Capitol).
This is The Beastie Boys' hits package that documents their rise from loud-mouthed teens to household names. Highlights include the band's peculiar take on Elton John's "Benny And The Jets".

Steven Mirkin

THE (ENGLISH) BEAT

Formed Birmingham, England, 1978; disbanded 1982.

Ultra-tight ska revivalists **The Beat** (marketed in the US as 'The English Beat') were formed in the aftermath of punk by **Dave Wakeling** (guitar/vocals), **Andy Cox** (guitar), **David Steele** (bass) and **Everett Morton** (drums). Early pub gigs garnered a devoted following, but also a reputation for privileging musicianship over soul. This was remedied by the recruitment of black rapper **Ranking Roger** (Roger Charlery) and a sixty-something Jamaican saxophonist known simply as **Saxa**, who had once worked with ska legend Prince Buster. They would add a much-needed element of fun.

The band's first break came in 1979, when **Jerry Dammers** of The Specials signed them to his 2-Tone label. Dammers had been attracted by their pumped-up bluebeat sound, but also by their stridently anti-racist politics – always an essential ingredient in the lyrics. Now The Beat were label-mates with not only The Specials but also Madness, The Selecter, and other very hip names, and were firmly associated with the burgeoning ska revival, a movement devoted to putting danceability back into 'alternative' pop. Their first single, a cover of Smokey Robinson's "Tears Of A Clown", went into the UK Top 10, and overnight turned the band into *Top Of The Pops* favourites: the mix of Wakeling's cool demeanour and the frantic energy of Ranking Roger would become a familiar sight on the programme in years to come.

The band now had some clout within the music industry, and parted company with 2-Tone soon afterwards. They came to an arrangement with corporate giants Arista to form their own subsidiary label, Go Feet, over which they would have complete artistic control – a way of both making money and staying 'indie' (something that 2-Tone had already achieved by becoming part of Chrysalis). The

singles released on the label in 1980 were incredibly successful, and included three upbeat Top 10 hits – "Hands Off... She's Mine", "Mirror In The Bathroom", and "Too Nice To Talk To".

Politics was still an important element. Benefit gigs for CND and organizations for the unemployed confirmed the band's radical lefty credentials – there was never any question that they would attract the same kind of National Front following as the unfortunate Madness. Their main vinyl contribution to the cause was the magnificent "Stand Down Margaret", a practical bit of advice to the (then) Prime Minister ('I see no joy, I see only sorrow: I see no chance of your bright new tomorrow...'), which became something of an anthem among Britain's politically aware youth.

The debut album, I JUST CAN'T STOP IT (1980), contained many of the hits, plus two excellent cover versions: Prince Buster's "Rough Rider", and the less obvious "Can't Get Used To Losing You", originally a hit for none other than Andy Williams. One of the finest pop LPs of the 1980s, it went to #3 in the UK.

But it was also the high spot for the band. By the end of 1980, the ska boom was losing its original punky edge, and the bands associated with it were testing new directions. Madness became more orientated towards the kids' market with their 'nutty sound', while The Specials experimented with darker soundscapes inspired by Dammers' interest in film themes. Similarly, The Beat chose to try out a new reggae-influenced approach. Things slowed down a great deal on the second album, WHA'PPEN (1981), a huge disappointment, with lyrics expressing paranoia and despair in place of the old anger. It nevertheless climbed to #3, and spawned the Top 30 single "Drowning"/"All Out To Get You".

Live, the band emphasized instrumental passages, and especially the saxophone breaks, though the ever-more-doddery Saxa retired in 1982, to be replaced by **Wesley Magoogan**. Guitarist Cox had also developed into a very individual player, though his rubber-legged dancing technique was an unsettling sight. Ranking Roger, meanwhile, looked increasingly lost. By now, things were clearly on the slide for the band, and as the hits dried up they decided to try to break America, where they toured as The English Beat, to avoid confusion with another outfit. They never achieved their goal, and the third and final album, SPECIAL BEAT SERVICE, was barren as far as hit singles were concerned, but nevertheless went Top 30.

Ironically, 1983 saw the band's biggest chart hit in the form of a remix of "Can't Get Used To Losing You", from the first album, which went to #3. But it was all too late, and Wakeling quit soon afterwards. He and Ranking Roger went on to form **General Public**, while Cox and Steele regrouped as **Fine Young Cannibals**. The Beat will probably be remembered as 'the third' 1980s ska band after Madness and The Specials, but to anyone who can recall the heady days of 250,000-strong CND marches, and sore-throated choruses of "Stand Down

Margaret", their music will always have a special resonance.

- **I Just Can't Stop It** (1980; Go Feet).
  A real classic, on which the tracks seemingly blend into each other.

- **What Is Beat?** (Best Of The Beat) (1983; Go Feet).
  Excellent compilation, with the added bonus of "Tears Of A Clown".

Roger Sabin

THE BEATLES

Formed Liverpool, England, 1957; disbanded 1970.

"Groups with guitars are on the way out." Decca executive after cancelling a Beatles audition, 1961

"I'd like to say thank you on behalf of the group and ourselves, and I hope we've passed the audition." John Lennon performing "Get Back" on the roof of Apple, 1969

The Rolling Stones may have rocked harder and Dylan may have been smarter, but neither could claim the cultural impact of **The Beatles**. Throughout the 60s, they were always in tune with the times, and in their bitter dissolution they reflected the fragmentation of pop culture at the end of the decade. The Beatles catalogue forms perhaps the most important body of work in popular music, representing not only the development of the musicians themselves, but also the development of the modern music business. They were the ultimate pop group and one of the few bands to transcend the limitations of their art to produce music that was universal. Yet at the heart of the Beatles odyssey is the story of two lads who became the best of friends and were split up by marriage. It could be any young man's rite of passage, except that the people involved happened to be two of the greatest songwriters of the late twentieth century.

Fate dealt the winning hand on July 6, 1957, when budding rocker **Paul McCartney** went to see a local band, **The Quarrymen**, at a church fête in Woolton. McCartney got talking to the rhythm guitarist, a certain **John Lennon**, and found they had a mutual interest in Eddie Cochran, Gene Vincent and Little Richard. McCartney was soon asked to join the band and started writing songs with Lennon, though most of their set consisted of the crowd-pleasing hits of the day. By 1960, they had acquired a new name, a manager and a fairly stable line-up of **George Harrison** on lead guitar, **Stu Sutcliffe** on bass and **Pete Best** on drums. That same year, The Beatles secured a residency in Hamburg, a favoured haunt for early British rockers, which proved to be the making of the band. The living was rough and wild, with the fresh-faced Liverpool teens exposed overnight to the pleasures of speed, existentialism, all-night drinking, fighting and the Reeperbahn's notorious red-light zone. Most importantly of all, their punishing schedule of three sets a night turned them into seasoned professionals within only a few months. The existentialist input came from Stu Sutcliffe's German girlfriend Astrid Kirchherr, who created much of the early Beatles look. On their second Hamburg stint, Sutcliffe himself dropped out of the band, leaving McCartney to take over on bass.

The Beatles returned to Liverpool in June 1961, to find that their frenzied playing went down a storm at home as well as in Germany. Within a few months they acquired a new manager, **Brian Epstein**, and a residency at The Cavern, where they soon became local heroes at the centre of Liverpool's beat boom. But with their horizons opened by their time in Europe, their eyes turned to London and a national record deal. Derek Rowe of Decca has gone down in history as the man who turned down The Beatles, but he certainly wasn't the only one to reject Brian Epstein's overtures. In fact, it was hit or miss as to whether EMI/Parlophone would sign them, but it seems that producer **George Martin** liked their sense of humour as much as their music (he had worked on comedy for Peter Sellers and many other acts) and decided to take a chance. However, one final and controversial change remained: next time The Beatles returned to London's Abbey Road studios in September 1962, **Ringo Starr**, previously of Rory Storm and the Hurricanes, was in the drummer's seat. The reason was as much musical as personal (whether it had anything to do with the fact that Pete Best was too good-looking for the others' liking is of course debatable), but the girls at The Cavern didn't see things this way and in one of the ensuing punch-ups George Harrison sustained a black eye. He was still sporting it as The Beatles struggled through their first commercial recording, a Lennon and McCartney composition called "Love Me Do".

Today it sounds like a pretty lightweight affair, but its refreshing directness made it stand out at a time when most British pop was compressed and reverb-laden in the Joe Meek school. It reached an unimpressive #17 and in the hope of the top slot The Beatles threw everything into their next effort, "Please Please Me". This time there was no doubt, as it smashed in at #1 following a live appearance on the *Thank Your Lucky Stars* TV show. Teenage audiences were mesmerized by this fresh new group with the long hair and the buttoned-down suits; slowly but surely, Beatlemania was spreading.

As luck would have it, George Martin turned out to be the perfect producer for the band. Acting on instinct, he decided to make their debut album something better than the usual cash-in of the time. PLEASE PLEASE ME, recorded in one marathon session, was a lively mix of their own compositions and standards from their stage act, including a frenzied version of "Twist And Shout". By now, the Lennon and McCartney hit machine was working in over-

Happy Days. The Fabs at work on "Let It Be"

drive, producing a string of singles that were both innovative and fiendishly catchy: "From Me To You", "She Loves You", "I Want To Hold Your Hand". By the time of the November 1963 release of their second album, WITH THE BEATLES, they were established as Britain's favourite group, on a scale that was previously unheard of. The obvious next step was America, and their fabled appearance on the *Ed Sullivan Show* on February 9, 1964, decided it. A country shocked by the recent assassination of JFK took the moptops to their hearts, so that by April The Beatles held the top five positions in the US singles charts and an unbelievable fourteen slots in the Billboard Hot 100. It was as if the visiting Brits had kick-started America's 50s rock explosion back and into a higher gear of intensity.

Returning to the studio, The Beatles produced the rousing "Can't Buy Me Love" and then, in a frenzied bout of recording and film-making, A HARD DAY'S NIGHT, the soundtrack to a brilliant study of Beatlemania directed by **Richard Lester**. The public were delighted to find that as well as being talented tunesmiths with a rowdy stage act, The Beatles also looked great on the screen. However, they were already starting to move beyond the confines of their beat group image, with both Harrison and Lennon showing a strong interest in Bob Dylan. The two key

forces in 60s music met for the first time that August in New York, when Dylan turned The Beatles on to the delights of dope.

BEATLES FOR SALE, their second album of 1964, offered a slightly more soulful variation of their usual fare, though Lennon's "I'm A Loser" showed a new emotional depth and hinted at new influences in their music. The catalyst arrived some time in early 1965, when The Beatles had their first encounter with LSD, an experience reflected in the density and sensual languor of their next single, "Ticket To Ride". The experimentation continued on their soundtrack album for their second film, *Help!*, which boasted the Dylanesque "You've Got To Hide Your Love Away" and McCartney's deathless ballad "Yesterday", as well as the superb title track.

After another hectic round of touring, including the Shea Stadium gig (yes, they gave us the horrors of stadium rock too), The Beatles found themselves pushed to match a batch of summer singles from the likes of the Kinks, Animals, Rolling Stones, and of course Bob Dylan, who'd just capped "Subterranean Homesick Blues" with the astonishing "Like A Rolling Stone". They rose to the occasion with RUBBER SOUL, the first of their classic albums, and one that showed a new maturity and complexity in songs such as "Norwegian Wood" and "Nowhere

Man". The accompanying single, "Day Tripper", backed with the brilliant "We Can Work It Out", reinforced the image of a band working at the peak of their powers.

Yet RUBBER SOUL was merely the base camp for the push that was to come, and following a final UK tour the band took three months off, relaxing and preparing for their next waxing. If RUBBER SOUL had opened minds, then REVOLVER, released in August 1966, was to blow them. As well as some of the finest pop songs ever recorded, it also contained two tracks that set out a manifesto for the psychedelic explosion of 1967. "She Said She Said", however lysergic, was at least a pop song, albeit one pushed to the limits; "Tomorrow Never Knows", however, was something completely different. On top of Ringo's hypnotic drums and a kaleidoscope of tape loops, John Lennon's mesmerizing vocal exhorted you to listen to the 'colour of your dreams'. It was the final delight on an album that took in everything from George Harrison's bitter "Taxman", to "Eleanor Rigby" and the obligatory singalongaRingo track, "Yellow Submarine". Even the advance single, "Paperback Writer", was a corker, backed by "Rain", The Beatles best ever B-side, propelled by yet more innovative drum work from Ringo.

Ironically, at a time when The Beatles were achieving new heights in the studio, they were packed off on a demoralizing world tour, which saw them physically assaulted in the Philippines (for allegedly insulting Imelda Marcos), then facing demonstrations and death threats in the States, following John Lennon's offhand remark that the band were now bigger than Jesus. Their last concert performance was at Candlestick Park in San Francisco: on their return to the UK, they made it clear to Brian Epstein that touring was now off the agenda. Apart from the hassles and threats, they couldn't even hear themselves play over the screaming, never mind attempt to reproduce the complexities of their new studio work.

With unlimited studio time available to them at Abbey Road, The Beatles set about topping their previous efforts. By this time, Lennon was so spaced out from the acid that McCartney had taken over as de facto leader of the group, but the old tensions in their relationship were pushing each of them to new heights, as could be heard on their next double A-sided single, "Penny Lane"/"Strawberry Fields Forever". Both were registered as Lennon and McCartney compositions, but the lazy psychedelic swirl of "Strawberry Fields" was as obviously Lennon as the bouncy melody of "Penny Lane" was McCartney. Astonishingly, it was their first single since 1962 not to hit the top slot: the great British record-buying public preferred Englebert Humperdinck's ballad, "Release Me". The single however, was merely a foretaste of The Beatles big statement, SERGEANT PEPPER'S LONELY HEARTS' CLUB BAND.

If ever an album perfectly summed up the times this was it. Acid-drenched from start to finish, it was

Not tomorrow – nine letters – begins and ends with Y...

the definitive crystallization of the mood of 1967's 'Summer of Love'. Though it had little real integrity as a concept album, bar the opening track and its reprise, the conceptual link was in the wash of echoed and reverbed sound, heavy with Harrison's Indian instrumentation, underlaid by the wet tea-towel clump of Ringo's drums to stop the whole thing levitating off the turntable. Songs like "Lucy In The Sky With Diamonds", "With A Little Help From My Friends" and "A Day In The Life" marked the culmination of five years of intense recording activity, but from these towering heights there could only be one direction – down.

The rest of the year was spent in a stoned reverie, although the hours of good-natured studio experimentation did produce two classics in the form of "All You Need Is Love", broadcast live as Britain's contribution to the first global satellite link-up, and Lennon's remarkable "I Am The Walrus", the product of a drug-twisted consciousness imploding into adolescent psycho-goo. The recording was given extra emotional bite by being made only a few days after the suicide of Brian Epstein, a sobering shock amidst the love and peace vibes of that hot, incense-scented summer. Without his leadership, The Beatles were left to their own devices, a situation that would lead to financial crisis in the following year and the ultimate collapse of group spirit.

In the immediate aftermath of Epstein's death, The Beatles decided to press ahead with *The Magical Mystery Tour*, a film project inspired by Ken Kesey's Merry Prankster's touring coach and by the chara-banc coach trips to Blackpool of their Liverpool youth. The somewhat amateurish results were screened on Boxing Day to a hostile reception, though today it comes over as an engaging period piece. *The Mystery Tour*'s destination turned out to be a disused airfield at West Malling in Kent, where the memorable "I Am The Walrus" clip was filmed with forty dwarfs and a military band.

Early in 1968 The Beatles decamped to Rishikesh, to the Maharishi's meditation centre on the banks of the Ganges. Predictably, Ringo was the first to tire of the endless prayer, chanting and vegetarian curry, but Lennon and Harrison stuck it out for a full three months, before realizing that the Maharishi was extremely attentive to the spiritual needs of his female devotees. Their stay might have ended in disillusionment, but it was to prove extremely productive in songwriting terms. Freed from the entertainments of Swinging London, they had come up with enough material for a double album.

Back in London, they resumed work at Abbey Road and set about developing Apple Corps, a company that was to handle all their collective interests. As McCartney said, it was to be 'a controlled weirdness... a kind of Western Communism'. Apple Records launched with a bang on August 11, with "Hey Jude", one of the finest Beatles singles. Yet, despite this testament to oneness, The Beatles were starting to come apart at the seams. If the demands of running a busi-

ness weren't enough to contend with, John's relationship with **Yoko Ono** (who was now present at most of their recording sessions) was another source of friction, which was to boil over during the making of the new album, officially called THE BEATLES, but more usually known as THE WHITE ALBUM.

Weeks of rancour culminated with the walkout of Ringo, who was of course persuaded to rejoin, though the bad vibes refused to go away. The album, however, was a fascinating display of the different facets of the group, often in the form of solo performances backed by the other three. As well as rockers such as "Back In The USSR" and "Helter Skelter", THE WHITE ALBUM was stuffed full of more reflective gems such as "Dear Prudence", "Julia" and "Blackbird", not to mention the complete one-off, "Happiness Is A Warm Gun". There was even a section of avant-garde *musique concrète* in the form of "Revolution No. 9", perhaps the most skipped-over track on any Beatles album.

The recording of THE WHITE ALBUM was such a lengthy bad-tempered affair that it left the group completely exhausted musically and close to breaking point. When the band reconvened in January 1969 the idea of returning to live performance was seen as a panacea for the group's ills. Various exotic venues were suggested before they settled on the idea of filming themselves rehearsing and recording a 'live' album/film, to be called GET BACK, in a freezing film studio in Twickenham. The sessions were a disaster, with McCartney and Harrison at each other's throats, while the beatific John and Yoko looked on dispassionately. Not even Ringo's good-natured humour could stop the rot. Fed up, Harrison walked out and the sessions ended in chaos. When everyone had calmed down, they returned to their Apple headquarters at Savile Row in the hope of better vibes, but it was obvious that the magic had gone. They struggled on with a mixed bag of material, enlivened as ever by some great songs, as well as the presence of organist **Billy Preston**. It was to be over a year, however, before the proceedings, edited down and controversially overdubbed by **Phil Spector**, reached the shops as the farewell album, LET IT BE (1970). However, January did produce one legendary performance, on the rooftop of Apple, to the delight of passers-by. The band gave it their best shot, until the arrival of the blue meanies put an end to the proceedings. It was to be the last live Beatles show ever.

The Beatles story was more or less over, but despite the aggravation they couldn't face bowing out with the shambles of LET IT BE. Later in 1969, George Martin was astonished to get a phone call from McCartney asking him to produce an album 'the way we used to do it'. He responded cautiously, but the ABBEY ROAD sessions proved to be astonishingly fruitful. Harrison contributed two of his best songs, "Something" and "Here Comes The Sun", and there was strong competition from Lennon's "Come Together" and from Paul, who contributed most of the "Long Medley" on the second side. George Martin's immaculate touch at the controls gave a glittering sheen to the whole set.

Such a return to form made the band's final break-up, announced by Paul McCartney on April 10, 1970, seem even more like the end of an era. All four Beatles pursued solo careers: John with the PLASTIC ONO BAND and IMAGINE albums, followed by a marked decline and disappearance into domesticity and drink; Paul with the less acclaimed but more commercially successful **WINGS**; George with a handful of albums followed by a steady career as sideman; and even Ringo was dragged away from the bar to bang out a few sentimental favourites. There was regular speculation about a reunion, but a decade of accumulated resentments and the Byzantine legal actions that dogged the affairs of Apple made it difficult to get all four in the same room together.

The final blow was the slaying of John Lennon in December 1980. A reunion had been unlikely, but now it was impossible – or was it ? Come Christmas 1995 and the eerie strains of "Free As A Bird" echoed around the Top 10 as John, Paul, George and Ringo were brought together by modern technology. Where they had once burst tunefully out of your radio, now they were a dirge-like memento mori, cynically promoting a nostalgic collection of inessential outtakes for baby boomers. In true Beatles style, "Free As A Bird" summed up the 90s *Zeitgeist* as perfectly as their original music had reflected the innocent joys of the 60s.

In the 90s, Apple's three-volume ANTHOLOGY series, to accompany the television history of the band, collected rarities, alternative mixes, demos and outtakes, plus the occasional unreleased track from The Beatles' archive. Harrison appeared in court as a Beatle again, reluctantly as ever, in 1998, when he came before judges in London to defend his position that an amateur recording of the Beatles from their time in Hamburg was unfit for human consumption. He won. Sadly, this was to be his final stand: Harrison died in 2001 of cancer.

And then there were two.

Please Please Me (1963; Parlophone). Captures the Fab Four in their first rush of glory. Fourteen tracks bashed out in thirteen hours, from the rocking wildness of "I Saw Her Standing There" to the climactic "Twist And Shout". Naive and brilliant.

With The Beatles (1963; Parlophone). The Fabs are still recognizably a Mersey Beat combo, but with talent to burn and a new level of refinement. Standouts: "All My Loving", "Roll Over Beethoven" and "Money".

Help! (1965; Parlophone). Not a particularly coherent album, but a great collection of tunes, including their most-covered number, "Yesterday".

Rubber Soul (1965; Parlophone). The first of a hat trick of classics, with a sound world that takes in everything from George Harrison's sitar experiments on "Norwegian Wood" to the Euro-sophistication of "Michelle" and "Girl".

Revolver (1966; Parlophone). Arguably The Beatles' best, this explosion of excellence pits classic pop against the metallic drone of the emerging psychedelia. Who else would have the nerve to preface the tortured self-examination of "She Said She Said" with "Yellow Submarine"?

Sergeant Pepper's Lonely Hearts' Club Band (1967; Parlophone). The 'Summer of Love' captured for eternity on magnetic tape. A kaleidoscope of psychedelic delights: but after all the fun and games, the haunting climax, "A Day In The Life", still sounds like the end of the world.

The White Album (1968; Apple). A sprawling double album of many moods, and even the upbeat numbers have an undertow of fragmentation. Lacks the polish of most of the other Beatles records, but makes up for it with the individual strands of brilliance – including George's best outing, "While My Guitar Gently Weeps".

Abbey Road (1969; Apple). Designed as The Beatles' swansong, ABBEY ROAD doesn't disappoint. There's "Come Together" from John, "Something" from George, "Golden Slumbers" from Paul and "Octopus's Garden" from lovable Ringo. All given a smooth once-over from George Martin.

Let It Be (1970; Apple). Not the way to go, sure, but any record with "Let It Be", "Across the Universe", "The Long and Winding Road" and "Get Back" retains at least four stakes to essential status.

Beatles 1963–1966 (1970; Parlophone). Superbly chosen compilation of singles and album cuts, charting The Beatles' journey into the national psyche. The effect of their seemingly inexorable progression is breathtaking.

Beatles 1967–1970 (1970; Parlophone). The other definitive collection, but this time following the journey from the psychedelic splendours of "Strawberry Fields Forever" to the resigned reflections of "The Long And Winding Road".

Iain Smith

THE BEAUTIFUL SOUTH

Formed Hull, England, 1989.

Boasting a couple of the disbanded **HOUSE-MARTINS** – **Paul Heaton** and **Dave Hemingway** (both vocals) – **The Beautiful South** had enough familiarity with the public to hit #2 with their first British single, "Song For Whoever", in May

1989. An ex-Housemartins roadie, **David Stead**, had been conscripted on drums, bassist was **Sean Welch**, and lyricist Heaton had found himself a new songwriting partner in guitarist **Dave Rotheray**. Most notably, the presence of female vocalist **Brianna Corrigan** helped extend the range of tunes and lyrics.

The irony of the band's name and the debut single's mockery of the big buck sentimental songwriting industry was furthered with the release of the first album, WELCOME TO THE BEAUTIFUL SOUTH (1989). Several chain stores took exception to the image of a woman holding a gun to her own mouth. Those too queasy to stock it were provided with an alternative version, featuring an inoffensive cuddly bunny and teddy bear.

The second album, CHOKE (1990), featuring perhaps their best-known single, the Brianna–Dave duet "A Little Time", and one of Heaton's finest vocal performances, "Let Love Speak Up Itself", a heartfelt portrait of a lived-in relationship. "Old Red Eyes Is Back" reintroduced the band in 1992 – a song about alcoholism from a band well noted for their drinking capacity. A promotional jaunt around Europe with the single proved too much for some: after a football match in Italy, Paul vanished in Sardinia, temporarily casting the band's future into doubt. On returning, though, another album appeared in the early summer of 1992, 0898 BEAUTIFUL SOUTH, which spawned another three singles, and has the privilege of still being liked by its creators.

Brianna Corrigan left to pursue a solo career shortly afterwards, and by early 1994 her raw, often plaintive voice had been replaced by the rich tones of new vocalist **Jacqueline Abbott**. Abbott was showcased on the singles, "Good As Gold (Stupid As Mud)" and the cover of Fred Neil's "Everybody's Talkin'" (made famous by Harry Nilsson's recording featured in the movie *Midnight Cowboy*). Both tracks were included on MIAOW (1994), which, though not a huge commercial success, was arguably their best album. Whilst still indulging in ironic twists, Heaton was also writing more straightforward, if edgy, lyrics, accompanying less sugary arrangements.

The release of CARRY ON UP THE CHARTS at the end of 1994 served to re-establish their status, and was put out in two versions, one containing the B-sides as well as the singles. The third-fastest-selling album ever in Britain, it confirmed their radio-fuelled popularity, though there was no shortage of critics ready to dismiss the band as whinging, twee, MOR fodder. Still, whinging, twee, MOR rock does sell and the band continued to smirk all the way to the bank off the back of 1996's BLUE IS THE COLOUR, another big-drinking, people-hating collection, topped by the wistful "Don't Marry Her" with Jacqueline Abbott's sting-in-the-tail closing line 'Don't marry her ... fuck me'.

Popularity still undimmed by their detractors, "Perfect 10" reached number two in the charts in 1998 swiftly followed by its attendant album QUENCH (1998), another jaundiced poke at life

which made many wonder how much longer they would be able to keep it up.

With PAINTING IT RED (2000) they pretty much pushed the cynical soul-pop formula to its limit. Mundanity may be appropriate subject matter for their barbed lyricism but when it spills over into the music – especially over nineteen tracks – it edges just that bit closer to tears of boredom, rather than tears of empathy. Even the presence of Heaton's former Housemartin colleague Norman Cook as 'rhythm consultant' did little to lift the set.

But, as ever, their fans were content, and the sales kept rolling on – a position further consolidated by the release of 2001's 'best of' collection, SOLID BRONZE. A better summary of the Beautiful South's career to date would be hard to conceive.

⊙ **Choke** (1990; Go! Discs).
The second and wittiest album, Heaton keeping a sharp eye on sickly relationships, free enterprise, success and deceptively angelic small children.

⊙ **0898 Beautiful South** (1992; Go! Discs).
There are some very sombre moments here, both musically and lyrically, marking something of a new direction.

⊙ **Miaow** (1994; Go! Discs).
Songs about love, both positive and bitter, and Heaton politically biting as ever on "Poppy".

Maria Lamle

BECK

Born Los Angeles, 1971

"I'm just bursting on the scene like a pathetic, gold-plated sperm."

The singer-songwriter and guitarist **Beck Hansen** was raised in Kansas, claiming that his self-styled 'punk-rock/folk' had originated in a childhood visit to an aunt, who introduced him to Leadbelly and Woody Guthrie records. At 17 he moved to New York's East Side, where he was influenced by a punk scene that was rediscovering country-blues and its obsessions with homelessness, hopelessness and drunkenness.

After a succession of dead-end jobs, a broke Beck relocated to Silverlake, in Los Angeles. He began performing and recording, releasing a number of independent singles – most notably "MTV Makes Me Want To Smoke Crack". Before very long, he was the focus of a record company bidding war. A contract with Geffen allowed Beck to release a collection of demos, co-produced by Karl Stephenson, who had worked with hip-hop act The Geto Boys, and the first single, "Loser", received massive play on MTV. This semi-rapped anthem to self-loathing combined a Dylan-tinged slide guitar, a psychedelic Dr. John sample and a rumbling hip-hop breakbeat, which backed the refrain, 'I'm a loser baby, so why don't you kill me?'.

The accompanying album, MELLOW GOLD (1994), combined a whimsical jumble of influences ranging from hip-hop and hardcore to psychedelia and folk,

THE BEAUTIFUL SOUTH • BECK

77

Beck: and you thought Marilyn Manson looked scary

1996's album ODELAY, which included such radio-and-TV-friendly outings as "New Pollution" and "Devil's Haircut", confirmed him as the world's most successful loser with regular appearances on the European Summer Festival circuit. If anything, his three subsequent, very different, album releases have merely furthered his reputation as one of the very few commercially viable artists in the world today who are prepared to take risks. MUTATIONS (1998), a low-key release with nods to Latin and alternative country, added emotional depth and a more mature level of songwriting to the mix, while MIDNITE VULTURES (1999) was a tense, priapic and triumphant celebration of funk and electronic influences that recalled both Prince and Kraftwerk. 2002's SEA CHANGE was even stronger, boasting some of his finest writing to date.

Mellow Gold (1994; Geffen).
This disordered rag-bag of rock, pop, folk and hip-hop is, by turns, tormented, despondent, hilarious and funky. It includes the mainstream successes "Loser" and "Pay No Mind".

Odelay (1996; Geffen).
MTV used to make him want to smoke crack but these days it helps him promote his album. Deeper and more considered than MELLOW GOLD, ODELAY draws influences and takes samples from wildly diverse sources, from country through to urban hip-hop. Irresistibly catchy, good-humoured and relaxed, a classy album for slacking to.

Midnite Vultures (1999; Geffen).
Funked up beats shuffle alongside blues guitar, heavy rock, and Motown swoon, banishing predictability from the music. Comparisons with Prince are justified – Beck has become an accomplished media showman.

Sea Change (2002; Geffen).
Here Beck sings in long aching yawns set against a backdrop of slow, country-tinged twangs and brooding storms of violin. The album's highpoint is "Round The Bend", which sounds like a long lost Nick Drake gem played at half speed.

Michael Andrews

resulting in a cohesive yet profoundly under-produced set. The often distorted countrified vocals painted a curious yet poignant picture of American lowlife – a world of the 'drive-by body pierce' and characters like the 'whisky-stained, buck-toothed backwoods creep' of "Truckdrivin' Neighbors Downstairs".

Following the success of MELLOW GOLD, two more Beck albums were released on independent US labels in 1994, both consisting of earlier recordings. STEREOPATHETIC SOUL MANURE (1994) was a primitive, half-baked collection of recordings from 1988 to 1993, and included the grungey "Thunder Peel", a send-up of Henry Rollins ("Rollins Power Sauce"), and the lazy country of "Rowboat". In contrast, ONE FOOT IN THE GRAVE was largely acoustic and less eclectic. The songs – which rarely exceeded two minutes in length – frequently displayed a mature cynicism, with highlights including the moody "I Get Lonesome" and the sardonic "Asshole".

Since then, Beck has toured the globe, consolidating his position, gradually building his fan base and bringing his twisted vision to a world audience.

JEFF BECK

Born Wallington, England, June 1944.

Influenced by the likes of Chet Atkins, Merle Travis and Cliff Gallup of Gene Vincent's Blue Caps, young **Jeff Beck** was looking for an opening in rock'n'roll while ostensibly studying at Wimbledon Art College. In 1961 he joined an all-purpose ensemble backing singers for a Hampshire promoter, then moved on to **The Crescents**, a quartet that imitated The Shadows, before sojourns with **Him And The Others**, **The Bandits**, **Kerry Rapid And The Blue Stars**, and **Screaming Lord Sutch**. After Rolling Stone Ian Stewart loaned him some R&B albums, Beck formed **Nightshift**, but his susceptibility to 'going off on a tangent' didn't go well with the rest of the band; he was to be similarly frustrated in his next group, **The Tridents**.

Beck's career got off the runway, however, when he succeeded Eric Clapton in THE YARDBIRDS after the first-choice replacement, Jimmy Page, chose to remain a session musician. No Clapton duplicate, Beck displayed eclecticism and unpredictability in compatible amounts – as shown in his stage solos and such hits as "Heart Full Of Soul", "Evil-Hearted You", "Shapes Of Things", from The Yardbirds' two-year golden age. Nevertheless, the attention given fretboard genius Beck contributed to the group's self-destruction – particularly after Page finally joined in 1966.

Guided by mainstream pop producer **Mickie Most**, Beck then entered the UK Top 40 three times, with "Hi Ho Silver Lining" (now a 60s nostalgia circuit singalong), "Tallyman" and 1968's schmaltzy "Love Is Blue". The lead vocal on "Tallyman" was shared with **Rod Stewart**, whom Beck had enlisted into The Jeff Beck Group for an outstanding US concert debut to promote a debut album, TRUTH – a blueprint set for Page's Led Zeppelin.

After the COSA NOSTRA BECK-OLA follow-up in 1969, Beck was branded as a straightforward heavy metal item (as Zeppelin were to be), a slur maintained even after he'd demonstrated his wider skills in 1974 on a TV guitar workshop, on which other guests included Julian Bream and John Renbourne.

On recovering from a serious road accident, Beck led another outfit for two albums – ROUGH AND READY and THE JEFF BECK GROUP – before linking up with Vanilla Fudge's **Tim Bogert** and **Carmine Appice**. However, this so-called 'supergroup' petered out mostly through lack of new material and Beck's growing dislike of heavy metal. In 1975, Beck's BLOW BY BLOW demonstrated a captivation with jazz-rock and, on declining a post with The Rolling Stones, he recorded WIRED (1976) with former Mahavishnu Orchestra keyboard player **Jan Hammer**, with whom he toured, surfacing as one of few rock guitarists who could handle fusion music convincingly.

After 1980's THERE AND BACK (with Hammer), and FLASH, an album more in keeping with passing trends, there came his assistance on the only album by **A Box Of Frogs**, an ensemble containing other former Yardbirds. At the decade's end there was a wonderful and bizarre liaison with **MALCOLM MCLAREN** on the latter's WALTZ DARLING and, in 1990, the more characteristic JEFF BECK'S GUITAR

SHOP, with drummer **Terry Bozzio** and keyboard player **Tony Hymas** from the THERE AND BACK period.

As gaps between projects increased, Beck thought aloud about an acoustic album, and one with a big band, before going full cycle with CRAZY LEGS (1993), a Gene Vincent And The Blue Caps tribute that recalled his long apprenticeship in the ballrooms.

CRAZY LEGS was not, however, just a holding action as some critics insisted. Besides paying tribute to one of Beck's major influences, rockabilly guitarist **Cliff Gallup**, it revealed the stylistic origins of the Brit legend's licks, albeit at a lower level of volume.

Jeff Beck maintained a high profile during this time, collaborating with **Jed Leiber** on the score for a movie, FRANKIE'S HOUSE (1992). The album was an atmospheric evocation of Eastern music, but despite an electrifying version of "Hi-Heel Sneakers" it was of little interest to the casual listener. Beck's guitar work also appeared on the movie soundtracks TWINS (1990) and LITTLE BIG LEAGUE (1994). A brutal update of "Train Kept A-Rolling" lit up the former while a faithful "Walk, Don't Run" graced the latter.

Beck then collaborated with **Seal** on a Jimi Hendrix tribute album, STONE FREE (1993). The duo tackled "Manic Depression" and came up with one of the most astonishing performances of Beck's career. The end of the decade found Jeff Beck entering his most prolific era since the late 60s/early 70s. In 1999, WHO ELSE? was released. The album was rife with sonic experiments, adding dashes of electronica and big beats to the usual mix of razor-sharp leads and harmonics. This was followed by YOU HAD IT COMING (2001), which echoed the previous album's formula of techno-flirtations in a hard rock context.

Of the three Yardbird guitarists (Eric Clapton, Jeff Beck and Jimmy Page), Beck is the least tied to his past, continually seeking to expand his sound and range. Unfortunately, this often comes at the expense of cohesiveness. Beck's turn-of-the-millenium work showed a band leader with little sense of direction. His guitar playing, however, was still impeccable.

⊙ **Truth** (1968; EMI).
A diverting mixture of workmanlike originals, revamped blues, 1950s classic rock, and oddities like "Greensleeves".

⊙ **Wired** (1976; CBS).
Purely instrumental and technically dazzling, this built on BLOW BY BLOW to create one of the great jazz-rock albums of the decade.

Alan Clayson

BELLATRIX

Formed Reykjavik, Iceland, 1992; put on ice 2001.

Iceland's music scene is finally gaining international momentum. There are precedents, of course; jazz-funk group Mezzoforte scored a worldwide hit back in the 80s with "Garden Party", while The Sugarcubes' eccentric blend of winsome pop and capricious rock tickled many ears later that decade.

But since the latter's lead singer Björk departed for solo stardom in the early 90s, a whole new generation of Icelandic artists have emerged, among them Gus Gus, ethereal vocalist Emiliana Torrini, Sigur Røs, and most excitingly of all, the lovable and otherworldly pop quintet **Bellatrix**.

Although it took until 2000 for them to issue a full-length album outside their homeland, the story of Bellatrix dates back to the early 90s when classically trained **Eliza Geirsdottir** (vocals/violin) and **Sigrun Eriksdottir** (keyboards/guitar), then both just sixteen, formed the duo **Kolrassa Krokridandi**. By 1993, following a name change to Bellatrix (a star in the Orion belt) and their first single release "Drapa", **Anna Hraundal** (guitar) and **Karl Gudmundson** (drums) had joined to complete the line-up.

Their following grew in Iceland, as their style developed from chaotic folk-rock to a more streamlined but accomplished brand of pop. By 1998, they had performed almost 700 concerts across Europe, as well as a few in the United States, but found that they were limited by the lack of opportunities in Iceland. They relocated to the UK, initially finding a recording contract elusive – they later claimed that most A&R departments were looking for Spice Girls clones – but Global Warming Records signed them, releasing the mini-album G (1998), consisting of demos recorded back in Iceland. Sell-out shows in London followed, coinciding with the recruitment of bass guitarist **Kristin-Kidda Thorisdottir**.

Bellatrix's profile was heightened still further when enthusiastic music press coverage helped lead to their signing with Fierce Panda Records in the summer of 1999, and the recording of their first album proper, It's All True, with Velocette producer **Dan Swift**. Released in 2000, as the band embarked on an extensive UK tour, it became a substantial success on the independent charts. In 2001 the group parted company with Fierce Panda, and then the various members decided to take a little time out to work on other projects. Though they have as yet not announced an official split, things are very, very quiet.

⊙ **It's All True** (2000; Fierce Panda).
A super-confident mix of the abrasive and the melodic. While the group as a whole impresses, it is Eliza's strident, gregarious and eccentric voice which dominates, punctuated by the bonus of her agile violin playing. All three singles – the playful "Jedi Wannabe", the infectious "Girl With The Sparkling Eyes" and "Sweet Surrender" – appear, but it's the more ambitious tracks such as "Always" that stand out.

Justin Lewis

BELLE & SEBASTIAN

Formed 1995, Glasgow, Scotland.

Sweet-sounding Scottish band **Belle And Sebastian** make music that is a virtual compendium of UK pop from the past 30 years. By mixing the lilting hippy melodies of 60s folk singer Donovan with the lush orchestral production of blue-eyed soul singers like Dusty Springfield and Tom

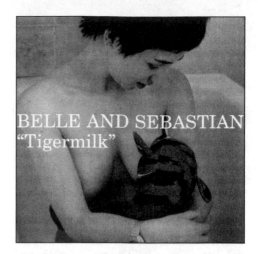

BELLE AND SEBASTIAN
"Tigermilk"

Jones, Belle And Sebastian's retro-hybrid sound has certainly struck a chord, and the group themselves acknowledge their stance: guitarist **Stuart Murdoch** sings on the band's second album IF YOU'RE FEELING SINISTER, 'Give me a song to set me free / nobody writes them like they used to / so it may as well be me.' By layering flutes, electric organs, vibraphone, strings, hand claps and more on top of bouncing rhythms, the band cleverly disguise a lyrical content as dark as the music is sunny. The songs' subjects run the gamut from homelessness to sexual perversion and racism, with Murdoch's reticent, high-pitched singing generally buried deep within the lush production. In addition to his skills as an arranger, Murdoch also has a way with a story.

The story of the band's formation begins at Stow's College, where a 1996 music class project evolved into the limited edition LP TIGERMILK. Despite being recorded in only three days and with only 1000 copies printed, the album's popularity ensured a follow-up set just a few months later.

As was the case on TIGERMILK, most of the songs on IF YOU'RE FEELING SINISTER were written by Murdoch. The album was an immediately success, aided by glowing reviews in the British press and an obsessive fan base. While Smiths-esque lyrics about schoolboy crushes and compulsory military service ("Me And The Major", an impressive mix of Bob Dylan and Dusty) caused some US critics to accuse Murdoch of fetishizing youth, Belle And Sebastian's growing stateside popularity allowed the band to briefly tour the US.

Perhaps this brush with fame was too much for Murdoch and company. The band's collective shyness was already well established – with publicity photos frequently featuring the band's friends instead of the band. In what was perceived as a reaction to the success of IF YOU'RE FEELING SINISTER, songs on Belle And Sebastian's third full-length album, BOY WITH THE ARAB STRAP, were not immediately catchy. Murdoch had also retreated within the band, allowing guitarist **Steve Jackson** to contribute two tracks, while violinist **Isobel Campbell** and bassist **Stuart David** (who also performs as **Looper**, releasing several peculiar lo-fi collections) also both contributed their own material. As demonstrated by Jackson's tragicomic ode to record industry magnate Seymour Stein (head of Sire Records), it seemed that Belle And Sebastian saw the dark side of fame, even as they were drawn to it.

In 1999 the band curated the inaugural Bowlie Festival in Camber Sands (later to become All Tomorrow's Parties). The following year Belle And Sebastian were back on top with their triumphant 4th album, FOLD YOUR HANDS CHILD, YOU WALK LIKE A PEASANT (2000). Again, songwriting duties were split amongst the group, with Jackson providing one of the strongest numbers – "The Wrong Girl". The set as a whole was drawn from a familiar Belle & Seb palette, but was infused with subtle, almost experimental musical effects; the lyrics were still strong, and the narrative visions dark. Meanwhile, Isobel Campbell had been slowly bolstering the reputation of her own band, **The Gentle Waves**. Perhaps a touch too sugary for some tastes, they released two albums, THE GREEN FIELDS OF FOREVER LAND (1999) and SWANSONG FOR YOU (2000), though have as yet failed to extricate themselves from the shadow of Belle And Sebastian.

In 2002 Murdoch et al returned with a soundtrack album to accompany Todd Solondz's film *Storytelling*. Though a pleasant enough diversion, it hardly made up for the absence of a new album proper and offered little in the way of musical development. The set was also the last to feature Campbell, who departed shortly after its release. Stuart David had by now also drifted away, to be replaced by **Bobby Kildea** of V-Twin fame.

⊙ **Tigermilk** (Jeepster; reissued 1999).
Quite simply one of the greatest debut albums ever. A beautiful, poetic masterpiece to match The Smiths at their best.

⊙ **If You're Feeling Sinister** (Jeepster; 1997).
Immediately hailed as a minor masterpiece, this is an album of delicate pop with a cutting lyrical edge.

⊙ **Fold Your Hands Child, You Walk Like A Peasant** (Jeepster; 2000).
Another fine collection: cellist Isobel Campbell's mournful "Beyond The Sunrise" is chillingly good and Jackson's "The Wrong Girl" has all the hallmarks of a pop classic.

Ken Miller and Peter Buckley

BELLY

Formed Boston, Massachusetts, 1991.

"We have a weird fan base. Wounded nerds everywhere are attracted to us, but I'd rather attract them than people who want to look up my skirt." Tanya Donelly

Tanya Donelly (vocals/guitars) had previously played in **THROWING MUSES** alongside her half-sister Kristin Hersh, and in **THE BREEDERS**, alongside Kim Deal. Her songwriting skills had been intermittently evident from the Muses' debut HUNKPAPA (1989) and blossomed with tracks such as "Too Soon" on their 1991 album THE REAL RAMONA. However, increasingly frustrated by these limited outlets for her songs, she formed a group of her own – **Belly** – along with fellow Muse, **Fred Abong** (bass), and brothers **Chris** (drums) and **Tom** (guitar) **Gorman**.

Having been firmly pegged as 'art-rock', Belly moved away from the somewhat fussy, over-embellished sound of Throwing Muses towards an alliance of strong tunes and poppy hooks. With Pixies producer **Gil Norton** at the controls, their first release, the SLOW DUST EP, displayed a capacity for brooding, haunting atmospherics, reminiscent of both Julee Cruise and the Cocteau Twins, offset by frenzied country-tinged rock playing. At the same time, Donelly's distinctive vocals could move from breathy sweetness to cracked fury in an instant, while her lyrics addressed the same sort of twisted child's-eye topics as Hersh's – endearing them to the same core audience of adolescent misfits that had propelled The Cure to superstardom.

They garnered critical attention from the music press on both sides of the Atlantic and the record made the American college charts, as well as reaching #1 in the British indie chart. Two further singles consolidated their position and "Feed The Tree", a song based around a Southern expression for a family graveyard, become a radio hit, making the UK Top 40. Their debut LP, STAR (1993), received good reviews from the rock press and regular newspapers, ensuring a smooth crossover to a wider audience, although they became firmly tagged as student favourites. The album entered the UK charts at #2, while in America it went gold and was nominated for two Grammy awards. They recorded a feisty cover of Jimi Hendrix's "Are You Experienced?" for a US tribute LP and Donelly was asked to write for Tom Jones when their entertaining cover of "It's Not Unusual" was brought to his attention.

The band's occasionally twee record sleeves, and Donelly's more childlike lyrics, led to accusations that they were peddling lightweight indie whimsy – an unfair charge, because, as Donelly pointed out, most of their songs were darkly hued. "Dusted", for instance, recounted the tale of a drug-addict rape victim, whilst "Slow Dog" described a practice where Chinese women were forced to carry a decomposing dog on their back as a punishment for adultery.

Their sound changed when Abong left soon after the LP's release. New recruit **Gail Greenwood** was less technically accomplished but soon became the dynamic centre of their stage act. Their shows became intentionally rougher, with layers of electric guitar well to the fore, a shock for fans who expected note-perfect renditions of the often ethereal LP.

Their second album, KING (1995), was produced by veteran rock producer **Glyn Johns**, and was more 'rock'. The rest of the band played a greater part in the songwriting than before, but it was a critical and commercial disappointment. Despite their popularity, the band were stuck in limbo between underground and mainstream acceptance, with one reviewer noting that Donelly seemed likely to 'abdicate as the queen of college rock'.

Whether her solo album LOVESONGS FOR UNDERDOGS (1997) counts as an abdication is debatable, as it treads the same paths followed by her previous musical incarnations and adds little to what she has said before. BEAUTYSLEEP (2002), on the other hand, was a mature, considered solo effort.

⊙ **Star** (1993; 4AD).
Fizzy pop gems and twisted lullabies, packed to bursting with hooks and tunes. The darker songs prove that the band aren't the inconsequential pop things that their detractors would have them be. Sold in the millions and quite rightly, too.

⊙ **King** (1995; 4AD).
Their much-vaunted looser approach sees the band edging perilously towards becoming just another pop-rock band. The usual second-album whinges about the music business are disappointingly present, but a brace of excellent tunes show that all is not lost.

Jonathan Holden

THE BELOVED

Formed London, 1984; disbanded 1997.

Formerly known as **Journey Through**, **Jon Marsh** (vocals/guitar), **Guy Gausden** (drums) and **Tim Havard** (bass) became **The Beloved** with the addition of Cambridge University mathematics graduate **Steve Waddington** (guitar/keyboards). Forming their own Flim Flam label, The Beloved released several singles in 1986–87, none of which hit the mainstream charts–although "Forever Dancing" (1987) was a big hit on the UK indie charts. The cult success of the album WHERE IT IS (1987) led to a deal with WEA, by which time their brief foray into jangly psychedelia had been replaced by a pop-dance hybrid reminiscent of New Order.

Gausden and Harvard left in 1988, and Marsh and Waddington, fired up by the rapid development of British dance music, replaced them with an electronic rhythm section. All the same, the first fruits of the WEA deal – "Loving Feeling" (1988) and "Your Love Takes Me Higher" (1989) – also failed to hit the charts. Thankfully, the elusive search for recognition ended with the Top 30 success of "The Sun Rising", one of the best singles of 1989. Its hypnotic female vocal sample and mellow rhythms also made it a favourite with TV advertisers.

The single's follow-up, the quirky "Hello", was a list of the band's personal heroes and villains. The postmodern juxtaposition of icons as diverse as "Freddy Flintstone, Fred Astaire" or "Charlie Parker, Charlie Brown", or even "Little Richard, Little Nell" attracted plenty of radio airplay, and saw The Beloved tipped as successors to the Pet Shop Boys. Both singles appeared on HAPPINESS (1990), as did a

remixed version of "Your Love Takes Me Higher", which became their third hit.

Waddington left The Beloved in 1991 to work with Steve Hillage's ambient collective, **SYSTEM 7**. Marsh's wife **Helena** (vocals) became his replacement, and work began on new material. The results achieved even greater commercial success: in early 1993 "Sweet Harmony" became The Beloved's first Top 10 single in the UK, and the album CONSCIENCE (1993) nearly hit the top of the UK charts a few weeks later. Unfortunately, while the songs retained the positivity of previous output, The Beloved, unlike dance music, had more or less stayed still for three years, and their sound and attitude had suddenly become dated. Lesser hits followed with "You've Got Me Thinking" and "Outer Space Girl", before Jon and Helena departed for a while. Their return in early 1996 with a single, "Satellite", and album, X, showed a minor improvement in the songwriting department, but overall the outmoded sound remained.

DJ-ing and remixing were fast becoming Marsh's favoured activities, and so he abandoned The Beloved's name in 1997. He went on to remix material by artists as disparate as Depeche Mode, The Creatures and Olive, but also released two mix albums under his own name: NITE LIFE 01 (2001) and FABRIC 03 (2002). While mainstream success with The Beloved was fleeting, they deserve credit for being one of the first rock bands of the late 80s to wholeheartedly embrace dance culture.

⊙ **Happiness** (1990; East West/Atlantic).
"Hello" kicks off this feel-good soundtrack to the early 90s pop and dance scene. Highlights include the exhilarating "Scarlet Beautiful", and "The Sun Rising", which remains their finest moment.

⊙ **Single File** (1997; East West/Atlantic).
A greatest hits compilation saves buying all those irritating digipaks, costs less and lets history decide which tracks are worth keeping forever. This album is a prime example.

Justin Lewis

BEN FOLDS FIVE

Formed North Carolina, c.1993; disbanded 2000.

There is no real musical reason why **Ben Folds Five**, guitarless purveyors of American MOR, should occupy a place in the hearts of alternative-rock fans – you will struggle very hard to find even a trace element of punk rock in their mild-mannered craft – but they do. Named after leader **Ben Folds**, their debonair pianist and vocalist, the group was not in fact a quintet but a trio completed by **Robert Sledge** (bass) and **Darren Jessee** (drums).

Folds had previously worked in publishing, on stage-shows (he played bass for a Broadway production of *Buddy*) and as a percussionist on Nashville sessions for Christian artists. Dissatisfied with this – and who could blame him – he eventually returned to his native North Carolina to hook up with Sledge and Jessee, who had been gainfully employed selling burgers and singing telegrams. Armed with Folds' off-kilter songs, they then set out to confuse audiences as support act at Heather Nova and Better Than Ezra concerts.

The group made its debut for Caroline Records in 1996 with a self-titled collection of songs which made no apology for the fact that its leader liked nothing better than a gentle tinkle on the ivories, nor for the fact that he was a songwriter rooted in mainstream traditions. Comparisons were made by some to the UK's Squeeze, by dint of crafted material such as "Jackson Cannery", a typical Folds vignette shot through with pathos. Despite their perceived gentility, the group could also muster a pretty intoxicating live set – Folds famously headbutting his microphone at London's 100 Club while singing "Satan is my master" to the tune of the Commodores' "Easy".

However, there was nothing remotely punk rock about Folds or the group (although Sledge once admitted to having been in a group who supported Suicidal Tendencies). Indeed, the group were once described as a "fuck you to the fuck you bands" (see songs such as "Underground" for further evidence of Folds' indifference to the US alternative scene). But mention the word 'kitsch' in their company at your peril. Even if they did sound more Barry Manilow than The Beastie Boys, Folds and company were entirely serious about their craft. And behind the easy tempos were hidden more confrontational lyrics than you might expect – drug overdoses and relationship meltdowns being favoured subjects.

Their 1997 album WHATEVER AND EVER AMEN, was even better than its predecessor. It was again largely written and recorded in café bars and Folds' home, with production by Caleb Southern, despite the fact that the group had just signed with Sony following a major-label bidding war. It was promoted by the single, "Battle Of Who Could Care Less", a typically Foldsesque account of good humour in the face of grunge defeatism. In 1998, prompted by their recent successes, an album of outtakes and singles was released, NAKED BABY PHOTOS, and later that same year Folds released a somewhat deranged solo album – FEAR OF POP: VOL.1 – which traded hallmark piano stabs for kitsch techno grooves and a narration by William Shatner.

The following spring a third album proper hit the shelves, THE UNAUTHORIZED BIOGRAPHY OF REINHOLD MESSNER (1999). With grand production and some blistering tunes this was the group's finest moment, and they knew it. Though tempted by the prospect of a cash-in follow-up, the Ben Folds Five bowed out gracefully, announcing their split at the end of 2000.

(•) **Whatever And Ever Amen** (1997; Sony).
Bear with it as Folds lulls you into semiconsciousness – then sticks you with the sort of line you won't find anywhere on a Manilow or Elton John album – neither of whom could have expressed a sentiment as succinctly as Folds does in "Song For The Dumped" ('Give me my money back, you bitch').

Alex Ogg

Born St Louis, Missouri, 1926.

"There was a time in my life where my only ambition was to play like Chuck." Keith Richards

Chuck Berry (vocals/guitar) has an almost unique importance in the history of rock-'n'roll, as one of its most individual early singer-songwriters, and as a seminal influence on second-generation rock. He was the author of compositional and instrumental styles which heavily influenced early Beatles, Dylan, The Beach Boys and The Rolling Stones, but his own musical career was patchy and prone to skirmishes with the law.

Berry was almost 26 before he gave his first paid performance, and didn't record until three years later. By the early 50s he was leading a blues trio which featured pianist **Johnnie Johnson**, while his influences ranged from the likes of T-Bone Walker, Charlie Christian and Les Paul, to Louis Jordan, and even Nat 'King' Cole, as well as the songwriter Don Raye, who wrote for Ella Mae Morse ("House Of Blue Lights", "Down The Road Apiece"). In 1955, under the supervision of blues giant **Muddy Waters**, Berry recorded a demo of "Ida Red", a song derived from a country and western record he had heard on the radio. Leonard Chess persuaded him to rerecord the track as "Maybellene", and the record quickly became one of the earliest rock'n'roll hits, soon followed by the immortal "Roll Over Beethoven", a statement of intent if ever there was one.

With nearly twenty chart hits between 1957 and 1960, Berry became famous for his examination of the adolescent experience, particularly on "Rock'N'Roll Music", "School Day" and "Sweet Little Sixteen". And, as the next decade was to prove, he was a figurehead and a role model for a generation of aspiring rock'n'rollers. He even made several big-screen appearances – *Rock Rock Rock*, *Mr. Rock'N'Roll* (both 1957) and *Go Johnny Go* (1959), while his live concert show was captured on film in *Jazz On A Summer's Day* (1960).

In 1959 Berry was convicted on an immorality charge concerning a teenage girl employed at his nightclub. His first conviction was quashed on appeal, but he was eventually sentenced and spent a total of two years in jail. By the time he was released, his early recordings were more popular than ever, thanks to his huge influence upon the new breed of white rock groups. In the UK, The Beatles and The Rolling Stones made his songs staples of their live repertoire and recorded their own versions on their early LPs. Dylan's first Top 40 single, "Subterranean Homesick Blues" (1965), obviously drew upon one of Berry's classic numbers, "Too Much Monkey Business". His first recordings upon leaving jail included "Nadine", "No Particular Place To Go" and "It Wasn't Me".

BEN FOLDS FIVE ▪ CHUCK BERRY

Paisley, Pah! Chuck stakes his claim to the ugliest shirt in rock'n'roll

In 1966 Berry signed to Mercury for a $50,000 advance; however, it is generally agreed that the five albums he recorded for the label are among his worst efforts. A return to Chess in 1970 yielded the BACK HOME album, which included "Have Mercy Judge" and "Tulane", two tales about getting busted.

But it was a live novelty single that gave him his only chart-topper on both sides of the Atlantic. While in the UK to record with 60s guitar legends on THE LONDON CHUCK BERRY SESSIONS (1972), he recorded "My Ding-A-Ling" with the help of **The Average White Band**. The record's success established Berry in the hearts and minds of a new, younger generation of fans and listeners, while his run-ins with the law continued. In 1979 he was sentenced to a hundred days' imprisonment for tax evasion.

His sixtieth birthday in 1986 was marked by a star-backed concert in St Louis, organized by Keith Richards of The Rolling Stones. This was filmed, forming the basis for the movie, *Hail! Hail! Rock'N'Roll*, which coincided with the publication of his autobiography (which, unusually for rock stars, he actually wrote). Promotional interviews for the autobiography suggested Berry's upcoming retirement; indeed the only subsequent Berry news has been bad news, with a further arrest in 1990 relating to allegations of involvement in pornography. Nevertheless, in 1993, he performed at President Bill Clinton's inauguration, and continues to make live appearances to this day.

Chuck Berry Onstage (1963; Chess).
Primitive, lo-fi but still sounding just great. Songs to get up and dance to, make love to and get drunk to.

The London Chuck Berry Sessions (1972; Chess).
A cast of legends assembled with the great man, in a similar format to earlier records by Muddy Waters and Howlin' Wolf, those other pioneers who turned white Brits on to the new beat.

Hail! Hail! Rock'N'Roll (1993; Charly).
Twenty-eight delightful slices of raw rock'n'roll in one neat package, licensed by reissue specialist Charly from the original Chess masters. Excitement, style, wit and musical ingenuity, this virtually defines rock'n'roll. A must.

Michael Sumsion

THE BETA BAND

Formed London 1996.

Whatever their other talents, **The Beta Band** are bona fide masters of anti-publicity. Besides susbscribing to the Joy Division/New Order policy of refusing interviews, the quartet also took a leaf out of Lee Mavers' book and rubbished their first album proper in the music press. The products of this counter-hype have been creditable sales and the sort of pop page column inches you'd usually only receive if you'd married Patsy Kensit and then an All Saint.

Fortunately, there's more to The Beta Band than quality anti-promotion. The group grew out of a gang of musicians that had been playing together since school in Scotland. By 1996 The Beta Band had come into being, eventually cementing into the line-up of **John Maclean** (decks/samples/percussion), **Steve Mason** (guitar/vocals/percussion), **Robin Jones** (drums/percussion) and **Richard Greentree** (bass/percussion), who arrived after the release of the group's first EP. Together, they boast a sound that is entirely their own. With eclectic tastes (their music pulls on everyone from Santana to Richard Thompson) and a preference for unusual instruments (biscuit tin and bottle percussion, smashed-up washing machines, etc.), the act's noise is so allusive that they are most accurately described as a jazz/folk/dub/rock/blues/psychedelic/dance combo.

Though they seem to operate with a highly laissez-faire approach – live, the group's members are frequently seen abandoning their regular stations to apparently play whatever instrument is closest to hand – their eccentric, incoherent, almost slapdash sound is highly composed. Though experimental, their techniques are exceptionally tight: few other bands could so perfectly synchronize the ending of an apparently improvised wall of noise the way these guys do. It was this combination of madness and control, along with some beautiful tunes, that turned The Beta Band into the darlings of the late 90s pop scene.

The Beta's unique beat first emerged on the 1997 EP CHAMPION VERSIONS, which had been partly written prior to the band's inception with longtime sonic cohort **Gordon Anderson** (who now performs as The Lone Pigeon). The EP also featured the bass of Steve Duffield, though he too never officially joined the troop. Although only 400 copies were pressed, the record proved such a hit with the critics that it became instantly collectable. The band's second EP, THE PATTY PATTY SOUND, saw the group's line-up stabilize with the appearance of Greentree,

and was also well received. By the time of EP number three, LOS AMIGOS DEL BETA BANDIDOS (1998), the group were such a cult phenomenon that their label, Regal Recordings, crammed their recordings to date onto a compilation album – The Three Eps. Although Regal promoted the LP as an altruistic venture designed to give fans a chance to hear the hard-to-get-hold-of CHAMPION VERSIONS, the rush releasing of THE THREE EPs was evidence of just how saleable The Beta Band had become. The group's fan base had also swollen to include such big names as Dr John, who asked the band to collaborate on one of his releases.

As they started to shift units, The Beta Band also began to sell out concerts. Much as they claimed to hate self-promotion, the group used the few interviews they attended to stress that fans had to undertake the Beta live experience in order to fully appreciate their music. As Maclean explained; 'It may not make you want to grin and take your shirt off. It may make you want to crawl around like a bug, but it will make you move.' Sure enough, the band were every bit as unique and infectious live as in the studio, and their gigs swiftly achieved must-see status.

The Beta Band raise the roof

THE BETA BAND

The Beta Band looked good and ready to attain crossover appeal when things started to go wrong. People had been getting excited about the group's first album proper since the release of THE THREE EPS, but by the time THE BETA BAND hit the shops in the summer of 1999, the record had been dismissed as underwritten, incomplete and poorly mixed. That these stings were delivered by the band themselves left the record-buying public in two minds; was this a cunning publicity stunt or was the album actually crap? The music press certainly weren't impressed, although it was hard to tell whether the critics were disappointed with the band for underachieving or with Regal for tampering with the record. There was also confusion over plans for the set to be accompanied by an additional hour-long ambient album which the group deemed to be unworthy shortly before it was due on the shelves. Anyway, for whatever reason, the record didn't sell like it might have and the band's relationship with their label reached breaking point.

Despite all these troubles, the dust eventually settled and the band found their feet, while Steve indulged in worthy side projects, releasing several excellent EPs as **King Biscuit Time**. The Beta Band eventually re-emerged in 2001 for HOT SHOTS II – a far more satisfying effort than their debut. The set arrived just in time to remind everybody what all the initial fuss was about. The collection's deft, accessible songs were rich with diversity and tender with soft-voiced surrealism: a satisfying balance between zeitgeisty beats, samples and idiosyncratic eccentric touches. Squelches, glugs, spaceship noises and mystical/comedy lyrics kept The Betas from sounding too self-consciously fashionable – as did their habit of sporting rabbit costumes and spacesuits.

2001 saw the release of "Squares", from HOT SHOTS II, as a single. The following year the group moved back to Scotland and, after a false start with a big name producer, returned to the studio to work on a new, self-produced album. What it will contain is anybody's guess.

⊙ **The Three EPs** (1998; Regal Recordings).
The band's first three releases, repackaged at a fan-friendly price (a set of the original vinyl EPs would set you back over £100).

⊙ **Hot Shots II** (2001; Regal Recordings).
A vast improvement on their debut. Even on the slower, less obtrusive songs, such as "Gone", Steve Mason's lamenting lead mobilizes the cuts into genuinely moving pop experiences.

Richard Luck

BETTIE SERVEERT

Formed Amsterdam, Holland, 1990.

In cover art or concert, **Carol van Dijk** always seems to be, in her own words, 'smokin' fags and feelin' cool'. As singer-songwriter for **Bettie Serveert**, she pens thoughtful lyrics about hooky-playing schoolgirls, female identity, and something

called 'Brain-Tag'. Her three bandmates – **Berend Dubbe** (drums), **Peter Visser** (guitar) and **Herman Bunskoeke** (bass) – add the distinctive wah-wah flavoured, layered guitars and vibe-conscious rhythm section that has helped to make an international name for these alt-rockers.

The band formed after the demise of **De Artsen**, a group of some note in which Dubbe and Visser had played. Dubbe found their new name browsing through an old tennis book; he came across a sexy picture of Dutch star Bettie Stove serving the ball, skirt aflutter, captioned Bettie Serveert ('Bettie Serves'). It was a decision they now claim to regret, since everyone calls van Dijk 'Bettie'.

The hip folks at New York's Matador Records got wind of the band's demo in 1992 and signed them up, releasing a quickie EP, TOMBOY, followed by PALOMINE, a sensational debut that became an instant darling of US alternative radio. "Kid's Allright" was the song American high-school kids related to, telling of a girl whose mum wished she had never been born, against a simple, falling-chord chorus. The album didn't have a weak tune in sight, from the building tension of "Tomboy" to the stops and starts of "Balentine". Throw in a Sebadoh cover ("Healthy Sick"), and you have an album which stands the test of time and is regarded as one of the great alt-rock albums of the 90s.

Unfortunately, the band failed to consolidate on such a spectacular beginning, releasing only singles culled from the album with throwaway B-sides over the next three years. The tricky second album, LAMPREY, (1995), was uneven and lacking its predecessor's punch. Sure, there were moments – the perfect pop and singalong chorus of "Ray Ray Rain" and the dark co-dependency narrative of "Something So Wild". Indeed "Re-Feel-It" may be van Dijk's best ever song but it broke little new ground and failed to generate PALOMINE's ground swell of support.

Bettie Serveert, however, toured hard, in the US especially, and got some (justified) credit. DUST BUNNIES (1997) built on their reputation as rock-'n'roll outsiders with titles such as "What Friends?" and "Geek". In 1998, they indulged themselves a little by releasing BETTIE SERVEERT PLAYS "VENUS IN FURS" AND OTHER VELVET UNDERGROUND SONGS and it was followed by a new studio album PRIVATE SUITE (2000), released on their own Palomine label. Produced by PJ Harvey collaborator **John Parish**, it showcased a richer sound with strings and keyboards to the forefront and completed Carol van Dijk's transformation from indie tomboy to torch singer. Her commanding stage presence and charismatic delivery could yet turn Bettie Serveert into true Dutch masters.

⊙ **Palomine** (1992; Matador).
A wonderful debut album: van Dijk's lyrics invoke zen koans ('You could travel for a lifetime/and still stay where you are'), while the band provides catchy, ringing riffs for her to soar above.

⊙ **Lamprey** (1995; Matador).
The sound remains the same, though things get a bit dicey when the songs grow more introspective and ponderous.

David A. Mills

THE BEVIS FROND

Formed London, sometime between 1968 and 1987.

If you imagined psychedelia turned up its toes at the close of the 70s, then you are almost certainly unacquainted with **The Bevis Frond**. The creation of one **Nick Saloman**, who writes all the material, plays just about all the instruments, and handles the recording and production to boot, The Frond have been standard-bearers of the genre for well over a decade. Quintessentially English and endearingly eccentric, they are worth their place in any rock book worth the name.

The Frond emerged in its present imago around 1986, but its chrysalis appeared around twenty years previously, when Saloman formed a band with two London schoolmates. The name 'Bevis Frond' dates from this early stage, though early incarnations appeared as the **Oddsocks**, and then, in a late-70s psychedelic punk manifestation as the **Von Trapp Family** and **Room 13** (each of whom released a single on Saloman's own Woroznow label).

A serious motorbike accident in 1982 forced Saloman into a period of recuperation and introspection, during which he recorded at home, abandoned all ideas of fame, and set himself the task of making a record to his own satisfaction. The result, created on his own, and issued in a printing of 250, was MIASMA (1987), his first release as The Bevis Frond. To Saloman's surprise, its power-pop melodies, virtuoso guitar solos, folk touches and a fluid psychedelic background gained a cult following, and more copies were demanded. Thus encouraged,

Saloman followed up with INNER MARSHLAND (1987), another solo effort in a similar vein, whose flashes of whimsy included Harry Corbett introducing Sooty and Sweep.

From the third album, TRIPTYCH (1988), on, Saloman has used other occasional musicians, particularly drummers **Martin Crowley** and recently **Andy Ward**. Albums have come thick and fast, including MAGIC EYE (1990), made as **Bevis And Twink** (with the legendary Pink Fairies drummer), and BEVIS THROUGH THE LOOKING GLASS (1988), with its Hendrix-style freakout jamming. The output has been patchy, and at times could be accused of losing the plot slightly, but Saloman's lyrics – with his surrealist stoned humour, sharp social comment, and personal observation – can usually rescue the day, while the music, at its best, has enough hooks to reel in a school of barracudas.

As the 1990s unfurled, Saloman upgraded his production, creating a crisper, more contemporary sound on albums like NEW RIVER HEAD (1991), a masterpiece of folk-punk sounds, with a flowing, quirky guitar sound that could have come from Mountain's Leslie West, and SUPERSEEDER (1995), a sharp blend of his electric and acoustic muse. The decade also saw sporadic live forays for The Frond with **Adrian Shaw** on bass, Martin Crowley, **Ric Gunther** or Andy Ward on drums, and some incendiary guitar duelling with Hendrix-influenced **Bari Watts** of the Outskirts Of Infinity. 1998's NORTH CIRCULAR was joined in the same year by the concert recording LIVE AT THE GREAT AMERICAN MUSIC HALL SAN FRANCISCO which saw Saloman achieve some measure of recognition in the wider musical world (he has subsequently seen one of his songs covered by Elliott Smith). Further albums have followed, including VALEDICTORY SONGS, which failed to live up to its title since 2002 saw the release of WHAT DID FOR THE DINOSAURS. This latest recording demonstrated a more acoustic side of The Bevis Frond but it would probably have been a mistake to think that Saloman had been mellowing in his dotage. Instead, it was merely the latest in a series of charmingly psychedelic musings on the world as seen from Walthamstow, London.

⊙ **Miasma** (1987; Reckless).
Lie back and let yourself be guided through some tunefully mind-expanding musical backwaters.

⊙ **New River Head** (1991; Woroznow).
This double album is Saloman's most mature and consummate work. An eclectic mix of delicate tunes and chunky riffs, with some measured extemporization.

Nick Edwards

THE B-52'S

Formed Athens, Georgia, 1976.

The story goes that when **Cindy Wilson** (vocals) and her brother **Ricky** (guitar) met **Fred Schneider** (vocals), **Kate Pierson** (vocals/organ/keyboard/bass) and **Keith Strickland** (drums, later guitar/keyboard) for a jam, things took off in a spontaneously haphazard way that set them on course to become house-party superstars **The B-52's**. They took their name from the slang term for the bomb-like, bouffant hairdos sported by the girls, while the music came from all over the place, mixing 60s pop, rockabilly and New Wave energy with some bizarre lyrics (often concerning interplanetary matters). The result was an instantly recognizable good-time sound that could inspire all but the most dedicated wallflower to dance.

Their first record was the instant classic, "Rock Lobster", privately issued in July 1978. This surreal marine adventure impressed Chris Blackwell enough to win them a deal in the UK with his Island label and the rerelease in July 1979 became a cult summer hit. The debut album, THE B-52's (1979), laid down their simple but effective formula: jagged guitar, piercing organ and insistent rhythm topped by the contrasting delights of Schneider's spirited chanting and the girls' soaring vocals, as heard on favourites such as "52 Girls", "Planet Claire" and "6060 842". The band made a colourfully eccentric attraction around the college circuit and at some large outdoor events, helping them to break through in the US when "Rock Lobster" became a hit in 1980 and the album went gold. Around this time they received the ultimate accolade when John Lennon was reputed to have said that it was hearing The B-52's that had inspired him to start recording again.

The second album, WILD PLANET (1980), kept up the high spirits on tracks like "Strobelight" and "Party Out Of Bounds", but on MESOPOTAMIA (1982), produced by David Byrne, they went for a more experimental approach. WHAMMY! (1983) showed their form intact, but their popularity fading, with the optimistic single "Song For A Future Generation" keeping party revellers happy, but failing to make the chart. In October 1985, tragedy struck when Ricky Wilson died from AIDS. Doubts about the whole future of the band were ended when BOUNCING OFF THE SATELLITES appeared in 1987 with session sax-meister **Ralph Carney**, but it made little commercial impact.

The real turning point came when the crack production team of Don Was and Nile Rodgers, along with former **GANG OF FOUR** bassist **Sara Lee**, were employed for COSMIC THING (1989), their first for Reprise. This included the hit singles "Love Shack" and "Roam", and showed the band perfecting the art of making intricate rhythms and harmonies sound simple and fresh. The band were suddenly back on the map, with plenty of airplay building a following beyond those who could remember "Rock Lobster" first time round. Kate Pierson's distinctive vocals even cropped up on **R.E.M.**'s hit of 1991, "Shiny Happy People".

Despite the departure of Cindy Wilson, the 1992 release GOOD STUFF kept up the standard. An impressive list of guest musicians now augmented the original trio, and Pierson and Schneider's vocal

exchanges sounded as exuberant and barmy as ever on "Tell It Like It T-I-Is" and "Is That You Mo-Dean?". In 1994 they were the inspired choice to perform the theme for the big-budget *Flintstones* film and sounded uncannily at home in a Stone Age cartoon world. In 1994 and 1995, Fred Schneider stepped outside the group to help write songs with a ghoulish theme for two albums by American TV's famous campy horror hostess, Elvira.

Cindy rejoined the band for a new round of fun and a further greatest hits compilation TIME CAPSULE: SONGS FOR A FUTURE GENERATION (1998), which also featured two new tracks – "Debbie", in homage to the queen of Blondie, and "Hallucinating Pluto". The band set out on their first full tour in almost a decade in the summer of 1998, co-headlining with The Pretenders. Their present seems fine and the future looks Day-Glo bright. In 2002, their status as one of the definitive New Wave bands was cemented by Rhino's excellent double-CD career retrospective, NUDE ON THE MOON.

⊙ **Cosmic Thing** (1989; Reprise).
Welcome return to the limelight with a few new tricks and flashy production but the basic recipe was still the same. And why change?

⊙ **The Best Of The B-52's: Dance This Mess Around** (1990; Island).
Best of the various compilations, including a worthy selection from the first four albums.

Nick Dale

THE BIBLE

Formed Cambridge, England, 1986; disbanded 1994.

"I think it's important that music should stop the idea that your inspiration dies at 22 and after that you just become a piece of flesh." Boo Hewerdine

The seeds of **The Bible** were sown in a Cambridge record shop, where aspiring singer-songwriter **Boo Hewerdine** found work after returning from London to his home town. Boo played a couple of his songs ("King Chicago" and "She's My Bible") to **Tony Shepherd**, a fellow shopworker, who agreed to play drums and keyboards on a demo. It was these self-financed sessions that resulted in WALKING THE GHOST BACK HOME (1986), an album released by local label Backs, and greeted with music press cries of 'The New Smiths'. The album also contained the first release of the much-loved "Graceland", which was to pop up again and again.

Supplemented by drummer **Dave Larcombe** and guitarist **Neil MacColl** (brother of Kirsty), The Bible were lured to London by Chrysalis Records, and **Steve Earle** was drafted in to produce a new album (after an earlier attempt had been scrapped).

The result, EUREKA (1988), was a less rocky affair, with pop, folk and jazz moments, and a marked development both lyrically and musically. Unfortunately, two singles, "Honey Be Good" and "Crystal Palace", failed to make any impact anywhere other than the bargain basements.

After previously relying on session musicians and friends, **Leroy Lendor** was recruited as bassist for the EUREKA tour and the recording of a third album. This line-up, however, dissolved when Chrysalis rejected the band's new songs and insisted on re-releasing old material (which at least saw a reissued "Honey Be Good" in the UK Top 40).

A couple of years of flirting with solo careers followed, then The Bible re-formed for four acclaimed gigs in December 1993. This led to a deal with Warners subsidiary Blanco y Negro, who released an EP of new Bible songs the following year. However, all the band members were active on other fronts. Two Hewerdine songs ("Joke" and the hit single "Patience Of Angels") were included on **Eddi Reader**'s self-titled 1994 album, while Tony Shepherd was playing keyboards with **Oasis**, and Dave Larcombe was giving their (former) drummer **Tony McCarroll** some lessons.

In December 1994, the band split up again, leaving an unfinished album which eventually saw the light as a second Hewerdine solo venture, BAPTISM HOSPITAL (1996), featuring additional contributions from, among others, Eddi Reader and **Richard** and **Danny Thompson**. It was arguably his best album to date but the record company seemed unwilling to promote it, and it made little commercial impact.

In 1995, Hewerdine and Derek Chapman, his old Backs Records associate, gained rights to The Bible's back catalogue, and reissued the two albums, together with a Nashville-meets-Mersey Beat collaboration with **Darden Smith**, EVIDENCE, and RANDOM ACTS OF KINDNESS, a singles collection. He continues to tour, usually in the company of percussionist **Rob Peters** (ex-Everything But The Girl), and often with **Neil MacColl**, and has been writing for Eddi Reader and Brian Kennedy. 1999 saw the release of THANKSGIVING, a new album which was followed in 2002 by ANON and the self-explanatory A LIVE ONE.

Neil MacColl, meanwhile, linked up with Gary Clark to form a band, initially called **Junk** and then **King L**, whose outstanding debut, A GREAT DAY FOR GRAVITY, was released in 1995, chalking up a number of places in 'record of the year' summaries, though few sales.

⊙ **Eureka** (1988; Haven).
The gorgeous second album, at last available again on CD.

⊙ **Random Acts Of Kindness** (1995; Haven).
A collection of rare and unreleased tracks, including the beautiful "Bubblehead", the rerecorded "Graceland", and great acoustic versions of "I'm So Lonely I Could Cry", "Motherless Child" and "On Broadway".

Martin Rowsell
With thanks to Andrew Bradley for update

BIG AUDIO DYNAMITE

Formed London, 1984; still bangin'.

When **THE CLASH** sacked their guitarist **Mick Jones** in 1984, he was more than prepared. Always up with the times, he had become convinced of the potential that technology offered music. He recruited former club **DJ Don Letts** as co-lyricist and keyboard player, together with **Leo Williams** (bass) and a second keyboard player, **Dan Donovan**. The line-up was completed by the arrival of drummer **Greg Roberts**, and **Big Audio Dynamite** became the first British band to respond to PiL's METAL BOX and to cross traditional guitar-based rock with the new electronic sounds, paving the way for the late-80s 'baggy' scene.

BAD released their first album in 1985. Called, with Jones's characteristic directness, THIS IS BIG AUDIO DYNAMITE, it was the first album by a British rock-orientated group to feature sampling, a technique that had only recently become possible. The most noticeable and effective samples on the album were taken from film, with Clint Eastwood's *Man With No Name* appearing on "Medicine Show", whose Wild Western feel was augmented by other samples from Ennio Morricone; Michael Caine turned up on "e = mc²", which reached #11 in the UK.

These two songs and "The Bottom Line" showed how the new technology could be harnessed, but heard today, much of the album sounds dated – its tinny drum loops and pointless scratching appear arbitrary and faddish. The album's importance is clearer when seen in context: the most popular British bands of the time were Wham! and Duran Duran; the premier electronic band was Depeche Mode; and the only person who had done something comparable to BAD was Malcolm McLaren, with "Buffalo Girls" and "Madam Butterfly".

The album sold moderately well and other LPs followed, but rarely amounted to more than the sum of their inadequate parts. Jones never learned to sing and rarely lightened up his sloganeering. He bumped into **Joe Strummer**, who helped produce and write No. 10 UPPING ST (1986), but if this is how The Clash would have sounded, be glad they left off when they did. More influences flowed into the melting pot – primarily funk and ska – for TIGHTEN UP VOL. 88 (1988) and MEGATOP PHOENIX (1989), but it was all a bit messy and leaden. Meanwhile, the group was coming under increasing strain. Donovan, already famous for being someone else's son (photographer Terence), became briefly celebrated as someone else's husband (Patsy Kensit), and promptly got divorced. Jones nearly died from pneumonia in 1988, leading to the delayed release of PHOENIX and contractual problems. The original line-up parted company and, although Jones recruited a new one, including **Chris Kavanagh**, the drummer from Sigue Sigue Sputnik, the records produced by **BAD II** – KOOL-AID (1990) and THE GLOBE (1991) – were of little consequence. Jones himself showed that he was still a dyspeptic force on Aztec Camera's single "Good Morning Britain", but BAD had been overtaken by the music they had helped to shape.

The band struggled on for a couple of years releasing HIGHER POWER (1994) under the name **Big Audio** (comprising Mick Jones, Nick Hawkins, Chris Kavanagh, **Andre Shapps** and **Mickey Zonka Custance**) and a single "Looking For A Song" – which made the UK Top 75. A further album, F-PUNK (1995) produced the single "I Turned Out A Punk", which also made the chart, and the compilation, PLANET BAD – GREATEST HITS (1995), together with the band's high-profile remixing service, helped keep the band visible. A further, utterly superfluous hits compilation SUPER HITS was released in 1999 to widespread disinterest.

⊙ **This Is Big Audio Dynamite** (1985; CBS).
This album falls away in its later stages, but you can see what Jones is trying to do – splice funked-up, late Clash to an electro beat. The result is a distinctly modern hybrid, not always successful but nonetheless worth listening to. And it has one outstanding track, "Medicine Show", that rates as one of the best pop songs of the decade.

James Owen

BIG BLACK

Formed Chicago, 1982; disbanded 1988.

Fanzine writer **Steve Albini** formed **Big Black** in the aftermath of the punk/hardcore explosion that had swept the US underground scene in the late 70s and early 80s. Reaching beyond the narrow parameters of hardcore, he looked to the liberating influence of avant-punk bands such as Wire, Pere Ubu and PiL to confront the listener with the senselessness of the modern American experience – Big Black's vision was of rock as an atrocity exhibition.

The first Big Black recording, the LUNGS EP (1982), was virtually an Albini solo production, laying the wiry minimalist clang of his guitar over the echoey thud of a Roland drum machine (at a time when a drum machine in a rock band seemed futuristic). These bones were fleshed out on the BULLDOZER EP the following year, when Albini was joined by **Jeff Pezzati** (bass) and **Santiago Durango** (guitar). The expanded line-up produced a more muscular effect, and songs like "Cables", about bored youth seeking amusement in an abattoir, demonstrated how far ahead of the scene the band were. The mini-album RACER X, and pile-driving single "Il Duce" followed in 1985, after which the funk-influenced **Dave Riley** replaced Pezzati on bass.

Big Black had become just about as big and black as it was possible to get, and in 1986 recorded their definitive statement, the howling whirlwind that was the ATOMIZER LP. Coruscating guitars, inhuman amp-distorted vocals and the relentless programmed detonations of the drum machine made this experience a little like being wired into the mains while being hammered to a pulp. Lyrically, the album con-

fronted the 'desperate entertainments' sought by those adrift in the empty monotony of small-town America: child abuse, corruption, ritual degradation and self-destruction.

The success and notoriety of ATOMIZER, together with the band's place in a burgeoning US 'noise' scene (Sonic Youth, Swans, Butthole Surfers, Scratch Acid, etc), brought Big Black increased media attention on both sides of the Atlantic – something their puritanical punk ethos made them deeply uncomfortable with. However, the success rolled on with the HEADACHE EP (1987), not so much four songs as four psychopathic streams of consciousness from the end of the American tether.

Durango's decision to enrol at law school, coupled with the band's determination to quit at its peak, ensured that SONGS ABOUT FUCKING (1987) would be their final album. It was possessed of the kind of scorching power only available to bands with time running out, and although it perhaps lacked some of ATOMIZER's density, the critics loved it. After a farewell tour, highlights of which were captured on the live LP, PIGPILE (1992), Big Black split up.

Durango released two excellent EPs under the name of **Arsenal** whilst Albini first formed the dubiously named and short-lived **Rapeman**, then the stupendous **SHELLAC**. He has also become a much-sought-after producer, notably for the Pixies, The Breeders, Nirvana and PJ Harvey, and has thrived as an all-round alt-rock celebrity: in 2002, with Shellac, he curated the *All Tomorrows Parties* festival in full comedic mode.

⊙ **The Rich Man's Eight Track Tape** (1986; Blast First/Touch & Go).
CD reissue of ATOMIZER, Big Black's masterpiece, plus the HEADACHE EP. In "Kerosene", a tale of the ultimate cheap thrill, Big Black distil their sound to its impure essence.

⊙ **The Hammer Party** (1987; Homestead/Touch & Go).
Big Black's first two EPs LUNGS and BULLDOZER gathered as one album, along with the Racer X mini-album.

⊙ **Songs About Fucking** (1987; Blast First/Touch & Go).
Big Black screaming hell for leather towards their own destruction, and it sounds like they can't get there soon enough. Includes a terse cover of Kraftwerk's "The Model".

Ian Canadine

BIG BROTHER & THE HOLDING COMPANY

Formed San Francisco,1965; disbanded 1972.

Though known primarily as the launching pad for **JANIS JOPLIN**, **Big Brother & The Holding Company** were very much a band in their own right. Admittedly, if Joplin hadn't joined them in mid-1966 their status in the San Francisco psychedelic sweepstakes would have been minor. All of their noteworthy recordings date from her two-year tenure with the group, and though these are erratic and occasionally grating, the best of their free-spirited romps embody some of the most good-hearted and liberating features of the San Francisco sound.

Amazingly, some band members were initially resistant when promoter Chet Helms, an all-round catalyst of the early San Francisco scene, hooked the musicians up with Joplin, who had recently moved back to the city from Port Arthur, Texas. As a concert recording from mid-1966 has demonstrated, Janis didn't even sing lead on about half the songs in the early days. But even at this juncture, her extraordinarily powerful, bluesy wailing was the group's strongest suit, especially as the band always leaned heavily on revamped blues and R&B material for the bulk of their repertoire.

Favouring crude, sometimes sloppy blues-rock with occasional freakout jams and storms of feedback from guitarists **Sam Andrew** and **James Gurley**, Big Brother was unknown outside of northern California until their electrifying appearance at the Monterey Pop Festival in June 1967. Their epochal performance of the classic downer blues, "Ball And Chain", was one of the event's highlights, attracting the attention of high-powered manager Albert Grossman and major labels. Before signing with CBS, however, the band had to extricate themselves from a shoddy contract with the tiny Mainstream label, which they signed when they needed some quick cash to get home after getting stiffed while on the road in Chicago. Recorded hurriedly, their sole Mainstream LP, BIG BROTHER AND THE HOLDING COMPANY (1967), didn't show them to their best advantage, and they never developed much songwriting acumen. But it still included some powerfully loose-limbed workouts, especially "Coo Coo" and "Down On Me".

By mid-1968, constant touring, their Monterey appearance and sheer word of mouth had ensured that their second album, CHEAP THRILLS, soared to the top of the US charts. Few listeners knew at the time that the LP had been a protracted, at times painful, affair. Originally planned as a live recording, that strategy was abandoned after satisfactory performances could not be captured. The ensuing studio sessions were so fraught that producer John Simon (most famous for his work with The Band) refused to be credited on the sleeve. Though a bit patchy, the result largely captured the band at its best. Joplin's vocals, especially on the hit single "Piece Of My Heart" and a radical rearrangement of "Summertime", are soulful and wrenching, while the fractured, distortion-ridden guitar frenzy on "Combination Of The Two" and "Ball And Chain", though dated, is spaced-out acid-rock at its best.

Behind the scenes, major rifts were tearing the band asunder; unsurprisingly, the press and public latched on to Joplin as Big Brother's focal point, whetting Janis's appetite for solo stardom and stirring the seeds of tension between her and the rest of the group. All the same, many fans were stunned when Joplin left to go solo in November 1968, just after the group had achieved superstar status. Everyone involved suffered from the split: Big Brother lost their biggest asset, and although Joplin's popularity continued to rise, she never found another group of musicians as sympathetic. Big Brother & The Holding Company, without Joplin, did resume operations for a time in the early 1970s, but by then everyone agreed that the magic had gone.

⊙ **Cheap Thrills** (1968; Columbia).
One of the most popular – and least polished – albums of the psychedelic era. Those who were there claim that Big Brother could generate more heat at their best, but "Piece Of My Heart", "Combination Of The Two", "Summertime" and "Ball And Chain" still pack a punch.

⊙ **Janis** (1993; Columbia).
In a discographical quirk, this three-CD Janis Joplin retrospective contains more Big Brother in one place than any Big Brother release. Featuring highlights from the first two albums, it also unearths some interesting studio outtakes and live material (including a great version of "Ball And Chain" from Monterey). The rest of the box, which presents Joplin's best solo recordings, ain't too bad either.

⊙ **Live At Winterland 1968** (1998; Sony).
Widely bootlegged, this is Big Brother & The Holding Company's finest hour. Janis is by turns sublime, tender, raving and genuinely frightening, especially on the ten-minute "Ball And Chain". Big Brother chug and flow to good effect and sling some quality licks. Dated for sure, but you'd need to be dead to avoid being moved by the best moments.

Richie Unterberger

BIG COUNTRY

Formed Dunfermline, Scotland, 1981; disbanded 2000.

"If anyone else asks me how I make my guitar sound like bagpipes, I'll flatten them!" Bruce Watson

Formed by **Stuart Adamson** (guitar/vocals) and **Bruce Watson** (guitar), shortly after the former's departure from **THE SKIDS**, the fledgling **Big Country** was not without its early setbacks. First there was the ignominy of being dropped from an Alice Cooper tour after only two dates as support, allegedly for being too weird. Then followed the swift dissolution of the original all-Scottish five-piece line-up, following Adamson's apparent discontent with the capabilities of the rhythm section. Nevertheless, Adamson's fastidiousness was to pay handsome dividends with the subsequent recruitment of the eminently capable London-based session team of **Tony Butler** (bass) and **Mark Brzezicki** (drums). Fortunately, their arrival did little to detract from the distinctly Caledonian sound that Adamson, with the assistance of Watson, had been busily honing. On the contrary, the presence of a rock-solid rhythm section was just the foundation that Adamson required to build a panoramic sound befitting the band's name.

Swiftly signed to the Mercury label, Big Country proceeded to ripple chart waters with the release of their debut single "Harvest Home", before making a truly big splash with "Fields Of Fire" and "In A Big Country". These, combined with considerable television exposure, were sufficient to ensure eager anticipation for THE CROSSING (1983), which duly reached the British Top 10 and the American Top 20.

That these early recordings constituted a continuation of The Skids' urgent, rousing style came as no surprise for those who recognized that it had always been Adamson's guitar that had shaped the sound of his former band. What did come as a surprise, however, was the spaciousness and emotional warmth, showcased on ballads such as "Chance" and "The Storm", which invested the band with a far greater appeal than The Skids could have hoped for.

STEELTOWN (1984), captured the band at the peak of their popularity, entering the UK album charts at #1. Disappointingly, though, the album failed to make any significant impact on the American charts, due in part to its somewhat bleak feel. If the first album represented the realization of the vast openness implied by the band's name, then STEELTOWN was its antithesis, a denser, nationalistic introspection redolent of a small country locked in the process of economic upheaval.

Unfortunately, Big Country's subsequent output was somewhat repetitive, making only superficial adjustments to a tried and tested formula of soaring guitars, galloping drums and singalong choruses. Despite further hit singles, and a third UK Top 5 album, THE SEER (1986), the band was rumoured to have split in 1988 following exhaustive touring, which brought to a head Adamson's ongoing conflict between family man and rock star.

A little rest and recuperation were enough to cause a change of heart in Adamson, but Mark Brzezicki decided he needed a fresh challenge and in 1989 he left the band in favour of a return to session work and a brief stint with The Pretenders. Brzezicki's departure was to prove only temporary, however: he rejoined the band in 1993 after the recording of THE BUFFALO SKINNERS, released by Chrysalis subsidiary Compulsion – drum duties on the album fell to **Simon Philips**.

After the set's relative commercial failure, 1995 witnessed a concerted effort to reverse sliding fortunes.

Successful tours in their own right, and as support to both The Rolling Stones and Page And Plant, confirmed that the band remained a force to be reckoned with live. Nevertheless, the poor chart showing of the attendant album WHY THE LONG FACE (1995) and the low-key live album ECLECTIC (1996) suggested that the band's protracted decline was irreversible. This did not stop them from releasing DRIVING TO DAMASCUS (1999), however, which featured songwriting contributions from **Ray Davies** and performances from **Eddi Reader**. If anything, the album proved that there was a great deal of creative fire left in the band – even if they had decided to call it a day by 2000. They announced their amicable dissolution with a final world tour: their swansong gig, in Malaysia, took place in October 2000.

Meanwhile, Stuart Adamson, inspired by his forays into American music during the mid-90s, had moved to Nashville where he joined forces with songwriter **Marcus Hammon**, and formed **The Raphaels**. A critically acclaimed first album entitled SUPERNATURAL showed plenty of promise for further releases, but such potential evaporated in December 2001, with the sad news of Adamson's death in a Hawaii hotel room at the age of just 43. Personal and professional tributes flooded in from friends, musicians and fans, and a career retrospective and tribute concert at Glasgow Barrowlands in May 2002 were planned. The former collected tracks from all periods of his varied career.

⊙ **The Crossing** (1983; Mercury).
The definitive Big Country album, selling over two million copies, and in the process cementing the band's image as check-shirted rockers with guitars that sound like bagpipes.

⊙ **Through A Big Country** (1990; Phonogram).
A 'best of' compilation which marked the end of a fruitful relationship with Mercury/Phonogram.

⊙ **Without The Aid Of A Safety Net** (1994; Compulsion).
Essentially a live greatest hits set, recorded in front of a distinctly partisan audience in Glasgow.

Ian Lowey

BIG STAR

Formed Memphis, Tennessee, 1972; disbanded 1975; re-formed 1992.

The unluckiest of all 70s bands, **Big Star** created two albums of classic pop-rock; both faintly reminiscent of The Beatles, The Kinks and West Coast pop, both almost totally overlooked at the time. **ALEX CHILTON** and **Chris Bell**, Big Star's founders and inspiration, were a class apart. How different it all should have been.

And how different almost all of it was. Chilton and Bell were joined by **Andy Hummel** (bass) and **Jody Stephens** (drums), named themselves after a supermarket chain, and produced one of the great debut albums, NO. 1 RECORD (1972). The acoustic beauty of songs like "Thirteen" and "Give Me Another

Chance" mingled effortlessly with harder snarling guitar rock on "Don't Lie To Me" and "Feel". Throughout the album wonderfully produced gorgeous tunes backed lyrics bemoaning unrequited love and lost innocence – notably on the classic "Ballad Of El Goodo", of which the self-effacing Chilton is still justifiably proud. Critics were ecstatic, the record was infinitely marketable, and it should have made Big Star very big stars indeed. That it did not was almost entirely down to record company incompetence – Ardent Records' distribution system and in-house squabbling effectively scuppered the album's chances of major success and, with hindsight, lost Big Star to the world.

The album's failure emphasized the strains inherent within Big Star. Chilton wanted to tour, Bell didn't. The upshot, inevitably, was Bell's departure, at the end of 1972, and a series of messy shows that did nothing to progress the band's cause. For all their songwriting genius, Big Star never made it as a live act.

Such was the acrimony between Chilton and Bell that the latter refused to take credit for any contribution to RADIO CITY (1974), an album that marks the pinnacle of Chilton's musical achievement. Raw and rasping pop at its best, RADIO CITY exuded a tension, an excitement and a power that perhaps its predecessor lacked. Wonderful tunes remained, of course, as on "September Gurls", "Way Out West" or "What's Going Ahn", but elsewhere – on "Mod Lang", for instance – the power of the performance and the erratic mix gave a sense of chaos which only added to the thrill. With the Ardent and Columbia labels at loggerheads, and distribution minimal, the record languished. Inevitably the critics loved it.

After all that, it is hardly surprising that Big Star fell apart. THIRD (1975) was a Chilton solo album in all but name. Strange, erratic and at times beautiful, this haunting collection became a legend in its own right. Unfortunately, it was the last Chilton collection to truly reflect his talent. Chris Bell's I AM THE COSMOS, recorded in 1975–76 but only released on Rykodisc in 1992, was similarly compelling, and a fine epitaph for Bell, who died in a car accident in 1979.

In the 90s, however, largely through the fandom of young British bands like Primal Scream and Teenage Fanclub, a new generation have been awakened to Big Star. The interest led to a brief reunion of Chilton and Jody Stephens, a tour and a live album, COLUMBIA: LIVE AT MISSOURI UNIVERSITY 4/25/93 (1993). Chilton's unabashed pure pop sensibilities bubbled to the surface once more in 1998 when, on the back of interest generated by a TV advertisement, the **Box Tops**, his earlier band reformed for an unexpected new album TEAR OFF! (1998).

- **No. 1 Record & Radio City** (1972 & 1974; Stax/Fantasy).
The first two albums reissued on one CD. The former is a mix of power pop and wondrous acoustic balladry to shame all contemporaries, while the latter is a brilliant union of artistry and imagination, inspired melodies and chaotic performances.

- **Third** (1975; Rykodisc).
More Alex Chilton than Big Star, but recognizable nonetheless. Wonderfully strange and haunting, it's hardly accessible but still well worth the effort.

Hugh Wilson

BIKINI KILL

Formed Olympia, Washington, 1990; disbanded 1998.

Washington quartet **Bikini Kill** – **Kathleen Hanna** (vocals), **Tobi Vail** (drums), **Billy Karren**, aka **Billy Boredom**, (guitar) and **Kathi Wilcox** (bass) – formed an integral part of the 'riot grrrl' movement, which in the early 90s briefly promised to do for the American rock scene what punk had done for a weary British scene in the 70s.

The movement's geographically remote axes were Washington DC in the east, and Olympia, capital of Washington State, in the northwest. The former city was the home of the Dischord label, founded by **FUGAZI** main man Ian MacKaye along the lines of the first wave of UK independents, and this operation influenced Olympia's K label (run by Calvin Johnson of Beat Happening), and the evolution of riot grrrl itself. Young women from these two cities began collaborating on ways to challenge the male domination of the rock world, bypassing the major labels, and established music press in favour of independent releases and cheap but passionately written fanzines.

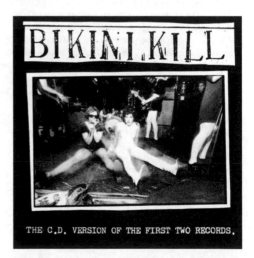

THE C.D. VERSION OF THE FIRST TWO RECORDS.

It is against this background that Bikini Kill's music must be heard. In Hanna, Bikini Kill had a truly magnetic frontwoman, able to inspire and infuriate in equal measures, with a powerful, penetrating voice, which somehow echoed Laura Logic's saxophone lines on old X-Ray Spex records. Bikini Kill, and Hanna in particular, were eager to accept the label of 'spokespersons for a generation'. This stance, coupled with a refusal to play the media game, detracted from the music – a thrashy sound, with disarmingly low production values, that owed more to the likes of Fugazi and the Californian punk band Black Flag than to any UK punk group, feminist or otherwise.

After the self-produced demo cassette, REVOLUTION GIRL STYLE NOW, Bikini Kill provided the stand-out track on the compilation, KILL ROCK STARS (1991), which commemorated Olympia's International Pop Underground Festival, with the atmospheric and lyrically dense "Feels Blind". This was despite the inclusion of an early Nirvana track. "Feels Blind" appeared in a different version on the Bikini Kill six-track mini-LP, co-produced by Ian MacKaye and featuring ferocious songs such as "Double Dare Ya" and "Suck My Left One". A second release was a split EP, YEAH, YEAH, YEAH, YEAH (1993), with London-based allies **Huggy Bear**, with whom Bikini Kill toured the UK in a confrontational double bill in 1992. These two releases later became available on a single CD issue, THE CD VERSION OF THE FIRST TWO RECORDS (1993).

Amid the waning interest in riot grrrl and a lukewarm response to PUSSY WHIPPED (1993) – despite the inclusion of the anthemic "Rebel Girl" which would later be rerecorded with riot mom Joan Jett behind the boards – Bikini Kill were looking for direction. The band scored headlines when Hanna showed up at the 1995 *Lollapalooza* tour, and was punched in the face by Courtney Love, but this was effectively the last gasp. REJECT ALL AMERICAN (1996) was just what the remaining fans wanted, but unfortunately they were no longer numerous enough to make the band commercially viable. Hanna announced in March 1998 that she was going off to graduate school and would perform in future as **Julie Ruin**.

With JULIE RUIN (1998), Hanna proved that she was no one-trick pony, transmogrifying the girlish pop-punk of later Bikini Kill into lo-fi electronica. Hanna's next project, **Le Tigre**, was originally going to be Julie Ruin's backing band, but the quirky electronic 'roller skate jams' and vox-pop politics that Hanna, **Johanna Fateman** and **Sadie Benning** (later replaced by **J.D. Samson**) produced proved too unique to be merely background sounds. The group's self-titled first album (1999) found Hanna reconciling anger, pleasure, body and mind in a sound that would herald New York's rediscovery of 80s New Wave, particularly on the fabulous "Hot Topic". FEMINIST SWEEPSTAKES (2001) offered more of the same.

The CD Version of the First Two Records
(1994; K Records).
The first two mini-LPs released on one CD. Aggressive, lippy and none too disciplined, it was never going to win any prizes for polemical subtlety, but it nonetheless managed to sound like a triumph of female bonding against the odds.

Owen James

THE BIRTHDAY PARTY

Formed Melbourne, Australia, 1978; disbanded 1983.

The **Birthday Party** were one of the most remarkable and challenging bands of the immediate post-punk era – and one of the most passionately followed. During their London years, at the onset of the 80s, there were fans who went to every Birthday Party gig. And why not? On a good night, their chaotic, menacing songs sounded like no one else on earth.

The band began life in Melbourne as The Boys Next Door, with a line-up, preserved more or less intact throughout their career, of **Nick Cave** (vocals), **Rowland Howard** (guitar), **Tracey Pew** (bass), **Phil Calvert** (drums) and **Mick Harvey** (everything). Their change of name – taking the title of a Harold Pinter play – was revealing of Cave's literary and artistic interests, and apt, in that the band's music shared Pinter's black humour, menace and grotesquerie (another tale has it that the band took its name from the Harvey/Cave song "Happy Birthday" and that the name change took place on the eve of their move to the UK, to underscore their new, more mature direction; yet another claims the name was suggested by the party scene in Crime And Punishment). The Birthday Party were as gothic as bands came in the post-punk era, although the humour that pervaded their records set them apart from more solemn contemporaries like their future label mates, Bauhaus.

This identity, carved out amid a noisy, feedback-drenched thrash – took a couple of albums to assert. THE BIRTHDAY PARTY (1980), the Australian-released debut album, was a fairly conventional affair. After their move to England, in 1981, however, they became ever more distinctive, claiming a cult classic with the single "Release The Bats". The Birthday Party sound was really forged, however, with a pair of albums, PRAYERS ON FIRE (1981) and, especially, JUNKYARD (1982), which was recorded for independent label 4AD. This was uncompromising music, the tracks often sounding on the point of collapse, with the band seemingly playing multiple different songs while Cave ranted and raged about lost souls and the grotesques who infested his imagination.

The black comedy of many of those songs – like "King Ink" and "Just You And Me" – led the music press to dub the band 'cartoonish', but, pretentious though it may sound, they were really more tragi-comic. Listen, for example, to "Hamlet Pow Pow" – Shakespeare-meets-Jimmy-Cagney, as Cave, in the guise of Hamlet, screeches, 'Wherefore art thou babyface?'. Some of their more extreme and violent imagery, though, was not for the fainthearted, like "6" Gold Blade": 'I stuck a six inch gold blade in the head of a girl'.

Given the nature of the band and its personalities, it was not surprising that tensions began to appear, particularly between Cave and Howard, over its future direction. Pew, imprisoned for drink-driving, was replaced for a while by **BARRY ADAMSON** (ex-Magazine), and Calvert was eased out (joining **PSYCHEDELIC FURS**) as the band shifted to the more congenial locale of Berlin, and its members devoted their energies to collaboration with **LYDIA LUNCH** and **EINSTÜRZENDE NEUBAUTEN**.

The band's fragmentation and divisions were starkly highlighted on their final EP, MUTINY! (1983). "Jennifer's Veil", featuring the Nick Cave croon for the first time, was in effect his first Bad Seeds solo outing, while the demented "Mutiny In Heaven" served as The Birthday Party's swansong, with Cave raving like a trooper over Blixa Bargeld's guitar. It was a superb epitaph for an extraordinary band.

The Birthday Party's permanent break-up was finalized by the death of Tracey Pew from drug-related complications in 1986, although he was supposedly 'clean' at the time of his death. Rowland Howard left to join the legendary **Crime And The City Solution**, and subsequently formed **These Immortal Souls**; he then released a solo album, TEENAGE SNUFF FILM (2000). Cave began a long and brilliant solo career as frontman of **NICK CAVE AND THE BAD SEEDS**, taking Harvey along for the ride.

⊙ **Junkyard** (1982; 4AD).
The final album, full of amazing songs – "She's Hit", "Big-Jesus-Trash-Can" and "Junkyard". Cave's megalomania is still held in check by the rest of the band, on top form here.

⊙ **Hits** (1992; 4AD).
This double-album compilation, chosen by Cave himself, is an excellent introduction for any unfortunates yet to experience the world of The Birthday Party. It covers their whole career, from "Mr Clarinet" to "Mutiny In Heaven", and includes all the really tasteless songs.

Chris Jenkins
With thanks to William Alberque for updates

ELVIN BISHOP

Born Tulsa, Oklahoma, 1942.

In 1965 a blues band made up of white musicians was still a novelty in America, though the British blues boom had come and almost gone by then. The pioneer was guitarist **Elvin Bishop**, in partnership with his University of Chicago friend **Paul Butterfield**. The band took harmonica player Butterfield's name, but by this time Bishop was a youthful veteran of the Chicago club scene, with an apprenticeship that included a stint with the late, great **Magic Sam**, who was an inspiration to younger performers such as Buddy Guy.

Bishop was soon joined in the Butterfield band by **Mike Bloomfield**, but when the latter went solo in 1968 Bishop stayed. Not for long, however: he too hankered after seeing his own name in lights and formed **The Elvin Bishop Group**, with **Steven Miller** (organ), **John Chambers** (drums) and **Art Stavro** (bass). In 1969 they recorded for the San Francisco label Fillmore, owned by Bill Graham, the man who ran the celebrated venue of the same name.

After a clutch of further albums on CBS, **Mickey Thomas** joined as featured vocalist in 1974, when the group moved to the Capricorn label for LET IT FLOW. A series of impressive albums decorated the rest of the decade, often in the Southern boogie style of the label's star attraction, The Allman Brothers, but the group ground to a halt in 1979 with the departure of Thomas to **JEFFERSON STARSHIP**. Since then, Bishop has maintained a comparatively low profile. Most of his work is out of catalogue, but worth keeping an eye out for in specialist shops.

⊙ **Tulsa Shuffle: The Best of Elvin Bishop** (1994; Legacy).
Not the only 'best of' but the only one still available, this collects Bishop's 1970s material, by which time he had broadened into Southern shuffle, country and rock as well as the blues material that made his name.

John Collis

BITCH MAGNET/SEAM

Formed Oberlin College, Ohio, US, 1987. Seam formed Chapel Hill, North Carolina, US, 1991.

One of the most underrated bands to come out of the post-punk era, **Seam** combine melancholy, rage and pure plaintive yearning to devastating effect. Steered by guitarist and vocalist **Sooyoung Park**, the band originated in the fiery ball of rage created by **Bitch Magnet**, an ironically monickered bunch of sonic terrorists. Bitch Magnet's first LP, STAR BOOTY (1987), combined sweet melody with sour, thrashing guitar and savage slices of bass and drums. Despite additional mixing by **Steve Albini**, the album's strengths were drowned in poor-quality recording and it was not until BEN HUR (1988) that the Bitch Magnet sound was crystallized.

BEN HUR's nine-minute epic opening track, "Dragoon", packed in an album's worth of hooks and riffs, yet was still followed by what can only be described as a controlled detonation of song delivered via Park's ferocious bass, **Orestes Delattore**'s jazz-influenced drumming and **Jon Fine**'s soaring guitar work.

Bitch Magnet hit their peak with the magnificent UMBER (1989), recorded in a mere two days. The album led you in with the pounding, jarring tracks "Motor" and "Big Pining" before closing with "Americruiser", re-creating a bystander's response to a car wreck over radio chatter and gently pattering drums. Park's vocals remained virtually incomprehensible throughout the dynamically astonishing album, at the bottom of a mix heavy in sparring guitars and crushed by the rhythm section.

In 1991, following the band's disintegration (largely due to further education commitments), the more melodic and restrained Seam broke gently over the world with two low-key singles and a tour with Hole. Sooyoung took on guitar duties, with Superchunk's **Mac McCaughan** and **Lexi Mitchell** on bass. Seam's first album, HEADSPARKS (1992), was a melodic, bittersweet treat, featuring guest vocals with a sense of longing from Velocity Girl's **Sarah Shannon**. The band grew into a four-piece as the music increased in complexity, with **John McEntire** joining on drums and **Bundy K. Brown** as second guitarist. Both were later founder members of **TORTOISE**.

At this point, Park decamped to Chicago to take a job as a computer programmer. Seam progressed slowly, content to ignore commercial pressures and to concentrate on their contemplative music. Their second album, THE PROBLEM WITH ME, was released in 1993, with a more cohesive and consistent sound than before. **Bob Rising** (Poster Children) contributed understated drums and **Craig White** played guitar (although Brown made an appearance to contribute some delicate E-bow work, notably on the crashing "Sweet Pea").

In 1995 Mitchell left the band, and **Chris Manfrin** (drums), **Reg Schrader** (guitar) and **William Shin** (bass) joined Sooyoung to record ARE YOU DRIVING ME CRAZY? (1995). The melancholic tinge was stronger than ever, making the listener fear for Park's sanity, holed up in freezing Chicago writing songs of love and regret. The fizzing guitars were joined by a trumpet and violin, contributing to the sombre mood. Things neither cheered up nor accelerated three years later, on the appropriately entitled THE PACE IS GLACIAL (1998), where Park's world-view had, if anything deteriorated.

Park moved away from love songs to concentrate more on his experience as a second-generation Korean-American. Songs such as "Little Chang, Big City" and "Nisei Fight Song", as well as Park's championing of Asian-American bands on his Fortune4 record label, made him something of a spokesman for a burgeoning scene.

As for Seam's future, the band is seemingly content to continue on a leisurely path, having earned the rightful respect of their peers. Park seems unsure whether the upheaval caused by concentrating full time on touring and recording will ultimately suit the band. Fans will just have to wait and see.

Bitch Magnet

- **Ben Hur** (1988; Glitterhouse) **& Umber/Star Booty** (1989; Communion).
Buy each on sight.

Seam

- **Headsparks** (1992; City Slang).
A fizzy, spirited debut.
- **The Problem With Me** (1993; City Slang).
Matches Bitch Magnet's fury with lyrical tenderness.

Jonathan Bell

BJÖRK

Born Björk Gudmundsdóttir, Iceland, 1965.

Born into a creative background, to parents who were members of a hippie-ish commune, **Björk** was encouraged to develop her talents to such an extent that she released her first record at the age of 11. It was quite a big Icelandic hit. From this point onwards, her childlike, otherworldly image, adopted so as 'not to threaten people', has belied an astute and canny approach to her life and career.

Throughout her childhood, she dabbled in music and other artistic activities, all quite punky and anarchic in approach, while singing in cover bands. By 1986 she was in a band called **Kukl**, half of which broke away to create **THE SUGARCUBES**, featuring **Thor**, the father of Björk's son Sindri, on guitar. They became Iceland's biggest export, and Björk's voice, with its full, strong range from whisper to screech, became familiar to many. U2's The Edge describes it as 'an ice pick through concrete'; he is a fan nonetheless.

The members of The Sugarcubes always had outside projects, and Björk was no exception, recording a jazz/swing LP with an Icelandic jazz trio in 1990 (GLING-GLO, rereleased by One Little Indian in 1998) and collaborating on two tracks with 808 State's **Graham Massey** on their 1991 album, EX:EL, including the single "Ooops". However, after The Sugarcubes' amicable split in 1992, her varied tastes became even more diverse, firstly with the release of her 1993 single, "Human Behaviour". A brooding commentary on an unfathomable species, it was her first taste of work with producer **Nellee Hooper**, the man behind Soul II Soul and Massive Attack. Happy with the result, the two ended up working together on a whole album's worth of material. The music on DEBUT (1993) veered between layered, percussive tunes, anthemic house and bare-bones acoustic numbers, with Björk's odd turn of phrase and pronunciation – pitched somewhere between Reykjavik and London – dominating proceedings. Boosted by the success of the single "Play Dead", from the soundtrack of the film *The Young Americans*, DEBUT achieved worldwide sales of 2.5 million – Björk had become something of a 'coffee table' pop star, acceptable in most quarters.

Throughout 1994, Björk was reported to be working with everyone from Madonna to The Beastie Boys. Apart from the dance-floor success of the remixed album track "Big Time Sensuality", however, all was quiet, until the April 1995 release of "Army Of Me". Co-written by old friend Graham Massey, whose menacing keyboard riff was quite fitting for the sinister lyrics, it featured in the movie *Tank Girl* and was later the opening track on POST (1995). More experimental and explorative than its predecessor, it requires work from the listener, but is worth the effort if you can handle songs that mutate and lurch from hard techno to orchestral arrangements. Legend has it that one song, "Cover Me", was even recorded in a cave.

Christmas 1995 saw Björk's hit revival of "It's Oh So Quiet", a remarkable vocal theatric, backed by string quartet The Brodsky Quartet and classical percussionist Evelyn Glennie. In 1996 she was awarded *Best Female International Artist* at the Brits, turning up and hiding behind boyfriend Goldie. However, the overreactive shyness (and perceived threat to her family's privacy) drove her to thump a TV camerawoman at Bangkok airport a few days later, helping to dispel the Björk-as-cuddly-elf myth.

Björk's 1997 album, TELEGRAM, was a remix project based on the POST tracks. However, as she rerecorded the vocals to fit the new music – provided by **Dilinja** and **Dobie**, with further aid from **Glennie** and the **Brodskys** – the result was effectively a completely new album. Despite adopting a lower public profile after being sent a letter bomb early in 1997, Björk continued to work throughout the year, with a new album, HOMOGENIC, being released in September. The new album, in many ways, reflected the strain in her personal life over the preceding twelve months, sounded angrier, older and wiser. The music followed darker paths, too, definitely not a singalong cash-in on the success of "It's Oh So Quiet". Standout tracks, "Hunter", "Jóga" and "Pluto" emphasize her skills as composer, singer and producer.

After the release of several remixed singles packages of HOMOGENIC material, all went quiet until the start of the new millennium. In 2000 Björk exploded back into the limelight, starring in the Lars Von Trier film *Dancer In The Dark*. This Palme-D'Or-winning moviemusical received mixed reviews on its release, but all agreed that Björk's accompanying soundtrack album, SELMASONGS (2000), was a triumph. Featuring many of her familiar musical elements – strings, brass, chaotic beats, etc – and guest vocalists such as Radiohead's **Thom Yorke**, this dynamic work hurls cacophonous orchestral charges against both explosive electronic rhythms and mellow lulls, with equally fine results.

Released only a year later VESPERTINE was an altogether quieter affair, to say the least. Words like 'intimate' and 'graceful' failed to capture the breathless fragility of the collection. Her genius at situating the listener in unfamiliar landscapes reached new heights in "Cocoon", while the sheer delicacy of "Aurora" evoked an exquisite sensuality. Serene and intoxicating,

VESPERTINE showed that without the vocal explosives or the cathartic gut-wrenching there is a level of subtlety to her work that approaches perfection.

⊙ **Debut** (1993; One Little Indian).
Contains several songs which had been written some years before, personal musings that Björk had wanted to do her own way, rather than share them with The Sugarcubes. Features probably the only song ever to have been recorded in the toilet of a nightclub.

⊙ **Post** (1995; One Little Indian).
Listeners of a nervous disposition should be warned: "It's Oh So Quiet" is one of those Hollywood, big-band numbers in which Björk is one second whispering, the next yelling 'Zing Boom!' at full-lung capacity. Tricky lends a hand in places, producing a club stormer in "Enjoy"; add to this harpsichords, strings and bizarre percussion, and it should keep you going for weeks.

⊙ **SelmaSongs** (2000; One Little Indian).
With the opening cuts, beautiful and swollen orchestrations and brass compositions seamlessly mesh with tumbling break-beats and fractured collages of industrial found sound. Though not her most commercial, SELMASONGS is Björk's most accomplished album.

⊙ **Vespertine** (2001; One Little Indian).
From the divine "Hidden Place" to the lush "Pagan Poetry" this is a sublime, extraordinary album that transports the listener to a fairy-tale world without resorting to twee cliché. Not without its dark moments ("An Echo, A Stain"), this is nevertheless a work of consummate beauty.

⊙ **Greatest Hits** (2002; One Little Indian).
This collection was compiled from a survey conducted on the lady's website. An essential retrospective.

Maria Lamle

BLACK

Formed Liverpool, England, 1980.

Based around songwriter **Colin Vearncombe** (vocals/guitars/keyboards), **Black** were formed during one of Liverpool's periodic ascendancies in pop culture. Vearncombe and an anonymous supporting cast released a single, "Human Features", on Rox Records, which sold out its initial pressing and brought them to the attention of Pete Fulwell, then manager of stalwart scousers Wah!. Bringing **Dave 'Dix' Dickie** (keyboards/guitars) into the fold, a follow-up single, "More Than The Sun", was put out on the Wonderful World of... label, which won them a support slot with The Thompson Twins.

Encouraging press reviews brought Black to the attention of WEA, who invested in a third stab at immortality, "Hey Presto". Unfortunately, WEA developed cold feet after the failure of this and the subsequent orchestral version of "More Than The Sun", and Black were unceremoniously dumped. Dix relinquished his full-time musical participation, to continue as engineer/producer. Then, in August 1986, after eighteen months of writing, rehearsing and unsuccessful attempts to get record deals, "Wonderful Life" made its first appearance on another local label, Ugly Man. A minor chart hit, it led to a deal with A&M, which produced a UK Top 10 success during 1987 for "Sweetest Smile", and then issued the reworked and improved "Wonderful Life", which duly repeated the trick around the world.

The ground was thus well prepared for Black's debut album, WONDERFUL LIFE (1987), a long-running best seller across Europe. (Its warm reception with press and public persuaded WEA to rush-release a compilation of early material, simply entitled BLACK). A second album-proper, COMEDY (1988), with Sade producer **Robin Millar** on board, had no turkeys but few stand-outs. The momentum had been lost, and it took the group a while to retrieve it, what with further line-up changes, sporadic all-star fests for Vearncombe, and even guest songwriting stints for the likes of Robert Palmer.

By 1991, Vearncombe had returned to the studio, producing BLACK (1991), which turned out to be his best effort yet, with Millar's imaginative arrangements supplementing some nicely sardonic ("Let's Talk About Me") and regretful ("Too Many Times") melodies. It was let down only by some unnecessary and, one suspects, A&R-inspired guest appearances from **Robert Palmer** and **Sam Brown**. While finding little favour beyond the critics in the UK, the album again performed well in Europe, and the single "Feel Like Change" was a hit in South Africa.

After three albums for A&M, Vearncombe's contract was up, and he retired to the heart of the Normandy countryside with new producer **Mike Hedges**. Here, they recorded ARE WE HAVING FUN YET? (1993), which was first issued via mail order only on Black's own label, nero schwartz, before its commercial release. A pleasantly self-indulgent affair, it boasted relaxed chug-along acoustic pop on "Don't Take The Silence Too Hard", by way of the Scott Walker pastiche "Swingtime", the mock-operatic "Ave Lolita" and the breezy, summery sound of "That's Just Like Love".

"Wonderful Life" enjoyed a third brief spell of chart action in 1994, after it had been featured in an insurance company's TV ad. A compilation album, HAUNTING HARMONIES (1995), brought the story to an end.

⊙ **Wonderful Life** (1987; A&M).
The title track is an instant classic and "Sweetest Smile" isn't far off. Vearncombe's distinctive honey-smooth tones compensate for the insipid 80s synth production.

⊙ **Black** (1991; A&M).
Topnotch arrangements, voice and writing on generally good form; just ignore the 'guest' contributions.

Lance Phillips

FRANK BLACK

Born 1965, Long Beach, California.

"I can't understand personal suffering. I have a good time making my records!"

B orn Charles Michael Kitteridge Thompson IV (naturally), **Frank Black** (aka **Black Francis**) was lead singer in the **PIXIES**, arguably the most influential group ever to emerge from Boston. He is, therefore, assured a place in the Rock and Roll Hall of Fame, even if it's just in the hallway.

In 1993, after five acclaimed albums, the Pixies had looked set to break into the mainstream in a big way. Weird, peculiar, angular and highly eclectic, their aforementioned influence filtered down into what would become America's highly lucrative alternative-rock scene, most notably with Nirvana, whose singer Kurt Cobain never missed an opportunity to namecheck Frank Black. But **Black Francis**, as he was then known, had had enough of sharing the limelight, and of band tensions – notably between himself and bassist **Kim Deal**. Francis announced the split – a shock to most in the music press – on the release (coincidentally enough) of his first solo album, FRANK BLACK (1993). While interviewers were hellbent on quizzing the singer about the split, all he wanted to do was talk about the future, but finding this impossible he vowed never to do another interview. The album, nonetheless, was widely celebrated for sounding like the Pixies, only more so: harder, faster, and heavy with gloriously askew melody, beefy horns and Iggy-ish metal riffing. It was imbued, too, with Black's characteristic off-centre humour and enduring fascination with UFOs. All, you might think, ample compensation for the death of the Pixies.

Surprisingly, though, it sold badly and, to rub salt into the wound, Kim Deal's new band, **The Breeders**, sailed into the charts with LAST SPLASH. Black, undeterred, returned to his Californian studio with **Eric Feldman** (ex-Captain Beefheart and Pere Ubu) adding keyboards and co-producing, emerging a year later with the gargantuan TEENAGER OF THE YEAR (1994). Herein, it appeared that our hero had, if not lost it exactly, certainly taken a wrong turning. The double CD's 22 tracks served to confound, bemuse and perplex listeners with guitar noise one minute, cod reggae the next, meandering instrumentals here and there, and a whole stream of consciousness pervading the abstruse lyrics. Black, meanwhile, did no press whatsoever, an action that could have been perceived as enigmatic but in reality served only to distance him from his old fan base. The record, inevitably, bombed.

But then something changed, as Black rediscovered ambition. He parted company with the cult 4AD label and signed to Epic and started courting the press again, welcoming journalists into his home, conviviality itself. Which is where THE CULT OF RAY (1996), his third solo album, came in.

Slimmed down to just thirteen tracks, RAY asserted itself as a far more streamlined affair than its wayward predecessor, confirming once more that Frank Black's off-kilter, 'alternative' American rock music really did rock. It also boasted the sweetest pop song he'd written in an age, "I Don't Want To Hurt You (Every Single Time)", proving that Black had never lost it at all. Of course he hadn't. He'd just got lazy.

Still, mainstream success did not follow, and nor did critical acclaim, with the music press comparing the new album to Tom Petty, and some going so far as to suggest that Black had become 'boring'. The hardcore fans, meanwhile, were convinced that this was an interim imitation-robot phase, and that the real Frank was up there with the aliens...

The recording industry panic that set in during 1998, when the major labels realized that they weren't shifting product in the same quantities as a few years previously, led to a number of prime babies being thrown out with the dirty bath water as acts were dropped worldwide. Frank and Epic went their separate ways, with a new album, FRANK BLACK & THE CATHOLICS (1998), coming out on a feisty independent. The new material was classic Black-style garage rock, the artist seemed happy with the product and with sexy stuff such as "Steak 'n' Sabre" coming out, it looked like the next chapter of Frank's life was going to be pretty interesting.

If anything, his next offering PISTOLERO (1999), again recorded with The Catholics, was seen as a return to form for many critics keen to lend kudos to a performer who increasingly seemed to be suffering from almost total commercial indifference. Though the set veered from beguiling lo-fi pop ("Skeleton Man") to the frankly dull ("Smoke Up", "I Want Rock'n'Roll"), more often than not Black was firmly in focus.

The 2001 follow-up, DOG IN THE SAND suffered from the same frustrating inconsistency while retaining the thread of Black's indisputable talent and vision. This time there was a welcome intrusion of both slide guitar and keyboards, which brought a dusty Americana vibe to the party. The next two Catholics' releases, BLACK LETTER DAYS and DEVIL'S WORKSHOP were both released in 2002, the latter, particularly, displaying enough twisted growl to appeal to the ever-loyal Pixies fans – indeed, the set featured Black's old Pixies cohort, **Joey Santiago**. One can't help feeling, however, that Black is yet to find that certain *je ne sais quoi* that turns a good album into a great one.

(•) **Frank Black** (1993: 4AD).
Black at his most rotund, musically speaking, laying the fattest of melodies on top of big, chugging guitars and those trademark vocals of his that sound like he's swallowed an egg. "Los Angeles", "Fu Manchu" and his cover of the obscure Beach Boys track, "Hang On To Your Ego", in particular, confirm that Black's hypnotically strange tunes are pretty much peerless.

Nick Duerden

THE BLACK CROWES

Formed Atlanta, Georgia, 1984.

The band formed as the **Greasy Little Toes** by brothers **Chris Robinson** (vocals) and **Rich Robinson** (guitar) went through a number of line-up changes and one more name (**Mr Crowe's Garden**) before settling down under the name The

Black Crowes. Their style was rooted in barroom R&B, a format that remains very resistant to change. The same can be said of The Black Crowes' career. They spent many years building up a loyal following in the Southern states, playing the music they grew up with, at a time when heavy rock internationally was mutating into thrash or overproduced stadium fodder. The Black Crowes appealed more to an audience that appreciated the truths of simple blues-based rock. Obvious influences were Free, The Faces and Aerosmith, as well as (naturally) Lynyrd Skynyrd.

In the late 80s, back-to-basics rock came more into fashion, and suddenly the record labels were looking for bands that would reflect the new mood. Nobody did it better than The Black Crowes, whose early 70s dress sense confirmed their suitability. In 1989 they were picked up by Def American, and SHAKE YOUR MONEY MAKER (1990), produced by **George Drakoulias**, proved a hugely successful debut, hitting the US charts and staying there for eighteen months.

The band had become a stable five-piece, supplemented by an occasional pianist, with the Robinsons backed by **Johnny Colt** (bass), **Steve Gorman** (drums) and 1988 arrival **Jeff Cease** (guitar). The music was simple and traditional, providing a hard but melodic backing to Chris Robinson's powerful and emotive vocals. Lyrically the preoccupations were just as traditional, with song titles like "Twice As Hard", "Jealous Again" and "Struttin' Blues" pointing the way.

In 1991 a storming version of Otis Redding's "Hard To Handle" made the singles charts on both sides of the Atlantic, and a 350-date US tour helped to keep them in the national consciousness. The Black Crowes proved equally popular in Europe, and a hectic touring schedule kept them out of the studio until the emergence of 1992's THE SOUTHERN HARMONY AND MUSICAL COMPANION, which was recorded in ten days between tour dates. By the time it was recorded, Cease had succumbed to the heavy touring schedule, to be replaced by ex-Burning Tree guitarist **Marc Ford**. The formula was given an added little shake by the addition of gospel backing singers and a cover of Bob Marley's "Time Will Tell".

The album confirmed The Black Crowes as one of the big acts of the new decade, and 1993 saw them playing Europe's major festivals, while continuing to release singles, most of which hovered just outside the Top 30. Three years in the spotlight, however, had failed to taint the deep-rooted, no-frills approach that had become the band's trademark, and they made all the right noises about the evils of image-making and corporate sponsorship (some pointed remarks along these lines got them booted off a ZZ Top tour). It was ironic, then, that The Black Crowes provoked a furore with the cover of the AMORICA album (1994), which depicted a close-up of a bikini bottom straining to hold its contents. Some shops in the US refused to stock it, but the album did solid business worldwide.

An eighteen-month tour began in September 1996, but it was cut short by ructions within the band. That year saw the release of THREE SNAKES AND A CHARM, a disappointing follow-up, which lacked AMORICA's guts and conviction. In 1997 recording sessions for a new album were disrupted by Marc Ford's departure. A month later Johnny Colt was also gone, to be quickly replaced by Atlanta bassist **Sven Pipien** (ex-Mary My Hope). **Eddie Harsch** was brought in on keyboards, leaving Rich in sole charge of six-string duties.

The album BY YOUR SIDE (1998) was a reaffirmation of what the Black Crowes had almost forgotten: they were a ROCK band. And this fact wasn't lost upon legendary guitarist **Jimmy Page** who hooked up with the Crowes for a charity concert at the Café de Paris in London on 27 June 1999. The response was nothing short of phenomenal and a US tour followed almost instantly. Within a mere six minutes the tickets for the first two shows at the New York Roseland sold out, and a third show sold out in eight minutes. The gigs consisted of reworked Led Zep classics along with some Crowes tunes and rock classics such as The Yardbirds' "Shape Of Things To Come", Page, of course, having been a former member of that outfit. As a testament to the brilliance of the shows, LIVE AT THE GREEK (2000) crackled with an energy seldom captured on record. Unfortunately the Crowes' next move was not quite so memorable and LIONS (2001) failed to roar with the same conviction, despite being produced by Don Was. The band also elected to tour, somewhat bizarrely, with **Oasis** on the *Tour of Brotherly Love*. Furthermore, things appeared to be less than harmonious within the group's fold – drummer Steve Gorman was eventually fired and the group were effectively put on ice while Chris Robinson decided to inflate his solo career with the release of the frankly unremarkable NEW EARTH MUD (2002).

For now, fans of the Crowes-proper will have to make do with 2002's GREATEST HITS and BLACK CROWES LIVE releases.

⦿ **Shake Your Money Maker** (1990; Def American).
The barroom blues style may be limited, but The Black Crowes' debut ranks them with the best exponents of the style.

⦿ **Amorica** (1994; American).
The lyrics may be a little more complex than on its predecessors, with the opposition to drugs more implied than explicit, but the music retains its simplicity while displaying more texture and originality than most bands in the genre.

Patrick Neylan-Francis

BLACK FLAG

Formed Los Angeles, 1977; disbanded 1986.

Hardcore punk rock was born of pure aggression, but many of its best practitioners eventually found it necessary to modulate this with elements of jazz (The Minutemen) or folk (Hüsker Dü), or even country (The Meat Puppets). Not **Black Flag** – they just got more aggressive. They only quietened down so **Henry Rollins** could read his poetry – an alternative form of assault – and they only slowed down to grind their audience's nerves with thudding heavy metal riffs. Say what you want about them, there's no way you can say they ever went soft.

Black Flag was the brainchild of **Greg Ginn**, a gawky, soft-spoken Californian with a rare, useful combination of musical talent and business sense – while he was leading and playing guitar in Black Flag, he also became the force behind SST Records, which sustained Southern Californian hardcore for years. Ginn, bassist/running buddy **Chuck Dukowski**, drummer **Robo** (replacing short-termer **Brian Migdol**) and singer **Johnny 'Bob' Goldstein** (a pseudonym for **Keith Morris**, later of the **Circle Jerks**) began recording and gigging when the likes of The Last and The Germs were starting to forge a local punk scene. Ferociously energetic and nihilistic, Black Flag fitted the scene perfectly.

To begin with, attempts to spread the word on vinyl were problematic: Goldstein quit during the recording of JEALOUS AGAIN, and his tracks were re-recorded with his replacement **Chavo Pederast**, who in turn was replaced by **Dez Cadena** by the time of the EP's release. Their early output was distinguished by the band's unrelenting attack and Ginn's guitar playing, which interspersed rapid block-chording with strangled riffs, making English punk leads of the time sound rather studied. Lyrics were predominantly teen-angst rants about being wasted, or a maniac, or having no values, etc – so unrelievedly grim that they verge on a sort of black comedy. The vocals were suitably harsh – Cadena, in particular, sounding as if he'd gargled battery acid before each take.

By 1981, the band, by now favourites of the burgeoning hardcore scene, sought a replacement vocalist, as Cadena became their full-time rhythm guitarist. They chose ice-cream store manager and longtime fan Henry Rollins, who debuted on the almost painfully earnest DAMAGED. The Rollins-era output was prolific by any standards: buoyed by a national network of fans, gigs, Ginn's label, and a gung ho full-time frontman, there were nearly two dozen Black Flag records issued in five years. By this stage, Rollins was also sharing songwriting credits (MY WAR), while the band backed his poetry readings (FAMILY MAN). Rollins's aggression was well balanced by his intelligence, which helped old and new material immeasurably; early classics such as "Room 13" and "Police Story" gained force and clarity, while goofy new tunes like "TV Party" and "Thirsty And Miserable", which might have sunk into mush with the group's previous frontmen, kicked the proverbial ass.

Nonetheless, the switch from goofy over-the-topness to just plain over-the-topness that characterized Rollins's reign did bear bitter fruit. The band developed a propensity for Sabbath-like dirges on SLIP IT IN and MY WAR, and in general the music began to serve the lyrics rather than (as previously) vice versa. By the mid-80s, Chuck and Robo had quit, and a new bassist, **Kira Roessler** – one of the few women in hardcore at the time – had signed up. The group, however, irredeemably split in 1986 after the release of the live set WHO'S GOT THE 10 ^{1}/$_2$?. Ginn went on to form his own instrumental group, **Gone**.

Black Flag's story has both musical and historical significance. Historically, they were key figures in forming a pocket of punk consciousness in California and in other mid-American communities. Their defiant, anti-establishment stance was inspirational, and musically the band carried the hardcore banner probably as far as it could be carried – every local-hero hardcore band sounds like a revival after them. Even after repeated listenings, their best songs – the clamorous "TV Party", "Slip It In" with its clever ritardando refrain, the beyond-despair "Annihilate This Week" – carry the anguish of youth into the realm of art. A useful companion to further study is Rollins's coffee-table book, *Get In The Van.*

◉ Damaged (1981; SST).
What people think of when they think of Black Flag. The funny stuff is funny; the angry stuff is funny. This is SoCal punk ethos frozen in vinyl for all time. Time-capsule nominee: "Six Pack" ('My girlfriend asked which I liked better/I hope the answer don't upset her').

◉ Everything Went Black (1982; SST).
A stopgap product issued during the Unicorn Records legal tussle, this early retrospective CD not only has table-pounders like "White Minority" and "Wasted" (some in multiple versions), but also a montage of vintage radio ads for Flag shows and records – punk audio theatre accompanied by the sound of roaring Marshalls, splintering wood and police helicopters.

◉ Who's Got The 10½? (1986; SST).
The band's last incarnation, live and at full bore. And the sound quality isn't even that bad.

Roy Edroso

BLACK GRAPE

Formed Manchester, England, 1993; disbanded 1998.

"John Paul knows I'm cool." Shaun Ryder responding to Vatican criticism

When **THE HAPPY MONDAYS** came to a predictable end, the biggest surprise was the speed with which **Shaun Ryder** (vocals) repeated the trick. Supposedly washed up, his drug abuse now common knowledge, he did the unthinkable. Instead of re-forming, rebirthing or dying, he created a new band fuelled by the same laddish enthusiasm and irreverence.

With fellow ex-Monday **Mark 'Bez' Berry** (official job description: 'vibes') in tow, Shaun formed **Black Grape** in his living room a couple of weeks after the Mondays' split, along with his flat-mate **Paul 'Kermit' Leveridge** (vocals), whose hard and fast rapping provided the perfect contrast to Shaun's drawn-out, druggy voice. Kermit and drummer **Ged Lynch** were formerly in the **Ruthless Rap Assassins**, while guitarist **Paul 'Wags' Wagstaff** previously played with the **Paris Angels**.

Friends since childhood, Shaun and Kermit have written most of Black Grape's material with **Danny Saber** and **Stephen Lironi**, who co-produced and played additional instruments on their acclaimed 1995 album, IT'S GREAT WHEN YOU'RE STRAIGHT... YEAH!. In promotional interviews, Shaun enthused about the virtues of having a writing partner for the first time, which probably helped the band to complete the making of the album in just seven weeks – a far cry from the meandering months spent in Barbados completing the Mondays' disastrous 1992 swansong YES PLEASE!. Preceded by a brace of singles, "Reverend Black Grape", which smashed into the UK Top 10 in the early summer of 1995, and "In The Name Of The Father", the album topped the British charts in the week of release.

Kermit somehow picked up a dose of septicaemia and was out of action till the middle of 1996. While he recovered, and once the previous convictions problems had been cleared with the US authorities, Black Grape recruited the likely-sounding **Psycho** in his place, ditched Bez and headed west on tour. The rest of the year saw a couple of single releases; "Fat Neck" and the soccer-hooligans-on-MDMA dirge "England's Irie" – a lousy song, like all football songs, despite the presence of **Joe Strummer** assisting on vocals.

STUPID, STUPID, STUPID (1997), their follow-up album, lacked the sheer drug-revivalist inspiration of IT'S GREAT WHEN YOU'RE STRAIGHT... YEAH!, but maintained that 'still dancing at dawn' feeling. Kermit was back on board by this time, the grooves were sufficiently groovy, the beats were meaty, but the music had lost something. 'Musical differences' is the kindest explanation for the disastrous remainder of 1997; by the end of the year, Kermit and Psycho had left (to press on together as **Manmade**), with the Grape continuing as the duo of Shaun and Danny.

Following 2000's Happy Mondays comeback tour, Ryder joined forces with the tenor **Russell Watson** for a decidedly bizarre remake of Freddie Mercury and Montserrat Caballe's "Barcelona". He then compiled his own mix CD for the 'Planet Groove' series, unearthing a suitable hotch-potch of favourites ranging from classic easy listening to reggae, house and gangsta rap selections.

Black Grape took their inspiration readily from all sources: "We try to steal, but without making it obvious, which was what we tried to do with the Mondays, rip off loads of stuff, right, but not make it obvious," Shaun once boasted. It was still fairly obvious, since casual plagiarism was partly what the Mondays were famous for, pioneering the freedom from anxiety of influence later heard in Oasis's work.

⊙ **It's Great When You're Straight . . . Yeah!** (1995; Radioactive).
The upbeat 'Madchester' sound is evident on tracks such as "Tramzi Parti" and "Kelly's Heroes", while "Big Day In The North" and "Shake Your Money" reveal a more soulful side. In the midst of all the Blur and Oasis hype, this was the British album of 1995.

Matthew Grant

BLACK REBEL MOTORCYCLE CLUB

Formed San Francisco, California, 1998.

The Bay Area music scene is a noted producer of rock acts that are preferred overseas and **Black Rebel Motorcycle Club** are no exception. They have fared best in the UK, being influenced by Brit bands like Joy Division, Ride, Loop and the Jesus & Mary Chain (to whom they bear an eerie resemblance). Deriving their name from the classic 1957 Brando movie *The Wild One*, the band dress in black, sport mop-fringed haircuts, and generally manage to look as dark and menacing as much of their music sounds. That said, the group's trademark layers of amped guitar and distortion are often the bedfellows of beautiful tunes and sumptuous acoustic backings (as was the case with the Mary Chain before them).

High school pals **Peter Hayes** (guitars/bass/vocals) and **Robert Turner** (guitars/bass/vocals) had started out as The Wave, an act Turner claims had no real songs but an appetite for psychedelic rock workouts: 'We'd just show up with equipment and start playing. Some songs lasted thirty minutes.' This attitude saw them team briefly with cult California indie act, The Brian Jonestown Massacre, before recruiting statutory Englishman, **Nick Jago** (drums)

ANGELA LUBRANO

BRMC's Peter Hayes

who, according to legend, won his spurs by leaping on stage one night, 'playing the tambourine and causing a ruckus'.

The Dandy Warhols, having hit big themselves with their second and third albums, were keen to have the band tour with them. The darkness of Black Rebel Motorcycle Club's sound perfectly contrasted with the askance observations of Courtney Taylor and co, and, needless to say, the support's profile began to gain serious weight from these gigs.

After two US 7" singles ("Red Eyes And Tears" and "Rifles") their eponymous debut album (2001), the bulk of which was reworked versions of the original demo that had so impressed The Dandy Warhols, signalled their arrival as part of the new rock scene. Regardless of this great leap forward in US distribution, it was Britain that gave the band the airplay essential to their breakthrough. While The Strokes and The White Stripes hogged *NME* front covers, BRMC ghosted into the UK rock audience's subconscious with the insidious "Whatever Happened To My Rock 'N' Roll? (Punk Song)", a powerful slice of slacker blues. "Love Burns", the following release, was another previous US single, and then, the most sriking of their work, "Jesus & Mary Chain" was also released and entered the UK Top Forty in January of 2002. The more commercial "Spread Your Love" took the band higher into the chart in

May, with "Whatever Happened…?" finally gaining the hit status it deserved a few months later.

As the album was certified silver, plaudits were forthcoming from a swathe of new BRMC converts, including Noel Gallagher, Johnny Marr and – yes – the Jesus & Mary Chain's Jim Reid.

A sophomore album recorded early in 2003 at London's Fortress and Mayfair studios, entitled TAKE THEM ON, ON YOUR OWN looks set to cement further Black Rebel Motorcycle Club's uncompromising position as rock's coolest outcasts.

⊙ **Black Rebel Motorcycle Club** (2002; Virgin).
No real boundary-pushing with this debut, but an enjoyably unadorned statement of intent from a focused band that wears influences with pride.

Jeremy Simmonds

BLACK SABBATH

Formed Birmingham, England, 1967.

"When we came out of The Exorcist we had to all stay in one room together – that's how black magic we were." Ozzy Osbourne

The definitive heavy metal band, **Black Sabbath** – **Ozzy Osbourne** (vocals), **Tony Iommi** (guitar), **Terry 'Geezer' Butler** (bass) and **Bill Ward** (drums) – emerged from the British Midlands to instant success, as their debut album, BLACK SABBATH (1970), stormed to #8 in the UK charts. As with all overnight success, it was somewhat deceptive. In an earlier incarnation, **Earth**, the band had clocked up ceaseless late-night miles and played more dates at Hamburg's Star Club than The Beatles. A reworking of their jazz-blues style and a change of name had caught the first wave of heavy metal – from the start the Sabs were in the metal premier league with the likes of Deep Purple and Led Zeppelin.

In the first half of the 70s, every Sabbath album approached metal classic status. PARANOID (1970) gave the band a UK chart-topping set, a hit single, and the stage favourite "War Pigs". Its sombre tone, and the Sabs' dark showbiz trappings, also forged the band's supposed reputation as 'satanists' – an absurd image, but one that received a boost when Ozzy bit the head off a bat (the boy from Beelzebub then had to be treated for rabies).

Still, PARANOID certainly saw the Sabs at the peak of their powers, and they remained there with a great trio of early 70s albums. MASTER OF REALITY (1971) was a riffmongous romp and VOLUME IV (1972) was little short of brilliant, combining matchless metal with instrumental passages, while the ballad "Changes" showcased Ozzy's vocal prowess in a chilling number that still retained an element of power. SABBATH BLOODY SABBATH (1973) was another masterpiece, with a title track that is arguably the best ever Sabs number.

With the mighty Warner corporation behind them, Sabbath stormed the US. Iommi's crunching riffs reworked basic blues at mind-numbing volume, while Ward and Butler held a solid backing track that left space for Ozzy's vocals to approach hysteria. The cynics might depict the Sabs as a bunch of dummies who had struck lucky, but this was music that made sense after three seconds of listening, appealed to the expanding FM rock radio market, and sent long-haired kids into guitar shops by the million.

From the mid-70s much of Sabbath's career would be beset by management and contractual problems, and by the all-too-predictable 'musical differences'. Basically, Iommi wanted to experiment and Ozzy wanted to party and stay basic. Geezer was largely behind Iommi, and Ward could knock back as many drinks as Ozzy. The tension could, on occasion, produce great music, but from SABOTAGE (1975) the music often had a self-conscious quality that undermined the strength.

Ozzy briefly left in 1977 and **Dave Walker** became the least successful in a string of Sabs vocalists who attempted the near-impossible task of replacing him. By 1978, Ozzy was back for NEVER SAY DIE (1978), but despite British hit singles and respectable business around the world he was gone again soon after. Unstable line-ups would become a Sabs feature from this point.

OZZY OSBOURNE's solo career would prove spectacular, bizarre and extremely lucrative, especially in the US. Sabbath, meantime, laboured to recapture former glories, a struggle centred mainly on the vocalists trying to fill Ozzy's shoes. **Ronnie James Dio**, who had a pedigree taking in Rainbow, and a definite sense of his own identity, avoided copying Ozzy's style on HEAVEN AND HELL (1980) and MOB RULES (1981). In the studio the band were managing solid if predictable heavy metal, but this came at a price and no one was surprised when the acrimony boiled over. Dio split amid accusations that he tampered with the mixes to LIVE EVIL (1983) to favour his vocals.

Ian Gillan had the vocal ability to lead Sabbath, but his stint out front marked the nearest any real metal band ever came to Spinal Tap. BORN AGAIN (1983) managed to make most of the right sounds but lacked the songs to suggest this line-up had a chance. Live, things got seriously strange on a US tour. The Stonehenge stage set was worrying enough and Gillan's sketchy grasp of Sabbath lyrics was undermined as swirling dry ice blocked his view of his cue cards. Classic metal songs were reduced to endless riffs and screams of 'yeah'. Tragedy and comedy were seldom so close together.

The classic line-up re-formed for a perfunctory turn at Live Aid, and Iommi then recruited several notable metal faces for the forgettable SEVENTH STAR (1986), the only Sab album that doesn't sound much like Sabbath. By the late 80s, however, Sabbath-inspired bands like Iron Maiden had taken the basic crunching style to new commercial and visual heights, and it seemed unlikely the Sabs could ever again be a major force.

Against all odds a contract with IRS saw the tide finally turning. New line-ups featured Iommi and a changing cast of dependable metal performers. A return to classic Sabs values of hard work, unpretentious riffing and a little of the occult finally paid off. **Tony Martin**'s impassioned vocals and **Cozy Powell**'s solid skin thrashing enlivened some of the band's best work and Iommi's riff invention seemed limitless. The title track to HEADLESS CROSS (1989) was an improbably simple stunner of a cut. TYR (1990) was a conceptual album dealing with Norse myths. Dio's gutsy larynx returned for DEHUMANIZER (1992), but Martin was back for CROSS PURPOSES (1994), where the band confidently put the Sabbath stamp on a range of metal sounds from the ethereal to the bluesy.

A year later, the HEADLESS CROSS/TYR line-up, perhaps the strongest Sabs crew since the original quartet, was reunited. By now Sabbath were once again established as a dependable and valued feature, appreciated by many as the band that set the metal agenda. There was little chance they could recapture former glories, but there was real fire in most of their work for IRS. There were some surprises, too – for example, the sparky FORBIDDEN (1995) featured an unlikely vocal from rapper **Ice-T**.

The biggest surprise of all, however, was Ozzy's agreement in 1997 to return for *Ozzfest 97*, a reunion tour. As ever in the Sabbath camp, humour and tragedy were bedfellows; when Ozzy's larynx failed him the rest of the Sabs took the stage at one date to play their greatest hits in tandem with the support acts. Predictably enough, the fans rioted and *Spinal Tap II* got a great plot idea. By the end of the year Birmingham experienced a great reunion as the Sabs – with Ozzy – sold out the NEC. The predictable live album had an uncharacteristically naff title – REUNION (1998). It also premiered two new studio cuts which would have done justice to any of the first four albums. Ward's health problems cast a shadow over the UK reunion but the demand for

action from the original line-up had a tempting financial angle that suggested this was nowhere near the end of Sabbath. This was borne out by the success of REUNION in the US where the album went platinum, a show of enthusiasm not reflected so closely in CD sales in the UK. Since then the band has reunited periodically to tour, but the topic which has most fans waiting with bated breath is the possibility of a new album. Thus far attempts to revive the old songwriting genius in the studio have failed to come up with anything deemed worthy of release – but the possibility remains.

⊙ **Sabbath Bloody Sabbath** (1973; Warners).
The album that improbably added synths to the sludge and came up trumps. Little did they know that this formula would create the likes of Bon Jovi and Def Leppard.

⊙ **The Sabbath Stones** (1996; IRS).
Best of the IRS years; faster tempos than classic Sabbath, but no less bludgeoning.

⊙ **We Sold Our Soul For Rock'N'Roll** (1998; Essential).
Welcome reissue of the 1976 GREATEST HITS package. Seventeen tracks of Midlands madness.

⊙ **Reunion** (1998; Epic).
The inevitable double collection from the home-town reunion gigs in December 97. Solid in the musical department and clearly great fun for the crowd. The Oz man is too intent on working up the crowd to roar into the mike in the hope of making a classic live album. Iommi, however, is as dependable as ever. The 'new' stuff – "Psycho Man" and "Selling My Soul" – wouldn't be out of place on this line-up's old albums.

Neil Nixon

BLAKE BABIES

Formed Boston, Massachusetts, 1987; disbanded 1992.

Juliana Hatfield (vocals/guitar), **John Strohm** (guitar/vocals) and **Freda Boner** (drums) were overshadowed for much of their career by their lustrous Massachusetts-based contemporaries Throwing Muses, Pixies, Dinosaur Jr, and The Lemonheads. As The Lemonheads and Blake Babies shared members throughout their careers, some people looked on the Babies as an **Evan Dando** sideline, or a mere preface to Hatfield's solo career. Neither view is fair.

1987's NICELY, NICELY on Chewbud Records was a premature shot at a full-length record. Shambolic and packed with song titles like "Swill And The Cocaine Sluts", it was clearly the sound of a band trying to find their way. Though more straightforward and tuneful than the Pixies or Muses, their folk-punk elements and Hatfield's squeaky-voice-gone-hoarse definitely resembled the latter's sound. Blake Babies emulated the Pixies and Muses when they recorded several songs with their producer **Gary Smith** at the Fort Apache studio. The result was issued in Britain as a mini-album on Billy Bragg's Utility label under the title SLOW LEARNER, while all seven songs were also included on the full-length US album EARWIG, which also contained an ironic cover of The Stooges' misogynist anthem "Loose".

Despite its truly dreadful sleeve, SUNBURN (1990) successfully moved with the spirit of the times and cranked up the guitars. Hatfield herself finally stepped in as permanent bassist, and gave a memorably assertive performance on "I'm Not Your Mother", while Strohm took a bow with the deceptively sweet-sounding perviness of "Girl In A Box".

It seemed like the band were finally getting somewhere. It had been a slow haul, but, just as the ROSY JACK WORLD EP (1992) and British tour picked up the acclaim that all their contemporaries had been getting for years, they prematurely broke up. Hatfield played bass for **The Lemonheads** while launching her solo career and becoming suddenly notorious as an ex-anorexic, self-proclaimed virgin and Evan Dando's alleged sometime girlfriend. Strohm and Boner formed **Antenna**, and then Strohm put together **Velodeluxe**, as well as playing guitar for The Lemonheads.

After a gap of more than ten years the Babies made a surprising return to the fray when drummer Freda Love Smith persuaded both Hatfield and Strohm to return to the studio. While time had made them less ingenuous, 2001's GOD BLESS THE BLAKE BABIES did benefit from more refined musicianship and an undoubted maturity.

⊙ **Sunburn** (1990; Mammoth).
Quality songs, but with a beefier noise behind them so no one will think you're a wimp for listening to it.

⊙ **Rosy Jack World** (1992; Mammoth).
The most critically successful effort, with a cover of Dinosaur Jr.'s "Severed Lips".

Marc Elliot

BOBBY BLAND

Born Memphis, Tennessee, 1930.

The most original and sensitive blues singer of the last forty years, **Bobby Bland** at his best is the last word in sophisticated, soulful passion.

He was born in a small town just outside Memphis, and began singing gospel songs as a teenager. In Memphis he performed with the **Beale Streeters**, a group which included **B. B. King** and **Johnny Ace**. Signed to Duke Records in the early 50s, he started getting hits in the R&B charts almost from the start. "Further On Up The Road", "I Smell Trouble", "It's My Life Baby" were hard blues in the B. B. King vein. But it was "Little Boy Blue", released in 1956, that would come to define the Bobby Bland style, a combination of quiet pleading and hoarse gospel shouts.

Duke Records teamed Bland with arranger and band-leader Joe Scott, who was instrumental in the creation of the singer's sound. Scott meticulously built big-band arrangements of horns, chunky guitar and a loping, funky backbeat around songs such as "Who Will The Next Fool Be?", "I'll Take Care Of You" and "I Pity The Fool". Carefully combining ballads, blues, jazz and country, Bland and Scott-

produced hits continued right through to the end of the 60s. The classic albums of that decade, TWO STEPS FROM THE BLUES (1961), CALL ON ME (1963) and AIN'T NOTHING YOU CAN DO (1964), were recorded in the midst of continuous touring around the soul circuit, 300 dates a year being the generally accepted work rate. During this time Bland was almost constantly in the R&B charts: "Share Your Love With Me", "Lead Me On" and "Call On Me" were all million-sellers.

Scott left Bland in 1968 and the hits began to dry up until the early 70s, when Bland signed with ABC Records. HIS CALIFORNIA ALBUM (1973), featuring "It's Not The Spotlight" and "If Loving You Is Wrong (I Don't Want To Be Right)", and DREAMER (1974), with "Ain't No Love In The Heart Of The City", were stunning returns to form. Two albums with B. B. King, TOGETHER FOR THE FIRST TIME . . . LIVE (1974) and TOGETHER AGAIN . . . LIVE (1976) were commercially successful but the Vegas showroom format didn't quite come off.

At the end of the 70s ABC tried to position Bland in the disco market, with predictably dire results, and it wasn't until 1985, when he moved to Malaco Records, that his fortunes were revived. This marvellous Texas label was devoted to recording classic soul singers in a basic R&B format. The results were reinvigorating, as is clear from FIRST CLASS BLUES (1988), a compilation from his first three Malaco sets.

Bland has particularly inspired a whole generation of British rock singers. Rod Stewart has covered several of his songs and Van Morrison's 1973 live album, IT'S TOO LATE TO STOP NOW, was virtually a Bobby Bland tribute concert. In 1997 he was justly awarded a *Lifetime Achievement Grammy*.

⊙ **3D Blues Boy** (1991; Ace).
The earliest singles, featuring the towering signature tune "Little Boy Blue". Try singing along to this one and you won't be able to talk for the rest of the day. The great man himself, understandably, declines to perform it these days.

⊙ **The Voice** (1991; Ace).
An exhaustive selection from the greatest hits of the 50s and 60s. Total magic from start to finish, this is some of the best soul music ever recorded.

Len Lauk

THE BLASTERS

Formed Los Angeles, 1980; disbanded 1986; re-formed 1994.

The **Blasters**, one of America's most famous 'unknown bands', were formed in 1980 by two brothers born and bred on the bedrock of all that is Music USA. **Phil** and **Dave Alvin** grew up in Downey, California, on an eclectic diet of sounds – surf from neighbourhood bands, a dash of country from an uncle's record collection, and side orders of rock'n'roll and blues. All fed into The Blasters' sound, which, for all the rockabilly, cowpunk and roots revivalist labels, the Alvins would never call anything other than 'American music'.

In the original line-up, Phil (lead vocals/harmonica/guitar) and Dave (lead guitar) were joined by **John Bazz** (bass) and **Bill Bateman** (drums). Home base was the early thriving punk scene in Los Angeles that spawned their peers: bands like X, the Circle Jerks and the Beat Farmers. In their early 80s heyday, The Blasters crisscrossed the country delivering a set-list of American classics and an ever-increasing number of originals written by Dave Alvin – songs about cars, girls, the working man and road dreams.

AMERICAN MUSIC, the band's debut album, was released in 1980 on the independent Rolling Rock label run by Ron Weiser in Los Angeles. Weiser wanted original songs and Dave Alvin, rising to the challenge, began to find it easier than 'copping lyrics off of Gatemouth Brown records'. The album produced two of the most well-known Blasters Tunes, "American Music" and "Marie, Marie". The first was an anthem, running through the entire stratum of the music that was near and dear to the hearts of the band. The latter became a staple for US bar bands and a hit in the UK for Shakin' Stevens. They were strong enough for Warners to move in, and to re-record them for THE BLASTERS album (1981), in versions supplemented by three new band members: the legendary **Lee Allen** (tenor sax), **Steve Berlin** (baritone sax) and **Gene Taylor** (piano, previously in Canned Heat).

The band's next studio release, NON FICTION (1983), saw Dave Alvin maturing into a great songwriter, most notably on "Long White Cadillac" (later popularized by Dwight Yoakam) and "Bus Station" – probably the best song Alvin wrote during his Blasters days and one that he still performs acoustically today. Two years later came HARD LINE, the last Blasters album recorded with both Phil and Dave Alvin, and featuring a substantially augmented line-up, including former Elvis back-up singers, **The Jordanaires**, the **Jubilee Train Singers**, **Richard Greene** (violin), **Stan Lynch** (vocals/percussion), **Larry Taylor** (bass) and **David Hidalgo** (mandolin).

The Alvin brothers' split, after HARD LINE, was in large measure down to Dave's increasing self-belief as a songwriter, and a desire to sing his own material, rather than craft it for Phil, who has one of those perfect, beautiful rock'n'roll voices. Dave's was rougher-edged, but brilliantly interpretative. The Blasters continued after Dave's departure, with **Michael 'Hollywood Fats' Mann** – until his death of a heart attack, age 32, in 1986. Dave Alvin showed his support by stepping in to meet touring commitments, but it was the end of the road for the band.

Post-Blasters, Dave guested on guitar with X, on their albums SEE HOW WE ARE and POOR LITTLE CRITTER IN THE ROAD (recorded as **The Knitters**), before launching a solo career in 1987. Phil Alvin also went solo, releasing UNSUNG STORIES (1986), with old pals Bazz and Bateman, before going back to school for a maths degree at California State University. Other erstwhile band members, meanwhile, cropped up on the roots revivalist scene, notably Steve Berlin, who discovered, fell in love with and joined **LOS LOBOS** in 1983.

In 1994, Phil Alvin re-formed The Blasters along with Johnny Bazz, LA guitarist **James Intveld** and drummer **Jerry Angel**. They toured the US in the spring and autumn of 1995, and recorded an album, COUNTY FAIR 2000 – an eclectic mix of originals, old blues and vaudeville – with guests **The Dirty Dozen Brass Band**, **Billy Boy Arnold**, **Mary Franklin** and **Cesar Rosas**.

⊙ **The Blasters Collection** (1991; Slash Records). The only pre-split Blasters material available on CD, this mix of studio and live songs shows just what made the band a vibrant, flat-out rockin' representation of American music. Includes, of course, "Marie, Marie", "Border Radio" and "Long White Cadillac".

Erica Wissolik

PETER BLEGVAD

Born New York City, August 14, 1951.

"Imagination, like a muscle, will increase with exercise."

Cartoonist, surrealist and musician, **Peter Blegvad** inhabits one of rock music's finest cul-de-sacs. In a field of jaded songwriters, he stands out as a maverick storyteller and song-philosopher, endowed with a world-weary voice and abundant imaginative powers.

Raised in New York, Blegvad moved with his book-illustrator parents to Britain in 1965. On and off, London would be his base for decades, the place where he would establish himself in what were loosely dubbed avant-garde or radical rock circles. With **Dagmar Krause** and **Anthony Moore**, he formed **SLAPP HAPPY** in 1971; and his three-album legacy with them, and later collaborators **HENRY COW**, communicates a flavour of that scene perfectly.

Blegvad went on to work with **The Lodge** (with former Cow member, **John Greaves**), Anton Fier's collective **THE GOLDEN PALOMINOS**, and **John Zorn** (on the Locus Solus project). His first 'solo' outing, KEW RHONE (1977), co-credited to John Greaves and **Lisa Herman**, was an oddity. Titles such as "Seven Scenes From The Painting 'Exhuming The First American Mastodon' By C. W. Peale" and the more straightforward "Three Tenses Onanism" megaphoned imminent intellectual pretension. But it had wit aplenty and some gorgeous moments.

After returning to Britain in 1982, Blegvad fashioned two further post-Cow creations – THE NAKED SHAKESPEARE (1983), produced by **Andy Partridge** of XTC, and KNIGHTS LIKE THESE (1985) – hit-and-miss cocktails of the complex and the word-choked. Back in New York, Blegvad threw in his lot with the

Golden Palominos collective for two years in 1985. Returning to England again, DOWNTIME (1989) was economy dictated by finances, recorded during unsociable hours or studio cancellations. Its simpler, poetic mood improved his songs immeasurably, and the promise turned to real fulfilment on the masterly KING STRUT & OTHER STORIES (1990). This was as articulate and insightful a collection of songs as a listener could desire or an artist dream up – less arty, better crafted, but as philosophically marbled as before. The songs were really short stories set to music or, as Blegvad put it, 'condensed narrative in rhymes'. The backing, including **Syd Straw** and **Danny Thompson**, had a light country feel that suited Blegvad's work perfectly.

Just when things seemed to be looking up, though, Blegvad found himself without a label again, and preoccupied with an opera project, *Camera*, for Channel Four TV, along with old Slapp Happy associates Krause and Moore. Fortunately, a change in career beckoned. For years Blegvad's doodles, calligraphic squibs, cartoons and cover artwork had brightened releases, and in 1992 he wangled himself a wonderland-ish, referential strip called *Leviathan* in the *Independent On Sunday* newspaper, which was to run for the next seven years.

Cartooning might have become the Sunday job for Blegvad in the 1990s but he continued playing occasional gigs, with **Eugene Chadbourne** and **Loudon Wainwright** among others, and teamed up with old Cow colleagues Chris Cutler and John Greaves for occasional tours as a trio. Greaves and Cutler became collaborators on disc, too. 1995 saw a joint Blegvad-Greaves project, UNEARTHED, spoken-word examinations of the human condition, and in more conventional singer-songwriter mode, Blegvad's own JUST WOKE UP. The latter was less immediate than KING STRUT, but full of extraordinary songs, like a kind of aural equivalent of the *Leviathan*.

As the 1990s drew to a close, Blegvad seemed to be getting critical if not commercial recognition.

Matt Groening sung the praises of the *Leviathan* strip (published as a book by Sort Of/Overlook Press), and the *New York Times*, no less, hailed his songwriting. There was a flurry of discs, too: a Slapp Happy revival with ÇA VA (1998) and two new solo outings, HANGMAN'S HILL (1998) – supported by Greaves and Cutler – and CHOICES UNDER PRESSURE (2001), a collection of acoustic reworks of numbers from his own and Slapp Happy's catalogue.

Since these albums, Blegvad has continued to tour, sporadically, while crafting a series of aural cartoons – 'eartoons' as he calls them – for the late-night Radio Four show, *The Verb*. In 2003 he also co-authored a new CD/book, *Orpheus, The Lowdown*, with Andy Partridge: 'a bit-part play for the fable-minded', as he described it, released on Partridge's low-key Ape label.

Truly, a unique talent.

Peter Blegvad

- **Downtime** (1989; ReR).
  Recorded between 1986 and 1989, DOWNTIME counterposed songs like "Model Of Kindness" and "Not Weak Enough", suffused with sensitivity and fellow feeling, with the brashness of "When The World Was New" with its 'I prefer my senses blurred', highly schooled braggadocio. He was on the right track.

- **King Strut & Other Stories** (1990; Whatever).
  If Jorge Luis Borges had written songs instead of prose, they would sound like these. Epiphanies, short stories, epigrams, quotable quips, and an absolute killer country-tinged composition in "Gold". One to hunt out in the secondhand racks.

- **Choices Under Pressure** (2001; Resurgence).
  A largely-unplugged Best of Blegvad that has charm aplenty, plus stand-out reworkings of "Gold", his country hit-in-waiting, and Slapp Happy's "Haiku".

Peter Blegvad and Andy Partridge

- **Orpheus, The Lowdown** (2003; Ape).
  Blegvad and Partridge is a fortuitous partnership, and this collection of spoken poems on the mythic lyre-ist's return to the 21st century, is a most peculiar delight (available from www.ape.uk.net).

Ken Hunt

BLINK 182

Formed San Diego, California 1992.

Stupidity and the celebration of general moronic behaviour have been accepted as worthy attributes in a rock'n'roll band since the time of Keith Moon. With a distinguished pedigree that links them back to Screaming Lord Sutch, Sir Sidney Vicious and the Dead Boys, **Blink 182** are aristocracy in the pop-punk kingdom; the 182, incidentally, stands for the number of times the word fuck is mentioned in Al Pacino's gangster masterpiece *Scarface*. Blessed from the start with a gift for idiocy, the band can be traced back to the early 90s when **Tom DeLonge** (guitars/vocals) and **Mark Hoppus** (bass/vocals) got together with **Scott Raynor** (drums) in a garage – where else? – to bash out a few punk tunes. The recorded result became FLYSWATTER (1992), a col-

lection of rough demos that gave an indication of where this trio were headed.

In a world where The Offspring and Green Day had yet to score heavily in the charts, they were surplus to market requirements and by the mid-90s they had managed only another couple of releases – BUDDHA (1994) and CHESHIRE CAT (1995) – released on indie labels that were willing to take a chance on three reprobates with questionable taste in rhyming couplets. With recording budgets even lower than the sound quality, there was still no mistaking the chirpy sing-along quality of the tunes, a fact not overlooked by MCA records, who, taking note of the pop-punk genre, threw them some major-label money and bundled them into a studio to cook up their full-strength debut. DUDE RANCH (1997) appeared adorned with cover art that said more about the band than reams of PR, featuring the anatomically detailed rear end of a cartoon bull.

Blink 182 had arrived, though a whole load of gigging and another album would be required before they would enter the super league. In the meantime Scott Raynor decided that he really ought to go back to school and ducked out of the band in 1998 to be replaced by **Travis Barker**, formerly of the Aquabats.

Whether Raynor regrets what he gave up or not isn't really clear but he's definitely the Pete Best of our tale: almost as soon as he'd gone, the band's career suddenly went multi-platinum stratospheric when ENEMA OF THE STATE (1999) hit town; it was recorded in their home town and at the production helm was Jerry Finn who had worked with Clash-alikes Rancid and Green Day. The album's three singles – "What's My Age Again?", "All The Small Things" and "Adam's Song" – took up residence on MTV and in a million or more teenage bedrooms across the globe. "All The Small Things" hit #2 in the UK charts and "What's My Age Again?" was a Top 20 hit.

They were puerile and dumb, they were foul-mouthed and naturally, they were stupendously

successful; they even appeared in crude teen comedy *American Pie*, a genius marketing move which appealed directly to their core audience; to ice their cherry pie they knocked out a swift one – a live album of 20 tracks THE MARK, TOM & TRAVIS SHOW (THE ENEMA STRIKES BACK) (2000).

When you've got so much of the teenage market spending its money on you, it's just foolish not to take things to the limit and Blink 182 decided to mine the business possibilities of their new brand status, launching clothing lines, endorsing skating goods and sticking their logo onto accessories; not only could the kids listen to the music, they could now wear the gear and risk a broken ankle on the skateboard. Such commercial ventures aside, the band were well aware their next magnum opus of cheerfully inane nonsense was due, and they devoted themselves to not thinking very deeply about writing it. They came up with TAKE OFF YOUR PANTS AND JACKET (2001) – just think about that title for a moment and let the punning possibilities sink in… got it? Good – where "The Rock Show" provided yet another chart friendly hit while anyone not completely offended by the liberal swearing and lyrics to "Happy Holidays, You Bastard" could always revel in the delicate acoustic strum-along of "Fuck A Dog". Wonderful.

⊙ **Dude Ranch** (1997; MCA).
This is where the indie albums had been leading. A more polished sound and some stoopid lyrics make 'Dude Ranch' the point at which most people ought to get to know the band.

⊙ **Enema Of The State** (1999; MCA).
This is the one that broke Blink 182 to the world. A multi-platinum-selling album, the production is bright and radio-friendly even if some of the lewd and crude lyrics are not. Filthy fun from beginning to end.

⊙ **Take Off Your Pants And Jacket** (2001; MCA).
If it ain't broke don't fix it – just crank out more of the same. Lots of cheery sing-along punk for kids who want to shock their parents with a little inventive swearing.

Essi Berelian

BLONDIE

Formed New York, 1974; disbanded 1982; re-formed 1998.

I t was in 1973, at New York's Boburn Tavern, that **Deborah Harry** (vocals) met **Chris Stein** (guitar). She was performing as one-third of **The Stilettos**, whose specialty was trashy girl-group tributes, and he was immediately besotted. Chris joined their drifting troupe of backing musicians (including **The New York Dolls**), but soon lured Debbie away to form a new group, recruiting **Fred Smith** (bass) and **Billy O'Connor** (drums), who was quickly replaced by **Clem Burke**. After using various names, they adopted the one that truck drivers shouted at Debbie in the street and, as **Blondie**, the band recorded a demo featuring "Platinum Blonde" and the Shangri-Las' "Out In The Streets".

When Smith left to join **TELEVISION** in 1975, only Burke's optimism prevented the group from folding. His enthusiasm was infectious, and with **Gary Valentine** (bass) and **Jimmy Destri** (keyboards) on board they resumed rehearsing. There was something of a setback when they were blacklisted from CBGBs for complaining after arriving for a booking to find another group playing. However, as Blondie returned to gigging dispiritedly in obscure places, CBGBs was to bring the big break, for it was there that Debbie collared veteran producer **Richard Gottehrer**.

The result was a perfect debut single, "X-Offender" (1976), released on Private Stock, with Debbie's spoken intro echoing Gottehrer's 60s hit production, "My Boyfriend's Back", plus manic drum rolls, a hail of tinny power chords and beach-movie harmonies. With confidence running high, they turned in some dynamic live shows and Private Stock asked Gottehrer to produce an LP. BLONDIE (1977) expanded everything that had been condensed into "X-Offender", while the video of "In The Flesh", starring the miniskirted 'Garbo of Punk', was the first of many to show Debbie and Chris as astute media manipulators.

The group toured the US and flew to the UK to play dates with **Television**. On returning home they signed to Chrysalis and recorded PLASTIC LETTERS (1978) with **Frank Infante** replacing Valentine on bass. Although "(I'm Always Touched By Your) Presence Dear" was one of the LP's highlights, another track, a cover of Randy And The Rainbows' 60s hit "Denis", was a British #2 hit.

After the recruitment of English bassist **Nigel Harrison**, Infante moved to guitar for the gruelling world tour that preceded the magnificent PARALLEL LINES (1978; reissued 1998; EMI). This album spawned four singles, "Hanging On The Telephone", "Picture This", "Sunday Girl" and "Heart Of Glass", the last of which was a #1 all round the world, even in the band's native America. Its follow-up, EAT TO THE BEAT (1979), generated a ground-breaking video album with a promo to accompany each track. The hits continued with "Dreaming", "Union City Blue" and the British #1 "Atomic", and then a one-off collaboration with disco producer **Giorgio Moroder**, "Call Me" (1980),

which returned them to the top of the US charts for six weeks and was featured in the movie *American Gigolo*. A lesser movie released the same year, *Roadie*, featured the band in front of the camera, where they performed Johnny Cash's "Ring Of Fire".

The cover of John Holt's "The Tide Is High" (1980) became Blondie's fifth UK #1 in two years, and was a taster for AUTOAMERICAN (1981), which also contained the early rap crossover single "Rapture". Both were American #1s, but the stand-outs were Chris's edgy filmic intro "Europa" and Destri's "Angels On The Balcony". By now many members of the group were becoming involved in solo projects and the end of Blondie seemed inevitable. However, Debbie Harry's solo album KOO KOO (1981), on which she teamed up with Chic's **Bernard Edwards** and **Nile Rodgers**, was a disastrous seller, and probably caused Blondie's re-formation in early 1982. THE HUNTER (1982) spawned the hit single "Island Of Lost Souls", but was otherwise unmemorable. After a poorly attended tour, the band split.

Clem Burke concentrated on live and session work, most notably with Eurythmics, and Jimmy

Debbie Harry getting back to her roots

Destri released a few solo albums. Chris Stein moved into production, and founded Animal Records, who went on to release several records by The Gun Club, whose frontman, Jeffrey Lee Pierce, had once been president of Blondie's fan club. However, in 1983, serious illness forced Stein to retire from the music business for a couple of years. After a role in David Cronenberg's futuristic horror movie, *Videodrome*, Debbie Harry also hid from the limelight to look after Stein.

By 1986, Stein had more or less recovered, and he helped Deborah Harry (as she was now known) to relaunch her variable solo career. Hits such as "French Kissin' In The USA" (1986) and "I Want That Man" (1989) helped keep her in the public eye.

Harry bubbled away in the classy jazz underworld until a series of press-only and invited-guest-only Blondie gigs took place towards the end of 1998. With wild audience reactions and frantic music press coverage, it was only a matter of time before the band returned to the studio, to surface with the well-received NO EXIT (1999) and a chart-topping single "Maria". The resulting tour was a massive success both in terms of audience reaction and press coverage – Blondie were back in a form that paid tribute to their earlier career and showed them to be equally relevant to the new millennium. Inevitably LIVID (2000), a cracking live set, emerged hard on the heels of the concerts and helped keep the band's profile high while they worked on new material.

⊙ **The Platinum Collection** (1995; Chrysalis).
A rewarding double-CD package, collecting all the hits, a few unnecessary remixes, a couple of obscure B-sides, an early outtake of "Heart Of Glass", plus some refreshing early demos featuring original bassist Fred Smith.

⊙ **No Exit** (1999; Beyond Music).
The return of the Blondie-machine with fourteen well-crafted pop tunes, guest appearances by Coolio, Candy Dulfer and James Chance. Stand-out tracks "Maria" and "No Exit" confirm Blondie's place in pop's pantheon.

Tony Thewlis

BLOOD, SWEAT & TEARS

Formed New York, 1967; disbanded 1980;
re-formed briefly in 1988.

Brooklyn-born **Al Kooper**'s place in the 60s Rock And Roll Hall of Fame is guaranteed for his part in a five-minute song generally regarded as one of the best singles of all time – Bob Dylan's "Like A Rolling Stone". However, the quasi-legendary status he gained for playing the electric organ on this record has served to obscure his own work, beginning with the ground-breaking white blues-rock outfit, **The Blues Project**, founded with singer/guitarist **Steve Katz**.

It was from the ashes of this short-lived but celebrated band that **Blood, Sweat & Tears** emerged, Kooper and Katz and drummer **Bobby Colomby** forming the nucleus of a group prone to frequent changes of its eight-to-nine-man line-up. Indeed, Kooper himself split in 1968 to record the huge-selling SUPER SESSION with another mid-60s Dylan stalwart, guitarist **Mike Bloomfield**, and **Stephen Stills**.

Kooper's contribution to the original Blood, Sweat & Tears sound is evident on their debut, CHILD IS FATHER TO THE MAN (1968). Untypical of the rock and jazz fusion with which they are normally associated, this showcased Kooper's musical roots in a hybrid of heavily orchestrated pop tunes, Motown, blues and jazz – an unwieldy mix that gave way to musical bombast.

David Clayton-Thomas took over vocal duties for BLOOD, SWEAT & TEARS (1969), a better outing by far, which spawned a trio of million-selling singles in quick succession: covers of Brenda Holloway's "You Made Me So Very Happy" and Laura Nyro's "And When I Die", and Clayton-Thomas's self-penned "Spinning Wheel". Although these were fine exercises in AM rock, they signalled an end to Blood, Sweat & Tears' self-conscious 'civilizing mission' amongst rock's excesses. Indeed, later albums were little more than a vehicle for Clayton-Thomas's overambitious vocal forays, rather than any ground-breaking musical experiments.

The third album, BLOOD, SWEAT AND TEARS 3 (1970), saw the rock-jazz fusion take on classical baggage, and all but their most devoted 'serious' rock critics, and not a small part of their former commercial following, beginning to fall away. Clayton-Thomas quit in 1972 to pursue an ill-fated solo career, his place filled by a series of vocalists – **Bobby Doyle**, **Jerry Fisher** and **Jerry Lecroix** – before a rather tired reunion on NEW CITY (1975).

From a self-declared musical revolution, Blood, Sweat & Tears had evolved into the preferred choice of more cabaret-orientated audiences – a fate confirmed by their nostalgic 1988 canter through the back catalogue.

⊙ **Child Is Father To The Man** (1968; CBS).
When the fusion project showed promise and Al Kooper's pop orchestrations arguably took their Beatles inspiration a step further.

⊙ **Blood, Sweat & Tears** (1969; CBS).
Million-selling, Grammy-winning collection that lives up to the band's reputation as one of the original rock-jazz fusion groups.

⊙ **What Goes Up!** (1995; Columbia).
A budget 32-track compilation featuring the memorable chart-toppers, the better tracks from their debut album, and a few more forgettable numbers culled from later albums.

Neil Partrick

THE BLUE AEROPLANES

Formed Bristol, England, 1984;
disbanded in the late 90s.

Easy to like but harder to love, **The Blue Aeroplanes** ploughed an idiosyncratic furrow after their conception in early 80s Bristol. They aimed to marry taut, angular guitar pop to **Gerard Langley**'s spoken-word poetry and to channel the result through performance art, adding backing tapes, slides and a dancer to their live shows. Although clearly Langley's creation, the band maintained a loose, collective spirit throughout its existence, with at least thirty people helping out over the years that followed their debut album, BOP ART (1984).

BOP ART, and its two successors, TOLERANCE (1986) and SPITTING OUT MIRACLES (1987), created the blueprint for The Blue Aeroplanes sound, a frenetic mélange of hurdy-gurdy, banjo, French horn, backing tapes, mandolin, dulcimers and surging guitar solos underpinning Langley's wordy monologues. While this heady brew was always capable of degenerating into art-school preciousness, by MIRACLES it had coalesced into an innovative proposition, embracing drone and feedback, and gorgeous pop music, in equal measure. In addition to Langley, the mainstays of the line-up during this period were **Nick Jacobs** (guitar), **Dave Chapman** (multi-instrumentalist), **John Langley** (drums), **Wojtek Dmochowski** (dancer), **Richard Bell** (guitar/piano) and **Ruth Cochrane** (bass/mandolin). However, MIRACLES had a total of sixteen collaborators, including an emerging **MICHELLE SHOCKED**.

The band secured a major label deal with Ensign in 1989, and proceeded to hone their eccentric appeal. After a UK support slot with R.E.M., two near hits, "And Stones" and "Jacket Hangs", tapped into the prevailing dance-rock sensibility. The following album, SWAGGER (1990), was enhanced by the guitar playing and songwriting of **Angelo Bruschini** and **Rodney Allen**, whose influence proved decisive in sharpening the sound into 'total poetic guitar bejewelled rock'n'roll folk art let's dance godstar unalloyed alchoholic genius', as the typically understated *Select* magazine would come to describe it. SWAGGER also benefited from more conventional lead vocals (including a guest spot from **Michael Stipe**), providing a respite from Langley's sometimes overwrought wordplay.

BEATSONGS, which emerged in 1991, invoked psychedelia and power pop and combined more commercial material with wired guitar dynamics. It was the band's most compelling effort to date, but lacked a hit single and foundered commercially.

1994's LIFE MODEL was a transitional album after a move to Beggars Banquet and the loss of key personnel, but a ten-year anniversary tour reunited the band with BOP ART-era colleagues, and although unfocused, 1995's ROUGH MUSIC offered glimpses of the band's vibrant pop sensibility and hints of possible new directions on the Andy Sheppard sax-driven experiment "Secret Destination".

These possibilities were never really explored. Stylistically, HUH! (1997) mainly reprised BEATSONGS and SWAGGER. A live album, FRUIT (1996) culled performances from a number of periods and sounded disjointed and cobbled together. It effectively acted

as an epitaph for an awkward band whose time never really came. They have now split up.

⦿ **Beatsongs** (1991; Ensign).
This neglected gem is the breakthrough album that wasn't to be – perfect pop music made at exactly the wrong time.

⦿ **Friendloverplane 1** (1988; Fire); **Friendloverplane 2** (1992; Ensign).
These two compilations of singles, B-sides and alternative takes offer a good overview of the band.

Nig Hodgkins

THE BLUE NILE

Formed Glasgow, Scotland, 1981.

"Wouldn't you say there's a strong case for putting out less material, not more?" Paul Buchanan

The Blue Nile have released few albums in the space of a career that has spanned over two decades. Not prolific, for sure, but not indulgent, either. This is a band who value quality songwriting and production, who are sought out for collaborative help by the likes of **Robbie Robertson** and **Michael McDonald**, and who have been covered by artists as diverse as Annie Lennox and Isaac Hayes, Rickie Lee Jones and Rod Stewart. Clearly they do something right.

The band began at Glasgow University as students **Paul Buchanan** (vocals), **Robert Bell** (bass) and **Paul Joseph Moore** (keyboards) self-financing a few recording sessions. An awed studio engineer passed their demo to RSO Records, who immediately offered them a deal, and released a promising single, "I Love This Life", in 1981. RSO, in a rather cruel twist of fate, collapsed just two weeks later, and both single and band disappeared from view. But good fortune struck a second time, when Linn, a hi-fi manufacturer, was given some Blue Nile demos to use as demonstration tapes for their products. They were so impressed they signed the band – only their second act – to their fledgling Linn Records.

A new single, "Stay", was released in early 1984, followed by A WALK ACROSS THE ROOFTOPS, the band's debut album. Its gorgeous ballads and sparse, delicate arrangements met with huge critical praise, and it reached #80 in the UK charts without so much as a tour or TV appearance. Singles chart success proved elusive, but the band seemed set to become major players on both sides of the Atlantic.

However, the group's insistence on controlling all aspects of their career delayed a return to the studio. When the band finally got in front of the mikes, writers' block struck and below-par songs were reputedly abandoned by the dozen.

Still, they eventually cracked it, and HATS, released in October 1989, proved to be the masterpiece everyone was waiting for. Paul Buchanan's uncanny ability to inject heartfelt meaning into well-worn phrases such as 'I love you' attracted rapturous praise. The album reached #12 in the UK and the following year the band set out for a press tour of America, supported by a new version of "Easter Parade" recorded with Rickie Lee Jones, with whom they appeared on stage in New York. Having overcome their fear of playing live, they returned home for a sell-out British tour, and with the help of a full backing band their polished sound was reproduced perfectly.

Typically, the band then disappeared from view, apart from fleeting appearances on Robbie Robertson and Annie Lennox records, and the odd mention on the gossip pages of Buchanan's affair with Rosanna Arquette. Finally, in 1996, Warners released the band's third album, PEACE AT LAST. It proved to be another triumph of musicianship and songwriting over music industry fashions and styles. Buchanan ranged through his familiar lyrical themes – family, religion, sex, music – with consummate skill, and the band matched him with meticulous arrangements. Despite a seemingly tortuous recording process, including stops in Dublin, Paris, Venice, Copenhagen and LA, and employment of brass and gospel choirs, the record maintained a breezy economy. 'Inexpressibly lovely', concluded Q, evoking Raymond Carver in the lyrics, Sinatra and Gabriel in the singing, and giving it the full five stars.

The one question that remains is, 'When next?'.

⊙ A Walk Across The Rooftops (1984; Linn).
Lauded as 'the best debut album of the last five years' by the *Glasgow Herald*. With luscious synths, funky bass and Paul Buchanan's beautiful lyrics of everyday romance, it's not difficult to see why.

⊙ Hats (1989; Linn).
A more polished affair but with no loss of passion. Five years in the making, virtually every song on this album is a piece of pop perfection.

⊙ Peace At Last (1996; Warners).
"At Last", indeed. The band prove themselves yet again on a stunning set, whose simplicity and control belied the long wait.

Joanna Severs

BLUE OYSTER CULT

Formed New York, 1969.

The roots of that strange, outlaw motorcycle band, **Blue Oyster Cult**, can be traced back to the smoky wisps of psychedelia, when they were known as **Soft White Underbelly**, **Oaxaca**, and eventually **The Stalk Forest Group**. The brainchild of rock journalist **Sandy Pearlman**, they were signed to Elektra, a deal that only yielded one single, the bizarrely compelling "Arthur Comics". Shortly afterwards, The Stalk Forest Group's lead singer, **Les Bronstein**, was replaced by **Eric Bloom**. He completed a line-up that also consisted of **Donald 'Buck Dharma' Roeser** (guitar/vocals), **Allan Lanier** (keyboards/guitar), **Joe Bouchard** (bass/vocals) and **Albert Bouchard** (drums).

Taking their new name from a Pearlman lyric, the Blue Oyster Cult earned a reputation as a fiercely exciting rock band, propelled by Roeser's raw chord dynamics, Pearlman's sinister lyrics, and an apocalyptic stage presence based on occult and Hell's Angels imagery. Pearlman moulded the sound and image of the band to evoke the spirit of Altamont. However, while The Stones dabbled with jet-set debauchery and satanic posturing, the Blue Oyster Cult seemed like the real thing: grizzly hedonists pursuing dark thrills and meddling in the black arts with psychotic glee.

The first-time album, BLUE OYSTER CULT (1972), remains a landmark of early 70s rock. The opening chords of "Transmaniacon M.C." captured the essence of the band – tight, loud, inventive heavy metal. On the other hand, "She's As Beautiful As A Foot", with its floating guitar solo, harked back to dreamy, off-centre psychedelia, illustrating the band's firm grasp of rock's lighter shadings. The follow-up – TYRANNY AND MUTATION (1973) – was just as good, mining the same rich veins of emotional bleakness and driving hedonism on tracks such as "O.D.'d On Life Itself".

Around the time of their third album, 1974's SECRET TREATIES, the band refuted allegations of neo-Nazism, their lyrics seeming too cryptic to have any simple political significance. Propelled by the Patti Smith song "Career Of Evil", the album outsold their previous efforts in the US.

The Cult's early albums retained a discipline, fluidity and clarity uncommon in the music of the period. Concert shows, in contrast, were more excessive, and overindulgent soloing characterized the group's first live album, ON YOUR FEET OR ON YOUR KNEES (1975). Walking the thin line between genuine force and empty bombast, the Blue Oyster Cult faltered for the first time, although sales remained high.

The leather-clad, S&M shock of the band was gradually fading and a more radio-friendly form of melodic hard rock provided them with their most successful album, AGENTS OF FORTUNE (1976). The odd malignant biker anthem apart, it offered a lighter worldview than previous efforts, with the set's "Don't Fear The Reaper" cut proving to be the band's defining moment. With two tracks co-written by Patti Smith, the album belatedly broke the band in the UK.

By the end of the 70s, however, the group had begun a slow limp towards self-parody, sadly evidenced by SPECTRES (1978). "R.U. Ready To Rock" was as dumb and obvious as their previous efforts had been cryptic. Subsequent albums, despite the occasional stand-out track – such as "Death Valley Nights" from SPECTRES, or "Joan Crawford" from FIRE OF UNKNOWN ORIGIN (1981) – seemed content to pander to the obsessions of their fan base. CLUB NINJA (1985) represented a nadir of sorts.

However, the band's next album, IMAGINOS (1988), was probably their strongest work of the decade. An ambitious exercise in multi-layered guitars (including Robbie Krieger) and trademark hooks, it was bolstered by bizarre lyrics about alien cults and sundry conspiracy theories. They surfaced again in 1992, scoring the movie Bad Channels, and, most recently, in 1994, soundtracked Stephen King's chiller, *The Stand*. On this last outing, Chuck Burgi joined on drums.

HEAVEN FORBID (1998) – BOC's first studio album since 1986 – apparently finds them in somewhat reduced circumstances: a new (small) label, less-than-pristine cover art, minimal promotion and no hype. The music, on the other hand, demonstrated a return to the sleek, charged hard rock and crazed, sinister lyrics of the band's heyday. Only Bloom, Dharma and Allan Lanier remained from those glory days, but the album resonated with the riff-laden, stripped-down boogie-evil. Their sales and profile remained low – CULTOSAURUS ERECTUS (1999), CURSE OF THE HIDDEN MIRROR (2001) and A LONG DAY'S NIGHT LIVE (2002) making few ripples – but with the band's edge of cool outsiderdom now fully resurrected, the time is ripe for a fully fledged re-emergence of one of the truly great heavy metal bands. If metal compels through brute force, then this band changed the equation, and at their best (1972–76) they brought a sharp, if chilling, intelligence to a generally unsophisticated genre.

⊙ **Blue Oyster Cult** (1972; CBS; remastered and reissued 2001).
Heavy metal for people who hate heavy metal: sleek, primal rock'n'roll music, filtered through unsettling, if thrilling, images of Altamont, drug dealing and murder.

⊙ **Tyranny And Mutation** (1973; CBS; remastered and reissued 2001).
More of a sonic bombardment than its predecessor, but a more cohesive proposition. Holding up a genre that was tailing off back towards the self-parody of Alice Cooper, this album succeeds through sheer conviction.

⊙ **Workshop Of The Telescopes** (1995; Sony).
This is the definitive compilation, with great sleeve notes and photos, and rare material from the classic 1971–73 period.

Nig Hodgkins

BLUES MAGOOS

Formed New York City, 1964; disbanded 1969.

In the late 60s, American bands seemed unable to mine the frenetic veins of psychedelia in the manner of their British counterparts. Not so the **Blues Magoos**. Though not as consistent as Syd Barrett's Pink Floyd, the Blues Magoos turned out two classic songs – one a pop-psych nugget and the other a galactic gem even the aforementioned quartet would have been proud of.

Consisting of **Ralph Scala** (keyboards/vocals), **Emil 'Peppy' Theilhelm** (guitar), **Ronnie Gilbert** (bass), **Michael Esposito** (guitar) and **Geoff Daking** (drums), the Blues Magoos burst out of the Greenwich Village scene in 1966, signed to Mercury, and recorded PSYCHEDELIC LOLLIPOP during the waning months of 1966, beating the Floyd to vinyl by a full six months.

The album contained a Day-Glo potpourri of songs, both originals and covers. The Blues Magoos' version of J. D. Loudermilk's Southern poverty anthem, "Tobacco Road", was anything but Mississippi blues. Rather it was Interstellar Delta. Using the same thudding arrangement as The Nashville Teens (who'd taken the song to the top reaches of the charts in 1964), the Blues Magoos went one step further: 'We added a freakout section in the middle,' said Daking in probably the understatement of the decade. When the band came to the bridge, Esposito began hitting his guitar with an iron bar, employing tape-delay effects and other production techniques to achieve lysergic discord.

The song became the warhorse of the band's visually stunning live set (they wore electric stage uniforms that actually lit up). "Tobacco Road" was slated to be their first 45, but, at more than four and a half minutes, it was deemed too long and Mercury released "We Ain't Got Nothing Yet" instead. The song stayed in the charts for fourteen weeks, peaking at #5 in the American charts in early January 1967. With a wonderful guitar hook, "We Ain't Got Nothing Yet" was an infectious, hallucinatory pop song that propelled the album to number 21.

The Blues Magoos sophomore effort, ELECTRIC COMIC BOOK, was released in March 1967. While it did not fare as well as their first LP (peaking at #74), the album was as powerful a psychedelic statement as the debut. The experimental sound effects of "Rush Hour" – feedback, squealing guitars and disembodied vocals – left the listener with a nauseous feeling of being caught in an aural traffic jam. Another highlight was "One By One", a more traditional pop song. The album packaging itself was a psychedelic masterpiece. Aside from the garish cover, it contained a comic-book insert advertising fan-club information, iron-ons and lava lamps. However, when the next single, a freakout version of Them's "Gloria", also failed to perform well, it seemed the balloon had burst.

With flower power waning, the Blues Magoos returned to basics. Hence the subdued sepia-tone album cover of their third and final effort, BASIC BLUES MAGOOS (1968). While the album contained some of their most noteworthy songs, the band was fracturing internally. They moved to the West Coast, but by the middle of 1969, the band was no more.

The Blues Magoos faded into the mist of psychedelia apart from lighting up Lenny Kaye's famed double album NUGGETS in 1972 with the shattering "Tobacco Road". Geoff Daking is still involved in the music business. Michael Esposito runs a bicycle repair shop in Upstate New York, plays bass with **Older Than Dirt** and is surprised that his guitar playing evokes respect so many years after the fact. 'Boy, it's something else, isn't it? Occasionally, somebody tracks me down and hands me an album to autograph,' he said, bemused.

One of those who recently tracked down the Blues Magoos was **Jon Weiss**, leader of 80s garage-revivalists the Vipers. Weiss organizes the world's premier garage extravaganza, Cavestomp, in New York City every year. For the 2000 show Weiss brought four of the five original Magoos together for the first time in three decades.

The reunion was highly anticipated. They churned out an endearingly sloppy set and Theilhelm even displayed his original electric suit on stage, though he could no longer fit into it. The crowd was charmed, demanding an encore, which none of the bands were supposed to get. They returned and stomped through the Psychedelic Nation's anthem, "Tobacco Road". As he left the Cavestomp stage, Esposito handed his guitar-battering metal bar to a fan and said he would never play again. Is this indeed it for the Blues Magoos?

⊙ **Kaleidescopic Compendium** (1992; Polygram). This compilation includes every important Blues Magoos song as well as some minor classics. Of course, "Tobacco Road" and "We Ain't Got Nothing Yet" highlight the set. An anaemic cover of the Move's "I Can Hear The Grass Grow" also appears on the CD.

⊙ **Psychedelic Lollipop/Electric Comic Book** (1999; Collectable Records).
This unification of the Blues Magoos debut and sophomore albums is the CD to get. Once again, "Tobacco Road" and "We Ain't Got Nothing Yet" are the apex of the band's recorded legacy. A slower-tempoed version of "One By One" is also included, while Esposito's personal favorite, the disconcerting "Rush Hour", rounds off this most satisfying CD.

Will Bedard

The Bluetones: suit you sir

THE BLUETONES

Formed Hounslow, England, 1994.

"We know our strengths. We're a two-car garage band." Mark Morris

Back in the mid-Nineties, before they had even committed a note to disc, **The Bluetones** had to deal with the pressure of being touted by the British music press as the 'next big thing'. The praise, and the comparisons, were unanimous: not only were they expected to shape the future of British indie music, they were also being hailed as the 'next Stone Roses', whilst being touted as a viable rival to both Oasis and Blur in the newly vitalized Britpop stakes.

The group's strengths lay in **Adam Devlin**'s jangly guitar and the fey, whimsical vocals of **Mark Morris**; completing the line-up was Mark's brother **Scott** on bass, and drummer **Ed Chester**.

Their first two singles, "Are You Blue Or Are You Blind?" and "Bluetonic", boasted an understated swagger and some wonderful throwaway lines. Wisely, the band resisted the temptation to rush-release a debut LP on the strength of this success, instead opting to introduce new songs live, via a series of low-key gigs. In January 1996 they released

their third single, "Slight Return", which smashed into the UK charts at #2. A stop-start affair with a glorious shuffling beat, it heralded their debut LP a month later. The collection was entitled EXPECTING TO FLY (1996), and it showed the band to be a serious proposition. There were echoes in the music of The Who's guitar riffery and The Stone Roses' effortless charm; there were even traces of folk and country, while the songwriting recalled the likes of Squeeze's Difford and Tillbrook. It was catchy as hell, despite its rather maudlin tone, and propelled The Bluetones straight to #1 in the UK album charts.

Apart from touring – which occupied most of the next year – little was heard of the band as they prepared for the second album release. RETURN TO THE LAST CHANCE SALOON (1998) took the cowboy imagery a bit far, lurching into sub-country'n'western twang territory at times and failing comprehensively to set the world on fire. The dust settled after their stormy ride into town, and little was heard of the group until the release of a third album in 2000.

SCIENCE AND NATURE saw the band pull out all the stops, incorporating everything from mariachi horn-stabs to reggae grooves. Sadly, though overflowing with ideas and quirks, the set was overblown and lacked clout.

The Bluetones have had the occasional moment

of glory and have even been around long enough to warrant a 'greatest hits' package – THE SINGLES (2002) – but when all is said and done, they're now just four British hombres, with nothing much to say, despite a pretty way of saying it.

⊙ Expecting To Fly (1996; Superior Quality Recordings).
A fine debut and altogether more introspective than had been hinted at by their early singles (two of which, "Bluetonic" and the smash hit "Slight Return", are included).

⊙ The Singles (2002; Superior Quality Recordings).
A motley collection of Britpop ditties that occasionally lives up to the appeal of the appetizing cover art.

Mark Hooper

BLUR

Formed Colchester, England, 1989.

Blur were formed by **Damon Albarn** (vocals), an art-school dropout working as a record studio tea-boy so that he could use the studio out of hours. He joined up with **Alex James** (bass), **Graham Coxon** (guitar) and **Dave Rowntree** (drums), and the band, talented beyond their station, were within a couple of years spearheading the Britpop scene – a collection of credible and accessible acts whose popularity did much to silence the predictions of the death of rock at the hands of video games and dance music.

The band played a few concerts as **Seymour**, and cult artist **Damien Hirst** pronounced them 'the best British band since The Beatles'. A demo tape then led to their signing to EMI subsidiary Food Records, although it was stipulated that they change their name. Their 1990 debut single "She's So High" graced the UK Top 50, revealing a band in thrall to the 'baggy' scene, although its backwards guitar and fey vocals had equally strong suggestions of Syd Barrett-era Pink Floyd. It was an enjoyable if slight record, but the boys were photogenic, funny and lippy, and soon became British music press darlings. Their formulaic indie/dance single, "There's No Other Way", duly entered the UK Top 10 as did their debut album LEISURE (1991). Lolloping baggy beats and distorted guitars made this very much a product of its time. Featuring some terrible lyrics, it is not fondly remembered by the band.

In contrast, 1992's excellent single "Popscene" flopped. Its punky, energetic and brass-propelled pop sound was at odds with the prevalent morose mood of grunge, whose popularity with the fickle music press left Blur looking like yesterday's men. Fruitless American tours led to group ructions, and when they returned home, drained and dispirited, they discovered that management wrangles had virtually bankrupted them. Worse still, their concert performances were poor and audiences stayed away. At a charity concert in London they played while drunk and rounded off the evening by accidentally injuring a security guard, which nearly caused Food to fire them.

Blur's 'last chance' was MODERN LIFE IS RUBBISH (1993), finally released after their American label had suggested that they rerecord it with Nirvana producer **Butch Vig**. Food had already rejected an entire album in 1992, feeling the new material lacked a hit single. Albarn's response was the single "For Tomorrow", a superbly catchy XTC-influenced song and minor hit.

Both album and single were cautiously reviewed, with praise for Albarn's vastly improved lyrics tempered by criticism of what some took to be a contrived new mod-influenced look and classically English sound – its roots this time firmly embedded in vintage Kinks. The album and subsequent singles performed disappointingly, although they atoned for previous live sins with some sterling performances, which recovered a fan base.

Within the year the band returned with a new single, "Girls And Boys", featuring an arcane synthesized pulse and an irrepressibly catchy chorus. A calculated attempt at a hit, it went UK Top 5 in March and was a radio mainstay throughout the summer. It also opened their widely acclaimed third album, PARKLIFE (1994), which topped the UK charts, sold two million copies worldwide and spawned three more hits. Music industry acceptance was confirmed with a record four *BPI* awards in February 1995 – best single, album, video and group.

By now, Blur's appeal stretched from the pre-teens to the over-thirties, hip in both teen and style-magazine circles. Unlikely pin-ups, they even appeared in a tabloid newspaper comic strip. Although their Englishness was thought to have hindered the album's performance in America, its 150,000 sales there were still nearly three times its predecessor's global total. Meanwhile, the band's growing domestic appeal was demonstrated in the autumn of 1994 when they played to 8000 people at London's Alexandra Palace. By the following summer they were playing to 20,000 at London's Mile End Stadium, prior to the release of their first UK #1 single, "Country House".

"Country House" was released in Britain amid a glare of publicity, as rival Britpop kings Oasis also issued a new single on the same day. The battle for the top of the charts centred on a clash between the northern working-class Oasis and the middle-class art-school Londoners Blur. In the event, "Country House" triumphed, helped by a video directed by old friend Damien Hirst, while THE GREAT ESCAPE (1995) topped the album chart soon afterwards. It consolidated the band's fascination with the heritage of British pop, encompassing punk, two-tone and psychedelia, and again produced a trio of UK #1 singles – Damon having become firmly established as the country's leading teen-dream pop star. Basking in his new fame, Damon got to sing with his hero, **Ray Davies**, duetting on an uncanny echo on The Kinks' classic "Waterloo Sunset" for TV show *The White Room*. And this was clearly a two-way tribute, which must have given the Blur songwriter immense satisfaction.

Blur moved away from pop superstardom towards, well, creative endeavour. THE GREAT ESCAPE was a little too dark for many of their younger fans, some of whom deserted for the more straightforward pleasures of rivals Oasis, while Brit-rock critics indulged in a bit of traditional backlashing at the band's expense.

The group pushed their repositioning to the limit with their fifth album, BLUR (1997), seen by many as a retreat to their early days of indie obscurity. Recorded in Iceland (always a good start for a 'serious' album), Damon and Graham Coxon put together a bleak, punkish, guitar-driven collection that made "Parklife" sound like a distant memory of a sunny day by the sea. With more than a tip of the hat to Pavement and the rest of the American 'lo-fi' underground, Albarn closed the door on pop with titles such as "Song 2", "On Your Own" and "Death Of A Party". 1998 saw the instantly collectable Japan-only remix album BUZZIN' AND DRONIN' released – now also available in the UK – and also Coxon's solo debut THE SKY IS TOO HIGH (1998) on his own Transcopic label. This marvellous solo effort was a darkly lo-fi amalgamation of acoustic Blur stylings and introspective cuts that nodded to the likes of Sebadoh and Daniel Johnston

Meanwhile, Damon worked on 'Granada A La Luna', a project composing music to accompany the work of Spanish poet Federico Garcia Lorca, before shepherding the boys once more into the studio for 13 (1999). Opening with the catchy, end-of-a-long-day single "Tender" (with vocal help from the **London Community Gospel Choir**) and produced by **William Orbit**, the album was characterized by a looser, ragged-at-the-edges feel; less poppy than PARKLIFE, less self-indulgently indie than BLUR. Other stand-out tracks include the frankly loopy "Bugman" (with its knowing tip of the hat to Bowie's "Suffragette City") and "Coffee & TV". Ultimately an intriguing, arty, satisfying album with plenty to offer – lots of noise, melodies, inter-

esting lyrics and one of Graham's paintings on the cover.

In 2000 Damon turned his attention to soundtrack composition, contributing to the movie score of *Ordinary Decent Criminal*; the year ended with a new Blur single "Music Is My Radar" and a sumptuously packaged greatest hits collection, BLUR: THE BEST OF. Meanwhile, Coxon released another solo album, the hardcore tinged GOLDEN D (2000), which was followed by CROW SIT ON BLOOD TREE (2001) and THE KISS OF MORNING (2002).

Insatiable as ever when it comes to new ideas, Damon hooked up with beat-master **Dan "The Automator" Nakamura** and Tank Girl cartoonist **Jamie Hewlett** to form **GORILLAZ**: a pleasant, and ongoing, diversion into hip-hop, dub and other left-field beats. And then he was off again, this time to Mali. Hooking up with local musicians, Damon produced the MALI MUSIC album (2002), hailed by many as his finest work.

But all was not well in the Blur ranks. Coxon and Albarn were increasingly at each other's throats, as revealed by Fat Boy Slim, who had been producing the new album. Coxon eventually jumped ship prior to the 2003-released "Out Of Time" single and its accompanying, disappointing THINK TANK album.

- ⦿ **Parklife** (1994; Food, reissued 1998; Food).
  Marvellous genre-straddling epic, ambitious and diverse yet entirely of a piece: laddish laughs with guest vocalist Phil Daniels on the beery title track, twitchy New Wave thrashes, cheesy disco, Gallic crooning, and finally a tour of the British Isles via the BBC Radio 4 shipping forecast and an evening down the pub on "This Is A Low". Essential.

- ⦿ **The Great Escape** (1995; Food; reissued 1998; Food).
  Staggeringly ambitious and not a little misunderstood: catchy pop tunes drew attention away from the album's bleak heart, and an overreliance on comic caricatures diluted its impact. But, at its best, it demonstrated that the band were in a different league to their Britpop rivals.

- ⦿ **Live At The Budokan** (1996; Food).
  Another album in the great tradition of live recordings in front of an adoring Japanese crowd, this documents the lads at the height of their powers, brushing aside the manufactured war with Oasis, at the time still raging at home, to completely ensnare the entire Budokan audience.

- ⦿ **Blur** (1997; Food).
  Less self-conscious than earlier albums, this grungy set hailed a newly democratized Blur sound.

Jonathan Holden

BMX BANDITS

Formed Bellshill, Scotland, 1986.

Though they were leading lights of the much-derided 'C86' or 'anorak' movement of the mid-80s, **Duglas Stewart**'s **BMX Bandits** have been classic underachievers. While ex-members of his band have gained critical and commercial success, BMX Bandits have consistently evaded the public's taste.

The band released their first single, "E102", in May 1986 on **Stephen Pastel**'s 53rd And 3rd label, with Stewart's camp Glaswegian vocals supported by **Sean**

Dickson (bass), **Jim McCulloch** (guitar), **Willie McArdle** (drums) and **Billy Wood** (backing vocals). This charming debut was followed up by a second single, "What A Wonderful World", by which time McArdle and Dickson had dropped out to be replaced by **Joe McAlinden** (bass) and **Francis McDonald** (drums). Dickson formed his own band, **THE SOUP DRAGONS**, whose success rapidly eclipsed that of his former group.

By the time the BMX Bandits released their debut album, the ironically titled C86 (1989), McCulloch had joined Dickson as a Soup Dragon, while Stewart and McDonald were joined by **Gordon Keen** (guitar) and **Norman Blake** (guitar) as well as the itinerant McAlinden. The rough production of this home-made LP could not obscure the quality of the band's Caledonian take on Jonathan Richman and the Lovin' Spoonful. C86 was followed by a live album, TOTALLY GROOVY LIVE EXPERIENCE (1989), which showed the band's self-deprecating humour, most notably in a bizarre version of the Dead Kennedys' "Nazi Punks Fuck Off", which has to be heard to be believed.

Another two-year hiatus followed, during which time Norman Blake's own band **TEENAGE FAN-CLUB** hit the big time, but he was still on hand to help in the production of STAR WARS (1991), along with guest guitarist and ex-Vaseline **Eugene Kelly** (guitar). The relative stability of the line-up made this set better thought out than its predecessors, and the band were noticeably outgrowing their C86 affiliations. A single, "Serious Drugs", won rave reviews, but, though it was released twice and supported by a tour with Shonen Knife, it failed to hit the Top 40. A disappointing mini-album, GORDON KEEN AND HIS BMX BANDITS (1992), followed before Kelly and Keen decamped to form **Eugenius**, who gained some notoriety by supporting Nirvana on a British tour.

The band that was signed to Creation Records for LIFE GOES ON (1993) was once more restructured to include **John Hogerty** (guitar) and Francis's brother **Finlay McDonald** (bass), with Blake, McAlinden and Jim McCulloch appearing as guests. A larger recording budget made this a much more listenable album, but there was no obscuring the downbeat feel of the finished product. However, the following record, GETTIN' DIRTY (1995), built upon its sonic improvements, and taken together with the follow-up, also on Creation, 1996's THEME PARK demonstrated the band's most mature and rewarding work. Ex-Soup Dragon **Sushil Dade** (bass) joined, allowing Finlay McDonald to play piano, and with the use of a string section the group's sound was embellished to almost Beach Boys dimensions. The songs maintained Stewart's twee style, whilst the lush backing confirmed what many had known all along: these boys have good record collections. This was reiterated by both 1997's HIDDEN AGENDA AT THE 13TH NOTE (a collaboration with **Kim Fowley**) and 1999's 53RD AND 3RD YEARS collection. Indeed,

you can summarize the Bellshill sound by way of a tribute, a heartfelt reference to what came before – the BMX Bandits and all their affiliated groups show a passion for music lacking in many of their more fashionable contemporaries.

⊙ **Gettin' Dirty** (1995; Creation).
Goodbye Bellshill, Hello LA! You can hear Brian Wilson, the Lovin' Spoonful, The Byrds, and even Burt Bacharach here, but most of all it's the BMX Bandits at their best. Proof that you have to have good records to make good records.

⊙ **53rd And 3rd Years** (1999; Avalanche).
A great collection of all those hard to find singles from the group's early days on 53rd And 3rd records.

James Wirth

BOARDS OF CANADA

Formed Scotland, around 1980.

"We always assume that the listener is the most intelligent person imaginable"

Michael Sandison and **Marcus Eoin** comprise the inscrutable duo **Boards Of Canada**. And as they rarely offer interviews, let alone explanations of their sound, it says a lot that their music has so profoundly struck a chord with so many listeners with broad-ranging tastes. Their comforting mix of dreamy electronics, hip-hop rhythms and Sesame Street-styled oddness has enough groove and universal charm to entrance twenty-somethings and thirty-somethings, indie-somethings and techno-somethings alike. They proffer contorted electronic memories of a 70s childhood, conjuring a Super-8 landscape of scorched grass, declarations of playground love and drowsy sibling squabbles in the back of the car.

During the 70s, as children, Michael and Marcus accrued their musical skills while moving between Scotland, the south of England and Alberta, Canada. By 1980, somewhere on the northeast coast of Scotland, an early incarnation of the band came into fruition, though Eoin was at the time absent. By 1986 Marcus had joined the troop playing bass; they gigged around their home town playing hard abstract electronic sets in support of an unlikely selection of glam-rock covers bands.

Inspired by, and eventually naming themselves in reference to the documentaries of the National Film Board of Canada, the fluid collective broadened its remit to include photographic projects and film-making. The works were cryptic and wistful, featuring experimental soundtracks of found sound and sampled TV excerpts. Though many had been involved over the years, by 1989 Boards Of Canada had reduced to a three-piece – Mike, Marcus and **Chris**. They built their own studio, initiated various 'happenings' and other audio/visual projects, and were soon the driving force of the Hexagon Sun collective, hosting 'Redmoon' nights in a ruin close to their studio. In 1995 the comrades' studio in the Pentland Hills was christened 'Hexagon Sun'.

Though several self-financed EPs and albums had already emerged within the confines of the collective (courtesy of the band's own Music70 imprint), the first to reach the outside world was a lo-fi selection of haunting melodies underpinned by stark rhythms entitled TWOISM (reissued by Warp in 2002). In 1996 a copy of TWOISM found its way to SKam records in Manchester; within a matter of hours Autechre's **Sean Booth** made contact with the Boards Of Canada, by then a two-piece: Mike and Marcus. December 1996 witnessed the pair's first release for SKam: the HI SCORES EP, a stunning six-track collection of effervescent beats nestling in vast clouds of serene melody.

The following year more tunes surfaced on two highly limited 12" compilations jointly released by SKam and Musik Aus Strom, a label based in Munich. The first of these MASK collections featured a new Boards Of Canada cut, while the second included a selection credited to a Boards Of Canada alter ego, **Hell Interface**. As interest grew in the band and their genuinely original take on electronica's excessively traced blueprint, the scene witnessed more Boards Of Canada live appearances – complete with Super-8 projections – and remixes; but it wasn't until early in 1998, after much speculation and rumour, that it was announced that the duo had signed to Sheffield's Warp Records and an album release was imminent.

MUSIC HAS THE RIGHT TO CHILDREN, jointly released by Warp and SKam in April 1998, was a masterpiece. The collection received rave reviews, drifted to the upper reaches of many end-of-year polls, and eventually peaked at #7 in the UK Independent Chart the following February. The praises continued to flow, Warp released the band's Peel session as an EP (originally aired by Radio 1 the previous year) and in May 1999 the *NME* cited MUSIC HAS THE RIGHT TO CHILDREN in a list of the *Top Psychedelic Records Of All Time*, alongside classics by the likes of The Beatles, Pink Floyd and Spiritualized.

A considerable period of silence followed, with only one EP being released in 2000: IN A BEAUTIFUL PLACE OUT IN THE COUNTRY. A second album didn't appear until 2002. GEOGADDI was another fine collection, though its grooves lacked the immediacy of the duo's previous set, favouring instead sonic abstraction and richly layered amalgams of found sound, lush synth chords and stark beats.

Boards Of Canada have done much to revive a genre that has tended to lazily follow the path of mediocrity. Their music is math, and so much more besides.

🔘 **Music Has The Right To Children** (Warp; 1998).
Quite simply a modern classic of psychedelic dance that filters thousands of scattered sonic shards through a soft-focus lens, the whole thing held in place by some irresistibly booming beats and sirenian melodies. Your collection is incomplete without this title.

🔘 **Geogaddi** (Warp; 2002).
Darker than its predecessor, but still rich with Boards Of Canada hallmarks: sampled documentaries and dreamy melodies abound.

Peter Buckley

BODAST

Formed England 1968; disbanded 1969.

Together for just eighteen months in 1968 and 1969, **Bodast** only recorded one short album – an absolute gem that then went unreleased until 1982.

The band formed as a power trio with **Steve Howe** (fresh from a stint as the guitar prodigy behind the psychedelic rockers **Tomorrow**), **Bobby Clarke** (drums) and **Dave Curtis** (bass and vocals), who had most recently worked in an early version of **Deep Purple**. Eventually they added **Clive Skinner** on guitar and **Bruce Thomas** on bass.

Despite landing a few prime gigs opening for Chuck Berry and The Who, Bodast didn't perform live very much, preferring to practise incessantly. It shows on their album – every song is wrenched tight, with none clocking in much over three minutes. The solos are note-perfect and never gratuitous; the sound is damn near perfect. "Beyond Winter" and "1000 Years" can stand up to many Bowie tunes, while "I Want You" lurches into a monster groove worthy of the Guess Who's "American Woman". "Mr. Jones" – perhaps the best song on the record – has a wonderful guitar line and tart lyrics that recall The Kinks.

Amazingly, the album sat in the vaults until 1982, when a minor record label released a small run of LPs; even then, it was missing two songs. The full album didn't come to light until 1990, when the C5 label released it on CD. Of course, it barely elicited notice on release – Howe's next band **YES** had, by this time been and gone; how it would have been received in 1969 will have to remain one of rock's many 'what-ifs'. We do have one clue, though: when Howe reused the guitar part from "Nether Street" in the Yes song "Starship Trooper", it quickly became one of that group's standards.

BOARDS OF CANADA TWOISM

After Bodast called it quits in December 1969, Howe hitched himself to the rapidly rising star of Yes. Later still, he would have commercial (if not critical) success with **Asia** and **GTR**. Each of the other members went on to record with other bands – most notably, bassist Bruce Thomas became a founding member of Elvis Costello's backing band, **The Attractions**.

⊙ **Steve Howe With Bodast: The Early Years**
(Recorded 1969, Released 1990; C5 Records).
'The Early Years' implies that there were 'Later Years' for this band; sadly, that isn't the case. This album is the sum of their output. The 1990 CD edition is preferable to the 1982 LP, or to piecemeal Howe compilations like MOTHBALLS.

Paul Collins

THE BODINES

Formed Glossop, England, 1985; disbanded 1987; re-formed briefly 1988.

Mike Ryan (vocals), **Paul Brotherton** (guitar), **Tim Burtonwood** (bass) and **John Rowland** (drums) formed their band, **The Bodines**, for that oldest of reasons – to escape the alternatives of the dole or a dead-end, small-town job. They soon built up a loyal following in the nearby city of Manchester, where they headlined at the Boardwalk venue in March 1986. The Boardwalk became a cornerstone of the briefly significant 'C86' scene, so-called after a tape released by the *NME* and featuring a host of 'jangly' guitar bands influenced by The Smiths.

At this point, the band seemed on the verge of success, but the vagaries of the music press decided otherwise. Within a few months of being hyped, 'C86' became the target of much abuse and disdain and was expunged from music history as an embarrassment, partly by the *NME* itself. It was a tough fate, for, while many of the bands involved were amateurish in the worst sense, The Bodines were in a different class. Their track "Therese" – The Bodines' second single – was the pick of the bunch, up against competition like McCarthy, The Wedding Present, Primal Scream and The Pastels – some of whom subsequently achieved success and longevity, although they may not wish to be reminded of their origins.

With its unforgettable refrain of 'It scares the health out of me', "Therese" deserved to transcend its origins. However, despite further single releases like "Heard It All" and continual reissues of "Therese" a commercial breakthrough remained elusive. The rapid decline wasn't helped by the late arrival of their sole album, PLAYED (1987). With cover photos of the lads at the beach, it tried to create the image of a classic summer pop album. Yet summertime is not the best time to release an album of any kind, and it sank without trace, as attention shifted away from 'C86' to American guitar bands.

The Bodines split soon afterwards, re-forming briefly at the end of 1988 for a one-off gig at The

Hacienda as a last hurrah. Mike Ryan resurfaced briefly with **Medalark 11**, who released one album, SHAPED UP, SHIPPED OUT in 1992 on Creation Records. And that was that, though footnote-ists might like to know that their manager **Nathan McGough** later looked after The Happy Mondays, while producer **Ian Broudie** found fame as **THE LIGHTNING SEEDS**.

⊙ **Played** (1987; Magnet).
The band's only LP has stood up quite well, with "Therese" still shining through.

Chris Jenkins

BOG-SHED

Formed Hebden Bridge, England, 1985; disbanded 1988.

Originally named after one of their songs – "The Amazing Roy North Penis Band" – **Bog-Shed** soon ditched that dubious moniker for something just a tad more commercial. After grabbing the attention of **John Robb**, of legendary noisy northerners The Membranes, they were signed to his Vinyl Drip label, which released the 12" EP, LET THEM EAT BOG-SHED.

The record set an odd blueprint: repetitive, rickety, seemingly unplayable guitar riffs, a monster bass sound bludgeoning its way from one groove to the next and, on top, **Phil Hartley**'s deranged vocal, sometimes crooning, sometimes screaming, always ludicrous but still strangely melodic, and crammed with vivid imagery, buzz words and slogans. It spent weeks in the UK indie charts, with lavish praise from radio DJ John Peel, who gave the band a couple of sessions on his show, previewing material from the upcoming LP, STEP ON IT BOG-SHED (1986). The album's lo-fi production gave it real character, while the sleeve art, designed by bassist **Mike Bryson**, depicted appropriately hideous cartoon characters.

Before long, however, Bog-Shed's association with the short-lived 'C86' boom was doing damage. A catchier single, "Morning Sir", sold disappointingly, and Hartley's move to Liverpool made writing and rehearsing more difficult. Hardcore fans were satisfied with a 12" EP of the John Peel radio sessions, TRIED AND TESTED PUBLIC SPEAKER, while the band began recording the second album, BRUTAL (1987).

Owing to printing difficulties, the brilliant sleeve, featuring almost-too-lifelike puppets of the band, took over six months to finish. On its eventual release, the *NME* and *Melody Maker* dismissed the album as student fodder, but the newly launched *Underground* magazine hailed it as a work of genius. Live shows were as vivid as ever, with Hartley's hand on hip, Bryson's blurring hands on the fretboard, and **Mark McQuaid** playing guitar and gurning at the same time.

Yet, by 1988's magnificent single, "Excellent Girl", Bog-Shed's sales were diminishing fast. Heavily in debt after its failure, the band shelved the next single, "Stop Revolving", and called it a day, but not before recording one final John Peel session, which contained some of the band's finest work. The seven-minute "Into Me" and the uncharacteristically garagey "US Bans" showed that the band were at their artistic peak, despite low morale.

Mike Bryson went on to take his ghoulish artwork into the world of animation, whilst **Tris King** drummed with **Jackdaw With Crowbar** and later **A Witness**. Phil Hartley has made a few unsuccessful attempts to launch a solo career.

⊙ **Step On It Bog-Shed** (1986; Shelfish Records). Kicking off with the sprightly "Mechanical Nun", Bog-Shed's first LP saluted the grimier side of life. Its finest moments, "Jobless Youngsters" and the small but perfectly formed "Little Car", provide a refreshing summary of the late 80s DIY scene.

Rhodri Marsden

BOMB THE BASS

Tim Simenon, born London, 1968.

Exploding onto the scene in 1987 with "Beat Dis", **Tim Simenon**'s **Bomb The Bass** proved that developments in sampling, sequencing and MIDI technology had made as much impact on the record industry as punk a decade earlier. Simenon's debut, the first tune he ever wrote, cost him a mere £300 to make, yet it reached #2 in February 1988.

A DJ at London's Wag Club, Simenon captured a defining moment in British hip-hop. Hot on the heels of M/A/R/R/S's 1987 chart-topper, "Pump Up The Volume", "Beat Dis" was very much a record of its time, incorporating elements that would become generic. From the JOURNEY INTO STEREOPHONIC SOUND samples to the acid-house smiley face sleeve it showcased elements that would soon become overexposed.

With appearances from Soul II Soul's **Jazzie B** and **Mark Moore** of S'Express, the accompanying album, INTO THE DRAGON (1988), showcased some of the major players of Britain's embryonic dance scene. Despite featuring two different mixes of both "Beat Dis" and the follow-up "Megablast", it was the cover of "Say A Little Prayer", with lead vocals by **Maureen Walsh**, that stood out. Co-produced by Bristol's Wild Bunch supremo **Nellee Hooper** (later to produce Björk, Massive Attack and Soul II Soul), it became Bomb The Bass's third consecutive British Top 10 single in November 1988.

Soon afterwards, Simenon co-produced **Neneh Cherry**'s worldwide hit, "Buffalo Stance", the first of countless outside projects. It would be 1991 before any fresh Bomb The Bass material would be released. The comeback single "Love So True", appeared during the Gulf War conflict and was released with Simenon's name as a tactful but commercially inopportune replacement.

With **Loretta Haywood** on vocals, elements of 1991's UNKNOWN TERRITORY (particularly the

single "Winter In July") anticipated the 90s trip-hop boom with smoky atmospherics and newly mature songwriting. However, by Simenon's own admission, it was a generally hit-and-miss affair. Even after such a long absence, he seemed to be treading water. His external collaborations with **Seal**, **Björk**, and even **Naomi Campbell** seemed to offer him equal stimulation.

His 1995 album CLEAR, released on his own label, Stoned Heights, emphasized this collaborative approach. An eclectic mix of soul, hip-hop and dub, it showed Simenon discovering his own true voice through working with the likes of **Sinéad O'Connor**, **Jah Wobble**, **Bim Sherman**, **Benjamin Zephaniah**, **Justin Warfield**, **Carlton** and writers **Leslie Winer** and **Will Self**.

Although there are plans for further Bomb The Bass records, Simenon, now A&R man for Stoned Heights, mostly uses his experience to nurture the next generation of turntable whizzkids in the club which spawned him.

⊙ **Clear** (1995; Stoned Heights/Island). The most coherent collection, fusing its disparate elements of soul, hip-hop and dub into a dark, menacing whole.

Mark Hooper

BON JOVI

Formed New Jersey, 1983.

Heavy metal is played by big ugly men with greasy hair and bad teeth. Or so everyone thought until **Bon Jovi** came along. Bon Jovi the band is barely distinguishable from **Jon Bon Jovi** (guitar/vocals), an energetic and photogenic frontman, who in 1983 assembled around himself a band of musicians somewhat older than himself – drummer **Tico Torres** is some nine years older than his boss.

The band's heritage lay with Springsteen and Southside Johnny (nowadays Jon's celebrity mates), but the early days of Bon Jovi were unquestionably poodle rock, with both the eponymous debut (1984) and the follow-up, 7800 FAHRENHEIT (1985), boasting hairstyles more memorable than the music. That pseudo-meaningful title – referring to the melting point of rock – said it all.

Nonetheless, these albums charted and paved the way for the arrival in 1986 of SLIPPERY WHEN WET, a #1 album that spawned two US #1 singles, "You Give Love A Bad Name" and "Livin' On A Prayer". In the US, SLIPPERY had some kind of wet T-shirt contest on its cover, instead of the dull raindrops perplexingly seen in Britain. It was a touch of raunch that sat uneasily with the Bon Jovi image. Cartoon rockers like Poison would make sledgehammer use of the rock-chick angle, but the lyrics to "Livin' On A Prayer" showed much more clearly what Bon Jovi were about. This was rock as romantic dream, the possibility of release from the humdrum by picking up a guitar. Bon Jovi was not a band racked by creative tension. It was moulded around Jon's boy-next-door good looks, the behind-the-scenes writing and production talents of **Desmond Child** and **Bruce Fairbairn** and a slick commercial organization.

The first single from NEW JERSEY (1988), "Bad Medicine", was deliberately commercial and became another US chart-topper but the album's sound showed a marked change. The 'pop metal' tag is one that will follow Bon Jovi for eternity, but it is only really true of SLIPPERY – NEW JERSEY was much more soulful, and rock'n'roll. "I'll Be There For You" also hit #1, but the fans' favourite was "Blood On Blood", a rousing ode to camaraderie. The closing "Love For Sale", a bluesy jam, brought Bon Jovi a million miles from "Let It Rock".

Then Bon Jovi went on hold as grunge briefly changed the geography of American rock. Jon made BLAZE OF GLORY, a solo album 'inspired' by *Young Guns II*, continuing a cowboy fixation already displayed on "Wanted Dead Or Alive" and "Stick To Your Guns". Its success, and sound, paralleled that of his band.

When Bon Jovi the band was resurrected in 1992, it was with some panache, but the excellent "Keep The Faith" single turned out to be a little deceptive. The album of the same name had cleaner production, but still clung to those old cock-rock clichés – check out "If I Was Your Mother". The album's slow-burning success may have ensured a new era for Bon Jovi, but the stodgy sentimentality of "Bed Of Roses" became the pattern.

Many were surprised at the success of CROSSROAD, the Bon Jovi 'best of' that held top spot for week after week and was the biggest UK seller of 1994. Bon Jovi's success in the singles chart was much greater than in their heyday, as well. As Jon cultivated the public image of the cosy family man – and even the tearaway part of the team (guitarist **Richie Sambora**) married and settled – their fan base broadened so much that in 1995 they finally graduated to stadium band in the UK.

JBJ's next solo project, DESTINATION ANYWHERE (1997), showed him prepared to experiment with his golden-egg-laying soft-rock lite that had kept him in designer jeans for more than a decade. Encouraged by Black Grape producer **Steve Lironi** to play around with drum loops and studio effects, there was a lighter, more modern feel to the whole album. Bon Jovi's attempts at balladry still failed in terms of lyrics, but there was no faulting the degree of emotion he squeezed into his voice. Tracks guaranteed to please the more conservative poodle-rock faithful included "Queen Of New Orleans" and "Midnight In Chelsea".

Despite JBJ refusing to commit himself to the possibility of Bon Jovi reforming in the late 90s – he instead insisted on cultivating his movie-actor alter ego – the temptation to hit stages worldwide proved to be far too great. The result was CRUSH (2000), the band's first album to be recorded entirely in their native New Jersey, which, as usual pulled no punches

when it came to big choruses and unashamedly commercial songwriting. After a massive stadium-bothering world tour, JBJ concentrated on life in front of the camera lens and was most recently spotted in the one-time hit, now-flagging, US show, *Ally McBeal*. He returned to the rock arena in 2002 with the power chord-laden BOUNCE.

⊙ **Slippery When Wet** (1986; Mercury). The classic, crunching, singalong pop-metal album, featuring "Livin' On A Prayer", "You Give Love A Bad Name", and their best song, "Wanted Dead Or Alive".

⊙ **New Jersey** (1988; Mercury). The hit-packed follow-up, which is more mature and rockier than its predecessor.

⊙ **Crossroad** (1994; Mercury). The big hits, plus Jon's solo "Blaze Of Glory" and a brace of new tracks. Quintessential mainstream hard rock.

Robert Jones

GARY 'US' BONDS

Born Jacksonville, Florida, 1939.

A lthough his time in the spotlight was brief, **Gary 'US' Bonds** was a pivotal figure of early 60s rock'n'roll. His biggest hits burst with exuberance, combining New Orleans-styled R&B, West Indian calypso rhythms, and raw, blurry production flourishes. His dirty, sax-driven riffs and joyful exhortations to party down were an obvious influence on early Motown, Dion's early 60s hits, and Bruce Springsteen, who eventually returned the favour by resuscitating Bonds' career in the early 1980s.

The unique qualities of Bonds' singles were due at least as much to producer **Frank J. Guida** as to Gary himself. Guida bought a local studio on the verge of bankruptcy in 1960, and enlisted local singer **Gary Anderson** to cut "New Orleans", although Gary didn't like the song. "New Orleans", co-written by Guida and local businessman **Joe Royster** (who would collaborate with Guida to write most of Bonds' hits), was a decent stomper, but what really made the record stand out in the teen-idol-dominated months of late 1960 was the pre-'wall of sound' production. Guida lacked the resources Phil Spector had at his disposal; what he could do was thicken Bonds' voice with echo and double-tracking. Intentionally or not, the layers of overdub and reverb resulted in a gritty, even muddy sound that sounded like nothing else around, and indeed like little else since.

Guida had Gary Anderson change his name to US Bonds, thinking that radio stations would mistake it for a public service announcement. Whether or not the ploy helped, the record made the American Top 10, and the name stuck, though Gary was able to tack his first name to the beginning of the billing on subsequent records. In mid-1961, he followed up his initial success with his best single, "Quarter To Three", a #1 hit with a genuinely live, rowdy party atmosphere, provided in part by fourteen kids that Guida took to the session. One of the most sponta-

Gary 'US' Bonds coiffed and bang on time for his greatest hit

CHARLIE GILLETT

restored Bonds to the Top 20 for the first time in nearly two decades. He was soon back on the oldies circuit again but he deserves his place in the rock-'n'roll pantheon for proving that rock was far from dead between Buddy Holly's death and the emergence of The Beatles.

Dedication (1981; Razor & Tie).
With considerable input from co-producers Bruce Springsteen and Steve Van Zandt, this comeback album manages to make Bonds sound reasonably contemporary without unduly diluting his original sound.

The Best Of Gary US Bonds (1990; Rhino).
All the big hits, plus quite a few minor hits and down-right misses. It's repetitive taken all at once, but the best is invigorating.

Richie Unterberger

BONGWATER

Formed New York, 1985;
disbanded 1992.

"Usually you figure the more embarrassed you are after a show, the more successful it's been." Ann Magnuson

Bongwater was conceived after Shimmy-Disc supremo and former **BUTTHOLE SURFERS** bassist **Mark Kramer** (instruments/vocals) met **Ann Magnuson** (vocals/lyrics) at her New York nightclub, Club 57, where he sound-engineered for her all-female percussion group **Pulsalamma**. The two collaborated on the single "Breaking No New Ground" (1987), which featured avant-garde favourite **Fred Frith**, and lead guitarist **Dave Rick**, who joined the duo full-time. Bongwater's idiosyncratic style was characterized by Magnuson's surreal satires on the Downtown scene's artistic conceits and decadence, accompanied by Kramer's psychedelic freakout backing. A cover of The Monkees' "Porpoise Song", a 1987 single, featured a typically celebrity-fixated narrative from Magnuson's dreams.

With drummer **David Licht** on board, they released the ironically titled DOUBLE BUMMER (1988). With four sides of vinyl allowing space for experiment, Bongwater indulged themselves and their audience. Along with covers ranging from Gary Glitter's "Rock & Roll Part 2" to Johnny Cash's "There You Go" and the bizarre "Dazed & Chinese" (Led Zeppelin's standard rendered into Chinese), Magnuson's stories and Kramer's eclectic music played off each other to create, as Magnuson put it, a veritable pop-cultural smorgasbord. DOUBLE BUMMER's jump-cut mix of styles and tone established Bongwater as a postmodern project that reflected the diversity and humour of New York, while satirizing the shallowness of media culture's celebrity fixation.

"Decadent Iranian Country Club" and "David Bowie Wants Ideas" stand out, miniature playlets poking fun at the entertainment industry's self-

neous and celebratory R&B/rock hybrids of all time, it helped spawn other live-party-in-the-studio soul classics by The Miracles ("Mickey's Monkey") and Sam Cooke ("Twisting The Night Away").

Other early-60s hits brought the slight West Indian influence of his first singles to the fore. Guida had spent three years in Trinidad during a stint in the military, and Bonds' Top 10 hits, "School Is Out" and "Twist, Twist Señora", were heavily indebted to the calypso rhythms and infectious vocal chants of West Indian music. Guida would employ the West Indian beat even more heavily with another of his protégés, **Jimmy Soul**, who went to #1 in 1963 with "If You Wanna Be Happy" as Bonds' star began to wane. Although he had successfully tapped into the twist craze for a few hits, his records began to sound like lesser repeats of themselves as the British invasion and the mid-60s soul explosion rendered his style passé.

Bruce Springsteen had appropriated much of Bonds' trademark style for his early recordings with the E Street Band, and in 1981 he gave Gary's career a huge boost by co-writing and co-producing Bonds' 1981 comeback album, DEDICATION, with E Street guitarist **Steve Van Zandt**. "This Little Girl", a slightly updated variation of the vintage Bonds sound

obsessed glamour, which Magnuson knew well from her acting role as a fashion magazine editor in a TV sitcom, *Anything But Love*, in addition to her part in Susan Seidelman's film *Making Mr Right* (1987).

Kramer, too, was a busy man, running Shimmy-Disc and collaborating with artists and groups such as **Dogbowl**, **Galaxie 500**, **King Missile** and (later) **Daevid Allen** of Gong. Perhaps because of their other commitments, the group's warmly received next album, TOO MUCH SLEEP, did not appear until 1990. Freed from the occasional longueurs of DOUBLE BUMMER, it was a laid-back, lo-fi classic, which refined the combination of eccentric covers and surreal spoken word to near perfection. The album worked as a seamless whole, with songs segued into fragmented dialogue, sampled answerphone messages and TV sound bites – dissecting, twisting and regurgitating kitsch Americana into an ironic collage of psychedelic urban country music and featuring some of the finest use of cheap drum machines and keyboards on record.

Having taken a break from Bongwater, David Licht returned to the fold for their next album, THE POWER OF PUSSY (1991), along with what turned out to be their last UK tour in the spring of that year. The new record continued where TOO MUCH SLEEP had left off, with more emphasis on feminist issues, sex and relationships, particularly (it seemed) that of Magnuson and Kramer themselves. It mercilessly parodied soft-core fantasies of sex, and the remnants of the permissive society. Despite a few irritants (such as an unnecessary cover of "Bedazzled"), the combination of Magnuson's and Kramer's harmonies was as bittersweet as ever, and "Kisses Sweeter Than Wine" is reinterpreted, Bongwater-style, as an elegy for people with AIDS.

Rick departed prior to the European tour of 1991, replaced by **Randolph A. Hudson III** (lead guitar), and live rhythm guitar was provided by Kramer's longtime colleague and friend, Dogbowl, who also supported (with the ubiquitous Kramer as his bassist). Their stage show was just that, a theatrical performance with Magnuson casting her discarded story notes into the appreciative audiences' waiting hands, while the boys rocked out under Kramer's tight control.

However, with the increase in the band's popularity came a decrease in ideas and a clash of personalities. As a result of their complicated personal relationship, Kramer and Magnuson's partnership came to a bitter end after the release of THE BIG SELL-OUT (1991). Since then, Ann Magnuson has released an album of her postmodern cabaret THE LUV SHOW (1995) and has collaborated with **John Cale** on his 1994 operetta *Life Underwater* while continuing her acting career. Kramer has since played live bass for **Ween**, joined **Penn Jillette** as **Captain Howdy** for TATTOO OF BLOOD (1995) and MONEY FEEDS MY MUSIC MACHINE (1997), and has now formed **Glen Or Glenda** with former soap star **Tammy Lang**.

The dissolution of the duo's partnership resulted in lawsuits from both parties and Shimmy-Disc's temporary closure. What had started as a fun side-project between friends degenerated into a vindictive argument over money and resulted in the disappearance of one of the most consistently eccentric record labels in the world. The label was ultimately acquired by Knitmedia and is now associated with Knitting Factory Records. In 1999 a line appeared to have been drawn under these disputes with the release of THE BOX OF BONGWATER, a 4 CD set containing the complete recordings of this unique and eccentric outfit. It seemed to signal an uneasy truce but also made the prospect of further collaborations unlikely. A shame.

⊙ **Too Much Sleep** (1990; Shimmy-Disc).
The quintessential Bongwater release – humorous, inventive and with a pastiche Quicksilver Messenger Service sleeve thrown in for postmodern quotation purposes as well. The cover of Slapp Happy's "The Drum" is the high point, while "Talent Is A Vampire" presages the acrimonious future of the band.

⊙ **The Power Of Pussy** (1991; Shimmy-Disc).
Mostly excellent penultimate release, with the epic "Folk Song" namechecking the coolest pop cultural icons, from Oprah to Butthole Surfers, with Dr Seuss, Led Zeppelin (again) and Richard Gere along the way.

Richard Fontenoy

BONZO DOG DOO-DAH BAND

Formed London, 1965; disbanded 1970.

T he ultimate in art-school bands, the **Bonzo Dog Doo-Dah Band** formed at Goldsmiths College, London, and their early performances resembled in-jokes more than paying propositions. Originally known as The Bonzo Dog Dada Band, their musical style was a mixture of highbrow anarchy and lowbrow nostalgia. Pegged as 20s revivalists, they turned out two flop singles in this vein, "My Brother Makes The Music For The Talkies" and "Alley Oop", before the defection of **Bob Kerr**, who built a career on just this kind of nostalgia, led them to broaden their act.

An appearance in The Beatles' *Magical Mystery Tour* film, singing "Death Cab For Cutie", led to a record contract with Liberty. The Bonzos' debut, GORILLA (1967), was probably the only album to be dedicated to King Kong, 'who must have been a great bloke'. If the Bonzos invited any comparisons, it was surely with early Mothers Of Invention, but they replaced anger and alienation with irony and affection, most memorably on the hilarious "The Intro And The Outro".

The posh tones, eccentric wardrobe and surrealist wit of singer, trumpeter and raconteur **VIVIAN STANSHALL** were dominant, but he led an outrageous bunch of English eccentrics: **Roger Ruskin Spear** (saxophone) seemed most intent on setting off explosions and programming robots; **Legs Larry**

Stanshall (right), Innes (holding leg), and the Doo-Dahs

The band had tightened up and become more rocky, with the (uncredited) electric bass of **Joel Druckman**, and the LP was interspersed with backwards tapes, the rhythms of the electrified trouser press, and various references to the 'underground' culture of the time. They were a major live attraction, a carnival of visual and musical mayhem with frequent changes of costume and mass instrument swapping. They were also frequent performers on John Peel's BBC Radio 1 show, and indeed UNPEELED, a CD of some of these sessions, was released in 1995. A fourth album, KEYNSHAM (1969), with **Dennis Cowan** on bass, was the Bonzos' swansong: a collection of funny and sad songs, it echoed the cult TV series *The Prisoner*, imagining a civilization where people were subdued in a materialist world which crushed all individual freedom.

The Bonzos imploded after an American tour in early 1970, whereupon Stanshall organized a pick-up band called **Bonzo Freaks**. With Who drummer **Keith Moon**, they recorded a legendary session for John Peel's radio show, which included the premiere of Stanshall's 'Rawlinson

Smith (drums) was a cross-dressing tap dancer; and **Neil Innes** (piano/guitar) looked most comfortable when wearing a duck on his head. Completing the line-up were **Rodney Slater** (saxophone), spoons player **Sam Spoons**, and the plainly named **Vernon Dudley Bohey-Nowell**, who tackled both the banjo and double bass.

The band found a mass audience on the late-60s TV show *Do Not Adjust Your Set*, on which they performed weekly musical deconstructions. (The show also featured future *Monty Python* members **Terry Jones**, **Eric Idle** and **Michael Palin**, who doubtless learned much.) The best songs from these shows were rerecorded for TADPOLES (1969), which was preceded by a 'proper' LP, 1968's THE DOUGHNUT IN GRANNY'S GREENHOUSE. Stanshall and Innes were now well into their songwriting stride, the former witty and acerbic like Lennon, the latter soft and sentimental like McCartney. Indeed, under the pseudonym **Apollo C. Vermouth**, Paul McCartney produced their biggest hit, Neil Innes's "I'm The Urban Spaceman".

End' saga. Contractual reasons then forced Stanshall, Innes and Legs Larry to re-form for the scrappy LET'S MAKE UP AND BE FRIENDLY (1972); they all seemed to be singing in different studios, and probably were: the album was the first to be recorded at The Manor House Studios in Oxford, owned by Virgin Records, and in addition to the interpersonal strains (headed off by games of cricket) there were technical teething troubles to contend with.

Neil Innes went on to work with *Monty Python*, as well as teaming up with Python member Eric Idle for the fabulous Beatles pastiche movie, *The Rutles* (1978). He also continued to record his own delicate and melancholic songs, the best of which are gathered together on the compilation CD, RECYCLED VINYL. Slater later became a psychiatric social worker, Legs Larry Smith tapdanced on stages round the world, while Spear continued to tour Britain with his exploding robots and musical nostalgia. Stanshall, a national institution, died a shocking and premature death in 1995.

⦿ **Cornology** (1992; EMI).
Available as a three-volume CD box set, or as separate discs, this unbeatable package comprises all five original LPs, plus rarities and lost singles. It also features Brian Hogg's authoritative history of the Bonzos' continuing saga, complete with rare photographs.

⦿ **Unpeeled** (1995; Strange Fruit).
A CD of radio sessions by the band recorded between 1967 and 1969. Here are looser versions of LP tracks, and two major discoveries: the John Lennon pastiche of "Give Booze A Chance" and the extraordinary "Craig Torso Show", which seemed to predict the worst excesses of junk TV.

⦿ **The History Of The Bonzos** (1997; Beat Goes On).
The classic all-time 'best of' compilation, at last available on CD.

Brian Hinton

THE BOO RADLEYS

Formed Liverpool, England, 1988; disbanded 1999

Schoolfriends **Martin Carr** (guitar) and **Simon 'Sice' Rowbottom** (vocals/guitar) would dream constantly of living the pop star's life, miming with tennis racquets and hairbrushes, acting out the descent from the plane to the tarmac and teeming hordes of fans. Adolescence failed to deliver the cynicism to quash these ideals and, inspired by the noisy melodies of such bands as The Jesus And Mary Chain, they took the first step to potential international fame.

Another schoolmate, **Tim Brown**, taught Martin to play guitar, and then took up bass himself. As Martin had always regretted the fact that he was unable to sing, this task fell to Sice. Taking the name **Boo Radleys** from the eccentric-outsider figure in *To Kill A Mockingbird*, they recruited drummer **Steve Hewitt**, and performed several 'dodgy' Merseyside gigs in 1988.

Demo tapes got no response from local labels, so Martin and Tim were obliged to take day jobs as civil servants. This bleak existence was brought to an end, and sanity restored, when independent label Action paid for the recording ICHABOD AND I (1990). Although the band weren't entirely pleased with the primitive production sound of the LP, it won them press attention and acclaim from DJ John Peel, who invited them to record a session for BBC Radio 1. They also signed to Rough Trade, changing drummers as they did so; **Rob Ceika** remained until the end.

The three EPs released through Rough Trade, later collected on one album, LEARNING TO WALK (1994), brought their distortion-coated pop to the attention of a wider audience. Regular *Single of the Week* judgements in the music press must have led the band to believe they were on the cusp of major stardom, but the demise of Rough Trade in 1991 left a completed album gathering dust. Fortunately, on hearing it, Alan McGee signed them to his Creation label, which finally released EVERYTHING'S ALRIGHT FOREVER in March 1992.

The album, along with its preceding EP, ADRENALIN, was clear evidence that the band were developing, adding strings and horns to the mix, and becoming less reliant on a staple diet of noise-fuzz guitars, though they had to bully their producers to let them take things as loud as they wanted to. Their appeal was gradually broadening, as they supported The Pale Saints – the two bands were often seen as Siamese twins, sound-wise – and getting consistent press coverage. Like other British indie groups, though, they were overshadowed at the time by the hugely popular wave of American grunge, and the excellent single, "Lazarus", was a commercial failure, despite its mixture of experimental sound and strong melody.

Undeterred, the band busied themselves in the studio, getting lost amid piles of samples, songs, melodies and discrepant ideas, resulting in GIANT STEPS (1993). Seventeen tracks strong, it effectively mixed a range of unlikely influences: dub-reggae bassline introductions to 60s-style pop melodies, jangly guitars squaring up to melodicas and explosions of brass, with odd samples peppering the lot. Critically, it was a smash and GIANT STEPS hit the Top 20, although the singles failed to do likewise.

For Martin, this was war. He wanted to hear his songs blaring out of radios on building sites, and the band ruthlessly set out to achieve this by releasing the infectious "Wake Up Boo!" in February 1995, which quickly became a radio favourite and major hit. Childhood dreams were fulfilled with an appearance on BBC TV's *Top Of The Pops*, while the follow-up album, WAKE UP! (1995), topped the UK charts – proof that they had finally made it to the pop heroes' club. Just in case anyone considered Carr the Boos' only capable songwriter, Sice Rowbottom released an extracurricular outing, FIRST FRUITS, under the name **Eggman**, and backed by various Creation artists, in summer 1996. It was a good filler for fans awaiting the next band release, revealing, if anything, even more of a Beatles influence.

The next release, C'MON KIDS (1996), wasn't, however, the pop-drenched cash-in that many had predicted. If anything, the album was a return to the quirky comfort of GIANT STEPS; no hit singles, just good-quality, mixed-influence, Liverpool seaside rock.

In 1998 another album emerged, the sprawling 14-tracker KINGSIZE. Once again it hit the spot with the fans, being heavily laden with both experimental blasts and tuneful pop, but it spawned no hit singles and by early 1999 the band had split. After a long period of silence Martin Carr resurfaced with a new group, **Brave Captain** (named after a Firehose song); in 2000 two albums were released, THE FINGERTIP SAINT SESSIONS VOL. I and GO WITH YOURSELF, both recognizable as having come from the Boos' camp.

⦿ **Everything's Alright Forever** (1992; Creation).
Martin wrote all the songs in ten days, under the influence of The Beatles' WHITE ALBUM and *Helter Skelter*, the biography of Charles Manson, amongst other things. He was also heard championing such early 80s heroes as The Human League and Haircut 100 – all of which goes some way to explaining the excellent pop tunes behind the array of effects pedals.

Giant Steps (1993; Creation).
Whether or not you had heard The Boo Radleys before, this would be something of a shock. A bit like going on a drive with a reckless driver through Jamaica, New Orleans, Glasgow and the Beatles Museum, and then down to the pub before last orders.

Maria Lamle

THE BOOMTOWN RATS

Formed Dublin, Ireland, 1975; disbanded 1985.

Having enjoyed a brief stint as a journalist for the *NME*, songwriter **BOB GELDOF** (vocals) formed a band with **Gary Roberts** and **Gerry Cott** (guitars), **Johnny Fingers** (keyboards), **Pete Briquette** (bass) and **Simon Crowe** (drums). Their original name was **The Nightlife Thugs** but Geldof came up with **The Boomtown Rats** from a Woody Guthrie biography, the phrase being a description of newcomers to the Oklahoma oilfields.

Playing a mix of R&B covers and original material, The Rats hit an immediate obstacle as there were few suitable venues in Ireland for their raw, uncompromising sound. However, they soon helped forge a new gig circuit across Ireland, and after seeing a Dublin performance Ensign signed them to its roster. In October 1976, the band moved to London to join its burgeoning punk scene. They blagged the opening slot on Tom Petty's UK tour in the summer of 1977 and saw their first single, "Lookin' After Number One", hit the British Top 20, closely followed by "Mary Of The Fourth Form" and a self-titled debut LP. The band's appeal ranged from star-struck schoolgirls to serious musos, who considered The Rats to be pretty good for a bunch of punks.

A string of hits followed these initial successes, including their first UK #1, "Rat Trap" (1978), taken from their second album, A TONIC FOR THE TROOPS (1978). Attempts to crack America in 1978–79 were fruitless, but while they were there a dramatic news item about a 16-year-old schoolgirl shooting her own classmates was to provide the basis for The Boomtown Rats' biggest hit song. With the glaring exception of the States, "I Don't Like Mondays" was a worldwide smash, and in the UK the single was certified gold in just ten days. The album from which it came, THE FINE ART OF SURFACING (1979), probably represented their finest hour.

Although The Rats returned to the Top 10 in late 1980 with "Banana Republic", and they continued to be a massive draw as a live act, the albums MONDO BONGO (1980) and V DEEP (1982) both flopped. Geldof became increasingly involved with other projects, including the lead role in Alan Parker's film of Pink Floyd's *The Wall*, before he famously created **Band Aid** and Live Aid.

Despite a phenomenal reaction to their performance at Live Aid in 1985, The Boomtown Rats' last album, IN THE LONG GRASS (1985), did nothing to reverse the downward trend. Unable to secure a new deal with a label, the band split up soon afterwards. Geldof's profile has remained reasonably high ever since, while Briquette's session work included appearances on Tricky's highly acclaimed MAXINQUAYE album in 1995.

The Boomtown Rats

A Tonic For The Troops (1978; Ensign. Reissued 1992; Mercury).
Expertly produced by Robert Lange, this shows the band to be a fine New Wave act. It contains the controversially titled "I Never Loved Eva Braun" and a pop at the press in "Don't Believe What You Read", but also finds room for the hits "She's So Modern" and Geldof's Springsteen tribute, "Rat Trap".

Bob Geldof And The Boomtown Rats

Loudmouth (1994; Vertigo).
Probably the best way to sample the hits.

Simon Ives

THE BOREDOMS

Formed Osaka, Japan, 1983.

A fusion of heavy metal, hip-hop and bubblegum-pop played in a free-jazz style by punk musicians – that's perhaps the best description of **The Boredoms**' style. Imagine the Butthole Surfers and Sun Ra, with a dash of Devo's absurdist slant thrown in.

The band was formed in the bedroom of **Yamatsuka Eye** (leader and arch vocal fiend), who was at first partnered by percussionist **Tabata** (also of Zevi Geva); together they produced the ANAL BY ANAL EP, and the LP, ONANIE BOMB MEETS THE SEX PISTOLS.

The present line-up – Eye plus **Toyohito Yoshikawa** (co-vocal fiend), **Hira Hayashi** (bass), **Yamamoto** (guitar), and drum duo **Atari** and **Yoshimi** (who also blows a 'little trumpet') – formed in 1986 and first produced the awesome SOUL DISCHARGE 99, eventually released outside Japan in 1989 on Kramer's New York label Shimmy–Disc. In the 90s, The Boredoms' output gathered apace, with the albums ROOTS (1992), POP TATARI (1993), WOW 2 (1993) and CHOCOLATE SYNTHESIZER (1994). Renowned for wild live appearances, ultra-wacky costumes and bizarre cover art (Japanese pop culture in a post-Dada style), The Boredoms became darlings of the New York radical music scene – and why not?

Though their profile has been somewhat lower since, the group has continued to be prolific, releasing a string of SUPER ROOTS albums, VISION CREATION NEWSUN (2001), and four volumes with the appellation REBORE. The collective have 'technically' changed their name to **V∞rdoms**, though they continue to use their old moniker so as not to confuse those of us that simply can't keep up.

Various band members have also collaborated on outside projects: Yoshimi has drummed for Sonic

Youth's Kim Gordon in her sideline band **Free Kitten**, while Yamatsuka Eye lent his vocal talents to John Zorn's **Naked City** project, and Bill Laswell's **Praxis** project. There was also a Boredoms thrash spin-off, **Concrete Octopus**, as well as Eye's band **Hanatarash**, whose live performances strived to create 'a visual experience of war'.

Eye has also played live improvisation with **Otomo Yoshohide**, creating a bewildering mix of turntables, voice and guitar, as witnessed on a Blast First/Disobey CD, LIVE IN MANCHESTER 95, and shared credits with John Zorn on NANI NANI (1996), an album self-described as 'ambient screams, hardcore surf, erotic Indian psychedelia and moronic samples'. All good stuff, indeed.

⊙ **Soul Discharge 99** (1989; Wiiija/Earthnoise).
Presumably recorded in Eye's bedroom. Whatever it lacks in sophistication it makes up for in inventiveness.

⊙ **Chocolate Synthesizer** (1994; Warners/Reprise).
In which The Boredoms totally abuse some state-of-the-art studio technology. Includes the tracks "Acid Police" and "Synthesizer Guide Book On Fire".

Ross Holloway & Peter Moyse

BOSS HOG

Formed New York City, 1990.

Boss Hog were born from the ashes of the celebrated Washington DC no-fi, neo-blues howlers, **PUSSY GALORE**. Before their implosion, Pussy Galore moved to New York, to the heart of the No Wave, post-punk, shock-rock scene that spawned Sonic Youth and Swans. Pussy Galore's one-time photographer and guitarist, **Cristina Martinez**, made the move with her boyfriend, lead singer **Jon Spencer**, until the band's notorious internal tensions caused her to quit. By 1990, Pussy Galore had split for good, and Spencer and Martinez were jobbing in various bands.

Boss Hog was cobbled together in order to fill a vacant support slot at legendary club CGBG's. The name was allegedly culled from a biker magazine, and

not the corrupt and corpulent governor in *The Dukes of Hazzard* TV show, as is generally assumed.

Taking their musical cue from the more solid, rhythmic aspect of Pussy Galore's trash aesthetic, and doubtless encouraged by the (then) prevalent NY trend for hard and fast retro punk rock, the Hog were an immediate success, mixing sexploitation and sleaze (Martinez allegedly performed the first show entirely naked) with fuzz-heavy riffs. 1989's mini-LP, DRINKIN', LECHIN' AND LYIN' was a collection of distorted bass and crunching guitar riffs, howled over by Jon and Cristina and expertly captured in Chicago by the ubiquitous **Steve Albini**. Most eyes were focused on the attention-grabbing cover, graced by Martinez clad only in boots, gloves and strategically placed lipstick.

Their second LP, COLD HANDS (1990), also featured a naked (but more artfully posed) Martinez, as well as the infamous Boss Hog 'All-Star' line-up that had graced the first album – **Kurt Wolf**, **Charlie Ondras**, **Jerry Teel** and **Pete Shore** (who, however, appeared on COLD HANDS only). Although Boss Hog had to coexist with the Blues Explosion's rising star, each band had become very much the personal project of their respective lead singers, by then husband and wife.

In 1992, following numerous 'All-Star' bust-ups and the unfortunate death of Charlie Ondras, Spencer and Martinez sacked the remaining members and recruited **Jens Jurgensen**, a German design student who had previously played third bass for the recently defunct Swans. The line-up was solidified by the addition of **Hollis Queens** on drums, despite her almost complete lack of experience. As a four-piece, 'more like a band and less like an indie super-group', according to Spencer, the group released their last offering on Amphetamine Reptile, the GIRL+ mini-LP (1993). With a far more structured, mature sound, the five songs featured brass and subtler dynamics and marked a turning point in the band's development. Its success led to a deal with DGC, the major label of choice for New York's finest alternatives. Spencer and Martinez, flushed with the success of their respective bands, jacked in their day jobs, working on magazines, to concentrate on the music full time.

In 1995, BOSS HOG was released, their Geffen debut – a raucous smattering of straight-on punk thrashes coupled with some more off-the-wall moments (such as the neo-gothic "Texas" and the Ike Turner cover, "I Idolize You"). Produced by Seattle master **Steve Fisk** and Spencer (and 'reduced' by Martinez), it looked for a while as if Boss Hog would be the commercially successful legacy of Pussy Galore. However, the Jon Spencer Blues Explosion's well-received major-label debut and hit follow-up, ACME, lent a perilous edge to the careers of alt-rock's second favourite celebrity couple (after Kim and Thurston). Indeed, despite the obvious potential present in Boss Hog's Geffen debut, nothing very much was heard from the band for nearly five years, mainly

boss hog
whiteout

due to their being dropped from the label during a buy-out. Nevertheless, they took time out to write some superior songs, hitch a ride with City Slang Records, recruit **Mark Boyce** (ex-Goats) as a keyboard player and return with WHITE OUT (2000), a blistering set that even managed to lend a seductive cut to a Levis jeans commercial.

As Boss Hog go from strength to strength, Geffen are probably wishing they had been a little less enthusiastic with their pruning.

⊙ **Drinkin', Lechin' And Lyin'** (1989; Amphetamine Reptile).
Positively spits monosyllabic riffs of fury. Check "Fix Me" for a harmonic-spiked, single-minded, full-on riff-o-rama.

⊙ **Girl+** (1993; Amphetamine Reptile).
The brassy, sassy "Ruby" showed there was more to the Hog than punk rock, as the sound fills out to encompass more than schlock rock.

⊙ **Boss Hog** (1995; DGC).
But not that much more. Nevertheless, as fine a 90s rock album as you're likely to hear, utterly bereft of bombast and pretension.

⊙ **White Out** (2000; City Slang).
This tightly crafted set employs the band's familiar garage-rock swagger whilst confidently slipping disco grooves and break-beats into the mix, complete with wall-of-sound production and funky Hammond-organ stabs.

Jonathan Bell

BOSTON

Formed Boston, Massachusetts, 1976.

On their multimillion debut album, **Boston**'s self-description in "Rock & Roll Band" read: 'We were just another band out of Boston/On the road and trying to make ends meet/Playing all the bars and sleeping in our cars'. The reality was more sinister: the revival of the beat combo as the puppets of a sullen studio-bound genius, the return of the boffin.

That boffin was design technician **Tom Scholz** (guitar/keyboards/percussion), who recruited studio musicians **Barry Goudreau** (guitar), **Fran**

Sheehan (bass), **Sib Hashian** (drums) and **Brad Delp** (guitar/vocals), whose inimitable howling helped make "More Than A Feeling" a band anthem, UK and US hit, and rock classic. "More Than A Feeling" was the Boston manifesto: its rock-solid riff threatening to dissipate into white noise, but saved by Delp's singing of how the power of rock made up for lost love. CBS executives believed that, in the boogie-soaked music scene of 1976, people would pay good money for this alternative. They were right – BOSTON (1976) sold eight million copies, while the band became the first to open in New York by playing Madison Square Garden.

Despite this breakthrough, Scholz's masterplan for world domination overlooked one key element: CBS president Walter Yetnikoff. While Scholz laboured over recording a drumbeat seven hundred times to find the sounds in his head, Yetnikoff soon fell out of love with his money-spinner: '[Scholz] told me from time to time I could go fuck myself. He'd complain about the colour of the sky, all sorts of things.' Scholz was displeased with BOSTON's advertisement slogan ('better music through science'); similarly, in 1978, when CBS rush-released DON'T LOOK BACK, Scholz put its disappointing four million sales down to its only being 'half as good' as he had wanted.

Nevertheless, Boston dragged a forty-foot-tall organ with them on tour, and Scholz began work on THIRD STAGE in 1979. Having compared his perfectionist streak to that of Mozart, Scholz manically devoted the time it took his hero to compose *The Magic Flute* to making guitars sound like violins. By the time the album was finally released he had made a fortune from inventing the Rockman Mini-Amp, while Goudreau had quit to form **Orion** with vocalist **Fran Cosmo**. In the interim, Yetnikoff had suspended Scholz's royalty payments, and demanded $900,000 in return for Boston's contract. Behind Yetnikoff's back, Scholz signed a fresh deal with MCA, which inspired CBS to sue, preventing the immediate release of THIRD STAGE. Scholz hit back and counter-sued them for malicious prosecution.

When THIRD STAGE finally hit the shops in 1986, it sold four million copies, and spawned an American #1 single, "Amanda", an ode to the anodyne. Another eight-year gap ensued before WALK ON was released in 1994. Scholz blamed its delay on litigation and his affirmation that "Boston will never knowingly release inferior product." Nevertheless, as Scholz locked himself back in the studio, the question remained as to why he continued to spend years crafting rewrites of the first album. Indeed, GREATEST HITS (1997) contained only three new songs, one of them being a version of "The Star Spangled Banner". The other two tunes, "Tell Me" and "Higher Power", failed to set the world alight. The next product to escape from the Boston sonic laboratory was 2002's CORPORATE AMERICA; though largely unremarkable, several cuts did find Delp's vocals recalling better days.

● **Boston** (1976; Epic).
The original and the best. Listening to the heavenly "More Than A Feeling" so affected one Kurt Cobain that he sold it to the 90s generation under the title of "Smells Like Teen Spirit".

Charles Bottomley

BOW WOW WOW

Formed London, 1980; disbanded 1984.

"Our main criticism of Malcolm is that he's too intellectual. We do have intellectual elements in what we do, but the music is basically about shagging." Leigh Gorman

After the Sex Pistols disintegrated in 1979, their manager **Malcolm McLaren** wasted little time in assembling a new band, which he christened **Bow Wow Wow**. Recruiting **Matthew Ashman** (guitar), **Leigh Gorman** (bass) and **Dave Barbarossa** (drums) from an embryonic **ADAM AND THE ANTS**. He then set about searching for a talented, charismatic, and preferably malleable frontperson. It didn't take him long to find what he was looking for in the shape of **Annabella Lwin** (vocals), a 14-year-old half-Burmese schoolgirl whom he encountered singing in a north London laundrette. She was recruited on the spot, completing a highly controversial line-up that would go on to produce some of the sparkiest, sassiest music of the early 80s.

Bow Wow Wow's eagerly awaited debut single emerged on EMI in July 1980. "C30 C60 C90 Go!" was a frantic, Burundi-driven homage to home taping, featuring the infamous line, 'Now I don't buy records in your shop/ I just tape them all!' Unsurprisingly, it enraged the BPI, alienated radio and, despite a barrage of hype, only scraped the UK Top 40. Undeterred, McLaren decided that the six-track follow-up EP, YOUR CASSETTE PET, would be issued on cassette only. It met with little enthusiasm from record buyers – a shame, as the EP, particularly the breathless sensuality of "Louis Quatorze", was far more representative of Bow Wow Wow than the first single.

A deal with RCA failed to improve the band's chart fortunes, even the melodic "Chihuahua" failing to chart. At this stage, the band were very much in the shadow of Adam And The Ants, whose more commercial version of the same Burundi-influenced sound and piratical image left little room. Although the music press favoured them for their provocative energy, the public tended to see them as Adam's poor relations, fronted by a pouting adolescent.

The release of the debut album, SEE JUNGLE! SEE JUNGLE! GO JOIN YOUR GANG! YEAH, CITY ALL OVER! GO APE CRAZY! (1981), caused a new furore when Lwin's mother objected to the proposed cover photo, which featured Annabella (still only 15) posing nude. When she won a temporary ban on the offending photo, a weary McLaren toyed with the idea of replacing her with **Lieutenant Lush**, who had already made guest appearances at a couple of gigs. It came to nothing, however, and Lush resurfaced a year later as **Boy George** in his own band, **CULTURE CLUB**. The storm over the album's packaging overshadowed the record itself – confident, energetic and spirited, with Annabella's voice having lost much of its early shrillness.

The album sold respectably, and was followed in early 1982 by the hit single, "Go Wild In The Country", an invigorating, zestful rampage of a song that still sounds fresh and exciting. A cover of the Strangeloves' "I Want Candy" went Top 10, but reinforced suggestions that the band were struggling for new material. A hastily assembled compilation album, unimaginatively entitled I WANT CANDY (1982), symbolized the beginning of a downward spiral. As McLaren began recording his own album, Bow Wow Wow were now in control of their own career, with Lwin making her first contributions as a songwriter.

The band finally re-emerged with "Do You Wanna Hold Me", a watered-down calypso number that had little of their old vitality and none of their old charm. The accompanying album, WHEN THE GOING GETS TOUGH, THE TOUGH GET GOING (1983), was poorly received, and the band split the following year amid growing tension, financial problems and general exhaustion. Gorman, Ashman and Barbarossa continued as **The Chiefs Of Relief** for several fruitless years before disbanding. Annabella embarked on solo work for RCA in the mid-80s, and in 1993 was briefly signed to Sony.

In 1994, shortly before his untimely death, Ashman was reported to have turned down an invitation to reform Bow Wow Wow. Eventually, though, the remaining members found the temptation too great: Bow Wow Wow was reborn with **Eshan Kadroo** replacing Barbarossa on drums, and **Dave Kalhoun** on guitar. US dates at the end of 1997 were well received, but perhaps it's best that we remember them as they were, full of the wide-eyed excitement of youth and self-discovery – not easy things to re-create more than two decades down the line.

● **See Jungle! See Jungle! ...** (1981; RCA; currently unavailable).
Not many pop albums from the early 80s have stood the test of time as well as this – a string of sharp and sexy songs, full of exuberance and tunes to die for. An underrated gem.

● **The Best Of Bow Wow Wow** (1994; RCA).
A definitive mid-price anthology of the RCA years, this includes their best songs ("Chihuahua", "TV Savage") and some lesser-known delights ("The Joy Of Eating Raw Flesh").

Jonathan Kennaugh

BOSTON • BOW WOW WOW

DAVID BOWIE

Born David Jones, London, 1947.

"I once asked Lennon what he thought of what I do. He said 'It's great, but it's just rock'n'roll with lipstick on'."

Before there was a **David Bowie**, there were David and Davie Jones. There were also the **King Bees**, the **Lower Third** and the **Nazz**. There was the South London bluesman, the mod and the hippie. In short, David Jones wanted to be a star. From the very beginning, he also had aspirations to be weird: he flirted with Buddhism, the Golden Dawn, mime and an atrocious Anthony Newley voice before settling down as your average everyday bisexual from Mars.

He recorded a swath of diabolical pop music for Decca/Deram in the mid-60s, before changing his name to avoid confusion with the Davy Jones from The Monkees and striking gold in 1969 with "Space Oddity", a Top 10 hit in the UK. The LPs MAN OF WORDS, MAN OF MUSIC (1969; reissued on RCA as SPACE ODDITY) and THE MAN WHO SOLD THE WORLD (1970) followed, and it's perhaps most charitable to say that they have not aged well. HUNKY DORY (1971; RCA), however, was a ready-made classic, Bowie's best work as a 'standard' singer-songwriter and featuring the prophetically titled "Changes" – the song that started his bid for stardom.

The real stuff, however, was to come, as, between HUNKY DORY and THE RISE AND FALL OF ZIGGY STARDUST AND THE SPIDERS FROM MARS (1972), Bowie completely redefined the term 'star' as applied to men in rock'n'roll. Prior to Bowie, you created an image and pretty much stuck to it: rock'n'rollers were mean, out-and-out heterosexual carnivores who'd kill you and eat you if they couldn't screw you. They certainly never wore dresses, never appeared in makeup off stage or recorded songs with titles like "Queen Bitch". The press was bored of leather-clad moodiness and Bowie knew how to manipulate a story. Journalists lapped up every word from the new waif in town with his orange hair and his eyes of many colours, a star who held court in elegant hotel rooms dressed in flimsy girly clothes.

With the creation of **Ziggy**, Bowie went internationally ballistic, providing the overgorging 70s with the perfect, hedonistic, Lurex-and-makeup superstar. The concerts to promote the album titillated the mainstream press by having David simulate fellatio on guitarist **Mick Ronson** while he was in mid-solo. This blatant disregard for the possibility of electrocution enraged the tabloids and sold untold numbers of records.

For the next few years, Bowie invented a new character for each of his LP releases. He retired Ziggy at the end of the 1973 tour; the character that replaced him was **Aladdin Sane**, and despite the lousy pun and the head-to-toe white greasepaint (apart from a red and blue lightning flash across his face), he was a more mature, fuller character than Ziggy. Bowie, Aladdin's alter ego, had toured the world and had developed a nervous twitch in his songwriting. ALADDIN SANE (1973) had a tinny, neurotic sound, like a Hollywood party where the cocaine ran out an hour ago.

But by 1974 and the release of DIAMOND DOGS, Bowie could barely put a foot wrong. Reverting to outer-space imagery, he borrowed from Orwell – the tour was originally to have been called 'The 1980 Floor Show' – and created a dark world of dictatorship, oppression and, ultimately, escape. "Sweet Thing" concluding the album by dragging us through the urban mire to 'buy some drugs and watch a band and jump in the river' – the ultimate rock'n'roll night out.

It was a confident period for Bowie and he used his confirmed status in the rock world to bring old acts like **The Stooges** and **Lou Reed** back to life – alas, completely screwing up the production on their records in the process. Still, he donated a superb song, "All The Young Dudes", to UK rockers **Mott The Hoople**, reinventing them as a glam group and making them all a small fortune in the process.

Bowie's image as an omnisexual Martian from a totalitarian future had been a brilliant success, but it was time for a change. Bowie kept the fans happy by issuing a slick stopgap concert album, DAVID LIVE (1974), and then, for reasons known only to himself, came down from the mountain as a white soul boy. Even worse, he wasn't even working with the gutsy, rootsy soul people of Stax or Atlantic records – he'd opted for the processed-cheese sound of Philadelphia. Yet "Fame", in collaboration with **John Lennon**, was a hit single, while its parent album, YOUNG AMERICANS (1975), was a Top 10 smash on both sides of the Atlantic.

Bowie had by now dropped his first name. He was spending a lot of time in Berlin, doing a lot to revive the city's reputation for divine decadence. Rumour had it that Bowie was indulging in serious drugs and dabbling with the dark secrets of art-rock. He certainly stopped smiling and lost a lot of weight; he also managed to alienate a good few of his old-time fans by making statements in defence of dictatorship and the stability offered by a strong leader. This was the birth of the **Thin White Duke** character mentioned in the title track of the next album, STATION TO STATION (1976) – pretty grim, serious stuff.

1977 saw the release of LOW, the first of three studio LPs put together in association with **Brian Eno**. Bowie had given up concept albums, and listening to side two of LOW you might believe he had given up rock'n'roll. Eno was the man who more or less invented ambient music; by getting him in on the act, Bowie made a complete break with his past images and reinvented himself as an exponent of experimental music.

HEROES (1977) filled out the arts department by getting **Robert Fripp** to join the band and add some strangeness to the sound. Although only the title track, which tells a story of lovers killed by border guards at the Berlin Wall, has any direct connection to the city, HEROES reeks of Berlin in the late 70s. During this period, Bowie appeared in the film *Christiane F*, the story of a teenage junkie Berlin prostitute, and there's an odour of narcotics abuse to all the Berlin recordings. Despite the frantic emoting in the vocals, you sense he doesn't truly care about what he's singing, particularly "Heroes" in German.

Perhaps he'd just picked up a bad attitude from **Iggy Pop**; in between fiddling around with synthesizers with Fripp and Eno, Bowie dragged Iggy into the studio and squeezed THE IDIOT and LUST FOR LIFE from his drug-ravaged frame. (Bowie borrowed the music from Iggy's "Sister Midnight" for a track on his 1979 LP LODGER and also later recorded a version of Iggy's "China Girl".) Whatever the reason, the music of this period, while sincere enough, lacked emotion.

STAGE (1978) was another live album, with material covering ZIGGY STARDUST to LOW. An interesting document of his act at the time, again it didn't really capture the excitement that he could generate in a crowd. LODGER, which followed, was more in the vein of LOW, with songs on one side and a series of moods on the other. The singles "Boys Keep Swinging" and "DJ" were a return to more general-issue rock music, with just a hint of mayhem in the vocals to show off his status as tortured artist.

Bowie and his fans had had enough of this artsy, intellectual fare by the end of the 70s. He went back to writing songs and came up with SCARY MONSTERS in 1980. He also dragged out the makeup box for the cover picture and the stunning video that accompanied the hit single "Ashes To Ashes". In this song, a British #1 single, he finally killed off the **Major Tom** character created for "Space Oddity" eleven years earlier. Fripp made magnificent guitar-

He took it all too far ... Bowie models the Ziggy pyjamas

based noises throughout, although Eno didn't appear at all, as Bowie ditched what he didn't need from the world of experimentation, and remoulded its remainder into his own new distinctive sound. "Fashion", another single from the album, ushered in the 'me decade' in self-satisfied style.

For the next LP, Bowie signed to EMI, and devised a commercial sound and clean-cut image. "Let's Dance", the title track of the 1983 album, was a huge success all around the world and perfectly matched the bland new Bowie with the middle-of-the-road audience he was chasing. He'd moved into direct competition with mainstream acts like Phil Collins, Dire Straits and the solo Mick Jagger and there was no longer any menace associated with him. LET'S DANCE went to #1, followed by another less-than-sparklingly innovative recording in 1984, TONIGHT. This sexless incarnation of Bowie was the kind of tanned, good-mannered, well-dressed suc-

cess that you were supposed to try to be during the 80s. Sure, the music was a financial success and, true, he was no teenager any more, but did he have to be so nice?

Although Bowie's work throughout the 80s was his most successful in terms of earnings, there was precious little soul, sincerity or good old-fashioned weirdness; his 1987 album, NEVER LET ME DOWN, gave him another single in the charts but was otherwise ignored. Bad, mid-80s AOR was available elsewhere from younger performers, with better teeth.

He finished the decade by creating a new sub-style in popular music – Superstar Pub Rock. He gathered together a couple of Iggy's old rhythm section, bolted on a worthy guitarist and revealed **Tin Machine**. Innumerable press conferences were held, and interviews given, stressing that David was 'just one of the guys in the band'. He insisted that they were a simple rock'n'roll band, wanting no special treatment and, after an initial flurry of interest, his wish was granted. Tin Machine put out a trio of albums before Bowie sent them back to their deserved obscurity.

In 1993, he went to the top of the UK charts with BLACK TIE, WHITE NOISE, which contained a brief revival of the old nasty Bowie. The title track and "Jump They Say" echoed his mad 70s days but his next recording, THE BUDDHA OF SUBURBIA (1993), was a series of throwaway songs merely filling space around the title song, written for a BBC TV drama series, adapted from the Hanif Kureishi novel of the same title.

Still going strong in 1997, Bowie moved into art of a different kind. An exhibition featuring his watercolours and other works opened to general hilarity when it was revealed that he also dabbled in wallpaper design. However, forays into acting over the years have been generally better received, from film roles in Nic Roeg's *The Man Who Fell To Earth* (1975), *Merry Christmas Mr Lawrence* (1982) and *The Hunger* (1982), to a successful run on Broadway as

John Merrick in *The Elephant Man* (1980). Bowie these days is more convincing as one of rock's culturati than as a musician.

He returned to collaborating with Eno on the critically lauded 1: OUTSIDE (1995), which harked back to the European influences of his late-70s output, with some contemporary dance-floor references, which were more fully developed on his 1997 EARTHLING. Panned by the young lions of jungle as an old man's attempt to reinvent himself with some new clothes and a sequencer, this was not really a fitting epitaph. The drum'n'bass warriors were, of course, absolutely correct to shun this elderly Johnny-come-lately; Bowie's most creative era was, to them, as distant as, say, Sinatra's had been to Ziggy's fans back in the 70s.

HOURS (1999) was missed by all but the most committed of his followers – hardly surprising given the excitement already generated by the digitally remastered reissues of his back catalogue – there's a limit to the amount of Bowie-mania that can be generated this far down the line. The old mixmaster blended the name of one of the great 60s British groups with a title borrowed from the Stooges in "The Pretty Things Are Going To Hell" and relaxed back into some quality songcraft on "Thursday's Child" and "Survive", but despite the generally favourable reviews, there was no way that HOURS would charm anyone away from jungle.

Nonetheless, Bowie has built up a catalogue of so many outstanding songs that, these days, he can afford to tour his 'greatest-hits' set, when and where he wishes. He appeared at Glastonbury 2000, conjuring up a 'will he play or won't he?' kerfuffle in the week prior to the show with a thoroughly convincing, if convenient, bout of laryngitis. He sang through his pain though, holding the gargantuan crowd in the palm of his hand, and was awarded 'man of the match' by the majority of attendees questioned afterwards.

As a prelude to 2002's HEATHEN album, Bowie spent the Summer acting as the curator of the eclectic Meltdown Festival at London's South Bank centre – interestingly, his choice of acts was neither as surprising or diverse as you might have thought. Perhaps he's finally relaxing that finger on the pulse – who knows it might bring some interesting results if he stops paying attention to what's going on in popular culture and starts contributing to it again.

The Rise And Fall Of Ziggy Stardust And The Spiders From Mars (1972; RCA).
Image aside, this is a fine, no-nonsense rock album, telling the title story in eleven perfect songs, highlighted by "Starman", "Suffragette City" and "Soul Love".

Diamond Dogs (1974; RCA).
More role-playing blending nicely with solid rock. Classic cut on the album is "Sweet Thing", where the space-alien-cum-cracked-actor from ALADDIN SANE has become jaded and more powerful – the list of decadent temptations culminates in the perfect rock'n'roll hot date, 'We'll buy some drugs and watch a band and jump in the river holding hands'. Bowie at his best.

Station To Station (1976; RCA).
Lots of synthesized sounds and studio effects create

an impersonal atmosphere at odds with the vocal pyrotechnics unleashed on a couple of tracks. Still, it provided a couple of hit disco singles – "Golden Years" and "TVC15" – and some heart-stoppingly beautiful love songs, "Word On A Wing" and "Wild Is The Wind".

- **Low** (1977; RCA).
The first part of this album is instantly accessible: the songs have words; some of the words tell stories. The second section has hardly any real words, just four pieces of music with voices. All very moody and atmospheric as Bowie meets Eno meets Berlin.

- **Heroes** (1977; RCA).
Featuring, in the title track, the best song of loneliness and love he ever wrote, this album reeks of dangerous liaisons with creatures of mystery, of barely concealed despair, and yearning. The Eno-influenced instrumentals, "V2 Schneider" and "Neuköln", too, paint haunting, bleak pictures of a crippled city.

- **Scary Monsters** (1980; RCA).
You need to listen to this album loud, preferably over headphones, to get the full thrill of its screaming Japanese lyrics, unexpected bursts of mad guitar, and the thread of alienation running through. Bowie was back on top, kicking, energetic form.

- **The Singles Collection** (1993; EMI).
From 1969's "Space Oddity" to the inferior "Day In Day Out" (1987), a 37-track portrait of one of the most consistent pop-singles artists of the 70s and, more surprisingly, the 80s (check out "Ashes To Ashes", "Let's Dance", his collaboration with Pat Metheny on "This Is Not America", and even "Absolute Beginners").

Al Spicer

THE BOYS

Formed London, 1976; disbanded 1982.

Good-hearted bandwagon jumpers of the punk era, **The Boys** never set out to change the world. They were happy to make three good albums interspersed with jolly singles, then give up and get themselves proper jobs after making one dire, final album.

Casino Steel, Norwegian proprietor of one of the worst pseudonyms in rock'n'roll, was between jobs in London when punk broke. Having previously gigged with **The Hollywood Brats**, London's sleaze-rock riposte to The New York Dolls, Steel was able to put his new band into clubs. Its line-up consisted of Steel, bassist **Duncan 'Kid' Reid**, guitarists **Matt Dangerfield** and **John Plain** and drummer **Jack Black**.

As the band's singer and lyricist, Reid gave the band its sense of humour. He was behind its thinly disguised alter ego **The Yobs**, who became notorious for a series of pure punk covers of classic Christmas records. If necessary, the fake-sincere deadpan delivery in love songs like "Backstage Pass" (from their second album) could turn into an off-the-peg punk snarl, giving the band a wider range than most of the competition.

John Peel's radio show helped build a market for their self-titled debut LP, which hit the streets in 1977. It was a fine set, although somewhat rushed; the gigs promoting the album featured a lot of newer material, most of which appeared on their follow-up album, 1978's ALTERNATIVE CHARTBUSTERS.

Casino Steel took the band back to a little town in Norway to make their third long-player. The town was called Hell and the LP was called TO HELL WITH THE BOYS (1979). Despite this millstone of a title, they managed to create a good-quality mid-career album which, like all their other recordings, did a lot more business in Europe than at home.

When Steel was deported in 1980, the rest of the band tried to continue without him, but produced an enormously bad album, BOYS ONLY (1981). Uncharacteristically, The Boys had the good taste at this point to realize that they'd lost whatever they'd had, and split up. Recommended only to devotees of bad taste is the 1980 LP release by their alter egos – THE YOBS CHRISTMAS ALBUM.

- **Alternative Chartbusters** (1978; NEMS; currently unavailable).
More subtle, more confident and more unified than their debut, this was the nearest they got to a hit album.

Al Spicer

BILLY BRAGG

Born Barking, Essex, England, 1957.

As with most British musicians of the 80s, **Billy Bragg** was inspired to pick up a guitar by punk – and more specifically a Clash gig in 1977. In true DIY fashion, he formed a band, **Riff Raff**, with his childhood friend Wiggy, who taught him how to play the guitar he'd just picked up. Riff Raff split in 1981, although Bragg's later video, *…Goes To Moscow*, contains a version of their seminal two-chord dash, "I Wanna Be A Cosmonaut".

Bragg's next, bizarre career move was to join the British Army – he wanted to drive a tank. He lasted just three months, got discharged and, fresh out of uniform, began to gig as a solo artist. After a year of touring, he came to the attention of music publishers Warner Chappell, who allowed him to record some demos in their studio. The results turned out to be a full debut album, LIFE'S A RIOT WITH SPY VS. SPY, released by Go! Discs in 1984.

It was a tour of Britain – through 1984 and 1985 – visiting communities torn apart by the miners' strike, that turned Bragg into the political songsmith of current legend. He began to play benefits and pen overtly political songs, some of which found their way onto the BREWING UP WITH BILLY BRAGG album (1984). Serious chart action was to follow in 1985, first with Kirsty MacColl's version of "A New England" (for which he wrote a new verse), and then with his own BETWEEN THE WARS EP (1985), for which he took a lone guitar, an amp and a checked shirt onto the image-dominated *Top Of The Pops* TV show, and into the Top 20.

1986 saw the political stakes raised with a leading role in *Red Wedge*, an organization and tour (also involving The Style Council, Madness, The Communards and Morrissey) that threw its weight

Billy Bragg – Playing for the workers

"Sexuality", the 1991 single that took Bragg back into the charts; its 12" version even boasted a dance remix.

For DON'T TRY THIS AT HOME (1991), a full band (still featuring Wiggy) was recruited, and augmented by guests such as R.E.M.'s **Michael Stipe** and **Peter Buck**. Bragg then took a break from the music business after the birth of his son Jack in 1993, popping up only to play alongside S★M★A★S★H at the Carnival Against The Nazis in 1994, and at the Glastonbury Festival in 1995. Always more than just a musician, Billy also assumed the role of political and social commentator, contributing to British newspapers and the *NME*, and fronting several documentaries for BBC radio and TV. Nevertheless, eagerly awaited new material and live work was not far away.

The new role of father was one that was to shape much of his next album, WILLIAM BLOKE (1996). A companion piece, "Bloke On Bloke" (1997), was followed by the *Blatant Electioneering Tour* running up to the general election, culminating on the night itself with an emotion-drenched London show. Fittingly, his first ever gig under a Labour government came at the union-backed May Day free festival in Finsbury Park. The politics of another period provided the basis for his next project, MERMAID AVENUE (1998). Backed by alt-country heroes **Wilco**, it took a collection of Woody Guthrie's lyrics and set them to new music. An immensely fitting combination, and one that drew high praise from all quarters, not least Guthrie's own daughter.

It was hard to imagine a more fitting musician to carry Guthrie's torch into a new millennium. The album sold more than 600,000 copies worldwide, was subsequently nominated for a *Grammy* and spawned an equally satisfying follow-up, MERMAID AVENUE VOLUME II (2000).

Backed by a new band, **The Blokes**, featuring keyboard player **Ian McLagan** (Small Faces, Rolling Stones, Bob Dylan) Bragg released a new album of originals ENGLAND, HALF ENGLISH in 2002. Taking its title from a collection of essays by writer Colin MacInnes (*Absolute Beginners*), the album delved into the sticky issue of identity in multicultural Britain – proof, if it were ever needed, that Bragg was still campaigning, still making great music and still as relevant as he ever had been.

⊙ **Back To Basics** (1993; Cooking Vinyl).
Part of a reissue series, this is Bragg's first two albums plus the BETWEEN THE WARS EP. All life is here – schoolboy crushes, the *Sun* newspaper, the Falklands, love, betrayal and a seventeenth-century revolutionary group. Short blasts of harsh guitar and frankly less-than-tuneful vocals.

firmly behind the Labour Party and unsuccessfully tried to make politics 'sexy'. Later in the year, Bragg released what was to be his first great single, "Levi Stubbs' Tears". The album that followed, TALKING WITH THE TAXMAN ABOUT POETRY (1986) – subtitled 'the difficult third album' – not only broadened the musical backdrop but saw a new and sharper lyricism that ranged from trade unionism to the pressures of young marriage. With pianist **Cara Tivey**, he recorded "She's Leaving Home", a contribution to an *NME* benefit album of Beatles covers, SERGEANT PEPPER KNEW MY FATHER (1988); released as a double A-side with Wet Wet Wet's "With A Little Help From My Friends", it topped the UK charts for a month, with all proceeds donated to Childline, an organization devoted to helping children in trouble.

'Capitalism is killing music' was the cheery message emblazoned on Bragg's next release, the accomplished WORKER'S PLAYTIME (1988), but the album's political element was kept to a minimum – essentially, this was an honest and beautiful set of love songs. 1990's THE INTERNATIONALE, on the other hand, focused on out-and-out socialist lyrics. The two were to mix on

● **Victim Of Geography** (1993; Cooking Vinyl).
Perhaps the two best albums so far, on one release. TALKING WITH THE TAXMAN ABOUT POETRY features "Levi Stubbs' Tears", a great story song, and "Greetings To The New Brunette", featuring Johnny Marr (then of The Smiths). WORKER'S PLAYTIME covers everything from relationships to the British penal system.

● **William Bloke** (1996; Cooking Vinyl).
Bragg's work reflects both his changing political and personal landscapes, examining the effect of parenthood on the radical mind. "Pict Song" is a Martin Carthy-esque nod to his folk roots, while the album closes with the sunshine ska of "Goalhanger". Not a total success, but at times untouchable.

● **Mermaid Avenue Volume II** (2000; Elektra).
The first volume's brilliance was tempered by a sense that the musicians were feeling their way with the nostalgic material. However, this second set glows with confidence, and the cohesion between the Bragg- and Wilco-led material is far greater.

Phil Udell

BRAINTICKET

Formed Switzerland, c. 1971.

"Advice. After listening to this record your friends won't know you anymore." *Sleeve of Cottonwoodhill*

Brainticket must surely rank as the most obscure band of all time; the kind you discover by accident, the most probable route being from one look at the extraordinary sleeve of their debut album, COTTONWOODHILL (c. 1971). Put it on the player (yes, there is an equally obscure CD reissue) and the first couple of tracks suggest woolly acidheads Gong, with their nasal vocals, trippy flutes and far-out lyrics laid over recycled Led Zeppelin licks. But keep going and you reach the astonishing 26-minute epic, "Brainticket". Eschewing the standard litany of wazziness associated with trip-rock, this track penetrates the descent into psychosis latent at the heart of the acid experience. A punishing guitar loop is overlaid with disruptive sounds of trains and crowds, while **Dawn Muir**'s plummy English voice degenerates into a kind of speaking in tongues. Like some weird mix of Quentin Crisp, Lydia Lunch and Diamanda Galas, it is genuinely devastating.

The band's second outing, CELESTIAL OCEAN (1972), was a concept album 'inspired from *The Book of the Dead* of the Ancient Egyptians'. Fair enough, but those of us not fired up by such things can content ourselves with some of the most visionary rock music of the time outside Can, Faust and Bowie. "Egyptian Kings" features a brilliant ponderous organ figure overlaid with wild effects, and "Jardins" boasts about the only use of the sitar in rock music that doesn't come over sounding like anodyne New Age (it sounds a bit like A. R. Kane's luscious unpicking of the guitar fretboard in fact). "Era Of Technology", meanwhile, could almost be Aphex Twin, while "The Space Between" approaches a kind of trance-techno.

Brainticket made at least two other full-length recordings – ADVENTURE (1979) and VOYAGE (1980) – but that, to the best of my knowledge, was it. For the record, apart from Dawn, the band included such names as **Cosimo Lampis** (who now runs a school of percussion in Sardegna, Italy), **Joel Vandroogenbroeck** and **Wolfgang Paap**. God knows what Joel and Wolfgang are doing now.

● **Brainticket** (c. 1971; Sound Solutions).
This CD reissue includes all of COTTONWOODHILL, and a few bonus chunks of CELESTIAL OCEAN for good measure. And no sleeve notes...

Ben Smith

GLEN BRANCA

Born Harrisburg, Pennsylvania, 1948.

Initially working in the arena of confrontational and experimental theatre while at college in Boston, **Glen Branca** moved to New York in 1976 to form a band, only to find punk rock uninvolving. Briefly continuing with the theatre, he formed a new outfit, at first called **The Statics**, later **The Theoretic Girls**. With their particular brand of loud experiment and peculiar tunings – Branca would frequently replace guitar strings with various kinds of wire – The Girls were popular performers in the burgeoning post-punk No Wave scene, until the scene split after Brian Eno released the controversial NO NEW YORK compilation.

Abandoning the band format for more experimental areas, Branca formed his **Guitar Army** (including **Lee Ranaldo** and, later, **Thurston Moore**, of Sonic Youth), with himself as composer and conductor on several low-budget tours of the alternative US scene. Relying on a wall of guitar sound and primitivistic percussion, Branca's unique soundscapes married consonance with dissonance in a form that soon bordered on the symphonic.

Branca's first single, "Lesson No. 1", was released in 1980 on 99 Records, and the following ASCENSION album sold over 10,000 copies – enough to finance him and the Army to tour for the next two years. The first stage of the trip across America comprised shows that caused havoc even with audiences used to the volume of punk and No Wave groups, with up to six guitarists generating seemingly endless amounts of feedback. The noise was incredible and Branca soon became a doyen of the avant-garde, and a patron of **SONIC YOUTH**, whose first EP he released through his own Neutral label in 1981.

Following a recording of music he composed for **Twyla Tharp**'s experimental dance piece *Bad Smells*, Branca took his group on their first European tour in 1983 to perform his SYMPHONY NO. 4, during which time he fell out with Ranaldo and Moore, when they used the opportunity to tour as Sonic Youth at minimal expense.

Returning to the US, Branca became more interested in the mathematics of musical composition, using complex formulas as the basis of much of his future work. His SYMPHONY NO. 1 (TONAL PLEXUS) and SYMPHONY NO. 3 (GLORIA), on the ROIR and Crepuscule labels respectively (both since rereleased on CD), did much to establish Branca in his chosen field, with only **Rhys Chatham** approaching the level of intensity generated by Branca's massed guitars. Since the early 80s, Branca has continued to explore the extreme possibilities of the electric guitar, and has found a congenial home on the British label Blast First since 1989's SYMPHONY NO. 6 (DEVIL CHOIRS AT THE GATES OF HEAVEN), which featured ten guitarists, as well as keyboards.

Though he will probably never belong to any mainstream, Branca has gradually worn down the distrust of his music often expressed in both the 'serious' and the rock music worlds, and has even been gaining a platform as a composer of contemporary highbrow music: his SYMPHONY NO. 9, for example, was recorded by a Polish orchestra in 1994. Continuing Branca's drift into the 'classical' world, the mood of the guitarless symphony more closely resembled Glass than No Wave. INDETERMINATE ACTIVITY OF RESULTANT MASSES (1996) was a live performance of his seminal 1982 work, while 2001's HALLUCINATION CITY: SYMPHONY FOR 100 GUITARS was a vast undertaking, performed on June 13, in New York City; both revealed an artist who seemed set on moving further still from the masses.

⊙ **The Ascension** (1980; New Tone. 2002; Felmay). CD rerelease of Branca's first and possibly most accessible LP. Each piece builds gradually to a crescendo of guitar noise, calms, and then returns for a final blast. The title track is Branca at his typically chaotic best.

⊙ **Symphony No. 6** (Devil Choirs At The Gates Of Heaven) (1989; Blast First). Branca at his most intense. Stepping into the same area of hypnotic repetition as Steve Reich and Philip Glass, Branca adds feedback and volume to the equation.

Richard Fontenoy

THE BREEDERS

Formed Boston, Massachusetts, 1988.

When the **PIXIES**' pioneering SURFER ROSA album appeared, guitarist/vocalist **Kim Deal** (aka **Mrs John Murphy**) received much acclaim for writing a radio-friendly track called "Gigantic", so it was only natural she would want to step out of Black Francis's creative shadow and try building up a following of her own. Drunkenly recruiting the commercially minded **Tanya Donelly** of **THROWING MUSES** (a 4AD stablemate and similiarly frustrated songwriter) during a night out in a Boston disco in 1988 seemed to be a step in the right direction, but the pair spent the next two years looking for time to record and going through countless line-ups. They called their outfit **The Breeders**, the name that Deal had used when she and her sister **Kelley** had run a truckstop-touring group in Dayton, Ohio. This recycling was indicative of the slightly retrogressive music they were about to make.

POD (1990), The Breeders' debut album, was rehearsed and recorded in three weeks with Slint's **Britt Walford** (appearing as **Shannon Doughton**) on drums and Englishwoman **Josephine Wiggs**, from old Pixies' support band The Perfect Disaster, on bass. Given a fashionably warts-and-all 'live' feel by **Steve Albini**, who also produced SURFER ROSA, POD wasn't quite as reminiscent of the Pixies as some critics made out – the backgrounds provided by Albini and the band for Deal's lilting, low-mixed vocal melodies were far too plodding for that. Yet its lo-fi guitars and lyrics about old Pixie standbys such as abortion ("Hellbound"), weird/bad sex ("Only In 3s", "When I Was A Painter") and a lover's death ("Fortunately Gone") did provide balm for purists who felt that the Pixies' album of that year (BOSSANOVA) was too solidly produced and science-fictional for its own good. Unhampered by a cool critical reception, POD outsold BOSSANOVA in 1990 and set a strong style on which subsequent Breeders' releases would build.

Unfortunately the bankruptcy of Rough Trade America meant the band lost most of their royalties on POD, a factor which – along with the other commitments of Tanya Donelly, who had been vital to the 'supergroup' image – pushed Deal back to the Pixies until their disbandment. With Donelly only playing on one more release (1992's SAFARI EP) before achieving success with her own band **BELLY**, The Breeders became a very different beast. **Jim Macpherson** – from Dayton's The Raging Mantras – was drafted in on drums, while Kim's sister Kelley Deal became the new guitarist, despite a total lack of experience in the part.

Kim really did seem to have gone back to square one when a ramshackle Breeders opened for Nirvana on the latter's July 1992 European tour. Amazingly, the next thing this line-up did was to step into a San Francisco recording studio with British co-producer **Mark Freegard** to record "Cannonball", turning out the band's most successful marriage of old-style Pixies guitar innovation ('exactly a dozen different aural effects in the first 57 seconds!' shouted one excited critic) with Kim Deal's own svelte melodies and lyrics about Sadian sexuality. Suddenly The Breeders were hot stuff again, and with "Cannonball" (backed by a cover of Aerosmith's "Lord Of The Thighs") added to MTV's Buzz Bin, its mother album THE BREEDERS' LAST SPLASH (1993) – a warmer but more rambling take on POD – went on to sell over a million copies in the States alone. The Breeders had seized that post-Pixies audience, and many others besides.

But by this time Kelley was working mainly with her own band, **Kelley Deal 6000,** releasing GO TO THE SUGAR ALTAR in 1996; and Josephine had the **Josephine Wiggs Experience**. Meanwhile Kim, along with MacPherson, formed **The Amps**, releasing the satisfyingly lo-fi album PACER in 1995.

It was only a matter of time before Kim Deal revamped the Breeders name but – bar some scattered live shows – it was to be several more years

before any new material surfaced. When MacPherson eventually left the band to join **GUIDED BY VOICES**, Kim was left in sole charge of the Breeders future.

A helping hand – at least financially – appeared when the Prodigy sampled "S.O.S" for their single "Firestarter". With Kelley back on board and writing with Kim, the possibility of a new album looked increasingly hopeful. Finally, with a new backing line-up on board – **Richard Presley** (guitar), **Mando Lopez** (bass) and drummer **Josh Medeles** – the Deals entered the studio with Steve Albini to record a long-awaited third album.

Finally released in 2002, TITLE TK (4AD) wasn't quite the miraculous, world-beating album fans had hoped for, but then again it wasn't half bad either. Recorded with what Kim refers to as the 'All Wave' philosophy, an approach eschewing modern production technology akin to the cinematic Dogme movement, the album trades more off the ramshackle aspirations of The Amps rather then the slick, innovative pop of LAST SPLASH.

⊙ **Pod** (1990; 4AD).
The Breeders' spacious and haunting debut often sounds naked alongside both The Pixies' output and The Breeders' later releases. Nonetheless, a great album.

⊙ **The Breeders' Last Splash** (1993; 4AD).
A listenable 25-minute album padded out with fairly pointless instrumentals ("Flipside", "S.O.S.") and draggy avant-garde mumblings ("Mad Lucas") to give it that classic Pixies' fifteen-track, 39-minute format. Still, singles "Cannonball" and "Divine Hammer" are excellent pop stuff.

⊙ **Title TK** (2002; 4AD).
The set's trump card is its simplicity: less is most definitely more. Cuts like "Sinister Foxx", "Off You" and "The She" (a masterpiece) all proffer a narcoleptic haven of cool tones, staggered rhythms and dream space.

Piers Clifton

BRINSLEY SCHWARZ

Formed London, 1969; disbanded 1975.

A**fter five poorly received singles in five years, Kippington Lodge** decided to call it a day.

Keyboard player **Bob Andrews**, guitarist **Brinsley Schwarz** and bass player/vocalist **NICK LOWE** found themselves a new drummer, American **Billy Rankin**, and in October 1969 launched themselves with a much more commercial name: **Brinsley Schwarz**.

They teamed up with Jimi Hendrix's former tour manager, **Dave Robinson**, who managed the band, co-produced their eponymous first album and orchestrated an infamous Fillmore East debacle in New York. To help promote the LP, 150 media people were flown out for one of the shows at the theatre. However, their plane was delayed, their 'reserved' seats occupied and several of them were thrown out when they protested. In this case, the maxim that 'all publicity is good publicity' was inappropriate: an angry press ignored both band and album, and BRINSLEY SCHWARZ duly flopped.

Now in debt and with little chance of stardom, Brinsley Schwarz began to take their music much more seriously. Renting a house near London, they spent eighteen months playing and listening to various types of music. The range of musical influences was obvious on DESPITE IT ALL (1970), which was released during this period, to be followed by SILVER PISTOL (1972), the first to feature new vocalist and guitarist **Ian Gomm**.

Then, in the summer of 1972, Brinsley Schwarz saw American band Eggs Over Easy performing at a London pub. As they watched, an idea formed – a way of gigging which didn't involve the expense of hiring huge PAs to fill vast halls. Amenable landlords were found and a circuit emerged in London that would last for many years, breaking innumerable bands. If the Brinsleys were not the founders of pub-rock they were certainly influential pioneers, and were soon followed by Bees Make Honey, Kilburn & The High Roads, Chilli Willi and Ducks Deluxe. Young audiences appreciated them and began to realize that virtuosity was inessential to get a gig and a recording contract, and by the mid-70s the seeds of punk had been sown in the pub-rock scene.

Throughout this period, the Brinsleys continued making excellent music across three LPs – NERVOUS ON THE ROAD (1972), PLEASE DON'T EVER CHANGE (1973) and THE NEW FAVOURITES OF BRINSLEY SCHWARZ (1974). Commercial success still eluded them as much as they themselves shunned the limelight, and in March 1975 the band played their last gig at London's Marquee before an amicable split.

Ian Gomm later re-emerged in 1978 with some solo success, while Brinsley and Billy joined a late incarnation of **Ducks Deluxe**, before Schwarz and Andrews teamed up with ex-Ducks guitarist **Martin Belmont** to form **The Rumour**, who became **GRAHAM PARKER**'s backing band. Most successful of all was Nick Lowe, whose solo career was to encompass performing and producing for himself and a variety of other acts.

⊙ **Surrender To The Rhythm** (1991; EMI).
A near-definitive twenty-track compilation put together by Mr Schwarz himself. Switching from live favourites like "Home In My Hand" and "Nervous On The Road", to the earlier, wistful "Last Time I Was Fooled" and "Silver Pistol", it also boasts six tracks from the final album, which showcase Lowe's fast-improving songwriting ability. Overall, though, it's the sheer quality of the music and the band's love of the material that shines through.

Simon Ives

THE EDGAR BROUGHTON BAND

Formed Warwick, England, 1968; disbanded 1976; re-formed 1978.

I f you wanted a sex symbol in 1970 you could have had glitter-boy Marc Bolan, cool androgyne David Bowie, or, if you wanted something hunkier, there was always Robert Plant. But whoever your pin-ups may have been, they weren't the terminally hairy **Edgar Broughton Band** – even Black Sabbath were better-looking.

The outfit was formed in 1968 by **Edgar Broughton** (guitar/vocals) and his brother **Steve** (drums) after their expulsion from public school, with **Arthur Grant** (bass) and **Victor Unitt** (guitar), who departed early for London, where he spent some time in **The Pretty Things**. The briefly fresh-faced trio came to London in 1968 in Mrs Broughton's van, and were soon regarded, along with Yes and Led Zeppelin, as one of the up-and-coming acts of the time. Signed to Harvest, their first album, WASA WASA (1969), mirrored their stage act in its rough-edged psychedelic aggression, and was a masterpiece of underground electric blues.

Broughton was possibly the only vocalist of his day who was audibly influenced by Captain Beefheart, while his guitar screeched like a cat sliding down a blackboard. His brother Steve used the skills he had learned wielding a sledgehammer during the building of the Warwick bypass on his drum kit. It was up to Art Grant's bass to bring some sense of order to it all, which it did occasionally.

1970 was the year they should have broken big, but bad management saw them miss their opportunity. SING BROTHER SING (1970) reached #18 in Britain, and two singles staged brief commando raids on the charts without breaking into the citadel of the Top 30. But it proved to be the apex of the band's success. The singles showed two sides of The Edgar Broughton Band's style. "Out Demons Out" (1970) was an audience sing-along, a chant exorcizing the evils of the day. The follow-up, "Apache Drop-Out" (1971), took Beefheart's "Dropout Boogie", added some new lyrics, and then shoehorned The Shadows' "Apache" into the instrumental sections. No one else would have dared.

Then, in 1970, Victor Unitt returned, bringing a drastic shift in direction. The head-on rock disappeared just as that kind of music was making fortunes for the likes of Deep Purple and Black Sabbath. In its place appeared more structured songs, tending towards ballads, with a strong political slant, and the band lost its commercial momentum. Three albums followed – THE EDGAR BROUGHTON BAND (1971), INSIDE OUT (1972) and OORA (1973) – before the band left Harvest for NEMS in search of better fortunes. Legal problems kept them out of the studio until BANDAGES (1975), by which time Unitt had been replaced by John Thomas.

The music was getting gentler, owing more to Roy Harper than the MC5, though the lyrics were sometimes more vitriolic. NEMS were expending most of their minimal energies pushing Black Sabbath and, although the band was popular in Europe, BANDAGES was never going to make any mark back home. "Speak Down The Wires", with its refrain, '...there's room at the shelter/Take food and warm clothing for Yesterday's Men', sounded uncomfortably close to home.

Still they refused to throw in the towel and get proper jobs. 1978 saw the release of LIVE HITS HARDER, followed by PARLEZ VOUS ENGLISH? (1979), by which time they had expanded to a six-piece under the name **The Broughtons**. Years of frustration led them to style themselves 'the band that would not die', but the studio album was a rather flaccid and toothless affair.

Low-level touring continued throughout the 80s, once again as The Edgar Broughton Band. A concept album, SUPERCHIP (1981; rereleased with extra tracks 1997), was an electronic, Orwellian nightmare of mind control. Various personnel joined and left the original trio, and the touring intensified into the 90s, by which time they had attained a kind of mythical status that conferred respectability. Sections of a bemused press finally began to acknowledge these indestructible hippies. The hair and beards had gone, the middle-age spread was showing, but the fiery intensity was if anything burning brighter, with Edgar railing ever more vehemently at the state of the world.

Art Grant finally left in 1994 because of family commitments (to be replaced by **Kris Gray**), while Edgar has been working with youth projects, introducing kids to Hendrix while getting 'heavily into dance acts, like the Chemical Brothers'. By 1997 the band was recording again (with Edgar's 18-year-old son **Luke** on keyboards and **Ian Hammond** on guitar), using electronics and some 'heavy things' with programmed drums. A new Edgar Broughton Band album, THE FIRST SUPPER, was released in 1999. The band that refused to die goes on.

⊙ **Wasa Wasa** (1969; BGO).
An album that grips, from the tense electric grind of "Death Of An Electric Citizen" to the head-on psychedelic assault of "Evil" and "Love In The Rain". Ragged and brilliant.

⊙ **Sing Brother Sing** (1970; BGO).
Taking the style of WASA WASA a step further, with lengthy experimental work like "Psychopath" and "There's No Vibrations But Wait!". Part of "The Moth" was inspired by a police raid on the studio, and there's also their other

'anthem', the raucous stomp-along "Momma's Reward (Keep Them Freaks A-Rolling)", beloved by hippies everywhere.

The Edgar Broughton Band/Inside Out (1993; Beat Goes On).
Back-to-back issue of the second and third EMI albums (1971 & 1972). Less of the raw and raucous stomp, particularly on the oponymous album, which features more textured material like "Mad Hatter" and "The House Of Turnabout", as well as "Poppy", an Edgar/Victor guitar/vocal duel. INSIDE OUT has more punch musically, employing the glam-rock thump in place of the faster attack of WASA WASA. Best tracks are "I Got Mad (Soledad)", "The Rake" and the single "Gone Blue".

Superchip (1981; EMI; 1996; See For Miles).
'Never before have so many been so subservient to so few...' This electronic album is about the mind-controlling 'superchip'. If the music is early 80s, the concept is frighteningly prescient. It works – most of the time – but don't expect "Love In The Rain". The album has been augmented by an new extra track ("The Virus") co-produced and co-written by Luke Broughton, 'as an antidote to the negative side of the album', but the pessimism still wins through. Luke's ambient 'secret track' takes The Edgar Broughton Band into a second generation.

Patrick Neylan-Francis & Guy Davies

ARTHUR BROWN

Born Whitby, England, 1944.

"It was 1968 and we were playing in Paris. Some girls had lost their clothes and were being carried over the top of the audience to the stage. It wasn't sexist like it would be today; they were enjoying it. It was part of the fun of being alive."

Thus **Arthur Brown** described **The Crazy World Of Arthur Brown** in their brief heyday, when "Fire" topped the UK charts, and when he was one of the prime movers behind the British progressive underground. Psychology graduate Brown was 'the god of hell-fire', fronting a group comprising **Sean Nicholas** (bass), **Vincent Crane** (keyboards) and **Drachen Theaker** (later replaced by **Carl Palmer**) on drums. Unusually for an R&B-based act, there was no guitarist.

A devout Christian, Brown always gave his work a strongly religious flavour, daubing his face with diabolic paint and starting his show by being lowered by winch onto the stage wearing his psychedelic robes and flaming 'fire-helmet'. Apart from a rip-roaring version of Screaming Jay Hawkins' "I Put A Spell On You", the centrepiece of the set was Brown's five-track mini rock opera about the conflict between the fear of hell and the comfort of sin, a sequence with the recurring refrain of 'Why is it so cold out here? Let me in!/The price of your entry is sin'.

The Who's **Pete Townshend** helped produce the debut album, THE CRAZY WORLD OF ARTHUR BROWN (1968) and **Charles Fox** of the *New Statesman* wrote the sleeve notes, enthusing that

Brown 'could easily be the first genuine artist to come out of our local underground'. Townshend of course was to produce his own rock opera the following year, and the brass sound used on THE CRAZY WORLD... would resurface five years later on The Who's QUADROPHENIA.

But it all went rather sour for Arthur Brown. He was sued for stealing the tune of "Fire", thus losing most of his royalties. Then, midway through the band's first US tour, Crane and Palmer quit to form **ATOMIC ROOSTER**, before Palmer once again moved on, this time to form **EMERSON, LAKE & PALMER**. Undeterred, Brown set up a new Crazy World and recorded STRANGELANDS in 1969, but it would not be issued until 1988. He had now abandoned R&B and was moving into more impenetrable experimental sounds. When he finally resurfaced in 1971, he was doing 'rock theatre', including his own on-stage crucifixion, with his new band **Kingdom Come**.

Kingdom Come had a rockier, progressive sound, but despite three fine albums, GALACTIC ZOO DOSSIER (1971), KINGDOM COME (1972) and JOURNEY (1973), with some excellent work from **Andy Dalby** (guitar) and **Mike 'Goodge' Harris** (keyboards), they never had much success and split in 1973. Brown went on to cut three more albums, all pretty dire, before disappearing to Texas to become a carpenter. There he recorded REQUIEM (1982), another concept piece, this time about nuclear war.

Arthur Brown – dressed conservatively, as ever

Brown resurfaced in 1993 to do a well-received fiftieth birthday tour ('carpentry didn't pay the bills'), and despite the absence of a fire-helmet he had lost none of his touch for showmanship. His voice still screamed and growled as powerfully as ever, and he must have enjoyed it all, because he was back on the road in late 1995. A live album, LEGBOOT, followed in 2002.

⊙ **The Crazy World Of Arthur Brown** (1968; Polydor). "Nightmare", "Fire" and "I Put A Spell On You" all display Brown's incredible voice to full effect, from a deep rumble to a piercing scream. Crane's manic keyboards complement it beautifully and, if Brown never made a better album, nor have many others. Every home should have one.

⊙ **Strangelands** (1969; finally issued in 1988; Reactor). The second Crazy World album; a confused, disjointed piece of psychedelic experimentation. Gong did it better.

⊙ **Galactic Zoo Dossier** (1971; Polydor). Brown's strange ideas are surrounded by tighter music, with all the tracks merging into one another. Harris's organ rocks magnificently on "Gypsy Escape" and "No Time", and it all ends with the surreal sound of running feet and someone jumping into the canal. Equally great when stoned or straight.

Patrick Neylan-Francis

IAN BROWN

Born Manchester, England, UK, 1971.

The ugly demise of Manchester favourites **THE STONE ROSES** in 1996 left many predicting the end for vocalist **Ian Brown**. Insiders considered Brown's former songwriting partner, guitarist **John Squire**, to have been the driving force in the Roses, while Ian was mocked in the press for his stoned manner and unpredictable voice. Squire's emergence in 1997 with the bland and retro Seahorses put the balance into greater perspective, and set the stage for Ian Brown's comeback.

Having completely disappeared from public view, Brown suddenly hit the upper reaches of the UK charts at the start of 1998 with his debut solo single, "My Star". In collaboration with the talented guitarist **Aziz Ibrahim**, Ian fashioned a surging slab of psychedelia which sounded like a lost classic Roses track recorded in a phone booth. The uneven but engaging UNFINISHED MONKEY BUSINESS followed, and revealed a tentative but ambitious singer trying his hand with all the styles and musical instruments available (including some truly archaic synthesizers). It also ushered in the now universally known tag of 'King Monkey' to describe its creator. The album's raw grooves pleased more Stone Roses followers than Squire's efforts had, spawning two more hits in the dance-floor friendly "Can't See Me" and the dark and spiteful "Corpses In Their Mouths".

Brown seemed truly back on track, when two separate incidents were to threaten his career. Returning to Manchester from Paris on British Airways, Ian was alleged to have threatened a stewardess. He awaited what appeared to be no more than a typical rock-star-gets-a-slap-on-the-wrist trial. Meanwhile, Brown's unwise comments to *Melody Maker*

regarding homosexuality suddenly placed him in the midst of a minor national furore that saw his image as a progressive and liberal thinker considerably tarnished. No sooner had the controversy begun to die down than Ian was given a harsh three-month sentence in Strangeways prison for his supposed 'air rage'; he was let out early for good behaviour.

The atmospheric "Be There", released by James Lavelle's progressive U.N.K.L.E. outfit after being reworked and given the vocal treatment by Ian, returned the 'monkey man' to the charts. Fired up by this non-guitar-based collaboration Ian set to work. Late 1999 saw the release of GOLDEN GREATS, created in tandem with programmer/composer **Dave McCracken**. An excellent record from start to finish, Ian had found his voice and his true musical home amongst the progressive sounds and carefully crafted songs, touching on the familiar themes of vitriol and devotional love. The bizarre "Dolphins Were Monkeys" returned him to the UK Top 5 (the flip side of which featured the unlikeliest of covers in Michael Jackson's "Billie Jean").

Having outlived his one-time Madchester contemporaries and out-performed his former Stone Roses compadres, Ian released the laid-back and critically acclaimed MUSIC OF THE SPHERES in 2001, charting at #3 in the UK. Its parent single, the orchestrated "F.E.A.R.", was thoroughly impressive, while the lush "Northern Lights" and "Shadow Of A Saint" were merely beautiful. A sister release, REMIXES OF THE SPHERES, followed in 2002.

Not likely to break out of the UK sales market, Ian is nevertheless one of the last true mavericks in the music business. King Monkey remains the coolest man in rock.

⊙ **Golden Greats** (1999; Polydor). Brit-pop meets House meets Northern Soul, and an infectious, joyous and angry record with great tunes results. Standout tracks include the hit "Love Like A Fountain" and the digital-riff-heavy "Golden Gaze", which will make you wonder why anybody would bother picking up a guitar.

⊙ **Music Of The Spheres** (2001; Polydor). Ian chills out and looks up at the stars for inspiration. "F.E.A.R." is mind-blowing, while the inside sleeve photo of Brown blowing smoke rings tells you all you need to know about the man they call 'King Monkey'.

R Tyndall

JAMES BROWN

Born Barnwell, South Carolina, May 3, 1933.

"That's when I hit on 'Papa's Got A Brand New Bag'. It was a slang that would relate to the man on the street, plus it had its own sound: the music on one-and-three, the downbeat, in anticipation."

With the exception of the work of the very greatest singers (Aretha Franklin, Al Green,

Marvin Gaye), pop music communicates mainly through the noise of its rhythm. Little Richard made the piano talk like a drum; Elvis made the high lonesome sound of country swing like a Memphis jook joint; The Velvet Underground turned rock's roll into a mechanical drone; Public Enemy remade the bounce of funk as the synaptic snap of information overload. No one, however, has done more with, and for, rhythm (and thus popular music) than **James Brown**. From his over-the-top, processed hairdo to the outrageous athleticism of his dancing, to the bone-rattling dexterity of his rhythms, Brown is all flash, energy and urgency.

Despite his status as the Minister of the Brand New Super-Heavy Funk, it was Brown's remarkably primal voice that first got him noticed. Brown's first record, "Please, Please, Please" (1956), was a culture clash between the urbanity of Louis Jordan and the grittiness of unacknowledged influences like Archie Brownlee of the gospel harmony group The Five Blind Boys Of Mississippi, and Clarence Fountain of The Five Blind Boys Of Alabama (compare their version of "Maybe The Last Time" with Brown's 1964 version). Despite the single's Top 10 R&B success, Brown was about a decade ahead of his time and released a string of lacklustre flops to compensate. On the brink of being dropped from his label, King-Federal, Brown came up with "Try Me" (1958). Another extraordinarily individualistic interpretation of pop balladry, "Try Me" set in motion a barrage of fifteen Top 20 R&B hits which included a cover of the 5 Royales' "Think" and the largely instrumental "Night Train", both of which featured stunning interplay between bass and drums that is the foundation of funk.

The finest moment of Brown's early career was the release of LIVE AT THE APOLLO (1963). The boss of Brown's label, Syd Nathan, was dead set against a live album, but Brown went ahead and paid for the recording himself. The American #2 chart success of the album not only vindicated Brown's self-belief, but, more importantly, it proved the validity of black self-sufficiency. In addition, it remains one of the greatest albums ever recorded: pure adrenalin, astonishing audience–performer interaction and breathtaking music. The only way it could get any better was if you could see James good-footing across the stage.

The man they call the Godfather

1965, though, was the beginning of Brown's golden age, a period of unprecedented innovation that would last until the mid-70s. "Papa's Got A Brand New Bag" (1965) was as insistent as any punk song, while its rhythmic sophistication changed the world by shifting the accent of the downbeat. Even more 'on the one' was "I Got You (I Feel Good)" (1965), which featured an undeniable hook for good measure. By 1967, Brown's emphasis on rhythm had become so streamlined that melody ceased to have any relevance to his best music. "Let Yourself Go" (1967) featured the definitive James Brown sound: the endlessly riffing 'chicken scratch' guitar played by **Jimmy Nolen** and **Alphonso 'Country' Kellum**. This was rhythm as groove in its literal sense; rhythm as a locked repetition; rhythm that was simultaneously hypnotic and kinetic.

Compared to everything else that was out at the time – Aretha Franklin's first recordings for Atlantic, Otis Redding's last recordings for Stax/Volt – "Cold

Sweat" (1967) was as shocking as Chuck Berry. This was simply the most purely physical record made up to that point and it is still hard to imagine anything that moves the way "Cold Sweat" does. Even the horns of the incomparable **Maceo Parker** and **Pee Wee Ellis**, which were usually used to fill out the sound, became percussion instruments subservient to the groove. Aside from being the first funk master-piece, "Cold Sweat" is also the keystone of hip-hop as it is the first important recording to feature a drum break, the DNA of hip-hop.

This primacy of rhythm was one of the cultural parallels of the emerging Black Pride movement. Again, Brown was years ahead of his time with the release of "Say It Loud, I'm Black And I'm Proud" (1968). Even though it was probably the first song to deal explicitly with the politics of race, "Say It Loud" didn't need an explicit text – the message was in the infathomably deep funk groove. After his next mas-terpiece, "Give It Up Or Turn It Loose" (1969), which turned the funk into a conglomeration of molecular grooves, Brown instigated the second dance craze of his career, the Popcorn. Although less significant than "Say It Loud" or "I Don't Want Nobody To Give Me Nothing" (1969), the Popcorn records featured some of Brown's band, the **JBs'**, most galvanizing grooves. Despite its relatively lowly chart peak, 1970's "Funky Drummer" is one of the most important records ever made. Its outrageously percussive drum break, played by **Clyde Stubblefield**, popularized the 'give the drummer some' interlude and twenty years later dominated the musical landscape of the late 80s/early 90s, appearing on records by Public Enemy, Sinéad O'Connor and Madonna.

"Funky Drummer" was the last important single released by the JBs before the bulk of the band walked out. Brown quickly turned to a group of teenagers who hung out at his Cincinnati studio. Based around the remarkable **BOOTSY COLLINS** and his brother **Phelps**, the group soon became the most rhythmically innovative band in the history of pop-ular music. Their first record, "Get Up (I Feel Like Being A) Sex Machine" (1970), was as kinetic as "Cold Sweat", with Bootsy's bassline popping and sliding and slithering in unimaginable ways. The new band reinvented music with the pure funk of "Super Bad" (1970), the almost unbearably electric "Get Up, Get Into It, And Get Involved" (1970), "Talkin' Loud & Sayin' Nothing" (1970), "Soul Power" (1971), and a stunning live remake of "Give It Up Or Turnit A Loose" (1971).

After Bootsy and co left in 1971, Brown con-tinued to re-imagine funk as the crossroads of physical ecstasy and droning trance. Songs like "Escape-Ism" (1971), "Get On The Good Foot" (1972), "Stoned To The Bone" (1973), "The Payback" (1974), "My Thang" (1974) and "Funky President (People It's Bad)" (1974) were little more than grinding, buzzing guitar riffs set to a deep funk bottom. Disco was coming, though, and Brown

couldn't keep up. With the exception of the hyper-kinetic "Get Up Offa That Thing" (1976), Brown didn't have a significant hit until the mid-80s. The Godfather didn't wither away, however. With the emergence of hip-hop in the mid-70s, Brown and his aesthetic of beats as the be-all and end-all of music became more important than ever. As usual, Brown was light years ahead of his time. His concept of rep-etition was perfectly in tune with a culture that was created almost entirely out of ready-mades. Hip-hop's debt to Brown was repaid in 1984, when Brown teamed up with **Afrika Bambaataa** for the underrated "Unity" single.

However, it was with Eric B. & Rakim's "I Know You Got Soul" (1987) – which sampled Brown's production of longtime sidekick Bobby Byrd's song of the same name – that Brown's music was truly acknowledged by hip-hop, and his rhythms became as elemental to music as the I–IV–V blues progres-sion. It is simply inconceivable to think of contemporary music without James Brown. Although words have always been subservient to the feel of a record in blues-based popular music, Brown made rhythm, tempo, groove, catalysis, energy and timbre everything. Brown was the first black artist to be in control of his career, and his loud and defiant presence was more important to race politics than any march ever could be. Typically, Brown's larger-than-life persona has got him into legal trouble and dodgy ideological territory. But Brown's gargantuan ego is the product of one of music's most gifted talents and a legacy that is the genesis of contemporary music, and will be for some time to come.

(•) **Live At The Apollo, Volume One** (1963; Polydor). One of the most purely energetic records ever released – you don't need the visuals to get a full image of the specta-cle of the Godfather at the height of his power.

(•) **In The Jungle Groove** (1986; Polydor). A great compilation of the JBs' early 70s funk mantras.

(•) **Star Time** (1991; Polydor). Yes, it's four CDs; yes, it's expensive; but if you don't own this, you shouldn't be reading this book. If you're not a believer and cannot under any circumstance afford a box set, then settle for

(•) **20 All-Time Greatest Hits** (1991; Polydor). A distillation of STAR TIME's highlights.

Peter Shapiro

JACKSON BROWNE

Born Heidelberg, Germany, 1948.

"I'm a Los Angeles writer. I cannot speak for Middle America."

Although born in Germany, **Jackson Browne** is the chronicler of post-surf California's good and bad times, its confessions and betrayals. A con-summate storytelling songwriter, he's been an admired figure for over thirty years, and a steadfast voice for America's liberal conscience.

Initially, Browne attracted the attention of **THE NITTY GRITTY DIRT BAND**, who recorded "Shadow Dream Song", "It's Raining Here In Long Beach", and "These Days", and drafted him into their ranks for a few months in 1966. He became **Nico**'s guitarist for a time, and through her met Lou Reed, who introduced him to bands such as Cream and The Who.

By the turn of the 70s, Browne had returned to California, where a demo tape found favour with David Geffen's newly founded Asylum label. A debut solo LP, JACKSON BROWNE: SATURATE BEFORE USING (1972), was a consummate southern Californian artefact, on which Browne was joined by **David Crosby** (vocals), guitarists **Albert Lee** and **Clarence White**, The Nitty Gritty Dirt Band's **Jim Fadden** (harmonica) and **Sneaky Pete Kleinow** (pedal steel). The Dirt Band and The Byrds both covered one track, "Jamaica Say You Will", while The Jackson Five hit the singles charts in 1973 with a cover of "Doctor My Eyes".

His status as media darling was reinforced by **The Eagles'** huge international hit, "Take It Easy", which Browne had written with **Glenn Frey**. It also appeared on Browne's 1973 album FOR EVERYMAN, which also featured "These Days" (memorably reworked by The Allman Brothers) and marked the beginning of a long-standing association with multi-instrumentalist **DAVID LINDLEY**. That same year also saw further commercially successful collaborations with The Eagles on DESPERADO.

LATE FOR THE SKY (1974) and THE PRETENDER (1976), consolidated his position as an AOR radio staple. The latter mixed the straight-ahead Californian soft rock of the title track with the Mexican tinges of "Linda Paloma" and the poppy "Here Come Those Tears Again", in which he duetted with **Bonnie Raitt** and **Rosemary Butler**. RUNNING ON EMPTY (1977), a patchwork of various performances over the years, had a looser, rougher-edged feel and led to Browne scoring a rare hit with a cover of the Maurice Williams classic, "Stay".

By the early 80s, Browne's career was increasingly reflecting his liberal politics. Browne allied himself with MUSE (Musicians United For Safe Energy), and appeared at a number of benefits, culminating in the triple LP and film, NO NUKES (1980). His strong positions on disarmament and Central America often threatened his career and it was an open secret that his phone was being tapped. Browne's political ideology perhaps lacked the radicalism and acid wit of Phil Ochs, but his activism was still notable for someone in his position. LIVES IN THE BALANCE (1986) featured Browne at his most coherent and eloquent, his blasts against Reaganite politics, set against more personal musings such as "In The Shape Of A Heart".

WORLDS IN MOTION (1989) lacked its predecessor's lyrical vehemence, and the early 90s heralded a quiet period for his solo work, although he did cover

Incredible String Band founder Robin Williamson's "First Girl I Loved" for Elektra Records' fortieth anniversary set, RUBÁIYÁT (1990).

Browne's return with I'M ALIVE (1993) was a faithful, if unremarkable, set of songs. Then, as he celebrated thirty years in the music business, he released LOOKING EAST (1996), which proved that, while his music was comfortable, his politics were anything but. If at times his conscience-probing songs have eclipsed his repertoire of love songs, then it is worth recalling the Scots singer Dick Gaughan's observation that a political song can be 'a different sort of love song'.

⊙ **For Everyman** (1973; Asylum).
From its opening "Take It Easy" and "Our Lady Of The Well" through "I Thought I Was A Child" to "Ready Or Not" (an uncomprehending tale of unplanned pregnancy and befuddled naivety), here was confirmation that a major talent had arrived.

⊙ **Late For The Sky** (1974; Asylum).
Another strong album, including "Fountain Of Sorrow", "For A Dancer" and "Before The Deluge", the last of which was covered by Irish group Moving Hearts on their self-titled 1981 debut LP.

⊙ **Lives In The Balance** (1986; Asylum).
Browne's most openly political album: messages melded to strong music, especially on the impassioned "For America".

⊙ **The Next Voice You Hear** (1997; Elektra).
Twenty-five years after the release of his debut album, this excellent compilation covers all the high points in Browne's career and features two tracks not seen elsewhere – "The Next Voice You Hear" and "The Rebel Jesus".

Ken Hunt

JEFF BUCKLEY

Born Orange County, California, 1966; died
Memphis, Tennessee May 29, 1997.

Jeff Buckley emerged in the mid-90s as one of the most gifted singer-songwriters of his generation; a remarkable feat considering it was achieved on the basis of just one album – and that everyone was comparing him to his late father, Tim, himself one of the most creative talents of the 60s.

Young Jeff made his first appearance in the early 90s, knocking about on New York's Greenwich Village club circuit, the reputation of his mesmeric multi-octave voice and striking looks quickly spreading by word of mouth. The LIVE AT SIN-É mini-LP, released by British independent label Big Cat in 1994, captured Buckley in a typical club setting, alone with his electric guitar. Two originals, "Mojo Pin" and "Eternal Life", highlighted his emerging talent, but it was on covers of Edith Piaf's "Je N'En Connais Pas Le Fin" and Van Morrison's "The Way Young Lovers Do" that Buckley really shined, on the latter scatting and improvising around the melody for a full ten minutes.

The debut album GRACE (1995), appeared a few months later, and duly bowled the music press over. Particularly impressive was Buckley's grasp of structure on the self-penned songs, employing a basic

Jeff Buckley in a heartbreak troubadour (not to mention Morrissey) mode

rhythm section behind his own guitar, augmented by sparse keyboards and strings. Buckley and his band showed themselves equally adept at creating dream-like reveries ("So Real" and "Dream Brother") and Led Zep-style riffing ("Eternal Life"), but the central feature of attention was Buckley's startling voice. Like his father, he dominated the mood and tone of a song: he could effortlessly cruise along, then suddenly veer away in a flight of vocal power and finesse – listen to the codas of "Grace" and "So Real".

Buckley cited heartbreak troubadours as his musical heroes and influences, and he possessed a lyrical depth and emotional honesty to match the best of them. Live appearances throughout the mid-90s saw an ever-increasing audience response to his music, and one that went well beyond the folk-club scene. Buckley triumphed, for example, at Elvis Costello's Meltdown festival alongside a broad spectrum of other artists and musical styles. Maybe he inherited from his father that adventurous stance towards musical boundaries and the capabilities of the human voice.

His death – he drowned on Thursday, May 29, 1997, in the Mississippi River outside of Memphis – brought his outstanding promise to an abrupt end. GRACE will stand as his finest testament, despite the awesome beauty evident in the posthumously released and unfinished follow-up (SKETCHES FOR) MY SWEETHEART THE DRUNK (1998), and the sporadically wondrous live set MYSTERY WHITE BOY (2000), which was compiled by his mother and his guitarist, **Michael Tighe**, from his group's 1994–1996 tour tapes. A further collection of rarities, SONGS TO NO ONE, appeared in 2002, credited to Jeff Buckley and **Gary Lucas**.

Grace (1995; Columbia).
An incredibly assured major-label debut – cuts like the title track and "Lover, You Should've Come Over" are astounding in the way they find the balance between power and delicacy.

(Sketches For) My Sweetheart The Drunk (1998; Columbia).
It's incredibly sad that Jeff isn't around to take these 21 unfinished tracks through to completion. The voice is as impressive as ever, the music still swims with those disconcerting stop-start rhythms, and the overall feeling is one of regret. The CD comes with a little interactive falderol for those of us who play CDs on our computers.

Mystery White Boy (2000; Columbia).
Even though many of the renditions are stifled by clumsy live arrangements, this set offers a beautiful, heartfelt and appropriate conclusion to Jeff Buckley's post-mortem release schedule.

Nicholas Oliver

TIM BUCKLEY

Born Washington DC, 1947; died 1975.

He did not always sing remarkable songs – at least a quarter were dull, dire or downright self-indulgent – but **Tim Buckley**'s voice was incendiary. And just as his voice could explode from a grumble to a falsetto shriek, stylistically he was forever bewildering his audience and record company – album after album presented new directions. For Buckley, songs were springboards for risk-taking, but at some point in his life he took to understudying oblivion too strenuously for comfort. Eventually he forfeited his life.

With high-school bands behind him, he slipped into folk-protest, folk-rock and kindred hyphenated folk permutations. During the 60s, Elektra had made massively important contributions to the folk scene, through the likes of Judy Collins, Tom Paxton and Phil Ochs. Tim Buckley was added to Elektra's folk roster in 1967, although it's interesting that when Elektra celebrated its fortieth anniversary with the covers compilation RUBÁIYÁT (1990), nobody attempted a Buckley cover, despite HAPPY SAD's prominence in the accompanying booklet.

Adhering to Elektra's usual policy of eponymous debuts, TIM BUCKLEY (1966) was fairly conventional 'folk' fare for the period. GOODBYE & HELLO (1967) was wordy soft-rock with Greenwich Village troubadour inflections, showing the strong influence of singer-songwriter Fred Neil, whose "Dolphins" would turn into a showcase for Buckley's vocal callisthenics. HAPPY SAD (1969) found him maturing as an artist, blending genres in arrangements using vibraphone, congas and marimba.

Signed to Straight Records, he began to reel off albums with a frenetic wilfulness that flouted the prevailing recording-promotion-recording catechism. BLUE AFTERNOON (1970) was followed just weeks later by LORCA (1970), named after the poet murdered by fascists during the Spanish Civil War. In hot pursuit came STARSAILOR (1971), which tested many fans' loyalties. Live shows made few concessions to expectations, dousing listeners in free-form workouts.

The vehemently electric GREETINGS FROM L.A. (1972) broke new ground, especially in its avowedly sexual lyrics, a coarse revelation cloaked in the garb of the sexual revolution. SEFRONIA (1973) was inessential, apart from "Dolphins" and "Honey Man", while LOOK AT THE FOOL (1974) proved an unseemly swansong. Less than a year later, Buckley was dead of a heroin overdose after playing a gig in Dallas.

Buckley's work began undergoing a reappraisal from the mid-80s onwards. A groundswell of interest built the artist as a young casualty, beginning with several bootleg recordings of concerts or radio broadcasts. Then, in 1990, came the unearthing of DREAM LETTER, recorded live in July 1968 between sessions for HAPPY SAD and BLUE AFTERNOON. A 1968 session for John Peel's BBC radio show was released in 1991 on Strange Fruit, and was reissued on a 1994 compilation, MORNING GLORY. That same year, LIVE AT THE TROUBADOUR 1969 further fed the stream, while HONEYMAN (1995), recorded in New York in 1973, drew on his SEFRONIA period and revealed performances superior to those available on bootleg.

Buckley's voice-as-instrument approach was often more engaging than his actual songs, and the lows of his output outweigh the highs. Nevertheless, hearing him imbue the same song with new emotional depth over several readings (prime examples being "Buzzin' Fly" or "Dolphins") confirms what a magnificent technician he could be. Better still, he could charge songs with extraordinary emotional depth, a trait that briefly flowered in the 90s through the son he barely knew, **JEFF BUCKLEY**.

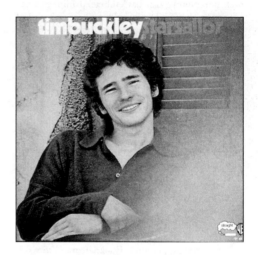

Happy Sad (1969; Elektra).
Transitional, experimental and perfectly in tune with the times, Buckley smoulders and emotes on "Strange Feelin'", "Buzzin' Fly", and the ten-minute "Love From Room 109 At The Islander (On Pacific Coast Highway)". The sexually charged "Gypsy Woman" ranks as his "Light My Fire", albeit more poetically realized than The Doors' hit. This is the place to begin.

Greetings From L.A. (1972; Rhino/Demon).
A holiday postcard about having a lovely time, and the relief that loved ones aren't there – an album that journalist Martin Aston described as being 'drenched in lust'.

Dream Letter (1990; Enigma Retro/Straight).
A live compendium of Buckley's early musical styles, straddling his singer-songwriter folk-poetry, soft-rock and jazz phases.

Ken Hunt

RICHARD BUCKNER

Born Fresno, California, 1964.

Listen to **Richard Buckner**'s debut album, BLOOMED, and you might wonder what qualifies him as a rock artist, rather than a country/folk one. His mournful laments placed him firmly in the camp of maverick Texas singer-songwriters such as Butch Hancock, Townes Van Zandt and Jimmie Dale Gilmore. The back-porch ambience of his ruminations evoked the prairies around Lubbock, Texas, the region that spawned Hancock and Gilmore, and whose awesome beauty and stultifying isolation fed the restless tension of their music.

Indeed, the unwary could be forgiven for assuming that Buckner was the newest master of the Lubbock country sound. He recorded his album there, for one thing, with **Butch Hancock** himself guesting on harmonica. The disc was produced by **Lloyd Maines**, a principal behind-the-scenes figure of modern country-rock, who has also worked with Hancock, Uncle Tupelo, Jimmie Dale Gilmore, and Joe Ely.

Yet Buckner was not a Texan, but rather a Californian-born wanderer, and it's the alternative-rock community that has embraced him, not the country audience. His sound may be composed of largely traditional elements, but he owes his allegiance to contemporary rock and folk singer-songwriter tradition rather than the pop factory of Nashville.

Buckner grew up in rural northern California in a family that moved frequently and split up occasionally, accounting for some of the wanderlust that can be sensed in his compositions. After a period in Atlanta, he began to make his name in the San Francisco alternative-rock scene of the early and mid-1990s. There he played fully arranged country-rock as the leader of **The Doubters**, who augmented the standard rock line-up with pedal steel and fiddle. He has cited expected influences such as Lucinda Williams, Townes Van Zandt and Peter Case, but also alternative-rock artists such as Giant Sand and Pavement, who bend musical conventions to suit their own needs.

For recording purposes, Buckner opted to work as a solo act, backed by Austin-based acoustic musicians. He originally planned BLOOMED as a sort of concept album built around his family, but ultimately scrapped the idea. If Buckner's weathered voice and bittersweet romantic compositions set the mood on BLOOMED, producer Lloyd Maines was the principal architect of the dusty musical landscapes, adding pedal steel, dobro, lap steel, slide guitar and banjo.

Comparisons to country-rock deities such as Gram Parsons are premature. He sings with authority and distinction, but some of his material can feel a little ordinary. His edgier songs ("Gauzy Dress In The Sun", "Rainsquall"), however, show considerable promise.

So far, Buckner has struggled to transcend cult status in the US. It didn't help that BLOOMED only came out in Germany on its original 1994 release, although it was subsequently picked up stateside by the small Texas label Dejadisc. More recently, tours supporting Butch Hancock in the UK and country-rockers Son Volt in the US have increased his visibility considerably.

A deal with MCA saw the release of a second album, DEVOTION AND DOUBT (1997), followed by SINCE (1998), both of which were recorded with fuller band arrangements, a move that may lead to Buckner's acceptance within the rock and pop audience. More releases followed with HILL (2000), IMPASSE (2002) and RICHARD BUCKNER (2003).

⊙ **Bloomed** (1994; Dejadisc).
Not an entirely representative reflection of the breadth of Buckner's vision, as he and producer Lloyd Maines choose to present a straight acoustic country/folk programme, without any overt rock elements. The album effectively places Buckner in the Lubbock, Texas songwriting tradition.

Richie Unterberger

BUFFALO SPRINGFIELD

Formed Los Angeles, 1966; disbanded 1968.

"There's something happening here/What it is ain't exactly clear." Stephen Stills' "For What It's Worth"

The best American folk-rock band of the 60s besides The Byrds, **Buffalo Springfield** mixed folk, country and British Invasion influences to produce some of the most enduring California rock of the era. Boasting sparkling harmonies and several excellent singer-songwriters, they were enormously influential for an act with a catalogue of just three albums. Besides establishing the careers of guitarists **NEIL YOUNG**, **Stephen Stills** and **Richie Furay**, their idiosyncratic hybrid of styles inspired numerous folk and country-rock acts throughout the 70s.

Like The Byrds, Buffalo Springfield were composed of renegade ex-folkies who were steered back to the rock'n'roll of their youth after the massive success of The Beatles. Stills, who had travelled the coffee-house circuit in New York City with Furay, moved to LA (where he unsuccessfully auditioned for The Monkees) and convinced Furay to join him. Trying to put a group together without much success, they were caught in a traffic jam on Sunset Boulevard when they noticed a hearse in front with Ontario licence plates. Stills was sure the driver was Neil Young, whom he had already met in Toronto, and indeed it was – with bassist and fellow Canadian **Bruce Palmer** in tow as well. With the addition of drummer **Dewey Martin**, who had played with the folk-bluegrass group **The Dillards**, Buffalo Springfield were born.

An immediate success in the highly competitive Los Angeles rock scene, the Springfield were excellent performers, but their greatest strengths were the songwriting smarts of Stills and Young, who created a healthy friction by egging each other on to give their band's repertoire a balance and diversity. Stills was the more straightforward, country-influenced and pop-driven of the pair; Young, then as now, favoured moody, eccentric, haunting tunes. But all of their material was gloriously melodic, delivered by the band with superb craftsmanship and versatility that could encompass get-down-and-dirty rock'n'roll as well as tender, wistful ballads.

Signed to Atlantic Records, they made a fine start with BUFFALO SPRINGFIELD (1966), divided almost evenly between Stills and Young compositions. Stills and Furay took most of the lead vocals at this stage, although Young would handle the singing on most of his subsequent Springfield material. Characterized by sumptuous interplay between electric and acoustic guitars, Martin's hard-driving snare drums, and gorgeous harmonies, it contained some of Stills' finest songs, and introduced Young's oddly brooding persona and enigmatic lyrics on cuts like "Out Of My Mind" and "Nowadays Clancy Can't Even Sing". It wasn't a big hit, but in early 1967 the group entered the US Top 10 with Stills' "For What It's Worth", inspired by teenage riots on LA's Sunset Strip. One of the best protest songs of the 60s, it remains the band's most famous recording.

Seemingly poised for a big breakthrough, the group was derailed in 1967 by major internal and external pressures, which found Young leaving, then rejoining, the band, and Palmer under constant threat of deportation back to Canada. An album, STAMPEDE, was never completed, and various musicians were drafted in for short periods to cover the absences. Young missed the band's celebrated appearance at the 1967 Monterey Festival, where **David Crosby** (then still with The Byrds) guested.

Amid all these difficulties, late 1967 saw them complete a second LP, BUFFALO SPRINGFIELD AGAIN, which, against all the odds, remains their best effort. Critics of the thinly produced debut, who felt it had diluted the sound of their live performance, were satisfied with this album's rich layers of electric and acoustic guitar, and seamless, at times elaborate, arrangements. Young's orchestrated opuses, "Expecting To Fly" and "Broken Arrow", rank among his greatest achievements, while "Bluebird" and "Rock & Roll Woman" are Stills' toughest rock songs. The LP also unveiled Furay as a songwriter of considerable promise, though his tunes lacked the brilliant edges of his colleagues'.

The group's personnel conflicts continued unabated, however, and their final album, LAST TIME AROUND, was released after their split in 1968. Young departed early in the proceedings, leaving behind a couple of excellent bittersweet songs, "I Am A Child" and "On The Way Home". His absence tilted the balance on the rest of the record towards Stills, with engineer **Jim Messina** enlisted as bassist to fill out the line-up. Their weakest overall LP, it still included a few first-rate tracks, especially Stills' Latin-influenced "Pretty Girl Why" and Furay's "Kind Woman".

After the split, Stills helped form **CROSBY, STILLS & NASH** (later joined for a while by Young), while Furay and Messina were mainstays of the original line-up of country-rock band **Poco**, before Messina teamed up with **Kenny Loggins** to form a soft-rock duo.

Buffalo Springfield had provided the foundations for the country-influenced California rock groups of the 70s, as well as acting as vital reference points for latter-day folk-rock groups like the Long Ryders and The Jayhawks.

⊙ **Buffalo Springfield** (1966; Atco).
Only a couple of weak moments on this masterful folk-rock debut, which presents almost fully matured songwriting skills. Contains their sole hit single, "For What It's Worth".

⊙ **Buffalo Springfield Again** (1967; Atco).
The Springfield at their peak, reflecting the influence of hard rock and psychedelia. Young provides the LP's most experimental triumphs, while "Mr. Soul", "Bluebird" and "Rock & Roll Woman" are masterpieces of economic, intelligent Californian 60s rock.

Richie Unterberger

BUFFALO TOM

Formed Boston, 1986.

As the 90s progressed, **Buffalo Tom** grew from being categorized as another college-rock three-piece of the Hüsker Dü/ Dinosaur Jr. lineage to critical acceptance as a genuine force that had somehow eluded the mainstream. The trio of **Bill Janovitz** (vocals/guitar), **Chris Colbourn** (bass/vocals) and **Tom Maginnis** (drums) formed at the University of Massachusetts in the mid-80s and gelled into a solid unit.

Financed by the MEGADISC imprint and then licensed to SST, their eponymous first album appeared in 1989 (reissued 1998) and relied on raw, fresh power chords, exemplified in the searing opener, "Sunflower Suit", and the dynamic but melodic "Impossible". There were ample signs of the songwriting talents of Janovitz and Colbourn and of the band's ability to vary the pace, but they were largely written off as a junior to Dinosaur Jr., a criticism given force by the fact that **J. Mascis** himself produced their early output.

They ploughed on regardless and secured a faithful following on the US college circuit and in indie circles on both sides of the Atlantic. They had the advantage of a strong camaraderie that showed in the special chemistry of their live shows. They even grinned and bore the stage-diving.

Their second album, BIRDBRAIN (1990; reissued 1998), showed the band – and Janovitz in particular – getting to grips with personal angst, while the shimmering sound and more complex rhythm structure of "Baby" previewed a broadening musical vision.

By 1992 the group had done some solid touring in Europe and other parts of the world and had signed to a major label, RCA, though they maintained their connection with MEGADISC. It was the release of LET ME COME OVER that year which raised the band's profile and attracted acclaim in the music press. Hardly surprising, as the record showed the increased maturity of the two songwriters and a lighter musical touch than the band had been thought capable of. "Taillights Fade", a power ballad with a soul-wrenching crescendo, became a standard request on alternative-rock stations, while "Mineral" had a wistful folkier strand woven round a delicious melody. Sadly, however, the album didn't sell as well as it deserved.

The following year saw the band take a fair break from touring to allow more time in the studio and they spent a couple of months in LA with the experienced **Robb Brothers** – who had worked with the likes of Rod Stewart and Steely Dan – producing BIG RED LETTER DAY (reissued 1998). A lot more trouble was taken over the production, yet somewhere amid all the careful layering and dubbing the band's passion was lost; it was as if they felt inhibited by big studio techniques. The material, however, was fine, in essence very similar to that of LET ME COME OVER, but without the high peaks.

In 1994 Bill Janovitz embarked upon a solo acoustic tour, with a set consisting wholly of Buffalo Tom songs and covers, all played with his natural humility yet magnetic force. In 1997 Janovitz further bolstered his solo career with the release of LONESOME BILLY – an exceptional and well-received solo effort; its highpoints included "Gaslight" and "Ghost In My Piano". He released a second solo collection in 2002, entitled UP HERE.

As for Buffalo Tom: SLEEPY-EYED (reissued 1998), was released at around the time of the band's excellent set at the Reading Festival in 1995. Recorded at Dreamland, a converted church in Woodstock, it struck a fine balance between crisp freshness, as in the opener and single, "Tangerine"; melodic pop sensibility, as in "Kitchen Door"; and passionate grandeur, displayed in full measure on "Sparklers" and the magnificent "Sunday Night". All this suggested that we hadn't heard the best of Buffalo Tom yet. As Chris Colbourn put it, 'Over the last couple of years we've stopped watching MTV and started realizing our own place in the world.' True to their word, SMITTEN (1998) was drenched in harmonic, confident tracks such as "Rachel" and "Postcard".

In 1999 the group contributed a cover "Going Underground" to the FIRE & SKILL Jam tribute album. The cut also featured on a double A-side single with the flip sporting Liam Gallagher and Steve Cradock's version of "Carnation" – it debuted at number six in the UK chart.

2000 also witnessed the release of a retrospective singles collection: ASIDES FROM BUFFALO TOM: 1988–1999. Summing up their career nicely, the collection featured many of their finest moments, including "Birdbrain", "Sodajerk" and "Taillights Fade". A punning companion release, BESIDES, followed in 2002.

⊙ **Let Me Come Over** (1992; RCA; reissued 1998; Beggars Banquet).
The mellower side of Tom comes into balance with the rockier, in a set of well-crafted material.

⊙ **Sleepy-Eyed** (1995; RCA; reissued 1998; Beggars Banquet).
Even greater maturity is in evidence here, as the ability to mix power, passion and subtlety reaches new heights.

⊙ **Asides From Buffalo Tom: 1988 – 1999** (2000; Beggars Banquet).
A superb document of the band's rise ; it features many of their early grunge stormers as well as much of the more rounded later material.

Nick Edwards

T-BONE BURNETT

Born John Henry Burnett, Fort Worth, Texas, 1945.

When **T-Bone Burnett** became involved in Bob Dylan's 1975 touring band, **The Rolling Thunder Revue**, he already had a considerable reputation as a producer and had recorded himself, most notably as **J. Henry Burnett** (releasing an album on Uni in 1972 – THE B52 BAND AND THE FABULOUS SKYLARKS). The Revue, a loose congregation of soloists and backing musicians, bringing together such diverse figures as Joni Mitchell and veteran Canadian rocker Ronnie Hawkins, gave him a taste for performing.

After completing his stint with Dylan, Burnett formed his **Alpha Band** in 1977, with fellow Revue members **Steve Soles** and **David Mansfield**. After a couple of late-70s albums, Burnett released his solo debut, TRUTH DECAY (1980), followed by a 1982 mini-album, TRAP DOOR. The Texan musical melting pot was evident from this early solo work, a high-energy form of rock'n'roll drawing on both blues and country traditions. Burnett often used both as a vehicle for social comment, as in bitter cameos such as "A Ridiculous Man" (from TRAP DOOR) and "Madison Avenue" (TRUTH DECAY). Furthermore, Burnett's committed Christian background did not prevent such driving rock songs as "Come Home" ('...went down to the nightclub the other night/It started with a drink, ended in a fight...') and "Pretty Girls", a lustful endorsement of Texan women.

For his next album, PROOF THROUGH THE NIGHT (1983), Burnett teamed up with **Ry Cooder** and **Pete Townshend**, before touring with **Elvis Costello** the following year under the name **The Coward Brothers**, who also released an excellent one-off single, "The People's Limousine" (1985). (This can now be found on Costello's 1987 compilation album, OUT OF OUR IDIOT.)

Burnett and Costello continued to work together, notably on The Costello Show's KING OF AMERICA album in 1986. Despite collaborations with **Los Lobos**, Burnett himself has recorded only occasionally since. All the same, the fleeting appearances have confirmed that his is a refreshing and highly individual rock'n'roll voice. The sparser textures of his 1992 comeback album, THE CRIMINAL UNDER MY OWN HAT, provided the backdrop to songs critical of the sentimental and the hypocritical, especially where politicians and evangelists were concerned.

Since the release of this comeback set, T-Bone has continued to focus on collaborations and production work with the likes of **Counting Crows**, **The Wallflowers** and **Jackson Browne**, amongst others.

⊙ **Truth Decay** (1980; Demon).
With a supporting cast including Billy Swan, this breakthrough album contained some of Burnett's finest rockers. Alas, hard to find these days.

John Collis

BUSH

Formed London, 1992.

About 99 percent of British music fans have probably no idea who **Gavin Rossdale** (vocals/guitar), **Nigel Pulsford** (guitar), **Dave Parsons** (bass) and **Robin Goodridge** (drums) are. By contrast, it's likely that 99 percent of US music fans could tell you all about **Bush**.

Originally named **Future Primitive**, they changed their name in honour of the London suburb of Shepherd's Bush, where they once resided. Bush then slogged round a series of London fleapits, consistently failing to attract any positive attention from record companies or to gain any kind of fan base to set them on an upward trajectory, and by 1994 the only regular gig available to the quartet was at the tiny Amersham Arms pub in southeast London. A depressing situation, but fortune, as so often is the case, was to shine on those who persevered.

In the final months of 1994 Gary Crowley, Capital Radio disc jockey, passed a copy of Bush's demo to a friend from a new American label, Trauma. This friend, one Rob Kahane, was so impressed that he turned up at the band's shabby rehearsal room in Harlesden and offered them a deal, the clincher coming in the form of a guarantee of total creative control.

Fortune continued to look kindly upon Bush once their debut album was in the can. Trauma distributed advance tapes to various radio stations in America. The highly influential K-ROQ in Los Angeles fell head over heels in love with the track "Everything Zen", and started giving it heavy rotation, even before the album had been released. A clamour for the band grew and grew, so Bush headed stateside, playing their first ever US gig in New York in January 1995. So SIXTEEN STONE (1995) was an eagerly awaited release, and it didn't disappoint.

America was sold on its power and passion; SIXTEEN STONE was on its way to quintuple platinum sales and Bush found themselves performing the arenas.

In Britain, however, all this gave the cynics a field day. Every review tossed the name 'Nirvana' liberally around, with the likes of Pearl Jam and Stone Temple Pilots also receiving regular namechecks, whilst some went so far as to suggest that Bush were only making waves in the States because Trauma was associated with the hip Interscope label, home of Trent Reznor and Nine Inch Nails. Rossdale and co had the good grace to suggest that comparisons with the grunge deities were actually complimentary, and eventually the British press started to accept that Bush had been around the pub circuit for too long to be mere bandwagon copyists.

In some ways the waves from across the Atlantic did count against Bush, but the four were perfectly content to work hard in their homeland, returning to the small venues to build from the grassroots – indeed they were relieved to be out of the American goldfish bowl for a while.

Bush – from W10 to Everything Zen

1997 saw the release, at last, of the follow-up to SIXTEEN STONE, the staggeringly confident RAZORBLADE SUITCASE. The album – produced by the golden boy of grunge, **Steve Albini** – sold millions of copies and made millions of dollars. DECONSTRUCTED (1997) was a remix album featuring radical reinterpretations of Bush favourites (Derek Dahlarge takes on "Everything Zen" anyone?). Not everything about the album worked perfectly but it succeeded in introducing the 'electronica' audience to British indie rock and vice versa. This more experimental direction led to THE SCIENCE OF THINGS (1999), a less commercially successful release, so for 2001's GOLDEN STATE, they returned to their riffing roots.

⊙ **Razorblade Suitcase** (1997; Trauma/Interscope).
The biggest surprise was perhaps the lack of surprises, either in the music, the critics' response, or the copious sales figures. In other words, it sounded much the same. The hacks hated it and the Yanks couldn't buy it quickly enough. Still, at least "Swallowed" gave them a Top 10 hit in the UK.

Hugh Hackett

KATE BUSH

Born Bexleyheath, England, 1958.

Kate Bush was a bit of a prodigy. By her fifteenth birthday she had already written more than a hundred songs, and in 1973 her precocious talent came to the attention of Pink Floyd guitarist **Dave Gilmour**. He was sufficiently impressed by her material to subsidize a demo tape, which in turn impressed A&R executives at his record company, EMI. As a result, a unique 'sponsorship' arrangement was set up in 1976 whereby Bush would spend a year honing her talent in return for an EMI advance of £3500. At the end of this period, the singer began recording at Abbey Road, and in January 1978 the first Kate Bush single, "Wuthering Heights", was released. It was a breathtakingly original piece of music, which showcased her four-octave voice to stunning effect, and it raced to the top of the UK charts. The song's impact was enhanced by an elaborate dance routine which Bush performed in the video and on her frequent *Top Of The Pops* appearances.

Two albums were released in quick succession, THE KICK INSIDE (1978) and LIONHEART (1978), which pressed a claim for Bush as Britain's most original female artist. The songs were deep and imaginative, covering subjects such as murder, incest, feminism and nuclear war with a degree of perception astonishing for someone so young. In January 1979 she embarked on *The Tour Of Life*, a gruelling 28-date spectacular that involved magic, mime, dance routines, and countless costume changes. It was a triumph, but the experience left her so drained that she has never toured since, preferring to express her visual creativity through video.

Another milestone came in September 1980,

when NEVER FOREVER became her first #1 album, and remarkably, the first ever by a British female artist. Its closing track, "Breathing", a six-minute epic about childbirth during a nuclear attack, was evidence of a new willingness to experiment with sound, and it became an unlikely Top 20 hit.

Encouraged by the experience of co-producing NEVER FOREVER, Bush felt ready to go it alone, and set to work on new material in 1981. The first fruit was "Sat In Your Lap", a frenetic, percussion-driven single which acted as a taster for her fourth LP, THE DREAMING (1982). Bush would later refer to this as 'my mad album', and it was certainly her most inaccessible, with its dense, uncompromising arrangements, radio-unfriendly songs, and bizarre contributions from **Rolf Harris** and animal impersonator **Percy Edwards**. For those willing to investigate beyond the surface weirdness, there was much to love about THE DREAMING, but it sold poorly and remains her commercial nadir.

At only 24, Kate Bush had to deal with failure for the first time in her career. Her response was to withdraw from public view for three years, during which time rumours of mental breakdown began to circulate. There was also speculation about her future with EMI, fuelled by the release of THE SINGLES FILE (1983), a box set of all her singles to date. The truth was that, having worked solidly for five years, she was enjoying the opportunity to take stock, and with a newly expanded home studio in place, she was now free to work at her own pace. Although this gave her the space to indulge her perfectionism, it slowed down her work rate so much that only three albums would be completed in the next ten years.

The long-awaited comeback began in August 1985 with a new single, "Running Up That Hill", whose mesmeric drum pattern and constant Fairlight synth drone gave her a first UK Top 3 hit since "Wuthering Heights". Its success heightened anticipation for HOUNDS OF LOVE (1985), which went straight in at #1 and quickly established itself as one of the albums of the year. To date it has sold close to a million copies in the UK and is widely regarded as her masterpiece. It also provided her with belated success in America, where "Running Up That Hill" became her first Top 30 hit.

Another four years would pass before the next album, but this time Bush's excuse was her involvement in numerous other projects. A singles collection, THE WHOLE STORY (1986), featuring a new song, "Experiment IV", and an inferior new recording of "Wuthering Heights", reached #1 and its companion video anthology was also a bestseller. She appeared as guest vocalist on albums by **Peter Gabriel, Midge Ure** and **Big Country**, and wrote new material for several film soundtracks, as well as making her acting debut in a Comic Strip TV special, *Les Dogs*. After all this extracurricular activity she returned with renewed enthusiasm to her own project, which would eventually become THE

Kate's first press call at EMI, 1978

Pleasure" and "You're The One" outstanding.

More years of silence followed, and 1999 – the 21st anniversary of Bush's explosive debut – dawned with no sign of new material. There was one minor diversion for fans in the shape of I WANNA BE KATE, a well-intentioned but amateurish tribute album featuring Bush tracks covered by a host of unknown Chicago bands, but perhaps unsurprisingly it failed to light any fires.

Over the last ten years, Kate Bush has found her monopoly of the "eccentric female soloist" market challenged by the likes of Björk, Tori Amos and Polly Harvey. She may well have to share the spotlight in future, but the popularity of this unique talent seems unlikely to fade – indeed, when she accepted a special award at the *Q Magazine Awards* of 2001, the plaudits were everywhere, including one from the unlikely figure of John Lydon.

⊙ **The Dreaming** (1982; EMI).
Her 'mad album' it may be, and there's certainly nothing here suitable for daytime radio, but there is enough edgy, fiery beauty to make this an (admittedly underrated) classic.

⊙ **Hounds Of Love** (1985; EMI).
Kate Bush at her creative and commercial peak. The first side is powerful and dramatic, while "The Ninth Wave" breathes new life into the dreaded concept-album format with an ambitious journey through the mind of a drowning woman.

⊙ **The Red Shoes** (1993; EMI).
Against a backdrop of personal loss, this is her most emotionally charged album, but it also contains some of her most accessible material for years.

Jonathan Kennaugh

SENSUAL WORLD (1989). This album saw Bush at her most thoughtful, its autumnal introspection a marked contrast to its more dynamic predecessor. The title track (a Top 20 single) was a shimmering, erotic delight based on James Joyce's *Ulysses*, while Balkan folk singers **Trio Bulgarka** brought a ghostly serenity to three songs, including the soaring "Rocket's Tail", which also featured Dave Gilmour on guitar.

Private trauma overshadowed the making of her seventh album, THE RED SHOES (1993). The death of her mother and the end of her long relationship with bassist **Del Palmer** contributed to the mood of her most personal record to date. There were moments of sheer exuberance – the opening single "Rubberband Girl" and the **Prince** collaboration, "Why Should I Love You" – but overall it was a painfully intense album, with "Moments Of

BERNARD BUTLER

Born May 1, 1970.

With the release of **SUEDE**'s eponymous debut album (1993) **Bernard Butler** landed a reputation as the most innovative British guitarist since The Smiths' Johnny Marr a decade earlier. The album confirmed Butler as a musician whose ambition and dexterity knew few bounds, but while the band became increasingly successful, Butler retreated in on himself, refusing to conduct interviews and shunning the limelight. The breaking point came towards the end of the recording of their second album, the magnificent DOG MAN STAR, in 1994, when Butler walked out.

A spell of 'guitarist for hire' followed (he played with **Sparks** and **Edwyn Collins**, amongst others), during which Butler's reputation for being a difficult character escalated. Eventually he got together with **David McAlmont** for a single, "Yes", in mid-1995. "Yes" instantly established itself as one of the most flamboyant and exquisite songs of the year, sounding like the best thing Phil Spector never produced. The pairing of David's wondrous falsetto and Bernard's six-stringed virtuosity pointed to a match made in heaven. A Top 10 smash, it encouraged them to record another single, "You Do". It was almost as perfect as its predecessor. However, things rapidly went wrong. In a drunken interview with the *NME*, McAlmont – interviewed alone because Butler still refused to speak to the press – claimed that the pair were having difficulties communicating, hinting that homophobia could well be the source of the problem. A week later, he issued an apology to Butler, retracting all his accusations.

Thereafter, neither of them deigned to speak to the press on the subject again, and McAlmont & Butler rapidly dissolved, leaving behind just one mini-LP, THE SOUND OF MCALMONT & BUTLER (1995), which collected together both singles, B-sides and studio outtakes.

Butler went on to guest on **Aimee Mann**'s I'M WITH STUPID, and on **Tim Booth**'s (ex-James) BOOTH & THE BAD ANGEL before being sounded out by **Richard Ashcroft** – in the middle of reassembling his band. In the event, Nick McCabe got his old job back in The Verve and Butler finally bit the bullet, and opted for a solo career.

First evidence, a single "Stay" (1997), demonstrated the restraint and delicacy that would set his solo material apart from the pyrotechnics of Suede and the flamboyance of his partnership with McAlmont. For PEOPLE MOVE ON (1998), Butler played the bulk of the instruments and showed himself equally at home with intimate, quiet acoustic numbers ("You Light The Fire") as he was with broader-palette 'production numbers' such as "Not Alone".

2000's FRIENDS AND LOVERS, one of the final releases on Creation Records, had its moments, although Butler's voice suffered against the predominantly excellent songwriting and intricate arrangements. Alan McGee's decision to wind up the Creation label later that year left Butler without a recording contract, but he continued to work with other artists, including **Bert Jansch**, **Heather Nova** and, in 2002, his old friend McAlmont – the duo hooking up for the release of BRING IT BACK.

People Move On (1998; Creation).
A far more modest and polite album than is usual from ex-rock-guitar gods gone solo. Thought-provoking lyrics, moments of tenderness and swirling orchestral beauty.

Nick Duerden & Al Spicer

Formed San Antonio, Texas, 1980.

"Oh no, no regrets at all. It took her about ten years, but my mom even says it now." Paul Leary on naming his band the Butthole Surfers

The evasive and unconventional **Butthole Surfers** were formed by vocalist **Gerome 'Gibby' Haynes** (accounting student and son of American children's TV presenter 'Mr Peppermint') and guitarist **Paul Leary**. A drummer, **King Koffee**, was soon recruited. In its early incarnations as **Ashtray Baby Heads** and **Nine Foot Worm Makes Home Food**, the band enjoyed little success, but a move to California resulted in a deal with Jello Biafra's Alternative Tentacles label. The group fitted well into the burgeoning 'art-punk' scene also inhabited by Big Black and Sonic Youth.

THE BUTTHOLE SURFERS, their eponymous debut, released in July 1984, was a more disparate affair than those released by their contemporaries, fusing Beefheart, PiL, hardcore and rockabilly influences. Leary was also beginning to develop a bizarre lyrical style, on "The Shah Sleeps In Lee Harvey's Grave" declaring... 'I smoke Elvis Presley's toenails when I wanna get high'.

After a rather uninspired mini-LP, LIVE PCPEP, their true originality flourished on PSYCHIC... POWERLESS... ANOTHER MAN'S SAC (1985) and the CREAM CORN FROM THE SOCKET OF DAVIS EP (1985). While many of their contemporaries merely aped their heroes, the Buttholes had begun to twist Sabbath, Zeppelin and the Grateful Dead into crazed and contorted compositions, a process which became increasingly apparent on their next LP, REMBRANDT PUSSY HORSE (1986), featuring a nagging, pounding version of Guess Who's "American Woman".

Such musical escapades culminated on the band's tour de force, LOCUST ABORTION TECHNICIAN (1987), an eclectic mixture of heavy metal, punk, prog-rock and Eastern rhythms. Gibby was now in possession of his legendary 'Gibbytronix' vocal effects unit, used to full effect alongside Leary's vastly improved guitar skills on the incredible Sabbath parody "Sweat Loaf" and the ethnic "Kuntz".

A visit to Britain followed with the band's line-up featuring **Jeff Pinker** on bass, a second drummer (Koffey's sister **Theresa**), nausea-inducing strobes, and a nude dancer named **Kathleen**. The newsworthy disturbances that broke out as several hundred were turned away from the Buttholes' London gigs were a sign of their increasing popularity.

HAIRWAY TO STEVEN (1988), with its Zeppelin piss-take sleeve featuring symbols of defecating stickmen and syringes instead of song titles, was not quite as awesome as its predecessor but was nevertheless a fine piece of work. After that, with the exception of the WIDOWMAKER EP, the band was silent until 1990, when they released an almost-commercial, light-hearted cover of Donovan's "Hurdy Gurdy Man" and the country-and-western-tinged LP, PIOUGHD. After the sheer madness of the first two sets, there was general disappointment at this relatively tame material, while critics seemed to be tiring of the drug-induced nonsense doled out at interviews.

Having provided perhaps the ultimate parody of hallowed rock'n'roll, in 1992 this band too sold out, signing to EMI. The result was INDEPENDENT WORM SALOON, produced by **John Paul Jones**.

The Buttholes then went into a period of hibernation during which King Koffey developed his Trance Syndicate label. The band were back, however, minus Jeff Pinkus for a single, "Pepper", in 1996, which saw them storm the American charts for the first time. "Pepper" fused rock and hip-hop beats with a typically uncompromising stance and sounded utterly contemporary. An album, ELECTRICLARRYLAND (1996) – the band's best since the 80s – followed and sold an amazing 750,000 copies in the US alone.

AFTER THE ASTRONAUT (1998) moved them closer still to the middle of the road. The humour had diminished and the vocals had been watered down to mainstream weirdness, though the mildly manic "Turkey & Dressing" helped save the day. The general verdict was 'could do better' – so they then proved they could with WEIRD REVOLUTION (2001). The clue was in the title as the group veered startlingly away from guitar-fuelled psychedelic juvenilia in favour of studio-generated beats and surreal electronica. Quite what their remaining fans make of this is anyone's guess, but it ranks highly as one of the oddest – and strangely effective – career moves of all time.

⊙ **Locust Abortion Technician** (1987; Blast First).
One of the scariest albums ever made. Brimming with special effects and samples, it moves from the heavy metal mayhem of "Sweat Loaf" to the nightmarish visions evoked by "Twenty Two Going On Twenty Three". Don't listen to this album when you're alone in the house at night.

⊙ **Hairway To Steven** (1988; Blast First).
The ridiculous sleeve exemplifies the Buttholes' rather perverted sense of humour and this album contains Leary's finest guitar work while subverting almost every form of rock music. Along with its predecessor this album is among the very best to emerge from the American alternative-rock scene of the 1980s, and one to which most grunge bands are indebted.

⊙ **Humpty Dumpty LSD** (2002; Latino Buggerveil).
This artifact pulls together home recordings and demos, largely instrumental, from 1982–94. As stews of crazed dirty sound go, this one tastes pretty fine.

Malcolm Russell, with thanks to the inestimable Jason, Omz and Mark Williamson for the update

BUZZCOCKS

Formed Manchester, England, 1976; disbanded 1987; re-formed 1993.

"I don't like most of this New-Wave music. I don't like music. I don't like movements." Howard Devoto

Like London, Manchester in the mid-70s had its own bunch of bored teenagers in search of an identity. **Peter Shelley** (guitar) and **Howard Devoto** (vocals/ lyrics) met and formed **Buzzcocks** in early 1976 – one of many bedroom bands spurred into activity after seeing the Sex Pistols. Recruiting a rhythm section of drummer **John Maher** and bassist **Steve Diggle**, they rehearsed like mad in a friend's kitchen, and leapt into the maelstrom, taking a raw Ramones-influenced fuzz-guitar sound and blending it with some of the purest expressions of adolescent torment and joy that pop music has ever seen. If the Sex Pistols were the shock troops of the new wave, then the Buzzcocks became the dirty tricks division, using catchy, poppy tunes to sneak into teenage bedrooms and take over the lives within.

The band played a list of seminal 1976 gigs including the infamous London 100 Club punk all-dayer – the gig where someone lost an eye, to the delight of the tabloid press – sharing the bill with Sex Pistols, The Clash, The Damned and an early incarnation of The Banshees featuring Sid Vicious on drums. Pete Shelley's sawn-off Woolworth's Audition guitar was a big hit with the influential music press of the period but the music was strong enough in itself – a unique blend of sardonic Mancunian humour with celebratory 'teenagers-for-ever' music, all played as fast as possible.

Buzzcocks' debut EP release, SPIRAL SCRATCH, was announced to the world in blotchy black-and-white advertisements in the back pages of the *NME* near the end of 1976. One of the classic punk records, it was self-financed by the band's own New Hormones label, and received extensive radio airplay from DJ John Peel. Some of the EP's lyrics declared a healthy interest in amphetamines, and it contained an early punk anthem, "Boredom". With this song, punk developed its first cliché, as it appeared that

Shelley, Maher, Diggle and Garth sampling the rock'n'roll high life

everyone had to address boredom: The Clash were 'bored with the USA', The Adverts were 'bored teenagers', and Alternative TV (ATV) were so bored that their 'love lay limp'.

Howard Devoto's gruff, vaguely menacing vocals had provided an essential ingredient to the Buzzcocks' overall sound. However, after they supported The Clash on their *White Riot* tour of the UK, Devoto's shock departure in 1977 – to form **MAGAZINE** – forced Shelley to replace him on lead vocals. As well as his flawed-genius guitar solos, Shelley also wrote most of the new songs, whose awareness of the romantic and sweaty sides of adolescence set them apart from the more overtly political and social concerns of groups like The Clash. Devoto's influence took time to wane, though, as Buzzcocks continued to play the hits from their early days, and the guitar line that carried their song "Lipstick" was identical to the introduction to Magazine's "Shot By Both Sides". There are still unresolved arguments as to who wrote which of the Buzzcocks' earlier hits.

At the end of 1977 the band signed to United Artists, with Diggle taking on the bulk of the guitar work and **Steve Garvey** joining on bass (after a brief tenure from the taciturn **Garth**). "Orgasm Addict" was their first, attention-grabbing release. With a gabbled high-speed vocal delivery, it was guaranteed to be played over and over again, if only to work out what Shelley was on about. (The way he managed to fit the words 'international women with no body

hair' into a space far too small to contain them was one of the vocal highlights of the year.)

Buzzcocks fans' love for the band was different from the respect accorded to the Sex Pistols, the devotion offered up to The Clash, or the 'all-pals-together' feelings shown for The Damned. Boys and girls alike developed a romantic fascination with the band. "What Do I Get?", in early 1978, was the band's first chart hit in the UK and showed what a fine songwriter Pete Shelley could be. Another teen anthem, its lyrics were favourably compared with those of the early Kinks, and it lifted above self-pity with its rushing guitars and irresistible enthusiasm.

United Artists wanted an LP and the Buzzcocks delivered them a masterpiece – ANOTHER MUSIC IN A DIFFERENT KITCHEN (1978), which stayed in the British charts for three months. Shelley's half-guitar had long gone, while the secondhand general-issue teenage-rebel clothes were ditched for a rather tasteful, all-in-black, silk-shirt styling. The LP came with its own carrier bag (sardonically labelled 'Product') and attracted universal acclaim in the music papers.

The band's golden years – 1978–79 – saw five further singles-chart entries, including their biggest seller, "Ever Fallen In Love (With Someone You Shouldn't Have)" – later successfully covered by Fine Young Cannibals in 1987. The album had shown an interest in more experimental music but the guys were moving steadily closer to a pop audience with their singles: the words of "Ever Fallen In Love", for example, were actually comprehensible on first hearing.

LOVE BITES, their second LP, saw the rest of the band brought into the songwriting department and a consequent widening of musical direction. Four-chord sketches such as "Just Lust" sat alongside longer workouts. It sold well but lacked the exhilaration of their first album. The recordings at this stage (such as "Everybody's Happy Nowadays") sometimes had a vaguely psychedelic feel to them as Shelley developed into a more mature lyricist and Diggle took over the bulk of the singles work.

Shelley's influence diminished a little during this period: at rehearsal, in the studio and on stage he was slowly beginning to release control of the song-writing and of the band. October 1979 saw the release of A DIFFERENT KIND OF TENSION, which was badly received, even by die-hard fans. The band had been on tour for the best part of five years, had produced three LPs and seven singles, and were showing the strain. In 1980, after three further, poorly received singles, Pete Shelley decided that the time had come for the split. He moved on to a solo career, collaborating with **Martin Rushent** – the band's longtime producer – and had a degree of success with recordings such as his HOMOSAPIEN (1981). Diggle and Maher put together **Flag Of Convenience**, who did little of significance and there the story ended, until early 1993.

To capitalize on the 'fifteen-years-on from punk' nostalgia boom, Buzzcocks re-formed, toured and released a comeback album, TRADE TEST TRANSMISSION, a good effort, but by a changed band. Shelley and Diggle were backed by master drummer **John Maher** and **Tony Barber** (bass), making madly delicious, danceable, punk-pop. They showed it up once again on ALL SET (1996), and on tour in the UK they showed younger bands where the 80s indie sound had its roots as well as giving their older fans a chance to show they'd kept the faith. For fans who didn't make it along, the band released a live album, FRENCH (1996), recorded at a Paris gig the previous year.

CHRONOLOGY (1997) was the 'lost tape from the back of the cupboard' missing Buzzcocks album. Pulled out and cleaned up at the insistence of Tony Barber, it gathered together the cream of the outtakes from the three United Artists albums – and even features the mysterious Garth.

Buzzcocks are still to be found on the road, with new releases popping out now and then (most recently with the 2003 studio effort BUZZCOCKS), and there's still an enduring interest in their classic material as shown by Mute's welcome CD reissue of the absolutely essential SPIRAL SCRATCH EP in the Spring of 2000.

⊙ **Another Music In A Different Kitchen** (1978; United Artists).
Singles aside, the band never bettered this debut album, which showed both their pop artistry ("Fast Cars", "Love Battery") and musical experiment in tracks like "Moving Away From The Pulsebeat".

⊙ **Singles Going Steady** (1981; EMI).
The definitive Buzzcocks compilation, featuring their first eight United Artists singles and their B-sides, all from 1977 to 1979. "Orgasm Addict", "Ever Fallen In Love" and "Noise Annoys" still sound lippy, crude and delicious.

⊙ **Time's Up** (2000; Mute).
Pulling together all eleven tracks recorded in the seminal Spiral Scratch session and boosted by footage from Buzzcocks' first ever gig, this set is unmissable. Devoto's vocals never sounded stranger, and Shelley's guitar was never chunkier.

Al Spicer

THE BYRDS

Formed Los Angeles, 1964; disbanded 1973.

As personalities **The Byrds** were elusive, and they built their name purely on a sound as beautiful and intriguing as any in rock music. The fact that none of the original members came from a rock background was crucial to the creation of that sound. The roots of The Byrds lie in folk, country, bluegrass, blues – even jazz.

In 1964, **Jim McGuinn** (guitar/vocals), **David Crosby** (guitar/vocals) and **Gene Clark** (vocals/tambourine) began playing folk music in coffee houses around Los Angeles, calling themselves **The Jet Set**. They eventually got a rhythm section – drummer **Michael Clarke** and bassist **Chris Hillman** – and changed their name to The Byrds, the spelling a homage to The Beatles.

They also got some canny management, who secured them a recording deal with CBS and, as their first single, suggested a cover of Bob Dylan's "Mr. Tambourine Man". The marriage of Dylan's lyrics to The Byrds' hypnotic, chiming swirl of guitar and voices was a breakthrough in rock. It opened the door for a new wave of American bands such as Buffalo Springfield, Jefferson Airplane, The Doors, Love and Jimi Hendrix, and had an immediate impact on the work of The Beatles (RUBBER SOUL, REVOLVER) and Dylan himself.

The Byrds' debut album, MR. TAMBOURINE MAN (1965), was every bit as good as the single. Featuring a few more Dylan covers ("Spanish Harlem Incident", "All I Really Want To Do", "Chimes Of Freedom") and some stunning Gene Clark originals ("Feel A Whole Lot Better", "I Knew I'd Want You"), the set was unlike any other group's, but was accessible and instantly appealing. The critics called their sound 'folk-rock' and the label stuck.

The single and album were huge hits and in Los Angeles the group began a residency at Ciro's night-club on Sunset Strip, a glamorous Hollywood hangout in the 40s that had recently been reopened. On stage they affected a studied West Coast cool. With their backs to the audience, they would start by tuning up, an almost endless process. McGuinn wore funny little granny sunglasses and a strange, crooked smile. Crosby had an enormous green suede cloak. Clark, standing in the middle with a tambourine, looked dark, brooding but nervous. Meanwhile in the audience were all sorts of strange-looking young people. Lots of new drugs and words like 'psychedelic' were floating about, and The Byrds' music was the perfect soundtrack. The California hippie era had begun.

The title track of their second album, TURN TURN TURN (1966), an inspired reworking of Pete Seeger's biblical folk tune, was their second #1 single. There were two more Dylan songs ("Lay Down Your Weary Tune" and "The Times They Are A Changin'"), two excellent McGuinn efforts ("He Was A Friend Of Mine", "It Won't Be Wrong") and, best of all, three new Gene Clark songs ("Set You Free This Time", "World Turns All Around Her" and "Wait And See").

Only a year after their debut The Byrds were being hyped as America's answer to The Beatles. They had both teen appeal and musical credibility. In the next few years, they would record four of the best and most influential records of the decade, but losing most of their audience along the way and undergoing a bewildering series of line-up changes.

Gene Clark's last major contribution was the lyrics for the band's finest single, "Eight Miles High". Even today this song sounds fresh and exciting, with its famous opening bassline, a guitar break inspired by John Coltrane, and Clark's queasy lyric about the band's first trip abroad to London. Radio stations banned it, claiming it was a drug song, but the single was #1 in a matter of weeks. Clark left shortly after recording their third LP, FIFTH DIMENSION (1966), an ambitious progression of The Byrds' sound, chiefly because of McGuinn's fascination with new studio technology.

While Hillman and Crosby were writing most of the songs for the next LP, YOUNGER THAN YESTERDAY (1967), McGuinn was tightening his grip on The Byrds' sound. The new album had room for everything from Hugh Masekela's trumpet to droning sitar-like riffs, a brew that may have been too rich for The Byrds' rapidly shrinking teen audience but was perfectly in tune with a new underground following who disdained hit singles but were coming to regard albums as major artistic statements.

Crosby and Clarke left the band midway through sessions for the next LP, THE NOTORIOUS BYRD BROTHERS (1968). Crosby had been spending most of his time hanging out with new groups like Buffalo Springfield and Jefferson Airplane, and was beginning to adopt some of the revolutionary rhetoric of the time. None of this went down well with the reserved McGuinn, and the two quickly fell out. (On the cover of THE NOTORIOUS BYRD BROTHERS, Crosby's place in the group photo was taken by a horse.) Despite these upheavals the album held together remarkably well. The blend of pedal steel guitar, brass horn sections and Moog synthesizer was worked seamlessly into a diverse collection of songs including Carol King's "Goin' Back" and "Wasn't Born To Follow". It wasn't a big seller but the studio-enhanced sound effects were irresistible to the hemp and headphones crowd.

His band now reduced to just two members, McGuinn perversely hit on the ambitious plan of recording a double album encompassing the entire history of American popular music. (It was also around this time that McGuinn changed his name from Jim to Roger in keeping with the teachings of an Eastern religion he was taken with.) The album concept was abandoned after the band drafted in the brilliant singer and songwriter **GRAM PARSONS** for their next LP, SWEETHEART OF THE RODEO (1968), an album of straight country music. The mixture of Dylan covers, original songs and traditional ballads was a marvellous corrective to the excesses of the psychedelic era, but the record was a shock to their fans. Although they had used elements of country music previously, they had never approached it in such a purist way.

Parsons lasted only five months as a Byrd, quitting on the eve of an ill-advised tour of South Africa. The band were assured they would be playing before an integrated audience but wound up with whites-only gigs. Their anti-apartheid comments met a hostile reaction in the country's press and The Byrds found themselves getting booed at the concerts. Hillman, disgusted with the tour and finding the band's financial situation in chaos, angrily quit. He and Parsons went on to form the **Flying Burrito Brothers**.

McGuinn, now the only original member, recruited, amongst others, the dazzling guitarist **Clarence White**, and carried on leading The Byrds for the next four years. Although they managed to establish themselves as a credible live act, the albums from here on were patchy.

There were a few more hit singles – notably the neargospel "Jesus Is Just Alright" (1969) and the lovely "Chestnut Mare" from UNTITLED (1970) – but after their last album for CBS, FARTHER ALONG (1972), disappeared soon after release, McGuinn brought The Byrds down for landing. However, there would be one more album. Unable to resist a lucrative offer from Asylum Records, the five original members reunited in 1973 to record THE BYRDS. It was a decent enough effort, with Gene Clark rising to the occasion with "Full Circle" and "See The Sky About To Rain", but the reviews were scathing. A planned tour was abandoned, and all went their separate ways again.

If you're planning to move your Byrds collection from vinyl to CD, it's worth pointing out that the reissues of THE NOTORIOUS BYRD BROTHERS, SWEETHEART OF THE RODEO, DR BYRDS AND MR HYDE and BALLAD OF EASY RIDER (all 1997; Columbia Legacy) have added value bolted on in the form of otherwise unobtainable tracks. That noted, it must be said that most of the bonus tracks are alternative versions of familiar songs, or rambling experiments lacking direction.

Mr. Tambourine Man (1965; CBS).
Dylan meets The Beatles on the title track and folk-rock is born. Also featuring perhaps the only rock cover of Vera Lynn's "We'll Meet Again", but in the CD age that can now be programmed out.

Len Lauk

DAVID BYRNE

Born Dumbarton, Scotland, 1952.

"I'm just an advertisement for a version of myself."

The cover of *Time* magazine once labelled **David Byrne** 'The Renaissance Man of Rock', which embarrassed him so much that he had to leave the country. But the label wasn't altogether crazy: as well as the usual rock-star activities of writing, performing, producing and running a record label, he has been an accomplished movie and video director, a highly regarded photographer, and has even written ballet music.

Having moved from Scotland to Canada then Baltimore as a child, Byrne enrolled at the Rhode Island School of Design in 1970. Here, he met future collaborators **Chris Frantz** and **Tina Weymouth**, and took courses in Bauhaus theory and conceptual art, but only lasted one year. Back in Baltimore, he started to play ukelele and violin with an accordionist, **Mark Kehoe**, in a duo called **Bizadi**, covering Sinatra standards and 60s pop.

In March 1972, Byrne moved back to Rhode Island and reunited with Frantz and Weymouth, eventually moving to New York and forming **TALKING HEADS** with them in 1975. His first project outside the group was MY LIFE IN THE BUSH OF GHOSTS (1980), a collaboration with the band's producer **BRIAN ENO**. The album sampled radio evangelists, Islamic chants and Egyptian popular singers to produce an absorbing sonic collage. It pointed the way to further one-off collaborations, and to his enduring interests in world music, fundamentalist preachers, and the similarities between religious ecstasy and rock'n'roll.

Throughout the 80s, Byrne's solo projects ran alongside his career as the frontman and creative force of Talking Heads. Next, he collaborated with choreographer **Twyla Tharp**, and wrote the music for her ballet *The Catherine Wheel*, premiered in September 1981 in New York to rave reviews. After producing the album MESOPOTAMIA for The B-52's in 1982, he devoted himself mainly to his Talking Heads work for a couple of years.

In January 1985, Byrne presented *The Tourist Way Of Knowledge*, a solo depiction of a trip across the US, at the New York Public Theatre, and, in September that year, released another solo album on ECM, MUSIC FOR THE KNEE PLAYS. It was a series of short pieces written for a horn quintet with some droll spoken narrative, designed to link the longer segments of **Robert Wilson**'s stage piece *The CIVIL warS*. This more playful side of Byrne's work had first emerged in the Talking Heads tour and film *Stop Making Sense* the previous year, and continued to appear in many of his subsequent projects. A further collaboration with Wilson, his neoclassical score for *The Forest*, was premiered in 1988 and commercially released three years later.

Byrne's appetite for everyday quirkiness and whimsy was in full flood in his 1986 movie *True Stories*: focusing on a bizarre small town, with Byrne playing the narrator, it charmed some reviewers and annoyed others, who found it patronizing. A soundtrack was released simultaneously with a Talking Heads album of songs from the film, and the following year, Byrne's score for Bertolucci's film *The Last Emperor* (a collaboration with **Ryuichi Sakamoto** and **Cong Su**) won an *Academy Award*.

In 1989, still officially a member of Talking Heads, Byrne released REI MOMO, on which he was backed by Brazilian musicians, and embarked on a solo world tour. His interest in Brazilian music led him to launch the Luaka Bop label (named after a kind of tea), dedicated to bringing world music to a wider audience. His personal compilations for the label, based on tapes made for friends, are as brilliant as any of his creations.

After Talking Heads formally split in December 1990, Byrne's next solo album, UH-OH (1992), sounded just like the next Heads album – pop/rock songs with quirky lyrics, enlivened by Latin horns and percussion. It didn't sell that well, perhaps because former Talking Heads fans now expected him to produce another foray into left-field weirdness.

In 1993, Byrne made some acoustic appearances, including duets with **Natalie Merchant**, **Lucinda Williams** and **Roseanne Cash**, before he returned once again to solo work. He recruited a much smaller band for 1994's DAVID BYRNE, which again achieved only modest sales. Still, he had little cause to worry: brimming with ideas, he still had complete artistic freedom, while countless other artists from different media queue up to work with him. His interest in finding the miraculous among the mundane continued in his book, *Strange Ritual* (1995), a collection of photographs of religious kitsch and assorted strange artefacts.

Back in the world of music, FEELINGS (1997) saw the eclectic Byrne bubbling through to the surface once again. After the back-to-basics approach of his 1994 album, this was a much richer collection, corralling influences from all the usual suspects and mixing in a touch of clubland magic. Following FEELINGS, Byrne indulged his more artistic leanings with a highly eclectic selection of exclusive and limited releases, all of which were more likely to attract long-time devotees than legions of new fans. First came THE VISIBLE MAN (1998), featuring remixes of some of its predecessor's more prominent tunes made available only through Internet outlets, and IN SPITE OF WISHING AND WAITING (1999), a soundscape composed for the Belgian dance outfit, **Ultima Vez**. When Byrne returned to his more accessible songwriting persona it was with LOOK INTO THE EYEBALL (2001), another rich collection of styles given a more unified feel through the use of strings, a horn section and, of course, Byrne's ever-present wry sense of humour.

But a real surprise was yet to come in the form of Byrne's collaboration with the house outfit **X-Press 2**: their "Lazy" (2002) single was both a monster UK hit and was actually very good, no doubt introducing a whole new generation to the distinct tones of Byrne's voice.

⊙ **Rei Momo** (1989; Luaka Bop/Sire).
In which Byrne immerses himself in his new love, Latin music, using top Latin players for a down-and-dirty backing to his lyrical whimsy. Check out the awesome power and precision of the horns on "Make Believe Mambo".

⊙ **David Byrne** (1994; Warners).
Musically stripped down, with lyrics that are at once confessional and oblique, this is a conscious return to the spare and twitchy style of Talking Heads before they lost focus.

Andy Smith

CABARET VOLTAIRE

Formed Sheffield, England, 1973;
disbanded 1987 and 1994.

The original Cabaret Voltaire lasted the length of 1916 before its creator, one Hugo Ball, dolled up in the cardboard outfit of a mystical bishop, called it quits. The name and spirit of his Dadaist venture was revived in the 'industrial band' **Cabaret Voltaire**, forged in 1973 by a trio of student electronic alchemists: **Stephen 'Mal' Mallinder** (bass/vocals), **Richard H. Kirk** (guitar/wind instruments) and **Chris Watson** (electronics/tapes). The three had started experimenting with tapes together in 1973, beginning with an a cappella version of Bowie's "Five Years", and in 1975, tired of playing to confederates in Sheffield University's music department, Kirk learned guitar and they blagged a live debut at a local club. A rioting audience sent them and their raincoated 'image' home in an ambulance, but they were only a couple of years too early. When punk broke, Sheffield kids such as Phil Oakey (The Human League) took off their Mott The Hoople earmuffs and savoured the 'no future' white noise of the Cabs and their detuned radios.

The band's first single was a fascist-baiting song, "Baader Meinhof" (1978), which also featured on the FACTORY SAMPLE EP. It sounded as German as the title and was not a hit. The following year saw work start in earnest, with the debut album, MIX-UP (1979), first in a seminal trilogy for Rough Trade that continued with the surf-jazz-soul-in-a-blender

VOICE OF AMERICA (1980) and RED MECCA (1981). The band also knocked out LIVE AT THE YMCA (1979), a techno-industrial racket that sounded like it had been recorded in the club's pool.

Watson left in October 1981 to work as a television sound engineer, form **The Hafler Trio**, and more recently record some delightfully odd field recordings of atmospheric radio waves. Exit the Dada influence, enter more commercial concerns as the remaining Cabs duo left their Sheffield stronghold to record THE CRACKDOWN in London, for Some Bizarre, taking scratching into the bedsit and into the UK Top 40 to boot. The Cabs drew still more attention through (the first of many) samplings of the Yemeni-Israeli singer Ofra Haza, on a single, "Yashar", which was a big indie and dance-floor hit.

Ironically, just as the Cabs-inspired Depeche Mode and Human League started climbing to fame, the original model fell into decline. MICROPHONIES (1984) and DRINKING GASOLINE (1985) sounded like Kirk and Mallinder were happier with their solo projects. THE COVENANT, THE SWORD AND THE ARM OF THE LORD (also 1985) saw a temporary return to form, but things had fallen apart again by CODE (1987). 'It had become stale', remarked Mal, who then formed **Love Street** with **Dave Ball** and **Ruth Joy** from **Soft Cell**. Kirk, meanwhile, continued an already active solo side-career.

Oddly, though, the defunct band was beginning to be name-checked on the developing house scene, by such technoheads as Steve 'Silk' Hurley and Mixmaster Morris. Almost unthinkable, but the Cabs were fashionable. Thus the duo had another outing, with house legend **Marshall Jefferson** lending assistance for the triumphant GROOVY, LAID BACK AND NASTY (1990), and **Pete Waterman** remixing their Top 60 hit "Keep On (I Get This Feeling)". They were back again in a more minimalist mode with PLASTICITY (1992), INTERNATIONAL LANGUAGE (1993) and THE CONVERSATION (1994), but it soon became apparent that Mallinder and Kirk had finally closed the Cabaret's shutters.

Mallinder moved to Australia and Kirk continued as a solo artist with numerous guises. Despite the band's inactivity, their influence on the dance scene has never vanished, and new retrospectives continue to sell respectably. 1998 saw the release of RADIATION, a stunning collection of BBC session cuts, while CONFORM TO DEFORM (2001), ORIGINAL SOUND OF SHEFFIELD (2001) and the box set METHODOLOGY 74-78 (2003) lavishly packaged the group's archive cuttings and 12" mixes for the enjoyment of the original fans and a new generation alike.

- **Red Mecca** (1981; Rough Trade).
  Mecca is Britain with the street signs rearranged, the windows blocked out and paratroopers choking the air. It weighs the dark heart of Thatcher's Britain and finds it wanting.

- **Eight Crepuscule Tracks** (1988; Crepuscule).
  Some of the Cabs' best work was done for the Belgian label that was closest to them in surreal spirit. "Yashar" and "Gut Level" both aim for the head, but hit below the belt.

- **Listen Up With Cabaret Voltaire** (1990; Mute).
  Excellent collection of Factory material and Crackdown castoffs. This is hell's rave.

- **Groovy, Laid Back And Nasty** (1990; Parlophone).
  The moment when the Cabs fell in step with the rest of the pack, this is nevertheless unashamed hedonism as formulated by the cream of 80s house, and given an arty twist by the Cabs.

- **Original Sound Of Sheffield** (2001; Virgin).
  It comes in a pretty box, courtesy of Design Republic, and it's crammed with brilliant 12"mixes, many of which have never before been squeezed onto the CD format. Essential Cabs listening.

Charles Bottomley

J. J. CALE

Born Oklahoma City, Oklahoma, 1938.

"People ask me why I don't do one o' them unplugged albums, and I go, well, that's what I did first."

It would be hard to find a more low-key rock artist than **J. J. Cale**. For a man who, as rock critic Barney Hoskyns put it, 'inhabits the same musical hinterland as The Band', and who pretty much devised the guitar sound that Mark Knopfler took to global success, he has remained a peripheral figure – a musicians' musician, with a loyal but never over-powering fan base. Even the basic facts of his life are forever misquoted: he was born plain John Cale, and the J. J. prefix (translated as Jean-Jacques in twenty years of press reviews) was devised by a California club owner to distinguish him from his Velvets' namesake.

Like his friend Leon Russell, and Bread's David Gates, Cale started out playing in school bands around Tulsa. After forming an ill-fated band of his own – **Johnnie Cale And The Valentines** – looking for session work and touring with **The Grand Ol' Opry Company** in Nashville, he moved to Los Angeles in 1964, where Leon Russell was already a key session player on many of Phil Spector's records. Before long, Cale too was in regular session work, and in 1967 teamed up with Liberty Records producer **Snuff Garrett** for a (now cult) album of psychedelic songs, A TRIP DOWN SUNSET STRIP (1967), trading under an absurd, ill-advised band name, **The Leather Coated Minds**. Three years later, Cale was hired for a tour by **Delaney & Bonnie Bramlett**, which proved his lucky break, for tagging along with the duo was **Eric Clapton**, then of tour-headliners and short-lived supergroup Blind Faith.

After the tour, as Cale returned to Tulsa, Clapton enjoyed a hit cover of Cale's classic, "After Midnight". Its success prompted Leon Russell to sign Cale to Shelter Records, a label he part-owned, and in 1972 released his debut album, NATURALLY, recorded by Cale with a team of prominent Nashville session players. Its sound was predominantly Southern country blues, with rocky edges, and Cale cast as the hobo drifter. Two things lent it charm and distinction: Cale's weary, throaty, sensual drawl, which drew on the clipped and mumbling blues tradition; and its effective blend of a shuffling, percussive rhythm – often piano-driven – with other sounds of the delta, such as fiddles and harmonicas. The sound of Cale's own guitar was notable for its purity.

Although a success, the album's follow-ups – among them REALLY (1972), FIVE (1979) and SHADES (1981) – were rarely as distinctive or diverse, as if Cale were satisfied with a uniformity of tone and emotion, close to MOR country-rock. There were exceptions to this rule, though. TROUBADOUR (1976) had a livelier, electric blues feel to it, and included another song made famous by Clapton, "Cocaine". And 1982's GRASSHOPPER found Cale at his most assured. All his stock ingredients were in evidence on titles like "Drifter's Wife" and "Can't Live Here", songs that were little blues homilies, evocative of the railroad and gas stations along the sluggish Mississippi. The set featured some fine crisp guitar-picking, while the novel sounds of steel drums and xylophones gave a sense of urgency.

J. J. Cale's career has been most significant for his impact on others, most obviously Mark Knopfler, but also Eric Clapton, whose gruff vocal style was clearly inspired by Cale. J. J. himself has never achieved great success; indeed, after poor sales of #8, he asked to be released from his contract with Phonogram, who, on his departure, released a rather ordinary compilation, SPECIAL EDITION (1984).

Cale has continued to record occasionally, releasing TRAVELOG (1989), CLOSER TO YOU (1994) and GUITAR MAN (1996), which adopted a more hi-tech, digital sound – closer, oddly enough, to his protege Knopfler's last few albums with Dire Straits. Mercury released an excellent two-CD career retrospective in 1997: ANY WAY THE WIND BLOWS, a fifty-track compilation of the best of the twelve studio albums he recorded between 1972 and 1996. More recent releases have been notable by their scarcity, although a LIVE set crept out in 2001, and a DVD title, THE LOST SESSION, arrived the following year.

- **Naturally** (1972; Mercury).
  This first album was as good as Cale ever got. In effect a showcase for his mellow style, composed of two parts croaky voice to one part sweet guitar. Included "After Midnight", but the outstanding tracks are "Call The Doctor", "Don't Go To Strangers" and "Magnolia".

- **Troubadour** (1976; Mercury).
  Another career peak, most notable for "Cocaine", which was representative of the album's rockier feel.

JOHN CALE

Born Garnant, Wales, 1942.

An awkward figure to pigeonhole, **John Cale** began his musical career in the classical field, studying viola and cello at London's Goldsmith's College before moving to Massachusetts. By 1963, now based in New York, he was being tutored variously by John Cage, Aaron Copland and La Monte Young. Cale remained a minor figure in the classical scene, but brought to rock music the forms and techniques of New York's high-culture avant-garde.

At college Cale performed with La Monte Young's **DREAM SYNDICATE**, making a proto-minimalist music of sustained single notes or chords. The Dream Syndicate still holds a legendary mystique, but from its obscurity rather than its influence: La Monte Young has refused to release the mass of tapes recorded, now stored in a nuclear bunker. But it was with The Dream Syndicate that Cale first sawed down the bridge of his viola and attached a pick-up to produce the amplified sound that characterized his most famous work as a violist, with **THE VELVET UNDERGROUND**. Cale met **LOU REED** in 1964 and was attracted to his wry, dark songs, but it was Cale's eagerness to experiment with noise and discord that transformed a garage band into an outfit that could create tracks like "Sister Ray" and "Black Angel's Death Song".

After Cale's departure from The Velvets in 1968, his classical background continued to inform his interest in experimentalism. His collaboration with **Terry Riley**, CHURCH OF ANTHRAX (1971), was an exciting, sprawling minimalist/jazz fusion, but THE ACADEMY IN PERIL (1972) was all but drowned out by uninspired cod-classical solo piano and orchestration. He also opened up another avenue of creativity, as the writer and singer of numerous unadorned songs infused with a haunting sense of melancholy and unease. The first set of such songs, VINTAGE VIOLENCE, appeared in 1970, followed by the exemplary PARIS 1919 (1972), FEAR (1974), SLOW DAZZLE (1974) and HELEN OF TROY (1975), all of which were dominated by sparse guitar/piano-based instrumentation and an impression of stillness maintained in a state of extreme tension. At occasional points, the music seemed to buckle completely, as on "Fear Is A Man's Best Friend", or a menacing cover of Elvis's "Heartbreak Hotel".

When this productive songwriting period dried up, Cale's music became frenzied and less articulate, as on the ANIMAL JUSTICE EP (1977) and the live LP SABOTAGE (1979), a set dogged by sloppy rock guitar clichés. Cale turned his hand to production, embracing the New Wave wholeheartedly and creating stunning sounds from the raw material provided by **The Stooges**, **Patti Smith**, **Modern Lovers**, as well as a whole bunch of UK punks such as **The Fall**, **Sham 69** and **Alternative TV**. With the new decade, however, he was back on form. On MUSIC FOR A NEW SOCIETY (1982) the music plotted out a bare landscape in which Cale's mournful voice strained to fill the space. Sandwiching this set were the unashamed pop of HONI SOIT (1981) and CARIBBEAN SUNSET (1983), glorious albums but unsuccessful as attempts at commerciality.

ROCKARCHIVE.COM

The frenzied and articulate John Cale

Middle age then calmed Cale, and his classical albums – WORDS FOR THE DYING (1989) and PARIS S'EVEILLE (1992) – were insipid and empty. More rewarding and restless were collaborative releases with Brian Eno on WRONG WAY UP (1990) and Lou Reed on SONGS FOR DRELLA (1990), which saw Cale revert to his stark, urgent piano playing. Unfortunately, 1994's abysmal LAST DAY ON EARTH, recorded with Bob Neuwirth, illustrated just how much Cale had changed, featuring largely vapid songs about fragmentation and despair from the standpoint of a detached observer.

He didn't scrape together another decent album until 1996's WALKING ON LOCUSTS, a collection of pop-flavoured pieces that featured ex-Velvet Underground colleague **Mo Tucker** and ex-Talking Head **David Byrne**, veering from the quirkiness of "Crazy Egypt" to the maudlin sincerity of "So Much For Love" (a tribute to another ex-Velvet, the late Sterling Morrison). With music like this and his self-explanatory 1997 release EAT/KISS: MUSIC FOR THE FILMS OF ANDY WARHOL still lurking up his sleeve, it was far too early to write John Cale off as a calmed-down grown-up. An Island anthology, CLOSE WATCH (1999) served as a reminder of his varied output, while the Velvets' debut album's rerelease in 2002 (including demos and rarities) underlined his undeniable influence on 35 years of rock music. A new EP, JOHN CALE 5 TRACKS, was released in 2003 as the prelude to a new album.

⊙ **Fear** (1974; Island).
Cale's best solo LP, achieving a clarity of vision and panorama of moods unmatched by his other records. The resignation to ruin in "You Know More Than I Know" is as chilling as his music gets.

⊙ **Music For A New Society** (1982; A&M).
An album of desperate abandonment, each song exactly prepared beforehand and then recorded in just one take. Unnerving and distressing, this is tortured and agonized music which never seeks to comfort the listener.

⊙ **Fragments Of A Rainy Season** (1992; Hannibal).
Recorded on his 1992 world tour, this is an excellent introduction to Cale. It features a selection of the finest from his oeuvre, stripped of any dated stylistics and reconstructed with the sparsest piano and acoustic guitar.

David Castle

CALEXICO

Conceived Los Angeles, 1990.

Many groups are inspired by the environment in which they live and work, but perhaps none so much as Tucson-based, **Calexico**. One of the standout groups to bear the increasingly meaningless term 'alt-country', they forge sublime music that incorporates Californian surf, Tex-Mex, funked-up jazz and spaghetti Western atmospherics, all infused with the flavour of the Arizona district they call home. With the Mexican border only 100 miles to the south, Calexico's musical platter underpins lyrics that reflect the uneasy society of the region.

The group nominally consists of **Joey Burns** (bass, vocals) and **John Convertino** (drums), with additional support from an extended family of players. While the pair's primary instruments define much of the Calexico style, their music is coloured by an awesome array of instrumentation: accordions, marimbas, banjos, mandolins and guitars all put in an appearance.

The two first met in Los Angeles in 1990. Convertino had been drumming with **Howie Gelb**'s experimental country-ists **GIANT SAND** since 1988; Burns was recruited by Gelb as an upright bassist for a European tour. The three eventually moved en-masse to Tucson, Arizona, when Gelb was trying to find a good school for his daughter.

Burns and Convertino began to experiment together and eventually hooked up with steel guitarist **Bill Elm** in the band **Friends Of Dean Martinez**, performing what can only be described as 'desert lounge'. The two left in 1996 and became a 'rhythm section for hire' working on recordings for Giant Sand (BACKYARD BARBECUE BROADCAST), Rainer and Richard Bruckner.

Meanwhile, they had also issued a low-key debut, recorded at their home studio and released on the German label, Haus Musik. SPOKE (1996) made enough of a dent to land them a bigger record deal but was nothing compared to their second offering.

Now settled on the name Calexico, the group issued THE BLACK LIGHT (1998), a more upfront set, where genres melted into one another – mariachi married Morricone, reverb-rich guitars backed Italian trattoria music. The album was rich in atmospheric instrumentals like the noirish "Gypsy's Curse", the heat-hazed and melancholy "Over Your Shoulder", and the spectacular end-credit "Frontera". There were dark tales to be had too, and though Burns' singing voice was less confident than on later releases, it still possessed an intriguing charm – he's a narrator rather than a performer, and on tracks such as "Stray" and "Bloodflow", he's a Tom Waits-styled storyteller.

The duo's next effort, HOT RAIL (2000), was perhaps a little more uneven, but where good, pushed the envelope even further – more mariachi, and more cinematic romps through the badlands complemented a seriousness about their musicality that elevated the band above mere kitsch. The collection kicked off with the blistering "El Picador" before launching into an English/French duet (Burns singing with **Marianne Dissard**), "The Ballad Of Cable Hogue". The extended street-jazz of "Fade" and the gritty Orbital-meets-cop show drum workout "Mid Town" were other highpoints.

Extensive touring and collaborations with **Neko Case** (on the beautiful BLACKLISTED), French duo **Amor Delhom** (working together as ABBC) and **Evan Dando** (the two helped out on the former Lemonhead's first solo album, BABY I'M BORED) filled the next couple of years until the return of Calexico.

2003's FEAST OF WIRE was the most perfectly realized version of their musical vision – from the accordion and twang of the opening track, "Sunken Waltz", to the sinister machine noise of the set's close. The album contained some of their most striking and sensitive music yet: "Across The Wire" communicated images of a flooded children's graveyard, while the strangely compelling suicide tale "Not Even Stevie Nicks" had an almost Flaming Lips quality to it. Elsewhere Mingus-styled big band ("Crumble"), mashed up beats ("Attack El Robot! Attack!"), and even echoes of dub ("Dub Latina") surfaced amid the collision of Latin and Americana. Dust bowl perfection.

⊙ **The Black Light** (1998; City Slang).
Feel the arid desert winds blow through you on this soundtrack to a postmodern cowboy flick that's begging to be written.

⊙ **Feast Of Wire** (2003; City Slang).
Just when you thought you'd worked out their musical style they go and push the boundaries back again; incredibly eclectic, yet it all makes perfect sense.

Derryck Strachan

TERRY CALLIER

Born 1945, Chicago.

Terry Callier albums can be found sectioned by record stores as either jazz, soul or folk, but the fact he can't be pigeonholed or his music easily defined has kept Callier from the mainstream success he deserves. Although Callier's first album, THE NEW FOLK SOUND OF, was released in 1968, it would be nearly 30 years before he started to sell records in any volume, thanks to TIMEPEACE in 1997.

Back in the 60s Callier's eclecticism confused both public and labels alike, Prestige making the first mistake with his acoustic debut; recorded in 1965 it was held back until 1968, by which time the folk boom was over and Terry had already begun to work with a fusion of styles that put him somewhere between Curtis Mayfield and Gil Scott Heron.

Three albums on the Cadet label, a subsidiary of Charly, received critical acclaim – OCCASIONAL RAIN (1972), WHAT COLOUR IS LOVE (1973) and I JUST CAN'T HELP IT (1975). Charles Stepney's production of the trilogy had allowed space for Callier's voice, subtle instrumentation and lyrics – an amalgam of politics and soulful meanderings. The nine-minute epic "Dancing Girl", with its numerous changes of pace, exemplified Callier's unsettling portrayal of deprivation and addiction; whereas "Ordinary Joe" (from OCCASIONAL RAIN) got fingers snapping and still opens Callier's wonderful live sets today. But, surprisingly, the label saw no future for Callier and the partnership with Cadet dissolved in 1976.

More quality followed with the Elektra releases FIRE ON ICE (1977) and TURN YOU TO LOVE (1978), both of which were ignored by the public. An enforced hiatus followed when Callier took custody of his daughter and, desperately in need of a steady income, ditched music in favour of computer programming.

Interest in Callier blossomed afresh when Charly Records issued the BEST OF album in the early 90s, at the height of the acid jazz boom; the record sold well. By 1996 Callier had signed to Verve. The following year he joined hip UK label Talkin' Loud who, in collaboration with Verve, issued the stunning TIMEPEACE. Finally critical and public taste coincided, and Callier could ditch computing and return to music, full time.

Callier has since dueted with **Beth Orton** and worked on remix projects with the likes of **Zero 7** and **Four Hero**. However, 1998's LIFETIME on Talkin' Loud failed to live up to the success of its predecessor and Callier moved to London-based label Mr Bongo. A live set, ALIVE (2001), and the disjointed SPEAK YOUR PEACE (2002) followed. The latter featured more collaborations with contemporary artists, among them **Paul Weller**; their duet, "Brother To Brother", continued Callier's social commentary and was apparently penned by the pair in a day.

Success took a long time to arrive for Terry Callier, but when it finally appeared, was richly deserved. Expect him to continue pushing the boundaries and striving for a better world.

- **What Colour is Love** (1972; Universal).
  This fine album of intelligent, tuneful jazz-folk features the immaculate "Dancing Girl".

- **Timepeace** (1997; Verve/Talkin'Loud).
  More beautifully constructed pieces full of soul and harmony.

- **Alive** (2001; Mr Bongo).
  This historic London live set covers his evolution, better than any 'best of' compilation could.

David Moreton

ROBERT CALVERT

Born Pretoria, South Africa, 1945; died 1988.

Having moved to England with his parents at the age of 2, **Robert Calvert** grew up wanting to become an RAF pilot, but this hope was dashed by the discovery that he had a defective eardrum. Instead he trained as a building surveyor, before his literary aspirations led him towards London's late-60s hippie movement. Soon he was writing for underground magazines.

After meeting **Dave Brock** in a London café, Calvert became a peripheral member of **HAWKWIND**, guesting in their stage act and reciting poems and dramatic monologues. His photograph was included on the cover of IN SEARCH OF SPACE (1971), and he co-wrote their million-selling hit "Silver Machine" (1972) with Brock, although Calvert's original lead vocal was replaced by the gruff tones of bassist and future Motörhead founder **Lemmy Kilminster**. Calvert's lead vocal survived on the release of the follow-up single, "Urban Guerrilla", which glorified the lifestyle of a terrorist, but an IRA bombing campaign in London led to the single's swift deletion.

The success of "Silver Machine'" enabled Hawkwind to take their 'Space Ritual' stage show on tour. The short-haired, clean-shaven and dapper Calvert, their 'resident poet', was a curious contrast to the other band members, but his inspired contributions, like "Sonic Attack", "In The Egg" and "Wage War", helped to make their gigs genuine multimedia performances. His work was well represented on SPACE RITUAL ALIVE (1973), but soon after he quit, just before their first US tour.

He immediately started work on his own solo concept album, CAPTAIN LOCKHEED & THE STARFIGHTERS (1974), about death-trap aircraft in the modern German air force. Many of his Hawkwind colleagues played on the album, along with **Brian Eno** and **Arthur Brown**, while the interspersed dramatic sketches featured **Vivian Stanshall** and Traffic's **Jim Capaldi**. It was popular with critics, as was LUCKY LEIF AND THE LONGSHIPS (1975), a lighter album about the Vikings' discovery of America. Impeccably produced by Brian Eno, it showed off Calvert's songwriting versatility.

After a guest appearance with Hawkwind at the 1975 Reading Festival, Calvert turned to playwriting in 1976 with *The Stars That Play With Laughing Sam's Dice*, an unsuccessful drama about Jimi Hendrix. He rejoined Hawkwind as vocalist/lyricist for QUARK, STRANGENESS AND CHARM (1977), giving the band's work an intellectual boost. After a European tour, though, Hawkwind split for a time, with Brock and Calvert forming **The Hawklords**. Their album 25 YEARS ON (1978) shared much of Hawkwind's idiosyncratic style, but was leaner and punchier, allowing Calvert's imagination more room. Calvert toured extensively with The Hawklords before they in turn disbanded about a year later.

While performing solo gigs, Calvert was working on a novel entitled *Hype*, about the cynical projection to fame of a rock performer named Tom Mahler. Following its publication, he released a spin-off album, also called HYPE (1982). Mostly straightforward rock, it was Calvert at his most accessible, but it also demonstrated his maturing songwriting talent.

Unfortunately, both album and novel went largely unnoticed, and Calvert's subsequent output drifted towards electronic and futurist minimalism. All but his most committed fans ignored FREQ (1984), a bleak, sparse but creditable album, concerned with automation in the workplace, industrial decline and unemployment, interspersed by sound footage of the 1984–85 miners' strike. TEST-TUBE CONCEIVED (1986) was equally intense, and can now be seen as the artistic culmination of work begun in the late 70s.

Robert Calvert died of a heart attack in August 1988. A few months later, Hawkwind played a benefit gig for his widow and son, fittingly staged at the same south London venue where most of SPACE RITUAL ALIVE had been recorded. Since those days, Calvert had more or less achieved his aim to be a 'true space-age oral poet'. One of the most intelligent lyricists working in the progressive-rock field, his recorded and published output consistently showed an informed and compassionate concern with social and environmental issues.

- **Hype** (1982; See For Miles).
  An accessible and astute exploration of the sociology and mythology of rock.

- **Test-Tube Conceived** (1986; Demi-Monde).
  Futurist in tone, this was Calvert's most disciplined release, examining in vitro fertilization, government surveillance, computer hacking and vivisection.

Martin Haggerty

CAMEL

Formed London, 1972; disbanded 1984; re-formed 1992.

Key players in the much-maligned genre of 1970s progressive rock, **Camel** eschewed a traditional lead singer and the grand theatrics of some of their contemporaries, going instead for precise ensemble work, indulgent soloing and epic masterworks. It's a style that hasn't aged well, but at its best the music's optimistic spirit and inspirational tunes could sweep you along.

The band formed when **Peter Bardens**, previously a keyboard player in Van Morrison's Them, teamed up with members of Philip Goodhand Tait's band: **Andy Latimer** (guitar/flute), **Doug Ferguson** (bass) and **Andy Ward** (drums). Their first two records, CAMEL (1973) and MIRAGE (1974), established Bardens and Latimer as the main writers, showing off their sound musicianship and penchant for a tricky time signature, but there was little to mark them out from similar bands in the field and they didn't sell well.

The anonymity of the early days was heightened by confusion with Peter Frampton's Camel and it took the chart success of THE SNOW GOOSE (1975) to put the band firmly on the map. This was a work of highly melodic, thematically linked instrumentals based on a Paul Gallico children's story (Gallico took action against the band for copyright infringement), and it has gone down as one of the definitive concept albums of its day.

Camel celebrated its acceptance into the elite of progressive rock in all too traditional fashion with a bash at the Royal Albert Hall with the London Symphony Orchestra. They maintained their success with MOONMADNESS (1976), which again showcased Latimer's full-blooded guitar and Bardens' busy Moog runs on tracks such as "Lunar Sea" and "Song Within A Song". The vocals remained weak and uninspired – they were never Camel's primary concern – but they improved with the arrival of **Richard Sinclair** (bass/vocals; ex-**CARAVAN** and **HATFIELD AND THE NORTH**) as a replacement for Ferguson. With **Mel Collins** filling out the sound with his seasoned sax playing, subsequent albums RAIN DANCES (1977) and BREATHLESS (1978) were more song-based and poppy, and even spawned a single.

The arrival of the New Wave barely affected Camel, who remained faithful to their pre-punk values and hairstyles. All the same, as their commercial fortunes declined, and both Bardens and Sinclair quit, the band's survival was in question. Now chief songwriter, Latimer led Camel into the 80s with new bass player **Colin Bass** (later a member of **3 MUSTAPHAS 3**) and a succession of keyboard players including **Kit Watkins** and old Caravan contact **Jan Schelhaas**. With **Rupert Hine** producing, the pop-orientated I CAN SEE YOUR HOUSE FROM HERE (1979) retained the familiar soaring guitar tones and dramatic arrangements, although there were a few contrived attempts at modernity. Such an accusation, however, could not be levelled at the concept album NUDE (1981), telling of a prisoner unaware that World War II had ended. The lyrics and concepts for releases since NUDE were provided by **Susan Hoover**, now Latimer's wife.

When Ward left, Latimer pressed on with guest musicians, producing THE SINGLE FACTOR (1982) and STATIONARY TRAVELLER (1984), but it was no surprise when the split was announced. Camel bowed out with the live LP PRESSURE POINTS (1984), recorded at their spiritual home, Hammersmith Odeon, and featuring a guest appearance by Bardens.

Latimer and Hoover decamped to California and, when record companies showed little interest in their new material, formed their own label, Camel Productions, eventually to release DUST AND DREAMS in 1992, based on John Steinbeck's book *The Grapes of Wrath*.

In 1994 Bardens joined forces with Ward and old Caravan hands for some live gigs reworking a few old Camel numbers and a live album trading as **Mirage**. But the Caravan contingent soon quit, plans for a new studio album never materialized, and by 1997 the project had folded.

The late 90s saw Camel run as a cottage industry based around Latimer and Bass. HARBOUR OF TEARS was released in 1996 – a story of Irish emigration to the new world – showing that, against the odds, the new concept album was alive and well in the broad church of 90s rock. COMING OF AGE (1998) was a double CD recorded on their 1997 tour – a grab bag of songs from THE SNOW GOOSE onwards – which was followed by two studio collections, RAJAZ in 1999 and A NOD AND A WINK in 2002.

⊙ **Rain Dances** (1977; Decca).
Camel's most varied album with newly installed bassist Richard Sinclair adding his defiantly English vocal to tracks like "Metrognome", some familiar epics like "Unevensong", and even a dreaded jazz workout on "One Of These Days I'll Get an Early Night".

Nick Dale

CAMPER VAN BEETHOVEN

Formed Redlands, California, 1984; disbanded 1990; reformed 2002.

Back in 1984, southern Californian's rock scene was hardcore to the point of tedium, so when **Camper Van Beethoven** got together they had one goal in mind – to make music that would irritate these guys. With a guitar, mandolin, violin, the kitchen sink, and anything else available, they set off playing folked-up versions of hardcore classics and Russian songs. This dastardly career plan mystified the locals at first, but the madness eventually caught on and 1985 saw the band set up in the studio (admittedly for just two weekends, on a $1500 budget), recording an album with help from LA-based Independent Project Press, the label owned by Bruce Licher of the band Savage Republic.

Camper musicians changed constantly from the onset, but the core members were **David Lowery** (guitar/vocals), **Chris Molla** (guitar), **Victor Krummenacher** (bass), **Jonathan Segal** (violin) and **Chris Pedersen** (drums). All featured on Camper's first album, TELEPHONE FREE LANDSLIDE VICTORY (1985), a cross-genre masterpiece with tongue-in-cheek originals ("The Day Lassie Went

To The Moon"), hardcore covers (Black Flag's "Wasted"), and, yes, Russian folk songs ("Vladivostock"), as well as a magimix of styles, encompassing polka, country, reggae, ska and metal-hearted rock. Overlaying it all, though, were David Lowery's catchy pop hooks and melodies, and some great musicianship, especially from Jonathan Segal.

Modest word-of-mouth sales led to a break on the college-radio circuit, when stations picked up on "Take The Skinheads Bowling", a wonderful anti-skate-rat romp. Suddenly, Camper had a college hit. And then the dreams took over. Lowery, lead singer and guitarist, received a call from one Michael Stipe, gushing with praise for the album, and Stipe proceeded to nominate TELEPHONE FREE in his top ten albums of the year in *Rolling Stone*. With no records left in the stores (the original printing was 1250), Camper signed a distribution and pressing deal with Rough Trade.

For all the plaudits, sales were not huge, and Rough Trade were cautious about putting out another album too soon, so CAMPER VAN BEETHOVEN II & III (1986) emerged as an independent release on the band's own label, Pitch-A-Tent (a name derived from the phrase 'she makes me want to pitch-a-tent in my pants'). It was in much the same vein as the first album – though Lowery's lyrics had become more cohesive and the band a bit tighter – but not the progression Camper needed, Lowery later referring to it as 'sixteen tracks of blazing duck decoy music'. Nonetheless, an album that included a ska song entitled "ZZ Top Goes To Egypt" had to be doing something right.

In 1986, Camper went out on the road with R.E.M., broadening their appeal to the college market, especially, and clocking up sales for THE THIRD LP (1986), a little more pop-orientated than its predecessors, and the intriguingly titled EP, VAMPIRE CAN MATING OVEN (1987). Again, these records didn't really go beyond the debut album, but Lowery and the band had a sure quality, and the majors came a-courting. Camper eventually chose to

sign with Virgin, for an impressive six-figure sum and promises of creative control.

Thus handsomely endowed, Camper recorded OUR BELOVED REVOLUTIONARY SWEETHEART (1988). This was a whole lot more focused, proving that extra budget (and a real producer) could make a fair old difference. The lyrics and the music were 100 percent tighter, while keeping a sense of Camper's reckless abandonment, and the album spawned a near-hit single in "Eye Of Fatima".

Though the band were still unable to crack the mainstream, they increasingly had the critics on their side, with KEY LIME PIE (1989), acclaimed in some quarters. The set was a real showcase for Lowery's maturation as a songwriter, which was at its best on another almost hit, "Jack Ruby" and "(I Was Born In A) Laundromat", probably Camper's strongest ever songs. It was a domination, though, that was creating turmoil in the band, and in spring 1990 the band split, Lowery going solo with **CRACKER**, all the others going off to form **The Monks of Doom**.

Cracker's successes have been characterized by a more straightforward, poppy guitar-rock sound. The Monks, meanwhile, have released one largely disappointing album, THE INSECT GOD (1992), and, according to one of our correspondents, a whole bunch of others that aren't too disappointing at all.

As for Camper, they came back together in 2002 for a series of live shows and the following year an album, TUSK, a bizarre, but wonderful collection of Fleetwood Mac covers – what a way to return.

⊙ **Telephone Free Landslide Victory** (1985; IRS).
The irresistible debut – which Camper never bettered. There was something right going on here, from the mix of all different styles of music to the humour, which runs rampant.

⊙ **Our Beloved Revolutionary Sweetheart** (1988; Virgin).
A great all-around album with an eclectic mix of old styles and major-label production. Includes an excellent cover of the old bluegrass classic tune, "O Death!".

Jeffrey S. Kaye

CAN

Formed Cologne, Germany, 1968; disbanded 1978/79; re-formed briefly 1986.

"We were never a normal rock group. Can was an anarchist community." Irmin Schmidt

There is a significant lobby among rock fans – and probably an even stronger one among musicians – that **Can** were the greatest band ever. They were, beyond any shadow of doubt, the brightest star in the Krautrock galaxy, or, as Julian Cope put it in *Krautrocksampler*, his book on the genre: 'every one of Can's members is a hero, a Wizard and a True-star.' Amazingly, thirty years on, they still sound ludicrously contemporary, both on their original discs and on an ever-burgeoning array of sampled treatments by others.

Can started out with pretty serious music credentials. **Holger Czukay** (bass) and **Irmin Schmidt** (keyboards) had both studied under the avant-garde classical composer Karlheinz Stockhausen, and the onset of 1967 found the duo, both in their thirties, involved in teaching (and, in Schmidt's case, conducting) modern classical music. It was then that **Michael Karoli** (guitar), one of Czukay's pupils, played him "I Am The Walrus", closely followed by choice albums by Hendrix, Zappa and The Velvet Underground. Enlisting **Jaki Liebezeit** – a free-jazz drummer, also in his thirties – a group was formed, initially called **Inner Space**.

True to the spirit of the May 1968 riots, the group's early live appearances were noisy and confrontational, and their relative lack of conventional technique on their chosen instruments allowed them to avoid the technical clichés of the era's progressive-rock groups. Can were not interested in impressing audiences with virtuoso skills and never suggested in their playing that they were great artists slumming it in rock music. And, although they gradually achieved more form, they would always create their pieces out of collective improvisation, becoming, in Karoli's words, 'a geometry of people'.

By the time they were ready to record their first album they had teamed up with an incredibly volatile black American artist called **Malcolm Mooney**, who'd played accordion, clarinet and percussion at various times and who'd also worked with his own a cappella singing group (The Six Fifths) at high school. By the time he hooked up with the band, Mooney had distilled his talents into the purity of scream-and-moan vocals. The first results of this collaboration were released as MONSTER MOVIE (1969), an album clearly influenced by The Velvet Underground but somehow rawer and more primal. All the early Can trademarks were in place: the unchanging two-note basslines, the metronomic, almost machine-like drumming, the distortions of guitar and keyboards. On top of this, Mooney's ravaged howl relayed disturbing babble or, on the slow-burning, almost tribalistic "Yoo Doo Right", sections from an intimate letter he had received.

Mooney's demented performances were part of Can's live appeal but it soon became clear that much of this dementia was real. Under a psychiatrist's advice Mooney returned to America, leaving Can without a vocalist again. Help was at hand when Czukay discovered one **Damo Suzuki**, a young Japanese traveller, busking outside a café and asked him to join.

Suzuki's unique vocalizing – an amalgam of Japanese, German, English and words culled from the very fringes of language – was introduced on THE CAN SOUNDTRACKS (1970), an album (in part, of film music) that witnessed the group perfecting its cyclical dance-floor groove. The real turning point, however, came at the end of the year, when Can set up at Inner Space, a studio in a castle outside Cologne, under the guidance of one **Conny Plank**. The immediate result was a quite extraordinary double album, TAGO MAGO (1971). The sound here

was less upfront and more controlled than before. The eighteen-minute locked groove of "Hallelujah" sounded like a shotgun wedding of the James Brown band and The Velvets playing "Sister Ray", while "Aumgn" and "Peking O" took rock music out to the limits: forbidding yet fascinating, dense and abstract yet intensely physical.

If the next album, EGE BAMYASI (1972), sounded rather humbled and subdued after its devastating predecessor, then 1973's FUTURE DAYS saw Can breaking away into entirely new territories. The overall sound was glacial and undulating, achieving a kind of blissful melancholia under which occasional, barely perceptible squalls of violence or euphoria made themselves felt.

In 1973 Damo Suzuki left Can to become a Jehovah's Witness. His departure did not seem to affect the band as much as Malcolm Mooney's and the following year they produced their final masterpiece, SOON OVER BABALUMA, with Karoli and Schmidt taking over the vocal duties. Its jagged but lush pulsations anticipated much of the club music of the 90s and, in the drifting vapour trails of "Quantum Physics", some of today's more eventful ambient music (Aphex Twin, for example).

Can's growing cult following brought them a contract with Virgin in 1975, which meant more money (one hopes) and better recording facilities. It also seemed to mark the end of Can as a 'geometry of people'. They would never truly become a normal rock group but they seemed to be getting close. LANDED (1975) and FLOW MOTION (1976) were great collections of off-kilter pop songs – FLOW's "I Want More" gave the band their only UK chart entry – but they lacked the sense of wonderment that characterized the 1969–74 releases. For that, though, fans could turn to two wonderful compilations of early rarities, issued as LIMITED EDITION (1974) and UNLIMITED EDITION (1976).

By 1976, Holger Czukay had begun to occupy an increasingly marginal position in the group. He was credited only as 'sound editor' on the proto-world-music release SAW DELIGHT (1977), and it was probably his lack of input coupled with the presence of two rather workmanlike session musicians – **Reebop Kwaku Bah** (ex-Traffic, bass) and **Rosko Gee** (percussion) – which gave that album a somewhat turgid feel. The group's final, Czukay-less LP, CAN (aka INNER SPACE; 1978), with its genuinely funny demolition of the "Can-Can", had an appealingly throwaway quality to it – almost a shrug of the shoulders at the realization that the group could never flourish within a major record company's conventional rock format.

Post-Can, **HOLGER CZUKAY** has produced some of the greatest, wittiest world music fusions, and collaborated with **JAH WOBBLE** (with **Jaki Liebezeit**), **DAVID SYLVIAN** and U2's **The Edge**; Irmin Schmidt returned to film work (Can fans should seek out his SOUNDTRACKS anthology); while both singers have occasionally stepped out fronting their own bands.

However, there was to be an encouraging group postscript, when in 1986 the core members of Can staged a one-off reunion in the studio with a more sedate Malcolm Mooney. Apparently, Mooney had found, down the back of a sofa, an air ticket the band had sent him in the US a decade before, and was prompted to renew contact. The most you can normally expect from reunions and comebacks is that if you grin and bear it the whole thing won't be too painful. However, when the resultant album, RITE TIME, was eventually released in 1989, it proved to be their finest since 1975.

Even if not as shockingly innovative as the 1969–75 work, RITE TIME was more in keeping with the essence of Can than most of their later albums. Can's true legacy to subsequent artists was an unquenchable source of inspiration and cheerful, but never exhibitionist, iconoclasm. For this reason, the remix album SACRILEGE (1997), must stand as the truest manifestation of the Can spirit since LANDED. Some of the mixes – like Sonic Youth/Wharton Tier's "Spoon" and Brian Eno's "Pnoom" – remain close to the originals, whilst others simply use them to construct new tracks – a very Can thing to do. The best pieces were A Guy Called Gerald's drum'n'bass overhaul of "Tango Whiskeyman" and Carl Craig's re-imagining of "Future Days" as Utopian techno. Suzuki's own stumbling into the light came about with the release of VERNISSAGE (1998) a marvellous 1990 live set featuring Damo's solo take on Can classics "Hallelujah" and "Mushroom".

The real thing has recently been made a lot more accessible by the 1997 reissuing on Spoon Records of seventeen (count 'em) Can albums from MONSTER MOVIE to SAW DELIGHT, including selected CANNIBALISM compilations. Enough for everyone. Presently, Malcolm Mooney is working with his new band – **The Tenth Planet** – in the San Francisco/Los Angeles area, while the rest of the guys made a rare live appearance in Berlin early in 1999,

at the Columbiahalle. Though the members were still speaking, it had been more than twenty years since Can had last played as a group and the evening progressed as a series of solo projects. The only time the four were actually on stage together was to take a bow as the evening came to an end.

- **Tago Mago** (1971; Spoon/Mute).
  From the autobahn joyride of "Oh Yeah" to the chasms of "Aumgn", panoramic is too small a word.

- **Future Days** (1973; Spoon/Mute).
  Perhaps their greatest moment. Psychedelic, and as natural as breathing.

- **Landed** (1975; Spoon/Mute).
  The finest of the later albums: four slices of astral glam-boogie, a pomp-rock burnout, and a thirteen-minute trail of sonic debris to finish.

- **Anthology** (1994; Spoon/Mute).
  All of Can's albums are readily available on CD, but for the uninitiated, uncertain yet curious, this compilation is a good place to start.

Ben Smith

CANNED HEAT

Formed Los Angeles, 1966.

Any vinyl junkie will feel a chill at the image of **Bob 'The Bear' Hite** hurling himself desperately at the shelves as a Californian earth tremor destroyed much of his priceless collection of blues 78s. It was his vast knowledge of the subject, together with the scholarship of co-founder **Al 'Blind Owl' Wilson**, that gave **Canned Heat** as much authenticity as a white, middle-class blues band could ever hope to have.

Hite (from Torrance in California) and Boston-born Wilson formed the band with drummer **Bob Cook**, guitarist **Henry Vestine** and bass player **Larry Taylor**. Their electric country-blues, along with the crisp rock'n'roll of John Fogerty's Creedence Clearwater Revival, provided a breath of fresh, downhome air in a late-60s music scene that was beginning to take itself a little too seriously. The two leaders also offered a vocal contrast between Hite's deep rasp and Wilson's falsetto.

Their first album, CANNED HEAT, was released in 1967, the same year that they were a hit at the Monterey Festival. By the time of its follow-up, BOOGIE WITH CANNED HEAT (1968), Cook had been replaced by **Adolpho de la Parra**. Canned Heat were also hitting the singles chart regularly, succeeding with "On The Road Again" and "Going Up The Country", arrangements of old blues standards. Their recording of the latter was adopted as a kind of theme tune for the *Woodstock* movie.

Following a half-studio, half-live double album, LIVING THE BLUES (1969), and an appearance at the Woodstock Festival, Vestine left, to be replaced by **Harvey Mandel**. 1970 brought their most successful single, a reworking of Wilbert Harrison's "Let's Work Together", but they were dealt a severe blow by the death of Wilson from a drug overdose in September that year. Although the band carried on,

CAN • CANNED HEAT

notably on HOOKER & HEAT (1971), a collaboration with **John Lee Hooker**, they had passed their peak.

There were further personnel changes – Vestine back for Mandel (until his untimely, though very rock'n'roll, death in a Paris hotel room during a tour with the band), **Antonio de la Barreda** for Taylor – and with the passing of the blues boom, Canned Heat became something of a marginal attraction, their later live appearances limited to bars and mini-festivals. Their career never quite recovered from Wilson's untimely death, and then Hite's, from a heart attack, in April 1981. Vestine himself died in 1997, shortly before the release of BLUES BAND (1998; Mystic). However, thirty years on, the band are still to be found on the road, and intermittently recording the blues.

⦿ **Let's Work Together** (Best Of Canned Heat) (1989; Liberty).
Canned Heat peddling their choogling white man's boogie – as distinctive and respectful an interpretation of the blues as was Peter Green's in the UK, and equally far from being a carbon copy or a sociological exercise. This is the most recent 'best of' to surface.

John Collis

CAPTAIN BEEFHEART

Formed Magic Band, Lancaster, California, 1964; disbanded 1982.

Captain Beefheart was born Don Van Vliet in Glendale, California, in 1941. A creative child, he spent most of his time sculpting in his room while his parents pushed food under the door. He recorded for the first time in 1959, after being encouraged to sing by one of his school friends, **Frank Zappa**. Sporadic collaboration with Zappa lasted until 1964, when Beefheart formed the first **Magic Band** in Lancaster, while Zappa moved to Los Angeles to form The Mothers Of Invention.

Beefheart and his band – featuring **Alex St Clair** and **Doug Moon** on guitars, **Jerry Handley** on bass and **Paul Blakely** on drums – attracted enormous local interest, largely due to their outrageous stage appearance: long hair, high-heeled boots and leather jackets. A single, "Diddy Wah Diddy", a Bo Diddley song, was released on A&M Records and was a local hit, but the next single, "Moonchild", was unsuccessful. When Beefheart delivered the tapes of an LP, SAFE AS MILK, to the co-head of A&M, Jerry Moss, it was declared to be 'too negative' and the company refused to release it. Disillusioned, the band split up.

In 1966, Beefheart was persuaded to re-form the Magic Band and rerecord SAFE AS MILK for Buddah Records. A new guitarist, **Ry Cooder**, was brought in to help with arrangements and **John French** joined on drums. The LP fused elements of delta blues, R&B, jazz and soul, and used rather unusual instrumentation – such as the theremin (the electronic instrument famously used by Brian Wilson for the distinctive opening to "Good Vibrations" from PET SOUNDS). Following the album's release,

The Captain finally settles the 'But Is It Rock' debate

Beefheart became the greatest underground find of the decade so far, and was proclaimed 'the greatest white blues singer'. Yet, while his voice was similar to that of Howlin' Wolf, his lyrics certainly weren't: verbs became nouns, adjectives became verbs, ants became the size of elephants, sounds became smells, sights became tastes.

Ry Cooder left the band before the recording of the next LP to pursue a solo career and was replaced by **Jeff Cotton**. STRICTLY PERSONAL (1968) saw a movement towards longer songs and a more intense form of blues. (Indeed, the four-track MIRROR MAN LP, recorded at the same time but not released until 1971, features some cuts over ten minutes in length.) However, after the triumph of the previous record, STRICTLY PERSONAL damaged Beefheart's reputation quite badly. The mixing of the record was done without his approval; it was littered with phasing and other 'spacey' effects by producer **Bob Krasnow**, and Beefheart was left with a psychedelic, acid-rock record that was certainly not what he intended. He disowned the album and, again, disillusionment set in. (Luckily most of it was reissued in 1992 in its 'unpsychedelic' state, on the CD I MAY BE HUNGRY BUT I SURE AIN'T WEIRD.)

His career resumed when he signed to Zappa's newly formed Straight label in 1968. The band was given freedom to come up with whatever they wanted and Beefheart used the opportunity to its full potential. While keeping Jeff Cotton (renamed 'Antennae Jimmy Semens') and French (renamed 'Drumbo'), he recruited two new amateur musicians, **Bill Harkleroad** ('Zoot Horn Rollo') and **Mark Boston** ('Rockette Morton'), who all began an intensive year of rehearsal that culminated in TROUT MASK REPLICA (1969).

This record was Beefheart's greatest moment, his most bewildering and fascinating record, at odds with all the developments of his previous LPs. It was a double LP in line with the fashions of the time, but it contained no less than 28 songs, an amazing concentration of thought. Lester Bangs, writing in *Rolling Stone*, was stunned by the result: 'TROUT MASK REPLICA shattered my skull, made me nervous, made me laugh ... it was a whole new universe, a completely realized and previously unimaginable landscape of guitars ... it hit like a bomb.'

After TROUT MASK REPLICA, John French was replaced by **Art Tripp III** ('Ed Marimba', on marimba and percussion), who appeared on the wonderful fifth LP, LICK MY DECALS OFF, BABY (1970). It was a much darker record than the previous one, addressing issues such as pollution and destruction of the planet. A Beefheart-directed promo video was immediately banned by a local TV station, and has since achieved legendary status, with many fans baffled as to why anyone should have banned footage of coins being flicked at a wall, a man in a mask using an egg whisk, and the Captain pushing over a tub of paint.

Claiming an interest in more commercial success, Beefheart moved on to the glum but sporadically inspired THE SPOTLIGHT KID (1972), the bright, effervescent though occasionally sickly CLEAR SPOT (1972), and the nasty and thoroughly sickly UNCONDITIONALLY GUARANTEED (1974). The drift towards American MOR rock was completed with BLUEJEANS AND MOONBEAMS (1974), which showed none of the old Magic Band traits whatsoever. In fact the LP was recorded with session musicians to fulfil a contractual obligation with Mercury Records after the old line-up had quit. Suitably perverse, Beefheart dismissed his last two LPs as 'horrible and vulgar' and urged the fans to go back to the shops for a refund.

Zappa gave Beefheart a job in The Mothers Of Invention for the BONGO FURY (1975) LP and tour, and set about producing for his next LP, BAT CHAIN PULLER (1978), with an entirely new Magic Band, featuring **Jeff Moris Tepper** and **Richard Redus** on guitars, **Eric Drew Feldman** on keyboards, and **Robert Williams** on drums. However, owing to a split between Zappa and his manager, the LP was halted by an injunction. It had to be rerecorded with a revised track-listing and eventually appeared as SHINY BEAST in 1980. Fans breathed a sigh of relief as the Captain returned to form, alternating between styles in the same way he had on SAFE AS MILK – from the poppy Latin sound of "Tropical Hot Dog Night", to the spoken-word "Apes-Ma" and the more impenetrable "Bat Chain Puller" itself (said to be based on the rhythm of Beefheart's car windscreen wipers!).

This LP was closely followed by DOC AT THE RADAR STATION (1980), for which John French rejoined on guitar and occasional drums, and the final LP, ICE CREAM FOR CROW, was released in 1982 (with **Cliff Martinez** on drums and **Richard 'Midnight Hatsize' Sneyder** on bass), at which point Beefheart retired to the Mojave Desert to continue his already lucrative painting career. These last two LPs showed a marked return to the TROUT MASK REPLICA style and, in fact, most of the material was first worked on at that time.

Captain Beefheart has remained a much-maligned character, often dismissed as creating weirdness for the sake of weirdness. Colin David Webb's book, *Captain Beefheart: The Man And His Music*, began with the words, 'Genius, charlatan, freakshow or egomaniac?'. It seems possible that Beefheart is all four, and there is no doubt that he is a very unusual man, highlighted by a 1999 television documentary involving fans as diverse as *Simpsons* creator and cartoonist Matt Groening and British DJ John Peel. Even Peel, although reluctant to be seen as contributing to the mythology surrounding Beefheart, recounted a story of his almost alien behaviour: 'If someone was going to phone him, he would know that they were going to phone, and he would go and wait by it for a few seconds until it rang! I know it makes me seem like some sort of hippie derelict, but he was quite simply the most extraordinary man I've ever met ... If anyone in the world of rock music really deserved to be labelled as a "genius", I think that he could be it.'

● **Trout Mask Replica** (1969; Straight Records).
Beefheart at his most exquisite. It kicks off with "Frownland", hammering out a frantic racket and, just when the gravelly voice and harsh discordancy are getting too much, a delightful note rings, exquisite chords appear and disappear, drums skip and miss a beat. Magic is not too strong a word.

● **Doc At The Radar Station** (1980; Virgin).
With his best album for ten years, Beefheart shrugged off any thoughts he might have had of making money from his music and got back to doing what he always did best. With fantastic production that TROUT MASK REPLICA deserved but never got, it combines the instantly recognizable Magic Band sound with keyboards, trombone, marimba and Chinese gongs. Through twelve marvellous songs, Van Vliet and his cohorts show up the New Wave bands as mere pretenders to his throne.

● **Zig Zag Wanderer – The Best of the Buddah Years** (1997; Wooden Hill).
An excellent starting point for anyone who's been stunned by TROUT MASK REPLICA and wants to know where the weirdness all began.

Rhodri Marsden

CARAVAN

Formed Canterbury, England, 1968;
disbanded 1982; re-formed 1990.

Caravan stood at the very heart of the 70s' Canterbury scene. Before coming together as Caravan, all four original members – **Pye Hastings** (guitar/vocals), **Richard Sinclair** (bass/vocals), **Dave Sinclair** (keyboards) and **Richard Coughlan** (drums) – had played in local pop band **The Wilde Flowers**, whose former blooms included Kevin Ayers, Robert Wyatt and Hugh Hopper.

At first seen as poppier counterparts to the Soft Machine, they employed tricky time signatures, their lyrics delighted in eccentricity, and Richard Sinclair's vocals had the same English irony and dropped Hs of the Softs' under-employed singer, Robert Wyatt. But as the Soft Machine edged more into instrumental jazz-rock, Caravan concentrated on extended songs, exuding a sense of dreamy melancholy, undercut by a heady regret for some lost paradise.

The original four-piece was remarkably ego-free, and worked as an ensemble. Hastings' guitar provided textures rather than dominance, while Sinclair laid down melodic leads. Their vocals were similarly matched, Hastings' high-pitched and ethereal against Sinclair's baritone. His cousin Dave's Hammond organ was the lead instrument, alternating washes of sound and solo breaks, while Coughlan's drums were precise and powerful, however complex the time signature. Keeping things in the family, they were sometimes joined by Pye's older brother **Jimmy Hastings** on flute and saxophone.

The band got started by borrowing equipment from the Soft Machine's tour with Jimi Hendrix, and as a result the first LP CARAVAN (1968; reissued 1997) was an unusually mature musical statement. Richard Sinclair remembers an indefinable magic during these days, when 'you'd turn up at a ploughed field with nothing but a mains wire sticking out', and a couple of hours later there'd be a concert. Adopted early by the hippie newspaper *International Times*, Caravan were as underground those days as it got.

Following a not-quite-hit single, the band signed to Decca and released IF I COULD DO IT ALL OVER AGAIN, I'D DO IT ALL OVER YOU (1970). Like SOFT MACHINE TWO, each side formed a continuous musical suite.

It was as good as their own whimsical version of prog-rock was to get, although run pretty close by the follow-up, 1971's IN THE LAND OF GREY AND PINK, produced in pinpoint clarity by **David Hitchcock**, with its perfect matching of Richard Sinclair's vocals and Dave Sinclair's lead organ.

Dave Sinclair then briefly left Caravan to join **ROBERT WYATT's Matching Mole** (where he co-wrote with Wyatt the band's heartbreaking single "O Caroline", as reworked by Gorky's Zygnotic Mynci). His replacement was **Steve Miller** from the blues band Delivery, whose electric piano gave WATERLOO LILY (1972) a jazzier, lighter atmosphere. Miller and Richard Sinclair then departed, the latter to form **HATFIELD AND THE NORTH**. In their place, **John G. Perry** joined on bass, and classically trained **Geoff Richardson** came in on electric viola.

FOR GIRLS WHO GROW PLUMP IN THE NIGHT (1973) saw the return of Dave Sinclair, and this new line-up established themselves as an excellent road band, with a rich and complex sound. October 1973 saw a somewhat pretentious live orchestral collaboration with the New Symphonia, arranged by Penguin Café Orchestra's **Simon Jeffes**. Still, every band makes mistakes.

CUNNING STUNTS was released the same year. For most, this was a letdown: with Mike Wedgewood now on bass, the band had become a little anonymous, lacking the mystery and majesty of their early sound. Dave Sinclair left again after the recording, to be replaced by **Jan Schelhaas** for BLIND DOG AT ST DUNSTANS (1976), a pale shadow of the past glories on show in a double-LP compilation, CANTERBURY TALES.

The band pressed on, attempting a more commercial sound, but were wildly out of kilter with the times and BETTER BY FAR (1977) and THE ALBUM (1980) are best glossed over, as is COOL WATER (recorded at this time but released a decade later). Dave Sinclair's solo album, MOON OVER MAN, also belatedly released, was merely a pleasant footnote.

In 1982 the four original players re-formed in a low-key way to produce BACK TO FRONT, recorded in Herne Bay and featuring some ironic reflections on lost fame and as the 90s dawned, they re-formed again for a late-night TV appearance, later released as CARAVAN LIVE, and some splendid concerts, supported by Ozric Tentacles, who could have been their children, both musically and in real time.

The spirit of Caravan refused to die. Richard Sinclair recorded a 1992 CD, CARAVAN OF

DREAMS, with Dave Sinclair and Jimmy Hastings, and the same line-up recorded a double live CD in Italy the following year. Meanwhile, Dave Sinclair and Jimmy Hastings joined brother Pye and the remnants of **CAMEL** – to record LIVE 14.12.94 under the name of **Mirage**. Then the band's original line-up, minus Richard Sinclair, but with **Geoff Richardson**, reconvened for enjoyable retreads THE BATTLE OF HASTINGS (1995) and ALL OVER YOU (1996). The BBC got in on the act too, with the release of LIVE IN CONCERT (1998), while TRAVELLING MAN (1998) was a good-value compilation of their more recent work, padded out with a few classics.

The band continue to play one-off gigs, now augmented by **Doug Boyce** on guitar, **Jim Leverton** on bass and **Simon Bental** on percussion.

Continuing interest in Caravan has led to the BBC combing its vaults for more previously unreleased material. SONGS FOR OBLIVION FISHERMEN (1998) features the original line-up on some priceless early sessions, including "Love Song Without Flute", as well as later, more languid, performances with Geoff Richardson on viola. ETHER WAY (1998) takes the band up to 1977, with three sessions recorded for John Peel. There is also a new four-CD series, CANTERBURIED SOUNDS, compiled by Brian and Hugh Hopper, which draws together previously unreleased performances by Caravan and their friends.

All these are nostalgic exercises, but what the hell, the Sex Pistols are at it, too. Musically, all the variants can be pleasing enough, though they miss the distinctive old Hammond organ of Dave Sinclair – now proprietor of a keyboard emporium – and, of course, the driving intensity of those early days is gone for ever.

⊙ **For Girls Who Grow Plump In The Night** (1973; Deram).
A more musically mature version of the band, driven along by John Perry's bass, as Dave Sinclair discovers the synthesizer, and a new interaction with the plangent viola of Geoff Richardson.

⊙ **The Canterbury Tales** (1976; Decca).
This double CD includes a couple of tracks from the original Verve LP, studio versions of "For Richard", "Nine Feet Underground" and "A Hunting We Will Go", and even some live new Symphonia tracks. As near to a 'best of' as is currently available.

Brian Hinton

THE CARDIACS

Formed Surrey, England, 1977.

There is no question about it – **The Cardiacs** aroused extraordinary feelings of malice from the music media. One editor of *NME* banned them outright from ever appearing on the mag's sacred pages, while *Smash Hits* delivered the relatively kindly verdict that they were 'completely bloody hopeless'. But these are the very Cardiacs who regularly pack out stomping grounds far beyond the capacity of London's latest media-crowned pop sensations. The Cardiacs inhabit a proudly subcultural world populated by obsessive fanzine readers and adventurous travellers following the word of mouth.

Lurking behind the ludicrously titled, mock-corporate Alphabet Business Concern is a band who have been through profligate name and personnel changes. By 1983, a semi-stable line-up had emerged around head Cardiac **Tim Smith** (guitar/vocals), **Jim Smith** (bass/vocals), **Tim Quy** (percussion/keyboards), **William Drake** (keyboards), **Sara Smith** (saxophone) and **Dominic Luckman** (drums).

Their maverick reputation was given a head start with the release of a series of cassette-only recordings: THE OBVIOUS IDENTITY (1980), TOY WORLD (1981), ARCHIVE CARDIACS – 1977–1979 (1983), THE SEASIDE (1983). Next came RUDE BOOTLEG (1986), which was a quite appalling recording of a Reading Festival performance that now has a certain rarity value. But they did put on an impressively theatrically Bonzo-esque stage show, and by the time that the first studio album proper, A LITTLE MAN AND A HOUSE AND THE WHOLE WORLD WINDOW (1988), was released, a distinctive sound had been developed – an acceptable dash of prog-rock, a hint of speed metal, some Edwardian-tinged psychedelia, a nod towards King Crimson, XTC and the Sex Pistols. It was just out of step with baggy, rave Britain, but A LITTLE MAN... was a corking album: Tim Smith's oh-so-English, pre-Suede mockney fronting grandiose Wurlitzer montages ("In A City Lining") and barn-storming flag-wavers ("Is This The Life?"). However, CARDIACS LIVE (1988) reinforced the view that you really had to be there – as, indeed, did 1990's ALL THAT GLITTERS IS A MARE'S NEST, which was recorded in Spinal Tap fashion in a church on Salisbury Plain.

Preceded by the departure of Sara Smith, Quy and Drake, ON LAND AND IN THE SEA (1989) is revered by die-hard Cardiac fans as the outstanding release, but to the less than fully converted it was a curiously one-dimensional affair, weighted far too heavily in favour of the furious rapid-fire style of "Two Bits Of Cherry" or "Baby Heart Dirt". A far better effort was SONGS FOR SHIPS AND IRONS (1989), which ranged from the exuberantly swashbuckling "Big Ship" and "Everything Is Easy" to the compelling "Burn Your House Down".

By 1992, with new guitarist **Jon Poole** on board, it had been decided to have a crack at what Tim Smith referred to as the 'established, proper music biz channels'. HEAVENBORN AND EVER BRIGHT (1992) was to be released through an alliance with Rough Trade and a new management deal was to sort out the still cynical press pack. But Rough Trade collapsed and the album sank without a trace. Leading Cardiacs immersed themselves in extracurricular duties, particularly Tim Smith, who assumed production duties for releases by Levitation and Sidi Bou Said, and formed **The Sea Nymphs**, a spin-off project involving himself, Sara Smith and William D. Drake.

By 1995, it briefly seemed that Britain's musical tastes were swinging in The Cardiacs' direction, as longtime fans Blur put them on the Mile End Stadium bill and the band's entire back catalogue was rereleased. Then in 1996 they broke cover with their first album in four years, the excellent SING TO GOD (PARTS 1 & 2). It took another three years before GUNS hit the shelves, sparking a rather green patch for Cardiacs fans as it was followed in quick succession by SONGS BY CARDIACS AND AFFECTIONATE FRIENDS (2001) – a compilation of old tunes and selections from various members' solo efforts – and the amusingly titled GREATEST HITS (2002).

⊙ **A Little Man And A House And The Whole World Window** (1988; The Alphabet Business Concern).
Shifts from relentless switchbacking assaults to pop show stoppers of the most conventional kind. Worth a tenner of anyone's money for "Is This The Life?" alone.

⊙ **Heavenborn And Ever Bright** (1992; The Alphabet Business Concern).
Made with the conviction that this would be the one, and the arrogant confidence of the title is bang on the nail. Best-sounding Cardiacs album by a mile as well.

⊙ **The Cardiacs Sampler** (1995; The Alphabet Business Concern).
Self-avowedly not a 'best of' compilation, though it would be hard to think how such an affair could improve on this. Also includes excerpts from The Sea Nymphs and one track from the (then unavailable) SONG TO GOD.

Lance Phillips

Nina Persson: no jacket required

THE CARDIGANS

Formed Jon Koping, Sweden, 1992.

After many years in the wilderness of musical credibility, the 1990s began to tolerate easy listening, but at a price: it carried with it the unnecessary tag of kitsch. For 'easy listening', read 'good tunes with lyrics that no one listens to', although the works of Bacharach & David, The Carpenters, Sinatra and Abba had often tackled complex, unnerving and adult concerns – obsession, loneliness, anxiety.

Caught up in this revival were a Scandinavian quintet whose very name had often been something of a hindrance, suggesting little more than whimsy and cosiness. Yet **The Cardigans** began as a 90s exercise in luring the listener with attractive melodies, only to share harsh and uncomfortable lyrical secrets. Their biggest hit single, "Lovefool" (1996), was misconstrued by countless radio programmers as a frothy, fluffy love song: pop at its most romanticized. However, it turned out to be nothing of the sort – here was a darker theme of love as an infatuation, or passion as an untruth.

At the beginning of their career, The Cardigans – **Nina Persson** (vocals), **Peter Svensson** (guitar), **Magnus Sveningsson** (bass guitar), **Lars–Olaf Johansson** (keyboards) and **Bengt Lagerberg** (drums) – were barely acknowledged in their Swedish homeland. Curiously, though, a debut LP, EMMERDALE (1994), became a cult success in Japan, a country that also fanatically embraced their follow-up album, 1995's LIFE. EMMERDALE was not released in Britain or the United States to begin with; both countries resequenced the track-listings of LIFE to feature highlights from its predecessor. With a sleeve-design pastiche of its magazine namesake, LIFE contained breakthrough hit singles in "Carnival" and "Sick & Tired", and even contained a masterly reworking of Black Sabbath's seemingly uncoverable "Sabbath Bloody Sabbath".

Despite having played their Sabbath card, and to The Cardigans' bewilderment, the release of FIRST BAND ON THE MOON in 1996 still generated the assumption that the band were featherweights. Those who checked the album's lyric sheet, however, or listened very carefully, discovered even starker, occasionally profane lyricism, concentrating on the neurotic and the erotic (often in the same song, as on "Happy Meal II"). This progression was slightly offset by the use of the admittedly excellent "Lovefool" on the soundtrack of the Baz Luhrmann movie *Romeo & Juliet*.

Gradually, impressive live performances began to erode The Cardigans' image of old, and the appearance of the rockier, harder-edged fourth LP, GRAN TURISMO (1998), showed they were not one-trick ponies. Daytime radio and the rock press appeared to agree – the compelling, but agitated, "My Favourite

Game" became a Top 20 single prior to the release of GRAN TURISMO, and helped them banish their one-hit-wonder status. Early 1999 found the band playing shows at London's Royal Albert Hall, and releasing "Erase"/"Rewind" as a single.

In 2001 Nina popped up with a new collective and album, both going by the name **A Camp**. Though Sparklehorse's **Mark Linkous** was at the production controls, the collection was undeniably Persson's show – and a fine show it was too, made all the more marvellous by the included cover of Daniel Johnston's "Walking The Cow".

In 2003 The Cardigans were back on and buttoned up for the release of LONG GONE BEFORE DAYLIGHT, which saw the group's sound fall more into line with the A Camp material; there was also a definite broadening of lyrical themes to include – shock horror – true, untainted 'love'.

The Cardigans

⦿ **Life** (1995; Stockholm/Polygram).
A wondrous mix of unforgettable pop-rock and down-beat neurotica. Call it 'easy listening' if you must, but only because everything is so consummately written and performed, especially the jerky "Sick & Tired" and the beautifully eccentric "Celia Inside".

⦿ **First Band On The Moon** (1996; Stockholm/Polygram).
The Cardigans cover Sabbath again ("Iron Man" this time), just one of a cluster of slightly less compromising gems. First-rate pop music.

A Camp

⦿ **A Camp** (2001; Polydor).
The first-person songs are well-defined constructions, largely of the sweet-soft-sad variety, but with a substantial sound that supports her lonely complaint. Where she sings her discomforting subjects of disappointment in love and bad comedowns her voice is clear, close and cruel over the undercurrent of strings, samples and melancholy country steel.

Justin Lewis

THE CARS

Formed Boston, Massachusetts, 1977; disbanded 1988.

The Cars represented the better instincts of the US New Wave movement. While the Knack were clearly faking it with their skinny ties and skinnier tunes, The Cars were given a cogent musical platform by singer/guitarist **Ric Ocasek** – incidentally, a pretty damned skinny guy himself.

Having moved to Boston from Cleveland in the early 70s, Ocasek began working with **Ben Orr** (bass/vocals) in sundry local bands before eventually founding The Cars alongside **Greg Hawkes** (keyboards/saxophone), **Elliot Easton** (guitar) and ex-Modern Lover **David Robinson** (drums), who gave them their name.

Punk was just beginning to happen in Boston and its favoured locale was the Rat Club, where the group honed talents that were already much more musical than some of the local opposition. Elektra

signed them in 1978 and put them to work with producer **Roy Thomas**. THE CARS (1978) was, alongside Blondie's PARALLEL LINES, the quintessential US New Wave album. Taking Ferry and Bowie as his obvious starting point, Ocasek also rooted his songs in older traditions – notably the hit single "My Best Friend's Girl" (with its quasi-high-school doo-wop rejoinder of 'And she used to be mine'). Even better was "Just What I Needed", a demo of which had originally attracted Elektra's attention: it was perfect for those who couldn't take punk's abrasiveness.

CANDY-O (1978) was even slicker, and though the singles remained strong (notably "Let's Go" and the heady "Double Life"), there was already something disinterested and removed about The Cars' work. Whereas everybody else was talking up alienation, Ocasek had already written the line 'Alienation is the latest craze' on the group's debut album, which kind of left him running down a blind alley.

By now The Cars were immensely popular throughout America, though their European popularity had dipped. PANORAMA (1980) stuck closely to the formula which had established the band, but lacked the great singles potential as Ocasek's lyrics veered into introspection and resignation. Much lighter in tone was SHAKE IT UP (1981), which returned to the uncluttered pop style of "My Best Friend's Girl" in "Think It Over" and the title track. Afterwards the group took a sabbatical while Ocasek released the solo collection BEATITUDE. The group reconvened in 1984 for the overtly commercial HEARTBREAK CITY; by now New Wave angst had been completely subsumed by studio polish and meaty pop hooks. It produced three substantial hit singles in "Magic", "You Might Think" and "Drive", the last incongruously reprised as accompaniment to 1985 Live Aid footage of starving Ethiopians.

By the time they returned to the studio once more for DOOR TO DOOR (1987), three other members of the band (Hawkes, Easton and Orr) had all completed solo albums, in addition to a second Ocasek effort. All offered interesting footnotes to the group's heavily orchestrated sound, but none was in any way essential. DOOR TO DOOR saw Ocasek take full control of the group, including all writing and production (having become an established 'name' producer with Suicide and Bad Brains). In reaction to the clinical assurance of the previous album, the songs this time favoured layered guitars rather than keyboards, though it proved the group's worst seller.

The Cars disbanded permanently thereafter. Ocasek continued his successful production career and also released a third solo album, FIREBALL ZONE, in 1991.

⦿ **The Cars** (1978; Elektra).
A pretty accomplished collection of New Wave pop songs, with the odd great moment.

⦿ **Greatest Hits** (1985; Elektra).
You will probably enjoy about half of this record, which balances the group's early new wave pop cool with the more overblown but superbly executed arena pop of the mid-80s.

Alex Ogg

CARTER USM

Formed London, 1986; split 1998.

"Our subjects are usually pretty downtrodden people. They're not glamorous. They haven't got any money. Other people don't write about them because people want records in the charts to be about having a good time." Jim Bob

Carter The Unstoppable Sex Machine, the self-mocking south London duo of **Jim Morrison** and **Les Carter** – aka **Jim Bob** and **Fruitbat** – formed out of the ashes of unsuccessful mid-80s popsters Jamie Wednesday. Their instantly memorable new name was a piece of deliberately misleading whimsy, for in Carter's world view England was a grey and unpleasant land.

Jim Bob and Fruitbat toured the pubs and clubs of London from 1987, with their dual punk-flavoured guitar assault augmented by the furious clatter of a cheap drum box. Songs wittily lambasted injustice, mixing puns with sociopolitical polemic – a method that won them as many converts as critics. Their debut single, "A Sheltered Life", appeared on Big Cat in August 1988 and was generally ignored. A year later, a second single, "Sheriff Fatman", crept out. An attack on money-grabbing landlords, the track began to get airplay, resulting in their selling out any venues they were playing. It later became Carter's first UK Top 40 hit when rereleased in the summer of 1991. The flip side's cover of Buzzcocks' "Everybody's Happy Nowadays" was only the first in a series of wry reworkings that saw everyone from Pet Shop Boys to Pink Floyd getting the Carter treatment.

The duo's growing reputation was bolstered by the debut album, 101 DAMNATIONS (1990). Mixing frantic guitars with samples, hip-hop beats, keyboard blasts and lyrics that namechecked south London haunts with alarming regularity, the LP revealed the band had ideas and energy to spare. As the rest of the country looked towards the 'Madchester' scene, Carter were starting a riot down south.

With music press support, "Rubbish" and the less frenetic "Anytime, Anyplace, Anywhere" appeared. In early 1991, Carter were extremely unlucky to miss the charts with the glam-rock-tinged tale of army brutality, "Bloodsport For All", which was denied any radio airplay owing to the simultaneous outbreak of the Gulf War.

Carter were not to be denied, however. In 1991 they released their breakthrough LP, 30 SOMETHING. It was Carter at their most approachable, and arguably their finest moment. Suddenly they were the name on everyone's T-shirt. Not even the demise of Rough Trade shortly after the LP's release could halt their rise, as they were signed to Chrysalis within days.

Carter's peak was probably their headlining appearance at the 1991 Reading Festival, where the strutting pair were introduced by their longtime compere, the ample-gutted Jon Beast, to the audience's beery chant of 'you fat bastard'. The only sour note that year was The Rolling Stones' lawyers slapping an injunction on their next single, "After The Watershed", which contained an audacious lift of "Ruby Tuesday".

After that they released "The Only Living Boy In New Cross", another uptempo roller coaster that summoned the diverse youth tribes that bought their records. It was followed by THE LOVE ALBUM (1992), which despite its name deployed the usual establishment-baiting rants. After touring Europe and the States with EMF, they returned in the autumn of 1993 with POST HISTORIC MONSTERS, which sold respectably but marked the beginning of their decline. A live album recorded in Zagreb, Croatia, was given away with initial copies of follow-up LP WORRY BOMB (1995) – but Carter weren't flavour of the month any more.

The duo tried to recapture their freshness by recruiting a drummer named **Wez** for the bouncy 1995 comeback single "Let's Get Tattoos", but WORRY BOMB was largely greeted with indifference. A series of compilation albums STARRY EYED AND BOLLOCK NAKED (1994), STRAW DONKEY: THE SINGLES (1995) and their instantly reissued, lacklustre 1996 work-out A WORLD WITHOUT DAVE (1997) suggested Carter's glory days were past.

I BLAME THE GOVERNMENT (1998) was their swansong, and like most bands that make the decision to bow out with a degree of credibility, they pulled it together for the occasion. Stand-out track "Growing Old Disgracefully" said it all. After a period of silence, both men assembled solo projects. Jim Bob released IN A BIG FLASH CAR in 2002 under the name **Jim's Super Stereo World**. Fruitbat released a solo single under the name **Who's The Daddy Now?** Both of these new projects were somewhat underwhelming although the pair have toured together and encored together with a few Carter classics. Maybe a reunion is on the cards.

- **30 Something** (1991; Chrysalis).
  The sound of a band at the peak of their powers: a dizzy Doc Marten-booted stage-dive from start to finish.

- **Straw Donkey: The Singles** (1995; Chrysalis).
  A compilation spanning the band's seven-year recording career from "A Sheltered Life" to "Born On The 5th Of November". They may be unfashionable, but this collection shows that Carter have achieved something many of their peers haven't – there's not one duff track.

Gavin Stoker

JOHNNY CASH

Born Kingsland, Arkansas, 1932.

Johnny Cash's stripped-down, unadorned 1994 set, AMERICAN RECORDINGS, confirmed his status as one of the most powerful interpreters of the

American experience in song, introduced him to yet another generation and brought his music full circle. Now in his seventies, Cash remains one of the most charismatic of performers, as capable of conquering the Glastonbury Festival as of wowing the country-music die-hards.

Born in the midst of the Great Depression to a guitar-playing mother, Cash won a talent contest in the neighbouring town of Dyess in 1948, took singing lessons and learned to play the guitar while serving with the American Air Force in Germany. By the time he was discharged in 1954, his elder brother Roy (who had played in a prewar hillbilly band) was working in Memphis, Tennessee; there he introduced Johnny to two local musicians, guitarist **Luther Perkins** and bass player **Marshall Grant**. Signed to the Memphis label, Sun Records, alongside Elvis Presley, Carl Perkins, Jerry Lee Lewis and Roy Orbison, the trio evolved the distinctive Cash sound, with simple, rhythmic electric guitar filled out by Cash's acoustic, a slapped upright bass, Cash's sombre, nasal, down-in-the-boots voice and a ton of echo. In 1955 they recorded such classics-to-be in "Folsom Prison Blues", "Cry Cry Cry" and "Hey Porter", followed in April 1956 by the first smash hit, "I Walk The Line"/"Get Rhythm", which established Cash in the pop charts.

Unlike his illustrious label mates, Cash stayed true to country music, resisting the lure of rock'n'roll, and his huge success on Sun and – from 1958 – on the major label Columbia (where he traded licks, songs and admiration with Bob Dylan), elevated him to a country trinity with prewar pioneer Jimmie Rodgers and the peerless songwriter Hank Williams.

By 1965 his friend **Carl Perkins**'s career was threatened by alcoholism, and Cash was struggling with pill addiction. The answer was for Perkins to join Cash's band, and for them to wean each other off their cravings. In 1969, the live album JOHNNY CASH AT SAN QUENTIN, including the huge hit "A Boy Named Sue", was another career peak; Cash

remained a chart force throughout the 70s with such titles as "A Thing Called Love" and "One Piece At A Time".

In 1981 Cash was reunited with Perkins and **Jerry Lee Lewis** for the SURVIVORS album, and in 1985 **Roy Orbison** joined in as well, back in the old Sun studio, for CLASS OF '55. In the same year another collaboration, this time with country 'outlaws' **Waylon Jennings**, **Willie Nelson** and **Kris Kristofferson**, produced a #1 in "The Highwayman". In 1986, somewhat bizarrely, Columbia dropped Cash from its roster, but a move to Mercury barely interrupted a career of stunning achievement and depth. A cameo on U2's ZOOROPA (1993), on the track "The Wanderer", introduced him to a new audience but his 1996 album UNCHAINED spoiled his attempt at winning this new team of fans by trying to make him all things to all men. Ill-advised covers (Johnny Cash sings Beck, anyone?) and age-hardened cheese ("I've Been Everywhere" and even "Memories Are Made Of this") watered down his seen-it-all, cynical image maybe too far even for the 90s generation. 1998's THE BEST OF was a good stab at the impossible task of summarizing a career such as Cash's on a single album, but missed too many essential tracks. HITS & CLASSICS (1998) was a better bet – an inexpensive package of classy material recorded at Sun Studios in the 1950s.

In the autumn of 1997, Cash collapsed during a concert and then announced, from the stage, that he had Parkinson's disease. Doctors later diagnosed him with a rare neurological disorder (Shy-Drager's Syndrome) with no cure. The singer was told he might have only a year left, and his deteriorating physical condition was hardly conducive to work. Consequently, it was a nice surprise when, in 2000, Cash not only released a three-disc set exploring his 46-year career (LOVE GOD AND MURDER) but also a terrific album of new recordings, AMERICAN III: SOLITARY MAN. Composed of both originals and interesting cover choices (by the likes of Neil Diamond, Nick Cave, and Will Oldham), the album shrewdly and inimitably examined life from the perspective of an ill, sixty-eight-year-old founding father of rock'n'roll. The similarly-formatted THE MAN COMES AROUND followed in 2002, this time featuring sublime covers of cuts by the likes of Depeche Mode and even Nine Inch Nails.

Cash remains one of the great folk poets, and continues to craft music that makes the hair rise on the back of the neck, and although in variable health the 'Man in Black' is still a force in the rock music picture.

American Recordings (1994; American Recordings). A superbly dark, bleak and earthy new set.

The Man in Black (1994; Columbia). A twenty-track chronicle of his two decades at CBS-Columbia, this features all the middle-period material, and his biggest hits.

Folsom Prison Blues (1995; Charly).
A sterling collection of the spare, resonating Sun classics that made his name.

Love God Murder (2000; Columbia).
Spanning forty years worth of material, the three sets weigh heaviest on his most fertile periods of the 50s and 60s. The best finds are the cuts that have been previously somewhat overlooked, such as the spooky "Hardin Wouldn't Run" and "Mr. Garfield" (the tale of the most obscure of American assassinated presidents).

The Man Comes Around (2002; Columbia).
A beautiful, at times fragile, collection of covers and original material. The title cut is mesmerizing, while only Cash could make such well-trodden numbers as "Bridge Over Troubled Water" and "I'm So Lonesome I Could Cry" sound fresh and compelling.

John Collis

CAST

Formed Liverpool, England, 1993;
disbanded, 2001.

When **THE LA'S'** debut (and only) album drew to a close, its crescendo of noise reflected the band's self-implosion. Amidst the cacophony, one line rang out: 'The change is cast'. And, lo, **Cast** the band was born, formed by The La's' bassist **John Power** – who had become increasingly frustrated with Lee Mavers' studio rambling – with **Keith O'Neill** (drums), **Liam Tyson** (guitar) and **Peter Wilkinson** (bass).

The timing of Power's re-emergence could hardly have been better: headed by Blur and Oasis, 60s-influenced Britpop had crossed over from the indie scene to huge commercial success. Noel Gallagher had singled out The La's as a defining moment in the development of his own style, mentioning them in the same breath as The Beatles, Bacharach and The Stone Roses. When he saw Power's new band play live, he likened the effect to a religious experience. Rave reviews followed Cast everywhere, and they proceeded to upstage any band naive enough to sign them up as a support act.

At a time when A&R men were falling over themselves to sign anyone with the right haircut, Cast arrived with a welcome and reassuring dedication to content over style. With The Beatles and The Who as obvious reference points, their two hit singles of 1995, "Fine Time" and "Alright", paved the way for the acclaimed Top 10 album ALL CHANGE (1995). A solid debut, it also contained their magnificent third single, "Sandstorm", which proved to be their first Top 10 single in January 1996. The only disappointment was that the album failed to reflect the full scope of Power's songwriting ability, opting for full-on stomping crowd-pleasers at the expense of subtler moments. Still, the melancholic "Walkaway" (their second UK Top 10 single) provided a welcome pause in proceedings, while the climax of "Two Of A Kind" cast a knowing eye over The La's' last moments.

MOTHER NATURE CALLS (1997) saw Power finally gaining the confidence to experiment – a little.

A fine, stomping example of the beauty inherent in playing simple tunes very loudly, there was room here and there for deeper emotions and even a hint of sensitivity.

With memories of Britpop now consigned to the dim and distant past, Cast's next offering, MAGIC HOUR (1999) struggled to find a place, and despite the brashness of the UK top 10 single "Beat Mama" their beat-rock formula now sounded anachronistic amid the pre-millennial rush of newer, brighter sounds. 2001's lacklustre BEETROOT effectively marked the end and with a sense that the band had run its natural course, announcements of a split followed soon after. However, while his days in Cast may be behind him, it is difficult to imagine someone as irrepressible as John Power staying away for long.

All Change (1995; Polydor).
A blistering first album. Highlights include the four singles and the multi-layered harmonies on the reflective "Four Walls".

Mark Hooper

CAT POWER

Chan Marshall born Atlanta, Georgia, 1972.

Chan Marshall at times sounds just like she looks: gentle, demure, almost frail. At other times her voice is resonant and powerful. But it is only with closer inspection that one picks out the darker aspects of her music. Chan's group, **Cat Power**, more often than not simply a one-woman-band, have produced bold but subtle collections of indie-blues with an evil eye. Chan's voice swoons with a velveteen croak around lyrics that chill as often as they delight.

After her parents' marriage ended, Chan (pronounced 'Shawn' and born Charlyn), discovered Aretha Franklin, dropped three letters from her name and before long had moved in with her sister in Atlanta at a time when Georgia's capital had a booming New Wave scene. All her friends were in bands and finally, at the age of twenty, Chan was persuaded to pick up the guitar in her bedroom and do it, too: Cat Power came into being. Her Atlanta days were, however, to be short-lived. After the deaths of two close friends Marshall felt the need to get away and wound up living in New York's East Village, where she played a few gigs opening for Liz Phair. The move proved a valuable one when Sonic Youth associate Wharton Tiers saw her perform and gave Chan a one-day session at his studio, with the tracks put down eventually making up the first pair of Cat Power albums.

But Marshall felt deeply at odds with the processes that defined the musical world she had entered: she felt that recording her music and even playing live had stripped the form of its art, an attitude that resulted in almost rueful stage appearances. There were occasions when Chan apologized profusely to audiences, and others when she made numerous false starts. Most infamous was an appearance with a

Chan Marshall, aka Cat Power

refurbishment of The Stones' "Satisfaction" is, however, an indisputable revelation of tainted, fragile blues – and gives the original a serious run for its money.

YOU ARE FREE (2003), the most recent full-length album, saw Marshall in an apparently upbeat mood – although all attempts to interpret her lyrics remained steadfastly futile. Zeitgeist producer Adam Kaspar (Queens Of The Stone Age/Foo Fighters/Pearl Jam) might have seemed an unlikely selection, but the results were soaring. In the face of across-the-board praise Chan remained remarkably humble: 'I'm not an artist, I'm a simple person. I'm so basic...'

⊙ **Moon Pix** (1998; Matador).
The piano-based "Colours And The Kids" might just be the most heart-stopping moment in Chan Marshall's career.

⊙ **You Are Free** (2003; Matador).
This is a far more sombre affair all round compared to MOON PIX, and though at times a little too flat, songs such as "I Don't Blame You" and "Half Of You" are too beautiful to be ignored.

Jeremy Simmonds

CATATONIA

Formed Cardiff, Wales, 1993; disbanded, 2001.

The source of **Catatonia**'s indelible spirit was vocalist **Cerys Matthews**, a brassy Boadicea of the mike-stand with a back-to-basics belief in drinking, and havin' a laffff. That's not to say that **Mark Roberts** (guitar), **Paul Jones** (bass; ex-member, together with Roberts, of Welsh-language punk band Y Cruff), **Owen Powell** (guitar) and **Aled Richards** (drums) didn't contribute greatly to a band who came across surprisingly well on record.

Roberts first discovered leather-lungs Cerys busking Jefferson Airplane songs outside Debenhams in Cardiff, and invited her to work on some songs with him. They took the name Catatonia (a type of schizophrenia characterized by periodic states of stupor) based on Cerys's experiences of working in a mental health institution in London. The songs they wrote delivered central messages of self-empowerment and personal liberation through the medium of guitar rock, but the band's ambitions stretched beyond the indie circuit. 'I can't understand all this ideology about independent music, cos it's a bit of an elitist thing. Bollocks!' pledged Cerys in one of Catatonia's first interviews in 1994. Nevertheless, it was the indie community that clutched the band to their hearts and who formed their initial fan base.

Catatonia set about securing their first gigs and drew the attention of Welsh label Crai Records. Their first release, "For Tinkerbell", was an attack on the all-pervading power of TV and became an *NME Single of the Week*. As well as original drummer **Dafydd Ieuan**, who subsequently joined Super Furry Animals, it also featured keyboard player

bewildered guitarist and percussionist (Two Dollar Guitar's **Tim Foljahn** and **Steve Shelley** of Sonic Youth) at New York's Knitting Factory where the singer screamed almost uncontrollably for what seemed an eternity.

The remainder of her story is, thankfully, dominated by a series of great records. The cuts recorded at Tiers' studio finally emerged: a mini-album, DEAR SIR (stand-out, the insistent, raucous "Itchyhead"), was released by Runt in 1995, with MYRA LEE surfacing through Smells Like in 1996. It was Matador Records, though, that put out brand new material with the very impressive WHAT WOULD THE COMMUNITY THINK?, also 1996. Sometimes in barely a whisper, sometimes approaching a wail, Cat Power juggled the shadowy worlds of Nick Drake and Lisa Germano in such draining confessionals as "In This Hole" and "Good Clean Fun".

1998's seminal MOON PIX, which drew heavily from traditional folk and country styles, but somehow remained utterly original, was the recording that made her name. Her next CD, THE COVERS RECORD (2000), contained none of her own material and split critical opinion. Marshall's complete

Clancy. The same line-up was also responsible for their second single, "Hooked".

By the time "Sweet Catatonia" was released in 1993 the group had cemented its line-up. 1995's "Bleed", released on Nursery Records, finally brought them the recognition that had escaped earlier singles. Signing to Blanco y Negro, they toured relentlessly with bands like Salad, who were initially considered a 'better bet' by the music press. Undeterred, Catatonia embarked on recording their debut album with producer **Stephen Street**. WAY BEYOND BLUE (1996) was a minor success, propelled by the track "You've Got A Lot To Answer For", which resulted in a huge injection of radio exposure when released on single, and a place in the Top 40. Catatonia could always count on a place in the gossip columns, too, thanks to the lagered-up antics of their boisterous lead-singer-about-town.

1997 was the group's breakthrough year. "I Am The Mob" – a charming narrative built on a succession of gangster clichés – was deemed too controversial by the radio authorities and only scraped the Top 40. It took the *X-Files*-inspired "Mulder And Scully" to really set the ball rolling. Climbing to #3 in the UK charts, it gave a huge commercial boost to the attendant album INTERNATIONAL VELVET (1998). A further single, "Road Rage", also reached the Top 5, as Catatonia left the indie ghetto far behind. Cerys's 1998 duet with **Space**, "The Ballad Of Tom Jones", became a huge radio and chart hit, leading to a duet with its titular hero and greatest living Welshman on Jools Holland's 1998 New Year's Eve TV show.

In the interim, INTERNATIONAL VELVET proved a strong seller and Christmas stocking-filler. On the back of their outstanding 1999 single "Dead From The Waist Down", and the haunting, confessional "Bulimic Beats", EQUALLY CURSED AND BLESSED (1999) stormed the British charts and the band jumped to the next level of stardom. Catatonia had soaked up the constituency of coffee-table music fans who bought Björk and Beautiful South records to demonstrate their left-field credentials.

But such fans were to prove rather fickle when there were so many more novel experiences to be had. Exhilarating and kooky Cerys Matthews may be, but there was too little substance or invention on 2001's PAPER, SCISSORS, STONE to spark any real interest. The jaded feel of the album clearly mirrored the feelings of the lead vocalist, as shortly after its release Catatonia announced their split, citing Cerys's exhaustion as a major factor. Since then the band have vowed to carry on without her, under a different name. Cerys, meanwhile, checked into rehab, sorted herself out, and then retreated to Nashville where she recorded a lulling, stripped-back, country-influenced solo album, COCKAHOOP (2003), with Bob Dylan's slide-guitarist, Bucky Baxter. Returning to the UK, Cerys toured the new material, heavily pregnant, seeming more than at home with her rejuvinated, mellower style.

⊙ **International Velvet** (1998; Blanco y Negro).
Although this was Catatonia's breakthrough album, for the first time they faced some nay-sayers in the press (including the *NME*). But it would take a hard-hearted cynic to begrudge the band their new fans. At least half the songs on display here are of the highest order, and Cerys's sheer, unadulterated joy in singing provides them with extra punch and life.

⊙ **Catatonia 1993/1994** (1998; Crai).
A useful compilation of their early material for local label Crai, including such delights as "For Tinkerbell", "Dimbran" and "Sweet Catatonia".

⊙ **Equally Cursed And Blessed** (1999; Blanco y Negro).
With a bigger sound and more leather-lunged anthems (particularly the rabble-rousing "Storm The Palace"), this should have taken the band to international stardom.

Alex Ogg

CATHERINE WHEEL

Formed Great Yarmouth, England, 1990.

The potential of **Catherine Wheel** – **Rob Dickinson** (vocals/guitar), **Brian Futter** (guitar/vocals), **Dave Hawes** (bass) and **Neil Sims** (drums) – was first spotted by Norwich indie label Wilde Club, who released two four-track EPs in early 1991 – SHE'S MY FRIEND and PAINFUL THING. The recordings were effectively demos, but despite the primitive production their distinctive blend of indie guitar and dark lyrics shone through, and both made inroads on the UK indie charts.

By the summer of 1991, Catherine Wheel had toured with Blur, Levitation, The Replacements, The Charlatans and The Lemonheads. Nevertheless, the music press were less than convinced with the band's lack of animation on stage, earning them the tag of 'shoegazers' (a brand of the year). Undeterred, and newly signed to Phonogram's subsidiary Fontana, they released a third EP, BLACK METALLIC, a menacing seven-minute epic, featuring a grotesque close-up of comedian Max Wall on the sleeve. This minor hit was followed by "Balloon", which with its "ba ba ba ba" chorus could conceivably have been called a breezy pop song.

And then came the debut LP FERMENT (1992), a Top 40 album in the UK. Produced by **Tim Friese-Greene** (who had previously twiddled knobs for Talk Talk), it displayed guitar wailing, feedback and wah-wah acrobatics aplenty. The lyrical content was unfathomably sinister, particularly on the title track's descent into the nightmare of drug addiction and self-delusion.

After a UK tour supporting Smashing Pumpkins, Catherine Wheel headed to the US for a nine-month tour, building on the success of FERMENT. While in America, they broke the UK Top 40 for the first time with "I Want To Touch You", a radio-friendly tale of obsession, and later in the year released a covers EP of material by Scott Walker and Hüsker Dü, 30 CENTURY MAN.

Further original material was aired in June 1993 at a gig in London's Finsbury Park, but the releases – a single, "Crank", followed by a second album,

CHROME (1993) – sold poorly. Production duties from Pixies and Belly producer **Gil Norton** could not disguise the fact that much of the material was comparatively lightweight. Still, tracks such as "Broken Head" and "Kill Rhythm" showed that the songwriting strengths of the debut LP were still in evidence, sometimes.

Further touring, including a second US jaunt with Slowdive, helped the band's survival, and finally rid them of the 'shoegazing' tag, and in 1995 a brooding single, "Way Down", signalled a return to form. Chart success still proved elusive, however, and their third LP, HAPPY DAYS (1995), saw them opening a door marked, in bold paint, 'Heavy Alternative Rock (US Division)'. Thundering along with furious guitar mutilation, it was effectively a relaunch; highlights included a duet with Belly's **Tanya Donelly** on "Judy Staring At The Sun". A collection of non-LP cuts, LIKE CATS AND DOGS (1996), made use of their new-found success.

By the release of ADAM & EVE (1998), Catherine Wheel had their feet firmly under the table in the US, and were sitting with their backs to England. Their UK label Fontana dropped the band as part of the late-90s cull that swept through the industry, but in the States they could do little wrong. Standout track "Here Comes The Fat Controller" may have lacked resonance in a country not brought up on *Thomas the Tank Engine*, but it still kept the alt-rock contingent happy.

Despite their continued relative lack of success at home – something that the band claim keeps them fresh and hungry – the new millennium brought with it a desire to deconstruct their usual way of working. The result was WISHVILLE (2000), named after the mythical destination the band were keen to arrive at – wherever that may be. Written over two years it was the culmination of each band member creating songs separately rather than together; the strain of working this way led to Dave Hawes being replaced by Glaswegian **Ben Ellis**, but the album was possibly their most creative yet.

⊙ **Ferment** (1992; Fontana).
Catherine Wheel's fiery debut sent indie kids reaching for their air guitars and everyone else calling out for earplugs. The album to (almost) put Great Yarmouth on the map.

⊙ **Wishville** (2000; Chrysalis).
The Tim Friese-Greene-produced WISHVILLE finds singer/guitarist Rob Dickinson sounding as vulnerable and energized as ever – witness the cracking opener "Sparks Are Gonna Fly". WISHVILLE is a complex and satisfying album.

Anna Robinson

NICK CAVE AND THE BAD SEEDS

Formed London, 1984.

After Australian band **THE BIRTHDAY PARTY** split in 1983, vocalist **Nick Cave** decided to launch a solo career, accompanied by a band he

Cave getting on down – in an Old Testament kind of way

dubbed **The Bad Seeds**. The Seeds' line-up has changed frequently over the years, though multi-instrumentalist **Mick Harvey** (also from The Birthday Party) and guitarist **Blixa Bargeld** (who maintains a night job with German noise-experimentalists **EINSTÜRZENDE NEUBAUTEN**) have, until recently, been constants.

At the outset, Cave, Harvey and Bargeld were joined by **BARRY ADAMSON** (ex-**MAGAZINE**; bass), **Hugo Race** (guitar) and, just in time for their first album, FROM HER TO ETERNITY (1984), sometime lyricist **Anita Lane**. Later notable Seeds included drummer **Thomas Wydler** (from 1986), guitarist **Kid Congo Powers** (ex-**CRAMPS/GUN CLUB**; from 1986), **Martyn P. Casey** (ex-**TRIFFIDS**; bass, joined 1992) and pianist **Conway Savage** (from 1992).

Cave and The Seeds' first single, a cover of "In The Ghetto" (1984), was evidence of a dual fascination – with Elvis and with cover versions. They went on to cover Leonard Cohen's "Avalanche" on the debut LP, FROM HER TO ETERNITY, and Dylan's "Wanted Man" on the follow-up, THE FIRST BORN IS DEAD (1985). Then, in 1986 came KICKING AGAINST THE PRICKS, an entire album of covers that peaked with "By The Time I Get To Phoenix", transforming the cheesy original into a powerful and angst-laden epic of love and loss.

1986 was a real stormer of a year for Cave, who produced arguably his own strongest material on YOUR FUNERAL ... MY TRIAL. This delivered his uncompromising ideology of Old Testament finality – people are good or bad and can do little about it. Significantly, Cave's band took its name from William March's novel *The Bad Seed*, about an apparently innocent young girl who is rotten to the core and comes from a long line of murderers.

Cave's work has been overwhelmingly based on such 'bad' souls – drunks, prostitutes, white trash and, in particular, murderers. The classic Cave hero, brutal but aware of the vulnerability behind his own bravado, is the protagonist of "The Mercy Seat" on TENDER PREY (1988). Cave's finest eight minutes, the song related the final moments of a convicted killer on Death Row, combining biblical imagery with music of relentless and inescapable repetition: 'And in a way I'm yearning/To be done with all the measuring of truth/An eye for an eye/And a tooth for a tooth/And anyway I told the truth/And I'm not afraid to die'. The cut was recently, and powerfully, covered by Johnny Cash as part of his continuing exploration of his own mortality.

Cave has frequently been charged with misogyny, and indeed several of his songs – both originals and covers – have been about the murder of women ("Hey Joe", "Long Time Man", "I'm Gonna Kill That Woman"). Yet some of his best songs have been love songs, such as "Straight To You" and "The Ship Song", a magnificent ballad on which Cave's crooning was worthy of Scott Walker. Many such items featured on Cave's 1994 album, LET LOVE IN, suggesting marriage and fatherhood might have mellowed him, while a debauched happiness pervaded his "Wonderful World" duet with **Shane MacGowan** (1992).

But longtime fans were doubtless relieved by MURDER BALLADS (1996), a ten-track litany of violent death featuring accomplices Shane MacGowan, **Polly Harvey** and – amazingly – soap personality and teenybop disco star **Kylie Minogue**, appearing as a girl who gets smashed with a rock and dumped in the river.

In THE BOATMAN'S CALL (1997) – vintage growly Cave and classic sombre Seeds, and the nearest we'll get to a collection of love songs from this bunch – Cave delivered a cold-blooded vivisection of this most fascinating emotion, separating the sacred from the profane to form another ghastly exhibit in The Bad Seeds' cabinet of horrors.

Other than a BEST OF collection (1998) and a spoken word set – THE SECRET LIFE OF THE LOVE SONG (2000) – all was quiet until the release of the stupendous NO MORE SHALL WE PART in 2001, an enchanting amalgam of beautiful love songs and rage. This set was followed in 2003 by NOCTURAMA, which was released shortly before Bargeld announced his intention to leave the Seeds and concentrate on his film and theatre work.

Cave still shows no sign of slowing down. He has dabbled in other media, appearing in the films *Wings Of Desire* (director Wim Wenders is a longtime fan) and *Ghosts Of The Civil Dead*, and in 1989 published *And The Ass Saw The Angel*, an impressive Faulknerian tale of everyday murder and incest. But his priority is still music, and Cave remains one of the most commanding and charismatic frontmen in the business.

⊙ **The First Born Is Dead** (1985; Mute).
Cave's second LP, but his first wholly consistent one. Highlights include a vigorous and witty version of Dylan's "Wanted Man", and the dramatic and intense opener "Tupelo".

⊙ **Your Funeral... My Trial** (1986; Mute).
A richer, more mature record, revealing more of The Bad Seeds' potential and versatility. Features the relentless "Hard On For Love", the powerful "Long Time Man" and the aching "Sad Waters".

⊙ **Let Love In** (1994; Mute).
Perhaps Cave's most accessible LP. The Bad Seeds show an effortless mastery of all forms. High point is "Red Right Hand", where Morricone meets Dostoevsky. As ever, it's all dominated by Cave's massive, brooding presence.

⊙ **Murder Ballads** (1996; Mute).
Almost a spoken-word album, with little for The Seeds to do as Cave's voice is counterposed with Kylie and Polly Harvey. At its best on "O'Malley's Bar", showing Cave's abiding love of language.

⊙ **The Best Of** (1998; Mute).
Perfect introduction, a handy accompaniment for that cross-country drive to slaughter a close relation or cheating spouse.

⊙ **No More Shall We Part** (2001; Mute).
Here Cave constructs a moving monument to oppression and passion. But after eleven albums, it's ultimately Cave that becomes exposed within the dark room of these songs.

⊙ **Nocturama** (2003; Mute).
Though far from being either Cave's most dashing of succulently morose collection, NOCTURAMA is another fine album that grows more compelling with every listen. The opening cut, "Wonderful Life", is a delight; "Still In Love" slithers to the swoon of a drunken violin; but the collection's highpoint is "Babe, I'm On Fire", which rocks like a mutha' for nearly fifteen minutes.

Chris Jenkins

EUGENE CHADBOURNE

Born Mount Vernon, New York, January 1954.

A true maverick virtuoso of modern American music, **Eugene Chadbourne** both undermined and energized the contemporary rock scene. He recognized none of the barriers that are placed between the genres of folk, blues, country, jazz and rock and was at ease playing not just these Western formats but also with Oriental and Middle Eastern styles and instrumentation.

This is somewhat surprising as Chadbourne grew up in relative cultural isolation in Boulder, Colorado (even now he is based in the boondocks of North Carolina). He was first inspired to take up the guitar after seeing The Beatles on TV and went on to play covers of Dylan and Hendrix songs in high-school bands. His key influence, however, was the protest singer Phil Ochs (an early rival to Dylan), whom the young Eugene saw in live performance and whose radical songs may have prompted him initially to choose journalism, rather than music, as a profession. Chadbourne's eventual decision to take up music full time was further delayed by his enforced exile in Canada, where he retreated to avoid the Vietnam draft.

Upon President Carter's amnesty for conscientious objectors, Chadbourne settled in New York and began to play and study music in earnest, making contact with others among the nascent 'loft scene' of avant-garde performers. His most significant collaborator was saxophonist **John Zorn**, who was similarly inclined to explore the possibilities of purely improvised music. Having forged further links with the improvisation scene in Britain, as well as allying with other US pioneers such as the West Coast guitarist **Henry Kaiser**, Chadbourne began to issue recordings of his and Zorn's work, notably the now hard-to-find vinyl releases SCHOOL and 2000 STATUES: THE ENGLISH CHANNEL.

As well as being a progenitor of the improv scene, Chadbourne rekindled his initial interest in the tradition of folk and protest song, taking a vocal stand against the iniquities of corporate America and the military-industrial complex, at times forsaking his instrumental sophistication for a hard-hitting approach that's true to his vision of rock as a revolutionary art form. Chadbourne has also made much room in his career for the often-ridiculed genre of 60s psychedelia, particularly with his cover versions – or rather 'deconstructions' – of songs by Tim Buckley, Love, Pink Floyd and others.

He has teamed up with the ex-Mothers Of Invention drummer **Jimmy Carl Black** virtually to rewrite the Frank Zappa and Captain Beefheart canon. Another intriguing collaboration was the power-trio **Shockabilly**, formed with proto-grunge guru **Kramer** (Bongwater), where Chadbourne tapped into the anarchic energy of the folk roots of rock music. This was also evident in his work with the younger country-psychedelic bands **Camper Van Beethoven** and the reunion with Zorn on the self-styled 'Free Improvised Country and Western Be-Bop' album THERE'LL BE NO TEARS TONIGHT (1980). Conversely, his collaboration with underground ethno-rock eccentrics **Sun City Girls** relied far more heavily on Eastern folk instrumentation and arrangements.

Chadbourne remains most compelling as a live performer, switching at ease from electric guitar to banjo, zipping through a tune that sounds totally improvised and yet recalls something buried in the collective folk memory, like a punk Burl Ives, whipping off his spectacles to scrape them down the fretboard, adding another dimension to his wonderfully pixilated sound.

Eugene Chadbourne

⊙ **There'll Be No Tears Tonight** (1980; Fundamental Music).
As it says on the sleeve – Hank Williams on LSD, Waylon Jennings meets the Sex Pistols.

⊙ **Pain Pen** (2000; Avant).
One of numerous stupendous improv freakouts available on CD, this one features Eugene with New York jazz stalwarts Mark Dresser and Susie Ibarra.

Eugene Chadbourne and Jimmy Carl Black

⊙ **Pachuco Cadaver** (1996; Fireants).
An effective and comprehensive set of Zappa and Beefheart reworkings.

Robert Murray

THE CHAMELEONS

Formed Manchester, England, 1981; disbanded 1987; reformed 2000.

Trying to decide the best band to come out of Manchester may be an impossible task, but the most underrated must surely be **The Chameleons**. **Mark Burgess** (bass/vocals), **Reg Smithies** (guitar), **John Lever** (drums) and **Dave Fielding** (guitar) emerged as Thatcherism was beginning to ravage the country's former industrial heartlands, as did many other bands in Manchester, Liverpool (Echo And The Bunnymen) and Leeds (Gang Of Four). Their powerful, exhilarating music was shot through with an anxiety and a yearning for the security of innocence, qualities captured perfectly on their debut release, the three-track NOSTALGIA (1981), made with the help of hottest producer of the time, **Steve Lillywhite**. It contained the concise and thrilling "In Shreds", with Burgess presenting himself as an individual ill at ease in an oppressive and dehumanized world. The record's atmosphere was reflected in its sleeve, too – a disturbing painting by Smithies, whose artwork was a notable feature of all their records.

Their first LP, SCRIPT OF THE BRIDGE (1983), built on the EP's promise, with the guitar-based sound and Burgess's forceful vocals enhanced by a judicious use of synthesizers. It was such an impressive record that The Chameleons would struggle to emulate it – and indeed the follow-up, WHAT DOES ANYTHING MEAN, BASICALLY? (1985), was as half-baked as the title. Swamped by synthesizers, Burgess was barely discernible at times, though his disaffection was noticeable on "Singing Rule Britannia (While The Walls Close In)", a tirade against mass unemployment.

The following year the band signed to a major label – Geffen – who released their third and last album, STRANGE TIMES (1986). Though an improvement, with a couple of terrific songs ("Mad Jack" and "Swamp Thing"), it suffered from an overly slick sound and a general lack of conviction. It was no great surprise when The Chameleons called it a day a few months later.

After the split, Burgess and Lever went on to

form **The Sun And The Moon**, while Smithies set up **The Reegs**, neither achieving very much success. Burgess then toyed with a solo career with backing band **The Sons Of God**, releasing ZIMA JUNCTION (1993), SPRING BLOOMS TRA-LA (1994) and a live album, MANCHESTER 93 (1994), before hooking up with **Yves Altana**, a songwriting partner. They released an album in 1995 called PARADYNING.

In 2000 The Chameleons reformed for a series of gigs at 'The Witchwood' in Ashton-under-Lyne, a favourite venue of the band. This success was followed by a new studio album, WHY CALL IT ANYTHING. Though the band are still officially together, progress the second time around is proving to be slow, partly due to Smithies' parenting commitments. So for now, keep a look out for Burgess's solo acoustic shows.

⊙ **Script Of The Bridge** (1983; Statik).
A long time in the making, but worth the wait. Standouts included "Don't Fall", "A Person Isn't Safe Anywhere These Days", which summed up Burgess's philosophy perfectly, and, arguably their best song, "Second Skin".

⊙ **The Fan And The Bellows** (1986; Imaginary).
A fine compilation aptly subtitled 'Classic early recordings'. It also includes all three tracks from NOSTALGIA.

Chris Jenkins

JAMES CHANCE AND THE CONTORTIONS

Formed New York, 1977.

A standard punk rock insult used to be that 'New York is ok if you like saxophones'. People stopped saying that around the time **James Chance** started bringing his horn and his No Wave band **The Contortions** to New York punk clubs in 1977. A refugee from the Milwaukee scene, Chance (given name James Siegfried) came to the Big Apple to play free jazz, and even studied for a while with saxophonist David Murray. At the time, though, a lot of buzz and energy was in the non-jazz avant-garde, where musicians like Glenn Branca were getting noticed by combining the formal strategies and expressive solos of 'serious' music with punk primitivism. The naturally aggressive Chance fell right into that scene. He took on his stage name, started wearing loud suits that recalled acid visions of early James Brown, and formed The Contortions, a five-piece that, abetted by **Adele Bertei**'s shrieking organ runs and **Pat Place**'s wobbly slide guitar work, pushed standard funk grooves to the edge of chaos.

Contortions gigs became semi-legendary, and not only for the music: when not blowing frenzied skronk sax or wailing ultra-negative lyrics ('Soon I'll feel nothing somehow') like a banshee, Chance would often wade into audiences and pick fights with spectators. Some audiences dealt with him playfully, in which case Chance's aggression became a kind of balletic contact-improvisation performance, but often Chance would piss off the wrong person and wind up bleeding all over his baroque hipster threads. Chance relished his belligerent role. When a reporter asked him if there was anything about the 60s he admired, he replied, 'I liked when they had riots'.

Chance was consistent in his self-destructiveness. When **Brian Eno** recorded The Contortions for his NO NEW YORK sampler of No Wave bands on Antilles, Chance refused to let the famous producer mike the amps. Presumably concerned with keeping control of the sound of the band, Chance only allowed room mikes to be used and the band did no overdubs. The sound was miserably bad, but you did get a sense of their electrifying 'live' sound. BUY THE CONTORTIONS, brought out on Ze in 1979, had better sound and some of the same energy.

No Wave was too abrasive to go anywhere, and as that scene dissipated Chance made another identity switch. He rechristened himself James White and formed **James White And The Blacks**, a sort of fractured funk group that leaned heavily on a pseudo-lounge-lizard repertoire, most amusingly in a version of Cole Porter's "Heat Wave". Albums of frayed-edge jazz, OFF-WHITE and SAX MANIAC, followed, but the manic energy of The Contortions days was largely gone and Chance/White soon faded from view.

Ageing NY hipsters recently got a pleasant shock, though, when the name 'James Chance And The Contortions' started turning up on club bills. The new Contortions featured Chance and fellow altoist **Luther Thomas**, backed by a bass/guitar/drums configuration. The new band continues to gig sporadically, touring in support of old records – Henry Rollins' Infinite Zero reissued BUY THE CONTORTIONS and brought out SAX MANIAC in 1996. Chance still skronks with the best of them, but he hasn't beaten anybody up yet.

⊙ **Buy The Contortions** (1979; Ze; reissued 1996; Infinite Zero).
The band is tight, though relatively subdued, and Chance gives a clear reading of his sex- and self-loathing in tunes like "Design To Kill" and "Contort Yourself". But you might have to have fond memories of being strung out on coffee and malt liquor at 5am in a East Village slum to get a lot out of this.

Roy Edroso

TRACY CHAPMAN

Born Cleveland, Ohio, 1964.

"I call myself a hopeful cynic."

Try to conjure up a sure-fire formula for rock stardom in 80s America. Chances are that a dreadlocked, jeans-clad black folk singer from Boston wouldn't be high on the list. Nonetheless, against all the odds, **Tracy Chapman** became an overnight international celebrity in the summer of 1988.

In her formative years, Chapman tried various instruments before settling on the acoustic guitar; her college yearbook joked that she was the student 'most likely to marry her guitar'. After several years playing clubs on the quiet folk scene of the mid-80s, she finally secured a major-label deal in the wake of Suzanne Vega's surprise platinum success in 1987.

TRACY CHAPMAN was issued by Elektra in early 1988 and quickly became a landmark record of the period. Producer **David Kershenbaum** constructed moody settings for Chapman's incisive and occasionally menacing social commentaries, setting the perfect tone for the starkly melodic material. Addressing subjects such as poverty ("Fast Car") and domestic violence ("Behind The Wall"), the album's ultimately positive message struck deep with a growing army of listeners, and Chapman's career began to take off.

Already pencilled in for the *Amnesty International Tour*, Chapman was invited to perform at the globally broadcast Nelson Mandela Seventieth Birthday Show in June 1988. Chapman's direct freshness was a revelation, and she was repeatedly called back to the stage. Almost overnight, her album soared to the top of the UK and US charts, while the single "Fast Car" pushed into the Top 10 on both sides of the Atlantic. It was a rare thing: a genuinely moving smash hit single.

Her second album, CROSSROADS, appeared in 1989, was written and recorded in a fraction of the time she had given to her debut, and followed the pattern of that first album a little too faithfully. But even though the songs were not as memorable, the momentum of her sudden, massive success carried CROSSROADS to #1 in the UK and #2 in the US.

Chapman was still seen as a real contender, but she took three years to prepare her next album, during which time her profile had dropped significantly. MATTERS OF THE HEART, released in 1992, was a merely adequate folk-rock record and it missed the US Top 50. A second long sabbatical eventually ended with the release of NEW BEGINNINGS (1995), but critics and public remained unconvinced. TELLING STORIES (2000) followed the same pattern, while TV ads for her 'best of' COLLECTION (2001) inevitably concentrated on the content of her 13-year old debut album. 2002's LET IT RAIN, however, was a slightly different kettle of fish. Having hooked up with producer **John Parish**, Chapman managed to produce a set that was restrained, compositionally innovative and, most significantly, forward-looking.

Perhaps Chapman will yet escape the albatross of her initial fame.

⊙ **Tracy Chapman** (1988; Elektra).
From "Fast Car" to "For My Lover" and "Across The Lines" – a flawless piece of songwriting and recording.

Neil Blackmore

THE CHARLATANS

Formed Wolverhampton, England, 1989.

"Being in the Charlatans is a long weekend, you know. And we're up to about Saturday morning at the moment." Martin Blunt

The **Charlatans**, despite having played under that name for a while, really came into being when their original singer left, and **Martin Blunt** (bass), **Jon Brookes** (drums), **Rob Collins** (keyboards) and **Jon Baker** (guitars) first rehearsed with **Tim Burgess** (vocals). After a failed attempt to get a record deal they set up their own label, Dead Dead Good, and released the single "Indian Rope" in January 1990. Its Hammond-organ pop-buzz sold out in a week and took them straight to the top of the indie charts.

Things moved fast as The Charlatans were co-opted with The Stone Roses, Happy Mondays and Inspiral Carpets into the 'Madchester' scene, when any band with loose clothes and a floppy haircut was snapped up by a public gone baggy-crazy. However, they were to far outlast lesser bands, thanks to their catchy melodies and the Jaggeresque looks of Tim Burgess, an achingly cool frontman.

Signing to Beggars Banquet in the spring of 1990, they released "The Only One I Know". It strutted its funky bass line and wah-wah guitar straight into the UK Top 10 and was soon followed by the equally baggy but moodier "Then". This singles' success was in turn eclipsed by the tune-filled debut album, SOME FRIENDLY (1990), which immediately topped the album charts, and went gold in its first week of release.

It was then that the bad luck that was to follow them reared its head. On their first American tour, they were forced to revise their name to The Charlatans UK, as an existing US band already owned the original name. In 1991, after the release of a third Top 20 hit, "Over Rising", the band's long-term future was in doubt as Blunt was suffering from severe depression, while guitarist Baker announced his departure the day after playing at London's Royal Albert Hall.

However, with replacement guitarist **Mark Collins**, they resumed touring and began work on a second album. By the time BETWEEN 10TH AND 11TH emerged, in the spring of 1992, the heady days of 'Madchester' had long gone, and the album was largely ignored by press and public. It was darker and less immediate than its predecessor, but it spawned a couple of great singles – the spooky "Weirdo" and the dancey "Tremelo Song".

After touring Japan in late 1992, disaster struck again, as keyboardist Rob Collins went out for a drink with an old friend and somehow got mixed up in an armed robbery. Eight months' imprisonment ensued. A week after his release in January 1994, he was back with the band and on a *Top Of The Pops* TV appearance performing the hit single "Can't Get Out Of Bed" – Collins had recorded his keyboard part while awaiting trial. It was a gloriously catchy track, Tim's lazy vocal perfectly summing up its title.

Despite the problems of Rob's incarceration, UP TO OUR HIPS (1994) was a seamless return to the soulful slouch of old, and included two more fine singles: the extravagantly titled "I Never Want An Easy Life If Me And He Were Ever To Get There" and "Jesus Hairdo".

Although Tim had also featured on tracks by **Saint Etienne** and **The Chemical Brothers**, by 1995 The Charlatans were still very much together, and working on a fourth album. The first products of these sessions were "Crashin' In" and "Just Lookin'"; the singles coincided with their biggest UK tour for three years, and the summer found them back in the charts with a Stonesy new single, "Just When You're Thinkin' Things Over", complete with a video casting the band as 60s-style gangsters.

It was followed by THE CHARLATANS (1995), which found them harking back to 60s pop; a surprise #1 in Britain, it was hailed as their best work to date. As always, the recording was not without its difficulties, mainly a few injuries for band members, then shortly afterwards, Rob's earlier brush with the law got them into more trouble with the sponsors of their planned American tour.

Rob Collins' tragic death in a car accident during the recording of 1997's TELLIN' STORIES (Beggars Banquet) obviously cast a pall, but, like the bad guy in a horror film, the rest of the band staggered once more to its feet and, against all the odds, produced an excellent, studied album. **Martin Duffy** was roped in from Primal Scream to complete the album and took The Charlatans' trademark Hammond-organ sound to a new level.

A new record deal with Universal and the band kept soldiering on, unswerving in their path to show that not only is it possible to stay the course but also

to remain convincing. But the group continued to be dogged by bad luck: this time their accountant was found to have defrauded them.

US AND US ONLY (1999) found echoes of Dylan and the Stones never far away, while lessons in the groove had clearly been learned from Burgess's work with The Chemical Brothers. The band's blend of dance and rock remained seamless, and totally authentic – from the dirty funk of "My Beautiful Friend" to the snarling "Forever". 2001's WONDERLAND edged marginally closer to the dance floor; it was a solid addition to their catalogue, although it lacked the character of some of their previous releases. Nevertheless, seven albums and a stream of great singles (and B-sides, collected on SONGS FROM THE OTHER SIDE) isn't bad for a band with a curse.

⦿ **Up To Our Hips** (1994; Situation Two/Beggars Banquet).
Here The Charlatans really come of age with a brace of hip-shaking, riff-heavy and effortlessly cool tunes.

⦿ **The Charlatans** (1995; Beggars Banquet).
The title smacks of self-belief, as well it might: the tracks contrast three-minute pop songs with extended jams, taking in snatches of disco, modish anthems, dirty riffs and stoned grooves along the way.

⦿ **Melting Pot** (1998; Beggars Banquet).
More than a simple 'greatest hits', this is best described as a 'story so far' album for those who might have missed the beginning. Rarities, favourites, a few odd remixes from the bug-eyed baggy days through to the nightmares of 1997.

⦿ **Wonderland** (2001; Universal).
This time around The Charlatans drew their inspiration from the canon of Sly Stone, with the beats sounding surprisingly funky.

⦿ **Songs From The Other Side** (2002; Beggars Banquet).
This B-side collection opens with the organ-fuelled instrumental "Imperial 109" (originally found on the flip of "The Only One I Know") before plummeting into "Everything Changed" and "Happen To Die", two of the band's strongest numbers and this collection's highpoints.

James Sutherland

CHEAP TRICK

Formed Rockford, Illinois, 1972.

Cheap Trick's spectacularly creative first blast earned comparisons with The Beatles – not all of them favourable, though at first they kept pace brilliantly, releasing five great albums. By the sixth, however, ALL SHOOK UP (1980), they were wilting badly, George Martin's production had sold the band short, and all this coincided with the loss of main writer **Rick Nielsen**'s magic touch. It was the beginning of a gentle downward-slide that ended in songs for the *Top Gun* soundtrack and stadium tours as second fiddle to Heart. Cheap Trick deserved better.

The association of guitarist Nielsen and bassist **Tom Petersson** dates back to a group called **Fuse**. FUSE was their only album, a slick, earnest, over-played hard-rock record. When the group broke up in 1969, anglophiles Nielsen and Petersson made a pilgrimage to England, and ran into **Todd Rundgren**, at London's Marquee Club. On their return to the US, the duo tracked down Todd's ex-bandmates, **Thom Mooney** (drums) and **Stewkey** (keyboards/vocals), and played for a few months under old names Fuse or **Nazz**, or as **Honey Boy Williamson and The Manchurian Blues Band**. By 1970, guitarist and bassist were on the move again, performing around Europe in a band called **Sick Man Of Europe** before a call from Stewkey brought them back to the States. Once demos had been recorded, travelling resumed, this time to Germany where contact was made with American drummer **Bun E. Carlos**. He became a founder member of Cheap Trick, along with Nielsen, in the summer of 1972. Petersson, still in Europe, was lured home by Neilson to play bass and Cheap Trick spent two years working the American Midwest.

Steady progress was consolidated by the arrival of **Robin Zander** (vocals/guitar) in 1974, and in 1976 the enthusiastic support of Aerosmith producer **Jack Douglas** helped clinch a deal with Epic. Douglas produced CHEAP TRICK (1977), the first album, but its brilliant melodies were submerged by a claustrophobic metal-fixated mix.

In May the band began work on a follow-up with Ted Nugent's producer **Tom Werman**. Werman applied an updated early-Beatles production approach to IN COLOR (1977), contributing a clean, punchy and well-ordered sound to the band's first, and greatest, pop masterpiece. The release of HEAVEN TONIGHT (1978) was brought forward for Japan, where the band were hugely popular, to tie in with an April tour. Unfamiliar tunes such as cryptic lead-off classic "Surrender" and a fantastic, over-the-top version of Fats Domino's "Ain't That A Shame" received a hysterical reception, recorded for posterity on AT BUDOKAN (1978).

With DREAM POLICE (1979), the international breakthrough was complete. It featured bigger production and "Voices", Nielsen's best ever ballad. However, seemingly poised for massive, long-term success, Cheap Trick stumbled. The two 1976/77 studio outtakes on 1980's odds'n'ends roundup, FOUND ALL THE PARTS, sounded far fresher than anything on ALL SHOOK DOWN, that year's new album.

Since 1980, Cheap Trick's fortunes have been varied. Tom Petersson left in 1981 and only flashes of brilliance illuminated ONE ON ONE (1982) and NEXT POSITION PLEASE (1983). STANDING ON THE EDGE (1985) was overproduced; technology-album THE DOCTOR (1986) was a disaster. Petersson returned for LAP OF LUXURY (1988), by which time professional hit-writers had been foisted on the group. They provided a US #1 power-ballad hit, "The Flame", but overall it was a distressingly bland affair. BUSTED (1990), slightly better, was also a big hit; WOKE UP WITH A MONSTER (1993), slightly better again, with a title song reaching for the spirit of the old uncorrupted Cheap Trick, was not.

Since 1993 though, there's been a reappraisal of the band by public and press. Their 1997 release for Red Ant records, CHEAP TRICK, captured much of the energy and excitement they put into the first CHEAP TRICK album, twenty years previously. In 2002 the band found redemption and reappraisal from an unexpected source as **Steve Albini** of Big Black and Shellac fame invited them to perform at the British rock festival All Tomorrow's Parties. Playing in front of a young and underground crowd, they were received with massive enthusiasm. A masterful comeback.

⊙ **Cheap Trick** (1977; Epic).
An intense, vicious record, quite unlike anything else the band ever recorded. Nielsen's wild guitar playing is amazing.

⊙ **In Color** (1977; Epic).
Cheap Trick's masterwork, running over with classic songs: "Come On, Come On", "Southern Girls", "Downed", "I Want You To Want Me". A perfect high-energy pop production.

Robert Coyne

THE CHEMICAL BROTHERS

Formed Manchester, England, 1989.

A similar taste in music led Manchester University history students **Tom Rowlands** and **Ed Simons** to form a DJing outfit called **The Dust Brothers**, a name chosen as a mark of respect to the American hip-hop production team of the same name. Six years on, though, Rowlands and Simons changed their name to **The Chemical Brothers** after legal action was threatened by their American counterparts.

In 1989 the duo had little intention of becoming recording artists: they were content to find and spin the loudest possible records, many of which featured big breakbeats and sirens, traits which would later surface on their own releases. Taking their inspiration from Justin Robertson, whose club they frequented, The Brothers started up their own night, Naked Under Leather, and then, in 1992, hit on the idea of recording a track they could play whilst DJing. Borrowing £300 from a friend, they recorded the aptly titled "Song To The Siren", a mesmerizing sound-clash of house and hip-hop. The record was soon snapped up by the Junior Boys Own label and given a wider release in February 1993, with a pair of remixes from one of the track's biggest fans, **Andy Weatherall**.

Up to this point Tom had been dividing his time between The Dust Brothers and post-baggy dance band **Ariel**, who had a minor hit with "Let It Slide" (1993). The success of "Song To The Siren", however, persuaded him to dedicate himself full time to The Brothers' commitments. During much of 1993 the duo kept busy with remix assignments for, amongst others, Justin Robertson's band Lionrock, Leftfield and The Sandals, and then in early 1994 THE 14TH CENTURY SKY EP arrived to an initially lukewarm reception from many DJs, who were unsure how audiences would react to the record's eclecticism. Despite this initial setback, the EP became a cult hit, especially the pulsating dance-floor favourite, "Chemical Beats", and further acclaim came a few months later with the instantly recognizable MY MERCURY MOUTH EP, as well as remix work for Primal Scream, The Prodigy and Saint Etienne.

Rowlands and Simons also started playing a few one-off live shows with the duo slouched over two samplers. Visually it did not add up to much, but the seamless live beats and noises made their gigs as impressive as many conventional rock concerts, and by the end of 1994 they were chosen as the DJs to warm up for Primal Scream on a British tour. They also began a regular DJ residency at the now-legendary Heavenly Sunday Social club night.

In 1995 The Dust Brothers became The Chemical Brothers, and after inking a deal with Virgin they released "Leave Home", closely followed by their debut album, EXIT PLANET DUST (1995), which gave ammunition to the sceptics, who had begun to question their limited recording formulas. Certainly much of EXIT PLANET DUST was dominated by the duo's trademark breaks and beats, but the slow, sweeping "Alive: Alone", featuring **Beth Orton** on vocals, and a cameo from The Charlatans' **Tim Burgess** on the hit single "Life Is Sweet", indicated new directions. A limited-edition EP, LOOPS OF FURY, sold out almost immediately in early 1996, while the rush-released LIVE AT THE HEAVENLY SOCIAL marched out of the record stores just as quickly.

Their second album proper, the epic DIG YOUR OWN HOLE (1997), confirmed their place at the top of the 'electronica' table. From its head-pounding opening "Block Rockin' Beats" through the clubland rebellion of "Setting Sun" (featuring **Noel Gallagher** of Oasis on groaning vocals) to the closing finale "Private Psychedelic Reel", this was one of the finest albums of 1997.

The duo reached their apotheosis with 1999's SURRENDER; it seemed like the full realization of everything their music was about – massive beats, psychedelia and songs that you could listen to as well as groove to. A rash of celebrity guests enhanced the sense that this was a genuine fusion of dance and rock – among them Noel Gallagher (again), **Bernard Sumner** and **Bobby Gillespie** (who collide in the delirious "Out Of Control"), Mercury Rev's **Jonathon Donahue** and **Hope Sandoval**, whose hauntingly erotic vocals provide one of the standout moments in "Asleep From The Day".

Three years later COME WITH US found the Rowlands and Simons axis treading water slightly – great tunes admittedly but it basically covered the same old ground. While the energizing, transcendent funk of "It Began In Afrika" and the cinematic caper "My Elastic Eye" were as good as anything they've done before, it was an all too familiar journey. Let down most significantly by "The Test" – a pale imitation of "Private Psychedelic Reel" featuring a

melody-free rant from **Richard Ashcroft** – there was a feeling that the album should have a been a real magical mystery tour. Instead everybody knew their destination from the outset.

⊙ **Exit Planet Dust** (1995; Junior Boys Own).
This impressive debut album picks up speed on its devastating quartet of "Song To The Siren", "Three Little Birdies...", "Fucked-Up Beats" and "Chemical Beats", a sequence designed to simulate their relentless live shows. Greater diversity can be found on the disturbingly effective pop song "Life Is Sweet", and "Playground For A Wedgeless Firm" would be perfect soundtrack fodder if anyone could make a movie scary enough to warrant its inclusion.

⊙ **Dig Your Own Hole** (1997; Junior Boys Own).
A more grown-up follow-up to EXIT PLANET DUST. From the barnstorming opening track through the introspective loops mid-album to the irresistible closing epic, this is a classy album from a pair of top-quality musicians.

⊙ **Surrender** (1999; Virgin).
Littered with guest stars, this collection seamlessly blends mashed-up beats, electro and – in "Hey Boy, Hey Girl" – one of the whackiest hip-hop/dance crossovers ever.

Jonathan Swift

NENEH CHERRY

Born Stockholm, Sweden, 1964.

The daughter of avant-garde jazzman Don Cherry, **Neneh Cherry** began her recording career in the early 80s with long-forgotten Bristol-based indie-funk experimentalists **RIP, RIG & PANIC**. It was to take the unlikely intervention of a group once described as 'the thinking woman's Wham!' to bring her to widespread public attention.

Morgan McVey were a mid-80s pop duo with backgrounds in fashion photography, video direction and modelling. **Jamie Morgan** had been highly influential as part of Buffalo, a styling team whose tough, streetwise look was all-pervasive in the British style mags of the time. His group's tribute to this look – "Buffalo Stance" – was a throwaway B-side in late 1985, but in 1988 Neneh Cherry rerecorded the song and watched it race to the Top 3 in the UK, before achieving Top 10 status in America and around the world in 1989. For the next year or so, Neneh Cherry seemed ubiquitous as her sassy outspokenness, exotic upbringing and sexy, hip-hop-flavoured funk endeared her to media and public alike.

More hits followed, beginning with "Manchild", in May 1989. This eerie ballad, featuring a full string section, was co-written by **Robert Delnaja** of Massive Attack and was a sonic precursor of the 90s Bristol scene. Startlingly dissimilar to "Buffalo Stance" in style and tone, "Manchild" was an indication that Neneh was prepared to take her music beyond the traditional concerns of the rapper or R&B artist. A proud mother, who provoked admiration and controversy by appearing on TV's *Top Of The Pops* in a tight Lycra outfit while obviously pregnant, she frequently addressed the topics of motherhood and childcare, particularly on tracks like

"Inner City Mama" and "The Next Generation".

Both songs were featured, along with her two Top 10 singles, on her debut album, RAW LIKE SUSHI (1989). Her future seemed assured. However, apart from a cover of "I've Got You Under My Skin" for the 1990 charity album RED HOT & BLUE, new material was not forthcoming. When she returned in 1992 with the lacklustre single, "Money Love", there was a distinct sense of anticlimax. It performed adequately enough in the charts, but hardly set the world alight. As such, it was a pretty good indicator of the forthcoming album.

While HOMEBREW (1992) was not bad by any means, it suffered in comparison to RAW LIKE SUSHI. Ranging from modish jazz (courtesy of rap outfit **Gang Starr**), to proto-trip-hop and featuring a vocal cameo from R.E.M.'s **Michael Stipe**, it seemed to lack the spark of its predecessor.

In the summer of 1994 she returned unexpectedly to the British Top 10 with "Seven Seconds", a multilingual duet alongside Senegalese artist **Youssou N'Dour**. Well received and universally successful (the song remained at the top of the French charts for seventeen weeks), "Seven Seconds" represented something of a turning point for Cherry, giving fresh momentum to her career and paving the way for MAN, released in September 1996.

A MORE diverse and spontaneous-sounding LP than its predecessors, MAN ranged in mood from the rocky, lascivious "Kootchie" to "Golden Ring", a traditional American Gypsy melody delivered as a flamenco-style ballad. Some tracks appeared a little half-baked, but there were enough high points to compensate, a prime example being "Woman", Neneh's wry take on James Brown's "This Is A Man's Man's World", which reached the Top 10 as a single in 1996.

Cherry kept a lower profile during the next few years, surfacing for the occasional concert (her appearance at Glastonbury in 1997 was particularly memorable) but steering clear of the recording studio to devote more time to her family.

⊙ **Raw Like Sushi** (1989; Circa).
Even having dated a little, this is still an irresistible burst of personality and cheekiness.

Robin Morley

VIC CHESNUTT

Born Georgia, 1965.

"Some day I'll be a paragon, like Louis Farrakhan"

A drunken teenage car smash left the offbeat singer-songwriter **Vic Chesnutt** confined to a wheelchair. He discovered he had not lost his instrumental abilities some months after the accident, when he was recovering from an acid binge, and soon afterwards moved from his parents' home in the backwoods of Georgia to the bright lights of nearby Athens, where he gained a residency at the 40 Watt Club. In October 1988, he was discovered by local hero **Michael Stipe**, who produced his first album, LITTLE, the following afternoon. Stripped-down in feel, it featured some gorgeous harmonica and arresting lyrical images on the opener, "Isadora Duncan".

The follow-up, WEST OF ROME (1991), again produced by Stipe, was darker and more focused. The songs were vivid snapshots: random messages written on gravestones and sidewalks, a friend's suicide in Florida ('there's no more perfect place to retire from life'), the first sight of a girlfriend naked. The instrumentation was still sparse, but drums, electric guitars, and haunting violin and cello added to the melancholy atmosphere.

The lyrics on the more electrified DRUNK (1994) hinted at a man's physical and psychological decline, scared of what he might do if he stuck around. Songs explored failed relationships, missed therapy appointments, out-of-body drug experiences and, of course, alcohol. Some respite came from the ruefully humorous delivery.

His finest set to date, IS THE ACTOR HAPPY? (1995), was a concept album loosely based around the idea of playing live, which allowed him to hit new levels of obscurity and quirkiness. The album's battle between the forlorn and the near-perky was encapsulated by "Gravity Of The Situation", a song inspired by an attack of stage fright prior to performing with legendary songwriters **Dan Penn**, **Allen Toussaint**, **Guy Clark** and **Joe South**. The Scared Skiffle Group, who backed him on this outing, brought a welcome tonal variation to complement Chesnutt's new-found way with a tune.

Chesnutt teamed up with Athens band **Widespread Panic** for NINE HIGH A PALLET (1996), which was released under the name **Brute**. Meantime, he announced an intention to work with Van Dyke Parks, and accepted a film role playing Dwight Yoakam's sidekick and kept himself busy by recording and releasing ABOUT TO CHOKE, his fifth album – as always, packed with the bitter ironies of life seen through folk-tinged spectacles.

Chesnutt was then to be spotted in a biographical documentary film called *Speed Racer* before releasing the much more soulful album SALESMAN AND BERNADETTE (1998), in collaboration with **Lambchop**.

After his time with Lambchop, Chesnutt resurfaced in yet another collaboration, this time with **Kelly** and **Nikki Keneipp**, a married couple with ties to Chesnutt compatriot Jack Logan. Released on the Keneipp's own Backburner Records, MERRIMENT (2000) showed Chesnutt in a typically pensive mood, wrapping his surrealist lines across the couple's steady – and heavy – backdrop. Chesnutt's next collaboration was a series of gigs with long-time friend **Kristin Hersh**, while there are rumours of a writing partnership with **Neutral Milk Hotel**, which has yet to come to fruition.

Vic Chesnutt

2001's Left To His Own Devices provided the requisite demos and outtakes collection in the Vic Chesnutt section of the record shop, featuring Chesnutt with just simple guitar accompaniment. Laid-back of delivery and idiosyncratic of lyric, this was head and shoulders above what, for most artists, would be just a release schedule filler.

Vic Chesnutt

⊙ **Is The Actor Happy?** (1995; Texas Hotel).
Beginners start here, although the earlier albums are worth checking out later. Stipe completists should check out the backing vocals on "Guilty By Association".

⊙ **Merriment** (2000; Backburner).
On this set Chesnutt moans over the languorous pianos, woodwinds and percussion of Mr and Mrs Keneipp. Like all the best support acts, the Keneipps know when to add frills and when to hold back, which is no bad thing, as Chesnutt's nostalgic muse needs all the space it can get.

Brute

⊙ **Nine High A Pallet** (1996; Capricorn).
Although officially a collaborative effort, this sounds like a regular Chesnutt album, only 'plugged'. The songwriting is as fine as ever, and there is also a cover of Hoyt Axton's "Snowblind Friend".

Andy Smith

BILLY CHILDISH

Born Chatham, England, 1958.

Earl of the Medway lo-fi punk rock scene since 1977, **Billy Childish** has been one of the most prolific recording artists ever, boasting over a hundred records, latterly on his own label, Hangman,

which has also published several volumes of his poetry. Too much perhaps, for a single idea, since all of Childish's bands have played the same style of self-consciously basic, blues-derived songs – witty, soulful and coarse paeans to lowlife subjects, performed with punk gusto. But what the hell, this is DIY rock. When the records weren't live they seem to have been recorded in some shed of a studio. And live, they eschew modern amplification in favour of trusty Vox amps and a weathered vocal PA.

Billy began his career as lead singer with punk rock upstarts **The Pop Rivets** from 1977 to 1979, and by 1980 he had taken up the guitar and formed the more accomplished **Thee Milkshakes** with **Mick Hampshire** (guitar/vocals), **Bruce Brand** (drums) and **John Agnew** (bass). These associates reappeared as members of **Thee Headcoats** – along with a cast of dozens – before the bands themselves mutated through incarnations such as **Thee Mighty Caesars** with Childish the only constant, on guitar and vocals. In 1995 he announced his retirement from the music business to concentrate on painting. He commemorated this event with a series of farewell gigs at the Wild West Rooms in London featuring all of his former bands and collaborators.

He dusted off the microphone for a day in 1998, though, when he reassembled Thee Headcoats for The Messerschmitt Pilot's Severed Head (1998), a splintered masterpiece of garage punk. However, 2001 saw the beginning of a major upsurge of interest in all things Childish. First, there was a widely publicized feud with artist and former lover Tracy Emin. Then, the bizarre possibility emerged that Childish was about to become fashionable, when **Jack White**,

singer of Detroit upstarts The White Stripes, appeared on *Top Of The Pops* with "Billy Childish" magic-markered on his arm. A new **Buff Medways** album was released in 2002 and became his most commercially successful work to date. Apparently the Earl of Medway has not yet been deposed.

Thee Milkshakes

⊙ **Thee Knights Of Trashe** (1984; Hangmans Daughter).
Valiant in their quest to bring you the true spirit of rock'n'roll.

Thee Headcoats

⊙ **Beach Bums Must Die** (1990; Crypt).
Quite simply – rockin'.

Ross Holloway

CHILLI WILLI AND THE RED HOT PEPPERS

Formed London, 1971; disbanded 1975.

Having first played together in Junior's Blues Band in the early 60s, **Phil Lithman** (guitar/piano/fiddle/vocals) and **Martin Stone** (guitar/mandolin/vocals) reunited a decade later to play simple, downhome music, combining blues, country and jazz in a seamless unity. The two had never lost touch, and Stone called Lithman over from San Francisco to join him at the Sufi commune where he was then living. In the intervening years, Stone had worked as a session guitarist for blues acts like **Savoy Brown**, before playing with the eclectic **Mighty Baby**. Stone's masterful guitar work for the latter's live take on John Coltrane's "India" can be found on the GLASTONBURY FAYRE triple LP, and the same small record label, Revelation, released the first album from **Chilli Willi And The Red Hot Peppers**, KINGS OF THE ROBOT RHYTHM (1972).

The first track announced 'we don't have no psychedelic show', and the album was a collection of largely acoustic, rough-and-ready country-picking. This genuinely harmonious music was enhanced by a backing group who comprised members of **Brinsley Schwarz**, and blues singer **Jo Ann Kelly**, as well as White Noise synthesizer player **Dave Vorhaus**, a more surprising choice. The album's packaging by Barney Bubbles was characteristically friendly and nostalgic, using early Hollywood cartoons and a cut-out C&W bow tie.

In late 1972, Chilli Willi became a touring band, with **Paul Riley** (bass) and **Pete Thomas** (drums), who in company with Stone had worked with Robin Scott, later to find fame as M and the hit single "Pop Muzik" in 1979. **Paul 'Dice Man' Bailey** (banjo/guitar/saxophone) joined from a bluegrass background, and **Will Stallibrass** (harmonica) became a part-time member.

The band's live reputation had improved still further by the release of their second LP, BONGOS OVER BALHAM (1974). With another post-hippie sleeve design, and the addition of backing vocalist **Carol Grimes**, the music was tighter than on the previous album, similar to the output of American bands like the Flying Burrito Brothers and Commander Cody.

Chilli Willi's tongue-in-cheek approach never managed to extend its fan base beyond ex-hippies, who were becoming increasingly discontented at their musical direction. Members of the entourage defected to become torchbearers for the New Wave: manager Andrew Jackman changed his name to Jake Riviera, and managed Elvis Costello, while Pete Thomas became a member of Costello's Attractions. Riviera also founded Stiff Records, for whom Barney Bubbles became a sleeve artist, while Riley became an engineer at Nick Lowe's studios.

After a one-off reunion concert in London in the early 80s, Chilli Willi's two founder members finally went their separate ways. Phil Lithman returned to California to work with cult band **THE RESIDENTS**, who christened him **Snakefinger** after his weird, upside-down and back-to-front style of guitar playing, and recorded five albums for the band's Ralph label. He died in 1987 of heart problems. Martin Stone had a brief stint with **The Pink Fairies**, left the music business altogether for a time, then made a comeback as **Les Homewreckers**, recapturing some of his old band's charm and spice.

1997's I'LL BE HOME (Proper Records) was a posthumous collection of nineteen previously unreleased tracks and a fine epitaph.

⊙ **Bongos Over Balham** (1974; Mooncrest).
Their most professional and exacting work. Songs like "Midnight Bus" and "We Get Along" still zing with happiness, and "All In A Dream" adds pathos and mystery to the mix.

Brian Hinton

THE CHILLS

Formed Dunedin, New Zealand, 1980.

Of all the indie bands that emerged from New Zealand's fertile post-punk scene in the 1980s,

The Chills were probably the most significant, and certainly the most well known on an international level. Just as influenced by 60s psychedelia, The Byrds and The Velvet Underground as by punk and New Wave, at their best they crafted an otherworldly mist of jangly guitars, floating organ, droning bass and evocative lyrics. Their preoccupation with mood over content, however, spelled trouble when it came to creating album-length statements, as their gooey soundscapes could became wearisome over the course of an entire disc.

The Chills were pretty much the project of singer-songwriter **Martin Phillipps**, the only constant member of their dozen or so line-ups, and the author of almost all of their material. The band grew out of a Dunedin outfit called **The Same**, which Phillipps helped form as a teenager. Renamed The Chills in 1980, they made their recording debut for New Zealand's most prominent indie rock label, Flying Nun, in 1982. (Phillipps had played keyboards on the very first Flying Nun single, The Clean's "Tally Ho", in 1981.) Since then, members of other Flying Nun outfits – such as **The Verlaines**, **The Clean**, **The Great Unwashed** and **Snapper** – have drifted in and out of the band: if you tried to draw a Chills family tree, you'd need a blackboard the size of a storefront.

Over the next few years The Chills released several Flying Nun EPs and singles of low-key, often charming and sometimes pedestrian modern psychedelia. The ghost of Syd Barrett/early Pink Floyd hovered particularly close to these early cuts, with their folky sing-alongs ("Satin Doll"), celestial organs and swooping guitar slides. Several of these early recordings were hits in the Kiwi charts, including "Rolling Moon", "Doledrums" and the goofy "I Love My Leather Jacket", but the best of the lot was "Pink Frost", a spooky lament penned for Phillipps's late friend **Martyn Bull**, who had drummed with the band for a while. The sparkling interplay between the incandescent guitars, cavernous bass rolls and Phillipps's whispery vocals remains the best realization of their ambitions to create a truly contemporary equivalent to psychedelia.

The Chills began to attract overseas attention in the mid-80s, landing a UK distribution deal with Creation, recording a John Peel session for the BBC in 1985, and making their first appearances in the US in 1987. But their first proper album, BRAVE WORDS, was a disappointment to both the band and their fans. The group felt that the record suffered from the hasty execution of the all-night sessions, but the harder reality was that Phillipps's songs weren't diverse enough to sustain interest and that his lyrical vagueness couldn't compensate for the sonic tapestries.

SUBMARINE BELLS, released three years later, saw the band coming to grips with high-quality production values more effectively. It was also their first effort for a major label (Slash/Warners), and some fans who'd been with them from the beginning bewailed their increasing sophistication. From most perspectives, however, it was a clear improvement over BRAVE WORDS, with less stress on the drone and more on Phillipps's lighter melodic qualities. The spacious arrangements brought out the pungency of their trademark glowing organ riffs, complementing them with instrumental and vocal harmonics in the spirit of Brian Wilson.

Phillipps and The Chills didn't exactly pump out product with the regularity of Elvis Costello, and SOFT BOMB was released in 1992. The band aimed for a more radio-friendly, modern-rock-conscious sound on this outing, with generally slight results, although Phillipps's ambitions remained high.

The Chills briefly got together again in 1996 to record SUNBURNT, released on Flying Nun. Since then only a collection of demo 'song-seeds', SKETCH BOOK: VOLUME ONE (1999), and a 3-CD rarities compendium, SECRET BOX (2001), have emerged.

⦿ **Kaleidoscope World** (1989; Homestead).
Nineteen tracks from early and mid-80s singles, EPs and compilations, showcasing the band at their most psychedelic and likeable. "Pink Frost" is the obvious highlight, but "I Love My Leather Jacket" and "The Great Escape" were also big favourites with the indie crowd.

⦿ **Submarine Bells** (1990; Slash).
The best of their three bona fide albums, achieving the most accomplished balance between polished production/arrangements and Phillipps' quirky melodicism.

Richie Unterberger

ALEX CHILTON

Born Memphis, Tennessee, 1950.

While still at school **Alex Chilton** began singing in bands with classmate **Chris Bell**. His breakthrough came in 1966 with Memphis soul outfit **Ronnie & The Devilles**. The following year, his new band were offered a song and a recording session with producer Chips Moman (though in the event Dan Penn showed up and did the magic instead), but were encouraged to change their name to **The Box Tops**.

The pop gem born of this session, "The Letter" hit #1 in America and the British Top 10 in late 1967. Founder members **Danny Smythe** and **John Evans** quit the group to return to full-time education, (being replaced by **Tom Boggs** and **Rick Allen**), leaving **Gary Talley**, **Bill Cunningham** and Alex as the founders and torch-carriers. They landed a series of engagements opening for The Beach Boys on their Canadian tours and for a few dates in the USA, while American hits continued for two years, most notably "Cry Like A Baby" and "Soul Deep".

After Cunningham's departure in September 1969, Chilton and Talley ploughed on with increasingly rapid line-up changes but it was only a matter of time before The Box Tops finally folded in 1970. Chilton made his way, via New York, to Memphis, where he was reunited with Chris Bell, joining his power trio, **Ice Water**. Changing their name to **BIG STAR**, they recorded two albums which, while unsuccessful at the time, have since had a huge influence.

After Bell's departure in 1974 – Alex was calling too many shots – Chilton pieced together the unfinished second Big Star LP, RADIO CITY, himself, while BIG STAR'S 3RD ALBUM (aka SISTER LOVERS) essentially marked the beginning of his solo career. It was a much more cerebral LP. "Holocaust" was all about pre-suicidal numbness, while the feedback of "Kangaroo" represented the nervous electricity of the first touch of a new love. Big Star's label, Ardent, was dumbfounded and the set wouldn't see release until 1978.

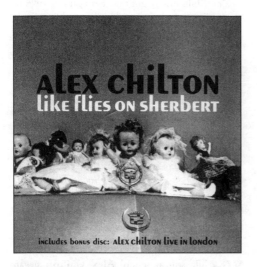

Meantime, Chilton recorded several tracks with **Jon Tiven** in Memphis, which emerged in various guises (notably the 1980 album BACH'S BOTTOM, featuring a fine take of The Beatles' "I'm So Tired" and a reworking of Big Star's "Jesus Christ"). In 1979, Chilton, **Chris Stamey** and **Richard Lloyd** briefly formed **Alex Chilton & The Cossacks** and relocated to New York, where they played the rounds with the Ramones, Television and The Cramps. Their (part live) ONE DAY IN NEW YORK CITY was released in 1979.

That same year saw Chilton's finest three minutes – "Bangkok" – recorded solo in London. Everything was drenched in slap echo, with guitars, machine guns and madcap laughs jutting in at Batman angles as Chilton sang of 'living on Chinese rocks'. It was a pre-emptive distillation of what was to come on his masterpiece, LIKE FLIES ON SHERBET (1979), featuring four original songs and some chaotically creative covers. Never has a record sounded so electric, with even the piano sounding as if powered by fusing neon, and rarely has so much human soul come over, warts, fluffed entrances and all. His UK label, Aura, shipped him over to London to promote it, playing to an awed audience at Dingwalls, backed by two **Soft Boys** and a **Vibrator**.

Chilton was having a frantic burst of creative energy around this point, producing the first **Cramps** records (after they stole a car and drove south to Memphis to find him), and teaming up with rock-'n'roll showman **Gustav Falco**, under the name **Panther Burns**. With his razor-creased pants, Little Richard pompadour and 'showbiz Hitler' moustache, Falco was an inspired striking partner for Chilton, and their collaboration gleefully transformed tracks like "Bourgeois Blues", "Brazil" and "Goldfinger" into gorgeous slabs of warped, ardent cabaret. An EP, TAV FALCO & THE PANTHER BURNS (1980), was followed up by the album BEHIND THE MAGNOLIA CURTAIN (1981), on which Chilton also played drums.

Despite sporadic touring in the early 80s, Chilton all but vanished until the release of Panther Burns' SUGAR DITCH REVISITED (1985). His solo rehabilitation began in earnest when he climbed on stage with **The Replacements** in 1986 (the band had released a single, "Alex Chilton", in his honour), following up with the solo album HIGH PRIEST in 1987, and some stunning work on another Panther Burns outing the following year, THE WORLD WE KNEW.

Since then Chilton has gigged and recorded on a pretty regular basis, reverting to his 'roots' in (fairly restrained) classy soul on record, while emitting flashes of his uncontrollable anarchic spark on stage. In 1993 he re-formed Big Star, whose influence on young bands on both sides of the Atlantic (notably **Teenage Fanclub**) was by now explicit, while 1995 saw the release of an unspectacular but consistent solo album, A MAN CALLED DESTRUCTION. Like much of his more recent output, its collection of R&B covers and quasi-rock'n'roll was enjoyable, if not quite so essential as before.

1998 got off to a great start, with Alex getting together with a re-formed original line-up The Box Tops, and calling in the **Memphis Horns** to record TEAR OFF! (1998), a marvellous album. Great production and a cheery, almost party atmosphere blend to make this a great 'good times' recording. SOUL DEEP: THE BEST OF (1998; Arista), pushed the year along nicely by pulling together eighteen of the best from The Box Tops' four studio albums. Only four Chilton compositions, but tremendous torch singing from the blue-eyed soul king. The re-formed group went on to tour the record extensively.

Alex Chilton

19 Years: A Collection Of Alex Chilton (1991; Rhino).
This has the best of BIG STAR'S 3RD ALBUM, LIKE FLIES ON SHERBET, HIGH PRIEST, and the cream of his EPs and singles (including the wonderful "Bangkok").

Like Flies On Sherbet/Live In London (1998; See For Miles).
The splendid SFM label does it again with this masterful reissue of his menacing studio album bundled with a troubled live set from the same period.

The Box Tops

Tear Off! (1998; Last Call).
The triumphant return both to form and to the studio that fans of Alex and The Box Tops had been waiting for.

Stand-out tracks include the 1998 cut of "The Letter", made all the more poignant by Alex's more mature vocals, standards such as "Flying Saucer Rock'N'Roll" and "Wang Dang Doodle" given that Memphis Soul Treatment, and the awesome closing track, "Big Bird" – for which the entire band pull out all the stops.

Tony Thewlis

THE CHOCOLATE WATCH BAND

Formed San Jose, California, 1964; disbanded 1970.

The appeal of the mid-60s 'garage rock' genre has survived all these years thanks to a resolute lack of both political conviction and weight of tradition. As one of its prime movers, **The Chocolate Watch Band** has inspired many a young guitarist to fake a lippy sneer, crank up a wah-wah pedal, and try to reproduce the same ripped-off, flash Chicago blues that captivated the US for a short, sweet period in 1965–67.

The line-up stabilized as **Dave Tolby** (lead guitar), **Dave Aguilar** (vocals), **Bill Flores** (bass), **Mark Loomis** (guitar/vocals) and **Gary Andrijasevich** (drums). Thieving shamelessly from The Stones, The Kinks and Them, they mixed in their own ingredients of fuzzbox, primitive raga rock mysticism, 'trippy' phasing and punky bravado. Their love of the British invasion was tempered by the rough, urgent production values of renowned producer and songwriting associate **Ed Cobb**.

The group widened their exposure by performing "Don't Need Your Lovin'" in the exploitation 'hippie-revolt' movie, *Riot On Sunset Strip* (1967). If the group's performance had shades of The Yardbirds in *Blow Up* about it, The Chocolate Watch Band lacked the headstrong self-assertiveness of such British counterparts. In truth, they were something of a manufactured creation, with Cobb having no qualms about using a host of session musicians to create the right sound. Indeed it is a matter of dispute exactly who played on some of the band's material, and a session vocalist, **Don Bennett**, featured sporadically, much to Aguilar's chagrin. However, it's hard to deny the driving urgency of "Sweet Young Thing" and "Let's Talk About Girls", whatever the personnel. As a point of interest, **Frank Zappa** also produced some of the group's early material, including the intriguingly titled but musically limp "Loose Lip Sync Ship".

Zappa's laboured whimsy was jettisoned for the first album, NO WAY OUT (1967), which tightened up the strutty Jaggerisms and sharpened the Yardbirds-style sonic fuzz into a compelling if derivative formula of slightly acidized R&B. Any departures were into the florid, string-laden territory of silly psychedelia, such as "She Weaves A Tender Trap", which hinted at a band in the throes of an identity crisis.

A single in June 1967, "Are You Gonna Be There (At The Love-In)", offered fresh contradictions.

Written for a film called *The Love-Ins*, its snarling confrontational tone seemed to satirize rather than celebrate the 'scene-capturing' youth-ploitation movies that the group were associated with. In the background the band fought for some semblance of artistic control, while Cobb sought a different direction as the direct, simple energy of 'garage rock' dwindled before psychedelia's loftier and more excessive acid visions, and the general shift towards hard rock and blues.

The strange fruits of this tension materialized in 1968 via the compelling and totally schizophrenic second album, THE INNER MYSTIQUE. Weaving Cobb's instrumental, blissed-out pieces of acid-awe wonderment ("Voyage Of The Trieste", "Inner Mystique") between thudding R&B standards like "Sitting Here Standing", the album created an ambience that was both awkward and beguilingly mixed up. In the confusion lay the charm, and if a punky cover of The Kinks' "I'm Not Like Everybody Else" looked fondly back to 'garageland', then the dreamily hypnotic "In The Past" blended mysticism and pop dynamics far more convincingly than many contemporaries.

THE INNER MYSTIQUE had its moments, but by the time of its release many of those moments were already dated. Frustrated by a lack of control, Aguilar decided to quit and the band struggled on to release their third and weakest album, ONE STEP BEYOND, in 1969, before splitting in 1970. By this time the garage/early psychedelic era – so lovingly captured on Lenny Kaye's seminal NUGGETS collection (1974) – had given way to confrontational politics, hard drugs and heavy rock. The Chocolate Watch Band and their contemporaries generally failed to convince within these new, tougher realities. Their amateurish musicianship starkly contrasted with the new virtuoso showmanship, their lyrical preoccupations were considered dumb high-school posturing, and their lack of political conviction made them look shallow compared to agitprop revolutionaries such as the MC5.

It would be tempting to label The Chocolate Watch Band as a minor footnote in 60s rock history, but at their best they provided a neat, unpretentious aesthetic that would resonate consistently, if marginally, through the next two decades.

THE INNER MYSTIQUE has since been remastered and rereleased by super-cool West Coast label Sundazed – a prime slice of lysergic wonderment.

⊙ **44** (1994; Big Beat Records).
  A sound compilation of the strongest three-minute moments, avoiding acid-awe in favour of aggressive R&B. The revved-up motorcycle engine at the start of "Blues Theme" somehow captures the dumb teenage excitement of a band who, thankfully, refused to grow up.

Nig Hodgkins

CHRISTIAN DEATH

Formed Los Angeles, 1979.

Christian Death managed to cultivate a large following in inverse proportion to press aversion. Frequently name-dropped by the likes of Trent Reznor and Marilyn Manson, the band was formed by **Rozz Williams**, **Rikk Agnew** (guitar), **James McGearly** (bass) and **George Belanger** (drums). They made their mark with ONLY THEATRE OF PAIN (1982): a collection of self-aggrandizing doom rock redeemed only by strong musicianship. This was the only full-length recording by the original line-up, although the DEATHWISH EP (1984), in fact recorded earlier than OTOP, had the same personnel. CATASTROPHE BALLET (1984) had similar lyrical themes and introduced the magnificently named **Gitane DeMone** on vocals/keyboards.

By the advent of ASHES (1985), Williams was backed by a new line-up. Although lyrically more convincing, the album was musically ponderous and appealed only to the already obsessed.

With the departure of Williams, the group became a trio (with none of the original line-up) for the EP, THE WIND KISSED PICTURES (1985), as **Valor Kand** took over the vocal and songwriting duties, and dictated the band's general direction. His chief aim seemed to be to castigate religious institutions at every possible opportunity – not in itself a bad thing, but it soon became abundantly clear that Kand was not up to the job.

Christian Death's lyrical pomposity was again to the fore on THE SCRIPTURES (1987), with its preposterous subtitle 'Translation Of World Beliefs'. Still, at least that album was semi-musical – the risible shock tactics of SEX AND DRUGS AND JESUS CHRIST (1988) had no such redeeming features. The cover picture of Jesus shooting up on the cross was profoundly childish in execution and intent, and the lyrics would have disgraced any self-respecting third-division satanic metal band.

ALL THE LOVE (1989) at least went against expectations, exploring various themes of 'love', but its accompanying release, ALL THE HATE (1989), concentrated on more familiar terrain, with its misjudged swastika cover and recorded samples from the Third Reich and KKK. By 1994, worse news followed for music fans: two Christian Deaths now walked the planet, each laying claim to the name. Williams committed suicide in April 1998, ending the controversy but depriving the music world of a true maverick.

⊙ **Jesus Points The Bone At You** (1992; Jungle).
A singles compilation for those who absolutely must.

Alex Ogg

CHROME

Formed San Francisco, 1975; still kind of extant.

Around the close of the 1970s, San Francisco cult industrial band **Chrome** created some of the most freaked-out music ever committed to vinyl. Their driving force was producer, drummer and sometime vocalist **Damon Edge**, who was part-

nered during this vintage period by lead vocalist and guitarist **Helios Creed**. Other original band members were bassist and violinist **Gary Spain** and guitarist **John Lambdin**.

Born of science fiction movies and a technological obsession with processing sound, Chrome's music fell into closer company with the writing of Philip K. Dick or William Gibson than with the output of other bands. It was music without regard for traditional song structures, and it was often hard to tell where individual songs began and ended, especially on their two finest LPs, ALIEN SOUNDTRACKS (1977) and HALF MACHINE LIP MOVES (1979).

Stylistically these albums bridged the apparently unbridgeable – a move from the 70s hippie rock of their 1975 album, THE VISITATION, to punk/New Wave. Undoubtedly, Helios Creed, who joined for ALIEN SOUNDTRACKS, the band's second LP, made a major impact. And that was some strange disc – a concept album, no less: music for a strip show set in a space-age totalitarian state. Don't let that put you off. The album sounded like The Stooges playing Can in cyberspace.

Originally released on the band's own label, Siren Records, ALIEN SOUNDTRACKS attracted enough attention to get the band signed to UK minor-league label Beggars Banquet for the follow-up, HALF MACHINE LIP MOVES. Here, Chrome were virtually a two-piece – Edge and Creed – and their sound had become less accessible. Being a two-piece meant that Chrome very rarely played live, and, working away in the studio, the music got gradually more industrial, notably on RAINING MILK (1983), the last Chrome LP to feature the talents of Edge and Creed. The duo gradually grew apart over the issue of live shows, finally splitting when Damon moved to Berlin with his girlfriend.

Damon Edge was still making Chrome albums up until his death in the summer of 1995, having won the legal right to use the name, but the band's spirit was more easily recognized in Helios Creed's grunge-industrial solo output for Amphetamine Reptile Records. The early work, meanwhile, developed quite a cult. In 1990 The Jesus Lizard released a single, "Chrome", that was a medley of songs from HALF MACHINE LIP MOVES, while New York noisesters Prong covered the song "Third From The Sun", from the album of the same name.

Since Damon's death Creed has again gigged and recorded with the Chrome moniker while also maintaining a healthy solo catalogue.

⊙ **Alien Soundtracks/Half Machine Lip Moves** (1977/1979; Touch & Go).
Chrome's two great albums on one CD. Weird craziness that includes "ST37", definitely the finest song ever written about sex with an android.

⊙ **The Chronicles 1 & 2** (1982; EFA).
Extended versions of the tracks from RAINING MILK. Nothing about aliens but lots of cyclical music and heaps of flanged and phased guitar and bass.

Ross Holloway

CHUMBAWAMBA

Formed Leeds, England, 1984.

Coming together in an anarchist squat in Leeds, **Chumbawamba** originally featured **Alice Nutter**, **Dunst** and **Lou Watts**. They recorded a song that appeared on an album alongside a song by a group called **Passion Killers – Harry Hamer** and **Mavis Dillon**. The two groups met, merged, and the line-up was complete.

Initially, Chumbawamba defined themselves by their opposition to Thatcherism and earned police raids for their trouble. During the miners' strike of 1984–85 they became street collectors, played benefits, picketed on the front line and recorded a three-track cassette that was sold to raise money for the miners' hardship fund. In 1985, as police clashed with travellers near the site of Stonehenge, Chumbawamba released their first single, "Revolution".

While Bob Geldof was receiving worldwide acclaim for organizing Live Aid, Chumbawamba released their debut album, PICTURES OF STARVING CHILDREN SELL RECORDS: STARVATION, CHARITY AND ROCK 'N' ROLL – LIES AND TRADITION (1986), lambasting the career-boosting aspects of such campaigns. They continued this theme in 1987 when, under the name **The Scum**, they released the single "Scab Aid" as a response to *The Sun* newspaper's celebrity single raising money for the victims of the Zeebrugge ferry disaster.

The group's second album, NEVER MIND THE BALLOTS ... HERE'S THE REST OF YOUR LIVES (1987) was rush-released to coincide with the general election of that year, with songs critical of all parties ("The Candidates Find Common Ground"). Next came an a cappella mini-LP, ENGLISH REBEL SONGS 1391–1914 (1989), which consisted largely of renditions of fourteenth-century anti-poll-tax protest songs.

1990's SLAP! couldn't have been more of a contrast, as Chumbawamba discovered the potential of sampling. But after an American tour, a planned album called JESUS H. CHRIST was banned before its release, as publishers refused to permit the group to cover songs by Kylie Minogue, Paul McCartney and Abba. Instead, the band explored censorship on SHHH (1992).

In 1993, after touring at home and abroad, the group teamed up with **Credit To The Nation** on the single "Enough Is Enough", a reaction against the worldwide increase in fascist activity. Its indie chart success helped make 1994's ANARCHY their most successful LP to date. Subjects under the microscope this time round included U2's *Zoo TV* concept, politicians dabbling in rock'n'roll culture, and the self-explanatory "Homophobia".

A live album, SHOWBUSINESS, issued in 1995, alongside rereleases of the band's entire back catalogue, paved the way for SWINGIN' WITH RAYMOND (1996), which found our anarcho-popsters exploring the concept album. Raymond was a man with LOVE and HATE tattooed on his knuckles – words that formed the two halves of the CD, the former recorded on an industrial estate adjoining a lard factory, and the latter on a Welsh farm. The slow "Love It!" side was an inspired slice of vapid pretentiousness (its lyric sheet peppered with quotes from Jeanette Winterson), but, of course, it was the "Hate It!" songs that suited the Chumbas better. Among these were the anti-fascist polemic "Hey! You! Outside Now!" and a glorious rant about pop stars' atrocious taste ("Ugh! Your Ugly Houses!").

In 1997, after a decade of righteous poverty, and free festivals, Chumbawamba signed to a major label. Having first checked that EMI were no longer selling instruments of torture to dodgy governments, they produced a chart-topping single "Tubthumping" from their chart-topping album TUBTHUMPER (1997) and the crowd went crazy; the anthem was adopted worldwide for sports coverage, TV trailers and game shows.

After a hectic six months of touring, promotion and harassing TV interviewers with their well-honed debating skills, the band returned to the charts with "Amnesia" and then took on the forces of sporting reaction with the only unifying anthem for a World Cup, "Top Of The World (Ole Ole)".

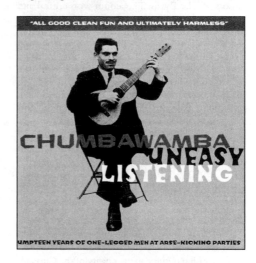

"ALL GOOD CLEAN FUN AND ULTIMATELY HARMLESS"

CHUMBAWAMBA UNEASY LISTENING

UMPTEEN YEARS OF ONE-LEGGED MEN AT ARSE-KICKING PARTIES

Endless touring kept the band out of the studio for much of 1999, though that year did witness the release of retrospective collection, UNEASY LISTENING, and "Tony Blair" their Christmas single – a lovesong to the British Prime Minister, given away to fans on their mailing list. There were no more chart-bothering releases until April 2000's WYSIWYG. Despite the business-inspired, and frankly ungrammatical 'COPYKILLSMUSIC' logo on the CD sleeve, this was a big slice of fresh anarcho-rock in the band's familiar style. It was followed in 2002 by READYMADES, another round of dance pop and political folk stomps.

- **Anarchy** (1994; One Little Indian).
  Pop, rap, folk, rock and dance – their most diverse set to date, as well as their best-selling album.

- **Showbusiness** (1995; One Little Indian).
  The live one which collects all the best tracks from a varied career – a good starting point for their back catalogue.

- **Swingin' With Raymond** (1996; One Little Indian).
  A concept album for the 90s. Splendid.

- **WYSIWYG** (2000; EMI).
  Another album of hard-hitting songs and acid vignettes – though with no anthemic lager-drinking songs this time round.

- **Shhhlap!** (2003; Mutt).
  Corporate repackaging anyone? This is a double CD collection of the albums SHHH and SLAP!

Martin Rowsell

CHURCH

Formed Sydney, Australia 1980.

The **Church** produced a formidable body of guitar-orientated ethereal pop tunes in their time. Initially they consisted of **Steve Kilbey** (bass/vocals), **Peter Koppes** (guitar) and **Nick Ward** (drums). Before recording their first album, they were joined by English tourist **Marty Wilson-Piper** on guitar.

OF SKINS AND HEARTS (1981) was a fresh slice of jangly guitar pop that saw the Church pegged as successors of The Byrds. The album won critical and commercial success in Australia with "The Unguarded Moment" – released as a single – hitting the Australian Top 30. Kilbey, who was writing almost all the songs, had already become unhappy with the band's direction and took steps with the next album, THE BLURRED CRUSADE (1982), to broaden their musical scope. Nick Ward had been replaced by **Richard Ploog** on drums and the new album was a more diverse and languid affair than its predecessor. However, the new direction triggered a downturn in commercial and critical success, with SEANCE (1983), REMOTE LUXURY (1984) and the SING SONGS EP (which included a questionable cover of Paul Simon's "I Am A Rock") all having their musical high points but also collectively failing to ignite the excitement and mystery of the first two sets. Kilbey's lyrics – at best described as off-centre – had, by SING SONGS, degenerated into obscure and pretentious rants.

A surprising upsurge in the quality of the Church's output came after they parted company with their label in 1985 and radically altered the songwriting process. 1985's HEYDAY saw a more collaborative approach based on the entire band jamming songs in the studio. New tracks such as "Tristesse" and "Tantalized" surged and throbbed with a power that harnessed the band's dual shimmering guitars alongside the sensual pulse of Kilbey's singing and bass playing.

STARFISH (1988), the band's fourth album, saw the Church at a commercial and artistic zenith they have since failed to regain. Relocating to Los Angeles to record helped them produce a beautifully mournful piece of work that still shines brightly today. The first single, "Under The Milky Way" – a song that simultaneously dealt with the not unreasonable longing to be in a hash bar in Amsterdam and with the story of former Australian Prime Minister, Malcolm Fraser, losing his trousers in Memphis – went Top 40 both in Australia and the US, whilst also winning Kilbey an *Australian Recording Industry Award* for songwriting. The band toured heavily throughout the US, Australia and Europe and built on their already sizeable cult following, although the LA music-business scene was starting to bring disillusionment.

The 1990 follow-up, GOLD AFTERNOON FIX, was a patchy and half-hearted affair. The band's attitude to it was clear in the opening couplet of the first track "Pharaoh", where Kilbey sings 'Hi to all the people that are selling me/Here's one straight from the factory'. PRIEST AURA (with drums now courtesy of **Jay Dee Daugherty**) was released on Arista in 1992 and, while it was met by indifferent sales, was in retrospect one of the band's most audacious and satisfying albums.

During this period Kilbey, Koppes and Wilson-Piper all trotted out solo albums and side-projects – most notably Kilbey, who took to producing as well as teaming up with an ex-member of the Go-Betweens, Grant McLennan, to record two critically acclaimed albums under the moniker of **Jack Frost**. After the disappointing performance of PRIEST AURA, Koppes left the band, but Kilbey and Wilson-Piper recorded another Church album (SOMETIMES, ANYWHERE; an experimental but directionless set) in 1994, joined by an army of guest musicians.

1994 also saw a greatest hits collection released (ALMOST YESTERDAY 1981–1991), which added to previous Church compilations; HINDSIGHT (a 1988 compilation of singles and B-sides) and A QUICK SMOKE AT SPOTS (a 1991 release of rarities and B-sides not otherwise available). Koppes then returned to the fold (which now also included drummer **Tim Powles**), joining in the sessions for their 1996 album, the underrated MAGICIAN AMONG THE SPIRITS, and accompanying the others on tour.

More releases followed: HOLOGRAM OF BAAL (1998), A BOX OF BIRDS (1999, which boasted several different cover designs by fans) and AFTER EVERYTHING NOW THIS (2002). The latter reappeared later the same year in remixed form as PARALLEL UNIVERSE.

- **Starfish** (1988; Mushroom/Arista).
  An album of rare depth and beauty. Encompasses all the Church's styles from jangly guitar pop ("Hotel Womb"), soundscape travel tunes ("Destination") and hard-riffin' rock ("Reptile"). "Under The Milky Way" remains one of the most affecting and well-constructed pop songs you could ever wish to hear.

- **Starfish** (1996; Griffin).
  Though slated by many at the time of its release, this is one of The Church's strongest, most full-sounding collections.

Benn Barr

CINDYTALK

Formed Scotland, 1984.

Gordon Sharpe first popped up as **The Freeze** in a John Peel session back in 1981. However, he first made waves with **THIS MORTAL COIL**, providing menacing backing on their 1983 EP, SONG TO THE SIREN, and contributing vocals to their IT'LL END IN TEARS album (1984), including a haunting performance of Big Star's classic "Kangaroo". He shared with This Mortal Coil – and others of the 4AD contingent, such as the Cocteau Twins and Dead Can Dance – a love of ethereality and melancholy, and an enthusiasm to get it across in something a bit less superficial than the prevailing superficiality of mid-80s pop.

Around 1984 Sharpe (voice and many instruments) formed **Cindytalk**. It was essentially a personal vehicle, and Sharpe its only 'band' member, though he used a range of studio musicians, notably fellow multi-instrumentalist **John Byrne**. He recorded sporadically through the 80s and 90s, with CAMOUFLAGE HEART (1984), a brooding industrial album, heavy on the guitar and bass, leading on to an exploration of pop's ambient possibilities with IN THIS WORLD (1988), a lighter record with strings and a mass of reverb; and THE WIND IS STRONG (1990), an intended soundtrack of atmospherics, which the Cindytalk website neatly summarizes as 'fucking yum'.

It was with 1995's WAPPINSCHAW, however, that Sharpe really mastered his musical canvas, creating a gorgeous elegy for his Scottish homeland. The record sought to align the Scots with Native Americans, alluding to deceased heroes from Wolfe Tone to Sitting Bull, and included readings by the novelist Alasdair Gray. Employing trumpets, strings, samples, bagpipes, guitars, and choir-like voices, it combined to harness a vision of dignified independence.

⊙ **Wappinschaw** (1995; Touched).
A passionate love for Scotland pervades this wonderful ambient concept album. Political angst never sounded so heavenly.

Michael Sumsion

CIRCLE JERKS

Formed Los Angeles, 1980.

In what seemed like a backlash against New York's art-punk scene of the 1970s, young rock acts on the West Coast came out of the decade parading a grittier, more working-class sound than their elitist forebears. The first band from this new wave to gain broad notoriety were the awesome **BLACK FLAG**. Flag's original singer, **Keith Morris**, left in 1980 to form his own band, **Circle Jerks**, a quartet initially completed by energetic guitarist **Greg Hetson** (formerly of **Redd Kross**), bassist **Roger Rogerson** and drummer **'Lucky' Lehrer**.

Their name was taken from an insalubrious frathouse initiation involving several young men and a milk bottle, and thus Circle Jerks found some labels a touch reluctant to sign them up. However, the hardcore-championing Frontier Records stepped in to issue the band's first album, the entertaining GROUP SEX (1980). This was a patchy attempt to free themselves from the 'Black Flag mark 2' tag, but nonetheless contained the elements of humour and satire that were to become a trademark of Circle Jerks' lyrics. Early classics such as "Wasted" and "Beverley Hills" could soon be heard echoing across West Coast campuses and the band became John Peel favourites in the UK.

In 1981 their potential was recognized by ex-Police manager Miles Copeland, who signed them to his own Step Forward/Faulty label in the UK, which issued the second LP, WILD IN THE STREETS (Frontier Records; 1982 in the US), and brought Circle Jerks to a wider audience. Along with a slightly tighter production, the label transfer brought about an unjustified backlash. Despite the carping, the album has aged reasonably well and includes a definite classic in the adrenalin-infused "Letter Bomb".

Circle Jerks' position at the forefront of US hardcore was strengthened by their inclusion on Jello Biafra's compilation LET THEM EAT JELLYBEANS, to which they contributed the popular "Paid Vacation". However, the appeal of early 80s US punk began to wane by 1983, and Circle Jerks' third album – the stale and regrettably named GOLDEN SHOWER OF HITS – took a critical pasting. Disillusioned, Rogerson and Lehrer disappeared from the scene, while Hetson moved on to work with hardcore contemporaries, the enduring **BAD RELIGION**.

Just as it seemed the Circle Jerks were to disappear without trace, the stalwart Morris and Hetson acquired a new bassist **Zandor Scloss** and drummer **Keith 'Adolph' Clark**. This breath of new life spawned WONDERFUL (1985), which showed the band maturing and moving with the times. Standout tracks included "Killing For Jesus", and, continuing the band's apparent fascination with incendiary devices, "Making The Bombs".

The new blood brought only temporary relief, however, and V1, a long-player which appeared almost to ridicule their earlier identity, sank without trace. Their last official releases, GIG (1992) and ODDITIES, ABNORMALITIES AND CURIOSITIES (1995), added little to the band's myth, although they appealed to the committed fans.

Although little has been heard of Circle Jerks recently, they continue to tour and their influence (and that of their contemporaries) is echoed in the sound and lyrics of such US crossover acts as Green Day, Offspring and Sum 41, while their satirical bite has natural descendants in, amongst others, Rancid, Royal Trux, SNFU and Ween.

⊙ **Oddities, Abnormalities And Curiosities** (1995; Frontier/ Mercury).
This fourteen-track CD (available in UK on import only) rounds up all remaining Circle Jerks cuts into one conveniently throbbing playpen. Included is the storming live favourite, "Teenage Electric".

Jeremy Simmonds

Born Ripley, England, 1945.

"Sex – when it's good, it's very, very good. When it's bad, it's still all right – and that's what listening to Eric Clapton is like."
Tom McGuinness

The blues masters idolized by young **Eric Clapton** didn't appear to be the stereotypical destitutes: they dressed in fine suits, drove fast cars with fast women, and exuded sexuality. In the course of his own forty-year career Clapton has come to emulate this image, which of course has brought its detractors, just as some have a problem with his being white, middle-class and, worst of all, English. Yet at heart Clapton has remained true to the emotional power and honesty of the blues, one of the most unsullied of popular art forms.

Clapton was one of many bitten by the blues bug in southern England in the early 60s, as the remnants of the venerable trad-jazz movement began to incorporate Delta and Chicago blues standards. Under the aegis of performers such as Alexis Korner and Cyril Davies, originals like Sonny Boy Williamson and Jesse Fuller were demonstrating first-hand that rock-'n'roll had its roots in the blues.

After brief stays with Tom McGuinness in R&B band **The Roosters** and Mersey Beat-style **Casey Jones & The Engineers**, Clapton's break came in late 1963, when he replaced lead guitarist Anthony Topham in **THE YARDBIRDS**. Within six months, dissatisfied with his new band's embrace of mainstream pop, Clapton quit, just as they were on the brink of major commercial success. Weeks later, he was invited to join fellow enthusiasts **JOHN MAYALL**'s **Bluesbreakers**. Mayall had heard the lead guitar playing on a minor Yardbirds recording, "I Ain't Got You", and was determined to have Clapton in his band. Committed to a purely blues format, Clapton found himself in what proved to be one of the most satisfying settings of his career; indeed, such was his impact that Clapton's name was added to the band's billing, both live and on record.

The 1966 album JOHN MAYALL'S BLUESBREAKERS WITH ERIC CLAPTON displayed Clapton's astonishing technique. Using a Gibson Les Paul, partly in homage to his hero Freddy King, he produced a round and mellow tone, but at high volume Clapton could coax more extreme sounds, ranging from an extraordinary sustained wail (which he called 'woman tone') to a gritty, harsh attack. A master of phrasing and dynamics, he scorned the single-string melodies of bands like The Shadows, whose style was previously considered to be about as advanced as the instrument was likely to get. Thus the definitive sound of the modern electric guitar was born.

A multitude of eminent musicians passed though Mayall's band, among them bass player **Jack Bruce**.

As Clapton announced his departure from Mayall's band in 1966, he was approached by drummer **Ginger Baker**, eager to form a blues trio in the fashion of Buddy Guy's combo. Because of previous altercations between them, Baker was initially reluctant to work with Jack Bruce, whom Clapton suggested as **CREAM**'s third member. However, professional relations between them settled for a time, as the virtuoso trio's three-year career expanded from twelve-bar blues to freestyle improvisation.

By 1969 Clapton was again restless, and became attracted to the lighter and subtler approaches of **Steve Winwood**'s **TRAFFIC**. Before long, Winwood and Clapton had joined forces with Ginger Baker and Family's bass player **Rick Grech**, to form **Blind Faith**, a short-lived supergroup that folded after just one self-titled LP at the end of 1969. The high quality of songs like "Can't Find My Way Home" and "Sea Of Joy" deepened the sense of disappointment.

An aimless couple of years saw Clapton performing with John Lennon's **Plastic Ono Band** in Toronto, and touring with young American couple **DELANEY AND BONNIE** Bramlett. For his debut solo LP, ERIC CLAPTON (1970), he was accompanied by the Bramletts and some of their band members, who would later join Clapton permanently – bass player **Carl Radle**, keyboardist **Dick Sims** and drummer **Jamie Oldaker**. It was a laudable effort by Clapton, who played down the virtuosity in favour of projecting himself as a band leader, songwriter and singer. Just as noticeable was the smoother, cleaner guitar sound of the Fender Stratocaster he now preferred to the Les Paul.

His quest for greater anonymity peaked with the formation of **Derek & The Dominoes**, with Radle, drummer **Jim Gordon** and keyboard player **Bobby Whitlock**. Unfortunately their live performances, while successful, were uneven and inconsistent, and much the same could be said of their double studio album, LAYLA AND OTHER ASSORTED LOVE SONGS (1970), although the highlights – above all, the seven-minute title track, a heartfelt love song for George Harrison's wife Patti Boyd, and the wonderful "Bell Bottom Blues" – could justify all of the dogs. The album's relative lack of success, however, and Clapton's unrequited love for Patti, quickened his journey towards heroin addiction.

Shunning the pressures of the music business for almost two years, Clapton was saved from almost certain self-destruction by The Who's **Pete Townshend**. Backed by Townshend, Steve Winwood and **Ronnie Wood**, he played a hesitant comeback show at London's Rainbow Theatre in 1973 (released as ERIC CLAPTON'S RAINBOW CONCERT), before beginning a tough addiction therapy programme. As the emotional effects of his experience made him a stronger and more confident man, so his music mellowed. Reuniting with Radle, Sims and Oldaker, Clapton filled the remainder of

Eric in his godly, loon pants period

moments of the four-CD retrospective, CROSSROADS 2 – LIVE IN THE 70s (1995). However, by the end of the 70s many pundits felt that his days of innovation and significance were over. He had finally won Patti Boyd, but the couple's marriage in 1979 was doomed, largely because of his prolonged absence on tour. Furthermore, having beaten heroin addiction, he fell into a similar quagmire with alcohol: recovery from a near-fatal perforated ulcer in 1982 led to a second detoxification programme.

A turning point came with Clapton's appearance at the Philadelphia leg of the Live Aid concert in July 1985, which kindled interest from a whole new generation of fans. A friendship with **Phil Collins** resulted in his producing two excellent LPs, BEHIND THE SUN (1985) and AUGUST (1986), the latter revisiting R&B to great effect, and even his personal life seemed complete – in 1986 his Italian girlfriend Lori Del Santo gave birth to a son, Conor.

1989's JOURNEYMAN found Clapton on top form as a guitarist (if not as a composer), and proved his biggest seller since the 70s, but tragedy was just around the corner. In August 1990, after a star-packed Blues Bonanza at Alpine Valley, Wisconsin, the brilliant young **STEVIE RAY VAUGHAN** and several members of Clapton's entourage were killed in a helicopter crash. And then, early in 1991, five-year-old Conor fell to his death from a window in his mother's New York apartment.

Years earlier, Clapton would have turned to heroin or brandy to ease the pain. Now he poured out the grief into his art. He wrote "Tears In Heaven" for Conor and included it in the set for his UNPLUGGED LP (1992), along with a delicious, laid-back acoustic version of "Layla" and a number of classic blues standards like Robert Johnson's "Malted Milk". 1994's FROM THE CRADLE suggested Clapton had come full circle. His playing on standards like Willie Dixon's "Groanin' The Blues" and Lowell Fulson's "Reconsider Baby" almost equalled the heights of his John Mayall days, and proved conclusively that the blues was not restricted by race or by nationality. PILGRIM, released in 1998, was Clapton's

the 70s with several competent, pleasant but unspectacular albums.

The predominantly acoustic 461 OCEAN BOULEVARD (1974) kicked off with some gorgeous moments, not least a spirited "Motherless Children" and a homage to Bob Marley on "I Shot The Sheriff", an American #1 single. It was followed by THERE'S ONE IN EVERY CROWD (1975), a weak set save for a cover of Elmore James's "The Sky Is Crying"; NO REASON TO CRY (1976), an outing distinguished by the presence of old friends **Bob Dylan** and The Band's **Rick Danko**; and SLOWHAND (1977), his best album of the decade, with a bit of blues energy back, and a standout cover of J. J. Cale's "Cocaine". Further LPs, BACKLESS (1978) and ANOTHER TICKET (1981), had their moments – respectively the blues "Early In The Morning" and "I Can't Stand It" (a Top 10 single in the US) – but to those with memories of his Bluesbreakers days it was all a little tame.

Live, Eric could still pull it off, with occasional flashes of blues genius, as could be heard on the 1975 live album E.C. WAS HERE (1975), and on the better

first album of originals in a decade – slickly executed, though uninspiring.

Recorded with long-term friend and influence **BB King**, 2000's RIDING WITH THE KING saw Clapton firmly in the passenger seat, an understated sideman to King's blues behemoth. In next to no time – in Clapton's terms anyway – he had followed up with another album, REPTILE (2001). New compositions were sprinkled among some surprisingly soulful covers (including a tremendous version of James Taylor's "Don't Let Me Be Lonely" with the Impressions on backing vocals); though on the whole a fairly bland affair, the set was rescued by occasional sparks of magic.

⊙ **The Cream of Clapton** (1995; Polydor).
And indeed it is. Eric's early albums never quite came off, but you'd never imagine such a thing from this disc. Nineteen wondrous and flawless cuts, from 1966 to 1981, including Cream's "Sunshine Of Your Love", D & The D's "Layla" and "Bell Bottom Blues".

⊙ **Crossroads** (1988; Polydor).
OK, this is the one for completists – a real honker of an anthology, whose four CDs trace the Artist Once Known As God from his Yardbird days to the mid-80s. It has most of the highlights you'd expect, and some unreleased gems to draw in hardened fans.

⊙ **August** (1986; Warners).
With the help of producer Phil Collins, this represented a perfect updating of Clapton's sound. Contains the hit single "Behind The Mask".

⊙ **Unplugged** (1992; Warners).
Here was the maturation of a well-rounded bluesman, the understated master of his craft, who had experienced the highest of highs and the lowest of lows. In acknowledgement from his peers, he was rewarded with six Grammys.

⊙ **Reptile** (2001; Reprise).
This project is rescued from MOR oblivion by a couple of deliciously soulful numbers, namely versions of Stevie Wonder's "Ain't Gonna Stand For It" and James Taylor's "Don't Let Me Be Lonely".

Phil Lynch

ANNE CLARK

Born Croydon, England; May 14, 1960.

Like many alienated teens, **Anne Clark** took refuge in art, books and music, until eventually, towards the end of the 70s, she was working at Bonaparte's – Bromley, south London's premier record store, independent label and punk mecca. By the early 80s she had taken the decisive step towards making music and, with backing provided by local band **A Cruel Memory**, she went on stage to recite poetry comparable to the work of earlier punk-scene spoken-word stars Patti Smith and John Cooper Clarke.

A Cruel Memory's moody keyboard/drum machine backing was a perfect match for Anne's tales of urban social decay and everyday angst (concerns she shared with other post-punk acts of the time, in particular The Raincoats, Gang Of Four and The Au Pairs) and soon led to a deal with Virgin group label Schallplatten GmbH.

Her first recording for the label, THE SITTING ROOM EP (1982), was a solid and solemn affair,

seven tracks of two minutes or less, with shadowy synths dominating the music. She then hooked up with a pal from her days booking bands for the Warehouse Theatre, keyboardist **David Harrow**, a collaboration that clicked immediately and resulted in CHANGING PLACES (1983).

The musical advance was startling, with Harrow's keyboards duelling with the cinematic guitar of Durutti Column's **Vini Reilly**. It also showcased Clark's new poetic maturity in "Wallies" and "Sleeper In Metropolis" – commentaries on narrow minds and the dreariness of urban living.

JOINED UP WRITING (1984), a six-track EP which blended SITTING ROOM's haunting atmosphere with the synth experiments of CHANGING PLACES, featured "Our Darkness" – a classic slice of pre-techno/rave keyboards and urban anger – that became one of her most notable successes. Virgin, however, decided that bigger sales were needed and Clark moved to 10 Records. There, she paired up with former Ultravox leader **John Foxx** to produce the more polished PRESSURE POINTS LP in 1985, which, unfortunately, still failed to sell in huge numbers. Undaunted, Clark went back to working with Harrow and new keyboardist **Charlie Morgan** to produce HOPELESS CASES (1987), a brilliant combination of spacious, muscular synths and Clark's on-target observations. Again, this was an artistic rather than commercial success. R.S.V.P. (1988), recorded live in Holland, was a good overview of her music, but when it failed to meet expected sales levels the split between Clark and the label was inevitable.

Having moved to Norway, she met classically trained musicians **Ida Baalsrud** and **Tov Ramstad**. This collaboration resulted in UNSTILL LIFE (1991), which conjured a mature classical/traditional atmosphere. Charlie Morgan contributed synths to several tracks but further planned collaborations were brutally terminated by his sudden death in 1992.

Clark returned to Ramstad and created her most sophisticated and satisfying work, THE LAW IS AN ANAGRAM OF WEALTH (1993), which combined her new Neoclassical leanings with moody synth sounds to brilliant effect. It was also her first album of cover versions, featuring dramatic readings (mixed with quality original music) of Friedrich Ruckert's poetry. This period also produced THE PSYCHOMETRY ALBUM (1994), recorded live in Berlin, in which she reinterpreted a selection of her earlier songs. Her final record for SPV, TO LOVE AND BE LOVED (1995), occasionally bordered on the maudlin but strong musicianship saved the day.

1997 saw the release of THE WORDPROCESSING – THE REMIX PROJECT, on which Clark's material was remixed by top European dance producers. Her finest moment came, however, with her sublime tribute to her personal literary hero: JUST AFTER SUNSET – THE POETRY OF R. M. RILKE (1998).

A new single, "Sleeper In Metropolis 3000", saw the light of day in 2003, and a book, *Notes Taken, Traces Left*, should be in the shops soon.

- **Hopeless Cases** (1987; 10 Records).
  A favourite among her fans. Sinewy synths work out as Anne deftly covers topics ranging from sexual healing ("Homecoming") to romantic frustration ("Hope Road"), and many points in between.

- **The Law Is An Anagram Of Wealth** (1993; SPV).
  A more mature piece of work music- and lyric-wise. The sombre elegance of old is now even more sophisticated and stunning.

- **Just After Sunset – The Poetry Of R. M. Rilke** (1998; Indigo).
  If you ever buy one musical tribute/cover version CD in your life (and for some people even one is too much), look no further than this disc.

Chris Lark

GENE CLARK

Born Tipton, Missouri, November 17, 1944;
died Los Angeles, 1991.

Gene Clark originally played folk music. Then he heard The Beatles while on a 1964 tour with his group **The New Christy Minstrels**, and reputedly played "She Loves You" on a jukebox fifty times in a row. He promptly moved to LA to look for a new band, found **Roger McGuinn** and **David Crosby**, and formed **The Jet Set**, the group that evolved into **THE BYRDS**.

Clark was the least known yet most talented of The Byrds' core trio. McGuinn would go the distance with the group and Crosby would achieve some kind of stardom with Crosby, Stills, Nash (and Young), but Clark always seemed destined to remain in the shadows. While the others cultivated an air of Californian indifference, he looked moody, nervous and seemed to wish he were elsewhere. However, his songs for the group were always strong, and with McGuinn and Crosby he co-wrote the first great shot of psychedelia, "Eight Miles High".

Like fellow Californian anomaly Brian Wilson, Clark found that life on the road held no allure. Citing a fear of flying and having no desire to enter into a three-way ego war with the others, he left The Byrds in 1966. Keeping his connections to the group's management and record label, Clark assembled an impressive cast of session musicians for his first album: country/bluegrass singers **The Gosdin Brothers**, keyboardists **Van Dyke Parks** and **Leon Russell**, guitarists **Glen Campbell** and **Clarence White** – and, from The Byrds, bassist **Chris Hillman** and drummer **Michael Clark**. With that special sort of bad luck that seemed to follow Clark around, GENE CLARK AND THE GOSDIN BROTHERS was released in February 1967, the same week as The Byrds' fourth LP, YOUNGER THAN YESTERDAY. America's Beatles duly hogged the publicity and Clark's first album of West Coast country-rock sank without a trace.

Signing to A&M in 1967, Clark teamed up with banjo player **Doug Dillard**. As Dillard And Clark, they released two albums – THE FANTASTIC EXPEDITION OF DILLARD & CLARK (1967) and THROUGH THE MORNING, THROUGH THE NIGHT (1968) – each of them a jingle-jangle of Byrds rock, R&B, country, folk and bluegrass. Gene Clark's first three post-Byrds records had all boasted irresistible hooks, unexpected chord changes, soul-searching (if cloying) lyrics, melancholy vocals and sweet harmonies. However, three years spent demonstrating an astonishing range had brought little commercial reward.

Studio sessions produced a great deal of material, but it languished in the vaults until a compilation album, ROADMASTER, was issued in 1986. More substantial developments occurred in 1971 with WHITE LIGHT, produced with guitarist Jesse Ed Davis for A&M. While not a major departure from previous work, its haunting arrangements of harmonica, organ and bottleneck guitar suggested that he was slowly finding his own cohesive musical identity.

Success, however, was still elusive, and an unhappy Byrds reunion in 1972–73 did little to rescue matters. Fortunately, in 1974, Clark – with new producer **Thomas Jefferson Kaye** – hit the bull's-eye with the NO OTHER album. His expressive and intimate vocals fronted a broad sweep of styles, mixing and matching soaring pop songs with country-rock, trippy jazz riffs, wah-wah funk grooves, gospel-like backing vocals and simple, resonant lyrics. An album of unique beauty, it remains Gene Clark's masterpiece.

Clark would never be so ambitious again. The pleasant but unmemorable TWO SIDES TO EVERY STORY (1977) was followed by two rather messy albums for Capitol with McGuinn and Hillman – MCGUINN, CLARK AND HILLMAN (1979) and CITY (1980). In the 80s Clark made guest appearances on recordings by the likes of The Long Ryders, Three O'Clock, and Textones singer **Carla Olson**, with whom he recorded SO REBELLIOUS A LOVER (1981) and a live album, SILHOUETTED BY LIGHT, recorded in the last year of his life.

Clark's influence on successive generations of musicians has always been large. Teenage Fanclub namechecked their hero on their third LP, THIRTEEN (1993). By then Gene Clark had been dead two years. He never matched the commercial success of The Byrds and his best work is still awaiting a bigger audience.

- **Echoes** (1967; Columbia/Legacy).
  CD rerelease of GENE CLARK AND THE GOSDIN BROTHERS, featuring Leon Russell's gorgeous orchestral arrangements, plus ten bonus tracks.

- **The Fantastic Expedition Of Dillard & Clark/Through The Morning, Through The Night** (1967 &1968; A&M).
  Now available on one CD, these Dillard And Clark blueprints inspired The Eagles in the 70s. The second album features one of the all-time great Beatles covers, "Don't Let Me Down".

- **No Other** (1974; Edsel).
  Stare in amazement as Gene enters the glam-rock era on the back cover. Get this record into your life now. Untouchable.

Len Lauk

JOHN COOPER CLARKE

Born Salford, England, 1949.

Teenage poet **John Cooper Clarke** began performing his work in Manchester folk clubs. There he met local musician **Rick Goldstraw** and began to gig with him and his band, **The Ferrets**. In 1977, having considered and dismissed a career as a club comedian, he was put in touch with new label Rabid, home to the likes of Ed Banger and Jilted John.

Clarke's high-speed, Salford-twanged delivery, based on the rhythms of rock and amphetamine sulphate rather than any conventional poetic metre, was the verbal equivalent of the headlong musical thrill of punk. Likewise, his subject matter was often lurid enough for punk, combining the bohemian sensibility of Kerouac or Ginsberg with the more whimsical wordplay of, say, Adrian Henri. His performances, though relentless and confrontational, were always good-humoured.

After radio and TV exposure for "Suspended Sentence" – a bleakly comic contribution to the capital punishment debate, taken from Clarke's debut EP, INNOCENTS (1977) – Clarke found himself dubbed 'The Punk Poet' by writers in search of a bard for the times. His look was appropriately startling – stick-thin, drainpipe trousers and jacket, winkle-picker shoes, backcombed black hair, and permanent shades.

Offered a support slot on the final Be Bop Deluxe tour in 1978, Clarke soon signed to CBS and released a summer single, "Post War Glamour Girl", a characteristic combination of the playful and the brutal. Despite the wincing pun of its title, his debut LP, DISGUISE IN LOVE (1978), showed Clarke at his most sophisticated and caustic, ranging from the strutting punk staccato of "I Don't Want To Be Nice" and the bloody live version of "Psycle Sluts" to the mellow tenderness of "The Valley Of The Lost Women".

Over the next year Clarke became ubiquitous on the punk and New Wave circuit. After supporting Elvis Costello on his breakthrough *Armed Forces* tour, he released the single "Gimmix!", which scraped the UK Top 40. The shortfall between his popularity as a live act and his disappointing record sales led Epic to release a live album, WALKING BACK TO HAPPINESS (1979), but this too sold underwhelmingly, even though it captured abrasive stalwarts of his live set, like the radio-unfriendly "Twat", dedicated to cabinet minister Michael Heseltine.

SNAP, CRACKLE AND BOP (1980) was a superior production, marrying dead-end realism with haunting, edgy arrangements on tracks such as "Evidently Chickentown" and the moving "Beasley Street". (A limited-edition book, *Poems*, was given away with initial copies.) Then followed his one and only tour with a backing band, as part of a formidable package featuring The Durutti Column and Pauline

Murray, with whom he shared the backing group, **The Invisible Girls**.

The inspiration now seemed to wane. A 'best of' album entitled ME AND MY BIG MOUTH (1981) was released to little fanfare, as was his swansong for Epic, 1982's ZIP STYLE METHOD, with only "Night People" arousing any real interest among the new material. Although Clarke appeared with Allen Ginsberg for the Poetry Olympics at London's Royal Albert Hall in 1985, his subsequent work has been restricted to low-key performances. For much of the 80s, Clarke had an on-off domestic arrangement with **NICO**, based largely on their mutual leisure pursuits. His talent was stalled by his lifestyle, but the late-70s scene had been all the funnier, and more literate, for his presence.

⊙ **Word Of Mouth: The Very Best Of** (2002; Sony). A twenty-track-strong compilation of highlights from the albums, with some singles and rarities thrown in for good measure. This is the best place to start.

Peter Mills

THE CLASH

Formed London, 1976; disbanded 1986.

"I'd like to say we're not boring. We play great music, jump about, and wiggle our bums." Joe Strummer

Just as The Rolling Stones in the 60s always had something to prove to The Beatles, **The Clash** were seen to be snapping at the heels of the Sex Pistols, and were obliged in the early part of their career to pull off something exceptional time after time. And that's just what they did, more or less defining punk's agenda in broadening teenage angst into the worlds of mainstream and revolutionary politics.

The legend of The Clash has its roots in the equally legendary **London SS**, a going-nowhere proto-punk band formed in 1975 by **Mick Jones** (guitar). The SS had an ever-changing line-up that featured **Nicky 'Topper' Headon** (drums), **Keith Levene** (guitar; later of **PUBLIC IMAGE LTD**) and **Paul Simonon** (later to emerge as bass player for The Clash). The SS faded away but the pursuit of rock'n'roll stardom continued and the line-up of what grew into The Clash was complete when Jones and Simonon recruited **Joe Strummer** (guitar/vocals) from pub-rockers, **The 101ers**. Before long, they had a charismatic manager, **Bernie Rhodes** – a man who reregistered his car to CLA 5H and who figured that the boys arriving at a gig in a military-armoured car could only be good for their image.

By the time they first came to major attention touring with the Sex Pistols on the infamous *Anarchy In The UK* tour, various problems had forced Levene's departure, and Headon joined him in

The late, great, Joe Strummer

jumping ship for a while. Sometime Clash member, the dependable **Terry Chimes**, stepped in at the last minute to drum on the studio sessions for the first album (receiving the wonderful pseudonym 'Tory Crimes' on the sleeve). THE CLASH, the best album of 1977, was completed in just three weekends. The music was angry, message-laden rock, played fast and furiously. A treble-heavy mix and production ensured that the lyrics were seldom incomprehensible.

They had signed to CBS, beating off any accusations of selling out to big business by swearing 'to corrupt them from within'. When their label sneaked "Remote Control" from the LP on to the market as a single without informing the band or their equally visible manager, The Clash responded with the "Complete Control" single. Their stance as the most honest band in the world was offset by some nagging doubts: even some of their true believers felt that Strummer (real name **John Mellors**) came from too privileged a background to be genuinely angry, while Jones's 'Sarf London' accent was considered suspect. The Clash certainly appeared to care about their fan base – they produced some remarkably inexpensive LPs and you could almost always afford a ticket when they toured – but their thinly veiled ambition at the time was to crack America, and that probably explained their acceptance of dubiously qualified Blue Oyster Cult producer **Sandy Perlman** to produce their second LP, GIVE 'EM ENOUGH ROPE (1978).

Having fired Rhodes in October 1978, they briefly hired *Melody Maker* journalist **Caroline Coon** as their manager, and set off for two successful American tours in 1979. During this time, the debut LP was finally released in America by CBS (albeit in a shortened form), who had previously shied away from its confrontational approach. Meanwhile, The Clash kept British fans happy with the release of the four-track COST OF LIVING EP, featuring a marvellous remake of "I Fought The Law" and a second version of their anti-playlist anthem "Capital Radio One".

December 1979 saw the release of LONDON CALLING, a double LP for the price of a single disc, recorded with veteran producer Guy Stevens. Critics and fans alike loved it, while the heavy-metallist accusations that had accompanied GIVE 'EM ENOUGH ROPE died away: the band's love of reggae showed in "Guns Of Brixton", they came over all historical with "Spanish Bombs", there was an R&B classic in "Brand New Cadillac", and even Mick Jones's weedy voice survived well on "Lost In The Supermarket". It also produced their biggest hit singles to date – the title track in Britain, and "Train In Vain (Stand By Me)" in the States.

After further chart success with "Bank Robber" in the summer of 1980, they released a triple album just in time for the Christmas market. SANDINISTA!, issued for the price of a double LP, once again showed them striving to expand their horizons. Reggae was welcomed as before, to be joined by brass bands, disgustingly syrup-voiced children, dance rhythms and even some C&W fiddle-playing. It was mauled by critics, and even old-time fans felt it was too long and sprawling, but it certainly had some marvellous moments – "The Magnificent Seven", the wonderful "Hitsville UK", the pacifist "The Call-Up" and the wobbly "Junco Partner".

In dire need of stable management, The Clash reinstated Bernie Rhodes in early 1981, but otherwise kept a low profile during much of the year, before touring the Far East and Australia for the first time. On returning to the UK in March 1982, they finished recording a new LP with producer Glyn Johns. COMBAT ROCK (1982), the final album with the original line-up, was substandard, but it succeeded in its commercial intent, particularly in America where both "Should I Stay Or Should I Go?" and "Rock The Casbah" reached the Top 10. Furthermore, on the eve of the band's *Know Your Rights* British tour, Strummer disappeared for three weeks, and the dates were postponed before it was revealed to be one of Rhodes' increasingly desperate publicity stunts. As Strummer returned to the ranks, Headon was fired, to be replaced once more by Terry Chimes.

Although there was a massively successful US tour in late 1982 – including a series of slots supporting The Who on their 'first farewell tour' – the rot had set in. Shortly after Chimes was replaced by **Pete Howard** in early 1983, Mick Jones was sacked, resurfacing in 1985 with **BIG AUDIO DYNAMITE**. By then, Strummer and Simonon had recruited guitarists **Vince White** and **Nick Sheppard**, and squeezed out the superfluous CUT THE CRAP (1985), of little interest bar "Dirty Punk" and "This Is England".

Months later, The Clash were no more, as Strummer embarked on a solo career. Their back catalogue has continued to sell, but they resisted the temptation to re-form and tour the stadiums, even after an unexpected #1 UK hit in 1991 with the reissued "Should I Stay Or Should I Go?", after featuring in a Levis 501s commercial. A sequence of often-shoddy compilation albums appeared, while the fan base waited for a live LP that finally appeared in 2001 in the form of FROM HERE TO ETERNITY (LIVE). Also worth checking out is Don Letts' film *Rude Boy*, put together from 1977–78 concert footage of the band, held together by a romanticized punk life story, for an idea of just how good they were.

During his post-Clash years Strummer dabbled with acting, and briefly sang with **The Pogues** before returning in 1999 with a new band, **The Mescaleros**. The group toured constantly, but, tragically, in December 2002, Strummer died at home in Somerset at the age of 50 after suffering a heart attack. Early the following year The Clash were inducted into The Rock And Roll Hall Of Fame.

⊙ **The Clash** (1977; CBS).
It's undeniably raw, but it's also pure, coming from a time when "I'm So Bored With The USA" hadn't become a cliché. THE CLASH is an indispensable document of early UK punk, full of inescapable guitar hooks and ready-to-wear slogans. "Career Opportunities", "White Riot", "What's My Name" and a cover of Junior Murvin's "Police And Thieves" ensured that every track was a wonderful manifesto.

⊙ **Give 'Em Enough Rope** (1978; CBS).
Opening with the awe-inspiring power-guitar riff of "Safe European Home", this shows a more considered approach, appreciating that louder doesn't always mean better. There's bitter humour in "Julie's Been Working For The Drug Squad" and "Guns On The Roof", with improvements in the narrative style of the lyrics.

⊙ **London Calling** (1979; CBS).
A mature and well-constructed album from the cover (a clever Elvis parody) to the running order, this is The Clash at their peak. On "Hateful" and "Koka Kola" they're happy to deal with sex'n'drugs'n'rock'n'roll, while on slices of everyday London life ("Lost In The Supermarket", "Jimmy Jazz", "Rudie Can't Fail") they equal anything by the likes of The Small Faces or The Kinks.

⊙ **Black Market Clash** (1980; CBS).
A stopgap compilation, but hardly a rip-off. As well as odds and ends from single releases, it features the excellent original version of "Capital Radio One", plus their glorious reggae/soul tributes, "Pressure Drop", "Time Is Tight" and "Armagideon Time". Well worth having.

Al Spicer

THE CLEAN

Formed Dunedin, New Zealand, 1978.

New Zealand has too often been overlooked in favour of its bigger brother Australia. But its music has played a serious part in alternative guitar pop/rock thanks to the Flying Nun label and **The Clean** – one of the first bands in NZ to play original material without leaning on a borrowed sound or covering British rockers such as The Beatles, Rolling Stones, Kinks or The Who.

They started out in 1978 in New Zealand with brothers **Hamish** (drums) and **David Kilgour** (guitar), plus **Peter Gutteridge** on bass. They had a scratchy, punky edge, which made a good combination with NZ punk legends The Enemy (who they supported in concert on many occasions). Gutteridge left the following year when Hamish and David moved to Auckland. David moved back to Dunedin in 1979, where he met **Robert Scott**, and they began jamming together. Hamish moved back too and The Clean were reborn.

By 1980, their new sound had a poppier edge and their concerts attracted a committed fan base. When one follower, **Roger Shepherd**, started record company Flying Nun, it was the natural home for The Clean's first single – The Velvets/Modern Lovers-tinged "Tally Ho!". With organ played by future Chills founder **Martin Phillipps**, the single did well on the NZ charts.

Hopes of a full-length Clean album were dashed when most of the engineers in NZ, taking fright at the punk word and fearing they might be difficult, refused to work with their material. Undaunted, they hooked up with former Toy Love leader, **Chris Knox**, and **Doug Hood**, and recorded the BOODLE, BOODLE, BOODLE EP (Flying Nun) to 4-track in 1982. The EP reached #4 on the NZ charts. Another EP, GREAT SOUNDS GREAT, followed in a quirkier style, but there were problems – resulting from all the usual rock'n'roll pressures – and the guys were rapidly getting sick of being "The Clean" day in, day out. By the time "Getting Older" came out in late 1982, The Clean were no more. Scott left to form **The Bats**; Hamish moved back to Christchurch with a 4-track, later followed by David to create **The Great Unwashed**. (Both bands ditched The Clean's aggressive pop style for a more folk-pop sound.)

The Clean reunited several times. In 1988, they drew large audiences with two concerts that led to a world tour and a five-song LIVE EP. Two years later the first full-length album VEHICLE (1990) appeared. They hooked up again for MODERN ROCK (1994), by which time, no longer content with their garage rock trio sound, they had added some rollicking keyboards and synths to the mix. UNKNOWN COUNTRY (1996) was even better, with more keyboards, mandolins and strings. Flying Nun put out a tribute album, GOD SAVE THE CLEAN, in 1997. Like Orange Juice and their short-lived label Postcard, The Clean and Flying Nun proved that guitar pop and witty lyrics still mattered, regardless of musical trends.

After The Unwashed, Hamish went on to form two more great bands – the even noisier **Bailter Space** and the more experimental **Mad Scene**. David later formed **Stephen** and had more critical success with his later solo albums.

In 2000, the Dunedin Arts Council persuaded the Clean to perform at a festival celebrating the history of New Zealand music. Thrust together once again the trio began working on a new album, GETAWAY, which emerged in 2001 on Matador. Only their fourth proper full-length offering, the set was sparsely melodic, betraying a hint of country twang amidst their intoxicating lo-fi: a welcome addition to their canon.

The Clean are now legends in the indie-rock genre. They've inspired everybody on Flying Nun and others, such as Pavement and Yo La Tengo.

(●) **Anthology** (2001; Merge).
On this double CD set you'll find the classic "Tally Ho!" and the funnier "Getting Older" (a chorus for the ages: "Why don't you do yourself in?") Imagine the Modern Lovers and PINK FLAG-era Wire meeting at a karaoke bar, getting drunk and jamming together.

Chris Lark

CLIMAX CHICAGO BLUES BAND

Formed Stafford, England, 1968.

A fter disbanding his hipster-image R&B outfit in 1967, **Colin Cooper** (vocals/guitar/saxophone) led the **Gospel Truth**, a sextet that adjusted to the late-60s blues boom with ease. To stress a style hinged mostly at the urban end of the spectrum, it also renamed itself the **Climax Chicago Blues Band**, solidifying into a line-up of Cooper, **Arthur Wood** (keyboards), **Richard Jones** (bass), **George Newsome** (drums) and singing guitarists **Derek Holt** and **Peter Haycock**.

Between 1969 and 1974, six albums – notably A LOT OF BOTTLE and SENSE OF DIRECTION – sold steadily if unremarkably as the band amassed a regular following via a hectic touring schedule. Inevitably, personnel fell by the wayside. The departure of Jones in 1970 was resolved when Holt volunteered to transfer to bass. Next out was Newsome, who was replaced by **John Cuffley**, and with Wood's exit in 1972 the group decided to continue as a less cumbersome four-piece, and drop 'Chicago' from their title to avoid confusion with the Windy City's own big band of that title.

A concentration on the US market paid off with 1974's FM LIVE, a New York radio concert offering with Los Angeles 'supersideman' Jim Price at the console. It lingered on the *Billboard* list for almost a year, then 1975's STAMP album compounded the breakthrough, enabling the lads to move from support act to headliners.

They embarked on a round-Europe trek in 1975, restoring popularity lost through long absences across the Atlantic. The following year, they even reached the UK Top 10 with "Couldn't Get It Right" from the TV-advertised GOLD PLATED, an album which did even better in the New World, thanks to exposure on FM radio, a medium which would remain amenable to the Climax Blues Band until the punk storm broke. When it did, the hirsute, denim-clad, expatriate Midlanders seemed suddenly outmoded – and even more so when they pursued a very middle-of-the-road route in the 1980s.

The group are still a going concern, with just Cooper left from the FM LIVE zenith – from which much of the present-day stage repertoire is still drawn. Haycock, meanwhile, formed the imaginatively titled **Pete Haycock's Climax** and was later to be found in a reincarnation of ELO.

(●) **25 Years: 1968 to 1993** (1994; Repertoire).
A streamlined but representative sample of the group's creative parameters and the general drift of university circuit rock in the early 1970s.

(●) **FM Live** (1974; Polydor).
On this night of nights, the band approached their set with the lucid attack that pre-performance nerves often inspire. Blues forms tackled range from the exquisite dirge of "Too Many Roads" to "Plight", a jazzy instrumental riven with tricky dynamic shifts and tempo refinements.

Alan Clayson

CLINIC

Formed Liverpool, 1997.

T hey can play funky, punky and even country, and like The Velvet Underground and The Fall, **Clinic** are a little more awkward than your average indie band, harder to pin down. Their songs are either edgy, scratchy and challenging, or sumptuously smooth and yielding. When you enter the musical world of Clinic and they offer you a chair, the chances are that your seat will be pulled out from under you and replaced by either a luxuriant beanbag or a cactus!

Clinic formed back in 1997 when **Ade Blackburn** (guitar, keyboards, vocals) and **Hartley** (guitar, keyboards) set aside their activities in other directionless ventures to concentrate on their own vision. Their previous project had been, in their own words, both 'ridiculous' and 'quite rock'n'roll', yet it wasn't until Clinic was calcified by the recruitment of **Brian Campbell** (bass, backing vocals) and **Carl Turney** (drums) that the band truly began to find their own wayward sound. In the autumn of 1997 Clinic threw down the gauntlet to the weekly music press with the brilliantly named debut EP "IPC Sub-Editors Dictate Our Youth". The title cut opened with a plodding, Phil Spector-ish beat that quickly shifted up a gear to become the drive shaft of a propulsive, krautrock-tinged blast of keyboards, bass and percussion, with Blackburn's monosyllabic skittering vocal pulling the whole thing together. Released on the group's own Aladdin's Cave Of Golf imprint and championed by John Peel, the single was a triumphant stab at indie music's tendency toward reductive conformity – the press lapped it up, and the punters' appetites were whet for more.

A second single followed, "Monkey On Your Back" (1998), and then a third, "Cement Mixer" (1998), both of which were voted single of the week by IPC's very own *NME*. The tunes were still chaotic, raw and energized, but also brilliantly infused with pop. The group soon found themselves hooking up with Domino records, who promptly released the three hard-to-come-by EPs as a CD compilation.

In 1999 the band surged forward with another single, "The Second Line", and then in 2000 a debut album proper, INTERNAL WRANGLER, which presented the expected mix of jagged songs, punchy beats and propulsive keyboards, all bolstered by a newly acquired rich production sound. The set also featured a strong dub element: on several cuts resonant chord organs and melodicas were pushed to the fore in true Augustus Pablo style. In the year that followed, the group were invited to join Radiohead on tour and also nabbed themselves a spot in Scott Walker's prestigious Meltdown festival.

At the start of 2002 a second album hit the streets. WALKING WITH THEE, co-produced with **Ben Hillier** (Blur, etc), was another set of stormy oddities and mashing guitars. But this time around, the whole thing felt a little more controlled, even mellow at times.

🔘 **Internal Wrangler** (Domino, 2000).
Combining the intelligent experimentalism of post-rock, the simplistic beauty of electro-pop, a punk snarl, and enough great hooks to sink a battleship, Clinic have created a debut set of original, yet compelling gems.

🔘 **Walking With Thee** (Domino, 2002).
Simple motifs, sparsely arranged, insinuate themselves effortlessly into songs to spellbinding effect. Walking With Thee lacks the grinding immediacy of Clinic's earlier music, but may prove all the more enduring for it.

Peter Buckley

CLOCK DVA

Formed Sheffield, England, 1980;
disbanded 1984; re-formed 1988.

While Throbbing Gristle got all the plaudits for the 'industrial revolution' that overtook post-punk sensibilities at the end of the 70s, **Clock DVA** were also a critical component of that movement. The band was formed in 1980 in Sheffield and, by the time they were ready to record, the line-up had settled on **Adi Newton** (vocals), **Steven Taylor** (bass/vocals), **Paul Widger** (guitar), **Charlie Collins** (saxophone) and **Roger Quail** (drums). Most had played in local underachievers – the **Studs**, **Veer** and **They Must Be Russians** – and Adi had, briefly, fronted **The Future**, an early incarnation of The Human League.

The group's debut release, WHITE SOULS IN BLACK SUITS, was recorded in cassette-only form for Throbbing Gristle's Industrial label in 1980. Entirely improvised, it fused white soul and funk with disorientating machine noise to produce a sound distinctively contemporary and definitively urban. THIRST (1981), an edgy album dominated by abrasive musical machinery, saw them move to the Fetish label, aware that the idea of being perceived as Throbbing Gristle's better-house-trained younger brothers was doing their critical profile no favours.

With his colleagues defecting to form the underrated **Box**, Newton recruited an all-new line-up – **Paul Browse** (saxophone), **John Carruthers** (guitar; ex-Banshees), **Dean Dennis** (bass) and **Nick Sanderson** (drums) – and secured an unlikely contract with a major label, Polydor. The result was ADVANTAGE (1983), the group's most accessible recording, coupling genuine musicianship with a recalcitrant streak of adventurism. It revolved around blissful, sustained rhythms, traumatized by folds of white noise and discordant trumpet. Newton's anxious vocals completed the emotional circuit.

Alas, the group didn't last. Sanderson and Carruthers departed (the latter rejoining The

Banshees) leaving Clock DVA to struggle on, briefly, as a trio. After they gave up the ghost, Newton turned to work on his video project, **The Anti Group**, working with multimedia producer/guru **Robert Baker** and other musicians on sporadic releases under that name. Then, in 1988, he re-formed Clock DVA, with Browse and Dennis, producing a couple of EPs for American label Wax Trax!, THE HACKER and THE ACT – tracks that proved the highlights of BURIED DREAMS (1989), a grandiose album themed on death and decadence. Further releases punctuated the next four years, though none had the intimacy or power of ADVANTAGE.

From 1993, Newton maintained Clock DVA as a duo with Robert Baker, producing the overly cerebral SIGN, BLACK WORDS ON WHITE PAPER and VIRTUAL REALITY HANDBOOK (all 1993), 150 EROTIC CALIBRATIONS (1994) and ANTERIOR (1995), for the Italian label Contempo.

⊙ **Advantage** (1983; Polydor).
Clock DVA's most sustained effort, a dextrous collage of sound underscoring their bleak intensity. Truly, a tripwired triumph.

Alex Ogg

Formed Germany, 1969.

Even amid the 90s renewal of interest in Krautrock, **Cluster** seemed marginalized. **Dieter Moebius** and **Hans-Joachim Roedelius**'s quarter-century career has been too often condensed to a dismissive 'Cluster: see Eno' reference in encyclopedias and record-store racks. They deserve more, especially for the contribution of their early work, which was as brilliant (and ahead of its time) as anything by groups such as Can and Faust.

The band began life in 1969 as a trio called **Kluster**, comprising Moebius, Roedelius and **Conrad Schnitzler** – the driving force behind Tangerine Dream's ELECTRONIC MEDITATION. This outfit (all of whom played piano, organ, synths and guitars) released two albums before Schnitzler left, when the duo anglicized their name to Cluster and signed to the Philips label. It was an oddly conventional home for one of Krautrock's wildest and most psychedelic albums, CLUSTER (1971).

There was a tension in all good Krautrock – a bargain struck between power and playfulness. That 1971 release was as near as Cluster got to letting sheer sonic immensity go to their heads, as Tangerine Dream were to do. As their career progressed, and as acoustic instruments mingled with their banks of electronics, Roedelius and especially Moebius gave their playful sides freer rein. CLUSTER II (1972), released on the legendary Brain label, began this process, and ZUCKERZEIT (1974) continued it, with **Connie Plank** sharing writing and production credits. It was ZUCKERZEIT that attracted Eno's attention, its bubbling vignettes inspiring his work on ANOTHER GREEN WORLD.

Next step for Moebius and Roedelius was a venture called **Harmonia** with **Michael Rother**, who had split from **NEU!** (their Brain label mates). This led to two albums, MUSIK VON HARMONIA and HARMONIA DELUXE, both of which rank in Julian Cope's '50 Greatest Krautrock Albums', distinguished, as he puts it, by that 'candy melody and simplicity of guitar licks that made all NEU! songs so austere and Joe Meek-ian'. Great as they were, though, the sales were tiny, and in 1976 Rother returned to NEU!.

Re-formed as a duo again, Cluster produced another quiet triumph, SOWIESOSO (1976), which contrived to be sensitive, sly and relaxing, employing for the first time what Cope brilliantly defines as 'darling Charlie Brown theme tunes' – quirky melodies which became a keynote on many of the duo's subsequent group and solo releases. GROSSES WASSER (1979) was more downbeat; still beautiful but somehow more serious. The fruition of the Cluster comedy came with a solo Roedelius album, JARDIN AU FOU (1979), a stunning, absurd rack of cuts that had movie narrative writ large. It remains Roedelius's best solo outing, overshadowing a series of too-often-bland New Age and ambient soundtrack recordings.

It was around this time that Cluster's first collaborations with **Eno** took place, resulting in the albums CLUSTER AND ENO (1978) and AFTER THE HEAT (1979). They were obvious moves all round, and, if not quite the ambient-Krautrock supergroup that could have been, produced some wonderful moments – above all, the eerie vocal coaxed from Eno on HEAT's "Broken Head".

Perhaps the most memorable collaboration, however, was that between Moebius and Connie Plank. Their two early 1980s albums – RASTAKRAUTPASTA and MATERIAL – stand among the most wildly inventive of the whole German scene. Plank and Moebius shared a whimsical pop sensibility and a desire to co-opt traditional melodies and rhythms into their far-out sound. On RASTAKRAUTPASTA, funny and brilliant at the same time, with **HOLGER CZUKAY** on bass, they funked out in unrivalled fashion.

In the 90s, Cluster's APROPOS CLUSTER (1993) saw a lost harshness return, as the duo shattered and scattered old-style tonescapes to unnerving effect. Naturally, though, their next record, ONE HOUR (1994), was their most placid – and, to be honest, unengaging – yet. The releases and collaborations have continued to come with yawnsome regularity, but there is little in the recent catalogue to rival the releases from their Krautrock heyday.

Cluster

- **Sowiesoso** (1976; Sky).
  Classic gentle Cluster, with its soft repetitions of acoustic guitar/keyboard phrases over deceptively simple electronic backdrops.

Moebius and Plank

- **Rastakrautpasta/Material** (1994; Sky). This is a great double-CD reissue, worth your money if only to hear (on "Tollkuhn") the invention of Goa trance in 1981!

Eno, Moebius, Roedelius and Plank

- **Begegnungen II** (1986; Sky).
  This compilation takes in tracks from Cluster proper, their solo records and their collaborations – though sadly nothing of HARMONIA.

Tom Ewing

THE COASTERS

Formed Los Angeles, 1955; ended in the late 60s, though 'Coasters' groups still surface on the oldies circuit.

The received wisdom has it that rock'n'roll was dying on its feet during the period between Buddy Holly's death and The Beatles' invasion of the US. However, the music that appeared during this time – the first rumblings of Berry Gordy and Motown, the infectious New Orleans rhythms of The Showmen and Huey 'Piano' Smith, and especially the comedy of **The Coasters** – was perhaps more joyous and more intensely rhythmic than anything by Elvis, Chuck Berry or Buddy Holly. This music was neglected partly due to subconscious racism, but also because it was producers' music *par excellence*, lacking an even remotely iconic presence. Nowhere was this more apparent than with the remarkable Coasters.

The Coasters evolved out of **The Robins**, a Los Angeles-based R&B vocal group who recorded for **Jerry Leiber** and **Mike Stoller**'s Spark records. The Robins had several hits in California, most notably "Riot In Cell Block #9" (sung by future "Louie, Louie" composer **Richard Berry**) and "Smokey Joe's Cafe". Impressed by the songwriting talents of Leiber and Stoller, who not only wrote The Robins' hits, but also the R&B staples "Hound Dog" and "Kansas City", Atlantic offered the duo an independent production deal. **Carl Gardner** (vocals) and **Bobby Nunn** (vocals) from The Robins joined Leiber and Stoller and recruited vocalists **Billy Guy** and **Leon Hughes** to become The Coasters. Their first single, "Down In Mexico" (1956), contained almost all of the elements that would characterize their style: novel rhythms, a prominent, honking sax, and a lyric that told a comically mysterious story in an exotic setting.

After a few lacklustre singles, The Coasters hit their stride with "Searchin'" (1957). Leiber and Stoller's lyric brilliantly combined a detective story with poetic boasting, but it was the music that pushed the song into the American Top 3. The feel was reminiscent of Fats Domino with a slightly less funky New Orleans rhythm and drunken piano, played by Stoller himself. The flip side, "Young Blood", went into the Top 10 in its own right and was the first example of the comedic style that The Coasters will be best remembered for.

"Yakety Yak" (1958) justly went straight to the top of the American charts on its release and has since become one of the classic rock'n'roll songs with a hilarious lyric, Nunn's basso profundo "Don't talk back" and King Curtis's glorious sax solo. This ubiquitous sax sound would reappear on "Charlie Brown" (1959), the utterly bizarre "Along Came Jones" (1959), and "That Is Rock & Roll" (1959). By this time, Hughes and Nunn had left and were replaced by a succession of singers, including **Will Jones** and **Obie Jessie**.

The Coasters ended 1959 with a string of remarkable songs. "Poison Ivy" abandoned the sax in favour of a harder, guitar-based rhythm and was constructed around a dazzling extended metaphor filled with over-the-top internal rhymes, while "What About Us", along with Chuck Berry's "Brown Eyed Handsome Man", pioneered rock'n'roll's exploration of race and class issues. "Run Red Run", meanwhile, was perhaps their best song. On the surface it was another one of Leiber and Stoller's comic playlets, but underneath was an extraordinary political statement. As Leiber puts it, 'once the monkey knows how to play [poker], he knows how to understand other things. And once he understands that he's being cheated and exploited, he becomes revolutionary.'

After 1959, the hits dried up, with the exception of "Little Egypt" (1961) and the wonderful "Shoppin' For Clothes" (1960), whose perfect depiction of cool has been sampled by both Barry Adamson and The Jungle Brothers. The Coasters continued until the late 60s with little success but Leiber and Stoller continued writing and produced hits for The Drifters, Ben E. King, The Dixie Cups and Elvis. As two of rock'n'roll's greatest songwriters and producers, Leiber and Stoller occupy a central position in the story of rock'n'roll's early evolution. They created many of its linguistic staples and much of its rhythmic language too.

- **The Very Best Of The Coasters**
  (1994; Rhino/Atlantic).
  The cream of the crop from Rhino's fifty-song retrospective, COASTIN' CLASSICS. This shows off Leiber and Stoller's enormous talent for mixing the comic and the political, and suggests why things like Red Wedge and Rock Against Racism are such abject failures.

Peter Shapiro

EDDIE COCHRAN

Born Albert Lea, Minnesota, 1938; died 1960.

In the 50s, rock'n'roll seemed it might be a fad with a limited life span, as ephemeral as hula-hoops. Despite his great talent and mould-breaking success, Elvis Presley was no great innovator musically, and never wrote his own material. It was the likes of **Eddie Cochran**, along with Chuck Berry, Buddy Holly, Little Richard and others, who saw rock's potential, developing the foundations of a cultural phenomenon.

Cochran was born in Albert Lea, Minnesota, and grew up in Oklahoma City, where he joined the school band on clarinet (he'd been rejected as a drummer and trombonist). However, he fell in love with the guitar and, listening to country and western music on the radio, taught himself to play. The family moved to California in 1953 and Eddie soon began playing in a local group, playing dance halls and parties before winding up in a duo with **Hank Cochran** (no relation). Then he met aspiring songwriter **Jerry Capehart**, and the two began a partnership. They recorded some tracks that were eventually picked up by the Liberty label, and Eddie was signed.

He appeared (on a TV screen) in the film *The Girl Can't Help It*, and the song "Twenty Flight Rock" was considered for the first single. But, going against his country and R&B roots, a bopalula ballad, "Sitting In The Balcony", was chosen instead. Still, it had the desired effect and was a national hit. Even then, Eddie was more interested in being a musician than a teen idol, hence his rather unenthusiastic vocal performance; asked how he'd feel if he lost his voice, he replied: 'I'd consider it a blessing.'

Cochran and Capehart failed to capitalize on their success, and spent most of 1957 looking for the song that would catapult them back into the big time. But Eddie, always a homely sort, didn't like the promotional work that went with stardom. Apart from another film, *Untamed Youth*, nothing was to happen until 1958, when Eddie started playing around with a rather tasty little riff he had made up. It struck Capehart that no one had written a song about the hassles teenagers faced during summer, and thus "Summertime Blues" was born, becoming a monster smash in the summer of 1958. Decades on, it's still almost universally recognized.

The follow-up was deliberately crafted around a similar theme, this time the hassles of trying to have a party, and the music again relied on a simple but heavy acoustic riff and hand-clap backing. Formula or no, "C'mon Everybody" hit the mark and has lasted the test of time almost as well as its predecessor.

Eddie was still more interested in the studio side of rock'n'roll and his reluctance to tour was intensified by the death of his friend Buddy Holly in February 1959. He wanted to marry, settle down and work with production and songwriting. If a great song like "Something Else" didn't hit the Top 10, it wasn't the end of the world.

But one more tour was planned, this time to Europe with Gene Vincent. Britain, in particular, was in the grip of rock'n'roll mania, and this was the first full tour by a genuine American rocker. Eddie suddenly became a star like he had never been back home, getting the kind of reception reserved there for Elvis. Although he decided this would be his last major tour, it was so successful that it was extended from five to fifteen weeks.

Homesick as ever, Eddie decided to visit home during a break in the action, and it was on the way to Heathrow Airport on the wet morning of April 17, 1960, that his taxi blew a tyre and crashed into a lamppost on the A4 near Bath. Eddie died in hospital that afternoon.

In the US his death attracted little attention, but in Britain it was traumatic, and served to solidify his reputation and influence in British rock. Kids like George Harrison had followed him from town to town, and his influence was felt throughout the 60s. That influence spread back across the water, and Eddie Cochran is now recognized worldwide as one of the most important figures of pre-Beatles music. He was inducted into The Rock And Roll Hall Of Fame in 1987.

Legendary Masters: Eddie Cochran (1990; EMI).
Along with Little Richard, Cochran is definitive proof that the power of rock'n'roll is in the attitude. "Summertime Blues" and "C'mon Everybody" show the clear line that extends from Cochran to the Sex Pistols, while the blues numbers show the line that extends to the past.

Rare'N'Rockin' (1998; Music Club).
An excellent collection that helps fill the gaps left by most other compilations.

Patrick Neylan-Francis

JOE COCKER

Born Sheffield, England, 1944.

"I've always done me little theatricality bit of throwing me arms about with the music."

The earthy white soul voice of **Joe Cocker** has proved more durable than much of the rock posturing of his late-60s and early-70s contemporaries. However, Cocker's first attempts to apply his gritty Ray Charles-influenced interpretation of soul and blues were not auspicious. A gas fitter by trade, Cocker fronted **Vance Arnold & The Avengers** during the 1963 beat boom, becoming well known as a warm-up for bands like The Hollies. Yet their excellent reworking of The Beatles' "I'll Cry Instead" (1964) flopped, forcing Cocker to return to the gas trade.

Two years later he founded British white soul and funk outfit, **The Grease Band**. For a couple of years Cocker, **Vernon Nash** (piano), **Dave Memmott** (drums), **Frank Myles** (guitar) and Cocker's future

The original air guitar: Joe Cocker at Woodstock

which featured **Henry McCullough** on guitar and contributions from Page and **Steve Winwood**. A follow-up album, JOE COCKER (1970), charted well on both sides of the Atlantic, and featured Leon Russell's "Delta Lady" – another strong example of the gospel/soul sound of which Cocker was increasingly becoming enamoured. Russell – who at that time was ploughing the same musical furrow with Delaney And Bonnie – encouraged Cocker to play more than sixty dates in two months on the *Mad Dogs And Englishmen* tour, for which he recruited many of Delaney And Bonnie's sidemen. A feature film and soundtrack album, MAD DOGS AND ENGLISHMEN (1970), caught the show's chaotic feel. Cocker, now declining physically and mentally, exiled himself on the US West Coast, where he furthered his decline with booze and drugs.

As Tommy Eyre re-formed The Grease Band for session work on the soundtrack of *Jesus Christ Superstar* and a few albums of their own, Cocker and Stainton reunited for a 1972 American tour, disappointingly reproduced on LIVE IN L.A. (belatedly released in 1976). After a short UK tour, Cocker was busted for drug possession in Australia, but Stainton stayed loyal and played a major role on the partly live showcase album, SOMETHING TO SAY (1973).

Cocker's last consistent album for some years, I CAN STAND A LITTLE RAIN (1974), produced hits in "Put Out The Light" and a memorable cover of Billy Preston's "You Are So Beautiful". It also featured a cover of Randy Newman's "Guilty" – with its confessional 'been through the mill' theme, it provided the perfect statement on Cocker's life at this point. His next notable work appeared in 1981, when he collaborated with **The Crusaders** on the minor torch-song hit, "I'm So Glad I'm Standing Here Today". It was a prelude to a remarkable comeback.

For SHEFFIELD STEEL (1982) he teamed up with Island Records supremo **Chris Blackwell** and a host of other famous 'friends' in Nassau. The following year he duetted with **Jennifer Warnes** on the million-selling "Up Where We Belong", the title song from the highly schmaltzy film *An Officer And A Gentleman*.

Although Cocker returned for a triumphant Sheffield City Hall gig in 1983, nothing followed for three years, when the disappointing COCKER (1986) was released. The title track of UNCHAIN MY HEART (1987), a minor chart hit, allowed Cocker to indulge in a personal tribute to his hero Ray Charles, and it remains an AOR radio favourite even today. NIGHT

musical mentor, **Chris Stainton** (bass), were engaged in arduous evening and weekend touring round the pubs and clubs of northern England. It finally paid off when legendary producer-manager **Denny Cordell** offered them a single deal, thanks to the efforts of Stainton.

The first single, "Marjorine" (1968), was a minor hit, and for the second, a radical reworking of The Beatles' "With A Little Help From My Friends", there was a new line-up of **Micky Gee** (guitar), **Tommy Reilly** (drums) and **Tommy Eyre** (keyboards), plus top session players like **Jimmy Page** and **B. J. Wilson**. A huge success in the charts and at Woodstock, it showed Cocker dispensing with the two-minute pop format, and prefigured his future direction in its gospel treatment.

US chart success followed with the debut album, WITH A LITTLE HELP FROM MY FRIENDS (1969),

CALLS (1991) featured a return to 60s pop covers with The Beatles' "You've Got To Hide Your Love Away" and the more surprising Blind Faith number, "Can't Find My Way Home", alongside lesser material like the dire Bryan Adams song, "Feels Like Forever".

A deluge of variable compilation albums hit the market before Cocker released HAVE A LITTLE FAITH (1994). It was somewhat pedestrian, and all the more so when contrasted with 1996's completist four-CD box set, THE LONG VOYAGE HOME – which was rendered incomplete almost immediately by the 1996 release, ORGANIC. This album, an intimate, low-key recording, mainly cover versions, saw Joe revisiting his own classic "Delta Lady" as well as exploring Van Morrison's "Into The Mystic".

More mainly fresh material was heard on the 1997 release ACROSS FROM MIDNIGHT, which was followed by greatest hits packages in both 1998 and February 1999, and in 2002 RESPECT YOURSELF, a mixed bag that featured a frankly brutal butchering of INXS's "Never Tear Us Apart".

⊙ **With A Little Help From My Friends/Joe Cocker**
(1969 & 1970; A&M).
Now both available on one CD, the former has help from Steve Winwood and guitarist Albert Lee, as well as Leon Russell and, of course, The Grease Band. The latter album features the excellent "Delta Lady" as well as Beatles covers and a version of Traffic's "Feelin' Alright".

⊙ **Sheffield Steel** (1982; Island).
Cocker's most vital and complete album, with impressive covers of Dylan's "Seven Days", Winwood's "Talkin' Back To The Night", Jimmy Cliff's "Many Rivers To Cross", and "Sweet Lil' Woman". Robert Palmer and Winwood form part of the superstar backup team, while Sly Dunbar and Robbie Shakespeare provide a solid, dependable rhythm section.

Neil Partrick

COCKNEY REBEL

Formed London, 1973; disbanded 1976; periodically re-formed as Steve Harley's backing band.

Fronted by ex-journalist **Steve Harley** (born Steven Nice; vocals/guitar), **Cockney Rebel**'s original line-up consisted of **Milton Reame-James** (keyboards), **Jean-Paul Crocker** (violin), **Paul Avron Jeffreys** (bass) and **Stuart Elliot** (drums). Their violin-tinged rock and Harley's strangulated but confident vocals gained an obsessive following after the release of their debut album, HUMAN MENAGERIE (1973).

As David Bowie flirted with American soul, Cockney Rebel stepped into the glam-rock void he had left behind. They achieved their first British hit with "Judy Teen" (1974) and their use of imagery plundered from the cult film *A Clockwork Orange* provided them with a legion of trenchcoated and gaunt-looking fans wearing one false eyelash.

"Judy Teen" had barely left the charts when the follow-up, "Mr. Soft", made the UK Top 10. The accompanying album, PSYCHOMODO (1974), was an uncompromising mix of convoluted literary lyrics, scratching avant-garde violins and heavy-handed operatics. An instant success, it fuelled Harley's self-destructive arrogance – he constantly feuded with the music press, who responded by printing ever more derisive reviews.

In response Harley broke up the band, and returned in early 1975 as Steve Harley & Cockney Rebel with Elliot still on drums, and a new line-up of ex-Family guitarist **Jim Cregan**, **Duncan Mackay** (keyboards) and **George Ford** (bass). Their first release was "Make Me Smile (Come Up And See Me)", a cynical lyric wrapped in a sugar-coated tune which became the band's only British #1 in March 1975.

Accompanying this masterstroke was an accessible third album, THE BEST YEARS OF OUR LIVES (1975), which found Harley at his lyrical best. However, other singles taken from the album proved too oblique to repeat the success of "Make Me Smile".

THE BEST YEARS OF OUR LIVES had become Cockney Rebel's best-selling album, but once again Harley engaged in another doomed war against the critics. He made himself a sitting target at a festival at Crystal Palace, where, dressed in white Messiah-like robes, Harley 'walked' across a water-filled moat between stage and audience. From then on Harley was a byword in the music press for bombastic arrogance.

The band continued touring and recording but the LPs TIMELESS FLIGHT and LOVE'S A PRIMA DONNA (both 1976) were only modest sellers. A cover of The Beatles' "Here Comes The Sun" returned them to the singles charts that summer, but then came the split.

Harley went to America and embarked on a slow-burning solo career. "Irresistible" narrowly missed the charts in 1985, then he had his biggest hit for ten years early in 1986, duetting with Sarah Brightman on the title song from *The Phantom Of The Opera*. (Harley was offered the lead role in the musical itself, although the part eventually went to actor Michael Crawford.)

Cockney Rebel was to make a macabre return to the news in December 1988, when bassist Paul Avron Jeffreys became one of the victims of the Lockerbie air disaster. Harley has occasionally re-formed his band and, as the titles of his solo LPs, YES YOU CAN (1995) and POETIC JUSTICE, attested, his self-confidence has remained intact.

The mid-90s saw the release of an intriguing collection of (mainly early) radio sessions for Radio 1 – 1995's LIVE AT THE BBC (reissued in 1998 as ON AIR) – and an emotive live recording made in 1989 at Brighton issued in a variety of disguises on super-cheapo labels, known generally as LIVE AND UNLEASHED!.

In 1997 Steve Harley performed some casual shows at the Edinburgh Fringe Festival consisting of music and chat about his career, accompanied only by instrumentalist **Nick Pynn**. The success of these led to Harley and Pynn playing over a hundred dates in 1998, performing under the explanatory tour-title *Stripped to the Bare Bones*. Tying in with the tour was the release of MORE THAN SOMEWHAT, THE VERY BEST OF STEVE HARLEY (1998), the mid-price reissue of most of the early catalogue, and an album entitled STRIPPED TO THE BARE BONES (1999), reissued as UNPLUGGED (2000).

It seems there's life in the old dog yet.

⦿ **Psychomodo** (1974; reissued 1998; EMI).
Now out on CD for the first time. Glam, goth and gauche, this is the Rebel at their most irresistible.

Tony Drayton

COCKNEY REBEL ■ COCTEAU TWINS

(left margin, vertical text)

COCTEAU TWINS

Formed Grangemouth, Scotland, 1982; split 1996.

Robin Guthrie (guitars/effects/tapes) and **Will Heggie** (bass) formed **Cocteau Twins** in 1982, recruiting **Elizabeth Fraser** (vocals), whom they had met in a local disco. Inspired by punk, the band recorded two demo tapes, one of which was sent to 4AD label manager Ivo Watts-Russell, and the other handed by Robin to BBC Radio 1 DJ John Peel. Nine days later, on a budget of just £900, the debut eight-track GARLANDS (1982) was completed. The music was a blend of ominous pulsating bass, stark TR808 drums, cyclical guitar and great screeching arcs of reverberating feedback, over which Liz alternated dry, brittle utterings with full-power, vocal gymnastics. GARLANDS was an immediate indie hit, and there was much speculation concerning the content of Liz's lyrics, which were mostly rendered unintelligible by her unique vocal style.

Resisting overtures from major record labels, the Cocteaus remained with 4AD and 1983 saw the release of the EP LULLABIES and the single "Peppermint Pig". Will departed but Liz and Robin returned to the studios to record the highly impro-vised second LP, HEAD OVER HEELS (1983). With this set the band began to ditch the spikiness of GARLANDS, as Guthrie developed a lush cascading guitar technique, creating a rich texture and other-worldly feel. A prime example was the finale "Musette And Drums", which gradually built layer upon layer of guitars, drums and vocals to create an enveloping soundscape and a spirit of resolution that would run through final tracks on all future LPs.

During this period the 4AD label project **THIS MORTAL COIL** made the album IT'LL END IN TEARS, featuring Liz and Robin's version of an old Tim Buckley track, "Song To The Siren". Released as a single, it remained in the indie chart for over a year.

In 1984, the Cocteaus became a trio again, as **Simon Raymonde** joined on bass, and they enjoyed their first entry into the national singles chart, with "Pearly-Dewdrops' Drops" reaching #29. The third album, TREASURE (1984), peaked at #28 and sounded like nothing anyone had yet heard. Creating a series of beautiful and disquieting emotional abstrac-tions and drawing on arcane Scots vocabulary, Fraser

used her voice primarily as another musical instru-ment. From this point on, music journalists found it impossible to describe the band's work without resorting to the word 'ethereal'.

1985 saw the production of two more albums, their first US release (the compilation THE PINK OPAQUE) and four EPs. During 1986, as Simon concentrated on This Mortal Coil's FILIGREE AND SHADOW, Liz and Robin busied themselves with the fourth Cocteau LP, the acoustic VICTORIALAND. In the previous year, the band had collaborated with American minimalist composer **Harold Budd** for a TV documentary, but as funds for the film dried up the music was released in 1986 as the non-Cocteau album THE MOON AND THE MELODIES. It was an artistic if not commercial success and was viewed as marking a move towards 'New Age' music. However, their last release for two years, the wall-of-sound LOVE'S EASY TEARS EP (1986) once again defied categorization.

The long-awaited BLUE BELL KNOLL (1988) was greeted rapturously by press and fans alike. As with HEAD OVER HEELS, there were the impressionistic layers of guitar, voice and bass, but the music was much cleaner and more energetic, Liz favouring the higher end of her vocal range for lyrics comprised totally of neologisms.

In 1989 the band opened their new London studio, September Sound; the single "Iceblink Luck" and LP HEAVEN OR LAS VEGAS were finally presented towards the end of 1990. The album was more con-ventionally structured than their previous work and easier to translate into live performance, as shown in the subsequent international tour, for which guitarists **Mitsuo Tate** and **Ben Blakeman** were added.

Splitting with 4AD, The Cocteaus signed a new deal with Fontana in 1992, but Liz was experiencing some vocal problems and it was a year before the album finally emerged. On FOUR-CALENDAR CAFE, for the first time the guitars sounded like guitars and the words sounded like words – Guthrie had come to feel that the layers and effects of the earlier records had made their music too claustrophobic, and so stripped them to a minimum. Despite some disappointment from diehard fans, the album maintained the band's record of commercial and artistic success.

The 1995 release of two EPs – the classical TWINLIGHTS and the ambient OTHERNESS (Liz's previous venture into ambience could be heard on the **Future Sound Of London**'s "Lifeforms" single, from 1994) confirmed the band's continued desire to push their music forward. However, MILK AND KISSES (1996) returned to familiar ground, prompting some journalists to suggest that stagnation had set in.

Shortly after the set's release the group announced their split. For the Cocteaus, innovation had always been essentially the by-product of fidelity to their own vision, which until the end saw them mining a rich seam of their own invention. In the years since, Guthrie has concentrated on his new **Violet Indiana** project, in collaboration with **Siobhan de Maré**. Frazer and Raymonde have similarly perused new paths, with Liz notably popping up to contribute vocals to Massive Attack's MEZZANINE album.

In terms of the Cocteau Twins' impact on British indie rock, they rank alongside New Order and The Smiths. A fact illustrated by the continued strong sales of the groups early catalogue – remastered and reissued by 4AD in 2003.

- **Treasure** (1984; 4AD; reissued 2003).
  From the crashing outset of "Ivo" to the monumental conclusion, "Donimo", this rich assortment of experimental patterns blazed a trail of musical options and remains the definitive album for many fans.

- **Victorialand** (1986; 4AD; reissued 2003).
  Limiting themselves to acoustics and vocals plus minimal percussion, the Cocteaus still manage to produce an astonishing array of textures, images and moods. A major forerunner to the ambient scene.

- **Heaven Or Las Vegas** (1990; 4AD).
  One of the group's warmer, more reflective offerings – Liz bringing a deeper, more intimate voice into pulsating electronic lullabies. Pure aural confection.

- **Milk And Kisses** (1996; Mercury).
  The band's latest album blends the rapturous energy of BLUE BELL KNOLL, the gothic thorns of TREASURE and the melancholy of VICTORIALAND with FOUR-CALENDAR CAFE's spirit of self-affirmation. Vocally, this is surely Liz Fraser's most accomplished work to date.

- **Stars And Topsoil** (2001; 4AD).
  This retrospective of the band's 4AD years is a great place to start if you're new to the angelic, crisp cloudscapes of the Cocteaus.

Link Hall & Ian Canadine

LEONARD COHEN

Born Montreal, Canada, 1934.

"All my writing has guitars behind it, even the novels."

If the biggest crime in the punk era was being a Boring Old Fart, **Leonard Cohen** was Public Enemy Number One. 'My name was basically used for comic relief in those days', Cohen recalled, but he was to have the last laugh when in 1991 post-punk and grown-up punk stars contributed cover versions of Cohen's songs on the tribute album I'M YOUR FAN.

Leonard Cohen first gained public attention in 1956 with the publication of an acclaimed collection of his verses, *Let Us Compare Mythologies*, which in turn led to his involvement in the film *Six Montreal Poets* and the release of a spoken-word album by Folkways Records. The line between poetry and music was blurred in the beatnik world of Cohen and his cohorts, and he often performed late-night recitals at the Birdland jazz club in Montreal backed by improvising musicians.

After travelling to London and to Greece, he returned to Canada to publish several more volumes of poetry, and the novels *The Favourite Game* (1963) and *Beautiful Losers* (1966), both stream-of-consciousness romps loosely based on episodes in his life. There was an existential ache in these pages, which found further expression as Cohen blossomed into a singer-songwriter.

Cohen decided to move to Nashville in 1966, planning to make a country and western album, but a stay in New York, then in the grip of the folk-rock boom, inspired him to change tactics. At the age of 34 he released his first album, simply titled SONGS OF LEONARD COHEN (1968). The music was basic, mostly Cohen's solo acoustic guitar, inlaid with mother-of-pearl lyrics distilled from twenty years' experience of writing poetry. It was a keynote album, with Cohen's sobriety providing an apposite commentary as the decade stopped swinging.

Recorded in Nashville, his second album, SONGS FROM A ROOM (1969), followed its predecessor into the British charts, a remarkable achievement for a 'difficult' artist unlikely to enjoy daytime radio support. Although SONGS FROM A ROOM was also a success in the US album charts, Cohen's following in Europe was more widespread, and in 1970 he toured the continent, where each show closed with "Please Don't Pass Me By". This deceptively simple folk refrain developed over thirteen minutes into a startlingly intense bray against complacency; some audiences found it cathartic, though a performance at the 1970 Isle of Wight Festival prompted one reviewer to dismiss 'this boring old drone'.

After the tour, Cohen returned to Nashville to record SONGS OF LOVE AND HATE (1971), another big pan-European seller, but not a great success in the US. He spent much of the next three years on lengthy tours, where he confounded his press image of a self-pitying depressive by developing a charming and witty stage persona. The LIVE SONGS album (1973) was a dignified stopgap release, but the reception for NEW SKIN FOR THE OLD CEREMONY (1974) was decidedly mixed. The flowing lyricism of previous releases had been replaced by more cynical texts and staccato phrasing, while an expanded line-up and more complex arrangements created an additional element of unconnectedness.

Leonard Cohen – a hip Frank Sinatra?

Having offered his services to the Israeli army in the 1972 war, Cohen played Jewish military bases, where he occasionally came under fire. These experiences formed the basis for much of NEW SKIN FOR THE OLD CEREMONY – military symbolism replaced biblical on "There Is A War", "A Singer Must Die" and the wonderfully enigmatic "Field Commander Cohen". The album's standout track, though, was "Chelsea Hotel", which concerned itself with a sexual encounter Cohen had experienced while staying there in the mid-60s.

As he entered his forties, Cohen spent three more years touring Europe, during which period an audaciously titled GREATEST HITS set filled the creative void. Then in 1977 came the much-troubled DEATH OF A LADIES' MAN, produced in strained circumstances by **Phil Spector**, whose trademarks were spattered across the album, burying Cohen's finely etched observations in vulgar backings, as on the mismatched "Don't Go Home With Your Hard On", which strangely enough featured **Allen Ginsberg** and **Bob Dylan**.

In subsequent years only one track from the album was ever played live, and Cohen appeared to distance himself further from the project with the publication of the subtly retitled poetry volume, *Death Of A Lady's Man* (1978). He then plunged into a strict regime of

Zen Buddhism and weight training and, with his body and soul replenished, released RECENT SONGS (1979), which was warmly received by critics as a return to form. Its clarity was exceptional, and a vastly expanded yet sympathetic array of musicians gave it a sophistication derived from jazz fusion and AOR.

Though he continued to publish prose and poetry, and made *I Am A Hotel* (1983), an award-winning movie based on five of his songs, Cohen's stock as a musician fell so low in the early 80s that, when he finally delivered a new LP, VARIOUS POSITIONS (1985), CBS America declined to release it. In contrast, in Europe he had acquired the status of a hip Frank Sinatra, attracting serious press comment and reverent audiences for concerts that mixed early classics with new material from VARIOUS POSITIONS, like the near-hit "Dance Me To The End Of Love" and the quasi-religious "Hallelujah".

Nearly twenty years after his debut album, he received long-overdue attention in the States when **Jennifer Warnes**' collection of Cohen covers, FAMOUS BLUE RAINCOAT (1987), hit the Top 10. The following year his own album, I'M YOUR MAN (1988), found him a whole new post-punk audience who, like the post-hippie listeners of twenty years earlier, began to demand more depth in their songs. The laconic Cohen reacted to this new-found commercialism with a four-year gap before his next solo release, although he did make occasional guest appearances, like on **Was (Not Was)**'s 1990 album, ARE YOU OKAY?. By the time the focused but overpolished THE FUTURE appeared in 1992, most of his back catalogue had been reissued on CD, as well as SO LONG MARIANNE, a compilation of early material. Since then there have been gap-fillers, such as COHEN LIVE: LEONARD COHEN LIVE IN CONCERT (1994) and a major-league but clumsy tribute album, TOWER OF SONG (1995). Two previously unreleased tracks were released as part of MORE BEST OF LEONARD COHEN (1997), but then, once more, there was silence.

Since 1997 Cohen has mainly resided at the Zen Centre of Mount Baldy near Los Angeles, where he is known as Jikan. Cohen promised fans a new album before the new millennium and 2001's TEN NEW SONGS belatedly fulfilled this promise. Fans weren't disappointed though – the ten songs in question, all co-written by **Sharon Robinson** (who provided the musical textures), found Cohen focused and erudite in his poetic musings. Clearly his spell of retreat had given him ample opportunity to hone his mind even further. More soon please, Len.

⊙ **Songs Of Leonard Cohen** (1968; CBS).
This great debut contains breathtaking imagery which remains unsurpassed in rock music, the words gaining extra resonance from Cohen's monochrome voice. High points include the much-covered "Suzanne" and "Sisters Of Mercy".

⊙ **Songs From A Room** (1969; CBS).
Opening with the famous "Bird On A Wire", this is a starkly uncompromising album with an undertow of religious imagery.

⊙ **Songs Of Love And Hate** (1971; CBS).
The first side captures a man's deep emotional turmoil and self-disgust, while the other side lightens up somewhat, especially on the classic song of cuckolded love, "Famous Blue Raincoat".

⊙ **I'm Your Man** (1988; CBS).
Opening with the line 'they sentenced me to twenty years of boredom', and continuing with favourites like the title track, "Tower Of Song" and "Everybody Knows", this is Cohen's most complete album in nearly twenty years, and was one of the best LPs of its year.

⊙ **Ten New Songs** (2001; CBS).
Five years in a retreat did not dull Cohen's perception. Here he throws religious imagery, love and longing, pain and passion together with almost complete abandon.

Tony Drayton

COIL

Formed London, 1983.

"...we've never held back from looking at imagery or subjects just because we were worried about what people would think. I mean our first album, Scatology, was about shit." -Peter Christopherson

Coil was conceived by **John Balance** as a solo side-project to **PSYCHIC TV** alongside his work in **Zos Kia** with **John Gosling**, but developed into a full-scale musical project in 1984, when he cemented a partnership with **Peter 'Sleazy' Christopherson**. A founder member of both Psychic TV and Throbbing Gristle, Christopherson had been experimenting with tape loops since the early days of TG, using the first crude computer samplers live on stage, and later pioneering experiments with the Fairlight. He had also been a member of graphic designers Hypgnosis, who produced covers for groups like Zeppelin and Floyd in the 70s.

The first Coil release was a seventeen-minute, one-sided 12" titled "How To Destroy Angels" (1984). Described on the cover notes as 'ritual music for the accumulation of male sexual energy', it was dedicated to the god Mars and used predominantly iron and steel instruments, such as swords and gongs. This theme was echoed on the group's debut album, SCATOLOGY (1984), on which Balance and Christopherson collaborated with **Stephen Thrower** (of Possession), **J. G. Thirwell** (aka **FOETUS**) and **GAVIN FRIDAY**. Concerned with the alchemical or spiritual process of transforming base material into gold, the album compounded a multitude of apparently banal non-musical sound sources, which were processed to create a momentum within changing rhythms. The result was an album of considerable intensity that varied from slow dramatic tracks like "At The Heart Of It All" to the ferocious celebratory bacchanalia of "Panic".

Coil's next release was a 12" single covering Soft Cell's version of "Tainted Love" (1984), with "Aqua Regis" (a restructured version of "Panic") on the B-side. Coil produced a video to accompany the single: featuring car crashes, hallucinogenic putrefaction and **Marc Almond** as the Angel of Death, it was widely banned, but the Museum of Modern Art in New York bought a copy.

Between 1984 and 1986 Coil collaborated with **Derek Jarman** on the film *The Angelic Conversation*, the soundtrack to which was reworked and remixed before release in 1994. In collaboration with **Boyd Rice**, Coil – as **Sickness Of Snakes** – released the split NIGHTMARE CULTURE (1986) album with **Current 93** (Balance is also a longtime member of C93); Coil then recruited Stephen Thrower as a full member of the band and released the album HORSE ROTORVATOR (1986) and the ANAL STAIRCASE EP (1986). HORSE ROTORVATOR combined Fairlight brass and clunky percussion with lyrics about sex, death and cannibalism. However, the album's most striking feature was Christopherson's sampling – notably on "Ostia", where a recording of grasshoppers on the Aztec pyramid at Chichen Itzá is used as the vehicle for a song about the film-maker Pasolini, who was murdered by a rent boy in Ostia.

These sets were followed by a mini-album, THE UNRELEASED THEMES FOR HELLRAISER (1987), a mix of tracks originally produced as a soundtrack for the Clive Barker film, plus a number of themes written for adverts. The *Hellraiser* tracks were sublimely atmospheric gothic instrumentals, with menacing undercurrents, while the advertising jingles featured everything from Satie-styled ambience to Thelonious Monk-influenced be-bop.

In 1987 Coil incorporated **Otto Avery** into the line-up and went through their archives to produce GOLD IS THE METAL, a remastering and remixing job that embraced a range of music wide enough to offend and inspire most people. Though self-consciously experimental, it stands out as one of their best albums in that it concentrates many of their obsessions – magic, bizarre and ambivalent sexuality, shifting states of consciousness, and alchemy.

This autobiographical summing up continued with the first volume of the UNNATURAL HISTORY retrospective (1990), after which there came a substantial change in musical direction, as Coil began a foray into the techno/rave scene with "Windowpane" and "Wrong Eye/Scope". These singles prepared the way for LOVE'S SECRET DOMAIN (1991), a large-scale multi-collaborator production that switched between psychotic dance tracks and freaked-out industrial experiments. It manifested an aural inferno, a sonic landscape where psychotropic experiences were played out against a backdrop of Blakean imagery.

A CD of outtakes was released as STOLEN AND CONTAMINATED SONGS in 1992, marking the last contributions of Thrower who left to join improvisers **Put Put** and to form **Cyclobe** with **Simon Norris** (ex-Death In June). LOVE'S SECRET DOMAIN opened the door to many fruitful collaborations and remixes, notably with Nine Inch Nails, whose Trent Reznor signed Coil to his Nothing label, though the BACKWARDS album, recorded at his New Orleans studio in 1996, remains unfinished and unreleased. A remix album of HOW TO DESTROY ANGELS even included a 'mix' of the blank B-side, "Absolute Elsewhere". 1994 brought the ecstatic club track "Protection", while as **Eskaton** they also released the dubbed-up "First Dark Ride/Nasa Arab", and in the following year, using the name **ElpH**, the reassuringly experimental ambient album WORSHIP THE GLITCH, which also saw **Drew McDowell** join the group.

The late 90s saw a further diverse set of releases under various names, including two more volumes of UNNATURAL HISTORY, the collaborative **Black Light District** project A THOUSAND LIGHTS IN A DARKENED ROOM (1996; Eskaton), a bargain reissue of WINDOWPANE/THE SNOW (1996) and the re-release of the noisy Zos Kia/Coil cassette TRANSPARENT (1997). The EQUINOX/SOLSTICE limited series (1998) of CD singles involved several improvised collaborations and brought the electric viola of **Bill Breeze** into the group.

A CD released as **Time Machines** (1998) consisted of 'four tunes to facilitate time travel'. This latter formed the basis of Coil's first live performance in April 2000 as part of fellow born-again pagan Julian Cope's Cornucopea festival at the Royal Festival Hall, with Simon Norris and Cope/Spiritualized multi-

instrumentalist **Thighpaulsandra** joining Balance and Christopherson in furry suits onstage. With ASTRAL DISASTER(1999) and MUSICK TO PLAY IN THE DARK VOLS. 1 & 2 (Chalice; 1999/2000) Thighpaulsandra brought his unique synth stylings to the group, marking a significant shift into a more spacious, intentionally 'feminine' sound, contrasting the releases of Coil's self-stated 'masculine' past. Further highly psychedelic live shows in 2000 indicated a departure into hitherto unexplored realms, echoing the angry analogue-heavy whirls of CONSTANT SHALLOWNESS LEADS TO EVIL (2000).

Coil have been at the forefront of European experimentalism and electronic music for two decades, and they remain outstanding innovators, always seeking to drag the mainstream into the darker margins of the occult.

⊙ **Horse Rotorvator** (1986; Force and Form). Coil move into the realms of the artificial, with almost every instrument synthesized. The songs are more epic in structure and conception than the somewhat cultish Scatology, and the sampling and sequencing are superb throughout.

⊙ **Love's Secret Domain** (1991; Torso). A hyperdelic odyssey that obliterates the boundary between dance and industrial, combining extremely dense sound-layering with trance-inducing rhythms to produce music that is at once catchy and subversive.

⊙ **Stolen And Contaminated Songs** (1992; Threshold House). Even Coil's outtakes are stunning; rolling jazzy instrumentals, a harshly effective mix of "Love's Secret Domain", the darkly humorous "Omlagous Garfungiloops" (with it's "Have you been exploding frogs again?" sample), and the disturbing "Who'll Fall?" making a fine album in its own right.

⊙ **Musick To Play In The Dark Vols. 1 & 2** (1999/2000; Chalice). Initially subscription-only, these releases find Coil transformed for a Lunar phase of waking dream-states and shivery synthesizer atmospheres. Balance's vocals have rarely sounded so impassioned or astute as on "Broccoli", "Tiny Golden Books" or "Paranoid Inlay".

Glenn Gossling
Thanks to Richard Fontenoy for updates

COLDPLAY

Formed London, 1998.

"Our music's much better than we are" Johnny Buckland

The radio ubiquity of **Coldplay** during 2000/1 and the borrowing of "Trouble"'s intro for a thousand mobile phones' ringtones, along with every television portrayal of regret, so overexposed the simple set of songs that was their debut, PARACHUTES, that these cuts are now weighed down by repetition and accolades. An A&R man's wet dream, Coldplay's rapid ascendancy and wide-ranging appeal conquered the pop world at the turn of the new century and paved an untroubled route to stardom for these boys who sing their pessimism so sweetly.

The four school-leavers, **Will Champion** (drums), **Guy Berryman** (bass), **Johnny Buckland**, (guitar) and **Chris Martin** (vocals and keyboards), met at University College London in 1996. Martin and Buckland's jamming sessions preceded the formal birth of the band in January '98 and despite Champion's utter lack of drumming experience, their first year saw them achieve a self-financed release of 500 copies of the SAFETY EP and a glowing NME live review. The follow-up BROTHERS AND SISTERS EP dented the Top 100 and precipitated a deal with Parlophone in mid-'99. Coldplay's public profile was on the rise. A Glastonbury appearance, Radio One live session and the winter's *NME Newcomers'* tour ensured good airplay for the "Shiver" single in 2000 and thrust "Yellow" into the UK chart at #4 just before the summer's release of PARACHUTES entered the UK album chart at #1.

The frenzy of two UK headline tours and a world tour alongside the *Mercury Music Prize* nomination and *Best Band* and *Best Album* Brit Awards consolidated Coldplay's position as men of the moment. It seemed nobody could get enough of the romantic, hands-in-pockets shy boys with their doomed lyrics and surf harmonies. At a time when it seemed there could be no more mileage in unrequited love songs, a record chock-full of them had appeared, with each track sounding like a potential single, and four of them succeeding.

In the summer of 2002 the hotly anticipated follow-up album surfaced in the form of A RUSH OF BLOOD TO THE HEAD, which was preceded by the single "In My Place". Lyrically, the set sounded as heartfelt as its predecessor, and compositionally the group had chosen to pull out all the stops, mixing styles and generally managing to produce a record that lived up to the high expectations.

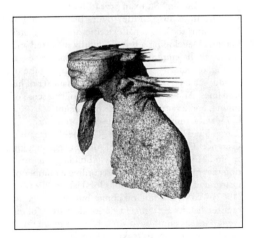

As the band's centrepiece, it is Chris Martin who embodies Coldplay's heartbreak persona. With a voice quaking with emotion and his high-cheek-boned good looks, it's easy to attribute the first-person songs to his lived experience, though songwriting credits are split four ways. Martin's emo-tional rawness is akin to Thom Yorke's, but more seductive to the mainstream. More original than the oft-likened Travis, and more likeable and believable than David Gray, Coldplay have reached a position to be envied: cool enough for the music papers, contemporary enough for a young audience, MOR enough for older followers.

⊙ Parachutes (2000; Parlophone).
A tender, shimmering classic that made the band into a household name.

⊙ A Rush Of Blood To The Head (2002; Parlophone).
Like its predecessor, this set is a real grower; songs such as "God Put A Smile Upon Your Face" and "Warning Sign" stand out.

Annebella Pollen

LLOYD COLE AND THE COMMOTIONS

Formed Glasgow, Scotland, 1983; disbanded 1989; Cole recording solo since 1990.

With their college degrees, black polo necks and pale complexions, **Lloyd Cole** and company created the template for a certain kind of 'intellectual' pop group. By-products of the band's success included such pretentious outfits as Frazier Chorus, Deacon Blue, Hue And Cry, and the many faces of Stephen Duffy. The plus points were the appearance of likeably alert acts such as Microdisney, The Verve and Gene.

Lloyd Cole And The Commotions came into being in the winter of 1983. After trying to get bands together in his native Derbyshire, Lloyd Cole (vocals/guitar) moved up to Glasgow. There he fell in with **Neil Clark** (guitar), **Blair Cowan** (keyboards), **Lawrence Donegan** (bass) and **Stephen Irvine** (drums), otherwise known as The Commotions. Within months of finding one another the band and Cole sealed a deal with Chrysalis Records.

Student support bolstered by extensive airplay on national radio helped take the band's first single, "Perfect Skin", into the Top 30, as Cole's stylish croon and Clark's jangly guitar led to comparisons with both Lou Reed and The Byrds. "Perfect Skin" and the band's debut album, RATTLESNAKES (1984), served notice that somewhere in Scotland there was a bunch of blokes who knew how to play, fronted by a guy with a voice Robbie Robertson would kill for, and a rare knack with intelligent lyrics.

When it came to songwriting, Cole trod the line between the intellectual and the pretentious, and on more than one occasion he wrote couplets that even Hue And Cry might have thought twice about: 'She looks like Eve Marie Saint, in On the Waterfront/She reads Simone de Beauvoir, in her American circumstance...' ("Rattlesnakes"). For every ponderous cultural reference, there was a cracking chorus or a genuinely witty piece of word-play, but the namechecks to French novelists and obscure screen actresses were a barrier to mainstream success. To many people, The Commotions came across as a band you needed a degree to enjoy.

As soon as the band began to fade out the pretension, they hit the big time. 1985 brought two Top 20 hits, "Lost Weekend" and "Brand New Friend", and a gold-selling album, EASY PIECES (1985). In the midst of this new-found success, Cole also became a rather unlikely teen heart-throb. No longer the angry young man, he now came across as an attractive and affable fellow, quite willing to answer important questions about acne and ice cream.

After the success of EASY PIECES, the band rather lost their way. The follow-up, MAINSTREAM (1988), was by and large a disappointing affair, the only standout tracks being "My Bag", which inexplicably failed to make the Top 40, and "Sean Penn Blues", the appeal of which owed an awful lot to its title. At the end of 1989, the band looked at their situation and decided to split up.

While the rest of the group went back to session work and day jobs, Cole gathered up Cowan and left for New York. Anxious to take his music in new directions, Cole recruited Lou Reed affiliates **Fred Maher** and **Robert Quince** before starting work on his debut solo album. The end result, LLOYD COLE (1990), met with mixed reviews and poor sales. Follow-ups DON'T GET WEIRD ON ME, BABE (1991) and BAD VIBES (1993) were greeted with similar indifference. Indeed, it was not until his fourth album, LOVE STORY (1995), that Cole was to receive anything approaching a positive critical response (the single "Like Lovers Do" was as charming as anything released that year). Looking back at these albums, you can see that Cole was really rather hard done by, as the first two solo sets in particular had things going for them.

Produced by **Stephen Street**, 2001's THE NEGATIVES broke the drought with Cole sounding comfortable fronting a new band despite his years of self-reliance. Commotion-esque, wry, and inward-looking – there's a lot in that title – the album found Cole self-deprecating as ever, taking task with himself over failed attempts at becoming more hip on "Too Much E" and "Tried To Rock".

PLASTIC WOOD (2001) found our hero trying out ambient works à la Eno and Aphex Twin and making a surprisingly accomplished effort for a man one would associate with a more wood'n'strings aesthetic.

For those wondering what Lloyd got up to during the 'dry' period between LOVE STORY and THE NEGATIVES (other than hanging out and being all bohemian), ETC (2001), a collection of outtakes and demos, explains a lot. Vacillating between urbane Cohen-esque folk and throwaway introspection, a handful of worthy tunes feature alongside an unfortunate version of Dylan's "You're A Big Girl Now", but there's an overall sense that it took Cole a few wrong turns to get to where he's at.

Lloyd Cole and The Commotions

⊙ **Rattlesnakes** (1984; Chrysalis).
The band's debut – profound or pretentious pop, depending on your mood.

⊙ **Easy Pieces** (1985; Chrysalis).
The Commotions' most successful release, featuring lots of delightful pop songs about people called Jesus, James and Jane.

Lloyd Cole

⊙ **Don't Get Weird On Me, Babe** (1991; Chrysalis).
Lloyd's second solo album shows that, while Cole without The Commotions isn't quite as impressive a package, the band's leading man still has it in him to write intelligent, articulate songs. And there is always that croon.

Richard Luck

ALBERT COLLINS

Born Leona, Texas, 1932;
died Las Vegas, Nevada, 1993.

"There's one cat I'm still trying to get across to people. His name is Albert Collins. He's a very smooth guitarist who plays around Texas. He's good – real good. One of the best guitarists in the world." Jimi Hendrix

Known variously as 'The Master Of The Telecaster', 'The Houston Twister' and 'The Razor Blade', **Albert Collins** had a tough haul to the top, despite his blistering technique, despite the homage of the likes of Hendrix, and despite growing up in the company of 'Lightnin'' Sam Hopkins (his cousin), Johnny 'Guitar' Watson, Eddie 'Cleanhead' Vinson and 'The Texas Twister' Johnny Copeland.

The clean, bright tone of the Fender Telecaster was well known through the finger-picking James Burton, rhythmic Stax-man Steve Cropper, and the strident Big Jim Sullivan (creator of the famous walking-note intro to the "James Bond Theme"). Yet Collins took its tonal extremes to even greater heights. Developing a brutal, slightly distorted and icy attack, he employed an unusual minor-key open tuning, enhanced into a higher register by the use of a capo, which served to augment the character of his lead lines. And to all this he added a brilliant sense of timing, and a remarkable sense of restraint.

Heavily influenced by the elder generation of Texan blues guitar players like 'T-Bone' Walker and Clarence 'Gatemouth' Brown, Albert began gigging around Houston in 1952, slowly building a reputation that eventually led to his recording a number of instrumental singles for various local labels. "Frosty" (1962) sold over a million copies but, as it failed to register in any recognized national chart, Collins went largely unnoticed and had to maintain a number of day jobs to make ends meet.

It was not until 1968 that he tasted real success, when he was sought out by Bob Hite of **CANNED HEAT**, the California-based blues-rock band, and was persuaded to move to Los Angeles. An immediate hit with a new young white audience, Collins was signed to Canned Heat's label, Imperial, but the three albums he recorded for the company – LOVE CAN BE FOUND ANYWHERE (EVEN IN A GUITAR) (1969), TRASH TALKIN' (1969) and THE COMPLEAT ALBERT COLLINS (1970) – curiously concentrated on contemporary soul/funk. His subsequent move to The Eagles' producer **Bill Szymczyk**'s Tumbleweed label gave rise to the superior 1972 release THERE'S GOT TO BE A CHANGE, but Collins was consigned to the club circuit once more when the company abruptly folded.

Finally, somebody had the good sense to secure Albert on a long-term contract, and that somebody was **Bruce Iglauer** of Chicago-based blues guardians Alligator Records. At last, Albert was able to pour out his 25 years of hard-currency experience in a totally conducive atmosphere. Backed by a carefully chosen support band, he issued a total of five studio and two live albums in fairly quick succession, all to remarkable acclaim. By 1985, he had appeared jamming with George Thorogood before 1.8 billion people at the Live Aid show from Philadelphia and had earned his first *Grammy award* for the album SHOWDOWN (1985).

Parting company with Alligator shortly afterwards, Collins took a break from recording, but his career went from strength to strength thanks to TV appearances, movie work and relentless touring. He appeared at Carnegie Hall in 1987 with **Lonnie Mack** and fellow Telecaster wizard **Roy Buchanan**, and accompanied **Eric Clapton** in his Albert Hall concerts in London. He signed to Virgin subsidiary Point Blank in 1991, releasing ICEMAN, which earned another Grammy nomination.

However, by the time COLLINS MIX was released early in 1993, Albert's health was deteriorating. He battled stoically against lung cancer, but ultimately succumbed quickly in November 1993. It was a shocking end for a master showman whose success had been a long time coming. Although the state of Texas continues to produce great blues guitar players in the shape of people like Jimmie Vaughan and Smokin' Joe Kubek, Albert Collins's shoes are impossible to fill.

⊙ **Showdown** (1985; Alligator).
A rollicking blues bonanza recorded with his Texan contemporary Johnny Copeland and his great protégé, Robert Cray. Albert's contributions to tracks like "Black Cat Bone" and the Muddy Waters standard "She's Into Something" became minor masterpieces of modern blues. A fascinating study in differing guitar styles – Cray's smooth, rounded tone and Copeland's breakneck, free-form approach are balanced by Collins's carefully phrased intensity.

⊙ **Deluxe Edition** (1998; Alligator).
The ultimate collection by the modern master of blues guitar.

Phil Lynch

EDWYN COLLINS

Born Edinburgh, Scotland, 1959.

J ust when the British public believed that former **ORANGE JUICE** frontman **Edwyn Collins** was

safely consigned to the box marked 'cult enigma', he became an indomitable presence in the charts of 1995, firstly with the worldwide hit, "A Girl Like You", and then with the attendant album, GORGEOUS GEORGE.

Both single and album had initially struggled upon UK release in the autumn of 1994, but the single had achieved healthy radio airplay, impressing a Belgian radio DJ who was holidaying in London at the time. Taking a copy back to his homeland, he began to play the record incessantly on his radio show. Huge public response led to its release throughout Europe, where it became a massive hit. Reissued in June 1995, "A Girl Like You" became one of the UK's biggest summer hits, and Collins was back in the charts for the first time since Orange Juice's 1983 hit, "Rip It Up".

Curiously, that song's insistent refrain of 'rip it up and start again' proved to be prophetic for Collins. Dropped by Polydor in 1985, his early attempts at securing a solo recording contract were dogged by his reputation as a stubborn and single-minded operator. Nevertheless, two sell-out London shows in the summer of 1986 induced Creation Records' Alan McGee to sign him up to his Elevation label.

The failure of Collins's Elevation singles "Don't Shilly Shally" and "My Beloved Girl" reflected the fortunes of the label, which folded in 1987. To compound matters, ill-feeling between Collins and McGee conspired to leave Collins once again without a record deal, as McGee brought Elevation's other aspirants – Primal Scream and The Weather Prophets – back into the Creation fold.

Eventually signing with Demon, Collins's fortunes recovered when, for a nominal fee, he was offered a recording session in Germany by a management team who turned out to be loyal Orange Juice fans. The fruit of this good fortune was the majestic HOPE AND DESPAIR (1989), which featured the tutored playing of latter-day Orange Juice producer and bassist **Dennis Bovell**, and Aztec Camera's **Roddy Frame** and **Dave Ruffy**. Collins's dark years in the wilderness were reflected in the album's sardonic portraits of broken relationships and crises of confidence, while the musical backing encompassed an impressive array of rootsy styles from twanging country to rattling rockabilly. HOPE AND DESPAIR went on to sell a respectable 30,000 copies.

HELLBENT ON COMPROMISE (1990) lacked its predecessor's tight, dense production, and its atmospherics too often gave way to an unsatisfactory sparseness. Still, the sensitive ballad "Graciously" ranked as one of Collins's best, and the use of sampled sitar brightened "Now That It's Love" and "Everything And More".

Having established himself as Demon's biggest-selling artist with his first album, Collins failed to boost his profile with his second, and this undoubtedly contributed to the absence of any new product until GORGEOUS GEORGE. Not that he was inactive in the intervening four years – on the contrary, he busily furnished his London studio with vintage recording equipment, while making live appearances and producing the likes of The Frank And Walters, A House, The Rockingbirds and occasional collaborator **Paul Quinn**.

Happily describing such acts as his guinea pigs, Collins's covert aim was to acquaint himself fully with production techniques to ensure the most vivid transference of his musical visions to tape. Recorded for under £10,000, the end result was GORGEOUS GEORGE, a captivating coupling of spacey, seductive melodies and a biting lyrical cynicism that marked the tenacious return of an errant songwriting genius.

Solo success had been a long time coming and few artists can claim to be have pursued it quite as determinedly as Collins. The multimillion-selling "A Girl Like You" was a tough act to follow, but, having secured the belated respect of the rock literati, Collins's future looked assured.

He capitalized on his new-found popularity with the disappointing I'M NOT FOLLOWING YOU (1997), a wide-ranging, though disjointed album. Borrowing freely (in some cases, almost note-perfect) from everyone from The Velvet Underground to The Eagles, he seemed to be looking for a voice of his own by rummaging through as many different styles as he could find. 1998 saw Collins seated behind the mixing desk producing Vic Godard's THE LONG TERM SIDE EFFECTS album, while 1999 found him, along with various members of his band, starring in a six-part TV comedy show – *West Heath Yard*; the show also starred Collins's pal **Bernard Butler**, one time Suede guitarist. Bernard and Edwyn came together again in 2001 for the release of a single, "Message For Jojo". It was a fine pop moment that raised many hopes about future releases, but 2002's DOCTOR SYNTAX was another disappointment. Like I'M NOT FOLLOWING YOU, it was an album that never quite seemed to know where it wanted to lay its hat.

⊙ **Hope And Despair** (1989; Demon).
Collins at his most accessible, helped by excellent arrangements and an impressive supporting cast.

⊙ **Gorgeous George** (1994; Setanta).
Guns N' Roses, grunge and summer festivals all feel the lash of Collins's caustic tongue on an album which initially left critics baffled. Sombre, rambling, scornful – and irresistible.

Ian Lowey

THE COLOURFIELD

Formed Coventry, England, 1983; disbanded 1988.

At the time of **The Colourfield**'s formation, **Terry Hall** (vocals) was one of the most successful frontmen in British pop. With **THE SPECIALS** he had introduced a new generation to the sound of ska, while with the **FUN BOY THREE** he had been an almost permanent chart fixture, and had set Bananarama on the road to becoming the most successful British female vocal group ever. With such impressive credentials, it was all the more surprising that his third band, The Colourfield, was such a commercial disappointment.

Comprising Hall, **Toby Lyons** (guitar) and **Karl Shale** (bass), The Colourfield's debut single, the doleful "The Colourfield", released in January 1984, missed the British Top 40, becoming Hall's first non-chart single in five years. A follow-up single that summer, "Take", fared equally badly and it was not until the following January that they finally made a significant chart impact with "Thinking Of You". With a nod to Burt Bacharach and Andy Williams, Hall and songwriting partner Lyons stated their intentions to the press that they wanted to write standards and not 'pop songs'.

Their debut album, VIRGINS AND PHILISTINES (1985), was superb: acoustic guitars and gentle string arrangements billowed around like butterflies, and Hall's notoriously flat vocal delivery was sweetened by tasteful harmonies. It was a less ponderous and uniquely English take on Scott Walker, whose brooding majesty was much in evidence, but in the age of 'big rock' – U2, Simple Minds and Big Country – the album was doomed to failure. A disastrous tour to promote it, with Hall seeming to be unduly keen to confront his audiences, only compounded the misery. Augmented by former **THE TEARDROP EXPLODES** drummer **Gary Dwyer**, they went off to America, after interest from college radio.

Back in the UK, a non-album single, the uncharacteristically jovial "Things Could Be Beautiful" (1986), failed to set the charts alight, and the group began to fall apart. Trimmed down to a duo of Hall and Lyons, they released a cover of Sly Stone's "Running Away" in early 1987, followed by the DECEPTION (1987) LP, which met with generally complimentary reviews, although the arrangements and production were rather cold and sterile. Hall reluctantly recorded the album in New York at the behest of his label, and has since confessed that he found walking in the park a far more attractive proposition than recording an album he had no interest in promoting.

DECEPTION nose-dived into the bargain bin, and The Colourfield vanished. In 1989, Terry recorded a promising single, "Missing", followed by a truly dreadful keyboard-cluttered album, ULTRA-MODERN NURSERY RHYMES (1990). Hall then took an extended sabbatical, emerging briefly to collaborate with Dave Stewart in Vegas, before enlisting the help of Ian Broudie of **THE LIGHTNING SEEDS** to write songs for his first solo album, HOME (1994). More recently, he has guested with Blur and with Tricky (on his NEARLY GOD project). A second solo album, LAUGH, was released in 1997.

⊙ **Virgins And Philistines** (1985; Chrysalis).
A painfully truthful study of everyday ennui, wrapped up in pseudo-easy-listening arrangements. Hopelessly out of time on its release, it has aged surprisingly well.

James Wirth

COME

Formed Boston, Massachusetts, 1990;
disbanded 1999.

Formed from the rubble of various experimental rock bands, **Come** – originally **Thalia Zedek** and **Chris Brokaw** (both guitar/vocals), **Sean O'Brien** (bass) and **Arthur Johnson** (drums) – specialized in frighteningly intense variations on the standard rock themes of love and despair.

The buzz surrounding Come's 1991 debut, the "Fast Piss Blues" single, was extreme, drawing comparisons to the bruised blues of The Rolling Stones – the flip side was a cover of The Stones' "I Got The Blues". On their first album, ELEVEN: ELEVEN (1992), Zedek's guttural voice made her lyrics sound like they were being dragged out of her larynx, while the guitars wrangled like two wolves fighting over a kill. In comparision, DON'T ASK, DON'T TELL (1994) found the band numbed: the music was muddier, its pace slower, its pall heavier.

Acknowledging the stagnation, Johnson and O'Brien decided to leave in mid-1995. Before their departure, however, the quartet served as backing band on **Steve Wynn**'s (ex-Dream Syndicate) solo album, MELTING IN THE DARK. Come's third album, NEAR LIFE EXPERIENCE (1996), which featured bassist **Tara Jane O'Neil** and drummer **Kevin Coutlas** (both formerly of **Rodan**), came from a totally revitalized band. Tighter, more focused songwriting, better overall musicianship and a readiness to trim the flab from the longer pieces resulted in a powerful album, ready to step outside the neo-blues framework towards a gentler, more reflective sound.

The new-found delight in melody and volume settings lower than eleven continued on their fourth full-length outing, GENTLY, DOWN THE STREAM (1998), with the introspection overwhelmed by rage and thrashing guitarwork often enough for maximum listener comfort. But soon after the band was no more. Since Come's disintegration, Zedek has released two solo collections: BEEN HERE AND GONE (2001) and YOU'RE A BIG GIRL NOW (2002).

⊙ **Eleven: Eleven** (1992; Matador).
If you are going to buy one Come album, this is it. The music and moods teeter precariously, erupting into violent explosions with little warning.

Julie Taraska

THE COMMUNARDS

Formed London, 1985; disbanded 1988.

After enjoying considerable success with **Bronski Beat**, vocalist **Jimmy Somerville** decided to split from the band in 1985 to form **The Communards** with keyboardist **Richard Coles**, who had trained at the Royal School of Church Music and had occasionally played for Bronski Beat on tour.

The Communards' first release, "You Are My World" (1985), was a joyously uplifting number whose swirling strings and piano marked a break from the synthesized sound of Bronski Beat. Their debut also hinted at a slight transition from dance-orientated music, but the next single, "Disenchanted" (1986), bore all the hallmarks of a classic Bronski track: a driving synth line coupled with the urgency of Somerville's lyrics.

Both singles just scraped into the Top 30. The third single, on the other hand, was an instant success. "Don't Leave Me This Way" (1986), a cover of the Thelma Houston and Harold Melvin number, was at #1 for four weeks and proved to be the second-biggest-selling single of 1986. The song featured **Sarah Jane Morris** as co-vocalist, and she was to become a regular face on tour with the band, duetting with Somerville as well as providing backing vocals. With a dedication to Ken Livingstone's Greater London Council, "Don't Leave Me This Way" revealed a consolidation of the band's political stance with that of the Labour Party – indeed the band confirmed their support for Labour in January 1986, when they participated in the Red Wedge tour with fellow lefties Billy Bragg and Paul Weller's Style Council. Somerville had clearly not mellowed in his political convictions and, while the new Bronski Beat line-up watered down their radicalism in favour of pure pop, Somerville and Coles continued to promote left-wing politics.

The eponymous debut album was a diverse collection, ranging from the Spanish bravado of "La Dola Rosa" and the Eastern promise of "So Cold The Night" to the dance-club sounds of "Disenchanted" and "Heavens Above". The tone of the album was split between bitter indictment of Thatcher's Britain (found on "Breadline Britain" and the moving ballad "Reprise") and the abandon of "Don't Slip Away" and "You Are My World". Somerville's experience of being persecuted for his sexuality was explored with dignity on "Forbidden Love", where he articulated a sense of alienation at not being able to express his homosexuality in public. A second album, RED, followed a year later, reaching #4 in the album charts, heralded by the Top 30 single, "Tomorrow". Returning to the successful formula of "Don't Leave Me This Way", The Communards then released a cover of the Gloria Gaynor classic, "Never Can Say Goodbye", which gave them a Top 5 hit in November 1987. RED featured a number of inspired piano-led tracks, notably "C Minor" and the poignant "For A Friend", written in honour of Mark Aston, a friend who died of AIDS. The upbeat "There's More To Love Than Boy Meets Girl", with its innocent melody, proved to be The Communards' swansong, as Somerville made the decision to go solo. Somerville on his own has continued to notch up chart success, and has also been a perennial champion of gay rights and AIDS awareness campaigns.

⊙ **Communards** (1986; London).
Continuing where he left off with Bronski Beat, Somerville's soaring falsetto explores a range of emotions on The Communards' debut, with strings and a horn section added to Coles' keyboards.

Every bit as accomplished as its predecessor, Red contains "Tomorrow", "Never Can Say Goodbye", "There's More To Love..." and "For A Friend", perhaps Somerville's most impassioned moment.

Mark Hooper

THE COMSAT ANGELS

Formed Sheffield, England, 1978; disbanded 1996.

Sheffield contemporaries of the synth-pop bands Cabaret Voltaire and The Human League, **The Comsat Angels** – formed by schoolmates **Stephen Fellows** (vocals/guitar) and **Mik Glaisher** (drums) with **Andy Peake** (keyboards) and **Kevin Bacon** (bass) – similarly based their sound on electronics. On the strength of a self-financed first recording, THE RED PLANET EP (1979), they signed to Polydor, before releasing their debut album, WAITING FOR A MIRACLE (1980). Combining a melodic pop sensibility and an air of brooding menace, it contained the original recording of their best-known song, "Independence Day". Their more accomplished follow-up LP, SLEEP NO MORE (1981), continued in similar if less poppy vein, eschewing conventional arrangements; on one of its stand-out tracks, "Darkest Parade"; the bass guitar, rather than underpinning the sound, provided the melodic hook.

Quality control was maintained for the third album, FICTION (1982), which included another Comsats favourite, "Ju Ju Money". But, critical acclaim notwithstanding, a lack of commercial success resulted in the group being dropped by Polydor – the first of several label changes. Throughout the mid-80s, they were cajoled into making ever more supposedly commercial LPs – LAND (1983), 7-DAY WEEKEND (1985) and CHASING SHADOWS (1987) – the last even featuring **Robert Palmer** on guest vocals. The band's problems came to a head when, after threats of legal action by the American Com Sat Corporation, they were forced to trade as the **CS Angels** in the US. Under pressure from their (then) record company, Island, the band changed its name to **Dream Command**, and released the album FIRE ON THE MOON (1990).

By now, though, Kevin Bacon had decided to quit the band. After a sabbatical, Stephen Fellows resurrected the original name, and tried to recapture the spirit and inventiveness of their earlier output. Bacon was temporarily re-recruited for MY MIND'S EYE (1992), issued on the independent Thunderbird label. A return to the moodier flavour of old, with a punchier, more guitar-orientated sound, it signified a serious return to form. The group subsequently toured with new members **Terry Todd** (bass) and second guitarist **Simon Anderson**, and released a new album, THE GLAMOUR, in 1995. Despondent at the album's poor sales however, the Comsats disbanded early in 1996.

Stephen Fellows has subsequently enjoyed considerable success in his role of manager of **Gomez**, also finding time to contribute some guitar parts to their first album.

● **Time Considered As A Helix Of Semi-Precious Stones** (1992; RPM).
A collection of tracks recorded for the BBC between 1979 and 1984, and easily the most worthwhile collection of Comsats material.

Keith Prewer

CONCRETE BLONDE

Formed Los Angeles, California, 1985; split 1993; re-formed 1997.

Johnette Napolitano, the driving force behind Concrete Blonde, delivered songs with loaded lyrics that come from the shadows and a jaded heart.

In 1985, Johnette Napolitano (bass, vocals), **James Mankey** (guitars) and **Harry Rushakoff** (drums) formed a band, originally calling themselves **Dream 6**, but when the group signed to I.R.S. they became Concrete Blonde, a name inspired by Michael Stipe. CONCRETE BLONDE (1986), their debut, established a foothold in the music market, with the single "Still In Hollywood" doing particularly well. FREE (1989), a self-produced effort, with singles such as "God Is A Bullet" and "Scene Of A Perfect Crime", added further dark moods to their palette.

However, it was the band's third album, BLOODLETTING (1990), inspired by Anne Rice's vampire novels, that gained the band international exposure, with powerful songs such as "The Beast" (a song about falling in love with the wrong person, the devil), "Tomorrow Wendy", (penned by **Andy Prieboy** of Wall of Voodoo, about a woman slowly dying of AIDS), and the single "Joey" (a song of a man in love with alcohol), which went to #1 in the US. **Paul Thompson** replaced Harry Rushakoff on drums, and Mankey played both bass and guitars.

Harry Rushakoff was reinstalled on drums and percussion for WALKING IN LONDON (1992), which continued the band's journey into the spectral world, but also displayed hints that they were falling apart. MEXICAN MOON (1993), the band's last studio effort, was a mess of overproduction and chaos, despite strong vocal tracks such as "Jenny I Read", "Mexican Moon" and "Heal It Up". As the year closed, Concrete Blonde split, subsequently releasing their epitaph STILL IN HOLLYWOOD (1994), a compilation of leftover studio B-sides and live versions of studio singles.

Johnette signed to Warner Brothers without a band, and two years later resurfaced as **Pretty & Twisted** – with **Marc Borland** on guitars and **Danny Montgomery** on drums – releasing an eponymous album in 1996.

Concrete Blonde re-formed the following year to record several tracks, predominantly in Spanish, and teamed up with the Latino band **Los Illegals**. With the album CONCRETE BLONDE Y LOS ILLEGALS

(1997), the band returned to the music underground. The fortunes of both Concrete Blonde and Pretty & Twisted, however, remain to be seen.

⊙ **Bloodletting** (1990; I.R.S.)
The album contains "Tomorrow Wendy", "Caroline", and "The Sky Is A Poisonous Garden". A must-have for goths.

⊙ **Recollection: The Best Of** (1996; I.R.S.)
This compilation album contains all the singles released between 1986 and 1993; it also has a live bonus track of a Janis Joplin cover, "Mercedes Benz". A good start for beginners.

David Morgan

RY COODER

Born Los Angeles, 1947.

"He sends shivers down my spine – comes out with this old tune your parents taught you, and it's like going back in time." Pop Staples

Arguably the finest blues guitarist of his generation, **Ry Cooder** attracts a following that cuts across most known boundaries. Earning his early blues dues with Taj Mahal and his rock credentials with Captain Beefheart's Magic Band, Cooder has, over the past couple of decades, made superlative rock, jazz and movie soundtrack albums, and crossed effortlessly into world music fusion with artists as diverse as Malian bluesman Ali Farka Toure, Okinawan group Nenes, and the Indian guitarist V. M. Bhatt. Indeed, it's in these ethnic fusions – and the soundtrack instrumentals – that Cooder seems most at ease, as a guitarist essentially. The songs and the vocals often seem a secondary concern.

Largely self-taught, Ryland Peter Cooder began playing guitar at the age of 3. Influenced by recordings of blues legend Josh White, he spent his teens at the centre of the Los Angeles blues scene, the Ash Grove, where he regularly took the stage from the age of 16. Encounters at the Grove led to musical experimentation. Conversations with the likes of Gary Davies and Jackie DeShannon made him take up both the banjo and the mandolin, and within a year he was playing both proficiently. It took him even less time to master bottleneck blues guitar, the style which would later become his trademark.

In 1964 **TAJ MAHAL** came to the Grove in search of new ideas and rehearsed extensively with Cooder, before the pair formed **The Rising Sons**, and began recording an album. With the record only half-finished, Taj Mahal disappeared, but, short-lived though their professional relationship was, Mahal's influence upon Cooder is still very apparent in his playing.

After years of live performances, Cooder finally entered the recording studio in 1968 to work on **CAPTAIN BEEFHEART**'s debut album. He was hired as a session musician, but his contribution to the project extended to his arranging a couple of tracks. On Beefheart's recommendation, Cooder went on to record successfully with Paul Revere And The Raiders, before travelling to England in 1969 for his first real brush with fame.

Once in England, Cooder set about writing the soundtrack for an upcoming motion picture, *Candy*. While working on this project, he was approached with an eye to recording with **THE ROLLING STONES**. By all accounts, Cooder thoroughly enjoyed the time he spent working on LET IT BLEED, but his experiences recording the CANDY soundtrack were to have the more profound effect on his career. Meantime, such was his reputation as a session player

Ry Cooder (note cunning extension of guitar strap as headband)

that he sealed a deal with Warner/Reprise, and released RY COODER (1970), a blues- and folk-inflected rock album, covering songs by the likes of Woody Guthrie.

Cooder's second album, INTO THE PURPLE VALLEY (1972), with the slide to the fore, was a big enough commercial success to allow him the luxury of experimentation. Later albums would see Ry try his hand at classical guitar on BOOMER'S STORY (1973), gospel music on PARADISE AND LUNCH (1974), and Dixieland jazz on JAZZ (1978), while a profound interest in Hawaiian guitar manifested itself on his fifth Warner release, CHICKEN SKIN MUSIC (1975).

These records just about covered their costs back in America, but Cooder enjoyed more substantial success in Europe. A big hit in Germany and Holland, Ry also found an audience in Britain, where his 1979 album, BOP TILL YOU DROP, made the Top 40.

However, it was in soundtrack music that Cooder made his mark. After contributing to the score of Nic Roeg's Borgesian thriller *Performance*, he went on to record numerous scores for Hollywood productions, notably with film director Walter Hill, with whom he has collaborated on Westerns and action movies from *The Long Riders* (1980) to *Geronimo* (1994). Other film work has included the soundtrack for the Jack Nicholson Western *Goin' South* and the much-praised score for Wim Wenders' haunting movie *Paris, Texas*.

Outside of his soundtrack work, Cooder drifted into a number of collaborations on the world music scene, notably on TALKING TIMBUKTU (1994), a collaboration with **Ali Farka Toure**, which stands as a benchmark for world fusions. It was a commercial success – huge by world music standards – but Cooder had also collaborated in a much lower-profile way with Hawaiian, Indian and Japanese musicians, and was soon to come up trumps in Cuba.

As a solo artist, Cooder made few albums after 1980's BORDERLINE – the noteworthy THE SLIDE AREA (1982) and GET RHYTHM (1987) both revisited old rock'n'roll terrain. He continued to tour sporadically, attracting equally devoted audiences in Europe and the US. In 1995 he teamed up for a brief tour with **DAVID LINDLEY**, one of the few guitarists who can match his technical ability and passion for a variety of instruments.

But it was Cooder's excursion into the studio that resulted in the BUENA VISTA SOCIAL CLUB (1997), which once again pulled him back into the public's attention. This multi-artist collaborative project dragging in a bunch of Cuban musical luminaries such as the venerable **Compay Segundo** (89 years of age at the time of recording), **Ibrahim Ferrer** (just 77) and young whippersnapper **Ruben Gonzalez** (a mere stripling, at 77 years of age).

He continues to produce and guest on albums for other artists; in 1999 he produced Jon Hassell's FASCINOMA, and contributed guitar to Terry Evans's WALK THAT WALK in 2000. More Cuban productions are also in the pipeline.

⊙ **Jazz** (1978; Warner/Reprise).
A brave, experimental album, proving that Ry was more than a mere jazz pretender.

⊙ **Why Don't You Try Me Tonight** (1986; Warner/Reprise).
A good compilation of Cooder's own songs, drawing on the first half-dozen albums.

⊙ **Music By Ry Cooder** (1995; Warner/Reprise).
This double CD features tracks from eleven soundtracks. It is a tribute to him that his brand of bottleneck blues has become a standard feature of road movies – just check out Thelma And Louise.

Richard Luck

ALICE COOPER

Born Detroit, Michigan, 1948.

"Just because I cut the heads off dolls, they say I must hate babies. But it's not true. I just hate dolls."

Preacher's son Vincent Furnier, aka **Alice Cooper**, the 'godfather of shock rock' was raised in Phoenix, where he formed The Earwigs in the mid-60s. On moving to Los Angeles in 1966, Cooper, **Glen Buxton** (lead guitar), **Michael Bruce** (rhythm guitar/keyboards), **Dennis Dunaway** (bass) and **Neal Smith** (drums) became The Spiders, intent on 'driving a stake through the heart of the love generation'. Swiftly dubbed 'the worst band in LA', they changed the band name to Alice Cooper in early 1969, and were signed to Frank Zappa's Straight label – Zappa figured that any band who could clear a club in seconds was worth endorsing.

Zappa's enthusiasm was not matched by record buyers, who sensibly steered clear of the acid-rock dirges on PRETTIES FOR YOU (1969) and EASY ACTION (1970). But in a remarkable reversal of fortune the band signed to Warner Brothers, hooked up with hot producer **Bob Ezrin** and promptly hit with the angsty "Eighteen" from LOVE IT TO DEATH (1971). Its success, however, was merely a dry run for the world-conquering KILLER (1972), SCHOOL'S OUT (1972), BILLION DOLLAR BABIES (1973) and MUSCLE OF LOVE (1974). While their albums were top sellers, it was the group's live shows that became really notorious: their gory and outrageous theatrics featured mock hangings, slaughtered chickens and bloody toy babies.

Cooper fired the rest of the band in mid-1974 and, while they formed **Billion Dollar Babies**, he began a variable solo career. Cooper was backed by Lou Reed's band and narrator **Vincent Price** on the classic WELCOME TO MY NIGHTMARE (1975), and for a while his career was sustained by a clutch of uncharacteristically tender hits, most notably "Only Women Bleed" (1976). His downfall came at the hands of disco and drink, with appearances on TV shows like *Celebrity Squares* and *The Muppets* adding to his indignity rather than his sales.

Determined to regain lost ground, Cooper produced a stream of releases in the late 70s and early 80s, but when admirably contemporary-sounding albums like ZIPPER CATCHES SKIN (1982) sank like a stone, he began touting a project called 'The Nightmare Returns'. Ironically, its first achievement was to trigger Aerosmith's comeback: alarmed by Alice's enlisting of **Joe Perry**, singer Steven Tyler poached the guitarist back for his own return-to-glory bid.

Emerging in 1986 on the MCA label, Alice came up with a couple of patchy albums, CONSTRICTOR (1986) and RAISE YOUR FIST AND YELL (1987), but his trump cards were the accompanying tours: an unashamed retread of his vintage cocktail of horror-style theatrics and shouty-chorused rock'n'roll. One show in April 1988 almost turned to grim reality when a stunt went wrong, and Cooper nearly hanged himself with a noose prop. The shows were a hit with the 80s heavy metal generation brought up on the similarly ghoulish Ozzy Osbourne and Motley Crue, and his next two albums, for Epic, TRASH (1989) and 1991's HEY STOOPID, were both hits. The former contained the smash hit single "Poison", his biggest chart success since "School's Out".

A period of self-imposed commercial exile followed, although Cooper made a few movie cameo appearances, most memorably in the 1992 comedy *Wayne's World*. Returning to the marketplace with THE LAST TEMPTATION (1994), Alice surprisingly chose not to tour the album – supposedly because the violent shows of yore were now uncomfortably close to reality. Declining ticket sales for metal in general no doubt played their part, too – Alice may be sick, but he ain't stupid.

The death of Glen Buxton (October 1997) from pneumonia brought a significant chapter in the band's history to a definitive close. The co-author of classic tracks such as "School's Out", "I'm Eighteen" and "Elected" will be missed by fans and musical associates alike. Alice said: 'I grew up with Glen, started the band with him, and he was one of my best friends. I think I laughed more with him than anyone else. He was an under-rated and influential guitarist, a genuine rock'n'roll rebel. Wherever he is now, I'm sure that there's a guitar, a cigarette, and a switchblade nearby.'

With the millennium fast approaching, what Alice did next flummoxed many, including longtime fans. First there was the extensive trawl through the recording crypt to unearth rarities for THE LIFE AND CRIMES OF ALICE COOPER (1999), a massive four-CD box set. Then followed BRUTAL PLANET (2000) and DRAGONTOWN (2001), two studio albums that showed Alice could not only swim with the sharks, but was the Great White that gave the nu-generation of metallers their nightmares in the first place. The records were boneshakingly heavy and lyrically horrific in places, taking in subjects such as wars in the Balkans and high-school shootings, with Alice proclaiming proudly in interviews that they made

WELCOME TO MY NIGHTMARE seem pretty and pastel in comparison. When last heard from, Alice was, bizarrely, concentrating on opening and developing a chain of restaurants.

⊙ **Trash** (1989; Epic).
Writer-for-hire Desmond Child (Bon Jovi, Kiss, Aerosmith) is hauled aboard for a ride on the ghost train. The result: garbage, but highly amusing garbage.

⊙ **The Beast Of Alice Cooper** (1989; WEA).
In which the theatrical trimmings take second place to the musical muscle. Includes "School's Out", although the definitive classic is "No More Mr Nice Guy".

Bruno MacDonald

THE COOPER TEMPLE CLAUSE

Formed Wokingham, England, 1998.

"We don't slag off other bands – we just make better music." Dan Fisher

It was in the sleepy Berkshire satellite-towns of Reading and Wokingham that Cooper Temple Clause emerged. According to guitarist **Dan Fisher**, Friday night was generally 'fight night', and having long hair, he was fair game for Wokingham's harder cases. Fisher recalls the time when he and multi-instrumental fellow-Clauser **Tom Bellamy** had to defend themselves with fast-food – anything – to combat the town's equally bored thugs. But while all this meant further monotonous aggro for some, for Dan and Tom – and other school band survivors **Ben Gautrey** (vocals), **Didz Hammond** (bass/guitar), **Kieron Mahon** (keyboards) and **Jon Harper** (drums) – it was the catalyst to play, and convert brooding revenge into lyric and song.

A lock-up adjacent to a pig farm became nerve centre for Cooper Temple Clause's creativity. Band members talked enthusiastically about influences as diverse as Simon & Garfunkel, Sonic Youth, Warp Records and Mogwai – but early fans and live attendants summed up the Clause sound succinctly as being that of 'a slightly-less-pissed-off Primal Scream'.

In August 2000, after just a handful of gigs, Cooper Temple Clause (the name allegedly pulled from dialogue in a Michael J Fox movie) signed a two-album deal with BMG. One month later, a 'homecoming' gig at Reading's Fez Club drew curious faces from across the industry: a couple of short UK tours then attracted a few more. By the end of March 2001, Cooper Temple Clause had something to give the radio stations – in the shape of limited edition EP, HARDWARE. It sold out within the week of its release.

The first single proper was the powerful "Panzer Attack", the headline track from the WARFARE EP, but it was September's "Let's Kill Music" that proved the breakthrough. Despite national airplay – and an

We're the Cooper Temple Clause – deal with it!

play by the rules of the music business, and more recently by an obsession with religious, arcane and ecological themes. At times, it seems that many people have cherished the *idea* of Julian Cope more than the music he has actually created.

To begin with, his music was very fine indeed. After the acrimonious split of **THE TEARDROP EXPLODES** in 1983, frontman Cope lost no time in salvaging the best of their unreleased material. Adding some fine new songs, he released WORLD SHUT YOUR MOUTH (1984), an exciting, charming pop album, with Cope given ultra-tight support by lead guitarist **Steve Lovell** and **Gary Dwyer** (ex-Teardrops) on drums. There was even a pastoral colouring, reminiscent of Kevin Ayers, thanks to **Kate St John**'s oboe. Unfortunately, its two singles – "Sunshine Playroom" (with a promo video directed by David Bailey) and "Greatness And Perfection Of Love" – both flopped.

Cope decamped to his base in the Midlands to lay low and (reputedly) take a lot of LSD. His second LP, FRIED (1984), featured Cope on the cover with a turtle shell on his back, looking decidedly unhinged; as for the music, it had a less polished and more frenetic sound, with several melodies being spiked with lysergic edges, as on "Reynard The Fox" and "The Bloody Assizes". Other tracks bore a dreamy suggestiveness, but its standout track, the warm, barmy love song "Sunspots", failed to chart. FRIED sold abysmally on release, and Cope's contract with Mercury was terminated.

With increasingly sloppy live performances, the future looked decidedly bleak for Julian Cope. Luckily, his next incarnation would be his most successful – he got his hair cut, bought a new leather jacket, and compressed his obsessions into tight three-minute power-pop sound bites on SAINT JULIAN (1987), his first LP for Island Records. If Cope did surrender charm for glory, it was soul-selling of the most discreet type, for even the most cold-hearted purist could not deny the vibrant insistency of singles such as "Trampoline" or "World Shut Your Mouth". Cope's live shows were a vast improvement – tight and disciplined, with the excellent **Donald Ross Skinner** on lead guitar. Yet Cope's 1988 release, the underwhelming MY NATION UNDERGROUND, lacked its predecessor's coherent punch. Apart from the pretty single "Charlotte Anne", most of the album suffered from a lack of identity, and represented his swansong as a commercial pop star.

Now keen to explore stranger terrain, he independently released two albums aimed at his fan-club members. DROOLIAN (1990) was a generally lazy, meandering indulgence, and, although the more forceful SKELLINGTON (1990) did include the marvellously titled "Out Of My Mind On Dope And Speed"; both albums were bogged down by a heavily stoned incoherence.

Thankfully, his next official album for Island, the double set PEGGY SUICIDE (1991), was his finest since

unlikely slot for the promo on MTV – the Clause narrowly missed the UK Top Forty.

This fledgling band's popularity was borne out by most end-of-year polls, and was comfortably augmented by the strong 2002 debut album SEE THIS THROUGH AND LEAVE with its brace of Top 30 singles: "Film Maker"/"Been Training Dogs" and "Who Needs Enemies?" These were songs that shifted the core of Clause's sound away from their dark early psychedelia into a wider pop arena.

Cooper Temple Clause may talk of 'pushing sonic boundaries', but this is a band that should embrace its position as clear leaders in the field of young commercial rock. They leave rivals for the position – such as Pontypridd's Lostprophets – some distance behind them.

⦿ **See This Through And Leave** (2002; Morning). Almost a mini-'Greatest Hits' package, the strong debut contains all the singles and a number of gig favourites.

Jeremy Simmonds

JULIAN COPE

Born Deri, Wales, 1957.

Though cast as both a maverick genius and a drug-addled loser, **Julian Cope** is probably too shrewd for the latter judgement, while his recorded output has been too uneven for the former. His career has been characterized by a general refusal to

his debut and proved to be a successful seller in the UK. The targets included chemical dumping, car pollution and the poll tax, while the music was rooted in rock'n'roll. "Hanging Out And Hung Up On The Line" was Stooges-era dementia, while "Safe Surfer" was a 70s-style guitar freakout nailed to a 90s paranoia – AIDS. Hidden in this audacious mixture was the minor but infectious hit single, "Beautiful Love".

If PEGGY SUICIDE balanced political convictions with the need to entertain an audience, its follow-up, 1992's JEHOVAKILL, forged ahead uncompromisingly with Cope's more esoteric spiritual concerns. Musically diverse, it introduced techno rhythms and trance-rock reminiscent of early-70s Can or Faust. Reviews opined that if Cope had an editor half as good as his record collection, then his output would be stunning. Certainly this was a frustrating album, bizarrely sequenced to unsettle and provoke, and it duly flopped.

Ignoring the poor sales, Cope toured Britain, before independently issuing yet another album – RITE (1993), a seventy-minute 'urban meditation groove' drawing on influences as varied as Sly And The Family Stone and German progressive head music. It was the last straw for Island Records, who fired him.

With no commercial backing, Cope returned to touring, and published his memoirs of his days in The Teardrops, entitled *Head-On*. It wasn't too long before the Echo label signed Cope, who then unleashed the wayward AUTOGEDDON (1994), an unholy marriage of spacey guitar dynamics and discordant ranting. As intended, it was a commercial disaster.

Meanwhile, the Arch Druid was once again honing his excessive musical talents, this time with a little more discipline, returning to the pop arena and the singles chart. The Top 20 hit "Try, Try, Try" echoed the tighter, more controlled edge of SAINT JULIAN, and it was followed by his best solo album for years – 20 MOTHERS (1995), which was toured extensively to hugely positive reviews. Cope himself described this as 'pagan rock'n'roll through sci-fi pop

to bubblegum trance music', a fair summary of its sprawling genius.

Ensconced in the countryside of Wiltshire, Cope remained a well-read, eminently quotable New Age Renaissance man. He wrote the admirable *Krautrocksampler,* a personal history of German 'Kosmische' rock, and his output remains varied and prolific. *The Modern Antiquarian* (1998; Thorsons) is one of the most comprehensive guides to megalithic Britain – the result of lengthy research of over 400 sites – and also contains a series of essays on the Landscape, the Goddess and the interpretation of monuments (plus a chapter on etymosophy, which Julian describes as a cross between etymology and philosophy).

On the recording front, Cope produced his most commercial solo effort to date late in 1996 with INTERPRETER. Named after a Roky Erickson song, the album crystallized the pop promise of 20 MOTHERS. The heart of the record was Mott-styled glam-pop, undercut by Cope's trademark sardonic wit and self-parody ("I've Got My TV And My Pills", "Cheap New Age Fix"): a refreshing attempt to debunk some of the myths surrounding his eccentric persona. In short, this was a very together record, and would have sold a lot better if Cope had released the standout potential single, "S.p.a.c.e.r.o.c.k With Me", first, instead of comparatively weaker numbers.

Island belatedly woke up to their erstwhile prodigy's hipness with a rather obsolete compilation of 80s material (B-sides and cover versions) entitled THE FOLLOWERS OF SAINT JULIAN. Cope proved himself to have cool taste in his choice of covers ("Levitation", "Non Alignment Pact"), but perhaps was a little unwise in choosing to record his performances of them. Some things are best kept in your record collection.

Cope has also released a mail-order four-track album of Urban Meditational Grooves (Cope's words) entitled RITE 2, in which he allows his Krautrock fixations to float in and out of a suitably trancey backdrop of Mellotron and free-form freakout. For the converted, both FRIED and WORLD SHUT YOUR MOUTH have been remastered and re-released with extra tracks. SKELLINGTON and SKELLINGTON 2 have also been rereleased as THE SKELLINGTON CHRONICLES.

1998 saw the release of the second **Queen Elizabeth** album QE2: ELIZABETH VAGINA – an experimental collaboration between Julian and his (and Spiritualized's) keyboard player **Thighpaulsandra**. Julian is currently working on a new album – CITIZEN CANED – and the follow-up to *The Modern Antiquarian*, called *Let Me Talk To The Driver*.

With his lecture tours, odd festivals and history books Cope is rapidly becoming a forebear of some theoretical millennial renaissance. His activities may seem disparate but there is a strange, intuitive synergy running through them.

Other recent musical projects have included ODIN (a 73-minute meditation on Silbury & Waden hill), **Brain Donor** – whose stoned Stooges garage groove made its album debut with LOVE PEACE & FUCK

(2001) – and **L.A.M.F.** The latter released AMBIENT METAL in 2001, on Cope's own Head Heritage label; the set was a freeform rock-sound splurge with one epic track called "The Death Of The Motherculture At Mona Mam Gymru The Wailing Shamanic Fury Of The Hoeurs And Druids And The Coming Of The Romansno". Cope's expanded musical vision came together nicely on CORNUCOPEA (2000), a CD compilation of highlights of his two-day festival at the South Bank.

While he remains endearingly prolific, no other artist could be as self-indulgent as Cope and be allowed to live.

⊙ **World Shut Your Mouth** (1984; Mercury).
A schizophrenic but lovably eccentric set, which also manages to be melodically focused at the same time.

⊙ **Peggy Suicide** (1991; Island).
An ambitious album that sounds great because of Cope's manic indulgences, rather than despite them.

⊙ **20 Mothers** (1995; Island).
St Julian returns to top pop form, venting his psychedelic spleen.

⊙ **Floored Genius – The Best Of Julian Cope And The Teardrop Explodes, 1981–1991** (1992/1995; Island).
Cope's aptly titled anthology trawls through the favourites. An ideal introduction, if lacking in the bizarre wayward indulgences that gave the original albums their unique appeal. Two further volumes have been issued to complete your set.

Nig Hodgkins

THE CORAL

Formed Wirral Peninsula, England, 1996.

The Coral are the band responsible for bringing the sea shanty back into popular music. More than just The Las-a-likes that certain quarters of the press have tagged them to be, The Coral are a band who would seemingly rather play the role of sonic pirates plundering each and every corner of music's history: their treasure chest overflows with everything from Beefheart-styled strangeness to elegant mariachi horns.

The Coral were – frighteningly – in their midteens when they first dropped anchor in the mid-90s. Their accents and dress sense suggested the next Cast, but their music was a whole new ball game. The band was conceived by two brothers, **James** (guitars/vocals) and **Ian Skelly** (drums), who jammed with keen, if not necessarily accomplished, mates **Nick Power** (keyboards), guitarists **Lee Southall** and **Bill Ryder-Jones** (also on trumpet duty) and **Paul Duffy** (bass and sax). Before long an unlikely residence as The Cavern's house band gave the story a strangely familiar twist.

Once a week, The Coral would pitch up at Liverpool's legendary venue and play three separate sets of crowd-pleasers – covering The Beatles (obviously) and Sam Cooke, and they also threw in an unlikely take on Bob Marley's "Get Up Stand Up". Performing original material at this stage was 'out'. One attendee who saw real promise in their reading of the classics was former Shack drummer Alan Wills, who liked the sextet's self-penned material and signed them to his Deltasonic label, recording the SHADOWS FALL EP (July 2001) and the rather less sparkling OLDEST PATH (December 2001). (Hardcore collectors would later find these two EPs on an ultra-rare CD snappily entitled EIGHT SONGS FROM THE WIRRAL TO LEND YOUR EARS TO.)

The next move was to prove a winning one: for The Coral's third EP on Deltasonic, April 2002's

The Coral still haven't upgraded their tour bus

SKELETON KEY, manager Wills employed peripatetic Liverpool face Ian Broudie to master the tracks, which included the impressive "Dressed Like A Cow". With something of a buzz now surrounding the band, the professional courtship of Broudie was established with his production of The Coral's much vaunted debut long-player.

Ahead of the release of the album, the first real hit emerged in the shape of the thumping "Goodbye", the group's most commercial offering to date (underlined by its UK #21 chart position). THE CORAL stormed into the UK Top Five on a tsunami of hype at the beginning of August 2002. The record was a revelation, particularly in light of the protagonists' ages: within its complexities there lurked echoes of Leadbelly, Motown, British psychedelia, but most of all, a definite flavour of the ocean! Opening cut "Spanish Main" swayed like a centuries-old seafaring standard. The sprightly "Dreaming Of You" was pulled as the next single in, and despite some unkind comparisons with Showaddywaddy, entered the chart at #13. Accolades came faster than anticipated, with a *Mercury Prize* nomination almost beating the album into the public domain and a brace of *BRIT* recommendations maintaining it in the consciousness at the start of 2003.

James Skelly's strongest composition yet, the Yardbirds-esque "Don't Think You're the First", took the band into the Top Ten for the first time in March 2003 – giving a taste of what to expect from The Coral's second collection. With Sony picking up the band for US distribution, one was left wondering just what an American audience might make of a bunch of straggly youths from the Wirral singing of the ocean.

⊙ **The Coral** (2002; Deltasonic).
From 1964 to 2002 in a leap of imagination that belies their few years, The Coral arrive with an album that exhales with an opium-fuelled sense of purpose. Just when you think you can hear jazz funk or Roy Orbison, they go all Dylan Thomas on you. Destined to be a classic.

Jeremy Simmonds

CORNERSHOP

Formed Leicester, 1991.

Fans of "Brimful Of Asha" who were inclined to investigate its authors further rapidly came to the conclusion that there were two versions of **Cornershop**. The early, determinedly lo-fi indie band added playful wit to inspired amateurism and came up with a bunch of enjoyable EPs and a debut album of Asian-English vaudeville. By the time they achieved chart success, however, leader **Tjinder Singh** (vocals/guitar) had immersed their sound much deeper in contemporary Asian reference points. Their first stab at the celebrity market came after they rebuked indie kingpin Morrissey over the content of some of his post-Smiths lyrics. Their anti-racist agenda was enshrined in a choice of name that was pointed but self-mocking, like much of their songbook.

The initial incarnation of the band featured Tjinder Singh, fellow guitarist/vocalist **Ben Ayers**, Tjinder's brother **Avtar Singh** (bass), **Anthony Saffrey** (sitar) and 'token honky' **David Chambers** (drums). The line-up was drawn from the ashes of Leicester underachievers General Havoc, whose sole release, the FAST JASPAL EP, was issued on Chapati Heat Records.

Cornershop's own debut EP, IN THE DAYS OF FORD CORTINA, announced a spirited realism and Tjinder's eye for detail at the margins of contemporary English culture. It also came on 'curry'-coloured vinyl, and tracks such as "Waterlogged", with elegant flute and sitar, provided a blueprint for the group's later sound. Signed to Rough Trade spin-off Wiiija Records, at this stage Cornershop were considered fellow travellers with London's emergent 'riot grrrl' scene. There was certainly little indication of their future chart status.

"Breaking Every Rule Language English", from the follow-up LOCK, STOCK AND DOUBLE-BARREL EP, demonstrated an ability to laugh at themselves that some of the riot grrrl bands did not share, by mocking Asian assimilation of the English language. HOLD ON IT HURTS (1994) provided an all-new selection of delights – the award for best song title going to "Born Disco, Died Heavy Metal". The album elicited great critical interest, especially in America, where world music champion David Byrne signed them to his Luaka Bop! label.

American interest in the band was cemented by the release of WOMAN'S GOTTA HAVE IT (1995), as they toured the continent three times, including dates on the Lollapalooza showcase. Chambers had now left, leaving the core duo of Tjinder and Ayers, though it was the former who had always been Cornershop's principal thinker, songwriter and spokesman. They also toured Europe as support to Beck – a dream billing for fans of rock nonconformity.

The first single to be taken from the group's breakthrough third album, WHEN I WAS BORN FOR THE SEVENTH TIME (1997), was "Butter The Soul". But it was "Brimful Of Asha" that won the day. Over an insistent, simple backing track (redolent of Jonathan Richman's "Roadrunner"), Tjinder paid tribute to Bollywood star Asha Bhosle. Originally released in August 1997, it was the Norman Cook remix that propelled it up the charts early in 1998, turning it into a huge dance-floor and mainstream pop hit. It followed the similarly unlikely success of Chumbawamba's "Tubthumping" the year before.

Strange days indeed, with two of Britain's most avowedly didactic groups giving the boy bands a run for their money at the paying end of the charts. While the latter slid into obscurity, Cornershop were merely resting, looking on while the Britpop world they helped to liven up a little fizzled into nothingness.

Some were wrong-footed by Ayres and Singh's next venture, **Clinton**; listening to the album DISCO AND THE HALFWAY TO DISCONTENT (2000) was either enlightening or utterly mystifying, depending on your point of view. Fully indulging in the kind of rinky-dink electronica that had begun to surface on WHEN I WAS BORN…, this was a cheeky, irreverent and, thus, entirely necessary step, an antidote to the poe-faced posturings that defined indie-dom.

A Cornershop album proper finally made its way onto the shelves in 2002. Widely acclaimed, HANDCREAM FOR A GENERATION framed Singh's cultural commentary within a context so ridiculously bright and breezy that it was guaranteed to bring a smile to your face. "Lessons Learned From Rocky I To Rocky III" should be required reading on any school syllabus; **Noel Gallagher** pops up playing dodgy sitar on the warped jam of "Spectral Morning" and veteran soul singer **Otis Clay** MCs on the intro "Heavy Soup".

⊙ **Hold On It Hurts** (1994; Wiiija).
The title of the lead-off track, "Jason Donovan/Tessa Sanderson", tells you a great deal about this collection, but not everything. There's enough grist in its shambolic indie sound to deserve repeat listens, and intelligence is at work throughout the lyrics. The Asian touches add another dimension – "Tella Mera Pyar" announces Singh's infatuation with Indian film, while "Where D'U Get Your Information" reveals its author to be as angry as he is amused.

⊙ **When I Was Born For The Seventh Time** (1997; Wiiija).
A completely different beast from its predecessors, with more melody, tonality and improved production. More importantly, Singh was now writing properly weighted songs: Cornershop's musicality was not always as considered as their lyrics. And there are some sublime arrangements of guitar, sitar and synthesizer, peppered with club rhythms. The two singles "Brimful Of Asha" and "Sleep On The Left Side" are obvious standouts, but check out the Punjabi version of "Norwegian Wood" for variety, or Allen Ginsberg's contribution to "The Light Appears Boy".

⊙ **Handcream For A Generation** (2002; Wiiija).
Armed with a bag of T-Rex albums, charity shop instruments, some ropey dance beats and a couple of guest stars, Cornershop here craft a most gloriously whacky pop culture meltdown. Smart and unpredictable – just the ticket.

Alex Ogg

COSMIC ROUGH RIDERS

Formed Glasgow, Scotland, 1998.

"It's amazing. Everything that's great about music is on this album." Norman Blake, Teenage Fanclub, on *Enjoy The Melodic Sunshine*

The career of **Cosmic Rough Riders** could prove to be one of the brightest and briefest sparks in recent British music history. As they hang suspended following the departure of charismatic founder member, vocalist and chief songwriter **Daniel Wylie**, the future seems uncertain for a band that once promised so much.

Wylie's prodigious talent came into its own in 1998, when he found the required empathetic minds in **Stephen Fleming** (guitars/vocals), **Gary Cuthbert** (acoustic guitar/vocals), **James Clifford**

(bass/vocals) and **Mark Brown** (drums/vocals). They duly put together a collection of smart pop songs called DELIVERANCE, released on the band's own Raft label in the summer of 1999. Early Wylie tunes such as "Baby, You're So Free" and "Glastonbury Revisited" became standards as the band began to pick up a local following. Cosmic Rough Riders (the convoluted name an amalgam of posters for Lee Cooper 'Rough Rider' jeans and Glasgow's 'Cosmic Wheels' club) were off and running.

A second Raft album, PANORAMA, was released in March 2000. Here the songs were further honed, with debts to fellow Scots, Teenage Fanclub and more obviously, R.E.M., whose writing Wylie had always cited as a major influence. ("You've Got Me", for example, could have been an outtake from MURMUR.) The record sold out in no time.

Most impressed by the Cosmic Rough Riders was Alan McGee, who, on seeing the band at Glasgow's Nice'n'Sleazy venue, secured them as one of the first names for his new Poptones label. Standout cuts from the two earlier albums were re-recorded for a debut album proper at the end of 2000. Their first single, "The Loser" emerged in October, with ENJOY THE MELODIC SUNSHINE released the following month. The set steadily gained critical momentum until it had secured a place on almost every magazine year-end poll for 2001. The record's classic, chiming guitars provoked superlatives across the board, evoking shades of The Beach Boys, Flying Burrito Brothers, Gin Blossoms, Blue Nile and, here and there, Buffalo Springfield.

Wylie's consummate pop and impressive lyric-writing had earned him the respect that he'd craved. But he had seemingly outgrown the band: in 2002, with several songs penned for a new Cosmic Rough Riders album, Wylie suddenly decided to pursue a solo career.

To date the fruits of his labour – and those of the surviving Riders – have yet to emerge, although an enjoyable compilation of B-sides, PURE ESCAPISM, was issued by the band in September 2002.

Enjoy The Melodic Sunshine (2000; Poptones). Neo-folk without peer. From the uplifting 71-second opener "Brothers Gather Round" onward, this set offers a sonic tableau of the purer, simpler things in life: regret, infidelity, and minor customs offences.

Jeremy Simmonds

ELVIS COSTELLO

Born London, August 25, 1955.

"There's one thing I wanna know. What's so funny about peace, love and understanding? ... "

Born Declan MacManus, **Elvis Costello** was raised in Liverpool within a fairly traditional musical environment. His father, Ross MacManus, was a singer with the Joe Loss Orchestra, and Declan's first proper band was a country combo called Flip City. Despite this, the angry young Costello of 1977 was very much of his time. He arrived on the music scene armed with a thrift-shop suit, a little black book of his enemies' weak spots, and a deal with Stiff Records – whose co-owner, Jake Riviera, had signed him on the strength of some demos played on Charlie Gillett's Radio London show. And although the main influences on his first album, the grainily produced MY AIM IS TRUE (1977), were more the Flip City favourites Gram Parsons and The Band than the Pistols or The Clash, the vitriolic songwriting was firmly rooted in the punk ethos. This was displayed most notably on songs like "I'm Not Angry" and the much-celebrated "Alison", both about obnoxious ex-lovers, as well as the first single, "Less Than Zero", which focused on English fascism, and climbed to #14 in the UK charts.

MY AIM IS TRUE and the subsequent hit single "Watching The Detectives" – a tale of domestic violence sung to a reggae beat – would become classic examples of Costello's clever marrying of snarly punk with other, less fashionable genres. With the release of THIS YEAR'S MODEL (1978) and ARMED FORCES (1979), he managed a more seamless synthesis of these forms. In tow by this time were his backing group, **The Attractions**, a tight combination of **Steve Nieve** (keyboards), **Pete Thomas** (drums) and **Bruce Thomas** (bass), who between them wowed audiences in America enough in 1978 to get their frontman's debut album into the US Top 40. Unveiled on the 1977 Stiff tour, which also featured Nick Lowe (the producer of Elvis's first five albums), The Attractions provided a retro guitar- and organ-based sound that was the perfect board for Costello's Dylan-esque punning in songs like "No Action" ('Everytime I phone you, I just want to put you down') and "Lipstick Vogue" ('Love is just a tumour, you've got to cut it out'). THIS YEAR'S MODEL, and in particular its two hit singles "Pump It Up" and "(I Don't Want To Go To)

Chelsea", represent Costello's spiky, intelligent pop at its best, while ARMED FORCES, though a less consistent record, became his all-time best seller, spawning the 400,000-selling monster hit "Oliver's Army", as well as lesser successes like "Accidents Will Happen".

Eager to move on musically, Costello scrapped several days of recording for his next album, and started again using a variety of Motown, Stax and Atlantic sounds, the result of which was the twenty-track mini-epic GET HAPPY!!. On this, for songs like "Opportunity", "Possession" and "New Amsterdam" he borrowed as boldly from The Supremes and Al Green as he had earlier done from 60s pop and R&B, and provided a brilliant and popular inauguration for Jake Riviera's new label F-Beat. It also paved the way for further experiments in Americana the following year, when Costello released an album of Nashville-produced C&W standards called ALMOST BLUE (1981) – "Sweet Dreams" and "Good Year For The Roses" were standout tracks. Despite featuring a warning sticker that its content 'may produce radical reaction in narrow-minded people', ALMOST BLUE sold twice as many copies as the superior TRUST, a curious hotchpotch, ranging from the funky "Strict Time" to the jazzily percussive "New Lace Sleeves" and the German cabaret-styled "Shot With His Own Gun".

Costello's response to accusations that he'd taken a step backwards with the dry, stripped-down sound of TRUST was to revert to his pop roots with the 1960s soundalike IMPERIAL BEDROOM (1982). Produced by former Beatles engineer and studio boffin **Geoff Emerick**, IMPERIAL BEDROOM was a broad-canvased and emotionally lyrical creation, but, while it was a hit with the pundits, the public stayed away in droves. Costello turned his magpie mentality to a more commercial pop sound on his next two albums, PUNCH THE CLOCK (1983) and GOODBYE CRUEL WORLD (1984), which were plastered with the radio-friendly pop sheen that producers **Clive Langer** and **Alan Winstanley** had made their trademark with bands like Madness. The souled-up Mersey beat of "Everyday I Write The Book" – from PUNCH THE CLOCK – was Elvis's biggest US hit, and with the deceptively sweetly rendered Falklands War lament "Shipbuilding" (from the same album, and originally recorded by Robert Wyatt), it figures amongst his best-loved compositions. GOODBYE CRUEL WORLD was less successful, its bland renditions of obviously heartfelt songs about his recent marriage break-up ("Home Truth", "The Only Flame In Town") meeting almost universal indifference.

Deciding it was time to make a break, Costello temporarily dumped The Attractions, and briefly tried his hand at acting, produced records for Philip Chevron, The Pogues and The Specials, and duetted with the likes of John Hiatt, Ricky Skaggs and Nick Lowe; he also found time to get married again, to the Pogues' bassist Cait O'Riordan. Most significantly, though, he released a single – "The People's Limousine" – with **T-Bone Burnett** (under the name **The Coward Brothers**). Burnett had supported Costello during the latter's US solo acoustic tour just before the release of GOODBYE..., and was later promoted to playing rock'n'roll covers on stage as second 'Coward Brother' – sharing as he did Elvis's interest in American roots music.

It was no big surprise, then, that Costello should ask Burnett to produce his next album, the rootsy KING OF AMERICA (1986). The Attractions only performed one track on this, "Suit Of Lights", and the line-up was instead a combination of Elvis Presley's old Vegas band, and session musicians like **Jim Keltner**, **James Burton** and **Jerry Scheff**, who provided just the right kind of understated roots-rock accompaniments for fragile and occasionally po-faced tunes like "Indoor Fireworks" and "Sleep Of The Just". KING OF

AMERICA was touted as a much-needed return to form, and Elvis's second album the same year, the Hammond organ-fest BLOOD AND CHOCOLATE, maintained the quality. Recorded with The Attractions and Nick Lowe, its powerful, rumbling songs ("Uncomplicated", "I Want You") suggested that Elvis could switch back on his talent whenever he pleased.

For many, Costello's second major downturn came when he signed with the corporate monster, Warner Brothers, at the end of 1987, ending a decade of indie releases on Jake Riviera labels. He'd already behaved strangely earlier that year, touring BLOOD AND CHOCOLATE with such unlikely acts as The Bangles and Tom Petty, appearing as a butler in Alex Cox's awful modern Western *Straight To Hell*, and, most unfashionably, collaborating with **Paul McCartney** on the ex-Beatle's FLOWERS IN THE DIRT album. By the time Elvis's first Warners release appeared, no one really knew what to expect. What they got was SPIKE (1989), a sprawling, densely textured mixture of Irish folk ("Any King's Shilling"), New Orleans gospel ("Deep Dark Truthful Mirror"), pure pop (US hit McCartney/MacManus composition "Veronica") and angry politicizing ("Tramp The Dirt Down"). It wasn't well received, and many felt that Costello should get back to his four-piece combo sound.

Featuring three keyboardists, two drummers and four guitarists often playing simultaneously, MIGHTY LIKE A ROSE (1991) further alienated listeners, who were unable to spot some great songs ("Couldn't Call It Unexpected No. 4", for example). By the time of THE JULIET LETTERS (1993), a sequence of songs recorded by Costello and **The Brodsky Quartet**, many had washed their hands of Elvis altogether. However, the next album, BRUTAL YOUTH (1994), recorded with all The Attractions back in tow and **Nick Lowe** as 'second bassist', was a development of the short, sharp songs Costello had speedily penned for chanteuse Wendy James's album NOW AIN'T THE TIME FOR YOUR TEARS. Borrowing heavily from the in-your-face dynamics of BLOOD AND CHOCOLATE, with added raucous guitar, a generally sunnier feel and great dollops of self-referentiality ("Just About Glad" was pure MY AIM IS TRUE), BRUTAL YOUTH seemed a sure bet for success in the nostalgia-obsessed 1990s. It was certainly Costello's most calculated effort to date and, for all his claims that he'd fallen back in with The Attractions in a very uncontrived way, it was perhaps an admission that he couldn't go on indulging his own interests for ever.

Costello then took The Attractions with him on a 'greatest hits' tour, prior to getting involved in a number of more offbeat projects. These included a solo support to Bob Dylan at Brixton Academy, and the release of a couple of not-great LPs: KOJAK VARIETY (1995), a covers album of some favourite Costello tracks recorded in 1991, and DEEP DEAD BLUE (1995), a set of old Costello songs played by himself and jazz guitarist **Bill Frisell**. If these

Elvis Costello: he's not angry

records prove anything, it's that one of Costello's favourite pastimes was the reinterpretation of songs, both his own and those of other writers. No surprise, then, that Elvis's next project with The Attractions was ALL THIS USELESS BEAUTY (1996), an album mainly covering songs he had written for other performers.

Next up came a five-CD box set collaboration with **Steve Nieve** entitled COSTELLO & NIEVE (1996) which disappeared off the shelves almost as soon as it was released. It wasn't until 1998 that Costello truly started to shift units again, thanks to the heavily crooned **Burt Bacharach** collaboration PAINTED FROM MEMORY. Though a little too cheesy to devour in one sitting, the set sold well and even earned Costello a Grammy for "I Still Have That Other Girl".

As has come to be expected, recent years have seen Costello with fingers in many pies, cropping up in concert and on disc with the likes of the **Fairfield Four** and classical singer **Anne Sofie von Otter**. But despite all these diversions, longtime fans were rewarded in 2002 with a fine pop collection in the form of WHEN I WAS CRUEL, where Costello recaptured the sound and twisted wit of his earlier guise, whilst still clinging to the eclectic habits he'd more recently picked up.

- **This Year's Model** (1978; Demon).
  The album that introduced The Attractions, and memorably consolidated Elvis's blend of crafty pop and sardonic observation on songs like "Lipstick Vogue" and "No Action".

- **Armed Forces** (1979; Demon).
  Costello's third album sees him refining the hard-edged sensibilities of his early work into a distinctive political pop sound, masterfully matched by Nick Lowe's at-his-fingertips production.

- **Imperial Bedroom** (1982; Demon).
  Less of an out-and-out pop record than Costello's early material, with a more sombre and more orchestrated sound. No single track stands out, except perhaps "Man Out of Time", but the overall feel of the album is that of a songwriter at his creative peak.

- **King Of America** (1986; Demon).
  This mainly acoustic set, recorded with T-Bone Burnett, is the most successful of Costello's 'experimental' albums. A controlled, focused sound, and some cracking good songs.

- **Blood And Chocolate** (1986; Demon).
  Lacking the focus of KING OF AMERICA, but a collection of great songs nonetheless, not least the relentless "I Want You" – one of Elvis's finest moments.

- **Brutal Youth** (1994; Warners).
  The phrase 'return to form' might have been coined to describe this renewal of the sound and straightforward writing that brought Costello to prominence. Perhaps it's no coincidence that The Attractions played on every track – the first time for eight years.

- **Painted From Memory** (1998; Mercury).
  A critically acclaimed collaboration with Burt Bacharach. Rich string backing – utterly timeless.

- **When I was Cruel** (2002; Mercury).
  Though the lyrics are at times a little over-egged, the production is tight and frequently harks back to the sound of Blood & Chocolate. Compared to his recent excursions, this collection stands to remind us that Costello can still churn out great twisted pop.

Piers Clifton

COUNTING CROWS

Formed San Francisco, 1991.

It was exactly that sentiment – 'help me believe in anything' – that made the music of **Counting Crows** so accessible when they burst onto the popular music scene in 1993 with the stunning debut AUGUST AND EVERYTHING AFTER (1993). Atop a musical mix of roots rock and hopped-up folk sensibilities, there was a vocalist/lyricist with a flair for the poetic turn of phrase, a lyricist who was clearly engaged in his own personal hunt for life's meaning.

Singer **Adam Durlitz**, an unassuming fellow with a powerful and passionate voice, churned out lyrics that seemed to have been written with a poetry club's open-mike night in mind. The music-buying public, it seemed, was enthralled with Durlitz's casual, quasi-storytelling style, and "Mr. Jones" became an enormous hit.

AUGUST AND EVERYTHING AFTER quickly became a word-of-mouth favourite, an antidote to the jittery, non-cerebral grunge fare filling the airwaves at the time. Several other songs on the disc also made an impact, most notably "Round Here", "Rain King" and "A Murder Of One". AUGUST AND EVERYTHING AFTER was picked apart and studied by practically every rock critic working at the time: it had been a very long time since a debut album had been filled with so many indispensable compositions.

But with such glorious success came the inevitable threat of the sophomore slump: could the album's successor ever be as good as this? It seemed, for a while, that the Crows were almost afraid to find out, and it took three years before RECOVERING THE SATELLITES (1996) was revealed to a world that had become a bit weary from the wait. During the hiatus, a sad fact had been discovered: Counting Crows had virtually no stage presence, and their live shows were dreary exercises in boredom, made all the more intolerable by Durlitz's constant extemporaneous singing. But RECOVERING THE SATELLITES was a very good album, which, whilst not reaching the heights of its predecessor, still saw the band expanding their repertoire of moods – folk gave way to grunge, rock gave way to country. It was a chronicle of a talented bunch of songwriters as they matured, grew and found their feet, and as such it is essential.

In 1998, Counting Crows inexplicably issued ACROSS A WIRE: LIVE IN NEW YORK, a plodding, almost lifeless two-CD live set, no doubt intended as a stop-gap release. While they remain expert crafters of folky, thought-provoking melodies, revisited on their next studio efforts THIS DESERT LIFE (1999) and HARD CANDY (2002), their lack of stage magic may ultimately consign them to the dustbin of studio-band history.

- **August And Everything After** (1993; DGC).
  All killer, no filler. This is in many ways a classic debut album, in that it uses up the band's stock of great ideas in one blast, leaving them scratching around for inspiration on subsequent recordings.

James Bickers

COUNTRY JOE AND THE FISH

Formed Berkeley, California, 1965;
disbanded 1970.

To the wider world, **Country Joe McDonald** (vocals/guitar) remains best known for his infamous 'Fish Cheer' in the *Woodstock* movie ('Gimme an F! Gimme a U! Gimme a C! Gimme a K! What's that spell?!'). This notoriety has tended to overshadow his band's substantial contributions to the halcyon days of psychedelic music.

Country Joe And The Fish started out as a folky jug band, cutting one EP which contained an original, acoustic version of the "I-Feel-Like-I'm-Fixin'-To-Die Rag". Turning electric in 1966, McDonald and **Barry 'The Fish' Melton** (vocals/guitar) were joined by **Bruce Barthol** (bass), **David Cohen** (electric guitar), **Paul Armstrong** (harp) and **John Francis Gunning** (drums). A second locally pressed EP was among the earliest recorded exhibitions of the best hallmarks of the San Francisco psychedelic sound: distorted guitars, Indian raga-influenced melodies, devil-may-care celebrations of free love, and impressionistic, drug-influenced lyrics. The hypnotic, six-minute instrumental "Section 43", with its duelling guitar-organ-harmonica riffs, was a particular highlight that they and other San Francisco bands would rarely match. A big success for an indie production of its type, the EP was an impressive underground seller in the region.

The Fish signed to Vanguard in late 1966 and mixed original songs with some recut material from early EPs for their debut, ELECTRIC MUSIC FOR THE MIND AND BODY (1967). It has remained their best effort by a considerable margin, although its heady mix of swirling organ (by Cohen), folk-rock, blues, jug band, all-out psychedelic instrumental passages, leftist politics and flower-power lyrics has dated. On the whole, however, the high-spirited, idealistic flavour of their eclectic sound has made it more than a period piece.

Like many California bands, Country Joe and The Fish were given a boost by appearing at the Monterey Pop Festival in June 1967 (they are seen playing "Section 43" in the documentary film of the event). Their second album, I-FEEL-LIKE-I'M-FIXIN'-TO-DIE (1967), was less impressive than their initial outing, but the title track was a highlight. A smart-aleck jug band-cum-folk-rock protest song against US involvement in Vietnam, it served as one of the anthems of the antiwar movement, and remained a staple at demonstrations for some years.

Chief songwriter McDonald made only a small contribution to TOGETHER (1968), and it showed; it may have been a big seller, and contained the famous soul parody "Rock And Soul Music", but it was largely disappointing. The core line-up disbanded shortly afterwards, McDonald and Melton borrowing bassist **Peter Albin** and drummer **David Getz** from **BIG BROTHER & THE HOLDING COMPANY**, and adding **Mark Kapner** on keyboards. However, the final two Fish albums – HERE WE GO AGAIN (1969) and C. J. FISH (1970) – were subdued, drab affairs, though the band managed a fairly memorable appearance at Woodstock, where McDonald was also summoned to entertain the crowd with his acoustic guitar when rain threats cleared electric instruments off the stage. His version of "Fixin' To Die" was a harbinger of his subsequent solo career, performing and recording mildly political, folk-and-blues-based music that hasn't held a candle to the glory days of The Fish at their peak.

1997 saw a low-key live album sneak almost unnoticed into the stores, but LIVE! FILLMORE WEST 1969 (Vanguard) – an essential document of what all the fuss was about – is a more worthwhile investment. Check out the full 38-minute version of "Donovan's Reef" for the full psychedelic experience. The best of Joe's solo work is lovingly compiled in SOMETHING BORROWED, SOMETHING BLUE (1998), with extra material in the form of rarities and demos to bulk out the package.

⊙ **Electric Music For The Mind And Body** (1967; Vanguard).
Contains most of the band's best songs, including the infectious, bluesy "Not So Sweet Martha Lorraine" and the uncharacteristically apocalyptic "Death Sound Blues". The re-recording of "Section 43" is slightly inferior to the original EP version, but all in all, this is one of the best San Francisco-area psychedelic albums.

⊙ **The Collected Country Joe And The Fish** (1987; Vanguard).
Intelligently compiled, this seventy-minute-plus CD has almost all of their essential material, leaning heavily on the first two albums. Also features highlights from the first two EPs (including "Section 43") and the best songs from their patchy final three LPs – most notably "Rock And Soul Music" and "Rockin' All Over The World".

Richie Unterberger

WAYNE/JAYNE COUNTY

Born Georgia, date unknown.

"When people talk about the English punk scene they don't mention me and it pisses me off because I made a big contribution to the thing."

Born **Wayne County**, the self-styled 'big-nosed boy from Georgia' took a Greyhound bus to New York City in the late 60s and kicked off a career in underground theatre before producing some of the lewdest gender-bending rock'n'roll ever. A performance artist as much as a rock'n'roller, always in the front line of radical culture, Jayne County is finally getting the recognition she deserves.

Introduced to the Warhol set by photographer Leee Black Childers, Wayne started in avant-garde theatre alongside such notables as Patti Smith and

Cherry Vanilla, as well as Holly Woodlawn and Jackie Curtis (both immortalized in Lou Reed's "Walk On The Wild Side"). Rod Stewart and David Bowie were among the rock glitterati who experienced these performances and worshipped at the altar of Queen Wayne. Theatre was Wayne's spiritual home, and a rock'n'roll backbeat was a natural progression.

In the early 70s Wayne formed his first band, **Queen Elizabeth**. Demos were made ("Stuck On You" and "Max's" among them) but never commercially released. Wayne would dress in a Dusty Springfield fright wig and carry a dildo on stage – 'ridiculous' theatre and the nascent genre of punk had collided, and Wayne had a foot in both camps.

As a scene emerged on the Lower East Side, with Patti Smith and Suicide grabbing the notices, Wayne rounded up **The Backstreet Boys**, featuring the future **Marky Ramone** on drums. The sound was loud, distorted and wild and Wayne And The Backstreet Boys became part of the burgeoning New York punk movement. Gutter-poverty posturing took over from the relics of glamour personified by The New York Dolls, and the leading lights of the revolution were four leather-jacketed street urchins, the Ramones. The time was ripe for shock tactics and thunderous back-to-basic rock'n'roll: Wayne County provided both and added deviant sex, cross-dressing, extreme vulgarity and heaps of bad taste.

The Backstreet Boys' proposed first album, which was to have included the infamous "(If You Don't Want To Fuck Me, Baby) Fuck Off" and "Rock & Roll Enema", never materialized commercially, although the band contributed tracks to the MAX'S KANSAS CITY album, which was released in the UK, coming to the attention of John Peel, who began to play tracks on the radio. Acts like the Ramones, Patti Smith and Blondie were signing record contracts in the US, but Wayne was considered too hot to handle and he decided that England would provide a more accepting audience.

In England, the band metamorphosed into **The Electric Chairs** and became regulars on the punk circuit. Wayne wore chiffon, fishnet stockings and a high white wig and was welcomed with open arms by the punk pioneers. The Electric Chairs toured ceaselessly, and Illegal Records opted to release an EP featuring a cleaned-up version of "Fucked By The Devil" called "Paranoia Paradise", which appeared on the soundtrack of Derek Jarman's *Jubilee*. Soon after came the release of the most renowned of Wayne's songs, "Fuck Off", which Safari Records wisely chose to release under the label pseudonym Sweet F. A. Wayne was wicked, witty, obscene and punky in the extreme and The Electric Chairs provided a wall of sound to back up his manic activities.

The Electric Chairs' second album, STORM THE GATES OF HEAVEN, was their most commercially successful and included the song "Man Enough To Be A Woman", mirroring Wayne's personal transition. But as punk began to lose its cutting edge, so

Wayne/Jayne's star dimmed. During the 80s Jayne spent time in the Berlin underground and faded from public view, but she entered the 90s in fighting form with a rewired set of Electric Chairs and an even more heightened image. DEVIATION, released in 1995, showed Jayne still as punky and as deviant as hell. Who else could possibly write a song called "Texas Chainsaw Manicurist"?

In 1996, County published an entertaining biography, *Man Enough To Be A Woman*, with Serpent's Tail; she is currently touring her new one-woman show.

⊙ **Blatantly Offensive** (1978; Safari).
This EP includes "Fuck Off" and "Toilet Love". Blatant. Offensive. Indispensable.

⊙ **Storm The Gates Of Heaven** (1978; Safari).
More of the same to rock your socks off.

⊙ **Deviation** (1995; Thunderbird).
The return of Queen Jayne. Inimitable.

Veronica Kofman

COWBOY JUNKIES

Formed Toronto, 1985.

"We used to have lots of ideas but couldn't always pull them off. Now we can do pretty much whatever we think of." Margo Timmins, 1996

While 'new country' music seems increasingly hidebound by the same cliched conventions of the genre which spawned it, **Cowboy Junkies** have managed to bring something fresh to the scene without resorting to irony. With their depictions of claustrophobic small-town life, **Michael Timmins** (guitar), his brother **Peter** (drums) and sister **Margo** (vocals), plus bassist **Alan Anton**, have put a good deal of soul back into country.

Released on their own indie label, Latent, the band's debut LP, WHITES OFF EARTH NOW (1986), was recorded in a friend's house and resonated with stark simplicity. Although decidedly lo-fi, it introduced the band's trademark style – whispered vocals and minimal backing, redolent of after-hours disillusion and heartbreak. As well as original material, the band also faithfully interpreted the blues of Robert Johnson and Lightnin' Hopkins, just as on their next album, the richly evocative THE TRINITY SESSION (1988), they carried the despair of Hank Williams' "I'm So Lonesome I Could Cry" into the 90s. Recorded on a single microphone in the Holy Trinity Church, Toronto, at a reputed cost of $250, this album sounded like a candlelit homage to the spectral influence of Williams and Patsy Cline, while its rendition of Lou Reed's "Sweet Jane" also proved that the band's spiritual range was as wide as it was deep.

Having sold a quarter of a million copies in the US without the benefit of serious hype, the band embarked on a year-long world tour that led to a European breakthrough in 1990. Live, the band fleshed out its sound with bottleneck and slide guitar, accordion and extra percussion, and showcased material from their third album, THE CAUTION HORSES (1990), which featured some excellent Michael Timmins originals, but perhaps overplayed its bleary-eyed melancholia. However, despite it's slight lack of range and dynamics, THE CAUTION HORSES sold well both in America and abroad.

A wider gamut of emotions was covered on the superior BLACK EYED MAN (1992), on which the bittersweet, storytelling tradition of country music was augmented by the charged electric spirit of folk and even, occasionally, rock'n'roll. The move towards a rougher-edged sound continued on the powerful follow-up, PALE SUN CRESCENT MOON (1993), though the band's trademark poise remained intact amidst the harsher textures of "7 Years" and "Crescent Moon". Sadly, neither of these more adventurous albums matched the commercial success of THE CAUTION HORSES.

1995 saw the end of the band's relationship with RCA and, as such, despite flawless playing and the Cowboys' trademark atmosphere, whispered beauty and foreboding, the double live album 200 MORE MILES had an air of contractual obligation about it. LAY IT DOWN (1996), their first album for Geffen was well received, although, with its lighter, crisper approach its appeal was a little less immediate than PALE SUN's.

The band toured extensively in 1996 and seemed keen to shrug off their rather desolate image as Margo Timmins interspersed the songs with friendly banter and amusing anecdotes. Tellingly, however, not all the shows were that well attended and it was the oldest numbers that were greeted with most enthusiasm.

Where earlier Junkies albums clung to the shadows, MILES FROM OUR HOME (1998) headed for light and space with a fuller, more fleshed-out sound courtesy of former Stone Roses producer **John Leckie**. Michael Timmins' guitar dominated the startling opener, "New Dawn Coming", then shimmered on through the gorgeous, aching "Blue Guitar", before punctuating the title track with wired, fractured bursts not too far removed from Tom Verlaine. Make no mistake: this was a ROCK album, albeit infused with the band's trademark care and sensitivity. Resolutely unfashionable, it was another fine album, with no desire to pander to expectation or to retread old paths. If the only Junkies album you have is THE TRINITY SESSION, then MILES FROM OUR HOME offers the ideal opportunity to renew your acquaintance.

Returning to their own Latent Recordings imprint, the group released RARITIES, B-SIDES AND SLOW SAD WALTZES (1999), the title being pretty self-explanatory. Since then a 'best-of', a RADIO ONE SESSIONS CD and a new studio album, Open (2001), have been added to their canon.

⊙ The Trinity Session (1988; RCA).
Late-night evocations of regret and heartbreak. Moving in a way that contemporary country rarely achieves.

⊙ Black Eyed Man (1992; RCA).
With the help of session heroes John Prine and Townes Van Zandt, the Cowboy Junkies' storytelling skills really take off in these vignettes of loss and love.

⊙ Studio (1997; BMG).
A selection of album tracks culled from all their albums through to LAY IT DOWN. Nicely sequenced and quietly released, and repackaged without hype or swagger. No real hits – only quality music – and a good place to start.

⊙ Selected Studio Recordings (1998; RCA).
Much more of a greatest hits album than STUDIO, this has all their essential tracks, from "Sweet Jane" (which accompanied one of the more tender moments in the movie *Natural Born Killers*) to the heart-wrenching "Cause Cheap Is How I Feel".

⊙ Open (2001; Zoe).
Opening with a blast of feedback, this collection offers another fine set of unhurried Cowboy Junkies charm.

Nig Hodgkins

KEVIN COYNE

Born Derby, England, 1944.

"I'll just have to steam in and sort a few people out. Do a bit of damage."

Kevin Coyne's image owes as much to his experiences as a social worker as to his abiding love of blues and R&B. Blessed with one of the most individual voices in rock, he worked as a therapist at a psychiatric hospital before forming **Siren** in 1968 with guitarist **Dave Clague**. Signed to DJ John Peel's Dandelion label, the band made two albums, SIREN (1970) and STRANGE LOCOMOTION (1972), and then, disillusioned by a poor public response, the group folded. Coyne embarked on a solo career.

He poured a lot of pain into his debut, CASE HISTORY (1972), which drew directly on his work with mental patients, a source of inspiration that he would return to throughout his career. The following year he left Dandelion for fledgling company Virgin, who offered him a long-term deal, with a chance to develop as a left-field artist. The first fruit of this relationship was the milestone release MARJORY RAZORBLADE (1973), an album that won great critical acclaim for its variety of disturbingly accurate character studies, delivered with a voice of astonishing range and volume.

During the rest of the 70s, Coyne consolidated his uncompromising reputation without gaining mainstream acceptance. A loose touring outfit was formed, featuring **Gordon Smith** (slide guitar), who played on a further fine album of solo and band performances, BLAME IT ON THE NIGHT (1974). Next, Coyne recruited a more heavyweight line-up of future **POLICE** guitarist **Andy Summers**, **Archie Leggett** (bass), **Peter Wolf** (drums) and **Zoot**

Money (keyboards), for MATCHING HEAD AND FEET (1975), a bit of a mixed bag, but one yielding a roaring highlight of Coyne's vocals in "Turpentine" and a gorgeous ballad in "Sunday Morning Sunrise", aided by Summers' effortless guitar work.

This new line-up was deservedly acclaimed for its live work, and by the release of HEARTBURN (1976) they were playing larger venues, which enabled Coyne to concentrate on presentation. Props and tapes of his monologues were used as a backdrop to the simultaneously disturbing and hilarious performances, the overall flavour of which was nicely captured on the double live LP, IN LIVING BLACK AND WHITE (1977).

As rock's early-70s complacency was swept away by punk rock, Coyne's regard for honesty at the expense of finesse fitted the emerging ethic perfectly. Johnny Rotten cited Coyne as a major influence, and he responded with DYNAMITE DAZE (1978), the title track of which was a direct response to the energy of the Pistols. MILLIONAIRES AND TEDDY BEARS (1979) continued his prolific solo period, and in June of that year he immersed himself in the production of a theatrical song-cycle, BABBLE (subtitled 'Songs For Lonely Lovers'), in which he was well matched by ex-Slapp Happy singer **Dagmar Krause**.

BURSTING BUBBLES (1980) was Coyne at his harshest and most uncompromising, as he continued to move away from conventional musical structures. The double LP, SANITY STOMP (1980), with backing from **THE RUTS** and **ROBERT WYATT**, marked the end of his association with Virgin, who had long since begun to pursue more commercially viable acts. Two albums for indie label Cherry Red, POINTING THE FINGER (1981) and POLITICZ (1982), indicated a loss of focus, partly induced by Coyne's alcoholism and his marriage break-up.

A subsequent relocation to Germany brought greater rewards; as well as German-only record releases, he had two books published, has exhibited his paintings, and has acted on television and on stage. Following the release of a CD of BBC recordings, THE PEEL SESSIONS (1990), Coyne now occasionally visits Britain to play to small but receptive audiences. A new album, CARNIVAL, was released in 2002. His acceptance as a multimedia artist abroad is Britain's loss and Germany's gain.

- **Marjory Razorblade** (1973; Virgin).
  Coyne sets out his stall, with themes ranging from the harrowing ("House On The Hill", "Old Soldier") to the humorous ("Karate King", "Eastbourne Ladies"). Its twenty-song spread remains a definitive collection of raw vocals and inspired lyrics.

- **In Living Black And White** (1977; Virgin).
  A set of fuelled live electric and acoustic performances that regularly surpassed their studio-recorded counterparts.

- **The Peel Sessions** (1990; Strange Fruit).
  Excellently recorded by the BBC, these sixteen tracks date mainly from 1973 to 1979, and offer a clear overview of Coyne's abilities, from reworkings of album material to daring one-take improvisational pieces like "Miner's Song" and "Dance Of The Bourgeoisie".

Steve Dinsdale

CRACKER

Formed Richmond, Virginia, 1991.

The Cracker story is a tale of endless side projects, more drummers than Spinal Tap and a ten-year-plus career as purveyors of quality rock with an order of quirky guitar pop on the side. Since their formation, the band have had two permanent fixtures – singer/guitarist **David Lowery** (formerly of Camper Van Beethoven) and guitarist **Johnny Hickman** (from 80s wild-west rockers The Unforgiven). After **CAMPER VAN BEETHOVEN** wound down in 1990, Lowery immediately began demoing new material with Hickman and bassist **Davey Faragher**, initially calling themselves the **David Lowery Band**.

Settling on the name **Cracker**, the trio found it difficult to find a permanent fixture to sit on the drum stool, making do instead with the services of redoubtable sticksmen **Rick Jaeger**, **Jim Keltner**, **Michael Urbano** and **Phil Jones** while recording their first two albums. 1992's CRACKER was a sterling debut, the opening three tracks in particular set out the group's brand values in no uncertain terms, dispensing with the wilful messiness of Lowery's previous band and ushering in a more traditional rock feel, albeit with a lyrical sting in the tail.

Notching up both significant sales and critical praise, their sophomore effort, KEROSENE HAT (1993) ensured the band's long-term survival. With a video starring comedienne Sandra Bernhard, the single "Low" brought them the MTV audience that had eluded Camper Van Beethoven, while the rest of the album, with its balance of unashamed sentimentalism, sturdy rockers and a touch of country twang, merited repeat listens.

It took three years to record a follow-up, by which time Faragher had departed for stints with John Hiatt and Sheryl Crow. THE GOLDEN AGE (1996) featured a new bass player (**Bob Rupe**) and another batch of drummers. Rather than duplicate the formula of KEROSENE HAT, Lowery et al widened their scope,

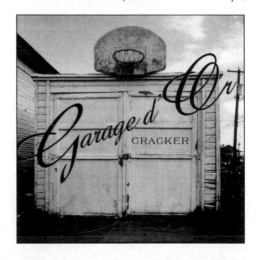

taking in country-rock, grunge, psychedelia and more skewed pop. It was an uneven ride that lacked the immediacy of its predecessor, but there were quiet gems buried beneath the overwrought guitars that begged to be sought out.

After THE GOLDEN AGE, Lowery turned his attention to studio work and has since been a prolific producer when not Cracker-ing; in recent years he's manned the controls for outings by Counting Crows, Sparklehorse, Lauren Hoffman and Vic Chestnutt.

1998's GENTLEMAN'S BLUES saw Cracker finally find a permanent drummer in the shape of **Frank Funaro**; they also picked up keyboard/accordion player **Kenny Margolis**. Jettisoning any ideas of teen-appeal, GENTLEMAN'S BLUES returned to American rock fundamentals with something approaching resignation, perhaps even nostalgia. There was a world-weariness that verged on bitterness in places, the irony spread thickly over reminiscences on fame, rock'n'roll and growing old ("The Good Life" and "Been Around The World"). After a long period with Virgin Records, the band found themselves out of a deal, signing off with 2000's wittily named compilation, GARAGE D'OR. This collection saw the unveiling of a new bass player, **Brandy Wood,** who got in just in time to record on the three new tracks that fleshed out the set.

A period of rest and recuperation followed, broken by sporadic touring, often featuring colleagues from Lowery's Camper Van Beethoven days. A live album was inevitable and duly followed. During this period Lowery officially reunited with Camper Van Beethoven for a series of live dates and more recently the bizarre TUSK (2003), an album of Fleetwood Mac covers.

As for Cracker, 2002's FOREVER was widely considered one of their best since KEROSENE HAT; even if the tracklisting did include some lame ducks – witness the pseudo-rap of "What You're Missing" or the limp "Merry Christmas Emily". Seemingly intent on making any biographer sweat for a living, all the members of Cracker are currently working on various other projects, while a new album, O' CRACKER WHERE ART THOU, was released through Pitch-A-Tent Records in May 2003.

⊙ **Kerosene Hat** (1993; Virgin).
The most coherent album and the most popular. "Take Me Down To The Infirmary" and "Sick Of Goodbyes" are worth the price of admission alone.

⊙ **Garage D'Or** (2000; Virgin).
A great sampler of ten years worth of material – especially if you manage to get hold of a copy with the bonus CD of rarities.

Derryck Strachan

CRADLE OF FILTH

Formed Ipswich, England, 1991.

Not many bands court controversy with the unfailing accuracy of this quintessentially English black metal outfit. Right from their inception, with the line-up of **Dani Filth** (vocals), **Paul Ryan** (guitar), his brother **Ben Ryan** (keyboards), **John Richard** (bass) and **Darren** (drums), there was something uniquely different about **Cradle Of Filth**'s approach to the darker side of metal. Three demos, respectively titled "Invoking The Unclean", "Orgiastic Pleasures" and "Total Fucking Darkness", showed a band gradually coming to grips with gothic imagery and the vampire myth. They aspired to writing full-blown operatic pieces drenched in blood and darkness, a goal they would achieve a little way down the line after their debut, THE PRINCIPLE OF EVIL MADE FLESH (1994). During this period the line-up shifted a number of times, finally settling down with drummer **Nicholas Barker**, guitarists **Paul Allender** and **Stuart**, keyboardist **Damien** and **Robin Graves** on bass.

Preceded by the mini-LP VEMPIRE OR DARK FAERYTALES IN PHALLUSTEIN (1996), DUSK & HER EMBRACE (1996) was a full-blown gothic epic of bloodcurdling proportions and featured yet another new guitarist, **Gian Piras**, replacing the departed Allender. The music was fully realized thrash-opera topped off with Dani Filth's trademark eardrum-popping screech – the singing equivalent of steel talons being dragged across the blackest of blackboards. Song titles included such gems as "A Gothic Romance (Red Roses For The Devil's Whore)" and "Beauty Slept In Sodom".

The band dressed as vampires, complete with ashen corpse face paint and were keenly aware that the best way to market themselves was with a nifty line in T-shirts. To call the designs offensive would be an understatement. The 'Vestal Masturbation' T-shirt, for instance, featured a semi-naked nun pleasuring herself on the front, whilst the back boldly stated 'Jesus is a Cunt'. Needless to say, the garment became one of their best sellers. In interviews, too, they went out of their way to offend everyone, from environmentalists to church groups. They were clearly having fun, though Damien left to be replaced by **Les 'Lecter' Smith**.

By the time of CRUELTY AND THE BEAST (1998), a concept album of sorts – based on the grisly story of sixteenth-century noblewoman Countess Bathory, who would preserve her beauty by bathing in the blood of virgin girls – the Filth's style was firmly established. Sweeping Gothic orchestration and passages of blistering thrash metal carried some of Dani Filth's most outrageously ornate and over-the-top lyrics. Such was their growing notoriety at this stage that they became the subject of an unintentionally humorous documentary in the BBC's *Living With The Enemy* strand, while month by month some new incident would result in press coverage. One marvellously farcical situation resulted from a photo shoot in the Vatican, when police armed with submachine guns took exception to Dani Filth's 'I (©) Satan' T-shirt and Lecter's customary vicar's dog collar.

These fun and games aside, the band's musical mission continued with a vengeance. The "From The Cradle To Enslave" EP was unveiled in 1999 as a precursor to 2000's MIDIAN – based loosely upon horror writer Clive Barker's *Nightbreed* story – which also featured *Hellraiser* horror actor Doug Bradley's ethereally spooky Cenobyte vocal contributions. By this point the band's notoriously fluid line-up had changed again to include Gian Piras (guitar), **Martin Powell** (keyboards), **Adrian Erlandsson** (drums) and Paul Allender (guitar), the latter back in the band after several years off. Robin Graves eventually left in 2001 to pursue other goals (to be replaced by ex-Anathema bass player **Dave Pybus**) while his band-mates busied themselves with a couple of cunningly punning titles – BITTER SUITES TO SUCCUBI (2001) and LOVECRAFT AND WITCH HEARTS (2002) – both compilations, of sorts, intended to plug the gap while the Filth prepare to release their first full-blown major label atrocity for Sony.

⊙ **Cruelty And The Beast** (1998; Music For Nations).
Don't expect subtlety, hit singles or poppy melodies; this is dark, savage, painful black metal played with frightening intensity and a complete disregard for prevailing musical trends.

Essi Berelian

THE CRAMPS

Formed Ohio, 1976.

S inger **Lux Interior** and guitarist **'Poison' Ivy Rorschach**, misfits with a shared taste in B-movies and obscure 50s and 60s records, originally formed **The Cramps** with voodoo-obsessed guitarist **Bryan Gregory** and his sister **Pam Balam** (drums). Their sound was a synthesis of rockabilly structure and punk rock intensity, centred on Ivy's Link Wray-influenced guitar, so heavy that no bass was needed. The image was intense: frenzied, frightening and funny in equal parts.

On moving to New York in 1979, they met **Miles Copeland**, manager of The Police, the band they incongruously supported at their first British appearance. With new drummer **Nick Knox** on board, Copeland's Illegal label issued the GRAVEST HITS EP (1980). With its much-reproduced graveyard photo session, this story-so-far singles collection set the tone for the 'rockabilly voodoo' image that was to influence dozens of dreadful psychobilly and goth bands.

The title of the debut album, SONGS THE LORD TAUGHT US (1980), was closer to the band's own assessment of the music, keeping faith with the sacred spirit of rock'n'roll. Its follow-up, PSYCHEDELIC JUNGLE (1981), recorded after Gregory's departure, showed the influences could come from further afield while keeping a primeval swampy sound. However, there were continual personnel problems – Gregory was replaced by a succession of short-lived guitarists – while record company wrangles culminated in a lawsuit against Copeland in 1983, eventually settled out of court.

Despite patchy studio output during this period, live recordings and numerous bootlegs kept the cult following happy, while the band's talent as musicologists did not go unnoticed. Their selections of arcane 50s and 60s songs fitted them so well it was hard to

believe they were not their own. A series of various-artist compilation albums, like SONGS THE CRAMPS TAUGHT US (Born Bad), dug up originals in homage.

The final Illegal/Castle release was the 1983 compilation OFF THE BONE, which gave the band their first British chart entry. Next, Big Beat released the live mini-album, SMELL OF FEMALE (1983), and the later A DATE WITH ELVIS (1986). The label-hopping continued in the 90s, with STAY SICK! (1990) on Enigma, LOOK MOM NO HEAD (1991) on Ace, FLAMEJOB (1994) on Creation and BIG BEAT FROM BADSVILLE (1997) on Epitaph. In contrast, the band's musical vision has settled down a little, as they left behind labels like 'trash aesthetic' and 'psychobilly', and followed their own individual rock'n'roll vision unfettered by fashion. To this end they decided to resurrect Vengeance Records in 2001, on which label they issued their first singles back in 1978, in order to rerelease various albums from their back catalogue in wildly coloured vinyl editions.

The Cramps remain at their most enjoyable on stage, with Ivy's ice-cool sexuality the perfect foil for Lux's hilariously unhinged frenzies. While their influence really peaked in the early 80s, their cult following remains, and probably always will, for as long as Lux Interior can groan and grovel at the altar of rock'n'roll.

⊙ **Off The Bone** (1983; Castle; reissued 1998; Zonophone).
Compilation bringing together the five tracks from the GRAVEST HITS EP (including "Human Fly"). It's worth hunting down the original Illegal LP release which came in a 3D sleeve.

⊙ **Rockinnreelininaucklandnewzealandxxx** (1987; Ace).
This self-released live album is a pounding, howling snapshot of the band. Contains a full range of wildlife references ("Chicken", "Do The Clam", "Birdfeed", and the infamous "Can Your Pussy Do The Dog"), with animal noises to match. Also included is The Cramps' anthem "Sunglasses After Dark".

⊙ **Stay Sick!** (1990; Ace).
The album that gave the band their one genuine hit, "Bikini Girls With Machine Guns". Sex, drugs and rock'n'roll are covered more explicitly than ever, a bit of country is thrown in, and you get one of the best song titles – "The Creature From The Black Leather Lagoon".

Penny Kiley

THE CRANBERRIES

Formed Limerick, Ireland, 1990.

At the end of 1993, **The Cranberries** were a fairly anonymous group of Irish musicians who toured relentlessly and were struggling for a hit. Two years later, they were a fairly anonymous group of Irish musicians who'd sold close to twenty million albums worldwide. Theirs has been a rags-to-riches story of epic proportions: four slightly unworldly rockers who refuse to compromise become Ireland's biggest musical export since U2 without anyone really noticing.

The story begins in 1990 in Ballybricken, a tiny village near Limerick. The Cranberry-Saw-Us, a cringesomely named all-male quartet, decided to ditch their frontman, and the three remaining members – **Fergal Lawler** (drums), **Noel Hogan** (guitar) and brother **Mike** (bass) – brought in local tomboy **Dolores O'Riordan** (vocals) as a replacement. The new line-up, now more sensibly calling themselves The Cranberries, wrote a few songs and produced a demo tape which excited the interest of several major UK labels, most notably Island, with whom the band signed a six-album deal in 1991. So far, so good. The problems began at the end of that year, when debut single "Uncertain" received a hostile reception from the previously enthusiastic music press, and interviews presented them as naive country folk who spoke with wide-eyed surprise about encountering black people during a visit to London. (The *NME*'s feature was painfully headlined 'Yo! Bumpkin Rush The Show'.)

The aptly titled debut single preceded a year of uncertainty in which O'Riordan considered quitting the band and anxiety grew over Island's apparent apathy. Managers and publicists came and went, and Stephen Street was drafted in to produce their debut album, EVERYBODY ELSE IS DOING IT, SO WHY CAN'T WE? (1993), which was delayed to tie in with a successful UK tour supporting Belly. Two tracks, "Dreams" and "Linger", were released but failed to take off, and the album struggled to #78. The band now turned their attentions to America, where their relish for gruelling tour schedules earned them support slots with The The and Duran Duran, as well as a now-famous joint venture with Suede, which marked a turning point in The Cranberries' career. Through word of mouth, thousands were turning up every night to watch these 'four little Irish leprechauns' (*Melody Maker*) shyly perform their winsome melodies. Sales of the album began to increase week by week, MTV and college radio latched onto the wistful charm of "Linger", and The Cranberries were suddenly Big in America.

The time was now right for a British reappraisal. Island gave "Linger" a second chance in February 1994 and this time it was an instant success, spending seven weeks in the Top 20 and setting the scene for a relaunch of the album. By now Britain and Europe were smitten too, and on June 25, 1994, it became only the fifth album in rock history to reach #1 more than a year after release.

Rationalizing such enormous success proved almost as troublesome as achieving it; it seemed that The

The Cranberries' Dolores demonstrates the D chord

Cranberries had stumbled upon a previously untapped global market for fey Celtic vignettes about lost loves and broken hearts delivered in a crystal-clear, defiantly Irish warble. Their strength lay in their ability as a band to create something musically uplifting from O'Riordan's bewildered, discontented lyrics, which occasionally veered towards fourth-form awkwardness: 'Totally amazing mind/So understanding and so kind/You're everything to me' ("Dreams").

With EVERYBODY ELSE... taking the scenic route to the top, NO NEED TO ARGUE (1994) seemed like a quicker follow-up than it actually was. For the cover shot, the band dug out the same sofa they'd adorned on their debut, emphasizing the continuity between the two records. And indeed NO NEED TO ARGUE was essentially more of the same, only "Zombie"'s angry grunge raising any eyebrows on another soothing collection. Written after the IRA bombing in Warrington, which killed two children, "Zombie" was O'Riordan's sole political moment, its aggressive lyric ("What's in your head, zombie?") delivered with uncharacteristic venom. It became their most popular track, a Top 10 hit in 25 countries, winner of the prestigious *MTV Song of the Year* award, and a hit all over again when turned into an unlikely rave anthem a year later. NO NEED TO ARGUE blazed a trail through 1995, spawning further hits and ending up, amazingly, as the world's bestselling album of the year by a European artist.

For their third album, TO THE FAITHFUL DEPARTED (1996), the band dumped Stephen Street in favour of Bon Jovi's producer **Bruce Fairbairn**, who toughened up the music and took them further down the route they'd explored with "Zombie". The new all-grown-up image was let down by O'Riordan's lyrics, which remained childishly gauche in places ("With a Smith & Wesson 38/John Lennon's life was no longer a debate"), but the album was nonetheless an instant success, debuting at #2 in the UK and #4 in the US.

With such planet-straddling success came, inevitably, relentless media coverage and speculation, most of it unwelcome. When O'Riordan chose to get married in little more than a net curtain in 1994, there was a frenzy of moral outrage in the Irish press, and through 1995 rumours circulated of a growing distance between band and singer. When the band cancelled its world tour and dropped out of sight, commentators were quick to assume it was on its last legs. However, the members were merely taking a first long break after five hectic years and O'Riordan was working on a production of her own – Taylor (born November 1997).

Their return in 1999 with BURY THE HATCHET demonstrated just how much things had moved on since O'Riordan's furrowed brow earnestness last ruled the video-waves. Though it lacked an obvious killer single along the lines of "Zombie" or "Linger", the compositions were as competent as any on their previous releases. The problem was that they seemed to be struggling to come up with a sound that would re-establish them as a relevant proposition.

With as much of a back-to-basics feel as multmillion selling purveyors of sophisticated adult rock are allowed to indulge in, WAKE UP AND SMELL THE COFFEE (2001) was an attempt to redress the balance – or perhaps just to put the brakes on the slide.

Despite finding it increasingly difficult to establish a comfortable place in the pop world, the Cranberries have come through it all with honesty and sanity intact. And, even after selling close to twenty million records in a two-year period, they remain genuine, occasionally awkward, and unpretentious.

⊙ **Everybody Else Is Doing It, So Why Can't We?**
(1993; Island).
A half-apologetic title ushers in a collection of uncertain yet emotional Gaelic-tinged three-minute pop songs. Although O'Riordan's girlish delivery inevitably dominates, the musicianship and discreet production contribute to a strangely powerful sound.

⊙ **No Need To Argue** (1994; Island).
The same serene charm pervades this second album. "Zombie" may have launched it into the sales stratosphere, but the real gem here is "Empty", which spins an enchanting orchestral web around O'Riordan's bruised vocals.

⊙ **To The Faithful Departed** (1996; Island).
Although by now one of the world's top stadium rock bands, The Cranberries tried to embrace a punk spirit on this vivid and aggressive third album. It doesn't always come off, but they deserve credit for tampering with a winning formula.

Jonathan Kennaugh

CRANES

Formed Portsmouth, England, 1988.

Emerging apparently from nowhere at the tail end of the decade, **Cranes** for a while seemed to perfectly encapsulate the twin tendencies of 80s art-rock: the foreboding industrial noise of bands like Einstürzende Neubauten, Swans and The Young Gods; and the ethereal vocal explorations of the likes of Cocteau Twins and Dead Can Dance. At their best Cranes made music so startlingly alien that it was impossible to tell if they were closer to the elegant bird or the ugly machine of their namesakes.

The band formed in Portsmouth around the partnership of brother and sister **Jim** and **Alison Shaw**, combining his multi-instrumental talents with her unsettling childlike vocal style. Their earliest work, the cassette-only FUSE (1988), was recorded on the lowest of budgets, and thus only did partial justice to their potential, with its harsh rhythms and indistinct cries and whispers. The pair were able to develop their sound substantially, with the backing of local label Bite Back!, for their first vinyl outing in 1989, the mini-LP SELF-NON-SELF. In a far more confident recording than FUSE, Jim's instrumentation carved out a mechanistic labyrinth of noise, constantly on the verge of overwhelming Alison's inarticulations of distress and abandon.

The album received favourable attention from the national music press, and the band gained further exposure with a radio session for John Peel. Their critical adulation owed much to the way their sound contrasted with the unrelieved ordinariness of the Madchester/baggy aesthetic that dominated the UK indie scene of the time. Cranes were not ashamed to produce art at a time when the idea was at its least fashionable.

Following the success of SELF-NON-SELF, Jim and Alison consolidated the band with two guitarists from the Portsmouth scene, **Mark Francome** and **Matt Cope**, and signed to larger indie label Dedicated. Over the period 1990–91 they released four EPs – INESCAPABLE, ESPERO, ADORATION and TOMORROW'S TEARS – which contained some of their best work. Songs like "Inescapable" and "Sixth Of May" emulated the geometric beauty of an Escher print, while the use of piano on "Adoration" and "Tomorrow's Tears" suggested some kind of autistic torch song.

This string of EPs led up to Cranes' first full album, WINGS OF JOY (1991), which slightly lightened the tone of their material with strings and hints of classical guitar. The exception was "Starblood", a live favourite, and a truly crushing piece of music. WINGS OF JOY achieved considerable indie chart success, and drew the attention of alternative stadium-rockers The Cure, who invited Cranes to support them on a US tour, offering exposure to a largely new audience.

Touring with The Cure proved to be an unfortunately influential experience for the band, and the subsequent LP, FOREVER (1992), saw them moving towards the kind of goth-lite territory Robert Smith's men had long made their own. While the tremulous ballads, like "Cloudless" and "Rainbows", were as perfect as ever, the note of menace was no longer there. This seemed to be reinforced with the "Jewel" single, which, though released in multiple remixes (by Robert Smith, Jim Foetus and 4AD big boss Ivo Watts-Russell), largely missed out on the experimental possibilities of the exercise.

Cranes tracks had previously been used to accompany a TV documentary and a perfume advertisement, and in 1994 this direction was continued when they provided the soundtrack for a British film *Scarborough Ahoy!*, which was voted best student film at Cannes. This work ran in parallel with the recording of LOVED (1994), an album very similar in tone to FOREVER, somehow too comfortable, though containing some echoes of the clang of old on "Reverie". Both 1997's POPULATION FOUR and 2001's FUTURE SONGS (the latter on the group's own Dadaphonic label), continued their theme of building wisps of melody around Alison Shaw's little-girl-lost voice.

⊙ **Self-Non-Self** (1989; Bite Back!).
'Nothing to fear, nothing to fear' croons Alison Shaw on "Joy Lies Within", like she's singing a nursery rhyme in hell. From the dysfunctional beauty of its sleeve to the claustrophobic construction of its soundscape, SELF-NON-SELF is an immaculately self-contained debut. Uneasy listening.

⊙ **Wings Of Joy** (1991; Dedicated).
Not as gripping as the EPs that preceded it, but nevertheless a fairly impressive collection, with Alison's vocals coming more to the fore.

⊙ **The EP Collection Vol.1 & 2** (1997; Dedicated).
A whole bunch of the early Dedicated EPs and remixes are present on this two-CD set documenting Cranes at their height.

⊙ **Future Songs** (2001; Dadaphonic).
More of the same, only this time around the gothic architecture of their sound has been stripped of the more pompous spires and mouldings. Future songs is an elongated cinematic collection that finds Alison Shaw's otherworldly voice still distinct, though mellowed a little with time.

Ian Canadine

CRASH TEST DUMMIES

Formed Winnipeg, Canada, mid-1980s.

Brad Roberts, linchpin and songwriter of Crash Test Dummies, formed the offbeat collective as a low-key bar band hustling covers of favourite hits, with no initial ambitions beyond huddling indoors playing music during Canada's harsh winters. Appalled by his singing voice, he concentrated on guitar until told by a singing teacher that he possessed a perfect bass–baritone range, whereupon he took on the role of rumbling vocalist. A lo-fi demo of original compositions – recorded while he was an English literature/philosophy student – courted enough attention to whip up a record-company bidding war. This was encouragement enough to divert Roberts from his intended academic career and flesh out the band's personnel to include **Michel Dorge** (drums), **Ellen Reid** (backing vocals/keyboards/accordion), **Benjamin Darvill** (harmonica/mandolin) and **Dan Roberts** (bass).

Following their debut, THE GHOSTS THAT HUNT ME (1991), the group recruited kindred spirit **Jerry Harrison** (Talking Heads) to produce a second album – the hugely successful GOD SHUFFLED HIS FEET (1993; reissued 1998), which spawned the hit single "Mmm, Mmm, Mmm, Mmm". It also boasted not one, but two ditties about going for a chest X-ray, a song about going out with artists, and the insidiously absurd "How Does A Duck Know?".

The 1996 release of A WORM'S LIFE, built on their reputation for quirky, unfathomable lyrics and added a deeper, more orchestral feel to the music. With admirable wit, Brad's booming, rumbling voice tickles round such delicate subjects as waking with an erection and having your teeth pulled.

The warped irony and delicate eccentricity of the group's work has surprisingly received commercial as well as critical success in both Europe and the US, and has invited comparisons with Talking Heads and the more esoteric, humorous moments of mid-period R.E.M. While their spirited cover of XTC's "The Ballad Of Peter Pumpkinhead" ended up on the soundtrack to the enormously successful comedy film *Dumb And Dumber* in 1994, more recent releases like GIVE YOURSELF A HAND, complete with improbable drum'n'bass influences, and 2002's festive JINGLE ALL THE WAY have enjoyed only limited appeal.

- **God Shuffled His Feet** (1993; Arista).
  A wry collection of bizarre storytelling and seductive vignettes, welding left-field playfulness to a fairly traditional musical framework. Full credit for staying clear of AOR clichés, but the Dummies are sometimes guilty of recycling an alternative formula.

Michael Sumsion

CRASS

Formed London, 1977; disbanded 1984.

"Do they owe us a living? Course they fuckin' do."

No other punk band ever approached the anger and integrity of **Crass**, the only outfit who tried to put 'anarchy in the UK' into practice. Although they shared political outrage with bands like The Clash and The Jam, theirs was an entirely different level of fury – they were more likely to barricade the street than sign a petition.

They'd always planned to split up in 1984 and this fixed life span pushed them to making the most of their time. As well as relentless touring and recording, they set up an anarchist commune in Essex where they published manifestos, established record labels, organized campaigns and helped the recording careers of several like-minded libertarian acts. They developed a committed following by dint of sincerity and refusal to compromise, and their message was always more important than the music that served to deliver it.

Formed by **Steve Ignorant** (vocals) and **Penny Rimbaud** (drums), by the early 80s Crass also consisted of vocalists **Eve Libertine** and **Joy de Vivre**, guitarists **N. A. Palmer** and **Phil Free**, backing vocalist (now film-maker) **Mick Duffield**, **G.Sus** (videos/artwork/lighting) and bassist **Pete Wright**. Constantly in trouble with the law, they dressed in black, used obviously false names, and mocked or abused authority whenever possible. Their fan base grew, writing intense amphetamine-fuelled letters pleading with them to never sell out. Crass stayed true, even daring to challenge the commitment of teenage rampage heroes The Clash on their second album, 1979's STATIONS OF THE CRASS.

By the time PENIS ENVY came out in 1981, they'd put the band's espoused feminism into effect, with Libertine and de Vivre taking full vocal responsibility, and the whole album protesting about society's treatment of women. They attracted much music-press interest in the wake of a sharp media prank. Posing as 'Creative Recording And Sound Services', they managed to get a subversive free disc given away with *Brides* magazine. (It is not known how many prospective grooms got cold feet after hearing the saccharine voice burbling, 'never look at anyone, anyone but me ... listen to those wedding bells, say goodbye to other girls, don't be untrue to me'.)

Crass could hardly be accused of selling out with the antagonistic title of 1982's CHRIST – THE ALBUM,

although its packaging – a boxed two-album set with accompanying booklet – was a little upmarket for their monochrome image. The music had also become more sophisticated, with the buzzsaw'n'-drum-roll sound augmented with strings, and the hectoring lectures smoothed over with poetry.

Crass were never short of targets for their vitriol, but when Prime Minister Thatcher took Britain to war in 1982 over the Falkland Islands, she became prime target for YES SIR, I WILL, released the following year. Blending raw punk with more experimental styles, it also spawned their only indie-chart-topping single, dedicated to Margaret Thatcher – "How Does It Feel (To Be The Mother Of 1000 Dead)?" – and showed the band at its deadly serious best.

True to its word, the band split in 1984, although Steve Ignorant later sang at a couple of gigs by Crass descendants, **Conflict**, and went on to form **Schwarzenegger** – who then became the **Stratford Mercenaries**. The Crass name lived on for a while, with Rimbaud and Libertine recording an album of romantic poetry, ACTS OF LOVE (1986), and, the same year, unleashing 10 NOTES ON A SUMMER'S DAY. They had kept the faith and split up before they became irrelevant, setting a standard that later bands would have to struggle to match.

- **Feeding The 5000** (1978; Crass).
  Opens with a brilliant, if controversial, dismissal of Christ and all the religions that have taken his name, all recited over a swelling feedback roar. The rest of the album is just as wickedly shocking, with lashings of strong but heartfelt language over raw guitar and boy's-brigade-band drumming.

- **Stations Of The Crass** (1979; Crass).
  Three studio sides and a live set, packed with punk venom. The band experiment on several tracks (even disco rhythms), and the live set captures the overcrowded, sweaty, beer-and-speed atmosphere of their gigs really well.

- **Best Before** (1989; Crass).
  A collection of twenty tracks previously released as singles, from the beautifully snotty 1977 version of "Do They Owe Us A Living?" to an equally angry recording from their swansong gig seven years later.

Al Spicer

ROBERT CRAY

Born Columbus, Georgia, August 1, 1953.

The most important and the most successful blues artist of his generation, **Robert Cray** is the spiritual heir to the great B.B. King. Like King, Cray produces a potent combination of leanly eloquent guitar and warm vocals, but he has also begun to throw off the shackles of the form and address its customary concerns in more modern fashion, reappraising the traditional themes of passion and despair as the products of male failings.

Cray formed his first band in high school in Tacoma, Washington. **One Way Street** were heavily influenced by Hendrix and Southern soulsters like Steve Cropper, until the young Cray heard the more urbane sound of Albert Collins. He and bass player **Robert Cousins** formed the **Robert Cray Band** in 1974 and within two years they were touring with Collins.

Their first album, WHO'S BEEN TALKIN' (1979), was cut in just two sessions for the struggling Tomato label. Merging the heritage of the Delta with the Chicago style of King and Buddy Guy, it gave immediate notice of Cray's ability. Partly because of Tomato's demise, four years were to pass before his next record, BAD INFLUENCE, which indicated Cray's increasing confidence as a songwriter.

Having come to the notice of British aficionados through an appearance on *The Old Grey Whistle Test* (Eric Clapton was later to record a version of "Bad Influence"), Cray recorded two albums in 1985 – the accomplished FALSE ACCUSATIONS and SHOWDOWN, a collaboration with **Johnny Copeland** and his idol **Albert Collins**.

The next year saw the band sign to Mercury and release the masterpiece, STRONG PERSUADER. Its storytelling lyrics, allied to Cray's beautifully clean guitar lines and the addition of **The Memphis Horns**, made it a crossover smash, the first blues album in thirty years to make the Top 20.

Saxophonist **David Sanborn** appeared on 1988's follow-up DON'T BE AFRAID OF THE DARK, an album whose polished tone occasionally slid into blandness. MIDNIGHT STROLL (1990) and I WAS WARNED (1992) similarly descended too often into a supper-club slickness. Technically, Cray had become the equal of B. B. King, although he lacked King's barrelling gruffness and emotional depth.

During the 90s Cray made a pleasing return to a barer, more sombre style. 1993's excellent SHAME AND A SIN ached with betrayal, relying less on rich arrangement and more on the force of Cray's voice and guitar. That he has come to terms with his talent and with the need to strike a balance between the past and future of the blues was further confirmed by SOME RAINY MORNING (1995), SWEET POTATO PIE (1997), TAKE YOUR SHOES OFF (1999) and SHOULDA BEEN HOME (2001).

It seems there is plenty of life in the young dog yet.

⊙ Who's Been Talkin' (1979; Charly).
Cray pays homage to his influences and proves he is as comfortable with a blues ballad like "The Welfare" as with funkier pieces like Willie Dixon's "Too Many Cooks". Raw and teeming with promise.

⊙ Bad Influence (1983; Mercury).
From the pleading urgency of the opening track, "Phone Booth", to the gleeful confession of the last, "I Got Loaded", this is a lesson in discipline. By turn resolute, sassy and aggrieved, Cray's expressive vocals are tightly underpinned by sparkling guitar.

⊙ Strong Persuader (1986; Mercury).
The full flowering of Cray's talent: from the blistering opening of "Smoking Gun" he shows he means business. Love is the basis of the songbook, and Cray ranges magnificently through it – "Right Next Door", the belated self-abasement of an adulterer, is perhaps the finest thing he has done.

⊙ Shame And A Sin (1993; Mercury).
An album that carries itself with the moody grace of a Southern belle and whose sound is that of a train hooting down the Mississippi by night. Darker than much of his earlier work, with muted brass, piano and xylophone complementing a more direct approach.

James Owen

CREAM

Formed London, 1966; disbanded 1968.

When **Cream** first came together in June 1966 they rightly regarded themselves as three equals, taking their name from **ERIC CLAPTON**'s boast, 'we are the cream'. Each was already known to the others on the blues circuit of the time. Lead guitarist Clapton had left **THE YARDBIRDS** for the purer blues air of **JOHN MAYALL**'s Bluesbreakers, where he had worked with the classically trained **Jack Bruce** (bass), most memorably on a terrific live rendition of "Stormy Monday". Bruce and self-taught drummer **Peter 'Ginger' Baker** had first met in Graham Bond's Organisation before the drummer sacked the bassist. In addition, Clapton and Bruce had worked together in The Powerhouse, a one-off studio band, which recorded two of Cream's future stage highlights, "Crossroads" and "Stepping Out". However, Cream finally came together when Baker sat in on a John Mayall concert in Oxford, and Bruce left his lucrative gig with Manfred Mann. Early rehearsals went so well that talk of recruiting Graham Bond and Steve Winwood was soon discontinued, and the first power trio was born.

The lack of a separate lead singer brought a focus on to the band's musicianship, and early gigs demanded total commitment from all three musicians: Clapton's screaming lead breaks were matched by Bruce's fearsome bass playing and piercing harmonica breaks, and Baker's thunderous drumming. Bruce, as lead singer and main songwriter, was in some ways the frontman, although Clapton's hypnotic soloing was what really captured the public's imagination.

Cream legendaries, Jack Bruce, Ginger Baker and Eric Clapton

Clapton's earlier decision to quit The Yardbirds as they became more commercial seemed highly ironic when Cream achieved similar chart success. They broke the attendance record at London's Marquee, made several TV appearances, signed up with pop impresario Robert Stigwood, and scored their first British hit with the relatively lightweight "Wrapping Paper", backed with the far more rootsy "Cat's Squirrel".

FRESH CREAM (1966) was a debut LP that mirrored their live set at the time. They had already outgrown Clapton's original game plan for the band as a strict blues outfit, or 'Buddy Guy with a rhythm section', and were soon to go much further. When the newly formed Jimi Hendrix Experience played its first official gig supporting Cream at the Central London Polytechnic, Hendrix joined them on stage for a version of "Killing Floor". The influence of Hendrix was clear on Cream's second LP, DISRAELI GEARS (1967), a far more psychedelic affair – and Clapton was now copying Hendrix's Afro perm. Underground magazine *Oz*'s cartoonist **Martin Sharpe** designed the album sleeve, as well as penning the lyrics to "Tales Of Brave Ulysses".

The recording of this second LP took place in New York, during Cream's first tour of America. They had left forever the round of English pub and blues-club gigs, and launched straight into an eleven-night residency at the Fillmore West. It was here that they released themselves into long improvisations, and virtually rewrote the lexicon of rock. The resulting WHEELS OF FIRE (1968), a two-record set, comprised one whole album recorded live at the Fillmore, with four extended tracks.

By the time of its release, the band had announced their imminent split, and undertook a fifteen-gig farewell tour of the States, followed by two final sell-out concerts at London's Royal Albert Hall. Cream's farewell LP, GOODBYE (1969), featured three live tracks from the LA Forum, each one written by a different band member. Clapton's "Badge" was co-written with **George Harrison**, who, as rhythm guitarist on the track, was credited under the pseudonym L'Angelo Misterioso.

As a tribute to Cream's dissolution, Jimi Hendrix broke unexpectedly into "Sunshine Of Your Love" when he appeared as a guest on Lulu's BBC TV variety show. Cream compilation albums followed,

CREAM

as did LIVE CREAM VOLUMES 1 and 2 (1970), two LPs mainly taken from US dates, the second of which was notable for a splendid "Stepping Out". The organizers of the 1970 Isle Of Wight Festival announced that a re-formed Cream would headline, but hadn't even discussed it with the band. The three would only reunite at Clapton's wedding reception, and at their induction into the Rock And Roll Hall Of Fame.

After Cream had split up, Clapton founded **Blind Faith**, before forming **Derek And The Dominoes** and embarking on a solo career. Bruce joined Tony Williams' **Lifetime**, a jazz-rock ensemble, and then enjoyed a sporadic solo career. Baker formed **Airforce**, later played with **Hawkwind**, and built a recording studio in Nigeria, which became one of the catalysts of what was later known as world music. All three record to this day, but, for impact and visceral excitement, Cream remains for each the most sympathetic landscape they have so far inhabited.

⊙ **Fresh Cream** (1966; Polydor).
Powerful and simple music, with half the songs drawn from Delta and Chicago blues. It opens with a trio of Jack Bruce songs, on which his emotionally bare vocals and thumping bass dominate, then Clapton stretches out on "Dreaming", "Spoonful", and the showcase near-instrumental "Cat's Squirrel". Clapton's penny-plain vocals on Robert Johnson's plaintive "Four Until Late" presage a later career.

⊙ **Disraeli Gears** (1967; Polydor).
Matched by Pete Brown's surrealistic lyrics, the music edges away from the blues into the riffing of heavy rock – "Sunshine Of Your Love", not least – and a fuller, multi-dubbed sound.

⊙ **Wheels Of Fire** (1968; Polydor).
A double album of two halves. "In The Studio" expands the instrumentation to include violas, trumpet, organ and hand bells, while lyrical concerns have changed from love to politics, alienation and post-hippie paranoia. "Live At The Fillmore" is by turns magical and overbearing, but who would dare make – or could carry off without studio trickery – music of such power and ambition today?

⊙ **Very Best Of** (1995; Polydor).
Twenty-track compilation which covers all the bases, apart from the lack of prolonged live improvisations.

⊙ **Those Were The Days** (1997; Polydor).
Four CDs' worth of prime, white-boy blues and neat, button-down pop. This collection blends their entire 'official' output with selected rarities and oddities (anybody remember the Falstaff Beer advertisement?). As always with retrospectives of this nature, there's no reason to splash out unless you're planning a major investment in Cream product – a decent 'greatest hits' like Polydor's own 1995 effort will adequately scratch most itches.

Brian Hinton

THE CREATION

Formed Middlesex, England, 1965;
disbanded 1968; re-formed 1994.

The influence of **The Creation** stands out of all proportion to their record sales. The group are treasured by a (mainly British) rock following as one of the great bands of the 60s, for a sound that combined the driving power of R&B with the explosiveness of psychedelia. And, strange to say, they resurfaced in the 90s as inventive as ever before, supporting Oasis, and recording for a label named in their honour. Strange and heady stuff.

The story begins – and eventually resumes – with the songwriting partnership of **Kenny Pickett** (vocals) and **Eddie Phillips** (guitar), who released four singles as **The Mark Four**, a mod-styled group. Their promise led to management by Robert Stigwood, production from Shel Talmy, who had already fashioned a powerful sound for The Who, and a new name, The Creation.

At this point the band were a four-piece comprising Phillips, Pickett, **Bob Garner** (bass/vocals) and **Jack Jones** (drums). Their debut single, "Making Time" (1966), made #49 in the UK charts and hinted at the power the band could create, with a stunning guitar break clashing with the distinctive sound of Phillips taking a violin bow to his guitar. It was innovative stuff, and Phillips' violin-bow antics – later appropriated by Jimmy Page – were just the start. Pickett had taken to spray-painting canvases on stage before torching them.

"Painter Man" (1966), the band's second single, was a 60s pop classic, and, peaking at #36, suggested The Creation were certainties for major success. On the verge of the breakthrough, however, they broke up. The collapse of their record company didn't help, but the real problems revolved around friction between Pickett and Garner. When Pickett arrived at a rehearsal to find Garner on vocals and **Kim Gardner** installed as a new bass player, he didn't bother to argue the toss. He just left, and so broke one of the most promising songwriting partnerships of the era.

The new line-up signed a deal with Polydor, and capitalized on their success in Europe. Germany, in particular had taken to The Creation with a passion. Further singles such as the ballad, "If I Stay Too Long" were followed by an album WE ARE THE PAINTERMEN (1967) which was only available on import in the UK and featured the now departed Pickett on most tracks. Rare to the point of serious value, it is prized to this day as a prime slice of British rock/pop. The band managed two more classic singles, "Life Is Just Beginning" (1967) and "How Does It Feel To Feel?" (1968), penned by the new songwriting team of Phillips and Bob Garner. Sadly, both stiffed in the UK.

Faced with German hits and UK indifference, the band again splintered, but when a three-week tour of Spain was offered, a scratch line-up of Pickett, Gardner, Jones and the mysterious 'Digger' duly obliged. When Phillips decided against rejoining the band, Gardner pulled in **Ron Wood**, a former member of his previous band **The Birds** who later found fame with The Faces and The Rolling Stones. A few more creditable singles followed before the band broke up again.

Sporadic reunions took place over the next three decades, until the one that really mattered in 1994. By this time the British indie scene contained many bands taking their cue from the visionary charge of The Creation's music. Indie label Creation had taken homage to the extreme of naming itself in honour of the legendary British band.

In the summer of 1994 the original band – Pickett, Phillips, Garner and Jones – returned to the studio and, on Creation Records of course, released an eponymous single. It was a stunning slice of power pop and, given their legendary status, the band picked up prestigious gigs, including a co-headliner with the emerging Oasis. POWER SURGE (1996) showed they were still capable of impressive new music but sadly, Pickett died unexpectedly in January 1997. Interest, however, remained consistent and new compilations continue to trickle out around the world. In the UK, OUR MUSIC IS RED WITH PURPLE FLASHES (1998) finally saw the release of "Ostrich Man", a crunchy pop gem from the great days.

- ⊙ **How Does It Feel To Feel?** (1990; Demon).
  Almost all of the classic single cuts along with some other seminal tracks, like an inspired reworking of "Hey Joe".

- ⊙ **Painter Man** (1993; Demon).
  A mid-price roundup. Some tracks duplicated from HOW DOES IT FEEL TO FEEL?, but some other cover versions available here only. Creation addicts find they can't survive without this as well.

- ⊙ **Power Surge** (1996; Creation).
  Back for the right reasons: because they wanted it and because they still had it.

- ⊙ **Our Music Is Red With Purple Flashes** (1998; Creation).
  A studious trawl through the back catalogue to produce a collection fit both for the curious and for the rabid. Twenty-four tunes including hits, genuine rarities and two previously unreleased tracks.

Neil Nixon

THE CREATURES

Formed London, 1981.

Siouxsie Sioux (born Susan Janet Dallion) and **Budgie** (born Peter Clark) make music as **The Creatures** that hinges on Budgie's drums, percussion, and Siouxsie's haunting voice.

The Creatures made their official debut in 1981 with a difficult-to-find EP, WILD THINGS. Originally, this material was intended for the **SIOUXSIE AND THE BANSHEES** album JUJU (1981), but was deemed superfluous. The Creatures first full-length, though spotty, album FEAST (1983), recorded in a two-week stretch on the lush islands of Hawaii, displayed a synthesis of goth, psychedelia and exotica. The album also featured brass players and Hawaiian chorus singers on several cuts. One odd track, "Miss The Girl" (released as a single), was based on J. G. Ballard's book *Crash*. Another single, not included on the original cut of the album, "Right Now!", a Mel Torme cover, received coverage from teen magazines such as *Creem* and *Smash Hits*, due in part to Siouxsie's gothic ice princess Cleopatra image in the accompanying video.

The Creatures returned to the musical scene with the pulse-pounding, erotica-driven, flamenco beats of BOOMERANG (1989). Recorded in Jerez de la Frontera, Spain, over a four-week period while Siouxsie and Budgie were on holiday, this sixteen-track album spawned two minor hits in the US. "Standing There" was described by Budgie as 'a ribald stab, a shout back at the attitude of some males in this world who gang together and ridicule and victimize the individual female mostly' and "Fury Eyes" – based on Philip Ridley's novel *In The Eyes of Mr. Fury*.

In 1991, Siouxsie and Budgie married and moved from London to the south of France in search of privacy and seclusion. Both appeared on Hector Zazou's SONGS FROM THE COLD SEAS (1994) – Siouxsie contributing keyboards and drum-programming, and Budgie providing the percussion on "The Lighthouse", their reworked portion of the Gibson poem, *Flannen Isle*.

In the past, Siouxsie and Budgie viewed The Creatures as a sort of 'working holiday' allowing them to create infectious dance-floor rhythms. By the time they returned to the home studio in 1998 to record ANIMA ANIMUS (1999), however – another collection of expertly crafted dance with black lace trimmings – the working holiday had become a full-time job.

The whole album gleamed with ideas and enthusiasm, with standout track "Exterminating Angel" gaining extra power from its classy **Juno Reactor** production. Ms Sioux, photographed by Pierre et Gilles, glowered from the cover as glamorously as ever. Another new Creatures set has been on the cards since then, with albums such as HYBRIDS REMIX (1999) – Creatures tracks given the electronic treatment by various artists – filling the gap. But with the Banshees resurrected for a major tour during 2002 it seems unclear when it will ever emerge. Mind you, the Creatures' website contains details of so many rare and Internet-only releases that it should keep fans more than happy for quite a while.

- ⊙ **Boomerang** (1989; Geffen/Polydor)
  This is the quintessential Creatures album, ranging from the blues-driven "Killing Time" to the campy interlude of "Speeding". If you only get one Creatures album, this is the one to buy.

David Morgan

CREEDENCE CLEARWATER REVIVAL

Formed Berkeley, California, 1967; disbanded 1972.

In 1971's *NME* poll, **Creedence Clearwater Revival** superseded The Beatles as the world's 'Top Group'. One of America's most important bands, they'd been together at least as long as the Fabs, having worked the high-school hop circuit of central California as **Tommy Fogerty And The Blue Velvets** from the late 1950s until 1965, when **Tom Fogerty** (guitar), his younger brother **John**

(vocals/guitar), **Stuart Cook** (bass) and **Douglas 'Cosmo' Clifford** (drums) signed to Fantasy, a local label that had hitherto specialized in jazz.

They were then called **The Golliwogs**, a renaming commensurate with a tardy attempt to cash in on the British Invasion. The Golliwogs' flop records – including "Don't Tell Me No Lies" and 1966's "You Came Walking" – preceded a compulsory spell in the forces for Doug and John, and a subsequent decision to go fully professional as Creedence Clearwater Revival.

Stylistically, the group harked back to the energy and many of the standard chord sequences of 1950s rock'n'roll without actually looking the part, and the likes of Dale Hawkins' "Suzie Q" and "I Put A Spell On You" by Screaming Jay Hawkins (no relation) formed the backbone of their repertoire. John Fogerty also found his feet as a writer. Though Californian by birth, his spiritual home seemed to be the Deep South, as exemplified in titles like "Born On The Bayou" and "Mardi Gras".

Initial domestic chart strikes came with 1968's eponymous debut album and its two spin-off 45s – and after 1969's "Proud Mary" came within an ace of a US #1 slot, the outfit reached a wider world as the twelve-bar "Bad Moon Rising" (from 1969's wonderful GREEN RIVER) topped lists in Britain and elsewhere. So began two years of chart-topping for singles such as "Travelling Band", "Up Around The Bend", "Long As I Can See The Light", plus attendant albums – particularly WILLY AND THE POOR BOYS and COSMO'S FACTORY – that met favour with the heavy-rock and mainstream-pop fan alike. Their verse–chorus succinctness was a refreshing contrast to the tendency of other rock bands to stretch out a solitary number for up to thirty po-faced minutes.

Whether battling with the PA system at Woodstock or miming their latest Top 20 smash on BBC TV's *Basil Brush Show*, it was all part of a day's work for Creedence, whose winning streak came to an end with the departure of Tom Fogerty in January 1971 after the issue of the disappointing PENDULUM. Following a world tour and a final album, the poorly

received MARDI GRAS, the trio threw in the towel in October 1972.

After that, John Fogerty alone achieved some commercial success – notably with "Rockin' All Over The World" (adopted as a signature tune by Status Quo) and 1985's CENTREFIELD album. His brother died in 1990 and in 2001 a stunning, but weighty, 6-CD Creedence box set slipped out, to the delight of fans.

⊙ **Creedence Clearwater Revival** (1968; Fantasy).
Resulting from years of rough nights in parochial dance halls, the proceedings are endearing for a rough-and-ready spontaneity that fame would not obscure.

⊙ **Green River** (1969; Fantasy).
The Creedence blueprint, with each member working at full capacity.

⊙ **Cosmo's Factory** (1971; Fantasy).
Containing no fewer than three million-selling singles, this was a courageous attempt to broaden their scope, with tracks such as a remarkable overhaul of "I Heard It Through The Grapevine". The gifted John proves no slouch on saxophone either.

Alan Clayson

MARSHALL CRENSHAW

Born Detroit, Michigan, 1953.

Jangle, twang, rockabilly or power pop, **Marshall Crenshaw**'s work in the early 80s was a pure distillation of lessons learned from musical giants and, while he may not have stood on the shoulders of men such as Holly, Fuller, Lennon and Chilton, he managed a pretty decent view. It is hard to fathom how Crenshaw's smart songwriting and ringing guitar failed to do battle with vapid synth-pop for chart respectability – he writes a potential hit every time he puts pen to paper. But they remain just that: while critics have been captivated, the music-buying public have not, condemning him to bounce between labels, and almost into obscurity.

Prior to his self-titled debut in 1982, Crenshaw had already been introduced to the music biz by playing John Lennon in the touring show *Beatlemania*. It was this break (answering a casting call in *Rolling Stone*) that brought him to New York, where he was to land a recording contract after a few years of polishing his songwriting abilities. MARSHALL CRENSHAW was everything a pop album should be – hook-laden, crisply produced, eminently listenable – and it was a hit with fans and critics alike (*Rolling Stone*, at the end of the decade, declared it the 72nd best album of the 80s). The first single, "Someday Someway", was a driving, Holly-esque hit, but the real key to the album was the playfully serious search for a "Cynical Girl". This self-effacing geek seemed like he just might have the stuff to find her.

He followed this success the next year with FIELD DAY, a murkier recording, but a strong one, highlighted by the winsome "Whenever You're On My Mind". It was becoming obvious what was always on Crenshaw's mind – girls, girls and, um, girls – but he could constantly make his yearning for them seem fresh. On DOWNTOWN (1985), his most consistent collection, the songs were maybe not so pure fun as his earlier work, but they were durable and on target. The lead tracks on each album side, "Little Wild One (#5)" and "Distance Between", were revelations, the former a simmering love/lust rocker and the latter a stirring paean to love lost. The best work of his career, it went largely unnoticed.

Warner Brothers, Crenshaw's record company for these three albums, as well as the next two, MARY JEAN & 9 OTHERS and GOOD EVENING, began to grow disenchanted as sales failed to build. Little marketing weight was put behind these two recordings, which were, admittedly, a bit lacklustre, if not without their moments. GOOD EVENING was a mishmash of vaguely competent originals and some covers of tunes by artists of greater emotional depth than he could manage. Sometimes Crenshaw seemed more craft than conviction, and never was it more apparent than during this ebb.

Nevertheless, this was a crucial time. Crenshaw appeared in two movies, *Peggy Sue Got Married* (1986) and *La Bamba* (1987), both with ties to Buddy Holly, with whom he had often been compared. Rather than shunting the comparison aside, he now seemed to embrace it, actually portraying Holly in *La Bamba* and turning in a very credible version of "Crying, Waiting, Hoping". His twin passions for movies and music merged further when he edited the insightful *Hollywood Rock*, a critical compendium published to acclaim in 1994.

Though Crenshaw's music has largely taken a back seat in the past five-plus years, he did manage one album for a new label, MCA/Paradox, in 1991. LIFE'S TOO SHORT was a minor triumph, particularly the daft "Fantastic Planet Of Love", but again it made no inroads. In 1994, a live album culled from performances over a twelve-year stretch was put out by Razor & Tie, a label which has made a name for its rereleases of minor-selling artists. LIVE ... MY TRUCK IS MY HOME was a worthwhile keepsake and a decent overview of some of his top material. And the covers hit the mark, with the Bobby Fuller Four's "Julie" and, even more telling, Abba's "Knowing Me, Knowing You", an understated rendition which fitted nicely with his song catalogue.

A little short of media attention these days, with no more burdens from major labels and nothing left to prove, Crenshaw's first studio album in five years, MIRACLE OF SCIENCE (Grapevine) was released in summer 1997. A low-key affair, still shiny pop, but with a more 'rootsy' feel, typified by his cover of 60s (and 70s) hit, Dobie Gray's "The 'In' Crowd", Crenshaw shows depths previously obliterated by the glare of the spotlight. He followed up in 1998 with THE 9 VOLT YEARS and BATTERY-POWERED HOME DEMOS AND CURIOS 1979–85, a sub-lo-fi collection taken, as the name suggests, from his own collection of rough drafts. Most interesting are the alternative versions of some of his best-known tunes ("Rockin' Around In NYC" and "Vague Memory" stand out), though the previously unreleased material (particu-

larly "Run To You" and "Stay Fabulous" – an awesome instrumental track) holds its own well in this high-class company. More great music followed: 1999 saw the #447 album, 2000 brought THIS IS EASY!, and 2001 was blessed with I'VE SUFFERED FOR MY ART ... NOW IT'S YOUR TURN.

A major pop talent, hopefully one day to receive the appreciation he deserves, Crenshaw is now free, like fellow Razor & Tie graduate Graham Parker, to cultivate his niche popularity while augmenting his legacy of memorable melodies for the non-masses.

⦿ **Marshall Crenshaw** (1982; Warners).
A breath of fresh air when it came out, and it hasn't staled since. Loaded with catchy hooks, headed by "Someday Someway", which reached the singles chart in the US, and "Cynical Girl".

⦿ **Downtown** (1985; Warners).
A close contender with his debut for career highlight, this one is more an exploration of a range of emotions than a collection of singalong singles.

⦿ **Live ... My Truck Is My Home** (1994; Razor & Tie).
The remarkably clean sound makes these live sets seem like a studio recording, but this could just be a reflection of the type of crowds he usually draws. Stellar versions of "Calling Out For Love (At Crying Time)" and "Fantastic Planet Of Love".

Andrew Rosenberg

CRIME AND THE CITY SOLUTION

Formed Sydney, Australia, 1978; disbanded 1992.

Although **Crime And The City Solution** had existed since 1978, when they were formed by singer **Simon Bonney**, it was in London in 1984 that the band took on its true shape. Bonney joined up with ex-**BIRTHDAY PARTY** members **Mick Harvey** (multi-instrumentalist) and **Rowland S. Howard** (guitar), together with Howard's brother **Harry** on bass, and released a self-produced debut EP, THE DANGLING MAN, in 1985. Though they were overshadowed by fellow Birthday Party veterans Nick Cave And The Bad Seeds (of whom Mick Harvey was also a member), Crime were slowly developing their distinctive sound, a blend of Tom Waits-style blues, swamp-rock, and the grand vistas of Ennio Morricone, perfectly complementing the existential romanticism of lyrics co-written by Bonney and his wife **Bronwyn Adams**.

With the addition of drummer **Epic Soundtracks** (ex-**SWELL MAPS**), the band showed signs of development on the dark but redemptive 1985 mini-album JUST SOUTH OF HEAVEN. They crystallized this aesthetic with their first full album – 1986's ROOM OF LIGHTS. Simultaneously despairing and uplifting, the record gave free rein to the epic ambitions of their music with Bonney's grainy voice perfectly complemented by Rowland Howard's often majestic guitar.

The original line-up's final act was to perform "Six Bells Chime" in Wim Wenders' classic Berlin love story, *Wings Of Desire*. Shortly afterwards, the Howard brothers and Epic Soundtracks left to form **These Immortal Souls**. The remainder of Crime stayed in Berlin, where ROOM OF LIGHTS had been partly recorded, and reinvented itself. Bronwyn Adams became a full-time member on violin, while **Chrislo Haas**, **Thomas Stern** and **Alexander Hacke** were recruited from the local avant-garde scene.

This new line-up produced SHINE (1988), Crime's finest album, and one of the most overlooked releases of its time. Howard's bluesy guitar had been replaced with a more restrained, almost Oriental, feel, while the blend of violin and organ smouldered like The Velvet Underground. The uplifting devotion of the folky "On Every Train (Grain Will Bear Grain)" and the heartbreaking nostalgia of "Home Is Far From Here" demonstrated Bonney and Adams' grasp of emotional intangibles.

SHINE was largely ignored on its release, but the undeterred Crime began work on THE BRIDE SHIP (1989). Perhaps inevitably, it lacked the delicacy of touch of its predecessor, but it did contain many fine moments, including a reworking of "The Dangling Man". THE BRIDE SHIP also revealed Bonney's growing interest in the narrative song-cycle as a method of developing themes – in its trilogy of the same name he addressed the idealism and disillusionment of the emigrant.

Crime's last album was 1990's PARADISE DISCOTHEQUE, which possessed some magical moments, such as the beautiful "The Dolphins And The Sharks", but also revealed a pompous loss of subtlety epitomized by Bonney's song-cycle "Last Dictator", a clumsy dissection of the Ceauşescu regime in Romania.

After contributing "The Adversary" to the soundtrack of Wim Wenders' ill-advised sci-fi venture *Until The End Of The World*, Crime were all but finished. Mick Harvey continued to work with Nick Cave, and later **PJ HARVEY**, while Bonney and Adams worked together on the former's excellent country-inflected solo album, FOREVER (1992), and the much less impressive follow-up, EVERYMAN (1996).

While Crime And The City Solution were generally critically lauded, they never quite managed to escape the circumstances of their genealogy. Nevertheless, they were genuinely spellbinding doomed romantics, and remain one of the great undiscovered bands.

(•) **Just South Of Heaven** (1985; Mute).
The first flowering of the Crime's early promise, the six tracks on this mini-album constitute blues of the darkest hue. Songs like "Rose Blue" examine destructive relationships and the temptations of damnation, while the delicate "Stolen & Stealing" is an aching evocation of loss.

(•) **Room Of Lights** (1986; Mute).
Howard's guitar and Bonney's voice combine to sublime effect and, while emotional quandary is still at the heart of their songs ("Right Man Wrong Man"), a glorious sense of hope suffuses the record.

(•) **Shine** (1988; Mute).
An unacknowledged classic, this evokes a world of yearning and possession to rival Van Morrison's ASTRAL WEEKS. Dark, intoxicating and life-affirming.

Ian Canadine

CROSBY, STILLS, NASH & YOUNG

Formed California, 1969; disbanded 1971 but re-formed at intervals since, mainly as a trio without Young.

"Thank you, we needed that. This is the second time we've ever played in front of people, man. We're scared shitless." Stephen Stills at Woodstock

Rock journalist David Hepworth memorably described **Crosby, Stills And Nash** as 'Three of the most conspicuously stoned individuals that ever fumbled with a finger-pick', a neat summary of a band that captured the imagination of a generation but too often failed to deliver due to the debilitating effects of drugs and ego. The fact that neither **David Crosby**, **STEPHEN STILLS** nor **Graham Nash** knows for sure when they first sang together gives some indication of the collective state of their heads in 1969.

Crosby's cosmic leanings had eventually finished his membership of **THE BYRDS**; Stills had been a member (with Neil Young) of **BUFFALO SPRINGFIELD**, who had delivered fleeting moments of brilliance but ended in a mixture of acrimony and apathy; and Nash's membership of English popsters The Hollies had faced similar pressures to Crosby's tenure as a Byrd. The trio first teamed up either at Joni Mitchell's or John Sebastian's house, when Nash spontaneously joined a Crosby/Stills jam, hitting three-part harmonies that were to become an enduring and spellbinding aspect of their music.

Recording their first album, CROSBY, STILLS AND NASH (1969), in London, partly to allow Nash to extricate himself legally from The Hollies, CSN were an instant hit. The record started a marathon run in the US charts and launched the group to international fame. Their only problem was an overreliance on Stephen Stills' instrumental skills, a problem solved with the recruitment of **NEIL YOUNG**. With Young in place, the quartet played Woodstock – their second gig; the recordings indicate they played a patchy set, but history records that they had arrived.

To American audiences who had seen The Beatles as mythical figures, CSNY seemed like the rightful successors to the crown. They wrote songs of insight and feeling, had the musical expertise to stretch out and dazzle audiences, and produced a four-part vocal sound that could wrap the most mundane lyric with beauty. Their live work combined acoustic sets of fragile beauty with storming electric workouts featuring the twin lead playing of Stills and Young.

The quartet's first album, DÉJÀ VU (1970), was a strong and varied set, laced with antiwar and anti-government sentiments, mainly from Crosby and Stills. By the time Young's song "Ohio", written in response to the killing of protesting students by the National Guard, had stormed the US Top 20 in the face of a radio ban, CSNY were near enough the official band of the hippie generation. All the more sad and ironic, then, that a band that seemingly represented the ideals of peace and love blew such a strong beginning on years of puerile ego battles that would have been beneath even most of the politicians they railed against.

Logging further big sales with the live album FOUR WAY STREET (1971), the quartet set about recording solo projects, in Young's case with phenomenal artistic and commercial success. The lack of future action as a foursome would be largely down to his solo career eclipsing the work of the other three. Stills worked through part of the 70s with the seven-piece Manassas, who could play up a storm on stage and managed to get some of this down on vinyl. Crosby and Nash worked on as a duo, basing recording and touring projects on close vocal harmonies and well-crafted, if rather unsubtle, songs.

A CSNY reunion in 1974 produced a stadium tour that swelled bank accounts to embarrassing levels for a bunch of hippies. The projected reunion album got as far as some promising sessions and the cover artwork. Further attempts at albums in 1975 and 1976 collapsed in interpersonal difficulties, and when the contributions of Crosby and Nash were wiped from the tapes of the 1976 reunion, Nash vowed he would never work with Stills or Young again. A year later, however, Crosby, Stills and Nash re-formed.

The late 70s and early 80s were marked by CSN projects that showed the harmonies in fine shape and the songwriting pretty much where it had been at the start. Both CSN (1977) and DAYLIGHT AGAIN (1982) satisfied the old fans and sold well – indeed Stills' "Southern Cross" from the 1982 album was arguably the best song the trio had ever recorded. Touring

behind the albums, CSN were now a respected if predictable fixture of the rock big league. Individually, none of the trio had the commercial or critical clout to play the same venues or sell as many records. Young on the other hand was continuing to outperform his former cohorts on both fronts.

Crosby's lack of input on DAYLIGHT AGAIN had been ominous, and following some failed drug cures a spell in jail in the mid-80s finally cleaned up his act. Young had promised a reunion if Crosby got straight, and the quartet did play together at Live Aid while Crosby was out on bail. The second CSNY studio album, AMERICAN DREAM, appeared against all expectations in 1988, but only Crosby emerged with real credit, as his song to his new-found spirit, "Compass", briefly dragged the band back to their earlier heights. However, there was to be no live reunion and things continued, more or less, as they had at the start of the 80s.

With FREEDOM (1989) Young hit awesome solo heights that put further albums by the trio into the shade. CSN's career became noted for studio work that relied heavily on session friends and some songs co-written with others. LIVE IT UP (1990) was also notable for one of the worst sleeves in rock history, featuring steeplejacks attending to giant cocktail sausages on the surface of the Moon. The trio seemingly had little to offer by way of new music; their live work was frequently superb, but nostalgia played a big part.

Crosby staged a low-key solo rally after signing to A&M with OH YES I CAN (1989), winning back a few old fans and critics. His most meaningful contribution to rock may turn out to be his autobiography, *Long Time Gone* (1989), a chronicle of unremitting drug abuse that makes the man's continued hold on life nothing short of miraculous. His voice and songwriting survived in better shape than his liver, which was swapped for a less damaged model.

Stills, Crosby, Nash, Mitchell and Young: too many names for the album cover

The 'Unplugged' sets for MTV donated by CSN and Neil Young provided something of a contrast in the mid-90s. CSN relied on faithful reworkings of the old stuff while Young managed to reinvent and surprise within the acoustic format. By this time the two acts seemed so far apart that any further CSNY action seemed unlikely, a situation underlined by the execrable AFTER THE STORM (1995), on which CSN were reduced to covering The Beatles "In My Life" for the album's high spot. By 1997 they were without a label but their gigs were still inviting praise. Young, by contrast, could still make the cover of the glossy rock monthlies.

If anything it was Young's continuing pulling power that brought 1999's LOOKING FORWARD a level of attention far in excess of what it actually deserved. Anything but forward-looking, this tired, insipid and dull album failed to catch any of the sparks that the quartet still – on a good day – let fly in the live arena, as demonstrated on their highly successful *CSNY2K* tour in the album's immediate aftermath.

These four players are still lumped together because their moment in the early 70s promised so much. That they would develop into the American Beatles was a possibility, given the talent on offer. It would be harsh to rate CSNY as a failure, but there have certainly been missed opportunities.

So Far (1974; Atlantic).
A stopgap compilation for a band that were, at the time, intended to go on to greater things. This is still the strongest single album credited to CSNY.

Crosby, Stills & Nash Box Set (1991; Atlantic).
Superbly remastered four-disc compilation covering 1968–90, including unreleased material and the best of the solo work as well. Some of it, like Crosby's "Tracks In The Dust" from the 1988 solo album, is every bit as good as CSN's best cuts.

Neil Nixon

SHERYL CROW

Born Kennett, Missouri, 1962.

Born into a musical family – both her parents were big-band musicians – **Sheryl Crow** started playing piano at the age of 6. By 14 she was writing songs, and has been singing and playing in bands ever since. She graduated from the University of Missouri with a degree in Music Performance, Piano & Voice, and moved to St Louis shortly afterwards, where she taught music by day and played in bands by night. For a while she sang in the city's black gospel choirs, in what she refers to as her 'born again phase'.

After singing on a television advert for a fast-food chain and earning more money from it than she'd made 'in two years of schoolteaching', Crow decided to try singing full time. Packing all her belongings into her car, she drove to LA, where she had a few friends, and set about finding work on the session circuit. By

chance, she heard that Michael Jackson was auditioning backing singers for his forthcoming *Bad* tour. Although the auditions were by invitation only, she turned up and landed a job on the eighteen-month world tour. Her career prospects rose remarkably, and she soon found herself doing backing vocals for Stevie Wonder, Don Henley and Sinéad O'Connor, among others. In between, she managed to find time to write songs for country star Wynonna Judd and pop-funk outfit Lisa Lisa & Cult Jam.

But her main concern was getting a solo career off the ground. Her next big break came in 1992, when Hugh Padgham, former producer of The Police, heard one of her demo tapes and passed it on to A&M Records, who signed her up. Crow and Padgham spent several months – and around $450,000 – working on what should have been her debut album, but she was not satisfied with the finished work, finding it 'too perfect'. Much to her surprise, A&M scrapped it and allowed her to start over again. This time, she called on her friend Bill Bottrell (producer and co-writer of Michael Jackson's hit "Black Or White"); together with drummer Brian McLeod and a few other musicians, they would meet on Tuesday evenings, have a few beers, bounce ideas off each other and jam for a while. The resulting album, TUESDAY NIGHT MUSIC CLUB, was released in September 1993, but it was the release of the single "All I Wanna Do", the following summer, that made Crow a household name, eventually earning a Grammy for *Record of the Year*, one of three that she won. Having two songs – "Strong Enough" and "No-One Said It Would Be Easy" – featured in the film *Kalifornia* increased her following.

Big appearances ensued. Crow, rappers Salt-N-Pepa, and gospel supergroup Sisters Of Glory, were the only female acts at the Woodstock 2 festival in the summer of 1994, and Crow accompanied Hillary Clinton on a tour of Bosnia, playing a number of acoustic gigs for the peacekeeping forces. She also contributed to the *X Files*-inspired SONGS IN THE KEY OF X album (1996), her first new recording in three years.

She finished the year with a second solo album SHERYL CROW, a more mature and introspective selection, spanning bitterness in "The Book" – reflections on betrayal of trust – to almost-unbridled joy in "If It Makes You Happy", easily the album's brightest track. Most of 1997 was spent touring in support of the album and winning over mud-spattered festival audiences to her own easy-going jam-rock. Her major hit single for 1997 was the theme song for the Bond film *Tomorrow Never Dies*. It wasn't her best work, nor was it a particularly memorable Bond theme (in fact, it sounded more like the old *Perry Mason* TV theme).

Crow continued to champion various worthy causes; her music was featured alongside that of several top female musicians in LEADING LADIES, a box-set compilation released for the National Alliance of Breast Cancer Organizations (NABCO) in 1997. The following year, she joined a star line-up in a charity concert for Tibet. Occasionally, her public-spiritedness got her into trouble; the giant American retailers Wal-Mart banned her self-titled second album because of the lyrics to the song "Love Is A Good Thing" – in which she sang about children killing each other 'With a gun they bought at Wal-Mart discount stores'.

Crow released her third album in September 1998. It was originally titled RIVERWIDE, but the title (and, with it, the album's whole direction), changed after she received a phone call from Bob Dylan's manager, offering her a song. The song, "Mississippi", was an outtake from Dylan's Grammy-winning TIME OUT OF MIND album, which he'd been dissatisfied with. Crow accepted the song and recorded it, along with two more tracks: "Anything But Down" and "Crash And Burn". She then renamed the album THE GLOBE SESSIONS, after the New York studio at which it was recorded.

After a patchy live album – 1999's SHERYL CROW AND FRIENDS LIVE FROM CENTRAL PARK – Crow returned to the studio before releasing C'MON C'MON in 2002. The set was warmly welcomed by press and fans alike, and garnered much airplay thanks to seasonal singles like "Soak Up The Sun". The set also saw Crow opening her address book to enlist a host of celebrity voices, among them Stevie Nicks, Liz Phair and, bizarrely, Gwyneth Paltrow.

⊙ **Tuesday Night Music Club** (1993; A&M).
A real 'vibe' album – so laid-back you could do your ironing on it.

⊙ **The Globe Sessions** (1998; A&M).
Looking back to the good-time boogies of The Rolling Stones. An album punctuated with well-crafted, more introspective songs and even a Bob Dylan cover. Less attention-grabbingly weird than SHERYL CROW, it's still her best work to date.

George Luke

CROWDED HOUSE

Formed New Zealand, 1985; disbanded 1996.

"We're the band people feel the need to apologise for liking." Neil Finn

When New Zealand band Split Enz broke up in 1985, **Tim Finn** went off and married actress Greta Scacchi and pursued a mildly successful solo career. His brother **Neil** decided on a different path: he formed a hugely successful group with drummer **Paul Hester** and bassist **Nick Seymour**. The group called themselves The Mullanes after Neil's middle name, then signed to Capitol Records, and finally moved to Los Angeles, where they played several gigs under the name Largest Living Things. However, as they were living in a rather **Crowded House**, they decided to change it.

Produced by Mitchell Froom, their debut album, CROWDED HOUSE (1986), was a multimillion seller in America, while one track, "Don't Dream It's Over", just missed #1 in the *Billboard* Hot 100. British interest was more muted, only paying attention when Paul Young covered that very song at the Nelson Mandela 70th Birthday Concert at Wembley Stadium in June 1988. (Young would also cover it on a hit single in 1991.)

Even less successful in the UK was the second LP, TEMPLE OF THE LOW MEN (1988), which also fared worse in America. A major rethink was needed, beginning with a temporary split. On re-forming, they ditched two albums' worth of material, and Tim Finn joined Crowded House as a songwriter and harmony vocalist.

The resulting third album, WOODFACE, was finally released in 1991, and after a slow start became a huge seller in the UK, especially after the Top 10 success of the single, "Weather With You" – a beautiful singalong number with touches of The Byrds and The Beatles about it.

During the tour that followed, Tim Finn quit the band after a reported bust-up with his brother. He returned to solo work and had a hit of his own with "Persuasion". Meantime, Neil Finn had become a hot songwriter, with further hits "Four Seasons In One Day" and "It's Only Natural", as well as Paul Young's cover of "Don't Dream It's Over".

For the fourth album, the first without Mitchell Froom as producer, they recruited British producer Youth, best known for his work in contemporary dance music. Instead of recording in a stuffy studio in LA or Melbourne, they headed off to Kare Kare, a remote coastal region of New Zealand. Crowded House were heading back to their homeland and roots, as they turned their back on the American and British sound that had influenced their previous works. They even recorded a Maori choir for the title track of the band's biggest seller to date, TOGETHER ALONE (1993), on which Neil Finn's writing demonstrated his funny, as well as his romantic, side. It spawned another sequence of hit singles, with "Distant Sun" and "Nails In Your Feet" reaching the Top 20. The album was only kept from #1 by the unexpected comeback of Meatloaf.

The 1994 American tour was to cause another personnel change – moments before a show in Atlanta, Paul Hester walked out, to be replaced by the support act's drummer for the rest of the tour. A sell-out UK tour culminated in their headlining 1994's Fleadh festival at London's Finsbury Park. After that the Finn brothers released FINN (1995), a one-off album project that produced two singles, a brief tour, warm reviews and moderate sales.

In 1996, Tim went back to his solo work and various collaborations, which included being a member of 'folk supergroup' **Alt**, together with Andy White, and Hothouse Flowers member Liam O'Maonlai. However, Crowded House got back together for a tour in the summer to promote a 'greatest hits' compilation, RECURRING DREAM, before announcing their demise in November 1996. "Don't Dream It's

Over", "Weather With You" and "Fall At Your Feet" remain rock radio staples to this day, and long-term fans were delighted by the arrival of 1999's AFTERGLOW, a compilation of rarities and previously unreleased gems.

⊙ **Together Alone** (1993; Capitol).
Again, the songwriting shines through, from the rock of "Locked Out" to the semi-acoustic "Distant Sun".

⊙ **Recurring Dream** (1996; Parlophone).
Most of the hits, well segued, if out of chronological order, together with three new songs, and a bonus live album.

Martin Rowsell & Nick Duerden

CUL DE SAC

Formed Boston, US, 1990.

Brought together by **Glenn Jones** (guitars and 'Contraption'; ex-Shut Up, 7 Or 8 Worm Hearts), **Robin Amos** (synthesizer; ex-Shut Up and The Girls) and **Chris Guttmacher** (drums; ex-Bullet Lavolta), **Cul de Sac** were joined by bassist Chris Fujiwara (from 10 Stolen Vibes) as a project for exploring Jones's interest in combining the finger-style guitar playing of John Fahey with the group's other influences, which included a shared love of Sun Ra and Captain Beefheart.

Marrying Neu!-style Motorik drumming, occasional sub-Hendrix guitar freak-outs and the unique sound of Jones's Contraption (a prepared lap-steel guitar played with cutlery), Cul de Sac's first recordings were the "Sakhalin"/"Cant" (Shock) and "Doldrums"/"His Teeth Got Lost In The Mattress" (Nuf Sed) singles, followed by the ECIM album, all of which were released in 1992 to critical approval in North American and European underground circles.

With its combination of psychedelic, avant-garde and Krautrock techniques, ECIM was several years ahead of the trend towards instrumental post-rock – which grew to become the late-90s rock underground standard. Featuring guest contributions from Boston punk legend **Dredd Foole** (vocals) and 7 Or 8 Worm Hearts members **Ed Yazijian** (steel guitar) and **Phil Milstein** (tape-collage and saws), it boasted a remarkable cover of Tim Buckley's "Song To The Siren" with Foole's increasingly strangled vocals, and "Nico's Dream", a piece combining tapes of the German singer's characteristic voice over the band's playing and Milstein's tape noise.

Despite the praise of critics in certain quarters, Cul de Sac virtually disappeared for several years. Guttmacher departed for the West Coast in 1993, though the band played occasional live shows – usually backed up by films made by A. S. Hamrah and Fujiwara – and they released two further singles, "K"/"Frankie Machine" (Lunar Rotation) and "Milk Devil"/"Rain Moths" (New World Of Sound), following their own path in happy obscurity.

Meanwhile, Guttmacher collected together several years' worth of rehearsal tapes which appeared as I DON'T WANT TO GO TO BED on Flying Nun/Nuf Sed in 1995. The album was a surprise success in a 'post-rock' climate – which had seen a revival of all things instrumental and progressive – with its blending of guitars, bass and drums with electronics and unusual musical structures. With the addition of drummer **Jon Proudman**, the group completed their second studio album, CHINA GATE (Flying Nun/Thirsty Ear), in one fifty-minute session the following year. Welcomed on both sides of the Atlantic, it featured in many Album Of The Year charts and brought Cul de Sac new fans around the world.

Spurred on by Thirsty Ear's Peter Gordon, Cul de Sac revived earlier plans to collaborate with the veteran cult American Primitive guitarist **John Fahey**, who had recently recovered from a serious illness. Despite clashes over their differing musical styles and approaches to recording, the turbulent recording session in late 1996 resulted with the 1997 release of THE EPIPHANY OF GLENN JONES. The album was radically different from Cul de Sac's previous efforts, and will be treasured by relatively few listeners, due to the collapse of Flying Nun in Europe and the album's lack of proper distribution outside America.

Fujiwara and Proudman departed in the fallout of the Fahey recordings, to be replaced by **Michael Bloom** and **Michael Knoblach** respectively. Proudman's last contribution was in to CRASHES TO LIGHT, MINUTES TO ITS FALL, which received glowing reviews on its release in 1999. The album was one of the group's finest to date, and was preceded by a lavishly packaged 7" radio session reinterpretation of Fahey's "Portland Cement Factory At Monolith, California" (1999). Cul de Sac's strength has always been their complete unconcern with trends or fashions; long may they continue to explore what are too often dismissed as the dead ends of music.

⊙ **ECIM** (1992; Capella/Northeastern).
A brilliant debut, which combines the trance-rock of "Death Kit Train" with a Faustian cover of Fahey's "The Portland Cement Factory at Monolith, California". A cruelly ignored classic, whose time has come around again.

⊙ **I Don't Want To Go To Bed** (1995; Flying Nun/Nuf Sed).
Raw, lengthy rehearsal pieces that recall Can's studio jams in intensity and invention.

⊙ **China Gate** (1996; Flying Nun/Thirsty Ear).
A combination of new versions of singles, a cappella show tunes and (post-) space-rock grooves, culminating in the wonderful "Utopia Pkwy".

⊙ **The Epiphany Of Glenn Jones** (1997; Thirsty Ear)
An unusual document of the meeting of a group with an unwilling idol; unabashedly experimental and occasionally hilarious.

Richard Fontenoy

THE CULT

Formed Bradford, England, 1982; disbanded 1995.

Bradford's aspiring punksters, The Southern Death Cult, were fronted by singer **Ian Lindsay**, a man whose image, heavily influenced by

American Indian culture and Aboriginal spiritualism, sat uneasily next to his band's collision of indie and punk. But they were distinctive enough at a time of great confusion for the British underground scene, then midway between the aggression of punk/New Wave and the triumphalism of indie rock. Generous press coverage and radio attention helped an album, THE SOUTHERN DEATH CULT, into the lower reaches of the charts during the summer of 1983.

It all fell apart later that year when Lindsay, having reverted to his real name of Ian Astbury, moved to London, where he met up with ex-Theatre Of Hate guitarist **Billy Duffy**. (Duffy had also played in Slaughter & The Dogs and The Nosebleeds, whose singer was future Smiths vocalist Morrissey.) Together with **Jamie Stuart** (bass) and **Ray Mondo** (drums), Astbury and Duffy formed The Death Cult, which brought their sound a little closer to the mainstream.

By mid-1984 their name had once more been trimmed to **The Cult**, and an album, DREAMTIME, was released that summer. Astbury indulged his shamanistic tendencies to the full, assisted by an ever more potent psychedelic infusion. It sold respectably, and a single, "Resurrection Joe", scraped into the UK charts, but the band would virtually disown the album later on.

1985 saw The Cult crashing into the mainstream with "She Sells Sanctuary", which spent months climbing the UK charts before it eventually peaked at #15. The album that followed, LOVE (1985), showed how they had fully absorbed the 60s psychedelic-rock influence into their heavy indie sound. Its massive domestic success provided a launch pad for similar recognition in the US.

The Cult sensed a gap in a market where thrash had become the acceptable face of metal. Heavy rock became an increasing feature of their music, and ELECTRIC (1987) displayed the sort of crisp, sharp boogie more usually associated with the likes of ZZ Top. Produced by Rick Rubin (Slayer, Run-D.M.C., The Beastie Boys), it spawned several hit singles, notably "Li'l Devil", which narrowly missed

the UK Top 10. SONIC TEMPLE (1989) consolidated their reputation as one of the prime attractions of the late 80s and, if the music showed little progression, their insistent groove was nonetheless a perfect foil to Astbury's full-throated assault.

The loss of bassist Jamie Stuart in the early months of 1990 rather took the cohesion out of the band. Stuart was replaced by **Mark Morris**, formerly of Balaam & The Angel, but a lack of any fresh ideas meant an inevitable decline for The Cult. By CEREMONY (1991), only Astbury and Duffy remained from the original line-up, and although the album still made the Top 10 it lacked staying power, while the singles "Wild Hearted Son" and "Heart Of Soul" were barely noticed. Drug and alcohol abuse compounded the problem as the output slowed, and finally, in 1992, Astbury and Duffy cut their hair short to emphasize that 'Rock is dead'.

After the compilation PURE CULT (1993), only one more album followed, which featured a wider use of keyboards and textures than their earlier output. Even so, THE CULT (1994) was largely ignored, and mere months later the band called it a day, with Duffy briefly teaming up with ex-Wonder Stuff singer Miles Hunt to form Vent, while Astbury formed a band called The Holy Barbarians. After lying low for a few years, Billy Duffy resurfaced in 1998 to join up with Mike Peters (ex-Alarm) in a project called **Colour Sound**.

Beggars Banquet then began reissuing the band's classic albums in their original format, with no bonus tracks. They were intelligently remastered and, if you're planning to move on from vinyl, they're a highly recommended purchase.

In the meantime Astbury has continued to flex his cod beat poetry leanings with solo projects such as SPIRIT/LIGHT/SPEED (2000), and as soon as Colour Sound's limited shelf life expired both he and Duffy found themselves back in the studio recording another Cult album – a project many thought would never get off the ground. BEYOND GOOD AND EVIL, the group's first studio effort in years was released in 2001; it marked a triumphant and heavy return to form.

⊙ **Electric** (1987; Beggars Banquet/Sire).
Veering between goth-rock and R&B, this encapsulates The Cult at their peak. Astbury's vocal is always at the edge of mania, and the simple tight arrangements keep it all uncompromisingly direct and upfront. Rock's pre-grunge alternative to thrash.

Patrick Neylan-Francis & Guy Davies

CULTURE CLUB

Formed London, 1981; disbanded 1986.

"I'm not a musician, I don't play anything and I don't care to." Boy George

A British tabloid newspaper headline in October 1982 echoed nationwide sentiments after

Culture Club's first *Top Of The Pops* TV appearance – "Is it a bird? Is it a bloke? No, it's Boy George of Culture Club!" The sight of this strapping six-footer mincing across the stage in white smock and dreadlocks caused much raising of eyebrows, but it represented an instant success story, which would burn itself out almost as quickly.

BOY GEORGE (George O'Dowd) had always wanted to be a star. His flamboyant and original style had made him a well-known face about town during the New Romantic era of the early 80s, and after performing under various guises – including Lieutenant Lush with **BOW WOW WOW** – he formed his own band, Sex Gang Children, in 1981. After changing their name briefly to In Praise Of Lemmings, they became Culture Club, with a line-up comprising former Damned member **Jon Moss** (drums), **Roy Hay** (guitar) and **Mikey Craig** (bass).

Impressed by an eclectic demo tape, Virgin took them on, and released two unsuccessful singles – "White Boy" and "I'm Afraid Of Me" – before the breakthrough with "Do You Really Want To Hurt Me", which soared to #1 in the UK, and did much the same in more than twenty countries. With the debut album, KISSING TO BE CLEVER (1982) quickly establishing itself in the Top 5, Boy George was a star overnight, and not just a pop star, either – his charisma, humour and penchant for one-liners made him an all-round celebrity and chat-show favourite.

For the next two years, Culture Club were on the crest of a wave, conquering Britain, Europe and the States with a string of perfectly crafted three-minute pop songs. Their great strength lay in Boy George's unerring ability to achieve massive mainstream success without compromising his natural eccentricity. His lyrics were often baffling ("Miss Me Blind" or "Church Of The Poison Mind"), but they were invariably married to joyously catchy tunes and soulful vocals.

Prime examples of this were "Karma Chameleon", #1 in both the UK and US, and its parent album, COLOUR BY NUMBERS (1983), which was packed with similarly effervescent melodies and emotive ballads, establishing them as one of the world's biggest-selling bands. Their lead singer's appearance, so initially outrageous to many, had also become widely accepted, as he cultivated an unthreatening, asexual persona. Although his infamous quote, 'Sex? I'd rather have a cup of tea', still haunts him, he opened the door to a host of fellow 'gender-benders', none of whom had his talent or staying power.

When Culture Club released their third album, WAKING UP WITH THE HOUSE ON FIRE, in November 1984, it appeared that the years of constant touring and promotion had taken their toll. It was a patchy collection, which lacked both conviction and, more importantly, good songs. The first single, "The War Song", reached #2 in the UK, thanks mainly to an expensive video, but it was universally ridiculed for its inane chorus of "war is stupid and people are stupid". Its follow-up, "The Medal

Song", was an improvement, but disastrously only reached #32 in the chart. The backlash had begun.

A long silence followed as the band took stock and resolved to bounce back stronger than ever, but Boy George's spiralling drug dependency and the breakdown of his four-year relationship with Jon Moss caused friction and acrimony on all sides. They managed to complete one final LP, FROM LUXURY TO HEARTACHE (1986), but it was an indifferent album full of polished but soulless songs, on which even George's vocals failed to shine.

In July 1986, as his heroin addiction was revealed by bloodthirsty British tabloids, Boy George's band disintegrated. Hay and Moss both went on to form new bands with little success, while Craig turned his hand to producing, but, inevitably, the vocalist's solo career has been most prominent. After his recovery from drug addiction, he enjoyed a #1 hit of his own in 1987, and has gone on to huge success as an in-demand club DJ.

When even the fans seemed to have forgotten them, in 1998 the band unexpectedly hid their old differences behind extra-thick make-up and jumped aboard the crowded 80s revival bandwagon. An American tour proved hugely popular, a new track "I Just Wanna Be Loved" put them back in the UK Top 5 for the first time in fourteen years, and they were soon bopping and bitching like the 90s had never happened. An surprisingly likeable album, DON'T MIND IF I DO, was released in 1999; it was followed by a retrospective box set and, in the years since, a blizzard of other compilations. A clearly delighted George summed up the comeback with a classic O'Dowd sound bite: "Culture Club is pure tabloid, a Joan Collins soap opera with extra shoulder pads. People have clearly missed us."

Colour By Numbers (1983; Virgin/Epic).
One of the definitive early-80s pop albums, with every track exuding confidence and style, and backing vocalist Helen Terry's raw passion adding spice to George's soulful vulnerability. If occasionally lightweight, it remains an important document.

Greatest Moments (1998; Virgin).
Wisely consigning low points like "The War Song" to the dustbin of history, this spruced-up compilation tells you all you need to know about the Club, while the inclusion of a couple of new songs suggests there may be another chapter or two still to tell.

Jonathan Kennaugh

THE CURE

Formed Crawley, England, 1976.

When schoolmates **Robert Smith** (vocals/guitar), **Lol Tolhurst** (drums) and **Michael Dempsey** (bass) formed **The Cure**, they were inspired not by the emergence of the Sex Pistols but by an ad in the music press, beckoning 'Wanna Be A Rock Star?'. It prompted the trio to trump up their fledgling ambitions and create a dreamy kind of pop that was quietly, uniquely potent in the lager-heady days of punk.

Original Cures Robert Smith, Michael Dempsey and Lawrence Tolhurst

Their response to the ad led to an uneasy alliance with the Dutch label Hansa and by 1978 they'd recorded "Killing An Arab", a Camus-inspired rant which fell on many an illiterate ear and provoked unwarranted controversy. But the band also caught the eye of New Zealander Chris Parry, who'd shepherded The Jam's career and knew he could do the same for The Cure. Parry promptly signed them to Fiction, a subsidiary of Polydor.

The sleeve for their debut LP, THREE IMAGINARY BOYS (1979), sent up their faceless image by substituting appliances in place of a group photo. While this tactic misfired (a new cover was quickly prepared for the US market), the music itself was heralded as a fine debut. The Cure were showing that doom-laden British rock was not strictly the domain of the industrial north.

Simon Gallup (bass/keyboards) replaced Dempsey in 1980, the beginning of a sequence of pretty but increasingly bleak records – SEVENTEEN SECONDS (1980), FAITH (1981) and PORNOGRAPHY (1982). When bitter rows led to Gallup's departure, Smith and Tolhurst (now a keyboard player) adopted a more whimsical stance with the single "Let's Go To Bed" at the end of 1982. Its accompanying video marked the beginning of a long association between the band and director Tim Pope. The growing darkness defined the band's style for the next few years and grew them a horde of waif-like followers, with the bleak "A Forest" from SECONDS repeatedly winning fan polls.

By the middle of 1983, The Cure seemed something of a part-time job for Smith. Despite their first major hits with "The Walk" and "The Lovecats", and the release of a compilation mini-LP of singles and B-sides, JAPANESE WHISPERS, Smith also joined **SIOUXSIE AND THE BANSHEES** as guitarist, to be featured on the single "Dear Prudence" (1983) and LP HYAENA (1984). He also formed a further sideline project, **The Glove**, with Banshees guitarist Steve Severin producing the 1983 album BLUE SUNSHINE. Smith returned to The Cure full time in spring 1984. An experimental new album, THE TOP, came out that year, but it wasn't until 1985's quirky, uneven THE HEAD ON THE DOOR that the band's line-up was expanded to include **Porl Thompson** (guitar/saxophone/keyboards), drummer **Boris Williams**, and Simon Gallup once more. The album spawned two big hit singles – the infectious "In Between Days" and the Motown pastiche "Close To Me", accompanied by a video which featured the band crammed into a wardrobe and toppling over the White Cliffs of Dover.

While The Cure's gloomy image was quickly becoming as claustrophobic as that wardrobe, they had become a sell-out stadium band. This high-profile popularity had inevitable side effects – at a 1986 performance in Los Angeles a loveless fan stabbed himself to death. 'We can't win, really,' commented Smith. 'We're either considered a really doomy group that inspires suicides or we're a bunch of whimsical wackos.'

The double LP KISS ME, KISS ME, KISS ME (1987) was the band's unlikely key to the American market, and their 1989 epic, DISINTEGRATION, furthered their stateside fan base – the summery single "Love

Staring At The Sea (1986; Fiction).
A fine retrospective of Cure singles, encompassing all the highs and lows, from jangly, bell-jarring pop to dire dirges.

Kiss Me, Kiss Me, Kiss Me (1987; Fiction).
Ambitious, fascinatingly overblown album. The hysterical image problem that is "Why Can't I Be You?" makes a strange bedfellow for "Just Like Heaven", the latter covered by Dinosaur Jr, who declared it 'the only listenable song on the LP'.

Disintegration (1989; Fiction).
This blinding collection of joyful love songs, psychedelics, and heart-ripping despair is not one to be missed. The opening title-cut alone is worth the price of admission.

Greatest Hits (2002; Fiction).
All the chart favourites from the last twenty years – uneven, but with some superlative moments. The two new songs featured – particularly the elegiac "Cut Here" – are full-strength Cure cuts and just about make up for the exclusion of "Killing An Arab", removed presumably due to the sensitivity of the time.

Susan Compo

Song" was a huge hit in the *Billboard* charts. By now, founder member Tolhurst had left to form the short-lived Presence, after furious clashes with Smith. (The battle continued in court in 1993 after arguments about songwriting royalties; Tolhurst lost the case.)

Tolhurst's replacement in The Cure was **Perry Bamonte** (keyboards/guitar), but new material would be a long time coming. Die-hard fans were less than enamoured with the stopgap compilation MIXED UP (1990), a curiously enjoyable LP of remixes that demonstrated how suitable their music was for the dance floor. Eventually, new material appeared in the shape of WISH (1992) and its smash hit single "Friday I'm In Love", before Thompson announced his departure in 1994. There was a further two-year gap before a new album, WILD MOOD SWINGS (1996), emerged – a rather staid release that saw no noticeable development on past triumphs. 1997's singles-sampler GALORE mined old turf, with the exception of new track "Wrong Number," a somewhat nondescript song which nonetheless put forward a beguilingly scrambled caller ID.

2000's BLOODFLOWERS aimed to carry on where DISINTEGRATION left off, but ended up sounding forced – an attempt to hark back to glory days perhaps? 2001's fully-fledged GREATEST HITS (which overshadowed the previous calendar's drab GALORE singles collection) showed just how much the band had changed over the years. While STARING AT THE SEA captured a coherent sound, this career retrospective captured The Cure's stylistic fits and starts, and for its many plus points demonstrated how difficult Smith has found it to balance his goth tendencies with his pure pop sensibilities.

Seventeen Seconds (1980; Fiction).
Though tinged with darkness, this stunning collection maintains a delightful buoyancy thanks to the crisp rhythms and Smith's great lyrics – "Play For Today" and, of course, "A Forest" stand out.

Faith (1981; Fiction).
This is the sound of The Cure in truly miserable mood. Pieces such as "All Cats Are Grey" and "The Drowning Man" sound haunted and endless. Not to be listened too if you're feeling a little glum.

CURRENT 93

Formed London, 1983.

Current 93 is the work of **David Michael Tibet**, who departed Psychic TV after the DREAMS LESS SWEET LP, collaborating with Coil's John Balance and 23 Skidoo's Fritz Haaman. Naming themselves Current 93 (after Aleister Crowley's secret religion) they released their first EP "Lashtal" for Laylah Anti-Records in 1983. This was followed a year later by the LP NATURE UNVEILED, a hair-raisingly unusual combination of warped voices (courtesy of Annie Anxiety, John Balance and Youth), orchestral tape loops and Tibet's own possessed cry. The LP also introduced Steven Stapleton (with whom Tibet had worked in Nurse With Wound and as **Dogs Blood Order**), who would be the band's other most frequent contributor.

Follow-up release DOG'S BLOOD RISING (1984) was an even noisier affair, this time with Tibet's Diamanda Galas-ish wailing to the fore. Tibet's extreme vocals and the stirring in of ex-Strawberry Switchblade Rose McDowall resulted in the next LP IN MENSTRUAL NIGHT (1986 United Dairies) being even more unusual and easily the best C93 album of this period. Things turned even stranger with the follow up single, the notorious "Happy Birthday Pigface Christus", ushering in a new 'apocalyptic folk' sound influenced by the melancholic singing of Shirley Collins. A core group of musicians – including Death in June's Douglas Pearce and Tony Wakeford of Sol Invictus – helped develop the group's sound through the hypnotic repeated chords found on IMPERIUM (Maldoror 1987), CHRIST AND THE PALE QUEENS MIGHTY IN SORROW (1988) and the sinisterly beautiful EARTH COVERS EARTH (United Dairies, 1988).

Each album revealed further aspects of Tibet's interest in Gnostic mysticism and impending apocalypse, and in 1987 he found himself in hot water over the title of C93's most famous album SWASTIKAS FOR NODDY – in part inspired by a bizarre vision of Enid Blyton's character crucified as a Gnostic deity. It has since been retitled as SWASTIKAS FOR GODDY. Many of Current 93's finest moments can be found here; the cover of Strawberry Switchblade's "Since Yesterday", a version of the Blue Oyster Cult's "The Summer Of Love" and adaptations of Isidore Ducasse's proto-Surrealist text *Maldoror* stand out in particular.

In 1992 Tibet set up his own label Durtro, and unleashed the incredible THUNDER PERFECT MIND double LP. Taking much inspiration from Tibetan Buddhism and Early Christian visions, the album set the direction for much of C93's subsequent output, including the shimmering OF RUINE OR SOME BLAZING STARRE (1994) triptych and the brilliant psych-rock diversion "Lucifer Over London" EP – latter in collaboration with Bevis Frond. The more autobiographical ALL THE PRETTY LITTLE HORSES (1996) brought much favourable mainstream press attention, ranking it alongside the work of **Nick Cave** (who appears on the album), while the piano-led SOFT BLACK STARS (1998) remains Tibet's own personal favourite release. Collaborative works with writer Thomas Ligotti (Tibet also runs vintage horror imprint *Ghost Story Press*) included the disturbing I HAVE A SPECIAL PLAN FOR THIS WORLD (2000), while Tibet and Stapleton also released three non-C93 albums together.

Current 93's stance has always been staunchly independent, distanced from the music industry as much as possible, and, alongside Nurse With Wound and Coil, they form part of a genuine underground. Their music is full of stark contrasts; on one hand gentle, lilting folk and uneasy ambient nuances and on the other violently noisy soundscapes filled with terrifying religious visions. C93's extensive back catalogue is eagerly collected; its most recent additions include SLEEP HAS HIS HOUSE (2000), which mixes layered drones with Tibet's moving reflections on the death of his father; the double CD ALL DOLLED UP LIKE CHRIST (2000), a comprehensive document of their powerful live sound; and CATS DRUNK ON COPPER (2001), another live artifact.

⊙ **In Menstrual Night** (1985; United Dairies/1994; Durtro).
A journey of sorts through the mind of a young girl, the album sculpts an eerie and dramatic ambience much like that of TAGO MAGO-period Can. The CD version also contains C93's 'disco-single' "Killykillkilly".

⊙ **Thunder Perfect Mind** (1992; Durtro).
A more personal turn in the obsessions of David Tibet, possibly Current 93's definitive moment. A musical Gnostic mystery tour from the "Descent Of Long Satan And Babylon" via a haunting cover of Sand's "When The May Rain Comes" to the apocalyptic imagery of "Hitler As Kalki".

⊙ **Emblems: The Menstrual Years** (1992; Durtro).
An essential two-CD collection of C93's work between 1982 and 1992, including some carefully edited versions of tracks from the first three LPs, plus a second disc containing some of their best songs – among them "Hooves", "The Signs And The Sighs Of Emptiness", "They Returned To Their Earth" and the famous "Happy Birthday Pigface Christus".

⊙ **All The Pretty Little Horses** (1996; Durtro).
Definitely their friendliest and most beautiful recording to date, it keeps the experimentation to an effectively sinister minimum. Here they craft some of their most memorable and melancholic tunes – "The Bloodbell's Chime", "The Inmost Light Itself", and, courtesy of Nick Cave, the beautifully rendered title nursery song.

⊙ **Soft Black Stars** (1998; Durtro).
A distillation into quietness of the central themes previously explored by Current 93 – childhood fantasy, waking dreams, loss and sorrow – set to Michael Cashmore's simple piano compositions.

Terry McGaughey & Richard Fontenoy

CURVE

Formed London, 1991; disbanded 1994; reformed 1998.

Described by one reviewer as like 'Debbie Harry colliding with Motörhead', **Curve** were focused on lead singer **Toni Halliday**, who enjoyed a misspent youth in various amateur bands. A local TV interview attracted the attention of Dave Stewart, who persuaded her to move from Sunderland to London and put a band together. The appallingly named **Uncles**, however, won few friends with their sole MCA release ("What's The Use In Pretending"; 1983) and split within months.

Undeterred, Stewart introduced Halliday to session bassist **Dean Garcia**, who had played on Eurythmics albums TOUCH and BE YOURSELF TONIGHT. In 1986 Garcia and Halliday formed **State Of Play**, a funk-pop band whose 'one druggy, horrific year' of existence was a financial disaster for their label, Virgin. Their one LP, BALANCING THE SCALES (1986), was justifiably forgotten, as Garcia and Halliday became involved in legal disputes with each other. Halliday turned to session work, notably on Robert Plant's NOW AND ZEN (1988), before making a bid for solo success with HEARTS AND HANDSHAKES (1989), which flopped completely and was conveniently ignored when her fortunes improved.

In a remarkable about-turn, given the aftermath of State Of Play, Halliday and Garcia reunited to form Curve, and signed to Dave Stewart's Anxious label. With guitarist **Chris Sheehan** and drummer **Monti**, they produced a sequence of thrilling EPs – BLINDFOLD, FROZEN and CHERRY (1991), FAIT ACCOMPLI and HORROR HEAD (1992). Each release married Halliday's glacial vocals to pile-driving industrial backing, and all topped the UK indie charts. Their discography celebrated its first year in March 1992, when the debut album DOPPELGANGER just missed a Top 10 album placing.

Though many critics felt the album did not live up to the EPs which had preceded it, Curve's reputation spread across the Atlantic, thanks to the UK version of the Lollapalooza tour, *Rollercoaster*, where they played alongside Spiritualized and The Jesus & Mary Chain. Fellow noisenik Trent Reznor of Nine Inch Nails offered to remix their next single,

"Missing Link", as a taster for the 1993 album, CUCKOO.

While impressively produced and played, Cuckoo displayed little creative progression. After its extremely brief chart career, difficulties with their label and the departure of new guitarist **Debbie Smith** for Echobelly, Curve were apparently finished.

Solo projects, meanwhile, were still most intriguing. In 1995, Halliday guested on Leftfield's excellent single "Original", before forming another new band, **Scylla**.

The mid-90s explosion of interest in 'electronica' won Curve's back catalogue renewed attention and when Dean was called in to help out on some of Scylla's material it was only a matter of time until the reunion was announced. COME CLEAN (1998), showed just how much the members of a band could benefit from some time to themselves: there was a rediscovered joy in the music that had previously been missing.

This glee and confidence was even more apparent on 2002's GIFT, an intense, dense mash of electronica, featuring a guest guitar assault by My Bloody Valentine's **Kevin Shields**.

⊙ Radio Sessions (1993; Anxious).
A good selection of early tracks and proof that Curve were as good live as in the studio. For the band at their best, however, search out the early EPs.

⊙ Gift (2002; Artful).
This set offers the best of Curve's 'second coming'; it's an intense listening experience, with Toni Halliday's silky snarls often engulfed by dynamic tides of noise.

Bruno MacDonald

CURVED AIR

Formed London, 1969; disbanded 1977.

They might be just a footnote in British rock history but the aspirations were high when **Darryl Way** and **Francis Monkman** formed **Curved Air** in 1969. Way was a graduate of London's Royal College of Music who had begun to experiment with amplification systems for violin; Monkman was studying keyboards at the Royal Academy of Music and investigating the possibilities of the electric guitar. It was a classic progressive-rock background. Unfortunately, though, the relationship between the two would provide as much acrimony as musical experiment.

Still, things had begun well. Having recruited Swedish-American **Sonja Kristina** as vocalist, the band set about doing everything you would expect of an aspiring prog outfit. John Peel sessions and club and university gigs were developing an interest and their manager had managed to sell the tapes of their first album to Warners, netting a £100,000 advance – huge at the time. Support dates on some prominent tours helped their first album, AIR CONDITIONING (1970), to #8 in the UK charts. Novelty played a part, too – it was one of the first picture discs, a psychedelic mandala nestling in a clear sleeve.

Way and Monkman could structure music that trashed much of the pretentious prog-rock competition, whilst Kristina's background as a stage performer (she'd been in *Hair*), and her neat line in costumes, gave the band a real impact in live work. The second album, SECOND ALBUM (1971), was tighter than the first, giving Way and Monkman one side each to display their compositional and instrumental talents. It was followed by a headlining UK tour and the "Back Street Luv" single, which hit #4 in the UK charts and helped the album to #11.

The band's musical pedigree suggested they could build on this start although, in truth, their spark depended on a fragile chemistry, and by the time the band were ready for a serious stab at the US, things were already falling apart. The American response was warm and Air still had a solid fan base in the UK, but the third album, PHANTASMAGORIA (1972), was problematic. Kristina fought to get her own composition, "Melinda More Or Less", onto the disc, for which the two main composers again split the sides for their own material. The album just scratched the Top 20 and proved to be the last chart entry, album or single, that the band would notch up in the UK. The rifts were sorted when both Way and Monkman left in an upheaval that split the classic line-up that had been completed by **Ian Eyre** (bass) and **Florian Pilkington-Miksa** (drums).

Recruiting two teenage prodigies, **Kirby Emerson** on guitar and **Eddie Jobson** on keyboards, Kristina toured a new album, AIR CUT (1973). This line-up was more cohesive than the previous crew, but the project smacked of some desperation and Kristina's sometimes trite and pretentious lyrics were exposed in music that moved towards standard 70s rock with frills. AIR CUT's opener, "Purple Speed Queen", was a case in point, ending with an overdose suicide and the line 'The doctor said, that she just couldn't take any more'.

Predictably enough, others plundered the musical talent on offer. Within a year Jobson had joined **ROXY MUSIC**, Kristina was back on stage in *Hair* and the others had gone their separate ways. Contractual problems had played their part in disbanding Air and they also forced a rapid reunion when an outstanding tax bill prompted a tour in late 1974. A revamped line-up including Way, Monkman, Kristina and Pilkington-Miksa once more headed around campuses. The album LIVE (1975) also generated some cash, after which Monkman and Pilkington-Miksa departed.

Way had an eighteen-month stint in the truly progressive and truly ignored **Wolf** behind him and Kristina had ambitions. Between them they recruited another line-up for the albums MIDNIGHT WIRE (1975) and AIRBORNE (1976). By this point the music press and rock market had moved on from the days when cosmic and classically based rock presented mind-expanding possibilities and mind-numbing advances from record companies. Nonetheless, the final Air crew, which toured as punk rock was getting started, was still a powerful proposition. From 1975 the live and studio work was fuelled by the percussive skills of **Stuart Copeland**, shortly to power **THE POLICE**. Copeland's massive sound and ability to combine a solid beat with the illusion that he was soloing gave the final line-up a live impact that kept them up with the competition. Copeland and Kristina also formed a relationship that would outlast the band, which was finally laid to rest at the start of 1977.

Copeland's post-Air success has eclipsed the others, whose disparate futures showed the band had always been saddled with 'musical differences'. Monkman went AOR when he helped to form Sky with classical guitarist John Williams. Jobson's CV includes some of Roxy Music's most lucrative work and guesting with Frank Zappa. Way worked with Wayne/Jayne County, among others, while Kristina's low-key solo career included her own band, Escape, and a hippiefied 90s comeback.

Curved Air retain a die-hard following, but it is a measure of their time-warped status that until recently a definitive 'best of' collection hasn't even been on the cards, though Warners are due to be putting things right very soon. In a curious footnote, Darryl Way's post-Air work has included the album FORTRESS (1995), on which he arranged the London Symphony Orchestra in covers of Sting and The Police.

⊙ **Air Conditioning** (1970; WEA); **Second Album** (1971; WEA).
These 1996 mid-price reissues of the first two albums showed the Air still had a nostalgic following.

⊙ **Live At The BBC** (1995; Strange Fruit).
These Radio 1 sessions date from 1970 to 1976 and include pretty much all the stage favourites – except "Back Street Luv" – and are often more immediate and spirited than the studio versions.

Neil Nixon

HOLGER CZUKAY

Born Danzig, Germany, 1938.

"Inability is often the mother of restriction, and restriction is the great mother of inventive performance."

Holger Czukay has contributed to some of the most influential records of the last quarter-century, both with **CAN** and as a solo artist. In his work is a direct link between the symphonic and avant-garde traditions and the rock world – one that has inspired many – while his seminal use of samples and world music deserves wider recognition, beyond his fellow artists and collaborators around the globe.

From an early age Czukay expressed a desire to be a composer and conductor. The only question mark hung over the music. He was disqualified from a 1960 jazz festival for 'unclassifiable' music, and two years later expelled from Berlin's Music Academy. He then studied composition under Karlheinz Stockhausen, an important experience, which taught not only attention to detail in each note but also the limitations of an overintellectual avant-garde. Taking up teaching himself, Czukay found himself exposed to The Beatles, The Rolling Stones and The Beach Boys by one of his pupils, Michael Karoli, and subsequently spent nine years playing with him, and Irmin Schmidt, in Krautrock supremos Can.

Around the same time as Can's first recordings, Czukay and his friend Rolf Dammers released an LP called CANAXIS 5 (1969), in a limited edition of 500, in which they pioneered both sampling techniques (using tape splicing) and interest in world music. The music was constructed from thousands of tape recordings from short-wave radio, notably two unknown Vietnamese singers on "Boat Woman Song", and mixed in with Czukay's bass playing. It is this technique that Czukay has refined over the past 25 years, to an extent with Can, and more overtly as a solo artist.

Czukay's first album, following his split from Can in 1977, was the highly influential MOVIES (1979; reissued 1998), which was rated #5 in that year's *NME* critics' poll, and gained its creator *Sounds Germany*'s vote as Musician Of The Year. It was a remarkable record, Czukay studio-editing short-wave radio sources – notably a gorgeous Iranian singer on "Persian Love" – against delicate guitar work and **Jaki Liebezeit**'s (ex-Can) usual superb drumming.

The record drew a lot of music-business attention, and Czukay was enlisted along with the renowned producer Conny Plank to work on the debut album by the then unknown Eurythmics in 1981. That year also saw him working with Jaki Liebezeit and **JAH WOBBLE** on the LP FULL CIRCLE and a single "How Much Are They", which, with Wobble's dubbed-out bass (both he and Czukay were fans of Lee Perry), became an 80s club hit. Wobble also introduced Czukay to Japanese singer Phew, and together with Plank and Liebezeit they recorded the LP PHEW (1982).

Czukay's own next solo outing, ON THE WAY TO THE PEAK OF NORMAL (1982; reissued 1998), was partly assembled from recordings with Düsseldorf band SYPH, and again collaborated with Jah Wobble. Its standout track is "Ode To Perfume", which Holger recommends for 'listening while rollerskating, driving or flying.'!

The next few years were spent chiefly in production work, but Czukay found time for two further solo albums, DER OSTEN IST ROT (1984), which featured a rhythmic reworking of the Chinese national anthem, and ROME REMAINS ROME (1987), featuring wittily treated samples of Pope John Paul II delivering his Easter Message on "Blessed Easter". Both albums had some success, adding to Czukay's reputation as a musical eccentric, a role in which he starred in a German TV special, *War Of Sounds*, in 1987.

Following a spell working with David Sylvian on the albums PLIGHT AND PREMONITION (1988) and FLUX AND MUTABILITY (1989), pleasant washes of sound lacking the bite and humour of Czukay's own work, Czukay helped re-form Can (for 1989's RITE TIME), and then returned as a solo artist with a 'live studio' album, RADIO WAVE SURFER (1991), an oddity, setting Sheldon Ancel's vocals and storytelling (Ancel is a member of Jaki Liebezeit's Phantom Band and former US Armed Forces Network announcer) over a rhythmic background (courtesy of Liebezeit), punctuated by Czukay on his favourite instrument, the French horn.

Since then, Czukay has been engaged in remastering the Can back catalogue for CD rerelease, while releasing the darkly atmospheric MOVING PICTURES (1993), also the first to feature the voice of partner **U-She**. Sadly, however, he didn't participate in the 20th anniversary 'not quite-reunion' shows in 1999. Now in his sixties, Czukay has plunged into electronic multimedia work, running an eccentric web-TV station and collaborating enthusiastically with a new generation of German and international musicians and DJs. His recent releases have included the double CD of off-kilter techno CLASH (1998), recorded live with Air Liquide's Dr. Walker in Cologne and America. His rate of solo output has also picked up recently, to include the Can-sampling atmospherics of GOOD MORNING (1999) – incredibly also his first record to use digital samplers – and LA LUNA (2000). Czukay has earned his place as an icon of Twentieth Century experimental music, and is well placed to continue developing into the new millennium.

Canaxis 5 (1969; Spoon).
A beautifully recorded and composed masterpiece of tape samples (recently rereleased on CD), with sleeve notes that rival Can in their absurdity.

Movies (1979; Spoon).
Czukay's finest hour, featuring the tremendous "Persian Love" – a track later used for a Japanese whisky commercial!

Rome Remains Rome (1987; Virgin).
Flip but engaging, with John Paul II on guest vocals. The CD rerelease includes highlights of DER OSTEN IST ROT.

La Luna (2000; Tone Casualties).
Recorded in a single session in May 1996, and subtitled an "Electronic Night Ceremony", this set rides on a ubiquitous electronic pulse.

Richard Fontenoy

DICK DALE

Formed Del-Tones, California, 1960.

"He's a crazy man. Any amplifier we ever made, the guy could blow up." Fender on Dick Dale

One of the hardest-working men in show business, **Dick Dale** has been on stage nearly every day of his life for the past forty years. He's known to all as 'The King Of The Surf Guitar', though he professes a dislike for all matters surfing. An oddball, you might say.

Still, Dale was the undisputed creator of surf music in the early 60s, in southern California, unleashing a blazing, beach-bonfire guitar style that generated dozens of surf groups within a couple of years. His blistering style was something of an anomaly – it didn't reflect the lull of ocean swells so much as herald the future of harsh skateboarding rips and riffs – but what the hell. Dale played guitar left-handed, choosing not to alter the strings, an effect which defined his sound as much as did a happy proximity and association with the Fender Instruments factory in nearby Santa Ana.

And then there was the reverb. Fender supplied Dale with the first portable reverb device, which allowed him to make sounds approximating an offshore earthquake. In September 1961, **Dick Dale & The Del-Tones** released "Let's Go Trippin'", the first 'surf' record. The Fender Reverb made its debut on 1962's "Miserlou", a cover which goes about as deep as you can get, and nods to Dale's Lebanese heritage.

SURFER'S CHOICE and its single "Surfbeat" came out in late 1962, hot on the heels of The Beach Boys' "Surfin' Safari". Capitol Records lured Dale to its ranks, where he released a bevy of records, among them "The Wedge" (1963) and the faddish hot-rod LP, MR. ELIMINATOR. His Capitol days ended in 1965, with a final LP, SUMMER SURF. Two of its tracks, "Tidal Wave" and "Banzai Wipeout", involved multiple tracking and a more sophisticated studio production. All the same, Dale, along with the entire surf music fad, disappeared in the mid-60s, although his popularity as a live act continued. He eventually resurfaced in 1987 to contribute to the nostalgia film *Back To The Beach*, while his recording of "Pipeline" with Stevie Ray Vaughan rose above the proceedings like a tsunami.

In 1994, "Miserlou" skidded over the opening credits of Tarantino's *Pulp Fiction* and the reverb was resurrected for at least another generation. Dale him-

Dick Dale (with plank, naturally) and Frankie Avalon

self got a recording contract again, too, releasing new material – TRIBAL THUNDER (1993), UNKNOWN TERRITORY (1995) and CALLING UP SPIRITS (1996) – which showed he had lost none of his thunderous vitality. When Jimi Hendrix, himself a Dick Dale fan, prophesied, 'You'll never hear surf music again', he was all too wrong.

⊙ **The Best Of Dick Dale & His Del-Tones** (1989; Rhino).
A drive-thru menu of Dale's consummate surf'n'turf music. The perfect ride without a wipeout in sight.

Susan Compo

DALEK I LOVE YOU

Formed Liverpool, 1977; disbanded 1985.

In his spellbinding autobiography, *Head On*, Julian Cope recalls the following: 'The middle of June [1978] we saw a group called **Dalek I Love You**. They played Eric's one night, with sofas and lamps on stage, and their set was a weird mixture of uncool and brilliant. Like the guitarist had a moustache. Uncool. And the bass player was a total sissy, with a lisp and cutesy fringe. But they had organ lines like the Seeds and Doorsy bass lines. The bullshit on stage didn't work, but along with the psychedelic guitar and Suicide drum machine, it all helped to create their own thing.'

Along with Cope's band The Teardrop Explodes, and their deadly rivals Echo And The Bunnymen, Dalek I Love You emerged from a scene based at Liverpool's Eric's club. The scene was fluid and its family tree a jungle. Guitarist **Alan Gill** and bassist **David Balfe** were refugees from punk, bailing out from Radio Blank to found the new band in November 1977. Gill wanted to call it Darling I Love You; Balfe preferred The Daleks, so they combined ideas, like Pink and Floyd. They added **Dave Hughes** on keyboards, and experimented with synthesizers and a drum machine, pioneering the New Wave synth-pop that would dominate the charts over the next few years.

Dalek released some influential synth-pop singles, before Balfe left to join Big In Japan (and later The Teardop Explodes). Thus it was that, by the time of their 1980 debut album, COMPASS KUM'PASS – with **Chris Hughes** on percussion and **David Bates** adding backing vocals – they had in a way already passed their prime. It was a decent enough album, but somehow lacked the appeal of, say, Orchestral Manoeuvres In The Dark, who were charting at this time with similar material. In fact, you could say that OMD (like The Teardrop Explodes) were as much Dalek as Dalek themselves, with Hughes defecting to them in 1980, and his Dalek replacement, **Malcolm Cooper**, taking his OMD place the following year. Gill, meanwhile, had joined Balfe in The Teardrop Explodes.

Still, a rejigged band of Daleks – **Gordon Hon** and **Kenny Peers** plus mates – got a deal with Korova, producing a rather messy follow-up album, DALEK I LOVE YOU (1993), and, in a last burst of activity, the cassette-only release, NAIVE (1985), as **Dalek I**, before consigning the group to the realms of rock legend.

⊙ **Compass Kum'pass** (1980; Fontana).
Divided into 'topsy' and 'turvy' sides, this is DIY music, with toytown synths and soundscapes straight out of Eno's green world. Boppy and poppy, it uses stereo in entertaining ways for the first time since primetime psychedelia, which "Heat" oddly resembles. The likes of Soft Cell and OMD took off from this compass point to find buried treasure. The Daleks walked the plank.

Brian Hinton

DALI'S CAR

Formed and disbanded London, 1984.

Dali's Car was a short-lived – one album – partnership between **Mick Karn**, ex-bassist with arty New Wave band **JAPAN**, and **Peter Murphy**, ex-vocalist with arty gothic punks **BAUHAUS**. They took their name from a Captain Beefheart song and that of their album, THE WAKING HOUR (1984), from the Maxfield Parrish painting that adorned its sleeve. (Parrish was a Paris-based poster artist of the 1920s, famous for his pseudo-classical style and ultra-bright light effects.) It was accompanied by a single, "The Judgement Is The Mirror", in which the duo styled themselves as skinny-tied 60s mods, inspired by Michael Caine in the Harry Palmer spy movies.

Multi-instrumentalist Karn handled virtually all the music, aided by **Paul Vincent Lawford** on percussion. As you might expect from a band who paid homage to Beefheart, the sound is pretty bizarre: jerky looping rhythms, gothic keyboards, Karn's complex fretless bass, and a dash of his Turkish Cypriot roots. Meanwhile, Peter Murphy gets all mystic and esoteric, his impenetrable lyrics out-weirding the weird efforts of his previous band. The result was unconventional, almost surreal music that still stands distant from its contemporaries.

Afterwards Murphy avoided talking about the album in interviews, moved to Turkey and enjoyed some solo success in the US. Mick Karn continued to make odd records, collaborating with his ex-Japan cohorts on various projects, and contributing his bass virtuosity to the likes of Bill Nelson and Kate Bush.

⊙ **The Waking Hour** (1984; Beggars Banquet).
A richly textured and unconventional album that now sounds of its time – Siouxsie And The Banshees stalwart Steve Churchyard produced – though still deeply original. The weirder King Crimson stuff is probably its nearest point of reference.

Ross Holloway

THE DAMNED

Formed London, 1976; disbanded 1978; re-formed 1978; disbanded 1988; reformed 1997.

The first version of **The Damned** emerged in early 1976 from the nascent punk scene that was

Damned if there's no Rat. From left: Dave Vanian, Capt. Sensible, John Moss, Lu Edmunds and Brian James

gathering force in London's nightlife demimonde. **Rat Scabies** (drums), **Brian James** (guitar) and **Ray Burns**, soon to become **Captain Sensible** (bass), had briefly backed *NME* journalist **Nick Kent** in his Subterraneans; Scabies and James had also flirted with the **London SS**, a proto-punk outfit which had included **Mick Jones** and **Tony James**, soon to find fame with The Clash and Generation X respectively. It was James who named the Rat; till then he had gone by the rather more prosaic name of Chris Miller.

By the time of The Damned's first gig, on July 6, supporting the Sex Pistols at the 100 Club, a handsome young man had been roped in to sing: **Dave Vanian** (real name Letts) hailed from Hemel Hempstead and was a regular at London gigs, cutting a distinctive figure in his Dracula-like garb. Brian James was the mainstay of this first version of the band, providing a string of brutally simple but effective songs dealing with standard rock'n'roll themes – S&M sex on "Feel The Pain", drugs on "So Messed Up", and generally behaving badly on "Neat Neat Neat" and "I Fall". The inclusion in the set of The Stooges' "I Feel Alright" was an indication of his main source of inspiration. The rest of the band were content to ride on James's coat-tails for the time being, although this unequal relationship held the seeds of their eventual downfall.

Apart from James's obvious talent for a good tune, The Damned got by in those early days on little more

than enthusiasm, gigs being noted mainly for their chaos and the furiously kinetic performance. The music press began to characterize them as a pantomime of punk buffoons, but this was unfair: they were an enjoyable addition to a scene that had its genuinely threatening element in the Pistols and its (relatively) articulate political spokesmen in The Clash. If The Damned had a problem, it was that they could never make up their minds what they were about: was James's rocker chic at the heart of the band, or was it Vanian's gothic obsession, or Sensible and Scabies' idiocy?

The Damned signed to the recently formed Stiff label in October and The First Ever Punk Single was quickly recorded and released. The classic "New Rose" (1976) was followed by The First Ever Punk LP, DAMNED DAMNED DAMNED (1977), a fine template for other aspiring punk bands. Nick Lowe's lo-fi, tinpot production augmented the songs perfectly, and the whole thing was a speed- and booze-fuelled oafish triumph.

The remainder of the year saw a slow decline in The Damned's fortunes, although their gigs remained as invigorating as ever and the single "Problem Child" indicated that the early standards might be maintained. A second guitarist, **Lu Edmunds**, joined in August at the behest of James, but the group became increasingly rent by internal tensions. Although he played on the second LP, MUSIC FOR

PLEASURE (1977), Scabies left in October, decrying James as a dictator, and demanding to be known in future as Chris Miller. The album was badly received, and it was not only the music press which savaged it – the band have generally dismissed it as well. Their early energy had dissipated, and producer Nick Mason of Pink Floyd was powerless to rescue things.

Events reached a nadir with a tour in late 1977, with **John Moss** (later to be seen as Jon Moss – without an 'h' – in Culture Club) standing in for Rat. Attendances were poor and The Damned collapsed early in 1978, leaving behind them a couple of classic singles, a great album, and the responsibility for starting one of punk's true rituals – gobbing.

After briefly working on various other projects, they re-emerged in September 1978 under the title The Dimmed, which became The Doomed, and finally The Damned again early the next year. Vanian still dressed as Dracula, and Sensible and Scabies remained the lunatic axis, but they were a radically different prospect from the first incarnation. Brian James had not been asked back; Sensible had switched to guitar and **Algy Ward** from The Saints had been drafted in on bass. Gigs were an irresistible draw for kids who had missed the band first time around, and all the rowdier for making up lost time. As in the early days, there was the occasional punch-up between band members to enliven the spectacle.

Musically there had been, if not a leap, then a hop forward. The songs were far more polished, as if the band had realized that punk did not necessarily have to be equated with an absence of a clearly discernible tune. Three great singles were released in 1979 – "Love Song", "Smash It Up" and "I Just Can't Be Happy Today" – followed by the excellent MACHINE GUN ETIQUETTE (1979) album, an adept mix of punk and pop, though still without much in the way of lyrics.

Ward left to be replaced by **Paul Gray** from The Hot Rods, and by late 1980 the band had reached a kind of post-punk creative peak with THE BLACK ALBUM (1980). This double LP lacked the outright aggression of earlier efforts and showed the band happy to explore some of pop's mellower areas. Vanian at last gave some substance to his gothic persona on "Dr Jekyll And Mr Hyde" and "13th Floor Elevator", while Sensible had a go at singing on "Silly Kids' Games". Most surprising of all was the seventeen-minute epic "Curtain Call", which occupied the whole of side three. The album was a riposte to those who had always written them off as a one-dimensional joke band who should have given up years previously.

Curiously, in the wake of Sensible's departure, The Damned enjoyed something of a resurgence with a line-up consisting of Scabies and Vanian, the improbably named **Roman Jugg** on guitar (he had previously played keyboards at the band's gigs), and **Bryn Merrick** on bass. PHANTASMAGORIA was released and several overblown hits followed – including a cover of Barry Ryan's "Eloise" (1986),

their biggest hit to date. One more album, ANYTHING (1986), followed, but in the late 80s the band ground to a halt. By then, connections with their early days had become so tenuous that 'The Damned' seemed just a brand name that could accommodate any number of personnel changes.

For much of the 90s it seemed as if the various members were content to do their own thing and just get together for the odd reunion gig to entertain nostalgic punks. They also churned out the occasional dodgy album; I'M ALRIGHT JACK AND THE BEANSTALK (1997) – also known as NOT OF THIS EARTH – was another bland slab cut from an apparently dead horse and it really did seem as if The Damned would never release a decent collection again. Until GRAVE DISORDER (2001) appeared, that is. Maybe they needed the money, maybe it was fate, but the band somehow landed a deal with US label Nitro (owned by **The Offspring**, who ironically covered "Smash It Up" to great acclaim), and Vanian and The Captain were reunited alongside ex-Sisters Of Mercy four-stringer **Patricia Morrison** (now Mrs David Vanian), keyboard player **Monty Oxy Moron**, and drummer **Pinch** (ex-English Dogs, The Wernt, and Janus Stark). The album, while not quite classic, was nevertheless a slick and stylish return to the kind of cartoon goth punk that The Damned had previously done so well.

Most recently SMASH IT UP: ANTHOLOGY 1976–1987 (2002) and THE STIFF SINGLES 1976–1977 (2003) have introduced the power of the group's back catalogue to a new generation who equate Blink 182 with punk.

- **Damned Damned Damned** (1977; Demon; reissued 2002; Castle).
  The first punk album – three chords and a cloud of dust. Naturally, an essential purchase.

- **Machine Gun Etiquette** (1979; Big Beat).
  First-rate power pop, including the anthemic "Smash It Up" and "Love Song".

- **The Black Album** (1980; Big Beat).
  A far more restrained, almost playful side to the band, somewhat offset by side four's mad live set.

- **The Stiff Singles 1976-1977** (2003; Sanctuary).
  This set features the group's first five singles for the legendary Stiff imprint. As well as cuts such as "New Rose" and Neat, Neat, Neat", this is the place to track down the ultra-hard-to-find gig-freebie track "Stretcher Case Baby".

Andy Lewis

DANDY WARHOLS

Formed Portland, Oregon, 1994.

For a quick introduction to simple guitar rock, you need something by The Velvet Underground, something by T-Rex, a bit of Neil Young, and then bring it up to date with some Jesus & Mary Chain, R.E.M., Ride, Blur and Oasis. Or just economize by getting a **Dandy Warhols** album. They gleefully take all these influences and mix them in a bucket with a bottle or two of tequila, in what *Rolling Stone* called 'the most exhilarating 60s-into-

90s excursion yet attempted by an American band' – and then **Zia McCabe** takes her clothes off. At last, someone's remembered that rock'n'roll should be fun.

Courtney Taylor (guitar/lead vocals/tequila) started out in The Beauty Stab and Nero's Rome before launching his own rock vision with **Peter Holmstrom** (guitar/vocals/tequila), **Eric Hedford** (drums/vocals and synthesisers/tequila) and the afore-mentioned Ms McCabe (keyboard/bass/percussion/vocals/tequila/occasional bra).

Gigs involving heavy drinking, fighting, striptease by various band members (with McCabe's most eagerly awaited) created a big buzz around their hometown of Portland, Oregon. Local label Tim Kerr Records snapped them up for their debut single, "Little Drummer Boy", in 1994, followed by a debut album, DANDYS RULE OK, the following year. The bright and catchy first single, "TV Theme Song", got them on to MTV and got a naked Taylor into *Rolling Stone*, with 'Kings of Pop' emblazoned across his chest in lipstick.

The major labels quickly hit the Oregon trail, 'so naturally we rode this pony for all it was worth,' as the band put it. 'Free meals, plane rides, hotel rooms and much much more. Eventually we ran out of A&R people willing to fund our entertainment.' So they signed to Capitol, with a big cash advance. Forty-eight hours and four large hangovers later, they found themselves still with a major deal, but without the advance: 'Everyone wrote about us saying that we were going to be the next big thing. Of course we fucked it up.'

When they finally delivered the album, Capitol delivered it right back with the unexpected stipulation that the album should include some 'songs'. Flat broke and on the brink of the abyss, the band retired to Taylor's basement to start again. Taylor stopped fighting with Hedford and wrote some new songs, and Capitol gleefully unleashed THE DANDY WARHOLS COME DOWN in 1997. It was a corker. First into the charts was "Not If You Were The Last Junkie On Earth", driven by its insistent drum track (cf. The Velvets' "I'm Waiting For The Man") and wry hookline 'Heroin is so passé'. Next up was "Every Day Should Be A Holiday", with one of the most infectious riffs of the year – an almost inevitable hit. Then came "Boys Better", with its heavy Neil Young-style guitar and vocal.

Hedford and Taylor never quite patched up their differences, with the drummer departing in March 1998 to pursue his solo ambitions as **DJ Aquaman**; he was replaced by Taylor's pal **Brent de Boer**. Meanwhile the group spent three years spawning a follow-up to COME DOWN. Taylor, curiously, doubled his name to **Taylor-Taylor** and promised a new album 'somewhere between ALL THINGS MUST PASS (George Harrison) and WORKINGMAN'S DEAD (Grateful Dead)'. THIRTEEN TALES FROM URBAN BOHEMIA (2000) certainly contained a sense of post-party ennui, but still packed a good few punches, not

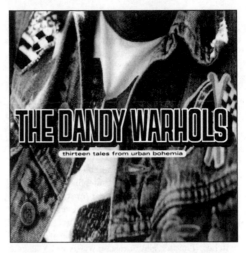

least the huge hit single "Bohemian Like You" which went Top Ten in the UK charts – the fact that it was used in a marketing campaign for Vodaphone helped more than a little. The single proceeded to roll out across Europe picking up Dandy's converts in its wake.

America has so far failed to come to terms with the shameless decadence of the Dandy Warhols, although the British have wholeheartedly embraced Taylor's credo. This situation may yet change, given the brilliance of 2003's WELCOME TO THE MONKEY HOUSE, which was co-produced by Duran Duran's Nick Rhodes and Toni Visconti, and even features a guest appearance from Simon Le Bon.

Dandies Rule OK (1995; Time Kerr Records).
"Ride", "Coffee and Tea Wrecks" and "Lou Weed" betray their influences in the titles, but the latter works in its own right as well as a parody/imitation. Just when you think it's running out of steam in the middle, there's the compulsive beat of "Nothing", making a whole song out of a Led Zep cadenza ("Babe I'm Gonna Leave You"), with its distorted, almost falsetto 60s-style vocal.

The Dandy Warhols Come Down (1997; Capitol/Parlophone).
With the gentle hippie intro to "Be-In", it sounds like the Dandies are coming down big time, but it builds into some swirling, pulsating rock, sustained by "Boys Better" and the immaculate "Minnesoter". "Good Morning" shows R.E.M. where they have gone wrong, but "Pete International Airport" could almost be Gong.

Patrick Neylan-Francis

DANIELSON

Formed Clarksboro, New Jersey, 1991.

Danielson (the family and group) produce a strange combination of art and psychedelic folk music, with a gospel element that, while central, does not limit their creativity. **Daniel Smith** created Danielson as part of his high-school thesis (receiving an 'A' grade), drawing on earthy country traditions of musical worship, learned from the knee of his uncle Lenny Smith (composer of Christian hymns), as well as through his membership of an art-noise band that railed against growing up in the nearby narrow-minded farming town of Clarksboro.

Daniel (vocals/guitar), sisters **Rachel** (keyboards/vocals), **Megan** (xylophone/vocals) brothers **David** (drums) and **Andrew** (drums/percussion), and honorary Smith **Chris Palladino** (organ) form the core of the Danielson family group, using different group identities for each occasion. **The Family** (also spelled 'Famile') specialize in energetic, semi-acoustic gospel; **Danielsonship** is the darker, choral group (with guests), while **Brother Danielson** foregrounds Daniel's heartfelt, singalong folk style – bizarrely, performed wearing a nine-foot papier-mâché tree.

As a group, the Family appear on stage in nurse's outfits (complete with hearts on sleeves), are often seen dressed as angels and also produce a range of Danny-themed goodies, including pillowcases and patches. The first album release was A PRAYER FOR EVERY HOUR (1995), based on the Danielson family's home-worship services and the art-rock propensities of Daniel. Including one of Lenny's hymns, simple acoustic numbers and more experimental, improvised, almost deranged moments amongst its mixed bag of 24 songs, the album showcased Daniel's falsetto voice and unusual songwriting style. Though based in religious practice, the effervescent, contagious energy of the young Daniel and siblings shone out from a patchy record.

By the time TELL ANOTHER JOKE AT THE OL' CHOPPIN' BLOCK (1997) appeared, Danielson and Family had recruited renowned producer Kramer to oversee the project. What is undoubtedly their best album so far benefited greatly from Kramer's production, at times revealing affinities to his Bongwater work, as well as fellow eccentrics The Holy Modal Rounders or God Is My Co-Pilot. Kramer drew great performances from the group, whose expanded instrumentation included flute, banjo, bass and trombone, bringing greater depth to their sound. Showcasing what Daniel calls 'vulnerary music', for the healing of spiritual wounds, TELL ANOTHER JOKE received rave reviews across America for its unusual blend of complex, yet joyful, noise with the emotional wranglings of Daniel's highly personal songs of doubt and faith. A small line-up of the band toured America with Soul Junk in the summer of 1997 (though whether the tree came too is not recorded).

The three Danielson incarnations released TRI-DANIELSON !!! (ALPHA) (1998), part one of a two-part expansion of their sound (OMEGA followed in the autumn of 1999). With a more rock edge to the Famile songs (even including electronics), comparisons to the Pixies were even made.

With these last two releases, Danielson achieved the almost unimaginable – the rehabilitation of Christian music from the realms of saccharine sermonizing into thoughtful, even mind-bending, and ultimately highly original music, a mission which was continued with the Steve Albini-engineered FETCH THE COMPASS KIDS (2001).

⊙ **Tell Another Joke At The Ol' Choppin' Block**
(1997; Tooth & Nail).
The essential Danielson album covering themes of how to be a spiritual person in an irreligious world, as well as tempatation, redemption and mother–child relationships. This album exudes the intensity of a gospel revival with a distinctly psychedelic twist.

⊙ **Tri-Danielson!!! (Alpha)** (1998; Tooth & Nail).
First part of a two-part, tri-fold expansion of the Danielson world. One-third shows Danielson's thoughtful, acoustic side; one-third, the rousing gospel choir typified by the emotional fireworks of "Body English"; and rocking tracks such as "Rubbernecker" and "Pottymouth". Most surprising, though, is the cover of jazz-eccentric Ken Nordine's "Flesh" in electro style.

Richard Fontenoy

DANZIG

Formed Los Angeles, 1988.

"A thousand angers have kept me alive." Glenn Danzig

Shortly after the dissolution of legendary punk/hardcore band **THE MISFITS**, its lead singer **Glenn Danzig** formed the darkly arty Samhain with bassist **Eerie Von**, creating an embryonic version of the band that would later adopt Danzig's surname. Immediately seized by producer, label chief and philanthropist Rick Rubin, **Danzig** evolved in 1988 with the addition of ex-**DOA**, **CIRCLE JERKS** and **BLACK FLAG** drummer **Chuck Biscuits** and guitarist **John Christ**. The quartet recorded their 1988 eponymously titled debut album before playing a single gig, although their solid-state sound and malevolent image had already been well crafted by frontman Danzig. Inspired by the crunch of death rock, 70s proto-metal swagger and a good old-fashioned dollop of the blues, the band produced an illicit musical union between Black Sabbath, The Doors and AC/DC.

Danzig's reign of terror continued with their second, more diverse and most accomplished effort, DANZIG II – LUCIFUGE (1990), a set fuelled by self-parodic incantations of evil (they just can't be serious) and a singer who alternately recalled the sensuality of Elvis Presley, the wounded sincerity of Roy Orbison and the growling bravado of Jim Morrison. Two years later, the more accessible DANZIG III – HOW THE GODS KILL, represented their first appearance in the US Top 40. It also marked the first time Glenn Danzig was able to wrest production duties from the adamantly hands-on Rubin.

In 1993 the band put out THRALL – DEMONSWEATLIVE, an EP featuring three studio tracks and four live tracks recorded at a 1992 gig. "Mother", originally emanating from the band's debut, was included on the live side. Thanks to radio and MTV exposure, it hit the charts, and success was consolidated with the release of 1994's DANZIG IV.

Shortly afterwards, Chuck Biscuits left the group (either over business differences or excess chemical abuse), to be replaced by **Joey Castillo**. Also that year, Glenn Danzig wrote the wonderfully dark "Thirteen", for label mate Johnny Cash, who recorded it on his phenomenal AMERICAN RECORDINGS album.

In 1996 the band released BLACKACIDEVIL, which was followed by SATAN'S CHILD (1999) and SACRIFICE (2000); all three failed to break any new ground, propelling them further into self-parody.

⊙ **Danzig** (1988; Def American).
Dark songs and darker imagery. Includes the Doors-ish "She Rides" and the sadomasochistic, yet catchy "The Hunter", which sounds like it could have been written by Spinal Tap.

⊙ **Danzig II – Lucifuge** (1990; Def American).
The band's best work, this includes the taut blues of "Killer Wolf" and the twelve-bar shuffle of "I'm The One". Tight ensemble playing by Biscuits, Von and Christ form the perfect platform for Glenn Danzig's fierce, impassioned vocals.

⊙ **Danzig III – How The Gods Kill** (1992; Def American).
Their most accomplished commercial effort. Danzig's vocals are less demonstrative and tortured than on earlier works. Likewise, the music is dynamically arranged, exploding from a whisper to a scream and vice versa, often within the space of the same song.

Ben Hunter

TERENCE TRENT D'ARBY

Born New York, 1962.

The unlikely name of **Terence Trent D'Arby** may first have come to the public's attention via the barnstorming, beseeching 'sweetheart, listen...' introduction to "If You Let Me Stay", but behind that lay years of obscurity and dues-paying. As a teenager, D'Arby had dabbled in boxing and journalism and spent three years in the US Army. He then joined German funk-rock band The Touch as lead vocalist in 1982 before heading for London, where he worked on solo demos, which finally led to a deal with CBS.

His first single, "If You Let Me Stay", stormed into the UK Top 10 in April 1987, boosted by music press approval and a series of eye-opening live shows. It all augured well for the eagerly awaited album, and INTRODUCING THE HARDLINE (1987) did not disappoint, brimming with rumbustious funk rockers and smouldering soul ballads, all delivered with the serene confidence that would become D'Arby's trademark. The album went on to sell eight million, reaching the *Billboard* Top 5 and topping charts across Europe.

The master plan according to CBS at this stage was to mould D'Arby as a Prince/Otis Redding hybrid, but they reckoned without their golden boy's ego and defiantly stubborn streak. In the first flush of success, he set out his stall during an *NME* interview, declaring: 'I think I'm a genius. Point fucking blank.' In 1988, he posed naked and crucified for publicity photos, alarming his record company and alienating many fans with his self-aggrandizing excesses. These proved to be the first steps on the road to commercial suicide.

The single-album-tour treadmill was given short shrift by D'Arby when he delivered his second album, the experimental and psychedelic NEITHER FISH NOR FLESH (1989), to baffled CBS executives. Won over by his unflinching self-belief, they agreed to his demands that there should be no preceding singles and timed its release for the Christmas market. Their concern at its lowly initial sales turned to panic when it vanished from UK and US charts within four weeks. Even the belated release of two singles – one of which D'Arby claimed had been sung to him in a dream by the late Marvin Gaye – failed to arrest its decline.

D'Arby spent much of the next two years licking his wounds before emerging from the wilderness with SYMPHONY OR DAMN (1993). Divided into two segments – 'Confrontation' and 'Reconciliation' – this was a dynamic comeback whose four Top 20 hits firmly re-established D'Arby's credibility. Although there was plenty of the old pretentiousness in evidence, there was also a new line in lyrical wit and self-deprecation. The critics approved and SYMPHONY OR DAMN reached the Top 5.

With his rehabilitation now firmly on track, D'Arby spent the next two years touring and working on material that became VIBRATOR (1995). It failed to live up to commercial expectations. Eyebrows were raised at the recruitment of former Bros star **Matt Goss** to perform guest vocals on one track, but D'Arby was typically unapologetic: 'I knew it would suitably annoy people. Too much attention is paid to credibility. No artist can be enslaved to any concept.'

After a long period in exile, and having untangled himself from CBS (by now part of Sony), D'Arby worked hard to reclaim some ground with the release of WILDCARD in 2003. By this time he was sporting the name **Sananda Maitreya**, a moniker that had apparently been delivered to him by a host of angels. Musically, the set was a powerful comeback and boasted several, standout, funky moments.

He is too intelligent and capricious to settle for the Simply Red coffee-table option, although his mellifluous voice and knack for a gorgeous chord sequence suggest that he could quite easily make his fortune along that path. It's much more likely that TTD will continue to baffle, fascinate, enthral and generally rock the boat for as long as he wishes to do so.

⊙ **Introducing The Hardline** (1987; CBS).
Almost entirely self-written, this scintillating debut announced in bold block capitals the arrival of a major new talent. The funky numbers are handled with the vigour of a youthful James Brown, while the ballads display a silky sensitivity which recalls Sam Cooke.

⊙ **Symphony Or Damn** (1993; Columbia).
Returns don't come much more triumphant than this sixteen-track cosmopolitan journey through a kaleidoscope of musical styles, all linked by an unobtrusive production, which allows each song to shine in its own right. The closing "Let Her Down Easy" is D'Arby at his tender, bewitching best.

⊙ **Vibrator** (1995; Columbia).
Stage two on the comeback trail forsakes the rainbow approach of SYMPHONY OR DAMN in favour of a Kravitz-esque rock guitar feel. It's all stylishly executed, but there is a coolness about it that makes you yearn for the panache of old.

Jonathan Kennaugh

THE DATSUNS

Formed Cambridge, New Zealand, 1995.

It's hard to believe that any country where sheep outnumber the inhabitants could produce a band hailed as the force to save rock'n'roll. But that's exactly what happened when New Zealand gave **The Datsuns**, originally named Trinket, to the world.

The story started with a bunch of kids meeting at school and forming a band, eventually adopting the group's name, in true Ramones style, as their surnames. In the mid-90s **Dolf Datsun** (bass/vocals) was caught up in the enthusiasm of the US pop-punk explosion spearheaded by the likes of Green Day and felt the urge to make some noise of his own. He grabbed his mate **Phil Datsun** and made him guitarist before they both approached the only kid in school with a drum kit, **Matt Datsun**, to be their sticksman. About a year later they bumped into **Christian Datsun** (lead guitar), a self-taught musician with a taste for the slabs of dusty vinyl he found in charity stores, who would prove to be the band's classic rock director. He reckoned he might enjoy a little guitar mayhem and the chance to see where luck and dedication might take him.

The band had a love of modern sounds but the writing sensibilities of an earlier generation of rockers. Live shows would find them indulging in all the preposterous shape-throwing of yesteryear but knocking out tunes that had all the immediacy of punk; it was bluesy hard rock delivered with the venom of youth. Having created their own label, Hell Squad Records, at the turn of the millennium they issued their first singles. Needless to say, the likes of "Supergyration" and "Fink For The Man" are now collectors' items.

As their reputation for Who-like, thrilling live performances spread across New Zealand and Australia they set their sights on Europe – in particular the UK. The handful of shows they played in early 2002 had the music business salivating. Having started the tour on a shoestring budget, by the end they had labels falling over themselves to sign them up and cover their hotel bills.

When THE DATSUNS (2002) finally emerged it featured everything a classic rock fan could desire: the raw riffery of AC/DC with the arcane splendour of "Machine Head"-era Deep Purple, all topped off with a healthy dose of punky brattishness.

The band have been building their fan base ever since, touring relentlessly with like-minded thrashers such as The Von Bondies and The Hellacopters. With the album now on American release it looks like The Datsuns will be winning further plaudits and adulation when they truly go Stateside.

⊙ **The Datsuns** (2002; V2).
Loud, raucous, unreconstructed blues rockers belted out with fire and fury. Anyone who remembers the first generation of heavy rock will love this, as will those brought up on MTV-approved pop-punk.

Essi Berelian

REDFERNS

The Datsuns'll huff and puff and blow your house down.

MILES DAVIS

Born Alton, Illinois, 1926; died 1991.

By the late 1960s, **Miles Davis** and his jazz contemporaries were drying up before the combined forces of white rock and the Afro-American avant-garde. To counter this, Miles looked outside the immediate jazz tradition and by 1969 was systematically demolishing rock, jazz, African and Asian sounds to create something that pitched his music towards the outermost fringes of intelligibility.

IN A SILENT WAY (1969), with its eddying pools of electric piano, and the even more expansive BITCHES BREW (1970) still had one foot firmly in the jazz camp and, for all their truly warping propensities, were merely tasters for further voyages out. 1970's soundtrack album, JACK JOHNSON, was his rockiest yet and managed to capture all of the sex and swagger of the boxing ring (plus some of the mess). However, it was on the huge live albums, AT FILLMORE (1970) and LIVE-EVIL (1971), that Miles really started to pull away. An incredible brew, concocted from Keith Jarrett's molten keyboard explosions and the guitar abrasions of **JOHN MCLAUGHLIN**, this music teetered on the brink of insanity, yet had a propulsively pelvic groove. When on LIVE-EVIL Miles first morphed his trumpet through a wah-wah pedal, he found some miraculous line that linked Tim Buckley's soul babble with Jimi Hendrix's pagan witness and uncoiled the trauma latent in both.

The studio album ON THE CORNER (1972) was like nothing else in recorded music. An endlessly repeated funk backbeat is given a feel of looped oppressiveness, in and out of which strange unlocatable sounds explode, implode and zigzag through studio-contrived infinity. The studio became Miles's main tool. The later albums (with the exception of two compilations, BIG FUN and GET UP WITH IT) may have been live recordings, but they were warped and distorted through the mixing desk in post-production.

On MILES DAVIS IN CONCERT (1972), Miles purged his band of its jazz roots by introducing an R&B guitarist and an electric sitar player. By the time he reached the extraordinary DARK MAGUS (1974) he had removed the keyboards almost entirely and built up a battery of three guitarists who cranked out convulsive funk riffs and savagely disfigured solos amid Miles's malevolent wah-wah-driven emissions. Faced with the hair-raising beauty of this tormented yet hedonistic music, audiences could only wonder if Miles's kinky-sex-'n'-speedballs midlife crisis had finally tipped him over the brink.

In a way it had. In 1975 he embarked on a five-year retirement so total that it was rumoured he had died. His final releases of the decade – the doubles AGHARTA and PANGAEA (1975) – betrayed a certain tiredness. The band were permitted to meander too often into undisciplined exhibitions of virtuosity and

Miles seemed detached, as though musing on some new musical development he no longer had the energy to realize.

As with most great music, the significance of Miles's electric years has been misinterpreted. Musicians from the fields of rock as well as mainstream and avant-garde jazz were frightened off by its vipers' pit of indefinable emotions and its only influence at the time seemed to be on the polite fusion of protégés like Weather Report and Return To Forever. On the other hand, most of today's representatives in hip-hop, experimental rock, techno, ambient and even funk-metal should feel glad of the demons that possessed Miles Davis from 1969 to 1975.

Columbia has come up with yet another essential recording for Davis's devotees with its release in 1998 of THE COMPLETE BITCHES BREW SESSIONS (AUG 69–FEB 70), a four-CD collection featuring a completely remastered BITCHES BREW, odds and ends from the BIG FUN, CIRCLE IN THE ROUND and LIVE-EVIL sets, plus nine previously unreleased tracks. A rarity amongst remastered reissues, this is well worth the price asked.

(•) **At Fillmore** (1970; CBS); **Live-Evil** (1971; CBS Japan).
Words cannot describe the unbelievable mix of funk-drenched street swagger and urban psychosis emerging . . .

(•) **Dark Magus** (1974; CBS Japan).
And this was the climax – an amazingly dense amalgam of free jazz and funk.

Ben Smith

THE SPENCER DAVIS GROUP

Formed Birmingham, England, 1963; disbanded 1969.

There will always be purists who insist that musical authenticity should be maintained by keeping its individual components distinct. Often, though, the result of intermixing is not a dilution of the source but creation of a whole new thing. Exactly that took place in a pub in Birmingham, early in 1963, when a folk-blues-jazz-soul mixed parentage produced an R&B band called **The Spencer Davis Group**.

The English folk circuit, somewhat unwittingly, had been turning out Delta blues devotees influenced by solo acoustic practitioners like Son House, Mississippi Fred McDowall, Blind Willie McTell (whence Ralph McTell took his name), Leroy Carr and Jesse Fuller. Meanwhile, the trad-jazz circuit was paying increasing homage to the blues of Memphis and New Orleans. When a young folk-blues guitar player called **Spencer Davis** happened to share the bill with The Muff Woody Trad-Jazz Band, he was impressed by their inclination towards a rawer, more soulful blues sound and was particularly taken with the band's guitarist, **Muff Winwood**, and his younger brother, pianist **Steve Winwood**, all of 15 years old. He suggested they join forces: Spencer on rhythm guitar, Muff switching to bass, and young Stevie extending his role to add harmonica, lead guitar and vocals. With the line-up completed by drummer **Pete York**, the group was soon gigging regularly on the Birmingham club circuit.

The band was spotted and signed by Chris Blackwell, who set about forming his own Island Records by licensing releases of the group's material through Fontana. The early singles, however, were only modestly successful. Four efforts – a remake of John Lee Hooker's classic "Dimples", "I Can't Stand It" (both 1964), "Every Little Bit Hurts" and "Strong Love" (both 1965) – failed to emulate the band's live success. Part of the difficulty, Blackwell felt, was that the group lacked an identity in its material. As no member of the group yet showed any propensity for songwriting, the answer was to commission stuff specifically for the group. It was a vindication of Blackwell's instincts when, in November 1965, they released "Keep On Running", a song written by a close friend of Blackwell's, Jackie Edwards.

A sure-fire hit with a distinctly soulful flavour and a plaintive fuzz-guitar riff, it proved to be the band's turning point. Not only did it reach #1 within a month of its release, it achieved perhaps the pinnacle of achievement by ousting a Beatles record, "Day Tripper", in doing so. The success of the single also boosted sales of the band's first two LPs, FIRST ALBUM (1965) and SECOND ALBUM (1966). The next single, "Somebody Help Me", was also written by Edwards and also went to #1, but far more significant was "When I Come Home", the seventh single, as it marked Steve Winwood's songwriting debut.

From the earliest days, Winwood had clearly been the exceptional talent within the band. In addition to his precocious instrumental ability, he had developed a mature and extraordinarily powerful voice, and now he was demonstrating some ability as a songwriter as well. But if Spencer Davis ever felt any resentment about Steve's pre-eminence, he never showed it – indeed the next single was a collaborative effort, and one which became the band's masterpiece.

"Gimme Some Lovin'", released in November 1966, was one of the great recordings of the 60s, covered by bar bands across the world. A pounding bassline (inspired by Ravel's "Bolero"), a crushing keyboard phrase (maybe a throwback to Ray Charles) and an electrifying vocal were enhanced by numerous layers of percussive accompaniment under the direction of engineer **Eddie Kramer**, who the following year would create more studio fireworks with Jimi Hendrix. Both this and its Winwood-composed successor, "I'm A Man" (1967), became Top 10 hits in both the US and Britain, and it was enough to give Steve, who had reached the mighty age of 18, the confidence finally to break free. In April he joined forces with Dave Mason, Chris Wood and Jim Capaldi, who had contributed some of the percussion and vocal backup to "Gimme Some Lovin'", and so **TRAFFIC** was born.

Without him, The Spencer Davis Group haltingly continued, but disbanded within a couple of years. Spencer Davis briefly re-formed the band in the early 70s, but he was its only original member, and it could never be the same. However, the legacy of the British R&B movement, in whose vanguard The Spencer Davis Group belong, continued long after the demise of the classic line-up. In the bands of the pub-rock movement of the early 70s, and those of the later punk movement, you can clearly hear the echo of the brash excitement of records like "Gimme Some Lovin'". Three not tremendously good albums from their long decline were re-released by Repertoire in 1998 – WITH THEIR NEW FACE ON, GLUGGO and LIVING IN A BACK STREET – while 2000 saw the more appealing live document SESSIONS & SHOWS 1966 – 1968 hit the shelves.

⊙ **Eight Gigs A Week – The Steve Winwood Years** (1996; Island).
The complete Winwood-era archive, including all the album tracks and singles, a rare EP, and unreleased live material.

Phil Lynch

DANIELLE DAX

Born Southend, England, birthdate unknown.

Brought up by her grandmother ('a medium with a vivid imagination'), **Danielle Dax** made her musical debut on keyboards as part of the seven-piece Amy Turtle & The Crossroads. Their career lasted just one ninety-minute performance at Reading University, with Danielle dressed in a green balaclava and lab-coat ensemble. It was not a roaring success, but did bring her to the attention of Karl Blake, who asked her to design the cover for an EP by his band, **The Lemon Kittens**. Within a week she was on stage with them.

Neither Dax nor Blake could actually play, but in the aftermath of punk they could claim to be experimental. Over the following three years they served their apprenticeship on a couple of challenging LPs, WE BUY A HAMMER FOR DADDY (1980) and THE BIG DENTIST (1982). However, The Lemon Kittens are not remembered for their music: stating that they thought it 'lazy to just walk onstage in the same crappy old clothes you've had on all week', the pair overcame the problem by not wearing any. (Actually, Karl would usually wear Bermuda shorts while Danielle covered herself in body paint.) Although they sold few records, gigs were usually well attended.

When The Lemon Kittens split in 1982, Karl Blake went on to form The Shock-Headed Peters and Danielle set about a solo career. She put her diverse collection of unusual musical instruments to good use, and recorded material on four-track equipment in a variety of settings, like a local church and her brother's bedroom. These basic recordings formed the beginnings of the surprisingly listenable album, POP-EYES (1983). Her intention had been 'to combine natural sounds with synths', using whatever instrumentation came to hand: on "The Wheeled Wagon", for instance, a guitar is combined with what sounds like a grumbling stomach. Speaking of churning stomachs, the album's sleeve was a grotesque facial collage put together from medical photographs. Suffice it to say that the nose appeared to have been represented by a rotting testicle.

Danielle's heavy makeup and big hair made her a natural for the then-thriving 'Batcave' scene, although she was always too colourful to be a real goth. In 1984, she gained a small but memorable role in Neil Jordan's film *The Company Of Wolves*, as well as in *Chimera*, a film by Holly Warburton, whose ornately beautiful photographs have graced the covers of many Dax records.

Named after a tabloid story, the mini-LP JESUS EGG THAT WEPT (1984) was a more polished record than POP-EYES. Future co-writer David Knight made his debut on a couple of tracks, and Karl Blake returned to make some noise on "Ostrich", but "Pariah" was the stand-out, allowing Danielle to show off a rather startling vocal range. Following this album, she recruited a band and again became a live draw, this time for the right reasons. A stream of singles appeared over the next few years on her own Awesome label – "Yummer Yummer Man" (1985), "Where The Flies Are" (1986), "Big Hollow Man" (1987), "Cat-House" (1988) and "White Knuckle Ride" (1989) – each building in confidence and commerciality, and in 1989 she was signed by Warners' subsidiary label Sire. Unfortunately, missing the point in the way only major labels can, Sire reasoned that, as Danielle's songs often shared the Eastern flavour of some Beatles compositions, she should cover "Tomorrow Never Knows". Inevitably, it flopped, as did its accompanying album, BLAST THE HUMAN FLOWER (1990).

Not surprisingly, artist and label soon parted company, and it was 1995 before Dax made a cautious return, reissuing much of her back catalogue on her new Biter Of Thorpe label. That she knows she has yet to live up to her potential is evidenced by the subtitle of a recent compilation: THE THWARTED POP CAREER OF DANIELLE DAX. Not that she's giving up – a new single, the "Timber Tongue", slipped out late in 1995. Dax is currently reported to be working as a garden designer.

(•) **Jesus Egg That Wept** (1984; Biter Of Thorpe).
A tastefully sleeved mini-album which contains two of her best songs in "Pariah" and "Ostrich".

(•) **Comatose Non Reaction: The Thwarted Pop Career Of Danielle Dax** (1995; Biter Of Thorpe).
A valuable compilation of all Dax's 80s singles and sundry obscurities.

Glenn Law

dB'S

Formed North Carolina, US, 1978; disbanded 1987.

Superior pop combo, the **dB's** started out life as The Sneakers, comprising **Chris Stamey** (vocals/guitar), **Gene Holder** (bass), **Will Rigby**

(drums) and **Mitch Easter** (vocals). Easter (later of Let's Active and a renowned producer) left in 1978, being replaced by **Peter Holsapple**, late of the H-Bombs and a previous collaborator with Stamey in Ritterhouse Square (a group who once wrote a song called "She Means More To Me Than My Gibson Les Paul"). This new line-up changed their name and moved to New York.

There, in 1978, the dB's issued a couple of singles, "I Thought (You Wanted To Know)" and "Black And White", neither of which whipped up much interest in the US. However, the UK label Albion liked what they heard and signed the band, funding a pair of Scott Litt-produced albums, STANDS FOR DECIBELS (1981) and REPERCUSSION (1982). These were lumped by reviewers with the emergent New Wave scene but in truth owed much more to the 60s pop of The Byrds, with Stamey and Holsapple creating eloquent, knowing pop songs – romantic travelogues edged with scattershot rhythms from the ever-inventive Rigby.

Both albums would become essential listening among such cognoscenti as R.E.M. and Bob Mould, with whom Holsapple and Stamey would subsequently work. However, commercial recognition was harder to come by. Perhaps sensing this, Stamey launched his solo career with IT'S A WONDERFUL LIFE (1983), and left the group before the third album, LIKE THIS (1984). Recorded as a trio, the album lacked Stamey's esoteric wit (he was, as critics pointed out, the dBs' Lennon to Holsapple's McCartney), but it was a fine disc nonetheless, with the songs beginning to betray Holsapple's country bent, and an expressive production from Chris Butler.

The band hooked up with bass player **Jeff Beninato** and gathered guests such as Syd Straw and Van Dyke Parks for one last album, THE SOUND OF MUSIC (1987). It had its moments – Straw's arresting duet with Holsapple on "Never Before And Never Again" – but sounded like a band at the end of its career, as indeed was the case. Shortly after its release, Holder left for The Wygals, and after one last tour the dB's called it a day, Holsapple playing with the **GOLDEN PALOMINOS** and becoming a near-permanent fixture of the **R.E.M.** entourage.

In the late 80s the original dB's re-formed to play a benefit for the homeless, which led to a Holsapple–Stamey project, MAVERICKS (1991), a poignant collection of songs marrying their disparate styles with amazing cohesion. With guest musicians including Elvis Costello/Tom Waits collaborator Michael Blair, it was fine compensation for old dB's fans.

(•) **Stands For Decibels** (1981; Albion; 1989; IRS).
Few who repeat the mantra of achieving the 'perfect three-minute pop song' get anywhere near as close as the dB's on this debut.

(•) **Repercussion** (1982; IRS).
The slightly more elaborate presentation detracts little from the group's overall impact; a second great American pop album from a band who, ironically, couldn't at the time get a US record deal.

Alex Ogg

Formed Cleveland, Ohio, 1976; disbanded 1980.

Often overlooked in chronicles of the New York punk scene, **The Dead Boys** were one of the most controversial bands playing at CBGB's between 1976 and 1979. Part of American punk's second wave, they were brash, nihilistic, aggressive, trashy, vulgar, threatening and, above all, outrageously provocative. Their legacy is perhaps summarized by the much-covered punk anthem, "Sonic Reducer", most famously revived live in the 90s by Pearl Jam, while "Ain't It Fun" was covered by Guns N' Roses on their 1993 album, THE SPAGHETTI INCIDENT.

The Dead Boys' line-up – **Stiv Bators** (vocals), **Jimmy Zero** (rhythm guitar), **Cheetah Chrome** (lead guitar), **Jeff Magnum** (bass) and **Johnny Blitz** (drums) – was drawn from two Cleveland bands, Rocket From The Tombs and Frankenstein. Taking the name from their song, "Down In Flames" ('Dead boy, running scared'), they relocated to New York in 1976, and their first CBGB's appearance was secured on their behalf by Joey Ramone, who had met them in Youngstown, Ohio. Impressed with Bators' outlandish and raucous behaviour, Ramone had a hunch that their music would be as impressive as Bators' personality.

The gamble paid off: abandoning all artistic pretensions, the band's motto was 'fuck art, let's rock'. They retained some cover versions from their previous bands, like Iggy Pop's "Search & Destroy" and Mott The Hoople's "Death May Be Your Santa Claus", and devised their own offensive songs ("Caught With The Meat In Your Mouth" being an apt example). An explosive and notorious image was offset by some extreme and disturbing visual imagery – swastikas, Nazi uniforms and other right-wing regalia, which offended the establishment but gratified the punk crowd's thirst for kitsch, shock tactics and rebellion. It wasn't long before Seymour Stein of Sire Records, who had recently signed the Ramones, invited The Dead Boys onto the label roster.

Opening for The Damned's CBGB's performances in April 1977, The Dead Boys were inspired by the headlining act's tight, concise and witty songs, but their own material, while spirited, lacked the spark, ambition and the discipline necessary for success. Like the Sex Pistols, they adopted a menacing posture and, like the Pistols, they produced one brilliant album. YOUNG LOUD AND SNOTTY (1977) encapsulated their anarchic, pile-driving, chaotic punk rock sound; it also represented the limits of their achievement. The title was perfect punk poetry, and every track offered a slap in the face for establishment respectability.

For a second LP, though, a fresh angle was required, and WE HAVE COME FOR YOUR CHILDREN (1978) revealed the band's shortcomings, with very little progression to speak of. Sire did not renew their contract and the band finally called it a day in 1980. Bators made two solo albums, and then formed **The Lords Of The New Church** with The Damned's Brian James. Bators died in a road accident in France in 1990.

The Dead Boys will be remembered and revered for one great album, some demented live performances, a host of brutal and insensitive imagery, and a unique frontman. Modern thrash bands owe them a particular debt of gratitude, and their young, fresh aggression can still be seen as quintessentially punk rock.

⦿ **Young Loud And Snotty** (1977; Sire).
Trashy and thumping, with a sleaziness matched only by Johnny Thunders, this is an essential album for any punk connoisseur.

Veronica Kofman

Formed Melbourne, Australia, 1981; split 1998.

Fitting the early-80s house style of Ivo Watts-Russell's seminal 4AD record label, **Dead Can Dance** found themselves nestling comfortably alongside the soundscapes of the Cocteau Twins, This Mortal Coil, Modern English, Colourbox, the Wolfgang Press and Xmal Deutschland.

Multi-instrumentalist **Brendan Perry** and classically trained singer **Lisa Gerrard**, both of Anglo-Irish extraction, met in Melbourne at the turn of the decade and, following just one recording (for Aussie cassette magazine, *Fast Forward*), decided to move to London, where their extraordinary marriage of music and ethereal vocals was soon to gain the attention of Watts-Russell. When DEAD CAN DANCE was issued early in 1984, it transpired that the name was not some facile goth reference point but was inspired by 'the transformation from inanimacy to animacy' (Perry) – a notion illustrated by the album's cover, which depicted a ritual mask from New Guinea. Brendan Perry placed a great deal of importance on his sleeve art, and himself produced the drawing for the duo's first 12" EP, the acclaimed GARDEN OF THE ARCANE DELIGHTS (1984). As well as these releases, Dead Can Dance also contributed two tracks to the This Mortal Coil compilation IT'LL END IN TEARS, which also featured most other names on the 4AD roster.

In 1985, a second album, SPLEEN AND IDEAL, promptly went to the top of the independent charts. The year after came WITHIN THE REALM OF A DYING SUN, a work with a more Baroque feel than the earlier albums: Perry said they had 'decided to work within the form of the classical idiom, and use classical instruments, with the aid of samplers, computers – and a few books on how to score'. A more tribal feel was prevalent in Dead Can Dance's two excellent contributions to the 4AD compilation LONELY IS AN EYESORE, released in 1987.

The album SERPENT'S EGG (1988) received a more muted critical response, with some feeling that Brendan Perry was stretching credulity with his hifalutin theories. Unabashed, he presented his interest

Lisa Gerrard of 4AD noisesters Dead Can Dance

continuing their spin around world music, kicking free of the Elizabethan experimentation and keeping a clear eye on their goth roots.

After nearly twenty years together the duo split in 1998 allowing Gerrard and Perry time to concentrate fully on their respective, burgeoning solo careers. Gerrard's soundtrack work has since expanded considerably – she has worked on such Hollywood Blockbusters as *Mission Impossible 2* and *Ali* as well as contributing to the Oscar-nominated score for Ridley Scott's *Gladiator*.

Brendan Perry's first post-DCD engagement was a collaboration with **Hector Zazou** on his unsettling exploration of Irish music, LIGHTS IN THE DARK (1998) before he contributed his production and arranging skills to former Dead Can Dance percussionist **Peter Ulrich**'s PATHWAYS & DAWNS. It was only a matter of time before a solo album emerged, and with 1999's EYE OF THE HUNTER he continued his long and fruitful association with 4AD.

Released in 2001, 4AD's masterful anthology DEAD CAN DANCE 1981 – 1998 was an extremely well-constructed document of the band's

in the secular music of the early Renaissance in AION (1990), for which reproduction Renaissance instruments were incorporated into the overall structure. The years 1991–93 saw Dead Can Dance working on numerous disparate projects across the world, including Lisa Gerrard's score for a production of *Oedipus Rex*, and music for the soundtrack of the film *Baraka*. 1991 saw the release of A PASSAGE IN TIME, a compilation of their finest pieces from ten years of European recordings.

In September 1993, 4AD released Dead Can Dance's sixth LP, INTO THE LABYRINTH, an extraordinary melange of the primitive ideas and the arcane, with tracks varying between straightforward ballads and profoundly motif-laden instrumentals. When queried as to how Dead Can Dance could realize their music in a live situation – a question frequently levelled at 4AD acts – Brendan Perry stated, 'We have a system where we introduce modal structures which allows room for improvisation ... You can achieve some dangerously beautiful musical moments by way of this process.' This was illustrated on the stunning 1995 release, TOWARD THE WITHIN, which was recorded live in Santa Monica, California. Accompanied by a 4AD video of the same name, this set showed Dead Can Dance at their stark best, drawing from Eastern influences, whilst maintaining their allusions to more familiar European pastoral themes. 1996's SPIRITCHASER saw Brendan and Lisa

progression over the years – a fitting summary of their remarkable musical ingenuity and ambition.

⦿ **A Passage In Time** (1991; Warners).
For an introduction to the extraordinary music of Dead Can Dance, look to this American import. The CD comprises a good selection of early material, as well as two tracks – "Bird" and "Spirit" – not available elsewhere.

⦿ **Toward the Within** (1995; 4AD).
A stunning live (and largely improvised) set.

⦿ **Dead Can Dance 1981 – 1998** (2001; 4AD).
As close to definitive as any collection could get, this 3-CD set is a balanced overview of their seven studio albums as well as the *de riguer* rarities.

Jeremy Simmonds

DEAD KENNEDYS

Formed San Francisco, 1978; disbanded 1986.

"Isn't a Dead Kennedys concert on 22 November [anniversary of JFK's assassination] in rather bad taste?" "Of course. But the assassinations weren't too tasteful either." East Bay Ray interviewed in 1979 by the *Vancouver Sun*

A crucial part of the burgeoning American hardcore punk scene in the late 70s/early 80s, the

Dead Kennedys were formed when vocalist **Jello Biafra** – having seen the Sex Pistols' final live performance at the San Francisco Winterland in January 1978 – answered a music paper advert placed by guitarist **East Bay Ray**. They were joined by bassist **Klaus Flouride**, drummer **Bruce Slesinger** (aka Ted) and a second guitarist known to posterity simply as **6025**. The latter soon departed, while Slesinger was replaced in 1981 by **D. H. Peligro**.

After a brief rehearsal period, the Dead Kennedys played their first gig in July 1978. Initially, their music was a fairly faithful reproduction of British punk rock, all beefy guitar sound, rumbling bass and enthusiastically whacked drums. Yet from the start there was obviously more to them than this: the band were quite clearly playing within their musical abilities, and there was a depth to the lyrics which raised the group above the average punk outfit.

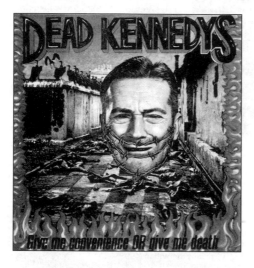

Biafra's main lyrical concerns were political and his polemical broadsides attacked any number of easy but nonetheless deserving targets – big-business skulduggery, the Reagan administration, atrocities perpetrated by the Klan, and the feeble response of liberals to such issues. Underpinned by an acute sense of humour and Biafra's extraordinary tremulous vocal, early songs such as "Let's Lynch The Landlord", "I Kill Children", "Chemical Warfare" and "Funland At The Beach" satirized the twin elements of extreme violence and conservatism which characterize much of American life. The Dead Kennedys' inflammatory name and provocative behaviour (in one 1979 prank, Biafra ran for mayor of San Francisco – and came fourth) attracted the attention of a number of far-right politico-religious groups. The band's problems with these self-appointed moral guardians were compounded by a confrontational relationship with US authorities, ensuring an aggressive police presence at most of their gigs. These associations scared off major record companies from signing the band, so their only option

was to release records on their own label – Alternative Tentacles – set up in 1979.

Early British singles were issued on indie label Cherry Red, beginning with "California Über Alles", a blistering attack on the Governor of California, Jerry Brown. "Holiday In Cambodia" followed and is perhaps the band's definitive moment – a perfect mix of hilarious yuppie-baiting lyrics and evil-sounding music. Almost as essential were "Kill The Poor" and "Too Drunk To Fuck" (remarkably, a British Top 40 single in 1981), but the debut LP, FRESH FRUIT FOR ROTTING VEGETABLES (1980), was largely sunk by unsympathetic production. Nevertheless, a British tour in late 1980 established the band as a figurehead for an audience long deprived of the Pistols and affronted by the alleged 'sellout' of The Clash, Biafra stage-diving to great enthusiasm.

The eight-track EP, IN GOD WE TRUST INC. (1981), took things further, boasting a speed and power that left most reviewers nonplussed and contemporaries trailing. There followed a lengthy hiatus before the album PLASTIC SURGERY DISASTERS appeared in late 1982. A vast improvement on FRESH FRUIT..., this fine collection of songs retained the trademark savagery and satire, but the musical content had diversified, even including such unexpected moments as Flouride playing clarinet.

After two years of touring, the more melodic FRANKENCHRIST (1985) appeared, marked by a frantic sense of desperation that reflected America's increasingly right-wing political landscape. As ever, the group ran into controversy, this time with the LP's accompanying poster, "Penis Landscape" by Swiss artist H. R. Giger. Detailing several rows of copulating genitalia, it provoked a legal offensive against the band, beginning in April 1986. As well as having his flat torn apart by the police, Biafra was charged with 'distributing harmful matter to minors', a charge which he repulsed on the basis of the First Amendment right to free speech, and which was finally overturned the following year.

The band, meantime, had taken the decision to disband in early 1986, before release of their final album, BEDTIME FOR DEMOCRACY (1986), which suggested their creative relationship had run out of steam.

Since the split, all the Kennedy members have remained active in music. Biafra immediately took off on a bewildering range of projects, including spoken-word performances and musical collaborations, most effectively as **Lard**, with **Al Jourgensen** and **Paul Barker** of Ministry. East Bay Ray worked on an album with Algerian rai legend **Cheika Rimitti**, and has formed a 'sinister cabaret band' called **Candyass**. Flouride has released a couple of idiosyncratic solo LPs, and Peligro has his own eponymous band. Klaus Flouride and East Bay Ray are currently playing in a surf instrumental band called **Jumbo Shrimp**.

In 1998 news leaked out of a rather squalid argument between Biafra and the rest of the band over money and the rights to the band's back catalogue. The various claims and counter-claims were put before the court in 1999, where it was found that Biafra had acted fraudulently with respect to payments made to be rest of the band: a very sad footnote to add to the band's history.

⦿ **Plastic Surgery Disasters** (1982; Alternative Tentacles).
Effectively trashes every promise of the American Dream and manages to be funny at the same time. The CD re-release includes the IN GOD WE TRUST INC. EP.

⦿ **Give Me Convenience Or Give Me Death** (1987; Alternative Tentacles).
A worthwhile compilation that revisits some of the band's early material and offers several miscellaneous oddities.

Andy Lewis
With thanks to East Bay Ray for updates

DEATH IN VEGAS

Formed 1994, London.

Zambian-born graphic artist and DJ **Richard Fearless** (born Richard Maguire) first forged his alliance with **Steve Hellier** (programmer) back in 1994; performing as **Dead Elvis**, the duo enjoyed a residency at The Chemical Brothers' near-legendary West London club night, The Heavenly Sunday Social. Following their triumphant performances, Dead Elvis committed the mighty floor-filler "Opium Shuffle" to vinyl as a single in early 1995, but, perhaps wisely, opted to change their name after unwitting fans of 'The King' turning up to gigs in search of karaoke-style eulogies to their hero.

Reincarnated as **Death In Vegas**, the band released a second single, "Dirt", in the spring of 1996; it became a club hit. This success led the duo to support Lionrock on a British tour, for which they assembled a backing band, rather than simply relying on tapes. "Rocco" was recognized by radio to some extent, but crossover success only really began with the appearance of the well-received debut album DEAD ELVIS (1997). The set contained an alluring

cocktail of break-beats, lounge-jazz and techno, its success triggered the reactivation of both "Dirt" and "Rocco" as singles later that same year, although neither broke into the Top 40.

With the departure of Hellier, a two-year silence followed, save for remixing duties for Spiritualized and David Holmes. Despite this hiatus, when Death In Vegas returned with THE CONTINO SESSIONS in September 1999 their following had not deserted them and the set received a rapturous response from press and fans alike. This time, Fearless was joined by keyboard player and programmer Tim Holmes, Ian Button (guitar), Matt Flint (bass guitar) and Simon Hanson (drums). The album could also boast vocal cameos by Dot Allison (formerly of One Dove), Primal Scream's Bobby Gillespie, and (most impressively of all) Iggy Pop on "Aisha". Perhaps surprisingly, given their varied and growing fan base, a major hit continues to elude Death In Vegas, but they have managed to find a place in British popular culture – "Claiming Marilyn" was featured in the 1998 movie of Irvine Welsh's cult book *The Acid House* and "Dirge" found its way into a Levi advertising campaign in 2000.

⦿ **Dead Elvis** (1997; Concrete/deconstruction).
Like The Chemical Brothers' DIG YOUR OWN HOLE, released at about the same time, this set marries techno and break-beat with a bewildering but playful array of influences: dub, blue-beat and lounge-jazz all make welcome appearances, as does a burst of Country Joe & The Fish on "Dirt". A brilliant white-knuckle ride of a record.

⦿ **The Contino Sessions** (1999; Concrete/deconstruction)
Menacing and provocative, this even heavier-sounding second album, recorded in New York and London, was feted by publications as diverse as *Muzik*, *Q* and *The Guardian*, and led to a Top 20 placing and a *Mercury Music Prize* nomination. Track titles like "Dirge", "Death Threat" and "Broken Little Sister" signal that this is not a record that embraces hedonism; nonetheless, it is exhilarating, powerful and unforgettable fare from the heart of darkness. A beautifully realized combination of the most contemporary styles of dance and rock.

Justin Lewis

DEEE-LITE

Formed New York, 1982; split 1995.

For many, the summer of 1990 is remembered most of all for the odd-looking cosmopolitan trio who single-handedly fused the psychedelia of P-Funk with the kitsch of 70s disco to deliver the anthemic "Groove Is In The Heart". But **Deee-Lite**'s history goes back eight years earlier, when vocalist **Kier Kirby** (otherwise known as The Lady Miss Kier) met Kiev-born **Super DJ Dmitry Brill** in a park in New York – the start of a relationship that would develop into a marriage. The trio was completed when they were joined by **Jungle DJ Towa Towa**, a computer expert from Tokyo.

Deee-Lite's debut single, "Groove Is In The Heart", featured guest appearances from Bootsy Collins and rapper Q-Tip from A Tribe Called Quest. It spent thirteen weeks in the UK chart, peaking at #2, but November's follow-up single, "Power Of Love", spent only seven weeks in the chart, peaking at #25. Their debut album, WORLD CLIQUE (1990), was a Top 20 hit, but none of the singles or albums that followed achieved any such success, or delivered anything near the innovation of "Groove". Having a remix of "Groove" on its B-side did not prevent "How Do You Say... Love" (1991) from being a flop.

Kier branched out into other creative areas and became a graphic artist, designing a number of album sleeves, including the one for the next Deee-Lite album, INFINITY WITHIN (1992). Like its predecessor, INFINITY WITHIN featured guests from the funk hall of fame, including Bootsy Collins, Maceo Parker and Fred Wesley, plus house favourite Satoshi Tōme. Though their oddball humour was again evident in a spoof sci-fi story that ended with a 'fax orgy', the album also made half-hearted attempts to address social issues such as the environment ("I Had A Dream I Was Falling Through A Hole In The Ozone Layer"), safe sex ("Rubber Lover") and political awareness (the half-minute "Vote Baby Vote").

A new member, **On-e**, joined the group and contributed to their third album, DEW DROPS IN THE GARDEN (1994), but by this time only their die-hard fans took any notice. In 1995, Towa Towa released a solo album, FUTURE LISTENING!, under his real name, Towa Tei. As 1996 drew to a close, the band announced that they were calling it a day. A compilation album, SAMPLADELIC RELICS & DANCEFLOOR ODDITIES (1996) was released the following January, made up of remixes of the best tracks from their back catalogue.

⊙ **World Clique** (1990; Elektra).
Quirky and kooky to the max, this remains one of the best dance albums of the 90s and maintains the perfect balance between house and funk.

⊙ **Infinity Within** (1992; Elektra).
Sadly overlooked second album, probably due to the fact that Deee-Lite had by now lost their novelty value. A shame, because they were still very much up to scratch. Besides, the great funk gods appeared in person, not via sampler.

⊙ **Sampladelic Relics & Dancefloor Oddities** (1996; Elektra).
The goofiness that made Deee-Lite so memorable is somewhat lacking but the drum'n'bass reworking of "I Had A Dream" more than compensates.

George Luke

DEEP PURPLE

Formed London, 1968; disbanded 1976; re-formed 1984.

The **Deep Purple** aesthetic was based on the British notion of squeezing and stretching the blues, turning up the bass and blasting volts through the speakers until your ears bled. It wasn't always pretty, but it had balls aplenty. The key to Purple's success was the flash and heat generated by the musical antagonism between classically trained organist **Jon Lord** and philistine guitarist **Ritchie Blackmore**, with drummer **Ian Paice** holding it all together and getting a long nightly solo.

Formed as Roundabout in 1968, briefly as a front group for former Searchers drummer Chris Curtis, they had some chart success in America, peddling poppy rock covers such as "Hush" and "Kentucky Woman" in the style of Vanilla Fudge. They made three albums, SHADES OF DEEP PURPLE (1968; reissued on vinyl 1998; EMI), BOOK OF TALIESYN and DEEP PURPLE (both 1969). After their US label Tetragrammatron went bust, however, the group decided to begin again from scratch, dumping singer **Rod Evans** and bassist **Nicky Simper** in 1969 in favour of two ex-Episode 6 men, **Ian Gillan** and **Roger Glover**.

The new Purple were looking for a heavier sound, with Glover in particular wanting to do something like Led Zeppelin; Jon Lord, though, still had ideas of expressing his classical leanings. They decided to try both approaches, so the first work of the new band was Lord's CONCERTO FOR GROUP & ORCHESTRA (1969), performed at the Royal Albert Hall in September. It sounds appalling – in retrospect – but was well received at the time. Nonetheless, the band thankfully dumped the classical pretensions, put in some solid touring and recorded an unalloyed heavy rock album, DEEP PURPLE IN ROCK (1970). This went Top 5 in the UK straight off, and stayed in the charts for six months. It opened (as it ended) with a loud crash of electrical abuse, subsiding into a quiet organ piece, before kicking into "Speed King", which threw the words of Little Richard into some punishing heavy rock. It also included "Child In Time", a gentle organ ballad with Gillan's soulful singing building into all-out screaming.

Purple's live shows were characterized by long improvised pieces in which Blackmore and Lord traded musical ideas, often stolen from blues or the classics (Bach was a particular favourite of Lord, while "Jingle Bells" often cropped up in Blackmore's solos). Musical magpie-ism wasn't confined to the stage. "Black Night", a UK #2 hit in November 1970, stole its catchy riff from Ricky Nelson's "Summertime".

"Strange Kind Of Woman" again went UK Top 10 in 1971, but albums and touring were Purple's mainstays. FIREBALL (1971) was notable for "The Mule", with its psychedelic organ track slave-driven by Paice's brutal drumming, but it was MACHINE HEAD (1972) that crowned their reputation. It was recorded on a mobile studio in the corridors of a hotel in Switzerland after the planned venue was burned down during a Zappa concert. "Smoke On The Water" told the story: its thumping power-riff was the classic that became a cliché.

The 1972 tour of Japan yielded the double live MADE IN JAPAN (1973), distinguished by some wonderfully indulgent Blackmore solos, and a *Guinness Book Of Records* credit as the world's loudest band. But the strain (four US tours that year) wore them down, and WHO DO WE THINK WE ARE? (1973)

Big flares, big hair, big personalized jet. Purple show how it was done in the 70s

sounded tired. In 1973 Deep Purple imploded, with Gillan and Glover leaving the band. When the dust settled, only the original trio of Lord, Paice and Blackmore remained in place.

At first, Paul Rodgers of Free was pencilled in as Gillan's replacement, but he eventually formed his own band, Bad Company. Purple finally settled on a man with a similar voice, the unknown **David Coverdale**, along with ex-Trapeze singer/bassist **Glenn Hughes** as a replacement for Glover. BURN (1974) saw the new band rejuvenated, with a more direct bluesy sound and elements of funk supplied by Hughes. But it didn't last. Blackmore and Coverdale loathed each other, and STORMBRINGER (1974) saw the guitarist largely absent.

Blackmore finally quit in 1975, to form **RAINBOW**, and Purple struggled on with ex-James Gang young blood **Tommy Bolin**. But his energy couldn't breathe new life into the dinosaur, and soon he and Hughes were getting deeper into a mire of drug use. In June 1976 Deep Purple finally collapsed. Bolin died of a heroin overdose six months later.

By the early 80s Lord, Paice and Coverdale had ended up in **WHITESNAKE**, Glover had joined up with Blackmore in Rainbow, and Gillan had fronted his own quirky but successful band before a Spinal

Tap-like stint in **BLACK SABBATH**. As Rainbow and Gillan ran out of steam, the pressure for a reunion began to build and in 1984 the mark 2 line-up of Blackmore, Gillan, Glover, Lord and Paice re-formed. In the event, Lord and Paice were reduced to being sidemen in a stadium-rock outfit: it was essentially Rainbow with Gillan singing, and Glover's heavy-handed production made PERFECT STRANGERS (1984) sound like it was soaked in treacle.

Purple in the 70s had played blues-based music, tidied up in the studio to make songs. In the 80s the music was straitjacketed into songs without the chance to develop or breathe, although Gillan's humour was intact. But Gillan was sacked for criticizing THE HOUSE OF BLUE LIGHT (1987) and **Joe Lynn-Turner** came in to make the band sound even more like Rainbow.

After a donkey of an album – SLAVES & MASTERS (1990) – better sense prevailed. Gillan was readmitted for his third stint, uncomfortably sharing stage and studio with Blackmore. The line-up remained stable while the band recorded THE BATTLE RAGES ON (1993), but Blackmore jumped ship once more during the tour that followed – billed as the 25th Anniversary Tour and resulting in the live album COME HELL OR HIGH WATER (1994). The tour was

DEEP PURPLE

completed courtesy of US guitar whizzkid **Joe Satriani**, who filled in so successfully that he returned to tour again in 1994. Contractual obligations, however, meant his tenure could only be short-term and Purple hurriedly enlisted **Steve Morse** (ex-Kansas) as his replacement to record PURPENDICULAR (1996). Setting off on tour again, they took a fresh look at their 70s repertoire; tour highlights were captured on LIVE AT THE OLYMPIA (1997), with forgotten favourites jostling for position against new material from the PURPENDICULAR set.

Suddenly they felt they could have fun again, and the concerts were enlivened by dropping old faves like "Lazy" and "Space Truckin'" in favour of new material and songs from the back catalogue that had seldom, if ever, been played (such as "Bludsucker", "No One Came" and "Rat Bat Blue"). Completists will also find ARCHIVE ALIVE (1997; Archive/Navarre) – a compilation of previously unreleased live recordings from the mid-70s – completely unmissable.

The fans keep the faith to this day, no longer dashing out in denim'n'leather droves perhaps, but in large enough numbers to warrant Gillan and the gang making regular tours and to release the occasional album. If you suffer from it already, then 1998's ABANDON (EMI) has all the classic rock attitudes, nasty guitars, pounding drums and driving bass to scratch that Rock itch. There's little to commend it to the non-converted, though. Alternatively, indulge yourself with the orchestral delights of LIVE AT THE ROYAL ALBERT HALL (2000), which does exactly what it says on the tin, and features the 30th anniversary live performance of Jon Lord's "Concerto For Group And Orchestra"; various special guests pop up, not least Ronnie James Dio.

⊙ **Deep Purple In Rock** (1970; Warners).
Dirty and loud; only Jon Lord has had a wash and shave, and even he sometimes gets his elbows in the grime.

⊙ **Machine Head** (1972; Warners).
The one with everything: power rock, storming R&B, and short sharp solos everywhere. Even Gillan gets a harmonica solo on "Lazy". If you hate early-70s rock you'll detest this, or it might just convert you.

⊙ **Made In Japan** (1973; Warners; reissued 1998; EMI).
The other one with everything: Purple are the consummate live rock band and this epic album shows them at their best. Worth the purchase price if only for the version of "Smoke On The Water" that launched a thousand bedroom guitarists.

⊙ **Abandon** (1998; EMI).
Tremelo-happy Steve Morse is hardly an inspired guitarist, but Purple's latest does thunder with some purpose. "Seventh Heaven", with its traces of Yes and offbeat riff, has a real edge, and there's some of Gillan's social conscience in "Watching The Sky" and "Fingers To The Bone". "Bludsucker" is almost as good as in 1970, but rather unnecessary (unless old pal Blackmore needed the royalty money).

⊙ **30: Very Best Of** (1998; EMI).
Purple compilations are seldom inspired, but at least this one contains something from every era except 1989–93. But what philistine faded "Child In Time" halfway through? Next time, take a closer look at MARK I & III and give the MARK II singles a rest.

Patrick Neylan-Francis
Thanks to Mike C and Essi for
updates and corrections

DEF LEPPARD

Formed Sheffield, England, 1977.

The roots of **Def Leppard** are to be found in the band Atomic Mass, who featured bassist **Rick Savage**, guitarist **Pete Willis** and drummer **Tony Kenning**. Into the picture soon came vocalist **Joe Elliott**, and the name Deaf Leopard, which was soon adapted to the now familiar misspelling. Second guitarist **Steve Clark** was recruited in time for the first set of gigs in the summer of 1978, before Kenning was replaced by Frank Noon. This line-up was responsible for the first Def Leppard recording – the three-track single "Getcha Rocks Off", released in a limited edition of just a thousand copies on the band's own Bludgeon Riffola label.

In 1979, the line-up settled when **Rick Allen** joined as drummer. Radio airplay and music press interest led to the band signing to Phonogram, which handled the debut album, ON THROUGH THE NIGHT (1980). Despite its Top 20 success, the press felt its overly polished sound was a deliberate ploy for American success, and the accompanying single, "Hello America", appeared to support the charge. Still, they toured the States to encouraging response, although British reactions were poor at the 1980 Reading Festival.

Back in the studio, they began a long-lasting partnership with producer Robert 'Mutt' Lange on HIGH'N'DRY (1981). It was a vast improvement on its predecessor, but its British success was once again overshadowed at the time by its US sales. Another personnel change was inevitable, as Pete Willis's drinking was becoming increasingly problematic; in 1982, he was replaced by **Phil Collen**.

PYROMANIA (1983) was the first real demonstration of both Leppard's songwriting ability and Lange's meticulous production. It was released to cautious praise in Britain, but in America it sold over seven million copies and spawned several major hits, especially "Photograph". Britain was starting to slowly take notice, but cruel fortune was ready to bring the band back to earth.

On New Year's Eve 1984, Rick Allen was involved in a serious car accident near Sheffield, losing his left arm. Amazingly the drummer refused to be beaten and set about working out how he could continue in the band, eventually succeeding with the help of a custom kit that allowed him to trigger rolls and fills with his feet. He was able to resume his duties for the recording of the next album, which took three years and cost a million pounds to make. Yet HYSTERIA (1987) proved to be an instant rock classic, and marked a spectacular breakthrough in the band's homeland. Its first spin-off single release, "Animal", hit the Top 10, while the LP was an immediate chart-topper, and a tour sold out. Stateside, Def Leppard became the first band ever to have successive albums sell over seven million copies.

With worldwide sales of HYSTERIA topping fourteen million, Def Leppard had a tough act to follow, but aimed to release a fifth album by the summer of 1991. However, Steve Clark's alcohol problems were worsening and, despite taking time off to sort himself out, such efforts were in vain. On January 8, 1991, Clark was found dead, aged just 30.

The remaining quartet threw themselves into recording ADRENALIZE, more polished and likeable commercial rock, which was released in March 1992. Weeks later, the band unveiled their new guitarist, ex-Dio and Whitesnake axeman **Vivian Campbell**, at the Freddie Mercury Tribute Concert. The world tour was yet another triumphant passage, including an emotional homecoming at Sheffield's Don Valley Stadium, by which time ADRENALIZE had sold over six million copies.

The usual epic wait for a new album was made bearable by stopgap releases: RETRO-ACTIVE (1993), a fine collection of B-sides, remixes and unreleased studio material, wrapping up Steve Clark's time in the band, and a greatest hits set, VAULT (1995). Finally, SLANG (1996) appeared, a bold, contemporary release, which combined the classic Leppard sound with the rootsiness of RETRO-ACTIVE. It was greeted with acclaim from fans and critics alike, proving again that the band's renowned perfectionism was very much worth waiting for. Despite this, a ground swell of opinion still hankered after the classic polished rock sound of yore. EUPHORIA (1999) was just that, with a fine balance struck between the rockers and the ballads. Following this return to form Collen and Elliot turned their attention to their **Cybernauts** side project, concentrating on Ziggy-era Bowie tunes. They then returned to the fold for the cunningly titled X (2002), as in the Roman numeral for ten.

⊙ **Pyromania** (1983; Bludgeon Riffola/Phonogram). Credit for this breakthrough album is often given to producer Lange, who co-wrote all the songs, but time proved that Def Leppard had plenty to offer in their own right: "Rock Of Ages" and "Photograph" remained great crowd-pleasers.

⊙ **Hysteria** (1987; Bludgeon Riffola/Phonogram). A masterclass in commercial hard rock. No duff tracks to be found, and at least half have already attained 'classic' status.

⊙ **Retro-Active** (1993; Bludgeon Riffola/Phonogram). The 'other side' of Def Leppard. Recorded in days rather than years, the songs are forced to stand up for themselves without the aid of huge production, and do very nicely.

⊙ **Slang** (1996; Bludgeon Riffola/Phonogram). The long wait well rewarded with Leppard's updated 90s sound.

Hugh Hackett

DEFTONES

Formed: Sacramento, California, 1989

Of all the bands lumped into the loose and ever-expanding alternative-metal scene, Sacramento's **Deftones** must be one of the most primal, powerful and experimental. The band's story

Deftones – complete with matching footware

began innocuously enough with school friends **Chino Moreno** (vocals), **Chi Cheng** (bass), **Stephen Carpenter** (guitar), and **Abe Cunningham** (drums) – who joined the band after the departure of their original drummer **John Taylor** – getting together to thrash out their adolescent angst at various neighbourhood clubs' pay-to-play nights. They quickly built up a local reputation through dishing out various demo tapes. The band's sound was raw and pitched together everything from hip-hop and punk to balls-out heavy metal. Chief in shaping their direction was Moreno's love of 80s pop, which brought a dark and brooding quality to his vocal style and would eventually lead to the band recording cover versions of songs by Depeche Mode and Duran Duran. However, anyone looking for an overt chart-friendly pop angle would have been disappointed with the early 'Tones – this was the sound of anger and frustration tempered by a melancholic vibe that made the band a unique entity on the heavy music scene.

The years of hard work eventually paid off when they were signed by Maverick Records – Madonna's music label. What had started as a bunch of mates making what they regarded as a fun noise was to turn into a scene-altering movement. In the post-grunge environment of the mid-90s, heavy music fans were ready for something that blew traditional metal clean out of the water and, for a while, following the release of ADRENALINE (1995), it was difficult not to mention Deftones in the same breath as the likes of Korn. The album was brutally aggressive in places, with Carpenter's abrasive down-tuned riffing and Moreno's tortured vocals delivering the kind of extreme gratification that the fans demanded. This force was balanced by an ability to pull back from the edge of the emotional precipice with quieter, more intricately wrought passages.

By the band's own admission, while the debut captured the spirit of the time, it was a less than fully focused debut. The follow-up, 1997's AROUND THE FUR, however, was much more tightly constructed and executed – in short, it was a monster. The opening "My Own Summer (Shove It)" not only received heavy radio airplay, but MTV picked up on the video, guaranteeing that the Deftones had truly arrived. Likewise songs such as "Be Quiet And Drive (Far Away)" proved that they could write more accessible tunes alongside the real scorchers. By now the band's live appearances had become legendary, with Moreno pouring so much into his performance it was almost exhausting just to watch him.

The band have since developed into one of the world's premier heavy rock acts, a fact underlined by the superb WHITE PONY (2000). This extraordinary and passionate album found the band pushing the sonic envelope even further – the rage and fire was still very much apparent but with a definite desire to make more of the arty and pensively ambient edge they displayed on previous efforts. And with the genre-bending advent of nu-metal their desire to pursue a unique sonic agenda has made them stand apart from the crowd, while being viewed as pioneers on the scene.

⊙ **White Pony** (2000; Maverick).
Relative to their first two sets, WHITE PONY is a mellow, occasionally futuristic affair. Cuts like "RX Queen" and the haunting "Digital Bath" supplement The Deftones' diet of beefy riffs with effect-saturated percussion, electronics and some very laid-back vocals.

Essi Berelian

DEL AMITRI

Formed Glasgow, Scotland, 1980.

Taking their name from the Greek phrase meaning 'from the womb', **Del Amitri** began their recording career in a Glasgow dominated by the post-punk of Orange Juice. Their early semi-acoustic efforts were in the same musical territory as Edwyn Collins and his band, stripping the passion of soul music down to a whisper, but **Justin Currie** (vocals/bass/piano) later acknowledged the influence of the swooning despair of Joy Division, the metallic attack of Gang Of Four and the brutality of The

Damned and The Clash. At the same time he made clear his determination to strike out on a different path: 'We never wanted to sound like that. We always wanted the guitars to be clean and undistorted.'

With a line-up completed by guitarists **Iain Harvey** and **Brian Tolland**, and drummer **Paul Tyagi**, Del Amitri gigged frequently with other young Glasgow bands, like The Casuals, an early incarnation of Lloyd Cole And The Commotions. In 1981 they shared a flexi-single with The Bluebells, before their own debut single, the largely acoustic "Sense Sickness" (1983), was released on indie label No Strings, which had been founded by The Jesus & Mary Chain cohort Nick Low.

They continued to play any venue in Scotland that would book them, and persistence paid off when major label Chrysalis snapped them up for their first, eponymous LP (1985). The album now sounds a little unformed, but at the time it fulfilled the initial promise of a band who had made a name for themselves supporting everyone from The Fall to The Smiths.

All seemed set for success when the band were summarily dropped by Chrysalis for demanding more creative input in their own records. Luckily, the relentless touring paid off as a hard core of fans helped them set up gigs. The band rented a van and toured the US, staying with members of the audience overnight. With this support mechanism in place, Del Amitri grew more confident, toughening and sweetening their sound until they were unique.

After a sabbatical of two years, during which Currie gigged in a country band with Ali McKenzie from The Cuban Heels and learned to simplify and focus his songwriting, Del Amitri signed to A&M, and achieved three hit singles. The 1989 album WAKING HOURS captured this new dimension to their work, a smooth blend of rock, country and blues with what rock critic Brian Hogg defined as 'a persistent air of melancholia'.

That the band was dominated by its two songwriters, Currie and Harvey, became clear when the other two members were replaced by **David Cummings** (guitar) and **Brian McDermott** (drums), with no appreciable musical change. This new line-up recorded the 1992 album CHANGE EVERYTHING, which further accelerated their transformation from an indie band to mainstream acceptance.

With the release of TWISTED (1995), Del Amitri had become live performers who were confident enough to pay homage to their musical roots. This encompassed not just the expected soft rock of David Bowie's "Oh You Pretty Things" but also an ironic version of Motörhead's "Ace Of Spades" and a medley of their own song "Start With Me" with Iggy Pop's "Lust For Life". The harder Del Amitri have got, the more interesting they've become.

"Some Other Sucker's Parade" (1997) continues their quest for the perfect grown-up pop song. Mark

Freegard was brought in as producer to toughen up the sound; not an acoustic guitar in sight. THE BEST OF: HATFUL OF RAIN reached the Top 10, a sign of the band's steady fan base, and testimony to their ability to marry a good tune to great words. (Early copies came with DRIVING WITH THE BRAKES ON, a bonus CD of B-sides.)

A long silence for Del Amitri ended in 2002 with the album CAN YOU DO ME GOOD, although guitarist Cummings had during the band's absence been enjoying a rewarding sideline as a comedy scriptwriter. He submitted sketches for the BBC's *Harry Enfield And Chums* and *The Fast Show* and, with star of both shows Paul Whitehouse, wrote the bitter-sweet comedy-drama series *Happiness* in 2001.

⊙ **Waking Hours** (1989; A&M).
Currie's questioning, ironic voice dominates the album's live sound, which is sweetened by keyboards and accordion. Friendly music.

⊙ **Twisted** (1995; A&M).
There are fangs behind the affectionate smile of this album, and Currie's intimate vocals plumb deep wells of sadness and regret.

Brian Hinton

DELANEY AND BONNIE

Formed Los Angeles, 1967; disbanded 1972.

"They were just down-home, ordinary cats. That's what I liked about them." Eric Clapton

S urely every artist or band suffering the various indignities of the grassroots circuit must want to make it to the big time? Who wouldn't happily forgo the wearisome life of the road in favour of the security of a one-album-a-year recording contract? Well, **Delaney And Bonnie** did make the breakthrough, and it proved to be their undoing, as they fell victim to the capriciousness of a wider public.

Delaney Bramlett met **Bonnie Lynn** in LA in 1967 and the two were married within a week. Both were seasoned musicians, he having worked with Leon Russell and J. J. Cale, and she with Ike and Tina Turner. Against the flow of the musical tide amongst white Americans (West Coast psychedelia and the East Coast folk revival), Delaney and Bonnie's musical leanings were towards blues, gospel, funk and soul, which they channelled into an ensemble soul-revue package, emphasizing brass, percussion and the pair's powerful vocals.

Their act was dynamic enough to secure a deal with Elektra, but the resulting debut, THE ORIGINAL DELANEY AND BONNIE (1969), attracted little significant attention. For their second release, HOME (1969), they switched to the legendary Stax label and although this, too, did not sell well, it did get them a significant break, as the opening act on the debut US tour by **Eric Clapton**'s shortlived supergroup Blind Faith.

It could have been a perfect opportunity for Delaney And Bonnie to evolve into a headlining act, but Blind Faith had simply not cemented together – they were underrehearsed and uneasy with the hype which had foreshadowed the tour. While Delaney And Bonnie had designs on rising to Clapton's level of celebrity, Eric was looking for an opportunity to escape the media madhouse. He was soon spending most of his time with the Bramletts, drinking with them, jamming with them, riding on the tour bus with them (while the other Faith members flew), and finally coming to serve as a fully fledged band member.

The Bramletts were ecstatic. Adding a fine blues guitarist to the close-knit band would in itself have been an astute move, and when the guitarist in question happened to be Eric Clapton they had every reason to be extremely self-satisfied. However, having a personality as big as Clapton in tow was always likely to prove a tough act, and the Bramletts were going to have to be exceptionally good to avoid melting in the intense glare of Clapton-worshippers.

Clapton, it must be said, had good intentions. During the remainder of 1969 he organized the 'Delaney and Bonnie and Friends' tour around England which, as well as attracting further guest appearances by the likes of Traffic's Dave Mason and even George Harrison, yielded an album, DELANEY AND BONNIE AND FRIENDS ON TOUR (WITH ERIC CLAPTON) (1970), which easily became their biggest seller. Clapton took the Bramletts with him to participate in John Lennon's Plastic Ono Band adventures; they also toured Europe. Finally, when Clapton suspected that the guitar-god nonsense had died down a little, he included the Bramletts and their band as an integral part in his first solo album, ERIC CLAPTON (1970).

After he left the band, Clapton felt that the Bramletts would have no difficulty in sustaining the impetus he had helped to create, but when the Delaney And Bonnie and friends band toured the US later that year, they found that audiences were staying away now that the star attraction was gone. What was worse was that most of the band members, perhaps for the most prosaic of economic reasons, decided to jump ship in favour of Joe Cocker's Mad Dogs And Englishmen or Clapton's Derek And The Dominoes.

Delaney and Bonnie continued to record together, with two singles becoming Top 20 hits in 1971, but both the act and the marriage proved impossible to sustain after the release of D & B TOGETHER (1972). Though both have subsequently recorded solo, and continue to play sessions with former associates, it was a disappointing end for one of the most underrated bands of the era. Bonnie has been concentrating on acting as a way of bringing home the bacon more recently, appearing in the film-biography of The Doors as well as in the US TV sitcom *Roseanne*.

⊙ **Delaney And Bonnie And Friends On Tour (With Eric Clapton)** (1970; Atco).
This would be a great record even without Clapton's name on the cover. The sophistication and energy of the act, as well as the strength of the material (such as "Only You Know And I Know" and "I Don't Want To Discuss It"), showed that D & B were a very classy soul band.

⊙ **Motel Shot** (1972; Atco).
D&B show that they are still a potent force without the superstar in the line-up. "Never Ending Song Of Love" went to #13 when released as a single – so why did people stop buying their albums?

Phil Lynch

THE DELGADOS

Formed Glasgow, 1994.

Though they have since been critically eclipsed by many of the acts on their own Chemikal Underground label (established in 1995), **The Delgados** can be posited as the group who lit the touch-paper of the Glasgow lo-fi scene that spawned the likes of Mogwai, Bis, Urusei Yatsura and Arab Strap. At a time when much of the UK's music scene was being channelled by the derivative posturing and media hype of Britpop, The Delgados were among a select affiliation of acts that looked to American bands like Pavement and Sebadoh for their inspiration. Made up of four graduates of Glasgow University - **Alun Woodward** (vocals, guitar), **Emma Pollock** (vocals, guitar), **Paul Savage** (drums) and **Stewart Henderson** (bass) – The Delgados craft consistently thrilling amalgams of distorted fuzz, guitar pop and, more recently, organ tones, orchestrations and samples, all overlaid with lazily spun, almost conversational, boy/girl lyrics.

In 1995 The Delgados (their name coming from one of the great Spanish cyclists, Pedro Delgado) released their debut single, the much-lauded "Monica Webster/Brand New Car". The music press were instantly hooked and, supported by the likes of John Peel and Steve Lamacq, the group went on to record a series of radio sessions that were later released as an album by Strange Fruit. Their vinyl debut was followed by a smattering of 7" and split-single releases, both on the infant Chemikal Underground imprint and labels like Radar, Boa and Japan's 100 Guitar

Mania. The best of the batch was "Liquidation Girl", a split single with **Van Impe** (who turned out to be a Delgado alter ego, the giveaway being that Lucien Van Impe was another famous *Tour de France* cyclist).

1996 saw the group cement their live sound with billings alongside Elastica and Sebadoh, and a slot at Glasgow's T In The Park festival. The time was ripe for the release of another single - the brilliant "Under Canvas Under Wraps" – and their debut album DOMESTIQUES (another cycling reference!). The set was critically acclaimed for its diverse sound and refreshingly playful swipe at indie pop norms; though a little ragged around the edges, the collection's eclectic sound set the scene for what was to come. The following year's Peel session previewed even greater things, much of which ended up on their self-produced, cycle-racing-monikered second album PELOTON (1998). Supported by two singles, "Everything Goes Around The Water" and the beautiful "Pull The Wires From The Wall", the collection built upon the US alternative-rock influences of DOMESTIQUES, with the band sporadically discharging vast sheets of noise over their indie pop ditties, placing them not a million miles away from Sonic Youth. Again the press were enchanted, but the group's sales were consistently overshadowed by the successes of peers such as Arab Strap and Mogwai.

Despite the brilliance of the self-produced material on PELOTON, for their next trip into the studio the group were more than happy to place themselves into the hands of Mercury Rev's Dave Fridmann in his New York Tarbox Studio. The resulting collection, THE GREAT EASTERN, was released in 2000 and received rapturous reviews; it was even nominated for a Mercury Music Award. With swooning blasts of brass, grandiose orchestrations, and countryfied gems like "Make Your Move", the set witnessed the band's most accomplished material to date. Two years later thay returned with another razor-sharp set, HATE (2002) – a peculiar title given that Pollock and Woodward had recently become parents – which was followed in 2003 by the single, "All You Need Is Hate".

While their live performances continue to accrue fans worldwide, and the Chemikal Underground label persists in going from strength to strength, we can no doubt expect further great things from The Delgados in the near future.

⊙ **The Great Eastern** (2000; Chemikal Underground).
This set realized The Delgados' awesome potential, a potential that their previous releases only hinted at. Like Mercury Rev's DESERTER'S SONGS, THE GREAT EASTERN documents a band not only blossoming, but bountifully bearing fruit.

Peter Buckley

DELTA 5

Formed Leeds, England, 1979; disbanded 1981.

Leading lights of the feminist new wave, **Delta 5** formed in the wake of second-generation

Leeds punk bands the Mekons and Gang Of Four. The three founding members, **Julz Sale** (vocals/guitar/bass), **Ros Allen** (fretless bass/vocals) and **Bethan Peters** (bass/vocals), initially started the band for fun, but it wasn't long before their raw brand of edgy funk had moved to the centre of Leeds' radical post-punk movement.

With **Alan Briggs** (guitar) and **Kelvin Knight** (drums), Delta 5 put out three influential singles on Rough Trade, the first of which, "Mind Your Own Business", was released in late 1979. Impressed critics made favourable comparisons with the funk-fuelled vitriol of Gang Of Four. Both groups were heavily involved in the Rock Against Racism movement, and shared firm political convictions, gigs, and even personnel – Knight had briefly taken over from Gang Of Four's regular drummer Hugo Burnham.

As band members were attacked in the street by right-wing thugs (Leeds produced a short-lived Rock Against Communism movement in the late 70s), Delta 5 built up an enviable reputation as torch-bearers for the post-punk radical dance faction, with a choppy, combative twin-bass rhythm section that gave them a truly individual sound. Much of their appeal lay in the fact that their songs evoked experiences shared with their audience: band members were on the dole, at college, living at home or squatting, situations from which they extracted both humour and political subtext. When their second single was released early in 1980, critics celebrated the feminist sentiments of "You" (a song cataloguing the hilariously banal defects of the singer's lover) and the infectious groove of "Anticipation".

Riding a wave of success, Delta 5 headlined more than twenty dates on a US tour in late 1980. Their two singles may only have appeared on import there, but punk audiences took to the band, and the tour gained momentum as their reputation spread. Fame came in greater measure than fortune – as the third single "Colour"/"Try" was released, post-tour profits were modest. Nonetheless, band members could afford to be paid a modest weekly wage upon their return, and they also successfully secured an album deal with Charisma's subsidiary label, Pre. Further touring at home supporting Pere Ubu and Gang Of Four saw Delta 5 accumulate promising reviews, but the tide began to turn against them with the release of their album, SEE THE WHIRL (1981). Crowded out with session musicians, the LP swamped their original sound with horns, keyboards and effects. The irrepressible "Anticipation" still shone, "Open Life' conjured up some of the deep, dubby brilliance which had invited comparisons with the Gang Of Four, but the critics were disappointed.

Leaving Rough Trade for the deeply indie Pre label, which they helped create, Delta 5 were trying to keep their heads above water in a political pop scene that favoured the smoother, more seductive grooves of Scritti Politti and Heaven 17. The move had little effect, and Delta 5 – and Pre – folded soon after, two of the many punk-orientated casualties of this period.

See The Whirl (1981; Pre).
Over-busy, with more ideas than hooklines, although tracks like "Anticipation", "Shadow" and "Journey" can still rattle the floorboards. Fans of feminist rock's vanguard should seek out a secondhand copy.

Huw Bucknell

DEPECHE MODE

Formed Basildon, England, 1980.

Andy Fletcher, **Martin Gore** and songwriter **Vince Clarke** originally formed as a guitar and synth trio at school in 1976. Vocalist **David Gahan** joined shortly afterwards, but it wasn't until leaving school that they decided to trade remaining guitars in for synthesizers. They changed their name to **Depeche Mode** after spotting a headline in a French style magazine (it loosely translates as 'fast fashion'), and plunged into London's 'new romantic' scene of the time – dressed-up boys with synths, like rivals Spandau Ballet.

Resident 'futurist' gigs followed around London, leading to interest from Some Bizarre label boss Stevo. He included a track of theirs, "Photographic", on a label compilation called SOME BIZARRE ALBUM (1980), but chose not to offer them a deal. That followed during a short tour in 1981 supporting Fad Gadget, when Depeche Mode accepted an offer from Daniel Miller's Mute Records. A debut single, "Dreaming Of Me", hit the lower reaches of the British charts, and extensive TV exposure sent the follow-up, "New Life", to #11 that summer.

The band's tuneful, if lyrically awkward, synth-pop looked set for great things. However, after a UK Top 10 single, "Just Can't Get Enough", and successful debut album, SPEAK AND SPELL (1981), Vince Clarke quit, weary of touring and unprepared for the trappings of fame. (Ironically, mere months after his departure, he hit the charts with vocalist Alison Moyet as Yazoo, before going on to form Erasure).

Martin Gore took over Clarke's songwriting role in Depeche Mode, and **Alan Wilder** joined to tour with the band during 1982, becoming a full-time member after the second album, A BROKEN FRAME (1982), which capped its predecessor in the UK charts, peaking at #8. The material, never particularly credible during this early period, grew progressively darker with the release of CONSTRUCTION TIME AGAIN (1983) and SOME GREAT REWARD (1984), with Gore's lyrics tackling subjects from racism to religion, and from capitalism to S&M. Oddly, perhaps, this did nothing to halt a run of hit singles.

By the mid-80s, Depeche Mode had begun to adopt a much lower profile, and a more enigmatic image. BLACK CELEBRATION (1986) reintroduced guitars to the band's sound, and increased their following in Europe, while MUSIC FOR THE MASSES (1987) broke them in America, with a sell-out 1988 world tour climaxing in a concert at the Pasadena

DELTA 5 ■ DEPECHE MODE

hits. Indeed, despite middling reviews, EXCITER lived up to its name, and ranked as one of the band's most rounded and fascinating releases to date. Though more Mode material is yet to appear, in 2003 Gore, now **Martin L. Gore**, released a second, and more impressive covers album, COUNTERFEIT 2, featuring reworks of classic cuts such as "In My Time Of Dying" and "Candy Says".

⊙ **Violator** (1990; Mute; reissued 1998; Mute).
Given that, by now, Depeche Mode had become a stadium phenomenon in the States, VIOLATOR seemed an oddly introspective way to sell six million units (the synth-rock single "Personal Jesus" was the exception to the rule). "Enjoy The Silence" was the big hit from the album, but ultimately the most rewarding tracks here were the slow-building "Clean" and the gorgeous "Halo".

⊙ **The Singles 86–98** (1998; Mute).
Radio play has been more muted and chart success less spectacular in recent years, but this greatest hits sequel to THE SINGLES 81–85 is actually more consistent, and benefits from its chronological approach, documenting a band gazing into the abyss but overcoming disaster.

Justin Lewis

DESCENDENTS

Formed Los Angeles, 1980; disbanded 1987.

After the Sex Pistols dragged punk's corpse across America during their ill-fated US tour, the remains settled in California's sprawling suburbia. Typical of a group of kids whose main problem was too much leisure time rather than dole queues and getting beaten up for wearing bondage trousers, bands like Black Flag, Fear and **Descendents** turned punk's political rage into hardcore's teen angst.

Like most of their contemporaries on the SST label, the Descendents – **Milo Aukerman** (vocals), **Bill Stevenson** (drums), **Tony Lombardo** (bass) and **Frank Navetta** (guitar) – were alienated kids from suburban Los Angeles who managed to turn their disaffection into hyperspeed, singalong anthems. What set the Descendents apart, though, was that their wounded masculinity was funnier and slightly less hateful than other hardcore bands, and would even develop into a pure pop sensibility later on. Their first recorded output, 1981's remarkable FAT EP, is among the best, and certainly most succinct, portraits of the male teenage loser since the first Modern Lovers album. The two best songs are about fast food ("Wienerschnitzel", clocking in at eleven seconds, and "I Like Food", sixteen seconds of 'I like food, food tastes good/Juicy burgers, greasy fries/Turkey legs, raw fish eyes/Teenage girls with ketchup too'), although there are also 36 productive seconds of Oedipal vitriol on "My Dad Sucks". Amidst all the frenetic guitar bleats, on "Mr. Bass" they take two minutes to serenade the only love object they understand – a fish.

The next year, they released one of hardcore's definitive moments, MILO GOES TO COLLEGE. MILO was the distilled essence of the genre – sexual frus-

We told you last time guys, send us a cheque and we'll find something less embarrassing

Rose Bowl stadium in California, which was captured on a double live album, 101 (1989). A huge following on both sides of the Atlantic ensured that VIOLATOR (1990) and SONGS OF FAITH AND DEVOTION (1993) were even bigger sellers.

Depeche Mode, in the 90s, attained the status of stadium-rock gods. The innocent futurist fashions of their early career had long since given way to an image that appeared to embrace the grunge movement. It wasn't to everyone's liking. Wilder left in 1994, after the world tour, and there were rumours of Fletcher's departure – and of a suicide attempt by Gahan in August 1995.

Following Gahan's well-publicized recovery, he reunited with Fletcher and Gore on the 1997 album, ULTRA. Highly impressive, but decidedly demanding, its effect on most listeners was one of an exhaustive chemical weekend. Contrastingly, a second singles compilation and accompanying tour in 1998 had an air of in-built triumphalism, underlining the band's resilience in the face of catastrophe, and Gore was busying himself with a solo release of covers entitled COUNTERFEIT.

With a new album, EXCITER, released in 2001, Depeche Mode confirmed their position as one of the few surviving bands from early 80s British pop not reduced to wringing nostalgia out of their early

tration, blind rage, guitar fury, bruised egos – combined with pop hooks and tunes. For a genre that was preoccupied with snarling, manic guitars, the Descendents' understanding of a percolating bass line ("Myage" and "Suburban Home") and quasi-melody (the intro to "Bikeage") was surprising, and injected a sense of levity. Unfortunately, the album title was prophetic and Milo's foray into higher education not only meant that the band was on sabbatical for three years, but, more importantly, signalled the exhaustion of hardcore.

When hardcore's moment ended in 1983, Hüsker Dü incorporated melodies and 'sensitivity' while The Minutemen added angular avant-garde-isms to their populist rants. The Descendents, however, settled for the easy way out by appropriating the production values, guitar licks and pacing from heavy metal. When the Descendents turned rock, all the fun was gone, leaving only the uneasiness and the dull certainty of formula. Their first post-academe effort, 1985's I DON'T WANT TO GROW UP, was a relatively successful stab at power pop. The songs were well crafted and Tony Lombardo was in excellent form, but the production was more professional, and the guitars – played by **Ray Cooper** – were heavier and less exciting. Their attempt at creating sunny, jaunty pop (they would even cover a Beach Boys song), however, was doomed to failure and the two subsequent studio albums, ENJOY (1986) and ALL (1987), both sound frighteningly similar to the surf-brat rock of Ugly Kid Joe. Milo departed after ALL, and Stevenson formed the boring, Californian rock outfit **All** with remaining Descendents **Karl Alvarez** and **Stephen Eggerton**.

MILO GOES TO COLLEGE

⊙ **Two Things At Once** (1987; SST).
Contains both MILO GOES TO COLLEGE and the FAT EP with two extra songs. It doesn't always work and its adolescent skid marks will probably make you cringe, but as a map of the beginnings of 'alternative' American rock – and in its own right – this makes for compulsive listening.

Peter Shapiro

dEUS

Formed Antwerp, Belgium, 1991.

dEUS announced themselves to a world conditioned to sneer at the very thought of Belgian rock'n'roll (think Plastic Bertrand, think Singing Nun) with two hugely successful 1994 singles, "Suds And Soda" and "Via". These elegant, uninhibited compositions were widely bracketed within the alternative-rock genre, but both contained much more than that categorization might indicate. Irreverent but energized, dEUS's music corralled elements of folk, punk and progressive rock into a sound that some called 'avant-grunge'. Others considered them 'The Levellers with O levels'.

Signed to the ever-vigilant Island Records after some low-key London gigs, the group revealed to a perplexed but enthused music press their origins as a Violent Femmes/Velvet Underground cover band. Taking all the more obtuse elements from those artists, their own original material placed them on a par with Captain Beefheart's more accessible moments – an opulent pop art soundtrack with libertarian attitudes to match. They had begun in earnest with a string of appearances at Antwerp's Music Box, a waterfront watering hole notorious for the artists, musicians and general hangers-on who frequent its environs. Some of its rampant bohemia had evidently rubbed off on the group.

Led by vocalist/guitarist **Tom Barman** (apparently his real name), dEUS additionally comprise **Steff Kamil Carlens** (bass), drummer **Julle De Borgher**, violinist **Klaas Janzoons** and guitarist **Rudy Trouvé**. Much of their European popularity rests on a live show which eschews pragmatic repetition of crowd-pleasing favourites for a flowing, improvisational show which is as close to free-form jazz as rock music comes. If they want to 'borrow' something from another tradition, they simply do so (for example, the line 'I skipped the part about love' on "Via" was appropriated from R.E.M.'s "Low"). It comes as little surprise, then, that each member also enjoys the pursuit of separate musical projects, such as Barman's house collective, **General Electric**, while Trouvé is an accomplished painter who provides the group with their distinctive artwork.

Harnessing those elements for a studio album was not the easiest task for a band for whom wanton experiment had been the abiding code. Yet WORST CASE SCENARIO (1994; reissued 1998) did an admirable job in translating their loose aesthetic into something more cohesive. Afterwards they defied Euro-sceptics further by announcing plans for their own porn movie as well as a mail-order-only album, MY SISTER IS MY CLOCK (1995).

By 1996 dEUS had begun to export their European popularity to the US, completing a full-scale tour with close friends Morphine. The push was to promote IN A BAR, UNDER THE SEA, released in October of that year. Again the group's American influences were to the fore here, ranging from The Velvet Underground and Tom Waits to The Captain Beefheart Band – fittingly, that group's long-standing keyboardist Eric Drew Feldman helped produce the record. However, despite their instinct for experimentation, the best song was the comparatively straight-laced pop effort, "Little Arithmetics".

Although they featured on the album, original guitarist Trouvé and bassist Carlens left the group to concentrate on their own projects. The band's refusal to compromise – building raw noise into the sweetest of tunes – has kept them on the fringes of rock with sufficient space to move and experiment, though it was their characteristically eclectic influences that continued to attract audiences to the 1999 album THE IDEAL CRASH and 2001's "Nothing Really Ends" single. A compilation, NO MORE LOUD MUSIC, hit the shops in 2002.

⊙ **Worst Case Scenario** (1994; Island; reissued 1998; Island).
From the singles to the mighty Tom Waits-like "Right As Rain", WORST CASE SCENARIO marked dEUS out as a band with a flair for compulsive pop tunes in directly inverse proportion to their charming lack of commercial ambition.

Alex Ogg

DEVO

Formed Akron, Ohio, 1972; disbanded 1985; re-formed 1987; disbanded 1991.

Industrial Akron's most famous band, **Devo**, grew out of the experimental work of songwriters **Mark Mothersbaugh** (vocals/keyboards) and **Gerry Casale** (bass). Deciding to form a band, they added their brothers – guitarists **Bob Mothersbaugh** and **Bob Casale** – along with drummer **Alan Myers**.

The group moved to LA in 1977, where they gained plenty of attention for their stage act, based around the idea of 'de-evolution' through the dehumanizing effect of modern technology. Mark would wear a baby-face mask to sing songs as his alter ego, Booji Boy, and the band's style and sound began to appeal to fellow musicians like Bowie and Iggy Pop (who included their song "Praying Hands" in his live set).

Devo's first single, "Jocko Homo" (1977), was a kind of explanation of the band's overall concept: 'They tell us that we lost our tails/Evolving up from little snails/I say it's all just wind in sails/Are we not men?/We are Devo!'. Released on the Booji Boy label in the States, and licensed to Stiff in the UK, the single, along with their stage act and a short film called *The Truth About De-Evolution*, led to lucrative deals with Warners in their homeland and Virgin in the UK.

Devo's first album, Q: ARE WE NOT MEN? A: WE ARE DEVO! (1978), was produced by Brian Eno. As well as featuring a rerecording of "Jocko Homo", it contained other staples of their live set, including "Uncontrollable Urge", "Sloppy" and "Praying Hands". Several tracks were lifted as singles, the most

popular being their reworking of The Rolling Stones standard, "Satisfaction", which coincided with a radical deconstruction of the very same song by fellow US oddball band, The Residents. In contrast, Devo's catchy and poppy reading of the song nearly hit the UK Top 40, despite all but abandoning the original's signature riff and backbeat.

The public liked the quirky guitar work, boiler suits and industrial shades, and the band toured the world promoting the album and its follow-up, DUTY NOW FOR THE FUTURE (1979). The band found particular success in Japan, where punk failed to establish itself with audiences who liked to see an original show. But by the time of FREEDOM OF CHOICE (1980), the Devo concept was beginning to wear thin and sales suffered – though one track, "Whip It", became their only significant US chart hit. Subsequent releases in 1981, DEVO LIVE and NEW TRADITIONALISTS, didn't stop the rot, nor did 1982's OH NO! IT's DEVO!, and after one more LP, SHOUT (1984), they disbanded. With new drummer **David Kendrick**, the band's brief return on the Enigma label with TOTAL DEVO (1988) and SMOOTH NOODLE MAPS (1990) merely sought to underline that the joke had worn thin. The obligatory 'best of' compilation, HOT POTATOES (1993), attempted to cover up their decline by largely avoiding a chronological track listing.

Devo get down to serious training

Q: Are We Not Men? A: We Are Devo! (1978; Virgin).
Devo's first and best, containing most of their hits – the manifesto of "Jocko Homo", the near hit "Satisfaction" and "Space Junk", an everyday tale of a guy who sees his girlfriend totalled by a piece of falling debris from a spacecraft. But the seeds of their own downfall are here, too: the vocals strain to keep their 'weirdness' intact and there is the occasional hint of a heavy metal riff.

Hot Potatoes (1993; Virgin).
A creditable nineteen-track compilation containing all the hits and several misses.

Simon Ives

DEXYS MIDNIGHT RUNNERS

Formed Birmingham, England, 1978; disbanded 1987.

Born in Wolverhampton of Irish parents, **Kevin Rowland** (vocals/guitar) began his musical career in a Birmingham punk rock group, The Killjoys. However, after one flop single, "Johnny Won't Get To Heaven" (1977), he and rhythm guitarist **Al Archer** left to form a group they called **Dexys Midnight Runners** – a name derived from the pep pill 'dexedrine' (oddly enough, given the band's code of 'no drink, no drugs').

The Dexys' idea was to pay homage to the soul music of the mid-60s; their image was derived from characters in Scorsese's *Mean Streets* movie. The original line-up comprised Rowland, Archer, **Pete Saunders** (organ), **Andy Leek** (keyboards), **Steve 'Babyface' Spooner** (alto saxophone), **'Big' Jimmy Patterson** (trombone), **Pete Williams** (drums), **J. B.** (tenor saxophone), and **Bobby Junior** (drums). In 1979, they gained a support slot on a UK tour with The Specials, and were signed to EMI by former Clash manager, Bernie Rhodes.

An excellent debut single, "Dance Stance", an attack on anti-Irish prejudice, scraped into the UK Top 40. But it was after Saunders was replaced by (future Style Council member) **Mick Talbot** that they hit the big time with a tribute to British soul legend Geno Washington. "Geno" reached #1 in the UK in May 1980, and the band, in an early example of behaviour earning the 'difficult' tag, instantly dropped the song from the live set.

Already, all was not well within the group's ranks. While recording their first album, SEARCHING FOR THE YOUNG SOUL REBELS (1980), Rowland seized the master tapes from producer Pete Wingfield, refusing to return them until better contract terms were granted. The group's instability created a difficult, if brave and intriguing, album, but the rifts grew deeper. Many of the band felt uncomfortable with the direction or material, and after the wilfully uncommercial single "Keep It (Part 2)" flopped at the end of 1980, Rowland and Patterson found the rest of the band departing to form **The Bureau**, who continued for a year or two with EMI.

By mid-1981, Rowland and Patterson had left EMI and signed to Phonogram, with their new

Dexys' line-up of **Micky Billingham** (keyboards), **Steve Wynne** (bass, soon replaced by Giorgio Kilkenny), **Billy Adams** (guitar), **Paul Speare** (tenor saxophone), **Brian Maurice** (alto saxophone) and **Seb Shelton** (drums). A single, "Show Me", with Bowie producer Tony Visconti at the controls, deservedly hit the UK Top 20, although the next release, the curious "Liars A To E" failed to chart. Then, after critically acclaimed London shows in late 1981 – *The Projected Passion Tour* – there was a crucial change of direction. This time, the soul revival element was accompanied by an Irish folk thread, forged through the addition of fiddle trio **Helen O'Hara**, **Steve Brennan** and **Roger Macduff**, collectively known as **The Emerald Express**. The band's image was to change too – from *Mean Streets* and tracksuits to dungarees and gypsy-dress. After this new line-up's first release, "The Celtic Soul Brothers" (1982), Speare and Maurice left, along with the long-standing Patterson, although he had already taken part in recording and co-writing the second Dexys' album, TOO RYE-AY (1982). Although fiddles, banjos and tin whistles were now integral to the sound, there was still a place for horns and pianos – the staple fare of the soul revival. Somehow it all fell into place, not least on the gorgeous "Come On Eileen", a #1 in Britain, and in the US the following year.

It was a success – commercial and critical – they would find hard to sustain, especially following the exit of co-writer Jimmy Patterson, with whom Rowland had fallen out. It would be a long three years before a new Dexys' album was released, and on DON'T STAND ME DOWN (1985) only Rowland, Adams and O'Hara were left from the previous line-up, augmented by guests. Neither a triumph nor a disaster, it was a baffling, brave and occasionally brilliant album – much more introspective and diverse than its predecessors. No single was issued before its release, however, which probably destroyed any chance of mainstream success. The following year, Adams left, while Rowland and

O'Hara had one final hit single with "Because Of You", the theme tune to a BBC TV sitcom, *Brush Strokes*, before calling it a day.

After the split, Rowland recorded a low-key solo LP, THE WANDERER (1988) before vanishing for some years, re-emerging for an exuberant TV appearance on Jonathan Ross's Channel 4 show *Saturday Zoo* in 1993, and, less successfully, a poorly received solo covers album, MY BEAUTY (1999), which was nevertheless feted by departing Creation boss Alan McGee. Though by now regarded as a spent force by some of the music press, Rowland's considerable creative powers were recalled with the 20th anniversary reissue of SEARCHING FOR THE YOUNG SOUL REBELS in September 2000 – it sounded as fresh in the new millennium as it did when it was first released.

⊙ **Searching For The Young Soul Rebels** (1980; EMI). Now finally available on CD, complete with extra tracks and a multimedia video clips. This is a debut that utterly deserves its status as a flawed masterpiece.

⊙ **Too Rye-Ay** (1982; Phonogram/Mercury). The most consistent of the three Dexys albums which manage to translate onto record the stirring Celtic soul of the band's unforgettable live performances. Features "Come On Eileen", a faithful cover of Van Morrison's "Jackie Wilson Said", and live favourites "Let's Make This Precious" and "Old". The 1996 reissue includes several extra live tracks.

⊙ **The Very Best Of Dexys Midnight Runners** (1991; Phonogram/Mercury). Very much compiled by the record company rather than the band. Luckily, non-album 45s like "Show Me" and "Let's Get This Straight (From The Start)" are present and correct, as are all the ones you'd expect.

Justin Lewis

THE DICTATORS

Formed New York, 1974; disbanded 1978; re-formed 1990.

Back when the New York scene was spawning the first punk rock bands in the early 70s, **The Dictators** were, except for maybe the Ramones, the most back-to-basics band existing, not to mention one of the first to come out with a record (beaten only by Patti Smith). Saluting cars, girls, TV, soda and junk culture, they took rock'n'roll back to the land of Chuck Berry with a smartarse twist to it.

While other New York groups were full of artsy pretention and most English bands had a political agenda, The Dictators stood as the real young, loud and snotty bunch of misfits that were supposed to make up the punk rock scene. They became spiritual daddies to other loud New York brats like the Beastie Boys and junk-culture denizens De La Soul and Brand Nubian.

Bassist/singer/writer **Andy Shernoff** started out with his *Teenage Wasteland Gazette* fanzine, getting other writers like **Richard Meltzer** and **Lester Bangs** to work out their rock obsessions. Shernoff teamed up with college buddy **Scott 'Top-Ten' Kempner**, local bar-band sensation **Ross 'The Boss' Funichello** and drummer **Stu King** to form the first version of The Dictators. Wrestling nut **Handsome Dick Manitoba** started out as their roadie but was elevated to singer for breaking too much equipment. Meltzer was chummy with Blue Oyster Cult (who Patti Smith was writing for) and got their production team of Murray Krugman and Sandy Pearlman to get them in good graces with Epic.

Fronting money for a band who had never even done a demo or rarely performed live, Epic put out the band's debut, GO GIRL CRAZY! (1975), just as the other New York punk bands were beginning to create a buzz. Their lack of musical finesse was more than made up for in their smarts and fun. Sadly, this grimy, sweaty masterpiece went largely unheard and, without an appealing gimmick like most of the other local bands had, The Dictators didn't make much headway with the radio or the public – even if they were packing CBGB's just as much as any other local band. Lack of record company support, lousy tour packages (they went from gigs with Kiss to gigs with Billy Preston and had Cheap Trick and AC/DC open for them at different times), internal problems and management problems didn't do much good for the band, either. King would also quit, replaced by **Richard Teeter**, and **Mark 'The Animal' Mandoza** joined them on bass.

After Epic dropped the band, it was two years before they came out with their follow-up, MANIFEST DESTINY (1977), on the Asylum label. Going along with more good times, more metal and maybe even some maturity, the album carried on the party mood of the debut. Unfortunately, Asylum were sceptical and the band managed to put out one more roller-coaster ride of raging rock, BLOOD BROTHERS (1978) – named after a Richard Price novel – before breaking up shortly afterwards.

The Dictators did some reunion gigs in New York in 1980 and 1981, which came out on disc as FUCK 'EM IF THEY CAN'T TAKE A JOKE (1981). After this, members started appearing in other groups. Kempner would later form The Del Lords, Mark 'The Animal' – who was around only for the second album – would strike gold in **TWISTED SISTER** and Ross the Boss played with metalheads **Manowar** for a while. Finally, in 1990, Manitoba, Shernoff and Ross reunited to make ...AND YOU? as **Manitoba's Wild Kingdom**, finding some solace in the metal bands that were popping up in their wake and proving something to the wannabes on the scene. After this heartening return, The Dictators themselves started to play gigs with Kempner back in the fold, showing everyone that they'd lost none of their power.

Tours of Europe and South America proved fruitful, as they were hailed as heroes much more than in their native country. The band are active again, old albums have been reissued, and in 2001 The Dictators finally unleashed a brand new album, DFFD.

⊙ **Go Girl Crazy!** (1975; Epic). One of the most vital platters ever released. Any real rock fan will need this or risk an empty, meaningless life. Their "California Sun" beats the hell out of the Ramones and their "I Got You Babe" is funnier and heavier than UB40 or Sonny and Cher.

⦿ **Manifest Destiny** (1977; Asylum).
Thanks to some heart-wrenching tunes and Andy's keyboards, this may sound like a maturity move from this bunch of perpetual adolescents, but "Science Gone Too Far" and their version of The Stooges' "Search And Destroy" showed that they could tear it up at will.

⦿ **Blood Brothers** (1978; Asylum).
The twisted "Baby, Let's Twist", another anthem called "Faster And Louder", "Stay With Me" (a raging love song) and the Flaming Groovies' "Slow Death" (were these guys a great covers band or what?), along with nods to whores and Meltzer all would leave track marks on any record player. A start-to-finish winner like the debut.

Jasen Gross

BO DIDDLEY

Born McComb, Mississippi, December 30, 1928.

"I still like Bo Diddley. If he ever gets outta the chord of E he might get dangerous." Jerry Lee Lewis

Guitar hero and rock'n'roll pioneer **Bo Diddley** (real name Ellas McDaniel) was born in Mississippi and grew up in Chicago. Dual careers beckoned: his teen training as an amateur boxer was where he reputedly earned his nickname (although it is also an inversion of a Southern folk instrument, the diddly bow). But he had been playing street-corner music since his schooldays, building his own electric guitar and basing his style on gospel and the blues.

By the beginning of the 1950s he and his band were playing electric blues/R&B in the Chicago clubs. The big break came in the spring of 1955, when the fledgling Chicago blues label, Chess, launched Bo Diddley's career along with that of fellow Chicago musician Chuck Berry. While Berry quickly earned a pop career, Bo's harder (and blacker) style kept him out of the mainstream, although both were to prove influential, particularly on the other side of the Atlantic. Bo's debut single, on Chess subsidiary Checker, set the tone for what was to come. "Bo Diddley" was a statement that put the man firmly centre stage, and a theme tune to keep him there for the rest of his career. It also introduced the rhythm that was to take his name. The syncopated signature, taken from Africa via New Orleans, once known as 'shave and a haircut/two bits', will never again be known as anything but 'the Bo Diddley beat'. Bo's popularizing of the rhythm left its mark on numerous pop songs down the years. The B-side was the heavy blues "I'm A Man", and both sides became hits in the R&B chart.

The career was moving: Bo played at the Harlem Apollo in August and in November shot to fame with an appearance on Ed Sullivan's TV show. His first American pop hit came in 1959 with the calypso-influenced "Crackin' Up", but Bo's biggest US pop hit was the novelty number "Say Man", which reached the Top 20 later that year. Hindsight sees the jive talk between Bo and his regular sidekick and maraca player **Jerome Green** as a forerunner of modern rap.

In 1963 he toured Britain for the first time, along with Little Richard, The Everly Brothers and The Rolling Stones. And it was the white pop acts who took over the Bo Diddley style and made it pay. Like much of American rock'n'roll/R&B, the records were bigger across the water than they were at home. Within one year, Bo had four hit albums in the UK, more than he would achieve at home: BO DIDDLEY (1962), BO DIDDLEY IS A GUNSLINGER (1961), BO

Bo Diddey (left) with The Duchess and Jerome

CHARLIE GILLETT

DIDDLEY RIDES AGAIN (1963) and the live BEACH PARTY (1964). During this period there were also British hit singles: "Pretty Thing" (1963) (which gave a band its name) and "Hey Good Lookin'" (1965). Other songs, like "Who Do You Love", "Road Runner" and "I'm A Man", provided the repertoire for a whole generation of British R&B bands and, following them, a new wave of American garage bands.

Soul and psychedelia killed rock'n'roll and Bo returned to the blues. In 1968 he recorded the SUPER BLUES BAND with Muddy Waters and Little Walter, following it with SUPER SUPER BLUES BAND with Muddy Waters and Howlin' Wolf. A new generation emerged and in 1979 Bo Diddley opened for The Clash on their first American tour. The early-80s rockabilly revival brought more work and his touring expanded worldwide. Most records during this period were live albums.

There were also some small acting roles, including an appearance on a television advertisement for Nike. In 1987 his position as living legend was confirmed when he was inducted into the Rock And Roll Hall Of Fame. His musical and technical innovation make him one of its worthier recipients. No one else mixed traditional rhythms and modern technology with his panache, and his work anticipated everything from heavy rock and psychedelia to rap and African pop. Instantly recognizable as much for his physical presence as for the distinctive rectangular guitar, Bo Diddley projects an identity – a sense of humour, a sense of threat and shameless self-promotion – that has stood the test of time.

Diddley continues to play live, still headlining and still looking pretty damn good. He has recorded sporadically, too, enlisting old mates like Keef and Ron, and Johnny Guitar Watson, for a blues workout, A MAN AMONGST MEN (1996). This was fun ('I'm sick! Sick! A lunatic!', he sings on the opener, "Bo Diddley Is Crazy") and dire ('Don't be takin' your mom and daddy's gun to school') in about equal measures. Welcome, though, all the same.

⊙ **I'm A Man** (1992; Charly).
There are numerous compilations around, but this budget-price 'best of' is a good, basic introduction. You get sixteen of his best-known numbers, including "Bo Diddley", "Pretty Thing", "Crackin' Up" and the title track – and lots of examples of that famous beat. Classic stuff and still sounding powerful after nearly forty years.

⊙ **Bo's Blues** (1993; Ace).
Themed compilation with the emphasis on blues, all from the Chess sessions of the 50s/early 60s. A varied selection ranging from traditional twelve-bars to stomping R&B, some lament, some bragging and some humour. And a chance to discover where The Rolling Stones got some of their best ideas.

Penny Kiley

DIDO

Born London, 25 December 1971.

As with most perceived 'overnight successes', **Dido Cloud Armstrong**'s rise to fame and

The ever-animated Dido

acclaim was anything but. A prodigious musical talent, she had mastered piano and violin by her early teens, and was educated at London's Guildhall School of Music. A day job in a publishing agency helped pay the bills while she was involved with her elder brother Rollo's new band Faithless. Contributing backing vocals to seven tracks of their debut album, REVERENCE (1996), it wasn't until the group's next album, SUNDAY 8PM (1998), that she got the chance to sing the lead, on the track "Hem Of His Garment". Dido also worked with cult dance act **Skinny** on their 1997 track "Failure".

However, her solo recordings were also taking shape, and soon emerged in the form of NO ANGEL. The album was glacial but intimate, and its success on American soil was undeniably assisted by three things: firstly, her appearance at the Lilith Fair festival in 1999, next the use of opening track "Here With Me" as the theme song for the hit TV series *Roswell* and, lastly and perhaps most significantly, the patronage of Eminem. By the time that NO ANGEL was released in the UK, the rap artist had borrowed the first verse of "Thank You" for the refrain of his worldwide number one hit, "Stan", which documented an eerie fable of obsessive fandom.

NO ANGEL topped the UK charts for several weeks in early 2001, spawned a clutch of major hit singles, and achieved the rare feat of being feted by just about every station in the UK's fragmented pop radio industry. The set taps into the neuroses of modern life – insecurity, betrayal, powerlessness – and offers tentative hope and reassurance. The album ended the year as Britain's best seller, while a series of TV appearances and gregarious live outings showed her to be nothing like the shrinking violet she had sometimes been portrayed as. Her extraordinarily high profile now meant that her vocal on Faithless's 2002 single "One Step Too Far" inevitably resulted in the group crediting the cut as 'Faithless featuring Dido'.

⊙ **No Angel** (Cheeky/BMG, 2000).
Credible pedigree, natural talent, and the ability to connect with millions of listeners – it would seem that Dido Armstrong has it all. Though a little uniform – mid-tempo, sincere, low-key songs abound – this collection is a fitting soundtrack to the early 21st century.

Justin Lewis

DIED PRETTY

Formed Sydney, Australia, 1984.

"The goatee brings out the devil in me. I think I should start wearing the cloven hooves to go with it."
Ronald S. Peno

One of the most original and enduring of Australian bands, **Died Pretty** were formed by a Brisbane indie scene trio – **Ronald S. Peno**, **Brett Myers** and **Frank Brunetti** – backed by **Chris Welsh** (drums) and **Mark Lock** (bass). If their name suggested image above content, such ideas were soon erased by the energy and originality of their early releases on prime alternative label, Citadel, under the production of that veritable godfather of Oz rock, ex-Radio Birdman Rob Younger.

The band came to prominence in 1985 with a four-track EP, Next To Nothing. This had elements of the jangly guitar sounds typical of 80s Aussie outfits, but an original trademark in Brunetti's swirling organ – a moody backdrop for Peno's vocals to metamorphose from gentle drawl to manic howl, counterpointed by Myers' intense guitar. The band's stage shows also attracted early interest due to the wild acrobatics and capers of Peno, a strange-looking, almost neckless figure, whose presence added excitement and anarchy to all proceedings.

The debut album, Free Dirt (1986), consolidated the band's reputation with a fine set of songs by Myers and Peno – the creative force then, as now. Ranging from poppy numbers like "Blue Sky Day" and "Through Another Door" to the dark brooding "Just Skin" and "Next To Nothing", the album has a rich yet raw sound, and fine guest playing on sax, mandolin and pedal steel. Extra instrumental input has been a factor ever since.

Two years on, the Lost album demonstrated a shift to a softer sound, though without losing power, and a clever pacing and mix of acoustic and electric elements. In "Springenfall", it featured one of the group's finest moments – a majestic track building on its melody through a strummed chorus to truly ecstatic crescendo. It ranks alongside the bouncy "Everybody Moves" (from the sadly unobtainable Citadel compilation Positively Elizabeth Street) as the zenith of Died Pretty art.

In 1990 **John Hoey** and **Steve Clark** took over on keyboards and bass, respectively, for the album Every Brilliant Eye, produced by Jeff Eyrich in LA. The less dominant keyboards and sharper production gave the album a lighter feel, even with Peno's insistent barking about the state of the world on the apocalyptic "The Underbelly". The same personnel maintained standards on the following year's Doughboy Hollow, although it didn't quite reach the heights of its predecessor.

By 1993 Robert Warren had come in on bass and background vocals, and the band tried London for the recording of a new album, Trace – a rather subdued effort that soon got deleted. However, just as it seemed Died Pretty might be slipping away, they got a new lease of life, recording Sold (1995), with Rob Younger back on production duties at Boston's Fort Apache studios – home of Dinosaur Jr., Buffalo Tom and The Lemonheads.

Next came the more experimental Using My Gills As A Road Map (1999), and in 2000 Everyday Dream, which successfully pulled together the group's classic sound with their newer digital leanings. The group still seem more than capable of maintaining their relevance.

⊙ **Free Dirt** (1986; Citadel).
A great debut full of vocal pyrotechnics, swirling keyboards and carefully balanced instrumental tensions.

⊙ **Sold** (1995; Columbia).
The band's latest offering displays their full range – pleading vocals, whining guitars, lush bass runs, soothing keyboards and acoustic tinges.

Nick Edwards

ANI DIFRANCO

Born Buffalo, New York, September 1970.

The most successful contemporary writer to meld the ideological and musical influences of folk and punk – Billy Bragg and Michelle Shocked aside – **Ani DiFranco** can boast a more fervent fan base than either. Her prodigious 90s output has exhibited sufficient character and literacy to distinguish her from a tidal wave of Alanis Morissette-styled angst-ridden young women. That she has achieved this distinction without recourse to the mainstream music industry and its inevitable compromises says much about her determination. That would count for little, however, were it not for the fact that her music displays frequent excellence and sporadic brilliance. Look beyond the tattoos and body piercings and DiFranco can match any of her more conventional folk peers in song composition and execution.

DiFranco first began releasing albums through her own Righteous Babe Records in 1989, with a self-titled debut that only hinted at her future stature.

Ani DiFranco – Commander in Chief of her one woman army

growing fan base, she recorded her first, self-titled cassette album. It sold out of its initial pressing of 500 copies quickly enough to convince her to repeat the experiment (she claims to have had some 100 songs to draw from already at this stage). A devotee of the DIY punk ethos, DiFranco founded her own record company, Righteous Babe, to distribute further recordings.

NOT SO SOFT followed in 1991, as DiFranco toured America coast to coast in her trusty Volkswagen. Clearly enamoured by the nomadic existence, she played gigs wherever she could get on the bill, slowly building a word-of-mouth following as a result. The upswing continued through IMPERFECTLY (1992), PUDDLE DIVE (1993) and OUT OF RANGE (1994) as she clocked up 200 gigs a year. But it was 1995's NOT A PRETTY GIRL that broke her out of the indie ghetto, picking up plaudits from a wide variety of media beyond the alternative and roots communities, including the *New York Times*. Some erstwhile fans were dismayed at 1996's DILATE – a suite of songs addressing a recent love affair with a man – but the contents were no less visceral for the retuning of subject matter. The double live set LIVING IN CLIP (1997) was a fans-only affair, before two major 1998 releases. Of the two, UP UP UP UP UP UP was the most consistently rewarding – not least for "'Tis Of Thee", the title track and "Angry Any More", the latter a powerful account of coming to terms with the demons that had driven her through her adolescence.

Difranco continues to perform and record, while her reputation with both fans and fellow musicians continues to grow: in recent years she has worked with the likes of Prince, Maceo Parker and Bruce Cockburn. TO THE TEETH (1999), REVELLING/RECKONING (2001) and EVOLVE (2003) were among her finest recordings to date, the latter particularly offering a double-CD spread of confessional, beautiful lyrics, minimal guitar and expansive jazzy arrangements.

Ani DiFranco (1989; Righteous Babe).
DiFranco's debut established the singer's forthright, confessional tone. Opening song "Both Hands" and "Every Angle" offer perfect examples of her directness.

Out of Range (1994; Righteous Babe).
More reflective than previous efforts, and boasting an increased variety of musical accompaniment (including brass), songs such as "You Had Time" leave behind some of her earlier, more didactic leanings.

Not a Pretty Girl (1995; Righteous Babe).
The record that broke her across America and Europe. Could be subtitled 'Not a Corporate Babe, either'.

However, it did serve to bookmark an individual voice. Her songs were openly lesbian in orientation, addressing a feminist agenda without resort to cliché or self-satisfaction. If her attempts to tackle difficult issues ranging from abortion to rape could sometimes seem haphazard, it would only be a short time before she rectified that and turned them into harrowing travelogues and confessionals. Musically, her vocal range has been much remarked upon – but she is also a very, very good guitarist.

DiFranco made her live debut at the age of 9, when she performed a set of Beatles covers at a local coffee house under the auspices of her guitar tutor. Though she was befriended by Michelle Shocked and Suzanne Vega, she temporarily gave up music for ballet, but returned to songwriting in 1984 at the age of 14. Within a year she'd left home to become a fixture on the Buffalo folk-club circuit, relocating to New York City in 1989. There, encouraged by a

⊙ **Revelling/Reckoning** (2001; Righteous Babe).
Musically, this set saw a bit of a departure for
DiFranco, but stick with it and you won't be disappointed.

Alex Ogg

DINOSAUR JR.

Awoke Amherst, Massachusetts, 1984.
Went back to sleep 1998.

"I actually contemplate suicide every day. My record sales would certainly go up." J. Mascis

After having played together in the hardcore punk band Deep Wound, **J. Mascis** (guitar/vocals) and **Lou Barlow** (bass) recruited **Patrick Murphy** (aka Murph) as the drummer for their new band, initially named Dinosaur. Their first release DINOSAUR (1985) brought them their first tour, supporting Sonic Youth across the US. The threat of legal action from a West Coast band, The Dinosaurs, forced them to add a suffix, and it was thus that **Dinosaur Jr.** released their second LP, YOU'RE LIVING ALL OVER ME, in summer 1987.

Through Sonic Youth, with whom Mascis collaborated on several recordings, the band were introduced to the UK label Blast First, resulting in a deal which led to their single "Freak Scene" (1988). The record topped the indie charts in Britain, becoming an anthem for the pre-grunge, pre-slacker generation. With their finely crafted mix of melody and full-on noise, Dinosaur Jr. soon took on the mantle of Sonic Youth as the premier American pop-noise group, prefiguring Nirvana's reconstruction of the rock'n'roll band. Indeed, in 1990 there were rumours that J. Mascis was about to join Nirvana on drums, the instrument he had started out playing in Deep Wound and various jazz orchestras.

Dinosaur Jr.'s third album, BUG (1988), which many fans consider their peak achievement, was released a month before Lou Barlow's acrimonious departure (to form **SEBADOH**). BUG's successful reception was followed up by what turned out to be Mascis's last recording for three years, a blistering and heartfelt cover of The Cure's "Just Like Heaven" (1988), with **Donna Biddell**, formerly of The Screaming Trees, taking over on bass. Mascis kept the band on hold for the next few years, producing Buffalo Tom, among others, and making guest appearances on various Sonic Youth projects as usual, as well as the Velvet Monkeys collaboration. A proposed label, Seaweed, did not materialize. However, Blanco y Negro offered Dinosaur Jr. a contract, and the resulting single, "The Wagon", was released at the start of 1991, featuring **Don Fleming** (guitar/vocals), ex-B.A.L.L., Half Japanese, Gumball and Velvet Monkeys), while **Jay Spiegel** (also ex-B.A.L.L. and Velvet Monkeys) assisted on percussion. This line-up did not last long, and the major-label debut album, the disappointing GREEN MIND (1991),

was mostly recorded by Mascis alone. Summer 1991 saw him recording the soundtrack to the film *Gas Food Lodging*, which was later released through Mute Records. However, he soon found a regular collaborator in bassist Mike Johnson (ex-Snakepit), who remains as the single other constant band member. Their first single, "Whatever's Cool With Me", marked his debut in 1992, with the album WHERE YOU BEEN appearing the following February to a favourable reception. However, while it was hailed as 'seminal' in some places, this set suggested that there were just two kinds of Dinosaur Jr. songs: tortured and self-pitying, and fast and shrieking.

J. Mascis unplugged – well, it worked for The Monkees

BLANCO Y NEGRO

The success of WHERE YOU BEEN marked a turning point for Dinosaur Jr., who were part of the so-called grunge explosion of 1990–91, as recorded in their appearance on the video 1991 – *The Year Punk Rock Broke*, with Sonic Youth and Nirvana. Mascis then slightly loosened up his notoriously uncommunicative public persona, and WITHOUT A SOUND (1994) brought them further popularity, and marked a partial return to the use of varied sounds and structures which made the band interesting in the first place. HAND IT OVER (1997), however, was a return to safer ground, with more real tunes and stories whipped up into a screaming frenzy by Mascis' wildboy guitar playing.

Mike Johnson has also released two solo albums, the most recent being YEAR OF MONDAYS (1996), while Mascis's own self-titled solo acoustic recordings appeared in 1996 as the album MARTIN + ME. Mascis was in danger of becoming a Neil Young figure for the 90s, with his blend of sad, painful songwriting and intense feedback-driven hardcore appealing to post-grunge thirtysomethings who still appreciated the rock–dinosaur paradigm: Dinosaur Jr. called it quits as a band in early 1998.

In 2000 Mascis resurfaced on the City Slang Label with an album, MORE LIGHT. Released under the name **J Mascis & The Fog**, and blessed by the production genius of My Bloody Valentine's **Kevin Shields**, the collection found J on powerfully good form. It was well received by the old fans and marked the beginning of a new chapter in the Mascis story. The new band, which also features **Mike Watt** (Minutemen, fIREHOSE) and toured extensively, being joined for many shows by onetime Stooge **Ron Asheton**, followed up with FREE SO FREE in 2002.

Dinosaur Jr.

Dinosaur (1985; Homestead).
A debut showing the band's progress from Cure-influenced tracks such as "Forget The Swan" to their trademark combination of melody and bursts of noise on "Does It Float" and "Pointless". Mascis's self-deprecating vocal style sustains the mood of warped awkwardness mixed with occasional moments of raw agony.

You're Living All Over Me (1987; SST).
Continues the melodic melancholic style, but with rather more fuzz-wah and a more coherent production. The final track, "Poledo", is virtually Lou Barlow's resignation speech.

Bug (1988; Blast First).
Dinosaur Jr.'s finest moment, virtually flawless from the opening hit single "Freak Scene" to the closing noisefest of "Don't". With titles like "Yeah We Know" and "Let It Ride", this is Mascis at his most slack and angst-ridden.

J Mascis & The Fog

Free So Free (2003; City Slang).
God Bless J. Mascis and long live the ghost Of Dinosaur Jr. Mascis, with Fog in tow, produces a fine collection of ear-throttling indie rock dappled with hallmark guitar solos, jaunty riffing and succulent melodies. Mascis still sings like a man who's having a belt tightened around his throat and he still rocks with a bizarre amalgam of narcoleptic laziness and axe-propelled energy.

Richard Fontenoy

DION

Born New York, July 18, 1939.

"I was raised in the Bronx; you could say I was forced up."

Of all the 50s rockers, **Dion DiMucci** has proved the most consistently creative; when Lou Reed inducted him into the Rock And Roll Hall of Fame in 1989 with the rhetorical question, 'Who could be hipper than Dion?', it was an acknowledgement that, more than thirty years after his first hit, he was still a vital artist.

He was discovered by a small New York label and scored some half-hearted flops before his producer saw a way to break through the singer's insecurity: 'You got any friends who can sing?' He did, and **Dion And The Belmonts** were born. Their debut release, "I Wonder Why", an up-tempo exercise in vocal harmonies, hit the Top 30 in America in 1958, and at the age of 19 Dion became the hottest property in white doo-wop.

A succession of hits followed – including the Top 5 "Teenager In Love" and "Where Or When" – on which Dion's sensitive tenor was increasingly emphasized over the street chants of The Belmonts. He was the prototype teen idol: a tough kid from the Bronx who sang like the tears were just a sax solo away, the loner whose heart was perpetually bruised.

The Belmonts split in 1959, not long after Dion had refused the offer of a seat on Buddy Holly's plane, and he began the process of reinvention. His solo singles "Runaround Sue" and "The Wanderer" were both written by an old friend from the Bronx, Ernie Maresca, and featured a new sound: a heavier, up-tempo stomp accentuated by hand claps and the moody braying of vocal group The Del Satins. Dion's voice too had changed – harder and more assertive, he sounded like he was swaggering. The records made #1 and #2 respectively in 1961.

For two years Dion's records climbed the heights of melodrama. Particularly startling were his own compositions "Little Diane", a kazoo-driven explosion of hate, and "Born To Cry", in which the angst-ridden teenager howls in existential pain: 'There's so much evil round us, I feel that I could die, and I know I was born to cry.' Switching labels, he had further hits with superior reworks of The Drifters' "Ruby Baby" and "Drip Drop", but the twin onslaughts of Beatlemania and his own heroin addiction were beginning to tell. A series of R&B singles came too early for the blues revival and failed.

Dion responded by cleaning up his drug problem and re-emerging in 1968 as a folk singer. His version of "Abraham, Martin And John", a tribute to the assassinated leaders of the 60s, made #2 and gave him a new lease of life, light years away from the nascent revival circuit. He did eventually re-form The Belmonts, but refused to trade on past glories, preferring new compositions and covers of Dylan and Gershwin.

Through the 70s and early 80s he released some outstanding albums that won over the critics, though they left a wider audience untouched. During the same period, he rediscovered Christianity and ventured into gospel with some success.

As music degenerated into spandex superficiality in the late 80s, the Kennedy-era heroes were reclaimed, and Dion again found critical acclaim. His 1989 album, YO FRANKIE, saw him boast of being the "King Of The New York Streets", and was hailed as a masterpiece of American rock from a man who seemed to have spent three decades making triumphant comebacks. DREAM ON FIRE, which appeared in 1992, was not highly rated and A ROCK & ROLL CHRISTMAS (1995) was little more than a competent cash-in.

⊙ **Born To Be With You** (1975; Phil Spector International).
Produced by Phil Spector, the epic arrangements bring out the monumental side of Dion's voice. The title track in particular was one of the most majestic singles of the 70s.

⊙ **Dion Hits** (1986; Ace).
Beautifully remastered collection of eighteen hits from 1958 to 1963, featuring The Belmonts and the early solo work. Not a surplus song, and a sound quality so perfect you wouldn't believe it was 35 years old.

⊙ **Yo Frankie** (1989; BMG).
The most recent return to form. His taste is still good enough to cover Tom Waits, while his voice is as powerful and authoritative as ever. Backing vocals by Lou Reed, k. d. lang and – regrettably – Bryan Adams.

Alwyn W. Turner

DIRE STRAITS

Formed Deptford, England, 1977;
put on ice in the mid-90s.

Their origins may have been the downmarket British pub-rock scene of the mid-70s, but **Dire Straits**' enormous success in the 80s rewrote the rules on superstar promotion by using innovations such as CD and MTV, as if 'they had been designed with them in mind' as one critic put it. Guitarist and songwriter **Mark Knopfler** had paid his dues in a Leeds pub band before moving south to London. Here he joined Brewer's Droop before teaming up with younger brother **David** (guitar), **John Ilsley** (bass) and **Pick Withers** (drums) to form Dire Straits, named after their habitual financial state.

They toured constantly and were discovered by London radio DJ Charlie Gillett. This led to a deal with Vertigo Records, and the release of their debut LP, DIRE STRAITS (1978), produced by Muff Winwood. It showcased a gentle bluesy sound, similar in style to Eric Clapton and J. J. Cale. One of its highlights was the single "Sultans Of Swing", a semi-autobiographical tale of a London pub band featuring superb guitar work and characteristic laid-back vocals, which hit the Top 10 on both sides of the Atlantic. Despite the prevailing trends of punk and disco, the album's well-crafted songwriting and skilled playing unexpectedly appealed to over seven million record buyers.

Their follow-up, COMMUNIQUÉ (1979), was a relative disappointment, although Bob Dylan was impressed enough to ask Knopfler and Withers to play with him. By now Knopfler was firmly in control of the group (David departed over his brother's assertion that he 'didn't practise enough'), and he and John Ilsley were the only survivors of a line-up that then changed according to touring or recording necessity.

MAKING MOVIES (1980) and LOVE OVER GOLD (1982) saw their sound change with the addition of **Alan Clark** (keyboards), and the successful introduction of rockier material, often in the style of Springsteen's lengthier narrative songs. They graduated to the worldwide stadium circuit for their live shows, high points of which can be heard on the excellent, double live LP ALCHEMY (1984). They hit the singles charts with "Romeo And Juliet" and the moody seven-minute "Private Investigations", while the EP TWISTING BY THE POOL (1983) saw a shift towards simpler material, ideally suited to pop radio.

BROTHERS IN ARMS (1985) exploited new CD and video technology to excellent results. Knopfler's slick production ensured that it became a must-have for people wanting to demonstrate their new players (leading the *NME* to sniffily declare that it was for 'compact dickheads only'), while "Money For Nothing", a sly dig at MTV propelled by an amazingly catchy rock guitar riff, introduced the channel to the world. Computer graphics transformed the resolutely unglamorous band into video stars. It was a global smash and uncool teenagers around the world bought both single and album, with many thinking that they were a hip American band. A two-hundred-date tour pushed the band's sales above fifteen million: in New Zealand they played to a tenth of the population, while an estimated one in ten British households owned a copy of BROTHERS IN ARMS.

Afterwards, Knopfler retreated from the limelight. Despite one-off charity concerts, his ambivalence towards the group led to rumours of a split. During the early 80s he'd branched out into production and soundtrack work and he continued both, with his charming score for the Bill Forsyth 1983 film *Local Hero* and production credits for Randy Newman and Aztec Camera amongst others. In 1990, he recorded NECK AND NECK, a collection of guitar duets with **Chet Atkins**, and he reassembled some of his collaborators from his pub-rock days in Leeds, under the name of **The Notting Hillbillies**, resulting in the low-key MISSING, PRESUMED HAVING A GOOD TIME.

ON EVERY STREET (1991) was an underwhelming comeback, and sold relatively poorly, although its double-platinum UK sales would represent a career best for most bands. A live stopgap, ON THE NIGHT (1993), documenting the following stadium tour, was an unworthy successor to ALCHEMY, too, suggesting a band in stasis. The release of Knopfler's solo album, GOLDEN HEART (1996) – a Dire Straits album in all but name – led to speculation that the band would not be re-forming, although Knopfler characteristically wouldn't be drawn on the subject in press interviews. He promoted the record by means of an enthusiastic tour of small-scale concert halls, where he clearly felt more comfortable than on the Dire Straits stadium gigs.

After another spate of soundtrack works – LAST EXIT TO BROOKLYN (1997), WAG THE DOG (1998), A SHOT OF GLORY (2001) – Knopfler released a new album proper, 2001's SAILING TO PHILADELPHIA. This well-crafted and personal collection further underlined the notion that the end really had come for Dire Straits.

Dire Straits

⊙ **Dire Straits** (1978; Vertigo).
This was a brilliant debut, with Knopfler's lyrics cleverly mythologizing London by using American country and folk idioms. The breezy "Sultans Of Swing" is an enduring highlight.

⊙ **Alchemy** (1984; Vertigo).
Unlike many live albums, this double set has no 'fixing and mixing'. Its longer songs like "Telegraph Road" and "Private Investigations" aren't just the fiddly fretwork their detractors make them out to be – they're lyrically clever and quietly dramatic, too.

⊙ **Brothers In Arms** (1985; Vertigo).
Though the much-vaunted production now seems overly glossy, it's hard to deny the mainstream appeal of "Walk Of Life", "Your Latest Trick" and "Money For Nothing". The less instant folky material on side two is ultimately more rewarding, though.

⊙ **Money For Nothing** (1988; Vertigo).
The obligatory greatest hits compilation, documenting the band's rise from finger-picking bluesy shuffles to multi-platinum glory.

Mark Knopfler

⊙ **Golden Heart** (1996; Vertigo).
The start of a post-Dire Straits career, this set offers little change on Knopfler's lightweight rockers, though the ballads, drawing on Celtic, Cajun and country influences, are more distinct.

⊙ **Sailing To Philadelphia** (2001; Mercury).
Featuring contributions from Van Morrison and James Taylor, this is a sensitive, blues-influenced collection.

Jonathan Holden

DISPOSABLE HEROES OF HIPHOPRISY

Formed San Francisco, 1990; disbanded 1993.

Originally an offshoot of the Beatnigs – a kind of avant-garde industrial jazz poets' collective – the **Disposable Heroes Of Hiphoprisy** were the champions of early-90s rap liberalism. In direct opposition to some of the extremes expressed in the lyrics of Ices T and Cube, the agenda of **Michael Franti** (vocals/raps) and **Rono Tse** (percussion/mixing) attacked the flippant sexism of the gangsta rappers, which led to Franti being eulogized as 'the new Gil Scott-Heron'.

Though the Disposables were subsequently vilified as an attempt to placate white objections to the street reportage of black, urban rappers, Franti remains one of the idiom's most articulate and compelling narrators. The group's best-known and most-often-quoted song, "Television: The Drug Of The Nation" (an old Beatnigs number), is one example, but several others littered HIPHOCRISY IS THE GREATEST LUXURY (1992). In "Language Of Violence", Franti inverted a tale of wanton homophobia into a morality tale about chickens coming home to roost; in "Socio-Genetic Experience" he documented his own rites of passage as a black man adopted by white parents but continually harassed by white peers; and in "Amos And Andy" he berated an educational system that foisted just two career alternatives on him – sportsman or entertainer.

Yet the group that spawned these songs never found a truly black constituency. After recording an album with William Burroughs, Franti disbanded the group, his relationship with Tse (often seen as little more than a bit player) having deteriorated. He returned with **Spearhead**, an attempt to redress his perceived distance from his own roots (or to 'get funky', as some critics had it).

⊙ **Hiphoprisy Is The Greatest Luxury** (1992; 4th And Broadway).
Deeply politicized and beautifully observed, Hiphoprisy is a brilliant engagement with the all too often latent agitprop possibilities of hip-hop.

Alex Ogg

Thanks to Dave Brecha for corrections

THE DIVINE COMEDY

Formed London, 1990.

Keith Cullen, founder of Setanta Records, must have been prescient when he signed the original incarnation of **The Divine Comedy**. Launched in June 1990 with the LP FANFARE FOR THE COMIC MUSE, they were a totally unremarkable, sub-R.E.M. guitar combo, comprising **Neil Hannon** (vocals/guitar), **John McCullagh** (bass/vocals) and **Kevin Traynor** (drums/percussion). It was only when the drummer and bassist returned to study in their native Ireland the following year, leaving Hannon telling Cullen 'I'll be fine by myself', that The Divine Comedy started on the road to pop brilliance. The atheistic, apolitical son of a Church of Ireland bishop, Hannon would go on to become one of the most distinctive singer-songwriters of a decade in which band after band were smugly touting the same influences and sound. Scott Walker, Nik Kershaw, ELO, Kraftwerk, F. Scott Fitzgerald, William Wordsworth, William Morris, French New Wave cinema, Audrey Hepburn – Hannon's palette had a place for them all.

It took a year of playing musical mix'n'match with his compositions before he came up with LIBERATION (1993), an album which eschewed the sound of old in favour of anything that seemed pertinent – harpsichords, pianos, French horns, organs, sampled train noises. Ornate but never busy, the music was always catchy enough to carry Hannon's knowing but rarely pretentious lyrics about such subjects as hay fever ("Pop Singers' Fear Of The Pollen Count"), children's TV ("Festive Rd"), 1920s flappers ("Bernice Bobs Her Hair"), and one-week relationships ("I Was Born Yesterday").

Unsupported by a tour or accompanying single release, LIBERATION wasn't a great commercial success, despite its excellent critical reception. Hannon, however, was encouraged enough to start work almost immediately on his next project, an attempt to destigmatize the 'concept album'. Called PROMENADE (1994), this collection of songs about the seaside was really no more than a hook on which Hannon could hang some favourite topics. And if some had trouble swallowing a list of authors as a song ("The Booklovers"), the music was a more than sufficient tonic: a mixture of strings, woodwind, acoustic guitar and piano, it was lush enough to have film-makers and TV producers knocking on Hannon's door. Neil wrote the theme tune for the cult British TV sitcom *Father Ted* and performed a 'Eurosong Contest' entry in one of the episodes. Although a spoof, it towered above most entries to the genuine Eurovision contest.

PROMENADE reached the indie Top 10, and, flushed with his taste of success, Hannon began work on an album he described as 'a 60s orchestral pop wig-out about lurve'. It emerged as CASANOVA (1996), a record that sounded a million pounds, and mixed what had become hugely trendy influences – Burt Bacharach, Scott Walker, even Barry White. Its pop melodies won rave reviews all over the place and Hannon took his vision, together with an orchestra, to West London's Shepherd's Bush Empire theatre where the follow-up, 1997's A SHORT ALBUM ABOUT LOVE, was swiftly recorded. Its seven swoon-making tracks indicated that major-league success was just a matter of time.

FIN DE SIÈCLE (1998) seemed to be the catalyst that would bring it about. Adding a little sharpness to his frequently saccharine compositions, Hannon addressed some of life's seamier side for once, tilting at, for example, tabloid soft porn, 90s hedonism, the end of the world and Sweden. The standout track, however, was Hannon's ode to the far-from-romantic British cousin of the Greyhound Bus – "National Express". The band's most recent collection, 2001's REGENERATION, saw the group take a significant leap sideways, and as a result, a giant leap forward. Having moved to Parlophone Records and now sharing a producer with Radiohead, the group unveiled a more electronic sound, with cuts such as the fine "Note To Self" almost sounding like outtakes from OK COMPUTER.

⊙ **Liberation** (1993; Setanta).
Tired of Britpop? Buy LIBERATION – right from the birdsong at the start, it really is a breath of fresh air.

⊙ **Promenade** (1994; Setanta).
LIBERATION with bells on – ballads like "The Summerhouse" and "Tonight We Fly" really are heart-stopping.

⊙ **Casanova** (1996; Setanta).
The label put the boat out for this gorgeous slice of pop.

⊙ **Regeneration** (2001; Parlophone).
Here the group trade their signature baroque flourishes for mournful electronic atmospheres.

Piers Clifton

DOA

Formed Vancouver, 1978.

Mainstays of Canadian hardcore punk, **DOA** have had a fluid line-up, starting with **Joey 'Shithead' Keithley** (vocals/guitar), **Randy Rampage** (bass) and **Chuck Biscuits** (drums). The last has been hardcore's best-known percussion stylist and would subsequently work with the Circle Jerks, Black Flag and Danzig.

After making their debut with the TRIUMPH OF THE IGNOROIDS EP in 1979, the SOMETHING BETTER CHANGE (1980) and HARDCORE '81 (1981) albums established DOA's dynamic formula of fast, rousing rock guitar and accusatory lyrics. Their message lacked the puritanical streak of peers such as Minor Threat, but placed a similar emphasis on social unrest and collapse.

The WAR ON 45 EP won the group new converts in Europe, before they moved to a new spiritual home at Alternative Tentacles. By this time the personnel had shuffled, with **Dave Gregg** now on guitar, **Gregg James** on drums and **Brian Goble** on bass joining Keithley.

After the career anthology BLOODIED BUT UNBOWED (1984), 1985's LET'S WRECK THE PARTY caught them at a peak, both in popularity and form. Here the clean, professional production showcased their trademark compressed rhythmic attack at its best. Unlike their rivals, however, DOA refrained from crossing the sonic and ideological borders between punk and heavy metal.

TRUE (NORTH) STRONG AND FREE (1987) was almost as good, and royalties from songs such as "Ready To Explode" were donated to the ANC. Topics broached included the domestic growth of fascism ("Nazi Training Camp") and Canada's cultural domination by the US ("51st State"). Long-standing guitarist Dave Gregg made way for **Chris Prohom** on MURDER (1990), which lacked none of the fire but some of the inspiration of old.

Though the same charge could be levelled at 1993's 13 FLAVOURS OF DOOM, the intervening TALK MINUS ACTION EQUALS ZERO (1991) was a more compulsive suite of songs. Also worth investigating is LAST SCREAM OF THE MISSING NEIGHBOURS (1990), a collaboration with **Jello Biafra**, particularly on the extended and sustained brutality of "Full Metal Jackoff". Despite the occasional slip, many hardcore fans would take a mediocre DOA over just about anyone else, and they retain the capacity to excel.

⊙ **Bloodied But Unbowed** (1984; CD Presents).
Fire-in-the-belly punk rock, full of charisma.

⊙ **Let's Wreck The Party** (1985; Alternative Tentacles).
The best representation of mid-period DOA, its juxtaposition of wholehearted political messages with wit and
self-mockery is a winning formula.

Alex Ogg

DR. FEELGOOD

Formed Canvey Island, England, 1971.

A powerful live attraction for over two decades,
Dr. Feelgood was one of a handful of bands
to thrive in both the British blues boom and the age
of punk. And deservedly so. Even today, playing
low-key gigs, and without their late-lamented singer
Lee Brilleaux, they can still kick up a storm.

The Feelgoods were formed by teenage R&B fan
Lee Brilleaux and guitarist **Wilko Johnson** (aka
John Wilkinson) after the former saw the latter performing in a jug band, and the pair were joined by
John B. Sparks (bass) and drummer John Martin,
the quasi-legendary **Big Figure**. Taking their name
from an old B-side by Johnny Kidd & The Pirates,
they started out on what was to become the London
pub-rock circuit, playing covers of Chuck Berry,
Sonny Boy Williamson and Elmore James. They also
periodically backed Heinz, formerly of The
Tornados. It was during these early gigs that recurrent bouts of violence among the teddy boy crowd
convinced the band to transfer their allegiance from
classic rock'n'roll to Brilleaux's and Sparks's preferred
R&B. It was not until three years into their career,
however, that they finally gave up their day jobs and
went pro.

Although their first two LPs, DOWN BY THE
JETTY and MALPRACTICE (both 1975) sold
respectably, it was their third album, the live
STUPIDITY (1976), that broke the band. A UK #1
album, it perfectly captured the sweaty anarchy of
their shows and the stripped-down 'in yer face' R&B
that would inspire up-and-coming punk bands such
as The Boomtown Rats and The Clash. The band's
'non-fashion' statement – all short hair, sober jackets
and no flares – made an impression, as did Wilko's
combined rhythm and lead guitar style, borrowed
unashamedly from Johnny Kidd's guitarist Mick
Green.

Despite the hard-earned success, all was not well
in the Feelgood camp. Following disagreements
during 1977 sessions for SNEAKIN' SUSPICION, their
fourth album, the band acrimoniously parted company with Wilko. In lesser bands, the sacking of your
only hit-maker and main visual attraction would be
seen as suicidal. Not so with Dr. Feelgood.
Recruiting guitarist **Gypie Mayo** (aka John
Cawthra) as Johnson's replacement, Brilleaux grasped
the opportunity to change the band's sound, giving
it a more polished, commercial edge. The public's
reponse quietened any fears Brilleaux might have had

– their next single, "Milk And Alcohol" (1979), produced by Nick Lowe, hit the UK Top 10, and
remains possibly the best-known Feelgood track.

Although Dr. Feelgood were never to better this
singles chart success, they were able to command
huge live audiences through the 70s and 80s, regardless of fickle fashions. One of the UK's
hardest-working bands, they would clock up around
250 gigs a year as well as churn out albums. In 1979,
they excelled themselves and released both AS IT
HAPPENS and LET IT ROLL.

The constant gigging was to claim its victims,
though. In 1980, Gypie Mayo retired from the band,
an event followed by the wittily entitled A CASE OF
THE SHAKES (again produced by Nick Lowe). Fellow
founder members The Big Figure and Sparko were
not far behind him, citing road fatigue as their decision to quit in 1982.

Undeterred, Brilleaux soldiered on under the
Feelgood banner, recruiting **Johnny Guitar**,
Gordon Russell and finally **Steve Walwyn** into the
guitarist's position. The replacement rhythm section
of **Phil Mitchell** (bass) and **Kevin Morris** (drums)
was the one Brilleaux would use right up until the
end of his life.

Showcasing the new line-up with DOCTOR'S
ORDERS in 1984, Brilleaux went on to cement his
leadership with BRILLEAUX (1986), released on the
Stiff label, which he had helped found a decade earlier. Bucking the prevailing singer-songwriter trend,
this triumphant return to form relied heavily on
material by other artists such as John Hiatt and, more
curiously, Johnny Cash.

Carrying on the Feelgood tradition of extensive
gigging into the 90s, the band released one of their
greatest live albums, LIVE IN LONDON, in 1990. With
Brilleaux's gutsy vocals to the fore, the band ably
demonstrated that they had lost none of their fire
with their mix of Johnson compositions and tasteful
choice of covers, ranging from material by B. B. King
to Bill Haley.

Brilleaux, the heart and soul of Dr. Feelgood for
over two decades, died of cancer in April 1994, aged
41. Shortly before his death, Lee recorded his swansong – an emotive live set recorded at the Dr.
Feelgood Music Bar in Southend, proving that, even
to the end, he had lost none of his star quality.

While Brilleaux's death would have seemed an
appropriate point to close the Dr. Feelgood story, the
band decided to recruit new singer **Pete Gage** and
continue the name. To add to the confusion, former
Feelgoods Gypie Mayo, Sparko and the Big Figure
have also been performing the band's back catalogue
as **The Practice**, sometimes being billed as 'Dr.
Feelgood's Practice'. Let's hope that neither band
sinks into the kind of mediocre pub rock which
Brilleaux's star qualities had for so long held them
well above.

⊙ **Stupidity** (1976; EMI).
Live recordings capturing a particularly raw version of
the band before Nick Lowe and modern recording techniques got to work.

🔘 **Live In London** (1990; Grand Records).
An energetic mean mutha of a live album, containing ballsy versions of all the hits from "She Does It Right" through to "Milk And Alcohol" and "Down At The Doctor's", plus some rockin' covers by the likes of John Lee Hooker.

🔘 **Down At The Doctor's** (1995; Grand Records).
Recorded three months before Lee died, this is an emotional and gutsy rendition of old and new favourites.

🔘 **25 Years Of Dr Feelgood** (1997; Grand Records).
An excellent collection covering the first quarter-century of vicious, dirty, Southend Rhythm and Booze. All their greatest hits and more.

Paul Morris

DR. JOHN

Born New Orleans, Louisiana, 1940.

"This is a testament to funk, to funksters, tricknologists, mujicians, care-rack-ters, who got music burning in their brains and no holes in their souls." Dr John, Under A Hoodoo Moon

Enigmatic New Orleans R&B artist **Dr. John** (born Malcolm Rebennack) began his recording career at 15, honing his skills with luminaries like bandleader Dave Bartholemew. Initially concentrating on guitar, he contributed sessions to a number of R&B hits during the late 50s and early 60s, as well as composing hits for artists including Lloyd Price and Art Neville. However, drug problems, a shooting incident involving a promoter and a thwarted attempt at swindling a record company culminated in a spell in jail.

Moving to the West Coast, Mac Rebennack shifted his speciality to piano and organ, gaining session work with Van Morrison and Sonny and Cher while he set about developing his own act, Dr. John The Night Tripper. Bearded and tall, the Doctor possessed a natural charisma which he emphasized with elaborate voodoo regalia, charms and carved walking sticks.

The album ZU ZU MAN (1965) on A&M proved unsuccessful, but the later Atlantic release GRIS GRIS (1968) was well timed, and its spooky blend of R&B, Creole and psychedelia earned Dr. John a considerable cult following. (The stand-out track, "She Walks On Gilded Splinters", has been covered by figures as diverse as Marsha Hunt and Paul Weller.) The same voodoo-rock formula was repeated on BABYLON (1969), REMEDIES (1970) and SUN, MOON AND HERBS (1971), the last notable for the contributions of Eric Clapton and Mick Jagger.

Still in demand as a session artist, Dr. John worked with legendary Memphis producer Jerry Wexler, and provided the organ on Aretha Franklin's "Spanish Harlem". Wexler then produced Dr. John's 'roots' masterpiece GUMBO (1972), described in his sleeve notes as 'a picture of the music that New Orleans people listen to, a combination of Dixieland, rock

and roll and funk'. Containing songs made famous by Professor Longhair and Huey Smith, its highlights included the heavily syncopated "Junko Partner" and the minor hit "Iko Iko".

IN THE RIGHT PLACE (1973), an album more accessible to rock audiences, was recorded with The Meters and the revered producer/songwriter Allen Toussaint (who, curiously, played most of the piano parts). Two US hits – the jerking funk of "Right Place, Wrong Time" and the jazzed-up waltz of "Such A Night" – came from the album, and the latter was reprised for The Band's movie, *The Last Waltz* (1976).

DESITIVELY BONAROO (1974) was in the same vein, being 'positutedly, honorificatedly, medicatedly, Doctoratedly' funky; yet it sold poorly, despite the guitar-clacking funk of "Can't Gitt Enuff" and "(Everybody Wanna Get Rich) Rite Away". Accompanied by his Rhythm & Blues Orchestra, Dr. John engaged rock producer Bob Ezrin for the live album HOLLYWOOD BE THY NAME (1974), a disappointing and too disparate release: the bizarrely rocky "Reggae Doctor" sat uncomfortably beside the over-sentimental cabaret cover of The Beatles' "Yesterday".

The Night Tripper in the right place

Retreating from live performance, Dr. John released the more relaxed CITY LIGHTS (1978) and TANGO PALACE (1979), both of which were co-written with songwriter Doc Pomus. The former included the charming unhurried shuffle "Dance The Night Away With You". His next collaboration was with British trad-jazz bandleader Chris Barber on the celebratory TAKE ME BACK TO NEW ORLEANS (1983), and the two later reunited for the live recording MARDI GRAS AT THE MARQUEE (1989).

The 80s saw Dr. John concentrate his energies on re-creating the spirit and style of past masters, and the much-acclaimed DR. JOHN PLAYS MAC REBENNACK (1981) was a collection of unaccompanied piano tributes to his New Orleans mentors. Another tribute album, IN A SENTIMENTAL MOOD (1989), was a set of Grammy award-winning smoochers that reached its zenith on the brassy duet with Rickie Lee Jones, "Makin' Whoopee".

GOIN' BACK TO NEW ORLEANS (1992) saw Dr. John back on GUMBO territory, in the company of The Neville Brothers, while TELEVISION (1994) brought a return to his inimitable brand of voodoo funk-rock, with a slow, sublime cover of Sly Stone's "Thank You (Falletin Me Be Mice Elf Again)" and a guest appearance from the Red Hot Chili Peppers' Anthony Kiedis.

Another collection of big-band seduction, AFTERGLOW (1995), received rave reviews upon release. It was followed by an intimate collection recorded at Ronnie Scott's in London, TRIPPIN' LIVE (1997). 1998's ANUTHA ZONE saw Dr. John reaching an ever wider audience, this time thanks to the collaborative input of various indie rock names: the list includes members of Portishead, Spiritualized, The Beta Band and Ocean colour Scene, as well as Paul Weller.

In the years since, the albums have just kept on coming, with recent highlights including DUKE ELEGENT (2000), a collection of Duke Ellington reworks, and CREOLE MOON (2001).

These later recordings confirm that Dr. John's longevity is the product of great talent, charisma and a profound grasp of New Orleans' rich musical heritage. Dr. John's autobiography, *Under A Hoodoo Moon* (St Martin's Press), was published in 1994.

⊙ **Gumbo** (1972: Atlantic).
One of the most comprehensive introductions to New Orleans music ever recorded. Includes 'Doctored' classics such as "Let The Good Times Roll" and Professor Longhair's "Tipitina".

⊙ **In The Right Place** (1973; Atlantic).
A flawless work: well produced, well arranged, well written and performed by the best backing band in New Orleans. Aside from the hits, it also features the Toussaint-penned stroll, "Life".

⊙ **The Very Best Of Dr. John** (1995; Atco).
This eighteen-track compilation makes a worthy attempt at representing every aspect of a long and varied career.

⊙ **Anutha Zone** (1998; Parlophone).
The gem of Dr. John's more recent catalogue, this set comprises a hypnotic blend of voodoo-rock, gospel and a willingness to embrace a broader palette of ideas.

Michael Andrews

DOCTOR NERVE

Formed New York, 1984

S ince 1984, **Doctor Nerve** – led by composer/guitarist **Nick Didkovsky** – has carved out a unique position in popular music. Unique for a lot of reasons but mostly because few other bands could do what they do and almost no other bands would want to.

Doctor Nerve combine instrumental arrangements so fiendish that perhaps only Frank Zappa in his 'Dance to this if you can, suckers' moments could match them, with the thrashiest of thrash metal. Its not such a bizarre idea – the energy and raw aggression of thrash combined with jaw-dropping virtuosity works like a charm. At their best Doctor Nerve have an intensity like no other band, but they can also be utterly exhausting to listen to.

Doctor Nerve's music seemed to have sprung fully formed Didkovsky's fevered imagination. Their trademark complex, angular time signatures, screeching guitar and honking brass were all in evidence from the very first album OUT TO BOMB FRESH KINGS (1984), now available on Cuneiform as a two-for-the-price-of-one package with ARMED OBSERVATION, (their second album). The line-up comprised of Didkovsky (guitars), **Greg Anderson** (bass), **Leo Ciesa** (drums), **Dave Douglas** (trumpet), **Yves Dubain** (soprano sax), **Rob Henke** (trumpet), **Michael Lytle** (bass clarinet) and **Marc Wagonon** (vibraphone electronics).

ARMED OBSERVATION (1987) was followed by a live album DID SPRINTING DIE? (1990), proving that they could play material in front of an audience and have it sound exactly like a studio release – a major achievement, given the awesome complexity of their compositions. The next studio collection was BETA 14 OK (1991). The set included 44 tiny musical snippets at the end, which you were supposed to play randomly to produce Cage-ian chance composition. That a bunch of fairly sensible composers actually did this and even put out a CD – TRANSFORMS THE NERVE EVENT PROJECT (1993) – aptly illustrated the respect in which Didkovsky was held.

The band was hardly known for its light and shade and it became increasingly apparent that the computer software Didkovsky used to generate many of Doctor Nerve's compositions resulted with music that sounded kind of samey.

But that all changed with SKIN (1995). Maybe Didkovsky's software got more sophisticated, maybe the band exploded one eardrum too many and drew back a little, but SKIN really did represent a change. There was much more variety of tone: sometimes it sounded like the heavy metal band from hell; at others, like something off Zappa's UNCLE MEAT; and there were even some quieter trio moments where, for once, the whole band was not steaming along at full volume. On these occasions the sheer brilliance of the compositions shone through without for a moment lessening the pure sonic thrill.

The next release was EVERY SCREAMING EAR (1997), which consists of live recordings and uses a couple of different ensemble groups. It was fine but not an utterly typical release. 2000 saw the group collaborate with the **Sirius String Quartet** for the release of EREIA, a peculiar, and only partly successful, blend of prog-rock, jazz and classical music. To this day the group continue to play together, while Didkovsky frequently crops up with side projects and collaborations.

⊙ **Skin** (1995; Cuneiform).
Simultaneously Doctor Nerve's most intense and most approachable moment. From the awesome metal of "Plague" to the strange reflective piano piece "Our Soldiers Are Soft Pianos", it doesn't put a foot wrong. This is what modern progressive music should sound like.

Graham Taylor

DR STRANGELY STRANGE

Formed Dublin, Ireland, 1967; disbanded 1971; re-formed briefly 1973 & 1982.

A band that could only have emerged and flourished in the hippie era, **Dr Strangely Strange** were an Irish counterpart of **THE INCREDIBLE STRING BAND**, and indeed appeared on their 1969 LP, CHANGING HORSES. String Band members Robin Williamson and Mike Heron had been early visitors to their communal home in Dublin, and Williamson covered their song "Strings In The Earth And Air" on his solo LP, MYRRH (1972).

Like The Incredible String Band, Dr Strangely Strange moved from an experimental folk base into an LSD-fuelled but tongue-in-cheek blend of mythology, childlike whimsy and unfettered imagination. Irishman **Tim Booth** (vocals/ guitar) had graduated from Trinity College, Dublin, where he met Englishman **Ivan Pawle** (vocals/bass/keyboards). They began gigging with friend Brian Tench, before they met **Tim Goulding** (vocals/keyboards/fiddle/whistles/recorder), an Irishman who had returned from school in England to be a painter.

The band lived and rehearsed in a house owned by Goulding's girlfriend, backing vocalist Orphan Annie (aka Annie Xmas), which was thus nicknamed 'The Orphanage'. Eventually Booth created a second Orphanage, which became the cradle for a new generation of Irish rock, with the likes of Thin Lizzy's Phil Lynott and Gary Moore hanging out there.

After initial doubts, The Incredible String Band's manager Joe Boyd signed them up and they recorded their first LP, KIP OF THE SERENES (1969). Touring Britain, they supported the likes of Fotheringay, but found they needed a heavier sound to fill concert halls. In true hippie style, they recruited drummer **Neil Hopwood** out of the audience during a gig in Wales.

On their second album, HEAVY PETTING (1970), one song declared 'Like a sunny breeze, I'm lost in winter', and the band duly withered away in the harsher winds of the early 70s. Goulding retreated to a Buddhist monastery, while Pawle and Booth joined

forces with Gay & Terry Woods for a brief tour, then disbanded.

Dr Strangely Strange reunited for a short Irish tour in 1973, and brought in synthesizers for some cameo appearances in the early 80s, the highlight of which was a live version of "Donnybrook Fair". They also provided the soundtrack for a film written by Tim Booth. The line-up stabilized in the early 80s as a good-time dance band, and has remained stable ever since.

In 1997, Dr Strangely Strange released a third album, probably the most unexpected treat of the year. ALTERNATIVE MEDICINE (1998), recorded more than a quarter of a century after their second album, understandably showed a few stylistic changes. It's an extremely Irish affair, tuneful and relaxed with some good instrumentals. While it lacks the sheer eccentricity of the band's late-60s work, there are enough hints in tracks like "Pulp Kayak" (its tune supposedly composed for a kayak convention) and "Epilog" (written in the studio and played once, one take) to keep things oddly normal. Gary Moore is back to add lead guitar on selected tracks.

They've been playing sporadic gigs at home in Ireland in the meantime, however, and the new album is recognizably from the same reliable vein of gentle folk that served so well before – beautiful melodies, tinged with the odd hint of the blues. Their lasting legacy to the Irish musical scene has been to show successors that you could write and play virtually anything as long as you were true to yourself. Dr Strangely Strange played music for a simpler, happier world.

⊙ **Kip Of The Serenes** (1969; Island).
A largely acoustic mixture of guitars, whistles, kazoos and harmonium, with drifting, and occasionally bitter, lyrics.

⊙ **Heavy Petting** (1970; Vertigo).
This toughens up the trio's sound with the help of Fairport Convention drummer Dave Mattacks, Brush Shiels on bass and Gary Moore on electric guitar. The music takes in a wider spectrum of blues, country, folk and gospel, with the stand-out track "Sign On My Mind", featuring a sleepy solo from Moore, paired with Andy Irvine on mandolin.

Brian Hinton

THOMAS DOLBY

Born Cairo, Egypt, 1958.

Born Thomas Robertson, **Thomas Dolby** began his varied career in late-70s London, where he worked as a sound mixer and sometime member of Bruce Woolley's Camera Club. While fascinated by gadgetry and technology, Dolby also found plenty of work as a session keyboard player, initially working with Lene Lovich, and in early 1981 he made his solo recording debut with "Urges", issued on the indie label Armageddon.

Within months, he had accepted a deal with Parlophone, and immediately scored a Top 40 single with "Europa And The Pirate Twins", which showcased Dolby's trademark combination of the charming and the gimmicky. For his next releases, he incorporated his own label Venus In Peril into the Parlophone deal, but his eccentric boffin image and diverse output made commercial success hit-and-miss.

Dolby's debut LP, THE GOLDEN AGE OF WIRELESS (1982), was a modest seller until the release of the single "She Blinded Me With Science" at the end of that year. The song and its accompanying video, featuring eccentric TV scientist Dr Magnus Pyke, became a firm favourite on burgeoning cable TV channel MTV, and even though few American viewers would have known of Pyke the single reached #5 in the US charts in the spring of 1983. In contrast, the single missed the British Top 40, perhaps a victim of the British suspicion of anyone 'too clever by half'.

Dolby's highest profile in Britain came in early 1984 with the chart success of the frenetic single "Hyperactive". However, this track was unrepresentative of his second LP, THE FLAT EARTH (1984), which included a haunting cover of Dan Hicks' "I Scare Myself" plus music that suggested aspirations towards film soundtrack work. This came to fruition within a couple of years, although perhaps Dolby would have preferred to have scored better movies than George Lucas's disastrous comedy *Howard The Duck* (1986) and Ken Russell's preposterous *Gothic* (1987). Fortunately, his 1986 collaboration with Ryuichi Sakamoto, "Fieldwork", was a triumph, and his long-standing role as producer of Prefab Sprout would continue into the 90s.

Thomas Dolby's move to Los Angeles in 1987 coincided with session work for the likes of Foreigner, Def Leppard and Belinda Carlisle. He also married Hollywood actress Kathleen Belier, who at the time was a regular in the TV soap opera *Dynasty*. Then, having already collaborated with George Clinton on the one-off "May The Cube Be With You" (1985), issued under the name Dolby's Cube, the two reunited on the funky ALIENS ATE MY BUICK (1988), for which Clinton wrote "Hot Sauce".

After a long silence, Dolby resurfaced on Virgin with ASTRONAUTS AND HERETICS (1992), his rockiest effort to date, trailed by the single "Close, But No Cigar", which became his biggest British hit since

"Hyperactive", which in turn was reissued (as a double A-side with "She Blinded Me With Science") as a trailer for a 'best of' compilation called RETROSPECTACLE (1994).

THE GATE TO THE MIND'S EYE (1994) – an album of experimental soundtracking – was nothing exceptional, but proved that Dolby could still be inventive. Dolby is currently ploughing his energies into the development of Internet radio technology, through his own company, Beatnik.

⊙ **Retrospectacle: The Best Of Thomas Dolby** (1994; EMI/Capitol).
A Dolby compilation is inevitably something of a mixed bag. While the earliest selections have dated, all in all this is a fine summary of an often underrated talent.

Justin Lewis

DOLL BY DOLL

Formed London, 1977; disbanded 1983.

B orn in Fife, Scotland, **Jackie Leven** first performed as a solo singer/guitar player under the name John St Field in the 70s, playing the club circuit and in support slots for the likes of prog-rockers Man. As the New Wave swept all before it from 1977, Leven formed guitar band **Doll By Doll**, enlisting **Jo Shaw** (guitar), **Robin Spreafico** (bass) and **David McIntosh** (drums).

While this voice/guitar/bass/drums setup appeared to fit the spirit of post-punk, the first album, REMEMBER (1979), revealed Leven's ambitions to cover a wider canvas. Though informed by R&B, the songs were lengthy, had comparatively complex arrangements, and melodically there was a Celtic folk influence – not to mention the distinctiveness of Leven's soaring vocals. By the time the more accessible and consistent follow-up GYPSY BLOOD was released a few months later, **Tony Waite** had replaced Spreafico on bass. For DOLL BY DOLL (1981), the mood had lightened on bouncy numbers like "Carita", which verged on disco, and the folky ballad "Main Travelled Roads". Doll By Doll were a volatile bunch, though; GRAND PASSION (1982) was recorded without Jo Shaw, and singer **Helen Turner** was brought in to embellish the group's sound.

But that was that for Doll By Doll – though another album was recorded, it was never released. The lyrics of Leven's songs of 'grand passion' were often demanding, if not downright obscure, which may, at least partly, account for why Doll By Doll's audience never increased beyond the devoted few. Though Jackie Leven continued to play music throughout the 80s, his energies were largely devoted to rehabilitation from drug abuse – firstly his own, and later that of many others – and he remains heavily involved in work helping drug users. It was to be ten years before another album was recorded. In the meantime there was the odd single, including "Uptown" (1984), and during the mid-80s he gigged with a couple of ex-Doll By Doll members, plus

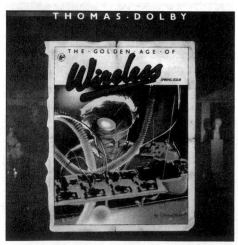

former Sex Pistol Glen Matlock, in the group CBI, though they never recorded.

After his long sabbatical post-Doll By Doll, Leven has been relatively prolific in the 90s. In 1994, he released a mini-album, available only in Scotland, SONGS FROM THE ARGYLL CIRCLE. Tracks from this were subsequently included on the full-length album, THE MYSTERY OF LOVE IS GREATER THAN THE MYSTERY OF DEATH (1994), on which he collaborated with the American poet Robert Bly (a leader of the 'Men's Movement', an interest which Leven shares). Leven's Celtic folk influences were still more to the fore on the subsequent FORBIDDEN SONGS OF THE DYING WEST (1995), THE ARGYLL CIRCLE – VOLUME ONE (1996) and FAIRY TALES FOR HARD MEN (1997).

Lyrically, Leven has continued to expound his theme of man's condition, with the music often interspersed with poetry recitation. Yet this seeming weightiness is continually offset by humour and his knack of throwing in a memorable melodic hook, never more evident than on the release, in 1998, of possibly his best solo outing to date, NIGHT LILIES. Meantime, Leven and his record company have been striving to secure the rights to the whole Doll By Doll back catalogue, to enable the long-overdue reissue on CD of their five albums.

Doll By Doll

Gypsy Blood (1979; Automatic).
Containing some of Leven's finest work, including "Teenage Lightning" and "Strip Show" (which dated from the John St Field days). It also features a couple of impressive songs by Jo Shaw, notably "Binary Fiction".

Grand Passion (1982; Magnet).
Arguably Doll By Doll's best record, this boasted another crop of memorable Leven tunes, not least the poignant closing track, "So Long Kid".

Jackie Leven

The Mystery Of Love is Greater Than The Mystery Of Death (1994; Cooking Vinyl).
You might find the recitations (by Robert Bly and ex-Waterboy Mike Scott) a little distracting. But the sheer power of tracks like the worksong "Farm Boy" and the sad lament "Heartsick Land", not to mention the slightly bizarre version of Burt Bacharach's "I Say A Little Prayer", more than compensates.

Night Lilies (1998; Cooking Vinyl).
A tuneful collection of reflective, but never self-pitying, songs about parting and loss. Without the poetry recitals, and enjoying a more cohesive 'rootsier' sound, this is Jackie's most accessible solo outing to date.

Keith Prewer

DONOVAN

Born Glasgow, Scotland, 1946.

"Electrical bananas is gonna be a sudden craze/Electrical banana is bound to be the very next phase/ They call me Mellow Yellow."

Although Scots-born, **Donovan Leitch** spent his childhood in the English county of

Every rock book needs a kaftan, modelled here by Donovan

Hertfordshire, before becoming a folk-club entertainer in his late teens. Influenced by Woody Guthrie, Jesse Fuller and, inevitably, Bob Dylan, he produced two singles in 1965, "Catch The Wind" and "Colours", which presented him as a beatific, non-political Dylan. However, an EP called UNIVERSAL SOLDIER, with its title song composed by Buffy Sainte Marie, and accompanied by a promotional film shot in World War II trenches, was a much more biting exercise in uncompromising pacifism.

A drugs bust, contractual difficulties and a lengthy sabbatical spent in a proto-hippie commune on a Scottish island delayed further releases for almost a year, but with producer Mickie Most he was back with a vengeance on "Sunshine Superman" (1966), which raced to #1 in America. A further move into psychedelic pop spawned another million-seller in "Mellow Yellow" – his best-known song – and was followed by three more hits: "There Is A Mountain", "Hurdy Gurdy Man" (all 1967) and the bilingual "Jennifer Juniper" (1968). The last of these was dedicated to Jenny Boyd who, with Donovan and The Beatles, was among seekers of nirvana at the Maharishi Mahesh Yogi's ashram on the Ganges in 1968.

"Atlantis" struggled in the charts in winter 1968, but a studio liaison with The Jeff Beck Group on "Goo Goo Barabajagal (Love Is Hot)" returned

Donovan to the Top 20 in early 1969. An unscheduled appearance at Blind Faith's free 1970 concert in Hyde Park was well received, though the same could not be said of his performance supporting Led Zeppelin at the Bath Festival later that year. Times were changing and the rock scene growing heavier.

Donovan still had enough admirers to push OPEN ROAD (1970) into the UK album list, while HMS DONOVAN (1971; reissued 1998; Beat Goes On), a collection of children's songs, was a critical if not commercial success. He was commissioned to pen movie soundtracks to *If It's Tuesday It Must Be Belgium* and 1973's *Brother Sun Sister Moon*, and even tried his hand at acting as the title role in *The Pied Piper Of Hamelin* and, later, a cameo in the Martin Sheen movie *Walking After Midnight*. Though COSMIC WHEELS (1973) was his chart finale, subsequent Donovan albums shifted sufficient quantities to make them worthwhile commercial exercises. Even so, it soon became transparent that many concert-goers merely wanted a retread of the glories of the 60s.

Now based in California with his wife and children, Donovan has clung on to his youthful looks and is far from a spent force as a creative artist. Indeed, there have been occasions when a return to contemporary prominence seemed imminent; a show at 1980's Edinburgh Festival was one such triumph, while RISING (1990) contained several items which equalled his 60s recordings. He was also seen at 1995's WOMAD festival, playing, entirely appropriately, and with great spirit, alongside Moroccan trance drummers The Master Musicians Of Jajouka. He returned to the studio for his 1996 album SUTRAS, a twenty-song collection of admittedly low-key workouts tastefully and sensitively produced by noisenik Rick Rubin. Since then, all has been quiet.

⦿ **Sunshine Superman** (1967; Pye/Epic; reissued 1997; EMI Gold).
The title track, "Hampstead Incident", the jazzy "Preachin' Love" and the much-covered "Season Of The Witch" all show a literate, watchful lyricist at a creative peak.

⦿ **A Gift From A Flower To A Garden** (1968; Pye/Epic).
Maharishi Mahesh Yogi adorns the cover of a double album bound forever to flower-power times past. However, fleetingly, you're convinced – as Donovan was – that God had 'seen all the ugliness that was being created and had chosen pop to be the great force of love and beauty'.

⦿ **Love Is Hot, Truth Is Molten** (1998; Raven).
Australian label Raven have done a splendid job here, compiling, remastering and packaging 23 classic tracks from the British Ur-hippie.

Alan Clayson

THE DOOBIE BROTHERS

Formed San Jose, California, 1970; disbanded 1982; re-formed 1988.

The Doobie Brothers' is the story of several bands, each with their own sound, and, at their peak in the early 70s, a deserved niche in rock history.

The original Doobies were created when **John Hartman** (drums), **Dave Shogren** (bass) and **Tom Johnston** (vocals/guitar) added another guitarist/vocalist, **Pat Simmons**, to their group Pud. They decided to rename themselves after a doobie, a slang term for a joint, and in 1971 released THE DOOBIE BROTHERS (1971), a laid-back affair, taking its lead from bands like America and Crosby, Stills, Nash & Young.

The record, however, stood totally at odds with The Doobies' live act, which bristled with a soulful funk, and was perfectly captured on TOULOUSE STREET (1973), for which the band had added a second drummer, **Michael Hossack**, and a new bassist, **Tiran Porter**, replacing Shogren a couple of tracks into the recording. The solid backbeat, raunchy interweaving guitar work and tight-knit harmonies of the group were all here in abandon, and displayed brilliantly on "Listen To The Music", which became their first major US single, followed by "Jesus Is Just Alright". Further American hits previewed what was perhaps their best LP, THE CAPTAIN AND ME (1973). From this, both "Long Train Running" and "China Grove" illustrated an ability to combine a tuneful lyric and a killer hook with a hard rock sound.

Keith Knudson (drums) and Little Feat keyboard player **Bill Payne** joined for The Doobies' fourth album, WHAT WERE ONCE VICES ARE NOW HABITS (1974), an overall disappointment despite the presence of their first US chart-topper, "Black Water". Newly redundant Steely Dan session players **Jeff 'Skunk' Baxter** (guitar) and **Michael McDonald** (vocals/keyboards) were then brought in to augment The Doobies' live sound as the band continued their gruelling touring schedule. They took time off to record STAMPEDE (1975), but it was not well received, even though it contained another hit with a cover of the Motown classic, "Take Me In Your Arms". Johnston, hit by health problems, now left the band, although he would return briefly in 1976.

TAKIN' IT TO THE STREETS (1976), LIVING ON THE FAULT LINE (1977) and a BEST OF... (1976) confirmed that The Doobie Brothers were stuck in a rut, and spurred McDonald into a change of style. By the release of MINUTE BY MINUTE (1979), the band's trademark guitar sound had all but vanished, keyboards dominating the mix along with a smoother vocal sound, albeit still augmented by fine harmonies. "What A Fool Believes" became the band's biggest selling single and was quickly followed up the charts by "Minute By Minute".

The group's new image didn't suit all the band members, and Baxter and Hartman left, leaving McDonald in sole control. For 1980's ONE STEP CLOSER, the band became a seven-piece, with the arrival of **Chet McCracken** (drums), **John McFee** (guitar) and former Moby Grape sax and keyboard player **Cornelius Bumpus**. The album spawned a Top 5 single in the States, "Real Love", but the inspiration had clearly gone and, after a farewell tour, The Doobie Brothers split up.

Johnston, Simmons and McDonald all embarked on solo careers, with McDonald gaining the most success, thanks to hits like "I Keep Forgettin'", "Sweet Freedom" and "On My Own", a duet with Patti Labelle. Then, in 1988, Johnston, Hartman, Simmons and Porter re-formed The Doobie Brothers, with former drummer Michael Hossack and **Bobby Lakind** (percussion). This line-up made two albums for Capitol – CYCLES (1989) and BROTHERHOOD (1991) – while a radical dance-floor reincarnation of "Long Train Running" in 1993 gave The Doobies their biggest ever British hit.

The group were back again in 2000 for a new studio effort, SIBLING RIVALRY, featuring a line-up of Hossack, Johnston, Knudsen, McFee and Simmons. Though it fell a long way short of being a masterpiece, the set was warm and dignified and showed that this ageing collective still had something.

⊙ **Listen To The Music – The Very Best Of The Doobie Brothers** (1994; Warners).
This is an excellent introduction to the band, charting all its changes, from the jangling guitars and tight harmonies of "Listen To The Music", to the exhilarating heavy rock intro of "China Grove" and the sublime white soul of "What A Fool Believes". Contains both the remix of "Long Train Running" and the original.

Simon Ives

THE DOORS

Formed Los Angeles, 1965; disbanded 1973.

"I am interested in anything about revolt, disorder, chaos, especially activity that seems to have no other meaning." Jim Morrison

In 1965, **Jim Morrison** (vocals) and **Ray Manzarek** (keyboards/bass pedal) were at film school in LA, working on projects together, when they realized they also shared an interest in music. After the classically trained keyboard player began to add Morrison's morbid poetry to a blues soundtrack, they joined garage rockers Rick & The Ravens. However, they soon discovered a more inspired backing from two drug buddies who had previously been employed by The Psychedelic Rangers. **Robbie Kreiger** (guitar) had been raised on a diet of Chicago blues and this, coupled with flamenco-style guitar tuition and exposure to R&B radio, had helped him to forge a unique style, while **John Densmore** (drums) was a would-be beatnik frequenting clubs such as Shelley Manne's Hole, listening to John Coltrane and the rants of Allen Ginsberg.

Taking the name **The Doors** from Aldous Huxley's *The Doors Of Perception*, the quartet put a year into rehearsal and songwriting, which led to bookings on Sunset Strip and eventually a residency at the Whiskey-A-Go-Go. Throughout 1966, The Doors played alongside the rising stars of the day, including The Byrds and Van Morrison's Them. The two Morrisons became close, jamming together and comparing notes on blues standards.

In the early months, Morrison tended to slink around in the shadows with his back to the crowd, but soon his acid-influenced musings inspired him to strike more heroic poses, such as using the mike-stand as a penile extension. This is not to say that the music was of lesser interest, though, and tracks like the cover of Howlin' Wolf's "Back Door Man" were of sufficient quality to impress the LA cognoscenti. Love's Arthur Lee recommended that Jac Holzman, head of Elektra Records, should witness the small-scale performances while he had the chance, and Holzman had to fend off Frank Zappa and Columbia Records in his bid to sign the band.

Made with the addition of bass player **Doug Labahn**, THE DOORS (1967) was hailed by a billboard on Sunset Boulevard – the first of its kind for a rock act. Holzman had discovered a hit-making team who, having won the affections of LA's alternative society, had set their sights on the FM radio audience. Much has been made of The Doors' dramatic delivery of poetic lyrics set to a classic rock beat, but from the beginning they were open to compromise, editing epics such as "Light My Fire" for single release. And though The Doors were mixing with the monarchs of drug culture, Jefferson Airplane, and sharing a press agent with The Beatles, who were entering their Maharishi phase, they remained largely untouched by the escapist philosophies embraced by lesser 'Summer Of Love' merchants.

By Christmas of 1967 they had emerged from Sunset Sound Studios with another strong album, STRANGE DAYS (1967), which did not stray far from the territory explored on the debut, though a more sophisticated style was becoming apparent. Ballads such as the title track and "Unhappy Girl" rested next to the more compelling single releases, "Love Me Two Times" and "People Are Strange", while the album also provided

Kreiger, Morrison, Manzarek and (behind the wire) Densmore give a clue to their drug of choice

employed by contemporaries such as The Beach Boys and Love sometimes paid off, notably on Kreiger's "Running Blue", where a horn section was given free rein to create an improvised jazz backing. However, the finished album was far from being the group's SMILE or SERGEANT PEPPER, and Morrison's frustration was apparent in a series of live fiascos, which culminated in March 1969 with what was to become known as the 'Flasher Incident'. The concert, in an over-crowded Florida auditorium, was seen as the beginning of the end for Morrison, who was arrested when he exposed himself and jumped into the audience. The police were probably the only ones sober enough to

a showcase for some of Morrison's schoolboy poetry in the shape of "Horse Latitudes". These songs confirmed that The Doors were not viewing life through the rose-tinted granny glasses of peace and love – their salvation came in the form of sex and death.

Labahn was replaced on bass by **Leroy Vinegar** for the more understated WAITING FOR THE SUN (1968), which nevertheless returned them to the #1 spot in the US album charts and gave them a second chart-topping single in "Hello I Love You". It was also noteworthy for its inclusion of the schismatic anthem, "Five To One", and the chant on the futility of war, "The Unknown Soldier". A version of the latter song was captured by a British TV crew, and became one of the highlights of the documentary *The Doors Are Open*.

The Doors consolidated their accomplishments on record with a succession of hectic tours, but Morrison in particular was tiring of their contradictory image – shamanistic leaders to some and teenybop idols to others. Elektra's original biography quoted Morrison's interests as 'revolt, disorder, chaos and any activity that seems to have no meaning' and, as the touring progressed, he backed this up with ever more negative behaviour. He soaked himself in alcohol and exposed his companions to temperamental outbursts: he blighted recording sessions by destroying equipment, and disrupted live shows with self-indulgent displays of mock sex and profanities.

Yet The Doors' musical creativity did not suffer as much as might have been expected. THE SOFT PARADE (1969) may have been their weakest effort, but attempts to emulate the experimentation

have seen anything but the charge of 'lewd and lascivious behaviour' resulted in a string of legal battles which were to haunt Morrison until his death.

The group retreated to the studio and returned to form with MORRISON HOTEL (1970). Producer Paul Rothchild recommended that they adopt a more instinctive approach, spending less time searching for the perfect take. The impression was of a band returning to their roots and it was fitting that their playing was complemented by some raw blues bass from the legendary **Lonnie Mack**. The more spartan sound was an unqualified success and the fears raised by the over-orchestration of the previous album were confounded.

The furore caused by the Miami bust had resulted in an enforced break in touring, but The Doors had made enough tenable recordings in the concert halls to justify a live album, and ABSOLUTELY LIVE (1970; re-released 1997) went some way towards capturing The Doors' live experience. While there was little of the hair-raising mid-60s material in its grooves, the medley of "Alabama Song", "Back Door Man" and "Five To One" was a fitting finale.

The Doors' recording renaissance continued apace with L.A. WOMAN (1971), which this time featured **Jerry Scheff** as bassist. This collection of visceral songs was an artistic success, but the band's leader was growing distant from his fellow Doors and at the turn of the decade they embarked on a tour of the Southern US which was to be their last. As Morrison's live performance became more erratic and his off-stage persona more introverted, it became an unspoken certainty that he was to leave.

In March 1971, Morrison and his girlfriend Pamela moved to Paris with the intention of starting a new life there. The couple were both dogged by drug and alcohol problems, and their stay reached a grievous conclusion on July 3, when the 27-year-old singer was found dead in his bathtub. Speculation abounded as to the exact cause of death – no autopsy was performed – but it seems likely that Morrison's body finally gave in to the rigours of his Nietzschean belief in 'delicious ecstasy'.

Morrison had collapsed when he removed himself from the support of the band, and the remaining Doors could not survive without their leader, though they kept the name alive for two more albums, OTHER VOICES (1971) and FULL CIRCLE (1972). Titles such as "I'm Horny And I'm Stoned" would not have seemed out of place in a Spinal Tap pastiche, and it was not long before they went their separate ways, Manzarek to concentrate on solo efforts, while his partners formed **The Butts Band**.

The surviving Doors were drawn together once more to record AN AMERICAN PRAYER (1978). Preempting The Beatles by almost twenty years, they took a selection of poetry which Morrison had committed to tape on his final birthday and spent eighteen months recording backing music for the album he had dreamed of making. The album was a valid project, even though Morrison's original intention was to compile an orchestral backing for this material, but The Doors' action was seen by many, including Paul Rothchild, as tantamount to artistic rape, and the resulting instrumental meanderings lacked direction.

After the Oedipal nightmare of "The End" was employed as a theme song for the 1979 movie *Apocalypse Now*, The Doors were held in near-mythical regard throughout the 80s. *No One Here Gets Out Alive*, the fawning memoirs of Morrison's young confidant Danny Sugarman, acted as a blueprint for countless rockers who wished to emulate their benighted The hero, while the music inspired countless bands like The Stranglers, Echo And The Bunnymen and The Cult.

The ex-Doors acted as consultants to Oliver Stone for the biopic *The Doors* in 1991, in which Val Kilmer played the role of Morrison. They have continued with musical ventures such as Manzarek's version of Carmina Burana and production work for bands such as X. Tribute bands such as The Australian Doors have attempted to re-create the original magic for cult audiences across the globe, but as far as The Doors themselves are concerned the music is truly over.

The Doors (1967; Elektra).
The quartet's varied background and influences all converge on this coherent debut. Their live set was plundered for showstoppers like the dodgy sex of "Back Door Man", the theatrical "Alabama Song" and the immortal "Light My Fire", but the highlight is "The End", Morrison's exhortation to generational patricide.

Morrison Hotel (1970; Elektra).
This album placed the band back on the map. From the boom and bust of "Ship Of Fools" to the sublime love song "Indian Summer", this offering captures the full range of The Doors' abilities.

L.A. Woman (1971; Elektra).
By now, Paul Rothchild had bailed out, to be replaced by new producer Bruce Botnick. Recognizing an opportunity to turn Morrison's despondency to everyone's advantage, Botnick captured an air of swampside lament on a set that tips its hat to masters of the blues like John Lee Hooker (as on "Crawling King Snake"), before finding rescue with the finale, "Riders On The Storm".

Stephen Boyd

LEE DORSEY

Born New Orleans, Louisiana, 1926; died 1986.

"If a smile had a sound, it would be the sound of Lee Dorsey's voice."
Allen Toussaint

Brought up in Oregon as lightweight boxing hopeful 'Kid Chocolate', **Lee Dorsey** served a spell in the navy then returned to his birthplace. There he worked as a self-employed car mechanic and part-time entertainer before being 'discovered' by Fury Records talent scout Marshall Schorn.

A debut single on Fury, "Lottie Moe", was an impressive seller, although it never quite broke into the pop charts. However, the follow-up was the self-penned million-selling "Ya Ya" (1961), which, as "Ya Ya Twist", was covered for the European market by Petula Clark. A calculated follow-up, "Do Re Mi", was less potent, and subsequent discs were so unsuccessful that Dorsey returned to his car mechanic business, until the jaunty "Ride Your Pony" provided him with a comeback hit in 1965. It also figured in the repertoire of countless garage bands worldwide, while Dorsey's unusual preoccupation with staccato rhythms appealed to hip white drummers like Ringo Starr and Robert Wyatt.

Making a more insidious impact, "Get Out Of My Life Woman", another composition by celebrated New Orleans producer **Allen Toussaint**, gave Dorsey his UK chart debut, while he scored a global smash with "Working In A Coalmine" (1966). Dorsey peaked commercially with "Holy Cow", the album NEW LEE DORSEY (1966), and an international schedule on which he was frequently backed by his regular studio accompanists, The Meters.

After 1969's "Everything I Do Gohn Be Funky (From Now On)" disappeared from the charts, Dorsey cut back on his stage work to run the auto business he had bought from his 60s royalties. "Ya Ya" enjoyed a revival in 1973 when it was featured on the soundtrack to the movie *American Graffiti*, while artists as diverse as John Lennon, Little Feat, The Pointer Sisters and The Judds covered his work.

Not so lucrative were Dorsey's own releases, although NIGHT PEOPLE (1977) marked his critical rehabilitation, and it was generally felt that his time could come again. He made a qualified stage comeback as a reliable support to James Brown, Jerry Lee Lewis, and even some famous New Wave acts, but died of a respiratory disorder on December 1, 1986.

⊙ **Yes We Can** (1970; Polydor).
Produced by Toussaint, this most adventurous of Dorsey albums switches smoothly from sections jittery with percussion to wordless choral passages that could have been lifted from some mellow New Age CD.

⊙ **Greatest Hits** (1974; Sue/Island).
Non-specialists can start right here with this encapsulation of Lee's best-remembered moments and his inimitable brand of New Orleans soul.

⊙ **Wheelin' & Dealin': The Definitive Collection** (1998; Arista).
The title pretty much says it all.

Alan Clayson

DOVES

Formed Manchester, England 1996.

Mancunian trio **Doves** may have only released two albums, but their history can be traced all the way back to the Madchester acid house boom of the late 80s, when they frequented the Hacienda club and rubbed shoulders with the likes of Mark E Smith and Happy Mondays. Although **Jimi Goodwin** and twin brothers **Jez** and **Andy Williams** had found common ground with their love of The Smiths and The Velvet Underground, it was the irresistible lure of dance culture that caused them to form a band. As **Sub Sub**, they landed several spots at the Hacienda, and after an aborted spell on Virgin's roster were taken on by New Order manager Rob Gretton for his Rob's Records label. With Melanie Williams on vocals they released a joyous tribute to diva-fronted disco – "Ain't No Love (Ain't No Use)" – which became a huge UK hit, peaking at #3 in 1993. The follow-up singles and album – FULL FATHOM FIVE (1994) – failed to connect in the same way. Then in 1995, a fire destroyed the Williams brothers' studio, and symbolically marked the end of Sub Sub; the time was right for the trio to complete reinvention of their sound and style.

With Jimi on vocals and bass, Jez on guitar and Andy on drums, Doves eventually surfaced in 1998 with a well-received EP called "The Cedar Room" and gigs supporting Badly Drawn Boy. But tragedy was to strike when the trio's long-term friend Gretton died in May 1999 of a stroke. His death was seen as an incalculable loss to Mancunian music culture – Doves dedicated their first album to his memory. Released in March 2000 and entitled LOST SOULS it was an adventurous, brooding rock collection, which earned them UK chart success and, later that year, a *Mercury Music Prize* nomination. The group showed they hadn't lost their knack for an unforgettable hook and melody since their Sub Sub days, witnessed by the bittersweet 60s pastiche "Here It Comes", and best of all, the glowing delight of minor chart hit "Catch The Sun". But the set was, over all, just a little too melancholy to spawn the chart-climbing single that was needed.

In 2002 the group returned with an even more stunning collection: THE LAST BROADCAST. Announced by the epic single "There Goes The Fear", this second set was even more accomplished than their first, and a lot chirpier. It sold well and has even been compared to the Stone Roses' colossal debut.

Doves – life and soul of the party

Lost Souls (2000; Heavenly/EMI).
The album's opener, "Firesuite", a majestic instrumental, sets the mood. Elsewhere Goodwin's vocals, often distorted or buried in the collision of samples and riffs, are treated as another instrument in the mix. Doves have made that rarest of things – a complex, heartbreaking and grown-up rock record.

The Last Broadcast (2002; Heavenly/EMI).
Featuring the single "There Goes The Fear": a mammoth seven-minute opus of guitars, enchanting melodies and drum loops. The remainder of the collection is just as good – destined to become a classic.

Justin Lewis

NICK DRAKE

Born Burma, 1948; died Tanworth-in-Arden,
England, 1974.

"You know, Nick Drake was the very best of all." Tom Verlaine

Singer-songwriter **Nick Drake** has had an enduring cult following for over twenty-five years now, with new fans falling in love with his intricate guitar work, introspective songs and understated English voice. All the more poignant then, that on his death (at the age of 26) Drake's talent was largely unrecognized.

Born to colonial parents in Burma, Drake moved to Britain at the age of 7, when his family settled in a village near Coventry, in the Midlands. He took up guitar at 16 – a refuge no doubt from the public school, Marlborough, where he was sent away to board – and by the time he reached Cambridge University he already saw himself as a singer-songwriter. One of the live sets he played there – singing and playing guitar, backed by a dozen female string players – was seen by Ashley Hutchings, Fairport Convention's bass player, who introduced him to their producer/manager, Joe Boyd.

Boyd, amazed and entranced, signed Drake to his own label, Witchseason Productions, whose other artists included Richard Thompson, John and Beverly Martyn, and The Incredible String Band. It would have been hard to imagine a more sympathetic home for the songwriter, whose work, as the retrospective CD sleeve notes put it, 'resonated with the fragile innocence of the 60s counterculture ... the hippy vision made permanent on vinyl'.

Drake's first album was released in 1969. FIVE LEAVES LEFT (the message near the end of a pack of Rizla papers) was a remarkably accomplished work from a writer yet to turn 21. Contemporary critics likened it to Tim Buckley and Van Morrison, although its pace and tone was more contemplative than either, and less declamatory than the latter. The beauty of Drake's sound lay in the intimacy of a voice at once purposeful and wistful, and the exceptional confidence and clarity of his guitar playing. The album was also notable for the warmth of its string arrangements – by Drake's Cambridge friend, Robert Kirby – and the maturity of his often elegiac lyrics, as in "Fruit Tree", a meditation on the posthumous acquisition of fame.

Drake dropped out of Cambridge a year early, moved to London, and did some painful tour dates, avoiding any eye contact with the audience. More productively, he set about work on a follow-up album, BRYTER LAYTER, which emerged in 1970: Boyd, its producer, and John Wood, its engineer, claim it is the one perfect record they have ever made. Drake's lyrics, always elliptic and personal, had acquired almost poetic form, and they were lent a sprightliness of rhythm and jazzier sound by the guitar of Richard Thompson (who had also appeared on the first album), John Cale's piano and organ, and Dave Pegg's bass. It received favourable reviews, though sales were disappointing, hampered by Drake's reluctance to play live. Without a hit single, exposure was difficult to create, and Britain lacked the FM radio that enabled Leonard Cohen to break through in the US.

Drake, always introverted, became dangerously withdrawn, submitting to a depression that, despite the efforts of his parents and friends, including Boyd, Wood, and Chris Blackwell (who had acquired Witchseason for his Island Records) necessitated psychiatric treatment. At one stage, however, Drake borrowed Blackwell's apartment on the Spanish coast, and, returning home, called John Wood to say he'd like to record a new album.

PINK MOON (1972) – like Van Morrison's ASTRAL WEEKS – was recorded in just two days, or more precisely nights, with Drake accompanying himself on guitar and piano, no band, no arrangements. Island were startled to receive the tapes, left by Drake at reception. It was a record of intense simplicity, the sound pared down to an austere combination of voice and acoustic guitar, occasionally relieved by piano. Again, it didn't sell, and Drake's depression deepened to anger. He thought of giving up music as a career, and even signed up as a computer programmer, though he didn't last the week.

In a state of apparently morbid depression, Drake recorded a further four tracks for a projected new album; they carried over PINK MOON's themes of uncertainty, apprehension and betrayal, and included "Black Eyed Dog", a bleak premonition of death. The record was left unfinished, but it seemed Drake then turned a corner. He went to Paris, lived on a barge, and decided to move there; intending to write, perhaps, for the chanteuse Françoise Hardy (she had asked him for songs a while back).

Tragically, he never went back. Home in England, briefly, staying at his parents, and learning French, Drake took an overdose – accidentally, it seems – of an antidepressant. He died on November 25, 1974.

Nick Drake's work has never been out of catalogue – a condition of Boyd's sale of Witchseason to Island – and periodic renewed interest in his music has led to the release of an album of early recordings and demos, TIME OF NO REPLY (on Boyd's Hannibal Records in 1986), together with a box set

The late, great Nick Drake

of all four albums – FRUIT TREE (1986) – and, in 1994, WAY TO BLUE, a compilation to mark the twentieth anniversary of his death.

⊙ **Bryter Layter** (1970; Island).
For Drake, a sunny sky of an album. His immaculate voice is at its most open and upbeat on songs like "Hazey Jane" and "Northern Sky", and most affecting on "At The Chime Of A City Clock".

⊙ **Pink Moon** (1972; Island).
Drake's sound is still warm and intimate here, but a little claustrophobic too. Admirably truthful and brave, but a bit like watching someone shaping up for a dive into an empty pool.

⊙ **Fruit Tree** (1986; Hannibal/Ryko).
This box set includes all four albums, copious sleeve notes and photos, and full lyrics.

James Owen

THE DREAM SYNDICATE

Formed Los Angeles, 1981; disbanded 1989.

Before forming **The Dream Syndicate**, **Steve Wynn** sang and played guitar in **THE LONG RYDERS**, the band put together by Sid Griffin in 1981. Despite common roots in the LA punk scene, the two musicians were pulling in different directions: Griffin inclined towards The Byrds/Flying Burritos tradition, whereas Wynn was into an earthier sound, with The Velvet Underground and Television being obvious influences.

Wynn had previously been in LA New Wavers The Suspects and formed The Dream Syndicate with another previous Suspect, **Kendra Smith** (bass); **Karl Precoda** on guitar and **Dennis Duck** on drums completed the line-up. Their first recording, a mini-album on Wynn's own Down There label in 1982, called simply THE DREAM SYNDICATE, was followed by the full-length THE DAYS OF WINE AND ROSES (1982). This early material had a basic approach, immediately distinct from the more polished sound of groups like The Rain Parade, whom critics had lumped with The Dream Syndicate in a movement they termed 'The Paisley Underground'. Moreover, Steve Wynn's songs were distinctly dark in subject matter, in contrast to the whimsy of many of his contemporaries.

Kendra Smith left in 1983 to pursue her own career (a solo album, FIVE WAYS OF DISAPPEARING, was released in 1995) and was replaced by **Dave Provost**. The new line-up moved to a major label, A&M, the first of several record company changes, and released what was arguably their finest album, THE MEDICINE SHOW (1984). With Green On Red frontman Dan Stuart, Wynn took time out in 1985 to record DANNY AND DUSTY, an album of rough-and-ready country-rock, which concluded with a rendition of Dylan's "Knocking On Heaven's Door".

Following a compilation of earlier material, THIS IS NOT THE NEW DREAM SYNDICATE (1985), the next Dream Syndicate album was OUT OF THE GREY (1986). By now, the band's former recording engineer, **Paul B. Cutler**, had replaced Precoda on guitar, and **Mark Walton** had taken over on bass.

Despite the high quality of the material, and its more mainstream sound, OUT OF THE GREY failed to achieve significant sales.

GHOST STORIES (1988) was another fine clutch of songs, dominated by themes of reminiscence and mortality. The group's swansong was the double live album LIVE AT RAJI'S (1989); recorded and released after GHOST STORIES, though oddly containing nothing from it, it was a useful trawl through the band's history.

Steve Wynn's first solo project, KEROSENE MAN (1990), continued The Dream Syndicate's approach, though with a greater variety of instrumentation and glossier sound. In 1993, Wynn teamed up with former Long Ryder, Stephen McCarthy, in the part-time band **Gutterball**, while continuing to record and tour under his own name. In 1995 he recorded MELTING IN THE DARK, with the assistance of Boston band **COME**, which was something of a return to the earthier sound of early Dream Syndicate, and in 1997 released SWEETNESS & LIGHT (a typically ironic title), followed by more studio sets: MY MIDNIGHT (1999), HERE COME THE MIRACLES (2001) and STATIC TRANSMISSION (2003).

An enthusiastic live performer, Wynn enjoys as much popularity outside the US as he does at home and continues to tour regularly (with and without a band) in Europe as well as in the States.

The Dream Syndicate

(•) **The Medicine Show** (1984; A&M).
The band's best album, musically and lyrically, with a tight, rocky feel, and reflective songs like "Merrtville", where Wynn's gloomy world-view is trained on small-town America.

(•) **Out Of The Grey** (1986; Chrysalis).
Syndicate fans are divided about the merits of this album, but it contains some of Wynn's best songs to date, including "Boston" and "Now I Ride Alone". This CD reissue offers as a live bonus track a surprisingly effective rendition of Clapton's "Let It Rain".

Steve Wynn

(•) **Take Your Flunky And Dangle** (1998; Innerstate).
A stunning collection of outtakes and rare recordings: sparse and raw.

(•) **Here Come The Miracles** (2001; Innerstate).
This expansive double-CD set rolls with feedback-damaged compositions and some great songs.

Keith Prewer

DRUGSTORE

Formed London, 1993.

> "I want it to sound like you're entering someone's bedroom and whispering right in their ear."
> Isabel Monteiro

Named after Gus Van Sant's film *Drugstore Cowboy*, **Drugstore** are a dark, twisted marvel. The husky whisper of petite Brazilian **Isabel Monteiro** (bass/vocals) spins tales of failing relationships, chemicals and death, while the backing mutates from the relative calm of the Cowboy Junkies to feedback-drenched The Jesus & Mary Chain and back again. They spent 1995 as critical darlings of the English music press – always a worrying position to be in, but they have the talent to ride out the inevitable backlash.

Isabel Monteiro arrived in London from São Paulo at the turn of the 90s. After serving time in various undistinguished bands, she teamed up to write songs with LA expatriate **Mike Chylinski** (drums). As Isabel hated her 'masculine' voice, they auditioned various unsuitable singers before she reluctantly decided to take on the vocal duties herself. Initially an indie-punk thrash outfit, their songs became slower and slower as they realized that, in Isabel's words, 'maybe a whisper was going to be a lot more powerful than a shout'.

Rather than trying to attract record company interest with demo tapes, they released their first single, "Alive", on their own Honey label in May 1993, gaining instant music press acclaim. Its follow-up, "Modern Pleasure", was another limited edition, released through Rough Trade's singles club in the autumn of that year. Finally, Drugstore signed to Go! Discs in the spring of 1994, as **Daron Robinson** became their permanent guitarist.

They toured heavily, supporting the likes of The Lemonheads, Tindersticks and Gene. The EP STARCROSSED, released at the beginning of 1995, was another critical smash – you get the idea if you imagine The Velvet Underground if Lou Reed had been a girl.

The band undertook their first headlining tour of the UK in early 1995. In the spring of that year, the album DRUGSTORE was released to further praise. The sound was deliberately raw-edged, concentrating on feel rather than polish, and intimacy was paramount, with Monteiro's voice smokier than ever.

Continuing their heavy schedule of live performances the money kept coming in whilst they extricated themselves from the mess left by the collapse of their record company, but the twelve-month delay in releasing WHITE MAGIC FOR LOVERS (1998; Roadrunner) had broken the momentum. More mature and self-assured than their first outing, WHITE MAGIC featured guest vocals from Radiohead's Thom Yorke but suffered from a flabby production job that crushed the excitement they generated in front of an audience. More record company shenanigans followed when Roadrunner ditched much of its non-metal roster. The band were soon hooked up with Global Warming Records, and in 2001 released SONGS FOR THE JETSET. Though arguably their most rounded release to date, the record still proffers the notion that Drugstore are a group capable of much more.

A collection of outtakes and demos, COLLECTOR No.1 was released in 2002, but it remains to be seen if they can transcend their influences and use more of their emotional and musical palette without losing the intensity that made them special.

(•) **Drugstore** (1995; Go! Discs).
Moments of sublimity light up a Velvety dark backdrop: Isabel waits to meet her maker with a loaded gun in "Favourite Sinner", and croons 'there's a star for everyone' in "Superglider". And how about the bit in "Accelerate" where she breathes, 'slow down honey...'?

Andy Smith

DUBSTAR

Formed Newcastle, England, 1994; split 2000.

With New Order a distant memory, the Pet Shop Boys in temporary retirement, and Saint Etienne pursuing solo projects, the time was right for another band merging pop-dance sensibilities with acerbic lyrics. That band would be **Dubstar**, formed by songwriter **Steve Hiller** (keyboards/programming) and **Chris Milkie** (guitar) when they met **Sarah Blackwood** (vocals), who was studying at college in Newcastle. A demo tape containing a startlingly contemporary cover of Billy Bragg's "St. Swithin's Day" soon resulted in a deal with Food Records, home to Blur and Jesus Jones.

Although Dubstar's debut single, "Stars", merely brushed the UK Top 40 in the early summer of 1995, it got rave reviews from several music press titles. A second single, "Anywhere", also attracted some interest, but it wasn't until their first album was unleashed that their sound won much of a public. DISGRACEFUL (1995) was to become a steady seller, although its sleeve, which depicted what can best be described as a vagina-shaped pencil case, alarmed one or two chain stores. (They heaved a sigh of relief when a second sleeve, showing a furry pink slipper, appeared in its place.)

With tracks produced by sometime New Order associate Stephen Hague, DISGRACEFUL earned the epithet 'escapist realism' for kitchen-sink mini-dramas like "Not So Manic Now", which broke into the UK charts in early 1996, closely followed by a remixed version of "Stars". The following year saw the acerbic "I Will Be Your Girlfriend" and the infectious "Cathedral Park" hit the UK Top 40, both from the long-awaited but rather formulaic second album GOODBYE (1997). Thankfully, a new album for 2000, MAKE IT BETTER, and a single "I (Friday Night)" found the trio back on form, if not in the top ten.

But that was, sadly, that. At the end of the year Hiller announced that his relationship with Sarah had become 'increasingly tested'. The group split. The end.

(•) **Disgraceful** (1995; Food/EMI).
A refreshing collection of deceptively simple pop songs, which manages to be joyous and melancholy at the same time. Particularly worthy of mention is their utterly modern transformation of Billy Bragg's "St. Swithin's Day".

(•) **Make It Better** (2000; Food/EMI).
While the charming single "I (Friday Night)" is undoubtedly the standout track, the remaining eleven songs also

manage to lodge in the mind. The lyrical content is quirky and engaging, and there's a sense that these are songs for thirty-something ex-clubbers, confirmed by the presence of "Mercury", written by Kirsty Hawkshaw of the early 90s positivist rave troupe Opus III.

Justin Lewis

STEPHEN DUFFY

Born Birmingham, England, 1961.

> "There's that quote: 'All you need to make a film is a gun and a girl.' But with pop music you don't even need a gun." Stephen Duffy

In 1979, **Stephen Duffy** formed a band with college friends Nick Rhodes and John Taylor. As **DURAN DURAN**, they would become one of the most successful groups in the world during the 80s. But by then Stephen Duffy was no longer in the band: after six months, either out of good sense or stupidity, depending on your viewpoint, he had left in search of a more fulfilling career. Ever since, his work has attracted a frustratingly limited following, despite critical accolades.

For a brief period, though, Duffy threatened to rival his old band's mainstream success. Under the name of **Stephen 'Tin Tin' Duffy**, his insidiously catchy dance-floor favourite "Kiss Me" (1983) was remixed and reissued in early 1985, whereupon it hit the UK Top 5. There was minor interest in an LP, THE UPS AND DOWNS OF... (1985), but after one more lesser hit, "Icing On The Cake", he disappeared from the charts.

When lawyers representing cartoon character Tintin's creator Hergé objected, Duffy was forced to drop his middle name, and retired to the countryside. It was here that he formed the suitably English band **The Lilac Time**, with brother **Nick** (guitar), **Michael Giri** (bass) and **Micky Harris** (drums). Their name was taken from the lyrics of the Nick Drake song, "River Man", and Drake's sensitive folk-rock influence became apparent in the band's quietly wonderful albums. THE LILAC TIME (1987), PARADISE CIRCUS (1989), AND LOVE FOR ALL (1990) and ASTRONAUTS (1991) were all largely acoustic efforts with strong melodies and perceptive, worldly lyrics.

Unfortunately The Lilac Time only attracted a small if loyal following, and label after label let them go. By 1992 the band had had enough, and once again Duffy embarked on solo projects, notably with Saint Etienne and even with violinist Nigel Kennedy.

In 1995, the time was indisputably right for a Stephen Duffy renaissance. Signed to the Indolent label, he formed **Duffy** with the American guitar band **Velvet Crush**. Together they headed down to North Carolina with one-time R.E.M. producer Mitch Easter, and emerged with possibly the best album of Stephen Duffy's career.

The therapeutic positivity of DUFFY (1995) belied the fact that it had been born out of a depression triggered by the death of his father two years earlier. Its lyrics – sharp, wry and eloquent – were typically Duffy, and one track, "London Girls", was his own affectionate poke at the Britpop phenomenon. He has even worked on a collaboration with Blur guitarist **Alex James**, the self-effacing combo choosing ME ME ME as their nom de guerre. Duffy released I LOVE MY FRIENDS in 1998, and then The Lilac Time re-emerged for the sparkling LOOKING FOR A DAY IN THE NIGHT (1999). This set was followed by the country-tinged LILAC6 (2001), with support from **Steven Page**, **Tyler Stewart** and **Kevin Hearne** of The Barenaked Ladies (a band that Duffy also writes for). In the same year a compilation of cuts from the earlier, long-deleted, Lilac Time albums was released, COMPENDIUM: THE FONTANA TRINITY.

Duffy

● **Duffy** (1995; Indolent).
Duffy's often delightful wordplay – particularly on "London Girls" and "Needle Mythology" – combines with delicate guitar flourishes to craft an album as sensitive as it is clever.

The Lilac Time

● **Compendium: The Fontana Trinity** (2001; Fontana).
The Lilac Time's Nick Drake-ian serenity was markedly out of step during the 80s, but today their charm and musical poise sound surprisingly fresh.

Nick Duerden

DURAN DURAN

Formed Birmingham, England, 1978; disbanded 1990; re-formed 1992.

Which one did you fancy? At a lot of schools, **John Taylor** (bass), the one with the two-tone wedge cut, got the edge over **Simon Le Bon** (vocals). Others held out for **Nick Rhodes** (keyboards), the ALADDIN SANE-era Bowie wannabe who not only had the best haircut, but, as evidenced by his production of Kajagoogoo's "Too Shy", was also **Duran Duran**'s chief theorist.

Naming themselves after a character in Roger Vadim's sci-fi sexploitation flick, *Barbarella*, Duran Duran spearheaded a movement of Chic-loving, British art-dandies who briefly invaded the American consciousness in the early to mid-80s. Their American success had nothing to do with their eyeliner, Italian shoes or silk scarves, much less their songs; it had everything to do with the emergence of MTV. Promotional videos were virtually nonexistent in the States during the early days of MTV, so the bulk of the programming was taken up by the likes of Blancmange, ABC, Bow Wow Wow, Adam And The Ants, Howard Jones, Thomas Dolby and, most successfully, Duran Duran. No one who went to high school in the 80s will ever forget the boys sailing off Antigua in the video for "Rio" or Le Bon hunting his 'exotic' love object in "Hungry Like The Wolf".

Hearts first began fluttering when the band was formed at the tail end of punk by Taylor, Rhodes, **STEPHEN 'TIN TIN' DUFFY** and **Simon Colley**. Colley and Duffy, who would eventually record the classic "Kiss Me", were soon replaced by **Roger Taylor** (drums) and **Andy Wickett** (vocals). With the addition of **Andy Taylor** (guitar) and Le Bon taking over vocal duties, the Fab Five were set for world domination and recorded the New Romantic anthem, "Planet Earth" (1981), which peaked at #12 in the British charts. Their eponymous debut album also contained the sub-Roxy Music decadence of "Girls On Film", whose ill-conceived soft-porn video somehow managed not to alienate their legion of teenage girl fans.

RIO (1982) saw the band ditch their futurism in favour of a pastel-hued, linen suit suavity that pre-dated Miami Vice by several years. "Hungry Like The Wolf", "Rio" and "Save A Prayer" – all of which featured ridiculously oblique lyrics and better hooks than, say, A Flock Of Seagulls – were all Top 20 hits on both sides of the Atlantic (Top 10 in the UK). RIO's success was followed by the British #1, "Is There Something I Should Know" (1983), which took Chic's stilted plain speech to its illogical conclusion with the immortal lyric, 'You're about as easy as a nuclear war'.

SEVEN AND THE RAGGED TIGER (1983) was nowhere near as innovative, yet proved to be more successful. "The Reflex" was stiff and mindless, "Union Of The Snake" was downright stupid, and "New Moon On Monday" was a pale imitation of "Save A Prayer". The unstoppable chart success continued with the inspired hook-up with ex-Chic guitarist and producer extraordinaire, Nile Rodgers. "The Wild Boys" (1984) saw Duran Duran adapt the brittle funk style that Chic had pioneered and was quickly turning into the sound of the 80s. The ultimate video band then released the pointless and wretched live album, ARENA (1984).

The following year saw the band pursue redundant side-projects. **Arcadia** was Le Bon and Rhodes' attempt at creating Japan-style art-pop, while **The Power Station** saw John and Andy repay their Chic debt by teaming up with the other members of that band – Tony Thompson and Bernard Edwards, plus Robert Palmer – to record impossibly slick, studio-hack dance rock. Duran Duran returned in 1986 as a trio without the excess baggage of the two sexless Taylors and released their best single, "Notorious". But the band had next to nothing to do with it – the sparse beats and jagged groove were created entirely by Rodgers.

A series of rapidly diminishing returns followed as the band, who were developing paunches by now, tried to get themselves taken seriously. The humourless, gutless, bloodless, anonymous schlock-funk that followed had even less character than Shakatak. Remarkably, out of nowhere, the band came back in 1993 with two US Top 10 singles, "Ordinary World" and "Come Undone".

The upturn in their sales figures gave them the clout to pursue one of the worst projects ever in the history of popular music. THANK YOU (1995) was an album of cover versions in tribute to the band's 'influences' – though just how they were influenced by Bob Dylan or Elvis Costello remains a mystery. They turned Grandmaster Flash's "White Lines", one of hip-hop's most important singles, into brat rock that would have embarrassed EMF, while Lou Reed's achingly melancholic "Perfect Day" became a vapid, lugubrious Steve Winwood ballad. The real crime, though, was their version of Public Enemy's "911 Is A Joke". If there was ever a song that could not be covered, it was surely this.

John Taylor then quit the group, leaving Le Bon and Rhodes to release MEDAZZALAND (1997), a workmanlike update of their New Romantic pop sound. EMI refused to release the set in the UK, and shortly afterwards the band's contract ended. Next came the defiantly rocky POP TRASH (2000) on the Hollywood label; though arguably the most interesting thing they'd done in years, the group now seemed doomed to earn their royalties from regurgitated best-of compilations.

⊙ **Decade** (1989; Capitol).
They weren't as good as ABC or Haircut 100, but they had better songs and better clothes than Haysi Fantayzee or Wide Boy Awake. This is the proof.

⊙ **Singles Box 1981 - 1984** (2003; EMI).
This thirteen-CD collection of singles features a ton of mixes that you won't have heard since the early 80s.

Peter Shapiro

THE DURUTTI COLUMN

Formed Manchester, England, 1978.

The story of **The Durutti Column** is essentially that of guitarist extraordinaire **Vini Reilly**, whose 'avant-garde-jazz-classical' style also incorporates elements of rock, pop, folk and electronic forms, rendered wholly distinctive by his chiming lightness of touch.

After a music-saturated childhood, illness forced him to decline an offer to play cabaret guitar on the QE2, and he stayed in Manchester. In 1976 Reilly joined the semi-serious punk band Ed Banger & The Nosebleeds, whose numbers also at one time included Morrissey. After one single, the truthful "Ain't Been To No Music School", their manager and local broadcaster Tony Wilson asked Reilly to join up with **Tony Bowers** (bass), **Phil Rainford** (vocals), **Dave Rowbotham** (guitar) and **Chris Joyce** (drums).

In January 1978, this line-up became The Durutti Column, taking their name from 1930s libertarian-anarchist Buenoventuri Durutti, who led a brigade in the Spanish Civil War, and their politics from the Situationiste Internationale. The new band played psychedelic-tinged pop, and cut two tracks for the inaugural Factory Records sampler EP, before breaking up. Chief songwriter Reilly retained the name, while the rest went off to the oblivion-bound Mothmen.

Interest generated by the album landed Reilly several support slots, notably with John Martyn, as well as with John Cooper Clarke and Pauline Murray's Invisible Girls. Busy live work took its toll on Reilly's health, and for the next two LPs, L.C. (1981) and ANOTHER SETTING (1983), he fronted a fuller-sounding band and favoured vocals over guitar. Here he was joined for the first time by former Alberto Y Lost Trios Paranoias drummer **Bruce Mitchell**, who remains the only other permanent member of The Durutti Column. Reilly's work rate was remarkable in this period: he improvised and recorded an entire album, AMIGOS EN PORTUGAL, in one day; contributed a side of material to The Factory Quartet album; sweetly covered "I Get Along Without You Very Well" as a single; and issued an EP, DEUX TRIANGLES, through Factory Benelux.

In November 1984 came Reilly's next major project, a TUBULAR BELLS-like two-part piece entitled WITHOUT MERCY, its title taken from Keats's *La Belle Dame Sans Merci*. Underpinned by a recurrent, mournful piano motif, plaintive violin and stirring brass, Reilly's delicate and often minimalist material brought him spectacular success in Japan; a live album recorded there, DOMO ARIGATO (1985), became one of the first albums to be released on CD only.

The melancholic shading of its follow-up, CIRCUSES AND BREAD (1986), had a translucent quality, especially on its dreamlike second side, where the tracks drifted and faded into each other. A more vigorously evocative side was revealed on the GREETINGS THREE EP recorded for the Italian label Materiali Sonori, while a trip to California yielded another EP, featuring a swirling, dynamic cover of Grace Slick's "White Rabbit", sung by LA punk queen Debi Diamond.

THE GUITAR AND OTHER MACHINES (1987) was a tightly focused collection on which brass and new technology were more widely employed. The loopingly arhythmic "When The World" saw light of day as a single, while Reilly's spectral vocals were heard for the first time in years on "Don't Think You're Funny".

Reilly was to taste rare mainstream chart success on **MORRISSEY**'s post-Smiths debut, VIVA HATE (1988), which gave the guitarist a chance to mix and match styles as diverse as heavy metal, Johnny Marr arpeggios, and his own trademark resonant echo. Thus interest was greater than usual in Reilly's next album, simply called VINI REILLY (1989), his best work in years, with astutely chosen and elegantly employed samples of Otis Redding and Tracy Chapman lacing "Otis", plus sombre yet defiant social comment on "My Country".

Further bouts of illness restricted Reilly's live work during this period, and OBEY THE TIME (1990) was a relatively routine release. Signed to Factory throughout the 80s, Reilly had rarely had to worry about the lack of commercial success, but when

Factory announced its bankruptcy in late 1992 his admirers wondered where else he might find such an appropriate setting.

Thankfully, in 1994 Reilly found a home at the chastened successor label, Factory Too. The Durutti Column album SEX AND DEATH was its first release, and despite the ominous title it contained rich and luxuriant textures, and even a wink towards Hank Marvin with the buoyantly optimistic "The Rest Of My Life". Reilly's next move was FIDELITY (1996) which deliberately juxtaposed acoustic instrumentation with shifting electronic rhythms to mixed effect, above all showing Reilly's, well, fidelity to continue experimenting. In late 1996 and through 1997, Factory reissued eight of the first nine Durutti Column albums as remastered, repackaged CDs, with stacks of extra cuts – WHY BREAD AND CIRCUSES missed the boat has never been established.

1998's TIME WAS GIGANTIC WHEN WE WERE KIDS bore a sense of renewal and refreshment and was as intensely melodic and sensuous as anything in Reilly's catalogue; it made much use of the strong, sweet vocals (and lyrics) of **Eley Rudge**, Bruce Mitchell's daughter and Durutti cover star since childhood. Another new album, REBELLION, followed in 2001; the set received favourable reviews, was unmistakeably Durutti fare, but also tried hard to embrace various modern trends. The next installment, SOMEONE ELSE'S PARTY (perhaps titled as a response to the Factory biopic *24 Hour Party People*) followed in 2003 and featured some truly beautiful and affecting moments, each song having been recorded in response to the illness and death of Reilly's mother.

The First Four Albums (1988; Factory).
A generous reissue from Factory of old vinyl material transferred to CD, containing THE RETURN OF THE DURUTTI COLUMN, L.C., ANOTHER SETTING and WITHOUT MERCY, each on an individual disc. Hard to find now, though Factory reissued the first two albums (with nice extras) on CD in 1996.

Vini Reilly (1989; Factory; reissued 1996).
Reilly's best individual album, combining his resonant, ringing echo-box-based style with sampling technology to remarkable effect throughout.

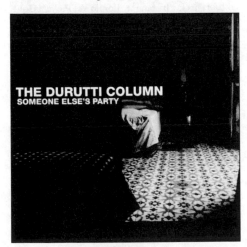

Someone Else's Party (2003; Artful).
A stunning home-recorded collection. The final cut, "Goodbye", features an answer-phone message from Reilly's mother that was left shortly before her death – the cut is staggeringly moving.

Peter Mills

IAN DURY

Born Billericay, England, 1942; died 2002.

One of the more unlikely stories of pop stardom occurred in 1977 when pub-rock veteran **Ian Dury** released his first solo album NEW BOOTS AND PANTIES, and established himself seemingly overnight as a much-loved and unmistakeable character of the British scene. Though his brand of cockney recitation over a solid backing was never punk, its success owed a lot to the New Wave's rough-and-ready values, for Dury had as much street cred as anyone around, plus twice as much wit.

Severely affected by polio at the age of 7, Dury progressed through art college, and took up a teaching job, before forming Kilburn & The High Roads in the early 70s. Although Dury honed his lyrical prowess in songs like "Billy Bentley" and "Upminster Kid", there was little commercial potential in this brand of beery bar-room racket. An album, HANDSOME, was released in 1975, but the Kilburns split up soon afterwards, with guitarist Keith Lucas going on to form **999**.

Undeterred, Dury signed a deal with the newly formed Stiff label, and teamed up with **Chas Jankel** (guitar/keyboards) to write songs for a solo album. Jankel's compositions suggested a move away from solid rock'n'roll roots towards a more lightweight jazzy style, anchored by funky bass lines. This new sophistication, topped with Dury's earthy delivery, jelled into a formula that was to produce some of his biggest hits. Most of the session work for the recording of these new songs was supplied by a collection of fine musicians who would later become **The Blockheads – Charley Charles** (drums), **Norman Watt-Roy** (bass) and **Davey Payne** (sax).

Dury's first solo single release was the definitive statement on the rock'n'roll lifestyle – "Sex And Drugs And Rock And Roll" in the summer of 1977. On its release, NEW BOOTS AND PANTIES was widely hailed as a brilliant debut LP, with Dury demonstrating a talent for a punchy couplet in music-hall parodies like "Billericay Dickie" and "Clever Trevor", while indulging the rough edge of his tongue on "Blockheads" and "Plaistow Patricia", and coming up with the ultimate rock'n'roll tribute on "Sweet Gene Vincent". The album went gold and this success was consolidated by a punishing touring schedule, with The Blockheads having added **Mickey Gallagher** (keyboards) and **John Turnball** (guitar) to the line-up. After providing some riotous nights alongside Elvis Costello, Nick Lowe and the galaxy of talent that was the first Stiff tour, they jetted

The late Ian Dury takes a break from sex and drugs

A change of label to Polydor, a reunion with Jankel and a new album, LORD UPMINSTER (1981), recorded with top-drawer rhythm section **Sly Dunbar** and **Robbie Shakespeare**, prompted great optimism. But an upbeat single, "Spasticus Autisticus" (1981), released for the Year Of The Disabled, was deemed offensive by radio stations and refused airplay. The album gained good reviews but registered few sales and this was just about the end of the road for The Blockheads. While Dury had thrived, like Costello, as a tangent of New Wave, his wit and charm was at odds with the new generation of 'serious' bands now on the rise.

From this point on Dury's musical forays were infrequent, but were always assured a warm reception. In 1984 he released the optimistic 4000 WEEKS HOLIDAY, and gigged with The Music Students, an outfit which included some Blockheads. He took on a variety of acting roles, including parts in Roman Polanski's *Pirates* and Peter Greenaway's *The Cook, The Thief, His Wife And Her Lover*. Dury's lyrical capabilities were still in evidence in a musical called *Apples*, written with Mickey Gallagher, and featuring Dury as Byline Brown, a tabloid hack. It ran at London's Royal Court Theatre, and spawned a soundtrack, released on WEA in 1989.

The death of Charley Charles motivated some nostalgic Blockheads reunion benefit gigs at the end of 1990. This encouraged Dury to sharpen his pencil once more for THE BUS DRIVER'S PRAYER AND OTHER STORIES (1992), its title track being a secular version of the Lord's Prayer based around London bus routes.

Little was heard from Dury until 1998 when, after being 'doorstepped by the tabloids' he took the story of his continuing struggle with cancer to the broadsheets. There followed a flurry of respectful interviews and articles. Dury came out promoting a new album MR LOVE PANTS (Ronnie Harris Records) and reunited with the old Blockheads. The album's bouncing arrangements met with the approval of fans, providing a backdrop to the playful

off to support Lou Reed in the States, a market that proved resistant to this very British band.

The first acquaintance with the UK singles chart came in April 1978 with "What A Waste", then in January 1979 came the big hit, the innuendo-laden "Hit Me With Your Rhythm Stick", which sat at #1 for two weeks. The keenly awaited follow-up LP, DO IT YOURSELF (1979), reached #2 in the chart, but its writing process hadn't been helped by a hectic gigging schedule and the pressure of matching the debut LP's high standards. The summer of 1979 was lightened up by the jazzy stream-of-consciousness single "Reasons To Be Cheerful (Part 3)", but from here on Dury's fortunes were waning.

After two years of frantic activity it was time to take stock, and Jankel decided to move on to solo work. Ex-Dr. Feelgood dynamo guitarist **Wilko Johnson** stepped in to become a Blockhead as the singles "I Want To Be Straight" (an antidote to "Sex And Drugs And Rock And Roll") and "Superman's Big Sister" and the LP LAUGHTER (1980) appeared to modest approval.

yet pointed lyrics on tracks such as "Jack Shit George".

At the end of 1999 Dury attended a ceremony inducting him into Q magazine's songwriters' hall of fame. Sadly, this was to be his final public appearance: on 27th March 2000 he succumbed to his cancer, leaving behind some of the most powerful, challenging and singular music ever recorded. His warmth and good humour will not be forgotten quickly.

⦿ **New Boots And Panties** (1977; Stiff).
The essential purchase and it still sounds rude. "Wake Up And Make Love With Me", "I'm Partial To Your Abracadabra", "Billericay Dickie", "Clever Trevor" – they're all here.

⦿ **Sex And Drugs And Rock And Roll** (1987; Demon).
Compilation especially worthwhile for the singles – "There Ain't Half Been Some Clever Bastards", "What A Waste" and "Hit Me With Your Rhythm Stick".

Nick Dale

BOB DYLAN

Born Duluth, Minnesota, May 24, 1941.

"Keep a good head and always carry a light bulb."

Robert Zimmerman first entered the public consciousness as a Greenwich Village folk singer back in 1961, two years after his reincarnation as **Bob Dylan**. The fragile young songwriter had started out as much a rocker as a folkie, but had cashed in his Mystery Train ticket to make it on the folk scene, the only thing happening in a music world caught in the doldrums between the advent of rock'n'roll and its 60s apotheosis. Dylan, frustrated by the stylistic McCarthyism of his audience, quickly began to experiment, first with forays into stream-of-consciousness writing and then, inspired by groups like The Beatles, The Animals and The Byrds, by going electric. The beards hated it, but the results were three of the greatest albums ever recorded, and status as the iconic spokesman for a generation. His obliquely revelatory lyrics, combined with a reclusive attitude to the press, and industrial-strength sunglasses, led to the creation of an enigmatic persona unique in popular music.

Until his legendary motorcycle accident of July 29, 1966, Dylan was up there with Elvis and The Beatles. Since then, his career has been somewhat less spectacular, though he still remains as refreshingly perverse as ever. Despite several creative droughts, he has produced more fine albums, most notably during the breakdown of his marriage in the 70s, though in recent years the focus of his art has shifted from the recording studio to the stage. Since 1988, he has been engaged in a so-called 'Never Ending Tour', perhaps as an attempt to rekindle the creativity he found during his early hectic touring years, but the returns seem to be diminishing fast. Not that this bothers his legions of obsessive believers, who can derive as much

meaning from the contents of his trash can as ancient Chinese astrologers could from examining the stools of a boy emperor.

Born in Duluth, Minnesota, he enjoyed a comfortable Jewish upbringing in Hibbing, a mining town close to the Canadian border. As a teenager, he took in everything from Hank Williams to Little Richard, with the emphasis on the latter. His first major performance at Hibbing High School set the pattern for future confrontations, with his ragged garage band, the Golden Chords, kicking up a storm in the school hall. Too big for his cage, Bob went to university at nearby Minneapolis in 1959. One of his first acts was to find a solo gig at local folk venue The Ten O'Clock Scholar, where, on the spur of the moment, the young Robert changed his stage name from Elston Gunn to the more rootsy Bob Dylan (generally thought to be in tribute to Dylan Thomas, though some sources have him gleaning the name from the Matt Dillon character in *Gunsmoke* – experts agree, though, that the rabbit in *Magic Roundabout* was named after our hero). Throughout 1960, he spent most of his time developing a style that would go down well in the local coffee houses. Indeed he pursued his reinvention with an unusual enthusiasm, and with his new name, a harmonica style copied from Jesse Fuller and a weather-beaten singing voice borrowed from Woody Guthrie, he soon felt ready to try his luck in New York's emerging folkie scene.

Bob Dylan arrived in the Big Apple in January 1961 in the middle of one of the worst winters in living memory. Immediately he sought places to play and places to stay, down in the boho hangouts of Greenwich Village. Like most rock genesis myths, this period has been romanticized ever since, but at the time there was definitely a magic in the air, as idealistic folk singers played to callow youths gathered around the pot-belly stoves of subterranean bolt holes, a-seeking shelter from harsh winter evenings. Or as Bob pictured it: 'words runnin' out in a lonesome hungry growlin' whisper that any girl with her face hid in the dark could understand'.

Dylan started off guesting in the clubs and bars but learned fast, and, with a talent for songwriting and self-promotion that was way ahead of his more purist peers, soon began to dominate the scene with his solo performances. He also achieved a personal ambition in 1961, when he met Woody Guthrie, then dying from Huntington's chorea. However, his friendships with Ramblin' Jack Elliott and Dave Van Ronk were to prove more influential on his early style. By autumn he was established as someone to watch and, following his session work on other people's albums and a favourable review from Robert Shelton, the folk critic in the *New York Times*, he was offered a deal by Columbia's John Hammond.

Dylan's eponymously titled first album of covers and a few originals, recorded with just voice and guitar in two days, turned out to be a hesitant start. But there was no mistaking the quality of his second outing, THE FREEWHEELIN' BOB DYLAN (1963). By

featuring I WANT YOU and
RAINY DAY WOMEN Nos. 12 & 35

engulfs the listener. Dylan's most angry political work is here, particularly on "With God On Our Side" with its bitter double punch line, but the detached desolation of "North Country Blues" conveys an equally powerful message, with a delivery that sounds more like the embittered voice of middle-aged redundancy than the young man in his twenties who recorded it. Romantic relief is provided by "One Too Many Mornings" and "Boots Of Spanish Leather", but even these are haunting songs of loss, however beautifully framed.

Yet, even as his star glittered brightly in the folk firmament, Dylan was beginning to tire of the whole circus. During a holiday in Greece, he wrote most of ANOTHER SIDE OF BOB DYLAN, an album of largely personal songs cut in one drunken evening in June 1964, that drew accusations of a lack of commitment from the protest movement. It was very much a transitional album, but many of the songs were excellent, and The Byrds were later to record no fewer than five of them with vastly improved arrangements. If the folkies had reservations about ANOTHER SIDE, they were to choke on his next recordings, as Dylan was now experimenting with rock'n'roll – a commercial medium they loathed, but which was about to become a vehicle for protest and self-expression more explosive than anything they had dreamt of.

One of the catalysts was, as ever, The Beatles. Dylan was impressed by their impact and had become envious of their success with armies of screaming girls, while he was stuck playing to the same old beards. Another revelation was hearing what The Animals had done to "House Of The Rising Sun". Dylan's version, on his first album, was a distinctly trad acoustic cut, whereas the Geordies had turned it into a menacing organ-driven rocker. The Byrds, too, were about to launch folk-rock with their chiming interpretation of Dylan's "Mr. Tambourine Man" demo. Dylan wasn't slow in seeing which way the wind was blowing and began jamming with likeminded musicians, an experience he found immensely liberating. However, it should be noted that he had already experimented with a rockabilly sound back in 1962 on the obscure "Mixed Up Confusion" single, a primitive rave-up that should have cleared up any confusion about where his musical sympathies truly lay.

That experiment had been quietly forgotten to avoid damaging his protest-singer image. This time, there was no going back and his audience were confronted with the startling "Subterranean Homesick Blues" 45, a revved-up torrent of bizarre drugs imagery. He fol-

this point he was churning out songs at a rate of knots and the track listing changed several times before becoming the folky classic we know and love. As well as the song that would make his name with a wider audience, "Blowin' In The Wind", the record was full of originals, both personal and political, that left no doubt that Bob Dylan had arrived.

He starred at the Newport Folk Festival, took part in civil rights events and played endlessly, all the time fitting in sessions for the album that was to be released in January 1964 as THE TIMES THEY ARE A-CHANGIN', easily the best of his four folk albums. Gone were the self-conscious postures of the debut and the occasional inconsistencies of FREEWHEELIN', to be replaced by a level of commitment that totally

lowed up with the superb half-electric, half-acoustic BRINGING IT ALL BACK HOME album (1965). If the electric side was an exciting step forward, the acoustic side was possibly an even greater triumph, pushing the boundaries of Dylan's solo work to the limit. More importantly, both sides showed Dylan with renewed energy, whether it was blasting out "Maggie's Farm" with childish glee or singing the beautiful stream-of-consciousness lyrics of "Mr. Tambourine Man", a musical evocation of Arthur Rimbaud's dictum that 'the poet makes himself a seer by a long, prodigious and rational disordering of the senses'.

Dylan was now performing at his very best, both with and without his band, and patenting a highly entertaining confrontational interview style to boot. But his daily regime of coffee, speed and no sleep was putting a great strain on his health and psyche. This manic lifestyle was captured perfectly on Pennebaker's brilliant documentary of Dylan's 1965 UK tour, *Don't Look Back*, a fly-on-the-wall portrait of a man on the brink of exhaustion. Incredibly, it seems that he was genuinely considering jacking it all in, when epiphany struck out of the blue on the plane home. He started writing a new song which became an unstoppable stream of frustrated psychobabble. After a bit of editing and one of his finest band performances, he had the ground-breaking "Like A Rolling Stone". With inspiration running on overdrive and the likes of Mike Bloomfield on guitar and Al Kooper on organ, he kept recording throughout July and August and came up with the fabulous HIGHWAY 61 REVISITED, surely his creative high-water mark. Rivals gasped in astonishment at the endless waves of expressionistic lyrics woven deep into the music's bluesy after-hours groove. With this album, Dylan effectively fused his folk-based sensibility to R&B, to create a rock-based music that went way beyond the traditional forms of Chuck Berry, The Beach Boys and even The Beatles.

However, Dylan's folk disciples were looking on aghast like jilted lovers, and the inevitable split finally came at July's Newport Folk Festival midway

through the HIGHWAY 61 sessions. Dylan came on stage with band in tow and proceeded to blow at maximum volume; large sections of the crowd booed vehemently, either because of his new music, the poor sound, the deliberately in-your-face performance, or maybe just because of the loud shirt. Whatever, it crystallized the folk movement's unease with the new Dylan and the jeering continued throughout his ensuing national tour with Canadian rockers The Hawks (later to become The Band). Dylan responded within four days of Newport with the supremely venomous "Positively Fourth Street" single. Bile has never sounded so good.

Dylan was now on a roll and only a few months later was back in the studio recording a new double album with an army of seasoned pros. The result was another *tour de force*, BLONDE ON BLONDE (1966), which pushed beyond HIGHWAY 61 to wilder streams of surrealist imagery, backed by superb band performances. This album defined 'the thin, wild mercury sound' that Dylan later claimed he was always seeking, the sound of staying up all night on coffee and ciggies. But the strain was again beginning to tell, with Dylan booked on to a punishing tour schedule and obliged to produce further albums, a book and another film, the legendary *Eat The Document*. His 1966 world tour with The Hawks exposed him to more hostile audiences, including the notorious 'Judas!' evening at the Manchester Free Trade Hall, and the accompanying tour madness once again left him drained. He had to get off the treadmill, and a convenient motorcycle accident in July 1966 provided the perfect excuse. Under the pretext of recuperation, he scrapped all commitments and dropped out of dropping out for eighteen months.

While his absence fuelled the mystique, Dylan was using his freedom to attend to his young family and chill out with The Band in the rural isolation of Woodstock. Tapes of these sessions were frequently bootlegged at the time, but didn't appear formally until 1975, as THE BASEMENT TAPES, an engaging collection of country-styled songs and fragments, including the original "This Wheel's On Fire" and the aptly named "Nothing Was Delivered". They form the missing link between BLONDE ON BLONDE and his comeback album, JOHN WESLEY HARDING, released in 1968. Though it raised eyebrows at the time, this album in its own quiet way was easily the equal of any of his earlier works. Dark, mysterious and laden with biblical imagery, it had a strong acoustic flavour, on material that varied from "I'll Be Your Baby Tonight" to the brooding enigma of "All Along The Watchtower". With the Band's MUSIC FROM BIG PINK (named after the house where THE BASEMENT TAPES had been recorded), it started the trend away from the psychedelic excesses of the mid-60s to a more rootsy country-rock style.

Dylan got even more C&W with his next album, NASHVILLE SKYLINE, which featured a duet with Johnny Cash. Yet, despite the sublime "Lay, Lady, Lay", it showed a marked decline in intensity that continued with a run of lacklustre albums, which varied from the boring to the unlistenable. Though still accepted universally as one of rock's elder statesmen, it seemed that Bob had lost it big time; or, as some critics suggested, was even deliberately trying to deconstruct his own myth.

Luckily, artistic resurrection was just around the corner, but it took the slow collapse of his marriage to get the creative juices flowing again. The first stirring was his film soundtrack for Sam Peckinpah's *Pat Garrett And Billy The Kid*. As well as contributing a memorable screen appearance as a drifter called Alias, he also wrote his finest song in ages with the elegiac "Knockin' On Heaven's Door". This was merely a taster for the thoroughgoing excellence of his best mature album, BLOOD ON THE TRACKS, released in January 1975. A masterpiece from end to end, it was packed with bittersweet observations from the eye of an emotional hurricane. Unlike most of the contemporary singer-songwriter turns, the songs on this album are supremely honest and direct, with no hint of self-pity. Dylan followed up with DESIRE, another batch of great songs about everything from an allegedly wrongfully imprisoned boxer, "Hurricane", to the grave-robbing shaggy dog story of "Isis" – and that was just the first two tracks. He also embarked on the famed 'Rolling Thunder' tour, a travelling circus of musicians and retainers that careered round the States like some hard-drinkin' rock'n'roll medicine show. Some of the magic was captured on the tour film, *Renaldo & Clara*, but, at getting on for four hours long, it had much of the excess too.

It was to be Dylan's last truly fertile period. 1978's STREET LEGAL was a fair collection, but seemed earthbound compared to the dizzying romanticism of DESIRE. And the call-and-response gospel stylings of the album prefigured a disastrous conversion to Christianity the following year. Being born again may have been good for Dylan's soul but it wrecked his muse, as a series of less than ecstatic evangelical albums were to prove. He spent most of the 80s in credibility limbo, but a pairing with hip producer Daniel Lanois in 1989 went some way towards restoring the faith of the discouraged. Lanois had produced the excellent Neville Brothers album YELLOW MOON, which featured spectacular reworkings of two Dylan songs from THE TIMES THEY ARE A-CHANGIN'. He scattered the same star dust over OH MERCY, Dylan's best collection in ages. Tasteful backings and plenty of studio trickery give Dylan's intriguing ruminations on failure and world weariness an extra edge. Sadly, he chose to follow up with two dismal acoustic collections that showcased an improved finger-picking style but also the deficiencies in his increasingly cracked and tired voice. It seems that unlike, say, Neil Young or Van Morrison, he has been unable to find a credible persona for changing times.

As a result, the most interesting Dylan item of recent years has been THE BOOTLEG SERIES, a thoughtful trawl through his massive back catalogue of unreleased songs and alternative performances. Apparently, there's plenty more in the vaults and more volumes are eagerly awaited. However, the biggest surprise of late was "Dignity", a thoughtful arrangement with a truly committed vocal, which was an unreleased song included on a 'best-of' album. More recent releases, however, have tended to be less than inspiring; 1997's TIME OUT OF MIND proved to be an exception and demonstrated that the old folky cannot yet be written off.

For what it's worth, the album earned him three *Grammy* awards, a fate also shared by its immediate successor, LOVE & THEFT (2001). If anything the latter was more deserving of the accolades. Without a doubt his best set for years, it was a looser, easier, more vibrant collection of ruminations on love, life and mortality. One could even have gone as far as to say Dylan sounded 'fresh'.

While two good albums in a row is perhaps too little to announce a full-scale reinvention, we can still live in hope.

⊙ The Times They Are A-Changin' (1964; CBS).
Ultra-bleak dust-bowl blues, with gritty cover to match. Contains some of his most directly political material alongside songs of plain desperation. It's hard to get more desolate than "North Country Blues" and "The Ballad Of Hollis Brown".

⊙ Bringing It All Back Home (1965; CBS).
A masterpiece that showcases both sides of the Dylan muse. The amped-up psycho-vomit of "Subterranean Homesick Blues" clears the folkies from the decks, but even the newly electrified Dylan cannot overshadow an acoustic side that starts with "Mr. Tambourine Man" and journeys through the wasteland of "Gates Of Eden" and "It's Alright Ma (I'm Only Bleeding)" to the broken dream of "It's All Over Now, Baby Blue".

⊙ Highway 61 Revisited (1965; CBS).
Consistent brilliance from a man at the peak of his powers, and with the band to match. Arguably the best Bob Dylan album ever, bookended by "Like A Rolling Stone" and "Desolation Row".

⊙ Blonde On Blonde (1966; CBS).
Though Dylan is slightly stretched on some tracks, this is a sonic universe all of its own, where classic tracks like "Visions Of Johanna" and "Just Like A Woman" pass by in an amphetamine rush of dazzling music and imagery.

⊙ John Wesley Harding (1968; CBS).
A quietly mysterious work, packed full of obscure religious imagery (there are allegedly 61 Bible references in total). The laid-back rootsy arrangements disguise songs of unusual depth and complexity – just compare the deadpan of the original "All Along The Watchtower" to the hysterical Hendrix freakout.

⊙ Blood On The Tracks (1975; CBS).
The classic divorce album, where beautiful music and poetic lyrics cloak the heartfelt emotion of Dylan's anguish. Songs like "Idiot Wind", "Shelter From The Storm" and "Tangled Up In Blue" add up to his best 70s excursion.

⊙ Desire (1975; CBS).
A wayward Tarot pack of an album, with "Romance In Durango", "Isis" and "Hurricane" standing out in the Major Arcana. His last truly great long player?

⊙ Oh Mercy (1989; CBS).
The best of his recent outings, given a trendy, atmospheric sheen by ambient producer Daniel Lanois. The songs may lack the violent inspiration of his earlier works, but "Man In The Long Black Coat" and "Everything Is Broken" harbour ghostly flickers of genius.

⊙ Love & Theft (2001; CBS).
A sparkling set that finds Lanois back at the controls, and Dylan howling like a man possessed.

Iain Smith

E

THE EAGLES

Formed Los Angeles, 1971; disbanded 1982; briefly re-formed 1994.

The Eagles – one of the biggest-selling of all 70s rock groups – were born out of Linda Ronstadt's backing group, and took their musical cue from The Byrds and Gram Parsons, creating yearning rock ballads with countrified harmonies. Although denigrated as AOR conservatives by the end of the decade, they were as hip as anyone around when they set out, and, judged on an album like DESPERADO rather than their all too-globally familiar mega-seller, HOTEL CALIFORNIA, their success seems pretty much deserved.

Bernie Leadon (vocals/guitar/banjo) was the shaping influence on the band's sound. Having previously played bluegrass with Chris Hillman (before Hillman joined The Byrds), Leadon had gone on to play country-rock in The Flying Burrito Brothers with former Byrds Gene Clark and Gram Parsons. Meantime, **Glenn Frey** (vocals/guitar) had recorded with J. D. Souther under the name Longbranch Pennywhistle, **Don Henley** (vocals/drums) was previously a member of Shiloh, while **Randy Meisner** had been a founder member of Poco before playing in Rick Nelson's backing band.

Signed to the newly launched Warners subsidiary, Asylum, they cut their eponymous debut LP in London with Faces producer, Glyn Johns. THE EAGLES (1972) went gold and featured three US Top 30 singles, most memorably "Take It Easy", written by Frey and Jackson Browne. This was followed in 1973 by the concept LP DESPERADO, on which the group drew parallels between bandits such as Bill Doolin and the modern-day Western desperado, the rock star. Arguably their finest hour, it introduced the standards "Tequila Sunrise" and "Desperado", soon to be covered by Judy Collins.

For ON THE BORDER (1974), Johns was replaced by B. B. King and J. Geils Band producer Bill Szymczyk, while the studio sound was fleshed out with the help of session guitarist **Don Felder**. This new, slightly harder-edged sound gave The Eagles their mainstream breakthrough. The album went platinum in America and contained the US #1, the lilting ballad, "Best Of My Love". The European and British market was cracked with ONE OF THESE NIGHTS (1975), including the hit single "Take It To The Limit".

With the departure of founder member Leadon for a career of solo and session work, and the recruit-ment of **JOE WALSH** (guitar/vocals), HOTEL CALIFORNIA (1976) completed The Eagles' transition from soft country to a harder, more electric main-stream rock sound. Its songs were mostly downbeat tales about coping with LA's rock-star lifestyle, but its title track, portraying California as a hedonistic prison, hit #1 in the US, as did "New Kid In Town" (written with J. D. Souther).

Meisner left for a solo career in 1977, and was replaced by **Timothy B. Schmit** (bass), who had previously succeeded him in Poco. **Joe Vitale** (keyboards) also joined for THE LONG RUN (1979), but despite another massive American hit with "Heartache Tonight" the LP was generally felt to be a disappointment. Following the obligatory live LP, EAGLES LIVE (1980), the disillusioned band officially split in 1982.

All the main ex-Eagles went on to pursue solo careers, most successfully Frey, whose singles "The Heat Is On" and "Smuggler's Blues" were hits on both sides of the Atlantic in 1985, while his LPs included THE ALLNIGHTER (1984) and SOUL SEARCHIN' (1988). Meanwhile, Henley had teamed up with Stevie Nicks on the 1981 single "Leather And Lace", before enjoying huge solo hits with "Dirty Laundry" (1982), "The Boys Of Summer" and "All She Wants To Do Is Dance" (both 1985), and the top-selling album, THE END OF THE INNOCENCE (1989). The appeal of The Eagles didn't dissolve with their break-up. Their back catalogue continued to sell throughout the 80s and 90s, and a one-off reunion between Frey and Henley on an MTV 'Unplugged' session in 1994 led to the release

of HELL FREEZES OVER (1994). This mixture of new material and rerecordings of old favourites unexpectedly returned them to the top of the US charts.

In 2000, just in time for Christmas, the box-set EAGLES SELECTED WORKS 1972-1999 was issued. This mammoth document pulled together the best of their career's work, topped off with a live recording from New Year's Eve 1999. The Eagles are now among the biggest selling artists of all time, they still tour and seem to be built to last.

- **Desperado** (1973; Asylum).
  An ambitious project, released at a time when concept albums were becoming increasingly ridiculous. Yet this well and truly established the group as leaders within their field, and the title track still soothes.

- **Hotel California** (1976; Asylum).
  The obvious choice. As well as appearing in many people's 'all-time greatest albums' lists, this set shifted nine million copies in its year of release.

- **Very Best Of The Eagles** (2001; Elektra).
  Impressive, no-frills collection containing all of their most enduring songs.

Michael Sumsion

STEVE EARLE

Born Fort Monroe, Virginia, 1955.

When Bobby Fuller wrote "I Fought The Law", he could have been penning an early biography of **Steve Earle**, the living model of the outlaw minstrel. Earle has had more than his fair share of run-ins with authority, but by his early teens was as handy with a Gibson guitar as he was with his fists. He frequented the clubs and bars of Dallas, mixing and picking with the local blues and country nobility, and became a protégé of the team of Texan songwriters headed by Guy Clark.

The struggling songwriter managed to acquire a number of publishing deals but, even though his work was acknowledged by Elvis Presley and recorded by Carl Perkins, he was forced to take day jobs to support his lifestyle and a succession of broken marriages. A small part in Robert Altman's film *Nashville* took him to Hollywood, but the magic of Tinseltown was not to last and he was soon back in Texas where he quipped, 'no one remembered me but the cops'.

1980 saw Earle back in the musical fray with the first incarnation of his group, **The Dukes**. Earle settled in Nashville with his third wife Carol, and parenthood ensured that Earle achieved the kind of stability necessary for progress in the music industry. With backing from his new publishers, Dea and Clark, he released an EP, and Nashville music journalist John Lomax soon became his manager, convincing Epic Records that they should buy the rights to this young rebel's songs. Unfortunately, Epic missed the point by a country mile, and in 1983 planted Earle in a studio, demanding material in an updated Gene Vincent style. Earle countered that he was more hillbilly than rockabilly, but Epic persisted

for two more years before both sides agreed to part.

With the arrival of the so-called New Country movement in 1985, Nashville A&R men were hot on the trail of the next Dwight Yoakam. MCA's Tony Brown, responsible for signing Lyle Lovett and Nanci Griffith, was first to get Earle to sign on the dotted line, and Earle's debut album, GUITAR TOWN (1986), set about reviving the tradition of dust-bowl folk, and dealing with injustices against the working man and the plight of minority groups. A high point was the country hit "Good Ol' Boy (Gettin' Tough)", a response to President Reagan's firing of air-traffic controllers during their mid-80s strikes.

The follow-up, EXIT O (1987), included more songs in a country vein, like the Farm Aid benefit number, "Rain Came Down", and gave little warning of the hard rock direction on the benchmark album COPPERHEAD ROAD (1988), which secured international recognition thanks to collaborations with The Pogues and Maria McKee. Earle set his sights on Europe, putting the band on the road for an arduous world tour.

Much of the remainder of the 80s was spent in Britain, where a rock audience warmed to Earle's new biker-with-a-heart image, especially in the Irish quarter of London, and in Belfast in Northern Ireland, where he worked with Energy Orchard. But Earle was living life to bacchanalian extremes, and his gruelling tour schedule was about to take its toll. Sensing signs of a depleted talent, MCA announced that, after THE HARD WAY (1990), they were only prepared to back him for one more album of live material.

The Dukes disbanded and Earle entered his wilderness years, occasionally surfacing for some remarkable acoustic shows in which he displayed a Dylanesque ability to reinterpret his own songs while also doing justice to tunes by his heroes from the Dallas days. Hunger for success led him to audition for the re-formed Lynyrd Skynyrd but, having managed to survive the 70s drugs scene, they were reluctant to take Earle and his drug dependency on board.

Finally, in 1994, he gave himself up to the police, pleading guilty to drugs charges, but although he was sentenced to a year in jail, he was later transferred to a detox centre where he received treatment for his methadone addiction. Out on probation in 1995, Earle released his first album in five years. An acoustic mixture of old and new material, TRAIN A-COMIN' was a remarkable return to form, which quickly topped the UK country charts, and showed he could not be written off yet awhile. His revival continued apace in 1996 with the release of the acclaimed I FEEL ALRIGHT album, and a return to the road with the **Viceroys**.

A succession of European jaunts highlighted the fact that Steve's songs could stand the spotlight on their own (notably acoustic triumphs at the Cambridge Folk Festival and on a tour where he was accompanied by his son), as well as the full band treatment from Buddy Miller and Brady Blades. In 1998 Earle retreated to Galway to work on new lyrics, maintaining his public profile with songs on the soundtracks to films such as *The Horse Whisperer* and *Psycho*. He continued to offer his services as producer to up-and-coming players on the Americana scene, as well as established artists like Lucinda Williams. The latter's most accomplished album to date, CAR WHEELS ON A GRAVEL ROAD, was produced by Twangtrust (co-conspirators Mr Earle and Ray Kennedy).

1999 saw the release of a bluegrass-flavoured album, THE MOUNTAIN, where Earle linked up with the **Del McCroury Band**. He was also heard on a tribute to Johnny Cash, DON'T TAKE YOUR GUNS TO TOWN, and harmonizing with his sister Stacey on her SIMPLE GEARLE album.

In 2000 Earle gathered his current edition of The Dukes for TRANSCENDENTAL BLUES. With songs informed by the Beatles and Springsteen as well as traditional Irish music, this multifarious album concluded with "Over Yonder (Jonathan's Song)", a tender, unflinching piece written for Jonathan Nobles, a victim of America's electric chair who Earle got to know through his work with anti-capital punishment groups. In addition to running the E-Squared record label, Earle now spends his scant non-musical (and non-activist) hours penning fiction – a collection of short stories, *Doghouse Roses*, was published in 2001, while 2002 saw the release of the SIDETRACKS CD, a collection of rare cuts and soundtrack contributions.

⊙ **Copperhead Road** (1988; MCA).
Few artists would betray the comfortable success of early albums in favour of a completely new sound – but then nobody ever accused Steve Earle of being predictable. From the opening pipelike drone of the title track, you know only to expect the unexpected. Tales of drug-running and Vietnam veterans gone astray show Earle's superb talent for storytelling.

⊙ **The Hard Way** (1990; MCA).
A musical continuation of COPPERHEAD ROAD, but the lyrical content is possibly even more potent: the spartan arrangement of the Death Row lament, "Billy Austin", would not have seemed out of place on Bruce Springsteen's NEBRASKA.

⊙ **Train A-Comin'** (1995; Winter Harvest).
Steve Earle's acoustic album, and his most credible to date, recorded with some of the greatest session players in Nashville – among them fiddler Norman Blake and Emmylou Harris.

⊙ **I Feel Alright** (1996; Warners).
Earle at his strongest, hardest and most brutally honest. From the evilly-accurate "CCKMP" ("Cocaine Cannot Kill My Pain") to the portrait of delinquency that is "Billie And Bonnie" to the departed love of "Now She's Gone", Earle declines to hold back and the power of his music blazes through.

Stephen Boyd

EASYBEATS

Formed Sydney, Australia, 1964.

Australia's postwar immigration boom saw many teenagers dragged out of Europe by parents hopeful of a new life. Potential stars to land in the migrant camps of Sydney in the late 50s included the likes of Barry, Robin and Maurice Gibb (later, sadly, to form the Bee Gees) and the guitar-playing **Young** brothers from Glasgow. Oldest brother **George** in the (southern) winter of 1964 soon linked up with fellow émigrés **Snowy Fleet** (drums) and **Harry Vanda** (guitar) from Holland, and **Dick Diamonde** (bass) and vocalist **Steven (Little Stevie) Wright** from England. Playing at suburban dances, the **Easybeats'** first gigs were often unpaid but their talent for composing high-quality originals soon drew the attention of manager Mike Vaughan, who sorted them out a deal with EMI. The band owed an obvious debt to the 'beat music' coming out of the UK at the time and comparisons can easily be drawn between their back-of-a-cigarette-packet sketches and those of The Kinks and The Small Faces in Britain.

Their earliest records were for Albert Productions and released on the Parlophone label. This proved to be a bit of a mixed blessing since Parlophone had no facility for marketing or the promotion of local records, and artists and managers were obliged to do it all themselves – visiting radio stations, glad-handing the DJs and handing out the records to get some airplay. A further stumbling block was the Sydney–Melbourne rivalry, which meant that Melbourne DJs would rarely play records by Sydney bands (and vice versa), with national Top 40 charts being meaningless as a result. The Easybeats' first single, "For My Woman/Say That You're Mine", sold few copies initially but their second, "She's So Fine/Old Oak Tree" hit #1 in the national charts in June 1965. The resulting interest in the band dragged their previous single up to #5 and they had two more hit singles before the end of that year including the manic one minute and fifty-eight seconds of "Wedding Ring".

The band made it big in Australia in 1966 with a series of regular TV appearances and two more Top 10 hits and two hit albums before leaving home for England in July. Their first English studio sessions proved to be the high point of their recording career, delivering the singles: "I'll Make You Happy" (#7 in Australia), "Sorry" (#1) and finally, the timeless Mod classic "Friday On My Mind" (#1), which broke the band internationally, reaching #6 in the British charts and, in 1967, #16 in the US. International tours followed. Back in Australia, original drummer Snowy Fleet was replaced by **Tony Cahill** and another six Top 40 hits followed in the next two years. Only "Hello, How Are You?", however, had any international success, reaching #20 in the British charts.

By 1969 the momentum had ebbed away and following a last local mega-hit, "Show Me The Way To St. Louis", the band split amicably. Vanda and Young stayed on with Albert Productions forming a production team that is still churning out local hits today, including some which they performed themselves as Flash And The Pan. They also helped two of George's younger brothers, Malcolm and Angus, form the next Australian superstar band, AC/DC. Cahill returned to England and Python Lee Jackson, Diamonde went to manage a pub in Brisbane and Wright continued with a solo career, having local success throughout the 70s. He was still performing in 1986 when The Easybeats re-formed for one more Australian tour that sold out every venue. Wright's story, however, has a less than happy ending: when last heard of he was living in a rented caravan in outer Sydney, forgotten, forlorn, and messed up.

⊙ **It's2Easy** (1966; Parlophone; reissued 1992). Again a fine studio album boosted to a satisfying plumpness with choice bonus tracks. A must for all Australian-guitar-pop fans.

⊙ **Friday On My Mind** (1967; Parlophone; reissued 1992). Buy this for the title track alone. The other eleven original tracks (now sixteen with the CD bonuses) are all groovy 60s rockers and worth a listen, but it's the title track that made the band heroes for anyone who's ever slaved in a hateful dead-end job.

Pierce Morgan

ECHO AND THE BUNNYMEN

Formed Liverpool, 1978;
defunct from 1992 to 1997.

"I know we're the best group in the world." Ian McCulloch

When **Echo And The Bunnymen** formed in Liverpool in November 1978, most people assumed Echo was the name of their singer. In fact it was the three-piece group's drum machine. Scouse schoolfriends **Will Sergeant** and **Les Pattinson** had met **Ian ('Mac') McCulloch** at Liverpool's Eric's club, where all had been members of groups with like-minded punks like Pete Wylie and Julian Cope. The hastily formed Echo And The Bunnymen played their first gig at Eric's as support to The Teardrop Explodes, with whom they were managed and recorded by Bill Drummond (later of the KLF) and his Zoo company. Their first release, "Pictures On My Wall", backed with the Cope co-written "Read It In Books", was released on Zoo in March 1979, and exhibited a frail semi-acoustic charm that bore no hint of what was to come.

Later that year, Echo was made redundant when **Pete de Freitas**, a public schoolboy from down south, joined as drummer. The band signed to WEA subsidiary Korova and its ramshackle sound grew quickly more aggressive. The Bunnymen's first single for the label, "Rescue", was released the following spring and followed by their debut album CROCODILES (1980), which made the UK Top 20. Now a fully fledged rock band, the Bunnymen were soon established as post-punk leaders, helped by McCulloch's ego-fuelled mouth, a powerful live reputation, and Drummond's wacky ideas about touring (camouflage chic, gigs in Iceland and 1984's madcap

'Crystal Day' in Liverpool). The band played as big as they talked, and their combination of melodrama and melody was rarely bettered by those they influenced. Along with Manchester counterparts Joy Division, they unwittingly set off a whole generation of doomy youth sporting long raincoats, big hair and carefully cultivated angst. And Mac's sex-symbol looks gave them extra credibility as pop stars.

The single "The Cutter" (1983) made the Top 10 in Britain and the US. The albums – the epic HEAVEN UP HERE (1981), the difficult yet powerful PORCUPINE (1983), and the masterful OCEAN RAIN (1984) – also charted Top 10 in Britain. But the band, whose eccentric, enigmatic image was not just music-biz hype, were never quite comfortable with their success and, while the Bunnymen-influenced U2 happily pursued world domination, they took a sabbatical from recording during 1984–85, a period in which WEA released the compilation album SONGS TO LEARN AND SING and Mac recorded a solo single, "September Song".

In 1986 Pete de Freitas abruptly left and headed to New Orleans, where he formed his own band, **The Sex Gods**. He was to rejoin the Bunnymen later that year while The Sex Gods (later renamed Balcony Dogs) continued without him. Echo And The Bunnymen continued, releasing their final (self-titled) album in 1987 and having a few more hits; the 1988 single, The Doors song "People Are Strange", from the soundtrack of *The Lost Boys*, went Top 40 in the

The Bunnymen's McCulloch – rarely seen onstage without a ciggie

E A S Y B E A T S ▪ E C H O   A N D   T H E   B U N N Y M E N

ANDREW CATLIN/SIN

UK, and again in 1991, when it was reissued for the UK TV showing of the film.

On April 26, 1988, the Bunnymen played their last gig: after months of rumours, Mac announced that he was leaving, on the eve of the group's tenth anniversary. To his surprise, the rest of the band decided to continue without him, keeping the name, but in June 1989, as they were auditioning singers, Pete de Freitas was killed in a motorcycle accident. The tragedy made itself felt in Mac's first solo LP, CANDLELAND (1989), a more personal work than the previous Echo And The Bunnymen material, while his former colleagues, now joined by singer **Noel Burke**, keyboard player **Jake Brockman** and drummer **Damon Reece**, released REVERBERATION (1990), an album that gave full rein to Will's psychedelic influences. Dropped by WEA, they set up their own label, Euphoric, and released the defiantly named single "Prove Me Wrong" in 1992, the same year that Mac released his second solo album, MYSTERIOSO.

Things went quiet from the Bunnymen after that, although Will, following the experimental leanings of his 1983 instrumental album THEMES FOR GRIND, surfaced occasionally incognito with ambient material – in the guise of **Glide**. Will and Mac were reunited in a new band, **Electrafixion**, and released an album, BURNED, in 1995, which received mixed reviews.

EVERGREEN (1997), by a re-formed Bunnymen with a 'proper' line-up came as a bit of a shock. The Bunnies' spooky sound no longer resounded with the atmosphere of deserted streets and lonely shopping malls, but was still recognizably their own – McCulloch's crooning cigarette-wracked voice over guitar and drums beamed in from another planet. Eminently disturbing and as compelling as a car crash, the Bunnymen were back.

The band's second coming was set in stone by 1999's WHAT ARE YOU GOING TO DO WITH YOUR LIFE?, and then in 2001, FLOWERS. Though the first of these two collections was a little gushing and overall disappointing, FLOWERS marked the haunting return of the classic Bunnies' sound, tweaked and polished for the new millennium. 2002 brought the release of LIVE IN LIVERPOOL, recorded the previous year. The set was, remarkably, the first official live Bunnies album, and with "Killing Moon" and "Seven Seas" among its tracks, it offered itself as a viable alternative to one of the regular 'greatest hits' packages in the shops. The band have since toured extensively with a line-up of Ian McCulloch, Will Sergeant, **Vinny Jamieson** (drums), **Ceri James** (keyboards), **Ged Malley** (guitar) and **Pete Wilkinson** (bass). Most recently McCulloch took another sabbatical for the 2003 solo release SLIDELING.

⊙ **Crocodiles** (1980; Korova/WEA).
A brilliant debut. There is toughness and tension on this record, and immense self-assurance. At the time it sounded astonishingly fresh; certainly it shows the band at their best, poised between early sensitivity and later melodrama. It also gives a hint of where U2 got their best ideas.

⊙ **Ocean Rain** (1984; Korova/WEA).
Orchestrated and ornamental; but, in contrast to the overkill of HEAVEN UP HERE and PORCUPINE, this has a feeling of understatement that harks back to the band's early days. A lighter touch is reflected in lyrics that are sometimes humorous, and at other times meaningless. Includes three hit singles: "The Killing Moon", "Silver" and "Seven Seas".

⊙ **Songs to Learn and Sing** (1985; Sire).
All the Korova A-sides in their original singles version, from "Rescue" to "Bring On The Dancing Horses". The closest thing to a real 'best of'.

⊙ **Ballyhoo – The Best Of Echo And The Bunnymen** (1997; WEA).
Ah, but this is a real 'best of' compilation. Recommended.

⊙ **Crystal Days 1979-1999** (2001; Rhino).
A mammoth box-set of rarities, B-sides, Peel session cuts and the like. One for the fans.

Penny Kiley

ECHOBELLY

Formed London, 1992.

As the American grunge influence neared saturation point in the early 90s, Britain responded with a flurry of activity at the grass-roots level. **Echobelly**, led by Anglo–Asian singer/writer **Sonya Aurora Madan**, were one of a package of bands (Suede and Elastica were others) who mixed attitude with power pop, establishing their credentials with a debut EP, BELLYACHE (1993), featuring powerful songs like "Give Her A Gun" and "Sleeping Hitler".

Live, too, Echobelly carried it off. Madan and **Debbie Smith** (guitar) had considerable presence, while Swedish co-writer **Glenn Johansson** (guitar), **Alex Keyser** (bass) and drummer **Andy Henderson** provided an agile wash of sound. The band were depicted by the music press as representing a new constituency that embraced women, gays (Smith is an out lesbian) and ethnic minorities, and Madan and Smith became alternative pin-ups, their opinions eagerly sought on just about every issue possible. Morrissey declared them his favourite band, and Echobelly's next singles "Insomniac" and "I Can't Imagine The World Without Me" continued the momentum. Their first album, EVERYONE'S GOT ONE, made the Top 10 in Britain.

The album, with its apposite acronym, EGO, was a fine debut. Songs like "Call Me Names" and "Father, Ruler, King, Computer" (a title culled from a piece by feminist Germaine Greer) encapsulated the band's fierce, punky, live-and-let-live attitude. Echobelly wore their politics on their sleeve. Continued gigging gained them high-profile fans, including R.E.M.'s Peter Buck and Madonna.

EGO's precocious breadth of material was reiterated with their second album, ON (1995). Produced by Sean Slade and Paul Kolderie, fresh from Hole and Radiohead projects, ON accentuated Echobelly's rough edges, its blur of energy tempered by deft writing and, as always, Madan's blend of strength and vulnerability. It peaked at #4 in Britain, and although it was spoken of as representing a swerve towards more poppy terrain, if anything the pop scene had, by then, changed to accommodate Echobelly's spiky, accessible music.

Bassist **James Harris** joined Echobelly in time to record "The World Is Flat" and LUSTRA (1997), their disappointing third album. Smith and Echobelly unexpectedly parted company before either record was released and she is rumoured to be working with former members of Curve and The Mekons; Madan herself had a side-project in a one-off single collaboration with Lithium, "Ride A Rocket' (1997). Echobelly returned to the festival circuit in 1997 and in 2001 released a new album, PEOPLE ARE EXPENSIVE: an uninspiring affair, the product of a band grappling with the onset of rigor mortis.

(•) **Everyone's Got One** (1994; Fauve).
A fine introduction to a band whose best moments were often in concerts. For all the singles' verve, don't ignore the more subtle but equally powerful songs "Call Me Names" and "Cold Feet Warm Heart".

(•) **On** (1995; Fauve).
A bigger album than the debut – more sound, more production, more fun – but its integrity remains untarnished.

(•) **I Can't Imagine the World Without Me** (2001; Sony).
Echobelly's best-of collection shows the group at its best: political, energetic and entertaining.

Louise Gray

ED GEIN'S CAR

Formed New York, 1982; disbanded 1987.

There's always been something a little funny about hardcore punk's unrelenting aggressiveness, but while HC pioneers like Warzone seemed oblivious to that angle, genre weisenheimers such as The Dickies and Murphy's Law positively revelled in it. Songs like the former's cover of "The Sound Of Silence" and the latter's "I Got The Bong" show a healthy sense of humour, but the sarcasm kings of the mid-80s were **Ed Gein's Car**. They seemed to take themselves the least seriously of any genuinely major hardcore ensemble.

Throwing surf, ska and blues licks into their mess, they played the old loudfast with exuberant disregard for 'authenticity' and the usual anti-authoritarian bromides. While other bands sang with strangled sincerity about 'the kids' and their ideals, EGC offered such lofty ideas as "Turning In Your Parents" for smoking pot ('They won't buy me ice cream ... this ain't Stalin's Russia, it's the good old USA/but if they don't get off my back, I'll turn 'em in today'). Hardcore fans got the joke and gave the Car a good ride for about four years.

The band started around 1982 when bassist **Tim Carroll** and guitarist **Eric Hedin**, then students at SUNY, New Paltz, formed a group with the says-it-all name Deadhead Assassins. They were quickly banned from every bar in town and moved to New York, where they linked up with a series of drummers and, most importantly, a wise-guy bicycle messenger named **Scott Weiss**, who became the snide soul of Ed Gein's Car, strolling slumped and shaven-headed around the stage in boxing trunks, T-shirt and sandals and rasping out the jacked-up tunes.

The band issued a single, "Brain Dead", in 1984, and followed up with a self-produced album,

MAKING DICK DANCE, which helped lift their profile considerably. They started selling out CBGBs and touring, tightening their stage-show, which is evident in their live CB's LP, YOU LIGHT UP MY LIVER, and on their contribution to ROIR's SCUM ROCK LIVE AT CBGB tape, "A Girl Just Like You", the band's noblest achievement ('I want a girl with a little class/I want a girl who can kick my ass').

Unfortunately the band really was serious about not taking things seriously, and proved it by disbanding around 1987. Scott Weiss carried the joke-rock torch a while longer as lead singer of **Iron Prostate** ('Loud, Fast, and Aging Rapidly', with *Rolling Stone* critic Charles M. Young on bass), and then became a painter. What remains? For some of us, fond memories; for bands like Green Day and The Offspring, proof that they didn't think of it first.

(•) **You Light Up My Liver** (1987; CBGB/Celluloid).
Wisecracks, power chords, bad sound. Fast/funny rules.

Roy Edroso

EDDIE AND THE HOT RODS

Formed Canvey Island, England, 1975; disbanded 1981; re-formed 1984 & 1995.

Guitarist of **Eddie And The Hot Rods**, **Dave Higgs** had played in a band called The Fix with Lee Brilleaux, Dr. Feelgood's frontman. When the Feelgoods hit the big time, Higgs formed the Hot Rods with bassist **Paul Gray**, **Steve Nicol** on drums, the manic **Lew Lewis** playing harmonica and **Barry Masters** as lead vocalist. The Hot Rods roared out of Canvey Island to hit the pub-rock scene in July 1975, when they secured themselves a gig at Kensington's Nashville Rooms. Their set comprised covers of 60s songs like "Gloria" and Creedence Clearwater Revival's "It Came Out Of The Sky", mixed with Dr. Feelgood-influenced R&B originals, all played at 100mph. The Rods' sheer energy made them stand out from the veterans of the pub-rock scene and they attracted a younger audience. Masters was a fine frontman, adept at winding up a crowd.

They signed to Island and released their first single in 1976, "Writing On The Wall"/"Cruisin' (In The Lincoln)", two originals co-written by Higgs and Ed Hollis. Hollis was a crucial figure for the Hot Rods, managing the band, co-writing much of their material and producing all their best records. The single wasn't the hit Island had hoped for and it was closely followed by a cover of "Wooly Bully" produced by Roxy Music's Andy Mackay and featuring the great man on saxophone. "Horseplay", another Higgs/Hollis collaboration and a stage favourite, was the B-side.

In March 1976 the Rods played The Marquee, supported by a new London band out to make a name for themselves. The two bands fell out, a stack of equipment got trashed and the Sex Pistols grabbed all the headlines. Around this time Lew Lewis was sacked. Prone to letting his enthusiasm get the better of him, he overdid it after one gig supporting The

Kursaal Flyers. He later fronted his own band for a while. The four remaining members then decided to try to capture one of their live sets, returning to The Marquee to do so. The subsequent live EP featured "96 Tears", Bob Seger's "Get Out Of Denver" and a version of "Gloria" that mutates into The Stones' "Satisfaction". For the first time the general public were able to appreciate the Hot Rods sound.

The record reached #45 in the charts and they saw out 1976 by releasing the TEENAGE DEPRESSION (1976) album and the title track as a single. In 1977 a second live EP was released (AT THE SPEED OF SOUND), they played five nights consecutively at The Marquee and took a new member on board. **Graeme Douglas** had been a founder member of The Kursaal Flyers but left due to that old favourite: 'musical differences'. His first gig with the Rods was at London's Rainbow and culminated with the crowd tearing up rows of seats. Liable for the damage, the band made nothing from the gig.

Douglas began writing with the band and eventually turned out their Big One. Based around a riff allegedly stolen from "Born To Run", Douglas and Ed Hollis wrote "Do Anything You Wanna Do", which rose to #9. All of a sudden the boys from Canvey Island were stars.

They headlined at the Reading Festival and toured the States during that year. After LIFE ON THE LINE (1977) became their only UK Top 30 album, they gigged relentlessly and tried to recapture the success of "Do Anything You Wanna Do". Ultimately they failed. THRILLER (1979) was a disappointment, and when Douglas left, the writing was on the wall. Island released a BEST OF... compilation and one album for EMI followed, FISH 'N' CHIPS, before they decided to call it a day.

Barry Masters sang with **The Inmates** for a while and Gray joined **THE DAMNED** and later **UFO**. Masters has twice re-formed the band, in 1984 and 1995, releasing a live LP, ONE STORY TOWN (1985), first time round, and, less forgivably, the rather desperately retro GASOLINE DAYS (1996) with the later incarnation. The band are still touring today, having released another stage set, LIVE AT THE PARADISO, back in 1998.

⊙ **The Best Of Eddie And The Hot Rods** (1994; Island).
The album to go for, including all the hits.

Simon Ives

DUANE EDDY

Born New York, April 26, 1938.

Well before the likes of Hendrix, Clapton, Beck and Page, one of rock's first guitar heroes would be known and loved not for rapid fingering, complicated chord structures or lengthy impassioned solos but for a throbbing, minimalist, rock-steady 'twang'. **Duane Eddy** was born in Corning, New York, in 1938 and by his early teens

had developed an interest in country music and guitar playing, first from singin' cowboy idols Roy Rogers and Gene Autry and later from many guitarists like Chet Atkins and Les Paul. After cutting a demo with some friends he caught the attention of local DJ **LEE HAZLEWOOD** (yes, the same one that worked with Nancy Sinatra). A further demo on Lee's Eb. X Preston label failed, but he finally landed up with a deal with Jamie Records, an indie label from Philadelphia. Although his first song for them, "Movin' N' Groovin'", didn't place high in the charts, Duane gained major attention with his third single, the unforgettable "Rebel Rouser".

"Rebel Rouser", with its hard driving rockabilly beat, raunchy sax and brilliant, moody, rumbling, guitar riff (Duane's 'twang' played on a heavyweight Gretsch 6120), introduced the instrumental single to late 50s rock'n'roll and burned a path in the mind of many a future guitarist. Duane continued his hit streak with unique instrumentals in a variety of styles and moods – the rock'n'roll/rockabilly one-two punch of "Ramrod" and "Cannonball", the slow and cinematic "The Lonely One" and the cool tempo country-blues of "40 Miles Of Bad Road". These singles and the remainder of Duane's output in the late 50s stand tall and proud alongside the material of Elvis, Eddie Cochran, Gene Vincent, The Everly Brothers, Roy Orbison and Buddy Holly from the same period. Lee Hazlewood's production work for Eddy helped build his legend next to other star producers such as Phil Spector, Joe Meek and Sam Phillips. Not surprisingly, Lee would go on to borrow some of Duane's rockabilly cool to add the finishing touch to his work with Nancy Sinatra.

Like other late-50s rock'n'roll stars Eddie Cochran and Gene Vincent, Duane's biggest fame came from overseas. Many British teens picked up guitars in the fallout from "Rebel Rouser" and began trying to copy his style (George Harrison and John Entwistle being two prime examples). By 1960 Duane had beaten Elvis in a *New Musical Express* readers' poll, and an admiration society The Duane Eddy Circle, based in Sheffield, continues to this day.

Duane persevered through the 60s as his popularity slowly declined. He spent most of the decade recording a series of increasingly gimmicky albums such as DUANE EDDY DOES BOB DYLAN, TWISTIN' WITH DUANE, SURFIN' WITH DUANE, and even one inexplicably called WATER SKIING. When not recording those, he delved into his American and country music roots with titles like PLAYS SONGS OF OUR HERITAGE and his personal favourite, 'TWANG' A COUNTRY SONG.

By the late 60s he had practically retired from the music business but resurfaced mainly thanks to continuing British interest. He recorded a syrupy top UK hit, "Play Me Like You Play Your Guitar" in 1975, then in 1986 UK experimental pop group **ART OF NOISE** worked with Duane for a cool yet still gimmicky remake of the theme from the TV show *Peter Gunn*, which went on to become a worldwide hit.

In 1987 he received some return at last on the dues he'd paid, being helped out by Paul McCartney, George Harrison and Jeff Lynne on another cool musical grab-bag LP simply called DUANE EDDY.

Duane's influence continues to make itself felt in the works of Ry Cooder (who has played with Duane in the past) and other guitarists, proving that a cool original can still challenge the fiery work of later guitar gods.

⊙ **Twang Thang – The Duane Eddy Anthology** (1993; Rhino).
An excellent two-disc introduction and currently the only collection on CD. All the hits from "Rebel Rouser" to the "Peter Gunn" remake, plus curiosities like the jazzy "Quiniela" and the country ballad "The Window Up Above". The informative booklet contains personal comments from Duane about the tracks, rare, previously unreleased, photos and a complete discography.

Chris Lark

EELS

Formed Los Angeles, 1995.

A trio who go by their first names only – **E** (guitar/vocals), **Butch** (drums) and **Tommy** (bass) – **Eels** have won a solid following on both sides of the Atlantic for their cultured and densely layered pop, replete with samples, breakbeats and vicarious/hilarious/bilious lyrics: 'Take a left down Echo Park/A kid asks do I want some crack/TV sets are spewing Baywatch through the windows into black'.

The man responsible for those words is E, already a veteran of two solo efforts before forming Eels, and their chief producer and songwriter. The group expansion, he says, was undergone in order to produce a fuller sound, more akin to the music of his hero, Randy Newman. He took his new project to Dreamworks, the label established by movie mogul Steven Spielberg, allegedly so that that he would be able to work with Mo Ostin, the man responsible for signing Prince and Jimi Hendrix. The most immediate critical comparison following the release of BEAUTIFUL FREAK (1997) was with fellow Los Angeles denizen Beck – whose music boasts a similar eclecticism. However, E was resistant to this charge: 'The only similarity is that we're white guys using samples. We're coming from a completely different angle.' That may be the case, but the similarities also extended to the audience Eels draw – a literate, post-modern set dissatisfied with the slacker culture – and there's also the fact that each of E's songs have a heartfelt, personal edge underpinning the humour – very Beck. Whatever, BEAUTIFUL FREAK's neat amalgamation of classic pop, country, rock and hip-hop provided one of the freshest new sounds of 1997.

With 1998's ELECTRO-SHOCK BLUES, the Eels came untethered from spurious comparisons with Beck as E's troubled life found its way more directly into his music. This extraordinary album, which dealt with the deaths of his mother, father and sister, had the potential to be one of the biggest misery fests of

all time, but the results were undeniably life-affirming and it was widely considered one of the albums of the year. Despite the bleakness of the song titles the album even spawned hit singles with "Last Stop: This Town" and "Cancer For The Cure" (which also featured in the film *American Beauty*).

Although it was released in 2000, the sequel, DAISIES OF THE GALAXY, was actually completed less than six months after ELECTRO-SHOCK BLUES. The set was lighter in tone without shedding any of E's uncanny ability to capture life's messy complications; it also saw a collaboration with R.E.M.'s **Peter Buck**, who co-wrote the title track.

SOUL JACKER (2001) turned the singer's vision (and facial hair) more outward; his vignettes captured the richness of the humdrum, while the rock-out moments – downright nasty in "Dog Faced Boy" – were tempered by almost impossible lightness ("Fresh Feeling"). It was the sound of a band that continue to grow with each record.

⊙ **Beautiful Freak** (1997; Dreamworks).
Featuring the ironic "Novocaine For The Soul", this album offers a surprisingly enjoyable halfway house between Nirvana and They Might Be Giants. Best moments? "Manchild", "Susan's House" and the icily sharp lyrics of "Guest List" – 'Are you one of the beautiful people?'

⊙ **Daisies Of The Galaxy** (2000; Dreamworks).
Compared to ELECTRO-SHOCK BLUES this is a light affair, worth the price of entry alone for the wonderful "I Like Birds".

Alex Ogg

EG AND ALICE

Formed London, 1989; disbanded 1992.

"If I write about nice things, I sound like Cliff Richard." Eg White

S omewhat to his chagrin, **Eg White** had been bass player with teen-pop heroes Brother Beyond. In 1989, deciding that he'd had enough of playing other people's songs, he left to write and record his own. Meanwhile, childhood BMX-champion-turned-fashion-model **Alice Temple** (she had starred in a campaign for Joseph) had grown uncomfortable with the modelling lifestyle and, knowing Eg as her elder brother's college friend, heard about his recording project, sat in on the sessions and eventually recorded a number of vocal tracks. When 24 YEARS OF HUNGER (1991) was issued, reviewers compared it to both Prefab Sprout and Prince; though, when questioned about their musical tastes, **Eg And Alice** named Lennon, Traveling Wilburys, Joe Jackson, Joni Mitchell and Curtis Mayfield.

While Q magazine nominated the album as one of 1991's finest, commercial reaction was more muted. Two singles, "Indian" and "Doesn't Mean That Much To Me", missed the charts despite a fair amount of broadcast exposure. Perhaps Eg's songwriting was a little too personal for mainstream acceptance at this stage, but interviews revealed that the duo had ambitions to tour and to make future releases sound less naive.

But there was to be no more from Eg And Alice. In 1992 Alice defected to the US, reportedly in search of grunge. There was a long silence from Eg, before he unexpectedly resurfaced in early 1996 with a solo album, TURN ME ON, I'M A ROCKET MAN, which maintained the high standards of his earlier release – indeed the songs sounded like he'd recorded them five weeks, rather than years, after his last outing – continuing a journey into the complexity of the male psyche.

Eg And Alice

(•) **24 Years Of Hunger** (1991; WEA).
From "Rockets" to "I Wish", a beautiful collection of quality pop music.

Eg

(•) **Turn Me On, I'm A Rocket Man** (1996; WEA).
A welcome return from solo Eg, unveiling his fresh collection of perfectly cut melodic pop songs.

Martin Rowsell

EINSTÜRZENDE NEUBAUTEN

Formed Berlin, Germany, 1980.

The key members of **Einstürzende Neubauten** – **Blixa Bargeld** (vocals/guitar) and **N. U. Unruh** (percussion) – had worked with various members of the Berlin underground music scene before recruiting Hamburg percussionist **F. M. Einheit**. Later joined by bassist **Marc Chung** and teenage guitarist **Alexander von Borsig** (aka Hacke), Einstürzende Neubauten (Collapsing New Buildings) became the pioneers of so-called 'industrial' music.

Fascinated with sound produced from non-musical sources, they set about recording the soundtrack of entropy and the world's descent into chaos. Bargeld's lyrics jarred together images of viruses and star sys-

tems, in an apocalyptic vision that drew on a rich German literary tradition. The approach was unequivocally brutal: for the early single "Thirsty Animal", featuring Rowland Howard and **LYDIA LUNCH**, Bargeld's ribcage was miked up to record the punishing rhythms as Einheit 'played' his body with his fists. Conventional drum kits were rejected in favour of salvaged metal, industrial springs and pneumatic drills. They played the walls of buildings, anticipating the cacophony with which the Berlin Wall would be brought down.

In live performances the band embodied the assault of their music. Bargeld, clad head to toe in leather, displayed a shocking mound of spiked blond hair; Hacke staggered round every inch of the stage, while Unruh and Einheit, laughing gnome and muscled warrior respectively, turned the metallic instruments into violent weapons. The band became notorious in Britain in 1984, when Hacke and Chung, with Genesis P. Orridge and Frank Tovey, performed in "Concerto For Voices And Machinery" in London's Institute for Contemporary Arts. Egged on by the audience, Hacke and Chung decided to see if they could reach one of London's myriad wartime tunnels by cutting through the stage. The management cut the power, and promoters ever since have twitched whenever a drill starts up during a Neubauten concert.

The first album, KOLLAPS (1981), was followed by DURSTIGES TIER and DRAWINGS OF PATIENT O. T. (both 1983), the latter set inspired by the occupational therapy drawings of a schizophrenic patient. Neubauten's popularity broadened with STRATEGIES AGAINST ARCHITECTURE (1984), a collection of singles, and HALF-MAN (1985). They were especially big in Japan, where they toured to great success, and made a video with Sogo Ishi. The B-side of the accompanying single, "Yu-Gang", featured the band at their most whimsical, with a cover version of Lee Hazelwood and Nancy Sinatra's "Sand".

FIVE ON THE OPEN-ENDED RICHTER SCALE (1987) saw Bargeld pen his first song in English, while back home they moved from cultural terrorists to ambassadors: they were West Germany's representatives at the 1986 Montréal Expo and were commissioned to compose for ballet and theatre in Germany.

Though Bargeld contributed scratchy blues guitar to **NICK CAVE AND THE BAD SEEDS**, Einstürzende Neubauten continued to pursue the sonic potential of anything they could lay their hands on: the nursery rhyme-like "Ein Stuhl In Der Holle" on HOUSE OF LIES (1989), for example, was sung over a rhythm of F. M. Einheit and an unidentified young woman tap-dancing. The song itself was based on a medieval German folk song, which, if the liner notes are to be believed, was found by Blixa in a cookbook. At the same time their lyrical content was becoming more politically engaged: the album's entire second half was recorded over a backdrop of riots – this was the year the Wall came down. "Headcleaner", on 1993's TABULA RASA, attacked the resurgence of the extreme Right. ENDE NEU, released in 1996, saw them heading, in a less frenzied way, towards a more introspective mood. Treated as always with snippets of found sound, Einstürzende Neubauten wove tune and rhythm into a series of powerful, expert compositions. A sister release, ENDE NEU REMIXED, appeared the subsequent year, boasting a rather too expected list of rejiggers, among them Kreidler, Alec Empire, Barry Adamson and Jon Spencer.

Though band members were becoming more and more sidelined by solo and collaborative projects, they found time to reunite for SILENCE IS SEXY (2000), a remarkable and surprising exploration of space and hush that built on the ideas laid down by ENDE NEU. This excursion was followed by a third installment of STRATEGIES AGAINST ARCHITECTURE (2001) and a limited edition double live CD, 9-15-2000 BRUSSELS. By this time Bargeld had amicably thrown in his towel with The Bad Seeds, reaffirming his commitment to Neubauten. The group is now an iconic institution of German music with a sound that has slowly drifted from abrasive aggression into a more considered, and occasionally noisy, form of elegance.

⊙ **Strategies Against Architecture** (1984; Mute).
The hard industrial sound on all the early singles and B-sides.

⊙ **2 x 4** (1998; ROIR).
Welcome rerelease for their 1985 classic live album. It still sounds like someone attacking sheets of metal with a pneumatic drill, which is exactly what it is.

⊙ **Silence Is Sexy** (2000; Mute).
Here, power tools and jet engines sit alongside violins and cellos, combining to contrive some quite beautiful music. Blixa Bargeld and company draw from cabaret, folk and rock in their attempt to redefine the song form, in turn leading the album to strange, sometimes contrary, destinations.

Dave Sewell

ELASTICA

Formed London, 1992; disbanded 1998; reformed 1999; disbanded 2001.

Formed by **Justine Frischmann** (vocals/guitar) and **Justin Welch** (drums), **Elastica** were nearly famous for all the wrong reasons. Frischmann, a former architecture student, had been a temporary feature in an early **Suede** line-up, but threw Brett Anderson over for Blur's Damon Albarn. As Suede and Blur became big, Justine's fledgling band attracted just the sort of publicity you'd expect from the worst kind of male journo.

But with **Donna Matthews** and **Annie Holland** joining on guitar and bass, Elastica quickly established themselves with a brittle, high-tempo sound and a collection of short, well-crafted Buzzcocks-influenced songs. "Stutter", the band's debut single for independent label Deceptive, was released in November 1993 and sold out in one day. Elastica were aided considerably by their more or less constant live appearances. Frischmann may not have been a Patti Smith, but her stage persona evoked something of the American singer's androgynous allure; delivering her vocals with a slightly bored insolence, she seemed colder than Echobelly's Sonya Aurora Madan, but had the same confident presence.

The band's second single, "Line Up" (1994), went straight into the Top 20, while its follow-ups – "Connection" (1994) and "Waking Up" (1995) – reiterated Elastica's punk origins, using uncredited lines from Wire's "Three Girl Rumba" and The Stranglers' "No More Heroes" respectively. The record credits were hastily rewritten (The Stranglers now get royalties from "Waking Up"), but it was clear with the release of ELASTICA in March 1995 that the band had sufficient vision and front to carry off even the most blatant retreadings. The album entered the charts at #1, and Elastica spent much of 1995 cracking the US. Line-up changes have inevitably occurred: a keyboard player (Dave Bush, formerly of The Fall) widened their range; Holland left the band in 1995 to be replaced first by Beck's bassist, Abby Travis, then by newcomer Sheila Chipperfield.

Although they played a few festivals following their album release, Elastica were not, as impatient fans noted, fast writers. As the Britpop bubble swelled and finally burst, Elastica disbanded and promptly disappeared off the map.

But this was not the end of the story. By the turn of the new millennium Elastica were back with a new line-up that saw Annie Holland reinstated and the addition of keyboardist **Dave Bush**, guitarist **Paul Jones** (of Linoleum) and keyboardist/vocalist **Mew** (from the band Heave). After what had seemed like an eternity, the group released a follow-up to their 1995 debut, in the form of THE MENACE (2000). Though it didn't achieve the same volume of sales as its predecessor, the set was just as bright and sparky. As well as their own numbers, such as the blinding "Your Arse My Place", the set featured an unforgettable rendition of Trio's 1982 hit "Da Da Da", while **Mark E Smith** popped up on "How He Wrote Elastica Man" to inject a little of his unique brand of magic.

But, sadly, this was not to be the rebirth the band had hoped for: a year of inactivity followed, with reportedly unproductive sessions spent in the studio. In October 2001 a relieved Justine announced that Elastica were to split after the release of a farewell single – a 7"-only release, "The Bitch Don't Work"/"No Good". This time the split was to be for good.

⊙ **Elastica** (1995; Deceptive).
Debut album containing all the singles, including the magnificent "Waking Up". Elastica never let the pace slip for a moment: guitar heaven with vocals by a slightly grumpy angel.

⊙ **The Menace** (2000; Deceptive).
A superb second album that stylistically bends and twists with the input of an expanded line-up. The Menace's charm stems from its rough and ready appearance – a stunningly raw slice of intelligent electro-indie-punk.

⊙ **The Radio One Sessions** (2001; Strange Fruit).
In light of their split, this collection of fast and furious two-minute songs can be seen as an alternative 'best of'. Comprising Radio One evening sessions and sets for John Peel and Mark Radcliffe from 1993 to 1999, there are favourites like "Line Up" and the electric "Waking Up" to remind you what all the fuss was about.

Louise Gray

ELBOW

Formed Bury, England, 1991.

"It's the most sensuous word in the world," utters the nurse as she tenderly treats the crippling scars of Dennis Potter's long-suffering *Singing Detective*. The word, in fact, is **Elbow**, and on discovering the gentle tones of **Guy Garvey** – whose group selected the name from this source – you immediately detect the connection. In the music, there are echoes of Blue Nile or Talk Talk – the better moments of King Crimson, even – but witnessing the guitarist and singer's almost anaesthetized intensity on stage is experience in itself

Garvey, along with affiliates bassist **Pete Turner**, percussionist **Richard Jupp** and guitarist **Mark Potter**, put together Soft, a Bury sixth-form college band, as early as 1991. The group was a Sly Stone-influenced chilled funk act, perhaps living a few years after the fact. A pivotal point creatively was the troop's return to Manchester itself, and the introduction of Mark's brother **Craig Potter**'s distinctive hovering organ tones, which began to drive the newly named Elbow's sound.

While the core of the group earned its crust working at Manchester's fabled Roadhouse venue, the name of Elbow was beginning to be bandied around as the 'next big thing'. But, although "Powder Blue" emerged early in 1998, it was still too soon for a major impact, and their signing to Island records turned out to be a false dawn. According to Garvey, what killed the deal with the recording giants was the band's sabbatical to rural France to write and record. What could have been a potential springboard ended as little more than one long, protracted argument. Elbow didn't really recover: the deals with first Island and then a hastily arranged lifeline with EMI crashed and burned.

Elbow's clean living Guy Garvey

In the event, they were to prove grateful to little-known Manchester independent, Ugly Man, which issued the group's "New Born" as lead track of an EP in August 2000. The track, a ballad that soon became something of a sleeping masterpiece, precipitated long-overdue exposure. A further EP, ANY DAY NOW consolidated Elbow's growing reputation in January 2001. Richard Branson's V2 soon proved keen to take the band on board, and by the end of April 2001, Elbow – extraordinarily and justifiably – had breached first the singles, and then the album Top 40.

When the single "Red" took its place at #36 in the UK, there was little clue as to the impact Elbow's debut album might make just one week later. In a rare moment of prescience and good taste, the British record-buying public sent ASLEEP IN THE BACK straight to #14, at once dissolving a decade of disappointment for the band. A sometimes brooding, sometimes uplifting mix of heart and gut, the album was a gem: a crush of guitars and strings, with monstrous howls released over bursts of manic percussion. Guy Garvey's clarion cries were, as ever, affecting and choked by the pain of his lyrics. His agonized vocal crescendos and wise whispers echoed in the instrumentation, only denser and darker. Featuring evocative newer songs such as live favourite "Coming Second" and revitalized early tracks such as "Powder Blue" (the next single), the set was quickly nominated for a *Mercury Music Prize*.

The start of 2002 saw a *Time Out* magazine award, a Top 20 single in "Asleep In The Back" and a successful tour of the USA. Indeed, the band's 'new born' confidence was such that when Guy Garvey contracted laryngitis in Atlanta, he was happy to sit back, allowing audience members to take the microphone and play 'Elbow Karaoke'.

You may at times be left disorientated by the dynamics of Elbow's sound, but their enraged harmonies and tender sighs offer somewhere to rest your head as well as lose it.

⦿ **Asleep In The Back** (2001; V2).
A decade of backbreaking, tear-stained cultivation yields an awesome crop. Fluttering drums, industrial scrapes and swirling synths layer and tangle into scribbled knots, creating an intriguing balance of pop and experimentation. From Talk Talk to vintage Peter Gabriel, Elbow thieve and weave a dense record which repeatedly compresses more emotional movement into a single song than other bands can deliver in ten.

Jeremy Simmonds

THE ELECTRIC FLAG

Formed Chicago, 1967; disbanded 1969; re-formed briefly 1974.

"The music you listen to becomes the soundtrack of your life." Mike Bloomfield

The Electric Flag were a 'supergroup' formed to combine the raw energy of blues and soul with psychedelic experimentalism. They were also one of the first bands, along with Blood, Sweat And Tears and Chicago, to use a horn section as an integral part of their sound, establishing a genre that has since been much reviled, but at the time was seen as a great innovation.

The group was formed by the legendary Chicago blues guitarist **Mike Bloomfield**, who served an apprenticeship both as a pop musician in Northside ballrooms and in a Southside blues-club house band with Charlie Musselwhite and Big Joe Williams. Still only 19, he began to work as a session man, backing Sleepy John Estes on a 1963 album and playing for a number of labels, notably Columbia, whose artistic director John Hammond signed him to a recording contract, as leader of The Group, with fellow Chicagoan blues enthusiast, songwriter **Nick Gravenites**. Nothing was to come of this, but he was recruited for a session with the newly formed Paul Butterfield Blues Band in early 1965, then made his name as guitarist on the Bob Dylan classic "Like A Rolling Stone" and other tracks on HIGHWAY 61 REVISITED; also at that famous session was keyboard

player Al Kooper, with whom he forged a lasting musical friendship.

Bloomfield later joined the **Butterfield Blues Band** as a full-time member, alongside guitarist **ELVIN BISHOP** who, with powerhouse harpist Paul Butterfield, had played with Howlin' Wolf. Despite their credentials as blues musicians, the group caused untold controversy at the Newport Folk Festival in June 1965, not just for performing on electric instruments, but also for backing Bob Dylan in his first appearance as a rock'n'roll artist. After a couple of albums Bloomfield left the group in early 1967 because its growing success had led to a punishing touring schedule; he suffered from chronic stage fright and insomnia, factors in his long-standing heavy drug dependency.

He wanted to form a band that would take the spotlight away from him and yet allow him to put new musical ideas into practice. While playing a session backing 'blue-eyed soul' singer Mitch Ryder, he linked up with keyboardist **Barry Goldberg** and found an appropriate showman in **Buddy Miles**, a 17-year-old, 300-pound drummer who could also sing. Next, a horn section was found, with **Marcus Doubleday** on trumpet, **Herbie Rich** on alto sax and **Peter Strazza** on tenor; on bass was **Harvey Brooks**, another veteran from HIGHWAY 61. Finally, Bloomfield's old friend Nick Gravenites was given lead vocal duties, and he wrote the group's first single, "Groovin' Is Easy".

The Electric Flag made their live debut at the historic Monterey International Pop Festival in June 1967 and were a big hit, displaying their R&B roots to good effect. Yet their first album, A LONG TIME COMIN', released the following year, also revealed Bloomfield's mastery of a new psychedelic style, on material like the ballad "Sitting In Circles" and the guitar freakout "Another Country". The blend of the traditional and experimental was evident on his score for the classic underground film *The Trip*, which was played by The Flag under the name The American Music Band, the contrast between the homely brass tones and the stinging fretwork being curiously effective for the cinematic subject.

But again Bloomfield could not come to terms with success and he left The Flag to the more ebullient Buddy Miles, who placed more emphasis on the group's soul roots. A second album, ELECTRIC FLAG, was released in 1969, but it was unsuccessful and the band, riven by its members' enthusiasm for unhealthy recreational habits, broke up. In 1974, an attempt to re-form similarly flopped on the misleadingly titled THE BAND KEPT PLAYING, despite the presence of Bloomfield and Gravenites.

Bloomfield regained enough courage to team up with Al Kooper for some live performances, confirming his status as a guitarist of great virtuosity and emotional power. However, he concentrated more on studio work, film scores and teaching. He made some accomplished solo albums, rediscovering the acoustic country-blues style he had played in his youth; his last live performance was as a guest at a Dylan concert in November 1980. In February the following year he was found dead in his car, apparently from an accidental overdose.

Gravenites went on to join **BIG BROTHER & THE HOLDING COMPANY** when Janis Joplin left, then received acclaim as a solo artist; Harvey Brooks played on the seminal BITCHES BREW album by Miles Davis. Buddy Miles teamed up with another ex-Wilson Pickett sideman, Jimi Hendrix, to form the **Band of Gypsies**, after his own **Buddy Miles Express** had initiated a form of psychedelic soul that was to be influential on the funk scene of the 1970s. Apart from a mid-70s stint with Carlos Santana, he did little else, but has recently released work on the Celluloid and Rykodisc labels, as well as appearing with a Hendrix tribute band.

⊙ **A Long Time Comin'** (1968; CBS).
The first and best album by The Flag, on CD reissue with four extra tracks.

Robert E. Murray

THE ELECTRIC PRUNES

Formed Woodland Hills, Los Angeles 1966; disbanded 1969.

Almost every town in mid-60s America had a clutch of teenage garage bands eager to spit out a three-chord thrash infected with cheesy Farfisa organ and topped with angst-ridden vocals. **The Electric Prunes** were just such a band, but one whose musical career took several strange turns.

Their classic line-up spanned 1965–67 and consisted of **Jim Lowe** (vocals), **Ken Williams** (guitar), **James 'Weasel' Spagnola** (guitar), **Mark Tulin** (bass) and **Preston Ritter** (drums). After a first gig in Seattle, Washington (leading to rumours that Seattle was their home town) and scuffling around the LA club circuit for a while, the band signed to Reprise, and in May 1966 a brash single appeared entitled "Ain't It Hard". Success was not immediate, but later that year The Prunes broke the charts with "I Had Too Much To Dream Last Night", a single that narrowly missed the US Top 10 and reached #49 in the UK. A classic of its genre, it featured a freaked-out, fuzz-drenched introduction and Lowe's snarling vocals narrating a psychedelic nightmare that numerous fans could empathize with during the heady excesses of 1967.

The third single, "Get Me To The World On Time" (1967), also enjoyed fair success on both sides of the Atlantic and was an equally effective slice of 60s punk, featuring a shrieking whistle-like sound effect reminiscent of the kind of primitive sonic experimentalism produced by Texas band the 13th Floor Elevators. Then, after recording a cheesy radio advertisement for the Vox wah-wah pedal, The Electric Prunes released their debut album I HAD TOO MUCH TO DREAM LAST NIGHT in April 1967 with most of the tracks by songwriting duo Anette

Tucker and Nancie Mantz. It sold surprisingly poorly but remains a fine document of the underground sound of mid-1960s America, dominated by upbeat buzzsaw guitar-driven punkers and more laid-back psychedelia.

By the time UNDERGROUND (1967) appeared, Lowe and Tulin had been permitted to make a greater contribution to songwriting duties and the music developed a more experimental edge, especially evident on the subtle acid-tinged whimsy of tracks such as "Antique Doll" and "Wind-Up Toys". The old Prunes style was still employed to full effect, however, on the storming "Long Day's Flight" single. Ritter left the band during the UNDERGROUND sessions. He was replaced by Quint, who had drummed in an embryonic version of the group. 1967 also found the departure of Spagnola; his replacement, **Mike Gannon**, was on board when the Prunes launched a European tour. A positively dazzling live performance by this line-up was caught on tape in Stockholm during December 1967, this legendary show finally saw the light of day as a CD in 1997.

In 1968 The Electric Prunes were joined by writer/arranger **David Axelrod**; the result was the ditching of all their previous punk sensibilities, and the bizarre MASS IN F MINOR (1968). A psychedelic excursion based around a Gregorian chant, this album was one of the first incarnations of that dubious genre the 'rock opera'. The opening track, "Kyrie Eleison", was featured in Dennis Hopper's *Easy Rider* in 1969, but this was the beginning of the end for The Electric Prunes. For RELEASE OF AN OATH (1968), there was a completely different line-up led by Dave Hassinger, with John Herren (keyboards), Brett Wade (bass/vocals), Richard Whetstone (drums), Mark Kincaid (guitar) and Ron Morgan (guitar). The crew was new, but the bloated pomposity was the same.

The dreadful JUST GOOD OLD ROCK'N'ROLL (1969) showed that lame bar-room rock was no antidote to the previous albums' pretentiousness. And that was it for the next quarter century. The mid-90s found James Lowe and Mark Tulin getting together to work on a retrospective of 23 classic Prunes tunes, three of which had never been heard before. The album, LOST DREAMS, was released in 2001 on the Birdman label.

Lowe and Tulin then tracked down Ken Williams and second Prunes drummer Quint via the Internet. Sadly, Mike Gannon had passed away several years previously. With the addition of **Peter Lewis** from the legendary Moby Grape, and a host of extras, the most legitimate line-up of the Electric Prunes since late 1967 was set to enter a studio for the first time in three decades. The resulting album, ARTIFACT (2001), was recorded in a garage studio in true analogue style. For the band it was the record that they should have made years ago.

In their original incarnation, The Electric Prunes were undoubtedly one of the true innovators in garage and psychedelic music. While their later more progressive material now sounds ridiculous and dated, the naive charm and energy of their first two albums have withstood the ravages of time.

- **Long Day's Flight** (1986; Edsel; currently unavailable).
  A compilation of early classic material. In San Francisco they may have had flowers in their hair, but in 1966–67 The Electric Prunes had some serious attitude.

- **Stockholm '67** (1997; Heartbeat).
  A punchy live performance from The Prunes' first and only European tour.

- **Lost Dreams** (2000; Birdman Records).
  This compilation boasts tracks that were personally remastered and selected by singer James Lowe. Consequently, this set is *the* definitive Electric Prunes album.

Malcolm Russell

ELECTRONIC

Formed Manchester, England, 1989.

Johnny Marr (ex-**SMITHS**/**THE THE**) and Bernard Sumner (ex-**JOY DIVISION**/**NEW ORDER**) were among the most influential British musicians of the 80s. Smiths songsmith Marr made quality guitar work fashionable again in the mid-80s and inspired people such as Noel Gallagher to start playing. Sumner came from a different background, making electro-techno dance music with New Order. The connection between the two Mancunians came out of Marr's keen interest in New York dance music as played at Manchester's Hacienda Club and his admiration for Sumner's work with New Order. Originally Marr was only to contribute to an intended Sumner solo album, but the two of them got along so well that forming a group together seemed only logical and thus **Electronic** – conceived as a part-time project – was born.

Their first release was a joint effort with **Neil Tennant** of the **PET SHOP BOYS**, "Getting Away With It", a beautifully lush pop tune and a continuation of both New Order's and the Pet Shop Boys' late-80s material. The critically acclaimed debut album ELECTRONIC (1991) came two years later and yielded two singles, including the Top 10 hit "Get The Message". A further single with the Pet Shop Boys, "Disappointed", also made the Top 10.

Electronic was placed on the back burner for a while, while the guys worked on and released albums with their 'full-time' groups. Declaring that Electronic would be their main activity in the future, Marr cut back on his collaborations with all other artists except the Pet Shop Boys.

A further two years of hard work resulted in the second album, RAISE THE PRESSURE (1996). A bit more dance-orientated than its predecessor and with Marr playing more guitar, the album also featured contributions from Kraftwerk's Karl Bartos. Three singles all found their way into the UK Top 40 and the group continued working on new material in preference to extensive touring.

Disappointingly, a third album, TWISTED TENDERNESS (1999) offered little progression from

the duo's dance-rock template. With both Sumner and Marr both involved in full-time bands once more (namely the re-formed New Order and Johnny Marr's Healers, respectively), further Electronic releases are unlikely to appear in the near future.

- **Electronic** (1991; Virgin/Warners).
  With a more open sound than on the debut, this album takes influences from 80s Euro dance music, soul and various guitar influences. Songs that are joyful and sombre at the same time.

Melvin Welters

JOE ELY

Born Amarillo, Texas, 1947.

For a while in the late 70s, against a background of small-venue punks and posing stadium-rockers, **Joe Ely** and his superb band were delighting audiences with good-time Mexican-inflected country ballads, jigs and polkas, blues and rock'n'roll. However, this early distinctive style was sacrificed in the 80s to a scarcely more commercial change of image, as Ely threw on his leather trousers and cranked out heavy-blues chords.

Ely grew up in the windswept west Texas town of Lubbock, home to Buddy Holly And The Crickets, and Delbert McClinton. It was here in 1971, after a brief spell as a solo singer and guitarist, that Ely formed The Flatlanders with Butch Hancock and Jimmie Dale Gilmore. They recorded an album, ONE ROAD MORE, in 1972, but it remained in the vaults until 1980, when the names of the three main members had become more widely known. (It was retitled MORE A LEGEND THAN A BAND for the American market.)

JOE ELY (1977) was to introduce him to an audience beyond the world of Texan clubs and colleges. His band was made up of drummer **Steve Keeton**, bassist **Gregg Wright**, steel guitarist **Lloyd Maines** and guitarist **Jesse Taylor**, soon to be joined by accordionist and pianist **Ponty Bone**, and they were responsible for the equally striking follow-up, HONKY TONK MASQUERADE (1978). Gilmore and, in particular, Hancock, featured among the writing credits. Further studio releases, DOWN ON THE DRAG (1979), MUSTA NOTTA GOTTA LOTTA (1981) and HI-RES (1984), were punctuated by 1980's LIVE SHOTS, recorded at small clubs in London, which encapsulated much of the Ely band's live exuberance. They also toured with Bo Diddley, and in 1981 even supported The Clash.

The change of direction for Ely came in the late 80s, with such releases as LORD OF THE HIGHWAY (1987) and LIVE AT LIBERTY LUNCH (1990). Many of the songs survived from the old days, like Hancock's beautiful "If You Were A Bluebird", but the attitude now was tougher, noisier and less subtle. Now based in Austin, Ely entered the 90s as one of the Texan greats, with influences from neighbouring Mexico and Louisiana permeating his rich musical stew.

Unfortunately, it hasn't made Ely any more of a household name, although a current acceptance of a marriage between country and rock suggests that perhaps his unique strengths could still yet be recognized. His 1995 set, LETTER TO LAREDO, thankfully suggested a return to a more 'unplugged' approach, kicking in with flamenco and steel guitars to fine effect. TWISTIN' IN THE WIND (1998) was consistent, but failed to break new ground.

⊙ **Joe Ely/Honky Tonk Masquerade** (2000; Beat Goes On).
These two records that introduced Ely to a wider audience still sound fresh as a Saturday night.

⊙ **Letter To Laredo** (1995; Transatlantic).
The Spanish-Mexican thread in Texan music unites this recent set, with its distinctive flamenco guitar figures. Many of Ely's former musicians and collaborators make guest appearances, and Bruce Springsteen is among the backing vocalists.

John Collis

EMBRACE

Formed West Yorkshire, England 1993.

Emerging in 1997, just as Britpop's so-called boom was beginning to subside, **Embrace** took the full force of the 'build them up knock them down' tactics favoured by the UK's music press. Described early on by some pundits (and, admittedly, the band members themselves) as the band to succeed Oasis or The Verve as the figureheads of British rock, it was not too long before they were dismissed as underachieving and unimaginative. Unsurprisingly, both readings of the group's output are a little unfair.

In a way, it was hardly remarkable that the press compared the band to Oasis: Embrace favoured epic, mid-tempo anthems; they shunned contemporary influences in favour of classic rock; and most significantly, they were fronted by two brothers whose sheer self-belief quickly became headline news. Whether or not they were trying to ape the Gallaghers – and critics did sometimes attribute their success to Oasis being 'on holiday' – Noel Gallagher himself was said to be a fan, as was Elvis Costello.

Richard McNamara (guitar) was a teenager obsessed with heavy metal, but he broadened his musical palette in his early bands; it wasn't long before his younger brother **Danny** (vocals) was by his side. With the addition of **Steve Firth** (bass) and **Mike Heaton** (drums), they became Embrace in 1993, but success was anything but instant – it was later claimed that record company A&R people could barely contain their laughter at the standard of Danny McNamara's vocals. Yet they began to attract positive reviews from the music press, to the point where a limited-edition 7" single of live favourite "All You Good, Good People", released in February 1997 on Fierce Panda, sold out its pressing of 1200 in a matter of hours. It led to a tour with The Longpigs, a recording contract with Hut, and the release of two EPs, FIREWORKS and ONE BIG FAMILY, both of which entered the British Top 40.

Danny McNamara – that plucker from Embrace

The band were now firmly established; their next singles, a rerecording of "All You Good, Good People", plus "Come Back To What You Know" and "My Weakness Is None Of Your Business", all reached the Top Ten – their debut LP could be held back no longer. Trailed by the McNamara brothers themselves with their now-trademark self-confidence, THE GOOD WILL OUT (released in July 1998) hit number one, although critics were concerned that Embrace had a very limited palette of songs – 'slow and half-slow', in the words of one reviewer. Nevertheless, the public loved them, and they headlined the second stage of the Glastonbury Festival that same summer.

As the tide of Britpop ebbed away still further, critics were less kind to the group's broader second album, DRAWN FROM MEMORY, released in early 2000 with keyboard player Mickey Dale promoted to a full-time band member; sales were underwhelming. Their next release, 2001's IF YOU'VE NEVER BEEN, sadly saw a major step backwards in quality; it contained none of the sense of adventurousness that flickered on their second set. One can only hope that inspiration strikes again next time round.

⊙ **Drawn From Memory** (2000; Hut/Virgin).
On the whole, a big improvement on their debut, and most impressive on the low-key piano-led title track, and the closing sigh of resignation "I Had A Time", which is refreshingly free of self-pity.

EMERSON, LAKE & PALMER

Formed London, 1970; disbanded 1978;
re-formed 1992.

"We were seen as the ultimate rock capitalists." Keith Emerson

The archetypal 70s prog-rock group, **Emerson, Lake & Palmer** were as successful as any band of the era, and suffered the biggest backlash of the lot, with critical resentment of their 'pomp-rock' reinforced by punk's casting them as dinosaurs to be culled.

The trio was a veritable supergroup when it formed, uniting former Nice keyboard player **Keith Emerson**, King Crimson's **Greg Lake** (vocals/guitar) and Atomic Rooster drummer **Carl Palmer**. After an unsuccessful collaboration with Jimi Hendrix and Mitch Mitchell, ELP (as they were known from the outset) made their debut at the 1970 Isle Of Wight festival. Amid exploding cannons, their arrival was a spectacular visual and musical experience, and the group's technical expertise quickly became hugely popular.

EMERSON, LAKE & PALMER, released in November 1970, demonstrated Emerson's penchant for translating classical themes into a rock context, featuring reworkings of Bartók and Janáček within the group's own compositions. Meanwhile, Emerson's Moog solo on "Lucky Man" was one of the first recorded examples of the synthesizer in rock.

Large-scale success came with TARKUS (1971), while increasingly spectacular performances culminated with a live recording of Mussorgsky's PICTURES AT AN EXHIBITION suite (1971). For some critics, this meeting of the rock and classical worlds bordered on desecration, but the studio-based TRILOGY (1972) consolidated the band's position as a premier progressive act. They also experimented with multitracking synthesizers to achieve a more orchestral sound.

After an eighteen-month break, another bestselling LP, BRAIN SALAD SURGERY (1973), showed ELP at the peak of their powers, with advanced use of synthesizers and electronic percussion, plus lyrical contributions from King Crimson's **Pete Sinfield**. A world tour spawned the triple live LP, WELCOME BACK MY FRIENDS TO THE SHOW THAT NEVER ENDS... (1974), which epitomized the overweening ambitions of 'prog-rock' with its overlong and overplayed arrangements.

Keith Emerson wired up for hot prog action

During their long absence from the scene as a group, Greg Lake had a seasonal solo smash hit with "I Believe In Father Christmas" (1975), but ELP only resurfaced in 1977 with the double set, WORKS VOL. I, which featured side-long solo offerings from each of the trio, plus two group efforts on the fourth side. One of the group pieces from the set, a reworking of Aaron Copland's "Fanfare For The Common Man", became a surprise British hit that summer.

ELP undertook a US tour, for which they employed a full orchestra, with mixed results. They didn't try this in their homeland, though, where the punk movement was threatening to sweep away both them and their peers. WORKS VOL. 2 (1977), a desultory series of outtakes and previously released singles, again suggested that the trio had run out of steam, and this was confirmed a year later with the release of LOVE BEACH (1978), an appalling attempt at mainstream pop. The group quietly disbanded, leaving IN CONCERT (1979) as a last memento.

Emerson embarked on film soundtrack work, while after brief solo projects both Lake and Palmer joined early 80s pop-rock group Asia, who briefly became a phenomenon in the American charts. Emerson and Lake returned with drummer **Cozy Powell** for EMERSON, LAKE & POWELL (1986), while AOR songwriter Robert Berry joined Emerson and Palmer for TO THE POWER OF THREE (1988), but neither album quite hit the mark.

With the advent of the 90s, and its 70s nostalgia boom, the original trio finally re-formed, recorded BLACK MOON (1992), and returned to live work, highlighted by three triumphant shows at London's Royal Albert Hall, where they delivered a crowd-pleasing set of their classics. The subsequent LIVE AT THE ROYAL ALBERT HALL (1993) capitalized upon renewed interest, but IN THE HOT SEAT (1994) seems set to be a last farewell, with Emerson announcing his retirement from the rock world. A fairly poor-quality compilation, THE RETURN OF THE MANTICORE (1993), WORKS LIVE (1993) and a splendid FLOWER HOUR (1997) on King Biscuit were the final twitches from a dead horse.

- **Tarkus** (1971; Victory).
ELP find their feet as a group. The lyrics may be loopy but the musical content is some of the best of its kind: its twenty-minute title track accommodates a startling number of ideas. Emerson even succeeds in making the Hammond organ sound like a real rock instrument.

- **Pictures At An Exhibition** (1971; Victory).
Recorded live in Newcastle before a rabidly enthusiastic audience, the album captures the breathtaking excitement of classical rock in full flight. Based on Mussorgsky's piano work, it gives the trio a chance to demonstrate the full range of their abilities.

- **Brain Salad Surgery** (1973; Victory).
Beautifully produced by Greg Lake, and dominated by technically and musically advanced synthesizers, this contains one of progressive rock's masterpieces, the three-part opus "Karnevil 9". After this peak, there was nowhere for ELP to go.

Steve Dinsdale

EMF

Formed Forest of Dean, England, 1989; split 1997; re-formed briefly 2001.

"The charge sheet: Ian's a dictator. Derry's a thug. Mark's a basket-case. James is paranoid. And Zac is obsessed with his knob." Select

The baseball-capped, baggy-shorted **EMF** – Epsom Mad Funkers or, in the words of their eponymously titled song, Ecstasy Mother Fuckers (the band could never quite make up their minds) – made their first attack on the UK music scene in the autumn of 1990 with the Jesus Jones-influenced Top 10 single "Unbelievable". Sampling hard-hitting US comic Andrew Dice Clay, the single was a catchy pop pile-up featuring fresh-faced vocalist **James Atkin**'s sneery schoolboy vocals, bandleader Ian Dench's swaggering rock guitar and a booming bassline, courtesy of **Zac Foley**. Mischief-maker **Derry Brownson** (keyboards) and **Mark Decloedt** (drums) completed the line-up.

'Madchester' had exploded in 1990, and every previously no-hoper band with half an idea sold their souls to hitch a ride on the ensuing 'indie dance' bandwagon. EMF's ideas were better formed than most, despite the fact that they had been signed by a major label (EMI/Parlophone) after only a handful of gigs. Denounced as beered-up party animals by some and cider-drinking country bumpkins who'd struck lucky by others, the group cultivated a hedonistic young-upstart image that ensured that they felt as at home on the cover of *Smash Hits* as they did in the *NME*.

Steered through these giddy times by the older, uglier, Svengali figure of guitarist and songwriter Dench, who had already enjoyed limited success with the band Apple Mosaic, the quintet quickly despatched identikit follow-up singles in "I Believe" and "Children", with little drop in quality or commercial impact. By this stage "Unbelievable" was breaking the band in the States, but their debut single's worldwide success was to hang heavily on their shoulders in years to come.

In May 1991 EMF released their debut album SCHUBERT DIP ('If ever I'm short of a chord sequence I nick one from Schubert', Dench was quoted as saying), which contained all the band's singles to date, and already felt like a greatest hits collection. Similarly it topped the charts, although the fourth single, "Lies", like much of the rest of the album (with the possible exception of slowie "Girl Of An Age"), paled in comparison with their initial batch of exuberant singles. It also drew attention from Yoko Ono's lawyers, who objected to the single's use of a sample of Lennon lyrics recited by her husband's murderer, Mark Chapman.

With SCHUBERT DIP becoming a million-selling album, the band took to hanging out in LA with such luminaries as Perry Farrell of Jane's Addiction, getting tattoos, getting high and talking big about making a 'real' rock record. When second album STIGMA appeared in late 1992, heralded by the noisy single "They're Here" and the UNEXPLAINED EP (containing a rowdy cover of The Stooges' "Search And Destroy"), it was interpreted by many as a deliberate attempt by EMF to distance themselves from their teenage fan base. Though they may have won some respect from the critics by going for a harder, less straightforward sound, the album wasn't received as well as hoped, sliding quickly out of the charts and selling only a fifth of its predecessor's total. The limitations of Atkin's voice were also readily apparent against the crunchier guitar backing. Perhaps the band had been partying too hard, and simply forgot to write some tunes; 'Around the time of STIGMA I was pumping myself full of anything', bassist Foley would later admit.

With the band either touring or doing nothing during 1993–94, there was a hiatus in the group's recording career, and many assumed that EMF had simply split up until the single "Perfect Day" appeared from nowhere in early 1995. Though it was the band's breeziest, grooviest single for a long while, it failed to recapture their previous fortunes, and the album that followed, CHA CHA CHA – from which Massive Attack/Neneh Cherry producer Johnny Dollar had walked out during the sessions – stubbornly refused to shift units. "Bleeding You Dry", the next single to be pulled from the album, seemed perversely appropriate.

The summer of 1995 saw the band abandoning promotion of the album and teaming up with comics Vic Reeves and Bob Mortimer on a karaoke cover of The Monkees' "I'm A Believer". Although this commercial move ensured the band appeared on *Top Of The Pops* again – wearing Mike Nesmith wigs and miming badly – many critics smelled the stench of desperation. Their self-promoted follow-up, "Afro King", seen in some quarters as a return to their poppy origins, and in others as too little too late, failed to do as well. The band were subsequently dropped by their label and, with no other offers forthcoming, called it a day.

EMF briefly regrouped in 2001 to promote a best of collection, but it was largely ignored. At the start of the following year Zac Foley died after a bout of New Year intemperance, further blighting the group's hopes for a significant return. James is now playing in a new band, Beauty School Dropouts.

⊙ **Schubert Dip** (1991; Parlophone).
EMF's debut might be a touch lightweight and of-the-moment, but classic pop music – as "Unbelievable" undeniably was – is as much about disposability as longevity.

Gavin Stoker

EMINEM

Born St Joseph, Missouri, October 17, 1972.

His views on bow hunting have yet to be recorded, but **Eminem** is nevertheless the leading contender to inherit Ted Nugent's title of 'Motor City Madman'. Born **Marshall Mathers**, Eminem grew up on the east side of Detroit in a predominantly black neighbourhood. Of course, it's no small irony that the main contribution to hip-hop of America's largest city with a predominantly African-American population has been a string of melanin- and skills-deficient rappers. Unlike Kid Rock and Insane Clown Posse, though, Eminem's got a lot more going for him than some recycled Aerosmith riffs and second-hand Kiss make-up.

Mathers began rapping in high school and he quickly acquired a rep for his freestyling abilities. In 1995 he released a single with fellow Detroit MC **Proof** on a tiny local label, which led to the INFINITE (1996) album on the Web Entertainment label. While Infinite showcased Eminem's abundant wit and rhyming ability, it was a muddled effort in a far different, more positive style than has become his familiar approach.

On the SLIM SHADY EP (1997), however, Eminem got his licence to ill, and on the extraordinarily nihilistic "Just The Two Of Us" (in which he talks to his daughter while her mother's corpse is in the trunk of the car they're driving) and "Just Don't Give A Fuck" he displayed the awesome skills and stoopidly mordant world-view that would make him multi-platinum on his next release.

After becoming a favourite on LA's *Wake Up Show*, Eminem signed to Aftermath and worked with **Dr. Dre** for THE SLIM SHADY LP (1999). Built on a kiddie-park calliope keyboard and a singsong bass line, "My Name Is" featured lines like 'Got pissed off and ripped Pamela Lee's tits off/And smacked her so hard it knocked her clothes backwards like Kriss Kross' and 'You know you blew up when women rush the stands and try to touch your hands like some screaming Usher fans' and became one of the singles of the year. The second single, "Guilty Conscience", was based on that scene in *Animal House* where Tom Hulce's conscience and id battle it out, with Dr. Dre playing the conscience, setting up Eminem's 'You're gonna take advice from someone who slapped Dee Barnes?' line. Aside from the three Dre tracks, though, the production couldn't match Eminem's gratuitously offensive wordplay and made THE SLIM SHADY LP feel too much like a novelty record.

Eminem was at his best, however, on indie singles like "Any Man" (1999), which featured on Rawkus's *Soundbombing II* compilation. Produced by **Da Beatminerz**, "Any Man"'s simple, raw and head-nodding beats suited Eminem's flow and rhymes far better than those on The Slim Shady LP.

With beats from Dre, **45 King**, **F.B.T.** and Eminem himself, THE MARSHALL MATHERS LP (2000) didn't improve the production any (their cartoonish quality still deadened the impact of both his rhymes and his flow), but Eminem's growing self-consciousness made the album compellingly disturbing. There was a trend for rappers claiming that they weren't role models in the early 90s, but Eminem's response to the moral panic surrounding

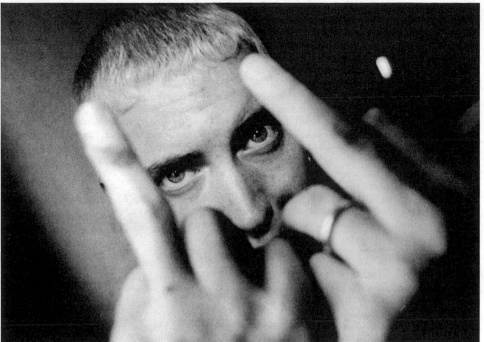

Eminem – as charming as ever

him and Marilyn Manson was both to get brooding and to hurl invective at Middle America. He talked about raping his mother, he adopted the persona of an obsessed fan whose letters he didn't respond to, and avers, 'There's a Slim Shady in all of us'. The first single, "The Real Slim Shady" was the only light relief: 'I'm sick of you little girl and boy groups/All you do is annoy me/So I've been sent here to destroy you'. If the beats were better, this would have been hip-hop's THERE'S A RIOT GOIN' ON.

After generating more controversy with his participation in the schlocky shock rap of D-12's DEVIL'S NIGHT (2001), Eminem returned in 2002 with THE EMINEM SHOW and his debut big screen role as a rapper from Detroit in *8 Mile*. The *8 Mile* soundtrack included four new Eminem tracks, including the excellent "Lose Yourself" and "Rabbit Run". THE EMINEM SHOW, meanwhile, more or less followed the same formula as THE MARSHALL MATHERS LP with the sing-song synth hooks, cheap (albeit funny) shots at lesser pop stars and an obsession with both the media circus that surrounded him and his dysfunctional family life, only this time without the morbidity. Instead, you got a couple of ballads, a godawful sex rap and an interpolation of Aerosmith's "Dream On" – maybe he doesn't have that much more going for him than Kid Rock after all.

⊙ **The Slim Shady LP** (1999; Aftermath)
Despite uneven production, the high points make this the most cathartic, teenage angst cartoon since Slayer's Reign in Blood.

⊙ **The Marshall Mathers LP** (2000; Aftermath).
Teeny-bopper pin-up angst at its most dark and disturbing and perceptive – if only George Michael had made a record this good.

Peter Shapiro

BRIAN ENO

Born Woodbridge, England, 1948.

Brian Peter George St. John le Baptiste de la Salle **Eno** was – despite the fanciful name – descended from three generations of postmen. An erstwhile glam-rock 'hero' and self-confessed non-musician, he has become known as the propagator of ambient and (most recently) computer-generated music, as an international video artist and latter-day futurist, and as producer for such acts as David Bowie, Talking Heads and U2. All the same, though, he did confess that his mother once asked him, 'Do you think you'll ever get a real job?'

Growing up near a US Air Force base in Suffolk, Eno's early influences included what he dubbed the 'Martian music' of doo-wop subculture broadcast on American armed services radio, as well as the first wave of rock'n'roll, and the lush tones of The Ray Conniff Singers. What all these influences shared was a lack of context – this 'mystery music' had seemingly arrived from 'outer space' (ie America), and sounded decidedly exotic amidst the English countryside.

Between 1964 and 1969 Eno studied at art school, involved in conceptual paintings and sound sculptures, as well as early experiments with tape recorders ('my first instrument'). He liked The Who and The Velvet Underground, but also developed a keen interest in the experimental music of composers such as La Monte Young, Cornelius Cardew, Steve Reich and John Cage. Their use of written instructions, chance, repetition and error as methods of composition caught his imagination, particularly Reich's proto-minimalist tape piece, "It's Gonna Rain" (1965). Eno formed an avant-garde performance group, **Merchant Taylor's Simultaneous Cabinet**, and sang and played the signals generator with improvising rock band **Maxwell Demon**. By 1969, he was to be found both in **Cornelius Cardew's Scratch Orchestra** (appearing on THE GREAT LEARNING, 1971) and on clarinet amid the ranks of the infamous **Portsmouth Sinfonia**, who achieved notoriety by recruiting non-musical members and offering concerts of the 'best bits' of popular classics like "The Blue Danube Waltz". Eno later produced their albums THE POPULAR CLASSICS (1973) and HALLELUJAH (1974).

Eno had also joined **ROXY MUSIC**, and appeared on their first two albums, ROXY MUSIC (1972) and FOR YOUR PLEASURE (1973). On stage, he donned feather boas and make-up and manipulated the band's sound via his synthesizer gadgetry. His stage presence rivalled that of Roxy's frontman Bryan Ferry, with a consequent clash of egos. After realizing in the middle of one gig that he was actually thinking more about his laundry, Eno quit, adding that Roxy Music had lost the important element of 'insanity'.

Eno's first release after leaving Roxy was a collaboration with King Crimson supremo **ROBERT FRIPP**, NO PUSSYFOOTING (1973), on which he treated Fripp's guitar via tape-loop delays, and created a layered sculptural ambience. The duo toured and produced a second collaboration, EVENING STAR (1975), while Fripp has featured on several subsequent Eno albums. 1973 also saw Eno's first solo outing, the wonderful HERE COME THE WARM JETS, its title an apparent reference to urinating. An uneasy marriage of idiosyncratic rock/idiot-pop and skewed urban-fairy-tale lyrics, it featured a host of musicians, including all of Roxy Music (less Ferry), with Eno himself credited for 'simplistic keyboards, snake guitar, electric larynx and synthesizer'. It reached the UK Top 30, but polarized the critics, who also didn't know how to respond to the subsequent release of a proto-punk single, "Seven Deadly Finns".

Eno, meanwhile, was suffering from ill-health, and a brief spell as frontman for **The Winkies**, in early 1974, ended five days into a British tour, when he was rushed to hospital with a collapsed lung. TAKING TIGER MOUNTAIN (BY STRATEGY), released in late 1974 saw Eno extending his stream-of-consciousness approach to writing lyrics and featured The Portsmouth Sinfonia on "Put A Straw Under Baby". The following year, the LP's cover designer Peter Schmidt joined Eno to produce 'Oblique Strategies', a set of cards bearing instructions, phrases and advice to solve dilemmas – akin to a latter-day I Ching. 1975

Eno post-Roxy, with a whole life ahead of him

saw the accidental birth of ambient music when Eno was convalescing in bed after being hit by a car. Unable to move, he couldn't turn up the volume on his amplifier after one visitor had put on an album of 'Virtuoso Harp Music'. The rain outside drowned out all but the loudest notes, and Eno realized that music could be used as one could use lighting or colour in a room. DISCREET MUSIC (1975) was in a sense his first ambient work, though primarily an extension of his interest in self-regulating systems. On the title track, Eno fed synthesizer phrases into a system involving two looped tape recorders, limiting his involvement to that of planner and programmer. Side two, meanwhile, employed instructions for a group of performers playing fragments of Johann Pachelbel's "Canon in D Major", resulting in a blurred slow-motion opulence. DISCREET MUSIC was part of a ten-LP series that Eno produced on his Obscure Records label (the Obscure series), a showcase for other experimental musicians like John Cage, Penguin Café Orchestra (genuinely experimental on their first album), Michael Nyman, Harold Budd and Eno's former art-school teacher, painter Tom Phillips. ANOTHER GREEN WORLD (1975) was arguably the most subtle and successful realization of Eno's experimental approach. It was widely perceived as his third 'song album' of the 70s, although only five of four-teen tracks had lyrics and "Becalmed" and "Spirits Drifting" continued his shift towards purely instrumental concerns. Where lyrics were used, they were more a part of this musical landscape, away from the convention of narrative song 'portraits'.

The slightly self-conscious and studied BEFORE AND AFTER SCIENCE (1977) was a wonderful summation of Eno's talents, with an energized first side and calmer second half, featuring "By This River", on which **Hans-Joachim Roedelius** and **Dieter Moebius** (of **CLUSTER**) appeared. The duo joined Eno for the slightly disappointing 1978 album CLUSTER AND ENO followed by AFTER THE HEAT (1978), notable mainly for its uneasy futuristic lyrics sung by Eno on "Broken Head", "The Belldog" and "Tzima N'arki". At this point New York post-punks **Talking Heads** caught Eno's attention. He went on to produce a trio of albums – MORE SONGS ABOUT BUILDINGS AND FOOD (1978), FEAR OF MUSIC (1979) and, most notably, REMAIN IN LIGHT (1980), where he and **David Byrne** were credited with writing all but one of the tracks. Eno's involvement caused increasing friction within the band but his collaboration with Byrne was a fruitful one, and resulted in an album, MY LIFE IN THE BUSH OF GHOSTS (1981). A blend of 'found sounds', frac-tured melodies and African-inspired dance rhythms, it presaged the world music–dance fusions made popular a decade later.

Eno's solo work had continued with the ambient MUSIC FOR FILMS (1978), parts of which were heard in Derek Jarman's films *Sebastiane* (1976) and *Jubilee* (1978). Indeed, by the 80s, Eno's music was crop-ping up everywhere, from TV documentaries and commercials to films like David Lynch's *Dune* (1984).

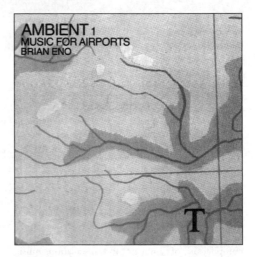

AMBIENT 1
MUSIC FOR AIRPORTS
BRIAN ENO

Music from APOLLO: ATMOSPHERES & SOUNDTRACKS (1983), made with Canadian musi-cian and producer **Daniel Lanois** and Eno's brother **Roger**, appeared in Al Reinert's 1989 documentary *For All Mankind*. This C&W-meets-ambient hybrid added a nostalgic 'frontier' edge to the evocative NASA moon-landing footage.

Eno's ambient music lends itself to visual analogies: he once referred to it as 'holographic' – where any given moment reflected the greater musical whole. His first excursions in the field, AMBIENT #1: MUSIC FOR AIRPORTS (1978) and AMBIENT #4: ON LAND (1982), could be listened to in the same way as one might occa-sionally look at a picture, without loss of continuity, and with details revealing themselves over time. The back cover of ON LAND had instructions for making an 'ambient' (third) speaker system, whilst the music had a decidedly environmental feel with the likes of "Dunwich Beach, Autumn, 1960" and "Lantern Marsh" recalling places from Eno's childhood.

Alongside these two releases in the 'ambient series' came AMBIENT #2: THE PLATEAUX OF MIRROR (1980), with Eno manipulating **Harold Budd**'s sparse piano playing, and AMBIENT #3: DAY OF RADIANCE (1980), containing **Laraaji**'s meditative zither music. Eno and Budd went on to record THE PEARL in 1984, produced by Eno with Daniel Lanois, while a collaboration with **Jon Hassell** on POSSIBLE MUSICS (1980) developed Hassell's theoretical genre of 'fourth world' music – a blend of 'first/third world' skills and instrumentation, overlaid with his breathy and haunting trumpet lines.

The late 70s had seen Eno working on three cel-ebrated **DAVID BOWIE** albums – LOW (1977), HEROES (1977) and LODGER (1979). Other classic Eno productions include **Devo**'s ARE WE NOT MEN? (1978) and a trio of albums for **U2**. Along with Daniel Lanois, he earned a *Grammy* for his work on ACHTUNG BABY in 1992.

MUSIC FOR FILMS III (1988) was a compilation of work by both Eno brothers, Lanois, Budd, Laraaji, Brook and Led Zeppelin bassist **John Paul Jones** –

all at the time connected to Eno's production company, Opal. One highlight, "For Her Atoms", was recorded in Moscow and featured **Lydia Theremin** (granddaughter of Leon Theremin, the inventor of the eponymous electronic instrument). Fostering such East–West creative links, Eno visited Moscow in 1988, producing an eponymous 1989 album by underground Soviet band **Zvuki Mu**.

In 1990, Eno's voice made a long-overdue return on an album of songs with **John Cale**, WRONG WAY UP. Musically, it was perhaps closest to BEFORE AND AFTER SCIENCE – clever and quite poppy. A solo album MY SQUELCHY LIFE was aborted and rejigged before appearing as NERVE NET in 1992. On the cover Eno outlined the contents as '… like paella, crunchy, godless, clockless …'.

There followed more serious instrumental experiments: THE SHUTOV ASSEMBLY (1992), a compilation of ambient and installation music recorded between 1985 and 1990, and the modal mystery of NEROLI (1993). They were counterpoints, perhaps, to Eno's rock work, which in 1996 saw a *Brit Award* for his production on Bowie's 1995 comeback album OUTSIDE. Eno also found time to create a perfect soundtrack for old associate Derek Jarman's memorial-like collection of home movies, *Glitterbug* (1994), which, worked over by **Jah Wobble**, emerged as SPINNER (1995).

Alongside his musical career Eno has, since 1979, developed an international reputation as a video and installation artist, with countless exhibitions of his work. His success in this field has gone largely uncredited by the British media, seeing such diversity as 'dilettantism' – Eno terms it interdisciplinary research. For instance, *Mistaken Memories Of Medieval Manhattan* was a vertical-format video (ie turn your TV sideways) that Eno made in New York in 1980–81, while other projects have included videopaintings of Christine Alcino (he released the gorgeous soundtrack to these, THURSDAY AFTERNOON, in 1985); a Shinto shrine inauguration in Japan (1989); and *Self Storage* (1995), created with **LAURIE ANDERSON** and a group of college students.

In the early months of 1996, Eno returned to the media's attention with projects in two new fields. The first was the publication of his 1995 diary, *A Year With Swollen Appendices* (Faber), a splendidly quirky flow of thoughts and observations. The second was a piece of software, *Generative Music 1* (released as a CD-ROM by Sseyo/Opal). This developed the idea of screensavers (ever-changing patterns on a computer screen) for sound, allowing the 'player' to feed in musical 'seeds' for a computer to 'grow'. THE DROP (1997) and DRAWN FROM LIFE (2001) continued his exploration of ambience and atmospheres.

Interviewed on these ventures, rock's Mr Cerebral expressed customary amazement at how unusual it was to have broad artistic and cultural horizons, theories and areas of interest. 'I don't think most people think about most things,' he mused, 'but I do. I think thinking is a bloody good idea.'

Brian Eno

- **Here Come The Warm Jets** (1973; EG).
  Glammed-up art-pop brimming with crude energy ("Needles In The Camel's Eye"), smarmy anxiety ("Dead Finks Don't Talk") and fanciful tales ("The Paw Paw Negro Blowtorch").

- **Another Green World** (1975; EG).
  A gem of accessible experimentation. Eno at his understated best, on this predominantly instrumental album of 'songs', just before he discovered the recipes he was using.

- **Ambient #1: Music For Airports** (1978; EG).
  "1/1", 2/1", 1/2", '"2/2" – no, not dance steps, but the titles off this seminal ambient album, which apparently became popular with airport employees. So perfect that you needn't listen to hear it.

- **Apollo: Atmospheres & Soundtracks** (1983; EG).
  The Eno brothers and Lanois present a glittering album of country/ambient moon-landing music. "Deep Blue Day" steals the show.

- **Nerve Net** (1992; Opal Records/Warners).
  Eno rematerialized in fine form with this 'Bleep & Booster' song assemblage. Robert Fripp (guitar) rips through the excellent "Distributed Being" into a labyrinthine "Web".

Brian Eno and David Byrne

- **My Life In The Bush Of Ghosts** (1981; Virgin/Sire).
  An agitated 'popular mechanics' futurism, trading obsolete lyrics for 'real life' – Middle Eastern singers, exorcists, radio phone-ins, gospel choirs. Plunderous and unmissable.

Ian Stonehouse

ENYA

Born Gweedore, Ireland, 1961.

New Age artist **Enya** (born Eithne Ni Bhraonain) has sold 30 million albums despite retaining a very low profile in an industry more comfortable with self-promotion, flamboyance and live performance. An intensely shy person, Enya has sold on the strength of her music alone, becoming one of the biggest-selling artists in the world today.

Classically trained on piano, Enya started out in her family's group, **Clannad**, in the early 80s, before being approached to compose the music for a BBC TV documentary series, *The Celts*. When it was finally issued on record in 1987, the reviews glowed, and soon afterwards she was signed to WEA, where she began working with producer Nicky Ryan and his lyricist wife, Roma, who would become long-term collaborators.

The result was WATERMARK (1988), which spawned the UK #1 hit single, "Orinoco Flow", a wall-of-sound production sung largely in Gaelic. The album caught on with listeners on a global basis, clocking up over a million sales in the UK and eight million worldwide. After extensive promotional work, Enya returned to the studio to begin work on SHEPHERD MOONS (1991), essentially a reprise of its predecessor's ethereal music and lush production. Not that this stopped it shifting nine million units worldwide, spending four years in the US album charts, and winning her a *Grammy*.

As THE CELTS was reissued by WEA at the end of
1992, Enya once more retired to the studio, but it
was late 1995 before she released her third album,
THE MEMORY OF TREES. Once again this did not
depart from the formula of her debut, offering more
examples of delectable mood music.

Quite clearly, Enya had joined the ranks of the
rock aristocracy, dispensing with a surname and
dwelling in a castle. Her music may be easy to dismiss as 'ambient for the armchair-bound' but,
whatever she does, she knows what her public likes:
her album A DAY WITHOUT RAIN (2000) was considered by many American radio programmers to be
the preferred accompaniment to the tragic aftermath
of September 11. More recently Enya's tones have
been heard on the soundtracks of the blockbusting
Lord Of The Rings trilogy, while a 4CD box-set collection, ONLY TIME, was released in 2002 to keep
her fans sedated while they wait for a new album
proper.

> ⦿ **Watermark** (1988; WEA).
> This music is all about majesty and calmness, with
> "Orinoco Flow" the clear highlight.

> ⦿ **Paint The Sky With Stars** (1997; WEA).
> Enya's greatest hits on one disc.

> ⦿ **A Box Of Dreams** (1998; WEA).
> A trawl through Enya's back catalogue on three CDs
> named OCEANS, CLOUDS and STARS.

Nick Duerden

ROKY ERICKSON

Born Dallas, Texas; July 15, 1947.

The demise of Texan psychedelics **13TH FLOOR
ELEVATORS** illustrated the precarious nature of
the counterculture lifestyle, especially the dangers of
running headlong into conflict with the authorities.
The forces of law and order in Texas were determined to do something about the group's behaviour,
not least lead singer and guitarist **Roky** (ROger
KYnard) **Erickson**'s public advocacy of the use of
hallucinogenics in the cause of spiritual enlightenment. When tried for narcotics possession, Erickson
announced that he came from Mars, but his plea of
insanity landed him an indefinite sentence at the
Rusk State Mental Institution.

After three years in a regime of shock treatment
and mind-corrective drugs, Erickson was released,
thanks partly to the intervention of family and
friends, and partly to his writing a book, *Openers*, that
affirmed his interest in the Christian religion. Its publication helped to convince the hospital authorities
that he was truly on the straight and narrow.

Once out of Rusk, however, Erickson formed the
band **Bleib Alien** – 'Bleib' being a corruption of
'Bible' – and initiated a self-created satanic
mythology of demons, vampires and zombies, an
arcane system of belief which would both energize
and hamper his comeback. Bleib Alien did not last
long, but by 1975 Erickson had started to make live
appearances with fellow Texan **Doug Sahm**, and

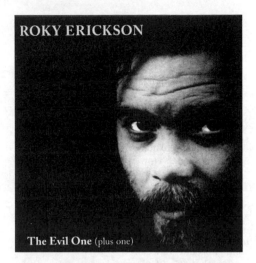

ROKY ERICKSON

The Evil One (plus one)

later with a series of pick-up bands eager to rekindle
the fire of the Elevators.

Erickson only returned to the recording studio at
the end of the 70s, resulting in a disappointing album,
given the official title of an untranslatable rune.
Comic-book schlock-horror imagery dominated on
"Don't Shake Me Lucifer" and "Cold Night For
Alligators", but such songs always sounded better in
live performance, with his most stable group **The
Aliens** and the later line-ups of **The Explosives** and
The Nervebreakers. There have also been some
solo acoustic performances which show the strength
of Erickson as a songwriter who has remained true
to his vision of the world, with songs like the stately
"I Have Always Been Here Before", which was also
covered by Julian Cope. Erickson's second proper
album, ALL THAT MAY DO MY RHYME (1995),
showed that he was far from being a burned-out case.
NEVER SAY GOODBYE (1999) and 2002's reissue of
The Aliens–era collection THE EVIL ONE (PLUS
ONE) offered further confirmation of the importance
and paranoid brilliance of Rocky's legacy.

> ⦿ **Gremlins Have Pictures** (1986; Demon).
> A useful introduction to Erickson's work as a solo artist
> and as a still-rampant live performer. The most widely avail-
> able of many collections of studio and live cuts.

> ⦿ **All That May Do My Rhyme** (1995; Trance).
> A collection that shows Erickson's strength as a solo
> artist, featuring new versions of some songs that he wrote in
> the early 70s.

> ⦿ **Never Say Goodbye** (1999; Emperor Jones).
> Largely recorded in the early 70s when Erickson was a
> resident of Rusk State Mental Institution, this set presents a
> stunning overview of Rocky's songwriting genius. Even the
> poor sound quality can't muffle his charm.

Robert Murray

MELISSA ETHERIDGE

Born Leavenworth, Kansas, 1961.

Gravel-voiced singer-songwriter **Melissa
Etheridge** studied at Boston's prestigious

Berklee College of Music prior to her discovery in California by Chris Blackwell. The Island Records boss backed his faith with the release of her debut album, MELISSA ETHERIDGE, in 1988. Etheridge's confessional, plain-speaking songs and blues-based sound (sounding like a distant echo of Janis Joplin or Rod Stewart) found a ready audience, and the album broke into the US Top 30.

Etheridge's next two releases, BRAVE AND CRAZY (1989) and NEVER ENOUGH (1992), duplicated her debut's impressive numbers, but failed to spawn any major hit singles. However, when Bill Clinton was elected president at the end of 1992, she appeared with her friend k.d. lang at a celebratory ball organized by the gay community. Her coming out at this event did her career no harm at all: indeed, 1993's YES I AM became her biggest seller to date, and contained the American hits "Come To My Window" and "I'm The Only One".

In early 1995, Etheridge paid tribute to Janis Joplin at the singer's posthumous induction into the Rock And Roll Hall Of Fame, also performing a solo-acoustic guitar rendition of Joplin's "Piece Of My Heart" at the same ceremony. Shortly afterwards, she performed on MTV's *Unplugged*, where she was accompanied by Bruce Springsteen on a version of his "Thunder Road". The end of 1995 brought with it a new album, YOUR LITTLE SECRET, as accomplished as ever, ploughing a classic Springsteen groove; while 1999's BREAKDOWN unshackled Etheridge's tones from rock to craft a far stealthier, confessional sound. Both recordings brought further massive chart success in the US, though the Brits still don't seem to get it.

⊙ **Melissa Etheridge** (1988; Island).
Her angry debut album includes the scathing "Similar Features", which cracked the US charts the following year.

⊙ **Yes I Am** (1993; Island).
Slickly produced and written by Etheridge, YES I AM's songs seep into your consciousness, even if they pack no great emotional wallop. And, of course, they achieved sales to die for.

Benjamin R. Hunter

EURYTHMICS

Formed London, 1981; disbanded 1990; re-formed 2000.

After four years as a couple, and four years as The Tourists, **DAVE STEWART** (guitar/keyboards) and **ANNIE LENNOX** (vocals/keyboards/flute) embarked on an experimental period of demos at Conny Plank's studio in Cologne, West Germany. These sessions – some of which included help from Can's Holger Czukay – formed the basis for IN THE GARDEN (1981), the first album by a band called **Eurythmics**.

The duo's new name was taken from the technique of one Emil Jacques-Dalcroze, which taught children music through movement. The new music had a European electronic sound – and it wasn't an initial success. The Tourists had been closely identified with power pop, racking up a handful of chart hits (notably "I Only Want To Be With You"), but this was by now desperately unfashionable, and the critics didn't know quite what to make of their new sound. It didn't quite fit with New Romanticism – the new fad. Still, some industrious touring with a band including Blondie drummer **Clem Burke** and backing vocalist **Eddi Reader** (later of Fairground Attraction) began to pick up a following.

Eurythmics' second album, SWEET DREAMS (ARE MADE OF THIS) (1983), continued their love affair with technology, although this time the songs themselves were more immediately commercial. They included "Love Is A Stranger", which had just missed the British Top 40 in late 1982, and was to become a Top 10 hit, after the album's stunning title track had reached #2 in the UK. The music had hit a chord: contemporary and hugely catchy, it was synth-and production-driven, yet it had a soul, melancholy and personal. It made most of their New Romantic contemporaries seem very clumsy indeed.

What Eurythmics did have in common with those contemporaries was their success with video. Heavy MTV rotation for "Sweet Dreams" helped it to #1 in America, although the cable channel banned the "Love Is A Stranger" promo for its transvestite imagery (Lennox played both female and male roles in the video). Throughout their career, Eurythmics' videos were to blur glamour and gender, reaching a peak when they teamed up with director Sophie Muller (notably on the video version of the SAVAGE album in 1987).

By the time TOUCH was released, near the end of 1983, Lennox and Stewart had become major pop stars, though without losing their enigmatic approach to music and image. Even a rare song of optimism, like the calypso pastiche "Right By Your Side", or a supremely extrovert series of sell-out live shows, didn't seem to harm their profile, and they kept notching up the hits with style – including the best cut on TOUCH, "Here Comes The Rain Again". All the same, the duo's relationship with RCA had its ups and downs – an ill-advised low-price album of remixes, TOUCH DANCE, was released against their will in 1984, as was a rushed video compilation.

As their worldwide profile heightened, Eurythmics were asked by film director Michael Radford to provide the soundtrack music for his remake of George Orwell's novel *1984*. The duo were unhappy that so little of their work got used in the film itself, but they ended up with a soundtrack album and a single, "Sexcrime", which became their sixth UK Top 10 hit in two years.

Eurythmics' fifth album, BE YOURSELF TONIGHT (1985), could best be described as paying homage to their roots, with its Stax, Atlantic and Tamla Motown motifs. Indeed, two of the LP's guest artists were Stevie Wonder ("There Must Be An Angel" – a UK #1 single in July 1985) and Aretha Franklin ("Sisters Are Doing It For Themselves"). Both were

Dave and Annie near the end of the road, and already seeing separate hairdressers

long-term heroes of Stewart and Lennox, although the original choice for guest vocal on "Sisters" was, admittedly, Tina Turner. Other collaborators included Elvis Costello on "Adrian". Less exciting was the duo's tribute to adult-orientated rock, as demonstrated on REVENGE (1986). Clearly an attempt to crack America, it ironically sold far fewer copies there than their earlier, more individual work, although it remains their best-selling album in Europe.

From this point on, critics were predicting a gradual artistic decline for Eurythmics, as they travelled around stadiums puncturing their old hits with unnecessary guitar solos. Yet SAVAGE (1987) was an extraordinary album. The duo had finally abandoned the traditional rock band approach in favour of a flexible guest cast, while Lennox had produced lyrics as forceful and feisty as the cover image of her in a rubber mask, flexing her muscles. It was a woman breaking out, and in retrospect it was the beginning of the end for the duo, whose relationship had been drifting apart.

By the release of WE TOO ARE ONE (1989) this was public knowledge, and the last song the duo collaborated on, "Don't Ask Me Why", chorused 'I don't love you anymore/I don't think I ever did'. After a final tour, Lennox and Stewart put Eurythmics behind them, and set out on solo careers, which showed them to be two musicians of startlingly different backgrounds, who, after their personal and professional breakdowns, had very little left in common. But their differences were not so great that they couldn't get it together again nearly a decade later for the appropriately titled PEACE. Though it had its moments, the idea of the album as a returning triumph was more interesting than the music, and the pair were soon swept back into the current of their respective solo careers.

⊙ **Touch** (1983; RCA).
Eurythmics at the very height of their songwriting capabilities, with "Right By Your Side", "Who's That Girl?" and "Here Comes The Rain Again".

⊙ **Greatest Hits** (1991; RCA).
The inevitable compilation, which shrouds the fact that Eurythmics should have had at least five #1 singles, rather

than just the one. The title is taken literally – there's nothing from In The Garden, unfortunately – but at least this means there's no filler here.

Justin Lewis

THE EVERLY BROTHERS

Formed Kentucky, 1955; disbanded 1973; re-formed 1983.

The Everly Brothers' teen hits brought to rock-'n'roll a tradition of close-harmony singing that stretched back through Appalachian country duos like the Louvin Brothers to centuries of Scottish and Irish folk music. It was essentially from this that their sharply observed – though sometimes maudlin – vignettes of girl or parent trouble gained their emotional whack.

Don (vocals/guitar) and **Phil** (vocals/guitar) were the sons of country singers with whom, from an early age, the boys appeared on local radio shows and tours of the South. Their earliest records, in that close-harmony style that was already becoming regarded as old-fashioned in 1956, sank without trace, but their fortunes changed the following year when their new manager, Wesley Rose, got them signed to Cadence Records. They began to record songs by Felice and Boudleaux Bryant, a middle-aged husband-and-wife songwriting team who had an unerring ability to catch the angst and self-absorption of the average teen.

The first Bryant song they released, "Bye Bye Love", had already been rejected by thirty other acts. However, this time the boys and their musical mentor, Nashville guitar supremo Chet Atkins (a friend of their father), had something new to add. The new Everlys sound kept the high, keening harmonies, but backed them with robust acoustic guitars and a rock'n'roll beat that owed something to Bo Diddley. The new sound – precisely arranged, whiny, compelling – was perfect for teenagers' portable radios. In June 1957 it hit #2 in the US

charts and became a million-seller. The next single, "Wake Up Little Susie", a wry tale of two teenagers who fall asleep at a drive-in until 3am, was another million-seller, as were "All I Have To Do Is Dream", the rocking novelty "Bird Dog", "Problems" in 1958, and "(Til) I Kissed You" (written by Don) in 1959.

In 1960 the brothers signed to Warners for a million-dollar, ten-year contract. Although this meant that they lost their production team and the Bryants' songwriting prowess, everything went well at first. Don's "Cathy's Clown" was their biggest-selling single, and Phil's "When Will I Be Loved", "Walk Right Back" and the morbid love-and-death ballad "Ebony Eyes", all did well in the US and UK charts. However, their career began to slow down in 1962 after a six-month stint in the marines; in November Don collapsed on stage during rehearsals for a UK tour, and Phil had to finish the tour alone.

As animosity between the brothers grew, the hits dried up in the US. In 1963 none of their releases made the US Top 100, although they remained popular in the UK into 1965, when "The Price Of Love" reached #2. Experiments with R&B and country-rock failed to set the world alight. Disagreements persisted through the late 60s and early 70s; in 1973, midway through a concert in Hollywood, Phil smashed his guitar and stormed off, and Don announced that The Everly Brothers had split. Ten years of solo career doldrums followed.

In 1983 the brothers reunited for a triumphant reunion concert at The Albert Hall. Three years later they were inducted into the Rock And Roll Hall Of Fame. The Everly Brothers were a massive influence on many acts, especially in the 60s. This is particularly noticeable in Simon And Garfunkel's harmonies, but The Beatles, The Byrds, The Hollies, Lovin' Spoonful, and even The Proclaimers, all built on their achievements.

⊙ **Golden Years Of The Everly Brothers** (1993; WEA). Twenty-four hits including both Cadence and Warners material.

⊙ **Original British Hit Singles** (1995; Ace). This is the best collection of the Cadence hits; lovingly remastered and with good sleeve notes.

Andy Smith

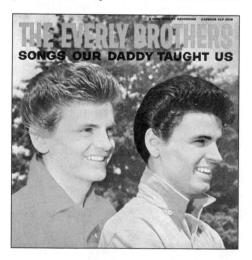

EVERYTHING BUT THE GIRL

Formed Hull, England, 1982.

Everything But The Girl was initially a sideline to the careers of Hull University students **Tracey Thorn** and **Ben Watt**. Thorn was a member of The Marine Girls, while Watt had released a couple of solo singles and collaborated with Robert Wyatt.

With Thorn and Watt already separately signed to the independent label Cherry Red, they took their collaborative name from a distinctly non-PC sign in a Hull shop window ('for your bedroom needs we sell everything but the girl'). Their debut single was a recording of Cole Porter's "Night And Day" (1982); the cool breeze of Thorn's rich, tender vocal and Watt's jazz-samba guitar was irresistible and the single was an indie chart success. Thorn's mini-LP A DISTANT SHORE followed, and in 1983 Watt released his NORTH MARINE DRIVE album, both big indie sellers. As EBTG they then recorded a version of Paul Weller's "English Rose" for a sampler cassette given away free with the *NME*. An impressed Weller invited the pair to contribute to **THE STYLE COUNCIL**'s 1984 debut album, CAFÉ BLEU, with Thorn taking the vocal on "Paris Match".

Still at university, but now operating full time as Everything But The Girl, Thorn and Watt signed to Blanco y Negro, and entered the UK Top 40 with the light and jazzy "Each & Every One", closely followed by the LP, EDEN (1984). It showed rapidly maturing talents at work, but further singles "Mine" and "Native Land" failed to chart, although the latter featured Smiths guitarist Johnny Marr on harmonica. By the time Everything But The Girl set out on their first UK tour in the autumn of 1984, Thorn had also contributed (again with Robert Wyatt) to the Working Week single "Venceremos".

For the duo's second album, LOVE NOT MONEY (1985), the chiming guitars of The Smiths had become a primary influence, while mid-80s indie rock had replaced the jazz-pop of EDEN. Touring took them far and wide: in July 1985, they joined a British Council trip to the Soviet Union, playing supposedly 'open' concerts which turned out to be mainly for Communist Party officials and their chosen few. Consequently, an EBTG album was released briefly in the USSR, one of the first by a modern British act, while the band became possibly the only UK act to play the USSR before the USA.

On their 1986 US tour, the undiluted emotionalism of real country music clicked with the pair, and the result was BABY THE STARS SHINE BRIGHT. This showcased Thorn's Patsy Cline-style vocal and Watt's bold (but sometimes overstretched) orchestrations, a tribute to both Burt Bacharach and Jimmy Webb, as well as Nashville.

A much sparser sound was favoured for the Top 10 album IDLEWILD (1988), considered by many to be their best. Augmented by drum machine, piano and percussion, some poised and confident material really shone, as did the sheer loveliness of Thorn's voice. Later in the year, their sweet and simple cover of Danny Whitten's "I Don't Want To Talk About It" hit #3 in the British charts, while the acoustic jazz styling of the accompanying tour's line-up gave the finest 'full band' concerts of their career.

Recorded in Los Angeles with soul producer Tommy Lipuma, THE LANGUAGE OF LIFE (1990) was slick and bright, but even with sax legend Stan Getz on the closing cut, "The Road", the result was somewhat faceless. Back home, Thorn and Watt considered the comforts of home and the tiring pleasures of touring on WORLDWIDE (1991). Early the following year, they played a series of acoustic sets at smaller venues, and drew on their stock of covers for an EP, led by a rare duet on a version of The Everly Brothers' "Love Is Strange".

After Ben Watt's severe year-long illness, in late 1993 the duo celebrated a decade of recording with the compilation album, HOME MOVIES. Responding enthusiastically to the cross fertilization of styles in EBTG's output, **MASSIVE ATTACK** approached the pair to collaborate on their album PROTECTION (1994). The result was two Thorn vocal cameos on "Better Things", and on the title track, a hit single early in 1995.

The claustrophobic spatial dynamics of PROTECTION were paralleled on EBTG's AMPLIFIED HEART (1994), their strongest set for some years. Enlisting the likes of Richard Thompson, Danny Thompson and Dave Mattacks, this set of lean songs combined the studio-bound atmospherics of dub with a confessional ambience reminiscent of Nick Drake. The sense of urgency was strong, markedly so on "Get Me" and the single "Missing", a massive worldwide hit in late 1995, when it was incongruously, if sensitively, remixed by DJ Todd Terry.

It was only when Massive Attack really broke on both sides of the Atlantic, however, that anyone other than loyal EBTG fans paid the band notice. Overnight, more or less, the group had been rescued from knocking reviews as bedsit bossa nova, and were, well, back at the cutting edge. Their 1996 album, WALKING WOUNDED, for new label Virgin, was a revelation, even to those who had spotted the signs on AMPLIFIED HEART, employing insistent drum'n'bass rhythmic backing for the duo's songs. It was trip-hop, it was cool, and it was still quintessential EBTG.

A lengthy lay-off followed, during which Ben and Tracey happily became the parents of twins. They returned to the fray via a collaboration with **Deep Dish**, the 1998 chart single "The Future Of The Future", which cropped up again on EBTG's 1999 album TEMPERAMENTAL, a set which confirmed their commitment to dance music whilst finding room for samples from Roland Kirk and Tommy Watt, Ben's bandleader father. Watt's club DJ residency at London's 'Lazy Dog' Sunday-nighter led to the 2000 release of a mix album with his collaborator **Jay Hannan**. The set spawned the 2001 single "Tracey In My Room": a mix of EBTG's "Wrong" (from WALKING WOUNDED) and Sandy Rivera's 1998 club hit "Come Into My Room". A further best-of collection, LIKE THE DESERTS MISS THE RAIN, cropped up in 2002. Always open to fresh ideas, don't bet against EBTG taking everyone by surprise again in the near future.

⊙ **Idlewild** (1988; Blanco y Negro/Warners). This luscious and languid collection conceals emotional turmoil ("Love Is Here Where I Live"), startlingly vivid autobiography ("Oxford Street"), vexed analysis of patriotic pangs ("Lonesome For A Place I Know") and tussles between the reasoning intellect and primal instincts ("Apron Strings"). Also contains the hit "I Don't Want To Talk About It".

- **Amplified Heart** (1994; Blanco y Negro/Warners).
  Sparsely arranged, the sounds and stories here are sometimes intimate, sometimes frightening, and often both.

- **Walking Wounded** (1996; Virgin).
  Whew, just spot the difference as Thorn and Watt roll on from Massive with a mightily atmospheric album on which drum'n'bass and jungle collide with glistening acoustic textures.

- **Like The Deserts Miss The Rain** (2002; Virgin).
  This 'best of' collection takes an interesting, around the houses route through the duo's career, taking in numbers from their early student bar crooner days right through to their mid-90s dance successes. It's made all the more worthwhile by the inclusion of some obscure mixes, B-sides and album cuts that nestle comfortably alongside expected smashes.

Peter Mills

THE EXPLOITED

Formed East Kilbride, Scotland, 1979.

They virtually owned the patent on krazy-kolor Mohican hairstyles, they wore their leather jackets to bed and they probably never washed. If that isn't enough to earn **The Exploited** your admiration, consider their best song, "Maggie", which minced no words on the subject of the ex-prime minister of Britain.

Back in the late 70s, when the anger of punk washed over Scotland and got mixed up with the rage of unemployment and frustrated nationalism, the resulting sludge was the ideal compost for a more twisted, mutant punk rock. This was the dawn of hardcore, when delicate, clever imagery gave way to stomping anthems, while gigs became beer-soaked tests of endurance.

When **Wattie Buchan** screamed and snarled over **Big John Duncan**'s guitar, and **Dru 'Stix' Campbell** (drums) and **Gary McCormick** (bass) added their little extra, The Exploited put out a very powerful noise. Consistently anti-establishment, they nailed their colours to the mast with their first single, "Army Life/Fuck The Mods/Crashed Out", released on their own Exploited label. This set the style for the next fifteen years, the first in a never-ending torrent of high-speed, buzzsaw acts of mayhem. Another brace of singles tided them over until the great PUNK'S NOT DEAD (1981), which peaked at #20 in the UK charts and made them lots of money.

The last thing a band like The Exploited needs is mainstream success, but they managed to struggle on in spite of it, releasing a dreadful live album, EXPLOITED LIVE ON STAGE (which sounded like the work of a drunk bootlegger who was sitting on the mike for much of the performance), and another couple of singles, before their even more successful second studio album, TROOPS OF TOMORROW

(1982). Anthems like "Sid Vicious Was Innocent" and "They Won't Stop", combined with a bit more cash spent on production, took them to #17 in the UK.

Big John moved on at the end of 1982 – he formed the impressively named but otherwise unknown **Blood Uncles** – and was replaced by **Billy**. Just Billy. The band now found themselves floundering in the middle of "Oi" – a misguided attempt to legitimize thugs acting tough to music – and recorded the now hugely embarrassing "Singalongabushell". (Bushell, once a rock journo, now a Tory hack, represents everything The Exploited despised.) The 'real' Exploited's final fling was the 1983 Falklands/Malvinas tribute album LET'S START A WAR (SAID MAGGIE ONE DAY). Since then The Exploited has essentially been Wattie – still raging at the moon and kicking against the pricks – plus whoever he can draft in and keep upright.

There was, however, a new Exploited album in 1985, HORROR EPICS, which might have been more metal than punk – a kind of low-rent Deep Purple on speed – but at least kept the tattered old banner of rebellion fluttering. Featuring the above-mentioned "Maggie", it's since been reissued as a two-for-the-price-of-one CD package, bundled with LET'S START A WAR (Loma).

In 1989 came DEATH BEFORE DISHONOUR, another less-than-great album, which even had Wattie stumbling around in a dub mix; and there was a 1991 offering entitled THE MASSACRE. They were pretty peripheral unless you'd decided to devote yourself to late-period punk rock and needed to brush up on Scottish rage.

What made The Exploited such a great band, and keeps them a great live act today, is Wattie's single-minded jugular-leaping hatred. They have a devoted following both in the UK and in the US, leather-clad aficionados of such titles as "Wankers", "Fuck Religion", "Treat You Like Shit" and "Jesus Is Dead". The Exploited had wit and venom in the right proportions, they let you know precisely where they were coming from, and they gave you the slogans, if not the intellectual backup, to deal with many of life's irritants.

- **Totally Exploited** (1984; Dojo).
  The obvious starting point, this compilation album would have been the ideal soundtrack to the poll-tax festivities. It has all their early hits bar "Maggie", and is the perfect beginning to a night spent prowling the streets in search of illicit thrills.

- **The Singles Collection** (1993; Cleopatra).
  Twenty-two tracks ranging from "Army Life" to "Singalongabushell". All the highs and, generously, some of the lows.

Al Spicer

THE FACES

Formed London, 1969; disbanded 1975;
played reunion gigs in 1986 and 1993.

**"We were barred from so many
hotels – the entire Holiday Inn
chain – that we had to check in as
Fleetwood Mac lots of times."
Ronnie Wood**

Formed in 1969 from the ashes of two seminal 60s bands – **THE SMALL FACES** and the **JEFF BECK** group – **The Faces** presented a perfect antidote to the serious virtuoso musicians who dominated the British rock scene of the time. Their creator was Jeff Beck's sacked bass player **Ron Wood**, who enticed **ROD STEWART** to leave Beck, and then joined forces with **Ian McLagan** (keyboards), **Ronnie Lane** (bass) and **Kenny Jones** (drums) – the remnant of The Small Faces after the departure of their frontman Steve Marriott to form Humble Pie with Peter Frampton.

Initially billed as The Small Faces, the group soon shortened their name as they began to shape their own brand of rock'n'blues, worlds apart from the mod pop that Marriott had crafted with Lane. Although the debut single from FIRST STEP (1969), the ethereal "Flying", received critical acclaim, the band's identity was better represented by the inspired sloppiness of tracks such as "Three Button Hand Me Down". (Incidentally, the song's opening bass riff would be used as an audition piece by Glen Matlock to gain entry to the Sex Pistols.)

While their next release, LONG PLAYER (1971), contained a proportion of mellow acoustic numbers such as "Richmond", the band were reinforcing their booze'n'blues image with concerts that became the ultimate lads' nights out, with Stewart kicking footballs into the audience, who were usually as plastered as the band. The addition of Stewart solo numbers such as "It's All Over Now" added to the band's popularity as a live act (his solo career had gone into overdrive with EVERY PICTURE TELLS A STORY); their live appeal has been effectively captured on several bootlegs such as THAT'S ALL YOU NEED and REAL GOOD TIME. The landmark LP, A NOD'S AS GOOD AS A WINK ... TO A BLIND HORSE (1971), epitomized the band: its sleeve featured them on stage in front of a heaving, largely male, mass, and the disc

Ronnie Lane (left) and Rod Stewart have a giggle over the latest Polaroids

F

was chock-full of good-time fare such as the staple "Stay With Me", "Too Bad", and a rousing version of Chuck Berry's "Memphis Tennessee". On numbers such as "Debris", Lane's more reflective songwriting provided a welcome foil to the yobbishness of the Wood/Stewart compositions, but the LP still bolstered the band's bad-boy image. Warner Brothers had to withdraw thousands of copies from sale after complaints from record dealers about a poster insert made up of hundreds of Polaroids that chronicled, among other things, the band's sexual conquests.

However, once Stewart's international success as a solo artist began to overshadow his band's achievements, the impetus of one of the UK's biggest live attractions gradually came to a halt. A below-par studio album, OOH LA LA (1973), was dismissed by Stewart as 'a bloody mess' – while the rest of the band accused him of absenteeism during recording. In late 1973, Lane, unable to work with Stewart any longer, left to form the ironically named **Slim Chance**, and two years later, Ron Wood graduated from part-time work with **THE ROLLING STONES** to become Mick Taylor's official replacement. The Faces' lack of cohesion wasn't helped by the release of the substandard live LP, COAST TO COAST/OVERTURE AND BEGINNERS (1974), although they did produce a wondrous final single in "You Can Make Me Dance, Sing Or Anything", which many rank among their finest work.

While Stewart's solo career and Wood's stint in The Stones continued, Kenny Jones joined **THE WHO** in 1979 as Keith Moon's replacement, and McLagan continued in session work. However, life was very different for Ronnie Lane. After some unsuccessful solo albums, and one fine collaboration with Wood (on 1976's MAHONEY'S LAST STAND), he began a long battle against multiple sclerosis. By the time of The Faces' 1986 reunion at London's Wembley Stadium, his condition had worsened so much that Bill Wyman had to play bass in his stead. Lane sadly died in 1997.

In the 90s, with Faces fever once again spreading thanks to a new generation of disciples, Stewart shrewdly attempted a second reunion in 1993 for that year's televised *Brit Awards*. Predictably the band's performance, again with Wyman on bass, was the highlight of the evening, as the past twenty years had thankfully done nothing to improve their lack of polish. Two live albums followed featuring band members: Stewart and Wood's acoustic UNPLUGGED ... AND SEATED, and Wood's own SLIDE ON LIVE (both 1993), on which he unearthed several Faces tracks, backed by McLagan among others. However, with both The Stones and Stewart often on tour, fans can expect a long wait before any more Faces reunions.

⊙ **A Nod's As Good As A Wink ... To A Blind Horse** (1971; Warners).
The essential purchase if you like your rock'n'roll loud and brash. Woody's guitar riffing never sounded so ballsy as on "Miss Judy's Farm", "That's All You Need" and the anthemic "Stay With Me".

⊙ **Snakes And Ladders (The Best Of The Faces)** (1977; Warner Brothers).
Only available as an expensive Japanese import, but the most representative Faces album, featuring the rockier moments "Silicone Grown" and "Stay With Me", singles such as "Pool Hall Richard" and "You Can Make Me Dance... ", and their quieter stuff, like "Flying", "Ooh La La" and "Sweet Lady Mary".

Paul Morris

JOHN FAHEY

Born Takoma Park, Maryland, 1939; died 2001.

Many guitarists on the East Coast folk club circuit of the late 60s were inspired by **John Fahey**'s country-blues instrumentals on his steel-stringed acoustic. His first love was country music, but in 1956 his discovery of country-blues marked a change of direction. The instant accessibility of BLIND JOE DEATH (1959; rerecorded in part or near-full for subsequent pressings in 1964 and 1967, with material from all three of these sessions reissued in 1996 as The LEGEND OF BLIND JOE DEATH CD) foreshadowed many of the elements that made 'New Age' so appealing in later years.

Fahey spent the 1960s travelling the Southern states with guitarist Henry Vestine of Canned Heat, researching the origins of the blues. In the course of these trips he rediscovered bluesmen Skip James and Bukka White, and collated sufficient material for an authoritative account of the life of bluesman Charley Patton.

Meanwhile Fahey had set up his own record label, Takoma, and released a string of albums, including a return to his old theme on his fifth album, THE TRANSFIGURATION OF BLIND JOE DEATH (1965). Featuring tunes like "I Am The Resurrection", "Transcendental Waterfall" and "On Doing An Evil Deed Blues", it was the template for later albums such as DEATH CHANTS, BREAKDOWNS & MILITARY TWO-STEPS (first issued in 1963, but almost entirely rerecorded for its 1967 edition) and REQUIA (1967; reissued 1998). On 1966's VOL. 4: THE GREAT SAN BERNARDINO BIRTHDAY PARTY he revealed a penchant for incorporating odd touches like backwards

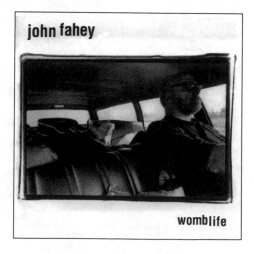

john fahey

womblife

tapes, ghostly organ, and flute into his sombre and slightly dissonant acoustic guitar instrumentals.

Despite the quality of these albums, sales through his own record label were poor, and in 1967 he signed to Sam Charters' Vanguard label, where he briefly achieved some sort of commercial acceptance with THE YELLOW PRINCESS (1969), on which he displayed his ability at synthesizing elements of country, blues and classical into his own style.

Although Fahey no longer recorded for his own label, he recorded guitarist Leo Kottke, who cut his ground-breaking SIX AND TWELVE-STRING GUITAR for Takoma; the relationship between the two would continue throughout the 70s, with Fahey producing albums for Capitol and Chrysalis. Fahey also worked with Robbie Basho and Mike Auldridge, who introduced the Dobro to a new generation of folk and country musicians.

After leaving Vanguard in 1969, Fahey was signed by Reprise, who hoped that the success of THE YELLOW PRINCESS was just the beginning of a commercial triumph. They were wrong. OF RIVERS AND RELIGION (1972) marked a return to the oblique mysticism of his debut. Other albums followed, but poor sales led to Fahey's departure from Reprise in 1974.

Returning to his own Takoma label, Fahey issued albums at regular intervals throughout the 80s. While albums like RAINFORESTS, OCEANS AND OTHER THEMES (1985) signified awareness of guitarists like Will Ackerman and Michael Hedges, the visceral urgency of his style still had more in common with that of the late Elizabeth Cotten. In the late 80s Fahey was signed to the Rounder label, for whom he made I REMEMBER BLIND JOE DEATH (1987); then, after several years of silence he returned in 1992 with the attractively titled OLD GIRLFRIENDS AND OTHER HORRIBLE MEMORIES and, after a further five-year gap, CITY OF REFUGE (1997) a 'concept album' for the end of the millennium.

Thanks to the likes of American underground producers like **Jim O'Rourke**, a new generation found Fahey, leading him to release several experimental albums on the obscure Table Of Elements label. In 2000 Fahey also published a collection of surreal autobiographical stories, *How Bluegrass Music Destroyed My Life* (Drag City Press). But despite his continued output, Fahey had for a long time been suffering with ill health. On 22nd February 2001, after undergoing heart surgery, Fahey passed away. In early 2003 his final recordings were released in the form of RED CROSS on his own Revenant Label, an imprint that he had been nurturing for some years and had earned three Grammys for its sumptuously packaged box set of Charley Patton recordings, SCREAMIN' AND HOLLERIN' THE BLUES. Fahey's influence and popularity continue to grow with music-lovers of all ages.

⊙ **The Transfiguration Of Blind Joe Death** (1965; Takoma).
More talked about than owned, this is the key to the John Fahey canon. The 1964 version was remixed and so has more clarity than the 1959 original.

⊙ **The Yellow Princess** (1969; Vanguard).
Could be described as Fahey's pitch for fame. Sellout? Not a bit of it. Just great tunes played with real verve and imagination.

⊙ **Of Rivers And Religion** (1972; Reprise).
Anticipating the emergence of New Age, this is Fahey at his most cerebral.

⊙ **Womb Life** (1998; Table Of Elements).
Produced by O'Rourke, this collection documents Fahey's true collision with the experimental. Slide guitar tones melt over loops and drones to craft exquisite spaces of sound.

⊙ **Red Cross** (2001; Revenant).
A beautiful collection of effortless picking and some stunning electric work – a fitting epitaph.

Hugh Gregory

FAIRPORT CONVENTION

Formed London, 1967.

S eminal folk-rockers **Fairport Convention** have one of rock's most complex histories, drifting through a myriad of personnel changes over a near thirty-year career. Established in a 60s London music scene where they straddled the folk club and hippie scene, they remain a much-loved fixture, reforming and performing, with associated personnel, at their annual Cropredy Festival.

The group originally comprised **Ashley Hutchings** (bass), **RICHARD THOMPSON** (guitar/vocals), **Simon Nicol** (guitar/vocals) and **Shaun Frater** (drums). After the first gig, Frater was replaced by **Martin Lamble** and later in the year the band recruited **Ian Matthews Macdonald** (vocals) and **Judy Dyble** (vocals). This line-up performed covers of Dylan and Joni Mitchell songs at London clubs, where they shared billing with Pink Floyd.

After the release of FAIRPORT CONVENTION (1968), Dyble left to join the proto-King Crimson group, Giles, Giles & Fripp, to be replaced by **Sandy Denny** (vocals) from **THE STRAWBS**. Denny brought with her a deep knowledge of British folk music, and this, coupled with Hutchings' growing interest in the genre, led to the excellent WHAT WE DID ON OUR HOLIDAYS (1969), an album that reworked traditional pieces, as well as introducing "Fotheringay", one of Denny's finest songs, and that durable Fairport favourite, "Meet On The Ledge".

Matthews left after this album to pursue his own career with Matthews Southern Comfort, a band that went on to top the UK charts with a cover of Joni Mitchell's "Woodstock". Fairport, meanwhile, recorded UNHALFBRICKING in early 1969, before setting out on a fateful UK tour – in which a road accident left Lamble dead. After much consideration they decided to continue, and released the finished album in July. It included "Si Tu Dois Partir" – a French translation of Dylan's "If You Gotta Go" – which became their one and only British chart hit, despite its somewhat eccentric instrumentation – piled-up canvas chairs acted as drums. (If you listen

The Fairports holding a convention

sound – and was replaced by **Bruce Rowlands**, formerly of The Grease Band. Then, by the time BONNY BUNCH OF ROSES was released in 1977, Denny, Lucas and Donahue had left and Nicol had returned. Denny died tragically from a brain haemorrhage in April 1978. She was just 31.

The commercial failure of BONNY BUNCH OF ROSES and its follow-up, TIPPLER'S TALES (1978), persuaded the band to call it a day in August 1979. Another contributory factor was that Swarbrick, allegedly Princess Margaret's favourite musician (she was said to receive a copy of anything he recorded), was suffering from increasing deafness and felt that he should switch to acoustic music.

Over the next six years the band limited their appearances to a once-a-year reunion at the village of Cropredy in Oxfordshire, where they were joined by guests including Thompson and Dyble. Attendances slowly grew year by year from 1500 to more than 15,000, and the event has become an annual fixture on the British folk-rock/roots scene. During the early 80s, meanwhile, Swarbrick formed **Whippersnapper**, Nicol recorded solo and Pegg joined **JETHRO TULL**.

Finally, in 1985, a new line-up started touring and recording. Pegg, Mattacks and Nicol were joined by **Martin Allcock** (guitar/strings) and **Ric Sanders** from a late variant of **SOFT MACHINE** (violin). Despite the totally different approach to the violin's role, and the fact that there was far less concentration on traditional songs – apart from the instrumental EXPLETIVE DELIGHTED (1986; reissued 1998) – the new band met with immediate success with fans and critics. Fairport continue to produce quality records, and live have actually been a more consistent outfit than in the earlier days of booze-fuelled gigs. Their musicianship was underlined, most recently, by OLD, NEW, BORROWED, BLUE (1996), an 'unplugged' album, recorded without Mattacks; and by WHO KNOWS WHERE THE TIME GOES (1997; Woodworm). For the latter, Allcock had been replaced by Chris Leslie. Soon after, Dave Mattacks left the band to pursue other musical interests, leaving the Convention once more a totally acoustic band. Stand-out track on an impressive recording is awarded to Richard Thompson for his impassioned vocals on Marvin Gaye's "I Heard It Through The Grapevine".

Their thirty years in the business were celebrated with massive gusto at the annual Cropredy Festival in 1997, which itself was commemorated in the three-CD CROPREDY box set; a live collection of the

carefully, you can hear them collapse towards the end of the song.)

Lamble's replacement on drums was **Dave Mattacks**, who joined along with **Dave Swarbrick** (fiddle), who had featured on their previous album's "Sailor's Life". Both figured on LIEGE AND LIEF (1969), generally considered to be the band's – and folk-rock's – most important album. It reached the UK Top 20, but then Denny, who wanted to play modern folk, and Hutchings, who preferred to continue with 'roots' folk, both left.

The Fairports recruited **Dave Pegg**, an old friend of Swarbrick who had also worked with Led Zeppelin's Robert Plant and John Bonham, for 1970's excellent FULL HOUSE, an album in the vein of LIEGE AND LIEF. It, too, charted in the UK, while the B-side of the subsequent single, "Now Be Thankful", gained a *Guinness Book Of Records* entry for its 38-word title. Thompson then left for a fruitful solo career, although he has occasionally reappeared as a guest at Fairport gigs.

ANGEL DELIGHT (1971) became a Top 10 album in the UK, and was followed by JOHN BABBACOMBE LEE (1971), an only partly successful concept album based on the true story of 'The Man They Couldn't Hang', as Lee described himself (the music was used in a BBC documentary about the outlaw). After its release, both Nicol and Mattacks left to form **The Albion Country Band**.

When Mattacks returned four months later, he brought with him guitarists **Trevor Lucas** (Denny's husband) and **Jerry Donahue**, and this line-up recorded ROSIE and FAIRPORT NINE (both 1973). Neither album was a great success, although the title track "Rosie" became part of the live repertoire.

In November 1973, Denny finally rejoined the band, but Mattacks left once more midway through sessions for RISING FOR THE MOON (1975) – a return to form, with a somewhat slicker, modern

best of the previous three decades. The band continue to play live and reissue discs and live oddities just keep on appearing.

◉ **Liege And Lief** (1969; Island/A&M).
The album that spawned 5000 bands and a new genre, but which has seldom, if ever, been bettered. Thrill to "Tam Lin", dance to the jigs and weep with "Crazy Man Michael".

◉ **House Full** (1986; Hannibal).
There are loads of live albums to choose from, but this 1970 recording offers the best representation of the early band.

◉ **Five Seasons** (1990; New Routes).
All of Fairport's last half-dozen albums are superb, but this has one of their best ever versions of a traditional song, "Claudy Banks", an intelligent folk song from ex-Slapp Happy member Peter Blegvad ("Gold"), and two songs that touch the heart ("Ginnie" and "The Wounded Whale").

Paul O'Brien

FAITH NO MORE

Formed Los Angeles, 1982;
mutual decision to stop 1998.

"We're not alternative, we're a rock group, we're mainstream, and there's a little bit of shame in that." Billy Gould

Faith No More's antagonistic attitude towards the world of corporate, stadium-rock whoredom has produced thrilling musical polarities. It has also been the main cause of endless angst and inter-band tensions, forever threatening the existence of this remarkable and uncomfortably 'mainstream' band.

The core of the band ever since its inception was **Mike Bordin** (drums), **Roddy Bottum** (keyboards) and **Billy Gould** (bass), but it was some time before they even approached contentment with the line-up and their repertoire. On their first gruesome 'transit van' tours of the States, they teamed up with **Chuck Mosely** (vocals) and **Jim Martin** (guitar), before releasing their debut album, FAITH NO MORE, on Mordam Records in 1985.

Their signing to Slash the following year leading to the release of INTRODUCE YOURSELF (1987), produced by Matt Wallace and Steve Berlin from Los Lobos. Building a hard-won name for themselves, they finally grabbed airplay and attention with the funk-metal groove of the single "We Care A Lot" – the shouty, snotty highlight of a largely lumbering album. By the time it hit the UK charts in early 1988, Mosely's days as singer were numbered, and he was soon dismissed, although he later joined **BAD BRAINS**. Mosley's replacement in 1989 was **Mike Patton**, whose remarkable vocal range and smouldering looks made him a pin-up and hypnotic frontman.

THE REAL THING (1989) was a spectacular breakthrough on both sides of the Atlantic, with its abrasive but stadium-friendly brand of melodic funk-rock. Jim Martin's guitar playing suggested he was

possessed, Patton whined and sulked his way through fearsome rock, and Bottum's keyboard hooks added pomp to "From Out Of Nowhere", "Edge Of The World" and the title track. As the band embarked on an intense US and European tour, 1990 brought Grammy nominations, plus chart success for "Epic" and "From Out Of Nowhere". While a much-expanded fan base awaited new material, they released LIVE AT THE BRIXTON ACADEMY (1991), recorded in London the previous year.

The gem that came out of a turbulent but triumphant 1992 was ANGEL DUST, a wilful splatter of noise and melody, aspiration and cynicism, beauty and brutality, a million miles away from the bratty adolescence of their earlier work. Patton in particular had developed from teetotal pin-up youth to a depraved subcultural ghoul, and a seam of disgust and satiety now ran through his lyrics. The music, meanwhile, was a manic rush across idioms from country to thrash via rap and dance. "Jizzlobber" and "Malpractice" spewed out screaming vocals, thrash guitars and a sense of entropy and alienation, while melodic funk underpinned "Midlife Crisis", "A Small Victory", "Be Aggressive" and "Caffeine".

Armed with this masterpiece, Faith No More embarked on a world tour supporting Guns N' Roses, and blew the headlining act away. This helped make ANGEL DUST their biggest-selling album so far, and a startlingly straight version of The Commodores' classic laid-back track, "I'm Easy", became their best-selling single early in 1993.

Headlining the Phoenix Festival to a UK audience of 50,000 should have been 1993's moment of triumph for Faith No More, but tensions, exhaustion and enervation embittered the success and the future of the band looked uncertain. The pressures finally erupted when Martin was fired early in 1994. The remaining members claimed his musical and song-writing contributions had been minimal since the days of THE REAL THING. His replacement was **Trey Spruance**, from Patton's part-time project, **Mr. Bungle**. Meanwhile, the old line-up had recorded "Another Body Murdered" with rap group Boo-Yaa T.R.I.B.E. as part of the soundtrack for the movie *Judgement Night*. It was a UK chart hit in late 1993.

Faith No More's fifth album for Slash, KING FOR A DAY ... FOOL FOR A LIFETIME (1995), was a less fractured affair than its predecessor. It marked Faith No More's mastery of what they do, revelling one moment in thrashing discordance and Patton's heavyweight ululations and, the next, in neo-Motown, gospel and 80s chart soul.

Having acquired yet another guitar player (new boy **John Hudson**) and a new record label, ALBUM OF THE YEAR (1997) screamed confidence from its title to its run-out groove. The by-now-traditional mix of poppy hooks, rock-star posturing and jazzy irony, riveted together by the Bordin and Gould method, works beautifully, with stand-out tracks like "Pristina" giving Patton room to wail and grunt to his, and our, heart's content.

The rumours of strife and discontent that had been circulating for some time were finally confirmed by Billy's press release of April 1998; 'After fifteen long and fruitful years, Faith No More have decided to put an end to speculation regarding their imminent break up ... by breaking up.' Fifteen years was probably long enough.

⊙ **The Real Thing** (1989; Slash).
Showcases the straight rock of "Epic", "The Real Thing" and the cover of Black Sabbath's "War Pigs".

⊙ **Angel Dust** (1992; Slash).
A marvellous mess of an album, with at least three definitive singles in "Midlife Crisis", "Be Aggressive" and "A Small Victory". A giant career leap.

⊙ **King For A Day ... Fool For A Lifetime** (1995; Slash).
Less bruising – but only just – what with the straight rock of "Digging The Grave", "Get Out", and traumatic "Cuckoo For Caca", though the mood changes dramatically on the mellow "Evidence" and the pomp-finale "Just A Man".

Andrew Stone

MARIANNE FAITHFULL

Born London, 1946.

The fascinating and often harrowing metamorphoses of **Marianne Faithfull** have seen her evolve from teen pop star and celebrated consort of one of the most famous entertainers of the century, through the depths of drug addiction and a stalled career, to reinvention as a battle-scarred survivor for the post-punk era. She is perhaps the only 60s icon who is a vastly more effective artist now than when she first became a household name.

Her growth as a songwriter and vocalist could never have been predicted when she began recording in 1964. The 17-year-old was discovered at a party by Rolling Stones manager Andrew Oldham, who convinced her that stardom awaited even though he had never heard her sing. What appealed to him was her angelic appearance. Like his idol Phil Spector, Oldham was convinced that producers could provide the musical content, which would be sold by the artist's image. And Faithfull undoubtedly had a look that was perfectly in tune with swinging London.

Commercially at least, things got off to a great start with "As Tears Go By," a simple but effective ballad donated by Mick Jagger and Keith Richards. Reaching the Top 10 in the UK and narrowly missing the US Top 20, this debut single remains her biggest international hit, and the song with which she is most frequently identified. (The Stones would have a big American hit with their own version a year later.) Other hits followed in 1965 ("Come And Stay With Me", "This Little Bird", "Summer Nights"), though she was a far bigger star in Britain than in America. With high, precious vocals backed by effete pop melodies and Baroque arrangements, her mid-60s recordings are essentially insubstantial but enjoyable period pieces.

In 1965, her career was slowed by marriage and a child but she indicated her unwillingness to live up to her virginal image the following year when she left her husband to live with her new lover, Mick Jagger. Their relationship was to keep the tabloids busy throughout the rest of the 60s – first as the storybook mod couple, then as the symbol of degenerate youth. Jagger's amphetamine bust in 1967 saw Marianne's musical career increasingly overshadowed by her notoriety, although she did establish herself as a film and stage actress during this time.

Her final single of the decade, "Sister Morphine" (1969), was her creative awakening, detailing the dark underside of drug addiction with a croaking voice that had seemingly lowered almost an octave since her teenage years. Co-written with Jagger and Richards, it marked the first glimpse of her lyrical talents. The single passed almost unnoticed and shortly afterwards, Faithfull suffered a miscarriage, nearly died of an overdose, and ended her affair with Jagger.

The 1970s were a mostly bleak time for Faithfull, finding her reduced to virtual destitution and deep heroin addiction. The 1977 album, FAITHLESS, was inconsequential, which made 1979's BROKEN

Dangerous acquaintance Marianne Faithfull

ENGLISH all the more shocking. This remarkable comeback saw Faithfull embracing New Wave attitudes and electronic-tinged rhythms and singing with a power that was, if anything, enhanced by her ravaged vocal cords. It also found her tackling subjects like sex and degradation with a frankness that was (and is) rare in rock'n'roll, and her acutely pained words won praise from Bob Dylan.

DANGEROUS ACQUAINTANCES and A CHILD'S ADVENTURE were erratic and disappointing follow-ups, as Faithfull compromised her uncompromising approach in search of mainstream approval. Drug and medical problems continued to dog her, as well as threats of deportation from America where she had relocated for a few years. However, this didn't prevent her from delivering another first-rate album. Consisting of cover versions of songs by the likes of Tom Waits, Dylan, Leadbelly and Jerome Kern, as well as a drastically different reprise of "As Tears Go By", STRANGE WEATHER (1987) recast Faithfull (with considerable input from producer Hal Willner) as a modern-day chanteuse in the spirit of Lotte Lenya and Edith Piaf. If BROKEN ENGLISH was Faithfull's greatest creative accomplishment, STRANGE WEATHER was her crowning achievement as a singer.

Faithfull's 90s output was largely disappointing. BLAZING AWAY (1990) was a live career retrospective that broke no significant ground. A far better move would have been a document of her bare-bones 1990 American tour, in which she gave stark and riveting shows, accompanied only by her long-time collaborator/guitarist, **Barry Reynolds**.

The mid 90s saw the publication of her autobiography, *Faithfull* (Mark Hodgekinson's more objective book is also worth reading). 1995 also saw her first album of original material in over a decade, SECRET LIFE, with Angelo Badalamenti as producer and co-songwriter. The combination promised more than it delivered, with Badalamenti's icy arrangements tending to blunt the force of Faithfull's still-compelling voice and words.

Now in middle age, Faithfull is not one to stand still. Her 1995 activities included film work, interpretations of Lotte Lenya songs at Brooklyn Academy and performances with **The Chieftains**. A concert of Kurt Weill songs at the New Morning club in Paris was released as 20TH CENTURY BLUES: AN EVENING IN THE WEIMAR REPUBLIC (1996). After a five year hiatus, a sampler of her solo work A STRANGER ON EARTH – AN INTRODUCTION TO MARIANNE FAITHFULL appeared in 2001 and the following year her rehabilitation seemed complete. KISSIN' TIME was an album of collaborations with various luminaries of contemporary pop. **Jarvis Cocker**, **Damon Albarn**, **Beck** and **Billy Corgan** were among the artists delighted to help confirm Faithfull's status as one of rock'n'roll's greatest survivors. Although her recordings are extremely erratic, each release remains, at the very least, unpredictable, which is not something you can say about many other veterans of the 1960s.

(•) **Broken English** (1979; Island).
With two decades of punk and post-punk outrage under the bridge, this sounds more mainstream than it did upon its release, but it's still one of the most unexpected victories of rock history. Faithfull remoulds herself as a toughened warrior on life's edges, unafraid of examining the most disturbing psychosexual wounds.

(•) **Strange Weather** (1987; Island).
Cabaret music for the end of the twentieth century. Haunting interpretations of a wide range of after-hours tunes, wisely selected and tastefully performed, with strong contributions from guitarist Bill Frisell and bassist Fernando Saunders.

(•) **Perfect Stranger** (1998; Polygram).
This marvellous, 35-track anthology is the ideal introduction to her long and illustrious career.

Richie Unterberger

THE FALL

Formed Manchester, England, 1977.

"You've got to have something to moan about, haven't you?" Mark E. Smith

Dubbed 'The Grumpiest Man in Pop', **Mark E. Smith** has been carving his jaundiced signature on the music scene for the past twenty years. Rarely tempted to celebrate the lighter side of life, Smith uses humour and horror to illuminate hypocrisy and injustice, and, on stage, works himself into a maelstrom of contempt that temporarily obliterates the flawed and imperfect world. Without **The Fall**, punk and its descendants would have turned out very differently; they've produced a huge volume of high-quality music over the last 22 years and their vast influence on independent music cannot be denied. Nor can their integrity and refusal to compromise.

The story of The Fall starts in the Manchester Docks, where sharp but cynical Mark E. Smith was holding down a tedious office job. Inspired by the early punk scene, he got together with **Martin Bramah** (guitar) and **Tony Friel** (bass) and set out on one of the weirder journeys in rock'n'roll. The trademark shambling though purposeful rhythms, the 'unusual' vocals – the whole scene started here.

The first line-up was completed by **Una Baines** (electric piano) and **Karl Burns** (drums). Legendary early gigs included a supermarket's staff Christmas party and a couple of resolutely traditional working men's clubs, where the band were not immediately appreciated. Still, the band progressed, and, after the first of what were to become a lifetime of sessions for John Peel, signed with Step Forward, a tiny London label run by ATV's Mark Perry.

Their debut release, 1978's BINGO MASTER'S BREAKOUT, was a three-track EP outlining Smith's manifesto: bizarre subjects minutely observed from unusual angles, a bleak, wry humour conveyed in a sardonic Manchester accent, and a disregard for the 'normal' rock approach. Even a bit of conventional

The ever sartorial, ever chirpy, Mark E. Smith

punk thrash like "Psycho Mafia" is rendered experimental by Smith's yelping as his voice wrestles for attention with the piano and guitar tracks. In its own distinct way, it was as arty and clever, and as coolly distanced, as prime Velvet Underground, who, along with Can, Smith cited as a prime influence.

Personnel changes were to be a recurrent feature of The Fall. By the time the band were recording their second single, "It's the New Thing"/"Various Times", Una Baines had been replaced by **Yvonne Pawlett**, and Tony Friel had given way to **Marc Riley**. The A-side was all chirpy sarcasm, the flip was a gloomy tale of backstreet Nazi Germany.

The Fall were being managed at the time by Smith's partner, Kay Carroll. Mark would often seek lyrical inspiration by picking arguments with her and recording them for analysis. With this level of disturbance in the mix, The Fall's first album, LIVE AT THE WITCH TRIALS, released in January 1979, was predictably angst-ridden, absorbing and deviant, placing Smith and his team at the screaming edge of rock.

By the summer of the year, Smith was already the only original founder member still recording with The Fall. Riley took on guitar in addition to keyboards, **Steve Hanley** replaced Bramah on bass, **Mike Leigh** took over on drums, and Pawlett was replaced by guitarist **Craig Scanlon**. The second album, DRAGNET appeared in 1979; it was less ragged than its predecessor and more experimental in terms of tempo and texture. Smith had grown more confident as a lyricist, coining outrageous rhymes and distilling complex themes into punchy, lasting images.

The Fall opened the 80s with one of Mark E.'s most searing caricatures, "Fiery Jack" (1980), a vicious, rockabilly-styled song about a beer-swilling, pig-ignorant fighting type. Then in May 1980 came the live album, TOTALE'S TURNS (IT'S NOW OR NEVER), their first release for Rough Trade.

Other than Mike Leigh's replacement on drums by Steve Hanley's brother, **Paul**, The Fall managed to maintain this line-up until early 1983 and record much of the band's finest and most complex material. First came a pair of singles rich in madness and exaggeration. "How I Wrote Elastic Man" delved into the world of a misunderstood songwriter while "Totally Wired" celebrated the joys of amphetamine sulphate.

With their following growing steadily, Smith and co released their third album, the masterful GROTESQUE (AFTER THE GRAMME) (1980). This matched inventive, uplifting music with lyrics depicting, in Hogarthian detail, the underbelly of poverty in English society. The album's epic extended track, "The North Will Rise Again", was a slow but determined saga of betrayal and insurrection.

SLATES (1981) came next, a 10" mini-album which maintained the band's trademark intensity while extending their musical parameters. "Leave The Capitol", for example, was deceptively jaunty but harboured an amusingly poisonous rant about a superficial and grotesque London. Following a move from Rough Trade to Kamera records, The Fall released a confident single, "Lie Dream Of A Casino Soul", and a masterful new album HEX ENDUCTION HOUR (1982). Recorded partly in Reykjavik, this was the apotheosis of the band's early work. Powered by a new two-drummer line-up (Karl Burns was back), it saw Smith broaden his lyrical range as the band reached new heights of inventive savagery.

Strangely, a short fallow period came next. A throwaway single "Look Know" was followed by ROOM TO LIVE (1982), an unfocused set which occasionally veered towards self-indulgence. The band returned to Rough Trade and Mark Riley and Kay Carroll departed. Fresh impetus was needed and it came in the shape of Smith's new girlfriend, **Brix**. She joined the band on guitar and vocals and eventually provided a lightness of touch which up to that point had never been present.

Perversely, Brix's first Fall outing, 1983's PERVERTED BY LANGUAGE, was a dark, claustrophobic affair. Smith's fascination with Nazi Germany surfaced again on "Garden", while the closing "Hexen Definitive Strife Knot" found our man in a state that could only be described as despairing defiance.

1984 saw a move to Beggars Banquet, a couple of singles and an album, THE WONDERFUL AND FRIGHTENING WORLD OF THE FALL which featured guest vocals from Virgin Prune **Gavin Friday**. The album showed the band maturing but perhaps lacked the range of certain Fall releases. It was followed by THIS NATION'S SAVING GRACE (1985), The Fall's biggest tilt towards the mainstream, which saw multi-instrumentalist **Simon Rogers** replacing Hanley. It was consistently excellent, with Brix's West Coast pop sensibilities pushed to the fore but with plenty of room remaining for oddball experimentation.

Another change to the line-up followed, as Karl Burns departed and was replaced by **Simon Woolstencroft**. Burns missed out on The Fall's best-ever drug song, and first UK chart entry (albeit peaking at #75), "Mr Pharmacist". This three-minute, amphetamine masterpiece proved the highlight of BEND SINISTER (1986), not a great album by Fall standards.

1988's patchy THE FRENZ EXPERIMENT introduced **Marsha Schofield**, on keyboards and vocals and propelled The Fall into the UK Top 20 albums chart. They had gone Top 50 a couple of months earlier with their cover of The Kinks' "Victoria" and had started to attract a new generation of fans. But, if fame and fortune beckoned, The Fall didn't exactly go for the jugular. Their next release was a 'concept album' in association with avant-garde ballet dancer (and Mark's longtime pal) **Michael Clark**, I AM KURIOUS ORANJ (1988).

The Fall ended 1988 in fine form, in the studio and on stage, as shown by SEMINAL LIVE (1989). However, serious personnel changes were afoot as Brix left with cheesy violinist Nigel Kennedy. Martin Bramah returned to play guitar and Mark's lyrics acquired a new level of cynicism. On EXTRICATE (1990), "Sing Harpy", the opening track, immediately let you know you were in for a rough ride, and if the other tracks held back from dealing overtly with the break-up, the overriding emotion was rage.

In spring 1990, Smith cut the band down to a four-piece unit, with only Craig Scanlon, Steve Hanley and Simon Woolstencroft keeping their jobs. Pausing only to pull in a fiddle player, **Kenny Brady**, he took the band out on the road again and then returned to the studio for SHIFT WORK (1991).

By now, The Fall were enjoying both chart success and credibility. Both CODE: SELFISH (1992) and THE INFOTAINMENT SCAN (1993) were treated with grudging respect by the music press and kept The Fall in the UK album charts. The former was as well crafted a collection of songs as Smith had ever devised, with **David Bush** (keyboards and 'machines') bringing a range of new sounds. The latter reached a dizzying peak at #9. Amid the usual mad rants, it contained a gorgeous cover of "Lost In Music" and, in "I'm Going To Spain", almost a romantic ballad. It was backed by the best shows they had given since touting HEX ENDUCTION HOUR more than ten years previously.

Smith guested on vocals for the **Inspiral Carpets'** 1994 single "I Want You" but went back to the day job later in the year with the caustic MIDDLE-CLASS REVOLT. This spawned no hits, with Mark returning to dark, cultish obscurity. Brix returned to the band for live performances and played on CEREBRAL CAUSTIC (1995), which saw Smith picking at the scabs of their broken marriage on prime sour cuts such as "Don't Call Me Darling" and "Feeling Numb".

Interviews had alluded to problems with the booze, and at the beginning of 1996 it seemed that Smith was treading water with the band. The year kicked off with SINISTER WALTZ (RECEIVER), alternating mixes of tracks from the 1990 EXTRICATE and 1991 SHIFTWORK sessions: a worthwhile addition to the collection while the miserable old git worked out where to go. Then came a live album, THE TWENTY-SEVEN POINTS (a double CD of, naturally, 28 tracks), featuring a wonderful version of "Lost In Music", before yet another label and line-up change for studio outing THE LIGHT USER SYNDROME. This offered encouraging stuff, with Brix performing her grain-of-sand role to Mark E.'s oyster, the resulting pearls including a mad Gene Pitney cover, drums'n'bass to knock the walls down, and the return of Mancabilly.

1998 opened with rumours of wild backstage behaviour on Mark's part; anonymous band members complained to the press, fans circulated stories on the Internet and finally Mark was arrested in New York for fighting with partner and keyboard player, **Julia Nagle**. The latest in a series of final straws, this caused Steve Hanley (the power behind the throne in the band), Karl Burns and Tommy Crooks to peel off and form a band of their own. Smith took time out to assemble the remarkable POST NEARLY MAN (1998; Artful), a 'spoken-word' collection. He then unveiled yet another line-up (himself plus Nagle, **Tom Head** on drums, guitarist **Neville Wilding** and bassist **Adam Halal**) and another 'proper album' THE MARSHALL SUITE (1999).

There followed a flood of archive recordings. Some had little or nothing to add to material avail-

able elsewhere, but a cache of classic Fall live albums, previously almost impossible to obtain, finally saw daylight in 1997 and 1998: THE LEGENDARY CHAOS TAPE, FALL IN A HOLE and LIVE TO AIR IN MELBOURNE 1982 (all on Cog Sinister).

More recently the market has been flooded by more live Fall collections, many of dubious worth, while the PEEL SESSIONS (1999) was a well-chosen seventeen-track set with sleeve notes by Peel himself.

The Fall saw off the old millennium with their strongest work in a decade. THE UNUTTERABLE reunited Smith with **Grant Showbiz** – known, to those who know such things, as the best live soundman in the UK, and one of the few producers with an understanding of what makes the band tick. Smith had again lined up Nagle, Halal and Wilding and, after the recruitment of **Tom Head** on drums, appeared to have stumbled across one of the most enduring line-ups in the band's history. Typically, the only surviving member of the band on The Fall's next album was Smith himself.

The enigmatic **J Watts**, **B Pritchard**, **S Birtwistle**, **E Blaney** and **B Fanning** were conjured out of nowhere to accompany our hero on 2001's ARE YOU ARE MISSING WINNER. Rough and dirty Kraut-rock-abilly and, on "Ibis- Afro Man", bizarre and inspired experimentation were the order of the day. 2002 saw 2G+2, a live performance from 2001 with some promising studio morsels thrown in, and also TOTALLY WIRED–THE ROUGH TRADE ANTHOLOGY.

Hopefully, he'll keep doing this for ever.

⦿ **Live At The Witch Trials** (1979; IRS).
Littered with attention-grabbing, lyrical images, the music builds up an atmosphere of deserted, windswept streets. Recorded in two days, it is clearly a masterpiece.

⦿ **Dragnet** (1979; IRS).
Continuing where TRIALS left off, this album reeks of hatred, injustice and fear. Strong stuff, best listened to in a cold, dimly lit room...

⦿ **Grotesque** (After The Gramme) (1980; Castle).
Smith dissects the underbelly of English society in the Thatcher years, but with some surprisingly catchy tunes.

⦿ **Hex Enduction Hour** (1982; Line).
A big, stomping, stumbling album, with everything mixed up louder than everything else on a sequence of drum-led songs and experimental interludes.

⦿ **Code: Selfish** (1992; Cog Sinister).
Smith as songsmith on an album that found a new musical dimension, though he still complains "Everything Hurtz" on the anthemic track.

⦿ **The Infotainment Scan** (1993; Permanent/Cog Sinister).
The Fall go Top 10. And why not, with these covers of "Lost in Music" and "Why Are People Grudgeful?'", plus two splendid versions of "The League of Bald-Headed Men".

⦿ **The Legendary Chaos Tape** (1997; Cog Sinister).
Their greatest live set, finally available everywhere. A magnificent celebration of everything that makes them such a great band, shambling rhythm, bizarre lyrics alternately yelled and whispered by a madman. Perfect.

⦿ **Peel Sessions** (1999; Strange Fruit).
From "Rebellious Jukebox" to "M5", seventeen tracks compiled by guitarman Steve Hanley, from the collection of the band's greatest fan.

Al Spicer

FAMILY

Formed Leicester, England, 1967; disbanded 1973.

The much-maligned genre of progressive rock occasionally produced bands who challenged people's perceptions about music and life. One such band was **Family**, formed by **Charlie Whitney** (guitar) at Leicester Art College. Once he'd recruited **Ric Grech** (bass), **Jim King** (saxophone), **Roger Chapman** (vocals) and **Rob Townsend** (drums), the five-piece moved down to London, where they were an instant success on the city's burgeoning underground music scene.

Reprise signed them up and hired Traffic's Dave Mason to produce their first album, MUSIC IN A DOLL'S HOUSE (1968). Featuring Whitney's unique guitar style, with Grech and King adding violin and flute to a mix topped by Chapman's distinctive rasping vocals, Family had a minor hit on their hands.

The second LP, FAMILY ENTERTAINMENT (1969), included the haunting "Weaver's Answer", a single release which earned them memorable TV appearances. A US tour followed, during which Ric Grech shocked the band by announcing he was quitting to join supergroup **Blind Faith** with Eric Clapton and Steve Winwood. **John Weider** was his replacement on bass and violin, but the States proved difficult for the band to break, a situation that wasn't helped by an alleged fist fight between Chapman and promoter Bill Graham.

Back in England, Jim King left and was replaced by **Poli Palmer**, who added keyboards and vibes to the band's impressive array of sounds. The Top 5 album A SONG FOR ME (1970) was followed later in the year by ANYWAY, which contained their biggest hit single, "In My Own Time". Unlike many of their contemporaries, Family were never afraid to show their working-class roots and rock out – 'art school' they were not.

OLD SONGS NEW SONGS (1971) came out, Weider left and was replaced by **John Wetton**, and the band at last was rewarded with some success in the States. FEARLESS (1971) maintained the high standard, but BANDSTAND (1972) was a largely disappointing collection, apart from the stomping stage favourite "Burlesque", and "My Friend The Sun", a simple acoustic ballad.

Family seemed to have reached a plateau. They moved on by switching labels from Reprise to Raft and replacing Palmer and Wetton with **Tony Ashton** (keyboards) and **Jim Cregan** (bass/guitar). The upshot was a fine album, IT'S ONLY A MOVIE (1973), on which Ashton's vocals often provided an effective contrast to Chapman's, as on the bar-room singalong hit, "Sweet Desiree". However, the album failed to sell, and Family broke up.

Cregan joined **Cockney Rebel** and later played with Rod Stewart; Ashton returned to session work; and Townsend is currently with **The Blues Band**. Chapman and Whitney formed **The Streetwalkers** and recorded five albums, the best of which was RED CARD (1976). Subsequently, Chapman fronted various bands to work in Europe, while Whitney formed **Axepoint** and cut a couple of albums for RCA. However, all are best remembered for Family – an inventive band whose appearances on the festival circuit are fondly remembered.

Both A SONG FOR ME and ANYWAY were dusted off, remastered and reissued in 1998, plus bonus tracks, on Essential records. The albums have dated – as has most of the prog-rock of the time – but they still have magic to offer the unprejudiced ear.

⊙ **Best Of Family** (1991; See For Miles).
A reissue of the Reprise greatest hits compilation originally released in 1974 – unquestionably the one to go for.

⊙ **Music In A Doll's House/Entertainment** (1968/1968; See For Miles)
The first two albums repackaged and reissued together at last.

THE FARM

Formed Liverpool, England, 1983; split 1995.

Twenty-one-year-old would-be vocalist **Peter Hooton** formed the original line-up of **The Farm** with his dole-queue pals – **Stevie Grimes** (guitars), **Phil Strongman** (bass) and **Andy McVann** (percussion) – with a view to voicing what he liked to describe as 'The Soul of Socialism'. While the rock press quickly turned against what it considered mere sloganeering, the burgeoning cult popularity of other left-wing bands such as the Newtown Neurotics, Three Johns, and the Redskins (whose distinctive horn sound they sought to emulate), gave The Farm reason to believe that their message could be heard – not least through a football-flavoured fanzine entitled *The End*, which Hooton was running at the time. By 1984, The Farm had the brass section it desired, in the shape of **Anthony Evans**, **Steve Levy**, **George Maher** and **John Melvin**.

Success, however, was delayed by the death in 1986 of McVann, killed in a car crash following a chase with the police. The group came through the trauma, and found a replacement sticksman in **Roy Boulter**. (Strongman, however, gave up his bass duties to new boy **Carl Hunter**.)

Losing its horn section, The Farm then adopted another new style by bringing in the keyboard skills of Benjamin Leach, which gave the band a synth-pop sound that changed the group's fortunes for the better. A spirited fourth independent single release, "Body And Soul" (1988), gained some attention, particularly on the dance floor. This was still not good enough for The Farm, however: the group now pursued success on its own label, Produce Records.

Early in 1990, Hooton and company approached fashionable producer Terry Farley to further 'dancify' their sound. The first result was a hypnotic, bottom-heavy reading of The Monkees' "Stepping Stone".

This single narrowly missed the Top 40, but grabbed the attention of the baggy/dance crossover scenesters, who began to show up at The Farm's gigs. In September, the band's seventh single – the enjoyable "Groovy Train"– entered the chart at #40 and, following a debut *Top Of The Pops* TV appearance, peaked at #6. This new-found pop star status was cemented by the anthemic "All Together Now" (1990), for which they boldly stole the melody from Pachelbel's famous *Canon In D*. The record became the band's best-selling 45, peaking at #4 and shifting over half a million copies in the UK.

The next year began on a high with SPARTACUS, the debut LP, entering the British album chart at #1 in the wake of its two hit singles. Lucrative deals with Sire and Sony followed, but a downward trend appeared to have set in: the next Farm single, "Don't Let Me Down", scraped into the charts; its rapid follow-up, "Mind", also failed to enter the Top 30. The fans' doubts were borne out by the next album, LOVE SEE NO COLOUR (1991), and its title-track single, which foundered at #58 while the album sank like the Titanic. After another flop single, the fading stars found some respite when asked to contribute a track to a covers compilation of 80s #1s. The Farm contributed an awful version of The Human League's "Don't You Want Me?" (1992), which somehow dragged the band back into the Top 20.

It was to prove a false dawn. The 1994 album HULLABALOO was given virtually no airplay in the UK, though it fared marginally better in the States thanks to the enthusiasm of Sire. Before long, though, the band had vanished. Since then the only reminders have been a couple of 'best of' compilations and a slice of fiction, *Powder*, written by the band's manager, Kevin Sampson.

⊙ **Spartacus** (1991; Produce).
This strong debut contains the hit singles "Groovy Train" and "All Together Now", as well as other notable cuts like "Hearts And Minds".

Jeremy Simmonds

FATBOY SLIM

Born Brighton, England 1963.

Darling of the mainstream dance scene, purveyor of student-friendly Big Beat and remixer to the stars, **Norman Cook**, better known under his **Fatboy Slim** moniker, has successfully crossed over from a low-key, after-club house-party ritual to daytime-radio megabucks. Cook is still riding high in the public eye, with eye-catching videos and richly layered intensely danceable pop singles boosting the album sales and pulling in remix and production requests by the sackload. He's an undisputed master of production and has an obsessive enthusiast's familiarity with popular music history that gives him the wide palette he employs both in the studio and at the decks.

The Fatboy used to be bass-slinger for dour northern British Marxists **THE HOUSEMARTINS**.

When that band folded in 1988 (spawning **THE BEAUTIFUL SOUTH**), Cook went on to explore a long-standing interest in hip-hop and dub reggae, releasing a couple of singles under his own name before surfacing as **Beats International** with the powerful "Dub Be Good To Me". This track, with its floor-shaking lift of the bass line from The Clash's "Guns Of Brixton", broke the band big time, and the album LET THEM EAT BINGO (1990) went gold. The dubbed-to-crazy follow-up, EXCURSION ON THE VERSION (1991) sold less well and, following a tour of Africa, Cook shelved the project and remained out of the limelight until 1994.

Reggae had proven to be a dead end, but the growing popularity and good-times hedonism of the dance clubs and DJ world finally attracted Cook's notice. And so, briefly, he was Pizzaman, serving slices of cheesy dance such as "Trippin' On Sunshine" and the handbaggy "Happiness". Overlapping with the Pizzaman was Wildski, Fried Funk Food and Freak Power, whose "Turn On, Tune In, Cop Out" (sampling heavily from War's "Low Rider") crossed over from being a club smash in 1993 to the soundtrack to a Levi's jeans commercial two years later. Their 1994 album DRIVE THRU BOOTY sold well enough but Cook was, by this time, finding more satisfaction (and a shorter journey home) DJing in the clubs of Brighton, his home town, and assembling floor-filling gems in his home studio.

Happy to leave the cerebral, introspective side of the music biz to the experts, Cook concentrated on the 'drink and dancing' aspects that he knew best, contributing "Magic Carpet Ride" – as Mighty Dub Katz – in 1995 before the Fatboy appeared with a series of uplifting and rushy singles "Everybody Needs A 303", "Santa Cruz" and the cheeky Who-sampling "Going Out Of My Head" (which also borrowed some John Bonham beats) as tasters to his thrown-together mishmash, BETTER LIVING THROUGH CHEMISTRY (1996). The album was a wild assemblage of styles, with bouncing breakbeats liberally drenched in humour, stealing from all flavours of dance music. Famously assembled in two weeks, and with scant attention paid to obtaining clearance for the hundreds of chopped and distorted samples from which it was constructed, the album perfectly complemented the innovative work he was doing as a DJ at Brighton's Big Beat Boutique. The album's ten tracks were all positive, uplifting dance grooves, with the crowd-pleasing Fatboy trademark structure (which he effectively described as 'foreplay, then you get into the rhythm and then you build and build and then you have the orgasm and then the cigarette afterwards') and built from his phenomenal magpie-like collection of samples, riffs and beats.

This eclectic approach defined Big Beat; a willingness to look beyond hip-hop rarities to pop music gems and unassailable rock classics as source material. The next full-length Fatboy Slim release, ON THE FLOOR AT THE BOUTIQUE (1998), was a DJ mix that

captured the genre-transgressing joy of one of Norman's club nights. The album, including smile- and boogie-inducing classics by the Jungle Brothers and Fred Wesley, was a classic rummage through the record collection that also featured snatches of "Louie, Louie", a bongo-band version of the Shadows' "Apache" and the apple-on-ecstasy computer vox of Christopher Just's "I'm A Disco Dancer".

The club attracted big-name DJs from as far as the US and gave Cook the perfect venue to try out his own new compositions as well as his wildly successful remixes; his version of Cornershop's "Brimful Of Asha", for example, was a hit at the club months before it crossed over (and went on to massively outsell Cornershop's original version), he did wonders on The Beastie Boys' "Body Movin'", and he turned Wildchild's "Renegade Master" into a huge club hit.

The success of both BETTER LIVING and ON THE FLOOR enabled Cook to charge £15,000 for a remix and led to his having fun and making money at the same time, with heroes such as Bootsy Collins hanging out in his bedroom studio. It also let him devote time and money to the crafting of YOU'VE COME A LONG WAY BABY (1998). Once again prefaced by the release of a chart-topping single – "The Rockafeller Skank" – it had stand-out tracks in the ska-tinted "Gangster Tripping", the vaguely disturbing "Love Island" and the Krautrock-meets-gospel of "Praise You", helped to chart success by one of the year's strangest videos.

By the end of 1999 Cook was a worldwide sensation – Britain's biggest artist in the US and winner of countless awards. But fame and the inevitable scourge of the tabloids began to have an effect. 'The pressure of being in the limelight all the time was beginning to take its toll,' he commented. 'For about three months my job was to go to awards ceremonies.'

This sentiment informed the title to Cook's third studio LP, HALFWAY BETWEEN THE GUTTER AND THE STARS (2000) – a move away from the tried and tested Fatboy formula that saw Mr Slim experimenting with his soulful side. Collaborations with Macy Gray, Bootsy Collins and Urban Soul's Roland Clarke sat alongside more traditional fare. Though not entirely consistent and perhaps a more downbeat affair than his previous sets, his third collection was thoroughly entertaining.

No rest from award ceremonies though for Mr Slim, as GUTTER AND STARS and its attendant singles furnished him with several more assorted gongs for his Brighton pad. In 2002 Norman was appointed as England's official World Cup DJ, while July saw the staging of a sonically triumphant Fatboy-hosted free gig on Brighton beach. The event had been staged the previous year, attracting around 30,000 people; this time around more than 250,000 people descended on the city causing absolute bedlam.

Despite this disaster and his wobbly marriage to radio DJ/presenter Zöe Ball, Fatboy Slim currently shows no signs of retiring.

- **Better Living Through Chemistry** (1996; Skint/ Astralwerks).
The dawn of Big Beat – cheeky, dance-inspiring, uplifting fun and games.

- **You've Come A Long Way Baby** (1998; Skint/ Astralwerks).
Big Beat in full flow – better production than BETTER LIVING with guaranteed enjoyment from start to finish.

- **Halfway Between The Gutter And The Stars** (2000; Skint/ Astralwerks).
Where's the Big Beat? More experimental, even mellow, this set finds the Fatboy trying some new shots and grappling with fatherhood.

Al Spicer

FATES WARNING

Formed Hartford, Connecticut, 1984.

Born in a musical era when heavy metal bands could still fill stadiums, **Fates Warning** have tinkered with the edges of the genre since their first album, NIGHT ON BROCKEN (1984). Although not their greatest artistic statement – fairly traditional metal with a distinctively Iron Maiden feel – it carried hints of the progressive work that was to come. THE SPECTRE WITHIN (1985), laden with thick, complex arrangements, saw their experimentation begin in earnest as vocalist **John Arch**'s wickedly unusual and technical melody lines played counterpoint to the instrumentation. The style was brought to full fruition on AWAKEN THE GUARDIAN (1986; Metal Blade), one of the band's best albums.

Still cherished by many fans, perhaps because it was Arch's last album, AWAKEN THE GUARDIAN was more accessible than THE SPECTRE WITHIN, and saw a new level of complexity in the band's songwriting. Undeniably heavy – the twin guitars of **Jim Matheos** and **Frank Aresti** form a thick, crushing aura – the songs are filled with more melody than expected from 80s metal, mainly due to the odd and compelling vocal lines.

On NO EXIT (1988; Metal Blade), vocalist **Ray Alder** joined the group and the songwriting took a drastic turn away from the thick, warm tones of AWAKEN THE GUARDIAN towards more of a crisp 'speed metal' sound. This album marked the beginning of a new period for the band for several reasons: the replacement of Arch with Alder, the drastic change in songwriting tempo and guitar sound, and a new focus on the progressive approach, with side two of the album consisting of a single, 21-minute song.

Less heavy than NO EXIT, the follow-up album PERFECT SYMMETRY (1989) is widely considered the band's most progressive release, carrying a seriousness and maturity that make it a stand-out. While songs still feature crunching guitars and Ray Alder's ungodly high vocals, the arrangements and mixing make the disc more suitable for 'non-metal' ears.

Their tendency toward a lighter sound continued with PARALLELS (1991), the first in a series of 'mellow' albums. To date the band's most financially successful album, each song was short (with the exception of "The Eleventh Hour", widely considered to be the album's best song) and filled with radio-friendly hooks. While PARALLELS was greeted with enthusiasm by the prog-metal community, the next release, INSIDE OUT (1994), was almost universally panned – even by the band themselves. More in the same style as PARALLELS, though without the heart, the only exceptional track is "Monument".

In 1997, the band shrank to a smaller core unit of guitarist Jim Matheos, singer Alder and drummer **Mark Zonder** – and once again set sail in search of more progressive songwriting. The result was A PLEASANT SHADE OF GRAY (1997), a *tour de force* album containing a single piece in twelve parts, almost an hour long, written by Matheos and produced by Rush veteran Terry Brown (with whom the band had worked on the previous two albums). The artistic success of A PLEASANT SHADE... was reflected in the double live album STILL LIFE (2000), which featured parts I to XII of the preceding album on the first disc. The excellence was maintained with DISCONNECTED (2001), with Dream Theater's **Kevin Moore** providing keyboards on the title track.

- **A Pleasant Shade Of Gray** (1997; Metal Blade).
Refreshing, original, progressive metal with brains as well as brawn.

James Bickers

FATIMA MANSIONS

Formed London, 1989; split 1996.

After the split of **MICRODISNEY**, **Cathal Coughlan** – the band's acerbic and political edge – surfaced with a new group and uncompromising vision. **Fatima Mansions**, named after a run-down Dublin housing estate, was to be a vehicle for his world-view, and **Andrias O'Gruama** (guitar), **Hugh Bunker** (bass), **Nick Allum** (drums) and **Zac Woolhouse** (keyboards) were enlisted for the supporting roles. Coughlan's lyrical fixations of religious bigotry, imperialism and death were spelled out in parables of increasing hysteria and black humour, while the safety of Microdisney's rock arrangements was abandoned in favour of an all-out aural assault. Fatima Mansions was to become a cult favourite for the 90s.

AGAINST NATURE (1989) was lauded as a startlingly well-rounded debut, establishing a broad territory from the driving single "Only Losers Take The Bus", to the synth-pop pastiche of "13th Century Boy", and the occasional brooding ballad like "Wilderness On Time". There was a new-found power and urgency in the vocal delivery, and an incisiveness to the sound, driven by Andrias's raw guitar lines. The single "Blues For Ceausescu" (1990) took the band onto a higher level of ferocity and invention, heralding the eighteen-track onslaught of VIVA DEAD PONIES (1990). From the opening track,

Fatima Mansion's Cathal shows he's as game for a
laugh as anyone

to the Manic Street Preachers' flip-side cover of
"Suicide Is Painless". While their uncompromising
style may have ruled out any greater commercial
success, their standing as a live act secured a support slot on a U2 tour. But Cathal refused to be on
best behaviour for the big occasion, infamously
causing a near riot on the Italian leg with some on-
stage Catholic baiting. Cathal continued his prolific
output by releasing 20 GOLDEN SHOWERS (1993)
under the name Bubonique, featuring compatriot
comedian Sean Hughes, followed by a new Fatima
Mansions album, LOST IN THE FORMER WEST
(1994). Once again this was not for the faint-
hearted, tackling international affairs with the usual
rage and humour. But there was a sense that the
format had become too well defined and that some
of the shock value of earlier works had been eroded
by familiarity.

In 1996 Cathal put out his first solo release,
GRAND NECROPOLITAN, in which he felt able to
wrap his lyrics in a more melodic music once more.
This proved to be Cathal's way of telling the world
that the Fatimas had now broken up. Since then
Cathal has continued to stitch away at his solo
tapestry: most recently BLACK RIVER FALLS (2000)
and THE SKY'S AWFUL BLUE (2002) both rejected
bluster and rock in favour of sparse folksy arrangements. Future developments are awaited with
interest.

⊙ **Viva Dead Ponies** (1990; Kitchenware).
Stylistically this has everything but the proverbial
kitchen sink: running the gamut from epic ballad ("The Door
To Door Inspector") to cathartic rant ("Chemical Cosh"),
there's something here for everyone.

⊙ **Bertie's Brochures** (1991; Kitchenware).
A mini-LP including some uncharacteristically measured vocal performances by Cathal, although he can't resist
an occasional bellow. Its title track is particularly fine.

⊙ **Valhalla Avenue** (1992; Kitchenware/Radioactive).
"1000%" is the riff-driven single, but much of the rest
has a doom-laden, if still alluring, quality.

Nick Dale

"Angel's Delight", which took the idea of light and
shade in a song to new heights of absurdity, this was
an ambitious roller coaster of an album, taking in a
huge range of styles and themes.

Meanwhile, regular gigging quickly built their reputation as an extraordinary spectacle, with Cathal
hurling his hulk around the stage like a man possessed,
while the band drove him on, with Andrias in
wraparound shades grimacing at the pain of his dis-
cords. In early 1991, Cathal performed some acoustic
gigs billed as 'Fatima Mansions Singular', showcasing
the control and mellowness of his voice – 'I know you
all think I'm a brute', he observed. Some of these more
restrained songs emerged on BERTIE'S BROCHURES
(1991), including covers of Scott Walker's "Long
About Now" and Richard Thompson's "The Great
Valerio", but this was no simple 'unplugged' effort and
included a barely recognizable dismemberment of
R.E.M.'s "Shiny Happy People".

Normal service was resumed with the release of
VALHALLA AVENUE (1992), which contained the
customary doses of rancour and strident guitar
riffing on tracks like "Evil Man" and "Go Home
Bible Mike". The album's ferocious tone did not
prevent it from becoming their biggest seller yet,
reaching #52 in the UK. They even had a surprise
Top 10 single later that year with a near-psychotic
reworking of Bryan Adams' "Everything I Do (I
Do It For You)", although this was largely down

FAULTLINE

Formed London, 1998.

O ne of the surprise successes of 2002 was the
Faultline album YOUR LOVE MEANS
EVERYTHING; it was a set that seemed to come
from nowhere, hiding behind an anonymous-
looking cover that depicted a plastic monkey
wrench, and containing a stunning collection of
heartfelt electronic torch songs, made all the more
marketable by the presence of several 'big name'
guest vocalists.

David Kosten is the one-man-band that comprises Faultline. The London DJ/producer came to
music through a childhood talent for the clarinet,
which saw him through to the National Youth
Orchestra. The classical influences of Kosten's background were not squandered during his forays into
electronica and pop. From his first single, "Control"

(1998), to his first album, CLOSER, COLDER on Leaf Records (1999), Kosten displayed his unique ability to fuse high-modern classical music with digital distortion. CLOSER, COLDER was a challenging record, chock-full of paranoia and claustrophobia, left-field intellectual noise and general sonic mayhem with no two tracks sounding alike.

Seemingly headed towards arty obscurity, it was then a surprise when Kosten signed to Blanco Y Negro and released a far more accessible follow-up, complete with its all-star guest list. YOUR LOVE MEANS EVERYTHING found Faultline in gentler mood, creating a touching record fit for post-relationship aural therapy. Kosten's choice of collaborators was inspired. The inclusion of Coldplay's **Chris Martin** on the beautiful opener "Where is My Boy?" and the closing "Your Love… Part II" held the record in place, with Martin's heartbreaking, intimate vocal style perfectly encapsulating the tender mood. Elsewhere, the coup of persuading his hero **Michael Stipe** to sing on a cover of the Brothers Four's 1960 song "Greenfields" payed off well for Kosten, with more lost love and longing effectively added to the mix. Other contributors – the Kosten-produced Sacramento singer **Jacob Golden**, **Wayne Coyne** of the Flaming Lips, and guest guitar from The Verve's **Nick McCabe** – provided direction, though Kosten's meandering instrumentals tended to be forgettable. Nevertheless, with a range of musical skills at hand, the accolades of musical heavyweights and his continuing production work – lately Ben Christopher's feted SPOONFACE album – David 'Faultline' Kosten enjoys the position of now only having golden opportunities to choose from.

⊙ **Your Love Means Everything** (2002; Blanco Y Negro).
A come-down album of the highest calibre. Electronic ache and hair-on-end vocals from Chris Martin, among others, provide a soundtrack of digital despair.

Annebella Pollen

FAUST

Formed Hamburg, Germany, 1971;
disappeared 1975;
re-formed 1992 and active sporadically since.

"There is no group more mythical than Faust." Julian Cope

A longside Can and Kraftwerk, **Faust** hold a place in the first division of German underground bands of the 1970s – "Krautrock", as it was dubbed. They have influenced, collectively, people like Julian Cope, Stereolab, and a lot of the more left-field modern dance acts. Nothing beat early-70s German bands for sonic experimentalism.

Faust was created in the summer of 1971, when music journalist **Uwe Nettelbeck** persuaded Polydor Records to advance him a large sum to capitalize on international success of German Krautrock groups such as Amon Düül II and Can. Building a studio in a converted schoolhouse in the country with the proceeds, Nettelbeck approached **Jean-Herve Peron**, **Werner 'Zappi' Diermaier**, **Hans Joachim Irmler**, **Rudolf Sosna** and **Gunther Wusthoff** as his core musicians, plus 'special equipment constructor' **Kurt Graupner**, and a tape of experimental music involving happenings and steamrams made its way to Deutsche Grammophon.

In conditions of secrecy and sometimes overbearing communal living (Nettelbeck had the only car and attempted to control all outside contact), they rehearsed the deconstruction of Anglophone rock-'n'roll and the creation of some outlandish improvised music based heavily on overdriven electronic instruments and a reinterpretation of other people's ideas, especially Zappa and The Velvet Underground. Nettelbeck recorded hours of tape, and painstakingly edited it to make a music unlike any which had come before, built around extended trance-like beats, with surreal lyrics ('daddy take a banana/tomorrow is Sunday') chanted like mantras, and occasionally a lapse into melancholic folk songs. It was 'such a catchy bizarre sound', as Julian Cope observes in his book, *Krautrocksampler*, 'like music from some parallel universe … played through the oldest radio'.

A staggeringly weird live performance for Polydor executives was thrown together hastily in Hamburg when the label demanded some sign of activity – the night set the stage for the chaos to come, disintegrating in a confusion of unprepared specially-built equipment and the destruction of a wall of tin cans by Zappi. Despite this, Polydor released their debut LP FAUST on clear vinyl in a transparent sleeve with a striking X-rayed fist motif. Though it was received with disdain in Germany, it was a big hit in Britain, where all things German and experimental were in vogue with the underground music scene. The follow-up LP, FAUST SO FAR (1972), was far more accessible, and was a success in Britain and Europe, as was the single cut of the title track. Again, it came lavishly packaged, all black this time, with an art-print illustration for each track by Munich artist Edda Kochl.

Developing their avant-garde links, Faust also recorded with violinist **Tony Conrad**, former member of The Dream Syndicate with John Cale and LaMonte Young. The result was OUTSIDE THE DREAM SYNDICATE (1972), a triumph of minimalism which was reviled and then ignored by the music press. Further collaborations included two LPs as **SLAPP HAPPY**'s backing band, SORT OF (1972) and ACNALBASAC NOOM (1973), the latter unreleased until 1982 when, at Virgin's insistence, it was re-recorded with session musicians.

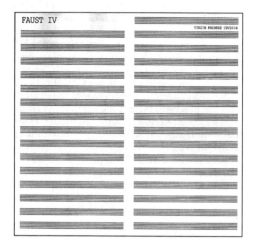

With the Polydor contract elapsed, Nettelbeck licensed Virgin to release THE FAUST TAPES (1973), a collage of the band's private rehearsal recordings. Sold at 49p, the price of a single, it sold in huge numbers and paved the way for Faust's legendary tour of France and Britain in 1973. Accompanied by a situationist manifesto, Faust stunned audiences with road drills, pinball-machine synthesizers and blinding lights in an era more accustomed to the comfortable avant-rock of support band Henry Cow.

FAUST IV (1973) turned out to be the band's last studio LP for 23 years, recorded following an unwise move to England. An audience by now accustomed to Faust's radical sound was disappointed by the relatively conventional pieces on the album, and after a brief period recording in Munich the band disappeared in 1975.

Faust's influence on late-1970s 'industrial' music was immense, with Throbbing Gristle, This Heat and Einstürzende Neubauten among those who followed their lead in the use of power tools, sheet metal and pure noise taken to new extremes. Faust achieved mythic status when avant-garde label Recommended rereleased the Polydor classics along with two collections of unreleased material, MUNIC & ELSEWHERE/RETURN OF A LEGEND (1986) and THE LAST LP (1989).

Faust finally resurfaced for a one-off gig in Hamburg. A single of this performance renewed interest in the band, and led to the astonishing, ramshackle return of Peron, Diermaier and Irmler to the Marquee in London in October 1992, complete with chainsaws and metal percussion. Touched by their enthusiastic reception, Peron and Diermaier embarked on a 1994 American tour with a group of guest musicians including Japanese guitar legend **Keiji Haino**, New Zealand's **Michael Morley** (Gate, The Dead C) and **Jim O'Rourke** (Gastr del Sol, Sonic Youth). Faust took the opportunity to realize some of their more spectacular performance ideas, with walls built, televisions smashed, railway lines amplified, and sheep brought on stage as calming influences following their liberal use of explosives.

Following the tour, tape-splicer extraordinaire O'Rourke worked on the live tapes, resulting in RIEN (1995), while Tony Conrad and Faust reunited for a mesmerizing performance at London's Queen Elizabeth Hall in February of that year. Further European tours brought concrete mixers, hay-blowing machines, live welding and nude action painting of record sleeves by Peron, but the band have, unfortunately, not yet realized their ambition to use helicopters to drop steel scrap as percussion.

Just before recording a soundtrack to the classic vampire film NOSFERATU (1997) and a live record of their 1997 EDINBURGH FESTIVAL appearance, Faust lost Peron to musical differences. This move didn't prevent Diermaier and Irmler, with **Michael Stoll** (bass/double bass/flute) and **Steve Lobdell** (guitar), from pursuing their own energetic brand of enthusiastic musical chaos, on RAVVIVANDO (March 1999) and as the incendiary highlight of Daniel Miller's Mini-Meltdown on London's South Bank in April 1999.

Thankfully, after thirty years, Faust show no signs of going away. Jean-Hervé made a return solo performance of classic-era songs at the London Musicians Collective's (LMC) Festival of Experimental Music in May 2000, while the rest of the band continued their progress into monster art-rock territory with tours of NOSFERATU and a succession of blisteringly heavyweight shows, captured on the LAND OF UKKO AND RAUNI double CD (2000). A RAVVIVANDO remix album, FREISPIEL, was released in 2002 and was soon joined on the shelves by PATCHWORK 1971-2002, a dissatisfying collection of overly brief snippets from the group's catalogue.

(•) **Tony Conrad With Faust – Outside The Dream Syndicate** (1972; Table Of The Elements).
More minimal than anything Steve Reich or Philip Glass could muster, Conrad's violin plays microtones, while Faust pound the drum and bass relentlessly for more than seventy minutes. A trance-inducing exploration of mathematical perfection, and a perfect party-clearer.

(•) **Faust IV** (1973; ReR).
Again, absolutely essential, including such delights as the reggae song, "The Sad Skinhead", as well as the full-on Faust sound of "Krautrock".

⊙ **The Wümme Years 1970-73: Boxset** (2000; ReR).
Long unavailable on CD outside Japan, the first three albums are here lovingly remastered with a booklet of interviews and a made-over 71 MINUTES OF FAUST, which previously collected much of the MUNIC & ELSEWHERE/RETURN OF A LEGEND and LAST LP material. Also on offer, and of most interest to long-term fans, is the BBC SESSIONS+ disc.

Richard Fontenoy

FEEDER

Formed London, 1995.

F ew bands are truly capable of harnessing a genuine sense of power and sweet pop melodies, but Feeder make the task appear ridiculously easy. The secret to this muscular but eminently commercial approach can be attributed to songwriter **Grant Nicholas (vocals/guitar)**, whose pre-Feeder career included a stint of studio engineering work during which time he obviously absorbed as many tricks of the trade as possible. Nicholas also learned a great deal by playing in a number of local bands in South Wales before teaming up with **Jon Lee (drums)** in an outfit dubiously dubbed Temper Temper. After the band fell apart a move to London for Nicholas led to a typically tortuous period trying to get things started before Lee was persuaded to join up again along with **Taka Hirose**, a bassist who had spent more than a few nights in various bands entertaining the metal-loving folk of Tokyo. Thus Feeder were born.

Signing to the Echo label in 1995 resulted in their debut release, the TWO COLOURS EP, which, along with the following year's SWIM mini-LP, gave a satis-fying indication of the sonic delights to come. While SWIM gave rock fans bored with the dour dronings of grunge some of the luscious pop buzz they craved, it was the band's first full album, POLYTHENE (1997), that truly showcased Feeder's penchant for gut-busting heaviness allied to a knack for awesomely addictive tunes. The record was voted *Album Of The Year* in *Metal Hammer* magazine and spawned a whole host of gig favourites, including "Stereo World", "Cement" and "My Perfect Day". Alongside these crowd-pleasing gems Feeder also managed to create something of a team anthem out of "High", which reached number 24 in the charts in the autumn of 1997.

The following year saw the band in a gigging frenzy – a situation that has remained fairly constant ever since – as a huge US tour was followed by a two-night stand at London's Astoria. In the midst of all this frantic live activity the band somehow found time to record and release YESTERDAY WENT TOO SOON (1999), which entered the album charts at #7 and found Nicholas expanding his songwriting repertoire to include a little sensitive balladry in the string-driven title track and minimally melancholic "Tinsel Town".

Then came the outrageously bouncy "Buck Rogers", which became a Top 5 hit and paved the way for ECHO PARK (2001), which, spookily, debuted at #5.

But disaster was to strike: in January 2002 drummer Jon Lee committed suicide in his Miami home. Despite this devastating news the group decided to stay together. Before the year's close they had released the touchingly titled COMFORT IN

Feeder, going underground...

SOUND, a powerful album that paid homage to their lost comrade and the feelings that the tragedy left behind.

⊙ **Yesterday Went Too Soon** (Echo; 1999).
This, the second album from Feeder, speeds through an energetic set of three-chord, angst-driven indie nuggets. For those who enjoyed the singles "Insomnia" and "Yesterday Went Too Soon" this album is a must.

⊙ **Echo Park** (Echo; 2001).
Songwriter Grant Nicholas' guitar and vocals dominate proceedings (as ever) and his ability to tout a hooky chorus yet again brings with it a fistful of aggravatingly catchy variations on the soft-loud-soft-loud blueprint.

Justin Lewis

THE FEEDERZ

Formed Phoenix, Arizona, 1977; disbanded 1987.

One of the most notorious punk bands to come from the American hardcore punk scene, **The Feederz** formed in Phoenix, Arizona in 1977. Starting with their first performance when guitarist **Frank Discussion** opened fire on the audience with an assault rifle (fortunately it was loaded with blanks), The Feederz were known to use outrageous provocations to underscore their music. The Feederz line-up at the time consisted of **Art Nouveau** on drums (now dead), **Clear Bob** on bass, with Frank on guitar and lead vocals.

Their music was eclectic, with influences ranging across rockabilly, classical, Captain Beefheart and Robert Fripp – although there was never any question of their punk allegiances. There was also no question of their intention to provoke, having 'the abolition of society' as their goal. In 1980 they released a 7" single, "Jesus", which was named after what was to become their most popular song "Jesus Entering From The Rear". It is also regarded by some as perhaps the most blasphemous song ever written.

After a local scandal in 1981, when 5000 students were handed official-looking documents announcing a fraudulent essay contest by their teachers, Frank Discussion was forced to leave Phoenix for San Francisco. He reformed the Feederz, with **Mark Roderick** on bass and **DH Peligro** on drums, recording the album EVER FEEL LIKE KILLING YOUR BOSS?, which became notorious for its sandpaper cover, created to damage any record it came in contact with. The Feederz also became known during this time for their situationist leanings and were considered "political" (although less naive than some other political bands such as the Dead Kennedys and MDC).

In 1984 The Feederz, now consisting of Frank Discussion and **Jayed Scotti**, released their second album, TEACHERS IN SPACE, the cover featuring a photo of the *Challenger* space shuttle disaster. The band quit playing in 1987 with Frank Discussion later being interviewed in the *Re/Search* tome and video entitled *Pranks*, wherein he was quoted as saying 'crime is honorable, art is a disgusting mess'.

Frank Discussion is living in Seattle at present and is a babalawo or high priest in the Santeria religion. He's also jumped back into the fray with the 1999 reissue of EVER FEEL LIKE KILLING YOUR BOSS?

⊙ **Ever Feel Like Killing Your Boss?** (1983; Flaming Banker Records; rereleased 1999).
Sandpaper cover. Classy US hardcore punk rock, dating back here and there to 1977. Titles such as "Burn Warehouse Burn", "Fuck You" and "Gut Rage" give only the merest hint of the venom contained. Classy poster, suitable for the office wall, too.

T. Frances Farmer

THE FEELIES

Formed Hoboken, New Jersey, 1977; disbanded 1991.

Although **The Feelies** reside in the Talking Heads wing of the punk rock museum, they were far from imitators. In fact, the band date back to the very dawn of New York's punk scene, rehearsing Velvets and Stooges covers in New Jersey garages, before crossing the river to brave city stages, defiantly projecting a hip-to-be-square approach. At the nucleus of the original (and subsequent) line-up was guitarist and songwriter **Glen Mercer**, with **Bill Million** providing first-string support in the early years.

The earliest Feelies gigs at CBGB's in the late 70s (with future Golden Palomino **Anton Fier** on drums) were a strange mix of garage and minimalist rock, mixing the energy of the former with the intense concentration and refinement of the latter. They dressed in natty thrift-store shirts and well-laundered slacks, deliberately eschewing the dramatic presence of their contemporaries, which made them seem more honest than other bands on the scene. Similarly, they had little interest in publicity, only playing shows on national holidays. When Stiff Records signed the band and released their debut LP, CRAZY RHYTHMS, in 1980, The Feelies refused to support it by touring, and even declined T-shirt sales. (A story from the period had The Feelies informing their label that a T-shirt was something one wore *under* a shirt.)

Aside from its punk-era sonic roughness, CRAZY RHYTHMS remains a very endearing record. Long lead-ins give numbers like "Forces At Work" and "The Boy With The Perpetual Nervousness" time to percolate, while briefer numbers like "Fa Ce La" show a predilection for pop largely missing from their live shows. Its directness also showed a willingness to experiment slightly, but critical praise wasn't matched by commercial success, and the band's first line-up folded soon afterwards.

As other members diversified into other bands, Mercer and Million became involved in a burgeoning New Jersey scene – firstly at Maxwell's, a club in Hoboken, and then with a new local label, Coyote. The duo began to collaborate with percussionist and songwriter **David Weckerman**, and contributed the beautiful, moody soundtrack to Susan Seidelman's film *Smithereens*.

As word spread to Athens in Georgia, R.E.M.'s Peter Buck travelled north to pay homage to his forebears, and to produce THE GOOD EARTH (1986). The sound was an improvement on CRAZY RHYTHMS, but it was still indistinguishable from almost any other modest college-radio platter that year. In fact one song, "Slipping Into Something", actually sounded much more exciting in an alternative version on the self-produced EP, NO ONE KNOWS.

The reinvigorated Feelies finally chose to tour, finding a new enthusiastic audience in Europe, and even landed a neat cameo as a high-school reunion band in Jonathan Demme's movie, *Something Wild*. But their two late-period records for A&M – ONLY LIFE (1988) and TIME FOR A WITNESS (1990) – exposed the limitations of their approach. The Feelies officially split again in the early 90s, although Mercer and Weckerman then surfaced with a new band, **Wake Ooloo**, and a string of albums, the best being 1994's HEAR NO EVIL.

⦿ **Crazy Rhythms** (1980; Stiff).
The definitive Feelies record. The long slow builds on "Boy With The Perpetual Nervousness" and "Forces At Work" catch some of their signature quality, and even the lyrics shine.

⦿ **No One Knows** (1986; Coyote).
Along with "Slipping Into Something", this also has the lovely "The High Road", as well as the wonderfully ridiculous knock-offs of Neil Young's "Sedan Delivery" and The Beatles' "She Said She Said".

Roy Edroso

FELT

Formed Birmingham, England, 1980; disbanded 1990.

As a child weaned on glam and punk, **Lawrence Hayward** dreamed of glitzy pop stardom. Through a combination of musical idealism and bad timing, he has never achieved his aim, although as leader of **Felt** he became a late-80s cult figure, with an impressive track record of Lou Reed- and Television-styled pop.

Hayward produced the first Felt single, "Index" (1979), alone in his bedroom using a portable cassette player. It consisted solely of one guitar, two or three thrashy chords and a bit of mumbling over the top, but by some quirk was hailed as a minimalist masterpiece by the music press. Hayward happily formed a band to carry the Felt banner, though his despotic habits meant that early line-ups were volatile (original drummer **Tony Race** was sacked largely for having curly hair). Still, a core trio eventually emerged – Hayward, **Gary Ainge** (drums) and guitarist **Maurice Deebank** – and signed to Cherry Red. They produced a string of three-minute singles, which were gathered in 1983 on the superlative mini-LP, THE SPLENDOUR OF FEAR, alternating with lengthier experimentation.

Felt's primitive sound was hardly suited to mainstream pop, but the delicate impressionistic blur was an antidote to the greyness of post-Joy Division New Wave, and they became darlings of the UK music press. Most attention was focused on Deebank's extraordinary guitar style: classically trained, he mixed Tom Verlaine, Durutti Column's Vini Reilly, and even a smattering of Hank Marvin, into a mercury cascade. Much was also made of Hayward's 'new puritan' stance, disowning drink, drugs and smoking in a rejection of post-punk fatalism.

After a patchy pop-song album, THE STRANGE IDOLS PATTERN AND OTHER SHORT STORIES (1984), Hammond organ whizzkid **Martin Duffy** joined the band, but the flare-ups continued (Hayward and Ainge once had to play a disastrous festival date as an improvising two-piece). Deebank vanished for good in 1985 after they had finished IGNITE THE SEVEN CANNONS with Cocteau Twins' Robin Guthrie. This dense and psychedelic album gave Felt a near hit with the six-minute swirl of "Primitive Painters", which was augmented with extra vocals from fellow Cocteau Twin Liz Fraser. Major labels still weren't keen, though, and the band ended up on Creation, then going through one of its purple periods.

Duffy was now the musical focus of a shifting line-up, and a series of lush and slightly Dylanesque releases followed. FOREVER BREATHES THE LONELY WORD (1986) was the peak, a wonderful album smeared with vocal harmonies. Hayward wriggled once again in the music-press spotlight, and his personality quirks – obsessive cleanliness and a pathological fixation with image – filled column inches.

A triumphant appearance at Creation's all-day festival, 'Doing It For The Kids', in August 1988, marked the pinnacle of Felt's popularity. This was despite the wilful uncommerciality of their current LP, TRAIN ABOVE THE CITY (1988), which consisted entirely of jazzy piano instrumentals by Duffy.

Next, a move to Cherry Red offshoot El Records yielded ME AND A MONKEY ON THE MOON (1989). Hayward decreed that this would be Felt's swan song, after realizing they'd now made ten albums and ten singles in ten years. (He suggested to the press that this had been a master plan cooked up in 1980.) A cycle of songs about growing up in the 70s, this final album was Felt's greatest achievement, restating all their musical ideas and featuring unexpectedly direct, honest lyrics. As the dust settled, Martin Duffy was welcomed into a career of rock-'n'roll debauchery with **PRIMAL SCREAM**, while Hayward laid low and immersed himself in 70s nostalgia. The result was **Denim**, a loose aggregation of session men and ageing glitter-rockers chosen more for their image than prowess. Their debut live appearance was reliant on backing tapes and the keyboard player's synthesizer was notable for not being plugged in. BACK IN DENIM (1992), however, with its glam and synth-pop influences, received brief acclaim, and was followed in 1996 by DENIM ON ICE and in 1997 by NOVELTY ROCK. These ploughed the same furrow, packed with insider references to bands and music journos, and parodying genres from New Romantics to pub rock.

⊙ **Bubblegum Perfume** (1990; Creation).
A mid-period compilation, concentrating mainly on short sharp, pop and brittle instrumentals (always a Felt strongpoint).

⊙ **Absolute Classic Masterpieces** (1992; Cherry Red).
A more straightforward collection of Felt's early output.

Chris Tighe

BRYAN FERRY

Born Washington, County Durham, England, 1945.

In the early 70s **Bryan Ferry** brought a note of sophistication into a vulgar pop world ruled by glam-rock. If Bowie was the chameleon, Ferry adopted the identity of the lounge lizard to complement his melodramatic croon, and embarked on a successful parallel solo career after barely a year in the limelight with **ROXY MUSIC**.

Growing up in a northeastern mining community, grammar-schoolboy Ferry preferred jazz and blues to rock'n'roll. His degree from art college gave him a grounding in pop-art experimentation that was to form the backdrop for his musical career, and he was influenced, too, by a spell on vocals with 'blue-eyed soul' band The Gas Board. Ferry's musical ambitions forced his move to London in 1968, where he worked as a ceramics teacher and planned the cultural phenomenon that was to become Roxy Music. At one point in 1970, Ferry even auditioned to replace Greg Lake in King Crimson, but his strained warbling was deemed unsuitable.

When Roxy Music broke in 1972, Ferry achieved iconic status so quickly that, after only two Roxy albums, he launched a tandem solo career with the release of THESE FOOLISH THINGS (1973). As an album of covers from the 60s and before, this was an adventurous departure from the rock convention that serious artists wrote their own material. (The idea caught on, with Bowie and Lennon soon following suit.) Ferry cast his net wide, selecting favourites like Dylan's "A Hard Rain's Gonna Fall" (which reached the UK Top 10), Smokey Robinson And The Miracles' "The Tracks Of My Tears", The Beatles' "You Won't See Me" and the title track, Eric Maschwitz's sentimental ballad from the 30s.

More revival albums were to follow. ANOTHER TIME, ANOTHER PLACE (1974) featured him posing as the languid aristocrat in a white tuxedo with musical selections to fit the image, like the hits "Smoke Gets In Your Eyes" and "The In Crowd", while the party pieces on LET'S STICK TOGETHER (1976) had an R&B emphasis set by Wilbert Harrison's title song.

With Roxy put on hold in the summer of 1976, what had been a casual sideline was to become the main event. Ferry produced his first album of originals, IN YOUR MIND (1977), and kept his profile high by charting with singles "This Is Tomorrow" and "Tokyo Joe". Though lighter in tone than Roxy Music, the songs and arrangements had a familiar feel thanks to the presence of **Phil Manzanera**, **John Wetton** and **Paul Thompson** in the band.

While Ferry was marking time, the punk rock explosion made his sophistication look dated almost overnight, and he faced his first commercial failure with the release of THE BRIDE STRIPPED BARE (1978), the title of which was inspired by a Marcel Duchamp artwork. Recorded following the highly publicized break-up with girlfriend Jerry Hall, the songs were far more intense and bleak than anything he had done before.

Re-formed Roxy received Ferry's undivided attention until the final split in 1982, after which he was

Brian Ferry – Oozing style even when in a plastic suit

REDFERNS

to bring a highly developed knowledge of studio techniques to the next phase of his solo career. The songs on BOYS AND GIRLS (1985) and BÊTE NOIRE (1987) were painstakingly constructed as complex soundscapes, and if the lyrical obsessions were familiar – take "Slave To Love", for example – Ferry's easy vocal style had fewer of the old crooning mannerisms.

Now a married man and father, but no longer a big star, Ferry the perfectionist laboured obsessively on new songs. Getting bogged down in the possibilities of the modern studio, he took a break and returned to his old hobby of recording covers, releasing the album TAXI in 1993, before completing an album of his own songs, MAMOUNA, in 1994. Like his 80s output, these had a meticulously polished production which captivated some, while alienating those who liked their rock'n'roll raw.

In January 1998 Ferry took part in a tribute concert commemorating a hundred years since Noel Coward's birth. The CD of the event, 20TH CENTURY BLUES: THE SONGS OF NOEL COWARD (1998; EMI), includes Ferry performing "I'll See You Again"; he then released another album of blissfully crooned covers, AS TIME GOES BY (1999). However, it took until 2002 for an album with fresh Ferry material to appear, namely FRANTIC. The album reunited Ferry with **Brian Eno** on the final composition, "I Thought", and also featured a guest spot by Radiohead's **Jonny Greenwood**. Despite all this activity, Ferry also found the time to briefly reform Roxy Music for a world tour and compilation album.

⊙ **These Foolish Things** (1973; Polydor).
In need of light relief after Brian Eno's departure from Roxy Music, Ferry began his solo career as a cover artist with this inspired collection of songs from his heroes, using most of Roxy in his backing band.

⊙ **The Bride Stripped Bare** (1978; Polydor).
This mix of covers and originals was poorly received, but Ferry rates this as one of his best.

⊙ **Bête Noire** (1987; Virgin).
One of his studio-bound labours of love from the later years, the mood swings from the dark atmospherics of "Zamba" to the slick beat of "Kiss And Tell", and an uplifting strut through "The Right Stuff", co-written with Johnny Marr.

Nick Dale

FIELDS OF THE NEPHILIM

Formed Stevenage, England, 1985;
disbanded 1991.

"How often do I have to say this?! We always walk around like this, but we're not cowboys!" Carl McCoy

Considered by many as a driving force behind the 80s goth movement, it is perhaps surprising that **Fields Of The Nephilim** never matched the success of their rivals, Sisters Of Mercy and The Mission. For a time, the fresh-faced line-up of **Carl McCoy** (vocals), **Paul Wright** (guitar), **Tony**

Fields of the Nephilim – rumours of crop-dusting in the dressing room were greatly overstated

Pettitt (bass), **Gary Wisker** (saxophone) and **Nod Wright** (drums) had serious potential.

Signing to newly formed Tower Release, Fields Of The Nephilim released their first venture into vinyl, the BURNING THE FIELDS EP in 1985. By 1987, although Wisker was gone, the band's debut LP, DAWNRAZOR, released on Beggars Banquet and Situation Two, marked a great leap forward. Containing their unofficial 'anthem', "Preacher Man", and the hauntingly aggressive "Volcane (Mr. Jealousy Has Returned)", some of the tracks were also used as backing music for the hit US television series *Miami Vice*, although this fact eluded the band itself at the time.

However, it was the release of their darker second album that ensured they got at least some of the attention they deserved. THE NEPHILIM (1988), featuring the rock-club favourite and unexpected UK chart hit "Moonchild", showed that McCoy's rougher vocal style had improved the sound, while the band's playing had become tighter and more sinister. Touring Germany as support to New Model Army helped gain a new legion of fans from the metal mainstream audience, as well as building up their gothic fan base.

In 1989, the band returned to the studio to record ELIZIUM (1990), a less aggressive performance all round, as the band opted for a darkly melodic and smoother flow in parts. The album still featured a couple of Nephilim belters, but on the whole the feel of the whole album was more muted than previous offerings.

By now, musical differences were becoming apparent, and this led to the band's break-up a year later, after the release of the live album EARTH INFERNO (1991). McCoy fired the rest of the band and carried on under the name of **The Nefilim**, while the others went on to form **Rubicon**. A very fine compilation REVELATIONS (1993), containing various rarer recordings, helped plug the gaps in most fans' record collections, but the trail went cold for much of the 90s with various rumours flying around about possible reunions.

In the meantime, McCoy's The Nefilim concentrated on a more brutal death metal-styled sound, a decision which dismayed many fans. The "Penetration" single gave a taste of ZOON (1996), which eventually proved to be a flop. The last anyone heard from Carl McCoy was the release of the "One More Nightmare"/"Darkcell AD" single in 2000, once more under the original Fields Of The Nephilim name; a compilation, FROM GEHENNA TO HERE (2001), pulled together much of the band's early output in one easily digestible chunk, but there was still no new album. There have been persistent rumours of a reunion since then, though the Wright brothers most recently resurfaced with **Last Rites**: they have one album, GUIDED BY LIGHT (2001), to their name.

Apparently a new Nephilim album has been recorded but for various nebulous reasons has yet to be released.

⊙ **Dawnrazor** (1987; Beggars Banquet/Situation Two). This album shows the band finding their feet and developing image as well as style. Dark and moody, highlights include "Preacher Man", "Volcane" and "Slow Kill".

⊙ **The Nephilim** (1988; Beggars Banquet/Situation Two).
Their best album overall, with strong vocals, tight musicianship and a compelling catalogue of musical and lyrical misery.

Richard Allan

FILTER

Formed Bay Village, Ohio, 1994.

O ver recent years the heavier end of the rock spectrum has been dominated by nu-metal, that bastard child of rap and metal, forever shot through with psychological poison and personal angst. So overwhelming has been its success that it has almost eclipsed the early-90s take on extremity – industrial metal as expounded by outfits such as Ministry and Nine Inch Nails.

From this stable came **Filter**, consisting basically of one man's vision plus a massive amount of technical know-how and equipment – so much so that although Filter's base is industrial it is almost impossible to really categorize their diverse and powerful sound. **Richard Patrick** (vocals, guitars, bass, programming, drums) was a touring member of Nine Inch Nails and thus well seasoned in the possibilities of technology crossed with music.

Having left Trent Reznor's gang, Patrick hooked up with a like-minded musical adventurer named **Brian Liesegang**. Ensconced in a small house in Patrick's Ohio home town, they recorded SHORT BUS (1995), an album of breathtaking energy and sweeping soundscapes, especially as it comes from the

imaginations of just two people. It was a small but significant victory for Filter, scoring a respectable hit when "Hey Man, Nice Shot" was picked up by alternative radio.

Liesegang left in 1997, but Patrick still saw Filter as a going concern and set about consolidating the band's modest success by putting together TITLE OF RECORD (1999). At the time hip-hop was at the root of many bands' metal ragings, but Patrick stuck to his industrial guns and the set was a diverse synthesis of fresh and dynamic electronic stylings with a polished metallic splendour, the perfect riposte to those who reckoned that Patrick had blown his creative wad on SHORT BUS and a minor hit single. Patrick's success relied in part on his ability to find the musicians to complement his abilities, and the line-up featured guitarist **Geno Lenardo**, drummer **Steve Gillis** and bassist **Frank Cavanagh**.

This unit grew stronger as time passed, the creative bond sealed during a mammoth two-year and four-continent tour. With a staggering number of live shows under their belt Patrick was able to relinquish some of the writing and control, and allowed other ideas to seep into the mix. So, by THE AMALGAMUT (2002) they had really grown into a creatively democratic band, although Patrick's individual stamp was still clear throughout. The theme of the record was the vast diversity of America's cultural heritage, one that Patrick had begun musing over during Filter's previous tour. Underpinning this notion were Patrick's hard-hitting lyrics which included takes on the tragic Columbine school massacre ("Columind"), commonplace school violence ("American Cliché"), and the 9/11 terrorist attacks ("The Missing"). Softer textures could be found on tracks such as "The Only Way (Is the Wrong Way)" and "God Damn Me".

THE AMALGAMUT has proved to be a crucial album for one of America's premier alternative bands, and promises well for the future.

⊙ **Short Bus** (1995; Reprise).
A broad and imaginative slab of industrial noise, distinguished by Patrick's ability with a strong hook and melodic

chorus. "Hey Man, Nice Shot" might have been the hit single, but there are more riches to be found within.

◉ **Title Of Record** (1999; Reprise).
Four years on and the improvement is remarkable. As if the first album wasn't dynamic enough this record incorporates some truly sensitive touches with raging anger. Amazing.

◉ **The Amalgamut** (2002; Reprise).
There's just no rushing some people. This took a year to write but the care that has gone into crafting the songs shows in its sweeping textures and moods.

Essi Berelian

54•40

Formed Vancouver, Canada, 1980.

"When we came out, nobody would play our records because there was no place for the kind of music we made ... now there's a place, but it's taken." Neil Osborne

In 1980 Vancouver bassist **Brad Merritt** was looking for a name. Along with **Neil Osborne** on vocals and guitar and **Ian Franey** on drums, he'd put together a rock group in the punk spirit of the day. He found his name in a slogan from the 1844 American presidential election. '54°40´ or fight!' were the words of James Polk, who won the '44 election; the phrase referred to the southern border of Alaska – 54°, forty minutes latitude – and indicated that Polk would try to seize all the territory that now makes up British Columbia. 54•40 evoked the subtly political integrity of the band.

54•40 recorded their first EP, SELECTION, in 1982; the following year, with **Phil Comparelli** as a second guitarist and a new drummer, **Darryl Neudorf**, who was soon replaced by fan **Matt Johnson**, they recorded a full-length album, SET THE FIRE. These critically admired college radio hits were later collected on a compilation CD, SOUND OF TRUTH.

By 1986, 54•40 had been signed by Warner Brothers on the strength of a new album. This self-titled disc, sometimes called THE GREEN ALBUM, produced singles in "Baby Ran" and "I Go Blind". The more polished follow-up, SHOW ME demonstrated the band's constant appetite for reinvention but despite a couple of successful Canadian singles, it failed to make the desired commercial impact.

1989's FIGHT FOR LOVE had a more stripped-down and acoustic feel but retained definite pop overtones. However, its commercial appeal was once again limited and Warner Brothers decided against re-signing the band. 54•40 signed with Sony Music Canada but didn't release another album until 1992.

A platinum-seller in Canada, and perhaps the group's most consistently excellent album, DEAR DEAR (which clocked in at exactly 54 minutes and 40 seconds) returned to a louder and more traditionally rock'n'roll sound, while retaining the band's trademark complexity and originality. Beyond powerful basslines and a restless electric guitar, the album also highlighted Osborne's maturity as a lyricist; whether recapitulating the essentials of human existence in "You Don't Get Away (That Easy)", or taking a dark look at domestic violence in "She La", Osborne displayed a natural ability as a songwriter and, as always, a willingness to take a stand.

1993 saw the group make an odd purchase: the neon sign from a Vancouver hot spot they'd played in their formative years. Their next album was duly named after the place, the SMILIN' BUDDHA CABARET, with the sign turning up on the cover. A darkly humorous album showcasing a more lo-fi, acoustic approach, it proved a challenging but enduring set. 1996's TRUSTED BY MILLIONS was focused around a similar mixture of laid-back attitude and dissonance but, as always, supported by strong song structures. Naturally, the next album would be totally different.

Described by the band as their 'heavy mellow' album, SINCE WHEN was produced by GGGarth Richardson, known for working with groups like L7 and Rage Against The Machine. Horns, violins and an antique piano helped to make SINCE WHEN the sweetest album of 54•40's career to date. It was followed by a tour of extra-long shows designed to function as a career retrospective.

A live double CD, HEAVY MELLOW, followed in 1999 and then a year later the self-produced CASUAL VIEWIN' surfaced; the latter found the group in a playful mood, sounding as vibrant as ever.

◉ **54•40** (1986; Warner Brothers).
By turns vigorous ("Baby Ran") and haunting ("Alcohol Heart"), the so-called green album still stands out among 80s alternative releases.

◉ **Sweeter Things** (1991; Warner Music Canada).
An excellent compilation of singles, solid album tracks, and some rarities.

◉ **Dear Dear** (1992; Sony Music Canada).
Influenced by blues-R&B sounds, an album with convincing authority.

◉ **Smilin' Buddha Cabaret** (1994; Sony Music Canada).
The second album takes as much arm's-length inspiration from punk as the first does from R&B. Both distort and play with their source material to the point where it's only vaguely recognizable.

◉ **Since When** (1998; Sony Music Canada).
Sweet and charming, and with a real – if ambiguous – emotional content, this is a pop album for people who hate pop albums.

Matthew Surridge

THE FIRE ENGINES

Formed Edinburgh, Scotland, 1979; disbanded 1981.

One of Scotland's foremost post-punk bands, **The Fire Engines** formed out of a band called the Dirty Reds. This included three of the future Engines: singer and guitarist **Davey Henderson**, bassist **Graham Main** and drummer **Russell Burn**, along with Burn's brother **Tam**. Splitting from the Reds, the trio teamed up with guitarist **Murray Slade**, taking their new name from a 13th Floor Elevators song.

The band recorded their debut single "Get Up And Use Me" in a cottage in Fife, and the finished article, complete with false start, established their trademark of urgent, tangling two-guitar discord. Henderson weighed in on top with a shrieking vocal command. It was an inventive mix and drew excited press response in the UK music mags. An LP, LUBRICATE YOUR LIVING ROOM, appeared in early 1981, packaged in a plastic carrier bag. It comprised eight largely instrumental tracks with the manic repetition, angularity and speed drive of the New York scene of a couple of years earlier, rather than the British punk movement. It was discordant, harsh, rhythmic noise-funk and defiantly against the grain.

As if they had worked their more difficult ideas out of their system, the band's next single, "Candyskin", was a wonderfully grating bubblegum pop classic with Davey Henderson's sickly vocals at last to the fore, and a string section adding an ironic twist. For an indie single it was huge. Its follow-up, "Big Gold Dream", with a sleeve shot of the band cradling raw meat, was a sneaky nod toward chart territory. It failed, though, despite the relatively controlled guitars and female backing chorus, and the group broke up soon after.

Henderson and Burn regrouped some years later with **Win**, who were signed to London Records, meeting minor success with an ambitious dance-orientated progression on their previous band's sound. Henderson re-emerged again in the early 90s with **The Nectarine No. 9**.

⊙ **Fond** (1992; Creation/Revola).
This CD gathers together all three singles and their B-sides, the LUBRICATE YOUR LIVING ROOM LP, and the infamous John Peel session cover of Heaven 17's "We Don't Need This Fascist Groove Thang". The convenient way to catch up on The Fire Engines' abrasive anti-pop.

James Robert

fIREHOSE

Formed Ohio, 1986; disbanded 1995.

When **Daniel Boon**, songwriter/guitarist of California hardcore trio **THE MINUTEMEN** died in 1985, his fellow band members **Mike Watt** (bass) and **George Hurley** (drums) declared the band defunct and withdrew for a while. They re-emerged the next year – having been recruited by Ohian guitarist and vocalist **Ed Crawford** – as fIREHOSE.

Their first work together was a single, "Into The Groove(y)", with Sonic Youth offshoot **Ciccone Youth**. They released their debut album, RAGIN' ... FULL ON, in 1987 on SST Records. It belied its title by providing an understated take on the hardcore

approach: Crawford had brought folk influences on board, and acoustic and semi-acoustic guitars were prevalent.

The overall sound was strong but basic, with little or no overdubbing. Like their previous incarnation, fIREHOSE relished disorientating tempo changes, which made them a folkier counterpart to the 'jazz-core' of bands like NoMeansNo. Choosing to avoid effects-driven guitar overload, they displayed a palette of articulation unavailable to most pure hardcore bands, and developed a dynamism of crushing riffs and light finger-picking. They also seemed more relaxed with themselves, perhaps in the light of Boon's demise (all fIREHOSE albums have been dedicated to him).

The album's underground success was followed by IF'N (1988), which built on the strengths of the debut, further developing the role of the acoustic guitar. Boasting a message of support from Creedence Clearwater Revival's John Fogerty, it also featured a double-edged R.E.M. tribute, "For The Singer Of R.E.M.", with an enigmatically meaningless lyric delivered in a parody of Stipe's vocal style. Elsewhere, Mike Watt began his half-narrated, abrasive and staccato bass-led contributions on "Making The Freeway".

Cult status was assured but a major breakthrough was still elusive. In 1989 they released their finest album, fROMOHIO, which incorporated instrumental interludes, the pure pop of "Time With You", the quasi-folk of "Liberty For Our Friend", and perhaps their loveliest song, "Understanding". In the best way possible, it was a very American record, rich in tradition and innovation.

Signed to major label Columbia, fIREHOSE next released FLYIN' THE FLANNEL (1991), a wry view of America during the Gulf War, with cover artwork that likened the stripes on the US flag to those on a plaid shirt. Their sound was tightened up for the caustic 1992 mini-album, LIVE TOTEM POLE, a mix of old and new material.

However, two cancelled European tours and no apparent increase in their popularity were an obvious concern for their label. MR. MACHINERY OPERATOR (1993) somehow gave the impression that they were stalling, despite a return to some of their jazz-folk stylings, and the sheer vigour of cuts like "Blaze", "Rocket Sled" and the curious "More Famous Quotes". Their laid-back style won them a loyal following but denied them crossover appeal, and in 1995 the band split.

⊙ **Ragin' ... Full On** (1987; SST).
fIREHOSE emerge fully formed. Crawford's dexterity amd grasp of pop, folk and jazz are the defining features, over the thunderous, magmatic rhythm section of Hurley and Watt.

⊙ **fROMOHIO** (1989; SST).
Their finest record by some way, where the players and their influences reached near-perfect interaction, notably on the reflective "Riddle Of The 80s" and the shimmering "Understanding".

Peter Mills

LARRY 'WILD MAN' FISCHER

Born Los Angeles, 1945.

"Will I end up a bum? Will I end up a crumb? Will I end up in Jesus? Will I end up in trees? Will I end up rich rich rich?"

Larry 'Wild Man' Fischer was a certified paranoid schizophrenic when his musical 'career' started in the mid-60s. Unhinged and out of step with mainstream culture, he embraced a hippie movement that had adopted the likes of Charles Manson and Tiny Tim. His stock in trade involved asking unsuspecting passers-by for spare change, and then rewarding them with a free-form musical rant.

With a voice ranging from a full-throated bellow to hysterical whoops, Fischer soon became a regular fixture on LA's Sunset Strip, and caught the attention of **Frank Zappa**, producer of his debut album. The cover portrait of a grinning Wild Man holding a knife to a cardboard cut-out woman suggested that AN EVENING WITH WILD MAN FISCHER (1968) would not be easy listening, and indeed it wasn't, mixing autobiographical monologues, live busking and experimental pieces amid Zappa's avant-garde soundscapes. It was hard to escape the feeling that everyone was partying at Fischer's expense, and the Zappa connection soon ended in acrimony.

By the mid-70s, after some TV and club appearances, generally as a kind of resident weirdo, Fischer was signed to LA indie label Rhino for a three-album deal. Rhino provided support in place of the smothering he had received at Zappa's hands and were rewarded with more focused albums, as well as a great commercial ditty ('Go to Rhino Records on Westwood Boulevard... '). WILDMANIA (1977) marked Fischer's critical and commercial high point, its skeletal rock backing and hoarse vocals satisfying hippies and stunned punks alike.

PRONOUNCED NORMAL (1981) and NOTHING SCARY (1984) teamed Fischer with oddball producer/performers Barnes & Barnes, already known for rock atrocities like "Party In My Pants" and "Boogie Woogie Amputee". They fashioned two albums of bizarre sound bites and minimal electronic backing for Larry's deranged nursery rhymes. The first of these included inspired rap in its title track, plus demolitions of The Beatles' "Yesterday" and The Beach Boys' "In My Room". The 1984 release, meanwhile, featured a cynical sideswipe at an exploitative music industry in "Music Business Shark" and the hilarious and terrifying "Oh God, Please Send Me A Kid To Love".

Sales were low but the legend grew, thanks in part to incidents like the one at a Rhino Records shop in LA, when Fischer took it upon himself to rip albums out of customers' hands, replacing them with copies of NOTHING SCARY. Predictably enough, he was banned from the shop owned by his own label, and no new record contract appeared.

Fischer's legend has proven a mixed blessing for the man himself. As each new generation of audio thrill-seekers tracks down the distinctive Fischer sound, he remains trapped in the role of rock's premier freak show. In addition, it remains almost impossible to encounter vinyl copies of Fischer's albums, while there's no sign of any CD reissues.

In the absence of genuine new product, recent years have seen mixed news for Fischer watchers. Oddball compilations like WORSE THAN SLIME (1989) have kept the odd track in print and Larry made a guest appearance on an album by former Beefheart drummer Robert Williams. The bootleg SING POPULAR SONGS (1997) was credited to 'Wild Man Fischer meets Smegma'. Despite the increase in activity the lovingly crafted Fischer websites have recently been reporting sightings of a homeless Larry drifting around East Hollywood.

Wildmania (1977; Rhino; currently unavailable). Shorter, punchier and slightly more structured than Fischer's debut.

Pronounced Normal (1981; Rhino; currently unavailable).
The Barnes & Barnes association starts here; be prepared for some truly odd cover versions.

Nothing Scary (1984; Rhino; currently unavailable). More of the same – all in all, to be recommended to bad-record junkies and anyone interested in musical extremes.

Neil Nixon

FISHBONE

Formed Los Angeles, 1982.

The ultimate 'nearly' men of the alternative-rock explosion, **Fishbone** have spent their existence on the fringes, defying definition and often comprehension. Their idiosyncratic mix'n'match of styles has been both their strength and downfall: it's hard to know quite who their jazz/hard rock/ska/funk was meant to appeal to. Not that this seems to concern Fishbone, who reckon if people can't take the eclecticism that's their problem.

The band were mostly still in their teens when they were signed by CBS in the early 80s as a sextet – **Angelo Moore** (vocals/sax), **Kendall Jones** (guitar), **Norwood Fisher** (bass), **Walt Kibby** (vocals/trumpet), **Chris Dowd** (keyboards/trombone) and the enigmatic drummer **Fish**. Their debut mini-LP, FISHBONE (1985), showcased the band's gift for melody, humour and youthful energy, with oddities like "Modern Industry" alongside the manic ska of "Party At Ground Zero".

An improved second LP, IN YOUR FACE (1986), failed to set the world alight but Fishbone's all-action live sets were rapidly becoming legendary, owing especially to Angelo's rooster haircut, walking stick and on-stage backflips. Although humour was an integral part of their sound, the music always carried enough weight to prevent intolerable wackiness.

The band followed the seasonal IT'S A WONDERFUL LIFE EP with the release of the more guitar-driven TRUTH AND SOUL (1988). As the black rock of Living Colour began to gain recognition, the time seemed ripe for Fishbone's breakthrough but despite much improved songwriting and the band's trademark versatility, commercial success still proved elusive.

Intensive touring led up to 1991's THE REALITY OF MY SURROUNDINGS, which saw **John Bigham** joining as a second guitarist, and Dowd's role became more prominent, as he shared some lead vocals with Angelo. The album sprawled and sparkled intermittently, but confirmed a growing feeling that Fishbone were destined to be remembered for their frequently outrageous live performances rather than their recorded output.

Two strong singles, the funky "Everyday Sunshine" and the blazing "Sunless Saturday" – with a video directed by Spike Lee – still failed to break the band, and then disaster struck in 1992. While recording a new album, the band lost Kendall Jones, who left to join a religious cult and denounced everything Fishbone had done. Kendall had latterly grown stranger and stranger, underlining quotes from the Bible as instructions to the rest of the band, and attempting to baptize his girlfriend by slashing a hotel water bed. In desperation, Norwood attempted to bring his friend back to reality but instead found himself in court, on kidnapping charges.

Unsurprisingly, this rather overshadowed the subsequent albums: GIVE A MONKEY A BRAIN & HE'LL SWEAR HE'S THE CENTER OF THE UNIVERSE (1993), CHIM CHIM'S BAD ASS REVENGE (1996) and THE PSYCHOTIC FRIENDS NUTTWERX (2000). Despite the odd moment of greatness, most of the tracks were overlong and forgettable. Touring continued, but even their live reputation was criticized for the never-ending 'jams'. It was clear that an essential part of the jigsaw was missing; after Jones' departure, Fishbone were never quite the same again.

⦿ **In Your Face** (1986; CBS).
More varied and polished than the debut: short, fun, and to the point.

⦿ **Truth And Soul** (1988; CBS).
The most focused Fishbone album, and the one that really should have broken the band worldwide. Listen to the likes of "Ma & Pa" and "Bonin' In The Boneyard" and wonder how it never happened.

⦿ **The Essential Fishbone** (2003; CBS).
A reasonable place to start if you want a taster of the group.

Mauro Venegas

MORGAN FISHER

Born London, 1950.

Experimental musician, neo-glam pop star, guru devotee, and curator of arguably rock's wackiest and most original compilation album, the MINIATURES LP, **Morgan Fisher** has straddled careers and idioms as diverse as they come in the rock world.

The story begins with Fisher on Hammond organ with 60s popsters **The Love Affair**, who had a UK #1 single, "Everlasting Love", in 1968. He then got hold of one of the first synthesizers, creating electronic scores for early-70s art movies, launched **Morgan**, a 'classical rock' band, with **Tim Staffell**, Queen's original singer, and did a spell with exotic hippie experimentalists **The Third Ear Band**. Then in 1973 he joined **MOTT THE HOOPLE** (on keyboards), staying through their abbreviated (in every respect) Mott years, after Ian Hunter and Mick Ronson had left the band.

At this time Fisher cut an eccentric sartorial dash – with his white suit, homburg and waxed moustache. However, nothing if not versatile, he turned his hand to punk sessions with Wayne County, the Dead Kennedys, Cherry Vanilla and others, and, inspired by the movement's rough entrepreneurial and artistic freedoms, set up an independent studio and label, Pipe Records.

One of Pipe's first releases was SLOW MUSIC (1980), a collaboration between Fisher and avant-jazz saxophonist Lol Coxhill that explored a similar ambient terrain to 90s electro-minimalism. It was, as Fisher says, 'a result of yearnings to play with sounds in the way countless musicians do effortlessly in the 90s with samplers; in those days it was a long-winded but wondrous process of recording single sounds on tape and making loops and varying playback speeds to create new sounds'.

Pipe were distributed by the open-minded London indie label Cherry Red, and a trio of Fisher projects around this time brought the label cult releases. First off was HYBRID KIDS (1979; reissued 1997, Blueprint), an apparent compilation album of unknown bands Fisher had 'found on his travels, doing punk remakes and art collage pop songs'. In fact it was all his own work, as was its bizarre sequel, CLAWS (1980), which reworked Christmas classics. The third project, however, MINIATURES (1980), was a genuine compilation. Subtitled 'A sequence of fifty-one tiny masterpieces', it presented the submissions of artists asked to provide a new work that ran to less than one minute. Contributions were brilliantly diverse, including Robert Fripp, The Residents, The Flying Lizards and Michael Nyman.

In 1982, Fisher toured with Queen, playing keyboards, before embarking on a three-year sabbatical, travelling through India and America, eventually settling in Japan. There he produced a series of ambient instrumental soundscapes, LOOK AT LIFE (1984 – 'ten instrumental responses to a beautiful world', dedicated to 'my beautiful master, Bhagwan Shree Rajneesh'), WATER MUSIC (1985) and, with Yoko Ono, ECHOES OF LENNON (1990).

Fisher returned to England in 1994 to play with Ian Hunter, Bowie and other 70s luminaries in a memorial concert for the late Mick Ronson.

Since then he has collaborated with numerous musicians and produced some impressive new work. Most interestingly, 2000 saw the release of MINIATURES 2 – having taken over six years to assemble, the collection was just as diverse and unforgettable as its predecessor.

⦿ **Miniatures** (Reissued 1994; Voiceprint).
Every home should have this breathless compilation.

⦿ **Slow Music** (1995; Voiceprint).
Proto-ambient soundscape with Lol Coxhill.

⦿ **Miniatures 2** (2000; Cherry Red).
Bizarre, compelling, disjointed; MINATURES 2 is all of these things and more. A 'veritable smorgasbord' is the only way to describe it.

Chris Brook

THE FLAMIN' GROOVIES

Formed San Francisco, 1966; disbanded 1979; re-formed briefly 1987.

"We had this great masterplan."
Chris Wilson

It's difficult to see the lack of success enjoyed by **The Flamin' Groovies** as being anyone else's fault. Seemingly driven by the imp of the perverse, they managed to make exactly the wrong career choice on two critical occasions, ignoring prevailing taste in favour of desperately unfashionable music destined for nothing more than cult acceptance.

Formed during the hippie heights of Haight-Ashbury, when just about any San Franciscan band could get signed at the drop of a tab, The Groovies turned their backs on acid-rock and psychedelia, and looked for inspiration from the late 50s/early 60s. Unable to attract record company support for their blend of garage rock'n'roll and white-boy R&B, they self-released their debut, SNEAKERS (1967), a mini-album that achieved respectable sales and started a slow-burning cult.

The band at this stage was focused on two frontmen, vocalist **Roy A. Loney** and lead guitarist **Cyril Jordan**. Loney brought a punk edge to the songs, while Jordan's interest in British beat added a melodic element. This conflict of interests was dynamic enough to steer the band through two classic albums for New York-based label Kama Sutra – FLAMINGO (1970) and TEENAGE HEAD (1971) – with a line-up completed by **Tim Lynch** (rhythm guitar), **George Alexander** (bass) and **Danny Mihm** (drums).

Sales were unimpressive, but critics – even then looking for an alternative to the excesses of the early 70s – were generally supportive, and there was talk of The Groovies as the new Rolling Stones. It was not an entirely convincing claim, as The Groovies lacked the trash glamour and showmanship that might have gained them a wider audience. In any case, they lacked a long-term record deal and, when signed to United Artists for over two years, just one EP was released – SLOW DEATH (1972). (By then, Loney had been replaced by **Chris Wilson**, and Lynch was substituted by **James Farrell**.)

The Flamin' Groovies really had more in common with the MC5, who deployed the same twin-guitar assault on white rock. Both would become regarded

'Could somebody please clear these wigs off the stage?'

as forerunners of the punk rock movement, setting the standards for The New York Dolls, and the later punk generation of 1976. In that year, The Groovies returned to Europe for a tour with new drummer **David Wright**, where, on some dates, they shared a bill with label-mates the Ramones. This was The Groovies' big chance to establish their credentials as New Wave godfathers. But Loney's departure a few years earlier had enabled Jordan and Wilson to indulge their fondness for 60s powerbeat. The 1976 album, SHAKE SOME ACTION, was produced by Dave Edmunds and showed the group sporting matching suits and purveying big, harmony-drenched guitar pop songs. Undeniably wonderful, but it was a world away from punk and as much out of time as their debut had been. The Groovies missed out on another audience.

A subsequent release with Edmunds, NOW (1978), was equally strong, but after one more album, JUMPING IN THE NIGHT (1979), the band faded, as Roy Loney formed **The Phantom Movers** with Mihm and Farrell. After Chris Wright joined **The Barracudas** in the early 80s, Cyril Jordan re-formed The Flamin' Groovies in 1987. Although several classic tracks were recorded for the anniversary celebration LP, ONE NIGHT STAND (1987), it more or less marked the end of the road.

Subsequent releases have varied in quality, being little more than compilations of outtakes and ageing, inessential live recordings. LIVE: IN PERSON (1997; Norton) however, deserves separate mention, being a top-quality recording of the band in their prime. Probably as good as it gets.

⊙ **Shake Some Action** (1976; Topic).
Alongside The Raspberries' STARTING OVER, and the first two Big Star albums, this is one of the milestones of power pop. And, despite covers of The Beatles, Paul Revere & The Raiders and Chuck Berry, the original title track remains the stand-out.

⊙ **Flamin' Groovies** (1990; Kama Sutra).
A CD reissue consisting of FLAMINGO and TEENAGE HEAD. The former album is probably the band's best work, a collection of blitzing guitar riffs, topped by Loney's hollering and sneering R&B voice. The latter is, well, more of the same.

⊙ **Groovies' Greatest Grooves** (1989; Sire).
A 24-track CD retrospective that focuses on the later incarnation as a beat group. As good a reworking of the Beatles, Stones and Byrds as was ever committed to vinyl.

⊙ **Yesterday's Numbers** (1998; Camden).
Splendid budget compilation with all of TEENAGE HEAD and the best bits from FLAMINGO plus a few tracks from STILL SHAKIN' (an earlier collection of outtakes).

Alwyn W. Turner

THE FLAMING LIPS

Formed Oklahoma City, Oklahoma, 1983.

Guitarist **Wayne Coyne** and his vocalist brother **Mark** formed **The Flaming Lips** with bassist **Mike Ivins** and drummer **Richard English**; none had any significant background in working bands, and the fledgling Lips began the long process of writing and touring. Although they could boast a range of influences – early Floyd, Zeppelin,

STEVE GULLICK

The Flaming Lips get the horn

punk, The Stooges – the group soon found their own mix of acid-drenched fantasies, tortured vocals, and outbursts of deranged guitar.

Before long Mark Coyne quit, and brother Wayne took over as singer. An early EP on their own Lovely Sorts Of Death label (later reissued by Reckless) gave some hints of the mayhem to come, and the two subsequent issues, HEAR IT IS (1986) and OH MY GAWD!!! (1987), were both definitive examples of their capabilities, with their sound suggesting a collision between The Jesus & Mary Chain, Black Flag and the Dead Kennedys. The latter album contained the recording of the stage favourite "Love Yer Brain", which climaxed with the destruction of a piano – to the accompaniment of a tape-loop sample of The Beatles' "Tomorrow Never Knows".

TELEPATHIC SURGERY (1989) maintained The Lips' growing reputation, right from the sleeve artwork, which included an eyeball held over a blood-spattered sink. The music continued to live up to the sonic assault of their live shows, in which a Who or Sonic Youth cover might make a sudden appearance. When English departed after this record, Coyne and Ivins spent a short period touring as a two-piece, then recruited new drummer, **Nathan Roberts**, guitarist **Jonathan Ponemann**, and **Johnathan Donahue** (guitars/vocals), who left in 1991 to form **MERCURY REV**. The sessions resulted in 1991's IN A PRIEST-DRIVEN AMBULANCE (WITH SILVER SUNSHINE STARES), which created further bafflement for the band's admirers. Still, several tracks suggested a new purpose and concision, like the punchy "Take Me Ta Mars" and the moody "Five Stop Mother Superior Rain".

The move to major label Warners did not harm the band one iota, although HIT TO DEATH IN THE FUTURE HEAD (1992) easily outsold its predecessors. After **Ronald Jones** (guitar) replaced Donahue and **Steven Drozd** (drums) replaced Roberts, 1993's TRANSMISSIONS FROM THE SATELLITE HEART was a comparatively conventional album, although quirky by most standards. By now more consistent and accessible than ever, they still had few equals when exploring the real meanings of the word 'psychedelic', though they received less general attention than some of their rivals and contemporaries. More of the same, though with increased confidence and devotion to detail, was on offer on their 1995 release CLOUDS TASTE METALLIC. Track titles such as "Kim's Watermelon Gun", "They Punctured My Yolk" and "Lightning Strikes The Postman" give an idea of the acid-stained lyrics and impenetrable imagery it contains, yet this remains by far their most self-assured, complex and appealing album to date.

Their next two sets occupied positions at opposite ends of the commercial scale. ZAIREEKA (1997) was an intriguing collection with the mix spliced between four separate CDs; so to hear the complete songs the discs needed to be played simultaneously on four CD systems. On the other hand, THE SOFT BULLETIN (1999) actually gained them a British Top 40 single with the gorgeous "Race For The Prize", and contained their warmest, most emotionally literate songs to date.

The latter very much set the tone for 2002's YOSHIMI BATTLES THE PINK ROBOTS. Part concept album, part Manga-styled fable, this collection told the story of a young Japanese girl fighting mechanical foes set against a backdrop of adventurous indie-rock and digital detail. Visually, the band also started to quantify their image, making several TV appearances and finding their way onto numerous journal covers. By this time Wayne Coyne had grown into a sudo-suave grey-flecked pin-up, while The Lips also managed to up their pop stock by recruiting Justin Timberlake to play bass for them on *Top Of The Pops* dressed as a dolphin.

⊙ **Oh My Gawd!!!** (1987; Restless).
Features early bizarre outpourings, like the nine-minute "One Million Billionth Of A Millisecond On A Sunday Morning", somewhere between a pastoral tone poem and an all-out assault on the brain cells. Meanwhile "Everything's Exploding" recalled the last hurrah of the MC5.

⊙ **In A Priest-Driven Ambulance** (With Silver Sunshine Stares) (1991; Restless).
Why is every song listed as clocking in at 3'26"? Why are some of them subtitled with the tag 'God Song' and a number? What brought about their cover of "What A Wonderful World"? A baffling but brilliant album.

⊙ **Hit To Death In The Future Head (**1992; Warners).
Another mix of uncompromising song titles, curious melodies and blazing riffs.

⊙ **Transmissions From The Satellite Heart** (1993; Warners).
A stunning amalgam of radio-friendly sing-alongs and psyched out weirdness.

⊙ **Clouds Taste Metallic** (1995; Warners).
A real delight – this set finds The Flaming Lips in masterful control of their sound, with fewer compositional quirks seemingly left to chance.

⊙ **Yoshimi Battles The Pink Robots** (2002; Warners).
This warm and inventive album finds The Lips in charge of a strange cartoonish universe where sonic colours melt together like the contents of some lost scene from *Fantasia*. A blinding coming of age.

Gerard F. Tierney

FLEETWOOD MAC

Formed London, 1967.

"Nothing ordinary ever happened to this band." Mick Fleetwood

The **Fleetwood Mac** story is usually described as the ultimate rock'n'roll soap opera, but even the most imaginative of scriptwriters would have a hard time dreaming up a comparable litany of success, failure, love, hate, alcoholism, disappearance, sex, drugs and rock'n'roll – and that was just 1971. Around the eternal nucleus of **Mick Fleetwood** (drums) and **John McVie** (bass), Fleetwood Mac have battled through triumph, disaster and countless personnel changes since their inception in 1967 and, amazingly, are still around to tell the tale.

The Mac history falls into two distinct periods. Its earliest incarnation comprised **Peter Green** (vocals/guitar) and **Jeremy Spencer** (guitar) alongside Fleetwood and McVie, both of whom had served a brief stint with John Mayall's Bluesbreakers, as had Green. Mac mark 1 rode the blues boom of the late 60s with a number of hit albums (most of which are now available again on CD reissues) and singles, most notably Green's haunting instrumental "Albatross", which gave them a British #1 and established them in the pop marketplace for the first time. The combined pressures of success, touring, money and LSD took their toll on Green, however, and he suddenly quit the band in the middle of a German tour in 1970, returning to England to live as a semi-recluse. Former Chicken Shack vocalist **Christine Perfect** (keyboards/vocals), who later married McVie, was subsequently added to a line-up which by now also included **Danny Kirwan** (guitar).

Another disaster followed during a major US tour in 1971, when Spencer left the band's LA hotel to go shopping and never returned. After four days of frantic searching involving psychics, Interpol and the FBI, he was finally tracked down to a warehouse occupied by religious sect The Children Of God, where a spaced-out Spencer calmly told his ex-colleagues of his new identity and refused to return to Fleetwood Mac. Facing ruin, the band made a desperate call to Green – now working as a grave-digger in Surrey – who reluctantly agreed to a temporary return, enabling the tour to go ahead.

Spencer was eventually replaced by American **Bob Welch** (guitar), a session musician who had worked with James Brown and Aretha Franklin. His straightforward rock style and Christine McVie's bittersweet love songs took Fleetwood Mac in a new direction, but the next two years brought further upheavals as growing tensions within the group proved impossible to suppress. The increasingly difficult Kirwan was dismissed in 1972, and his replacement **Bob Weston** was fired after a very public affair with Fleetwood's wife Jenny. Exhausted and confused, the band cancelled a US tour, prompting their furious manager Clifford Davis to send a group of impostors to perform in their place. Unsurprisingly, the bogus outfit was quickly sent packing by disgruntled punters, but the ensuing legal battles saw Welch depart and the real Fleetwood Mac relocate en masse to California.

It was at this point that the group's fortunes began to change. Visiting an LA studio in 1974, Fleetwood had a chance encounter with **Lindsey Buckingham** (vocals/guitar) and his girlfriend **Stevie Nicks** (vocals), who performed together as Buckingham Nicks. Impressed by the duo's music and image, Fleetwood invited them to join his band as replacements for Welch, completing the tenth Mac line-up in eight years. This time, though, the band chemistry generated a spark of excitement that had been missing since Green's departure, and the new energy quickly translated into commercial success. It began with FLEETWOOD MAC (1975), whose breezy West Coast feel, offset by Nicks' mystical musings, was an embryonic version of what was to come. It went to #1 in the States.

However, just at the point where confidence should have been high, the follow-up was recorded in what Fleetwood would later describe as 'an emotional holocaust'. The fragile Buckingham/Nicks relationship had ended in bitterness, the McVies' marriage was over, and Fleetwood himself was in the middle of a painful divorce. Six stifling, cocaine-crazed months of claustrophobic tension resulted in RUMOURS (1977), a record which launched Fleetwood Mac into stratospheric superstardom. Its achievements remain

phenomenal – more than 25 million copies sold, a Grammy award winner, #1 in the UK (where it spent a staggering 450 weeks in the Top 100), 31 weeks at #1 in the States, and, until Michael Jackson's THRILLER, the best-selling album in rock history. The secret of its success has been the subject of much speculation over the years, with Fleetwood himself suggesting that the public appreciated the (then unusual) presence of two women at the forefront of a white rock band. It was certainly true that the variety of songs and lead vocals on the record set RUMOURS apart from its monolithic AOR contemporaries.

Anxious to avoid the trap of churning out more of the same ad infinitum, Buckingham insisted on a more experimental approach on the follow-up, TUSK (1979), which at the time was tagged as the most expensive album ever made. A diverse and eccentric collection, its four sides allowed each contributor the space to develop, sowing the seeds of the solo careers which would blossom once the massive TUSK world tour drew to a close. Stevie Nicks went on to top the US chart in 1981 with BELLA DONNA, but later that year Fleetwood Mac reconvened to produce MIRAGE, a tuneful, breezy attempt at updating the radio-friendly sound they had seemed to have left behind. It was a partial success, with four hit singles and a brief run at the top of the American chart, but the revival was short-lived as Nicks and Buckingham returned to solo projects without committing themselves to a Mac tour.

It took Fleetwood's inexplicable bankruptcy to bring the band's most popular line-up together for the last time. The result was TANGO IN THE NIGHT (1987), a surprise monster hit whose ringing harmonies and immaculate production fitted in perfectly with the CD revolution of the late 80s. Energized by yet another renaissance, the band called an emotionally charged meeting later that year in the hope of persuading the reluctant Buckingham to agree to a lengthy tour, but it ended in tears and recriminations. After a violent confrontation with Nicks, Buckingham quit the band altogether, bringing to an end the most successful era of Fleetwood Mac's history. **Billy Burnette** (vocals) and **Rick Vito** (guitar) replaced Buckingham, but without his creativity the band floundered. Momentum took BEHIND THE MASK (1990) to #1 in the UK, but the snappy tunes and clear direction of old were absent and, tellingly, it produced no hit singles.

When Nicks, enraged by Fleetwood's 'tell-all' biography, left the band in 1990, it seemed that the glory days were finally over. It took US President (and longtime Mac fan) Bill Clinton to reunite Buckingham and Nicks with their former colleagues when, having used "Don't Stop" as his campaign theme song, he asked the five of them to perform it at his inauguration party in January 1993. The invitation was accepted, but afterwards both ex-members were quick to scotch any hopes of a permanent reunion. Meanwhile, the McVies and Fleetwood struggled on, recruiting new faces **Bekka Bramlett** (vocals) and ex-Traffic frontman **Dave Mason**

(guitar). Although both added something new to the Mac mix, the spark failed to re-ignite on TIME (1995), a country-tinged affair that leaned more heavily than ever on the songwriting skills of Christine McVie. Crippled by a surprising lack of support from Warners, the album bombed, failing to chart or generate much interest on either side of the Atlantic.

A 1997 album, THE DANCE (WEA), came from shoehorning the "Don't Stop" line-up into the studio once again (this time for a one-off MTV special) and brought forth five new tracks, none of which set the world on fire. The remainder of the album was filled with by-the-book renditions of "Tusk", "Go Your Own Way", "Landslide" and "You Make Lovin' Fun", leaving an uninspired and vaguely unpleasant taste in the mouth when compared to the fresh sparkling originals. Fleetwood Mac then found themselves in the unaccustomed position of being dismissed as an irrelevance. And yet the album coasted effortlessly up the charts, the world tour was a massive success and, although cynics could write this off as just another megabuck bandwagon, Ms Nicks herself assures us, 'It's rock'n'roll, and everybody's in love again'.

Peter Green then reappeared performing a number of low-key gigs in the UK with **The Splinter Group**. Working with Nigel Watson, he also brought out an excellent album, THE ROBERT JOHNSON SONGBOOK (Artisan, 1998), bringing the accumulated experience of breakdown and recovery to Johnson's already darkened, brooding visions.

2003 brought with it a rejuvenated Mac, minus Christine McVie, for the brand new studio set SAY YOU WILL. Though the cynics were aching to get their knives out, the album was by no means a mundane final stand. The set boasted some beautiful songs and rich textures that easily stood up to comparison with their classic catalogue material. They've still got it.

(•) **Greatest Hits** (1972; Sony).
A concise mid-price collection which rounds up the key moments of the band's blues era, cutting through the flabby self-indulgence that often marred their early albums. Essentially a showcase for the genius of Peter Green – the billowing beauty of "Albatross" alone makes this an essential purchase.

(•) **Rumours** (1977; Warners).
One of the legendary albums of music history, RUMOURS found its inspiration in the unravelling relationships within the new-look Mac, but this is much more than an album about Californian divorce. Almost every song creates its own distinct mood – hazy melancholy on "Dreams", cool euphoria on "You Make Loving Fun" – but they jell together brilliantly to create a 'soft rock' blueprint often copied but never bettered.

(•) **Tusk** (1979; Warners).
This monument to late-70s rock excess (even the inner sleeves had their own inner sleeves!) may lack the collective focus of RUMOURS, but it contains some sublime moments of individual inspiration in much the same way as The Beatles' WHITE ALBUM. Lindsey Buckingham's maverick genius is in full flow throughout, but the highlight is Stevie Nicks' masterpiece "Sara", on which the aching sadness of her vocal is backed by an ocean of angelic harmonies, acoustic guitar and subdued percussion to create a moment of thrilling beauty.

(•) **Tango In The Night** (1987; Warners).
By now considered something of a spent force, the Mac stormed back with their most disciplined work in a decade. All three main songwriters are in fine form – Buckingham contributes the rampant, breathless "Big Love",

while Nicks' touching "When I See You Again" and McVie's dreamy "Everywhere" rank among their most memorable songs.

Jonathan Kennaugh

FLIPPER

Formed San Francisco, 1979; disbanded 1984; re-formed 1991; split again 1993.

In San Francisco, January 1978, Johnny Rotten ended the Sex Pistols' career with the words: 'Ever get the feeling you've been cheated?' Well, yes, a growing legion of San Francisco punks felt exactly that way, and within months the city was awash with bands – the Dead Kennedys, the Avengers, the Mutants, and, somewhat less celebrated, a bunch called Negative Trend, whose singer, Rozz, overdid the Iggy impersonations and injured himself too seriously to continue. He was replaced by one **Rickie Williams**, who renamed the band **Flipper**. A legend was about to be spun.

By mid-1979 the band – Negative's rhythm section, **Will Shatter** (bass) and **Steve DePace** (drums) – had found another new vocalist, **Bruce Loose**, and added Vietnam vet **Ted Falconi** on guitar. Announcing that they were playing a new form of music called 'PET Rock' ('not a joke, and, if it were, it wouldn't be funny'), they were signed to a new independent label, Subterranean, appearing on a four-band sampler EP, SF UNDERGROUND (1979), which launched the label. Flipper's contribution, typically perverse, was a slow, grinding number about spine-free mud-munchers called "Earthworm". The band also appeared on the following year's SF punk scene LP, LIVE AT TARGET.

By now, Flipper's logo of a line drawing of a fish with sharp teeth bared, and motto (Flipper Rules OK?) were appearing on walls all over San Francisco. The Flipper sound, meanwhile, had jelled, with a simple, repetitive bass line upfront, guitar feeding back and improvising in the background, and a mad shouty bloke shouting madly over the top. "Love Canal" (1981), their first single, also demonstrated a love of echo and, on the flip side, "Ha Ha Ha", deranged chaos. Its follow-up, "Sexbomb" (1981), overlaid the whistle of a bomb falling earthwards whilst Will Shatter screamed incoherently, occasionally breaking off to bark the intricate lyric 'She's a sex bomb, yeah', before ending without warning mid-scream.

The first Flipper album emerged in 1982, entitled ALBUM – GENERIC FLIPPER. Unclassifiable then and now, it crystallized the band's slow, rhythmic sound (when all around the scene had turned to thrash), though closing with a near-apocalyptic, saxed-up version of "Sex Bomb". It was followed up with another great single, "Get Away", whose B-side was a wild Flipperization of "The Old Lady Who Swallowed A Fly".

After a two-year hiatus, Flipper reappeared with the humungous GONE FISHIN' album (1984). Only

The Stooges' FUNHOUSE comes close to the demented wonder of this record. The music seems skewed, out of time, out of tune, even, but – it's perfect. No other band ever sounded like this. The only problem was that Flipper had split up before its release. All that was to be heard for the next few years were the posthumous live collections BLOW'N CHUNKS (1984) and PUBLIC FLIPPER LTD. (1986).

Then in 1991 an orange vinyl 7" single, "Some Day"/"Distant Illusion", materialized. The 'perky porpoises of punk' (as they billed themselves) were back, sadly without bassist and driving force Will Shatter, who had died during the lost years and to whom the single was dedicated, but with a great sound still and a new bassist, **John Dougherty**. Strangely, a decade on, it was better appreciated. Grunge had arisen from the roots of punk, and several of its main men credited Flipper as a major inspiration; Kurt himself sports a Flipper T-shirt on the sleeve of IN UTERO.

So, welcomed back, Flipper became unlikely label mates to The Black Crowes and Johnny Cash on Rick Rubin's Def American label, and in 1993 released the splendidly titled AMERICAN GRAFISHY. It couldn't be described as a return to form, since this was a band who had never been off form, but it hung right in there with earlier releases, a little more straightforward, perhaps, but what the hell.

Flipper bit the dust after the failure of this corporate-sponsored resurrection and a car crash which forced Bruce to retire. Steve is still functioning, care of Subterranean Records, but John died of a heroin overdose in 1997. Concert albums LIVE AT CBGB's (1997) and BLOW 'N' CHUNKS (2001) rounded out the band's history by capturing some of the manic bliss of Flipper in full effect. All Flipper recordings are in print, though distribution difficulties have made them difficult to locate. Well worth having your friendly record store order them in for you, and also well worth badgering the suits at Warner Brothers to release the band's mythical fifth studio album.

⊙ **Album – Generic Flipper** (1982; American Recordings).
Reissued, this is a must for any weirdcore collection.

⊙ **American Grafishy** (1993; American Recordings).
More straightforward than its predecessors, sure, but Flipper's idea of straightforward, nonetheless.

⊙ **Sex Bomb Baby** (1995; Infinite Zero).
This recent CD gathers all of Flipper's singles and EPs on Subterranean plus various compilation appearances. An excellent introduction, though. If you can find the original release (1988 on the band's own label), then you'll appreciate the vastly superior (ie more outrageous) artwork.

Glenn Law

FLOWERED UP

Formed London, 1989; disbanded 1993.

On first appearance in 1989, **Flowered Up** were regarded as a kind of bastard London offspring of the Happy Mondays and their Manchester 'baggy' sound. There was certainly no denying the inspiration behind their indie-funk, and the two bands appeared to share the same preoccupations with white-meets-black groove, as well as an 'outlaw' mentality; Flowered Up even boasted their own version of the Mondays' Bez in the shape of dancer **Barry Mooncult**. However, their promising career never matched that of the Mondays, nor, really, fulfilled its potential, largely due to the group's artistic and personal waywardness.

The band's constant line-up consisted of **Liam Maher** (vocals), **Joe Maher** (guitar), **Tim Dorney** (keyboards), **John Tuvey** (drums) and **Mick Leader** (bass). Signed to London indie label Heavenly, their first two singles, "It's On" and "Phobia", were attempts at moulding a post-acid-house crossover sound. Pitched somewhere between the hedonism of Primal Scream and the obtuse rantings of the Mondays, both releases typified the early 90s *Zeitgeist*.

"It's On" reached the British Top 40 during the summer of 1990, and the group embarked on UK tours the following year. In 1991, their records began to be distributed by London Records, who proceeded to delay the release of the warmly received album, A LIFE WITH BRIAN (1991), and then refused to release the next single, "Weekender". Recognizing the anthemic quality of this twelve-minute opus, Heavenly Records boss Jeff Barrett welcomed the band back and released "Weekender" in April 1992. Dedicated to 'sufferers of Saturday night fever everywhere', it crystallized the reality of living the ecstasy/clubbing lifestyle in an aggressive, funky moment of pop perfection. From its sleeve's brazen hotel room iconography to its hedonistic lyrical sentiments, this remains the ultimate document of rave culture. It even inspired a twenty-minute film, which played in some cinemas, and was later issued on video.

As "Weekender" became a Top 20 hit in the UK, Andrew Weatherall issued a brilliant and even longer remix. Flowered Up made contributions to an Anti-Nazi League project, and recorded a wonderful cover of "Don't Talk Just Kiss" for a Right Said Fred tribute EP in late 1992 (also released on Heavenly). However, in 1993 it was announced that the band had split up, and that was it, bar a 7" single, "Better Life", which unexpectedly appeared (and disappeared) the following year.

⊙ **A Life With Brian** (1991; London).
Cheeky, wide-eyed and irreverent snapshot of urban London. Delight in tales of scallywag casuals and Camden Town chemicals – if you can decipher Liam Maher's scowling whine.

Michael Sumsion

FLUX OF PINK INDIANS

Formed Hertfordshire, England, 1980; disbanded 1987.

One of the most musical of the early-80s punk bands, **Flux Of Pink Indians** were inspired by Crass Records' marriage of punk and politics, similarly regarding musical technique as secondary to ideological discourse.

Flux Of Pink Indians were originally a primal punk group called The Epileptics, who later changed their name to Epi-X, after complaints from the British Epilepsy Association. Singer **Colin Birkett** and his bassist brother **Derek** (founder of One Little Indian Records) were the core members; they were eventually joined by **Martin Wilson** (drums) and **Kevin Hunter** (guitar), but it was an earlier formation that debuted with the NEU SMELL EP on Crass Records, which included the group's best-remembered song, "Tube Disasters". Built on a punchy pop riff borrowed from Johnny Kidd, and with ghoulish lyrics about the fun of derailments on the London Underground, it was in stark contrast to the more po-faced fare usually produced by the anarcho-punk tribe.

More typical of their peers' output was their first album, STRIVE TO SURVIVE CAUSING LEAST SUFFERING POSSIBLE (1982), released on the group's own Spiderleg label. Behind its impressive monochromatic packaging lay songs railing against consumerism and punk conformity, with musical accompaniments dominated by guitar feedback.

Predictably, most chain stores banned THE FUCKING CUNTS TREAT US LIKE PRICKS (1983), another cacophony of anarcho-punk – indeed, copies were seized from Manchester indie record store Eastern Bloc, who were charged with displaying 'obscene articles for publication for gain'. Chastened but unbowed, the final offering from the abbreviated Flux was UNCARVED BLOCK (1986). The level of musicianship had improved, and fierce funk rhythms had become a major influence, but it contained largely uninteresting instrumental tracks, complete with sound effects and free-form improvisation.

⊙ **Strive To Survive Causing Least Suffering Possible**
(1982; One Little Indian).
A near-militaristic musical barrage of sociopolitical messages, coupled with the welcome addition of the NEU SMELL EP tracks.

Alex Ogg

FLYING SAUCER ATTACK

Formed Bristol, England, 1992.

"The quests for some form of musical beauty and ideal, an otherworld, and our interests in strange phenomena such as UFOs, is perhaps reiterating indirectly that maybe life is a crock of shit, just like you thought it was." Dave Pearce

Formed in Bristol by **Dave Pearce** and **Rachel Brook** after they split from Lynda's Strange Vacation, **Flying Saucer Attack** was initially a studio-based (or more accurately, four-track) project for the pair to give vent to their art-psychedelic influences, most notably Can, Syd Barrett, Wire, John

Coltrane, Nick Drake, Roy Harper, A. R. Kane, and (especially) Krautrockers Popul Vuh.

FSA's first release was "Soaring High/StandingStone", a 7" single on their own FSA label (and VHF in America). Released in March 1993, it was followed in June by "Wish/Oceans" and a vinyl-only album, FLYING SAUCER ATTACK, in November 1993; notorious for covering Suede's "The Drowners" in a storm of fuzz guitar, it sold out rapidly. These too sold like hot cakes to audiences starved of Spacemen 3 and My Bloody Valentine – quality feedback-drenched psychedelia – and led FSA to sign to Domino Records in order to press greater quantities of discs.

1994 saw FSA's first live outings, including appearances at London's Rough Trade record shop (various recordings of these were released in 1996 on New Zealand's Corpus Hermeticum label – confusingly enough, also entitled FLYING SAUCER ATTACK!) and with Stereolab. These consisted of ramshackle half-hour improvisations, featuring **Matt Elliot** (also known as **THIRD EYE FOUNDATION**) and **Kate Wright** (both ex-Lynda's Strange Vacation), among others.

Back on the FSA trail, Domino released "Land Beyond The Sun"/"Everywhere Was Everything" in October 1994, followed by DISTANCE in November, a CD compilation of their first few singles and some unreleased tracks, emblazoned with the oxymoronic statement that 'CDs destroy music!' Fuzzy, elemental and gloomily atmospheric, each track is a still-life approximation of a waking dreamstate – drumless and post-rock.

The group's next 'new' album, FURTHER (1995), retained their militantly lo-fi credentials, being recorded at home to four-track as per usual, without digital assistance. Opening with a siren-like wail of feedback over heavily delayed clattering percussion, it proceeds through a more acoustic, pastoral approach, to use of overpowering samples of FSA playing live. It was followed by the "Outdoor Miner" single, a Wire cover backed with "Psychic Driving", an experiment in rhythm that pointed at some relaxation of the group's fervent anti-digital position.

CHORUS appeared at the end of 1995, and pulled in material both from before and after FURTHER, radio sessions and singles. Tracks like "There" and "There Dub" used computers in the mix to once again belie FSA's reputation as technophobes. The group itself declared that it marked the end of phase one of their existence, and hinted at mysterious things to come. In the interim, a 25-minute collaboration with **Roy Montgomery**, GOODBYE, appeared, along with the **Tele:Funken** project DISTANT STATION, an hour-long CD made up from FSA samples in two lengthy parts.

The promised FSA phase two turned out to be NEW LANDS (1997), an album featuring even more use of samples, and produced by Pearce alone, as Brook had decided to concentrate on his other band, **Movietone**. Essentially more of the same, NEW LANDS revealed a gradual change in method, rather than a radical departure from the entropic essence of FSA. 2000's MIRROR, however, found Pearce retreating into a far folksier sound with stunning results.

Flying Saucer Attack

⊙ **Distance** (1994; Domino).
This compilation of rare self-released singles and other material is FSA at their very best, at moments as original and as moody as their heroes, Popul Vuh.

⊙ **Further** (1995; Domino).
Again, astonishing, with its folk songs and feedback sculptures.

Tele:Funken/Flying Saucer Attack

⊙ **Distant Station** (1996; Domino).
Two tracks of increasing intensity, abstracted and nearly unrecognizable from the FSA material.

Richard Fontenoy

FOCUS

Formed Amsterdam, 1969; disbanded 1978.

Based around the technical mastery of **Thijs Van Leer** (keyboards/flute/vocals) and **Jan Akkerman** (guitar), the largely instrumental music of **Focus**, and their uncommercial Dutch origins, should have been a recipe for obscurity. However, Van Leer and Akkerman's superior blend of classical influences, inventive rock, jazz improvisation and sumptuous melodies, and a couple of startlingly catchy singles, won them a decade of international stardom.

Amsterdam music student Van Leer had been backing various Dutch singers with **Hans Cleuver** (drums) and **Martin Dresden** (bass), before recruiting Akkerman from Brainbox to form Focus at the end of 1969. Their first booking was backing the Dutch production of *Hair*, but the band's chemistry was successful enough to get a deal with Sire Records. Their debut LP, IN AND OUT OF FOCUS (1970), revealed the embryonic Focus sound, with the lead shared between Akkerman's singing guitar lines and Van Leer's flute, swirling organ, and occasional vocal. Jan also played the meanest lute in rock. Their work had the seriousness of progressive rock, while avoiding the pomposity and lyrical pretensions which dogged the genre.

Focus achieved their first modest success with the flute-driven Baroque pop of "House Of The King", a big seller across Europe. After **Pierre Van Der Linden** (drums) and **Cyril Havermans** (bass) were drafted in as the new rhythm section, they released the more ambitious MOVING WAVES (1971). It featured the 22-minute epic "Eruption", and the hit single "Hocus Pocus", complete with Akkerman's definitive riffing and soloing, and Van Leer's extraordinary lead yodelling.

With another new bassist, **Bert Ruiter**, a busy period of international touring established Focus as a formidable live act, and laid the foundations for their arrival as unlikely rock stars. The double album FOCUS III (1972), plus the exuberant guitar melody of its extracted single, "Sylvia", were both hits in early 1973. At the same time, MOVING WAVES and "Hocus Pocus" were both reissued and reached the charts in Britain and the US.

The frantic activity had drained the band and recording sessions in mid-1973 failed to produce a new album, although some of this work was later released as SHIP OF MEMORIES (1977). A live LP, FOCUS AT THE RAINBOW (1973), was issued to keep up the momentum and represented the band at their commercial peak. But 1974's HAMBURGER CONCERTO, with new drummer **Colin Allen**, was a major letdown, especially in its lengthy, overfamiliar title opus.

A move to a lighter jazz-infused sound on MOTHER FOCUS (1975) failed to halt their declining fortunes, and they were dealt a terrible blow when a disillusioned Akkerman decided to leave, to concentrate on his solo career. He has since released many albums, mainly indulging his classical inclinations and his passion for the lute, although he returned with the more mainstream THE NOISE OF ART (1990). Meanwhile Van Leer had enlisted respected jazz-rock guitarist **Philip Catherine**, and yet another drummer, **Steve Smith**, but they were to release just one more album. This was a bizarre collaboration with veteran trouser-splitting rocker **P. J. Proby** on FOCUS CON PROBY (1978). It marked the end of Focus, although the line-up from the FOCUS III sessions reunited in 1990 for a special performance on Dutch television.

⊙ **Moving Waves** (1971; Polydor).
The breakthrough album with stand-out tracks "Hocus Pocus", "Janis" and "Focus".

⊙ **Focus III** (1972; Polydor).
The melodies are now in full flow on "Sylvia" and "Round Goes The Gossip", and Jan even gets to play his lute on "Elspeth Of Nottingham".

⊙ **Hocus Pocus – The Best Of Focus** (1994; EMI).
A useful, mid-price compilation, mainly from the first three albums.

Nick Dale

FOETUS

Conceived London, 1980.

"This isn't the melody that lingers on, it's the malady that malingers on." Clint Ruin on "Cold Day In Hell"

Jim Thirlwell – aka **Foetus** – is a true original. If God has 1000 names, then Thirlwell must be well on the way to demi-god status. Philip & His Foetus Vibrations, Foetus Über Frisco, You've Got Foetus On Your Breath and The Foetus All-Nude Revue are just a few of the names he's worked under. To the relief of record-shop shelf-fillers everywhere, 'Foetus' always crops up somewhere... except, when he's calling himself Stinkfist, Flesh Volcano, Wiseblood, Clint Ruin, Frank Want and suchlike.

Hailing from Melbourne, Australia, Thirlwell moved to England in 1978. After abortive attempts to sell the Foetus concept to a record label, he started his own, Self Immolation, in 1980, and set to recording, subsidizing his efforts with a job at a Virgin record store.

The embryonic Foetus sound was of the tape-looping noise-fetishist industrial underground of the time, and not immediately popular. Indeed, after records such as **Foetus Under Glass**'s OKFM (1981), his first release, and the longer-running **You've Got Foetus On Your Breath**'s DEAF (1981) and ACHE (1982), his following was probably still in single figures and he was hopelessly broke. However, as luck would have it, one of Foetus's few fans was Stevo of the Some Bizarre label. Thirlwell manfully accepted their offer of a deal, though insisting that they took his favourite band Einstürzende Neubauten on board at the same time.

Thus financed, Thirlwell was able to move from working with eight-track to 24-track recording. First born was **Scraping Foetus Off The Wheel**'s HOLE (1984), an extraordinary record, written, performed and produced by Thirlwell in the guise of Clint Ruin, the ultimate mirror-shaded, cowboy-booted, wasted rock star making music to be listened to 'just before they drop the big one'. It mixed satanic surf music, sampled movie dialogue and World War II sound effects with devilish wordplay, metal-banging, crunching drums, guitars, synth-noise and incongruous samples and quotations. Death metal groups would have sold their souls to sound this evil.

HOLE was followed by a 12", CALAMITY CRUSH (1984) and the unexpectedly electro-orientated **Foetus Art Terrorism**, For a while, Thirlwell seemed to be everywhere, recording with (amongst others) Marc & The Mambas, Annie Hogan and Nurse With Wound. He even turned up on *Top Of The Pops* playing sax with Orange Juice. Clint Ruin also joined Nick Cave, Marc Almond and Lydia Lunch to form **The Immaculate Consumptive**, who performed a couple of wild US shows. Ruin's contribution consisted of dancing on a piano keyboard prior to trashing it.

By now a Foetus house style had been established: record covers were a distinctive combination of black, red, grey and white, Japanese calligraphy, and black and white militaristic pictures. The design had its finest hour when, in 1985, Some Bizarre released THE FOETUS OF EXCELLENCE box set. That same year, NAIL, by Scraping Foetus Off The Wheel, revealed a mellower side to Thirlwell's music, with a pair of pseudo-soundtracks, "From Pigdom Come", providing temporary relief from percussive, scraping scream-alongs. 'Say what you mean and say it mean', rasped Ruin, and he did just that when he informed presenter Muriel Gray that 'a woman's place is on my face' during an interview on UK TV music show, The Tube.

In 1986, Thirlwell relocated to New York, in part to be near his kindred spirit Lydia Lunch. He kept up the work rate, forming **Wiseblood** with former Swans percussionist **Roli Mosimann**, producing the album DIRTDISH (1986). During spare moments, he put together soundtracks for transgressive New York film-maker Richard Kern and made the odd willy-waving appearance on screen himself (most memorably with Lunch in a sequence during *Right Side Of My Brain*, which brings a whole new meaning to 'blowing one's cool').

Thirlwell has continued a relentless release schedule with records such as **Foetus Corruptus**'s RIFE, **Foetus Interruptus**'s THAW, **Foetus Inc**'s SINK and (live) MALE, as well as a couple of LPs under the name **Steroid Maximus**. While no Foetus issue is boring, these lacked the shock value of his mid-80s records. More recently, the likes of Ministry and Nine Inch Nails have taken many of the ideas Thirlwell pioneered to both critical and commercial success. Do you reckon he gives a damn, though? Releases such as his joint project with the Cardinal of Camp, **MARC ALMOND**, FLESH VOLCANO/SLUT (1998), tend to suggest not.

(...) Foetus (...)

- **Hole** (1984; Self Immolation).
  This is arguably the best Foetus album: a screaming bloody noise featuring Ronald Reagan, the Batman theme and the outbreak of World War II.

- **Gash** (1995; Big Cat).
  One of the best recent Foetus CDs – head-banging music for people who enjoy whiplash injuries.

Wiseblood

- **Dirtdish** (1986; K.422).
  A thumping record in every sense.

Glenn Law

FOGHAT

Formed London, 1970; disbanded 1984.

Sledgehammer Chuck Berry retreads were **Foghat**'s stock in trade, and the sheer dependability of their approach was the band's greatest strength and weakness. Attempts at diversification, usually into the realm of MOR balladry, were generally unsuccessful, and, when Foghat finally went full tilt for a different sound in an effort to move with the times, they became an authentic, albeit rather undeserving, punk rock casualty.

After playing for a while with Switzerland-based group Les Questions, guitarist/vocalist **'Lonesome' Dave Peverett** returned to England to join Savoy Brown, whose fluctuating line-up, marshalled by dictatorial guitarist Kim Simmonds, also included drummer **Roger Earl**, and, later, bassist **Tony Stevens**. In 1970, having helped steer Savoy Brown toward bona fide boogie, Peverett, Earl and Stevens left to form Foghat, picking up slide-guitar specialist **Rod Price**, who, like Free's Paul Kossoff and Simon Kirke, had previously played in Black Cat Bones.

Foghat warmed up with a two-week UK tour supporting Captain Beefheart, then secured a deal with Albert Grossman's Bearsville label via a Todd Rundgren-produced demo tape. Their debut album, FOGHAT (1972) established the long-running blues-metal formula, right from its opener, a savage cover of Willie Dixon's "I Just Want To Make Love To You", emphasized by a clever volume leap after the intro (Dave Edmunds taking a bow on production here).

It was Foghat's definitive moment, and narrowly missed the US singles chart. Meanwhile, a well-received appearance in Wisconsin, soon after the album's release, was the first date of a US tour, endlessly extended as the band rapidly built a following. Sales of FOGHAT gradually advanced to the million mark, and the follow-up, FOGHAT (ROCK'N'ROLL) (1973), sold respectably in the US, too. It was a little less effective, "Ride, Ride, Ride" and "Long Way To Go" standing out on a set that (like most of its successors) walked a fine line between boogie excitement and boogie nod-out.

Although interest remained muted in their homeland, Foghat went from strength to strength in America, racking up gold and platinum discs. ENERGISED (1974) was probably their best release of this mid-period, featuring the frenetic "Honey Hush", a fine "That'll Be The Day", and a comical but enjoyable funk bash, "Step Outside".

By now, Peverett had begun to dominate the songwriting, and the band's career curve was approaching its peak with ROCK AND ROLL OUTLAWS (1975), after which Stevens left the band. The album's producer **Nick Jameson** took his place on FOOL FOR THE CITY (1976), which contained a couple of classic tracks in its Kiss-like title track and "Slow Ride".

Jameson quit after the album, to be replaced on NIGHTSHIFT (1976) by **Craig MacGregor**. A woolly-sounding greatest hits live album, FOGHAT LIVE! (1977) was nowhere near as entertaining as might have been hoped, but still sold a million, while back in the studio (with Kiss producer Eddie

Kramer), Foghat turned out STONE BLUE (1978), featuring the hard-rocking "Easy Money" and another strong title song.

BOOGIE MOTEL (1979) and its country-pop singalong, "Third Time Lucky", suggested Foghat were on the slide and groping for a new direction, and the awful truth was confirmed by TIGHT SHOES (1980), on which the band sounded appropriately cramped and uncomfortable. Peverett's songs were at best mediocre, while the production sounded ugly, modern and over-bright. Price left in 1981, replaced by **Eric Cartwright**, but although several more albums followed – GIRLS TO CHAT, BOYS TO BOUNCE (1981), IN THE MOOD FOR SOMETHING RUDE (1982) and ZIG ZAG WALK (1983) – Foghat failed to regain their raunch or popularity.

In 1994, however, the band reformed with all the original members to release the relatively refreshing blues/rock collection RETURN OF THE BOOGIE MEN – the fans who hadn't forgotten Foghat's earlier triumphs were more than happy, though there wasn't enough there to stop Price from once again jumping ship, only to release a solo album, OPEN (2000). As for Foghat, Price was replaced by Bryan Bassett, a live album followed in 1998, ROAD CASES, and over the next couple of years several incarnations of the same mid-Seventies live material, THE KING BISCUIT FLOWER HOUR (aka HITS YOU REMEMBER LIVE or LIVE 2000), also appeared in stores.

Sadly, early in 2000, Dave Peverett died from cancer-related complications. It seems unlikely that the band will ever reform without Lonesome Dave, though the loyal fans are kept happy by the sporadic rerelease of old material and live recordings.

⊙ **Anthology** (2000; Essential).
A well-selected, 24-track anthology that will probably do the trick for most tastes.

Robert Coyne

FOLK IMPLOSION

Formed Massachusetts, 1993; split 1999; rekindled 2002.

I t's ironic that what began as a side project is now better known than the main attraction. As the driving force of **SEBADOH**, **Lou Barlow** was behind the wheel for several indie gems and yet the closest he has been to mainstream recognition was as one half of **Folk Implosion**'s original incarnation. More specifically, fame came a-courting thanks to the band's unforgettable contributions to the soundtrack of *Kids*.

In 1993, in the aftermath of Sebadoh's BUBBLE & SCRAPE, Barlow received a tape of songs from fellow Massachusetts songwriter **John Davis** who was then working in the very un-rock'n'roll world of librarianship. Their first release was the seriously low-key cassette-only 1993 EP WALK THROUGH THIS WORLD WITH THE FOLK IMPLOSION, recorded in the ultra-

lo-fi surroundings of Davis's house and released on the almost invisible Chocolate Monk label; the cuts were very much in the Sebadoh/Sentridoh tradition.

1994's TAKE A LOOK INSIDE expanded the duo's vision; with fourteen tracks in a mere twenty-two minutes it reined in many of Barlow's tendencies for lengthy wig-out instrumentals or noise barrages. Within the sometimes exhaustingly unrefined sound there was a nascent pop sensibility waiting to surprise the patient listener.

Although Sebadoh were starting to reach a wider audience with 1995's BAKESALE, and both bands were invited to contribute, it was the Folk Implosion that ended up providing the linchpin cuts on the soundtrack to Larry Clark's controversial movie Kids; the duo duly coughed up the trippy, electronic single "Natural One", and could also be found lurking in the soundtrack's grooves under the moniker of the **Deluxx Folk Implosion** (you guessed it: Lou, John, and members of the band Deluxx).

Picked up by alternative radio, "Natural One" charted on both sides of the Atlantic, enabled Davis to give up his day job and apparently even appeared on karaoke lists. With its fluid bass line and insistent drum-machine backing, "Natural One" was described with most un-Barlow-like adjectives such as "sexy" or "funky".

1997's DARE TO BE SURPRISED eschewed the production values of "Natural One" in favour of a 'back to basics' approach. Where most bands would have attempted to emulate the sound of their hit, the Folk Implosion chose to stick to their guns, resulting in their most coherent album. It was hook-laden indie-rock, but where Sebadoh had sometimes squashed good songs under walls of noise, here a sense of melody flourished, albeit in a quirky, thrift-store kind of way.

But with 1999's ONE PART LULLABY you get the sense that Davis and Barlow almost wished they'd cashed in when they had the chance. There was more electronic toying on this release, and certainly a nod toward radio acceptance, but the glossy production didn't suit, and the songs seemed, in places,

remarkably flat. The duo were floundering, trying to recapture the elusive magic that only messing around can create – only this time, with Sebadoh rapidly becoming redundant, in the pressurized environment of a major-label deal.

Despite widespread good reviews, Folk Implosion effectively called it a day after ONE PART LULLABY. Davis quit; Barlow claimed his partner had 'never really fully embraced being a musician as a lifestyle', although he had managed to release four solo albums during his time with Folk Implosion, including 2000's I'LL BURN.

2003's THE NEW FOLK IMPLOSION marked something of a new start for Barlow. Asked by the Melvins to support them on tour, Barlow recruited former Sebadoh drummer **Russ Pollard** and guitarist **Imaad Wasif** (who were both working together as **Alaska!**), recorded a new album and reactivated the Folk Implosion name.

Compared to previous Folk Implosion releases, the new set featured fewer weird noises and drum machine activation, and it also bypassed Sebadoh's draining cacophony; instead, the group were content to supply little more than a selection of good tunes – the almost Zeppelin-esque epic "Releast" and the introspective "Pearl" being the best of the bunch.

But there was also a tangible lack of enthusiasm, and with lyrics such as 'what I thought was fun isn't fun anymore' (from "Easy") one wondered whether Barlow needed something to rekindle the fire. But for someone as apparently obsessed with the recording process as he is, it can only be a matter of time before he stumbles across another daringly lo-fi outlet for self-expression.

Folk Implosion

🔘 **Dare To Be Surprised** (1997; Communion).
The sweeter side of experimentation, lo-fi with a heart and one of Barlow's finest releases.

Various Artists

🔘 **Kids** (1995; London).
It's rare to find a soundtrack collection as dazzling as this. As well as the Implosion's "Natural One" and their mesmerizing, Satie-sampling "Wet Stuff", the set features contributions from, among others, Daniel Johnston and Slint.

Derryck Strachan

FOO FIGHTERS

Formed Seattle, 1994.

The Foo Fighters crashed spectacularly into view following the untimely demise of **NIRVANA**. Few people realized that behind the Nirvana drum kit lurked a man of such prodigious musical talents. Prime mover **Dave Grohl** (guitar/vocals) played guitar before he took up the drums, and had served time with a number of hardcore groups, including the legendary Scream.

Throughout the roller-coasting nightmare of fame and fortune that was Nirvana's short lifetime, Grohl

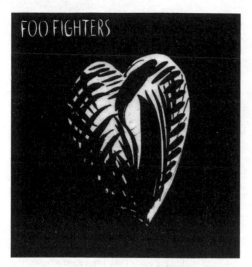

FOO FIGHTERS

nurtured a desire to create his own music. During periods off the road he took time out to write his own material, an example of which, "Marigold", emerged as the low-key B-side to Nirvana's penultimate single, "Heart Shaped Box". Following the period of confusion after Cobain's suicide, Grohl decided to do what he had always wanted to do since he recorded his first song all by himself.

In September 1994 he booked himself into a studio and recruited a band: **Nate Mendel** (bass) and **William Goldsmith** (drums) from short-lived Sub Pop hopefuls Sunny Day Real Estate, plus old acquaintance **Pat Smear** (guitar), who had joined Nirvana on their final tour. Taking their name from the jargon used by World War II fighter pilots to describe UFOs, a new phenomenon was born: cool songs combined with supercool B-movie imagery.

The record company (Capitol) and media circus were salivating at the prospect, and the anticipation was such that the first single, "This Is A Call", sailed into the upper reaches of the chart in June 1995. In the same month, FOO FIGHTERS was released on the Roswell label (to keep the UFO theme running), to near-universal acclaim. The brilliance of the single was no fluke: drawing on his early punk influences, Grohl had crafted twelve euphoric shots of hardcore melody and layered vocal harmonies. The lyrics were impenetrable but no one cared; it was the sound of the summer, earning them the label 'the hardcore Beach Boys'. Naturally the Nirvana tag was wheeled out time after time, but the ragged Foo Fighters sound owed little to the heavier Nirvana vibe.

The subsequent US tour was a major blast, then late August brought them back to the UK for the Reading Rock Festival, where, in a move that defies explanation, they were booked to play the small Second Stage tent, a venue that couldn't contain all the punters who wanted to see them – havoc naturally ensued. The remainder of the year brought the release of two fur-

ther singles ("I'll Stick Around" and "For All The Cows") and more very successful live shows.

Whereas the first album was essentially a recording of Grohl alone, THE COLOUR AND THE SHAPE (1997) was a genuine Foos album. The band had changed drummers – exit Goldsmith, enter **Taylor Hawkins** – and Grohl himself took the drummer's stool for most of the recording as well as writing most of the music. THE COLOUR AND THE SHAPE did little to dispel the band's growing reputation for 'grunge-lite' in the eyes of the press but it sold well enough. In part autobiographical, and with a good deal of cathartic screaming, the album made few radical departures from standard grunge (itself in danger of becoming as formulaic and dull as the big-hair metal bands it had virtually blown away). However, stand-out pieces such as "Everlong", "Walking After You" and "New Way Home" – the three closing tracks of the set – were enough to reaffirm one's faith in loud guitars as the road to salvation.

During the European leg of the 'Colour and the Shape Tour', rumours began to circulate that Smear was leaving the band after a backstage row with Dave Grohl. The stories were dismissed by Grohl as 'a bunch of internet crap' but they persisted and on September 4, during the *MTV Awards* in New York, Smear bowed out and his replacement, **Franz Stahl**, was introduced.

Despite the blip encountered with Smear's departure, 1998 proved to be a highly successful instalment in the Fighters' ongoing tale. Grohl indulged himself with a spot of movie soundtrack writing by scoring *Touch* with a little help from Veruca Salt songstress **Louise Post**. A contribution to *The X-Files* movie soundtrack provided the band with a minor hit single, but it was their appearance on the UK leg of the monster Ozzfest rock festival that proved they had the staying power to maintain their position as one of the most popular post-grunge bands of the decade, a status underlined by their contribution to the *Mission: Impossible 2* soundtrack – a particularly rabid version of Pink Floyd's "Have A Cigar" recorded with Queen's **Brian May**. And then came 1999's superbly accomplished THERE IS NOTHING LEFT TO LOSE album. As well as some great singles, such as "Learn To Fly", the album spawned several hilarious videos that to this day regularly lighten MTV's stodge.

More recently the Foos have toured extensively, while Grohl has found time to drum for **QUEENS OF THE STONEAGE**. The Foos returned again in 2002 with ONE BY ONE, another blinding slice of their own, unmistakeable brand of rock. Successfully exorcizing the ghosts of the past, the Foo Fighters continue to prove that there is life after Nirvana.

⊙ **Foo Fighters** (1995; Roswell/Capitol).
A brilliantly paced and infectiously catchy debut. Distortion, melody and attitude merge to make this one of 1995's essential releases.

⊙ **There Is Nothing Left To Lose** (1999; Roswell/RCA)
The opening track – "Stacked Actors" – bursts into life with a driving power, the band's energy focused to a diamond point. The album throbs with confidence, with catchy

numbers like "Learn To Fly" and "Gimme Stitches" standing out in a way that Foo Fighters' songs never have before. These compositions chop and snarl, gliding from anthemic grunge to country ballad.

⊙ **One By One** (2002; Roswell/RCA).
As catchy, punky and propulsive as ever, this set fails to broaden the Foo Fighter's sound, but, nonetheless offers stunning cuts such as "All My Life" and "Times Like These (One-Way Motorway)".

Essi Berelian

FOUNTAINS OF WAYNE

Formed New Jersey, US, 1995.

Songwriting duo **Adam Schlesinger** (vocals/guitar) and **Chris Collingwood** (bass guitarist) had been in bands for the best part of a decade – from Woolly Mammoth to the improbably named Three Men When Stood Side By Side Have A Wingspan Of Over 12 Feet. However, the first real signs of success came when, as a member of **Ivy**, Schlesinger found himself the composer of the theme behind the Tom Hanks 60s beat-group movie *That Thing You Do!* in 1996.

By then, Schlesinger and Collingwood had joined forces once more, this time as **Fountains Of Wayne**. (Like Everything But The Girl, their name was derived from a shop – in this case a store in the New Jersey town of Wayne, which dealt exclusively in fountains.) With a line-up completed by **Jody Porter** (guitar) and **Brian Young** (drums), the foursome based themselves in New York and set to work on a debut album.

Released on Atlantic Records, FOUNTAINS OF WAYNE (1997) was economical but richly tuneful, inventive but joyous, and populated by eccentric, complex characters in gems such as "Leave The Biker" or "Sick Day". Reference points were varied, from Jonathan Richman to The Eagles via The Beach Boys, but, like Eels or Ben Folds Five, Fountains Of Wayne have been resourceful and innovative enough to breathe new life into post-grunge American pop-rock.

Critical reactions to the album were largely encouraging, and sometimes euphoric, while the duo received beneficial coverage from American college radio. Public response, though, was relatively muted, although "Radiation Vibe" and "Survival Car" tickled the lower end of the UK singles charts, and they achieved their biggest chart success in December 1997 with that rarest of feats, a highly listenable Yuletide release entitled "I Want An Alien For Christmas". The follow-up album came in 1999 – UTOPIA PARKWAY was, again, a critically cherished, but largely ignored set. Perhaps their brand of Posies-styled power-pop sat a little too out of step with the times, but since then, nothing has been heard.

⊙ **Fountains Of Wayne** (1997; Atlantic).
A first-class batch of short, sharp, radio-friendly songs, just about all of which manage to sound both familiar and refreshing. Quite an achievement in this day and age.

Justin Lewis

KIM FOWLEY

Born Los Angeles, July 27, 1942.

Cult rocker **Kim Fowley** has carved a unique and often strange path through four decades of rock. Singer, songwriter, producer, dancer, manager, poet and hired musical hand, he organized 'love-in' events in the 60s, shamelessly blagged his way into many fashionable underground situations, and generally acted as a catalyst for some of the most celebrated music of the 60s and 70s, forging a music scene in Los Angeles at a time when the only scene going was linked to the film industry. He has also cut a stack of albums and has a singles catalogue stretching into three figures. Die-hard fans continue to champion him as a true original who embodies the very essence of underground cool. Detractors see him as a self-indulgent maverick without the discipline to build a career on his musical talents.

Fowley's early work revolved around duties as musician, writer and producer. In 1960 he helped shape the Hollywood Argyles, who hit the US #1 spot with "Alley Oop", then in 1962 both the US and UK gave in to the infectious novelty stomp of "Nut Rocker" by B. Bumble And The Stingers, a Fowley production. Given Fowley's touch at this stage the future seemed to promise everything for a prodigy who was still not yet 21. Artists as diverse as Cat Stevens, Soft Machine, The Mothers of Invention and The Byrds were later to benefit from Fowley's input as producer and/or writer.

From the mid-60s onwards Fowley also pursued an on/off solo career, creating his own brand of garage rock. Like The Stooges and the MC5, he straddled 60s underground and 70s New Wave, although his early work, especially the first solo album LOVE IS ALIVE AND WELL (1967), had a strong hippie influence. Nothing he did generated many sales, but albums like INTERNATIONAL HEROES (1973) and SUNSET BOULEVARD (1978) gained reverential press and are still treasured by fans. A collection of some of his most obscure and crazy rarities from this time, OUTLAW SUPERMAN (1997), including his lost, thought-provoking, punk rock masterpiece "What If Boys Got Pregnant?", is essential.

Fowley also masterminded the launch of all-girl group, **THE RUNAWAYS**. In a breathtakingly blatant exercise in teenage glam-metal exploitation, The Runaways had their tender ages printed on the sleeve of their first album, a scam that launched the careers of **Joan Jett** and heavy guitar queen **Lita Ford** and generated more column inches than most of Fowley's projects.

A more bizarre and lucrative twist to the Fowley saga saw the man working on albums of music for live sports events. Realizing that "Nut Rocker" was making regular appearances while speed skaters and basketball teams were strutting their stuff, he set about applying his production skills to updating the formula.

During the 90s Fowley's stock fell, with only the slightest cult following still appreciative of his sparky slabs of anarchic rock. Despite this, the man continued on his own idiosyncratic path and still cuts records that grind and hum with a vengeance. HIDDEN AGENDA (1997) took Fowley's sound back to the melodic folk-tinged style of The Byrds; THE TRIP OF A LIFETIME (1999) hooked our hero up with the likes of Teenage Fanclub and even Roni Size; while HIDDEN AGENDA AT THE 13TH NOTE documented a live appearance with the BMX Bandits.

With his matchless pedigree, Fowley should – at the very least – be in A&R work until his ears give out. Nonetheless, he may remain a mere footnote in rock, confined to fanzines, websites and classified ads in *Goldmine*.

⊙ **Outrageous/Good Clean Fun** (1995; Creation).
Two-albums-on-one CD reissue of a couple of seminal late-60s albums. Unless your local record shop is the size of the Graf Zeppelin, you'll have to order this.

⊙ **Mondo Hollywood** (1996; Rev Ola).
More riveting, seminal 60s weirdness.

⊙ **The Trip Of A Lifetime** (1999; Resurgence).
A bizarre and compelling amalgam of styles, post-techno oddness and guest appearances. In Fowley's own words, this set ' …is better than death because it screams, stomps and salivates all over itself like a volcano.'

Neil Nixon

PETER FRAMPTON

Born Beckenham, England, 1950.

"I'm the guy who does the live thing."

Apart from death and taxes, one of the few certain things in life is that in pretty much every secondhand record store you'll find a copy of FRAMPTON COMES ALIVE, the double album that remains the best-selling live pop record of all time.

Its creator, **Peter Frampton**, had his first taste of success singing and playing guitar with The Herd, a teen group who had three UK hits in 1967–68. The band was directed by Ken Howard and Alan Blaikley, Britain's most successful non-performing songwriting duo, and put out pseudo-psychedelic popcorn designed not to upset radio programmers, whilst giving teenyboppers a taste of 'alternative' music. Under normal circumstances, the combination of craftsmanlike songs and Frampton's prettiness would have ensured a couple of years of big hits and then a move into cabaret. But Frampton had higher ambitions and, as The Herd's third single hit the Top 10, he took his leave, hooking up with Steve Marriott to form **HUMBLE PIE**. This much heavier, more blues-orientated act allowed Frampton to showcase his skills

and develop a reputation as a drop-dead gorgeous guitar hero and songwriter.

When he left the Pie in 1971, after five albums, his solo career was not expected to amount to much, critical opinion being unanimous that Marriott was the real talent in the group. His decision to jump ship just after the Pie had released what would go on to be one of the best-selling live albums ever – LIVE AT THE FILLMORE. There's no reason to revise this verdict now, but it has to be added that Frampton was a good guitarist and was prepared to work hard for his success. He hung out with the rock aristocracy (playing session on George Harrison's ALL THINGS MUST PASS) and concentrated on breaking really big in America.

A succession of four albums (two credited to the group **Frampton's Camel**) steadily built up sales and critical tolerance and culminated in the gold-selling FRAMPTON (1975). Meanwhile he was touring relentlessly through the States, an effort that paid off in trumps when FRAMPTON COMES ALIVE (1976) ended up shifting fifteen million units (trumping Humble Pie's FILLMORE album in the process) and yielding three hit singles: "Show Me The Way", "Baby I Love Your Way" and "Do You Feel Like We Do" – all originally on FRAMPTON in superior versions.

It was interesting timing, for as punk appeared the following year Frampton became the epitome of everything to kick against: semi-acoustic pop bloated into stadium rock that sacrificed everything for the lowest common denominator. As detractors would have it, Frampton had nothing to say and no new ways of saying it (apart from the voicebox on his guitar). Nonetheless, his follow-up, I'M IN YOU, went platinum, despite an unprecedented critical battering.

It was a vacuous record, however, and must have turned off most of the fans from FRAMPTON COMES ALIVE. And worse was to come as Frampton was signed up to play Billy Shears in the film of SGT PEPPER'S LONELY HEARTS CLUB BAND, a dismal venture, in which (the indignity) he was outstarred by the Bee Gees. His career damaged by these poor records, the advent of New Wave and a serious car crash, Frampton entered the 80s with little to commend him. He eventually got rid of the 70s curly hairdo, but a succession of bland albums failed to take off, and a bit part in Bowie's band for the *Glass Spider Tour* (he had attended the same secondary school as the former David Jones) coincided with the artistic low point of Bowie's career. It looked nothing short of desperate when he released FRAMPTON COMES ALIVE II in the mid-90s, while 1999's self-titled effort could be described as 'mature', in the lacklustre MOR sense of the word.

⊙ **Frampton Comes Alive** (1976; A&M).
If you must own a Frampton album on CD, this is the one – as FRAMPTON is still awaiting rerelease. It may prompt you to wonder if the world went mad in the mid-70s and, in particular, why so many people fell for such a dreadful version of "Jumping Jack Flash".

Alwyn W. Turner

THE FRANK & WALTERS

Formed Cork, Ireland, 1990.

Named after a couple of tramps in their home town, Cork, **The Frank & Walters** first came to attention through a deal with the Brit-based Setanta label. The aptly named EP.1 (1991), embodied the band's self-confessed quirkiness in titles like the breezy lead track "Fashion Crisis Hits New York". **Paul Linehan** (vocals/bass), brother **Niall** (guitar) and **Ashley Keating** (drums) specialized in celebrating the mundane and unfashionable, breaking down the barriers between fan and 'artiste', and exploring their self-proclaimed 'hippy diddly crazy world'.

With interest building after the release of EP.2, Setanta repackaged the two EPs on one budget-priced CD and signed a deal with the larger Go! Discs, who, it was felt, could give the band the push they deserved. Their first release for their new label was the HAPPY BUSMAN EP, which was produced by **EDWYN COLLINS** and told the tale of an eccentric local bus driver. It narrowly failed to chart but drew comparisons to The Undertones and The Wedding Present and indicated that intelligence and maturity lay beneath the band's trademark silliness.

Their next single, "This Is Not A Song", an anthemic yet tender celebration of life itself, again stopped short of the UK chart, but shortly afterwards the trio sold out their first major headline date, at London's Astoria Theatre. In October 1992, The Frank & Walters released their debut album, TRAINS, BOATS AND PLANES. It charted at #36 but felt like an anticlimax as it contained many tracks already available. Desperately in need of a hit single, they teamed up with Lightning Seed **Ian Broudie**, who remixed the LP track "After All". It almost made the UK Top 10, and was followed by a rerecording of "Fashion Crisis Hits New York", again produced by Broudie. By this stage, fans were beginning to feel cheated by the lack of new material and the band's relentless tomfoolery was in danger of becoming irritating.

They returned in 1996 with THE GRAND PARADE, which delighted their old fans but failed to win them any new support. The album had its moments but the fizzing enthusiasm and wide-eyed innocence was beginning to wear thin. The group continued to record, releasing BEAUTY BECOMES MORE THAN LIFE (1999), GLASS (2000), and an excellent self-titled best-of in 2002. Their perseverance remains admirable, and certain quarters of the press continue to champion them, but, their sales are meagre and, all in all, they remain a chirpie reminder of a golden age of indie-pop.

⊙ **Trains, Boats And Planes** (1992; Go! Discs).
A collection of The Frank's lovable and whimsical pop ditties: "This Is Not A Song", "Walter's Trip", "After All" the infamous "Trainspotters", "Happy Busman" and, of course, the endlessly recycled "Fashion Crisis Hits New York".

Gavin Stoker

THE FRANK CHICKENS

Formed London, 1982.

"She'd never thought there'd come a day like this, She'd have to give her only daughter a goodbye kiss."

Papa didn't suspect anything, but Mama Hohki had seen the look in Kazuko's eyes and knew that the journey her daughter was starting was not to be just the three-month vacation they had been planning. Kazuko's trip turned into a four-year absence from her native Japan, during which she brought all the joys of Japanese youth culture to the jaded London punk scene. Along with **Kazumi Taguchi** and **Moriko Iwatsudo**, **Kazuko Hohki** created **The Frank Chickens** and took avant-garde pop from the bargain bins of the 1980s towards the next millennium. Using fashion, art and electronics, The Chickens pioneered future pop.

A racing dance groove in which Bruce Lee meets Nureyev, "We Are Ninja" and it's pioneering remix, "We Are Ninja (Not Geisha)", made the indie top 10. With **Steve Beresford** and **David Toop** providing state-of-the-art production, their first album, WE ARE FRANK CHICKENS (1984), crossed the Yellow Magic Orchestra with Talking Heads. With confidence growing, their next single "Blue Canary" (Kaz Records) became an all-time John Peel favourite. Taken from the Izumi Yakimura hit, it cheekily mixed Japanese folk and karaoke to infectious and celebratory effect.

Their brilliant use of simplistic drama, fast wit and spontaneity led to a support slot with The Smiths. A second collaboration with Beresford and Toop (plus **Grant Showbiz** and **Justin Adams**) produced the excellent GET CHICKENIZED (1987) with subject matter even more mind-bending than before. It included tales of runaway lesbians and female wrestlers, ironic rap ("Yellow Toast"), and a traditional tune from Japanese street advertisers, the *Chindon Ya.*

CLUB MONKEY (1987) was both a successful album and stage musical, based on the Chinese allegory Monkey King. Geisha ghosts and Kabuki kung fu augmented show-stopping tracks such as "Dead Dog", "Night Drain" and title track "Club Monkey". CLUB MONKEY became not only a top album but a favourite haunt of hip Londoners and one of the best multimedia events of the period. 1987 also saw Hohki launch a successful acting career which was to include a cameo in the film *90 Days Tottenham Pub.* The soundtrack, THE 90 DAYS – THE ORIGINAL SOUNDTRACK (Virgin Japan), included three new Frank Chickens tracks including the future show stopper, "Gochamaze".

1992 saw the release of the ironic and personal PRETTY FRANK CHICKENS, which featured delights such as "Sayonara Rockefeller" and "Yummy

Yummy Yummy" and won them the *New Collaborations* award from the Arts Council of Great Britain when they took it on tour.

The witty and infectious YUKASITA-UNDERFLOOR WORLD followed in 1994 and was followed in 1996 by a dub version by producer Grant Showbiz, ANNABELLA/DIFFERENT (THE REMIX COLLECTION). It was mightily effective and maybe just a little ahead of it's time.

After a collection of essays, *London Kai Kai*, Hohki released her first solo album, KAZUKO HOHKI CHANTE BRIGITTE BARDOT, a compilation of old hits recorded between 1987 and 1991. Further solo material appeared on 1992's LOVE IN RAINY DAYS, less surreal than the Bardot album with cool electronic grooves lurking behind the vocals.

In addition to her solo work, Hohki contributed to Dutch improvisational musician **Teo Joling**'s CONCERT FOR EYES album (1984) and collaborated with **Kahonda Style**, a British improv unit known for using indigenous Thai and Japanese instruments. She also produced a poignant drama, *Toothless*, a one-woman show telling the story of Kazuko and her relationship with her mother.

The Frank Chickens' live events have become multimedia extravaganzas, mixing DJs and VJs with live performances from the band in which Hohki is assisted by **Atsuko Kamara**, **Chikama Kagawa** and **Ray Hogan**. Issues – such as arranged marriages, visa problems and the world of Japanese allegories – are put on the big screen and juxtaposed with live renditions of Frank Chickens favourites. More film work and collaborations with Coldcut's Ninja Tunes label means that the future continues to look lively.

⦿ **Get Chickenized** (1987; Flying Lecords; reissued 1998; Resurgence).
Art pop at its glittery, classy peak, taking inspiration from Bowie, Godzilla and Monty Python.

⦿ **Club Monkey** (1987; Flying Lecords; reissued 1998; Resurgence).
One of indie music's more intriguing children.

Tyrone Thomas

FRANKIE GOES TO HOLLYWOOD

Formed Liverpool, England, 1980; disbanded 1987.

A tale of sudden phenomenal success, rewards and excesses, and an equally sudden return to obscurity, the career of **Frankie Goes To Hollywood** typifies the time and place which spawned them – 1980s Britain.

Taking their name from the caption to a newspaper photograph of Frank Sinatra, the band had spent much of the early 80s playing nightclub gigs with a mixed gay and straight line-up of former Big In Japan bass player **Holly Johnson** (vocals), **Mark O'Toole** (bass), **Peter 'Ped' Gill** (drums), **Brian Nash** (guitar) and **Paul Rutherford** (vocals/dancing). Their energy and provocative stage shows gained sufficient notoriety to win them a slot on the weekly TV pop show *The Tube* in early 1983. Here, playing a raw version of "Relax", they were spotted by ABC and Malcolm McLaren producer Trevor Horn, who signed them to his new label, Zang Tuum Tumb (ZTT).

Horn, a notorious perfectionist, recorded four full versions of "Relax" before arriving at the finished product, a throbbing disco track played entirely by computer and driven by an insistent monotone bass line. Released in November 1983, "Relax" progressed up the UK charts very slowly until national radio DJ Mike Read objected on air to its 'overtly obscene lyrical content' – i.e., 'Relax, don't do it/When you wanna come'. Within hours BBC Radio 1 banned it, although it had already been played over seventy times on the station. The ban made no difference: a #1 in the UK for five weeks, it stayed in the Top 40 for most of 1984, and sold the best part of two million copies. A second Frankie single was an urgent priority. "Slave To The Rhythm" was originally slated as the follow-up, but failed to jell and later become a hit for Grace Jones. Its replacement on the Frankie schedule was "Two Tribes", a simplistic antiwar number promoted by a video depicting Reagan and Chernenko look-alikes fighting in a wrestling ring. Horn's arrangement and production was unprecedentedly sophisticated – a mad, crushing cacophony of orchestral stabs, rock guitars and high-energy rhythms, and vocal samples, all fed through the then-ubiquitous Fairlight sampler. Released in eight different versions, from June 1984 "Two Tribes" was a British #1 for nine weeks, and was joined at the #2 spot by the revitalized "Relax" for a few of those weeks. Even Frankie T-shirt sales were phenomenal, so it was hardly surprising that by October 1984 they had a #1 LP with the double set, WELCOME TO THE PLEASURE DOME. The album featured the two million-selling singles, backed up with the gorgeous Christmas ballad "The Power Of Love" and the epic, Coleridge-inspired title track. But there was also a good deal of padding across its four sides, notably some inessential cover versions like "Born To Run", "Ferry Cross The Mersey" and even "Do You Know The Way To San José?". More entertaining than the music, in many ways, were ZTT co-founder Paul Morley's pseudo-intellectual sleeve notes, featuring offers for Frankie merchandise such as the 'Kurt Weill sweatshirt', the 'Edith Sitwell bag', even the 'Jean Genet boxer shorts'.

After "The Power Of Love" completed a hat trick of British chart-toppers, 1984 was going to be an impossible year to top. Sure enough, in 1985 their live shows, though popular, were a little too scrappy for a public used to the sophistication of the records. As their teenage audience moved on to Wham!, Madonna, and even A-Ha, the Frankies chose to adopt a more adult, stadium-rock sound for their second album. Produced by Horn's deputy, Steve Lipson, the project soared way over budget, and by the time LIVERPOOL was finally released at the end of 1986, the band's days were numbered. While the album managed to spawn three Top 30 hits – most significantly, "Rage Hard" – it was generally devoid of the humour and personality which had characterized Frankie in their earlier years.

The band eventually split in the spring of 1987. Paul Rutherford went on to pursue a solo career, scoring two minor hits, "Get Real" and "Oh World". Holly Johnson, meanwhile, embarked upon a long and bitter courtroom battle with ZTT in an attempt to free himself from his recording contract; in 1988 he won the case. Two solo albums were released by MCA, the first of which, BLAST (1989), returned him to the top of the UK album charts. Johnson has written extensively about his years in Frankie Goes To Hollywood; his widely acclaimed autobiography *A Bone In My Flute* (1994) contained many acute reminiscences, as well as the announcement that he had been diagnosed as being HIV-positive.

The growing trend in the 80s revival market has resulted in countless television companies borrowing anthemic soundbites of "Relax" and "Two Tribes" for use on cosy, nostalgic documentaries. Equally, every few years has seen the hottest club DJs doing their worst in diluting Frankie singles with tepid, dull remixes. Yet the fact remains that Frankie Goes To Hollywood were, for a brief period in the mid-80s, one of the most subversive and exciting of British pop acts.

⊙ **Welcome To The Pleasure Dome** (1984; ZTT).
Sprawling and patchy, but with moments of brilliance, this is by far the best memento of Frankie at their opulent, self-indulgent best.

⊙ **Twelve Inches** (2001; ZTT).
They took a long time in coming, but finally all the band's original, exceptional single remixes have found their way onto CD.

Robin Morley

FREE

Formed London, 1968; disbanded 1973.

For much of the 70s it was damned near impossible to be at a party without hearing **Free**'s "All Right Now", a song first released in 1970 but forever rereleased, its chunky chords, catchy chorus and funky bass line seemingly impervious to the dictates of fashion. Above all, "All Right Now" encapsulated the raw energy that made Free the blueprint for just about every subsequent hard rock outfit.

The band was formed by singer **Paul Rodgers**, who had come to London from Middlesbrough to front a band called Brown Sugar, with guitarist **Paul Kossoff** and drummer **Simon Kirke**, who were playing in a band called Black Cat Bones, also going nowhere. The trio recruited 16-year-old bassist **Andy Fraser** from John Mayall's Bluesbreakers to complete a line-up which debuted at the Nag's Head pub in Battersea, in 1968, under a name suggested by

British blues guru Alexis Korner, who also helped secure a record deal with Island.

Free started as a blues band heavily influenced by Hendrix and Cream and, to their eternal credit, never attempted to soften their rough edges or indulge themselves in the kind of overextended soloing which made many of their contemporaries so tedious. The first album, TONS OF SOBS (1968), a heavily bluesy set, allowed Kossoff the opportunity to show off his distinctively fluid guitar style. Kossoff soon developed into one of the most expressive guitarists in rock, using sustain and feedback in a way that reflected the inner torment of his essentially fragile character. In time he fell prey to the pressures of success and became heavily involved with heroin.

By the time of their second album, FREE (1969), the band had established a following attracted as much to the rock work-outs of songs like Albert King's "The Hunter" as to reflective ballads like "Lying In The Sunshine". Unkempt and wasted, their image reflected the post-Woodstock era perfectly, and the beat of "All Right Now" was a sure-fire hit when it was released in the summer of 1970. The accompanying album, FIRE AND WATER, was acclaimed by critics and public alike and remains the band's most successful LP. Perhaps the most powerful voice in rock, Rodgers applied his gravel'n'honey vocals to delicate numbers like "Oh I Wept" (showing the influence of his mentor Otis Redding) and to more raucous numbers like "Mr. Big".

By August 1970, Free were big enough to be one of the headliners at the Isle of Wight festival, playing to over 500,000 people (a performance available on Island's *Free* video). However, a new single ("Stealer") and album (HIGHWAY) failed to sell as well as expected, even though the latter contained some of the band's finest ballads, such as "Soon I Will Be Gone" and "Be My Friend". The set failed to capture the energy of their stage performance, and so a warts-and-all live album, FREE LIVE (1971), was released to showcase the band at their very best. By this stage, though, gruelling tours of America and the Far East had brought ego conflicts to a head and Free decided to call it a day.

Rodgers and Fraser both went on to form ill-fated bands (**Peace** and **Toby**), while Kossoff and Kirke enjoyed minor success with an LP recorded with Japanese bassist **Tetsu** and Texan keyboardist **Rabbit**. The original Free line-up regrouped in 1972 to record FREE AT LAST, a patchy LP which nevertheless spawned a hit single in "Little Bit Of Love". However, Kossoff's increasing drug dependence made the future seem bleak, and he was too out of it even to get on stage on the first date of the subsequent UK tour.

He was only well enough to attend half the sessions for HEARTBREAKER (1973), an album which contained the sublime "Wishing Well", Rodgers' heartfelt plea to Kossoff to pull himself together. Andy Fraser had already left to form Sharks by the time it was recorded, and it was a surprise that it emerged as one of the band's strongest recordings. From the agonized blues of the title track to the gentle piano runs of "Easy On My Soul", the LP was varied and powerful. It sold well, but ego conflicts persisted and Free finally disbanded in late 1973.

Talk of further reunions continued for some time, but when Kossoff's drug-racked body finally gave out on a plane above the Atlantic in March 1976 the final chapter in the band's history was closed for ever. After Free, Fraser went into semi-retirement, while Rodgers and Kirke formed the instantly successful **BAD COMPANY**. Most recently, Free's back catalogue has been given a digital spring clean and repackaged for a new generation of music fans. Even hoary old rockers might want to check out these reissues, as each album comes with a whole host of bonus tracks and rarities.

(•) **Fire And Water** (1970; Island/A&M).
An indispensable mix of blues and bravado, Rodgers' emotive singing and a 'less is more' attitude to production ensuring this cult status. Contains "All Right Now" and a clutch of slow numbers that can only be described as white soul.

(•) **Free Live** (1971; Island/A&M).
Pure raw energy that nevertheless contains some deft, gentle and even funky moments, such as Fraser's gargantuan bass solo on "Mr. Big", and Kossoff's wailing on "Be My Friend".

(•) **Heartbreaker** (1973; Island/A&M).
A powerful return to form. Kossoff appears only fitfully on this, Free's swan song. Rodgers hits his stride on "Wishing Well" and allows Rabbit's piano to give much of the material an understated feel.

(•) **Anthology** (1993; Island/A&M).
Two-disc collection that includes all the hits and some solo Kossoff tracks.

Chris Coe

GAVIN FRIDAY

Born Dublin, 1959.

As lead singer of **THE VIRGIN PRUNES**, **Gavin Friday** (born Fionan Hanvey) was the guiding force of one of the darkest and most challenging (if sometimes inscrutable and self-indulgent) Irish bands to arise from the punk/New Wave movement. Working as a solo artist since the late 1980s, he's turned toward a more theatrical, cabaret-ish style that continues to grapple with the time-honoured themes of sex, death and tense relationships. Sometimes infuriatingly overblown and overambitious, he's never been boring.

Born a few blocks away from Bono (a longtime close friend), Friday formed The Virgin Prunes in an effort to create, in his words, a cross between the Sex Pistols, The New York Dolls and Salvador Dali. When The Virgin Prunes disbanded in 1986, Gavin took up painting, and mounted an exhibition in Dublin with Bono, ex-Virgin Prune Derek 'Guggi' Rowan and Charlie Whisker.

Friday has claimed to have made more money during this time than he did during The Prunes' entire tenure with Rough Trade, but he felt the urge to return to showbiz, starting a cabaret in Dublin, the Blue Jaysus. It was here that Gavin met pianist **Maurice Roycroft**, whom he adopted as his collaborator, renaming him **The Man Seezer**. A demo tape landed the duo a contract with Island in 1987, and the following year they recorded their debut album with producer Hal Willner.

Not released until 1989, EACH MAN KILLS THE THING HE LOVES reflected Friday's deepening interest in the darkly inviting music of such European singers and songwriters as Edith Piaf, Kurt Weill, Bertolt Brecht and Jacques Brel (whose vicious satire "Next" was covered on the record). Gavin's singing, as it had with The Virgin Prunes, evoked inevitable comparisons with Bowie, though his approach was considerably more menacing. Similarities with Marianne Faithfull's contemporary brand of noir-ish pop were not accidental: Willner was fresh from overseeing Faithfull's STRANGE WEATHER, and re-employed a couple of the musicians from that album (guitarist **Bill Frisell** and bassist **Fernando Saunders**) on Friday's recording. Guitarist Marc Ribot, drummer Michael Blair and jazz cellist Hank Roberts also played strong parts in weaving a sonic tapestry for the funhouse-flavoured observations of Friday and Seezer.

1992's ADAM 'N' EVE was a less impressive follow-up. Though the singer continued to explore the dark side of human nature, musically he retreated from the eclecticism of his debut into a far more rock-orientated sound, bringing his campy glitter-trash Bowie-isms much closer to the forefront (though these are leavened somewhat by guest appearances from ex-Lone Justice vocalist Maria McKee on a couple of tracks). At times veering uncomfortably close to cheap rock-star moves (complete with thudding, booming drum'n'bass tracks), ADAM 'N' EVE sounded diffuse and confused, perhaps partly because the production chores were divided among three handlers – Willner, Flood and Dave Bascombe.

In 1993, Friday gained his greatest public exposure to date when he and Seezer composed three songs with Bono for the soundtrack of Jim Sheridan's film, *In The Name Of The Father*; Bono and Friday also shared the vocal chores on two of these tracks.

After almost a year of delays, Friday's third solo outing, the self-described 'science fiction cabaret' SHAG TOBACCO, appeared in the late summer of 1995. Seezer was still aboard as Gavin's co-composer and primary instrument collaborator for a work that struck a balance between the dark carnival of his debut and the camp-rock of the follow-up. The lyrics, as usual, were a funhouse of frustrations. Friday seemed to have a lot on his mind as regards sex and media (often both together), though it was unclear quite what.

THE BOXER (1998; MCA) was another soundtrack album, to the film of the same name starring Daniel Day-Lewis. After further collaborative efforts with

Roycroft, Friday was forced to lay low for much of 2002 following spinal surgery. He has since recorded a charity project, *Peter And The Wolf*, and completed a soundtrack for Jim Sheridan's *East Of Harlem*. Though erratic and self-important, Friday's work is always of interest, as he continues to challenge himself without undue concern for amassing an audience.

⊙ Each Man Kills The Thing He Loves (1989; Island).
Arguably, this is Friday's best work, either on his own or with The Virgin Prunes. A definitive 'difficult-but-rewarding' album, mixing the smoky ambience of European cabaret with late-twentieth century angst, amplified by an accomplished and imaginative cast of supporting musicians.

⊙ Shag Tobacco (1995; Island).
Less fully developed than EACH MAN, but not as annoying as ADAM, this is a sort of uneasy compromise between Friday's cabaret aspirations and thumping Eurorock.

Richie Unterberger

ROBERT FRIPP

Born Wimbourne, England, 1946.

"My solo guitar work is based around delay, repetition and hazard, an approach introduced to me by Eno, directly and without explanation in September 1972."

Since 1969 **Robert Fripp** has fronted incarnations of the band **KING CRIMSON** as well as producing a large amount of solo and collaborative work. Arguably, it is as a guest, within others' sound-scapes, that he really shines, unhindered by his own technical perfectionism.

His has been an eclectic and cerebral career. While active with the original Crimson, one of the few enduring 70s prog-rock bands, Fripp had outings on guitar for Van Der Graaf Generator, and produced jazz composer Keith Tippett's SEPTOBER ENERGY album and Robert Wyatt's LITTLE RED RECORD. And after the collapse of the 1972 Crimson he drifted into a partnership with one **Walli Elmark**, a witch. Their joint album, COSMIC CHILDREN OF ROCK, was never released but the occult interest became part of Fripp's enduring quest to explore esoteric philosophical practices.

Sharing EG Management with Roxy Music led to a collaboration between Fripp and **BRIAN ENO**, 1972's NO PUSSYFOOTING. Comprising just two twenty-minute tracks, it provided a first real stage for Eno's 'treatment' experiments with Roxy. Free-form soloing by Fripp with 'The Fripp Pedalboard' was stretched and looped through Eno's VCS3 synthesizer and modified tape recorders, producing an entirely new form of electronic music. A sequel, EVENING STAR, appeared in 1975 and the duo performed a few live dates, partners in a self-described 'small, mobile and highly intelligent unit'.

Fripp was to develop this electronic sound template into the omnipresent 'Frippertronics' of later solo tours and recordings, and the Eno partnership was to produce almost a decade's worth of recordings. The unique tones of Fripp's 'restrained lead guitar' techniques were used to gorgeous effect on "I'll Come Running' and "St. Elmo's Fire" on Eno's album, ANOTHER GREEN WORLD (1975), and prefaced a

Robert Fripp (right) shares a joke with ex-Policeman Andy Summers

major contribution to the **DAVID BOWIE** album HEROES (1977). Fripp appeared at Berlin's Hansa Studios after a short-notice summons from Bowie and Eno, listened to the backing track and creating the elliptical swirl of the title song in one take.

The end of the 70s saw major change for Fripp, with a move to New York and his first real solo album, 1979's EXPOSURE. It's a curious record, referring constantly to the 'retreat' he attended between the King Crimson split and his re-emergence through the HEROES sessions. It featured the crackling voice of the late **J. G. Bennett**, founder of the 'self-improvement' centre Fripp studied at – intoning his maxims in a gentle sepulchral voice on the title track.

The album was intended as part of a trilogy, along with, oddly perhaps, a Daryl Hall album (which Fripp produced but RCA turned down) and PETER GABRIEL II. Both artists feature on the album, along with Barry Andrews (ex-XTC), Brian Eno and Peter Hammill, but the main influence on the album is Fripp's growing friendship with Debbie Harry and Chris Stein of Blondie. He guested on the band's "Fade Away" and "Radiate" and tracks like "You Burn Me Up I'm A Cigarette" rock out in New York New Wave style.

The early 80s saw Fripp working with Bowie again, producing deliriously lurching solos on SCARY MONSTERS, and on a 1981 tour with a punked-up/funked-out variant of Crimson, **The League Of Gentlemen**, featuring Barry Andrews and Sarah Lee.

An album of Frippertronics, LET THE POWER FALL, was released in 1981; the promised 'discotronics', alas, failed to appear. Instead a guitar duet album with Police guitarist **Andy Summers**, I ADVANCE MASKED (1982), emerged, not quite living up to the mystique of its title, followed by a return to the King Crimson drawing board, a solo tour of pizza restaurants, and a TV documentary. Meanwhile, Fripp had settled down with pop-punk **Toyah Willcox**, producing a pair of albums with her, THE LADY AND THE TIGER (1986) and NETWORK (1987). The former was a companion album to Robert Fripp and THE LEAGUE OF CRAFTY GUITARISTS LIVE! (1986). Both featured students tutored by Fripp in acoustic guitar courses held in West Virginia.

As the 90s unfolded, collaborations with pioneers of ambient techno seemed logical. Fripp recorded with The Orb's **Alex Patterson** as **FFWD>>**, improvised with **Future Sound Of London** and played with **No-Man** and **The Grid**. He also collaborated with **DAVID SYLVIAN** (notably on 1994's DAMAGE), played London's Royal Albert Hall with yet another reincarnation of the Crimson King, and performed a day-long ambient work of 'soundscape' guitar treatments as part of a New Music/New Media London festival in 1996.

Fripp has also run – since 1994 – his own label, Discipline Global Mobile, featuring related artists past and present such as Peter Hammill and Adrian Belew, along with his own Soundscape albums. SOMETIMES GOD HIDES – THE YOUNG PERSON'S GUIDE TO DISCIPLINE (1996) features a comprehensive overview of this output. While he continues to work with King Crimson, one of the most recent, and bizarre, artifacts to appear was ROBERT FRIPP … UNPLUGGED (2000), a collection of interviews and conversations between Fripp and 'Fripp … the sister'.

Fripp may seem the eccentric polymath, yet a pervading wit and warmth continues to lend a rewarding accessibility to his work.

Fripp and Eno

(•) **Venture: The Essential Fripp & Eno** (1994; Virgin). The birth of Frippertronics, featuring the main body of No Pussyfooting and Evening Star, plus four new pieces.

Robert Fripp

(•) **Exposure** (1979; EG/Virgin). Extreme and exciting songs and musical collaborations unique within the Fripp canon.

(•) **Radiophonics, Soundscapes And Gates Of Paradise** (1995–96; Discipline Global Mobile). A new progression for Frippertronics is evident on this live trilogy, employing a dual-loop sound system to veer even further away from recognizable guitar shapes. For information on Discipline Global Mobile, write to: PO Box 1533, Salisbury SP5 5ER, England.

Chris Brook

FRED FRITH

Born Heathfield, England, 1949.

Fred Frith is not exactly a rock star. We're talking about a founder member of **HENRY COW**, here, arguably the least accessible 'rock' group of the 70s, and a man whose nearest brush with rock-biz glamour came in 1974 when he played violin on Robert Wyatt's cover of "I'm A Believer", appearing with Mike Oldfield on an *NME* cover, flanking Wyatt, seated in solidarity in wheelchairs. And since that time, Frith has moved steadily further from any rock sensibility, a prolific guitar virtuoso at the vanguard of that avant-rock, experimental, 'new music' scene that nobody quite knows how to describe.

Undoubtedly, Frith was shaped by his first bands: Henry Cow, then the merged group with Slapp Happy, and the Art Bears trio with vocalist Dagmar Krause and Cow percussionist Chris Cutler. Each was a seedbed for Frith's apparent life mission: to extend and mutate the place of the electric guitar in music, and to seek out ever more radical fusions of noise-making. To this end, he has worked with just about everyone on the avant-rock scene, both in London and New York.

His own early interests took in close composition work for electric and acoustic resources, tape work, 'concrete' constructions, songs and noise-art improvisations, all of which are evidenced on the wryly titled GUITAR SOLOS (1974), issued by Virgin's cheap-and-weird offshoot, Caroline, when he was still in Henry Cow. The themes found later expression, at the end of the 80s, in Frith's work creating a youth orchestra in Marseille, and in compositions for a String Quartet and Guitar Quintet. The most commercial he got was a collaboration with **BRIAN ENO** on BEFORE AND AFTER SCIENCE (1977), for which he jointly arranged, and contributed 'cascade guitar' to a Harold Budd tribute, "Through Hollow Lands".

In the 80s and 90s, Frith worked in New York as a part of **John Zorn**'s avant-jazz Naked City project and performed and recorded with **Bill Laswell** (on bass) and **Fred Maher** (drums) as **Material** and later **Massacre**, a kind of experimental power-thrash trio. He also recorded as a trio/quartet with **Henry Kaiser**, **John French** and guest **RICHARD THOMPSON**, and performed a huge number of one-off events, too, with bands like Red Balune, 2 Aksak Maboul and The Muffins.

Frith is currently professor of composition at Mills College, California, but continues to create new music; ACCIDENTAL (2002) was his last eclectic offering, its title suggesting exactly the principles behind the compositions. Created for a dance piece it took elements as diverse as improvised mandolin and random radio tunings and assembled them into a mesmerizing whole. The newer works have been complemented by a series of reissues from Frith's own archive, with 1980's GRAVITY being the first.

Fred Frith

● **Step Across The Border** (1994; RecRec Records). Retrospective compendium of work covering many strains and styles.

Massacre

● **Killing Time** (1981; RecRec Records). Intense guitar power punk-funk with Bill Laswell and 16-year-old Fred Maher.

French, Frith, Kaiser and Thompson

● **Invisible Means** (1990; RecRec Records). More creative guitar textures.

Chris Brook

FU MANCHU

Formed Southern California, 1990.

For most people the 70s was a decade of hideous fashion disasters and poor taste. But it was also the decade of classic rock, Evel Knievel, skateboards, demolition derbies, and Cheech & Chong movies. It was the time when **Scott Hill** (guitar/vocals) was growing up, so when he came to start a band it was only natural to delve into the good times of sun and fun, when hair was long and rock bands would lay waste with poly-decibel stadium-based extravaganzas featuring extended guitar jams and towering amplification. **Fu Manchu** is about all these things and more, making them a prime stoner band.

Of course, stoner is a lazy catch-all for any outfit with even a hint of Ozzy-led Black Sabbath to their groove, but Fu Manchu have never been about doom – rather, they borrow the power and grind of the classic metal-from-Brum template and inject it

with their own unique Californian twitch. Few bands manage to combine their musical output so successfully with the look and feel of their artwork and graphics. The synthesis of the visual with the aural is arguably what makes Fu Manchu such a long-lived and creatively fascinating outfit.

Alongside Scott Hill, the earliest recorded incarnation of Fu Manchu featured **Ruben Romano** (drums), **Greg McCaughey** (bass) and **Glen Chivens** (vocals) on the stupendously hard-to-find "Kept Between Trees" single. A further clutch of singles and a line-up shift or two preceded the classic NO ONE RIDES FOR FREE (1994) album and a slightly more stable line-up that featured **Eddie Glass** (guitar) and **Mark Abshire** (bass). By the time of the following year's DAREDEVIL album **Brad Davis** had joined on bass. This line-up remained solid for 1996's IN SEARCH OF…, a storming album with a foxy lady poised to start a custom car race gracing the sleeve.

Each of these albums found Hill praising all that made the 70s fun – the cars, the girls, the vast quantities of weed – and all in his characteristically nonchalant vocal style. The band were striving for that killer combination of riff-laden nirvana and stylistic edge, and they achieved it with THE ACTION IS GO (1997), though by now Hill had had enough of dealing with Romano and Glass, who left to form **NEBULA** – a far more spacy and psychedelic take on stoner – and brought in ex-**KYUSS** member **Brant Bjork** (drums), and **Bob Balch** (guitar). The excellent sleeve art featured cult 70s skateboard hero Tony Alva in mid stunt, a huge set of headphones clamped to his afro'd head.

Fu Manchu now turned into something of a touring behemoth, with only a couple of stopgap releases holding up their relentless pursuit of rock-'n'roll on the road. KING OF THE ROAD (2000) and CALIFORNIA CROSSING (2002), however, found them modifying their sound a touch, the latter album especially. The band seemed to be easing off the speed a little and concentrating just a little more on pop melodies. With the new album on the shelves

Bjork decided it was time to go solo and another ex-Kyuss member, **Scott Reeder**, stepped into the fold.

⊙ **In Search Of...** (1996; Mammoth).
Cars, girls, rock'n'roll; this one has it all. Hill drawls out his tales of gasoline and grass consumption over a thundering selection of taut, muscular riffs.

⊙ **The Action Is Go** (1997; Mammoth).
A new start for the band with Bjork and Balch on board. The subject matter is the same but it's attacked with even more relish than before.

⊙ **California Crossing** (2002; Warners).
A slight easing off in speed is detectable, though everything else is as fuzzed up and tough-sounding as before. Hill shines as a seasoned architect of the pummelling riff.

Essi Berelian

FUGAZI

Formed Washington DC, 1987.

"I think anger is a really beautiful thing when it's put to work." Ian MacKaye

Taking their name from US military jargon for 'fucked up situation', **Fugazi** originally comprised **Ian MacKaye** (vocals/guitar), **Guy Picciotto** (vocals/guitar), **Brendan Canty** (drums) and **Joe Lally** (bass). They distilled the various trends that influenced the Washington hardcore scene, with a melodic rhythm section that combined the funk-punk of The Minutemen/fIREHOSE with the irrepressible ska sound of bands like the Beat. Over this they continue to lay a diverse range of guitaring that ranges from staccato machine-gunning to power chords, lead breaks and experimental scratchings. Add vocals and what you have is an ascetic aesthetic that generates the maximum power with the minimum excess.

Ian MacKaye began his musical career back in the early 80s with the Slinkees, Teen Idles and **MINOR THREAT**. He and Jeff Nelson (Teen Idles and Minor Threat) set up Dischord Records in 1981, and soon Minor Threat were being credited with starting the 'straight edge' movement, courtesy of the song "Straight Edge", which raged against the use of drink and drugs. Putting out material by many of the most innovative and influential groups from the Washington scene, Dischord became to Washington what Sub Pop was to Seattle, and is still run from MacKaye's home, embodying a principle of self-reliance that pervades the way that Fugazi go about everything.

After Minor Threat called it a day in 1983, MacKaye formed **Embrace** and then **Pailhead** (with Ministry's Al Jourgenson). During the summer of 1985, as numerous post-hardcore bands rapidly split, formed other bands and split again, Picciotto and Canty played together in Rites Of Spring, who metamorphosed into One Last Wish, then Happy Go Licky and then finally Fugazi.

The first the world outside Washington knew of

the new outfit was the superb FUGAZI EP (1988). It won the band instant acclaim but at the time was seen in the shadow of Minor Threat. In the early days Fugazi were very much a live band, whose Washington concerts were organized by Positive Force, a kind of punk rock promotion and grassroots activist group. Throughout the late 80s and early 90s they played numerous benefit gigs, in venues that were chosen as an attempt to break away from the conventions of the rock industry. They have played church basements, an old Safeway store, an old roller-skating rink, Lafayette Park, soup kitchens and Lorton Correctional Facility, to name but a few.

In 1989 they released the MARGIN WALKER EP, toured Britain, and issued a single, "3 Songs". In 1990 came REPEATER, the album with which Fugazi established themselves. They kept their tight rhythms and added a little New York experimentalism, but kept their urgency and rage. Every track on the album burst with passion, energy and innovation.

The commercial success of FUGAZI attracted a lot

of attention from major labels but Fugazi remained staunchly uninterested – the cash the album brought in enabled Dischord to subsidize the production of material by lesser-known bands from the Washington scene. The offers for gigs flooded in and Fugazi henceforth were on tour for almost six months of the year. Perhaps in reaction to this schedule of performances, Fugazi's songwriting became less anthemic and more personal on the next album, STEADY DIET OF NOTHING (1991). The music and the lyrics refused to settle into comfortable grooves; but, for all the fragmentary structure of the songs, the set was sustained by a tension between silences and explosions of energy.

Following STEADY DIET OF NOTHING they worked almost to a standard rock industry format – an album every two years, with tours between. 1993's IN ON THE KILL TAKER, had it been released by a major label, would have made Fugazi one of the biggest bands in the world. As it was, the album was acclaimed in the music papers and topped the European indie charts for weeks – an awful lot of success without even one video.

RED MEDICINE (1995) did not really move in a new direction, but refined and developed their sound. As usual there were awesomely contorted and controlled rhythms, oblique lyrics and so much anguish and rage it made you wonder why they didn't explode. END HITS' (1998) unwelcome experimentation did little to please the fans. INSTRUMENT (1999) kept away from hardest of hardcore, showing a broader-minded approach. In 2000 Canty teamed up with **Lois Maffeo** to release THE UNION THEMES on Kill Rock Stars; though musically accomplished and critically acclaimed it certainly wasn't one for Fugazi's 'straight edge' fans.

THE ARGUMENT, the follow-up to INSTRUMENT, appeared in 2001. It was the band's most expansive and subtle album yet, perhaps attributable to an enlarging line-up that included **Bridget Cross** from Unrest, Bikini Kill's **Kathi Wilcox** and **Amy Domingues** of Ida. Both pop and experimentation seemed to have become permanent elements in the Fugazi sound, though it remains to be seen what their devotees will make of this broadening vision.

Fugazi

⊙ **13 Songs** (1989; Dischord).
CD compilation of their first two EPs, FUGAZI and MARGIN WALKER. Classic stuff, from the ska end of Fugazi's musical scope.

⊙ **Repeater** (1990; Dischord).
One of those extremely rare, truly brilliant albums that hook into the brain on first listening, yet never cease to be fresh and immediate.

⊙ **In On The Kill Taker** (1993; Dischord).
Fugazi at their best. An aural hand grenade.

⊙ **Red Medicine** (1995; Dischord).
A mature album from one of the very few bands from the hardcore generation who still have the power to astound.

Lois Maffeo & Brendan Canty

⊙ **The Union Themes** (2000; Kill Rock Stars).
This unlikely musical pairing features Brendan's guitars, drums and stabbing piano lines forcefully accompanying Lois's acoustic guitar and powerfully sung songs of stormy love.

Glenn Gossling

FUGEES

Formed South Orange, New Jersey, 1989.

Aside from maybe Hootie & the Blowfish, the **Fugees** were the biggest pop group of the 90s. They formed in South Orange, New Jersey in 1989, with vocalist **Lauryn Hill**, multi-instrumentalist **Nel Wyclef Jean** and his cousin, keyboardist **Prakazrel Michel**, and parlayed their warm grooves and gentle politics into a global market share even Michael Jackson would be envious of nowadays.

Their first album, BLUNTED ON REALITY (1994), was a frugged album that attempted to shed light on

the political situation of Haiti, from where Wyclef and Pras are refugees (hence the name). It was a laudable album, though it lacked personality, coming to life only on the remix of "Mona Lisa" and "Vocab".

The group took over production for the second album and the ensuing blend of Caribbean lilt, alterna-rap and supper-club soul became a worldwide phenomenon. Sporting a cover based on the posters for *The Godfather*, THE SCORE (1996) earned global respect and success very quickly. To date, the album has sold over eighteen million copies worldwide, which is fairly remarkable considering that, aside from the massive singles "Killing Me Softly", "Ready Or Not" and "Fu-Gee-La", and the cover of Bob Marley's "No Woman, No Cry", THE SCORE was a dark, down-tempo album comprised of sound bites from a Kingston dancehall, wafting vapour trails from an East Harlem air shaft and samples of doo-wop group The Flamingos.

While Hill stole the show with her rich vocals and not-bad mic skills, Wyclef's solo album, THE CARNIVAL (1997) showed that she didn't have a monopoly on the group's talent. Though nowhere near as good as THE SCORE, THE CARNIVAL had Clef collaborating with the Neville Brothers and Celia Cruz and not embarrassing himself. He'd save that for his duet with Bono, "New Day" (1999). ECLEFTIC: TWO SIDES OF A BOOK (2000), however, showed that THE CARNIVAL was a fluke: the cast of stars on ECLEFTIC included Kenny Rogers, and "However You Want It" proved that Canibus was right about blaming Wyclef for the failure of his album. A shocking collaboration with Brian Harvey from East 17 and a third solo album, MASQUERADE (2002), didn't help his reputation any.

Pras's GHETTO SUPASTAR (1998) album had him living up to his **Dirty Cash** alias by including ten-plus minutes of celebrity endorsements from the likes of Elton John, Sting and, of course, Donald Trump. The real solo album action, however, was to be found on Hill's THE MISEDUCATION OF LAURYN HILL (1998). Looking back to 60s and 70s soul's age-old virtues, referencing 70s sitcoms, reminiscing about mid-80s hip-hop, dabbling in reggae and dancehall and digging in the crates like the best 90s beat-freaks, THE MISEDUCATION OF LAURYN HILL was the black bohemian equivalent of a Beastie Boys album, but from a woman's point of view. Replacing the wisecracks and cheap laffs of the Beasties with a sense of personal triumph (that, granted, occasionally crept into self-righteousness), Hill made the ultimate cross-over album of the hip-hop era. That self-righteousness would become full-on 'messiah complex' on the car crash that was MTV UNPLUGGED NO. 2.0 (2002), which saw Hill croak through mostly new songs, with her acoustic guitar and some tortured soliloquies being the only accompaniment.

Fugees

⊙ **The Score** (1996; Ruffhouse/Columbia).
Perhaps the bravest, grittiest and certainly the best mainstream hip-hop album to date.

Lauryn Hill

⊙ **The Miseducation Of Lauryn Hill** (1998; Ruffhouse/Columbia).
It's not perfect, but, at its best, the soaring music – the string stabs, the upful drums, the scratches, the grain of her voice – transmits the album's message more potently than the lyrics, turning clichés into words that hit like the gospel truth.

Peter Shapiro

THE FUGS

Formed New York, 1964; disbanded 1969.

"We had no idea of the impact these songs would have, nor illusions about fame or legacy. We thought we were just obeying the dictates of our generation – demand more freedom, have fun through art, and sniff the winds of freedom." Ed Sanders

Predating even The Mothers of Invention and The Velvet Underground, **The Fugs** were arguably the first self-consciously underground rock band, writing openly about sex, politics and drugs. They also challenged the limits of censorship by using words deemed obscene and profane. They achieved all this with the help of an outrageous humour and keen satirical bite, which ensured that the best of their recordings have survived as more than mere curiosities.

Ed Sanders (vocals/guitar) and **Tuli Kupferberg** (percussion/vocals), beatnik-type poets in New York's Lower East Side, formed The Fugs more as a free-floating ensemble of underground poets and folkies than a band with any sort of serious aspirations to stardom. Neither of the pair had anything in the way of instrumental confidence or

conventional vocal skills, but with the assistance of local musicians like **Peter Stampfel** (guitar/banjo/vocals) and **Steve Weber** (guitar) of the **HOLY MODAL ROUNDERS** they set their whimsical ditties to music with crude, energetic jug band-like arrangements.

The result was the self-explanatory THE FUGS FIRST ALBUM (1965), released on Folkways (and later picked up by ESP). Sanders later regretted the more juvenile, sex-obsessed lyrics on some of these early songs, although items like "Slum Goddess" and "Supergirl" were legitimately funny, parodying pop and rock conventions with affectionate subversion.

The Fugs were best experienced live, and at long runs at off-Broadway venues in Greenwich Village they infused their sets with spontaneous agitprop performance art – as seasoned post-Beat poets, this came naturally to them. Back in the studio for THE FUGS SECOND ALBUM (1966), they recruited more experienced electric musicians, which suggested they were taking studio sessions more seriously than before. Released on ESP, a label known chiefly for its avant-garde jazz recordings, it was their best album, balancing antiwar satirical pieces with paeans to open-hearted lust, hard folk-rock declarations of personal independence, and a couple of surprisingly pretty ballads. It even made the *Billboard* Top 100 album chart, although it also attracted the attention of the FBI for its bad language.

After an aborted album for Atlantic, The Fugs jumped to the majors by signing with Reprise in the late 60s. Musically more conventional and accomplished, with a lyrical content that remained untamed, their Reprise material nonetheless lacked the overall edge of their ESP output. Along with drummer **Ken Weaver**, Sanders and Kupferberg were now the only constants in The Fugs line-up, which may have been the reason for the lack of direction in the band's output.

More than almost any other rock group of the era, The Fugs translated their lyrical convictions into action, appearing at antiwar demonstrations at the Pentagon and the 1968 Democratic convention, and fighting for their rights to free speech in the face of harassment from government authorities. Since the band's demise, Sanders has diversified into investigative journalism, poetry and political activism, while Kupferberg is still a prolific, if little-read, poet and a political cartoonist. Besides issuing sporadic solo material, the pair reunited The Fugs in the mid-80s for some low-key live dates and good-hearted, if inessential, albums of new material.

They reunited again in 1994, with a line-up of Sanders, Kupferberg, **Coby Batty** (drums/vocals), **Scott Petito** (bass/keyboards) and **Steven Taylor** (guitars/vocals) to subvert Woodstock 2, appearing with Country Joe and Allen Ginsberg in an upstate New York barn to bash out poetry, satire and rock-

'n'roll. The gig, commemorated on a live double CD, THE REAL WOODSTOCK FESTIVAL, showed no advances in the musical department.

⊙ **The Fugs First Album** (1965; Big Beat).
Shambling but ticklish slices of Greenwich Village bohemia, saved from musical anarchy by the contributions of Stampfel and Weber of The Holy Modal Rounders. The CD reissue adds nearly a dozen unreleased live and studio tracks from the same era, some of which ("CIA Man", "The Ten Commandments", the Sanders/Allen Ginsberg collaboration "I Saw The Best Minds Of My Generations Rock") count among the better efforts of their first sessions.

⊙ **The Fugs Second Album** (1966; Big Beat).
A tighter, more riff-driven band and much harder rocking arrangements did nothing to blunt the sardonic wit of "Kill For Peace", "Frenzy", "Dirty Old Man" and "Doin' All Right" on their best outing. The CD reissue adds previously unreleased tracks from their aborted 1967 Atlantic LP, and a couple of live cuts.

Richie Unterberger

FUN BOY THREE

Formed Coventry, England, 1981; disbanded 1983.

THE SPECIALS had become one of the most popular bands in Britain at the turn of the 80s, but by 1981 vocalists **Terry Hall** and **Neville Staples**, and guitarist/vocalist **Lynval Golding**, felt restricted by the format of the band's music, and in particular by the firm grip Jerry Dammers had maintained. They announced their departure from the band after a second US tour and their biggest British hit, "Ghost Town".

Fun Boy Three first hit the UK charts with "The Lunatics (Have Taken Over The Asylum)" in late 1981, and then teamed up with girl trio **Bananarama** on two hit cover versions – firstly a reworking of the 30s standard "It Ain't What You Do (It's The Way That You Do It)", then a revival of The Marvelettes' US 60s hit, "Really Saying Something". Both hit the British Top 10 in early 1982, but although Fun Boy Three's self-titled debut LP (1982) received good reviews, it was a patchy affair.

Their second album, WAITING (1983), was much more the ticket. **David Byrne** of Talking Heads had been brought in to produce it, while among the backing musicians was Specials horn player, Dick Cuthell. Kicking off with the jaunty instrumental "Murder She Said", it was swiftly followed by the sadly neglected single, "The More I See (The Less I Believe)", with Hall's distinctive strained vocals expressing despair at the average person's lack of interest in the problems of Northern Ireland. The rest of the album dealt with similarly 'difficult' material, featuring booming drums and dramatic strings.

Further hit singles followed with "Tunnel Of Love" and "Our Lips Are Sealed", the latter co-written with **GO-GO**'s guitarist **Jane Weidlin**. However, tensions were growing within the band, aggravated by a punishing touring schedule to try to break the group in America. Including The Doors'

track "The End" in their set may not have been the wisest move they ever made, especially when they climaxed it by burning an American flag.

The band split in the summer of 1983, as Hall went on to form **THE COLOURFIELD**, **Terry Blair & Anouchka and Vegas**, and to record as a solo artist. Golding and Staples formed **Sunday Best**, but soon disappeared from the scene. A Fun Boy Three greatest hits – BEST OF THE FUN BOY THREE (1987) – showed their transition from post-Specials ska to more complex pop.

⊙ **Waiting** (1983; Chrysalis).
One of the great 'undiscovered' albums, this is an absolute treat from start to finish, ranging from the joylessness of celebrity lifestyles ("We're Having All The Fun") to an account of a drugs raid on a cannabis farm ("The Farm Yard Connection"), and thoughts on child abuse ("Well Fancy That!").

Simon Ives

FUN LOVIN' CRIMINALS

Formed New York, c.1991.

"We would turn on MTV and watch four videos, and all four videos in a row there would be someone screaming at you. We didn't want to be screamed at."

Next to The Beastie Boys and Luscious Jackson, fellow New Yorkers **Fun Lovin' Criminals** are about as fun as white rap gets. Loath to reveal their real names, ex-Marine **Huey** (vocals/guitar), **Steve** (drums/programming) and **Fast** (bass/keyboards/harmonica) met at New York's Limelight nightclub – thereby providing an extra dash of underworld authenticity. They purloined their name from a friend's graffiti crew in nearby Queens, and, jointly inspired by gangster movies and hip-hop, they set about writing material.

Their first sets were also played at the Limelight, where Huey worked as a barman and Fast was a cashier – and it was here they were spotted by an

Stick 'em up Punk, it's the Fun Lovin' Criminals

EMI A&R scout. While many groups have attempted to blend hip-hop with the intensity of De Niro's film noir persona, none have done so with the vibrancy or instinctive musical qualities of Fun Lovin' Criminals. Drawing on rock and blues as well as hip-hop, that musical chassis is completed with spray-painted film samples to produce a seductive, distinctively urban groove.

Despite the peculiarity of their geographical origins, the group established their initial popularity in the UK (where their album spent over thirty weeks in the chart and sold 200,000 plus) rather than America. Indie DJs, in particular, fell in love with songs like the deliciously fruity "The Grave And The Constant" and "Scooby Snacks", included on their 1996 EMI debut, COME FIND YOURSELF. "Scooby Snacks" is one of a clutch of songs they have built around the theme of drugs – in particular, their relentless quest for them. Indeed, Huey claims the use of marijuana to be medicinal and therapeutic rather than merely recreational.

The trio quickly became one of the sure-fire pulls on the UK concert circuit with their souped-up, jazzy beats and well-heeled grooves. Theirs was the set that lit up Phoenix 97, proving that hip-hop can be at least as big a crowd-pleaser as trad indie. However, the wisdom of supporting U2 on one of their latest globetrots was harder to evaluate.

1998's 100% COLUMBIAN delivered the Crim's gangster manifesto in an easily digestible form, the jazz licks and late night grooves ("Love Unlimited") fitting nicely among rougher fare ("Korean Bodega" and "Big Night Out"). The album also saw the departure of drummer Steve, though a replacement, Maxwell Jayson, was found for a slew of bodacious festival dates throughout the summer of 1999. With its timely pre-Christmas release, MIMOSA, a "lounge" album, proved to be a variable pick 'n' mix of covers (with Ian McCulloch guesting on a version of Sinatra's "Summer Wind") and remixes, but served to keep fans keen throughout 2000.

Despite continuing support in the UK, FLC are still struggling to make any impact in their native US. The release of LOCO (2001) with its beer-endorsing title track has done little to remedy this fact, but provided ample evidence of the increasing musical ingenuity that hides behind a comic-book image.

Come Find Yourself (1996; Silver Spotlight/EMI). Peerless post-gangsta, intelligent hip-hop, with "Smoke 'Em" and the irresistible "Scooby Snacks" the highlights. Prominent brass fuels the haze, while a comparatively low sample count (let's not comment on the inclusion of Lynyrd Skynyrd on a hip-hop record) allows the songs to breathe in their own right.

Mimosa (1999; Chrysalis). A lounging album with a film noir slant. It includes the group's covers of Louis Armstrong's "We Have All The Time In The World", and 10cc's "I'm Not In Love".

Loco (2001; Chrysalis). This set weaves retro-chic with innovative twists and turns, in particular on "There Was A Time" – one of their most interesting tracks yet. With music this cool, a little beer-fuelled tomfoolery can be forgiven.

Bag Of Hits (2002; Chrysalis). A great party collection made all the more viable by the inclusion of a bonus disc of remixes.

Alex Ogg

FUN-DA-MENTAL

Formed London, 1991.

British multiethnic band **Fun-Da-Mental**, proponents of hard-hitting songs for hard-hit people, have created a new rock form that draws on Indian, West Indian and Afro-American music forms – bhangra, ragga, rap, hip-hop and whatever else assists their message. While the rap element in their music has sometimes stalked cliché, their use of sound bites and samples is as original as it comes. Songs sample Pakistani village field recordings, the mournful cry of the sarangi (the North Indian stringed instrument that most closely captures the nuances of the human voice), snatches from Malcolm X speeches, mutated *filmi* (Indian film) music and, perhaps most notoriously of all in "Dog War", the unmuzzled howl of a neo-Nazi Combat 18 racist whose hateful diatribe flows as unstaunched as diarrhoea.

The band came together a week prior to the Notting Hill Carnival in London, in 1991, where they made their debut. At this point they comprised **Bad-Sha Lallaman**, **Propa-Gandhi** (both of Pakistani extraction), **Man-Tharoo** (an Indian born in Uganda, later known as **Goldfinger**) and **DJ Obeah** from Barbados. An early press release defined their stance: 'The philosophy, which forms an integral foundation of the band – the Fundamentals – is to highlight the various forms of traditional classical Asian sounds and rhythms whilst incorporating hardcore rap and ragga-dancehall, promoting the beauty of Islam, Sikhism and Hinduism whilst highlighting corruption, oppression and degradation promoted by the western powers-that-be.'

This initial line-up lasted for about eighteen months, becoming along the way a vehicle for Propa-Gandhi, the guise in which Aki Nawaz masquerades. The band's direction was also shaped by punk – Propa-Gandhi had drummed for Southern Death Cult circa 1984 – and black music forms. Their music contains vehement messages refuting the stereotypes of Indian civility, conservatism and passivity. Over their first five years their voice has grown ever stronger and ever more adroit at handling bigotry in British society, especially the demonization and scapegoating of Islam in Western societies. What many would regularly take as aggression, they view as sincerity.

Their debut single, "Janaam – The Message", came out in May 1992 followed, later in the year, by "Gandhi's Revenge" and a cassette anthology, PEACE, LOVE OR WAR. On these and ensuing releases they were tilling fertile musical soil usually left untouched, and with "Countryman" (1993), described as 'the story of an Asian man', the message broke into the mainstream, receiving considerable airplay on MTV. The credits, by this time, were listed as **Amir Ali** (lyrics) and **Inder Matharu** (lyrics/percussion), Propa-Gandhi (music), **Dave 'D' Watts** (additional samples) and **Count Dubulah**

(bass and guitar). Lallaman and Goldfinger departed in summer 1993 to form Det-Ri-Mental, to be replaced by **M C Mushtaq** and **Hot Dog Dennis**. To keep matters confusing, after touring South Africa, Watts took on the identity of **Impi-D** (Impi being a name for 'warrior' he learned there).

1994 saw the release of SEIZE THE TIME, the band's album debut proper. A double CD, it contained many of their most coherent testaments, among them the posture-free rap of "Dog War", and "Mother India", with poet Subi Shah listing notable women in Indian history before broadening matters to an incantatory tribute to Universal Woman, over a clever pastiche of sampled sitars and track-panned *filmi* strings.

WITH INTENT TO PERVERT THE COURSE OF INJUSTICE!, released the following summer, said it all in the title – a handy epigram to describe the band's purpose, philosophical stance and the spirit of their music. By the end of the year, however, a new direction was evident as the core group of Propa-Gandhi and Impi-D launched into a series of dates with Aziz Mian, a *qawwali* (Sufi devotional) singer, and phased down their rap content in favour of heartfelt Indian subcontinent shadings. Their sampling had become increasingly sophisticated, too, and collaborations with the sort of musicians they once had sampled were reducing (in Propa-Gandhi's words) their 'sample thieving'. EROTIC TERRORISM (1998) and THERE SHALL BE LOVE (2001) continued the sonic attack on racists, fascists and all the other bad guys.

⊙ **With Intent To Pervert The Cause Of Injustice!**
(1995; Nation).
A simple 'Instrumental fusion of Peace, Love, Confusion and Extremism' is how it is described on the cover. Stand-outs include "Dog War" and "Mr Bubbleman", alongside some exceptional samples and passion.

Ken Hunt

FUNKADELIC

Formed Detroit, Michigan, 1969.

What's a **Funkadelic**? Take R&B, mix heavily with LSD, and season with rock, gospel and psychedelia: the resulting Parliafunkadelicment Thang is perhaps the longest-lasting, most complicated and most influential brew in the history of rock. Coming into existence essentially to get out of a legal ruck, Funkadelic centred on **George Clinton** and an extended group of friends and musicians. Funkadelic survived because of an almost constant state of flux, exacerbated by deaths, prison sentences, marriages, army drafting, business fall-outs, overnight drug psychosis and side-projects.

Funkadelic emerged from the rubble of Clinton's vocal group, The Parliaments, in 1969. When The Parliaments refused to fulfil their contract to Revilot, Clinton arranged a new contract for Funkadelic, with him and other musicians from The Parliaments initially playing as 'guest' artists. At this point, a holding company called Parliafunkadelicment Thang Inc. was

Clinton (as Napoleon) assembles the troops

ment. Funkadelic, meanwhile, continued orbiting the inner space of Clinton's dementia with FREE YOUR MIND AND YOUR ASS WILL FOLLOW (1970). The band really hit their stride with the classic MAGGOT BRAIN (1971), where the psychedelic/funk fusion jelled on tracks like "Hit It And Quit It", "Can You Get To That", "Super Stupid", and the inspired anti-racist jibes of "You And Your Folks, Me And My Folks". By this point, **Eddie Hazel** (guitar), **Bernie Worrell** (keyboards) and **Gary Shider** (guitar) had all joined the Parliafunkadelicment Thang.

AMERICA EATS ITS YOUNG (1972) should have been one of the greatest albums ever made. It blended Clinton's scatology, an explicit political comment, Hendrix guitar jams washed in acid, and brutal parodies of Sly Stone and The Temptations to create a record of unmatched ambition. Unfortunately, whether it was the drugs or the sheer scope of the project, it failed to deliver on its promise. COSMIC SLOP (1973) was an inspired mix of bizarre religion and antiwar sentiment, featuring the outrageous "No Compute", which tackled racial stereotypes head-on with its pro-oral-sex message. STANDING ON THE VERGE OF GETTING IT ON (1974) was slightly more R&B and less LSD, while LET'S TAKE IT TO THE STAGE (1975) took Clinton's view of sex to its thorny limit on "No Head, No Backstage Pass".

registered in Detroit by Clinton with frontmen **Grady Thomas**, **Calvin Simon**, **Fuzzy Haskins** and **Ray Davis**. Another important change happened with the new name. Clinton and his cohorts abandoned their neat suits and slicked-back-hair look and plunged headlong into the psychedelic era. The traditional soul vocal-group sound was combined with Hendrixian rock histrionics and the stripped-down rhythmic arrangements of James Brown and Dyke And The Blazers.

Funkadelic's self-titled debut in September 1970 gained Clinton and his P-Funk mob their first serious recognition. Emerging alongside the Bootsy Collins-led JBs, FUNKADELIC was the heavy, narcotized, depth-charge flip side to the catalytic conversions of "Sex Machine" and "Super Bad". By now heavily into LSD, Funkadelic's stage show expanded with their minds, becoming increasingly surreal and theatrical, while musically dominated by long jams and guitar solos.

PARLIAMENT re-emerged at this point, dropping the definite article and the 's' from their name, and released the Funkadelic-style OSMIUM (1970) before becoming the dance-floor side of Clinton's twin-tiered attack on narrative, 'the placebo syndrome', The Doobie Brothers, puritanism, and the govern-

More damaging for the band than any drug problem was Clinton's decision in 1976 to make himself the sole owner of Parliafunkadelicment Thang Inc., putting everyone else on fixed salaries. Not surprisingly, band relations deteriorated rapidly from that point and, in June 1977, the other four original members quit, later to form their own band, also to be known as Funkadelic. The replacements included **Mike Hampton** (guitar), **Maceo Parker** (saxophone), **Fred Wesley** (horns) and **Jerome Brailey** (drums). The real Funkadelic's last album for Westbound was TALES OF KIDD FUNKADELIC (1976) which, despite its hurried release and slapdash organization, contained epochal Funkadelic tracks like "The Undisco Kid" and "Take Your Dead Ass Home".

Funkadelic's debut for Warners, HARDCORE JOLLIES (1976), was as far out as any of their previous records. The more straight-ahead funk sound of their groove numbers presaged the awesome ONE NATION UNDER A GROOVE (1978). It was the best amalgam of Clinton's politicized scatology

("Promentalashitbackwashipsychosisenema Squad" and "Doodoo Chasers") and his de-essentialism ("Who Says A Funk Band Can't Play Rock"), while the title track was (and still is) one of the most galvanizing grooves ever committed to wax. The follow-up, UNCLE JAM WANTS YOU (1979), was a return to the cryptic logic of old. The record's highlight was the extended funk jam of "(Not Just) Knee Deep", later sampled by De La Soul among countless others. The final Funkadelic album, THE ELECTRIC SPANKING OF WAR BABIES (1981), was a spaced-out, failed masterpiece that featured the return of Sly Stone.

Historians and completists will no doubt be fighting over copies of LIVE – MEADOWBROOK, ROCHESTER, MICHIGAN 12TH SEPTEMBER 1971 (1997) to get their hands on the wonderful, sizzling versions of "Maggot Brain" and "All Your Goodies Are Gone" which it contains. The late-70s collection ULTIMATE (1998) is, however, destined for bargain bins around the world.

⊙ **Maggot Brain** (1971; Westbound).
The best of the early Funkadelic albums. The title track features the best guitar solo the band ever put down. Fusion never sounded so good.

⊙ **One Nation Under A Groove** (1978; Charly).
As funky as the Godfather, as spaced-out as Hendrix, as rigorous as Einstein, as scabrous as Redd Foxx.

⊙ **Music For Your Mother** (1993; Westbound).
Contains all of the Westbound-era singles and B-sides. The only drawback is that some of their best material never appeared as singles.

⊙ **The Very Best Of ...** (Charly; 1998).
A double CD that gives a perfect introduction to the band at their best.

Matthew Grant

FURNITURE

Formed London, 1981; disbanded 1991.

Formed by **Jim Irvin** (vocals), **Tim Whelan** (vocals/guitar/piano) and **Hamilton Lee** (drums/percussion), **Furniture** must go down in rock history as one of the most unfortunate of bands, and a salutary lesson for any young hopefuls being courted by minor labels.

The band started out with a lot of promise, signing to the Survival label after submitting a demo of a beautiful Irvin/Whelan composition, "I Miss You", and releasing a self-financed mini-LP, WHEN THE BOOM WAS ON, in 1983. By that time, the band had augmented to a five-piece, with the addition of **Maya Gilder** (keyboards) and **Sally Still** (bass). After a further few singles had been released, these and their flip sides were collected to form a second album, THE LOVEMONGERS, which was released by Survival for the Japanese market only. Part of this collection was "Bullet", which grew from just a few words – originally recorded in 1981 with the help of a Swedish busker – into a thirteen-minute tape loop.

Furniture's move to Stiff Records in 1986 produced "Brilliant Mind", one of the most distinctive singles in a thin year for pop. Their first and only hit, it reached #21 in the UK chart, although the band presumably received further royalties in 1987, when it was featured on the soundtrack to the John Hughes movie, *Some Kind Of Wonderful*. The follow-up was a rerecorded "Love Your Shoes", but within weeks of release Stiff Records went into liquidation, and the pieces were left to be picked up by ZTT. Worse still, just thirty thousand copies of Furniture's third album, THE WRONG PEOPLE (1986), were pressed before it was abruptly deleted. Storytelling songwriting at its best, it included a brilliant reworking of "I Miss You", the Madness soundalike "Let Me Feel Your Pulse", and the jazzy "Pierre's Fight".

Thereafter, three years of court battles followed, as Furniture tried and eventually succeeded to free themselves from ZTT. In 1989, newly signed to Arista, they gained more plaudits for FOOD, SEX AND PARANOIA (1989), though this fourth album flopped completely, as did its two single offshoots, "Slow Motion Kisses" and "One Step Behind You".

After the departure of Maya Gilder in 1990, the remaining quartet continued to tour for a time, but they decided to split early in 1991. A compilation, SHE GETS OUT THE SCRAPBOOK – THE BEST OF FURNITURE, was released on Survival in 1991, a posthumous summary of much-neglected talents. Both Irvin and Still went into music journalism (Still under the name of Sally Margaret Joy), working for British weekly *Melody Maker*. Irvin then formed the short-lived Because, who released an album in 1992 called MAD SCARED DUMB AND GORGEOUS, before returning to journalism, notably for monthly magazine *Mojo*.

⊙ **She Gets Out The Scrapbook – The Best Of Furniture** (1991; Survival).
The only Furniture album likely to be still available, this is a complete career study, from the original demo of "I Miss You", through "Brilliant Mind" and "Love Your Shoes" to a couple of new songs, including "Farewell", which was nearly recorded as the band's last single.

Neil Nixon

NELLY FURTADO

Born Victoria, British Columbia, Canada, 1978.

One of the most promising new talents to appear in 2001, **Nelly Furtado** (named after the great Russian gymnast, Nelly Kim Furtado) initially came to the attention of her Canadian homeland, and then across the world with the chart hit "I'm Like A Bird", while her debut album WOAH, NELLY! was a zippy, witty hybrid of pop, hip-hop and R&B, which gained a considerable critical following, as well as respectable sales.

Nelly grew up in British Columbia with her parents, both of whom had migrated from the Azores, off the Portuguese coast. Her musical upbringing seems in retrospect to have epitomized the eclectic vision of her work, even down to the instruments she

Nelly – flapping like a bird

chose to study: ukulele, trombone, and later, guitar and keyboards. Meanwhile, she was absorbing and appreciating numerous musical styles, most notably hip-hop, R&B and rock.

At the age of sixteen, a visit to her ancestral homeland of Portugal led to the discovery of a highly colloquial and improvisational vocal style, which would later be central to her own distinctive technique. Similarly, a compilation of Brazilian music was hugely influential on the teenage Furtado: 'It was African and Portuguese music coming together. The emotion and the romanticism comes from the Portuguese side; the rhythm and groove and energy come from the African side.'

By 1996, Furtado had met **Gerald Eaton** and **Brian West** from hip-hop group The Philosopher Kings, who later became her composing and production collaborators, although at this early stage the three had barely finished one demo before she set off for a year of travelling across Europe and tackling a creative writing course. Finally tempted back to Toronto, she resumed writing and recording, and the results impressed the mighty Dreamworks corporation, who signed Furtado in late 1999.

First released in North America in late 2000, WOAH NELLY! showed an influence of Beck and Cornershop, who for their own albums had plundered equally disparate sources, while the set's standout cut, the global smash "I'm Like A Bird" was undoubtedly the sound of the summer.

If Furtado's work was not quite of the same remarkable standard as the aforementioned Beck, on the evidence of her first flush of success, she deserves to outlast most new artists of her age.

Woah, Nelly! (2001; Dreamworks).
A jazzy, witty hybrid of pure pop, soul and disparate world styles.

Justin Lewis

PETER GABRIEL

Born Cobham, England, 1950.

W hen in 1975 **Peter Gabriel** left **GENESIS**, the band he had co-founded and dominated through its first seven albums, he expressed doubts about returning to rock music. The band split not only because of tension between him and the other members, but also due to the strain of life in the public eye, the long tours, and record company pressures. And though only 25, Gabriel was married with children, and prematurely alienated from rock's celebration of youth.

In the event, Gabriel was back inside two years but on distinctly new terms. On stage, he ditched the overblown theatrics, costumes and make-up of his Genesis days. Likewise, his first four solo albums were all titleless, distinguished only by his name and a partially obscured face on the cover.

Gabriel saw a solo career as a chance to create more personal music. As the albums progressed, his art became more (and more effectively) confessional. Relatively little was evident on PETER GABRIEL [I] (1977), which despite moments of beauty (notably "Solsbury Hill", one of his best songs, about the Genesis break-up) was bombastic power rock – due in part, perhaps, to the chosen producer, Bob Ezrin, whose credits included Alice Cooper and Kiss.

For the follow-up, PETER GABRIEL [II] (1978), Gabriel enlisted **ROBERT FRIPP**, who should have been a more sympathetic spirit but had his own agenda, intending the record as part of an 'MOR

trilogy', with Daryl Hall's SACRED SONGS and his own EXPOSURE (whose title track was a more severe version of a song on Gabriel's album, and which also contained a sublime cover of "Here Comes The Flood" from GABRIEL [I]). To experimentalist Fripp, MOR must have been an adventure, but it was hard to see Gabriel's songs for the incessant funk. The one real stand-out was "On The Air".

Part of the problem was that Fripp had a different method of working to Gabriel, his inventiveness often the result of improvisation, while Gabriel's (as Fripp observed) was – and is – essentially 'compositional'. It was an approach that led Gabriel towards a more minimal and sensitive music, which emerged properly on PETER GABRIEL [III] (1980). This set saw Gabriel installed in his own studio, at liberty to experiment, and, at a financial low, forced to draw on the skills of a small group of friends – notably **Phil Collins**, Robert Fripp, **Tony Levin** (his regular bassist) and **Larry Fast** (keyboards). It meant a lot more artistic control, while Steve Lillywhite, the new producer, brought fresh ideas from work with new post-punk bands such as Siouxsie And The Banshees and XTC.

The music on this third album was revolutionized also by new technology – specifically the Fairlight CMI, an early sampler perfectly suited to Gabriel's 'compositional' method, and a drum machine, which allowed him to build songs around rhythm. Equally crucial, Gabriel was discovering non-Western musics, sampling South African funeral drumming and chanting for the brilliant, anthemic "Biko" (one of his few overt political songs), and marimbas for "No Self Control". All in all, it was quite an advance and, led by the radio-friendly single "Games Without Frontiers", the album topped the UK album charts, and reached #22 in the US.

On PETER GABRIEL [IV] (titled SECURITY in the US; 1982) the world beat was even more prominent, with Ethiopian pipes employed on "The Family And The Fishing Net", Brazilian rhythms on "Kiss Of Life", and Ghanaian drums on "Rhythm Of The Heat". The new sounds and rhythms were proving a liberation for Gabriel. He managed another hit single, "Shock The Monkey", and followed "Biko" with another impressive political song, "Wallflower".

World music was to play an increasingly major role in Gabriel's working life. In the summer of 1982 he helped present the first ever WOMAD (World of Music and Dance) festival, showcasing musicians from such places as Pakistan, Burundi and Indonesia. Ahead of its time and organized with little commercial consideration, it left a £200,000 debt, which Gabriel was able to clear, drawing on his old band's goodwill to play a one-off fund-raising concert with Genesis. Rescued, WOMAD has gone from strength to strength, spreading to events worldwide, and with Gabriel a highly active figurehead, both for the festival and in particular its affiliated world music label, Real World, which is based at Gabriel's studio in the village of Box, near Bath.

The early 80s also saw Gabriel's first forays into film work, contributing a track to Spielberg's *Gremlins* and a song, "Walk Through The Fire" for Taylor Hackford's *An Officer And A Gentleman*. More significantly, he wrote the entire soundtrack for Alan Parker's 1985 film, *Birdy*, building it in large part from his previous two releases, remixed to superb effect as instrumentals. The BIRDY soundtrack album remains one of the highlights of his career, very much tighter than the albums from which it was drawn, though it was headily eclipsed by PASSION (1989), Gabriel's album of haunting music for Martin Scorsese's *Last Temptation Of Christ*.

SO (1986), announced to a receptive radio audience by the catchy and upbeat "Sledgehammer", propelled Gabriel back to pop stardom. He had finally allied rhythm and texture with the hook of a strong melody, and unscrambled his lyrics into the bargain. Giving the album a title may have helped, too, as did the shirking of past self-effacement on the sleeve. The biggest credit, though, is probably owing to **Daniel Lanois**, in whom Gabriel had finally found a totally appropriate producer.

After SO, Gabriel was as busy as ever, promoting Real World (and spreading fairy dust around the WOMAD artists), recording and playing live with his friend the Senegalese superstar **Youssou N'Dour**, and in the late 80s, especially, championing human rights on behalf of Amnesty International. He did this not just with benefit concerts but with major tours (*Conspiracy of Hope*, 1986; *Human Rights Now*, 1988), with **Sting**, **Springsteen** and other artists.

During the early 90s, his non-soundtrack outings included US (1992) – a record he has described as his 'dark' album, reflecting his own divorce and personal angst – and SECRET WORLD LIVE (1994), a frankly bland live recording. On the former, "Digging In The Dirt" (like "Red Rain" from SO) was an expression of his interest in Jung and his belief that we diminish our problems if we recognize and name them. Although less commercial than SO, the album charted at #2 on both sides of the Atlantic.

In 1994 he produced a CD-ROM, XPLORA, and soon after was working on putative plans for a Real World theme park with Brian Eno and Laurie Anderson. At the end of 1997 Gabriel was invited to create a show for London's Millennium Dome. After over a year of brainstorming and writing, the resulting *Ovo* show was premiered on the first day of the new millennium and was followed later in the year by a CD soundtrack. This diverse album – which documented the unraveling tale of a mythical society grappling with issues of technology, ecology and race – featured an army of guest musicians and singers, including **Neneh Cherry** and **Elizabeth Fraser** of the Cocteau Twins.

Gabriel followed with a new solo album, UP (2002), that featured contributions from **Nusrat Fateh Ali Khan**, **Danny Thompson**, **Peter Green** and **Blind Boys Of Alabama**. Also new to his catalogue was LONG WALK HOME (2002), the haunting soundtrack album to the Australian film *Rabbit Proof Fence*. In addition, a timely series of reissues brought all Gabriel's solo albums to light once again.

Gabriel continues to pour his energies into Real World, whilst also maintaining an active interest in various environmental and human-rights projects.

⊙ **Peter Gabriel** [IV]/Security (1982; Charisma/Geffen). The fourth album hosts Gabriel's most adventurous and consistent songs, as a world of sounds collect, pattern and dissipate to a backdrop of Jerry Marrota's fantastically heavy drumming.

⊙ **So** (1986; Virgin/Geffen). Daniel Lanois, world music and upbeat spirits produced an accessible set, including the hits "Sledgehammer", "In Your Eyes" and "Big Time".

⊙ **Passion** (1989; Real World/Geffen). Gabriel has a rare sensitivity for foreign musics, weaving his sources together and overlaying his own synthesizers without any hint of force or clumsiness. The music appears both immediate and accessible, and also alien and endlessly fascinating.

⊙ **Us** (1992; Virgin). OK, clear the couch for group therapy, as Gabriel unleashes a highly personal sequence of songs that make Phil Collins sound like, well, Phil Collins.

⊙ **Ovo** (2000; Real World). Hip-hop beats, pop hooks, drum'n'bass breaks, folk melodies, Eno-styled ambient striations, and even a River Dance-ish jig all creep onto Gabriel's hallmark palette of plundered ethnographic colours.

David Castle

GALAXIE 500

Formed Boston, Massachusetts, 1986.

Galaxie 500 seemed to appear out of nowhere with their 1987 debut album, TODAY. Its sparse lo-fi sound was almost anti-rock, certainly out of line with the dictates of US indie-pop and the fearsome racket of the Pixies and Dinosaur Jr. Although influential on the UK 'shoegazing' scene and US 'slow-core' crawlers like Codeine, their extraordinary brand of atmospheric minimalism had no real inheritors until relatively recently, with the rise of groups such as Low.

The trio of **Dean Wareham** (guitar/vocals), **Naomi Yang** (bass) and **Damon Krukowski** (drums) – helped by producer and Shimmy Disc boss **Kramer** – created a hypnotic psychedelic wash obviously indebted to The Velvet Underground and The Modern Lovers. Wareham's guitar and vocals sounded oddly frantic despite the band's constant restraint in the tempo department.

Galaxie's languid, rolling pace soon became a trademark, particularly on their feverishly awaited follow-up, ON FIRE (1989). This saw the band crafting expansive mini-epics in tiny boxes – like all their recordings of the time, it was made in Kramer's apartment studio. Marked by Wareham's bizarrely gauche lyrics and frazzled solos, songs built to heady climaxes then dissipated like vapour trails; the whole LP dripped mystery and a vaguely unsettling glacial beauty. The album thrilled several music press writers in the UK, but some sections of the US press took such umbrage at Wareham's vocal 'limitations' that the band was effectively sidelined.

With a title filched from an old Ornette Coleman album, THIS IS OUR MUSIC (1990) fared even less well, attracting accusations of being too formulaic and ornate for its own good. In retrospect, Kramer's embellishments of organ and flute seem like a logical refinement rather than the desperate ploy of one-trick fakers caught in a corner. All aesthetic problems soon became academic when Wareham unexpectedly and acrimoniously fled the band in early 1991. After a stint playing on and producing art-pop experimentalists Mercury Rev's astonishing CAR WASH HAIR EP (1991), he released a sole solo single, the frustratingly throwaway "Anesthesia", before going on to form the minor-league supergroup Luna 2 – later known simply as **LUNA** – in 1992.

Meanwhile Yang and Krukowski immediately set about disproving the popular assumption that Wareham was the sole architect of the Galaxie sound: as **Pierre Etoile** and then as plain old **Damon And Naomi** they came up with a warmer, more elegant take on their old band's style, while also appearing as the rhythm section for the little-known **Magic Hour**. Still together today, and now signed to Sub Pop, Damon And Naomi continue to keep the Galaxie 500 sound alive with albums like WITH GHOST (2000), a collaboration with the Japanese band **Ghost**, and SONG TO THE SIREN (2002) with **Michio Kurihara**.

Since the demise of Galaxie 500, Rykodisc have continued to carry the torch with a fine boxed set of all the group's releases and in 1998 a best-of entitled THE PORTABLE GALAXIE 500.

⊙ **On Fire** (1989; Rough Trade).
Housed in a gorgeous sleeve adorned with Kramer's stream-of-consciousness notes, this package of icy songs is utterly entrancing. The highlight, "Snowstorm", captures the uneasiness of a kid confronted with something both cool and dangerous. Keep looking.

⊙ **Galaxie 500 Box Set** (1997; Rykodisc).
This makes everything a whole lot easier; a deluxe four-CD collection containing all three impossible-to-find albums, bundled with a disc of rarities.

⊙ **The Portable Galaxie 500** (1998; Rykodisc).
This is a great place to start, but no substitute for the whole catalogue. The set does, however, feature an enhanced video track of "Blue Thunder".

Chris Tighe

RORY GALLAGHER

Born Ballyshannon, Ireland, 1948; died 1995.

One of the most respected and able musicians among the blues and rock fraternities, **Rory Gallagher** managed to maintain both his popularity

and his integrity for all of his lengthy career.

Cutting his teeth as a besuited guitarist playing Chuck Berry songs in The Impact and The Fontana Showband, Gallagher formed the original incarnation of **Taste** in 1965. Extensive gigging around their native Ireland ensured that the trio were soon building a healthy reputation for their pioneering brand of free-form blues-rock. Gallagher would regularly astound audiences by swiftly changing from guitar to saxophone mid-song; later on in his career he would show similar dexterity with the mandolin and harmonica.

Signing to Polydor, Taste, comprising Gallagher plus **Richard McCracken** (bass) and **John Wilson** (drums), recorded their eponymous debut in 1969, which featured live favourites such as "Same Old Story". Both TASTE and its follow-up, ON THE BOARDS (1970), were well received by the public. However, despite US tours with Blind Faith and Delaney And Bonnie, as well as supporting Cream at their Royal Albert Hall farewell gig, Taste became dogged by management and financial problems, resulting in an acrimonious split in early 1971. They left behind LIVE TASTE (1971), which included their set at the 1970 Isle Of Wight festival, surprisingly unaffected by the fact that their equipment had just been stolen.

Always the main attraction at Taste gigs, Gallagher had little trouble launching a solo career. RORY GALLAGHER (1971) reached the UK Top 40, then LIVE IN EUROPE (1972) and BLUEPRINT (1973) did even better. A blues purist, admired by rock aristocrats like John Lennon, Gallagher was a natural choice to join the all-star session band for Muddy Waters' and Jerry Lee Lewis's two LONDON SESSIONS albums (1972 and 1973), which also featured the likes of Steve Winwood, Peter Frampton and Jimi Hendrix Experience drummer Mitch Mitchell. Indeed, Waters was so impressed with Gallagher's style that he employed him again on his LONDON REVISITED album of 1974 – the year Gallagher was touted as a replacement for Mick Taylor in The Stones.

But it was for his live shows, with bassist **Gerry McAvoy** as the only constant fixture of his backing band, that Gallagher was most loved throughout his lengthy solo career. He would regularly enthral audiences with 150-minute-long sets, featuring impassioned readings of blues standards and Gallagher compositions such as "A Million Miles Away" and "Walk On Hot Coals". Shunning gimmicky guitar pyrotechnics, Gallagher's approach was a breath of fresh air compared with the lengthy self-indulgence of acts such as Led Zeppelin.

Capitalizing on his stage reputation, Gallagher released several live recordings over the years, ranging from the raw blues-based hit albums LIVE IN EUROPE (1972) and IRISH TOUR '74 (1974) to the more rock-orientated STAGE STRUCK (1980) – all while keeping up a solid touring schedule.

After JINX (1982), Rory took a five-year recording sabbatical, but DEFENDER (1987) showed he could still deliver the goods. The follow-up, FRESH EVIDENCE (1990), featuring Nine Below Zero harmonica player Mark Feltham, again displayed a refreshing bluesy approach which had been temporarily exchanged for a rockier sound on the previous albums.

In early 1993, the first signs of drink-induced ill health were evidenced during a live set at London's Town & Country Club. Heckling fans made Gallagher curtail his set, vowing that he would never play London again. His words were to be an all-too-accurate prediction; although he regained his composure for the otherwise unremarkable Portsmouth Blues Weekend later that year, by Christmas 1994 his touring plans had to be shelved.

Contracting pneumonia after a liver transplant, Rory died in June 1995, aged only 47. In true blues tradition, he had already delivered his epitaph twenty years before, on the IRISH TOUR '74 album, when he sang J. B. Hutto's "Too Much Alcohol".

⊙ **Irish Tour '74** (1974; Demon).
One of the few artists to regularly play Northern Ireland during the troubles, Rory and the boys were treated like conquering heroes at every appearance. On listening to this album, you can hear why.

⊙ **Edged In Blue** (1992; Demon).
Culled from his live and studio albums, this is a good introduction to Gallagher, although his rawer live recordings are sadly missing, as is the exemplary "Bullfrog Blues". Still, besides his time-honoured blues covers (Muddy Waters' "I Wonder Who" is particularly outstanding), Gallagher proves he was a sterling songwriter on numbers like "The Loop" and "Loanshark Blues".

⊙ **The G Men Bootleg Series Vol.1** (1992; Castle Communications).
A triple-CD compilation, with more volumes apparently in the pipeline, this presents the pick of Rory Gallagher's live material. Vintage recordings of "Country Mile" and "Bullfrog Blues", at an affordable price – but the vague, minimal sleeve notes leave a great deal to be desired.

Paul Morris

GALLON DRUNK

Formed London, 1991.

At a time of when shoegazing was rife, **James Johnston** (vocals/guitar/keyboards) and **Mike Delanian** (bass) knew pomade was the future. Bequiffed, they walked in snakeskin boots, cigarette mashed between lips, eyes blackened from last night's punch-up. **Max Decharne** (organ) of the Earls Of Suave fitted the picture, and with **Nick Combe** (drums) they formed **Gallon Drunk**, beating out mile-high rockabilly – with an echo of The Birthday Party – when not scraping a living in Soho bookshops.

Combe was replaced by My Bloody Valentine alumnus **Joe Byfield**, with his fistful of maracas and his ability to make the snare drum sound like the entire kit was falling over. Singles on their manager's Massive label brought acclaim, but their debut album, YOU, THE NIGHT AND THE MUSIC (1992), had a bigger kick. On "Eye Of The Storm" and "The Tornado", the guitars screamed like out-of-control cycles hitting the speedwall in a typhoon of highballs.

Decharne battered frantic Morricone triplets on an under-mud piano while Byfield became a jungle tribe preparing for war. Johnston's 'singing', a collection of grunts, moans and 'C'mon!'s, could have been recorded at the bottom of a drain.

FROM THE HEART OF TOWN (1993) was their masterwork. Horn supremo Terry Edwards had joined the band, Johnston had assumed the tunesmithing, and he courted London as his muse, celebrating the glory and grimness of her smelly streets. After that Johnston became a Bad Seed, touring for Lollapalooza 94, and both Edwards and Johnston provided an eerie musical backing for DORA SAUREZ (1994), a spoken-word album with crime writer Derek Raymond. A prolonged silence from Gallon Drunk, during which Blur stole their subject matter, ended with the release of THE TRAITOR'S GATE EP (1995), a more swinging effort than previous, with new additions **Ian Watson** (guitar/trumpet), **Andy Dewar** (percussion) and **Ian White** (drums).

Come 1996, and the Drunk squeezed on their brothel creepers again, poured themselves a stiff one, and stalked the mean streets of the capital one more time with IN THE LONG STILL NIGHT, featuring more guitar, even more brass and yet more percussion. Seen by many as a return to form, the album preceded a rash of live activity – and then a well-earned break.

It didn't take a big leap of the imagination to comprehend their next step as **The Drunk**, returning with a soundtrack for Greek director Nikos Triandafyllidis' thriller *Black Milk* – in which they also appear. FIRE MUSIC, a new album proper, arrived early in 2002; an upfront, funked-up gem whose ideology placed them firmly in their rightful place alongside fellow new Bohemian travellers Tindersticks and Nick Cave.

⊙ **From The Heart Of Town** (1993; Clawfist).
A man stared into a Piccadilly puddle, and this is what he heard: a mad dance of marimba, squawking saxes, and a gee-tar that howled the rage of any spirit trapped in the metropolis.

Charles Bottomley

GANG OF FOUR

Formed Leeds, England, 1977; disbanded 1984; re-formed 1990 and briefly in 1995.

Taking their name from a radical Chinese Communist faction, three students and one truck driver formed the **Gang Of Four** in Leeds, although guitarist **Andy Gill** and vocalist **Jon King** had been in bands together while at school in Sevenoaks, in southern England. Drummer **Hugo Burnham** and **Dave Allen** (bass), one of the most powerful rhythm sections of the era, completed a line-up.

King's Marxist-intellectual lyrics drew much attention, but it was the band's overall sound which startled – punky in its minimalism and attack, but made distinctive by Gill's choppy, stroppy guitar style, involving lashings of feedback – sometimes brilliant, sometimes awful – which were fully incorporated into the songs, rather than as a mere climax to the performance. (This technique anticipated the sonic assault of The Jesus & Mary Chain in the mid 80s.) Of equal importance to the Gang's sound was the inventive drumming of Burnham, and Allen's rich, driving bass, which provided a watertight 'martial funk' basis for freewheeling voice and guitar. The overall effect was of Dr. Feelgood and Sly And The Family Stone rehearsing in the same room.

The first release, the DAMAGED GOODS EP (1978), released on the fiercely independent label Fast Product, featured sweaty sexual politics and feedback-strewn ramblings, and led to the band signing, amid some rumblings about ideological contradiction, to major label EMI.

However, any objections soon vanished with the arrival of the dazzling and self-deprecatingly titled ENTERTAINMENT! (1979). The use of Marxist epigrams and 'subversive' collage-imagery on an EMI record sleeve was satisfying enough, but the music's directness and sense of vision created a terrifyingly effective masterpiece. As the LP charted, they were invited onto TV chart show *Top Of The Pops* to promote the single "At Home He's A Tourist", but refused a request to alter the song's reference to condoms, and so did not appear.

As the band toured widely and played numerous benefit concerts for Rock Against Racism, it took two years for a second LP to appear. Largely murky and disappointing, SOLID GOLD (1981) was redeemed by the sparse and edgy "Paralysed" and "Cheeseburger", a snapshot of America taken from a tour bus. Otherwise, though, Gang Of Four's rock-funk template was being widely adopted by everyone from Talking Heads to The Pop Group, and they began to lose their original momentum. During a US promotional tour, Allen acrimoniously quit, later returning to the scene with Barry Andrews (formerly of XTC) under the name **Shriekback**.

The final single made by the original Gang Of Four line-up, the stirring "To Hell With Poverty", took the feedback experiments to their logical extremes. Then, in 1982, with new bassist **Sara Lee** (later a top session player, notably for The B-52's),

The Gang Of Four, from left, Hugo Burnham, Dave Allen (mouthing), Andy Gill and Jon King

they released the far more controlled and successful SONGS OF THE FREE. The Falklands War between British and Argentinian troops was the subject of "Call Me Up" and the near hit "I Love A Man In A Uniform", while "We Live As We Dream, Alone" was a career highlight.

In late 1982, Burnham quit the band, subsequently backing Bryan Ferry and, more bizarrely, the model Samantha Fox. In his absence, led by Gill, Gang Of Four recorded as a trio with a drum machine, and with HARD (1983) they made a deliberate stab at commercial success, with strings and session players making its overall sound reminiscent of American studio-funk. The album failed to make the desired impact but it did have its moments, like the diamond-hard funk of "Is It Love", or the cold signing-off of "Independence".

The early to mid 80s was not a good time to be a Marxist pop group in the UK and, after a short tour, the band split in the spring of 1984. Although a live album, AT THE PALACE, emerged later that year, it appeared that Gang Of Four's time was up.

However, by 1990, THE PEEL SESSIONS, recorded for BBC Radio DJ John Peel's show between 1979 and 1981, had finally been issued, closely followed by a compilation album, A BRIEF HISTORY OF THE TWENTIETH CENTURY (1990). This reawakening of interest led Gill and King, now based in the US, to resurrect Gang Of Four for MALL (1991). As the title suggests, the album reflected aspects of American consumer culture, but despite Gill's undiminished guitar work it remained a muted affair, and they were dropped from Polydor's roster.

In the light of the long-awaited CD reissue of ENTERTAINMENT! in 1995, Gill and King reactivated the band once more. SHRINKWRAPPED (1995) returned to the four-piece approach of their early recordings. These songs nearly all began life as the soundtrack to the 1994 movie *Delinquent*; the album was destined to duplicate the film's commercial obscurity however, and Gill and King dissolved the band once more. In 1996 Gill began work with Michael Hutchence, as co-writer and producer of his solo album, and was placed in editorial control and given responsibility for the completion of the project after Hutchence's death in November 1997.

A 1998 2CD anthology, 100 FLOWERS BLOOM, presented the familiar, but welcome, live, unreleased, rarity and remix cocktail, adding further fuel to the argument that the Gang Of Four were one of the great bands of the late 70s and early 80s, with a sound and approach that was quite distinctly their own. Their influence will surely grow.

(•) **Entertainment!** (1979; EMI/Warners; reissued 1995). Outrageously good, from the opening salvo against media brainwashing, "Ether", to the sublime "I Found That Essence Rare". They never bettered this essential work. The CD reissue contains three extra cuts.

(•) **Songs Of The Free** (1982; EMI/Warners; currently unavailable). This almost matches their debut for attack, wit and commitment. The arrangements have also become increasingly sophisticated, with special mentions for "We Live As We Dream, Alone" and the modestly titled "The History Of The World".

(•) **A Brief History Of The Twentieth Century** (1990; EMI). A serviceable selection from Gang Of Four's entire catalogue does justice to their range and scope, and even boasts sleeve notes by American rock academic Greil Marcus, who had become a belated advocate of the band.

Peter Mills

GANGWAR

Formed London, 1989.

"I don't really want to play the same sort of music for years and years. I like to evolve. Musical progression is very important to me." James Ray

In 1989 **James Ray** moved from his previous incarnation in **James Ray And The Performance** to a new project, bringing the heavy goth-influenced rhythms of his previous work to a new trance/dance-orientated sound. Already established on the Merciful Release label, James Ray had sung on Eldritch's (of Sisters Of Mercy) side-project The Sisterhood's album GIFT, a collaboration that added to his reputation. With **Karl Harrison** of The Performance, he released the compilation album A NEW KIND OF ASSASSIN in 1989, characterized by driving rhythms overlaid with Ray's heavy, mesmerizing vocals.

When this project disbanded, Ray formed James Ray's Gangwar with **Damon Vingoe** (bass/keyboards), **Travis Earl** (guitars) and **John Bainbridge** (guitars). Gangwar are a very strong team who share the writing, producing and performing duties. Beginning to gig in late 1989, *Melody Maker* described hearing them live as 'like discovering sex for the first time'.

The band created sounds that crossed the decades, consistently offering something new and exciting. They reached a peak with the truly outstanding PSYCHODALEK album in 1996, characterized by steady, up-tempo dance rhythms and an infectious subterranean musical structure. The lyrics reflected Ray's concerns with social and political matters and regularly involved Christian iconography, samples, American kitsch and European social decay. The band's gothic is always visible and its convergence with synth-based 80s sounds and 90s techno and trance creates a complex, intoxicating sound that has been described as 'technogoth', 'electrogoth' and 'New Age Techno'.

While working in Gangwar, James Ray has produced two solo albums under the name **MK Ultra** – THIS IS THIS and BELUGA POP, both on Merciful Release Records – and has also written novels and screenplays. When asked about his opinion on trance music he responded by stating 'Trance is modern goth without the horror.' It is this ability to broach boundaries, see connections and meld the diversities of life into something new and whole that makes James Ray a creative artist of some note.

When PSYCHODALEK was released, *Melody Maker* dubbed Ray 'one of the coolest curmudgeons' in the rock business, a title which is arrogantly worn by the man behind the music. Ray has described himself as an 'electroassassin' and a 'cyberchrist', but his canny observations of the contemporary music scene are impossible to ignore.

Gangwar then split temporarily and Ray proved to be rather elusive, while Bainbridge went on to exercise his techno skills as **Volatile Headspace**. Currently, it looks as if Gangwar's back catalogue is to be reissued by Infinity Records, and there are rumours that new material may soon see the light of day. Better not hold your breath, though.

⊙ **Third Generation** (1993; Surgery).
A major step forward in Gangwar's evolution. Dance music dominates, while sampling and percussion loops enrich each track. "Cobalt Blue", "Sinner" and "Third Generation" don't let go once they've got their hooks into you. A synth feast.

⊙ **Psychodalek** (1996; 24:24).
With John Bainbridge taking full control of the production, this is Gangwar's finest creation. Hypnotic and powerful it marks itself out as representative of things to come – a cyberpunk creation.

Valerie Palmer

GARBAGE

Formed Wisconsin, 1993.

"We're a totally collaborative, psychotic, dysfunctional unit – just like any band." Butch Vig

Garbage are the warped techno-grunge brainchild of one-time Nirvana, Sonic Youth and Smashing Pumpkins producer **Brian 'Butch' Vig** (drums/noise/fx), in league with fellow studio tricksters **Duke Erikson** (guitars/keyboards) and **Steve Marker** (guitars/bass/samples). Owners of a successful studio, yet frustrated by their mixing-desk-bound jobs and the relative failure of previous band incarnations Spooner and Firetown, the trio searched for a vocalist and found one when they saw singer **Shirley Manson** fronting **GOODBYE MR MACKENZIE**. Impressed by Manson's darkly humorous ad libs during an informal audition, the band welcomed her to their fold.

Despite Vig's insistence that the band was a democracy, Garbage's early press attention focused on the influence he had on their polished, poppy, grunge sound – largely because rock critics were still salivating over Vig's production on Nirvana's NEVERMIND. Garbage's early output also attracted collectors, as they issued a series of limited-edition singles, beginning with "Vow", which came in a metal box. "Vow" was a dark, distorted slice of angst,

nearer to the entertainingly pseudo-goth theatrics of Nine Inch Nails and Curve than any of grunge's most popular exponents. Nevertheless, here was a band who clearly wanted – and warranted – attention.

Packaged in a startling rubber sleeve, the follow-up single, "Subhuman", was a dark, but spirited piece of gothic grunge, plundering pop history for a sound that seemed at once alien and familiar. It was backed with another version of "Vow", for those who missed the band's hard-to-find original.

By the summer of 1995, Garbage were receiving support from the music press on both sides of the Atlantic, closely followed by a Top 40 entry in Britain for their third single, "Only Happy When It Rains". Poppier and cockier than the first two releases, it seemed to cock a snook at the doom-laden merchants of rock – 'I'm riding high on a deep depression ... pour your misery down on me', sang Manson, while guitars bent themselves out of shape.

Expectation for Garbage's self-titled debut album was running high, especially among UK critics desperate to escape the burgeoning Britpop scene. Its release, in early October 1995, displayed an impressively varied range, topped with angst-ridden lyrics, weird studio-induced samples, and punchy pop hooks. The collectors' market was not forgotten, either: a limited edition came in the form of six colour-coded singles, all packaged in a cardboard box.

As the band prepared for a one-off British live appearance later in the year, the radio-friendly album track "Queer" was released as a single. A comparatively ambient number, with Manson sounding seductive yet threatening, it became their first Top 20 hit in the UK, although reports of the live show in London were mixed. Abandoning the album's techno-trickery, the band favoured a 'straightforward' live rock sound, which was suiting some of their repertoire but lost some of their inimitable freshness. "Stupid Girl" crashed into the Top 10, in 1996, bringing the name and image to a wider public and becoming Garbage's biggest hit to date. Relentless touring, followed by a round of record-company shenanigans, held up the release of any new product for some time. The logjam was finally broken by the release of VERSION 2.0 (1998; Mushroom/Alma). Stand-out tracks "When I Grow Up" and "Hammering In My head" show a willingness to move beyond the conventional boundaries of neo-gothery and and drew more willing converts to the Church of Garbage.

After becoming a strikingly appropriate choice to provide the title theme for the James Bond film *The World Is Not Enough*, Manson et al reconvened for the 2001 single "Androgyny", a taster for their third full-length excursion which was accompanied by a brand new Tintin haircut for Shirley. BEAUTIFULGARBAGE (2001) smelt of a band at ease with itself; terse, honed and beautifully tooled, it was less jagged than the other two sets, while retaining that instinctive feel for a pop hook that makes the group so compelling.

Garbage (1995; Mushroom).
Twelve tracks of techno-goth posturing, rock mayhem and ambient-pop oddities. A mix with something for everyone.

Version 2.0 (1998; Mushroom/Alma).
No great surprises, no tremendous disappointments. The second album builds on the rock-solid underpinning laid down in the first album, with Manson's little-girl-gone-wrong confessional vocals well to the fore.

Beautifulgarbage (2001; Mushroom/Alma).
A glossy record, but thanks to the intervening arrival of nu-metal's rawness, this set sounds like the choice of aging goths.

Gavin Stoker

JERRY GARCIA

Born San Francisco, 1942; died 1995.

"There are lots of spaces between the Carter Family, Buddy Holly and Ornette Coleman, but Jerry Garcia filled them all." Bob Dylan

The future lead guitarist of **THE GRATEFUL DEAD**, Jerry Garcia was named by his musician father after the Broadway songwriter Jerome Kern. His earliest musical influences came through his grandparents, however, with whom he lived after his father drowned in 1948. They instilled in him a fondness for country music, and when his older brother introduced him to the likes of Chuck Berry and T-Bone Walker, Garcia's soundscape was mapped for ever. Hooked, he took up the guitar.

After a miserable stint of army service, in the early 1960s Garcia wound up in Palo Alto, home of Stanford University, south of San Francisco. He drifted into the folk scene – the era's happening music – and joined The Warlocks, who, after going electric, became The Grateful Dead. With LSD (which future Dead lyricist Robert Hunter had sampled as part of a Stanford medical trial) prevalent, and still legal, this was a deeply psychedelic scene, characterized on and off stage by long jam sessions. Garcia, nicknamed Captain Trips, developed an improvisatory ability to magic musical solutions.

Parallel with his day job in The Dead, Garcia produced an enormous body of work as a session musician or soloist on the San Francisco scene. He shaped songs for Jefferson Airplane (SURREALISTIC PILLOW, 1967), contributed signature guitar to albums by David Crosby (IF ONLY I COULD REMEMBER MY OWN NAME, 1971), Paul Kantner (BLOWS AGAINST THE EMPIRE, 1970) and jazzman Ornette Coleman (VIRGIN BEAUTY, 1988) and, perhaps most famously, played the pedal steel solo on "Teach Your Children" on Crosby, Stills, Nash & Young's DÉJÀVU (1970).

As a soloist, Garcia debuted on Antonioni's film *Zabriskie Point*, creating a number called "Love Scene" as accompaniment to a desert orgy; it appeared, alongside **PINK FLOYD** material, on the album ZABRISKIE POINT (1971). Soundtrack work remained a source of interest and revenue his whole life long, and on Philip Kaufman's remake of *Invasion Of The Bodysnatchers* Garcia even got a cameo role, the second time fleetingly as a dog's face! Up until the end he was dreaming celluloid dreams, as shown on Wayne Wang's *Smoke* (1995).

Garcia's first 'solo' album was HOOTEROLL? (1971), a set of jazz-tinged instrumentals co-credited to keyboardist Howard Wales. It was followed by GARCIA (1972), a more decisive work with only Hunter (tape-foolery) and Bill Kreutzmann (drums) assisting. The same hectic period saw his first collaboration with keyboard player Merl Saunders, beginning with Saunders' HEAVY TURBULENCE (1972) and FIRE UP (1973) albums. This relationship would prove an enduring one, with a trio of live albums recorded together over the years – LIVE AT KEYSTONE (1973), KEYSTONE ENCORES (1988) and, best of all, BLUES FROM THE RAINFOREST (1990).

A characteristic of Garcia's career was a profusion of offshoot groups, playing diverse repertoires – pop and rock standards, jazz, experimental music, bluegrass and country. GARCIA (aka COMPLIMENTS OF GARCIA, 1974) presented a song bag dipping into Dr. John, Irving Berlin, Van Morrison and Peter Rowan. Garcia's love of bluegrass found expression in OLD AND IN THE WAY (1975), one of his most successful creative and commercial outings. Back on a more rock track, REFLECTIONS (1976) returned to original songs including the immaculate "It Must Have Been The Roses". Propelled by the energy that had created BLUES FOR ALLAH, this featured The Dead, drummer Ron Tutt (from Elvis Presley's band) and Rolling Stones session pianist Nicky Hopkins. CATS UNDER THE STARS (1978), credited to the Jerry Garcia Band, was a more polished work – and Jerry's own favourite – its most notable song the Hunter/Garcia composition "Rubin And Cherise".

RUN FOR THE ROSES (1982), by contrast, was a rather marginal release, reflecting Garcia's 1980s slide into hard drugs, junk food and road life, which cul-

minated in him falling into a diabetic coma in 1986. When he regained consciousness five days later, he had no musical memory. He owed his rehabilitation to Merl Saunders, who began slowly and painfully reacquainting Garcia with his musical skills, starting with scales and favourite tunes like "My Funny Valentine". By 1989, he was not only back with The Dead but recording a side-outing, ALMOST ACOUSTIC (1989), with Dave Nelson and Sandy Rothman from the old Palo Alto folk scene, to produce something similar to The Dead's RECKONING album.

Garcia bands came and went in the early 90s, a fine version being captured on the live double CD, JERRY GARCIA BAND (1991), playing covers of songs from The Band, Dylan, Los Lobos, Allen Toussaint, and the like. Garcia also hitched up again with the mandolin virtuoso David Grisman, who had worked with The Dead in the early 70s, producing JERRY GARCIA/DAVID GRISMAN (1991), a fluent testimony to their virtuosity (and a good seller, helping to float Grisman's Acoustic Disc label); NOT FOR KIDS ONLY (1993), a children's album bound to create a new race of Deadheads; and SHADY GROVE (released posthumously in 1996).

Tragically, though, Garcia had returned to old habits, and on August 10, 1995 he was found dead by an attendant at a Forest Knolls (California) rehab centre. He had died of a heart attack in his sleep. The tributes flooded in, both for his musicianship and for his warmth and humanity; as Joan Baez recalled, 'He did every benefit I ever asked.' He was impressive in other ways; as much a cultural icon for his generation as Kurt Cobain was for his. But whereas Cobain's flight was brief, Captain Trips sustained a thirty-year career, with a music reflecting his intellectual playfulness and catholic tastes. There were highs to be had from too many musical sources to tally, which was perhaps why Garcia's playing at its best – whether on guitar, banjo or through a MIDI system – approached the celestial. Whatever he achieved was due to dedication to his craft and the challenge of the new.

Since his death, Jerry's been rather prolific, with several albums having been issued in his name postmortem. The Jerry Garcia Band continues without the captain, shortening their name to JGB.

Jerry Garcia

⊙ **Garcia** (1972; Grateful Dead Records).
Garcia's debut solo album used just Bill Kreutzmann on drums plus an uncredited Robert Hunter, who supplies the nonsensical narration about Oppenheimer et al. on the sound-collage, tape-loop extravaganza "Spidergawd".

⊙ **Old And In The Way** (1975; Rykodisc).
The marketing ploy behind this was making something that would appeal to two different camps. As well as bluegrass fare such as "Pig In A Pen" and Grisman's "Old And In The Way", there's the Jagger/Richards "Wild Horses" and Rowan's American mystic "Land Of The Navajo".

⊙ **Cats Under The Stars** (1978; Grateful Dead Records).
This was Jerry's own favourite, and shows him at his tightest, both for songwriting and on guitar, with fine backing on keyboards.

Jerry Garcia and David Grisman

⊙ **Jerry Garcia/David Grisman** (1991; Acoustic Disc). Masterful music in an acoustic setting.

Merl Saunders

⊙ **Blues From The Rainforest** (1991; Summertone). Garcia plays on two-thirds of the tracks here, juxtaposing field and studio recordings in ambient, jazz and world music settings.

Ken Hunt

GASTR DEL SOL

Formed Chicago, 1993; disbanded 1998.

Gastr Del Sol were one of the greatest practitioners to emerge from the avant-garde rock scene that flourished in Chicago throughout the 1990s. Together for a mere five years, the band – principally **David Grubbs** and **Jim O'Rourke** – sailed a variety of the stylistic craft that floated around their city's trendier waters, often setting these vessels adrift on strange, unfamiliar sonic seas. With acoustic guitars they defined soporific tonal circles that invoked the playing of both classical players and folk outsiders such as John Fahey; electronic excursions yielded gnawing squeals and drones more familiar to fans of electronic sound pioneers than contemporary techno; by the end of Gastr's run, the pair had introduced jubilant horns and strings to the mix, foreshadowing the indie-pop records that would later emerge from their respective solo careers.

The immediate origins of Gastr Del Sol can be traced back to the less brainy **SQUIRREL BAIT**, a noisy punk group that Grubbs played in as a Louisville teenager. After that band's short run, Grubbs released a handful of masterful records under the tag **Bastro**; he eventually snagged bassist **Bundy K. Brown** and drummer **John McEntire** (both future members of Tortoise) in the early 90s to form Gastr Del Sol. In 1993 this short-lived line-up released THE SERPENTINE SIMILAR, a quiet, largely instrumental record with a soft spot for tinkering piano lines and sparse guitar work. The album that is seen by many as the band's debut proper, however, did not appear until O'Rourke entered the fray the following year. Already known to arty ears as a precocious young improviser, this stocky Chicago musician proved the ideal foil to Grubbs (who had initially contacted his new partner with questions regarding a semiotics term paper). Whereas David Grubbs developed Gastr Del Sol as he was moving away from rock'n'roll, Jim O'Rourke was headed in the opposite direction: away from the avant-garde and towards more crowd pleasing sounds. During the brief period when their paths crossed – or perhaps collided – they were unmatched.

1994 brought CROOKT, CRACKT, OR FLY, an acoustic album of gentle guitar circumlocutions, isolated pianos and Grubbs' abstruse wordplay. Though interesting, this minimal collection ultimately suf-

towards O'Rourke's sort-after mainstream sound. But with such stark, recondite songs as "Blues Subtitled No Sense Of Wonder" and "A Puff Of Dew", it's certainly no pop-rock set. "The Seasons Reverse" bounces about with aggressive electric chords, a throbbing organ, and steel drums; "Black Horse," a Vietnamese folk song that Grubbs and O'Rourke had been playing live as an acoustic-guitar duel, reappears surrounded by sprightly strings, French horn, clarinet, and a dippy bass line. Perhaps most telling is the album's finale, "Bauchredner", which begins with classical guitar picking, then trots off into a music-for-the-masses sunset, as McEntire's rapid-fire drums kick the listener through a horn arrangement that wouldn't feel out of place in a blaxploitation movie.

The pair's respective post-Gastr work showed them pursuing their separate interests. Grubbs, a Ph.D. candidate at University of Chicago, found time to record a string of solo records (2000's THE SPECTRUM BETWEEN being his finest) featuring his delicate backdrops and introspective vocals, while O'Rourke, free to explore the chipper world of pop, became the 'it' boy of Chicago's scene. As a producer, he established a sound identifiable by gushy strings and wind instruments, often played by the same coterie of musicians. In addition to working with Chicago's Bobby Conn, Edith Frost, Smog, and the Aluminum Group, the fledgling producer got plucked to breath new life into recordings by rockers like Stereolab, Superchunk, and **SONIC YOUTH** (who O'Rourke subsequently joined as a full-time member). While his solo albums included extended flirtations with *musique concrète* (1995's TERMINAL PHARMACY) and guitar experimentation (1997's HAPPY DAYS), with the instrumental BAD TIMING (1997) O'Rourke reinvented himself as an indie-pop teddy bear whose overt influences leaned more towards Van Dyke Parks and Scott Walker records than, say, John Cage essays. EUREKA (1999) and its follow-up EP (HALFWAY TO A THREEWAY, 2000) even found the formerly tight-lipped musician singing: his voice is soft, a bit shaky, and surprisingly, pretty nice, even when covering Burt Bacharach. While the current stylistic incarnations of these two artists may seem pretty far apart, every note struck by either O'Rourke or Grubbs bears the inimitable mark of a Gastr Del Sol man.

fered from a heart as cold as ice. Later that year the duo refined their formula with MIRROR REPAIR, a five-song EP drenched in an eerie, post–nuclear meltdown vibe. With songs ranging from the acoustic folk snippet "Photographed Yawning" to the nine-minute piano work-out "Eight Corners" and the clamorous math-rock explosion "Dictionary Of Handwriting", this little record established Gastr as a force to be reckoned with. The following year their position in the alternative US scene was solidified by a seventeen-minute orchestral release (THE HARP FACTORY ON LAKE STREET), and collaborations with notorious drone artist **Tony Conrad** (in both a tour and "The Japanese Room At La Pagode", a split 7") and the reawakened **Red Krayola** collective. They also started a record label, Dexter's Cigar, dedicated to releasing lost treasures of experimental music by the likes of Circle X, Derek Bailey, Henry Kaiser, and Loren Mazzacane-Connors.

In the wake of this profusion of activity, Gastr Del Sol struck gold with their next album, UPGRADE & AFTERLIFE (1996). With string contributions from Conrad, horns from **Mats Gustafsson** and **Gene Coleman**, plus O'Rourke's tape cut-ups and white noise squeals, the record offered a cinematic amalgam of layered textures and atmospheric mood swings. This particularly held true for the album's lengthy bookends: the opener, "Our Exquisite Replica Of 'Eternity'", wheezes, cackles and, ultimately, bursts into a grand cry of horns; at the end of the set "Dry Bones In The Valley (I Saw The Light Come Shining 'Round And 'Round)" beautifully reworks a Fahey song and concludes with a hypnotic coda replete with a Conrad violin drone. UPGRADE & AFTERLIFE presented challenging musical concepts and juxtapositions in a fashion that was never overwhelming, rarely dull, and too darn lovely to be considered pretentious.

Completed just before O'Rourke dissolved the partnership, 1998's CAMOFLEUR took further steps

(•) **Mirror Repair** (Drag City, 1994).
Despite its meagre status as a five-song EP, MIRROR REPAIR opened the curtain on Gastr Del Sol's glory period. Cleanly recorded by Steve Albini, the arty set has moments of introspective folk as well as electric math rock and a stupendous nine-minute piano piece.

(•) **Upgrade & Afterlife** (Drag City, 1996).
Considered by many to be Gastr's finest moment, UPGRADE & AFTERLIFE opens with an ominous, cackling drone and closes with a smooth, lulling drone. It also contains the duo's most beautiful song – a cover of John Fahey's "Dry Bones In The Valley" – and finest album cover: a striking photograph of water exploding forth from a pair of Wellington boots.

(•) **Camofleur** (Drag City, 1998).
The band's final album is both their most pop-orientated and most peculiar. Bursting with frisky horns, strings,

organs and, on one song, a steel drum, CAMOFLEUR shows Gastr making the kind of crowd-pleasing music inattentive listeners assumed they would scorn.

Jay Ruttenberg

MARVIN GAYE

Born Washington, DC, April 2, 1939;
died April 1, 1984.

"Beyond sex is God."

The most talented of Motown's superstars alongside Stevie Wonder, **Marvin Gaye** was one of the greatest singers, songwriters and eclectic visionaries in all of soul music. Unlike most soul greats, he maintained an artistic evolution (albeit sometimes erratically) over the course of three decades, moving from hard-driving soul-pop to funk and dance grooves and, along with Wonder, Curtis Mayfield and Sly Stone, he was one of the few soul pioneers to craft lyrically ambitious, album-length singer-songwriter statements. While his temperamental nature fuelled his artistic innovations, it also contributed to a tumultuous private life that eventually culminated in a tragic death.

Born Marvin Gay, he began singing in doo-wop acts as a teenager in the mid-1950s. With the help of Bo Diddley, one of his early groups, The Marquees, recorded a flop single for the Okeh label. Harvey Fuqua, leader of the popular 50s doo-woppers The Moonglows (most famous for "The Ten Commandments Of Love"), made The Marquees into Moonglows in 1958, using them to replace the previous Moonglows line-up en masse. As a member of The Moonglows, Marvin sang backup on a few of their final Chess sides in the late 50s, taking lead on just the one number, "Mama Loocie".

Around the beginning of the 60s, Fuqua dissolved The Moonglows, but kept Marvin in tow. The pair relocated from Chicago to Detroit, where Fuqua married into the family of Motown boss Berry Gordy Jr, and joined the label's staff. At virtually the same time, Gaye also married one of Gordy's sisters, Anna, and started playing Motown sessions as a drummer (that's him on the Marvelettes' "Please Mr. Postman").

The close family ties couldn't have hurt Gaye's prospects at Motown, and by 1961 he was recording for the label as a solo artist. Surprisingly, he didn't debut as a soul/R&B singer, or even a doo-wop one, but as an urbane jazz crooner in the mould of Nat 'King' Cole. According to Smokey Robinson, Gaye harboured aspirations of becoming the black Sinatra, and Marvin would periodically persist in following that dream on stage and in the studio over the following few years.

A 1961 album in that vein flopped, as did his first few singles. He may have been on the verge of being dropped from the label when he gave in and recorded a gritty early soul number, "Stubborn Kind

Of Fella", in 1962. That single became his first R&B Top 10 hit, and "Hitch Hike", "Pride And Joy" and "Can I Get A Witness" followed in short order, establishing Gaye in both the R&B and pop markets. These songs were also some of the earliest and best examples of Motown's combination of gospel fervour and pop polish, though Marvin would lean more toward the funkier side of that equation than most of Motown's stars.

In hindsight, Gaye would complain that he only sang rock'n'soul as a last resort, and that his heart lay in pop-jazz. Everyone but Gaye himself, however, seems to agree that he was a great soul singer, and a mediocre jazz vocalist. This seems to be one case where the pressure to be commercial made a great artist out of an also-ran, rather than vice versa.

In the mid 60s, he reeled off a first-class string of tough-tender hits, including "How Sweet It Is", "I'll Be Doggone", "Ain't That Peculiar", "One More Heartache" and "You're A Wonderful One". He also became the partner of choice for Motown's leading ladies, recording hit duets with Mary Wells, Kim Weston and, especially, Tammi Terrell (who died in 1970 at the age of 24). More than most Motown artists, however, Gaye's talents became constrained by the label's more formulaic practices. Although he had helped pen several of his early hits, he was usually assigned outside material in the last half of the 1960s. He also had his own ideas about production, which didn't always jibe with the staff producers who oversaw his sessions.

By the end of the 1960s, Gaye's records began to take a more progressive turn under the auspices of producer Norman Whitfield (who was bringing Motown into the psychedelic and funk age via his work with The Temptations). Their best and most innovative collaboration, "I Heard It Through The Grapevine", was initially rejected for release by Berry Gordy. After Gladys Knight & The Pips made #2 with their version, Gaye's ominous reading was issued, and only a year after Knight's rendition Marvin's topped the charts, becoming the best-selling Motown single of the decade.

By the early 1970s, Gaye wanted total creative control of both his material and his production. That wasn't the way Berry Gordy did things, and the Motown chief also didn't think Gaye's new songs – addressing not just romance, but ghetto life, ecology and social confusion – were sufficiently commercial. Gaye threatened to leave Motown before Gordy relented and released WHAT'S GOING ON in 1971. One of the great soul albums, it was one of the first to be organized as a flowing, wall-to-wall statement. It was also a big commercial success, making the Top 10 and spinning off three monster hits, "Inner City Blues", "Mercy Mercy Me" and the title track.

With WHAT'S GOING ON Gaye had finally found a way to vent his passion for jazz by using jazz elements to serve the soul-funk groove, rather than trying to pretend he was a jazz singer. Gaye took the groove into even jazzier, more introspective categories on the early 70s singles, "Trouble Man" and "You're The Man", but by the time of 1973's LET'S GET IT ON he had refocused his attentions on sensual pleasures, albeit without scaling back the sophistication of his production. The result was his most commercially successful effort – the album went to #2 in America, and the title track became his second #1 single.

Critical opinion on the rest of Gaye's work is divided, but most would agree that he never matched the consistency and lyrical poignancy of WHAT'S GOING ON again. That didn't mean that he couldn't produce interesting material. 1977's "Got To Give It Up" was one of the best disco hits, and his final chart-topper. 1978's HERE MY DEAR was one of the few avowed concept albums in black pop. The double-album chronicle of his divorce from Anna Gordy, however, was not his best or most subtle music. Nor was its motivation wholly artistic – it was recorded after a judge ordered Marvin to give Anna the proceeds from his next album, as part of their divorce settlement.

In the early 1980s, Gaye's personal life was in rough shape. A second marriage had failed, and his substance abuse (particularly with cocaine) was escalating. Owing the Internal Revenue Service millions of dollars, he moved to Europe, where he recorded IN OUR LIFETIME in 1981. This and the more successful MIDNIGHT LOVE (released on Columbia in 1982, ending his twenty-year association with Motown) saw Gaye's music take on more of a spiritual hue, and he continued to mix and match funk and pop in unusual fashions, though without as much freshness as his work of the early 1970s.

The huge hit "Sexual Healing" was MIDNIGHT LOVE's best track, and indeed the highlight of Gaye's final years. Gaye seemed to be riding a remarkable artistic and commercial comeback, but his life was spiralling out of control. His drug problems worsened, as did his depression, and he threatened suicide several times. Much of his final months were spent in the Los Angeles home of his parents, and marked by increasing conflict with his father, with whom Marvin had feuded throughout his life. On April 1, 1984, just one day before his 45th birthday, Gaye was shot dead by his father, ending a career as remarkable as any in the history of African-American music. His story is best told by David Ritz in the biography *Divided Soul*.

Since his death, Marvin's recorded legacy has been fairly extensively plundered with more than twenty full length albums – of varying quality – released in the last two decades. Those who haven't yet discovered just how good Marvin could be are sure to be won over by ANTHOLOGY, Motown's 1995 tribute.

⊙ **What's Going On** (1971; Motown).
Good and important though it is, this album is just a bit overrated. The hits ("What's Going On", "Mercy Mercy Me" and "Inner City Blues") tower over the rest of the tracks, which sometimes give way to meandering introspection. Overall, though, it's easily his best non-compilation album.

⊙ **Anthology** (1995; Motown).
Double-CD retrospective crammed with Gaye's big hits of the 60s and 70s, as well as some choice obscurities. Also includes his hit duets with Mary Wells, Kim Weston, Tammi Terrell and Diana Ross.

⊙ **The Master 1961–1984** (1995; Motown).
This four-CD retrospective includes all of the essential hits and duets, some interesting B-sides and unreleased material, and key album tracks. Most fans are better off with ANTHOLOGY, but those with the budget and interest for more won't be disappointed.

⊙ **Early Classics** (1998; Spectrum).
The title says it all. Gaye himself may have rated his own 70s material more highly than the 60s Tamla-pop featured here, but there's not a single forgettable track on this collection.

Richie Unterberger

GAYE BYKERS ON ACID

Formed Leicester, England, 1986; disbanded early 90s.

From great beginnings, when they provided a world of hip-hop beats married to psychedelic guitars and rockist lyrics, **Gaye Bykers On Acid** lapsed into chaos, uncertain which trend to pursue. Still, theirs was a four-year career of wit and craziness worth a place in any contemporary rock book.

The band was fronted by flamboyant vocalist **Mary Mary** (aka Ian Garfield Hoxley), aided and abetted by **Robber** (Ian Reynolds; bass), **Tony** (Anthony Horsfall; guitar), **Kevin Hyde** (drums) and **DJ Rocket Ronnie**. Like Crazyhead and Pop Will Eat Itself, they became key players in the so-called 'grebo' scene, which mixed traditional rock structures with psychedelia and dance. The Bykers pioneered the 'crusty' style favoured by many British alternative bands in the early 90s, and fraternized with members of similar subcultures, such as The Mutoid Waste Organisation, who built a special vehicle for them out of recovered scrap metal. There were also their alter egos to contend with, namely the Lesbian Dopeheads On Mopeds (allegedly from New Zealand), and Rektum, the 'Eastern European Thrash Metal Band'.

The Bykers received music press support for a few months after the release of the EP NOSEDIVE KARMA (1987), the main selling point of which was its driving hip-hop beat, then unheard of in the world of indie rock. As a result of the publicity they were signed to Virgin, at a time when the major labels could do no right in the eyes of the indie community.

Their first LP, DRILL YOUR OWN HOLE (1987) – a vinyl release which encouraged you to do just that – was eagerly awaited, but proved to be a letdown. The basic sound of the EP proved incapable of sustaining itself throughout the course of an album, although a few tracks stood out. It was also clear that the Bykers were unhappy in the role of a major-label band, and soon they returned to making records on their 'own' independent label, PFX. PFX also became an alternative moniker for the band, releasing dubby, dancey records such as SPACE and PERNICIOUS NONSENSE.

This direction had been indicated by the style of their later releases as Gaye Bykers On Acid, which sampled dub bands like Tackhead, and featured extended dance remixes. Singer Mary Mary also did a stint as vocalist in **Pigface**, and concentrated more on dance music, until he eventually became a club DJ. Subsequent releases were increasingly desperate until the Bykers eventually disintegrated, and the various members assimilated into the clubland culture they had once skirted.

⊙ **Drill Your Own Hole** (1987; Virgin; currently unavailable).
Something of a missed opportunity, but there you go.

⊙ **Everything's Groovy** (2001; Cherry Red).
A collection of the pre-Virgin stuff – a great way to remember them.

Jonathan Bell

BOB GELDOF

Born Dun Laoghaire, Ireland, 1954.

Bob Geldof, co-writer of the best-selling single ever, and orchestrator of the world's biggest rock concert and TV music event, began as a journalist for the *NME*, then became the extrovert, angry frontman with **THE BOOMTOWN RATS**, an Irish New Wave outfit whose popularity had begun to wane by the early 80s. In addition he was known as a mouth-on-a-stick, a dedicated self-publicist, and an occasional actor, notably in Alan Parker's movie of Pink Floyd's *The Wall* (1982).

Since becoming 'the only person to receive a knighthood for saying "fuck" on television' – referring to his impassioned pleas for donations during the broadcast of Live Aid in July 1985 – Geldof has married and divorced journalist and TV presenter Paula Yates, written his autobiography *Is That It?*, recorded four albums, gone on countless mini-tours, and co-founded a youth-orientated TV production company, Planet 24.

While *Is That It?* was a bestseller, and Planet 24 has been an unabashed success, Geldof's musical output has been less so, and has seldom been as hard-hitting as his personality. A year after Live Aid, he joined forces with **Dave Stewart**, who produced his debut solo LP, DEEP IN THE HEART OF NOWHERE (1986). Its critical and commercial reception was lukewarm, but he fared better with a single, "The Great Song Of Indifference" (1990), on which he poked fun at his public persona, singing 'I don't care if a nation starves' and doing an irreverent Irish jig in the video. Both the song – and the year's album, THE VEGETARIANS OF LOVE – hit the British charts and might have been taken for the beginnings of a comeback, but his 1992 album, THE HAPPY CLUB, again flopped.

The tenth anniversary of Live Aid in 1995 coincided with a fresh bout of media clamour around Geldof when Yates left him for the late **INXS** frontman Michael Hutchence. To cap it all, Yates then initiated divorce proceedings on the grounds of Geldof's adultery. The harrowing saga was to develop yet another tragic dimension in September 2000 with the discovery of Yates's body at her London home.

Geldof, who had taken time out of recording for several years, returned in 2001 with a new album, SEX AGE AND DEATH. Although even considerable media promotion could not propel it into the charts, its lyrical directness suggested a cathartic experience in its composer. Meantime, Planet 24's success with *The Big Breakfast*'s ten-year run on British television was to expand into worldwide recognition with the reality game show *Survivor*. Geldof himself has remained politically active, not least in his campaigns of awareness over the Third World debt crisis.

Bob Geldof

⊙ **The Vegetarians Of Love** (1990; Mercury/Atlantic).
The description 'folksy' covers every track on the album, yet there is a considerable range evident here – the notion of mixing Cajun music with Irish is almost certainly a first.

Bob Geldof and The Boomtown Rats

⊙ **Loudmouth** (1994; Vertigo).
A useful compilation of solo and group projects.

Matthew Grant

GENE

Formed Watford, England, 1993.

Gene came into being after a motorway accident involving aspiring band Spin left their bassist badly injured. Soon after, the group disbanded, and after a period of adjustment and convalescence, guitarist **Steve Mason**, whose brother had been so badly hurt, and drummer **Matt James** decided to continue their careers in music. **Kevin Miles**, a bassist friend of Matt's, moved down to London and the three set about finding a singer. The search proved fruitless, until Steve spotted fey Welshman **Martin Rossiter**, possessor of a voice 'as pure as a choirboy'.

The next year was spent rehearsing and writing songs before embarking on gigs that were enough to persuade journalists Keith Cameron and Roy Wilkinson to set up their own Costermonger label specifically to release Gene's debut single, "For The Dead". Issued in April 1994, it was a haunting elegy, displaying a deft craftsmanship and songwriting skill, and almost all 1994 copies sold out on the day of release.

With Britpop rivalry high on the agenda in the summer of 1994, Gene had chosen the best and worst time to emerge, and reactions to them were either highly complimentary or equally derisive. Unfavourable comparisons with The Smiths were to haunt them; but, undeterred, the band persisted in producing gentle songs of introspection, revealing a maturity not often seen in the cartoon antics of their contemporaries.

"Be My Light, Be My Guide", an uplifting song to a London cabbie, became an independent #1 in the UK in July 1994, a success that resulted in Gene being courted by dozens of labels before signing with Polydor for the rest of the world and staying with Costermonger in their homeland. High-profile gigs followed, and critical acclaim accompanied the release of "Sleep Well Tonight' in September 1994. Indeed, by early 1995, Gene were honoured at the NME BRAT Awards for *Best New Act*.

After another single, "Haunted By You", Gene's debut album, OLYMPIAN (1995) was released to a mixed reception, the general consensus being that they had almost made a fine record. A series of soaring anthems and soothing ballads, it was sensitive without sliding into limp sentimentality. It reached the UK Top 10, while the title track was later issued as a single in its own right.

1996 began with a stopgap compilation, TO SEE THE LIGHTS, made up of B-sides, rerecordings and live numbers, and some were still uncertain whether Gene were anything more than a Smiths convention for the 90s. However, DRAWN TO THE DEEP END (1997) was a magnificent, lush return to form.

Apart from some low-key touring, Gene kept their heads down throughout much of 1998 as they worked on their new album. Martin became a father in 1999 and also began sporting a severe skinhead haircut. A new single, "As Good As It Gets", was released in February 1999. A sly attack on New Labour, the band saw it as representing their more political side, although its later use as the theme tune to the characterless TV sitcom *Sam's Game* (2001), starring *Big Brother* host Davina McCall, suggested that such connections had been somewhat over-looked by the programme's producers.

Their most mature recorded statement, REVELATIONS (1999) captured their raw, live-sounding approach, but wasn't commercially strong enough to stop them being dropped by Polydor. It was two and a half years before the appearance of their fourth album LIBERTINE (2001) – released on their own Contra Records – shortly after a singles compilation entitled AS GOOD AS IT GETS had hit the shelves.

⊙ **Olympian** (1995; Costermonger/Polydor).
Listen and enter a world of 'cheap, dead rooms' and unrequited love. A collection of delicate murmurs and sporadic rock-outs that aspires towards poetry and sometimes touches it.

⊙ **Libertine** (2001; Contra).
LIBERTINE does little to alter the band's stroke, but like all Gene sets it does manage to speak directly to anyone who's ever suffered the indignity of being dumped by a partner they still love. The standout here is the heart-rending first single "Is It Over".

Maxine McCaghy

GENE LOVES JEZEBEL

Formed London, 1981.

An odd bunch of vagabonds, **Gene Loves Jezebel** migrated from Wales to London in 1981 to join a thriving post-punk scene that included the likes of The Cult, Spear Of Destiny, Love And Rockets, and Flesh For Lulu. Signed to Situation 2

Records after their first gig, the band – then comprising identical twins **Jay** (guitar and vocals) and **Michael Aston** (vocals), **Ian Hudson** (guitar), **Julianne Regan** (bass) and various drummers – released the obscure single "Shaving My Neck". Opening slots with Nico and UK Decay were followed by a BBC Radio 1 appearance (soon after which Julianne Regan left to form **ALL ABOUT EVE**). Their second single "Screaming (For Emmalene)" landed them their first real tour, opening for X-Mal Deutschland.

The band's sound at the time boasted screeching guitars against a tribal exchange of vocals between Jay and Michael, with firm and pounding bass and drums filling in the edges. PROMISE (1983), their first LP, secured them a John Peel session, which was followed by extensive touring of the UK and Europe. While on tour they caught the eye of John Cale, who whisked the band off to New York for recording sessions (never released). Returning to the UK, and now joined by **Chris Bell** (drums) and **Peter Rizzo** (bass), the Jezebels recorded a well-received album, IMMIGRANT. This infused a new element of pop, and even dance, into the chaos, and reached #2 in the independent charts. During the following tour **Marcus Gilvear** replaced Chris Bell.

The Jezebels recorded their last single for Situation 2, "Desire", before touring the United States. Ian left midway through the tour, replaced by **James Stevenson** (ex-**GENERATION X**). 1986's LP DISCOVER followed, its sound even more pop-injected with a heavy Mick Ronson influence discernible in James's guitar playing. The singles "Sweetest Thing", "Heartache", and "Desire" all received good airplay, with "Desire" being included in the movie *She's Having A Baby*. After the tour Marcus left the band and Chris Bell returned.

THE HOUSE OF DOLLS (1987) included three splendid singles – "Gorgeous", "The Motion Of Love", and "Suspicion". Another US tour with New Order and PiL resulted in the (by now customary) loss of a band member – this time Michael – leaving the band with Jay as the sole vocalist. 1990 saw the release of KISS OF LIFE, featuring "Jealous", their most successful single. The band then signed for Savage Records and released HEAVENLY BODIES (1992), featuring "Josephina", a major European hit. During their promotional tour of the US, Savage Records folded, leaving the Jezebels without a record label.

Michael re-emerged in 1993 with the band **Edith Grove** and a single, "Rivers Edge", followed by a solo acoustic record, WHY ME, WHY THIS, WHY NOW. He also assembled a Jezebel double live album, IN THE AFTERGLOW, featuring complete sets from shows in 1988 and 1993. A brief 'reunion' tour featuring the two brothers and a backing band was followed by a more official, and successful, reunion that included Peter Rizzo and James Stevenson. Confusingly, Michael has also been known to play under the name Gene Loves Jezebel (featuring

Michael Aston) with members of the backing band he and Jay used on the first leg of the reunion.

Jay's solo album, UNPOPULAR SONGS (1998), made with help from James, displayed a new maturity in his songwriting. UNPOPULAR SONGS became the foundation for the latest Jezebel album, VII (1999) – initially released as the fan-club album YOU'LL LOVE IT. VII is probably the least dance/pop-orientated album they have released since PROMISE – the rocky leading tracks "Love Keeps Dragging Me Down", "Welcome To LA" and "Who Wants To Go To Heaven?" typifying the band's new sound.

In late 1998 Gene Loves Jezebel (now featuring Jay, James and Peter, but without Michael) made their return to the UK stage with their first London appearance in years. 1999 saw the release of a tribute album, DESIRE, with remixes from the likes of The Mission, Spahn Ranch, Kevin Haskins (Love And Rockets), Leather Strip, and Rosetta Stone, while Beggars Banquet issued VOODOO DOLLIES, a solid 'best of' set. All this activity, however, didn't alter the fact that the band was still in a peculiar state of duality with the twins releasing various albums under the Gene Loves Jezebel tag. Most recently, Michael's version of the band released GIVING UP THE GHOST (2000), while Jay's version issued ACCEPT NO SUBSTITUTE (2002), a double-CD live collection concentrating on their greatest hits.

⊙ **The House Of Dolls** (1987; Beggars' Banquet/Geffen).
A step up from the excitement caused by DISCOVER. This, the last album to feature both brothers, is a glam-driven, tongue-in-cheek, pop experience. Perhaps the best 'summer' album ever recorded.

⊙ **Heavenly Bodies** (1992; Savage).
An extension of the direction taken on the HOUSE OF DOLLS album. Glam-pop mixed with the addition of more gentle moments.

⊙ **VII** (1999; Robison).
Lacking in the pure pop that coloured their early hits, but still possessing a solid core of strong writing. Brilliant.

Ryan Michael Painter

GENERATION X

Formed London, 1976; disbanded 1981.

Punk band **Generation X** were formed by vocalist **BILLY IDOL** (William Broad), one of the 'Bromley Contingent' of Sex Pistols fans based in South London, along with ex-Chelsea members **Tony James** (bass) and **John Towe** (drums). After recruiting guitarist **Bob Andrews**, they debuted in December 1976, securing a regular spot at seminal London punk club The Roxy.

These were very hip beginnings, but the band was always a little too rock'n'roll to find a place in the hearts of purist punks. Most bands were spat at out of 'respect''; Generation X received the treatment because they were genuinely despised. Idol himself was a bleached-blond strutting peacock, spouting cod-hooligan lyrics about fights between punks and

teds. The band's sound was no more endearing: a weedy commercialized form of punk that exhibited little of the menace of other bands on the circuit. In retrospect, the songs were enjoyable, well-played power pop, but in the context of punk rock's first wave, Generation X were simply too tame.

Still, almost from the beginning, they were wooed by the major labels, and in July 1977 they signed to Chrysalis and released their first single, "Your Generation". A minor UK chart hit, it was a typically supercharged adolescent rant about a war between young and old: 'The end must justify the means/Your generation don't mean a thing to me!'

By now, the Idol–James songwriting partnership had become prolific, while Towe had been replaced by former Subway Sect drummer **Mark Laff**. Live, the band were improving dramatically, and a residency at London's Marquee saw them garnering a large, if mostly very young, following. Indeed, whereas many of their contemporaries proved unable to maintain their initial momentum, Generation X seemed to go from strength to strength, fitting smoothly into the less confrontational post-punk New Wave movement.

1978–mid-1979 were vintage years. The GENERATION X (1978) album charted, while the single "Ready Steady Go" confounded punk fans by eulogizing the 60s. An almost teenybop piece of fluff, it contained references to bands from the period, and a chorus celebrating the TV show hostess 'Cathy McGow-ow-ow-ow-an!' The band's finest song from this period, "Kiss Me Deadly", was not a hit, but was a perfectly structured mix of vocal melodies and power chords, and demonstrated just how professional they had become since their Roxy days. (The song was also featured in Lech Kowalski's 1981 movie *DOA*.)

1979 also saw the band's biggest hit single, the banal "King Rocker", while the second album, VALLEY OF THE DOLLS (1979), was produced by Mott The Hoople's Ian Hunter. However, their fortunes began to wane in 1980, as they changed their name to Gen X – always the favoured moniker among their fan base. Despite releasing the excellent "Dancing With Myself", a lively pop tune with lyrics referring to masturbation, the single only scraped into the lower reaches of the charts.

Soon afterwards, Laff and Andrews quit, to be replaced by **Terry Chimes** (ex-Clash) and **James Stephenson** (another former Chelsea man). One last album, the less than brilliant KISS ME DEADLY (1981), disappeared almost immediately, and led to a bust-up between Idol and Chrysalis over creative control. In disgust, Idol left for the US and a solo career, Chimes rejoined The Clash, while Tony James re-emerged in 1985 with the overhyped 'art-prank' band **Sigue Sigue Sputnik**.

⊙ **Generation X Perfect Hits, 1975–1981** (1991; Chrysalis).
With a track listing thoughtfully selected by Idol and James, this compilation of the band's finest moments also features some unreleased treats, including a radio session version of "Day By Day" from 1977.

Roger Sabin

GENESIS

Formed Godalming, England, 1967.

Opinions divide pretty strongly over **Genesis**. The archetypal progressive-rock band of the 1970s – and, as such, the model for everyone from early Queen to Supertramp to Marillion – they mutated over the next decade into a distinctly unprogressive but hugely successful soft-rock giant: prog-lite, if you will. It is an odd tale and one mirrored in the side-careers of the band's two (ex-)vocalists. **PETER GABRIEL**, domineering and quirky when he was in the band, became a great pop singer and patron saint to the world music community, whilst **Phil Collins** turned out to be Elton John.

The group formed in 1967 at Charterhouse, one of England's oldest public (by which is meant private) schools. **Tony Banks** (keyboards) and **Mike Rutherford** (bass) teamed up with Peter Gabriel (vocals), **Anthony Phillips** (guitar) and **Chris Stewart** (drums). With the help of Charterhouse oldboy and novelty hit-maker Jonathan King, they were signed to Decca, who issued their first two singles, "The Silent Sun" and "A Winter's Tale", in early 1968. Flower-powery ditties, they disappeared without trace, though the label showed faith, financing an (unremarkable) debut LP, entitled, presaging their development of the concept album, FROM GENESIS TO REVELATION (1968). By this time Chris Stewart (whose parents felt he might better himself staying on at school) had been replaced on drums by **John Silver**, who in turn gave way to **John Mayhew**. The album failed to fit the pop format demanded, and Decca and King soon lost interest.

At this point Genesis came close to folding due to a lack of commercial appeal. Bottom of the bill on

the college circuit, they limped into 1970, before coming to the attention of Tony Stratton-Smith, then in the process of creating his own label, Charisma, future home to a roster of prog-minded hippie bands. Genesis happily signed up and, given some artistic control and a helpful producer, John Anthony, began work on what they came to see as the first proper Genesis album in the summer of 1970. Released the following year, TRESPASS proved a substantial cult and critical success. Its style seems extraordinarily dated now but it showed the group experimenting with song structures (the very hub of prog) and elaborate lyrical themes. It had some good tunes, too – prog but catchy – and a first rocking anthem in the nine-minute workout, "Knife".

The band prepared to tour, having first replaced Phillips and Mayhew with ex-child actor and Flaming Youth drummer Phil Collins and ex-Quiet World guitarist **Steve Hackett**. The classic Genesis line-up was now in place and their 1971 tour has entered fan legend. It took rock into a new level of theatricality, Gabriel appearing in huge papier-mâché masks and clownish make-up, and reciting stories aloud, with theatrical improvisations, between songs. He would push these effects further and further with each new tour, and so would his imitators, but at this moment it all seemed wondrously original.

After Gabriel broke his ankle during a show, the group took time out to write and record a new set of songs, issued in 1971 as NURSERY CRYME. It showed the new line-up jelling (Hackett and Banks to fine effect with guitar–organ interplay), and composing songs that (if not yet quite a concept suite) more or less followed each other as movements. Helped by the band's live following, it edged into the UK Top 40.

It was with FOXTROT (1972), however, that Genesis scored their first major critical success. The album signalled the group's move from cult to chart success in Britain, reaching #12, and led to their first major headline tour, as well as some successful US club dates. Genesis had arrived and, at this stage, they were quite disarmingly hip.

Capitalizing on their enviable live reputation, the band issued GENESIS LIVE (1973), which went Top 10 in the UK, then took a break from their exhausting touring schedule to record new material. Eagerly awaited, this emerged in October as SELLING ENGLAND BY THE POUND. It charted at #3 in the UK, allowed Gabriel to show off his radical shaven forehead look and provided the group's first UK hit single, "I Know What I Like (In Your Wardrobe)".

As efficient new management from Tony Smith forged a successful US tour in early 1974, rock superstardom seemed imminent. Genesis went for the grand gesture, releasing at the end of the year a double album 'rock opera', THE LAMB LIES DOWN ON BROADWAY. Many fans see this as the group's finest moment, and the culmination of Gabriel's genius, for he alone wrote its songs, telling of a New York street hustler character called Rael. It was an impressive performance, and again had some strong songs – "Counting Out Time", "The Carpet Crawlers" – which propelled it to #10 in the UK album charts and a best-so-far #41 in the US. But LAMB was grandiosity personified, and a 102-date world tour, where each and every night they played the whole record live, was probably not a good idea, exacerbating the pressure between Gabriel (now appearing fairly nutty, with his shaven hair now grown back to jaw-length) and the rest of the group.

In May 1975 Gabriel announced his departure from the group and the music press began writing their obituaries. In the event, they were (at least) twenty years premature, as the remaining members regrouped, auditioned for a new singer, and ended up propelling Phil Collins from the drum stool. In retrospect it seems an obvious move, though few at the time shared the confidence of Charisma boss Tony Stratton-Smith, who gushed: 'He sounds more like Peter Gabriel than Peter Gabriel!'

In early 1976, Collins debuted on TRICK OF THE TAIL, which matched SELLING ENGLAND by reaching #3 in the UK, and saw a steady rise in the US, peaking at #31. The band, clearly, were more than Gabriel, and set out to show they could still do it live, too, with Collins surrendering drumming duties to **Bill Bruford** (ex-Yes, King Crimson) on tour. Collins, amazingly, had no problems matching Gabriel's vocals on the old favourites.

WIND AND WUTHERING (1977) continued the same musical direction as TRICK – still essentially theatrical prog-rock, with little hint of the AOR pop to come. It was promoted with a massive seven-month tour, replete with a light and laser show, on which **Chester Thompson** (ex-Weather Report) took over on drums. His brief tenure is recorded on a second live set, SECONDS OUT – the most appealing of the group's several concert albums.

The tour over, Steve Hackett left to embark upon a solo career, leaving the line-up – Phil Collins, Tony Banks and Mike Rutherford – that remained until

GENESIS

SELLING ENGLAND BY THE POUND

1996. This proved a crucial move as the trio moved swiftly from their prog-rock origins towards a light rock sound, of the type that would dominate the charts in the 1980s. It was partially a response to the tidal wave of punk across British pop, which Genesis was lucky to survive. But the change also derived from the easier, more relaxed mood of the group post-Gabriel and Hackett. In 1978 they released their most accessible set so far, AND THEN THERE WERE THREE. This included a significant chart single, "Follow You Follow Me", and was, overall, a successful shift to atmospheric adult-pop.

Old prog fans left the story here, but a lot more arrived to take their place as DUKE (1980) began a series of UK chart-topping albums, abetted by quality singles, in this case "Turn It On Again" and "Misunderstanding". DUKE was an unrepentant step toward a state-of-the-art commercial rock direction, using drum machines and synthezisers in tight but weightless AOR arrangements. Ever more confident in this new mode, Genesis quickly recorded the album, ABACAB (1981), the title punning on their gleeful acceptance of conventional song structure. It was their first home-made album, recorded at their own studio, The Farm, in Surrey, and used session musicians for the first time, including the Earth, Wind And Fire horn section on the hit "No Reply At All". Yet another live release, the perfunctory THREE SIDES LIVE (1982), capitalized on their now massive success.

Genesis were finally big-time rock stars after a decade of work. But, having hit on a formula that sold, they would not develop one inch in the next decade, at least with the band. During the 1980s, all of the members became involved in spin-off careers: Phil Collins with AOR pop; Rutherford as **Mike + The Mechanics**; Banks with movie soundtracks. The Genesis Saturday job, meanwhile, continued with GENESIS (1983), their first platinum-rated US hit, selling over three million copies worldwide, and spawning the single "That's All" and another highly professional world tour. INVISIBLE TOUCH (1986), although calculated and oddly emotionless AOR, sold even better, spending four months in the US Top 10 and producing a full hand of Top 5 US singles. Hits like the title track or "In Too Deep" were by now barely distinguishable from Collins' songs as a solo artist, but the fans lapped it up, three million witnessing the group's ten-month world stadium tour.

When Genesis released WE CAN'T DANCE (1991), after a five-year break, it headed straight up the charts worldwide, and the fans were happy to shell out for two more live albums, THE WAY WE WALK – THE SHORTS and THE LONGS, in 1993. The former consisted mainly of the 80s singles; the latter, if you listened closely amid the medleys, still betrayed a hint of old prog roots, including a 90s rendition of "Musical Box" from NURSERY CRYME, half a lifetime away.

In March 1996, when Collins announced he had left the band, it looked like the end. However, Banks and Rutherford continued the Genesis name and auditioned new vocalists for a projected album – 'darker, heavier and back to the old melodrama' – released in spring 1997. The lucky vocalist, **Ray Wilson**, was plucked from obscurity (he'd previously been the frontman for **Stiltskin**) and the album he sang, CALLING ALL STATIONS, had all the promised gloom and despondency, drummed to perfection by **Nir Z**.

Since then things have been relatively quiet and low-key on the band front, with the only new product being the result of a thorough root around the vaults, as is currently the fashion with artists boasting a mature and wealthy fan base. Two beefy multi-CD retrospectives – ARCHIVES VOL 1 1967-75 and ARCHIVES VOL 2 1976-92 – covering the Gabriel and Collins periods, emerged in the late 90s. The later material was then neatly summed up by 1999's TURN IT ON AGAIN.

- ● **Trespass** (1971; Virgin).
  The early Genesis style: extended musical work-outs, fantastic lyrics, and the then-fashionable attempt to make rock sound more English.

- ● **Foxtrot** (1972; Virgin).
  The most successfully realized and appealing example of golden-age Genesis, at their prog peak on the likes of "Supper's Ready" and "Watcher Of The Skies".

- ● **Selling England By The Pound** (1973; Virgin).
  OK, some prefer this to FOXTROT, and it does feature "I Know What I Like (In Your Wardrobe)", their first real pop song.

- ● **And Then There Were Three** (1978; Virgin).
  A lesson in rock survival. With Gabriel and Hackett gone, and clearly forgotten, the stripped-down pop-rock of these songs suggested a brighter future than anyone could have expected.

- ● **Archive 1967–1975** (1998; Virgin).
  Mammoth four-CD collection, with one entire disc comprising rare demo and radio session material; one of live recordings from the SELLING ENGLAND era; and – recorded live on January 24, 1974 at the Shrine in Los Angeles – the full LAMB LIES DOWN extravaganza. Not the ideal introduction for the casual browser but a prize for any committed fan.

Neil Blackmore & Almo Miles

GENTLE GIANT

Formed Portsmouth, England, 1969; disbanded 1980.

Gentle Giant were formed from the ashes of Simon Dupree and The Big Sound, who had hit the UK Top 10 in 1967 with the psychedelic "Kites". Giant were a more adventurous and idiosyncratic outfit, featuring the **Shulman** brothers – **Derek** (vocals), **Ray** (bass) and **Phil** (horns) – alongside **Gary Green** (guitar), **Kerry Minnear** (keyboards) and **Martin Smith (**drums).

Their debut LP, GENTLE GIANT (1970), set the tone for an eclectic and complex musical career, boasting eccentric time signatures and a wide range of instrumentation (strings, recorders, saxophones) with a subtle heaviness never far behind. ACQUIRING THE TASTE (1971) and THREE FRIENDS (1972) consolidated the style, gaining them a small but fervent

following. The music was a little too eccentric and uncompromising for mass acceptance; though, on the plus side, it avoided the pomp of many of their peers, approaching complicated material with a playful, personal and often humorous touch.

In 1973, the band decided on new drummer **John Weathers**, but a fourth album, OCTOPUS (reissued by Mercury in 1997) showed business pretty much as usual, and a Roger Dean cover ensured their reputation as a 'progressive' band. Their next, IN A GLASS HOUSE (1973), ran into a minor problem when Capitol considered it too offbeat for US release, though ironically it became one of America's top import albums, indicative of a growing fan base, and 1974's THE POWER AND THE GLORY (1974) actually broke into the US Top 50. FREE HAND (1975), showing the Giant at their most consistent and accessible, was followed by INTERVIEW (1976) and a world tour, later captured on a live album, PLAYING THE FOOL (1977).

With punk spearheading an attack on the old prog dinosaurs – and 'Gentle Giant' was as prog-dinosaur a name as any in the business – the band responded with THE MISSING PIECE (1977), a collection of concise and relatively populist songs, though retaining the band's cleverness and sensitivity. GIANT FOR A DAY (1978), however, suggested that the band were uncomfortable with this new direction: weak and insipid, it displayed little of their past intricacy or commitment. It was followed by a stronger and darker release, CIVILIAN (1980), after which Gentle Giant broke up.

Ray Shulman went on to become a producer for indie bands (notably The Sugarcubes), while his brother Derek became head of A&R at Phonogram. Meanwhile, most of Gentle Giant's output has been rereleased on CD, and their intimate, virtuosic and challenging music is still worth investigating.

- ● **Edge Of Twilight** (1996; Vertigo).
  An exemplary collection of digitally remastered tracks, compiled by a fan for Vertigo. Frustratingly, the material is solely from five of their first six albums, but still manages to cram a double CD with excellent and accessible examples of their versatility and talent. Can't wait for Volume II ...

- ● **Live On The King Biscuit Flower Hour** (1998; KBFH).
  Recorded in 1975, this features some prime cuts from GG at their peak.

Adam Kimmel

GERMS

Formed Los Angeles, 1977; disbanded 1980.

The Germs are too often seen as little more than a historical footnote to guitarist **Pat Smear**'s revitalized career in the 90s, firstly with **NIRVANA** on their swansong live album, UNPLUGGED, and then with **FOO FIGHTERS**. This, unquestionably, is a travesty.

The Germs were formed by **Darby Crash** (aka Jan Paul Beahm; vocals), a combination of Johnny Rotten and Sid Vicious rolled into one obnoxious blast of phlegm and fury, along with Smear, **Lorna Doom** (bass) and future **GO-GO'S** girl **Belinda Carlisle** (drums). Carlisle was subsequently replaced by numerous sticksmen (notably Don Bolles) as the quartet set about their brief but chaotic career, playing the seediest of seedy holes and assaulting any audience who dared enter. The music, a vulgar rock-'n'roll roar, was as confrontational as the disturbed high-school dropout who fronted it.

The group only recorded one proper album, GI (1979), but in so doing built a bridge for American punk between the New York No-Wavers such as Television and the LA hardcore movement spearheaded by Black Flag. Produced by Joan Jett, the album's savagery lay in the combination of Smear's staccato riffing and Crash's absolute possession by the music, articulating his spiritual horror in maniacal vocal spasms.

Many critics have compared the significance of GI with that of the Sex Pistols' NEVER MIND THE BOLLOCKS. This may be an overstatement, but there was little doubt that Crash was committed to the cause of punk rock, and the risks that came with it: the singer was found dead of a heroin overdose on the eve of John Lennon's assassination in 1980.

The rest of the Germs' discography consisted of barely listenable live recordings and cobbled-together studio outtakes. A more worthy research project would be to search out a copy of Penelope Spheeris's film on punk, *The Decline Of Western Civilization*, where Crash's apocalyptic visage can be sampled visually.

⊙ **GI** (1979; Slash).
"Forming", "We Must Bleed", "Lexicon Devil" – here is a hymn book for American punk rock. Black Flag starts here, as do Hüsker Dü, Nirvana and Green Day.

Alex Ogg

GIANT SAND

Formed Tucson, Arizona, 1980.

The unpredictability of **Giant Sand**'s multi-instrumental mainman **Howe Gelb** has delighted his admirers for over fifteen years. In addition to using an ever-changing cast of collaborators in Giant Sand, he has run a sideline 'country' project called The Band Of Blacky Ranchette, as well as issuing a solo recording, DREADED BROWN RECLUSE (1991).

Giant Sand was formed by Gelb as Giant Sandworms, with **Rainer Ptacek** (guitar), **Billy Sed** (drums) and **Dave Seger** (bass). This line-up recorded an EP in New York, and another with **Scott Gerber** in place of Seger on bass, before Gelb grew restless and dismissed the rest of the band. Thus by the mid-80s, Giant Sand had largely become a one-man operation.

A distinctive instrumentalist and songwriter, often bracketed with fellow Arizonians and 'desert bands' Green On Red and Naked Prey, Gelb soon attracted press coverage with his perceptive, witty and poignant commentaries on modern life. There was plenty of wild guitar exploration in his music too (Neil Young is frequently cited as a reference point), and fine piano playing to boot.

It was difficult to maintain a release schedule that could keep up with Gelb's whims; in 1986, albums by Giant Sand (BALLAD OF A THIN LINE MAN) and Blacky Ranchette (HEARTLAND) came out on the same day, although his Blacky alter ego was then rested until 1990, and the release of SAGE ADVICE. Giant Sand recordings continued to dazzle: STORM (1988) captured an astonishing near-live feel, notably in the guitar parts; THE LOVE SONGS (1988) boasted more studio technique, though some parts were based on home recordings. Gelb was also happy to throw in the occasional cover, like "The Weight" and "All Along The Watchtower", and a splendidly quirky "Is That All There Is?"

During the late 80s, Gelb briefly moved to Los Angeles, but soon returned to the Arizona desert once more. Temporary band members included bassist **Paula Jean Brown**, once of The Go-Go's, ex-Green On Red guitarist **Chris Cacavas**, country singer **Lucinda Williams** and septuagenarian bartender **Pappy**. One of Gelb's most enduring collaborations was with **CALEXICO**'s **John Convertino** – LONG STEM RANT was a particularly incendiary testimony to this phase.

Gelb continued to surprise, providing guitar tuition for one *Bill & Ted* movie, and putting together another sprawling live ensemble, **Fruit Child Large**, with **THE LEMONHEADS**' Evan Dando. Meanwhile, his sterling contribution to KEROSENE MAN, a solo album by Dream Syndicate's Steve Wynn, was a favour returned by Wynn for Giant Sand's SWERVE (1991). The latter album also featured a cameo by **Rainer Ptacek**, the engaging songwriter Victoria Williams, and R.E.M. associate Peter Holsapple.

With previous American deals having foundered, some 90s material like SWERVE and RAMP (1991) was released in the US on Gelb's own Amazing Black Sand label, but was licensed in Europe. Sadly, some recent material, like GLUM (1994), is already deleted, but Gelb and Giant Sand's catalogue continues to grow. 1996 saw the release of BACKYARD BARBECUE BROADCAST on the Koch label, compiled from two radio shows transmitted in New York, while in 1997 the first two albums were rereleased by Diablo on one disc.

Issued after Ptacek's death (he appears fittingly on the album's closing instrumental "Shrine"), CHORE OF ENCHANTMENT (2000) weaved image-rich Americana over an underlying sense of pained melancholy, while Gelb's weathered, road-weary voice was as evocative as ever. With the exception of a few misfiring excursions into punk this was a satisfying trip.

Ever happy to spring a nice cover now and again (see above), Gelb obliged us with a full album's worth of other people's songs, acquisitioning material from sources as varied as Nick Cave and Johnny Cash. The opener of COVER MAGAZINE (2002), a medley of Marty Robbins "El Paso" and Neil

Young's "Out On The Weekend", nutshelled Giant Sands' ethos while a skewed version of Sonny Bono's "The Beat Goes On" transformed easy-listening shtick into sleazy lounge-a-billy.

⊙ **The Love Songs** (1988; Demon).
Perhaps the most assured of Gelb's early Giant Sand albums, including dynamic versions of many enduring favourites.

⊙ **Center Of The Universe** (1993; Restless).
Another terrific display of songwriting and instrumental skills.

⊙ **Chore Of Enchantment** (2000; Thrill Jockey).
Sprawling, vibrant, moody and dense, CHORE OF ENCHANTMENT provides an apt metaphor for the continuing career of Giant Sand.

Gerard F. Tierney

THE GIGOLO AUNTS

Formed Boston, Massachusetts, 1992.

The Gigolo Aunts formed as the sound of electric guitar-wielding boys was regaining 90s currency. However, their chirpy, effervescent sound clashed against the fashionable 'slacker' noise of Cobain and the grunge crowd, which owed more to the raw power of Black Sabbath and The Stooges than to the wide-eyed pop of The Beach Boys, Love, The Beatles, The Byrds, and Simon And Garfunkel.

Their debut LP, FLIPPIN' OUT, was released in 1993 to muted reception. Containing the catchy though anodyne "Where I Find My Heaven", it was uncomplicated, infectious soft-rock, full of big guitars, harmonies and vintage mid-60s songwriting. Ironically, it took the appearance of "Where I Find My Heaven" in the appalling *Dumb And Dumber* to break the band into the charts. Flushed with the success of the song as a single, in 1995 Fire Records promptly reissued the band's debut as a double-set package with a six-track fan-club CD, FULL-ON BLOOM. For the worst of reasons, a fine band was at last on the road.

All went quiet for five years until MINOR CHORDS AND MAJOR THEMES appeared in 1999. A competent release, but rather uninspired. Barely detectable on its release, PACIFIC OCEAN BLUES (2002) proved to be stunningly out of time with the prevailing pop climate – perhaps if they wait a little longer they might just be in fashion again.

⊙ **Flippin' Out/Full-On Bloom** (1995; Fire).
Goofy, flippant, undemanding guitar pop ploughing a furrow not a million miles away from that of The Raspberries, Teenage Fan Club, and fellow countrymen Velvet Crush. No concessions made to popular music developments after 1966.

Michael Sumsion

CLASSIC GIRL GROUPS

There were one-hit female vocal bands in the 50s, such as The Chantels and The Teen Queens, but the heyday of the **harmonizing girl group** was that extraordinarily fertile period in American music between the collapse of rock'n'roll and the rise of The Beatles: the years of Kennedy pop.

The group who launched the genre were **The Shirelles**, four young black girls who had started singing together in imitation of the male doo-wop bands of the late 50s. Signed by Florence Greenberg – mother of one of their high-school friends – to her own Decca-licensed label, they had a minor hit with their composition "I Met Him On A Sunday". Things really picked up in 1959 when Greenberg decided to take control of the marketing and launched a new label, Scepter, with "Tonight's The Night". (In so doing, she became one of the most influential, if uncelebrated, record company bosses, taking on Bacharach and David in A&R and signing Dionne Warwick, The Isley Brothers and The Kingsmen.) The result was a sequence of seven Top 20 hits over three years, including "Will You Love Me Tomorrow" and "Soldier Boy".

Much of the essence of the girl-group sound was present in these early Shirelles records. Drawing on Leiber & Stoller's work with The Drifters, the accompaniment was much fuller that it had been on doo-wop, with softly insistent rhythms and simple string lines, while the voices hovered between naivety, resignation and a yearning for a better life. **Shirley Owens**, the group's star, was a wonderfully expressive singer, with an ability to sound almost (but not quite) out of tune, giving the records a sense of innocence and striving.

Admittedly the words weren't the most sophisticated ever committed to vinyl, but their simplicity barely concealed the subtexts: "Tonight's The Night" was as enthusiastic about having sex for the first time as Buddy Holly's "Oh Boy", whilst "Tomorrow" asked whether respect, trust and sex could coexist. This was to become characteristic of the best girl-group records: a sometimes formulaic but nonetheless genuine depiction of reality for young women of the time, addressing teen problems from a female viewpoint that had previously been absent from pop. They did so, too, within a specifically female environment, in which girls talked to girls: the subject of the records tended to be 'he' not 'you'.

After "Tomorrow" hit #1 in America – the first record by black women to do so – the floodgates opened and a legion of girl groups were unleashed by small labels and independent producers. Most famous of those producers was, of course, **Phil Spector**, who left Leiber & Stoller's employ to branch out on his own. His first girl-group production, The Paris Sisters' "I Love How You Love Me" (1961), was highly derivative of The Shirelles, but the same year he signed **The Crystals** and began the studio experiments that were to make his name.

The Crystals' "Uptown" (their second single) was a major hit in 1962 and one of Spector's great moments. Written by Barry Mann and Cynthia Weill, the most socially conscious of the songwriting teams of the time, it picked up on The Drifters' use

Ronnie (centre) and the Ronettes

of Latin rhythms, and then added an enormous arrangement. Where a song like Ben E. King's "Spanish Harlem" (co-written by Spector) had featured a percussionist playing a light beat, a simple string counterpoint and a delicate Spanish guitar, Spector went overboard with a battery of percussion, a full orchestra and what sounded like dozens of guitars.

He repeated the trick later that year with "He's A Rebel", which hit #1 in the US. Written by Gene Pitney – who originally offered it to The Shirelles, but was turned down because of the subject matter – "Rebel" introduced a new element to the iconography of the girl groups: the tough-but-tender biker boyfriend. It also indicated a new development in the recording process, for none of The Crystals were invited to participate. Instead Spector used **The Blossoms**, a West Coast vocal band, as session singers. It was undoubtedly the right artistic decision, since it introduced the world to the glories of **Darlene Love**, possibly the finest female singer of her time, but it did suggest that the groups had become mere tools for manipulative producers.

The 'real' Crystals did get to sing on their next release, "Da Doo Ron Ron", which became one of Spector's most famous pieces, but it was not a patch on its predecessors: a bigger production, certainly, but no emotional content, no heart, almost as though he were losing interest.

Meanwhile, many others were picking up on the new genre. 1963 saw **The Angels** score their biggest

hit with "My Boyfriend's Back" (in which the boy rebel went beyond tough-but-tender into overt violence), and The Chiffons reached #1 with arguably the genre's best ever song, "He's So Fine" (later subconsciously reprised by George Harrison as "My Sweet Lord"). The Chiffons had actually started back in 1960 with a rival version of "Tonight's The Night", but found their own voice with a series of songs concerned with the acquisition of boyfriends. There was an assertiveness and a self-confidence about their material and their delivery that represented a major break with the passive female sexuality of 50s rock.

1963 also saw Spector reach the pinnacle of his career, with The Ronettes. Where earlier groups had been largely faceless studio-bound outfits, **The Ronettes** were a real band. Heavily made up with lashings of mascara and vast quantities of hair, they were not so much a girl group as a gang. The image (if not the reality of Ronnie Bennett's marriage to Spector) was of sexually independent, maybe even predatory women, powerful enough to survive the tempests of love, lust and passion. The records matched the scale of the hairdos: huge swirling melodramas of sound pierced by Ronnie's pure, inflected voice.

The Ronettes were not actually very successful commercially – one Top 10 hit with "Be My Baby" was a poor return on the amount of time and talent invested in the masterpieces they issued. The tracks now remembered as classics, like "Baby I Love You" and the awesome "Walking In The Rain", didn't make the big time. The reason was possibly the tone: breaking from The Shirelles' approach, 'he' became 'you', a more disturbing prospect for a record industry still nervous of radicalism. It did, however, work wonders for boys not normally used to being spoken to with such power by bouffant goddesses, and The Ronettes went down a storm on stage, particularly when supporting the likes of The Rolling Stones.

Though the British Invasion is sometimes believed to have killed the girl groups, the most successful label was not even launched until 1964. Leiber & Stoller set up Red Bird specifically to explore the genre, and hit gold immediately with **The Dixie Cups**' #1 "Chapel Of Love", a charming if old-fashioned record. The group later managed to take the voodoo sounds of "Iko Iko" into the Top 20.

More impressive were **The Shangri-Las**, the last great girl group and the first discovery of producer George 'Shadow' Morton. Records like "Remember (Walking In The Sand)", "Leader Of The Pack" and "Past, Present And Future" were as melodramatic as anything by Spector, but featured a much sparser sound in which the gaps that Spector would have filled with timpani and half a dozen grand pianos were exploited for even more intense emotional effect. The lyrics, meanwhile, headed straight into daytime soap, reaching a peak with "I Can Never Go Home Anymore", an unbearable tragedy in which a teenager's parents are heartbroken by her leaving home.

The Shangri-Las brought together all the strands of girl groups – the assertiveness, the female solidarity, the love of bad boys, the heightened emotion – in such style that there didn't seem anywhere else to go. After their peak in 1965, the genre effectively withered away. There was one last hit for The Chiffons in 1966 with "Sweet Talking Guy", but significantly the production on it sounded more like Motown, where the lessons of the girl groups had been assimilated into more durable vehicles like The Supremes.

Most of the big groups – Shirelles, Shangri-Las, Chiffons – have greatest hits releases in abundance, and versions of the groups have plied the revival circuit over the past couple of decades. Be warned, however, that most bands rerecorded their best work to diminishing effect; only The Shangri-Las, who never worked the revival circuit, can be guaranteed to be the original material. If you'd rather go for a compilation of the whole genre, those below are highly recommended.

⊙ **Leaders Of The Pack** (1993; Polygram).
This 23-track compilation doesn't have Spector's work and goes beyond straight girl groups into Motown and early 60s female vocalists generally (even Lulu gets a look in), but it's still the best introduction.

⊙ **Kiss 'N Tell/Early Girls Vol 1: Popsicles And Icicles** (1993 & 1995; Ace).
Two generous compilations – 30 and 28 tracks, respectively – featuring less obvious choices but demonstrating the vast depth of talent unleashed in the wake of The Shirelles. Famous names like Carole King and The Chiffons nestle alongside forgotten gems like The Aquatones and the should-be-legendary Bonnie Guitar.

Alwyn W. Turner

GIRLS AGAINST BOYS

Formed Washington, DC, 1990.

The members of **Girls Against Boys** could all boast strong hardcore credentials prior to the group's formation. **Scott McCloud** (vocals/guitar), **Alexis Fleisig** (drums) and **Johnny Temple** (bass) were all part of Soulside, who recorded two albums for the acclaimed Washington independent Dischord Records before breaking up. They were joined in Girls Against Boys by their former sound engineer, **Eli Janney** (bass).

Girls Against Boys came about as the result of studio 'noodling' sessions between Janney, McCloud and various members of Fugazi and Fire Party. The duo enlisted their former Soulside colleagues in time to record their debut NINETIES VS. EIGHTIES EP – a post-punk skin graft onto a muscular pop/rock torso. A debut album, TROPIC OF SCORPIO (1992), followed for Adult Swim, before the group moved over to Touch & Go for "Bulletproof Cupid". A slightly bleak, slightly desperate record, it left critics agog in both the US and the UK as Girls Against Boys translated punk's three-chord anxiety rush into something far more complex and alien. VENUS LUXURE NO. 1 BABY (1993) was another fine achievement, the group shifting from dark melancholia to incendiary swaths of atmospheric bottom-end noise.

The slightly sordid but ultimately noble CRUISE YOURSELF (1994) relied more on simplicity than had previously been the case. The most stunning item was "(I) Don't Got A Place", McCloud finding the perfect mode of address for his world-weary lyrics (he later confessed to finding the idea of being sexy 'far more appealing than being angst-ridden'). HOUSE OF GIRLS VS. BOYS (1996) expanded his unique take on sexual decadence further still – the murky atmo-

spherics of the group's double-bass sound was retained and distilled with the integration of almost subliminal dance rhythms. It was their last independent release before the group moved on to a new contract with Geffen Records. The new deal gave the band the opportunity to rediscover what they did best; hard, urgent rock tinged with gloom and darkness.

The resulting album FREAK★ON★ICA (1998), with intense, snarling tracks like "Exorcisto" and "Black Hole" was, like a first hit of acid, simultaneously frightening and attractive. But their next set of songs, YOU CAN'T FIGHT WHAT YOU CAN'T SEE, issued in 2002 on the independent label Jade Tree, found them in the more comfortable environment of the underground scene.

⊙ **Cruise Yourself** (1994; Touch & Go).
An elemental slew of primal post-punk blues from the isolation epic "(I) Don't Got A Place" to the shallow security of "Tucked In" and the apoplectic single, "Sexy Sam". CRUISE YOURSELF is Girls Against Boys' most complete album.

Alex Ogg

GIRLS AT OUR BEST!

Formed Leeds, England, 1979; disbanded 1982.

In 1979 local Leeds punk heroes **James Alan** (guitar) and **Gerald Swift** (bass) recruited art student **Judy Evans** (vocals) and formed the ramshackle The Butterflies. About to give up the ghost, they responded to a half-price recording offer at a recording studio in Cambridge, where, with **Chris Oldroyd** (drums), they cut two tracks, "Warm Girls" and "Getting Nowhere Fast". The tapes were accepted by Rough Trade, who in March 1980 distributed the songs as the debut single of **Girls At Our Best!** – the new name being taken from a line in "Warm Girls".

"Getting Nowhere Fast" was a bright, confident noise, which mixed the directness of punk with a natural pop flair, and Evans' piping voice and highly 'proper' diction made for a striking mix with the artless vigour of the band. Immediate cult success and rave reviews led Girls At Our Best! to junk all their repertoire from their days as The Butterflies. Augmented by session drummer Paul Simon, they released their second single, "Politics", in the autumn of 1980. A bouncy satirical examination of American-style campaigning, the single followed its predecessor to the top of the UK indie charts.

In 1981, having recruited **Carl Harper** from Leeds band The Expelaires, the band finally played their debut gig in York, then had a third indie hit on Happy Birthday Records, "Go For Gold", in turn followed by their sole LP, PLEASURE (1981). Although it developed the mix of pop invention and dry wit that had characterized the earlier material, the album didn't sell, perhaps because the determinedly independent post-punk attitude had been succeeded by the arch, eager-to-please ambitions of acts like ABC and Haircut 100.

Girls At Our Best!'s career seemed to grind to a halt after their album's release, with not even an official announcement of their split. They have stayed quiet ever since, although an EP of radio sessions was issued in the late 80s, and in 1994 PLEASURE reappeared on CD.

At an early stage, Girls At Our Best! became weighed down with the burden of expectation, but still made some dynamic and breathtaking pop records – most memorably "Politics" – while their style can now be seen as having paved the way for bands like The Sundays and The Cranberries.

⊙ **Pleasure** (1981; Vinyl Japan).
The full album and all their singles, plus their final recording, a powerhouse version of the traditional "This Train".

Peter Mills

THE GO-BETWEENS

Formed Brisbane, Australia, 1977; disbanded 1989; reformed 2000.

Formed by friends **Robert Forster** (guitar/vocals) and **Grant McLennan** (bass/guitar/vocals), **The Go-Betweens** were to become one of the most consistent songwriting teams ever to emerge from Australia. Their melodic songs of love and loneliness were adored by the critics, yet they never achieved the expected crossover into the mainstream.

Forster's decision to eschew universal songwriting themes in favour of 'my feelings in the bedroom, Brisbane, driving my car and anything from overheard conversations', was swiftly followed by a debut single, "Lee Remick"/"Karen". Released on the Able label, both songs were reminiscent of Bob Dylan. This was followed by the wonderful keyboard-dominated "People Say", a personal favourite of Forster and the band's debut LP, SEND ME A LULLABY (1981), which was picked up for release in the UK by Rough Trade.

Augmented by drummer **Lindy Morrison**, The Go-Betweens moved to London. McLennan was by now emerging as a songwriting force and the band's second album, BEFORE HOLLYWOOD (1983), included his haunting "Cattle And Cane", and the tear-jerking "Dusty In Here". The arrival of bass player **Robert Vickers** coincided with the band's signing to Sire, and releasing the excellent SPRING HILL FAIR (1984), which boasted the gorgeous "Bachelor Kisses" and the bitter "Draining The Pool For You".

However, for the critically acclaimed LIBERTY BELLE AND THE BLACK DIAMOND EXPRESS (1986) The Go-Betweens were on yet another label, Beggars Banquet. The breezy pop of "Spring Rain" even helped put the band on the brink of chart success, but radio airplay for the follow-up singles, the melancholy "Right Here" and the catchy "Bye Bye Pride", could not achieve a sales breakthrough.

By now the group was becoming disillusioned, despite the arrival of violinist **Amanda Brown**, and was on the verge of splitting. The sunny-sounding 1988 single "Streets Of Your Town", which belied its subject matter of wife-battering, received some airplay but again failed to chart. The same was true of The Go-Betweens' swan-song LP, 16 LOVERS LANE (1988), a polished affair with effortless driving pop like "Love Is A Sign" and "Dive For Your Memory".

After the band's dissolution, Forster and McLennan set about building solo careers. Forster was first off the mark with DANGER IN THE PAST (1990), which had a sound not too far removed from that of The Go-Betweens. It was followed with CALLING FROM A COUNTRY PHONE (1993) which, as the title suggested, featured a heavy country influence. His most recent solo recordings were I HAD A NEW YORK GIRLFRIEND (1994) – an album of covers, which Forster admits came about as a result of a period of writer's block – and WARM NIGHTS (1996).

McLennan recorded an experimental album under the name JACK FROST (1990) before releasing WATERSHED (1991) as G.W. McLennan, which was followed by FIREBOY (1993), the acclaimed HORSEBREAKER STAR (1995) and, in 1997, the even better IN YOUR BRIGHT RAY. In 1996, all the group's albums were rereleased on Beggars Banquet, and in 1999 a best-of collection, BELLAVISTA TERRACE, followed.

2000 saw Mclennan and Forster reunited as The Go-Betweens for the release of the superb THE FRIENDS OF RACHEL WORTH on the Circus Label. With a backing band that included all the members of **SLEATER KINNEY**, the set marked a triumphant comeback that recalled some of the group's finest pop moments and was followed strongly in 2003 by the equally marvellous BRIGHT YELLOW BRIGHT ORANGE. Whatever emerges in the future, Robert Forster and Grant McLennan will leave behind them a strong body of work much loved by their devoted following.

(•) **Send Me A Lullaby** (1981; Beggars Banquet).
The barest of The Go-Betweens' albums and a debut that marked McLennan and Forster out as fine writers of traditional pop.

(•) **Liberty Belle And The Black Diamond Express** (1986; Beggars Banquet).
The most commercial of the band's albums, this won loud praise and a host of new followers.

(•) **The Friends Of Rachel Worth** (2000; Circus Records).
Considering the blinding quality of their early material, this comeback collection does well at living up to the name. The album has many highpoints, though Forster's closing number, "When She Sang About Angels", is particularly lovely.

Andrew Mosley

THE GO-GO'S

Formed Los Angeles, 1978; disbanded 1984; re-formed briefly 1994.

It seems unlikely now that you could find a connection between Kurt Cobain and **Belinda Carlisle**, but there is at least one. Pat Smear, once of notorious LA punks **GERMS**, played with Nirvana on their last tours, while Carlisle was once, albeit briefly, a member of Germs. In fact the spoilt, wealthy girls who became **The Go-Go's** were as hard-living as anyone in California's nascent New Wave scene. Far from embodying the all-American girl image they later adopted, Carlisle (vocals), guitarists **Jane Wiedlin** and **Charlotte Caffey**, **Margot Olivarria** (bass) and **Elissa Bello** (drums) put as much work into drug-taking and sick practical jokes as into trying to get their shambolic, Buzzcocks-influenced band off the ground.

Still, they had enough natural pop sense to get noticed ahead of their more hardcore contemporaries. London's Stiff Records, then home of Madness, decided to give The Go-Go's a chance to make a record. With **Gina Schock** now on drums, they made "We Got The Beat", a raucous New Wave track that was more pop than punk. The Police's manager Miles Copeland signed them to his IRS label and, with **Kathy Valentine** (bass), a debut LP was recorded – BEAUTY AND THE BEAT (1981). Full of twangy surf guitars, it mixed upbeat pure pop with enough paranoia and cynicism about the LA lifestyle to keep them on the right side of saccharine. Best of all, it had their first hit, "Our Lips Are Sealed", a masterpiece of mistrust written by Wiedlin and The Specials' Terry Hall, who later recorded a version with Fun Boy Three.

The Go-Go's were perfectly suited for the early days of MTV, and the video for "Our Lips Are Sealed", with the five members jumping around in a fountain, was rarely off the air. They had become a rarity for the US charts – a successful all-female vocal and instrumental pop band. They were indebted to the way punk had freed bands from the technical virtuosity that had made early 70s rock so turgid.

As its title suggested, VACATION (1982) was even chirpier than their debut. Its title track became another big American hit, and probably remains The Go-Go's' epitaph: poppy, unashamedly corny and getting away with it in style. But five years of excess were beginning to cause trouble within the ranks. They managed to record a third album, TALK SHOW (1984), which made some generally unsuccessful attempts at a mature sound, but did include one last brilliant single, "Head Over Heels".

The tour that followed brought the end of the band in December 1984, as rehab and solo careers beckoned. Belinda Carlisle later became the epitome of the aerobicized, face-lifted Reaganite corporate rock star, but although the other band members never rivalled such success, Jane Wiedlin did suggest that she had been responsible for much of The Go-Go's' spirit and talent with her hits "Blue Kiss" and "Rush Hour".

An early-90s reunion to promote a greatest hits album was accompanied by a benefit concert for the anti-fur trade organization, PETA. Further benefits occurred in 1994, when they reunited once more to promote a new, improved compilation, RETURN TO THE VALLEY OF THE GO-GO'S (1995). They did a world tour and, more surprisingly, released a top-notch single, "The Whole World's Lost Its Head", a slightly harder re-creation of their old sound. The Go-Go's obviously have a place in pop history as female pioneers, but their concerns have shown that they are more than simply a pop group.

⊙ **Beauty And The Beat** (1981; IRS).
Cheery Californian paranoia, including the immortal "Our Lips Are Sealed".

⊙ **Vacation** (1982; IRS).
A top holiday-romance album, complete with a fab title track and the ridiculous "Beatnik Beach". To be listened to in very bad shirts.

⊙ **Return To The Valley of The Go-Go's** (1995; IRS).
All the hits, and some wonderfully incompetent early punk demos.

Marc Elliot

GOD IS MY CO-PILOT

Formed New York, 1990.

"We won't take your attention without giving some back."

Craig Flanagin (guitar) and **Sharon Topper** (vocals) formed the core of **God Is My Co-Pilot** out of the feeling that 'We can find very little that we want to listen to, so we'll get up there and do it ourselves.' After buying himself a guitar, Flanagin soon discovered an inimitable style of playing – choppy, detuned, completely rhythmic but totally improvised, with no attention paid to chord shapes or other established patterns. You can hear precedents in Half Japanese, Gang Of Four and Big Flame, but with their twin-drum assault and meandering bass playing, GIMC created something far less screwed-up and far more breezy and fun, influenced by everything from hardcore through avant-jazz to Jewish music.

Their first LP, I AM NOT THIS BODY (1992), was the beginning of an astonishingly prolific output,

with six further albums, eleven singles, and over three hundred shows in more than a dozen countries to date. For these recordings and performances, Flanagin and Topper have been surrounded by a floating membership of around ten people, enabling them to achieve much more than a fixed line-up could. According to Flanagin: 'it's more fun for me to look at every show and every recording as a specific puzzle to solve so that it yields maximum enjoyment'.

This approach has led them to work with many people from other bands, such as Marion (Dog Faced Hermans), Margaret (Laika), Jer (Dawson) and John Zorn, and they have built up a reputation as one of the most hard-working and interesting bands on the circuit. Their lyrics and general 'attitude' have created as much fuss as their extraordinary music, addressing issues of gender, feminism and homosexuality, and challenging assumptions about how music is produced and consumed.

⊙ **I Am Not This Body** (1992; Making Of Americans Records).
Opening quietly with an ode to fist-fucking, GIMC move through more palatable territory – being instantly killed while out on a bike, passing peas around the table, etc – but always with the stop-start rhythm that's essential to life as we know it, and with such a sense of fun that you could actually be right there in their playground.

⊙ **Speed Yr Trip** (1992; reissued 1995; DSA).
More songs about sexual encounters, practices, deviancy and love.

⊙ **Best Of God Is Not My Co-Pilot** (1996; Atlantic).
The perfect introduction to an alternative lifestyle.

Rhodri Marsden

THE GODFATHERS

Formed London, 1985.

The **Godfathers** came about following the break-up of nihilistic south London punks The Sid Presley Experience, who released two indie singles ("Hup Two Three Four" and a cover of John Lennon's "Cold Turkey") in 1984. After a failure to keep control of the name, brothers **Peter** (vocals) and **Chris Coyne** (bass) set about contriving a band with a vaguely threatening image, loosely based on the Kray Twins, with new cohorts **Kris Dollimore** (guitar), **Mike Gibson** (guitar) and **George Mazur** (drums).

The name was a good start. Early material – generally rollicking R&B with titles like "This Damn Nation", "I'm Unsatisfied" and "I Want Everything" – was also promising, loaded as it was with venomous frustration and crude, chant-along choruses. A clutch of singles, released on the band's own Corporate Image label and collected on HIT BY HIT (1986), led to comparisons with Dr. Feelgood, and as The Godfathers' profile increased, and the superb "Love Is Dead" single showed signs of their chart potential, CBS stepped in and signed them.

Expectations were high after the signing – Peter Coyne went on record predicting that The Godfathers' major-label debut would outsell label-mates George Michael and Michael Jackson, although this was in all probability a rare moment of playfulness. The album, which was eventually titled, with typically blunt nihilism, BIRTH, SCHOOL, WORK, DEATH (1988), was the high point of the band's career, featuring some fine pop moments, characteristic rabble-rousers, and even a dose of psychedelia ("When Am I Coming Down?"). A few column inches were also gained when the sleeve design for "Cause I Said So" – featuring a picture of Margaret Thatcher done up to look like Hitler – was banned, but the single was not a hit. Disappointingly, the rereleased "Love Is Dead" also failed to chart, despite being the best pop song the band would ever come up with.

The next single, "She Gives Me Love" (1989), was strong, although the subsequent album, MORE SONGS ABOUT LOVE & HATE (1989), failed to break new musical ground. The speed-fuelled "Walking Talking Johnny Cash Blues" was among the highlights on a record which suggested that The Godfathers were either playing it safe or had simply run out of ideas. Losing the suits wasn't a great move, and a bizarre attempt to gain dance-floor credibility through Keith LeBlanc remixes of "She Gives Me Love" went largely unnoticed. At the end of the 1989 tour, Kris Dollimore, always an influential member, quit the band and went on to front **The Brotherland**.

There was reason for optimism at the start of 1991, with a replacement for Dollimore, Chris **Burrows**, the big St Valentine's Day Massacre gig at the Brixton Academy, and at least some attempt at moving with the times with the strangely funky "Unreal World" single and the album of the same name. Nods were given to baggy and there was a bit less of the old pub rock; the album stiffed, however, and CBS finally ran out of patience and dropped the band.

Worse was to come, as Gibson and Mazur also quit the band in 1992, and The Godfathers were left to contemplate no record deal, a dwindling line-up and a dwindling fan base. An independent live album (DOPE, ROCK 'N' ROLL & FUCKING IN THE STREETS) was a sensible move – The Godfathers had always been about playing live – and plugged the gap while the band figured out what to do next. Out of touch with the musical *Zeitgeist*, and riddled with bad luck, the Coyne brothers have soldiered on, although it has become impossible to keep up with all the guitarists and drummers. 1996 saw the release of another studio album, AFTERLIFE (Intercord), to predictably little attention. You can still, however, catch them live every February 14 – no number of setbacks can ever stop this peculiarly British institution, it seems.

⊙ **Birth, School, Work, Death** (1988; Sony).
Peter Coyne's vocal limitations are all too clear on the gentler material, but the best material shows a band ahead of their time (Nirvana, et al), and rocking out to huge effect on "Love Is Dead" and the anthemic title song.

⊙ **Dope, Rock 'N' Roll & Fucking In The Streets** (1992; Corporate Image).
Probably the best Godfathers album, for the simple reason that they always made more sense live than on record. Apart from the omission of "Love Is Dead" and "I'm Unsatisfied", the tracklisting is spot-on.

Mauro Venegas

GODFLESH

Formed Birmingham, 1988.

"I hate people, not in a physical way, so I express it through the music." Justin Broadrick

After their stint in Fall Of Because, **Justin Broadrick** (guitars/vocals; ex-**NAPALM DEATH** and Head of David) and **G.C. Green** (bass) formed **Godflesh** aiming to combine influences ranging from Black Sabbath to free jazz to Swans and Throbbing Gristle. Their eponymous debut EP was released independently in 1988, leading to a deal with Earache Records and a full-length album, STREETCLEANER, the following year. The GODFLESH mini-LP was also rereleased by Earache with two extra tracks.

With the heaviest of metal riffs, slowed down to a crushing, claustrophobic pace and backed by a drum machine, Godflesh created a relentless, alienating wall of sound overlaid with feedback, samples and Broadrick's misanthropic vocals. This album and a US tour with Napalm Death made their reputation in the industrial rock scene they helped to define. A further tour with Loop led to the release of the Loopflesh/Fleshloop 7″, each band covering the other's songs.

Dissatisfied with the limitations of grindcore's metal origins, the trio added hip-hop and techno influences, resulting in the SLAVESTATE EP in 1991. This was accompanied by a remix EP, which, along with their Sub-Pop single "Slateman/Wound '91", would eventually emerge as the SLAVESTATE LP. Following this release, Neville was replaced by **Robert Hampson** of the recently dissolved Loop. The "Cold World" single was followed by PURE (1992), which incorporated ambient/isolationist elements into their increasingly electronically influenced sound. Hampson then departed to concentrate on **Main**, for whom Green occasionally guested on bass.

Following a successful North American tour with Skinny Puppy, Godflesh was put on hold while Earache sorted out a financial and licensing deal with Columbia. Broadrick did production work, and collaborated with **Techno Animal**, **Ice**, **Scorn**, **John Zorn** and **Bill Laswell** among others.

Broadrick's series of experimental ambient recordings as **Final** (started when he was 12) have recently featured Green as well, while Broadrick has also set up the hEADdIRT and Lo Fibre labels, the latter releasing his Solaris techno 12″s from 1996 onwards. Finally, the MERCILESS EP emerged in 1994, 'biomechanically' remixed from material dating back as far as the mid-1980s.

Re-sampling, editing and processing the Godflesh sound into entirely different shapes, this was their most radical release yet, and preceded that September's disappointing SELFLESS. The growing popularity of Godflesh with American metalheads led to a US tour with Danzig in Spring 1995, and attempts to recruit Broadrick into **FAITH NO MORE**.

Godflesh's fourth album, SONGS OF LOVE AND HATE (1996), developed their established sound with the addition of **Brian Mantia**'s live (and occasionally funky) drumming. By now highly influential in metal circles, they toured Europe with Ministry, **Ted Parsons** of Prong taking over on drums. 1997's self-remixed LOVE AND HATE IN DUB came hot on the heels of a series of rereleases designed for American audiences who were just starting to catch up. US AND THEM (1999) and HYMNS (2001) continued to carry the Godflesh torch, grinding the skulls of all who dipped in.

⊙ **Pure** (1992; Earache).
The most accomplished and eclectic of the group's album releases, from the skyscraping "I Wasn't Born To Follow" via the hip-hop-based title track to the rhythmically varied "Baby Blue Eyes" and "Don't Bring Me Flowers". CD release has "Pure II", a 21-minute ambient companion piece to Main's "Thirst", and "Love, Hate (Slugbaiting)", which uses a live Fall Of Because recording as its basis.

⊙ **Selfless** (1994; Earache).
Godflesh's breakthough into metal acceptance has a tendency towards mechanical, headbanging sameness, though the excellent "Crush My Soul" (released as a single) is based around an asthmatically weaving sample loop. Once again, the CD has a menacing twenty-minute-plus bonus track, "Go Spread Your Wings".

⊙ **Songs Of Love And Hate** (1996; Earache).
More traditionally metal-sounding than hitherto, though retaining the passionate, crushing intensity. Songs like "Sterile Prophet" and "Time Death And Wastefulness" express the frustration with futile existence, which is Godflesh's speciality.

Richard Fontenoy

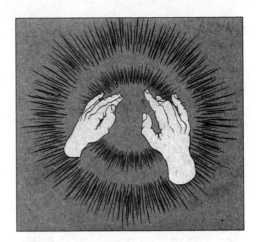

GODSPEED YOU! BLACK EMPEROR

Formed Quebec, Canada, 1994.

Godspeed You! Black Emperor – named after a Japanese biker gang – seek to describe a near apocalyptic collapse of society and state. Godspeed craft a thunderous musical amalgam of paranoid fantasy, social dissent and architectural desolation through their beautiful, epic soundscapes and sampled monologues.

The original ensemble of two, **Efrim** (guitar) and **Mauro** (bass), surfaced in Mile End, Quebec, playing illegal bring-a-bottle shows in defiance of the local clubs' pay-to-play policy. Operating from a poky studio-cum-venue called Hotel2Tango (named after the postcode, and not, as rumour has it, some apocalyptic call-sign), the duo released a cassette, ALL LIGHTS FUCKED ON THE HAIRY AMP DROOLING. Limited to only 33 copies, few have heard this debut set, which featured titles like "Perfumed Pink Corpses From The Lips Of Ms Celine Dion" and "Loose The Idiot Dogs", though it is reportedly even more chaotic and volcanic than their later releases.

Choosing to shun media attention early on, an enlarging line-up of Godspeed You! Black Emperor made the decision to remain as anonymous as possible, refusing to offer the press any personal information that didn't directly relate to the group's sonic agenda. Interviews were often carried out by email and only conducted on the band's own terms: Efrim once volleyed a question from the *NME* by saying 'If I want to have an awkward conversation with people about things I hold to be self-evident, I'll go to my parents' place for the holidays.' Supported by the equally nonchalant Constellation label, the ploy worked well and served to focus all eyes on the group's artistry rather than members.

By the time that Godspeed's debut proper was recorded, the ensemble had toured the east coast of Canada and expanded to include violin, cello, percussion, tape-loops, drones, glockenspiel and even bagpipes. Originally released in 1997 as a vinyl edition of 500 on Constellation (released the following year on the Kranky imprint as a CD with extra material) f#a#∞ was a menacing but beautiful debut collection of cinematic drones, guitar twangs, swooping strings, fierce crescendos and haunting monologues. Appearing at a time when post-rock was fragmenting into scattered shards of lo-fi electronica and horrifyingly retro prog, Godspeed's combination of beauty, anger, mystery and classicism grabbed the press's attention and entranced a wide variety of music fans: like the group Rachel's, Godspeed take as much from Beethoven and Satie as they do from their direct heritage of disgruntled hardcore and airy space-rock. The vinyl version was sumptuously packaged with individually assembled covers that featured pasted photographs of urban skylines and decaying locomotives; in every sleeve could be found a penny, flattened on the rail tracks that run behind Hotel2Tango. The CD art was even bleaker – a single grainy image of three lonely antennas and a blurred signpost, dwarfed by a stormy sky.

In 1999 an EP was released, SLOW RIOT FOR NEW ZERO KANADA, which built a denser sound than that of their debut. Its drowning drone opener, "Moya", with its heavenly strings that give way to strummed guitar lines and pounding drums, remains their most powerful recording. Now solidified into a nine-piece – **Aidan** (drums, percussion), **Bruce** (drums, percussion, glockenspiel), **Mauro** (bass), **Thierry** (bass), **Dave** (guitar, tapeloops), **Efrim** (guitar, tape-loops), **Roger** (guitar), **Norsola** (cello) and **Sophie** (violin) – the group strove to present a unified musical voice, which inevitably complicated the group's recording sessions and in turn intensified their sound. As media interest grew, Godspeed concentrated on developing their live sound through a succession of exhausting tours and maintaining their defiant and principled stance – the collective democratically opting to turn down a considerable amount of money from a bank that wanted to feature one of their cuts in a commercial.

The following year, Efrim, Thierry and Sophie took time out from Godspeed to form **A Silver Mt. Zion** and release the piano-led mouthful HE HAS LEFT US ALONE, BUT SHAFTS OF LIGHT SOMETIMES GRACE THE CORNERS OF OUR ROOMS… (2000). Later that year Godspeed released their epic double CD LEVEZ VOS SKINNY FISTS COMME ANTENNAS TO HEAVEN. Keenly anticipated, the set was a triumphant menagerie of howling guitars, stampeding percussion and growling chords; it sold well and attracted critical acclaim.

Recorded by **Steve Albini**, 2002's YANQUI U.X.O. witnessed a further drenching episode in the Godspeed story. The album's five tracks embraced both the sound of the band at their most explosive and thunderous while also revealing their masterful ability to map music's quieter, melancholy foothills.

Despite all the apparent doom and gloom, Godspeed's music is fundamentally about empowerment and, in their own words, 'hope and endurance in the face of real economic and emotional adversity'. Having already fortified their position and delivered some hefty musical artillery, it looks like Godspeed's campaign has only just begun.

Godspeed You! Black Emperor

⊙ **f#a#∞** (1998; Kranky).
A stunning debut collection of extended sound sculptures, playful instrumental experiments, and dark visions of decaying architecture.

⊙ **Levez Vos Skinny Fists Comme Antennas To Heaven** (2000; Kranky).
Godspeed's second album proper combines the group's hallmark cinematic suites with waves of percussion and found sound – harvested from across the continent. This collection reflects much of the group's finely honed live sound.

A Silver Mt. Zion

⊙ **He Has Left Us Alone, But Shafts Of Light Sometimes Grace The Corners Of Our Rooms…** (2000; Constellation).
A Silver Mt. Zion keep things wonderfully simple, with meandering rivers of piano, and barren flood-planes of contrebass and violin. The pieces are recorded with a sumptuously lo-fi, compressed sound – tonally reminiscent of early shellac-cut classical 78s.

Peter Buckley

GOLDEN EARRING

Formed The Hague, Holland, 1961;
still going strong…

"I've been drivin' all night my hand's wet on the wheel." Radar Love

Golden Earring's origins are a tad convoluted. The band – which still exists – was formed in 1961, as The Golden Earrings, by teenagers **George Kooymans** (guitar), **Rinus Gerritsen** (bass/keyboards/harmonica), and ran through various early line-ups before settling down as a quartet in 1967, with **Jaap Eggermont** (drums) and Indian-born **Barry Hay** (vocals/saxophone/flute/guitar). It was with this incarnation that they scored the first of many Dutch #1 hits, with "Dong Dong Di Ki Di Gi Dong" (1968), a title worthy of entry in the Eurovision Song Contest.

The band were by now touring as Golden Earring, and had begun to gain an international following, particularly in the US. In 1969, **Cesar Zuiderwijk** replaced Eggermont on drums, and since that time the line-up has remained essentially stable, although during the 70s they would occasionally be augmented by a fifth member – firstly with **Robert Jan Stips** on keyboards and then **Eelco Gelling** (guitar).

Earring's unusual mix of hard rock and breathy, slow flute and saxophone breaks led Pete Townshend, an old friend of the band, to invite them on The Who's 1972 European tour as support. The success they enjoyed culminated in their being signed to The Who's own label, Track, and Top 20 success on both sides of the Atlantic with "Radar Love" (1973), a single most rock fans around at the time can still hum effortlessly today. Taken from the MOONTAN album (the band's eighth, issued in 1973), this hard-rock song with its fast shuffle beat became a highlight of the band's stage shows and featured a protracted drum solo by Zuiderwijk, which ended with him vaulting over his drum kit.

Having achieved international success, the band failed to capitalize on it with a disappointing follow-up album, SWITCH (1975), although it did at least contain the memorable single "Kill Me, Ce Soir". Their 1977 LIVE album recaptured some of the onstage excitement, though, with live readings of much of MOONTAN, as well as a superb cover of The Byrds' "Eight Miles High".

Unfortunately, the live album served to highlight the lack of good new material. Occasional tracks stood out, such as "Roxanne" from 1979's GRAB IT FOR A SECOND, and the SECOND LIVE LP (1981) again reflected their considerable performing capabilities, but thereafter the only studio album to rise above mediocrity was CUT (1982). It should have been a more distinguished career for a band who share with Focus the distinction of being the only Dutch acts to chart in the UK and US, and who are among a very few groups from the continent to sound convincingly English.

Still, Golden Earring's following has always been healthy in their homeland, and they have long had fans in the US, where they charted again with Twilight Zone in 1983. After a fallow period, between 1986 and 1989, when Hay tried a solo career with the album VICTORY OF BAD TASTE, the band got back together again, and have kept rolling since. Their status is shown by their refusal to support Deep Purple on a US tour in 1996, believing that they had little to prove or to gain.

They have, at last count, issued some forty-plus albums, all adhering to a straightforward hard-rock formula, if rarely with the catch of "Radar Love".

⊙ **The Best Of Golden Earring** (1992; Connoisseur). This has about all you need of the Earring, including "Radar Love" (of course) and the excellent "Vanilla Queen" from MOONTAN, plus "Eight Miles High" and "Twilight Zone".

Paul O'Brien

THE GOLDEN PALOMINOS

Formed New York, 1982.

The Golden Palominos were formed principally by **ARTO LINDSAY** (guitar/vocals) and **Anton Fier** (drums), following their departure from the jazz-based Lounge Lizards. They were names that immediately bracketed the band amid New York's avant-funk scene, and it was from these quarters that The Palominos' personnel were drawn, both for recording (they have always been a largely studio band) and occasional live work.

BILL LASWELL, **Jamaladeen Tacuma**, **John Zorn** and **David Moss** all guested on the 1982 debut, THE GOLDEN PALOMINOS, a bewildering musical soundscape that was dominated by Lindsay's neurotic screech and extraordinary guitar stylings. By the time of 1985's VISIONS OF EXCESS, however, radical changes were afoot. Lindsay appeared only on the closing track, and a stellar cast of hired hands had joined Fier and Laswell – among them **Richard Thompson**, **Carla Bley**, Funkadelic's **Bernie Worrell**, and ex-Raybeat **Jody Harris**. Even more extraordinary was the cast of vocalists assembled: **Jack Bruce**, **John Lydon**, **Michael Stipe** and **Syd Straw** all participated. Highlights of the set included the three openers – "Boy (Go)", the neo-psychedelic "Clustering Train", and Skip Spence's "Omaha" – all of which featured Stipe. "The Animal Speaks", opening with a thunderous belch, was Lydon's impressive contribution.

A lesser but still very curious cast was assembled for BLAST OF SILENCE (1986), a record that kicked off with "I've Been The One", a Lowell George song from the first ever Little Feat album, sweetened by the pedal steel guitar of Sneaky Pete Kleinow. Ex-Slapp Happy man **PETER BLEGVAD** shared writing credits on most of the tracks, along with Fier, Robert Kidney (writer of that Lydon track), Matthew Sweet

and Syd Straw, while T-Bone Burnett, Don Dixon and Jack Bruce also cropped up.

This period was a high point for Fier's project. The next album, A DEAD HORSE (1992), was based around two distinct composer credits: Kidney contributed three songs, while four were written by Fier with singer and keyboard player **Amanda Kramer** and guitarist **Nicky Skopelitis** (a frequent Laswell collaborator). Indeed Fier, Laswell, Kidney, Skopelitis and Kramer were listed as The Golden Palominos on the sleeve, and a relatively small supporting cast was appended. Those helping included Mick Taylor and Chuck Leavell, The Allman Brothers' keyboard player, though you'd hardly have guessed from the melancholic, almost doom-laden music, pleasant in execution but devoid of many of the flashes of inspiration that had so enlivened the earlier recordings. This impression was reinforced by the subsequent Palominos releases: DRUNK WITH PASSION (1991) and THIS IS HOW IT FEELS (1993).

Kramer was still heavily involved with the first of these, but by the second was in the B-team, with Fier, Laswell, **Lori Carson** and **Lydia Kavanagh** the new core unit. Carson was a key voice on PURE (1994), which had a greater willingness to experiment with rhythmic texture, Fier and Laswell using restructured samples of their improvised bass and drum parts as a back-up to the sensual vocals. The fact that musicians as diverse as Skopelitis and Bootsy Collins could both contribute to the overall picture showed there was still room for Palomino experimentation. DEAD INSIDE (1996) suffered from the lack of Carson's voice – though replacement **Nicole Blackman**'s voice fitted the gloomy introspection of the new songs perfectly – and an obvious musical direction. Intriguing, nonetheless, and if Fier keeps shuffling the personnel over the next few years more good things seem bound to emerge.

⊙ **Visions Of Excess** (1985: Celluloid). It's hard to imagine any rock fan not wanting to hear the combinations of musicians on this album. Clearly essential.

⊙ **A History** (1986–1989) (1992; Metrotone). A CD reissue of most of BLAST OF SILENCE and A DEAD HORSE.

Gerard F. Tierney

GOLDFRAPP

Formed London, 1998.

The mid 90s were an interesting time for UK music. While the Britpop debacle ensued a whole other generation of musicians were taking to the studio armed with a vision of welding hip-hop beats to John Barry records – with far more exciting results than any of their Dad-rock contemporaries.

Artists such as Massive Attack, Björk, Tricky and Portishead sculpted soundtracks that defined a genre. It was from this musical heartland that **Goldfrapp** emerged in 2000 with the startling FELT MOUNTAIN.

Alison Goldfrapp's two backing singers do a runner...

It must have been a difficult task to create something new in the genre, what with such earth-shattering musical statements preceding them, but Goldfrapp succeeded in carving their own niche without being derivative or repetitive. Björk had her quirky abstractions, Portishead their damaged torch songs, Tricky his apocalyptic rantings. Goldfrapp occupied a kind of erotic dreamspace, a lush utopia that sat (atmospherically) somewhere between *Cabaret* and *Goldfinger*.

The group consists of vocalist **Alison Goldfrapp** and composer **Will Gregory**. Alison made her first appearance providing vocals on Tricky's MAXINQUAYE in 1995 and then popped up on Orbital's SNIVILISATION and Add N To X's AVANT HARD shortly afterwards. Gregory, a composer and multi-instrumentalist, spent the 90s as a sax player on a host of albums by everyone from Spiritualized to The Cure, and arranged strings on Peter Gabriel's OVO release.

The two signed to Mute in 1999, releasing FELT MOUNTAIN the following year to widespread acclaim. While the opiate bliss of its sound was enough to recommend the album to the ear (it conjured up the same liquid sexuality as the music to *The Story Of 'O')*, it was Alison Goldfrapp's vocals that earned most of the attention. By turns she could be baby-cute, alien or even operatic, and was certainly a worthy peer of Beth Gibbons (Portishead) or Björk, though far more stately than either. Contributions on the album from Portishead's **Adrian Utley** drew the comparisons even closer to home, while "Lovely Head" recalled Garbage at their most soporific.

The album earned a *Mercury Prize* nomination and led to a touring frenzy throughout 2001 and 2002. Alison also found time to tour Europe as a DJ with an eclectic set that incorporated everything from Baccara to Motörhead. As for the band, Goldfrapp's live encore of Olivia Newton John's "Physical" perhaps gave some hint as to the new direction unveiled, eventually, in 2003 on BLACK CHERRY.

Life at the cutting edge has its difficulties and following up something as sublime as FELT MOUNTAIN without treading the same ground was always going to be difficult. BLACK CHERRY saw Goldfrapp attempting a stylistic leap but, uncomfortably, in too many simultaneous directions. They had lost the focus of their debut, opting instead for an onslaught of drum machines, which sometimes obfuscated the chilling intensity of Goldfrapp's voice.

There was a harder agenda on the set's modish excursions into electro, such as on the Moroder-esque "Crystalline Green" or the bruising "Train". Gone was the dreamy sexiness, replaced by a darker view on the fairground bunk-up "Twist" or the S&M fantasy "Strict Machine". The title track, however, allowed Goldfrapp's vocal to shine, while "Deep Honey" and "Hairy Trees" were breezily euphoric. While it lacked some of the soul of FELT MOUNTAIN the set was a brave attempt to move on – they nearly pulled it off, but there remained a sense of unresolved transition. Perhaps their next release will manage to pin down the group's brave new world.

GOLDFRAPP

Felt Mountain (2000; Mute).
There's a glacial quality to this album that is completely transfixing. Like Zero 7's SIMPLE THINGS or Lemon Jelly's LOST HORIZONS this is utterly of its time.

Derryck Strachan

GOMEZ

Formed Southport, England, 1996.

"It's not a crime to put some country music in a pop tune!" Ian Ball

Perhaps **Gomez** exist simply to show that rock-'n'roll dreams really can come true. In the spring of 1998 they were unknowns, fresh out of university, but by the end of the summer they had won the Mercury Prize and had the world at their feet.

Ben Ottewell (vocals/guitar), **Tom Gray** (vocals/keyboards), **Paul Blackburn** (bass), **Olly Peacock** (drums) and **Ian Ball** (vocals/guitar/harmonica) breathed new life into the faltering body of Britpop with a health-bringing injection of the blues. Their meteoric rise was in no small part due to two stunning live performances, firstly on *The Jools Holland Show* on British TV, then at a rain-lashed Glastonbury Festival. In both cases, the audience had to suspend their disbelief that such a nerdish-looking bunch of 20-year-olds could produce such a hoary sound that seemed like the missing musical link between the Mississippi Delta and Manchester.

Their debut, BRING IT ON, was recorded in their communal house in West Yorkshire and, like the singles, featured hallmark cover artwork by Reggie Pedro. The album brought comparisons with any number of 60s rock heroes, whilst they admitted the influence of Joni Mitchell, Hendrix, Marvin Gaye, J. J. Cale and The Doors. The set has a freshness all of its own, however, and its quirky humour and lo-fi production value owe as much to Beck as to any of the elder statesmen of rock. Nevertheless, singer Ben's gravelly voice does sound like it comes from another age, particularly on the opener "Get Miles", and gives the album a bluesy gravitas unmatched by any contemporaries.

The band is blessed with two other fine singers (Ian Ball and Tom Gray), whose good humour is infectious, particularly on anecdotal tracks like "Whippin' Piccadilly" and "Get Myself Arrested". Only when starry-eyed romanticism gets in the way, as on the wince-inducing "Tijuana Lady", does the album sound laboured.

At the close of 1998 Gomez featured strongly in the media's end-of-year round-up, being hailed by both *Q Magazine* and the *NME* as the "Best Newcomer", while the sales of their debut continued to go through the roof. Early in 1999 the band toured America; they were greeted rapturously, with BRING IT ON receiving impassioned reviews across the board. Returning to England, the group recorded their eagerly anticipated sophomore album LIQUID SKIN (1999). Where their debut is a stupendous mesh of downhome styles, LIQUID SKIN is even more richly textured and accomplished. "Rhythm & Blues Alibi" encompasses eccentric electronic beats and tides of aural lunacy, while the familiarly titled single "Bring It On" offers a stylistic vaulting horse from the earlier material. Like the first, this set was warmly received and – clothed in more of Pedro's striking cover art – it helped to solidify Gomez's growing fan base.

The new millennium saw the release of ABANDONED SHOPPING TROLLEY HOTLINE, a playfully indulgent but wonderful odds-and-ends collection, on which their determination to have a good time is cheering.

Settling comfortably into their third album, IN OUR GUN (2002), Gomez managed to strike a fine balance between evolution and retaining their core sound. The use of electronic paraphernalia was more obvious in the mix while the connection with LIQUID SKIN was anchored by a horn section that sounded like it had been played in a pub back room. Gomez's trick – and one that they continue to employ with considerable aplomb – is in turning quite standard songs inside out, taking unexpected turns and making throwaway melodies into almost spiritual experiences.

Bring It On (1998; Hut)
A hip strum-athon of melodies that steals from so many classic rock albums that comparisons with the living or dead seem purely of academic.

Liquid Skin (1999; Hut)
Repeated plays reward with a richness of hooks and textures, uncovering a genuinely eclectic set of influences, including blues, roots, dance and rock. Highpoints include the hypnotic single "We Haven't Turned Around", and the vocoder-led epic finale "Devil Will Ride".

Abandoned Shopping Trolley Hotline (2000; Hut)
Compiling radio sessions, previously lost cuts from deleted singles, unreleased nuggets and a clinky clunky remix of "Emergency Surgery", this set is often deranged, loose and likely to confound the uninitiated, but it is certain to delight existing fans of Gomez's wayward genius.

Chris Coe

Gomez
Liquid Skin

GONG

Formed Paris, France, 1970; faded away 1975; reactivated 1990.

"I was in the position of being a psychedelic usher at the cinema of the French mind." Daevid Allen

No other band has such immediate word association with 'hippies' as **Gong**, the psychedelic vision of Australian beatnik **Daevid Allen**. This was a group who emerged in the full flood of psychedelia, appearing on stage in 'pothead pixie' hats, and provided a space-metal soundtrack for getting stoned to – a notion that informed many of their songs, along with a breezy eroticism and sub-Tolkien allegory. Twenty years on, the old albums stand up surprisingly well, especially compared to the earnestness of many of their prog-rock counterparts.

The story of the self-styled Planet Gong is essentially that of Daevid Allen who fell in with the Canterbury scene in England in the late 60s, playing guitar for the embryonic **SOFT MACHINE**. After just one single with the Softs, Allen left the band, having been refused re-entry into England after a French tour. He settled in Paris, where he set up a proto-version of Gong, recalled as 'a large number of musicians and singers improvising around nothing for hours on end, completely stoned'.

From this community of drugged-out hippies, Allen began shaping the Gong blueprint, with his partner, poet **Gilli Smyth**. An early influence was minimalist composer Terry Riley who inspired Allen's technique of 'glissando guitar' and the tape textures that gave a base to Gong's pioneering 'stratified' rock. This was in evidence right from the band's first recording, a film soundtrack entitled CONTINENTAL CIRCUS (released in 1970), which Allen and Smyth had worked on around the time of the Paris 1968 uprising. Branded 'cultural agitators' by the authorities, they had left France in a hurry, and were not allowed to return until 1971.

During this period, Allen and Smyth released two albums on the French Byg label: MAGICK BROTHER, MYSTIC SISTER (1970) and BANANA MOON (1971). The music recalled Soft Machine but lyrically, all the Gong ingredients were in place – whimsical surrealism ("Fred The Fish"), sexual fantasy ("Pretty Miss Titty"), and, of course, drugs ("Stoned Innocent").

When Allen and Smyth returned to France in 1971, Gong's first stable line-up convened in a rural farmhouse commune to record CAMEMBERT ELECTRIQUE 'during the full moon phases' of the summer. This began both Allen's wacky wordplay with the names of his musicians, and the idea of Gong as a planet. Gilli Smyth became **Shakti Yoni**; **Didier Malherbe** (sax/flute) transmuted into **Bloomdido Bad De Grasse**; and one **Venux De-Luxe** emerged as switch doctor and mixmaster; the line-up was completed by **Pip Pyle** (drums and breakage). The album itself was an abandoned piece of space-funkery, too stoned for its own good at times, but zesty enough to attract the attentions of the embryonic Virgin Records, who signed the band and, echoing their promotional trick with THE FAUST TAPES, rereleased the album as a 69p ($1) bargain buy.

Allen moved Gong to a new commune, back in England, so as to more easily use Virgin's production facilities. Thus endowed, the band launched into a shamelessly psychotropic triptych of albums, FLYING TEAPOT and ANGEL'S EGG (both 1973) and YOU (1974). These wonderfully trippy albums offered a sequence of songs and proto-ambient layers of electronics well ahead of their time. **Steve Hillage**'s guitar and **Tim Blake**'s synth provided a serenely mantric backdrop for Malherbe's eclectic sax patterns and delayed flute codas. The rhythms were tight, too, with Mike Howlett (bass) and Pierre Moerlen (drums) giving Allen and Smyth's ethereal poetry its tightest structure ever. Live, the band were even better, an astonishing spectacle utilizing lasers, and dressed and lit like a mummer's play. Allen described the band live as like a 'more feminine version of Hawkwind'.

Tea with the pothead ones: that's Hillage with the guitar and Allen on bongos

GONG

Unfortunately for this extended family of Utopian dreamers and deviants (now including Hillage's partner, keyboard player **Miquette Giraudy**), the times were about to change. In 1973, funded by the success of Mike Oldfield's TUBULAR BELLS, Virgin could indulge its hippie iconoclasts. But Allen never became 'the Beefheartian cult figure' of Virgin's imaginings, and as the decade progressed, punk would tar Gong with the same prog-rock brush as Genesis, ELP et al.

Allen and Smyth pre-empted it all, jumping ship for Spain in 1975 – Allen maintaining he had been prevented from appearing on stage one night by a 'force field' of unspecified origin. Gong continued for a while, with Hillage and Giraudy fronting SHAMAL (1975), produced by Pink Floyd's Nick Mason, before finally docking into dry jazz-rock terrain as Pierre Moerlen's Gong, with Moerlen and Malherbe alone remaining from previous incarnations. Their albums, GAZEUSE/EXPRESSO and EXPRESSO II (1977 and 1978) were Gong in name alone.

The spirit was kept alive more by **STEVE HILLAGE**, whose spaced out solo albums were marketed successfully by Virgin alongside the Sex Pistols. Oddly, Allen and Smyth returned to England much more in key with the times, re-forming as Planet Gong and enlisting musicians from punk–hippie hybrid **Here & Now**. The LIVE FLOATING ANARCHY tour along with thinking punks Alternative TV followed. The music (commemorated by a live disc) was a howl of psychedelic, urban squat polemic, going a little lighter on the space whisper.

It's at this stage that the Planet Gong annals get confusing. Allen moved to New York around 1978, made a few solo albums, and instigated a **New York Gong** project with **BILL LASWELL**, before returning to Australia, where he wound up driving taxis. A compilation of his post-NY Gong work, DIVIDED ALIEN CLOCKWORK BAND, featuring a spoken-word run-through of the Planet Gong mythos, was released on Blueprint in 1997. Gilli Smyth, meanwhile, recorded and toured as Mother Gong, producing a trilogy of cosmic feminist tracts, often accompanied by Malherbe. Tim Blake briefly joined Hawkwind, before basing himself in France and recording and performing as Crystal Machine. Hillage and Howlett became Virgin's in-house producers (Simple Minds, Martha & The Muffins, among others), before the former returned to the limelight with The Orb and his own System 7.

In 1988 Allen returned to England, settling in Glastonbury. He was a largely forgotten figure, but Gong material was beginning to be sampled by acid-house producers, and he reclaimed sufficient momentum to get a band together again, touring in 1992 as Gongmaison, with Malherbe back on reeds, and with tabla percussion and techno-esque electronics reflecting how many of the original musical tenets of golden period Gong had come back into

play. He went on to record with Bongwater and Shimmy Disc mainman Kramer for 1993's WHO'S AFRAID album.

In October 1994, Allen hosted a 25th birthday party for Gong at London's Forum, headlining a bill featuring some of the many spin-offs that had continued through the years. It was a testament also to the Gong Appreciation Society (GAS), which has been assiduously reissuing much of the extended Gong catalogue.

A 1997 release, SHAPESHIFTER (Viceroy) brought a lot of graduates from Allen's university back to the alma mater to show what they'd learned along the way. It was complemented by the release of GONGYOUREMIXED PHASE1 & PHASE2 in which 'electronica' acts such as The Orb, The Shamen and 808 State got their hands on the YOU master tapes and wreaked havoc with the magic therein. The remixes vary widely in their faithfulness to the originals, but are none the worse for that.

To this day the group's catalogue continues to swell, with more and more recordings being unearthed: 2002's GLASTONBURY 1971 is essential, as is much of Allen's newer solo material.

Camembert Electrique (1971; Charly).
Gong's best early album, infused with the experience of Paris 1968 and trippy psychedelics.

Flying Teapot (1973; Charly);
Angel's Egg (1973; Charly); **You** (1974; Charly).
The Radio Gnome Trilogy is definitive Gong – elegant, ethereal soundscapes, shimmering electronics and effusive musicianship. Essential stuff, but if you're unsure, the trilogy's finer moments (plus slices of Camembert) are gathered on The Best Of Gong (1998; Reactive).

Live Floating Anarchy '77 (1977; Charly).
Allen, Smyth and Here & Now performing with garage-punk fervour as Planet Gong. Rough, wild, angry and spacey.

The Birthday (1994; GAS/Voiceprint).
Double live CD featuring Gong's Virgin-period line-up playing together for the first time in twenty years.

Chris Brook

GOODBYE MR MACKENZIE

Formed Bathgate, Scotland, late 1970s;
finished up 1996.

Despite a number of try-out line-ups, **Goodbye Mr Mackenzie** didn't truly come together as a band until **Martin Metcalfe** (singer/guitarist) and **Derek Kelly** (drums) met at college in Edinburgh in 1981. Named after Metcalfe's favourite novel, *After Leaving Mr Mackenzie* by Jean Rhys, the band gigged around Edinburgh, featuring on one side of a single released on a college label in 1984. This single, "Death Of A Salesman", sold out its 1000 run and was played on Radio 1, suggesting good times ahead.

They struck their first deal with the Precious Organisation in Glasgow in 1985 and this led to their first serious release, an uptempo rocker titled "The Rattler". It was a hit in the independent charts, sold 6000 copies and got the Mackenzies on to the coolest pop show of the time, Channel Four's *The Tube*. A BBC Radio 1 session was recorded in November 1986, but their failure to gain a major deal led to a change in management at the turn of the year.

Their next single, "Face To Face", described by Martin Metcalfe as 'commercially suicidal', was the harrowing tale of the torments of a rape victim in court. Although not ideal material for a band seeking mainstream success, the single again scored heavily in the independent charts. Constant gigging paid off later in the year in the shape of a deal with Capitol Records.

By now, the personnel had jelled to Metcalfe, Kelly, **Fin Wilson** (bass), plus **Shirley Manson** and **Rona Scobie** (together providing backing vocals and keyboards) who Martin had met at a theatre club in Edinburgh. The line-up was completed shortly after the Capitol deal with the arrival of **'Big John' Duncan**, formerly of legendary Scottish thrash-punks **THE EXPLOITED**. His guitar skills allowed Metcalfe to take over as lead singer. A tour with Aztec Camera reinforced their popularity and the stage was set for their debut major label release. The album Good Deeds And Dirty Rags reached #26 in the UK charts and a rerecording of early hit "The Rattler" cracked the Top 40 singles chart. Three other singles from the album also charted, but cracks in the relationship with Capitol began to appear. Capitol put out Fish Heads And Tails – a compilation of covers, rarities and live tracks – but this was to be their last release on that label before being shifted sideways onto Parlophone.

In 1989, the band decamped to Berlin to record Hammer And Tongs. They soaked up the atmosphere of the fall of the Berlin Wall and produced an incredibly strong and up-beat album. Better still, they were offered the support spot on Deborah Harry's tour of the UK and Europe. And to crown everything, Goodbye Mr Mackenzie played a set at Europe's biggest ever outdoor gig (at the time) in front of 250,000 people in Glasgow. However, new single "Love Child", released in June 1990, just missed out on the Top 50 and "Blacker Than Black", which followed later in the year, also failed to excite radio stations, peaking at #62. Parlophone were tired of the Mackenzies' failure to become an instant smash, and accepted an offer from MCA to buy out their contract. The Mackenzies joined new label, Radioactive, run by Deborah Harry and Talking Heads manager Gary Kurfirst. The band returned to Berlin to record the single, "Now We Are Married", but once again this failed to chart despite being rated by Metcalfe as 'one of our best records'.

On the eve of a gruelling fifty-date tour of Europe, Rona Scobie announced her departure. Undaunted, the five-piece drafted in their producer as temporary replacement. However, the band's relative failure led to a loss of confidence by MCA. The Mackenzies' response was to form their own label, Blokshok Records, and to release their first live album, Live:

On The Day Of Storms, and a new studio album, Five (both 1993).

For Five, keyboards and sweet backing vocals were ditched in favour of a new, harsher sound. Martin had been pushing Shirley to perform lead vocals on some of the new songs in an attempt to produce a 'Velvet Underground & Nico'-type album. The results led Radioactive to try and sign Shirley (as a solo artist), and to offer the Mackenzies the former Talking Heads Chris Frantz and Tina Weymouth as producers. Recording had already started on a new album Angelfish (1994), when John was called upon by **NIRVANA** to tour with them.

Meanwhile, Angelfish had been completed and was selling well enough in the US for the "Suffocate Me" video to be aired on MTV. It is allegedly at this point that Nirvana producer Butch Vig spotted Shirley and dragged her away to superstardom in **GARBAGE**. With their chief asset gone, the remaining members (reunited with John) returned to Scotland and recorded The Glory Hole (1995) before deciding to wind the band up in December 1995. After an extra farewell gig in Aberdeen in January 1996, Goodbye Mr Mackenzie finally came to an end.

For a short time John was involved with a splatter-punk band called **Gin Goblins**, but was most recently seen on Channel 4's *Young Person's Guide To Being A Rock Star!*

Kelly saw the future and set himself up as a website designer; spending some time in Berlin continuing to unite with Martin and Fin for occasional gigs and fan-club only releases. Initially they recorded as **Fishhead**, the group then became Angelika and most recently Cactus. A permanent home on the web for Kelly's design skills and Metcalfe's musical outings emerged in 2000 with the launch of www.blokshok.com, a site which published the first new tunes from the ex-Mackenzies in years.

⊙ **Hammer And Tongs** (1991; Radioactive). Long-deleted masterpiece, which still surfaces now and then in the secondhand stores.

Nick Dillon

GORILLAZ

Formed London, 2000.

Sure, they were merely the pomo version of 70s cartoon bands like The Banana Splits, The Archies and Josie & The Pussycats, they insisted on doing interviews in character, and they weren't nearly as clever as they thought they were, but with their blend of dub, hip-hop and spectral indie-rock the **Gorillaz** were the acceptable face of pre-fab studio pop at the turn of the millennium. Even your little sister would agree that **Murdoc**, **Noodle**, **Russel** and **2D** were considerably more 'real' than stiffs like Westlife.

With Gorillaz, producer **Dan "The Automator" Nakamura** probably realized the

● **Gorillaz** (2001; Virgin).
Similar in many senses to James Lavelle's ego trip, UNKLE's PSYENCE FICTION, this attempt to have your cake and eat it too is by turns brilliant, irritating, relentlessly boring and forgettable wallpaper.

Peter Shapiro

GORKY'S ZYGOTIC MYNCI

Formed Carmarthen, Wales, 1990.

dream of every studio Svengali since the recording desk was invented: get a bunch of friends – rather than untalented prima donnas – together, record music that you actually like, hide behind the mask of cartoon characters and make it commercially viable by wrapping it up in a media-friendly, animated package. Of course, having friends like Blur's **Damon Albarn**, *Tank Girl* creator **Jamie Hewlett**, rapper **Del Tha Funkee Homosapien**, DJ **Kid Koala**, **Miho Hatori** from Cibo Matto, Tom Tom Club and Buena Vista Social Clubber **Ibrahim Ferrer** doesn't hurt either.

Gorillaz debuted in November 2000 with the TOMORROW COMES TODAY EP. The title track featured Albarn making like Augustus Pablo with a melodica and wailing in a vaguely Thom Yorke-ish, undynamic fashion way; "Rock The House" finds Del rapping over a facsimile of the theme from *Are You Being Served?*; "Latin Simone" is an uncomfortable union of a Cuban danzón and scratchy hip-hop beats; and "12D3" sounds like "Want To Be Free", but, of course, Albarn could never be that direct.

The self-titled album followed in the spring of 2001 and was more of the same writ large: intriguing dub experiments like "Clint Eastwood" and superb postmodern pop like "19/2000" sitting uncomfortably next to the wan indie rock of "Re-Hash" and the unconvincing thrash bash of "M1 A1" and "Punk". And, inevitably, the website and the videos were better than the album itself. With all of the pan-stylistic globe-trotting, smart-ass media tactics, self-referentiality and high concept schtick, it was the usual problem: too much of everything still isn't enough.

G-Sides (2002), a collection of remixes, was largely pointless, with almost no one adding anything to the originals. They then collaborated with rapper Redman for the almost funky (Albarn's spectral backing vocals destroyed the flow) "Gorillaz On My Mind" from the *Blade II* soundtrack, while LAIKA COME HOME (2002) found Gorillaz getting the remix treatment from Space Monkeyz. Oh, and don't forget the interactive game on Sky Digital television in the UK.

Welsh-language rock, anyone? At the onset of the 1990s the idea seemed pretty absurd to anybody outside the Gwynedd-based Ankst label and their clique of musicians and followers. A decade later, well, it's almost a reality, with **Gorky's Zygotic Mynci** frequently charging up the UK indie charts and Super Furry Animals wearing the crowns of kings. Stranger still, we are talking Welsh hippie-psychedelia here, with both bands namechecking the likes of Kevin Ayers as musical influences.

The Gorky crew were formed at school in Carmarthen, South Wales, by **Euros Childs** (vocals/organ), **Richard James** (bass) and **John Lawrence** (guitar), expanding before long to include **Euros Rowlands** (drums) and **Megan Childs** (violin). Singing in Welsh more often than English, they recorded a series of bedroom demos, silly and gorgeous by turn (they were later released as a mini-CD, PATIO), and then in 1992 debuted with a 10″ single, "Patio". This got curiosity reviews in the music press but it was a support slot with The Fall in London in 1994 that brought them wider attention. They looked like they were still at school but they sounded unique – quirky, melodic, a little Velvet-ish and, uhh, Welsh.

The band's first album, TATAY (1994) followed, setting out its store with both Welsh and English covers of Robert Wyatt's best ever song, "O Caroline", and a track entitled "Kevin Ayers" in homage to the 'creator of the best LP of all time', SHOOTING AT THE MOON'. That credit – to Ayers' most experimental outing – was significant, for the band clearly liked their pop a bit experimental, creating sumptuous piano-based melodies and piling all number of strange effects from violin, guitar and keyboards on top. The arrangements were so interesting that you could forgive the odd splashes of indulgence, which, of course, is how most of the British audience would class the Welsh lyrics. Not so, of course, the nationalist Welsh, one Cardiff club being so unhappy about Welsh alternating with English that they immediately placed the band on a blacklist.

The album was accompanied by a rush of singles, notably the LLANFWROG EP (1995), featuring the delicious "Miss Trudy", which notched up a slot as *NME* Single of the Week. The buzz was growing, concerts were getting sold out, and the band were looking more and more like hippies. On the sleeve of their second album, BWYD TIME (1995), they appear like some latter-day Incredible String Band – an influence, no doubt, although it was a love of The Beach Boys that shone through strongest (Childs had owned up to this on a live recording of "Merched Yn Neud Gwallt Eu Gilydd", howling the closing section of "Good Vibrations"). Amid the racket, still rough-edged and charming, were other glimpses of Beefheart, The Fall and early Soft Machine, as they wove their web of sound around the catchy tunes.

The band set out on a major British tour, following the album's release, hitting the summer festival circuit in both 1996 and 1997. BARAFUNDLE (1997) was a beautiful summer's album in a wet and dismal year, but its melodies haunted the brain and the wilful weirdness of the tunes managed to get the sun to come out even when played inside.

After 1998's disappointing GORKY 5 album, the band parted company with Polygram and signed to Mantra records. The following year they delivered the excellent SPANISH DANCE TROUPE, their most consistently satisfying album to date, in which they finally appeared comfortable with their calling as a radiant, quirky and experimental folk band. In 2000, after a triumphant appearance at the Reading Festival, they released a mini-album, THE BLUE TREES, which saw the group truly transcend their influences and establish a sound all of their own. It was followed in 2001 by an extraordinarily rich examination of nostalgia, HOW I LONG TO FEEL THAT SUMMER IN MY HEART.

⊙ **Tatay** (1994; Ankst).
Irresistible stuff, from the bizarre vocals of the opener, "Thema O Cartref", through "O Caroline", and into all manner of Welsh wackiness.

⊙ **Bwyd Time** (1995: Ankst).
The melodies are stronger, the playing's a superbly balanced racket, and the stand-out single, "Miss Trudy", is sing-it-in-the-shower exquisite.

⊙ **Spanish Dance Troupe** (1999: Mantra).
This is a roller-coaster ride of hybrid rock and kindergarten ballads. Brass and strings playfully intermingle with the band on tracks such as "She Lives On A Mountain", while a solo violin tiptoes through "Don't You Worry".

Mark Hughes

GRANDADDY

Formed Modesto, California, 1992.

Though they had been around since the early 90s, **Grandaddy**'s distinctive warped-out-country sound didn't really click with the record-buying public until the stage had been set by the likes of Mercury Rev and The Flaming Lips.

A former professional skateboarder, guitarist **Jason Lytle** put together a three-piece version of Grandaddy as long ago as 1992: in his home town of Modesto, in California's San Joaquin Valley, an industrial 'nowhere'. Lytle began goofing around with music in between skateboarding. On hand were fellow boarders, **Kevin Garcia (**bass) and Arizonan percussionist **Aaron Burtch**. Early initiatives included the construction of a studio in the Lytle's home, situated among farmhouses, where the

Grandaddy's Jason Lytle

recording of the US-only album COMPLEX PARTY COME ALONG THEORIES was self-produced by the band. Just 200 copies of this 1994 release were pressed, the record's disjointed title and accompanying DIY artwork setting the stall for the band's better-known subsequent works.

Grandaddy live weren't straying too far from Modesto, but were frequently supported by guitarist **Jim Fairchild**; such was his affinity with the trio that he soon left his own band and teamed up as a permanent fourth member. In 1995 they were joined by Fairchild's regular jam-buddy **Tim Dryden** on keyboard. The first studio result from this new, improved Grandaddy was the seven-track EP A PRETTY MESS BY THIS ONE BAND, released in 1996. It included four songs from COMPLEX PARTY COME ALONG THEORIES. The band's sound had taken a significant leap forward, the music returning fresher and brighter than before.

Further early tracks resurfaced on UNDER THE WESTERN FREEWAY (reissue via V2), the first collection proper, which increased interest in the group, though did not achieve hit status.

Grandaddy toured during 1999, and with little time to record fresh material issued the compilation THE BROKEN DOWN COMFORTER COLLECTION. This was good news for those without the earlier EPs that it comprised – and probably worth it alone for one of Jason Lytle's finest-ever compositions in "Wretched Songs".

A summer spent playing the festival trail saw Grandaddy previewing material from their 'difficult' second album, THE SOPHTWARE SLUMP, which duly arrived in 2000. Though displaying a largely more considered approach than its predecessor, THE SOPHTWARE SLUMP still trotted out the odd glam-rock riff to accompany tales of abandoned machinery ("Broken Household Appliance National Forest"), but when not doing this the set was still able to wrench at the soul with a series of David Lynch-styled anecdotes from the suburbs and beyond that echoed those found on Mercury Rev's DESERTER'S SONGS. The press loved it. *The Independent* cited the record as 'easily the equal of OK COMPUTER' perhaps unwittingly drawing a comparison in lyrical inspiration. Where Radiohead had penned the alienation standard of the 90s in "Creep", then, with the glorious "He's Simple, He's Dumb, He's the Pilot", Lytle and co. had arguably composed a self-examining anthem for the new millennium. (With the commercially beguiling cut "The Crystal Lake", meanwhile, Grandaddy broke the UK Top 40 in February 2001.)

A sequel came in SUMDAY (2003) As before, the group submitted a delicious collection of ambling, silver-lined indie rock that recalled the swooning keyboard pop of bygone bands such as ELO. On cuts such as "I'm On Standby" and "OK With My Decay" Lytles' lyrics soldered despair onto a circuit board of beautifully contrived computer metaphor, though musically, the band disappointed many by wholeheartedly failing to progress.

At times, Grandaddy bridge the same post-hippie, pre-prog divide as Neil Young, at others, they trace the sketchy ruminations of Will Oldham. What is undeniable, though, is that this band always fashion a recognizable form of their own that is timeless and always evocative.

⊙ **Under The Western Freeway** (1997; V2).
The dysfunctional "Summer Here Kids", earworm "AM 180" and self-effacing muse of "Laughing Stock" are the stand-out moments here. Initially a curio demanding closer attention, this set proves to be one of the decade's essential debuts.

⊙ **The Sophtware Slump** (2000; V2).
Eccentric and questioning while never heavy-going, this second collection proper brings Grandaddy closer to the mainstream, without selling any of their precious originality downriver.

Jeremy Simmonds

GRANT LEE BUFFALO

Formed Los Angeles, 1991; disbanded 1999.

The talents of **Grant Lee Buffalo** were first brought to the attention of the British public thanks to R.E.M.'s Michael Stipe, who announced that the band's album FUZZY (1993) was one of his picks of the year. R.E.M.'s 1995 world tour featured Grant Lee Buffalo as support, and when their own drummer Bill Berry collapsed, and was hospitalized, he was replaced by Grant Lee Buffalo's **Joey Peters**.

The genesis of Grant Lee Buffalo can be traced back to the summer of 1986, when Peters, who had worked with John Lee Hooker, met **Grant Lee Phillips** (vocals/guitar). Bass player and pianist **Paul Kimble** arrived in 1989, but it was 1991 before the trio became Grant Lee Buffalo. Phillips explained, 'One night we'd be Sorta GoGo Futurists, then it was Dustbowl Dandies. But at the end of the night the music we'd always come back to is the stuff that became Grant Lee Buffalo.'

That stuff, as FUZZY showed, took folk and country influences and mixed them with hard-edged rock in a manner that hadn't been heard since Neil Young – a debt acknowledged on the band's subsequent live EP, BUFFALONDON (1993), which included a superb version of Young's "For The Turnstiles". The song was a perfect fit for Phillips' acoustic/grunge guitar sound, and for the passion with which he sings. The Doors were another discernible influence, and, as critics never tire of pointing out, Phillips shared Jim Morrison's background in having attended film school at UCLA.

Constant touring meant that it was the tail end of 1993 before the trio began work on their second album. MIGHTY JOE MOON (1994), which was based, Phillips explained, 'on a creature of our own invention ... a character who embodies the spirit of the band in his sheer defiances of law and reason'. The trademark acoustic swirl and raging feedback guitar remained dominant, but the trio had expanded their instrumentation to take in organ, cello and pedal steel, with Kimble revealing a notable dexterity on keyboards. It was a perfect summer album, with its dreamy, cinematic songs.

During 1995, the band set to work on that difficult third album, which emerged as COPPEROPOLIS. This was again produced by Paul Kimble, and featured an even more bewildering array of instruments – this time including marimba, pump organ, Mellotron and strings. It was a leap forward, both musically (with the expanded palette beautifully controlled, and the R.E.M. influence less overt) and lyrically (with Phillips painting a canvas of dust-bowl life in songs about transition, loss and the human spirit). It yielded a great single, too, in "Homespun", expressing the shock felt by Americans at finding the Oklahoma massacre 'a homespun violent sound'.

Kimble left the band after COPPEROPOLIS - leaving the bassist's and producer's berths empty - and Phillips and Peters moved into experimenting with different sounds and instrumentations. The result was JUBILEE (1988), a move back to instant pop with fourteen songs, including crashing classics such as "APB". Under the production of Paul Fox (10,000 Maniacs), and including contributions from **Michael Stipe, E** from Eels and **Robyn Hitchcock**, it was a stunning return to form. However, it proved to be their swansong, with the group splitting in the summer of 1999.

⊙ **Fuzzy** (1993; Slash/London).
The band's intentions are revealed right away on "The Shining Hour", a bar-room acoustic number with a skiffle

influence. Neil Young and Doors comparisons abound on "Stars & Stripes", while the single release "Jupiter & Teardrop" is a gorgeous ballad about a mismatched couple in an uncaring world.

⊙ **Mighty Joe Moon** (1994; Slash/London).
Perhaps the best example of the range of moods and sounds the band are capable of, from the full-on rock of "Lone Star Song" to the Ry Cooder-esque country-picking style "Last Days Of Tecumseh".

⊙ **Copperopolis** (1995; Slash/London).
A triumphant third album, introducing a richer, more sweeping sound, and some stunning songs full of wild, enduring images.

⊙ **Jubilee** (1998; Slash/London Records).
A bewildering array of traditional instruments, but Phillips' voice is at its glorious, clear, dry best on this collection.

Mike Martin

THE GRATEFUL DEAD

Formed Palo Alto, California (as the Warlocks), 1965; formally disbanded in December 1995 but live on as a diversified business organization.

"Our audience doesn't come to see theatrics ... they realize we're not performers, and that we're a group that's earnestly trying to accomplish something, and we don't quite know what it is." Jerry Garcia

The Grateful Dead, San Francisco's most mythic musical constellation and deliverers of the straight dope on musical Americana, sprang from the union of the bohemian, literary, musical and psychedelic in 1960s California. They epitomized Haight-Ashbury American hippiedom and their trip went on longer, and grew weirder, than any band in rock history.

The band's history is incomparably convoluted, though their origins were similar to those of the other Bay Area groups that filled San Francisco's dance halls in the so-called Summer of Love of 1967. As with Jefferson Airplane, Quicksilver Messenger Service, Big Brother And The Holding Company and Country Joe And The Fish, they drew on elements of folk, blues and jug-band music (America's skiffle). These and other folky roots would later be collected on THE MUSIC NEVER STOPPED (1995), a source set of tracks from such as Obray Ramsey ("Rain And Snow"), Bobby 'Blue' Bland ("Turn On Your Love Light"), Bonnie Dobson ("Morning Dew") and the Pinder Family ("I Bid You Good Night").

The Dead's foundations were laid by the 1961 meeting of the band's core partnership: their defining lyricist Robert Christie Burns, known as **Robert Hunter**, and the guitarist and banjoist **JERRY GARCIA**. They shared an interest in folk and country music, had both recently been discharged from the US Army, and, based in Palo Alto, the site of Stanford University, began working as a two-guitar duo. The US government was funding a research programme

at Stanford to assess the effects of hallucinogenic drugs. Among the guinea pigs who signed up for trials were Hunter and the novelist Ken Kesey. It was a crucial moment in the history of American psychedelia.

Before long, Hunter and Garcia found themselves at the centre of a clique of like-minded musicians and proto-hippies, whose number included **Ron (Pigpen) McKernan** and **Bob Weir**. They drifted in and out of various short-lived folk combos until 1964 when two key events took place. Garcia went off in search of bluegrass, taping shows (a portent of the Deadheads' later, obsessive recording of the band's gigs) for the future Dead circle to digest. And Ken Kesey formed the Merry Pranksters, a busload of psychotropic improvisers who crossed the continent, wired on acid (which was not banned in the US until 1966), filming the reactions of a slack-jawed America. Private Prankster parties at La Honda in California expanded into the Acid Tests – and the Acid Tests needed a party atmosphere. Cue The Dead in their early incarnation as the Warlocks.

The Warlocks had evolved out of a number of folk, blues and jug bands, but had gone electric as a result of hearing The Beatles' A HARD DAY'S NIGHT. They comprised Garcia (vocals/lead guitar), Pigpen (organ/vocals) and Weir (rhythm guitar), along with **Bill Kreutzmann** (drums) and **Phil Lesh** (bass). It was 1965 and The Dead were on their way.

The Acid Tests were chronicled for posterity in Tom Wolfe's *Electric Kool-Aid Acid Test* (1968), and they undoubtedly helped the Warlocks roll back the musical boundaries. The band's name change, too, was assisted by drugs. Smoking DMT one day at Lesh's place, the band decided to try Valentinian chance – fortune telling using a randomly selected passage from a book, in this case, Funk and Wagnell's *New Practical Standard Dictionary*. 'Grateful dead' was a folkloristic term for earth-tethered spirits freed from their earthly ties through human intervention. As a metaphor for what The Dead would do, it was perfect.

In 1966 the first Dead record, "Stealin'"/"Don't Ease Me In", emerged on the local Scorpio label. It was essentially electric jug-band music and thus a new – Grateful Dead – identity. The band also recorded with jazz veteran **Jon Hendricks** for the *Sons And Daughters* soundtrack, creating enough confidence for Warners to step in and finance March 1967's frenetic, speed-laced THE GRATEFUL DEAD.

A credo of 'longer and louder' meant that The Dead evolved their live act through improvisation. And evolve they did, spurred by the arrival of a second drummer, **Mickey Hart**, who transformed the sound, and by the reappearance of Hunter to add lyrics. The sound of this sextet can be heard on TWO FROM THE VAULT (recorded 1968, released 1992). Their repertoire already included "Dark Star", "The Eleven", "Saint Stephen", "The Other One" and "New Potato Caboose" – the last two songs were to be core elements of their next Warners release.

Augustus Owsley Stanley III, an LSD magnate nicknamed The Bear, underwrote the band's finances

GRANT LEE BUFFALO ▪ THE GRATEFUL DEAD

at this critical juncture, joining them at work in Los Angeles. For ANTHEM OF THE SUN (1968) Warners again paired them with producer Dave Hassinger but they parted company midway, and, at Garcia's suggestion, the project took a new turn, deploying live and studio performances collage-fashion. The Dead ranks had by now been swelled by keyboard player **Tom Constanten**. Having studied under Berio, Boulez, Pousseur and Stockhausen, he was well versed in the piano's alternative voices – as shown by ANTHEM's prepared piano and gyroscope-on-piano-strings death rattle.

Constanten was an even more significant mover on the next album, AOXOMOXOA (1969), a densely textured, experimental work. His harpsichord on "Mountains Of The Moon" was a minor miracle for a rock album of the time, while the electronic dribble of "What's Become Of The Baby" took experimental rock down a new paisley-primrose path. Pigpen and Weir were gradually being found wanting, ill-equipped to cope with the band's new experimental rock incarnation. In 1968 both had been excluded from the short-lived improvisatory offshoot, **Mickey Hart & The Hartbeats**.

The Dead were still a cult group at this stage, with a Bay Area following that wasn't matched across the States or abroad. Lacking the vocal harmony of Jefferson Airplane, or the rude dynamics of Big Brother, it was hard for those who hadn't seen the band to understand what all the fuss was about – until the release of LIVE DEAD (1970). One of the most telling live rock albums ever released, this was acid-jazz twenty years before the term was coined, flambéed with extemporized feedback (Weir's redemption) and seasoned with Pigpen's salacious funk on "Turn On Your Lovelight". "Dark Star", a launch pad for majestic instrumental improvisations, debuted on this LP as a live staple.

The summer of 1969 saw the birth of another off-shoot, the **New Riders Of The Purple Sage**, born out of Garcia and Dave Nelson fooling around, jamming on country material while Garcia improved his pedal steel playing. Garcia and Hart both guested on their debut and their songs also went through The Dead's Ice Nine Publishing imprint. Eventually NRPS found members who could devote their exclusive energies to this country-inflected music.

In January 1970, Constanten bowed out of the group, although he travelled with The Dead to New Orleans that month, where all but he and Pigpen were charged with drug offences (subsequently dismissed), inspiring a key verse of "Truckin'". Constanten went on to arrange for The Incredible String Band, co-found Touchstone, compose for the Kronos Quartet, become a professor and play keyboards in diverse settings. His autobiography, *Between Rock And Hard Places* (1992), puts many arcane aspects of The Dead into context.

The stage was set for something less experimental, and WORKINGMAN'S DEAD (1970) heralded this change. Heavily rehearsed to minimize studio time, it was a reaction to mounting debts, with the band,

inspired by Crosby, Stills and Nash, dusting down their country, blues and folk roots and, strengthening their vocals. Also key to their development was the maturing of the Hunter/Garcia partnership. Hunter's wry homilies were as staunchly demotic as they were philosophical, fluent where once they had been stiffly poetic. "Cumberland Blues" typified their new approach. White blues with bluegrass leanings, its turbulent tutti arrangement masks the arrival of Garcia's bubbling banjo to the extent that its presence registers retrospectively. Garcia dubbed this 'sneak music' in a *Swing 51* interview. The debacle of Altamont, the 1969 festival at which Hell's Angels murdered a hapless bystander while The Rolling Stones pranced, was revisited in "New Speedway Boogie". Post-Altamont, The Dead's image had been tarnished since they had associated with the Angels since the Acid Tests and people were eager to apportion blame.

AMERICAN BEAUTY (1970) was a continuation of WORKINGMAN'S DEAD. Beautifully crafted songs such as "Ripple", "Box Of Rain" and "Friend Of The Devil" showed The Dead approaching true greatness. HISTORY OF THE GRATEFUL DEAD (VOLUME ONE) BEAR'S CHOICE (1973), however, was a disappointment. Recorded at the Fillmore East in 1970, it had few stand-outs beyond Weir's prettily sung "Dark Hollow". Listening to DICK'S PICKS VOLUME FOUR (1996), of the same provenance but the surreal McCoy, it seems all the more puzzling.

In 1971 Mickey Hart left The Dead, shaken by revelations of his manager-father, Lenny Hart's, protracted embezzlement of their finances – Hunter's gentlemanly 'You know better/But I know him' would later resound through "He's Gone". Reverting to their core quintet line-up, the band released the live double GRATEFUL DEAD (1971), introducing "Wharf Rat", one of Hunter's best tales of the underdog, and including covers of Chuck Berry ("Johnny B. Goode") and Kris Kristofferson ("Me And Bobby McGee"). The bland title was Warner's choice, after rejecting The Dead's provocative SKULLFUCK. They were rewarded with The Dead's highest chart appearance at #25 in the US. (This era is also captured on DICK'S PICKS VOLUME ONE [1995], selected by The Dead's archivist Dick Latvala.)

By 1972 The Grateful Dead were the last surviving icon of the San Francisco music scene and still ascending. EUROPE '72 (1972), a triple vinyl album went Top 30. By now there was a bewildering cast of Hunter cameo characters (later, of course, familiars), like Annie Bonneau in "Black Peter", Benson in "Candyman" or Shannon in "Jack Straw". HUNDRED YEAR HALL (1995) documents the Frankfurt leg of this tour, showcasing what Lesh described as one of their best concert tours ever. The tour also featured new members, **Keith** and **Donna Godchaux** (respectively keyboards/vocals and vocals).

This was an important time for solo and session activities. Garcia had taken the first steps with the soundtrack albums ZABRISKIE POINT and HOOTEROLL? (both 1971) and the notable GARCIA (1972). The atoning Hart released ROLLING THUNDER (1972), a masterpiece of weirdness and channelled energy with members of The Dead, other Bay Area bands, and the Northern Indian classical tabla maestros Alla Rakha and his son Zakir Hussain in attendance.

Although credited to Weir, ACE (1972) was generally viewed as a band album. Reprising "Playing In The Band" from GRATEFUL DEAD, it also debuted a new writing combination, with Weir working alongside **John Perry Barlow**, an oddball visionary active in Freemasonry and Republican politics. "Cassidy" and "Looks Like Rain" were exquisite and the Barlow/Weir partnership forever shifted the songwriting balance. Although still prolific, Hunter would henceforth get ever fewer songs on Dead albums.

In March 1973 Pigpen died of cirrhosis of the liver. An era had passed. That July, BEAR'S CHOICE doffed its cap to him, and bade farewell to the band's contract with Warners. In their place came Grateful Dead Records – own labels being highly fashionable in the wake of The Beatles and Apple. Their first self-release, WAKE OF THE FLOOD (1973), would be remembered for Hunter/Garcia's moving ballad "Stella Blue", and Weir's "Weather Report Suite", co-written with Eric Andersen and Barlow. Sadly, counterfeit copies cut a swathe through profits, reducing revenue at a critical stage in the label's development. Undeterred, the group also launched a subsidiary label, Round, in May 1974, debuting with Hunter's TALES OF THE GREAT RUM RUNNERS and COMPLIMENTS OF GARCIA. That month The Dead also unveiled a three-storey-high sound system.

FROM THE MARS HOTEL (1974) unveiled a new songwriting partnership in Lesh and Bobby Petersen, who had made a minor contribution to ANTHEM. Their "Pride Of Cucamonga" and "Unbroken Chain" were two of the album's highlights, emblematic songs cut from the Grateful Dead cloth. Sadly, the partnership was cut short by Petersen's death in 1987. MARS HOTEL also premiered the classic Dead songs "China Doll", "Ship Of Fools" and "Scarlet Begonias".

In October 1974, road-weary and ground down by the cost of touring their "Wall Of Sound", The Dead filmed their Winterland dates. After Woodstock's success, rock films were considered to have big potential; however, The Dead got it wrong, with their planned movie gobbling up finances for years to come. Off the road, they put together a new repertoire – as ONE FROM THE VAULT (1991 but recorded in the summer of 1975) showed – which debuted in their repertoire for BLUES FOR ALLAH (1975), a tight and spirited release on the band's own label which topped previous Dead albums with a #12 placing in the US charts.

Financially, The Dead were a mess and they signed with United Artists, releasing the heavily compromised STEAL YOUR FACE (1976). It was intended as the film's aural counterpart, but the movie remained in limbo until the following year. Frustrated, the band again changed labels, this time to Arista, and enlisted Keith Olsen – who had assisted the relaunch of Fleetwood Mac – to produce TERRAPIN STATION (1977). It was a mixed bag, ranging through Barlow/Weir's muscular "Estimated Prophet", Weir's fey cover of Martha And The Vandellas' "Dancin' In The Streets", and the lushly poetic Hunter/Garcia "Terrapin Station" suite.

Despite their fanatical live following – DICK'S PICKS VOLUME THREE (1995) captures a set of this period – record companies want bestsellers. The Dead succumbed to pressure from Arista, who paired them with Lowell George from Little Feat for SHAKEDOWN STREET (1978). 'Nothing's happening on Shakedown Street', they sang ominously. Only the title track and the final emergence of an old song, "Fire On The Mountain", suggested otherwise. However, in the true spirit of The Dead, the year ended on a high, as they finagled permission to play a series of dates at the pyramids of Cheops in Egypt – including one that coincided with an eclipse. A different shade of darkness was manifested in Hart's film score for Coppola's *Apocalypse Now* (1979).

The Godchauxs were dispatched after SHAKEDOWN STREET (Keith died in 1980 in a road accident) and **Brent Mydland**, who had been playing in Bob Weir's band, Bobby And The Midnites, moved in to expand the palate with piano, organ and synthesizer. He made his debut on GO TO HEAVEN (1980), which was given a radio-orientated sheen by producer Gary Lyons and added "Feel Like A Stranger" and "Althea" to their live repertoire. Spurred by the active trade of concert tapes among Deadheads, Arista followed up with two live sets, the superior, acoustic RECKONING and the electric DEAD SET (1981).

Around this time, Garcia was sinking into a slough of self-indulgence with cocktail drug-taking and a junk-food diet for company. Heroin staunched his flow of creativity and a nadir was reached when he fell into a diabetic coma in 1986. Afterwards he had to be taught the rudiments of music by Merl Saunders, a keyboardist who had guested on the 1971 vintage GRATEFUL DEAD and worked extensively in solo, session and Garcia offshoot band contexts.

With Garcia back in the fold, The Dead returned to the studio for IN THE DARK (1987), one of their most enduring works and their most commercially successful (reaching #6 in the US). Its songs had been toured for years and consequently were 'jammed in'. "Touch of Gray"/"My Brother Esau" charted, with an imaginative video for the MTV generation despite its defiant oldie viewpoint. "Hell In A Bucket" and "Throwing Stones" were magnificent. A Dead revival ensued, buoyed by touring with Bob Dylan. The souvenir of this collaboration, however, DYLAN & THE DEAD (1989), recorded in July 1987, successfully desecrated two legends in one go.

BUILT TO LAST (1989), despite a couple of good songs – "Victim Or The Crime" and "Picasso Moon" – proved another unmemorable studio

Sleep of the Dead (from left): Garcia, Pigpen, Kreutzmann, Godchaux, Weir and Lesh

adventure. Another live album WITHOUT A NET (1990), almost made up for it, culled from shows with jazz saxophonist Branford Marsalis, renewing an association dating back to "Eyes Of The World" on WAKE OF THE FLOOD.

The scale of The Dead's success as a live band brought rewards as well as problems. In an era of stadium rock The Dead could generate enormous sums of money, and in the 90s they featured in *Forbes* magazine's annual list of entertainment industry high-fliers as a multimillion-dollar business. A proportion of this wealth was channelled back into the arts, via the **Rex Foundation**, whose wide interests included funding recordings of living classical composers Elliott Carter and Robert Simpson, and a dead one, Havergal Brian, and by Rex Radio, co-created by Lesh in 1987 on KPFA-FM to air new non-commercial music or, as Lesh commented, 'the stuff that falls between the cracks'. Lesh was also a prime mover behind GRAYFOLDED (1995), one of the best Dead offshoots, in which dozens of "Dark Star" recordings were reconfigured and resequenced by John Oswald.

Although The Dead continued to tour in the early 90s, and fellow artists such as Elvis Costello, Lyle Lovett and Dr. John paid their respects with a covers album, DEADICATED (1991), darker clouds were gathering. Mydland was killed by a cocaine and morphine speedball in 1990. In the wake of his death, **Vince Welnick** joined the band, and **Bruce**

Hornsby (keyboards) helped them through tours of Europe and the US. Archive work (the DICK'S PICKS series) and solo projects predominated, Hart, notably, winning a Grammy in the 'World Music' category for a rhythm extravaganza called PLANET DRUM (1991), featuring African, Caribbean and Indian percussion maestros.

Most fans must have sensed that the end, when it came, would be when Garcia died and on August 9, 1995, Captain Trips succumbed in his sleep to heart failure at a rehab centre. Over the subsequent months, The Dead considered replacements, short-listing several and argued over the wisdom of even attempting to replace Garcia. Wisdom prevailed. In December 1995 they announced their formal decision to disband.

It was an honourable close to proceedings. The Dead had become a national institution as they evolved from state-of-the-cool, though the butt of anti-hippie wit, to recognition as a unique musical institution, and they had supported uncounted good causes along the way, playing untold fund-raising benefits for environmental, community, health and welfare causes. The obituaries for both Garcia and The Dead were heartfelt, and even the obligatory GREATEST HITS album (1996) managed a suitable degree of reverence.

After the disbandment, Hart continued to work on world music projects and was the first to release a new solo album, THE MYSTERY BOX (1996). This had been years in the making and confounded expectations, his voice growling through songs counterpointed by the tight vocal arrangements of English female vocal group, the Mint Juleps. Longtime Dead associate Bob Bralove and Constanten, meanwhile, created a remarkable piano duo called **Dose Hermanos**, and Weir put together **Rat Dog** for a summer tour. A new trip had begun.

DOZIN' AT THE KNICK (1997) was the first post-Captain Trips product to make the stores. Another live album to stack up next to the hundreds already on the shelves, this shows Grateful Dead Incorporated in their 1990 finery and stretches over three CDs. Another addition to the Dead's awesome live catalogue was FALLOUT FROM THE PHIL ZONE (1997), a double-CD selection of live tracks showing The Dead at their greatest from vintage '67 space-noodlings through to 1995's version of Dylan's "Visions Of Johanna" featuring the legendary Jerry.

⊙ **Two From The Vault** (1992; Grateful Dead Records). Recorded on foreign turf in Los Angeles in 1968, this captures a fiery performance by the sextet of Garcia, Hart, Kreutzmann, Lesh, McKernan and Weir.

⊙ **Live Dead** (1970; Warners). One of the supreme psychedelic testaments, genuinely revealing of the experience. "Dark Star" into "St. Stephen" into "The Eleven" into "Turn On Your Lovelight" reveal a cosmos of possibilities. For the first time, The Dead's reputation made sense for those who had never had the opportunity to see them live.

⊙ **Workingman's Dead** (1970; Warners). The first of two folk-styled beauties, this ranks as a peak achievement. Odd to recall that in the midst of all this beauty "Casey Jones" fell foul of airtime programmers because of its 'Drivin' my train/High on cocaine' couplet and "Uncle John's Band" because of 'goddamn'. Pigpen was also to be heard in his element in the hard-driving "Easy Wind", showing what a powerful vocalist and how steeped in the blues he was.

⊙ **American Beauty** (1970; Warners). Like WORKINGMAN'S DEAD, another folky series of gems (including Hunter's biographical tale, "Truckin'", with guests such as David Grisman, Ned Lagin, Dave Nelson, Dave Torbert and Howard Wales, all of whom would bob in and out of The Dead circle over the years.

⊙ **Dick's Picks Volume Four** (1996; Grateful Dead Records). This triple-CD set, recorded over two nights at the Fillmore East in 1970, offers a snapshot of history, with elaborate jams segueing into song after song. Check the pure magic of "Dark Star" into "That's It For The Other One" into "Lovelight".

⊙ **Blues For Allah** (1975; Grateful Dead Records). This studio album revealed a Dead that had been wood-shedding while off the road. Strong material prevailed, played by the Garcia, Godchauxs, Kreutzmann, Lesh and Weir line-up – with Hart augmenting, credited with percussion and crickets.

⊙ **Reckoning** (1981; Arista). The acoustic face of The Dead playing originals and covers from the Warfield in San Francisco and Radio City Music Hall in NYC. As Blair Jackson wrote in his book *The Music Never Stopped*, 'The remarkable thing about the record is that the Dead are able to pull off the same kind of dynamic shifts and intricate jams as an acoustic group as they do as an electric powerhouse.'

⊙ **In The Dark** (1987; Arista). With this album, The Dead reached out and shepherded home a new audience. "Touch Of Gray" was a Top 10 charting single, and on its back this excellent album did good business.

⊙ **Fillmore East 2.11.69** (1998; Grateful Dead Records).
Maintaining an anywhere-near-complete set of Grateful Dead releases is beyond the scope of all but the most dedicated and well-heeled fan. This live recording from the band at their late-60s peak, however, wins a place on every Deadhead's shelves, being one of the five best Dead releases of all time.

Ken Hunt

DAVID GRAY

Born 1968 Manchester, England.

If there's one contemporary British recording artist who epitomizes the maxim that perseverance pays, it's singer, guitarist and songwriter **David Gray**. With his career seemingly over in the mid-90s, after his first three albums had failed to trouble the chart compilers in his homeland, long-overdue and unexpected success was still to come after the release of album number four, 1998's WHITE LADDER.

Gray's musical career began after his family moved to Pembrokeshire in Wales. As a teenager, inspired by punk rock and The Smiths, his first band **The Prawns** (renamed The Vacuums) performed at school events to equal levels of bemusement and irritation from classmates. But Gray's determination was considerable even then, and by the time he had embarked on a course at the Liverpool College of Art, he had begun songwriting in earnest, forming a group called Waiting For Deffo. Although a demo tape reached Orbital's manager Rob Holden, Holden was only prepared to sign Gray, not his band. With Waiting For Deffo no more, Gray moved to London, whereupon he signed a deal with Virgin's indie subsidiary Hut Records.

A Celtic-flavoured debut A CENTURY ENDS (1993) and the following year's grungier FLESH were poor sellers in the UK, but the day after Virgin dropped him in early 1995, he was offered a deal by an A&R man from EMI America. The making of the resulting album, Sell Sell Sell (1996), was a traumatic process for Gray and a new collaborator known simply as **Clune**

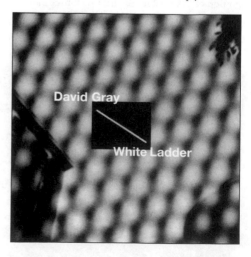
David Gray
White Ladder

(bass/percussion), after disastrous sessions with Grant Lee Buffalo's **Paul Kimble** as producer. The finished album (completed by the duo themselves) was released to near indifference, all the more punishing when Gray was at the time reaching a live audience, opening for Radiohead and The Dave Matthews Band on their US tours. Shortly afterwards, both his recording and publishing deals were terminated.

At least it couldn't get any worse. Back in London, Gray and Clune worked on numerous new songs, some of which would end up on LOST SONGS 95-98 (2000). But by the time that collection had seen the light of day, two of Gray's songs had been included in the 1999 British romantic comedy film *This Year's Love*, and WHITE LADDER, first released on his own IHT label, had finally established him as a multi-million selling artist in the UK, Ireland and the USA. Described by its creator as "the antithesis of big-budget sterility", after a slow start it even spawned two hit singles: "Babylon" and "Please Forgive Me".

2002's follow-up, A NEW DAY AT MIDNIGHT was a darker, more emotional affair (Gray had recently lost his father and gained a son). Gray was now confident with a variety of styles: "Freedom" was a heartfelt gush sung through a cracking voice, while "Real Love" rocked with big production.

Despite his dispiriting experiences in the music business, at long last David Gray was widely recognized – critically and commercially – as a performer and writer of considerable skill and depth. Even when tackling the work of others – as with his cover of Soft Cell's "Say Hello Wave Goodbye" – he is capable of remaking a song as one of his own. After several years as a well-kept secret, Gray has well and truly established himself, and shows no signs of fading away.

◉ **Lost Songs 95-98** (IHT/EastWest; 2000)
Recorded over ten days in October 1999, LOST SONGS finds Gray in intimate but defiant mode. Texturally sparse – though occasionally Gray's vocal-guitar is fleshed out with sensitive bursts of piano and rhythm section – this is a whisper of understatement in a blustering world.

Justin Lewis

MACY GRAY

Born Canton, Ohio, 1970.

Macy Gray, her of the big hair and loony stare, was born Natalie McIntyre with a 'funny voice' that kept her self-conscious and quiet for much of her childhood. Despite her early avoidance of singing, a musical career was kept in sight during seven years of classical piano training. Moving to Los Angeles to study screenwriting at college, Gray began writing songs for a musician friend. It was only when she was forced to step in as a replacement vocalist because a session singer didn't show that her remarkable voice made itself known. As the ensuing tape circulated, it was Gray's Eartha Kitt/Tina Turner style that demanded attention. Picked up by a local jazz band, Gray earned her stripes singing standards in hotel piano bars, and later moved on, with friends, to open a late-

REDFERNS

Macy Gray standing tall

night coffee-house and venue in LA, where her audience grew. Record companies took notice of her blending of styles, and in 1997 she signed to Atlantic.

A rock-leaning album was recorded but never issued and a disillusioned Gray, with a divorce and three children in tow, headed back to Ohio. It took just a year for her fortunes to change. A deal with Epic in 1998 gave Gray the opportunity to put ON HOW LIFE IS together for release the following summer. Mixing old-school soul with hip-hop and an overriding ghetto-superstar flavour, the autobiographical album of sex and violence was a hit with black and white audiences on both sides of the Atlantic, netting Brit awards for *Best International Newcomer* and *Best International Female Solo Artist* in 2000, and a Grammy in 2001 for *Best Female Pop Vocal Performance* on the flagship single, "I Try". Gray's reputation was cemented when Fat Boy Slim employed her for vocals on two tracks of his album HALFWAY BETWEEN THE GUTTER AND THE STARS (2000), including the hit single "Demons".

With outrageous taste in trash-glamour clothes, the self-titled freak waved her flag to an adoring public, but then rumours of drug abuse abounded. Speculation was inspired by her shambolic performance of "The Star Spangled Banner" at a football game in her home state in August 2001, where she stumbled over forgotten words – not the best precursor to her second album's release the following month. While THE ID sold pretty well, there were no resulting singles of the calibre of "Why Didn't You Call Me?" or "I Try". Although joined on record by Mos Def, Angie Stone and Erykah Badu (for the duet "Sweet Baby"), the record lacked cohesion and was little more than a slice of corporate soul.

Macy was back in 2003 with another album, the apologetically titled THE TROUBLE WITH BEING MYSELF, and a stomping party single "When I See You". Unfortunately, the remainder of the set lacked the single's drive, and was, like THE ID, largely forgettable. Perhaps Gray will yet pull a rabbit out of her hat and match the sparkle and soul of her debut, but until that happens her public will have to make do with well-buffed but unexciting corporate product.

⊙ **On How Life Is** (1999; Epic).
Though Gray has become a victim of her own hype, this sparkling debut still stands as a solid, funky collection.

Annebella Pollen

AL GREEN

Born Forrest City, Arkansas, April 13, 1946.

More than any performer of his generation, **Al Green** symbolizes the secular/sacred divide that gives soul music its emotional power. Green's journey across the battlefield of sexual release and spiritual transcendence began in 1960 as a member of his brothers' gospel quartet, The Greene Brothers. After a few years of modest success in Grand Rapids, Michigan, Green tried his hand at pop music with the 1967 single, "Back Up Train", which would become a US R&B Top 10 hit.

With this taste of the big time, Green decided to move south to Memphis, where he hooked up with Willie Mitchell, in-house producer for Hi Records. Their first collaboration, the muddled GREEN IS BLUES (1969), showed glimpses of the formula that would make Green one of the most accomplished soul singers of the 70s, subdued, soft soul textures heightening Green's quiet, introspective tone. It was in 1970, though, with the defection of the sublime drummer Al Jackson from cross-town rivals Stax/Volt, that Green's persona and music began to take shape. On AL GREEN GETS NEXT TO YOU (1970), Green combined the Southern rawness of Otis Redding with Marvin Gaye-style smooth moves and the tenderness of Smokey Robinson. It was a composite portrait of the soul man, both funky ("I'm A Ram For You") and forlorn ("Tired Of Being Alone").

Green distilled this emotional range into his next release, "Let's Stay Together" (1972), a perfect pop single that conveyed the pain and joy of love and sex in one sing-along chorus. The 1972 album of the same name was weighed down by material that failed to live up to the single, although his version of The Bee-Gees' "How Can You Mend A Broken Heart?" was a remarkable redemption of the original. Green's

ROCKARCHIVE.COM

The Reverend Green and his combo

other 1972 release, I'm STILL IN LOVE WITH YOU, was a deceptively simple album laden with unforgettable hooks, anchored by Al Jackson's sublimely economical drumming (his stunning intro to "I'm Glad You're Mine" was sampled by Massive Attack on "Five Man Army"). The gorgeous title track presaged the preoccupation with the bittersweet melancholy of love that would be writ large on the next album.

CALL ME (1973) was Green's masterpiece. A sad, painful, but ultimately uplifting exploration of loss, it was at once the best break-up, and the best make-out, record ever made. His sensuous voice turned Willie Nelson's "Funny How Time Slips Away" from a cry-in-your-beer mourn to a warm embrace of good memories. The album ended with "Jesus Is Waiting", a track which acknowledged the spirituality in sexuality and the physicality of religious devotion. This theme continued with "My God is Real" on LIVIN' FOR YOU (1973), but whereas CALL ME had focused on the exquisite pain of loss, the new album was a testament to the optimism of great sex and new love.

AL GREEN EXPLORES YOUR MIND (1974) suffered from weaker material, and music that retreated to the formula of subtle drum figures and nearly acoustic instrumentation. The one stand-out, though, was "Take Me To The River", a mixture of sexual and baptismal metaphors that is perhaps the ultimate expression of the conflict between the pleasures of the flesh and the ecstasies of the spirit. After AL GREEN EXPLORES YOUR MIND was recorded, Green had a vicious fight with his lover, who threw a bowl of boiling grits in his face and then killed herself. The incident pushed Green closer to God and created a musical fallout which resulted in three lacklustre and frequently bizarre albums that saw him searching for his voice and his vision.

The breakthrough came when Green parted company with Willie Mitchell, whose formula had become ossified, particularly after Al Jackson died in 1975. Green's first self-produced album, THE BELLE ALBUM (1977), made sense of what had happened to him and of the body/spirit split that had created soul in the first place ('It's you that I want, but it's Him that I need', he sang on "Belle"). Featuring Green's most emotional and dynamic singing since CALL ME, the album was boldly built around his often inspired acoustic guitar riffs. The same daring that pushed Green to make an acoustic soul album in the age of disco saw him cover "I Say A Little Prayer" on his next album, TRUTH 'N' TIME (1979).

The 80s were ushered in with Green's defection to the gospel label, Myrrh. With a couple of exceptions, most notably TOKYO ... LIVE! (1981; Cream) and HIGHER PLANE (1981), this period saw Green descend into genre exercises that combined pop stylings with gospel lyrics.

Green made a brief return to secular singing on 1995's YOUR HEART'S IN GOOD HANDS, a passable effort but really only a shadow of his former glories.

He is still undoubtedly a great singer, but, past his prime, his unforceful style doesn't lend itself to gospel the way the more stately style of Mahalia Jackson did. For past glories, he picked up a *Lifetime Achievement Grammy* in 2002, and continues to tour to this day.

⊙ **Call Me** (1973; Hi).
One of the best soul albums ever made. Languorous and sexy, holy and sinful, it is the epitome of the musical and lyrical concerns of the soul genre.

⊙ **Livin' For You** (1973; Hi).
Not quite CALL ME, but nearly there. More upbeat than its predecessor, but no less effective at creating and exploring a mood.

⊙ **The Belle Album** (1977; Hi).
Another essential release. The poignant work of a man torn between God and sex. BELLE features some of the best singing by perhaps the most beautiful male voice in black music.

⊙ **Al Green's Greatest Hits** (1975; Hi).
A faultless selection of his best-known songs and a great compilation of his styles.

⊙ **Love And Happiness** (Boxset) (2001; Hi).
A great 3-CD collection of singles, B-sides and select album cuts.

Peter Shapiro

GREEN DAY

Formed Berkeley, California, 1990.

"I do declare I don't care no more I'm burning up and out and growing BORED." First line from "Burnout"

As much phenomenon as punk band, **Green Day** grew out of Berkeley's 'progressive' Gilman Street punk clique. They were formed by **Billy Joe Armstrong** (vocals/guitar) and **Mike Dirnt** (bass/vocals), who had been playing together in garage bands from childhood, with **John Kiffmeyer** (drums), and traded initially under the name Sweet Children. As such they were signed by Gilman Street alumnus Larry Livermore's Lookout Records. The adoption of Green Day ('a stupid name', Livermore remembers saying) came just before their debut, 1000 HOURS, an EP of vast youthful vitality.

Impressed, Livermore gave the boys studio time to record 39/SMOOTH (1990). It was completed in a single day, printed up in green vinyl (original pressings are now worth much mullah), and immediately referenced the band with such as the Ramones, Undertones and Stiff Little Fingers, a musical template Green Day have stayed faithful to ever since. The songs, which still litter their live set, focused squarely on hormonal issues.

Following a national tour, Kiffmeyer left to concentrate on college studies (and subsequently the Ne'er Do Wells). In came **Frank Edwin Wright III**, better known as **Tre Cool**, a nickname given him by Livermore, who had employed him in the (recently deceased) Lookouts as a 12-year-old. This signalled the classic Green Day line-up, heard for the first time on KERPLUNK (1992), an unashamed return to a late-70s British punk sound, which became an underground alternative-rock success. Lyrically, Armstrong shied away from advocacy of anything beyond alternative, grassroots lifestyles, though he did tell one journalist that what was needed in contemporary America was 'Less sports, more painting. Less Joe Montana, more Van Gogh!'

At this time the group still split its loyalties between various collaborative projects, including such delights as Pinhead Gunpowder and Screaching Weasel. Armstrong also co-wrote "Radio, Radio, Radio" for another breaking punk band from the same region, Rancid. However, the major labels were now swarming, and Green Day opted for Reprise/Warners, whose A&R man Rob Cavallo would produce their third album, DOOKIE (1994).

Reprise must have expected a return on their investment, but they could hardly have envisaged DOOKIE's commercial ascendancy (it would eventually sell over ten million copies worldwide – an astonishing feat for what in essence remained a basic pop-punk record). Appearances at Lollapalooza and Woodstock helped spread the news, as did MTV, though British critics could hardly contain their bewilderment. Perhaps they just missed the distinctions. As Armstrong told Vox, much of the band's appeal resided in the fact that their songs were 'about being a sucker but never a dweeb'.

Inevitably, INSOMNIAC (1995) was hard-pressed to repeat its forerunner's success, but it was another strong effort in a market now saturated with blistering three-minute punk pop songs. It was of course a market Green Day had played no small part in creating. NIMROD (1997) tried to turn around the chilly reception of INSOMNIAC and was more experimental. The album has some great ideas, but overall many felt that Green Day had been left to run on too long.

After a three-year silence, Warning (2000) – another experiment – was released: a half-hearted folk-infused album with heavy leanings towards The Levellers. Despite the single release of the set's most hardcore track ever, misfit anthem "Minority", Green Day seemed to have lost their three-minute credentials. A thought which might have occurred to many fans who picked up the far more appealing INTERNATIONAL SUPERHITS (2001). Despite being a 'best of' cash-in, it nevertheless cut out some of the band's later, more muddled efforts in the studio to concentrate on what made them great in the first place. But, alongside relative newcomers such as The Bloodhound Gang and Blink 182, even die-hard fans might think Green Day have started to sound like dweebs.

(•) **1,039/Smoothed Out Slappy Hours** (1991; Lookout).
A hearty compilation of the group's early releases for Lookout.

(•) **Dookie** (1994; Reprise).
Ten million pogoing punk rock fans can't be wrong. A record for basket cases everywhere.

Alex Ogg

GREEN ON RED

Formed Tucson, Arizona, 1979.

One of the most successful of the groups of the so-called Paisley Underground, **Green On Red** were formed by **Dan Stuart** (guitar/vocals), along with **Jack Waterson** (bass), **Chris Cacavas** (keyboards) and **Van Cristian** (drums). The last was replaced by **Alex MacNicol** prior to the debut GREEN ON RED album of 1981, released on the Down There label founded by Steve Wynn of The Dream Syndicate. Like the Syndicate, Green On Red's most apparent influence in the early days was The Velvet Underground, with a thin garage-band organ sound also much in evidence.

After their second LP, GRAVITY TALKS (1983), the group was joined by guitarist **Chuck Prophet IV**, whose arrival marked a significant change in direction. With the addition of Prophet's raw but fluid guitar, and the organ sound of Cacavas considerably beefed up, Green On Red's most obvious mentor had become Neil Young in his electric rock incarnation, as evident on GAS FOOD LODGING (1985), which was particularly well received in the UK. (Like several of their Paisley Underground contemporaries, Green On Red were to find more success in Europe than the States.) Where their debut is hesitant in style and derivative in content, GAS FOOD LODGING is packed with powerful, original songs, like "The Drifter" (about a serial killer), which paint a characteristically bleak picture of America.

In 1985 Dan Stuart took time off to put out THE LOST WEEKEND, a collection of bar-room rockers released under the name **Danny & Dusty**. Recorded with Steve Wynn, the backing came from various members of the Green On Red, Dream Syndicate and Long Ryders fraternity. One song from the album, "Down To The Bone", subsequently became a staple of Green On Red's live act.

Back with Green On Red, NO FREE LUNCH (1986) saw a significant shift towards country music, a move which set the agenda for much of the band's subsequent material. But their country-orientated songs carried a strong suggestion of parody: on "Time Ain't Nothing" you were never quite sure whether Dan Stuart's homilies to family and the simple life were meant to be taken seriously. Similarly, the cover of Willie Nelson's "(Gee Ain't It Funny How) Time Slips Away" bordered on satire.

THE KILLER INSIDE ME (1987), and its accompanying tour proved to be a turning point in the band's career. Green On Red had now begun to sound contrived, and at Stuart's instigation the group was whittled down to a duo, comprising himself and Prophet. Jack Waterson recorded the album WHOSE DOG (1988), and erstwhile keyboard player Cacavas became singer and guitar player of his own group, **Chris Cacavas & Junkyard Love**, releasing a fine self-titled album in 1989.

Meanwhile Stuart and Prophet were supplemented by session players, on stage and on record. HERE

COME THE SNAKES (1989) was characterized by a raw 'take no prisoners' approach, and dominated by brash rockers like "Zombie For Love" and "Rock'N'Roll Disease". Live, the group performed as a simple four-piece, generating a buzz captured on LIVE AT THE TOWN & COUNTRY CLUB (1989). Stuart and Prophet continued with various temporary musicians on THIS TIME AROUND (1989) and SCAPEGOATS (1991), albums that revealed a greater emphasis on country almost-parodies, but also continuing experimentation. SCAPEGOATS included the extraordinary "Hector's Out", an elaborately arranged song full of dramatic tension.

Since TOO MUCH FUN (1993), Green On Red have been inactive due to the blossoming of solo careers. By 1997, Prophet, offering his own brand of low-slung guitar rock, had released his fourth solo album, HOMEMADE BLOOD, with further releases THE HURTING BUSINESS and NO OTHER LOVE emerging in 2000 and 2002 respectively. Stuart recorded RETRONUEVO (1994), with Tucson barband leader **Al Perry**, and the solo set CAN O'WORMS (1995), but since then has been pursuing other interests, devoting his attention to writing a film script.

- ⊙ **Gas Food Lodging/Green On Red** (1992; Mau Mau/ Demon).
  A reissue of the first and third albums on one CD.

- ⊙ **Little Things In Life** (1991; Music Club).
  An excellent low-price compilation of the band's later output, which also contains a fair chunk of their LIVE AT THE TOWN & COUNTRY CLUB 1989 set.

- ⊙ **The Best Of Green On Red** (1999; China).
  A comprehensive and thoughtful overview of the band's career.

- ⊙ **Archives Volume I: What Were We Thinking?** (1998; Normal).
  Fine collection of rarities, demos and radio sessions, spanning the band's heyday of 1980–87.

Keith Prewer

GREEN RIVER

Formed Seattle, 1984; disbanded 1988.

Deep in the mists that hang over the early Seattle grunge scene lie the origins of one of the key rock groups of the early 80s: **Green River**. They never really became commercially fruitful, but their records epitomized the Seattle sound, and they would later spawn two more successful groups – **MUDHONEY** and **PEARL JAM**.

In the beginning there were The Limp Richards, Mr Epp and The Ducky Boys – three bands churning out variations of hardcore punk, influenced by British new wave and American heavy metal. The personnel situation was extremely fluid if not downright incestuous, but two key players in all three bands were **Mark Arm** (guitar/vocals) and **Steve Turner** (guitar), who created Green River in late 1984. They were joined by **Alex Shumway** (drums) and Montana-born skate-punk **Jeff Ament** (bass). Green River's sound took in all the usual influences and

then spat them back as splintered, fuzzed-up punk. Add to this a taste for bizarre imagery and what you have is a beast that would later be named grunge. They were so impressive live that alternative-set darlings Sonic Youth would specially request their presence on the bill whenever they played the area.

The summer of 1985 saw the addition of another ex-Ducky Boy, **Stone Gossard** (guitar), allowing Mark Arm to concentrate on vocals. Although they had already been featured on a compilation record called DEEP SIX (1985), it was this line-up that eventually recorded the group's first true solo effort. The mini-LP COME ON DOWN (1985) was released on the Boston-based Homestead label, and from the opening title track to the closing "Tunnel Of Love" it captured the raw fury of the band's live sound. Following its release, Steve Turner soon left the fold, and would later reunite with Mark Arm in Mudhoney. Taking on replacement **Bruce Fairweather** (guitar), this line-up remained constant during the following bouts of success and internal strife.

June 1986 saw the band record their first EP for the now-legendary Sub Pop label, though a record label cash crisis delayed release until July 1987. DRY AS A BONE (1987) was a direct distillation of the Seattle scene ethos and the distinctive Sub Pop sound. These five gut-wrenching tracks were arguably as important as Nirvana's BLEACH in gate-crashing the collective rock consciousness; people began to notice Seattle at last.

Following this success they began work on an album. Laying down a version of David Bowie's "Queen Bitch", they ploughed on with their own original material. However, by the time REHAB DOLL (1988) had hit the shelves, conflict within the band had reached crisis point. Three records and three tours down the line they split. According to Mark Arm, it was a typical conflict between art and commerciality – punk versus the major-label deal. After a furious gig at LA's Scream Club, Arm wanted backstage passes for their friends, but Ament had already given them to record company A&R men who didn't even bother to turn up. Arm accused Ament of abandoning their principles and split.

This spectacular implosion resulted in the creation of three bands that have etched their identities even more deeply on the world of rock: the short-lived **MOTHER LOVE BONE**, Pearl Jam and Mudhoney.

- ⊙ **Come On Down** (1985; Homestead).
  This vicious six-track mini-LP is akin to a snapshot of the embryonic Seattle scene. Energy, distortion and alienated attitude make this a classic example of proto-grunge.

- ⊙ **Dry As A Bone** (1987; Tupelo/Sub Pop).
  This EP alone went a major way towards building Sub Pop's international reputation as the home of weird alternative rock. Uncompromising and angry, these five tracks mark an important point in the creation of a sound that would become a worldwide phenomenon.

- ⊙ **Rehab Doll** (1988; Sub Pop).
  The band had split by the time this came out, but it gave an indication as to where the various members would be heading.

Essi Berelian

GROOVE ARMADA

Formed London, 1996.

A duo united by the precision of dance music and the spontaneity of jazz, **Thomas Findlay** and **Andy Cato** are producers and multi-instrumentalists who, like Massive Attack, favour the genre-hopping type of dance album. Findlay's formative years had been spent in jazz bands playing trumpet, as well as absorbing recordings and live sets by the likes of Keith Jarrett and Bill Evans. Visits to raves in Leeds introduced him to the delights of dance, and his meeting with Cato led to their founding of a club night in London called **Groove Armada**, at which they showcased their favourite house, jazz, funk and soul influences.

When the time came to move into recording, Findlay and Cato took their club night moniker as their group name, and released several singles for the Tummy Touch label during 1997: "Captain Sensual", "M 2 Many", an EP called FOUR TUNE COOKIE and an embryonic version of "At The River" were collected on 1998's NORTHERN STAR. All were edgy and raw examples of underground dance music, and although chart success eluded the duo at this point, a second album, VERTIGO (1999) was to change all that. Prior to its inclusion on a thousand 'chill-out' compilations of varying quality, a new version of "At The River" was to take them into the UK Top 20 for the first time, closely followed by a **Fatboy Slim** remix of the arch study of dance-floor etiquette, "I See You Baby", complete with a superb mocking vocal from **Gramma Funk**.

Norman Cook was by no means the only one who had spotted Groove Armada's potential: they were asked to contribute mixes to Madonna's "Music" single, and were even invited by Elton John to appear as his opening band for a series of shows that same year. Increasingly high-profile spots at Los Angeles clubs helped their reputation in America, and 2001's GOODBYE COUNTRY (HELLO NIGHTCLUB) boasted cameos from **Nile Rodgers** and **Richie**

Havens. And when a vocal sample from Brandy on "My Friend" could not be cleared, an earthier replacement vocal from **Celetia Martin** demonstrated that Groove Armada, when freed from a sample-centric culture, could still produce something creative and sensual. Barely a year later the group were back with another album, LOVEBOX (2002), which, again, featured Richie Havens as well as contributions from **Neneh Cherry**.

- **Northern Star** (1998; Tummy Touch).
  Like many dance acts' debut albums, this is a fine collection of singles and oddities, and if it lacks the fluidity of their later work, it's still an enlightening and entertaining record.

- **Vertigo** (1999; Pepper/Zomba).
  Hypnotic and virtuoso dance music which could not be diluted even if it were featured in a trillion car commercials.

- **Goodbye Country** (Hello Nightclub) (2001; Pepper/Zomba).
  Packed with guest stars from Nile Rodgers to Richie Havens, this is their smoothest (and just occasionally, most innocuous) album, but their extraordinary skill and versatility cannot be underestimated.

Justin Lewis

THE GROUNDHOGS

Formed London, 1963; disbanded 1966; re-formed 1968; disbanded 1975; re-formed briefly 1976; re-formed 1984.

One of the more experimental musicians of the British blues boom, **Tony McPhee** (guitar/vocals/keyboards) has been leading **The Groundhogs** in various incarnations for more than three decades. Originally called The Dollar Bills, McPhee formed the first group with brothers **John** (vocals/mouth harp) and **Pete Cruickshank** (bass), **David Boorman** (drums) and **Tom Parker** (piano). They changed name to John Lee's Groundhogs in 1963, in honour of a song by blues giant **JOHN LEE HOOKER**. Despite working with blues legend Champion Jack Dupree, the original line-up split in 1966 with only a paltry two singles to its credit, though a (rare) retrospective album, LIVE AT THE AU GO GO (1973), captured the band in full swing.

McPhee subsequently teamed up with John Cruickshank in the aptly named Herbal Mixture, and enjoyed a brief tenure with The John Dummer Blues Band, before re-forming The Groundhogs, this time minus the John Lee prefix, in 1968. The new line-up featured Pete Cruickshank, plus drummer **Ken Pustelnik** and harmonica player **Steve Rye**. Flattered by their enthusiasm for his music and ability to cope with his idiosyncratic timing, John Lee Hooker insisted on The Groundhogs backing him on another prestigious UK tour, which also featured Dupree, Aynsley Dunbar and Joanne Kelly, with whom McPhee would periodically collaborate.

Reduced to a three-piece, following Rye's departure after their debut SCRATCHING THE SURFACE (1968), the band entered their most creative and suc-

GROOVE ARMADA
Vertigo
G★

cessful period. BLUES OBITUARY (1969) set the scene, but it was their third album, THANK CHRIST FOR THE BOMB (1970), which broke the band nationally, reaching #9 in the UK album charts. In addition, their burgeoning reputation was greatly enhanced by British and US tours supporting The Rolling Stones, and by their appearance at the 1970 Isle of Wight festival.

Skilfully blending social commentary with progressive rock, the McPhee songwriting machine could do no wrong – SPLIT (1971) reached the UK Top 5, a peak almost equalled by WHO WILL SAVE THE WORLD (1972). Although other releases such as HOGWASH (1972) and SOLID (1974) were equally well received, the initial rumblings of punk in the mid-70s, coupled with management problems, brought about the Groundhogs' second dissolution.

Undaunted, McPhee found new sidemen for two more albums under the Groundhogs' banner, CROSSCUT SAW and BLACK DIAMOND (both 1976), before finally calling it a day. He then formed Terraplane, named after the Robert Johnson song "Terraplane Blues", and recorded with blues legends Billy Boy Arnold and Little Walter. He also put out a couple of solo albums, the most interesting of which was THE TWO SIDES OF TONY MCPHEE.

Renewed interest in the band led to yet another Groundhogs re-formation in 1984, for the album RAZOR'S EDGE, with bassist **Alan Fish** and drummer **Mick Kirton**. More albums have followed, including 1988's excellent live set, HOGS ON THE ROAD, featuring the most stable line-up of recent years, ex-**HAWKWIND** bassist **Dave Anderson** and drummer **Mick Jones**.

Bolstered by a loyal fan base, especially in England and Germany, The Groundhogs remain a firm fixture on the pub-club circuit. The BBC radio sessions released in the ON AIR series (1998) demonstrated their awesome electric wizardry. In addition, McPhee also continues to regularly play stunning solo acoustic blues shows.

⦿ **Hogwash** (1972; BGO).
One of the band's more bluesy outings, this features McPhee's chilling rendition of Robert Johnson's "Me And The Devil", as well as self-penned masterpieces such as "3744 James Road" and "Mr. Hooker, Sir John". But quite why McPhee credits himself on the sleeve notes as having written traditional numbers like the aforementioned "Me And The Devil" or Son House's "Death Letter" is something of a mystery.

⦿ **Hogs On The Road** (1988; Demi-Monde/Magnum).
This live album from a 1987 German tour showcases the great man's guitar histrionics and composition on favourites such as "Express Man" and "Back Against The Wall".

Paul Morris

THE GUESS WHO

Formed Winnipeg, Canada, 1962; disbanded 1984; re-formed sporadically since.

From their roots as Chad Allan And The Reflections, **The Guess Who** rose to become the most popular Canadian rock band of their generation. **Chad Allan** (aka Allan Kobel; guitar/vocals), **Randy Bachman** (guitar), **Jim Kale** (bass), **Bob Ashley** (piano) and **Garry Peterson** (percussion) released their first single, "Tribute To Buddy Holly", in 1962, and followed it with further singles for Quality and Reo. Changing their name to Chad Allan And The Expressions in 1965, they achieved a #1 single in Canada with a cover of Johnny Kidd And The Pirates' "Shakin' All Over".

Ashley was then replaced on keyboards by **Burton Cummings**, who also contributed joint lead vocals. The name 'Guess Who' was an attempt to deceive buyers into thinking that the group was a 'name' English outfit; Quality Records printed these two words on the cover of the group's 1966 debut album, SHAKIN' ALL OVER. The following year, Allan left and was briefly replaced by **Bruce Decker**. The Guess Who elected to persevere as a quartet with Cummings' vocals and songwriting shaping the group into something far more dynamic.

Substantial Canadian success followed, with brief forays into the UK charts including 1967's "His Girl". Albums such as IT'S TIME (1966) and A WILD PAIR (1967) were increasingly successful, but it was 1968's WHEATFIELD SOUL that really established them as a commercial force. "These Eyes", reached the top of the domestic charts and earned the band a more lucrative American contract with RCA. Singles such as "Laughing", "Undun" and "No Time" provided further hits.

The band's only US #1, "American Woman", followed in March 1970. An album of the same title (1970) also entered the US Top 10 and is widely considered to be The Guess Who's finest achievement. However, Bachman, a devout Mormon, was tiring of the group's lifestyle and he departed to form **BACHMAN-TURNER OVERDRIVE**. He was replaced by **Kurt Winter** and **Greg Leskiw**, but they failed to bridge the gap his departure had left. Despite further success with the upbeat, cosmopolitan rock of "Share The Land" and "Rain Dance", by 1972 Leskiw and Kale had also departed to be replaced by **Don McDougall** (guitar) and **Bill Wallace** (bass). McDougall lasted until 1974, when **Domenic Trobiano** (ex-James Gang) was drafted as the group's sole guitarist, Winter having also left. These extensive line-up shuffles inevitably undermined the group's progress, although Canadian success continued. They enjoyed their last hit in 1974 with "Clap For The Wolfman", but Cummings disbanded The Guess Who the following year. After a million-selling debut single, "Stand Tall", he has produced an uneven but occasionally enthralling sequence of solo albums, the best being his debut, 1976's BURTON CUMMINGS.

Several unsuccessful reunions were attempted in his absence until 1987, when Cummings and Bachman toured together as The Guess Who for the first time in years. However, when Kale and Peterson enlisted a few helping hands to record LONELY ONE (1995) as the first new Guess Who album in fifteen years, the critical reaction was venomous, with *Goldmine* magazine describing it as 'pathetic and desperate'. It wasn't much of a welcome back. 2002's RADIO 1 SESSIONS was, thankfully, far more warmly received.

⊙ **Track Record: The Guess Who Collection** (1988; RCA).
This comprehensive double-album collection takes in all The Guess Who standards, from "These Eyes", "Laughing" and "American Woman" to "Clap For The Wolfman".

Alex Ogg

GUIDED BY VOICES

Formed Dayton, Ohio, 1986.

Although singer-songwriter **Robert Pollard** formed **Guided By Voices** in the mid 80s, it wasn't until the mid 90s that their work gained any recognition outside the Ohio state borders. Originally consisting of Pollard, his brother **Jim** and **Tobin Sprout**, this trio later became a sextet with the recruitment of **Mitch Mitchell** (guitar), **Kevin Fennell** (drums) and **Don Toohey** (bass).

After limited-edition albums and singles all sold out, a breakthrough was achieved with their seventh LP, VAMPIRE ON TITUS (1993), their first for New York label Matador, and their first release in the UK, packaged on one CD with the album PROPELLER. It contained all their essential musical elements – extremely brief songs with impenetrable titles and lo-fi sound quality. Though as hit-and-miss as its predecessors, tracks like "Wished I Was A Giant", "Jar Of Cardinals" and "Gleemer" hinted at finer things to come.

While scarcely any more accessible, many of their more recent albums, BEE THOUSAND (1994), ALIEN LANES (1995) and UNDER THE BUSHES UNDER THE STARS (1996), have benefited from the greater resources available to them. MAG EARWHIG (1997)

came about after Sprout had departed and demonstrated heavy influences from garage band Cobra Verde, who provided Pollard with heavier backing. 1999's DO THE COLLAPSE was even more accomplished and polished; it found the band for a short time signed to the ill-fated Creation Records.

Something like a cross between The Beatles, Pavement and Sebadoh, Guided By Voices have been summed up by Robert Pollard as 'a pop band but a strange pop band. We're other worldly' Catchy melodies are often undercut by bizarre or unsettling lyrics, as on the ALIEN LANES song "My Valuable Hunting Knife". Sometimes a single image resonates – "Striped White Jets" are 'in their hangars bleeding/Cover them all in black' – while in other songs the meaning is only clarified at the conclusion.

Guided By Voices' expansive catalogue had always attracted the obsessive fan, a resource that in 2000 allowed the band the indulgence of an enormous 4CD collection of outtakes, SUITCASE – FAILED EXPERIMENTS AND TRASHED AIRCRAFT, a package that is not recommended to the idle listener. 2002's UNIVERSAL TRUTHS AND CYCLES, though, was a mesmerizing addition to their catalogue. With various solo careers, side projects, and future collaborations in the offing, expect great things from the GBV camp in the future.

⊙ **Bee Thousand** (1994; Matador).
Imagine the soundtrack to an episode of *The X-Files* written by Lewis Carroll, and you can get some idea of this album. Highlights include "I Am A Scientist" and "Buzzards And Dreadful Crows", where Pollard sings 'There's something in this deal for everyone.'

⊙ **Alien Lanes** (1995; Matador).
On which Guided By Voices make a heroic attempt on the world record for most songs on a single album – 28. Their pop sensibility is to the fore in songs like the terrific "Game Of Pricks" and "Motor Away".

⊙ **Universal Truths And Cycles** (2002; Matador).
A great set that finds the band, as ever, sounding raw, flustered and slightly shambolic. "Wire Greyhounds" and "Wings Of Thorn" shine.

Chris Jenkins

THE GUN CLUB

Formed Los Angeles, 1980; disbanded 1985; re-formed 1987; ended 1996.

Initially and mistakenly seen as poor relations to the likes of Black Flag, the first incarnation of **The Gun Club** comprised **Kid Congo Powers** (aka Brian Tristan; guitar), **Rob Ritter** (bass), **Terry Graham** (drums) with the uncompromising figure of **Jeffrey Lee Pierce** (vocals, guitar) at the helm.

Ruby Records were the first to pick up on their distinctive fusion of punk, Delta blues and rockabilly, and released the powerful FIRE OF LOVE (1981). This strident opening salvo included startling arrangements of blues standards "Cool Drink Of Water" and "Preaching The Blues". Pierce, with occasional help from Powers, penned the rest of the material, including the vibrant "She's Like Heroin To Me" and the disturbing "For The Love Of Ivy", with its redneck lyric and howling vocal. Powers briefly defected to **THE CRAMPS**, and was substituted by **Ward Dotson** for the recording of the album.

FIRE OF LOVE was well received on both sides of the Atlantic, but MIAMI (1982), rush-released on Blondie guitarist Chris Stein's label, Animal, was a disappointment. Kid Congo Powers' return at this point did little to help The Gun Club's progress, and the next LP, DEATH PARTY (1983), was patchy, to say the least.

The following year saw a brief change in fortunes, with Pierce seemingly over the worst of his alcoholism. LAS VEGAS STORY (1984), was a great improvement, recalling the fire and ambition of the debut LP – especially on "Walking With The Beast".

A prolific period for The Gun Club continued with the solid and stirring, THE BIRTH, THE DEATH, THE GHOST (1984). Presumably on the strength of its title, it attracted a new audience from the British goth scene. Indeed, bass player at the time, **Patricia Morrison**, later joined **SISTERS OF MERCY**. Nevertheless, by 1985's live release, DAS KALINDA BOOM, Pierce was back to his self-destructive habits, and disbanded the group. A 1985 compilation, TWO SIDES OF THE BEAST, appeared to have tied up all the loose ends.

Despite his drink problems, Pierce embarked upon a short-lived solo career, which resulted in a handful of bizarre live appearances, and the intelligently conceived LP, WILDWEED (1985). The time spent apart seemed recuperative to The Gun Club, and they surprisingly re-formed in 1987.

The critically acclaimed MOTHER JUNO (1987) introduced the new line-up of Pierce, Powers, **Romi Mori** (bass/lead guitars) and percussionist **Nick Sanderson**, with help from the likes of **EINSTÜRZENDE NEUBAUTEN** frontman Blixa Bargeld. Produced by Robin Guthrie of Cocteau Twins, it offered a lusher, more textured variant on the band's familiar sound. Although some purists derided this new strain, there was little denying the power of songs like "Port Of Souls" and the standard "Bill Bailey". For the first time since their debut LP, the band found themselves in the ascendant.

After a three year hiatus, PASTORAL HIDE AND SEEK (1990) saw yet another change in direction. The maturing sound was equally in evidence on 1991's DIVINITY, the release of which saw the departure, for the third time, of Kid Congo Powers. He resurfaced in 1993 as a member of **KILLING JOKE**. Their story finishes with the magnificent LUCKY JIM (1993), which saw the band return to the hard blues sound that had made their name in the first place.

Jeffrey Lee Pierce released a further solo album in 1992 – RAMBLIN' JEFFREY LEE & CYPRESS GROVE WITH WILLIE LOVE – but his health was deteriorating. His death, from a stroke in April 1996, was a sad end for a powerful, soul-searching band.

⊙ **Fire Of Love** (1981; Beggars Banquet/Ruby; currently unavailable).
This wild-eyed, unrestrained record was surely one of the finest US rock debuts of the 80s. Its primitive production and subject serve only as a harrowing reminder of West Coast backwater attitudes. A shame the band could not repeat the effect.

⊙ **Divinity** (1991; New Rose/Red Rhino).
One of the few Gun Club albums available on CD, this interesting release contains both studio and live tracks.

Jeremy Simmonds

GUNS N' ROSES

Formed Los Angeles, 1985.

"We're like a fuckin' grenade and it's like everybody's struggling to hold the pin in!" Slash

One of rock's most exciting, visceral and dangerous live acts, **Guns N' Roses** formed from the debris of several rock bands floating around the scuzzier neighbourhoods of LA. Vocalist **Axl Rose** (anagram of 'oral sex' – real name William Bailey) had previously been part of Hollywood Rose, and an early incarnation of LA Guns; **Izzy Stradlin** (aka Jeff Isabelle; guitar) had known Axl since 1979, while **Michael 'Duff' McKagan** (bass) was a veteran of the LA punk and hardcore scene. Guitarist **Slash** (aka Saul Hudson) and drummer **Steven Adler** had previously put together an outfit called Road Crew.

Generally regarded as the band's definitive line-up, this quintet played their first gig at LA's Troubadour Club in June 1985 after only two days' rehearsal. It preceded the aptly named Hell Tour, during which they suffered transport breakdowns and atrocious ticket sales – only twenty people turned up to their first gig. However, before long their residency at the Troubadour was coinciding with a glam and sleaze revival, and they were marked out as one of the hottest attractions on the LA circuit.

Major label Geffen signed the band for a mere $75,000 in March 1986, but the money vanished soon on drugs and debts. In the summer of 1986, they unleashed a self-produced, limited-edition EP LIVE ?!★@ LIKE A SUICIDE, containing four tracks: tacky covers of Rose Tattoo's "Nice Boys" and Aerosmith's "Mama Kin", along with two originals, "Move To The City" and "Reckless Life". Its fury and raw energy ensured that all 10,000 copies sold out within four weeks.

The band's reputation for sex, drugs and violence followed them to the UK in June 1987, as Axl tried to pick fights with hecklers, while Slash and Izzy staggered nonchalantly around the stage under the influence of something stronger than Jack Daniel's.

It was not until the release of APPETITE FOR DESTRUCTION (1987) that the band proved their importance. From the shuddering riff and police-siren scream of the opener "Welcome To The Jungle" to the closing swagger of "Rocket Queen", each song was nailed home with murderous precision. The album was studded with instant classics: "Mr. Brownstone" was pure, shuffling sleaze; "Out Ta Get Me" was all paranoid posturing; and "Sweet Child O' Mine" proved they could write hit singles. The cover – a Robert Williams painting of a robot

REDFERNS

Axl (with rock'n'roll baggage) Slash (with cigarette)

humour, but it was the final track, "One In A Million", that found the band courting controversy again. Written from the point of view of a hick white kid arriving in LA, Axl made references to 'niggers' and 'faggots'. This resulted in the band being slung off an AIDS benefit gig in New York, but the album was another big seller.

Their self-destructive image continued to grow. When supporting The Rolling Stones at the beginning of their 1990 world tour, Axl threatened to quit if his band-mates didn't tone down their chemical excesses. His vitriol was primarily aimed at Slash, who within a year had broken his heroin habit, but Adler found it harder to wake from the nightmare and, was eventually replaced by ex-Cult drummer **Matt Sorum**.

Sorum and new keyboard player **Dizzy Reed** made their Guns N' Roses debut at the Rock in Rio festival in January 1991, before the band confounded expectations by starting work on a new album. It was a gargantuan affair, with thirty tracks spread across two separate volumes. After Axl's hatred of Bob Clearmountain's mix led to everything being scrapped, the project was resumed with Bill Price, who had previously worked with the Sex Pistols, at the controls.

"You Could Be Mine", also included in the Arnold Schwarzenegger movie *Terminator 2*, was released as a taster in July 1991, with USE YOUR ILLUSION I & II following in September. The hard rock and honky-tonk blues numbers were effortlessly convincing, but they lost the plot with some bloated ballads, pointless cover versions and childish rants. Two epics, "Civil War" and "Coma", were outstanding cuts of focused quality, but generally it all lacked the lean, live feel of their debut.

On the subsequent world tour, the performances were much less chaotic than previously, but Axl's prima-donna tendencies continued to surface, with some shows being delayed for up to three hours. Izzy Stradlin quit in late 1991 to begin a solo career and was replaced by **Gilby Clarke**. Duff came up with a side-project of his own at around the same time, releasing BELIEVE IN ME (1992).

A covers album, THE SPAGHETTI INCIDENT? (1993), provided an interesting insight into the group's influences, featuring songs by The Damned, Sex Pistols, The Stooges and, provocatively, Charles Manson.

Since their hit cover of The Rolling Stones' "Sympathy For The Devil" (1994), recorded for the soundtrack of *Interview With The Vampire*, they have remained silent. Clarke left in the wake of his solo release, PAWN SHOP GUITARS (1994), but Slash officially stayed with the Gunners, despite his sideline project, Slash's **Snake Pit**, and a 1995 album, IT'S FIVE O'CLOCK SOMEWHERE (1995).

However, it has become increasingly clear that G N' R really stands for Axl Rose plus hired flunkies. High-profile band members were gradually ousted from the next album and Axl began to bring in col-

raping a woman – caused even more controversy than the expletive-laden songs. Only initial quantities were shipped with the original cover and subsequently the Gunners' cross logo was used. To date it has sold seventeen million copies worldwide.

They promoted the album by supporting The Cult and Motley Crüe in their homeland, and when, on a UK tour with Aerosmith, the headliners unexpectedly pulled out, the Gunners went ahead with the tour anyway, which culminated with a near sellout gig at London's Hammersmith Odeon. The following summer, they were on the bill at the Donington Monsters Of Rock but their appearance ended in tragedy as a surge towards the stage resulted in two young fans being crushed to death.

The release of LIES (1988) was more a holding operation than a true follow-up, comprising their first EP, plus four new acoustic numbers. "Used To Love Her (But I Had To Kill Her)" was pure black

laborators from outfits as diverse as the Vandals and Nine Inch Nails. By the end of 1998 the sessions were apparently well under way, but various reports suggested that when any new material saw the light of day there would be no tour.

By the summer of 2000 Slash had put together an actual band for his second Snakepit album, AIN'T LIFE GRAND. As Snakepit became more of a permanent proposition, the occasional rumours of a reunion G N' R tour seemed less and less likely. Axl meanwhile seemed to be constantly on the verge of releasing an album oddly titled THE CHINESE DEMOCRACY with a supposedly more industrial flavour to it – witness the single track "Oh My God" that emerged on the *End Of Days* soundtrack. Other ex-G N' R-members (Clarke, Stradlin, McKagan) continue to

occasionally knock out solid if unexciting solo efforts. In 2002, however, a G'N'R reunion began to seem possible as it was announced that the band would be headlining at the UK's Reading Festival.

Appetite For Destruction (1987; Geffen).
A foul-mouthed debut on which the Gunners shamelessly recycle rock's scarier moments. Derivative but frighteningly good.

Use Your Illusion I & II (1991; Geffen).
The overindulgent production masks the energy of the songs, and some material fails to hit the mark. However, in amongst the dross lurk some fine songs.

The Spaghetti Incident? (1993; Geffen).
A trawl through the band's personal record collections – worth hearing for Axl's hilarious attempt at an English accent on a rendition of UK Subs' "Down On The Farm".

Essi Berelian

HALF JAPANESE/JAD FAIR

Formed Maryland, 1977.

Armed with a voice shrill enough to shatter his trademark eyeglasses and the unique ability to turn his most minute fascination into a riotous, cranky love song, **Jad Fair** has been clinging to rock's fringes since the late 1970s. Despite his expressed desire to pen the most popular song the world has ever known, one gets the feeling that the margins are where Fair most likes to hang his hat.

Never was Jad's yelp more piercing or guitar less tame than on the early recordings of **Half Japanese**, the Maryland bedroom band he starred in alongside his brother **David**. After two obscurely released 7" EPs – CALLING ALL GIRLS (1977) and NO MONO/NO NO (1978) – an expanded line-up debuted the knockout triple-LP 1/2 GENTLEMEN/NOT BEASTS (1979). With this collection the band rode the fury of punk rock with the wide eyes of Richman's Modern Lovers and a desire to pour every mood swing and passion, every guitar burp and vocal wheeze, onto a cheap tape-deck – a recording method that would become ever more popular among lo-fi indie rockers over a decade later. In the spirit of Royal Trux's TWIN INFINITIVES or even Lou Reed's METAL MACHINE MUSIC, Half Jap's long-winded debut was only digestible in bits and pieces. Nevertheless, hearing the Fairs wail about all the girls they couldn't get is a viscerally thrilling, albeit occasionally disturbing, experience.

Although the brothers' development as songwriters didn't compare to say Jonathan Richman's (the duo broadly sticking to a formula of 'love songs' and 'monster songs'), the Fair pair left the Eighties with decidedly smoother edges than they had at the start of the decade. 1981's LOUD, considered their masterpiece by some, presented a more focused version of its predecessor. 1984 saw the simultaneous release of SING NO EVIL, which showcased Jad songs like "Firecracker Firecracker", and OUR SOLAR SYSTEM, on which David unleashed creepy lyrics like 'Little girls have to be home early/They can't stay out late at night/To tease me and kiss me'.

In the mid-80s, label troubles forced this prolific band to take something of a hiatus. Eventually MUSIC TO STRIP BY appeared in 1987, while the release of CHARMED LIFE was pushing back to 1988. Featuring surprisingly catchy songs such as "One Million Kisses" and "Said And Done", CHARMED LIFE showed Half Japanese (which, at the time of the album's 1985 recording, included Gumball's **Don Fleming**) at the height of their powers. Unfortunately, David Fair didn't stick around too long to bask in his band's glory, and several of the albums Jad recorded in the immediate wake of his brother's departure – both as Half Japanese and under his own name – suffered from David's absence. From this period, the solo effort BEST WISHES (1987) offers a full helping of oddball instrumentals, while Half Japanese's THE BAND THAT WOULD BE KING (1989) – which carried the same name as a wonderful Half Jap documentary movie – at times seemed a bit too smooth.

Over the years Fair has sought refuge from his solo career in a series of collaborations. The list is impressive. He's shared records with **The Pastels**, **Daniel Johnston** and **Kramer**, and has also invited members of **Sonic Youth**, the **Velvet Underground** and **Dinosaur Jr.** to play on his albums. **The Stinky Puffs** teamed Jad with his son and, briefly, members of **Nirvana**. 1996 brought DQE AND JAD FAIR, an interesting collaboration with Dairy Queen Express's **Grace Braun**, in which Fair whinnied over Braun's junky guitar stylings. The same year he joined forces with his brother David for JAD AND DAVID FAIR: BEST FRIENDS (1996), and two years later 26 MONSTER SONGS FOR CHILDREN (1998). A pair of albums with the Shapir-O'Rama (1997's WE ARE THE RAGE and 1999's I LIKE YOUR FACE) have Fair yelping lyrics he wrote with co-bellower **Kim Rancourt** while a five-piece band stages what amounts to a musical riot.

The 90s also saw Jad hooking up with **Steve Shelley** (Sonic Youth) and **Tim Foljahn** (Two Dollar Guitar) to form **Mosquito**. The trio released a handful of singles and several great collections of chaotic, scratchy miniatures that present some of Fair's most energized moments. The best of the batch are TIME WAS (1993) and UFO CATCHER (1993).

Best of all, however, was 1998's collaboration with **Yo La Tengo**, STRANGE BUT TRUE, which featured 22 songs inspired by supermarket tabloid headlines such as "Helpful Monkey Wallpapers Entire Home" and "Feisty Millionaire Fills Potholes With Hundred-Dollar Bills." Though the collection sold well thanks to the presence of the lauded Hoboken trio (who provide the loosely structured instrumentation), the LP's unsung heroes are lead vocalist Jad, and his brother David, who penned the very funny lyrics ('Glad it's a watch and not a cuckoo clock', the narrator shrugs in "X-Ray Reveals Doctor Left Wristwatch Inside Patient"). Released on Matador to critical acclaim, the record led to a subsequent tour with Yo La Tengo that found Jad serenading listeners half his age. While most in the audience seemed unaware of Fair's history, their record collections no doubt bore the influence of this aggressively nerdy middle-aged guy who, at least in spirit and spunk, may as well have been the youngest kid in the club.

The late 90s witnessed even more activity with the release of Half Jap's thrilling BONE HEAD (1997), while Jad released a series of extremely anarchic and obscure sets with the likes of **Jason Willett** and **Gilles Rieder**, while also putting in an appearance with **Teenage Fanclub** for WORDS OF WISDOM AND HOPE (2002). It seems unlikely that Jad Fair will hang up his battered, hand-painted guitar just yet.

Half Japanese

(•) **1/2 Gentlemen/Not Beasts** (1979; Armageddon. Reissued 1993).
The audacious triple-album debut of Half Japanese brims with all the good things that made punk rock tick: sexual frustration, hostility towards mainstream heroes, technical incompetence and youthful innocence.

(•) **Charmed Life** (1988; 50 Skidillion Watts).
Perhaps the most approachable of the band's records, this mid-career effort could be tagged Half Japanese's *Rubber Soul*.

(•) **Greatest Hits** (1995; Safe House).
An ironically titled two-CD collection looking back at eleven albums and fifteen years. With a nice mix of the old (NOISY AND CHAOTIC) and new (noisy and chaotic), this is the ideal Half Japanese starting point.

Jad Fair and Yo La Tengo

(•) **Strange But True** (1998; Matador).
This one-off teamed Fair's voice with his brother's lyrics and Yo La Tengo's back-up. All songs are based on strange-but-true headlines from supermarket tabloids – an admittedly easy target, which the co-conspirators nail with subtle wit.

Jay Ruttenberg

HALF MAN HALF BISCUIT

Formed Birkenhead, England, 1984;
disbanded 1986; re-formed 1990.

A band as savage as they are whimsical, **Half Man Half Biscuit** provide an unexpected dessert for those British post-punk teenagers who lament the demise of bands with bite. **Nigel Blackwell**'s inimitable songwriting on the minutiae of life, football and TV celebs quickly garnered cult status; particularly live, where fans could eagerly chant back his wise words.

The singer and rhythm guitarist, Blackwell formed HMHB along with his brother **Si** (lead guitar), **Neil Crossley** (bass/vocals) and **Paul Wright** (drums). Keyboard player **David Lloyd** joined midway through recording their debut album, BACK IN THE DHSS (1985). Championed by DJ John Peel, it was the best-selling indie album of 1986, and set the tone for all subsequent HMHB discs, with references galore to minor celebs and the everyday tedium of contemporary Britain.

Further indie chart-topping success came with the 1986 EP TRUMPTON RIOTS, the title track of which could almost have made it as a punk anthem a decade earlier. Nevertheless, hard-line anarchists might have had trouble coping with Blackwell's tongue-in-cheek approach, which satirized rock and pop attitudes as much as our cosy images of childhood.

The band displayed an indifferent attitude towards success and stardom. Twice offered national TV exposure on Channel Four's live pop show *The Tube*, they preferred to watch their underachieving football team, Tranmere Rovers. Such modest ambition largely explained their decision to split in October 1986, just as they were enjoying a second indie #1 single with "Dickie Davies' Eyes". Although the band's popularity was very much in the ascendant, Nigel Blackwell was already tiring of the rock'n'roll lifestyle.

Half Man Half Biscuit addicts got what seemed to be a 'final fix' when a compilation of B-sides, radio sessions and new songs was issued in 1987. BACK AGAIN IN THE DHSS followed its predecessor to the top of the indie chart, replete with lyrical gems like 'There is nothing better in life than writing on the sole of your slipper with a biro' ("The Best Things In Life"). It was reissued on CD in 1988, called ACD, with nine additional live tracks.

By 1990, the Blackwell brothers and Crossley had re-formed, to the relief of a diminished but no less enthusiastic fan base. A new album, MCINTYRE, TREADMORE AND DAVITT (1991), displayed a marked progression in songwriting and performance, with a fine mix of hard rock and soulful ballads, and another memorable title – "Outbreak Of Vitas Gerulaitis".

Two further albums – THIS LEADEN PALL (1993) and SOME CALL IT GODCORE (1995) – were then issued, both continuing the twin obsession with

mundanity and hilarity. Meanwhile, since a triumphant live return at the 1990 Reading Festival, the band have operated on a 'two gigs per month' basis, while continuing to record session material for John Peel's Radio 1 show. Recent works include the not-terribly-arty ENO COLLABORATION EP (which, naturally, didn't feature Britain's most musical polymath), the magnificently foolish VOYAGE TO THE BOTTOM OF THE ROAD (Probe Plus) (1997) and the wry CAMMELL LAIRD SOCIAL CLUB (2002). Their work is becoming more polished and sophisticated, but they retain their sour sense of the absurd.

⊙ **Back In The DHSS** (1985; Probe Plus).
The definitive chart-topping Half Man Half Biscuit album, containing tirades on snooker referees, clubbing seals and irritating TV stars ... and it's anyone's guess what The Velvet Underground thought of "Venus In Flares".

Patrick Thorne

PETER HAMMILL

Born London, 1948.

"There comes a point when you realize that now is not a permanent state. All this shouldn't just be about youth culture."

If Britain ever sets up its own Rock'n'Roll Hall Of Fame, **Peter Hammill** should have a place, perhaps on an obscure floor, sought out by the faithful and stumbled upon by the curious. In different circumstances, Hammill's success might have paralleled that of the likes of Peter Gabriel. Like Genesis, Hammill's band, **VAN DER GRAAF GENERATOR** were art-prog-rock, with a theatrical, wordy and peculiarly English appeal. Stardom never came knocking for Hammill, and instead his is a voice that has permanently sung and recorded outside the mainstream.

Hammill's solo career stretches over 25 years and 25 albums: a prodigious output by any standards, given that virtually every album is a song cycle. At the outset, there was little to distinguish Hammill solo from his Van Der Graaf Generator (VDGG, hereafter) output. His first trio of releases – FOOL'S MATE (1971), CHAMELEON IN THE SHADOW OF THE NIGHT (1973) and THE SILENT CORNER AND THE EMPTY STAGE (1974) – all featured old band-mates (the first also enlisted label mate Robert Fripp), and the tone was vintage VDGG: melodramatic, emotionally charged prog-rock. SILENT CORNER was the best of the three: a heady mix of songs, the content and voice as ever switching from harsh to calm, outrage to introspection, wistful to anthemic.

IN CAMERA (1974) signalled a change, as Hammill reworked his anguished poetry to a then-novel soundscape of tape loops and sampled effects. Then came a much greater departure, NADIR'S BIG CHANCE (1975), in which our cerebral hero of old gave way to a hard-rocking alter ego, Rikki Nadir, on a sequence of 'beefy punk songs, weepy ballads and soul struts'. It was a startlingly pertinent vision of the coming New Wave and it garnered some highly un-prog admirers, among them Johnny Rotten and David Bowie, both of whom have namechecked Hammill over the years.

After re-forming Van Der Graaf for a couple of years, Hammill went solo again with OVER (1977), a record detailing the breakdown of his marriage. It was soul-bearing and maudlin, beautiful and self-indulgent, in pretty much equal measures. Still, it must have done him good, for he returned the following year with his strongest solo release to date, THE FUTURE NOW (1978) which favoured short, bare-boned songs, on which Hammill tackled virtually all the instrumental parts, using tape-loops and synthesized rhythm tracks to back up his vocals. After the angst of OVER, the lyrics, too, were maturing, addressing issues such as age (a perennial from here on), futility and (a rare venture into non-personal politics) apartheid.

The album's stark feel was revisited on PH7 (1979), another strong outing, before he took time off to contribute vocals to **Robert Fripp**'s EXPOSURE album. In 1980, he reappeared with the raw, bleak A BLACK BOX. By now the punk rock explosion had swept away many contemporaries, but Hammill maintained a hugely committed following through his music's integrity, intelligence and passion.

In 1981, Hammill formed **The K-Group** with ex-VDGG members **Guy Evans** (drums) and **Nic Potter** (bass), and ex-Vibrator **John Ellis** (guitar), to produce SITTING TARGETS, arguably his most focused and formidable 'band album' to date. Its follow-ups, ENTER K (1982) and PATIENCE (1983), sounded, inevitably, a little muted by comparison.

Hammill also recorded the largely instrumental, experimental solo album, LOOPS AND REELS, in 1983. It was SKIN (1986), however, that the followers had been waiting for: a furious, rocking confessional. It was followed by a quieter release – Hammill recently declared he was alternating 'Quiet' and 'Loud' releases – in ANDCLOSEASTHIS (1986), for voice and keyboard only.

Through the late 80s and early 90s Hammill produced an album most years, often self-issued on his own Fie! label. He also made sporadic live appearances, usually with old VDGG cohorts Ellis, Potter and Jackson.

The studio records themselves were erratic. IN A FOREIGN TOWN (1989) and OUT OF WATER (1989) retrod old ground, while THE FALL OF THE HOUSE OF USHER (1991) was a brave but ill-advised revival of rock opera, based on the Edgar Allan Poe story. FIRESHIPS (1992) was utterly becalmed. Hammill then seemed to be returning to form. THE NOISE (1993) was a fiery affair with streaks of malicious wit; his songwriting remained taut and compelling on ROARING FORTIES (1994) and X MY HEART (1996) was a stunner. Although EVERYONE YOU HOLD (1997) and THIS (1998) frustratingly never reached these heights, they still had moments of brilliance and beauty, undermined by a tendency towards tuneless and lugubrious indulgence. Unfortunately, these were the sole qualities he brought to NONE OF THE ABOVE (2000), a turgid and tragic waste of talent and arguably his worst album, ever.

2002's acoustic CLUTCH and THE THIN MAN SINGS BALLADS were thankfully more compelling.

⊙ **Nadir's Big Chance** (1975; Virgin).
In which Hammill shed his skin, claiming to be possessed by one Rikki Nadir, a 'loud, aggressive, perpetual sixteen-year-old' and his 'distorted three-chord wonders'. Discontented and discordant, it was painfully simple on one hand, and seething with anger and frustration on the other.

Try to track down the vinyl: Virgin's CD reissue inexcusably omits Hammill's cover notes.

⊙ **Sitting Targets** (1981; Virgin).
A driving, demon-fuelled slice of Hammill at his best and, entirely coincidentally, at his most accessible. The songs have an immediacy and intensity but are still shot through with Hammill's edgy ambiguity. Chilling and exhilarating, it's a cruise through the heart of darkness – with the top down.

⊙ **X My Heart** (1996; Fie! Records).
Hammill's 26th album release was his best outing in fifteen years, highlighted by the a cappella "A Better Time", and with old VDGG colleague David Jackson lending stalwart backing to other tracks on sax and flute.

Adam Kimmel

THE HANDSOME FAMILY

Formed Chicago, 1993.

Like their contemporaries Wilco, Lambchop and Ryan Adams, **The Handsome Family** have taken the threads of Americana and woven them into music that reinvigorates the traditional forms of country while sounding contemporary. Their song-stories are true American gothic, where people's lives are slippery, and sex, death and drink blend into surreal narratives.

The Handsome Family are husband and wife duo **Brett** and **Rennie Sparks**, supported occasionally by guest musicians. Texan Brett and New Yorker Rennie met in Chicago and began to make music together, recording all their material in their living room, with Rennie handling lyrics and Brett the music. Their first album, ODESSA (1995), released on

The Handsome Family's Brett and Rennie Sparks

Carrot Top in the US, revealed the edginess of Rennie's lyrics – uncomfortable, elusive, and with a vein of humour. At that stage they still carried a good dose of garage rock, but MILK & SCISSORS (1996) was far more distinctive, and widely acclaimed, with Brett's baritone drawing comparisons to Nick Cave. The set perfectly captured their off-kilter vision.

It took a while to record their next album, THROUGH THE TREES (1998); this was largely due to Brett's depression, a condition that informed lyrics like 'this is why people OD on pills and jump off the Golden Gate Bridge, anything to be weightless again'. But while the songs weren't exactly cheering, they were infused with a melancholy that was too oblique to be seen as merely personal catharsis. THROUGH THE TREES again distilled a perfectly creepy, *Twin Peaks*-meets-*Blair Witch* atmosphere.

In 2000 came a compilation, DOWN IN THE VALLEY, which put favourites such as "Drunk By Noon" and "Woman Downstairs" alongside "Don't Be Scared", a taster for their next offering, IN THE AIR. Featuring contributions from fellow travellers Squirrel Nut Zippers's **Andrew Bird** and Wilco's **Jeff Tweedy**, IN THE AIR (2000) was a lighter affair, though it hadn't lost all of the insidious spookiness of its predecessor. "When The Helicopter Comes" sounded like bluegrass Armageddon, while "Poor Lenore" told the story of a girl carried to the top of a tree by crows. The sinister place inhabited by The Handsome Family was crystallized once more on 2001's TWILIGHT, where songs took the listener into the space between sleep and wakefulness. Its release marked the end of an era for the Sparks, as they left Chicago after twelve years to move to New Mexico.

The Handsome Family's recorded output is only half the story, as anyone who has witnessed their live shows will testify. And so, for those who haven't experienced it, 2002's LIVE AT SCHUBA'S TAVERN captured the full on-stage ambience – marital bickering'n'all – as well as being a fair 'greatest hits' selection into the bargain.

⊙ **Through The Trees** (1998; Loose).
Dark, disconcerting, but also strangely uplifting. Distils a century of American folk music tradition into 13 unsettling and lovely songs.

⊙ **Twilight** (2001; Loose).
The most supernatural of their releases – unhinged, but with a sense of humour.

Derryck Strachan

HANOI ROCKS

Formed Finland, 1980; disbanded 1985.

Finnish punks **Hanoi Rocks** launched themselves onto an unsuspecting Scandinavian audience with the album BANGKOK SHOCKS, SAIGON SHAKES, HANOI ROCKS in 1981. It was a mixed bag, in terms of quality, but it defined the glam-punk-

metal style of a group that – despite their geographical provenance – belonged firmly in the New York Dolls/MC5/Alice Cooper school of decadence.

The group's founding member Rocks were **Gyp Casino** (drums), **Sam Yaffa** (bass), **Nasty Suicide** (guitar/backing vocals), **Andy McCoy** (lead guitar/backing vocals) and **Mike Monroe** (lead vocals/piano/sax/harmonica). McCoy was the band's chief songwriter, while Monroe, blond and glamorous, gave the group its distinctive image, and provided a focus for the fans.

Appearances at London rock clubs gave Rocks their first exposure outside Scandinavia, where they had topped the charts with "Love's An Injection", and around the time of their second LP, ORIENTAL BEAT (1982), they moved to the UK and shed Casino in favour of British drummer **Razzle** (Nicholas Dingley). The album did OK, but an indulgent filler follow-up of outtakes and B-sides, SELF-DESTRUCTION BLUES LP, was panned, and their next album, BACK TO MYSTERY CITY (1984), was released only in Scandinavia. However, in one of those odd rock'n'roll quirks – could the name perhaps have attracted attention? – it attracted a following for the group in the Far East. The band promptly signed a three-album deal with CBS, and relocated to the US.

There, ex-**MOTT THE HOOPLE** leader **Ian Hunter** was drafted in as lyricist for new material, released in July 1984 as TWO STEPS FROM THE MOVE. This turned out to be a polished album of uncompromising, high-voltage power rock, and its stand-out track, a cover of Creedence Clearwater Revival's "Up Around The Bend", just missed the UK singles chart. However, the year ended disastrously for Hanoi Rocks as Razzle was killed in a motor crash (the other driver involved, Motley Crue's Vince Neil, was convicted of manslaughter). A swift live recording, ALL THOSE WASTED YEARS (1985), captures the decadent swagger of the band on stage at London's Marquee Club.

A few months later, Hanoi Rocks folded, and little has been heard of the Finns since. Monroe embarked on a short solo career, while songwriter McCoy and Suicide formed **The Cherry Bombz** with former Toto Coelo vocalist **Anita Mahaderlan**.

⊙ **Hanoi Rocks** (1996; Castle).
Yes, a 'greatest hits' compilation, but filled with gems of the purest sleaze.

Michael Sumsion

HAPPY FLOWERS

Formed Charlottesville, Virginia, 1983.

Happy Flowers – comprising **Mr. Anus** and **Mr. Horribly-Charred-Infant** – inhabit a nightmare world of insecurities and uncertainties, as seen through the eyes of a pair of emotionally disturbed hyperactive children. They appeared on the scene in the summer of 1984 with two EPs, SONGS FOR CHILDREN and NOW WE ARE SIX, both of which featured ferociously pummelled and heavily distorted instruments, over which the sound of screaming, wailing, pleading infant voices could be discerned. To listen to the records was like spending an entire day in a supermarket observing dysfunctional children trying to communicate with their equally dysfunctional parents, while a very noisy rock festival was held in the car park.

Unsurprisingly, the Happy Flowers found favour with many in the late 80s US hardcore scene, and played with such luminaries as Big Black, Killdozer and Pussy Galore, as well as receiving attention and praise from bands such as Sonic Youth. They were often likened to the early Butthole Surfers, although their approach to recording was more haphazard and relied almost entirely on improvisation. Their chosen method was to decide upon a lyric, or theme, and then set it to music.

Their themes were inevitably concerned with the terrifying incidents of youth. Titles like "Mom, I Gave The Cat Some Acid", "The Vacuum Ate Timmy", "Mom And Dad Like The Baby More Than Me" and "Jenny Tried To Kiss Me In Recess" gave some indication of the extent of their genius. "Find The Rising Mittens" detailed the horrific experience of having one's hair brutally cut off and then facing prolonged taunting, which only ceases with the threat of extreme physical violence involving power tools. A similar cautionary tale, "Left Behind", told of being stranded at the gas station, as Mom and Dad drove off unawares for a family picnic, while "These Peas Are So Green" was, predictably, a diatribe against the sensationally green nature of peas, and how unpleasant it was to eat them.

The duo were most recently spotted supporting Yo La Tengo in 2000, though their appearances are few and far between, especially since Mr. Anus received his doctorate in economics (presumably making him Dr. Anus).

Sadly, most of the Happy Flowers' albums are hard to track down these days; although, if you can find them, I Crush Bozo, Making The Bunny Pay, Oof and Lasterday I Was Been Bad are all recommended. Moreover, it would seem that Happy Flowers' extreme contributions to the bland landscape of music have been largely forgotten.

⊙ **Flowers On 45** (date unknown; Homestead).
A handy 35-track singles compilation, featuring "They Cleaned My Cut With A Wire Brush", alongside other classics of psychotic and troubled youth.

Jonathan Bell

HAPPY MONDAYS

Formed Manchester, England, 1984; disbanded 1993.

Named after New Order's hit song "Blue Monday", the **Happy Mondays** consisted of five scruffy Mancunian clubbers – **Shaun Ryder** (vocals/lyrics), his brother **Paul** (bass), **Paul 'PD' Davis** (keyboards), **Gary 'Gaz' Whelan** (drums),

bummed

and **Mark 'Moose' Day** (guitar) – each of whom wanted to take his interest in dance music a step further. Before long, they had recruited a new member, **Mark Berry** (percussion/dancing), better known to everybody as **Bez**.

Like their hometown heroes Joy Division and New Order, the Happy Mondays sprang to success on the back of a talent contest, a 'Battle Of The Bands' at Manchester's Hacienda club; unlike their idols, the Mondays won a rigged event. On the back of this devious success, they were offered a deal with Manchester independent label Factory Records, whose chairman Tony Wilson was to help mastermind their phenomenal rise. Wilson's masterstroke was his insistence that the band work with established producers and remixers, but the band's success also had much to do with their authenticity – they were genuine, hedonistic, sexist, druggy louts, out to have a good time, all the time.

Former Velvet Underground luminary John Cale produced their debut LP, the catchily titled Squirrel And G-Man Twenty Four Hour Party People Plastic Face Carnt Smile (White Out) (1987). Acclaimed by the British music press, it hit controversy within weeks; although the Happy Mondays would always liberally borrow riffs and lyrics from other sources, it was felt that "Desmond" was a little too similar to The Beatles' "Ob-La-Di, Ob-La-Da". The LP was withdrawn, and later reappeared without the offending track.

The Happy Mondays teamed up with Factory's inhouse producer Martin Hannett for 1988's brilliant Bummed, which presented a slightly more accessible mix of rock and funk, most impressively on the near hit "Wrote For Luck". After this had been remixed for dance-floor appeal by Erasure's Vince Clarke, Wilson arranged for the band to be produced by Manchester DJs/remixers Paul Oakenfold and Steve Osborne. Out of this collaboration emerged the group's distinctive 'Manchester' noise. The subtle change in their sound brought the Happy Mondays closer to mainstream success. An inspired performance on BBC TV's *Top Of The Pops* guaranteed Top 20 success for the MADCHESTER RAVE ON EP (1989), led by the anthemic "Hallelujah". For a couple of years afterwards, the British music scene was dominated by Manchester acts like the Stone Roses, the Inspiral Carpets, James and 808 State, perhaps the most exciting movement to hit British music since the Two-Tone explosion of the early 80s.

Further hits followed, most notably the cover of John Kongos' early-70s hit, "He's Gonna Step On You Again", which was shortened to "Step On", and became a Top 5 single. Like its follow-up singles, "Kinky Afro" and "Loose Fit", it was included on their third (and biggest-selling) album, PILLS 'N' THRILLS AND BELLYACHES (1990).

By now, the Mondays were playing sell-out stadium concerts, which were baffling events, with the various band members looking as if they each belonged in other bands. Sometimes these unpromising scenarios were transformed into magical, if incoherent, spectacles, and the double LP LIVE (1991) captured some of the highlights from Leeds' football stadium, Elland Road.

However, as the Happy Mondays hit a peak in 1989–90, stories of their drug addictions and boorishness filled the tabloid press, while the music press, once so supportive, turned against them. They hoped to reclaim lost ground with a new album, recorded in the Bahamas with producers Chris Frantz and Tina Weymouth from Tom Tom Club and Talking Heads. The result – YES PLEASE (1992) – at a costly quarter of a million pounds, was a critical and commercial failure. As if all this weren't bad enough, a disastrous UK tour to promote the album succeeded in boosting support act The Stereo MCs, but sinking the Mondays. Shaun's inability to kick his heroin habit exacerbated the band's problems, and after Factory Records filed for bankruptcy in November 1992 the Happy Mondays were all but finished.

When Shaun Ryder left, there were rumours that backing singer **Rowetta** would replace him on lead vocals, while keyboard player Davis would take over as songwriter. Neither came to fruition, and in March 1993 the Mondays officially announced their split. Ryder went into rehab, and silence reigned until he reunited with Bez, and **Kermit** from the Ruthless Rap Assassins, to form **BLACK GRAPE**.

⦿ **Bummed** (1988; London).
The band's best album. Raw and raucous, fresh and funky, it epitomizes their sound prior to their encounter with Messrs Oakenfold and Osborne.

⦿ **Happy Mondays: Greatest Hits** (1999; London).
As fine a hits package as you could hope for.

Richard Luck

ED HARCOURT

Born East Sussex, England, 1978.

Ed Harcourt's musical output inhabits the same kind of bedroom bohemia as Badly Drawn

Boy, a world in which E.L.O sit comfortably alongside Tom Waits and Joe Jackson, and where it's OK to like Elton John (well, the more acceptable 70s stuff anyway). And like Badly Drawn Boy, Harcourt's sound has matured quickly and easily from the bedroom to a bigger stage. He's prolific too – claims abound that he's got more than 300 songs to his name, which isn't bad for a songwriter still only in his mid-twenties.

As early as 1997, Harcourt, while still in his teens, fronted brash adolescent punk outfit Snug. Signed too early by WEA, the group bristled with home-counties cleverness and youthful exuberance; while their hook-laden guitar pop didn't manage to endear them to a particularly large audience, the wryness of the lyrics betrayed something of Harcourt's later musical direction.

After the disintegration of Snug, Harcourt retreated to the comfort of his home and using a 4-track set about recording his remarkable debut – six tracks of subtlety and depth that were issued soon after as the MAPLEWOOD EP (2000) by Heavenly Recordings. Harcourt wrote, produced and performed the lot (with some help with the horns by **Hadrian Garrard**) – his musical tastes catholic enough to take in piano, guitar, banjo, programmed drums and trumpets.

Two tracks from the EP, "Hanging With Wrong Crowd" and "Apple Of My Eye", deservedly made it onto Harcourt's debut album, HERE BE MONSTERS (2001), a justly acclaimed full-length effort that managed to absorb 70s rock riffs, abstract lullabies, and bombastic piano-driven epics like "She Fell Into My Arms" and "Shanghai".

Harcourt devolved some of his performing responsibilities to new band members **Arnulf Linder** (bass) and **Nick Yeatman** (drums), but nevertheless had a hand in producing the album along with Death In Vegas' Tim Holmes, while some sure-handed engineering was handled by Gil Norton (Pixies, Belly) and Dave Fridmann (Flaming Lips, Mercury Rev). The album featured some genuinely sublime love moments ("Wind Through The Trees"), song-writing with real sensitivity and ambition (check out the stand-out "She Fell Into My Arms"). In its diversity of influences the set was never confusing, always tasteful.

A *Mercury Music Prize* nomination followed – deservedly – while tours with the likes of Beth Orton and Sparklehorse occupied Harcourt's time until recording for his second album began. A limited edition single (a version of a 'lost' Brian Wilson song "Still I Dream Of It") issued at the tail end of 2002 kept his fan base interested in the interim.

Drawing the Tom Waits comparisons even closer, Harcourt hooked up with production veteran Tchad Blake (Waits, Crowded House) and headed to the rural idyll of Peter Gabriel's Real World Studios and began work on FROM EVERY SPHERE (2003). It was a step away from his previous effort, that sacrificed some of those endearing bedroom qualities in favour of bigger 'rock' efforts ("Watching The Sun Come Up"), terse radio pop tunes ("All Of Your Days Will Be Blessed") and faux-abstract pieces like "Ghost Writer".

⊙ **Here Be Monsters** (2001; Heavenly).
Melancholy and anguish flourish on Harcourt's debut album proper. Songs like "Beneath The Heart Of Darkness" say it all with a mix of drifting calm and exploding guitars.

⊙ **From Every Sphere** (2003; Heavenly).
The album opens with the jangly, Harrison-esque "Bittersweetheart"; elsewhere the set slips into a darker mood, with "Ghost Writer" standing out as reminder of Harcourt's power over the hairs on the back of your neck.

Derryck Strachan

TIM HARDIN

Born Eugene, Oregon, 1941; died 1980.

With his sobbing voice and introspective, almost reticent compositions, **Tim Hardin** was one of the more memorable singer-songwriters of his day. A cult figure who never really broke through to a wide following, he is now chiefly remembered via cover versions of his best songs, especially "If I Were A Carpenter" and "Reason To Believe". His failure to become renowned for performing his own work is mainly attributable to his heroin habit, which helped cripple his career after a couple of promising albums in the late 1960s.

Hardin moved to the East Coast in the early 1960s after leaving the Marines, doing time in the folk scenes of Greenwich Village and Boston. While he was based in Boston, he was contacted by producer Erik Jacobsen (most famous for handling Lovin' Spoonful) to do some demos for Columbia. Hardin was pretty much a white blues singer at this point, with a repertoire dominated by blues covers and thinly veiled rewrites of blues standards. He claimed in one interview (probably falsely) that 'I'm a better singer than Ray Charles, and Ray Charles told me so.' In fact, not only were blues and R&B not really his forte, but fellow Greenwich folkie Fred Neil (with whom the higher-voiced Hardin shared some

similarities) did blues-folk substantially better, as the many derivative early demo tracks demonstrate.

However, by the time Hardin debuted on Verve with TIM HARDIN 1 (1966), he'd found a more pop-folk songwriting voice. His backing band included Lovin' Spoonful leader **John Sebastian** on harmonica and jazzman **Gary Burton** on vibes, but Hardin claimed to be so upset by the strings that were overdubbed on some tracks without his consent that he cried when he first heard them. Still, it was a strong set with a tender low-key, confessional tone, and contained some of his best compositions, such as "Misty Roses", "How Can We Hang On To A Dream", and especially "Reason To Believe", which became something of a signature tune.

Strings also occasionally graced Hardin's next LP, TIM HARDIN 2 (1967), in a more subtle fashion. Another solid collection in much the same vein as the debut, it contained perhaps his most famous song, "If I Were A Carpenter", which was taken into the US Top 10 in a faithful cover version by Bobby Darin.

These two albums, sadly, represented the apex of Tim's career; almost all of his best work is contained on them, although he was to live another dozen years. Heroin problems and general irresponsibility often made him miss shows or perform poorly; he suffered from pleurisy in 1968, and a tour of England the same year had to be cancelled when he fell asleep on stage at the Royal Albert Hall, shortly after dismissing his backing group in front of the audience. The live TIM HARDIN 3 (1968) was a decent set with jazzy backing musicians that introduced some new material along with reprises of previously recorded favourites. But Hardin didn't record another set of fresh songs in the 60s, although he performed at Woodstock, where he lived for a while (his performance, however, didn't make it onto the film of the event).

Hardin recorded a few albums in the early 1970s that were not without bright moments, but, whether due to dope or other factors, his muse seems to have withered: the 1973 record PAINTED HEAD didn't even contain a single original composition. TIM HARDIN 9 (also 1973) was his last LP; after years of bouncing around England and the West Coast and fighting health and psychological problems, he died in Los Angeles in 1980, at the age of 39.

⊙ **Live In Concert** (1968; Polydor).
A CD reissue of TIM HARDIN 3, plus three previously unreleased tracks from the same gig. This fine live set contains interesting interpretations of some of the best songs from his first two albums, and half a dozen other compositions, notably "Lenny's Tune" (a eulogy for Lenny Bruce).

⊙ **Hang On To A Dream: The Verve Recordings** (1994; Polydor).
The definitive retrospective of his earliest and best work, this double CD contains all 47 songs he recorded in the mid 60s for Verve, including the first two albums in their entirety. Disc two consists of his early blues demos.

⊙ **Simple Songs of Freedom: The Tim Hardin Collection** (1997; Columbia).
A seventeen-track collection – Columbia's reply to the Polydor compilation – this encapsulates the cream of the songs he recorded during his three album stay.

Richie Unterberger

HARMONIA

Formed Germany, 1971.

"The most important rock music being produced today...the music of the future." Brian Eno

Harmonia started out as a result of a chance meeting when **Michael Rother** and **Klaus Dinger** – members of a short-lived incarnation of **KRAFTWERK** – happened to be on the same bill as **Cluster** in 1971. The following year Rother and Dinger, who had formed **NEU!** in the meantime, were offered a tour of England. Because Neu! was a two-piece, they started to look round for musicians with whom they could re-create the sound live. Rother had been impressed by the CLUSTER II album, and so, armed with a guitar, he spent Easter with **Roedelius** and **Moebius**. The three soon discovered a musical understanding, so Rother decided to put Neu! on hold while Roedelius and Moebius did the same with Cluster. Their first album, MUSIK VON HARMONIA, was recorded in 1973 in their own Harmonia studio and was released in 1974, accompanied by tours of Germany, Holland and Belgium.

In April 1974 **Brian Eno** came to see a Harmonia concert in Hamburg, joining the band on stage at the end of the show, and was given an open invitation to visit their place in the Weserbergland, an invitation that bore fruit a couple of years later.

DELUXE, the second Harmonia album, with **Mani Neumaier** of Guru Guru guesting on drums and Conny Plank producing, was released the following year to great critical acclaim. This failed to translate into sales, and in 1976 the band decided to go their separate ways, with each releasing a solo album.

They remained friendly and continued to share the same house, and Eno's visit in September 1976 encouraged them to record together once more. The workshop atmosphere gave each of them an opportunity to experiment with ideas and concepts, with no initial thought of releasing an album. After twelve days Eno left to work with David Bowie, intending to come back later that year, but by the time he returned, the success of Rother's solo album FLAMMENDE HERZEN meant he was fully occupied elsewhere. Eno and Cluster decided to record albums without him.

Eno took the tapes of the Harmonia sessions with him, and for nearly twenty years they were believed lost. However, Roedelius discovered them in 1995 and used modern technology to polish the somewhat primitive recordings. Moebius and Rother were satisfied with the results, and the album was released as HARMONIA 76 (TRACKS AND TRACES) in November 1997 through Rykodisc and Sony Music. It was nominated for the 1998 Independent Music Award in the US.

(•) **Harmonia 76** (Tracks and Traces) (1998; Sony).
All three albums are worth a listen, but the earlier two are more difficult to get hold of. A mixture of electronic

rhythms and thoughtful, pensive pieces, with some of the feel of Satie or Debussy, as on "Almost". The album reaches its high point on "Luneburg Heath", where Cluster's electronics, Eno's voice and Rother's yearning guitar combine to create an eerie, otherworldly effect.

Paul O'Brien

BEN HARPER

Born Inland Empire, California, 1969.

While almost every contemporary songwriter lays claim to being eclectic, few draw on such good sources as **Ben Harper**. His best work is as politically shrewd as Gil Scott-Heron, as resonant as Muddy Waters and as humane as Bob Marley – esteemed company, but there are few more articulate songwriters on the modern American music scene.

Harper grew up in a musical family in Inland Empire, a town east of Los Angeles, playing guitar as a child, and graduating to the distinctive 'Weissenborn' – a lap slide guitar with a hollow neck that emits a distinctively elastic, ringing tone. In the early 90s he was performing alongside Taj Mahal and bluesman Brownie McGhee, carefully assimilating their music and world-view, and in 1994 he signed a contract with Virgin America.

His debut album, WELCOME TO THE CRUEL WORLD (1994), made an immediate impact with the critics, as did the single, "Like A King", which juxtaposed two figures in the black struggle who shared a surname – 'Well Martin's dream/Has become Rodney's worst Nightmare'. Typical of Harper, anger and resentment at this state of affairs was subordinated beneath sadness and regret at its continuance. Another song on the album, "Don't Take That Attitude To Your Grave", again echoed the impact of the Rodney King beating with the lines, 'So you can move your court case/Way across town/You can move it across the whole wide globe'.

Harper then made an apparently odd career move by providing the music to Morgan Freeman's narration on a children's film, *Follow The Drinking Gourd*, before turning back to his own songs. For his second album, FIGHT FOR YOUR MIND (1995), J. P. Plunier returned as co-producer, with **Juan Nelson** joining on bass and **Oliver Charles** on drums. Songs such as the string-laden "Power Of The Gospel" added spiritual convictions to his regular theme of urban oppression but musically the dominant concept remained 'less is more', the simplicity of execution amplifying the essence of Harper's themes.

THE WILL TO LIVE (1997) and BURN TO SHINE (1999) dealt with similar issues and had their weaker moments; occasionally lyrically gauche and musically meandering. However, when the music was tight and the words sharp and focused, he remained compelling. He returned in 2001 with LIVE FROM MARS, a double-CD set that provided a comprehensive overview of his back catalogue and saw him covering songs by artists as diverse as The Verve and Marvin

Gaye. It was enjoyable enough but generally an underwhelming way to return after a long absence. Harper's wide-ranging and committed fan base awaited new material, and were rewarded in early 2003 by DIAMONDS ON THE INSIDE.

⦿ **Fight For Your Mind** (1995; Virgin)
If you like your moral sentiments hard-boiled but your music with a little sweetener, then uncluttered, direct songs like "Ground On Down" and "Another Lovely Day" will charm and engross you.

⦿ **Diamonds On The Inside** (2003; Virgin)
Moving in lyrical breadth, and rich with experimental musicality, this is perhaps his most accomplished set yet.

Alex Ogg

ROY HARPER

Born Manchester, England, 1941.

One of Britain's greatest singer-songwriters is **Roy Harper**, a unique, unruly talent, whose output and audience hovered between folk and rock (not, mind you, folk-rock) in ways that record companies could never quite fathom how to sell. Although famous mates – **Jimmy Page**, notably – helped out on his records in the 70s, both studio and stage often saw him spliffed to the gills or in wilfully anti-commercial mode, and he's never progressed much beyond a cult following. He deserves wider recognition, both for the lyrical expressiveness and fine musicianship of his best work, and for a rare integrity, imagination and charisma.

Harper's youth was a torment. His mother died in childbirth and he was brought up in Blackpool by his stepmother, a Jehovah's Witness, an experience he claims 'drove me mad and filled me with a lifelong hate for any form of religion'. At age 15 he joined the Air Force but found this regime equally unbearable, and, discharged on the count of insanity, was placed in a mental hospital and given electroconvulsive therapy. He escaped and lived on the streets for a while, before being apprehended and sent to prison for a year.

These were experiences that shaped Harper's songs, which – early on, especially – stand right on the edge, powered by personal insecurity, deep distrust of authority, celebration of individual liberty, anger against cruelty, and reckless self-indulgence. They were aired first on the London folk-club circuit, when Harper, having returned to England from busking around Europe, secured a residency at the legendary Les Cousins, building a reputation as a stoned hippie singer-songwriter of uncompromising radicalism and emotional intensity.

His first album, THE SOPHISTICATED BEGGAR, was released in 1966. Most of the songs were firmly in the conventional folk protest mould, but the set concluded with "Committed", a harrowing representation of helpless suffering under psychiatric treatment, delivered against a quirky pop backing. On the next two albums, COME OUT FIGHTING, GENGHIS SMITH (1968) and FOLKJOKEOPUS (1969),

Harper further demonstrated a willingness to experiment with songwriting forms, and by the end of the 60s he had become established on the underground music scene.

Signed by Peter Jenner, the manager of Pink Floyd, to EMI's Harvest label, Harper began moving towards a more rock sensibility. Jenner himself produced the 1970 album, FLAT, BAROQUE AND BERSERK, a milestone in Harper's musical development. Alongside pieces like "How Does It Feel" and "Feeling All The Saturday", which could have come from the earlier albums, were songs that show the flowering of an exceptional talent. Angry yet beautiful, "I Hate The White Man" is possibly the most cogent condemnation of British imperialism ever put in a song; "Don't You Grieve" sympathetically represented Judas's position in the betrayal of Christ; while poignant depictions of vulnerability in love, "Tom Tiddler's Ground" and "Another Day", evinced an uncanny ability to handle well-worn themes in an original and exciting way. This lost masterpiece was rereleased in 1997 on Science Friction Records.

Still working mainly with acoustic guitar, though often backed on record by Jimmy Page, this creativity was maintained through STORMCOCK (1971), LIFEMASK and VALENTINE (1974), each of which produced a wealth of passionate, evocative songs as well as the occasional embarrassment when Harper overreached himself. Many of the best numbers (and some embarrassments, too) can be heard on FLASHES FROM THE ARCHIVES OF OBLIVION (1974), a double album of live recordings which faithfully reflected his mercurial personality on stage.

HQ (1975) came as a surprise to many. Although Harper's earlier albums were directed mainly towards a rock audience, and he had occasionally used a backing band, this presented his case for recognition as a major rock musician according to the usual terms of the genre. It kicked off with "The Game", an epic hard-rock track accompanying a fine lyrical rant on civilization's debasement of the human spirit and destruction of the planet. Then, shifting through a multitude of styles, the set concluded acoustically with "When An Old Cricketer Leaves The Crease", the essence of England encapsulated in a cricket match. A distinguished cast of backing musicians included **David Gilmour**, **John Paul Jones** and **Bill Bruford**. Now emphatically established as a rock performer, Harper released BULLINAMINGVASE (1977), his most successful album commercially (#25 in the UK) and yielding a minor hit single, the elegiac "One Of Those Days In England".

Punk rock had arrived, however, and Harper became increasingly unsure of his role. He was never again as prolific or inventive as in the early 70s, and his confidence in new work only gradually returned. Albums like THE UNKNOWN SOLDIER (1980) and WORK OF HEART (1982) showed more bitterness than fire, but had two or three excellent songs apiece. After a couple of rather uncertain albums for shoestring labels, Harper teamed up again with Jimmy Page to produce WHATEVER HAPPENED TO JUGULA (1985) for Beggars Banquet. It was a fine set and, no doubt due to Page's involvement, brought a revival of interest in Harper's work, a #44 slot in the UK, and a moderate increase in the cult following.

In 1988, Harper returned to EMI/Harvest to record DESCENDENTS OF SMITH, a bleak collection of songs, after which they parted company again. Subsequent new releases have been on the small Awareness label, which is also gradually reissuing all of Harper's early albums. ONCE (1990) showed Harper to have gained a quieter but more certain confidence in his own worth and improved vocal and guitar-playing techniques, while his most recent outing, DEATH OR GLORY? (1992), demonstrated that he could still deliver the goods.

Six hours' worth of archive material covering the years 1969 to 1978 was recently rescued and began to surface on the excellent ROY HARPER LIVE AT THE BBC series. VOLUME I (1997) had two *Top Gear* sessions from 1969 and 1970, with an *In Concert* from 1971 and his first *Bob Harris Show* session from 1973. VOLUME II (1997) was a full *In Concert* from 1974. Essential purchases for the committed. For the merely curious, AN INTRODUCTION TO... (1994) was a fine, thirteen-track skimming of the cream off Harper's career. RETURN OF THE SOPHISTICATED BEGGAR (1997) was a revised version of his debut, boosted with four new tracks, while TODAY IS YESTERDAY (2002) was an interesting collection of early oddities and singles.

⊙ **Valentine** (1974; Awareness).
An impressive collection of love songs covering adolescent awakening, the casual yet meaningful fling, the wish for reunion, and the desire for permanence. Less earnestly, there are songs about male chauvinism and sexual perversion, and a luscious version of "Girl From The North Country", which compares very favourably with Bob Dylan's.

⊙ **HQ** (1975; Awareness).
Harper's most eclectic album and brilliant from beginning to end. "When An Old Cricketer Leaves The Crease" is perhaps the best song ever written about Englishness, with a fine performance from the Grimethorpe Colliery Band.

⊙ **Live At The BBC** (1997; Science Friction).
Six hours of Harper classic sessions. Unmissable.

Martin Haggerty

EMMYLOU HARRIS

Born Birmingham, Alabama, 1947.

"I've always been a left-field artist ... they just don't know what to do with me ..."

Dubbed the 'solo songbird of country' by American radio, **Emmylou Harris** has rarely been truly solo and never exclusively country. As a student at the University of North Carolina she sang in a folk duo, before following the singer-songwriter trail to the clubs of Greenwich Village. Playing second fiddle to the likes of Jerry Jeff Walker failed to provide her with the audience she had hoped for, and a one-off album deal with Jubilee resulted in the debut GLIDING BIRD (1969), which met with a decidedly underwhelmed public.

Yet her initial foray into the music business had made enough of an impression to gain bookings in Nashville, where the climb to stardom was to begin. She was a known face on the honky-tonk circuit when the first of several domestic upheavals impinged on her career. Her first marriage failed and she retreated with her daughter to her parents' home in Washington.

Emmylou was playing a regular slot in a bar near the family home when she was approached by The Flying Burrito Brothers' Chris Hillman, who asked her to become the first sister in his band. The Burritos' mainman **GRAM PARSONS** was the alchemist who turned Southern boogie into the much-maligned genre of country-rock, and when he decided to do this under his own steam he took Emmylou with him. Over the next couple of years the duo were to produce two landmark albums, G. P. (1972) and GRIEVOUS ANGEL (1973), although both were credited to Parsons alone. These works featured some of the greatest duets ever recorded and were to prove an inspiration to the ever-growing list of performers requesting backing vocals from Emmylou.

The early 70s saw her on the road with Gram Parsons and The Fallen Angels for a highly successful tour, but she was thrown into despair once more by the news of Parsons' death in 1973. Still reeling from the loss of her partner, she began rehearsals with **The Angel Band**, but it was to be a couple of years before the release of her first Warners album, PIECES OF THE SKY (1975), and its supporting single, "Boulder To Birmingham", which was to become her signature tune.

By the time ELITE HOTEL (1976) was released, Emmylou had achieved transatlantic success and a high chart placing. She had also been invited by The Band to appear in the film of their swan-song performance, *The Last Waltz*, as they believed that she was a true representative of a genre which had originally inspired them. Now one of country's foremost songsters, Emmylou had worked with established stars like **James Burton** and **Albert Lee**, but her mission to bring the best of traditional music to a mass audience also involved the fostering of new talent. Singing sisters The Whites and bluegrass bomber **Ricky Skaggs** were amongst those to benefit from an apprenticeship with her **Hot Band**.

In the 80s Emmylou was at the height of her commercial success, charting on duets with **ROY ORBISON** and Don Williams. She drew on a broad array of favourites, peppered with a selection of originals, to produce at least one album a year. Her ambitions stretched to recording a concept album, THE BALLAD OF SALLY ROSE (1985), with assistance from her then-husband Paul Kennerley and her two close friends **Linda Ronstadt** and **Dolly Parton**, who were to accompany her on her next project, TRIO (1987). As any marketing expert could have predicted, it became a bestseller.

Towards the end of the 80s, Emmylou's sales went into decline and, sensing the need for a change, she disbanded The Hot Band and opted for the rootsy sounds of **The Nash Ramblers**. The 1992 tour saw them stoking up some sterling performances, but a change in style earned a poor response from her record company, leading to a relocation to London-based Grapevine Records. Any fears that Emmylou might have lost her touch as an interpreter of emotionally charged music were dismissed by the release of the highly acclaimed COWGIRL'S PRAYER (1994) and, even more so, by WRECKING BALL (1996), which saw a masterful production by Daniel Lanois.

As well as being one of the most prolific recording artists in the industry, Emmylou Harris is also the curator of a rich musical heritage. Serving as president of the Country Music Foundation, she has been instrumental in the discovery and release of recordings by her heroes, Hank Williams and the Louvin Brothers. Despite her achievements, she remains an intensely modest individual, and she is as likely to be discovered singing harmonies with her friend **Dolores Keane** in a Galway pub as she is to be seen amongst the rhinestones and spandex at a Country Music Foundation awards ceremony.

The mid 90s saw Emmylou Harris adopting a more relaxed attitude to her output. She claimed to have reached the realization that there were some tours and albums that should not have seen the light of day, and she recognized the need to be 'quiet and still'. Her record company chose to cover up the quiet period with a three-CD retrospective (featuring only six previously unavailable tracks), PORTRAITS (1996; Reprise Archives). A much more fitting tribute to the quality of Emmylou's back catalogue was her own reinterpretation of some of her best work, SPYBOY. This live album featuring Buddy Miller and Brady Blades also forms the basis for a film.

Recent projects have shown that the 'Gliding Bird' does not intend staying still for too long. She has recorded a version of Jimmy Rogers' "My Blue Eyed Jane" with **Bob Dylan** and contributed to Nanci Griffiths' book *Other Voices: A Personal History of Folk*. 1999 saw Harris returning to the studio with her old friends Dolly Parton and Linda Ronstadt for the release of TRIO VOL. 2, which featured a beautiful rendition of Neil Young's "After The Gold Rush".

Emmylou Harris

(●) **White Shoes** (1983; Warners).
Maintaining a preference for quirky songs, Emmylou came up with some tales of material girls, including a remake of "Diamonds Are A Girl's Best Friend".

(●) **Live At The Ryman** (1992; Reprise).
Working with The Nash Ramblers, Emmylou opens with a rocking version of Steve Earle's "Guitar Town". Dominated by a fresher, semi-acoustic sound, this shows a different approach to the standard country rock style.

(●) **Wrecking Ball** (1996; Grapevine).
A current of electricity and reinvention runs through this wonderful album, with Daniel Lanois helping to give a contemporary feel to vintage tracks such as Dylan's "Every Grain Of Sand". The record was produced 'live' in the studio, with contributions from Neil Young, Steve Earle and the McGarrigles.

Harris, Parton and Ronstadt

(●) **Trio Vol. 1 & 2** (1987 & 1999; Warners).
Both volumes offer a delight of sweet harmonies and restrained instrumentation.

Stephen Boyd

GEORGE HARRISON

Born Liverpool, England, February 25, 1943; died Los Angeles, November 29, 2001.

"Being a Beatle was a nightmare."

George Harrison began to emerge from the shadows of his **BEATLES** songwriting colleagues Lennon and McCartney when "Something", his contribution to ABBEY ROAD (1969), went to #1 in the US. Lauded by Sinatra as 'the most beautiful love song ever written', it was the first Harrison track to be released as a single, and suggested there might be a productive solo career when the Fabs finally called it a day.

In fact the quiet Beatle had already become the first of the group to start a solo career, with his WONDERWALL (1968) film soundtrack – the album that gave a title to Oasis's most famous song, nearly thirty years on. The following year's ELECTRONIC SOUNDS (rereleased in 1996 on Apple to cash in on the interest in all things Beatle-esque) was the kind of meandering tosh that flourished after the invention of the Moog, but having been forced to stockpile songs while with The Beatles, it was only a matter of time before Harrison made an impact with a solo outing.

That came with ALL THINGS MUST PASS, a triple-album project on which friends, including **Eric Clapton** and **Bob Dylan**, lent a hand. Released in late 1970 to favourable reviews and massive sales, it marked the full flowering of the spirituality and introspection that had been present in Harrison's Beatle work since REVOLVER. If three discs was perhaps more than the album merited, it was certainly worth two, with songs like the title track, an exquisite cover of Dylan's "If Not For You", and "My Sweet Lord", which topped charts around the world when released as a single the following year. "My Sweet Lord", however, set problems in store, with allegations that its tune plagiarized The Chiffons' "He's So Fine", leading to a long-running legal case.

Still, in retrospect, 1971 was Harrison's greatest year, with his crucial role in organizing a massive Madison Square Garden benefit, CONCERT FOR BANGLADESH (1971) – a gig which provided a high-profile return to live work for himself, **Ringo Starr**

George Harrison – 'the quiet Beatle'

wasn't a happy time: Harrison's marriage had disintegrated (courtesy of Eric Clapton), an event picked over in self-pitying fashion on "Bye Bye Love", while songs like "Ding Dong" showed that the creative juices weren't flowing too well. The response to the tour was equally poor.

Subsequent albums – EXTRA TEXTURE (1975), THIRTY-THREE AND A THIRD (1976), GEORGE HARRISON (1979) – dwindled into mere competence, boasting the odd superstar guest spot but taking little account of changing tastes. However, Harrison made a massive contribution to the entertainment industry in 1978 when he founded Handmade Films, the company responsible for many of the best British films of recent years, including *Monty Python's Life Of Brian*, *The Long Good Friday*, *Time Bandits* and *Mona Lisa*. As for the music, "All Those Years Ago" – a tribute to the murdered Lennon, featuring the other surviving Beatles – saw a chart placing around the world in 1981 and dragged the accompanying SOMEWHERE IN ENGLAND (1981) album into the Top 20 on both sides of the Atlantic. However, GONE TROPPO (1982) seemed again to be Harrison just going through the movements.

Help from another friend, **Jeff Lynne**, aided a return to form in 1987 when Harrison's cover of Ruby Clarke's R&B classic, "Got My Mind Set On You", went to #2 in the UK and stormed to the top of the US charts. Lynne's masterful production of the CLOUD NINE (1987) album made it Harrison's most successful work in over a decade. With pressure on for a follow-up, Harrison and Lynne began rehearsals in Bob Dylan's roomy garage, when chance encounters with **Tom Petty** and **Roy Orbison** led to the Harrison solo project being scrapped in favour of the first of two albums by **THE TRAVELING WILBURYS**, projects that returned Harrison's commercial and critical profile to its 70s levels.

The death of Orbison and his mooted replacement Del Shannon put the Wilburys into mothballs and Harrison tried some gigs of his own, with Eric Clapton supporting on guitar, for the ever-respectful Japanese fans. The resulting LIVE IN JAPAN (1992) showed he could still deliver the goods, but didn't mark any major return.

Beatle activities based around the Anthology reissues provided some interesting Harrison moments. Harrison's own solo demo for "While My Guitar Gently Weeps" on ANTHOLOGY 3 was a delicate gem

and Bob Dylan. The resulting album was another triple LP and another massive seller, topping the UK charts and hitting #2 in the US, and Harrison's single, "Bangladesh", was a success, too, both critically and commercially, though administrative problems diminished the effect of the revenue in famine relief.

Harrison was at this point outselling his old colleagues, and chalked up another massive-selling album, LIVING IN THE MATERIAL WORLD (1973), on the back of the US #1 single, "Give Me Love (Give Me Peace On Earth)". But, success notwithstanding, it marked the start of a critical backlash, with Robert Hilburn's lengthy consideration in the *LA Times* par for the course, describing it as 'Hardly the level of work we'd expect from a major artist'.

Harrison wasn't managing the levels of activity expected from a major artist, either, though in 1974 he started his own Dark Horse record company and announced a North American tour on the back of his new album, the toothless DARK HORSE (1974). It

that stole the album from his colleagues. He was in court as a Beatle again, reluctantly as ever, in 1998, when he came before judges in London to defend his position that an amateur recording of The Beatles from their time in Hamburg was unfit for human consumption. He won. But his gaunt appearance at this event and the memorial service for Linda McCartney raised fears about Harrison's own health.

Indeed, Harrison's final years were largely traumatic ones. At the end of 1999 he was assaulted by an intruder at his Henley-On-Thames mansion, two years after the revelation that he had had swollen lymph nodes removed from his throat. However, a diagnosis of brain cancer in 2001 sadly proved to be inoperable.

George Harrison's tragic death in a Los Angeles hospital at the age of fifty-eight left millions of fans mourning around the globe, leading to a repromotion of his best-loved songs. "My Sweet Lord", reissued as a single in early 2002, hit number one for the second time in the UK, while the *Concert For Bangladesh* film, now widely available on DVD, served as a reminder that Harrison was always more concerned with the state of the world than his own celebrity status.

2002 also saw the release of Brainwashed, a collection that Harrison had begun prior to his death; the set was completed by producers Jeff Lynne and **Dhani Harrison** (his son) based upon extensive notes made by Harrison in the months before his death.

- ⊙ **All Things Must Pass** (1970; Parlophone).
  This sprawling epic is arguably Harrison's masterpiece. Now remastered, repackaged (check out the additions to the colourized inner-sleeve artwork) and expanded to include extra cuts, this is essential listening.

- ⊙ **The Best Of George Harrison** (1976; Parlophone).
  This includes the early-70s hits, with the bonus of great Beatle cuts like "While My Guitar Gently Weeps".

- ⊙ **Brainwashed** (2002; Parlophone).
  With restrained, precise production, and some of Harrison's most interesting lyrical work, this posthumously released set sounds fresh and warm. A worthy epitaph.

Neil Nixon

GRANT HART/NOVA MOB

Grant Hart's date of birth unknown;
Nova Mob formed Minneapolis, Minnesota, 1990.

When **HÜSKER DÜ** folded in 1987, **Bob Mould** formed **SUGAR**, while his songwriting partner **Grant Hart** was left to battle with a drug problem and a hesitant solo career. His difficulties were increased when he decided to play lead guitar rather than drums.

In the event, he played just about everything on his solo debut, INTOLERANCE (1989), a ragged but engagingly eclectic affair which made a virtue out of simplicity. The Dylanesque "Now That You Know Me", with its driving melody and frantic harmonica, was infectious, while "Twenty-Five Forty-One" was

a moving reminiscence on Hüsker Dü's impoverished early days. The album also spawned a mesmerizing single, "All Of My Senses".

Commercial acceptance proved elusive, and Hart parted company with Hüsker Dü's old label SST in 1990. That year, he formed **Nova Mob** with **Tom Merkl** (bass) and **Michael Crego** (drums). Their first album, THE LAST DAYS OF POMPEII (1990), was melodically strong and lyrically intriguing, with Hart weaving references to the Apollo moon landings and Hitler's dictatorship into his skewed world-view. Resembling a lighter, poppier Hüsker Dü, it contained a stunning pop song in "Over My Head" and the album deserved far wider exposure than a struggling Rough Trade label could afford.

Moreover, the album drew mixed reviews, as Hart's slightly abstract lyrical sensibility and 60s musical stylings did not connect with the emerging Nirvana generation. The 1991 live shows proved problematic too, as Hart grew impatient with demands for Hüsker Dü songs.

A near-fatal car accident involving the band delayed further recordings for three years, a silence broken in 1994 with NOVA MOB, for World Service Records. Hart continued the high standard of songwriting but lost out on some of the earlier edge and eccentricity. The recording wasn't helped by a thick, indistinct production, and the addition of a second guitarist, **Chris Hesler**, for a twin-guitar attack further muddied the water. Again, sales were weak, and later in the year it seemed the band was over, when, allegedly, the other members failed to turn up for a show that was to be recorded for a live album.

As a result, Grant Hart issued ECCE HOMO (1996) under his own name, playing acoustic at Washington's Crocodile Café. It was nothing short of a marvel, with Hart battling through audience indifference to deliver poignant, raging versions of Hüsker Dü classics and solo favourites. It remains his last release and sank without trace. ECCE HOMO's failure must have hit hard but Hart has proven himself resilient to a catalogue of suffering – some self-inflicted, some not – and will almost certainly continue to gnaw away at prevailing trends with his future work, which will doubtless continue to be criminally overlooked. Bloodied but unbowed, one hopes that persistence will eventually reap dividends, and Hart will gain the acclaim he deserves.

- ⊙ **The Last Days Of Pompeii** (1990; Rough Trade).
  An overlooked pearl. Odd and fiercely melodic, it moves away from the self-obsession of 'grunge' into its own strange, uncharted territory.

Nig Hodgkins

JULIANA HATFIELD

Born Boston, Massachusetts, 1967.

When the alliance between **Juliana Hatfield** and her **BLAKE BABIES** partner **John Strohm** broke down, she was invited by another ex-

Juliana Hatfield minus two

there were plenty of hook-laden gems here, it was difficult to avoid the impression that, in aiming to make a commercial record, Hatfield had allowed the producers to stamp out her originality. The Boston musical mafia, so instrumental in her rise to semi-stardom, seemed too musically conservative to allow Juliana Hatfield to stretch out and prove to the public that she is much more than a singer with famous friends.

BED (1998) was a far more mature piece of work, with Hatfield grabbing the reins to a large extent and showing greater confidence all round. Her lyrics still catered to the lonely, bedsit crowd, but they were bitter and angry rather than wistful.

In 2000 Juliana split the two aspects of her muse across a pair of discs: JULIANA'S PONY was harsh and ravishing, reportedly having been recorded in a week, while BEAUTIFUL CREATURE was far more acoustic and restrained. Both sets made a point, but would have benefited from a little pruning and integration. After the reunification of the Blake Babies at the start of the new millennium, Hatfield unleashed a greatest hits package, GOLD STARS, in 2002.

⊙ **Become What You Are** (1993; East West).
All of her songs may sound alike, but the template's as good as they come. US pop-punk at its naive best.

⊙ **Beautiful Creature** (2000; Zoe).
This collection finds Hatfield unplugged and restrained, at times achingly beautiful music is revealed, though the regularity of the tunes is the album's downfall.

James Wirth

Blake Baby, **Evan Dando**, to play bass on his band, **THE LEMONHEADS**' breakthrough album IT'S A SHAME ABOUT RAY (1992). However, rather than ride The Lemonheads' wave to stardom, Hatfield dedicated her time to recording a solo LP.

On HEY BABE (1992), Hatfield took on most of the guitar and bass duties herself, and was supported by a number of local luminaries – the ubiquitous Dando, one John Wesley Harding, and various members of Bullet Lavolta. The hallmark Boston sound – a kind of jingly-jangly take on punk rock – was stamped all over the record, and, though Hatfield has since stated her disappointment with the album's naivety, her talent for confessional songwriting and her Karen Carpenter warble managed to raise HEY BABE above the MTV mass.

With a permanent backing band – **Dean Fisher** (bass) and **Todd Philips** (drums) – the **Juliana Hatfield Three** (as they were to be known) toured extensively to promote the album, although press coverage (as 'Dando's dame') was more into muck-raking than the musical content. In reaction to this invasion of privacy, Hatfield's second album, BECOME WHAT YOU ARE (1993), was much more oblique than its predecessor, although her ability to write punchy pop tunes was still much in evidence.

After a year off, Hatfield re-emerged in early 1995 with a single, "Universal Heart-Beat", and a third album, ONLY EVERYTHING. The album received favourable reviews for its gutsier sound, but although

HATFIELD AND THE NORTH

Formed Canterbury, England, 1972; disbanded 1975; re-formed for a series of gigs in 1989–90.

Technically accomplished, jazz-influenced **Hatfield And The North** were the acceptable face of 70s prog-rock: a band who didn't take themselves too seriously, played (and sung) songs with ridiculous titles, and had honourable guest appearances from the likes of Robert Wyatt – always a good sign. Their origins lay in the late-60s Canterbury scene which evolved out of Soft Machine and Caravan, and spawned such notables as Gong and Kevin Ayers' group, The Whole World.

Formed in November 1972, the Hatfields (their full name was taken from the A1 motorway signs in North London) comprised **Richard Sinclair** (bass/vocals; ex-Caravan), **Phil Miller** (guitar; ex-**ROBERT WYATT**'s Matching Mole), wonder-drummer **Pip Pyle** (ex-Delivery and Gong), and

Dave Stewart (keyboards). Stewart – not to be confused with the half-Eurythmic – had previously worked with **STEVE HILLAGE**, before collaborating with the avant-garde duo Egg and Khan. A fine arranger, his keyboards gave the Hatfields their distinctive sound, along with Sinclair's Wyatt-influenced deadpan English vocals.

The band, signed to the fledgling Virgin label, belonged to that 70s coterie of hippie experimenters, finding a place somewhere between the stoned extrapolations of Gong and the earnest politico-rock of Henry Cow. They improvised at length, employed a trio of female backing singers – **Barbara Gaskin**, **Amanda Parsons** and **Ann Rosenthal**, aka **The Northettes** – and roped in jazz-wise associates such as Cow members Lindsay Cooper (oboe) and Geoff Leigh (saxes/flutes). Less poppy than Sinclair's old band, Caravan, the band walked a line between avant-garde inclinations and accessibility.

Frequent gigging led to modest airplay and attention from a small clique of music journalists. 1974 saw the release of a debut album, HATFIELD AND THE NORTH. A whimsical offering, it included a few engaging Sinclair songs and daring instrumental passages. However, it was the subsequent single, "Let's Eat (Real Soon)"/"Fitter Stoke Has A Bath", released at the end of 1974, that showed what the Hatfields could do, mixing catchy riffs with meandering breaks. It bombed, of course – this was an album band in an era of pap chart 45s.

Dave Stewart was pretty busy around this time, recording sessions for Steve Hillage's solo album, FISH RISING (1975), and even re-forming Egg for the LP, THE CIVIL SURFACE (1974). However, a second Hatfields LP, THE ROTTERS' CLUB, emerged in 1975, consolidating their reputation, with Sinclair's subtle and witty lyrics, sympathetic arrangements and some fine jazz-rock instrumentals. The album charted very briefly in the UK, but, believing their following to be limited, the band agreed to split months after its release. A compilation LP was issued in 1980.

After the band's demise, most of the crew resurfaced in **NATIONAL HEALTH** (formed 1975), alongside members of Gilgamesh. Richard Sinclair joined **CAMEL**, returned to Caravan for a time, and most recently resurfaced with his Caravan Of Dreams. Dave Stewart did session work for Bill Bruford's first two solo LPs, before hitting unexpected pop stardom in 1981, firstly with a revival of Jimmy Ruffin's "What Becomes Of The Broken Hearted?", with ex-Zombies singer **Colin Blunstone**, and then with former Northette, Barbara Gaskin, on a radical cover of Lesley Gore's "It's My Party" – which topped the UK charts and was followed by several diverting, if less successful, singles. Stewart also ventured into writing music for television, and formed a short-lived Hatfield successor called **Rapid Eye Movements**, who, needless to say, had nothing whatsoever to do with R.E.M.

The Hatfields themselves re-formed for a series of gigs in 1989–90, with the original line-up, minus Stewart, whose place was taken by **Sophia**

Domanich, and some fine new numbers alongside the old material. A live album – LIVE 1990 – emerged in 1993 to commemorate the event.

⊙ **The Rotters' Club** (1975; Virgin).
With its sophisticated yet melodic compositions, and astute playing, this was the Hatfields at their most cohesive and creative.

⊙ **Afters** (1980; Virgin; currently unavailable).
Compiled by Dave Stewart, this is a representative selection of material from Hatfield's two albums, along with some live tracks. Well worth a CD rerelease ...

Martin Haggerty

RICHIE HAVENS

Born Brooklyn, New York, 1941.

"I'm not in showbusiness and never was. I'm in the communications business."

Singer-songwriter **Richie Havens** has brought his idiosyncratic guitar style and soulful voice to bear on a wide range of material, from his early days on the Greenwich Village folk circuit, to later interpretations of contemporary songwriters like Sting and Tom Waits. If one thing unites his output, it's his commitment to the ideals of the 1960s.

Havens' roots were in gospel and doo-wop, before graduating onto the coffee-house circuit of the early 60s alongside singers like Bob Dylan and Gordon Lightfoot. Already a popular performer, he developed his trademark open-chord guitar tuning at this time, providing an urgently rhythmic backdrop to his voice.

Early demos for Douglas Records were issued in 1967 as A RICHIE HAVENS RECORD and ELECTRIC HAVENS. Both showed Havens' ability as a folk singer, but it was his major label debut, MIXED BAG (1967), that provided the blueprint for his subsequent career: its outstanding tracks were versions of Dylan's "Just Like A Woman" and Lightfoot's "I Can't Make It Anymore".

SOMETHING ELSE AGAIN (1968) went gold despite being more intense in its music and lyrics (notably "The Klan"), while the double album RICHARD P. HAVENS, 1983 (1969) was an excellent mix of originals and covers, with a darker, brooding feel. The latter also bore witness to Havens' compelling ability as a live performer, but his finest three hours came with his performance at Woodstock in 1969. The image from D. A. Pennabaker's documentary, of a sweat-drenched, kaftan-clad Havens improvising his final song "Freedom" (from the traditional "Motherless Child"), encapsulated the event's spirit.

American chart success followed, firstly with a Top 20 cover of The Beatles' "Here Comes The Sun", and then with its parent album, ALARM CLOCK (1970). Its predecessor, STONEHENGE (also 1970), had featured his cover of The Bee Gees' "I Started A Joke", which showcased Havens' ability to transform the unlikeliest material. Subsequent albums continued in the same vein, most notably THE GREAT BLIND DEGREE (1971) and PORTFOLIO (1973) for the Stormy Forest label, MIXED BAG II (1974) for Polydor, and MIRAGE (1977) for A&M. There was also the live set, RICHIE HAVENS ON STAGE (1972), which kept his live following going even when reactions to his later, mellower recordings became indifferent.

An honest and earnest musician, and a diligent campaigner on ecological issues, Richie Havens survived the musical excesses of the 70s and 80s to see the emergence of a new breed of similarly inclined singer-songwriters, like Ben Harper and Freedy Johnston. Best captured live, he remains one of the most distinctive and powerful survivors from the 60s. CUTS TO THE CHASE (1994), despite some questionable rock arrangements, contained excellent covers of Sting's "They Dance Alone" and Jackson Browne's "Lives In The Balance". 2002's WISHING WELL was equally accomplished, and was hailed by many as his most accomplished work since the 70s.

⊙ **Mixed Bag** (1967; Verve).
The only early Havens record currently available on CD, this is still probably the best illustration of his abilities as an interpretative singer-songwriter.

⊙ **Résumé: The Best Of Richie Havens** (1993; Rhino).
Usual excellence from Rhino, with an illustrative selection of Havens' material from the late 60s to the early 70s, backed up by in-depth sleeve notes, featuring commentary by Havens himself.

⊙ **Wishing Well** (2002; Evangeline).
An exceptional set that finds Havens still more than capable of filling his music with pure heart and soul.

Nicholas Oliver

SCREAMIN' JAY HAWKINS

Born Cleveland, Ohio, 1929; died, France, 2000.

"I went to a place called Nitro, West Virginia. this is 1950. There was a big, big huge fat lady at the bar … she was downing scotch and Jack Daniel's at the same time and whenever she looked up at me she shouted, 'Scream, baby, scream'." Screamin' Jay on how he got his name

Plumbing the depths of morbidity while scaling the heights of originality, **Screamin' Jay Hawkins** was one of showbiz's most singularly demented talents. Without him, we might never have seen the antics of Arthur Brown, Ozzy Osbourne or Alice Cooper.

Born Jalacy J. Hawkins, Jay spent his early years in an orphanage, before enrolling at high school to study piano, tenor sax and opera. 1944 saw him enlisted in the army, then the air force, where he began entertaining GI audiences at service clubs in the US, UK and Japan. He was also a middleweight boxer of some repute.

Demobbed in 1952, Jay found civvy clubs crawling with fledgling jump-blues and R&B out-

CHARLIE GILLET

Screamin' Jay – He Put a Spell On You

fits. He experimented with a succession of bands before joining **Tiny Grimes & His Rocking Highlanders** on vocals, sax and keyboards. Following a very brief stint in **Fats Domino**'s band – Jay was fired for upstaging the boss by wearing a gold and leopard-skin outfit and turban – his solo career began in earnest with "Baptise Me In Wine" (1954). A slew of session recordings from this time show Jay's early promise, his voice and humour cutting through the primitive R&B backing.

September 1956 saw Jay cut the vinyl that would change his life. He'd already recorded one version of "I Put A Spell On You" (according to a DJ in Cleveland where the session was held, Hawkins was so drunk that when the song later became popular he had to relearn the words from the disc), but it was the challenge by Columbia's A&R department to make it scary that really pushed him over the edge. As producer Arnold Maxim got together the best session men of the day, Jay became so drunk for the session that he had no subsequent recollection of it. Refusing to believe that it was *his* bloodcurdling baritone on the recording, he burned a copy when confronted with photographic evidence.

This legendary version of "I Put A Spell On You" was deep and primal, the distant sound of drums coming from a nocturnal jungle. No wonder rumours of cannibalistic ritual circulated, even to a 50s audience who were becoming more comfortable with rock'n'roll's wild antics. For Jay it was the first time he'd managed to commit his flamboyant and frightening stage act to vinyl. His notoriety ensured that it sold a million copies, but it was mysteriously absent from the *Billboard* charts.

By now Jay was starting gigs from inside a coffin, dressed in a cape, and surrounded by stage fireworks and a cigarette-smoking skull stick called Henry. His performances brought – and sometimes sent – audiences running. Encouraged by his friend, the DJ Alan Freed, Jay singlehandedly invented 'ghoul-rock' – tongue-in-cheek horror meets Little Richard. With such a charismatic image, it was only a matter of time before Jay would make his movie debut. He was booked to feature in Freed's 1957 movie, *Mister Rock And Roll*, but his appearance – in a loincloth, and with white shoe polish on his face – ensured that his singular celluloid contribution was consigned to the cutting-room floor.

1957 also saw Jay back on record with the quirky "There's Something Wrong With You", but as the 60s loomed only a Hawaii club residency with Shoutin' Pat Newborn was keeping his career alive. However, he was back by 1962 with the storming, disturbed single, "I Hear Voices", as well as the introspective "Ashes", which was recorded with the volatile Newborn. Her services were dispensed with, however, after she knifed Jay for meeting the woman who became his wife.

For much of the 60s Jay's career stumbled along in a series of fits and starts. After Nina Simone covered "I Put A Spell On You", Jay wrote "Poor Folks"/"Your Kind Of Love" for her in 1965. She refused to record them, and Jay was left to do so himself in typically macabre fashion. He returned to Hawaii in 1966, but by the end of the 60s success in the UK meant that he was signed to the Philips label and he released the LP WHAT THAT IS (1969). Tracks included the cannabalistic "Feast Of The Mau Mau" and the tasteful "Constipation Blues", replete with predictable sound effects.

Although Jay has often been labelled a one-hit wonder (because of an apparent reliance on "I Put A Spell On You"), his career has actually been far more diverse. As well as touring, and occasionally recording, with The Rolling Stones, he has continued to beat the bounds of voodoo R&B, whilst influencing the stage-shows of ghoulish musical descendants. He has even been more fortunate in surviving cinema's ruthless editing process with two Jim Jarmusch movies – in the second, *Mystery Train* (1989), he played a comically laconic hotel concierge.

Signed to Demon Records in the 90s, Jay returned to the charts with "Heart Attack And Vine" (1991), which was also featured in a Levis jeans advertisement, while his ground-breaking stage show continued to tour Europe. But in early 2000, having undergone surgery to treat an aneurysm at the age of 70, Jay passed away. He had often been quoted as saying, 'when I go, I don't want to be buried. I've been in too many damn coffins already!'

Black Music For White People (1991; Demon).
A knowingly titled mixed bag, this contrasts a swampy blues reading of Tom Waits' "Heart Attack And Vine", a full-throttle version of "Ol' Man River" and an ill-judged dance mix of "I Put A Spell On You".

Stone Crazy (1993; Demon).
Proof that Hawkins' career is back on an even keel, this contains a homage to *Twin Peaks* actress, "Sherilyn Fenn".

Portrait Of A Man (1994; Edsel).
Probably the best overview of Screamin' Jay Hawkins' career, from "Little Demon" (1956) right up to "Scream The Blues" (1994).

Alligator Wine (1998; Music Club).
A positive ghoul-fest of scream and gurgles, with twenty tracks spanning a long career.

Simon Whittaker

HAWKWIND

Formed London, 1969.

The **Hawkwind** collective began as The Famous Cure, changed to Group X and then became Hawkwind Zoo – a title taken from a Michael Moorcock story. After one final name change, Hawkwind signed to Liberty Records and released their self-titled debut album in 1970.

Famed for playing the free-festival circuit (their obscenity trial resulted from a performance where the band were alleged to have appeared naked on stage, handed out contraceptives and encouraged 'free love'), main songwriter **Dave Brock** (vocals/guitars/keyboards) was the pivot around whom the innumerable line-up changes occurred. After their debut, co-founder **Huw Lloyd-Langton** (lead guitar/vocals) left the band for nine years, while two bass players were recruited before the follow-up, X IN SEARCH OF SPACE (1971).

This marked the beginning of a high-profile and prolific period for Hawkwind – five albums in four years, characterized by tribal drumming, atonal electronic excursions, sci-fi poetics, heavy blues and rock'n'roll riffs and a distant snorting saxophone. The hit single "Silver Machine" (1972) and its accompanying album, SPACE RITUAL (1973), gained them a wide audience. The addition of **Simon House** (violin/keyboards) in 1974 mellowed the musical assault, but with **Lemmy** on bass the demands of heavy rock would always be satisfied. So, too, the demands of sci-fi fans, as the seminal WARRIOR ON THE EDGE OF TIME (1975) with its narration by Michael Moorcock proved.

Lemmy was forced out after a drugs bust in 1975 – forming **MOTÖRHEAD** soon after – and the same year also saw a label switch, to Charisma, and the arrival of vocalist and lyricist **Robert Calvert**. ASTOUNDING SOUNDS, AMAZING MUSIC (1976), saw a cleaner, clearer sound, as well as a rather more intelligible lyrical content. "Kerb Crawler" was even remixed for single release by Pink Floyd's Dave Gilmour.

Even so, the end seemed in sight by 1977 as punk rock arrived and legal squabbles over the Hawkwind name threatened to undermine the band's existence. Linchpins Dave Brock and Robert Calvert were forced to tour as The Sonic Assassins, and to record as The Hawklords for 1978's 25 YEARS ON album.

After producing the contract-filling PXR-5 (1979), Brock re-emerged with a new Hawkwind line-up, minus Calvert but with Lloyd-Langton back in the fold, with old hands **Simon King** (drums) and **Harvey Bainbridge** (bass), and **GONG**'s **Tim Blake** on keyboards. The resulting Live Seventy-Nine (1980) captured the energy of punk and featured the minor hit, "Shot Down In The Night". It paved the way for 1980's awesome Levitation (1980), which featured **CREAM**'s **Ginger Baker** on drums.

After three moderately successful LPs for RCA – including Sonic Attack (1981) and Choose Your Masques (1982), the band began a half-life with independent labels. Tours still sold out and Flicknife records released the band's best studio album of the 80s, The Chronicle Of The Black Sword (1985), based on Michael Moorcock's *Elric* novels. Although Live Chronicles (1986) ranked alongside the very best live albums, The Xenon Codex (1988) only hinted at former glories by trying to follow the Warrior On The Edge Of Time format.

Arguments about royalties, Lloyd-Langton's second departure and Calvert's death from a heart attack in 1988 seemed to point to the end of Hawkwind. But with yet another new line-up, Space Bandits (1990) emerged to acclaim and touring continued. **Bridget Wishart** survived two albums on vocals, while her dancing was reminiscent of the legendary **Stacia**, who had accompanied the tours of the early 70s, with painted breasts aflutter.

Now signed to Castle, a line-up of Brock, **Alan Davey** (bass/vocals/keyboards) and **Richard Chadwick** (drums/vocals/keyboards) recorded the excellent hi-tech Electric Tepee (1992), improved their already phenomenal live shows, and reaped the benefit of a rising generation of festival bands like Ozric Tentacles. 1993's It Is The Business Of The Future To Be Dangerous (1993), was a meandering affair, however, featuring their only cover version to date, a radically reworked "Gimme Shelter", originally released on a compilation for homeless charities.

A fine live album, The Business Trip (1994), followed, before Alien 4 (1995), a sci-fi concept album

that succesfully edged the band back to the days of Calvert, with a new vocalist, **Ron Tree**.

Incredibly, as the band's thirtieth anniversary approached, the grizzled old veterans played the '12 Hour Technicolor Dream All Nighter' at Brixton Academy and, with Ambient Anarchists (1998), the masters of the universe demonstrated they were ready to pilot spaceship Earth into the new millennium. Since the turn of the century, official Hawkwind projects have been thin on the ground. For the truly addicted, though, there has been a plethora of compilations and live bootlegs and, of course, the band continues to tour.

⦿ **Space Ritual** (1973; EMI).
This sprawling double live album acted as a testament to all things riff-laden and unutterably heavy. The current CD reissue, lovingly repackaged, includes three rare extra tracks.

⦿ **Warrior On The Edge Of Time** (1975; Dojo).
Bizarre musical landscapes, pumping rock songs, Michael Moorcock, two drummers and Lemmy's final album. A masterpiece.

⦿ **Levitation** (1980; Castle Communications).
A mellow and extraordinary album, glinting chrome production, Ginger Baker on drums and glistening songs.

⦿ **The Chronicle Of The Black Sword** (1985; Dojo).
Hair-tearing exercise that exceeded all expectations. Heavy rock songs, anti-drugs messages and throbbing instrumentals. The American edition on Griffin has lyrics and an extra song.

⦿ **Live Chronicles** (1986; Castle Communications).
An essential double live album; the UK version was reissued as one CD, but the US double-CD set has six extra songs, a lyric booklet and a short story by Moorcock.

⦿ **Live At The Chicago Auditorium March 21, 1974:** The 1999 Party (1998; EMI).
Well, if you weren't there, this might help push you over the edge into a drug-ravaged hallucinatory flashback. Take two of these and call me in the morning.

Duncan Harris

ISAAC HAYES

Born Memphis, Tennessee, 1942.

Isaac **Hayes** is now acknowledged as one of the most prolific, multi-talented singers, songwriters, arrangers, musicians and producers that America has ever spawned. Yet he has never quite experienced the mainstream success of those who followed him (Barry White, for example), and his career has taken some disastrous turns over the years.

Born in Memphis, Hayes was exposed to a broad spectrum of musical styles, notably gospel, jazz and even country. His first instrument was the saxophone, and before too long he was doing horn arrangements for the likes of **Sam Phillips**. After auditioning for Stax Records three times, he met **Dave Porter**, with whom he began a successful songwriting collaboration. They wrote for Carla Thomas, Otis Redding and, perhaps most famously, **SAM & DAVE** ("Hold On I'm Comin'", "Soul Man"). Hayes played on sessions for all these artists, as well as for Wilson Pickett, Don Covay and The Emotions.

DOREMI FASOL LATIDO

Some jamming sessions at these dates inspired an album, PRESENTING ISAAC HAYES (1967), sometimes reissued under the title BLUE HAYES. This was followed by a further six albums in the years 1969–73, extending the jamming influences of his debut to their logical conclusion. Typically, many of his albums from this period consisted of only four to six tracks, many lasting over ten minutes, with lush orchestral arrangement and occasional vocal breaks.

Hayes himself remarked that 'My composing depends a lot on my mood. I'm kinda lazy when it comes to lyrics, but I find the music comes pretty easy.' Hence the somewhat unorthodox structure of his work from this period, in which he extended the structure of his own songs and stretched to the limit other people's works, usually to great effect. Jerry Butler's "I Stand Accused" (on THE ISAAC HAYES MOVEMENT, 1970), Bacharach and David's "The Look Of Love" (from TO BE CONTINUED, 1971), and "I'll Never Fall In Love Again" (from BLACK MOSES, 1971) were all tremendous reworkings.

With Hayes' fondness for mood music, it was only a matter of time before he would be offered film soundtrack work. His soundtrack for the blaxploitation movie *Shaft* (1971) won a Grammy, while "Theme From Shaft" not only hit #1 in America and #4 in Britain, but also won an Oscar in 1972. This success was mirrored by Curtis Mayfield's *Superfly* soundtrack (1972), while Hayes himself produced two further soundtracks for Stax – TOUGH GUYS and TRUCK TURNER (both 1974).

Isaac Hayes models his own unique range of evening wear

After the brilliance of his 1973 album JOY, Isaac Hayes' career started to slip as he left Stax for the ABC label. His disco output of the mid-70s was largely undistinguished – atmosphere was now less important than a beat and an instant hook, which Barry White understood when he borrowed Hayes' styles for his own three-minute hits. Despite albums of duets with **Dionne Warwick** (1976) and **Millie Jackson** (1979), Hayes was bankrupt by the early 80s, and also spent a short time in jail for drug offences.

During the 80s, Hayes' acting career took precedence, notably in the movie *I'm Gonna Git You Sucka* (1987). More significantly, his reputation as a musician began to improve once again, as British DJs started to sample Hayes' past glories – the "Shaft" riff was particularly in evidence on Bomb The Bass's 1988 debut single "Beat Dis". But it was the early 90s before Isaac Hayes' work was properly re-evaluated. Massive Attack's "One Love" (from their 1991 landmark debut BLUE LINES) was based around horn and piano riffs from "Ike's Mood". Then, by chance, in 1995, a string sample from "Ike's Rap 2" appeared on two separate hit singles – Portishead's "Glory Box" and Tricky's "Hell Is Round The Corner". The time was right for a new Isaac Hayes album and he responded with possibly his best album in twenty years. BRANDED (1995) was a mixture of covers (including Sting's "Fragile" and Lovin' Spoonful's "Summer In The City"), and new readings of old songs like "Soulsville" from SHAFT. At long last, the maverick genius of Isaac Hayes was back in fashion.

Furthermore, Hayes reached a new audience in the late 90s when he voiced the character of Chef in the cult TV cartoon series *South Park*. Satisfied that his fervent belief in Scientology would not be lampooned by the show's writers, he turned his attention, naturally enough, to the musical content of the show. High spots have included "Love Gravy" – already a live favourite, inspired by the near-legendary moment in the show when a drunken pig was encouraged to 'make sweet lurve' to an equally inebriated elephant – and "Chocolate Salty Balls", cannily released as a 1998 Christmas single.

Since then, Issac has branched out, releasing not another best-selling album, but a kitchen tome (*Cooking With Heart & Soul*) as well as the 'I Like Barbecue' barbecue sauce.

⊙ **Hot Buttered Soul** (1969; Stax).
The prototype for Hayes' late-60s/early-70s catalogue, this is best remembered for his eighteen-minute epic reading of Glen Campbell's "By The Time I Get To Phoenix", although the highlight is probably his own extraordinarily titled "Hyperbolicsyllabicsesquedalymistic".

⊙ **Black Moses** (1971; Stax).
The definitive example of Hayes' multi-layered approach to arrangements – horns, strings, backing vocals, the works. A double album, it contains all the "Ike's Rap"s, along with covers including "They Long To Be Close To You" and "Never Can Say Goodbye".

⊙ **Isaac's Moods: The Best Of Isaac Hayes** (1988; Stax/ Ace).
For the full-length versions, check out the original albums. But as a starter for the 1969–73 period this compilation will do just fine. Contains "Shaft", "Joy", "Soulsville", and edited versions of "Walk On By" and "I Stand Accused". An unusual but effective collection.

Justin Lewis

LEE HAZLEWOOD

Born Mannford, Oklahoma, 1929.

As record producer, **Lee Hazlewood** discovered Duane Eddy and helped the guitarist develop his influential 'twang' sound in the late 50s; nearly a decade later, he made **Nancy Sinatra** a star with "These Boots Are Made for Walkin'". As label honcho, Hazlewood supported the early work of Gram Parsons. And as singer, Hazlewood unleashed his deep, deep throat in a variety of settings, from solo acoustic storytelling to funky duets with female foils such as Sinatra and **Ann-Margret**, all while boasting one of the inarguably cool moustaches of modern times. While his work can be lighter than the air it glides on, it comes rife with an amiable, humorous, and very distinct edge that continues to endear the singer to adventurous country-pop listeners.

Hazlewood was already entrenched in the biz when he released his first solo album, 1963's TROUBLE IS A LONESOME TOWN. Although recorded primarily to showcase his songs for more popular singers, the album was an amusing listen, with sparse

acoustic songs and spoken narration detailing the happenings of a mythical town called Trouble. These tales about town denizens like Ugly Emery Brown and Sleepy Gilloreeth ("The Best Dressed Man In Trouble") initiated a projected trilogy of records: THE N.S.I.V.I.P.S followed, while a promised third entry still remains unwritten.

In the mid-60s, Hazlewood hooked up with Nancy Sinatra, who – despite her parentage, record contract, and legs – had yet to score an American hit. This all changed in 1966 when the pair concocted "These Boots Are Made For Walkin'". Hazlewood also joined Sinatra for a series of country duets that would be collected on the album NANCY AND LEE, which included some of Hazlewood's finest and most popular songs, such as "Some Velvet Morning", a dusty, mysterious piece that one can only wish had been added to *Pulp Fiction*'s soundtrack.

Of course, such inclusion would have meant the type of widespread acceptance to which Hazlewood never really aspired. After his success with Sinatra, Hazlewood took off for Europe. ('I move every year,' he recently told a newspaper, 'It keeps you from getting too close to anybody.') Living in London, Paris, and, finally, Sweden, he continued to record, albeit on a relatively minor commercial scale. Although a reunion with Sinatra proved less dynamic than their initial fling (as would a second reunion 25 years later), his string of solo work was enticing. 1969's THE COWBOY AND THE LADY teamed the singer with actress Ann-Margret for a set of oddball country covers. The next year brought both REQUIEM FOR AN ALMOST LADY, a

Lee Hazlewood (he's the one in the middle!)

handsome acoustic outing about failed romance, and also COWBOY IN SWEDEN, the first of Hazlewood's collaborations with director **Torbjörn Axelman**,

Much of Hazlewood's quirky and varied solo output has been restricted to the ears of record collectors and Lee Hazlewood fanatics who track down the original vinyl copies. The recordings were given a new life in the late 90s when Smells Like Records (a New Jersey indie operated by Sonic Youth's drummer, Steve Shelley) began a series of reissues. In addition to reissuing many of the singer's rarities, the label released FARMISHT, FLATULENCE, ORIGAMI, ARF!!! AND ME, a new album of Tin Pan Alley standards. Recorded in Arizona in the late 90s with Al Casey (who played on Hazlewood's earliest productions), the album found the musician applying his trademark baritone to songs such as "It Had To Be You" and "I Can't Get Started" with a fan's ardour.

Riding on the back of the renewed interest in his work, 2002 saw the release of an outtakes collection, FOR EVERY SOLUTION THERE'S A PROBLEM, as well as a tribute album, TOTAL LEE, which saw the likes of The Tindersticks, Lambchop and Calexico paying their respects. While the ageing cowboy may have lost his moustache and maiden, his throat and flair ride on.

Fairy Tales & Fantasies: The Best Of Nancy & Lee (1989; Rhino).
A perfect starting point, this disc collects the finest fairy tales and fantasies growled and purred by the duo, including "Sand," "Some Velvet Morning," and a Sonny and Cher–styled cover of "You've Lost That Lovin' Feeling."

Cowboy In Sweden (1970; Smells Like).
The soundtrack to a Swedish television programme of the same name, this album paired Hazlewood with the singers Nina Lizell and Suzi Jane Hokom. With deep-throated country rambling, a relatively dark lyrical edge, and gooey strings worthy of a Bacharach recording, the album is prime Hazlewood.

Requiem For An Almost Lady (1970; Smells Like).
A sombre concept record that finds Hazlewood reviewing a series of failed romances over a sparse backdrop of almost folksy acoustic instruments.

Jay Ruttenberg

HEART

Formed Vancouver, early 1970s.

It must have seemed like an A&R man's dream when **Heart** were 'discovered' in the mid-70s playing up to four sets a night in the Pacific Northwest and Canadian club circuits. Two glamorous rock-chick sisters with a Led Zep fixation, great vocals, a handful of hard-rock tunes with melody, and a tight band – success was assured … up to a point.

Evolving out of a Seattle-based band known as The Army, then as White Heart, the line-up of **Nancy Wilson** (guitar/vocals), her sister **Ann** (lead vocals), **Steve Fossen** (bass), **Roger Fisher** (guitar), **Michael Derosier** (drums) and **Howard Leese** (keyboards) changed their name to Heart when they

based themselves in Vancouver. They signed to local label Mushroom Records, for whom they recorded DREAMBOAT ANNIE (1976), a mixture of folk and hard rock.

Picked up by Epic Records for the American market, DREAMBOAT ANNIE hit pay dirt in the States, and spawned the hit singles "Crazy On You" and "Magic Man", relatively subtle rock/pop tunes that were probably their finest moments. They initially enjoyed minor success in Britain (helped by occasional TV exposure), but their sound soon proved dated for European tastes dominated at the time by the New Wave.

Contractual and legal problems plagued the early years of their career, but the hit singles "Barracuda" and "Even It Up" cemented their reputation as major FM-friendly stadium-rockers, while well-crafted acoustic ballads like "Keep Your Love Alive" and "Dream Of The Archer" (from 1978's LITTLE QUEEN) demonstrated a more gentle side. They lacked originality, but it was hard not to be impressed by the range and power of Ann Wilson's voice, while the band's twin guitar attack was calculated to inspire air-punching devotion.

By the early 80s, Fisher, Fossen and Derosier had left, to be replaced by **Mark Andes** (bass) and **Denny Carmassi** (drums). With the arrival of MTV, the Wilsons stocked up on an extravagantly gothic wardrobe, signed to Capitol and won a wider, international audience with heavily rotated videos of synthesized power ballads like "What About Love" (1985), "These Dreams" (1986) and "All I Want To Do Is Make Love To You" (1990). They only occasionally allowed their harder edge to resurface, as on the menacing title track to their million-selling album BAD ANIMALS (1987), which also contained the slickly produced "Who Will You Run To" and the American #1 and worldwide hit "Alone".

After the poor response to the live album ROCK THE HOUSE LIVE (1991), Ann and Nancy Wilson returned to their native Seattle and began jamming in clubs with the likes of Alice In Chains, Soundgarden and Pearl Jam. All the same, there were no apparent grunge influences on their next album DESIRE WALKS ON (1993), which contained the usual mix of rockers, soft-rock ballads, and acoustic numbers like "Back To Avalon" and an overwrought version of Dylan's "Ring Them Bells".

Extracurricular activities have included a stint as acoustic alter egos **The Lovemongers** for the soundtrack to the movie *Singles* (directed by Nancy's husband, Cameron Crowe) and an EP that included a cover of Led Zeppelin's "Battle Of Evermore", that also turned up on THE BRIDGE CONCERTS (1997), an all-star charity disc produced by Neil Young. Having covered Zep songs in their live sets for over twenty years, it was fitting that their unplugged THE ROAD HOME (1996), was produced by Zep bassist John Paul Jones. It revealed a surprising depth in some of their best-known songs, and perhaps points to a possible new phase in their career – assuming they ever decide to get Heart pumping again.

In the meantime Heart put things on hold in the late 90s as the Wilsons decided to focus on the Lovemongers, resulting in the release of WHIRLYGIG (1997) and HERE IS CHRISTMAS (1998), the latter title speaking volumes about what you would expect to find within. Nancy then went on to release her first solo effort, LIVE AT MCCABES GUITAR SHOP (1999), while in 2001 Ann participated in the star-studded *A Walk Down Abbey Road: A Tribute To The Beatles* tour.

⊙ **The Essential Heart** (2003; Sony).
This double-CD set includes early hits "Magic Man", "Crazy On You" and "Dreamboat Annie", as well as the thudding riffs of "Barracuda".

Chris Coe

HEARTBREAKERS

Formed New York, 1975; last seen 1990.

Bad attitudes, black leather, loud'n'snotty rock-'n'roll music, drug habits and good-looking in a wasted kinda way, the **Heartbreakers** were everything your parents were scared you might become interested in when they bought your first record player.

The band was formed in New York, from the remnants of **THE NEW YORK DOLLS** – **JOHNNY THUNDERS** (guitar/vocals) and **Jerry Nolan** (drums) – together with **RICHARD HELL** (ex-**TELEVISION**; bass/vocals) and **Walter Lure** (guitar/vocals). They got a brief set of lowlife classics together (including the wonderful "Chinese Rocks", an ode to the trials of feeding a habit, co-written by Johnny Thunders

and **Dee Dee Ramone**), played a few gigs and promptly headed for England to record their first album and check out the heroin-maintenance programme offered by the National Health Service. Arriving just as the UK punk scene was building momentum, they developed a cult following by playing some storming gigs in and around London, signed up with Track, fixed up the tracks on their arms and hit the studios.

The resulting album, LAMF (1977), featured all the Heartbreakers' best live songs but somehow managed to lose most of the excitement. The original mix – although later repaired by Johnny Thunders and **Tony James** (ex-**GENERATION X**) for the 1985 reissue LAMF REVISITED – was bad enough to cause Jerry Nolan to leave the band. By this point, the band had also lost Richard Hell – replaced by **Billy Wrath** (bass/vocals) – so Johnny took control (to the best of his chemically challenged ability) and was deported, for his trouble, together with his boys, back to New York.

In some form or another **Johnny Thunders & The Heartbreakers**, as they'd become, tarted themselves around New York City's clubs until 1991, playing for cash to feed the various interests of the band. Walter Lure's guitar playing improved, as did his backing vocals, and the band were still occasionally setting crowds on fire even towards the end of Thunders' life. The music failed to develop and the live shows increasingly featured songs he'd performed with The New York Dolls or taken from his solo material. His death in 1991 was ultimately related to his extreme way of living – evidently coming about due to a methadone overdose – and came as little

Heartbreakers (from left): Billy Wrath, Jerry Nolan, Johnny Thunders and Walter Lee

shock. The industry predictably cashed in with numerous 'bootleg' and 'studio demo' compilations, not one of which is really worth the money asked.

- (•) **Live At Max's Kansas City** (1979; Max's Kansas City).
Back on his home turf, Johnny and the gang swagger and snarl their way through a monstrously powerful set, stopping only to hurl abuse at the paying customers.

- (•) **DTK LAMF** (1984; Jungle).
Must-have twin pack, featuring the remastered studio album bolted onto a 1977 live set from London's Speakeasy club. Both recordings sensibly let Johnny's scrawny junkie-whine and his rock-god guitar playing run the show. The initials, by the way, stand for 'Down To Kill, Like A Motherfucker', evidently an old New York gang challenge.

Al Spicer

HEAVEN 17

Formed Sheffield, England, 1980; disbanded 1989.

Ian Craig Marsh (synthesizer/saxophone) and **Martyn Ware** (synthesizer) spent the mid- to late 70s in various electronic bands, from the obscure (Musical Vomit) to the near-legendary (the original line-up of **THE HUMAN LEAGUE**). In 1980, however, after two Human League LPs, the duo left – planning to abandon touring for good. To begin with, they developed **BEF** (British Electric Foundation), an experimental project using guest singers and musicians as needed. Then they recruited vocalist **Glenn Gregory** and named themselves **Heaven 17**, after one of the fictitious groups in Anthony Burgess's *A Clockwork Orange*.

Heaven 17's debut single, "(We Don't Need This) Fascist Groove Thang", was one of the grooviest and most overtly political singles in British pop history. A witty, confrontational slice of driving electronic funk, it was denied radio play and missed the Top 40, but created plenty of interest for the trio's first album, PENTHOUSE AND PAVEMENT (1981). A record as intelligent as it was danceable, this was named *Record of the Year* by *Melody Maker*, but chart success still eluded the band, and they spent much of 1982 concentrating on their BEF sideline project. One BEF track, a cover of "Ball Of Confusion" recorded with **Tina Turner**, effectively began her revival of the 80s and 90s, and Marsh and Ware went on to produce Turner's hit cover of Al Green's "Let's Stay Together" (1983), and also contributed to her 1984 album, PRIVATE DANCER.

By then, though, Heaven 17 had firmly established themselves as a chart group. "Temptation", a Motown pastiche featuring the soaring vocals of session singer Carol Kenyon, reached #2 in the UK singles charts, and its companion album, THE LUXURY GAP (1983), continued to marry memorable pop hooks with its predecessor's political edge. HOW MEN ARE (1984) was perhaps more ambitious, and one track's royalties ("Five Minutes To Midnight") were donated to CND.

But by 1986 the bubble had burst. ENDLESS (1986), a collection of dance mixes, failed to sell, and

the fourth album proper, PLEASURE ONE (1986), seemed to have abandoned electronica, along with the melodic and lyrical treats of earlier works. It flopped, as did TEDDY BEAR, DUKE AND PSYCHO (1988).

Martyn Ware's reputation as a producer has continued to flourish, through his work for Terence Trent d'Arby and Des'ree. Meanwhile, Heaven 17 experienced a short revival in 1992, as "Temptation" reached the UK Top 10 in a remixed version by **Brothers In Rhythm**.

A new album BIGGER THAN AMERICA (1996) witnessed a reasonable return to form, but its sales were barely measurable. Like many of their contemporaries, they were on safest ground when revisiting old material – and in 1998 they issued a double set of remixes entitled RETOX/DETOX, on which their classic hits were reincarnated with the help of backroom boffins like **Adrian Sherwood**, Dubstar's **Steve Hillier** and even **Giorgio Moroder**.

In 2000 Ware hooked up with Vince Clarke for an album of largely uninteresting ambient compositions, recorded in '3d surround sound'. PROTENTIOUS was released by Mute under the banner of **The Clarke & Ware Experiment**; a sequel, SPECTRUM PURSUIT VEHICLE, followed in 2001.

- (•) **Higher And Higher: The Very Best Of Heaven 17** (1993; Virgin).
Heaven 17's artistic and commercial fortunes nosedived in the late 80s, so this singles compilation sensibly avoids a chronological track-listing. Helpfully contains the original and updated versions of "Temptation" and "Fascist Groove Thang".

Justin Lewis

HEFNER

Formed Kent, England, 1992.

Hefner are perhaps the greatest survivors of a bygone age of indie-pop. Their sound owes much to the Sarah Records/C86 school of guitar janglers, but the group's brilliance can also be seen in their ability to imbue their music with touches of country, rock, The Beach Boys' harmonies, humour, and not forgetting the hip-swinging sexiness of Pulp. Their songs are warm, magical, vividly imaginative, and often a little tortured. They cover sex, love, pubs, the comforts of a big city's anonymity, and the general emotional flotsam and jetsam of modern life.

Having each already played in hosts of direction-less bands, singer/guitarist **Darren Hayman** and drummer **Anthony Harding** met in 1992 while attending art school in Kent – Hefner was conceived. A couple of years later the duo found themselves in London where they recruited bassist **John Morrison**, Darren later stating that 'it never really felt like a band until John joined'.

In 1996, shortly after the two became three, Hefner recorded their debut single "Another Better Friend". This fine slice of organ-tinged balladry was made all

Hefner's Darren hayman pooring his little indie heart out

the more amazing by the fact that when recorded it was only the second time they had played together as a trio. Having attracted the attention of the Too Pure imprint with an early rendering of "Christian Girls", Hefner found themselves on the label, and soon after recorded a 10", THE HEFNER SOUL (1998), and their first album BREAKING GOD'S HEART (1998). Both were recorded at the Ca-Va studio in Scotland with Belle And Sebastian's producer **Tony Doogan**. Also present at the session was Belle And Sebastian's Stuart, who played on the 10"'s "More Christian Girls". Proceeded by the Steve Lamacq-championed "Pull Yourself Together" (1998), BREAKING GOD'S HEART was a conquering debut of bouncing indie grooves ("The Sad Witch") and brooding mellow cuts ("A Hymn For The Postal Service" and "Tactile"), all wrapped up with Hayman's great lyrics.

Two singles emerged from the album – "Love Will Destroy Us In The End" (1998) and "The Sweetness Lies Within" (1998) – and soon Hefner discovered that they had gathered quite a following of obsessive indie devotees. The music press now loved them; they were being regularly wheeled out for BBC radio sessions, and their gigs were consistently entertaining and packed out.

Next came THE FIDELITY WARS (1999). Produced by the BBC's **Miti**, who had befriended the trio during their radio session work, this second album had a much more rounded sound. All the band's familiar elements were there, and everything still hinged on Hayman's poignant and witty songs of emotional butchery and bedsit romance. The set was warmly embraced by both fans and the press, the

group amassing comparisons with everyone from Elvis Costello, The Modern Lovers and The Smiths to Billy Bragg and The Violent Femmes. Again the collection's highpoints were stylistically oceans apart: the punky opener, "The Hymn For The Cigarettes", spat jagged guitars over a ranting Jarvis Cocker-style chorus, while the piano-led "Every Little Gesture" was a ballad of striking and fragile beauty. THE FIDELITY WARS also saw the group's sound enriched by brass, a Wurlitzer, additional backing vocalists and, on "Don't Flake Out On Me", the guitar work of The Wisdom Of Harry's **Peter Astor**.

In 2000 there was even more activity: "Christian Girls" made a splash as a single; a collection of session cuts and deleted singles was released, BOXING HEFNER; as **Ant**, drummer Anthony Harding presented an acoustic solo mini-LP CURES FOR BROKEN HEARTS; and the autumn witnessed the release of the group's third studio album WE LOVE THE CITY. With a newly recruited band member, **Jack Hayter**, this record served up more of Hefner's winning recipe, garnished with glorious moments of shining indie pop and – on numbers like the album's title cut – thrilling compositional experiments, crescendos and richly layered production. WE LOVE THE CITY was Hefner's finest concoction yet.

Before anyone had a chance to catch their breath, Hefner were back again with DEAD MEDIA (2001), which peddled more wry, witty lyricism with sparky indie tunes, though for this outing the band seemed to be a little less agitated than on previous missions.

Thanks to their near-constant stream of single releases, phenomenal live sound, and doggedly obsessive fans, we can expect to hear more of Hefner's lovingly penned and sophisticated musings in the near future.

⊙ **Breaking God's Heart** (1998; Too Pure).
A blinding debut filled with raw emotions, raw production and confident wit.

⊙ **Boxing Hefner** (2000; Too Pure).
All the best moments from their singles and radio sessions. Featuring the awesome "Christian Girls" and the previously unrecorded gig favourite "Twisting Mary's Arm".

⊙ **We Love The City** (2000; Too Pure).
A humorous, sexy, sophisticated and brilliant third studio effort, peppered with catchy tunes, brass and twanging guitars.

Darling Bell

RICHARD HELL

Born Kentucky, October 2, 1949.

Of all those who lay claim to the invention of punk, **Richard Hell** may have the strongest case. He wandered through 70s New York acting as a general catalyst to the scene there, forming three of its most important bands, and unwittingly inspiring the British scene.

Born Richard Meyers, he was a troublesome youth and was expelled from every school he attended. On moving to Virginia, his desperate mother sent him to a boarding school in Delaware, from which he promptly absconded with a like-minded 'slum-kid with big visions', **Tom Miller**. Meyers moved to New York in 1967, followed later by Miller. After time spent writing poetry and working in bookshops, the pair formed **The Neon Boys** with drummer **Billy Ficca**. This first attempt to fuse Meyers' poetic sensibilities with Miller's love of 60s rock and free jazz saw Meyers pick up a bass for the first time. During their brief existence in 1972–73, The Neon Boys produced a demo, which included an early take of the seminal "Love Comes In Spurts".

A year later the trio added second guitarist **Richard Lloyd** and became **TELEVISION**. Meyers cultivated a wasted rock-star look of ripped clothes and short, spiky hair – 'Rimbaud looked like that.' To complete the picture, Meyers became Richard Hell and Miller became Tom Verlaine. Television, alongside Patti Smith, kick-started the New York New Wave, but Verlaine became irked by Hell's manic stage antics, not to mention his unsophisticated bass playing. One by one, Hell's songs were dropped from the set, and when the last, "Blank Generation", disappeared, so did Hell. At Hell's final Television gigs two things happened. First, then-manager of The New York Dolls Malcolm McLaren, fascinated by Hell's look, attempted to lure him across the Atlantic to front a band he was putting together. Hell refused, but within a year both that look and the Sex Pistols would be big news in England. Second, he got together with equally disillusioned Dolls' guitarist **JOHNNY THUNDERS** to form the **HEARTBREAKERS**.

Hell lasted a year with the Heartbreakers before deciding to form his own band to realize his view of rock'n'roll as 'an outlet for passions and ideas too radical for any other form'. During that year, Hell co-wrote the classic "Chinese Rocks" with Dee Dee Ramone, about the trials of heroin addiction. The song was autobiographical for both its authors, and Hell's taste for junk had not been helped by twelve months in the company of 'the Dean Martin of heroin', Johnny Thunders.

Robert Quine was an old friend who also happened to be a phenomenal guitarist, capable of playing everything bar the predictable. Together, they nicked drummer **Marc Bell** from Wayne County and found second guitarist **Ivan Julian**. This bunch were dubbed **The Voidoids**, after a novel Hell had been writing. With remarkable speed they recorded the BLANK GENERATION EP (1976), finally committing one of the defining songs of the era to vinyl.

Soon after making their first live appearances in late 1976, they signed to Sire and commenced work on their debut album. The recording was complicated by record-company politics and by the time BLANK GENERATION (1977) was released, Hell was questioning his commitment to music. His mood wasn't helped by a nightly gob-drenching during a British tour supporting The Clash.

Back in the States, The Voidoids left Sire and recruited a bass player so that Hell could concentrate on being a front man. The next two years saw the band playing sporadically and releasing one single, "The Kid With The Replaceable Head"/"I'm Your Man" (1978). Hell's heroin-exacerbated tendency to view himself as a doomed poet was by now taking a real toll. Quine remarked that Hell couldn't decide whether 'to be a rock star ... or just go die' and left at the end of 1979 when it became obvious that neither a record deal nor a second album were forthcoming.

After a two-year hiatus, a cleaned-up Hell managed to summon up enough enthusiasm to record a second Voidoids album, DESTINY STREET (1982). Response was muted and Hell disappeared from the music world for a decade, filling his time with writing and acting (notably alongside Madonna in *Desperately Seeking Susan*).

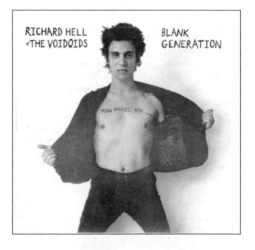

In the 90s he returned to recording with a new band, **Dim Stars**, backed by **Don Fleming** of Gumball, and **Steve Shelley** and **Thurston Moore** of Sonic Youth. He also gave occasional spoken word performances and published his mid-70s novel, *The Voidoid*. Despite these diversions, the studio beckoned and in 2000, after over two decades apart, The Voidoids' original line-up came together to record a single, "Oh", which was distributed over the Internet by Musicblitz.com.

In 2002 American label Matador released TIME, a long-overdue document of Hell's demos, outtakes and live cuts; at around the same time a book of essays, notes and poems, *Hot And Cold*, ensured that Hell's influence and energetic spark would not be forgotten.

⦿ **Blank Generation** (1977; Sire).
Poetic nihilism à gogo with "Blank Generation", "Love Comes In Spurts" and "The Plan", a paean to incest. Despite an ill-advised struggle through Sinatra's "All The Way", it still holds its own against any New York art-punk record, past or present.

⦿ **Destiny Street** (1982; Danceteria).
Well worth a listen and contains a version of the killer single "The Kid With The Replaceable Head".

⦿ **Time** (2002; Matador).
An essential and raw double-CD archive of Hell's glory days.

Glenn Law

HELLACOPTERS

Formed Stockholm, Sweden, 1994.

In the world of rock'n'roll, the more things change the more some bands strive to revive the spirit of the past. And, for some strange reason, Sweden has produced many bands that borrow wholesale from the likes of the Stooges, the MC5, New York Dolls and just about every other down and dirty garage band you'd care to name. Such was the case when **Nick Royale** (guitar/vocals), **Kenny Håkansson** (bass), **Robert Eriksson** (drums) and Backyard Babies' lead guitarist **Dregen** decided to take on the world with a fistful of 7" singles. Royale's day job at the time involved pounding the skins for twisted metal crew Entombed, but the lure of snotty rock won over as the **Hellacopters'** stock rose.

The four-man unit was snapped up by independent label White Jazz and their debut, SUPERSHITTY TO THE MAX (1996), emerged to almost unanimous praise. It was a rip-snorting, hi-octane sonic adventure recorded in a mere 26 hours with cues cheekily pinched from the band's many obvious US influences. The following year found the band expanding their line-up by recruiting **Bobby Lee Fett**, aka Boba Fett (piano/keyboards). This injected their second album, PAYIN' THE DUES (1997) with a more honky-tonk revved-up Rolling Stones vibe.

By this time Dregen was feeling the pressure of splitting his time between two bands, and Backyard Babies were beginning to generate enough heat on

their own to keep him busy. Something had to give – and it was him. So in early 1999 **Robert 'Strings' Dahlqvist** (guitar/vocals) stepped in, giving the band a more complex and bluesy flavour. In May of the same year Hellacopters released their third album, GRANDE ROCK (1999), which proved to be yet another scorching slab of bad boy boogie.

Thus far the template had comprised speed and melody in equal measure, but with Dahlqvist's more polished and fluid style the Hellacopters were ready to make the leap with HIGH VISIBILITY (2000). Recorded in three weeks – a relative eternity for a band that prefers life on the road – the album was a tour de force of intense melody and high impact delivery. Most recently the vinyl-only rarities collection HIGH ENERGY ROCK'N'ROLL (2001) and the storming BY THE GRACE OF GOD (2002) have kept the Hellacopters' name at the forefront of Swedish trash rock.

⦿ **Supershitty To The Max** (1996; White Jazz).
A berserk sprint through some of rock's sleazier, trashier moments. This is what New York Dolls might have sounded like with Lemmy in their ranks. They even released a vinyl cut of "Its Too Late", a New York Dolls cover, to reward those fans with turntables.

⦿ **High Visibility** (2000; Universal).
A more professional production job makes this brace of songs truly shine. Dahlqvist's blues-directed style certainly gives the Hellacopters' usual bluster a powerful bar-room swagger.

⦿ **By The Grace Of God** (2002; Mercury).
This underrated band keeps getting better and better: a smokin' rock'n'roll collection, "By The Grace Of God" and the equally good "Rainy Days Revisited", allow this album to not only better its predecessors but live up to live performance at its best!

Essi Berelian

HELMET

Formed New York, 1989. Disbanded 1999.

A band synonymous with the most obstreperous, distorted guitar noise, **Helmet** were founded by **Page Hamilton** (guitar/vocals), who first moved to New York to study jazz. He started out playing with the **Band of Susans**, then linked up with bassist **Henry Bogdan**, classically trained drummer **John Stanier** and Australian guitarist **Peter Mengele** (ex-New Christs).

This quartet debuted as Helmet in 1989 with a series of singles and the BORN ANNOYING EP for cult indie label Amphetamine Reptile (they also contributed to that label's epochal DOPE, GUNS, 'N' FUCKING IN THE STREETS compilation). While the ear-splitting volume and cranium-impairing guitar playing shared much with the nascent Seattle scene, Helmet refused their place at the slacker dinner table by dint of short crops and an almost militaristic dress code. These guys, in common with the New York hardcore bands who preceded them, were disciplined.

By STRAP IT ON (1990) Helmet had perfected what was to become their trademark sound: a short-fused barrage of chords deployed in a manner where density rather than linear purpose was the key. The distinguishing point was that Helmet, unlike many of their peers, knew that a rigidly delimited sound spectrum offered ample opportunity for the thorough exploration of a single riff – an approach once advocated by The Fall and heard to best effect here in tracks such as "Sinatra". For MEANTIME (1992), their major-label debut for Interscope/Atlantic, Helmet roped in Steve Albini as producer, suggesting they were less than hellbent on compromise. It was a tightly condensed record, its appeal having much to do with the band's recognition that less can indeed be more.

Mengele left the band in 1993 to be replaced by **Rob Echeverria**. BETTY (1994) saw Helmet branch out a bit and featured the group's collaboration with House Of Pain, "Just Another Victim", which was used on the soundtrack of the film *Judgement Night*. Another track, "Milquetoast", recorded with Butch Vig, featured on The Crow. Arguably the best cut, however, was the post-apocalypse blues of "Sam Hell".

By the time AFTERTASTE (1997) hit the stores, the band were back in disciplined step with the approach to rock that made them famous – turn the volume up, turn the vocals up, yell the lyrics like they were escaping from your body against your will and do it all as fast as possible – an example of texture, not flavour, being all important. The inevitable bout of touring followed, but by early 1999 it was becoming evident that the band were running out of steam and they decided on an amicable split. The various members headed off to pursue different projects. Hamilton is, apparently, creating a solo album but is also keeping himself busy working with other artists as well, not least Nine Inch Nails.

Meantime (1992; Interscope/Atlantic).
One of the great, hard-ass intensity records. Parts of it make Rollins sound like a lounge singer.

Alex Ogg

JIMI HENDRIX

Born Seattle, 1942; died 1970.

"If I seem free, it's because I'm always running."

Though **Jimi Hendrix** is one of rock's icons, it is hard to think of another artist who has been so often misrepresented. To the media and public alike, Hendrix was the wild man of rock, the chief advocate of the drug generation, uncontrollable, undisciplined and inarticulate. Many saw his career in terms of a rise to megastardom with flashy guitar histrionics, followed by a squandering of his talents and an ugly death from an overdose of the drugs that ruled his life. Yet the real Hendrix was a sensitive, soft-spoken and shy man; above all he was an instinctive musician and songwriter who was admired, not just by his contemporaries in rock but also by those in the jazz, folk, soul and blues worlds.

The real quality of his playing has been obscured by his showmanship. His skill was extraordinary, drawing his raw technique from blues giants like Albert King, and mixing in the subtlety and melody of jazz, and the dynamic rhythms of soul and R&B. With his uncluttered dexterity, he was as comfortable producing a crisp acoustic sound as he was with the brash, sometimes free-form electric delivery and breathtaking volume often considered his trademark. It is well known that the generation of feedback became an integral part of his sound, but few realized that he used to orchestrate it, allowing the higher-register strings to feed back while harmonizing with the lower-register ones.

Hendrix's rise was not meteoric. Despite demonstrating a flair for the instrument at a very early age, he was already in his early twenties before he made his first serious attempt to earn his living through music. By the summer of 1966 he had spent a tough period touring America with The Isley Brothers and Little Richard. Though he would later recall the frustration of playing 'Top 40 standards' night after night, there is no doubt that paying his dues in this way made his playing tighter, as well as expanding his stage skills. Many of Hendrix's predecessors, from 'T-Bone' Walker to Chuck Berry, had learned from the same experiences – you had to entertain people to survive on the live stage.

After passing through countless bands of varying quality, Hendrix wound up in New York, penniless. Adopting the stage name Jimmy James, he formed his own band, but it lacked the finesse and direction to attract serious interest; auditions for record companies were unsuccessful, as bosses failed to recognize any potential in the young guitarist whose talent must have outshone the abilities of his backing band.

However, The Animals' bassist-turned-manager and producer **Chas Chandler** saw Hendrix and was so impressed that, in September 1966, he persuaded him to return with him to England. Chandler's timing was impeccable – The Beatles had ceased touring in favour of recording, and the UK scene was set for an extravagant new talent – and he understood how to direct his new charge both visually (the white guitar and tie-dyed clothes looked totally new in the 60s) and musically, without in any way compromising him. While there was never anything contrived about Hendrix's talent or style, there was still a need to fashion his image for maximum effect, and Chandler knew what would work. Even small touches such as suggesting that Hendrix should spell his name Jimi proved to be spectacularly astute. Chandler also encouraged Hendrix's earliest attempts at songwriting.

The Jimi Hendrix Experience, formed with bass player **Noel Redding** and drummer **Mitch Mitchell**, quickly became a sensation in the British club circuit, but still failed to attract interest from a major label, despite the respect he drew from the contemporaries with whom Chandler had shrewdly arranged for Hendrix to mingle.

It was a new company, Track Records, part owned by The Who's manager Kit Lambert, that snapped up the talent that the biggest fish of the recording world had overlooked. Work began quickly on the band's first single, "Hey Joe" (1967), which, along with the subsequent "Purple Haze", managed to capture the bright essence of the shows which were electrifying audiences throughout the land. But it soon became clear that Hendrix also had an affinity with the

growing sophistication of studio techniques, even if his experimentation with overdubbing on the debut album ARE YOU EXPERIENCED? (1967) almost went unnoticed in the excitement surrounding the release of The Beatles' SGT PEPPER just three weeks later. Equally importantly, Hendrix's assimilation of his various influences placed an unmistakeable stamp on EXPERIENCED?: "Can You See Me" was reminiscent of a Yardbirds number; "Love Or Confusion" sounded like an extract from The Beatles' REVOLVER; and "Remember" evoked Otis Redding.

Fuelled by their success in England, it was time for The Experience to take on America, where they made their explosive debut at the Monterey Festival in June 1967. Although they were billed to appear immediately after The Who, Hendrix was determined not to be upstaged, and finished his set by spraying his guitar with lighter fluid and incinerating it. The gesture shot him to overnight fame, even if part of his audience felt uneasy with the flamboyance.

After Monterey the pace became frenetic: with limited radio play and low singles sales, The Experience's live work was still the best source of revenue, and so they toured incessantly to fund Hendrix's vision of more complex albums. AXIS: BOLD AS LOVE (1968) was clearly more of a 'studio' album than its predecessor, encompassing intricately crafted songs like the classic "Little Wing", as well as a great deal of experimental electronic effects. The double LP ELECTRIC LADYLAND, released in October 1968, represented a further progression in technique and innovation, but its release came as The Experience fell apart. Chandler, decreasingly influential as Hendrix's success grew, had departed in September 1968, and relationships within the trio had reached breaking point. Redding quit when Hendrix suggested expanding the line-up – a rather insensitive move by Hendrix, demonstrating how much he missed the guidance of Chandler.

Hendrix asked an old friend, **Billy Cox**, to be Redding's replacement and used the opportunity to jam extensively with a diversity of musicians. It was this new incarnation, tentatively called Gypsies Suns And Rainbows and featuring extra percussion, keyboards and a second guitar, which accompanied him on stage at Woodstock. Hendrix, as ever, performed with total commitment – "The Star Spangled Banner" was for many fans the greatest single moment of his career – but the band was under-rehearsed and, lacking cohesion and direction, lasted only a few months.

Next came **The Band Of Gypsies**, which retained Cox and added drummer **Buddy Miles**. Early performances were impressive, although they were deliberately toned down by a Hendrix intent on making his music speak louder than his showmanship. The album BAND OF GYPSIES, released in April 1970, yielded some of the most complex and introspective work of his career, but he was becoming incapable of dealing with his business manager, Michael Jeffrey, who insisted on taking more control over Hendrix's artistic direction.

Jimi picks up a Penguin

A frustrated Hendrix became more insular and sought an escape through more frequent drug use. Meanwhile, seeking to rekindle the money-making success of The Experience to finance Hendrix's new Electric Lady studio in New York, Jeffrey set about firing Miles and rehiring Mitchell. Redding was originally slated to return too, but Cox was ultimately reprieved.

Opinions as to Hendrix's state of mind at this point vary: some say Jeffrey's restrictive management sapped his motivation; others felt that the opening of Electric Lady made him confident and optimistic. The recorded evidence of The Experience during the summer of 1970 does not dispel either possibility, demonstrating some of the very best (Berkeley) and very worst (Isle of Wight) extremes of Hendrix's performances.

While the tour was in Europe, Billy Cox suffered a breakdown and the rest of the dates were cancelled. Hendrix went to London to see Chandler, possibly with a view to reinstating him as his manager, following which he planned to continue to New York to work in his new studio. Hendrix swallowed nine sleeping pills at around 7am on September 18, 1970, and crawled into bed. He never woke up. Instead, he vomited in his sleep, slipped into unconsciousness and suffocated. His girlfriend, possibly afraid that the marijuana in her apartment would be discovered by the emergency services, failed to summon medical help in time to save him. Though his system had been weakened by drug abuse, it had not, contrary to popular belief, directly caused his death.

He was just 27. In a career of scarcely four years' duration, Hendrix had become a consummate master of the guitar, an adventurous explorer of different musical terrains, and an inspirational figure for black artists and for the civil rights movement. As the appetite for Hendrix reissues and rarities demonstrates, there is no argument about his place in the rock pantheon. Honoured in London in 1997 by a 'blue plaque' on the house he used while in town, and with the increased influence of the Hendrix Family Foundation on the back catalogue, fans can look forward to seeing his reputation — somewhat damaged by years of poor-quality material slipping onto the market — increase as his legend grows.

The Legendary Hendrix at work

Are You Experienced (1967; Track).
This remains the classic Hendrix showcase: there's the lively funk of "Foxy Lady" and "Fire", the deep blues of "Red House", the heavy, driving riff of "Manic Depression", and the ballad "The Wind Cried Mary", to show how delicate his playing could be.

Axis: Bold As Love (1968; Track).
Hendrix's astonishing virtuosity is retained, while the stylistic experiments begin, notably on the ground-breaking "Little Wing" and the psychedelic "If 6 Was 9".

Electric Ladyland (1968; Track).
A sprawling but monumental double, containing some of Hendrix's most personal material ("Gypsy Eyes", "1983") and most exploratory recording techniques – particularly the overdubbing on "All Along The Watchtower". All in all, the perfect swan song for The Experience.

Band Of Gypsies (1970; Track).
Recorded live at the Fillmore with Cox and Miles, Hendrix shows that the evocation of turmoil was not confined to his rendition of "The Star Spangled Banner" – the feedback-dominated "Machine Gun" is just as violently effective.

The Ultimate Experience and Voodoo Soup (1993 & 1995; Polydor).
The best in a long line of Hendrix repackages, the former collects together all the hit singles, plus the finest album tracks; the latter is an excellent remastering exercise.

Hendrix: Blues (1994; Polydor/MCA).
An excellent compilation, notable for two tracks in particular: first is the acoustic version of "Hear My Train A Comin'", which illustrates that Hendrix was, first and foremost, a superb guitarist. The other is the Berkeley version of the same song – perhaps the single best example of Hendrix on record.

BBC Sessions (1998; MCA).
A long-awaited, 37-track collection spread over two CDs, with the cream of the BBC's crop of Hendrix masterpieces. An essential, despite mono sound.

Philip G. Lynch

JIMI HENDRIX

HENRY COW

Formed Cambridge, England, 1968;
fused with Slapp Happy 1974;
metamorphosed into Art Bears 1978;
disbanded 1981.

**"Others experimented with drugs;
we did it with radical politics."
Chris Cutler**

Among Richard Branson's peculiar cache of signings to his fledgling Virgin Records in 1973 was the lean and hungry beast of **Henry Cow**, the militant tendency of the avant-garde, strident, aesthetic experimentalists producing striking jazz/noise/improvisation, yet often within seethingly complex, scored, compositional pieces. Far from the established conventions of 'rock music', they were nevertheless a sturdy stitch in rock's rich tapestry, if only to sketch and stretch debates over what the band itself saw as the stultified nature of existing musical categories.

Fred Frith (guitar/violin) and **Tim Hodgkinson** (reeds) formed the band while at Cambridge University, giving their first performance supporting Pink Floyd at an Architects' Ball in (appropriately) May 1968. The duo recruited **John Greaves** (bass) and **Chris Cutler** (drums) in 1970, followed by **Geoff Leigh** (sax), later replaced by **Lindsay Cooper** (woodwind), beginning a career of defiantly lateral direction which, some thirty years on, can be seen to have fuelled an immense European genealogy of the avant-garde, manic margins of music. According to Tim Hodgkinson, the name 'Henry Cow' simply appeared at the same time as the group was formed; there was no connection between the two. He says that the name was 'in the air' in 1968, and it seemed like a very good name for the band that he and Fred Frith had just formed. The story that the group was named after left-field composer Henry Cowell is thus, alas, discredited.

Like most radical British bands, the Cow owed their initial airplay to DJ John Peel. After winning a Peel-sponsored radio contest in 1970 they headed for London, working with various theatre projects, and hosting their own series of 'Cabaret Voltaire' concerts at Kensington Town Hall. The serious, formal components of their music, odd instrumentation and collective commitment to far-left politics gave them a distinctly different flavour to the prevailing prog-rock conventions. When they joined Virgin in 1973 they had a growing live reputation, but they were the label's least commercial signing, beyond even the likes of Faust or Ivor Cutler.

Cow's first two albums, the punning HENRY COW LEGEND (1973) and UNREST (1974) were predominantly instrumental, full of weird time signatures and discordance – uneasy listening with odd moments of beauty.

They won few fans outside avant-garde circles, but Robert Wyatt pronounced them 'me favourite band',

and **SLAPP HAPPY**, who had just recorded a Virgin album of quirky songs (but had a distinctly experimental past), felt so drawn to the band that they proposed a merger. Thus the short-lived Happy Cow was born, with Slapp Happy's **Peter Blegvad** (guitar/vocals), **Anthony Moore** (piano) and **Dagmar Krause** (vocals) adding their talents to the pool.

The bands agreed to alternate as 'lead' artists and composers on a pair of discs. DESPERATE STRAIGHTS (1974) was credited to Slapp Happy/Henry Cow, and was written mainly by Moore and Blegvad. Its cerebral musings on the decline of the West, or Occident as they had it, were often terrific, with Blegvad and Krause excelling as vocal and lyrical counterpoints.

This process continued with IN PRAISE OF LEARNING (1975), which was credited purely to Henry Cow, Moore and Blegvad having left before the album's release. It was in a way a return to pre-Happy days, free-forming along with Messiaen-esque organ passages, but making strong use of Dagmar's extraordinary voice, employed for lyrics mixing apocalyptic despair with calls for class action (John Grierson's dictum 'Art is not a mirror – it is a hammer' is quoted on the sleeve).

It was with LEARNING, perhaps, that the Cow really defined their ethos: that radical politics demand radical language. Hence the group's defiantly anti-pop(ulist) musical aesthetic, which was to escalate over the years ahead. The group parted with Virgin, after a live album, CONCERTS, which featured the voices of both Dagmar and **Robert Wyatt**, and turned mainly to live work, gigging relentlessly, often in Italy and France at the behest of those country's radical left-wing groups. Financial problems, however, took their toll and in 1978 the Cow disbanded, promising, 'We will not settle into the role of being Henry Cow and reproducing our past to earn our pensions.'

Frith, Cutler and Krause – the core of the band – formed the **Art Bears**, a slightly more song-friendly trio. Their first album, HOPES AND FEARS (1978), released on Cutler's Recommended Records (ReR), was Cow in all but name, with guests Hodgkinson, Cooper and Blegvad helping to produce a torrent of short, sharp, bleak songs, propelled by the voice of Krause. WINTER SONGS (1978) was more esoteric with lyrics based on French cathedral carvings. Musically it used a vast array of moods and resources, from punk-thrash swaths of electronics and backward nightmare tapes to an antique, acoustic gentleness. The Art Bears made a final turbulent statement with THE WORLD AS IT IS TODAY (1981), a cathartic sonic examination of their vision of 'Democracy, Law, Peace, Freedom – corpses in the mouths of the bourgeoisie', although similar personnel surfaced on the groups **Duck And Cover** and **News From Babel**, the latter producing WORK RESUMED ON THE TOWER (1984) and LETTERS HOME (1986).

Almost all of Henry Cow's players are still working solo and collectively amid the global experimental/avant-garde music community, where boundaries have become a great deal more blurred between classical, rock and jazz than in Cow's day. As to individuals, **FRITH** and **BLEGVAD** each have their own entries in this book, while Cutler, who played with **PERE UBU** in the late 80s, has turned Recommended Records into a vital networking label and distribution service for experimental music.

Henry Cow

(•) **Concerts** (1975; ESD).
This double album was as accessible as the Cow ever got, containing a Peel session and a concert with Robert Wyatt and Dagmar Krause on vocals, while the CD reissue throws in the Cow's side of the 1973 GREASY TRUCKERS disc. Compared to the intricate studio recasting of ideas, this is a soaring journey beyond rock's left field, featuring wonderful Frith guitar work ("Nirvana For Mice") and Wyatt's Matching Mole agitprop anthem, "Gloria Gloom". Newcomers should start here.

Art bears

(•) **Winter Songs and The World As It Is Today** (1978 & 1981; ReR).
CD reissue of the two finest Bears albums.

Chris Brook

JOE HENRY

Born Charlotte, North Carolina, December 2, 1960.

"I just don't believe in treating a song like it's a fragile bird in your hand.'

Joe Henry's music doesn't stay in one place for long. He's let the rock'n'roll sparks fly plenty of times, but he's also toyed with bare-bones acoustic arrangements and steel-guitar country. He's cut some albums in weeks; for others he's spent a year tinkering in his home-built studio. Musically, his taste runs from Dylan to Ray Charles, Merle Haggard to Edith Piaf; just when you think you have him pegged – as on SHORT MAN'S ROOM and KINDNESS OF THE WORLD, both of which leaned toward country and had critics drooling – he goes and redecorates the cottage. Which only serves to keep his music interesting, gripping and very much alive.

Henry's striking lyrical style has always been central to his talent. Although presented in the first person, the songs are works of fiction and retain what he calls 'a healthy respect for mystery' instead of attacking his subjects head-on.

After a period of touring, Henry landed a deal with Profile Records who released his debut album, TALK OF HEAVEN in 1986. It had its moments but was largely unfocused – the jangle-rock feels dated, and the voice-and-piano numbers immature.

Henry signed to A&M after moving to New York. 1989's MURDER OF CROWS is his most rock-'n'roll album to date but it proved an unsatisfying experience as he lost all the arguments over arrangements and mixing. The sound was too big and the album was generally forgettable.

Henry reacted to CROWS by paring things down to a bare minimum on SHUFFLETOWN (1990), which was recorded live to two-track using only acoustic instruments – including trumpet played by jazz legend **Don Cherry**. Produced by **T-BONE BURNETT** (who's remained a friend and collaborator ever since), it's an intimate record in no hurry to go anywhere. A&M, however, didn't know what to do with it, and before long Henry was dropped. Which is just as well, because, suddenly free to do as he pleased, he produced one of the most straightforward, and finest, records of his career, SHORT MAN'S ROOM. (He also moved to LA with his wife, and they've stayed put ever since.)

Released by Mammoth Records in 1992, SHORT MAN'S ROOM finally got Henry noticed. It was packed with brilliantly written songs like "Diving Bell", "King's Highway", and the title track, all propelled by spare arrangements which shifted his music in a more country-folk direction. **The Jayhawks** were his backing band on the album – which was planned as a series of demos – and they lend the songs an easy-going country-rock vibe. A year later came KINDNESS OF THE WORLD, which wasn't as deliberately rural but still felt country-informed. Like SHORT MAN'S ROOM it was cut quickly and informally – eight days in Daniel Lanois's New Orleans studio.

Henry really outdid himself with his 1996 album, TRAMPOLINE. Recorded in the studio Henry had built in his garage, it was more about drum loops than steel guitars. The lyrics were as sturdy as ever, but the music was more texturally complex than any of his previous releases.

After touring in 1998 with members of the **Wallflowers**, Henry released FUSE in the spring of 1999, which was even more studio savvy and sonically adventurous, but retained his characteristic grounded honesty. 2001's SCAR was equally fine, at times calling to mind the instrumental clunk of Tom Waits.

(•) **Shuffletown** (1990; A&M; reissued 1994; Mammoth).
The piano, trumpet, violin and other acoustic instruments give this a laid-back, late-night vibe. Definitely worthwhile.

(•) **Short Man's Room** (1992; Mammoth).
A proud collection of rurally driven narratives – some dark and lonely, others funny and strange – that come to life with a spare country-rock sound courtesy of the Jayhawks.

(•) **Trampoline** (1996; Mammoth).
An adventurous, edgy and absolutely engaging new direction for Henry, with a heavier emphasis on rhythm. It's a very textural album, too, with ghostlike murmurs and other sonic mysteries drifting in from every corner.

(•) **Fuse** (1999; Mammoth).
Henry feels even more at home in the studio environment this time around. Drummer Carla Azar is his rock, and T-Bone Burnett his spiritual guide. Trip-hop? Almost, but that would be too easy.

Kurt Wolff

MATTHEW HERBERT

Born London, 1973.

Matthew Herbert, though not as well known as Richard James or Boards Of Canada, has become an important figure in electronica and the various genres of its bushy family tree; he is both a prolific and mysterious character, with numerous pseudonyms that allow him to ease from wild 'found-sound' experimentalism to deep house and jazz without a hitch.

Herbert began playing violin and piano at the age of four and as a teenager played in a Glenn Miller-type ensemble. His father was a BBC sound engineer, which no doubt sparked him to collect musical and recording equipment throughout his teens – girlfriends were presumably not a priority. It was at college that his distinctive sonic experiments with environmental sound began in earnest. In Glasgow, 1995, Herbert premiered a live set using a sampler and a crisp packet; and this was way before that irritating Pringles ad was first aired. Since those early days his sampling and reworking of everyday sounds – from breaking bottles to rushing blood – has formed an integral part the material Herbert has been responsible for.

Herbert's move to London prompted the release of the first three of his projects in 1996. As fond of pseudonyms as he is of pushing musical expectations, Matthew released RADIO as **Wishmountain** – everyday sounds and radio static incorporated into quirky electronica; "Ready to Rockit" as **Doctor Rockit** – a more electro-jazzy sound with vocal snippets; and "Part One" as, simply, **Herbert** in a house style. As Herbert, Matthew produced a series of EPs in the same year, PARTS 1-6, and two albums, PARTS 1-3 and 100LBS, on the Phono label. The PARTS REMIXED album followed in 1997. His Doctor Rockit persona was similarly active, releasing THE SOUND OF MUSIC in 1996 on Clear records. Wishmountain also, produced two EPs, VIDEO and BOTTLE (no prizes for guessing their content), before the 1998 album WISHMOUNTAIN IS DEAD, LONG LIVE RADIO BOY. As **Radio Boy**, Matthew changed tack and kept the source of his found sounds hidden, attempting to incorporate them more cohesively into the music. A run of Radio Boy EPs followed, as did further Herbert albums, 1998's AROUND THE HOUSE and WE ALL NEED LOVE for Phonography. These latter 'Herbert' releases were his most accessible and soulful takes on a deep house theme, and were tragically ignored by all except the most persistent of followers.

When several of the independent labels (Clear, Antiphon and Phonography) that had supported Matthew folded, he established labels of his own: Soundslike, Lifelike and Accidental records, named after his philosophy, 'Accidents are encouraged'. Always concerned with pushing musical boundaries, in 2000 Matthew composed a manifesto for his musical ambition. Entitled "Personal Contract for the Composition of Music", it was born out of his abhorrence of drum machines and the sampling of other people's music. In his manifesto, Matthew stringently demanded that there be no replication of traditional acoustic instruments if the possibility of a using a real one exists, and also prescribed that 'remixes must be completed using only the sounds provided by the original artist'.

The 2000 Doctor Rocket release INDOOR FIREWORKS (Lifelike) included a piece written for Yves Saint Laurent, film music from *Human Traffic* featuring a thirty-piece orchestra, and "Hymnformation", which incorporated the conversations of twenty of his slightly drunk friends discussing political matters.

Unafraid to show his political colours, Herbert's most sophisticated and mature release to date, BODILY FUNCTIONS (2001), came with sleeve-note advice, 'Get sanctions lifted from Iraq', and a reading list. The record itself showed Herbert's skills in jazz piano and the gorgeous, sensual voice of his partner **Dani Sicliano** on songs based on samples ranging from laser eye surgery to the scratching of a mouse trapped in a wastepaper basket. 2001 also saw the release of the anti-capitalist themed THE MECHANICS OF DESTRUCTION by Radio Boy, only available in free MP3 download or free CD by post.

Matthew continues to tour the world, make music for film, and record under his many names. Most recently he forming **The Matthew Herbert Big Band,** featuring four trumpets, four trombones and four saxophones.

Matthew Herbert

🔘 **Bodily Functions** (2001; K7/Soundslike).
Never have the sounds of digestion sounded so melodic. Heartbroken lyrics, soulful vocals and jazzy piano mingle harmoniously with the bleeps and whirrs of slamming train doors and a foetus in the womb. Totally original.

Annebella Pollen

JOHN HIATT

Born Indianapolis, Indiana, 1952.

Although still far from a household name, **John Hiatt** is one of the world's finest craftsman songwriters, with a skill for tapping into universal concerns that has led to his being sought out by artists in need. Like many, Hiatt was inspired by Bob Dylan. He tells of hearing "Like A Rolling Stone" while sitting in the car waiting for his mother and worrying that she would no longer recognize him. In 1970, he moved to Nashville and signed to Epic Records, for whom he made two unsuccessful LPs. By the mid-70s he had relocated to Los Angeles and MCA Records, where SLUG LINE (1979) and TWO BIT MONSTERS (1980) found favour on the New Wave scene, and helped a critical reputation to grow.

His early-80s stay with new label Geffen created two sure-footed albums, RIDING WITH THE KING (1983) and WARMING UP TO THE ICE AGE (1985), which mixed new keyboard sounds with an R&B feel. Both albums edged towards commercial success, but only slowly, despite excellent songs like "She Loves The Jerk", which showed the influence of Elvis Costello (who put in an appearance on WARMING UP TO THE ICE AGE).

Subsequently dropped by Geffen, and almost penniless, Hiatt planned to sell his songs to raise money leading his horrified publishers, Bug Music, to attempt to save him by buying him a house. But the real turnaround came with a second piece of generosity: UK label Demon gave him a free hand to make a record, whereupon Hiatt assembled a remarkable band for the sessions consisting of **RY COODER** (guitar), **NICK LOWE** (bass) and session giant **Jim Keltner** (drums).

This line-up was featured on BRING THE FAMILY (1987), which marked his maturity and brought instant acclaim. The touching "Lipstick Sunset" and the country-rock of "Thing Called Love" exemplified everything Hiatt had been striving to achieve. Its follow-up, SLOW TURNING (1988), mined the same vein, but was recorded in Nashville for true authenticity. Much as Springsteen's later work would do, Hiatt's music now reflected his new found domesticity. Both albums were dedicated to his family, and daughter Georgia Rae was the subject of a raucous ode on SLOW TURNING.

After the solid but unremarkable STOLEN MOMENTS (1990), Hiatt, Cooder, Lowe and Keltner became **Little Village** and released a self-titled album in 1992. Hiatt's influence on LITTLE VILLAGE was paramount, both as vocalist and songwriter, especially on "Solar Sex Panel" and "Don't Think About Her...". Patchy, but still worth a listen.

Energized by the Little Village experience, Hiatt broke new ground on a solo album, PERFECTLY GOOD GUITAR (1993). The use of Faith No More producer Matt Wallace indicated Hiatt's new direction, as did the use of musicians culled from the post-R.E.M. underground of guitar groups. Hiatt was 'raging for the meek and mild', and the album, while touching on a familiar lyrical blend of the mundane and the romantic, did so in a more crunching fashion than before.

Hiatt's next outing, WALK ON (1996), for Capitol, his sixth record label, was written and recorded on tour, and its fragment-like songs reflect the restless, rootless life of the road. Dark and moody, with some great rocking mandolin, it showed he was still evolving as an artist. It was followed the next year by LITTLE HEAD, his fourteenth album and one with a more rock'n'roll feeling. With his trademark good-quality, hand-crafted guitar pop, Hiatt takes an affectionate, self-mocking look at middle age on the outstanding title track and "Graduated". Short on surprises but comforting as a result.

Hiatt continues to record and tour; his most recent album, BENEATH THIS GRUFF EXTERIOR (2003), found him at ease with his muse and still more than capable of delivering the goods.

- **Perfectly Good Guitar** (1993; A&M).
  Hiatt adapts to the 90s with exuberant success.
- **Walk On** (1996; Capitol).
  Hiatt's road movie – just waiting transition to celluloid use, so he gets the fame he deserves.

Robert Jones

THE HIGH LLAMAS

Formed London, 1992.

Pundits were quick to categorize **The High Llamas** as 60s revivalists. The band distil a range of retro influences from the ornate virtuosity of Brian Wilson and early Van Dyke Parks, the cool precincts of Steely Dan-style jazz-pop and the gentler end of Krautrock, even acknowledging the craft of Burt Bacharach. These comparisons provide some pointers, but they don't really tell the full story, because, essentially, The High Llamas sound like no one else at all.

The roots of the band can be traced back to the seductive, polished grooves of the cult 80s band **MICRODISNEY**. Formed by Irish duo **Cathal Coughlan** and **Sean O'Hagan** in 1980, the group balanced heavily orchestrated and lushly arranged pop with angrily political lyrics, prior to splitting in early 1988.

Initially Coughlan emerged with the plaudits and a new outfit – the **FATIMA MANSIONS**. O'Hagan, on the other hand, took several years to gain any kind of recognition. After collaborating with an outfit called The Twilight, he concentrated on solo work, releasing an album entitled, somewhat confusingly, HIGH LLAMAS (1990). The album's luscious melodies signalled the embryonic High Llamas sound, and reintroduced O'Hagan's singularly obsessive pop sensibilities, summed up thus by *NME* writer John Mulvey – 'This is a man in love with the highest, most intoxicating music, chasing the holy sounds in his head with a perfectionist's zeal.'

By the time of the follow-up, APRICOTS (1992), O'Hagan had decided to call his group The High Llamas. This mini-album further develops O'Hagan's trademark soaring harmonies and dreamy orchestra-

tion on stand-out tracks such as "Travel" and "Birdies Sing".

After a brief collaboration with pop **Stereolab**, O'Hagan returned with the superlative High Llamas album GIDEON GAYE, released in 1994 and re-released to belated acclaim and sales in 1995. Costing only £4000 to make, this almost trance-like album has a sublime ebb and flow all of its own, laden with influences but never slipping into pastiche.

An extended High Llamas line-up – comprising GIDEON GAYE nucleus **Jonathan Fell** (bass), **Marcus Holdaway** (keyboards), **Rob Allum** (drums), **John Bennett** (guitar) plus O'Hagan (vocals/guitars/keyboards) – acted as **Arthur Lee**'s backing band in 1994, faultlessly re-creating Love classics for ecstatic audiences. Two well-received tours, playing with Mercury Rev and The Connells, took GIDEON GAYE out to the provinces, where audiences were small but reaction was enthusiastic.

The next High Llamas album, HAWAII, appeared in spring 1996, taking the lush, song-cycle ambience of GIDEON GAYE to new extremes, with kitsch, easy-listening, tape loops and orchestration introduced into the Llamas' sound. The general consensus was that HAWAII saw O'Hagan overreaching himself, as the audacious scope was scuppered by unmemorable melodies which often veered too close to pastiche and kitsch.

O'Hagan's next project was a one-off studio collaboration with Stereolab's Tim Gane called TURN ON. Described variously as 'inessential instrumental lab rock' and 'abstract sculpture', the self-titled album (on Duophonic) finds O'Hagan further demonstrating a preference for soundscapes (as opposed to songs) that pulse with strange drones, ambient noodling and sonic bursts. Though undeniably experimental, it is also a little smug and indulgent for such a proven songsmith. O'Hagan remained in demand as a producer and played live with Stereolab.

COLD & BOUNCY (1998) reflected O'Hagan's growing interest in obscure analogue synthesizers, with a mix of blissful harmonies and gorgeous instru-

mentals, glued together with jolly little fills from his latest electronic toys. Whilst unarguably king of his own cul-de-sac, he has so far proven unable to throw off the weight of his influences to properly follow up the talent hinted at on GIDEON GAYE.

The commercial failure of 1999's SNOWBUG signalled the band's departure from the V2 label. and despite adventurous breakthroughs by previously obscure American bands such as Mercury Rev and the Flaming Lips, the High Llamas failed to rise to the challenge. If anything, the Llamas were seen as a little too esoteric and experimental to threaten a mainstream that had once warmed to the strong melodies of GIDEON GAYE.

BUZZLE BEE, released in the autumn of 2000, again regurgitated the artsy sound and kitsch meanderings that had once appeared novel; but now the retro experimentation sounded jaded and formulaic. It was hard to escape the conclusion that the further the band travelled from their early reference points of multi-layered 60s harmonies and honed 70s pop, the less interesting they became.

◉ **Gideon Gaye** (1994; Alpaca Park).
An inspired album whose unique brand of otherworldliness is built upon a rich texture of sound – strings, organ, harpsichord and soaring vocal harmonies. Its melodies – light but never fey – have a habit of creeping under your skin and staying there.

◉ **Hawaii** (1996; Alpaca Park).
A slightly faltering attempt to build on the success – and sound – of GIDEON GAYE. There are many great moments, though you can't help but feel the album would be almost perfect were it fifteen minutes shorter.

◉ **Cold & Bouncy** (1998; Alpaca Park).
Revisiting some of the same terrain as previously – horns, piano and vocals echoing the pristine (if rather dotty) splendour of late-60s Beach Boys, orchestral flourishes lounging somewhere between Bacharach and Morricone. All of which could become rather precious and mannered in less skilful hands than O'Hagan's.

◉ **Retrospective, Rarities And Instrumentals** (2003; V2).
A great 2CD collection with enough of the group's older material to make it worth investing in.

Nig Hodgkins

STEVE HILLAGE/SYSTEM 7

Born England, 1951; formed System 7 1989.

The rise, fall and revival of **Steve Hillage** illustrates, as well as any career, the vagaries of rock fashion. As **GONG**'s guitarist, Hillage was the archetypal hippie musician, floating into the 80s on a cloud of New Age vibes that had the post-punk music press gagging. Yet twenty years on, after a spell in the background as a producer, Our Hero finds himself revered by the dance-trance crowd, and forming a band, **System 7**, that attracts guests from The Orb, Killing Joke and Detroit's techno scene. Too much – as the man might once have said.

Hillage began his celestial twanging with **Uriel**, a band that existed briefly in 1967–68, then went off to college in Canterbury – the home base of Soft

Machine and Caravan – before moving to London, in 1971. There he formed **Khan** with ex-Uriel keyboard player, **Dave Stewart** (later of **HATFIELD AND THE NORTH**), and recorded SPACE SHANTY (1972), a derivative slice of prog-rock whose only interest lay in introducing Hillage's enduring obsession with guitar echo and delay. The band didn't last – Stewart was also fronting Egg – and Hillage was enlisted by **KEVIN AYERS**, previewing his BANANAMOUR album on a 1972 tour alongside Daevid Allen (like Ayers, a Soft Machine original) and Gong. Hillage ended up joining Gong (and duly became 'Steve Hillside-Village' for the duration of his stay), honing their sound on the 'Radio Gnome' trilogy (1972–75), weaving electronic atmospherics, as evocative as it was then state-of-the-art, in conjunction with synthesizer player Tim Blake.

These were the days when Gong were part of the embryonic Virgin Records label, who, courtesy of Mike Oldfield's hugely successful TUBULAR BELLS, were happy to indulge in post-Softs (and Krautrock) experiment. (Hillage actually stepped in for the reclusive Oldfield for a live performance of BELLS and its follow-up, HERGEST RIDGE, in 1974. He was ever a skilled technician.) As Gong split, Virgin promoted Hillage as a solo artist, and with some success. FISH RISING (1975), recorded with his partner **Miquette Giraudy** (keyboards), various Gong musicians and Dave Stewart, was a more guitar-focused version of Gong, with its Utopian and spiritual ideals intact. It was followed by L (1976), a lavishly psychedelic album produced in New York with **Todd Rundgren** and featuring his band Utopia, plus the great jazz trumpeter **Don Cherry** for the "Lunar Musick Suite" ('recorded exclusively at full moon'). This album was also notable for Hillage's out-hippieing of the comparatively straight-edge Donovan in his cover of "Hurdy Gurdy Man" and for ripping the spiritual fripperies from George Harrison's "It's All Too Much" to reveal the pharmaceutical maelstrom the song so accurately celebrates.

In 1977 Hillage released MOTIVATION RADIO, this time produced on the West Coast of America by Malcolm Cecil – the man behind an influential early electronic project, his self-built studio-synthesizer, T.O.N.T.O. The album saw Hillage continuing to sing (never his strength) about being an Electrick Gypsy, Saucer Surfing, and how 'the light shone from our hearts and from our minds'. It wasn't going to make the Aquarian Axeman many friends in the new punk order, and he was by now more or less the last remaining link with Virgin's hippie past, the label having by now signed the Sex Pistols. Hillage, however, pressed on with admirable integrity, helping to organize the first revival of the Glastonbury Fayre in 1979, as well as producing a last clutch of space-rock albums – GREEN (1978), RAINBOW DOME MUSICK and OPEN (both 1979), and FOR TO NEXT (1983). The sales were modest, and few among the music press bothered to review such out-of-time work. RAINBOW DOME MUSICK, for example, was recorded by Hillage and Giraudy to be played in a dome at a London 'Mind, Body & Spirit' festival; a (welcome) instrumental outing, it featured two sublime drifts of ambient synths, sequencers and Tibetan bells.

Hillage spent the next decade producing, including credits on albums by Simple Minds, Robyn Hitchcock and The Shamen. Then, in 1989, apparently forgotten as a musician, he walked into the ambient room at the Land of Oz club, to hear RADIO DOME MUSICK chilling them all out. He introduced himself to **Alex Paterson**, and suddenly found himself out of limbo. The meeting led to Hillage working with Paterson's band, **THE ORB**, and was the genesis of a new Hillage-Giraudy band, System 7 – a credible, hip, dance-trance collective for the 90s.

The band's debut album, SYSTEM 7 (1991), was an accessible, if in retrospect untypical, release. Hillage and Giraudy were yet to settle into their after-hours, dreamy, chill-out style, and the record featured vocals by **Olu Rowe** reminiscent of Seal. It was the follow-up, 777 (1993), that saw their blissed-out trance textures and rhythms take over; released at the peak of ambient fervour, it reached the UK Top 40. Next out was POINT 3 (1994), released in two versions: THE FIRE ALBUM, which featured heavy rhythm workouts, and THE WATER ALBUM, which comprised drumless mixes of the same tracks. Both were accepted eagerly on the dance scene, where by now System 7 were fixtures, gigging at clubs such as the Whirly-y-Gig.

Hillage and Giraudy then proved themselves capable of changing direction again. POWER OF SEVEN (1996) took a trip to Detroit, employing the mixing skills of **Carl Craig** and **Derrick May** to produce hard-edged ambient techno. This took them on to 1997's GOLDEN SECTION, pushing their apparently contradictory blending of hardcore techno with formless ambient to new extremes, while 2001's SEVENTH WAVE witnessed a refreshing collaboration with Paterson.

Steve Hillage

⊙ Fish Rising (1975; Virgin).
These archetypal Hillage guitar soundscapes stand up OK, though the vocals less so.

⊙ Rainbow Dome Musick (1979; Virgin).
New Age ambient meditations – chill-out music long before its time.

System 7

⊙ Point 3 (1994; Big Life).
With its Balinese samples and peerless list of collaborators, this is one of the high points of S7's career – or rather, two high points, as the rhythm-heavy FIRE ALBUM and the drum-free WATER are quite different.

⊙ Power Of Seven (1996; Butterfly).
Deep and hard techno, avant-garde drum'n'bass in the company of Detroit luminaries Carl Craig and Derrick May.

Candy Absorption

HIS NAME IS ALIVE

Formed Livonia, Michigan, 1987.

**"My parents used to always say that I should have a regular job and just do music as a hobby because what if lost one of my hands in an accident or something like that?"
Warren Defever**

Formed by **Warren Defever** at the age of 16, His Name Is Alive's initial output was a series of cassettes with titles such as RIOTOUSNESS AND POSTROPHE and I HAD SEX WITH GOD. Constantly recording, Defever recruited friends **Damian Lang** (drums) from **Elvis Hitler** (a band Defever had also played with), **Jymn Auge** (guitars; ex-Bone Machine), with **Karin Oliver** and **Angie Carozzo** to sing his disturbing, if adolescent, lyrics in particularly haunting style, and sent the tapes to various labels, landing a contract with 4AD in London. Label boss Ivo Watts-Russell and producer John Fryer mixed the raw material into LIVONIA, released in June 1990 to unexpectedly widespread acclaim for its atmospheric, American Gothic feel and the striking harmonies of the two singers.

The follow-up, HOME IS IN YOUR HEAD (1991), consisted of short songs slipping from experimental miniatures into typically disturbing treatments of schizophrenia, dreams and mescalin via bouts of grinding guitar squalls. The album was a strange continuation of Defever's particularly eclectic recording process, with **Denise James** taking Carozzo's place as second vocalist, **Melissa Elliott** playing guitar and other guest musicians making various contributions. THE DIRT EATERS EP of April 1992 was a stunning release, featuring "Are We Still Married," accompanied by a disturbing Brothers Quay animated film, and an amazing interpretation of Rainbow/Dio's bombastic heavy metal opus "Man On The Silver Mountain" in a ghostly chorale style.

The same month the next year saw the release of the group's third album, MOUTH BY MOUTH, with the core group of Defever and Oliver supplemented by drummer **Trey Many**. Apparently more conventional, the album still plunged into riffs, skewed song arrangements and a more upbeat feel, even featuring guitar solos among the ever-diverting production values. Defever spent the next three years working on side-projects and collaborations including **Princess Dragon Mom**, the **Mystic Moog Orchestra**, the electronica of **Control Panel** and a string of ESP-titled groups, including the **ESP Beetles**, **-Family, -Summer** etc, while the Perdition Plastics label released a compilation of HNIA private tapes as KING OF SWEET (1994). Many of these releases and live HNIA tapes are available as limited editions direct from Defever's own Time Stereo basement.

The result of prolonged concentration on early dub, surf and Chicago blues influences was the bizarrely wonderful UNIVERSAL FREQUENCIES EP (1996), a remarkable cover/sequel which was the result of a week solid spent absorbing The Beach Boys' "Good Vibrations", and STARS ON ESP (1996), which was soon hailed as a definitively twisted pop classic by the music press. Accompanied by a bizarre live tour which included the band appearing variously dressed as Kiss or in whale suits, via CCTV or ignoring their own songs in favour of free noise arrangements, the gospel choir hired to sing on the track "Last One" also provided new recruit **Lovetta Pippen** (vocals). Bass player **Chad Gilchrist** and second drummer **Scott Goldstein** completed the group for the next few releases: a single "Can't Always Be Loved" (featuring a stunning seventeen-minute rock-out) and FT. LAKE (1998), while ALWAYS STAY SWEET (1999) collected a decade's worth of their very weirdest hits.

But in 2001 the world was in for a shock with 4AD's release of SOME DAY MY BLUES WILL COVER THE EARTH. The collection saw Lovetta's hypnotic gospel vocals pushed well and truly to the fore, with Defever's production easing into a template of minimal, almost R&B-like stylings. The press were enchanted, and cuts like "Write My Name In The Groove" and the set's blinding rendition of the blues standard "Solitude" seemed to signal a new era, and a new audience, for His Name Is Alive. These themes spilled over into 2002's LAST NIGHT, another sublime collection of haunting, funky blues.

Though the core of the band's work was appearing through 4AD, hard-to-find releases have popped up on smaller independent labels – among them FINER TWILIGHTS (1997), GOLDEN CITY (1998) and WHEN THE STARS REFUSE TO SHINE (2000). Equally, Defever has released his own solo efforts: 1999's grainy I WANT YOU TO LIVE ONE HUNDRED YEARS and 2002's WHEN FLOWERS COVERED THE EARTH.

⊙ **Livonia** (1990; 4AD).
Dark and strange as they come, a very peculiar album indeed. Spooky noises and weird production make for a disturbingly ethereal record topped off by haunting vocals.

⊙ **Mouth By Mouth** (1993; 4AD).
Like a 70s heavy-rock album produced by a hyperactive and easily distracted child with an interest in trying every possible effect, level and mixing technique, this is a baffling noise assault on the very idea of rock'n'roll.

⊙ **Stars On ESP** (1996; 4AD).
Featuring country-tinged psychedelic ballads, cod-70s dub reggae and an unsuspecting gospel choir singing over an ESP Family 7" in a warped version of the standard "I Ain't Got No Home In This World Anymore", this is pop music put through a blender.

⊙ **Ft. Lake** (1998; 4AD).
An expansive blend of seemingly every style from gospel to surf via pop harmonies and a dash of dub and free noise, which just goes to show that they were on the right track all along, as the world seems to have caught up with them at last.

⊙ **Someday My Blues Will Cover The Earth** (2001; 4AD).
A radical change in direction with breathtaking results: a captivating blend of blues, soul and haunting electronica.

Richard Fontenoy

ROBYN HITCHCOCK

Born London, 1953; went solo in 1981.

Only **Robyn Hitchcock** could write a song called "Sleeping With Your Devil Mask", or "Listening To The Higsons", or "Eaten By Her Own Dinner". But such flights of fancy are all in a day's work for a man who has made a career out of carrying on where Syd Barrett left off. For years, his eccentricities have condemned him to a lonely existence on the fringes of the music world. Now, following the sponsorship of R.E.M., he finds himself a major draw on the US college circuit, yet still a minority taste in his homeland.

Robyn Hitchcock first came to light as leader of 70s cult band **THE SOFT BOYS**. When they split in 1981, he went straight into the studio with his mates to record his first solo album, BLACK SNAKE DIAMOND ROLE (1981). Though it was very much a low-budget quickie, it did contain some excellent songs, including offbeat Syd tribute "The Man Who Invented Himself" and the legendary "Brenda's Iron Sledge".

Unfortunately, Hitchcock's next album, GROOVY DECAY (1982), was fairly disastrous. Made with hired musicians with whom he had little rapport, it was then mummified by a production job courtesy of Steve Hillage (before his rehabilitation with System 7). Although Hitchcock has since virtually disowned it, a few gems shone through the murk, most notably the haunting "St. Petersburg". But after The Soft Boys debacle, it was one failure too many, and Hitchcock decided to pack it in.

Luckily for the record-buying public, his urge to be weird was obviously too much to contain and two years later he returned with I OFTEN DREAM OF TRAINS, a supremely atmospheric album of vocal, acoustic guitar and piano. Hitchcock was obviously on a roll and contacted the original Soft Boys rhythm section of **Morris Windsor** (drums) and **Andy Metcalfe** (bass) to form **Robyn Hitchcock & The Egyptians**.

Their first album together, FEGMANIA! (1985), was superb, with "The Man With The Lightbulb Head" and "Egyptian Cream" standing out amid the good-humoured lunacy. Also, for the first time in his career, Hitchcock was getting some press attention and TV exposure. A wave of American 'Paisley Underground' bands had achieved cult status in Britain, in particular The Rain Parade and The Long Ryders, and the time was right for his quirky guitar-based style. The Egyptians followed up with GOTTA LET THIS HEN OUT! (1985), a live album, and ELEMENT OF LIGHT (1986), less immediate and more downbeat than FEGMANIA!, but full of fine compositions like "Winchester" and the completely loopy "Bass".

After years of being an obscure cult act, Hitchcock finally made it onto a major label with 1988's GLOBE OF FROGS, thanks largely to the recommendations of R.E.M., who had been Hitchcock fans since his Soft Boys days. GLOBE was an excellent set that became very popular on US college radio and an important step in cementing his American success. However, his next two albums for A&M, QUEEN ELVIS (1989) and PERSPEX ISLAND (1991), were both overproduced and featured unnecessary contributions from moonlighting R.E.M. members **Peter Buck** and **Michael Stipe**. The totally acoustic EYE (1990) veered away from this overproduced sound, being pretty much an eighteen-track companion piece to I OFTEN DREAM OF TRAINS.

Yet just when it seemed that Hitchcock's American success was destroying his much-loved Englishness, he returned to form on RESPECT (1993). A showcase for his unique brand of folk-rock psychedelia, the set opened in style with "The Yip Song", a manic tribute to Vera Lynn, which harked back to Hitchcock's earliest days in The Soft Boys. Other highlights included "When I Was Dead", a haunting, acid-tinged drone reminiscent of mid-period Beatles, and an evocative solo guitar piece, "Serpent At The Gates Of Wisdom". And there was "Wafflehead", a bizarre coda to an album that stayed consistently weird but always accessible. MOSS ELIXIR, his 1996 release for new label Warner Bros, was a continuation of his eccentric Englishman theme, with song titles like "A Happy Bird is a Filthy Bird".

It seems that Hitchcock has now returned to solo performing, but who knows what turn his eccentric career will take next? For the first time, virtually everything he has recorded is now available on CD, and popularity in his homeland continues to grow. Latest releases include UNCORRECTED PERSONALITY TRAITS (1997) – a twenty-track compilation of his earlier work from the 1980s before he signed to A&M – STOREFRONT HITCHCOCK (1998), a soundtrack to the movie by Jonathan Demme, and LUXOR (2003), with its blinding opening cut "The Sound Of Sound".

With the current music scene more open to his psychedelic song-craft than at any time since the late 60s, he can only go from strength to strength.

- **I Often Dream Of Trains** (1984; Sequel).
  Explicitly Barrett-esque acoustic album, suffused with an engaging melancholia. An underlying strain of gender confusion is apparent on "Sometimes I Wish I Was A Pretty Girl" and "Uncorrected Personality Traits".

- **Fegmania!** (1985; Sequel).
  The definitive album from Hitchcock's independent years, bursting with psychedelic pop whimsy.

- **Globe Of Frogs** (1988; A&M).
  Hitchcock's first major-label effort, boasting some of his most frenzied efforts in the song-title department. Only Captain Beefheart could possibly rival "Tropical Flesh Mandala".

- **Respect** (1993; A&M).
  Robyn Hitchcock & The Egyptians' most finely crafted work to date. The songwriting is superb, John Leckie's production is sympathetic, and the unusual acoustic/electric arrangements are comparable only to Love's legendary 1967 opus FOREVER CHANGES.

Iain Smith

THE HIVES

Formed Fagersta, Sweden, 1993.

The Hives may very well be yet another bunch of over-hyped, well-styled Knack wannabes, but there are some crucial differences between them and their skinny-tied brethren from New York. For a start, these rock scenesters have actually paid their dues: they didn't emerge straight from finishing school in Switzerland with a bunch of cash for stylists and PR agencies (see The Strokes).

This five-piece (who all have ridiculous names befitting a speed metal band – **Vigilante Carlstroem**, **Dr Matt Destruction**, **Howlin' Pelle Almqvist**, **Chris Dangerous**, **Nicholaus Arson**) hail from Fagersta, Sweden, from where they released a couple of albums and EPs of sharp, punky retro New Wave. They wear all black aside from white ties and shoes – exactly the sort of thing that five guys from a town whose only claim to fame is one of the biggest vintage American car clubs in Europe would think is cool, and wholly unlike what a high-paid stylist from London would think is cool.

The group released their first EP in 1996, the six-song OH, LORD! WHEN? HOW?, on Sidekicks Records. This EP featured all of their trademarks, albeit without any of the edges smoothed out as on later records. There were blistering Stooges guitar chords tempered by a Buzzcocks semi-pop sensibility, English-as-a-second-language lyrics, a hell-for-leather tempo and the first of many fabulous titles: "Some People Know All Too Well How Bad Liquorice, Or Any Candy For That Matter, Can Taste After Having Laid Out In The Sun For Too Long – And I Think I Just Ate Too Much".

Their first album, BARELY LEGAL, followed the next year, and would succeed in being even more

The Hives go undercover

rambunctious despite a slicker sound. This was garage rock as Lester Bangs had intended when he laid down the canon of punk: snotty, moderately talented kids from Nowheresville turning themselves into minor stars by sheer force of will, attitude and an allegiance to the eternal virtues of three chords and a cloud of dust. The breath taking A.K.A. I-D-I-O-T EP (1998) managed to outdo the album with a concentrated, six-song blast of pure pop-punk energy.

VENI VIDI VICIOUS (2000) added more pop nous to their febrile energy, with power pop hooks galore on the titanic "Hate To Say I Told You So" and "Main Offender". The group was generating a lot of buzz in the rock underground and garnering celeb testimonials which led to Alan McGee signing the band to his Poptones label. Poptones released a retrospective, YOUR NEW FAVOURITE BAND (2001) (essentially the best bits from VENI... and the A.K.A. EP) to rapturous press; the hype machine went into overdrive. What this album amply displayed, though, was the most crucial distinction between The Strokes and The Hives: they may both be just a collection of punk and power pop references from 1979–82, but the Hives still rock.

⊙ **Your New Favourite Band** (2001; Poptones). Probably the easiest of their records to find, it's a darned good, old-fashioned garage punk rave-up.

Peter Shapiro

Courtney lives through it

HOLE

Formed Los Angeles, 1989.

Well before her fabled union with **NIRVANA**'s **Kurt Cobain**, **Courtney Love** and her band **Hole** had already laid a foundation of harsh, angst-fuelled music that begged comparison with that of her future husband, as well as with that of many other like-minded peers in Seattle. Unfortunately, her marriage and subsequent widowhood have rather obscured her own musical achievements, giving the impression that she inherited Cobain's mantle of premier punk poet of pain as a matter of hereditary succession. But Hole's 1994 breakthrough, LIVE THROUGH THIS, showed that if Love learned a thing or two from Nirvana about making angry music pop-friendly, she also has her own well of distinctive images, and a band with sufficient musical resources to realize them.

Love (Michelle Harrison) was born in 1964 to rather granola parents: her mother was a New Age therapist, and her father was a writer and part-time entrepreneur who sometimes managed bands and was briefly involved with The Grateful Dead (The Dead's Phil Lesh is Love's godfather). Love's parents separated and her early life was nomadic and troubled; she was eventually sent away to school, during which time she first became acquainted with punk rock. After school, she became an exotic dancer, then a rock photographer, before landing a few minor movie roles (*Straight To Hell, Sid & Nancy*).

From here, she gravitated to the music scenes in different cities, initially as a fan, later as an aspiring performer. In Minneapolis she met **Kat Bjelland**, with whom she played in a few bands, including a short-lived and volatile prototype of **BABES IN TOYLAND**. After Bjelland fired her, Love even became part of **FAITH NO MORE** for a short time in 1989.

Then Love moved permanently to Seattle and wasted little time assembling her own band. After guitarist **Eric Erlandson** answered her want-ad, she enlisted him immediately as her musical accomplice. It was a fortuitous alliance – Love's direct and traditional punk influence was balanced by Erlandson's stylings, which became Hole's trademark: classic full-bore rock chording, alternating with sweetly plangent, ringing intervals. With the addition of **Jill Emery** (bass) and **Caroline Rue** (drums), Hole quickly emerged on the nascent Seattle scene, putting out an EP (RETARD GIRL, 1990) and a single ("Dicknail", 1991) on prestigious local label Sub Pop before recording their first LP for Caroline, PRETTY ON THE INSIDE (1991).

Hole's early titles and lyrical hooks coerced the listener into sharing Love's anguish ('I gave you plenty, what do you want, more?/Baby why are you a teenage whore?'). Although musically it tended to drone, there were poetic turns of phrase that not only suggested a style forming, but indicated a lyrical affinity with Kurt Cobain. Cobain and Love married in February 1992, at the floodtide of Nirvana's epochal success. Their daughter, Frances Bean, was born in August 1992.

During this bright period, Love rejigged the rhythm section again, settling on **Patty Schemel** (drums) and **Kristen Pfaff** (bass). Now more strongly supported, Love focused on her stage persona: dressed in ragged baby-doll dresses, heavily made up, she alternated between dreamy indolence and hurricane-force fury. The band was still powerful and harsh, but new elements of melody and counterpoint were creeping into the music. The result, LIVE THROUGH THIS (1994), was their first album for major label Geffen, but it was overshadowed by Cobain's suicide in April 1994. Only two months later, Pfaff was found dead of an overdose.

Love and Hole were hardly in shape to work, but the success of the album did their work for them. From the first ringing chords of "Violet", it was clear that if anything could put Love's scabrous images over, this album could. The music was clearer than before, the furious passages no longer collapsed inward, and Love's voice was so well matched to the moods of the songs that even her full screech mode was relatively easy to listen to.

LIVE THROUGH THIS won several music polls and commendations (not just in indie precincts but also from the *New York Times* and the *Village Voice*), and the entire band's profile was raised dramatically. But while Hole soldiered bravely on, with **Melissa auf der Maur** on bass, for obvious reasons their output slowed. The 1995 EP, ASK FOR IT, was really a holding operation, ready for Love's next move. MY BODY THE HAND GRENADE (1997; City Slang UK) was another stopgap, comprising outtakes from the shouty riot-grrrl days of PRETTY ON THE INSIDE and a few pieces from the *MTV Unplugged* show they did in 1995 – not essential, and not good enough.

In the meantime, Love had been ploughing her energies into acting (*The People Vs. Larry Flynt*, *Feeling Minnesota*, etc), further bolstering the notion that Hole was no more. But in 1998, assisted by **Billy Corgan**, the group recorded and released CELEBRITY SKIN. The set rocked and received positive reviews, but soon after Schemel departed to be replaced by **Samantha Maloney**, formally of Shift. Hole hit the road, but even a successful tour didn't stop Auf Der Maur jumping ship to join the then-active **Smashing Pumpkins**. Around the same time Love was voicing her dissatisfaction with the way her record company were handling the group's releases. In an attempt to free herself from a limiting contract, and fight the cause for artists everywhere, Love filed a lawsuit against the Universal Music Group, who had already attempted to sue Love and Erlandson for failing to deliver contracted albums. More legal wranglings followed, this time between Love, Dave Grohl and Krist Novoselic, concerning Nirvana's estate; once again Hole, the group, seemed to vanish off the map.

In 2001 Hole's future became even more uncertain, when Love unveiled her new band, **Bastard**. With reports of an imminent signing to Epitaph Records, the group – comprising Love, **Louise Post** (Veruca Salt), **Gina Crosley** (Rockit Girl), with Schemel back in the picture on drums – laid plans. But there were no Bastard releases, and the group's few gigs either received a lukewarm reception or degenerated into a platform for Love's viscous tongue.

At the time of writing, Love is assembling a touring band to support the release of a solo album. Whether this means the end of Hole remains to be seen. But despite the commotions she continues to fuel, Courtney Love is undoubtedly a talented and important presence on the music scene, and there are thousands of fans out there content to sit through all the news stories and courtroom dramas in anticipation of the next musical chapter of her story.

⊙ **Live Through This** (1994; Geffen).
Love's persona is a tightrope act – she needs balance to stay aloft. Hole gives her maximum help on this record. The sound is well modulated and the sentiments gain unforced entry to the consciousness; now female rock fans, drinking at the bar after a break-up, pump dollars into the jukebox for "Violet" and "Miss World", new anthems of pissed-off and suffering girlhood.

⊙ **Celebrity Skin** (1998; Geffen).
This album confirms that, despite all the turmoil of the group's history and associations, Hole are a stunning outfit capable of crafting both ear-splitting rock anthems and more subtle rock-pop constructions. Polished and essential.

Roy Edroso

BUDDY HOLLY

Born Lubbock, Texas, 1936; died 1959.

One of the most influential rock'n'roll stars of the 50s, singer, guitarist and songwriter **Buddy Holly** (Charles Hardin Holley) drew on influences as varied as rockabilly, country and western, blues, gospel and pop, to create a large body of classic work in a too-brief career. Also an innovator in the studio, Holly's records were as notable for their warmth and delicate emotional complexity as for their simple but unforgettable melodies.

Holly was already playing country and western music in his teens, but the emergence of Elvis Presley led him to plunge full-tilt into mid-50s rockabilly, and in 1956 he landed a contract with Decca. His earliest songs are fine enough, but Holly didn't truly find his métier until the 1957 smash single "That'll Be The Day". His classic descending guitar line and trademark hiccuping vocals made Holly an instant international star. It and its follow-ups, like "Peggy Sue", "Oh Boy", "Maybe Baby" and "Rave On", have become rock'n'roll standards. Unlike many of his performing peers, Holly also left behind many outstanding album tracks and B-sides, including some driving, exciting R&B covers.

Holly cut most of these sides with **The Crickets** – **Niki Sullivan** (rhythm guitar), **Joe B. Maudlin** (bass) and **Jerry J. J. Allison** (drums) – whose brash and full-bodied sound helped establish them as the rock-band prototype. As a composer, he was breaking entirely new territory, peppering his rockabilly-flavoured material with insinuating hooks, moving away from early rock's basic R&B chord progressions, without in the least compromising his energy and passion. Working with producer Norman Petty in New Mexican studios, he helped pioneer recording techniques that would shortly become commonplace in the pop world – double-tracking his vocals, miking his vocals and guitars to maximize his power and, in his latter sessions, using string sections. Holly's most enduring qualities, however, lay in the uncluttered joy of his song-writing and arrangements. While his lyrics seemed at first simplistic, they actually illuminated the euphoria, sorrow, doubt and melancholy of love with a verve, subtlety and expressiveness that have rarely been matched.

Although The Crickets and Norman Petty were integral to Holly's early commercial and artistic success, he was soon longing for greater creative freedom, especially in the studio. In late 1958 he broke with his band and producer, for myriad personal and professional reasons, and relocated to New York. His final sessions have been interpreted as signposts to more pop-orientated productions, especially his final hit, the Paul Anka-penned "It Doesn't Matter Anymore", which featured dancing violins. Others have argued that Holly's songs were becoming more personal, introspective and complex, heralding enormous possibilities. However, such speculation was rendered redundant by his death at the age of 22 on February 3, 1959, when a private plane – also carrying Ritchie Valens and The Big Bopper – crashed during a tour of Midwest America.

As it is, Buddy Holly's legacy is invaluable. Along with Chuck Berry, he was an undoubted influence on subsequent British rock, especially The Beatles and The Rolling Stones, whose revival of Holly's "Not Fade Away" gave them their first major hit single. He was also one of the first rock stars to tour Britain, one of the first to take firm control of his material and production, and one of the first to front a self-contained band that generated their own material.

From The Original Master Tapes (1985; MCA).
A faultless twenty-track best-of, featuring all the hits and most of the famous compositions.

The Buddy Holly Collection (1993; MCA).
A few good songs are missing, but this two-CD, fifty-track collection is almost unerring in its selection. Contains all of the hits, and many other more obscure tracks that are just as good, including "Words Of Love" (covered by The Beatles), "Wishing" and "Love's Made A Fool Of You".

Richie Unterberger

HOLLY AND THE ITALIANS

Formed Los Angeles, 1978; disbanded 1981.

"Holly is an underrated genius."
Joey Ramone

Though commercially outshone by their American punk contemporaries, **Holly And The Italians** rate as one of the era's most original and feisty outfits. With as much attitude as Chrissie Hynde, as arresting an image as Siouxsie Sioux, and as unique and powerful a voice as Debbie Harry, frontwoman **Holly Beth Vincent** (guitar/vocals) revealed an understanding of rock's roots that took her beyond the strict confines of punk. She and her band deserve a champion to secure their place in the punk hall of fame, like Kurt Cobain did for The Raincoats.

A committed Anglophile, Vincent took her band – **Mark Henry** (bass) and **Steve Young** (drums) – to London to kick off their career. They signed to the Oval label, and in 1979 released "Tell That Girl To Shut Up" (later the victim of a cover version by Transvision Vamp). Holly And The Italians cut their teeth on the English pub and club scene, before finally gaining recognition through some support dates for Blondie and The Clash.

Signed to Virgin, the band issued two punk/New Wave gems – "Miles Away" and "Youth Coup". The debut album, THE RIGHT TO BE ITALIAN (1981), was tuneful pop-punk with a depth often lacking in the sociopolitical assault of British punk (with the honourable exceptions of the Buzzcocks and The Undertones).

After two further singles, the band broke up and Vincent released a solo effort called, confusingly, HOLLY AND THE ITALIANS (1982). A darker, more introverted album, it revealed a wealth of influences – 60s psychedelia, garage rock and art-school intellectualism – that earned her comparisons with the similarly kooky and knowledgeable Jonathan Richman. In the same year Virgin released her duet with longtime friend **Joey Ramone** – their rendition of Sonny and Cher's "I Got You Babe" was as arresting in its own way as the earlier offbeat cut of the same song by punk forerunners The Dictators. 1995 saw the release of VOWEL MOVEMENT, Holly's eclectic collaboration with Johnette Napolitano.

The Right To Be Italian (1981; Virgin).
A lost masterpiece. What a female-fronted Ramones would sound like.

Veronica Kofman

DAVID HOLMES

Born Belfast, Northern Ireland, 1969.

The career of **David Holmes** illustrates just how quickly a fantasy can become a reality. From his earliest releases, he has used the drama and tension of cinematic music and combined it with the most contemporary dance-floor genres, resulting in his being offered actual movie soundtrack work.

The cinematic element in Holmes's output was evident on a single back in 1993, when he teamed up with fellow DJ **Ashley Beedle** under the name **The Disco Evangelists**. "De Niro" borrowed liberally but cleverly from Ennio Morricone's soundtrack to ONCE UPON A TIME IN AMERICA. At the same time, Holmes's reputation as a club DJ in his native Belfast led to remix work for the likes of Saint Etienne and Sabres Of Paradise, where he epically restructured material designed to delight both the feet and the brain.

The filmic influences continued to infiltrate his work: his first single under his own name, "Johnny Favourite" (1994), was partly inspired by Alan Parker's thriller *Angel Heart*, while the following year's "No Man's Land" was a gripping response to the recently released *In The Name Of The Father*. As the very title of his debut album suggested, THIS FILM'S CRAP LET'S SLASH THE SEATS (1995) was a collection of tracks in search of the perfect film. (His wish would be granted in 1997 when several tracks on the album were used in a British TV drama called *Supply And Demand*.)

Holmes decided to take a logical next step, and 'direct' his follow-up album: in August 1996, he packed a DAT machine and headed for New York City, where he wandered the streets in search of stories from the people whose voices are rarely heard. The resulting interviews – some disturbing, others eccentric – made up the interludes between the new tracks that the stories inspired. Unlike many movie soundtracks, which seem like a record company trawl through back catalogues and leftovers, Holmes wanted to create a seamless blend of often unsettling tales and dark, menacing soundscapes. LET'S GET KILLED, finally released in August 1997, was justifiably popular with clubbers and critics and, significantly, with movie-makers, who started to flood him with offers for soundtrack work. He has since written and recorded material for the motion pictures *Resurrection Man* and *Out Of Sight*, as well as scoring the TV thriller serial *Killer Net*.

But his most ambitious project was the edgy, but equally cinematic 2000 release BOW DOWN TO THE EXIT SIGN, which may have made for decidedly uneasy listening, but only underlined his commitment to the extension of dance music's possibilities. With more critical acclaim mounting at his door, Holmes took on the task of scoring Steven Soderbergh's remake of the Rat Pack classic *Ocean's Eleven*. His contributions were stunning: a mix of club grooves and cool jazz, that fitted perfectly alongside cuts by Perry Como and Percy Faith. Hot on the heels of Ocean's release came a mix album, COME GET IT I GOT IT (2002), released on the 13 Amp imprint. The set was a mouth-watering pick'n'mix of obscure R&B, soul and Holmes's own contributions, credited to the pseudonym Free Association.

Considering his extraordinary maturity as a composer and producer, it may well transpire that, given time, a new name may join the hallowed list of film music legends. Herrmann, Schifrin, Quincy Jones ... David Holmes? Stranger things have happened.

⊙ **This Film's Crap Let's Slash The Seats** (1995; Go! Beat).
Holmes's prodigious talent for dramatic tension exploded on to the music scene with this sophisticated collection equally suitable for dance floor and front room. He's no slouch at tunes, either – check out the desolate "Gone" with an appropriately ghostly vocal from Saint Etienne's Sarah Cracknell.

⊙ **Let's Get Killed** (1997; Go! Beat).
A set of jet-black brilliance, with wicked funk and techno introduced by the inhabitants of New York's heart of darkness. (Some tracks were reworked for the 1998 vinyl-only release STOP ARRESTING ARTISTS.)

⊙ **Bow Down To The Exit Sign** (2000; Go! Beat).
Taking its lead from intense and iconoclastic movies like *Performance* and *Midnight Cowboy*, this set includes notable highlights like "Sick City" (featuring Primal Scream's Bobby Gillespie) and the blues-rock nightmare "Bad Thing" (assisted by Jon Spencer). Unsettling, funky, and often disorientating – a fine addition to Holmes's catalogue.

⊙ **Come Get It I Got It** (2002; 13 Amp).
Though the segueing of tunes that should stand alone can become a little annoying, this is a fine mix set that saves the rest of us the bother of trawling secondhand stores for those obscure soul gems.

Justin Lewis and Peter Buckley

THE HOLY MODAL ROUNDERS

Formed New York, 1963; disbanded 1965; re-formed 1968, and on and off from 1981 into the Twenty-First Century.

"People ask us what kind of music we play – and most have not understood when we explain that no one has ever played music like us before." Peter Stampfel

The **Holy Modal Rounders** were formed in New York in 1963 by **Peter Stampfel** (vocals/fiddle/banjo) and **Steve Weber** (guitar/vocals). Both shared a background in – and love of – folk, country and blues, in particular influenced by the recordings on Harry Smith's vital ANTHOLOGY OF AMERICAN FOLK MUSIC (1952). Stampfel had been playing in a multitude of Greenwich Village folk and country groups as well as with folk legends Luke Faust and (naturally) Bob Dylan. Weber had perfected his guitar technique busking around the streets: fable has it that he once played "La Bamba" nonstop for eighteen hours. When the pair first played together they didn't stop for three days, and they have been together ever since; they now lay modest claim to being the oldest surviving American group in an original line-up.

Finding in each other a perfect musical counterpart, the duo set about playing folk clubs, book stores, acid tests, free festivals and almost anywhere else in a constant round of psychedelic happenings, collaborating with an ever-changing group of Greenwich Village Beat musicians and poets. Their music was a free-form collation of traditional folk songs, improvised yodelling, bluegrass, pop tunes – anything, in fact, that could be performed by an acoustic duo in the melting pot of New York in the early 60s. Having experimented with such marvellous word-crashing names as The Total Quintessence Stomach Pumpers, and after lengthy wooing from a number of major labels they finally signed, as the Holy Modal Rounders, with Prestige, evidently on the grounds that their producer on that label was a dope-smoking giggler too.

Their first album, THE HOLY MODAL ROUNDERS, was released on Prestige Records in 1964, followed by VOLUME 2 in 1965. Having reasonable success with these LPs, the duo then met up with the highly irreverent and scatological FUGS, guesting on two lengthy, chemical-crazed sessions recorded for Folkways in early 1965. Stampfel and Weber floated in and out of The Holy Modals, until in July 1965 the unit foundered on Weber's growing eccentricities and lack of inspiration.

With playwright **Sam Shepard** on drums, Stampfel formed **The Moray Eels**, a more rock-based group who also included **Dave Levy** (guitar) and Stampfel's wife **Antonia Duren** (lyrics/vocals). When Weber sorted himself out in 1967, the pair were reunited in the merged Moray Eel/Holy Modal Rounders.

Releasing INDIAN WAR WHOOP (1967) as The Holy Modal Rounders, and then THE MORAY EELS EAT THE HOLY MODAL ROUNDERS for Elektra in 1968, the group gained huge counterculture success when Antonia's "Bird Song" featured in the first minutes of the cult film *Easy Rider*. Festival appearances and a spell recording in California followed, but the mainstream was never ready for The Rounders' sound, and they returned to their unique brand of folk weirdness on albums such as GOOD TASTE IS TIMELESS (Metromedia 1971) and ALLEGED IN THEIR OWN TIME (1975).

With the exception of Stampfel, the band upped sticks to Portland Oregon in the early Seventies, playing local gigs together with Jeffrey Fredericks and Jill Gross of Les Clamtones, becoming The Holy Modal Rounders at the show that featured Weber. The current bass player **Dave Reisch** returned east to form the **Unholy Modal Rounders** with Stampfel and **Michael Hurley**. The whole gang (Michael Hurley, The Unholy Modal Rounders, Jeffrey Fredericks & The Clamtones) reconvened in

1975 to record HAVE MOICY! for the aptly named Rounder Records.

LAST ROUND (Adelphi, 1978) and STAMPFEL AND WEBER: GOIN' NOWHERE FAST (Fantasy, 1981) were the group's last albums before the pilot light eventually went out and distance forced a split. Stampfel formed dreadful, but short-lived hippie rock group **The Bottlecaps**, and then turned up playing guest banjo to great effect on Bongwater's version of "Kisses Sweeter Than Wine" in 1991. Weber returned east in 1996, and with Reisch on bass, the Holy Modal Rounders made a revitalized album TOO MUCH FUN FOR ROUNDER in 1999. This was followed in 2001 by I MAKE A WISH FOR A POTATO, a collection made up of familiar tracks intermingled with some obscurities and an unpalatable attempt at disco.

◉ **Indian War Whoop** (1967; ESP).
The HMR gleefully dissect traditional songs such as "Sweet Apple Cider" and "Bay Rum Blues" under the influence of psychoactive drugs. Positively reeks of the 60s and addled, inspired craziness.

◉ **The Moray Eels Eat The Holy Modal Rounders** (1968; Elektra).
The high point of The Rounders' folk-acid strangeness period, from the opening "Bird Song" to the closing sardonic interpretation of the Pledge of Allegiance. Reissued on CD in 2002.

◉ **The Holy Modal Rounders 1 & 2** (1998; BigBeat UK).
First-ever CD release for the first two albums, here packaged nicely back-to-back with a couple of bonus tracks. Two anarchic classics bubbling with bohemian humour. Essential.

◉ **Too Much Fun** (1999; Rounder).
Sounding as fresh as on their earliest recordings, the original folk nutters have never sounded better. Their infectious enthusiasm still remains intact.

Richard Fontenoy

HOME

Formed Tampa, Florida, 1992

Home were one of the most exciting post-grunge bands to appear in the 90s, riding a wave of public interest that was set rolling by the quirkier members of the US alternative scene – Grandaddy, Thinking Fellers Union Local 282, Mercury Rev, et al. The group formed in 1992 when the longtime collaborative duo of **Eric Morrison** (piano) and **Andrew Deutsch** (guitar) were joined by **Brad Truax** (bass) and **Sean Martin** (drums). They recorded at a startling rate, and in less than a year released eight full-length cassettes (numerically titled from one to eight, reissued, in part, as the CD HOME ISSUES: EXCERPTS FROM I - VIII), distributed via their local record shop The Blue Chair. Patrons of the store soon became familiar with the 'Screw Music Forever' cookie jars that housed the cassettes, and as time went on Screw Music Forever flourished in its own right as an independent label, releasing 7" singles and CDs by local bands like Meringue, IMA and Vacation Bible School.

The band's earliest recordings were made with crude equipment, the finished product being soni-

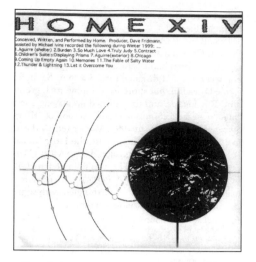

and marvellous tunes. The timing couldn't have been better for the UK release on Cooking Vinyl – Fridmann was the press's flavour of the month, and post-grunge psychedelic stalwarts Mercury Rev had already set the musical context with DESERTER'S SONGS; Home's European tour was duly well received.

Though there are no firm release plans for album number fifteen (Morrison has been busy becoming a father and recording an orchestral album with the **100% Storms Ensemble**), Home's timetable suggests that as their releases become more infrequent, their brilliance will multiply exponentially.

⊙ **XIV** (2000; Cooking Vinyl).
The music bounces through a dense matrix of shifting tempos, competing melody lines, churning guitar strings and pitter-pattering showers of digital detail. The album's many highpoints include the brilliant "Burden" and the blistering Floyd-ish stormer "Thunder & Lightning".

Peter Buckley

cally stifled (or enhanced, depending on your lo-fi aesthetic) by the double-tapedeck dubbing process. An experimental, erratic blend of prog-rock, folk, country and blues, the music was too often tuneless yet was powerful and peculiar enough to attract the attention of Relativity Records, who in 1993 put up enough money for the group to buy an 8-track porta-studio and rent a mobile home in the Florida backwater town of Plant City. Here, assisted by Brad Kopplin, Home enthusiastically recorded IX (1995) – their first release to cross the stateline. Much to the band's surprise the album travelled well, prompting positive feedback across the United States.

By 1995 the group had several tours under its belt, but had lost drummer Sean. With a succession of local drummers and new recording premises in a central-Tampa photographic studio, Home set about recording with an upgraded 16-track setup; the resulting album was unsurprisingly to be titled X. By the time the twenty weighty recordings from these sessions were mixed, Relativity Records had shifted its focus toward all things urban and closed its rock department; this cleared a path for the Jet Set and Emperor Jones labels to step in and release the material as X (1996) and XI ELF:GULFBOREWALTZ (1996) respectively.

The group relocated to Queens, New York, where they started to pen new material (much of which would end up on XIV) and recorded the spontaneous, superb studio construction 13 (NETHEREGIONS) (1998) to fulfil contractual obligations with Jet Set. Next they shifted to the Arena Rock Recording Company, enticed by producer Dave Fridmann (whose credits include Mercury Rev and The Flaming Lips). In early 1999 Fridmann and Home, assisted by The Flaming Lips' Michael Ivins, recorded the majestic XIV (2000) in only two weeks. Fuelled by Fridmann's enthusiasm and technical abilities the band crafted the most cohesive and compelling set of their sprawling catalogue, combining hallmark experimentation with exquisite songs

THE HOODOO GURUS

Formed Sydney, Australia, 1981; disbanded 1997.

Dave **Faulkner** (vocals/guitar) and **James Baker** (drums) spearheaded Perth's punk rock scene with The Victims, a band that dissolved in 1978 and briefly re-formed in 1980 for a highly acclaimed one-off gig. Baker and Faulkner then moved to Sydney, and recruited guitarists **Rod Radalj** (formerly of The Scientists) and **Kimble Rendall**. The quartet named themselves **Le Hoodoo Gurus**, feeling that the 'le' gave them class.

With no bass player, and three guitars, Le Gurus' onslaught was different from any other. Songs like "Dig It Up" drew comparisons with The Cramps, but other tracks like "Tojo" crashed out tiny variations of one single chord, which elevated their sound to an extraordinary power level. Faulkner also crafted delicious pop tunes to match – "My Girl", "True To You", "Zanzibar" and their debut single "Leilani" (1982).

However, Rendall bowed out after "Leilani", Radalj left to form The Johnnies soon afterwards, and when **The Hoodoo Gurus** returned (having wisely translated the French definite article) it was with former Super-K members **Brad Shepherd** (guitar) and **Clyde Bramley** (bass). It was this line-up that recorded the band's debut LP, STONEAGE ROMEOS (1983) – basically their live set, but with a little studio interference to smooth over the three-guitar roughness.

By the release of the second album, MARS NEEDS GUITARS (1985), Baker had also been ousted (he went on to form The Dubrovniks with a couple of ex-Scientists), to be replaced by **Mark Kingsmill**. The record had some success in the US, helped by college-radio hit singles "Like Wow Wipeout" and "Bittersweet". MAGNUM CUM LOUDER (1985) and BLOW YOUR COOL (1987), with its single "Generation Gap", also created some crossover interest in the UK.

A further personnel change came in 1987, Bramley being replaced by **Rick Grossman**, since when the group have continued to enjoy considerable college success in the US (with every album bar KINKY topping the college charts), while their good-time retro image has served them well in Australia. They have released KINKY (1991); CRANK (1994), overseen by Ramones producer Ed Stasium, and with a refreshingly rougher sound; and a seventh LP, IN BLUE CAVE, appeared in 1996. The following year the group decided to quit while they were ahead and embarked on their 'Spit the Dummy' farewell tour. Since the band's demise Shepherd has resurfaced with **The Monarchs** and several Hoodoo retrospectives have appeared: the best of the crop being 2000's AMPOLOGY and 1999's BITE THE BULLET 3CD set.

⊙ **Ampology** (2000; Acadia).
It's a shame that The Gurus' material is undersold as some 60s throwback or tribute, as this fine compilation shows. Faulkner is a master of the throwaway pop single, although some of his parodic material, like "Miss Freelove 1969", could be horrendously misunderstood.

Danella Taylor

JOHN LEE HOOKER

Born Clarksdale, Mississippi, 1920; died 2001.

Raised near the birthplace of the legendary Robert Johnson, the original blues brother, **John Lee Hooker**, first encountered music, like many bluesmen, by singing gospel in church. After trying to make his first instrument from an inner tube attached to a barn door, Hooker was taught guitar by his stepfather, William Moore.

Running away from home to seek his fame at the tender age of 14, Hooker first moved to Memphis, where he had formative encounters with several older bluesmen. It was from one such figure, Tony Hollins, that he appropriated the song "Crawlin' King Snake", which later became one of his many hits. On the whole, though, the experience was a fraught one, with Hooker too young to be admitted to blues clubs, or scorned by musicians for moving in on their spot.

Disillusioned, for the next decade Hooker virtually abandoned performing the blues, choosing instead to move north to Cincinnati and sing with gospel groups. Then, lured by the motor industry boom, he moved to Detroit in 1943, where he relaunched his blues career. It was thanks to local entrepreneur Joe Van Battle, who had built a recording studio behind his record store, that Hooker began his recording career there.

Finally, at the age of 28, Hooker enjoyed the first in a long line of hits. Recorded for

Battle's rivals Sensation Records, "Boogie Chillen" (1948) hit the black R&B charts. Singing with the accompaniment of his open-tuned guitar and Coca-Cola bottle-tops attached to his shoes, Hooker shaped a unique, gutsy sound that marked a major departure from the standard blues shouter field hollers.

Hits such as "Crawlin' King Snake" and "Shake, Holler And Run" quickly followed, while Hooker recorded under numerous pseudonyms for rival labels. Some, like John Lee Booker or John Lee Cooker were barely disguised, while The Boogie Man, Johnny Lee and Delta John were less obvious. He even worked as a local DJ, where he could promote his own products still further. However, in the best blues tradition, there was a price to pay for all this sudden material gain. Allegedly a wicked womanizer, Hooker almost died in 1950 after an aggrieved individual poisoned his whisky. (Twelve years earlier, Robert Johnson had not been so fortunate.)

With more sophisticated players like **B. B. KING** eclipsing his popularity by the early 50s, Hooker was astute enough to move with the times. Signing to Veejay in 1955, Hooker adopted on record the band format that he had been using live for some years. Once again he struck gold, setting the R&B and pop charts alight with classics like "Boom Boom" and "Dimples".

Similarly, as white college students longed for authentic blues styles, Hooker obliged by delving back into his past for THE FOLK BLUES OF JOHN LEE HOOKER (1959) and THE REAL FOLK BLUES (1966). Indeed, by the time of the mid-60s blues boom, the name of John Lee Hooker was one of those foremost on converts' lips. UK tours and sessions, backed by the likes of The Spencer Davis Group and The Groundhogs (who had taken their name from Hooker's "Ground Hog Blues"), brought his music to a whole new audience. Numerous white rock

The late John Lee Hooker at home with his awards

groups such as MC5, The Doors and The Animals also paid tribute to their hero by covering his songs, but the most significant recognition came from blues enthusiasts **Canned Heat**, who teamed up with him on the superb 1970 double LP, HOOKER'N'HEAT: THE BEST OF PLUS. A tour also proved to be a natural and lucrative pairing for both parties.

Bar the odd festival appearance and appropriate casting in the cult film *The Blues Brothers* (1980), Hooker was unusually silent for much of the 70s and 80s. However, aged 69, and aided by lifelong fans like **Santana** and **Bonnie Raitt**, Hooker's comeback album THE HEALER (1989) put him, and the blues, well and truly back on the map. If anything, the follow-up, MR. LUCKY (1991), was even better. Hooker found himself in the record books as the oldest artist to have reached the Top 3 of the UK album charts.

In addition to extensive touring, and collaborating with the likes of **Pete Townshend**, he returned in 1995 with the excellent album, CHILL OUT. In 1997, he trumped himself with the awesome DON'T LOOK BACK, having cut down on the famous friends and pared his boogie back to the bone.

But sadly, Hooker died on Thursday, June 21, 2001 of natural causes at the age of 83. His legacy and influence on both blues and rock will not be forgotten quickly.

John Lee Hooker

⊙ **John Lee Hooker Plays And Sings The Blues** (1989; Chess).
Plenty of examples of authentic Hooker, and at an affordable price too.

⊙ **Mr. Lucky** (1991; Silvertone/Charisma).
With the help of his superstar disciples, Hooker updates milestones like "This Is Hip" and "I Want To Hug You", while retaining his inimitable sense of pizzazz.

⊙ **The Ultimate Collection:1948–1990** (1990; Rhino).
Expensive but comprehensive, even including the collaborations with Canned Heat and Bonnie Raitt.

⊙ **The Early Years** (1991; Tomato).
If you like your blues raw and dirty, this is perfect. Two CDs feature all his classics, both solo and with a band.

⊙ **The Essential Collection** (1998; Half Moon).
Latest in a series of excellent JLH collections. But with a back catalogue of such quality, spanning forty years, it would be hard to put together a bad compilation.

John Lee Hooker and Canned Heat

⊙ **Hooker'N'Heat: The Best Of Plus** (1989; See For Miles).
The old boy is clearly enjoying the musical chemistry here, as he and the band run through a range of swingin' blues-soaked Hooker boogies.

Paul Morris

LIGHTNIN' HOPKINS

Born Centreville, Texas, 1912; died 1982.

Revered as one of the last great country bluesmen, **Sam 'Lightnin' Hopkins** had a career which spanned five decades and more than 600 recordings. He first made his name while still in his teens. After a long stint backing his cousin Texas Alexander in a travelling duo, the young Sam Hopkins teamed up with barrelhouse pianist Thunder Smith, adopting the nickname 'Lightnin' to complement his partner's. When Hopkins moved to Houston, he soon became the city's leading musical light, more or less singlehandedly putting it on the blues map. With a prolific recording output between 1946 and 1953, he at last enjoyed the hits he had worked so hard to achieve.

However, by the time folklorist Sam Charters located him in 1959, Hopkins' fortunes were declining. It was thanks to Charters' involvement that a remarkable resuscitation took place, with the release of the ground-breaking THE ROOTS OF LIGHTNIN' HOPKINS (1959). Hopkins then went on to produce hundreds of sessions for a multitude of major and smaller labels.

Hopkins had an unorthodox but very gritty style which was peculiar to Texas. The lyrical content of his songs and commentaries – on local events and international issues – together with the hypnotic intensity of his guitar, endeared him to an audience created by the American folk boom of the early 60s. As a kid he'd played to passengers on buses; now he could now count venues such as the Carnegie Hall among his gigs. Though the arrival of electric blues bands temporarily reduced Hopkins' popularity, as did his tendency to put out too much material, he showed he could still move with the times by issuing a 'progressive' electric album, THE GREAT SHOW AND DANCE (1968).

A film documenting his life and music, *The Blues Of Lightnin' Hopkins*, won the Gold Hugo Award at the 1967 Chicago Film Festival, and throughout the 70s he continued to capitalize on his by now legendary status. Tours of America, Canada and Europe were supplemented by regular radio, television and movie appearances.

He also carried on recording, teaming up with **Taj Mahal** and **Sonny Terry**, although Hopkins' cantankerous nature began to mar live performance. He retired at the end of the 70s due to ill-health, and he died of cancer in the early weeks of 1982.

⊙ **Texas Blues** (1989; Arhoolie).
Recorded during the early 60s, this is a superb introduction to Lightnin's music.

⊙ **Lightnin' Hopkins 1947–1969** (1992; Wolf).
A single CD covering some of Lightnin's most productive years, as well as his attempts at other areas of music, with songs such as "Jazz Blues". One of the best among a bewildering number of compilations on the market.

⊙ **The Complete Prestige/Bluesville Recordings** (1991; Prestige/Bluesville).
A seven-CD document for the converted and affluent.

Paul Morris

HOT TUNA

Formed San Francisco, 1969.

Initially a genial acoustic outfit, specializing in the cool economy of rural and Depression-era blues,

Hot Tuna came into being when **JEFFERSON AIRPLANE** lead guitarist **Jorma Kaukonen** and bassist **Jack Casady**, tiring of their regular band's divisions, established an offshoot project. Their creation provided a welcome antidote to the indulgences which had initially energized the blues genre, but, by then, were simply bastardizing it. After the Airplane mutated into the airbrushed soft rock of Jefferson Starship in 1973, Hot Tuna, conversely, were becoming more experimental, foraying into good-time boogie and country-blues, as well as – rather less impressively – into louder, more obvious, rock music.

In truth, the blues was what Kaukonen and Casady had always wanted to play, ever since the Washington-born duo had started performing together as **The Triumphs** in 1959. Indeed, by 1963, Kaukonen, now based in San Jose, could be found playing lead guitar for unknown blues singer **JANIS JOPLIN**. However, from the mid 60s, the duo's blues predilections were largely eschewed in favour of folk-rock, psychedelia and strident politicizing. As part of Jefferson Airplane, Kaukonen's charged but fluid alliance of fuzz and feedback, underpinned by Casady's dexterous bass lines, helped embody the San Francisco sound. Nevertheless, as early as February 1969, the seeds of Hot Tuna were sown; the release of the Airplane's peerless BLESS ITS POINTED LITTLE HEAD live LP featured the duo interrupting the dense improvisation and acid-drenched sonic assaults with the incongruous blues standard "Rock Me Baby".

By the end of that year, Hot Tuna were regularly supporting the Airplane with an assortment of stripped-back acoustic blues covers like "Hesitation Blues", "Wining' Boy Blues" and "Death Don't Have No Mercy". One performance recorded at Berkeley, and featuring **Will Scarlett** on harmonica, became their debut LP, HOT TUNA (1970). A refreshingly clear and simple slice of rural blues, complete with an endearing after-hours ambience of loose, genial interplay, it hit the US charts and set a standard which few subsequent releases would match.

With the addition of Airplane fiddle player **Papa John Creach** and **Sammy Piaza** (drums) in 1971, Hot Tuna raised the decibel level, concentrated on new Kaukonen material and began the slow process of shedding their charm. By the time Kaukonen and Casady finally left the Airplane in 1973, their Hot Tuna project had become prolific to the point of carelessness. Most of their releases exhibited the twin failings of inconsistent material and an increasingly reverential attitude towards the blues. BURGERS (1972), THE PHOSPHORESCENT RAT (1973), AMERICA'S CHOICE and YELLOW FEVER (both 1975) were often slaves to authenticity, invoking blues ghosts rather than recasting them.

Surprisingly, the straightforward rock of HOPKORV (1976) was popular with fans, and propelled Hot Tuna, now a five-piece with a second guitar and keyboard player, towards a higher profile, which culminated in their supporting Led Zeppelin at Knebworth in 1979. The previous year they had issued DOUBLE DOSE, a live recording which managed to balance their acoustic poise with new-found aggression and textural variety.

Hot Tuna's studio work dried up in the 80s, though they still performed sporadically. Casady embarked upon a series of ill-advised ventures, including a flirtation with punk, and the formation of **The Kantner Balin Casady Band**. Kaukonen kept a low profile, providing session work for Robert Hunter and performing solo gigs, captured on MAGIC (1985) and TOO HOT TO HANDLE (1986).

In late 1989, Kaukonen and Casady featured in the line-up on the patchy but underrated **Jefferson Airplane** reunion album and tour. Suitably revitalized, the duo recorded PAIR A DICE FOUND (1990), the first all-new Hot Tuna album in almost fifteen years. An inconsistent set, dominated by rock styles, it reawakened their partnership, which then blossomed due to an upsurge of interest in acoustic, 'unplugged' music.

Two well-received albums of live acoustic material followed – LIVE AT SWEETWATER VOLS. 1 & 2 (1992 & 1993) – and the additions of **Michael Falzarano** (guitar) and **Pete Sears** (ex-Jefferson Starship; keyboards) proved popular in live shows. It was a deservedly happy outcome to a saga of dogged persistence, allied to a generous desire to popularize the work of others. The remainder of the 90s saw a torrent of live recordings, reissues and Kaukonen's solo efforts in the shops; to this day the group continues to tour with an apparently boundless energy.

⊙ **Hot Tuna** (1970; Edsel).
The band's best overall album. Its organic warmth has aged well, and it provides a fine testament to the charm of spareness.

⊙ **Live At Sweetwater Vol. 1** (1992; Relix).
Hot Tuna come full circle with this rootsy live album, intimately recorded and echoing the ambience of their early material. The band mingle old ways and new tricks to beguiling effect.

Nig Hodgkins

HOTHOUSE FLOWERS

Formed Dublin, Ireland, 1985;
quiescent since 1993.

"We could get a party going at a bus stop." Liam O'Maonlai

Gaelic speakers **Liam O'Maonlai** (vocals) and **Fiachna O'Braonain** (guitar) met at school, where they were introduced to traditional Irish instruments like the tin whistle and the bodhran. (Liam went on to become the all-Ireland champion bodhran player). The pair formed punk band Congress, featuring future members of **MY BLOODY VALENTINE**, and later busked as The Incomparable Benzini Brothers, whose street performances earned them 1985's *Dublin Street Entertainers of the Year* award.

Meanwhile, they had also formed a rock band, the **Hothouse Flowers** with **Peter O'Toole** (bass), **Jerry Fehily** (drums), **Leo Barnes** (saxophone) and **Maria Doyle** (backing vocals). *Rolling Stone* called them 'The best unsigned band in the world', and it wasn't long before the British music press also took notice. Appearances on Irish television followed, one of which was seen by U2's Bono, who invited them to record "Love Don't Work This Way" for his band's label, Mother. Its release resulted in a swarm of A&R staff descending on Dublin in search of a deal, the lucky suitors being Polygram subsidiary, London.

By now, Maria Doyle had left the band to have a baby (she would later resurface with husband Kieran Kennedy in The Black Velvet Band, and with a starring role in the Alan Parker movie, *The Commitments*). The remaining Flowers, meantime, had already become second only to U2 as Ireland's biggest band, and success abroad was not far away. Their first single for London, "Don't Go", was released in May 1988, after being performed in an interval for that year's Eurovision Song Contest.

"Don't Go" was a major British hit, and a similarly successful album, PEOPLE (1988), coincided with the band's first UK tour. It was 1990 before any further material appeared, but the single "Give It Up" proved that the group was still capable of producing the goods, while HOME, inspired by their traditional backgrounds, was another big hit album.

After supporting INXS at their 1991 Wembley Stadium concert, Hothouse Flowers supported Dire Straits on the Australian leg of their tour. However, their third album, SONGS FROM THE RAIN, did not appear until 1993. Its songwriting was an improvement, while veteran producer Stewart Levine gave the record an overall sheen. A couple of the songs, including the single "An Emotional Time", were co-written with Dave Stewart.

SONGS was a respectable seller, if not quite up to the sales of its predecessors and for many it seemed the band had reached the end of the road. In 1995 Liam O'Maonlai joined Andy White and Tim Finn to form **Alt**, while various Flowers have appeared on tracks by acts including Indigo Girls, Michelle Shocked, Maria McKee and Sinéad O'Connor.

But this was not the end of the story. In 1998, having shed drummer Jerry Fehily and Leo Barnes's sax, Hothouse Flowers returned as a three-piece with a new album, BORN. Though the set by no means changed the world, it marked a welcome return, with Liam – minus golden locks – sounding gloriously on form. A BEST OF collection was released by London Records in 2000, without the involvement of the band; the selections were largely culled from the first two albums. The band are planning to release a new album some time soon, while VAULTS 1, a collection of rarities is to be made available via the group's website.

(•) **People** (1988; London).
While some feel that "Don't Go" has never been bettered, there are other delights here, with rockers like "I'm

Sorry", "Feet On The Ground" and "Love Don't Work This Way" lying next to the gorgeous "Forgiven" and "If You Go".

(•) **Home** (1990; London).
Another first-rate combination of rockers and ballads, while CD bonus tracks like the tear-jerking "Trying To Get Through" and the thrilling "Dance To The Storm" capture the band at their very best.

Martin Rowsell

THE HOUSE OF LOVE

Formed London, 1986; disbanded 1993; re-formed 2002.

The House of Love came together in early 1986, the brainchild of **Guy Chadwick** (vocals/guitar). Chadwick's previous band, Kingdoms, had enjoyed a one-single career on RCA, and in their wake he found himself with a batch of songs, but no band and no label. He placed an ad in the music press and recruited **Terry Bickers** (guitar), **Chris Groothuizen** (bass) and **Andrea Heukamp** (guitar/vocals), alongside old friend **Pete Evans** (drums). The House of Love was born.

They sent a bunch of demos to Creation label boss Alan McGee, who was persuaded to release "Shine On" as the band's debut single in May 1987. The charming simplicity of its chorus ensured favourable reviews, but the follow-up was something of a disappointment. Where its predecessor almost glided along, "Real Animal" was a routine rocker.

Tired of the constant touring in the latter half of 1987, Heukamp had left the band before the release of their third single, "Christine", a foretaste of the debut LP. A haunting, almost mesmeric, guitar soundscape from Bickers provided the perfect backdrop to Chadwick's pained vocals, a recipe repeated to great effect on THE HOUSE OF LOVE (1988). Thrust into the media spotlight, Chadwick and his cohorts suddenly could do no wrong. A compilation of the first two singles plus two unreleased tracks, intended for release abroad, was imported back into the country and sold well. A fourth single, "Destroy The Heart", ensured the boom continued.

HOTHOUSE FLOWERS • THE HOUSE OF LOVE

Offers arrived thick and fast before the band eventually agreed to sign for Phonogram/Fontana in late 1988. No sooner had they put pen to paper, however, than things started to go wrong. Overriding the wishes of the band, Fontana issued "Never" as the A-side of the next single, demoting "Safe", the band's choice, to the B-side. Despite knocking at the door of the Top 40, "Never" failed to impress the critics.

Having decided to rerecord their second album (four different producers eventually received credits), the band released "I Don't Know Why I Love You" in November 1989. It, too, failed to crack the Top 40 and a year of torment came to a dramatic end with Bickers' departure – he went on to form **LEVITATION** (and, recently, Cradle). **Simon Walker** was brought in to play guitar on tour and remained with the band as they finally enjoyed chart success with a rerecorded version of "Shine On", a single released in no fewer than seven different formats.

The second album, FONTANA, was eventually released in February 1990 and catapulted the band back to the top. It peaked at #8 in the UK and was the prelude to a gruelling six-month tour of Europe and America. In order to maintain the band's profile at home while they attempted to crack the US, at the end of 1990 Fontana released an album of outtakes from the aborted 1989 sessions, alongside previously unreleased tracks recorded in 1988 and 1990. Entitled A SPY IN THE HOUSE OF LOVE, it got lost in the Christmas rush.

It was almost twelve months before any new material was forthcoming, as spending the best part of a year on the road took its toll on Chadwick. "The Girl With The Loneliest Eyes" was eventually released in October 1991 but sank almost without trace, as the media, who had hailed The House of Love as great white hopes just eighteen months previously, began to look to America and the grunge phenomenon for their front-page stories.

As Chadwick struggled to find the sound he was looking for in the studio, six months passed before "Feel" was released, but it couldn't crack the Top 40. "You Don't Understand", rush-released to give a much-needed publicity boost in advance of the now completed third album, failed in its task.

BABE RAINBOW (1992), released nearly two and a half years after FONTANA had stormed into the Top 10, received largely tepid reviews and spent only two weeks in the chart. Despite long deliberations in the studio, the band's sound had lost the edge that had distinguished The House of Love's earlier releases. Accordingly, Chadwick announced his intention to return to the band's roots, and within a year AUDIENCE WITH THE MIND was in the shops. The motives behind the album were entirely honourable and the sound was noticeably less polished than it had been at any time since the band's days on Creation, but the songs were lacking in any real substance. The album spent one week in the chart and no single was forthcoming to promote its release.

Thinking that The House of Love were no longer a viable proposition, Chadwick consigned the name to rock's heritage and retired for a four-year battle with his muse. He returned with an album of love songs, LAZY, SOFT & SLOW (1998; Setanta) – a surprisingly descriptive title. The lyrics verged on the trite and contained no major insights but the music was adorable.

In late 2002 the story took an unlikely twist when Guy and Terry announced that they were again working together under the name The House Of Love. Within a few months they had been joined by Pete Evans and a new bass player, **Matt Jury**. Live dates quickly followed, and new recorded material is well on the way.

⦿ **1986-1988** (2001; PLR).
This retrospective pulls together the early singles and the band's debut LP – undoubtedly their best. Uncluttered production allows the fragile beauty of such songs as "Man To Child" and "Touch Me" to shine through, whilst Bickers' guitar battles with Chadwick's emotive vocals on tracks such as "Salome" and the classic "Christine".

⦿ **Fontana** (1990; Fontana).
Begins in almost anthemic fashion with "Hannah" and goes on to deliver a thoughtful set.

⦿ **The Peel Sessions 1988-1989** (2000; Strange Fruit).
A great collection, full of raw and majestic versions of many of the group's better-known numbers.

Andy Lowe

THE HOUSEMARTINS

Formed Hull, England, 1984; disbanded 1988.

S elf-deprecatingly promoted as 'The Fourth Best Band in Hull', **The Housemartins** came about through the efforts of Sheffield-born singer-songwriter **Paul Heaton**. When Heaton moved to Hull, he placed an advert in his front window, in search of other musicians. His neighbour **Stan Cullimore** (guitar) replied, while **Hugh Whitaker** (drums) and **Norman Cook** (bass) soon entered the frame.

Heaton tapped into his lyrical potential with "Flag Day", which poured contempt on shallow charitable gestures and the royal family in one fell swoop. Its clear socialist content won the band plenty of support, and it became their debut single for independent label Go! Discs at the end of 1985. Meanwhile, their live shows won over the less seriously committed, with styles ranging from quality pop to gospel harmonizing, augmented with awkward and endearing dance routines.

The Housemartins' breakthrough came in 1986 with the release of their third single, "Happy Hour", an eloquent attack on casual sexism. Boosted by a memorable video, in which the band members were represented by Plasticine figures, the single raced into the UK Top 5, as did their debut album, LONDON 0, HULL 4 (1986), which demonstrated their gifts to the full.

Christmas 1986 saw The Housemartins become true family favourites, as they topped the charts with an a cappella treatment of The Isley Brothers' little-known "Caravan Of Love". Such success was dampened by a furious tabloid press campaign, denouncing the band for being fake working-class, gay, and a threat to the Queen of England. If anything, this adversity made them less compromising and more uncomfortable than ever.

Since then, Heaton and Hemingway have achieved even greater success with **THE BEAUTIFUL SOUTH**, Cook has become a major figure on the UK's dance music scene, and Cullimore has embarked on a writing career, including children's books and a guide to the music business.

⊙ **London 0, Hull 4** (1986; Go! Discs/Elektra).
Songs to make you smile, songs to make you think and songs to make you weep, possibly all at the same time. Marvel at Heaton's ability to deliver a demon harmonica solo, and admire the 'influential guitar break' and 'middle bit of some repute', as listed on the album's lyric sheet.

⊙ **The People Who Grinned Themselves To Death**
(1987; Go! Discs/Elektra).
Though still trading with infectious pop tunes and affecting melodies, the lyrics have become much more vicious, spewing bile in several well-deserved directions.

Maria Lamle

H. P. LOVECRAFT

Formed Chicago, 1967; disbanded 1969.

Named after the great horror writer, **H. P. Lovecraft** fashioned a hybrid of acid-folk-rock and oddly striking vocal harmonies from two contrasting sources. Founder **George Edwards** had been a folk troubadour whose repertoire included covers of The Beatles' "Norwegian Wood" and Dylan's "Quit Your Low Down Ways", while vocalist/keyboard player **David Michaels** could boast a classical training and a four-octave range.

After covering The Troggs' "Any Way That You Want Me" with members of Chicago band **The Rovin' Kind**, Edwards and Michaels became the creative force behind H. P. Lovecraft. They recruited **Tony Cavallari** (lead guitar), **Mike Tegza** (drums) and **Jerry McGeorge** (bass), and a debut album for Philips, H. P. LOVECRAFT, soon followed. Featuring a nine-piece orchestra, its eclecticism was extraordinary, juxtaposing covers of Dino Valentine's hippie anthem "Let's Get Together", the Randy Newman ballad "I've Been Wrong Before", and lame vaudeville psychedelia in "The Time Machine". Most notable, however, was a musical tribute to their novelist namesake; based on one of his short stories, "The White Ship" was drenched in hallucinatory harmonies, droning feedback, baroque harpsichord passages and the chiming of a genuine 1811 ship's bell.

This album, and the single release of "The White Ship", established H. P. Lovecraft on the West Coast scene and they became regulars at San Francisco venues like Fillmore West and Winterland, where they appeared alongside luminaries like Jefferson Airplane and The Grateful Dead. These experiences were reflected on H. P. LOVECRAFT II (1968), a set

steeped in an LSD afterglow and, including "At The Mountains Of Madness", another adaptation of a Lovecraft text.

By this time McGeorge had been replaced by **Jeff Boyan**, whose previous project had the arresting name of Dalek/Engam: The Blackstones. His extra power enhanced their live appeal, captured on a set of 1968 live recordings, which were eventually issued in the US in 1991, under the title LIVE AT FILLMORE WEST. Containing songs from both earlier albums, the performances here revealed a new-found dynamism and intensity, and the album remains a vibrant testament to a band whose experimentation was often out of step with the times.

H. P. Lovecraft in its original form dissolved in 1969, but Edwards and Tegza subsequently returned with a new line-up as **Lovecraft**. An album, VALLEY OF THE MOON, was released, but it bore scant resemblance to the earlier sound.

⊙ **At The Mountains Of Madness** (1990; Edsel).
This is deleted but it's the CD to look for: H. P. Lovecraft's first two albums – retitled WHITE SHIP: THIS IS H. P. LOVECRAFT and SPIN, SPIN, SPIN – plus "Any Way That You Want Me".

Chris Brook

THE HUMAN LEAGUE

Formed Sheffield, England, 1977.

"What we're about is tunes, and to a lesser degree rhythm and lyrics, but really tunes – just the same as Abba or Michael Jackson or Rod Stewart." Phil Oakey

Influenced more by the pioneering electronic sound of Kraftwerk than the nihilism of punk, computer operators **Ian Craig Marsh** (synthesizer) and **Martyn Ware** (synthesizer) formed a band called Dead Daughters in 1977. After taking on projectionist **Adrian Wright** (synthesizer/slides) and hospital porter **Phil Oakey** (vocals/synthesizer), they became The Future and finally **The Human League**.

The band quickly built up a following through their visually impressive live performances, mixing covers of Righteous Brothers and Gary Glitter songs with strong original material (if let down by pretentious lyrics). They signed to Virgin in 1979, and released two albums within twelve months – REPRODUCTION (1979) and TRAVELOGUE (1980). By the second release, they had become sufficiently well known to merit a mention in The Undertones' hit "My Perfect Cousin".

Growing artistic differences within the League came to a head in October 1980 when Marsh and Ware quit on the eve of a European tour. (They resurfaced the following year with BEF and Heaven 17.) Oakey, meanwhile, recruited teenagers **Joanne Catherall** and **Susanne Sulley** (both vocals) in a last-ditch attempt at saving the band, when he was out drowning his sorrows at a local nightclub. The

THE HUMAN LEAGUE
DARE

tour went ahead with the addition of **Ian Burden** (synthesizer/bass), while **Jo Callis** (ex-Rezillos; guitar/synthesizer) joined in 1981 to complete the definitive Human League line-up.

With producer Martin Rushent, The Human League's new-found upbeat electronica became a global success during 1981. A string of hit singles taken from the album DARE (1981) defied the lingering misconception that synthesizers were only capable of producing cold, emotionless music. The album's biggest hit was "Don't You Want Me", #1 on both sides of the Atlantic, and one of the most enduringly popular songs of the 80s. It even led to belated Top 10 success in early 1982 for the four-year-old oddity, "Being Boiled".

The next two years were hardly prolific, although two singles – "Mirror Man" (1982) and "(Keep Feeling) Fascination" (1983) – both hit #2 in the UK charts, and even a stopgap remix album, LOVE AND DANCING (1982), sold remarkably well. However, following up DARE would prove difficult, and by the time HYSTERIA appeared in 1984, the band, inevitably, had lost its momentum. Even so, it yielded three Top 20 singles, including "The Lebanon", a questionable attempt at political commentary. However, all three singles were easily outsold by Oakey's "Together In Electric Dreams", a 1984 collaboration with producer Giorgio Moroder, which even led to a dispensable album in 1985.

The Human League, meanwhile, had lost ground by not touring to promote HYSTERIA, while Callis's departure in 1985 coincided with the scrapping of a whole album's worth of material. They left for Minneapolis to collaborate with dance producers and writers Jimmy Jam and Terry Lewis, who were also working with Janet Jackson and Alexander O'Neal. The manufactured and characterless result, CRASH (1986), was a hurried affair, which found the band swamped by a tide of thumping bass lines and mechanical arrangements. The one highlight was "Human", an outstanding song of betrayal and regret which was their biggest worldwide hit, and first US chart-topper since the release of "Don't You Want Me".

After CRASH, Burden and Wright left the band, leaving the nucleus of Oakey, Catherall and Sulley to go it alone. A singles collection, GREATEST HITS (1988), fared predictably well, but it was 1990 before any new material emerged in the shape of ROMANTIC?, a strangely listless album which, apart from the minor hit "Heart Like A Wheel", was almost completely ignored. Its failure led to financial troubles, depression and a parting from Virgin after twelve years.

At this point, it seemed that The Human League were heading for the permanent obscurity shared by so many early-80s pop stars, but the band had proved its resilience in the past and would do so again. Head of A&R at East West Records, Ian Stanley, signed them in 1992, and produced the seventh League album, OCTOPUS (1995). It was a sparkling return to form, with plenty of the old magic and enough state-of-the-art danceability to attract the younger end of the market. Its best songs were the hits "Tell Me When", a sassy, hook-laden stormer, and "One Man In My Heart", a lush synth ballad which recalled Abba at their most melodic. With a successful comeback tour, and a repackaged greatest hits set, OCTOPUS confirmed that the simple Human League ethos of good tunes, love and dancing was still as valid as it had been in the heady days of 1981.

2001's SECRETS has some nice tunes, when Oakey actually gets to sing, but the group are out of their element when it comes to crafting instrumentals – seven in total. One presumes they were mostly aimed at the dance floor but they miss by a mile. Luckily they still seem to be able to fashion a pop hook without breaking a sweat – the exhilarating opener "All I Ever Wanted", in particular, is one of their best in years. Time for a third revival?

- **Travelogue** (1980; Virgin).
  A fine document of the group's pre-split, pre-girls, pre-pop sound. Essential electronic listening.

- **Dare** (1981; Virgin).
  One of the best-loved and most successful British pop albums of all time. Hugely commercial, but never crass, positively glowing with joyous melodies and upbeat lyrics, it remains the band's greatest achievement.

- **Octopus** (1995; East West).
  This was hardly a radical departure from their early 80s work, but its best tracks show that The Human League's instinct for catchy, clever pop has still not deserted them.

- **Greatest Hits** (1995; Virgin).
  An essential compilation of some of the most glittering pop songs of the decade. The highs are all here ("Love Action", "Louise", "Human"), the lows ("I Need Your Loving") mercifully absent, and there's just one iffy choice – Snap!'s remix of "Don't You Want Me".

Jonathan Kennaugh

HUMBLE PIE

Formed London, 1969; disbanded 1975; re-formed 1980; disbanded again 1982.

Designed as a joint vehicle for **SMALL FACES** singer **Steve Marriott** (vocals/guitar) and The Herd's **PETER FRAMPTON** (guitar), **Humble Pie** didn't evolve quite as expected. The restrained influence of Frampton made for pleasant listening on albums such as AS SAFE AS YESTERDAY IS and TOWN AND COUNTRY (both 1969), but it was Marriott's blues-shouter boogie that defined the Humble Pie sound, evident on their debut single and UK Top 10 hit "Natural Born Bugie" (1969).

Encouraged by the band's new manager, Dee Anthony, to follow the trend for hard rock, Marriott gradually regained the laddish exuberance which had dominated The Small Faces, and he soon virtually ousted Frampton as band leader. Further albums like HUMBLE PIE (1970) and ROCK ON (1971) confirmed Marriott's gift for blistering rock-'n'blues, but their quintessential sound was captured on the ground-breaking live double LP, PERFORMANCE: ROCKIN' THE FILLMORE (1971). On this, Marriott, the consummate showman, employed his gutsy baritone to spine-chilling effect on lengthy and thrilling reworkings of both originals and blues standards.

Frampton left in 1971 to be replaced by ex-Colosseum guitarist **Dave 'Clem' Clemson**. He fitted in seamlessly, and the band continued to move in a heavier direction with SMOKIN' (1972), but success outside Britain and the States was limited, and the band found themselves in a worse financial state than ever. After a change in direction to encompass soul music on the unsuccessful double studio/live album EAT IT (1973), and a return to rock on THUNDERBOX (1974) and STREET RATS (1975), the band folded.

Following solo touring and recording, Marriott went on to an ill-fated Small Faces reunion in 1977 before he re-formed Humble Pie once again in 1980. Although the resultant albums, ON TO VICTORY (1980) and GO FOR THE THROAT (1981), were respectable enough, the stardom of the earlier years proved elusive and the band split up for a second time in 1982.

Marriott continued to play pubs and clubs with various groups, usually with ex-Humble Pie colleague **Jerry Shirley** (drums). There was even talk of Marriott and Frampton working together again, but after short-lived recording sessions in April 1991, Marriott lost interest, and flew home from New York. Sadly, there were to be no more opportunities; just one day later, he died in a fire at his home in Essex. A final testament to his talent was the 1989 solo album, THIRTY SECONDS TO MIDNITE.

⦿ **Performance: Rockin' The Fillmore** (1971; A&M). One of rock's most powerful live albums. Features Marriott at his most impassioned and Frampton at his most virtuosic.

⦿ **Humble Pie In Concert** (1995; King Biscuit). More of the same, from the 70s, with the band augmented by The Blackberries in a perfect fusion of hard rock and gospel.

⦿ **Hot'N'Nasty: The Anthology** (1994; A&M). The most representative of many compilations available, this covers the choicest singles and album tracks throughout the band's chequered career.

Paul Morris

HÜSKER DÜ

Formed Minneapolis, Minnesota, 1979; disbanded 1987.

Grant Hart (drums/vocals) met **Greg Norton** (bass) when they were applying for the same job in a Minneapolis record store. Norton was successful, but Hart got a job nearby, in a shop frequented by **Bob Mould** (guitar/vocals). As **Hüsker Dü**, the power trio formally got together in early 1979, and decided to sidestep the corporate whoring that had penetrated the New Wave music scene by creating their own record label, Reflex Records. They produced some of the most vital and absorbing music of the 80s.

Their early output was ferociously hardcore, forsaking melody for pile-driver aggression. The band honed and tightened their approach, playing in small local bars, unleashing raging adrenaline rushes, often built upon mantra-like shouting, and overlaid by Mould's feedback-drenched guitar and Hart's manic drumming.

Early albums LAND SPEED RECORD (1981) and EVERYTHING FALLS APART (1982) were relentless and hard to take, although the band's ferocity could work well within the single format, as testified by "In a Free Land"/"M.I.C. (Military Industrial Complex)" (1982). The title misleadingly hinted at a political dimension to a band who, according to Terry Katzman (their sound engineer at the time), preferred to 'power communicate *beneath* the surface of their music, as their songs asked real and personal questions'.

Excessive touring widened the group's exposure, and eventually they were signed to seminal punk label SST. Here, they produced the much-improved METAL CIRCUS EP (1983). It featured Hart's first real stand-out track – "Diane", a traumatized dirge about rape and murder. The double LP, ZEN ARCADE (1984), was a further leap forward with stronger, surging melodies starting to gain the upper hand. If sporadically self-indulgent, it was still punctuated with greats such as Mould's "Chartered Trips", or Hart's anthemic "Turn On The News" and harrowing overdose tale "Pink Turns To Blue". In addition, their cover of The Byrds' "Eight Miles High", released as a single, served notice of a love of classic psychedelia.

NEW DAY RISING (1985) set a songwriting pattern, with Mould contributing more material, but Hart usually submitted at least half of the stand-out songs on each album. (Generally, whoever sang lead vocal on a song had written it.) Development continued with FLIP YOUR WIG (1985), the band's last independent release and an accessible pop masterpiece throughout.

Although they had a rabid, if narrow, live following, the band still failed to break through commercially, despite material – such as Mould's "Makes No Sense At All" (a 45 rpm single off FLIP YOUR WIG) – that was crying out for radio play. Perhaps their overall intensity was at odds with a rock music scene dominated by stadium bands. Within this context, even a relatively melodic Hüsker Dü sounded taut, hemmed in and claustrophobically produced. Loosely speaking, it may have been pop music, but it was played as if their lives depended upon it.

When Hüsker Dü signed to Warners in 1986, suspicions that they would lose these trademark qualities disappeared with the release of CANDY APPLE GREY. Mould chose reflection over anger on tender acoustic laments such as "Too Far Down" and "Hardly Getting Over It", both of which demonstrated his fascination with the work of Richard Thompson. Echoing the dark corners of the Thompson psyche, they replaced sombre and arcane Englishness with urban, American despair. Meanwhile, Hart provided the strongest pop moments on the album – his "Sorry Somehow" and "Dead Set On Destruction" were vibrant highlights.

The album drew rave reviews, but alienated the band's hardcore following, who failed to appreciate the slower numbers. Tensions within the band also began to surface due to management problems and Hart's addiction to heroin. These events notwithstanding, the band released the double album WAREHOUSE: SONGS AND STORIES (1987), mixing jazz, power pop and psychedelia, while retaining a startling depth and cohesion. Its lyrics were by turns bleak, tender, hallucinatory or filled with the charm of a powerful parable, and the entire set would act as a touchstone for a whole generation of bands.

Nevertheless, the album's sleeve notes revealed a weariness at odds with the ecstatic music, showing a band increasingly suffering from tension and burnout. It proved to be Hüsker Dü's final album, and their split left a welter of tales surrounding their demise; the shocking suicide of their manager David Savoy Jr was one likely explanation.

Post-Hüsker Dü, Norton left the music business, while **HART** later formed **Nova Mob** and Mould formed **SUGAR**, although both also embarked on respective solo careers. By the early 90s, Hüsker Dü had received belated recognition, reflected in a substantial CD reissue campaign and an excellent live document, THE LIVING END (1993).

No new releases now or planned, no remastering (pity, as the Warners' Hüsker sounds a lot less than brilliant on CD) and no box-set retrospectives. They remain unfairly lumped in with usual suspects for the Great Anti-Grunge Backlash. However, true talent always rides over the slings and arrows of outrageous fortune, doesn't it?

⊙ **New Day Rising** (1985; SST).
Hüsker Dü's first truly convincing blend of pop and hardcore introduced an ironic sense of humour in Hart's caustic hippie put-down, "Books About UFOs". Elsewhere, there's some primal screaming over the title track, and even an acoustic guitar on the poignant "Celebrated Summer".

⊙ **Candy Apple Grey** (1986; Warners).
An excellent starting point for the uninitiated, as well as setting out the contrasts between Mould's and Hart's songwriting.

⊙ **Warehouse: Songs And Stories** (1987; Warners).
One of only a handful of genuinely consistent double albums, and an unforgettable swan song.

Nig Hodgkins

THE ICICLE WORKS

Formed Liverpool, England, 1980; disbanded 1990.

The **Icicle Works** were formed by **Ian McNabb** (vocals/guitar), **Chris Layhe** (bass) and **Chris Sharrock** (drums), and took their name from a short story by Frederick Pohl – "The Day The Icicle Works Closed". Their style was idiosyncratic power rock, and for a time they were one of Britain's finer pop groups.

They debuted with the singles "Ascending" (1981), a guitar-heavy outing, "Nirvana" (1982), and "Birds Fly (Whisper To A Scream)", an indie chart success in the summer of 1983. The latter was enough to secure a contract with Beggars Banquet, who issued "Love Is A Wonderful Colour" later in the year and saw it sail into the mainstream UK charts, peaking at #15.

THE ICICLE WORKS (1984) album followed, charting Top 30 on both sides of the Atlantic, though a US tour failed to achieve a breakthrough into the major league. Its follow-up, THE SMALL PRICE OF A BICYCLE (1985), ditched the Neil Young-style guitar influences for a more soulful sound; McNabb had trailed the album by namechecking The Walker Brothers, prompting reports of a forthcoming disaster. But it turned out an accomplished piece of pop, and with a more overtly political edge to songs like "All The Daughters (Of Her Father's House)" and "Seven Horses".

A compilation album, SEVEN SINGLES DEEP (1986), gathered a new legion of fans as The Works moved into a harder rock territory, although the singles "Who Do You Want For Your Love?" and "Understanding Jane" (both 1986) surprisingly failed to chart. IF YOU WANT TO DEFEAT YOUR ENEMY SING HIS SONG (1987) was a moderately successful collection of anthemic pop songs, "Evangeline" standing out, but the group was soon to flounder with the departures of both Sharrock (to **THE LIGHTNING SEEDS**) and Layhe after the patchy LP BLIND (1988).

For a while, Ringo Starr's son **Zak Starkey** filled the drummer's stool – one of many personnel changes. **Dave Green** (keyboards) and **Roy Corkhill** (bass) joined from **BLACK**, and in 1989 McNabb and Corkhill recruited **Dave Baldwin** (keyboards), **Mark Revell** (guitar/vocals) and **Paul Burgess** (drums). This new line-up, however, was to be short-lived as The Icicle Works bowed out with 1990's PERMANENT DAMAGE, a somewhat desperate set redeemed by the excellent single "Motorcycle Rider".

McNabb returned as a solo artist with the triumphant TRUTH AND BEAUTY (1993), a collection of classy guitar songs that included the lavishly praised "Great Dreams Of Heaven" single, and a lifelong dream became reality when Neil Young's band Crazy Horse backed him at Glastonbury and played on tracks of his disappointing HEAD LIKE A ROCK album (1994). McNabb has recently re-emerged with MERSEYBEAST (1996), a far better outing, which suggests he may still be a player.

Fans of the old-time Icicles, though, will have to content themselves with The BEST OF... (1992; Beggars Banquet) – a respectable two-CD collection featuring all their best-known material bundled with B-sides, live and rare tracks – and BBC LIVE IN CONCERT (1994; Windsong/BBC) – a 'slice of life' taken from a gig in 1987.

⊙ **The Small Price Of A Bicycle** (1985; Beggars Banquet).
A classy collection of politcally inspired songs, almost all of which were good enough to appear as singles. Includes the astute political comment of "Rapids".

Andrew Mosley

IDLEWILD

Formed Edinburgh, Scotland, 1995.

"The best way to be miserable is to be really, really noisy about it."
Roddy Woomble

'**L**ike a flight of stairs falling down a flight of stairs', said the *NME*; 'Like being chased down the road by a swarm of pissed bees', said the *Melody Maker*. The band causing the UK's oldest music organs to wax this lyrical about their live performances were **Idlewild** – young Scotland's 'most likely to' as rock'n'roll stared into the 21st century.

Idlewild – named after a place in the singer's favourite book, *Anne Of Green Gables* (as opposed to the original name of JFK airport or an LP by Everything But The Girl) – was the impressive result of a university Christmas party meeting between Sonic Youth and Stooges fans **Roddy Woomble** (vocals), **Rod Jones** (guitar) and drummer **Colin Newton**.

Just three weeks into their life, Idlewild played their first gig at Edinburgh's Subway club, having taken on bass player **Phil Scanlon**. The show was, reportedly, chaotic: 'we couldn't really play to start with', says Jones. The remainder of 1996 saw the group, who, bar Roddy, had all dropped out of college, play a further seventeen live shows in and around their hometown and Glasgow. In the meantime, Woomble frantically composed songs, one of which, "Queen Of The Troubled Teens", emerged in March 1997 on Edinburgh's Human Condition label, thanks in part to some creative use of student loans.

Picking up airplay locally, and in turn on DJ Steve Lamacq's influential BBC Radio 1 *Evening Session*, this opening salvo went on to become a collector's item within two years: copies are believed to be changing hands already for as much as £50.

These early days were not without hiccups, however. Scanlon was dismissed, bizarrely, for his 'bass-punching' antics, and replaced by the even more energetic **Bob Fairfoull**. Rejuvenated, Idlewild picked up impressive support slots, including one in August at the Cas Rock Café with no less than Mark E. Smith and The Fall. The turn of the year saw Idlewild hit the studios with producer Paul Tipler to record for two separate labels. In December, Simon Williams' successful Fierce Panda Records (home to early recordings by Placebo and The Bluetones, among others) put out the 7", "Chandelier", and in January the mini-album CAPTAIN was released on Deceptive.

However, by this time, Idlewild had snubbed all other offers, signing to Blur's label, Food Records. London's fledgling alternative station, Xfm, 'A'-listed the excellent track "Satan Polaroid" from CAPTAIN, the *NME* gave the album 8/10, and all seemed set for a bright 1998.

The music world picked out Idlewild, along with Wakefield's Ultrasound, as the big hopes for 1998, but it was the former's fast-growing reputation as a concert treat that really set them apart. Early in 1998, on tour with the *Evening Session*, Roddy's possessed barefoot performances prompted *Melody Maker* to describe Idlewild as the 'best live band in the UK'. (Indeed, the band's performances were so exuberant on this tour that Bob Fairfoull accidentally destroyed his rare hand-crafted bass guitar, believing it to be a cheap alternative.)

It wasn't until April that the first Food material appeared, but the single "A Film For The Future" was well worth the wait. This dramatic offering heralded the first chart action for the group. Diverse airplay helped the track up to #53 in the UK – an impressive achievement for what was essentially a debut single. Further singles "Everyone Says You're So Fragile" and "I'm A Message", plus a relatively low-key appearance at Glastonbury, continued the curve, and by the end of October a bona fide debut album was in the shops.

HOPE IS IMPORTANT (1999) showed a band confident and proud; stand-out tracks include "S'nese", "Lowlight", and the band's first Top 20 hit, the carousel-chorused "When I Argue, I See Shapes".

As the old century gave way to the new, Idlewild stabilized and found themselves a solid place in the UK's alternative-rock establishment. Further chart hits "Little Discourage", "Actually It's Darkness" and the worried, insistent "These Wooden Ideas" pre-

100 broken windows

viewed their sound second album on Food, 100 BROKEN WINDOWS – though detractors felt that it was time the group reignited the tinders of their triumphant debut pyre.

As if in answer, the group, amid a flurry of live activity, pulled out all the stops with "You Held The World In Your Arms", a UK Top 10 single and their biggest hit yet. The accompanying album, THE REMOTE PART (2002) was just as spellbinding. The group were grown up, confident and more lyrically intelligent than they'd ever been before.

⦿ **Captain** (1998; Deceptive).
Still readily available, CAPTAIN perhaps features Idlewild's finest recorded moments thus far. "Satan Polaroid" and the frenetic "Last Night I Missed All The Fireworks" recall the peak of a band best enjoyed live.

⦿ **Hope Is Important** (1999; Food).
What the debut album proper lacks in light and shade, it more than makes up for in sheer zeal. All Food singles to February 1999 are included, making it well worth the purchase.

⦿ **100 Broken Windows** (2000; Food).
Furnishing the expected three-chord anthems are some sublime pop moments and some thoroughly polished production. The album's finest song, "Roseability", combines the group's hallmark angsty thrash with a glistening perfect pop sensibility.

Jeremy Simmonds

BILLY IDOL

Born Stanmore, England, 1955.

"The biggest misconception people have about me is that I'm stupid."

After the disintegration of **GENERATION X**, lead singer **Billy Idol** (born William Broad) moved to New York, where Kiss manager Bill Avioin launched him onto a solo career. Signed to EMI, he debuted with a cover of Tommy James's 60s classic, "Mony Mony", produced by Giorgio Moroder associate Keith Forsey. A chaotic call-and-response

Life's been good to Billy Idol

collision of riffing and grunting, it broke Idol in the States, where he became one of the earliest discoveries of then-new MTV.

With Forsey and guitarist **Steve Stevens**, Idol pioneered a seamless marriage of techno and metal. "White Wedding" (1982) was a quintessential example, with Idol's vocals oscillating between purrs and roars, while synths and guitar riffs rose and fell from the pulsing bass line. Further hits "Rebel Yell", "Hot In The City" and "Flesh For Fantasy" boosted his profile, and saw REBEL YELL (1984) sail into both US (#6) and UK (#36) album charts.

Idol's move to California in 1986, in search of new and better musicians, resulted in WHIPLASH SMILE (1986), later dismissed by its maker as 'one of the most soulless pieces of shit I think anybody could make'. His studied 'rock'n'roll rebel' image began to turn against him, and recordings started to dry up. Despite a collaboration with **Joni Mitchell** on her track "Dancing Clown", Idol was in trouble, prone to acts like trashing the offices of his UK label Chrysalis, and scrawling the words 'Why are there

no Rebel Yells here?' over the walls. Matters came to a head on February 6, 1990, when he was involved in a near-fatal motorcycle crash in downtown LA. Ironically, he was on his way to pick up the masters for the forthcoming album, CHARMED LIFE (1990), which at $1.5m, was one of the most expensive albums ever made. It was also to be his masterpiece.

Featuring **Mark Younger-Smith** as a replacement for the departed Stevens, Charmed Life contained the very essence of Billy Idol on "Cradle Of Love", but also featured confessionals like "Mark Of Cain" and "Trouble With The Sweet Stuff", as well as "Prodigal Blues", which was a tribute to Idol's father, who had dismissed his entire career. On the down side, it also contained a dreadful cover of The Doors' "LA Woman", but overall, here was a record where, for once, Idol appeared to be sincere.

The public, especially in Britain, were less than impressed. Idol's rock'n'roll lifestyle seemed to be at an end, with cancelled tours, a support slot with rising stars Bon Jovi and, worst of all, a disastrous concept album, CYBERPUNK (1993). Even with Steve Stevens back on board, the album, like Idol, sank into oblivion.

Those interested in the early days of London's punk scene might like to take a look at Hanif Kureishi's book *The Buddha Of Suburbia*, which features a character by the name of Charlie Hero.

⊙ **Rebel Yell** (1984; Chrysalis).
In which Idol becomes a rocker draped in the Confederate flag. "Eyes Without A Face" and "Flesh For Fantasy" exemplify a cold and spooky mood.

⊙ **Idol Songs: Eleven Of The Best** (1988; Chrysalis).
A greatest hits package that defines the MTV generation. Bombastic rather than passionate, but if you can't sing along to it, then you can't rock.

⊙ **Charmed Life** (1990; Chrysalis).
When Idol stopped pretending to be Billy Fury and discovered the blues, he also made the album of his career. Zero hits, simply a clutch of heartfelt tunes and tales from the Betty Ford Clinic that finally peeled off the leather and revealed the man.

Charles Bottomley

THE INCREDIBLE STRING BAND

Formed Glasgow, Scotland, 1965; disbanded 1974; re-formed 2000

The **Incredible String Band** played acoustic folk music, but assimilated elements of rock, blues and jazz, as well as Indian and African traditions. This fusion embodied the spiritual concerns of hippie culture, and for its time was an offbeat and exhilarating project albeit something of an acquired taste.

The Incredibles originally comprised **Mike Heron** (guitar/vocals), **Robin Williamson** (assorted instruments/vocals) and **Clive Palmer** (banjo). They took their name from Palmer's Incredible Folk Club in Glasgow where the band had begun performing together. Initially playing a mixture of country and folk, they secured a contract with Elektra and made an unremarkable, eponymous album (1966). Palmer subsequently left, and Heron and Williamson's compositional talent began to blossom.

With THE 5,000 SPIRITS, OR THE LAYERS OF THE ONION (1967), they introduced their wide-ranging hybrid of styles and instrumentation: in addition to their twin acoustic guitars, Heron and Williamson played sitar, bowed gimbri, flute, harmonica and all sorts of exotic percussion, and were accompanied by **Danny Thompson** of Pentangle (bass) and one **Licorice 'Liccie' McKechnie** (backing vocals). Its stylistic fusions were quite remarkable for their time, as Indian and British folk styles, honky-tonk blues and mystical, Dylanesque vocals made the album an essential component of any hip record collection.

For a while, ISB managed to straddle both the folk and underground music scenes. In one week they appeared on the same bill as Shirley Collins at the Queen Elizabeth Hall and Pink Floyd at the Savile Theatre. Their next album, THE HANGMAN'S BEAUTIFUL DAUGHTER (1968), widely regarded as their classic, went even further in terms of eclectic experimentation. "A Very Cellular Song" incorporated pastoral ballad, Negro spiritual, shifting narrative passages backed by any combination of harpsichord, cello, fiddle, xylophone and guitar, a short ska section, and a hymn-like, mantric chorus. ISB's most successful album commercially as well as artistically, it reached #5 in the UK charts.

Also released in 1968, the double album WEE TAM AND THE BIG HUGE was nearly as brilliant, but at times fell into the pretentiousness that had always been latent in ISB. Highlights included the eerie and suggestive "The Circle Is Unbroken".

The band were now at the peak of their popularity, touring Europe and making their first US appearance at the Fillmore West in San Francisco. Liccie began playing violin in addition to her backing vocals and **Rosie Simpson** became the group's full-time bassist. Both were proficient musicians, as well as being Heron's and Williamson's partners. Rosie later went on to become Mayor of Aberystwyth – an event probably unconnected with the time she spent in the band.

ISB's involvement in the alternative arts scene then led to the 1970 album U which was the soundtrack to a stage-show which ran at London's Roundhouse Theatre before touring the USA. The music was good but the acting, dancing and choreography were terrible and arguably damaged their reputation. In 1971, ISB moved to Island Records and recorded BE GLAD FOR THE SONG HAS NO ENDING, the soundtrack for a film which combined concert footage with fantasy sequences.

As ISB became more cultish, their albums showed a gradual loss of creativity, though LIQUID ACROBAT AS REGARDS THE AIR (1971), made as a trio in Simpson's absence, recaptured some of the old inspiration and added reggae and traditional fiddle music to their repertoire. The band acquired an extra vocalist, **Malcolm Le Maistre**, for EARTHSPAN (1972), and **Gerard Dott** (keyboards/saxophone/clarinet) joined for NO RUINOUS FEUD (1973). ISB adopted conventional rock instruments for this and their final album, HARD ROPE AND SILKEN TWINE (1974), after which Heron and Williamson announced the end of their musical partnership.

Williamson began studying Celtic folklore and formed the harp-based **Merry Band**. He is now a highly respected Celtic storyteller on the festival circuit and plays the odd acoustic set. Pig's Whisker Music have recently reissued some of his non-ISB work; THE MERRY BAND'S FAREWELL CONCERT AT MCCABE'S, DREAM JOURNALS 66–76 and MIRRORMAN'S SEQUENCES 61–66. Heron, who had made a solo album whilst with ISB – SMILING MEN WITH BAD REPUTATIONS – continued in a similar electric folk vein with a new band called Mike Heron's Reputation, and a series of solo albums, the most recent of which, WHERE THE MYSTICS SWIM (1996) showed him returning to a style reminiscent of the ISB. After the welcome reissue in 1998 of BE GLAD FOR THE SONG HAS NO ENDING (Edsel), the soundtrack to their 1969 in-concert film/documentary, the group reformed for 2000's *Peel Sessions Live* at London's Royal Albert Hall. Now minus Williamson, replaced by multi-instrumentalist and singer **Fluff**, the group renamed themselves **incrediblestringband2003** and are today back on the road.

The Hangman's Beautiful Daughter
(1968; Hannibal).
ISB at their best. Exuberant, continually surprising, and intensely mystical, this is one of the quintessential works to emerge from late-60s British hippie culture.

Martin Haggerty

INCUBUS

Formed Calabasas, California, 1991.

What is alternative rock? Are we talking grunge? Nu-metal perhaps? Or how about rap-metal? For **Incubus** it is all these things and more. They love to be uncategorizable in a world that loves to pigeonhole. Formed by high-school mates **Brandon Boyd** (vocals), **Mike Einziger** (guitars), **Alex Katunich** (bass) and **Jose Pasillas** (drums), the band went through their rock rites-of-passage, years were spent honing their live skills and building a fan base on the Californian club scene, but for the most part Incubus were searching for a sound they could call their own.

But derivation was the order of the day. In 1995 FUNGUS AMONGUS emerged as a rough and ready amalgam of funk, rock, and wilful weirdness that merely hinted at what Incubus would go on to produce. Likewise the ENJOY INCUBUS mini-LP – also featuring **DJ Lyfe** and bassist **Dirk Lance** – showcased a band with a singer whose vocal style came uncomfortably close to that of Faith No More crooner Mike Patton and a guitarist keen to make like the Chili Peppers' John Frusciante.

Much better and far more accomplished was S.C.I.E.N.C.E (1997), which ironed out the wrinkles and gave the band a much smoother, groove-orientated sound. Splashes of funk were offset with driving riffage and spiky turntable shrapnel, while, Boyd's lyrics began to encompass a more intellectual world-view than your average rock star. A staggering two years of touring followed, during which Incubus shared the stage with the cream of both the new and the old – Limp Bizkit, Ozzy Osbourne, Black Sabbath and Korn among many others.

Incubus's next album proved to be their breakthrough and the moment when they transcended comparisons with their peers and carved a niche for themselves. The title, MAKE YOURSELF (1999), alluded to the general direction of lyrics that encouraged their fans to shape and direct their own destinies – not exactly an original message,

but light years ahead of the girls, booze, and angst peddled by the competition. Boyd had also progressed immeasurably as singer, rather than simply remaining a vocalist who indulged in occasional snappy rapping. The overall success of the set was also, doubtless, down to the sterling production of **Scott Litt** and the introduction of **DJ Kilgore**. A slot at 2000's Ozzfest ensured the album was still floating buoyantly in the charts a year later.

The next logical step was for Incubus to ditch the studio environment and apply the free-spirited approach to life they espoused to their own recordings. Hence MORNING VIEW (2001) was recorded in a Malibu mansion with breathtaking views – beauty to feed the creative spirit. A free-flowing and fluid exercise in musical invention, MORNING VIEW was the band's most fully realized take on their artistic vision.

⊙ **Make Yourself** (1999; Immortal/Epic).
Poetic, positive and powerful, Incubus finally take all their disparate influences and create something cohesively dazzling.

REDFERNS

Incubus's Brandon Boyd

Morning View (2001; Immortal/Epic).
A spontaneous and immediate sounding album, absolutely dripping with melody – the rocky bits rock very hard and the relaxed bits are quite gorgeous.

Essi Berelian

INDIGO GIRLS

Formed Atlanta, Georgia, 1986.

Singer-songwriters **Amy Ray** and **Emily Saliers** released early self-financed singles, but major-label interest in the literate songs and acoustic guitar performances of **Indigo Girls** was nonexistent until the successes of Suzanne Vega and Tracy Chapman. Signed to Columbia in 1987, their debut LP, STRANGE FIRE, employed their trademark harmonies but was slight and unfocused in comparison to later works.

INDIGO GIRLS (1989), produced by Scott Litt, and featuring contributions from R.E.M. and Hothouse Flowers, was a strong acoustic collection, their delicately melodic songs covering familiar folkie themes with style and intelligence. Netting a Grammy for *Best Folk Recording*, and scoring a hit single with "Closer To Fine", INDIGO GIRLS sailed into the US Top 30.

NOMADS INDIANS SAINTS (1990), which featured contributions from **Mary Chapin Carpenter**, **Jim Keltner** and **Benmont Tench**, failed to go Top 40, but the Girls threw themselves into intensive touring schedules, often at benefit performances. A fine concert recording, BACK ON THE BUS Y'ALL, was released in 1991.

As they slowly connected with an army of American thirty-somethings, the arrival of RITES OF PASSAGE (1992) showed Indigo Girls' familiar formula in its most favourable light yet. Sterling guest performances from Sara Lee (bass; ex-Gang Of Four), **Lisa Germano** (violin) and **JACKSON BROWNE** – plus strong production, complex arrangements and well-written songs – earned a gold disc. The similarly well-crafted SWAMP OPHELIA even cracked the US Top 10 in 1994, followed by 1200 CURFEWS (1995; Epic), a gorgeous collection of spirited live performances recorded during the Swamp Ophelia tour.

A timely compilation, 4.5 (1995), confirmed their good taste, and SHAMING THE SUN (1997; Epic) confirmed their reputation as the folkies it was cool for intellectuals to like, but fresh inspiration may soon be necessary. 1999's COME ON NOW SOCIAL was a little overambitious, trying to be too many things to too many people, but 2002's BECOME YOU was a beautifully crafted return to form.

Indigo Girls (1989; Epic).
Two voices, two guitars, great songs – the definitive Indigo Girls album.

Rites Of Passage (1992; Epic).
Marimbas, Irish fiddles, cellos and fine material are thrown into the familiar brew with excellent results.

Become You (2002; Epic).
A beautiful document of complex emotions, politics and an almost perfect unification of voices and instruments.

Neil Blackmore

INKUBUS SUKKUBUS

Formed Cheltenham, England, 1989.

"I was always a dreamy child ... I tended to drift off into dream worlds filled with goblins and witches." Candia Ridley

Tony McKormick (guitars/vocals/keyboards/programming) and **Candia Ridley** (lead vocal) – originally art college students with a dark, yet optimistic musical vision for the world – are the heart and soul of **Inkubus Sukkubus**. The pair, intrigued by paganism and vampirism, and followers of the Wiccan religion, infuse their lyrics with Candia's unbridled sensuality, coupled with pagan and gothic elements. The band was formed as **Incubus Succubus** in the summer of 1989.

The first full-length album, BELTAINE, taking its title from the first single, was released on cassette in 1991. Joined by **Bob Gardner** (drums), **Adam Henderson** (bass), **Kevin Gladwell** and **Jake Ridley** (both play the bodhrán), it was a dark look at persecution and damnation with songs such as "Burning Times", "Church Of Madness" and "In Defence". BELLADONNA & ACONITE (1993), their second release, further explored their fascination with the netherworld and introduced **Howard Worf** (bass), and **Jamie Gardner** (keyboards). Soon, Incubus Succubus were being hailed as Britain's premier pagan rock band.

Having formed their own label in 1993, they began releasing music more frequently. WYTCHES (1994) was a mixture of new songs and material from their first album. CORN KING was a five-song EP released in 1994, followed by the uneven HEARTBEAT OF THE EARTH (1995) which was recorded by the band's original line-up.

For numerological reasons, the band was reborn as Inkubus Sukkubus in 1995 and went through a musical metamorphisis – a different line-up included a drum machine and full backing from sequencers, giving the live band a richness and diversity of sound and emotion previously found in the recorded band.

Appearances on compilation CDs followed, including a cover version of "Spellbound" on the tribute album SIOUXSIE AND THE BANSHEES: REFLECTIONS IN THE LOOKING GLASS (1996), and "Vampyre Erotica" was included on the third and final Vampire Guild release WHAT SWEET MUSIC... R.I.P. Having built a recording studio in their home, Tony and Candia recorded their fifth album, VAMPYRE EROTICA (1997), whose highlights included a masterful cover of The Rolling Stones' song "Paint It Black", the ballad "Sweet Morpheus", and "Whore Of Babylon", notable for Candia's sublime screams.

Very much still on the road, Inkubus Sukkubus continue to tour, reissue their catalogue and present new material (most recently 2002's SUPERNATURE).

The future is wide open to their refreshing, albeit surreal, musical landscapes.

● **Belladonna & Aconite** (1993; Resurrection Records).
The fourteen-song CD contains three bonus tracks from BELTAINE, their first LP, as well as the powerful title track.

● **Vampyre Erotica** (1997; Resurrection Records).
As well as the magnificent title track, this album features "Paint It Black" and "Hell-Fire".

David Morgan

INSPIRAL CARPETS

Formed Oldham, England, 1987; disbanded 1995; reformed 2003.

"When we get to the gates of Heaven we'll get our just rewards. Saint Peter will call us up and say, 'Inspiral Carpets – good songwriters, strong melodies and fine harmonies. Dodgy middle-eights, but we'll let you off. In you go.'" Clint Boon

The early days of **Inspiral Carpets** saw a number of personnel changes, but the first line-up to record consisted of **Clint Boon** (organ), **Craig Gill** (drums), **Graham Lambert** (guitars), **Dave Swift** (bass) and **Steve Holt** (vocals). They quickly gained a local live reputation, so it came as no surprise when their debut EP, PLANECRASH, sold out almost immediately on its release in the summer of 1988. Unfortunately, a second EP was delayed by the bankruptcy of their label's distributor Red Rhino.

As the band set up its own label, Cow Records, Holt and Swift left at the end of 1988, and were replaced by **Tom Hingley** (vocals) and **Martin 'Bungle' Walsh** (bass). The TRAINSURFING EP (1989), containing four slabs of Hammond-driven pop, was followed that summer by the live favourite "Joe", and the punky garage of "Find Out Why". Now the third biggest band on the 'Madchester' scene, behind The Stone Roses and Happy Mondays, Inspiral Carpets were in danger of being more famous for their merchandise than their music: one T-shirt bore the legend 'cool as fuck', and landed several fans under arrest for breaching the obscenity laws.

The release of "Move" (1989) fell just short of the charts, but a deal with Mute Records led to a big hit in early 1990 with the plaintive ballad "This Is How It Feels". Unlike their 'Madchester' contemporaries, the Inspirals had never really dabbled with dance rhythms, but a lively, melodic debut album, LIFE (1990), fitted the times perfectly, and only just missed #1 in the UK charts.

"She Comes In The Fall", another slice of great pop, married a marching beat to a frenetic tune, and coincided with several headlining dates, including top billing at the 1990 Reading Festival, where they were surrounded by an explosion of fireworks and a full troop of drum majorettes. They built on this following with the subtler EP ISLAND HEAD in late 1990, but anyone expecting a jaunty second album on the basis of the single "Caravan" was in for a surprise. THE BEAST INSIDE (1991) hit the UK Top 10, but its darker moods, epic ballads and grisly lyrics met with very mixed reviews.

The organ-dominated "Dragging Me Down" gave them their biggest hit yet in early 1992, and heralded a move away from the grimmer concerns of THE BEAST INSIDE, but their much brighter third album, REVENGE OF THE GOLDFISH, was their worst seller yet in Britain. Fortunately, they were becoming big stars abroad, especially in Argentina and Portugal.

A long silence on the UK charts, broken only by the summer 1993 release of "How It Should Be", finally ended in early 1994 with one of the Inspirals' finest singles – the soaring "Saturn 5", a paean to space rockets, moonshoots and all manner of 60s imagery. It put them firmly back in the charts and paved the way for a moment of pure genius – they rerecorded the album track "I Want You" with The Fall's Mark E. Smith on guest vocals. The result was a ferocious punky babble that made the original version seem dull.

The album DEVIL HOPPING (1994) spawned a third hit single in "Uniform", but proved to be their last album for Mute. The group split the following year. Since their departure a sixteen-track singles compilation has been released, THE SINGLES 1995, and in 1999 a collection of Peel Session cuts found its way into the shops. 2003 also witnessed a gruelling 3CD boxset, COOL AS, and – shock horror – a reunion tour!

● **The Beast Inside** (1991; Mute/Sire).
Largely introspective and brooding, with lyrics revolving around revenge, regret and domestic violence, this is a little pompous and long-winded in places, but it makes up for it with some fine eerie ballads.

● **Revenge Of The Goldfish** (1992; Mute/Sire).
A return to the poppy sound of LIFE, but with a steadier hand at the controls. Full of busy organ dashes, squelchy bass, Tom's soaring vocals, harmony-packed ballads and more hooks than the average cloakroom.

● **Devil Hopping** (1994; Mute/Sire).
Here the Inspirals branch out three ways into all-out pop gems like "Saturn 5", melancholic slower moments such as "Just Wednesday", and punkier churns like "Cobra". Their fullest-sounding album to date, it makes their enforced departure from Mute all the more mysterious.

James Sutherland

INTERPOL

Formed New York, 1998.

New York's **Interpol** began life over a mutually admired vintage pair of Doctor Marten's – a staple for those fixated with style, and an indication of the key position of nostalgia in the band's developing image: where The Strokes pulled a fitting pastiche of New York's art-punk past, Interpol were to become a living, breathing entity nurtured on the UK's New Wave legacy.

Interpol's fresh New Wave perspective

In 1998, London-born guitarist **Daniel Kessler** was a freshman at NYU when he was drawn to the shoes of philosophy student **Carlos D (Dengler)**. Aside from sharing Daniel's love of 'airwear', Carlos also had a passion for music. Legend has it that Daniel had a spare bass which Carlos was happy to take up in the interests of forming a band, percussion temporarily coming in the shape of Daniel's room-mate, **Greg Drudy**.

Kessler then chanced upon Essex-born singer and writer **Paul Banks** wandering around New York, having lost touch with him after studying together in Paris some years before. Interpol became the act's working title once Paul had signed up, with the name coming from his own childhood nickname.

The following two years were spent in dingy city rehearsal rooms, where the band developed their Northern European Urban style: hours were spent nurturing the angular sound for which the band would be praised. But so singular was the creative vision that not all members were comfortable with it: Drudy left 'for artistic reasons' in April 2000, to be replaced by yet another former acquaintance of Kesslers, drummer **Samuel Fogarino**.

Containing three tracks that had originally appeared on a 1999 Interpol demo cassette, "fukd id #3" emerged via the ever-sharp-eyed UK independent Fierce Panda, in December 2000. The lead track was the compelling "PDA" – it was a stabbing, penetrative guitar thrust that would become a staple of the band's live show and future singles and compila-

tions. (Indeed, "PDA" and "Precipitate" reappeared almost immediately on the USA-only self-released INTERPOL EP, while "PDA" was again issued as leader on the group's debut for Matador in 2002.)

It was a blessing to Interpol that fellow New Yorkers, The Strokes, were claiming the column inches at this time, giving them occasion to rack up live dates as support and hone their knife-edge sound. Self-financed tours opening for And You Will Know Us By The Trail Of Dead, The Delgados and band favourites, Arab Strap, cemented Interpol's reputation in 2001. The band was beginning to wrest some of those headlines from their peers. By the spring of 2002, Interpol had headlined their own show at NYC's prestigious Bowery Ballroom, following in the summer with their first album proper, TURN ON THE BRIGHT LIGHTS.

Recorded at the tail end of 2001 at the Tarquin Studios, Connecticut (formerly a children's home), the debut sent immediate waves across the industry – mainly for its crisp retro emotionality. The press quickly cottoned to a fresh new version of the post-punk blueprint as set out by Joy Division, almost ignoring that what Interpol may have held in common with their Manchester forebears was far from the complete sum of the band's worth. TURN ON THE BRIGHT LIGHTS – which was mixed by **Pete Katsis** and **Gareth Jones** (of Depeche Mode and Clinic fame) – had real guts; it was a taut, filler-free compendium of the band's compact output to date. There were many apparent reference points:

"Roland" and "PDA" favoured a Joy Division sound that recalled UNKNOWN PLEASURES, the brooding sci-fi love song "Obstacle 1" was drenched in the sound of Television circa MARQUEE MOON, and "Say Hello To The Angels" boasted a near-jaunty Johnny Marr-style riff. The album – the title, a lyric from the band's wonderful "NYC" – had shifted almost 70,000 copies by the end of 2002.

Before long, theirs was the new whisper in the air of New York's music scene. They were no longer alone: LCD Soundsystem were gathering up and fielding a few Mark E Smith-isms, while Radio 4 and The Rapture had begun to serve stinging slices of Gang of Four/ACR-styled agit-funk.

So let's hope the US rock scene is ready for another seismic shift. If so, Interpol could become the first stadium art-rock band of the new millennium.

⊙ **Turn On The Bright Lights** (2002; Matador).
As much the askew smile of Bowie circa BERLIN as it is Joy Division. However, add Interpol's unerring style and hugely disquieting sense of delivery, and you have 2002's most arresting debut.

Jeremy Simmonds

INXS

Formed Sydney, Australia, 1979.

"I love being famous ... it makes me feel wanted and loved and noticed." Michael Hutchence

As a Sydney high-school boy, **Michael Hutchence** (vocals) was prone to getting into fights, one of which was broken up by **Andrew Farriss** (guitar/keyboards). Thereafter, the two were united, and, finding a shared love of music, they formed a band, **The Farriss Brothers**, with **Jon** (drums) and **Tim Farriss** (lead guitar), **Kirk Pengilly** (saxophone/guitar) and **Garry Beers** (bass). Extensive touring of the pub-rock circuit followed before they became **INXS** in 1979.

In May 1980 their debut single, "Simple Simon (We Are The Vegetables)", was released. Heavily influenced by ska and punk, it was notable mainly for its title, but their first Australian hit, the standard rock tune "Just Keep Walking", followed soon afterwards, and won a legion of hard-rock fans for the debut LP, INXS (1980). A second hit album, UNDERNEATH THE COLOURS, surfaced in 1981, previewed by the single, "Stay Young". Throughout this time, INXS continued to tour, often playing seven nights a week, sweating their way through every Australian hellhole, gaining fans as they went.

It was the third LP, SHABOOH SHOOBAH (1982), that introduced INXS's 'dance rock' element, and supported by a world tour it became a worldwide hit. Then in 1983 they signed to Atlantic in America, and – helped in no small part by Hutchence's feline looks – gained heavy MTV rotation with the single, "The One Thing", which reached the US Top 30.

Produced by Nile Rodgers, the sultry, whispering "Original Sin" (1984) went #1 in several countries, and became their first minor hit in the UK, to be followed by the album THE SWING (1984). Stadium-sized success was not far away by July 1985, when the band played at the Sydney leg of Live Aid, but it was the release of LISTEN LIKE THIEVES (1985) that catapulted INXS into the superleague. By this time, Hutchence had become the preening, posturing frontman, a perpetual party-goer with one model after another on his arm, though somehow he also found time to make a surprisingly effective acting debut in the movie *Dogs In Space*. The rest of the band, private family men, faded in the dazzle of Michael's glory, and the frontman's fame was underlined by the release of KICK (1987), an album that secured global success. Boosted by a world tour, it went on to sell ten million copies worldwide, while in September 1988 the band swept the board at the MTV awards.

INXS took a sabbatical at the end of 1988, enabling Hutchence to join forces with **Ian 'Ollie' Olsen** in the duo **Max Q**. An album of the same name appeared in late 1989, before INXS returned in 1990 with the "Suicide Blonde" single and album X. Hutchence had now discovered his own 'suicide blonde' in the form of the previously squeaky-clean **KYLIE MINOGUE**. Another year-long tour spawned the live LP, LIVE BABY LIVE (1991), but WELCOME TO WHEREVER YOU ARE (1992) was a clear attempt by the band at something different, including a sixty-piece orchestra on The Beatles soundalike hit, "Baby Don't Cry".

Trying to return to their rock roots, INXS began a tour of the dives they were forced to play in their early days, from which background emerged the raw, stripped-down rocking album, FULL MOON, DIRTY HEARTS (1993). It was not a critical or commercial success, and prompted the release of INXS: THE GREATEST HITS (1994), which contained the new song, "The Strangest Party". The band took a break from the studio and the stadium, and Hutchence was once again a subject of the tabloid gossip columns. His relationship with Danish supermodel Helena Christiansen ended, as he became known as the man who broke up the marriage of Bob Geldof and TV presenter Paula Yates.

ELEGANTLY WASTED (1997) was another formulaic, guitar-driven, good-times album, with Hutchence again getting most of the attention. His unexpected death in an Australian hotel room in November 1997, where he was staying while rehearsing with the band for a planned tour, saw him once again grabbing headlines around the world.

Since Hutch's death, INXS have played occasional shows with the likes of **Jimmy Barnes**, **Terence Trent D'Arby** and, most recently, **Jon Stevens** (of Noiseworks) taking centre stage. With an album of new material expected soon, it looks like the INXS story is likely to run and run.

⊙ **Kick** (1987; Mercury/ Atlantic).
A funky, confident collection, containing such hits as "Need You Tonight", "New Sensation" and "Devil Inside".

Welcome To Wherever You Are (1992; Mercury/
Atlantic).
INXS attempt to throw off their rock-god postures in favour of
experimentalism. Patchy in places, but it showed an
admirable willingness to escape the stadium-rock genre.

Shine Like It Does - INXS Anthology (2001;
WEA/Rhino).
A great double-CD collection of singles and remixes.

Maxine McCaghy

IRON BUTTERFLY

Formed San Diego, California, 1966; disbanded
1971; re-formed briefly 1974–75, 1983 and 1988.

It is widely believed that the term 'heavy metal' was
coined to describe the less than delicate sound of
Iron Butterfly, a band vilified when they first
emerged and still not accorded the respect they
deserve. Whereas Led Zeppelin and other metal gods
took their pioneering heavy sound and made it tighter
and sharper, Iron Butterfly turned out to be more of
an evolutionary dead end than a seminal influence.

The band was founded by **Doug Ingle**, who had
learned the organ from his father (who played in the
local church in San Diego), together with drummer
Ron Bushy, singer **Darryl DeLoach**, guitarist **Jerry
Weis** and bassist **Jerry Penrod**. Removing to Los
Angeles, they played the local clubs and cut an organ-
dominated album for Atlantic, HEAVY (1967), which
spent the best part of a year in the charts on the back
of a touring schedule in support of The Doors.
Penrod and Weis soon left to form Rhinoceros, as did
DeLoach, to be replaced by bassist **Lee Dorman** and
17-year-old guitarist **Erik Braunn**.

Iron Butterfly's debut LP, as well as the first side of
their second album, IN-A-GADDA-DA-VIDA (1968),
could best be compared with the psychedelic pop of
Strawberry Alarm Clock, especially with song titles like
"Flowers & Beads" and "Are You Happy?" The single
"Unconscious Power", which made the US charts, was
more a signpost to future direction. Although The
Doors and The Who had already begun experimenting
with extending the rock format beyond its four-minute
straitjacket, it was Iron Butterfly who made the big
leap. With a title referring to a stoned-speak of 'In the
garden of Eden', the second LP's entire second side
consisted of the crushing seventeen-minute title track,
complete with lengthy drum solo. The album was a
million-seller, while a four-minute edit of the title track
hit the US singles charts.

It was followed by BALL (1969), which continued
their journey towards heavy rock. By the turn of the
70s, guitarists **Mike Pinera** (of frequent support band
Blue Image) and **Larry 'El Rhino' Reinhardt** had
joined the fold. Shortly afterwards Braunn left to form
Flintwhistle with Penrod and Weis and the band
moved from Atlantic to Atco. Cracks were starting to
show, and although METAMORPHOSIS (1970) maintained the standards of previous offerings, the fact that

it was credited to 'Iron Butterfly with Pinera &
Rhino' gave some indication that all was not well.

This was typified by the fact that Iron Butterfly
were being swamped by a new British invasion of
heavy rock, which was quickly eroding their fan base.
Butterfly might have blown San Francisco's folkies
away, but Black Sabbath were a different proposition.
METAMORPHOSIS was to prove their swansong, and
in May 1971 they split, five weeks after IN-A-GADDA-
DA-VIDA had finally dropped out of the album charts.

An attempt was made to relight the fire in 1974
when Braunn and Bushy teamed up with **Phil
Kramer** (guitar) and **Bill de Martines** (keyboards).
In keeping with the times the music was even heavier,
but two albums for MCA – the excellently heavy
SCORCHING BEAUTY (1975) and its follow-up SUN &
STEEL (1976) – failed to make sufficient impact, and
the band split soon afterwards. There was another re-
formation in 1983 when Ingle, Bushy and Dorman
got together to record an album, but it was dismissed
as a failed attempt by three ageing hippies to relive lost
glories. Finally, in 1988, Ingle, Braunn, Bushy and
Dorman reunited for a one-off show in Los Angeles
which turned into a fifty-city tour of the US.

Metamorphosis (1970; Repertoire).
The last throw of the dice for the original Butterfly.
"Easy Rider" and "Butterfly Blew" are the prototypes for 70s
American heavy rock bands like Journey and Styx.

Sun & Steel (1976; MCA).
Heavier than its predecessors, tracks like "Scion"
demonstrate a penchant for the five-minute assault of power
chords and riffs; elsewhere, "1975 Overture" and "People Of
The World" epitomize mid-70s US rock music. Worth the
investment, if you can find it.

Patrick Neylan-Francis & Guy Davies

IRON MAIDEN

Formed London, 1976.

Originally leaders of the so-called 'New Wave
of British Heavy Metal', and now recognized
as one of the all-time greats of the genre, **Iron
Maiden** were formed by **Steve Harris** (bass), **Dave
Murray** (lead guitar), **Paul Di'anno** (vocals), **Doug
Sampson** (drums), and were named after a medieval
instrument of torture.

Iron Maiden's sound was an unprecedentedly
heavy mix of screeching guitar, barked vocals and frequent time changes, owing much to influences such
as Deep Purple and Black Sabbath, but also to punk.
Although Harris later claimed that the band was
formed to keep metal alive in the face of the onslaught
of bands like the Pistols and The Clash, the debt was
clear: the speed and energy of performances was similar, while Di'anno even looked like a punk (he had
short hair and wore leathers and studded wristbands).
Heavy metal had never been this aggressive.

The band worked up a fanatical following in
London, with their set including such early eardrum-
puncturing offerings as "Sanctuary", "Charlotte The
Harlot", "Running Free", "Prowler" and "Iron
Maiden", plus the occasional crowd-pleasing cover

like Montrose's "I've Got The Fire". Despite a lyrical inadequacy – respect for women was, notably, not a strong suit – the sheer power and volume of their delivery was a revelation.

In established punk fashion, Iron Maiden's debut EP, THE SOUNDHOUSE TAPES (1979), was released on their own label, and distributed via mail order, in the absence of major-label interest. Consisting of demo versions of "Prowler", "Iron Maiden" and "Invasion", it became a hit at the growing network of British heavy metal clubs. Its cult success, along with the band's increasing following, led to a deal with EMI.

The band's debut single, the pounding "Running Free" (1980), broke the UK Top 40, and when they refused to mime the song for TV show *Top Of The Pops* they became the first band to play live on the show since The Who some seven years earlier. Their debut LP, IRON MAIDEN (1980), shot into the British Top 5, but, while it included all their early live anthems, it was marred by an overtly 'clean' production. The biker anthem and second single "Sanctuary" also hit the charts, and caused some controversy when its sleeve, depicting band mascot Eddie knifing Prime Minister Margaret Thatcher, was censored and modified. At some point in 1980, the band was joined by **Adrian Smith** who was 'regarded one of the best guitarists in the metal genre with his melodic solos and stunning songwriting'. He stayed till 1990.

A number of duff singles followed – "Women In Uniform", "Twilight Zone", "Purgatory" – plus a rushed second album, KILLERS (1981), a half-live, half-studio album with four new tracks. Nevertheless, even with numerous personnel changes involving various rhythm guitarists, and the hiring of new drummer **Clive Burr**, Iron Maiden had already become a huge live draw across the world.

They only really started losing their way when Di'anno left in 1981. He was replaced by the far less street-credible **Bruce Dickinson**, an affable product of public-school education and army training. His lyrics were thankfully less sexist, but concentrated on the equally traditional heavy metal obsessions of myth, legend and the occult, which probably helped their rise in the US.

The story hereafter was one of consistent commercial success, and vast stadium and festival gigs. Their first of many UK Top 10 singles came with "Run To The Hills" (1982), which became an MTV video favourite, while the very patchy album THE NUMBER OF THE BEAST (1982) hit #1 in Britain. For PIECE OF MIND (1983), a platinum-seller in the States, Burr was replaced by ex-Trust drummer **Nicko McBrain**.

POWERSLAVE (1984), another massive seller, was promoted by the 200-date 'World Slavery Tour'. Highlights were collected for the double album, LIVE AFTER DEATH (1985). Some were surprised by the melodic, synthesized approach on 1986's SOMEWHERE IN TIME, but the dismal concept album SEVENTH SON OF A SEVENTH SON (1988) was to revitalize their chart profile – especially in the UK, where it hit #1 and

spawned four consecutive Top 10 singles. This incredible track record, making Maiden one of the all-time top-selling rock acts, hid the fact that, post-Di'anno, little of their original creative spark remained.

In the early 90s, EMI, well aware of their enormous fan base, repackaged all Maiden's previous singles across ten mini-albums, while the decision to package the 1991 single "Bring Your Daughter To The Slaughter" in several limited formats rewarded band and label with a UK #1 single. It was featured on the 'back to metal roots' album NO PRAYER FOR THE DYING (1990), which did at least boast some intelligent songs tackling subjects such as AIDS and big-business corruption.

Guitarist **Janick Gers** joined the band to co-write the hit single, "Be Quick Or Be Dead", and to perform on the highly polished FEAR OF THE DARK album (1992). This was Dickinson's final album with Iron Maiden, and he left amicably to pursue a solo career, which had begun in 1990 with TATTOOED MILLIONAIRE. His replacement was former Wolfsbane mainman **Blaze Bayley**.

"Man On The Edge" was an impressively hard single by the new line-up, and the chart success of the 1995 album THE X-FACTOR proved that the band's appeal was not on the wane. The follow-up, VIRTUAL XI (1998), pressed all the right buttons and was a respectably heavy slab of British metal. However, they were now in fierce competition with countless younger bands, mostly exploring speed, and thrash-metal genres. And yet, with the touring for VIRTUAL XI complete, the seemingly unthinkable happened – Bayley was replaced by Bruce Dickinson in a reconciliation most thought would never happen, with the former singer going off to found his own band, Blaze. Equally amazing was the reinstatement of guitarist Adrian Smith, which returned the line-up to that of the classic 80s albums. With the services of guitarist Janick Gers still in favour, Maiden found themselves with an unprecedented triple-guitar attack which they put to terrific use recording BRAVE NEW WORLD (2000), an album many hailed as their best work since NUMBER OF THE BEAST.

The positive vibe of the last couple of years was dampened more recently, however, by the news that Burr was diagnosed with multiple sclerosis. As a result Maiden opted to rerelease "Run To The Hills" from their ROCK IN RIO (2002) live set and play a string of shows at London's Brixton Academy in order to raise money for his trust fund. The single went Top 10 almost instantly and resulted in the band raising the roof at the BBC for a spirited appearance on *Top Of The Pops* in front of a near-rabid crowd of fans.

⊙ **Iron Maiden** (1980; EMI/Harvest).
Their first and best album from the Di'anno period, and consequently the best of their career.

⊙ **No Prayer For The Dying** (1990; EMI/Capitol).
The outstanding LP of the Dickinson era.

⊙ **Brave New World** (2000; EMI/Capitol).
The hunger, vitality and sheer energy of this album far exceeded expectations. A spectacular return to form – and then some.

Roger Sabin

CHRIS ISAAK

Born Stockton, California, 1956.

The son of a fork-lift operator, **Chris Isaak** harboured professional boxing ambitions at college as well as musical ones. The legacy of the former was a distinctly squashed nose; of the latter, a rockabilly band in the shape of **Kenney Dale Johnson** (drums) and **James Calvin Wilsey** (guitars), both of whom were to play on his first four albums.

Long years of gigging followed before a deal was secured with Warner Brothers, and a debut LP, SILVERTONE, followed in 1984. Isaak's influences and preoccupations were clear from the beginning – a countrified R&B sound set to a rocking tempo, and the theme of heartache. His voice harked back to that of the 50s crooner, an impression reinforced by Wilsey's chiming guitar which positively shimmered with vibrato. This was retro-America, a country of cars laden with chrome, of headlights in the rain, and of broken-hearted prom queens. Isaak moved through a moody, sometimes mysterious landscape, from Vegas to the voodoo of New Orleans and back to his home town of Stockton.

The tone of CHRIS ISAAK (1987) was pure West Coast smoothness; indeed the cover shot, by Bruce Weber, consciously played up Isaak's resemblance to Chet Baker. Like Baker, Isaak is no innovator, and few could claim that his style has really developed since his debut, but this fidelity to his chosen ground has made him inimitable – these acts of homage are where his touch is surest. His voice is most often compared to that of Roy Orbison (whose touchstone was also the pain of memory), and indeed there is a similarity when Isaak slips into the upper register, but he lacks Orbison's sense of drama. A more accurate comparison would be with the Presley of "Mystery Train", at its most obvious on a track like Isaak's "Blue Hotel", which is haunted by his ghost.

Even though CHRIS ISAAK failed to establish him, he was now acquiring a reputation for his vibrant live performances, complete with satin suits, at which his relaxed, ironic personality was at its best. His adept put-downs of hecklers – 'I remember my first drink too' – caused one *NME* reviewer to wail, 'Why isn't this man a star?'

HEART SHAPED WORLD (1989) was unrepentantly in the same slick vein, but found him at his brooding best in the perfectly paced "Wicked Game", which, in 1990, when lifted from the soundtrack of David Lynch's *Wild At Heart*, gave him a long-awaited hit and valuable exposure. Its success led to the release of a repackaged compilation drawn from the three albums. WICKED GAME (1991) leaned heavily towards his ballads, but amply demonstrated his uniquely moody sound.

It is apt that Lynch should have provided him with his breakthrough – he too is a dark romantic and chronicler of small-town disaster. Isaak has also pursued a cameo acting career, appearing in films such as *Married To The Mob*, *Little Buddha* and *The Silence Of The Lambs*, in which he led the SWAT team hunting the escaped Hannibal Lecter.

SAN FRANCISCO DAYS (1993) shifted slightly from T-Birds to the surf, and allowed a glimmer of brightness in his sound, while its successor, FOREVER BLUE (1995), still found him in melancholic spirits, but veering back towards his rockabilly roots. The stopgap 1996 outing, THE BAJA SESSIONS, showed an even more laid-back side to his music, had few new tunes to offer and had him tackling such ghastly 'standards' as "South Of The Border, (Down Mexico Way)" and Orbison's "Only the Lonely" as well as numbers from his own back catalogue. Similarly, 2002's ALWAYS GOT TONIGHT offered more of the same old sad songs and strums. Though he persists in producing albums that aren't bad, Isaak now seems to do little more than simply mark time.

⊙ **Heart Shaped World** (1989; Reprise).
Isaak at the epic peak of his moodiness. It's not blues by any stretch of the imagination, and he's too gentlemanly to sound sour, but these are the lush sounds of the Dream that went wrong. In short, Boy Loses All-American Girl.

⊙ **San Francisco Days** (1993; Reprise).
The title track and "Can't Do A Thing (To Stop Me)" are as good as anything he's done. The rest falls pleasantly into well-established grooves.

James Owen

THE ISLEY BROTHERS

Formed Cincinnati, Ohio, early 1950s.

One of the longest-running acts of the rock era, **The Isley Brothers** are also among the most eclectic groups in the history of R&B and soul. Their harmonies betray a heavy dose of gospel but the exuberance of their best work has been pure rock'n'roll, while along the way they have helped cultivate the talents of a very young **Jimi Hendrix** and performed original versions of rock standards that would enjoy greater commercial success on covers by white groups such as The Beatles.

The Isleys, like so many soul greats, received their primary musical schooling in the church. **Ronald**, **Rudolph** and **O'Kelly Isley** were already performing in a family gospel quartet in the early 1950s, with piano accompaniment by their mother (a fourth brother, **Vernon**, died in an auto accident in the mid 50s). In 1956, the trio moved to New York to enter the R&B business, recording flop singles for several labels before "Shout" gave them their first hit in 1959. "Shout" was call-and-response gospel, transfigured into rock'n'roll with added instruments, a fast tempo and the sheer glee of the vocals. Lulu covered the song in 1964 for her first big British hit, and a version by The Beatles surfaced on their 1995 ANTHOLOGY release.

Throughout the early 60s, The Isleys shifted from label to label; their output during this period was pretty erratic. When they hit the mark, though, few could match their energy or their sense of reckless

fun. "Respectable" was covered by The Yardbirds and would become a much tamer Top 20 hit for the American pop-rock group The Outsiders in the mid 60s. Ditto with "Nobody But Me", a winningly absurd dance-craze number that would give the Human Beinz their only big hit in 1968.

"Twist And Shout" (1962) was the Isleys' first Top 20 hit, and their early signature tune. Later, of course, it was a huge international hit for The Beatles, who probably got much of their inspiration for their moptop-shaking 'wooh!'s from The Isleys. Though the mid-1960s found The Isleys struggling and hitless, they continued to innovate, writing much of their own material, briefly running their own label (T-Neck), and using Jimi Hendrix in their backing band (he's heard to best effect on the uproarious 1964 single "Testify"). It wasn't all frenetic rave-ups, either: tracks like "The Last Girl" and the original bossa nova version of "Who's That Lady" testified to their talents at handling ballads and soulful harmonies.

When The Isleys signed with Motown in the mid 60s, it may have seemed as if their moment had arrived, but in the event it was a mixed blessing. Their first single for the label, "This Old Heart Of Mine", became their second Top 20 hit (and, a few years later, an even bigger smash in the UK), but the idiosyncratic Isleys were patently unsuited for the in-house production and songwriting of the Motown production line. Some good tracks were released, but The Isleys had no more hits for Motown, and by the late 1960s they had left to resuscitate their T-Neck label.

The Isleys wrote and produced their next hit, "It's Your Thing" (1969), themselves. Reaching #2 in the US, it also heralded a new, decidedly funky direction. Adding brothers **Marvin** and **Ernie** to the line-up, the band that had once employed Jimi Hendrix was now drawing inspiration from his thick, distorted guitar lines, and turning to material by Eric Burdon, Stephen Stills and Bob Dylan for some of their singles. 1973's 3+3 album was probably their best hard rock/funk synthesis, featuring the Top 10 single "That Lady" (a remake of their mid-60s single, "Who's That Lady").

But while The Isleys were pioneers in the sense that they were a self-contained band that combined rock, soul, funk and pop, their 1970s albums weren't terribly strong. Nor, after a while, were their singles. 1975's "Fight The Power" was a dance-funk landmark, but generally even the hits became less and less distinguishable from the R&B/pop mainstream, eventually following the disco beat in the late 1970s.

Founding member O'Kelly Isley died in 1986, and Rudolph departed for the ministry, but the group have remained more or less continuously active, guesting for Quincy Jones, R. Jones, and on various rap soundtracks, and occasionally generating side and solo projects as well. Their most recent album – delivered by Ron, Marvin and Ernie – was MISSION TO PLEASE (1996), a lite-soul workout with the odd great guitar break. Sony's Legacy imprint has recently reissued four classic albums on CD (scratched vinyl copies had been changing hands at outrageous prices): THE BROTHERS: ISLEY, GET INTO SOMETHING, GIVING IT BACK and BROTHER, BROTHER, BROTHER, with the last two being the pick of the bunch. Enthusiasts will be delighted, but the rest of the world will be delighted with one of their many greatest hits compilations.

The Isley Brothers Story, Vol. 1: Rockin' Soul
(1959–68) (1991; Rhino).
Marvellous twenty-track distillation of their best early work. Includes "Shout", "This Old Heart Of Mine", "Twist And Shout", the original versions of "Nobody But Me" and "Respectable", and little-heard gems like "Testify", the original version of "Who's That Lady", and "Behind A Painted Smile".

The Isley Brothers Story, Vol. 2: T-Neck Years
(1969–85) (1991; Rhino).
Two-CD retrospective of the funk and hard rock-influenced years, beginning with "It's Your Thing", and on through the 70s and 80s, including "That Lady" and "Fight The Power".

Shout! (1998; Camden).
Bumper CD reissue of their classic album from 1959, with an extra seventeen tracks from their golden age for good measure.

Richie Unterberger

J

JOE JACKSON

Born Burton-on-Trent, England, 1954.

After graduating from London's Royal College of Music, **Joe Jackson** spent time in the National Youth Jazz Orchestra, and then joined up with future cohort **Graham Maby** in Arms And Legs, a pub-rock outfit whose three singles disappeared without trace. After a stint as musical director for Coffee And Cream, winners of TV's *Opportunity Knocks*, he headed for London in 1978 to record demos that would secure him a deal at A&M with David Kerschenbaum, a future co-producer.

Those demos became the basis of LOOK SHARP (1979), Jackson's debut album; its jazz-inflected melodies saw it enter both the UK and US charts. The subsequent I'M THE MAN (1979), promoted by the wry single "It's Different For Girls", continued in similar vein, with spiky sentiments underpinning strong melodies. It demonstrated Jackson's growing strengths as a writer and brought comparisons with Elvis Costello. However, Jackson has always been more direct and less concerned with polemic than Costello.

Given the chance to self-produce, Jackson tried to steer away from his earlier sound with BEAT CRAZY (1980), an album credited to the **Joe Jackson Band**, which – as with the previous two albums – featured Graham Maby (bass), **Gary Sanford** (guitar) and **Dave Houghton** (drums), with Jackson himself handling lead vocals, harmonica and piano. A darker, edgier record, BEAT CRAZY was let down by an over-reliance on studio trickery, but it established precedents for future releases in its willingness to adopt other musical styles. This shift was dramatically accelerated by JOE JACKSON'S JUMPIN' JIVE (1981), an exuberant re-creation of a Louis Jordan 1940s swing-jive outfit. After the neurosis of BEAT CRAZY, the Joe Jackson Band was now unequivocally enjoying itself in an engagingly witty exploration of jazz influences.

Next came the 1986 double album, BIG WORLD, which was recorded direct to stereo two-track in an attempt to avoid the piecemeal process of multi-tracking. It was recorded in three days with a fairly orthodox rock line-up, and was a much more conventional album than one might have expected from Jackson at this stage. Tracks like "Home Town" and "Fifty Dollar Love Affair" were well up to standard, but it seemed a curiously impersonal affair. Next came WILL POWER (1987), which devoted the whole of its second side to a "Symphony In One Movement", a laudable attempt at orchestration which achieved little commercial success.

LIVE 1980/1986 (1988), a rearrangement of past hits, and TUCKER A MAN AND HIS DREAMS (1988), a big-band soundtrack to Francis Ford Coppola's film, kept Jackson busy until he delivered BLAZE OF GLORY (1989). Recorded with a ten-piece line-up, this was the best-realized of all Jackson's multi-influenced fusions. Structured as two six-song sequences, it ran through all of his stylistic phases, from the brash bluster of "Me And You Against The World" to the full-on orchestration of "The Human Touch". Recorded in a conventional studio and reinforced by a bright, hi-fidelity production, it was stuffed with cracking songs, notably the title track and "Nineteen Forever", and gave Jackson his best chart position in years. He followed it with a compilation, STEPPIN' OUT – THE BEST OF JOE JACKSON (1990) and entered the 90s in seemingly rude health.

LAUGHTER AND LUST (1991) was by-the-book Joe Jackson, and although it contained the sardonic "Hit Single", its sales reflected this. The far more consistent NIGHT MUSIC (1994) saw him extend the classical influence first seen on WILL POWER with a series of compositions entitled "Nocturnes Nos. 1–4" alongside two strong new songs, "Flying" and "Sea Of Secrets".

1997 dragged Jackson to the brink of overblown pop-dinosaur status with HEAVEN AND HELL (1997), a full-blown concept album dealing with the seven deadly sins. Dangerous waters indeed, and, despite attempts at resuscitation from **Jane Siberry** (appearing as Envy) and **Suzanne Vega** (as Lust), the album flounders and noisily expires.

A skilful writer and arranger, Jackson has continued to widen his range despite criticism from the sort of critics who see any deviation from pop's three-chord trick as some sort of betrayal. Ironically, however, many of his finest moments have been written largely according to the rules. A fact demonstrated by 2003's JOE JACKSON BAND VOL.4.

⊙ **I'm The Man** (1979; A&M).
A gem of a recording, with at least one class single and a strong supporting cast.

⊙ **Joe Jackson's Jumpin' Jive** (1981; A&M).
Much more than mere pastiche, Jackson pays respect to the Louis Jordan/Cab Calloway style of jazz – the kind 'played in whorehouses not Carnegie Hall'.

⊙ **Blaze Of Glory** (1989; A&M).
Jackson's personal musical history encapsulated in twelve easy lessons. Sharp pop, pretend classical, berserk Greek instrumental, lush AOR, all seamlessly constructed.

⊙ **This Is It – The A&M Years** (1997; A&M).
As good a starting point as any for those new to his work; containing 37 tracks, it includes all his best-known pieces, and steers clear of his more overblown orchestral material.

Lance Phillips

THE JAM

Formed Woking, England, 1973; disbanded 1982.

"There were actually three people in The Jam. And two of them weren't Paul Weller." Bruce Foxton

Though **The Jam** were apparently born from the one-dimensional anger of punk, the style and determined individuality of guitarist and lead singer **Paul Weller** always set them aside from the movement – and the New Wave of the late 70s. By the time of their dramatic finale in 1982 they had attracted the most devoted fan base in the country through the raw excitement of their performances and the consistent quality of quintessentially English songs imbued with the vanity and integrity of the working-class mod ethic.

Schoolmates Paul Weller, **Bruce Foxton** (bass/vocals) and **Rick Buckler** (drums) recruited guitarist **Steve Brookes** to form The Jam (as in 'jam session') and began by performing mostly covers in local working men's clubs. By 1976, the debut year of the Sex Pistols (for whom The Jam played one gig as support), they were getting somewhere, playing storming gigs at The Marquee; but this was also the year of their first setback – a rejection by EMI.

By the end of the year Brookes had left, but the band, now clearly led by Weller, were gaining a reputation for powerful live performances of short, fast and punchy R&B, influenced by Chuck Berry, The Who and the Pistols. Managed by Weller's dad, ex-boxer John, they signed to Polydor in 1977. An aborted tour with The Clash followed, prior to the release of IN THE CITY and its title track as a single, plus a headlining UK tour.

Weller's attitude was already obvious in the album's lyrics, brutally driven guitar sound and raw vocals. Despite accusations of revivalism and the obvious influence of The Who, it went to #20 in the UK chart, and more sell-out

gigs brought pressure for a hasty follow-up. THE MODERN WORLD, released in December, was to be the group's lowest creative moment, and it received no favours from the critics. Though the title track has stood the test of time, based as it is on one of Weller's most engagingly arrogant lyrics ('Even at school I felt quite sure, that one day I would be on top'), THE MODERN WORLD featured some of his most simplistic work, like the teenage rebellion song "Standards". Again mimicking The Who, the album closed with a cover of the Wilson Pickett standard "In The Midnight Hour".

In 1978 The Jam tried to break America the quick way, supporting Blue Öyster Cult in 20,000-seater venues. The ploy backfired (on one occasion they were booed throughout the set), and they were never to become popular in the States, partly owing to Weller's affected dislike of American culture. But

Weller in trademark Jam-days boilersuit

later that year came the pivotal ALL MOD CONS, an album that surfed the wave of the mod revival, expressing both a disillusionment with the nihilism of punk and Weller's ambivalence towards fame. Their most commercial offering so far, it was less derivative than the previous two albums, and showed that Weller had developed as a songwriter of breadth and confidence, with aching ballads like "Fly" and the stunning "English Rose" (from which The Stone Roses were to derive half of their name). "Down In The Tube Station At Midnight", meanwhile, documented a racist attack with well-observed detail.

The Jam's first world tour in 1979 included another unsuccessful attempt to woo America. Still, this was also the year the group began to make its reputation as Britain's best songsmiths. Though still heavily influenced by bands like The Kinks and The Beatles, Weller's writing was becoming increasingly politicized, as was revealed in the band's fourth album, SETTING SONS, on which the anthemic "Eton Rifles" concisely articulated the class war with which Weller now seemed obsessed: 'What chance have you got against a tie and a crest?' Some tracks were more personal, however. "Girl On The Phone" expressed Weller's discomfort with his new status as rock god and the subsequent invasion of his privacy by fans, while "Thick As Thieves" concerned a childhood friendship. The album went to #4 in the UK, but still only #137 in the US.

In March 1980, while touring in Texas, the band learned that their next single, "Going Underground", had entered the UK chart at #1. This now-classic song combined their early taut pace with Weller's maturing melodic skill and talent for pithy tales of social disenchantment. Polydor jumped on the song's success and rereleased six of The Jam's earlier singles, all of which charted for a second time. The next new single, "Start!", which followed "Going Underground" to #1 in September 1980, sailed pretty close to The Beatles' "Taxman" but, to be fair, Weller always admitted to practising the ultimate form of flattery.

With yet another UK and European tour on the horizon, The Jam put out a fifth album, SOUND AFFECTS (1981), a funkier work than anything previously attempted. With the brassy "Boy About Town", the ska-influenced "Music For The Last Couple" and Weller's magnum opus "That's Entertainment", the band achieved a consistency befitting the levels of adoration they were now receiving in the UK and, particularly, in Japan. A quieter period followed in 1981, though the singles "Funeral Pyre" and "Absolute Beginners" both reached #4 in the UK, and the year ended with The Jam winning just about every award in the *NME* poll for the second successive year.

In 1982 the band returned to #1 in the UK singles chart as the chunky bass-driven "Town Called Malice" revisited the angry urban landscape of "That's Entertainment" with a touch of Motown. The track graced THE GIFT, an album that had a

warm, 'live' rock/soul sound and sourced its rhythms from black music styles like calypso and Motown. "Happy Together" was an optimistic highlight on a set frequently bogged down with idealistic pleas for unity.

THE GIFT was promoted by a tour complete with backing singers and a brass section, but that was to be the end of the line: Foxton and Buckler were informed by Weller in June 1982 that he was leaving the group. Appropriately the next single released was the intentionally trite love song "The Bitterest Pill", a duet which featured Belle Stars vocalist **Jenny McKeown**. A lengthy farewell tour followed, and The Jam's final single, "Beat Surrender", entered the UK chart at #1, coinciding with the band's emotional last gig at The Brighton Centre on December 12.

Obliged by Polydor for one further album, The Jam provided DIG IN THE NEW BREED, a live anthology which didn't quite capture their power and intensity. Polydor also rereleased all thirteen Jam singles, which in a remarkable feat reached the UK Top 100 simultaneously. A greatest hits package, SNAP, served as conclusive proof of the band's consistent quality over seven years, although completists will no doubt prefer the luxurious DIRECTION REACTION CREATION set (1997), five CDs worth of every studio track (in nice, neat chronological order) bundled together with 22 tracks never previously released.

Weller almost immediately formed **THE STYLE COUNCIL** with ex-Merton Parkas keyboard player **Mick Talbot**, who had earlier joined The Jam on tour. Bruce Foxton released a single inspired by the life of the Elephant Man, called "Freak", and a solo album, before ending up with fading punks **STIFF LITTLE FINGERS**. Rick Buckler attempted to continue a musical career with **Time UK** before running a studio and finally his own furniture restoration business. Since the split, Weller has refused to speak to either of his former friends.

All Mod Cons (1978; Polydor).
Coinciding with the height of the mod revival, this projected The Jam to new levels of popularity and critical acclaim by combining the intensity and verve of earlier R&B work with a new maturity.

Setting Sons (1979; Polydor).
From the anthemic violence of "Eton Rifles" to the perkiness of "Wasteland", this shows Weller firmly settled in the 'Voice Of A Generation' hot seat.

Sound Affects (1981; Polydor).
The epic "That's Entertainment" is only one of many highlights of this, the archetypal Jam album.

The Jam Collection (1996; Polydor).
A fine 25-track anthology spanning the band's career.

Michael Booth

JAMES

Formed Manchester, 1983.

"James just wanted to wake people up. That was why we improvised so much on stage; it was a way of scaring ourselves awake as well."

James were formed in 1982 when would-be musicians **Gavan Whelan**, **Jim Glennie** (bass) and **Paul Gilbertson** (guitar) spotted **Tim Booth** dancing at Manchester University (where he was studying drama), and asked him to join their band. Over the next few years James made their name on the Manchester scene, with two EPs on the city's Factory label – JIMONE (1983) and JAMES II (1985) – and a tour supporting The Smiths.

In 1985, Gilbertson was replaced by **Larry Gott**, and the band signed to Sire, setting to work on a debut album. STUTTER (1986), produced by legendary New Yorker Lenny Kaye (guitarist with Booth's hero Patti Smith), confirmed them as contrary, cultish and unique. The track "Johnny Yen", with its themes of exhibitionism, despair and violence, set the tone for years to come and became an enduring highlight of the band's live appearances. And it was as a live band that James were making their reputation, building a following strong enough to see them through more setbacks than most.

1988's STRIP MINE followed the course set by STUTTER with its off-kilter folk influences, but added some simple singalong choruses which anticipated hits to come. But neither band nor label were happy, and they now parted ways, leaving James to finance their live album for Rough Trade, ONE MAN CLAPPING (1989).

The album made the top of the indie charts, but Rough Trade never saw James as a commercial band. They could not have been more wrong. In 1990 a revamped James – Gavan Whelan had been replaced by **David Baynton-Powell**, who was joined by **Saul Davies** (violin), **Andy Diagram** (trumpet) and **Mark Hunter** (keyboards) – signed to Phonogram, released the anthemic GOLD MOTHER

album and had three minor hits in "How Was It For You", "Come Home" and "Lose Control".

Then there was "Sit Down", the rerecorded version of a 1989 single which gave James their breakthrough. It was the middle of the 'Madchester' boom. They had just supported the Happy Mondays (co-leaders of the scene), and their increasingly baggy (and big-selling) T-shirts were looking like fashion items. The band's rhythmic sense and indie sensibility, present from the start, suddenly fitted into the indie/dance crossover sound that was making all the waves.

An anthem for outsiders, "Sit Down" got to #2 in the spring of 1991 and James were on a roll. By now they were playing big venues, even supporting David Bowie at Manchester's Maine Road stadium, and it all seemed perfectly natural. But there was a down side to all this. The first time an audience sat down for "Sit Down", it was something special. The twentieth time, it was a hollow ritual and the one thing that the band had always tried to avoid. So they upturned expectations with unpredictable live shows full of new songs, with the hits in the wrong places. The audience didn't know what to make of it, and the press backlash followed with SEVEN (1992), an album widely dismissed as 'stadium rock'.

James' Tim Booth – All that sitting down gets tiring

IAN TILTON/S.I.N

But the big sound had gone as far as it could. 1993's album LAID, produced by **Brian Eno**, had a subtle, stripped-down sound and improvisational feel, closer to the early days. The LAID sessions also produced a series of experimental, ambient jams which later surfaced on the WAH WAH album (1994). Tim Booth recorded an album, BOOTH AND THE BAD ANGEL (1996), with the American composer **Angelo Badalamenti** (of *Twin Peaks* fame).

Meanwhile, James, still misunderstood at home, turned their back on the backlash, toured the US, and went back into the studio, preparing WHIPLASH (1997). Not the most risk-taking of releases, the album had James tentatively meandering back to the style that got them into the stadiums – anthemic, singalong rock. It went gold and laid the ground for 1998's JAMES... BEST OF (Mercury).

Although the greatest hits album was carelessly sequenced, and trailed by a clunky dance remix of "Sit Down", it was a huge seller. So it came as a disappointment when their 1999 album MILLIONAIRES did not yield huge hit singles, despite effortless soaring tracks like "I Know What I'm Here For" and "Just Like Fred Astaire". A lengthy hiatus was broken by PLEASED TO MEET YOU (2001), which marked Brian Eno's return as co-producer, but the finished product was less impressive than its predecessor, and also failed to sell in large quantities. The same year also saw the release of an odds-and-ends collection, B-SIDES ULTRA, which was strictly for the fans.

Toward the end of 2001, Booth announced his imminent departure from the group, though he hung around long enough to finish a farewell tour. Jim announced that the band would continue in one form or another, though whether they can succeed without Tim's flamboyance and showmanship remains to be seen.

⊙ **Gold Mother** (1990; Fontana).
A triumphant blossoming for the new seven-piece James. This is as idiosyncratic and intelligent as before, but into the mix come rhythm and a brassily buoyant pop feel. The lyrics are business as usual: politics and parenthood, sex, sin and stress. Rereleased following the success of "Sit Down", with that track and "Lose Control" replacing "Crescendo" and "Hang On".

⊙ **Laid** (1993; Fontana).
This looks back to the folk-or-frantic choices of the early days but with a looser, dreamier feel. Pop moments include the soaring "Sometimes", "Low Low Low" (James's surprising attempt at a football anthem) and the risqué, radio-unfriendly title track.

Penny Kiley

ELMORE JAMES

Born Richland, Mississippi, 1918; died 1963.

Despite his brief career – spanning little more than a decade before his early death – bluesman **Elmore James** affected rock in a way that few of his contemporaries can lay claim to.

Profoundly influenced by blues guitarists such as Kokomo Arnold and the legendary **Robert Johnson**, who taught him to play bottleneck, James began playing on an instrument he had made from a lard can. He spent his apprenticeship in the company of the harmonica player **Sonny Boy Williamson II**, who had changed his name from Rice Miller to capitalize on the success of a namesake bluesman. Together, the pair did the rounds of Mississippi juke joints in time-honoured blues fashion, working at sawmills by day and playing by night.

After a spell in the US Navy between 1943 and 1945, James's next break came in 1947, when he played the prestigious *King Biscuit Time* radio show. With the help of Williamson, he secured his first recording contract, and relocated to Chicago. From then on, the legend of Elmore James was created. Fixing his steel guitar with an electronic pick-up, James and his backing group **The Broomdusters** stormed the R&B charts throughout the 50s. His remake of Robert Johnson's "Dust My Broom", a hit in 1952, set the style for which he is most remembered – passionate, amplified bottleneck guitar and intense, powerful vocals. Initially James was reluctant to grab the limelight, preferring instead the quieter life of a session musician, but his attitude soon changed when the royalties started flowing.

Tasting success, James exploited his "Dust My Broom" formula to the full-on songs such as "Dust My Blues" and "I Believe" (basically "Dust My Broom" with the first verse removed). However, he was also responsible for more original gems, which were to have an equally strong effect on the next generation of blues musicians. Songs such as "Shake Your Moneymaker" and "Bleeding Heart" were later to be adopted by Jeremy Spencer from Fleetwood Mac and Jimi Hendrix respectively, while "Done Somebody Wrong" proved to be a natural vehicle for the slide guitar of Duane Allman in The Allman Brothers Band. The Rolling Stones' Brian Jones was so taken with James's guitar style that for a while he adopted the pseudonym of Elmo Lewis in tribute to his hero. But perhaps the greatest acknowledgement of James's craft came from fellow blues giant B. B. King, who readily admitted to adopting aspects of James's style in his own playing. Strangely for a sound that is so hard to master, "Dust My Broom" also appeared with unceasing regularity on the set-lists of countless pub bands up and down the States, a flattering if sometimes discordant testament to James's influence.

James's dominance of the Chicago R&B scene was unfortunately to be short-lived. Dropped by his record company when his popularity began to wane, and blacklisted by the American Federation of Musicians for using non-union players, James became ill and he turned to the bottle for solace. It was then that fate dealt him the cruellest blow of all. In May 1963, on the verge of a comeback, he died of a heart attack at the home of his cousin, Homesick James. He was 45. Had he lived, Elmore James would have certainly enjoyed the sort of international acclaim and fortune enjoyed by bluesmen such as Muddy Waters and Howlin' Wolf.

JAMES GANG

Formed Cleveland, Ohio, 1966; disbanded 1976.

Although formed around drummer-vocalist **Jimmy Fox** as a 'British Invasion'-inspired group, the **James Gang** were in reality the product of a thriving Cleveland music scene. They were formed in 1966 by Fox, **Tom Kriss** (bass) and **Glenn Schwartz** (guitar), though it was after the latter was replaced by **JOE WALSH** (vocals/lead guitar/keyboards) the following year that the band got their break. This came in the form of a support slot for Cream in Detroit, when the trio were spotted by ABC/Bluesway staff producer and talent scout Bill Szymczyk.

The Gang's debut release, 1969's YER ALBUM, included pretty but powerful originals like "Take A Look Around", "Collage" and "Fred", an inspired reading of Buffalo Springfield's "Bluebird", and several minutes of charming tomfoolery interspersed between the songs. Cream's influence was apparent, especially on a lengthy run through The Yardbirds' "Lost Woman", though "Stop" was more than over-long at twelve minutes. An encouraging beginning, it scraped into the US Top 100, and the James Gang received further valuable publicity from The Who's Pete Townshend, who proclaimed Walsh as 'about the best guitarist I've seen' after they were on the same bill at a Pittsburgh show.

Following Tom Kriss's curiously timed departure for session work in early 1970, the James Gang recorded their second LP with new bass player **Dale Peters**. RIDES AGAIN (1970), one side of group-credited hard rock, one of softer, mostly acoustic guitar-based material written by Walsh, was a total success. "Funk #49", a sequel to YER ALBUM's "Funk #48", coupled a favourite Walsh guitar riff with catchy call-and-response vocals. "Tend My Garden" resembled a pastoral Who, while the lovely "Ashes, The Rain And I" concluded the LP's gradual slope into introspection, fading out on rising strings scored by Jack Nitzsche.

Perfectly paced and flowing, RIDES AGAIN set James Gang a high standard they were unable to match on the disjointed THIRDS (1971). Songwriting was rigidly divided – four songs for Walsh, two each for Fox and Peters, and a collaborative effort on the slight instrumental "Yadig?" Walsh's mournful but compelling sensitivity was supported by Peters' chirpy country contribution "Dreamin' In The Country" and Fox's "Things I Could Be". Although

THIRDS produced a second Top 30 placing in the US, Walsh left the Gang in November 1971.

The thin and weary LIVE IN CONCERT (1971), recorded before Walsh's departure, was hardly a fitting memorial, but it was preferable to STRAIGHT SHOOTER (1972), recorded by a new line-up that barely resembled the old one in sound or substance. New members **Roy Kenner** (vocals) and **Dominic Troiano** (guitar) dominated the writing, while Jimmy Fox contributed very little.

Walsh prospered with new band **Barnstorm** as the James Gang's fortunes went from bad to worse. After PASSIN' THRU (1972), Troiano left to join **THE GUESS WHO**, and was replaced by future **DEEP PURPLE** member **Tommy Bolin**. By the time of Bolin's departure in late 1974, the band had released BANG (1973) and MIAMI (1974) on Atlantic. Fox and Peters recruited **Richard Shack** (guitar) and **Bubba Keith** (guitar/vocals) for one final LP, the optimistically titled NEWBORN (1975), but they split the following year, in stark contrast to Walsh, who joined **THE EAGLES** for the million-selling HOTEL CALIFORNIA.

 James Gang Rides Again (1970; BGO).
A warm combination of power, subtlety and melody, which jell perfectly, especially on the acoustic cuts.

Robert Coyne

JANE'S ADDICTION

Formed Los Angeles, 1986; disbanded 1991; re-formed 1997.

"Good taste stifles creativity."
Perry Farrell

Leaving behind his first band, Psi-Com, vocalist **Perry Farrell** set about fulfilling his personal vision of rock as art through **Jane's Addiction**. When he recruited **Dave Navarro** (guitar), **Eric Avery** (bass) and **Steve Perkins** (drums) from the LA club scene, he chose from the city's alternative musical elite to create one of the most demonic groups of the last ten years. The aural equivalent of a psychopath's nightmare, Jane's Addiction set about their mission to corrupt and enlighten with refreshing honesty, shaped by Farrell's perverse and arrogant artistic sensibilities, and superlative all-round musicianship.

The group's first release was the live recording JANE'S ADDICTION (1987), on the Triple X label, which succinctly displayed their unique acid-tinged fury in songs like "1%", "Whores" and "Pigs In Zen". Early live performances reflected their desire to create a hedonistic and toxic twin to the mainstream posing of LA's cock-rock scene. Their first manager was a prostitute who would greet punters topless; inside was a freak-show carnival of transsexual strippers, fire-eaters, snake-dancers and sleazy porn flicks – a mind-trip topped off by the band's skull-crushing, hypnotic presence.

NOTHING'S SHOCKING (1988), released on Warner, was nothing short of terrifying: the cover featured a sculpture of naked Siamese twins with their heads on fire, and initial quantities were issued in ribbed rubber sleeves, intended, perhaps, to protect the innocent. Yet this first studio effort, packed with looping and mesmerizing rhythms, scorching guitars and Farrell's processed staccato vocals, has become one of the most important rock albums of recent years. The beguiling opener, "Up The Beach", drew the unwary listener into the pandemonium of "Ocean Sized". There were lighter, psychedelic moments like "Summertime Rolls" and the acoustic "Jane Says", while the anti-conformist funk of "Idiots Rule" featured **Flea**, of Red Hot Chili Peppers, in the horn section. No one before had created a record of such danceable, brooding perfection, and live performances matched the album's violent and mystical atmosphere. Farrell magnetized audiences with his shamanistic poise, and baited them with vitriolic insults, while the others assailed each song at chest-crushing full volume.

The artwork for RITUAL DE LO HABITUAL (1990) also caused censorship problems. This time, Farrell had created a sculpture of himself and two women lying naked on a bed, surrounded by occultish trinkets and icons representing the Santarian religion (a belief system incorporating voodoo). The cover was banned from several American chain stores, leading Farrell to design an ironic substitute about freedom of speech: a plain white cover with the First Amendment printed on it.

The music was another breathtaking, corrosive fix. Scalding numbers like "Ain't No Right" and the British hit "Been Caught Stealing" nestled up against fragile moments such as "Classic Girl". The album's outstanding cut, though, was the rolling rush of "Three Days", an epic of emotive passion. First-week sales alone of the new album outstripped those of its predecessor, and it hit the US Top 20 and UK Top 40.

It looked as though the group were ready to enter the major league of stadium rock. However, tensions within the band, previously a source of dynamic creativity, were growing unchecked. Similarly, although the band had attributed much of their creative inspiration to extensive drug use, reliance was now becoming problematic.

Farrell announced that he was tiring of group activities, and persuaded Warners to fund a film entitled *The Gift*. Then, after a tour of the UK and Europe in early 1991, he began to organize the Lollapalooza tour, featuring a diverse cast of supporting bands, including Ice-T, Henry Rollins and Living Colour. What should have been a triumphant headlining performance for Jane's Addiction became a disaster of public self-destruction on the tour's first date in Arizona. The band members were so wasted that they could barely play, while additional technical failures resulted in a startling punch-up between Navarro and Farrell.

Although the final few gigs were, fortunately, a return to their previous brilliance, they effectively marked the end of Jane's Addiction, the band bowing out, as all great bands should, leaving their audience wanting more (Lollapalooza would continue to be

an annual US festival tour for a few years afterwards, before finally grinding to a halt in the late 90s).

Farrell and Perkins resurfaced in **PORNO FOR PYROS**, but failed to match their former deadly splendour and spectacle, splitting up after only two releases, a self-titled debut (1993) and its follow-up, GOOD GOD'S URGE (1996). Navarro had an on-off relationship with **THE RED HOT CHILI PEPPERS**, that was ultimately put aside after a single album, the lacklustre ONE HOT MINUTE (1995), for a 1997 Jane's Addiction re-formation. Navarro brought Flea with him from the RHCPs when it became clear that Avery had turned down the invite, as a collection of demos and live tracks surfaced, KETTLE WHISTLE (1997). The album also included two newly recorded songs by the new line-up (themselves re-recordings of tracks written more than six years earlier), and while the success of the reunion tour sparked rumours of Jane's coming out of retirement permanently, its members went their separate ways upon its completion.

1999 saw the release of a Perry Farrell career overview; REV included hits and rarities of Jane's Addiction and Porno For Pyros, and a pair of newly recorded solo tracks. Two years later, both Farrell's and Navarro's solo debuts were released (SONG YET TO BE SUNG and TRUST NO ONE, respectively), which were followed up with the announcement of another Jane's Addiction reunion tour, this time with former Porno For Pyros bassist **Martyn Lenoble** taking the place of Avery. A new album, STRAYS, was released in 2003.

⊙ **Jane's Addiction** (1987; Triple X).
A taut and fearsome debut.

⊙ **Nothing's Shocking** (1988; Warner Bros).
Art-rock at its scariest. An essential studio effort where the band show a versatility and a knowing confidence.

⊙ **Ritual De Lo Habitual** (1990; Warner Bros).
Music with as much colour and style as the perverse cover art – "Three Days" is worth the admission price alone.

Essi Berelian

JAPAN

Formed London, 1974; disbanded 1982; re-formed briefly 1991.

"I'm neither ashamed nor proud of what Japan did, it's just history." David Sylvian

Brothers **DAVID SYLVIAN** (vocals/lyrics/guitar) and **Steve Jansen** (drums) formed **Japan** with schoolfriends **Mick Karn** (bass) and **Richard Barbieri** (keyboards). They played some disastrous early gigs while still at school, but got serious around 1977, after adding **Rob Dean** (guitar). London's music business was wrestling with its confusion over the burgeoning punk rock scene, and Japan's curious glam-metal funk was not the most obvious product. However, the band won a talent contest sponsored by the German Ariola-Hansa label, and secured a recording deal.

The result was ADOLESCENT SEX, released in 1978 to universal derision, alongside a single – a glam thrash through Barbra Streisand's "Don't Rain On My Parade" – that reflected a deeply uncertain musical direction. Still, Ariola showed faith, financing and releasing OBSCURE ALTERNATIVES (1978), a small improvement, with a quiet instrumental, "The Tenant", that pointed to Japan's later musical direction.

The band seemed doomed to a life of brief obscurity but someone had the idea of sending them on tour to their namesake country. Japan loved them, and even bought the records in chart quantities. It was a lifeline, which saw them through another dismal experiment, attempting disco on the Giorgio Moroder-produced single, "Life In Tokyo" (1979), before their distinctive sound began to emerge on their third LP, QUIET LIFE.

Recorded with Roxy Music producer John Punter at the helm, QUIET LIFE (1980) saw Dean's guitar toned down in favour of Barbieri's synthesizer, and Sylvian's voice shifted from the strangulated screeching of the debut to a style reminiscent of Bryan Ferry. The band had also changed image, with suave suits and a debonair stance replacing the gaudy clothes and cocky attitude. The album was well received in Britain – where New Romanticism was tossing its pretty head – and made a modest chart appearance at #53.

Hansa's patience was exhausted, however, and it was Virgin who underwrote the fourth LP, GENTLEMEN TAKE POLAROIDS. Released late in 1980, this reached #45 amid an ever-more-accepting New Romantic environment. Japan were suddenly in vogue, and their former label, anxious to recoup its losses, began rereleasing old material; "Quiet Life" (taken off the album) became their first UK Top 20 single in August 1981.

The band's fifth and final album, TIN DRUM (reissued 1998; Virgin), was released later that year. Japan's unique sound had by now become rooted on the synthesizer, which caused Dean's departure before recording began. However, the new style was held together perfectly by Karn's melodic bass and Jansen's tightly structured drumming style. The years spent in the Far East had also proved highly influential, both musically and lyrically, on the likes of "Visions Of China". As 1982 progressed, Japan's stock soared, with Virgin and Hansa releases competing for chart placings. The eerie "Ghosts" became a UK Top 5 hit single, and manager Napier-Bell (he of Wham! fame) contemplated world domination.

However, the seeds of Japan's demise had been sown. All four band members were working on solo projects, and some were reportedly dissatisfied with Sylvian's dictatorial ways. Sylvian, for his part, had become increasingly uncomfortable with the demands of pop stardom, especially when labelled 'the most beautiful man in the world' by the tabloids, and at the end of 1982 he announced the band's break-up. A farewell tour, which ended in Japan, was sampled for the live LP, OIL ON CANVAS (1983), while a compilation, EXORCISING GHOSTS, appeared in 1984.

Post-Japan, Sylvian achieved the most success as a solo act. Karn made two solo albums and collaborated with **Peter Murphy** in **DALI'S CAR**; Jansen and Barbieri recorded two ambient albums and formed the dreadfully named **Dolphin Brothers**.

Then, in 1991, the foursome unexpectedly returned as **Rain Tree Crow**, with an album of the same name; Sylvian, to the others' annoyance, refusing to resurrect the name Japan. Ranging from the gorgeous ballad "Blackwater" to the excesses of muso-jamming on "New Moon At Red Deer Wallow", RAIN TREE CROW was a critical rather than commercial success, but even by its release, disagreements had torn the band apart again, with Sylvian pointedly doing separate press interviews.

Since then, Jansen, Barbieri and Karn have continued to work both on solo projects and with the critically acclaimed pop group **No Man**. Sylvian collaborated on an album and tour with **ROBERT FRIPP**, and then embarked upon a solo retrospective tour, playing "Ghosts" live for the first time in thirteen years. Perhaps another reunion is not as unlikely as it would seem!

Japan

(•) **Quiet Life** (1979; Hansa).
Perfect – from the guitar squeals of "Halloween" and the surprisingly sleazy cover of The Velvet Underground's "All Tomorrow's Parties", to the quiet ballad "The Other Side Of Life". David Sylvian regards it as the only 'complete' Japan album.

(•) **Gentlemen Take Polaroids** (1980; Virgin).
This is more polished and atmospheric, with Dean's guitar used sparingly but to great effect on poppier tracks such as "Swing". The obligatory piano ballad, "Nightporter", a homage to French composer Erik Satie, is a moving tale of lost love.

(•) **Tin Drum** (1981; reissued 1998; Virgin).
Using syncopated keyboard melodies underpinned by complex drumming patterns, TIN DRUM might lack the warmth of previous albums, but it showcases Japan at their best, from the white-boy funk of "The Art Of Parties" to their pinnacle, "Ghosts".

Rain Tree Crow

(•) **Rain Tree Crow** (1991; Virgin).
More reminiscent of Sylvian's solo work than any previous Japan album, the stunning vocal tracks tower over the largely ponderous instrumentals, with the notable exception of the brilliant "Big Wheels In Shanty Town".

Joanna Severs

JAWBOX

Formed Washington, DC, 1989; split April 1997.

"It's always been a big concern of ours to marry noisy aggression with melodies and pop song structures." Bill Barbot

P illars of Washington, DC's early-90s hardcore scene, **Jawbox** never had the cachet of Dischord label mates Fugazi, but over the course of their eight-year career they crafted a legacy of explosive and remarkably clear-eyed post-punk. A Molotov cocktail of jagged rhythms and literate verse, Jawbox earned plaudits from fans and critics alike.

The band's entrée was the 1989 single "Bullet Park" (featured on the Maximum Rock'n'Roll compilation THEY DON'T GET PAID, THEY DON'T GET LAID...), which boasted a line-up of ex-Government Issue bassist **J. Robbins** (guitar/vocals), **Kim Coletta** (bass) and **Adam Wade** (drums). Jawbox's first full-length record, GRIPPE (1991), was a cry of resistance, brimming with songcraft ("Consolation Prize" being the stand-out) and Robbins' pithy lyrics. Also, the band's esoteric choice of cover versions – as in their startling make-over of Joy Division's "Something Must Break" – hinted at Jawbox's willingness to step outside the genre for inspiration. With GRIPPE, Jawbox established themselves as an intelligent and visceral rock outfit.

In conscripting guitarist **Bill Barbot** for 1992's NOVELTY (Dischord), the band broadened the scope of their sonic wallop. The new partnership between chief songwriter Robbins and Barbot spawned some fine results – "Cutoff", "Static" and the staggering "Tongues", for example – but NOVELTY occasionally stalled, with comparatively ordinary songs like "Channel 3" and "Chump".

In the spring of 1992, Wade left to join Shudder To Think. Jawbox replaced him with **Zach Barocas**, a whirlwind drummer with distinct jazz leanings. The band was excoriated by many fans for their lack of indie solidarity when it decided to sign with Atlantic and spat back a searing sonic retort – FOR YOUR OWN SPECIAL SWEETHEART (1994) – which remains the band's most difficult and ultimately dazzling record. The album scored a blissful balance of hardcore abrasion and sweet pop songcraft, emerging as one of the premier post-punk records of the decade. The single "Savory" most accurately illustrated the band's prickly disposition: a dissonant guitar figure and roaring rhythm section provided the backbone for Robbins' vehement censure of the objectification of women. An exercise in intensity, FOR YOUR OWN SPECIAL SWEETHEART offered pop gilded with barbed wire.

JAWBOX (1996) was a bit less caustic, though that shouldn't read 'more commercially palatable'. Reflecting on the more temperate feel, Barbot said, 'We were a bit shy about our melodic side in the past. It shows in a lot of places, but especially on FOR YOUR OWN SPECIAL SWEETHEART. Because it was our major-label debut, we wanted to make sure we didn't make a record that sounded like a major-label record. We didn't want it to sound syrupy and radio-friendly because we knew that in our heart of hearts that wasn't what we were really all about.' JAWBOX delivered ingenious sing-alongs like "Mirrorful" and "Spoiler" while harbouring ear-shredders like "Chinese Fork Tie" (an old Jawbox nugget and long a live favourite) and "His Only Trade". As an added bonus, the album contained an unlisted cover of Tori Amos's "Cornflake Girl", delivered with customary vigour.

Atlantic and Jawbox parted company in 1997; the band split up later that same year. A career retrospective, MY SCRAPBOOK OF FATAL ACCIDENTS (1998), was more than a mere 'best of' package, offering unreleased material, both studio and live (including a rousing Peel session), as well as gathering the band's sundry covers.

Barbot and Coletta continue to run the DeSoto label (home to Compound Red, Shiner, the Dismemberment Plan and others), while Robbins has become a sought-after producer (Braid, Kerosene 454, the Promise Ring). In 1998, Robbins and Barbot (now on bass) formed **Burning Airlines**, a three-piece with ex-Wool drummer Peter Moffett.

⊙ **Grippe** (1991; Dischord).
Over the span of more than forty minutes GRIPPE maintains the agitated thrum of a hydro wire after a rainfall. A heady combination of intelligence, guts and incendiary playing, this would be the shape of noise to come.

⊙ **For Your Own Special Sweetheart** (1994; Atlantic).
As good an album as the genre has spawned. In spite of Robbins' and Barbot's lacerating guitar work, the brilliant underlying pop craft is what sticks with you. A flawless execution.

⊙ **My Scrapbook Of Fatal Accidents** (1998; DeSoto Records).
An essential summary of a fine, if noisy, career.

Andre Mayer

THE JAYHAWKS

Formed Minneapolis, Minnesota, 1985.

"I guess it's like folk music, only really loud." Mark Louris

The Jayhawks may well have saved both rock and country music from themselves. In the dark days of the mid 80s, what was left of rock music was drowning in a sea of synths and bad-hair bands, while country music was watching its older legends (Haggard, Nelson, Cash) self-destruct and fade into oblivion. A rare hope of salvation lay in Minneapolis, where bands like Hüsker Dü, The Replacements and Soul Asylum were plugging DIY attitude into their amps, cranking up $100 guitars to '11', and producing ground-breaking albums.

The Jayhawks were an integral part of this scene, but rather than adopting the punk ethos of their peers they created their own blend of country-rock, reviving the genre and the tradition of such acts as Gram Parsons and the Flying Burrito Brothers. Minneapolis native **Mark Olson** (guitar/vocals) grew up listening to traditional folk and blues music, which he would later incorporate into his own songwriting. Circa 1985, he hooked up with **Marc Perlman** (bass) and **Norm Rogers** (drums). In the audience for one of their gigs was pedal steel guitarist **Gary Louris**, formerly of rockabilly band Safety

Last. He joined the fold in February 1985, and the band's line-up was complete.

A year of steady gigging developed the band's sound, which filtered the local rock scene's aggression through acoustic instruments – a seamless blend delivered in perfect harmony by Louris and Olson. They issued a debut album, THE JAYHAWKS (1986), on the vanity label Bunkhouse Records, which included such country titles as "Six Pack On The Dashboard". It was warmly received by roots-rock enthusiasts but sounded dated to major labels, who were unwilling to take the band on unless they compromised their sound. Louris and Olson were having none of it and, while hanging on to their day jobs, kept songwriting and recording demos.

By 1988, however, fame and fortune were as far away as ever and the band was drifting apart. Rogers had left in the summer and when in autumn 1988 Gary Louris was involved in a car accident, he too called a halt. Which would likely have been the end of the tale were it not for a gold-eared A&R man at the seminal Midwest label Twin Tone Records, home to The Replacements and Soul Asylum. He heard the raw Louris–Olson demos, and released them, with just a few overdubbed vocals, as BLUE EARTH (1979).

The album was a huge critical hit, and thrust the then-nonexistent Jayhawks into the national spotlight. They quickly re-formed, picking up yet another drummer, **Ken Callahan**, and began an endless tour. But while critics raved and the band gained a cult following, mainstream success remained elusive. Cue another flourish of the magic wand. As legend has it, producer extraordinaire George Drakoulias, on the phone to Twin Tone, overheard BLUE EARTH playing in the background, and was blown away. Phone calls and offers followed and The Jayhawks found themselves on their way to Drakoulis's home label, Rick Rubin's (Def) American Records.

Back in the studio, with Drakoulias behind the board, the band recorded their very own classic, HOLLYWOOD TOWN HALL (1991; reissued 1999). Masterful songwriting incorporated louder guitars into the mix, while maintaining a country heart, and the melodic, potent mixture of sounds was given added depth by organist **Benmont Bench** and Rolling Stones keyboard associate **Nicky Hopkins**. The songs were poignant and bittersweet, for the most part, but included a perfect single, "Waiting For The Sun", which made it to MTV and the charts.

Launching into an eighteen-month tour, the band added **Karen Grothberg** on keyboards, further rounding out their sound. They then took a year break, during which members made guest appearances with Uncle Tupelo, Counting Crows and others, while continuing to write. In the spring of 1994, they were ready to return to the studio, having made their annual drummer-change, this time introducing **Don Heffington**. Drakoulias again produced and, to everyone's credit, TOMORROW THE GREEN

GRASS (1994; reissued 1999) tore the old sound apart. "Seen Him On The Street" evoked golden-era Nashville country, while "Ten Little Kids" and "Miss William's Guitar" kicked up bar-band rock'n'roll. To further confound things, the band added strings to the single, "Blue", and dug way back for a smoking cover of Grand Funk Railroad's "Bad Time". Although it wasn't the country-rock masterpiece of its predecessor, TOMORROW stood as an impressive album in its own right. The critics loved it, sales were solid, and the future looked bright.

In 1995 the band again hit the road, both as an opening act for Tom Petty and as headliners, then Olson announced he was leaving. After some soul-searching, the rest of the band decided to remain together in one form or another, though no plans were immediately announced for further recording or tours, as Gary Louris ventured off for a successful side project, **Golden Smog**. By mid-1997, however, Louris had emerged as the new de facto leader of the Jayhawks and had herded them into the studio to assemble SOUND OF LIES (1997). In early 2000 the Louris-led squad developed their shifting sound with the critically acclaimed SMILE – a radio-friendly country/rock/pop hybrid – and then with RAINY DAY MUSIC in 2003. Whether the new sound, which has moved away from more or less straight country, will keep the old fans happy, or whether this is their first step towards winning a new team of supporters, remains to be seen.

- **Hollywood Town Hall** (1991; reissued 1999; American).
  Country-rock at its finest. Any record with Nicky Hopkins on is worth listening to, and songs like "Take Me With You (When You Go)" are instant classics.

- **Tomorrow the Green Grass** (1994; reissued 1999; American).
  Their finest album to date. More varied and colourful even than the previous album, and packed with strong melodies, exemplary playing and harmonies like lovelorn coyotes.

- **Smile** (2000; American).
  At times grungy, at times distorted and atmospheric, and even at times instilled with disco grooves, and there are even several polished Americana ballads to massage the ears of their original devotees.

David Fenigsohn

THE JAZZ BUTCHER

Formed Northampton, England, 1982.

L umbered with the 'English eccentric' tag along with the likes of Julian Cope and Robyn Hitchcock, **Pat Fish** (guitar/vocals), the creator and mainstay of various **Jazz Butcher** manifestations, has displayed a good deal more depth and breadth during his career than he's been given credit for. As a student of classics, though, he is no doubt aware, unlike most of his critics, that 'idiot' is derived from the Greek for 'a private person', a master of his own property.

Born in London in 1957 but reared mostly in Northampton, Fish (real name Patrick Huntrods) started playing while studying in Oxford in the latter half of the 70s, fronting bands named Nightshift and **The Institution**, who merged with **The Sonic Tonix** to become the nucleus of the first solid Butcher line-up. The Jazz Butcher persona was not devised by Fish until 1982, by which time he was back in Northampton, writing songs and playing on his own. He got a deal with Glass Records and recorded BATH OF BACON later that year, with the help of his erstwhile Oxford colleague **Max Eider** and others. The album, despite a lightweight production, was an interesting debut, with Fish playing an array of instruments and singing a bunch of off-beat but often catchy numbers like "Poisoned By Food" and "Love Zombie". His penchant for sharp social observations was clear from the word go.

In 1984 the Butcher line-up stabilized with a third Oxford cohort, **Owen Jones** (drums) and ex-**BAUHAUS** bassist **David J.**, also from Northampton, joining Pat and Max. This foursome set about recording SCANDAL IN BOHEMIA, a fine set ranging from classic guitar pop through sing-along bar-stool blues to darker and more innovative material. The opener, "Southern Mark Smith", was a true gem, a wry piece that somehow made the ephemeral seem timeless; another version of this song appeared on the collection of singles, GIFT OF MUSIC.

Faced with tepid popularity at home, the band set out on a couple of European tours in 1985 and went across the Atlantic in 1986, where they achieved a broader fan base, especially in Canada. The Englishness of The Butcher's appeal went down well there, whereas it seemed to stick in the throat of the British to have their wackiness pointed out to them. Indeed, Fish was more a commentator on eccentricity rather than a perpetrator of it, as seen on "Holiday" from 1985's SEX AND TRAVEL, an album on which the full mellowness of his voice and the ability to write romantically without being sickly became evident. David J. then left to form **LOVE AND ROCKETS**, but the others carried on in the same vein.

After another good Velvets-inspired single, "Hard", and a decent German-released live album, various ructions led to a period of instability and a patchy and poorly received studio album, DISTRESSED GENTLEFOLK. At this stage Max Eider went solo, showing his fondness for swing and jazz on his album, THE BEST KISSER IN THE WORLD, and Owen Jones sought pastures new in Hamburg, where he has proved himself an able singer-songwriter as leader of Shakespeare And The Bible.

In 1987 The Jazz Butcher signed to Creation and received a new lease of life under the auspices of Alan McGee, who was happy to allow Fish a free rein. The first release, FISHCOTEQUE, contained some good poppy material, put together mainly by Fish and new guitarist **Kizzy O'Callaghan** prior to the formation of a relatively stable group with **Alex Green** on sax, **Laurence O'Keefe** on bass and **Paul Mulreany** on drums. A further period of creativity

led in 1989 to BIG PLANET SCAREY PLANET, which included an acidic lash at Thatcherite greed and cultural degradation on "New Invention" and a hilarious poke at the 'new Brit family' on "Bicycle Kid". 1990's CULT OF THE BASEMENT was a more complete overall collection, stitched together by the recurring bohemian sleaze of the opening track. Among the delights in this subterranean nest were the catchy "She's On Drugs", heartfelt pop ballads "Pineapple Tuesday' and "Girl Go", and the humorous "Mr Odd". The sound was confident and mature without sacrificing freshness, and there was also the killer couplet: 'I was in my room watching *Blind Date* with Cilla/When in crashed the wall – fuck me – Godzilla!'

The early 90s saw further popular US tours and continuing indifference at home, more transience in the line-up and a couple of reasonable if not wholly satisfactory albums in CONDITION BLUE and WAITING FOR THE LOVE BUS, before hooking up again with David J., as producer of 1995's ILLUMINATE. A low-key but surprisingly consistent feel was achieved, considering the album covered the full range of Fish's muse from anti-Tory rants to surrealistic fantasy and pure romance. And at that point Fish decided to hang up his cleaver and played a farewell London gig just before Christmas 1995. Ever the maverick, he took over the vacant drum-stool of the **Stranger Tractors**, while he planned a new Aquarian incarnation. In 2000 he was back alongside Eider and Jones with a new album, ROTTEN SOUL.

- (•) **Scandal In Bohemia** (1984; Glass).
  Successful confluence of styles and an interesting glimpse into the mind of Fish, with the classic first line-up.

- (•) **Sex And Travel** (1985; Glass).
  Short but sweet, featuring a more mellifluous sound and bags of wit.

- (•) **Cult Of The Basement** (1990; Creation).
  A full and rich production adds a cultured air to another collection of unique scaly creations.

Nick Edwards

JEFFERSON AIRPLANE/STARSHIP

Formed San Francisco, 1965.

"If you can remember anything about the 60s, you weren't really there." Paul Kantner

In San Francisco's psychedelic hippie cosmos of the mid-60s, **Jefferson Airplane** were the yin to the Grateful Dead's yang. Whereas you could feel comfortable bathing in the warm solar vibes of The Dead, there was something dark and unpredictable about the Airplane which was both uplifting and scary. Both were hugely influential.

The band were initiated by **Marty Balin**, a folk singer who, inspired by The Beatles' US tour, wanted to experiment with electric music and earn enough to get to Europe. He spotted guitarist/singer **Paul Kantner** at a hootenany, then enlisted folk/blues lead guitarist **Jorma Kaukonen**, before persuading the latter's friend and experimental bassist **Jack Casady** to come west and join in the fun. Along with singer **Signe Anderson** and guitarist-turned-drummer **Skip Spence**, the prototype Airplane was ready. The band's name had been inspired by Kaukonen's hero, bluesman Blind Lemon Jefferson.

They debuted in August 1965, at the Matrix, a club started by Balin and friends because nowhere else would accomodate such weird-looking people. They soon acquired a loyal following and attracted the attention of promoter Bill Graham, whom Balin had met in the early 60s. By the end of the year a contract had been arranged with RCA and their name had crossed the Atlantic thanks to **Donovan**, who sang their praises on "Fat Angel".

1966 was a year of growth and change. After a couple of singles, debut album JEFFERSON AIRPLANE TAKES OFF appeared in May, a promising start, encompassing folk, blues and Byrds-style chiming guitar. But the real take-off occurred after two crucial personnel changes later in the year. Spence left to pilot **MOBY GRAPE** and Anderson quit to concentrate on motherhood. They were replaced by drummer **Spencer Dryden** and **Grace Slick**, vocalist with fellow Matrix band The Great Society.

Not only did Slick possess a stupendous voice, raucous and angelic by turns, but her songwriting ability also proved a crucial addition to the Balin and Kantner partnership. Most great bands have a double creative input, so it's no surprise that three such prodigious talents should have gone on to make such exceptional music. The band scored their only two hit singles with songs brought by Grace from her old band. Both tracks, "Somebody To Love" and "White Rabbit", featured on the landmark second album, SURREALISTIC PILLOW (1967), which was recorded in two weeks with Jerry Garcia as 'spiritual adviser'. Although the band's folk roots were still evident, the balance was tilting towards the drug-induced sounds of "She Has Funny Cars", "Plastic Fantastic Lover" and the aforementioned psychedelic anthem, "White Rabbit", whose Bolero-style cresendo encouraged you to 'feed your head'.

The Airplane made many appearances at Graham's Fillmore West during this period and often participated with The Dead in the Acid Tests, which had been set up by Ken Kesey and his Merry Pranksters. LSD was legal in the US until the end of October 1966, and the drug's passing from legality was marked by a party in Golden Gate Park, to coincide with Slick's 27th birthday. Legend has it many cops turned on and turned in their badges that day.

The parties didn't stop: the 'Gathering Of The Tribes – The First Human Be-In' on January 14, 1967, paved the way for the Summer Of Love. In the autumn, after the Monterey Pop Festival, the group set about recording the follow-up to the successful PILLOW. Ensconced in a luxurious mansion in Beverly

Hills, the band took a lot longer than two weeks to come up with AFTER BATHING AT BAXTER'S (reissued 1998; RCA). Self-indulgence notwithstanding, it worked – BAXTER'S appeared in January 1968, and for many, remains the archetypal acid-rock album. Anarchic and free-flowing, it somehow achieved an almost divine order in its chaos of soaring vocal harmonies, complicated rhythms, melodic songs, whining guitars and inspired jamming. Excellent from start to finish, it culminated in "Won't You Try"/"Saturday Afternoon", a lysergic hymn to the first Be-In.

BAXTER'S uncompromising nature made it far less commercially successful than its predecessor and the band struck a happy medium between the two on 1968's CROWN OF CREATION. Opening with Slick's atmospheric "Lather", featuring Kaukonen's unique haunting-cry guitar break, it progressed through a series of melodic and low-key songs to an electric second side, including Grace's vitriolic "Greasy Heart" and the final apocalyptic vision of "The House At Pooneil Corners".

In the summer of 1968 the Airplane finally visited Europe, playing two legendary gigs with The Doors at the Roundhouse in London as part of their tour. The 1969 live album BLESS ITS POINTED LITTLE HEAD, captured the Airplane in full flight during this period. Later that year, VOLUNTEERS (reissued 1998; RCA), the last album to be recorded by the line-up which convened in 1966, showed a more overtly political slant, exemplified by the anthemic "We Can Be Together" and the beautiful antiwar song "Wooden Ships", co-written by Kantner, David Crosby and Stephen Stills.

The swan song of the band's most creative period, their early-morning stint at the Woodstock Festival in August 1969 was unfortunately not recorded on film, although three numbers did make it onto the album. They were filmed supporting The Rolling Stones at the ill-fated Altamont Stadium concert in September (*Gimme Shelter*), where Marty Balin was knocked unconscious while trying to quell the escalating violence.

Major changes followed. Balin departed, feeling increasingly frozen out by Kantner and Slick, who had just had a child together. Spencer Dryden left to form The New Riders Of The Purple Sage, and was replaced by **Joey Covington**, drummer with Kaukonen and Casady's more blues-based side project **HOT TUNA**. In turn, he was soon replaced by **John Barbata**. Senior blues violinist **Papa John Creach** also joined. The band started their own Grunt label, but the last two studio albums, BARK and LONG JOHN SILVER, were disappointing. The last album under the name of Jefferson Airplane was another live effort recorded in 1973. THIRTY SECONDS OVER WINTERLAND was not as potent as the earlier live set but showed the band's gradual evolution into **Jefferson Starship** mode, exemplified by an elevating version of "Have You Seen The Saucers?"

In fact the Starship concept dated back to the very start of the 70s, specifically to a Paul Kantner science

This record, comprising mostly love songs, saw the Starship making a move to enter AM airspace with silky production techniques and a smooth ambience reminiscent of Fleetwood Mac's RUMOURS. The album sold better than any Airplane album and topped the US charts for four weeks. The line-up remained constant for three more years of touring and recording, despite the personal split-up of Kantner and Slick. The two albums from this period, SPITFIRE (1976) and EARTH (1978), contained a satisfactory blend of media-friendly romantic numbers and expressions of the band's continuing environmental concerns. The Airplane were no longer at the cutting edge, but there was enough lucidity and flowing music to make for enjoyable listening.

An abrupt change came during a tour of Europe in 1978, when Balin and Slick left, closely followed by drummer Johnny Barbata after a car crash. The new drummer was **Aynsley Dunbar** (ex-Mothers of Invention and **JOURNEY**), while vocal duties went to **Mickey Thomas**, who himself would not have sounded out of place in Journey. The resultant album, FREEDOM AT POINT ZERO (1979), was the only Jefferson album to lack a female singer, and yielded a worldwide hit single in "Jane".

It also signalled the awakening of Kantner the hippie from his mid-decade slumber. The increasingly torpid melodies were ditched in favour of heavy rock, while Kantner's lyrics were suddenly a lot sharper and more plentiful. "Lightning Rose", seemingly a paean to the spirit of Slick, summed up his mood: 'I've been too long in the green fields of rapture; I've been too long without being on the run'. Those who prefer the harder sound would argue that this is as good as the Starship got.

Slick made a guest appearance on 1980's MODERN TIMES, which also featured Chaquico's only notable guitar solo on "Save Your Love" and "Stairway To Cleveland", with its memorable refrain, 'Why don't you sound like you used to; in '65, '69, '75 ... Fuck You, We Do What We Want!'. As usual the appearance of an appalling Jefferson album, WINDS OF CHANGE (1982, with Slick returning full time), signalled the appearance of a more interesting Kantner solo project, this time a sequel to BLOWS AGAINST THE EMPIRE, called THE EMPIRE BLOWS BACK, under the name of **The Planet Earth Rock'N'Roll Orchestra**. The Airplane's old hippie acolytes were there, with **JERRY GARCIA**'s collaboration outstanding on the haunting "Mountain Song".

NUCLEAR FURNITURE (1984), on which Dunbar was replaced by **Donny Baldwin**, was filled with

fiction project involving a wide range of West Coast luminaries, including Jerry Garcia, **David Crosby** and **Graham Nash**. This emerged as BLOWS AGAINST THE EMPIRE, which contained some fine early space-rock. Indeed, the artistic decline of the Airplane during that period was in large part due to Kantner and Slick saving their best work for their joint ventures. SUNFIGHTER (1972), credited to Kantner and Slick, and BARON VON TOLBOOTH VS THE CHROME NUN (1973; reissued 1998; RCA), credited to them plus David Freiburg, were both excellent albums.

Eventually Casady and Kaukonen split to make Hot Tuna a full-time venture. They were replaced by ex-Quicksilver Messenger Service bassist/vocalist **David Freiburg** and young lead guitarist **Craig Chaquico**, and the official metamorphosis to Jefferson Starship was complete. The fine Starship debut, DRAGONFLY, came out in 1974, preceded by Slick's ambitious and only partly successful solo album, MANHOLE. The accomplished keyboard work of Englishman **Pete Sears** was now adding an extra dimension, and, despite lacking the originality of Kaukonen, Chaquico's virtuoso guitar complemented Creach's fiddle to flesh out a collection of great songs, including the up-tempo "Ride The Tiger" and another metaphysical Slick epic, "Hyperdrive". Even Balin joined in the renaissance with his ballad "Caroline", and was back in the band as a full-time member by the time the second album, RED OCTOPUS, was made in 1975.

apocalyptic visions of social, political and religious anarchy under the shadow of nuclear war. Kantner summed up the hippie ethos: 'I always used to think if we could sing loudly enough ... all of this madness would disappear,' before departing, taking with him (after a court battle) the Jefferson name and old pal David Freiburg. Apart from losing its soul, the Starship also lost its most accomplished songwriting team in Pete and Jeannette Sears. Chaquico, Slick, Thomas and Baldwin carried on regardless.

Aiming unashamedly at the MOR market, the surviving **Starship** was not without popular acclaim during the latter half of the 80s. "We Built This City On Rock And Roll" and "Sara" topped the US singles chart in 1985 and 1986, and the following year "Nothing's Gonna Stop Us Now" was a worldwide hit as MTV conquered the planet. At least Grace showed she could still sing better than most of her younger rivals.

The story ended with Jefferson Airplane's ill-received eponymous comeback album in 1989. Slick had left Starship and, with the exception of Dryden, the album featured the entire 1966–70 line-up. It had its moments, but musically and lyrically fell into the pit of nostalgia. A better bet was JOURNEY – THE BEST OF JEFFERSON AIRPLANE (1996) – a compilation that sensibly concentrated on the band's 60s heyday. Other partial reunions followed over the next decade, notably to mark the death of Papa John Creach in 1994, and Hot Tuna also continued to make sporadic appearances. It all served mainly to introduce a few youngsters to the band and to prompt some forgetful old hippies to delve into their dusty archives and rediscover the halcyon days when Grace could claim: 'It's a wild time. I'm doing things that haven't got a name yet.'

- ⊙ **Surrealistic Pillow** (1967; reissued 1998; RCA). Ground-breaking fusion of folk, blues and psychedelic elements; one of the Summer Of Love's most memorable soundtracks.

- ⊙ **After Bathing At Baxter's** (1968; reissued 1998; RCA). A wonderful and inspired acid scramble that weaves a golden thread through a web of melodic harmonies and experimental electric jamming.

- ⊙ **Crown Of Creation** (1968; reissued 1998; RCA). A mature combination of drug-induced haze and crystal-clear songwriting.

- ⊙ **Dragonfly** (1974; Grunt). The first and most inspired work under the flag of the Starship.

- ⊙ **2400 Fulton Street** (1987; RCA). A pretty comprehensive compilation of the Airplane's finest moments.

Nick Edwards

THE JESUS & MARY CHAIN

Formed East Kilbride, Scotland, 1983; split 1998.

Brothers **Jim** (vocals/guitar) and **William Reid** (guitar/vocals) apparently took the name **The Jesus & Mary Chain** from a line of Bing Crosby

film dialogue. Whether fact or fiction, the choice was certainly an improvement on Death Of Joey, the name they had earlier adopted after the demise of their pet budgerigar.

With their howling, nihilistic and feedback-dominated sound, the Reids found local gigs hard to secure at first, and so chose to concentrate on their recorded output. Playing by this time with **Douglas Hart** (bass) and **Murray Dalglish** (percussion), The Jesus & Mary Chain's demo tapes attracted Alan McGee, head of London independent label Creation. Although previous Creation releases had specialized in one-offs or efforts by his friends, McGee felt that there was more to this band than pure noise: 'I had to sign them ... They were either the best or the worst band I'd ever seen ...'

As Dalglish was replaced by the equally inept **Bobby Gillespie**, McGee persuaded the band to move to London. Here, he set about getting The Jesus & Mary Chain known, with the help of fifteen-minute sets and other juvenile publicity stunts. The group's real potential was realized by the first single, "Upside Down", released to huge critical acclaim in October 1984. A Ramones and Status Quo-inspired slice of mid-80s anti-pop, it was backed by an almost unrecognizable rendition of Syd Barrett's "Vegetable Man". At around the same time, a stunning session for John Peel's BBC radio programme was transmitted, containing "In A Hole", "Taste The Floor" and "You Trip Me Up".

Early 1985 saw massive music press coverage for The Jesus & Mary Chain, and a move to Warners subsidiary label Blanco y Negro, whose offices they allegedly trashed. What with this, and a staged riot during a gig at the North London Polytechnic, the next single could not come out quickly enough. "Never Understand" was similarly well received, but bore more than a passing resemblance to its predecessor, and failed to sell in quantities.

Further excellent singles, "You Trip Me Up" and the sumptuous "Just Like Honey", followed, showing that they possessed great pop sensibilities, but the major breakthrough still eluded them. Thus they embarked on a multitude of gigs in the summer of 1985, including one with Creation cohorts The Bodines, as well as Gillespie's sideline project **PRIMAL SCREAM**. Finally, in November 1985, The Mary Chain's long-awaited debut album, PSYCHOCANDY, was unleashed. It may have sounded slightly predictable at the time, but it has since become a bedsit classic, and remains the band's finest hour.

In early 1986, Gillespie left to concentrate fully on Primal Scream's activities, and was replaced by **John Loder**. Loder appeared in their live shows (now of an acceptable length), as well as the Top 20 single, "Some Candy Talking", which ran into trouble with some radio DJs, who objected to the apparently drug-orientated lyric.

There were no such objections to the next 45, "April Skies" (1987), which drew unexpected plau-

dits from British daytime radio and BBC TV's chart show *Top Of The Pops*. Its Top 10 placing in turn led to a Top 5 placing for their second LP. With new drummer **John Moore** on board, DARKLANDS (1987) had a very different feel from their debut, but was in its own way a sombre delight, and contained two further hits.

With Hart spending more of his time working on video production, The Jesus & Mary Chain became essentially the Reid brothers plus other musicians as needed. A one-off single, "Sidewalking", was followed by a compilation of rarities, B-sides and new songs, BARBED WIRE KISSES (1988). Later that year, the Reids also turned up to provide the backing on a remix of **The Sugarcubes**' single "Birthday". Apart from the highlight of the excellent single "Blues From A Gun", the third album AUTOMATIC (1989) was disappointing, while the low-profile EP ROLLERCOASTER (1990) was largely ignored.

A year away refreshed the brothers, and in 1992 they made a brief but striking return to the UK singles charts with "Reverence". The LP HONEY'S DEAD (1992) followed, spawning further hits (albeit minor ones) in "Far Gone And Out" and "Almost Gold". Opinion was divided on the album's quality: while many felt it was patchy, others suggested that it presaged a change in direction.

This feeling was confirmed by 1993's SOUND OF SPEED EP and the expectedly 'country-flavoured' set STONED AND DETHRONED (1994), which spawned the hit single "Sometimes Always". On this, Jim's vocals were shared with William's girlfriend **Hope Sandoval** of **MAZZY STAR**. Sadly, this LP alienated all but the most die-hard of British Mary Chain fans, although it seems to have finally opened up US interest in the band.

Bored with their diminishing public profile – not to mention diminishing returns – The Jesus & Mary Chain took time away from the music and concentrated on touring. During this period, the group returned to its original stable at Alan McGee's Creation. Unlike a decade before, however, their press at this time was almost unnoticeable, although

William managed some brief notoriety in 1997 thanks to his turbulent relationships with both brother Jim and girlfriend Hope.

Finally, new product arrived early in 1998 with the tremendous, typical Mary Chain 45, "Cracking Up". This saw the band back in the UK Top 40 (for a week), and was duly followed by their very consistent fifth studio album, MUNKI. This set included some classic murky moments, as well as the hastily released (and ironically titled) next single, "I Love Rock'N'Roll" – which showed that this group did, after all, possess a sense of humour.

Tensions within the group, however, saw to it that William and Jim finally went their separate ways at the end of 1998, although fans at their sell-out gigs appeared to enjoy the spectacle anyway.

In 1999, while Jim worked with friends **Death In Vegas**, William Reid caused a fuss with the artwork for his debut album – which featured a shot of himself, stark naked, in what can only be described as a state of advanced arousal. Creation was quickly forced to drop the item, which contravened just about every obscenity law in existence. With revised artwork William set up his own label, Hot Tam, and released the spiritedly self-indulgent FINBEGIN (1999), which was followed in 2000 by a second solo release, SATURDAY THE FOURTEENTH. Both albums saw William sporting the kind of ear-splitting experimentation that had not been heard since the early B-sides, such as "Head" and "Cracked", alongside introspective lo-fi acoustic ballads.

While his brother was busy getting undressed and messing about with a camera, Jim formed a new band, **Freeheat**, who have now released two EPs and are definitely worth catching live.

The new millennium also saw Strange Fruit release a collection of all the Mary Chain's Peel Sessions – a stunning set that rekindled memories of the group's early angst-ridden beauty.

The 21 SINGLES compilation of 2002 suggested a full stop to the Mary Chain's story, but it remains unclear whether the Reid brothers' separation will be permanent. After all, when was anything predictable in the domain of The Jesus & Mary Chain?

⊙ **Psychocandy** (1985; Blanco y Negro).
An essential debut of the mid-80s, it still sounds dangerous fifteen years on.

⊙ **Some Candy Talking** (1986; Blanco y Negro).
This rare gatefold 7" single is well worth seeking for its exclusive acoustic versions of Mary Chain masterpieces – "Cut Dead", "Psycho Candy", "You Trip Me Up" and the title track.

Jeremy Simmonds

JESUS JONES

Formed London, 1988.

The origins of **Jesus Jones** can be traced back to 1986 and the Wiltshire town of Bradford-on-Avon, where **Mike Edwards** (vocals), **Gen**, aka Simon Matthews (drums), and **Al Jaworski**, aka

Alan Doughty (bass), formed Camouflage. Within two years, the trio had relocated to London and formed a band whose rock and techno hybrid would help shape the musical climate of the early 90s.

Augmented by guitarist **Jerry de Borg** and **Barry D**, aka Iain Baker (keyboards/samplers), Jesus Jones signed to EMI indie offshoot Food Records in 1988 and released their debut single "Info Freako" early the following year. It bubbled under the UK charts, but their profile had been heightened by Edwards' propensity for predicting their own swift ascent into megastardom. And so began a rise to the top which lasted until 1993, when they ducked out of view for an extended lay-off.

Jesus Jones' arrival was perfectly timed to coincide with the growing integration of indie rock and underground dance music facilitated by the likes of The Stone Roses and Happy Mondays. Their debut album, LIQUIDIZER (1989), intertwined the kind of head-on rock assault Nine Inch Nails would later be famed for, along with bass-heavy and frantic techno beats, and poppy, infectious melodies. Whilst LIQUIDIZER only reached #32 in the UK album charts, the single "Info Freako" was recognized by several music press titles as one of the tracks of the year. Edwards became the acceptable face of pop megalomania, pontificating on the benefits of fame and the future of dance music.

In 1990 their popularity was broadened by touring territories as far-flung as Japan, the US and Romania, where they played some of the first rock shows since the Revolution. Back in the UK, two brand-new singles, "Real Real Real" and the magnificent "Right Here, Right Now", were released either side of their triumphant Reading Festival appearance.

The early weeks of 1991 saw the peak of Jesus Jones' popularity in Britain, as "International Bright Young Thing" gave them their first Top 10 hit, before DOUBT (1991) hit the top of the album charts. Merging screaming guitars with samples, white noise and techno dynamics, the album met with mixed reviews, but, by that summer, Jesus Jones had repeated their British success in the US. Their first album had reached the Top 5 of the alternative chart there the previous year, but, as the Gulf War was raging, patriotic Americans had adopted "Right Here, Right Now" as a flag-waving anthem, and the track was used as background music to news footage. Such moves understandably bemused Jesus Jones, who watched the song reach #2 in the *Billboard* chart, which was headed by "Unbelievable" by fellow Brits EMF.

Immediately there was talk of another invasion of the US charts by British bands. This failed to materialize but even so, Jesus Jones sold a million albums in America during 1991, and supported INXS at Wembley Stadium.

However, in 1993, PERVERSE, the band's third and most extreme album, was released to largely derisive reviews. Concocted mostly on Edwards' home computer, its vision was unquestionably bold, but listening to it was more difficult. At the end of another successful world tour, Edwards put Jesus Jones on hold for a time, while he became immersed in other projects, including writing and remixing for artists as diverse as ex-porn star Traci Lords and Bon Jovi.

The band returned in 1997 with ALREADY, but its marginally more accessible tracks failed to make any real impact. By the following year, the band had parted with their record company and saw their back catalogue reissued in a cut-price attempt to claw in a last few dollars.

⊙ **Liquidizer** (1989; Food).
   A frenetic fusion of dance meets rock. Distorted vocals, roaring guitars and mutant melody lines instantly made this a favourite with those who thought themselves daring. It remains the band's best work.

Nick Duerden

THE JESUS LIZARD

Formed Chicago, 1988; split 1999.

Long before the band's formation, members of The Jesus Lizard were veterans of the US underground. Vocalist **David Yow** had been an aficionado of the infant American punk scene, and in the early 80s had teamed up with fellow Texan **David Wm. Sims** (bass) as noted Austin-based band **Scratch Acid**. After two LPs, Yow and Sims moved to Chicago, where Sims briefly joined Steve Albini's provocatively named Rapeman, then began working with Cargo Cult guitarist **Duane Denison**.

With the addition of Yow, The Jesus Lizard came into being, and although a debut EP, PURE (1989), was recorded with a drum machine, it wasn't long before Phantom 309 drummer **Mac McNeilly** was recruited full time. The foursome's primordial, often indigestible stew of blues and punk drew comparisons with The Birthday Party, but The Jesus Lizard

were no mere plagiarists and have consistently managed to reinvigorate a genre often in danger of extinction or self-parody.

Almost from the beginning, David Yow became the face of the band. Ever unpredictable in live performance, with his disembodied voice howling his tales of violence, bodily corruption and decay from within the crowd, he has endured serious self-inflicted injury on several occasions. This, as well as performing naked, has made for some unforgettable gigs, notably at a London show in which, declining the generous offer of a blow job on stage, he proceeded to piss himself, head-butt the monitors and demolish the ceiling.

Yow's stage persona belied the startling, if mostly impenetrable poetry of his lyrics, one of the most important facets of the band. The first two albums – HEAD (1990) and GOAT (1991) – revelled in some grotesque and provocative imagery, but the group really hit their stride with LIAR (1992), which had producer Steve Albini describing his charges as 'The greatest currently active rock'n'roll band on the planet'. Albini's production was all-pervasive on the early efforts, but during the recording of DOWN (1994), The Lizard risked his wrath by daring to tell him what to do. Though enraged, Albini accepted the order and his subordinate role resulted in an easier album – on the ear if not the mind, for the wretched images of dirt and decay persisted, and Yow's vocals were given an alarming new clarity.

The Jesus Lizard's particular brand of rock'n'roll excess could hardly be sustained indefinitely, and a 1994 quote from Yow bears this theory out: 'I can't imagine doing this in five years. It seems to me that the four same people are likely to come to a dead end eventually.' Still, in 1995 the band signed to major label, Capitol, to record SHOT (1996), another wedge of death-metal-grunge that showed little sign of burnout, and equally little sign of mainstream chart success.

Mac MacNeilly left the band sometime in 1997 and was replaced on drums by **James Kimball**, who had played in Detroit's Laughing Hyenas and Mule. The album BLUE was released in April 1998, and although the Andy Gill-produced project was possibly their most melodic and challenging for a long time, the band eventually split a little over a year after its release.

⊙ **Liar** (1992; Touch & Go).
Scarcely easy listening, but strangely enthralling. Highlights include the harrowing "Slave Ship", focusing on some poor unfortunate baking alive in a ship's hold. Elsewhere, "Rope" details the twisted corpse of a suicide, and "Zachariah" heralds a small town's terrified reception of a fire-and-brimstone preacher.

⊙ **Down** (1994; Touch & Go).
Dubiously surreal in places, but predominantly up to standard. The high point is the slow and cinematic "Horse", telling of a dysfunctional hillbilly clan's descent into murderous violence. Prostitutes, disgruntled employees and corrupt politicians populate the rest of the songs. Literate yet primitive, and grimly compelling.

Andy Lewis

JETHRO TULL

Formed Blackpool, England, 1967.

Beginning as an unpromising blues group who travelled to London seeking gigs under various names, **Jethro Tull** adopted their definitive title (the name of an eighteenth-century agriculturalist) after they were finally rebooked at The Marquee under that identity. The original line-up was **Ian Anderson** (vocals/flute/harmonica), **Mick Abrahams** (guitar), **Glenn Cornick** (bass) and **Clive Bunker** (drums).

After being unexpectedly well received at the National Jazz & Blues Festival, they were signed to Island Records, and released THIS WAS (1968). Comprising mostly self-penned blues material, it became a major underground and then mainstream hit in the UK, eventually reaching the Top 10.

Abrahams and Anderson had been equal contributors to the band's material, but Anderson assumed full control after Abrahams, realizing that their musical aims were incompatible, left in 1969 to form **Blodwyn Pig**, and later **The Mick Abrahams Band**. Jethro Tull briefly replaced Abrahams with future Black Sabbath guitarist **Tony Iommi**, who was in turn replaced by **Martin Barre**, a band member to this day.

Anderson's histrionic flute playing was the main visual attraction (he was self-taught, inspired by jazz virtuoso Roland Kirk), but he had also become a fine songwriter by the time the band made STAND UP (1969). This superb album extended the band's range, featuring a jazzy interpretation of a piece by J. S. Bach, and examples of Anderson's penchant for heartfelt and satirical lyrics. Like all good progressive-rock bands, Tull recorded singles separately from album material, and for a time they were spectacularly successful in both formats: "Living In The Past", "Sweet Dreams" (both 1969) and the double A-side "Teacher"/"Witches Promise" (1970) all reached the UK Top 10. Jethro Tull was a headlining rock act, packing large venues in Europe and, soon afterwards, America.

Jethro Tull's line-up was augmented by **John Evan** (keyboards) for BENEFIT (1970), which became their second consecutive US #1 album. Cornick was replaced by **Jeffrey Hammond** on the multimillion-selling AQUALUNG (1971), a powerful concept album dedicated partly to the experiences of a tramp, and partly to Anderson's religious views. By now, Jethro Tull was being seen by many chiefly as a vehicle for Anderson.

Bunker was replaced by **Barriemore Barlow** on drums around this time, while the double-LP compilation LIVING IN THE PAST (1972), their first for new label Chrysalis, was fleshed out with substandard previously unreleased material. The critical acclaim enjoyed by the band was to end with THICK AS A BRICK (1972; reissued on vinyl 1998; EMI), which consisted of just one enormous track, concerning a

Tull's Ian Anderson, codpieced as ever

'dinosaurs of rock', his response was aggressively defiant.

Still, Jethro Tull's fortunes improved somewhat, with the chart success of the EP, RING OUT SOLSTICE BELLS, before Anderson's English and Celtic folk influences were emphasized on the exuberant and engaging SONGS FROM THE WOOD (1977), their biggest album success in five years. Its concerns were developed more seriously on HEAVY HORSES (1978), which examined rural and environmental issues. After a successful world tour, captured on the double LP LIVE, BURSTING OUT (1978), they appeared on a live New Year's satellite transmission from Madison Square Garden. Glascock was missing from the line-up, hospitalized with a coronary complaint, and in early 1979 he died after heart surgery.

Anderson took over on bass guitar for the uneven STORMWATCH (1979), although **FAIRPORT CONVENTION**'s **Dave Pegg** assumed this role on the following tour, while remaining a member of both bands. Anderson, Barre and Pegg were joined by new members **Eddie Jobson** (keyboards/electric violin; ex-**CURVED AIR** and **ROXY MUSIC**) and **Mark Craney** (drums). Conceived as a solo project for Anderson, A (1980) became an official Jethro Tull release, but both Jobson and Craney left afterwards; their replacements were **Peter-John Vettese** (ex-Altered Images; keyboards/backing vocals), and former Richard Thompson and Sandy Denny collaborator **Gerry Conway** (drums).

Produced by former Yardbirds bassist Paul Samwell-Smith, THE BROADSWORD AND THE BEAST (1982) was in part a historical fantasy of the type associated with Rainbow or Uriah Heep. Anderson then embarked on the solo LP, WALK INTO LIGHT (1983), a thin and bloodless production, and the next group project, UNDER WRAPS (1984), satisfied only the most loyal.

A throat infection kept Anderson and the band out of action until 1987's return to form, CREST OF A KNAVE. Its two uncharacteristically rip-roaring tracks, "Steel Monkey" and "Raising Steam", were sufficient for them to win a Grammy for *Best Hard Rock Album* in 1988. Returning to touring, they found new fans across Eastern Europe, but their recorded output reached a low point with ROCK ISLAND (1989), then improved slightly with CATFISH RISING (1991), which verged on stadium rock.

Thankfully, a varied career was neatly summarized on a semi-acoustic world tour, for which the band was joined by Fairport Convention drummer **Dave Mattacks**. The results were recorded on A LITTLE LIGHT MUSIC (1992), a fine retrospective. A 25th anniversary tour in 1993 was accompanied by the

boy's growth into manhood. Even less popular with the press was A PASSION PLAY (1973), which explored life after death. Yet although it was panned for being obscure and pretentious, the critical response wasn't mirrored by the public, particularly in the States where, like THICK AS A BRICK, it became a chart-topping album.

The variable WAR CHILD (1974) emerged from an abortive film project and, while far from the band's best work, contained the US hit "Bungle In The Jungle". Anderson also took time out to produce Steeleye Span's 1974 album NOW WE ARE SIX, before Tull's MINSTREL IN THE GALLERY (1975) gave free rein to Anderson's fantasy about being a latter-day Tudor troubadour. The press hated it.

The band's orchestrator **David Palmer** (keyboards) and former **Chicken Shack** bassist **John Glascock** joined for the tedious 1976 album, TOO OLD TO ROCK'N'ROLL: TOO YOUNG TO DIE. Its hackneyed theme was that of a faded rocker who suddenly finds himself fashionable again. In interviews around this time, Anderson appeared nervous about the phenomenon of punk rock, and as the music press began to attack Tull as one of the

release of a four-CD set, before Anderson's religious concerns were reiterated on the palatable instrumental album DIVINITIES: TWELVE DANCES WITH GOD (1995).

Jethro Tull then reconvened, with bass players Pegg and Steve Bailey, for the entrancing studio album ROOTS TO BRANCHES (1995), which marked a return to Anderson's prominent flute playing. It confirmed their status as one of the more important of all progressive-rock bands, both lyrically articulate and musically astute – a fact also underscored by J-TULL DOT COM (1999), an album which not only hinted at their embracing of the Internet age but which displays all the expected Tull songwriting twists as well as one or two new ones. Meanwhile the live vitality of the band was displayed to full effect on LIVING WITH THE PAST (2002), their first official live album since A LITTLE LIGHT MUSIC.

⊙ **Aqualung** (1971; Chrysalis).
Possibly Jethro Tull's greatest achievement – a concept disc that comes off, with both compassion and scepticism to the fore. Recently remastered and issued as a 25th-anniversary special.

⊙ **Songs From The Wood** (1977; Chrysalis).
An exuberant representation of British folklore and the force that, through the green fuse, drives the flower.

⊙ **Heavy Horses** (1978; Chrysalis).
Following on stylistically from the previous album, this sophisticated collection acknowledges the darker side of nature.

⊙ **A Little Light Music** (1992; Chrysalis).
Superb live reinterpretations of such songs as "Someday The Sun Won't Shine For You", "A New Day Yesterday", "Nursie" and "Living In The Past".

⊙ **Roots To Branches** (1995; Chrysalis).
Reasserts Anderson's creative power and the instrumental virtuosity of the whole band in an excellent collection of new material.

Martin Haggerty

JOAN JETT & THE BLACKHEARTS

Formed Philadelphia, Pennsylvania, 1980.

When all-female teenage glitter-punk band THE RUNAWAYS ground to a halt in 1979 after three and a half years, it appeared that the career of co-founder **Joan Jett** was over. Depressed and eager for a change of scenery, she left her adopted home town of LA for London, where ex-Sex Pistols Steve Jones and Paul Cook had accepted her invitation to produce and play on a wonderful version of Lesley Gore's "You Don't Own Me", issued as a one-off European release on Vertigo.

Unfortunately, the single did little to advance her cause, and Jett returned to California to work on a cheap and nasty film project, *We're All Crazy Now*, intended as a vehicle for The Runaways. Thankfully, it was never released, but her fortunes changed when she met bubblegum rock mainstays Kenny Laguna and Richie Cordell, who were hired to help with the movie soundtrack. They went on to work on ses-

sions for JOAN JETT (1980), which was initially only released in Europe, on the Ariola label.

As Laguna became her manager, Jett toured solidly with her new band **The Blackhearts**, who eventually comprised **Ricky Byrd** (guitar), **Gary Ryan** (bass) and **Lee Crystal** (drums). They were musically powerful and uncomplicated, but steadily increasing crowds and gathering radio support failed to impress the American record industry. In desperation and frustration, Laguna and his co-manager wife Meryl funded the American release of JOAN JETT, which soon rewarded them with a reissue on Boardwalk in 1981, retitled BAD REPUTATION.

For the follow-up, recorded between gigs, Jett returned to "I Love Rock'N'Roll", which she'd first tackled in the London sessions. The well-drilled band combined with Cordell and Laguna's terrific production to execute Joan's glittery vision perfectly, and the anthemic single raced to the top of the US charts, as did an album, also entitled I LOVE ROCK'N'ROLL (1981).

The moment of triumph was marred by the untimely death of Boardwalk Records chief Neil Bogart, and The Blackhearts signed to MCA. ALBUM (1983) benefited from a looser feel, as well as a more intricate production and a wider range than I LOVE ROCK'N'ROLL. Equally strong was GLORIOUS RESULTS OF A MISSPENT YOUTH (1984), but the band were beginning to lose momentum, partly due to trouble with the label.

A switch to CBS and Cordell's departure from the production team coincided with 1986's GOOD MUSIC. The following year, Jett branched out into acting, with an impressive performance in the movie *Light Of Day*, starring Michael J. Fox. The Blackhearts even reached the US Top 40 with a rendition of Bruce Springsteen's title song.

Key personnel changes saw seasoned pros **Kasim Sulton** (bass) and **Thommy Price** (drums) replacing Ryan and Crystal. The results were solid but unspectacular album releases like UP YOUR ALLEY (1988) and THE HIT LIST (1990), although each had its moments: the former contained the US Top 10 rabble-rouser "I Hate Myself For Loving You", while the latter, a covers album, featured a supercharged reading of ZZ Top's "Tush".

Sulton was not replaced when he did not appear on NOTORIOUS (1991), for which subtlety and zip were restored, but collaborations with members of L7, Bikini Kill and Babes In Toyland on the Warners release PURE AND SIMPLE (1994) generally blunted Jett's attack. However, like close spiritual relative Keith Richards, Jett has retained her magic, and she remains one of the more dependably exciting figures in rock-'n'roll – and something of a figurehead for female rockers.

⊙ **Bad Reputation** (1981; Blackheart).
An effective meeting of rock'n'roll, angst-ridden melodrama and upbeat glam-pop.

⊙ **I Love Rock'N'Roll** (1981; Blackheart).
Harder-edged and less varied than its predecessor, but enjoyable enough.

Robert Coyne

DAVID JOHANSEN

Born Staten Island, New York, 1950.

"If you're gonna be a pop artist and really understand what pop is then you have to camp on it … that's part of what pop is."

nlike the street-punk firebrands he joined in **THE NEW YORK DOLLS**, **David Johansen** did not come from the most rock'n'roll of neighbourhoods, growing up in the New York suburbs. Still, he became a teen terror on the streets of Greenwich Village in the mid-60s, when he formed his first band The Vagabond Missionaries, and he followed up with a stint in Fast Eddie & The Electric Japs, who played wild shows in wilder places.

A frequent club-goer, Johansen was soon spotted by bass player Arthur 'Killer' Kane, who invited him to rehearse with his band **Actress**. In 1971 they changed their name to The New York Dolls, and Johansen was soon leading them through a bizarre series of image changes, from the bangles and face-paint which accompanied TOO MUCH TOO SOON, to the communist chic of RED PATENT LEATHER. The band was a central component in the lineage from the modernist rock of The Velvet Underground to the nihilistic revolution of punk.

After The Dolls split in 1975, Johansen attempted to re-create the glory years with various stand-ins – featuring among them Blackie Lawless, future lead singer of WASP – before recruiting his own band. First in was ex-Doll and longtime collaborator **Syl Sylvain**, but a new line-up was formed with the help of drummer **Frankie LaRoka**. Called **The Staten Island Boys**, they consisted of LaRoka, **Thomas Trask** (guitar), **Johnny Rao** (guitar) and **Buzz Verno** (bass). As shown on DAVID JOHANSEN (1978) and the Mick Ronson-produced IN STYLE (1979), here was an able band who could conjure up a multiplicity of styles, ranging from the British Invasion sound to the Motown soul of The Four Tops.

For 1981's HERE COMES THE NIGHT and the live LP, LIVE IT UP (1982), Johansen was joined by **Blondie Chaplin** (guitar/vocals), **Ernie Brooks** (bass), **Tom Mandel** (organ), **Bobby Blain** (piano) and **Tony Machine** (drums), but although both albums attracted interest, Johansen longed for some of the flamboyance of old. He achieved his wish in 1987 when he reinvented himself as **Buster Poindexter**, an ethnomusicologist from the Deep South. Drawing from the well of R&B greats and Johansen's rich discography, Buster first came to light in a series of mid-80s loft gigs with The Uptown

Horns and, decked out in tux and pompadour, he can be seen at Bottom Line shows to this day. A self-titled album with **The Banshees Of Blue** appeared in 1988.

Buster was the most successful creation of a play-acting career that began as a teenager, when Johansen trod the boards in Charles Ludlum's *Whores Of Babylon*, and has since featured film and TV appearances in *Scrooged* and *Miami Vice*. Johansen's Poindexter was then subject of much interest from TV bosses after he launched the opening ceremony for the 1994 Soccer World Cup. His wide-ranging love for music is undimmed, and he is equally at home on a soundtrack to a Kurt Weill documentary as providing some righteously stomping mouth harp for Marc Almond.

Stephen Boyd

ELTON JOHN

Born Pinner, England, 1947.

lton John is one of the pop world's less obvious icons. Born Reginald Kenneth Dwight in the nondescript suburban town of Pinner in Middlesex, he became a star by celebrating his ordinariness, and then as the 1970s progressed he took on the most glam-pop-kitsch mantle yet conceived. It seemed out of time, even then, owing more to the showmanship of Liberace than the androgynous sexuality of glam-rock peers like David Bowie. And, of course, for all the rock theatrics, John was (and is) essentially a singer-songwriter, bashing out the tunes on piano to the oft-nonsensical (but ever-rhyming) lyrics of writing partner Bernie Taupin.

Reg Dwight's rise to fame began in the early 60s when he gave up a place at London's Royal College of Music, just two weeks before his final exams, and took a job as messenger and tea boy at a music publishing company. He made modest extra earnings performing in bars, solo or with his semi-pro band **Bluesology**, who supported name soul acts like Patti Labelle and Doris Troy, and later were themselves fronted by the R&B singer Long John Baldry. Baldry's middle name plus the first name of sax player

Elton in "Crocodile Rock" levitation routine (with original hair)

Elton Dean gave Reg his stage name. (Some years later, he would add the middle name 'Hercules' by deed poll.)

Elton and Bluesology's first taste of chart success came in the autumn of 1967 when they backed Long John Baldry on the schlocky "Let The Heartaches Begin". Shortly after, answering a small ad in the *NME*, Elton John was teamed with the lyricist **Bernie Taupin** by Dick James, an old hand at getting together promising performers and writers, a job he had performed to some success at Northern Songs. James signed them at £10 a week for his new record label DJM (Dick James Music), where John and Taupin set about writing pop standards. Before long, their composition "I've Been Loving You" was short-listed to be performed by Lulu as the UK entry for the 1969 Eurovision Song Contest. The song didn't win (it was rejected in favour of the eventual winner, "Boom-Bang-A-Bang") and instead John and Taupin, with the help of producer Steve Brown, recorded a batch of new songs, one of which was released by Columbia. Entitled "Skyline Pigeon", it would later be recognized as a classic; at the time, however, it was one of several Elton John singles ignored by the record-buying public; only "Lady Samantha", released shortly afterwards, achieved any kind of sales.

Although some critical favour followed the release of Elton John's first album, EMPTY SKY (1969), it was a commercial disaster. However, DJM remained faithful, envisaging Elton and Bernie as part of the singer-songwriter boom. Meanwhile, Elton played piano on several sessions for **The Hollies**, most notably on their 1969 classic, "He Ain't Heavy He's My Brother", and recorded cover versions of contemporary pop hits for release as supermarket soundtracks – a desperate measure that was recently reissued by RPM International under the title CHARTBUSTERS GO POP.

For the second album, ELTON JOHN (1970), production duties were overseen by the later long-term producer Gus Dudgeon. With the aid of orchestral arranger Paul Buckmaster, it helped give Elton his first real commercial success, the single "Your Song", which reached the British and American Top 10.

In 1970 contractual obligations forced Elton to release three albums. One of these, FRIENDS, a British TV soundtrack recorded prior to Elton's explosion of fame, went gold in the US album charts, though it was nothing special. The second was a live LP, 17-11-70 (1970), a dull and self-indulgent release, though showcasing the recruitment the same year of **Nigel Olsson** (drums) and **Dee Murray** (bass) from the defunct Spencer Davis Group. The best of the trio by far was TUMBLEWEED CONNECTION (1970), which highlighted Elton and Bernie's shared obsession with Wild West mythology. Shortly after its release, Olsson and Murray were joined by **Caleb Quaye** (guitar), and then by **Davey Johnstone** (guitar), forming the nucleus of what later became known as **The Elton John Group**. Meanwhile, the Dudgeon/Buckmaster production partnership was augmented by Ken Scott, engineer to Bowie and Supertramp.

The first fruits of this combo were MADMAN ACROSS THE WATER (1971), a somewhat overblown and overcooked production that drowned some promising songs amid Paul Buckmaster's grandiose string arrangements. However, HONKY CHATEAU (1972) was a huge improvement and, aided by a well-timed smash hit in "Rocket Man", went #1 in the US and #2 in the UK. It was a strong set all round, and introduced another long-term favourite, "Honky Cat", as well as a more rock-friendly sound.

DON'T SHOOT ME I'M ONLY THE PIANO PLAYER (1972) consolidated Elton's success in a big way, reaching #1 on both sides of the Atlantic, and unleashing "Daniel" and "Crocodile Rock" to an ever bigger audience. It firmed up the sound, too, into a faster-paced, show-band style that melded Bluesology's cabaret feel with its blues and soul roots. And by now Elton was rocking out on stage with ever more gay abandon.

The huge-selling GOODBYE YELLOW BRICK ROAD (1973) demonstrated still further that Elton had become the hottest commercial property of the time, with a plethora of hit singles and classic songs, not least the title track and the hardy perennial "Candle In The Wind", though there was plenty more besides on this sprawling double album. Somehow, Elton even had time in 1973 to launch his own record label, Rocket Records, which, after a faltering start, soon became home to his protégée **Kiki Dee** and MOR favourite Neil Sedaka.

Overexposure and overwork were perhaps to blame for the half-baked CARIBOU (1974), though this did produce the stirring hit single, "Don't Let The Sun Go Down On Me", and Elton helped **John Lennon** back into the limelight, playing on his comeback single, "Whatever Gets You Thru The Night", and having him as a guest (on what turned out to be Lennon's last stage appearance) at a Madison Square Garden show.

The next year saw the much more ambitious album, CAPTAIN FANTASTIC AND THE BROWN DIRT COWBOY (1975), which chronicled the early years of the John-Taupin partnership, and had a stand-out song in "Someone Saved My Life Tonight". Then, however, the quality dropped again. ROCK OF THE WESTIES (1975) grooved along nicely but had few decent songs, while the live HERE AND NOW (1976) and the double-album BLUE MOVES (1976) were still less memorable. Meanwhile, the apotheosis of Elton as rock monster, feeding off his own fame and glory, came with a cameo appearance as the Pinball Wizard in Ken Russell's suitably overblown film version of *Tommy* (1975). Elton had, quite simply, become too big for his boots.

After notching up his first ever British #1 single, with the Kiki Dee duet, "Don't Go Breaking My Heart" (1976), Elton split from Bernie Taupin and retired from the music business to concentrate on his chairmanship of English football team, Watford. It was a well-earned rest, though unfortunately timed. When he returned to the recording studio, punk was the dominant force in pop music, and A SINGLE MAN (1978), a collaboration with unknown lyricist Gary Osborne, made little impact. A low-key release, the album made reference to the autobiography of cele-brated homosexual writer Christopher Isherwood in its title but was largely lightweight, although it did provide the minor hit, "Part Time Love".

Struggling to find the right muse after Taupin, Elton teamed up with disco producer Thom Bell for the ill-fated album, VICTIM OF LOVE (1979), but hastily reverted to musical type with the largely uninteresting 21 AT 33 (1980). Greater favour was found with THE FOX (1981), for which Bernie Taupin wrote three songs, Chris Thomas produced, and Tom Robinson even penned "Elton's Song". On TOO LOW FOR ZERO (1983), Taupin had returned as full-time lyricist and, with Thomas at the production desk, the team knocked out a formulaic series of albums through the decade.

A revamped sound could not disguise an essentially bland collection of songs on BREAKING HEARTS, released in 1984, and worse was to come as Elton tried his hand at conventional marriage – to Renate Blauel – and gave the British tabloid press a field day. His personal life reached an all-time low in late 1986 when he collapsed on stage in Australia and had to undergo throat surgery, allowing the tabloids to speculate that he had throat cancer. After other lies had appeared in Rupert Murdoch's *Sun* newspaper during 1987, John took them to court and won substantial damages.

This won widespread sympathy and Elton was back at the top of the UK album charts with SLEEPING WITH THE PAST (1989), largely on the back of "Sacrifice", his only solo #1 single in Britain. A live duet with **George Michael** on a 1991 revival of "Don't Let The Sun Go Down On Me" also topped the charts, and proved a highlight at the Freddie Mercury Tribute Concert in April 1992. This was later featured on DUETS (1993), a patchy collection of collaborations with artists ranging from Leonard Cohen to PM Dawn, released the same year as a tribute album, TWO ROOMS, which highlighted the quality of his earlier songs – Sting, notably, re-interpreting "Come Down In Time".

If Elton was by now confirmed MOR, he was at least proving a master of the genre – witness his work with lyricist Tim Rice on the Oscar-winning soundtrack to Walt Disney's *The Lion King*. That was followed by a CBE – for services to music and charity – proof, if it were needed, of just how much of a British institution Elton has become. But it was proof of Elton's songwriting capabilities that would have been more welcome, as three rather average albums of new material were all that followed – THE ONE (1992), MADE IN ENGLAND (1995) and THE BIG PICTURE (1997).

Elton's status as rock'n'roll royalty was confirmed by his performance of "Candle In The Wind" at the funeral of his friend Princess Diana following her tragic death in a car accident. A newly written verse identified the song more closely with Princess Diana, rather than its original subject Marilyn Monroe, and propelled the song into popular consciousness throughout the world in a way even Elton couldn't have predicted. Within days of release the song had become the fastest selling single ever and eventually shifted more than 33 million worldwide with all proceeds going to Diana's favourite charities.

Reunited with Tim Rice, Elton next began work on another Disney project, a Broadway adaptation of *Aida* (1999). An album featuring versions of the songs performed by such luminaries as **The Spice Girls** and **Lenny Kravitz** added absolutely nothing to Elton's kudos other than a few more stodgy, unit-shifting AOR songs. A stopover scoring the Albert Brooks film, *The Muse*, and providing songs for Dreamworks animated flop, *The Road To Eldorado*, raised few eyebrows, other than indicating that Elton seemed much more comfortable working in show-business than pop music.

2001's SONGS FROM THE WEST COAST was an attempt to redress the balance, and with Bernie Taupin back on board it promised a return to the warm, feel-good melodies of his 70s heyday. While it was undoubtedly his best 'proper' album in years, there was a lack of feeling even in emotional ballads like "American Triangle" that fell short of expectations.

Elton's recent success on stage and screen has shown that his immense talent for creating popular songs is undiminished, but for the time being he seems unable to capture the public imagination in the pop arena with the same consummate ease that originally brought him fame.

⊙ **Elton John** (1970; Rocket/MCA).
Many Elton fans reckon this is the best album he ever made, featuring "Your Song", expressive vocal performances, and adventurous string arrangements by Paul Buckmaster.

⊙ **Goodbye Yellow Brick Road** (1973; Rocket/MCA).
Recorded at the height of Elton's fame, this is a double album that oozes tunes and influences, featuring everything from glitter-pop anthems like "Bennie And The Jets" to the fast-paced pop-rock of "Love Lies Bleeding" and orchestrated schmaltz of "I've Seen That Movie Too". There's even a disastrous attempt at reggae.

⊙ **Captain Fantastic And The Brown Dirt Cowboy** (1975; Rocket/MCA).
Expensive packaging and much hype accompanied the boys' musical autobiography. Despite all that, it's not as self-indulgent as you might expect, with some of Elton's best tunes complemented by lyrics that are among Bernie's most honest and insightful. "Bitter Fingers" and a genuine torch ballad, "Someone Saved My Life Tonight", steal the show. The CD reissue adds the excellent Lennon tribute single from 1975, "Lucy In The Sky With Diamonds", and its B-side, "One Day At A Time".

⊙ **The Very Best of Elton John** (1990; Rocket/MCA).
The best Elton compilation on the market, including all the hit singles and a host of highlights.

Neil Partrick

JANIS JOPLIN

Born Port Arthur, Texas, 1943; died 1970.

"On stage, I make love to 25,000 people – then I go home alone."

Born into a Texas oil community, **Janis Joplin** developed an early interest in folk and blues

music and began a low-key involvement with the local Waller Creek Boys. Her early recordings, released after her death, were unremarkable. It was an encounter with Chet Helms, poet and general man about the California scene, that launched Janis on her way to greater fame.

On a visit to his home state, Helms chanced on a Janis performance. He saw potential in the singer, who was delivering fairly standard renditions of fairly standard songs, and brought her to California, where she picked up occasional work as a singer and fairly regular doses of liquor and drugs. The drug abuse soon required hospital treatment, but Joplin soon bounced back to work with **BIG BROTHER & THE HOLDING COMPANY**, a blues outfit who could party better than they could play. The results far exceeded all expectations.

The Holding Company's shortcomings included an inability to keep complex tracks together, but Janis managed to scream and howl over the top in a way that made their ragged blues sound both primitive and awesome. Delivered in advance of their slot at the 1967 Monterey Pop Festival – where Joplin excelled herself – BIG BROTHER AND THE HOLDING COMPANY (1967) was too sloppy to match the live show. A year later, though, CHEAP THRILLS (1968) proved to be one of Joplin's two great albums. The band kept it basic and jelled into a powerful unit behind Joplin's vocals, which leaped from the speakers with an energy that still shocks to this day. Featuring the desperate "Piece Of My Heart", an inspired rendering of "Summertime" and the stage favourite "Ball And Chain", the album stayed at the top of the US charts for eight weeks and "Ball And Chain" entered the US Top 10.

The pressures of success and the fact that Joplin had gone from being a good way of getting gigs to being an undoubted star soon split Big Brother & The Holding Company. In an attempt to give Joplin a band that could provide music of the same intensity as her vocals, **The Kozmic Blues Band** was formed. From the outset the crew was dogged by the problem of being too large and unwieldy; and cluttered arrangements only made matters worse. The idea had been to develop a sound with the strength of Stax soul records, but their debut, at the Stax convention in Memphis in December 1968, was a disaster. Their one album, I GOT DEM OL' KOZMIC BLUES AGAIN MAMA (1969), had its moments, most notably "Little Girl Blue", in which, for once, the horns managed a level of restraint that allowed Janis to wrap an understated blues vocal around a simple sad tale.

Stripping down the backing line-up, Joplin recruited some of the Kozmic Blues sidemen to help with **The Full Tilt Boogie Band**, which was a return to the sound of Big Brother. The drug and alcohol intake remained dangerously high, however, and Joplin was found dead with fresh needle marks in her arm on October 4, 1970, a day before she had been due to record a vocal for "Buried Alive In The

Blues". Unfinished as it was, the posthumous PEARL (1971) was the second great album of her career, boasting arrangements that had been developed solely to show off her vocal talents. A ragged reworking of Kris Kristofferson's "Me And Bobby McGee" gave Joplin her first chart-topping single in the US, while the album managed nine weeks on top of the US charts and even crept into the lower reaches of the UK lists. The predictable reissues soon followed; some scraped the barrel, others – most notably IN CONCERT (1972) – provided testament to a great talent.

Two months before she died, Joplin had bought a headstone for the grave of blues singer Bessie Smith. Her death, like that of Smith, was sad and preventable. The real tragedy is that PEARL offered so much: its direct and uncluttered arrangements suggest that Joplin could have gone on to outshine the likes of Joe Cocker as a blues/rock performer of huge range and power. As it is she remains a noted talent, and sympathetic management of the back catalogue keeps her reputation alive. Big Brother & The Holding Company's much-bootlegged LIVE AT WINTERLAND 1968 (1968) and a budget two-CD package THE ULTIMATE COLLECTION (1998) have recently been added.

- **Pearl** (1971; Columbia).
  Given the room to breathe, Joplin shines on this, the best album released under her own name.

- **Live At Winterland 1968** (1998; Sony).
  Widely bootlegged, this is Big Brother & The Holding Company's finest hour. Janis is by turns sublime, tender, raving and genuinely frightening, especially on the ten-minute "Ball And Chain". Big Brother chug and flow to good effect and sling some quality licks. Dated for sure, but you'd need to be dead to avoid being moved by the best moments.

- **Box Of Pearls** (1999; Columbia).
  This five-CD retrospective is the definitive anthology, including great material from her solo LPs as well as the recordings with Big Brother & The Holding Company.

- **The Essential Janis Joplin** (2003; Sony).
  If the box set seems a little too meaty, then try this decent compilation of the highlights.

Neil Nixon

JOURNEY

Formed San Francisco, 1972; disbanded 1988; back together again in the 1990s.

America in the 80s was dominated by soft rock. Bands like Air Supply, Foreigner, Asia, Styx and REO Speedwagon wrote the muzak that made the whole world smile stupidly. But the genre's most singularly successful exponents – and perhaps the only ones with any real saving graces – were **Journey**.

Hand-picked by manager Herbie Herbert, the group came from a variety of sources. **Ross Valory** (bass) and **George Tickner** (guitar) had played in Bay Area band Frumious Bandersnatch, while **Gregg Rolie** (vocals/keyboards) and teenage guitarist **Neal Schon** joined from **SANTANA**. After **Prairie Prince** (drums) left to join **THE TUBES**, he was replaced by **Aynsley Dunbar**, a veteran of The Bluesbreakers and Mothers Of Invention.

The band set out playing jazz-rock, but CBS advised them to find a proper lead singer, and pressed the claims of Canadian **Steve Perry**, whose own band, Alien Project, had disintegrated in the wake of a fatal car accident. Perry had a unique brand of hollering – influenced by an unsteady alliance of Ozzy Osbourne and Sam Cooke – which could veer from raspy alto to screeching soprano and, along with Queen producer Roy Thomas Baker, set about getting Journey to eschew jazz-rock in favour of powerful guitar riffs. INFINITY (1978), his first album – and the band's fourth – had a platinum touch, reaching #21 in the US album charts.

Nonetheless, despite a fine slow blues given life by Perry's Sam Cooke impersonation on "Lovin', Touchin', Squeezin'", by the release of EVOLUTION (1979) Dunbar had left (to resurface with **JEFFERSON STARSHIP**), being replaced by **Stevie Smith**, and for the promotional tour of DEPARTURE (1980), a US #8 album, **Jonathan Cain**, formerly of The Babys, took on keyboard duties. Cain was well aware of the potential gold mine and helped Journey to achieve phenomenal success with songs like "Don't Stop Believin'" and "Who's Crying Now", from the band's US chart-topping album, ESCAPE (1981).

Although filling stadiums, Journey never lost their sincerity, refusing corporate sponsorship for their tours throughout the 80s. All the same, these triumphs epitomized an era, with their polished sheen and besuited metal. The success of the ESCAPE album brought with it a Journey video game, while MTV embraced the crisp raunch of FRONTIERS (1983), on which Cain employed a battery of sequencers for "Separate Ways", while Perry demonstrated he was a world-class singer in love with drama, a reputation confirmed by his solo album, STREET TALK (1984), and its mega-hit single, "Oh Sherrie".

By 1986's RAISED ON RADIO, however, Perry, Schon and Cain were the only remaining members, and they called it a day in 1988. Schon disappeared into the folds of sessioneering when his solo album LATE NIGHT/SCHON stiffed, and Perry went similarly quiet. Journey were largely forgotten or dismissed for their slickness; yet, vacuous though they could be, they played a crucial role in the development of pomp metal – and Bon Jovi, for one, bear their influence. Latterly, there was a revival of their hit ballad "Open Arms", when it was covered by Mariah Carey in 1996. Although their greatest work undoubtedly came during the 1980s, their most recent material has its adherents.

Journey

- **Journey's Greatest Hits** (1988; CBS).
  Screaming and supremely polished riffing. Airbrushed but irresistible.

Steve Perry

- **Street Talk** (1984; CBS).
  Steve Perry's solo album is the greatest record Journey never made. Features the mega-hit "Oh Sherrie", which reached all the parts the average Journey power ballad couldn't.

Charles Bottomley

JOY DIVISION

Formed Manchester, England, 1976.

"I used to work in a factory and I was really happy because I could day-dream all day." Ian Curtis

The hugely adored, cult-followed **Joy Division** had classic punk origins, being formed after an inspirational Sex Pistols gig at Manchester's Free Trade Hall, by two friends – **Bernard Albrecht** (guitar/keyboards/vocals) and **Peter Hook** (bass/percussion/vocals) – who had no musical experience at all. The pair bought copies of the Palmer/Hughes tuition guides to bass and guitar and, as Albrecht remembers, 'we got to page 27 and we decided to bring in a singer'.

The man they plumped for was friend and fellow concert-goer **Ian Curtis** (vocals/lyrics/guitar), and the band's line-up was completed when **Steven Morris** (drums) replied to an advert placed in a Macclesfield shop window. Morris's first meeting with the band was in the car park at Strangeways prison. Said Morris: 'I remembered thinking to myself, have they really just got back from holiday or have they just been inside?' Whatever their first impressions, the four were soon rehearsing on a regular basis. And rehearse was pretty much all they did during the early part of 1977.

The band's first working title was The Stiff Kittens (a name suggested by their friend and Buzzcocks frontman Pete Shelley), but by the time of their first gig, supporting the Buzzcocks at Manchester's Electric Circus on May 25, 1977, they had plumped for **Warsaw** instead (the early guitar-driven recordings made by the band under this name were finally given an official release in 1995 on Intermusic Movieplay Gold). After a nervous, shaky performance, they disappeared back into the rehearsal room for a further four months, emerging only on SHORT CIRCUIT, an EP released in June 1978 showcasing the talents of Manchester acts like Buzzcocks, The Fall and Slaughter And The Dogs. Warsaw's contribution, "At A Later Date", began with Ian Curtis bellowing at the audience, 'you all forgot Rudolf Hess!' The fascist implications of this outburst haunted the band for years afterwards, aggravated by a change of name to Joy Division – the term used by the Nazis for the Jewish women kept in concentration camps as prostitutes.

As Joy Division, the band's real breakthrough came in December 1978, when they entered an indie-label contest run by Stiff/Chiswick at Manchester's Rafter's club. The contest itself was a pretty chaotic affair, with Joy Division, scheduled to appear at midnight, not taking the stage until two in the morning. Nevertheless, it was through Stiff/Chiswick that the band found themselves a manager and mentor, Rafter's DJ Rob Gretton, and won themselves a recording deal with Manchester label Factory. Two of the factors that would propel the band to greatness were now in place. The third and most crucial – Curtis's quality as a lyricist and stage

Joy Division's Ian Curtis (dancing), with Bernard Albrecht and Peter Hook

performer – was becoming ever more apparent with each song he wrote and every gig he performed.

It was a package that was perfectly suited to the times, and Joy Division swiftly acquired a cult following, made up largely of lookalikes of the band, young men in their late teens or early twenties with short hair and long coats. With this solid fan base and their debut album, UNKNOWN PLEASURES (1979), garnering excellent reviews, the group looked set for great things. Curtis's lyrics, which reflected the band's obsessions with deprivation, isolation and claustrophobia, were always delivered with memorable intensity. "Digital", in particular, set the tone: 'I feel it closing in/Day in, day out!/I see you fade away, don't ever fade away...' The breakthrough was imminent and plans for a tour of the US had almost been finalized when, as Paul Morley wrote, 'just as Joy Division were heading off into their own sensational rock adventure, Ian Curtis, snagged on the jagged edge between the pleasure of it all, and the pain, killed himself. This was some end.'

Details of Curtis's death are hazy. According to Tony Wilson, then chairman of Factory, Curtis watched the Werner Herzog film *Stroszek*, the last line of which is 'there's a dead man in the cable car and the chicken's still dancing', listened to some Iggy Pop, and then put a rope around his neck. Whatever the truth of this, the fact remains that on May 18, 1980, the singer of one of the most influential bands of their generation took his own life. Contrary to what the tabloids might like to believe, the death had nothing to do with drink or drugs. A diagnosed epileptic with a marriage that was going to the wall, Curtis found life simply too much to take.

As Pete Hook revealed, 'the great tragedy of Ian's death was that all he really wanted to be was successful. And he missed it ... by a week.' On June 28, the band's latest release, "Love Will Tear Us Apart", entered the singles charts, and went on to become a Top 20 smash. In fact, in the eighteen months following the death of their singer, Joy Division enjoyed their most lucrative period. The band's second album, CLOSER (1980), and a live release, STILL (1981), both sold well. "Love Will Tear Us Apart"

re-entered the UK charts in 1980 and made the Top 20 again. The band drily joked that Curtis's suicide had been a brilliant publicity stunt.

While the press undertook lengthy postmortems, Hook, Morris and Albrecht – soon to be renamed Bernard Sumner – were busy reinventing themselves. Sumner took over on lead vocals, they added a new female member, and started to develop a new sound as **NEW ORDER**. Their progress had been prefigured by the fundamental changes they had undergone when Curtis was alive, as the harsh guitar-based rock sound of a track like "Warsaw" gave way, via the electonic bleepings of "Transmission" (1979), to the sweeping keyboards and crooning of CLOSER. Curtis's influence over the band's change in direction is undeniable. As Sumner once told Paul Morley, 'Ian used to play Kraftwerk records to us, saying "listen to this, this is something new, something fantastic." Maybe he knew and maybe he was showing us the way.'

⊙ **Unknown Pleasures** (1979; Factory).
Joy Division's best work and one of the finest – and most influential – albums of the post-punk era. At its best perhaps on the hypnotic "She's Lost Control", which was released as a single.

⊙ **Closer** (1980; Factory).
A darker, more introspective work but definitely a step forward, with a more distanced, electronic feel and Curtis's lyrics at their most chilling.

⊙ **Still** (1981; Factory).
One of the few surviving documents of the Joy Division live experience. Not entirely satisfying, but the version of "Ceremony" is worth the asking price alone.

⊙ **Heart And Soul** (1997; London).
A four-CD instant collectors' item. All you'd expect, plus a disc worth of rarities.

Richard Luck

JUDAS PRIEST

Formed Birmingham, England, 1969.

Metal magnates **Judas Priest** have been one of the driving forces of the British scene, huge through the last two decades, and synonymous with the biker image of leather, chrome and aggression. The music, of course, has been a flawless match: pounding drums and duelling guitars providing inspiration for a whole generation of rock-god wannabes.

The band's origins lay in the Midlands, where in 1969 singer **Alan Atkins** and drummer **John Ellis** had a short-lived band called Judas Priest, before joining forces with guitarist **Ken 'KK' Downing** and bass player **Ian Hill**. In 1971 Atkins and Ellis left, and vocalist **Rob Halford** and drummer **John Hinch** stepped in from defunct Birmingham-based band Hiroshima, bringing in rhythm guitarist **Glenn Tipton** in 1973 as they began touring the pubs and clubs, looking to make their mark.

The work paid off when Priest were signed to Gull Records to release their debut album ROCKA ROLLA (1974). The production, however, left a lot to be desired and the album flopped; Hinch left and was

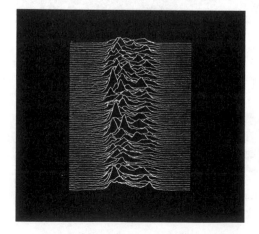

replaced by **Alan Moore**, who had previously drummed for Priest as a fill-in between Ellis and Hinch. Moore only stayed with the band for one album, though, leaving after SAD WINGS OF DESTINY, recorded in 1976 and released the following year. By then, Priest had left Gull for CBS, who gave them a £60,000 advance for SIN AFTER SIN (1977), which edged into the UK charts at #23. It was 1978's STAINED CLASS, however, that saw the band really firming up their style – and which was to become notorious for other reasons seven years on. At the time, it was a modest seller, peaking in the UK at #27.

Following KILLING MACHINE (1978) and the live LP UNLEASHED IN THE EAST (1979), Judas Priest's next landmark release was 1980's BRITISH STEEL, which introduced new drummer **Dave Holland**, as well as the hit singles "Living After Midnight", "Breaking The Law" and "United". It reached #4 in the UK and #34 in the US, establishing Priest as an international metal act.

1981's POINT OF ENTRY was followed by what is probably Priest's definitive work, SCREAMING FOR VENGEANCE (1982), which also became their biggest-selling album to date. But after the release of DEFENDERS OF THE FAITH (1984) and its accompanying tour, something occurred that plunged heavy metal into the media spotlight. In 1985 two teenage Judas Priest fans killed themselves with a shotgun in a deserted playground in Nevada. The parents of the boys decided to bring a lawsuit against the band, claiming that their music had been responsible for the suicides.

As the case gathered momentum, the band recorded TURBO (1986) and embarked on a 'Fuel For Life' world tour, during which the PRIEST ... LIVE! (1987) album and video were made. Then, with the release of RAM IT DOWN (1988), the Nevada case went to trial, just as the US pro-censorship society, the PMRC, headed by Nancy Reagan and Tipper Gore, launched an offensive against heavy metal music. However, the media circus disintegrated in August 1990 when Judge Jerry Whitehead threw the case out of court – the prosecution had presented a flimsy case, and there was evidence from the defence that the dead boys' surroundings had been 'violent and depressed'.

Priest bounced back in style with the release of the PAINKILLER album (1990) and yet another world tour, both of which featured new drummer **Scott Travis**, an American formerly with metal band Racer X. The tour reached Britain in March 1991, with Canadian thrashers Annihilator playing support.

Halford and Travis formed a sideline project called Fight in 1992, featuring an otherwise unknown line-up. The band became increasingly important to Halford, and in early 1993 he announced his departure from Priest. The announcement coincided with the release of the Priest anthology album METAL WORKS 73–93 (1993), but the rest of the band were keen to emphasize that this was not an obituary and, although currently without a singer or drummer, Priest would be back.

With the gaping hole in their line-up Judas Priest went on the hunt for a new mike man. Who better to replace him than someone who already fills his shoes in a Judas Priest tribute band? That's what the band figured, and pretty soon **Tim 'Ripper' Owens** took over the screaming duties. JUGULATOR (1997), with track titles such as "Blood Stained", "Dead Meat" and "Burn in Hell", was sufficient to convince the metal-buying public that the boys were still on the right track. Naturally, what all Priest fans wanted to know was whether Ripper could cut it live: '98 LIVE MELTDOWN provided ample evidence for any fans unable to see the band on tour. By the new millennium the constant rumours that Halford might return to the fold were crushed when the band emerged with the devastatingly heavy DEMOLITION (2001), which found Ripper not only hitting the high notes but developing his own style.

British Steel (1980; CBS).
Priest come of age with an album worthy of a place in any metaller's record collection. High-octane tracks such as "Rapid Fire" and "Breaking The Law" carry the album along at a faster pace than previous Priest offerings, while "Living After Midnight" became a live mainstay for years afterwards.

Screaming For Vengeance (1982; CBS).
From the opening crunches of "Hellion"/"Electric Eye" through to the echoed ending of "Devil's Child", an amazing, relentless ride.

Painkiller (1990; CBS).
New drummer Scott Travis opened this masterpiece with the rapid-fire double bass drums of the title track. No fillers here – an album that goes for the throat and doesn't let up.

Richard Allan

K

KELIS

Born New York, 1980.

The first psychedelic R&B sex queen of the new millennium announced herself with the most outrageous hook in living memory and the wildest haircut this side of the guy with the rainbow afro wig who held up the "John 3:16" signs at American sporting events in the 1970s. However, as everyone from Little Richard to Pete Burns could tell you, such a combination of outrageousness and genius is almost impossible to maintain and **Kelis** has been caught in a downward spiral ever since her outlandish debut.

Born in Harlem to a Pentecostal minister father and a clothes designer mother, Kelis Rogers grew up around jazz and immediately gravitated towards the unique vocal style of Betty Carter. As well as enrolling at the Fiorello H LaGuardia High School for Music, Art and Performing Arts (yes, the same school on which *Fame* was based), she began modelling at age 13. She quit school and left home at 16 to pursue music full time. She landed a vocal spot on the second album by the shock rap supergroup **Gravediggaz** and was one-third of an aborted girl group project called BLU (Black Ladies United), but her career took off when she met the up and coming hip-hop/R&B production team The Neptunes. Kelis sang the hook on their calling card, Ol' Dirty Bastard's "Got Your Money" (1999), and quickly bcame the duo's diva of choice, providing hooks for everyone from **Foxy Brown** to **Noreaga**.

It was the hook to her own debut single, however, that caught the ears of radio programmers the world over. "Caught Out There" (aka "I Hate You So Much Right Now") was a fairly typical, albeit excellent, R&B tune, but Kelis literally screaming the catch phrase made it one of the most unique singles in a genre based almost exclusively on its stylization of love and heartbreak; it was perhaps the most direct expression of female rage this side of Bikini Kill. **The Neptunes**-produced KALEIDOSCOPE (1999), inevitably, couldn't maintain "Caught Out There"'s momentum, but tracks like the rousing "Good Stuff", the pizzicato "Get Along With You" and "Mars", which in a better world would have been the love theme of *Logan's Run*, transcended the conventions of contemporary R&B.

Despite its shortcomings, KALEIDOSCOPE was successful enough to allow Kelis to hobnob with Moby and jet set around Europe with U2 (where she would cover Nirvana's "Smells Like Teen Spirit" live) and German trancemeister Timo Maas. WANDERLAND (2001) suffered from her newfound celebrity, as well as that of The Neptunes who had seemingly produced every other song that made it to radio since her debut album. By this point The Neptunes signature sound had become a rote formula, with only the heavy-handed rock posturing of the lead single, "Young, Fresh 'n' New", sounding in the least bit original. Kelis insisted on writing most of the album (The Neptunes had written most of KALEIDOSCOPE) and didn't do herself any favours by collaborating with **No Doubt** and, er, **Fieldy** from **Korn**. Of course, if the music thing doesn't work out, there's always the Miss Rebel fashion line which she launched at the end of 2001.

⊙ **Kaleidoscope** (1991; Virgin).
With its basic sleazy beats, eerie piano intros, builds of warm bass, hook stabs and acid licks, this album is as much The Neptunes' as Kelis's. On the hilariously manic "Game Show", the suitably offbeat "Roller Rink" and the melancholic "Get Along With You", the Neptunes marry their slightly crazy musical ethos to the flame-haired siren's surreal imagery, producing a fantastic blueprint for modern, sci-fi R&B.

Peter Shapiro

KILLING JOKE

Formed London, 1979.

Britain's post-punk era threw up some strange groups, but few as extreme as **Killing Joke**. Emerging at a time of Cold War tension, their savage meltdown of punk, heavy metal and dub was the perfect delivery system for frontman **Jaz Coleman**'s gleeful celebrations of forthcoming Armageddon. As much a way of life as a band, they generated an astonishing intensity in live performance, studio recordings and notoriously confrontational interviews. Despite splits and personnel changes, the band are still going strong, with a more refined sound but a world-view that remains as bleak as ever.

Forged in a Notting Hill squat, the original line-up comprised Jaz (vocals/synths), **Geordie** (guitar), **Youth** (bass) and drummer **Big Paul**. Their first break came supporting Joy Division at London's Lyceum, and after releasing a self-financed EP via Island they signed to art-rock label EG for their 1980 debut album, KILLING JOKE. A brutalist classic, it featured their essential singles "Requiem" and "Wardance", and – like all their early record releases – came with unsettling artwork that perfectly complemented the music. On stage, the band were developing a reputation for memorable, uncompromising performances. One of their legendary early gigs was at a CND rally in London's Trafalgar Square where Jaz Coleman introduced a performance of "Wardance" with the inspiring message: 'I hope you realize that your efforts today are all quite futile.'

Yet KILLING JOKE sounded like a mere collection of demos compared to the full-on assault of their second LP, 1981's WHAT'S THIS FOR?. This was the definitive manifestation of their early spirit on a record that started off intense with "The Fall Of Because" and never slackened the pace. Yet, despite the release of an enigmatic third LP, REVELATIONS, the band's spell was breaking. Early in 1982, Jaz Coleman jumped ship for Iceland for bizarre occult reasons perhaps best left unexplained, and the band made a legendary TV appearance with a mannequin substituting for the renegade singer, before opting to follow. Amidst the toing and froing, Youth left to pursue a new career with **Brilliant**, and ultimately as a top-flight dance producer.

Back in London, the band decided to continue with **Raven** newly installed at the bottom end and released HA, a stopgap live EP, at the end of the year. The fourth album, FIRE DANCES, showed a return to form, but it was 1985's NIGHT TIME that captured Killing Joke at an all-time best. Here was all their menace and intensity honed into a tight set of well-structured, almost commercial songs that raged with a savage energy. "Love Like Blood" released in January 1985 was their biggest hit yet, reaching #16 in the UK, and the accompanying tour was just as successful, with a string of messianic performances cementing the bond between band and disciples.

The follow-up, BRIGHTER THAN A THOUSAND SUNS, showed an increasingly keyboards-dominated sound, though "Chessboards" and "Rubicon" maintained the power of old. But by the time of OUTSIDE THE GATE, the music was verging on the point of progressive rock, reflecting Coleman's developing classical aspirations. The band fell apart, only to return in 1990 for the much underrated EXTREMITIES, DIRT AND VARIOUS REPRESSED EMOTIONS album, with one-time PiL drummer Martin Atkins behind the traps on such monolithic anthems as "Inside The Termite Mound" and "Age Of Greed". But entropy set in once again and Killing Joke dispersed to the four corners of the world; or, to be more specific, the US, Ecuador and New Zealand. It seemed that they just couldn't get far enough apart from each other.

However, against all the odds, 1993 saw Jaz, Geordie and Youth reconvening and trooping off to the King's Chamber of the Great Pyramid to record "Exorcism", a psychotic rant that featured what appeared to be the sound of Coleman vomiting ectoplasm into the mike. The new album, PANDEMONIUM, proved to be the Joke's biggest seller yet, with the title track and "Communion" standing out amidst the Nietzschean über-grind, all packaged within a trendy New Age chaos-theory-style sleeve. Killing Joke were back with a vengeance and were now seen as a major influence on US hardcore, industrial and grunge acts, particularly Nirvana, whose "Come As You Are" bore an uncanny resemblance to Killing Joke's frighteningly powerful "Eighties".

DEMOCRACY (1996) consolidated the sound of PANDEMONIUM, as the band moved ever closer to the mainstream, or the mainstream moved closer to them. Youth spent most of the 90s adding monumental bass and production skills to a growing number of dance-orientated acts, while WAR DANCE (1998), was a patchy at best remix album.

Since then the band have effectively been put under wraps (though 2003 saw the release of a rarities compilation, UNPERVERTED PANTOMIME) while the various members have indulged whatever solo activities they deemed worthy of their time. Most notably Jaz Coleman has been developing his classical leanings and has reworked the likes of Pink Floyd, Led Zeppelin and most recently The Doors for orchestra – RIDERS ON THE STORM: THE DOORS CONCERTO (2000) found him working with violinist Nigel Kennedy, a move which might satisfy his creative needs, but will surely flummox most hardcore Killing Joke fans.

What's This For? (1981; EG).
Industrial-strength assault that captures the early Joke at their malicious best. With titles like "Tension", "Unspeakable" and "Madness", you know exactly what to expect.

Night Time (1985; EG).
Their most accessible album and many would say their best. Refined production and a more commercial edge produced hits with "Love Like Blood" and "Kings And Queens".

Pandemonium (1993; Butterfly).
Their most commercially successful outing to date, showing a strong dub influence bubbling away under the surface. Geordie's exotic fills barely disguise a developing heavy metal tendency.

Laugh, I Nearly Bought One (1992; EG).
Handy compilation of many of the band's best-known tunes, from debut "Turn To Red" onwards. Most of the essentials, including "Requiem", "Follow The Leaders" and "Love Like Blood", are present and correct.

Iain Smith

CAROLE KING

Born Carole Klein, Brooklyn, New York,
February 9, 1942.

In addition to being the most successful female songwriter of all time, **Carole King** also ranks as one of the most distinctive musical voices of the late twentieth century. She grew up with Neil Sedaka as a near neighbour, and was tutored in piano and singing by her mother from the age of 6. By high school she had formed the vocal quartet the **Co-Sines**. She began to write professionally after meeting Paul Simon, teaming up with local pharmacy worker **Gerry Goffin**, who later became her husband. Together they took an office in New York's famed Brill Building, working for Aidon Music. Her own recording career began in 1959 with "Baby Sittin'" for ABC and two singles for RCA – "Short-Mort" and "Oh! Neil" – her retort to Neil Sedaka's hit "Oh! Carol" that immortalized her. She then put her recording career on hold and concentrated on writing for the next six years.

The first breakthrough for Goffin/King came in 1961, when **The Shirelles** hit the top with the epoch-defining "Will You Love Me Tomorrow". Had she never written another note in her lifetime, this would have reserved King's place in the annals of pop music. In fact, the creative stream was ready to go tidal. Other major successes of that year included a second #1 with "Take Good Care Of My Baby" recorded by **Bobby Vee**, and the **Drifters**' "Up On The Roof". Their hit-making abilities proven, **Goffin and King** became one of the dominating songwriting partnerships of the 60s, writing "The Locomotion", "Go Away Little Girl", "Pleasant Valley Sunday", "Chains" (covered by The Beatles), "(You Make Me Feel) Like A Natural Woman" by **Aretha Franklin**, and dozens of others, including the controversial **Crystals**' song, "He Hit Me (And It Felt Like A Kiss)".

King's "It Might As Well Rain Until September" was intended for Vee until Aidon co-owner Don Kirshner persuaded her to record her own version. She split both professionally and romantically from Goffin early in 1967, starting her own label, Tomorrow Records, with journalist Al Aronowitz. As well as her own material, the label was home to the **Myddle Class**, whose bassist **Charles Larkey** became her second husband. With Larkey (and guitarist **Danny Kortchmar**) she released a 1968 album credited to **The City**, but that band never performed live and split up soon after its release.

In 1970 she added piano to **James Taylor**'s breakthrough album, SWEET BABY JAMES (he would later score a #1 with King's "You've Got A Friend"), and also recorded her own debut, WRITER:CAROLE KING which failed to cause many ripples. But TAPESTRY, recorded just six months later in October 1970, turned that around and by May of the following year "It's Too Late" had reached the top of the American chart. TAPESTRY followed it there by June and went on to

sell 15 million copies and stayed in the charts for over 300 weeks. Carole King was the first superstar of the 70s, and TAPESTRY the *de rigueur* bedsit album for the post-60s comedown.

1972's MUSIC again scaled the top of the American charts, as King overcame her stage fear and toured domestically and in Europe. RHYMES AND REASONS, released at the end of the year, was only marginally less successful. Her first entirely self-written collection of songs, FANTASY, produced by Lou Adler, followed in August 1973. Less successful than expected, she chose to employ lyricist **David Palmer** for WRAP AROUND JOY (1974), which returned her to the top of the charts.

THOROUGHBRED (1976) featured guest vocals from **Graham Nash**, James Taylor and **David Crosby**, and saw her reunited with ex-husband Goffin. Her third husband was **Ric Evers**, who became her next co-writer. He was also a member of Capitol artists **Navarro**, who were employed as King's backing band on her 1977 release SIMPLE THINGS and 1978's WELCOME HOME. However, shortly before the release of the latter, Evers died from a drug overdose. King's own fortunes were in decline, too. Punk had swept aside the traditional singer-songwriters, and her albums were now struggling to gain a foothold in the charts.

Truth to tell, King's 80s output was patchy, the nadir coming with a soundtrack album for the *Care Bears* movie in 1985. She was inducted, alongside Goffin, into the Songwriters Hall Of Fame in 1987. Released at the end of the decade, CITY STREETS was her first new work for six years. Despite high-profile guest stars including **Eric Clapton**, nobody was buying. In the early 90s King turned to environmental causes (she had moved to Idaho a decade earlier), and played at President Clinton's inaugural ball. A 1993 collection, COLOUR OF YOUR DREAMS, featured two collaborations with Goffin. A year later she made her stage debut, appearing in the Broadway musical *Blood Brothers* at the age of 52.

Most recently, King has entered her sixth decade of writing and performing with the star-studded, if somewhat glutinous release, LOVE MAKES THE WORLD (2001), on which she shares the mike with **Celine Dion**, Aerosmith's **Steven Tyler**, trumpeter **Wynton Marsalis** and, most satisfyingly, **k d lang**.

⊙ **Tapestry** (1970; Ode/CBS).
"So Far Away", "I Feel The Earth Move", "It's Too Late" – just three of the songs everyone remembers from this epochal 70s album.

⊙ **Music** (1972; Ode/CBS).
Another #1 collection, attended by hit single "Sweet Sensations". "Some Kind Of Wonderful" is another stand-out.

⊙ **Thoroughbred** (1976; Ode/CBS).
The album that reunited King with Goffin. Note also the appearance of friends J. D. Souther, James Taylor, Graham Nash and David Crosby. The stand-out track is "Only Love Is Real", but this is solid rather than spectacular stuff. and contrived.

⊙ **Live At Carnegie Hall** (1996; Legacy).
A good opportunity for fans to immerse themselves in nostalgia at the delights of the King songbook.

Alex Ogg

KING CRIMSON

Formed Bournemouth, England, January 13, 1969;
disbanded 1974; re-formed 1981;
disbanded 1984; re-formed 1992.

"King Crimson was one of the only gigs for a rock drummer where you could play in 17/16 and still stay in decent hotels." Bill Bruford

Prime movers of progressive rock, **King Crimson** were a musically pioneering outfit who avoided many of the pitfalls which grounded lesser exponents of the genre. In **ROBERT FRIPP**, their guitarist and principal composer, they had perhaps the genre's most intelligent musician and, over a series of incarnations, Fripp augmented his band with some of the best players in the business. These were hippies who practised their art.

The band was conceived in late 1968, following the failure of **Giles, Giles and Fripp** – Mike Giles (Drums), **Pete Giles** (Bass) and **Robert Fripp** (Guitar) – to break through with a quirky pop album, THE CHEERFUL INSANITY OF GILES GILES AND FRIPP (1968). Pete Giles left, **Greg Lake** (vocals/bass), **Ian McDonald** (reeds/keys) and **Pete Sinfield** (lyrics/lights) joined, and as King Crimson the band made an immediate mark on the bill of The Rolling Stones' Hyde Park concert, in front of London's 650,000 most happening folk.

Bringing jazz, folk and classical influences to bear on a rock framework, the group's debut LP, IN THE COURT OF THE CRIMSON KING (1969), was acclaimed as a masterpiece by both the British and American music press. Its extremes of scary heavy rock contrasted dynamically with gentler, almost impossibly quiet sections, while the drama was heightened by dark swaths of Mellotron – a proto-sampler that would remain central to the Crimson sound. On top of that, Pete Sinfield's apocalyptic lyrics gave the album another distinctive quality, which captured the imagination of a hippie audience.

The success of the album – it went Top 30 on both sides of the Atlantic – perhaps did the band more harm than good, as by the end of the year, after an arduous American tour, McDonald and Giles left the band. Greg Lake's departure during the recording of IN THE WAKE OF POSEIDON (1970), to join **EMERSON, LAKE & PALMER**, compounded Fripp's problems, leaving him to complete the album with previous members helping out as session musicians whilst floundering around for replacements (both Elton John and Bryan Ferry reputedly failed singing auditions). Although musically as impressive as its predecessor, the album followed the blueprint too closely.

For the next year and a half, King Crimson existed only as Fripp and whoever was available to play on the records. LIZARD (1970) presented a new and unique sound, the suite on side two particularly being one of Fripp's most cohesive works, using jazz musicians **Keith Tippett** and **Marc Charig** alongside a nucleus of **Mel Collins** (reeds), **Gordon Haskell** (bass/vocals) and **Andy McCullough** (drums).

Fripp eventually assembled a live unit, retaining Collins and bringing in **Ian Wallace** (drums) and **Boz Burrell** (bass guitar/vocals), who were able to put Crimson back on the road to promote ISLANDS (1971). Although a little directionless, this contained one of Fripp's finest moments in the masterful instrumental "Sailor's Tale", and moved the jazz-rock fusion up a notch. It became clear, however, that the band fell short of Fripp's expectations and King Crimson once again fell apart after a US tour that saw the other members' less sophisticated approach increasingly at odds with the reserved, thoughtful guitarist. The live EARTHBOUND (1972) distinguished itself only by being one of the most poorly recorded live albums ever.

The third incarnation of Crimson, which emerged in late 1972, was initially a five-piece featuring Fripp, ex-**FAMILY** man **John Wetton** (bass/vocals), **David Cross** (violin/Mellotron), and the twin percussive assault of **Bill Bruford** (lured from the highly successful **YES**) and **Jamie Muir**. Eschewing old material for largely improvised music, they immediately won acclaim for their anarchic live work, percussionist Muir hurling chains, bouncing around the stage like a madman and running through the audience spitting blood. LARK'S TONGUES IN ASPIC (1973) was a landmark album which showed a transformed King Crimson losing much of the pomp that had sometimes blighted them and gaining a harder, clattering edge.

Shortly after the release of the album, Muir left to join a monastery. Bill Bruford, who had learned much from Muir's free approach to percussion, incorporated these elements into his own playing and the band continued as a four-piece. The following fifteen months were the most stable yet in the band's history and saw them establish a reputation in Europe and America as an awesome live outfit. STARLESS AND BIBLE BLACK (1974) demonstrated this power and continued to break new ground.

When their American tour ended in July 1974, David Cross was edged out of the group, and then Fripp split King Crimson completely, saying it was all over for 'dinosaur bands' (a very early use of the phrase). The posthumous studio album RED (1974) was as strong as any by the band, the elegiac closing piece "Starless" being a fitting conclusion.

Fripp went into semi-retirement, issuing the live USA (1975) and the retrospective A YOUNG PERSON'S GUIDE TO KING CRIMSON (1975), before going on to work on various projects with a multitude of artists between 1975 and 1981. Wetton joined **ROXY MUSIC**, and Bruford had short spells with various luminaries including **GONG**, **ROY HARPER** and **GENESIS**.

Fripp having unequivocally stated that Crimson was over, it came as a surprise when, in 1981, he reconstituted the band with Bruford and Americans **Adrian Belew** (guitar/vocals) and **Tony Levin** (bass/vocals). This was no revivalist exercise. Gone were the reeds, violin and Mellotron of past Crimson line-ups, as the new band forged ahead with a minimal guitar-led mesh of sound fronted by the confident vocals of Belew. The outfit actually sounded more contemporary than they were given credit for, most critics being unable to see beyond the associations conjured up by the name. The aptly titled DISCIPLINE (1981) was a hypnotic blend of patterned guitars and intricate rhythm work which also succeeded in being concise and commercial. BEAT (1982) was a less essential but stylistically similar effort, which saw the band exploring early guitar synthesizers and electronic drum kits. THREE OF A PERFECT PAIR (1984) continued this line of experimentation but suffered from a lack of substance. King Crimson once again ground to a halt towards the end of 1984.

Mainstay Robert Fripp, always the catalyst, re-formed the band after another seven-year interlude spent on other projects. It was again emphasized that there was no nostalgia associated with the decision, but that 'music was flying by that only King Crimson could play'. This time the DISCIPLINE-era line-up was expanded to a 'double-trio' format by the addition of **Trey Gunn** (bass/vocals) and **Pat Mastelotto** (percussion).

EPITAPH: LIVE IN 1969 (1997) was a fifteen-track, two-CD collection of live sessions from the band's classic line-up, progressing from their first radio appearances to their last show at the Fillmore West. For all devotees of Robert Fripp, an essential recording. The group are still very much alive with albums and live shows continuing to flow.

⊙ **Lark's Tongues In Aspic** (1973; EG).
Robert Fripp emerges with the most dynamic line-up yet. Predominantly instrumental in its focus, the album showcases Fripp's improved compositional skills while allowing the percussive mayhem produced by Muir and Bruford free rein. The two-part title track, which book-ends the album, particularly demonstrates the textural range that the players could achieve, from crunching guitar and bass riffs to searing violin and layered percussion.

⊙ **Red** (1974; EG).
An excellent final set from the mid-period line-up. The instrumental title track is a prime example of Crimson's menacing heavy rock, while "Starless" moves effortlessly from Mellotron-led melancholy through intense jazz to reach a suitably grand conclusion.

⊙ **Thrak** (1995; Virgin).
A stunning reassertion of the institution that is King Crimson. Archetypal instrumental terrorism, THRAK incorporates the finer elements of both the 70s and 80s versions of the band, while continuing to break new ground.

⊙ **The Nightwatch: Live At The Amsterdam Concertgebouw** (1998; Discipline Global Mobile).
Not really the band at its best, as Fripp emphasizes in the sleeve notes which come as part of the two-CD package, but still majestic and at times heart-stoppingly beautiful. Much better quality than the many bootlegs of the set already in circulation.

Steve Dinsdale

KING MISSILE

Formed New York, 1987.

Everyone knew a few **John S. Hall** types in college: whimsical, vaguely artistic guys who usually wound up as whimsical, vaguely artistic ad executives. In fact, you might say that Hall became, during **King Missile**'s heyday, the mischievous alter ego of all the young would-be-JSHs who went that way. It helped that Hall also has real gifts, both for stream-of-consciousness poetry and for picking musicians.

Hall had long been poeticizing aloud as part of the 'anti-folk' scene evolving at The Fort in New York's East Village, where the earliest incarnation of King Missile (or, as it was called then, **King Missile Dog Fly Religion**) came about when Hall got his buddy **Dogbowl** to back his poetical ramblings on guitar, and his girlfriend, local guitarist **Rebecca Korbett**, to back him up on drums. (You can hear some of his rants on the out-of-print BROOME CLOSET ANTI-FOLK SESSIONS, on which future major-label acts Paleface, Maggie Estep and Roger Manning also have cuts.) Hall's style was emblematic: a slightly dour elf, he wandered the stage swinging from coffee-bar blasé to corner-preacher manic.

He prevailed upon producer **Kramer** (of Bongwater) to produce a series of three albums on his Shimmy Disc label. The first, DOG FLUTING ON THE HUMP (1987), was a primitive affair – "Sensitive Artist", in which Hall portrays an artist so sensitive that he can't look at paintings because they hurt his eyes, was backed with a sloppy version of "Guantanamera". The second release, THEY (1988), added slightly more ambitious musical backing – **Stephen Danziger** replaced Korbett on drums, and Kramer added synthesized horn parts and other effects that offered a suitably whimsical counterpoint to Hall's words. On the third, MYSTICAL SHIT (1989), **Chris Xefos** took over on bass and **Dave Rick** replaced Dogbowl on guitar. This ensemble added more solid, rock-orientated grooves to support Hall's act.

Atlantic Records got interested and gave King Missile their major-label shot. The first Atlantic disc, THE WAY TO SALVATION (1991), did well enough to warrant another, HAPPY HOUR (1992), which featured the number that got King Missile into heavy rotation and on *Beavis And Butthead* – "Detachable Penis", in which Hall mused on the relative merits and drawbacks of a removable member ('Now and then I go to a party, get drunk, and for the life of me I can't remember what I did with it'). It was, for self-evident reasons, a college-rock hit, but unfortunately gave Atlantic the idea that King Missile should be a novelty band, which Hall wasn't up for. The eponymous follow-up got no support and tanked, and the band folded its tent, though Hall has had occasional thoughts about re-forming.

They (1988; Shimmy Disc).
Do you miss mid-80s college rock in all its sophomoric sweetness? Do you remember the Dead Milkmen? This set features Hall's most genuine and appealing love song, "I'm Open".

Mystical Shit (1989; Shimmy Disc).
The Xefos/Rick debut, featuring the Zen drone, "There Is No Point", and King Missile's first taste of indie fame – "Jesus Was Way Cool" ('He turned water into wine!/That's so cool!').

Happy Hour (1992; Atlantic).
The one about the breakaway dick notwithstanding, this is a solid, cheerful effort with an appropriately manic salute to Martin Scorsese ('If I ever meet him, I'm gonna grab his fucking neck and just shake him ... then stomp on his face forty or fifty times 'cause he makes the best fucking films').

Roy Edroso

KINGS OF CONVENIENCE

Formed Bergen, Norway, 1997.

The **Kings Of Convenience** look like very nice boys, and they sound even nicer, in a kinda twee, acoustic, Norwegian way. As well as becoming figureheads for a whole scene of acoustically biased bespectacled pickers and singers, the duo have also managed to transpose their sounds onto the dance floor, thanks to the help of a few, well-chosen, DJ mates.

Eirik Glambek Boe (guitar) and **Erlend Oye** (guitar) first met at the age of 11 at an inter-schools geography competition in their home town of Bergen, Norway. They didn't meet again until they were sixteen, by which time they both had acoustic guitars. The pair duly formed the indie-influenced **Skog** with two mates, and got as far as releasing an EP before disbanding in the mid-90s to get proper jobs, join the army, or in Boe's case, to study psychology.

Oye continued to play music in Bergen with **Peachfuzz**, then he and Boe relocated to England, where Boe continued his studies. It was at a gig at the Poetry Place in Covent Garden that the duo came up with their name, for what could be more convenient that having no more equipment than yourselves and a couple of amp-free acoustic guitars?

The pair were not to enjoy much recognition until they visited Manchester to perform as part of the In The City music festival. They stayed in a house owned by the cellist from the band Alfie and found themselves amongst a like-minded community that included Badly Drawn Boy – a community that would come to be known as 'the new acoustic movement'.

The Kings of Convenience released their first two singles for Ellet in 1999 and then recorded an eponymous debut album for the American Kindercore label (2000). The breakthrough came when they signed to Source and brought out QUIET IS THE NEW LOUD in 2001. Produced by **Ken Nelson** (Coldplay, Badly Drawn Boy) and borrowing six songs from their first album, this record was a shy, simple and fragile set.

Comparisons with Simon and Garfunkel were not misplaced, although the gentle humour of the lyrics had perhaps more in common with Belle And Sebastian. The same year Virgin released an album of remixes of songs from QUIET IS THE NEW LOUD, entitled VERSUS, which enjoyed crossover appeal in the DJ fraternity. The record was a hit-and-miss affair, with some tracks sounding little different at all, while other remixers (such as Ladytron) wholly changed the atmosphere; the best cuts came from contributors who had continued with the less-is-more atmosphere, as Four Tet did with "The Weight Of My Words".

Erlend obviously enjoyed life with beats, as he released his own solo collection of collaborations, UNREST, in 2003; the set featured ten songs and ten comrades, among them Morgan Geist and Schneider TM. Overall, the collection had a lot going for it, and has helped to ease the Kings Of Convenience out of the nose-dive that was by then killing the new acoustic movement.

(By the way, Oye won the geography competition.)

Quiet Is The New Loud (2001; Source/Astralwerks).
Nick Drake you can dance to, Belle and Sebastian hitting the right notes, Elliot Smith with jokes: the gentle duo prove that physical weakness is the new emotional strength.

Annebella Pollen

THE KINKS

Formed London, 1964.

"People always said The Kinks would never last – but we survived the silly 60s, the sordid 70s and the hateful 80s." Ray Davies

Formed as an R&B band by guitarist **Dave Davies**, **The Kinks** soon became the vehicle for the songs and singing of his elder brother, **Ray**, one of the most acute and witty social observers in the history of British rock. The first hit (#1 in 1964) was "You Really Got Me". It was the heaviest British recording yet made, driven by a distorted garage riff and delivered by Ray in an excitable shout. Over the next two years a succession of hits took the band towards a softer, more reflective sound: the playing was still elementary, but Ray's songwriting was developing faster than anyone else's. "All Day And All Of The Night", "Tired Of Waiting For You", "Set Me Free", "Till The End Of The Day" and "Dedicated Follower Of Fashion" all hit the Top 10, establishing The Kinks as the most English of pop groups.

When The Beatles rewrote rock with SGT PEPPER, The Kinks found the perfect response: a retreat into the past. Their 1967 album, SOMETHING ELSE, offered a self-deprecating title that matched its contents. While rock was enjoying a chemical world, The Kinks celebrated "Afternoon Tea" and tobacco. A collection of short stories and character sketches, the album climaxed with the glorious "End Of The Season", end-of-pier melancholia that sounded like the closing theme to the archetypal British movie. As an encore came "Waterloo Sunset", still their most cherished work and showing the band at an absolute peak. A simple statement of love in the city, its effortless delivery and valedictory atmosphere made it almost unbearably poignant.

SOMETHING ELSE remains the most influential Kinks album, but the next two were nearly as impressive. THE VILLAGE GREEN PRESERVATION SOCIETY (1968), the first Kinks concept album, took the fashionable dalliance with music hall seriously, in a wistful tribute to the lost simplicities of Edwardian England. ARTHUR, OR THE DECLINE AND FALL OF THE BRITISH EMPIRE (1969) was originally written for television, and presented a darker mood. As the subtitle suggested, the theme was the crumbling self-image of Britain, with the shadow of war ever present – if it weren't for some of Ray's most beautiful tunes, it would have been thoroughly depressing.

By now The Kinks were having image problems. The musicianship was so rudimentary that, though Ray wanted to go beyond hit singles, they were never going to make sense in a market dominated by

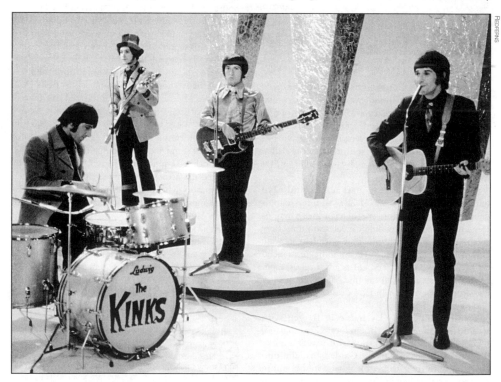

REDFERNS

60s beat combo The Kinks mime for TV: from left, Mick Avory, Dave Davies, Peter Quaife and Ray Davies

the likes of Cream. Nor was Davies' respect for 'ordinary' people entirely acceptable in the political atmosphere of The Stones' "Street Fighting Man". The Kinks fitted into neither pop nor rock, the album sales tailed off, the hit singles became scarcer, and the band entered the 70s looking confused. The situation wasn't helped by some terrible concept albums. The problem with English music hall was that most of it was dreadful, and so too were The Kinks' albums of the 70s. Even when they released strong singles such as "Supersonic Rocketship", the gender-bending masterpiece "Lola" and "Celluloid Heroes", they failed to storm the charts. In America, however, the band retained a loyal following, and LOW BUDGET (1979) reinvigorated their career. Their version of American rock was convincing enough to launch them onto the stadium circuit, too, and strong enough to proffer hopes for a return to form. High-profile covers such as Bowie's stab at "Where Have All The Good Times Gone?", "Stop Your Sobbing" as reinterpreted by The Pretenders and The Jam's version of "David Watts" also helped raise their stock.

It was a false new dawn. The 80s saw a couple of excellent singles ("Better Days", "Don't Forget To Dance") and their biggest US hit, "Come Dancing", but they were outposts on lacklustre albums. Still, the band remained an effective live outfit, where the quality of the songs, low-budget showmanship and shambolic energy could still work wonders, as witnessed by TO THE BONE (1996), which mixed live cuts with unplugged recordings – including an irresistible Tex-Mex take on "Apeman".

In the mid-90s the tide had turned again in Britain, as Ray Davies was namechecked as a major (and very obvious) influence by Blur's **Damon Albarn**. Davies and Albarn did a TV show together; The Kinks got a retrospective TV special of their own; and both Davies brothers published autobiographies, Ray's – *X-Ray* – proving typically overambitious, infuriatingly messy and occasionally brilliant.

1998 saw the reissue of some of their greatest albums: LIVE AT KELVIN HALL, THE VILLAGE GREEN PRESERVATION SOCIETY, ARTHUR, OR THE DECLINE AND FALL OF THE BRITISH EMPIRE; PART ONE, LOLA VERSUS POWERMAN & THE MONEYGOROUND and PERCY, all on Essential Records, and KINKS, KINDA KINKS, THE KINK KONTROVERSY, FACE TO FACE and SOMETHING ELSE BY... all on Castle, presenting the spirit of classic 60s English pop to yet another generation.

⊙ **Something Else** (1967; PRT).
The Kinks' finest hour. Ray's lyrics were increasingly about the struggle to maintain humanity and individuality in the modern world, and here his vision achieved its perfect realization. The Jam's SOUND AFFECTS and Blur's PARKLIFE owe a lot to this album.

⊙ **The Best Of The Kinks: 20 Classic Tracks** (1994; Kaz).
There are many compilations, all with the same obvious selections. This is the most recent and acceptable.

Alwyn W. Turner

KISS

Formed New York, 1972.

From The New York Dolls they took the glamour, from Alice Cooper the theatrics, and from Slade the stomp-along songs. Thus did **Kiss** – the bastard creation of New Yorkers **Gene Simmons** (bass) and **Paul Stanley** (vocals) – conquer the world...

Not that it all happened overnight. Early Simmons and Stanley bands – including Rainbow (not the Ritchie Blackmore one) and Wicked Lester – disappeared without trace, before they formed Kiss in 1972, recruiting **Peter Criss** (drums) and **Ace Frehley** (guitar). The quartet's self-promotion attracted the managerial eye of TV producer and label boss Bill Aucoin, whose credit card allegedly funded a gruelling sequence of tours promoting early albums, KISS, HOTTER THAN HELL (both 1974) and DRESSED TO KILL (1975).

The latter hovered around the Top 30 in the US, but it was the ALIVE! double live album (1975) that was the breakthrough, propelling the band into the Top 10 and the imaginations of a generation of wannabes (stand up Skid Row, Anthrax and Guns N' Roses). Buoyed by encroaching superstardom and greater support from their Casablanca label (home also to Donna Summer), Kiss took America by the throat: blood-and-thunder stage shows, overkill merchandizing and a prolific output combining to eclipse even Led Zeppelin in rock's heavyweight division, 1975–77.

It was a success that flew in the face of pretty much universal critical hostility, howls of protests from the moral majority, and – apropos the lightning-bolt 'S's of the band's logo – accusations of Nazism ('An interesting feat for Jews', observed Stanley). Strangely, too, bearing in mind their Neanderthal lyrics, many of Kiss's most loyal fans were (doubtless still are) women, and Simmons himself achieved gossip-column status by dating Cher and Diana Ross, neither renowned for meek obedience. At the cheaper end of the celeb scale, Stanley took an interest in UK pin-up starlet Samantha Fox.

Kiss's platinum period took in DESTROYER and ROCK AND ROLL OVER (both 1976), the former reaching a career peak #22 placing in Britain, and LOVE GUN (1977), before ALIVE II (1977) brought the era neatly to an end. Then the band went crazy and, in 1978, simultaneously released four solo albums. None had the energy and wild lack of restraint of their collective efforts, and many date the decline of the band from this point. It was of course punk time, and a new generation was stepping on up.

After a hit with the band's return album, DYNASTY (#9 in the US), and its disco-fied single "I Was Made For Loving You" (1979), chart placings plummeted and the band began to fall apart. Criss went in 1980, being replaced by **Eric Carr** (drums), and after THE ELDER (1981), a commercially disastrous rock opera, he was followed by Frehley.

Still, there was life in the beat and, revitalized by new guitarist **Vinnie Vincent**, Kiss recorded CREATURES OF THE NIGHT (1982), an album which, in Stanley's words, 'you put on when you want to turn your mind to jelly'. Further rejuvenation followed the ditching of their trademark war paint, and the appearance of LICK IT UP (1983), which went to #24 in the US and #7 in the UK, though multi-platinum record sales were now the domain of Motley Crüe, who vainly claimed that their lurid image was not Kiss-derived.

Subsequent upheavals included Vincent being fired and rehired, then replaced by **Mark St John**, who was himself ousted in favour of **Bruce Kulick**. The latter – now Kiss's longest-serving guitarist – had impeccable credentials: his brother Bob had deputized (uncredited) for the incapacitated Frehley in 1981, and he had concluded his association with former employer Michael Bolton by throwing an effects pedal at the crooner's head.

With this new line-up, the band's sales were big, if not mega, and as fashion had it they were now more popular in Britain than the States, with CRAZY, CRAZY NIGHTS (1987) hitting #4 in the UK. Meantime, Simmons – by his own admission the least able to cope without the make-up – widened his interests, notching up production credits for, among others, Wendy O. Williams's superb WOW album (boasting cameos from Stanley, Frehley and Carr), and appearing in a scene-stealing role alongside Tom Selleck in *Runaway*. Less successful were attempts to launch his own record and management companies – first client, Liza Minnelli.

1990 saw Kiss return to the US Top 10 singles chart with "Forever", and the appearance of a tribute album, HARD TO BELIEVE, which boasted a then-obscure Nirvana among acts paying homage. After two decades of Kiss-tory, it was finally OK to drop the band's name outside the metal fraternity. (KISS MY ASS, a second tribute album in 1994, yielded even more implausible contributors in Garth Brooks, Stevie Wonder and The Lemonheads).

Eric Carr died from a cancer growth in 1991, shortly before the band scored a major hit with "God Gave Rock And Roll To You" (1991), written for the film *Bill & Ted's Bogus Journey*. Eric Singer took over the drum stool and, denouncing most of their post-CREATURES discography, the band pursued metallic bliss once again with REVENGE (1992) and ALIVE III (1993).

1995 saw a much-mooted reunion of the original quartet for the obligatory 'Unplugged' performance, while the current line-up entertained US revellers with acoustic sets at a Travelling Kiss Konvention. Then in 1996 a fully-fledged revival tour – Frehley, Criss, make-up and all – became one of the summer's hottest tickets, featuring seriously over-the-top pyrotechnics and special effects. Kiss were officially back and just in case you doubted it, the official merchandise machine began to go into overdrive as well. The success of the tour was undeniable and the band thought the time was right to release PSYCHO CIRCUS (1998), an album which was meant to harness the magic of their heyday but which was in reality rather less focused. Nevertheless, this could not dampen the ardour of their fans who turned out in their thousands for what was rumoured to be the band's final world tour. Things did not go as smoothly as they might have towards the end of this gargantuan undertaking as on the eve of their Japanese and Australian stint in 2001 Pete Criss left the band following an apparent wrangle over money. In his stead **Eric Singer** stepped in and donned Criss's Cat-man make-up.

And just in case you thought that Kiss had finally been consigned to the annals of rock history, consider this – what band in their right mind would shut down such a lucrative merchandising machine so utterly and completely? You can expect to see Kiss duvets, wine, chocolate bars, underwear and crockery for a good few years yet – even if the band haven't got an album to promote.

Destroyer (1976; Casablanca).
The fans' favourite. "God Of Thunder" and "Shout It Out Loud" are the anthems, "Beth" is the weepie and "Do You Love Me" was the one Kurt covered.

Double Platinum (1978; Casablanca).
The only hits compilation worth bothering with.

Creatures Of The Night (1982; Casablanca).
A very metal muthafucker. "I Love It Loud", indeed.

Bruno MacDonald

KITCHENS OF DISTINCTION

Formed Amsterdam, The Netherlands, 1987; split 1996.

The Kitchens of Distinction liked to shroud their origins in multiple myths. Sometimes they said that they met in a Turkish sauna; sometimes in a satanist temple in Amsterdam; sometimes – most credibly – at a Dutch gig by the reggae legend Burning Spear. Drummer **Dan Goodwin** had been involved with East London experimentalists AR Kane; guitarist **Julian Swales**, had, it was said, been in an early incarnation of fluffy goth types **ALL ABOUT EVE**. But singer and bass player **Patrick Fitzgerald** was not, as was often assumed, the punk poet of the same name: he had been a doctor before deciding to chance it in the world of pop.

The Kitchens' first single, "Last Gasp Death Shuffle", was *Single of the Week* in the *NME*. "Prize", which followed in October 1988 on One Little Indian (the label made trendy by The Sugarcubes), was a very fine single, a mixture of the tuneful jangliness that had been indie pop's staple since Orange Juice, and bigger, more ambitious noises that suggested both the Cocteau Twins and dub-reggae. But "Prize" was also one of the first explicitly gay guitar-pop records. Apart from the dabblings of Lou Reed and David Bowie in the early 70s, most openly gay pop had been disco – the Kitchens' candid reflections on queer promiscuity were at odds with the very basic boy-loses-girl agenda of most indie records.

Another cracking single, "The 3rd Time We Opened The Capsule" (1989), preceded the release of the debut album, LOVE IS HELL. It picked up good reviews with its mix of lush effects-saturated guitars and dubby rhythms – a harder, more emotional approach than the easily washed away waffles of AR Kane. The autumn's ELEPHANTINE EP impressed with its title track, and the anti-Thatcherite "Margaret's Injection", plus the impressive reggae-rooted and vast sounding "Anvil Dub". Their live shows were fine too, their down-to-earth wit undercutting any cathedrals-of-sound tendencies in the music. Although they were never consensus music press favourites and were a long way from the Manchester lads who were starting to dominate the charts, it all seemed a matter of time before the Kitchens hit the big time.

Alas, the next single, "Quick As Rainbows", failed to turn them into popular heroes, and 1991's album, STRANGE FREE WORLD, despite providing another fab single in "Gorgeous Love", was somehow flat and lifeless. The Kitchens had become a very poor man's Psychedelic Furs. Even the distinctive, slightly kitsch packaging of their previous records had been dumped for a distinctly humour-free Japanese wave painting.

Still, the band played on, and although Britain had given up on them, America seemed more promising, with college radio play keeping them touring the US. DEATH OF COOL (1992), however, was neither a commercial or qualitative advance. After 1994's COWBOYS AND ALIENS hit the bargain bins without a backward glance, One Little Indian quietly dropped the band. Undeterred, the Kitchens picked themselves up, shortened their name to Kitchens OD, and signed to the small Fierce Panda label, for one more push.

The group did manage to achieve one more *Single of the Week* with "Feel My Genie" in 1996, but soon after decided that it was time to split.

Love Is Hell (1989; One Little Indian).
Like a spacey Smiths, full of gloomy joys: revel in the dubby "Shiver", the poppy "The 3rd Time We Opened the Capsule" and the hugely melodramatic "Prize".

Elephantine (1989; One Little Indian).
Buy this EP for the Tory-dissing "Margaret's Injection" but mostly for the immense "Anvil Dub", a testament to what might have been.

Mark Elliot

THE KLF

Formed as The Justified Ancients Of Mu Mu, Scotland, 1987; became KLF 1989; disbanded 1992.

"I'm not interested in songs about seventeen-year-old angst and drugs. I'm 38. These days I'm interested in songs about how difficult it is to get baby-sitters."
Bill Drummond

Bill Drummond (vocals/keyboards/programming/sampling) was a major figure on the British music scene long before **The KLF** (Kopyright Liberation Front) had even been thought of. A founder member of punk band Big In Japan, he had helped set up the Zoo Records label and had managed Echo And The Bunnymen and The Teardrop Explodes. In between times, he worked as an A&R man for WEA, where he signed a dance band called Brilliant, featuring the talents of Scots guitar player **Jimmy Cauty**. In 1986 Drummond left WEA and Cauty left Brilliant, and a year later the two teamed up to form **The Justified Ancients Of Mu Mu**. Strange days were on the horizon.

The JAMs were not so much a band as a concept. After a decade spent working in the industry, Drummond was heartily sick of the music business, and conceived The JAMs as the world's first anti-music pop stars. Instead of instruments, the band created their sound by sampling extracts from other people's records. Their first album, 1987 – WHAT THE FUCK IS GOING ON?, lifted bits from such illustrious names as The Beatles, Led Zeppelin and Abba, but The JAMs' failure to observe the legal niceties resulted in legal action from the Swedish stars, forcing Drummond and Cauty to destroy the 500 copies they had pressed. They did so by catching a ferry to Sweden and throwing the albums overboard. Years later, they were to pull stunts that made this escapade seem mild.

After recording a second album, WHO KILLED THE JAMS? (1988), the JAMs renamed themselves **The Timelords**, and before they knew it they had a UK #1 record on their hands, "Doctorin' The Tardis", sampling the *Doctor Who* theme tune, a bit of Sweet, a touch of Gary Glitter and a smearing of Harry Enfield's Thatcherite yob Loadsamoney. The duo explained their success in a self-published booklet called *The Manual (Or How To Have A Number One Without Really Trying)*, an astute study of the science of hit-making, which claimed that anyone could enjoy chart success if they stuck to the golden rules that the band had identified – with the proviso that 'sticking to the golden rules is boring'. After their brush with success, they promptly broke the very rules they had drawn up and released another novelty record, "Kylie Said To Jason". It was a massive flop.

From #1 to number nowhere, Cauty and Drummond turned their attention away from the mainstream and concentrated, instead, upon ambient music. While Cauty founded **THE ORB**, CHILL OUT (1990), an album still regarded highly by dance-trance aficionados, was released by the band under the new name of The KLF. Sadly, like the other records the band released during their ambient phase, it didn't sell particularly well.

What did sell, though, and in big numbers, were the so-called 'Stadium House Trilogy' dance singles – "What Time Is Love?", "3am Eternal" (a UK #1 and US #5) and "Last Train To Transcentral", which were released in various 7" and 12" dance formats and were catchy as hell. They were collected on the

album, THE WHITE ROOM (1990), which transformed the anti-pop stars into the biggest-selling artists in Britain (again #1) and did good business pretty much everywhere else (#39 in the US). The group celebrated their new success with a trip to the Shetlands to set light to a *Wicker Man*-style effigy. In the months and years to come, **King Boy D** and **Rockman Rock**, as Drummond and Cauty now referred to themselves, would waste a lot more on similarly extravagant pranks – most explicitly when they (quite literally and on film) burned one million pounds in banknotes.

On record, the band furthered their perversity when they teamed up with the Queen of Country, Tammy Wynette. "Justified And Ancient" (1991), the fruit of this collaboration, went huge in both Britain and the States – somehow Drummond and Cauty had managed to make country music hip. Prior to this outing, they also resurrected The Justified Ancients for a one-off single, "It's Grim Up North", blending an A–Z of northern English towns with an orchestral arrangement of "Jerusalem" for another improbable smash. A gloriously overproduced remix of "America: What Time Is Love?", released in early 1992, charted massively, too.

However, the duo were growing tired of their golden touch and set out to make themselves as uncommercial as possible. February 12, 1992 was the day The KLF were scheduled to self-destruct. Invited to perform at the annual BPI awards ceremony, Drummond and Cauty saw their chance to pull off an appalling anti-publicity stunt: they would cut up a dead sheep on stage in front of the big nobs of British music and a projected TV audience of nine million. They were only stopped from going ahead by the protests of their co-performers for the evening, thrash-metal merchants and vegetarian anti-fascists, Extreme Noise Terror. The lads knew that they had failed when The KLF won the Brit award for *Best Band*.

They went strangely silent for a while, but for an appearance at a BBC Radio 1-sponsored stock car

rally. Numerous celebrities attended the event in privately owned vehicles; The KLF turned up in an armoured car. Then, on May 14, the biggest-selling band of 1991 announced they were quitting the music business and deleting their entire back catalogue. As the music press went into meltdown, Drummond and Cauty departed for Mexico and the band's albums began to disappear from record shops. People began to conclude that this time The KLF might not have been kidding.

It is now over three years since The KLF quit the music scene. In that time, their main foray into the art world occurred when, under the name **The K Foundation**, Drummond and Cauty awarded artist Rachel Whiteread £40,000 for 'House' – a plaster cast of the interior of a London dwelling – as the worst work of art of 1993. Days earlier, Whiteread had picked up Britain's prestigious Turner Prize for the selfsame work. As for the music, The KLF remained silent save for an anonymous appearance on the HELP charity album (1995), mixing the "Theme From The Big Country" with spooky tapes from Serbian radio. They launched a brief guerrilla raid on the media when their 'Fuck The Millennium' campaign was revealed in a one-off show at London's Barbican Arts Centre in September 1997. Supported by the striking Liverpool Dockers they drew attention to the obscenity they perceived in spending a billion pounds of public money on millennial celebrations whilst rereleasing "What Time Is Love?" as "2K..." dressed in institutional pyjamas and wheeling themselves around madly on stage in powered wheelchairs. Fans were delighted to see the reappearance of their famous rhinoceros-horn headdresses.

Drummond now seems to be concentrating on writing, and has said that he would be quite happy if he never heard another dance record in his life, but was happy to lend his name to yet another novelty record, Solid Gold Chartbusters' "1-2-1", which sent up users of mobile phones and promptly flopped. Such is The KLF track record that only a fool would imagine we have heard their last – though as time goes by the waiting turns to resignation.

Shag Times (1988; KLF Communications).
Sit back and gasp as The JAMs take on Samantha Fox, Dave Brubeck, The Beatles, Whitney Houston, Petula Clark and Sly And The Family Stone, and win!

Chill Out (1990; KLF Communications; reissued by TVT).
A post-club ambient classic where sheep, Elvis and Tibetan monks somehow manage to sit happily side by side by side. The reissue is easy to pick up, but expect to pay big money for an original.

The White Room (1990; KLF Communications).
In effect a 'greatest hits' release, this contains "What Time Is Love?", "3am Eternal", "Last Train To Transcentral" and an early, Wynette-free, rendition of "Justified And Ancient". Unlike most KLF releases, this is still relatively easy to get hold of.

America: What Time is Love? (1992; KLF Communicat-ions).
A spoken introduction, screaming guitars, Gregorian chants and ex-Deep Purple frontman Glenn Hughes – the single that gave overproduction a good name.

Richard Luck

KORN

Formed Bakersfield, California, 1993.

Korn could never have existed without grunge. Amongst the pioneers of the alternative metal explosion of the mid 90s, Korn combined a whole host of metal and hip-hop influences with the anti-rock stance of grunge to create a fresh angle on a familiar sound. The original line-up consisted of **James 'Munky' Shaffer** (guitar), **Brian 'Head' Welch** (guitar), **Reginald 'Fieldy' Arvizu** (bass) and **David Silveria** (drums), all of them members of California band LAPD. It wasn't until singer (and bagpipe torturer) **Jonathan Davis**, who worked by day in a mortuary, joined from local band Sexart that Korn began their controversial career in earnest.

As ever, the early days involved the band working as pizza chefs, furniture movers, and cleaners whilst building a demo and a local following. In Davis they possessed an individual who was not afraid to recount personal stories of trauma and abuse in his lyrics, and when this hard-hitting subject matter was combined with the band's ugly, downtuned sound the result was quite unique. The music was brutal, yet the cathartic rage and rhythmic pulse saw them dubbed unimaginatively as 'funk metal' and Davis's unusual style varied between singing, half-rapping and breathless shrieking. Apart from the music the band also developed an early visual sense; here was a band so concerned about street cred they needed no encouragement to wear not just the trainers but the entire athletic wardrobe – enough to make a sportswear manufacturer hyperventilate.

Signed to Epic's Immortal imprint and decked out in flashy Adidas gear, the band produced KORN (1994). The underground buzz on the band grew steadily but it took tours with Ozzy Osbourne, Megadeth and Marilyn Manson eventually to send the album platinum. Even less sonically palatable and more disturbing, not least because of Davis's bagpipe playing, was LIFE IS PEACHY (1996), which was a more instant success producing a hit in "No Place To Hide". Other notably unpleasant tracks included such sing-along ditties as "Porno Creep", "A.D.I.D.A.S" (All Day I Dream About Sex) and a thorough mauling of the War classic "Low Rider".

By the time of FOLLOW THE LEADER (1998), featuring cover art by hot comic artist **Todd McFarlane** (creator of *Spawn*) and hit single "Got The Life", Korn were truly secure at the vanguard of alternative metal, a position that was maintained with the devastatingly good ISSUES (1999).

For many Korn had kick-started the nu-metal onslaught that was by then galloping at full speed, and by the time of UNTOUCHABLES (2002) it seemed that they could do no wrong. The set was intense, threatening, polished, and guaranteed to annoy parents everywhere.

Korn (1994; Immortal/Epic).
Sludgy, nasty heavy metal, replete with lyrics covering all manner of unsavoury topics. No hit singles, just plain old-fashioned raging throughout.

Follow The Leader (1998; Immortal/Epic).
Displaying a hitherto unsuspected sense of dynamics, the big production job made Korn one of the biggest alternative bands to cross over into the mainstream consciousness.

Essi Berelian

LEO KOTTKE

Born Athens, Georgia, September 11, 1945.

The inclusion of **Leo Kottke** in a rock book is justified more through his influence than his own records – or sales. Kottke's skill on the six- and twelve-string acoustic guitar has had an incalculable effect on other serious players, and his status as a cult figure seems sure to endure well into the future.

Kottke developed an early interest in blues and played his first live dates in the mid-60s while checking out the gigs of any credible blues figure within travelling distance of his home. His first recordings were largely folk-based material for obscure US labels, but by 1971 manager Denny Bruce had organized a deal with Capitol Records.

Kottke's time with Capitol and Bruce was characterized by some friction, as his own idiosyncratic ideas often grated against commercial wisdom, but his work for the label was always interesting and frequently exceptional. His debut Capitol album, MUDLARK (1972), placed him uneasily in the singer-songwriter category (he has described his voice as being like 'geese farts on a muggy day'), but displayed his amazing ability to exploit the varied sounds of the acoustic guitar, being equally at home pulling fast flurries of notes from a twelve-string or dragging the last lingering second of a note from a slow composition.

In the early to mid-70s, using backing musicians and throwing in some surprising cover versions, Kottke began to gain low chart places. Stand-out albums from this period included the live MY FEET ARE SMILING (1973) and CHEWING PINE (1975), the latter reaching the US Top 50 for the first time. 1975 also saw significant success outside the US, including a headlining appearance in the UK at the Cambridge Folk Festival, but despite growing commercial success, Kottke and Capitol parted company in 1976, and the guitarist signed to Chrysalis.

Sales dwindled, but this didn't seem to worry Kottke, who produced an eclectic and increasingly confident series of albums for Chrysalis, including another superb solo live effort, LIVE IN EUROPE (1980), the exquisitely crafted GUITAR MUSIC (1981) and TIME STEP (1983). The last album was a very accessible collection that used a strong rhythm section on some tracks and benefited from a clear and unfussy production from T-Bone Burnett.

Kottke was voted Best Acoustic Guitarist five years running in *Guitar* magazine, but his powerful technique had caused pains in his right hand that hampered his playing. Kottke remodelled his technique along the lines normally associated with classical performers before signing to Private Music, a label launched by former Tangerine Dream electrowizard Peter Baumann.

His releases for Private Music, which began with A SHOUT TOWARD NOON (1986), showed a more reflective quality and an even greater appreciation of tone. Ensuing albums continued his eclectic mix of folk, country, blues, bluegrass and jazz influences, and showed his eagerness to work with a wide array of musical talent – Lyle Lovett appeared on GREAT BIG BOY (1991), while PECULIAROSO (1994) benefited from the production skills of Rickie Lee Jones. His 1997 outing, STANDING IN MY SHOES (the title track here being an oldie lifted from his own Mudlark album), featured one of the most arresting tunes in his career, "Across The Street". The remainder of the album was jaunty enough and masterfully performed, concentrating on six-string pieces.

As the century ended Kottke played dates in prestigious venues – such as Harvard University – more used to classical events, and staged a brief Alaskan tour. In an era when 'unplugged' means 'honest, emotional and accomplished', Kottke sets standards few can match. He continues to enthral a devoted audience and the current availability of his Takoma, Capitol and Chrysalis catalogue should allow the cult to grow further. Anyone wishing to explore his unique style could also do worse than check out ONE GUITAR, NO VOCALS (1999), and his recent collaboration with Phish bassist **Mike Gordon**, CLONE (2002).

⊙ **A Shout Toward Noon** (1986; Private Music).
This instrumental album is eloquent, beautiful and atmospheric – the sort of thing that gets New Age music a good name.

⊙ **Leo Live** (1995; Private Music).
A timely live collection, with some exceptional playing throughout.

⊙ **The Best** (1994; Beat Goes On).
A compilation of the best of the Capitol work, with great sleeve notes and a considered selection that shows the range of Kottke's abilities. A double CD at a single CD price, this is the finest introduction you're likely to get.

⊙ **Standing In My Shoes** (1997; Private).
Surprisingly lively and accessible set from the increasingly eclectic Kottke.

⊙ **1971–1976 Did You Hear Me?** (1998; Beat Goes On).
Splendid compilation of live and studio material.

Neil Nixon

KRAFTWERK

Formed Düsseldorf, Germany, 1969.

"We play the machines but the machines also play us ... We try to treat them as colleagues so they exchange energies with us."
Ralf Hütter

Ralf Hütter and **Florian Schneider** met at the Düsseldorf Conservatory in 1968, where both were studying music. Schneider went on to play flute in a band with jazz saxophonist Klaus Doldinger and future members of Amon Düül II, before joining Hütter in an outfit called Organisation. In 1970, Organisation produced an album that encapsulated the current trend in German music for free-form improvisation laid over a relatively simple rhythm, using Eastern influences to break away from standard European chord progressions.

After its release, Hütter and Schneider left to form **Kraftwerk** (German for 'power station'), recruiting **Klaus Dinger** and **Thomas Hohman** to record their first album KRAFTWERK (aka HIGHRAIL). This was followed by a series of personnel changes – from which came the formation of the seminal **NEU!** – leaving Hütter and Schneider as a duo. Their second album, KRAFTWERK 2 (VAR), was less successful, but at this point Hütter and Schneider became friendly with musician/artist **Emil Schult**, playing some jam sessions and concerts with him and his associates. It was Schult who masterminded the group's change of image into a blend of Germanic romanticism and formal, stark modernity.

With the third album, RALF AND FLORIAN, the overlays of electronic effects and conventional instruments pointed the direction they were to follow. Arrival at their destination was marked by the release of AUTOBAHN (1974), on which they worked with **Wolfgang Flur** (electronic percussion) and **Klaus Roeder** (electric violin). A frigid and mesmerizingly repetitive synthscape, AUTOBAHN took off in both the US and Britain, where a generation of synthesizer minimalists were to derive inspiration from the Kraftwerk sound. The album reached high positions in the charts on both sides of the Atlantic, and in early 1975 an edited version of the title track similarly scaled the singles charts. Just as audiences were losing interest in the more avant-garde manifestations of Krautrock – such as Can, Amon Düül II and Faust – Kraftwerk captured a new constituency with pulsing, driving electronica that was to galvanize the dance scene as well as mainstream rock artists such as David Bowie and The Human League.

Hütter, by now the group's spokesman, began to conjure with the idea of electronic instruments which could tour by themselves while he and Schneider sunbathed and pushed buttons to start the gig. RADIOACTIVITY (1975) was released shortly after **Karl Bartos** (more percussion) joined the outfit, replacing Roeder and furthering the hi-tech vision. At some points the only sound was that of radio interference and static – a direction that ex-Can man Holger Czukay was simultaneously exploring – while many of the vocals were synthetic. Despite its innovations, the album didn't do well, in part because of Kraftwerk's perceived support for nuclear power, a stigma they would find hard to get rid of in Germany.

During this period, Hütter and Schneider met up with Bowie, prompting rumours of collaborations that never materialized. The only concrete results were the use of Kraftwerk's music as 'entrance music'

Impeccably coiffed and uniformed, Kraftwerk chart a new course for Eurodisco

at Bowie concerts, the track "V2 Schneider" on HEROES, and namechecks for Bowie and Iggy Pop on Kraftwerk's next album, TRANS-EUROPE EXPRESS (1977), a record that did much to restore their reputation and provided fuel for countless future samplers. (Afrika Bambaataa's "Planet Rock" was a sample too far, and became the subject of a lawsuit.)

The next release, THE MAN MACHINE (1978), took the machine-as-master concept a stage further – the opening track, "The Robots", summed it all up. The only track referring to a human, "The Model", became a #1 single in the UK, while numerous electronic bands plundered the album for inspiration. Meanwhile, Kraftwerk live shows featured robots on stage and ended with music playing without apparent human intervention.

With COMPUTER WORLD (1981), however, the ideas had come to seem overworked and the band seemed to be running out of steam. This was underlined by another long silence, broken only by the release of a single, "Tour De France" (1983). The album from which it was taken was scrapped, and it wasn't until 1986 that ELECTRIC CAFE was released. Again Kraftwerk were disappointing, with a set that appeared to be little more than their response to disco music. THE MIX, released in 1991, featured successful remixes of some tracks (notably "Radioactivity") plus less successful versions of others, and ignored numerous pieces that could have been successfully updated, such as "Tanzmusik" from RALF AND FLORIAN.

During the recording of THE MIX, both Bartos and Flur departed, feeling that they were superfluous. In 1998, after a long silence, the band suddenly embarked on a worldwide series of concerts. Despite occasional hiccups (they agreed to pull out of one gig because time would not allow them to set up their equipment), they were rapturously received, and the presence of a couple of new pieces raised hopes of a new recording to accompany the release of a live concert (recorded at the time of AUTOBAHN). However, given their notorious secrecy (no phone in their studio, no visitors, no mail answered, virtually no interviews and few photographs), it seemed dangerous to make assumptions. Patience was rewarded, to a degree, in 2000 by the release of a new single, "Expo 2000". It's slightly limp electronic ambience hardly heralded a triumphant return, but who knows what this surprising band have yet to unleash.

● **Autobahn** (1974; EMI).
The first definitive Kraftwerk opus. An electronic epic with man and machine in perfect harmony.

● **Trans-Europe Express** (1977; Cleopatra).
A journey through a dehumanized global village.

● **The Man Machine** (1978; Cleopatra).
The apotheosis of Kraftwerk's robomusic, allied to their most attractive tunes. "The Model" is the most hummable electronic single ever.

Paul O'Brien

LENNY KRAVITZ

Born New York, 1964.

Jewish-Bahamian **Lenny Kravitz**, the son of a TV producer father and actress mother, began his rise to fame as a teen actor, but his big break came in 1984, when he met Henry Hirsch, who shared a predilection for late-60s rock and pre-digital recording. With Hirsch a background collaborator, mixing and playing keyboards, and Kravitz doing more or less everything else, they set about reinventing music to the tune of 1967.

Few artists have prompted such extremes of euphoria and resentment as Kravitz did with his first album, LET LOVE RULE (1989). According to which magazine you were reading, he was the saviour of modern music or a waste of space with a good record collection. The only point of agreement was on his wild hippie dress sense, which nobody could fathom. Kravitz put a clean and sharp guitar sound through a valve amp and mixed it with Fender Rhodes, simple drum patterns, rubbery bass, a smattering of horns and strings, and howled peace and love over the top. The effect was never meant to be original: Jimi Hendrix, Curtis Mayfield and John Lennon were named in the reviews almost as often as Kravitz himself. Some cried plagiarism, but many were happy enough with Kravitz's own explanation that, if the best music was being written twenty years earlier, there was nothing wrong with going back to the same ingredients and trying it again. Besides, the themes went beyond flower-power retrogression, to encompass racism ("Mr. Cab Driver") and religion in adversity ("Rosemary"). He went to some lengths to demonstrate his seriousness to a cynical public: the single of "Let Love Rule" appeared with the sheet music printed on the sleeve.

A successful tour followed, and enough publicity had been created by now to make MAMA SAID a talking point on its 1991 release. Kravitz had become a father between albums and was in the process of breaking up with his wife, the actress Lisa Bonet. A melancholy, confessional tone dominated the new collection, a prime example being the 70s soul pastiche "It Ain't Over 'Til It's Over", wistfully aimed at Bonet. Released as a single, the track hit #2 in the US, while the album brought Kravitz his first US gold disc and spent half a year in the UK charts.

Not content with doing almost everything on his records short of pressing the vinyl himself, Kravitz was also appearing on everyone else's records; having already worked with Curtis Mayfield on the SUPERFLY II soundtrack, and Madonna on the "Justify My Love" single, he now duetted with Mick Jagger, co-wrote with Aerosmith and produced for Al Green. He even wrote an entire album for French singer Vanessa Paradis in 1992 – with ego still cheerfully out of control, he titled one track "Lenny Kravitz".

The third album, ARE YOU GONNA GO MY WAY (1993), was a commercial success, but whereas the previous records had been skilful reworkings of old styles this collection seemed closer to parody, or plain imitation. The title track, all wild guitars and attitude, brought Kravitz a worldwide hit, but the rest of the album, like CIRCUS (1995) and the even blander follow-up 5 (1998), didn't develop a given style, it simply impersonated it.

Despite this lack of imagination, an inevitable GREATEST HITS (2000) package contained a single new track, "Again", which at least showed that Kravitz was still capable of penning a decent tune when he put his mind to it. Fortunately LENNY (2001) found Kravitz reverting more to the psychedelic pop-rock of his earlier work; though it still lacked some of his initial naïve charm, it was at least more palatable than his last couple of studio efforts. Hopefully Kravitz will have realized that there's only so far you can go while looking backwards.

⊙ **Let Love Rule** (1989; Virgin).
Doesn't so much pay homage to the 60s as swallow it whole, which is either its greatest strength or its downfall, depending on how you look at it.

⊙ **Mama Said** (1991; Virgin America).
Felt by most to be the best album to date, broadening the themes and styles of the first release with more strings and horns and a job lot of angst thrown in.

Chris Wright

KREIDLER

Formed Düsseldorf, Germany, 1994.

Initially starting out as a backing band for spoken-word performers, and following on from their Deux Baleines Blanches incarnation, **Andrew Reihse** (synthesizer/sampler/stylophone), **Thomas Klein** (drums) and **Stefan Schneider** (bass) formed **Kreidler** in the spring of 1994. Recruiting DJ **Detlef Weinrich** (sampler/stylophone/rhythm boxes) after their first gig, the band set out playing clubs and performance spaces on Germany's growing electronic underground circuit.

Their debut was the cassette-only RIVA (1994), followed by a vinyl-only mini-LP the next year, produced by Matthias Arfmann of veteran industrial dub outfit Kastrierten Philosophen. Released on the small Finlayson label, these releases brought Kreidler attention from around Germany and a distribution deal for their Kiff SM label with the German branch of Belgian independent Play It Again Sam.

The result was WEEKEND (1996), an album that received praise at home and abroad, placing them firmly in the growing cluster of new electronic bands appearing from the edges of the German techno scene. Like Mouse On Mars and **TO ROCOCO ROT** (in which Schneider also plays bass), Kreidler mix dub, rock and electronica in a style similar to (but identifiably different from) such British and American (so-called) post-rockers as Ui, Tortoise or Seefeel. Comparisons have also been made to 1970s German legends Can and Kraftwerk but Kriedler's sound draws more from 80s pop influences while remaining utterly contemporary. However, Reihse made an natural connection with the group's precursors when he joined former **NEU!** legend **Klaus Dinger**'s La! NEU? for both live and studio albums in 1997.

An awesome live act, Kreidler followed the success of WEEKEND with annual European tours, including a support slot for warped electro-funksters Red Snapper, Kosmische Club-sponsored UK gigs and a showcase on London's South Bank with To Rococo Rot and the legendary Faust. A 7" single "Kookai" and the RESPORT remix album in 1997 for Stewardess in Düsseldorf preceded the excellent 12" EP FECHTERIN, taking them further into the realms of abstracted electronics and analogue rhythmic hybridization. The group's second album proper, APPEARANCE AND THE PARK (1998), revealed a broadly developed sound and a comprehensive grasp of the late 90s' interface of post-rock and electronica.

Having established their own studio in a disused post office behind Düsseldorf's main railway station, Kreidler recruited **Alex Paulick** to replace Schneider on bass when the latter decided to concentrate on playing with To Rococo Rot. In late 2000 the first fruits of the new line-up appeared: the CIRCLES EP and a self-titled album of abstract pop; the releases were supported by a tour with mischievous intellectual underground legend Momus – who guests on the album. In 2002 they returned, as creatively restless as ever, with the mini-album EVE FUTURE, which added horns, chimes and an increasing ear for melody to their ever-evolving rhythmic flair. Kreidler have shaken off the post-Rock tag and taken a dive into the gleaming waters of electronica to shimmering, but no less inventive effect.

⊙ **Weekend** (1996; Kiff SM/Play It Again Sam).
Looped bleeps and loping dub bass, occasional telephones and unidentifiable sounds fused into highly developed instrumental trance-outs. A classic of the European flavour of post-rock.

⊙ **Resport** (1997; Stewardess).
Various remixers, including To Rococo Rot's Robert Lippok and the unusually named Erik >>>; MMM, reconstruct non-album material into dub and art-breakbeat formats. An admirable companion to Kreidler's own releases.

⊙ **Kreidler** (2000; Mute).
More classic lush pop with deeply-drawn production and a mellow vibe. KREIDLER untwists languorously with an assured glamour, while leaving the group's hallmark electronic strings and deftly manipulated sounds intact.

Richard Fontenoy

ED KUEPPER/LAUGHING CLOWNS

Ed Kuepper born Germany, 1955; Laughing Clowns formed Sydney, Australia, 1979; disbanded 1985.

When **THE SAINTS** fell apart towards the end of 1978, guitarist **Ed Kuepper** returned from their London base to Australia, looking to continue his exploration of new ideas. Taking over vocals himself, Kuepper assembled **Robert Farrell** (tenor sax), **Ben** (piano) and **Dan Wallace-Crabbe** (bass) and **Jeffrey Wegener** (drums), at the outset of a turbulent stop-start career for the band, which only Wegener and Kuepper lasted.

The band's songs, though not entirely uncommercial, were founded on difficult time signatures, brass arrangements that were soaring and bizarre by turns, and Ed's stinging guitar phrases and sleepy vocals. The whole became an angular but melodious jazz-rock collision as far from the accepted fusion of the genres as from any other recognizable form.

Touring Australia extensively, **Laughing Clowns** received fair critical acclaim, but failed to reach their potentially large audience. They released a series of EPs, singles and an Australian LP, MR. UDDICH-SCHMUDDICH GOES TO TOWN (1981), before briefly relocating to London, at which time the British label Red Flame assembled two compilations of their output to date, LAUGHING CLOWNS and LAUGHTER AROUND THE TABLE.

Now with the relatively stable line-up of Kuepper, Wegener, **Louise Elliot** (trumpet/saxophone), **Chris Abrahams** (piano), and **Peter Walsh** or **Paul Smith** on bass, they became something of a live draw. Yet, even after the positive reception enjoyed by two further studio albums, LAW OF NATURE (1984) and GHOSTS OF AN IDEAL WIFE (1985), Laughing Clowns split up, still very much a cult band.

Ed Kuepper didn't kick his heels at home, and the guitar-based ELECTRICAL STORM (1985), on which he played nearly all the instruments, heralded the beginning of a prolific solo career. It was followed by ROOMS OF THE MAGNIFICENT (1986), EVERYBODY'S GOT TO (1988), TODAY WONDER (1990), HONEY STEEL'S GOLD and BLACK TICKET DAY (both 1992), SERENE MACHINE (1993), CHARACTER ASSASSINATION (1994), two mail-order-only albums, A KING IN THE KINDNESS ROOM (1995), and FRONTIERLAND (1997), and a couple of live recordings – WITH A KNAPSACK ON MY BACK (1998), recorded in Hamburg in 1997, and LIVE! (with the Playboys; 1998).

Each release experimented with a different instrumental setup, new musical styles and sounds, but it was rare that quality control suffered. From 1986 until 1995, drummer **Mark Dawson** stayed close at hand, since when Ed has worked with his drily monikered touring band, **The Oxley Creek Playboys**, and just as frequently, alone. Kuepper also found time, between 1991 and 1992, to recapture the spirit of the early Saints on SLSQ: VERY LIVE!, ASCENSION and AUTOCANNABALISM, with his high-octane guitar burnout group, **The Aints**.

Still recording and performing regularly, though to little commercial success, Ed's albums have met with huge critical acclaim, and he has twice received awards for *Australian Indie Album Of The Year*. In recent times, he has embarked on film soundtrack work, and this forms part of an ongoing mail-order-only CD series for the discerning fan, so far delivering I WAS A MAIL-ORDER BRIDEGROOM and EXOTIC MAIL-ORDER MOODS (both 1995), STARSTRUCK (1996) and CLOUDLAND (1998). THE WHEELIE BIN AFFAIR (1998), THE BLUE ROOM (1999) and SMILE PACIFIC (2000) are his latest postcards from the edge of madness.

Laughing Clowns

⊙ **History Of Rock'N'Roll Volume 1** (1984; Hot).
Of all the puzzling Laughing Clowns compilation configurations, this is as comprehensive a view of their first four years as you'll find. Includes the majestic "Everything That Flies" and anthemic, brass-heavy "Theme From 'Mad Flies, Mad Flies'".

Ed Kuepper

⊙ **Electrical Storm** (1985; Hot).
The first solo Kuepper album is all gutsy, guitar-driven rhythm and crashing drums, with his untutored nasal vocal well to the fore. The title track is a Kuepper classic.

⊙ **Today Wonder** (1990; Hot).
A shimmering stereo acoustic guitar album accompanied only by Mark Dawson's spooked percussion. "Horse Under Water" is a slow pulsating piece of spellbinding rhythm. Also includes the ballad "Everything I've Got Belongs To You", surely a million-seller in the hands of a mainstream artist.

⊙ **Serene Machine** (1993; Hot).
An astonishing record. Backward drones sit back to back with mock-gospel choruses, a traditional song is set alight by guitar pyrotechnics, and John Lennon's ghost is conjured up on this unclassifiable jamboree.

James Robert

KULA SHAKER

Formed London, 1993; disbanded 1999.

All bands have a story to tell about their formation. While most fall into the 'we met at school then gigged until someone noticed us' category, the tale behind the **Kula Shaker** genesis was coloured with LSD-fuelled cod mysticism, Indian religious philosophy and copious quantities of self-conscious psychobabble.

The prosaic facts are lost in the mists of time and obscured by repeated telling, but it all essentially began with **Crispian Mills** (guitar/vocals) and his introduction to Indian mysticism at a very early stage in his life. This led naturally to an infatuation with 60s psychedelia which, according to those around him at the time in the late 1980s, made him pretentiously insufferable. According to bassist **Alonza Bevin**, who joined early in the band's career, Mills looked like a 'twat' in his dodgy shades and Cuban heels. After five years of getting precisely nowhere, Mills decided he had to get away and headed for India in 1993 with **Mathura** – a 'freelance' traveller and mystic – in order to study the ancient teachings of one Chaitanya. This period was apparently an epiphany for the young Mills, who had by now tuned himself into the vibrations of the universe and could see how to align himself most fortuitously with the forces of the cosmos.

He duly formed **The Kays** upon his return, along with Bevin (of course), **Paul Winter-Hart** (drums) and **Saul Dismont** (vox). The latter did not stay long, but was also partly responsible for the path the band would follow for the next few years. Also around this point **Jay Darlington** (keyboards) became responsible for their trademark Hammond-organ sound. More dabbling with occult teachings ensued as they explored the magical connotations of

the letter K and pondered upon the writings of Aleister Crowley. According to Mills, at this stage they believed they were knights in the stables preparing for Armageddon. Glastonbury 1993 saw the band play a set at the Krishna tent in front of a drug-addled and amused audience, following an extraordinary brush with the local constabulary during which Mills and (yet another) mystical companion, Don Pecker, were almost arrested.

Things appeared to be moving along now, albeit slowly. It was not until Mathura materialized at their Swiss Cottage flat with still another magical consort, **Kula Shakhar**, that things began to take shape. Legend has it that the original Kula Shakhar was a ninth-century mystic and emperor. Thinking that they could do with a little regal patronage, his name was adopted by the band and within three months they had a deal. It was the quickest deal Columbia had ever turned around but it had to be clinched in such a manner that almost jeopardized the whole thing; the contract had to be signed at 10.10pm on St George's Day with the moon in its fourth quarter.

The release of "Grateful When You're Dead"/"Jerry Was There" was merely a precursor to the major summer hit of "Tattva". This in turn was a mere hint of the psychedelic wonders to behold upon K (1996), which rapidly became the last word in fashionably swinging retro 60s sounds. Bright young things the length and breadth of the land fell for the swirly multicoloured, Hammond-encrusted vibe and sent the singles which followed spiralling up through the charts.

The release of their long-awaited follow-up to K was preceded by a tantalizing single entitled "The Sound Of Drums". The album didn't materialize until 1999, titled PEASANTS, PIGS AND ASTRONAUTS. Once again the mysticism of the Indian subcontinent was prevalent throughout, as the band continued to exploit this particularly rich vein of psychedelic rock. However, sales of the album quickly fell away, as the band suddenly announced their dissolution, with Mills implying that a solo career was pending.

⊙ **K** (1996; Columbia).
An astonishingly accomplished debut owing as much to the spirit of the Beatles as it does to the flavours of the East. The spiritual vibe is ever-present and one or two of the tunes have apparently been liberally adapted from traditional Indian compositions.

⊙ **Peasants, Pigs And Astronauts** (1999; Columbia).
A lengthy gap between albums might suggest the band are trying to formulate a new approach. Not so in this case – there's plenty of acid-tinged psychedelia here to keep even the most jaded hippie feeling nostalgic.

Essi Berelian

KYLIE

Born Melbourne, Australia, 1968.

Kylie Minogue's biography sounds more like a collection of statistics than a life story. Vital or otherwise, she's certainly small, and big, and record-breaking. With an appeal that leads British newspapers to refer to the antipodean as 'our Kylie', she's fondly

The woman's success seemed infallible: her first thirteen single releases had formed thirteen consecutive hits and 1989 brought ENJOY YOURSELF, the second unchallenging album. 1990s RHYTHM OF LOVE, featuring the "Better The Devil You Know" single, however, saw Ms. Minogue take a new turning. Famously quoted as saying, 'Now I want to sing about sex', Kylie chalked up co-writing credits, whilst more noticeably losing the curls and coyness. Despite the risk involved in changing a successful formula after 20 million album sales, Kylie's new style was embraced and, due in part to her high-profile relationship with the late Michael Hutchence, Kylie's rock'n'roll status was raised. LET'S GET TO IT (1991) was the last of her Stock, Aitken and Waterman albums; after this split from the pop establishment, Kylie signed to Deconstruction Records' dance division in 1994 for the release of her more mature eponymous album.

An unlikely pairing with fellow Australian **Nick Cave** for "Where The Wild Roses Grow", from his 1996 MURDER BALLADS, gave Kylie both a European-wide million-seller and more credibility. Inspired by public acceptance of her new directions and Cave's mentoring, Minogue went into production with **Brothers in Rhythm, Dave Ball** from The Grid and **The Manic Street Preachers** for her 1997 'indie' album. Despite selling well in her home country, IMPOSSIBLE PRINCESS (retitled KYLIE MINOGUE in its British release, due to the death of Princess Diana), was critically ridiculed and Kylie was subsequently dropped by Deconstruction.

Pop was what made her career, and pop is what had sold her the most records. So it came as no surprise that for her 1999 comeback, LIGHT YEARS on Parlophone, Kylie opted for the high-pop template once more. The album's dance-floor anthem "Spinning Around" set the stage for the follow up, FEVER (2001). This album wore its credentials on its sleeve, displaying influences from Gallic dance through to early 80s electronica. The collection was unbelievably successful, largely due to its "Can't Get You Out Of My Head" single and the accompanying video, which saucily marketed Kylie's latest future-diva incarnation.

The musical Kylie could barely exist without visual accompaniment, and as she moves through her thirties, Kylie seems as popular as ever, having managed to top polls of most fanciable female in both 2002 and 1989 alike. Public opinion may be divided over whether the surgeon's knife has had a hand in shaping the Kylie body that the tabloids display daily, but as a resilient survivor of the fashions of three decades, it looks like we'll have plenty of time to contemplate the diminutive superstar yet.

held in public regard by women as well as men, by musos as well as pop tarts. As with so many enduring pop acts, the astonishing longevity of Kylie's career is due in part to her frequent and chameleon-like reinventions of self. From tomboy soap star and wholesome girl-next-door to indie-princess, gay icon and buttock-wielding vixen, her name is now superfluous as she has become a symbol of good clean fun and the purity of pop in a messy, changing world.

The British public first became enamoured with the pouting, pint-sized star-to-be during her two-and-a-half-year stint on Aussie soap *Neighbours*. She first appeared in 1986, when the show was at the height of its popularity. A cast performance of Little Eva's hit "Locomotion" for a local charity benefit led to Kylie pursuing her nascent singing career. Under the capable guidance of the Stock, Aitken and Waterman hit factory, Kylie's first British release was the terminally catchy "I Should Be So Lucky" in 1988, which spent five weeks at #1 in the UK chart. "Got To Be Certain" followed soon after, peaking at #2, and by the summer, Kylie had left Ramsey Street to concentrate on music. In July, her debut album, KYLIE, was released and entered the UK chart at #2, providing Minogue with the highest-ever chart entry positions for a female artist in both the single and album charts. The best-selling album of the year, KYLIE offered a world of smiley, superficial pop which two million purchasers wanted a part of. Adding to this, the highly plastic "Locomotion" single and the risible and saccharine duet with her Neighbours co-star and boyfriend Jason Donovan, "Especially for You", saw that 1988 was definitely Kylie's year.

(●) **Greatest Hits** (1999; Mushroom).
This is the place to find all those early grinning pop hits.

(●) **Fever** (2001; Parlophone).
Despite featuring the blinding hit single "Can't Get You Out Of My Head", complete with inescapably catchy la-la-la chorus, FEVER is a record embarrassingly low on charm and originality. This is what bandwagon music sounds like: Kylie clicked that the Daft Punk / revisited-Kraftwerk sound was the one to pursue.

Annebella Pollen

KYLIE

KYUSS

Formed Palm Desert, Southern California, 1990; disbanded 1995.

For some bands, notoriety and fame arrive only when their body of work becomes acknowledged as having influenced a whole generation of noise-makers. Such was the fate of **Kyuss**, whose initial line-up included **Josh Homme** (guitarist), **John Garcia** (vocalist), **Nick Oliveri** (bass) and **Brant Bjork** (drums). Formed by Homme in his teens, Kyuss became infamous for dragging their equipment and a whole load of recreational pharmaceuticals into the deserts around Palm Springs for now-legendary gigs of free-form rock, borrowing heavily from the legacy of bands such as Blue Cheer and Black Sabbath.

From these ferocious jam sessions sprang the band's first album, WRETCH (1991), which failed to do them justice but did manage to pique the interest of **Chris Goss**, singer and guitarist with Masters Of Reality, themselves no slouches when it came to interpreting 70s rock.

Goss helped the band shape BLUES FOR THE RED SUN (1992), a record now lauded by many as the template for 21st century bands that have followed in the pioneering wake of Kyuss. The distortion, doom and psychedelia they captured was nothing short of awesome, and with its down-tuned sludgy guitars and thundering drums the signature sound of 'stoner' rock had finally found its way onto record.

Almost as groundbreaking was WELCOME TO SKY VALLEY (1994), which was again shaped under Goss's guidance. However, Oliveri had by now departed to be replaced by **Scott Reader**.

At this point the group's reputation as a rock phenomenon was beginning to percolate through the underground and everything seemingly pointed to Kyuss becoming the leaders of the stoned-out pack. Behind the building momentum, though, internal tensions were beginning to grow. Eventually **Alfredo Hernandez** stepped in to take over from Bjork and ...AND THE CIRCUS LEAVES TOWN (1995) proved to be their last collection. As a swan song it was far from distinguished; at this point they were just treading water, waiting for the axe to fall.

Several formidable new groups emerged from the wreckage: Bjork turned up in **FU MANCHU**, while Garcia went on to form **Unida**. Most significantly though, Oliveri, Homme and Hernandez turned up in **QUEENS OF THE STONE AGE**, an outfit that are now being hailed as one of the most innovative rock bands on the face of the planet.

⊙ Blues For The Red Sun (1992; Elektra).
This is the one, the album almost always cited as the germ of modern stoner. Potent and towering, the set showcases a sound hewn by the desert wind and baked to a white hot intensity by the sun.

⊙ Welcome To Sky Valley (1994; Elektra).
More of the same gut-wrenching metal that made the band's name, shot through with the style of the 70s and more than a hint of willful eclecticism.

Essi Berelian

L

L7

Formed Los Angeles, 1986.

Grrl group **L7** stood out from the pack of pseudo-macho posturers – and then some. Whereas Suzi Quatro just sneered, and **THE RUNAWAYS** and Heart put heavy rock riffs beneath nice girlie harmonies, L7 stripped on TV and threw used tampons at the audience from the stage. Rock and, defiantly, roll.

The band was born out of various all-female punk-metal acts in mid-80s LA. Bassist **Jennifer Finch**'s early partners in crime included Kat Bjelland of Babes In Toyland and Courtney Love of Hole, but the great inspiration was a band called Frightwig, who built up a big live following without ever managing to escape the local club circuit.

Finch, **Donita Sparks** (guitar/vocals), **Suzi Gardner** (guitar/vocals) and, briefly, **Anne Anderson** (drums) formed L7 in 1986 and began to build up a following in LA. Their tongue-in-cheek metal set-list included such monster classics as "Bite The Wax Tadpole" and "Metal Stampede". Unavoidably, they became labelled as a 'grrrl' group, despite having the unmistakeably male **Roy Kolltsky** on drums (though this was rectified when **Dee Plakas** joined – an event that coincided with the band moving to Seattle as the LA scene grew stale.

The band's debut album, L7 (1988), pointed to their future direction and they followed it with a long bout of touring. 1990's mini-album, SMELL THE MAGIC, on Sub Pop showcased a growing repertoire which helped secure them a deal with Slash (a division of London), and they toured with new stable mates Faith No More. This led to BRICKS ARE HEAVY (1992), an enormous leap forward which established L7 as the foremost female rockers of the early 90s. A single, "Pretend We're Dead", even penetrated the Top 30 in Britain, where the band found a more receptive market than in the States. Ironically, it was the most American of songs: a militant call to arms against corporate US society and coca-colonialism.

Still, politics wasn't all. There were plenty of fans attracted more by the band's notorious reputation rather than their message. Sparks' impromptu strip on British TV was better publicity than any amount of late-night airplay, and L7 show no sign of mellowing. On HUNGRY FOR STINK (1994) they were as hard-edged as ever and rewarded for it by a #26 place in the UK album charts.

Tremors were felt at the departure of Jennifer Finch in 1997, but a fourth album, THE BEAUTY PROCESS – TRIPLE PLATINUM appeared later that year although the lack of a bassist meant they only managed one UK show in 1997, incongruously backing Kiss in Finsbury Park. Touring remained the mainstay activity; L7 seemed to have cemented their position as one of the foremost live bands of the 90s, with LIVE: OMAHA TO OSAKA (1998) driving the point home.

Since then the group have released a further pounding studio album, SLAP-HAPPY (1999), and a greatest hits package entitled THE SLASH YEARS (2000).

⊙ **Bricks Are Heavy** (1992; Slash Records).
An album dripping in vitriol, with statements about men and society that are concise to the point of bluntness.

⊙ **The Beauty Process – Triple Platinum** (1997; Slash Records).
Though slightly less heavy metal and slightly more angst-rock, the familiar features are still here. The toe-tapping "Off The Wagon" offers the usual L7 preoccupations, all revolving around serious drinking. "The Masses Are Asses" is self-explanatory, but there is also a bizarre cover of Joan Armatrading's "Me Myself I".

Patrick Neylan-Francis & Guy Davies

THE LA'S

Formed Liverpool, England, 1986; bowed out in 1994.

The La's revitalized a moribund Liverpool scene in the late 80s with breezy 60s-influenced pop and, despite a tiny output, they're fondly remembered.

The band's original line-up comprised **Lee Mavers** (guitar/vocals), **John Power** (bass), **Paul Hemmings** (guitar) and **John Timson** (drums). Garnering a reputation as a fine live act, they signed to Go! Discs, who issued the single, "Way Out" (1987), an arresting waltz-time debut. With **Chris Sharrock** (ex-Icicle Works) replacing Timson, they followed up with "There She Goes" (1988), a chiming, euphoric treat.

The failure of "Way Out" to chart (it stopped at #59 in the UK) shocked the band, its label and the music press, and further progress was scuppered by Mavers' first outbreak of obsessive perfectionism. A third single, "Timeless Melody", in the spring of 1989, was another winner, but Mavers was disappointed by the end product and a serious rethink ensued.

When The La's re-emerged in 1990, Powers and Sharrock had been replaced by **Peter Cammell** (guitar) and Lee's brother **Neil** (drums). Sessions with

La la la, la la, la la la la...

producer Steve Lillywhite for the debut LP descended into trauma as Mavers' mania for authenticity led to his insistence on hiring a 60s mixing desk. Songs were recorded over and over again, but could never meet his exalted expectations, and the live favourite "Callin' All" was never even attempted. In October 1990, exasperated by the cost and delay, Go! Discs issued THE LA'S in any case. Mavers vented his spleen in music press interviews, dismissing the album as unfinished and below par, though everyone else heard a great collection of heartfelt pop, owing much to the Fab Four but with a jaunty personality all of its own. And it sold in fair numbers, reaching #30 in the UK, alongside a new version of "There She Goes", which finally became a Top 20 hit in the singles charts.

The music press, eager to find a new focus after the early-90s Manchester scene, proclaimed The La's as ambassadors of a new 'Scouse pop', and predicted great things. However, the band fractured, and The La's were presumed dead by the end of 1991. They reappeared, unexpectedly, in 1994, playing a smattering of low-key gigs, though with no new songs and a line-up that shambled through interminable blues jams.

In the meantime, Power had popped up in **CAST**, whose sound was a carbon copy of prime La's. A new breed of La's-influenced bands, like The Bluetones,

have since been happy to claim the vacant throne left by The La's demise.

⊙ **The La's** (1990; Go! Discs/London).
According to Lee Mavers, half this album consists of shoddy demos with guide vocals only. If this was the quality of the demos, the intended final tracks would have been wonderful.

Chris Tighe

LABRADFORD

Formed Richmond, Virginia, 1992.

"I was one of those kids who thought we'd all be taking trips to the moon by now ... " Mark Nelson

LaBradford were formed as a duo by **Carter Brown** (synthesizers) and **Mark Nelson** (guitars/tapes/vocals). Their debut single "Everlast" (1992) positioned them firmly in the emerging US post-rock scene of the mid-90s, and their take on Krautrock-influenced atmospherics was part of the mood of rediscovered futurism sparked by bands like Stereolab and Main.

The band's debut album, PRAZISION (1993), produced by Rob Christiansen (Eggs/Grenadine), was a drumless wash of Moog, guitar and tape loops, reflecting Carter Brown's fascination with early classical music and holy minimalist Arvo Pärt, as well as ambient Krautrockers Cluster, and even the droneside of Spacemen 3. The tracks were composed rather than improvised, and were recorded live – their consistent methodology to date. They interspersed ambiences with ultra-low-key songs, low-mix vocals supplying texture rather than narrative. "Gratitude", for example, thanks the record label and equipment suppliers in words spoken through a vocoder over a droning Moog.

The record led to a Peel session, live guest appearances with Stereolab, Main and (in Britain) Spectrum, and a slot on the influential Virgin album ISOLATIONISM (1994), compiled by the ever-active Kevin Martin (of God/Techno Animal/Ice). Brown and Nelson, however, felt that LaBradford's sound lacked depth, with only the pair of them handling instrumentation, and **Robert Donne** (ex-Breadwinner) was recruited on bass guitar.

The new line-up's first recording, A STABLE REFERENCE (1995), was released to wide acclaim, particularly in Britain, where it eased its way into a number of Albums of the Year charts. Inspired by the abandoned promise of the space programmes, the album was, well, both spacey and spacious, intermixing fuzzy Moogs and ominous rocket-like sounds on "Mas" and a life-support hum on "Eero". Slow and gracious, and moving too at times, it occupies a similar dreamspace to Flying Saucer Attack's cloudy soundscapes. It was again produced by Christiansen and benefited greatly from Donne's precise bass additions to the mix.

In early 1996, LaBradford released "Scenic Recovery/Underwood 5ive", a 10" single on Stereolab's Duophonic label, and their first recording with a drummer. A successful live (and loud!) tour of Europe left audiences there wanting more of their serene take on modern spiritual drones, and this appeared with November's LABRADFORD (1996).

Recorded in the space of a few weeks, their eponymous third album uses the textures of the instruments to melancholic, though never gloomy, effect, and features guest violin by Chris Johnston. His contribution (to "Midrange" in particular) adds further atmospherics, while the percussion is subtly restrained.

With their extended line-up, LaBradford's sound could have become cluttered; instead it has expanded yet again to take advantage of the space created between each instrument. The experimentation continued with the addition of Johnson's string section on MI MEDIA NARANJA (1997), an almost wholly instrumental album accompanied by several atmospheric concerts, including a landmark performance by candlelight at a disued synagogue in Whitechapel, East London.

A show on the roof of the South Bank Centre in London launched their now annual and highly successful Festival of Drifting in 1998. They have brought together musicians and writers including Michael Moorcock, Iain Sinclair, Bruce Gilbert of Wire, Pole, Matmos, Pan Sonic, David Pajo (Arial M/Papa M), Chris & Cosey, Sigur Rós and Robin Guthrie of The Cocteau Twins.

While Nelson has released two noted albums as **Pan American** (PAN AMERICAN and 360 BUSINESS/360 BYPASS), Donne also worked as one half of **Aix Em Klemm** with Stars Of The Lid's **Adam Wiltze**. They released a self-titled album in 2000 on the Kranky imprint. Various Labradford collaborations and remixes have appeared with Matmos, composer Harold Budd and (again) Stars Of The Lid. All this extramural activity meant that their next set, E LUXO SO, didn't appear until 1999, but it was well worth the wait, as was 2001's FIXED::CONTENT.

Recorded by Steve Albini, this most recent, and haunting, album found Labradford stripped back to a trio; as ever the music was liable to set the listener drifting off into a mesmerized altered state.

⊙ **Prazision** (1993; Kranky/Flying Nut).
A brooding ambient mix that originally closed with the track, "Skyward With Motion", the band's most 'Isolationist' piece, recalling a David Lynch movie. The CD reissue on Flying Nun adds the single "Everlast".

⊙ **A Stable Reference** (1995; Kranky/Flying Nun).
The band's nostalgic exploration of the space programme – a theme made explicit in the music of tracks such as "Star City, Russia", and "El Lago" – named after Neil Armstrong's Houston suburb home during the time of the Apollo mission.

⊙ **Mi Media Naranja** (1997; Kranky/Blast First).
Subtle touches, such as restrained strings and a child's voice, complement the translucent compositions of the perfected LaBradford sound.

⊙ **E Luxo So** (1999; Kranky/Blast First).
One of those records that eases the dull throb of life's little (and big) problems; there's something comfortingly hypnotic about the record which makes everything seem much brighter as the peaks and troughs drift along.

Richard Fontenoy

LAIBACH

Formed Trbovlje, Slovenia (then Yugoslavia), 1980.

Laibach was the old German name for Ljubljana, the capital of Slovenia: adopting the name was a calculatedly defiant gesture which set the group in opposition to the (then) state of Yugoslavia. They were formed in 1980 as the music wing of an art collective, NSK (Neue Slowenische Kunst – New Slovene Art), whose members, in a parody of the Communist model of totalitarian industrial production, voluntarily renounce their individual names, tastes and convictions in joyful subordination to the NSK's collective identity and political programme.

If that suggests to you a vision of bleak, industrial music, mutant disco beats, and postmodern humour, then you're spot on. Laibach have always seen themselves more as ideological offensive than rock group. They view disco, for example, as an idealized expression of technical production: an archetype to stimulate automatic movement and industrial consciousness.

Laibach's earliest music, in the period between 1980 and 1984, was rudimentary as well as experimental. They drew on the electronic minimalism of groups like Kraftwerk and DAF, and the industrial experimentalism of Einstürzende Neubauten and early Test Department. An abstract soundscape was constructed by layering electronic beats, repetitive noises and tape loops (ready-made musical matter) with vocals, additional percussion and bass or guitar lines. The group's first concert took place in September 1980, as part of an NSK exhibition in Ljubljana, which was promptly banned by the police and city officials.

The group disbanded temporarily in 1981, due to its members' compulsory military service, but re-formed the following year for their (provocative) 'tour of three capitals' – Ljubljana, Zagreb and Belgrade. Following the Zagreb concert, **Tomaz Hostnik**, Laibach's original singer and spokesman, committed suicide, but the band continued, making its first studio recordings, and launching an electronic subgroup, **Germania**.

1983 saw Laibach gigging with experimental British bands, Last Few Days (on the 'Occupied Europe' tour of the Eastern Bloc) and 23 Skidoo, and, bizarrely, signing a contract with the state record company for their first LP, Nebo Zari (The Sky Glows). The contract was pulled, however: the Yugoslav authorities were uncertain how to view the band, and indeed NSK as a whole (Were they fascists, proponents for an end to the unitary state?). The band gave only the most enigmatic clues, and in June a Laibach TV interview precipitated a ban throughout most of Yugoslavia.

In spite of playing almost no concerts and releasing only one 12" EP, Sila/Boji/Brat Moj (1984), released through a Belgian production company, Laibach were beginning to generate European media interest, and in 1985 played a series of art showcases in London and Germany. They also gained a UK label, Cherry Red, for the release of Die Liebe Ist Die Grosse Kraft. They were finding a home as avant-garde artists, rather than as the cult rock group

of later years, and the mid-80s saw them taking part more often in art events, combining theatre (with NSK's Red Pilot Group), dance (with Michael Clark at Sadler's Wells, London) or visual art, than in 'rock concerts'.

Musically, however, the group began a shift as the 80s progressed, from out-and-out experiment – words repeated until made meaningless, music crossing from symphonic thrash to minimalism – to a more overt rock sound. Signing to Mute, they released Opus Dei (1987) and Let It Be (1988), still their best-known albums. These remixed rock classics – The Stones' "Sympathy For The Devil", The Beatles' last album – in industrial/disco soundscapes, with extra lashings of Wagner and heavy metal. Opus Dei actually spawned a UK chart single, "Life Is Life" – reworking the Euro-disco number. Meanwhile, the group remained active in theatre and film work, and with Macbeth (1990) seemed at last to have found a perfect subject match, producing a soundtrack brooding with a brutish occult ambiance.

In 1990, of course, the group's political backdrop changed irreversibly. Laibach's tenth anniversary concert coincided with Slovenia's declaration of independence from Yugoslavia – the trigger of that nation's civil war. NSK and Laibach apparently actively welcomed the State's dissolution, declaring their own non-national state and issuing passports, currency and stamps.

Kapital (1992) moved Laibach on a decade, musically, with the creation of Teutonic techno (Wagnerian opera house?), but Trans-Slovenia Express (1994), cover versions of Kraftwerk tracks, seemed to be standing still. NATO (1994) also went down the usual Laibach cover song route but reflected the group's preoccupation with the turmoil in Eastern Europe by including such tunes as Status Quo's "In The Army Now"; the subsequent tour was captured on Occupied Europe NATO Tour 1994-95 (1996), a live CD and video box set. The same year also brought Jesus Christ Superstars, a more straightforward collection of originals – assuming with Laibach there can be such a thing – peppered with a handful of cover versions. Since then new material has been less forthcoming and the group have concentrated on performing live – they appeared at the Expo 2000 Exhibition in Hanover, just days after celebrating their twentieth anniversary on 1 June 2000. A new album is allegedly being forged in the burning heart of the collective.

Opus Dei (1987; Mute/Elektra).
An album that takes the rock format beyond its limits with anthems like "Leben Heiß Leben" (Life Is Life) – the Laibach hit single! – and suggests fascistic roots at the heart of the rock spectacle. The enormity of sound that they produce is phenomenal.

Let It Be (1988; Mute/Elektra).
The Beatles will never sound the same once you have heard what Laibach do to them. Amid the radical deconstruction, there is one of the most remarkable guitar solos of all time on "One After 909".

Macbeth (1990; Mute/Elektra).
This music from the production of the Shakespeare play returns Laibach to their experimental roots but incorpo-

rates the production values of a big-budget pop record. The result is atmospheric, moving and perhaps the best thing the group have done.

⊙ **Kapital** (1992; Mute/Elektra).
Laibach's invasion of techno is their most intense work to date. Tackling the collapse of Western capitalism, it deploys multi-layered sampling on a symphonic scale and includes guest rappers to boot.

Glenn Gossling

LAIKA

Formed London, 1993.

Laika – named after the dog the Soviets left in space – are one of a handful of contemporary British bands filtering their rock-based songs through the rigours of digitally mutated studio space. They were formed by **Margaret Fiedler** and **John Frenett**, refugees from a band called Moonshake, whose obsession with the dark byways of city life they continued to share. However, augmented by producer and multi-instrumentalist **Guy Fixen**, they opted for a more feline, club-orientated flow.

Laika open their music outwards, incorporating some of the sound-source warping of jungle and dub to co-opt whatever comes their way. Their first album, SILVER APPLES OF THE MOON (1994), was a subtle masterpiece of urban menace, showing an understanding of dance music's dynamics reminiscent of early Public Image Ltd. "Red River" and "Let Me Sleep" were explosions of pent-up, looped chaos shredding the listener's nerve endings with sudden ejaculations of flutes and bongos, while "Honey In Heat" and "Coming Down Glass" were sticky with near-pornographic sleaze. It wasn't all a wallow in perversity though: "Marimba Song", "If You Miss" and "Sugar Daddy" were almost like lullabies, and all the more affecting for being situated in the midst of such grotesquery.

Laika's use of the studio-as-prism is one of the few viable alternatives to mainstream indie rock's fixation with grave-robbing the past. But rock, for all its past

.LAIKA/LOST IN SPACE

volume one (1993 - 2002)

glories, has always harboured a tendency towards insularity, and bewildering hybrids such as Laika will always lose out when there are so many more amenable bands on offer.

The band were on tour in the States during 1995, minus John Frenett, who left a while after the release of SILVER APPLES in search of financial stability. They returned to the public eye in 1997, slimmed down to a core duo of Fiedler and Fixen, with SOUNDS OF THE SATELLITES (Too Pure), a calmer, more considered take on Laika's view of the world, though still capable of pitching a few surprise curve balls. The three years between Laika's albums had also seen a whole batch of other rock outfits, such as Ui and Tortoise, very successfully catching on to the studio-as-prism idea. Heard in this context, SOUNDS OF THE SATELLITES couldn't match the subtle blast of its predecessor – even though, viewed on its own merits, it was a very fine slab of lunar funk.

Next came GOOD LOOKING BLUES (2000), a confident, swirling collection of jazz and funk grooves all wrapped in an almost sugary, dreamy coating. The album was warmly received by the press and is arguably their finest moment, though 2003's rarities collection, LOST IN SPACE VOL.1, also boasts some stunning, and truly out-there offerings.

⊙ **Silver Apples of the Moon** (1994; Too Pure).
Neither pop nor avant-garde, this set is impossible to classify, but was one of the best releases in a great year for maverick albums.

⊙ **Good Looking Blues** (2000; Too Pure).
A glorious set of mutating rhythms, textures and wry lyrics. "Badtimes", an ode to a particularly vicious computer virus, has got to be one of the greatest undiscovered gems of rock history.

Ben Smith and Peter Buckley

LAMB

Formed Manchester, 1994.

In the years following the emergence of Portishead, some detractors of the so-called 'trip-hop' boom suggested that a coupling of bluesy or jazz-influenced female vocalist with male techno boffin(s) was a sure-fire formula for a huge-selling LP. One example of this prediction failing to deliver the financial goods, concerns British duo **Lamb**, whose 1996 debut album LAMB showed a rare breadth of mood and depth of sound. Although the album received enthusiastic reviews, if limited space, relatively low sales suggest that it remains one of the 1990s' best kept secrets.

Lamb are **Louise Rhodes** (vocals) and **Andy Barlow** (keyboards). Rhodes came from a folk music background, but despite exposure to hip-hop and R&B she was sidetracked into fashion photography. Barlow had also been engaged by the rhythms and textures of hip-hop during his teenage years living in the United States. By 1994 he was a studio engineer back in Manchester, and working on sporadic musical projects of his own under the moniker of The

Lamb's Louise Rhodes tries to keep it undercover

leaving many of the tracks devoid of emotional punch.

2001's WHAT SOUND ironed out many of those difficulties. The breaks and beats were no less powerful – and at times were intensely oblique – but there was a soulfulness again. The album was also rounded out by an intelligent choice of guests, including **Michael Franti** and guitarist **Arto Lindsay**. One of the most interesting acts to emerge from the loosely defined 'trip-hop' scene, it still feels as though Lamb's edgy electronica could spin off in all sorts of interesting directions.

⊙ **Lamb** (1996; Fontana/Mercury).
Their sound has been described as 'like ten points on a compass all pointing in different directions', but if that suggests a lack of focus nothing could be further from the truth. This is a fluid, complex, strong and occasionally fiery LP.

Justin Lewis

LAMBCHOP

Formed Nashville, Tennessee, 1993.

The mid-90s saw a spate of acts playing country music, or country-rock, but aiming for the heart of the alternative-rock audience – Son Volt, Freakwater, Wilco, Richard Buckner. But, with the arguable exception of Palace, **Lambchop** were the weirdest of the lot. While most latter-day alternative country-rockers were determined to draw from the rootsiest sources possible, Lambchop make no bones about their love for smooth and sleepy Nashville pap. It's doubtful, however, that many Garth Brooks fans will cotton on to the group's slyly subversive tales of suicide, downtrodden losers, and anonymous proletarians struggling to make it through another mundane day.

Lambchop boast a large, unwieldy line-up more akin to the spirit of an improvisational jazz collective than the classic country combo. Roughly ten members inhabit the stage at their live performances; and even more participate on the group's two albums. Country staples like acoustic and steel guitars are prominent but share the spotlight with saxophones, tin whistles, clarinets and even 'open-end wrenches, lacquer-thinnercan' (credited to one C. Scott Chase on their second CD).

Yet the Lambchop linchpin is most definitely guitarist **Kurt Wagner**, who writes almost all of the material, and delivers it in a world-weary sing-speak that sounds, oddly enough, a little like Tindersticks. The comparison extends further, in that both groups are lyrically preoccupied with rambling interior monologues. You often get the feeling you've walked in on the middle of a movie scene, without enough context to follow the action.

Musically, Lambchop have an obvious affection for syrupy steel guitars and string-laden Nashville country in the Chet Atkins mould, but they draw just as much from the well of post-punk irony. That ethos is prominent on their 1994 debut, I HOPE YOU'RE SITTING DOWN (also, confusingly, entitled

Hipoptimist. At this stage, he was reputedly reluctant to include vocal lines in his work, which he felt could be intrusive. An impromptu telephone call from one Louise Rhodes, followed by several creatively promising meetings, helped to change his mind.

The first recorded fruits from Lamb arrived in late 1995 with the appearance of the excellent single "Cottonwool", which attracted a cult dance-floor following. A second single, "Gold", also received much positive press, but the real breakthrough was to come at the turn of 1996/97 with the release of LAMB itself, and the haunting six-minute single "Gorecki" (whose length did not prevent it entering the UK Top 40). Meantime, Rhodes had provided vocals and lyrics for **808 State**'s hit "Azura" (1996).

With their initial impact now dissipated through familiarity with the band's house style, the weaknesses of FEAR OF FOURS (1999) were laid bare. By no means a failure, their second effort nevertheless felt laboured, with Rhodes' after hours diva vocals beginning to grate and Barlow's over-intellectual beat-making taking a turn toward pure mathematics,

JACK'S TULIPS), which occasionally breaks up the mournful country arrangements with shambling near-thrash drums and Velvet Underground-like guitar lines and shaky organ. The songs, meanwhile, reflect Wagner's penchant for the bizarre ("Breathe Deeply" is about a deodorizer), and an apparent fixation with suicide, though just as often he just seems to be talking to himself, trailing off into inaudibility, about some routine activity – drinking beer, say, or shopping.

The second Lambchop album, HOW I QUIT SMOKING (1995), owed much more to mainstream country. It is surely one of the few underground records (if not the only one) influenced by the glossy 70s Nashville productions of Billy Sherrill (the man who sweetened the sound of Charlie Rich, Tanya Tucker and Tammy Wynette). Washes of strings were provided by arranger John Mock (who has also worked with straight country singer Kathy Mattea), though the lyrical weirdness remained intact, with song titles like "The Scary Caroler" and "Your Life As A Sequel".

There's a limit to how much Nashville Country pap even the most tongue-in-cheek bands can take, however, as evidenced by Lambchop's third full-length outing. THRILLER (1997) is a far more rock-influenced and wilfully obscure album (three of the eight tracks being East River Pipe cover versions. The two opening tracks, "My Face, Your Ass" (classic 'funny' answer to the question 'Got a match?') and "Your Fucking Sunny Day", show the more aggressive direction the band has taken.

All of which might make Wagner and Lambchop out to be more interesting than they really are. The albums have kept on coming, WHAT ANOTHER MAN SPILLS (1998), NIXON (2000) and IS A WOMAN (2002) all achieving critical praise and good sales, but wholeheartedly failing to broaden the band's palette. While the absurdity of setting existential angst in bold relief against weepy, off-centre country music clichés can be appreciated by anyone with a taste for artsy postmodernism, listening to Wagner on record can be a bit like sitting next to a commuter talking to himself on the bus. And you don't always want that seat.

⊙ **How I Quit Smoking** (1995; City Slang).
An inventive backdrop of Nashville country arrangements provide an intriguing foil for Wagner's drawled weirdness.

⊙ **Hank** (1996; City Slang).
A more accessible outing, recorded at festivals during 1995, and with a more relaxed feel than their studio cuts.

Richie Unterberger

THE LAMBRETTAS

Formed Brighton, England, 1979; disbanded 1982.

The Lambrettas were part of Britain's so-called mod revival of the late 70s/early 80s, which emerged in the wake of punk rock, spearheaded by The Jam. Formed by vocalist/songwriter **Jez Bird** and guitarist **Doug Sanders**, the line-up was completed by **Mark Ellis** (bass) and **Paul Wincer** (drums).

They signed to Elton John's Rocket Records in the summer of 1979, after the label had placed ads in search of new bands. A self-penned single, "Go Steady", also appeared on the Rocket sampler album 499 2139, where it was joined by tracks from other successful candidates. The single failed to chart, although it was a typical slice of New Wave – choppy guitars, busy drumbeat and studiedly English vocals. In fact, while The Lambrettas were to be the most commercially successful of this crop of mod revivalists, three of their rivals – Secret Affair, The Chords and The Merton Parkas – beat them to a place in the UK Top 40.

Still, The Lambrettas' second single, a cover of the old Coasters hit "Poison Ivy", reached the Top 10 in 1980. Hated by the music press, it was more reminiscent of the ska and two-tone boom than the mod one. The confusion was heightened by the sleeve pastiche of the 2-Tone logo, replacing the usual rude-boy with a mod figure, and bearing the moniker '2-Stroke'. 2-Tone objected and the offending design was withdrawn, though not before The Lambrettas had benefited from the publicity. After another Top 20 entry, "D-a-a-ance", the band were in trouble again with their next single, when tabloid newspaper *The Sun* objected to its title, "Page Three". A change of title to "Another Day (Another Girl)" cost Rocket Records a four-figure sum, which was unlikely to be recouped by a single that barely dented the charts.

Boosted by their raw and energetic live shows, The Lambrettas' debut album BEAT BOYS IN THE JET AGE (1980) sold well enough. This represented their commercial peak; by the end of the year the mod revival had run its course, and a second LP, AMBIENCE (1981), was an unashamedly poppy attempt to be seen as part of the mainstream. It failed, due to uninspired material coupled with a bland production.

The Lambrettas called it a day in 1982, consigned by an unsympathetic music press to a footnote in one of the many short-lived fads thrown up in punk's wake.

⊙ **Beat Boys In The Jet Age** (1980; Dojo).
Although not exactly classic material, this debut nonetheless retains some enjoyable hits and period charm.

Joe Nahmad

k. d. lang

Born Consort, Alberta, Canada, 1961.

Born deep in the heart of Canada's prairie lands, Kathy Dawn Lang – **k. d. lang** – has had a career riven with paradoxes. A former performance artist, she conquered the deeply conservative Nashville scene and brought country music into the mainstream market of the late 80s. Moreover, she has developed from a geeky, spiky-haired kid into a sleek, openly lesbian singer-songwriter, earning in the process Madonna's oft-quoted endorsement, 'Elvis is alive – and she's beautiful.'

k. d. lang, nobody's ingénue

lang – the avoidance of upper-case letters has been career-long – started out playing guitar as a 10-year-old, developing into a quirky rockabilly performance artist, and reinventing herself as the reincarnation of 50s country singer, Patsy Cline. With The Reclines, a band whose name was an obvious tribute to Cline, lang quickly drew vociferous audiences for her languorous love songs and her full-bodied voice. The outfit made their recording debut in the early 80s on Canadian independent label Homestead, releasing a single, "Friday Dance Promenade", and album, A TRULY WESTERN EXPERIENCE (1984).

Signed to Sire in 1985, lang and a different line-up of Reclines unveiled ANGEL WITH A LARIAT. Produced by Dave Edmunds, it was an energetic affair, although one of its finest moments, a version of Eddie Miller and W. S. Stevenson's "Three Cigarettes In An Ashtray", was an altogether more sombre song, which pointed towards lang's future development.

For SHADOWLAND (1988) the producer's chair was filled by Nashville's famed Owen Bradley, whose presence was lang's endorsement from the country establishment. The Presley-quiffed Canadian's acceptance was sealed with guest vocals from Loretta Lynn and Brenda Lee, and the album earned her *Rolling Stone*'s 'Critic's Pick' for Best Female Vocalist. Elsewhere, a duet with Roy Orbison on a remake of his single, "Crying", won the duo a Grammy. lang

won a second Grammy for her third album, ABSOLUTE TORCH AND TWANG (1989).

Meanwhile, lang's profile was increasing outside Nashville. Her androgynous appearance and a teasing reluctance to be drawn on details of her personal life ('I am a L-L-Liberace fan', she would tell audiences) drew the attention of fashion editors and a growing lesbian fan base. It was perhaps just as well; in 1990 lang managed to alienate country music's natural constituency and many fellow Canadians by appearing in an (unbroadcast) advert for People for the Ethical Treatment of Animals: 'If you knew how meat was made, you'd lose your lunch', she said. 'I know. I'm from cattle country and that's why I'm a vegetarian.'

Her horizons were expanding rapidly. She made an acting debut in Percy Adlon's 1991 movie, *Salmonberries*, and, in March 1992, released her most successful album to date, INGÉNUE. Produced by Greg Penny with longtime collaborator **Ben Mink** (guitar) and lang, it was a lusher, more reflective album – the product, apparently, of an unhappy love affair. Another Grammy award-winner, it represented lang's breakthrough on a global scale. Songs like "Miss Chatelaine", for which she swapped her increasingly sober suits for a glammed-up femme look, showed that she hadn't lost any sense of humour. For the most part, though, the mood of the album was best defined by songs of yearning, principally on the single, "Constant Craving".

Confident in this success, lang came out as a lesbian in prime US gay magazine the *Advocate*, and appeared on the cover of *Vanity Fair*, sitting in a barber's chair to be wet-shaved by scantily clad supermodel Cindy Crawford. After EVEN COWGIRLS GET THE BLUES (1993), a soundtrack to Gus Van Sant's movie of the same name, her range broadened still further on the more relaxed ALL YOU CAN EAT (1995). For the first time, she permitted the subjects of her songs a specific gender, on quietly raunchy songs like "Sexuality" and "Get Some", while the album's title track exuded a new confidence.

DRAG (1997) was, at last, a concept album with a truly rock'n'roll concept – smoking. Though deeply unfashionable, potentially fatal and regarded in most circles as being on a social par with clearing your nostrils into the gutter, smoking, in the sunglasses-after-dark wonderland of rock music, is still cool. Whether that'll ever lift a cover version of the Hollies' "Air That I Breathe" from being deservedly forgotten is debatable but, in DRAG, arguably k. d. lang's 'loungecore' album, she's breathed new life and meaning into a flip-top pack of unfiltered country-tinged magic. Including songs penned by Peggy Lee and Roy Orbison and "Hain't It Funny" (written by Jane Siberry especially for lang), it was, though highly polished, an album of few surprises.

The news that lang was back on a very singular form came with 2000's INVINCIBLE SUMMER album. Its name taken from an Albert Camus quote, the set sounded just as its sun-drenched sleeve photos looked: hazy and sensual. Irrepressibly romantic, the emotional landscape was also different, with lithe ballads of contentment replacing the big number dramas of before. With **Damian LeGassick** at the controls and Ben Mink contributing lush arrangements, lang's new band included **Wendy Melvoin** (one half of Prince's Wendy & Lisa fame), all pointing the singer towards a mature, confident style.

2001's LIVE BY REQUEST effectively consigned her greatest hits onto silicon while neatly satisfying fans' demands for a live album. Culled from a series of US TV specials, where stars and nobodies alike called in to request their fave k. d. moments, the set included unsurprising takes on "Constant Craving", "Crying" and – more successfully – "Miss Chatelaine".

If lang's early career was spent establishing her 'new country' credentials, her most recent output has shown her ability to cross over into poppier styles in a highly engaging and individual manner.

⊙ **Shadowland** (1988; Sire).
This was the album that established the singer's top-flight country credentials. Lushly orchestrated in parts, but lang's powerfully emotive tones and phrasing are never lost.

⊙ **Ingénue** (1992; Sire).
A worldwide success, this is a brooding, heartbreaking album filled with skilfully penned music – and a truly magnificent voice.

⊙ **Invincible Summer** (2000; Warners).
Songs like "Consequences Of Falling" and "Summerfling" reveal a skilful lightness of touch and offer two of the album's many highpoints.

Louise Gray

THE LAST POETS

Formed Harlem, New York, 1969.

"We was born in bebop, we was raised in doowop, we put the hip in hip-hop." Jalal

As the 60s ended, Martin Luther King and Malcolm X were dead, black anger was rising, and the white establishment was becoming alarmed at the spectre of organized black rebellion. This riot-torn America was the setting for **The Last Poets'** tirades.

US Army paratrooper **Jalal Mansur Nuriddin** had reasoned that anything was preferable to Vietnam, and so had got himself jailed, where he converted to Islam, learned to rap ('It was called your spiel ... expounding your virtues'), and met **Omar Ben Hassen** and **Abiodun Oyewole**.

On their release in 1969, the threesome hooked up with Harlem's East Wind poetry workshop. Inspired by the black consciousness movement, they gave street performances and adopted a name from South African poet Little Willie Copaseely, who had said that this was the last age of poets before guns took over. The Last Poets honed their performance on the same streets as **GIL SCOTT-HERON**, and having been spotted on a TV soul show in 1970 they were signed by jazz producer Alan Douglas.

Produced by Douglas, THE LAST POETS (1970) was an exorcism of 'years of oppression'. Both white duplicity and black complacency were lambasted to the stark beat of an African drum on tracks like "Niggers Are Scared Of Revolution". It sold 800,000 copies purely by word of mouth and made the US Top 10, but before they could tour they lost Abiodun Oyewole, sentenced to fourteen years for robbery.

The second LP, THIS IS MADNESS (1971), carried on from the first album, forming 'a composite sketch of life during the Johnson and Nixon administrations'. They didn't escape the notice of those administrations, their name turning up on Nixon's Counter-Intelligence Programme lists, amid rumours that the FBI was discouraging promoters and hampering record distribution.

When Omar Ben Hassen left to join a religious sect in the south, Jalal replaced him with Korean War veteran and one-time jazz drummer **Suliaman El Hadi**, who performed poetry to his own conga accompaniment on street corners. Suliaman's influence became apparent on CHASTISEMENT (1972), when backing singers and bass were added to percussionist **Nilaja**'s African rhythms for the first time, marrying The Poets' 'spoagraphics' to a jazz-funk style to create 'jazzoetry'.

Back in 1970, Jalal had become acquainted with Jimi Hendrix at a free gig in Harlem. Hendrix was much taken with The Poets and Jalal was soon jamming in the studio with him. The result, unreleased until 1984, was DORIELLA DU FONTAINE. Recorded under the alias Lightnin' Rod, it related the cautionary tale of good-time gal Doriella over a jazzy Hendrix riff.

In 1973, Jalal revived Lightnin' Rod for the superfly HUSTLER'S CONVENTION. Effectively a blaxploitation movie without the visuals, it told the story of Sport, a gambler, and his friend Spoon, on the streets of 1959 New York. It seemed to epitomize what the extremely moralistic Last Poets usually opposed, but the moral at the end of the tale brought it back into line, as Sport was exposed as a 'nickel and dime hustler' while 'the real hustlers were ripping off billions/from the unsuspecting millions'. Amongst others, Kool & The Gang, Eric Gale, Billy Preston and King Curtis supplied the leopard-skin flare-flapping musical backing.

The next official Last Poets LP, AT LAST (1974), saw them reciting poetry over free-form jazz, the music becoming more strident as the messages became less so. After this record, longtime percussionist Nilaja left, and record-company complications meant little was heard again until DELIGHTS OF THE GARDEN (1977), which contained Jalal's 66-verse epic "Beyonder", concerning post-apocalyptic survival. The duo's words were set to a delicious funk groove, with the pulse provided by cover-credited drummer **Bernard Purdie**.

Languishing without a deal, The Poets only resurfaced in 1984 when they signed to Bill Laswell's Celluloid label. With the rise of rap in the intervening years, their albums had become prized and expensive items. The two Celluloid albums, OH, MY PEOPLE (1984) and FREEDOM EXPRESS (1988), while not as raw as their early albums, still made for distinctly uneasy listening.

After another lengthy hiatus, two different groups released records under the name of The Last Poets in 1995. One incarnation, featuring Jalal and Suliaman, released "Scatterrap"/"Home" on the French Bond Age label, while original members Abiodun Oyewole and Umar Bin Hassan (sic) reclaimed the name for HOLY TERROR, featuring guest stars Bootsy Collins, Grandmaster Melle Mel and George Clinton. Another Laswell production in 1997, TIME HAS COME, featured cameos from Chuck D, DXT, Bomb Squadder Keith Shocklee and Pharoah Sanders.

If you want to know the full story, track down a copy of *On A Mission: Selected Poems And A History Of The Last Poets*, written by Oyewole. The Last Poets were a product of their time, and have continued 'spreading the news by way of the blues' ever since. Their influence on rap and hip-hop culture is immense, and no one since, with the exception of Public Enemy, has musically reflected black outrage with such clarity.

(•) **Hustler's Convention** (1973; Celluloid).
This jive-talkin', wah-wah wig-out is best heard complete, though these days it can be hard to find.

(•) **The Best Of The Last Poets** (1995; On The One).
Two volumes comprising the whole of their history, including Lightnin' Rod's Hendrix collaboration and extracts from HUSTLER'S CONVENTION.

Glenn Law

BILL LASWELL

Born Detroit, 1950.

"I appropriate music from everywhere. To me, we're all playing the same stuff."

A prime exponent of the cut'n'mix aesthetic, **Bill Laswell** has ingeniously and, occasionally, brilliantly appropriated largely non-Western ideas and dressed them up for the intelligentsia. Laswell was a minor player in New York's mid-70s avant-garde, with a love for Miles Davis, and William S. Burroughs and a knack of making the right connections. A key moment in his career was the realization that Burroughs' literary cut-up technique equated to hip-hop's breakbeat archeology. Rhythm is the key to Laswell's 200-plus albums of genre-shifting music, as both producer and instrumentalist. When his music works, it is because his ideas and his rhythms gel; when it fails, it is because his music becomes rhythm about rhythm, funk without being funky.

Laswell first came to prominence as the bassist in the avant-rock-jazz-punk-disco fusion band, **Material**. With **Michael Beinhorn** (keyboards), **Fred Maher** (drums) and **Fred Frith** (guitar), Material was the house band for New York's multicultural, hybridizing avant-garde of the very late 70s and early 80s. Their own first LP, TEMPORARY MUSIC (1981), was a startling mixture of punk and funk. MEMORY SERVES (1982) was better still, with guests Sonny Sharrock, Henry Threadgill and Billy Bang creating the unholiest meeting of jazz and rock since Miles Davis. ONE DOWN (1983) was their finest moment. Made in collaboration with prime movers from NYC's jazz and disco scenes, ONE DOWN was a perfect evocation of the strange glamour of the Big Apple.

On a similar vibe, Laswell produced two albums for the disco diva, Nona Hendryx, and Herbie Hancock's brilliant FUTURE SHOCK (1983), which spawned the electro hit, "Rockit". For the Celluloid label, Laswell worked with African bands such as Toure Kunda from Senegal, Gambia's Mandingo Griot Society and Nigeria's Fela Kuti. Laswell's remix of Fela's ARMY ARRANGEMENT (1985), which featured Bernie Worrell from P-Funk and constant Laswell collaborator Aiyb Deng, expanded upon Fela's limited, James Brown-influenced Afro-pop, much to Fela's dismay.

Meanwhile, as a member of **Last Exit** – with guitarist **Sonny Sharrock**, saxophonist **Peter Brötzmann** and drummer **Ronald Shannon Jackson** – Laswell churned out some of the most explosive music ever made – free jazz as nihilistic punk rock.

Laswell's appreciation of hip-hop and new technology, his willingness to mix genres, and his identifiable sound made him a sought-after mid-80s producer. During this time his credits included albums for Laurie Anderson, Mick Jagger, Yoko Ono, Ryuichi Sakamoto, Ramones, Iggy Pop and PiL. His best outside production, though, was Sly And Robbie's RHYTHM KILLERS (1987). By uniting the Jamaican rhythm section with rappers Rammelzee and Grandmixer DST, percussionists Deng and Daniel Ponce, avantists Threadgill and Nicky Skopelitis, and funkateers Mudbone Cooper and Bootsy Collins, Laswell made an album that fulfilled his fusion/fission concept.

Unfortunately, this became something of a Laswell blueprint. On albums such as Material's THE THIRD POWER (1991), the Axiom Funk all-star project FUNKCRONOMICON (1995), the Bahia Black project's RITUAL BEATING SYSTEM (1992) and numerous releases on his Black Arc label, Laswell's melting-pot groove failed to become more than the sum of its parts.

His interest in Burroughs and poet Brion Gysin led him to immerse himself in Morocco's mystical trance music. His recordings of the musicians of Jajouka, APOCALYPSE ACROSS THE SKY: THE MASTER MUSICIANS OF JAJOUKA (1990), and the Gnaoua brotherhood, GNAWA NIGHT – MUSIC OF THE MARRAKESH SPIRIT MASTERS (1991), were both definitive documents of these musical styles, while THE TRANCE OF SEVEN COLORS (1994) was an intriguing pairing of saxophonist **Pharoah Sanders** and trance musician **Maleem Mahmoud Gania**. Laswell's Moroccan interests inevitably led to Paul Bowles, too, and he created backing sounds for Bowles' readings of his stories and poems on the 1995 project, BAPTISM OF SOLITUDE.

Meanwhile, his interest in trance music continued in takes on ambient. Laswell has taken his experience with Brian Eno into collaborations with Pete Namlook and Tetsu Inoue, as well as ambient reworkings of the releases on his Axiom label. His most recent album, AMBIENCE DUB VOL 1 (1997) is a superb expression of this new direction. 1998's OSCILLATIONS 2 (SubRosa) continued the Burroughs connection with a track called "El Hombre Invisible", but concentrated more on drum'n'bass experimentation.

Laswell's third label, Subharmonic, is the home for his most out-there recordings. The best of these is EXECUTION GROUND (1994), the third album by **Painkiller**, his noise trio with saxophonist **John Zorn** and ex-Napalm Death and Scorn drummer **Mick Harris**, on which din-scapes were processed and looped by co-conspirator **Robert Musso**. In 1998 he released SONGS OF FREEDOM: ambient reworkings of Bob Marley dubs which was patchy but occasionally inspired. PANTHALASSA (1999) was a less successful attempt to similarly interpret the music of Miles Davis. 2001's RADIOAXIOM: A DUB TRANSMISSION was a fine example of Laswell at his best, this time paired with that other master bass technician, **Jah Wobble**. Conversely, BOOK OF EXIT: DUB CHAMBER 4 (2002) found Laswell easing off the dub pedal with surprisingly uplifting results.

Laswell treats music as pure sound to be manipulated any which way. The results are often rewarding but equally often, overly academic and stifled. His music is the product of a brilliant mind which often forsakes the pleasures of the body for exercises of the intellect.

Material

⊙ **One Down** (1983; Restless).
Featuring Nile Rodgers' instantly recognizable, chicken-scratch guitar riffing, gratuitous vocoders, brilliant horn charts, and two of 80s disco's greatest voices – Bernard Fowler and Nona Hendryx – this is the best non-Chic Chic album ever made (and there were an awful lot of them). "Memories", with a pre-star Whitney Houston and Archie Shepp, is one of the most beautiful ballads ever.

Sly and Robbie

⊙ **Rhythm Killers** (1987; Island).
In which some of the finest dance musicians in the world jam on two side-long grooves that imply that New Orleans R&B, 70s funk, hip-hop and ragga are all part of the same continuum.

Bill Laswell

⊙ **Deconstruction: The Celluloid Recordings** (1993; Restless).
A collection of Laswell's successful and unsuccessful 80s recordings with the wide-reaching Celluloid label. Moving from Afro-fusion to art-punk to conceptual hip-hop to bruising jazz massacres, this album provides a neat overview of Laswell's cut'n'paste artistry.

Peter Shapiro

PETER LAUGHNER

Born 1953; died 1977.

One of those semi-legends of the underground whose records have only been heard by rock critics, **Peter Laughner** was one of the prime movers of the mid-70s anti-scene in Cleveland, Ohio. As a music scribe, songwriter and member of **Rocket From The Tombs** and a very early incarnation of **PERE UBU**, Laughner created one of the earliest incarnations of the punk ethos with a sound that combined the folksy righteousness of Bob Dylan, the urban verité of Lou Reed, the bored, alienated squall of fellow Rust Belters MC5 and The Stooges, and a nihilistic streak scarier than those of his mentors.

Laughner began his musical career in the early 70s as an acoustic troubadour who would drop Velvet Underground songs in between his Richard Thompson and Ramblin' Jack Elliott covers. After gigs with dead-end blues bands and twisted glitter bands in and around Cleveland, Laughner joined **David Thomas**'s art terrorists Rocket From The Tombs in 1974. Along with **Gene O'Connor** (guitar), former bassist with local legends The Mirrors, **David Bell** and **Johnny Madansky** (drums), Laughner (guitar) and Thomas (vocals/keyboards/saxophone) shaped Rocket From the Tombs into perhaps the fiercest of all the American proto-punk bands.

The band's only existing material is a radio broadcast from February 1975 on Cleveland's WMMS, which has most recently been released as a limited-edition album called Life Stinks (1990). The covers of The Stooges' "Raw Power" and "Search And Destroy" made clear that their guitar shock tactics had their origins 150 miles up the road in Detroit; they stole riffs from The Who and Mick Ronson, but it was their original material that was so startling. Thomas's "Final Solution" remains one of the scariest songs ever written, while Laughner's "30 Seconds Over Tokyo" and "Life Stinks" weren't far behind.

Rocket From The Tombs broke up in the summer of 1975 with O'Connor (metamorphosing into Cheetah Chrome), Madansky (aka Johnny Blitz) and Stiv Bators forming THE DEAD BOYS, while Laughner and Thomas formed Pere Ubu. Rocket From The Tombs material would feature strongly in both early Ubu recordings (their first two singles were "30 Seconds..." and "Final Solution", while "Life Stinks" appeared on their first album) and on Dead Boys records ("Down In Flames", "What Love Is" and "Ain't It Fun", later to be covered by Guns N' Roses).

After Pere Ubu's first two singles, Laughner left the band to form his own short-lived project Friction, and briefly to become a member of TELEVISION. One of the great poets of self-destruction, Laughner's wretched excess caught up with him in 1977 and he died of pancreatitis at the age of 24. Aside from the Rocket material, his legacy is a self-titled mini-album of demo tapes and live recordings released posthumously in 1982 that showcases his folky tendency (odes to poets Baudelaire and Sylvia Plath), and the 1994 collection, Take The Guitar Player For A Ride, which collects all of his existing songs and scribbles.

Rocket From The Tombs

⦿ **Life Stinks** (1990; Jack Slack).
Only 600 or so copies of this double album exist, but these radio broadcasts of Rocket From The Tombs represent some of the finest punk rock ever recorded.

Peter Shapiro

CYNDI LAUPER

Born New York, June 22, 1953.

When an unknown American shot to the top of the charts on both sides of the Atlantic in early 1984, it looked like a classic case of overnight success. For **Cyndi Lauper**, though, it was the reward for nearly ten years spent paying her dues singing on street corners, in anonymous clubs and bars and for second-rate cover-version bands such as Flyer, known for their spirited attempts at Led Zeppelin and Joni Mitchell classics.

After losing her voice almost totally during 1977 and spending her enforced downtime working on her writing skills, she returned to front **Blue Angel**, a standard late-70s rock band formed with her friend John Turi. The band were briefly signed to Polydor and had a minor hit in Holland (a cover of Gene

Pitney's "I'm Gonna Be Strong") before their acrimonious dissolution.

Lauper was declared bankrupt in 1982 but had by now tasted success. Returning to bar work, she had a chance encounter with David Wolff, an aspiring manager whose music industry contacts eventually led her to a deal with CBS subsidiary Portrait in 1983. Thus it was that her first solo album, appropriately entitled She's So Unusual (1984), emerged, preceded by the rabble-rousing single "Girls Just Want To Have Fun", which shot to #2 in Britain and America. Lauper's Day-Glo hair, abstract make-up technique and colourful costumes, as well as her unique vocal style, earned her a reputation as a lovable eccentric, and the song quickly became an anthem for bored teenagers and young feminists. The album, an off-the-wall mix of energetic pop and thoughtful ballads, with outside assistance from Rob Hyman and Eric Bazillian of The Hooters, sold by the million and earned Lauper a Grammy award for *Best New Artist*. A second single, the vulnerable ballad "Time After Time", confirmed that Lauper's voice, technically efficient but sometimes shrill at full throttle, was most effective on slower material.

Having overcome a sticky moment when right-wing American pressure groups objected to her third single "She Bop" on the grounds of its supposed promotion of female masturbation, Lauper spent much of 1985 working on her second album, though she took time out to pick up a Grammy and MTV awards, to record a track for Spielberg's movie *The Goonies* and to appear on the USA For Africa record "We Are The World". Although True Colors (1986) was essentially another lively pop album, there were some moments of introspection, including a cover of Marvin Gaye's "What's Going On", on which Lauper's earnest vocal was surprisingly effective, and "Boy Blue", a poignant song written after the death of a close friend. The album's title track, a worldwide hit single, also served notice of a new, less frenetic direction.

A two-year sabbatical – during which Lauper managed female wrestlers, appeared in her first movie (*Vibes*), and became a born-again Christian – ended with the release of A Night To Remember (1989). Her best-selling album in the UK so far, it produced another Top 10 single in "I Drove All Night", but it signalled the beginning of a commercial decline in her homeland. The album had an overwhelming sense of sadness, with almost every track dealing with separation or isolation, reflecting the end of her long relationship with David Wolff. Publicity photos showed her looking glamorous and moody, suggesting that she was keen to leave behind the zany, scatterbrained image of old.

A largely unsuccessful foray into acting kept her busy at the start of the 90s, while her musical output was confined to one-off charity fund-raisers, including a part in Roger Waters' 1990 Berlin performance of *The Wall*. After her 1991 marriage to actor David Thornton, her fourth album, Hat Full Of Stars

(1993), emerged to a cool reception. A wistful and low-key record, it was a poor seller, despite an illustrious list of collaborators ranging from Mary Chapin Carpenter and The Hooters to Junior Vasquez. It also spawned a minor hit single, "That's What I Think".

1994 brought a mini-revival when a big-budget hits collection clumsily entitled 12 DEADLY CYNS ... AND THEN SOME (1994) was a bestseller in Britain, as was a lumpy cod-reggae remake of "Girls Just Want To Have Fun". The success of this compilation suggested that the public still retained its affection for Lauper.

SISTERS OF AVALON (1997) had major contributions from Lauper's English-born keyboard player **Jan Pulsford**. One of the most diverse albums of the year, the songs ranged from grungey rock ("Love To Hate") to dance anthems ("Ballad Of Cleo & Joe") and boasted "You Don't Know", a chart success in Europe, where she maintains a high profile. Lauper's energies were then shared between her son, Declan, recording MERRY CHRISTMAS AND HAVE A NICE LIFE for Sony and bashing out a 90s version of kitsch classic "Disco Inferno". Most recently, she released an EP, SHINE (2002), which featured the stunning ballad "Water's Edge".

Perhaps the biggest obstacle in her career has been the ever-present phenomenon of Madonna, whose chart career began the very same month. But, while Madonna has been a single-minded pursuer of success and celebrity, Lauper has been an idealist who has valued her art more than platinum discs – and she wouldn't have it any other way.

⊙ **She's So Unusual** (1984; Portrait).
Ten years of experience went into this fresh and vivacious debut, which outsold Madonna's first effort and is on its way to five million sales worldwide.

⊙ **True Colors** (1986; Portrait).
Lauper breezes through the 'difficult' second album by toning down the wackiness and adding a dash of angst, courtesy of her greater lyrical input.

⊙ **Time After Time** (2001; Columbia).
This collection serves as a useful introduction for those who loved "Time After Time" or "I Drove All Night", but it does no more than scratch the surface of Lauper's unique talent.

Jonathan Kennaugh

LED ZEPPELIN

Formed London, 1968; split up 1980.

"Way down inside/I'm gonna give you my love/I'm gonna give you every inch of my love ... "Whole Lotta Love

As gigantic a presence as their name would suggest, **Led Zeppelin** transcended the hard rock/heavy metal label slapped on them by some. Indeed, they epitomized the synthesis of multiple influences that characterized the best of 70s rock, while producing music that was stamped with their own dynamic identity.

The story really began in the summer of 1968, when guitarist **Jimmy Page** was left as the only person interested in preserving **THE YARDBIRDS**, the influential London-based R&B band that had also showcased the talents of Eric Clapton and Jeff Beck. He soon recruited experienced keyboards player **John Paul Jones** from the London sessions circuit and then went in search of a singer. His first choice, Terry Reid, had other commitments and put him on to young Midlands vocalist **Robert Plant**, who had played with a number of local pub outfits, including Band Of Joy, whose drummer was **John Bonham**. Plant, at the time treading water with Hobbstweedle, jumped at the chance, and eventually persuaded Bonham to join up, too.

The other key figure in the group's formation was manager Peter Grant, a larger-than-life jack of all trades who was often referred to as the fifth member, such was his influence. After some Scandinavian and British dates in August/September 1968 as The New Yardbirds, the Zep monicker was adopted, apparently after a quip by Keith Moon that they were 'so heavy they should go down like a lead zeppelin', although Who bassist John Entwistle has claimed the idea was his. Soon the 'a' was dropped to avoid confusion over pronunciation.

The early Zeppelin sound was heavily blues-based but with more emphasis on chunky riffs, plus a classical touch in Jones's keyboard work and even a slight West Coast influence in some of Plant's high-pitched vocals – his shrieks sometimes sounded uncannily like Janis Joplin. The eponymous first album (1969), reportedly recorded in just thirty hours, was one of the most stunning debuts of all time. It incorporated raunchy numbers with catchy riffs, like "Good Times Bad Times" and their live magnum opus "Dazed And Confused", the break-neck speed of " Communication Breakdown", a couple of heavy blues standards, and signs of the diversity to come in the acoustic instrumental "Black Mountain Side" and the outstanding "Babe, I'm Gonna Leave You". Page had played Joan Baez's version of this traditional folk song to Plant during one of their first meetings, and here they transformed it into a hypnotic shuffle, a delicious confluence of acoustic and electric elements.

With a brilliant debut tucked under their belts and critical acclaim on the British underground circuit, the dynamic Grant formulated his plan for world domination, the key to which clearly lay in conquering the US market. He'd already made an exploratory visit to New York and set up a lucrative five-year deal with Atlantic, which gave full control to him and the band, ensuring that nobody would interfere with Page's production. Now he seized the main chance and got the band on an American tour supporting Vanilla Fudge, when the Jeff Beck Group pulled out at the last minute. They debuted in Denver on December 26, 1968, and then went round blowing everybody off stage, from Country Joe And The Fish to Iron Maiden.

John Paul Jones, Jimmy Page, Robert Plant and John Bonham perch on some classic British metal

Their incendiary stage show lasted up to four hours, kept fizzing by the chemistry that had developed between the four and filled out with lengthy solos, a hallmark of the epoch. Bonham's mammoth effort during "Moby Dick" allowed those not into half an hour of heavy-duty percussion to take a breather, but few went missing for Page's virtuoso guitar showpiece, violin bow and all, during "Dazed And Confused".

Zep returned to England for more small-venue dates early in 1969 but their stateside reputation ensured they were headliners when they recrossed the Atlantic in the spring. Although the critics were more unanimous in their praise in the UK, the big audiences were on the other side of the pond, and Grant concentrated their efforts there. They toured almost incessantly for two and a half years, filling ever bigger venues, while Grant worked to cultivate an 'underground' image, releasing hardly any singles and avoiding big publicity campaigns.

LED ZEPPELIN II was put together while the band were on the road in 1969 and recorded with the help of engineer Eddie Kramer at several different studios. It was this album that glued the 'metal' tag to Led Zep, especially in the minds of those who only heard the driving riff of "Whole Lotta Love", an edited version of which reached the US Top 5. The track was not released as a single in the UK, where no official Zeppelin singles ever came out (until 1997 when, to coincide with the band's entire back catalogue being moved to the mid-price bracket, "Whole Lotta

Love" came out as a CD digipak single) but a softer version by CCS was for years used as the signature tune to the BBC's *Top Of The Pops* show.

1970's LED ZEPPELIN III, prepared by Page and Plant at a cottage retreat in Snowdonia, then rehearsed at a run-down mansion in Hampshire, showed more diversity than ever before. The first side was very electrified, opening with the thundering "Immigrant Song", a fine display of Plant's eerie Valhallic wail, but on the other side the tone was much more melodic and acoustic, featuring their arrangement of the traditional folk song "Gallows Pole", Plant at his mellowest on "That's The Way" and Page's finest love song, "Tangerine". The album was panned by critics, who had come to expect something more rowdy.

Zeppelin's reputation as a great live act continued to grow, as 'progressive' British rock groups like Zep and Jethro Tull started to fill huge arenas in the US. They also developed the 'bad boys on the road' image by trashing hotel rooms and so on, an image that accrued a nastier edge due to Page's fascination with the occult, particularly Aleister Crowley, whose Scottish mansion he bought in 1970. Their gigs during this period sometimes degenerated into riots, thanks to fans, stoked by the Princes-of-Darkness image and various substances.

The next release was not until late 1971, with the album known to all as LED ZEPPELIN IV, though no title nor any kind of name appeared on the cover – just four runic symbols. The band wanted the music to speak for itself, and that it did with "Stairway To Heaven". No 70s party was complete without the air guitars coming out to this one, and it is still the album track most frequently requested on radio. Not that it was a one-track album. The opener, "Black Dog", contained one of Page's most inventive riffs, "Misty Mountain Hop" paid joyful homage to hippie days and "The Battle Of Evermore", complete with mandolins and Sandy Denny's angelic vocal harmonies, emphasized the band's penchant for mystical folk-rock. Atlantic's fears about the lack of name proved unfounded as it became a mega-seller, but the subsequent British tour, including two dates at Wembley Empire Pool that sold out overnight, proved to be the last on home ground for nearly four years.

During the early 70s Zep eased up a little on the intensity of touring but increased its scope, graduating to world tours encompassing the growing Japanese market. HOUSES OF THE HOLY did not appear until spring 1973 and broke with tradition in actually having a title. Although it contained several great tracks in the majestic string-driven "The Rain Song", lovely semi-acoustic "Over The Hills And Far Away" and the Jones-dominated "No Quarter", the attempt at broadening the horizons fell flat with the ill-advised reggae piece "D'yer Maker" and the downright abysmal try at funk on "The Crunge", their worst ever moment.

The group's own Swansong label was officially launched in May 1974, a year of relative calm, with no gigs, some time in the studio, and opportunities for band members to rest, pop up for the odd guest appearance or get involved in other projects. One interesting sideline was that Zep helped finance the film *Monty Python And The Holy Grail*.

When the group finally took to the road again at the start of 1975, they were greeted as returning prodigals by old and new fans alike – hundreds queued all night to get tickets for the May gigs at London's Earl's Court. It's a shame these performances were not recorded on film because what emerged the following year on the rockumentary *The Song Remains The Same* was some lacklustre footage from end-of-tour gigs in 1973, plus some self-congratulatory behind-the-scenes clips and rather silly fantasy sequences. Overall the film was unsatisfactory, though it did well enough at the box office.

The album that had preceded the film soundtrack in the spring of 1975 was a return to form: entitled PHYSICAL GRAFFITI, it was the band's only studio double album and their last great piece of work. Although the tracks are by no means all classics, between the staccato riff of "Custard Pie" and the closing bars of "Sick Again" the album contained some stunning material, like the epic version of the trad blues "In My Time Of Dying", the whimsy of "The Rover" and party fave "Trampled Underfoot", with its semi-funk beat. Indeed, much recent dance music owes more than a little to this display of Bonzo Bonham's drumming. The most enduring piece, however, was "Kashmir", the song that lit a thousand joss sticks.

From there on, although there was some worthy stuff on the last two proper albums, PRESENCE (1976) and IN THROUGH THE OUT DOOR (1979), things went downhill. In the wake of the punk explosion Led Zeppelin were numbered among the dinosaurs that the new generation had come to blow away – though, interestingly, this negative attitude did not work in reverse, as both Page and Plant made positive noises about what the young bands were doing. To make matters worse, Plant had a serious car accident on the Greek island of Rhodes in August 1975, which laid him up for the best part of two years, and this was followed by the sudden death of his young son Karac in July 1977, just after the first US comeback tour. This drove him into retirement for a further year and rumours circulated that the group had split. In fact they made a dramatic return in 1979 with an appearance at the Knebworth Festival in England. Although critical acclaim was muted, they had proved they could still pull in the crowds. IN THROUGH THE OUT DOOR topped the US album charts for a record seven weeks, and it seemed they had come through their sticky patch.

In 1980 they toured extensively again in Europe, and more activity was lined up, when John Bonham was found dead after a binge at Page's house on September 25. The decision to call it a day was immediate, but the announcement didn't come until December. As a postscript, CODA, a collection of previously recorded material, came out in 1981 to fulfil contractual obligations, but it was only relevant to die-hard fans. Later in the decade Plant embarked on quite a successful solo career and there were a couple of reunion gigs, with Bonham's son on drums. More recently, CD compilations REMASTERS and the LED ZEPPELIN box set, digitally remixed by Page, have brought them renewed popularity. **PAGE AND PLANT** have also since reunited, but that is another story.

Meanwhile John Paul Jones has only recently got round to releasing solo albums – although one gets the distinct feeling that he would love to work with Page and Plant again. ZOOMA (1999) got the ball rolling and THE THUNDERTHIEF (2002) was a diverse collection of instrumentals, vocal-led tracks and downright weirdness featuring guitarists Adam Bomb and Robert Fripp. Of course, what everyone is waiting for is some sort of Led Zep reunion but with all these solo projects flying around and Page and Plant's curious reticence there's no telling how long we might have to wait.

⦿ **Led Zeppelin I** (1969; Atlantic).
A dynamic and spontaneous debut, heralding the archetypal 70s hard-rock sound from its bluesy 60s base.

⦿ **Led Zeppelin II** (1969; Atlantic).
The heaviest Zep album, but showcasing Plant's growing confidence as a songwriter, with his Tolkienesque mystical side to the fore on "Ramble On", and sensitive romanticism on "Thank You" and "What Is And What Should Never Be". The debut, too, of that unmistakeable riff – "Whole Lotta Love".

⦿ **Led Zeppelin III** (1970; Atlantic).
The band's most reflective album stands, in retrospect,

as a superb mix of electrification, blues and reflective folk-rock.

⊙ **Led Zeppelin IV** (1971; Atlantic).
This, of course, is the classic Led Zep album, blending metallic riffs and tuneful mysticism, from "Stairway To Heaven" on.

⊙ **Physical Graffiti** (1975; Swansong).
A mature and diverse set of great power and cohesion – and, historically, one of the last great pre-punk heavy rock albums.

⊙ **Led Zeppelin** (1990; Atlantic).
Well-organized and thoughtfully remastered four-CD set, covering the career and introducing previously unreleased material.

⊙ **Led Zeppelin** (2003; WEA DVD).
A blinding DVD collection of classic live Zep from the 70s.

Nick Edwards

LEFTFIELD

Formed London, 1989; split 2002.

Leaving their teen years of punk behind, **Paul Daley** and **Neil Barnes** both sampled the merits of dub, industrial and funk before latching on to the emergent house scene. When they linked up as a duo in 1989, they took the name **Leftfield**, hinting at a punk subversive attitude, and went on to earn themselves a place in the 'progressive house' camp, alongside the likes of Orbital and Sabres Of Paradise. For this crew, reinterpreting musical influences is more important than merely cranking up the beat.

After two independently released singles, "Not Forgotten" (1990) and "More Than I Know" (1991), Leftfield were signed to the Hard Hands label in 1992. Two more singles, "Release The Pressure" and "Song Of Life" (both 1992), became underground dance classics, but they really caught the public consciousness with the release of 1993's "Open Up", which featured John Lydon on guest vocals. With vitriolic lyrics like 'Burn Hollywood burn!/Burn down, Tinseltown', it made sufficient impact to become a Top 20 single in the UK, and was widely regarded as one of the year's finest releases.

When their eagerly awaited first album, LEFTISM, was released in January 1995, Paul stated that it marked their emergence from the underground scene. Much of it was effective dance-floor filler, without toppling into the pit of handbag house, but the quieter, more exploratory moments made this an album as suitable for the front room as for clubland. Several tracks featured guest vocalists to give the package something of a focus in the midst of the sequencers and samplers – as well as John Lydon's rant, also present were reggae vocalist Earl Sixteen, African rapper Djum Djum, Manchester poet Lemn Sissay, and Curve's Toni Halliday, whose track, "Original", was released as a single.

Considerable critical acclaim and UK Top 10 success greeted the album, and within a few months it had been nominated for the annual *Mercury Music Prize*. Though it didn't win, the ensuing publicity did them no harm; neither did their acclaimed soundtrack contributions to the British films *Shallow Grave*, *Shopping* and *Trainspotting*, the last of which contained the otherwise unavailable "A Final Hit" (1996).

Leftfield followed on with RHYTHM AND STEALTH (1999), a darker set than its predecessor that featured the Guinness-surf-ad-hyped "Phat Planet". Having successfully found their place in the mainstream dance arena, the duo presented a collection of remixes the following year. Though they continued to ride a seemingly unbreaking wave, in early 2002 Daley and Barnes announced that Leftfield was no more, adding that '…the end is just the beginning'. Both are now working on solo projects.

⊙ **Leftism** (1995; Hard Hands/Sony).
Apocalyptic visions finish off this album – Lydon's damnation of Hollywood is pursued by Lemn Sissay's despairing question, 'How may homes set alight till we fight?' It's by no means all doom and gloom, though, thanks to fascinating techno tracks like "Space Shanty" and "Song Of Life".

Maria Lamle

LEGENDARY PINK DOTS

Formed London, 1980.

The **Legendary Pink Dots** were formed by **Edward Ka-Spel** (lyrics/vocals/instruments) and Philip Knight, aka **The Silver Man** (keyboards/tape/samples). They're a cult band with a prolific, home-made output, starting with a series of cassette-only releases on their own Mirrordot label, and moving on to at least eighteen official LPs/CDs released mainly through Belgian label Play It Again Sam, plus many more cassettes.

Though initially based in England, the Dots moved to Nijmegen in Holland after the first three LPs, BRIGHTER NOW (1982), CURSE (1983) and THE TOWER (1984), which collected much material from early tapes. Initially following in the footsteps of such luminaries of British psychedelia as Gong and Julian Cope, the Dots added influences from the industrial and goth scenes (particularly in their use of electronics), spicing the mix with the uncanny lyrics of Edward Ka-Spel, whose delivery ranged from the wistful storytelling of "Hanging Gardens" to the more paranoid "City Ghosts" (both on BRIGHTER NOW).

The basic line-up in the early 80s consisted of Ka-Spel and The Silver Man, plus **April Iliffe** (vocals/keyboards), **Stret Majest** (guitars), **Roland Calloway** (bass) and **Patrick Wright** (violin/keyboards/vocals) and, from 1985, **Graham Whitehead**. Keeping track of Legendary Pink Dots personnel, however, requires decoding their many pseudonyms, with Ka-Spel alone appearing as D'Archangel, Che Banana, The Prophet Qa'spel (or Sepel) and Edward Ka'spel over the years.

With FACES IN THE FIRE (1984), the Dots launched themselves as one of Play It Again Sam's most active acts, with fourteen subsequent albums during their ten years on the label. 1984 also saw the release of Edward Ka-Spel's solo "Dance China Doll" and LAUGH CHINA DOLL, the first of eleven solo albums, many of which feature members of the Pink Dots, along with Elke Ka-Spel, Edward's wife.

ASYLUM (1985) was one of the Dots' defining moments. It was disturbing, humorous, theatrical and downright weird, particularly the charging cavalry of "So Gallantly Screaming", the backwards voices of "Go Ask Alice", and the near-psychopathic melodies of "Fifteen Flies In The Marmalade". Subsequent releases ISLAND OF JEWELS (1986), ANY DAY NOW (1987) and THE GOLDEN AGE (1988) were of variable quality, and late 1987 had seen another change of personnel with **Hanz Myre** (sax/flute/electronics) and **Bob Pistoor** (guitar/bass) joining The Silver Man, Ka-Spel and Wright in a band biased towards sequenced keyboards.

This line-up toured the US with some success, promoting a compilation album, STONE CIRCLES (1987), while Edward Ka-Spel played New York and Canada with a band consisting of present and former Dots members. Ka-Spel and The Silver Man also collaborated with industrialists Skinny Puppy (with whom they had toured) in the Tear Garden project.

The Dots spent 1989 rerecording, mixing and compiling older material and live recordings, along with some new tracks, into various formats, notably the LEGENDARY PINK BOX (1989) triple LP/double CD. Their next studio album, CRUSHED VELVET APOCALYPSE (1990), combined atmospheric electronics with Ka-Spel's ever-excellent lyrics, plus the eccentric reeds of **Niels van Hoornblower** (sax/flute/clarinet), to produce their biggest success to date. It was a fine Dots era, followed up with the breathtaking THE MARIA DIMENSION (1991), which reinvented the genre of space-rock. The band's planned US tour was cancelled, however, when they were refused visas due to 'a lack of artistic merit'; curiously, their next album, THE SHADOW WEAVER (1992), was deemed of a quality sufficient to impress the US Immigration Department, as well as their growing fan base.

MALACHAI (SHADOW WEAVER PT. 2) followed in 1993, with bass guitar duties on both records performed by **Ryan Moore** (also of Tear Garden), while **Martijn de Kleer** took over on guitars. What turned out to be the Dots' last CD for Play It Again Sam, 9 LIVES TO WONDER (1994) featured **Cevin Key** of Skinny Puppy on drums, adding yet another dimension to the Pink Dots sound.

From 1995 on, the Dots resurrected their own label, Terminal Kaleidoscope – the first fruit being

Legendary Pink Dots show their dark side

FROM HERE YOU'LL WATCH THE WORLD GO BY (1995). They have also embarked on an extensive programme of CD releases of tape material, most notably the CHEMICAL PLAYSCHOOL VOLUMES 8 & 9 (1996) and UNDER TRIPLE MOONS (1997) collections, and recruited a new guitarist **Edwin** (aka Atwyn) for the all-new HALLWAY OF THE GODS (1997) and their biggest North American tour yet.

Still more popular in Europe and America than in their (mostly) unresponsive homeland, and still very prolific, they continue to happily do their own thing, stranger than most and as legendary as ever.

⊙ **The Maria Dimension** (1991; Play It Again Sam). The Dots space out, freak out and sow confusion everywhere. Almost every track is perfectly mixed and composed.

⊙ **The Shadow Weaver** (1992; Play It Again Sam). The throbbing electronics and spacey guitars on "City Of Needles" are among the Dots' best yet, while "Guilty Man" is Ka-Spel's intensely paranoiac guilt trip of several lifetimes. "The Key To Heaven" is existentialism on a stick.

⊙ **9 Lives To Wonder** (1994; Play It Again Sam). Cevin Key guests on drums and adds an organic, occasionally almost dubby, flavour to the Pink Dots sound. Almost faultless.

Richard Fontenoy

THE LEMONHEADS

Formed Boston, Massachusetts, 1986.

> **"A lot of girls scream and go, 'Oh my God!' ... I don't really like it, I wanna be one of the punters."** Evan Dando

Formed while at school in Boston, **The Lemonheads** originally comprised **Jesse Peretz** (bass), **Ben Deily** (vocals/guitar) and **Evan Dando** (vocals/guitar). Dando – the only survivor

MARION LEEMAN

from those beginnings – drummed on and co-wrote the band's self-financed debut single, "Laughing All The Way To The Cleaners" (1986), which introduced a harsh sound strongly influenced by British New Wave. The boys then headed off to college, although Dando soon dropped out, and instigated a record deal for The Lemonheads with Boston indie label Taang!. He also guested on bass with **BLAKE BABIES** alongside his girlfriend **JULIANA HATFIELD**, while the Babies' John Strohm became one of a series of short-lived Lemonhead drummers.

The Lemonheads honed their sound on a trio of Taang! releases – HATE YOUR FRIENDS (1987), CREATOR (1988) and LICK (1989) – slowly establishing themsleves on the US college circuit. At the same time, Dando gradually moved centre stage, both in performance and in the songwriting, where he and Deily became bitter rivals. This resulted in increasingly schizophrenic records, until Deily left in 1989, threatening legal action if Dando played a note of his material.

LICK had begun a move toward softer sounds (exemplified by a romp through Suzanne Vega's "Luka") which was furthered on LOVEY (1990), their debut for Atlantic Records. Released as a single, "Luka" drew promising press coverage but a spot of writer's block led to a temporary split and an awful Dando solo EP called FAVOURITE SPANISH DISHES (1990), which featured a cover of New Kids On The Block's "Step By Step".

After spending time in Australia, Dando reformed The Lemonheads, recruiting **David Ryan** (who had drummed on LOVEY) and Juliana Hatfield (on bass) for IT'S A SHAME ABOUT RAY (1992). This was a snappy country-tinged album with an accessibility that stemmed from Dando's affection for the mellow and unpretentious Australian music scene. His more relaxed approach shone through on the album's narrative songs, many of which were co-written with Australian Tom Morgan. Another friend from Sydney, **Nic Dalton**, soon joined the band on bass.

Despite good reviews, the album stalled in the low 60s of the US and UK charts. However, shortly after its release, the label issued an enjoyable, if slight, guitar-heavy cover of Simon & Garfunkel's "Mrs. Robinson", which charted worldwide and revived the band's fortunes. Dando's hippie-ish good looks soon made him a teen pin-up, a minor film star (*Reality Bites*) and the media's favourite 'slacker', epitomizing the perceived mood of laid-back twenty-somethings across the world.

The band's next LP, COME ON FEEL THE LEMONHEADS (1993), however, was delayed by Dando's spiralling personal problems. Critical and commercial success in Britain – where a cover of The Love Positions' "Into Your Arms" became their biggest hit single – was counterbalanced by poor sales in the US, where Dando was seen as a lightweight 'bubblegrunge' star, an insult which infuriated him. His substance abuse worsened and the group's future

was cast into doubt. Later in the year, however, he managed a solo acoustic tour of the US.

Dalton departed in early 1995, and Dando hit a new low point at that year's Glastonbury Festival, inspiring boos from an angry crowd who had been kept waiting for ten hours. A period of rehab followed before Dando's accumulated experiences from this period were honed into the sharpened beauty of CAR BUTTON CLOTH (1996), which featured a new band, comprising **John Strohm** and **Murph** (ex-Dinosaur Jr). Titles such as "Hospital", the truth-laden "If I Could Talk I'd Tell You" and the cathartic, Kurt Cobain-tinged yelling behind "There's Something Missing From My Life" illustrated the many miles of bad road that he'd trodden since the quirky, happy days of "Mrs. Robinson". Soon after Dando vanished, and in 1998 a BEST OF… collection appeared, suggesting that the end had come.

Dando reappeared in 2000 with a rejuvenated Blake Babies before embarking on a solo tour (LIVE AT THE BRATTLE THEATRE being released in Australia in 2001). A solo album proper followed in 2003. BABY I'M BORED was a mature set that boasted some of Dando's strongest material yet – and with rumours of another new band, **The Virgins**, circulating, Evan's future looks rosy.

⊙ **It's A Shame About Ray** (1992; Atlantic).
Superb narrative skills applied to guitar pop gems, this is laid-back but snappy enough to appeal to grunge kids. It may be uncommonly brief at just 29 minutes, but it boasts more tunes and hooks than most double albums.

⊙ **Come On Feel The Lemonheads** (1993; Atlantic).
The guitar pop songs are better than the rockers and some songs are rather inconsequential, although most are so short it hardly matters. Flawed, but nonetheless fine.

⊙ **The Atlantic Years** (1998; Atlantic).
Highlights from the four studio albums recorded on Atlantic, padded out with B-sides and rarities.

Jonathan Holden

JOHN LENNON

Born Liverpool, England, 1940;
died New York, 1980.

"Why is everybody telling me to do it? I already did it."

The solo career of **John Lennon** effectively began in May 1968. By then, with SGT PEPPER behind them, **THE BEATLES** seemed to be running out of steam, and the death of their manager, Brian Epstein, in August 1967, had added to an air of confused disillusion.

Lennon, in retrospect, had already had his turning point when, in 1966, he attended an exhibition by the Japanese conceptualist **YOKO ONO**. The artist cropped up in his life again, over the next year, and on May 19, 1968, with his wife Cynthia away, John invited Yoko over to his Surrey mansion. They slept and recorded together, producing a work entitled

UNFINISHED MUSIC NO. 1: TWO VIRGINS. It was the start of a twenty-year relationship, and the birth of John Lennon, ex-Beatle.

Artistically and politically charged by each other, John and Yoko embarked on a decade of activism and art events, beginning with the planting of 'acorns for peace' at Coventry cathedral. Predictably, the press and many Beatles fans – not to mention his old buddies in the band – reacted badly to John's new partnership, while John's conviction for possessing cannabis gave further fuel to his many critics.

When John and Yoko released TWO VIRGINS in November 1968, the same month as The Beatles' WHITE ALBUM, the assault intensified. Issued in a brown paper bag to hide the notorious cover shot of the couple standing naked (EMI, it is said, lamented that it wasn't Paul – 'the pretty one'), the album was panned in the same terms as the 'unlistenable' "Revolution No.9" on the new Beatles LP.

Lennon didn't seem too bothered and in March 1969 became the first Beatle to return to live work, accompanyng Yoko at a Cambridge University avant-garde jazz concert. The art crowd hated it because Beatle John had no right to make 'art', the rock crowd felt Lennon had betrayed his roots, and the jazz crowd dismissed the howling guitar feedback because it wasn't jazz.

John and Yoko – as their "Ballad" (issued as a late Beatles single) would record – fled to Paris, got married in Gibraltar on March 20, and spent their honeymoon in bed in Amsterdam, where the 'Bed-In' became another headline-grabbing advert for peace. John was refused a US visa for a planned 'Bed-In' in New York, but, after he had changed his middle name to Ono and the couple had released UNFINISHED MUSIC NO. 2: LIFE WITH THE LIONS (1969), he and Yoko bedded-in at a Montreal hotel, where an impromptu version of "Give Peace A Chance" was recorded with all those who happened to be around their bed at the time. Credited to 'The Plastic Ono Band', it became a hit on both sides of the Atlantic in July 1969.

A real **Plastic Ono Band**, featuring **Eric Clapton**, ex-Manfred Mann bassist **Klaus Voorman** and drummer **Alan White**, was cobbled together for a 'Rock'N'Roll Revival' concert in Toronto. The show was later released as LIVE PEACE IN TORONTO 1969. It was a tough time for the Lennons, Yoko having suffered a second miscarriage in eighteen months, and their music reflected it, with John giving vent to his raw, primal singing and songwriting. The best-known track from this period was The Plastic Ono Band's "Cold Turkey", a rough, tough and heavy single. John and Yoko, however, also released a WEDDING ALBUM, packaged complete with slices of wedding cake and containing recordings of their heartbeats from the Amsterdam 'Bed-In'.

For Christmas, The Plastic Ono Band – now featuring Clapton, George Harrison and The Who's drummer Keith Moon – played a UNICEF benefit at London's Lyceum Ballroom. Billboards across the

Without Lennon this would be a shorter book by far

world declared: 'War Is Over! If You Want It. Happy Christmas from John and Yoko' – a message later repeated as the title of that endlessly reissued single. At the time it had a message, and John signed off from the 60s in rebellious spirit, returning his MBE in protest against Britain's stance towards Biafra and Vietnam.

Lennon began the 70s amid further uproar, with a London exhibition of lithographs that were deemed obscene and withdrawn from view, and a film of his penis. There were rushes of musical creativity, too, as John wrote and recorded "Instant Karma" in a single day, with producer **Phil Spector**; ten days later, it was in the shops. Then, in April 1970, Paul McCartney announced his departure from The Beatles. John's response was to fly with Yoko to Los Angeles for primal therapy, which he followed with the release of JOHN LENNON/THE PLASTIC ONO BAND (1970). A stark, brutal, beautiful, honest record – the primal therapy was clear to see – it was again produced by Phil Spector, though he proved his genius by not putting his usual stamp on it.

1971 began with myriad entanglements involving The Beatles, ex-wives and ex-husbands, their accountants and lawyers, but Lennon continued providing material for slogan chants with "Power To The People". That summer, Spector and The Plastic Ono Band were assembled again at John's studio for the recording of IMAGINE (1971), sessions later documented in David Wolper's film of the same name. As well as the title track, the album contained Lennon's infamous attack on Paul McCartney, "How Do You Sleep?" Written in retaliation against Paul's dig at John on "Too Many People", its bitterness was emphasized by Harrison's blisteringly pointed solo. "Imagine" aside, the album's most memorable cut was a remake of a song John had written for the WHITE ALBUM three years earlier: the original lyrics – 'Underneath the mountain ranges/Where the wind that never changes/I'm just a child of nature ...' – were thankfully suppressed, and the piece was rewritten as "Jealous Guy".

John and Yoko moved to New York in September 1971, and John was never to return to England. The pair were immediately adopted by the Greenwich Village underground, and became involved in numerous political campaigns, as commemorated by the live album, SOME TIME IN NEW YORK CITY (1972), which tackled such subjects as the IRA, the Attica Prison riots, and feminism (on the single "Woman Is The Nigger Of The World"). Despite Spector's powerful production, the album dated quickly, as indeed did the more enduring example of sloganeering, "Happy Xmas (War Is Over)", which became a major hit later that year.

After a spell of court battles over US government refusal to extend the Lennons' visas because of the earlier drug conviction, John returned to themes of peace, love and understanding on MIND GAMES (1973), which featured the raucous "Meat City", the poignant "You Are Here" and the title song, a hit single. However, the rest of the album seemed a little too uniform, even stagnant. Personally, John was all over the place and, having split up with Yoko, moved in early 1974 to LA to make an album of rock'n'roll favourites with Spector.

Although John had asked the producer to dictate the show as if he were a Ronette, discipline wasn't on the agenda, and the sessions lapsed into madness. John was living with Ringo Starr, Harry Nilsson and Keith Moon, a gang that led a hard-drinking, hell-raising, rock'n'roll lifestyle. Drunken brawls spilled over into the studio, guns were fired, and by the time John emerged from the alcoholic haze Spector had barricaded himself in his mansion fortress with the master tapes and refused to come out or give them back.

Abandoning the project, John pulled together a sane Plastic Ono Nuclear Band for the LP WALLS AND BRIDGES (1974). The material contained messages to Yoko ("Bless You"), a nod at companion May Pang ("Surprise Surprise"), a remake of "How Do You Sleep?" for Allen Klein ("Steel And Glass"), and the self-pitying but touching "Nobody Loves You (When You're Down And Out)". Elton John played on the more upbeat single "Whatever Gets You Thru The Night", and Lennon promised to appear live with him if it made #1 in the States. When it became his first US solo chart-topper, he duly gave what turned out to be his last public performance – with Elton John at Madison Square Garden. Yoko was in the audience and within a month they were reconciled and living together at the Dakota.

His confidence back, John recovered the ROCK'N'ROLL tapes from Spector. Although much was unusable, his enthusiasm for the project returned, and he finished producing the album within a week. Finally released in February 1975, the disc featured slowed-down versions of "Bonie Moronie" and "You Can't Catch Me", which emphasized the power of both singer and songs, and a cracking rendition of "Stand By Me". It is a shame that electrifying examples of the original Spector/Lennon concept (like "Be My Baby" and "Angel Baby") were left off the final running order.

When Yoko became pregnant in early 1975, plans for any further records were shelved, and after his son Sean was born, on his own 35th birthday, John opted for a role of fathering and domesticity. Notoriously, he turned Paul McCartney away when the latter turned up at the Dakota with a guitar, explaining he had the kid to look after.

After a five-year sabbatical, John was eventually inspired to return to recording while holidaying with his son. The result was an optimistic, slap-echoed Lennon hiccuping his way through "(Just Like) Starting Over", and a John and Yoko LP, DOUBLE FANTASY, in late 1980. It had its dodgy moments – too much sentimentality, for sure, with the likes of "Beautiful Boy" – but included some of his most direct and contented output, including a nice riposte to the critics, "Watching The Wheels".

It seemed as if Lennon was now ready to return to regular recording commitments, and he began work on a follow-up LP with Yoko, called MILK AND HONEY. But on December 8, 1980, Lennon was shot dead in the street by Mark Chapman, to whom he had given an autograph just hours earlier. "(Just Like) Starting Over" became a posthumous #1 in both the UK and US, and preceded a massive reactivation of Lennon's back catalogue. The incomplete and insubstantial MILK AND HONEY set, meanwhile, was eventually released in 1984.

● **John Lennon/The Plastic Ono Band** (1970; EMI/Geffen).
Lennon's finest solo album – honest and beautiful, with stripped-down production that emphasizes his power.

● **Imagine** (1971; EMI/Geffen).
More quintessential Lennon, including perhaps his best post-Beatles song, "Jealous Guy", as well, of course, as the title track. It was reissued on vinyl in 1998 (Apple).

● **The John Lennon Collection** (1981; EMI/Geffen).
Contains John's half of DOUBLE FANTASY, plus the pick of the output from 1969–1974, though only "Stand By Me" is added from ROCK'N'ROLL.

● **Lennon** (1990; EMI/Geffen).
This comprehensive four-CD box set collects 73 tracks from "Give Peace A Chance" to MILK AND HONEY. All the best singles, plus B-sides and a gorgeous outtake from ROCK'N'ROLL, the Spector-produced, mantra-paced version of The Ronettes' "Be My Baby".

Tony Thewlis

THE LEVELLERS

Formed Brighton, England, 1988.

I f those who live by the sword can also die by it, then it is also possible to be given a good beating with your own principles. Just ask **The Levellers**. Few bands have been so strongly accused of 'selling out', but then few bands have adopted such an outsider stance.

Their ascent to stardom was an unusual one. **Mark Chadwick** (vocals/guitar), **Charlie Heather** (drums), **Alan Miles** (mandolin/guitar/vocals), **Jeremy Cunningham** (bass/vocals) and **Jon Sevink** (violin) united through a love of punk and folk, and a mistrust of authority. In those golden pre-Criminal Justice Act days there were plenty of places for a young punk-folk band to get a gig, and The Levellers became a fixture on the free festival/squat circuit.

Two EPs on manager Phil Nelson's Hag label, CARRY ME and OUTSIDE INSIDE (both 1989), were perhaps the only studio recordings ever to truly capture the energy that the band created in even the most toilet-like venues. These eight songs may sound crude to ears accustomed to the band's later work, but they are well worth searching out.

A WEAPON CALLED THE WORD (1990), issued on Belgian label Musidisc, was a calling card for a wider public, but there was growing internal friction leading to Miles being replaced by **Simon Friend** (mandolin/guitar/vocals), sometime Red

Sky Coven member and a seriously talented songwriter. After some complicated legal wranglings, the band left Musidisc to sign to the more sympathetic China.

A tour with kindred spirits New Model Army followed, which increased their profile dramatically and this translated into sales with the release of "One Way" (1991), their most commercial moment. Success continued with a massive nationwide tour and a top ten album, LEVELLING THE LAND (1991).

"Fifteen Years" (1992) ushered in a year of prolonged hugeness. The band made their first appearance on that doyen of anti-punk, *Top Of The Pops*, albeit on a ropey 'live via satellite'-type affair. After selling out Brixton Academy they made a triumphant appearance at Glastonbury, where they played with all the passion, fire and drive that they'd shown those tiny clubs. At the end of the year they moved the festival vibe indoors with the Birmingham and Brighton 'Freak Shows', featuring a full supporting cast including Chumbawamba and Back To The Planet.

The following year was not quite so heart-warming. THE LEVELLERS (1993) topped the charts, but the band became increasingly paranoid, establishing a war with the music press. Gigs took place in cavernous sports halls, failing to capture the atmosphere of earlier days. The Levellers seemed to be taking independence to the point of isolation.

1994 saw more festival appearances and also the fronting, funding and coordination of the musical campaign against the Criminal Justice Act. The return to action saw them far more amenable to the music business as natty threads replaced dreads and ZEITGEIST (1995) topped the UK indie charts. ZEITGEIST was a surprisingly 'up' album, the first release to be recorded at the Metway, home to the band's offices, fan club and bar as well as the anti-CJA Justice organization and several local businesses. The tour that followed spawned a live 'best of' album and the video HEADLIGHTS, WHITE LINES, BLACK TAR RIVERS (1996), which conveyed the full Levellers live experience to the stay-at-homes. It won them many new fans prior to their wild barnstorming of Glastonbury 1997.

A cameo appearance as **The Leveller Mutineers** on Rev Hammer's FREEBORN JOHN Cromwellian concept album followed, part of a cast that included Maddy Prior, Eddi Reader, Justin Sullivan and Rory McLeod. Towards the end of the year The Levellers dropped their definite article to become, simply, Levellers. They were reunited with Reader on MOUTH TO MOUTH (1997), but the album is, at best, patchy.

1998 marked the band's tenth anniversary and they celebrated with more touring, a book (*Dance Before The Storm*) and a greatest hits album, ONE WAY OF LIFE. Two years on, the Levellers returned to the studio to record HELLO PIG (2000). Sales were slow and, coupled with a disappointing response to the Single "Happy Birthday Revolution" suggested that the band were merely preaching to the converted and are now unlikely to ever enlarge their fan base. The band worked hard to promote the album, with a huge acoustic European tour and a full British tour. By 2003 the band were keeping themselves busy organizing a new summer festival, Beautiful Days.

Having thrilled, provoked, inspired and frustrated us for over a decade, there is always the hope that when the Levellers return again they may have recaptured some of what made them so special in the first place. But, now seemingly unable to convert the passion of their live shows into quality albums, perhaps the end of the road is in sight.

⊙ **Levelling The Land** (1991; China).
The breakthrough album. A couple of moments are slightly weak, but "The Game", "Boatman", "Sell Out" and the inspiring "Battle Of The Beanfield" ensure classic status.

⊙ **Zeitgeist** (1995; China).
A lightening of attitude and a new spirit resulted in this sparkling set of punk-pop.

⊙ **One Way Of Life** (1998; China).
A singles-only best-of, so it misses many of their greatest moments. Nonetheless, the new version of the title track breathes life into an overplayed song, and the later stuff sounds a lot better away from its parent albums.

Phil Udell

LEVITATION

Formed London, 1990; probably disbanded 1994.

I n 1990, **Terry Bickers** quit THE HOUSE OF LOVE after a much-publicized bust-up with lead singer Guy Chadwick. Unhappy with the constraints placed upon his guitar playing, and irritated by Chadwick's mainstream approach, he left to follow his own rather untidier instincts, forming **Levitation** with fellow space cadets **Robert White** (keyboards/guitar), sometime-Cardiac **Christian 'Bic' Hayes** (guitar), **Dave Francollini** (drums) and **Laurence O'Keefe** (bass).

Levitation set about shaking up the scene with some chaotic and incendiary live shows, while Bickers talked up prog-rock revivals, as well as flying saucers, reincarnation, bacchanalian revelry and Egyptology, in music press interviews. The band's debut, COPPELIA, arrived in April 1991, a stunning EP – opening with the breathless and shimmering "Nadine", getting looser and more reflective on "Rosemary Jones", producing some of the most vigorous and exhilarating riffing imaginable on "Paid In Kind", and coming over anthemic on "Smile" – which has become a firm live favourite.

A second EP, the even more expansive AFTER EVER, followed that summer, and in 1992 the two records were gathered together, with some live cuts, and the wonderful "It's Time", on a mini-LP compilation, COTERIE. This, however, was merely a taster for the explosive NEED FOR NOT (1992), the band's finest hour on disc, which appeared just a few months later. Its ferocious sound went far to matching the band's intense live performances.

Levitation then blotted their copybook with the pompous WORLD AROUND EP, which prophetically featured a donkey on its front cover, and in mid-1993, after the release of the stale "Even When Your Eyes Are Open" (the band's debut for major label Chrysalis), Bickers suddenly quit, refusing to discuss the whys and wherefores of the decision. The remaining line-up limped on to record MEANWHILE GARDENS (1994), an Australia-only release on the Festival label. It included rerecordings of old material, as well as pacey, if patchy, new offerings. The stand-out track was "King Of Mice", which featured a brass section, some strings and the precisely enunciated tones of newly recruited vocalist **Steven Ludwin**, but lacked the spark of the original line-up.

Since the end of 1994 Levitation have remained silent, though Bickers has recently popped up again in the reanimated House Of Love.

⊙ **Need For Not** (1992; Rough Trade).
Produced by The Cardiacs' Tim Smith, this was Levitation in excelsis. Sometimes lamentable, sometimes majestic, but always intense.

Andy Shields

HUEY LEWIS AND THE NEWS

Formed San Francisco, 1979.

I n their prime, **Huey Lewis And The News** represented the down-to-earth, unpretentious side of commercial rock, and drew record buyers in their millions. Later, as the moment passed, they tried hard to adapt, but lost their honesty in the process, and consequently much of their following.

It all began in 1979 when **Huey Lewis** (vocals/harmonica) joined forces with session players **Johnny Colla** (guitar/saxophone), **Chris Hayes** (guitar/vocals), **Mario Cipollina** (bass), **Bill Gibson** (drums/vocals) and **Sean Hopper** (keyboards/vocals). They signed to Chrysalis under the name Huey Lewis & American Express, but soon changed the suffix due to copyright fears. A thin-sounding debut LP, HUEY LEWIS AND THE NEWS (1980), had little impact, but a growing live following led to a breakthrough single, "Do You Believe In Love", early in 1982, and attendant success for the album PICTURE THIS, which charted in the US at #13.

As America showed interest, the band delivered with SPORTS (1983), which eventually topped the *Billboard* album chart, and produced four hit singles. The band's success was partly down to an intelligent grasp of video. Consistently bright, funny and inventive, they kept pace with the rise of MTV, and by 1985 had become icons of mainstream America, where they were at the heart of the USA for Africa project.

Their appeal had also extended to Europe, where "I Want A New Drug" became a massive hit, and Japan, where they had a strong live following. However, these successes paled into insignificance when Steven Spielberg, on the lookout for a soundtrack for *Back To The Future*, asked Lewis for a contribution. After apparent initial reluctance, Lewis agreed, and delivered an absurdly infectious slice of guitar rock, "The Power Of Love". The song was the first of three US #1 singles ("Stuck With You" and "Jacob's Ladder" followed), and it charted just about everywhere else in the world, too. FORE! (1986), the album containing these hits, represented the band's commercial peak.

On its follow-up, SMALL WORLD (1988), ecological and family concerns abounded, and a sense of cosiness permeated the band's sound, albeit with elements of jazz, reggae and ska thrown in. It fared less well than FORE!, almost inevitably, and with HARD AT PLAY (1991) The News tried to recapture their rock credentials. They succeeded on "Build Me Up" and the single "Couple Days Off", but elsewhere found themselves in a backwater of middle-aged sentiments.

Unable to resurrect the friendly-superstar image, the band switched to Elektra and tried to rediscover their roots. However, both FOUR CHORDS AND SEVERAL YEARS AGO (1994) and PLAN B (2001) offered professional but undistinguished rock/pop. Trapped in the 80s *Zeitgeist*, it seems The News' hour has been and gone.

⊙ **Sports** (1983; Chrysalis).
A defining moment and a major hit album, including "Heart And Soul", the hard-rocking "I Want A New Drug" and the bluesy "Bad Is Bad".

⊙ **Fore!** (1986; Chrysalis).
Their warmest, richest album, which comes closest to capturing their live feel.

Robert Jones

JERRY LEE LEWIS

Born Ferriday, Louisiana, September 29, 1939.

"I was a kid. I didn't really know what was going on. Probably still don't. I never was the smartest person in the world."

Despite his oft-expressed claims, **Jerry Lee Lewis** was never really the king of rock'n'roll – he's just lived the life better than anyone else. Pumped full of pills and liquor, flashing firearms and chasing women at every opportunity, he has spent forty years seemingly bent on his own destruction, playing concerts that vary from drunken farces to barnstorming spectacles.

Like Elvis, Jerry Lee grew up as poor white trash in the Deep South, listening to country, gospel and blues. The arrival of rock suggested a way of bringing the disparate strands together, but he probably would have arrived at the same conclusion anyway. His first records for Sun in 1956 – "End Of The Road" and "Crazy Arms" – demonstrated a fully fledged style, driven by his piano playing, with his left hand pumping out simplified boogie patterns while the right hammered the keys with a relentless ostentation that bordered on arrogance.

Jerry Lee Lewis – he ain't preachin', boy

The next two singles were the foundations on which his musical legacy rests: "Great Balls Of Fire" and "Whole Lotta Shakin' Goin' On" were international smashes in 1957, announcing the arrival of an awesome talent. Like a man possessed by demonic self-belief, Lewis hollered the songs as bacchanalian celebrations of untameable energy. With his cousin, Jimmy Swaggart, he had trained to be a Pentecostalist preacher, and he brought the same sense of fervid passion to his music. Swaggart, of course, thought he had fallen under Satan's spell, and he was probably right.

With further hits and a movie under his belt, Lewis took his message abroad in 1958, only to meet his nemesis in England, where the press discovered his wife was not only his cousin, but just 13 years old to boot. Lewis couldn't see the problem – he had only been 14 when he first married – but in Britain such behaviour was unacceptable, and he was hounded out as a child molester. In Middle America, too, it was beyond the pale and, shunned by an industry seeking respectability, Lewis saw his career all but collapse.

There were minor hits over the next few years, still on Sun, and the concerts were as exciting as anything rock could offer, but it was not until 1966 that Jerry Lee returned to public favour. When he did, it was on Mercury as a country star, though the style had hardly changed. Some of the excesses were trimmed in the studio, but the essence remained. The choice of material (he has never written his own songs) was almost irrelevant – everything he touched ended up sounding like a Jerry Lee Lewis number.

Even today the spirit remains undimmed by time, self-abuse, tax troubles and a disastrous personal life (two ex-wives dead in strange circumstances, two children dead). Though his music hasn't changed over the years, neither has the quality of his performances dimmed. 1995's album, YOUNG BLOOD, showed him potent as ever and the rerelease of two of his classic albums in 1998 (SINGS THE ROCK'N'ROLL CLASSICS and THE COUNTRY COLLECTION) were warmly welcomed by Q magazine, who memorably described him as a cross between Jools Holland and Lemmy.

Lastly, Nick Tosches' biography of Lewis, *Hellfire!* and his own autobiography, *Killer*, are simply the best rock books ever. Read them and you'll have difficulty believing the man is still alive, still sane (possibly), and still at liberty.

⊙ **Live At The Star Club, Hamburg** (1963; Bear Family).
Backed by the Nashville Teens, Jerry shows a German audience the meaning of rock'n'roll. 'Primitive' is too mild a word to describe the results.

⊙ **Great Balls Of Fire** (1989; Charly).
There are legions of Jerry Lee compilations, but the rule of thumb is that anything on Charly is an original recording. This features thirty greatest hits from the Sun years.

⊙ **The Sun Years** (1989; Charly).
For those who need more, an eight-CD collection of everything Lewis recorded for Sun.

⊙ **Young Blood** (1995; Sire).
A new label, a new producer and a new lease of life. Back on form, particularly the cover of "I'll Never Get Out Of This World Alive" by Hank Williams, one of the few artists Lewis considers to be his equal.

Alwyn W. Turner

THE LIBERTINES

Formed Bethnal Green, London, 1996.

At a time when so many new bands nurtured a sound based in garage rock'n'roll in the hope of being hailed by the *NME* as 'the year's best', it would have been easy for **The Libertines**, with their bombastic, japey take on the genre, to be overlooked. Which would have been a shame – mainman **Carl Barat** possesses an exuberant, do-or-die mentality, and a way with lyrical delivery that at times resembles a punkier Jarvis Cocker (Pulp) or a less sulky David Gedge (The Wedding Present). Like Supergrass or even, erm, The Monkees, The Libertines possess an energy and humour far too often left out of rock's cookbook. Thankfully though, first Bernard Butler and then Mick Jones of The Clash 'got it', and then it all happened for Barat and his band.

The history of The Libertines is almost impossible to recount, so many faces have been a part of the tapestry. Suffice to say the nucleus of the band came into being when muso Carl was introduced to **Peter Doherty** (guitars/vocals). The pair quickly discovered a mutual love of music, and that their individually penned, half-finished songs actually con-

REDFERNS

The Libertines' Carl Barat sans trousers

nected – the band was born. So convinced was Barat that The Libertines would break, he ditched his job and shifted with Doherty to a doorless squat in Camden to craft the songs for which they felt labels would bite their hands off. Naturally, it was nowhere near that straightforward: "Death On The Stairs", from their debut, later documented the rejection Barat and Doherty had occasionally felt.

London pubs provided the backdrop for most of the group's performances at this point. Temporary members at the time included two frontmen known only as **Steve** and **Scarborough Steve**, and a drummer called **Zack**, who left Carl and Peter high and dry, preferring to join the unfortunately-monikered Cactus Camel, and subsequently disappearing without trace. The band was eventually completed by **John Hassall** (bass) and drummer **Gary Powell** – who himself replaced the original 54-year-old percussionist **Mr Razzcox**! Stability was finally achieved.

With Carl established as band leader, The Libertines entered a new phase. In 2001, as Rough Trade stepped in to sign the band, **Bernard Butler** appeared, enthusiastic to produce their first single. When "What a Waster" was finally released in 2002 it stunned everyone involved by not only making *NME Single of the Week*, but also cracking the Top Forty. One person impressed by the track was ex-Clash man **Mick Jones**, who became their next producer and loudest-hailing fan. With Jones, The

Libertines recorded the debut album UP THE BRACKET. It was a short, sharp shock of adrenaline, but in stark contrast with much of the austerity that surrounded the new rock'n'roll vogue, possessed a good measure of humour, as witnessed by the title track – another corking single. With the ship-steadying hands of both Butler and Jones, the band found itself facing stardom, with various TV appearances as well as a tour opening for natural mentors Supergrass and yet more single success with "Time For Heroes" (2003).

This is an act that can, and surely will, push much further.

⊙ **Up The Bracket** (2002; Rough Trade).
In years to come this set of blistering indie punk rockers will hopefully be looked upon as very much a 'starting point' for The Libertines. They certainly hint that they are no one trick pony, check out the delightful, acoustic "Radio America".

Jeremy Simmonds

THE LIGHTNING SEEDS

Formed Liverpool, England, 1988.

When **Ian Broudie** (vocals/guitar) formed **The Lightning Seeds** in the late 80s, he had already been in the music business for over ten years. He began his career in 1977 with the near-legendary post-punk band **Big In Japan**, where he worked with future KLF instigator Bill Drummond, Budgie (later of Siouxsie and The Banshees) and Holly Johnson (later of Frankie Goes To Hollywood).

After Big In Japan split in 1979, Broudie joined **The Original Mirrors**, whose eponymous debut LP appeared the following year. Then in 1982 he created **Care** with Wild Swans vocalist Paul Simpson, with whom he made several singles over the next couple of years. After that his interest in production took over, as he was commissioned to work with The Fall, Echo And The Bunnymen, The Icicle Works and Wah, among others.

Hankering after a return to the limelight, Broudie formed The Lightning Seeds as a solo operation, employing other musicians and performers when necessary. His songwriting ideals were to strike gold first time out: the first Seeds single, "Pure" (1989), was the perfect summer soundtrack and reached the UK Top 20 before hitting the Top 40 in the US. Its parent album, CLOUDCUCKOOLAND (1990), released on independent label Ghetto, attracted major-label interest, and in 1992 Broudie signed to Virgin.

The Lightning Seeds' second album, SENSE (1992), contained more of the same crisp, catchy pop, yet failed to chart, despite the inclusion of two fine singles: its title track, co-written with Terry Hall of The Specials and Colourfield, and "The Life Of Riley". The latter title was only a minor hit, but later captured public attention when its instrumental version accompanied BBC TV 'Goal of the Month' football action.

Broudie signed to Sony for JOLLIFICATION (1994), with a strawberry-adorned sleeve hinting at the sweet tuneful pop within. After initial commercial indifference, several tracks charted as singles, and eventually the album began to sell in its own right. As well as featuring cameos from Terry Hall (on the single "Lucky You"), Alison Moyet, and former Icicle Works singer **Ian McNabb**, Broudie also recruited co-producer and multi-instrumentalist **Simon Rogers** (once of The Fall), **Chive Layton** (organ) and **Marina van Rody** (vocals).

To promote the album, Broudie set out on tour with **Ali Kane** (keyboards), **Martin Campbell** (bass) and **Chris Sharrock** (drums). The shows were generally well received, although some felt that they suffered from a heavy-handed rock-orientated approach, which tended to drown out the more melodic side of Broudie's songs. Even so, it maintained momentum for new material throughout 1996, notably the hit singles "Ready Or Not", and the extraordinarily successful "Three Lions", written and performed with comedians Frank Skinner and David Baddiel as an anthem for England's soccer team in that summer's European football championships, and reworked for the 1998 World Cup Finals. The team may have been unsuccessful on both outings, but the single's fortunes were spectacular: "Three Lions" became the first song since "Bohemian Rhapsody" to hit the British #1 spot on two completely separate occasions.

In the meantime, Broudie ensured that the hits continued, thanks to DIZZY HEIGHTS (1996), an album crammed to the rafters with catchy tunes and hooks, this time collaborating with Manic Street Preachers' Nicky Wire and Baby Bird's Stephen Jones on a couple of tracks. With a predictably huge-selling LIKE YOU DO: THE BEST OF (1997), and a joyous series of accompanying live shows, it seemed that The Seeds' next return would yield further smash hits.

However, the more dance-orientated TILT, released prior to Christmas in 1999, was lost in the rush of bigger sellers and sold very poorly. Even Broudie's collaborations with **Mike Pickering** (M People), **Baby Bird** and **Terry Hall** failed to reel in the punters. Still, Broudie has such a gift for melody, it would take a brave individual to completely write off his commercial standing. His time may well come again, but for now the long silence has only been broken by, of all things, a third reissue of "Three Lions" in 2002.

⊙ **Jollification** (1994; Sony).
A stunningly consistent and catchy pop album, which spawned four major hit singles in "Lucky You", "Change", "Marvellous" and "Perfect".

⊙ **Pure Lightning Seeds** (1996; Virgin).
Broudie's songwriting capabilities are equally prominent on this compilation of material from CLOUDCUCKOOLAND and SENSE.

⊙ **Like You Do: The Best Of** (1997; Epic).
The ultimate collection from the acceptable face of AOR.

Justin Lewis

Formed Jacksonville, Florida, 1994.

The rise of **Limp Bizkit** has been instrumental in focusing attention on the disparate collection of bands lumped into the nu-metal camp, with its emphasis on aggressive metal stylings welded securely to rap's street-level credibility. While bands such as Slipknot have gone on to emphasize the thrashier, more metallic end of the spectrum, bands like Limp Bizkit reflect the rap side of things.

Still, none of this was apparent in the early 90s when **Fred Durst** was wallowing within the confines of his middle-class upbringing. He was undistinguished as a scholar and had spent a period of time in the navy; his family background cast him as a God-fearing kind of guy but within him was the urge to create the devil's music.

His most significant early outfit was Malachi Sage, where he met **Sam Rivers** (bass). River's cousin **John Everett Otto** (drums) was soon to join the like-minded pair and he knew of a young artist, **Wesley Louden Borland** (guitar), who was also frontman of a local metal band called Goatslayer. Borland joining the band would allow Durst to ditch guitar and concentrate on fronting, something for which he clearly had a gift. A band was forming that merged the power and ferocity of metal with the style and sass of hip-hop; Durst indulged his penchant for potty-mouthed ranting and Borland brought a trademark theatricality to their shows with his love of weirdly coloured contact lenses, body paint and bizarre attire

Their first major break came not through any musical effort, however, but through Durst's day job as tattoo artist. Rising stars Korn happened to be passing through town and their love of needlework meant that Durst ended up befriending Fieldy (bass) and Head (guitar). A tape eventually changed hands and ended up with Korn producer Ross Robinson, who loved the music and began talking them up in the music industry.

The ball had finally started rolling. Their first national tour found the Bizkit opening for hip-hoppers House Of Pain during which time they befriended **DJ Lethal**. With House Of Pain stuttering towards their demise, Limp Bizkit eventually gained their turntablist in 1996. This and the studio help of Robinson was to make them into stars.

THREE DOLLAR BILL Y'ALL$ (1997) contained all the stylistic elements that would appeal to the late-90s MTV generation: tough riffs, plenty of expletives and a readily identifiable vein of angst. But it sold poorly at first, largely because it seemed to confuse the conservative, format-led radio stations: they were neither metal, nor rock, nor rap. The radio industry needed something familiar, which came in the shape of "Faith", a cover of George Michael's solo hit. The band had been knocking this around for a few years but when Michael was arrested for lewd

behaviour in a public lavatory, Limp Bizkit's version took on a previously missing sense of irony. They had their first hit, which launched an inevitable bout of touring. By the time SIGNIFICANT OTHER (1999) emerged, the band were leaner and much meaner sounding, though the record was carefully crafted with a radio-friendly polish: a host of big, names from Korn's **Jonathan Davis** to Stone Temple Pilots's **Scott Weiland**, turned up on the disc – Weiland had acted as vocal coach, tuning up Durst's rather rough approach to the mic.

Bizarrely, around this time Durst was also made a senior Vice President at **Interscope**. Taking a tip from the best, Durst then decided that they should emulate The Beatles, U2 and other classic rock luminaries by playing a series of impromptu rooftop gigs around the US to advertise their new record. The plan didn't always work – they were usually stopped by the cops a few songs into their set – but it was enough to kick the record into the upper reaches of

Head Bizkit Fred Durst

the *Billboard* chart. Limp Bizkit had arrived – big time.

The release of CHOCOLATE STARFISH AND THE HOT DOG FLAVORED WATER in 2000, marked Limp Bizkit as megastars with hits such as "Take A Look Around" (from the soundtrack to *Mission Impossible 2*, borrowing the riff to **Lalo Schifrin**'s original theme). Durst himself had become a tabloid celebrity and the idol of a generation of disaffected, media-savvy youth. The band also spearheaded the 'nu-metal' breakthrough in Europe, with "Rollin'" topping the UK singles chart for two weeks in January 2001.

Since, things have gone quiet. One blow to the Bizkit stock came when Borland opted to leave the band in October 2001 after releasing the ill-fated DUKE LION FIGHTS THE TERROR!! from his **Big Dumb Face** project (also featuring ex-**Goatslayer**s, **Scott Borland** – his little brother – and **Kyle Weeks** amongst others). Subsequent tours followed, although the reviews were not good.

As for Bizkit founder Durst, he put out NEW OLD SONGS, Limp Bizkit's first remix album on his Interscope Records label with personnel drawn mostly from the hip-hop world: **Timbaland** added a dark industrial edge to "Take a Look Around"; **P. Diddy** amped up the bass line on "My Way"; while **Butch Vig**'s version of "Nookie" had a decidedly 80s electronic flavour. Best of all, though, was the **Neptunes**' take on "N2gether Now". It was the cheeriest thing that Fred Durst had ever been involved with.

- **Three Dollar Bill Y'All\$** (1997; Interscope).
  Rough and ready, this is a genre-defining album. Durst is limbering up the bad-boy image that will serve him in good stead over subsequent albums.

- **Significant Other** (1999; Interscope).
  Fred really lets rip on this one, with the polished production giving the band's already powerful sound that little extra boost. A professional and imaginative album.

- **Chocolate Starfish And The Hot Dog Flavored Water** (2000; Interscope).
  A mega album from a mega band. Packed with angst and ace musicianship, this one has it all.

Essi Berelian

DAVID LINDLEY

Born Los Angeles, 1944.

David Lindley, sometime bandleader, songwriter and sought-after session guitarist, has appeared in so many contexts and combinations that a complete discography would take on book form. Jackson Browne, Leonard Cohen, Ry Cooder, Little Feat, Maria Muldaur, Graham Nash, Dolly Parton, Rod Stewart and Warren Zevon are just a few of those whose albums have been graced by the Lindley touch. His playing reflects a voracious appetite for musical experiences – and ones as diverse as possible – coupled with a remarkable ear for idiom. Unfamiliar stringed instruments from around the world garnish his session credits, while apparently

unplayable guitars of the sort dumped in thrift shops contribute to the aura of mystery.

Fired initially by the South's mountain music, Lindley passed through various West Coast old-time and string bands before appearing on Elektra's STRING BAND PROJECT (1965) and co-founding the Los Angeles-based Kaleidoscope in 1966. A psychedelic-folk-cum-world-music rock group, **Kaleidoscope** had a protean line-up that settled on Lindley (guitar/fiddle/banjo/vocals) plus **Chris Darrow** (guitar/vocals), **Charles Chester Crill** (fiddle/harmonica/keyboards/vocals), **John Vidican** (drums) and **Soloman Feldthouse** (guitar/various exotic instruments/vocals).

While, to some degree, other Bay Area bands such as The Grateful Dead and Jefferson Airplane had roots in the coffee-house folk and blues scenes, and thus played amplified Anglo-American and Afro-American music, Kaleidoscope augmented these influences with flamenco and Middle Eastern music. This catholic approach resulted in three inspired visions – SIDE TRIPS (1967), A BEACON FROM MARS (1968) and INCREDIBLE (1969) – while, alongside The Dead, John Fahey and Pink Floyd, they contributed to the soundtrack to Antonioni's *Zabriskie Point* (1970).

After a spell in England, where he became acquainted with ska and reggae, Lindley established himself as a session musician, becoming most closely associated with Jackson Browne and Ry Cooder, through whom he garnered soundtrack credits on *The Long Riders*, *Alamo Bay* and *Paris, Texas*.

Lindley also formed his own group, **El Rayo-X** (named after a Mexican matinee idol), debuting with EL RAYO-X in 1981. Apart from Lindley's skills, the album also fanfared the talents of **Frizz Fuller**, whose songs – like "Quarter Of A Man", "Ain't No Way" and "She Took Off My Romeos" – were packed with arresting angles on the life of the homeless and destitute. WIN THIS RECORD! (1982) followed, by which time the nucleus of the group was **Jorge Calderón** (vocals/bass/percussion), **Bernie Larsen** (vocals/guitars/percussion) and **Ian Wallace** (vocals/percussion/baritone guitar). Their brilliance as a live act was caught on the EL RAYO LIVE (1983) – one of rock's finest live albums ever – though Lindley fell victim to Warners' roster purges in the 80s, and out he went, along with Van Morrison, Bonnie Raitt and others.

He hung on to a contract in Europe, however, recording MR DAVE (1985), an album wired with synthesizer and drum-machine technology, and unveiling techno-Lindley tracks such as "Pretty Girl Rules The World", "Hurt So Bad" and "Alien Invasion". Back in the US, Linda Ronstadt, aghast that Lindley had lost his recording deal, intervened to produce his VERY GREASY (1988).

In the early 1990s Lindley worked with the American multi-instrumentalist **Henry Kaiser** on a series of Madagascan and Norwegian releases, playing with local artists, and toured as a duo with Ry

Cooder. Always an adventurous player, he also collaborated (along with Cooder) on the shakuhachi (Japanese bamboo flute) player Kazu Matsui's WHEELS OF THE SUN (1994), an oddball album mixing Cooderesque New Age with instruments with *Grove Encyclopedia*-style names. It was par for the course for somebody who could mix Middle Eastern modes, Okinawan chunk, zydeco, ska, reggae, Tex-Mex, polka and rock without compromising his integrity.

In 1994 Lindley released LIVE IN TOKYO PLAYING REAL GOOD, a duo album with percussionist Hani Naser. It was followed by LIVE ALL OVER THE PLACE PLAYING EVEN BETTER. They encapsulated what he did best: making weird music for the nonconformist mind.

Kaleidoscope

- **Blues From Baghdad** (1993; Edsel).
  Gourmet Kaleidoscope compilation, featuring rarities and major tracks from the first three albums.

El Rayo-X

- **El Rayo Live** (1983; Elektra).
  If you only buy one El Rayo-X disc, make it this. Three venues and six cuts, including "Spodie", a song 'dedicated to all the spermatozoa who have died in the line of duty'.

David Lindley

- **Very Greasy** (1988; Elektra).
  "Papa Was A Rolling Stone", "Do You Wanna Dance", Frizz Fuller's "Tiki Torches At Twilight", and "Werewolves Of London", all put through the multicultural blender.

Ken Hunt

ARTO LINDSAY

Born Brazil, 1950.

Few, if any, artists have travelled a more indiosyncratic path in popular music than **Arto Lindsay**. Beginning his career in New York's impossibly avant-garde No Wave movement of the late 70s/early 80s, Lindsay then moved on to create startling fusions of lilting Brazilian tropicalia and grey, urban 'skronk'.

After Sonic Youth's Thurston Moore, Arto Lindsay is the most influential and original of the noise guitarists. His strikingly rhythmic and intense technique – he bashes and slashes his instrument, but with more strategy than this description might imply – was developed during his stint with No Wave bands DNA and (with a little more restraint) with The Lounge Lizards.

DNA (Lindsay, drummer **Ikue Mori** and keyboardist **Robin Crutchfield**) appeared on Brian Eno's justly celebrated NO NEW YORK (1978) compilation, alongside Mars, The Contortions and Lydia Lunch's Teenage Jesus And The Jerks, in a celebration of the physicality of pure noise. Crutchfield was replaced by funkier bassist **Tim Wright** before their only studio recording, A TASTE OF DNA (1981), a stunning EP of guitar splinters, intricate drums,

strange pulses, and Lindsay's remarkably expressive, primitivist vocals.

Lindsay then joined John Lurie's post-jazz troupe, **The Lounge Lizards**, for their eponymous debut LP. Lindsay's guitar shaped The Lizards' self-conscious jazz reinterpretations into something substantially more angular than postmodern pastiche.

After a brief spell with underground progressivists **THE GOLDEN PALOMINOS**, Lindsay formed **Ambitious Lovers** with **Peter Scherer** (keyboards). Their first album, ENVY (1984), moved from pure dissonance to sweet Brazilian pop at the drop of a hat, and suddenly the source of Lindsay's unique technique was made obvious – he was trying to replicate the rhythms and noises of an entire samba school on his guitar.

GREED (1988) continued this fusion with slicker production values and a more dance-orientated groove. Guitarists Bill Frisell and Vernon Reid guested to provide a more discernible shape to Lindsay's abstractions, while Lindsay's voice trembled and wailed emotively, if not cogently. Unsurprisingly, LUST (1991) followed suit with a more sultry take on the same musical theme.

If Lindsay and Scherer manage to continue their exploration of the seven deadly sins, then the future of samba–funk–noise fusion looks promising, because the most interesting ones are yet to come. Meantime, fans of Lindsay's Brazilian face got the record they had been waiting for in 1996 with the release of O CORPO SUBTIL (THE SUBTLE BODY), an album of unalloyed, unplugged bossa nova – or at least Arto's conception of bossa – featuring collaborations with, among others, Ryuichi Sakamoto and Brian Eno. A sublime, seductive set, understated and dreamy, it showed how much Lindsay had observed from recent production sessions with Caetano Veloso, Marisa Monte and fellow Brazilian enthusiast David Byrne.

MUNDO CIVILIZADO (1996) featured Lindsay blending his more recent pop-tinged outings with the 'new prog' of intelligent drum'n'bass. Less embarrassing than Bowie's similar dabblings, Lindsay managed to bring new life to his cover of TAFKAP's "Erotic City".

The years that followed witnessed more delightful Brazilian-tinged experiments: NOON CHILL (1998), PRIZE (1999) and INVOKE (2002). Lindsay is now also known for his production work, and has even been commissioned by choreographer Richard Move to produce music for dance and theatre. His unique talent continues to delight all those who come into contact with it.

- **A Taste Of DNA** (1981; American Clav).
  At under ten minutes, it might not provide enough quantity to justify the staggering amount of money you'll probably have to pay. The quality, however, is amazing. A unique record.

- **Greed** (1988; Virgin).
  Although Brazilian funk and distorted guitar squawk might not seem like the most auspicious of pairings, this album distils the best of both worlds into brilliantly crafted, if not immediately accessible, pop songs.

○ **O Corpo Subtil** (1996; Bar None/Ryko).
Arto finally yields to the Brazilian within, unplugging the thrash guitar, and crooning his own inimitable brand of bossa nova. Sublime.

○ **Prize** (1999; Bar None/Ryko).
Recorded in New York and Bahia, the album is infused with the Brazilian sound. Arto continues to sing partly and sublimely in Portuguese (check "Modos" and swoon) and to employ bossa nova forms, which are stripped down and reassembled into a near-ambient heat-mist of programmed sound.

Peter Shapiro

LINKIN PARK

Formed Southern California 1998.

Rap metal has come a very long way since Mike Patton rhymed his way through the Faith No More mega-hit "Epic" in 1989. It would take almost another ten years before the synthesis of rap and rock would hit the mainstream in such a way as to dwarf the efforts of the pioneers and provide a fresh success for the vast umbrella genre known as nu-metal.

Linkin Park's story starts unassumingly enough with school buddies **Rob Bourdon** (drums), **Brad Delson** (guitar), and **Mike Shinoda** (MC/vocalist) dreaming of musical superstardom. **DJ Joseph Hahn** eventually entered the equation and Xero was born, which was soon followed by the name Hybrid Theory. As soon as Arizona native **Chester Bennington** joined as frontman and focal vocalist, everything fell into place – Linkin Park was born. Of course, no label would touch them with a barge pole at this stage and the band spent some time as gigging regulars around Los Angeles while being turned down by various record companies. No one, it seemed, could see the appeal of their streamlined, angst-ridden metal, featuring Bennington's massive singing voice and Shinoda's street-savvy style of rapping. It wasn't until Warner Bros signed the band in 1999 that the wheels were set in motion.

Within a few months they were in the studio recording their debut album. When HYBRID THEORY (2000) emerged – named after their earlier

incarnation – no one knew it would prove to be such a monster-selling album. In the UK alone it spawned five hit singles, peaked at #4 in the album charts, and spent a massive 60 weeks in the Top 40. In the US it became the biggest-selling album of 2001 and the second biggest seller around the world. The band was also nominated for various Grammys and won the category of *Best Hard Rock Performance* for "Crawling", their profile no doubt raised by an extremely punishing touring schedule that put them on stage over 300 times during 2001.

By 2002 they were officially massive. So what did they do? They bided their time by issuing the REANIMATION (2002) remix album, which placed them at the mercy of an army of DJs and producers. The results were hit and miss but packaged in a very appealing and arty manner with the track listing presented in a 'modern' (and irritating) text message style: "Paper Cut" became "Ppr:Kut", "Cure for the Itch" became "Kyur4 th Ich", "Crawling" became "KRWLNG".

METEORA (2003) was a return to the blueprint laid down by their debut – 'if it ain't broke, don't fix it' clearly being the order of the day. The only change in the Linkin Park camp was the official addition of **Phoenix Farrell** on bass, otherwise it was business very much as usual for one of the world's biggest rock bands.

○ **Hybrid Theory** (Warners; 2000).
Take equal parts of metal and rap, fuse them together with epic production and you get this glossy, huge-sounding debut studded with hit singles. A perfect point from which to take over the world.

○ **Meteora** (Warners; 2003).
Back to the debut for inspiration, this album is chock full of big riffs, smooth beats and silky rapping. Give them what they want and they'll give you what you want – lots of lovely money.

Essi Berelian

LITTLE ANGELS

Formed Scarborough, England, 1987; disbanded 1994.

It's as well that **Little Angels** never became superstars, since success would have removed the vital spirit of the underdog from their very British rock music, and made self-destruction inevitable. Nonetheless, they had a narrow escape.

The first line-up – **Toby Jepson** (vocals/acoustic guitar), brothers **Jimmy** (keyboards/vocals) and **Bruce Dickinson** (guitars/banjo), **Mark Plunkett** (bass/vocals) and **Dave Hopper** (drums) – formed at sixth-form college, and played many of their early gigs in schools, because Jimmy Dickinson was too young to get into licensed clubs. Their music was fairly standard hard rock, with a strong dose of The Kinks and The Who.

After an impressive debut mini-LP, TOO POSH TO MOSH (1987), the recruitment of new drummer **Michael Lee**, and a London support slot with the little-known Guns N' Roses – the Angels signed to Polydor. The first fruit was the 1989 album, DON'T PREY FOR ME, which unleashed two feisty singles, "Kicking Up Dust" and "Radical Your Lover". The title track was an outstanding example of Jepson's songwriting, and remained prominent in the band's set right up to their demise.

YOUNG GODS (1991) promised major success, and prompted rock monthly *Vox* to proclaim them the 'new stripling hopefuls' of British rock. Songwriter Jim Vallance, former collaborator with Bryan Adams, contributed to the album, and Jepson's songs had also improved, showing a spirited defiance that set the band apart from maudlin rock balladry.

Lee was replaced by **Mark Richardson** at the end of 1991 after having been discovered auditioning for The Cult, The band clearly intended to go all the way, and resented being used as a stepping stone. In July 1992 they cultivated a celebrity mate in Bryan Adams, when they appeared at his Wembley Stadium sell-out show. Little Angels always fared well in support slots – they would later support Van Halen and Bon Jovi – and the chance to win over 80,000 new fans was an opportunity not to be missed.

JAM, the final and most accomplished album, was a surprise UK #1 in early 1993, showing that the Angels had absorbed commercial textures and sounds from the likes of Bon Jovi and Aerosmith. Consequently, nobody really understood the band's decision to split, especially given the evidence of Polydor's closing 'best of', LITTLE OF THE PAST (1994), which showed a band growing steadily in stature.

Perhaps uncomfortable with success, the Dickinson brothers and Richardson retreated into a lower-profile band, **b.l.o.w.** Meanwhile, Jepson and Plunkett, the two 'pretty boys' of the band, seem to have vanished from the music business. It seems something of a waste: while Little Angels hardly changed the face of rock music, they were a consistently improving band whose continuing survival could have have done British rock a lot of favours.

⊙ **Young Gods** (1991; Polydor).
A more rounded and professional effort than the debut, but still with some great vacuous sing-alongs. An excellent summer rock album – try it.

⊙ **Jam** (1993; Polydor).
The strongest album, with a varied set of bluesy touches, highly paced rock, and a real garage-band Kinks cover.

Robert Jones

LITTLE FEAT

Formed Los Angeles, 1969; disbanded 1973; reformed 1974; disbanded 1979; re-formed 1987.

"Lowell George is the best singer, songwriter and guitar player ever, hands down." Bonnie Raitt

Guitarist **Lowell George** began his career playing for The Factory, which also featured **Richie Hayward** on drums. The band split and George sang for Frank Zappa's Mothers Of Invention for a while before meeting keyboards player **Bill Payne**. Hayward, meantime, had joined The Fraternity Of Man and recorded "Don't Bogart That Joint" for the *Easy Rider* soundtrack.

The three got together with another ex-Mother, bassist **Roy Estrada**, and **Little Feat** was born. Signed to Warners, they released their eponymous debut album in 1970. It only hinted at their potential, but George's songwriting skills were already blossoming, as on "Truck Stop Girl" and "Willing", the latter later covered by The Byrds, Commander Cody and Linda Ronstadt. His ability as a guitarist, especially on slide, was also unquestionable.

A tour supporting Ry Cooder and Captain Beefheart followed, before Little Feat returned to the studio to record SAILIN' SHOES (1972), the first of their albums to feature the striking artwork of Neon Park. It was a big improvement on its predecessor, boasting material that would feature in their live sets for many years, but it sold badly and Estrada left to join Beefheart. New bassist **Kenny Gradney** and **Sam Clayton** (congas) were recruited from Delaney And Bonnie, together with **Paul Barrere** (second guitar).

The new line-up toured the States extensively, but another LP, DIXIE CHICKEN (1973), was almost universally ignored – its classic status came years later. George's warm seductive vocals were complemented by a rolling boogie backdrop, augmented by Payne's inventive keyboards, and biting guitar work from Lowell and Barrere. Faced with low sales and an unappreciative public, the band split up. Payne went on the road with The Doobie Brothers, Hayward joined Ike Turner, while George worked on sessions for the likes of Carly Simon, Robert Palmer, Bonnie Raitt and Nilsson.

Within a year, though, Little Feat were back together, recording another minor masterpiece, FEATS DON'T FAIL ME NOW (1974). At long last, Warners began to realize the band's potential, and more promotion led to better live gigs. Live, Little Feat were in their element; on a British tour as part of a Warners package in 1975, they consistently blew headliners such as The Doobie Brothers off stage. More commercial success came with THE LAST RECORD ALBUM (1975), although by now George's songwriting was being overtaken by the influence of Payne and Barrere, which continued with 1977's TIME LOVES A HERO. This was primarily Barrere's baby, and led to rumours of personality clashes, while a long-awaited live double LP, WAITING FOR COLUMBUS (1978), failed to capture the legendary fire of their live set, which had previously been heard on bootlegs.

The inevitable split finally came during the recording of DOWN ON THE FARM (1979), when George left to promote his solo album, THANKS, I'LL EAT IT HERE (1979), with an eight-piece touring band. And then, on June 29, 1979, Lowell George died of a heart attack, aged just 34.

A double album, HOY, HOY (1981), was a valuable Little Feat retrospective, in that it contained unreleased tracks, early demos and live material. More easily available on CD, though, is AS TIME GOES BY (THE BEST OF LITTLE FEAT), which was released in 1986. The following year, the band ill-advisedly re-formed with **Fred Tackett** (guitar) and ex-Pure Prairie League singer **Craig Fuller**. They have recorded several albums since – including LET IT ROLL (1988), REPRESENTING THE MAMBO (1990) and SHAKE ME UP (1991) – but none of them have approached the standard of their original output. Their 1995 album, AIN'T HAD ENOUGH FUN, was released in the UK by Zero Records.

Far more satisfactory was 2001's box set, HOTCAKES AND OUTTAKES, which no true fan should be without.

⊙ **Dixie Chicken** (1973; Warners).
Featuring stage favourites like "Two Trains", "Fat Man In The Bathtub" and a simmering cover of Allen Toussaint's "On Your Way Down", the high point is the title track, which exemplifies George's ironic songwriting style.

⊙ **Feats Don't Fail Me Now** (1974; Warners).
The live show-stopping medley of "Cold, Cold, Cold" and "Tripe Face Boogie" was actually bettered in this studio performance, as the former's typical Feat funk segues into a driving version of the latter. Two verses in, congas and piano kick-start a jazz improvisation section, interspersed with synths, before a sizzling finale. Elsewhere, there's the opening trio of classics, "Rock'N'Roll Doctor", "Oh Atlanta" and "Skin It Back".

⊙ **Hotcakes And Outtakes** (2001; Rhino).
No less than 84 cuts here; there are some fine live selections and a handful of stunning demos included.

Simon Ives

LITTLE·RICHARD

Born Macon, Georgia, December 5, 1932.

"Awopbopaloobopawopbamboom!"

His daddy sold moonshine, and **Little Richard** distilled rock'n'roll into a ten-syllable yawp still yelled by latter-day androgynes like Bowie, Prince and Michael Jackson. It was the manifesto of a career that was to include some of the greatest records of all time.

Little Richard was born Ricardo Wayne Penniman to a middle-class family in Macon, Georgia – home also to disciples James Brown and Otis Redding. Richard sang, hung out with the local drag queens, and toured with B. Brown and Sugarfoot Sam (with whom he sang in a dress) at age 14. His vocal technique was Sunday-school gospel, and his performing style was straight voodoo, a riot with a six-inch pomp and a face covered in Pancake 31, declaring: 'This Little Richard, King of the Blues, and the Queen too!'

After false starts with RCA and Peacock Records (where his extracurricular debauchery led to a brawl with manager Don Robey), Little Richard was signed to Specialty Records by Robert 'Bumps' Blackwell. Bumps was looking for a new Ray Charles, but found instead 'this cat in this loud shirt, with hair waved up six inches above his head... talking wild.' Richard choked at the September 1955 recording session with Fats Domino's band. During a break, Bumps and Richard went to a local hangout, where Richard leaped on stage, a-wop-bam-booming an obscene ditty called "Tutti Frutti". The lyrics were cleaned up at the studio by Dorothy LaBostrie (substituting for 'Tutti Frutti, good booty' the Dada poetry of 'Tutti frutti, aw rootie'), but then Richard wouldn't play in front of her. Bumps pleaded. So he faced a wall and – voice raw from recording – all hell broke loose.

Elvis had forged the miscegenated rocking'n'rolling in July 1954 with "That's All Right". Little Richard was all wrong: swooping from belting to screeching, speaking in tongues, pounding his piano to matchsticks, playing as if The Bomb was about to drop, partying like it was 1999. Most remarkably, as a performer who was black, bisexual, deformed (one leg was longer than the other), and boasted an effeminate demeanour and a pompadour that broke zoning laws in several states, Little Richard was as marginalized as they come. "Tutti Frutti" spent 22 weeks in the R&B chart, reaching #2, and peaked in the pop charts at #17, lighting a fuse under Perry Como. The breakthrough was reserved for preacher Pat Boone's cover, which went to #1.

Elvis sold his soul to the Colonel, but Little Richard was an impish Lucifer who celebrated his bright stardom with a fistful of raucous hit singles, running amok on stages around the land amid a blizzard of cocaine and flying panties. He played the piano with that little foot and orchestrated backstage orgies where he exercised his voyeuristic predilections. Elvis wanted you to "Love Me Tender" on his cloud in the 1956 movie, but Little Richard squealed "The Girl Can't Help It" to Jayne Mansfield as she clutched two milk bottles to her enormous bosom in the Frank Tashlin film of the same name.

Richard continued to mine rock's primitive seam and the hit singles, many co-written by him, piled up.

"Long Tall Sally", about a bald-headed vamp, peaked at #6 – NBC's censor asked, 'How can I restrict it when I can't even understand it?'; John Lennon heard it and wept when he realized there was someone better than Elvis. "Rip It Up" reached #17, and "Lucille" #21. Richard always carried his earnings on his person, flinging a wad of bills at James Brown when he discovered his tour bus stranded on the side of the road. The excess stalled in the middle of an Australian tour in October 1957, when Richard had a revelation on the night the Russians launched the Sputnik satellite. Seeing a ball of fire above the stage, he walked off and converted to Christianity as promoters and Specialty boss Art Rupe prepared to sue the hell out of him.

Rupe kept the coffers filled with releases of sides deemed too uncommercial to release during the Queen's reign. "Keep A Knockin'", with Richard struggling to remember the chorus, made #8. "Good Golly Miss Molly" charted at #10. It was later covered by Mitch Ryder and the Detroit Wheels, who pulled off the trick of playing the song twice as fast.

The struggle between sin and salvation wouldn't go away, and in 1959 Richard again answered rock's call. He had defined the parameters in the white heat of his glory days, but now contentedly paced the cell. He rerecorded his hits, made soul masterpieces like "I Don't Know What You Got, But It's Got Me" (lost at #92 in 1965, as the Richard-influenced Beatles and Stones ruled the charts), and flaunted a beehive hairstyle. Changing fashions didn't affect him. He was science fiction to begin with. He hired and fired Jimi Hendrix in 1964 for having too many effects pedals, and upstaged both Janis Joplin in Atlantic City in 1968 and The Plastic Ono Band's 1969 debut in Toronto, shedding his mirrored suit at every show.

The rockers kissed his feet in Hamburg, but he and his band ended up playing in Chitlin and Vegas hells. Rock'n'roll revival shows have kept him in loose change, punctuated by further conversions to Christianity. He emerged from chat-show purgatory to appear in *Down And Out In Beverly Hills* and graced the bikini paradise of Baywatch – a pale shadow of hedonism, mixing a drink he called the "Tutti Frutti".

◉ **18 Greatest Hits** (1985; Rhino).
The business on one disc, this is an album guaranteed to turn your party into an outtake from La Dolce Vita.

Charles Bottomley

LIVE

Formed York, Pennsylvania, 1990.

Grunge had the same galvanizing effect on the US that punk had had in Britain a decade before. The overblown, airbrushed music scene of the 80s crumbled, and suddenly rock music became a democratic movement: all you needed was a few chords, a few pairs of torn jeans and a long streak of angst. In the Capra-esque town of York, Pennsylvania, four friends, barely out of their teens, got together to have a go at it under the somewhat confusing moniker of **Live**. They comprised **Ed Kowalczyk** (vocals/guitar),

Chad Taylor (guitar/vocals), **Patrick Dahlheimer** (bass) and **Chad Gracey** (drums).

A local following – who could resist Live live – led to gigs at the legendary CBGB's in New York City and a deal with the Radioactive label, who enlisted one-time Talking Head Jerry Harrison to produce Live's first album, MENTAL JEWELRY (1991). Although lyrically naive, musically this was an astonishingly sophisticated debut, the band displaying a tightness and an ambition that boded well. Gracey's superlative drumming and Dahlheimer's versatile bass created a solid foundation and structure, with Taylor's guitars, never obtrusive or flashy, powering everything along behind Kowalczyk's heartfelt vocals. The result was closer to R.E.M. than Nirvana, though they were not striving to imitate.

It was three years before the follow-up, THROWING COPPER (1994), appeared, a denser, darker and altogether rockier release. It made a curious kind of history by lurking around the music charts for a full year before clawing its way up to #1 in the US, via a video directed by Jonathan Demme, a full touring schedule and sheer persistence. Live became one of America's top-selling bands, and broke through in the UK, too, with a storming stint at the 1995 Glastonbury Festival.

Unfortunately these promising steps forward were followed three years later by one huge step back, SECRET SAMADHI (1997), a plodding, generic and often incoherent slab of grunge/rock. With Live not being a band who'd fiddle with a winning formula, it predictably picked up where the eight-million-selling THROWING COPPER had left off and put them firmly back in the Bush league. Never heedful of the critics, however, the band pushed on, and their next release, THE DISTANCE TO HERE (1999), turned out to be a vibrant, engaging and impassioned collection of tunes that marked them out as a band to watch.

Unfortunately, V (2001) was a heavy handed clunker, overproduced and overblown. BIRDS OF PRAY (2003), on the other hand was a far more restrained affair: the keyboards and effects of V had gone, to be replaced by straight-ahead rockin' and quality songwriting.

◉ **Throwing Copper** (1994; Radioactive).
A sprawling and ambitious album, moody and crowded (perhaps overcrowded) with noise and ideas. It's a difficult piece to sit through in one go, but it's rescued by the power and ripped-through emotion of songs like "Selling The Drama", "I Alone" and "Lightning Crashes".

Adam Kimmel

LIVING COLOUR

Formed New York, 1985; disbanded 1995.

"We're black. We play rock and roll. Now maybe everybody will give that a rest." Corey Glover

Vernon Reid, one-time guitarist with jazz-influenced bands Defunkt and Decoding

Society, formed **Living Colour** with drummer **William Calhoun** and bassist **Muzz Skillings**, taking the band's name from the NBC TV announcement, 'The following programme is brought to you in living color.' Vocalist **Corey Glover** joined late in 1985, having just finished work on the Oliver Stone film, *Platoon*.

Living Colour's fusion of hard rock, jazz, dance and soul, although similar to that of Cheap Trick and the Red Hot Chili Peppers, was distinctive in that it was being made by an all-black band. This became a platform for strong social comment on black issues: Reid was a founding member of the Black Rock Coalition movement, formed with journalist Greg Tate to combat racial stereotyping in music, and his band drew music-press journalists as an ever-quotable act.

Their route to success was helped by a very useful contact – Mick Jagger, who saw one gig at CBGB's and invited them to play on his 1986 album, PRIMITIVE COOL. He produced two demos of the band's own songs and was a considerable factor in their signing to Epic, the label which put out the debut album, VIVID (1988).

VIVID was a critical favourite, and in the US a commercial one too, reaching #6 and staying in the charts for a full year. Driven by hard-rock backings and characterized by Reid's skilfully untidy guitar work, it was among the more thoughtful of late-80s rock albums. The opening track and first single, "Cult Of Personality", began with a sampled Kennedy speech played under a biting lyric, while "Open Letter (To A Landlord)" took a swipe at the negative aspects of gentrification. "Which Way To America" contrasted the idealism of the American Dream with the black America that 'looks like hell/Tell me where to go to get to your America'.

Living Colour maintained a high profile by supporting a diverse selection of acts on tour (Robert Palmer, Cheap Trick, Anthrax and Billy Bragg) and collaborating with other artists, like Reid's appearances on Keith Richards' TALK IS CHEAP and Bernie Worrell's FUNK OF AGES. In 1989 they took three MTV awards – Best New Artist, Best Group Video and Best Stage Performance – then received similar accolades the following year from *Rolling Stone* and at the Grammy Awards.

They headlined huge benefit concerts across America, wrote tracks for B. B. King, and set about recording the next album, with Jagger, Little Richard, Queen Latifah and Carlos Santana all happy to help out. Released in September 1990, TIME'S UP was an award-winner and a chart success on both sides of the Atlantic. It featured their best-known single, the wry "Love Rears Its Ugly Head", but the sheer eclecticism made it an interesting rather than a listenable experience.

The BISCUITS mini-album, which followed in August 1991, failed to make any waves, and in November Skillings left the band, to be replaced by ex-Tackhead bassist **Doug Wimbush**. STAIN (1993) was an indisputably solid rock album, and was another strong seller, but despite flawless musicianship and intriguing lyrics it made no further ground on the previous releases. In any case, Reid's extracurricular activities – sessions for Garland Jeffreys and the Ramones, as well as a photo exhibition – hinted at an artist in transition.

It seems that Living Colour's career came to a halt in early 1995 with the retrospective PLAY IT LOUD! (1997) pulling together some of their better known tracks. They were a ground-breaking black group, but perhaps such status was a distraction for a band that basically wanted to be known for making great music.

Vivid (1988; Epic).
Samples, engaging and provocative lyrics, and great rocking make this one of the 80s most enduring albums.

Time's Up (1990; Epic).
An advance in some ways, but self-indulgent and inspiring by turns. "Elvis Is Dead" proved controversial with fans of the King, who thought it a bit flippant to say 'Elvis has left the building'.

Play It Loud! (1997; Epic).
A great little retrospective – "Cult Of Personality" stands out.

Chris Wright

ALEX LLOYD

Born Sydney, Australia 1975.

Like Beck and to an extent David Gray, to whom he is frequently compared, **Alex Lloyd** manages to combine the best of technology with 'real' instruments, to often startling effect. While he has attained enormous success in his native Australia, Lloyd remains largely undiscovered in the UK and the US where his albums have met with a large measure of critical acclaim but with very little public recognition.

Born Alex Wasiliev in 1975, Lloyd left school early to concentrate on his music, paying his dues on the tough Sydney live circuit and finding his first regular engagement with indie-rock hopefuls Mother Hubbard. Released in 1996, the group's first album, YOU ME HIM SHE did little business, but it was genuine musical differences rather than poor sales that split the band – Lloyd had begun introducing programmed beats and other electronic additions to the music, that would later become a trademark of his songs.

Lloyd took the material he'd written for the second Mother Hubbard album and returned to the studio to begin work on tracks that, after a long gestation period, became BLACK THE SUN. Three years in the making, the album was eventually finished in Santa Monica with former Psychedelic Fur **Ed Buller** (sometime producer of Blur, The Boo Radleys and Suede).

BLACK THE SUN (1999) was a near-perfect fusion of technology and tradition, that deserved favourable comparisons with the ear-friendly song-craft of Crowded House on one hand and the more angsty

Alex Lloyd puckers up

Once again the album was massive in Australia but made little dent in Europe or the States; it was undoubtedly a crowded market but every fan of Coldplay, David Gray, Turin Brakes, or even R.E.M. deserves an Alex Lloyd album in their collection. Whereas in Oz Lloyd headlines arenas, over in the UK he's stuck with support slots for the likes of Toploader. With two albums that combine such originality and accessibility in equal measures – and a third currently being recorded in Sydney – it should only be a matter of time before that situation is remedied.

◉ **Black The Sun** (1999; EMI).
Every bit as exuberant and heart-felt as Gray's WHITE LADDER, but with an experimental twist that'll reassure you that you're not turning into your parents just yet.

Derryck Strachan

NILS LOFGREN

Born Chicago, 1951.

It's hard not to like **Nils Lofgren**. An evergreen streetwise kid, he is now entering his fourth decade in the recording industry and yet no one's got a bad word to say about him. What's more, lots of people want to work with him, because there's the small matter of his being one of the top guitarists in the business.

Born in the blues-infested city of Chicago, his first instrument was the accordion but he switched to guitar, influenced by The Beatles and Jimi Hendrix. Anyway, the back somersaults that characterize his stage performance might have looked a trifle bizarre with a squeeze-box.

Debunking to New York in the late 60s, he formed **Grin** with **Bob Gordon** (bass) and **Bob Berberich** (drums), and while in the city gatecrashed one of **NEIL YOUNG**'s backstage gatherings. His impromptu busk persuaded Young to draft him into the band that recorded AFTER THE GOLDRUSH (1970); he featured on **Crazy Horse**'s debut the next year. Indeed, he might have joined Crazy Horse permanently but for Danny Whitten's heroin problem, which cast doubt on the band's future.

Instead he and Grin began touring in earnest, and a record deal with Spindizzy saw two excellent albums, GRIN (1971) and 1+1 (1972), hit the stores to acclaim, but poor sales. The band's disappoinment at their lack of commercial success was apparent on the jaded third album, ALL OUT (1972). With Grin increasingly moribund, Lofgren toured with Neil Young, before returning to a reconstituted Grin to record GONE CRAZY in 1974. This also flopped and Grin folded, leaving Lofgren at a loose end. More session work followed on Young's TONIGHT'S THE NIGHT (1975) – including his own favourite solo (perhaps the best guitar solo ever) on "Speakin' Out" – before he set out on his own.

1975 saw the release of Nils' first solo album, NILS LOFGREN. This time he cracked it – here were

experimentation of Radiohead on the other. In his homeland he was lauded by critics and public alike, who rewarded Lloyd with multi-platinum sales and two ARIAs (the Australian Grammy's) for *Best New Artist* and *Best Male Artist*.

Lloyd chose to record his next album in London, working with producer **Magnus Fiennes** (brother of actors Joseph and Ralph; his previous credits include All Saints and Spice Girls). Leaning more toward the contemporary AOR of Del Amitri or R.E.M., WATCHING ANGELS MEND (2002) was a far less gruelling affair for Lloyd than its predecessor, taking only five months to complete.

Where Radiohead fed off the dramatic tension in life's low points, Lloyd here captured the energizing emotions of its high points, not least in the desperately joyous opening track, "Everybody's Laughing" (which featured backing vocals from Powderfinger's **Bernard Fanning**) and the slow-burn "Busride" – both standout moments. A host of guest stars lent a hand – UK pedal steel player extraordinaire, **B.J. Cole** popped up on "My Friend", while elsewhere Black Grape/Joe Strummer percussionist **Ged Lynch** provided rhythmic colour.

twelve tracks that showed his full potential. Among the best songs was "Keith Don't Go", a homage to his hero Keith Richards, who was then facing jail in Canada, while his debt to Hendrix was also visible in songs such as "Be Good Tonight". He also showed his versatility with some fine piano work on a version of Carole King's "Goin' Back". Once again, it failed to chart.

The follow-up was the moody, blues-inflected CRY TOUGH (1976), which consolidated his reputation and reached #8 in the UK and #32 in the US, but 1977's I CAME TO DANCE was a weaker offering. With punk and New Wave in the ascendant, Lofgren's melodic, well-crafted blues-rock was out of step with the times, and the promise of a platinum future evaporated.

Apparently washed up at age 26, he waited two years before bouncing back with NILS, an altogether stronger album that put him back on the rails, though again missing out on a chart placing. The next five years saw constant touring and a series of competent albums. It was a measure of the affection he generates that when *Sounds* reviewed the 1979 single "Shine Silently", they said, 'Please give this guy a hit before he disappears.'

In 1984 he began playing with **BRUCE SPRINGSTEEN**, and in 1985 he came as close as he was ever to come to major success with FLIP and the tour that accompanied it. A single, "Secrets In The Street", even graced the UK Top 30 but it was his last flourish as a full-time solo artist before an eight-year stint in Springsteen's E-Street Band as Miami Steve Van Zandt's replacement.

In the 90s Lofgren played live with **Ringo Starr**'s All-Stars as well as his own band (with **Levon Helm** handling vocals and harmonica). The albums SILVER LINING (1991) and CROOKED LINE (1992) were 'as raw and live as possible'. DAMAGED GOODS (1995) was solid and melodic, though failed to set the world on fire. But Lofgren's guitar work remained as distinctive as any in the business. NEW LIVES (1998), a compilation taken from three shows he did for BBC Radio 1's *In Concert* in 1985, 1987 and 1991, showed him at his masterful live best, while 2002's BREAKAWAY ANGEL revealed a slightly mellower side to Lofgren's art.

Now in his early fifties he can afford to play the part of one of rock's elder statesmen, though his youthful looks and exuberance still set him apart from some of his more grizzled contemporaries. He gives the rare impression of someone who genuinely cares, be it his espousal of the Vietnam veterans' cause or the concern he shows for real people's lives. A new album is perpetually promised, as is further work with Springsteen.

⊙ **Nils Lofgren** (1975; A&M).
A hot platter in a bad year for rock music. Tracks like "Back It Up" and "Keith Don't Go" are more melodic than the barnstorming live versions.

⊙ **Cry Tough** (1976; A&M).
Probably the best showcase for Nils' guitar skills, particularly on the title track and the cover version of The Yardbirds' "For Your Love". Not surprisingly, the songbook sold well.

⊙ **Flip** (1985; Towerbell).
Some of Nils' hardest rock ("Sweet Midnight", "King Of The Rock") and slickest production, and some of his most sensitive lyrics as well – 'Tryin' your best/Don't mean being Number One'.

⊙ **Damaged Goods** (1995; Ryko).
Lofgren does without superstar guests and sticks with a three-piece band – 'My heart told me to do something raw, emotional and honest' – and he returns to singing about the flawed and the dispossessed, dropping his voice an octave and parading influences from Neil Young and Hendrix to country sounds and 60s harmonies.

Patrick Neylan-Francis

THE LOFT/WEATHER PROPHETS/THE WISDOM OF HARRY

The Loft formed London, 1980; disbanded 1985.
Weather Prophets formed London, 1986;
disbanded 1989.
The Wisdom Of Harry formed London, 1996–97.

The Loft got together in 1980 when News Of Birds singer/guitarist **Pete Astor** met **Bill Prince** (bass) and **Andy Strickland** (guitar). The trio hit it off, were soon joined by drummer **Dave Morgan**, and set out performing live – initially as The Living Room, a name shared by a London venue owned by Creation Records boss Alan McGee, who signed the band.

Live shows gained approval from the music press, and The Loft's driving guitar sound, later to influence indie acts like Ride, was well displayed on the debut single "Why Does The Rain?" (1984). After that came the fabulous "Up The Hill And Down The Slope" (1985), but despite valuable TV exposure The Loft were soon disbanded. All their tracks were collected for a 1989 compilation, ONCE AROUND THE FAIR.

Andy Strickland pursued a career in music journalism and formed The Caretaker Race, who attracted record-company attention but failed to win public interest. Bill Prince was no more successful with The Wishing Stones, but Pete Astor and Dave Morgan's formation of the **Weather Prophets** was a more lucrative proposition.

For this project, the duo were joined up with **Greenwood Goulding** on bass and **Oisin Little** on guitar. Their debut single, the classy and laid-back "Almost Prayed" (1986), immediately gained a cult following, and was followed by a rerecording of The Loft's "Why Does The Rain?" (1987). Three creditable LPs also appeared – DIESEL RIVER (1986), MAYFLOWER (1987) and JUDGES, JURIES AND HORSEMEN (1988) – but band tensions were to resurface, and in 1989 the Weather Prophets split.

Peter Astor embarked on a solo career with the albums SUBMARINE (1990) and ZOO (1991), while Dave Morgan joined the **Rockingbirds**.

After a period of disillusionment with both the music industry and the group-based musical pro-

Peter Astor aka The Wisdom Of Harry

cess, the blossoming electronica and drum'n'bass scenes reawakened Astor's passions. By the mid-90s he had constructed his own Bigfoot studio and was gaining attention for his electronically flavoured work as **Ellis Island Sound** (remixing Regular Fries) and **The Wisdom Of Harry**, releasing a series of obscure vinyl-only singles on fledgling post-rock labels like Wurlitzer Jukebox, Lissy's and Motorway. In 1999 a compilation album appeared, STARS OF SUPER 8, which documented these tragically under-pressed 45s. Having signed to Matador and played live with the likes of Andy Weatherall and Cornelius, The Wisdom Of Harry released a debut proper – HOUSE OF BINARY (2000). Confidently drawing together the ambience of bedroom electronica and Astor's distinct voice, the set sold well and was warmly embraced by the press. The Wisdom Of Harry's future looks bright and further releases from the Bigfoot studio are hotly anticipated.

The Loft

🔘 **Once Around The Fair** (1989; Creation).
A compilation of The Loft's entire output. Hard to find now, but worth the effort. Listen and wonder why Pete Astor is not a regular feature in the pop charts.

Weather Prophets

🔘 **Temperance Hotel** (1989; Giant/Rockville).
US-released greatest hits compilation that'll answer the questions of the curious.

The Wisdom Of Harry

🔘 **House Of Binary** (2000; Matador)
A fine debut. Lo-fi electronica brushes shoulders with friendly beats, comfortable chord swoops and songs that stay true to Astor's pop passions.

Andrew Mosley & Peter Buckley

LONG RYDERS

Formed Los Angeles, 1981; disbanded 1987.

Cowpunks or part of the Paisley Underground? The **Long Ryders** sent out mixed messages, and so their take on country-rock never quite took hold, except with a cult audience. An all-American band – their songs and playing suffused with Americana – they spent a great deal of their time playing and recording in Britain, where they were championed by DJ Andy Kershaw. Founding eminence **Sid Griffin** still lives in London.

The Long Riders (as originally named, from the Walter Hill movie) were formed in LA in 1981. Three members had previously been in The Unclaimed: singer/guitarist Sid Griffin, bassist **Barry Shank** and drummer **Matt Roberts**. Their first guitarist, **Steve Wynn**, soon left to form his own band, the spooked Velvets- and drone-influenced **DREAM SYNDICATE**. His replacement, **Stephen McCarthy**, saw things through to the bitter end, as did Griffin.

The original rhythm section decamped, and the 1983 mini-album 10.5.60, featured **Des Brewer** on bass, soon replaced by **Tom Stevens**, and **Greg Sowders** on drums. Its punkish roots were sweetened by instruments familiar from C&W – steel guitar, autoharp, mandolin – though these were approached robustly, and the band's vocals were the very antithesis of Nashville smooth. If the Gram Parsons-led Byrds had approached country with respect, almost awe, this was a drunken, full-tilt attack. The rough-and-ready nature of the album – and the band's early live appearances – linked them with other members of the Paisley Underground, like

Rain Parade, Bangles, Green On Red, and Blood On The Saddle, all of whom wanted to re-create the best of 60s rock with trippy guitars and honest singing.

Their second LP, NATIVE SONS (1984), was a far more ambitious and cunning affair. The cover art was a remake of that commissioned for Buffalo Springfield's mythical, unreleased STAMPEDE, while the back sleeve placed steel and pedal steel guitars, a banjo and an autoharp alongside the Vox amp, drums and Rickenbacker. A tour jacket emblazoned 'Sin City' invoked the ghost of Parsons, the sense of desperation and hidden pleasures which ultimately destroy. As if to cement the Byrds angle, Gene Clark added his high, lonesome voice to the proceedings.

THE STATE OF OUR UNION (1985) saw the band move to a major label, Island, and to England to record what turned out to be a hard-hitting and surprisingly political collection. TWO FISTED TALES (1987), recorded back in Hollywood, was more user-friendly, though it too had a political bite. Like the best of Robbie Robertson's songs for The Band, the settings were often historical, as in "Harriet Tubman's Gonna Carry Me Home", a song about an escaped slave described by Griffin as 'the Nelson Mandela of her time'. This album seemed a springboard for further success, but internal tensions among the band drove them to split up in late 1987.

There has been a long-term rerelease programme of their original albums, with bonus tracks. Sid Griffin is now as well known as a rock historian – Gram Parsons a speciality – as for his work with the Coal Porters. Greg Sowders now works for Warner Brothers in music publishing. Tom Stevens released a cassette-only album and lives back in Indiana. Stephen McCarthy now tours with Steve Wynn. With country music retreating into a commercial, politically inert blandness, the rough enthusiasm of the Long Ryders had become a spectre at the feast.

(•) **Native Sons** (1984; Frontier/Zippo).
Still fresh as new paint: tight playing, good tunes and memorable lyrics. One of those records with no loose ends.

Brian Hinton

LOOP

Formed London, 1986; disbanded 1991.

"On first listening you could register our music as very much a hammer in the face type of thing but there is a lot going on in there. It can even be quite soothing when it's played quiet."
Robert Hampson

Loop kingpin **Robert Hampson** was into the idea of trance music, but detested the 'tea with gnomes psychedelia' aspect. He set out to introduce

a harder edge – 'more of the garage', as he put it – with a band that held surprise cards up their frayed sleeves.

Their debut was HEAVEN'S END (1987), a trance-grunge album featuring Hampson on guitar and vocals, bassist **Neil MacKay** and drummer **John Wills** – who described the effort as being 'held together by Sellotape – total hit or miss'. FADE OUT (1989) confirmed Loop's music as a deadly nightshade antidote to the 'baggy' scene, sure as their skin-tight black jeans, stiff belts and tangled fringes. A dark side to rivals Spacemen 3, Loop conjured southeast London's derelict landscapes with malignantly hypnotic riffs (Hampson claimed to know only four chords), uneasy percussion and aggressively whispered vocals.

THE JOHN PEEL SESSIONS (1987-90)

Just after FADE OUT's release, the band turned down a logical, scene-stealing support slot on an upcoming Cult tour – a bad career move. By the time A GILDED ETERNITY (1990) was released, they had reached their shining hour and gained a press perception as 'difficult'. The line-up likewise failed to solidify, despite the addition of guitarist **Scott Dawson**. A John Peel sessions album, WOLF FLOW, was released in 1991.

The combustible pioneers fragmented into two camps: Robert and Scott formed the trippy, intelligent **MAIN**; Neil and John, the **Hair And Skin Trading Company**. Neil eventually resurfaced in **Juicy Eureka** with wife **Kim** and **Peter** of Scaredycat; he is now working with John again under the moniker **If You Meet Your Anti-self Don't Shake Hands**.

(•) **Fade Out** (1989; Beggars Banquet).
A dark and powerful collection of droning rock that set the template for bands such as Black Rebel Motorcycle Club.

(•) **A Gilded Eternity** (1990; Beggars Banquet).
It begins with "Vapour", the musical equivalent of decanting dry-ice decadence from *I Dream of Jeannie*'s bottle, then drifts into "Afterglow", a melancholy Molotov cocktail. "Breathe Into Me" foreshadows Cobain and co and reduces them to Nerdvana. Masterpiece or what?

Susan Compo

LOS LOBOS

Formed Los Angeles, 1977.

They started as a Top 40 cover band, but **Los Lobos** have evolved into one of the most talented, original ensembles working today. In the late 70s, as the futility of playing covers became evident, the quintet decided to go back to their Chicano heritage and recorded an acoustic album of traditional Mexican-American songs. They soon recognized the limitations of this approach, so they plugged in and began writing songs in earnest.

Led by primary composers **David Hidalgo** (guitar/accordion/banjo/vocals) and **Louie Perez** (drums/vocals), and augmented by multi-instrumentalists **Cesar Rosas** (guitars/mandolin/vocals), **Conrad Lozano** (bass/guitarrón/vocals) and **Steve Berlin** (saxes/percussion), the many-faceted band quickly earned a rabid following on the LA club circuit. After gigging relentlessly, they signed with Slash Records in late 1982, releasing an EP, ... AND A TIME TO DANCE (1983), one track from which, "Anselma", won a Grammy for *Best Mexican-American Performance*.

Their first LP, HOW WILL THE WOLF SURVIVE? (1984), featured the first recorded evidence of the band's eclecticism, displaying influences ranging from folk and jazz through Tex-Mex to 50s rock. It also showed the band happy with a whole array of tempos, able to rock out on "Don't Worry Baby", but equally at home on the ballad "A Matter Of Time". The wolves' next release, BY THE LIGHT OF THE MOON (1987), contained another gorgeous ballad, "River Of Fools", though it was shackled by a lofty if well-intentioned social commentary, and a self-conscious attempt to homogenize the disparate sound.

Unexpectedly, Los Lobos's contributions to the *La Bamba* soundtrack (1987) took America by storm, and the title track hit #1 in the pop charts, catapulting Los Lobos to mainstream success. Many longtime fans cried 'sellout', and the group, characteristically, responded with LA PISTOLA Y EL CORAZON (1988), an album of traditional Mexican songs.

THE NEIGHBORHOOD (1990), however, was a resounding return to rocking form, kicking off with menacing clavinet figures from Steve Berlin, and including the frenzied swirl of "I Can't Understand". This set the stage for the band's crowning achievement, KIKO (1992), a rootsy, mysterious album that was concurrently tense, tough, tender and melodic. In short, a masterpiece.

In 1993 the band released JUST ANOTHER BAND FROM EAST LA, a 41-track anthology, while the following year Hidalgo and Perez joined Mitchell Froom and Tchad Blake (KIKO's producer and engineer) for a fantastically distinctive album called LATIN PLAYBOYS.

In 1995 Los Lobos further diversified their catalogue by recording a children's album, before rocking out again with COLOSSAL HEAD (1996), another fine set, with the Mexican roots given a more contemporary (and restrained electronic) sheen by Froom. THIS TIME (1999) was another metaphysical masterpiece, while GOOD MORNING AZTLAN (2001) saw the group working with producer John Leckie (Radiohead, The Fall) who helped to craft the Los Lobos sound into an even stronger creative form. In a world where artistic integrity and commitment have been devalued, the Lobos continue to succeed on their own terms.

⊙ Kiko (1992; Slash/Warners).
Both visceral and heady, this gem runs the stylistic gamut from rollicking blues ("That Train Don't Stop Here") to seamless pop ("Reva's House") and somnolent soul ("Kiko"). Buy this album even if you're down to your last few dollars.

⊙ Just Another Band From East LA: A Collection (1993; Slash/Warners).
A fine overview, compiling tracks from every studio album plus five previously unreleased songs and ten live recordings.

Ben Hunter

LOTION

Formed New York, 1991.

"Rock and roll remains one of the last honorable callings, and a working band is a miracle of everyday life. Which is basically what these guys do." Thomas Pynchon

OK, how many bands get Thomas Pynchon to stump up the sleeve notes for their album? My recollection is a round zero – and that, if nothing else, makes Lotion a lil' place in rock'n'roll history.

The guys with the honours are Tony Zajkowski (vocals/guitar), Bill Ferguson (bass) and Rob Youngberg (drums), who met at Syracuse University in the late 80s and after a good deal of thought, and, joined by Bill's brother Jim (guitar/vocals), they threw in their New York media day jobs and took that honourable path.

Their early inspirations were the Manchester baggy bands, the Happy Mondays and The Stone Roses, but by the time their first single, "Head", was released on the Kokopop label, such tendencies had disappeared, most critics talking up R.E.M., though the band themselves preferred to cite the rather more obscure Miracle Legion. After a second single, Lotion left Kokopop for Spin Art (in the US) and Big Cat (in the UK), that combination releasing their debut album, FULL ISAAC (1993), a disc that exercised a familiar pack of influences – Hüsker Dü, Buffalo Tom, R.E.M. – but with such subtlety that they escaped the post-grunge backlash. They then proved that they had some kind of sense of humour by singing the words to Hüsker Dü's "Flip Your Wig" over the tune to R.E.M.'s "Gardening At Night" on their AROUND EP, a gesture that was both a nod and a raised middle finger to the critics.

In the very best cult bands tradition, their finest effort to date is also their most obscure. Asked to contribute to CHAIRMAN OF THE BOARD (1994), a charity compilation of US alternative rock bands doing Frank Sinatra songs, Lotion avoided the cheap noisy jokes offered by most of the other bands. Instead they produced an utterly sincere and rather beautiful version of "Fly Me To The Moon", showing taste and talent well beyond their hardcore contemporaries.

1995's NOBODY'S COOL indicated this was no fluke; the big guitars were still in place, but the melodies were pushed right to the front, and "Rock Chick" was the best song that Lotion had written so far. But more attention was paid to the album's sleeve notes, written by fastidiously reclusive novelist Thomas Pynchon (*V*, *Gravity's Rainbow*). Lotion remained tight-lipped about how they found him, but the connection helped their highly hip reputation no end, and was followed by a Pynchon Q&A interview with the band in Esquire.

THE TELEPHONE ALBUM (1998) was further confirmation of the skills the band has to offer. The R.E.M. comparisons were still unavoidable but, unlike their more successful Athens colleagues, Lotion sounded sincere. Little has been heard of the band in recent years, though Tony is currently playing in a new group, **Schizo Fun Addict**.

Full Isaac (1993; Big Cat).
So named in tribute to the ever-cheery bartender from TV's *Love Boat*, this is a bag of NY-noise ingredients served in a whole new way.

Nobody's Cool (1995; Big Cat).
One of the finest of the whole rash of post-Hüsker Dü records. Worth having for "Rock Chick" alone, signalling the bright birth of loungecore.

Marc Elliot

LOVE

Formed Los Angeles, 1965; disbanded 1974.

"Love were LA's baddest sixties group." Dave Marsh in *The Heart Of Rock And Roll*

Nothing if not versatile, **Arthur Lee** began his career in the pre-Beatles novelty-hit era playing surf music, Booker T.-style organ workouts, dance numbers ('do the Slow Jerk, baby!'), soul ballads, the lot. And then, in late 1965, The Grass Roots – Lee's folk-rock band – evolved into **Love**, as Lee and guitarist **John Echols** were joined by ex-Surfaris bassist **Ken Forssi**, **Alban 'Snoopy' Pfisterer** on drums and, most significantly, ex-Byrds roadie **Bryan Maclean** on guitar and vocals. They were the first rock band to join Jac Holzman's Elektra label and success was instantaneous.

The first LP, LOVE, included a cover of "My Little Red Book", which reached #52 in the States, but overall the album lacked cohesion and suffered from

an Englishness that sounded stiff and awkward. That said, the bad attitude and street suss that truly embodied the spirit of Love did emerge from time to time, as on Lee's "Signed D.C.". Love appeared on *American Bandstand*, with Lee confessing to be 'as nervous as a long-tailed cat in a room full of rocking chairs'. However, despite this breakthrough, the band's refusal to tour outside LA hampered wider exposure.

DA CAPO (1967) might have had a title translating as 'return to the beginning', but the second album bore no relation to the tenuous artefact that was the debut. Fleshed out with horns and a second drummer, the tone was bright and warm, and the music was ingenious and eclectic – this time in a way that consolidated the band's pop sensibility rather than confusing it. The album was weakened somewhat by "Revelation", an ambitious but ultimately indulgent blues jam that took up the whole of the second side, but three fine singles were taken from side one, the biggest hit – "7 And 7 Is" – being a quintessential proto-punk rocker with keen, surreal lyrics.

Yet DA CAPO wasn't a huge success, peaking at #80 in the US. The band were living in a decaying Hollywood mansion previously used as a horror-movie set. Within this cloistered setting, Love started work on their most famous album – and foundational rock text – FOREVER CHANGES (1967). This embodied the schizophrenia of the Aquarian Age, with music that was by turns ecstatic ("Alone Again Or"), spiteful ("Live And Let Live"), blissful ("And More Again") and deranged ("A House Is Not A Motel"). Warm and open brass sounds added to the froth, only for the reverie to be undercut by malevolent soloing. The album hit #24 in the UK, but failed to sell in the States, peaking at #154. Disillusioned, Love retreated into their Hollywood mansion and commenced their acrimonious implosion.

Only a solitary single, "Laughing Stock" (notable for its masterly B-side, "Your Mind And We Belong Together"), was released prior to the emergence of the fourth album, FOUR SAIL, towards the end of 1969, by which time only Lee remained from the FOREVER CHANGES line-up. Lee's original title – LOVE FOR SALE – hinted at the pressure on the group to produce commercial music, and indeed he and **Jay Donnellan** (lead guitar), **Frank Fayad** (bass) and **George Suranovich** (drums) did come up with a very solid – occasionally brilliant – straight rock album. The opening track, "August", was as heavy as Love had got, but for all its urgent jamming and ringing chords, it retained a keen melodic edge. If FOREVER CHANGES had sounded studio-bound, FOUR SAIL was equally raw and live, and "Good Times" and "Singing Cowboy" would become live standards over the coming years.

Again, though, it had little success, peaking at #102 in the US, and Elektra opted not to renew the contract. OUT HERE, released on Blue Thumb only

four months later, comprised songs from the FOUR SAIL sessions. A sprawling, sometimes ragged affair, with strong short songs nestling alongside interminable workouts, it was followed in 1970 by FALSE START, which had a certain sly charm but lacked a sense of direction. It was an album of moments – guest star **JIMI HENDRIX**'s guitar on "The Everlasting First", and the psychedelicized surf music of "Ride That Vibration" – undercut by a sloppy frivolity.

With Love's commercial stock at a low ebb, Lee began to drift out of the public eye, and into the realm of myth and tragedy. Despite some underrated work – the 1972 solo album VINDICATOR, the funky moments of Love's last album, REEL TO REAL (1975) – Lee was caricatured as an acid casualty who had lost the plot, trapped in his role as the acid visionary of FOREVER CHANGES. He toured sporadically in the mid- to late 70s with various incarnations of Love, reunited with Brian Maclean for gigs in 1978, and released a weak solo effort, ARTHUR LEE, in 1981. During the rest of the 80s he played rarely and did not record at all.

From 1989, Arthur Lee started to pick up the pieces. More regular tours, often backed by eager young disciples, were greeted ecstatically, while another solo album, ARTHUR LEE AND LOVE (1992), also raised his profile despite offering only sporadic glimpses of his wayward talent. The two-CD retrospective, LOVE STORY (1996), crystallized a resurgence of interest in Lee and the band, which, augmented by deliriously received live shows by Lee in 1996, seemed to promise great things. However Lee's saga over the last thirty years has more often symbolized the darker, brooding corners of the California Myth, and his subsequent arrest and a twelve-year prison sentence for a firearms offence was just the latest example of his ability to self-destruct.

While Lee was banged up in a jail in southern California, his first solo album was rereleased to belated acclaim. VINDICATOR's ramshackle ebullience has worn well and the A&M reissue is lovingly remastered by Sid Griffin (of Long Ryders) who

found some interesting outtakes in the vaults. Bryan Maclean has re-emerged with lengthy interviews and the promised release of solo material recorded in the 60s, including acoustic versions of Maclean songs such as "Alone Again Or" and "Old Man".

Interest in Love seems to increase year on year, with the band's legacy enticing a devoted, not to say cultish, fan base. An excellent single, "Girl On Fire", appeared in 1994, and Lee earned more money from the royalties of Mazzy Star's version of "Five String Serenade" than all his Love royalties put together.

In 1997, Bryan Maclean's collection of unreleased studio tracks, IFYOUBELIEVEIN, proved a fragile, delicate affair, with early versions of "Old Man" and "Orange Skies", and Maclean was promising an album of all new material shortly prior to his untimely death on Christmas Day 1998. While it was undeniable that the light, pretty, songs of Maclean needed Arthur Lee's more aggressive output to provide balance over the course of an album, it was also true that Lee needed Maclean as a natural foil to his own dark, unruly temperament. Many would contend that Love never attained the same heights following the acrimonious implosion of the band and Maclean's sacking late in 1968. This can be confirmed, to some extent, by the 2001 double-CD release of FOREVER CHANGES, complete with several extra tracks.

⊙ **Da Capo** (1967; Warners).
The first side of DA CAPO pushed hard to be the best pop music of its day. "7 And 7 Is" reminds us that the Aquarian Age mingled proto-punk angst with its Utopianism – in its early days at least.

⊙ **Forever Changes** (1967; Warners).
An album that remains more than a psychedelic time capsule with a sublime mix of textures that steadfastly refuses to date. Demented and essential.

Nig Hodgkins

LOVE AND ROCKETS

Formed Northampton, England, 1985.

A couple of years after the split of **BAUHAUS**, Daniel Ash (guitar/vocals), **David J** (bass/vocals) and **Kevin Haskins** (drums) reunited without Peter Murphy as **Love And Rockets**. In the intervening years, Ash and Haskins had been busy making music with longtime associate Glen Campling in Tones On Tail, while David J had briefly joined Northampton band **JAZZ BUTCHER**, before recording several solo records – most memorably THIS VICIOUS CABARET, a song from Alan Moore's *The Watchman* comic.

From the band's first single, a cover of The Temptations' psychedelic soul classic "Ball Of Confusion", it was clear that Love And Rockets were not going to be Bauhaus Mark 2. Rather, they had forged fresh roots in the English psychedelic tradition as represented by (early) Pink Floyd and (late) XTC.

SEVENTH DREAM OF A TEENAGE HEAVEN (1985), the debut album, had a shadowy melancholia not in evidence on later works, while with EXPRESS (1986) the group's prevalent themes of transcendental mysticism and all things celestial came to the fore. This and all subsequent records were dominated by a positive vibe – none more so than on a one-off single released by their alter egos, The Bubblemen.

AFTER EARTH, SUN, MOON (1987), an album with a somewhat Beatles-esque sound, Love And Rockets turned to hard rock for a fourth album, LOVE AND ROCKETS (1989); a top seller in America, it featured the *Billboard* Top 3 single "So Alive". The band then took a lengthy break while Daniel Ash and David J made solo records, and Kevin Haskins worked on production for Trans-Global Underground's Natacha Atlas. Then, in 1994, they returned with the album HOT TRIP TO HEAVEN, in which they embraced dance music, reaffirming their ability to move forward and innovate. SWEET F.A. (1998) was more than a little gloomy and LIFT (1998) once again delved into the experimental electronic beats of HOT TRIP TO HEAVEN. A live album, SO ALIVE, saw the light of day in 2003.

⊙ **Earth, Sun, Moon** (1987; Beggars Banquet).
Love And Rockets' finest outing to date: concise, wistful and personal.

Ross Holloway

LYLE LOVETT

Born Klein, Texas, November 1, 1957.

An appearance in Robert Altman's 1991 film, *The Player*, in which he played a private investigator, confirmed **Lyle Lovett** as one of the more idiosyncratic members of the New Country movement. His sardonic lyrics and willingness to branch off in different music directions mark him out from the Nashville crowd, as does his predilection for the album format over the singles that are the staple of the country market. However, rock audiences have yet to come to terms with the country authenticity of his output, and he remains a cult figure in an increasingly conservative market.

After leaving school, Lovett studied German at the Texas A&M University before moving into journalism and starting to write songs. Inspired by writers like Guy Clark and Townes Van Zandt, he met a larger-than-life country musician called Buffalo Wayne while in Europe in 1979. In 1983, Wayne booked Lyle for a show he was organizing in Luxembourg, where he met keyboards man **Matt Rollings** and guitarist **Ray Herndon**, both of whom would play a central role on his later albums.

On his return from Europe, Lovett hit the Texas club circuit, where he met Nanci Griffith, who was so impressed by his songs that she covered "If I Were The Woman You Wanted" (later recorded by Lyle himself as "If I Was The Man You Wanted") on her 1984 album ONCE IN A VERY BLUE MOON. By 1986, on the strength of Guy Clark's recommendation, Lyle was signed to MCA by producer Tony

Brown. The resulting album, LYLE LOVETT (1986), quickly aligned him with the burgeoning New Country movement, and the single "Cowboy Man" became a Top 10 country hit. The album featured other strong material, such as "Closing Time" (later covered by Lacy J. Dalton) and "If I Were The Man You Wanted" and "This Old Porch", co-written with Robert Earl Keen.

After a tour of Europe, accompanied by cellist John Hagen, Lovett's second studio album, PONTIAC (1987), was released, confirming through songs like "If I Had A Boat" and "She's Hot To Go" that he was one of country's more offbeat performers. This reputation deepened further with the 1989 release of LYLE LOVETT AND HIS LARGE BAND, which featured a horn section, a female vocalist (Francine Reed), and some of his strongest songs yet. Critics drooled over Lyle's eclecticism and sense of humour; Nashville, on the other hand, was slightly put out by the ramifications of his cover of Tammy Wynette's "Stand By Your Man".

In 1990 Lyle moved to more cosmopolitan Los Angeles, where he cut his next album, JOSHUA JUDGES RUTH. Though tinged with gospel overtones, as you'd expect from an album named after three books of the Old Testament, it seemed to be geared more towards rock audiences, in common with other exponents of so-called New Country, such as Nanci Griffith and k. d. lang. This audience shift was confirmed by his selection to open for Dire Straits on their 1992 world tour.

The following year he married the actress Julia Roberts, after meeting her on the set of *The Player*, a coupling which both intrigued the media and solidified Lovett's move into the mainstream. His next album, I LOVE EVERYBODY (1994), received warm reviews, and showed that his move to Los Angeles had done nothing to dampen his irony. It was followed by a well-publicized divorce from Roberts, a hurt that seemed to permeate his 1996 album, THE ROAD TO ENSENADA. Not that this was a self-pitying release – in fact, quite the contrary. With its upbeat Texan dance-floor feel, and stunning range of sound, breezing through bossa nova, Cajun and honky-tonk, this was perhaps Lovett's most accessible outing to date. 1998 saw the release of STEP INSIDE THIS HOUSE – a double album of covers – slick, atmospheric and distinctly Lyle Lovett. No fresh material, other than soundtrack work, appeared until the release of SMILE (2003). Though the set was again slick and well ranging in style, it couldn't hold a candle to this Texan's earlier collections.

⊙ **Lyle Lovett** (1986; MCA).
Lovett's debut remains an intriguing New Country classic.

⊙ **Lyle Lovett And His Large Band** (2001; MCA).
This collection of strong and soulfully delivered songs is a fine example of someone bucking the odds and winning. Lovett's version of "Stand By Your Man" puts others in the shade.

⊙ **The Road To Ensenada** (1996; MCA).
A superb album, whose styles are even more eclectic than usual, and matched by compelling narrative songs. Randy Newman guests to fine effect on the witty opener, "(You Can Have My Girl). But Don't Touch My Hat".

◉ **Anthology, Vol 1: Cowboy Man** (2001; MCA).
Collecting together a number of songs from his first three albums, this set is full of Lovett's gentle satire and clever conceits. This is the sound of a man who enjoys what he does.

Hugh Gregory

LENE LOVICH

Born Detroit, 1949.

Before punk, most extravagantly dressed anti-hero types in the music biz tended to be male. **Lene Lovich**, together with Poly Styrene of X-Ray Spex, Gaye Advert of The Adverts and the entire cast of The Slits, helped kick the traditional mould to pieces and gave girls all over the world a suitably inspiring role model.

Lene specialized in shrieked vocals, spooky wide-eyed stares, and voluminous black clothing. She signed up with Stiff Records in the UK and charted with "Lucky Number" in 1979. It was a classic novelty hit: listen to it once and it stuck to your brain like chewing gum. After a few months of scaring the kids on TV music programmes she released an album, STATELESS.

Despite the comparative success of another single, "Say When", the Lene Lovich industry never really took off. Remixing the album for US release was a good notion, but too little, too late. 1980's FLEX followed a similar musical path, but, whereas STATELESS bounced along, with the songs carried by the sheer novelty of Lovich's eccentricity, FLEX aimed instead to rely upon better studio work. Understandable, particularly considering the criticism generated by the production on the first album, but a bad move: lacking spontaneity and sparkle, FLEX dragged along like a Hallowe'en hangover.

NEW TOY (1981) was another novelty, a multi-track EP at a time when a cycle of singles and albums was the norm. It was followed by NO MAN'S LAND

(1982), another album of limited appeal. Lene Lovich's spooky-cutesiness was by this point starting to grate like an 8-year-old's party trick; the eight-year wait for the next album, MARCH, gave her and **Les Chappell** (partner, guitar player and co-songwriter) the opportunity to refine their vision and hope the rest of the world would catch up. They are still writing and recording, but after nearly twenty-five years in the music business Lene'N'Les have yet to give complete satisfaction.

◉ **Stateless ... Plus** (1979; Rhino).
Remixed reissue of STATELESS, the best Lovich album so far, plus five extra tracks. Has the classic vocal tricks, novelty sax playing, lots of fun and the occasional stab at serious musical statement.

Al Spicer

THE LOVIN' SPOONFUL

Formed New York, 1965; disbanded 1969; re-formed 1991.

Initially a two-piece, **The Lovin' Spoonful** grew out of the early-60s folk-club circuit. **John Sebastian** (vocals/guitar/autoharp/harmonica) and **Zal Yanovsky** (guitar/vocals) began collaborating after being part of a larger pool of musicians which included Mama Cass Elliot, Maria Muldaur and Judy Collins. Their folk-club and café stint was initially so unsuccessful that the duo were on the point of folding when a final injection of cash from manager Bob Cavello and record producer Erik Jacobson produced the unreasonably optimistic "Do You Believe In Magic", Recorded with **Steve Boone** (bass/vocals) and **Joe Butler** (drums/vocals), this raised their profile and eventually led to a deal with Kama Sutra.

Although they were passed over for roles in the TV series *The Monkees*, success came quickly for The Spoonful. From the summer of 1965 until the end of 1966, the group enjoyed seven Top 10 US singles, and "Summer In The City" and the lazy gem "Daydream" both broke the UK Top 10. The Spoonful also cranked out three hit albums in quick succession, while sustaining a punishing live schedule.

Perhaps overwork explains the band's sudden falling-away, but at the time it seemed to owe a great deal to a drug bust that left Yanovsky in an impossible situation. As a Canadian he had to choose between deportation and informing against his supplier. He opted to keep his career and home in the US, but the incident lost Yanovsky his credibility, and in 1967 he was forced to leave the band. Also, the band's tightly crafted songs were increasingly out of sync with the folk-rock

Lene Lovich looking spooky

HUMS OF THE LOVIN' SPOONFUL

⊙ **Greatest Hits: Remastered** (2000; Buddha).
Tells you all you need to know, and includes both "Summer In The City" and "Daydream".

Neil Nixon

LOW

Formed Duluth, Minnesota, 1993.

Low, like Codeine before them, craft an elegant guitar sound that is most frequently noted for its… erm… slowness. Low's music more often references the ticking of clocks and the movement of tides than any other band currently churning out tunes, though it would be fair to say that Low's earliest work was heavily influenced by Brian Eno and Joy Division. At the heart of the group is a practising Mormon couple: **Alan Sparhawk** and his wife **Mimi Parker,** who added percussion and chilling harmonies to her husband's voice and guitar.

The door opened for the duo when a demo cassette was chanced upon by underground New York producer, **Kramer**, who drafted Sparhawk and Parker in to record an album at Noise, New Jersey. I COULD LIVE IN HOPE was issued in 1994 on Vernon Yard, and bravely eschewed conventional songwriting in favour of mood and movement, at a time when grunge was king. An EP, LOW – often referred to as the SUMMERSHINE EP – was also issued around this time.

On the first album, bass guitar had been supplied by temporary member **John Nichols** (now of Best Boy Electric), but for the second album, LONG DIVISION (1995), Low added the full-time services of **Zak Sally**. Sally's input added to Sparhawk's minimal guitar and Parker's one snare and cymbal, which made for a set less heavily reliant on the distinctive reverb found on the group's debut; this, coupled with producer Kramer's Mellotron, ensured that LONG DIVISION, with its grasp of gentle melancholy and babe-cooing melody, was even more of a dark joy than its predecessor. Low were subsequently pigeonholed into a supposed new scene that they were to dub 'slowcore'.

The next releases were the EP TRANSMISSION (showcasing Low's Joy Division cover, one of many the group have undertaken) and the third album, THE CURTAIN HITS THE CAST (1996), recorded in Seattle with producer **Steve Fisk**. Fisk also contributed keyboards to what was Low's richest work to date, featuring UK single cuts "Anon" and "Over The Ocean". It was, however, to be the band's last recording with Vernon, although the compilation OWL – REMIX LOW emerged from the label in July 1998.

Low produced themselves on the next release, the 6-track SONGS FOR A DEAD PILOT (1997), which featured some interesting touches from **Flag Day Strings** and emerged on Kranky Records. It was, however, the high profile and inimitable touch of **Steve Albini** that brought Low's music to a wider

---

scene. Neither as cosmic or rootsy as The Byrds, nor as edgy as Buffalo Springfield, the Spoonful were soon passé.

Whatever the reason, things fell apart quickly and the first album without Yanovsky, EVERYTHING PLAYING (1967), lacked any real spark and stalled at #118 in the US charts. Sebastian quit the band in October 1968, summing up their career as 'two glorious years and a tedious one'. Ironically his replacement was Yanovsky, who had struggled to start a solo career. Sebastian had written all the major hits and in his absence, the band rambled to an ignominious end after the forgettable REVELATION: REVOLUTION '69 (1969).

A mixed bag of solo projects soon followed. Sebastian's ceaseless beaming smile and John Lennon glasses can be seen in festival films and photos from the late 60s/early 70s. He appeared at Woodstock and the Isle of Wight, and dominates the *Festival At Big Sur* movie, due to his lengthy acoustic jams with **Steve Stills**. Sebastian was the only member of the band to achieve real commercial success, getting another week on top of the US singles charts with the TV theme "Welcome Back" in 1976. He continued into the 90s, cropping up in all sorts of unlikely places: for example, penning songs for the *Care Bears* movie. Despite failing to capitalize on his brief period of fame, Sebastian resisted offers to reform The Spoonful, although they did briefly reunite for a cameo appearance in Paul Simon's movie, *One Trick Pony*, in 1980.

The band members then went their separate ways until 1991 when Boone, Butler and **Jerry Yester** (who had replaced Zal after his drugs bust) re-formed The Spoonful. Sebastian maintained a solo career, and is still resisting the temptation to hit the nostalgia circuit using the Spoonful name. The 'classic' line-up was reunited for a memorable edition of British TV's *Rock Family Trees* in 1998, in which they retold stories of their glory days with evident pleasure. On a sadder, final note, Zal Yanovsky died at the end of 2002 – all future Spoonful activity is to be dedicated to his memory.

Low

⊙ **Secret Name** (1999; Tugboat).
Low meet Albini in a triumphant collision.

⊙ **Trust** (2002; Rough Trade).
With TRUST the group have awakened their rhythms with some hard-hitting electronic percussion, turned up the gain, and generally twisted the Low sound into some very interesting and welcome new contortions.

Jeremy Simmonds

NICK LOWE

Born Woodbridge, England, 1949.

Known throughout the music industry as Basher, **Nick Lowe** has enjoyed a lively and varied career since early days in pub-rock attractions Kippington Lodge and **BRINSLEY SCHWARZ**. These days he's known largely as a producer, a path he began when early engagements on records by The Kursaal Flyers and Dr. Feelgood led him to help set up Stiff Records with Jake Rivera and Dave Robinson in 1976. He became an early advocate of punk, piloting influential records by The Damned and Elvis Costello, including nine of Stiff's first 21 singles, although his own solo excursions attracted less attention.

The best of these solo outings came in the mid-70s, starting with the single "So It Goes" (1976), and followed by "(What's So Funny 'Bout) Peace Love And Understanding", which Elvis Costello made a standard. Soon after, Lowe formed Rockpile with other seasoned pub-rock veterans, including **Dave Edmunds**. The highlight was JESUS OF COOL (1978; PURE POP FOR NOW PEOPLE in the US), an exemplary collection of pop/rock songs, which even included an all-too-rare (UK) chart dalliance with "I Love The Sound Of Breaking Glass". A second almost-hit, "Cruel To Be Kind", followed in 1979, as did the album LABOUR OF LUST. Soon afterwards, Lowe married Carlene Carter, daughter of Johnny Cash and later a country star in her own right. She too would undergo his production tutelage.

Nick Lowe's association with Elvis Costello continued well into the 80s, while other production credits included Paul Carrack, The Men They Couldn't Hang, The Redskins, The Katydids and John Hiatt. By this time the nickname 'Basher' was well established, attributed to his creative impulse to 'bash it out' whenever faced with musical complexity in the studio. Among his many notable singles productions was "Stop Your Sobbing", the debut 45 from The Pretenders, a band whose career Lowe took some credit in launching, even though he would never work with them again.

Throughout this period, he continued to release albums, mostly of a high quality, although none became commercially successful. Even the formation of **Little Village** with **RY COODER**, **Jim Keltner** and **JOHN HIATT** in 1992, and the release of an eponymous album, failed to change Lowe's fortunes. But just when no one, except die-hards, expected it, Lowe released THE IMPOSSIBLE BIRD (1994). Among the highlights on this mature, thoughtful effort were

audience, primarily on their fourth album proper, 1999's SECRET NAME. Although very much a Low creation, the record owed much to Albini's steely-edged production, the overall sound evoking mid-period Neil Young. Universally acclaimed, SECRET NAME was one of the more inspired releases of a year that culminated in the group's CHRISTMAS EP, which found the group at their poppiest on the jingle-bell-laden, Spector-esque "Just Like Christmas".

Low returned in 2000 with their undoubted masterpiece, THINGS WE LOST IN THE FIRE. Albini was again in the hot seat for this set, which featured Low's best-known track, "Dinosaur Act" and the marvellous, disquieting "In Metal".

The band continues to give stirring live performances, perhaps the most memorable a collaboration with Godspeed You! Black Emperor in Chicago at the tail end of 1998; more recently, 2002's triumphant All Tomorrow's Parties performance lit up the UK's annual Camber Sands weekender. In tandem with studio releases, Low have issued various albums of their live work, the best being ONE MORE REASON TO FORGET, which featured versions of "Over the Ocean" and the popular "Do You Know How to Waltz?". TRUST (2002) was another magnificent release, though starker than previous sets – almost aggressively so at times. Everything about this record, from the stark red/black artwork to the set's thundering sonic innards, suggests that the previously lulling Low have taken time out to absorb the Swans' back catalogue.

Sparhawk has also found time for a number of eclectic side-projects. Among them **Hospital People**, with Zak Sally – described as a 'homage to bands like Kraftwerk and OMD' – and **Tooth Fairies**, featuring the pair with **Sean Erspamer**, as a heavier, almost metal-sounding act. Where Low travel next is anybody's guess, but that they'll take new disciples with them is guaranteed.

⊙ **I Could Live In Hope** (1994; Vernon Yard).
This beautiful collection shows the humility of Low in contrast with the more majestic works of recent years.

"The Beast In Me", a song written for and recorded by (now ex-father-in-law) Johnny Cash and the sardonic "12-Step Program (To Quit You Babe)".

DIG MY MOOD (1998), was a more reflective album than usual, with a mood that was more Roy Orbison than Dr. Feelgood – all broken hearts and bitter tears. Meanwhile, "What's So Funny 'Bout (Peace, Love And Understanding)", still his best-loved composition, earned him a few shekels (a cheque for just over a million bucks, to be precise) when Curtis Stigers covered it on the soundtrack to the film *The Bodyguard*. His most recent set, THE CONVINCER (2001), continued the run of high quality product and found Lowe stylishly crooning like never before. Lowe continues to tour and record, and recently went back to production work with The Mavericks, but despite his millions he continues to live in Brentford.

⊙ **Jesus Of Cool** (1978; Demon).
Its alternative title, PURE POP FOR NOW PEOPLE, says it better. Lowe may never have written or recorded a defining moment in pop history, but tracks like "Heart Of The City" consistently hit the mark.

⊙ **20 All-Time Lowes** (1984; Demon).
Although it reprises great chunks of the debut album, this is the only other must-have collection from Basher's catalogue.

⊙ **The Impossible Bird** (1994; Demon).
More soulful, personal and unashamedly ballad-orientated than previous Basher material – and the dark melancholia of the songs provides Lowe with a new and suitable environment.

Alex Ogg

LUNA

Formed Boston, Massachusetts, 1992.

With former members of **GALAXIE 500** (guitarist/vocalist **Dean Wareham**), **THE FEELIES** (drummer **Stanley Demeski**) and **THE CHILLS** (bassist **Justin Harwood**), **Luna** were indie rock's first supergroup. Although there were times when they sounded perilously close to some Velvet Underground tribute band playing the university circuit, at their best Luna managed to dispel any memories of Blind Faith or Crosby, Stills And Nash with artful songs comprised of immediately appealing melodies and a bizarre lyrical sensibility.

Musically, Luna took their cues from VU's eponymous third record: slowly propulsive guitar drones, loping bass lines and simple, straightforward drum patterns. But where Lou Reed's characters either took a bite out of the Big Apple or choked on its worm-eaten core, lyricist Dean Wareham's New York was a place of childish whimsy and wide-eyed innocence. Initially known as **Luna²** (appearing with the superscript due to copyright difficulties), the group's first album, named after Coney Island's original amusement park, exuded a laconic, listless boyishness. LUNAPARK (1992) began with the line, 'You can never give the finger to the blind', and such skewed lyrics prevented the band from sounding merely like The Feelies on sedatives.

Adding guitarist **Sean Eden**, the band – now firmly ensconced as plain old Luna – released the excellent SLIDE EP in 1993. With two of the best tracks from LUNAPARK and covers of The Velvets' "Ride Into The Sun", Beat Happening's "Indian Summer" and The Dream Syndicate's "That's What You Always Say", SLIDE neatly encapsulated the band's influences and got the ratio between languor and pep exactly right.

With a guest appearance from VU's Sterling Morrison, BEWITCHED (1994) was the epitome of Luna's Velvets obsession. While tracks like "Friendly Advice" and "Going Home" kicked up mesmerizing two-chord drones, the dishevelled confessional, "California (All The Way)", and the trite hipster kiss-off, "I Know You Tried", were less becoming. PENTHOUSE (1995) continued this trend and was largely the sound of men lazing around in stripy T-shirts and scruffy jumpers, delaying the onset of adulthood for as long as possible. That the record's bright spots came from guest spots was telling: **Tom Verlaine** donated one of his classic guitar solos to "23 Minutes Over Brussels", while Stereolab's **Laetitia Sadier** played Brigitte Bardot to Wareham's Serge Gainsbourg on a cover of Gainsbourg's "Bonnie And Clyde". The tired LUNA EP (1996) didn't help matters any.

PUP TENT (1997), THE DAYS OF OUR NIGHTS (1999) and ROMANTICA (2002) were all packed with rich, classy music and well-constructed lyrics. By the time of ROMANTICA the group's line-up had shifted, and now comprised Wareham, Egan, **Lee Wall** (drums) and **Britta Phillips** (bass); the resulting set was by far the most accomplished since LUNAPARK. Most recently, Wareham and Phillips have released the Lee & Nancy-styled romantic collection L'AWENTURA (2003). Dean Wareham's reinvention now seems complete: he's a left-field cult hero for a new audience, to whom Galaxie 500 mean absolutely nothing.

⊙ **Slide** (1993; Elektra).
Before the rot set in, Luna combined the urban drone of Lou Reed and the cuddle-core of Calvin Johnson with sharp songwriting – a strange melange – which found its pinnacle on this six-track EP.

⊙ **Bewitched** (1994; Elektra).
On which former Velvet Underground member Sterling Morrison is lured out of retirement to smear his trademark guitar chatter over Wareham's finest 45 minutes. The jaunty "Tiger Lily" and diaphanous, transfixing "Sleeping Pill" will melt even the sternest doubters.

⊙ **Romantica** (2002; Jetset).
Solid tunes, upbeat arrangements and sing-along chorus dapple this breezy set of summery, driving rock/pop.

Peter Shapiro

LYDIA LUNCH/TEENAGE JESUS AND THE JERKS

Born Lydia Koch, Rochester, New York, 1959.

Lydia Lunch was the original angry woman in a babydoll dress. Known for her collaborative work with the likes of Sonic Youth and The Birthday Party, she arrived on the New York scene in 1976, fronting the seminal No Wave band **Teenage Jesus And The Jerks**. The nucleus of the band comprised Lunch (guitar/vocals) and **Bradley Field** (drums), who described their work as 'a means of violent expression and reaction against the stagnancy of music and culture'. Sharp spiky songs rarely made it beyond the two-minute mark, while the band's inflammatory live sets barely lasted ten minutes. Its life span was suitably short, leaving behind a clutch of seminal singles and a quarter of the No NEW YORK album.

By 1978 Lydia was playing guitar in another short-lived New York band, Beirut Slump, before launching a solo career with the brooding and jazzy QUEEN OF SIAM (1980). She then led the excellent **Eight Eyed Spy**, a band featuring the unique bass-playing talents of **George Scott III**, whose untimely death halted their career. Spy's burlesque style has an all-too-small legacy – a hastily recorded, self-titled LP on the Fetish label, plus a one-off single and a live cassette.

On her journeys across the world via LA, London, Berlin and New York, Lunch recorded with **THE BIRTHDAY PARTY** and wrote fifty one-page plays with their frontman **Nick Cave**, before making an album with the band called HONEYMOON IN RED. Recorded just before the band's dissolution, it sounded like the product of extensive drug use, and did not appear officially until 1987.

During the same period, she collaborated with The Swans' Michael Gira on HARD ROCK (1983), a spoken-word performance, fronted **EINSTÜRZENDE NEUBAUTEN** on THIRSTY ANIMAL (1981), sang with Die Haut and Rowland S. Howard on SOME VELVET MORNING (1984), and appeared with **SONIC YOUTH** on DEATH VALLEY 69 (1984). Unfortunately, her now-legendary tour project with Nick Cave, **Clint Ruin** and **Marc Almond** – *The Immaculate Consumptives* – never made it to tape.

Lunch's solo work was similarly prolific, and her 1982 album, 13:13, recorded in California, was her most accomplished album to date. She joined forces with **Thurston Moore** for her mini-LP, IN LIMBO (1985), and made an eerie and twisted instrumental tribute to film noir called THE DROWNING OF LUCY HAMILTON, from the underground film of the same name.

In the mid-80s, Lydia Lunch starred in a clutch of underground movies and co-wrote two further films about the No Wave scene with photographer **Richard Kern**. Hardly family entertainment, both were unintentionally funny, especially in their exploration of some psychosexual themes. *In The Right Side Of My Brain*, Lunch was pursued by Henry Rollins and a host of New York music personalities, while in *Fingered* she got intimate with a gun, and very grubby and intimate with long-term partner and musical cohort, **JIM FOETUS**.

In 1989 Lydia Lunch toured again, and formed the sonically aggressive **Harry Crews** with Sonic Youth's **Kim Gordon**, and a raw drummer and part-time wrestler called **Cindy**, and recorded the album, NAKED IN GARDEN HILLS. The same year, she also worked with Clint Ruin again, making two EPs under the name of **Stinkfist**. She once again teamed up with former Bad Seed Rowland S. Howard in 1991 for the bluesy and morbid mini-LP, SHOTGUN WEDDING. Lunch has also written several books, often on the topic of censorship, and has performed spoken-word shows with ex-X singer **Exene Cervenka** – an album of which, RUDE HIEROGLYPHICS, was released on Rykodisc in 1995. Lunch continues to be the queen of all media, with numerous film, book, spoken-word, screenwriting, photography (including four permanent exhibits at the Museum of Erotic Art in Paris) and musical projects, the most recent of which was CHAMPAGNE, COCAINE, NICOTINE STAINS (2002), an album she recorded with German alt-cabaret band, **Anubian Lights**. And if you want to hear Lunch at her spoken-word best, check out 2000's DEVIL'S RACETRACK.

13:13 (1982; Line Records).
Scary stuff, often regarded as Lunch's best album, and now reissued on CD.

Hysterie (1986; Widowspeak).
Double album with essential sides by Teenage Jesus And The Jerks, Eight Eyed Spy, Beirut Slump, and a track each with Die Haut, Rowland S. Howard and Sort Sol.

Harry Crews (1989; Big Cat).
The two leading ladies of No Wave slug it out on this sonic thriller, adapted from stories by cult US writer Harry Crews.

8-Eyed Spy (1997; Atavistic).
Reissued masterpiece from 1981.

Widowspeak (1998; New Millennium Communications).
A carefully selected compilation of the 'musical' collaborations of Lydia with Sonic Youth, Shockheaded Peters, Clint Ruin and other noisy troublemakers from the left field of the avant-garde. An excellent introduction and a prime selection for any long bank-holiday drive.

Ross Holloway

THE LURKERS

Formed London, 1977; disbanded 1990;
re-formed 1996.

As 1977 progressed, the UK punk scene had one startling gap: there was no home-grown version of the Ramones. Happily, **The Lurkers** were prepared to don the mantle and from the start they were just perfect, with **Pete Stride**'s guitar sound and **Howard Wall**'s shorthand epic songs of life on the London scene.

The band's first single, "Shadow", issued on the fledgling Beggars Banquet label, was their statement: a faster-than-a-speeding-bullet, raw-punk story of love gone wrong, featuring the names of all concerned; a brief summary of the story and reactions to it; three choruses and a guitar solo – all in under three minutes. The next twelve months saw them hitting the UK singles charts with "Ain't Got A Clue' and "I Don't Need to Tell Her", the same kind of tragic love stories that were being told by the Buzzcocks, but with a harder edge. You listened to Pete Shelley when your boyfriend/girlfriend dumped you, but you put The Lurkers on before you went out to get a replacement.

The original line-up, with Howard and Pete, backed by **Arturo Bassick** (bass) and **Manic Esso** (drums), lasted only as far as the release of "Shadow". By the time the first album came out, the band had been through a couple of bass players and perfected the 'London's answer to the Ramones' sound – the guitar/drum thrash was, if anything, even more cranked-up than the New York boys, and the lyrics, though not exactly sensitive, had a little more to say. The live show was never much to look at (apart from Howard's atrocious 70s disco-boy taste in clothing), but there was so much untamed excitement pouring from the PA that no one seemed to care. They toured the UK, put out two fine albums and five singles, played anywhere there was a stage, and still remained pretty much a secret.

As the 1980s began, the band splintered. Although various line-ups released singles and a couple of albums as late as 1990, and a Lurkers band was on the road again in 1996, the spark had died ten years before.

⊙ **Greatest Hit, Last Will And Testament** (1980; Beggars Banquet).
A fine compilation from FULHAM FALLOUT and the second album, GOD'S LONELY MEN.

Al Spicer

LUSCIOUS JACKSON

Formed New York, 1991; disbanded 2000.

When The Beastie Boys set up their Grand Royal record label in the early 90s, **Luscious Jackson** were their first signings: a surprise to some, who had expected hardcore black urban rap or white punk. Luscious Jackson, with their bass-dominated hip-hop rhythms and spacious, loping pop-song con-structions, were a very different proposition. However, there was a link in drummer **Kate Schellenbach**, who had played with The Beasties in their early punk incarnation.

Comprising **Jill Cunniff** (vocals/bass) and **Gabrielle Glaister** (vocals/guitar), alongside Schellenbach, Luscious Jackson's hypnotic textures were premiered on their 1993 debut, IN SEARCH OF MANNY. A sassy seven-track mini-album, released almost unabridged from the group's first demo tape, this won acres of press in both the US and UK.

Their debut album 'proper', NATURAL INGREDIENTS (1994), was somewhat less impressive. Whereas MANNY had focused on life on the streets, the thrust here was the trio's relationship with the opposite gender and their own self-image, leaving no doubt about what was expected of either party – "Energy Sucker" featured the line 'I'm a Goddess, not your mother'.

FEVER IN FEVER OUT (1997) was a much more satisfying effort. With the group now augmented by multi-instrumentalist **Vivian Trimble**, it was recorded in New Orleans and Schellenbach's New York loft. This time the material was more personal – 'You could say we've moved past the "Men Suck!" phase', said Cunniff, half-jokingly. Daniel Lanois was an interesting ally in his role as the group's producer, inviting along Emmylou Harris and N'Dea Davenport as guest vocalists. It was also obvious to anyone attending their Astoria gig in London in the spring that there was still nothing hipper on planet pop than Luscious Jackson – with the guest list backing up hundreds of yards along Charing Cross Road.

Trimble left in 1998 to pursue other projects including an involvement with Josephine Wiggs (ex-**BREEDERS**) in **Dusty Trails**. The remaining trio issued ELECTRIC HONEY in 1999, only to find that their kudos had greatly diminished during their absence – despite production from Tony Visconti and guest appearances from Debbie Harry and Emmylou Harris (again). A pleasant but inconsequential release, it was to be their last album: the group disbanded the following year.

⊙ **In Search Of Manny** (1993; Grand Royal/Capitol).
Raw New York street sketches with seductive hip-hop undercurrents and plenty of attitude. One of the debuts of the 90s.

⊙ **Fever In Fever Out** (1997; Grand Royal/Capitol).
Skip over NATURAL INGREDIENTS for this. Still big on attitude, self-awareness and audience confrontation, on this occasion Luscious Jackson have the cocky songs to match their stage demeanour. The best moments include the intuitive "Mood Swing" (a natural successor to "Deep Shag") and "Water Your Garden".

Alex Ogg

LUSH

Formed London, 1988; broke up 1996.

Having collaborated on a short-lived fanzine called *Alphabet Soup*, schoolfriends **Emma Anderson** and **Miki Berenyi** (both vocals/guitar),

The Lush pretenders to the Britpop crown – Miki Berenyi wears the #77

King – who had played in both Felt and Biff Bang Pow!. In January 1992 Lush's debut full-length album, SPOOKY, was released. The British music press were unimpressed, criticizing its dependency on Guthrie's overpowering production, which threatened to drown the tracks in a pool of reverb and chorus. Still, it did pretty well, reaching #7 in the UK album charts.

After a lengthy period of touring, which included Lollapalooza in America, the band set to work on their second album, SPLIT (1994). With Mike Hedges producing, best known for his early work with The Cure, it marked a return to a more natural, less processed sound. However, it was woefully under-promoted and hovered briefly in the lower reaches of the UK Top 20 – a two-year break followed.

formed **Lush** with **Chris Acland** (drums) and **Steve Rippon** (bass). They were a striking crew – Miki has the unusual distinction of being half-Japanese, half-Hungarian – and after some well-reviewed live shows secured a deal with 4AD in early 1989.

The band's debut six-track mini-album, SCAR (1989), was a surprise commercial success, and its stand-out track, "Thoughtforms", characterized their approach to the traditional bass/guitar/drums setup, with layered harmonies and processed, chiming guitars. Press acclaim for their wistful, ethereal sound was highly positive at this stage, and Lush were quickly bracketed into the 'shoe-gazing' scene. It was a promise that seemed to be confirmed by the MAD LOVE EP (1990), produced by Robin Guthrie of label mates Cocteau Twins, and with a revamped version of "Thoughtforms" given sparkle and added bounce by Guthrie's experienced hand. The next single, "Sweetness And Light", combined a more upbeat backing with greater vocal clarity – and, as the 1990 singles compilation album, GALA, showed, Lush had developed a distinctive and unique sound.

Success in America and Japan followed, amid some relentless touring, and Guthrie returned to production duties for the 1991 EP BLACK SPRING. This contained the awesomely slow-burning "Monochrome", along with a bossa nova reading of Dennis Wilson's "Fallin' In Love", complete with Jane Birkin-style breathy vocals.

Towards the end of 1991, Steve Rippon left the band, to be replaced by ex-*NME* journalist **Philip**

1996 got off to a good start with UK Top 20 success for "Single Girl" and the release of a new album, LOVELIFE. This was a strong set of songs and Lush had finally achieved a really individual sound to accompany it.

The follow-up single, "Ladykillers", was also a success, and the band's next video, for the jaunty "500", saw the members larking about in the cheery little Fiat of the title, acting a million miles from the wispy shoe-gazer tag that had dogged their career.

After Chris Acland tragically took his own life at his parents' home in October 1996 the band faltered, unable to continue without this founding member. The final single, "Ciao!", ironically featured **Jarvis Cocker**, whose high profile may have gained the band the recognition they deserved. Instead, Lush quietly disintegrated. Emma Anderson later emerged with a new project, **Sing Sing**, and Phil King was spotted touring on bass with **THE JESUS & MARY CHAIN**. A sad ending for a band who sparkled with promise.

◉ **Gala** (1990; 4AD).
An ideal introduction to the band, collecting their first singles and the SCAR mini-album. Opening with the sprightly "Sweetness And Light", it then follows their back catalogue in reverse chronology, with the added bonus of a cover of Abba's "Hey Hey Helen".

◉ **Lovelife** (1996; 4AD).
Six years on, and six years more sophisticated. Well-crafted songs and Miki in confident vocal form. A fitting epitaph.

Jonathan Bell

LYNYRD SKYNYRD

Formed Jacksonville, Florida, 1966;
disbanded 1977; re-formed briefly 1987 & 1991.

"Cause I'm free as a bird now and this bird you cannot change."
Freebird

They will forever be associated with the Southern Rock revival of the early 70s, but **Lynyrd Skynyrd** in fact drew on far more disparate influences. The band was the brainchild of singer **Ronnie Van Zant**, who was reared to the strains of swamp blues and Merle Haggard, but was later beguiled by The Rolling Stones. Van Zant recruited friends **Bob Burns** (drums), **Gary Rossington** (guitar), **Allen Collins** (guitar) and **Larry Junstrom** (bass), later replaced by **Leon Wilkeson**.

Sessions for Shade Tree Records, featuring future Blackfoot singer Ricky Medlock on drums, produced one single, "I've Been Your Fool" (1971), although other material later resurfaced on the compilation First ... And Last (1978). Then, in 1972, they were signed to MCA by producer Al Kooper; joined by ex-Strawberry Alarm Clock bass player **Ed King** and pianist **Billy Powell**, they recorded Pronounced Leh-Nerd Skin-Nerd (1973). (The band's name was derived from school coach Leonard Skinner, with whom long hair had proved contentious.)

A loud, impassioned debut, the LP was blues-rock with a Southern coating, topped by Van Zant's dramatic vocals, best heard on the accusatory "I Ain't The One", the countrified semi-balladry of "Tuesday's Gone" and the succinct stomp "Things Goin' On". It is probably best remembered, though, for the popular Duane Allman tribute, "Freebird", on which Kooper's penchant for overdubbing led to a third melodious guitar part being added to Collins's extended climactic solo.

Ed King had switched to third guitar and Leon Wilkeson had rejoined on bass for Second Helping (1974), which instantly gained press attention for its hit opener, "Sweet Home Alabama". The song was inaccurately perceived as a redneck response to Neil Young's "Alabama" and "Southern Man", when in fact it had been composed with tongue firmly in cheek. Elsewhere, tracks like the groovy jig "Swamp Music" and the punky "Working For MCA" (which predated the Sex Pistols' infamous "EMI") created a hit album, and established Lynyrd Skynyrd as a major act.

After opening for The Who on several 1974 shows, they embarked on gruelling tours before an exhausted Bob Burns quit amid tales of drinking, hotel-wrecking and fist fights during performances. New drummer **Artimus Pyle** came on board for the contemporary rock sound of Nuthin' Fancy

(1975). The solo of the anti-gun "Saturday Night Special" was introduced by a torrent of synthesized atmospherics, while on "Made In The Shade" Van Zant saluted his blues mentors. The Tom Dowd production of Gimme Back My Bullets (1976) had a richer and fuller sound, highlighted on the triumphantly funky cover of J. J. Cale's "(I Got The) Same Old Blues" and the gospel-drenched chorus of "Double Trouble". Backing singer **Cassie Gaines** was to introduce the band to her younger brother **Steve** (guitar), who more than compensated for the departure of Ed King.

Ever popular as a stage act, Lynyrd Skynyrd released a live LP, One More From The Road (1976), which included readings of Robert Johnson's "Crossroads" and Billy Rogers' "T For Texas", reflecting a new direction for a band that was mellowing with family life. They began rediscovering the origins of country music, and the result was the laid-back honky-tonk of Street Survivors (1977), released just days before a plane crash took the lives of Ronnie Van Zant, and Steve and Cassie Gaines. The brass-accompanied single "What's Your Name?" became a worldwide hit, although the album itself lacked the vitality of earlier work.

The band split in 1977, many joining **The Rossington-Collins Band**, who recorded two mediocre albums in the early 80s. Ten years on, a 'tribute' tour and live album Southern By The Grace Of God (1988) reunited remaining band members, with **Johnny Van Zant** succeeding his brother on vocals. They re-formed yet again shortly after the death of Allen Collins in 1990 for Lynyrd Skynyrd (1991), a credible if slightly clichéd release which also included an attempt at rap. The Last Rebel (1993) strove to re-create the formula of earlier success, but was overproduced and poorly arranged. However, the acoustic set of reworkings, Endangered Species (1994), was released to some US interest and 1997's Twenty (SPV Records) – named for the twenty years since the plane crash – followed suit.

In 1995 Ed King retired from the band due to heart problems and more recently Leon Wilkinson died at the age of 49. The only two original members still in the line-up are Rossington and Powell.

⊙ **Second Helping** (1974; MCA).
Arguably the band's most accomplished work, recorded at their creative peak. It features the 'wah-wah' workout "Needle And The Spoon" and the celebratory jam "Call Me The Breeze".

⊙ **The Definitive Lynyrd Skynyrd** (1991; MCA).
The highest music industry accolade – a 47-track lavishly packaged box set with additional unreleased rarities, like the sultry "Was I Right Or Wrong?", the raw demo "Junkie", plus the original recording of the legendary "Freebird".

⊙ **Freebird – The Best Of** (1994; MCA).
The most recent of countless compilations, including the inevitable "Freebird" and "Sweet Home Alabama".

Michael Andrews

KIRSTY MACCOLL

Born Croydon, England, 1959;
died December, 2000.

Kirsty MacColl was too often referred to as being the daughter of Ewan MacColl and Peggy Seeger, or the wife of producer Steve Lillywhite, or as the guest vocalist on The Pogues' "Fairytale Of New York". A little credit in her own right, especially in light of her untimely death, is very overdue: there have been few musicians with the breadth of her songwriting and vocal abilities.

Signed to Stiff Records in 1979, MacColl made her first mark with a self-penned single, "They Don't Know"; it flopped, though became a big hit for actress Tracey Ullman four years later. By then, MacColl had made the UK Top 20 in her own right,

with her 1981 Polydor release, "There's A Guy Works Down The Chip Shop Swears He's Elvis". Unfortunately, these two songs gave MacColl the aura of a gimmick act, and worse was to follow when she toured Ireland and suffered from stage fright, singing her songs so fast she ran out of material and had to repeat an agonizing performance.

Still, by 1985, MacColl was back at Stiff – married to Steve Lillywhite and pregnant – and scored a third UK chart hit with a cover of Billy Bragg's "A New England", for which Bragg wrote an extra verse. The follow-up, "He's On The Beach", inexplicably missed the charts, though, and it was around this time that MacColl became even more heavily involved in backing vocals, mostly for albums Lillywhite was producing. With perfect pitch, she could go into a studio completely cold, give the song a quick listen and slot the backing voice in perfectly.

REDFERNS

The late, great Kirsty MacColl

Billy Bragg, Happy Mondays, The Smiths and countless others benefited from her expertise, but the song that won MacColl international recognition was **THE POGUES'** "Fairytale Of New York", a 1987 Christmas hit, in which her soaring voice clashed with Shane MacGowan's alcohol-soaked roar before joining in a glorious chorus. As well as gaining her a new fan base, the song helped MacColl's stage confidence, as she joined The Pogues on tour.

It was MacColl's KITE (1989) album that at last established her as an artist in her own right. Produced by Lillywhite, it expressed both anger (railing against Thatcherite politics and the position of women in Britain's class-ridden society) and tenderness in equal parts, and to equally strong effect. Her sense of humour was very much intact, too, as "Don't Come The Cowboy With Me, Sonny Jim", a light but effective put-down of macho values, showed.

In 1991, the former Smiths' guitarist **Johnny Marr** returned favours on MacColl's single, "Walking Down Madison", which saw a move into dance territory. The follow-up album, ELECTRIC LANDLADY (1991), featured songwriting collaborations with Fairground Attraction's **Mark E. Nevin**, notably the Latin-tinged "My Affair". MacColl even returned to live performance, too, at the 1992 Glastonbury Festival, with a glittering set of her own songs plus a few choice covers of songs by artists such as Billy Bragg, The Clash and The Smiths. (The high-quality bootleg of this performance is an essential collector's item for fans.)

Unfortunately, ELECTRIC LANDLADY, despite a healthy critical reception, was not a big seller, and MacColl was dropped by Virgin. However, she was soon snapped up by ZTT for the 1993 album, TITANIC DAYS, and her greatest hits package, GALORE (1995), introduced many to her output, as well as to a wonderful new song, "Caroline", described by MacColl as 'Jolene's Reply'. Typically, she ended the compilation with yet another cover, a gorgeous take on Lou Reed's ironic "Perfect Day", in duet with The Lemonheads' **Evan Dando**. WHAT DO PRETTY GIRLS DO? (1998) was a splendid collection of MacColl's better-known songs, with a few surprise inclusions to spice up the mix, recorded in session at the BBC between 1989 and 1995.

Other highlights of her latter career included the melancholy classic "Dear John" (presumably a thinly veiled farewell to Lillywhite, from whom she divorced) recorded by Eddi Reader on her 1994 album, and the song "As Long As You Hold Me", a hidden gem from the 1995 MAD LOVE film soundtrack written for Kirsty by Billy Bragg.

In 2000 she reappeared with the brilliant TROPICAL BRAINSTORM on the V2 label. The album saw a marvellous blend of her distinctive lyrics and Latin-pop stylings inspired by her newfound love of South America where she had spent time absorbing the culture and music. But sadly it was to be her swan song. Toward the end of 2000 she was tragically hit and killed by a speedboat while swimming in Mexico.

MacColl's career had been patchy, with much time spent hopping from one label to another, but she deserved to win wider acclaim than a couple of singles and a greatest hits package. Tragically, it was her final album that witnessed her most accomplished work, and it is this set that stands as a testament to what might have been if she had lived to pursue her musical passions.

⊙ **Galore** (1995; Virgin).
This collection showcases her ability to be simultaneously funny, charming and coruscating. "Free World" is an unusually melodic example of an anti-Thatcherite diatribe: 'In this free world, baby/You've got to take, gotta grab it/Gotta get it up and shag it'. It's not the MacColl that casual visitors to the charts would recognize, but then that was her all over.

⊙ **Tropical Brainstorm** (2000; V2).
Having spent five years marinating in the juices of Cuban and Brazilian culture, Kirsty MacColl released this startlingly wonderful collection of Anglo-Latin pop ditties. The production is flawless and the array of South American musical ingredients is exquisitely combined with pop-hooks and even hip-hop scratches.

Mike Martin & Peter Buckley

SHANE MACGOWAN AND THE POPES

Formed Britain, 1994.

Rumours of the death of **Shane MacGowan**, following his departure from **THE POGUES**, proved somewhat exaggerated. Despite drink and drug ingestion on a scale that would have floored even William Burroughs, MacGowan continues intact, albeit retaining a 'next-one-for-the-obituaries' appearance. Post-Pogues, MacGowan first cropped up duetting with **Nick Cave** on Louis Armstrong's classic, "(What A) Wonderful World" in 1992. It was a gloriously shambolic sing-along, the duo staggering through the verses like a couple of drunks, and posted a note of fine things to come with its B-side: Cave covering "Rainy Night In Soho" while MacGowan ripped into Cave's "Lucy", both splendid and touching affairs.

Drunken TV appearances seemed to confirm critics' fears of a very short career, but MacGowan proved them all wrong when **The Popes**, the band he had talked of forming, finally materialized in 1994. A shifting group of musicians, the band's first album recording line-up, for THE SNAKE (1995), comprised **Paul McGuinness** (guitars/vocals), **Berni France** (bass/vocals), **Danny Pope** (drums), **Tom McAnimal** (tenor banjo), **Kieran 'Mo' O'Hagan** (guitar/vocals) and **Colm O'Maonlai** (whistles). Guests drifted in from The Dubliners, along with stray Pogues **Jem Finer** and **Spider Stacey**, while film star **Johnny Depp** guested on the debut single, "That Woman's Got Me Drinking".

THE SNAKE was a return to the finer moments of The Pogues, and an extended 1995 rerelease was better still, featuring more of MacGowan's songwriting alongside contributions from **Sinéad O'Connor** and **Maire Brennan** (of Clannad). "Victoria" and "I'll Be Your Handbag" were raucous, bitter love songs, complemented by the cover of Gerry Rafferty's self-deprecating "Her Father Didn't Like Me Anyway". Making the myths of Ireland all the more sexy, "Donegal Express" and "Snake With Eyes Of Garnet" were further high points. THE CROCK OF GOLD (1998; ZTT) was a less satisfactory album, however, with MacGowan verging, on occasion, dangerously near to self-parody. All involved sound weary of the whole business of rock'n'roll, in contrast to the uplifting rebellion and mayhem that characterize the band on stage.

If Shane and The Popes can bring the excitement of their storming live performances into the studio, then their future promises a great deal.

⊙ **The Snake** (1995; ZTT).
The extended rerelease. Corking tunes, with all the sex, religion and romantic spirit that marked the best of MacGowan's contribution to The Pogues.

Duncan Harris

MADDER ROSE

Formed New York, 1991.

Even more than most New York bands, **Madder Rose** seemed haunted by the ghosts of Andy Warhol and The Velvet Underground. Formed in the early 90s, the band consisted of **Billy Coté** (lead guitar), **Mary Lorson** (vocals/guitar), **Johnny Kick** (drums) and **Matt Verta-Ray** (bass/backing vocals). Lorson, a Manhattan-based singer, had busked around Europe before auditioning for a guitarist. Coté answered the call, and he brought

in Verta-Ray, with whom he had worked in a print shop; the store's main client was Andy Warhol's Factory.

The band's first tracks, recorded in Verta-Ray's makeshift home studio, were compared to The Velvets, with good reason. Coté said of their precursors, 'they had psychotic rock-out songs back-to-back with beautiful lullabies, which is something we've always tried to achieve – to be able to play a really beautiful, vulnerable song, and follow it with a song where the guitars are really loud and you can hardly hear the words'.

College airplay and word of mouth drew labels, and the band opted for Seed Records, a subsidiary of Atlantic. Their first album was the thirteen-song BRING IT DOWN (1993), produced by Dumptruck guitarist Kevin Salem. Coté's guitar was a wall of volume and distortion pedals, providing stark contrast with Lorson's more melodic guitar and lovely, high voice. The Velvets were again the obvious comparison, but the band's tastes were broad enough to include the gorgeous, country-rock ballad, "Waiting For Engines", with its languid voice and slide guitar. BRING IT DOWN gained widespread critical acclaim, and the band embarked on American tours with The Sundays and Juliana Hatfield Three.

The EP SWIM followed in September 1993, featuring "Swim" plus three new songs, all with the (by-now) characteristic Lorson harmonies and Coté grinding guitars. Madder Rose's next album, PANIC ON (1994), revealed the band's multi-talented line-up in its full glory, with Coté and Lorson sharing the songwriting duties. The opening, "Sleep, Forever", showed them at full power, Coté's blistering guitar sound fighting with Lorson's vocals. The ethereal influence of their touring partners The Sundays also made itself felt.

By the time Madder Rose made it to Britain to tour in 1994, Verta-Ray had quit to pursue his solo projects. Former Eve's Plumb bassist **Chris Giammalvo** replaced him in time for the tour, and played a low-key role in the performances which centred around Lorson and Coté. TRAGIC MAGIC (1997) was a fine professional album released after three years' silence. With a new trip-hop/skunk-rock sensibility to the album, it showed Coté keeping in touch with the new ideas necessary to stay alive in the alternative-rock field.

A parting of the ways with the record company led to a long hiatus, and by the time the band returned to England they were supporting Soul Coughing, hardly a step forward. A lack of direction revealed itself in some of the new songs and their next album was a US-only release.

By 1999, Madder Rose had signed a UK distribution deal with Cooking Vinyl and TRAGIC MAGIC was released in the UK, with three extra songs not included on the US version. It was classified as a compilation for chart purposes and certainly has its inconsistencies. However, the brooding, excellent "Jailbird" and gorgeously catchy "Float To The Top" showed glimpses of what the band could still pull off. Later that year came HELLO JUNE FOOL, a wondrous return to form that showed just how comfortable the band were with their new label home.

Already having released a limited solo 7" ("Keep An Open Mind"/"Anywhere") on Easy!Tiger back in 1998, the new millennium saw Lorson release an eponymous solo set under the moniker **Saint Low**. A sumptuously mellow affair, SAINT LOW previewed the glut of Lorson's material that was deemed too laid-back for Madder Rose releases. 2000 also witnessed AMATEUR SOUL SURGERY, Coté's US-only solo album, released under the name **Jazz Cannon**. Currently Mary is penning screenplays, working on her first short film and, in collaboration with Coté, writing scores (the pair released the haunting, 'imaginary-soundtrack' PIANO CREEPS in 2003). Though there are currently no firm plans for a new Madder Rose release, let's hope this is not the end.

Madder Rose

(•) **Panic On** (1994; Atlantic).
Catchier than the band's debut release, but retaining the power and strong guitar sound. "Car Song" opens with a country-tinged guitar pattern, and has an almost stream-of-consciousness feel to it; "What Holly Sees" is a classic male/female harmony ballad with more hooks than a fisherman; and "Drop A Bomb"'s opening battle of the riffs offers a direct comparison between Lorson and Coté's guitar as they take turns to play the same chord.

Saint Low

(•) **Saint Low** (2000; Cooking Vinyl).
At times the uncluttered compositions and Lorson's pure vocal melodies recall early Suzanne Vega recordings. This is a fine little album, and an essential purchase for all Madder Rose fans.

Mike Martin

MADDESS

Formed London, 1978; disbanded 1986; re-formed for one-off gigs in 1988 and from 1992 on.

The Invaders, a bluebeat-obsessed north London band, numbered **Mike Barson** (keyboards), **Lee 'Kix' Thompson** (saxophone/vocals), **Chris 'Chrissie Boy' Foreman** (guitar) and **Chas Smash** (aka Cathal Smyth; bass) among its personnel. Formed in 1976, they were joined a couple of years later by lead vocalist **Suggs** (aka Graham McPherson), **Mark Bedford** (bass) and **Dan 'Woody' Woodgate** (drums). As Smash moved to horns, backing vocals and on-stage lunacy, The Invaders made their debut – as **Madness** – on that fateful day in May 1979 when Margaret Thatcher was elected British Prime Minister.

Madness's musical roots were in ska, reggae's faster-paced precursor, which in Jamaica and Britain

in the 60s had been a witty, satirical and danceable vehicle for social comment. However, the group were creating something uniquely their own, a trademark 'nutty sound' that blended authentic ska with Barson's Western saloon piano, in songs that offered perceptive observations on growing up in 70s London.

Signed to ska-revival label 2-Tone, Madness released their debut single, "The Prince", an infectious tribute to ska giant Prince Buster, in August 1979. It became the first in a line of 21 UK Top 20 singles. After its release, the band continued to tour with fellow 2-Tone acts, like The Specials and The Selecter, but switched labels to Stiff Records, for whom they released their debut LP, ONE STEP BEYOND... (1979), alongside a Top 10 single of the same name.

Early Madness gigs were marred by fascist audiences; skinheads from the racist National Front, in one of those odd British quirks, had always been into ska themselves. Madness got their support, presumably, because – unlike The Beat and The Selecter – they were an all-white band, and their music was less overtly political. Understandably annoyed by this unwanted attention, the group included an anti-NF track on the WORK REST AND PLAY EP (1980), a set that also included their classic song "Night Boat To Cairo".

In the early 80s, just about everyone who bought records in Britain liked Madness. Transparently good-humoured and exuberant, they became the country's consummate singles band – which is not to detract from first-rate LP tracks like "Bed And Breakfast Man" (on ONE STEP BEYOND...) or "Benny Bullfrog", from 1981's SEVEN album. The band's success was aided by Suggs's iconic presence and jerky, boxer-like stage moves, and by a series of increasingly funny and inventive videos. One of the most fondly remembered moments occurred in the promo for their ode to their schooldays, "Baggy Trousers" (1980), in which sax player Lee Thompson was briefly airborne.

Their finest moment was probably 1982's "House Of Fun" (oddly, their only UK chart-topper), a magnificently surreal tale of coming of age and adolescent misunderstandings at the chemist's. A more melancholy side to their work had surfaced in the gloomy "Grey Day" (1981), while radio was reluctant to play the anti-stress fable "Cardiac Arrest" (1982), which consequently became one of the band's smaller hits. As time went on, this world-weary, reflective strain became more pronounced, especially after Barson got fed up with the rock'n'roll lifestyle and went to live in Holland at the end of 1983.

Barson's retirement was the beginning of a (slow) end for Madness. He had been responsible for most of their good musical ideas, and the record-buying public began to lose interest. The band's own label, Zarjazz, launched in 1984, started off well enough with hits for Madness themselves and ex-Undertone Feargal Sharkey, but soon hit financial problems. Meanwhile, new Madness songs such as "Yesterday's Men" (1985) sounded lacklustre, while a ham-fisted cover of the Scritti Politti classic, "The Sweetest Girl" (1986), was their lowest-charting single yet. In July Madness played their final gig. As a swan-song single, "Welcome To The Ghost Train" briefly returned them to the UK Top 20.

In 1988, Suggs, Thompson, Foreman and Smash re-formed as **The Madness**, but a self-titled album was almost completely ignored, and they parted again by the year's end. Suggs then turned to stand-up comedy and TV work before managing and producing The Farm to a #1 album and several hit singles; Thompson and Foreman returned to their ska roots with **The Nutty Boys**; Smash became an A&R man for Go! Discs; Bedford turned to graphic design; and Woody worked with **VOICE OF THE BEEHIVE**.

And that would have been that, except that in 1992 the group's greatest hits collection, DIVINE MADNESS, suddenly shot to #1 in the UK. It was obvious that there were a lot of fans still out there, so in August 1992 the whole band, including Barson, re-formed for two triumphant concerts at London's Finsbury Park. An alarming proportion of the audience, some decked out in "Night Boat To Cairo" fezzes, knew all the songs word for word.

In 1995 Suggs released a debut solo album, THE LONE RANGER, which spawned Top 10 hits in the UK for his covers of The Beatles' "I'm Only Sleeping" and Simon & Garfunkel's "Cecilia", and an elegiac song, "Green Eyes", that was the equal of old Madness efforts. Finally, after thirteen years away from the studio, a fresh Madness collection was unveiled in 1999. WONDERFUL was just that, and equally as jolly and catchy as anything from their back catalogue; the duet with Ian Dury, "Drip Fed Fred", was especially marvellous. And then to top it all, the band's story was, in a roundabout way, captured in a box office-breaking West End show, *Our House*.

◉ **Divine Madness** (1992; Virgin).
All the hits, which makes it one of the best singles albums of all time.

◉ **Madstock!** (1992; Go! Discs/London).
Recorded at the Finsbury Park concerts, this is predominantly a live version of the above, complete with a word-perfect audience.

◉ **The Business** (1993; Virgin).
An exhaustive three-disc box set including B-sides, radio jingles and rarities.

Andy Smith

MADONNA

Born Bay City, Michigan, August 16, 1958.

"I won't be happy until I'm as famous as God."

It goes without saying that **Madonna** (Madonna Louise Veronica Ciccone) is the most successful woman in the history of popular music. Many would argue that she is far more than this, that she was the most significant pop artist of the 80s: Michael Jackson sold more records, Prince was more critically lauded, but nobody changed people's lives the way Madonna did.

There was nothing in Madonna's early years to suggest what was to come. She won a dance scholarship to the University of Michigan, dropped out and went to New York at the age of 20, where she struggled with various dance companies and bands to no great effect. A brief visit to Europe as backing vocalist/dancer to French disco star **Patrick Hernandez** didn't get her much further and she returned to New York.

Even when she did get a record deal, with Warner Bros through Sire, there wasn't much on the first album, MADONNA (1983), of any real substance – she seemed to be no more than just another disco singer. With some pushing from club DJs, "Holiday" was a US hit, followed by "Borderline" and "Lucky Star", but even after the album had sold three million copies in eighteen month it still sounded like little more than factory fodder.

Over the next two years, though, Madonna exploded into the world's consciousness. She appeared at Live Aid, released her second album, LIKE A VIRGIN (1984), and appeared in two films, *Vision Quest* and *Desperately Seeking Susan*, each of which yielded a massive hit ("Crazy For You" and "Into The Groove" respectively). The near-simultaneous success of the latter movie and the "Like A Virgin" single propelled La Ciccone onto a different plane – the juxtaposition of Madonna's street-vamp image and the word 'virgin' was sufficient to make her a centre of obsessive media interest, a development that she proved capable of handling better than anyone before her.

The second single from the VIRGIN album, "Material Girl", had a video re-creating Marilyn Monroe's "Diamonds Are A Girl's Best Friend" routine that had the mainstream media in thrall, seeing in the song an encapsulation of the wealth-obsessed

80s. But Madonna was only playing with the Marilyn iconography – the emerging feature of her career was her ability to manipulate the machinery of show business to her own advantage.

If those first hits sold largely on the strength of the video imagery and of the dance production, first by Jellybean, then by Nile Rodgers, by the time of the third album, TRUE BLUE (1986), Madonna was emerging as a more than competent songwriter and had abandoned the squeaky voice. Even so there were plenty of doubters who believed her success was built on hype rather than talent.

Such arguments collapsed with LIKE A PRAYER (1989), on which Madonna was able to achieve a level of pop perfection while exploring all sorts of explosive subjects – Catholicism, sex, family, female identity – often in conjunction with one other. "Like A Prayer", "Express Yourself" and "Cherish" were the biggest hits, but the album showed a new-found daring from beginning to end. It also included a collaboration with **PRINCE** ("Love Song"), the reigning king of mixing the sensual with the spiritual.

The next year, Madonna delivered two more gems: the Hollywood-obsessed smash "Vogue", off the otherwise forgettable quasi-soundtrack I'M BREATHLESS (music inspired by the Warren Beatty movie she starred in, *Dick Tracy*); and "Justify My Love," one of two new tracks (the minor hit "Rescue Me" was the other) on her 'best of' album, THE IMMACULATE COLLECTION. "Justify" was accompanied by a racy video that provoked much controversy, while the retrospective demonstrated just how far she had come with her music. And her 1990 *Blonde Ambition* world tour (filmed as *Truth Or Dare*, aka *In Bed With Madonna*) was no slouch either, an imaginative take on the staging of a stadium gig.

If this period finally established Madonna as the ultimate modern pop star, 1992 produced the inevitable backlash. With hysterical levels of hype, a misconceived coffee-table book, *Sex*, was launched, featuring soft porn photos and barely literate texts. The ridicule heaped on the book obscured the simultaneously released abum, EROTICA (1992), which was

actually a pretty decent record; a little samey in its subject matter, admittedly, but with two great singles in "Rain" and "Bad Girl".

As a career move, the *Sex* episode was nigh on disastrous. To a large extent Madonna's appeal had derived from the space she left for fans to project their fantasies onto her, enabling her to win audiences as diverse as teenage girls and lust-driven boys, gay men and postfeminist career women. Central to her reinvention of herself as ultra-celebrity was the fact that the masks she wore concealed an absence of authenticity. By stripping away much of the mystery that she had created, she ran the risk of rendering herself ordinary, particularly since the contents of the book were so banal. How could she be a star if her imagination was so humdrum?

By 1993 the acceptable critical position had become one of feigned boredom. But the preceding decade had shown again and again her drive to survive, and the next single, the atmospheric "I'll Remember", was one of her best ever, showing her ability to stay in touch with, and adapt to, musical developments.

The 1994 album, BEDTIME STORIES, failed to grip the public imagination, but did contain one classic in "Take A Bow", a US #1 when released on single. That song turned up again on the 1995 compilation, SOMETHING TO REMEMBER. Although she had made her name with dance-floor hits, Madonna had evolved over the years into an excellent ballad singer, and SOMETHING TO REMEMBER featured the best of her slower pieces; the new single taken from it, "You'll See", was another big hit. Her promotional appearances showed a more restrained image – the jeans and T-shirt a far cry from the halcyon 80s days of Gaultier metal bras – as though she were determined to let the music take centre stage for a while.

1996 signalled yet another major year in the Madonnalogue. Two long-publicized desires of hers became realities: she had a baby, Lourdes, fathered by personal trainer Carlos Leon; and she starred in the role of her lifetime (or so she thought), as the title character in the film version of Andrew Lloyd Webber's *Evita*. Though her movie career had previously produced two excellent supporting roles (in *Susan* and *A League Of Their Own*), there was nothing to suggest that she could carry a film on her own. There still really isn't, unless she gets to sing her way through. In fact, the musical may be her perfect medium. *Evita* was fairly well received; Madonna was conspicuously, though unsurprisingly, snubbed by the Oscars. The soundtrack was, well, the soundtrack: solid performances and Lord Andrew Lloyd Webber's material. For 1998's RAY OF LIGHT, the newly maternal Madonna picked up a superstar spirituality, took her ideas from William Orbit and, with the desperation so often seen in ageing pop stars, reinvented herself once again as a goth/witchy hybrid, swathing herself in Siouxsie Sioux's cast-off clothes. The music on the album was the usual up-to-date pop dance stuff, selling millions and short on surprises.

MADONNA)|| *ray of light*

In 2000 the chameleon-like Madonna transformed herself into a glittering rhinestone cowgirl for her surprise single smash "American Pie" – a cover of Don McLean's classic – and a new album entitled MUSIC. Produced by William Orbit and French deep-house technician Mirwais, the collection, like its predecessors, impressively straddled the pop and dance markets. Despite pre-release problems with Internet piracy, the collection sold phenomenally well, ensuring that Madonna remained, well and truly, in the limelight.

With her second child – a baby boy Rocco, born to English film director Guy Richie (who she married in 2000) – and her flourishing Maverick record label, she certainly had a full basket. And the live dates surrounding MUSIC proved her popularity had once again reached a peak, especially in the UK where she now lived and had benefited from associations with credibility enhancing projects such as the *Turner Prize* and appearing on stage in the West End. She also (allegedly) developed a stage school Brit accent. A second batch of greatest hits appeared (GHV2) toward the end of 2001, rescuing tracks from her early-90s slump and pasting them alongside more recent triumphs from her Orbit-sponsored resurrection. It was less essential than IMMACULATE COLLECTION but worth acquiring for completeness' sake, as well as MUSIC's blinding title track. Fresh material arrived in 2003 with AMERICAN LIFE, which offered more Mirwais-tinkered electronic disco settings.

Her ability to impact public consciousness is matched only by her capacity to successfully reinvent herself – now she's even writing children's books. What can be said with certainty is that she's unlikely to disappear. And for that, she should take a bow.

● **Like A Prayer** (1989; Sire)
Again, a winner through and through; a more mature voice can be heard on "Express Yourself" and "Oh Father", plus there's the scintillating title track.

● **The Immaculate Collection** (1990; Sire).
A trawl through the works up to and including "Justify My Love", this stakes Madonna's claim to be the best singles act of the 80s.

● **Erotica** (1992; Maverick).
A much better record than anyone was prepared to admit at the time, this has a consistency of texture and mood that justifies its title.

● **Something To Remember** (1995; Maverick).
Who would have thought that the pushy little upstart who bounced her way through "Holiday" would become such a mature and sophisticated performer? Well, she did probably, but on some of these slower songs she even sounds like she might occasionally entertain the odd moment of self-doubt.

● **Music** (2000; Maverick).
Here Madge mixes pop and house with a healthy dose of rhinestone country glamour and even experimental electronica. This album sees Madonna reunited with old favourite William Orbit for several songs, but the finest cuts come courtesy of Mirwais.

● **GHV2** (2001; Maverick).
This set presents an overview of the evolution that Madonna and her sound have undertaken between EROTICA and MUSIC.

Alwyn W. Turner

MAGAZINE

Formed Manchester, England, 1977; disbanded 1981.

In 1977, vocalist and lyricist **Howard Devoto** quit his band, **BUZZCOCKS**, leaving behind him one of punk's anthems, the tetchy "Boredom" from the SPIRAL SCRATCH EP. Later the same year he hooked up with guitarist **John McGeogh** and formed **Magazine**, with **BARRY ADAMSON** (bass), **Bob Dickinson** (keyboards) and **Martin Jackson** (drums). The band played their first show at the final night of Manchester's infamous punk venue, the Electric Circus, although they were not billed and had to borrow Buzzcocks' equipment to play. On the strength of a handful of demos, however, they secured a deal with Virgin, and made their 'official' debut at Manchester Rafters in October 1977.

"Shot By Both Sides" (1978) was an astonishing single – a gritty ode to alienation that built to a shuddering conclusion through McGeogh's expansive guitar work. Both this and the self-confident album that followed, REAL LIFE, received rave reviews. Featuring **Dave Formula** on keyboards (Dickinson quit before recording sessions), REAL LIFE demonstrated a maturity that sounded like the band had been together for years, with tracks like "The Light Pours Out Of Me" twisting the riff of Gary Glitter's "Rock And Roll (Parts 1 & 2)" into something threatening and edgy.

Following a UK tour, and a change of drummer, **John Doyle** picking up the sticks, Magazine recorded SECONDHAND DAYLIGHT (1979), an album dominated by Formula's lush keyboards (something viewed with suspicion in the aftermath of punk) and what many critics viewed as misanthropic lyrics from Devoto: 'I will drug you and fuck you/On the Permafrost' (from "Permafrost") was not untypical. The band's first single of 1980, "A Song From Under The Floorboards", continued the mood: featuring an icy Martin Hannett production, and a lyric derived from Dostoevsky's *Notes From The Underground* (classic Devoto territory), the song was simultaneously eerie, euphoric and terrifying.

Three further singles, including a minor hit in "Sweetheart Contract", and a strong LP, THE CORRECT USE OF SOAP (1980), proved the song was no fluke, although Devoto later claimed he felt Magazine had bowed to commercial considerations after SECONDHAND DAYLIGHT – indeed 1980 saw the beginning of the end for Magazine. McGeogh had been moonlighting with New Romantic club guru Steve Strange's **Visage** (who also featured Adamson and Formula), as well as **SIOUXSIE AND THE BANSHEES**, and in July he quit to work with The Banshees full time. He was replaced by former Neo and vox guitarist **Robin Simon**, who toured the USA and Australia with the band, and can be heard on a patchy live album, PLAY (1980).

Magazine's Devoto, Adamson, Jackson, McCeogh and Formula

MAGIC MURDER AND THE WEATHER (1981) proved to be Magazine's swan song. Featuring guitarist **Ben Mandelson**, an old friend of Devoto's who joined the band when Simon quit in late 1980, this was a lacklustre affair apart from the excellent title track. Its release was also overshadowed by Devoto's announcement in May that he was quitting the band.

The post-Magazine career of **HOWARD DEVOTO** began with JERKY VERSIONS OF THE DREAM, and continued with his band **Luxuria**, who released two albums – UNANSWERABLE LUST and BEAST BOX. None set the world alight, and Devoto now seems to have retired from the music business to work in publishing.

Of the others, McGeogh and Adamson have fared best. After The Banshees, McGeogh joined **The Armoury Show**, a band formed by former Skids men Richard Jobson and Russell Webb, and later **PUBLIC IMAGE LTD**. Adamson joined **NICK CAVE AND THE BAD SEEDS** before embarking on a solo career.

⊙ **Real Life** (1978; Virgin).
One of the great post-punk albums, an LP that threw down the gauntlet to those who still thought three chords and an attitude were enough.

⊙ **The Correct Use Of Soap** (1980; Virgin).
Despite Devoto's criticism of this album, it stands the test of time. Adamson and Doyle anchor proceedings, McGeogh's guitar and Formula's keyboards play well off each other, while Devoto provides some of rock's oddest and most effective lyrics.

⊙ **Rays And Hail 1978–1981** (1987; Virgin).
The best possible introduction: a compilation put together with Devoto's input and featuring the best tracks from the LPs.

⊙ **Magazine (Maybe It's Right To Be Nervous Now): Boxset** (2000; Virgin).
If you are feeling a little more adventurous, try this 3CD set of choice cuts, alternative mixes and Peel Sessions.

Jonathan Wright

MAGMA

Formed near Paris, France, 1969; disbanded 1983; occasionally re-formed.

"For me, music is everything ... But I could work on a theme for fifteen years before I find the exact expression." Christian Vander

Though often dismissed as the pinnacle of prog-rock pretensions, **Magma** have transcended other groups of the genre through the sheer strength and weirdness of the musical vision of its founder, drummer and vocalist **Christian Vander**. The son of a jazz pianist, Vander obtained his first set of drums through the dubious offices of Chet Baker and, modelling his style on that of Elvin Jones from the classic John Coltrane quartet, set about playing with a variety of R&B and jazz combos. It was then that he conceived the musical and philosophical project that has since underpinned his career: a spiritual-ecological vision of the destiny of the planet, to be performed in **Kobaïan**, his own invented musical and lyrical language.

To realize this concept, Vander set up what was in effect a jazz-rock commune just outside Paris, where he persuaded a collection of talented musicians to join him. His recruits – then, and over the years – have included the vocalist **Klaus Blasquiz**, the fusion maestro bassists **Francis Moze** and **Jannick Top**, and his wife **Stella**. Blasquiz's exquisitely modulated screeches provided the outstanding characteristic of the early Magma sound, as he helped to develop and shape the Kobaïan language into a working compositional device.

After eight months of intensive rehearsals, the outfit released the debut MAGMA album (1970). A double LP, it described the flight of mankind from a degenerated planet, its arrival on the Edenic Kobaïa, and subsequent conflicts with the corrupt earthmen and their descendants leading to eventual reconciliation with the deity, Ptäh, and the achievement of cosmic harmony.

The story continued on 1001° CENTIGRADE (1971), and MEKANÏK DESTRUCTÏW KOMMANDOH (1973). The latter, led by Jannick Top's bass, has remained a pivotal part of Magma's repertoire, its original menace becoming more enchanting over the years as its melodic qualities have been brought out through the complex texture of its vocal arrangement.

The group had some success in Britain and the US, where they toured in the early 70s, but Vander was unable to retain the communal ideals of the group, partly through lack of financial reward. Magma thus retreated from the wider public gaze, and from the mid-70s operated almost exclusively in France. There, Vander has seen his influence spread among a vast network of bands formed by ex-Magma members – there have been 28 line-ups over the years – including, notably, **Art Zoyd** and **Univers Zero**, though Magma offshoots have appeared in places as far-flung as Sweden (Ensemble Nimbus) and Japan (Happy Family and Ruins).

From 1983 to the present, Vander himself worked mainly with an acoustic version of the band, **Offering**, in which he forsook much of the mystical trappings of the 1970s for a more direct expression of his love for Coltrane. However, a recent project, **Les Voix De Magma**, is aimed at regenerating the early works with renewed emphasis on their vocal quality. They made a rare and treasured appearance in London in 1988, somewhat bizarrely at the instigation of British snooker player and long-term Magma-head, Steve 'Interesting' Davis.

⊙ **Live** (1975; Seventh Records).
This double CD from Seventh Records of France (who have rereleased Magma's entire back catalogue) is the best introduction for the uninitiated, having clearer sound and more material than the version more commonly available on Decal/Charly.

Robert Murray

THE MAGNETIC FIELDS

Formed Boston, Massachusetts, 1990.

Stephin Merritt, kingpin of **The Magnetic Fields**, once described his music as 'bubblegum and experimental music, and nothing in between'. That, combined with his avowed love for Abba and the fact that critics have compared his music to that of Joy Division and Gary Numan, might send less electro-pop-orientated rock fans running for cover – which would be a shame; Merritt boasts shrewd pop-rock instincts that are more in line with Brian Wilson and Phil Spector than any of the aforementioned influences.

The Magnetic Fields are not merely a front for Merritt. They are an actual band that has occasionally played live: **Sam Davol** (cello/flute) and **Claudia Gonson** (percussion) have been in the rotating cast all along, and **Susan Amway** took lead vocals on their first two albums. It's Merritt, though, who is the auteur, writing the songs, playing many of the instruments, crafting the imaginative arrangements as producer, and (of late) singing too. Their five albums (as well as Merritt's side-project, **The 6ths**) have presented indie synth-pop with a human face, achieving as much bittersweet warmth, symphonic grandeur and diversity as the form can allow.

Merritt developed his do-it-yourself studio ethic and technological expertise early, starting to record on a four-track in 1978, around the time he was entering his teenage years. The world didn't get to hear any of his music, however, until the first Magnetic Fields album, DISTANT PLASTIC TREES, originally released in 1990 in the UK only.

At this point Susan Amway's pristine, cool vocals piloted Merritt's odd combination of uplifting, soothing melodies and enigmatic, almost free-associative lyrics of romantic longing and loneliness. He was already sculpting complex synth-pop, squeezing an unusual variety of nuances and buzzes out of his Casios. Through the years the group has also tinkered with all manner of percussion effects, an arsenal that would eventually include a Slinky toy, a plastic bell, a sheet of aluminium, and other unexpected devices.

The influence of vintage symphonic pop-rock like Phil Spector/The Ronettes' "Be My Baby" was immediately evident on the follow-up, THE WAYWARD BUS. The production had more shimmer and depth, as well as Merritt's most gorgeous melodies, attaining an effective balance between natural and synthetic instruments.

Thereafter Merritt opted to sing his own material, to mixed effect. His dark and tremulous delivery is more in keeping with the private, brooding tenor of his compositions than that of Amway's, but her glistening purity gave the material a much-needed counterpoint. On HOLIDAY and the more narrative, less engaging THE CHARM OF THE HIGHWAY STRIP, Merritt's deep tones recalled the classic British electro-pop vocals of (for example) David Bowie and Ian Curtis.

The arrangements of these were also in a more burbling synthetic mould than the group's earlier outings, though care was taken to vary these in imaginative ways. Those who are wary of synth-pop that leans toward hollow, icy textures might want to approach

The Magnetic Fields' latest effort, GET LOST, with caution, as it's the most electronically minded of their releases to date. That doesn't mean that it's totally unapproachable for those not steeped in Kraftwerk and the Pet Shop Boys. Merritt's insinuating pop melodies, ingenious arrangements and humane lyrics are still out in force. And when he slows down the rhythms and mutes the gizmos for a bit (as on "Don't Look Away"), he projects a fetching melancholy that's not dissimilar to vintage Scott Walker.

Considering that Merritt views himself primarily as a producer/arranger/songwriter rather than a singer, it may make sense for him to pursue more projects like The 6ths' WASPS' NEST album (1995). Merritt wrote, produced and arranged everything on this alternative-rock tribal gathering, but sang only one of the tracks himself, employing a different guest vocalist (including **Barbara Manning**, **Lou Barlow**, and members of Air Miami, **Superchunk**, **Yo La Tengo**, **Luna**, the **Bats**, and **Helium**) for each of the others. This unusual project yielded unusually successful results, with Merritt's glowing, imaginative arrangements and catchy pop melodies as strong as ever.

1999's triple-CD set 69 LOVE SONGS was the biggest achievement of Merritt's career – not just in its conception, but in its execution too. To have created so many carefully tooled love songs is admirable enough, that those same songs run the gamut of the emotion from the bittersweet to the celebratory is remarkable. Most artists struggle to produce one album's worth of decent material yet Merritt runs to three, taking in an obsessive number of pop references, all orbiting central influences like Scott Walker, Leonard Cohen and Brian Wilson.

⊙ **The Wayward Bus/Distant Plastic Trees** (1995; Merge).
The two 90s albums recorded with Susan Amway as vocalist, thoughtfully combined onto one CD. THE WAYWARD BUS is considerably more developed and pungent, but both are worth hearing.

⊙ **Holiday** (1994; Feel Good All Over).
It's really a matter of taste as to which of the Magnetic Fields albums with Merritt on vocals is the best. HOLIDAY is the most listener-friendly of these, though listeners with a yen for heavier electro-pop textures might prefer to try GET LOST.

⊙ **69 Love Songs** (1999; Circus).
Expansive and beautiful, there's hardly any filler in over three hours of music. This is a panoramic sweep through fifty years of pop culture and love, love, love.

Richie Unterberger

MAIN

Formed Croydon, England, 1991.

"With Main, the physical side has been totally eradicated." Robert Hampson

Robert Hampson and **Scott Dawson** formed **Main** from the ashes of **LOOP**, and in a series of extended EPs and mini-albums explored the traces

left by sound as it recedes into nothing. "Suspension", from their debut EP HYDRA (1991), is typical, beginning with a crashing chord before fading over nine minutes with a series of noises that sound like guitars dying. Main have been described as ambient, but there is little to link them with other bands grouped in that category. Lacking orthodox dynamics, their music is highly uneasy listening – not intended for spliffed-out consumption.

The concurrent release in 1993 of the DRY STONE FEED mini-album and the FIRMAMENT EP displayed contrasting yet complementary sides of the Main sound. The former was not a million miles from Loop and in places it sort of rocked in a roundabout way. FIRMAMENT, on the other hand, followed a path into the deepest troughs of abstraction which, unlike the meanderings of most ambient groups, was a daunting voyage rather than an escapist retreat. With only the vaguest hint of rhythm, it seemed to track the traces of a rock band that barely existed.

MOTION POOL (1994) served as a useful digest of the band's concerns, but the real move into darkness came with FIRMAMENT II (also 1994). Consisting of just two 25-minute pieces, it sounded as if it wasn't created by humans and wasn't intended to be heard by them. Fascinating but deeply alienating, this music appeared almost to consume itself into a state of extinction.

The most approachable of their recent recordings remain LIGATURE (1994), a mini-album of remixes released between MOTION POOL and FIRMAMENT II, and HYDRA-CALM (1995), another hybrid of two earlier EPs. The presence of other hands – drafted in from the fields of improvisation and modern composition rather than rock, dance or ambient – opened the sound out and made it more inhabitable.

Through 1994 and 1995, the band were also working on a series of ambient works entitled Hz: six mini-albums, which were collected and boxed, alongside an equally abstract booklet, in 1996. Heard together, they were quite a revelation, each demonstrating a different facet of the band's work.

Inevitably, Main were something of a minority interest, and only a loyal few waited with anticipation for FIRMAMENT III (1996), DELIQUESCENCE (1997) and FIRMAMENT IV (1998). Scott jumped ship in 1996 leaving Hampson to work alone; with no collaborators or a band to take on tour, Hampson turned DJ with the **Main Active Sound System**, cutting remixes and vinyl oddities into glacial layers of sound. Since then, little has been heard of either Main or Hampson.

⊙ **Firmament** (1994; Beggars Banquet).
Drones, ghosts of rhythms, vague murmurings. Cryogenic rather than chilled out.

⊙ **Motion Pool** (1994; Beggars Banquet).
More variety here than on FIRMAMENT, which makes it easier but less intense.

⊙ **Ligature** (1994; Beggars Banquet).
It's great to hear the strange configurations which can be formed from Main's rough-hewn sounds. Mixers are Paul Schütze, Jim O'Rourke and Paul Kendall, plus Main themselves.

◉ **Firmament II** (1994; Beggars Banquet).
Infuriating, depending on mood, this takes music out to a remote crossroads where rock, sound sculpture and improvisation meet.

Ben Smith

THE MAMAS & THE PAPAS

Formed St Thomas, Virgin Islands, 1964.

Easy-listening architects of the summer of love, **The Mamas & The Papas** were as central to the 60s soundtrack as Jimi Hendrix or Janis Joplin, overlaying first-class contemporary pop songwriting with enchanting, prismatic folk-rock harmonies. Yet, despite their more demure sound and image, this was a band volatile enough to rival either of those celebrated peers.

The group evolved after **John Phillips** had recorded three albums with the **Journeymen**. Based in the Virgin Islands, in 1965 he teamed up with new wife **Michelle Gilliam**, and **Denny Doherty**, formerly a member of the Halifax Three and the Mugwumps. The trio worked to fulfil contractual obligations, before recruiting former Big Three singer **'Mama' Cass Elliot** (also a former Mugwump). After a handful of concerts in St Thomas, the quartet relocated to California.

Introduced to Dunhill Records' owner Lou Adler by Barry McGuire (of "Eve Of Destruction" fame), they worked initially as backing singers on his THIS PRECIOUS TIME (1965). That album included the first recording of John Phillips' enduring composition "California Dreamin'", which became The Mamas & The Papas' debut 45 in December (it was chosen ahead of projected debut "Go Where You Wanna Go" by Adler). Inspired by Michelle Gilliam's homesickness, it subsequently broke the US Top 5. That paved the way for their chart-topping second effort, "Monday Monday", another Phillips original. An accompanying debut album, IF YOU CAN BELIEVE YOUR EYES AND EARS (UK title: THE MAMAS AND THE PAPAS), also hit the top, eventually spending over a hundred weeks in the chart.

In July 1966 "I Saw Her Again" became their third consecutive US Top 5 hit. But there was trouble in the ranks. "I Saw Her Again" was, allegedly, inspired by Michelle's affair with Doherty. She was also dating Gene Clark of The Byrds around this time, seemingly in a single-handed attempt to justify the era's reputation for living and loving freely. Unsurprisingly, Gilliam and Phillips split, resulting in **Jill Gibson** (girlfriend of Jan Berry of Jan &Dean) replacing her for a month. It was the first sign of the group's instability, in contrast with their homely-hippie image. With the married pair reconciled, Gibson was ousted in time for the group's appearance at New York's Carnegie Hall and their fourth single, "Look Through My Window", which stalled at #24. Second album THE MAMAS AND THE PAPAS (UK title: CASS, JOHN, MICHELLE AND DENNY) fared marginally better.

Cass Elliot enjoyed her first real moment in the spotlight on "Words Of Love", another million-seller, released in January 1967. A third album, THE MAMAS AND THE PAPAS DELIVER, featured their affecting revival of The Shirelles "Dedicated To The One I Love", which reached #2. Shortly afterwards, Elliot gave birth to daughter Owen Vanessa. "Creeque Alley", documenting the group's history on song, provided further success in the singles chart.

In June 1967 came the group's engagement at the Monterey pop festival, immortalized in D. A. Pennebaker's movie, *Monterey Pop*. It was the last time the original quartet would perform together on stage. Phillips, meanwhile, was building a reputation for songwriting outside of the group – penning ex-Journeyman **Scott McKenzie**'s hippie anthem, "San Francisco (Be Sure To Wear Some Flowers In Your Hair)". McKenzie later joined a 90s touring version of the band.

1968 brought a second group birth – Phillips and Gilliam's daughter Chynna – who, alongside Brian Wilson's offspring, would later become one third of Wilson Phillips. Yet all was not well in the camp. The new mother received a letter from the other members of the band in June informing her that her services were no longer required. The group's own dissolution followed rapidly after the release of ...PRESENTING THE PAPAS AND THE MAMAS (1968). Messy contractual differences with Dunhill ensued, as Mama Cass made an immediate impact with her live recording of "Dream A Little Dream Of Me". Booked to play a six-week season at Caesar's Palace in Las Vegas, she was forced to cancel due to a throat haemorrhage and resulting operation. Her debut solo album, DREAM A LITTLE DREAM, foundered as a result, as did a subsequent batch of 1969 releases.

Phillips, meanwhile, scored some solo success in 1970 when "Mississippi" accompanied his debut album, JOHN PHILLIPS (JOHN THE WOLFKING OF L.A.). By October his divorce with Gilliam had come through. She leaped from the frying pan into the fire by opting for eight days of wedded bliss with actor Dennis Hopper. Doherty made his solo bow in 1981 with the flop, WATCHA GONNA DO? With Elliot's commercial fortunes also fading, The Mamas & The Papas reunited in November 1971 for PEOPLE LIKE US. Panned by the critics, they split again shortly after its release. There was simply no appetite for the group any more, and the nostalgia cycle had yet to turn in their favour. Even worse news was around the corner. On July 29, 1974, Elliot was staying at singer Harry Nilsson's flat when she suffered a fatal heart attack after choking on her food.

Of the remaining members of the band, Michelle Gilliam, under her original married name, Phillips, enjoyed the most colourful career acting in several films (including Ken Russell's *Valentino* and a clutch of Dennis Hopper-directed efforts) and becoming a regular character in TV soap *Knot's Landing*. There was some patchy solo output and she was sentenced to a five-year jail term for possession of cocaine (most of the sentence eventually suspended). Her 1986 autobiography, *California Dreamin'*, makes for a good read.

By 1982 Phillips and Doherty had reformed a touring version of The Mamas & The Papas, with new female vocalists **Spanky McFarlane** (ex-Spanky & Our Gang) and Phillips' daughter **MacKenzie** (of *American Graffiti* fame). A non-recording venture, they have worked on and off ever since, with varying line-ups since Doherty departed to pursue a film career (the 1998 line-up featured no participating original members). John Phillips, meanwhile, enjoyed one further notable chart success, when he co-wrote The Beach Boys' 1988 #1, "Kokomo". He'd also worked (abortively) with **Mick Jagger** and **Keith Richards**, and helped score *The Man Who Fell To Earth*.

⊙ **If You Can Believe Your Eyes And Ears aka The Mamas And The Papas** (1966; Dunhill/RCA).
The debut album features the two Phillips originals, which established the group at the forefront of the Summer of Love – "California Dreamin'" and "Monday Monday". There's also a winning interpretation of "The In Crowd". The best place to sample the group's delicious four-part harmonies.

⊙ **The Mamas And The Papas aka Cass, John, Michelle And Denny** (1967; Dunhill/RCA).
A solid follow-up, with further excellent songwriting from John Phillips in the shape of "Trip, Stumble And Fall" and "I Saw Her Again".

⊙ **Deliver** (1967; RCA/Dunhill).
The third of a trilogy of essential studio collections – "Look Through My Window" and "Creeque Alley" have both aged well.

⊙ **Farewell To The First Golden Era** (1967; Dunhill).
The group's last gold album during their life span – a workmanlike overview that has been supplanted by more recent, comprehensive compilation packages.

⊙ **Presenting The Papas And The Mamas** (1968; RCA/Dunhill).
Though you would hardly know from listening, the band was tearing itself apart during recording, and the songs lack the punch of their previous studio work. And "Meditation Mama (Transcendental Woman Travels)" is as bad as its title suggests.

⊙ **People Like Us** (1971; Dunhill).
The 'comeback' album. Though not as bad as some critics suggest, the songwriting pales in comparison to their first brace of studio albums. The single, "Step Out", is a slight exception.

⊙ **Creeque Alley: The History Of The Mamas & Papas** (1991; Probe/Dunhill).
An expansive compilation that contains everything you need by the band, including previously unreleased archive material (not all of it very good).

Alex Ogg

MAN

Formed Merthyr Tydfil, Wales, 1968; disbanded 1977; re-formed 1992.

Over the years **Man** have been through fourteen different line-ups and recorded thirteen albums. The one member to survive all of the various incarnations is guitarist and vocalist **Micky Jones**.

The band surfaced on the Pye label in 1969, with the albums REVELATION and TWO OUNCES OF PLASTIC WITH A HOLE IN THE MIDDLE, attracting attention in Britain mainly because they were just about the first Welsh band on the rock circuit. Along with Micky Jones, this original Man included **Deke Leonard** (guitar/vocals), enlisted from the 'other' Welsh band around, **The Dream**. He was shortly followed by fellow Dreamers **Martin Ace** (bass) and **Terry Williams** (drums), and the quartet that produced two solid, if unspectacular, albums – MAN (1970) and DO YOU LIKE IT HERE NOW, ARE YOU SETTLING IN? (1971) – and began acquiring a devoted live following.

The band was certainly at its best on stage, improvising with a growing flair, as was demonstrated in LIVE AT THE PADGET ROOMS (1972), their debut for United Artists, a company that was prepared to put some money behind them. Their line-up, however, remained in a state of flux, as Leonard and Ace left to pursue solo projects, and were replaced by **Phil Ryan** (keyboards/vocals) and **Will Youatt** (bass).

This group, along with Williams, Jones and another Man origina, **Clive John** (keyboards/guitar/vocals), went to Dave Edmunds' Rockfield Studios and came back with their first truly excellent record. BE GOOD TO YOURSELF AT LEAST ONCE A DAY (1972) re-created the band's live appeal, roaming through four extended tracks with evident influence from West Coast bands like Love and Quicksilver Messenger Service. There were great vocal harmonies, subtle changes of pace, and guitar solos – lots of them. While the music was heavily guitar-based, the keyboards brought an important element of contrast and Williams' excellent drumming drove the band on.

By the time of their next recording, a double called BACK INTO THE FUTURE (1973), Clive John had bailed out again. The first disc featured the remaining four, while the second was a live set from London's Roundhouse, with **Tweke Lewis** on guitar – plus the Gwalia Male Voice Choir on "C'mon". Choirs and orchestras were an aberration of the mid-70s in Britain. It was the band's first UK chart album, and reached their all-time peak at #23.

After another round of touring, Ryan, Youatt and Lewis were replaced by **Malcolm Morley** (keyboards) and **Ken Whaley** (bass) and a returning Deke Leonard for RHINOS, WINOS AND LUNATICS (1974). Leonard's harsher vocal and guitar sound made an excellent contrast to Jones's style, and the album was probably the best of their studio work, reaching #24 in the UK charts. Almost as good was the follow-up, SLOW MOTION (1974), made by the same line-up, less Morley, though it sold less well.

Soon after its release, the band met one of their all-time heroes, Quicksilver Messenger Service's legendary guitarist **John Cippolina**, who showed up at a rehearsal one day when they were in the States, and asked to sit in. The band refused to believe it was the great man himself until he had played half of QSM's repertoire. He later joined them on tour – including a London Roundhouse set released as MAXIMUM DARKNESS (1975), though rumour has it that Cippolina's guitar was so badly out of tune that Micky Jones overdubbed it for the album.

After a fine studio album, THE WELSH CONNECTION (1976), which failed to chart, and a farewell live set, ALL'S WELL THAT ENDS WELL (1977), Man called it a day. Terry Williams went on to drum with Dave Edmunds' Rockpile, **NICK LOWE** and **DIRE STRAITS**. Leonard and Micky Jones fronted their own bands for a while, then 'retired'.

It couldn't last, of course. In the 90s, Leonard and Jones were gigging again, reassembled the band as Man, with Martin Ace and a new drummer – line-up number fourteen – and put out THE TWANG DYNASTY. Finding they were still popular in Germany, they got themselves a fresh record deal with Hamburg label, Hypertension Music. The fruits of this, recorded in Seattle but sounding like they'd never been away, were released as CALL DOWN THE MOON (1996). But in the same year disaster struck: Deke suffered a stroke, and was forced to keep a low profile while he recovered.

In the meantime there was an unexpected treat for fans of the Welsh west-coast music scene when in 1997 Point Records in the UK started to make a whole swath of old or previously difficult-to-obtain material available once more. The infamously awfully titled bootleg BRAZILIAN CUCUMBER MEETS DEKE'S NEW NOSE reappeared, thankfully retitled as LIVE IN LONDON. In the same series, amongst others, came CHRISTMAS AT THE PATTI, THE OFFICIAL BOOTLEG, TO LIVE FOR – TO DIE FOR (the first Man bootleg from 1970, atrocious quality with most of the vocals missing, but still...), FRIDAY 13TH (live at London's Marquee club in 1983), THE GREASY TRUCKERS PARTY (previously only available on double vinyl, this set – a United Artists' showcase from 1972 – also features a couple of Hawkwind and Brinsley Schwarz tracks) and RARE MAN (a collection of rare single sides and studio finds), together with reissues of studio albums ALL'S WELL THAT ENDS WELL, THE WELSH CONNECTION, MAN (from 1970) and DO YOU LIKE IT HERE NOW, ARE YOU SETTLING IN?. All told, a vast catalogue of spiralling, magical, trippy guitar solos and floaty psychedelic lyrics to hold and cherish forever.

After several attempts to get back into the studio, hindered by family commitments and touring, the group released ENDANGERED SPECIES (2000) and then UNDRUGGED (2002), though fans were divided by the collections' sound. The group are to this day still together and gigging.

○ **Be Good To Yourself At Least Once A Day** (1972; Beat Goes On).
Included here are studio versions of three songs that were to become stage favourites. "C'mon" sees the band at their most spaced out; "Life On The Road" is a trucking boogie, while "Bananas" features the immortal lyric, 'I like bananas 'cause they've got no bones/I like marijuana 'cause it gets me stoned'.

○ **Maximum Darkness** (1975; Beat Goes On).
The album that captures best their live presence, as the band run through some of their best material, finishing with a blistering version of "Bananas".

Simon Ives

MAN... OR ASTRO-MAN?

Formed 21st century; time travelled to Earth 1992.

Trying to list the details of the Astro career goes against the Astro philosophy. This is an act from another reality – quite literally, they would have us believe. In terms of their approach to the outside world, the band are closer to The Residents than any other act in this guide. In sonic terms, their psychotic-surf blast uproots the ram-raiding style of Dick Dale and transplants it into a surreal world of samples and sci-fi references.

The recording Astro crew currently line up as **Star Crunch** (guitar), **Birdstuff** (drums) and **Coco The Electric Monkey Wizard** (samples/special effects). **Dexter X** (bass/guitar) helps out on stage. Coco's birth certificate probably disagrees but Astro lore claims him as a cybernetic life form with portions of an Atari 2600 in his brain. Coco takes the blame for their current residence in Alabama because it was his antimatter conversion bladder which malfunctioned, causing the destruction of the Astro ship. This ship was the band's intended means of transport back to the 21st century – a period in which they claim they have already sold a billion records. These 21st-century records are evidently so incredibly advanced that the Astro crew came back to the present century to record a sound bridge to help mankind cope with the revolutionary sounds and instruments they would encounter. You get the picture.

Like The Residents, **Man... Or Astro-Man?** have set up an alternative reality in which to mangle a section of popular music for their own ends. Most sounds and compositions are originals, although the occasional hint of external inspiration is seen in the odd familiar riff or occasional cover version, such as their all-out, surfed-up mangling of The Rezillos "Destination Venus".

A trawl through the facts shows a series of recordings starting with the single "Possession By Remote Control" in 1993 and including more than half a dozen albums. The best of these are the short, in-your-face YOUR WEIGHT ON THE MOON and the longer, more convoluted MADE FROM TECHNETIUM (1997), which adds some off-the-wall lyrics and plays games with production, while sustaining a series of changing moods remarkably well, considering the collection is built on a completely exaggerated approach to surf guitar. Then again you may prefer A SPECTRUM OF INFINITE SCALE (2000), a sublime and esoteric manifesto for the new millennium.

The band are strong live performers and, whilst their hard-core following remains small, they have the power to win over the most resistant audience. Probably best encountered by accident, the band can even liven up a jaded mid-afternoon British summer rock festival crowd, and their regular appearances on John Peel's BBC radio show always stand out from the competition by virtue of sheer, full-on, passionate weirdness.

With their instant surf attack, lunatic simple riffs and breakneck pace, Man... Or Astro-Man? are infectious. Their failure to sell a billion in the twentieth century as they will (have?) in the 21st lies both in the limits and cultishness of the surf style, and in the recent fragmentation of the music world into self-contained micro-genres with little common ground. Many who value them as an alternative to self-important festival headliners or sour-faced kings of pretension fail to make that vital trip to the record store and so they remain a typical cult act, many people preferring the band as concept to the band as music-makers.

Despite its near-invisibility in terms of radio and press coverage, surf guitar has been around for decades and the occasional bubbling to the surface of mutant forms such as Psychobilly has shown its continued appeal. Though big names like Dick Dale and Link Wray get all the credit, they also obscure the generations of breakneck twangers who have sweated it out for the benefit of the faithful in tiny, sweat-drenched venues all over the world. Astro-Man's genius has been the conscious addition of intelligent and comic elements to the basic formula.

Why Man... Or Astro-Man? The question mark at the end of the name is directed at the audience. Although the phrase was lifted from a film, it now works as a challenge, rather like the hook on the classic Devo song, "Are We Not Men?" If you're merely a Man you may pick holes in the whole concept and ask why a futuristic sound bridge should rely on the retro style of surf guitar or what will happen to the billion record sales of the future if the Astro crew fail to build the said sound bridge, but that's wilfully missing the point. Astro-Men don't question such things.

Whatever, the current state of operations has seen a recent cloning operation which resulted in various versions – Alpha, Beta and Gamma line-ups – treading the boards. They may have been cloned from the originals but one line-up looked curiously female! What was once a band is starting to look like a movement.

● **Experiment Zero** (1996; One Louder).
Pushing the surf envelope still further, by turns this is totally weird and wonderfully inspired.

● **Made From Technetium** (1997; One Louder).
About as coherent as collections of lunatic surf guitar can get. Samples, introspection and humour, 21st-century cosmic prog-surf, anyone?

Neil Nixon

THE MANIC STREET PREACHERS

Formed Blackwood, Wales, 1986.

"Our songs are about cultural alienation, boredom and despair."
Richey Edwards

The **Manic Street Preachers** were first and foremost a gang, who in 1986 were inspired to form a band by the tenth anniversary of the Sex Pistols. It took another two years for **James Dean Bradfield** (vocals/guitar), **Nicky Wire** (bass), **Sean Moore** (drums) and a certain **Flicker** (rhythm guitar) to start putting their ideas into practice. At the end of 1989, shortly after the release of a self-financed raging single, "Suicide Alley", Flicker was replaced by original gang member and schoolfriend **Richey James Edwards**.

The NEW ART RIOT EP (1990) was a second self-financed slab of retro-punk, which led to plenty of media coverage, even if much of it was disparaging. The Manics themselves, spraying 'I am a slut' on their blouses, sporting make-up and spouting situationist slogans, resembled a head-on collision between The New York Dolls and George Orwell. Heavenly Records released the next two singles – "Motown Junk" and "You Love Us" (both 1991) – the latter of which was a two-fingered salute to a music press that failed to see the band as anything more than cartoon punk.

In May 1991 Richey and journalist Steve Lamacq were heatedly discussing the 'authenticity' of the band when Richey decided to make his point by calmly carving the words '4 REAL' across his forearm with a razor blade. Widely regarded as a publicity stunt at the time, the incident has since been reappraised as an alarming early sign of his deteriorating condition.

After signing to the Sony label, "Stay Beautiful" became the Manics' first Top 40 single in July 1991, followed in early 1992 by a reissued version of "You Love Us", which cracked the Top 20. From here on, they began to attract a devoted, even obsessional fan base, while insisting that their debut LP would be their last – there would be no opportunity to sell out. In the event GENERATION TERRORISTS (February 1992; reissued 1999) was not followed by a split. After a rash of singles – including a cover of "Suicide Is Painless", which hit the Top 10 in September 1992, as they embarked on a US tour – a second LP, GOLD AGAINST THE SOUL (1993), revealed a more polished, anthemic sound. The anger remained, however, as did the 'them and us' stance, with motormouth Nicky berating everyone from New Age travellers to R.E.M.'s Michael Stipe.

A downward spiral for the Manics began in December 1993 with the death from cancer of their co-manager, publicist and close friend, Philip Hall. Richey's predilection for self-mutilation was getting out of control as well: at one gig in Thailand, he appeared on stage with his chest slashed by knives given to him by a fan. Back home, alcoholic and anorexic, he reached a dangerous level of depression, and spent several weeks recovering at a private clinic. The remaining Manics played several high-profile live performances as best they could.

Richey's situation was imprinted on the lyrics of the band's bleak but beautiful third album, THE HOLY BIBLE (1994). The songs were compact and poppy, but with blistering lyrics that explored man's

cruelty, both global and domestic. The album was critically acclaimed, and in October Richey rejoined the band for some European dates. He spoke candidly of his illness and insisted that suicide had never entered his head. However, on February 1, 1995, the eve of an American tour, he checked out of his London hotel, and has not been seen since. His abandoned car was found two weeks later at the Severn Bridge, near the English–Welsh border. The police searched for a while, but, despite some apparent sightings, eventually called off the hunt.

Although the three remaining members initially stated that they could not continue the band without Richey, they finally got back together to record EVERYTHING MUST GO (1996), which turned out to be their most rounded and sophisticated release yet, complete with quasi-Phil Spector productions and string arrangements. Both came together on "A Design For Life", which preceded the album's release as their biggest hit, peaking at #2 in the UK. A quotation from Jackson Pollock on the sleeve summed up the album's stoic optimism: 'The pictures I contemplate painting would constitute a halfway state and an attempt to point out the direction of the future – without arriving there completely.'

Such optimism was realized in the 1997 *Brit Awards* where the Manics won both *Best Group* and *Best Album*. Now almost part of the rock 'establishment', they quickly retreated to work on their next album. "If You Tolerate This Your Children Will Be Next", possibly one of the longest-titled singles in rock history, was released in August 1998. It was an elegant, understated account of Welsh volunteers in the Spanish Civil War that went straight to the top of the charts.

Wales, its history and its people dominated THIS IS MY TRUTH TELL ME YOURS (1998). The first album without any input from Richey, it was Nicky Wire as sole lyricist who shaped its very psyche. A work of subtle passion and measured introspection, it still contained The Manics' anthemic quality but with a more refined tone. A BBC documentary on the band was broadcast on TV in September 1998, featuring frank interviews with each member: it was a compelling journey through the band's history so far.

The Manics' entry into the rock hierarchy was complete when they won *Best Act in the World Today* at the Q Awards in November 1998, an event that brought a slightly embarrassed Nicky Wire face to face with a previously berated but forgiving Michael Stipe. No champagne was spilt. Like so many rebels, The Manics appear to have become part of what they previously raged against. Yet, despite their success, they are still angry and awkward enough to retain some of the spirit of the gang they once were.

Launched with a gig in Cuba, marked not only by the attendance of Fidel Castro but also with their first ever encore, KNOW YOUR ENEMY (2001) tried hard to kick against the Manics' establishment status, but with tracks like "So Why So Sad" and "Ocean Spray" they still had a careful ear on the mainstream. Despite the occasional embarrassing sixth-form lyric it harked back reasonably successfully to former glories – "Dead Martyrs" and "Found That Soul" in particular were stinging reproofs to those who underestimated their continuing ability to thrill. A 'best of', FOREVER DELAYED, cemented the group's status in 2002.

⦿ **Generation Terrorists** (1992; Sony; reissued 1999).
A spirited clutch of punk anthems raging against everything from Queen and country to high-street banks. The music may be 'sixth-form' – and Richey is rumoured not to have played a note – but there's an enduring fascination in the confrontational cut-and-paste lyrical style.

⦿ **The Holy Bible** (1994; Sony).
A work of relentless horror with strangely hummable tunes. Sharp, short and savage, as epitomized on "4st 7lb", an examination of anorexia.

⦿ **Everything Must Go** (1996; Sony).
Remarkably, this is their most consistent album to date, with highlights ranging from the hit "A Design For Life" to the seemingly gentle "Small Black Flowers That Grow In The Sky", one of five contributions from Richey.

⦿ **This Is My Truth Tell Me Yours** (1998; Sony).
From the words of Aneurin Bevan that gave the album its title, to the poem of R. S. Thomas that adorns the sleeve, this is a record set deep within the band's political and cultural identity. It is a work of gentle beauty and is at times intensely personal from the hearth-and-home subject matter of "My Little Empire" to the reflection on the band's career in "The Everlasting".

⦿ **Know Your Enemy** (2001; Epic).
This collection finds these contrary little socialist muffins back on savage form, with terse guitar lines and wayward sloganeering pushed to the fore. "Let Robeson Sing' salutes the communist singer, while "Miss Europa Disco Dancer" is a sardonic, Ian Dury-ish slice of funk.

Maxine McCaghy

AIMEE MANN

Born Boston, Massachusetts, 1960.

Aimee Mann arrived as a singer and writer of instantly engaging pop songs when her debut album WHATEVER was released to glowing critical approval in 1993. She came packaged with some familiar points of reference: the vocal delivery sounded like an introspective Chrissie Hynde, the ballads were like Suzanne Vega in Doc Martens, guest guitarist and ex-Byrd **Roger McGuinn** provided a direct link to the heyday of guitar pop, and Elvis Costello gave it his seal of approval.

She hadn't turned up out of the blue, however, having achieved commercial success as singer with Boston band **'Til Tuesday**. Their debut, VOICES CARRY (1985), was a big seller in the 'soft rock' record racks of mid-80s America. Two more albums followed as Aimee gradually took up the writing duties. By the time of the highly rated EVERYTHING'S DIFFERENT NOW (1989), Mann's distinctive way with a driving pop tune was central to the band's sound. But the band's fortunes declined and she became increasingly frustrated with a record company which she felt was out of touch with her aspirations. A three-year struggle to unravel contractual commitments ensued before she was free to launch a solo career.

The success of WHATEVER (1993) was down to the simple and direct guitar-based arrangements which gave the songs centre stage. Whether in the accusatory mood of "I Should've Known" and "Say Anything", or in the self-analysis of "4th of July", it was the personalized lyrics that gave the songs their edge. On "Stupid Thing" and "I Know There's A Word", she came close to the conversational style of her singing idol, Colin Blunstone from The Zombies.

No sooner had she generated an audience keen for more, than Mann's record company, Imago, went bust, leaving her to crawl from the contractual wreckage for a second time. Depressed by the delay in getting a new album out, she threatened to quit but was finally able to release I'M WITH STUPID on Geffen at the end of 1995. This proved to be a continuation of the assured style of her debut, with Jon Brion still present as producer and musical collaborator. If anything, the guitar arrangements were denser and the lyrics, which had hints of Costello's tricky wordplay, were more vitriolic, but the melodies were as compelling as ever on songs like "You Could Make A Killing" and "Ray", while the familiar harmonies of guests **Chris Difford** and **Glenn Tilbrook** from Squeeze drifted through the mix on "That's Just What You Are".

Mann's protracted legal wrangling with Geffen continued through 1999, but it obviously had little effect on her creativity. A walk-on appearance in the film *The Big Lebowski* as a German nihilist preceded a more prestigious cinematic involvement with director Paul Thomas Anderson. Her music played a key role in the narrative of *Magnolia*, Anderson's acclaimed follow-up to *Boogie Nights*, with the song "Save Me" – one of eight featured in the film – receiving a nomination for an Academy Award.

Finally in 2000, Mann wrested control of her third album, BACHELOR NO.2, from Geffen and was able to release it independently. Seen by many critics as her best work, it nevertheless met with disappointing sales. Unsurprisingly Mann's frustration with record companies emerged in tracks such as "Nothing Is Good Enough" and "Calling It Quits", although typically her lyrics were sophisticated enough to express far broader themes. LOST IN SPACE (2002) was just as good, with Mann seemingly back on top, and fighting.

While Mann has been criticized for being too narrowly focused with her writing, it is apparent that her goal has never been to push the frontiers of invention. Rather, her work is concerned above all with perfecting the modern pop song, a task she undertakes with a consistently uncompromising – though never unapproachable – stance.

⊙ **Whatever** (1993; Imago).
Superb solo debut with thirteen expertly crafted and beautifully realized songs. There's a total absence of histrionics or swagger – the songs don't need it.

⊙ **I'm With Stupid** (1995; Geffen).
The long-awaited follow-up has a darker tone, caustic lyrics and Bernard Butler's fuzzy guitar, but the tunes still flow. Labour MP Tony Banks is said to be an unlikely influence on "You're With Stupid Now".

⊙ **Magnolia Soundtrack** (2000; Reprise).
A beautiful collection dappled with orchestrated compositions and blessed by Mann's turmoilsom voice.

⊙ **Bachelor No. 2** (2000; Superego).
Freed from major label hell, Mann releases perhaps her most consistent work yet. Sharp, mature and focused.

Nick Dale

MANO NEGRA

Formed Paris, France, 1986; inactive since 1994; Manu Chao solo since 1995.

"I'm a thief: if I like something, I take it, then I go to market."
Manu Chao

Named after an Andalusian anarchist organization and strongly influenced by the rock-rebel iconography of The Clash, **Mano Negra** produce a blend of punk ethics and global musical styles that embodies the multicultural realities of modern France. They emerged from the ashes of rockabilly group **The Hot Pants**, and draw on the same reservoir of Parisian street musicians and indie types that gave rise to Les Negresses Vertes.

The group's core trio – vocalist **Manu Chao**, his brother **Tonio Chao** (trumpet) and cousin **Santiago Casiriego** (drums) – were of Spanish descent, while the remaining band members were a mixture of North Africans and Frenchmen recruited from the buskers of the Paris métro. Quickly earning a reputation as energetic live performers, Mano Negra mixed rock, rap, rai and flamenco to cook up a high-energy post-punk stew which they themselves dubbed 'Patchanka', a term derived from 'patchanga', a pejorative Spanish term for cheesy dance-hall music.

1988's independently released debut PATCHANKA

yielded a first French indie hit, "Mala Vida", and earned the band an international deal with Virgin. 1989's follow-up, PUTA'S FEVER (Dominican slang for VD caught from a prostitute) confirmed Mano Negra as France's principal alternative act and also launched the band abroad. Despite an enthusiastic press response and a spate of sell-out London shows, however, chart success in rock's Anglo-American heartlands remained elusive.

1991's KING OF BONGO bore a heavier rock sound and a higher proportion of titles sung in English, but this compromising of the group's roots was short-lived. They returned to the original concept of a travelling troupe of multicultural anarcho-punks, and in 1992 embarked on the 'Cargo Tour', a journey round the port cities of South America performing on a stage built into the ship's hold. Although subsidized by the French Ministry of Culture, Mano Negra were unlikely ambassadors, on one occasion trashing an Argentine TV studio when asked by a chat show host to explain precisely what 'anarchy' meant. To mark the 500th anniversary of Columbus's 'discovery' of America by debunking the myth of European cultural superiority, the group teamed up with performing arts group **Royal De Luxe** in an irreverent pageant of French history on the streets of Caracas, Rio de Janeiro and Buenos Aires.

Mano Negra were back in South America in 1993, this time travelling by rail from Colombia's Caribbean coast to the capital Bogotá, giving free concerts at stations along the way. Subsequently described by Santiago Casiriego as being 'more like Napoleon's retreat from Moscow than a rock'n'roll tour', the expedition was fraught with logistical problems, not least the need to negotiate with both the government and local guerrillas in order to ensure the train's safe passage.

The musical influences picked up on their Latin American tours were distilled onto 1994's CASA BABYLON, an energetic musical travelogue that moved effortlessly through salsa, mambo, merengue and ragga. Despite being the group's most accomplished and inventive album to date, CASA BABYLON sold only moderately well in continental Europe, and was never granted a UK or US release. This was largely due to the group's declining interest in conventional touring, and a growing disdain for the kind of promotional activities their record company expected of them.

Mano Negra remain a loose agglomeration of friends with no plans to record again. Manu Chao retired temporarily from the scene in 1995, devoting his time to solo work. CLANDESTINO (1999), his first outing under his own name, was the result of his spending the intervening four years wandering the world with a portable studio, attempting to capture the spirit of locations which inspired him. Stand-out tracks on this constantly surprising album include "Bongo Bong", an English-language lightweight reggae, the title track itself and the unstoppably danceable "Luna Y Sol". He followed up with two more cross-genre classics: PROXIMA ESTACION: ESPERANZA (2001) and RADIO BEMBA SOUND SYSTEM (2002).

⊙ **Puta's Fever** (1989; Virgin).
Applying punk aesthetics to a hochpotch of Mediterranean musical traditions, this album captures the band at their most joyfully energetic.

⊙ **Casa Babylon** (1994; Virgin).
Recorded in Buenos Aires and sung mostly in Spanish, this is a frenetic and occasionally deranged homage to the band's Latin roots.

Jonathan Bousfield

MANOWAR

Formed New York, 1980.

"Death to false metal!"

Man-mountains on a crusade to bring True Metal to the world – whether we want it or not – and the result of reading too many Conan the Barbarian comics, **Manowar** came into existence as the vision of one **Joey DeMaio** (bass). Legend has it that this one-time roadie for Black Sabbath found a like-minded soul in **Ross 'The Boss' Friedman** (guitar) backstage at Newcastle City Hall; DeMaio was working for Sabbath whilst Friedman was a member of support act Shakin' Street. Back in New York they recruited **Eric Adams** (vocals) and **Donnie Hamzik** (drums) into their heroic quest to expunge wimpy music from the face of the earth.

Theirs was the sound of testosterone and machismo run rampant, of leather, chains and instruments wielded as weapons: DeMaio famously possessed a bass guitar adorned with so many switches and controls it was affectionately dubbed 'The Enterprise'; the thunderous output from the bass amps, meanwhile, eventually earned the menacing title 'The Black Wind'. With former Kiss manager Bill Aucoin behind them, BATTLE HYMNS (1982) was their first skirmish with the forces of False Metal. The album is worth listening to if only to enjoy Orson Welles' ripe and dramatic voice-over for the track "Dark Avenger".

Having been dropped by their first label, and having brought in a new drummer in the formidable shape of **Scott Columbus**, they inked a new deal with Megaforce – using their own blood. INTO GLORY RIDE (1983) truly launched the era of furry loincloths, leather strides and bare chests. Were these guys for real? You bet. Ridiculously loud and proud of their uncompromising vision, the second stage of their campaign was truly under way. HAIL TO ENGLAND (1984) was immensely heavy and dedicated to the Army of the Immortals, those who had bothered to turn up for the first tour. A rapid follow-up, SIGN OF THE HAMMER (1984), spawned their major classic and succinct mission statement "All Men Play On Ten", the correct volume setting for True Metal.

The next album did not emerge for another three years, as the band toured solidly, headlining in Europe and performing as many support slots as possible in the States, not that easy because it was only the mighty **Motörhead** who weren't afraid of being blown away by them. FIGHTING THE WORLD (1987) was still as awesomely over-the-top as when the band first started, and the *Spectacle of Might* tour had the band go down in the *Guinness Book of World Records* as the loudest band ever, with their phenomenal 160-decibel show.

Unfortunately Friedman did the unthinkable and quit the band in 1988. Finding a replacement seemed like a genuinely Herculean task, but a mean hombre going under the moniker of **Death Dealer** (we kid you not) stepped into the breach. Dave Shankel, as he is known to his mum and dad, appeared on KINGS OF METAL (1988) – an album which also has DeMaio unleashing a blistering bass solo, clocking in at 208 bpm, called "Sting Of The Bumble Bee".

With the introduction of the rampaging **Rhino** on drums for TRIUMPH OF STEEL (1992), DeMaio and his sonic barbarians collectively presented their raised middle fingers to the grunge phenomenon. Of late the band have been somewhat selective about releasing the likes of LOUDER THAN HELL (1996), which emerged only in Germany, the gargantuan double-live helping of HELL ON WHEELS (1997) and WARRIORS OF THE WORLD (2002).

Beware all those who mock the warriors of True Metal; Manowar are far from finished with you. They shall return – the holy war against False Metal is a timeless and never-ending one ... or something like that.

- **Battle Hymns** (1982; Liberty).
  Stand aside you weak and feeble rabble; make way for the awesome majesty of Manowar, meat-eating, axe-wielding, womanizing saviours of metal.

- **Triumph Of Steel** (1992; Atlantic).
  The fight goes on. Words alone cannot convey the sheer metallic nature of this magnificently overblown, stupendously heavy, utterly focused album.

- **Warriors Of The World** (2002; Nuclear Blast).
  Epic-sounding and raw. This riffing monster snarls from its opener, "Call To Arms", until the speeding final sound of "Fight Until We Die".

Essi Berelian

MARILYN MANSON

Formed Fort Lauderdale, Florida, 1990.

"Love thy neighbour ... unless they deserve to be destroyed."

Few bands of recent years have been controversial by design: the notoriety so many groups crave as a means to shift lacklustre records often comes by accident. Not so with Mr Manson and his ghastly crew, where it is integral to the band's make-up.

Following a sickly childhood and an exclusive Christian education, the young **Brian Warner** shaved off his eyebrows, took all his frustrated rage and channelled it into the creation of **Marilyn Manson** (vocals), the self-styled 'God of Fuck'. Brian met future bass player **Twiggy Ramirez** at the local mall and they formed the fake Christian death-metal bands **Satan On Fire** and **Mrs. Scabtree**. After releasing a few singles but receiving limited airplay, the duo disbanded. Manson went to work on a newspaper covering the local music scene. A chance meeting with guitarist **Daisy Berkowitz** led Manson to form a new band, initially called **Marilyn Manson And The Spooky Kids**. The star-crossed serial-killer line-up was completed by **Madonna Wayne Gacy** (keyboards) and drummer **Sara Lee Lucas** – sadly, the magnificently named **Olivia Newton Bundy** (bass), **Gidget Gein** (also bass) and **Zsa Zsa Speck** (keyboards) got off the bus before the band hit the headlines.

The concept was simple: to see just how far America could be shaken to its conservative foundations by a band supposedly distilling and reflecting back all of the country's moral cancers. A key player in the band's ascendancy was **Trent Reznor** of Nine Inch Nails. Local recognition was almost immediate, with the band being nominated for *Best Heavy Alternative Band* and *Band Of The Year* at the South Florida rock awards, and winning the *Best Heavy Metal Band* award in *New Times* magazine. Releasing self-recorded tapes in small quantities, the band began to become increasingly more successful, and when Trent Reznor launched his own Nothing Records label he asked the band to be the first to sign. Reznor offered a support slot to Manson's fast-developing schlock-horror show and has been involved in producing and partly shaping each subsequent Manson release. The music itself owed a great deal to the likes of underground goth weirdos Alien Sex Fiend and industrial-noise pioneer Jim Thirlwell (aka Foetus), and first surfaced on PORTRAIT OF AN AMERICAN FAMILY (1994). By Manson's own admission, however, the writing and appearance of the band at this time were too cartoonish for the kind of outrage he was trying to provoke.

By the time the SMELLS LIKE CHILDREN (1995) mini-LP arrived as a stopgap production, America was finally waking up to Marilyn Manson's full gaudy horror. They scored an MTV hit with a cover of Eurythmics' "Sweet Dreams" and suddenly Manson's surgical-corseted, bloody-bandage chic was invading every American home. To complete the degenerate image, a single pale contact lens gave his leering visage an extra cataracted twist of the knife. Such cod-horror theatrics were nothing new to the generations who had witnessed Alice Cooper at his peak, but predictable waves of hysteria came from fundamentalist religious groups, the main target for Manson's vicious lampooning. He was instantly dubbed a child-molesting, drug-abusing son of Satan, making him even more attractive to the fans.

The concept album ANTICHRIST SUPERSTAR (1996) brought a line-up change, with replacement members **Ginger Fish** (drums) and **Zim Zum** (guitar) joining the Manson family. The new album

One of Rock music's showmen and a great role model for the kids – Marilyn Manson

posedly shocking stage antics. A fact underlined by HOLYWOOD (IN THE SHADOW OF THE VALLEY OF DEATH) (2000), a record created in the wake of the Columbine school shootings tragedy. Manson found himself the target of vilification because the two young perpetrators of the massacre were allegedly fans of his music; conservative elements branded him as somehow complicit in the blood-letting. Naturally, these events provided more than enough material for Manson to create an album that focused on, as he saw it, the degenerate and contradictory values at the heart of American society. What Manson has demonstrated so well up to now is how, in the MTV culture that passes for a modern music scene, cheap sensationalism and outrage are the lifeblood of rock'n'roll.

It was only a matter of time before Manson's showbiz aspirations took him into the cinema, firstly covering Soft Cell's "Tainted Love" for the Johnny Depp film *From Hell* then providing the authentic goth rock for vampire rock star wannabe **Lestat** in the screen adaptation of Anne Rice's *Queen Of The Damned*. A foray into composing for the theme to Zombie flick *Resident Evil* and a role in the murder/drugs/transvestism film *Party Monster* don't really expand Manson's aesthetic vision much – can we suggest a romantic comedy next?

Even being mired in legal proceedings following an alleged assault of a security guard didn't stop the Manson pen flowing – quite the opposite, it allowed him to increasingly see himself as an artistic crusader victimized by censorship. By this time comparing himself to the Marquis De Sade, he released another album, GOLDEN AGE OF THE GROTESQUE, in 2002. By now his music was betraying an accessibility that contradicted much of what had gone before, though on "Vodevil", Brian maintains his stance, snarling 'This isn't a show/This is my fucking life.'

had all the focus that their debut lacked and brought with it a live show guaranteed to offend Middle American sensibilities. At one point the venue would be transformed into a mock Nazi rally; red, white and black flags bearing the international shock hazard symbol would appear whilst the band donned steel helmets and Manson ordered the crowd to worship them. Nothing new to David Bowie or Pink Floyd fans (the album even features a 'wormboy' character) but such coarse irony made Manson a wanted man on every redneck fundamentalist's hit list. The band were banned from various towns as undesirables; ironically when the banning orders were challenged in court, many of them were lifted.

As a practised manipulator of the press and public opinion Manson knew a change of image could only be good as the band launched full-scale into a period consolidating the commercial success of the preceding two years. With the release of MECHANICAL ANIMALS (1998), Manson was no longer the bizarre-looking spawn of Satan; suddenly he adopted a scary, cold female android look which meshed seamlessly with the new writing approach. Outrage was still very much the name of the game but an obvious softening had occurred in the sound, which was occasionally compared to the glam electro-dabbling of twenty years earlier.

Still best known for their publicity-seeking live shows and adamant anti-Christian behaviour (while promoting ANTICHRIST SUPERSTAR, they were besieged by assorted religious and parents' groups, and many states attempted to ban the band), Marilyn Manson are actually an accomplished act, whose successive releases have demonstrated a high level of development of both ideas and performance ability. But the test will be whether Manson can maintain the same level of interest on his shamelessly manipulative and derivative mission; certainly there is nothing new to either the band's sound or the sup-

● **Antichrist Superstar** (1996; Interscope/ Nothing). Do we laugh at him or allow Mr Manson to take us for a ride? Nothing new here for industrial metal fans, but you have to admire the bare-faced cheek of the rip-off. That aside, behind the goth-shock treatment lurk some excellent tunes, particularly the glam-metal stomp of "The Beautiful People".

● **Mechanical Animals** (1998; Interscope/Nothing). Anyone who thought ANTICHRIST SUPERSTAR was a neat bag of tricks might be a tad disappointed with this. In reality, however, the writing is much better and the album provides a more seamless and cohesive listening experience. Never has shock rock sounded quite as accomplished as this.

Essi Berelian & Craig Joyce

MANSUN

Formed Chester, 1995; disbanded 2003.

One of the major success stories of 1996, **Mansun** enjoyed a charmed career trajectory. Comprising **Paul Draper** (guitar/vocals), **Stove King** (bass), **Andy Rathbone** (drums) and **Dominic Chad** (guitar), the group's starting point came at Wrexham Art College in 1995. After completing their degrees, they relocated to Chester to put the band on a more permanent footing.

There they honed new material before embarking on a demanding touring schedule, which saw writers from both the *NME* and *Melody Maker* become early converts. This gave much-needed publicity to their initial batch of recordings, issued as EPs on their own Sci-Fi Hi-Fi label. "Take It Easy Chicken" and "Skin Up Pin-Up" piqued the interest of several major labels as well as the press. With a publishing deal through Polygram under their belts, they eventually chose to make Parlophone their new home. The clinching factor was, apparently, Parlophone's willingness to underwrite Mansun's touring schedule of more than 200 gigs through 1996 – plus the uncontested option to continue releasing EPs and to self-produce their debut album.

Parlophone were rewarded for their faith with the instant success of "Stripper Vicar" (a cross-dressing member of the clergy providing Paul Draper with typically obtuse lyrical ammunition), which brought the group to the Top 20 and *Top Of The Pops*. Their debut album, ATTACK OF THE GREY LANTERN and a further single, "Wide Open Space", another Top 20 hit, followed in 1997. The album also included some genuine stinkers – "Tax Loss" being a prime example, which entered the UK charts at #1, a real achievement for a group disinclined to follow the traditional verse-chorus-verse framework. Even with this success some critics found their efforts at creating the thematic grandeur of a Suede or Gene a little troublesome, but the comparison cited most often was Radiohead.

Their 1998 album SIX leant towards a harder, heavier sound, with the title track, and the ear-splitting "Negative" being the stand-outs. A greater willingness to experiment with longer pieces showed a more mature band stomping into the future. Their new prog-ish sound received a lukewarm reception from many quarters, but also delighted obsessive fans. 1999 saw Mansun tour extensively, while 2000 witnessed the release of their third album, LITTLE KIX, on the back of more chart success with the single "I Can Only Disappoint U". The set was far more restrained and accessible than SIX, and was hailed by many as their finest collection, though it lacked the endearing pomp that enriched their earlier releases. The group spent much of 2002 working on new material, but it was never released; the group split in 2003.

Attack Of The Grey Lantern (1997; Parlophone).
Opening with "The Chad Who Loved Me", a 90s Bond theme with full orchestral interplay, this is a widescreen rock debut with trace elements of glam, punk and garage-pop. It started life as a concept 'to explore the undercurrents of British society' and offers a clearly Morrissey-derived set of clever-clogs references. However, the way the songs segue into each other actually works well. The closet melodrama of "Dark Mavis" and the already released "Egg-Shaped Fred" are stand-outs.

Little Kix (2000; Parlophone).
Having largely shed the orchestrated Brit-pop guise of GREY LANTERN and the pseudo-prog pomp of SIX, the Chester quartet draw upon, rather than replicate, a far wider selection of kitsch, 80s and Bowie-esque influences to construct a distinct, yet compromised sound. Highpoints include "Forgive Me" and the opener, "Butterfly".

Alex Ogg

MARILLION

Formed Aylesbury, England, 1978.

Marillion emerged in the early 80s as the standard-bearers of what the British music press disbelievingly referred to as the 'New Wave of Progressive Rock'. In the wake of the punk revolution, bands like this, dressed in their kaftans and loons, and with a name abbreviated from a bad Tolkien novel (*Silmarillion*), simply should not have existed. But they found a following and, in 1982, a major label – EMI.

The line-up, by this time, comprised **Fish** (his real name, Derek Dick, was worse; vocals), **Mark Kelly** (keyboards), **Steve Rothery** (guitar), **Ian Moseley** (drums) and **Peter Trewavas** (bass). Heavily influenced by Genesis and suchlike prog-rockery, Marillion produced long, complex, orchestrated songs with intricate, wordy lyrics. The first two albums, SCRIPT FOR A JESTER'S TEAR (1983) and FUGAZI (1984; reissued 1998), showcased the sound well enough, and came in cover artwork to give heart to Roger Dean. The fans loved it all. The music press sneered.

In truth, the albums were a tad overcomplicated, even indulgent, but live Marillion were a revelation. While their dinosaur predecessors had a yen for saving the lost city of Atlantis dressed as Trojan spacemen, Marillion's charismatic singer, Fish, would bounce on stage in wild face paint, produce pints of beer from beneath the drum kit, and banter merrily with the audience as he acted out the songs in a mad theatrical whirl.

On disc, it was with the MISPLACED CHILDHOOD (1985) that Marillion fulfilled their potential. This was – yes – a concept album, drawing its themes from the loss and regaining of childhood innocence. The whole band was in its element, segueing mood pieces and pop/rock songs, and Fish dropped earlier wordy pretensions to pen two straight-from-the-heart, honest love songs, "Kayleigh" and "Lavender". These surprised everyone by entering the UK singles charts, propelling Marillion into the uncharted waters of *Smash Hits* magazine.

The band by now had launched themselves into a rock mainstay and, as if on cue, Fish developed a full-blown ego, alcohol and drug problem – all too evident in the maudlin lyrics of CLUTCHING AT STRAWS (1987). The rest of the band, meanwhile, found themselves ever more uncomfortable with their new pop status, playing second fiddle to Fish in a band that had prided itself on its democracy. During sessions for the fifth studio album, Fish left amongst acute acrimony.

The press promptly wrote Marillion off, and the release of a below-par live album, THE THIEVING MAGPIE (1988), looked like a swan song. However, the band surprisingly regrouped around vocalist **Steve Hogarth** – formerly of European. His fluid, sensuous, almost casual vocal style signalled a considerable shift in style from Fish's fire, bitterness and shout. But the band adapted, providing lush walls of sound which Hogarth's voice could match on the 'comeback album', SEASON'S END (1990). On the subsequent tour, Hogarth won over the residual suspicions of much of the hardcore fan base, though stalwart prog-rockers parted company, taking one listen to the single, "Hooks In You", a standard, riff-heavy rock track, and calling it a day.

The album was not the popular (or critical) success the band were expecting, and neither was its follow-up, the more radio-friendly HOLIDAYS IN EDEN (1991; reissued 1998). The mainstream music scene, too, was further apart than ever, with the emergence of grunge. Again, it looked all over for Marillion. After something of a hiatus, however, they returned, defiantly, with BRAVE (1994), a seventy-minute concept album. This allowed the band to do what they do best – experiment with sonic textures. The multi-layered soundscapes ranged through ambient, rock, jazz and folk terrains, as Hogarth gave a startling and heart-rending vocal performance. The band, amazingly, took it on the road – on the aptly named *Brave Tour* – showing huge musical assurance, while Hogarth indulged in some very Fish-esque theatrics.

Revitalized, Marillion released a new CD within months. AFRAID OF SUNLIGHT (1995) returned to a more standard format of a half-dozen extended tracks, but with a few surprises – not least "Cannibal Surf Babe", which sounded like The Beach Boys on very bad acid. The album repeatedly touched on the divisive nature of fame and offered sympathy to the Kurt Cobains of this world, unable to cope in the increasingly mad and unreal world of the music industry. It was followed by a live set, MADE AGAIN, which effectively chronicled the Hogarth years and brought the EMI contract to a close.

The valiant Hogarth and his crew pressed on in their own neo-progressive manner, eventually coming up with THIS STRANGE ENGINE (1997) which, far from being yet another cod-Genesis workout, showed just how many new strings the band had added to its collective bow. Tracks such as "One Fine Day" verged on being plain-vanilla pop,

and "Hope For The Future" was positively jaunty. The band looked reassuringly glum on the cover, however, and enthusiasts found it all highly satisfactory. Which was also true for subsequent studio efforts RADIATION (1998) and MARILLION.COM (1999), with the latter reigniting the passion of prog aficionados by including the epic "Interior Lulu". As the title also suggests the band were exploiting the possibilities of the Internet during this period. Not only did a disappointed message posted by Mark Kelly on the band's website in 1997 relating to the financial impossibility of touring the US result in fans raising $60,000 to fund the transatlantic jaunt, but ANORAKNOPHOBIA (2001), was also presold over the web, thus covering the production costs in advance.

A million insults can be aimed at Marillion (and they probably have been), but for all the press abuse, the band have kept an integrity about them, surviving purely on the strength of their music. And nearly twenty years into their career, they're in good shape – Hogarth has made the lyrical side of the band his own, shaking off the shadow of Fish, and the band have set up their own label, Intact.

Meantime, Fish himself has become a full-time maverick, producing deeply introverted projects for a cottage record industry he has set up in his native Scotland. He has been dogged by legal wrangles with record companies and a less-than-stable backing band, and some of his work seems to have lacked flair, specifically the numerous live albums he has released to keep the rest of his business afloat.

⊙ **Script For A Jester's Tear** (1983; EMI).
Although lacking the grace and polish of later releases, Marillion's debut album is a remarkable statement of intent. Their trademark intricate mood swings and theatrical flourishes are there from the very first bars. Love it or hate it, in the midst of 80s electro-pop, you have to admire Marillion's audacity.

⊙ **Brave** (1994; EMI).
This dark concept album is a spectacular exercise in multi-layered music, with Hogarth howling away in compassion for the album's ill-fated heroine. To these ears, not just Marillion's masterpiece, but prog-rock's finest moment; Roger Waters' THE WALL sounds petty, misogynous and whingeing beside it.

Richard Butterworth

JOHN MARTYN

Born Glasgow, Scotland, 1948.

O ver the course of his career, **John Martyn** has ranged through folk, blues, jazz and rock, always giving it his trademark identity – cool, laid-back vocals (veering to ambient in the late 70s) and a guitar style that seems to unlock the ingredients, putting them back together with a mesmerizing echo and roll. While never reaching the heights of commercial success, his stature as an artist is reflected in a list of collaborators that reads like a *Who's Who* of rock.

A natural with the guitar, Martyn started performing on the London folk circuit in 1967. The teenager was spotted by Chris Blackwell and signed to Island, who released his debut, LONDON CONVERSATION, in February 1968. It was basically Martyn's folk set, recorded solo and acoustic. THE TUMBLER, which followed in December, saw Martyn pursuing a more jazz and blues direction, with session men enriching the sound on bass, guitar, sax and flute.

These records sound restrained and light compared to Martyn's later work, but by the standards of the day they were an adventurous step outside the unwritten rules of folk – which Dylan had broken to such uproar with his 'electric' recordings. Martyn continued in this direction on his next pair of albums, recorded in (musical and marital) partnership with the singer **Beverly Kutner**. On the first of these, STORMBRINGER (1970), a full band of seasoned American session players produced a more expansive style and helped widen his audience. For the second, ROAD TO RUIN (also 1970), double-bass player **Danny Thompson** (then of **PENTANGLE**) was drafted in. Thompson shared Martyn's musical vision and love of liquor, and was to become a long-term associate.

Martyn went 'solo' again for BLESS THE WEATHER (1971), which was recorded with Danny Thompson and the (unrelated) **RICHARD THOMPSON**. The latter provided an additional depth to the guitar sound, enabling the dreamy, laid-back Martyn style to really take shape. Tracks like "Head And Heart" had a jazz lilt, with Martyn's acoustic guitar style becoming more percussive, while his voice was now being employed as an extra instrument, the words slurring and sliding between notes. "Glistening Glyndebourne", meanwhile, contained a first glimpse of his echoing guitar.

By SOLID AIR (1973) Martyn, now a favourite on the British college circuit, had crystallized this style, with a bolder bluesy vocal delivery and more electric guitar – again aided and abetted by Richard Thompson. The rhythm section, too, was more to the fore, courtesy of **FAIRPORT CONVENTION**'s **Dave Pegg** (bass) and **Dave Mattacks** (drums). The album's strength is reflected by the endurance of its songs in Martyn's set, among them the title track – written for friend and fellow songwriter Nick Drake – and "May You Never", later famously covered by Eric Clapton.

Martyn had travelled a long way from the folk scene by this stage, playing to rock audiences and attracting stellar collaborators from the rock sphere. He was joined by **TRAFFIC**'s **Steve Winwood** and **Chris Wood** on INSIDE OUT (1973) and former **FREE** guitarist **Paul Kossoff** on SUNDAY'S CHILD (1975). Both extended the vein of SOLID AIR, developing Martyn's use of guitar effects (notably on the latter's "Root Love"). It was ONE WORLD (1977), however, again working with Winwood, that consolidated the style, creating a wonderful echoing and meditative soundscape, especially on the title track, unveiling possibly Martyn's finest song, the reflective "Couldn't Love You More", and rocking out with bigger-than-ever rhythms on "Dealer" and "Big Muff".

ONE WORLD was a pretty drugged-out record, as its lyrics reflected, and Martyn's personal life was in crisis. When he returned to the studio, three years later, for GRACE AND DANGER (1980), the songs had reached an unprecedented level of intensity, reflecting the breakdown of his marriage. Martin Levan was perhaps the ideal choice as producer, as he coaxed some fine performances from Martyn and special guest **Phil Collins** (drums/backing vox).

Collins was drafted in as producer after Martyn moved to WEA, influencing the almost mainstream rock arrangements of GLORIOUS FOOL (1981) and adding backing vox, piano and his trademark 'gated' (electronically doctored) drum sounds. This and WELL KEPT SECRET (1982), its successor, became Martyn's first UK Top 30 releases. But, despite extensive touring to showcase his new rock direction, Martyn still didn't break through to the wider audience now being reached by friends and contemporaries like Phil Collins and Robert Palmer. Perhaps both the songs and the voice were just a fraction too low-key to be really commercial.

Martyn maintained a loyal live following through the 1980s – his live sets can be compared on LIVE AT LEEDS (1975 vintage), PHILANTHROPY (1983) and FOUNDATIONS (1987) – but released just two further studio albums, back on Island. SAPPHIRE (1984), employing a host of session players, seemed to be reworking too-familiar territory, but PIECE BY PIECE (1986), on which he celebrated a new marriage, had a spirit and contentment that helped edge Martyn back into the UK Top 30.

At the end of the decade, Martyn went through another period of heavy drinking, which seriously threatened his health, and he found himself without a major record deal. But he emerged with a strong new set of songs on THE APPRENTICE (1990) and the jazz-infused COOLTIDE (1991), both released on Permanent Records. There followed a period of regular touring and a flurry of compilation and live albums. COULDN'T LOVE YOU MORE (1992) was a collection of re-recorded Martyn favourites, but he disapproved of the overproduced final mixes and set about another collection, this time recorded to his satisfaction on NO LITTLE BOY (1993). It wasn't until 1996 that an album of new material, entitled AND, was released on the Go! Discs label, but despite the gap there was a clear stylistic link to the groove of COOLTIDE, with the voice ever more cracked and indistinct. This was followed by THE CHURCH WITH ONE BELL (1998), an idiosyncratic covers album of what could loosely be defined as blues classics, ranging from Billie Holiday's "Strange Fruit" to Portishead's "Glory Box", all made uniquely his own. Next came GLASGOW WALKER (2000), which successfully married Martyn's musicality to a drum machine alongside more traditional instrumentation. He has continued to tour and record with a mastery of his genre and a voice that has grown ever richer with the years; a new live recording is expected soon, though other material may be some way off: Martyn recently underwent serious surgery resulting in the amputation of his leg below the knee. His recovery is likely to be long and difficult.

- **Solid Air** (1973; Island).
  A much-loved landmark album with a fresh-faced Martyn finding his voice and direction on tracks like "Don't Want To Know" and "Solid Air".

- **One World** (1977; Island).
  Reflecting a period of crisis, this includes some of Martyn's most powerful and enduring songs, swinging from the carefree "Dancing" to the impassioned work-outs of "Dealer" and "Big Muff".

- **Grace And Danger** (1980; Island).
  Island delayed the release of this album, worrying over its 'dark tone', but many Martyn followers reckon it's among his finest, with Levan lending a crisper production that captured the desperate mood of JM and his company of fabulous session musicians.

- **Cooltide** (1991; Permanent).
  Latter-period Martyn with a lighter jazz feel throughout. Plenty of fluttering sax and lush keyboard, and a raising of the tempo for what could be his theme song, "Jack The Lad".

- **Sweet Little Mysteries: The Island Years** (1995; Island).
  A 34-track collection of the main moments from "Bless The Weather" to "Piece By Piece".

- **Serendipity** (1998; Island).
  Billed as; 'An Introduction to John Martyn', this presents a modest selection of seventeen tracks from the Island years.

Nick Dale

CASPAR BRÖTZMANN MASSAKER

Formed Berlin, Germany, 1987.

"It's not head music. It's body music." Caspar Brötzmann

The term 'the new Hendrix' is on a par with 'the new Brando' or 'the new Smiths' as an example of critical shorthand laziness. In **Caspar Brötzmann**'s case, though, it is almost true – not because he sounds like Hendrix, but because his guitar playing has the same sense of terminal reinvention.

With **Danny Arnold Lommen** (drums) and **Eduardo Delgado Lopez** (bass), Brötzmann formed the trio **Massaker** in 1987, and their impressive debut album, THE TRIBE (1987), followed in the same year. Lommen and Lopez laid down rhythms both monolithic and pliant, but the real draw was Brötzmann's monstrous guitar playing: swooping, dive-bombing, setting up dirty great smears of sound, like the mutant issue of Black Sabbath's Tony Iommi and some malfunctioning piece of heavy industrial machinery.

Even better was DER ABEND DER SCHWARZEN FOLKLORE (1992), as its four longer tracks allowed more space for rhythmic and structural development. On "Bass Totem", the opening's stuttering beats gradually mutated into a irregular but steady Sabbathesque throb. The strung-out, razor-blade blues of "Sarah" provided the build-up for a Brötzmann solo of yowling, tormented intensity. 1993's KOKSOFEN represented the trio's best work to date, its vast expanses of sound laying to rest any misconceptions about the band's alleged 'primitivism'.

Massaker have been bracketed alongside the likes of Einstürzende Neubauten, Glen Branca and Swans. HOME (1995), the only album to capture some mainstream press attention, did not show the band at their best, though it did feature a truly bestial reworking of "Massaker" from their debut album. On tracks like this, Massaker seemed to be harking back to the therapeutic rage of prime 60s free jazz, as well as the essence of unadorned heavy metal, to create sounds many times more urgent than the cosmetic 'extremism' of any industrial band. A 1996 outing with **Page Hamilton** (one of Branca's protégés), ZULUTIME, once again failed to deliver the trademark menace and strangeness that their audience demanded. MUTE MASSAKER (2000), recorded with **Ottmar Seum** (bass) and **Robert Dammig** (drums), was simultaneously more explosive and hushed than anything previously released; it received favourable reviews, but failed to inflame a new audience. Predictably, mass acceptance has hardly been forthcoming.

- **Der Abend Der Schwarzen Folklore** (1992; Our Choice).
  With a title roughly translated as 'The evening of black folk stories', Brötzmann's portentous singing does threaten to spoil the brew a little, but the sheer sense of physical release is the dominant factor.

- **Koksofen** (1993; Big Cat).
  An almost indescribable mesh of brute force and poise – the best place to start.

Ben Smith

MASSIVE ATTACK

Formed Bristol, England, 1991.

"If a thing's worth doing, it's worth doing slowly." 3-D

There were two distinctly British flavours of hip-hop in the mid 90s: jungle – the screaming, twisted, nine-million-bpm sound – and **Massive**

Attack, whose music picked up the make-do labels 'ambient hip-hop' and the rather catchier 'trip-hop'. Unlike rave and most rap music, the Massive sound admits to, and explores, an inner world, a much slower groove that finds and strokes your musical hot spots. You don't dance to Massive Attack: you sit, lay or sprawl, and you listen.

Massive Attack's history goes back to 1983 and the Wild Bunch. One of the first sound-system/DJ collectives in the UK, they rapidly made themselves a reputation for their mixing up of styles and for their sound-system parties, which became so unmissable that the posse was accused of wrecking the local live-music scene by stealing the audiences. Developing a sound that took advantage of the soul/punk/reggae cross-fertilization seen in the early 80s, the hardcore trio of **3-D** (Roberto Del Naja), **Daddy-G** (Grant Marshall to his mum) and **Mushroom** (aka Andrew Vowles) decided to move on from playing records to making them, and Massive Attack was born.

Ditching the spraycans and packing in the break dancing proved an excellent career move. Their first album, BLUE LINES (1991), commanded respect and attention, and spawned three stylish singles, including one, the magnificent "Unfinished Sympathy", which bobbed around in the deep end of the Top 40. With its hard urban lyrics and hypnotic beats, dusted with samples from all your favourite songs and wrapped up in a smooth production job, it became audio accessory of the year.

Three guest vocalists featured on BLUE LINES – the superb **TRICKY** (who later went on to develop his reputation as a solo performer), the unmistakeable **Horace Andy** (the angst-ridden voice that suggests its owner is forever looking nervously over his shoulder) and **Shara Nelson**, whose smoking, powerful voice was Massive's most immediate hook.

When Nelson moved on to put together her own career, it was easy to write off Massive Attack as another good act dying young. Losing a manager and a co-producer was further carelessness, and changing the name of the band just when things were beginning to take off might have been thought unwise – 'Massive', their new handle, was chosen to avoid any implication of support for the United Nations' policy towards the Iraqi government (Bomb the Bass did something similar). They then crowned all this with a fairly disastrous attempt to conquer US stadiums with a club-scale sound. It's easy to see why there was a three-year gap between recordings.

Nonetheless, a spell of 'Bristol time' gave Massive's sound a chance to grow up a little. 1994's seductive masterpiece PROTECTION saw their music pinned down to the 90bpm region – that sparsely populated area between reggae and hip-hop – and beaten gently into shape by their old Wild Bunch pal **Nellee Hooper** (1995's most-wanted producer since his work with Soul II Soul and Björk). There was less sampling and a wider range of guest vocalists, star of the show being the remarkable **Nicolette**, whose school-of-Billie-Holiday voice was so fragile and

MASSIVE ATTACK
MEZZANINE

beautiful that it seemed dangerous to breathe when she sang (her lost treasure of an album, NOW IS EARLY, recorded with Shut Up And Dance, was a collection of torch songs to tear your heart out). Further stand-out contributions came from surprise team member **Tracey Thorn** of **EVERYTHING BUT THE GIRL**, whose bittersweet vocals let rip on the title track, and the vintage reggae voice of Horace Andy, whose "Spyglass" brought in a refreshing burst of paranoia.

In late 1994, Massive Attack (the name now back to full length) went on tour in the UK. They took acetate pressings of the various tracks on Protection with them, together with the whole Wild Bunch crew, packed each venue full with enormous speakers and mood-altering lights, and did the album live. People came, inhaled and fell over, beaten down to the ground by a bass that turned your knees liquid. South London's own Mad Professor reggae producer came along on certain dates and constructed a dub strong enough to fly off the turntable. His dub mix of "Protection" – released as "No Protection" (1994) – was an awesome, bass-heavy brew, dressed up with Ariwa Studio's Sunday-best technology. The band's appearances at UK summer festivals were celebratory and extraordinarily effective (for example, having a curtain fall away to reveal a full orchestra at the climax of "Unfinished Sympathy"). World tours took them far from home and ultimately had an influence on the music.

MEZZANINE (1998), their third album, was pure darkness. Horace Andy was still on board, providing the voice of bitter experience, and the female vocal side of things was jointly held up by **Liz Fraser** of recently defunct Cocteau Twins fame and **Sara Jay**. The music reflected the make-do attitude of the experienced gigging band, with raw guitar sounds being blended into the smooth mix of samples. The round of promotional interviews was peppered with references to hotels, world travel and the difficulties in connecting with one another any longer. The three break-dancing funsters that were the Wild

Bunch had grown older, wiser and perhaps a little more serious.

In fact, the pressure became too much for Mushroom who announced he was leaving the group in 1999, despite the trio apparently being well under way with a new album. Though they had been very active making tracks (including "I Against I" featuring rapper **Mos Def**) available to fans via their website, at the end of 2001 there was still no sign of an album, with 3D – now known by his real name **Roberto Del Naja** – admitting that they were having to rework much of it following Mushroom's departure. Uncertainty surrounding the group had reached such a level that their future was beginning to look in doubt. This uncertainty was further fuelled by the announcement of Marshall's 'extended sabbatical', which, to all intents and purposes, had left Del Naja to complete the new album alone.

When it finally arrived, 100TH WINDOW (2003) proved to be a weaker offering. Though its sound was dark and menacing, and the beats were, as ever, competently chilled, the overall collage – augmented by Horace Andy and **Sinéad O'Connor** – had the feel of an extended commercial for a family saloon. The set's release was also marred by Del Naja's arrest for alleged Internet child pornography offences; all the charges were quickly dropped, but the whole experience left Del Naja feeling 'shattered'.

Whatever their future holds, Massive Attack's coming-together of funk, rock and dub-reggae, tinged with the attitude that flavoured punk in the 70s, produced some of the 90s' greatest recordings. However, the corporate money, boosted by enormous worldwide album and ticket sales, continues to roll in, and is now, sadly, reflecting in the music, resulting in spiritless, mechanical recordings.

⊙ **Blue Lines** (1991; Wild Bunch Records).
A thoroughly urban album, with lyrics well aware of the darker side of city life but in no way ready to exchange it for the gorgeous rolling boredom of the English countryside.

⊙ **Protection** (1994; Wild Bunch Records).
Their music has become more confident, with fewer samples and an increased reliance on their own stock of sounds. Lyrics float around in the mix, looking for a way into your mind.

⊙ **No Protection** (1994; Wild Bunch Records).
Classic, old-school dub, with Mad Professor extracting the very essence of the original album and weaving it into a version from another planet.

⊙ **Mezzanine** (1998; Wild Bunch Records).
Whispered lyrics laid gently over a soft bed of samples and 'real instruments'. A compelling collection of songs, deep and disturbing, with the weary air of having done too much, too soon. A more guitar-heavy album than before, adding some welcome rough edges to the mix.

Al Spicer

ERIC MATTHEWS

Born Portland, Oregon, 1969.

A former student at the San Francisco Conservatory of Music, and latterly half of Cardinal (with Richard Davies), **Eric Matthews** started his musical career with ambitions of becoming a concert trumpeter, but has switched to singing in a breathy, tender style reminiscent of Nick Drake. He is blessed with a caressing voice and a near genius for slotting trumpets, strings and oddities like recorders into his expertly woven arrangements.

Weaned on a mixture of classic 60s pop (Beatles, Beach Boys, Zombies) and the melodic artisans of the 80s (The Smiths, ABC, Cocteau Twins), Matthews was already supporting himself at the age of 19 by playing trumpet in small ensembles and orchestras. However, he claims that he never wrote so much as a jingle until he was into his twenties, and that even now he can hardly play his guitar properly.

Inspired by the warm critical reception afforded to the 1995 Cardinal single, "Dream Figure", Matthews decided to go solo and cut demo recordings for an orchestral pop project. On the strength of these, he landed a Sub Pop contract and soon after released his debut single, "Fanfare", and its parent album, IT'S HEAVY IN HERE (1995), both of them real departures for the primarily grunge-based Sub Pop. Recalling not just Nick Drake but also the narcotic beauty of The Blue Nile, the contemplative poetry of Scott Walker, and the studio innovations of Lennon and McCartney, Brian Wilson and Bacharach, the album immediately won plaudits for its dreamy melancholia and lush, autumnal poignancy.

THE LATENESS OF THE HOUR (1997) consolidated the acclaim, with its beautifully melodic material and its more professional delivery, revealing an artist who was maturing very nicely.

But for the time being this is the end of the story. Though he continues to work as a session trumpeter and write his own material, Matthews is currently without a label – a state of affairs that will hopefully not last too long.

⊙ **It's Heavy In Here** (1995; Sub Pop).
Matthews' pensive, artful, fragile songs gain an impressionistic sheen from the lush but sinewy arrangements. Like The Boo Radleys and Colin Blunstone hooking up with George Martin for a raid through the Goffin/King songbook.

Michael Sumsion

JOHN MAYALL

Born Macclesfield, England, November 29, 1933.

R ock'n'roll owes a great debt to writer, interpreter, singer, keyboardist, guitarist and harmonica ace **John Mayall**. Wielding the music of Sonny Boy Williamson and J. B. Lenoir like scripture, Mayall became an ad hoc teacher and proselytizer of the blues in the early 60s, enlisting many young players who would go on to become future rock superstars.

Mayall's first unit, which came together in February 1963, included bassist **John McVie**, who after graduating from Mayall played an integral role in bringing **FLEETWOOD MAC** into existence. Two years later Mayall welcomed a fledgling guitarist who had just left The Yardbirds because of their pop-music leanings – **ERIC CLAPTON**. This version of Mayall's group also included bass player **Jack Bruce**, with whom Clapton would eventually form **CREAM**. It was this configuration that recorded the legendary BLUESBREAKERS WITH ERIC CLAPTON (1966).

Clapton departed in June 1966 and his replacement came in the form of another monstrous blues guitar player, **Peter Green**, who would later found Fleetwood Mac with fellow Mayall alumni McVie and Mick Fleetwood. Another great young guitarist, future **ROLLING STONE Mick Taylor**, would replace Green in May 1967, making his mark on BLUES FROM LAUREL CANYON, a concept album of sorts, exploring Mayall's relationship with Los Angeles. Mayall's next album of new material, THE TURNING POINT (1969), was an all-acoustic set, recorded live at the Fillmore East in July 1969, and included his best-known song, the harmonica-drenched "Room To Move", alongside mellow, drumless blues-based songs.

It was in some ways the end of an era at the cutting edge of blues and rock. Mayall released a spate of albums in the 70s and 80s, but they were generally unremarkable. It was not until 1993 that Mayall briefly returned to form, releasing WAKE UP CALL, featuring the talents of **Coco Montoya** on guitar. Subsequent albums such as BLUES FOR THE LOST (1997) and STORIES (2002) have tended to show an introspective, backward-looking bluesman, prone to wallowing in nostalgia whilst still wringing a mean flurry of notes from the neck of a suffering guitar.

Mayall's earlier albums remain his most riveting, but all of them provide interesting snapshots of his sidemen at their various stages of musical development. Though he has never been highly successful from a commercial standpoint, Mayall must be mentioned in the same breath as rock's primary movers and shakers.

◉ **Bluesbreakers With Eric Clapton** (1966; London).
A quintessential 60s blues album, this helped put both Clapton and Mayall on the map. It remains a compelling piece of work, with rock-solid performances of blues standards and Clapton's burning axe work.

◉ **Crusade** (1967; London).
Featuring Mick Taylor, John McVie, drummer Keef Hartley and sax player Dick Heckstall-Smith, this album was Mayall's first appearance in the American charts. The teenage Taylor, especially, shines on standards like Willie Dixon's "I Can't Quit You Baby".

◉ **Wake Up Call** (1993; Silvertone).
Mayall's best work in years features Coco Montoya ripping up songs like Chris Smithers' "Mail Order Mystics" and Jimmy Reed's "Ain't That Lovin' You Baby". Special guest appearances by Albert Collins, Buddy Guy, Mick Taylor and Mavis Staples make this one well worth the price of admission.

Ben Hunter

CURTIS MAYFIELD

Born Chicago, June 3, 1942;
died December 26, 1999.

"You know, to talk about the 60s almost brings tears to my eyes. What we did. What we all did. We changed the world."

As a guitarist, singer, producer and, especially, as a songwriter **Curtis Mayfield** was one of the titans of popular music. The former owner of the purest falsetto in soul, his influence extends through generations of soul singers and the beginnings of Jamaican ska to rap.

The gospel-trained Mayfield joined The Roosters, a Chicago quintet, in 1957, as a guitarist. On signing to the Vee-Jay label the following year, they changed their name to **The Impressions**, and had an immediate hit with "For Your Precious Love". The group in this form was short-lived, as their success persuaded their lead singer, Jerry Butler, to go solo, and for a while Mayfield made a living playing guitar and writing songs for Butler. But in 1959 Mayfield reformed The Impressions, and they moved to New York, signing to ABC/Paramount shortly after.

The Impressions soon developed a distinctive style, based on Mayfield's rolling, Pops Staples-influenced guitar sounds, their gospelly vocal interplay, and the distinctive horn arrangements of producer Johnny Pate. Like the Motown sound, the so-called 'Chicago sound' was sweet enough to cross over to mainstream radio stations – and hence the US charts – without sacrificing its integrity. Their first hit, the atmospheric "Gypsy Woman" (1961), was the first of a string of R&B successes. Things really took off, however, after they moved back to Chicago in 1963, when "It's All Right", their biggest hit, reached #4 in the US chart. During this time Mayfield also wrote and produced for other R&B artists, notably Major Lance and Gene Chandler.

The narrative strength of Mayfield's lyrics was influenced by his gospel training and in turn greatly influenced ska pioneers like Prince Buster. A sense of collective salvation and social awareness was increasingly apparent in his work, reaching its highest expression in the classic "People Get Ready" (1965), a song with dozens of covers. When Mayfield founded his Curtom label, he was even more upfront about social issues in songs like "This Is My Country" and "Mighty, Mighty, Spade And Whitey". The approach, however, was always tempered by his irrepressible optimism.

In 1970 Mayfield left The Impressions for a solo career, but continued to collaborate with the group as a writer and producer. His debut album, CURTIS (1970), contained the classic "Move On Up", his only UK hit. CURTIS LIVE!, with The Impressions, and his second studio album, ROOTS, followed in 1971, then in 1972 he released his *tour de force*, the platinum-selling blaxploitation movie soundtrack, SUPERFLY!, which yielded the million-selling US hits "Freddie's Dead" and the title track. This album signalled a preachy new bleakness in Mayfield's work, a well-timed antidote to a cuteness that some critics had begun to find grating. The impact of the lyrics, many of which read like modern rap, without the expletives or misogyny, was all the stronger for being delivered over deceptively light, string-washed funk. This trend continued with BACK TO THE WORLD (1973), but by the time of THERE'S NO PLACE LIKE AMERICA TODAY (1975) the public were beginning to lose interest. Perhaps Mayfield overextended himself in the mid 70s, working with Gladys Knight, the Staple Singers and Aretha Franklin, and a slip in quality control became more noticeable on disco-styled albums like DO IT ALL NIGHT (1978), which he released in a vain attempt to recapture success.

After Curtom hit difficulties in 1979, Mayfield moved from label to label before re-establishing himself as an R&B artist with LOVE IS THE PLACE (1981), featuring the sublime "She Don't Let Nobody (But Me)", a hit revived in the 90s by ragga duo Chaka Demus And Pliers. He followed this with HONESTY (1982), his most critically acclaimed album of the decade, and including a great song of political scandal, "Dirty Laundry". It failed to make the charts, however, and after the death of his old associate, Neil Bogart, who ran the Boardwalk label, Mayfield found himself without a recording contract.

Still, Mayfield's career looked set for a revival, as a new generation of musicians for whom he was an inspirational figure (the Blow Monkeys, Ice-T), began to queue up to work with him. But at an outdoor concert in Brooklyn in August 1990 tragedy struck – a lighting rig fell, leaving him paralysed from the neck down and unable to sing. Mayfield kept busy running his indie rap label, Conquest, waiting for the advances in computer technology to enable him to make music again. His return, with 1997's NEW WORLD ORDER, was heart-warming certainly, but more importantly, it was a fine album of good-quality music – the gorgeous toffee-dipped-in-honey voice was still strong and sweet and, despite the lack of guitar input from the man, the vocal collaborations with Aretha Franklin and Mavis Staples make the album a true delight. Tragically, this would be Mayfield's last contribution to music; he died in 1999 after a decade of poor health.

⊙ **Love Is The Place/Honesty** (1996; Sequel).
This two-for-one CD combines Mayfield's 1981 and 1982 albums, worth the price for "She Don't Let Nobody (But Me)" alone.

⊙ **People Get Ready! The Curtis Mayfield Story** (1996; Rhino).
This lavish three-CD set pulls all the highlights from The Impressions through to the disco years.

⊙ **The Very Best of...** (1996; Castle).
The distillation of an amazing talent into one unmissable 78-minute collection.

⊙ **Superfly!/Shorteyes** (1998; Sequel).
Far transcending the film it soundtracked, SUPERFLY! is Mayfield's masterpiece, and this is a great-value double pack. SHORTEYES is the soundtrack to a lost prison picture from 1977.

⊙ **Give It Up – The Best Of The Curtom Years 1970–77** (1998; Music Club).
An excellent budget-priced compilation, though with notable gaps ("Freddie's Dead", for example, is omitted).

Andy Smith

MAZZY STAR

Formed Los Angeles, 1990; split 1997.

Though **Mazzy Star** managed the neat trick of updating psychedelia for the 1990s without sounding dated, if you're looking for blissed-out music with a happy smile on its face, you might want to think twice before taking the plunge. When guitarist **David Roback** wrapped his shards of feedback and drawn-out crescendos of reverb and distortion around **Hope Sandoval**'s laconic vocal delivery, the results could indeed be trance-inducing. But their music was as much a disengagement from real life as an investigation of alternative realities, and the druggy states they evoked were comfortably numb rather than euphoric.

Mazzy Star's roots in the California Paisley Underground movement of the 1980s are deep. Roback, along with his brother Steve, was one of the main architects of leading LA psychedelic revival band, the **RAIN PARADE**. Leaving that band after their first LP, he founded the dreamier **Opal** in the mid 80s with ex-**DREAM SYNDICATE** bassist

Kendra Smith. Opal's quasi-psychedelic ruminations, with their guitar drones and hints of blues and folk, weren't far off the map that Mazzy Star would follow, and indeed Roback met Sandoval through Smith, who was a friend of Hope's.

Sandoval, still in high school at the time, was playing in a duo called **Going Home** with **Sylvia Gomez**; Kendra was impressed enough to make a tape of their music and pass it on to Roback, who produced a still-unreleased album by the pair (although 4AD has plans to issue the recording eventually). When Smith left Opal under cloudy circumstances in the middle of an American tour with The Jesus & Mary Chain, Sandoval was tapped as her replacement. After that tour and a jaunt through Europe were completed, Opal disbanded, and Roback and Sandoval decided to continue collaborating in Mazzy Star. Though theoretically a full band, Mazzy Star was very much Roback and Sandoval's show. They wrote all of the material, and although other musicians (including ex-Clay Allison drummer **Keith Mitchell**) were given minimal credits (no instruments are listed) on their albums, their backing players remained virtually anonymous to the public.

Their 1990 debut on Rough Trade, SHE HANGS BRIGHTLY, was a post-punk take on the kind of dark, long-winded psychedelia practised by The Doors on "The End", as well as the hypnotic massive guitar drone woven by The Velvet Underground on "What Goes On". That's only about half of Mazzy Star's world, though; most of the rest of their material comprised dusty, haunting acoustic-flavoured ballads with heavy blues and folk elements. Sandoval's detached, sing-speak vocals betrayed a slight country-folk twang, but were seemingly less concerned with piloting the songs than reflecting their fuzzy, sedate states of free association.

The American branch of Rough Trade folded in 1991, but Mazzy Star's contract was picked up by Capitol, who reissued the first album and put out the follow-up, SO TONIGHT THAT I MIGHT SEE (1993). Similar to the debut, but a bit more forceful in construction and execution, the emphasis remained on mood and texture, rather than melodic variety or clever messages. The languorous laments and pulsating waves of guitars could be very seductive, but the lack of diversity at times became monotonous. Roback and Sandoval might have done better to devote more space to the melancholy of their acoustic laments, and less to driving around the cul-de-sac of slow-burning guitar drones.

A year after its release, SO TONIGHT THAT I MIGHT SEE yielded a hit single, the whispy "Fade Into You". The album, seemingly destined for the cut-out bin, began an unexpected ascent into the US Top 40, and Mazzy Star were suddenly stars in sales as well as name. Make that anti-stars: Roback and Smith were notoriously difficult interview subjects, responding to most questions with monosyllables or silence. Their subsequent release, AMONG MY SWAN (1996), confirmed them as out-and-out champions of the mournful – their enigmatic public personas seemed less a cultivated pose than a complement to the shadowy, brooding mystery of their simultaneously frustrating and entrancing soundscapes. Though it seemed that the duo could do no wrong, soon after their third album, Mazzy Star were no more.

Sandoval made her solo debut in 2001 with BAVARIAN FRUIT BREAD, ostensibly backed by the **Warm Inventions**, though really this was a pairing with **Colm O'Ciosoig** (once of My Bloody Valentine), with folk legend **Bert Jansch** popping up with his six string on the beautiful "Butterfly Mornings" and "Charlotte". Largely written by Sandoval, the set plunged further into a languidly erotic, narcoleptic haze than even Mazzy Star could manage, the latter's spacey guitar rejected as possibly too energetic for the collection's country/folk saturated sleepiness. Adorable.

Mazzy Star

⊙ **She Hangs Brightly** (1990; Capitol).
The debut was pigeonholed by some critics as a 'Child Of Opal' exercise, but Roback and Sandoval do much to stake out their own territory here. Pleasing layers of acoustic and electric guitars dominate these reflective dream states, and if the vista seems a bit desolate and barren that's probably by design.

⊙ **So Tonight That I Might See** (1993; Capitol).
Overall, a slightly stronger, harder-edged effort than the debut, though the rootsy acoustic tunes outshine the electric rave-downs.

Hope Sandoval & The Warm Inventions

⊙ **Bavarian Fruit Bread** (2001; Rough Trade).
Hope swims dreamily through this extended adult lullaby. An exquisite delight.

Richie Unterberger

MC5

Formed Detroit, Michigan, 1965; disbanded 1972.

L ike The Velvet Underground, the **MC5** have attracted a huge amount of retrospective critical

MC5 kickin' out the jams

acclaim, far outweighing their original popularity, and now stand as one of the true innovators in rock music.

The band personnel got together in 1965 while still at school in Detroit – the city that inspired their name (Motor City Five). Initially **Rob Tyner** (vocals), **Wayne Kramer** (guitar), **Fred 'Sonic' Smith** (guitar), **Bob Gaspar** (drums) and **Pat Burrows** (bass) were essentially a covers band that played the bars of Detroit and Ann Arbor. Things began to heat up with the addition of **Michael Davis** (bass) and **Dennis Thompson** (drums) in late 1965. The band began to develop an interest in free improvisation rather than being limited by the confines of three-minute garage pop, although their first single was a version of Van Morrison's garage standard "I Can Only Give You Everything" (1966).

Their reputation as an explosive musical and would-be revolutionary force began to develop following an association with local radical, DJ and jazz critic John Sinclair. He became the band's manager in early 1967 and nurtured their love of the free-jazz experimentalists Pharoah Sanders, Sun Ra and Archie Shepp, who sought to fuse their art with a quest for spiritual freedom. These influences provided the MC5 with the inspiration for an extended distortion-drenched improvisation known as "Black To Comm", which formed a staple part of their live set.

Sinclair also had a massive ideological influence on the band, as he was the head of the subversive Trans Love Energies organization and connected with the White Panther Party, whose aims included 'an assault on the culture by any means necessary, including dope and fucking in the streets'. With their thirst for raw freedom of expression, MC5 were a fitting figurehead for the movement, and their music formed a far more apt soundtrack to the urban riots and student unrest of late-60s America than the drippy flower power of the West Coast.

At first, their antics made MC5 simply too hot to handle, but in late 1968 they signed to Elektra, the home of The Doors. The result was the incredible live album, KICK OUT THE JAMS (1969), which captured the band at their most powerfully confrontational. Recorded on their home turf, the album kicked off with a radical rap from **Brother J. C. Crawford** and then exploded into some of the most demented high-octane rock'n'roll ever made. Also included was an example of the band's wrecking crew approach to rock/free-jazz fusion, a razed, white-noise version of Sun Ra's "Starship".

Not surprisingly it was a controversial release, with some stores refusing to stock the album, claiming it was obscene. After the band took out newspaper ads criticizing Michigan's largest record dealer ('Fuck Hudson's'), they were sacked by Elektra.

The band's days as a revolutionary force were numbered, however. The lure of commercial success caused the breakdown of their relationship with

Sinclair and a deal with Atlantic led to BACK IN THE USA (1970). Produced by the 'discoverer' of Bruce Springsteen, Jon Landau, this was another classic, containing the excellent, hard-hitting "Shakin' Street" and "Lookin At You". But, probably due to the over-production, the album was a commercial flop. The band's third album, HIGH TIME (1971), attempted to return to their earlier style, but again with only limited success.

MC5 split in 1972 after a criminally short career. Subsequently, Kramer led a number of bands and was jailed for cocaine dealing, Fred 'Sonic' Smith married Patti Smith (and died in 1994), and Rob Tyner was found dead in September 1991. The MC5 were louder, brasher, angrier and downright heavier than their rivals and well deserve their legendary status as forefathers of the punk movement of the 70s.

Virtually everything they did that ever made it to tape has been reissued in one form or another in the intervening years, one of the latest additions to the discography being BABES IN ARMS (1998), a worthwhile collection of rarities, including a magnificent, uncensored "Kick Out The Jams". A full-length feature documentary film on the band and their legend, *MC5 – A True Testimonial!* hit screens in 2002 after spending over two years in production; it delivered a riffing political-rock extravaganza and is well worth seeing.

◉ **Kick Out The Jams** (1969; Elektra).
OK, so the lyrics are occasionally horrendous and the Sun Ra-inspired freakout is nowhere near as good as The Stooges' similar white noise meltdown. However, this has an irrepressible energy that overcomes the dated nature of the material.

◉ **Back In The USA** (1970; Rhino).
More pedestrian, but the MC5 were still out-rocking the competition. And who can resist a track named "The Human Being Lawnmower"?

Malcolm Russell

PAUL MCCARTNEY/WINGS

Paul McCartney born Liverpool, England, 1942.
Wings formed 1971; disbanded 1980.

"People say domesticity is the enemy of art ... but I made my decision and I feel okay with it. Ballads and babies – that's what happened to me."

After **THE BEATLES** split in 1970, **Paul McCartney** turned to a solo career which was to be far more commercially successful than those cut out by his three former colleagues. It's had some moments to match The Fabs, too, going well beyond Macca's self-deprecating claims of turning out a few simple 'ballads'. Indeed, it would be as wrong to dismiss McCartney's solo career, as many are prone to do, on the basis of "Mull Of Kintyre" as Lennon's on "Happy Xmas (War Is Over)."

The solo path started in promising, if low-key fashion with MCCARTNEY – released in April 1970, just ahead of The Beatles' swan song, LET IT BE. Spearheaded by the wonderful "Maybe I'm Amazed" – arguably Paul's best song, and unarguably his best vocal performance, outside of The Beatles – it was a fresh, spontaneous set, albeit with some sketchy songs and instrumentals. It shot straight to the top of the charts.

Due to the ex-Beatles' protracted litigation, it wasn't until the following February that Paul's gentle "Another Day" became his first solo hit, setting the tone for a career rich in melodic pop. RAM (1971) appeared soon after, the only LP to be credited to Paul and first wife, **Linda McCartney** (keyboards/vocals). Another UK #1 (and US #2), the album also produced McCartney's first solo US #1 single, "Uncle Albert"/"Admiral Halsey".

RAM introduced New Yorker **Denny Seiwell** on drums, and with the addition of **Denny Laine** (guitar/bass/vocals) from The Moody Blues, the core of Wings was in place. It was a brave move from McCartney, setting up a new 'group' career, though the band's lightweight debut album, WILDLIFE (1971), was critically panned. Undeterred, McCartney took the group on an unannounced college tour of the UK for his first live shows since 1966. **Henry McCullough**, former guitarist with the Grease Band, joined for the tour, and remained as the protest single "Give Ireland Back To The Irish" charted in the spring of 1972. Overtly political, in the wake of "Bloody Sunday", it was banned from radio play, prompting a swift riposte from McCartney in the form of "Mary Had A Little Lamb" – a nursery-rhyme follow-up.

The next Wings single, and their most substantial release to date, was the rocker "Hi Hi Hi". Again a radio ban ensued, this time for sexual references (it was actually more of a drug than sex song), but its whimsical B-side "'C'-Moon" became a hit. The album which followed, RED ROSE SPEEDWAY (1973), again disappointed, though the ballad "My Love" charted highly and was followed into the charts by "Live And Let Die", Paul's song for the James Bond film of the same name, and among his most impressive since The Beatles imploded.

Some months later, on the eve of a recording trip to Nigeria, Seiwell and McCullough quit, leaving Denny Laine with the McCartneys as the heart of Wings, a situation that would endure until the band's demise. Surprisingly, the resultant BAND ON THE RUN (1973), which was made under considerable duress, became Wings' most acclaimed LP, winning several awards and producing two Top 10 singles, "Jet" and the title track.

In mid 1974, guitarist **Jimmy McCulloch** (ex-**THUNDERCLAP NEWMAN** and Stone The Crows) and drummer **Geoff Britton** joined the group, who released a song written by Paul's father, "Walking In The Park With Eloise", under the pseudonym of **The Country Hams**. The rousing "Junior's Farm" was the only proper Wings release with Britton on board. He was replaced by an American, **Joe English**, on VENUS AND MARS (1975), a flawed attempt to revive the concept album formula. "Listen To What The Man Said" provided another hit, though the subsequent failures of "Letting Go" and "Venus And Mars"/"Rock Show" in the UK showed that McCartney's name no longer guaranteed a best-selling single.

The five-piece Wings embarked on a thirteen-month world tour, largely concentrating on material from VENUS AND MARS and the work-in-progress WINGS AT THE SPEED OF SOUND (1976), but also – for the first time – a handful of Paul's Beatles songs. SPEED OF SOUND was to be a patchy affair, hindered by the leader's democratic decision to hand each member a lead vocal spot, but it nonetheless produced "Silly Love Songs" and "Let 'Em In", each going Top 3 on both sides of the Atlantic.

In January 1977, the triple set WINGS OVER AMERICA (recorded on the US leg of the world tour) was unveiled, and went on to become the biggest-selling triple LP of all time. A version of "Maybe I'm Amazed" from the album went Top 10 in the US, just prior to the launch of Paul's peculiar orchestral LP THRILLINGTON (1977) – a souped-up instrumental version of RAM, released under the name of Percy 'Thrills' Thrillington.

McCulloch and English left Wings in September, but once again the reduced line-up came up trumps – commercially, at least. Recorded with a full Scottish pipe band, "Mull Of Kintyre" (a homage to McCartney's Scottish island home) was derided by critics yet broke the UK sales record held by The Beatles' "She Loves You", staying at #1 for two months. Strangely, its flip side ("Girls' School") was promoted instead in the US and barely caused a ripple.

After the disappointing LONDON TOWN (1978), Wings expanded to a five-piece once more. Guitarist **Laurence Juber** and drummer **Steve Holly** completed a line-up which attempted to capture the mood of the current disco boom with "Goodnight Tonight". It was backed with one of McCartney's strongest post-Beatles songs "Daytime Nighttime Suffering". BACK TO THE EGG (1979), which followed, proved to be the band's swan song. It didn't muster a major hit single and received a harsh battering from the media, even though it was arguably more diverse than anything previously attributed to the band.

After a UK tour and a drug possession charge for Paul in Japan, Wings disbanded. Nonetheless, little more than four months later, the pop-funk "Coming Up" and the ballad "Waterfalls" (both 1980) put McCartney straight back in the charts. Both appeared on MCCARTNEY II (1980), where synthesizers replaced the acoustic guitars of its 1970 predecessor.

After the death of John Lennon in December 1980, McCartney kept his longest-ever silence – not insignificant. He reappeared in spring 1982 with "Ebony And Ivory", a slushy racial-harmony duet with **STEVIE WONDER** that topped the charts on both sides of the Atlantic. This marked the beginning of a series of collaborations over the next decade: both TUG OF WAR (1982) and PIPES OF PEACE (1983) were chock-full of celebrity guests, while "The Girl Is Mine" (1982) and "Say Say Say" (1983) saw **Michael Jackson** and Paul guesting on each other's records and scoring international hits together. Their relationship would sour some time after when Jackson bought the rights to McCartney's Beatles compositions.

If many of Paul's solo projects had met with luke-warm responses, few had suffered the savaging handed out to GIVE MY REGARDS TO BROAD STREET (1984), a film (a 'musical fantasy drama' yet) and album consisting of half-baked back catalogue reworkings. Apart from a rare appearance singing "Let It Be" at the Live Aid concert, little was heard of McCartney again until 1986, when PRESS TO PLAY – a mix of catchy mid-tempo pop and ballads – spawned a handful of singles of varying quality.

Promisingly, however, "Back On My Feet" (1987), the B-side to "Once Upon A Long Ago", marked the beginning of a writing partnership with **ELVIS COSTELLO**. McCartney's 1989 album FLOWERS IN THE DIRT again used Costello's talents, and Paul's first collection of fresh material for three years was reckoned to be his strongest in a long while; songs like "My Brave Face" and "This One" displayed a hunger many thought was long lost.

In 1991, a well-received acoustic MTV performance from McCartney became the first of its kind to make it onto record, entitled UNPLUGGED – THE OFFICIAL BOOTLEG. As if to stress that he was exploring different avenues, his next project, LIVERPOOL ORATORIO (1991), conducted and co-written by Carl Davis, saw him moving into classical musical modes. The popularity of the work again exasperated his critics, and they were given fresh ammunition by the weak OFF THE GROUND (1993), a set featuring the same personnel as FLOWERS IN THE DIRT, but lacking the spark. Nonetheless, another world tour ensued, and an album, PAUL IS LIVE (1993), unapologetically reared its head at the end of it.

In another tangential move, McCartney teamed up with an unlikely collaborator, producer and **KILLING JOKE** founder member **Youth**, for a dabble in ambient-techno. Using the alias **The Fireman**, presumably to protect the guilty parties, STRAWBERRIES, OCEANS, SHIPS, FOREST (1993) caused barely a ripple, but it was a project Paul would revisit for RUSHES, released in 1998. Then, after years of rumour and counter-rumour, it was announced that a TV and video anthology of The Beatles would have the three surviving members recording together again for the accompanying three-part ANTHOLOGY album series, which was launched in 1995. The attendant praise and high-public profile which the project gave him seemed to energize McCartney, who in 1997 turned out two major releases. First, along with receiving a knighthood (without rumours of a quiet smoke in the toilets this time round, however) he produced a warmly received new solo record, FLAMING PIE, with assistance from **STEVE MILLER**, **Ringo Starr** and Paul's son. (Beatles fans will pick up immediately on the title, lifted from one of Lennon's early ventures into prose, writing for *Mersey Beat* magazine: 'Many people ask what are Beatles? Why Beatles? Ugh, Beatles, how did the name arrive? So we will tell you. It came in a vision – a man appeared in a flaming pie and said unto them "From this day on you are Beatles with an A". Thank you, Mister Man, they said, thanking him.'). Already recognized as the most successful songwriter of all time, he then forged ahead with STANDING STONE, an ambitious 'symphonic poem' that employed a large orchestra and chorus, and talents from the classical world such as Richard Rodney Bennett, John Harle and David Matthews.

The following year, after a long battle with cancer, Linda McCartney died. After a period of mourning for his partner of three decades, Paul oversaw the release of WODE PRAIRIE, a lovingly compiled collection of music Linda had recorded over the years. Other than pledging to continue his late wife's work on environmental issues, McCartney laid low for some considerable time before seemingly plunging headlong into a particularly creative patch. Both RUN DEVIL RUN and WORKING CLASSICAL emerged in rapid succession in 1999, the former a collection of classic rock'n'roll cover tunes, the latter another of his periodic orchestral excursions. Then came THE LIVERPOOL SOUND COLLAGE (2000), which harked back to McCartney's Fireman alter ego, and most recently DRIVING RAIN (2001), a collection of fresh McCartney compositions featuring a couple of new tunes co-written with his son **James** – the first McCartney and McCartney songs to appear on record. While the album displayed the kind of proficient commercial songwriting for which McCartney is renowned, the release of charity single, "Freedom!", written in the wake of the terrorist attacks on New York in September 2001, set the fuse for what would turn into a kind of latter-day Maccamania, at least in the States. The song became a major hit and with the announcement that McCartney would be embarking on his first tour for almost ten years – documented on BACK IN THE WORLD (2003) – fascination with one of the two surviving Beatles peaked to unprecedented levels.

⊙ **McCartney** (1970; Apple).
Under great weight of expectation, McCartney's first solo record turned out to be a collection of largely acoustic home recordings. With "Maybe I'm Amazed" given its first airing, this charming album has lasted where more ambitious efforts have dated.

⊙ **Band On The Run** (1973; Apple).
This rightly remains his best-known post-Beatles work. The title track and "Jet", with its blasting horns, were enormous singles, and the album barely has a duff track.

⊙ **Flowers In The Dirt** (1989; Parlophone).
McCartney's most substantial LP since Wings split, and the one that got him back on the road for the first time in years. Displays a raw edge missing from other sets, and stinging hooks to boot.

⊙ **All The Best!** (1987; Parlophone).
A compilation of Wings and solo singles – seventeen tracks and seventeen years' worth. An object lesson in pop songwriting craft.

James Robert

MARIA MCKEE/ LONE JUSTICE

Born Los Angeles, 1964.

I t was always likely **Maria McKee** was going to be an entertainer of some sort – her grandparents were tightrope walkers, her stepbrother Bryan Maclean was in the 60s group Love, and actor Nicolas Cage was a schoolfriend. She started performing professionally at 16, and in 1982 formed the country-rock band **Lone Justice** with guitarists **Ryan Hedgecock** and **Tony Gilkyson**, **Marvin Etzioni** (bass) and **Don Heffington** (drums).

Signed to Geffen, the group released their debut LP, LONE JUSTICE, in 1985, a set that showed they were trying to put some energy and youth back into country music. It was warmly praised by Mick Jagger, while Tom Petty and Bob Dylan offered to write material for them. McKee, the band's songwriter, had her song "A Good Heart" taken up by **Feargal Sharkey**, who scored a UK #1 with it later in the year.

McKee was joined by a new line-up on the follow-up album, SHELTER (1986), but she felt dissatisfied by the band's image and uncomfortable with their heightening profile in the States. Lone Justice supported U2 on their 'Joshua Tree' tour, but by the end of 1987 were no more, as McKee went 'solo' with guitarists Shane **Fontayne** and **Bruce Brody**. Her live shows became famous for their overwhelming emotiveness – one of them inspiring Ricky Ross to write "Real Gone Kid", a hit for his band **Deacon Blue** in 1988.

Largely self-penned, the 'solo debut', MARIA MCKEE (1989), featured several songs inspired by the plays of Tennessee Williams and the books of vaudeville history inherited from her grandparents. It was clearly the album that McKee had always dreamed of making, but its failure in her homeland dampened her spirits, and she relocated to Dublin. There she hung out with the Hothouse Flowers, U2, The Waterboys and Gavin Friday, while she contemplated her next move.

It was during this sabbatical that she received a tape of what was intended to be the title song of a new Tom Cruise film. Unenthusiastic at first, she agreed to record it on the condition that she was allowed to rewrite the lyrics. The film's producers relented, and so "Show Me Heaven" became the love theme for *Days Of Thunder*, and a UK #1 for four weeks in September 1990. It gave Geffen the excuse to reissue her album in 1991, and sell to a wider audience.

The next Maria McKee venture came when she teamed up with dance producer Youth in 1992. A one-off single, "Sweetest Child", was an experiment with pop–dance styles, but McKee then concentrated on creating a grander sound for her second LP. Released in 1993, YOU GOTTA SIN TO GET SAVED saw her reunite with several members of the original Lone Justice line-up. This time, three covers formed part of the set – two by her longtime hero **VAN MORRISON,** and one by **CAROLE KING**. The first single from the album, "I'm Gonna Soothe You", became a minor hit in the UK, but the album barely made any more impact than the first.

Still, another movie was to resurrect her name in 1994, when the spooky "If Love Is A Red Dress (Hang Me In Rags)", originally recorded for the second album, appeared on the *Pulp Fiction* sound-track. Perhaps prompted by this hip link, LIFE IS SWEET (1996) forsook formative influences for a remarkable meld of post-Nirvana punk squall and a rococo European chanson sensibility, suggesting something akin to Edith Piaf fronting Sonic Youth. It was hit-and-miss but typical of her work, in being highly theatrical and as original as you get.

Despite, or perhaps because of this startling quality, LIFE IS SWEET failed to sell in any great quantities and McKee was dropped from the Geffen roster. Out of contract for the first time in a decade she withdrew to take stock, surfacing only for the occasional live show and a hyper-sensual, supercharged guest vocal performance on "No Big Bang" on the 1996 David Byrne-less **TALKING HEADS** (now The Heads) reunion album NO TALKING JUST HEAD. Rounding off this stage of her career, an approved 'best of' album, drawn from Lone Justice and solo work, emerged in 2000 on US label Hip-O. New solo material finally surfaced in 2003 in the form of HIGH DIVE, released on her own ViewFinder label. At its best the set offered some fine, Lone Justice-sounding gems, but was largely bogged down by overly tin-kered production.

While many bands – The Dixie Chicks, for example – openly admit a debt of influence to McKee, she continues to follow her own path.

⊙ **Maria McKee** (1989; Geffen).
McKee at her best, from the yodelling country of "I've Forgotten What It Was In You (That Put The Need In Me)" to the mad rock-out of "Drinkin' In My Sunday Dress".

⊙ **You Gotta Sin To Get Saved** (1993; Geffen).
Having recruited Black Crowes producer George Drakoulis, and musicians like The Jayhawks and several of the Lone Justice cohorts, McKee comes up with a rockier effort, with the country influences overtaken by rock, pop and gospel.

⊙ **Life Is Sweet** (1996; Geffen).
McKee follows family circus tradition with this daring high-wire act of in-your-face vocals, caustic guitar, and walls of sound. McKee survives and the title cut is a stone-cold classic.

Peter Mills

MALCOLM MCLAREN

Born London, January 22, 1946.

The Revised Swindle: the ten-point career of punk Svengali **Malcolm McLaren**:

1. Go To The Right Schools. Young Malcolm went to a series of art schools out of sheer boredom. He sat out the 1968 Paris riots at Croydon College, but absorbed its radical ideas. In 1969, he embarked on a film about the history of Oxford Street, then hocked Goldsmith College's camera to raise money for his and Vivienne Westwood's first boutique. He finished the movie, *The Ghosts of Oxford Street*, in 1992.

2. Open A Shop. 'Selling things became an art in itself,' said McLaren. 'The art of provocation.' 240 King's Road throughout the years played host to Let It Rock, a teddy-boy haven that became too violent for McLaren; Sex, a rubber'n'leather outlet whose house band became the **SEX PISTOLS**; Seditionaries, boasting suede guerrilla gear; and World's End, a Wonderland with a backwards-running thirteen-hour clock. In turning consumerism into an act of rebellion, these stores were arguably McLaren's greatest achievements.

3. Play With Dolls. As **THE NEW YORK DOLLS** bought a ticket marked 'Drug'n'Booze Oblivion', McLaren approached the band with a new image: chuck the scarves for red patent leather, use the word 'red' at least six times in every song, and go 'Maoistic'. For McLaren, rock had become a means to a revolutionary end. The Dolls were just looking for the next hit. **JOHNNY THUNDERS** left the band in a Florida dive to go score some Cuban blond available only on 42nd Street. The NYD soldiered on, but as **Bob Gruen** observed, 'You get beat up for being a fag, but you get killed for being a commie.'

4. Take Credit For The Sex Pistols. Malc wasn't much for reading, but he saw a link between French anarchist theory and New York trash, and then turned it into hype for art's sake. Just don't ever think he had anything to do with the music.

5. Take Credit For Boy George, Adam Ant and Bow Wow Wow. And why not? The latter were a very wonderful pop creation indeed.

6. Find The Fad. Impressed by the New York hip-hop scene he 'discovered' when he brought Bow Wow Wow to America, McLaren decided to make the first postmodern album. DUCK ROCK (1983) brought the world both its music (the South African jive "Soweto") and scratching (the timeless cut-up "Buffalo Gals"), seamlessly produced by Trevor Horn and hideously sung by McLaren. Unhappy with Charisma's claims that he nearly bankrupted the company, the Shylock of Rock rereleased the album as D'YA LIKE SCRATCHIN'? (1984), and rereleased that as ROUND THE OUTSIDE, ROUND THE OUTSIDE to ever-diminishing returns.

7. Pillage The Classical World. With FANS (1984), McLaren turned to opera, synthesizing Puccini and the blues – at times to wonderful effect – in a soundtrack to an alleged musical about groupies kidnapping their idol. Five years on, he hit on the idea of combining classical dance music and funk with WALTZ DARLING (1989), a melange of Strauss, Bootsy Collins and six producers all trying to play waltzes in 4/4 time. He missed the 'vogueing' craze by a year that time, but his soundtrack to the fad that never was cost a million dollars and it sounded it. A hit that missed.

8. Go Legit. In 1988, the New Museum of Contemporary Art paid tribute to McLaren's status as 'tastemaker and professional litigant'. He was now being sued for unpaid royalties by the record company whose Zulu band he used on DUCK ROCK.

9. Get Into Movies. In spring 1985, as head of development at CBS Theatrical Productions and lover of Lauren Hutton, Malcolm had the following brainstorms: a beauty-and-the-beast fable starring Calvin Klein; the self-explanatory *Heavy Metal Surf Nazis*; Oscar Wilde discovering rock'n'roll in Texas in the 1890s (Spielberg got this pitch); and a Led Zep biopic, with Jason Donovan playing Robert Plant. To date, none of these films has been made, and in November 1985, CBS Theatrical Productions folded.

10. Raise The Barricades. McLaren moved to Paris to record PARIS (1994). Malcolm talked dirty over Lee Gorman's weak global techno, and nicked from Satie and Gainsbourg in an attempt to celebrate a city even more complicated than himself. A big success in Europe, it was sneered at by the Brits, ignored in the US, and later reissued as an ambient dance album. Oh, and Jacques Chirac asked McLaren to write his election theme tune. The circle was complete.

Duck Rock (1983; Charisma).
McLaren gets to jive before Paul Simon, rap before The Beasties, and record one of the all-time great comedy records on the hillbilly "Duck For The Oyster". A museum piece.

Fans (1984; Charisma).
As Malcolm realized, Puccini was some tunesmith, and the romance shines through on the best of these cuts.

Waltz Darling (1989; Epic).
It's hard to resist "Blue Danube" funked up by Bootsy

Collins, with guitar work from Jeff Beck. And nor should you. The great McLaren album.

Paris (1994; No!).
OK, this has some very tacky moments, but "Paris Paris" is defiantly gorgeous.

Charles Bottomley

JOHN MCLAUGHLIN AND THE MAHAVISHNU ORCHESTRA

John McLaughlin born Yorkshire, England, January 4, 1942. Mahavishnu Orchestra formed 1971; disbanded 1976; re-formed 1984; disbanded 1986.

He has become Britain's most renowned jazz guitarist, but **John McLaughlin**'s reputation was forged in the late 1960s with the fusion of modern jazz and heavy rock in the once hugely popular **Mahavishnu Orchestra**, the fastest, tightest jazz-rockers ever.

McLaughlin began playing piano and violin and only took up guitar to experiment with flamenco. By the time he was 21, though, he was a professional guitarist, serving a rigorous apprenticeship in bands led by **Georgie Fame** and **Alexis Korner**, seminal figures on the British R&B scene. He first gained notice playing straight-ahead jazz in a group led by **Graham Bond** which included **Jack Bruce** and **Ginger Baker**, later of **CREAM**. He was also a session musican and played on recordings by Duffy Power and The Rolling Stones.

By the mid 60s, McLaughlin had become interested in free jazz and spent time in Germany, playing with multi-instrumentalist **Gunter Hampel**. His first solo album, EXTRAPOLATION (1969), was recorded with fellow British avant-gardists **John Surman** (saxes) and **Tony Oxley** (drums), although it was notable for his mastery of classic jazz guitar styles founded by players such as **Charlie Christian** and **Wes Montgomery**. The subtlety of his playing caught the attention of drummer **Tony Williams** who, having made his name with Miles Davis, was about to form his own group, **Lifetime**, which at first reunited McLaughlin and Jack Bruce and initiated the jazz-rock fusion movement.

McLaughlin became more involved in this new direction in jazz when he was recruited by **MILES DAVIS** himself to play on the ground-breaking IN A SILENT WAY and BITCHES BREW albums. His funk-tinged, staccato riffing provided a framework around which Miles's trumpet could explore greater depths of emotional expression: in effect, he was taking the place intended for Jimi Hendrix in the cruelly frustrated collaboration between the two giants of black American music. McLaughlin adopted a heavier approach in his playing, placing greater emphasis on the blues style common to rock guitarists of the time, as evident on his second solo album, DEVOTION (1970).

At the same time, McLaughlin was developing a more reflective idiom as he forsook the lifestyle of a New York-based musician and became a follower of the Bengali mystic Sri Chimnoy, who gave him the name Mahavishnu, the name of an Indian god, meaning 'divine compassion, strength and justice'. His third solo album, MY GOAL'S BEYOND (1971), showed an interest in Eastern musical scales unmatched by anybody in jazz since John Coltrane. The eight-piece group featured veterans **Charlie Haden** (bass) and **Airto Moreira** (percussion), Panamanian-born drummer **Billy Cobham** and violinist **Jerry Goodman**.

McLaughlin retained Cobham and Goodman as the basis of his first Mahavishnu Orchestra, along with Czech keyboard player **Jan Hammer** and Irish bassist **Rick Laird**. A purely instrumental band, Mahavishnu were touted on the rock circuit chiefly due to the intensity and speed of McLaughlin's playing. Although always a self-effacing person, he attracted further attention from the rock press with his all-white dress and advocacy of clean living, as well as his custom-built double-necked guitar, which enabled him to reproduce the droning effect of a sitar while he soloed and whacked out the power chords. The group's first album, INNER MOUNTING FLAME, was released in 1972 and reflected McLaughlin's spiritual orientation, often at the expense of the subtlety that was his trademark.

Despite their excursions into wild fusion territory, the Mahavishnu Orchestra were adept at capturing a real rock sound. Two more albums followed in the next year, BIRDS OF FIRE (1973) and the live BETWEEN NOTHINGNESS & ETERNITY, the latter featuring new compositions that stretched the musicians' skills to the point where there was nothing much left to say.

The original line-up split, whereupon McLaughlin made a much-derided collaboration with fellow Chimnoy devotee Carlos 'Devadip' **SANTANA**, LOVE, DEVOTION, SURRENDER (1973), before forming a new Mahavishnu Orchestra with **Narada Michael Walden** (drums) and **Jean Luc Ponty** (violin), among others. This version released three lacklustre albums, and then McLaughlin renounced electric instrumentation, along with his previously unshakeable devotion to Chimnoy. He joined **Shakti**, an Indian classical group that featured violinist **L. Shankar** and percussionist **Trilok Gurtu**, with whom he later extensively collaborated.

In 1978, McLaughlin went back to playing electric guitar, initially with **The One Truth Band** and then with a third Mahavishnu Orchestra in the mid 80s. However, the attempts to redefine fusion were only occasionally successful, as McLaughlin seemed swamped by the array of electronic gadgets at his disposal, and he often reverted to earlier formats.

More recently, McLaughlin has found a balance in the Free Spirits trio, with **Dennis Chambers** on drums and **Joey DeFrancesco** on organ. He recorded a 1996 album, THE PROMISE, with these and a myriad of other cohorts. REMEMBER SHAKTI was released in 1999, and THE BELIEVER the following year, both were albums full of technically perfect, precision playing. With the resurgence of fusion in the form of dance and electronic music, who knows what the future holds for one of the genre's progenitors?

Inner Mounting Flame (1972; CBS). One of the classics of fusion, this features McLaughlin's fiery guitar melting into Billy Cobham's enormously influential funk drum patterns.

Robert Murray

MEAT LOAF

Born Marvin Lee Aday, Dallas, Texas, September 27, 1947.

"I am the Nureyev of rock and roll."

The career of **Meat Loaf** is remarkable for two reasons: first, his discovery of a profitable if improbable musical niche somewhere between light opera and heavy rock; and second, the way he managed to engineer his own rediscovery a decade after being consigned to the wings.

The young **Marvin Aday** allegedly acquired the Meat Loaf nickname from a gym teacher, at home in Texas, before he moved to Los Angeles in 1967, where his group **Popcorn Blizzard** backed Ted Nugent. Stardom was not forthcoming and he moved to New York, appearing in off-Broadway musicals before landing a part in the ubiquitous *Hair*. There he met singer **Stoney**, and together they recorded the unnoticed STONEY AND MEAT LOAF (1971) for Berry Gordy's Rare Earth label. When Hair folded in 1974 he toured in the *National Lampoon Road Show*, *More Than You Deserve* and *Never Land*, a show based on Peter Pan, the last two being written by **Jim Steinman**. His break came with the role of Eddie in a 1975 production of the cult musical *The Rocky Horror Show*. Meat also appeared in the movie version.

Steinman, who was involved in *Rocky Horror*, soon realized that in Meat Loaf he had found the perfect vehicle for his lyrics. He recruited some of the **E Street Band** to his cause, and **Ellen Foley** from the show to sing backing vocals. Then he persuaded Todd Rundgren to produce some tracks he had written; the outcome was BAT OUT OF HELL (1977). In 70s parlance it was a concept album, but basically it was a pantomime, marrying the camper excesses and imagery of the metal genre – lengthy songs, motorbikes, teenage girls and demon kings – to those of Broadway. By turns bombastic, sentimental and irresistibly jolly, it was carried off solely by the exuberance of Meat Loaf's performance. There were four show stoppers, each of which did well as singles, partly because all were tuneful and none approached

Meatloaf responds to his critics

their particular lapses of taste. The only real highlight was a greatest hits album, HITS OUT OF HELL (1984). It looked as if the curtain had fallen.

In 1992, however, Meat hooked up again with Steinman to have a go a repeating the old winning formula. Perhaps the most extraordinary thing about BAT OUT OF HELL II (1993) was that Meat Loaf was able to mine the same vein as the first album, yet still sound fresh doing so. Pleading vocals, cod metal guitar, anthemic tunes – even the album's cover was designed to revive memories of the original BAT. Almost equally impressive was the faith shown by Virgin in the reunited team, stumping up for a vastly expensive promotional video (in which Meat gets to play "Fat Man Of The Opera") before having heard the record.

The gamble worked, partly thanks to a corporate rock machine that was more professional and cynical than that of a decade before, but also through the indefatigable PR efforts of Meat, who showed himself to be a trouper without equal. The single "I'd Do Anything For Love" strode to the top spot in the UK and proved immovable. The album sold by the yard, leading to a reissue of a remixed (and utterly redundant) BAT I.

The second BAT album also, of course, repeated the problem of how to follow up. In the event, WELCOME TO THE NEIGHBORHOOD (1996) was a more than creditable attempt, with Meat romping through a couple of leftover Steinman songs, "Original Sin" and "Left In The Dark", and new producer Ron Nevison guiding him through some high-voltage metal workouts and big-passion power ballads with **Diane Warren**.

Nothing more was heard until 2003, when COULDN'T HAVE SAID IT BETTER presented another huge slab of rock-operatic pie ... with all the trimmings.

heavy metal – in fact, with hand-claps, sleigh bells and cooing female backing, a song like "You Took The Words Right Out Of My Mouth (Hot Summer Night)" was nothing more than souped-up Del Shannon.

The album sold well, particularly in the UK, where it hit #7. The half of the nation that wasn't making Sid Vicious and Boy George rich bought five million copies of the record, keeping it in the charts for a record eight years. It took four years for a reprise, the overblown DEAD RINGER (1981), to appear. Steinman knew he was onto a good thing, but this was too much of it. The title track, which featured a dynamic duet with Cher, was fine, but the rest lacked imagination and humour.

There was tension within the team and soon Steinman and Meat fell out. The former left to produce Bonnie Tyler's "Total Eclipse Of The Heart", the latter to star in *Roadie* with **Deborah Harry**. Foley, whose backing was integral to the sound of the first album, also got on with her acting career – she appeared in *Fatal Attraction*.

Meat Loaf remained popular enough in the years that followed, particularly as a live act, but the albums confirmed the law of diminishing returns, and were distinguished from each other by little more than

Bat Out Of Hell (1977; Sony).
An unlikely mix of air guitar and doo-wop, this is an album that knew it was being silly and played it for all it was worth. A disc literally jam-packed with stand-outs, from the title track on, which Loaf delivers with such verve that you can hear him stumble on one chorus in his eagerness to get the words out.

Hits Out Of Hell (1984; Sony).
What it says, including the best bits of DEAD RINGER. Sadly, it was released too early to include "Rock And Roll Mercenaries".

James Owen

MEAT PUPPETS

Formed Tempe, Arizona, 1981.

"We've never lost our taste for playing weird shit." Derrick Bostrom

Brothers **Curt** (vocals/guitar) and **Cris Kirkwood** (bass/vocals) taught themselves to play guitar by listening to Black Sabbath and ZZ Top, but it was the desert around Arizona, with its coyotes, creeks and empty spaces, that had the greatest effect on their music. Impelled to action by the early US punk movement, they roped in friend **Derrick Bostrom** (drums), and rehearsed by throwing small electrical appliances at each other. This kind of behaviour was almost guaranteed to gain **The Meat Puppets** a deal with LA's seminal hard-core label SST, who signed them in late 1981.

1982's MEAT PUPPETS was quirky, noisy and mainly unlistenable, a lesser version of what the Butthole Surfers would later call their own. The album's highlight was the fifty-second trashing of cowboy novelty classic "Tumblin' Tumbleweeds", which remains a live stalwart. It received some press and radio support, but gave only the sketchiest clues of what was to follow.

A deeply dull title could not prevent MEAT PUPPETS II (1983) from being their finest overall album, ranking alongside Hüsker Dü's ZEN ARCADE as one of the key proofs of hardcore's growing sophistication. Their debut's crudity had been replaced by a sparse and surreal country-rock, typified by "Plateau", which commented on the Arizona desert's curious beauty. The Minutemen's cover of "Lost" on their final album (3-WAY TIE FOR LAST), and the versions of "Plateau", "Oh Me" and "Lake Of Fire" the Kirkwoods played with **Kurt Cobain** on **NIRVANA**'s UNPLUGGED, are testaments to the quality of these songs.

UP ON THE SUN (1984) was different again: the spaces and short songs had been replaced by a lusher sound and a rather alarming musical virtuosity. The band's only reward for this burst of creativity was a seemingly never-ending college tour of the States.

There was something for everyone on OUT MY WAY (1986), which paid subtle tributes to ZZ Top and Gram Parsons, and contained a violent rendition of Little Richard's "Good Golly Miss Molly". This cleared the way for MIRAGE (1987), their most tuneful and polished album, which retained the Arizona mysticism of their early work. A commercial breakthrough was predicted, but it bombed and the band responded with HUEVOS (1987), a doomed attempt to make a rawer record. The Meat Puppets were becoming increasingly bitter at the big record contracts signed by contemporaries like R.E.M. Nevertheless, their last album for SST, MONSTERS (1989), had its moments, and the 1990 compilation, NO STRINGS ATTACHED, gave critics a chance to pay tribute.

London Records finally provided the long-hoped-for major-label deal, but they had to wait for the goods. FORBIDDEN PLACES (1991) was tired and unimaginative, and TOO HIGH TO DIE (1994) showed little improvement. However, NO JOKE (1995) turned in a set of anarchic, punky alternative rock that included some distinctly radio-friendly songs, notably "Taste O' The Sun". And it sold – notching up a cool half million units in the States.

During the next five years nothing was heard of the band due to a period of prolonged misery that saw Cris battling with drug addiction and the death of Curt's wife. Then in 2000 a new line-up emerged, still with Curt at the helm, for the release of GOLDEN LIES. The set was a droning, explosive, cranky return to form that showed a broader vision than had been seen in the band's work for a long while. A live DVD, ALIVE IN THE NINETIES, followed in 2003. After two decades, the Meat Puppets might yet just make it huge.

- ⊙ **Meat Puppets II** (1983; SST).
  Holy Ghosts and talk-show hosts are planted in the sand, to beautify the foothills. Very strange, spooky and funny, an adventure in cactus-filled places only previously explored by Captain Beefheart.

- ⊙ **Out My Way** (1986; SST).
  Ever imagined ZZ Top sounding liquid and funky? Just one of the illusions managed on this very clever mini-album.

- ⊙ **Mirage** (1987; SST).
  Melancholy, drifting yet concise country music. A surreal, sad, humorous attempt to come to grips with the desert, including the wonderful "Confusion Fog". Their last great record.

Marc Elliot

MEDICINE HEAD

Formed Stafford, England, 1968; disbanded 1976.

Before his obsession with The Fall, the influential British DJ John Peel had shown more loyalty to **Medicine Head** than to any other act. Their first three albums had come out on his own Dandelion label, and the debut, NEW BOTTLES OLD MEDICINE (1970), was produced by 'Peel, Pig and friends'. Peel has never been noted for nostalgia but the odd Head cut, especially "His Guiding Hand", still gets airplay on his show.

Medicine Head's mainstays, **John Fiddler** (vocals/guitar/keyboards/bass drum) and **Peter Hope-Evans** (harmonica/jew's-harp), went through school and art college together. Playing at parties extended to crashing gigs and, eventually, a meeting with Peel. Their first single, "His Guiding Hand" (1970), was lifted directly from a demo tape forwarded to the DJ. The single epitomized the band's approach, blending basic, rowdy blues with Fiddler's gift for finely crafted melodic songs. With solid radio support, especially from Peel, Medicine Head were soon a fixture of the British rock scene.

Working as a two-piece, the band became regulars on the college and club circuit and noted openers for bigger acts. As a duo they were an easy act to stage, with Fiddler playing guitar, pedal-thumping a bass drum and singing, Hope-Evans jigging along beside him. However, beginning with HEAVY ON THE DRUM (1971), Head developed a more subtle sound that was more difficult to reproduce as a live duo. This problem would dog the band for much of their career.

Former Yardbird **Keith Relf**, who had produced the 1971 album, briefly joined a three-piece version of the band when Hope-Evans quit following the minor hit single "(And The) Pictures In The Sky" (1971). By mid-1972, 'Harpo' was back and the most lucrative period of Head's career began. A seemingly throwaway number written between takes in the studio, "One And One Is One" (1973), was released as a single at Fiddler's urging. With its odd title and catchy slide-guitar riff, it reached #3 in the UK charts. Tony Ashton's production on the ONE AND ONE IS ONE album (1973) gave the band an even greater range in sound, featuring hippie folk in "Instant Karma Kid", the reggae-esque anthem "All The Fallen Teenangels", and a furious live reworking of "Blue Suede Shoes".

Within a year, **Roger Saunders** (guitar), **Rob Townsend** (drums) and **George Ford** (bass) had all joined the band. The new five-piece notched up two further hit singles: "Rising Sun" (1973) and "Slip And Slide" (1974), works of real merit in the increasingly formularized glam era. "Rising Sun" was described as 'psychedelic reggae' by *Disc*, whilst "Slip And Slide" featured some brilliantly underplayed harmonica and a largely spoken vocal intercut with an improbably simple and catchy guitar riff.

THRU' A FIVE (1974) recycled old blues progressions and other rootsy influences into a thick pop/rock sound with catchy riffs in abundance, in an effort to create a hit album. Critical opinion was divided, the album failed to chart, and things fell apart with disturbing speed.

Signing up to the ill-starred WWA organization, Head turned in some more superb radio work and one blinding single, "Mama Come Out" (1975), before stumbling to a halt along with their record company. By 1976 they had re-formed as a duo and signed to Chas Chandler's Barn label, cutting TWO MAN BAND (1976), a mellow album with strong romantic lyrics and some fine instrumental work. It may have been up there with their best, but by this time the Pistols' "Anarchy In The UK" had been released and Head had a mountain to climb to regain their place in the rock market. One more superb single, "Me And Suzy Hit The Floor" (1976), closed the account.

Fiddler soon turned up along with ex-Mott The Hoople members in **The British Lions**, who made solid glam-metal noises at a time when the music was threatened by punk. By the early 80s, he was earning respect and some money in **A Box Of Frogs**, in which he fronted a line-up composed mainly of ex-Yardbirds. In the early 90s he re-emerged as a solo act and briefly recruited a band to tour a new set of songs interspersed with the old hits. RETURN OF THE BUFFALO (1995) was an astonishing solo album capturing the charge and vision of the early work, and it gained good reviews. Fiddler's solo gigging increased around this time and the late 90s looked more promising than many of the preceding years and, following a stint in Arizona, Fiddler returned to the UK full-time to set up his own studio.

Hope-Evans shared a guru with **Pete Townshend** and did his most notable post-Medicine Head work on Townshend's EMPTY GLASS and WHITE CITY albums. Today, he gets a regular namecheck as a correspondent in *Fortean Times*, the cult journal of strange phenomena. The climate may be against him, but his songwriting abilities and the strength of the recent work suggest some possibilities for a comeback.

⊙ **New Bottles Old Medicine** (1970; See For Miles). A reissue with bonus cuts is for old hippies or those who wish they'd been there. A period piece for sure, but stuffed with naive charm and a real feel for music.

⊙ **Best Of Medicine Head** (1990; Polydor). Contains all the hits and the best of the cuts from the albums DARK SIDE OF THE MOON and THRU' A FIVE.

Neil Nixon

JOE MEEK

Born Newent, England, April 5, 1929; died February 3, 1967.

Joe Meek recorded Margaret Thatcher's favourite record – but don't let that put you off. "Telstar", by his studio ensemble, **The Tornadoes**, has proved to be popular with millions of other listeners since its release in 1962 and holds an important place in pop history, for being the first 45 by a British group to top the US charts. As the UK's first independent producer, Meek pushed back the boundaries of studio technique in Britpop's pre-Beatles Dark Age, with hits from umpteen acts both real and imaginary. But, however bizarre his records, few could match the psychotic flamboyance of their maker.

After starting his career working for the major labels, Joe Meek set up his own makeshift studio in London, in a dingy flat over a leather shop at 304 Holloway Road. Here he recorded songs using an inspired mixture of the latest electronic gimmickry and inspired amateurism, to an accompaniment of furious neighbours banging on the walls. His first independently produced #1, and perhaps the classic example of the Joe Meek Sound, was John Leyton's "Johnny Remember Me", released in July 1961. Composed by his Ouija-toting sidekick **Geoff Goddard**, it was a mournful lament for a dead lover, given an incredibly eerie quality by Meek's generous use of echo and reverb – the backing refrain in particular sounded like it was coming from beyond the grave. Leyton was just one of the many young hopefuls who crowded around Meek's circle hoping for a shot at the big time: amongst the singers and session players you would also have found, at one time or another, were Rod Stewart, Ritchie Blackmore, Mitch Mitchell and even the young Tom Jones.

One of Meek's big obsessions was space travel, which inspired the first ever outer-space concept album, I HEAR A NEW WORLD (1960), and the famous "Telstar", a track named after an American communications satellite. Dreamt up overnight after Meek had watched the first ever live satellite TV transmissions from the US, it was recorded the next day by Meek's session band. The tinny space-age sound caught the public imagination and was a major hit in summer 1962, topping the charts on both sides of the Atlantic. Indeed, it still remains Britain's best-selling instrumental single worldwide.

Less commercial were his gothic death discs, including The Moontrekkers' "Night Of The Vampire" (complete with creaking coffin lids) and the hysterical "'Til The Following Night" by Screaming Lord Sutch. All of them were banned by the BBC as being 'unsuitable for people of a nervous disposition'.

The age of innocence for British pop was soon to come to an end with The Beatles and the new professionalism they threw up in their wake. Although Meek still had hits with the likes of the Honeycombs' infuriatingly catchy "Have I The Right", his once futuristic sound was beginning to sound old hat. Not that Joe would accept it, of course. Beset by dodgy business dealings and black-mailers threatening to reveal his fast-living gay lifestyle, he was showing all the signs of an imminent nervous breakdown. His legendary tempers became more volcanic and musicians would often escape, pursued by large items of recording equipment hurled after them down the stairs. Some even claimed that Meek was psychically besieged by the spirits he conjured up at his endless seances, including the Great Beast himself, Aleister Crowley. Worst of all, the hits were drying up fast and by 1966 he was looking like a has-been.

On February 3, 1967, the anniversary of the death of his hero, Buddy Holly, Meek got into a heated dispute with his landlady. In a fit of rage, he shot her dead then blew his own head off, leaving a tangle of legal actions, unpaid debts and a legend that survives to this day; for, despite his personal failings, Joe Meek was a pioneer of the punk DIY ethic and a patron saint of home recordists everywhere. His original records are now highly desired collectors' items, and even the awful ones are accepted as retro-camp classics. Interest in his work keeps on growing, encouraged by a fabulous 1990 BBC documentary that even included Joe's midnight recording of a talking cat in a Brentford cemetery and a continuing series, currently at volume five, of THE JOE MEEK STORY (Sequel Records). Meek also developed many studio innovations, such as close-miking, studio isolation, multitracking and phasing, all now standard practice. With today's tech-nology at his disposal, who knows what kind of sounds he could have conjured up?

⊙ **The Musical Adventures Of Joe Meek** (1994; Kenwest).
An excellent introduction to his work, featuring most of his best-known tracks, including "Telstar", "Johnny Remember Me" and "Have I The Right", plus lesser-known gems by the Blue Rondos, the Cryin' Shames and the Fabulous Flee-Rakkers.

⊙ **Intergalactic Instros** (1997; Diamond).
This is part of Diamond's excellent JOE MEEK COLLECTION, 32 tracks of inspired madness, though of interest mainly to collectors and completists.

Iain Smith

MEGADETH

Formed San Francisco, 1983.

"The band's name means the act of dying, but, like, really mega!" Dave Mustaine

It's said that **Dave Mustaine** (lead guitar/vocals) left **METALLICA** in a bit of a hurry, prior to the recording of KILL 'EM ALL, reason being an altercation between him and **James Hetfield** that resulted in a collision between his boot and Hetfield's dog. He swiftly joined forces with **David Ellefson** (bass), guitarist **Chris Poland** and drummer **Gar Samuelson** to form **Megadeth**, whose debut album, KILLING IS MY BUSINESS ... AND BUSINESS IS GOOD!!! (1985), offered a thrashier, faster kind of heavy metal, which Mustaine classed as speed metal.

The original line-up lasted one more album, PEACE SELLS ... BUT WHO'S BUYING? (1986), after which Poland and Samuelson left the band – Poland recorded the solo album RETURN TO METALOPOLIS, Samuelson disappeared from the music scene. Their replacements were guitarist **Jeff Young** and drummer **Chuck Behler**, who did the business on SO FAR, SO GOOD ... SO WHAT? (1988), the album that really pushed the band into the limelight with tracks such as "Mary Jane" and a thrash version of the Sex Pistols' "Anarchy In The UK" (a staple of the Megadeth live set), both singles making a respectable dent on the UK charts for a US metal act. With success in the bag, Mustaine launched himself into what was to be a recurring frenzy of drug and alcohol consumption.

Young and Behler, like Poland and Samuelson before them, didn't last long. After the promotional tour for the album, the two were booted out by Mustaine, who replaced them with guitarist **Marty Friedman** and drummer **Nick Menza**. This line-up was first featured in the 1990 album RUST IN PEACE – which gave the band yet another British hit single with "Hangar 18", but one which paled next to their Top Twenty cover version of Alice Cooper's "No More Mr. Nice Guy" from the soundtrack to *Shocker* – and proved to be the most popular manifestation of the band.

After tours of major venues, including the Clash Of The Titans at London's Wembley Arena (with Slayer, Anthrax and Suicidal Tendencies), the band went on to release COUNTDOWN TO EXTINCTION (1992), which featured their mega-hit single, "Symphony Of Destruction", plus "Skin Of My Teeth", Mustaine's reflection on substance abuse and his several near misses with death. Megadeth had slowed down their music a little, and the end result was a heavier, more solid album which indicated that the band was developing and maturing.

The band recorded the track "Go To Hell" for the film *Bill & Ted's Bogus Journey* and then set off again on tour, announcing to the music press that Mustaine was now a rehabilitated family man, complete with baby son. 1993 also saw the end of the feud between Mustaine and Hetfield when Megadeth were invited to play as second on the bill at Metallica's Milton Keynes concert.

Having contributed the track "99 Ways To Die" to the compilation album THE BEAVIS AND BUTT-HEAD EXPERIENCE (the new-look dried-out Mustaine had regained his sense of humour), Megadeth reinforced their standing with YOUTHANASIA (1994) and its spin-off single "Train Of Consequences". The album's cover art – a computer photograph of an old woman pegging out babies on a washing line – provoked controversy, and a ban in Chile.

The follow-up, CRYPTIC WRITINGS (1997) had Mustaine dabbling in the occult craft of synthesizer-wielding and, unlikely as it may seem, brought a more thoughtful Megadeth to the fore. Thrash there was aplenty, together with lashings of evil imagery and much waving of long hair. This new direction, however, eventually led to the appropriately titled RISK (1999), which confused many fans with its more melodic approach. Megadeth seemed to be losing their way and it wasn't until THE WORLD NEEDS A HERO (2001), featuring guitarist **Al Pitrelli** and drummer **Jimmy DeGrasso**, that they rediscovered their sense of aggression. Sadly this rebirth was very short-lived because in early January 2002 Mustaine sustained serious nerve damage to his left arm and hand, effectively putting Megadeth out of action until such time as he could make a full recovery. Shocked fans were forced to find solace in the live offering RUDE AWAKENING (2002).

⊙ **So Far, So Good ... So What?** (1998; Capitol).
The lads in their element on the best of their early albums. Heavy, pounding tracks such as "Mary Jane" are matched by fast-paced numbers such as "Liar". A valuable component of any thrash collection.

⊙ **Countdown To Extinction** (1992; Capitol).
Megadeth reach maturity. A slower-paced (but still fast) album, with lyrics exploring weighty issues like – uhh – death, war and the destruction of the planet.

⊙ **Youthanasia** (1994; Capitol).
Gone are the artificial stimulants – this is Megadeth undrugged. Again the social concerns are present and again the tracks are serious yet catchy. The best of the albums so far, without a doubt.

Richard Allan

THE MEKONS

Formed Leeds, England, 1977.

Perhaps the most surprising thing about **The Mekons** is their longevity. A mixed bag of art students, who thought it might be a laugh to mess around with the Gang Of Four's equipment while they were in the pub, they eventually outlived not only their mentors, but pretty much every other New Wave band as well.

Formed in the incendiary atmosphere of Leeds' 1977 race riots, The Mekons served their political apprenticeship with fellow Rock Against Racism stalwarts Delta 5, Another Colour and the Expelaires. Racist violence at their early gigs crystallized an uncompromisingly radical attitude, which remains intact despite innumerable line-up changes, musical shifts and record labels.

The Mekons' first single, "Never Been In A Riot", written in response to the sloganeering bravado of The Clash's "White Riot", placed the band's down-to-earth humour in opposition to the posturing of many London New Wave outfits. Lo-fi even by punk standards, it encapsulated the punk ethic of 'everyone can do it', which The Mekons carried through to their live performances by allowing anyone to pick up an instrument and join them on stage.

At one point, band membership is thought to have numbered over twenty, although by the release of the first album, THE QUALITY OF MERCY IS NOT STRNEN...(1979), it had consolidated around the creative nucleus of **Andy Corrigan** and **Mark White** (vocals), **Tom Greenhalgh** and **Kev Lycett** (guitars), **Ros Allen** (bass) and **Jon Langford** (drums). The album featured an eclectic mix of punk-related styles, from the angular groove of "Trevira Trousers" to the formulaic bubblegum of "Dan Dare". If it disappointed the critics (and The Mekons' record company, Virgin), for lacking the shambolic spontaneity that characterized the live appearances, it did nothing to prepare them for its follow-up – the proto-gothic soundscapes of THE MEKONS. Released the following year, it set a benchmark for wilful New Wave obscurity. Oblique and impenetrable, it endeared them to no one.

Although The Mekons didn't formally split, its members' interests diversified into spin-off projects – of which Jon Langford's involvement in **THE THREE JOHNS** is most noteworthy. They had virtually ceased live performances by 1980, and an appearance at an Anti-Nazi League benefit in the summer of 1981 marked the end of the first chapter of The Mekons' history.

Drawn into the turbulent political wake of the 1984 miners' strike, The Mekons eventually re-emerged as a tightly focused and highly motivated outfit. Whereas punk had spiralled down into the constipated rhetoric of Oi! music, The Mekons regrouped in a musical territory that no one else would have had the nerve to occupy, their remarkable 1985 album, FEAR & WHISKEY, revealing them as a fierce, kick-ass country band, rolling along with an unstoppable alcoholic impetus. They gigged incessantly, spreading the word at benefits up and down the country, and lent tracks to compilations in support of the homeless, the stricken National Union of Mineworkers, Pro-Choice campaigns and AIDS charities.

If subsequent albums failed quite to capture the frustration and self-destructive impulse of FEAR & WHISKEY, they did at least reflect an increasing cohesiveness in Langford and Greenhalgh's writing. Sleeve notes and lyrics painted the picture of a nightmarish Mekonville, a beer-soaked frontier town peopled by the unemployed and dispossessed, the ghosts of dead revolutionaries and the fetishized icons of another era – Hank Williams, John Wayne and Elvis.

New recruits **Susan Honeyman** (fiddle) and **Sally Timms** (vocals) added a new dimension to The Mekons' infectious dance sound, and this eclecticism saw the band gracing the WOMAD (world music festival) stage. 1988's SO GOOD IT HURTS experimented with elements of Cajun, Hawaiian and English folk music. Although ambitious, the venom of old was lacking, and the album was criticized as lightweight. No such accusations were levelled at 1989's MEKONS ROCK'N'ROLL, which, from the brutal opening assault of "Memphis, Egypt" to the final strains of Tom and Sally's suicide-pact ballad "When Darkness Falls", was an unflaggingly passionate work, and seemed particularly exceptional amidst the dazed hedonism of the late 1980s.

Throughout the 1980s, despite a diversifying fan base, The Mekons had maintained strong links with Leeds and the north, often recording there, and littering songs with references to their home town. However, partly due to the attentions of *Rolling Stone* and *Village Voice* rock critic Greil Marcus, they also attracted something of a cult following in the USA, and the turn of the decade saw half of the band relocating permanently to the States.

From this atomized state, The Mekons continued to periodically regroup, attaining sporadic artistic (if not commercial) successes with THE CURSE OF THE MEKONS and I LOVE MEKONS in 1991 and 1993 respectively. They rose above the parapets again in 1996, releasing PUSSY-KING OF THE PIRATES, a startlingly off-kilter album backing the spoken-word novel narration of postfeminist American writer Kathy Acker, and their April 1996 release MEKONS UNITED – a book-cum-art-show catalogue, accompanied by a 32-track CD of new material. Last seen on the album OOOH (2002), recorded in Chicago, The Mekons look set to join the ranks of the great unkillable rock eccentrics.

(•) **Fear & Whiskey** (1985; Sin).
Mekonstein's Monster – a head of folk, a body of country and a heart of purest punk. At times, passion outstrips musical ability in the race to the end of a song, but there are some glorious moments, not least on "Hard To Be Human" and "Last Dance".

(•) **The Edge Of The World** (1986; Sin)
Following hard on the heels of FEAR & WHISKEY, this was good, if not better. The Mekons further explore their alternative country/folk universe. Contains the beautiful "King Arthur", which personalizes the British miners' defeat in the strike of 1984/85, using it as a metaphor for a soulless world.

(•) **The Mekons Honky-Tonkin**
(1987; Sin/Cooking Vinyl).
Further examines the warped psyche of 80s British society to great effect. "I Can't Find My Money" is both funny and sympathetic, whilst "'Prince of Darkness" is sumptuously doomy.

(•) **Mekons Rock'N'Roll** (1989; Blast First).
Their finest moment on record. Vicious and magnificent, a decade's worth of pent-up frustration reaches flash point. Alternately furious and agonized, the disenfranchized Mekons offer fourteen blistering tracks, many of which still feature in live appearances.

(•) **Mekons F.U.N. 90** (1990; Blast First).
A fine version of The Band's "It Makes No Difference" accompanies some more experimental material that marks a move away from country – although not totally, as later releases testify.

(•) **The Curse Of The Mekons** (1991; Blast First).
Subtle, atmospheric and criminally underexposed, featuring Sally Timms' incandescent voice on "Secrets" and "Waltz".

(•) **Retreat From Memphis**
(1994; Quarterstick/Touch And Go).
A 'rock' album, probably the weakest in The Mekons' catalogue, as failure to edit out the weaker tracks tends to obscure such gems as "The Flame That Killed John Wayne".

Huw Bucknell

JOHN (COUGAR) MELLENCAMP

Born Seymour, Indiana, 1951.

Tales of square-peg musicians and the round-hole record industry are not exactly scarce. Rarer are those of musicians who emerge with both artistic credibility and commercial viability intact. Step up **John (Cougar) Mellencamp**.

After cutting his teeth with the appallingly titled Crepe Soul and Snakepit Banana Barn, the then plain John Mellencamp sent a solo demo to David Bowie's management company, Main Man, which led to a deal with MCA and the release of his album debut, CHESTNUT STREET INCIDENT (1976). Two shocks were to follow for the artist, however: one, he found himself renamed on the disc Johnny Cougar; two, he was to participate in an open-top motorcade through his home town as part of 'Johnny Cougar Day'. Mellencamp parted company with Main Man the following year.

Dropped by MCA, too, after poor sales for KID INSIDE (1977), Mellencamp signed to Rod Stewart's manager Billy Gaff and his Riva label. JOHN COUGAR (1979) and NOTHING MATTERS AND WHAT IF IT DID (1980) followed – pleasant, lightweight pop-rock but hardly enough to warrant the 'new Springsteen' tag conjured up by Gaff. AMERICAN FOOL (1982) was at first glance more of the same, but proved the breakthrough, climbing to #1 in the US album charts – as did its prime cut, "Jack And Diane".

With his career on the up, John began to reassume control of his affairs. Despite record company protestations, UH-HUH (1983) became the first album to be credited to John Cougar Mellencamp. It was also, and perhaps this is not such a coincidence, the first to show signs of any real spirit. If at times a touch lyrically dumb ('this is a serious business/sex and violence and rock'n'roll), tracks like "Pink Houses" were nevertheless an indication of what was soon to follow.

The transition to serious artist was under way. Turning down a Live Aid appearance, Mellencamp instead concentrated on the money- and consciousness-raising Farm Aid, and his next album, SCARECROW (1985), focused on the crisis hitting the Midwest's agricultural community. With his long-term band in sparkling form and finally given weighty material to get stuck into, this was a harsher album, yet still yielded a brace of US hits.

Firmly ensconced in the album–tour–album treadmill, it was to be two years until THE LONESOME JUBILEE (1987). With an extended band, Mellencamp's music took on a rootsier feel and, although the lyrics often dealt with characters in states of turmoil, the music was life-affirming in spirit. The results were perhaps only to be expected – a Top 10 US album plus hit singles to follow.

Quite how long Mellencamp could comfortably exist in the world of stardom was to be answered by BIG DADDY (1989). From the opening single, "Pop Singer", it was a far less joyous affair. The band remained the same but took on a far more downbeat, folk feel. As for the man himself, the anger and frustration that he had aimed at America on the previous albums was now turned upon himself. There was no tour to support the record and the music business would have to do without John Mellencamp's company for the best part of the next two years.

When he did come back, after immersing himself in painting, and making a screen acting debut, the roots dimension had been abandoned in favour of a return to the stripped-down, hard-hitting style of UH-HUH. WHENEVER WE WANTED (1991) and HUMAN WHEELS (1993) both saw Mellencamp back on the road and back in the charts. By the time DANCE NAKED (1994) came around, the old enthusiasm was back in full effect.

In 1996 he confounded expectations by teaming up with ace dance producer **Junior Vasquez**. The album born of this unlikely union, MR HAPPY GO LUCKY, thankfully avoided Mellencamp reinventing himself for the MDMA generation, though it did see a novel twist applied to his familiar scenes of everyday life in a blue collar. Despite the best efforts of the music business machinery, this peg is still kinda squarish.

1999 saw him signed to a new label for the release of JOHN MELLENCAMP (Columbia). Although he still kept his hand in with the dance-orientated stuff, he'd suffered a heart attack since the release of MR HAPPY GO LUCKY, and looked more to his soft-rocking past than to the dance-floor for inspiration. Furthermore, there can't be many artists who lured **Trisha Yearwood** and **Chuck D** into the same recording

John Mellencamp

sessions, but Mellencamp did just that on 2001's CUTTING HEADS.

⊙ **Scarecrow** (1985; Riva).
From the harsh opening clank of metal on metal, this is the album that saw Mellencamp get serious. "Scarecrow" paints a picture of a Midwest seemingly dying on its feet, and a longing for the good old days permeates.

⊙ **The Lonesome Jubilee** (1987; Mercury).
A further re-examination of the American Dream through a series of vignettes. The juxtaposition of the hope-lessness of Mellencamp's characters and the band's spirited performances leads to an oddly uplifting record.

⊙ **Big Daddy** (1989; Mercury).
The final part of the trilogy, and the most personal. The odd character pops up, but much of the album is written in the first person: "Void In My Heart" is his life story down to the last detail. An unhappy journey for the artist; almost a feeling of intrusion for the listener.

⊙ **The Best That I Could Do 1978–1988** (1998; Mercury).
Excellent career retrospective for the million-selling master of Midwestern frustration.

Phil Udell

THE MELVINS

Formed Seattle, 1984.

The Melvins were the godfathers of the auspicious Seattle grunge movement, yet they will probably never claim a fraction of Pearl Jam's market share. A decidedly unsafe band, The Melvins are what Sabbath would sound like with Captain Beefheart as chief songwriter. Both Nirvana and Soundgarden have cited them as their creative muse; however, not even **Kurt Cobain**'s production and vocal credit on their 1993 release, HOUDINI, could endear the band to the millions who patronize Seattle's moribund music scene.

Four years before Nirvana formed, The Melvins were serving up the heaviest meat-and-potatoes rock in town. From their inception, they put the 'power' into power trio, with vocalist/guitarist **Buzz Osbourne**, bassist **Matt Lukin**, and a lulu of a drummer, **Dale Crover**. This early incarnation is documented on live album 10 SONGS (1986) and on GLUEY PORCH TREATMENTS (1987). Matt moved on to the fledgling **MUDHONEY** in 1987, and Buzz and Dale saw two more bass players leave the fold before **Mark D** joined up in 1994. Ironically, The Melvins' sound is so dense that a bass is oftentimes made obsolete by the basso profundo of Buzz's detuned riffing and sepulchral vocals.

The next full-length recording, released in 1989, pays a Faustian debt to Black Sabbath's "Master Of Reality" while avoiding most of the clichés of the heavy metal heritage. In lieu of the lyrical treacle and satanic clap-trap of similar-sounding bands, The Melvins took great pains to ensure the content of their songs concerned, well ... nothing at all. Surrealism abounds with song titles such as "Heater Moves And Eyes", "My One Percent Shows Most", and lyrics which owe more to Dada than the Devil.

Perfectly content to confuse those fans who understand the world only as it relates to the iconography of heavy metal, BULLHEAD (1991) was a brutal exercise in doom and vroom; the record jacket sports a righteous watercolour of a fruit basket. Even more conceptually obtuse was BULLHEAD's successor, an unnamed recording with no track listing. The Melvins started to shuffle off their metal coil with 1994's STONER WITCH, which showcased their dual allegiances to industrial noise and Southern rock. Tracks such as "Revolve" and "June Bug" bristle with a ZZ Top groove, while "Lividity" and "Goose Freight Train" recall the drunk-in-a-metalshop work of Tom Waits.

STAG, released in 1996, upped the ante still further; folded into the sound recipe are, among other ingredients, trombone solos, fuzz-tone drums, and vocal tracks tweaked at 78 rpm. All the while, they out-rock, out-metal and outrage the competition. Their novel approach to hard rock notwithstanding, The Melvins were dropped by Atlantic in 1996. They stormed back in early 1997 with HONKY, on Amphetamine Reptile. Though not as convincing as their previous efforts, HONKY forded new waters for the group with an intriguing, albeit somewhat mannered, attempt to resurrect the feel of Syd Barrett-era Pink Floyd.

In 1999, the band decided to go with ex-Faith No More singer Mike Patton's new Ipecac label; there followed a particularly prolific patch of releases. They

embarked on their most ambitious work to date, the *Trilogy*, with THE MAGGOT (1999), THE BOOTLICKER (1999) and THE CRYBABY (2000) all being released over the space of nine months. And, shortly after re-releasing GLUEY PORCH TREATMENTS with a bunch of extra tracks, THE COLOSSUS OF DESTINY (2001) followed. Amazingly, fans were given yet more material to gorge themselves upon with HOSTILE AMBIENT TAKEOVER (2002).

The same year also saw the release of the sludge-surfing live set MILLENNIUM MONSTERWORKS, a collaboration with Mike Patton's quirky metal combo Fantomas, released under the fairly self-explanatory appellation **Fantomas Melvins Big Band**.

- ⊙ **Ozma** (1989; Boner).
  The greatest hits of Black Sabbath – sans any references to God, wizards or pot – as written and performed by The Melvins.

- ⊙ **Bullhead** (1991; Boner).
  Slow, slower, slowest. Ferocious guitar and drum work. In a more aesthetically perfect world, legions of callow youth would raise cigarette lighters to doom rockers "Anaconda" and "It's Shoved".

- ⊙ **Stoner Witch** (1994; Boner).
  Fifty-foot guitars bob and weave on grim boogie numbers like "Sweet Willy Rollbar" and "Queen". Dale Crover leaves nobody pining for John Bonham.

Bruce Laidlaw

THE MEMBERS

Formed Camberley, England, 1977;
disbanded 1983.

For a brief moment in early 1979, **The Members** were contenders for the British music-press Flavour of the Week, injecting much-needed entertainment to an ever-more serious scene.

The creation of diminutive singer **Nicky Tesco**, bassist/vocalist **Chris Payne** and guitarist **J. C. Mainman** (aka Jean-Marie Carroll), with **Adrian Lillywhite** (drums) and **Gary Baker** (guitar/vocals; soon replaced by **Nigel Bennett**), the band's initial break had come in early 1978 when Stiff Records offered them a one-off single deal. "Solitary Confinement" was a roaring bedsit-land romp of laddish chaos, and it led to a contract with Virgin later that year. With lyrics like 'I've got it sussed, she's got a 40-inch bust', they were seen as a bit of a novelty act, but soon honed their sound and improved the content. It was their anthem, "Sound Of The Suburbs", released in January 1979, a crash through a Sunday of boredom and escapism in residential Surrey, that provided the break. Taken to the hearts of young commuters everywhere, it reached the UK Top 20.

The follow-up, "Offshore Banking Business", wasn't nearly as well received or successful – a slab of white, plastic reggae, its subject matter was far too clever for mass appeal, while its sound was second-rate. However, the debut album, AT THE CHELSEA NIGHTCLUB (1979), got good reviews, a stylish disc produced by Steve Lillywhite (Adrian's brother, later to produce Big Country and U2), featuring humorous and offbeat offerings like "Love In A Lift", which documented the ups and downs of a romantic interlude.

Alas, The Members' high-profile period was already over. Subsequent singles "Killing Time" and "Romance" failed to recapture their initial promise and Tesco's departure in 1980 was the beginning of the end. A post-Tesco single, "Working Girl", received some radio play, but the fan base was dwindling, and after GOING WEST (1983) the band signed off.

⊙ **Sound Of The Suburbs: A Collection Of Their Finest Moments** (1995; Virgin).
A comprehensive collection. The naivety can be a tad irritating at times, but the quirkier tracks – "Soho A Go-Go", "Phone-In Show" – are offset by more serious material – "Gang War", "GLC" – and even some attempts at metropolitan reggae.

Pip Southall

MEN AT WORK

Formed Melbourne, Australia, 1978; split 1985.

Astring of #1s, begun by "Who Can It Be Now?" made **Men At Work** one of the most successful rock groups of the early 80s. In their four years in the limelight, they racked up record-breaking success around the world, including a simultaneous top single and top album with their debut BUSINESS AS USUAL, which ended up spending fifteen straight weeks at the top of the charts, at that time the longest run for a debut LP. In all, the album stayed in the US *Billboard* charts for ninety weeks and sold more than fifteen million copies worldwide. The following year, their second single, "Down Under", immortalized their homeland as the place 'where women glow and men chunder' and, once again, topped charts around the world.

With this kind of trajectory, it's no surprise that the Men were viewed suspiciously as an 'overnight success', but the truth is somewhat different. A young **Colin Hay**, who had emigrated from Scotland when he was 14 years old, met guitarist **Ron Strykert** in 1978, and they started playing pubs as an acoustic duo. Soon after, they joined forces with **Greg Ham**, an impish saxophonist/flautist/keyboardist; **Jerry Speiser** drummer; and **John Rees** (bass). The group remained nameless until – according to legend – on the way to a gig and still without a handle, Ham spied a construction sign, and Men At Work was born. After a few years slogging away on the Australian pub scene – training ground for such bands as Midnight Oil, INXS, Angels, Icehouse, The Divinyls and The Eurogliders – they put together a trial single for CBS Australia and hit the big time.

Suddenly, the fivesome found themselves airlifted out of the Aussie pub scene and deposited into huge American arenas, opening for Fleetwood Mac on what was supposed to be a short jaunt. Instead, it turned into a gruelling headlining tour with no time off for bad behaviour. At one point, Colin, Greg, Ron, John and Jerry found themselves in Edmonton, Canada, freezing in their summer clothes, so the Canadian Company hastily made them up cosy jackets with a discreet, embroidered message inside which read "To Men At Work, for selling a shitload of records". Meanwhile, the tongue-in-cheek humour of their self-scripted video for "Who Can It Be Now?" made it MTV's most-requested video of 1983, and alienation – the song is about hiding out at home – was never more popular.

In February 83, they won the Grammy for *Best New Artist*, and a few weeks later CARGO (1983) was released, quickly jetting into the Top 10. An exhausted band then embarked on their second major headlining tour of North America.

Nothing in their homeland – which tended to savage people who believed their own press – could have prepared them for the perils of the star system in America. Band members who had once happily toured 'in a fired-out combie' and roomed together in cheap motels now started snapping at each other and demanding seperate limos. The boys – Men overworked – were homesick and getting 'crispy', as they called it; wives, girlfriends, and even parents, were flown into the New York show.

Under this kind of pressure, Men At Work became Men At Play. A year off stretched into two and, when faced with starting it all up again, drummer Jerry Speiser and bassist John Rees bowed out and session musicians sat in for them on the third LP, TWO HEARTS (1985). Although the album eventually went gold, it featured no Top 40 singles and next to the huge multiplatinum success of the first two records it was considered a colossal disappointment. Unfortunately, strong songs such as the title track and the beautiful ballad "Maria" went by unnoticed. Soon after, Men At Work, or what passed for them at that stage, called it quits – apart from a flurry of excitement caused by a 1996 reunion. Hay continues to record, and act, under his own name.

⊙ **Business As Usual** (1981; CBS).
This was the album with the most hits, such as "Who Can It Be Now" and "Down Under".

⊙ **Contraband: The Best Of Men At Work** (1996; Sony).
A collection of their best songs.

⊙ **Men At Work – Brazil: (Greatest Hits Live!)** (1998; Columbia Legacy).
Product of a cash-in reunion and their first live album, this is a far better record than it ought to be. The thirteen-year gap between this album and their previous one has been kind to the voices and musical abilities of all concerned.

Eran Breiman

THE MEN THEY COULDN'T HANG

Formed London, 1984; disbanded 1991, re-formed 1996.

The shadow of The Pogues pursued **The Men They Couldn't Hang**. At first they were seen (wrongly) as a second-division copy of Shane and his drunken revellers; as their music developed, they were then criticized for not sounding the same. In fact, when not bringing songs from the folk clubs into a rock context, The Men They Couldn't Hang boasted a songwriter who, like MacGowan, wrote songs which will one day enter the tradition.

True men (and one woman) of the people, they formed by complete mischance when they got on stage at the Alternative Country Festival, to play a set of crap songs as a kind of in-joke – "Donald Where's Your Trousers?", "A Boy Named Sue", "Where Have All the Flowers Gone". The joke was on them when they went down a storm, and were immediately offered more gigs.

All were known professionally by one curt name – for audience identification, or more likely for fear of a DHSS investigation. Welsh singer (Stefan) **Cush** had met bassist **Shanne** when he was busking in Shepherd's Bush. They were joined by guitarist **Paul** (Simmonds) from Southampton – who was to provide most of the band's lyrics – Scottish guitarist and singer **Phil** (Odgers), known as **'Swill'** for reasons one dare hardly guess at, and his brother **Jon** on drums.

They became part of the brief fashion for 'cowpunk' with bands like the Boothill Foot-Tappers and the Shillelagh Sisters, and were signed by Elvis Costello – himself then rediscovering roots music – for Demon Records. The first LP, Night Of A Thousand Candles (1985), was produced by Tony Poole, himself once of the country-rock band Starry Eyed And Laughing. The melancholy cover version of Eric Bogle's antiwar classic "Green Fields Of France", released in October 1984, had already become a hit single on the alternative charts. The follow-up, Simmonds' own "Ironmasters", was more up-tempo, but just as hard-hitting politically.

Following their third single, "Greenback Dollar", produced by Nick Lowe, the band were signed by a major label, MCA. 1986 saw the release of How Green Is The Valley, which failed to break through to a mass market, and which the band themselves described later as 'a compromise and a mistake'. However, Simmonds' lyric writing had the bite of genuine poetry rather than inspired doggerel; "Dancing On The Pier" had the same mixture of melancholy and sprightliness as the best work of Ray Davies.

MCA decided to drop them, and they moved to the even less fashionable Magnet Records, where they produced perhaps their best work. This included the catchy single "Island In The Rain" and the eminently listenable Waiting For Bonaparte (1988). **Ricky McGuire** was now on bass, and session man **Bobby Valentino** provided strings. When WEA took over Magnet and demanded a change in name, the band left, reincarnating The Men They Wouldn't Sign, until Andrew Lauder, mastermind of the first wave of English country-rock, signed them to Silvertone.

The band amply justified his faith in them and soon released another classic 12" single, "Rain, Steam And Speed", and an album, Silvertown, both 1998.

1990's The Domino Club, however, was to be their final studio effort, produced by Pat Collier of punk band The Vibrators, and adding keyboard player **Nick Muir**.

Shortly afterwards, they disbanded, but they lived up to their name in February 1991, when the Men re-formed for an emotional night at the Town and Country Club in London. The resulting vinyl document Alive Alive O (1991) saw the band back in their true element, live on stage with an audience going berserk.

The Men split again after this one-off, to be mourned and missed sufficiently that, in 1996, by popular demand, they rejoined forces once again for Wasn't Born To Follow and set off on another rabble-rousing series of blood-stirring gigs – with a new mini-CD, six tracks at just over a pound each, on the self-explanatory Six Pack. The compilation Majestic Grill (1998) gathered together all their greatest bits from "Green Fields Of France" to the post-reunion material. The band are still on the road, and a new album, The Cherry Red Jukebox, was released in Germany at the start of 2003.

⊙ **Night Of A Thousand Candles** (1985; Demon).
An invigorating blend of acoustic punk-thrash, straight-ahead rock and slow ballads spat out rather than crooned. The band finds its true voice on such brooding and heavily political songs as "The Green Fields Of France" and "Ironmasters".

⊙ **Waiting For Bonaparte** (1988; Magnet).
Paul Simmonds has matured into a major songwriter here, his lyrics full of ghosts, midnight trains, smugglers and bounty hunters. Musically, the band has become subtler, while not losing the amphetamine rush.

⊙ **Silvertown** (1989; Silvertone).
Paul Simmonds' trump card here is the pursuit of 'changing history' through to modern times: docklands development in "Blackfriars Bridge", corporate muscle in "Company Town", football bullyboys in "Rosettes".

Brian Hinton

MERCURY REV

Formed Buffalo, New York, 1988.

When they first appeared on the music scene, **Mercury Rev**'s startling mixture of whacked-out, psychedelic droning and breakneck guitar noise seemed to be the work of Martians attempting to play pop music without the rule book. One of America's most successfully experimental groups, they are secretive about their early history, claiming they met while all were psychiatric patients at the same hospital.

After lengthy rehearsals, **David Baker** (vocals), **Jonathan Donahue** (guitar/vocals), **Sean Mackiowiak** (guitar), **Suzanne Thorpe** (woodwind instruments), **Dave Fridmann** (bass) and **Jimmy Chambers** (drums) broke cover in 1991 with the album Yerself Is Steam. Though making little impression in the States, the album was greeted with awe in the UK. The band's brand of sonic exploration was virtually unprecedented (except per-

haps by **THE FLAMING LIPS**, with whom Donahue had previously been involved), and they were favourably compared to My Bloody Valentine.

Early live appearances were fascinating, shambolic, volatile and unpredictable. The band would argue on stage and drag out the hypnotic "Very Sleepy Rivers" for what seemed like days. After it was revealed that YERSELF IS STEAM had taken three years to complete and that infighting had escalated, doubts about the group's ability to hang together ran rife. A single, "Car Wash Hair", recorded with **GALAXIE 500**'s **Dean Wareham**, was a spiralling beauty, but no other new songs surfaced, fuelling further speculation about the band's future.

The unexpected second album, BOCES (named after a school for wayward youth), slipped out in mid-1993 and, astonishingly, possessed all the comatose beauty of its predecessor. Its lurches into self-indulgent silliness were balanced by an increasingly acute sense of melody. Shortly afterwards, Baker was ejected for wanting to be too noisy, and the slimmed-down Rev began to travel a less confrontational road, one signposted by Donahue's love of strung-out jazz and Broadway show stoppers.

1995's SEE YOU ON THE OTHER SIDE was instantly accessible, echoing PET SOUNDS-era Beach Boys, New Orleans brass bands, and even acid-jazz. It was a huge leap into the blue and an exhilarating success. However, the darker "Peaceful Night", which closed the album, showed their ghosts were not yet all exorcized, as did a scary B-side link-up with **SUICIDE**'s **ALAN VEGA**.

Meantime, David Baker had adopted the name Shady for a solo album, WORLD. Augmented by star collaborators (including members of **THE BOO RADLEYS** and **SWERVEDRIVER**), it was inspired if ultimately unfocused, too often substituting arresting screechy noise for tunes. Fans of the Rev will already be aware of the band's alter-ego **Harmony Rockets**, whose forty-minute-long one-track-album PARALYZED MIND OF THE ARCHANGEL VOID first stunned college-radio listeners across the USA before receiving a CD release in 1998.

DESERTERS SONGS, also 1998, unveiled a new Mercury Rev in all their skewed majesty; this collection was their most complete to date, moving away from the chaotic splurge of their earlier work to sublime, fragile pocket symphonies helped along by the presence of legendary arranger Jack Nitzche. The album was a massive hit, was hailed as a classic, and saw the group cross over from indiedom into the mainstream.

Darker, more insidious, ALL IS DREAM (2001) was in some ways a more sophisticated work, sacrificing the immediacy of its forebear for an edgier, more disturbing viewpoint. As a result it failed to capture the public's imagination in the same way that its predecessor had. That said, both collections were almost two sides of the same coin, with the schoolroom instrumentation of ALL IS DREAM employed to more sinister effect on cuts such as the lucid nightmare "Tides Of The Moon" and the overwhelming "The Dark Is Rising".

Mercury Rev

Yerself Is Steam (1991; Mint Films/Jungle).
A crashing, head-mangling, yet beautiful collection. Among the album's many highpoints, the epic "Very Sleepy Rivers" twinkles then vanishes like a melting glacier. One of *Melody Maker*'s top four albums of 1991. An essential.

See You On The Other Side (1995; Beggars Banquet).
The indispensable album. Flutes, trumpets, wobbly noises and crashing chords have rarely meshed into such a marvellous whole. The delirious joy of "Racing The Tide" and "Sudden Ray Of Hope" will put you in a good mood for days.

Deserter's Songs (1998; V2).
An organizing of the unconscious into subtle, startling compositions replete with architectural string arrangements and weird noises.

All Is Dream (2001; V2).
The set opens with the cinematic orchestrations of "The Dark Is Rising" before diving into the velveteen psyche torrent of "Tides Of The Moon". The remainder of the cuts drip with dramatic production, the arrangements are stunning and the spaces created by shimmering numbers like "Lincoln's Eye" and "Spiders And Flies" are simply beautiful.

Harmony Rockets

Paralyzed Mind Of The Archangel Void (1998; Big Cat).
A psychedelic sonic onslaught of guitars, sitars and, well, a whole bunch of unrecognizable clatter. Unmissable.

Chris Tighe
Thanks to Brett in Melbourne
and Derryck Strachan for additional info
and updates

METALLICA

Formed San Francisco, 1981.

"We don't mind you throwing shit up at the stage, just don't hit our beers – they're our fuel, man!"
James Hetfield

Though synonymous with the term 'heavy metal', **Metallica** have over the years consistently blurred the boundaries between mainstream

Jason Newsted and James Hetfield in Beavis and Butthead tribute

rock and the extreme end of the metal spectrum with shots of melody and mixers of aggression.

As with most fledgling bands, their initial line-up was very fluid. In October 1981 Danish-born **Lars Ulrich** (drums) recruited **James Hetfield** (guitar/vocals) through a classified advert. With **Lloyd Grant** on guitar, they recorded a version of "Hit The Lights" for the METAL MASSACRE compilation album. Grant didn't last long, but the addition of **Dave Mustaine** (guitar) and **Ron McGovney** (bass) brought stability to the line-up.

Following the recording of their legendary seven-track demo, NO LIFE TILL LEATHER, McGovney was replaced by **Cliff Burton** (bass) from fellow Bay-area thrashers **Trauma**. Then Mustaine in turn quit after a series of bitter clashes with Hetfield and Ulrich in early 1983, going on to form **MEGADETH**. His replacement was **Kirk Hammett** (guitar; ex-Exodus). Things settled down.

Finding fresh momentum after all the infighting, the band wasted no time in directing their energies into their initial release, KILL 'EM ALL (1983). This was a true heavy metal album with a sleeve that proclaimed 'Bang that head that doesn't bang'. The songs run the gamut of metal clichés – life on the road, war, death and violence – but the overall sound was energizingly fresh. There was even a spot of virtuosity in the form of Burton's bass solo, "(Anaesthesia) Pulling Teeth".

The early promise was confirmed with their second release, RIDE THE LIGHTNING (1984). Fleming Rasmussen's production, which harnessed

their original aggression, heralded the group's sonic trademark: thick, heavy bass crunch. The opening track, "Fight Fire With Fire", lulls you into a false sense of security with a mock-classical intro before plunging headlong into a cauldron of relentless, speeding guitars. Metallica took another sure step towards world domination by signing to Def Leppard's management, Q-Prime.

Clearly on a roll, the band released what is generally regarded as their master work in 1986. MASTER OF PUPPETS hit #29 in the US charts and #47 in the UK, all without a single promotional video or hit single. With Rasmussen again producing, they took the winning formula of their previous effort to its logical conclusion. The bludgeoning opener, "Battery", had a classical intro, while "Welcome Home (Sanitarium)" was their token mellow number. There was even another instrumental in the shape of the sublime "Orion". For six months, they supported Ozzy Osbourne on the huge *Ultimate Sin* tour. They seemed invincible: even when Hetfield broke his wrist skateboarding, they continued with roadie **James Marshall** playing while Hetfield sang. However, tragedy struck on the Scandinavian leg of their own world tour, when their tour bus crashed and Burton was killed.

Remarkably the band regrouped within a couple of months, taking on the less flamboyant **Jason Newsted** (bass) from thrash band **Flotsam & Jetsam**. Wasting little time, the remainder of the tour was completed before the band launched into their next off-the-wall project, jamming on cover versions of their favourite British metal songs in Ulrich's garage. The result of the sessions, THE $5.98 EP – GARAGE DAYS RE-REVISITED (1987), featured stripped-down vibrant versions of bone-crunchers by Diamond Head, Budgie, Killing Joke and The Misfits.

The next album, ... AND JUSTICE FOR ALL (1988), saw the Metallica bandwagon thunder on: it entered the UK chart at #4, and stayed in the US chart for a year. Unfortunately, a truly bizarre production sound shoved the drums so far to the front of the mix that the bass was reduced to a wallowing rumble. This was compounded by overly complex arrangements, which robbed the songs of their immediacy. Despite the criticisms, the band showed that they were capable of re-creating their former glories in the shape of "Dyer's Eve", "Harvester Of Sorrow" and the monumental "One".

As record sales soared, the Bay Area boys were awarded Grammys for *Best Metal Performance* in 1990 (for "One") and 1991 (for a cover of "Stone Cold Crazy"), and with the arrival of the eponymous METALLICA (1991) the group made a leap into the rock superleague. By recruiting Bob Rock as producer, they turned out an album which had a clean commercial edge but still appealed to veteran fans, even if Rock's penchant for string arrangements turned the already slushy sentimentality of "Nothing Else Matters" into elevator music.

The following three years brought an extensive touring schedule, including a tastefully titled live album, LIVE SHIT: BINGE AND PURGE (1993), and a prolonged period in the studio putting together their next magnum opus, LOAD (1996). Released amid an Apple computer-sponsored Internet 'Metallicast', this was melody-metal supreme, swaggering through the riffs, and with Hetfield re-staking his claim as the genre's best contemporary practitioner. It was released to hugely positive reviews – 'the only heavy metal band that adults can listen to without feeling their IQ diminishing', said one grateful critic – and with predictably huge sales. RELOAD (1997) was more than a sequel thrown together from leftovers – the RELOAD set was finished off during the *Load* tour. It had its patchy moments, but was, on the whole, a satisfying plateful of Southern badness.

Having decided that they would avoid indulging in binge bouts of recording followed by vast stretches of touring, the band opted for a more productive schedule following the LOAD sessions. Therefore almost exactly one year after the release of RELOAD they knocked out GARAGE INC. (1998). The double album consisted of the previous long-deleted GARAGE DAYS EP plus a whole host of other B-side cover versions, whilst the second disc contained a clutch of newly recorded covers from artists as diverse as Thin Lizzy and Nick Cave. The sound was rawer and more spontaneous, making for a welcome change from their often anal studio dabbling. But just to keep the LOAD albums firmly on the agenda a state-of-the-art concert video, CUNNING STUNTS (1998), was released directly afterwards.

And then it all went a little pear-shaped, at least as far as the average heavy metal fan was concerned. With bank balances bulging once more the band decided that it would be a great idea to reinterpret their live set with full orchestral support. To this end conductor/composer **Michael Kamen** was recruited along with the San Francisco Symphony Orchestra for a blast through the Metalli-repertoire, complete with sweeping strings and the conventionally amplified Hetfield and co. doing their best to drown out everyone in the process. The mixed results could be sampled on S&M (1999). After that the band slipped into their old ways; they dropped out of circulation while working on a new album and navigating through a few problems, among them Hetfield's adventures in rehab and the loss of Newsted, who eventually decided he had taken as much as he could of the Metallica machine. 2003 brought ST. ANGER, a rawer return to an older Metallica sound, though fans were divided over the 'under produced' nature of the material.

- **Ride The Lightning** (1984; Vertigo).
  The first glimmerings of greatness. Big fat riffs, delivered with technical precision. Hetfield's vocals sound meaner and more mature. Definitely a spandex-free zone.

- **...And Justice For All** (1988; Vertigo).
  Surely the prizewinner in the 'Most Complex Riffing' category. It consists of mainly Hetfield/Ulrich tunes with so many parts they're in danger of disappearing up their own backsides. High points include the two hit singles "Harvester Of Sorrow" and "One".

- **Metallica** (1991; Vertigo).
  Big rock production values made this slick and predominantly mid-paced – nonetheless, a landmark metal release of the 90s.

- **Load** (1996; Vertigo).
  You want doomy metal? Ace-heavy balladry? A lone acoustic ballad? Metallica show they can do the lot better than anyone around.

- **Garage Inc.** (1998; Vertigo).
  Forget about tracking down those elusive B-sides and grab this double album. When the covers work, this is splendid stuff, and even when they don't (check out the unintentionally hilarious version of "Whisky In The Jar") it's still tons of fun.

- **S&M** (1999; Vertigo).
  For the most part Metallica's thunderous symphonic bludgeon is well served by arranger and conductor Michael Kamen, with such live favourites as "Enter Sandman" and "Sad But True" putting in an appearance. Also present are two new numbers – "No Leaf Clover" and "Human" – which, written with the classical dimension in mind, work particularly well.

Essi Berelian

THE METERS

Formed New Orleans, 1966; split up late 1970s with sporadic reunions since.

The **Meters** became New Orleans legends right up there with Professor Longhair and Dr. John (two artists they've even played with) for their rejuvenation of the R&B sound – incorporating jazz and 60s soul elements to create funk.

They're closely linked to other New Orleans music legends, **THE NEVILLE BROTHERS**. **Art Neville**, keyboards, started The Meters from home rehearsals with local musicians in the early 60s for a new generation of his 50s band **The Hawketts**. He finally found a tight rhythm section with guitarist **Leo Nocentelli**, bassist **George Porter Jr.**, and drummer **Joseph 'Zigaboo' Modeliste**. They started out as the seven-piece group **The Neville Sounds** with Art and his brother **Cyril** on vocals, and began touring the local black clubs, then Art reduced the personnel and toured with Modeliste, Porter Jr. & Nocentelli as **Art Neville & The Neville Sounds** and finally as just **The Meters**.

Art's new band wasn't just the average bar band. Second only to Booker T And The MGs (a group the band members had idolized) for tight musicianship planted firmly in R&B roots, the new Neville Sounds brought an ever bigger following and attention from local music producers (and New Orleans legends) Allen Toussaint and Marshall Sehorn. They became the main session musicians for Allen's studio backing tracks for **LEE DORSEY**, Earl King and Betty Harris, and later in the 70s they would put the fire into hits by Dr. John ("Right Place, Wrong Time" and "Such A Night" from IN THE RIGHT PLACE) and **ROBERT PALMER** (on SNEAKING SALLY THROUGH THE ALLEY).

Deciding to branch out into recording their own music, they got a new name, signed to a record label – Josie – and scored immediately. Their first two hits, "Sophisticated Sissy" and "Sissy Strut" (both 1969), charted highly and became prime examples of what would become funk. The sizzling backbeat of Modeliste, Porter and Nocentelli's limber riffing and Neville's percussive keyboard playing anchored a whole slew of funk classics: "Chicken Strut", "Look-Ka Py Py", "Ease Back", "Hand Clapping Song" and "Message From the Meters". Their first three albums for Josie – THE METERS (1969), LOOK-A-PY-PY and STRUTTIN' (both 1970) – all provided a delicious stew of styles from the Caribbean laid-back feel of "Ease Back" to the fatback funk of "Stretch Your Rubber Band".

The success of those albums encouraged The Meters to evolve their style and hook up with major label Reprise in 1971. They introduced vocals back into the mix and used new studio effects. They also developed their songwriting skills, as evidenced by classic tracks such as "People Say". Reprise unfortunately didn't know how to promote The Meters, and their albums for the label – CABBAGE ALLEY (1972), REJUVENATION (1974) and TRICK BAG (1975) – largely fell by the wayside. They were still a vital live act, playing for a Paul McCartney and Wings album-release party (now released as UPTOWN RULERS! LIVE ON THE QUEEN MARY), earning the opening act slot for The Rolling Stones in 1975 and participating (with Neville's uncles) in the ode to Mardi Gras culture, THE WILD TCHOUPITOULAS (1976).

By the late 70s, The Meters were beginning to tear apart. TRICK BAG was their last with producer Allen Toussaint. They tried one last time with a new producer (Jeff Cohen) in San Francisco, for an album called NEW DIRECTIONS (1977). But it flopped and The Meters were no more. By then Neville was devoting more time to his brothers' new band, The Neville Brothers. The Meters reunited briefly in 1980, 1984 and in 1988 (this time without Modeliste). Their legacy, although not as well known as some other New Orleans figures, remains well respected and their songs are standards for most R&B players and even now are heavily sampled.

◉ **Funkify Your Life – The Meters Anthology** (1996; Rhino).
A brilliant introduction/career retrospective to The Meters. Hip-hop fans will especially love the first disc's mainly instrumental funk as most of it has been practically sampled to death by East and West Coast hip-hop artists (one example: the drum break at the end of "Here Comes The Meter Man" for "Long Live The Kane" by Big Daddy Kane). Fans of New Orleans R&B will more likely prefer the second disc.

◉ **The Very Best Of The Meters** (1997; Rhino).
Cool, concise and chronological compilation of their hits (and easier on the wallet than their two-CD ANTHOLOGY set.)

◉ **Uptown Rulers! Live From The Queen Mary** (1987; Rhino).
The Meters doing their thang live back in 75 (believe it or not for a Wings album-release party on the SS Queen Mary). Vital because it's the only live document of the band.

Chris Lark

GEORGE MICHAEL

Born London, June 25, 1963.

"Everybody wants to be a star. I certainly did, and I worked hard to get it. But I was miserable, and I don't want to feel that way again."

The well-documented transformation of **George Michael** from ugly-duckling teenager to perma-tanned Adonis with 80s pop kings **Wham!** is something he prefers not to talk about these days. Although it all seems like an eternity ago in the light of his current line in po-faced angst, those early days bear re-examination as the formative steps on what has proved a glorious, if rocky, road to the megastar league.

Born Georgios Panayiotou, to a Greek Cypriot father and English mother, George was an ungainly figure until befriending the more stylish and confident **Andrew Ridgeley** at Bushey Meads Comprehensive in 1975. Several years, a diet and a makeover later, he had become George Michael, songwriting half of boisterous teen duo Wham! After signing a hasty (and ultimately litigious) deal with fledgling label Innervision in 1982, the band achieved enormous UK and US chart success with a whole string of youth-orientated singles dealing with unemployment ("Wham! Rap"), possessive girlfriends ("Young Guns") and parental aggro ("Bad Boys"). After a UK #1 album, FANTASTIC (1983), Michael and Ridgeley broke free of the restrictive Innervision deal and signed up with the mighty Epic label.

The mid 80s proved a carousel of platinum discs, plastic surgery, countless awards, a historic tour of China, and several US and UK #1s, all of which ensured that Wham! were never far from the front pages or the top of the charts. During these years of dominance, Michael also released two solo singles. The first of these, "Careless Whisper" (1984), was a tuneful but bland smoocher; the second, however, "A Different Corner", was more revealing, its stark, introspection contrasting sharply with Wham!'s jitterbuggin' high spirits. It topped the charts in 1986, just as Wham! announced their decision to split, going out with a bang with a farewell concert at Wembley and a singles collection, both under the banner THE FINAL (1986).

Michael began work on his first solo album, but if he was out to cultivate a grown-up image as a songwriter and singer, his first single proved a serious error of judgment: with its facile lyric (and ludicrous 'Huuaargh, sex!' background vocals), "I Want Your Sex" had all the sensuous subtlety of a giggling schoolboy. It was an embarrassing start, but the lost ground was made up when its long-awaited parent album, FAITH (1987), topped the charts on both sides of the Atlantic. One listen to its power ballads and sleek pop numbers confirmed that this was an album aimed squarely at the US market, and its performance did not disappoint. The awards (including a Grammy) rolled in as FAITH soared towards eight million sales in America alone, boosted by four #1 singles there in nine months.

FAITH may have attracted precious metal like a magnet, but as a decade of virtually unparalleled success drew to a close, the increasingly private Michael felt dissatisfied with the pressures and trappings of stardom. For his second album, which he somewhat optimistically christened LISTEN WITHOUT PREJUDICE VOL. 1 (1990), he resolved not to give any interviews or appear in any videos, a move which inevitably lowered his media profile and affected sales of what was a difficult, soul-searching record. It was here that the seeds were sown of Michael's bitter dispute with Sony, whom he claimed did little to support or promote the album in order to punish him for his new direction.

By October 1992, Michael had decided to bring a restraint of trade action against Sony in a bid to free himself from a company he now described as 'a giant electronics corporation which appears to see artists as little more than software'. It was the start of three years of costly and acrimonious legal wrangling which came close to ending Michael's recording career.

Eventually coming to court in October 1993, the case rumbled on for a full eight months before the judge delivered his verdict on June 28, 1994. Ruling that the Sony deal was 'reasonable and fair', he blamed the singer's management team for the rift and concluded that Michael 'expected that the consequence of his new direction would be a loss of sales. He cannot blame Sony for the fact that he was right.'

Left facing a legal bill in the region of £5 million ($7 million), Michael resolved never to record another note for Sony, a bitter stalemate which was finally broken in July 1995, when Sony agreed to release Michael from his contract in return for the rights to a greatest hits package, a share in the profits from future albums, and a £25 million ($40 million) lump sum from his new labels, Virgin in the UK and Dreamworks in the US.

The first fruit of his new deal came in January 1996, when "Jesus To A Child", a mellow but meandering seven-minute single, entered the UK chart at #1, as did its follow-up, the much sprightlier "Fastlove". Their success heightened anticipation for his third album, OLDER (1996), a solemn but hugely marketable record which became one of the world's bestsellers for that year, as well as the first album ever to yield six singles to make the Top 5. The platinum discs and industry awards began to roll in all over again, and with a mega-budget greatest hits package (OLDER AND UPPER; 1998), followed by the double-CD LADIES AND GENTLEMEN, it was as though he'd never been away at all.

Despite almost no promotion, his covers album SONGS FROM THE LAST CENTURY (1999) was a strong, if short-term seller, featuring his reflective versions of "My Baby Just Cares For Me", "I Remember You", "Wild Is The Wind" and Sting's "Roxanne". Perhaps surprisingly, his spiky comeback single of spring 2002, "Freeek", failed to beat the various winners of the heavily promoted TV contest *Pop Idol* to the top of the singles charts, but it would be nothing short of foolish to write Michael off just yet.

⊙ **Faith** (1987; Epic).
This solo debut is not without soul, but much of it is airbrushed out by sterile arrangements that result in an album too glossy for its own good. Still, the gorgeous, 2am jazz-club feel of "Kissing A Fool" hits the mark.

⊙ **Listen Without Prejudice Vol. 1** (1990; Epic).
The cover of this watershed project depicts a sea of anonymous faces in a crowd, mirroring Michael's disenchantment with the pop-star game. The songs are impressive and at times moving ("Mother's Pride" was adopted as a Gulf War anthem), but the relentless navel-examination and whingeing about the horrors of success makes it a difficult album to love.

⊙ **Older** (1996; Virgin/Dreamworks).
Putting six years of professional turmoil behind him, Michael strode back into the limelight with this melancholy yet confident collection.

Jonathan Kennaugh

MICHELLE SHOCKED

Born Gilmer, Texas, 1962.

I n the 1980s **Michelle Shocked** (Karen Johnson) seemed to be carrying the torch of the political singer-songwriter, once borne by the likes of Phil Ochs. She seemed to her first fans a kind of punkier version of Suzanne Vega – a woman folkie with bite. Since then, she's confused everybody with pretty much annual reinventions of her style and material.

The singer's background was true-blue, only-in-America weirdness: hippie father, fundamentalist mother, dropping out of college, a spell in a psychiatric hospital, squatting-chic in San Francisco, radical politics and imported Doc Marten boots. Adopting her stage name to signify how shell-shocked she was by the system, she was spotted at the Kerriville Folk Festival in 1986 by Pete Lawrence of the UK indie label Cooking Vinyl. And, in true folk-star tradition, she initially resisted Lawrence's pressure to compile a live album from tapes he had made on a cassette player.

But she relented in the end and the resulting TEXAS CAMPFIRE TAPES (1986), which topped the UK indie charts in 1987, showed what Shocked excels at: simple, witty songs about how things should be. Her proclaimed loathing of big business then receded sufficiently for her to sign a $50,000 deal with the PolyGram money machine, the new label reissuing TEXAS CAMPFIRE TAPES in the US with the gleeful press release statement: 'It holds the distinction of being the only major label LP that cost less to make than it does to buy!'

Michelle Shocked's first studio album, SHORT SHARP SHOCKED (1988), wore a sleeve photograph of her in a police stranglehold at a demonstration. Shocked is not one to keep her mouth shut, and this, her best work, was a great example of confrontational folk-pop. Her political commentary on "Graffiti Limbo", concerning the murder in police custody of a young graffiti artist, was intelligent and scathing; elsewhere her material had an affectionately humorous edge, too.

She had the sort of antagonistic media-friendliness to make SHORT SHARP SHOCKED a strong seller, but failed to build on her early promise. CAPTAIN SWING (1989) used big-band stylings but the idea was not well realized and her right-on-ness began to wear with the critics. Nor did her reputation for unreliability help in an industry which indulges its drug-fuelled guitar heroes in return for strict obedience. Still, the British fans kept faith and the album reached a UK career high at #31.

Another good concept formed the core of ARKANSAS TRAVELER (1992), for which Shocked travelled all over America recording with various blues, folk and bluegrass musicians. Again, it was patchy. Her lyrical tone was occasionally hectoring, and she slipped into flattering but not entirely earth-shattering jam sessions with the likes of Hothouse Flowers and The Band. Again, though, there were great moments, not least a duet with young bluegrass fiddler and vocalist **Alison Krauss** on "Cotton-Eyed Joe", in which she tackled the abortion debate in a fresh way. Alas, sales were down across the board, and her record company were so unimpressed by the bleak follow-up, KIND HEARTED WOMAN (1994), that they turned it down, and she released it herself. In a heart-warming, rock-biz fairy tale, Shocked sued Mercury to get out of her contract, invoking the 13th Amendment to the US Constitution (the one against slavery) and won.

Many of rock's 'folk stars' of the 80s have been sucked down the same path as those of the 60s: stuck in an all-consuming search for 'sincerity' they stagnate, becoming irritating parodies of themselves in the process. While Michelle Shocked is unlikely to regain the high profile she earned in the late 80s, her low-key album of 2002, DEEP NATURAL, did demonstrate her standard flair for melody and attitude.

⊙ **Short Sharp Shocked** (1988; Mercury).
The title says it all about these tight songs: the 'shell-shocked' singer pours scorn onto The Men In Suits. As well as intense political commitment, there's also the brilliantly crafted and touching "Anchorage", and sterling production by Pete Anderson.

Neil Blackmore

MICRODISNEY

Formed Cork, Ireland, 1980; disbanded 1988.

Built around the songwriting partnership of **Cathal Coughlan** (vocals/keyboards) and **Sean O'Hagan** (guitar/harmonica), the early **Microdisney** took a while to develop their distinctive style, experimenting with sundry line-ups as they evolved the blend of melodic rock spiked with sneeringly bitter lyrics that became their hallmark. Defying categorization and splitting opinion, they remained on the verge of big-league success for much of the mid-80s.

An early formation, with **Mick Lynch** (bass) and **Rob Mackahey** (drums), released two singles on the Kabuki label, including "Helicopter Of The Holy Ghost" (1982), a song which gave an early indication of Coughlan's preoccupation with the Irish Catholic Church. Other early recordings were collected together on the wonderfully titled WE HATE YOU SOUTH AFRICAN BASTARDS (rereleased in post-apartheid days as LOVE YOUR ENEMIES), which emerged, in 1984.

By this time O'Hagan and Coughlan had moved to London, recruiting a new rhythm section in **Ed Flesh** (bass) and **Tom Fenner** (drums), and playing pub gigs to music-press acclaim. A deal with Rough Trade followed, and the band's first 'proper' LP, EVERYBODY IS FANTASTIC (1984) set out their stall as pedlars of finely crafted pop hooks, with O'Hagan's country guitar twang subverted by the invective of Coughlan's delivery.

Further releases underlined the split personality of the band, not least the infectiously poppy single "Birthday Girl", which was paired with the brooding menace of the Suicide-influenced "Waiting For The Trams". A second Rough Trade LP, THE CLOCK COMES DOWN THE STAIRS (1985), provided the strongest statement yet of their unique style, and the inevitable succession of Peel sessions, and regular appearances on the circuit, built up a faithful cult following – driven, not least, by the ferocious power of Coughlan's stage performances.

The band's growing reputation secured a big-league deal with Virgin Records, the first fruits of which appeared as CROOKED MILE (1987), with Flesh replaced on bass by **Steve Pregnant** and **James Compton** augmenting the sound on keyboards. The band's rougher edges had been sanded down, to mixed effect, but the jaunty single "Town To Town" hovered around the UK Top 50 and for a while it seemed possible that Microdisney could fool their way into the mainstream.

However, album sales remained disappointing, and the next single, "Singer's Hampstead Home" (1987), another irresistible melody alongside a wry commentary on the fall from grace of label-mate Boy George, didn't do well. A final album, 39 MINUTES (1988), had its moments, but was unconvincingly delivered and a pale imitation of the untamed live band.

With their fortunes declining, the band split up in the spring of 1988. Coughlan went on to give full-blooded voice to his angst in his new band, **FATIMA MANSIONS**, while O'Hagan has indulged his melodic instincts in the **HIGH LLAMAS**, a group that (soundwise at least) remain closest to the vision of one of the great cult bands of the 1980s. He has also provided string arrangements for **STEREOLAB** on their albums EMPEROR TOMATO KETCHUP and DOTS AND LOOPS.

⊙ **Everybody Is Fantastic** (1984; Rev-ola).
The band's great debut LP, melodic yet brooding. A fistful of stand-outs include "Dolly", "Moon" and "Escalator In The Rain".

⊙ **The Clock Comes Down The Stairs** (1985; Rev-ola).
Slightly lighter and more accessible, this was perhaps the best representation of the band's balance of West Coast pop and angry angst on classics like "Birthday Girl" and "Genius".

⊙ **Big Sleeping House** (1995; Virgin).
A budget compilation of material from CLOCK, CROOKED MILE and 39 MINUTES.

Nick Dale

MIDNIGHT OIL

Formed Sydney, Australia, 1976.

Rob **Hirst** (drums) and **Jim Moginie** (guitar/keyboards) – old schoolmates in Sydney – had been together as a band called Farm since 1971. With **Andrew 'Bear' James** on bass, they were best known for performing along the coast during summer holidays. Then in 1975 they advertised in a newspaper for a lead vocalist and had just one response – **Peter Garrett**, law student and former member of the band Rock Island Line. They signed him up, scratched up **Martin Rotsey** (guitar) from somewhere, renamed themselves **Midnight Oil**, and hooked up with local entrepreneur Gary Morris, who became their manager. It was the beginning for one of Australia's finest bands – and one of the few groups in the last two decades to combine strong political lyrics with mainstream chart success.

The early Midnight Oil played sporadically around Sydney's northern beaches during 1977, expanding their reach after Garrett received his Law degree that summer. By 1978, they were gigging five nights a week and had found support in 'alternative' radio station 2JJ. Record companies were less adventurous, and after being turned down by all the major labels in Australia the band formed their own, called Powderworks, recording their debut, MIDNIGHT OIL (1978), in an economic ten days. It was a fine declaration, establishing a rootsy pop sound.

Following its release, the band's militant, socially active side began to emerge. They played an anti-uranium mining benefit, and went on to gig in support of Greenpeace and the Tibet Council. In 1979, they turned their attention to business practices in the local live music circuit. Unhappy with the monopoly operated by local promoters and agents, they formed their own booking agency, blacklisting any venues they felt overcharged the public.

HEAD INJURIES (1979), their second album, went gold in Australia, helped by a national hit single, "Cold Cold Change". After a personnel change – James left the band in 1980 due to ill-health, and was replaced by **Peter Gifford** – a mini-album, BIRD NOISES, followed, again achieving gold status in Australia. Then came PLACE WITHOUT A POSTCARD (1981), recorded in Britain with producer Glyn Johns, but drawing heavily on Australian history in its lyrics. It went platinum at home and yielded a major chart single, "Armistice Day".

Armed with a sheaf of politically charged songs, the Oils returned to Britain late in 1982 to record the 10, 9, 8, 7, 6, 5, 4, 3, 2, 1 album. The crowning glory of this trip was a night supporting The Who. However, they turned down their hosts' offer to support on an upcoming US tour, and headed back home, where the album spent a staggering two years in the Top 40.

Following 1984's RED SAILS IN THE SUNSET album, Garrett took his political involvement a stage further, announcing that he was going to stand for a seat on the Australian Senate, on a Nuclear Disarmament Party slate. He received 200,000 votes and was only very narrowly defeated. After participating in the Artists United Against Apartheid project in 1985, Garrett focused his attention on racism closer to home, writing a track for a documentary about the Aborigines, and taking the band on the 'Black Fella White Fella' tour along with Aboriginal group, the Warumpi Band.

These experiences provided the subject matter for the DIESEL AND DUST (1987) album, which went gold in a day and platinum in three in Australia, and had the largest ship-out in the history of the country's record industry. Its stand-out track, "Beds Are Burning", reached the US and UK Top 20, too, drawing attention for a world tour (with New Zealander **Dwayne 'Bones' Hillman** replacing Gifford on bass).

After the tour, they returned with BLUE SKY MINING (1990), which was as biting as any previous release, its title track written for the thousands of

Australians who had contracted cancer while working as blue asbestos miners. The following year, the band was back on the road, rocking out to mass enthusiasm, as evidenced by a great live album, SCREAM IN BLUE (1992).

They returned to the UK and US charts with the 1993 album, EARTH & SUN & MOON, cementing their reputation as one of the most enjoyable, honest and committed acts around. BREATHE, their tenth album – recorded in Sydney and New Orleans – was released in 1996. The following year, the band celebrated their sixteenth anniversary with the release of a compilation titled 20,000 WATT R.S.L., which gave fans, in addition to sixteen of their best old songs, a sneak preview of things to come, with two tracks from their next 'proper' album, REDNECK WONDERLAND (1998). The single "White Skin Black Heart" was dubbed 'too controversial' for airplay on Australian radio for its attacks on the government, but by now the band were more than used to raising a little dust with their deliberately provocative lyrics. THE REAL THING (2001), an Australia-only collection of new material, live cuts and an *MTV Unplugged* session, kept the fires of indignation burning for CAPRICORNIA (2002), their most recent slab of uniquely impassioned protest rock.

⊙ **Head Injuries** (1979; Powderworks).
A more focused work than the rush job their debut MIDNIGHT OIL was, this established them as a major player in their home country.

⊙ **Place Without A Postcard** (1981; Powderworks).
It has been described as their most Australian album – despite the fact that it was recorded in Surrey and produced by a Brit, Glyn Johns, best known for his work with The Who.

⊙ **Diesel And Dust** (1986; Powderworks/1987; Columbia).
The one that secured them worldwide success – again despite the fact that its subject matter was very much focused on issues at home.

⊙ **Earth & Sun & Moon** (1993; Columbia).
Their decision to go for 'real' instruments rather than rely on studio gadgets made for an album with more of a raw feel to it.

⊙ **Breathe** (1996; Columbia).
After a three-year absence, the Oils returned to brilliant form with this offering. It was well worth the wait.

⊙ **20,000 Watt R.S.L.** (1997; Columbia).
The perfect summing-up of the Midnight Oil story so far, plus a glimpse into the near future. Looks bright from here.

George Luke

STEVE MILLER

Born Milwaukee, Wisconsin, October 5, 1943.

"I'm a joker/I'm a smoker/I'm a midnight toker ..." The Joker

Many are the fans of Eddie Van Halen and the like tempted into rash purchases of **Steve Miller Band** albums on the strength of the man's 'guitar hero' status, only to be left clutching an air guitar that played no solos for an entire album. Miller has always been a guitar stylist, and his best work relies on a solid grasp of chord sequences, effective arrangements and the ability to deliver a good melody without complications.

Already a veteran of high-school and college bands when he went to Chicago in the mid 60s, **Steve Miller** used his time in the city to pick up tips on recording and playing from the very best. He then moved to California in time to pick up on the mass signing of the bands involved in the growing hippie scene. A set at the Monterey Festival as **The Steve Miller Blues Band** led to a lucrative deal with Capitol.

An accomplished musician with a strong band, Miller showed style, substance and class from the start. His first five Capitol albums – CHILDREN OF THE FUTURE (1968), SAILOR (1969), BRAVE NEW WORLD (1969), YOUR SAVING GRACE (1970) and NUMBER 5 (1970) – were all characterized by strong songs with a blues base, and a skilful use of electronic keyboard and sound technology. The choice of accomplished backing musicians was another feature throughout Miller's recording career – some, such as **Boz Scaggs** and **Ben Sidran**, were to carve good solo careers.

Dependable recordings and a tough touring schedule put The Steve Miller Band (he dropped the 'Blues' soon after Monterey) amongst the respectable US chart performers. By 1972 the band were playing throughout Europe but a broken neck and hepatitis sidelined Miller for the final six months of the year. With time on his hands, Miller made a considered attempt to turn his obvious ability into serious cash by writing "The Joker" (1973) – a sly piece of pop craftsmanship that hit #1 in the US. The album of the same name was also a hit, reaching #2 in the American charts in early 1974, finally delivering on the promise that Miller had shown since the start.

Oddly, the massive hit preceded a low point in Miller's career. He retreated to a farm in Oregon following bust-ups with business partners and his girlfriend. A two-year lay-off led to some doubts about his appetite for the rock business, but Miller's return was blistering, as the monster FLY LIKE AN EAGLE (1976) spawned a welter of US hit singles, including "Rock'n Me", "Take The Money And Run" and the title track. It even gave him a chart breakthrough on both lists in the UK.

The winning formula involved a simpler sound than before, relying on strong chord structures and some skilful keyboard string effects. Miller's vocals had softened slightly and lyrically he managed an appealing mixture of rootsy observation and accessible hippie mysticism. It was just what the American FM stations wanted – perhaps he'd spent two years on the farm listening to the radio. The fans got more of the same a year later, when BOOK OF DREAMS (1977) achieved similar success. Miller had laid down the two platinum albums in one almighty set of sessions.

After another extended retreat, Miller produced a solid collection, CIRCLE OF LOVE (1981), while

"Abracadabra" (1982) put him back on top of the singles charts worldwide. The album of the same name showed more collaborative songwriting than the fans were used to, and some definite attempts to mine a radio-friendly pop formula. The latest incarnation of the band toured around the world and turned in the workmanlike LIVE (1983). Miller then headed off to record the commercially disappointing ITALIAN X-RAYS (1984), an album of great sounds in search of a winning tune.

Another period of obscurity followed, but this time the question was not whether Miller could come back, but whether he wanted to. The return was low-key and probably his most honest move of the 80s. BORN 2B BLUE (1988) was an album of exemplary blues-based music crafted by a man in full command of his art. It made no attempt to hit commercial targets and earned respect rather than dollars, though that mattered little as "The Joker", rereleased in 1990 on the back of its use in an advert, reached #1 again, this time in the UK charts. Meanwhile, Miller emits sporadic, ultra-low-key releases and continues to work with others. He contributed some fine guitar to Paul McCartney's FLAMING PIE set in 1997, by which time his back catalogue was beginning to rematerialize in a steady series of remastered rereleases, bringing him another wave of respect and an always-useful bulge in the bank balance.

Miller celebrated thirty years of recording with a massive feel-good summer trek around the US in 1998; international dates followed, as did an archive live album, KING BISCUIT FLOWER HOUR PRESENTS THE STEVE MILLER BAND (2002).

⊙ **Fly Like An Eagle** (1976; Mercury).
An uncool item, but the whole point about Miller is that he made mainstream rock exciting. If the likes of Michael Bolton and Phil Collins could put this much life and talent into their radio-friendly fodder, the whole world would be a better place.

⊙ **The Very Best Of Steve Miller** (1991; Sony).
Capitol/ Mercury/Sony's willingness to reissue Miller product whenever it rains has probably given Steve the best-fed cows in Oregon. It has also left die-hard fans with some serious track duplication in their collections. The excuse for this UK collection was probably "The Joker"'s stint at #1 in 1990. It includes a succession of Miller's memorable best.

⊙ **Greatest Hits** (1998; Polygram).
A sympathetic digital remastering with sleeve notes by the great man himself. A well-considered collection with many fan-favoured album tracks getting a look-in.

Neil Nixon

MINISTRY

Formed Chicago, 1981.

"I'm just a very well-paid juvenile delinquent." Al Jourgensen

Ministry started out as a vehicle for multi-instrumentalist **Al Jourgensen** – though the group also involved drummer **Stephen George** and sundry guests. They were inspired in early days by

Depeche Mode-styled synth-pop, releasing their debut, "Cold Life", through Chicago's Wax Trax! label (in which Jourgensen was a partner) in 1982. Several more forgettable singles followed, along with a 1983 album entitled WITH SYMPATHY (WORK FOR LOVE in Europe).

Jourgensen later distanced himself from all this stuff, having changed direction dramatically in 1984 while on a tour of the US with Belgian hardbeat group Front 242. Adopting a more industrial sound, Ministry recorded a dark, harsh album, TWITCH (1985), which benefited from production assistance from **Adrian Sherwood** of On-U Sound fame. It was an entirely new beginning.

During this period, Jourgensen became involved in numerous side-projects for Wax Trax!: among them **REVOLTING COCKS** (RevCo), **1000 Homo DJs**, **Acid Horse**, **Lard** (with Jello Biafra of **DEAD KENNEDYS**) and **PTP**. Most of these alter egos took European hardbeat for inspiration and mixed in whatever struck Jourgensen and friends at the time, including country (RevCo), and metal (1000 Homo DJs). However, a deal with Sire in 1991 limited his prolific output and led him to abandon his stake in WaxTrax!

Adopting influences and collaborators from RevCo, Ministry developed into a band featuring **Paul Barker** (bass), **William Rieflin** (drums), and occasional vocals from **Chris Connelly**, formerly of Finitribe. 1988's THE LAND OF RAPE AND HONEY, featuring the club hit "Stigmata", mixed metal with hardbeat, using sampling technology to create a dense, vicious sound which also owed a considerable debt to fellow Chicagoans, Big Black.

The follow-up, THE MIND IS A TERRIBLE THING TO TASTE (1989), was the apogee of death disco – abrasive and loud, bringing nihilism into the sampling era on stand-out tracks "So What?" and "Thieves". Along with Nine Inch Nails, Ministry became the most visible and popular of the burgeoning industrial dance bands of the early 90s, with Jourgensen gaining a reputation for living the rock lifestyle to the full while remaining elusively behind shades and leather in public.

The industrial psychobilly of 1991's "Jesus Built My Hotrod" 12" stormed into the clubs, featuring deranged vocals from **BUTTHOLE SURFERS** vocalist **Gibby Haynes**, and extensive sampling of John Huston's classic Southern Gothic film, *Wise Blood*. This unholy alliance was followed the next year by PSALM 69, a blast of industrial metal which was in turn followed by Ministry's appearance on the Lollapalooza 1992 festival tour where Jourgensen's bone-encrusted mike stand was one of the visual highlights. Complete with double-necked guitars and all-black gear, Ministry brought their live experience to Britain for the first time in November 1992, but without the bones, thanks to customs officials.

Ministry have since relocated to Texas, where Jourgensen also set up a country-music label to show that it's not all rhinestones and sentimentality. With a new line-up – **Rey Washam** (ex-Scratch Acid, **THE JESUS LIZARD**) on drums, **Mike Scaccia** and **Louis Svitek** (guitars) and **Duane Buford** (keyboards) – they released a new album, FILTH PIG (1996), hitching their sound firmly to the metal wagon train, a feat they repeated with DARK SIDE OF THE SPOON (1999). Indeed, SPHINCTOUR (2002), a live album product of the band's signing to Sanctuary Records, celebrated their more recent metallic leanings to great effect. A new album, ANIMOSITISOMINA, saw the light of day in early 2003 and, as promised, was even darker – if such a thing were possible – than their previous outings.

⊙ **The Land Of Rape And Honey** (1988; Sire).
The opening track, "Stigmata", was Ministry's finest moment until 1992. With eclectic sampling, including the Middle Eastern-influenced "Hizbollah", this is Ministry in their element.

⊙ **Psalm 69** (1992; Sire).
With several tracks later released as singles – "N.W.O." and "Just One Fix" (with William Burroughs) – Ministry reaches beyond the hardbeat influences of earlier years, redefining metal along the way. "Scarecrow" is perhaps their most ominous track to date, and "Corrosion" takes them back to the scraping sheet-steel territory of industrial music.

⊙ **Filth Pig** (1996; Warners).
The metal dominates on this heavy-duty album, which manages to turn Dylan's "Lay Lady Lay' into a stadium angst-anthem.

⊙ **Animositisomina** (2003; Mayan/Sanctuary).
Faster, scarier, and way more intense than anything they previously recorded, here Jorgensen and Barker touch down with a collection of extreme, room-clearing menace.

Richard Fontenoy

MINOR THREAT

Formed Washington DC, 1980; disbanded 1983.

Minor Threat, fronted by **Ian MacKaye**, offered a cohesive, disciplined ethos through music which displayed those same attributes. Their 'Straight Edge' was a philosophy which demanded abstinence from tobacco, alcohol and drugs, advo-

cating instead personal responsibility and communal action. Not quite the usual conventions of rock'n'roll as we know it.

The group's first two EPs – released on their own Dischord Records in 1981 and later compiled as the MINOR THREAT album – were statements brimming with belief, energy and passion. With a sound stripped to its essentials, MacKaye, alongside **Lyle Preslar** (guitar), **Jeff Nelson** (drums) and **Brian Baker** (bass), ripped through songs such as "I Don't Wanna Hear It" and "Minor Threat" – required listening for any reading of the hardcore phenomenon. Few bands have ever achieved a similar level of intensity or provoked such allegiance among fans, who quickly adopted the Straight Edge creed.

The musical precision of 1983's OUT OF STEP, a thematic and musical refinement of their earlier releases, revealed a stunning progression. MacKaye's lyrics offered a high yield of ideas over rhetoric, informing, accusing and motivating his growing audience.

With only one 'proper' album to their name, Minor Threat had said all that was required of them and much more besides. The group disbanded and its members joined a succession of allied groups such as **Senator Flux**, **Meatmen**, **Dag Nasty** and **Junkyard** (some of whom would also record with Dischord, an operation still overseen by Nelson). MacKaye himself joined **FUGAZI**, where the presence of a similarly talented co-writer and singer, Guy Picciotto, helped dissipate the cult of personality which he clearly reviled.

⊙ **Complete** (1988; Dischord).
As the title suggests, an all-encompassing compilation of Minor Threat's compelling early EPs, sole album, and the final "Salad Days" release.

Alex Ogg

THE MINUTEMEN

Formed San Pedro, California, 1980.

When The Minutemen (formerly Reactionaries) arrived on the greater-LA hardcore scene it was instantly clear that this was not your average hard/fast trio. Though they seldom played out of 4/4, driven by **George Hurley**'s drums, their accents and syncopations – not to mention **D. Boon**'s guitar chords and **Mike Watt**'s bass scales – were jazzy. What made them acceptable to the HC community were their energy and speed (their earliest songs usually lasted less than sixty seconds, hence the name), and their fury: Boon's committed if highly personal leftism informed most of his lyrics, and he howled them out as if trying to overpower the Republican tidal wave of the 1980s with sheer volume (he is credited on an early Minutemen EP as 'guitars, yelling').

While, generally speaking, Boon was the zealot and Watt the goofball (Boon would sing about the masses, Watt made lyrics out of a landlord's note

asking him not to use the shower), each had a healthy respect for the other's predilections. Their first EPs – PARANOID TIME, JOY and BEAN SPILL – reflect all these aspects, mixing the abstract ("Futurism Restated") with the evangelical ("Joe McCarthy's Ghost") and the absurd ("If Reagan Played Disco"), played with a rough angularity guaranteed to put off non-fans. After the fourteen-song 12" THE PUNCH LINE, and their first album, WHAT MAKES A MAN START FIRES? (1982), they were finding their stride (evident in the catchy opener, "Bob Dylan Wrote Propaganda Songs"), and the follow-up EP TOUR SPIEL (released on Bob Mould's Reflex label) even sported a respectful cover of Creedence's "Green River". Both were live songs from their Campaign Trail tour in the summer of 1984.

1983's BUZZ OR HOWL UNDER THE INFLUENCE OF HEAT EP marked a real step forward: though still fast and quirky, the cuts here sounded more like songs than inspired fragments, and there was a depth to the sound and the arrangements that could find a path to a non-aficionado. A single sharp guitar note leapt out of the churning murk of "Cut" with the force of a killer rock riff, and the way "Little Man With A Gun In His Hand" alternated between choppy refrains and gently bubbling verses presaged the method by which many latter-day alternative-rockers would engage Top 40 consciousness.

In 1984 a long touring gap was filled with POLITICS OF TIME, a feature-length outtake session (including an old Reactionaries tune "Tony Got Wasted In Pedro"). The band followed with a powerful one–two punch, recorded in two two-day sessions, one at the end of 1983, the other in April 1984. DOUBLE NICKELS ON THE DIME was their first coup – a four-sided LP ('Take that, Hüskers' – a reference to Hüsker Dü's recent double LP ZEN ARCADE – was scrawled on the play-out groove), it sported forty-something cuts with not a loser in the batch, lurching from the drunk-groove "Jesus And Tequila" to the agit-funk "Toadies" to the all-time definitive version of Steely Dan's "Doctor Wu" (with Watt singing the words on one vocal track and

blithely reading the lyrics as bad poetry on the other). Soon after, THE PROJECT MERSH EP, boasting horn parts and the epic "The Cheerleaders" ('Can you hear them call your name?/Can you count the lives they'll take?'), reshuffled their musical deck whilst picking them up more valuable kudos.

Their godhead in HC circles established, the band took things a little slower on the 1985 LP THREE-WAY TIE FOR LAST, their trademark kick-ass style relaxing (slightly) into warmer grooves. Fun experiments like Watt's (Henry Rollins-inspired) "Spoken Word Piece" were cushioned by forthright guitar tunes like "The Big Stick" (pretty rockin' for a song about US imperialism in Central America) and a great Watt-sung version of Blue Oyster Cult's "The Red And The Black". It was great, it was forward-looking – it was the end. During a Southwest tour, The Men's van got into an accident in Arizona on December 22, 1985, and Boon's spine snapped, ending his life at age 27 – a tragedy that, said critic Robert Christgau, 'for wasted potential has Lennon and Hendrix for company'.

He was right. No one filled The Minutemen's shoes. Watt and Hurley did great stuff with **FIREHOSE**, and Watt's solo career (notably BALL HOG OR TUG BOAT?) has had its moments, but while many latter-day hard rockers subscribe to Boon's beliefs, and some even evince his passion, no band has translated these into anything like The Minutemen's kind of rock – studied but swinging, precise but full of life and fun. The marriage of jazz and hardcore appears to have died with Boon and The Minutemen.

- **Post-Mersh, Vol 3** (1988; SST).
  This CD reissue has the early history – the first three EPs and POLITICS OF TIME. Over the hour-plus, you can hear the sound forming, from the mordant "Tony Got Wasted In Pedro" to the unrelenting Urinals cover "Ack Ack Ack".

- **Double Nickels On The Dime** (1984; SST).
  The Minutemen's enduring 40-plus-track masterpiece, criminally neglected by the masses. Just get it.

- **Ballot Result** (1986; SST).
  THREE-WAY TIE FOR LAST came with a ballot with which fans could vote for songs they'd like to see on a compilation. RESULT consists of previously unreleased versions of the winning songs. A good selection – and the existence of so many alternate takes is a testament to the obsessive work ethic of the band.

Roy Edroso

MIRACLE LEGION

Formed, Connecticut, 1984.

Miracle Legion started life as a four-piece, and though the rhythm section has undergone many personnel changes or, on occasion, been dispensed with altogether, **Mark Mulcahy** (singer) and **Ray Neal** (guitar) have remained at the heart of the band.

Miracle Legion first came to prominence in 1985; a year when British music journalists were falling over themselves in an attempt to unearth the American band that would justify the hype surrounding the faltering Paisley Underground movement. Despite the attempt at pigeonholing, anyone who bought the band's debut mini-album THE BACKYARD expecting a dose of New Psychedelia was instead greeted by a sound steeped in the traditions of melodic American rock. This inevitably led to R.E.M. comparisons, but Mulcahy boasted a lyrical simplicity and directness that was far removed from Michael Stipe's oblique speak, and was later cited by Radiohead's Thom Yorke as a key influence. The set's title track in particular, a fond remembrance of times and people past, is simply stunning.

After the positive impression created by THE BACKYARD, the band's first album proper, SURPRISE SURPRISE SURPRISE (1987), was disappointingly restrained. "Mr. Mingo" was the stand-out track, but the overall impression was of a band operating at less than full throttle. Their next release GLAD (1988) redressed the balance. The studio side included the wonderful "A Heart Disease Called Love", while **Pere Ubu** joined in a wild stomp through "Closer To The Wall" (from The Backyard) on the live side recorded at a New York concert.

By the release of ME AND MR. RAY (1989), Mulcahy and Neal were operating as a duo. Some of the band's most heartbreakingly beautiful songs ("You're The One Lee", "Gigantic Transatlantic Trunk Call") are to be found on this album, and it's only the presence of some less distinguished fillers that robs it of true classic status.

Returning as a four-piece with the addition of **Dave McCaffrey** (bass) and **Scott 'Spot' Boutier** (drums), Miracle Legion seemed on the verge of a commercial breakthrough in 1992 with the release of DRENCHED. Though lacking the emotional warmth of its predecessor, DRENCHED was a bold, confident album, and positive reviews led to the band appearing on MTV and *The David Letterman Show*. However, just as the band had earlier been caught up in the fallout from the Rough Trade collapse, now their relationship with their new label, Morgan Creek, ran into difficulties. Attempts to record a new album were thwarted, and when the band failed to secure a release from their contract they left the matter in the hands of their lawyers and went their separate ways.

After a three-year hiatus – during which time the band minus Ray recorded tracks under the name **Polaris** for a children's television programme – Miracle Legion released PORTRAIT OF A DAMAGED FAMILY (1996) on Mark's Mezzotint label. Freed from record company wrangling, Miracle Legion finally delivered the unassuming masterpiece they had always promised. As ever, it was the quieter songs dealing with bittersweet affairs of the heart that shine, but tracks such as "6 Months" and "KKM" also revealed the harder social edge of Mulcahy's lyrics.

The band have continued to play the occasional gig, but the release of Mulcahy's debut solo albums, FATHERING and SMILESUNSET, made the future look uncertain. Those who have been listening to date will definitely stick around in anticipation of another low-key triumph.

⊙ **Portrait Of A Damaged Family** (1996; Mezzotint). If you can find them, THE BACKYARD and ME AND MR. RAY should be snapped up, but the band's most recent release is also their finest.

Tom Tierney.

MIRANDA SEX GARDEN

Formed London, 1991.

An unlikely amalgam of classical harmonies, art-rock and convent-girl submission fantasies, the **Miranda Sex Garden** have become the preferred soundtrack for rubberwear parties across the nation. Following on in the strict tradition of The Velvet Underground's "Venus In Furs" or mid-period Siouxsie, they have spent years putting the S&M into R&B, and are probably still appearing at a punishment dungeon near you, despite lead singer **Katharine Blake**'s chart action with the **Mediaeval Baebes**.

The initial vocal trio of Blake, **Kelly McCusker** and **Jocelyn West** met at London's Purcell Music School. After being spotted busking on the Portobello Road, they were signed to Mute and released "Gush Forth My Tears", a techno update of a sixteenth-century madrigal. Disappointingly, they reverted to the traditional sound for their first album, MADRA, recorded in Southwark's' renowned Henry Wood Hall. All this changed in 1992 when **Donna McKevitt** replaced West and the vocal trio's impeccable harmonies were fleshed out with the menacing arrangements of **Ben Golomstock** (guitars) and **Trevor Sharpe** on drums. The new line-up released IRIS, a superb mini-album that showcased their exotic taste in original material, with the added bonus of a frenzied cover of the old folk fave, "Lovely Joan".

Next album, SUSPIRIA (1993), saw the full flowering of the Sex Garden sound, with tracks such as "Open Eyes" and "Sunshine" skilfully exploiting the clash between the beautiful voices and the harsh dissonant music. They also found a natural home for their bizarre live performances on London's underground fetish club circuit, an ambience reflected on perhaps their definitive statement, 1994's FAIRYTALES OF SLAVERY. Not everyone's cup of meat perhaps, but this grinding hymn to bondage provided a welcome alternative to the derivative Britpop that was cluttering the charts at the time.

In 1995 the band left their label but still carried on as a live draw. Blake was developing a second career with the Mediaeval Baebes, a vocal troupe pitched somewhere between a Pre-Raphaelite flower bower and a Hammer vampire flick. It was a return to the unadorned vocals of MADRA, but this time the formula paid off with big sales in the classical charts. Whether or not the Miranda Sex Garden ever return to the studio, their spirit lives on in the poisoned vision of the Baebes, latterly on UNDRENTIDE (2000) and THE ROSE (2002).

Iain Smith

THE MISFITS

Formed New Jersey, 1976; disbanded 1983;
re-formed 1996.

Despite a spectacular failure to sell any records during their existence, **The Misfits** went on to achieve cult status and the dubious distinction of becoming huge business on the bootleg circuit, mainly after metal giants such as Metallica and Guns N' Roses tackled their songs.

They were formed by **Glenn Danzig** (vocals) and **Jerry Only** (bass) in New Jersey, along with one **Manny** – the first of a succession of ill-fated and largely inept drummers. Notoriety of any description hardly seemed on the cards when they released their debut single, "Cough Cool"/"She" on their own Blank label in 1977. A Misfits anomaly, the single's keyboard-driven sound was soon replaced by some of the most crudely and brutally recorded punk guitar of all time with the introduction of **Bobby Steele**.

Their second single, "Bullet" (released on the band's Plan 9 label in 1978), with **Mr Jim** on drums, was prototype Misfits: fast, basic and subtlety-free. Glenn Danzig, whose full, distinctive voice (his main influences were Elvis and Roy Orbison) lent the band's sound much of its accessibility, took care of lyrics, music and Plan 9, while the rest of the band kept their day jobs. His interest in low-grade gore/splatter films gradually began to dominate – their next two singles were "Horror Business", apparently recorded in a haunted house, and "Night Of The Living Dead", which they released on Hallowe'en in 1979.

By this time The Misfits had acquired a certain reputation – but only as one of the worst-playing but most exciting live bands in existence. However, Glenn's poppy melodies and the band's enthusiastic three-chord racket was a winning combination when captured on vinyl. An unsavoury experience in Britain inspired Glenn to write "London Dungeon", the lead track on 1981's 3 HITS FROM HELL EP, which displayed a more atmospheric aspect to the band's thrash-punk arcana. That year they also released "Halloween", having ditched Bobby Steele for **Doyle**, whose guitar playing was technically incompetent – though he more than compensated by his sheer style. The B-side, "Halloween II", was some sort of attempt at sounding spooky. Needless to say, hampered as ever by minimal recording budgets and mangled by minimal musicianship, it naturally failed to scare anyone but, like Alice Cooper

and the Damned before them, the Misfits' take on horror was to make it a part of the entertainment.

Having previously aborted an album's worth of material, The Misfits worked out a distribution deal with Slash Records and finally managed an LP (a full 26 minutes) in 1982. WALK AMONG US featured some of their best, most hilarious, material. It remains unclear whether there was any comic intention behind tracks like "I Turned Into A Martian", but it is hard to imagine the band could have kept a straight face on "Braineaters" ('Brains for dinner/brains for lunch ... why can't we have some guts').

Still, it was downhill from there on, as they somehow saw fit to release a horrendous live EP, EVILIVE (1983), and as the humour slipped away they gradually lost their penchant for melody in their desire to be as brutal as possible. Their subsequent albums, EARTH A.D. (aka WOLF'S BLOOD; 1983), were collections of tuneless thrash with little to recommend them. The drumming, courtesy of 'legendary' punk producer **Robo**, was worse than ever.

In 1983 Glenn Danzig disbanded The Misfits, thoroughly fed up with being the only member of the band with any talent. He went on to form **Samhain**, who indulged in more 'spooky' sound effects and, in 1987, Sabbath-rockers **DANZIG** – neither were anything like as much fun as The Misfits. Bobby Steele formed **The Undead** after his dismissal, and they are still, sporadically, at it.

Metallica's championing of The Misfits' cause in the 80s resulted in a resurgence of interest on a scale they could only have dreamt about. Cheekily jumping on the bandwagon, Only and Doyle 're-formed' The Misfits (with Glenn replaced by vocalist **Michale Graves**), took the band around Europe in 1996 and recorded AMERICAN PSYCHO (1997). Guaranteed to please the 14-year-old brat in all of us, the album piled on the spookiness, dug up the rotting corpse of Duane Eddy's guitar and twanged through a brand-new set at lightning speed. 1999 brought another offering from beyond the grave, FAMOUS MONSTERS, which, as the title suggested,

romped its way through a ghoulish movie catalogue of inspiration. Song titles such as "Kong Unleashed" and "Hunting Humans" should give you an idea…

(•) **Beware** (1980; Cherry Red).
Seven-track compilation featuring all the early classics ("Last Caress", "Attitude") later popularized by metal stadium-rockers. Much sought-after, and likely to cost an arm and a leg.

(•) **Walk Among Us** (1982; Slash/Ruby).
Fast, fun, brutal yet still melodic, this is the band's only 'proper' album. Thirteen anthemic tracks, and the greatest two-note guitar solo Doyle ever played on "Hatebreeders".

(•) **Misfits** (1987; Plan 9).
Twenty-track compilation spanning their whole career, probably the best buy. Sing along with "Teenagers From Mars" and "Skulls", marvel at how they managed to make the guitars on "Vampira" sound like wind, and try to work out what on earth Glenn is singing on "Wolfsblood". Hours of fun.

(•) **Cuts From The Crypt** (2001; Roadrunner).
This compilation is a punky, funny, spine-tingling introduction to The Misfits' post-Glenn reincarnation.

Mauro Venegas

THE MISSION

Formed Leeds, England, 1985.

The most successful of all goth bands, **The Mission** were formed after **SISTERS OF MERCY** split in 1985. **Craig Adams** (bass) and **Wayne Hussey** (guitar/vocals), annoyed by the limited lyrical contribution they had been allowed to make, walked out while working on songs with Sisters leader, **Andrew Eldritch**, in Hamburg. After linking up with **Simon Hinkler** (guitar/keyboards) and **Mick Brown** (drums), they rehearsed a set comprising mainly Sisters rejects and covers (The Stooges, The Doors, Neil Young) and hit the road, supporting The Cult and initially calling themselves The Sisterhood – a stunt designed to annoy Eldritch. Soon after they became The Mission, a move that prompted more brickbats from Eldritch, who claimed they had lifted the name from the Sisters Of Mercy's projected new album, LEFT ON MISSION OF REVENGE.

The first recorded evidence, "Serpent's Kiss", was a far rockier affair than anything from their old band. After a second single, "Garden Of Delight", came their major-label debut, GOD'S OWN MEDICINE (1986), the beginning of The Mission's chart success as well as the first example of its overblown rock dream. They achieved their commercial breakthrough with "Wasteland", which reached #11 in the UK on the back of a tour with All About Eve.

The live shows and beery camaraderie gained them a large following, but cracks appeared on their 1988 tour of the US, when Craig Adams suffered a nervous breakdown and temporarily left the band. CHILDREN (1988) smacked into the UK album charts at #2 on the back of the windswept melody and passion of "Tower Of Strength", but it was a rather stilted and shallow affair, even with the cover of Aerosmith's "Dream On" and production by Led Zeppelin bassist, John Paul Jones.

Fans were invited to the recording sessions for their third album and asked to choose the track-listing from the fifteen or so songs available. The new directness of CARVED IN SAND (1990) was exemplified by the divertingly melodic and pretty "Butterfly On A Wheel", which dealt with the break-up of Simon Hinkler's relationship with All About Eve vocalist, Julianne Regan.

The band toured widely following the album's success and again it was the US leg that thwarted the band: midway through, Simon Hinkler smashed his guitar, walked off stage, and quit, later to surface with a new project, **Mindfeel** (with **Robin Downe** and **James Bacon**). To fill the gap, Mercury asked for a new album. After dusting down the previous leftovers and recording a few new songs, the remaining band members released GRAINS OF SAND (1990), which contained "Hands Across The Ocean" – a message to Simon Hinkler that asked for, and offered, forgiveness.

A new chapter began in 1991, spurred on by the dance explosion. The truncated three-piece recruited session musicians for the experimental, defiantly non-gothic MASQUE (1992), featuring the thundering dance-rock of "Never Again" and the songs co-written with Miles Hunt of The Wonder Stuff. The album's lyrical simplicity was summed up by the beautifully upbeat love song, "Like A Child Again", on which Fairport Convention violinist **Ric Sanders** was allowed full rein. The result was a perfect pop song but it disappointed many Mission fans.

After SALAD DAZE: RADIO 1 SESSIONS (1994) and SUM AND SUBSTANCE (1994), Craig Adams jumped ship to join **THE CULT** (who split up soon after), and it was left to Wayne Hussey and Mick Brown to reconfigure the band, recruiting **Andy Cousin** (ex-**ALL ABOUT EVE**) to play bass, **Rik Carter** (ex-Pendragon) on keyboards and a new guitarist to augment the sound.

A curious but occasionally successful album, NEVERLAND (1995), was released and marked a return to more guitar-based work, though with little commercial impact. It was followed by BLUE (1996) and AURA (2001), both lacklustre efforts, that added little new, and with the songwriting sounding ever more stretched.

Simon Hinkle, meanwhile, moved to New Mexico (USA) in 1996 with his wife and dog. Mindfeel managed to release a couple of singles, but by 1999 had vanished without trace.

(•) **God's Own Medicine** (1986; Mercury).
A defining moment of goth. A more human version of the Sisters Of Mercy with love songs, sex songs and fey rock songs. The vocals are a little strained but the sound is fully fledged.

(•) **Carved In Sand** (1990; Mercury).
A soundscape of intimacy and universal emotion. The singing is sublime and the music uplifting. This is the album on which their reputation should rest.

(•) **Grains Of Sand** (1990; Mercury).
The Mission's most direct album, ranging from the pure pop of "Hands Across The Ocean" to the full-blown orchestral ballad "Sweet Smile Of A Mystery" and the audacious "Heaven Sends You".

Duncan Harris

MISSION OF BURMA

Formed Boston, Massachusetts, 1979;
disbanded 1983.

Mission **Of Burma** were as significant to the development of the US alternative music scene as the Buzzcocks were to the UK's. The group formed in 1979 when **Roger Miller** (guitar) and **Clint Conley** (bass) arrived in Boston from Ann Arbor and New York respectively. Hooking up with tape-loop manipulator **Martin Swope** and drummer **Peter Prescott**, they quickly perfected the most agitated, displaced post-punk sound of the period.

The group's debut single, "Academy Fight Song", was pure sonic confrontation. Nowadays most readily recognized as an R.E.M. encore, it should be a primary source for all rock historians. The SIGNALS, CALLS, AND MARCHES EP (1981) excavated still lower layers of alienation and urban paranoia, notably in Conley's acidic "That's When I Reach For My Revolver", as surly an epistle as anything The Only Ones recorded. If anyone had expected their debut album, VS (1982), to tone things down, Mission Of Burma were keen to disappoint. Instead, songs such as "Einstein's Day" and "Fun World" married caustic and coruscating lyrics to music of heart-stopping intensity. However, the years of playing at maximum volume in minuscule rehearsal rooms took its toll early. With the decline in Miller's hearing, Mission Of Burma were forced to call it quits.

But the residual interest in the band showed no signs of abating, largely due to namechecks by R.E.M. and others. Of the glut of reissues and compilations, the best is the one reviewed below, though the live collection, THE HORRIBLE TRUTH ABOUT BURMA (1985), is worth hearing for its covers of Stooges and Pere Ubu material (two good reference points to the group's lineage). Miller headed into quiet obscurity with **Birdsongs Of The Mesozoic** (who also featured Swope) and **No Man**, while Prescott continued to tour with the **Volcano Suns**. Conley has subsequently produced for Yo La Tengo, among others.

⊙ **Mission Of Burma** (1988; Rykodisc).
This CD contains everything that all but the maddest completist could desire: the group's still incendiary debut single, "Academy Flight Song", the SIGNALS, CALLS, AND MARCHES EP and their sole studio album, plus various singles and live cuts. Mission Of Burma were never more than a brief flash point in music's evolution, but here you can detect their influence on everything from Hüsker Dü to Sonic Youth.

Alex Ogg

JONI MITCHELL

Born Fort McLeod, Alberta, Canada, 1943.

In 1963, **Roberta Joan Anderson** – a struggling painter and art student – could be found playing folk music in the coffee bars of Toronto for a few dollars. Folk music was the new currency of white middle-class youth at the time, its mixture of naivety and strident Utopianism touching a chord among the disaffected and educated. Mingling light radical protest and acoustic balladry (often rooted in Dust Bowl-era social commentary), it was a style that proved a perfect vehicle for Anderson's blossoming talents as a singer and guitarist.

After playing at the Mariposa Folk Festival in 1964, she married Chuck Mitchell, started calling herself **Joni Mitchell**, and committed herself to a career that would eventually establish her as one of the foremost singer-songwriters in America. Such recognition was some way off, although Mitchell's subsequent life in Detroit with Chuck, her divorce, her move to New York in 1967, and her subsequent short foray to England with producer Joe Boyd, all provided inspiration for key early songs such as "Both Sides Now", written during this period of upheaval. Initially, however, her songs became known through being covered by others, not least Buffy Saint-Marie and, in the UK, Fairport Convention.

It wasn't until her third album, LADIES OF THE CANYON (1970), that she really broke outside her homeland – in the UK it reached #8, while the single from it, "Big Yellow Taxi", managed #11. The album also contained a song that became an anthem for the hippie generation, "Woodstock", although its casting of her as spokesperson for a generation was at odds with the deeply personal songs she was then playing: the rest of LADIES OF THE CANYON was full of lyrical and introspective songs that touched raw nerves in their listeners.

She consolidated her position with BLUE (1971), an emotional flood of recollections and bittersweet observations perfectly complemented by a stripped-back production on tracks such as "The Last Time I Saw Richard" and "All I Want". BLUE proved a draining experience, and Mitchell took time out to travel and recharge before returning late in 1972 with a transitional album, FOR THE ROSES – a more confident and robust work than its predecessor, with a more expansive 'band' feel, partly created by the jazz arranger and musician Tom Scott. COURT AND SPARK (1974) marked a further move away from the rather virginal ambience of the early music. Chic and sassy, it was a cosmopolitan melange of reed, woodwind, trumpet and other jazzy colourings that was utterly relaxed and self-assured.

COURT AND SPARK proved to be Mitchell's most successful album to date, reaching #2 in the US and #14 in the UK, and she followed it with an extensive tour with Tom Scott and The LA Express – a tour that was captured on the double live album MILES OF AISLES (1975). Her Wembley appearance (with CSN&Y and The Band) reaffirmed her rock celebrity status.

With her next album, THE HISSING OF SUMMER LAWNS (1975), she moved further towards social commentary, particularly on the commercialism of American culture. Some fans felt alienated by her band's rock and jazz fusions, and some felt the lyrics

were becoming too wordy, but Mitchell stuck to what she saw as her musical progression, and the next album, HEJIRA (1976), rounded off a remarkably consistent run of albums. Written during car journeys between New York and Los Angeles, it took Mitchell into hitherto unexplored territory: propelled by **Jaco Pastorius**'s bass, her voice revelled in sinuous, spacious textures on songs that were long and light and seemingly spun out of air. It was a fascinating, beautiful record.

If HEJIRA showed Mitchell's explorations of jazz at their best, her subsequent albums – the double DON JUAN'S RECKLESS DAUGHTER (1977) and the jazz tribute MINGUS (1979) – were generally deemed to stray too far from her home ground, and were coolly received.

As with many of her contemporaries, Mitchell seemed out of place in the 1980s, and this was exacerbated by financial and health worries. All of the albums were patchy during this decade, although purists rallied round the Thomas Dolby-produced DOG EAT DOG (1985), an angry and despairing work that at least offered glimpses of conviction. There have recently been more positive signs of a creative awakening, notably on 1991's NIGHT RIDE HOME, which echoed some of the after-hours, hypnotic insistency of HEJIRA. A collection of her paintings was well received at exhibitions in London and Edinburgh, and examples of her art were featured on the cover and sleeve of TURBULENT INDIGO (1994), her seventeenth album. This was perhaps her most compelling work since the mid 70s, trenchantly confronting issues such as rape and wife-beating.

Mitchell played a rare one-off British gig in Kensington in late 1994 to promote the album, her first British appearance for five years. She described the album as 'songs about trapped women'. An intriguing pair of compilation albums, HITS and MISSES (1996; both on Reprise), reassessed her career in terms of songs that had been successful for Mitchell herself or as performed by other artists; and songs that she considered 'commercially viable' but which never made it as singles.

Joni Mitchell's personal life has dominated more than her music of late. In April 1997 the papers were full of her being reunited with her adopted daughter after 32 years, and her new-found family may account for her absence from the recording studio. She is also rumoured to be fighting cancer. She did find time to refuse to attend her admittance into the Rock And Roll Hall Of Fame, due to being asked to pay $1500 dollars for extra tickets – another laudable statement against Corporate Rock shenanigans.

Four years after TURBULENT INDIGO, Mitchell released TAMING THE TIGER (1998), a worthy addition to a canon of work that is arguably more consistent than Dylan's and Young's, and captures an artist still intent on risk taking. "TAMING..." is one of Mitchell's more exotic and beguiling offerings, confidently propelled by **Wayne Shorter**'s sax towards an array of different styles, wrapped around typically deft, sometimes acerbic lyrics. The album made lukewarm sales, despite warm critical reviews – nothing new, as Mitchell has hardly been a major unit-shifter since the 70s. She has settled instead for a role some way between major cult figure and reluctant elder stateswoman, and has offered longevity and consistency – one of only a handful of 60s heavyweights with any real shred of artistic credibility.

The 90s' revival of the female singer-songwriter genre put Mitchell's music into fresh focus, with artists as diverse as Beth Orton, Shawn Colvin, Fiona Apple, Liz Phair and Sheryl Crow, to name a random sample. The effect was an upping of the stakes for Mitchell, assuming she still wants to talk to a generation other than her own. Recent releases have all oozed the trademark Mitchell class, but they have been mature works, eschewing pain and emotional entanglements for a broader spectrum of concerns. Among the most interesting were the orchestral BOTH SIDES NOW (2000) and TRAVELOGUE (2002), but Mitchell does need to deliver something a little special next time if she is to avoid being feted purely for her 70s output. That said, Joni Mitchell remains rightly regarded as one of the finest singer-songwriters of the last forty years.

Court And Spark (1974; Asylum).
Cool and sweet, lyrical and musical, this album finds Mitchell displaying a new sophistication that enhances the introspective nature of most of the songs.

The Hissing Of Summer Lawns (1975; Asylum).
Another classic, banishing any lingering cheesecloth folksims with startling and innovative jazz rhythms and hypnotic sound textures, and scathing social portraiture in the lyrics.

Hejira (1976; Asylum).
Inspired by the possibilities of the open road, this offers a psychic journey and an exploration of dreamlike musical textures. Mitchell was communicating through sound as much as through words during this stage of her career.

Hits (1996; Warners).
This compilation is a good starting point for the casual listener; the companion CD, MISSES, is an intriguing second port of call, but not essential.

Nig Hodgkins

Born New York, 1966.

"Everything is wrong ... I know more about idiot actors in Hollywood than I do about the woman who lives next door to me (and who is probably more interesting)."

Richard Melville Hall was nicknamed **Moby** after *Moby Dick*, the great novel by his namesake and, so it is claimed, distant ancestor, Herman Melville. Unlike the novel's antihero, however, Moby is more inclined towards saving whales than hunting them. This philosophy graduate is as well-known for his veganism, his anti-drug declarations and his Christian faith as for his music. Once labelled 'the Iggy Pop of techno', Moby's music has now evolved into a slick blues-based 'product' that comfortably graces countless corporate advertisements.

Born in New York but raised in Connecticut (where his weekends were spent in hippie communes), Moby started learning classical guitar at the age of 10, and widened his taste, as a teenager, to encompass punk, New Wave, hip-hop, reggae and speed metal. He played in a number of bands, including **The Vatican Commandos**, hardcore band **FLIPPER** (while their lead singer was in jail), and 4AD recording artists **Ultra Vivid Scene**, for whom he played guitar.

At the end of the 80s, Moby went solo, and turned his attention to the acid-house and rave scene; his debut single, "Go", released in October 1991, was a radical reworking of a theme from David Lynch's cult TV series, *Twin Peaks*. Other hit singles followed – "I Feel It", "Move", "Hymn" and "Everytime You Touch Me".

His adventurous attitude was always in evidence. "Thousand", the B-side of "I Feel It", was listed in *The Guinness Book Of Records* as the fastest single ever – at one stage it attained 1015 beats per minute. Furthermore, while the average live techno performance was anonymous and characterless, Moby became known for 'surfing' on his keyboards, climbing up banks of speakers, stage-diving and occasionally trashing equipment.

After three unofficial albums had been released by US label Instinct, Moby's 1995 album EVERYTHING IS WRONG was the first to be released with his full consent. Quoting Einstein, Thoreau, Albert Schweitzer and St Francis of Assisi in the sleeve notes, Moby outlined his objections to modern life, organized religion, and environmental destruction. The music, meanwhile, ranged through house chaos to chill-out.

Not that EVERYTHING was Moby's first attempt to use his records to get a message across. His singles have usually carried the inscription, 'animals are not for eating. Love to Jesus Christ', and in 1994, when a car manufacturer had used a cover version of "Go!" for a TV commercial, he rereleased the track 'to set the record straight', and donated the royalties to the eco-charity Transport 2000.

In some quarters, ANIMAL RIGHTS, his 1996 album release, was considered a misplaced step rather than the expected confident stride forward – his reputation for experiment was badly dented by the album's retro, nosebleed-techno, lightning pace – and many commentators decided to write him off. He came back, and wrong-footed his critics once again with the dubiously titled I LIKE TO SCORE (1997), a collection of instrumental pieces for cinema. Surprise stand-out track is the Joy Division cover "New Dawn Fades". But Richard 'Moby' Hall – like his big, bad, cetacean namesake – was destined to return, unbowed and undiminished.

Noone quite expected just how enormous Moby's next album would become, least of all the man himself. It was easy to forget the consistent brilliance of PLAY (1999), given how ubiquitous it became, with every track licensed for use in an advert or film. It was a testament to the genius of the compositions that they were so fluid, so amorphous in their creation of atmosphere that the album became the soundtrack of a year in a way no other had before.

A follow-up was always going to be a difficult proposition and perhaps inevitably 18 (2002) fell short of the mark. Considered on its own it was everything you'd expect from a Moby album – more blues samples, a bit of swirling ambience and some swooping strings – but it lacked the direction of its predecessor. For a man with so many ideas though, it won't be long before he springs another surprise on us.

⊙ **Everything Is Wrong** (1995; Mute).
Everything is in, more like, on this unusually eclectic album. One minute orchestral pianos create a peaceful atmosphere; the next, you're launched into full-throttle metal, and there are other dalliances with jungle and ambient.

⊙ **Play** (1999; Mute).
Delta blues meets multimedia magnificence in a staggeringly coherent work – every track, from the gritty "Find My Baby" to the heavenly "Porcelain", is an absolute gem.

George Luke

MOBY GRAPE

Formed San Francisco, 1966; disbanded 1969; re-formed occasionally since then.

Few California bands of the 1960s exhibited as much promise or versatility as **Moby Grape**; few burned out as quickly or as ignominiously. Perhaps too talented for their own good, the Grape boasted the tightest instrumental and vocal empathy of all the psychedelic San Francisco groups, with the arguable exception of Jefferson Airplane. With their sure-footed hybrid of rock, blues, folk and country, as well as a line-up of no fewer than five skilled songwriters, they seemed poised for a long career after their near-classic 1967 debut, MOBY GRAPE. But commercial and management pressures, combined with the group's personal instabilities, were to short-circuit their potential.

Much of the group's combustible chemistry can be attributed to the fact that the band hadn't known each other long before they entered the studio. San Francisco rock impresario Matthew Katz (who had managed the first incarnation of the Jefferson Airplane) pieced together the Grape from young veterans of obscure West Coast surf and bar bands. The one member who'd already done time with a nationally known outfit was **Skip Spence**, who drummed on the Airplane's first album (he subsequently left or was fired). Spence returned to his first instrument, the guitar, when he hooked up with Moby Grape, joining fellow axemen **Jerry Miller** and **Peter Lewis** to form an unusual and thrilling triple-guitar front line, anchored by **Bob Mosley** (bass) and **Don Stevenson** (drums).

Creating a buzz in the emerging Haight-Ashbury rock scene, and instigating a bidding war among hip young A&R men only months after they formed, the band signed with CBS and released MOBY GRAPE just in time for the Summer of Love. The disc upon which the bulk of their reputation rests, it showcased fluid guitar interplay, soulful locked-in harmonies, and a knack for far more concise songwriting and disciplined arrangements than the typical San Francisco ensemble of the time. The record's good-time cheer and occasionally spacey lyrics fitted in well with the city's psychedelic vibe and, though not every song was a gem, cuts like "Someday", the mournful "Sitting By The Window", "Lazy Me" and, above all, Spence's celebratory "Omaha", were among the more enduring highlights of late-60s California rock.

Columbia's eagerness to promote the band, however, backfired badly when the company released five singles from the album at once – one of the most renowned rock critics of the period, Lillian Roxon, was moved to dub them a psychedelic version of the Dave Clark Five, a wholly unwarranted accusation. More seriously, three members of the group were arrested for consorting with underage girls. The band were embroiled in a dispute with manager Katz as well, and the hassles drained their creative energy as they prepared a follow-up.

The group could be their own worst enemy as well: as the sessions for the LP dragged on, Lewis quit for a time, and Spence, never the most grounded of personalities, flipped while the band were recording in New York, brandishing a fire axe in the studio and getting committed to Bellevue Hospital. Pieced together from sessions in Los Angeles and New York, the album that finally surfaced in 1968, WOW, showed a lack of focus, deteriorating songwriting and occasional excesses – exemplified by the bonus disc of meandering jams that came with the LP. The group seemed to be succumbing to the torpor and cloudy visions that typified the worst traits of psychedelic music.

And WOW pretty much ended Moby Grape's brief run as a top-flight band. The original line-up, minus Spence, reverted to rootsier and more countrified sounds on MOBY GRAPE '69 (1969). Mosley shocked the hippie community by joining the Marines shortly afterwards, and only Miller, Stevenson and Lewis were available to play (with Nashville session bassist **Bob Moore**) on TRULY FINE CITIZEN (1969). Both of these LPs had some classy country-rock and folk-rock tunes amidst the bombastic boogies, and the group remained capable of delivering the goods live. But their original momentum had dissipated, and they disbanded in 1969.

Re-forming and recording periodically over the next 25 years, none of the members produced music of note outside of the Grape, except Spence, who released a brilliant spaced-out acid-folk album, OAR, in 1969. To add insult to injury, when they have chosen to reunite, they've usually been prohibited from using the Moby Grape name by Matthew Katz – a sad footnote to the career of a group that combined all-out rock'n'roll with American roots sounds as well as almost anybody.

⦿ **Vintage: The Very Best Of Moby Grape** (1993; Columbia).
This excellent double-CD, 48-track compilation is one-stop shopping for everything you need by the band: the entire first album, the best tracks from their other 60s LPs, and some fine demos, outtakes and previously unreleased live material.

Richie Unterberger

MOGWAI

Formed Glasgow, Scotland, 1995.

"The best band of the 21st century." Stephen Malkmus, Pavement

I f you've ever felt that a dreadful vocal line ruined your favourite music, then Glasgow's **Mogwai** might just be the band for you. Not for this group such hackneyed notions as verses and choruses: a typical Mogwai gig will feature searing noise, instrument abuse, band members bleeding from the ears and – in some instances – tears, or a mass exodus by the bewildered punters. Mogwai aren't the first to dabble in such sonic terrorism – they themselves cite MC5, My Bloody Valentine and Fugazi as influences – but they just might be among the last to deal with basic rock'n'roll in such a way.

Mogwai came to be when longtime friends and Joy Division fans **Stuart L Braithwaite** (guitar/occasional vocal) and **Dominic Aitchison** (guitar) decided that, in the midst of the mid-90s Britpop scene they so disliked, they had to fashion their own 'serious music'. A drummer, **Martin Bulloch**, and a third guitarist, **John Cummings**, were drafted in, adding weight and power to the group's stance. Mogwai proceeded to issue a handful of 7" singles, versions of which are available in one form or another, on the Rock Action compilation, TEN RAPID. This ushered the band's

Mogwai's young team

signing to Glasgow guitar act the Delgados' label, Chemikal Underground: by summer 1997, Mogwai (christened after the cute creature in the movie *Gremlins*) was the name to drop.

An EP, 4 SATIN, picked up promising reviews as Mogwai launched into their first proper tour. Support on the dates came from **Macrocosmica**, whose multi-instrumentalist **Brendan O'Hare** (formerly of Teenage Fanclub and the much underrated Telstar Ponies) proved so popular with the band that they asked him to tour with them and help out on the debut album, MOGWAI YOUNG TEAM.

An enormous statement, MOGWAI YOUNG TEAM was built around two vast pieces, the sinister, dominating "Like Herod" (originally entitled "Slint" in homage to another of the band's influences), and the fifteen-minute leviathan "Mogwai Fear Satan". The album, described by *NME* as having 'fire and grandeur, melancholy and madness', went on to shift more than thirty thousand copies in the UK.

Bolstered by this interest in their sonic visions, the group was soon involved in a variety of recorded projects. In January 1998, **David Holmes** had Mogwai remix his "Don't Die Just Yet" track (which saw Mogwai credited with a Top 40 hit). Two months later they, and label-mates Magoo, were covering Black Sabbath numbers for the Fierce Panda label. Mogwai themselves then became the subjects of remixing on the excellent KICKING A DEAD PIG, which included the work of such luminaries as Third Eye Foundation, Kid Loco and Atari Teenage Riot frontman Alec Empire.

The band named its next EP, NO EDUCATION = NO FUTURE (FUCK THE CURFEW). It featured what was arguably Mogwai's finest moment, the eleven-minute "Christmas Steps", but another track fell foul of legal authorities by utilizing a football commentary without permission.

Some semblance of normality fell into Mogwai's world when they were asked to support the Manic

Street Preachers on their 1998 tour. The second album proper followed early in 1999, and did not disappoint. Like their debut, COME ON, DIE YOUNG was named via Glasgow street-gang lingo, and, if anything was even more uncompromising. Pre-release press had suggested that all manner of diverse dance and vocal styles appeared on the set. Opening track "Punk Rock", however, dissolved all such preconception and set the tone for the whole collection: it contained a sample of Iggy Pop drawling: 'What sounds to you like a big load of trashy old noise is in fact the brilliant music of a genius.'

A small change of direction was heralded by ROCK ACTION (2001), an album that bucked the trend of previous releases by clocking in at under forty minutes and boasting bona fide vocal tracks. This fresher, lighter take on non-conformity boasted a couple of contributions from Super Furry Animals' frontman **Gruff Rhys** – a longtime friend and admirer. A new album, HAPPY SONGS FOR HAPPY PEOPLE, was released in 2003; the band claimed that the set contained 'forty-one minutes fifty seconds of total unadulterated brilliance', though closer inspection revealed a slightly lighter-weight incarnation of the Mogwai sound that was far from convincing.

Whatever one may feel about their 'no sell-out' stance (their dalliance with clothing manufacturer Kappa possibly poses a few questions on that front), the music of Mogwai has largely lived and breathed by itself; whether anyone is still prepared to listen, remains to be seen.

Ten Rapid (1997; Rock Action).
The crushingly rare sound of a single-minded young band, 'Ten Rapid' represents a convenient place to keep all those early singles.

Mogwai Young Team (1997; Chemikal Underground).
With feedback and melody fading in and out of the mix, the overall sound is occasionally beautiful and sometimes downright corrosive, but is never less than compelling.

⦿ Come On, Die Young (1999; Chemikal Underground). '
CODY features the masterpiece "Christmas Steps", while pointing to a fascinating future for a band still - remarkably - regarded as unknowns, even in their own native Scotland.

⦿ Rock Action (2001; Southpaw).
Mogwai throw off the dark mantle, exposing fragility and cold calculation in equal doses.

Jeremy Simmonds

MOLDY PEACHES

Formed New York, 1994.

Leading lights of the so-called 'anti-folk' scene, **Adam Green** and **Kimya Dawson** were, despite the spurious sub-sub-sub-genre nomenclature, really just the latest in a long line of faux naïf indie kids that extends at least as far back as the mid 70s and the 'I don't wanna grow up' antics of Jad Fair and Half Japanese, if not Moe Tucker of The Velvet Underground. Unfortunately, in place of the wit and charm of the best of these groups – say, The Vaselines and Beat Happening – **Moldy Peaches** replace their search for wonder with exactly the kind of cynical, 'I'm going to hide behind a wall of irony' aesthetic stance that these groups were trying to challenge in the first place.

Green and Dawson first met each other at a record shop in the suburbs of upper Westchester County, New York when Dawson was 21 and Green was 13. Soon after, the two hooked up with friends and started to sing nursery rhymes and songs about Beat Happening's Calvin Johnson while surrounded by rubber chickens. Some time in 1998 this rag-tag group made a CDR they called FER THE KIDS. In the summer of 2000 Dawson, Green, bassist **Brian Piltin**, drummer **Brent Cole** and guitarist **Jack Dishel** started to gig around the cafés of New York's East Village as **Moldy Peaches 2000**, with Green and Dawson often dressed as Robin Hood and a bunny rabbit. **Steven Mertens** replaced Piltin and the group recorded a demo CD that found its way to

Rough Trade's Geoff Travis, who released THE MOLDY PEACHES (2001), effectively a 'greatest hits' album that combined their new material with stuff recorded back in Green's parents' house years earlier. The halted, I've-had-two-lessons guitar strumming and no-fi production values were good and fine, but their toilet humour lyrics and jaded, hipster 'jokes' (at their worst on songs like "Who's Got the Crack" and "Downloading Porn With Dave"), combined with their icky childishness that went far beyond cutesy to something rather more unsettling, dragged the album down. The one exception was "NYCs Like A Graveyard", which managed to craft something that verged on the anthemic. UNRELEASED CUTZ AND LIVE JAMZ 1994-2002 (2003) didn't help matters any.

⦿ The Moldy Peaches (2001; Rough Trade).
If lyrics about turds and 70-year-olds giving blowjobs are your idea of a pop revolution, then buy this record.

Peter Shapiro

MOLOKO

Formed Sheffield, England, 1994.

One evening at a party in Sheffield, in 1994, multi-instrumentalist **Mark Brydon** overheard Irish-born **Roisin Murphy** (vocals) incessantly chanting the phrase, 'Do you like my tight sweater?' That same night, the duo went off and used the phrase as the basis for their first recording, and within a year it was to appear as the (absurdly catchy) title track on their debut album. It was released under the author-name **Moloko** (Russian for 'milk'), which the duo, who had become personal and musical partners, had adopted as a working identity.

Previously, Brydon had worked with Sheffield funk groups **Chakk** and **Cloud 9**, though he had grown weary of their tight approach; Murphy had recently quit art school, bored of endless theorizing and analysis. Their styles and spontaneity were thus well matched. They shared a fascination with how the sound of words can trigger off further associations in the mind – as "My Tight Sweater" indicated – and a readiness to cast ideas to the wind. The DO YOU LIKE MY TIGHT SWEATER? album (1995), for example, was planned as a largely instrumental set, but turned out dominated by Murphy's bewildering array of vocal identities.

Following on the album's critical and commercial success, (winging into the indie chart), the duo bumped up their live shows from intimate two-handed affairs to celebratory events, complete with a six-piece band. This allowed them to develop further, mixing and matching elements drawn from the complex and diverse pop-funk of Talking Heads, early Grace Jones or Prince, as well as the British dance scene of the mid-90s. Perhaps inevitably they were compared with Portishead, but their flexibility was at odds with the Bristol group's monochromatic mood music, or as Brydon and Murphy put it, 'They're one sentence and we're a book.'

With "Fun For Me" edging its way into the UK Top 40 during the summer of 1996, Moloko seemed well placed for mainstream appeal, but the underwhelming I AM NOT A DOCTOR (1998) suffered from over-fussy arrangements and vocals that had become a little too mannered. Luckily, German producer Boris Dluglosch rescued the ponderous "Sing It Back", remixing it into one of the definitive pan-European dance anthems of summer 1999. A canny reworking, it raced into the British top three, as did its follow-up "The Time Is Now", which heralded the duo's third album, THINGS TO MAKE AND DO (2000).

Moloko had not simply been saved from obscurity, they were now making better records than ever. Even though ALL BACK TO THE MINE (2001), a retrospective set of remixes, was diverting but inessential, 2003's STATUES managed to balance the up-tempo groovers with a newly discovered taste for orchestrated melancholia. New material is eagerly awaited.

🔘 **Do You Like My Tight Sweater?** (1995; Echo).
Released in the largely retrospective shadow of Britpop, here is a British album keen to embrace the present and future. If the playful and infectious single "Fun For Me" is a stand-out track, much of this album's remaining content is danceable, thoughtful and occasionally baffling in the lyrical department. All in all, a colourful and addictive debut.

🔘 **Things To Make And Do** (2000; Echo).
This time round, the self-consciously clever has been transformed into the spontaneously smart. This intoxicating blend shows the duo maturing while retaining their playfulness; this is a captivating record that improves with every play.

Justin Lewis

MOMUS

Nick Currie born Paisley, Scotland, 1960.

"I want to shock myself as much as anyone else." Nick Currie

The songs of **Nick Currie**, aka **Momus**, have a wordiness that has perhaps alienated as many people as it's attracted, but if you like three-minute gems with the lyrical intensity and scope of a condensed Penguin Classic, then step this way. By turn confessional, cruel, camp and contrary, Currie has established himself as one of the most thoughtful and articulate songwriters around, with a readiness to tackle any subject, however unlikely or ill-advised.

Currie has drawn on the atmosphere and dynamics of European songwriters, most notably Jacques Brel, about whom he wrote a fine nutshell-biography for the *NME* in 1986 – 'Jacques Brel was and still is more thrilling and dangerous than a thousand Jesus & Mary Chains.' Fittingly, the first Momus EP, THE BEAST WITH NO BACKS (1985), was recorded in Belgium, Brel's own country.

It paved the way for Momus's first Creation album, THE POISON BOYFRIEND (1987), which began in a subdued manner, reminiscent in places of Nick Drake, but with the opening track of side two, "Flame Into Being", burst into life. The mock-Motown of "Situation Comedy Blues" then segued into "Sex For The Disabled", an account of the swerve in priorities imposed by Margaret Thatcher, set to a Spectoresque slab of sound – which, in turn, melted into "Closer To You", a claustrophobic and uncomfortably personal exploration of obsession and longing. A magic creation.

'I think exploring taboo areas has a lot to do with being ashamed of my proper, middle-class upbringing,' declared Currie, whose next two albums, THE TENDER PERVERT (1988) and DON'T STOP THE NIGHT (1989), explored death, paedophilia, incest, murder and bestiality. Just as effective, however, were songs like "Maoist Intellectual (In The Music Industry)", so sly in its self-deprecation, or "The Beshonin", a Samurai myth transported to Scotland and set to a Euro-chug.

The scatological HIPPOPOTAMOMUS (1991) was dedicated to French singer-songwriter and prime lecher, Serge Gainsbourg, and received a notable panning from the *NME*, who awarded it 'nul points' out of 10. Perhaps as a consequence, the next release, VOYAGER (1992), was somewhat muted in comparison, concentrating on creating atmospheres rather than opting for the narrative route. Later that year, THE ULTRACONFORMIST, which drew on the darker aspects of vaudeville and music hall, most successfully defined the Momus oeuvre – all march and waltz time, sleazy first-person vignettes. There was more than a hint of Brecht and Weill's *Threepenny Opera* in the foggy London-based atmosphere of fine songs like "The Ladies Understand", "The Mother-In-Law" and "Cape And Stick Gang".

THE PHILOSOPHY OF MOMUS (1995) and SLENDER SHERBERT (1995), a reworking of classic material, are the latest instalments by this intriguing writer who, at times, is capable of being utterly thrilling and dangerous. Cherry Red reissued his otherwise-impossible-to-find debut CIRCUS MAXIMUS in 1997. In 1998 Momus made an extremely successful tour of the States, and appears to be on the brink of major recognition there.

Sounding more like a proper album than a release-schedule space-filler, the rarities and demos collection 20 VODKA JELLIES (1996) included a must-hear version of Buzzcocks "Orgasm Addict", while the massive stylistic range of PING PONG (1997) – everything from Jacques Brel to disco – sowed the seeds of another magnum opus for the Scottish cultural polyglot. LITTLE RED SONGBOOK (1998) launched his self-named 'analogue baroque' style – which means it sounds like Bach played on a ZX Spectrum, all harpsichord and analogue snyths with sex, suave and wit all there in equal proportions.

All the tracks on 1999's STARS FOREVER were commissioned by individuals who had to pay $1000 for the privilege of having a song specially written to their guidelines. Those who coughed up included Jeff Koons and Cornelius, helping Currie through a difficult lawsuit that prevented the release of LITTLE RED SONGBOOK in the US.

Another nifty ideological construct followed: 2001's FOLKTRONIC found digital technology embracing Appalachian folk music via Japanese pop and more sexual musings. A strange, astonishing hybrid and yet it made perfect sense in the hands of the literate and irreverent Momus.

⊙ **The Tender Pervert** (1988; Creation).
Currie's masterpiece, a breathtaking sequence of narrative songs with an impossible scope. Nastiness, erudition and charm in equal measures.

⊙ **Monsters Of Love** (1990; Creation).
Perhaps the most uncompromising and unlikely compilation of singles ever released. Gloomier and darker in its overall atmosphere than any of the true albums.

⊙ **The Ultraconformist** (1992; Cherry Red; reissued 1997).
A welcome return to form for Currie as sleaze voyeur, with a mock-live feel and bursts of very black humour.

⊙ **Forbidden Software Timemachine** (2003; Analog Baroque).
A meaty double-CD collection that documents Momus's stint with Creation between 1987 and 1993.

Ada Wilson

THE MONKEES

Formed Hollywood, California, 1965; disbanded 1970; re-formed 1986.

"I rammed my fist through a door. I told the man, 'That could have been your face', and walked out. We did the instrumental work on the next album." Mike Nesmith

The brainchild of director Bob Rafelson and Bert Schneider, **The Monkees** – **Mike Nesmith** (guitar/vocals), **Peter Tork** (keyboards/bass/guitar/vocals), **Micky Dolenz** (drums/vocals) and **Davy Jones** (vocals) – were formed on the back of The Beatles' movies *Hard Day's Night* and *Help*. The notion of an American Beatles – four young men sharing a carefree lifestyle full of wall-to-wall humour and an innocent sexuality – appealed to

executives at Columbia Pictures who saw big $-signs and decided to cash in by manufacturing a band to fit the image.

An ad in *Variety* prompted 437 hopefuls to audition. Of the rejects, Charles Manson was never really in with a shout, but Stephen Stills (later of Crosby, Stills & Nash), who had played in a band with Tork, came close. Of the four successful applicants, Dolenz and (English-born) Jones were basically singing actors with little musical ability, whilst Tork and Nesmith had come through the coffee-bar folkie route. The four were given the corporate makeover and scripts before getting down to serious work in March 1966. On September 12, the first of 58 half-hour episodes of *The Monkees* was screened in the USA.

The basic format of the show involved the day-to-day adventures of a pop group. The musical strategy was to get dependable young writers and session musicians to do most of the work and then add vocals from The Monkees. This allowed a rapid turnaround time on records and left the four free to rake in more cash for Columbia from TV shows, tours and other spin-offs. As a business enterprise it was a staggering success worldwide. The show stayed high in the ratings for over two years while the band chalked up three #1 singles and four #1 albums in the States, plus seven UK singles hits and two UK #1 albums in 1967 alone. The first three of these singles – "Last Train To Clarksville", "I'm A Believer" (both 1966) and "Daydream Believer" (1967) – were, and remain, classics.

The group's success, however, backfired when the ceaseless interviews and attention exposed the fact that they hadn't actually played on these singles, nor indeed either of the first two albums. This was a point that had rankled with the group, especially Nesmith, whose fist finally won the battle with the Columbia executives. Thus the debates about The Monkees' musical standing hinge on the next four, self-performed albums: HEADQUARTERS (1967), PISCES, AQUARIUS, CAPRICORN AND JONES LTD. (1967), THE BIRDS, THE BEES AND THE MONKEES (1968) and INSTANT REPLAY (1969).

Dismissed by many as the hackwork of a bunch of hired hands, these records are celebrated by others as a pinnacle of trash culture, mixing poppy psychedelia, catchy folk rock, and Tork's tape-loop sound bites. Almost by accident Columbia had fashioned a credible band. True, Nesmith was the only musical heavyweight, but Tork's journeyman musical skills added colour and some humour, while Dolenz and Jones were troupers who could be relied on to give it everything they had – and the Dolenz composition "Alternate Title" ranks as one of the most inventive pop hits of the late 60s. However, though the first of these four albums sold well, the later pair showed diminishing returns.

With their pop crown lost, the band were never likely to make it with the rock crowd, and they used their last throw of the dice to create a bizarre coun-

No expense spared for the futuristic sets: Monkees Micky Dolenz, Peter Tork, Mike Nesmith and Davy Jones

terculture monument. The movie *Head* (written by Rafelson and one Jack Nicholson) had been contracted way in advance and The Monkees now found themselves with a film to deliver and a management that didn't give a toss what it looked like. With a cast that included Victor Mature, boxer Sonny Liston and Frank Zappa, *Head* aped the drug culture and took side-swipes at the manufactured nature of the band's history. The movie and its accompanying soundtrack album were too self-conscious in places, but bizarrely inspired in others. It was the end of the line in commercial terms, but *Head* gave The Monkees another hold on permanent cult popularity.

The band struggled through more TV, tours and albums, gradually falling apart in the process. By May 1970, only Davy and Micky were around to record the totally ignored CHANGES. The post-Monkee careers were predictable. Mike soon earned respect as a country performer and songwriter. Peter dropped out, hung out, and formed a band called **Release** who could party pretty well. Davy and Micky got back to business as much as their Monkee pasts would allow: Micky became a respected TV director while Davy kept acting. A greatest hits package featuring Micky, Davy and two of the band's songwriters created some TV interest in 1976, and then came a three-way reunion in the 80s.

The MTV generation loved the TV reruns – The Monkees were arguably the first MTV band – and came in droves, along with their parents, as Davy, Peter and Micky turned on the old magic. It might have been three middle-aged men in coloured suits dancing their way across the stage at the Brentwood Arena, but it was great fun for two hours, and by this point the strength of the songs was acknowledged all round. The accompanying 80s albums were spirited but hardly essential.

The band, which, both with and without Mike, had produced sporadic and hardly essential recordings, continued to attract fans from increasingly younger generations, enraptured by the dated psychedelia of the vintage TV shows still cropping up in schedules round the world. Nesmith remained sniffily aloof from all this showbiz hoo-ha, having a career of his own as a serious musician to pursue. He said he'd never do it, but in 1996 he was back on board for the thirtieth-anniversary tour, which generated serious nostalgia dollars. JUSTUS (1997) – the resulting album – was a disappointment for all those who expected the band to be as zany and teenaged as they'd been thirty years previously. However, the foursome blended to some effect, in an AOR sort of way, under Nesmith's direction. Three-quarters of the band now seem happy to trade – at least partly – on their ex-Monkee status and the future seems likely to hold more Monkee business.

⊙ **Headquarters, and Pisces, Aquarius, Capricorn And Jones Ltd, The Birds, The Bees And The Monkees and Instant Replay** (1967, 1968 & 1969; Rhino). Almost thirty years since the *Variety* ad that started it all, Rhino put out the whole catalogue with bonus tracks at budget price. If you want to check out the band at their peak, any of these four will do. When the dust had settled on the late 60s, The Monkees stood up as a credible pop band who could really play.

⊙ **The Definitive Monkees** (2002; Warners). A 29-track collection that more or less lives up to its title, with all the hits plus the cream of the albums.

Neil Nixon

THE MONKS

Formed Germany, 1964; disbanded 1967;
briefly re-formed 2000.

**"We chucked melody out the
window and used feedback and
dissonance instead." Eddie Shaw**

Forget The Yardbirds: the most innovative group
of the 1960s were five American ex-GIs.
Swathed in black, with their heads shaven in tonsures,
The Monks – Gary Burger (lead guitar/vocals),
Larry Clark (organ/vocals), **Dave Day**
(banjo/vocals), **Roger Johnston** (drums/vocals) and
Eddie Shaw (bass/vocals) – played over-beat music
in Germany's sweaty dives and beer-drenched venues.
They demolished accepted notions of song structure,
developed arbitrary arrangements, introduced key
changes galore, added clashing harmonics, wielded
gales of feedback, spat out strangled vocals, and substituted dissonance for melody. All this ten years
before the advent of punk.

Initially called the Torquays, the band played the
standard beat music of the day – R&B covers, surf
music and Chuck Berry tunes. Soon, however, they
tired of these formats and began experimenting with
rhythmically orientated music. Dave Day abandoned
the guitar in favour of chording a horse-gut-strung
banjo, which provided a crude clacking sound. Gary
Burger, meanwhile, had discovered guitar feedback
independently of the numerous and supposed inventors of said effect.

A residency at Hamburg's fabled Top Ten Club
solidified the band's musical approach. Audiences
were as amazed by the music as they were by the
image. Occasionally, irate Germans or American ser-
vicemen swarmed on stage, attacking the band for
various reasons. The Germans were appalled by the
seeming blasphemy of the Monks' image and the GIs
were enraged by the group's theme, "Monk Time,"
which damns the escalating war in Vietnam. 'I had a
German jump on stage and begin strangling me,'
Gary Burger said. 'I busted him in the chops with my
guitar neck. That settled the matter.'

In late 1965, the Monks entered Polydor's studios
to record their only album, BLACK MONK TIME
(1965). A sonic *tour de force*, it harbours twisted songs
of love like "I Hate You", bizarre odes to chaos such
as "Higgle-Dy-Piggle-Dy", and the pre-heavy metal
"Complication", released as a single though it failed
to chart. The album, released in early 1966 to critical
rave reviews, also failed to make any chart headway.

The Monks slogged on, touring Germany and
Scandinavia for another year and embracing more
traditional pop on their next single, "I Can't Get
Over You"/"Cuckoo", which might be the weirdest
attempt at commercial music ever. "I Can't Get Over
You" comes across as a lost Velvet Underground
song, while "Cuckoo" is just downright eccentric:
The Monks' rhythmic attack is evident, but the lyrics

and vocal delivery are reminiscent of Spike Jones on
LSD. "Cuckoo" did actually make a dent in the
lower regions of the German charts.

The band released one more single, which had
hints of psychedelia. Failing to chart, it effectively
sealed their fate. Disillusioned and dismayed at the
prospect of an upcoming tour of war-torn Vietnam,
The Monks broke up.

Their legacy survives, however, thanks to artists such
as The Beastie Boys, The Fall (who recorded their own
version of "Monk Time") and Henry Rollins.

In 1997 BLACK MONK TIME was rereleased on
Infinite Records; the renewed interest led to the band
established a website, attracting novitiates from the
world over. The band's rekindled fame reached a
peak when a movie company optioned a book
written a few years earlier by bassist Eddie Shaw.
Naturally enough entitled *Black Monk Time*, it told
the Monks' incredible story; Andy Bienen, who won
an Oscar for his *Boys Don't Cry* screenplay, began
work on a script, but as yet no movie has emerged.

In November 1999 the original demos that became
BLACK MONK TIME were released as FIVE UPSTART
AMERICANS. The set was stunningly stark, making the
previous album's production sound extravagant by
comparison. A few days later the Monks played live,
something they hadn't done since 1967. It was their
first gig in America to boot. The band was joined on
stage by **Mike Fornatale**, who provided lush Xerox
copies of Gary Burger's original falsetto harmonies.
The Monks' convoluted love ballads and odes to confusion had finally come home. The patriarch of the
garage revival, NUGGETS' compiler Lenny Kaye,
could only shake his head and smile. And that was it.
The Monks disappeared again. A live CD of the
reunion show was released in October 2000, LET'S
START A BEAT, but the group itself was silent. Were
the faithful going to have another 32-year wait? If
their previous history is any indication, the Monks
story will grow stranger yet indeed.

⊙ **Black Monk Time** (1965; Polydor).
Recorded in late 1965, The Monks' debut album has-
n't aged one iota. If anything, it's gotten stranger. The
in-your-face "Shut Up" remains pertinent today, while "We
Do, Wie Du" is still as nonsensically surrealistic as it was thirty
years ago. The reissue also contains the two singles released
after the album, a mesmerizing live track and two unreleased
demos.

⊙ **Five Upstart Americans** (1999; Omplatten).
One listen to "I Hate You" confirms that The Monks,
not the Rolling Stones, were the anti-Beatles. These essential
early recordings illuminate The Monks' unique sound.

Will Bedard

THE MONOCHROME SET

Formed London, 1978; disbanded 1985;
re-formed 1989.

The **Monochrome Set**, a quintessentially
English band, and eclectic to their core, were
perhaps better respected within the industry than

outside it. They emerged in 1978 from The B-Sides, whose members **Andy Warren**, **Max** and **David Tampin**, and **Stuart Goddard**, went off to form **ADAM AND THE ANTS**. The Monochrome Set comprised the other two Sides – singer **Bid** and guitarist **Lester Square** – along with **J. D. Haney** (percussion) and **Charlie X**, soon replaced by **Simon Croft**.

Signed to Rough Trade, the band recorded three singles in 1979 – "He's Frank", the superb "Eine Symphonie Des Grauens", and signature tune "Monochrome Set" – this time with **Jeremy Harrington** on bass. After a tour of the USA, Harrington, too, quit and was replaced by Andy Warren, who had by now fallen out with his fellow Ants. April 1980 saw the release of the band's debut LP, STRANGE BOUTIQUE, and its title track as a single. The album gained favourable reviews and reached the low 60s in the UK charts. The band's prolific output continued unabated that year with "405 Lines", the sardonic "Apocalypso", and the LOVE ZOMBIES album – which flopped, and lost the interest of a second record label, Dindisc.

Despite Spinal Tap-like line-up changes, a deal with Cherry Red and the ELIGIBLE BACHELORS (1982) album marked a significant return to form. By this stage The Set were featuring keyboardist **Caroline Booth**, and a fresh guitarist named simply **Foz**. Mid-1983 saw the issue of the tongue-in-cheek single "Jet Set Junta", which nodded to the previous year's Falkland Islands conflict, becoming a big indie hit and garnering extensive play.

In 1984 Mike Alway abandoned Cherry Red to start the WEA subsidiary, Blanco y Negro. He took Monochrome Set with him, issuing "Jacob's Ladder" (1985) as one of the new label's first 45s. The positive reaction to this much poppier affair gave the band renewed confidence, though the single missed the chart, as did the equally well-received "Wallflower" later in the year. When the subsequent LP, the pleasing LOST WEEKEND (1985), also made little headway, the disillusioned Set decided to go their separate ways.

The unlikely happened in late 1989 when Lester Square, Bid and Andy Warren re-formed the band with guitarist and keyboardist **Orson Presence**. Almost unnoticed, they released a series of quirky albums, among them TRINITY ROAD (1995) and CHAPS (1998), a rather splendid two-CD career retrospective. By the end of the 1990s, Cherry Red had reissued most of their back catalogue, with BEST OF THE MONOCHROME SET following in the year 2000.

⊙ **Volume, Brilliance, Contrast** (1983; Rough Trade). Gathers up all the Monochrome Set outings on Rough Trade and serves as a useful introduction to the band's music.

⊙ **Colour Transmission** (1987; Dindisc). Pulling together mid-period Dindisc material, this compilation is well worth seeking out on CD.

Jeremy Simmonds

MONSTER MAGNET

Formed New Jersey, 1989.

At the forefront of the movement that has been dubbed 'stoner rock' you'll find the incomparable **Monster Magnet**, led by leather-trousered, devil-whiskered, arch space cadet **Dave Wyndorf**.

Wyndorf was already an established, albeit relatively unsuccessful, musician when the Magnet were formed in 1989, having released a number of singles and albums while trying to find that all-important outfit to launch his career into orbit. Steeped in everything from the trashy rock ethic of The Stooges to the imponderable drone of space-rock stalwarts Hawkwind, Wyndorf (guitar/vocals) had a unique vision which was realized when he assembled **Tim Cronin** (vocals), **John McBain** (guitar), **Joe Callandra** (bass), and **John Kleinman** (drums). Their first feedback-soaked psycho-rock outing was a self-titled mini-LP released in 1990.

Afterwards Wyndorf decided to take the spotlight and full lead singer duties, a move which allowed him to indulge his wild'n'dangerous rock persona without hindrance. The band then focused on their first full-length album for independent label Caroline. SPINE OF GOD (1991), a raw and rolling slab of punk-suffused psychedelia was followed by the space-jamming mini-LP TAB (1992). Having attracted the attention of A&M, McBain was then replaced by **Ed Mundell** and the band concentrated on creating what would become the titanic SUPERJUDGE album. Released in 1993, it finally proved that Monster Magnet's very own chauffeur-driven UFO had landed. Gone were the more self-indulgent, jam-orientated and feedback-inspired trimmings, and in their place was a leaner more metallic and riff-based power. Even with the excesses stripped away the band still sounded like an outfit trapped in an alarmingly psychedelic time-warp, while the world was being rocked by the dour power of grunge.

THE MONOCHROME SET ■ MONSTER MAGNET

The perpetual outsiders, Wyndorf and crew decided to continue towards their rendezvous with the mothership at warp factor nine, pausing only to polish their production efforts for 1995's DOPES TO INFINITY. Nestling within the stoned-out grooves of that particularly heavy record was the band's first major hit single "Negasonic Teenage Warhead", a song with the requisite weirdness and appeal to break the band into the wider public consciousness. Despite this the albums themselves were simply not selling, even though the critical reaction was good. It was time for a new plan, so Wyndorf slunk into hotel-room exile in Las Vegas to reshape the band's direction. Who knows what stellar deities visited Wyndorf during this period, or what substances proved to be an inspiration, but from the nonstop glitter and neon of Sin City was born the quintessential retro-glitz of POWERTRIP (1998), a sleek and glamorous album positively bulging with Wyndorf's customary tales of cosmic strangeness. At last the band were on a sustainable course – presumably with the controls set for the heart of the sun – and the formula was refined and repeated to greater success with their latest album, GOD SAYS NO (2001). The group are currently in orbit working on some new songs and dabbling with soundtrack material; hopefully they will attempt re-entry again sometime soon.

⦿ **Dopes To Infinity** (1995; A&M).
A space-rock collection of quite impeccable credentials, this boasts the titanic "Negasonic Teenage Warhead". Simply sublime, baby.

⦿ **Powertrip** (1998; A&M).
The ultimate stoner trip – and then some. When Wyndorf tells you he's a freakin' Space Lord you have no choice but to believe him.

⦿ **God Says No** (2001; A&M).
Sleek, streamlined, stunning; Wyndorf pulls together a gloriously over-the-top acid-fueled psychedelic binge of colossal proportions. This is your gateway to the stars.

Essi Berelian

MORCHEEBA

Formed London, 1994.

There's a lot to be said for forming a band in which every member involved can offer a different musical background. Certainly, many of the groundbreaking British albums of the 1990s – BLUE LINES, MAXINQUAYE, SCREAMADELICA, for example – resulted from some startling collisions between genres with little apparent common ground. To such a list, we might add the output of south London trio **Morcheeba**, who quietly seduced an increasing band of listeners with their intoxicating stew of roots, funk, hip-hop and dub.

Morcheeba came into being when hip-hop fan **Paul Godfrey** (keyboards) and his brother **Ross** (guitar) – who worshipped the blues and Hendrix – encountered jazz- and folk-influenced vocalist/lyricist **Skye Edwards** at a warehouse party. Any musical differences were intriguing, not distracting, and it wasn't long before the trio were songwriting and recording

at the Godfreys' studio. An excellent single, "Trigger Hippie", surfaced at the end of 1995, and then in the spring of 1996 came a languid, compelling album WHO CAN YOU TRUST?. It sold promisingly, but to those who concentrated on the promotional treadmill, Morcheeba the band remained an enigma. Was their sound aimed at the dance market, or at a particular kind of music fan? No one seemed sure, but after the trio collaborated on several tracks for **DAVID BYRNE**'s 1997 album, FEELINGS, Skye's distinctive vocals would be recognized by a huge audience when she was just one of the cast on the BBC's promotional version of Lou Reed's "Perfect Day". When released as a single due to enormous public demand, it became one of 1997's biggest sellers.

Skye's voice was now known to millions, and the release of BIG CALM in the spring of 1998 only introduced it to a wider audience. If the album's mood was even more downbeat than its predecessor, the critics were deservedly unanimous in their praise, and despite the lack of a major hit single, domestic album sales passed the quarter-million mark by the end of that year. A third long-player, FRAGMENTS OF FREEDOM (2000) was disappointingly bland in comparison, but nevertheless gave the trio their first UK Top 10 album. More promisingly, though, the group made an excellent contribution to the BACK TO MINE mix album series with a 2001 brew which featured Dr John, Jim White and Lambchop. The inclusion of the latter collective led to a collaboration with its mainman, **Kurt Wagner**, on CHARANGO (2002).

⦿ **Big Calm** (1998; Indochina).
Unlike many of their contemporaries, whose debuts tended to exhaust all their original ideas, Morcheeba had far more to say than that. BIG CALM piles on the influences, from folk ("Over And Over"), reggae ("Friction"), hip-hop (the title track) and even Cajun on the near-hit "Part Of The Process". Stimulating, dramatic and essential listening.

Justin Lewis

ALANIS MORISSETTE

Born Ottawa, Canada, 1974.

Attaining international recognition as a singer-songwriter before the age of 21 may be read as a story of precocious success, but **Alanis Morissette** had already been on the ladder a long time by then. She was writing songs at the age of 9, releasing a single the next year on her own label in her native Canada, and had added a couple of poppy albums to her repertoire by the age of 18. After landing a part in an American cable television show, her face also became known outside Canada.

A move from Ottawa to Toronto and then to Los Angeles while still a teenager may have been what Morissette needed to free her from her upbringing in a fairly strict Catholic household. The shift was signalled by the first 'real' Alanis Morissette single, "You Oughta Know", a vitriolic and sexually frank diatribe against an ex-boyfriend, on which the radio-friendly version had the now-infamous line 'Are you thinking of me when you fuck her?' unsubtly edited out. The track's explicit nature prompted comparisons between Morissette and her boss – she is signed to Madonna's Maverick label. It was no doubt through Madonna's influence that **Flea** and **Dave Navarro** of **RED HOT CHILI PEPPERS** were persuaded to lend a bit of musical clout (and instant credibility) to that first single, matching the lyrics with some raucous bass and guitars.

Unsurprisingly, her stern upbringing has provided rich subject matter. "Forgiven" dealt with the indoctrination and deep-seated guilt of a Catholic schooling – a far cry from the first song Morissette wrote back in her pre-teen years, "Faith Stay With Me". Another track, "Perfect", conveyed the 'undue parental pressure on offspring' syndrome fairly well. Both of these songs were on the 1995 album JAGGED LITTLE PILL, which took America, and then pretty much the rest of the world, by storm.

A couple of hard years' touring followed, eventually resulting in worldwide sales of 30 million – the highest ever sales for a debut album. The follow-up album, SUPPOSED FORMER INFATUATION JUNKIE (1998), and the single, "Thank U", both reflect the enormous changes in Morissette's life since 1995. Stand-out tracks include the single, the spine-tingling "Front Row" and "Baba". She has yet to find a male audience, but with 30 million women already on her side she can probably afford to do without them.

Madonna has said that Morissette reminds her of herself when she first started out – forthright, but a little bit awkward at the same time. However, Alanis has not voiced any plans to attempt artistic world-wide domination on the same scale as her boss.

Adopting a more light-hearted approach for 2002's UNDER RUG SWEPT, Morissette ended up sounding rather trite, although she maintained a wit and intelligence to her writing throughout. Coupled with some deft melodic touches it made for good, listenable pop, gleaming with a radio-friendly production sheen. Though at times it was a little too ingratiating, it was to her credit that she seemed to be charting her own course, apparently unburdened by any responsibility to live up to her own extraordinary success and with any doubts as to her capacity to endure thoroughly assuaged.

⊙ **Jagged Little Pill** (1995; Maverick).
Basically rocky and straightforward in its lyrics, but with moments of greater subtlety to stop all the songs rolling into one. The breakthrough single, "You Oughta Know", is the most immediate stand-out track, though "Wake Up" is something of a grower and "Head Over Heels" marks a different lyrical direction. Not brilliant, but definitely interesting.

Maria Lamle

MORPHINE

Formed Boston, Massachusetts, 1992;
disbanded 1999.

Though **Morphine** were formed in 1992 in Boston, they had little in common with the country-tinged grunge of other local bands of that

Morphine's Mark Sandman

time, like Buffalo Tom and The Posies. Their unusual sound, best described as a cross between Tom Waits and modern blues, was produced by a highly original instrumental line-up. Formed out of the ashes of a punk-blues outfit called Treat Her Right, Morphine featured three men who, at the time of the group's conception, had no idea of the acclaim that their music would invite, or the tragedy that would in 1999 cut short a promising career.

Billy Conway played jazz-influenced, very tight drums, but crucially left plenty of spaces for the other two to make their noise. **Dana Colley** played baritone sax, which gave the music its jazz/blues flavour, sometimes even playing two saxes at the same time on stage. But it was lead singer **Mark Sandman**'s contribution that made Morphine such a distinctive band. His laid-back vocal style could be wickedly sensual, lowering itself to a whisper on occasions and his guitar playing was something else. Sandman used a weird-looking Premier bass with just two strings, both usually tuned to the same note. As if that weren't strange enough, he used a metal slide on his fingers to create an awesome, heavy sound that doubled as bass and distorted lead guitar. He claimed to be the only bass player using this setup, and he probably was. For the band's 1997 album, he unveiled the 'tritar' – one part bass to two parts guitar, with mashed sounds squeezed from it by the ubiquitous slide.

To complete the equation, there were Sandman's playful lyrics, showcased on Morphine's five studio albums: GOOD (1992), CURE FOR PAIN (1993), YES (1995), LIKE SWIMMING (1997), and THE NIGHT (2000). "Sharks", from YES, was one of their best songs: an allegory of modern life, it had a blues riff, a typical overlay of gorgeous tenor sax, and Sandman warning 'Sharks patrol these waters/don't let your fingers dangle in the water/Don't you worry about the dayglo orange life preserver/it won't save you, it won't save you'. In "Super Sex" his lyrics painted a picture of a druggy, seedy, alcohol-soaked backstreet America of motel rooms, whisky bottles and casual sex, sung in a Waits–like drawl with plenty of distortion.

But then it all came to a sudden end: in July 1999, shortly after the trio completed the stupendous, self-produced THE NIGHT, Mark Sandman died of a heart attack. Though Morphine were no more, THE NIGHT was released to critical acclaim, and then later that year an official live bootleg album, BOOTLEG DETROIT (2000), was released, a portion of the proceeds from which were donated to the newly founded Mark Sandman Music Education Fund. A BEST OF… collection followed in 2003, while the remaining band members reconvened as **Twinemen** with a self-titled CD the same year.

Morphine were a mightily powerful band and Sandman an incredible talent. Thankfully the albums that Morphine did release go some way toward documenting the development of Sandman's musical vision.

⊙ **Yes** (1995; Rykodisc).
On mid-tempo and slower, bluesier numbers, all the components are in place: Colley's saxes wail away while Conway provides an understated trap that holds the whole thing down. There's even a surprise in store in the form of the last track – a lovely acoustic ballad about a lost love.

⊙ **B-Sides And Otherwise** (1997; Rykodisc).
Includes brilliant songs from the soundtracks of *Get Shorty* and *Things To Do In Denver When You're Dead*, emphasizing the widescreen nature of Morphine's music. A more varied, if obviously more patchy, collection than the studio albums proper, and therefore perhaps more fun.

⊙ **The Night** (2000; Rykodisc).
The Night is easily Morphine's most accomplished album: It was self-produced and recorded over two years in the band's own loft studio. Their hallmark bass and saxophone-led sound is lushly accompanied throughout by piano lines, string arrangements, and even Middle Eastern drones. A fine collection and a fitting tribute to Sandman's memory.

Mike Martin

VAN MORRISON

Born Belfast, Northern Ireland, August 1945.

"I think I'm a loner, an outsider, not because I want to be … I found I had to be if I didn't play along with the music-business bullshit."

A professional musician since the age of 15, **Van Morrison** made his name as an R&B singer in the beat boom of the early 1960s, and by the end of the decade had found his own voice as a singer, song-writer and performer. Producing work rooted in the bedrock of popular music – blues, country, gospel and jazz – he has followed a fairly consistent career pattern since. When he has written enough songs for an album he records them, delivers the product to his record company and, with varying degrees of grumpiness or enthusiasm, tours to promote the release. Sometimes, invariably without enthusiasm, he also grants press interviews, performing in a manner conveying awkwardness, boredom, ill-temper and a poor opinion of his interlocutor. He feels, not without reason, that what he has to say is delivered on record and on stage.

Morrison was born into a working-class Protestant community in East Belfast, in the shadow of the huge cranes of the area's main employer, the Harland and Wolff shipyard. His father George worked there as an electrician, and was an enthusiastic collector of the work of blues musicians such as Leadbelly. While at school, Morrison had already set his mind on a career in music, and he left as soon as he could, serving his apprenticeship in local skiffle groups such as Deanie Sands And The Javelins. Gaining a reputation as a wild stage performer, Morrison played guitar and harmonica, and was soon to learn the saxophone.

A fluency on these instruments, together with his strong voice, led him towards a professional career on the showband scene, which, with its emphasis on slick cover versions of current hits and country standards, was fast becoming the dominant form of musical entertainment in Northern Ireland. Along with schoolfriend **George Jones**, a former Javelin and still a showband leader today, the 15-year-old Morrison formed **The Monarchs**, a showband that tried its luck first in Scotland, then London, and finally Germany, playing six-sets-a-night clubs in the red-light districts of Hamburg and other cities.

By November 1963 The Monarchs were back in Belfast, where they promptly split up. Two of them, Morrison and **Billy McAllen**, then formed **The Manhattans**, and started the shift towards R&B. Gigs at Irish clubs in England proved to Morrison that the music he loved was growing in popularity. Returning once more to Belfast, Morrison played briefly in **The Golden Eagles** before seeing an announcement in the local paper launching an R&B club at the Maritime Hotel. He chanced upon a band called The Gamblers, who became **THEM**, with Morrison joining in as vocalist and harmonica player. Their first gig was in April 1964, and their Friday-night residency at the Maritime has entered rock'n'roll legend.

Morrison left Them in the summer of 1966 to begin writing songs and sort out a solo deal. A call from the band's former producer, Bert Berns, who now had his own label, Bang, took him to New York for sessions that produced two albums, neither of which had the artist's approval – BLOWIN' YOUR MIND (1967) and THE BEST OF VAN MORRISON (1968) – although the first resulted in a 1967 hit, "Brown Eyed Girl", and an underground classic in

"TB Sheets". However, Berns died suddenly at the end of the year, and Morrison fulfilled his contractual obligations with track after track of inane and insulting gibberish (an intriguing set, in retrospect, released in 1994 as the Charly album, PAYIN' DUES).

A new deal with Warner Brothers resulted in the breakthrough album, ASTRAL WEEKS (1968). Though a modest seller at the time, this stunning collection of songs, backed by a jazzy flow of guitar, strings and acoustic bass, is now established as one of the most remarkable albums of the era, and songs like "Madame George" (previously recorded in a prototype version for Bang) and the autobiographical "Cypress Avenue" established him as a heavyweight artist.

The next set, the punchier, horn-led MOONDANCE (1970), was more of a commercial success, while the next two albums – HIS BAND AND STREET CHOIR (1970) and TUPELO HONEY (1971) – consolidated the jazz-folk orientation of ASTRAL WEEKS with strands of jump-jazz, country and Celtic music. Morrison also had a string of hit singles, scoring with "Come Running", "Domino", "Blue Money", "Call Me Up In Dreamland", "Wild Night" and "Tupelo Honey". ST DOMINIC'S PREVIEW, released in 1972, continued this run of success; it demonstrated the sheer versatility of Van Morrison, with songs ranging from the joyous white soul of "Jackie Wilson Said (I'm In Heaven When You Smile)" to the dark musings of "Listen To The Lion" and "Independence Day".

1973's HARD NOSE THE HIGHWAY, and the 1974 double live set, IT'S TOO LATE TO STOP NOW, marked the climax of the winning streak, the latter superbly capturing Morrison and arguably the finest of all his bands, the Caledonia Soul Orchestra, in a dynamic résumé of his career so far – blues by Sonny Boy Williamson and Willie Dixon, call-and-response gospel by Ray Charles, and his own songs from "Gloria" to the epic "Listen To The Lion". It remains one of the great live albums.

A holiday exploring the Irish countryside inspired his next album, 1974's low-key VEEDON FLEECE, which stressed the Celtic pulse of his music. This was followed by a barren period before a somewhat hesitant return with A PERIOD OF TRANSITION, released in 1977. The soulful WAVELENGTH (1978), and mystically inclined INTO THE MUSIC (1979), saw out the 1970s in more confident form. Among the highlights of the former were the punchy "Kingdom Hall", probably inspired by memories of his mother's brief flirtation with the Jehovah's Witnesses, while the latter boasted some of Morrison's best songs for quite a while – notably the jaunty, commercial "Bright Side Of The Road" and the more overtly Christian "Full Force Gale". On this record, especially, the principal elements of Morrison's music – spiritual yearning, a feeling for landscape and his Celtic heritage, a love of blues, jazz and gospel – jelled perfectly.

Whereas INTO THE MUSIC was largely enhanced by Morrison's interest in Christianity, the next record, COMMON ONE (1980), was by comparison half-baked – a concoction of meditative tunes wrapped around lyrics of New Age mysticism and poetic name-dropping. BEAUTIFUL VISION (1982) continued in the same vein, being coloured by his burgeoning interest in Scientology, whose founder, L. Ron Hubbard, got a 'special thanks' credit on the next album, the almost universally panned INARTICULATE SPEECH OF THE HEART (1983).

Morrison's journey continued waywardly on A SENSE OF WONDER (1984), but in 1986 he released the defiantly titled NO GURU, NO METHOD, NO TEACHER, which served as an answer to those who felt that he had fallen under the spell of psychobabble. Morrison's creative impulses seemed to have been reawakened: NO GURU was his best piece of work so far in the 80s, and was followed up strongly by the deft jazz and Celtic doodlings of POETIC CHAMPIONS COMPOSE (1987).

Morrison's more recent work has been nostalgic, above all emphasizing his native traditions – notably in collaborations with **The Chieftains**, preserved on 1988's IRISH HEARTBEAT, and also on studio albums such as AVALON SUNSET (1989). The latter was a successful record which pulled many styles together, perhaps most famously in a duet with **Cliff Richard** (of all people) on "Whenever God Shines His Light", which gave Morrison his first UK hit since the days of Them.

The following year's ENLIGHTENMENT didn't really hold anything new, although Morrison's collaboration with organist **Georgie Fame** rekindled his appetite for live performance – something powerfully confirmed on 1994's A NIGHT IN SAN FRANCISCO. The next studio set, HYMNS TO THE SILENCE (1991), was another wonderful outing, revisiting the spirituality of POETIC CHAMPIONS, summoning up ghosts from Van's Belfast childhood, as well as producing some of his best ever gospel fare. It showed again, too, what a great guitarist and harmonica player Van could be.

TOO LONG IN EXILE (1993) was barely more than a handful of covers stitched together with a revival of "Gloria", but Days Like This (1995), while a welcome, upbeat release, lacked real stand-outs. On the live How Long Has This Been Going On (1996), recorded with Fame at Ronnie Scott's in London, Van's voice was on impeccable form, and he proved his versatility again, swinging through a lightweight but enjoyable set of jazz (and Morrison) standards.

His 1997 release, The Healing Game, a beautiful, soft-pedal invocation of his distant Belfast childhood, was another effortless classic by the master of the genre, with high-class support from the likes of Georgie Fame, **Pee Wee Ellis** and **Katie Kissoon**. A collection of rarities, The Philosopher's Stone (1998), helped fill the gaps in many collections, and spanned 1971–1986, his most exciting and productive years.

1999's Back On Top offered typical, excellent-quality Morrison fare. Opening with stand-out bluesy vamp "Goin' Down Geneva", the album was filled with elegant and eloquent songs with a theme of loneliness. He had surrounded himself with the usual gang of high-class musicians, who provided the kind of faultless backing he and his fans have come to expect.

In 2000 Morrison teamed up with **Lonnie Donegan** and **Chris Barber** for the triumphant The Skiffle Sessions, and later that year he paired up with Jerry Lee Lewis's sister, **Linda Gail**, for an album of trad rock'n'roll with a country twist – You Win Again. Though seamlessly performed, the collection was full of the kind of nostalgic visitations that Morrison would do better to confine to his undiminished live performances. 2002 witnessed the release of Down The Road, which seemed to follow naturally on from Back On Top; this time, Van's band featured long-time-comrades such as **David Hayes** and **Mick Green**. While his existing fans rejoice in his continuing productivity, Morrison seems hellbent on making his mark on the new millennium.

⊙ **Astral Weeks** (1968; Warners).
A free-flowing roll of songs, superb in every way. Morrison's voice has rarely sounded better, and is perfectly complemented by Richard David's reverberating upright bass and the soft shuffles of Connie Kaye's percussion.

⊙ **Moondance** (1970; Warners).
Morrison shifted to R&B for this second classic, introducing "Into The Mystic" and "Caravan", while going for a straighter jazz sound on the wonderful and enduring title track.

⊙ **It's Too Late To Stop Now** (1974; Warners).
The singer's first great live album, reinterpreting everything from Them cuts through much of Astral Weeks, Moondance, Tupelo Honey, Saint Dominic's Preview, and Hard Nose The Highway. This was the golden early period.

⊙ **Into The Music** (1979; Warners; reissued 1998; Polydor).
A neglected gem from the end of the 70s, which breezed through gospel and R&B on a great set highlighted by "Angelou" and "Bright Side Of The Road".

⊙ **Irish Heartbeat** (1988; Mercury).
Van combines with The Chieftains to stunning effect on traditional Irish songs. Resist singing along to this and you've a heart of steel.

⊙ **Hymns To The Silence** (1991; Polydor).
A double set characterized by nostalgia (Van reliving his Belfast youth "On Hyndford Street") and gospel (including an all-time great rendering of "Just A Closer Walk With Thee", with Georgie Fame on revivalist organ).

⊙ **A Night In San Francisco** (1994; Polydor).
A double-CD offering, with Van joined by Georgie Fame, daughter Shana duetting on "Beautiful Vision", John Lee Hooker (on "Gloria"), and a very fine band. The Man rolls through his hits, and toys with fragments of the blues that formed his musical education.

⊙ **The Best Of Van Morrison** (1990; Polydor).
Every home should have more than one Van album, but this 'best of' should fill in gaps if you're not going for the full monty. The selections run from Them's "Gloria" through to 1989's gospel hit with Cliff Richard, "Whenever God Shines His Light".

⊙ **The New York Sessions 1967** (1998; Recall).
A two-CD collection of the recordings that resulted in Blowin' Your Mind (1967) and The Best Of Van Morrison (1968), with the two albums in their entirety padded out with the seventeen tracks that Morrison was contractually obliged to supply. The extra tracks are amusing once or twice, but are really of interest only to the completist.

⊙ **The Skiffle Sessions** (2000; Exile/Virgin).
With the addition of long-time collaborator Chris Barber, and Lonnie Donegan, the completed trio energetically rattle through fifteen cuts of foot-tapping skiffle. Donegan takes the lead on tracks like "It Takes A Worried Man" and the laid-back "Outskirts Of Town", while Morrison, in fine voice, steps up to the microphone on "I Wanna Go Home" and "Good Morning Blues".

John Collis

MORRISSEY

Born Manchester, England, 1959.

"I'd like all that vilification to end now and just the love to come through, and feel, for 24 hours a day, unbridled support from you all."

Probably the greatest surprise surrounding the break-up of **THE SMITHS** in 1987 was the speed with which Steven Patrick **Morrissey** returned to the studio. Viva Hate (1988), his remarkable solo debut, entered the UK chart at #1 and fulfilled most expectations of his devoted fans, who had wondered whether, without Johnny Marr, Mozza could pull it off. Assuredly he could: co-writing with his producer **Stephen Street**, and coupling his ambiguous, acid lyrics with the expert musicianship of Durutti Column guitarist **Vini Reilly**.

That first Morrissey album was previewed by "Suedehead", a dramatic song that swept into the UK singles charts (peaking at #5) on a wave of critical acclaim. However, the song that had fans and critics pricking up their ears was "Bengali In Platforms", a condescending warning to immigrants that 'life is hard enough when you belong here'. A plea of conscious irony was offered by many in Morrissey's defence, but it was a bizarre affair, and one that led to a perhaps more rigorous and less trusting regard for the songwriter than in Smiths days.

Following VIVA HATE (reissued 1998; Parlophone) Morrissey offered his followers a trio of singles: the camp, upbeat "Last Of The International Playboys", the ecstasy-inspired "Interesting Drug", and "Ouija Board, Ouija Board", the last being something of a critical low. He then dumped what seems to have been half a completed second album before releasing a stopgap compilation, BONA DRAG (1990). This was superb in most respects, with guest appearances from **Kirsty MacColl** and **Suggs**, and something of a new direction in Morrissey's lyrics with the advent of character-led compositions like "Piccadilly Palare" and the wonderfully titled "Hairdresser On Fire".

Morrissey's next product, KILL UNCLE (1991), was an altogether different affair, heavily influenced by glam-rock and with songs co-written by Mark Nevin. "Asian Rut" apparently sought to apologize for the offence caused by "Bengali In Platforms" but much of this tepid 33-minute offering sounded pasty and rushed, and left Mozza in the odd position of embarking on his first solo world tour to promote a weak album. He found support in fans still fanatically tuned to The Smiths, especially in the US, where he still has a massive following, but it was a warning sign.

All the more relief for everyone, then, when the Mick Ronson-produced YOUR ARSENAL (1992) emerged, and did good business in both UK (#4) and US (#21) charts. The critics were bowled over too, applauding Morrissey's new pairing with rockabilly guitarist and co-writer Alan Whyte. With subject matter ranging from working-class fascism ("The National Front Disco" at last nailing the racism issue), to the plight of the obese ("You're The One For Me Fatty"), the songs showed their creator no more the petulant pseudo-adolescent, but a consummate narrative-writer, producing such aching fare as "I Know It's Gonna Happen Someday" (later to be covered by Morrissey's hero Bowie) and "Seaside, Yet Still Docked", which would appeal to anyone who voted "Heaven Knows I'm Miserable Now" among their list of all-time great songs.

All wasn't quite the love-in Morrissey might have liked, however, with ignominy striking when the singer was booed and pelted supporting Madness, unwisely cloaked in a Union Jack, in London's Finsbury Park. On his home ground, though, Mozza remained supreme, as documented by BEETHOVEN WAS DEAF (1993), an exemplary live album, focusing mainly on songs from YOUR ARSENAL, recorded in Paris and London.

Over the following year Morrissey lost three close friends – Ronson among them – but regained one as he and **Johnny Marr** reacquainted themselves, and for a while looked set to collaborate again. Perhaps as a result, that year's album, VAUXHALL AND I (1994), was his most personal and understated work, and quite possibly his best. The record was rooted in Morrissey's nostalgic fascination with London's underclass – Vauxhall is a downbeat area of South London, best known for a gay drag club – and continued his development as a writer of character-led songs. Impeccable

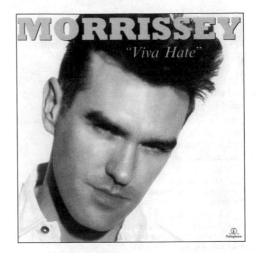

production by Steve Lillywhite provided a lush backdrop for emotionally open songs like "Hold On To Your Friends" (this from the notably 'difficult' Morrissey), and "I Am Hated For Loving", which showed the springs of self-pity were still productive. "Spring Heeled Jim" and "Billy Budd", meanwhile, wriggled with almost teenage vivacity, not to mention camp frivolity (although our hero requested 'not to be seen as a Kenneth Williams figure').

If THE WORLD OF MORRISSEY (1995) compilation – four tracks from VAUXHALL, three from BEETHOVEN, plus a recent trio of singles – was a perplexing filler, Morrissey's next release furrowed even more brows. SOUTHPAW GRAMMAR (1995 – for his new label RCA), revealed a predilection for the boxing world with songs like "Dagenham Dave" and "Reader Meets Author", which unfortunately said little new and, worse, were mired in hopelessly self-indulgent musicianship. Again, Morrissey set out on tour with a poor record to promote, supporting Bowie on an unsympathetic circuit of stadium tours, ending it hospitalized with an undisclosed illness.

MALADJUSTED (1997) didn't do a great deal to boost Mozza's flagging reputation. On this album, Morrissey delighted his legion of fans by doing exactly what he always did – scratching his neuroses for our entertainment, till they bleed. Still stinging in the wallet area after the Smiths royalties case, and no doubt a tad upset at being called 'truculent and devious' by the judge, Mozza had a full portion of chips on his shoulder and served them up with his trademark air of dissatisfaction and regret. Apart from another of those disturbing 'cheery' songs he occasionally dredges up from the bile in his soul ("Roy's Keen", the tale of a window-cleaner, was less funny than George Formby's ukulele masterpiece on the same subject), the album was standard Manchester drizzle – marvellous if you like it, dreary if you don't. Equally dismissible were 1998's MY EARLY BURGLARY YEARS, a hand-picked collection of B-sides and live cuts, and UNDER THE INFLUENCE (2003), an odd compilation that saw Morrissey turn

DJ (does anybody have a noose handy?) to shoehorn some of his favourite tracks by the likes of New York Dolls and The Ramones onto a CD. Neither set made up for the lack of fresh Moz material.

Today, Morrissey is living the life of a millionaire recluse in the Hollywood Hills, without a record deal, and without any forthcoming plans to present fresh offerings anytime soon. He'll pull it round, of course. After all, Morrissey is one of the finest songwriters and singers Britain has produced – a fact acknowledged by his receipt of an Ivor Novello Award in 1998 for *Outstanding Contribution to British Music*.

⊙ **Viva Hate** (1988; EMI).
Morrissey and Street confounded the vultures with this superb debut, epitomized by the vitality of "Suedehead" and the fantastic misery of "Late Night, Maudlin Street".

⊙ **Vauxhall And I** (1994; EMI).
Arguably the finest work of his career. Emotionally broad, musically polished and vocally effortless, with an appeal far beyond bedsit-land.

Michael Booth

MOTHER LOVE BONE

Formed Seattle, 1988; disbanded 1990.

"If he could have been anybody, he'd have loved to have been Freddie Mercury." Stone Gossard on Andy Wood

Following the demise of rockers **GREEN RIVER**, **Stone Gossard** (guitar), **Bruce Fairweather** (guitar) and **Jeff Ament** (bass) set about creating a new outfit. Along the way they recruited **Greg Gilmour** (drums), but their final addition, **Andy Wood** (vocals), was their ace and joker rolled into one. Former frontman of contemporaries, **Malfunkshun** who specialized in glam-punk and outrageous outfits, Wood was a born star and his contribution twisted **Mother Love Bone** into something unquestionably unique.

Wood was far from a perfect singer, but his presence on record cannot be underestimated. His lyrics were bizarre and overblown, displaying a unique vision that shaped the band's sound. The first studio outing issued on Mercury, the SHINE EP (1989), had Wood's personality firmly stamped on it. These six outstanding cuts excited a huge amount of interest, and were quickly followed by their first full-length album, APPLE (1990). With titles like "Stardog Champion" and "Holy Roller", Wood conjured up a mythical image for the whole band, while the rest of the group matched the lyrical hyperbole with a hard-rock sound straight out of the 1970s. The guitar histrionics were totally convincing on tracks like "Come Bite The Apple."

The future looked promising but tragically Wood died from a heroin overdose just as APPLE was due for release in March 1990. After such a crippling blow, the group elected to disband; they had, in any case, been dropped by their record company. In

recognition of the group's importance, the beautifully swirling "Chloe Dancer"/"Crown Of Thorns" found its way onto the soundtrack of Seattle-set romantic comedy, *Singles*.

Following Wood's untimely death, his friend **Chris Cornell**, of **SOUNDGARDEN**, began work on the **Temple Of The Dog** tribute project using various members of Mother Love Bone and Soundgarden, and the then-unheard-of **Eddie Vedder**. This was the beginning of **PEARL JAM**.

⊙ **Mother Love Bone** (1992; Mercury).
A posthumous release following the huge success of Pearl Jam, this is a double-CD compilation of the band's previously released material, along with the unsanctioned inclusion of the unreleased "Lady Godiva Blues". Hard to beat.

Essi Berelian

MOTÖRHEAD

Formed London, 1975.

"If we moved in next door your lawn would die." Lemmy

One of the most single-minded and intense rock bands to strike fear and loathing into the hearts of clean-living folks the world over, **Motörhead** were the creation of bass-playing, gravel-throated **Ian 'Lemmy' Kilmister**, the son of a vicar. A self-confessed speed freak, Lemmy spent much of his youth kicking around in various bands (The Rockin' Vickers, The Motown Sect) and roadie-ing for the likes of Jimi Hendrix and Pink Floyd. Following a four-year stint with psychedelic rockers **HAWKWIND**, the next logical step was the creation of his own band. Taking the name from a Hawkwind song he had penned himself, Lemmy bolted Motörhead together in 1975 with **Larry Wallis** (guitar) and **Lucas Fox** (drums).

Brazenly displaying their love of blues and boogie, the initial line-up produced only one album, ON PAROLE (1979), recorded in 1976 but held back by a hesitant record label. Fox and Wallis were then replaced by **'Fast' Eddie Clarke** (guitar) and **Phil 'Philthy Animal' Taylor** (drums) to create the definitive 'Head line-up. The result was a string of classic albums and notorious live performances. OVERKILL and BOMBER (both 1979) represented muscular, deadly rock'n'roll, screaming disrespect for authority figures and the status quo ("Lawman", "All The Aces", "Talking Head"). It's hard not to believe Lemmy when he claims to have invented thrash metal as the likes of "Overkill" and "Bomber" hurtle past at a whiplash lick. In the nihilistic punk landscape of the late 70s, the band found themselves in the unique position of being accepted by both long-haired rockers and punks who could not tell what they were listening to if they kept their eyes shut.

ACE OF SPADES (1980) showed Lemmy and the boys at the peak of their powers. Its title track (a hit single) was a cut guaranteed to make your teeth rattle and your nose bleed, and the rest of the set celebrated the staples of the rock'n'roll life: women ("Jailbait"), the road ("We Are The Road Crew") and general antisocial mayhem ("The Hammer"). To complete the cartoon outlaw image, the cover showed the band clad in bandit-black leathers. The follow-up, NO SLEEP 'TIL HAMMERSMITH (1981), recorded on the 'Ace of Spades' tour, careered into the UK charts at #1 and captured their sound more fully than a dozen studio albums would have done. Fan favourites like the grinding "Capricorn", "No Class" – with a boogie riff stolen from ZZ Top's "Tush" – and the Hell's Angels anthem, "Iron Horse"/"Born to Lose" were spat out at relentless, paint-stripping volume. The whole band played as tightly as a clenched fist, while Lemmy threw his head back and sang as though he had had razor blades and meths for breakfast.

Motörhead looked unstoppable and an unholy liaison with **Girlschool** produced the appallingly mixed, but hugely successful ST VALENTINE'S DAY MASSACRE EP. The roll did not last and IRON FIST (1982) did not match the metallic brilliance of their previous efforts, due mainly to the flat production, provided in part by Fast Eddie. He soon departed to form **Fastway**, and **Brian 'Robbo' Robertson**

(ex-**THIN LIZZY** and Wild Horses) was drafted in to take over guitar duties. ANOTHER PERFECT DAY (1983) was glossier, and Robertson's playing brought a hint of subtlety, space and melody to the usual terminal head-spin of rioting guitars. Unfortunately, Robertson was never truly accepted by the fans, as his approach failed to capture the warts-and-all glory of old Motörhead. Coupled with personality clashes in the band, his stay would be a short one.

Lemmy re-formed the band with two new guitarists, **Michael 'Wurzel' Burston** and **Phil Campbell**, and Philthy moved on to be replaced by **Pete Gill** (ex-**SAXON**). A new era dawned: the double compilation album NO REMORSE (1984) contained twenty classics and four new cuts, including the unstoppable, rolling thunder of "Locomotive" and the gonzoid "Killed By Death". In true Motörhead style, limited quantities were released in a tasteful, gold-embossed, black leather sleeve. Pete Gill remained for the release of ORGASMATRON (1986) and the band's Donington Monsters of Rock appearance, but Philthy returned to the fold for ROCK AND ROLL (1987) and the long-promised second live volume, NO SLEEP AT ALL (1988) – the latter proudly displaying the legend 'Everything Louder Than Everything Else'. The new

The boys: Lemmy (left) and Fast Eddie (right) sort out their musical differences with Philthy Animal

songs were not bad – but they were not brilliant either. The band seemed to be treading water.

A new management team and a move to Los Angeles produced 1916 (1991). With the bastard breakneck boogie of "Going To Brazil" and the bloodshot rattle of "Make My Day", the band were back on form again. In an unprecedented show of sensitivity, the title track featured a cello backing Lemmy's cracked voice as he told the tragic story of a young soldier's life cut short.

After Philthy's second departure in 1992, **Mick Brown** (better known as **Mickey Dee**) took over on drums. MARCH OR DIE (1992), BASTARDS (1993), SACRIFICE (1995), OVERNIGHT SENSATION (1996), SNAKE BITE LOVE (1998), WE ARE MOTÖRHEAD (2000) and HAMMERED (2002) all featured outstanding moments, but mostly it was business as usual. Live, however, Motörhead remained unique: not many rock bands of recent years can come close to the adrenaline rush and red-eyed savagery of full-force Motörhead; witness the reissued double-CD version of No SLEEP 'TIL HAMMERSMITH (2001), which featured seventeen rollicking unreleased classics in addition to the original running order.

(•) **Ace Of Spades** (1980; Castle Communications). No-holds-barred, no-frills rock'n'roll; the best of their early period. The re-released version includes a number of hard-to-find bonus tracks, making it even more indispensable.

(•) **No Sleep 'Til Hammersmith** (1981; Castle Communications).
Setting the standard for rock live albums, this contains proven crowd-pleasers throughout. Lemmy and the boys have rarely sounded this dirty and incisive on record. As with the other early album rereleases, this version contains a number of excellent bonus tracks. A lesson in how to make something great even better.

(•) **Orgasmatron** (1986; Castle Communications). An excellent comeback album after a fallow period. Lemmy sounds truly warty, while the title track has become a grinding live favourite.

(•) **1916** (1991; Epic). Another outstanding album, particularly for the diversity of material. The title track is surprisingly moving, and elsewhere ("Love Me Forever", "Nightmare/ Dreamtime") the band experiment with arrangements and production techniques to great effect.

(•) **Take No Prisoners** (1998; Recall). A 36-track marathon that concentrates on the glory days of Lemmy, Philthy and Fast Eddie from 1976 to 1982. All their best bits, including their joint hit with Girlschool, "Please Don't Touch".

(•) **Snake Bite Love** (1998; SPV). Possibly the strongest studio album Lemmy and the boys have come up with since 1916. Tracks such as "Love For Sale" just go to prove that the Lemster still has a fine ear for commercial melody, whilst the title track is a pleasantly nasty effort.

Essi Berelian

THE MOTORS

Formed London, 1977; disbanded 1980.

The term 'one-hit wonder' could have been coined for **The Motors**, a band remembered – if at all – for "Airport", four glorious minutes of pop perfection.

The band came together in 1977 when **Nick Garvey** (guitar/vocals) and **Ricky Wernham** (drums), previously of The Snakes, hooked up with Peter Bramall, aka **Bram Tchaikovsky** (guitar/vocals) and **Andy McMasters** (bass) – a former sidekick in another Garvey band, Ducks Deluxe, along with Dave Edmunds. Signed up to Virgin after a performance at The Marquee in March, they released a debut single, "Dancing The Night Away", which flirted very briefly with the UK Top 50, as did the album from which it was taken, MOTORS 1 (1977). Main songwriters Garvey and McMasters pursued a resolutely English style of pub rock with a hint of guitar metal, much in the same vein as the more established Dr. Feelgood and Eddie And The Hot Rods.

The next six months saw the band established as a fine live act, although singles releases "Be What You Wanna Be" and "Sensation" came and went, out of step with Britain's New Wave. Consequently the band underwent some sort of a conversion, ditching the more sweaty aspects of their sound and writing songs – or at least a song – which stuck firmly to New Wave principles: plenty of 'exciting' synth sounds, Metropolis-style mechanical backing vocals, and a chorus that could be whistled by the most tone-deaf milkman. The result was a Top 5 UK hit, "Airport", released in 1978.

Like the insubstantial "Sensation", it was included on APPROVED BY THE MOTORS (1978), an album that failed to emulate this deserved success, although a third single, "Forget About You", a rather bland affair with a smattering of Tamla in the chorus. did reach #13. "Today", a final attempt at squeezing the last drop of success from this set, proved a flop and The Motors' grip on the nation's affections was lost forever.

1978 saw the replacement of key personnel: Bram Tchaikovsky and Ricky Wernham left, and **Martin Ace** (bass) and **Terry Williams** (drums; ex-**MAN**, ex-Rockpile) came in. These changes did little to improve the band's fortunes, and it was March 1980 before the release of TENEMENT STEPS, the last Motors album. Although this was certainly no worse than APPROVED BY THE MOTORS, even producing a reasonable single in "Love And Loneliness", neither release saw the sunny side of the Top 50 and, after the failure of two further 45s, "That's What John Said" and "Metropolis", the band split up.

Nick Garvey went solo, releasing one album, BLUE SKIES (1982); and Terry Williams joined **DIRE STRAITS**. Virgin issued a 'best of' album in 1981, self-mockingly titled (by the record company if not by the band) MOTORS' GREATEST HIT; Caroline's 1995 package, however, is currently the easiest 'hit' collection to track down.

(•) **Airport – Greatest Hits** (1995; Caroline). "Airport" is naturally the stand-out cut. The rest doesn't quite match up, but there's no disgrace in tracks such as "Tenement Steps" or "Dancing The Night Away".

Lance Philips

MOTT THE HOOPLE

Formed Herefordshire, England, 1969; disbanded 1974.

In the early 70s **Mott The Hoople** were one of the few bands to successfully straddle the widening gulf between the English rock underground (prog-rock) and the new pop-star mentality encapsulated by *Top Of The Pops* (glam-rock).

Though they seemed to burst into the charts in 1972 as overnight sensations with the David Bowie-penned hit "All The Young Dudes", they had been discovered and developed by madcap visionary Guy Stevens. Working as Island Records' A&R man in 1969, Stevens was impressed by the demo tapes of a band named The Doc Thomas Band and made them a far-reaching offer. If they would agree to replace lead singer Stan Tippens and change their name to one of his choosing, he would not only sign them but become personally responsible for their inevitable rise to the top. Tippens agreed to be sidelined (though receiving credits in one way or another on most album sleeves) and Stevens instructed them that their new name was to be that of a book by Willard Manus, *Mott The Hoople*.

The musicians, **Dale 'Buffin' Griffin** (drums), **Pete 'Overend' Watts** (bass), **Verden 'Phally' Allen** (organ) – who was to leave after the recording of "All The Young Dudes" – and **Mick Ralphs** (guitar/vocals) all knew each other from various local bands, such as The Inmates, The Buddies, The Anchors and The Silence. An ex-bass player for Screaming Lord Sutch won the audition for lead vocalist. With his long curly locks and permanent dark glasses, **Ian Hunter** gave the band the rock-'n'roll image they were lacking and Stevens was seeking.

Their first three albums, produced by Stevens and the band, were muddled concoctions of Dylanesque sagas from Hunter and pondering rock-outs from Ralphs. Only the occasional song, "Rock & Roll Queen" or "Walking With A Mountain", suggested the force that, through continual touring, was gaining them a fervent following. Island threatened to pull the plug on Guy Stevens' project after the fourth and final album of the deal, which emerged as BRAIN CAPERS (1971). Both sides started with storming new rockers, "Death May Be Your Santa Claus" and "Sweet Angeline", but then descended into the murky sludge that blighted their previous releases.

Early in 1972, having been duly kicked off Island and crippled with debt, the band were on the verge of splitting when, backstage at Guildford, they had a most auspicious visit. Overend Watts had written to David Bowie explaining that Mott The Hoople were splitting and enquired if he needed a bass player. In response, Bowie, very much in the ascendant and already having persuaded CBS to take on one of his starving idols, Iggy Pop, offered his 'favourite band' a song he'd written, the opportunity to record it, and

his services as producer. Despite misgivings, Mott The Hoople recorded first the song, then soon afterwards an album produced by Bowie, and paid for by his management. Presented with the tapes, CBS paid a £25,000 advance and released the song, "All The Young Dudes", that summer. (The first song Bowie offered was "Suffragette City", and they turned it down.) "All The Young Dudes" gave Mott The Hoople, and especially Ian Hunter, what they'd been grasping for – an anthem that displayed what one music paper recognized as 'the solidarity of the disaffected'. It also didn't sound anything like Mott The Hoople: Bowie was using Hunter's more aggressive stance to deliver a clarion call for a 'glam-rock army' to kick out the old and begin the new. Mott were in no position to complain. Thanks to Bowie's intervention they were catapulted from backroom boogie oblivion to the lights and glamour of *Top Of The Pops*.

The album, also titled ALL THE YOUNG DUDES (1972), revealed Bowie's understanding of Mott The Hoople's qualities – stripping away prog-rock jamming to reveal hook lines and choruses without losing a lively, spontaneous feel. The single climbed to #3 in the charts, the album became their biggest success so far and briefly entered the Top 20. However, seeds of discontent were discernible in the songs written by Ralphs and Allen – their virtuosic yet pointless soloing driving obstinately along the prog-rock cul-de-sac.

After a couple of spin-off singles from the album came "Honaloochie Boogie" (1973), a jaunty, full-on rock affair complete with distorted vocals and addictive saxophone, courtesy of Andy Mackay from 'rivals' ROXY MUSIC. It was a Top 20 success and relieved the pressure, and the release of MOTT (1973) saw them stake a place as prominent members of the credible glam-rock club. After Bowie refused them the song "Drive In Saturday", they countered with "All The Way From Memphis", a roaring song about their own American experiences, lost guitars and rock'n'roll, which both started the album and became their third UK Top 20 hit.

Mott had three hit singles in 1973 and, though the tunes were classics, their *Top Of The Pops* appearances increasingly alienated them from the 'serious' rock fan. The career-saving adoption of a tongue-in-cheek glamouflage was becoming a glittering straitjacket. Mick Ralphs looked increasingly out of sorts and out of place, and it all proved too much for him during the recording of "Roll Away The Stone", a single intended to be the consolidation of Mott's position as supreme pop and rock stars. In amongst a mish-mash of Spectorish, echoing walls of sound, sharp guitars and sha-la-la choruses, Ian Hunter's vocal varied between theatrical camp and leering laddishness. New members **Ariel Bender** (guitar) and **MORGAN FISHER** (piano) were chosen, if publicity is to be believed, more for their eccentricity than for their musical accomplishments. As "Stone" carried on up the charts and the new-look Mott The Hoople cavorted on *Top Of The Pops*, their future success seemed assured. Yet within a year they were to split apart in acrimony.

Recorded in January 1974 and preceded by the Spectorish-sounding "Golden Age Of Rock & Roll", their third CBS release, THE HOOPLE, became the focus for a backlash against their overly glam mannerisms and demeanour, a reception that sent the group, and CBS, into a panic that was to prove terminal. This was a pity because some of the songs were brave attempts to develop the genre – and the cod-theatrical "Marionette" was as good as anything previously released. The panic wasn't helped, however, when that same month Ralphs' new band, **BAD COMPANY**, leapt into the charts and swept America with their debut single, which used an old Mott song structure, and an album that sounded like the Mott album Mick Ralphs always wanted to make.

After a LIVE (1973) album, Bender was replaced by **MICK RONSON**, from Bowie's Spiders, and Hunter knocked out "Saturday Gigs", another anthemic confessional, attempting to combine the best bits of "Roll Away The Stone" (sha-la-la choruses) and "All The Young Dudes" (documentary lyrics). It was the last Hoople release with Hunter, who left to form a new band with Ronson, and was, in fact, intended as their farewell single – as the repeated 'Goodbye' refrain at the end testifies. The remaining members auditioned and found a new vocalist, **Nigel Benjamin**, and guitarist, **Ray Majors**, and, under the shortened name **Mott**, managed two albums, DRIVE ON (1975) and SHOUTING AND POINTING (1976). These signalled an ironic return to roots – from the Herefordshire pub-rock beginnings they had come full circle and were once more a very average rock band.

⊙ **The Ballad Of Mott: A Retrospective** (1995; Columbia Legacy).
This is the essential purchase for a history of Mott The Hoople's popular years: everything you ever wanted to know, including a twenty-page booklet and previously unreleased tracks and B-sides.

⊙ **Mott The Hoople, The Island Years 1969–1972** (1998; Spectrum).
Likewise, a wonderfully crafted anthology of the less travelled path.

Tony Drayton

MOUNTAIN

Formed New York, 1969; disbanded 1973; re-formed 1974; disbanded 1975; re-formed 1981; disbanded 1988.

Although **Mountain** will probably be remembered only for the anthemic "Mississippi Queen" and the seemingly endless "Nantucket Sleighride", **Felix Papparlardi** (bass/keyboards) and **Leslie West** (guitar/vocals) were the musical fuel of a band that, along with Blue Cheer and Black Sabbath, pioneered the bottom-heavy sludge that would become heavy metal.

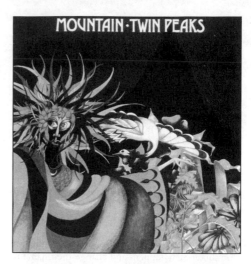

Papparlardi was already nearing 30 and settling down to life as a respected producer when he was given the assignment of pushing the knobs on the first serious recordings by The Vagrants in 1968. The Vagrants offered nothing to Papparlardi's muso ears, but he saw potential in the fat kid playing guitar. West's inevitable parting from his second-division partners was followed by a solo album, LESLIE WEST – MOUNTAIN (1969), on which Papparlardi fashioned the same meaty soundscape he had offered Cream on albums like DISRAELI GEARS and GOODBYE. West was greeted as a serious new talent and from nowhere Mountain became a major force.

West's solo album had provided the blueprint, and the first Mountain line-up, including **Steve Knight** (keyboards) and **Norman Smart** (drums), set about gigging. Their fourth show saw them pounding the ears of half a million stoned hippies at Woodstock. Critics might accuse them of being 'more Cream than Cream', but audiences tended to ignore such comments and by 1972 Mountain had chalked up four chart-placing albums – MOUNTAIN CLIMBING (1970), NANTUCKET SLEIGHRIDE (1971), FLOWERS OF EVIL (1971), and LIVE: THE ROAD GOES ON FOREVER (1972) – and an American Top 40 single in "Mississippi Queen" (1970).

The Mountain sound combined gargantuan rock riffs with a thick and punchy wash from bass and keyboards. **Corky Laing** (drums), who joined in late 1969, added a solid beat with the ability to cut loose and keep things interesting, crossing the tub-thumping of John Bonham with the lunatic fills of Keith Moon. Mountain's strengths lay in a level of skill that would allow extended work-outs based on the simplest rock structures and a readiness to turn up the volume to suicidal levels. The relentless crunching blues assault made the most sense in front of a sun-dried festival throng or a packed rock club full of people who had no commitments for the next three days.

However, by the mid-70s rock had moved on. Mountain were unwilling or unable to cut the excesses, and a new generation of fans opted for the less demanding crunch of bands like Black Sabbath. Papparlardi quit road work after THE ROAD GOES ON FOREVER, his return to full-time production work putting Mountain out of action. West and Laing made an opportunistic and, perhaps, too honest, move in teaming up with former **CREAM** bassist **Jack Bruce**. West, Bruce and Laing turned out three albums –including the rather good LIVE AND KICKIN' (1974) but couldn't really live in the shadows of their collective past. A Mountain reunion seemed to make the best business sense and Papparlardi duly returned to a new line-up. The vinyl output was maintained with 1974's TWIN PEAKS and AVALANCHE both coming out on CBS.

When AVALANCHE and the subsequent live commitments had run their course, West embarked on a solo career with Laing usually somewhere close by, and that was more or less the end for Mountain. Felix Papparlardi earned himself a couple of footnotes in the book of rock excess: he was declared 'legally deaf' as a result of Mountain's fearsome sound system; and in 1983 he was shot dead by his wife.

Mountain made their last high-profile appearance in 1985 when West and Laing recruited bassist **Mark Clarke**, ex-Uriah Heep and Rainbow, to record GO FOR YOUR LIFE (1985). It is a mark of how far the band's stock had fallen that it wasn't until 1995 that the definitive CD retrospective hit the shops. OVER THE TOP (1995) saw West and Laing putting down two bonus tracks with the bass skills of **Noel Redding**. The 90s spandex, heavy metal generation didn't recognize Mountain's nuclear-amped blues as heavy metal and it was difficult to see their influence in any category of the market.

Mountain's music is stuck in a timewarp and remains as massive and changeless as its name indicates. West keeps this spirit alive with storming blues sets to a faithful audience. He has also been involved in guitar design, and in 1997 took Joe Walsh to court after the sometime Eagle pulled out of a string of joint dates. The damages in the case – tens of thousands of dollars – suggested West still made a good living.

⊙ **Over The Top** (1995; Columbia).
This serious retrospective (with some decent sleeve notes) tells you all you need to know about Mountain – two CDs, 34 tracks and enough crunching riffs to take you back to 1970, for good.

Neil Nixon

MOUSE ON MARS

Formed Germany, 1993.

"Some people should have the job of driving around giving us random sound-loops." Jan St. Werner

Taking their cue from Can and Neu! as much as from the obvious influence of Kraftwerk, **Jan St. Werner** and **Andi Thoma** (who share home towns of Cologne and Düsseldorf with those bands) drifted together from rock and rap production respectively, having met at a death-metal gig. Not content with the limitations of Germany's massive techno scene, the duo formed **Mouse On Mars** as an electronic group who also utilize the more traditional guitar, drums and bass, both live and in the studio, often processed beyond recognition.

Initially working in TV music production, the duo sent a tape to fellow genre-avoiders Seefeel, in England, whose label Too Pure liked it so much they released the debut single "Frosch" in 1994. Mixing the riff-based electronica of the title track, the digi-dub of the excellent "Schnee Bud," plus the atmospheric "7000", the single instantly established Mouse On Mars in the emerging cross-genre scene which included label-mates Seefeel, Laika and Pram, all using rock methods in conjunction with electronics to surprising effect.

The duo's first album, VULVALAND, appeared later in the year, the vinyl edition accompanied by a 12" EP of remixes. Trancey and eclectic, it sold well and received wide critical acclaim, though suffering from a slight lack of coherence. Compilation appearances and remixes of other artists followed, including one for experimental CD-abusers Oval, whose **Markus Popp** joined St. Werner as **Microstoria** for the INIT DING release (1995).

St. Werner and Thoma's own 1995 release, IAORA TAHITI, was a wondrous melange of easy-listening exotica, post-Motorik trance rhythms and deep dubby bass, with guest drums by **Wolfgang Flür** (ex-**KRAFTWERK**) and **Dodo Nkishi**, and a suitably 'exotic' introduction in Japanese by **Nobuko Sugai**. The release was accompanied by live shows, including a brief tour with Stereolab, where St. Werner and Thoma joined the group on stage for improvised encores. Their own performances were similarly spontaneous, using the sequenced skeletons of tracks as backdrops for live instruments, tape loops and radio noise fed through echo boxes. A single from the album, "Bib", also appeared, along with a vinyl-only remix of the Latin-influenced "Saturday Night World Cub Fieber".

1996 found Mouse On Mars scoring the soundtrack to US indie-rock film *Glam*, while the pair also found time to join Flür as **Yamo** on the album TIME PIE. Microstoria released their second album, _SND, and its follow-up, REPROVISERS (1997), included mixes by, among others, Ui, Oval and Stereolab. Further collaborations with the latter resulted in **Laetitia Sadier** and the late **Mary Hansen** providing vocals for Mouse On Mars' single "Cache Coeur Naif". Returning the favour, the duo produced several tracks on Stereolab's DOTS AND LOOPS album in mid-1997. Jan Werner has also released several solo outings of minimal glitch-electronica under the name **Lithops**.

The third Mouse On Mars full-length outing surfaced the same year in the form of the highly praised AUTODITACKER, while links with the UK post-exotica scene expanded to include a High Llamas remix of their "Twift" single. The vinyl-only LPs INSTRUMENTALS (1997) and Microstoria's live IMPROVISERS (2000) were also released on Sonig before the band decamped to Domino for NIUN NIGGUNG in 1999. Showing no sign of moderating their eccentricities, the album propelled Mouse On Mars to further popular success, with Nkishi now joining the band as a full-time member. MODEL 3, STEP 2 (Thrill Jockey 2001) likewise kept Microstoria on course for limited crossover success.

Recent tours have leaned more and more toward rock, while further consolidating their reputation for energetic live performances. IDIOLOGY (2001) found their menagerie of sounds sprawling into prog-rock, hinting that the finest of the resurgent wave of German electronic bands may possibly have started to falter.

Mouse On Mars

⊙ **Vulvaland** (1994; Too Pure).
Melodic electronic compositions including the pedal steel-accompanied chug of "Chagrin" and the clattery radio babble of "Die Seele Von Brian Wilson".

⊙ **Autoditacker** (1997; Too Pure).
The inventive eclecticism of track titles like "Tamagnocchi" and "Twift Shoeblade" is as curiously (and appropriately) bewildering as the music to which they refer.

⊙ **Instrumentals** (1997; Sonig).
A laid-back, slowly unwinding release which acts as a meeting point between Mouse On Mars' and Microstoria's approaches to sound shaping. Vinyl only.

⊙ **Idiology** (2001; Domino/Thrill Jockey).
Here things drift between acoustic piano tinkling, electro noise and a perverse resemblance to the prog-operatic excesses of Jon & Vangelis on the glitchy melodies of "Presence".

Microstoria

⊙ **Init Ding** (1995; Mille Plateaux).
Combining the CD-scratch-and-paint manipulations of Oval with the surround-soundscapes of Mouse On Mars was one of the better collaborative ideas of the decade. Werner's bassy synth manipulations work well with the randomized jitters of hideously abused CDs, creating subtle machine music well beyond ambient.

⊙ **_snd** (1996; Mille Plateaux).
More of the above, refined and reprocessed, with further remixing and shuffling mutated into REPROVISERS (1997; Mille Plateaux) by various friends and relations.

Richard Fontenoy

MOXY FRÜVOUS

Formed Toronto, Canada, 1989.

It is impossible to pigeonhole the Canadian foursome **Moxy Früvous**. Their unique music blends aspects of rock, folk and a cappella, along with humour and political satire – not a regular combination in the 90s. The group consists of **Mike Ford** on guitar and piano, **Dave Matheson** on guitar, banjo and accordion, drummer **Jean Ghomeshi**, and bassist **Murray Foster**; all four handle the complex four-part vocal harmonies.

Starting out as buskers in Toronto back in 1989, Moxy Früvous (nobody has let on what the name means) gained an early notoriety for their highly entertaining blend of comedy and musicianship, illustrated by such songs as "King Of Spain" and a pseudo-rap version of Dr. Seuss's "Green Eggs And Ham". By 1992, they had festival and concert support slots under their belt for names as big as Bob Dylan and Bryan Adams, and had recorded their first EP, an indie release that went gold in Canada. Their first album, BARGAINVILLE, followed the same year and went platinum. It was a deserved success: many of the songs were mainstays worked on since busking days and the recording captured the band's live energy.

After a heavy touring schedule, promoting the record in the US, Moxy went back into the studio to record a follow-up. This emerged as WOOD (1995), the title nodding towards the 'earthier' sound the band had gone for. The songs, this time around, took a somewhat more serious approach. "Horseshoes" lamented about a lost love; "Poor Mary Lane" recounted the story of a woman accused of murder (as told by her accomplice). Musically, on "Misplaced" and other tracks, there was more of a tendency towards country/folk; indeed, throughout the album the band featured violin, banjo and piano.

The band's live shows remained unchanged (check out LIVE NOISE, released in 1998) and Moxy Früvous began developing a strong following in the US. As a Canadian band, with overt and frequent references to Canadian politics and life, this was no mean achievement. The B ALBUM (1996) was a compilation of unreleased songs, old and new, that re-emphasized the satiric side of the group, highlighted by a jab at Rush Limbaugh titled "The Greatest Man In America". It was followed by the Yank-stabbing YOU WILL GO TO THE MOON (1997), and THORNHILL (1999), which brilliantly transposed the group's live exuberance and ironic patter onto disc; both collections managed to make full use of the newly earned US respect and distribution deal to bump up sales. Most recently, the C ALBUM (2000) continued the Moxy story, but was only available at gigs and online.

⊙ **Bargainville** (1993; WEA/Atlantic).
A showcase of earlier songs from Moxy's busking days, highlighting their innovative four-part harmonies.

⊙ **Wood** (1995; WEA).
Country-flavoured, slightly more serious songwriting still displays the trademark Moxy sound.

Jim Dress

MS. DYNAMITE

Born 26 April, 1981, West Sussex, England.

Every few years a black musician from a genre that was formerly a pariah comes along that the mainstream press can latch onto and turn into that most loathed figure in contemporary pop music – the 'role model'. For UK garage that musician was **Ms.**

Ms. DYNAMITE, A LITTLE DEEPER

Dynamite, an outspoken MC/singer who deplored the violence, machismo and materialism that seemed endemic to the scene.

Ms. Dynamite was born Niomi McLean-Daley and at first didn't particularly care for the music that would make her a star. She started to MC on a dare when she was 17 at a local garage club, her courage boosted by booze. Her mic skills impressed the club's DJ, **Sticky**, who would eventually produce her debut single, "Booo!" (2000). Compared to the vast majority of garage's male MCs who couldn't rap their way out of a paper bag, Dynamite could not only flow and ride the stop-start beat, but she was capable of sustaining a train of thought for more than two bars. "Booo!" got more than just Bronx cheers on London's dance floors, eventually reaching #12 in the UK charts in the summer of 2001. With her girl-next-door good looks, refreshing womanist lyrics and accessibility, the stage was set for her R&B/pop-rap make-over – she was the UK's answer to Lauryn Hill.

Working with Fugees producer **Salaam Remi**, Dynamite reversed out of the garage by embracing a middle-of-the-road R&B style for her debut album, A LITTLE DEEPER (2002). Thankfully, her lyrics didn't always follow suit, and there was still room for her to scold iced-out players with shockingly forthright lines like, 'How many Africans died for the baguettes on your Rolex?' ("It Takes More"), and to let a little humour creep in by interpolating Musical Youth on "Dy-Na-Mi-Tee". With their complete lack of understanding of the music, the mainstream press lapped it up, and when they discovered that she turned down a place at university to pursue music, her career as a talking head on current affairs programmes that wanted to discuss 'urban violence' seemed inevitable. Her success and media profile was further established when A LITTLE DEEPER won the *Mercury Music Prize*.

⊙ **A Little Deeper** (2002; Polydor).
The singles ("Dy-Na-Mi-Tee" and "It Takes More") are great, but at times the flaccid music and occasional whining self-righteousness just drag.

Peter Shapiro

MUDHONEY

Formed Seattle, 1988.

Named after a Russ Meyer film, **Mudhoney** set out with a fine pedigree. Both vocalist/guitarists **Mark Arm** and **Steve Turner** had played in **GREEN RIVER** – the Seattle band that had included Stone Gossard and Jeff Ament, later of Pearl Jam – while **Dan Peters** (drums) and **Matt Lukin** (bass) had done a stint for their celebrated yet unlistenable rivals, **THE MELVINS**. So, when the first wave of Seattle bands were showcased on the SUB POP 200 compilation, Mudhoney (contributing "The Rose", a heartfelt cover of the Bette Midler number) were right up there with Nirvana and Soundgarden.

Their own debut release was SUPERFUZZ BIGMUFF (1989), a mini-album named after their favourite distortion pedals. The new wave of Seattle bands often treated the dumb tradition of hard rock and heavy metal with a good deal of irony. But Mudhoney, though smart, were not afraid to play dumb, and in the lack of sophistication of many of their songs you could trace an affectionate homage to avowedly superficial bands like the Ramones.

The single "Touch Me I'm Sick" – a classic confection of stuttering drums, fuzzed-out guitars and screamed vocals – was followed by a tour accompanying Sonic Youth in 1989. Then came "Sweet Young Thing Ain't Sweet No More", a slow menacing drawl of a song, and a split single with Sonic Youth that confirmed their acceptance into the alternative-rock scene.

The first full-length album, entitled simply MUDHONEY, was greeted with less enthusiasm than SUPERFUZZ BIGMUFF, many feeling it revealed that the band had few musical tricks up their sleeves. The next offering, EVERY GOOD BOY DESERVES FUDGE (1991) – Mudhoney have always had a way with titles – was a more uncompromising effort and went down better, but it also marked the beginning of the band's disillusionment with Sub Pop, mainly over money. The sudden worldwide success of Nirvana raised interest in Seattle bands to fever pitch, and in March 1992 Mudhoney succumbed and signed to Reprise.

Their major-label debut, PIECE OF CAKE, was released in late 1992 to lacklustre reviews. It seemed that Mudhoney were dulled by the Warners money honey trap, and an increased budget had overglossed the raw sound of the band, removing all that had made them good in the first place. The band seemed to sense this themselves and their 1993 mini-album, FIVE DOLLAR BOB'S MOOK COOKER STEW, was an attempt to recapture the energy and buzz of their earlier releases.

Mudhoney spent 1994 recording with Jack Endino in Seattle, hoping that the man who produced the city's seminal grunge albums had kept the fairy dust. In the event, MY BROTHER THE COW (1995) was a defiant restatement of the old formulae,

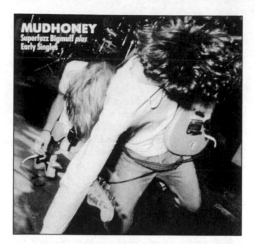

and at times it worked, as on the stand-out "Generation Spokesmodel".

The band has stuck doggedly to a tried-and-tested formula, and could never be accused of combining their prolific output with a commitment to innovation and experimentation. Celebrating ten years of existence with a constant line-up, TOMORROW HIT TODAY was released in September 1998, produced in Memphis with legendary session pianist **Jim Dickinson** (who played on The Rolling Stones' "Wild Horses"). The album received generally lukewarm reviews, perhaps because it marked a step towards a more competent, though hardly commercial, sound.

Truly veterans of an all-but-vanished scene, the band returned to the road after a long lay-off, supporting mentors Pearl Jam. In the meantime, the indie nostalgia market was fed several retrospectives, the double-CD set MARCH TO FUZZ (2000) and THE RADIO SESSIONS (2000) being the best of the bunch. It wasn't until 2002 that the group re-emerged with fresh material on disc, though having shed bassist Matt Lukin in favour of **Guy Maddison**, who'd formerly rocked with both Bloodloss and Lubricated Goat. SINCE WE'VE BECOME TRANSLUCENT (2002) marked a glittering return for Mudhoney and received rave reviews, while Turner's 2003 solo effort, the no-frills gem SEARCHING FOR MELODY, added an interesting, pensive strand to the band's tale. But despite all this activity, it seems unlikely that the group will again enjoy the kind of adulation that they earned in earlier days.

⊙ **Superfuzz Bigmuff** (1989; Sub Pop).
   Their greatest moment, this fast-paced mini-album was, for a few weeks in 1989, the record to have. The raw production and carefree guitar playing were without equal.

⊙ **Boiled Beef and Rotting Teeth** (1989; Tupelo).
   A collection of the early Sub Pop singles and B-sides, coveted at the height of Seattle fever. Includes "Sweet Young Thing" and "Touch Me I'm Sick".

⊙ **Every Good Boy Deserves Fudge** (1991; Sub Pop).
   The sound of a band coming to terms with its strengths.

⊙ **Tomorrow Hit Today** (1998: Warners Reprise).
   Corporate punk rock.

⊙ **March To Fuzz** (2000: Sub Pop).
   This set is not only a greatest hits package, but also a definitive rarities and B-sides collection. As well as angsty favourites like "Touch Me I'm Sick", "Hate The Police" and "Sweet Young Thing Ain't Sweet No More" you'll find the long-deleted 7" side "You Stupid Asshole" and their methadone-inspired cover of Spacemen 3's "Revolution".

Jonathan Bell

MULL HISTORICAL SOCIETY

Formed Glasgow, Scotland, 1999.

Born and bred in Tobermory on the Isle of Mull, off Scotland's west coast, **Colin MacIntyre** (singer, songwriter, guitarist and producer) developed a fascination with rock music through watching his uncle's covers band running through the standards, a mantle that the teenage MacIntyre took up himself under the name **Trax**. This group, made up of family members and friends (including bassist **Alan Malloy**) then became **Lovesick Zombies**, a Bowie/Clash covers act that would rehearse in Tobermory's old distillery on the harbour front.

It was only on moving to Glasgow that MacIntyre and Malloy became exposed to contemporary music and put together a couple of gigging bands in the shape of **7-11** and **Smells Like Marzipan**. Although this was creatively more fulfilling than the copy bands of the duo's island days, MacIntyre had a problem getting bookings when his opening gambit was 'this is Colin from 7-11'. Another name was sought, and so the pair agreed on **Mull Historical Society**, an unwieldy moniker inspired by the real Mull Historical Society's column in the local paper.

By November 2000 (by which stage MacIntyre had allegedly penned 300 songs) radio listeners on the mainland were being seduced by a track called "Barcode Bypass", issued on Rough Trade's Tugboat Records. It might seem hard to imagine how a song about a traditional shop-owner pressured by a newly

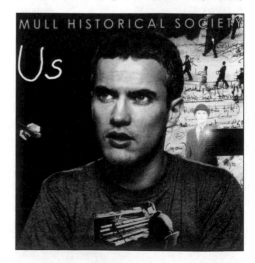

opened supermarket might tug at the heartstrings, but this charming tale of past-meets-present found its way into the consciousness of BBC programmers, and even MTV began rotating the single's charming snowbound promo.

This was a significant breakthrough, and MacIntyre promptly took his band – Malloy plus drummer **Tony Soave** and keyboard player **Colin 'Sheepy' McPherson** – on the road with Travis, The Strokes, Tindersticks and Elbow. At the same time Mull Historical Society signed to Blanco y Negro, who in 2001 issued further singles "I Tried" and "Animal Cannabus". LOSS, the debut album for Blanco, released the same year, was a pleasing collection of classic pop and windswept ballads, displaying a sound not heard since the days of Postcard Records in the Eighties. Exposure on mainstream radio and TV pushed "Watching Xanadu" into the Top Forty in 2002, further extending the fanbase of the Mull Historical Society.

In 2003 MacIntyre's troop followed up with US, another collection of magical bedroom tales, this time backed by far richer production, and polished with an attention to detail worthy of Brian Wilson. By this time Blanco y Negro had turned up the dial on their hype-ometer, and were to all intents and purposes marketing Mull as a one-man-show. As a result, the band suddenly had a very public face – and a face, it would seem, that was more than capable of shifting units.

🔘 **Loss** (2001; Blanco y Negro).
A brave and personal debut. The minimal oddness of "Barcode Bypass" is compelling, while "This Is Not Who We Are" shifts into a higher gear and rocks – kinda.

🔘 **Us** (2003; Blanco y Negro).
Here, MacIntyre and company make light work of 'that difficult second album'; the results have been hailed by many as the group's definitive PET SOUNDS moment.

Jeremy Simmonds

MUSE

Formed Teignmouth, UK, 1993.

Histrionic operatic shrieking and high-speed guitar noise might not be what you associate with the delights of impoverished wind-swept British seaside resorts, but **Muse**'s origins are to be found in such a setting and, somewhere along the line, these disaffected Devon teenagers decided to transform their lot through spiky hair and musical rage.

As thirteen year olds, **Matthew Bellamy** (vocals, guitars, keyboards), **Chris Wolstenholme** (bass) and **Dominic Howard** (drums) first began to make noise under the distinctly teenage moniker of Gothic Plague, later renamed Fixed Penalty, then Rocket Baby Dolls and finally Muse. Playing to half-empty pubs and refusing to cover the 60s pop their rural punters desired, the maturing Muse were determined to make it. Coming of age to discover all their friends had left for university and their day jobs as labourers and loo cleaners did not quite fit the rock'n'roll

dream, Muse signed a management deal that kicked off an intense promotional drive, saw them release two EPs (MUSE and MUSCLE MUSEUM) on Dangerous Records, and then garnered the boys four recording contracts within the year; most notably a very special Christmas present from Madonna – a signing to her Maverick label on Christmas Eve.

Muse's high-anxiety sound of primal screams over fully inflated guitar led to easy comparisons with, inevitably, THE BENDS-era Radiohead and even Queen. Borrowing Radiohead's former producer, John Leckie, for their 1999 debut, SHOWBIZ, helped draw attention to the band, and as it was attention they wanted, it was attention they got. While being hailed in the UK as *Best Newcomer* at 2000's *NME* Awards, Muse were racing around Stateside stages opening shows for Foo Fighters and Red Hot Chilli Peppers and rising to the daunting challenge of arena audiences. Assisted by further up-front, ear-splitting performances at the Reading and Glastonbury festivals, SHOWBIZ sold more than a million copies worldwide and each of the five singles released nudged a little higher up the British charts, with the fifth, "Unintended", breaking into the Top 20.

If 2000 was an astonishing year for the three lads from the backwaters, then 2001 was even better. The follow-up album, ORIGIN OF SYMMETRY, attempted a broader range, with high-camp rock arias, non-cerebral thrash, and even a dash of Euro disco and a cover of blues-singer standard "Feeling Good" tossed in. Muse were by now loved by metallers (*Kerrang!* crowned them *Best British Band* in this year), the charts also adored them and all four of the set's singles made the Top 20. "Bliss" saw Ibiza anthems mingle with mosh-pit violence, while the radio favourite "Plug In Baby" managed to combine a riff seemingly borrowed from Bach with rock guitar heroics, whilst still offering a chorus catchy enough to sing along to.

After achieving main stage and headline positions across the 2002 festival circuits, Muse consolidated their legend for blistering live shows with the double DVD/CD release of Hullabaloo, which featured live performances and B-sides. The record companies were certainly wringing every last drop of value for money out of these purveyors of a rags-to-riches rock dream.

⊙ **Showbiz** (1999; Mushroom).
Twelve tracks of dense, enraged rock and howling, like a lobotomized Radiohead – in a good way.

⊙ **Origin Of Symmetry** (2001; Mushroom).
Identity-making, ambitious, pompous and beguiling, Muse find their own high-pitched voice amidst theatrical metal.

Annebella Pollen

THE MUSIC

Formed Leeds, England, 1998.

By the end of 2002, **The Music**, with their defiantly retro-indie Roses-meets-Zeppelin sound, had gone from being the 'best unsigned band in Britain' to one of rock's top live draws in the UK. Having embarked upon a punishing schedule of gigs as school leavers in 2001, the speed with which this still-largely teenage band made their name was little short of alarming.

To wannabe rock god **Robert Harvey** (vocals, guitar) school dinner times in Leeds represented an opportunity to rehearse with stooges **Adam Nutter** (guitar) and **Stuart Coleman** (bass). From nearby Garforth, drummer **Phil Jordan** left his former band to complete the picture early in 1999. Before finishing their obligatory studies, The Music already had a couple of live performances under their belt, and had impressed the astute Simon Williams to the point that he was prepared to put their debut, "Take the Long Road and Walk It", out on his Fierce Panda label.

Although the entire band was collecting plaudits, it was the singer who caught the greatest amount of attention. Harvey's delivery was clearly influenced by Robert Plant while his look and stage presence drew comparisons with a younger Richard Ashcroft. The rest of the band also seemed eager to wear their influences on their sleeves: Nutter dived in and out of blues-influenced rock styles, while the rhythm section was unafraid to venture into funk bass lines and big-beat-heavy rhythms (the band, it transpired, were all huge admirers of The Chemical Bros). All in all, The Music were always likely to be targeted as a 'boys' band'.

Hut Records managed to capture the fledgling act's 'live' sound on record, the first EP to emerge on the label being "You Might As Well Try To Fuck Me" in November 2001. Needless to say, the cut's title raised shackles and prevented The Music from attaining the daytime airplay they needed. The real breakthrough was The People EP (with its demonic lead track) – which scratched the UK charts in 2002, and was followed by a reissue of "Take The Long Road And Walk It" which hit #14, signalling The Music's arrival as major contenders.

After several high-profile festival appearances, plus support slots with The Charlatans, New Order, Coldplay and Doves, the blistering eponymous debut album arrived at the end of the summer. The Music, produced by Jim Abbiss, cemented the group's reputation as the UK's leading new rock act by entering the album chart at #4. The album's stand-out cuts "Getaway" and "The Truth Is No Words", provided The Music with further hits, despite the former being on release for just one day.

In 2003, The Music continued to ride the tsunami of their success, even managing to tease a few understated words from the ever-reliable *NME* … 'There's desperate need for a group to come through and tear away the apathy and complacency – The Music are that group. The Music are going to change everything.'

⊙ **The Music** (2002; Hut).
The Music pushes all the right rock'n'roll buttons and gets the anorak-wearers dancing. With four barnstorming singles in place, it's a remarkably resolute debut for such a young band.

Jeremy Simmonds

The Music sittin' pretty

MY BLOODY VALENTINE

Formed London, 1986.

"It's actually the opposite of rock'n'roll. It's taking the guts out of it; there's no gut, just remnants." Kevin Shields

Educated rock primitivists, **My Bloody Valentine** started out as a fairly mundane indie band. The 1987 debut single "Strawberry Wine" and SUNNY SUNDAE SMILE album – produced by **Kevin Shields** (guitar/vocals), **Bilinda Butcher** (guitar/vocals), **Colm O'Ciosoig** (drums) and **Deb B. Googe** (bass) – did little more than hint at the extremities of thrash-pop and ethereal beauty that were to follow. Still, it caught the imagination of Alan McGee's Creation Records, and under his wing MBV reinvented themselves wholesale, finding totally new approaches to the electric guitar and the love song.

An MBV performance, in the late 80s, comprised forty minutes of slowly gyrating feedback distorting every frequency known to science, from which would emerge the sighing cross-harmonies of Shields and Butcher, or just the latter's fragile melancholia. Lyrics didn't need to be audible in this heavenly fog. On record, they were a little more discernible, the overall sound being meticulously layered and composed.

The 1988 EP, YOU MADE ME REALISE (featuring the mind-blowing B-side "Slow", a homage to oral sex) and accompanying album, ISN'T ANYTHING, were dark explorations of sex, love and languor; the collection was an instant underground classic, standing alongside The Jesus & Mary Chain's PSYCHOCANDY as a vehicle for some of the most exquisite and erotically charged guitar music to appear since the time of The Velvet Underground. However, years were to pass before the next album, as the increasingly perfectionist working methods of Shields led to a succession of broken deadlines. In the interim, the GLIDER EP (1990) appeared, a tongue-snogging close-up on the cover suggesting old themes, though its contents were a freshly expanded kaleidoscope of textures. The title heralded the use of a 'glide guitar' technique, whose swaths and surges of noise weren't obviously traceable to the physical acts that caused them. "Don't Ask Why", a soft hallucinatory neo-ballad, revealed Shields as a lyricist of heartbreaking substance. But it was the EP's opener, "Soon", that caused jaws to drop: its seven-minute journey through a glacial landscape of noise was backed by a more than funky groove that went hand-in-hand with the Primal Scream/Andy Weatherall collaboration "Loaded", released at around the same time. A Weatherall rework of "Soon" was quickly released, backed by an unedited version of GLIDER's disorienting title cut.

My Bloody Valentine's zone on the avant-pop soundscape by now accommodated a clutch of generic 'shoe-gazing' bands (The Boo Radleys, Slowdive, Chapterhouse, etc), whose derivations of Valentine dynamics were to underline just how far MBV had transcended the demimonde. When the

Valentines (from left): Deb B. Googe, Bilinda Butcher and Kevin Shields

LOVELESS album finally arrived in 1991, its elephantine gestation period was rumoured to have cost Creation a figure shadowing £200,000 in studio time. Eighteen engineers got a credit on the cover, including Shields and O'Ciosoig – both also listed as 'samplers'. Some might have accused the band of self-indulgent preciousness, but this colossal, mesmeric work proved they knew exactly what they were doing. "When You Sleep" produced one of rock's great clarions of joy; "To Here Knows When" sounded like whales pirouetting to the tones of a string quartet in E, before Butcher's lush vocals swept in over Philip Glass motifs and an echoplexed bagpipe.

MBV toured the album as part of 1992's 'Rollercoaster' tour with The Mary Chain, Blur and Dinosaur Jr., and moved from a financially beleaguered Creation to Island. Since then, the only MBV offering to surface was a cover of Wire's "Map Ref 41°N 93°W" on the Wire tribute album, WHORE (1996). Googe left the band in the meantime, to drive a cab for a while before forming **Snowpony**, while O'Ciosoig turned up with **MAZZY STAR**'s **Hope Sandoval** on her 2001 release BAVARIAN FRUIT BREAD.

Kevin Shields has contributed to productions by **Experimental Audio Research** (a project also featuring God's Kevin Martin, ex-Spaceman 3 Sonic Boom, and Eddie Prevost of AMM) and has frequently been spotted playing for, and remixing, **PRIMAL SCREAM**. Future directions for My Bloody Valentine are anybody's guess.

⦿ **Isn't Anything** (1988; Creation).
My Bloody Valentine managing to sound disembodied and raucous, rampant and ethereal all at the same time.

⦿ **Loveless** (1991; Creation).
Incandescent and essential.

Chris Brook and Peter Buckley

NAPALM DEATH

Formed Ipswich, England, 1982.

The prejudice of the mainstream rock press against thrash, speed and death metal has obscured the innovation and importance of the outer limits of the genre. In particular, the sonic invention of **Napalm Death**, the fearsome creators of grindcore, has been unjustly ignored.

Napalm Death's assault on the senses gained momentum in 1986, when the band began making an impact via Peel sessions and constant touring. The uncertainty of the period saw two line-ups produce one side each of the album SCUM (1987). Side one was produced by **Mick Harris** (drums), **Justin Broadrick** (guitar) and **Nick Bullen** (bass/vocals), side two was the work of Harris, **Lee Dorrian** (vocals), **Bill Steer** (guitar) and **Jim Whitely** (bass). Their agenda was to reduce heavy metal to a basic rolling grind, speeded up to burnout and shot through with demonic, growling vocals. The lyric sheet was essential and showed a political and social slant to the whole operation.

Despite being treated as a joke by some in the musical establishment, the band quickly gained a solid following, influencing an entire generation of metalheads and finding favour around the world. Death's influence is out of all proportion to their record sales: aside from spawning a host of grindcore imitators, the band has developed a broad palette of sound-manipulation techniques, particularly Harris's remarkable drum style, which has forever altered the drum kit's erstwhile role as rhythm machine.

For FROM ENSLAVEMENT TO OBLITERATION (1988), bassist **Shane Embury** replaced Whitely. This album took the short sharp formula to the limit by offering a whopping 54 tracks, some clocking in at a few seconds of noise and screaming; it made Slayer sound like Take That. (The ultimate thrash single came free with the compilation GRIND CRUSHER, when Death and The Electro Hippies both recorded one-second tracks, taking a side each of the world's shortest single.) After ENSLAVEMENT, Dorrian left to form **Cathedral**, while Steer moved on to form **Carcass**. Carcass took thrash to new extremes by wallowing in medical terminology and producing a concept album, REEK OF PUTREFACTION, that followed the detailed aspects of bodily decay after death. Shane Embury also appeared in **Unseen Terror**, a band that took thrash soundscapes into new areas and prompted legions of lo-fi, scuzz riffmongers.

HARMONY CORRUPTION (1990) saw Napalm Death moving towards fast heavy metal and experimenting with songs that approached a normal length. The album, with new guitarists **Jesse Pintado** and **Mitch Harris**, and vocalist **Mark Greenway**, featured a sound so radio-friendly that the band made progress in the US. Death themselves were unimpressed with the sound, and their MASS APPEAL MADNESS EP (1990) was an instant grindcore wonder, recorded quickly in a small local studio.

Before the recording of UTOPIA BANISHED (1992), Mick Harris departed to join ground-breaking, ambient dub combo **SCORN**. His old band, meanwhile, recorded FEAR, EMPTINESS, DESPAIR (1994), which finally communicated their phenomenal stage power while remaining strong as a collection of songs. By now, the critical tide was running in their favour, and the following year the band found themselves in the US Top 10 as part of the soundtrack of *Mortal Kombat*.

Napalm Death consolidated upon this deserved success, issuing a mini-album, GREED KILLING (1995), as a prelude to the solid and accomplished DIATRIBES (1996), which took the ferocious riffing of Pintado and Harris to a new level.

Death continued to perfect their craft with the live BOOTLEGGED IN JAPAN (1998), showcasing ten years of unrepentant noise classics, and WORDS FROM THE EXIT WOUND (1998), blending some surprisingly melodic touches into the sonic assault to provide one of their most accomplished studio collections. ENEMY OF THE MUSIC BUSINESS (2000) was just as essential, showing that the group were still producing the most extreme grind on the scene.

Earache Records has also been a major player in the expansion of thrash and its offshoots, supporting such talents as **Lawnmower Deth**, who have added a lunatic and comic element to music that was already on the cutting edge – their trashing of The Osmonds' "Crazy Horses" is one of the few rock covers that manages to reinvent a standard and totally wreck it at the same time. In short, with their own music and with their nurturing of the scene, Napalm Death, now twenty years into their career, have single-handedly instigated and propagated some of the most extreme music ever recorded, and their appetite for touring – especially in the US – suggests they won't stop until the whole world has had a thrashing.

⦿ **Fear, Emptiness, Despair** (1994; Earache).
This is a well-structured, focused and credible collection of tracks. It is also true to the power and guts that have been at the centre of this music since the start.

⦿ **Bootlegged In Japan** (1998; Earache)
It's surprising it took them so long – it's predictable that

this thing roars from the speakers with every intention of taking out the supporting walls in your house. Prompted, apparently, by the availability of bootlegs of this 1996 Tokyo show and all the better for a trawl of material from every incarnation of the band.

⊙ **Words From The Exit Wound** (1998; Earache).
Another great title, another roaring collection of anthems with shifting undertones and strength in sequence. "None The Wiser" stumbles into positively mellow territory in places, and the deft use of second vocals – with words you can make out! – lends a clarity and breadth to the whole affair.

⊙ **The Complete Radio One Sessions** (2000; Fuel).
There are some real classics here from three different line-ups of the band.

Neil Nixon

THE NAZZ

Formed Philadelphia 1967; disbanded 1970.

Too self-conscious, not enough quality control, impressive rather than likeable, out of step with the times: these have always been the knocks on the career of one-time 'studio whizkid' **TODD RUNDGREN**. His first group to gain any notoriety, **The Nazz**, were no exception.

Guitarist Rundgren formed The Nazz with bassist **Carson Van Osten** after they had quit blues purists Woody's Truck Stop. Recruiting drummer **Thom Mooney** and vocalist/keyboardist **Stewkey** (né Robert Antoni), Rundgren and Van Osten named the group after The Yardbirds' song "The Nazz Are Blue" and quickly landed a slot opening for The Doors in Philadelphia.

Taken under the wing of producer John Kurland, the group moved to New York and were moulded into a semi-teen-pop band. While the rest of the country was growing beards and turning on and tuning out, The Nazz were wearing foppish clothes and inventing power pop, ignoring The Beatles' psychedelia in favour of their harmonies and symphonic pretensions. The group's self-produced debut single, "Hello It's Me" (1968), was pretty, but hopelessly lugubrious and it wandered all over the place; tightening up the song considerably, Rundgren turned the cut into a radio standard in 1973. The flip, "Open My Eyes", however, was stunning. Starting off like The Who's "Can't Explain", then moving through proto-heavy-metal riffing, bongo fills, Mitch Ryder organ and hand-claps to a weird sheen courtesy of some of the most gratuitous phasing ever recorded, "Open My Eyes" was the perfect transition record from the 60s to the 70s. It was the best moment on their self-titled debut album (1968) which was mostly produced by Kurland and had too much Anglophilia and too many traces of their blues bore past to be as innovative as "Open My Eyes".

NAZZNAZZ (1969) was largely produced by Rundgren, but was bogged down by the weight of his pretensions, especially the eleven-minute-plus symphonic "A Beautiful Song". Power pop fans, however, were thrilled by rockers like "Under The Ice" and "Hang On Paul" and ballads such as "Letters

Don't Count" that ushered in the 70s' most odious trend. The album was originally conceived of as a double, with Rundgren taking over lead vocals for roughly half the tracks. The group, however, weren't happy with the direction and shelved his tracks – Rundgren quit in late 1969.

For NAZZ III (1970), Stewkey erased Rundgren's vocals from the shelved tracks and rerecorded the vocals himself. Tracks like "Only One Winner" and "Some People" betrayed the influence of Laura Nyro, while "Loosen Up" was a dreadful parody of Archie Bell & The Drells and showed the arrogance and fear of groove that always scarred the power pop project. The album went nowhere and what was left of the group joined **Fuse**, the band that would eventually mutate into power pop titans **CHEAP TRICK**.

⊙ **Open Our Eyes: The Anthology** (Sanctuary; 2002).
Most of the first two albums and a healthy selection from NAZZ III testify to the expulsion of the blues from the power pop blueprint.

Peter Shapiro

NEBULA

Formed California, 1997.

One of the more entertaining developments in rock of recent years has to have been the growth of 'stoner', led indubitably by godheads **KYUSS** and their desert-influenced brand of spaced out weirdness. For stoner think plenty of hair, probably beards, enough weed to give the munchies for about twelve years straight, and effects pedals the size of small cars. Oh, and lots of amplification, not to mention the Black Sabbath back catalogue from the Ozzy period. We're talking about raising the riff to an art form and lowering the bottom end to an earth-shifting rumble. Aside from the now defunct Kyuss, chief exponents of the genre are **FU MANCHU**, from whose ranks **Eddie Glass** (guitars/vocals) and **Ruben Romano** (drums) split off to form **Nebula**.

While Fu Manchu specialized in a driving Sabbath-esque groove, Glass and Romano wanted to bring a touch of space rock to the party, though ultimately to

label something as eclectic as Nebula's music simply as stoner would be far too lazy. They needed a bassist able to deliver rhythms heavy enough to anchor a battle-ship; at first they called upon Kyuss four-stringer Scott Reeder but when he couldn't commit they found their man in **Mark Abshire** and created LET IT BURN (1998), a dirty, feedback-drenched album of drug-fuelled psychedelia and basic rock'n'roll. True, some of the songs could well have featured on a Fu Manchu record, but already Glass was making his mark as a songwriter: Nebula's trajectory began to diverge sig-nificantly from that of their previous band.

One thing they retained, however, was a love of touring. Glass had started out playing drums in a band called **Olive Lawn** back in the early 90s before switching his attention to guitar, and his addiction to life on the road was deeply ingrained. Nebula didn't just tour, they became road animals, loving the freedom that live gigs gave them to reinterpret studio-written songs.

Next came a split mini-LP with **Lowrider** and the SUN CREATURE EP, but the recording sessions were crammed in while the band burned rubber touring around the States. These 1998 recordings were even-tually done justice by combining them into the DOS EPs (2002) album, where more powerful mixes and a clutch of new cuts elevated their previously rushed work into something bordering on the cosmic.

However, TO THE CENTER (1999), produced by old friend **Jack Endino**, was the first pure indication of the band's ability to crank out some truly aston-ishing rock. Titles such as "Synthetic Dream" and "Fields Of Psilocybin" gave a clear idea of where Glass and co. had come from and where they were going; the cover art, a mixture of amateurish lettering and a fish-eye lens photo of the band's stage setup captured baking in the desert sun, gave a flavour of the scorching potential contained within. This potential was fully realized on CHARGED (2001), a crackling slab of primal blues-based fuzz rock, dripping with feed-back and pulsing with psychedelic prowess.

● **To The Center** (1999; Sweet Nothing).
A stunning groove-laden journey into the recesses of chief writer Eddie Glass's mind, all played out in epic space rock tradition.

● **Charged** (2001; Sweet Nothing).
The cover art featuring huge generator pylons gives the game away. This positively throbs with feral rock power, from the opening rush of "Do It Now" to the crunching closer "All The Way".

● **Dos EPs** (2002; Sweet Nothing).
Two early records rejigged, remixed, added to and unleashed. It's all here from AC/DC-style boogie to Sabbath-esque doom, a worthwhile retrospective exercise.

Essi Berelian

NEGATIVLAND

Formed Berkeley, California, 1979.

In an age of information overload, collage seems the most appropriate of art forms, and **Negativland**

employ it to the fullest extent. Where popular music has too often settled for pastiche, this is a group that have pushed the limits beyond breaking point to expose the contradictions that underlie cultural con-sumption. It sounds like heavy going, but at their best Negativland are both hilarious and thought-pro-voking.

The group were formed in 1979 by **Mark Hosler**, **David Wills** and **Richard Lyons**, who started out using tape loops to create rather formless cut'n'paste exercises. In 1982 they began to host *Over The Edge*, a chaotic live radio show that featured skits, music, phone-ins and sampling. Tape manipulator extraor-dinaire **Don Joyce** joined soon afterwards and Negativland's mix-and-match noise sculptures grew into what they called 'culture jamming'. Its first appearance on disc was OVER THE EDGE VOLUME 1: JAMCON '84 (1984), an edited version of one of their radio shows, comprising a mix of looped noise, pranks, bad puns, tape manipulation, copyright infringement and general media shenanigans.

ESCAPE FROM NOISE (1987), continued along sim-ilar lines, but its theme (the cynical use of desire by the media) made it more cohesive. The best 'song' on the album, "Christianity Is Stupid", became central to the prank that first brought the group to widespread attention. After coming across a news item about a teenager who murdered his parents with an axe, the band circulated a phony press release stating that the song influenced his killing spree. The press took the release at face value and the story escalated out of control, which was exactly what Negativland wanted.

Next off was HELTER STUPID (1989), a comment on the state of the media, both troubling and scathingly funny. The second half of the record mitigated this queasy ambivalence with "The Perfect Cut", a send-up of 'oldies radio' that mixed samples, old radio jingles and the smarmy Dick Vaughn character, who would also appear on OVER THE EDGE VOLUME 4.

The following year, the band attracted more noto-riety with its U2 EP, containing parodic versions of that band's "I Still Haven't Found What I'm Looking For". U2 forced the record's recall because of copyright infringement, though they eventually dropped the case – and indeed used similar working methods on their *Zoo TV* tour.

Despite the encounter, Negativland continued to trample all over copyright laws in an attempt to expose media hypocrisy. Since the U2 affair, most of their recorded output has consisted of material in the Over The Edge series, though their full-length outing Dispepsi (1997) was an ode to a fizzy brown drink loved by millions. Happy Heroes (1998) and The ABCs Of Anarchism (1999, recorded with **Chumbawamba**) offered more expert sampler anarchy. Their media terrorism is not likely to remain underground for long.

⊙ **Escape From Noise** (1987; SST).
   Including "Christianity Is Stupid", this is a rigorous assault on cultural consumption that never lets its analysis obscure its humour.

⊙ **Helter Stupid** (1989; SST).
   Half a scathing satire on the gullibility and duplicity of the press, and half a satire on formulaic commercial radio and the 'moribund music of the 70s', this is probably their best and most accessible album.

Peter Shapiro

LES NEGRESSES VERTES

Formed Paris, 1987.

Les Negresses Vertes are that rare beast: a rock band achieving international success working in a language other than English – and French, to boot. So what's the claim for 'The Green Black Women' (the name came from abuse hurled at the core members by French bikers at a party)? Well, multiculti madness for one. Formed in Paris in 1987, the band drew members from working-class, immigrant areas of the city and from the Camargue area of southern France, and combine elements of French folk, Algerian rai, ska, rock, flamenco and waltz, plus a lashing of punk and plenty of spirit. It's an infectious, good-time mix.

The original line-up was nine strong – **Helno Rota de Louracqua** (vocals), **Braham** (trombone), **L'Ami Ro** (piano), **Stefane Mellino** (guitar), **Paulo** (bass), **Mathieu Caravese** (accordion), **Gaby** (drums), **Michel Ochowiak** (trumpet) and **Iza Mellino** (backing vocals) – and, as if that wasn't expansive enough, it was augmented on records and gigs by more horns and backing singers. The group arose out of friendship and hence were a very tightknit unit; additionally, many of the members were new to their instruments, producing gloriously unorthodox stylings and a dramatic, romantic punk-folk sounding like nothing else on earth.

Signed by an expat Scot, Peter Murray, to his Paris-based independent label, Off The Track, the group's first release was a hardcore punk protest song, "200 Ans d'Hypocrisie" (1989). A volley directed against the French Revolution bicentennial celebrations, it was a conscious echo of the Sex Pistols' anti-Jubilee "God Save The Queen". Helno, with his spluttering vocals (and speed-rotted teeth), recalled Rotten, or Joe Strummer, or Shane MacGowan.

Mlah (North African Arabic for 'everything's cool'), the band's first album, followed in 1989, causing an immediate splash with its punk attitude, lewd flamenco and rai rhythms, ska-soul horn arrangements, riotous choruses and, most of all, for its warmth, sensuality and deep Frenchness. Yet it was somehow pan-cultural too: Francophones could relish the outrageous double entendres in "Zobi la Mouche", or the satiric lament of "Voilá l'Et" about those left in scorching Paris in August during the *grandes vacances*, and the rest of us could dance.

Les Negresses Vertes – Une famille heureuse

"Zobi" was, bizarrely, made *Record of the Week* by two English Radio 1 DJs, but the single, like the album, fell just short of a UK chart placing.

In summer 1989 the Negresses made their British debut via sold-out gigs at Ronnie Scott's and won plenty of friends in the then-burgeoning world music constituency with a blistering performance at WOMAD. They also undertook a bold trip to play in Beirut. The band's stage show dazzled with the variety of their backgrounds and influences; the band, all sharp dressers, could be seen leaping around among moth-eaten Persian rugs, with backing singers belly-dancing, Helno strutting drunkenly at the front of the stage, and accordion player Caravese refusing to stir from his tatty wooden chair stage right, as if in a favoured bar seat. The effect was something between bordello, boozer and bazaar.

The Negresses contributed a gleeful take on Cole Porter's "I Love Paris" to the RED HOT AND BLUE AIDS benefit LP (their only non-French-language recording) and played several French antiracism 'Don't Touch My Friend' events, before returning to the studio for their second album, the aptly named FAMILLE NOMBREUSE (1991), featuring a new drummer, **Ze Verbalito**. Helno's copious drug habit was by now interfering with his ability to write, and the (French-Algerian) Stefane Mellino had become the dominant creative force. The album was a roaring success in France, and in Britain the ska-styled single "Famille Heureuse" only just missed out in the charts. Other highlights included Mellino's "Face à la Mer" and "La France à ses Dimanches", a joyous harangue in waltz time. Soon after this, Helno died of an accidental overdose. The extended family of LNV was hit hard, and withdrew to consider their next move. A stopgap album, 10 REMIXES 87–93 (1993) was issued, featuring remixes by the likes of Massive Attack, William Orbit and Norman Cook; "200 Ans d'Hypocrisie" also made its album debut, in honour of Helno. Alas, along the way, most of what made the songs danceable in the first place was sacrificed to bpm.

This would have been a dismal finale, so it was with pleasure that the band's admirers welcomed the all-new ZIG-ZAGUE (1995) album. The band was scaled down to just five of the original members. Produced by **Rupert Hine**, the sound was more studio rock, but Mellino, now undoubted frontman and leader, contributed "Mambo Show" and "Après la Pluie" in best LNV tradition. GREEN BUS (1996), a magnificent double album of live recordings, captured something of the sheer, wild glee of their best stage performances, including a glorious, ripped and torn version of the Sex Pistols' "Pretty Vacant".

This live summation of their work to date seemed to represent a line drawn under the original vision of LNV. Excepting the contribution of "La Gadoue" to Jane Birkin's 1999 album VERSIONS JANE, four years passed before the next release. Even checking Howie B's production credit, no one could have predicted TRABENDO (2000), an initially perplexing but

rewarding exploration into pure rhythm, that mixed slurred trip-hop with the crispness of Franco-Latin syncopation.

Many felt LNV had sacrificed their identity, but plenty more were thrilled by the creative adventure, to say nothing of the charms of the hypnotic, Eschersque spirals of "Ce Pays" and the classic-yet-radical-LNV cut "Leila". It was just this kind of creative restlessness that the band's advocates had recognized and responded to in the first place, and it is this which suggests that LNV's best is still to come. Meantime, an acoustic selection of favourites, ACOUSTIC CLUBBING, released at the end of 2001, kept fans content.

⊙ Mlah (1989; Virgin).
Imagine The Pogues, a troupe of French troubadours, Madness, rai-king Cheb Khaled, Joe Strummer and The Gipsy Kings, trapped together in a lift between floors on their way to a very wild party indeed. Et voilà: MLAH.

⊙ Famille Nombreuse (1991; Razzia/Delabel).
A more considered performance for this second album, but they still rip it up with "Hou! Mamma Mia" and the comic squint at traditional French folk on "Get Some Wood" – which, despite the title, but in common with everything else they have written is sung entirely in French.

⊙ Trabendo (2000; Virgin/Delabel).
Greeted by several 'Judas' cries in the press, this set soon revealed itself to be a slow, sensual, uncoiling investigation into the true meaning of rhythmic multiculturalism. Everything they were loved for is still here; you just have to listen differently.

Peter Mills

NEKTAR

Formed Germany, 1971; disbanded 1980; re-formed 2000.

Hard prog-rockers **Nektar** were a British band who spent most of their career in Germany, where they recorded for the Bellaphon label. The line-up consisted of **Roye Albrighton** (guitar/vocals), **Derek 'Mo' Moore** (bass/vocals), **Allan 'Taff' Freeman** (keyboards) and **Ron Howden** (drums), with additional credits, in typical 70s prog fashion, to **Mick Brockett** for his 'Liquid Lights'. They were that kind of band, drenched in drug imagery and with a tendency towards obscure and often pretentious concept albums. But they also had a robust approach that eschewed the pseudo-classical meanderings of so many of that genre for something heavier and more Hendrix-orientated.

Their first two albums, JOURNEY TO THE CENTRE OF THE EYE (1971) and a year later, A TAB IN THE OCEAN, were fairly typical 70s fare, with all the trappings you'd expect: surreal visions, pleas for universal peace and understanding, and lapses into rambling trippiness. Bubbling below this, however, was a bluesier tendency, and it was this willingness to rock out that set Nektar apart from many of their contemporaries. Albrighton was a ferociously inventive, versatile guitarist and he was backed to the hilt by Moore's sturdily flowing bass lines and Howden's tight, no-frills drumming, while Freeman's keyboards, never flashy, added texture and even a touch of funk to the mix. This was a band who enjoyed playing off each other, as was confirmed by 1973's ...SOUND LIKE THIS – a double album of rough and heavy songs, created and recorded in just three days. Later that year, they came out with a more conventional studio album, REMEMBER THE FUTURE, which got substantial airplay on American radio, along with release on the Passport label. It was a breakthrough of sorts, acquiring them a cult following among college students throughout the States, and they consolidated this in 1974 with DOWN TO EARTH, which featured some of their best, tightest and most accessible work.

After a year of touring came RECYCLED, for which they were joined by **Larry 'Synergy' Fast**, a synthesizer player who would later go on to play with **PETER GABRIEL**. The album was a moderate success but somewhere along the line the ballsy interplay had gone, and what was left was standard synth-progrock. Reduced to that, the band quickly unravelled. Albrighton left, to be replaced by **Dave Nelson**, who contributed an anonymous guitar style to their next LP, MAGIC IS A CHILD (1977), an insipid and bland affair. Albrighton cropped up in 1979 with his own version of Nektar, playing clubs in New York, and released MAN IN THE MOON in 1980 to little effect. Nektar drifted away without waiting for punk to kill them off, leaving in their wake some nuggets that deserve to be excavated.

Years of silence and fond memories followed, with the individual members taking their own personal and professional paths. Albrighton put solo work out and then, after recovering from a near-fatal liver condition, once again linked up with Freeman. Recruiting **Ray Hardwick** on drums, they revived the Nektar name, and the resultant album, THE PRODIGAL SON (2001) was better than anyone except the staunchest fan dared hope: a shade too slick, perhaps, but brimming with tuneful, accessible pieces and carried off with grace, confidence and energy. Not exactly progressive, but a gratifying surprise, nonetheless.

The band headlined Nearfest 2002, a prog-rock festival in America, with a full reunion of their original line-up including Larry 'Synergy' Fast. GREATEST HITS LIVE, recorded at the Nektar reunion concert in Trenton, New Jersey on June 29 2002, was released as a Classic Rock Production. NEKTAR LIVE DVD (2002) was filmed at the reunion concert; it also featured bonus footage of *Remember The Future*, filmed for German TV in 1973.

Recently, Nektar enjoyed playing loads of live gigs and festivals; they were one of the headlining acts at the 2003 Burg Herzberg Festival in Germany and the special guests at the Adirondack Mountain Music Festival in New York. No rest for the wicked!

⊙ **Remember The Future** (1973; Bellaphon).
Despite the Bosch-like cover and the bizarre concept (an everyday story of an extraterrestrial bluebird who comes to earth and befriends a blind boy), this is a beautifully wrought, seamless album, with moments of real power.

⊙ **Down To Earth** (1974; Bellaphon).
While not as consistent as its predecessor, this is somewhat more accessible, forgoing the cosmic concepts in favour of songs loosely grouped around the theme of a circus. The monster instrumental, "Nellie The Elephant", even has an undertow of funk in it.

Adam Kimmel

NEU!

Formed Düsseldorf, Germany, 1971;
disbanded 1972; re-formed briefly 1975 and 1986.

After six months with KRAFTWERK, **Klaus Dinger** (vocals/drums/guitar/keyboards) and **Michael Rother** (guitar/bass/electronics/piano) formed NEU! in 1971. Their first self-titled album emerged on German label **Brain** early the following year, having been recorded over four days and nights in December with the aid of Can producer **Conrad Plank**. It was a surprise hit in West Germany, where some 35,000 record fans were drawn to its plain cover emblazoned with the single word 'NEU!', like a slogan for a new washing powder.

While their former partners in Kraftwerk were busy laying the groundwork for the pure electronic pop music that would bring them global fame, Dinger and Rother were part of a German scene largely ignored elsewhere. Determinedly distancing themselves from the American and British notions of rock, they mixed heavily phased fuzz guitars with Dinger's trance-inducing beat (later dubbed 'Motorik' or 'Apache') in songs that could take ten minutes or more to reach their destination. Their pieces invited concentration on sound rather than lyrics, with vocals providing another instrument rather than narration.

Later in 1972, with the help of **Uli Trepte** and **Eberhard Krahnemann** of Guru Guru, the duo attempted a series of disappointingly received live appearances before returning to the studio in early 1973 to work on NEU! 2. Due to a lack of cash, studio time was short, and when the album emerged the tracks "Super" and "Neuschnee" appeared remixed at 16rpm and 78rpm several times on the second side, an expedient which worked surprisingly well, producing a quite disorientating effect, unintentionally presaging a time when remixes and versions would be the norm. Once again, the sleeve was a triumphant pre-punk minimalist comment on consumerism – the large NEU! of the first album over-sprayed with a fluorescent pink '2'.

Following the modest success of NEU! and NEU! 2, and the "Super/Neuschnee" single (released at normal speed) which followed, United Artists released both LPs in Britain to rave reviews. Lacking any inclination to tour, NEU! back-pedalled for the next few years while Dinger set up the short-lived Dingerland label. Rother joined **Dieter Moebius** and **Joachim Roedelius** of CLUSTER as HARMONIA, releasing MUSIK VON HARMONIA and

DELUXE for Brain; a third LP, a collaboration with Brian Eno titled HARMONIA: TRACKS & TRACES, saw light of day twenty years later.

1975 saw Rother and Dinger reunited, along with Klaus's brother **Thomas** and **Hans Lampe**, both playing drums. This quartet recorded the stunning NEU! 75 to complete their contract for Brain, with **Conny Plank** co-producing the LP in his soon-to-be legendary studio. The album proved to be a fitting end to NEU!'s short career. Dinger and Rother each took creative control of one side of the LP, witnessing a significant divergence of styles. On the first (Rother's) the band continued the exploration of their quieter tendencies, with the last track "Leb Wohl" slowing to an achingly sluggish halt in a subtle blend of rim-shots and occasional piano, accompanied by Klaus Dinger's forgetful lyrics. The Dinger-led second side, however, was the final fling of the characteristic propulsive NEU! sound: aggressive, mesmerizing and with a dose of biting scorn from the vocals of "Hero".

With the album complete, NEU! went their separate ways, Michael Rother to pursue a continuing solo career with ten albums to his name, while the Dingers and Lampe became **La Düsseldorf**, continuing the NEU! tradition with additional synthesizers and a sound that Bowie drew on heavily for his BERLIN album. What little mainstream recognition NEU! had was soon forgotten, but they emerged as a significant influence on the likes of Sonic Youth, Loop, Death In Vegas and especially Stereolab – who adopted the NEU! template wholesale for their early releases. NEU! also stand as a heroic presence in Julian Cope's book *Krautrocksampler*, which helped revive interest in the sound of German 70s music.

Two disappointing archive recordings, 72 LIVE (actually a tape of rehearsals) and NEU!/4 (recordings the duo made in 1986) were released in 1996 by Dinger via **Captain Trip** Records in Japan. The three NEU! albums proper were lost to legal wrangles for 25 years, appearing as imperfect CD bootlegs mastered from original vinyl pressings. All three finally appeared on German pop star **Herbert**

Grönemeyer's label **Grönland** in 2001 by mutual agreement between Rother and Dinger.

Dinger reappeared in the 90s with Die Engel des Herrn and La! Neu?, while Rother continues his solo career and an excellent electronic partnership with Moebius. He also contributed a new track to the A HOMAGE TO NEU! Compilation (1998) which also featured the likes of Autechre, Legendary Pink Dots and System 7. A reunion of Dinger and Rother – other than for the remastering sessions – seems unlikely, but remains hoped for by fans worldwide.

⊙ **NEU!** (1972; Brain, reissued 2001).
With its stark sleeve and blasts of road-drills and feedback, NEU! was a pre-punk, preindustrial slap in the face for the prog-rock-laden early 70s. Anarchic and raw, Dinger's stripped down, relentless 4/4 beat is an incredible companion to Rother's searing wah-ed guitar.

⊙ **NEU! 2** (1973; Brain, reissued 2001).
The money-saving idea of recording different-speed versions of side one on the flipside probably seemed like a good idea at the time, and as artistic statements made up on the spot go, it's quite good.

⊙ **NEU! 75** (1975; Brain, reissued 2001).
One of the greatest rock albums ever, with more experimentation on "Isi", more phase on "E-Musik" and more ennui in "Leb' Wohl" than anything since Can's "Mother Sky".

Richard Fontenoy

THE NEVILLE BROTHERS

Formed New Orleans, Louisiana, 1978.

The **Neville Brothers** comprise **Art** (born 1937; keyboards/vocals), **Charles** (born 1938; saxophones), **Aaron** (born 1941; vocals/keyboards) and **Cyril** (born 1948; drums/vocals). They formed the family-named group in 1978 but had been playing in various New Orleans groups for the previous two decades. In fact, in many ways, they represent the whole spirit of New Orleans R&B sound, along with Dr. John and Allen Toussaint. Since so much of their best work was done pre-Nevillization, it's worth delving a little into the dynastic history and back catalogue.

The story begins in 1954 when a group called **The Hawketts**, featuring Art Neville on keyboards and vocals, went into a local radio station, WWEZ, and, using minimal facilities, cut a song that would make history. Its title was "Mardi Gras Mambo" and over the years it became a virtual anthem for the New Orleans carnival, constantly re-pressed and anthologized. Equally crucial, Art Neville's first brush with the record business had him hooked, and with New Orleans, the Crescent City, as base, The Hawketts set out to work around Louisiana and Mississippi.

The band made a move towards fame around 1956, when Specialty Records began an association with Art Neville that would lead to regional hits like "Cha Dooky-Doo", "Zing Zing" and "Ooh-Whee Baby". Session work, with **LITTLE RICHARD** among others, stretched Art further and he developed his intuitive musicianship, capable of 'head arrangements' and those splashes of sound that transform black vinyl

into gold discs. Then, at the decade's end, Art was called up by the Navy, and his younger brother Aaron took on vocals. He was a natural, graced with one of the purest, loveliest voices America has produced – a tremulous, ululating shiver that really came into its own on torchy romantic soul ballads. In 1960 he had his first solo hit with the Sam Cooke song "Over You", but it was seven years before he hit the big time (#2 in the US) with the aching "Tell It Like It Is" – still the most perfect match of song and singer, and still in The Nevilles' set.

Through the 1960s, Art and Aaron continued to work at Specialty, independently of each other, with Allen Toussaint producing a string of local hits. (Louisiana has a very strong regional music scene, with US pop hits often rerecorded for local tastes.) Around 1967 Art began putting together a new group called, in turn, **Art Neville And The Neville Sounds**, **The Funky Meters**, and finally just **THE METERS**, who would become one of America's greatest session teams.

After a couple of hit singles around 1969 and 1970 with dance-craze cash-ins "Sophisticated Cissy" and "Cissy Strut", and despite The Meters' succession of very funky and critically well-received albums for Reprise, brother Cyril stepped into the frame, around 1975, reinventing the band as psychedelic soulsters for NEW DIRECTIONS (1977), shortly after which they broke up (though they would periodically reunite during the 1990s, and key Meters tracks like "Big Chief" and "Voodoo" would haunt later repertoires).

The backcloth was painted and in position for a new group. In 1972 a new Indian tribe had come about in the Thirteenth Ward of the city. They were called the **Wild Tchoupitoulas** and, since The Nevilles' uncle was **George Landry** (whose Indian name was Big Chief Jolly), there was a personal connection, a family tongue and groove. The Wild Tchoupitoulas' self-titled debut (1976) was cut in Allen Toussaint's Sea-Saint studio, and distilled the essence of Mardi Gras in such enduring songs as "Brother John", the totemic "Meet De Boys On The Battlefront" and "Hey Hey (Indians Comin')". For the first time, too, the four brothers were performing together, Charles having thrown in his lot with his brothers after pursuing a sideman's career in jazz and blues.

In 1978 the group adopted the **Neville Brothers** name, signed to Capitol Records and issued a surprisingly tame debut, THE NEVILLE BROTHERS, which fell by the wayside. They were cut loose but signed to A&M for FIRE ON THE BAYOU (1981), a quantum leap featuring versions of the tried-and-tested "Fire On The Bayou", "Brother John" and "Iko Iko". NEVILLE-IZATION (1984) followed on Black Top, recorded at one of New Orleans' finest clubs, Tipitina's. Transferring the thrill to disc had hitherto proved elusive and – just as The Grateful Dead had hammered home the point with LIVE DEAD when three studio albums had left vinyl listeners cold – this was the breakthrough. It presented Aaron's greatest hit, "Tell It Like It Is", alongside

Ellington's "Caravan", the evergreen "Fever", and the brothers' own "Fear, Hate, Envy, Jealousy" and a scorching version of "Africa", pinpointing The Nevilles' skill at spinning out a syncopated groove.

Inexplicably, it failed to make much impression, and NEVILLIZATION II (1987), overdubbed to oblivion, did them no favours. At this stage The Nevilles' career was a mess but then Rhino Records stepped in with a historical anthology, TREACHEROUS (1986), a glorious celebration of the various groups of the past thirty years. Those who heard it understood and became firm fans. Still, progress was uncertain, and UPTOWN (1987) was an anaemic affair, despite guests of such stature as **Jerry Garcia**, **Keith Richards** and **Carlos Santana**. The band's association with EMI America lapsed and they fell back again on live work.

In 1989, however, the brothers re-signed to A&M and at last translated their spirit to the studio with the Daniel Lanois-produced YELLOW MOON (1989), reaching #66 in the US album charts, and a single, "With God On Our Side", milked to a peak of emotion by Aaron, charting in both the US and UK. Aaron had made a bit of a splash the previous year with a song on Hal Willner's Disney covers album, STAY AWAKE, and a new generation had rediscovered "Tell It Like It Is" from the New Orleans police corruption thriller, *The Big Easy*. "Yellow Moon" itself aired on *The Mighty Quinn* movie and, suddenly, after all those years, The Nevilles were regarded as funky and cool, Aaron's solo star continuing to climb, too, with two hit singles duetting with Linda Ronstadt – "Don't Know Much" (1989) and "All My Life" (1990) – and a solo album, WARM YOUR HEART (1991), elevating him heavenwards. Charles, meanwhile, released the jazz-flavoured CHARLES NEVILLE AND DIVERSITY (1990).

In the midst of all this solo activity The Nevilles also released BROTHER'S KEEPER (1990), a strong album which included Aaron's reading of "Bird On A Wire" (the Leonard Cohen chestnut used in the film of the same name that year). FAMILY GROOVE (1992) was less memorable, and Aaron Neville's SOULFUL CHRISTMAS (1993) is only for the most devoted. Still, by this time the group had financial security and could perhaps afford to sit back awhile, pleasing old and new fans alike with LIVE ON PLANET EARTH (1994), a live session, doing what they excelled in – whipping up a crowd, while Aaron released another sublime set, THE TATTOOED HEART (1995). 1996's MITAKUYE OYASIN OYASIN/ALL MY RELATIONS, however, was that rare beast – an excellent Nevilles studio outing, with Aaron warbling at his tremulous best on Bill Withers' "Ain't No Sunshine".

The next Nevilles product, WITH GOD ON OUR SIDE (1997), a 35-track two-CD compilation, was far from excellent: it mixed one or two soul-filled bursts of song into a collection of no-class filler emphasizing just how much mud you have to dig up to find a diamond. VALENCE STREET (2001) was more palatable, though far from essential: its most interesting moment came with "Mona Lisa" a collaborative croon with **Wyclef Jean**.

The dynasty, incidentally, has not stopped with The Neville Brothers. Several offspring are making music, the most prominent of them Aaron's son, **Ivan Neville**, who has been playing with the parent group, worked with Keith Richards and his X-Pensive Winos, and launched a solo career with IF MY ANCESTORS COULD SEE ME NOW (1988) and most recently SATURDAY MORNING MUSIC (2002).

The Neville Brothers

- **Neville-ization** (1984; Black Top/Demon).
  The live album that demonstrated the power of The Nevilles' live act on home territory.

- **Treacherous** (1986/1988; Rhino).
  Originally released as a double vinyl album, the expanded CD reissue takes the listener from The Hawketts through the Toussaint years ("Waiting At The Station" and "Wrong Number (I Am Sorry, Goodbye)" are essentials) and solo work ("Tell It Like It Is" is present and correct) through to The Neville Brothers.

- **Yellow Moon** (1989; A&M).
  The road to recovery should forever be paved with works like this! New life is breathed into songs such as Dylan's "The Ballad Of Hollis Brown" and "With God On Our Side", and Sam Cooke's "A Change Is Gonna Come". They sit well beside originals such as "My Blood", "Voo Doo" and Cyril's rap-inflected civil rights history lesson of "Sister Rosa".

Aaron Neville

- **Orchid In The Storm** (1986; Rhino).
  Originally a 12" EP, but thankfully reissued, this was one of Aaron's great outings.

- **Warm Your Heart** (1991; A&M).
  The full majesty of Aaron's voice with buffed and polished arrangements, and sparkling vocal performances of songs by John Hiatt, Randy Newman, Allen Toussaint and others. "Ave Maria" is a lone error of judgement ("Ave Maria" and rock'n'roll do not go together).

Ken Hunt

NEW FAST AUTOMATIC DAFFODILS

Formed Manchester, England, 1988.

The scene: Manchester, 1988. Three young men share a vision. A band – with **Justin Crawford** (bass), **Dolan Hewison** (guitar) and **Perry Saunders** (drums) – would get exposure on the indie scene, a modicum of recognition in the *NME*, some gigs around Manchester, and true happiness would be theirs. All that was missing was someone to sing and front the band.

Dolan dreamed one night of meeting a man who not only wore glasses and fell off his bike, but was also able to sing. And so, when **Andy Spearpoint** turned up to audition having seen an advert in the paper, wearing his specs and apologizing for his inability to stand up properly as he'd just come off his bike, jaws dropped in unison.

Andy more than lived up to expectations – his strong, spoken–word-style vocals squared up well to the others' often fast-and-furious rhythms, while his

talent as a lyricist soon became apparent. His songs were intriguing and engaging, though often obscure. The name, **New Fast Automatic Daffodils**, was filched from an experiment by Liverpool poet Adrian Henri, who crossed a car maintenance manual with Wordsworth.

After a few local gigs, percussionist **Icarus Wilson–Wright** joined the band in time to appear on their breakthrough single, "Big" (1990). With its highly infectious bass line, odd lyrics and melodica, "Big" could hardly fail to catch on. The band acquired a collection of glowing reviews and a solid live reputation – they were dubbed 'the fastest men in pop' for the speed at which they'd belt through their sets. This kind of drive set them apart from the 'Madchester' scene of the time; the FADs were too busy to hang out with scenesters.

The end of 1990 saw the release of their well-received debut album, PIGEONHOLE, but it would be two years of slow writing and heavy touring before another album was finished. BODY EXIT MIND (1992) was musically moodier and lyrically more caustic and direct than its predecessor.

Again, it was around two years before any fresh material was unleashed on the public. During this period, the FADs had become more interested in music technology, which previously had been the domain of the various remixers of their singles. Icarus spent a few months programming drum tracks, and producer Jeremy Allom, who worked on Massive Attack's BLUE LINES, was brought in to add rhythmic precision on the next LP. LOVE IT ALL came out in 1995, attended by general critical approval, which failed to have any noticeable impact on the sales figures. As usual, the band were unperturbed by this state of affairs, having developed very thick skins.

Their ideas continued to develop in different directions, with Justin working on an extracurricular project under the guise of **Only Child**; he released the excellent SATELLITES AND CONSTELLATIONS in 2000 and then SOLITAIRE in 2003.

- **Pigeonhole** (1990; Playtime Records/Play It Again Sam).
  By turns bright, choppy, danceable and mesmeric, the music pulls together all kinds of source material from traditional guitar-based music to dub, without sounding patchy.

- **Body Exit Mind** (1992; Play It Again Sam).
  This album has a much angrier feel to it than PIGEONHOLE, which has as much to do with the brooding pace of guitar and percussion as with the lyrical content.

- **Love It All** (1995; Play It Again Sam).
  Melodies aplenty, distorted drums, some fine acoustic moments, and a whole stock of great lines from Andy Spearpoint. You'll find it difficult to pick a favourite.

Maria Lamle

NEW MODEL ARMY

Formed Bradford, England, 1980.

Formed at a time when Britain was reeling under the first blows of Thatcherism, **Justin 'Slade**

The Leveller' **Sullivan** (guitars/vocals), **Stuart Morrow** (bass/guitar) and **Robb Heaton** (drums/guitar) took their name from the Thomas Fairfax/Oliver Cromwell revolutionary army and set themselves up in direct opposition to the onset of the greed culture. Their particular brand of anti-Tory folk-punk, rebel chic and concern for the environment attracted a large and fanatically loyal fan base, arguably the first wave of the crusty phenomenon that would be spurred on to new heights with The Levellers.

Their first full album, VENGEANCE (1984), was an angry, taut assault on Thatcherism in all its forms. After releasing a number of singles and scoring a #2 indie-chart hit with "The Price", they forged a highly unlikely partnership with major label EMI; the band explained the move by stating that they used the label, in effect, as a bank. The move was instrumental in obtaining them a higher profile with NO REST FOR THE WICKED (1985) and THE GHOST OF CAIN (1986), **Jason 'Moose' Harris** taking over on bass. The enhanced recording budget allowed them to produce equally impassioned but increasingly experimental records. The percussive, battle-cry-led minimalism of their debut was gradually transformed into a lusher-sounding folkiness and they enjoyed a string of twelve UK chart singles between 1985 and 1991. Despite their commercial success they never shied away from outspoken confrontation; one memorable incident saw the band running into trouble for appearing on *Top Of The Pops* wearing T-shirts sporting the slogan 'Only Stupid Bastards Use Heroin'. By now Sullivan and Heaton were considered the band's foundations, whilst various second guitarists helped fill out the live sound; amongst this number was a young **Ricky Warwick**, who eventually went on to form **The Almighty**.

Following the self-explanatory RADIO SESSIONS (1988), THUNDER AND CONSOLATION (1989) saw them finally achieve a perfect balance between the personal and the political. A passionate and emotional collection of songs, it contains everything from the all-out rage of "Stupid Questions" to the violin-driven "Vagabonds". The release of IMPURITY (1990) brought a sense of stability with the newly recruited **Nelson** eventually becoming their longest-serving bassist, whilst the live RAW MELODY MEN (1991) was as close as they could get to capturing the incandescent fervour of their concerts.

A move to Epic for 1993's THE LOVE OF HOPELESS CAUSES saw them maintain the excellence of their studio efforts – if anything it brought out a more considered, but no less complex, set of songs. As a band always concerned with the quality of their material, the collection B-SIDES AND ABANDONED TRACKS (1994) brought together material every bit as intense and fiery as the better-known album tracks, and proved that for them there really were no half-measures when it came to songwriting.

Following the release of the B-SIDES compilation the band seemed to disappear from sight for such a long period that people assumed they had split. Appearing only occasionally to perform the odd gig, they reappeared with STRANGE BROTHERHOOD (1998) just to prove that they weren't through with the business of rebellion. Though lacking the instantaneous energy of earlier releases it showed that they had lost none of the old charm when it came to poignant lyrics and rousing choruses.

2000 saw the release of EIGHT, with a line-up that consisted of Sullivan and Nelson, with the addition of **Michael Dean** (drums), **Dean White** (keys) and **Dave Blomberg** (guitar). The set was far more stripped back, leaner sounding than older releases, and all the better for it. Since then NMA's output has consisted of collections and twentieth anniversary live offerings, though Sullivan did put in an appearance with a solo album, NAVIGATING BY THE STARS, in 2003; he also continues to work with **Joolz** and **Rev Hammer** as **Red Sky Coven**, peddling a quirky combination of live music, stories and jokes.

⊙ **Raw Melody Men** (1991; EMI).
This live album gives a decent impression of the intensity and passion of New Model Army in their element.

⊙ **B-Sides And Abandoned Tracks** (1994; reissued 1998; EMI).
Most groups use up second-division material to back their singles. What we have here is a compilation of some truly stunning songs that would not be out of place on any of their albums.

⊙ **Strange Brotherhood** (1998; Eagle Records).
A little more laid-back than usual, this is nevertheless a damn fine collection for the dedicated urban warrior.

Essi Berelian

NEW ORDER

Formed Manchester, England, 1980.

"I've always wanted to be a drum machine." Stephen Morris

Formed by the surviving members of **JOY DIVISION**, after the death of Ian Curtis in 1980, **New Order** initially comprised **Bernard Sumner** (who took over on vocals, and continued on guitar), **Peter Hook** (bass), **Stephen Morris** (drums) and an additional member – Morris's girlfriend, **Gillian Gilbert** (keyboards).

At the time, many felt that Curtis's death meant the end of the road for the group. Few could have predicted that New Order would become one of the seminal groups of the 80s, making a series of albums that would compare well with anything Joy Division had produced, and embracing club culture a good ten years before most of their contemporaries.

The initial signs, however, were inauspicious. Early singles were credited to Joy Division, and were generally seen as pale copies of previous glories, as was the group's first LP, MOVEMENT (1981). However, inspired by groups like Kraftwerk, and the electro music that they had heard in New York's clubs, New Order began to experiment with newly

TV and a cuppa – the homely New Order, from left: Bernard Sumner, Gillian Gilbert, Stephen Morris and Peter Hook

available computer technology, adding synthesizers and sequencers to their sound on minor hits like "Temptation" and "Everything's Gone Green". Then came the breakthrough, "Blue Monday," which became the best-selling 12" single of all time. Its rhythm track had been written while trying to fathom out the workings of a new drum machine, but the cutting-edge dance beats, subtle melody and introspective vocals attracted a wide cross-section of fans – more, certainly, than Sumner's description of their audience as 'spotty students and football hooligans'.

The modernist approach of New Order extended to their record sleeves. "Blue Monday" was packaged like a computer disk, a futuristic item for 1982, and in general very little, if any, information was given on New Order packaging, giving the record buyer the thrill of buying something that was impenetrable to all but the most devoted. The idea of New Order being a band apart was fuelled by their refusal to grant interviews (they didn't want to talk about Curtis) or play encores (they preferred to play all of their somewhat erratic set in one go).

The accusations of fascism that had dogged Joy Division continued to haunt New Order: their name was taken somewhat naively by manager Rob Gretton from Pol Pot's murderous Cambodian Army of Liberation; the bold simplicity of their sleeves had fascistic undertones; and, perhaps most damaging of all, footage of the Holocaust (from an episode of the TV series, *The World At War*) was projected at the Hacienda nightclub they co-owned with their record label, Factory. Some were satisfied by Sumner's

protests that he was so politically unaware he didn't even know what 'right wing' and 'left wing' meant.

POWER, CORRUPTION AND LIES (1983), in effect the first proper New Order LP, was a qualified success, though sales were hindered by the band's refusal to release any singles from the album, a policy encouraged by Factory. The decision to include "505", an early demo of "Blue Monday", instead of the track itself, also hurt sales and weakened the LP. However, the group did record a single, "Confusion", with respected hip-hop producer Arthur Baker (well known now, but unheard of then). LOW LIFE (1985) refined and extended their formula, containing aggressive rock alongside relentless dance rhythms. It received ecstatic reviews, and became a blueprint for later rock/dance LPs by groups like U2 and Primal Scream.

The follow-up, BROTHERHOOD (1986), broke no new ground, although it contained some good songs, including one of their finest singles to date, "Bizarre Love Triangle", though this failed to break the Top 40. Tensions flared, with Sumner unhappy with their more rock-orientated direction. Stephen Hague, fresh from working with the Pet Shop Boys, produced "True Faith", a seamless techno-pop hit which accompanied a singles collection, and now Hook expressed his unhappiness at this more commercial approach. They released another single, and a remix of "Blue Monday", before vanishing amid internal strife and rumours that their already prodigious drug use had got out of hand during a US tour.

The group returned with TECHNIQUE (1989), at a time when dance music was gaining credibility. Part

of the album was recorded in Ibiza, when the island was the centre of a new ecstasy-fuelled wave of club culture, and the band were inspired by the house music that they'd heard there. It was far more dance-orientated than previous work and received rave notices. A one-off single, "World In Motion", followed, and was fully in keeping with the ambience of drug-inspired exuberance, although, bizarrely, it was written as the England World Cup song. It was co-written by comedian Keith Allen, as Sumner was unable to think of anything to say on the subject, and featured rapping by Liverpool and England star John Barnes. Perhaps unsurprisingly, it went to #1.

In the early 90s the group dispersed to various solo projects. Hook recorded as **Revenge** to spectacular critical and commercial indifference. Sumner collaborated with **Johnny Marr** and the Pet Shop Boys as **Electronic**, netting a string of minor hits and a couple of albums, most recently the much-praised RAISE THE PRESSURE. Gilbert and Morris contined their intermittent soundtrack work – including the theme to *America's Most Wanted* – and recorded as **The Other Two**, although their commercial prospects were scuppered when the release of their enjoyable THE OTHER TWO AND YOU (1993) was held up for two years when Factory went bust.

New Order – who famously never had a contract with Factory – resurfaced before long with REPUBLIC (1993), the album they had been making during the course of Factory's demise. It was released on London Records, with attendant fanfare, and netted four hit singles. However, tensions surfaced again in the group interviews to promote the record, and when they eventually made their last appearance at the Reading Festival it was clear that both rock thrills and cutting-edge dance music were to be found elsewhere. A 1994 'best of' collection reinforced their popularity, but the group did nothing at all to promote it – and rumours of a split were neither confirmed nor denied.

Morris and Gilbert got married, Hook played in a house band for his then-wife Caroline's comedy show, *Mrs Merton*, and Sumner cheerily extolled the

virtues of the antidepressant Prozac, prior to the release of yet another remix LP, (THE REST OF) NEW ORDER (1995). Though New Order still appeared to be in a state of limbo, Hook was busy with another new band, **Monaco**, while Sumner worked on a second Electronic album.

In 2000 a taste of fresh New Order material appeared in the form of "Brutal" on the soundtrack to the movie *The Beach*. The group's first album proper in over eight years, GET READY, followed in the Autumn of 2001, and it was a stormer.

◉ **Low Life** (1985; London).
An epic album in every sense of the word, with in-your-face production, and detours into both ambient and country and western. Despite these stylistic excursions, however, it sounds more of a piece than its predecessors, and is essential listening for anyone with even a passing interest in the group.

◉ **Technique** (1989; London).
A seamless blend of house rhythms and fierce group playing, together with Sumner's melancholy musings on life and love, this album has a depth that many other 'Madchester' acts just didn't possess. A fun record, too, not least for the cod-Barry White monologues, and bleating sheep samples of "Fine Time".

◉ **Republic** (1993; London).
Glossy and polished, but lacking the tensions that made LOW LIFE and TECHNIQUE so thrilling. Yet singles like "Regret" and "World" are as good as anything the group have ever done.

◉ **The Best Of New Order** (1994; London).
Concentrating on late-period New Order and unnecessarily remixed, but it does include the otherwise unavailable "World In Motion", "Touched By The Hand Of God" and the remix of "1963".

◉ **Get Ready** (2001; London).
A stunning return to form after a long absence.

Jonathan Holden

THE NEW YORK DOLLS

Formed New York, 1971; disbanded 1976.

"The Dolls were like a gang who turned over to instruments instead of guns." Jerry Nolan

Fronted by nightmare Mick'n'Keith clones **DAVID JOHANSEN** (vocals) and **JOHNNY THUNDERS** (guitar), **The New York Dolls** took the glitter and glam of the early 70s to its extreme. Like a head-on collision between The Stones and The Shangri-Las on a road out of Iggy Pop's Detroit, The Dolls produced a mangled mess of blues, doo-wop and sonic excess.

The group came together when Thunders asked Johansen to join the remnants of his band Actress, then comprising **Sylvain Sylvain** (guitar), **Billy Murcia** (drums) and **Arthur 'Killer' Kane** (bass). They rehearsed through the winter of 1971 in Rusty Beanie's Cycle Shop, where they would be locked in overnight so that the owner could be sure they wouldn't make off with any of his stock. By the summer of 1972 the band had started playing out, securing a residency at the less than salubrious Mercer

Arts Center in SoHo. It didn't take long for the hipsters of New York to latch on to their bizarre, arrogant image and hybrid rock'n'roll rumble.

With only a few demos recorded, the band were invited to support The Faces on a UK tour. After playing to 13,000 people at Wembley, disaster struck. Billy Murcia drowned in the bath he'd been placed in to recover after passing out drunk. Back in New York the group recruited **Jerry Nolan** as their new drummer and got ready to start recording their debut LP, after signing with Mercury. Recorded and mixed in under a week, THE NEW YORK DOLLS (1973) contained such proto-punk classics as "Trash", "Jet Boy" and "Looking For A Kiss", but, though it received much critical praise, the band were unhappy with the sound that produceer Todd Rundgren had given them. Worse disagreements were soon to follow.

For TOO MUCH TOO SOON (1974), Johansen secured the services of Shangri-Las' producer Shadow Morton (his original choice for the debut LP), much to the annoyance of Thunders, who wanted to produce it himself. Morton completely failed to understand The Dolls' music, and what on paper appeared to be a fascinating combination resulted in comprehensive failure. After the album's poor reception the band began to fall apart. Thunders and Johansen argued constantly and Kane's descent into alcoholism meant that he was only capable of miming his bass parts at live shows.

Enter **MALCOLM MCLAREN**, who arrived as the band's manager in late 1974, so desperate to salvage something from the disintegrating Dolls that he even took on a job as a window cleaner to help fund Kane's detox bill. McLaren devised a new look for The Dolls with the help of his partner Vivienne Westwood. The band started appearing in red patent leather on a stage, draped in Russian and Chinese flags. But while McLaren hoped that this commie roadshow would outrage patriotic Americans and rejuvenate The Dolls with an injection of controversy, all that his manipulations succeeded in doing was to split the band. Thunders left midway through

a tour of Florida in 1975, returning to New York with Nolan and a growing heroin addiction to put together the **HEARTBREAKERS**.

After ejecting Kane, Johansen and Sylvain dragged a last version of The Dolls through a short tour of Japan, finally laying the group to rest in December 1976.

⊙ **The New York Dolls** (1973; Mercury).
Delicious, sneering rock'n'drawl which, despite the poor production that dogged Thunders throughout his career, ranks as one of the truly great rock'n'roll debuts. Just looking at the sleeve makes you wonder what planet these people beamed down from. A primitive blueprint for punk rock.

⊙ **Human Being (Live)** (1982; Clay Records; reissued 1998; Receiver Records).
Recorded live in Vancouver after TOO MUCH TOO SOON, it shows just what a great bunch of entertainers the boys could be, provided someone pointed them towards the stage. Jerry Nolan and David Johansen shine, Thunders and Sylvain get extra points for trying, but Kane will have to stay behind after class.

⊙ **Mercer Street Sessions** (1990; ROIR).
The demos that landed them the Faces tour. Essential for the committed but, objectively, not the best rock album ever.

⊙ **Rock'N'Roll** (1994; Mercury).
Compilation of the best tracks from the two studio albums and some unreleased oddities. As near essential as any rock CD can be.

Kirk Lake

RANDY NEWMAN

Born New Orleans, November 28, 1943.

During the 1970s heyday of confessional singer-songwriters, **Randy Newman** established a niche for himself with deeply ironic tales of racists, slave traders and all-American perversity. A bracing corrective to the introspective tweeness of the sensitive superstars of the time, Newman mixed his lyrics with a sophisticated grasp of traditional American pop music and a vocal style once described as Jewish blues.

Born in New Orleans and raised in LA, Randy came from a music family; his uncle, Alfred Newman, was an Oscar-winning Hollywood composer. Randy, along with everyone else his age, preferred rock'n'roll, specifically Fats Domino. He began writing songs professionally at 16, emulating Brill Building writers such as Carole King and Gerry Goffin with some success. "I Think It's Gonna Rain Today" was recorded by Judy Collins in 1966 and Alan Price had a UK hit in 1967 with "Simon Smith And His Amazing Dancing Bear".

His first album, RANDY NEWMAN (1968), was overproduced and a bit cloying, and he had yet to find the sly vocal style of later records, but the songs were quirky. Probably the best known is "Davy The Fat Boy", an outrageous bit of cruelty sung in the voice of 'Davy's only friend', who keeps a deathbed promise to the boy's parents to take care of him – then puts him in a freak show. Clearly any hopes

Newman had for mass commercial acceptance were delusional.

The follow-up 12 SONGS (1970) was an immeasurable improvement. The arrangements and orchestrations were more muted and subtle, while guitarist **RY COODER** added real bite to the sound. The new songs had a blues edge perfectly suited to Newman's deadpan delivery: "Suzanne" was a twisted love song about a potential molester; "My Old Kentucky Home" described, with admirable nonchalance, a Southern family of alcoholic derangement; Three Dog Night's cover of "Mama Told Me Not To Come" went to #1 later that year.

With his wife and family and big house in southern California, Newman acquired the title of King Of The Suburban Blues Singers. Life may have been good but Newman's songs were as dark and complex as ever. His next album, SAIL AWAY (1972), was his most fully realized work yet. The title track's seductive melody and majestic orchestration masked a lyric sung in the voice of a slave trader luring Africans on to a ship bound for America. "You Can Leave Your Hat On", later a hit for Joe Cocker, was a sleazy love song set in a low-rent motel room. SAIL AWAY was only slightly more successful than 12 SONGS, but Newman was getting lavish praise from the critics, and after three albums had secured a small but loyal audience.

Newman's next release, GOOD OLD BOYS (1974), was an evocative collection of songs about the American South. Once again Newman created characters to give voice to some disturbing thoughts: "Rednecks" was a racist's attack on Northern liberals, "A Wedding In Cherokee County" was about a backwoods farmer on his wedding day contemplating his hateful bride and his impotence. But best of all was "Louisiana 1927", a beautiful and touching song about the effects of a massive flood on poor Southern farmers.

Newman finally cracked the charts with GOOD OLD BOYS, but his next album, three years later, would be his first proper hit. LITTLE CRIMINALS (1977) was his weakest record in almost every way but contained a novelty hit of dubious humour – "Short People" with its refrain 'short people got no reason to live'. BORN AGAIN (1979) was slightly better, but where Newman was once ironic and subtle he was now more sarcastic and smug. The music too was becoming generic West Coast easy listening. TROUBLE IN PARADISE (1983) was loosely based on the concept of the less-than-sunny reality behind Cape Town, Miami and Los Angeles. "I Love L.A." was improbably adopted as the city's theme song despite its line about the town's attractions including the sight of bums throwing up in the street.

The family business of film soundtracks has not been neglected by Newman. He contributed songs to *Performance* (1970) and wrote scores for *Ragtime* (1979) and *The Natural* (1984). He co-wrote the script and several songs for the comedy western *Three Amigos* in 1986, where he made a memorable screen debut as 'The Singing Bush' in the inevitable campfire scene. Most recently he worked on songs for *Monsters Inc.*, winning an Oscar in the process.

In 1988 he made his best album since GOOD OLD BOYS. Co-produced with Dire Straits' **Mark Knopfler**, LAND OF DREAMS featured for the first time Newman singing as himself instead of in character. "Dixie Flyer" and "New Orleans Wins The War" were autobiographical songs about growing up in the South.

Newman then concentrated on film and TV work, while hatching up a project of vast ambition – a rock opera treatment of Goethe's FAUST. This emerged on disc in 1995, replete with choirs and orchestra, and featuring **James Taylor** as God, **Don Henley** as Faust and **Elton John** as a bitter Englishman. Newman of course played the Devil – for the Devil always has the best songs. A whole lot better than Lloyd Webber, too, come to that. Still, one suspects Newman's following would exchange it all for another side of SAIL AWAY. Check out the four-CD box retrospective released in 1998 – GUILTY: 30 YEARS OF RANDY NEWMAN – and 1999's studio set BAD LOVE.

⊙ **Lonely At The Top** (1989; Warners).
22 tracks spanning the whole career. This is the essential introduction to a true pop master, California's own Gershwin.

Len Lauk

NICO

Born Cologne, Germany, October 16, 1938; died July 18, 1988.

Born to a German mother and a father who had his marriage annulled before his daughter was born, Christa **Päffgen** spent much of her youth modelling in Paris where – adopting the name **Nico** – she socialized with Hemingway, Sartre, and Fellini, who provided her with a walk-on role in *La Dolce Vita*. Her statuesque beauty gained her work as a *Vogue* cover girl, and it was at this time that she met Alain Delon, the father of her son and the man she always referred to as 'husband'.

In 1965 Nico moved to England and, having secured a deal with Immediate (the label run by The Stones' manager Andrew Loog Oldham), released "I'm Not Saying", a song phrased in a Marianne Faithfull mode. It failed to make any impact. Shortly after this, she took the advice of a record executive who predicted that girl-fronted bands would be the next big thing, and relocated to New York in search of musical backing.

During her stay at the low-rent bohemian sanctuary, the Chelsea Hotel, she was introduced to Andy Warhol. Nico became one of Warhol's 'Superstars' and appeared in his long non-film, *Chelsea Girls*. While the film was in production, Warhol was considering the future of his rock protégés, **THE VELVET UNDERGROUND**, and came to the conclusion that it would be to everyone's benefit if the band were to be augmented by the European chanteuse, thus satisfying Nico's desire to be in a band and providing **LOU REED** with a charismatic foil. She appeared in The Velvets' multimedia presentation, *Uptight*, in February 1966, and on the ensuing classic VELVET UNDERGROUND & NICO, but the album did not surface until a year later, by which time Nico had been ousted.

During 1966–67 Nico played a series of gigs at New York's Dome, where she was introduced to Jackson Browne. The budding songwriter presented her with a selection of songs, which were to augment The Velvets' songs in her repertoire and become the basis of her first LP, CHELSEA GIRL (1968), which was completed with assistance from Reed and **JOHN CALE**.

During 1967's Summer of Love Nico developed an interest in psychedelic drugs and, as she turned her attention to her second album, began experimenting with LSD. She made drug-fuelled trips into the California desert with her lover, Jim Morrison, under whose influence she moved to LA to produce THE MARBLE INDEX (1969). Nico hoped that this would be the album to establish her as a singer-songwriter, but critics found her desolate soundscapes inaccessible and, without a manager to promote her as a touring performer, she went into retreat.

The 70s proved to be a period of transition for Nico, who enjoyed the support of Patti Smith, but was unable to cope with punk's pandemonium. In 1981 she teamed up with **Alan Wise**, who was able to provide her with enough live work to make her final years the most productive. Over a seven-year period, she played more than one thousand concerts, but much of the financial reward went on feeding her heroin habit and only two studio albums were released.

Wise found his charge a home in the north of England and hired musicians from the 'Manchester Mafia' to back her up on tours with John Cooper Clarke and solo. Towards the end, she talked of relinquishing her role as 'Nico' and returning to acting as 'Christa', but such dreams were never realized. During a holiday in Ibiza with her son she was found lying at

the roadside by her overturned bicycle, in a dazed state. Lack of treatment for what was later identified as a cerebral haemorrhage resulted in her tragic death.

Since her death, Nico has moved in high circles – having been elevated to the status of 'dead rock'n'roll junkie' – and there's a growing interest in the work she left behind. NICO-ICON (1997) has no connection, and is no comparison, with the excellent film of the same name.

John Cale worked on four of Nico's solo albums and declared in his autobiography that the final versions of MARBLE INDEX, DESERTSHORE (1971) and CAMERA OBSCURA (1985) are 'as complex and unique today as the day they were released'. Inspired by their days of fighting, laughing and crying in the studio, and with a deep respect for her craft, Cale joined forces with the Scapino Company to stage a ballet to Nico's memory in 1998.

⊙ **Chelsea Girl** (1968; Polydor).
The most complete of all Nico's work, her Teutonic voice cutting a clean swath through the folksy strings.

⊙ **Behind The Iron Curtain** (1986; Castle).
Almost every aspect of the singular splendour that Nico's live work had to offer is sampled here. Backed by James Young's band, Nico presents interpretations of songs by Lou Reed, her 'blood brother' (Jim Morrison) and the jazz standard "My Funny Valentine", which betrays a certain humour beneath the impassive vocal. Contrary to the sleeve notes, it was recorded in Rotterdam, by the way.

Stephen Boyd

THE NIGHTINGALES

Formed Birmingham, England, 1980;
disbanded 1986.

Singer and lyricist **Robert Lloyd** formed **The Nightingales** out of the ashes of punk band The Prefects, a collective whose only release, "Going Through The Motions", was culled from a John Peel radio session. Peel's patronage continued to serve Lloyd well through The Nightingales' career, as they were to record for his show on seven occasions before the DJ wrote the sleeve notes for their WHAT A SCREAM retrospective in 1991. Reviews were quick to make comparisons with fellow Peel favourites The Fall, but, while The Nightingales were kindred spirits and Lloyd's lyrical maelstrom rivalled Mark E. Smith's spew of ideas, the group's unfashionable, clanking twin-guitar rock'n'roll made them something like the Beefheart of their age to The Fall's Velvet Underground.

Unfortunately, by the time their Rough Trade debut "Idiot Strength" (1980) had hit the racks, the line-up which recorded it, with **Joe Crow** on guitar and **Eamonn Duffy** on bass, was already collapsing, leaving Lloyd and Prefects mainstay **Paul Apperley** (drums) to push on. The single was an excellent, if straightforward, pop song, but it bore little relation to all that would follow. Before the USE YOUR LOAF EP appeared on Cherry Red the next year, The Nightingales had installed a two-guitar attack that would endure for most of their career. **Nick Beales**

and **Andy Lloyd** (no relation to Robert) swapped psychotic repetitive riffs and lead lines to great effect, racing around the stage during the band's live shows, while Robert squinted out through trademark NHS spectacles and danced in his own ungainly style.

With **Steve Hawkins** on bass, this line-up recorded the PIGS ON PURPOSE LP, a summation of their live set, but it was let down by a flat production that didn't do justice to the duelling guitar thrust. A self-titled EP culled from a Peel session was more representative, and found Robert Lloyd on top form.

A sharper follow-up album, HYSTERICS, and subsequent singles showed The Nightingales' sound branching out, with use of keyboards here, a banjo there, a barely-in-control slide guitar somewhere else. Perennial live favourite "The Crunch" was rerecorded for an EP, and was a substantial improvement on the lacklustre PIGS version. During this period, **John Nester** briefly replaced Hawkins, but he too soon left, and Nick Beales also moved on, forming Pig Bros. Longtime fan and multi-instrumentalist **Pete 'Tank' Byrchmore** joined the group, chiefly on guitar and keyboards, and **Howard Jenner** took over on bass.

These changes ushered in a less jarring, almost radio-friendly Nightingales, evident after the first fruit of the new line-up, a repetitive rumble called "It's A Cracker". However, Andy Lloyd and Paul Apperley each made their final bows on the WHAT A CARRY ON EP, the lead track of which was a perky tune that boasted an eyebrow-raising dub version to boot. Robert Lloyd now drafted in **Ron Collins** on drums and **Maria Smith** on violin, adding an extra dimension to what proved to be the final line-up. After IN THE GOOD OLD COUNTRY WAY (1986) – easily their most polished work – Lloyd's involvement in his own Vindaloo record label took over his time, alongside managing the briefly successful We've Got A Fuzzbox And We're Gonna Use It. After a fleeting appearance with Lloyd's new protégées on *Top Of The Pops*, The Nightingales split.

With the continued enthusiasm of John Peel to back him up, Robert Lloyd embarked on a short solo career with Virgin, before the label realized he wouldn't fit into any marketing bracket.

⊙ **Pissed & Potless – The Best Of...** (2001; Cherry Red).
This serviceable anthology is currently the best way into The Nightingales.

James Robert

NINE INCH NAILS

Formed Cleveland, Ohio, 1988.

"The goal was to create a record that, ultimately, you'll like – but probably not the first time you hear it." Trent Reznor

Nine Inch Nails is essentially a one-man band – masterminded by **Trent Reznor**, whose journeys into despair and destruction have been charted by the band's hi-tech, raw-edged aural assaults.

A classically trained pianist, Reznor started his musical working life in a recording studio in Cleveland, as a general assistant, which basically amounted to making the coffee. At the age of 23 he forged the foundations of what was to become Nine Inch Nails, writing the traumatized and haunting songs that emerged on PRETTY HATE MACHINE (1989), the album that inaugurated industrial music's trek to the mainstream. Although industrial music had its roots as far back as the late 70s and was sustained throughout the 80s by bands such as Ministry, it wasn't until the early 90s that the genre took off as a commercial proposition, thanks in part to MTV's repeated showing of the video for "Head Like A Hole", the opening track from PRETTY HATE, which was released as a single in 1991.

1992 saw the release of an EP, BROKEN, produced by Flood, better known for his work with British pop-rock band Depeche Mode. A stronger piece of work than the album, BROKEN was also much more tormented and painful. Reznor generated controversy with the film that accompanied the track "Happiness In Slavery": shot in black and white, it featured performance artist and 'supermasochist' Bob Flanagan being tortured by a machine – a scene that ran foul of the British film censors. 1992 also saw the release of the FIXED EP, a remix of BROKEN by Reznor, J. G. Thirwell and Butch Vig, among others. The year also saw Reznor appearing in the line-ups of other industrial bands such as **Pigface** and **REVOLTING COCKS**, headed by the **MINISTRY** pair of **Al Jourgensen** and **Paul Barker**.

In 1993 Nine Inch Nails expanded into a full band for a live tour and recorded a cover of Joy Division's "Dead Souls" for the soundtrack to the Brandon Lee film, *The Crow*. Bigger things were just round the corner, for in 1994 Oliver Stone commissioned Reznor to work on the soundtrack for *Natural Born Killers*. The resultant album featured two Nine Inch Nails songs – "A Warm Place" and a remix of PRETTY HATE's "Something I Can Never Have" – alongside tracks from Lard, Rage Against The Machine and Leonard Cohen.

The same year also saw the release of the second Nine Inch Nails album, THE DOWNWARD SPIRAL, recorded in the LA house where Charles Manson and his mob murdered Sharon Tate and her guests. Journalists accused Reznor of pulling a ghoulish stunt, but Reznor denied knowing the house's history until work had already commenced – and the publicity did no harm to an album that was a smash on both sides of the Atlantic, backed up by powerful singles such as the violent "March Of The Pigs" and the seductive "Closer". In August, the year peaked for the band with a set at Woodstock 2, broadcast live on American TV.

A follow-up extended EP titled FURTHER DOWN THE SPIRAL was released in 1995, consisting of remixes of various tracks from THE DOWNWARD SPIRAL, and the band thrust themselves further into the limelight by landing the support slot on David Bowie's US tour – on which Bowie accompanied Reznor for the Nails' cover of his own "Scary Monsters" and for the Nails' "Hurt" and "Reptile". A series of EPs, such as 1997's PERFECT DRUG remixes, finally ended with FISTED (1999) – a UK-only box set (comprising two CDs of MARCH OF THE PIGS, the CLOSER 1 & 2 discs and FIXED).

The next instalment came with THE FRAGILE (1999), an epic collection of big production and overblown theatrics. Whether Reznor continues to move on up remains to be seen.

⊙ **Pretty Hate Machine** (1989; TVT/Island).
A stunning catalogue of anguish and despair. Check out "Head Like A Hole" and "Something I Can Never Have" – the latter is the ultimate 'I've just been dumped' track.

⊙ **The Downward Spiral** (1994; TVT/Interscope/Island).
A near-perfect album that completely immerses you in its misery then spits you back out into reality at the end.

Richard Allan

NIRVANA (UK)

Formed London, 1965; disbanded 1972.

There was a **Nirvana** years before Cobain, as he found to his cost when they resurfaced through their lawyers. Still, that's hardly the best way to remember the 60s group. Formed by songwriting partners **Patrick Campbell-Lyons** (vocals/guitar) and **Alex Spyropoulos** (piano), who came together from Dublin and Athens respectively, with **Ray Singer** (guitar), **Brian Henderson** (bass) and two classical musicians – **Sylvia Schuster** (cello) and **Michael Coe** (viola/French horn).

They secured a contract with Island Records, who were helping to create a market for psychedelia with groups like Traffic and Spooky Tooth. Their first single, "Tiny Goddess" (1967), emphasized their romantic approach but failed to chart; its follow-up, "Pentecost Hotel" (1967), was a paean of devotion to Island and featured the shimmering string sound and ethereal vocal style characteristic of their work.

Nirvana's debut album, THE STORY OF SIMON SIMOPATH (1967), was conceived as a science fiction song-cycle, and was, it seems, rock's earliest concept album. Yet the charm of their music did not capture the imagination of the British record-buying public and even their one acknowledged classic, "Rainbow Chaser" (1968), could only reach #34 in the UK chart. However, the record was #1 in several European countries, prompting an infamous appearance on French TV with Salvador Dali, who splattered the sextet with paint, a good enough validation of their credentials as a psychedelic combo.

By the end of 1968 the group was pared down to the original duo, who now used a variety of session musicians for their work. Their second album, ALL OF US (1968), moved towards a heavier sound, while

retaining the earlier chamber-music approach. Another album, BLACK FLOWER, was held back from release by Island boss Chris Blackwell and sold back to the duo, who remixed it as NIRVANA – TO MARKOS III (1969). Unfortunately, the US label that was to release it went bust, and it didn't hit the stores until 1994, by which time, of course, they weren't the Nirvana people knew.

Dispirited, the duo split. Campbell-Lyons released a solo album under the Nirvana name, LOCAL ANAESTHETIC (1971), on the fledgling Vertigo label, for whom he later worked as a producer and A&R man. Spyropoulos became a recluse but still continued to write. The two resumed collaborating in the 1980s, producing a score for a musical entitled *Blood*, which still awaits release.

⊙ **Travelling On A Cloud** (1992; Island).
A collection of early material, featuring "Rainbow Chaser".

Robert Murray

NIRVANA

Formed Aberdeen, Washington, 1986; disbanded 1994.

"All in all, we sound like The Knack and the Bay City Rollers being molested by Black Flag and Black Sabbath." Kurt Cobain

Like nearly every other musical icon from Elvis to James Brown to John Lennon to Michael Jackson to Madonna, **Kurt Cobain** had a psyche that was too big for one body. He was a passionate fan, but hated fame; he wrote and sang songs about male murderers, but identified with their female victims; he endlessly baited his audience, but became the symbol of an age. While this tortured universality enabled **Nirvana** to break through the corporate stagnation of American rock, it also, ultimately, killed him.

Kurt Cobain unplugged

The embryonic Nirvana formed in late 1986, in the trailer-park, limbo-hell of Aberdeen, eight miles from Seattle. Comprising Cobain (guitars/vocals) and **Chris Novoselic** (bass), they went through a succession of drummers before finding a suitable hard-hitter in **Chad Channing**. Encapsulating the rage and alienation of Seattle's youth, they rapidly became an act to watch out for. Novoselic, a wild and lanky player, had a penchant for hurling his bass around stage, while Cobain developed a taste for trashing equipment in true nihilistic style. Together they churned up a heavy, thrumming, pop sludge that took in influences as diverse as Aerosmith and the Butthole Surfers.

Having gained the interest of the hip Seattle label Sub Pop, they recorded their first single in June 1988. "Love Buzz" (a sonically bastardized Shocking Blue cover version) was the epitome of the grunge sound: thick and claustrophobic with stabs of near-smothered melody. BLEACH (1989) followed soon after and cost a mere $606 to record. As the band were broke at the time, the money was coughed up by new member **Jason Everman** (guitars). Far from a perfect debut, BLEACH showed the band trying hard to balance their influences against their label's hipness. Cobain's lyrics were thrown together quickly, but his vocal style and phrasing turned the minimal verses into catchy hooks. "About A Girl" was unashamedly melodious and acted as a lighter contrast to the

spartan genius of "School" or the leaden crush of "Blew".

A full US tour allowed the band to hone their live technique: if it was a great gig they would destroy their equipment through sheer euphoria; if it was a poor gig they would destroy it in frustration. As few gigs fell into the ordinary category, they spent a lot of time making repairs. About this time, tensions were growing with Everman, whose overt metallist tendencies grated with the others, and he departed soon after.

Down to a three-piece they toured with Tad after the release of the BLEW EP (1989). Conditions on their European tour were abysmal, with both bands crammed into a minuscule tour bus – all 6'7" of Novoselic and 300-plus pounds of Tad Doyle. Never having experienced total good health, Cobain's already crippling stomach problems got worse and he retreated behind a wall of sleep. Rome proved to be their nadir when a paranoid Cobain suffered a near-breakdown on stage.

Over the next few months their bad luck with drummers continued; Channing left and his replacement **Dan Peters** lasted exactly one gig (although he was involved with writing the bass-heavy "Sliver"). At the time **Dave Grohl** was a member of explosive hardcore band Scream. His power and precision was so impressive that it became obvious they had found the vital third member they had been searching for. With their fan base growing, Cobain was confident that their next record would be a milestone production. They finally settled on Geffen for a deal, but during the grey depressing winter of 1990 Cobain started his self-destructive heroin habit.

With the release of NEVERMIND (1991), it became clear that records would soon be classified as pre- or post-Nirvana. The songs were superb: "Smells Like Teen Spirit" bizarrely owed more to Boston's "More Than A Feeling" than to any alternative mentors, while "In Bloom", "Lithium" and "Come As You Are" were all instantly memorable. The acoustic "Polly" and the confessional whisperings of "Something In The Way" complemented the intensity of "Breed" and "Territorial Pissings". Andy Wallace's mixing rendered their previously plodding sound into something glistening and sleek.

Nirvana, and particularly Cobain, had unwittingly filled a musical gulf. They took a hard-headed, punk-influenced stance and fused it to a more mainstream, hard-rock sound. Somewhere in this mix, Cobain was voicing the emptiness felt by the youth of 90s America. The media would soon coin a catch-all phrase to capture this phenomenon: 'Generation X'.

Suddenly it was not just alternative kids who were tuning in, but everyone, including those they positively despised: jocks, misogynistic metalheads, racist, homophobic rednecks. Nirvana were appalled by their broad appeal, and none of their new-found audience seemed to appreciate the degree of hate they inspired in their new idols. Their success drove them to extremes of obnoxiousness. They felt indestructible, and tried to infuriate and alienate their audiences by being as offensive as possible: Cobain would wear dresses, they would kiss each other on stage, equipment was destroyed even before sets were finished.

In 1992, amid rumours of the band's self-destruction through heroin and health problems, Nirvana turned in a fevered performance at the Reading Rock Festival. Cobain turned the rumours inside out by arriving on stage dressed in a white hospital gown, pushed in a wheelchair. By the end of the set, the stage was a no-man's land of howling feedback and splintered fragments of equipment. Towards the end of the year INCESTICIDE (1992) was released and drew together earlier material previously available only on rare releases and bootlegs. A similar and very-hard-to-find release, HOARMOANING (1992), was prepared for the Japanese market.

The studio follow-up to NEVERMIND, IN UTERO (1993), was recorded by Steve Albini, who was famed for his raw, honest approach to production. Geffen hated the result because it lacked the metallic polish of its predecessor. Although melodies were still in evidence, they were buried under a ragged, thicker sound – a blend of BLEACH's smothering bludgeon and NEVERMIND's diamond-hard swirl of guitars.

The subsequent tour saw **Pat Smear** (guitar), of seminal punksters the **GERMS**, join the band to fill out their live sound. However, the European leg of the tour nearly brought tragedy. Cobain had managed to give the impression of control, but in March 1994 he almost ended his own life in Rome through a toxic cocktail of depressants and alcohol. Back home in Washington, Cobain committed suicide in April, leaving behind him an air of disbelief and miserable confusion. His songwriting and performing genius was commemorated on the UNPLUGGED IN NEW YORK (1994) session, recorded in late 1993.

From the remains of Nirvana, Dave Grohl was the first member to produce any new music: he formed **FOO FIGHTERS**, for which he recruited Pat Smear. Meanwhile, after a protracted break from the scene, Noveselic returned in 1996 with a new band, **Sweet 75**.

The UNPLUGGED set released in 94 showed the band at its quietest. The 1996 FROM THE MUDDY BANKS OF THE WISHKAH set, on the other hand, should come boxed with ear-protectors. This is the Nirvana that swept the world: a raw, angry and phenomenally LOUD band. At last, with a live recording of "Smells Like Teen Spirit", speeded up to full-punk full-throttle to balance the sweet depression of "Pennyroyal Tea", there was a document of this three-headed monster, standing tall and roaring.

○ **Nevermind** (1991; Geffen).
Slick rock production meets grunge. Cobain's songwriting is assured and scathing. A defining moment in rock music.

○ **In Utero** (1993; Geffen).
Not an instant classic, but more honest in feel due to the scuzzier production. The lyrics are coloured with images of disease and sickness, an expression of the pressures felt by the band.

○ **Unplugged In New York** (1994; Geffen).
The band clearly show their influences by jamming on covers by artists as diverse as David Bowie and Leadbelly. Original material is delivered with a clarity and force of emotion rarely heard; "Pennyroyal Tea" has never sounded so ethereal and cleansing.

○ **Nirvana** (2002; Geffen).
A stunning 'best of' collection with one exclusive cut, "You Know You're Right".

Essi Berelian

THE NITTY GRITTY DIRT BAND

Formed Orange County, California, 1965.

Originally a jug band who met at McCabe's guitar store, **The Nitty Gritty Dirt Band** was a complement of layabout hippies who turned into musical pioneers, reinvigorating the deep wells of country music. Somewhat bizarrely, George Bush, when questioned on pop music, named them his favourite group – though he couldn't quite get the name right.

Founder members **Jeff Hanna** and **Jimmie Fadden** were joined for a few months by a youthful **Jackson Browne**, whose songwriting they mined long after his departure; he was replaced by their manager's younger brother, **John McEuen**, and bassist **Les Thompson** completed the line-up. Their early LPs were a strange mix of jug-band songs and gorgeous classical pop, rich in harpsichords, with an almost spiritual quality that continued to invigorate later releases. On stage, they sported straw hats, double-breasted suits and neat collars and ties. Hardly what you'd call psychedelic.

After two LPs, they were joined by **Chris Darrow** from the legendary **Kaleidoscope**, who brought a more solid songwriting base, missing since Browne. A freak hit single, "Buy For The Rain", led to the group headlining concerts featuring The Doors and Jefferson Airplane – not bad for a band that was barely amplified. Following a performance in *Paint Your Wagon* – how's that for rock credibility? – the band split in 1969, to no one's great sorrow, and that seemed to be that.

Hanna and Darrow joined Linda Ronstadt's backing band, while McEuen played guitar with, of all people, Andy Williams. A chance meeting in the Golden Bear in Huntington Beach led to Hanna saying to McEuen about the bar band playing, 'Listen to that bunch of clowns ... we could wipe them out.' And so they did, with original colleagues Les Thompson and Jimmie Fadden, plus new recruit **Jim Ibbotson**, whose country roots were to prove influential. Greatly influenced by The Band, and with more upfront drums, they released UNCLE CHARLIE AND HIS DOG TEDDY, their first consistent LP, in 1970. It spent six months in the US charts. The following year saw ALL THE GOOD TIMES, an eclectic mix of rock'n'roll, country, folk and Cajun, but the best was still to come.

The band had moved out of LA to Aspen, Colorado, and this rural setting saw the birth of the ground-breaking triple LP, WILL THE CIRCLE BE UNBROKEN (1973), featuring country greats like **Doc Watson**, **Earl Scruggs** and **Merle Haggard**, with The Nitty Gritties functioning almost as a backing band. Rednecks and hippies met, and found they had more in common than they had ever realized.

Thompson left at this point, and the remaining four recorded another concept LP, STARS AND STRIPES FOREVER, in 1974. The next year saw another album, DREAM, in which the individuals gathered influences ranging from country, through sailors' hornpipes, to straight-up rock. A year later, they shortened their name to the **Dirt Band**, and toured widely, including a month-long trip to the USSR. Their music had flattened out to an easy-going country-rock, and has continued in that vein ever since, without hitting the peaks of the early 70s. One example of their near-universal acceptance saw them playing a bluegrass festival one day, and the next appearing with Aerosmith.

In 1983, they reverted to their full name for LET'S GO, which spawned a US country Top 10 hit, "Dance Little Jean". The following year's PLAIN DIRT FASHION included "Long Hard Road", which topped the country chart. Shortly afterwards, John McEuen left the band for a solo career. Jeff Hanna was now the band's undisputed leader. Ex-Eagle **Bernie Leadon** joined briefly, for WORKING BAND, and was also featured on 1989's WILL THE CIRCLE BE UNBROKEN, VOLUME TWO, where they revisited their greatest triumph, this time with the assistance of a mixture of the new and old waves in country music. Chet Atkins and Johnny Cash met Emmylou Harris and Ricky Scaggs, with the presence of two former Byrds, Roger McGuinn and Chris Hillman. BGO then began a reissue programme on CD, remastering as they went, which was followed in 2002 by another all-star set, WILL THE CIRCLE BE UNBROKEN, VOLUME THREE.

⊙ **Uncle Charlie And His Dog Teddy** (1970; Liberty).
A classic country-rock album (with the emphasis on rock), which mixes band originals with covers of the best songs of their contemporaries. Most of human life is here – psychedelic phasing, chicken imitations on the fiddle, accordions and washtub bass, and a supercharged version of Buddy Holly's "Rave On". Durable good-time music.

⊙ **Will The Circle Be Unbroken** (1973; United Artists).
A triple album now contained on two CDs. As well as its purely historical importance, this is also a fully satisfying suite, which takes the country experiments of Gram Parsons and The Byrds of SWEETHEART OF THE RODEO back to their source.

⊙ **Dirt, Silver And Gold** (1976; One Way).
The best of the many compilations of the band's long musical career.

Brian Hinton

MOJO NIXON

Born Chapel Hill, North Carolina, 1957.

Perhaps the most fascinating thing about wildman **Mojo Nixon** is that he's maintained a national career and not slid off into curio status. While his popularity fluctuates, his presence as music's premier sex, drugs and rock'n'roll enthusiast persists.

Mojo burst onto the San Diego music scene in 1984 as the jabbering half of **Mojo Nixon And Skid Roper**. Roper played washboard, tub and whatnot; Mojo played acoustic guitar with a lack of finesse that Johnny Ramone would appreciate, and in a lascivious hillbilly accent delivered high-octane songs/sermons extolling drugs, drink and fornication (as in 'fornication nation', Mojo's preferred term for his fan base).

Restless/RBI released the duo's demo tape as MOJO NIXON AND SKID ROPER in 1985. Lead cut "Jesus At McDonald's", a "Roadrunner"-style paean to psilocybin and Americana, generated college airplay and morbid interest, which was augmented by the follow-up college-airplay hit, "Stuffin' Martha's Muffin", a smutty love song to clueless MTV VJ Martha Quinn.

Mojo followed up with several records on Enigma, but it was MTV that brought Mojo's high jinks to a national audience. The network aired videos of "Burn Down The Malls", "Elvis Is Everywhere" (a hallucinogenic ululation roughly based on Chuck Berry's "Tulane") and "(619) 239-KING", and even ran promotional shorts scripted by and starring Mojo. He became a star of sorts, a poster boy for old-fashioned rock'n'roll mischief on the increasingly homogenized network. But when MTV banned his "Debbie Gibson Is Pregnant With My Two-Headed Love Child" video (despite a stellar performance by Winona Ryder in the title role), Mojo renounced his MTV Nation citizenship, preferring to relinquish the coast-to-coast stage it had given him rather than accept the network's increasingly onerous constraints.

Determined to hold his broadened audience without MTV, Nixon split with Roper in 1989, assembled an all-star band and made what could have been his 'break-out' album, OTIS (1990). But Enigma went bust soon after its release, which not only dashed the album's hopes, but condemned Mojo to spend the next few years suing to regain control of his own music (though in this period he did work on other projects, including the notorious HORNY HOLIDAYS CHRISTMAS LP on Triple X in 1992 and his excellent 1994 joint production with **Jello Biafra** of Dead Kennedys, PRAIRIE HOME INVASION). By 1995 the legal hassles were resolved and a bloodied-but-unbowed Mojo released WHEREABOUTS UNKNOWN.

Today, Mojo has gained a few pounds and learned to play decent guitar, but otherwise little else has changed: he still thinks 'McDonald's is putting something in our food to make us weak', still solicits sex from MTV VJs from the stage ('Kennedy, get your fat ass up here'), and is still given to eccentric, oddly touching gestures such as the acoustic cover of Elvis Presley's "If I Can Dream" that closes WHEREABOUTS UNKNOWN, and the bizarre ballad "When Did I Become My Dad" from 1999's THE REAL SOCK RAY BLUE. It may even turn out that the time is at last ripe for Mojo: judging from the ascension of anti-music, anti-fun killjoys, it may be that music needs all the Mojo it can get.

⊙ **Bo-Day-Shus!** (1987; Enigma).
Leads off with the epic rant "Elvis Is Everywhere" (and, Mojo adds, in everybody – except Michael J. Fox). Thereafter he declares "I Ain't Gonna Piss In No Jar" and "I Don't Want

No Foo-Foo Haircut On My Head", and asks his mama what she did with his Lincoln Logs. Shambling and sweet-tempered.

⊙ **Otis** (1990; Enigma).
The meaty sound of this first post-Skid Roper CD gave Mojo musical power to match his verbal onslaught. Features the great anti-mellow-rock anthem "Don Henley Must Die" ('Don't let him get back together with Glenn Frey!'). Other noble sentiments: "I Wanna Race Bigfoot Trucks", and "I Took Out The Trash And Never Came Back".

⊙ **Whereabouts Unknown** (1995; Blutarski).
Eric Ambel (Long Ryders) production adds heft, but Mojo's approach ("Tie My Pecker To My Leg") remains consistent.

⊙ **Gadzooks!!!** (1997; Needletime).
Every car stereo needs its Mojo and this fine seventeen-track career retrospective – with titles such as "I Like Marijuana", "I'm Drunk" and "Winnebago Warrior" – is the ultimate driving-under-the-influence collection.

Roy Edroso

NO DOUBT

Formed Anaheim, California, 1986.

In many ways, **No Doubt** are more of a cartoon band than, say, Gorillaz. They bounce and boinngg to a pop-ska groove behind a media-flirting ready-made star with a hairstyle that's re-etched and coloured for every TV appearance and magazine cover pose.

Eric Stefani (keyboards) formed No Doubt with his sister **Gwen** (originally on backing vocals) in 1986. Neither could play any instruments, but both wanted to have a bash at imitating the music they loved, British ska. They were joined by high-school friend **John Spence** on vocals and, soon after, **Tony Kanal** on bass.

Spence's suicide in 1987 left the band shaken, but determined to continue. Joined by **Tom Dumont** (guitar) and **Adrian Young** (drums), No Doubt carried on playing energetic live sets of two-tone covers and Eric's own songs to their enthusiastic local following. Meanwhile, Gwen took over lead vocals and began a relationship with Kanal that was to last seven years. The band's recording contract with Interscope lead to the release of their eponymous debut album in 1992, which sold poorly.

Legal wrangling with Interscope contributed to No Doubt's next record – THE BEACON STREET COLLECTION (1995) – being self-financed, self-produced and recorded in a garage. During this period, Eric quit the band to pursue a career as an animator (later notching up credits for *The Simpsons*) and consequently missed the group's pinnacle of achievement. In 1996, Trauma/Interscope released TRAGIC KINGDOM which took everyone by surprise, selling fifteen million copies worldwide. Featuring the singles "Don't Speak", a Spanish guitar-tinged power ballad, and the Gwen Stefani theme-tune "Just A Girl", the album made No Doubt's name. The following year, the British market was won over – "Don't Speak" went to #1 and "Just A Girl" to #3. The peroxide posturing of Stefani and her bouncy

REDFERNS

Stefani strikes a pose

tinued to peddle ska-sodden, subtlety-free, persistently poppy music. The "Hey Baby" single entered the UK charts at #2 and hooked itself into the memory of all that heard it. Collaborations such as ROCK STEADY's "Waiting Room" with **Prince**, and Gwen's appearance on **Moby**'s "South Side" single proved that No Doubt had many admirers and a taste for experimentation, though as a band they continue to milk the winning formula of hi-adrenaline pastiche ska.

⊙ **Tragic Kingdom** (1996; Trauma/Interscope).
Bubblegum, boot-stomping, party pop. Ten years after their formation, No Doubt go massive.

Annebella Pollen

NOMEANSNO

Formed Victoria, British Columbia, Canada, 1980.

NoMeansNo (the name comes from an anti-rape slogan) are, to all intents and purposes, the brothers **Rob** and **Jon Wright**, who formed their band in 1980. Over the past twenty years they have established themselves as Canada's finest indie band (more of a compliment than it may sound), acquiring legendary status.

The Wrights come from Victoria, an unenthralling seaside town on Vancouver Island, three hours across the straits from Vancouver, centre of Canada's alternative scene. NoMeansNo could benefit from Vancouver's resources, yet remain detached from the media, a detachment they maintain by running their own label, Wrong Records. Their music is like no other band's: their songs are based around Rob's bass and Jon's drumming, with guitars for colour and emphasis (reversing the guitar-centric norm), and they display a seemingly effortless ability to change direction in the course of a song, so that one piece may sound like three or four slammed together – and they last a long time. If three-minute pop, feel-good music is your thing, look elsewhere.

Although the band recorded their first album, MAMA, back in 1982, they established themselves in the late 80s, with a series of five releases: SEX MAD (1987), SMALL PARTS ISOLATED AND DESTROYED (1988), WRONG (1989) and 0+2=1 (1991) – bleak, challenging and discomforting works, painting a picture of a world rife with deceit and stupidity. 'What if every fourth person in the world/Is a DUMBFUCK?', they asked on 0+2=1. The approach saw its best in a song like "Body Bag" (on SEX MAD), where the pounding bass dominates an effective and astute attack on American foreign policy, or "Small Parts Isolated And Destroyed" (the album's title track), which twists and turns its jagged critique through the failure of punk radicalism.

Like so many of their songs, "Small Parts" was concerned with honesty, truth and lies; with the need to be as honest and truthful as possible, while recognizing the difficulty and rarity of this, especially in

fun-punk band were hard to forget once seen, and media coverage made the group's catchy/tacky novelty even harder to escape.

Stefani's high-profile relationship with Gavin Rossdale of US-beloved Brit band Bush may not have raised her street cred in the UK, but globally her pop-icon status was fixed. Although it would be four years until the next No Doubt album, the band toured relentlessly and, unsurprisingly for such a cartoon-style group, featured on the soundtrack of *Beavis And Butthead Do America*, and also teamed up with **Elvis Costello** to perform "I Throw My Toys Around" in the 1998 *Rugrats* film.

THE RETURN OF SATURN (2000) album (its title referring to Gwen's astrological coming-of-age at 29) was suitably more reflective. With musing on maternal desires and the public airing of her relationship with Rossdale, Stefani's songwriting contributions were more noticeable and personal. Artificially sweet and irritatingly infectious, the band's energy remained at full kilter – a manic homage to Stefani's all-time favourite band, Madness.

With the release of ROCK STEADY in 2001, No Doubt celebrated their fifteenth anniversary and con-

personal relationships, where betrayal and manipulation are ubiquitous. An even starker expression of the theme was to be found in "All Lies" (on WRONG), a song that shears through the bone.

THE WORLDHOOD OF THE WORLD (AS SUCH) (1995), was something of a disappointment, though it still contained flashes of bite, like "My Politics" ('I love to hate/That's fucking great'). 1998's DANCE OF THE BOURGEOISIE re-embraced the credibility of earlier releases and was a marked return to form. 1999's IN THE FISHTANK EP (In The Fishtank Records) was again strong, but by 2002 the band had split from their primary label, Alternative Tentacles. Since then no recordings have emerged, though the band continues to play live.

⊙ **Small Parts Isolated And Destroyed** (1988; Alternative Tentacles/Wrong):
NoMeansNo's third LP and their best to that point – perhaps the best of all – revealing the full range of their talents on such brilliant songs as the stunning title track and the deeply ironic and disturbing "Real Love".

⊙ **Why Do They Call Me Mr Happy?** (1993; Alternative Tentacles/Wrong).
NoMeansNo maintain their high standard. "The River" has incredible intensity, driven along by the best drumming you'll ever hear.

Chris Jenkins

STINA NORDENSTAM

Born Fisksatra, Sweden, 1969.

"The only possible happiness I can have is one with the pain and darkness in it"

Raised in the northern Swedish port of Fisksatra by music-obsessed, politically active socialist parents, the enigmatic, retiring **Stina Nordenstam** is one of the most original and unexpected voices to have emerged in recent years.

As a schoolgirl her evenings were divided between the Swedish Young Communist League and absorbing her father's jazz collection. She fell heavily for the wilder shores of John Coltrane (legend has it that she spent days transcribing his more frantic solos and reworking them for piano, as well as works by Bartok, Martinu and Satie). When it came to her songwriting, she brought the free spirit of jazz into her volatile mix: the juxtaposition of apparently antagonistic elements remains her creative dynamic.

Musically precocious, she joined a jazz group, **The Flippermen**, at 15; though less than half the age of fellow band members, she quickly became the undisputed band leader. Tiring of the local jazz scene, she eventually holed up on an island outside Stockholm to write and record for Swedish label Telegram Records. All this and still a teenager.

This period yielded the material MEMORIES OF A COLOUR (1991); a remarkable debut it was picked up by EastWest for worldwide release. Her voice was sensual yet childlike, half-sung and half-whispered, while the songs exhibited edgy jazz touches, classical undercurrents and pop singer-songwriter stylings. The songs — all written in English — drew comparisons with Rickie Lee Jones, Kate Bush and Jane Siberry. Yet for a while she considered quitting music, until Klas Lundig (Telegram boss), her first and firmest advocate, persuaded her to travel to London and record some demos for British record label 4AD. The sessions did not work out, but, consequent exposure to the music of such bands as This Mortal Coil, Talk Talk and Red House Painters reawakened her passion, leading her to begin work on what would become AND SHE CLOSED HER EYES (1993).

The breathtaking range, scope and depth of this set (on which she is backed by Swedish group **Popsicle**) made her debut seem juvenile by comparison. The jazz and classical influences were sublimated into a vivifying mix of acoustic, ambient and atonal elements tied to cinematic narratives and vertigo-inducing bittersweet melodies. Her vocals, too, had changed – now claustrophobically close-miked and dizzyingly high in the mix. "Little Star", released as a single, was a tragically beautiful song effectively a suicide note spliced by a confession sung in Latin by a schoolboy choir. Elsewhere, the sweet, bright optimism of "Something Nice" and "Hopefully Yours" stand in the shadows cast by the dark tales of "Crime" and "Fireworks".

Ever stage-shy, Nordenstam refused to tour in support for the album, performing only one nerve-racking show at London's Jazz Café in 1994. Nevertheless, the acclaim garnered by the collection brought her into contact with a wider audience and in 1995 she collaborated with soundtrack-meister **Vangelis** on the exquisitely understated "Ask The Mountains"/"Slow Piece" single.

The fractured, beatbox-heavy textures of AND SHE CLOSED HER EYES anticipated the atmospheres of her next set, 1996's startling DYNAMITE. The album's instrumentation consisted primarily of a super-distorted fuzz-tone single guitar being simultaneously

Stina Nordenstam
And She Closed Her Eyes

caressed and assaulted with Nordenstam's vocals again looming in the foreground, while 'industrial' rhythms rose and fell like a sonic tide. The songs, notably "Mary Bell" and "Under Your Command", told of betrayal, murder and failed love; they sounded all the more troubling for being delivered in her childlike, confidential whisper. A remix of the title track, issued as a single, offered an almost unrecognizably transformed piece, clothed in a dramatic, wide-screen film-noir orchestration.

Meanwhile, "Little Star" was featured on the heavily Swedo-centric soundtrack of Baz Luhrmann's *Romeo + Juliet* in 1996. The financial rewards brought by the film's success gave Nordenstam some capital to pursue her own creative agenda, which included photography (examples of which surfaced in British hipster mag *Dazed and Confused*), and directing video and short films.

Her next musical move was PEOPLE ARE STRANGE (1998) – an album of covers, deconstructed to the point where the majority were beyond recognition. It was strong stuff: her mesmeric "Purple Rain", chilling 30-second sliver of "Love Hurts" and one-note take on "Sailing" were hard to forget and placed leagues of clear water between herself and the mainstream.

Stina returned in 2001 with her unique vocal style for THIS IS STINA NORDENSTAM. **Brett Anderson** of Suede (sounding quite unlike his usual camp, mockney self) added to her fragile vocals on a number of tracks and gave them a totally new dimension, with the Beatlesque sound of "Keen Yellow Planet" working particularly well. A film compilation, of ten music videos by various directors was released to accompany the album: featuring vomiting ballerinas, trips to cartoon space and Stina herself, disguised as ever in a black wig, serenely walking through motorway traffic, it perfectly illustrated the diversity of the concepts behind her songs. "Welcome To Happiness", a heady mixture of riffs, muted guitars and child-like voices was released as a single, but since then Stina has gone a bit quiet. No doubt she won't be quiet for long.

(•) **And She Closed Her Eyes** (1993; EastWest).
Nordenstam delivers a song-cycle that measures innocence against experience. The bright acoustic surfaces and melodic intensity almost disguise the angst of her vision.

(•) **Dynamite** (1996; EastWest).
Narratives of luminous beauty and the deepest hideousness coexist in these startling, brutal and exquisite songs. Uneasy listening, for sure, and a drastic change in style, but it's utterly compelling.

(•) **This Is Stina Nordenstam** (2001; Independiente).
A truly modern masterpiece – a melting pot of sounds and styles that should leave you wanting more.

Peter Mills

HEATHER NOVA

Born Bermuda, 1968.

The teenage years of singer-songwriter **Heather Nova** were spent with her family sailing around the West Indies. Home was a forty-foot boat with no electricity, no TV and no official schooling, and they sailed wherever the current took them. Her time was spent learning the guitar and listening to the collected works of Neil Young and The Beatles. At 19, she moved to Rhode Island to study film, before heading to New York in search of a record contract.

London was next; going everywhere with her guitar, playing wherever possible, she eventually met up with **Youth** (ex-Killing Joke), who released GLOWSTARS (1993), a collection of her demos, on his own Butterfly label. Sounding as delicate and fey as All About Eve, the album didn't establish much of an identity, but through continuing hard work Nova managed to land several high-profile support slots, appearing with the fledgling Cranberries, and Bob Mould. And here, armed with only a guitar, she excelled.

Nova came into her own when she released her first 'proper' album, OYSTER, in 1995. Passionate, exquisitely sultry, and drenched in a lyrical poetry, the Youth-produced OYSTER placed its author somewhere between the confessionals of Jeff Buckley and the other-worldliness of Tori Amos. One track in particular, "Island", caused a stir: it exposed the emotional undercurrents of domestic abuse, and on stage she dedicated the song to Nicole Brown Simpson, the murdered wife of O. J. Simpson, which provoked mixed reactions from audiences, not least in Los Angeles.

Nova continued to tour heavily throughout Europe with the likes of Neil Young and Pearl Jam for the rest of the year, and this helped OYSTER sell well over 400,000 copies. At the beginning of 1996, she found herself a 'priority act' in the US, a term which basically meant that the record company (in this case, Epic) were going to make 'it' happen. SIREN appeared in 1998 and further heightened Nova's profile with singles such as "London Rain" and memorable album cuts "Valley Of Sound" and "I'm The Girl". The release fuelled an arduous schedule of tours and festival appearances that culminated with the release of a live album entitled WONDERLUST (2000).

A fourth studio album, SOUTH, released in the autumn of 2001, displayed a new-found pop dimension to add to her characteristically passionate and intense sound, and helped to further establish her in the United States.

(•) **Oyster** (1995; RhythmKings/Epic).
A sensual and mature album, mixing the traditions of folk with the swelling emotions of power ballad. Two tracks in particular, "Walk This World" and "Maybe An Angel", give goose bumps all down your back.

(•) **Wonderlust** (2000; V2).
Recorded in Germany, this is a well-recorded document of Heather Nova's live sound. The majority of the cuts are faithfully rendered versions of numbers from *Oyster* and *Blow*, but there is one surprise – a cover of Bruce Springsteen's "I'm On Fire". Her backing band shine, but it's Nova's smooth-then-jagged vocals that steal the show.

Nick Duerden

GARY NUMAN

Born London, 1958.

There can be few artists in popular music history to have so successfully cultivated critical loathing. The futuristic songs. The hair transplant. The silly aeronautical stunts. And, worse than any sex and drugs and rock'n'roll caper, **Gary Numan** broke the ultimate taboo by publicly endorsing Margaret Thatcher.

Gary Webb had previously been inspired by the more outlandish characters of 70s rock and pop – Bowie, Bolan and Ferry – and had taken the name 'Numan' from a plumber in a telephone directory. As a hopelessly introverted child, he saw pop music as a way to circumvent his own shyness, and set about inventing a persona (a sort of confused space orphan) to match his new name. He formed his own group, **Tubeway Army**, who initially masqueraded as a punk act, and by 1977 they had signed to the independent Beggars Banquet.

The group's eponymous debut album featured typically grandiose themes ("The Dream Police", "My Love Is A Liquid") and stalled commercially. However, Numan discovered fresh career impetus when the single, "Are 'Friends' Electric", became a surprise UK #1. An atmospheric, almost frigid-sounding monologue spliced over creepy after-dark synthesizers, it had not a hook or chorus in sight. Tubeway Army's subsequent album, REPLICAS (1979), also hit the UK #1 spot.

By the end of that year Numan had ditched Tubeway Army and reverted to solo billing (though bass player **Paul Gardiner** was retained). Numan's best song, and easily his most successful, followed. Whether "Cars" was eulogy or apocalyptic warning about the crammed arteries of Britain's roads is difficult to ascertain, but it was the closest this particular android was going to get to great pop. Both follow-up singles, "We Are Glass" and "I Die: You Die", were listenable but too evocative of Numan the pretentious nerd to impress the critics. Other parties were less grudging – both THE PLEASURE PRINCIPLE (1979) and TELEKON (1980) were #1 albums in the UK.

By the turn of the decade Numan had started mounting the most grandiose shows ever to grace a British stage. No expense was spared, but by this time Numan could afford to 'treat' his fans. These included New York's electro/hip-hop progenitors, who seemed to consider Numan the coolest man on Planet Pop. While subsequent releases failed to storm the charts (he complained of infrequent airplay), Numan was always able to count on a personal following who consumed everything he released. The love affair between the parties has hardly abated in nearly twenty years, but only the most besotted supporters should invest in the later albums.

DANCE (1981), a series of dance tunes that only an alien mutant could possibly dance to, was the last to be a major success. I, ASSASSIN (1982) sounded ridiculously dated, and the preposterous WARRIORS (1983), which saw him adopt the leather look, was the first album since the Tubeway Army debut to miss the UK Top 10. By 1984 and BESERKER Numan had founded his own record label, Numa. Both THE FURY (1985) and STRANGE CHARM (1986) were greeted by deafening silence, and various live albums hardly raised his profile. OUTLAND (1991) was his best album of the 90s, but even Numan owned up to the fact that MACHINE AND SOUL (1992) was fairly odorous. SACRIFICE (1994) was comparatively jolly, featuring some old-fashioned rock'n'roll guitar in addition to the usual mess of synths and would-be-ironic lyrics.

Still, he did have a comeback hit in 1996 when a British beer advert used "Cars" as its soundtrack. And

New York greeted Gary Newman as the coolest man on Planet Pop

there he was again, peering at us out of tinted contact lenses on *Top Of The Pops* like he'd never been away. Since the booze industry cash-in, though, things have quietened down for Numan, with his most recent release, EXILE (1998), causing few ripples in the ether.

The 1998 reissue of large sections of his back catalogue (TUBEWAY ARMY, REPLICAS, THE PLEASURE PRINCIPLE and TELEKON, all Beggars Banquet; plus THE NUMAN YEARS, a fine box set on Eagle Records) are all given added value in the form of bonus tracks and well-presented sleeve notes – a worthwhile investment for all the Numanoids planning to go digital.

Even in the 21st century, Numan has experienced yet more revivals, not least due to his work being heavily sampled by contemporary artists. Armand Van Helden and The Sugababes have both partially relied on Numan's number one hit successes to achieve their own chart-topping singles across Europe, while in turn keeping Numan's sound alive.

(•) **Premier Hits** (1999; Beggars Banquet).
The best-packaged of a number of compilations on the market, this also concentrates on Numan's early period, which is a relief; though the presence of two verions of "Cars" on a career restrospective does suggest a somewhat limited oeuvre.

Alex Ogg

NURSE WITH WOUND

Formed London, 1978.

Under the name **Nurse With Wound**, the prolific **Steven Stapleton** has been at the centre of London's post-industrial experimental scene, as evidenced by the number of similar artists who appear on NWW recordings: **David Tibet** (**CURRENT 93**), **Douglas P** (Death In June), **John Balance** (**COIL**), **Andrew McKenzie** (Hafler Trio), **David Jackman** (Organum), **Tony Wakeford** (Sol Invictus), **Annie Anxiety**, **Edward Kaspel** (**LEGENDARY PINK DOTS**), **James Thirwell** (**FOETUS**), **Peter Christopherson** (**THROBBING GRISTLE**), etc.

Starting with CHANCE MEETING OF A SEWING MACHINE AND AN UMBRELLA ON A DISSECTING TABLE (1979), Nurse With Wound have released a large number of utterly non-commercial, extremely avant-garde albums on Stapleton's United Dairies label. Early albums utilized electronics, improvisation, and tape collage with a Dada-esque sense of humour, to create patchworks of disorientating music (or some would say non-music) that veers from quiet to sudden bursts of noise, from irritating to soothing, combined with disjointed spoken phrases, laughter and very strange noises punctuating the tracks.

Surreal album covers, usually created by the multifaceted Stapleton, mirror the music within. From the harsh distorted noise shrieks of 150 MURDEROUS PASSIONS (1981) to the contemplative atmospheric soundscapes of SOLILOQUY FOR LILITH (1988), Nurse With Wound's music has covered the whole map,

with no two albums sounding very much alike. AUTOMATING VOL. 1 (1986) and VOL. 2 (1988) gathered material from various compilations. LIVE AT BAR MALDOROR (1986), recorded from 1984 to 1986, proved NWW were not just studio tricksters – live they can be just as jarring with their improvisational intuitive music. A SUCKED ORANGE (1989) consisted of 29 short snippets that were not as memorable as the longer, more conceptual pieces, while THUNDER PERFECT MIND (1992) was at times almost ambient. By the release of ROCK AND ROLL STATION (1994) NWW had become far more rhythmic, as if Stapleton were trying to make an electronic dance album without losing any of the NWW eccentricities.

NWW have also put out several albums with other artists, including CRUMBDUCK (1996) with **STEREOLAB** (which contains the Krautrock-inspired masterpiece "Animal Or Vegetable"), and the quite beautiful, melodic and haunting ACTS OF SENSELESS BEAUTY (1997) with violinist **Aranos**; most of these collaborations retained NWW's extremely bizarre flavour, and the best of such joint efforts are collected on THE SWINGING REFLECTIVE (1999).

NWW's most recent dip into the abyss, SALT MARIE CELESTE (2003), was a dark, brooding masterpiece of modern electronic music. One never knows what to expect from Stapleton next, but most of his stuff is recommended for the adventurous.

(•) **The Sylvie And Babs Hi-Fi Companion** (1985; Laylah).
Using 1950s lounge music and snippets of dialogue, along with the usual weird noises and a large number of guests, this is one of NWW's best collage works.

(•) **Large Ladies With Cake In The Oven** (1993; United Dairies).
This CD compiles three amazing EPs from 1983–84, including BRAINED BY FALLING MASONRY, which has Clint Ruin crooning demonically over an appropriation of Brainticket's ultra-trippy theme song.

(•) **Who Can I Turn To Stereo** (1996; United Dairies).
With a dozen songs segued together as one piece, this is more accessible (if anything by them can be considered as such), with some more rhythmic stuff as well as plenty of weird sounds and voices.

(•) **Salt Marie Celeste** (2003; United Dairies).
An hour-long tapestry of drone and found sound; NWW's finest ambient moment.

Rolf Semprebon

LAURA NYRO

Born Brooklyn, New York, October 18, 1947; died April 8, 1997.

The songs of **Laura Nyro** (pronounced 'Nero' to rhyme with 'Hero' or 'Zero') inhabit the boundary between the poetic and the precious, the sensual and the sentimental, the intense and the overwrought. Drawing on folk, soul, jazz and gospel, she pulled them into a kind of harmony through her piano-driven rhapsodies and reveries.

Of Italian-Jewish parentage, her father was a jazz trumpeter and she attended the New York High

Gonna take a miracle
Laura nyro
and Labelle

School of Music and Art then began singing in local clubs, before spreading her wings to San Francisco and a residency at the Hungry I nightclub. The impetus from this led to a contract with Verve/Folkways in 1966, but her relationship with the San Francisco counterculture was often troubled – at Monterey in 1967 she was booed off the stage, causing stage fright that lasted for several years. She never really connected with the hippie generation – perhaps because it was never as spiritually open or musically eclectic as it liked to think it was.

Nyro's first two albums – MORE THAN A NEW DISCOVERY (1966) and ELI AND THE 13TH CONFESSION (1968), on CBS – failed to break through commercially, though her songs were successfully covered by others, such as the Fifth Dimension, Blood, Sweat And Tears, Barbra Streisand and Three Dog Night. By the third album, NEW YORK TENDABERRY (1969), Nyro was starting to sell records in her own right. It perfectly embodied her fusion of poetry and white soul, with the piano following or leading Nyro's vocal through dark, thundering passages and delicate, heartbeat-like codas.

CHRISTMAS AND THE BEADS OF SWEAT (1970) further consolidated her position, and 1971's GONNA TAKE A MIRACLE (featuring vocals from black girl group Labelle) proved her most accessible offering to date – a honey-sweet, joyous homage to the street-soul sounds of her youth. Marrying, producing a son, Gil, and moving to rural Connecticut, Nyro then retired from music for three years, re-emerging in 1975 with SMILE and a tour that found her audience undiminished and her critical standing high. However, subsequent releases in the late 70s failed to connect to changing tastes. She released only one studio album in the 80s, the disappointing MOTHER'S SPIRITUAL, although a live album from 1989 showed glimpses of a wayward talent. The 90s – despite spo-

radic live appearances and a well-received 'come-back' album in 1994 – found Nyro's profile dipping to that of a minor cult artist.

STONED SOUL PICNIC (CBS), a definitive two-CD set appeared early in 1997 and offers the best retrospective available. Reviews were very positive and Nyro appeared to be on the verge of being rediscovered, prior to her tragic death from ovarian cancer in April 1997. Her death prompted a deluge of affection and reawakened interest in her work, and PICNIC has acted as an ideal starting point for the curious and a fine summation for the already converted. Less positively, articles have also sought to define Nyro's pivotal trilogy of albums (ELI AND THE 13TH CONFESSION, NEW YORK TENDABERRY and CHRISTMAS AND THE BEADS OF SWEAT) in terms of her turbulent sexuality (from heterosexual to homosexual love) and alleged drug use. Such conjecture added little to this most private and dignified of artists, who had latterly diverted a lot of her energies to animal rights, feminism and ecology – topics that do not sell so many copies of rock'n'roll magazines.

Prior to her death Nyro had been working with her six-woman harmony group and preparing songs for a new album. Her death galvanized devoted obituaries from more recent generations of female singer-songwriters such as Suzanne Vega, Jane Siberry, Rickie Lee Jones and Shawn Colvin, all acknowledging Nyro as a key icon. This admiration manifested itself somewhat unwisely in the tribute album, TIME AND LOVE – THE MUSIC OF LAURA NYRO (1997), which featured artists as diverse as Phoebe Snow and Rosanne Cash struggling through a selection of Nyro songs. Viciously described as 'a party of dwarves playing idly around the toes of a giant' by *Uncut* magazine, it undeniably suffers from the lack of coherence that always dogs this most tired of formats. Seek out STONED SOUL PICNIC for the ideal tribute to Laura Nyro, the high priestess of metropolitan angst and sweet devotion, the fount of stylized longings and deep, deep, beauty.

Her output had often been adventurous and not always successful: sometimes overwhelmed by erratic changes in tempo and volume, at others obscured by wordy grandiloquence. The contradictions in her work – the jazz phrasing versus the urban folkie, the sweet soul voice grappling with disconcerting rhythms – would always preclude mass acceptance. However, Laura Nyro's integrity and her willingness to take risks has ensured that her mystique remains intact. Both were much in evidence on a live set, THE LOOM'S DESIRE, released in 2002.

⊙ Stoned Soul Picnic (1997; CBS).
The best of Nyro's peak years. Inconsistent, far out and occasionally marvellous, it offers the best initiation for the curious.

Nig Hodgkins

OASIS

Formed Burnage, England, 1991.

"If there's no song I'm not interested – I can't stand endless soloing." Noel Gallagher

Whatever one might think of them, **Oasis** are more than just a rock band. Their phenomenal international success in such a short space of time bears homage to the band's self-belief – and the instinctive vision of Creation records boss **Alan McGee**. Indeed, nowadays, any utterance at all of even the word 'oasis' immediately conjures up an image of Britain's best-known brothers, along with mental soundbites of the soaring, anthemic guitar sound which became their trademark. In 1997, the band had such a stranglehold over the record-buying public's consciousness that the third album shifted some two million units in the UK – while topping the charts in eleven other countries – within a month of its release.

The limitations of his position as technician to Manchester's Inspiral Carpets kick-started the career of **Noel Gallagher**. Something of a tearaway when younger, Noel was an impressionable guitarist with more than a passing interest in the music business and a belief that he could do it better. Following the Inspirals' 1991 US tour, Noel approached his younger brother **Liam**'s band, **The Rain**, offering songwriting and musicianship on the condition that he had full artistic control over the group's output. Making one of rock history's better decisions, vocalist Liam – along with longtime friend of the Gallaghers, rhythm guitarist **Paul 'Bonehead' Arthurs**, bassist **Paul 'Guigsy' McGuigan** and drummer **Tony McCarroll** – said 'yes'.

Noel wrote many early Oasis compositions during the day while somehow holding down a humdrum desk job with British Gas; the first Oasis gig finally took place at Manchester's Boardwalk in October 1991. The quintet was to spend a year or two supporting local bands before capturing the attention of McGee. The Creation Svengali became an instant Gallagher convert on attending their Glasgow support slot to long-time (but now defunct) former Creation act, **18 Wheeler**. On their signing initial media response to 'yet another Creation band' was muted, perhaps in the wake of the much rebuked 'shoe-gazing' scene with which the label were connected. It soon became apparent, however, that Oasis were to have far greater com-

mercial potential. Supported by growing music press interest, the band's debut single – the cool and cocksure "Supersonic" – charted at #31 early in 1994. The distinctive melody and vocal sneer (which some compared unfavourably to John Lydon's) along with a humorously lazy lyric, were arresting, to say the least. When the hurriedly released follow-up – the apparent New Seekers homage, "Shakermaker" – trounced its predecessor by crashing the chart at #11 in its first week of release, Oasis were being proclaimed as the year's most promising newcomers.

In the music press, the Gallaghers were now known faces. The contrived arguments and laddish brawls were fast becoming a trademark, and other band members professed to having lost count of the times that one or other had quit the group. Despite this, it was drummer Tony McCarroll who became the first casualty of the squabbling, making way for **Alan White** – brother of Paul Weller percussionist, Steve. (A hotly-disputed court case in 1999 saw McCarroll walk away with £500k.) The Gallagher brothers' public feuds continued: one particularly fearsome episode was made available on the single release, "Wibbling Rivalry".

Oasis proved themselves as the UK's leading new rock act with the release of a remarkable third single in the summer of 1994. "Live Forever" had critics in raptures and duly presenting the band with its first Top Ten hit. Accompanied by an equally memorable video, the song – a stretched-back-in-the-sun paean to the joy of sharing self-belief with a kindred spirit – is still the band's most sublime moment.

With the music world seemingly at their feet, Oasis unleashed their eagerly anticipated debut LP at the close of summer. Its instantly accessible mix of powerful pop-rock work-outs and moodier musings saw DEFINITELY MAYBE heralded a classic by all sections of the press; the ever-effacing Liam could only retort 'That's nothing – our kid's got 200 more (songs) just as good…'. The album topped the chart in its first week, quickly going platinum in Britain, while further hits, "Cigarettes And Alcohol" and "Whatever", saw Oasis also closing in on the top of the singles chart. The only criticisms at this point were allegations of plagiarism, at which the Gallagher brothers were quick to scoff – and have since appeared to make a virtue.

In May 1995 Oasis stole a march on all of their rivals by topping the singles listings with "Some Might Say" – remarkably, their sixth hit in a little over a year. At Blur's label, Food records, the gauntlet had been thrown down…

OASIS

When it was announced that the next Blur single would be released on the same day in August as that of Oasis, the popular press were more than ready to build up a 'battle of the bands' hype. Beatles/Stones comparisons abounded (although who was supposed to have been whom is anybody's guess), and mild insults began flying between the two camps. Noel and Liam, however, remained unamused by the entire farrago. They had made little secret of their dislike of Damon Albarn and his band, and were annoyed by an apparent upstaging when Blur's somewhat trite "Country House" pipped their own "Roll With It" to the #1 position.

But this setback seemed to make Oasis stronger, and the following month saw them release one of pop's all-time classic albums in WHAT'S THE STORY (MORNING GLORY). This second outing – a mix of Beatle-esque rock and the occasional towering anthem like "Champagne Supernova" and the timeless "Wonderwall" – effortlessly trounced all others, and went on to become the year's best seller. The latter track became a single in its own right, spending some five months in the charts, even prompting a rapid easy-listening cover version by the Mike Flowers Pops. (This time the Gallaghers saw the joke and even attended one of the kitsch orchestra's concerts in London.)

Noel Gallagher's now flourishing reputation as one of Britain's top songwriters was enhanced by his much-reported friendship with fellow Beatles-obsessive **PAUL WELLER**. Fans attending Weller's London shows at the end of 1995 were treated to an acoustic support set from Noel that seemed to cement this regard. The pair even managed to play alongside **PAUL MCCARTNEY** (as the **Smokin' Mojo Filters**) on the one-off cover of "Come Together" for the charity CD, HELP!

As 1996 began, Oasis's astonishing rise and rise continued with a sweep of the Brit awards and a second #1 single in "Don't Look Back In Anger". Even more significantly, a US tour broke them effortlessly into the big time across the Atlantic, with "Wonderwall" and both LPs hitting the chart – a breakthrough unmatched by any other new generation UK rock act until Radiohead in 2000.

Success, however, brought with it all manner of problems. Whilst Oasis's music was widely revered, the Gallagher brothers themselves courted much media controversy. Liam seemed to thoroughly enjoy his newly gained reputation as rock music's bad boy: during 1996, he appeared unable to pass up any

Manchester's favourite sons borrow Pink Floyd's best-known backdrop

opportunity to swear, spit and quarrel with his brother – or get busted for cocaine possession. If the swearing and spitting caused no little outrage in the USA when the band were there to tour, then the arguments with Noel – and particularly the protracted drug use – came very close to curtailing the career of Oasis. On the eve of shows in Chicago, the tour was sensationally pulled at great expense to the band. Meanwhile, although slightly more sedate in behaviour than his younger brother, Noel was never far away from controversy. Various comments on parliamentary drug use, the 'corporate pigs' of the music industry and the notorious AIDS remark about Damon Albarn (which he later sensibly retracted) were widely quoted – whether in or out of context. Indeed, the only actual recorded output that materialized at this point was "Setting Sun" – a **CHEMICAL BROTHERS** single featuring Noel's vocals. It went to #1 in October 1996.

When the furore of the abortive US tour had calmed, both brothers found karma in the Abbey Road recording studio (where the third LP, BE HERE NOW, was recorded), and also at home. Liam married actress Patsy Kensit early in 1997 (a relationship not without tempest); Noel then tied the knot with his long-time sweetheart, media butterfly Meg Matthews.

After eighteen record-free months, the much-vaunted comeback single, "D'You Know What I Mean?" was issued in 1997. The record – which gave Oasis a third British chart-topper – did not, for once, please all the critics. Some felt it showed little headway after such a long wait, while others found it turgid on first listening.

As a precursor to the LP, the single gave many clues – although virtually the entire story was given away in the weeks prior to the album's release: Creation's elaborate 'teasing' of the media by carefully drip-feeding the tracks to Radio 1 worked a treat, as did a slightly contrived television special on the eve of the LP's release. The record, in truth, was nowhere near as strong as its predecessors, but had its moments: "Stand By Me" (a #2 single) was warm and well arranged, "Fade In/Out" offered great neo-psychedelia, and the punchy "My Big Mouth" showed previously unseen self-deprecation. But there were many disappointments, mainly in the shape of lyrical deficiencies and elongated self-indulgence. Nevertheless, "All Around The World" (the group's poorest single by some distance) returned the band to the top of the chart in January 1998.

Criticism, however, was at this time virtually pointless: Oasis were without any doubt the most significant rock act the country had produced since their idols some thirty years before. The furious paparazzi following of (mainly) Liam ensured 24/7 coverage in the media, but Noel appeared to mellow somewhat following the response to BE HERE NOW. Press interviews saw him disclaim the album as something of a mistake, and – to the consternation of all Oasis die-hards – he even admitted that Blur had a few good tunes!

By this time both brothers had discovered the delights of parenthood. But the joys of family life didn't last long and by the end of 2000 both Noel and Liam had separated from their respective spouses.

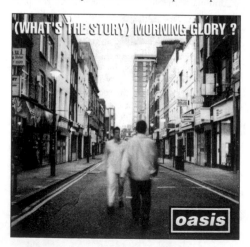

Liam went on to father a child with All Saint Nicole Appleton, while Noel cited the reason for his split as Meg's incessant partying – a bizarre turnaround from one who had previously been such an advocate of the rock'n'roll lifestyle.

Noel's involvement with dance music throughout 1998/1999 spawned collaborations with Goldie, Chemical Brothers (the single "Let Forever Be", a sequel to "Setting Sun", reached the top ten) and a remix for Beastie Boy Mike D's contribution to the UNKLE album.

Boasting a track listing partly chosen by fans over the Internet, 1998's B-Side collection, THE MASTERPLAN, arrived as a breath of fresh air and a reminder of just how vital a songwriter Noel Gallagher could be. With the early singles at least, the extra tracks had been a major selling point, with tunes such as the beautifully subtle concert favourite "Acquiesce" and the poignant "Talk Tonight" standing among their best efforts.

With Noel claiming to have eschewed narcotics in favour of mineral water, Oasis were back in the studio in 1999 working on their fourth studio album. But the group were about to be torn apart when, in August, they were hit by the departure, in quick succession, of both Bonehead and Paul McGuigan – though both finished recording their parts for the album before leaving. A new line-up featuring rhythm guitarist, **Gem Archer** (formerly of Heavy Stereo) and bassist **Andy Bell** (formerly of **RIDE** and Hurricane #1) alongside Noel, Liam and drummer Alan White made their debut in Philadelphia in December 1999.

The turbulence didn't end there however. Creation boss Alan McGee announced the closure of the Creation label shortly thereafter, prompting Oasis to form their own imprint, Big Brother records. The arrival of the album STANDING ON THE SHOULDER OF GIANTS in February 2000 was signalled by the single "Go Let It Out". This somewhat trite affair gave the band a fifth UK #1, proving there were still plenty of party faithful left.

With a title misappropriated from the Isaac Newton quote on the side of a British two-pound coin, STANDING ON THE SHOULDER OF GIANTS was a partial return to form; Noel's much-touted experiments with dance music imbued the set with new textures, though it was far from the radical departure promised. And finally the musical hegemony of the elder Gallagher was broken as Liam made his writing debut with the sweetly naive "Little James".

The inevitable touring followed with Noel making a surprise departure, announcing that he was to quit overseas touring. A hasty replacement was found in **Matt Deighton**, former leader of Mother Earth. The Oasis monster plodded on.

A live album, FAMILIAR TO MILLIONS, recorded at Wembley Stadium was released in November 2000. With trademark self-aggrandizement, this double CD documented their summer shows and captured some of their bombastic stage presence, although some cynics re-christened the record

'Over-familiar to Millions'. Needless to say, the selection of songs was heavily weighted in favour of their early material.

Despite the band's nostalgic indulgences, their legions of fans are clearly still enjoying the rock'n'roll circus the band has become. February 2002's "Hindu Times" returned the Gallaghers once again to the chart summit in the UK as fans anticipated a fifth studio album, the curiously-titled HEATHEN CHEMISTRY. "Hindu Times", and the follow-up, "Born On A Different Cloud", were vast improvements on the selected singles from the previous album, although with the album itself a familiar Oasis blueprint was still adhered to. The suggestion of any radical departure now seems buried forever.

⊙ **Definitely Maybe** (1994; Creation).
Featuring the great, anarchic, twisting "Supersonic" and the effortless cool of "Live Forever" and "Slideaway", this was possibly the most assured pop debut of the past twenty years.

⊙ **(What's The Story) Morning Glory?** (1995; Creation).
The rapid maturing of a band never afraid to wear its influences on its sleeve. On its way to becoming the best-selling LP *ever* in this country, this record has seduced audiences right across the musical spectrum – with its faultless mix of Beatles-eque melodies and towering, timeless anthems.

⊙ **Standing On The Shoulder Of Giants** (2000; Big Brother).
The big-beat incisions of "Fuckin' In The Bushes" and "Go Let It Out" are refreshingly successful; Liam's writing debut, "Little James", offers a simplistic and heart-felt moment, and "Sunday Morning Call" unearths stark and honest depths in Noel's voice.

⊙ **Familiar To Millions** (2000; Big Brother).
This set steers clear of newer tracks in favour of the classics. The good things about Oasis are here in spades – the crowd-pleasers, Liam's ripped-flesh vocals – and they easily outweigh the bad.

Jeremy Simmonds

OCEAN COLOUR SCENE

Formed Birmingham, 1989.

D read practitioners of bombastic 'dad-rock', over-musicianly and overbearing, or a classic rock act who borrow only from the best sources – where do you stand on the great **Ocean Colour Scene** debate?

There was a time, of course, when adopting any such position was entirely irrelevant. Formed in the late 80s, Ocean Colour Scene were widely viewed as one of the more anonymous of the anonymous scene bands known collectively as 'shoe-gazers'. Inspired by The Stone Roses and their effects pedals, the Ocean Colour Scene of early 90s vintage was as generic an indie band as you could hope to avoid. **Simon Fowler** (vocals), **Steve Craddock** (guitar), **Damon Minchela** (bass) and **Oscar Harrison** (drums) recorded their debut single, "Sway", for independent label Phffft in 1990.

The band were soon under the wing of a major, Fontana Records, who reputedly paid over a million pounds for the privilege. The quartet set about recording an album, but initial sessions (recorded with The Rolling Stones' producer Jimmy Miller) were rejected, and new producer, Primal Scream associate Hugh Nicholson, was drafted in. He too had to be replaced, this time by Tim Palmer, before the finished album, OCEAN COLOUR SCENE, finally emerged in 1992. Despite the cameo from **Alison Moyet** and some kind reviews, Fontana were distinctly unhappy over the commercial returns on their large investment. When the group returned from an American tour they were cut adrift.

It's hard to pinpoint exactly what caused the turnaround in their fortunes. Approving nods from Noel Gallagher of Oasis ('Best band in Britain', he said) probably helped, as did Craddock and Minchela's work with **Paul Weller**. These high-profile liaisons helped to suck the group back into the mainstream, and this time they had a product with which the mainstream could sit happily – namely, "The Riverboat Song". One of the first fruits of a new deal with MCA Records, the single crashed into the UK Top 20 on the back of committed support from DJ Chris Evans (it was swiftly installed as the incidental music to his student-orientated TV show, *TFI Friday*). Quickly followed up by the massively promoted MOSELEY SHOALS (1996), OCS soon established themselves as an acceptable acronym of the rock music world. Peaking on entry at #2 in the UK, and earning several platinum discs, the album and the undeniable slog of touring put in by the band had seen them 'arrive' by the end of the year.

A collection, B-SIDES: SEASIDES AND FREERIDES (1997) was rushed out to keep interests high, whilst the third 'proper' album, MARCHING ALREADY (1997), was being put together. Released in another storm of publicity, the set broke no new ground, serving mainly to reinforce their position as retro-rockers for the new millennium, and the same could be said of ONE FROM THE MODERN (1999). By the release of 2001's MECHANICAL WONDER, *TFI Friday* had been axed, and even their so-called 'mentors', Weller and Gallagher, were experiencing a dip in popularity. The album made a respectable chart showing, as did 2003's NORTH ATLANTIC DRIFT, but the band's time is almost up.

⊙ **Moseley Shoals** (1996; MCA).
With nothing else as compulsive as "The Riverboat Song" aboard (which, in itself, was pretty much superior Status Quo), there is plenty of ammunition here to aid and abet Ocean Colour Scene's detractors. Conversely, there are people out there who bristle with excitement at the words 'blues' and 'jam'.

⊙ **Songs For The Front Row** (2001; Island).
This 'best of' compilation charts the career of a band that, despite waning audiences, have remained defiantly loyal to their retro, English sound.

Alex Ogg

PHIL OCHS

Born El Paso, Texas, 1940; died April, 1976.

A s a topical songwriter, **Phil Ochs** may have been second-best to Bob Dylan, but he was a talent all his own, exploring political hypocrisy and injustice with a keen (at times savage) wit, warm melodicism and intense personal commitment. Like Dylan, Ochs hungered for mass acceptance, eventually crossing the line from acoustic folk to electric rock to facilitate it. Stardom eluded him, however, and this failure sowed the seeds of his artistic and psychological demise.

When Ochs arrived in New York in 1962 after dropping out of Ohio State University, he was one of a crowd of acoustic folk singers packing Greenwich Village in Dylan's wake. Dubbing himself 'the singing journalist', Ochs was soon applying his light, quavering tenor to original material addressing all sorts of leftish concerns. While his earliest recordings tended toward the drily didactic, he'd developed both his wit and melodic chops by the time of his 1964 debut for Elektra, ALL THE NEWS THAT'S FIT TO SING. Overseen by future Doors producer Paul Rothchild, and featuring future Blues Project member **Danny Kalb** on second guitar, Phil kept his songs (dealing with Cuba, Vietnam, political prisoners, civil rights, and more) from becoming too strident, adding touches of idiosyncratic humour.

Ochs' second LP, I AIN'T MARCHING ANYMORE (1965), also produced by Rothchild, explored similar territory, and gave the burgeoning anti-Vietnam War movement a couple of anthems with the title cut and "Draft Dodger Rag". 1966's PHIL OCHS IN CONCERT, though, was by far his best acoustic material, as he started to trade in his reporter's notebook for more personal statements. His views of US imperialism retain a chilling relevance, his critique of organized religion ("Canons Of Christianity") remains capable of stirring controversy, and "Love Me, I'm A Liberal" is his best satirical tune, but the highlights were some melancholy ballads that forsook sociopolitical territory entirely, including "When I'm Gone", the love song "Changes", and "There But For Fortune", which became a British hit in a cover version by Joan Baez.

By the time IN CONCERT came out, electric folk-rock had revolutionized pop, and Ochs – as well as every other folkie of note – knew that he had to follow suit. Having tested the waters with an excellent, if commercially overlooked, electric version of "I Ain't Marchin' Anymore", he decided to go the whole route by relocating to Los Angeles and leaving Elektra for A&M, where he recorded with electric instrumentation under the direction of producer Larry Marks.

Ochs' late-60s albums are among the most frustrating of the era. Phil apparently had much less of an idea of how electric accompaniment should sound than Dylan did, and, with no permanent band established, he and Marks veered between orchestral string and flute arrangements, Dixieland, cocktail jazz, and session-men-dominated, laid-back El Lay rock. The songs remained purposeful and his intentions noble and forceful, but the arrangements were just as likely to detract from his vision as to amplify it. On the occasions when the compositions and the arrangements complemented each other, the results could be stunning: the eight-minute indictment of the bourgeoisie, "The Party", is his best long track; "The War Is Over" is a perfect combination of droll antiwar commentary with jaunty, martial flute-dominated backing; and "Outside Of A Small Circle Of Friends", the deadpan Dixieland-ish portrait of social apathy, became his most famous song.

A tireless idealist, Ochs often lent his efforts to activist causes, raising money through benefits and appearing at protests at the 1968 Democratic Convention. But the lack of a commercial breakthrough, the constant battering against the status quo, and the constant battering of his highest ideals by politicians, and society at large, may have worn Ochs down by the end of the decade. His first album of the 1970s, the sardonically titled GREATEST HITS, betrayed a loss of inspiration. His next effort, GUNFIGHT AT CARNEGIE HALL (recorded in 1970, initially released in Canada only in 1975), was a puzzling affair; performing in a gold lamé suit, he alternated between some of his more popular compositions, covers of "Mona Lisa" and "Okie From Muskogee", and medleys of Buddy Holly and Elvis Presley, to jeers from the audience.

Ochs, however, was suffering from much more than artistic misdirection. The 1970s were brutal for him: he suffered writer's block (GREATEST HITS was his last album of original material), damaged his voice in a mysterious incident in Africa, and was prone to alcoholic binges and increasingly serious depression. He managed to cut a few obscure singles during this time, but his hopeless spiral ended when he hanged himself in his sister's home on April 9, 1976. His influence lingers, however, in the work of all folk-rock troubadours who try to do more than entertain themselves and their audience. Like Billy Bragg – who wrote sleeve notes for an Ochs reissue CD – he demonstrated that you could address social maladies in song without sounding like a sap.

A career retrospective, AMERICAN TROUBADOUR (1997), whilst omitting a couple of his best-known songs, is a great introduction to this talented American.

Phil Ochs In Concert (1966; Elektra).
Although it was eventually revealed that these 'in concert' recordings were actually doctored performances cut in an empty hall, this is the best set of material from his acoustic troubadour period. Features several of his best songs, including "There But For Fortune", "Changes", "Love Me, I'm A Liberal" and "Cops Of The World", as well as some acerbic between-song patter.

The War Is Over: The Best Of Phil Ochs (1988; A&M).
Not precisely the best, but a good selection from his erratic A&M records. (The best Ochs compilation is the out-of-print A&M double LP CHORDS OF FAME, which includes the highlights of the Elektra and A&M years, plus rare singles and live material.)

There And Now: Live In Vancouver, 1968 (1990; Rhino).
Unreleased during Ochs' lifetime, this acoustic set offers a good cross-section of some of his best mid- and late-60s material, with committed interpretations that sometimes differ considerably from the studio versions.

Richie Unterberger

SINÉAD O'CONNOR

Born Glengeary, Ireland, 1966.

"Don't read your press, weigh it."
Andy Warhol

The controversial and mercurial **Sinéad O'Connor** first sang in public at the age of 14, performing Barbra Streisand's "Evergreen" at a schoolteacher's wedding. The positive reaction to her voice inspired her to run away to study music in Dublin, where she later joined local band Ton Ton Macoute before being spotted by U2 guitarist **The Edge**, who asked her to sing on his solo album. After that she was quickly snapped up by Ensign Records, and in November 1987 her solo debut, THE LION AND THE COBRA, was released.

A month later, O'Connor exploded onto British TV screens when the success of the "Mandinka" single earned her a memorable debut appearance on *Top Of The Pops*, where, shaven-headed and unsmiling, she stamped all over the show's stage to the bewilderment of the assembled kids and DJs. The song was catchy enough to give her a Top 20 hit, but it would be another two years before this 'bald-headed banshee' (*The Sun*) came within sniffing distance of the charts again. During that time, O'Connor toured extensively, particularly in America, where the raw beauty of THE LION AND THE COBRA attracted considerable college-radio support.

One song – and a cover version at that – transformed her career at the beginning of 1990. Until then, "Nothing Compares 2U" had been a little-known Prince track, but the combination of Nellee Hooper's stately arrangement, O'Connor's heartfelt delivery, and a stunning video in which she famously wept unscripted tears, helped her interpretation become the first global megahit of the new decade. With a huge army of new fans behind her, O'Connor's second album, I DO NOT WANT WHAT I HAVEN'T GOT (1990), went to #1 in almost every major territory on its way to six million sales.

The ferocious anger of her debut had by now simmered down to a brooding disquiet, particularly about England and her own misrepresentation ('I never said I was tough/That was everyone else/I really am soft and tender and sweet'). America, and in particular MTV, took her to their hearts, but the affair came to a sudden end when O'Connor refused to perform at a show which opened with the American national anthem, a display of defiance for which she was never forgiven. In the furore that followed, concert boycotts and ceremonial record-burnings were organized, and Frank Sinatra memorably threatened to 'kick her ass'. With her controversial image now snowballing, she snubbed the Brits and Grammy award ceremonies, claiming that pop stars were allowing themselves 'to be portrayed as being in some way more important, more special than the very people we are supposed to be helping'. Superstardom, it was clear, was resting uneasily on her shoulders.

Sinéad confides in her public

An inactive 1991 saw the release of just two singles, one of which, "My Special Child", was a harrowing lullaby to the baby O'Connor had miscarried the year before. This was the first sign of a move away from the generalized target practice of old that led to a more personal, confessional approach. On the way came that self-indulgent of rock-star enterprises, the covers album. AM I NOT YOUR GIRL? (1992), enjoyed mixed reviews and briefly re-established O'Connor in the UK and US charts. But controversy again overshadowed the music. Appearing on American NBC's *Saturday Night Live*, she ripped up a photo of the pope and invited the audience, in no uncertain terms, to 'fight the real enemy'. The strength of American public feeling against her was made brutally clear a fortnight later, when she was jeered off the stage at the Bob Dylan Tribute event at Madison Square Garden. It was a grotesque and painful spectacle, but the *NME*'s conclusion was typical: 'A gigantic, misguided ego is at work here.'

1993 was spent away from the public eye, but O'Connor's graphic revelations of childhood abuse at the hands of her mother (who died in 1985) led to a bitter, seismic rift with her father and brother. Distraught, she suffered a breakdown and made a half-hearted suicide bid in September. From this experience came a new optimism: she began writing and recording again, her mind alive with ideas, which would eventually become the 1994 highly strung and harrowingly confessional UNIVERSAL MOTHER, a cathartic record that catalogued her demons against a backdrop of serene Celtic-tinged melodies. Despite considerable critical acclaim, the album was no great commercial success, although the single "Thank You For Hearing Me" later charted.

The next five years brought only sporadic output – the sparse GOSPEL OAK EP charted briefly in 1997 – but yet more personal upheaval ensured that O'Connor remained catnip to the ever-predatory British tabloids. An unseemly and traumatic battle for custody of her second child Roisin, a skirmish with Sinn Féin, her appointment as a priest and a flirtation with lesbianism all generated predictable derision from the press and O'Connor, just as predictably, took it to heart. There were reports of an overdose and an anguished fax to music magazine *Q* in which she sounded closer than ever to a breakdown: 'I CANNOT take any more. Stop trying to kill me!'.

Finally emerging from all the turmoil, O'Connor parted company with Ensign and signed to Atlantic for FAITH & COURAGE (2000), her most self-assured record to date. By now the hit singles had all but dried up and this sometimes lightweight album did nothing to change that. Equally, 2002's SEAN NOS NUA, a collection of traditional Irish folk numbers (the title translates as 'Old Songs Made New'), was a little too obscure to climb the charts. O'Connor's recent output has confirmed the popular view that – while no one would wish her any more troubles – musically at least, O'Connor is at her most vivid and exciting when she's fired up and taking on the world.

⦿ **The Lion And The Cobra** (1987; Ensign).
A melting pot of ideas and styles which struggled to find a place on the musical agenda of the late 80s. O'Connor rages at everyone from indifferent boyfriends to her ex-headmaster on a collection of songs that crosses every musical border from pseudo-hip-hop ("I Want Your Hands On Me") to fuzzed-out psychedelia ("Just Call Me Joe"). A brilliantly provocative debut.

⦿ **I Do Not Want What I Haven't Got** (1990; Ensign).
This found its way into six million homes by virtue of its multiplatinum Prince cover, "Nothing Compares 2U". Sadness and frustration permeate all ten songs, but O'Connor's haunting voice and some striking orchestral arrangements (notably on "Feel So Different") lift the pervading gloom.

⦿ **Universal Mother** (1994; Ensign).
Years of private and public anguish found a release on this harrowing but hopeful record. There are moments of self-indulgence, but enough inspiration to suggest that O'Connor's best is yet to come.

⦿ **So Far...The Best Of** (1998; Chrysalis).
Though O'Connor's albums are all strong in their own right, this career retrospective shows just how consistently good her work has been for the last decade.

⦿ **Faith & Courage** (2000; Atlantic).
Dave Stewart adds sheen to the production and there's a fruitful union with Wyclef Jean on "Dancing Lessons", which, with the frail and confessional "Emma's Song" and the sparkling Rasta-influenced update of "Kyrie Eleison", forms the emotional core of the album.

Jonathan Kennaugh

OFFSPRING

Formed California, 1984.

An embryonic version of **Offspring** was formed in 1984 when singer **Dexter Holland** (Brian to his folks) met **Greg K** (Kreisel), in the high school cross-country running team in Garden Grove, California. Holland had shown a penchant for punk through his interest in underground bands, particularly the likes of T.S.O.L, The Adolescents, The Vandals and Agent Orange. Holland roped in Kreisel to form a band after they failed to get into a Social Distortion gig. Unfazed at the obstacle of neither of them being able to play any musical instrument, the pair got together with two fellow cross-country runners and formed Manic Subsidal.

Learning guitar to survival level, Holland turned his hand to songwriting. Their first recording looked to be jeopardized with the departure of one of the original guitarists. A replacement was found, however, in the form of ex-graduate, then-janitor **Kevin 'Noodles' Wasserman**. Breaking the athletic mould, Wasserman wasn't much into cross-country running, preferring to spend time practising guitar and drinking beer.

By 1987 **Ron Welty** had moved to Garden Grove and joined as drummer. That year the band invested in the pressing of a 7" single called "Born To Kill", a lightning-paced fusion of power-chord metal and can't-stand-still punk, which was to earmark the style of much of their later material. Unable to pay the extra 25 cents per copy to paste the front cover to the back of the record sleeve, they purchased a couple of glue sticks and did the task themselves. Singer Dexter recalls that they didn't hold very well.

It was over two years later that the band signed a record deal with Nemesis, a small underground label, and released the single "Baghdad", and their debut album, THE OFFSPRING. By 1992, the band had switched to Epitaph Records, run by ex-Bad Religion guitarist, Brett Gurewitz, to release the energetic but patchy IGNITION.

Having been, until now, a fairly well-kept secret, **The Offspring** exploded onto the rock scene with three successive singles: "Come Out And Play (Keep 'Em Separated)", "Self Esteem", and "Gotta Get Away", their widespread success being the snowflakes that preceded the avalanche of global recognition. With the US-media interest in punk-style bands – a by-product of the grunge explosion – Offspring (now mysteriously 'The'-less) were well placed to release the album SMASH (1994), an irresistibly tuneful offering, which crossed both genres. The album sold over nine million copies, making it the most successful independent record ever sold.

In 1997 Offspring signed to Columbia Records, picking up a multimillion-dollar advance for their next record, IXNAY ON THE HOMBRE. Whilst not as fresh and catchy as SMASH, the sound remained as frenetic as any past offering by the band. During the changeover they apparently decided they sounded better with the 'The', and became THE Offspring again.

The album was preceded by the single, "All I Want" (which also contained a cover of The Damned's "Smash It Up", as featured on the BATMAN FOREVER soundtrack album). AMERICANA (1998) finally cracked the previously unconvinced British market. The band took their chart-topping single "Pretty Fly (For A White Guy)" onto *Top Of The Pops* in a masterpiece of marketing crossover. Along with subsequent album releases such as CONSPIRACY OF ONE (2000), it was all good punky stuff – though these days it's rumoured the band no longer glue their own record sleeves. A new set, CHINESE DEMOCRACY, is expected soon.

Ⓟ **Smash** (1994; Epitaph).
Multimillion-selling, chart-topping, raw and noisy, this album might provide the missing link between punk and heavy metal.

Richard Dodd & Matt Saldana

MARY MARGARET O'HARA

Born Toronto, withholds date of birth.

"I have a long history of being told I have no rhythm, and of people saying 'I've heard chickens sing better than that'."

A composer and singer of exceptional ability and originality, **Mary Margaret O'Hara** received critical acclaim and the beginnings of a cult following after the release of her debut album in 1988. Unfortunately, very little new material has emerged since then, but it has sufficed to keep alive hopes that, given time and label support, she will produce further classic albums.

After graduating from Ontario Art College, O'Hara got occasional acting parts and began singing in a soul-pop group called Dollars, covering material by the likes of Etta James. In 1976 she joined the rock band (**Songship**, whom she later persuaded to rename themselves **Go Deo Chorus**) as lead singer, and composed for them many of the songs that would feature on MISS AMERICA. O'Hara had soon become the focus for the band, developing an increasingly out-there stage performance, ad-libbing songs into gibberish, flapping one arm around like a flag while the other hung limp.

O'Hara left the band in 1983, but it was a Go Deo Chorus demo tape, surreptitiously sent around by a friend, that attracted the attention of Virgin, who signed her as a solo artist the following year. She went into the studio that November, accompanied by several members of her old band, and with Andy Partridge (ex-XTC) on production duties; he was phased by O'Hara's methods, however, and left after just one day. Her approach was indeed unorthodox. As guitarist **Rusty McCarthy** recalls, 'she might have her rhythm section switching beats, bass playing backward... or bass in 3/4 time and drums in 4/4', with his guitar bridging the intersections. These sessions yielded lots of tracks, but only four of them ("A New Day", "When You Know Why You're Happy", "Keeping You In Mind" and "You Will Be Loved Again") made it onto the album. Virgin wanted a marketable product, and relations with O'Hara became stormy.

Over the next three years, O'Hara remained on contract to Virgin and recorded more than enough material for an album. But the tapes were unmixed (or not mixed to everyone's satisfaction) and it was looking as if the project was going to die. In October 1987, however, the experimental guitarist and composer Michael Brook saw O'Hara and **Hugh Marsh** performing as a duo in Toronto, and undertook to help mix and co-produce the Virgin material. It was the perfect combination.

MISS AMERICA finally appeared in 1988 and it was astonishing – flouting conventional rules of arrangement and delivery in a manner that invited comparison with Van Morrison, Tom Waits or Tim Buckley. And, as with these artists, there was a strong sense of musical tradition behind the experimentation: "Keeping You In Mind" seemed like an old standard, as if Billie Holiday had sung it previously, while "Not Be Alright", musically the most unorthodox piece on the album, combined reggae and country forms, creating a jerky momentum to carry its lyric of calamity and breakdown. The emotional candour of the set was undiluted by cliché: for example, "You Will Be Loved Again", in which O'Hara was accompanied only by acoustic bass, combined the superficial characteristics of a bar-room song and a church anthem, but O'Hara's incredibly pure voice bent the notes and flew in unexpected directions, as every possible nuance of feeling was squeezed out of the simple lyric.

The album garnered ecstatic reviews in Britain and Canada – more hesitant ones in the US – but Virgin were still unhappy about their product, especially when it failed to chart, and a US tour left most audiences bemused: 'Dementia's not something a crowd expects of a singer-songwriter', one critic observed.

Since then, O'Hara has appeared mainly as a guest for other artists or one-off projects. She contributed a track to the PAUL HAINES ALBUM (1993), which used the poet's work as lyrics; provided vocals for **MORRISSEY**'s 1990 single, "November Spawned A Monster"; and she has sung in concert with the Lost Dakotas and Blue Rodeo. She has also worked in film, acting alongside Tom Waits in *Candy Mountain* (1986), and both acting and providing a soundtrack for *The Events Leading Up To My Death* (1991). More recently, she worked on the score and soundtrack of the film *Apartment Hunting* (2001).

Although O'Hara's work is greatly admired by rock figures such as Michael Stipe and Tanita Tikaram, and her songs have been covered by the Cowboy Junkies and This Mortal Coil, among others, her career seems on hold, at present, as far as a non-film-related album goes. She performs some new songs at her occasional gigs in Toronto, however, and says she's also interested in producing an instrumental record. Whatever, there's a contingent out there waiting, convinced of her genius.

⊙ **Miss America** (1988; Virgin/Kotch).
Just the one album, but definitely a classic, so get hold of a copy as soon as you can.

Martin Haggerty

MIKE OLDFIELD

Born Reading, England, May 15, 1953.

"They put me in the New Age slots in the record shops. It's not New Age. New Age Music is something session musicians do in their spare time."

The problem for **Mike Oldfield** was that he did the lot in his teens. In 1968, aged 15, he and his sister **Sally** (vocals) recorded a folk album, SALLYANGIE, for major label Transatlantic. At 16 he was playing bass with Soft Machine founder **KEVIN AYERS**' band **The Whole World**, an eclectic ensemble featuring avant-garde classical arranger **David Bedford** and radical jazz saxophonist **Lol Coxhill**, and a year later he was their lead guitarist. At 19 he had recorded TUBULAR BELLS, the rock instrumental icon whose sixteen-million-worldwide sales floated the fledgling Virgin Records towards its eventual corporate waters. Not a bad CV so far for a

shy-to-the-point-of-reclusive hippie multi-instrumentalist.

TUBULAR BELLS (its working title was 'Opus 1') was the first release on Virgin Records in June 1973. It was recorded in studio time gifted by Richard Branson (then a mail-order record retailer) and had been rejected by every label Branson had suggested, prior to hitting on the idea of launching his own label; yet its release was greeted with acclaim just as hyperbolic as the retrospective backlash. Basically an instrumental collage built within a sphere familiar to rock sensibilities, its great achievement – especially for a first composition – lay in its sustained intricacy and intuitive development.

The key to Oldfield's composition was looping clusters of notes – played on a variety of instruments mainly by Oldfield alone – which were built to a grandly cumulative, strangely emotional, climactic coda with a cod-thespian narration by the late Bonzo Dog man **Viv Stanshall**. It had tunes, too: you could whistle to it, have sex to it (a popular pursuit in the mid 70s), and even set it up as a movie soundtrack, as William Friedkin was to do for *The Exorcist*.

Despite the personal multitracked nature of his beast, BELLS was clear and taut enough in structure to allow Oldfield the opportunity to conduct ensemble renditions a month after its release at London's Queen Elizabeth Hall (a 'classical' venue) and on TV. On these occasions he was joined by a host of underground/progressive-rock luminaries, including old mates Kevin Ayers and David Bedford, Gong's **Steve Hillage**, and even **Mick Taylor** from The Stones. It's odd to reflect how hip the whole enterprise was back then.

Inevitably, it was a hard act to follow. HERGEST RIDGE (1974), the second Mike Oldfield creation, was unveiled to an expectant world and a British music press ever ready to shoot down yesterday's heroes. The new album, named after the remote part of Herefordshire its author had retreated to, was in reality a slightly more mature, avant-garde offspring – more serene and sedentary, less rocky, but with similar genesis. The critics began to sneer, but it again sold in crateloads, dislodging its predecessor from the top of the UK album charts, where it had resided over a year.

In retrospect, Virgin did little to offset the backlash, milking BELLS dry, releasing a wholly inappropriate 'classical' orchestral version with the Royal Philharmonic Orchestra, and – in 1975 – a futile but then fashionable quadrophonic version for people with four ears.

That year also saw Oldfield negotiating the difficult 'third-opus syndrome' in the form of OMMADAWN (1975). Surprisingly, given the pressures of fame at this point, it transcended its predecessors on every level, and stands perhaps as the fruition of Oldfield's abstract ambition. It marked a departure both in working methods and creative styles. Other musicians were involved in aspects of composition and arrangement, and the hypnotic, slowly unfurling

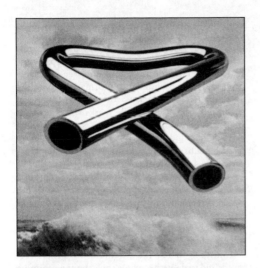

themes had distinct moods supplied by the folk musics of Eastern Europe, Africa and Ireland – the latter enhanced by the presence of Chieftains maestro **Paddy Moloney** on uillean pipes. It was way out there, ahead of its time – a pre-sampler, proto-ambient, ethno stonker – and Oldfield's electric guitar was sublime, shimmering, gliding and rising to a frenzy without a hint of self-indulgence.

Its creator, however, was a troubled 22-year-old, and all the more bemused amid punk's cull of hippies old and young. Virgin kept Oldfield on its books, as well they might, but they were moving with the times, signing up the Sex Pistols, hitching up their boards to surf with the New Wave. Though hardly a vacuous, progressive/pomp-rocker (that, ironically, would come later), Oldfield suddenly felt himself beached. 'Punk diluted the musical abilities of practically a whole generation. You were machine-gunned to death in the pop press if you really could play', he lamented. The whole cultural thrust of the age eluded him.

A three-year hiatus of retreat and therapy followed, before a disturbingly extrovert and hair-shorn Oldfield emerged, apparently having come to terms with peaking too early in life. Between 1978 and 1981 he returned to the album-a-year schedule. First came INCANTATIONS (1978), which continued side-long symphonic rock ideas, but gave a nod to the pop world with a single, "Guilty"; both charted. PLATINUM (1979) quoted from minimalist composer Philip Glass's "North Star", but also featured real songs – with vocalist **Wendy Roberts** crooning Gershwin's "I Got Rhythm". QE2 (1980) dispensed with the trademark long stuff altogether and, as if to celebrate, covered Abba's "Arrival", sung by (now regular) collaborator **Maggie Reilly**.

Oldfield was to continue in this pop-melody vein for some time, co-writing and performing now with Reilly and a core group, and combining gratingly twee hits – "Moonlight Shadow" reached #4 in the UK in 1983 – with more serious stuff on CRISES (1983). Accessibility at all costs seems to have been

his credo: a robust response to the post-punk realignment of the record business but one that clearly dissipated his strengths. In 1985 there was some return to form with the film score for *The Killing Fields* – soundtracks could have proved a rewarding byway for Oldfield – but in general he seemed altogether too distracted and swamped by new Fairlight technology, which rendered albums like ISLANDS (1987) and EARTHMOVING (1989) airbrushed and sterile.

In 1992 TUBULAR BELLS II appeared, in good time for the following year's twentieth-anniversary concerts. Oldfield had been quiet for a while, and there was a genuine sense of occasion, as what appeared to be the original BELLS – only perhaps played backwards – was premiered with live TV transmission from the Edinburgh Festival. Sold-out runs at the Royal Albert Hall and Carnegie Hall in New York followed. It wasn't a great work, but an eloquent celebration of earlier grooves, and, with ambient music in fashion, an Orb remix of the track "Sentinel" provided this perennial outsider with fresh credibility.

Oldfield has issued another two albums since: THE SOUND OF DISTANT EARTH (1994), a suite named after the Arthur C. Clarke work, based on his longstanding interest in the writer's work, and VOYAGER (1996), a Celtic-tinged New Age affair. To catch the few isolated tribespeople and rugged survivalists who hadn't picked up a copy from passing travellers, Virgin had original engineer/producer Simon Heyworth give the masters a little spit and polish and reissued TUBULAR BELLS in 1998; this classic popped up again in 2003 as a box set after Oldfield applied his own expertise to a complete studio rework of the original material.

⦿ **Tubular Bells** (1973; Virgin).
The length, the meanders, and the bells, the bells ... An overdub-fest that, surprisingly, stands up well enough.

⦿ **Ommadawn** (1975; Virgin).
The record Mike Oldfield was put on the earth to make.

⦿ **XXV – The Essential** (1998; WEA).
A sampler of Oldfield's greatest bits, brutally cut into easy-to-manage excerpts.

⦿ **Tubular Bells 2003** (2003; WEA).
3 CDs, 1 DVD, and a much fatter sound all around, assuming your hi-fi can tell the difference.

Chris Brook

WILL OLDHAM

Born Louisville, Kentucky, 1971.

Palace, **Palace Brothers**, **Palace Music**, **Palace Songs**, and now **Bonnie 'Prince' Billy**? The name changes, but the song remains the same. The mastermind of all of these projects is singer-songwriter **Will Oldham**, who is Palace in the same sense that Mark E. Smith is The Fall. Reaching back into the spirit of Appalachian Mountain music for his unique brand of post-punk solipsism, Oldham has been labelled 'the lo-fi Neil Young' and 'the American Nick Cave', but these tags

bonnie 'prince' billy
master and everyone

don't do justice to his distinctively addled vision, delivered in a thin but expressive voice that seems unable to make it through a single take without cracking.

Oldham was well on the way to making a name for himself in the film world before he began recording music. At the age of 16, he had a prominent role as a miner in *Matewan*, John Sayles' 1987 movie about an Appalachian mining community. Since then, he's appeared in several other independent movies and TV productions. But, characteristically, he doesn't like to talk about them.

His present-day focus is his musical career, which was effectively launched in 1993 with THERE IS NO-ONE WHAT WILL TAKE CARE OF YOU, his debut album and the most unremittingly bleak item in the Palace discography. Oldham would never exactly lighten up, but he did recognize the value of expanding his musical range. The 1994 six-song HOPE will hold the most appeal for Neil Young fans (albeit adventurous ones), fleshing out his bone-weary delivery with more harmonies, keyboards and electric guitar. Other times, Palace can appear as essentially Oldham unplugged, delivering a bare-bones sermon with nothing but acoustic guitar and vocals.

Oldham has been heralded as a leading light of the 'lo-fi' movement, which is understandable in the light of the spartan arrangements of his music, in which the spirit of the moment is valued much more highly than the polish of the product. But perhaps Oldham grew weary of the label, because he employed top producer Steve Albini to work on 1995's VIVA LAST BLUES. The project must have been a bit of a stretch for both men – Albini needing to restrain in-your-face sonics, Oldham having to make an effort to make his textures richer – but the result was a success, adding a little oomph to Oldham's songs without danger of veering into slickness.

The supply of his music will always exceed demand, as Oldham's vision is too twisted and down-beat for mass consumption. The man himself cultivates the air of an enigma. He'll give interviews in which he'll discuss films in depth, but resolutely refuse to discuss his music or biography. For a time he identified himself as Push, and his record sleeves often disclose absolutely no information about the accompanying musicians or circumstances of recording (though he usually works with Louisville musicians, including former members of the obscure, now-defunct indie band **SLINT**). Most of his albums feature full band arrangements, but live concerts are often solo acoustic affairs; when he does take a band on the road the results are often overwhelming and strangely out of time, appearing more like an 80s Beach Boys roadshow than a shy, retiring alternative country collective. His first live gig, however, consisted mostly of on-stage belching, as opening act at CBGB's for the notorious Rapeman.

And then there's the enigma of his bittersweet words and melodies. A whole song about performing intercourse with a mountain, a ballad of recollections of getting drunk at the pulpit, a composition titled "I Am A Cinematographer" – none use run-of-the-mill singer-songwriter imagery, even by alternative-rock standards. At the same time, there is a spiritual, quasi-biblical feel to much of Oldham's work, demonstrating a concern with redemption and dignity that steers his music well clear of the doom-and-gloom camp.

Praise for Oldham has poured in from mainstream sources such as *Newsweek* and the *New York Times*, but it's unlikely he will ever be out to please anybody but himself. His 1996 one-man (Palace) release, ARISE THEREFORE, was as raw as anything previous, its rough, unpolished sound echoed on the sleeve – a black-and-white drawing of a house in a forest – and a crudely typed lyric sheet with scribbled changes. The lyrics told of love gone awry (song titles included "You Have Cum In Your Hair" and "Your Dick Is Hanging Out") to a dubby soundtrack of piano, strummed guitar, bass drone and primitive drum machine. Once again, it enhanced Oldham's oddball reputation and growing cult following. Two compilations followed, LOST BLUES AND OTHER SONGS (1997) and GUARAPERO (2000), which together offered a worthwhile summary of Oldham's career to date and a good starting point for the curious.

Around this time Oldham shifted away from the Palace tag to release the seminal I SEE A DARKNESS (1998) under the moniker of **Bonnie 'Prince' Billy**. The set was one of the best yet: rich in dark imagery and musically focused, featuring fine numbers such as "Minor Place", "Death To Everyone" and the spellbinding title cut, which has since been covered by Johnny Cash. Two more Bonnie… albums followed, EASE DOWN THE ROAD (2001) and MASTER AND EVERYONE (2003), both equally as solid as the first.

On top of all this 'day job' output, Oldham has found time to dabble with film scores and side pro-

WILL OLDHAM

jects, releasing BLACK RICH MUSIC (1998), the instrumental ODE MUSIC EP (2000), an album with **Ryan Murphy** (ALL MOST HEAVEN, 2000), GET ON JOLLY (2000) with the Dirty 3's **Mick Turner** and, most recently, a soundtrack collaboration with **DAVID PAJO**, issued under the name **Continental Op**

Palace

(•) **There Is No One What Will Take Care Of You** (1993; Drag City).
This is the collection that set the ball rolling. From the peculiar opening clunk of "Idle Hands Are The Devil's Playthings" through to the blinding "O Paul", this set is a dust-blown gem.

(•) **Hope** (1994; Drag City).
Along with VIVA LAST BLUES, this six-song EP is Palace's most accessible effort. Hardly an insignificant detour (as many EPs are), this is bar-room country-rock for the truly alienated.

(•) **Viva Last Blues** (1995; Drag City).
Palace become a bit warmer and listener-friendly with help from Steve Albini. Much of this constitutes Oldham's best work to date, especially "The Brute Choir", "Old Jerusalem" and the goofy "The Mountain Low".

Bonnie 'Prince' Billy

(•) **I See A Darkness** (1998; Drag City).
Augmented by warm piano melodies, this set is far more wholesome than many of Oldham's earlier lo-fi country offerings.

Richie Unterberger

OLIVIA TREMOR CONTROL

Formed Athens, Georgia, US, 1995.

Listen to the press hype surrounding this band and you could be forgiven for thinking that they plug into the same well-worn sockets marked "Strawberry Fields Forever", "Good Vibrations", "See Emily Play". You might reflect that we don't really need another guitar band with unhealthy 60s obsessions cranking out thirdhand psychedelia. But then maybe you haven't heard the **Olivia Tremor Control**, formerly one of the better-kept secrets to emerge from Athens, Georgia.

Although the band certainly throw the usual ingredients into the blender – backwards guitar, echo, treated piano, phasing, sound effects, whimsical notions of 'concept', dreamy vocals – they then (to stretch the metaphor) actually bother to switch the blender on. With numerous artists treating psychedelia as a 'style' rather than an 'attitude', the pop arena is filled with the sound of astute pop students reading history rather than making it. The OTC, on the other hand take the route of alchemy, moulding the basic reference points into a more precious commodity.

The band consist of **Bill Doss**, **Eric Harris**, **Will Hart** and **John Fernandez** (all multi-instrumentalists). Their initial recordings appeared on their own Elephant 6 Collective, a loose collection of likeminded (if little known) free spirits such as The Apples (In Stereo), Neutral Milk Hotel, and The

Clay Bears. A debut EP, CALIFORNIA DEMISE, introduced the trademark splintered sound, complete with guitar effects and Beach Boys vocal harmonizing. A second EP, GIANT DAY, appeared on the Drug Racer label, its multi-layered pop sensibility segueing seamlessly into their fully realized magnum opus, DUSK AT CUBIST CASTLE: MUSIC FROM AN UNREALIZED FILM SCRIPT (1996): some 70 minutes and 27 tracks of wayward genius, detailing a day in the life of an imaginary town. The album resonated with the same warped pop vision and spooky derangement of cult 60s artists such as Skip Spence and the West Coast Pop Art Experimental Band; tantalizing glimpses of melody broke up and re-formed inside a single song. The effect was kaleidoscopic. This was a band more interested in reinvention than revivalism. Psychedelia was meant to challenge, to distort and shape perception – it was never meant for fey easy listening nor meandering cosmic jams and neither crime is committed on DUSK...

Tours with Beck and a good level of press coverage proved that music with a skewed, experimental edge could push open the door towards mainstream acceptance. Following a UK tour with Gorky's Zygotic Mynci in 1998, the band released a limited-edition 'experimental' second album, THE OLIVIA TREMOR CONTROL VERSUS THE BLACK SWAN COLLECTIVE. Featuring two lengthy drone-tinged instrumentals; the venture was far from successful.

With the wholesale pillaging of the 60s becoming a little tedious, the Olivia Tremor Control seemed intent on offering some fresh routes down psychedelia's well-worn pathways. Consequently, BLACK FOLIAGE (ANIMATION MUSIC VOLUME ONE) (1999) had a keen experimental edge – more "Revolution No.9" than "Sergeant Pepper". At times it was a mess, at other times it was a beautiful trip. An acid-drenched roller-coaster ride for the senses, BLACK FOLIAGE left you dizzy and exhausted, and is strictly for those who prefer their psychedelic intake in heavy doses.

The band entered the 21st century with PRESENTS: SINGLES AND BEYOND (2000), which, as a 'best of', ditched some of the more avant-garde features of its predecessors, to concentrate still further on the songwriting.

(•) **Dusk at Cubist Castle** (1996; Flydaddy Records/Blue Rose; rereleased 1997).
27 varied tracks over 70 minutes, and yet no sense of sprawl invades OTC's distinctive debut. However, even if you do find DUSK occasionally collapsing under a flurry of ideas, don't worry. Relax. Put on disc two – a collection of ambient dreamscapes designed to help you sleep. Dogs bark, crickets chirp under the moon (no, really, it was recorded at night on their back porch), occasionally a strange ripple of acoustic noise eddies through and then, well, not much else happens. Sublime, and can be played in tandem with disc one to achieve a suitable state of sonic bliss. Feed your head.

(•) **Presents: Singles And Beyond** (2000; Emperor Norton).
A great little collection and a great place to start if you're new to the group. And for the fans, this set offers a chance to catch up with long-lost gems such as "Beneath The Climb".

Nig Hodgkins

TARA JANE O'NEIL

Born Chicago, 1973.

Back in 1991, **Tara Jane O'Neil** was the bass guitarist of the influential **Rodan**, playing alongside **Jason Noble** (guitar/vocals), **Jeff Mueller** (guitar/vocals) and **Kevin Coultas** on drums. With their sprawling, post-rock sound, the band garnered much acclaim from the indie community for their only album, 1994's RUSTY (named after their beloved sound engineer, Bob 'Rusty' Weston of Shellac).

When the group broke up, only a year after the record's release, Noble altered his trajectory drastically with the semi-classical collective Rachel's, while Mueller resurfaced in June Of 44. The pair were eventually reunited in 1997 in the band Shipping News. (More recently both Noble and Mueller have released solo recordings on Monitor Records.)

Coultas continued to collaborate with O'Neil in her new band, the moody, string-driven **Sonora Pine**. Here O'Neil took on the roles of singer, songwriter, as well as guitarist. The project developed as a result of O'Neil's 1994 relocation to New York City with guitarist/vocalist **Sean Meadows**, from home town Louisville in Kentucky. Sonora Pine (featuring Meadows, Coultas, O'Neil and **Samara Lubelski** on violin) released their eponymous debut in 1995 and the follow-up, II, a year after. Concurrently, O'Neil's prolific creativity led her into an acting role in the cult film *Half Cocked* (1995) where she met and entered into partnership with **Ruby Falls**'s **Cynthia Nelson**. The song they recorded together for the film's soundtrack marked the beginning of a well-matched musical love affair. Under the name of **Retsin**, the duo were joined by **Greta Ritcher** (drums) and **Todd Cook** (bass) and have been responsible for three intimate acoustically leaning albums, 1996's EGG FUSION, 1998's SWEET LUCK OF AMARYLLIS and the dark, pastoral CABIN IN THE WOODS (2000).

O'Neil has long specialized in collaborations, recording and performing with **Ida** and **Come**, amongst others, in the incestuous post-rock, post-folk musical communities of Chicago and New York. After a decade of accumulating multi-instrumental skills and experimenting with diverse styles, O'Neil's first solo release, PEREGRINE (2000) saw her work achieving fruition. Displaying her incredible range, O'Neil played most instruments herself (including thumb piano and balalaika), wrote all the songs and painted the cover art. The mysterious peregrinations of her acoustic sonic sculptures through whispery, twisting jazz routes showcase her relentless innovation and refusal to compose songs that conform to expectation. IN THE SUN LINES followed in 2001 and featured old friends and new noises, while MUSIC FOR A METEOR SHOWER (2002), a collaboration with **Daniel Littleton** of Ida, found Tara in a far looser, instrumental mood. The same year also witnessed the release of an EP, THE JOY

OF..., on the Acuarela imprint, which is well worth tracking down for "Ahn Fahr", a blinding cover of Springsteen's "I'm On Fire".

With the promise of further solo work and more from the very much extant Retsin, O'Neil's maturing talent looks to be attaining its potential at last.

Rodan

(•) **Rusty** (1994; Quarterstick).
A classic slab of progressive hardcore. This set stands alongside Slint's SPIDERLAND as one of those records that defined a genre. Essential.

Retsin

(•) **Egg Fusion** (1996; Simple Machines).
This wonderful album is mournful and meandering, but also tense, at times discordant. Sweet melodies twist in and around country twangs, etching grooves into the sparse arrangements like a rake in a sandbox. "Kangaroo" and "Loon" provide the set's poppier moments, while "Bodega" is beautifully broken-hearted.

Tara Jane O'Neil

(•) **Peregrine** (2000; Quarterstick).
Hush and atmospheric, thronging instrumentation and private confessionals, O'Neil's debut solo groups together everything she does best.

Tara Jane O'Neil & Daniel Littleton

(•) **Music For A Meteor Shower** (2002; Tiger Style).
This brooding collection of improvised music was conceived after the duo watched a meteor shower together in New York. Though the playing style is familiar, the overall feel is far more spacious and meandering than on Tara's other releases. If you're after her songs, look elsewhere; but if it's a soundtrack to astral phenomena you're after, look no further.

Annebella Pollen

THE ONLY ONES

Formed London, 1976; disbanded 1981.

It's traditional, when writing about original UK punks **The Only Ones**, to mention that they could actually play their instruments. Despite this obvious disadvantage, they still came out with some of the best, most sordid rock'n'roll in history. What set them apart was the bleakness of their subjects, and the tortured delivery of **Peter Perrett**, singer, guitarist, songwriter and centre of attention.

Perrett had 'rock star' written all over him. He was good-looking, waif-like in his fake fur knee-length on-stage coat, dangerously angry about something and struggling hard to say it. A classic, too-much-too-young rock'n'roll junkie icon like Johnny Thunders or Keith Richards, Perrett came alive in front of an audience but seemed pretty lost when the lights went out and the people went home. Though it was Perrett who formed The Only Ones after the demise of England's Glory, they were not just 'Perrett's band' – **Mike Kellie**, who had previously drummed for Spooky Tooth and Peter Frampton, and bassist **Alan Mair**, who had been in bands as far back as the 60s, both brought experience to the outfit, and guitarist **John Perry** had a youthful exuberance to balance the team. Together they put together a powerful, New-York-Dollsy live set and released their first single, "Lovers Of Today", on their own Vengeance label in the summer of 1977.

By the end of the year, The Only Ones had built up a dedicated London following and were attracting attention just at the time when the major record companies were trawling for the next Squeeze or Dire Straits. They signed to CBS and in 1978 released THE ONLY ONES, which contained the beautiful love poetry of "Another Girl, Another Planet" amongst other gems of sleaze and bad living. They toured extensively, spreading the word as best they could amidst the blizzard of new bands swirling around the UK and making the most of the album's entry into the lower 50s of the UK chart.

A swift return to the studio followed, resulting in the excellent self-produced EVEN SERPENTS SHINE in 1979. There was a distinctive edginess to the sound of the whole album and a raw, unfinished feel to some of the tracks – reflecting, perhaps, the internal disagreements which were becoming more heated as

the royalties, and the pharmaceutical fringe benefits, rolled in. Despite roping in Colin Thurston to produce and **Pauline Murray** (of Penetration) to sing on a couple of tracks, their third album, BABY'S GOT A GUN (1980), wasn't really that good and led to the band being dropped by CBS and ultimately splitting up.

Perrett later said that he spent most of the 1980s sitting in a room taking drugs. He was also rumoured to have been working as a cab driver in south London, back where he started. For ten years, all that came out was a couple of compilations of previously unreleased material (REMAINS and ALONE IN THE NIGHT – both for serious devotees only) and a video of promos and live recordings. Eventually, though, he started to save the royalties instead of turning them into powders, strapped on his guitar again, and began performing with his new group, **The One**, in 1995, and trekking back to the studio for WAKE UP STICKY (1996), a record Q greeted as 'the album he should have made sixteen years ago'. Still, it was good to hear his laconic voice drawl its way over a lyric once again.

○ **The Only Ones** (1978; CBS).
This is the one. Buy this album, make yourself something really decadent to enjoy and listen to this album on your own, while you enjoy it.

○ **Special View** (1979; Epic).
A remarkably premature 'greatest hits' compilation, this combines bits of the first and second albums and throws in "Lovers Of Today" for good measure.

Al Spicer
Thanks to John Perry for corrections

YOKO ONO

Born Tokyo, Japan, 1933.

"Yoko is the most famous unknown artist in the world. Everyone knows who she is, but nobody knows what she does." John Lennon

Few artists polarize opinion quite like **Yoko Ono**. In the late 60s her blend of defiant feminism, avant-garde pretension, musical amateurism and art terrorist shock tactics would alone have been enough to elicit consternation from a white, macho music press. Obviously, being held responsible for the break-up of The Beatles didn't help either. Even now, Ono seems largely beyond the pale of critical rehabilitation, although Rykodisc reissued virtually all her solo and John and Yoko material in 1997. And recently Yoko finally seems to be rocking a little happier with her son Sean.

Ono's privileged upbringing in New York paved the way for her involvement with the early-60s art scene. She formed part of the Fluxus movement, a loose conceptual umbrella for various 'happenings' and mixed-media events. One of her early performances was called 'Cut Piece' in which members of

the audience were invited to come on stage and cut off pieces of her clothing. In another performance Ono's body was wired up to amplifiers so that the movement of her clothing created a kind of music. All of which might have led to a career on the fringes of the art world were Yoko not to have met one **JOHN WINSTON LENNON** in the Indica Gallery in London on November 9, 1966. Their relationship – and the music borne out of the hothouse atmosphere of their mutual obsession – provided fascination and irritation in equal measure to a bemused public.

The first published fruits of their union were not encouraging. UNFINISHED MUSIC NUMBER 1: TWO VIRGINS FROM LATE '68 featured tape loops, guttural wailing and John and Yoko trying to hold notes for as long as possible, topped off by a cover featuring a naked John and Yoko. It was adventurous, sure, but collapsing in on itself in a welter of ego and conceit. It got worse – MUSIC NUMBER 2: LIFE WITH THE LIONS (1969) rambled between primal screaming, bad jazz, and the sound of a baby's heartbeat (John and Yoko suffered a miscarriage in the autumn of 1968). THE WEDDING ALBUM from October of the same year, featured, among other delights, the couple shouting each other's names for twenty minutes.

LIVE PEACE IN TORONTO released late in 1969 was greeted as a half-decent album. Unfortunately, Yoko features on the other half – a cacophony of discordant wails and feedback, leaving the impression that Lennon and a shit-hot rock'n'roll band were indulging an errant child. It set a pattern in that Lennon's output would often completely overshadow his wife's, a situation compounded by the fact that they would often release albums at the same time. Lennon's only great solo album, JOHN LENNON/PLASTIC ONO BAND, drew all attention away from Yoko's first solo album and intended companion piece, YOKO ONO/PLASTIC ONO BAND (both 1970). This is a pity, as the album has moments amidst the largely improvised chaos, notably the proto-punk "Why", with its blistering guitar from Lennon and Yoko's aggressive vocalizing.

From then on Yoko's albums got better and her husband's got worse. Her five solo albums of the 70s document an avant-gardist's gradual education in pop music. Admittedly, FLY (1971) was less than great, but the dissonant free jazz guitar on "O Wind" seemed to offer a sense of liberation and the overall feel is almost cohesive. And Yoko always had a way with a song title – "What A Bastard The World Is" and "I Felt Like Smashing My Face In A Clear Glass Window" being prime examples from the improved double album APPROXIMATELY INFINITE UNIVERSE (1972) and "Woman Power" from FEELING THE SPACE (1973). Both efforts reflect stronger songwriting from Yoko as she attempted to escape the long shadow of John. Indeed, Yoko managed some of the better moments on the generally dismal joint venture with Lennon, SOME TIME IN NEW YORK CITY (1972), an album dated badly by dog-eared political sentiments

and stodgy musicianship courtesy of the awful backing band, Elephant's Memory.

Following periods of separation and seclusion, John and Yoko returned to the spotlight with DOUBLE FANTASY in 1980. Lennon's murder a few weeks after its release conferred an elevated status on the album that is largely undeserved. Lennon's muse was effectively shot by then and, ironically, it was up to Yoko to offer the freshest music on the album, noticeably the urgent funk-punk of "Kiss, Kiss, Kiss".

John Lennon's death had the unwelcome side effect of casting disproportionate media glare on Ono's powerful 1981 single "Walking On Thin Ice", which featured her husband's lead guitar recorded a few days before he was shot. Such ghoulish fascination aside, SEASONS OF GLASS, her 1981 solo album, remains her strongest work to date – Yoko's almost conventional vocals creating an effective backdrop to a collection of strong, original material, including a stand-out ballad, "Even When You're Far Away".

Yoko's subsequent output in the 80s was hardly prolific. IT'S ALRIGHT – I SEE RAINBOWS (1982), despite the positive title, proved a mournful affair. STARPEACE (1985) was a rather bombastic error of judgement, laden down by pseudo-cosmic philosophizing.

The 90s proved more fruitful, with Yoko's blend of uncompromising noise and poetry seen as a pivotal influence on the post-grunge Riot Grrrl scene, and a more liberal rock press willing to listen afresh to albums that had been largely ignored at the time of their release. NEW YORK ROCK, a musical written for the stage by Yoko and featuring songs from her whole career, was surprisingly well received. Ono's 1995 album, RISING – featuring **Sean Ono Lennon** – sounded noisy and almost 'contemporary' in a climate of indie rock noise pollution. In another bizarre twist, "Walking On Thin Ice" appeared as a single in 2003, complete with a gaggle of club-friendly remixes. Not a bad achievement for a pensioner.

Walking On Thin Ice (1992; Rykodisc).
A good starting point, compiled by Yoko and favouring her more accessible work over the more difficult pieces.

Plastic Ono Band (1970; Rykodisc).
For those who find early Sonic Youth a touch too MOR, try a full-volume exploration of this seminal slice of noise chaos.

Nig Hodgkins

ORANGE JUICE

Formed Glasgow, Scotland, 1979; disbanded 1985.

From the tear-stained faces that greeted the announcement of their dissolution at London's Brixton Academy on January 19, 1985, it was clear that **Orange Juice** had commanded a rare devotion.

Beginning as the punk-inspired Nu-Sonics in late 1976, the band which eventually comprised **EDWYN COLLINS** (guitar/vocals), **James Kirk** (guitar), **Steven Daly** (drums) and **David McClymont** (bass) became Orange Juice in early 1979, adopting the name and a collectively fey demeanour as a reaction against the machismo into which punk had degenerated. It was still as a Nu-Sonic, though, that Collins befriended a young botany student by the name of **Alan Horne**, whose enthusiasm for the band was not only to keep them together through the troubled times of their rebirth as Orange Juice, but also to provide them with an outlet for their music through the founding of the Postcard Records label.

Initial releases on the new Glaswegian label proved to be a shared triumph of vision over musical ability and financial resources. "Falling and Laughing", recorded for under £100, and with an initial pressing of 1000, reaped immediate critical acclaim, as did the subsequent singles "Blueboy", "Simply Thrilled Honey" and "Poor Old Soul". However, although Postcard was eventually to establish itself an impressive roster of acts that included Aztec Camera, Josef K and the Go-Betweens, the label imploded with the loss of Orange Juice to Polydor in 1981.

It was an advance from Polydor which enabled them to complete the recording of their debut You CAN'T HIDE YOUR LOVE FOREVER (1982; reissued 1998; Polydor), an album which for many was a negation of the purity of vision which had characterized the band's previous output and the whole Postcard ethos. In retrospect it retains an endearing naivety, exemplified by a rather ambitious rendition of Al Green's "L.O.V.E." Notably, though, the album featured guitar work from **Malcolm Ross** (ex-Josef K), whose inclusion into the band's line-up was to force a split with Kirk and Daly (who left to form the less-than-successful Memphis). Daly was replaced by Zimbabwean refugee **Zeke Manyika**, an altogether more accomplished player but one whose presence closed the door on all foreign touring options because of his status as an illegal immigrant.

Presumably this was considered a price worth paying as Manyika's rhythmic mastery undoubtedly enabled Collins to better realize his funk/pop aspirations. Certainly, RIP IT UP (1982; reissued 1998; Polydor) proved an altogether more purposeful affair, despite its odd shifts of pace, veering from the uplifting African-influenced "Hokoyo" to Velvets-inspired ballads such as "Louise Louise". It also delivered the band's one UK Top 10 single, by way of the title track, a catchy slice of pure-pop tomfoolery built around an elastic toe-tapping bass line.

Yet the album itself failed to better the chart placing attained by its predecessor, and when subsequent singles failed to chart either, Polydor's commitment to the band began to waver. Indeed, relations between Collins (in particular) and Polydor were fast reaching an impasse, and to make matters worse the group fragmented again in mid-1983, with McClymont and Ross decamping in pursuit of their own projects (Ross eventually surfacing in **AZTEC CAMERA**), though not before the recording of a six-track mini-album with reggae producer Dennis Bovell. Though brief, TEXAS FEVER (1984; reissued 1998; Polydor) was far from insubstantial, with

Bovell's dubby production showcasing to great effect the fast-maturing songwriting talents of Collins and the confident musicianship of the band.

Down but not quite out, Collins fulfilled touring commitments with a makeshift band before returning to the studio to record THE ORANGE JUICE (1984; reissued 1998, Polydor), a dark, brooding classic in which his songwriting was by turns wry, downbeat and disarmingly autobiographical – its most upbeat number proclaiming that he was 'going through a lean period'.

Polydor not surprisingly showed little interest in the work, and when the two singles "What Presence" and "Lean Period" stalled, the label acted to terminate Collins's contract. Curiously, Manyika was retained as a solo artist, whereupon he gained a degree of critical favour but little in the way of commercial success. Edwyn Collins meantime pursued a solo career, which blossomed into chart success.

⊙ **The Esteemed Orange Juice** (1992; Polydor).
This compilation will have to suffice, due to the unavailability of the above-listed albums. Still, a thorough overview of the band's years with Polydor.

⊙ **The Heather's On Fire** (1993; Postcard).
Lovingly compiled by Horne and Collins, this is a collection of Orange Juice's four Postcard singles and B-sides, together with tracks culled from BBC sessions. A fine introduction to what is arguably the band's best and most influential work.

Ian Lowey

THE ORB

Formed London, 1989.

Back in the days of punk, some warned that the hippies would return one day, but the truth is that they never really went away. With the rise of the rave scene, they resurfaced under the label of ambient, and leading the field were **The Orb**, a sort of latter-day Pink Floyd array with other influences, including reggae, dance music, punk, The KLF's approach to sampling, and more way-out hippie bands such as Gong. The Orb's psychedelic stream has become the sound with which to chill out from the hard sounds of dance, like punks chilled out to reggae in the 70s.

The Orb's one consistent member is **Alex Patterson**. A rave enthusiast and amateur DJ in the early days of London's acid-house explosion, he worked as an A&R man for the EG label, the original home of ambient music, whose clients included Brian Eno, and who were publishers for **Jimi Cauty** of The KLF. Alex also did stints as a roadie for punk bands Killing Joke and Basement 5 ('the black Public Image', as some called them). The Orb ignited from these cross-connections, their first spark being a track by Patterson and Cauty called "Tripping On Sunshine", which appeared on a compilation album put together by Killing Joke's **Youth** called ETERNITY PROJECT ONE (1988).

The four tracks on their first EP, KISS (1989), were based on samples from New York's Kiss FM black music radio station. Only a thousand copies were pressed and the record is now a collector's item. In the meantime, Patterson was taken on by Paul Oakenfold as resident DJ in the chill-out room at his Land of Oz club. One evening, while playing a **STEVE HILLAGE** track, he discovered that Hillage was there listening; the result was Patterson's early collaboration on Hillage's band, **System 7**'s, releases while Hillage joined The Orb for occasional live performances.

The Orb's next release, based on samples from Minnie Ripperton's 70s soul classic "Loving You", was entitled "A Huge Ever Growing Pulsating Brain That Rules From The Centre Of The Ultraworld" (1989). The record was eventually a hit, but its greater significance lies in its claim to being the first ever ambient house record: it was taken up in chill-out rooms across Britain, and led to The Orb's first session for John Peel. First time round, The Orb had failed to obtain permission for the Minnie Ripperton sample, so the record was deleted after a pressing of only 3000, but rereleased on Youth's Big Life label the following year, after the legalities had been sorted out.

In early 1990, Dave Stewart asked The Orb to remix his "Lilly Was Here". The new mix hit the UK Top 20, and suddenly the Orb found themselves in demand to remix tracks by artists as diverse as Depeche Mode and Bill Laswell. They released their own single called "Little Fluffy Clouds" (1990), with samples from the likes of Steve Reich and Ennio Morricone. This was a Patterson/Youth collaboration, with help from a new figure on the scene, a young sound engineer called **Thrash**. Jimi Cauty was now devoting more of his time to **THE KLF**, finally leaving The Orb altogether in the summer.

Patterson was still holding down his full-time A&R job, only making music on the side. In early 1991, he quit to devote himself full time to the band, with Thrash replacing Cauty. Steve Hillage on guitar completed the line-up for a live gig in aid of CND at London's T&C2, a major success that was followed by the release of the first album, a double entitled THE ORB'S ADVENTURES BEYOND THE UNDERWORLD (1991). It was a massive hit with the critics, perhaps because they were put into flotation tanks to listen to it. The album was originally to have been a triple, but the third record was released separately as a Christmas special called AUBREY MIXES, THE ULTRAWORLD EXCURSIONS. Deleted on the day of release, it sold enough to make the UK chart.

The next album, UFORB (1992) spawned the 39-minute "Blue Room", the longest single ever released. It again reached the UK Top 30, allowing the band to appear on BBC TV's *Top of the Pops* playing chess to its strains. A third Peel session followed in which The Orb, unusually, took the form of a rock four-piece, doing a version of The Stooges' "No Fun".

In 1993, following a money-related disagreement with Youth, Patterson left his Big Life label to sign up with Island, releasing LIVE 93, an assembly of material from gigs worldwide. In 1994, having played Woodstock 2, The Orb collaborated with German technoist **Thomas Fehlmann**, releasing the album POMME FRITZ, which stormed to #6 in the UK album charts and has been the zenith of their success in terms of sales so far. The following album, ORBVS TERRARVM (1995), also hit the chart's Top 20. However, 1997's ORBLIVION and 2001's CYDONIA carried the quirky ambient banner a little further, but failed to advance Patterson's musical vision.

The Orb, meanwhile, developed a live show that was more event than gig. Rather than have a support band, they built up with a series of house and techno DJs (the likes of Andy Weatherall, Darren Emerson and Paul Oakenfold) prior to a set featuring Patterson on the mixing desk with a varying crew on guitars, keyboards and electronics. Patterson still DJs himself, playing a mix of genres, particularly dub-reggae and ambient house along with the odd dance tune (check out the Orb's mix-album contribution to the BACK TO MINE series, released in 2003).

Perhaps more successfully than any other band, The Orb have united the influences of three generations of music: hippie, punk and rave. In the form of ambient house, they have provided an answer to a question all three generations have asked: When you're too knackered for the hard stuff, and too wired to sleep, what do you do? The answer is, you listen to The Orb.

⊙ **The Orb's Adventures Beyond The Ultraworld** (1991; Big Life).
The Orb's prototype, establishing a formula they have had little cause to vary since. The album contains a version of "A Huge Ever Growing ...", and two of "Little Fluffy Clouds", as well as a large number of natural samples (water, birds, insects), and slow funky grooves. Some tracks, however, sound like a random collection of samples: fine as background, but not serious listening.

⊙ **Blue Room** (1992; Big Life).
If you only get one Orb record, this is the one to go for. In spite of its vast length, it was the obvious choice for a single from the album UFORB, with a beat running through most of it and a reggae-influenced bass line supplied by Jah Wobble.

⊙ **Pomme Fritz** (1994; Island).
With more percussion and upfront beats, this is The Orb's least ambient album. The collaboration with Thomas Fehlmann gives the record a techno edge that makes it almost danceable.

⊙ **UF Off** (1998; Island).
Though it's filled with 'edits' of the group's sprawling pieces, this is a fine 'best of' that works well as an introduction to Patterson's Orb-ish mind.

Daniel Jacobs and David Wren

ROY ORBISON

Born Vernon, Texas, April 23, 1936; died December 7, 1988.

"I am blessed with a terrific voice. It's a God-given thing."

Like all early white rockers, **Roy Orbison** began as a country singer. By the early 50s he was performing professionally under the guidance of Norman Petty (later Buddy Holly's manager), though his break came when Johnny Cash put him in touch with Sun Records. Orbison sent a tape of "Ooby Dooby" and got himself a deal.

A rockabilly classic, "Ooby Dooby" was a hit in 1956, and was followed by several similar records. Although Orbison favoured ballads, these early releases are worth pursuing: his melodic tenor cuts across the rock beat with strange grace. Amongst the best were "Domino", covered by The Cramps, "Problem Child" and the weird-as-hell "Chicken Hearted", a raw semi-instrumental in which Orbison boasts of his cowardice in seemingly the wrong key.

Even at this stage, however, Orbison was looking beyond rockabilly. Amongst his first compositions were "Claudette", a hit for The Everly Brothers, and "Down The Line" for stable-mate Jerry Lee Lewis. He was invited to move to Nashville as a songwriter and after signing a contract with Monument, he struck gold with his self-penned third single, "Only The Lonely", in 1960. Reaching #1 in Britain and #2 in America, the record established Orbison as the premier balladeer of the Kennedy years.

Before he left Monument in 1965, Orbison enjoyed massive chart success, with melodramatic epics such as "Cryin'", "Dream Baby", "It's Over" and "In Dreams". Insistent Latin rhythms and swooping strings provided a backdrop for Orbison's phenomenal vocal range: from semi-spoken introductions, the songs would build into ever-bigger choruses utilizing his extraordinarily powerful falsetto. If Phil Spector created 'little symphonies for the kids', Orbison wrote three-minute operas, complete with maximum self-dramatization and excess.

What made the songs even more stunning was his performance. Wearing a plain dark suit, with jet-black hair and shades, Orbison would stand motionless, apparently powerless to control the pain, able only to stand and wail of tragedy. But real tragedy almost finished his career. In 1966 his wife Claudette was killed in a motorbike accident. Two years later, a house fire killed two of his three children. The double blow destroyed Orbison's creativity, and he abandoned songwriting altogether. For years he concentrated on gigs, particularly in Europe and Britain, where his popularity had always been massive. In America he was forgotten, but in Britain a greatest hits album could still top the charts in 1976.

By the late 80s, his stock had begun to rise worldwide. Covers of his classics by the likes of Linda Ronstadt, Don McLean and Van Halen assisted the cause, but essentially it was a process of American rock discovering its lost heroes. In 1987 a televised concert in Los Angeles saw, among others, Bruce Springsteen and Elvis Costello line up to pay tribute. The accompanying soundtrack album, BLACK AND WHITE NIGHT (reissued 1998), contains marvellous versions of "Crying", "It's Over" and a Springsteen-assisted "Oh Pretty Woman".

Further success came as part of the studio supergroup **THE TRAVELING WILBURYS**, with a revival of "Crying" (duetting with **k. d. lang**), and subsequent solo releases. The music was too bland to challenge his 50s and 60s classics, but the voice was still wonderful and he was getting some recognition again – which made his premature death in 1988 even sadder. A posthumous album, MYSTERY GIRL (1989), was inevitably his biggest seller.

Roy Orbison (1989; Laserlight).
A sixteen-track compilation of the Sun recordings, available at a budget price. Designed to trap the unwary, who are looking for the famous stuff, this is actually superb value for any rockabilly fan.

Golden Days (1981; Sony).
There are several compilations of the Monument years, all with much the same selection. This was the first on CD and collects twenty of the best-known songs, at least half of which are beyond compare – the rest are superfluous stabs at R&B, high-school pop and country.

Alwyn W. Turner

ORBITAL

Formed Sevenoaks, Kent, England, 1989.

"We're like two old geezers tinkering in the shed at the bottom of the garden."Phil Hartnoll

Named after London's capital-encircling motorway, cruised weekly by 1988's acid-house rave surfers, **Orbital** began through the shared interest of brothers **Phil** and **Paul Hartnoll** in early 80s experimental electro, Hi-NRG, and Crass/Dead Kennedys-style anarcho-punk. Using primitive keyboard, drum machine and four-track recording equipment, they produced the quintessential dance anthem of 1989 in "Chime", a joyful yet gently melancholic burst of embryonic techno-riffing.

Released originally on diminutive label Oh Zonc, it got a full release in 1990 on FFRR, which catapulted it to #17 in the UK charts and led to Orbital's memorably minimalistic *Top Of The Pops* appearance, with the shiny-domed pair standing static over their synths, wearing 'No Poll Tax' T-shirts. The subsequent single, "Satan", again broke new ground, sampling and looping the hardcore sonic nihilism of the Butthole Surfers onto relentless dance-floor beats that framed wilder warps of steamy oscillation.

Orbital's meteoric rise from dance-trance chancers to the UK's foremost electronic instrumental 'band' owed as much to their prolific live appearances as to their recordings. Loading component parts of their compositions into sequencers, and creating a situation where the programs and on-stage mixing created a new genre of improvisation, Orbital trashed any notions of techno as a sterile, studio-based exercise. Performing regularly at events which celebrated the merging of ex-punk/hippie free-festival activists with post-acid-house dance-party agitators, they provided a perfect meltdown soundtrack with their liberating synthesis of climactic riffs and long, trance-nurturing voyages of electronic excess.

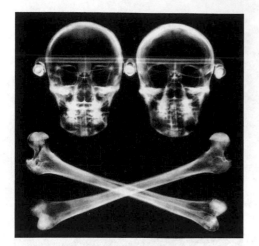

On top of that, their trademark welding goggles and their penchant for playing atop scaffolding platforms – 'in the round' – and alongside multiscreen video installations, made them one of the most visual live acts of any genre. **Giles Thacker** and **Luke Losey**'s projection and light construction were to become integral overtures and, unlike the formless psychedelics of their contemporaries, provided eerie images from the vaults of social realism. Deservedly, Orbital headlined the Glastonbury Festival in 1994 and 1995, and they were one of the few British acts invited to appear at the Woodstock 2 anniversary.

The band's first two albums – UNTITLED (ORBITAL I) (1991) and UNTITLED (ORBITAL II) (1993) – charted a sometimes graceful, sometimes skewered instrumental terrain. Astute editing and finely honed shifts of mood and dynamics were characteristic, but there was a tautness and tension in this music that set Orbital apart from much of the meandering chill-out school of abstract electronics. An intuitive romanticism never seemed too far away. On the third album, SNIVILISATION (1994), dissent and cynicism prevailed over escapism, the focal point being the increase of state power as represented by that year's Criminal Justice Bill, whose many new enforcements included an attempt to curb the rave scene.

In spring 1996, Orbital presented a 28-minute single, "The Box" – a gloriously contrived mutation of very English B-movie 'Hammer Horror' weirdness and spy intrigue harpsichord, uhh, riffs. It reached #11 in the UK charts, and preceded the much-anticipated fourth album, IN SIDES (1996). This was an equally scientific and symphonic excursion, presenting a music that had clearly transcended the creaking definitions of techno or dance. The band's seditionary stance also found expression through the recording of one track, "The Girl With The Sun In Her Head", using solar power from the Greenpeace generator, Cyrus.

Orbital's techno-to-the-masses lap of honour culminated in an extraordinary performance at London's Royal Albert Hall in May 1996. The brotherly technicians had come a very long way in a short time, and

were also much in demand for both soundtrack and remix work. They wove a sweaty minimalism into Madonna's BEDTIME STORY and also loaned their talents to acts including Meat Beat Manifesto, Underworld and The Drum Club.

THE MIDDLE OF NOWHERE (1999), saw a welcome element of humanity introduced into their work, with strings and sound effects mellowing the harder beats. Next came THE ALTOGETHER (2001), which boasted more electronic experimentation, a live favourite – the duo's interpretation of the *Dr. Who* theme – and menacing X-ray cover art of the brothers' heads complete with trademark DJ lamps. The set was far more adventurous than its predecessor, taking in samples from all over the shop; the results were labelled by some as 'techno skiffle', and the presence of vocal guest spots from **David Gray** and **Naomi Bedford** added a further dimension to the album's sound. Since then, the only release to surface has been a retrospective collection, WORK (2002), which relied too heavily on 'short' and 'edit' versions to be of any real interest. None the less, it did remind many just how stunning singles such as "Chime", "The Box" and "Lush" were.

The pair continue to work hard, both in the studio and on the road; a new album is expected soon, as well as a score for the British film *Octane*.

Untitled (Orbital I) (1991; FFRR Records).
Glacial extensions of chilly and soothing techno, featuring a live version of "Chime" and an effects-strewn impression of the Gulf War on "Desert Storm".

Untitled (Orbital II) (1993; Internal).
Designed for a single-session listen, this is seamless but ever-expanding, as didgeridoos, flutes and samples from Australian pedestrian crossings all mesh in a sweet, sexy, sonic maelstrom.

Snivilisation (1994; Internal).
A white-bearded God on the inner sleeve introduces us to an oblique look at the myth of civilized society. More leftfield experimental than the earlier albums, with "Attached" a vaporized hallucination made in heaven.

In Sides (1996; Internal).
The zenith of electronic anti-formalism, this is an album streaming with innovation and humanism. "Out There Somewhere" adds new dimensions to the description 'spatial'.

The Altogether (2001; FFRR Records).
Their most daring set to date; here Orbital are flying lower than usual, skimming the surface of punk and rock to produce some eclectic, daring compositions.

Chris Brook

ORCHESTRAL MANOEUVRES IN THE DARK

Formed Liverpool, 1978.

"We needed a name that would show people immediately that we weren't a punk band." Paul Humphries

Orchestral Manoeuvres In The Dark (OMD) are often regarded as cheerful electro-pop companions to The Human League or Depeche Mode – and, like them, lingering on, past their prime. They can be gimmicky and insubstantial, certainly, but OMD have a brilliant knack for catchy singles, and the music on the albums of their first seven years was constantly ambitious and brimming with ideas.

OMD were formed by **Andy McCluskey** and **Paul Humphries** in 1978, out of the fragments of an unwieldy eight-piece called **The Id** (OMD's first album consisted entirely of songs by The Id). Andy and Paul were drawn to music-making by the radical possibilities of synthesizers. Eno was an influence, but it was to Kraftwerk that they owed their greatest debt, taking up the Germans' project of creating an aesthetic for the technological age through the exact and pure sound of analogue synths. However, OMD's approach to science and technology was historically reflective rather than futuristic: radio, radar and atom bombs were their abiding images.

The first two albums – ORCHESTRAL MANOEUVRES IN THE DARK and ORGANISATION – were released in quick succession in 1980. Both were packed full of crisp, bright electro-pop, but sound a little tinny compared to the band's string of immaculately produced early 80s albums: ARCHITECTURE AND MORALITY (1981), DAZZLE SHIPS (1983), JUNK CULTURE (1984) and CRUSH (1985). These were the real fruits of partnership between McCluskey and Humphries, which was beginning to break down by the time of PACIFIC AGE (1986), a rather weak epilogue.

Humphries went on to form The Listening Pool – with long-standing OMD touring/session musicians **Malcolm Holmes** (percussion) and **Martin Cooper** (saxophone) – though with little commercial success. McCluskey meanwhile revived **OMD** (now down to the initials) as his solo project, producing the rather bland SUGAR TAX (1991) and LIBERATOR (1994). A further album, UNIVERSAL, appearing in 1996 and showed a return to the more comfortable floaty moods of OMD's heyday, with melody and atmosphere triumphing over raw electronica. More recently, McCluskey saw his stock rise as the songwriting brain behind the hits of girl-group **Atomic Kitten**.

◉ **Dazzle Ships** (1983; Virgin).
This austere evocation of modern alienation is the classic OMD album. Excellent use of samples and incredible synths on strong, melodic and above all highly intelligent pop music.

Dave Castle

BETH ORTON

Born Norwich, England, 1971.

"If I'm living in an ugly world with no justice then I'll create my own beauty and justice through my songs."

Beth Orton seemed to appear from nowhere, her blend of acoustic folk pop mingled with spacey trip-hop vibes adding light and colour to numerous festivals during the summer of 1997. In fact, for an overnight sensation, Orton had been around for a long time, initially discovering the dance/rock crossover at first hand when she was involved in videos for Primal Scream's SCREAMADELICA album in 1990, at the age of 19.

Later she sang on **William Orbit**'s STRANGE CARGO albums in 1992 and 1993, guested with **Red Snapper** on their first two singles, and courted even wider exposure with her guest vocals on **The Chemical Brothers**' EXIT PLANET DUST album in 1995. As such she eased, rather than forced, her way towards wider recognition. However, despite her own, virtually unknown, debut album – SUPER PINKY MANDY, co-produced by Orbit in 1993 – she remained best known as a collaborator and backing vocalist, rather than a solo performer.

In the summer of 1995 she worked on new material with **Andrew Innes** and **Martin Duffy** of Primal Scream, before finally forming a band of her own. A 1996 tour with **John Martyn** proved to be a turning point, with Orton establishing a strong identity in her own right. The shows also proved that her talents – like Martyn's – could touch a variety of audiences, with the siren-like hypnotism of "She Calls Your Name" captivating the most narrow-minded 70s folkie, and the loping bass and skittering drums of "Touch Me With Your Love" providing a blissed-out chill zone for the most hedonistic clubber.

Whilst Orton, at face value, would seem to echo the cheesecloth folkisms of the clutch of early-70s singer-songwriters, the soul of her music remained far more beguiling and mysterious. Though acoustic guitars have provided the bare bones of her albums, Orton and collaborators such as **Andy Weatherall** have woven an array of 'techno-lite' twists and turns, bending and shaping the sound into something far less conventional.

All of these qualities were in evidence on Orton's startling album, TRAILER PARK (1996), which achieved wider prominence (and a Mercury Prize nomination) the following year. Fleshed out by strings, cello and double bass, and with Andy

Weatherall remixing three of the tracks, the album perfectly blended the rustic reveries and spacier cosmic effects into a coherent package. The prevailing warmth and fragile sense of light and space counteracted the perceived wisdom that dance-based music was to find its truest expression in the dark, edgy ambience of urban paranoia. Orton's music is more informed by a sense of awe and wonder. She has often cited Ry Cooder (and the *Paris, Texas* soundtrack in particular) as a key influence and parts of TRAILER PARK resonated with the same shimmering and other-worldly filmic qualities.

Her EP BEST BIT with veteran US jazz-folk singer **TERRY CALLIER** – which included duets on their own songs plus a version of Fred Neil's "Dolphins", a song most famously covered by Tim Buckley – was quietly released on Heavenly, managing elegantly to raise her profile. Orton's involvement in the major US female singer-songwriter tour known as 'Lilith Fair' (dubbed the female Lollapalooza) then widened her exposure in the States, although she remained suitably pragmatic about her perceived outsider status within the 'movement', describing the tour as 'Loads of birds with long straight hair and guitars – and me.'

In terms of structure, her next release, CENTRAL RESERVATION (1999), rarely strayed far from the winning formula of its predecessor, although the songs were stronger and more richly textured and the employment of six different producers led to a slightly varied sound across the set. Beth found herself in some heavier company, though, notably **Dr. John**, **Ben Harper** and **Ben Watt** (Everything But The Girl). Even **David Roback** (Rain Parade, Mazzy Star) took a turn on "Devil Song", adding to the more varied feel of the twelve songs on offer.

Orton began the 21st century by winning a Brit Award of her own (for *Best British Female Artist*) and providing backing vocals on **Beck**'s MIDNITE VULTURES. Her long-awaited third solo LP, DAYBREAKER, was released in 2002; it was another pleasant collection of chilled ballads, orchestrations and beats, but didn't really manage to forward her cause. More interesting were her guest vocals on COME WITH US, the fourth LP by her old friends The Chemical Brothers. Notwithstanding her unfortunate susceptibility to acute mystery illnesses (she once went blind for a week – for no apparent reason – and has periodically suffered from serious bowel disorders), Beth Orton's future releases and tours are bound to be viewed with growing interest.

⦿ **Trailer Park** (1996; Heavenly Records).
Gorgeous, dreamy and delicate, yet retaining a strange edge of weirdness that draws the listener in and doesn't want to let go. A quiet revolution, perhaps, but for some TRAILER PARK was the sound of 1997.

⦿ **Central Reservation** (1999; Heavenly Records).
CENTRAL RESERVATION reminds you of your most intense, personal records – try ASTRAL WEEKS or Tim Buckley's BLUE AFTERNOON – yet still stands out as a unique proposition, perfectly capable of understanding the difference between mellow and mellifluous.

Nig Hodgkins

JOAN OSBORNE

Born Anchorage, Kentucky, 1963.

"Sexuality and spirituality are so closely related that, to me, it's no contradiction to put the two right next to each other in a song."

An overnight success who'd been paying her dues for nine years, **Joan Osborne** was nominated for five Grammy awards in 1996 on the strength of her hit song, "One Of Us" – a mainstream but quirky showcase for her powerhouse vocals, depicting the Almighty as a working stiff. It followed on from one of the 90s top-selling albums, RELISH, which – at last – had put Osborne up there in the panoply of women rock stars.

The child of lapsed Catholics, Osborne grew up idolizing soul divas like Etta James and Mavis Staples, as much for the attitude they projected – sexy, strong, funny – as for their music. At first she had no ambition to sing, and she moved to New York in the early 80s to study film at NYU. Then, one night she and a bunch of friends wandered into a local bar at the tail end of an open-mike session. Encouraged by her mates, Osborne got up and sang a Billie Holiday number and was asked to come back the following week. She became a regular, with a raw, emotional voice that was reminiscent of Bonnie Raitt or a more sorted Janis Joplin. So began years of working the sticky-floored blues-bar circuit, making friends among the musicians she hung out with, and building up a critical reputation.

She released an album, SOUL SHOW (1991), featuring covers of "Son Of A Preacher Man" and "Lady Madonna" as well as some rough-edged originals, and an EP, BLUE MILLION MILES (1993), on her own Womanly Hips label. She was then 'discovered' by pop producer Rick Chertoff, who had already delivered the goods with Cyndi Lauper and Sophie B. Hawkins.

Despite the disparity in their preferred styles, Osborne agreed to spend a week trying things out with Chertoff's favourite players, **Eric Bazilian** and **Rob Hyman** of The Hooters, which resulted in two singles ("Pensacola" and "Dracula Moon") and an album, RELISH (1995). Much of the power of the album derived from the contrast between the bluesy force of Osborne's voice and the pop-rock of the backing, which had a sheen and professionalism absent from many 'debut' albums.

Mixed with creditable covers of Dylan's "Man In The Long Black Coat" and Sonny Boy Williamson's "Help Me", her own songs were tales of lowlife or bizarre 'what-ifs?': What if God lives unrecognized among us and can't get home? What if Ray Charles regains his sight and consequently gives up singing? Ironically, her breakthrough hit, "One Of Us", almost didn't make it onto the album; it was written by Bazilian, and Osborne was worried that as a pop hit it would give people the wrong idea about the album. Luckily, she changed her mind, and in 1995 and 1996 it made her a star. She followed up with RIGHTEOUS LOVE (2000) and a set of covers, HOW SWEET IT IS (2002); both albums were again strong, while RIGHTEOUS LOVE broadened Joan's musical palette with the introduction of Indian raga ornamentations.

The pre-star Osborne was revealed on a collection of live material previously released on Womanly Hips: EARLY RECORDINGS (1996). If nothing else, the comparison between this and, say, RELISH showed the difference a good producer can make.

⊙ **Relish** (1995; Mercury).
A powerful display of blues-flavoured womanhood, from the raunchy "Right Hand Man" to the delicacy and restraint of "Crazy Baby" and "Lumina".

Andy Smith

OZZY OSBOURNE

Born Birmingham, England, 1948.

"I couldn't believe those videos – I looked like Elvis."A dried-out Ozzy on his former stage presence

Y ou can't say he didn't warn us. **Ozzy Osbourne** raised the curtain on his solo career with the splendidly infectious "Crazy Train", with its chorus, 'Mental wounds still bleeding, driving me insane – I'm going off the rails on this crazy train'.

The gleeful song was born of genuine despair. Fired from **BLACK SABBATH** by Tony Iommi in 1978, Ozzy sank further into the booze and pills that had contributed to his sacking. However, he was rescued by **Sharon Arden** (now his all-suffering celebrity wife), daughter of rock manager Don, who laid plans to relaunch him as 'Son of Sabbath' (a handle nixed by Ozzy in a rare moment of clear-headedness).

BLIZZARD OF OZZ (1980) got things off to a splendid start. Fuelled by hot string-slinger **Randy Rhoads** (formerly of LA no-hopers Quiet Riot), the album blew away everything Ozzy had done since Sabbath's SABOTAGE in 1975. Its clutch of classics included "Suicide Solution" – later the subject of one of the few controversies not of the madman's own making. The record and accompanying tour made Ozzy a superstar in the US – fuelled by his infamous dove – and bat-chomping escapades. Rhoads, meanwhile, was heralded as the best metal guitarist since Eddie Van Halen.

To the delight of fans and press officers, war was declared between Ozzy and the revitalized Sabbath (now fronted by the diminutive Ronnie James Dio – who got lost in the dry ice during his stage debut). Such was the enmity between the camps that, still reeling from Rhoads' death by plane crash in March 1982, Ozzy was persuaded to record a live album of Sabbath tracks, SPEAK OF THE DEVIL (1982), in a bid to screw his ex-colleagues.

Still, the sour taste of that disc was dissipated by BARK AT THE MOON (1983). Backed by new guitar foil **Jake E. Lee**, Ozzy scored with the album's title track, and set off on another triumphant US jaunt. He was drinking to constant excess, however, and the best efforts of Sharon (by then Ozzy's wife) to keep the booze in check were comprehensively demolished by support act Mötley Crüe, whose mock-Satanic trappings and appetite for destruction fitted seamlessly into the world of Oz. It was during this tour that the infamous Alamo incident took place in San Antonio. Sharon, to prevent Ozzy drinking, had locked away his clothes. Ozzy solved the problem by putting on one of her evening dresses, downed a bottle of Courvoisier and, needing a piss, made use of an old wall nearby. It turned out to be the Alamo, and Ozzy was charged with defiling a national monument.

The remainder of the 80s was equally event-filled: an emotional homecoming at the 1984 Castle Donington festival; a reunion with Sabbath at Live Aid; lawsuits over a fan's enactment of "Suicide Solution"; a 1986 tour with Metallica that catapulted the latter into rock's premier league; ill-fated sojourns at the Betty Ford Clinic; even a couple of new albums before the decade ended.

By the 90s, Ozzy – now an estate-owning family man – had tired of the rock'n'roll lifestyle (witness

STEVE GULLICK

Ozzy – the original, the great, the only Monster of Rock

his self-mocking appearance in Penelope Spheeris's metal documentary *The Decline of Western Civilization Part II*) and kicked the booze, replacing it with a strict regime of exercise and Prozac. He announced that the tour supporting the excellent No MORE TEARS (1991) album would be his last, and concluded the trek on a legendary note by inviting Sabbath to join him on stage for two nights in November 1992.

The inevitable attempts at a fully fledged reunion collapsed, but Ozzy returned to the road in his own right on the 'Retirement Sucks' tour. Despite metal's commercial decline, US fans gave him a heartfelt welcome and sent his new album, the splendidly titled OZZMOSSIS (1995) into the Top 10. Since then, he's been promoting and getting involved in the *Ozzfests* – a series of one-day metal events showcasing the 'nu' generation of the sons of Sabbath, usually culminating in a live set from the grizzled old monster himself and a reincarnated version of Black Sabbath. Ozzy's transformation from Dark Prince to Clown Prince was completed by MTV's disarmingly charming reality series, *The Osbournes*, which depicted Ozzy as a real life Homer Simpson trying to cope with lap dogs, satellite TV and a family even more insane than him. The show was more successful, on both sides of The Atlantic, than anyone would have thought possible, and propelled Ozzy, Sharon and their kids into the realms of super celebrity stardom.

- **Blizzard Of Ozz** (1980; Jet).
  Sprightly stomp that stands the test of time.

- **Live And Loud** (1993; Epic).
  Expletive-packed, de facto 'best of', with yet another guitar prodigy, Zakk Wylde (latterly of Pride & Glory and, briefly, Guns N' Roses).

- **The Ozzman Cometh** (1998; Epic).
  A two-CD collection, with one disc of greatest hits and one of the Ozzman interviewed.

Bruno MacDonald

JOHN OSWALD

Born Berlin, 1953, probably. But 'I have been listed as having been born in more than one country and I really appreciate the confusion and will do nothing to alleviate it.'

The music of Toronto-based **John Oswald** bears only tenuous links to rock music, yet in a way defines its essence. He's a composer, really, though re-composer might describe him better. He takes pop songs and rock tracks – most recently The Grateful Dead's "Dark Star" – and re-creates them as soundmaps, distorting and reorganizing his sources, yet capturing something crystalline that even casual acquaintance with the original can detect. His work also has comparisons with the samplers of the rock world, in that it totally upends concepts of intellectual ownership and copyright.

Oswald first came to public notice with PLUNDERPHONIC (1989), the actualization of his ideology published as *Plunderphonics, Or Audio Piracy As*

A Compositional Prerogative (1986). To say PLUNDERPHONIC rearranged commercial recordings by acts such as The Beatles, James Brown, Bing Crosby, Glenn Gould and Michael Jackson would be a profound understatement. It was little less than iconoclastic vivisection. A sex-changed Dolly Parton transforms into a gravelly voiced man singing "The Great Pretender", while The Beatles are glimpsed through a veil of psychedelia and mutant raga-rock. With Michael Jackson, however, Oswald went a little too far, perhaps, reworking both his music and his identity, depicting him on the cover wearing panties – with a detectable blush of period. The CRIA (Canadian Recording Industry Association), acting on a complaint from CBS and Jackson, waded in, threatening writs and demanding the destruction of the master tapes and all undistributed copies. Around 400 copies survived and since there was no encodement to disable copying, PLUNDERPHONIC sprang into life again and again, circulated samizdat-fashion in defiance of the record industry.

Previous to this venture, Oswald had committed many more conventional – or not – ideas to tape in the so-called Mystery Tape Laboratory, producing ALTO SAX (1980), SALMONMOOSE (1980) and SPOORS (1983). In the pre-digital era, he took manual techniques for reassembling and collaging sonic fragments about as far as they could go. Once in the digital domain, sampling technology began to match Oswald's imagination.

Post-PLUNDERPHONIC, Oswald received a commission from Elektra to commemorate the label's fortieth anniversary with an alternative RUBÁIYÁT (1990), and he jumped at the chance to use Elektra's sophisticated equipment. He began by doctoring The Doors, whose legal eagles jumped at the opportunity to gather full royalties, so the album became a limited-edition radio promo. PLEXURE (1993), a commission from John Zorn, would advance the cause further, plunderphonicizing swatches of Kate Bush, Peter Gabriel, Genesis, Public Enemy, U2 and others. In the process, hybrid acts were born, illustrated by morph christenings such as Marianne Faith No Morrisey and Sinéad O'Connick Jr. Rock had never been like this before! The same year, Oswald's "Spectre" piece sat alongside John Zorn's "Cat O' Nine Tails" on the Kronos Quartet's SHORT STORIES (1993).

Oswald had reached a point where his work was being taken seriously and, having come to the attention of Phil Lesh (The Grateful Dead's experimental music junkie), he received a fresh commission. This was to reinterpret "Dark Star", one of the band's key pieces. For it, Oswald was allowed access to the band's library of tapes to assemble a composite of their most iconic compositions. Performances were 'folded' – that is, compressed again and again to make them denser – and performances of entirely different vintages were juxtaposed, digitally spliced to make a seamless new creation – the birth of a new star. The resultant TRANSITIVE ASHES (1994) met with such a reception, aesthetically and commercially, that a sequel went ahead under the name of Mirror Ashes (1995), issued collectively as Grayfolded (1995). In a gnarled sense it represented an exorcism of The Dead's spirit while invoking the very same. Oswald continues to thrive on musical contradiction and rebirth.

- **Plexure** (1993; Avant).
Advanced plunderphonics. Not quite as fun as the original, but available without proscription.

- **Grayfolded** (1995; Swell/Artefact).
From the close encounters of the young and old Jerry Garcia duetting with each other, Oswald conjures the spirit of a supernova.

Ken Hunt

JOHN OTWAY

Born Aylesbury, England, October 2, 1952.

"Beware Of The Flowers (Cos I'm Sure They're Going To Get You, Yeh)."

Never a man to do the expected, **John Otway** once rejected Pete Townshend as the producer of his first album. He also warned his departing girlfriend Paula Yates that she would never again get the chance to date a rock star. John Otway has never quite seen things the way most other people do.

He first came to prominence in the mid 70s with his on/off partner **Wild Willy Barrett**. Developing a stage act that pitted the considerable musical abilities of Barrett against the manic mixture of lunacy and pathos that became the Otway trademark, the duo rapidly gathered a following. Technically speaking, what they did was folk and rock, but this description doesn't really get the essence of an act that was closer to the punk spirit than many middle-class kids in state-of-the-art bondage trousers. Barrett would slowly ramble round the stage playing an improbable home-made guitar as Otway flailed, cavorted and generally acted like some terminal dementia case from a B-movie. Otway originals like "Beware Of The Flowers (Cos I'm Sure They're Going To Get You, Yeh)", "Cor Baby That's Really Free" and "Oh My Body Is Making Me" trod the line between inspiration and lunacy. Yet, as the heartfelt ballad "Geneva" showed, there was a serious and ambitious side to the operation as well.

Otway and Barrett parted, re-formed, parted, and so on. They had a modest hit with "Really Free" (1977) and another with "DK 50-80", which ambled into the lower reaches of the Top 50 in 1980. In 1982 Willy Barrett's "Headbutts" was the last real attempt at a big single by the duo. It provoked controversy from do-gooders, who were worried it would encourage headbutting, but none of this helped sales. Established as a stage favourite from the start, the song encouraged Shure Microphones to sponsor Otway: if Shure's hardware could withstand headbutts from Otway, not to mention drop kicks

and any other random PA abuse he could dream up, they were good enough for your average rock band.

By the mid 80s Otway, usually without Barrett, was an established fixture on the college and club circuit, the lack of Barrett's musical presence leaving Otway as more of a straightforward showman. Otway gigs were sometimes breathtakingly honest, frequently hilarious, with slowed-down reworkings of standards like "Green Green Grass Of Home" and "Blockbuster" adding a new and comical dimension to their trite lyrics. Otway's take on the sublime "Cheryl's Going Home" was a fuzzed-out triumph of overacting and acrobatics.

Otway went on to control his own recordings and tours, and wrote an autobiography, *Cor Baby That's Really Me* (1990), an endearingly frank tale of missed opportunities and dauntless integrity. Terminally ambitious, he followed his sell-out two-thousandth gig with plans for a show at the Royal Albert Hall and the vague promise of an album of love songs. In a self-promotional orgy he headlined at the Royal Albert Hall in October 1998, having enlisted the help of others – including the cult comic *Viz* – to promote the gig. Short of becoming a regular *Viz* character, there didn't seem to be any obvious way to top this achievement. However, Otway was certain to think of something! And he did, in the form of the album Cheryl (2001), a ludicrous and tear-jerking tale of lost love and trainspotting.

- **Cor Baby That's Really Me** (1990; Strike Back).
The consideration of any musical worth starts here. Gathered together, Otway's best original musical moments show a solid awareness of classic songwriting strengths and an unflinching willingness to experiment.

- **Under The Covers And Over The Top** (1992; Otway Records).
If you've ever had problems taking rock images and ideas at face value, check this out. Cover versions with a sense of the ridiculous, from the poetry that is "Blockbuster" to Radio 2 anthems drowned in a sea of overwrought emotions.

Neil Nixon

OUTKAST

Formed Atlanta, 1992.

Just as The Pharcyde and Freestyle Fellowship represented the avant garde response to G-Funk in LA, Atlanta's **Dungeon Family** (OutKast, **Goodie MOb**, **Witchdoctor**, **Cool Breeze**, **Lil' Will** and the **Organized Noize** production crew) were the Dirty South's arty alter ego. Unlike SoCal's commercial pariahs, however, these Southern alchemists working in their dungeon managed to turn their spiritual and semi-mystical vibes into gold and platinum.

A partnership that began at Tri-Cities High School (Atlanta's version of Juliard), OutKast (**Antwan "Big Boi" Patton** and **Andre "Dre" Benjamin**) is one of the most impressive acts in hip-hop. Without sacrificing hip-hop's main pleasure principle, Dre and Big Boi have managed to grow and shift directions over the course of their career – a

Outkast's Dre wigging out

cheque to cheque/If you don't move your feet, then I don't eat, so we like neck to neck', the amazing "Elevators (Me & You)" was one of the first Southern singles to go nationwide. Elsewhere, they got more explicitly political on tracks such as "Babylon" and "Mainstream", and tried to incorporate George Clinton's P-Funk vision, and not just the synth lines, into hip-hop.

Their masterwork, though, was AQUEMINI (1998). Opening with a song called "Return Of The 'G'", AQUEMINI set you up for some big ballin' and shot callin', but then hit you with lyrics like, 'Return of the gangsta thanks to/Them niggas who got dem kids, who got enough to buy an ounce/But not enough to bounce dem kids to the zoo/Or to the park so they grow up never seein' the light/So they end up being like your sorry ass/Robbin' niggas in broad ass day light'. Other highlights included the hoedown "Rosa Parks" (complete with harmonica break from Dre's pastor) and the mind-blowing "Liberation".

Largely taking over production themselves, STANKONIA (2000) was just as good and became one of the biggest critical successes of recent memory. Anchored by two mind-blowing singles – "B.O.B.", Miami Bass meets Mississippi Pentecostal, and "Ms. Jackson", an apology letter to 'all the baby mamas' mamas' that has the guts to admit both tenderness and responsibility – STANKONIA was an epic that echoed the dichotomy at the heart of the group (and the heart of their biggest influence, P-Funk): Big Boi, the eloquent pimp who should know better, working off of and against Dre, the radical Afrodelic space cadet. Their wrestling may sometimes come off as contradictory, but it's also a fascinating testament to the complexity of life and the source of the group's electricity, and you wouldn't want it to change.

⦿ **Aquemini** (LaFace, 1998).
It's conflicted and drags in places, but this is nevertheless one of the most impressive hip-hop records in years.

Peter Shapiro

OZRIC TENTACLES

Formed Stonehenge Free Festival, England, 1983.

With a shared interest in psychedelic, high-flying space music and a penchant for playing the free festivals of the hippie circuit, brothers **Ed** (guitars/keyboards) and **Roly Wynne** (bass) had been gigging on and off since schooldays. As the 1983 Stonehenge event approached, the brothers and synth player **Joie Hinton** pondered a psychedelic-cereal name for their new band: Gilbert Chunks and Malcolm Segments were frontrunners before they opted for **Ozric Tentacles** and a line-up that contained practically two of everything (except bass players).

The first taste of the fast, floating nature of the band. ERPSONGS (1985) was embryonic in many ways, lacking the flutes, hi-tech keyboard setups, and

unique feat in hip-hop. Their debut album, SOUTHERNPLAYALISTICADILLACMUZIK (1994), sought to subvert the Southern stereotype of playa music. With gangsta-leaning production from Organized Noize (Rico Wade, Pat "Sleepy" Brown and Ray Murray) that was rich, deep and detailed, but never as seductive or crowd-pleasing as Dr. Dre's, SOUTHERNPLAYALISTICADILLACMUZIK was a melancholy depiction of the game that never shied away from its consequences: the album's sonic trademark was a truncated homunculus of the 808 clavé sound so characteristic of booty music; the chorus of "Crumblin' Erb" went, 'There's only so much time left in this crazy world/I'm just crumblin' herb'; "Player's Ball" had a Curtis Mayfield-styled falsetto undercutting its depiction of 'black man's heaven'; "Call of Da Wild" was the story of a G who had voices in his head like the Geto Boys; and the spoken "True Dat" had the brusque put-down: 'If you think it's all about pimping hoes and slammin' Cadillac doors/You probably a cracker or a nigga who think you a cracker'.

ATLIENS (1996) was probably more "mature", but their acquired wisdom was never thrown in your face and it didn't shackle their vision, fun or grooves. With lines like, 'I live by the beat like you live

much of the squalling glissando guitar that was to cement their reputation. Containing both jam sessions and instrumental songs, TANTRIC OBSTACLES (1986) continued this free-form style: apart from Ed Wynne, each member appeared to just float in and out of the group as required.

LIVE ETHEREAL CEREAL (1986) was a crowning moment: a series of live songs taped at various festivals around the country, it was the band's first world-class recording. The same year, THERE IS NOTHING (1986) documented their first proper sessions in the studio: elements of reggae, world music and jazz filtered in, broadening the sound. With its more guitar-driven direction, the addition of **'Jumping' John Egan** on flute, and the increased use of Middle Eastern, Indian and East Asian themes, SLIDING GLIDING WORLDS (1988) sealed the definitive Ozrics sound.

The first six albums were initially released on cassette only; the last of these, THE BITS BETWEEN THE BITS (1989), a collection of unreleased recordings from the whole life of the band, was put out as the precursor to the band's first proper album, PUNGENT EFFULGENT (1989). The cover artwork by Blim, a defiantly psychedelic scene of pixies casting spells, described the music perfectly: strange dreamscapes of power-packed instrumental sound suffused with moments of incandescent splendour.

ERPLAND (1990) was a landmark album that the band would find it hard to live up to. A double album combining beautiful slow movements with masterful playing and headlong space rushes, it featured the band's one and only vocal 'song', "Iscence", a reggae love ballad. Blinding instrumental trips and memorable melodic hooks gained the band greater attention and, when STRANGEITUDE (1991) appeared, it charted.

A massive student following had built up by this time, based primarily on the band's occasional ambient, acid/rave leanings. Both Joie Hinton and drummer **Merv Pepler** wanted to continue in that direction, so they formed **Eat Static** to allow them to pursue it without changing Ozric Tentacles.

JURASSIC SHIFT (1993) leapt into the UK charts at #11, surprising many people, not least the music journalists who had ignored the band for a decade. A curious hybrid of invention and formulaic retreads, it came wrapped in paper made from hemp, a relative of marijuana; it had no narcotic qualities, but created a stir.

They also got into trouble with their next project, the six-CD box set of the first six albums, VITAMIN ENHANCED (1993). In keeping with the origin of the band's name, Blim had designed the box to look like a cereal packet, and Kellogg's were not amused. A blink-and-you'll-miss-it limited edition swayed the company, and the band promised no more boxes would be made available ever again. Their next release, ARBORESCENCE (1994), was their best album for some time, ranging from the colossal guitar riff of "Myriapod" to a title track offering the calmness of midnight at an oasis. **Zia** was fully established on bass, having seen Roly disappear to various other bands and projects, and all looked well.

Unfortunately, a financially disastrous US tour, on top of the VITAMIN box debacle, contributed to the bankruptcy of the band and their label, Dovetail, and for a while it looked like the end. They laid low for a while, though, and raised the cash to buy back their rights and label. When they emerged, it was with a new drummer, **Rad Prince**, and **Seaweed** on keyboards and bubbles, Hinton and Pepler having left to concentrate on Eat Static (although the free-form family nature of the Ozric Tentacles means a return at some stage isn't precluded).

The band fully re-established themselves with BECOME THE OTHER (1995), an album that sounded almost like an ambient flip side to ARBORESCENCE, and gained encouraging reviews in the British music press. With CURIOUS CORN (1998), WATERFALL CITIES (1999), THE HIDDEN STEP (2000) and OAKUM (2001) providing the most recent doses of space-jamming, it seems that nothing can stop them providing their space food for a few more years yet.

⊙ **Live Ethereal Cereal** (1986; Dovetail).
Monstrously inventive live document showcasing the stunning improvisational abilities of the band with lengthy live jams and wild, crazy, extended versions of some early classics. Six songs in an hour should give you some idea of what they're doing.

⊙ **Pungent Effulgent** (1989; Dovetail).
A Hawkwind-influenced tour de force with guitars spiralling crazily, keyboards bubbling insanely and John Egan trying to babble words in edgeways. Now available as a double pack with STRANGEITUDE.

⊙ **Erpland** (1990; Dovetail).
A classic of ethnic space-trance dub-rock. Psychedelic rock touching base with reggae, and all sounding complete and highly individual.

⊙ **Become The Other** (1995; Dovetail/Pinnacle).
An entirely instrumental album of rave grooves, mixing in Spanish and Indian influences to fine effect.

Duncan Harris

P

PAGE AND PLANT

Formed 1994.

"Jimmy Page carries a total sense of vision. He is the Stravinsky of rock guitar." Carlos Santana

When **LED ZEPPELIN** folded, on the death of drummer John Bonham in 1980, they were probably the biggest rock act in the world, despite the onslaught of the New Wave. For the next decade, however, both singer **Robert Plant** and guitarist **Jimmy Page** more or less eschewed the Zeppelin legacy in order to carve out new and largely low-key careers. When the pair finally started playing together in earnest again in 1994, few could have predicted that their comeback would be so widely acclaimed.

Page, in particular, had seemed somewhat lost in the years following the Zeppelin split, and rumours that he was dogged by 'ill-health' were rife. His 1981 soundtrack to Michael Winner's *Death Wish 2* was hardly an inspired return to the spotlight, and it wasn't until 1984 that he got back into the fray, joining the ARMS tour of the USA in aid of multiple sclerosis research, with Clapton, Jeff Beck and ex-Free/Bad Company vocalist **Paul Rodgers**. This led to Page and Rodgers' The Firm, a partnership that promised far more than it delivered, sticking to a rigid hard-rock format. Page's solo outing, OUTRIDER (1988), was disappointing too, though it contained a clutch of intriguing instrumentals. By contrast, his guest spots, with The Rolling Stones ("One Hit To The Body"), Box of Frogs (on the LP STRANGELAND), and Stephen Stills ("50/50"), showed him still to be a stunningly inventive soloist. For the first few years of the 90s, Page kept a low profile, then teamed up with Whitesnake singer **David Coverdale** for COVERDALE/PAGE (1993); it pandered to every heavy rock cliché going.

Plant's solo career was always more determined and focused than that of Page. From the outset, the leonine locks were chopped, and crowd requests for old Zep numbers ignored, as he launched into a couple of solo albums of highly polished AOR, and a hit single, "Big Log" (1983). Encouraged by Atlantic supremo Ahmet Ertegun, Plant then cut a mini-LP of vintage R&B hits with help from Page and Beck, THE HONEYDRIPPERS VOLUME 1 (1984), which was a huge American success and provided him with a US Top 10 single in the shape of "Sea Of Love", originally a hit in 1959 for Phil Phillips.

1985's SHAKEN 'N' STIRRED was a brave, but flawed, attempt at experimentation, but Plant hit the big time with the more mainstream NOW AND ZEN (1988) and MANIC NIRVANA (1990). Backed by a young new band – and in full hippie garb once again – Plant gave full rein to his vocal technique on tracks like "Heaven Knows", "Tall Cool One" (complete with Zep samples), the acoustic "Liar's Dance", and "Watching You", a song sampling Egyptian diva Oum Khalsoum with a throbbing Eastern drumbeat – exciting stuff that hinted at the Arabic leanings of the Page/Plant project to come.

FATE OF NATIONS (1993) was the album that consolidated this renewed success with a variety of moods and textures, and included contributions from artists as diverse as classical violinist Nigel Kennedy and Fairport Convention guitarist Richard Thompson. Folk influences predominate and a convincing stab at country-rock ("29 Psalms") and a cover of the standard "If I Were A Carpenter" were released as singles.

Over the years there had been frequent rumours of a Page/Plant reunion. They had played underrehearsed sets together at Live Aid, the Atlantic Records Fortieth Anniversary bash, and Knebworth 1990, not to mention guesting on each others' solo albums. Then, in 1994, MTV came knocking.

The original proposal was for a Led Zeppelin 'Unplugged' show. However, this was clearly going to be no mere nostalgia fest, and when the results of the Page And Plant partnership were heard on NO QUARTER – UNLEDDED (1994), they were startling. Featuring Arabic and Celtic rhythms, the sound was augmented by a sixteen-strong Egyptian ensemble and a string orchestra. The CD really excelled on

songs infused with the sounds of an Asian or Moroccan bazaar – "Friends", "Four Sticks", the epic "Kashmir", and "The Battle Of Evermore". The last featured the haunting vocals of British-Asian star **Najma Akhtar** complementing Robert's best muezzin wail. The four new songs owed very little to the Western rock tradition, and drew heavily on the music of Marrakech, where three of them were actually recorded.

1997 saw another burst of activity with the release of WALKING INTO CLARKSDALE, a studio album that immediately won widespread critical acclaim. Once again, a heavy Eastern influence was in evidence, but many Zeppelin fans were dismayed by **Steve Albini**'s hard-edged production and the determined absence of guitar solos (except on the fiery "Burning Up"). Echoes of Roy Orbison, Dick Dale and The Grateful Dead could be heard, although the music had very much its own character, far removed from the monster riffs and folk-rock of yesteryear.

Page and Plant went into promotional overdrive, appearing on TV shows the world over (and even premiering the single "Most High" on *Top Of The Pops*), followed by another massive world tour, which took in such unlikely places as Zagreb and Istanbul. With a set made up largely of Zeppelin classics, the response was invariably ecstatic and revealed the pair at the height of their powers.

Few good things can last long, however, and by 1999 Plant had seemingly decided that the way of the road was not for him and any further touring plans were put on ice, despite the fact that the duo had recently been awarded a Grammy for *Best Hard Rock Performance* with "Most High". Page then proceeded to hook up with **The Black Crowes** to keep the rock flowing and Plant occupied his time with **Priory Of Brion**, formed with his old friend **Kevyn Gammond** of Band of Joy, before moving on to create another outfit called **Strange Sensation**. Whether Page and Plant resurrect their partnership remains to be seen, but with such a mutually successful period coming as a result of the collaboration surely it is just a matter of time.

The Honeydrippers

⊙ **The Honeydrippers Volume 1** (1984; Es Paranza).
Plant teams up with Page and Jeff Beck for a brassy, brilliantly produced mini-album of R&B classics such as Roy Brown's "Rockin At Midnight".

Robert Plant

⊙ **Fate Of Nations** (1993; Atlantic).
Plant's finest solo moment, taking in country-rock ("29 Psalms"), Arab-tinged hard rock ("Closer To You") and folk ("If I Were A Carpenter"). Eclectic, sophisticated and intriguing.

Page and Plant

⊙ **No Quarter – Unledded** (1994; Fontana).
'As I see it,' Robert Plant said, 'rock'n'roll is basically folk music.' Here's the supporting evidence as Page and Plant reposition hard rock in an Arabic/world music setting (or, perhaps, vice versa).

Chris Coe

THE PALE FOUNTAINS

Formed Liverpool, England, 1981; disbanded 1985.

"I just want to write classic songs." Michael Head

If there were any justice, **Michael Head** would be an acknowledged giant in any British rock history – but, alas, he and his band, The Pale Fountains, never quite made it beyond footnote status. Looking back, it's hard to resist the conclusion that Head's lovingly crafted, Latin-tinged pop songs – with their light, breezy choruses evoking the sunny optimism of the mid 60s and the orchestrated arrangements of Burt Bacharach – were released a decade too early.

Still, things looked promising at the outset, as the Fountains – Head (guitar/vocals/songwriting), **Chris McCaffrey** (bass), **Thomas Whelan** (drums) and **Andy Diagram** (trumpet) – were snapped up by Virgin for a staggering £150,000 after issuing a solitary single, "(There's Always) Something On My Mind"/"Just a Girl" (1982), on an indie label. The Liverpool-born Head was already – and a tad prematurely – being talked of as a new Lennon for the 80s.

The group's debut 45 for Virgin, "Thank You" (1982), was a lavish affair, and featured the string section from The Geoff Love Orchestra and an everything-but-the-kitchen-sink production. Its release was accompanied by confident forecasts of an instant Top 20 smash, with the band's publishers even wagering their Bentley on it. However, the record peaked at a rather more modest #48, a position which was, sadly, to be the pinnacle of the band's commercial achievements.

Further problems lay ahead. The Pale Fountains' first album, PACIFIC STREET (1984), took the best part of a year to record, with the band hiring and firing a succession of producers before finally opting to produce it themselves. Unfortunately, by the time of its release, the hullabaloo which had preceded and accompanied their big-money signing with Virgin had long since died down, and the reception was distinctly muted. With its bossa nova beats, acoustic guitars and strident exotic brass, PACIFIC STREET exuded a summery charm which was perhaps a touch too unassuming for mass acceptance. It failed to dent the UK Top 75.

With Ian Broudie (later of The Lightning Seeds) installed as producer, FROM ACROSS THE KITCHEN TABLE (1985) was a far more robust effort, and saw the band dispensing with their distinctive jazz inflections in favour of a much straighter guitar pop sound. But too much was sacrificed and overall the record lacked identity. Still, it produced a gloriously catchy, semi-orchestrated single, "Jean's Not Happening", which once again should have ascended the charts, and – like the album – bombed. The writing was clearly on the wall and, having lost the confidence of their record company, the band finally split amid much frustration and acrimony.

Following their untimely demise, Head returned to Liverpool where, with his brother John on guitar, he formed **Shack**. Their first album, Zilch (1988), made no impact, and its follow-up, Waterpistol, was scuppered by the collapse of Ghetto Records, and not released until four years after its recording – in 1995 on the German Marina label. The *NME* justifiably hailed its release as the rediscovery of a 'lost gem', which set the scene for Head's solo album The Magical World Of The Strand (1997), which performed well in many end-of-year polls. Another Shack release, HMS Fable, followed in 1999. Though little has been heard since, we may yet see the restoration of a talent that initially faltered under the weight of unrealistic expectations.

The Pale Fountains

⊙ **Pacific Street** (1984; Virgin).
Despite a brace of fine singles, The Pale Fountains never quite cut it over the course of a whole album. But Pacific Street has its moments, and has the merit of being true to the band's original ethos.

⊙ **Longshot For Your Love** (1998; Marina).
A splendid collection of John Peel sessions, *Old Grey Whistle Test* BBC TV performances and other assorted rarities.

Shack

⊙ **Waterpistol** (1995; Marina).
An album that more than makes up for the unfulfilled promise of The Pale Fountains. At times Shack bear an uncanny resemblance to the early Stone Roses, but whereas The Roses drew heavily upon 60s psychedelia, Head draws upon that decade's classic pop arrangements to create a sound which is moody, evocative and utterly contemporary.

Ian Lowey

PALE SAINTS

Formed Leeds, England, 1988; disintegrated 1995.

Pale Saints – **Ian Masters** (bass/vocals), **Graeme Naysmith** (guitars) and **Chris Cooper** (drums) – emerged in the wake of American guitar bands such as Sonic Youth, Throwing Muses and the Pixies. These last two bands had signed to 4AD in 1986–87 – as that label sought to change an image overly linked to the Cocteau Twins and their ilk – and they were followed by Pale Saints, who signed up in 1988, along with **Lush**.

The label released the Saints' debut EP, Barging Into The Presence Of God, and LP, The Comforts Of Madness (1990), in quick succession. They were interesting in that they combined the two 4AD styles, mixing harsh guitars à la Pixies with more dreamlike passages and Ian Masters' rather distracted vocals. It was music that had to be taken as a piece rather than as a string of songs, and it was best experienced live, where Pale Saints performed intense and unbroken sets.

Unfortunately for Pale Saints, the records appeared just as the 'Madchester' scene – Happy Mondays and their imitators – was at its height, manufactured by bored journalists who found they had no time for

groups such as Pale Saints. Thus, in 1990, *Melody Maker* trashed the band as 'overrated, generic sub-1988 indie rockers and ugly as fuck to boot'. At least Lush had the fallback of a luscious singer for males of all ages to fantasize about.

So Pale Saints' career failed to advance as hoped, and their second album, In Ribbons, didn't appear till 1992. In the interim they had taken note of their critics and made the obvious move for any struggling, ugly band – they'd added a female singer/guitarist, **Meriel Barham**, to share the vocals. And by their third album, Slow Buildings (1994), Masters himself had been replaced by **Colleen Browne** (bass/vocals).

These changes pushed Pale Saints into Cocteauland, with titles such as "Babymaker", "Featherforms" and "A Thousand Stars Burst Open" giving the game away. Here the Pale Saints' story ends, and Masters' begins. While his former band were busy vanishing without trace, Masters was collaborating with ex-A.C. Temple player **Chris Trout**. Their union as **Spoonfed Hybrid** spawned an eponymously titled album of intriguing oddness in 1993 on the 4AD sub-label Guernica. Next, Masters teamed up with **Warren Defever** of **HIS NAME IS ALIVE** to release a glut of obscure material under the monikers **ESP Continent** and **ESP Summer**. From this period, the most rewarding release was 1996's Mars Is A Ten. Masters continues to record and has released his work under numerous titles and aliases; if you want to track down his newest material, try tapping 'Friendly Science', 'Oneironaut' or 'I'm Sore' into your local search engine.

⊙ **The Comforts Of Madness** (1990; 4AD).
Easily their best record largely due to the presence of easily their best song, "Sight Of You". Indie-by-numbers perhaps, but they are the right numbers for once. Play very loud.

Chris Jenkins

ROBERT PALMER

Born Batley, England, January 19, 1949.

His image as the consummate smoothie belies the fact that **Robert Palmer** possesses a voice that ranks alongside other great British belters such as Rod Stewart, Joe Cocker and Paul Rodgers. And despite a 25-year career and international stardom, he has never achieved the critical acclaim that should have been his, largely because of his tendency to grab the tail coats of passing trends rather than be a trend-setter himself. His lounge-lizard image, however, has remained impervious to the variety of musical changes he has embraced: unlike most of his peers, Palmer has never harboured any working-class-hero pretensions.

Born in Yorkshire, Palmer spent much of his childhood in Malta, returning to the UK in his teens and joining the **Alan Bown Set** at 19, followed by a stint with Dada, a twelve-piece Stax-style outfit. This band evolved into the more rock-orientated **Vinegar Joe**, who built up a following supporting the Who and Hendrix.

When Vinegar Joe split in 1974, Palmer recorded an infectious solo album, SNEAKING SALLY THROUGH THE ALLEY (1974), with help from The Meters and Little Feat. The latter's "Sailin Shoes" opened proceedings and unfolded seamlessly into "Hey Julia"/"Sneaking Sally", fifteen minutes of some of the most joyous white funk ever recorded. The second half of the album, however, was disappointingly restrained and prevented the whole from being a true classic.

1975's PRESSURE DROP saw Palmer tackling reggae with distinction on the title track (written by Toots And The Maytals). The next year he moved to Nassau in the Bahamas, where he continued to build the feel of the islands into his music. By 1978's DOUBLE FUN, Palmer was confidently writing fine reggae tunes himself, like the title track and "Love Can Run Faster", an intelligent, soulful tune. The rest of the album was consistently excellent, laden with desire and sexual tension, and containing some fine jazzy R&B like "Every Kinda People", his first major hit single.

SECRETS (1979) betrayed a more populist, hard rock approach that paid off with the success of "Jealous" and "Bad Case Of Loving You", radio favourites to this day. For CLUES (1980), Palmer teamed up with electro-pop star Gary Numan, presumably to give himself a more contemporary edge. As a result, the album now sounds the most dated of his earlier LPs, but does include the dance-floor hit, "Looking For Clues", as well as "Johnny And Mary", now annoyingly familiar as the soundtrack to the Renault TV ads. It was back to a hard-rock approach for POWER STATION (1985), a collaboration with Andy and John Taylor from Duran Duran, plus the Chic team of Tony Thompson and Bernard Edwards; it spawned a huge hit with a loud rerun of Marc Bolan's "Get It On".

Never a confident live performer, Palmer has nevertheless become a star of the video age. Much of this success stems from the Terence Donovan-directed "Addicted To Love" (1986), which showed Palmer backed by a band of gyrating, leggy lovelies.

Shamelessly un-PC, it was an unforgettable if obvious image, and subsequent Palmer videos have kept to the same blatant formula.

Despite his growing popularity as a hard-rock singer, Palmer still experimented with a variety of styles. HEAVY NOVA (1988) contains perhaps the world's only example of Afro/yodelling fusion on the sprightly "Change His Ways", as well as exploring lush, romantic orchestrations on "She Makes My Day" and "It Could Happen To You". He was to return to this approach on RIDIN' HIGH (1992), a homage to the big band era. 'Ridin' High took seven years to conceive', he said. 'It was my hobby on the side, the only time I recorded a concept album.' In theory it should have been a winner, but in practice it was curiously unengaging and unloved.

Over the years, Palmer has lost none of his vocal skills and has kept his matinee-idol looks. And in the process of dabbling in soul, reggae, techno, hard-rock, funk, big-band and African sounds, he has attracted a huge international following. As the 1990s progressed, however, he seemed increasingly out of touch and an attempt to revive the POWER STATION formula in 1997 attracted little interest and smacked of desperation. Most recently, DRIVE (2003) was a more back-to-basics and invigorated affair, but for many he will always be 'the guy in the suit in that video with the girls.'

⊙ **Double Fun** (1978; Island).
Palmer's most consistently classy album. 'There's no profit in deceit', Palmer sings on Andy Fraser's gorgeous, jazzy "Every Kinda People", and the whole album has an honesty that is absent from his more contrived later LPs. Palmer's songwriting excels, and rarely have lyrics seemed so heavy with desire as on "Come Over" and "You Overwhelm Me". The reggae "Love Can Run Faster" is probably his finest song.

⊙ **Addictions Volumes I & II** (1995; Island).
A double-CD compilation that gives a reasonable overview of the career from "Sneaking Sally" onwards. Far preferable to the remixed, bass-heavy VERY BEST OF ROBERT PALMER, a Christmas hit in 1995, which virtually ignores his pre-80s work and seems to have been put together with the office party in mind.

Chris Coe

PANTERA

Formed Dallas, Texas, 1981.

To the uninitiated it would seem that **Pantera**'s ugly and twisted presence appeared in the world of rock at the start of the 90s. The grisly truth, however, is that they have been around a lot longer.

Having played together in their high-school jazz band of 1980, **'Diamond' Darrell Abbott** (guitars), **Rex 'Rocker' Brown** (bass) and **Vinnie Paul Abbott** (drums) formed the original Pantera with **Terry Glaze** (vocals/guitars). In those days they were firmly of the tacky, glam-influenced school – all Kiss-type anthems, poodle-perm hair and dubious spandex trousers. For the curious, the period can be sampled on METAL MAGIC (1983), PROJECTS IN THE JUNGLE (1984) and I AM THE NIGHT (1985).

Although each album was progressively heavier than the last, they were still light years away from their later blistering extreme metal sound.

Glaze departed in the late 1980s and for a while **David Peacock** took over. But it wasn't until he was replaced by the wild **Phil Anselmo** that the band began mutating into the Pantera of today. Their last flirtation with 80s-style metal came with POWER METAL (1988), which went some way towards securing their future career path. Recorded at the Abbott brothers' father's studios, it was mixed and marketed by the band themselves and, despite the extremely cheesy cover art ('We looked like dorks'), it managed to shift 35,000 units.

Having finally attracted the attention of a major label, the band signed to Atco, and the rest of the puzzle fell neatly in place. Ditching the glam and the cock-rock posturing, the band went for a distinctly more aggressive image and a stripped-down heavy sound. COWBOYS FROM HELL (1990) was a forearm-smash of an album: Anselmo's powerful voice teetered on the edge of mania, while the riffs on "Primal Concrete Sledge" and "The Art of Shredding" gave established bands like Metallica a run for their money. With an already dedicated fan base ready to lap up their new fierce sound, success was assured for their steroid-fuelled power groove.

With the help of Terry Date in the studio, VULGAR DISPLAY OF POWER (1992) established Pantera in the extreme metal vanguard. The band's offensively muscular stance was again borne out with tracks such as "Fucking Hostile" and "Mouth For War"; the guitar sound often edged towards melt-down, and it became self-evident why Vinnie Paul was known as 'The Brick Wall', so crushing was the drum attack.

By the time of FAR BEYOND DRIVEN (1994) they had pushed their sound even further. The trademark sonic squeals were ever-present and the whole thing had an unrelenting over-the-edge atmosphere in its tales of hate, fear, paranoia and brutalized existence. Perhaps realizing the unsuitability of his name, it was at this point that 'Diamond' Darrell became the equally unlikely 'Dimebag' Darrell.

The summer brought an appearance at the Donington Monsters of Rock Festival, the inevitable touring schedule, and the recording of an old Poison Idea song ("The Badge") for the soundtrack to the film *The Crow*. With FAR BEYOND DRIVEN having gone platinum in the US, the band took the opportunity to indulge themselves with a variety of solo projects and guest appearances. 'Dimebag' Darrell provided guitars for Anthrax's STOMP 442, while Anselmo was instrumental in putting together **Down**, a brutal and thundering side-project featuring various members of Crowbar and Eyehategod.

Having taken a well-deserved break from the mayhem of live shows and recording, the band stepped back into the heavyweight arena with possibly their most savage offering to date. THE GREAT SOUTHERN TREND KILL (1996) was an album of towering stature, psychotic mood swings and battering rhythms. The all-out rattling speed that had characterized their previous efforts was still in evidence but the band had tempered their approach with mellower textures in "Suicide Note Pt. 1" and the doom-laden "Floods".

In 1997 OFFICIAL LIVE: 101% PROOF came storming out to show just how hard'n'heavy the band could be. Having been out of action for such a long time, the band even made an appearance on the UK leg of the *Ozzfest* rock festival alongside other extreme heavyweights such as Slayer and Soulfly. Never ones to push themselves too hard when it came to getting new work into the CD stores, REINVENTING THE STEEL appeared three years later and was followed by a flurry of solo activity, most notably from Anselmo: his Down and **Superjoint Ritual** projects got back into full swing, allowing him to indulge in an altogether more sludgy, doom style of stoner metal.

From poodle-rockers to behemoths of the metal scene, Pantera's transformation has been totally successful and uncompromisingly deadly. One of the hardest and heaviest rock bands in the world, their influence can be heard in the work of many second-generation extreme metal bands, such as Korn, Fear Factory or Machine Head.

⊙ **Cowboys From Hell** (1990; Atco).
From the roots of a glam band grew a mad and mutated monster. COWBOYS positively bristles with jagged riffs and solid rhythms. Clearly influenced by 80s thrash, it took the standards of the genre and forged a vicious new sound for the 1990s.

⊙ **Vulgar Display Of Power** (1992; Atco).
Even more foul-mouthed and antisocial than their major-label debut, this album simply rages.

⊙ **Far Beyond Driven** (1994; Atco).
Dark and brooding, the band continued to explore the outer realms of the metal genre. Fearsome stuff.

⊙ **The Great Southern Trend Kill** (1996; Atco).
Just when it seemed that things couldn't get any nastier or heavier ... Anselmo once again sounds like he is on the verge of madness, while melodic guitar solos weave with some of the harshest, most menacing riffs ever recorded.

Essi Berelian

PAPA M/DAVID PAJO

Pajo born Texas, 1968.

"My goal has always been sovereignty, self-sufficiency." David Pajo

David Pajo has referred to himself as a 'band whore', and certainly his presence in the American indie music machine could be seen as promiscuous, with credits popping up for his vocals, playing, remixing and artwork on releases by many of the best-known post-rock and alt-country bands around. More than this, Pajo has worked alone to great effect, displaying his multi-instrumental abilities under a range of aliases and with a selection of styles.

While the first known recording from Pajo was a 1981 single for the quickly forgotten New Wave band **Church Of The American Astronauts**, it was not until the formation of Louisville's **SLINT** with **Brian McMahan**, **Britt Walford** and **Ethan Buckler**, that the world sat up and took notice. The attention gained with their two album releases, TWEEZ (1987) and SPIDERLAND (1990), was well deserved. Drawing on soft and loud in new ways, the tender watercolours of Slint's plucked melodies and voice-over were interrupted by violent impasto strokes of rock-with-intent, with Pajo's guitar at the very centre of the picture.

With the demise of Slint in the early 90s, Pajo did not become idle. Quite the opposite: he lead his guitars to **Stereolab** and McMahan's **The For Carnation**, played bass with **Royal Trux**, drums with **King Kong**, made his many talents available for use by **Will Oldham**, and replaced Bundy K. Brown in **TORTOISE** in 1996. However, by the time Tortoise's album TNT (1998) was released, Pajo had already left the group and launched headlong into his solo 'M' projects.

Although Pajo had released the first single, "M Is The Thirteenth Letter", under his **Papa M** guise back in 1995, his first full-length solo release did not appear until 1997. Now calling himself **Aerial M**, he released an eponymous instrumental album for Domino records that demonstrated his ability at constructing slow-burning guitar atmospheres. A remix album followed, POST-GLOBAL MUSIC (1999), featuring a lengthy homage from Bundy K. Brown.

Settling with the name Papa M in 1999 Pajo released the double album, LIVE FROM A SHARK CAGE, which took his instrumental complexity to new heights, assisted by his single-minded vision and painstaking attention to every detail of composing, performing and recording. Given his established reputation, it was with surprise that fans greeted the 2001 release of PAPA M SINGS. With no familiar Pajo reference points on display, the record did exactly as it said on the can, and presented Pajo singing, for the first time, on lo-fi country songs (three of seven by Jerry Jeff Walker) in a style reminiscent of Will Oldhams. It wasn't terribly good, but the 'official' Papa M album, WHATEVER, MORTAL (2001), made much more sense, marrying Pajo's instrumental abilities with more honed vocals and frank childlike lyrics.

Pajo's days of collaboration were not over: recently, he has paused from touring to record with a new band **Zwan**, fronted by ex-**SMASHING PUMPKIN** **Billy Corgan** (guitar and vocals), with **Jimmy Chamberlin** (another Pumpkin; drums), **Matt Sweeney** (vocals/guitar), formerly of Chavez, and **Paz Lenchantin** (bass) formerly of A Perfect Circle. The man with many names keeps himself busy and his fans guessing.

Papa M

Whatever, Mortal (2001; Drag City/Domino). He sings, he jokes, he rocks. With contributions by Oldham and Tara Jane O'Neil, skilfully fusing all of his influences, Pajo combines twisted country and sculptured noise with fresh charm.

Annebella Pollen

GRAHAM PARKER

Born London, 1950.

In the early 70s, London had a thriving pub–rock scene, populated by bands with an uncomplicated approach based on the traditions of 50s R&B. Most of these were destined to remain playing for their pints but there emerged a handful of bigger and more enduring talents, chief among them the soon-to-be-huge Dire Straits, but including lesser lights Dr. Feelgood, Chilli Willi And The Red Hot Peppers ... and **Graham Parker And The Rumour**.

It was from a composite of leading pub-rock bands – Chilli Willi And The Red Hot Peppers, Brinsley Schwarz, Ducks Deluxe, and Bontemps Roulez – that the original Rumour was formed. The group comprised **Brinsley Schwarz** (guitar), **Bob Andrews** (keyboards), **Martin Belmont** (guitar), **Andrew Bodnar** (bass) and **Steve Goulding** (drums). Under the auspices of studio owner (and future Stiff Records founder) Dave Robinson they were to become Parker's backing group.

Their debut album, credited to Graham Parker And The Rumour, was HOWLIN' WIND (1976). Produced by another pub-rock veteran, **NICK LOWE**, it was released to rapturous acclaim from the British music press, oozed passion and commitment, and introduced the Parker standards "Hey Lord, Don't Ask Me Questions" and "White Honey". Its follow-up, HEAT TREATMENT (1976), was similarly suffused with urgency and energy.

STICK TO ME (1977) marked the end of Parker's honeymoon with the critics, despite quality songs like "Problem Child" and "Soul On Ice", and was followed by a ramshackle live album, THE PARKERILLA, that seemed to have 'contract filler' written all over

it. It was enough to get Parker dropped by his American record company, Mercury, with whom he was unhappy.

Parker's 1979 album, SQUEEZING OUT SPARKS, was credited to him alone, although The Rumour were still in place. Produced with a crisp immediacy by Jack Nitzche, it dropped the brass instrumentation, which had been used to supplement the band's sound on previous studio albums, and was arguably Parker's best yet collection of songs, from rip-roaring opener, "Discovering Japan", to the bitter closing track, "Don't Get Excited". Deservedly, it charted in both the UK (#18) and US (a best-thus-far #40).

THE UP ESCALATOR (1980) sold well, too, and had the memorable songs, "Empty Lives" and "Stupefaction", but it sounded a little too much as if the group had found a formula and were sticking to it. It was a missed chance, considering the presence of **Nicky Hopkins** on piano, **Danny Federici** of the E Street Band on organ, and even a guest appearance from Springsteen. It was also to be Parker's last album with The Rumour, who had already recorded two albums without him and went off to make one more before breaking up.

Parker's 1982 'solo' outing, ANOTHER GREY AREA, suggested that session men (including, again, Hopkins) could do The Rumour as well as the original band. It was an almost seamless continuation of THE UP ESCALATOR, and opened in fine style with one of Parker's best ever songs, "Temporary Beauty". His subsequent 80s albums, however, moved away from the old R&B sound, alongside a mellowing of the anger and cynicism of his earlier compositions. All had their moments, but none were as consistent as his Rumour output, and sales dropped, with Parker's US label, Elektra, dropping him after STEADY NERVES (1985), which ironically had spawned his only US Top 40 single, "Wake Up (Next To You)".

THE MONA LISA'S SISTER (1988) was perhaps Parker's best late-80s outing, sparsely arranged and energetic, featuring fine songs like "OK Hieronymus" and "Success". It was followed by HUMAN SOUL (1989), STRUCK BY LIGHTNING (1991) and BURNING QUESTIONS (1992), all of which had flashes of brilliance, the last album including, for example, a superb paean to 60s producer Joe Meek, "Just Like Joe Meek's Blues", and the lovely folkish "Long Stem Rose".

By now Parker was often playing live with just acoustic guitar accompaniment, and two albums captured these performances: LIVE! ALONE IN AMERICA (1989) and LIVE ALONE! DISCOVERING JAPAN (1993). In 1995 he released the disappointing 12 HAUNTED EPISODES, playing most instruments himself on a mellow, almost pastoral set.

Then in 1996 came another live album, LIVE FROM NEW YORK, which showed Parker right back in the driving seat. He had new backing from a drums, bass and keyboards trio, The Episodes, who breathed new life into the old songs, and allowed him to chance new ones with confidence – including a wonderful, sneering rendering of Nirvana's "In Bloom".

He followed up the next year with ACID BUBBLEGUM, a continuation of his theme of wasting his flashing razor and glittering bottle of vitriol with a stale pub-rock backing band, standing outside the tent pouring scorn on those inside. Since then, Parker's releases have concentrated on live performances: SQUEEZING OUT SPARKS/LIVE SPARKS (1996) combined remastered studio recordings with a hard, driving live set and THE LAST ROCK'N'ROLL TOUR (1997) was a 22-track set recorded during his 1996 tour.

Aficionados of vintage Parker are directed immediately to the awesome piece of sonic weaponry NOT IF IT PLEASES ME (1998), a storming live set dating back to 1977 that has been crudely bolted on to a prime collection of John Peel session tracks recorded in 1976.

In 2001 Parker popped up with a new album, DEEPCUT TO NOWHERE, backed by old pal Steve Goulding and **Pete Donnelly** (The Figgs). The remainder of **The Figgs** joined Parker to tour the set. Though far from his finest moment, the album had several sparky moments. Hopefully more will follow.

(●) **The Best Of Graham Parker And The Rumour**
(1992; Vertigo/Mercury).
This is a compilation drawn from Parker's first three Vertigo albums, including generous lashings of HOWLIN' WIND and HEAT TREATMENT.

(●) **Live From New York** (1996; Nectar Masters).
The best Parker outing for many a year, strolling afresh through old territory with The Episodes' new arrangements.

Keith Prewer

PARLIAMENT

Formed 1955; disbanded 1981.

"I learned how to make a record with any two minutes of noise I've got." George Clinton

It was in **George Clinton**'s barbershop in Plainfield, New Jersey, pretty much at the dawn of rock and roll, that **Parliament**'s journey across the mind–body divide began. Enamoured with the harmonies of the East Coast doo-wop groups, the future Dr. Funkenstein formed The Parliaments as a straightforward vocal group. After years of unsuccessful releases on minor labels, he moved the group – including future P-Funk stalwarts **Clarence 'Fuzzy' Haskins**, **Grady Thomas**, **Raymond Davis** and **Calvin Simon** (all on vocals), and **Eddie Hazel** (guitar) – to Detroit, with dreams of recording for Motown. However, it turned out to be Motown's rivals Revilot that Clinton signed up with, and who released "(I Wanna) Testify" in 1967. With its fuzzy guitar and spaced-out bridge, the record was a prescient precursor to The

Clinton (centre) and Bootsy (far right) assemble The Parliament – on skates, naturally

Temptations' recordings with Norman Whitfield and reached the US Top 20.

In the ensuing three years, while The Parliaments were involved in legal wrangles over their name, Clinton fell in with the scene surrounding the MC5 and The Stooges, forty miles down the road in Ann Arbor. During this period, the numerous strands of Clinton's vision would coalesce as he discovered Sly And The Family Stone, LSD, Jimi Hendrix and conspiracy theory. Just as the sociopolitical fallout from Detroit's race riot was driving a thin blue stake into the heart of what once was the model city of the American Dream, both Clinton and the White Panther Party (the political wing of the MC5) were attempting to merge funk and rock, sex and politics, black nationalism and hippie-speak as the opening salvos in a war against the squares who ran America.

In an effort to resolve his legal disputes, Clinton renamed his group Parliament and released OSMIUM (1970; later reissued as RHENIUM) for Holland-Dozier-Holland's Invictus label. Along with **FUNKADELIC**'s debut album – recorded by the same crew for Westbound – OSMIUM was the first expression of Clinton's twisted, parodic, scatalogical rewiring of black music clichés. On tracks like "I Call My Baby Pussycat", the funk is definitely present, but it shares space with bagpipes, psychedelic nuances, strings and the rock histrionics of "Red Hot Mama". With less emphasis on the groove, OSMIUM was more like the schizophrenic fissions of a Funkadelic album, but the difference between the two outfits would become apparent with the release of the next Parliament album.

With the monolithic groove of its title track and its reworking of "(I Wanna) Testify", UP FOR THE DOWNSTROKE (1974) heralded Parliament's role as the dance-floor deconstructionists of the African-American musical tradition. CHOCOLATE CITY (1975) combined the hipster jive of 50s and 60s black radio DJs with a surreal, strength-in-numbers, political fantasy to make an oblique concept album about America's neglected inner cities. By this time, ex-James Brown saxophonists **Fred Wesley** and **Maceo Parker**, plus bass player extraordinaire **BOOTSY COLLINS**, had joined fellow Funkateers **Gary Shider** (vocals/guitar), **Cordell 'Boogie' Mosson** (bass), **Michael Hampton** (guitar), **Glenn Goins** (guitar/vocals), **Jerome Brailey** (drums), percussionist **Gary 'Mudbone' Cooper** and keyboard wizard **Bernie Worrell** to form the core of Clinton's Parliafunkadelicment Thang.

Parliament's other 1975 album, MOTHERSHIP CONNECTION, was one of the most strikingly original records ever made. Clinton's mind-boggling fusion of history and science fiction (he rededicates "Swing Low Sweet Chariot" to a spaceship on the title track) rode on top of the instrumental inventions of Bootsy and Worrell to create a powerful re-imagining of blackness. Aside from Clinton's inspired lunacy, Bootsy and Worrell were the two key factors to Parliament's uniqueness: Bootsy had an instinctive rhythmic feel every bit the equal of his former boss, while, in addition to reinventing the synth lexicon, Worrell co-arranged the horn parts with Wesley into space-age blues riffs.

Clinton's conceptual synthesis of the past and the future reached its zenith on FUNKENTELECHY VS. THE PLACEBO SYNDROME (1977). Clinton used the interpretation of black music as a revolutionary weapon as his central trope in this sci-fi tale of cloning and social control. Inhabiting the 'zone of zero funkativity', Sir Nose D'Voidoffunk is engaged in a battle to the death with 'the protector of the pleasure principle', Star Child, whose weapon against 'urge overkill' is the 'bop gun'. When the album comes to a raucous close with "Flashlight", Sir Nose is defeated by a groove so kinetic that it would make Tony Blair shake his rump.

Despite its cartoon voices, comic book characters and squiggly keyboard effects, the next studio album, 1978's MOTOR BOOTY AFFAIR, was as theoretically dense as any of Clinton's records. With its aquatic theme and oblique lyrics, MOTOR BOOTY AFFAIR was a series of riffs on the age-old racial stereotype that 'blacks can't swim'. It was during this time, though, that the P-Funk phenomenon began to unravel.

Rather than attempting a Berry Gordy-style self-sufficiency, Clinton tried to take the established record industry for all it was worth. The unfortunate side effect was the burnout of his musicians. While Parliament was signed to Casablanca and Funkadelic to Westbound (and later Warners), Clinton signed Bootsy's Rubber Band to Warners and Brides of Funkenstein to Atlantic, worked on projects with Parlet, Fred Wesley And The Horny Horns, Incorporated Thing Band and ex-Spinners singer Philippe Wynne, and arranged spectacular live extravaganzas complete with giant flying saucers.

Parliament as such fizzled out with two lacklustre albums, but Clinton kept the P-Funk spirit (and musicians) with solo albums like the marvellous COMPUTER GAMES (1982) and his P-Funk All-Star project. Parliament's influence on contemporary music is unavoidable: the funk-rock synthesis inspired both Living Colour and Red Hot Chili Peppers; without Clinton's conflation of sex and politics, Prince wouldn't exist; and P-Funk's subaquatic, stratospheric, nitrous-oxide, bordello-shaking sound lives on as the spinal column of hip-hop. With its firmly rooted, futuristic reinterpretation of the transcendence offered by black spirituals and its embrace

of the sound-bite hook of hip-hop, Parliament at once encapsulates and reconceives the history of popular music.

⊙ **Mothership Connection** (1975; Casablanca).
Thankfully, all of Parliament's output is available on CD. When they sing 'Swing down sweet chariot, stop and let me ride' on the title track, the most moving moment on any Clinton record yields the entire Parliament concept.

⊙ **Funkentelechy Vs. The Placebo Syndrome** (1977; Casablanca).
"Flashlight" might be the most audacious groove ever committed to vinyl or aluminium oxide. The rest of the album is both hilarious and insightful, and "Bop Gun" might be the second most audacious groove ever.

⊙ **Tear The Roof Off 1974–1980** (1993; Polygram).
This has all the obvious highlights from all the albums and is probably the best introduction to the P. But to really get 'on the one', you need the original albums and their concepts.

Peter Shapiro

GRAM PARSONS

Born Winterhaven, Florida, 1946;
died September 19, 1973.

Country music was regarded as reactionary, white and 'establishment' before **Gram Parsons** came along. Inspired by Hank Williams, George Jones, Bobby Bland, and especially Elvis Presley, Parsons had a musical vision. He called it American Cosmic Music, but everyone else ended up calling it country-rock.

Wealthy, alcoholic and suicidal, the Parsons family could have walked straight out of a Tennessee Williams play. Gram carried himself always with the bearing of an old Southern aristocrat and a trust fund gave him lifelong financial independence from the precariousness of the music business. He started his first band, The Shilos, in 1961 with some high-school friends, who wore suits and ties and played traditional folk music mostly around the Florida club circuit. After graduation Gram was dispatched north to Harvard and a degree in theology, but he barely made it through the first term. He quickly fell in with the local music scene, meeting the members of his next group, **The International Submarine Band**.

Inspired by Bob Dylan's move into rock music, the group went to New York and began gigging in the folk clubs of Greenwich Village – the idea being to play country music with a rock'n'roll attitude – and eventually moved to Los Angeles, where they landed a deal with Lee Hazelwood's LHI label. Their only album, SAFE AT HOME (1968), was recorded in the midst of constant line-up changes and by the time it was released the band had broken up. The record included songs by Merle Haggard and Johnny Cash, a couple of country standards ("Miller's Cave" and "Satisfied Mind") and four Parsons originals, notably the classic "Luxury Liner".

Although the album was unsuccessful, Parsons had become well-known on the LA scene, and in 1968 he was invited to join **THE BYRDS**. Parsons was with them for just five months but he was the driving force behind their move into a pure country sound that would breathe new life into one of America's biggest bands. The only album he recorded with The Byrds, SWEETHEART OF THE RODEO (1968), featured several Parsons originals, including one of his best songs, "Hickory Wind", an intense ballad about a country boy lost in the big city.

Parsons quit The Byrds at the end of 1968 on the eve of a tour of South Africa – he was advised against going by his new friends Mick Jagger and Keith Richards. While the rest of The Byrds certainly couldn't claim any moral high ground in the affair, the timing of Gram's departure caused maximum bad feeling. The tour turned out to be an unmitigated disaster and, on arriving back in Los Angeles, bassist **Chris Hillman** also quit.

Parsons and Hillman quickly patched things up and began to write songs and lay down plans for the greatest country-rock band of all time, **The Flying Burrito Brothers**. They were joined by **Sneaky Pete Kleinow** (pedal steel guitar), **Chris Ethridge** (bass) and **Jon Corneal** (drums), and with this lineup Parsons felt free to pursue a vision to bring together his love of country, R&B, rock and soul. Their first album, THE GILDED PALACE OF SIN (1969), was their finest hour. As evidenced on songs like "Sin City" and "Christine's Tune", which were filled with disillusionment about the evils of city life, Hillman and Parsons had established a prolific songwriting partnership. There were covers of the great Memphis songwriter Dan Penn's "Do Right Woman" and "Dark End Of The Street". Best of all, though, were two of Parsons' finest compositions, the unfortunately titled "Hot Burrito No. 1" and "Hot Burrito No. 2" – love songs of rare depth and passion.

If The Burritos sounded unlike anyone else around at the time, they also looked the part. For their stage act they got decked out in new suits from Nudie Of Hollywood, a shop specializing in outfits for traditional country stars like Buck Owens and Porter Wagoner. Parsons' suit was decorated with green marijuana leaves and naked women on the lapels. With the rest of the band similarly attired, The Burritos hit the road, but outside of Los Angeles they were met with puzzled indifference. They ended the year as part of the bill of The Rolling Stones' disastrous concert at Altamont, and can be seen singing "Six Days On The Road" in the film of the event, *Gimme Shelter*. Parsons began to hang out almost constantly with The Stones around this time. With a regular entourage of crazies, Gram and Keith frequently went out to a favourite spot in the California desert, loaded up on drugs, and watched the night sky for UFOs.

Perhaps deflated by the band's reception, Parsons' last album with The Burritos, BURRITO DELUXE (1970), was a disappointment. There were some very good Parsons/Hillman songs ("Older Guys" and "Cody Cody"), new member and future Eagle, **Bernie Leadon** (guitar/ vocals), contributed "God's Own Singer", and there was a fine version of The Stones' "Wild Horses", but the sound had lost its edge. Parsons lost interest in the band and left shortly after the album's release.

While The Burritos band replaced Parsons with singer Rick Roberts and went on to make several solid if fairly bland albums, Parsons was living in France with Richards and was rumoured to have participated in the recording of The Stones' last great album, EXILE ON MAIN STREET. At any rate, both Jagger and Richards have acknowledged that Gram was a heavy influence on The Stones' frequent excursions into country music.

Parsons returned to LA in 1972 and began work on his first solo album. He hired Elvis Presley's backing group (guitarist **James Burton**, keyboardist **Glen D. Hardin** and drummer **Ronnie Tutt**) and introduced a harmony singer of astonishing purity, **EMMYLOU HARRIS.** GP (1973) replaced The Burritos' exuberant, warped humour with melancholic songs steeped in Parsons' Southern childhood. On "We'll Sweep Out The Ashes In The Morning" and "New Soft Shoe", Parsons and Harris complemented each other with perfect sweetness. The sound and performance were richer and deeper than anything Parsons had done previously. But while The Eagles were selling millions with a watered-down version of Parsons' country-rock, GP sold poorly, barely making the charts. Undaunted, Parsons formed The Fallen Angels, a backing group including Harris on vocals and guitar, and set out on a barnstorming tour of America. A recording of a live radio broadcast was later released as GRAM PARSONS AND THE FALLEN ANGELS LIVE 1973 (1982).

Country soul, a phrase Parsons had been using for years, exactly describes the relaxed warmth and passion of what would be his last album. GRIEVOUS ANGEL (1974) was Gram Parsons' masterpiece. His quavering yet controlled vocals and Harris's pristine harmonies were offset wonderfully on an aching version of "Love Hurts" and on the elegiac "In My Hour Of Darkness". "Brass Buttons" and "$1000

Dollar Wedding" were precisely observed tales of loss and heartbreak, while "I Can't Dance" and "Ooh Las Vegas" added a Burritos-style boisterousness to an otherwise bleak air of finality.

By the time GRIEVOUS ANGEL was released, Parsons had been dead for four months. A lifetime of drink and drug abuse had ended in a motel room in the California desert in September 1973. He was 26 years old. In his time, Gram Parsons had completely redefined contemporary country music but his influence had always been greater than his fame.

The International Submarine Band

⊙ **Safe At Home** (1968; Magnum).
The blueprint for everything that follows. Parsons' much-covered "Luxury Liner" would secure him a place (posthumously) in the Country Music Hall Of Fame.

The Flying Burrito Brothers

⊙ **The Gilded Palace Of Sin** (1969; Edsel).
Crazy name, crazy band. No one else would play country-rock with such flash and swagger. One hippie boy's story of being lost in America with love in his heart and a spliff on his lips.

Gram Parsons

⊙ **GP/Grievous Angel** (1973 & 1974; Warners).
Both classic albums on one CD. Gram follows the patented Hank Williams road to immortality, but not before rewiring country music into his own beautiful vision.

Len Lauk

THE PASTELS

Formed Glasgow, Scotland, 1982.

"We knew we'd get laughed at because of our musical ability, but we didn't care." Stephen Pastel

Unambitious yet highly influential, **The Pastels** were the prime movers in a resurgent Scottish 80s rock scene, both in their own right and through their chief architect **Stephen Pastel**'s involvement with the 53rd & 3rd label. In that quarter, he was to prove a significant factor in the careers of a host of Scottish indie bands, including The Shop Assistants, BMX Bandits, The Soup Dragons, and The Jesus & Mary Chain.

The Pastels themselves began recording shortly after their formation, issuing a debut single "Songs For Children" in October 1982. Eventually comprising **Stephen McRobbie**, aka Stephen Pastel (guitar/vocals), **Brian Superstar** (guitar), **Martin Hayward** (bass) and **Bernice Simpson** (drums), the band were happy to learn their art in public, and were soon feted as the fathers of 'Shambling', a mildly derogatory term coined by the British music press – and which reached its apogee with the *NME*'s C86 compilation of (in large part) musically inept groups. Shambling was ultimately to do The Pastels a great disservice in filing them with contemporaries who shared only the band's wilful amateurishness and none of their sense of purpose.

With band members split between the Scots universities of Strathclyde and St Andrew's, The Pastels' progress was haphazard, with an LP not forthcoming until early 1987. In the meantime there was a series of increasingly accomplished singles, and label changes aplenty. The debut was on Whaam Records, the follow-up, "I Wonder Why" (1983), on Rough Trade, and they cemented their growing reputation on the fledgling Creation label with "Something's Going On" (1984), "Million Tears" (1984) and "I'm Alright With You" (1985). Eschewing the bright pop production of "I Wonder Why", the Creation singles saw the band's frail melodies blurred beneath a multi-layered drone, which evoked the ghost of The Velvet Underground at their most dissonant.

The Pastels split with Creation in 1985, surfacing again on the rather more nondescript Glass label. There, augmented by ex-Shop Assistant **Aggi** on keyboards, they embarked on a spell of intense creativity, releasing three singles and a debut album in just over a year, and enjoying their most commercially successful period to date. The driving, up-tempo "Truck Train Tractor" (1986) was hailed for its clean sound and breezy harmonies, suggesting the band no longer felt the need to hide their deficiencies in a soup of noise. The subsequent "Crawl Babies" and "Coming Through" confirmed their growing confidence, while the vaguely retrospective UP FOR A BIT WITH THE PASTELS (1987) charted a course back to their Creation work with the inclusion of remastered versions of "Baby Honey" and "I'm Alright With You".

Seeking to gain some return on their earlier association with The Pastels, Creation released what was to have been the band's original debut in the form of SUCK ON THE PASTELS (1988), an album which, despite its obvious immaturity, served to maintain the band's profile during a largely unproductive 1988.

With 1989's SITTING PRETTY – featuring vocals from **Eugene Kelly** (ex-Vaselines) and guitar work by another former Shop Assistant, **David Keegan** – it seemed that The Pastels were becoming a halfway house for refugees of defunct Scottish indie bands. Instead, the album was to prove to be a swan song of sorts for the long-established Pastels' line-up, with the band eventually slimming down to a core of Stephen Pastel, girlfriend Aggi, and multi-instrumentalist newcomer **Katrina Mitchell**, with David Keegan remaining on the periphery as an auxiliary.

The Pastels threesome moved forward, collaborating with the American primitivist **Jad Fair** (**HALF JAPANESE**) on JAD FAIR AND THE PASTELS (1991). They then worked with **Gerard Love** (**TEENAGE FANCLUB**) and **Dean Wareham** (**GALAXIE 500**) on the EP, OLYMPIC WORLD OF PASTELISM (1994), before releasing the MOBILE SAFARI (1995) and ILLUMINATION (1997) albums on Domino. All were fine sets, and further testimony to The Pastels' erratic but multifarious talent. With a well-received remix of ILLUMINATION (entitled ILLUMINATI: PASTELS MUSIC REMIXED) featuring such influential names as Stereolab, My Bloody Valentine and Third Eye Foundation, they proved themselves to be open to a little experimentation.

In recent times the group have been busy running the independent label Geographic, writing a score for David McKenzie's film *The Last Great Wilderness*, and helping to set up a new record store in Glasgow. A new album is also in the pipeline...

⊙ Up For A Bit With The Pastels (1987; Paperhouse). Almost a continuation of where they left off with Creation – a thin crystalline production brings to the fore the band's fragile melodies and a surprising musical dexterity.

⊙ Sitting Pretty (1989; Chapter 22). Benefiting immensely from a roughshod production, SITTING PRETTY is a typically uneven LP which nevertheless showcases some of the band's best ever work, in the form of the poptastic "Nothing To Be Done" and the epic viola-driven "Ditch The Fool".

⊙ Truckload Of Trouble 1986–93 (1993; ZTT). An eighteen-track compilation of singles, B-sides and previously unissued material that serves as an effective introduction to the world of The Pastels.

Ian Lowey

PAVEMENT

Formed Stockton, California, 1989; split 2000.

"Jaded pop is one of the worst curses in the world." Stephen Malkmus

The duo of **Stephen Malkmus** (vocals/guitar) and **Scott 'Spiral Stairs' Kannberg** (guitar) formed the nucleus of the lopsided, clattering, crooning beast that was **Pavement** at the tail end of the 80s. The SLAY TRACKS EP, released on their own Treble Kicker label in 1989, was the first thing to emerge from their Stockton studio/garage and, together with the EPs, PERFECT SOUND FOREVER and DEMOLITION PLOT (both on Drag City), created a lo-fi buzz on the US underground scene. The warmth and jagged melody of tracks like "Debris Slide", "From Now On", and the gorgeous opening fuzz of "Heckler Spray", set them apart from other bands, despite the precarious recording quality and the primitive technique of drummer **Gary Young**.

Touring sporadically around the US with an additional drummer, **Bob Nastanovich**, the band went down a storm, creating a staunch following. Their first album, SLANTED AND ENCHANTED (1992), despite initially seeing light of day in a roughly edited, unmarketed cassette version, effortlessly caused the media stir it so deserved, dwelling one moment in sweetly shaded avenues of melody like the single "Trigger Cut", then shrieking down experimental culs-de-sac the next. The album shone amid the angst-fuelled grunge prevalent at the time, borrowing from classic stuff on both sides of the Atlantic (Pixies, Sonic Youth, The Fall); indeed Malkmus's early singing style (like their early album covers) has been accused of borrowing a little too closely from The Fall.

Pavement embarked on their first full US tour to promote the album, followed by their first (sell-out) European dates, this time with the addition of **Mark Ibold** on bass. Live, Pavement were a swoonsome treat, making all this melodic discord look easy, and utilizing drummer Gary Young's one-man circus of drumstick stunts and impromptu handstands. However, they were most certainly more than a novelty band, and chart success quickly followed, with both album and single topping the indie charts throughout Europe. John Peel was, needless to say, a big fan.

They released four new tracks on the WATERY DOMESTIC EP at the end of 1992, and undertook a tour of Australia and the Far East. Meanwhile sales of the album topped 100,000, and the release of their sought-after early releases on WESTING BY MUSKET AND SEXTANT (1993) tied a big red ribbon on their success. The only hiccup was the forced departure of the erratic Gary Young, who was replaced by Malkmus's childhood friend **Steve West**.

After the often ear-taxing fuzz and hiss of their first releases, Pavement's next album, the resplendent CROOKED RAIN, CROOKED RAIN (1994), was strikingly accessible, with intriguing country leanings and some straight-in-your-face melodies. A single from the album, "Cut Your Hair", was an indie-chart hit, and the band's subsequent tour gained rave reviews. Around this time, Malkmus was moonlighting with **Silver Jews**, led by **David Berman**. Their debut release, STARLITE WALKER (1994) was a beautiful collection of alternative country oddities. This fine band continue to record to this day, but even though the group is primarily Berman's affair, the occasional presence of Malkmus has frequently meant that the Jews are dismissed as a Pavement side-project.

Three intense weeks recording in Memphis at the start of 1995 saw Pavement cut almost thirty tracks, eighteen of which saw the light of day on their third

studio album, WOWEE ZOWEE (1995), a less immediate work than its predecessors, but with a breadth and depth that repaid repeated listening. The stop-start experimentalism of old was still there, as was the languid, almost careless feel to many of the songs. But there was more diversity than before, ranging from the breathtaking Nirvana-like fury of "Flux = Rad", to the poignant melodies of "Motion Suggests" and "Father To A Sister Of Thought", which featured pedal steel guitar to die for. It was a strong, lasting statement, backed up with some terrific and much less chaotic live performances, and, together with the storming beauty of BRIGHTEN THE CORNERS (1997) confirmed Pavement's status as one of the most original, sincere and distinctive bands of the decade.

During the following year, however, the seeds of Pavement's eventual demise were sown, as both Kannberg and Malkmus played solo gigs. When TERROR TWILIGHT (1999) arrived it drew praise from virtually every corner, but the fact that it contained no Kannberg material made the inevitable seem, well, even more inevitable. Sure enough, the end of the TERROR TWILIGHT tour brought an announcement that Pavement would officially cease to exist. Since then solo and side projects have proliferated from the various members, the most significant coming from Kannberg and his **Preston School Of Industry**, who released ALL THIS SOUNDS GAS (2001), and Malkmus who emerged with STEPHEN MALKMUS (2001) and a follow-up, the excellent PIG LIB (2003), released under the banner of **Stephen Malkmus & The Jicks**.

Pavement

- **Slanted And Enchanted** (1993; ZTT).
  Nuggets of melody, storms of noise. An irresistible debut. Now reissued with an additional CD of rarities and live cuts.

- **Crooked Rain, Crooked Rain** (1994; Big Cat).
  Peerless, flawless pop, featuring the starry-eyed singles "Cut Your Hair", "Gold Soundz" and "Range Life".

- **Wowee Zowee** (1995; Big Cat).
  A less well-rounded album than its predecessors, but more profoundly satisfying for its initial obliqueness. Features the lovely single "Rattled By The Rush" and too many more to mention.

Preston School Of Industry

- **All This Sounds Gas** (2001; Domino).
  The graceful opener "Whalebones" deals with the Pavement split, but after that it becomes clear that Kannberg has moved on. He generally avoids the textural and rhythmic detours of Pavement and instead plays strong, memorable and slightly melancholy rock anthems. A promising new beginning.

Stephen Malkmus

- **Stephen Malkmus** (2001; Matador).
  The smooth production of the set is much easier on the ear than say SLANTED AND ENCHANTED, and yet the boy-to-man passage hasn't resulted in the total abandonment of lo-fi principles – healthy doses of dissonance and twang can be found within these more conventional cuts.

Andrew Stone

ANNETTE PEACOCK

Born Brooklyn, New York, 1941.

The visionary singer, keyboardist and composer **Annette Peacock** inhabits that little-visited but important territory where jazz meets the avant-garde, incorporating elements of performance art and poetry into her work. Her influence on rock, mediated via clued-in would-be collaborators like Bowie and Eno, is subtle and oblique, but she certainly helped pave the way for performers like Laurie Anderson.

She pitched into the middle of the jazz vanguard back in 1962, becoming friendly with Albert Ayler and the poet LeRoi Jones (later Amiri Baraka). She had a spell in Ayler's band but left in the midst of a European tour, returning to New York to concentrate on developing her own 'free-form song-form' style. The next crucial step came in 1967 when she was given a prototype modular synthesizer by its inventor, Dr Robert Moog. Peacock found a way to put instruments and her own voice through the synthesizer to alter their tonal qualities, and pioneered recording and performing using the synthesizer – an unmanageable beast measuring eight feet by five feet, it had previously only been used in the studio.

While the rest of her generation were discovering psychedelia in 1968, Peacock recorded her album REVENGE, which featured the ahead-of-its-time 'rap', "I Belong To A World That's Destroying Itself". The album was not released until 1971. In the same year she recorded I'M THE ONE, a low-key, slow-burning *tour de force* of treated vocals and soulful piano which, in a strange example of parallel evolution, echoes the albums THERE'S A RIOT GOIN' ON and FRESH that Sly And The Family Stone were recording around the same time.

In 1972 Peacock attracted the interest of David Bowie and signed up with his manager, Tony de Vries, playing the Lincoln Center along with fellow MainMan signing Iggy Pop. Bowie invited her to play synth on his ALADDIN SANE album, an offer she declined, deciding instead to enrol in the prestigious Juilliard School Of Music to study composition. In 1974 she left New York and came to England, where she lived on the breadline for the next four years while continuing to work on her compositions. After recording a solo gig in 1976, Brian Eno offered to produce her – another offer she turned down.

In 1978 she released the critically acclaimed X-DREAMS, an album of jam sessions with the likes of Chris Spedding, Bill Bruford and Mick Ronson. Both that album and the follow-up, THE PERFECT RELEASE (1979), featured her rapping about incest, masturbation, exploitation, promiscuity and 'ecological masochism'. She set up her own label, Ironic Records, in 1980, furthering the electro-rap experiments on the melodic SKY-SKATING (1982), BEEN IN THE STREETS TOO LONG (1983) and I HAVE NO FEELINGS (1986), the last exploring the move from the tyranny of emotion to serenity. In 1988 she released ABSTRACT-CONTACT, a sparsely arranged album (keyboards, bass and drums) containing moments of great poignancy.

Peacock was largely out of the music business for the following eight years, concentrating on bringing up her daughter. In December 1995 she moved back to rural bliss in the US, and is once again writing and recording, aiming to make her music as widely heard as possible. Yet her records remain only patchily available – track them down by contacting Ironic at PO Box 58, Wokingham, Berks RG11 7HN, England.

⊙ **Abstract-Contact** (1988; Ironic).
Probably her most accessible recording, featuring the fourteen-minute "Elect Yourself" (a jazz rap about the need for revolution) and "Happy With My Hand", a paean to the delights of sexual self-sufficiency.

Andy Smith

PEARL JAM

Formed Seattle, 1990.

"I'm still that surfer gas station guy that plays music. So I write fans back a normal letter and find myself becoming part of their lives." Eddie Vedder

The genesis of **Pearl Jam** was rooted in chance and tragedy. **Stone Gossard** (guitar) and **Jeff Ament** (bass) had both been members of seminal grungers **GREEN RIVER**, and later **MOTHER LOVE BONE** with ex-Malfunkshun member, Andrew Wood, on vocals. When Wood died of an overdose, his longtime friend Chris Cornell (of Soundgarden) put together a tribute project called TEMPLE OF THE DOG (1991) – Gossard, Ament and new recruit **Mike McCready** (guitar) were roped in, as was **Eddie Vedder** (vocals), who had provided some vocals for a demo tape put together by the others.

Once TEMPLE OF THE DOG was in the can **Dave Krusen** (drums) joined the other four. Flirting with different names on the way (Mookie Blaylock and Reenk Roink), they eventually settled on Pearl Jam, after an allegedly hallucinogenic recipe belonging to Vedder's grandmother. By spring 1991, Pearl Jam had begun to play live shows in the Seattle area supporting the likes of Alice In Chains. As the word spread about the Seattle scene, the band signed to Epic and their debut TEN (1992) was rushed out. Although it was recorded speedily, it distilled the pain and attitude of the disaffected, but injected it with an electric, classic rock feel. Gossard and McCready's playing owed as much to Jimi Hendrix as to any punk band. Vedder's lyrics and vocals carried a rare, raw emotion, and the soaringly poetic "Evenflow", "Alive" and "Jeremy" took elements of his own traumatic childhood and transformed them into universal experience.

Just as TEN entered the US charts, Krusen left to deal with personal problems and was replaced by **Dave Abbruzzese**. Fresh recording sessions pro-

duced "State Of Love And Trust" and "Breathe" for the soundtrack of *Singles*, a teen-romance comedy based on the Seattle music scene, starring Matt Dillon. Three of the band members even managed to make cameo appearances as part of Dillon's grunge combo, Citizen Dick. Despite this media exposure, the press were less than kind to Pearl Jam, reviews equating their driven sound with the rock dinosaurs of the 70s, while Kurt Cobain fuelled the controversy by calling them a corporate band (conveniently forgetting their lengthy apprenticeships for some of Seattle's finest). The fans on the other hand could not have cared less; TEN outstripped NEVERMIND in the US metal charts and outsold it worldwide in 1992.

A new album was planned for late 1992, but touring schedules slowed things to a crawl. Gossard kept himself fresh by working on SHAME (1993), the sole product of his Brad side-project; it was a mellow, danceable mix of psychedelia and funk rhythms. The summer of 1993 saw Pearl Jam providing support for **NEIL YOUNG** and tearing into soulful, breathtaking versions of old favourites along with fresh punk-inspired material. They joined Young for a powerful version of "Rockin' In The Free World", a song they reprised later in the year at the MTV Awards. A new and important alliance had been forged.

Evil-eyed Eddie Vedder

When Vs. (1993) finally saw the light of day, the fan response was awesome, and it entered at #1 in the *Billboard* charts. The guitars and rhythms raged more freely, and Vedder displayed his vocal and lyrical diversity, with songs of raw, blood-curdling anger ("Go", "Animal", "Blood") balanced by mellower textures ("Daughter"). Overall, it sounded more caustic, accomplished and mature than TEN.

Pearl Jam had always gone out of their way to be as accessible as possible; if fans wrote they would usually get a personal reply. This dedication to the public took a new turn in 1994. While continuing to tour, and make occasional appearances with Neil Young, they weighed in against the corporate might of the Ticketmaster booking agency, which they accused of raising prices beyond the spending power of their younger followers. They were joined in their protest by such artists as R.E.M., Aerosmith and, of course, Neil Young, and were to stay in dispute with the agency for the next two years.

To show their faith in vinyl, VITALOGY (1994) was first released on record, and then on CD, which saw it rocket to the top of the Billboard charts. Tracks like the searing "Spin The Black Circle" and the belligerent threats of "Not For You" delivered the usual doses of mayhem. However, tracks such as the pointless "Stupid Mop" dragged on the album's momentum.

Apart from McCready's **Mad Season** side-project, 1995 saw Pearl Jam's partnership with Neil Young flourish, their encore jams developing into the poignant, broad sweep of the MIRROR BALL (1995) album. Recorded in a mere four days, the record was a potent blend of Pearl Jam's hard rock influences and Young's poetic meanderings, oiled with doses of teeth-grating, overdriven feedback. Unfortunately, in a fit of marketing pique, Young's record company refused to allow Pearl Jam's name to appear on the cover.

Meanwhile the band, true to their word, continued to make a stand against Ticketmaster by touring less-established venues. Progress was hampered by forced cancellations and security problems, but when things went well audiences were treated not only to Pearl Jam, but to Young joining in on songs from MIRROR BALL.

The following year saw the band lose Dave Abbruzzese and finally focus their collective attention on a new studio effort. NO CODE (1996) was steeped in the all-American tradition of garage punk but instead of lunging headfirst into a soundscape of heaving guitars the songs marked out a more thoughtful approach. Opening track "Sometimes" was a slow burner and it wasn't until "Hail Hail" that things kicked off in familiar style. What the album lacked in pace it made up for in poise and moving, troubled lyrics. Overall, though, it received a less-than-ecstatic reception and the band turned back to what they knew best for YIELD (1998) and the live opus LIVE ON TWO LEGS (1998), straight-ahead hard

rocking. While LIVE ON TWO LEGS featured former Soundgarden drummer Matt **Cameron** (replacing **Jack Irons**) as part of the live set-up, he actually contributed to the writing of new LP BINAURAL (2000). As ever it was a *tour de force* showcase of the band's subtlety and power, addressing both social and personal issues with a deft touch. Later that same year, as if to emphasize the band's punk credentials, they opted to release a series of 25 official live bootleg CDs, all of them recorded, warts'n'all, during their European tour.

2002 brought with it RIOT ACT, another blast of rock, Vedder-style. The guitars sounded big and the armchair politics was, as ever, pushed to the fore. As far as we know, Ticketmaster's MD hasn't bought a copy.

⦿ **Ten** (1992; Epic).
The album that forced a complete reappraisal of the Seattle grunge sound.

⦿ **Vs** (1993; Epic).
Vital and powerful, shot through with a melodic core, pulsing with feral, snarling attitude.

⦿ **Vitalogy** (1994; Epic).
The band's love affair with punk continues with this roller-coasting release. Occasionally brilliant, this recording features the band making a stab at "Better Man", a song from Vedder's days with Bad Radio.

⦿ **No Code** (1996; Epic).
More thoughtful and focused than its hit-and-miss predecessor. A controlled and emotive collection of rock songs that concentrate more on quality than high-octane thrills. Vedder takes most of the writing credits and it shows in the moody textures and introspective tone.

⦿ **Live On Two Legs** (1998; Epic).
While the band's studio output has proved to be rather hit and miss, Eddie and the boys still excel in a live context, as can be experienced on this characteristically taut and lean concert set. It even makes some of their less worthy tunes bearable.

⦿ **Binaural** (2000; Epic).
Full-tilt tracks such as "Breakerfall", "Insignificance" and "Evacuation" ought to sate those who feel that the Jam have been easing off the gas pedal rather too much of late. Meanwhile the darker aspects of the collection benefit immensely from Vedder's ever-moody vocal introspection.

Essi Berelian

ANN PEEBLES

Born East St. Louis, Missouri, 1947.

Ann Peebles ranks alongside Aretha Franklin, Etta James and Irma Thomas as one of the greatest female singers of Southern soul music. She grew up singing gospel in her father's Baptist choir, idolizing and occasionally backing the legendary Mahalia Jackson. Peebles' secular music career began with an impromptu performance at the Rosewood club in Memphis in 1969, which caught the attention of famed producer Willie Mitchell of Hi Records. This began eleven years on the Hi label, resulting in seven albums and twenty-four singles, nineteen of which landed on the Billboard R&B charts. After spending some time raising a family, Peebles returned to the recording studio in the late

1980s, recording several albums for Bullseye/Rounder.

Peebles' first major hit, a cover of Little Johnny Taylor's "Part Time Love", typifies her style. It's a tough, bluesy slab of Southern funk sung with grit, intensity and passion. Mitchell's production is impeccable, with blasting horns and pounding rhythm courtesy of the amazing Hi rhythm section, who sound much funkier than when backing label-mate Al Green. During the period 1969–72, Peebles recorded one incredible song after another. Among the best are the strutting autobiographical "99 Pounds", the desperate "Breaking Up Somebody's Home", and a scorching cover of Bobby Bland's "I Pity The Fool". When Peebles rides the beat hard on the chorus of "99 Pounds", the combination of swagger and spunk is irresistible. On "I Pity The Fool", her rage simmers through much of the song, finally exploding as she shouts: 'Look at the people, I know you wonder what they're doing, they're just standing there watching you make a fool of me.' It's a version that stands as one of the all-time great performances by a female soul singer, up there with Aretha Franklin's "Chain Of Fools" and Etta James' "I'd Rather Go Blind".

In 1973, Peebles recorded her best-known album, I CAN'T STAND THE RAIN. Although the record is marred by the dreariness that crept into Mitchell's productions in the mid-70s, it contains two classic and often-covered songs, the ominous "I'm Gonna Tear Your Playhouse Down" and the heart-wrenching title track – recently used by Missy Elliott for her smash single "The Rain (Supa Dupa Fly)". The original proved to be Peebles' biggest chart success, reaching #6 in the R&B chart and #38 in the pop chart.

Her final three albums on the Hi label rarely reach such heights, but still include many great songs, like the excellent "Come To Mama", which is propelled by a hard funk groove. Other strong tracks from the period 1975–78 include the bluesy "The Handwriting Is On The Wall" and tough funky numbers like "Love Played A Game" and "I Got The Papers". The albums from the 1990s were not as strong as her Hi recordings, although there's a wonderful cover of Robert Ward's "Fear No Evil" on FULL TIME LOVE (1992).

- **Part Time Love** (1970; Hi).
  This album contains several tracks from the debut, as well as some even stronger material such as the driving title track.

- **Straight From The Heart** (1972; Hi).
  Peebles' best, a classic of Memphis soul with every track a gem. Five stars.

- **I Can't Stand The Rain** (1973; Hi).
  Although it contains the classic title track and "I'm Gonna Tear Your Playhouse Down", this highly regarded album suffers from an excessive emphasis on ballads.

- **Full Time Love** (1992; Bullseye/Rounder).
  A strong comeback, with good originals, good covers of Robert Cray and Robert Ward, but some misguided covers (like The Stones' "Miss You").

David Zingg

PENETRATION

Formed Newcastle, England, 1976; disbanded 1979.

Despite being one of the most promising of the early punk groups, **Penetration** never achieved their full potential. **Pauline Murray** (vocals), **Robert Blamire** (bass), **Gary Chaplin** (guitar) and **Gary Smallman** (drums) were all from Ferryhill, a small pit village close to Newcastle. Inspired by the Sex Pistols, they came together in mid-1976 and played several local gigs before a loss-making support slot for Generation X at London's Roxy in April 1977. Having survived that, they played regularly in the capital throughout that crucial year, making waves in London and building up a large following throughout the country.

The band was basically built around Murray, whose strong vocals and energetic performances rivalled those of Siouxsie (of the Banshees), and drew greatly from the example of Patti Smith – indeed Penetration's set at the time included a fine version of Smith's "Free Money". However, despite their success at grassroots level, their singles for the Virgin label – the excellently angry "Don't Dictate" (1977) and "Firing Squad" (1978) – didn't gain general acclaim.

In March 1978 Chaplin left, and was replaced by **Neal Floyd** as guitarist. **Fred Purser** joined as lead guitarist in July, drawing ludicrous criticism from some quarters that the band was flirting with heavy metal. Yet, by the summer of 1978, Penetration were beginning to make a name for themselves, if only because Murray made them stand out from the crowd of Pistols soundalikes. They were booked to play the Lyceum with The Fall in August 1978, and the Reading Festival a few weeks later. However, neither event went well, and the band seemed nervous of making the jump to bigger venues.

Their debut album, MOVING TARGETS, released in October 1978, was well received at the time, but seems in retrospect a rather bland, unfocused record, for all the strengths of Murray's voice. A slow decline in morale and direction began. Innumerable tours were undertaken, including a five-week jaunt around the States, which culminated in their coming to blows in San Francisco.

Added to this was Virgin's inexorable demand for recorded material. Penetration were pushed back into the studio to record COMING UP FOR AIR (1979), the album that proved to be their undoing. Too similar to TARGETS, it received lukewarm reviews and the band decided to split after completing a last, poorly attended British tour.

- **Moving Targets** (1978; Virgin).
  A bundle of ideas rather than an album of songs, played without the conviction the band brought to their live shows. Even "Free Money" sounds relatively tame, though the album does include the fine single release, "Life's A Gamble".

Andy Lewis

THE PENGUIN CAFE ORCHESTRA

Formed London, 1976; disbanded, 1997.

Released in 1976, MUSIC FROM THE PENGUIN CAFE, the first album by **The Penguin Cafe Orchestra**, opened up a world of startling possibilities. Predating by the best part of a decade the world-music phenomenon and WOMAD festivals, the record's 'invented folk music' introduced to British rock audiences a plethora of global styles and rhythms. And they came in mature form, housed within deceptively simple, cyclical frameworks that opened onto meandering passages of compelling strangeness. Gregorian chant, minimalist drones and dissonant operatics rubbed shoulders with snatches of ukelele-fuelled café jazz, polkas and Celtic reels. Holding the thing together was an almost nursery-rhyme simplicity and – a Penguin keynote – an emphasis on repetition rather than development.

The controlling maestro was composer and arranger **Simon Jeffes**. His writing held everything in check, ensuring an aching melody was never far away, and hinting at an accessibility that would be capitalized upon in future years. At launch, however, it was little short of revolutionary, and emerged as part of Eno's stable of ambient electronic adventurers on the dome-headed one's Obscure label. The group, although named on the record, was in essence a game for Jeffes and his friends, and maintained an air of anonymity personified by surreal sleeve paintings of suited penguins. They hardly ever played live – and made an event of it when they did, taking over a café (of course) as house band.

Simon Jeffes, meanwhile, was becoming an ever-more-sought-after producer, brought in by Malcolm McLaren to transform Adam And The Ants from a sluggish second-division punk outfit to a major chart band, with a music underpinned by the cunning deployment of Burundi drumbeats. Jeffes was also working at this time with the Yellow Magic Orchestra, whose own Ryuichi Sakamoto was later

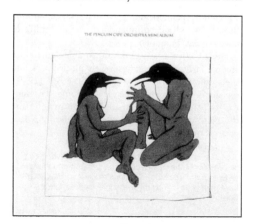

to exhibit in his solo work a comparable penchant for space and spare classical melodies. And he put the strings on Sid Vicious's last will and testament, "My Way".

The Penguins' second LP, five years on from the first, was entitled simply PENGUIN CAFE ORCHESTRA (1981). This time Jeffes was pursuing his agendas on strictly 'natural' instruments – piano, acoustic guitar and, most prominently, violin, with the odd spinet and cheng, and telephone and rubber band, thrown in. It was more tune-based than before, though eccentric as ever.

As the 80s progressed, the Penguins' music seemed to make sense to a wider audience, as world music got aired on the radio, and was assimilated into the pop mainstream via the likes of Paul Simon, Sting, Peter Gabriel and David Byrne. Jeffes' crew polished up their act accordingly, losing the rough edges (and abandoning any whiff of the avant-garde) as they developed into a consummate touring outfit. The music retained its sense of whimsy – and it might be said that any group playing 'rock music' as a chamber orchestra had originality – but the third album, BROADCASTING FROM HOME (1984), at times steered too close to MOR. Still, the audiences multiplied, and in 1988 the ensemble recorded a live album, WHEN IN ROME, in front of a packed and appreciative Royal Festival Hall – one of London's largest classical music venues – and the same year were the subject of a prestigious *South Bank Show* on British TV. The following year the Penguins headed further into the classical establishment, collaborating with the Royal Ballet and the BBC Concert Orchestra on a work entitled STILL LIFE.

The Penguins then toured intermittently, with a line-up that included **Peter McGowan** (violin), **Geoffrey Richardson** (once of **CARAVAN**; viola and clarinet), **Helen Liebman** (cello), **Barbara Bolte** (oboe/cor anglais), **Ian Maidman** (bass/percussion), **Stephen Fletcher** (piano/harmonium), **Annie Whitehead** (trombone), **Neil Rennie** (ukulele), and Jeffes playing mainly piano and guitar.

Their 1995 album, CONCERT PROGRAM, exemplified the modern sound: twenty Jeffes compositions, all quirkily Penguin, but in no way shocking, unless you count Annie Whitehead's unannounced trombone bursts or the sudden slides in tempo. They played seamless coffee-table music really, but the fact that they did indicates not just a shift from where Jeffes and co started off, but also in listeners' ears.

The untimely death of Simon Jeffes from a brain tumour on December 11, 1997 left the café with no one to write up the day's specials, though in 2000 a posthumous collection of Jeffes compositions appeared, PIANO MUSIC. This fitting final chapter of the Penguins' story was compiled by Jeffes' closest friends from disparate recordings; some of the cuts were written very late in his life while others dated back to the 70s. He will be missed.

PENTANGLE

Formed London, 1967; disbanded 1973; re-formed briefly 1982; re-formed intermittently 1988–93.

The blokishly titled BERT AND JOHN (1966) album – by **Bert Jansch** and **John Renbourn**, two of the leading acoustic guitarists of the time – provided the impetus for the **Pentangle** project, in which folk was fused with elements of blues and jazz. The band was formed when this nucleus was augmented by folk singer **Jacqui McShee** (vocals), who had already worked with Renbourn on the acclaimed ANOTHER MONDAY (1967), and **Danny Thompson** (bass) and **Terry Cox** (drums), two experienced members of the jazz and blues scene and graduates of Alexis Korner's Blues Inc. band.

Pentangle's debut album, THE PENTANGLE (1968), met with great acclaim – not least from a youthful John Peel, who wrote the sleeve notes – and laid the groundwork for a career of consistent popularity. The double-album follow-up, SWEET CHILD (1968), provided a perfect showcase for the band's talents, featuring one disc of live performance and another recorded in the studio, and, like its predecessor (and the rest of their 60s releases), it was produced by Shel Talmy, who (in sharp contrast) helped create the raw rock sound of The Who and The Kinks.

By the following year, Pentangle had reached a wider audience courtesy of the BBC TV series *Take Three Girls* (starring a young Joanna Lumley), for which the band wrote the theme song, "Light Flight". The album whence it came, BASKET OF LIGHT (1969), remains Pentangle's biggest-selling and most enduring record. It seemed the band could do no wrong, and their live performances were taking them to such varied but equally prestigious venues as Carnegie Hall and the 1970 Isle of Wight Rock Festival.

In many ways BASKET OF LIGHT proved to be Pentangle's musical swan song. Jansch and Renbourn wisely maintained their solo projects, which from 1970 onwards garnered more critical plaudits than Pentangle's. By the time of CRUEL SISTER (1970) and SOLOMON'S SEAL (1972), the musical dexterity could not disguise an idea that had seemingly run its course.

Danny Thompson went on to work with John Martyn, among a host of other credits; Jansch returned to the solo circuit; Jacqui McShee teamed up with John Renbourn in his band between 1974

and 1981; while Terry Cox provided percussion for the French crooner and one-time sex symbol, Charles Aznavour.

1982 saw these original members stage a Pentangle reunion with the OPEN DOOR album and a low-impact European tour. Then in 1988 Jansch and McShee again reconvened the group, enlisting **Nigel Portman-Smith** (bass/keyboards), **Gerry Conway** (drums) and **Mike Piggot** (guitar – later replaced by Lindisfarne founder member **Rod Clements**). They released a couple of albums, the enjoyable IN THE ROUND (1988) and slighter SO EARLY IN THE SPRING (1989), then again lapsed. A third 1991 revival, with **Pete Kirtley** taking on guitar duties, produced ONE MORE ROAD (1993), before the band finally seemed to throw in the towel.

However, in 1995 Jacqui McShee unveiled a semi-Pentangle outfit, teaming up with the band's last drummer, Gerry Conway, and recruiting keyboard player **Spencer Cozens** for an album entitled ABOUT THYME. Despite the title's weak pun, the album contained strong material which drew on the original band's disparate musical elements but with a more contemporary feel. Dubbed 'McShee's Pentangle', the new band toured throughout 1997, combining new songs with a reworking of some old material.

PERE UBU

Formed Cleveland, Ohio, 1975; disbanded 1982; re-formed 1987–95 and sporadically since then.

Pere Ubu originated in Cleveland with a discordant brand of urban angst and dense industrial sound that mirrored the city's troubled 70s soul. Their nucleus was formed from Rocket From The Tombs, a band heavily influenced by Detroit groups such as The Stooges and The MC5, and featuring **DAVID THOMAS** on vocals and **PETER LAUGHNER** on guitar. They became Pere Ubu in 1975 – taking the name from a proto-surrealist play by the French writer Alfred Jarry – and initially retained some of the Rocket's sonic bombardment, albeit with an infusion of wit.

The early line-up of Thomas, Laughner, **Tom Herman** (guitar/bass/organ), **Tim Wright** (guitar/bass), **Allen Ravenstine** (synths) and **Scott Krauss** (drums) produced a unique assemblage of art-

and garage-rock trash: disjointed synth whines, heavy loping bass, cut-ups of tape loops, atonal howling and chronic distortion. Their first two singles – "30 Seconds Over Tokyo" and "Final Solution", both released on Thomas's Hearthan label – were good examples of this dark, unorthodox mix, and created enough waves for the band to play Max's Kansas City in New York in early 1976.

As wider recognition beckoned, Laughner left to form **Friction** (he died in 1977 from severe alcohol and drug abuse), while Tony Maimone (bass/piano) replaced **Tim Wright** (who joined DNA). With Laughner's departure, Pere Ubu lost some of their nihilism, but his ghost hovered over their astonishing debut, THE MODERN DANCE (1978), a collage of avant-garde surrealisms, leavened with humour and some of the most exciting rock music of its time. The album echoed Beefheart and Eno-era Roxy Music but never buckled under the weight of its influences, operating on a strange frequency all its own, expressing, as Thomas put it, 'the abstractness of the words and the concreteness of the instruments'.

The follow-up, DUB HOUSING, released later the same year, further explored Ubu's off-centre rhythms and fractured sensibility. Its cryptic impenetrability almost swamped the melodies, but Ubu remained resolute within the chaos, maintaining their rock-'n'roll energy.

The band twice toured Britain in 1978, and, although they perhaps didn't live up to the expectations of an audience reared on US punk bands like The Ramones and The Dead Boys, they had a definite impact on post-punk bands like Joy Division. Thomas himself had nothing but disdain for a UK punk scene that he saw as antisocial and childish.

With NEW PICNIC TIME (1979), Pere Ubu drifted into unintelligible waters, provoking the loss of their contract with Chrysalis, and the crucial departure of Tom Herman, who was replaced by **Mayo Thompson** (ex-Red Crayola). The next two albums, THE ART OF WALKING (1980) and SONG OF THE BAILING MAN (1982), were equally obtuse and poorly received, and, after the second the band

split up, David Thomas going on to solo work with a new group, **The Pedestrians**.

Surprisingly, Pere Ubu reconvened in 1987 and the following year released the excellent THE TENEMENT YEAR, which they supported with dates in the US and UK. The new record bore scant relation to the scary creation that had lurched across the boundaries of late-70s punk, being characterized instead by a vibrant pop sensibility. The band had, in effect, traded challenge for enchantment, but only the most mean-spirited purist could complain.

Subsequent albums, none of which sold in any great numbers, mined the same rich vein of melodic, idiosyncratic pop – almost as if the band were intent on destroying their reputation as industrial-rock poseurs. It was a position made defiantly, or resignedly, explicit in the sleeve notes to their intended farewell album, RAYGUN SUITCASE (1995): 'Don't Expect Art/We allowed ourselves to lose control/We were content to follow the herd/No more'. For all that, RAYGUN was a wonderful and unique creation.

RAYGUN resonated with a dark, urban claustrophobia but its follow-up, PENNSYLVANIA (1998), was its cousin from the backwoods – a trippy travelogue through lonely diners, gas stations and endless white-line horizons. Thomas used this more rustic backdrop to ruminate on the dreamier, stranger slices of Americana whooshing past his windscreen in the late 1990s. "Woolie Bullie" set the scene – an incessant driving beat, buzz-saw guitars slicing through Thomas's beautifully bizarre observations. The album was an adventurous sprawl with room for a wide range of styles – from the delicately acoustic "Highwaterville" to the ghostly atmospherics of "Silent Spring" and the slide-guitar noisefest of "Mr Wheeler".

Despite commercial indifference in America, Pere Ubu's influence continued to gnaw away at the margins of European music-making. "Industrial Noise" remains the genre they are most often credited with restyling, but Ubu's pop vision is far wider and more humane than that. The band are currently enjoying a high-profile live renaissance, but anyone wishing to check out the Pere Ubu of old should track down THE SHAPE OF THINGS (2000), an official bootleg recorded way back in 1976 and only available via the Internet. Meanwhile, the band show no signs of grinding to a halt and ST ARKANSAS (2002) was possibly their darkest and most dramatic piece of work yet.

The Modern Dance (1978; Blank/Mercury).
This album took the rock world into uncharted territory, and made a lot of the competition seem decidedly adolescent.

Dub Housing (1978; Rough Trade).
A creepy soundtrack of dark thrills and surreal world-view, this is one of the great overlooked albums of the 70s.

The Tenement Year (1988; Fontana).
An unexpected pop delight, after a long silence, as Ubu decide to dance to a different beat. Few bands ever come back with credibility, but Ubu managed it with ease and charm.

⊙ **Raygun Suitcase** (1995; Cooking Vinyl).
From the most challenging rock band in America to the most overlooked? This is playfully weird and decidedly wonderful, with its slide guitar and electronics glimmering with melancholy.

⊙ **Terminal Tower** (1998; Cooking Vinyl).
This disc of rare odds and ends – including the seminal "30 Seconds Over Tokyo" – is the essential Ubu collection.

Nig Hodgkins

CARL PERKINS

Born Tiptonville, Tennessee, April 9, 1932;
died January 19, 1998.

"One day I was listening to a DJ play Presley's 'Blue Moon of Kentucky'... I turned the radio up and shouted, 'That sounds just like us playing!' At last someone was recording country music with a beat."

The beat was black, the country music was white and their marriage became known as rockabilly. **Carl Perkins** wrote its anthem, "Blue Suede Shoes", and when Elvis moved on to the army, Hollywood and operetta tunes like "It's Now Or Never", it became clear that Carl had been the uncrowned king of the music all along.

Racism was an irrelevance in Carl Perkins' childhood: everyone, white or black, was half-starved and working for the man. Carl picked cotton, the black kids picked cotton, but when he went to the movies with his best friend Charlie they had to sit in different sections. Like the great country pioneers Jimmie Rodgers and Hank Williams, Carl Perkins grew up among black people, and this helped give his music its unique quality. The sentiments, the cadences and the harmonies were white, but they were driven by a black engine.

As a teenager Perkins formed a trio with his brothers **Jay** (rhythm guitar) and **Clayton** (bass fiddle), playing at weekends to fit around their day jobs in Jackson, Tennessee. They had built a solid local reputation when they heard Elvis on the radio, and immediately they drove to the studio that had recorded him: Sun in Memphis. The song that eventually convinced studio boss Sam Phillips was a Perkins original that had won him a talent contest prize at the age of 13, "Movie Magg".

The Sun studio has since passed into rock legend. Though set up in the early 50s to record and lease songs by local blues artists like Howlin' Wolf, often to the Chess label in Chicago, it was the extraordinary roster of white talent coming together on Sun in the middle of the decade that made its name. Perkins shared the tiny premises with **Presley**, **Johnny Cash**, **Jerry Lee Lewis** and **Roy Orbison** – an informal recording of a jam session (and lively religious debate) involving Presley, Lewis, Cash and

Perkins has long been known as 'The Million-Dollar Quartet'. It was the raw rockabilly sound created by Perkins, combined with his chiselled good looks, that made Phillips feel easy about selling Presley's contract. After all, he had a replacement model ready to go.

"Blue Suede Shoes" should have been the passport to fortune. Most unusually, it was a smash hit in all of the three charts existing at the time: as well as peaking at #4 in the US pop charts, it reached #2 in both the Country and the R&B lists when released in 1956. But as the Perkins Brothers drove to New York to appear on the all-powerful networked TV shows hosted by Perry Como and Ed Sullivan, a crash put them in hospital. Jay broke his neck (he was to die of cancer two years later) and Carl himself was out of action for a long time. Meanwhile, Elvis covered "Blue Suede Shoes" and Perkins wasn't around to capitalize on his initial success. By the time he was fit again he had become a one-hit wonder in chart terms, while Elvis was now the biggest phenomenon in pop.

Perkins continued to feature in the country charts, though, and with singles like "Boppin' The Blues" he also nudged the Hot Hundred. Among those aware of the genius of his music – the spiky, urgent guitar style that epitomized rockabilly as surely as did Chuck Berry's for black rock'n'roll, the Saturday night fever of his lyrics, the relentless rhythmic drive – were The Beatles, who recorded three Perkins songs early in their career: "Honey Don't", "Everybody's Tryin' To Be My Baby" and "Matchbox". Perkins himself, though, was in premature decline, due in large part to a struggle with alcohol – though it was some years before he struggled too much.

In 1964 a tour of the UK with Chuck Berry revived his career, and a year later his friend and old label mate Johnny Cash, by this time the biggest star in country music, invited Perkins to join his roadshow as guitarist and featured artist. Slowly, Cash conquered his addiction to pills and Perkins dried out – they did it together, daring the other to weaken. Perkins wrote the Cash hit "Daddy Sang Bass", and began to feature once more in the country charts in his own right, with songs like "Restless" and "Cotton Top".

In 1977 Perkins' career received another boost courtesy of the UK, when he was signed to the Jet label and given a big promotional push for his comeback album, OL' BLUE SUEDE SHOES IS BACK. At this time rockabilly was undergoing a big and youthful revival in Britain, and Perkins was re-established as its king. One particular tour during this time, shared with Chicago legend Bo Diddley, was a glorious celebration of the black and white roots of rock'n'roll.

Perkins credits his religious faith for pulling him through the successive onslaughts of poverty, catastrophic injury and bereavement, failure and alcoholism – his 1978 autobiography is called *Disciple In Blue Suede Shoes*. But anyone who heard that song in 1956 – or, twenty years later, an equivalent masterpiece called "Put Your Cat Clothes on", which, mysteriously, had remained on the shelf all that time until rediscovered by the UK company Charly – knows that the music would have secured his place in rock'n'roll history even if he had succumbed. His death in 1998, preceded by a series of strokes, came as little surprise, but was still newsworthy enough to be reported around the world. The story of rock would be incomplete without Perkins' contribution. And when it comes to surrendering to the music, to passing 'that ol' fruit jar' and forgetting the consequences, he penned the ultimate advice – 'Pick your toenails up tomorrow'.

⦿ **Boppin' Blue Suede Shoes** (1995; Charly).
Here are those essential, pioneering, Southern rockabilly tracks on Sun in their latest CD format. Alternatively, there's a Charly box set that offers all the Sun cuts.

John Collis

PET SHOP BOYS

Formed London, 1981.

"We may have had the occasional scam but we never had any grand plans." Neil Tennant

Once every few years a happy confluence of talent unites two songwriters: Lennon and McCartney, Jagger and Richards, Morrissey and Marr. Then there's the 'Odd Couple' of British pop, **Neil Tennant** and **Chris Lowe**, the **Pet Shop Boys**, who for twenty years have consistently produced catchy, melodic synth-based pop songs that have enjoyed both critical and popular success around the world.

Tennant was assistant editor of *Smash Hits* magazine when, in 1981, aged 27, he met Lowe, three years his junior, in a King's Road hi-fi shop. Two years of unsuccessful demos followed until a chance meeting with disco producer Bobby Orlando resulted in the charting of their debut single, "West End Girls" (1984), albeit only in France and Belgium. The band arranged to be managed by the effervescent Tom Watkins, and in 1985 they signed to EMI. Their second single, the Thatcherite satire "Opportunites (Let's Make Lots Of Money)", again failed to chart at home, though it was central in forging the band's image as the arch ironicists of pop.

It wasn't until January 1986 that they finally arrived, as the rereleased "West End Girls", now produced by Stephen Hague, crept to #1 in both the UK and US charts. A debut album, PLEASE (1986), fleshed out the band's musical manifesto: resolutely unfashionable synthesized disco/pop, happy/sad tunes and compulsive choruses, all reminiscent of a past songwriting age. It's not impossible, for example, to imagine Dietrich or Brel rasping through more sympathetic arrangements of "Tonight Is Forever" or "Later Tonight". "I Want A Lover", on the other

hand, would have been perfect for Grace Jones. A speedy follow-up mini-album, DISCO (1986), showcased various idiosyncratic remixes.

Ivor Novello and Brit awards were showered on the duo in 1987, the year of their huge-selling second album, ACTUALLY (1987). More lavishly produced than their debut, it featured "It's A Sin" (another UK #1 single) and the wistful nostalgia of "It Couldn't Happen Here", a track enhanced by a John Barry-style arrangement of haunting sadness. **DUSTY SPRINGFIELD** also benefited from the duo's talents with their song "What Have I Done To Deserve This?", which she took to #2 on both sides of the Atlantic. Earlier in the year the pair had performed a cover of "Always On My Mind" for a TV tribute to Elvis. By Christmas, that also had hit the top of the UK chart.

The slightly more eccentric INTROSPECTIVE (1988) covered a wider musical landscape, encompassing a remix of "Always On My Mind" and the sunny pop of "Domino Dancing". 1989 saw further recording collaborations: with Springfield (on the film soundtrack for *Scandal*); with Liza Minnelli; and with Bernard Sumner (New Order) and Johnny Marr (The Smiths) in their **Electronic** project. That year the Pet Shop Boys were also persuaded to embark on a world tour which, despite the duo's lack of obvious visual appeal, succeeded through the theatrical use of dancers, costumes and sets.

Working with producer Harold Faltemeyer, the Pet Shop Boys' next album was about as different as could be expected. Though still blending synths with orchestra, the downbeat, muted ballads of BEHAVIOUR (1990) included little that was radio-friendly. Instead it expressed more personal and intense emotions in an effectively understated way, with only the odd, saccharine slip-up.

More touring followed in 1991, as did a witty cover of U2's "Where The Streets Have No Name", deflating the song's pomposity by mixing it with Frankie Valli's "Can't Take My Eyes Off You". Rumours of a split abounded after a year of inactivity and another Tennant collaboration with Electronic, but then a new album did emerge, perhaps even surpassing their previous delights. Just about every track on VERY (1993) would have made a hit single – a moving, gorgeous album, and conclusive proof (if it was needed) that synth-pop didn't have to be plastic. The first 15,000 copies of the CD came with a six-track masterpiece – RELENTLESS, a techno-inspired, sinister, insistent dance album that was the perfect counterpoint to VERY.

Their 1996 release, BILINGUAL, moved away from VERY's potent blend of sex, emotion and high camp, in favour of booming drums. Apparently inspired by the PSBs' tour of Latin America, they treated us to "Se A Vida E", "Red Letter Day" and "Metamorphosis", as warm as the weather they found, and as full of life and joy as a São Paolo street party. By now their releases, while fervently received by a select fan base, tended to have disappointing reactions from casual record buyers. 1999's NIGHTLIFE only spent three weeks in the British album chart (their early albums were huge sellers over an eighteen month to two-year period), although "You Only Tell Me You Love Me When You're Drunk" (funny, sad and beautiful) became their twentieth top ten single.

Mixed reviews came with Tennant and Lowe's 2001 musical *Closer To Heaven*, a collaboration with playwright **Jonathan Harvey**, although the positive notices acknowledged its contemporary voice in West End theatre. The musical's opening coincided with the reissues of their first six albums, each enhanced by a bonus disc of remixes and rarities, as well as copious sleeve notes. RELEASE (2002), a ten-track album of new material, largely eschewed electronic dance rhythms in favour of adult guitar-pop anthems, but despite heavy promotion, its sales peaked and fell rapidly. Still, tracks such as the single "Home And Dry" demonstrated that the duo's gift for four-minute pop genius had not abandoned them.

⊙ **Please** (1986; Parlophone).
Innocence tinged with English realism ensured that this disco-Kraftwerk release had both instant and enduring appeal.

⊙ **Discography** (1991; Parlophone).
This gorgeous singles compilation is a comprehensive review of the Pets' career to BEHAVIOUR.

⊙ **Very** (1993; Parlophone).
The Pets' masterpiece, showing themselves forever as masters of the pop song and the possessors of impeccable dance sensibilities.

Michael Booth

TOM PETTY & THE HEARTBREAKERS

Formed New Orleans, Louisiana, 1971.

Tom Petty & The Heartbreakers are a real band: tied by the '&' and creating music from a dynamic, principally that between **Tom Petty** (guitar/vocals) and **Mike Campbell** (guitar). The two came together in 1971, forged by a devotion to Brian Wilson, Woody Guthrie, The Byrds, The Band and Bob Dylan. The original Heartbreakers line-up was completed by **Ron Blair** (bass – later replaced by **Howie Epstein**), **Stan Lynch** (drums) and **Benmont Tench** (keyboards).

Like Ry Cooder – another of their heroes – Petty & The Heartbreakers made it big in Europe before finding acceptance in their homeland. Their debut album, TOM PETTY & THE HEARTBREAKERS (1976), sold well in Germany and France and reached the Top 20 in the UK, but was not to chart in America for another year. Impressed by their European success, the band headed over to tour Britain and Germany – performances that cemented the band's reputation as worthy successors to The Byrds, while creating a reputation for Petty as yet another 'new Bob Dylan'.

On the back of these sell-out dates, the Heartbreakers returned to the US and massive acclaim. Their follow-up, YOU'RE GONNA GET IT

The Southern-accented Tom Petty

(1977), combined artistic acceptance with impressive sales (#23 in the US), and by the third album, DAMN THE TORPEDOES (1979), the Heartbreakers were amongst the biggest acts in the States. (Bizarrely, Petty had been forced to file for bankruptcy shortly before TORPEDOES, but his label stuck by him and helped him through.) Post-Vietnam, post-Watergate, America was ripe for some folksy, home-grown, neo-country-rock to confirm its self-image, and with their familiar sound and gifted vocalist The Heartbreakers were able to provide just that.

Without changing their style dramatically, Petty & The Heartbreakers tangled – through the 80s and into the 90s – with disco, funk, punk, house, indie and grunge. They flourished throughout, helped in large measure by Petty's recognition of the importance of video. His first foray into video, the Lewis Carroll-inspired promo for "Don't Come Around Here No More" (1985), in which he played a deliciously sinister Mad Hatter, continues to receive extensive airplay on MTV and its adult-orientated sister station VH-1. It helped ease SOUTHERN ACCENTS (1985) to an all-time-best #7 US chart placing, and Petty repeated the trick to keep up the profile for the live album, PACK UP THE PLANTATION (1986) and LET ME UP (I'VE HAD ENOUGH)(1987).

The latter – as its title suggested – was the prelude to a break for the band, as Petty teamed up with Dylan, Orbison, Harrison and Jeff Lynne as **THE TRAVELING WILBURYS**, before going 'solo' with FULL MOON FEVER (1989), a US #3 chart success co-written and produced with Jeff Lynne.

REDFERNS

In 1991, however, Petty was back with the original Heartbreakers, releasing INTO THE GREAT WIDE OPEN, which borrowed generously from both R.E.M. and Hüsker Dü. A fairly representative greatest hits album was released in 1993, with its new single, "Mary Jane's Last Dance," accompanied by another weird, eye-grabbing video. Starring Petty as a morgue worker and actress Kim Basinger as a corpse, the video was voted *Hip Clip of the Year* by MTV in 1994. Late in 1994, Petty released the pleasant and fairly restrained WILDFLOWERS, which went triple platinum in the US. The 1996 follow-up, MUSIC FROM THE MOTION PICTURE *SHE'S THE ONE*, gave Petty a chance to rediscover himself as a songwriter while safely locked away within the well-defined boundaries of a movie soundtrack. An ill-advised cover apart (Beck's "Asshole"), this was vintage Petty, telling a single story – no more and no less – in each song, and telling it perfectly. ECHO (1999) was a sparse, regretful but effective album from the band, while ANTHOLOGY: THROUGH THE YEARS (2000) was an excellent summary of a varied career.

Tom Petty remains a great music-business pragmatist, but above everything else, he appreciates that no matter how good your publicity machine the music is still the thing that matters. For all of their thirty years together, The Heartbreakers have given good value and, while they have taken new influences on board, the band has essentially stayed true to the vision and ideals of their early hero, and the granddaddy of modern American music, Woody Guthrie. Their impressive live rendition of Guthrie's "This Land Is My Land" is a testament to the great man's influence upon Petty and his cohorts.

(•) **Tom Petty & The Heartbreakers** (1976; MCA).
A wonderful, rough-sounding album, a million miles away from countless 'beer-and-lifestyle' bands it spawned.

(•) **Damn The Torpedoes** (1979; Shelter).
A faultless album of rockers, including what is probably The Heartbreakers' finest three minutes' on "Refugee".

(•) **Greatest Hits** (1993; MCA).
A wonderful selection of sixteen prime Petty tracks. All the hits, from "American Girl" right up to Petty's gorgeous cover of Thunderclap Newman's "Something In The Air".

(•) **Playback** (1996; MCA).
This six-CD set fills in all the gaps, including three discs of unreleased tracks.

Richard Luck

LIZ PHAIR

Born Winnetka, Illinois, 1967.

Liz Phair followed a highly accelerated career path in the mid 90s, rocketing from modest home recording projects to national stardom with hardly so much as a performance in between. She has charted a confessional songwriting mode that many contemporary female rockers – perhaps terrified of sounding like Joni Mitchell – won't touch, and her voice has a conversational quality that eases you along

even when her subjects are oblique. And from her DIY origins she has retained a refreshingly unorthodox approach that makes even her trad three-chord rockers sound slightly exotic.

The adopted daughter of prosperous professionals, Phair banged around the Chicago scene in the early 90s, recording cassettes as Girly Sound. One of these tapes came to the attention of Brad Wood and Casey Rice, who got her a contract with Matador Records, supported her as players and engineers, and helped her concepts blossom into 1994's EXILE IN GUYVILLE. Its originality and style won immediate glowing reviews and radio airplay, and within months Phair was being championed as the new female figurehead of US alternative rock.

The album was fascinating, jumping recklessly from rock stomps to girl-and-guitar plainsongs, but with Phair's voice and persona coursing through its eighteen songs. These appeared to chart the decline of a relationship and Phair's exploration of a new way of life, worrying over her freedom and her passion as if they were new to her. The sprawling style of the album mirrored the confusion that accompanies sudden liberation. She mocked ("Soap Star Joe") and rebuked ("Never Said"), but in "Shatter", when she sang 'I don't know if I could drive a car/fast enough to get to where you are', the subject was heartbreak, albeit so unsentimentally expressed that few saw the thematic similarities to Patsy Cline.

The wobbly charm of EXILE touched a nerve nationwide, winning or nearly winning polls in *Village Voice* and *Rolling Stone*. In an era of riot grrrls and unsatisfying pretenders, Phair seemed to fulfil a yearning for a really strong, really modern female singer-songwriter.

The lukewarm reaction to her follow-up, WHIP-SMART (1995), might have led you to believe that she had dropped the ball, and some rather timid public appearances that accompanied the album's release didn't help her cause. But in some respects WHIP-SMART was actually a better record than EXILE, albeit less spectacular. Critics seemed to prefer the earlier *Sturm und Drang* to the happier life described in WHIP-

SMART, but the new record had some great lines, arrangements that tightened up the EXILE method, and one song that satisfied by any reasonable pop standard, "Jealousy", a propulsive tune in which Phair finds some photographs in her new man's drawer and loses it ('I can't believe you had a life before me/I can't believe they let you run around free').

She took time out to have a child and, with the new mother's typical disbelief that the rest of the world cared, named her subsequent recording WHITECHOCOLATESPACEEGG (1998) after her kid's bald head. The songs hinted at a slow return to the form she'd shown on EXILE, with intriguing subjects (such as back-seat masochism in "Dr. Feelgood") and wonderful titles ("Shitloads Of Money"). A follow-up has as yet not emerged, although her vocals can be heard on Sheryl Crow's 2002 album C'MON C'MON.

⊙ **Exile In Guyville** (1984; Matador).
Not since the singer-songwriter heyday of the 70s has such an atmospheric debut gained such attention. Though the frankness of her sex talk has been a popular hook for male critics, Phair is most interesting when she treats feelings that are harder to pin down: when she sings (in "Mesmerizing") 'He tossed the egg up and I found my hands in place, boy', the sexual metaphor isn't as important as the sense of astonished discovery.

⊙ **Whip-Smart** (1995; Matador).
This album shows more musical and thematic consistency than the debut, and its hooks (like the 'When they do the double-Dutch' refrain in the title song) are pop-friendly without betraying the singularity of her song-making.

Roy Edroso

PHISH

Formed Vermont, 1983.

The oft-touted 'successors to The Grateful Dead' (we'll come to that later), **Phish** were formed at the University of Vermont in 1983 and three of the early members – **Trey Anastasio** (guitar/vocal), **Jon Fishman** (drums) and **Mike Gordon** (bass/vocal) – survive to this day. Originally releasing home-recorded tapes, they didn't have an official release until LAWN BAY in 1989. Their live shows proved appealing to those in need of an alternative community and they soon became part of the whole HORDE touring scenario (Blues Traveller, Spin Doctors, Aquarium Rescue Unit) – an alternative Deadhead scene that didn't sound too, well, alternative.

Multi-setted long meanderings were the order of the day, as was eccentricity the norm – dressing up for New Year's Eve gigs (now where did they get that idea?), jumping around on trampolines on stage and playing whole 'classic' albums like QUADROPHENIA, THE WHITE ALBUM and REMAIN IN LIGHT on Hallowe'en sets being just a few examples. Townsend, McCartney and Byrne's views on this dubious form of tribute are not known.

Signing to Elektra in 1988, various albums have come and gone. RIFT in 1993, and HOIST in 1994 both had their moments and the trademark Phish

sound – loose and genial jazzy jamming, interspersed with pretty acoustic noodling, both often in search of a song. The live double album, A LIVE ONE (recorded in 1994 and released the following year) brought in Horns to beef up the sound, while **Page McConnell**'s keyboards added some textural variety. Phish is a touring phenomenon first and foremost, and A LIVE ONE (1995) gives more space for the music to breathe and, in so doing, makes most sense to the converted. To the uninitiated it can seem something of a long haul, although Anastasio's long and circular leads can weave some pretty patterns through the sometime rather stodgy ensemble playing, as on "You Enjoy Myself", one of their earlier numbers.

By 1996 and with The Dead no more, Phish were inexplicably one of the largest live draws Stateside, and with the release of BILLY BREATHES they finally released an album that appealed on its own merits to those not necessarily already in the know. Tracks like "Theme From The Bottom", "Swept Away" and the title track are beautifully crafted psychedelic pop to blow away the pre-millennium blues. Obviously, within days of its release some fool had described it as Phish's 'American Beauty'.

The Grateful Dead, through their music, their way of life and their 'philosophy', nurtured and developed a self-sustaining relationship with their fans over the course of three decades. Phish have tried too hard to create their own scene as a replacement or alternative to the Dead's, and to these ears the music just doesn't stand sensible comparison. True, there are moments – particularly in BILLY BREATHES – where the talents of these eternal sophomores are allowed to mature and blossom, but to misquote 1992 Vice-Presidential candidate Lloyd Bentson, 'I knew the Grateful Dead and you're no Grateful Dead.'

It's impossible to deny the fact that the sound of the band is primarily locked into the fusion escapades of mid-period Dead – BLUES FOR ALLAH seeming a key reference point. What's lacking in the band's sets are those moments of sonic daring – bass and lead guitar darting through percussive crescendos to achieve some kind of indescribable transcendence – that characterized The Dead at their peak. But The Dead aren't the only reference point – the band have provided backing to Santana and their sound often seems to find a spiritual home in that band's loose blend of samba and rolling lead guitar.

Until they produce an album halfway as interesting as even one of the lesser works of The Dead (and 1997's SLIP, STITCH AND PASS is not that album), Phish will forever be known as nearly-rans. They've got their reason to exist – the fans, the philosophy, the whole Phish 'movement' – now all they need is the music. Tantalizing glimpses suggest they might, just might, make it. In the meantime, Ben & Jerry's Ice Cream (Vermont's other neo-hippie-capitalist organization) has waded into the shallow end of the music industry with their Phish Phood and Phish Stick products.

Phish's brand of prog-Psychedelia continues to cut a swath through the live arenas of North America, soaking up the ex-Deadhead market who remain eager for lengthy jamming, musical showmanship and a 'feelgood vibe'. If a Phish show lacks the genuine spiritual element of a Dead concert, the band make up for it with versatility above and beyond the call of duty – from witless flashiness, to quiet jazzy bits, to ethereal country picking, to reggae, and even 'Cigarette Lighters Aloft' balladry. All these elements and more adorned THE STORY OF THE GHOST (1998) and FARMHOUSE (2000), which both wrapped up the pieces in some weird conceptualizing nonsense worthy of Gabriel-era Genesis. It sold laughably poorly.

During the next two years the band fractured as each member pursued a variety of solo projects that saw collaborations with the likes of Leo Kottke, Primus's Les Claypool, ex-Policeman Stewart Copeland, Oysterhead and the superbly named Pork Tornado. When the band regrouped for ROUND ROUND (2003) they were sounding distinctly refreshed and vital, having produced one of their finest collections in less than a week!

As for ticket sales, Phish continue to fill the vacuum left by The Dead with indisputable professionalism.

⊙ **A Live One** (1995; Elektra).
This double album does much to pump some warm blood around this previously cold-blooded reptile.

⊙ **Billy Breathes** (1996; Elektra).
Phish-heads worship the band as much to rekindle a 60s spirit as to hear something new, and if long, flashy soloing, pretty acoustic picking, and genial good-timey ambience are what you are after then look no further.

Nig Hodgkins

WILSON PICKETT

Born Prattsville, Alabama, March 18, 1941.

Wilson Pickett is a fully paid-up member of that elite club, The Great Soul Legends, an august body whose entrance qualifications involve more than just the possession of a fearsome voice and a Cadillac full of storming records. For better and for worse, his is a near-textbook soul-singer career.

A move to the fast-ascending commercial heart of R&B, Detroit, led to initial singing duties in a variety of gospel choirs. Then, in 1961, he teamed up with Mack Rice and Eddie Floyd in **The Falcons**, who had a US hit with the Pickett-penned "I Found A Love" in 1962. Securing himself a solo deal on Lloyd Price's Double L label, one of the many thriving independents catering for Detroit's burgeoning soul and blues scene, Pickett released a further three singles, two of which ("If You Need Me" and "It's Too Late") breached the middle ranks of the charts. This brought him to the attention of the mighty Atlantic Records, with whom he signed in 1964.

Pickett's first Atlantic recordings were met with indifference, which led famed label head Jerry

Wexler, in some desperation, to send him to the Stax studios in 1965. Here he made an inspired choice of collaborator in **Steve Cropper**, guitarist with **BOOKER T AND THE MGS**. The results were instantly fruitful, with "In The Midnight Hour" an immediate soul standard, breaking the Top 20 in the US and UK. Between September 1965 and November 1966 the pairing produced a string of great singles – notably "Don't Fight It", "634 5789 (Soulsville USA)" and "Land Of A 1000 Dreams" – and some of Pickett's finest albums.

IN THE MIDNIGHT HOUR (1965) established Pickett as a leading light in the continued R&B assault on mainstream pop with an energetic and irresistibly danceable sound. On the subsequent THE EXCITING WILSON PICKETT (1966) and THE WICKED PICKETT (1967), the Cropper–Pickett partnership was further enhanced by the production and engineering presence of Rick Hall, owner of Muscle Shoals' Fame Studios, where Pickett decamped in 1966. Despite some unnecessary duplications, these collections were a canny combination of Pickett's co-compositions with straight-up crowd-pleasing covers such as "Barefootin'", "Knock On Wood" and "Mustang Sally". Easily shifting from a soul/R&B sensibility into white mainstream acceptance, Pickett easily stood comparison with some of his more illustrious stable mates, such as Otis Redding.

1968 saw a new writing and production partnership begin with **Bobby Womack**, which provided the second 'Midnight' hit, "I'm A Midnight Mover", plus "I Found A True Love" and the LP MIDNIGHT MOVER. A more interesting (though less lucrative) alliance came with ill-fated Duane Allman on HEY JUDE (1969), arguably Pickett's most bizarre release (and there's some competition for that prize).

By now, the sound of soul was changing in a slicker, sweeter direction; clearly aware of this, the next Pickett move was to Philadelphia, home of the hit production team of Kenny Gamble and Leon Huff. WILSON PICKETT IN PHILADELPHIA (1970), featuring "Engine No. 9", "Don't Let The Green Grass Fool You" and "Knock My Love" carried all the Philly Sound trademarks, with Pickett seemingly at home with the pervading sound of disco. On the other hand, chart positions were becoming few and far between and his normally sure-footed choice of covers was beginning to look less and less convincing ("Sugar, Sugar" anyone?); in effect, the Gamble and Huff years actually represented his last stab at credible pop.

From the mid-70s onwards, Pickett acted out other parts of the 'Soul Man' role: arrests in 1974 for threatening behaviour with a gun, and again in 1993 for fatal drunk-driving; a succession of compilations, live albums and label changes (United Artists, Liberty, EMI America, Motown); endless touring in 'soul revues' on the chicken-in-a-basket cabaret circuit (Pickett had always been a top-drawer live act); and appalling remixes of his classics (a dub version of "Midnight Hour" in 1987!).

So the passage of time has not been kind to Wilson, whose longevity has robbed him of the glamour of Redding, Sam Cooke and Marvin Gaye, without bringing a career resuscitation of the sort Ben E. King has enjoyed on the back of TV ad campaigns and Hollywood soundtracks. But for a while, with an impeccable choice of co-writers, producers and material, in the most happening studio environments available, and backed by some of the very best house bands, The Wicked Pickett delivered a set of records to fully justify his membership.

⊙ **In The Midnight Hour** (1965; Rhino).
Pickett's exciting debut, introducing the world to a full-on throat and some of the most infectious dance music of the day. The epitome of tight mid-60s Atlantic R&B.

⊙ **The Sound Of Wilson Pickett** (1967; Rhino).
This single CD brings together Pickett's three albums with Steve Cropper – and as such is more than a by-the-book greatest hits. Of all the partnerships, this was the one that worked the best, Cropper's stripped-down arrangements allowing Pickett the space to display a maturing range of vocal styles.

⊙ **A Man And A Half** (1993; Rhino).
A 44-track, double-CD survey, trawling the dross as well as all the gems. Anything up to 1967 is indispensable, anything after is, well, interesting.

Lance Phillips

THE PINK FAIRIES

Formed London, 1967; disbanded 1973; re-formed and disbanded several times 1975–87.

"My favourite old wave rock band."
John Lydon

Originating amid the hippie community of Ladbroke Grove in West London, **The Deviants** (for a while the Social Deviants) were a loose-knit band who gravitated around **Mick Farren** (vocals) and usually featured **Paul Rudolph** (guitar/vocals), **Duncan Sanderson** (bass/vocals) and **Russell Hunter** (drums). Others who guested in the early days included Steve Peregrine Took and Marc Bolan of neighbours Tyrannosaurus Rex, and various musicians from Group X, soon afterwards renamed Hawkwind.

The Deviants made three albums, best of which was the third, THE DEVIANTS (1969), a set by turns psychedelic, anarchic and silly, evincing the influences of The Fugs, Zappa and The Doors. They then embarked optimistically on a US tour, at the end of which Farren quit to become a journalist – though he was to resurface occasionally with music projects, and supplied his old band with lyrics in later years. Returning to London, the group teamed up with **Twink** (aka John Alder) – a vocalist, songwriter, drummer, and one-time member of **THE PRETTY THINGS** (he had participated in their seminal 'rock opera' album S. F. SORROW) – working on his solo album, THINK PINK. It led to a permanent partnership, with Twink renaming the band **The Pink Fairies**.

The Pink Fairies were an underground band at this time – indeed, they never really ceased to be – and usually played gigs for free, often with Hawkwind, for whom they sometimes supplied musicians. Their reputation for drug taking and general debauchery spread faster than knowledge of their music, until they secured a contract with Polydor and released NEVER NEVER LAND (1971). Encompassing the breakneck "Do It!", the honest rock'n'roll of "Say You Love Me", and the visionary "Heavenly Man", "The Dream Is Just Beginning" and title track, this was the most far-out, decadent and poetic album that The Fairies would make, and is best enjoyed with a cocktail of illegal substances.

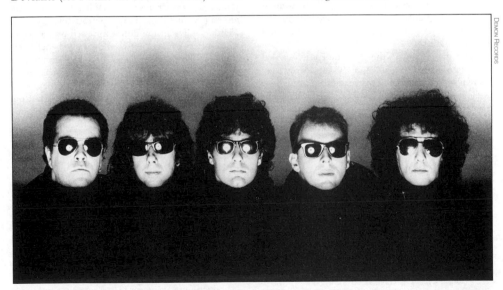

A bunch of sweeties: the Fairies' Wallis, Culquhon, Sanderson, Twink and Hunter

Twink left after this album and The Fairies continued as a trio. Their next LP, WHAT A BUNCH OF SWEETIES (1972), was another impressive offering, its highlight being "Walk Don't Run", a track beginning with salacious languor, punctuated by crashing chords, before it launched into high-energy rock-'n'roll and culminated in a long instrumental passage. Other outstanding numbers included "Pigs Of Uranus", which had a zany lyric set to rockabilly, and a creditable version of The Beatles' "I Saw Her Standing There". WHAT A BUNCH spent one week at #48 in the UK album chart, the nearest The Fairies ever came to commercial success.

When Rudolph left to join **HAWKWIND** on a full-time basis, the band used a series of temporary guitarists until **Larry Wallis** from **UFO** agreed to throw in his lot with them. The new line-up made KINGS OF OBLIVION (1973), for which Wallis wrote or co-wrote all the material, shifting The Fairies' style towards hard rock – indeed "City Kids", a Sanderson–Wallis number, was later covered by **MOTÖRHEAD** as the B-side of their own eponymous hit single, and Wallis was to serve in the original incarnation of that band. Continuing management and financial hassles had destroyed the band's morale, however, and despite Twink's brief return they split up before the end of the year.

The Fairies were in abeyance until early 1975 when, with the line-up of Rudolph, Wallis, Sanderson and Hunter, they reunited for a gig at London's Roundhouse. Encouraged by their reception, they subsequently tried to relaunch their career, but without much success. For the rest of the decade The Fairies passed through innumerable line-up changes and short disbandments, while their recorded output was limited to occasional singles on small labels. In 1978 Twink rejoined to make an EP, featuring a new version of "Do It!" as well as "Psychedelic Punkaroo", which harked back to The Fairies circa 1971 for its take on the current youth phenomenon.

With the coming of the 80s, The Fairies seemed to have gone forever, until in 1987 suddenly they were playing gigs again. They made an album, too – KILL 'EM AND EAT 'EM – but it was well past its sell-by date, and the band's subsequent demise was cause for little sadness. By fans there at the time, they are still fondly remembered, as much for their ethos and lifestyle as for their music – though at their best they were a bloody good rock band.

The 90s saw a resurgence of interest in the London underground and the reissue of both the second Deviants album, DISPOSABLE (1998), and the magnificently titled Pink Fairies compilation MANDIES AND MESCALINE ROUND AT UNCLE HARRY'S (1998) cobbled together from studio and live sessions.

⊙ **Pink Fairies** (1973; Polydor).
Polydor's selection from their three fairies albums, biased towards the shorter and more accessible tracks, but also including a previously unreleased quality number, "The Snake". Deleted in 1994, but with perseverance it can still be found.

⊙ **Live At The Roundhouse** (1991; Chiswick).
Besides a recording of the famed 1975 gig, this fine Fairies memento includes the 1977 "Do It!" numbers and a further ten unreleased tracks.

Martin Haggerty

PINK FLOYD

Formed London, 1965.

"I was in a pub when in walked Dave Gilmour saying 'I've just got the gig with Floyd and I'm getting £325 a week!' I thought, enjoy it while you can, because without Syd that band's going nowhere ... " John Etheridge

Exploding on to the Swinging London scene at the height of flower power, the original **Pink Floyd** walked a tightrope between the chart action of their psychedelic singles and the super-hip credibility of their free-form electronic freakouts. Then, almost as soon as they'd arrived, **SYD BARRETT**, their charismatic singer, lead guitarist and songwriter, suffered an LSD-induced total burnout. Most bands would have called it a day, but with the substitution of steady hand **Dave Gilmour** on guitar and vocals, and the subsequent ejection of Barrett into deep space, the Floyd carried on to become one of the biggest bands on the planet, endlessly recycling their private mythology of madness and loss. Despite a second crisis with the departure of **Roger Waters**, the lyricist and chief architect of DARK SIDE OF THE MOON and WISH YOU WERE HERE, the band continues under Gilmour's steady direction.

The Floyd story begins in early 1966 when Peter Jenner, a manager in search of a band, checked out an embryonic Pink Floyd performance at The Marquee Club in London. Impressed by the weird instrumental passages between their psychedelic versions of "Louie Louie" and "Road Runner", he swiftly introduced himself and offered to make them 'bigger than The Beatles'. It was an offer they could hardly refuse, and they quickly progressed from experimental freakouts in Notting Hill to playing the *International Times* benefit at the Roundhouse in December 1966, as the house band of London's burgeoning underground scene.

The early Floyd were very much the creation of Syd Barrett. He was the frontman on vocals and lead guitar, he wrote all the songs, and he even invented their name, a compound of two of his favourite blues artists, Pink Anderson and Floyd Council. Barrett was an art-school student – Waters (bass), **Rick Wright** (keyboards) and **Nick Mason** (drums) had studied architecture – and was keen on exploring the idea of 'music in colour'. Floyd were way ahead of their time in integrating music with visuals, as well as in their introduction of avant-garde free-jazz elements into a rock context.

They forged a legend with their residency at the UFO Club in London's Tottenham Court Road, where, cloaked by a dizzying light show, the Floyd stunned audiences with extended versions of their psychedelic anthems, "Interstellar Overdrive" and "Astronomy Domine". But as well as entertaining the acidheads of the UFO, Syd also nursed ambitions to make it onto *Top Of The Pops*.

Early in 1967, Pink Floyd signed to EMI and released a debut single, "Arnold Layne". Compressing all their hip weirdness into a crisp three-minute cut, it reached #20 in the UK charts, not bad for an underground 'art' group. Meanwhile, back in Underground London, Pink Floyd were chosen to top the bill at the *14 Hour Technicolour Dream*, an all-nighter held on April 29 at Alexandra Palace. Having already played in Holland the same day, it is unlikely that the Floyd were at their most inspired, but with most of the 20,000 audience out of their heads on acid, nobody was disappointed. The real breakthrough, however, came the following month at the Games For May concert at the Queen Elizabeth Hall, where punters were promised 'space-age relaxation for the climax of spring, with electronic compositions, colour and image projections, girls and the Pink Floyd'. It was their first major solo presentation, and the first concert to feature 'sound in the round' by using an extra pair of speakers at the back of the hall.

"Games For May" was also the title of a piece specially written for the event. With a new title and a bit of nip and tuck, this emerged as their second single "See Emily Play". A UK Top 5 hit, it was one of the best British singles from the 'Summer Of Love' and a superb taster for Pink Floyd's debut album, THE PIPER AT THE GATES OF DAWN, released in August 1967. One of the most original LPs of the 60s, it combined the innovative soundscapes of the group's avant-garde experimentation with the cream of Barrett's eccentric but brilliant songcraft.

Sadly, though, the pressures of writing and recording, constant touring and wanton experimentation with LSD were taking their toll on Syd's eggshell psyche. Dave Gilmour had noticed him acting strangely as early as the recording of "See Emily Play" in May. By autumn, he was freaking out with a vengeance. His long-awaited third single turned out to be the shambolic "Apples & Oranges", his contributions to the second album (including the often-bootlegged "Vegetable Man") were too disturbing to be used and his on-stage performance declined to playing the same note all evening. Worst of all was an abortive American tour, which had to be pulled after only a few dates due to Barrett's worsening condition. His last major gig with the group was at Olympia that December; early in the New Year, David Gilmour was asked to join as second guitarist. There was a five-piece Floyd for a brief interval until Barrett was finally given the push, to begin his bizarre solo non-career.

As an old friend, Gilmour was the perfect choice to keep the group together, though at first his role was merely to play all Barrett's parts and to help salvage the recording sessions for what was to become the Floyd's second album. A SAUCERFUL OF SECRETS (1968) turned out to be a surprisingly successful collection and, along with a confident performance at the Hyde Park Free Concert in June 1968, it did much to silence the critics who claimed that the Floyd were dead without Barrett.

After a couple of flop singles, the group decided to concentrate on weighty album material that would more accurately reflect the extended improvisations of their stage act. Perversely though, their first completely Barrettless work was MORE, a much underrated 1969 soundtrack album for French film director Barbet Schroeder. Banged out in only a week, it consisted of relaxed instrumentals, intercut with simple but atmospheric gems such as "Cirrus Minor".

That year's magnum opus, however, was UMMAGUMMA, a double album whose mystical-sounding title turned out to be a Cambridgeshire fenland euphemism for sex. One album was live, the other featured 'avant-garde' solo compositions from each member of the group. The latter were not a great success, and from this point on the band started moving away from their underground pretensions towards a more conventional rock sound. The next three albums, ATOM HEART MOTHER, MEDDLE and OBSCURED BY CLOUDS (another Schroeder soundtrack), chart this progression clearly, though none has aged particularly well. Of the three, MEDDLE has the most to offer, with the "Echoes" suite boasting some moments of real power, and unfortunately an equal number of longueurs.

However, in 1973, all the searching for new directions finally came together with the release of DARK SIDE OF THE MOON, one of the best-selling albums of all time. With its dominant themes of ageing, madness and death, the band had finally come up with something meaningful to hang their musical ideas on. It was an album so well integrated that it was hard to imagine any of the songs played without the context of the others.

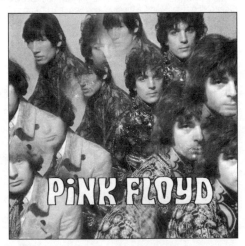

There was a two-year wait for WISH YOU WERE HERE. Recording it was sheer torture and the band almost split under the pressure, but their efforts produced some of their strongest music, their most affecting lyrics and undoubtedly one of the most intriguing album sleeves ever. The key piece was the superb "Shine On You Crazy Diamond", a lengthy tribute to Syd Barrett, whose spirit still seemed to haunt the band. Inspired by Gilmour's melancholic guitar theme, Waters came up with some of his most poignant lines. The album's title said it all.

Once again, Pink Floyd lapsed into a creative torpor, only to re-emerge in 1977 with ANIMALS, perhaps best known for its sleeve picture of a flying pig over Battersea power station. Two of the tracks, "Sheep" and "Dogs", were over three years old, being rewrites of songs rejected from WISH YOU WERE HERE, and although the album featured some stinging guitar work from Gilmour it lacked the thoroughgoing excellence of the previous two.

ANIMALS came out at the height of punk, when Pink Floyd were generally reviled as dinosaur rockers, yet many of Waters' lyrics expressed a bitterness and cynicism that should have been recognized by self-proclaimed nihilist punk groups. These strands were prominent in THE WALL (1979), a hopelessly ambitious album, concert tour and film project (directed by Alan Parker and starring **Bob Geldof** as the alienated central character), first inspired by Waters' hatred of the whole stadium-rock concept. Self-indulgence was the word here, but the conceit of literally walling off the audience during the live performance was surprisingly effective.

During this period Roger Waters began to withdraw behind a wall of his own. He took over more and more control of the creative process, treating the others as glorified session musicians and allegedly engineering the departure of founder member Rick Wright. The next album, THE FINAL CUT, was subtitled, 'By Roger Waters, Performed By Pink Floyd'. Like ANIMALS, it was largely made from reheated leftovers (in this case spare bricks from THE WALL), but this time the result was decidedly half-baked and brought about the band's final collapse.

In 1986, Roger Waters announced that he had left the band, assuming that the Pink Floyd would be finished without him. He had reckoned without the determination of Dave Gilmour, who decided to press ahead with Mason, a newly rehabilitated Rick Wright and an army of session musicians. Waters was furious and commenced a campaign of legal actions and slanging matches in the press, all to no avail. He had forgotten that, just like Barrett before him, he might have been the leader of the band, but to the public he was a distant, faceless figure on stage, half-hidden behind the dry ice, lights and inflatable pig. And, as Gilmour has pointed out, Waters might have created the concepts and lyrics, but Gilmour was behind most of the music.

The new Gilmour-led Floyd sounds infinitely more 'Floydian' than Roger Waters' dirge-like solo albums. But their first effort, A MOMENTARY LAPSE OF REASON, showed that without Waters' lyrical input the new Floyd were pretty toothless. They followed this up in 1988 with THE DELICATE SOUND OF THUNDER, a rather uninspired live album, though a copy was taken by cosmonauts up to the Soviet Mir space station in 1988, thus justifying the Pink Floyd's 'first in space' T-shirt claim. Most disappointing of all was SHINE ON, an expensively priced box set that merely repackaged seven Floyd favourites plus a bonus CD of the early singles, which annoyingly remains unavailable separately.

In 1994, Floyd mark 3 finally hit their stride with a new studio album, THE DIVISION BELL. Almost a concept album, it had a general motif of poor communications and, unlike A MOMENTARY LAPSE OF REASON, it featured significant musical contributions from Wright and Mason, amidst the session men. The accompanying world tour featured an astonishingly elaborate light show and complete performances of DARK SIDE OF THE MOON, all captured on the live CD, P.U.L.S.E.. However good their live *son et lumière*, though, the new material still lacked the emotional punch of the old, and unless Gilmour could find another songwriting partner of Roger Waters' calibre Pink Floyd seemed destined to trade off past glories. A fact not lost on anyone who splashed out on either ECHOES: THE BEST OF PINK FLOYD (2001) or IS THERE ANYBODY OUT THERE: THE WALL LIVE 1980-81 (2000), the latter a visually and sonically lavish box set commemorating the twentieth anniversary of THE WALL.

The Piper At The Gates Of Dawn (1967; EMI).
A psychedelic classic that sounds as fresh today as when it was first released. Contains two space-rock anthems and a clutch of brilliant acid-pop songs, all liberally smattered with Syd's deconstructed guitar genius.

A Saucerful Of Secrets (1968; EMI).
Surprisingly successful ragbag of fragments recorded during the period of transition from the Barrett Floyd to the Gilmour model. Contains the memorably mysterious "Set The Controls For The Heart Of The Sun" and Barrett's chilling sign-off, "Jugband Blues".

Relics (1971; EMI).
A fine compilation of early album tracks and obscure 45s. Includes "Arnold Layne", "See Emily Play" and "Julia Dream", plus the best two tracks from MORE.

Dark Side Of The Moon (1973; EMI).
Floyd's big statement. Though now familiar to the point of expiry, it remains the concept album par excellence. A 30th anniversary edition appeared in 2003 with new artwork and surround sound.

Wish You Were Here (1975; EMI).
This is the mature Floyd at their best, particularly on the lengthy but always engaging "Shine On You Crazy Diamond". Also sports the busker-friendly title track and the supremely cheerless "Welcome To The Machine".

The Wall (1979; EMI).
Awesomely grim double album that's just too miserable to play end to end, but superb in parts, particularly "Comfortably Numb" and "Run Like Hell".

Iain Smith

PINK MILITARY/
PINK INDUSTRY

Formed Liverpool, England, 1978; disbanded 1989.

The salient features of **Pink Military** were the distinctive vocal properties of singer **Jayne Casey** and her heavily experimental approach to pop music. Casey had initially worked as part of the Big In Japan collective, a group rewarded with scant sales but who later became famous because of their component elements – they also included Bill Drummond, later of The KLF, David Balfe (ex-Teardrop Explodes and Echo And The Bunnymen and Food Records' founder), Siouxsie And The Banshees' drummer Budgie, producer and Lightning Seed Ian Broudie (also ex Original Mirrors and Wild Swans) and Holly Johnson of Frankie Goes To Hollywood. After their demise in 1978, Casey recruited **John Highway** (guitar), **Wayne Wadden** (bass) and **Paul Hornby** (drums) to form Pink Military, and Budgie played with the group on occasion, such as their November 1979 John Peel session.

Their first release was the blink-and-you'll-miss-it single "Pink Military Stand Alone", followed soon after by an EP, BLOOD AND LIPSTICK (1979), released on Liverpool independent label Eric's. A recording contract with Virgin ensued, while Hornby was replaced by **Chris Joyce** and Wadden by **Martin Dempsey**. Other musicians credited on the resultant DO ANIMALS BELIEVE IN GOD? (1980) included **Neil Innes** (congas), **Charlie Gruff** (guitar/piano) and **Nicky Cool** (synthesizers). It was a genre-defying outburst of creativity whose charm was at least partly due to its shambolic recording, but it failed to sell well.

Altering the name to **Pink Industry**, Casey then joined future Frankie Goes To Hollywood member **Ambrose Reynolds** for a single, "forty five?" (1982), and an album, LOW TECHNOLOGY (1983), for which they were joined by guitarist **Tadzio Jodlowski**. An evocative melange of ethnic scales, found sounds and innovative arrangements, LOW TECHNOLOGY was the perfect base for Casey's assertive vocals. WHO TOLD YOU YOU WERE NAKED (1983) was more abstract still, with densely layered electronics that were never as mechanical as those perpetrated by other synthesizer exponents of the early 80s.

Two years passed before the release of NEW BEGINNINGS and the accompanying single, "What I Wouldn't Give". Casey then elected to concentrate on her television career and other activities. Sporadic live appearances for Pink Industry continued in small venues in Liverpool in the late 80s.

(•) **Do Animals Believe In God?** (1980; Eric's).
Agenda-setting debut, featuring strong songs such as "Back On The London Stage" and "After Hiroshima".

(•) **Low Technology** (1983; Zulu).
A sumptuous suite that makes new technology sound both resonant and intimate.

Alex Ogg

PIXIES

Formed Boston, Massachusetts, 1986; disbanded 1993.

It is ironic that when Charles Michael Kitteridge Thompson IV – later known as **Black Francis** (vocals/guitar) – decided to form a band in 1986, it was at the expense of a trip to New Zealand to view Halley's Comet, visible from earth only once every 76 years. For Thompson's obsession with outer space would become a key component of his band's songs.

Thompson dropped out of his human anthropology course at the University of Massachusetts and persuaded his roommate **Joey Santiago** (lead guitar) to do the same. The pair moved to Boston, where they placed an advert in a local paper for a bassist 'into Hüsker Dü and Peter, Paul and Mary'. **Kim Deal** (bass) was the sole respondent. Deal suggested they recruit **David Lovering** (drums) and the **Pixies** (originally known as Pixies In Panoply) were born – the name having been chosen by Santiago after leafing through a dictionary.

The band performed around the Boston club scene in late 1986 and became pioneers in a sound which combined a heavy, brooding bass line with melodic surfcore guitar. It was topped with the frantic half-spoken, half-screeched vocals of Black Francis, plus Deal's breathy harmonies. This was music to frighten the grown-ups.

The Pixies sent a demo tape to English label 4AD through Ken Goes, manager of recent signings Throwing Muses. When 4AD boss Ivo Watts-Russell flew to Boston to see the Muses perform at the Rat Club, he decided to sign the Pixies on the strength of their support slot. The result was an eight-track mini-album, COME ON PILGRIM, released in 1987. The title stemmed from Christian folk singer Larry Norman, whose catchphrase was 'Come on pilgrim, you know He loves you.' But this was not a record to play at the church youth club: tales of death, evil, whores, incestuous union and Lou Reed filled the grooves, married to furious Spanish rhythms. It received rave reviews, topped the indie chart, and led to a US support tour with Throwing Muses.

In March 1988 came the SURFER ROSA album, produced by Steve Albini of **BIG BLACK** fame. A natural progression from their debut, it demonstrated Black Francis's emerging songwriting talent and became an alternative classic, making #1 in the UK indie chart. The following month, the band played their first UK gig, a sell-out show at London's Mean Fiddler supporting Throwing Muses on a European tour, and were courted by several US record labels. With "Gigantic" (1988), written and sung by Deal, the Pixies scored an indie hit single which coincided with their first headline British tour.

In April 1989 the Pixies began a successful partnership with producer Gil Norton, which eventually brought them mainstream acceptance. DOOLITTLE

remained true to the band's roots but demonstrated a growing pop know-how and crashed into the UK Top 10, peaking at #8. The Pixies' debut release on Elektra in the US, DOOLITTLE enjoyed a six-month chart residency there, while the single "Monkey Gone To Heaven" (1989) became an underground anthem as Black Francis tackled the subject of pollution and lamented the earth's impending destruction. Its immediate follow-up, "Here Comes Your Man", was almost throwaway sing-along pop, complete with yodelling.

A 150-date world tour was in full swing and on the European leg, christened 'Sex and Death', the band delivered an outstanding performance at the Glastonbury Festival. However, it was not long before a split in the ranks became evident. With ex-Throwing Muse Tanya Donelly, Kim Deal had formed her own band, **THE BREEDERS**, as an outlet for her own songwriting, and their debut LP, POD (1990), produced by Steve Albini, achieved considerable success.

Nevertheless, the Pixies' rise continued. The hit single "Velouria" (1990) was a love-struck ditty and a perfect introduction to the otherworldly weirdness of BOSSANOVA, released the following month. Hailed as a surf science fiction classic, the album peaked with "The Happening", inspired by an LA radio show which invited listeners to phone in with their UFO sightings. The album reached Top 3 status in Britain (and a chart-best #70 in the US), although the second single, "Dig For Fire", failed to make an impact.

By the summer of 1991 the Pixies were filling stadiums across Europe and had embraced a harsher, dirtier sound. "Planet Of Sound" was a throwback to their raw and violent ancestry, while October's TROMPE LE MONDE was less well received by many critics, who claimed the band had turned their back on commerciality in favour of 'heavy metal'. Black Francis's obsession with outer space and aliens continued, spawning some of the Pixies' most accomplished songs.

The Pixies toured with U2 in early 1992, but by the autumn Black Francis was in the studio working on a solo project and hopes of a sixth album began to evaporate. On January 14, 1993, Black Francis announced that he had officially disbanded the Pixies, following record company and management pressure to deliver another album, plus increasing disagreements with Deal. The other members were apparently informed of the split in a New Year fax.

Thompson, changing his name to **FRANK BLACK**, has achieved limited commercial success with subsequent solo albums, aided by Santiago. Deal continues her career with The Breeders, while Lovering has recorded with **Nitzer Ebb** and was last seen as drummer in **Cracker**.

⊙ **Surfer Rosa** (1988; 4AD).
Seedy tales of lowlife set to a punishing metallic grind. This was COME ON PILGRIM part two but with extra relish, and included the terrifying trio of "Gigantic", "Where Is My Mind" and "River Euphrates".

⊙ **Doolittle** (1989; 4AD).
Fifteen eclectic tracks ranging from pop ("Here Comes Your Man") through punk ("Debaser") to the slightly ridiculous ("La La Love You") and back again.

⊙ **Bossanova** (1990; 4AD).
Songs about surfing ("Ana") and outer space ("Velouria", "The Happening") delivered with grungey aplomb as the Pixies reach their peak. The band even used a theremin on two tracks, which had not been done since The Beach Boys and Led Zeppelin. A near-perfect record reissued in 1998.

⊙ **Trompe Le Monde** (1991; 4AD).
The Pixies' final release, also reissued in 1998, was considered scrappy and self-indulgent by some BOSSANOVA-era converts. But they had not lost the magic, nor the UFO conspiracy theories ("Motorway To Roswell"), and we can only wonder what might have followed.

⊙ **Complete 'B' Sides** (2001; 4AD).
Another posthumous artefact. As well as a wealth of long-unavailable Pixies-penned B-sides, you'll also find among these selections two brilliant Neil Young covers ("I've Been Waiting For You" and "Winterlong"), and a couple of smouldering live recordings ("River Euphrates" and "Vamos") thrown in for good measure.

Anna D. Robinson

PJ HARVEY

Born Corscombe, Dorset, October 9, 1970; P J Harvey formed 1991.

T he intricate mechanics of man-woman relations – the sort of stuff that interests, say, Liz Phair – are not evident in **Polly Jean Harvey**'s work. She writes in a broad, almost abstract way about women's sexual desire and power, strength and weakness. Men in her songs are only of interest for the primordial effect they have on her. They are accompanied by a musicianship of rare expansiveness and passion.

Polly Harvey was born to a sculptor mother and quarryman father. As her mother was deeply involved in the local music scene, there were always players hanging around the Harvey household, and young Polly Jean got the opportunity to experience and experiment with a lot of different styles and instruments. In her first teenage bands, **Bologna** and

Automatic Dlamini, Harvey was a sidewoman, playing saxophone and only occasionally contributing a song. Considering that she was always writing, this couldn't last. Eventually she hooked up with bass player **Steve Vaughn** and began working out what would become **P J Harvey** the band.

The whole thing coalesced when drummer **Robert Ellis** joined and the trio released "Dress" and "Sheela Na Gig" on the Too Pure label in 1991. Together these singles established Harvey's ambiguous self-image: on the one hand powerful and proud ('Look at these, my child-bearing hips ... Look at these, my work strong arms'), on the other looking to men for validation ('Must be a way that I can dress to please him'). When Too Pure issued the first P J Harvey album, DRY, in 1992, the picture was more fully filled in. There was a strange, almost disconcerting use of sexual imagery, with breasts as 'dirty pillows', and imprecations like 'I'm happy and bleeding for you'. The music, in complement, was rigorously stripped down – no leads, simple riffs, but the rhythms were swinging and comfortable.

The follow-up, RID OF ME (1993), gave Harvey's vision a harder edge. Producer Steve Albini thoroughly indulged his taste for elementary dynamics – very loud to very soft, very sharp to very soft, with little in between. The title track, in which a woman refuses to relinquish a departing lover ('I'll make you lick my injuries ... Till you say don't you wish you never never met her'), set the tone for an album that was all mood swings between dominance and submission, with ferocious sexual avowals and brags ('Sweet babe let me stroke it ... I'll rub it till it bleeds') alternating with miserable admissions of weakness, as in the seduction-and-abandonment fable "Hook".

Then Harvey, who has more than once referred to herself as a 'dictator', reorganized her band and spent a year or two working on a new approach. The intervening release of a CD of some of her demos, which showed the elemental, raw gut-howl origins of some of her songs, served to confirm that P J Harvey the band was in fact P J Harvey the solo artist. Around this time she also started playing with her physical image, appearing in ballgowns and make-up – which was rather disorientating, since on her thin and fragile-looking frame the diva drag made her look like a little girl playing dress-up.

1995's TO BRING YOU MY LOVE, recorded with a new five-piece band and lushly produced by Flood (U2, Tom Jones), showed greater coherence than the previous albums: the Harvey character seemed to be working from strength and confidence even in her bleaker moments. Thus, though she was pleading in "C'mon Billy", the force of her objection ('Don't you think it's time now/You met your only son') is emphasized rather than her abject state. There was even some room for playfulness, as in the all-out rave "Meet Ze Monsta", where she played out a seductive fantasy image till it became a little ludicrous. Musically the record was more ambitious as well, with tasteful strings and cleverly chosen effects.

Polly Harvey on stage

A 1996 work, DANCE HALL AT LOUSE POINT, had her reunited with an old crony from Automatic Dlamini days, **John Parish**, for a collection of pieces to accompany a dance work performed in 1997. Though Harvey had implied that she was nearing the end of her musical career, she re-emerged in 2000. Mellowed and devoid of glitz she released one of her finest collections to date, STORIES FROM THE CITY, STORIES FROM THE SEA. The make-up-clad waif image had been well and truly buried, and consequently Harvey's music and writing finally received the attention it deserved in the serious press. Musically the album was more stripped down, like her earliest efforts, and the lyrical content was broad. Vocally Harvey still packs a mean punch; more self-assured than ever, she continues to follow her own path; in 2003 she played numerous festivals and even performed a special show at London's Tate Modern gallery as part of the *Tate & Egg Live* season.

Rid Of Me (1993; ZTT).
There are moments of tenderness, as with her keening in "Missed", but on the whole this is very harsh, powerful music.

To Bring You My Love (1995; Island).
One of her fullest statements yet, with a broad aural palette that ranges from the muzzy, half-whimpered "Working For The Man" to the bluesy, majestic title track.

Stories From The City, Stories From The Sea (2000; Island).
This is a well-balanced, mature set. The instrumentation is often sparse, never trying too hard to come to the fore it leaves Harvey's voice ample space to fill. On "This Mess We're In" – a duet specifically penned with Thom Yorke in mind – Harvey's tones only occasionally surface to add dressing to the Radiohead frontman's distinctive purr.

Roy Edroso

PLACEBO

Formed London, 1994.

"Brian is a genital eraser. Rubbing away the barriers." Steve Hewitt

One of the more interesting groups thrown up in the wake of Britpop, **Placebo** originally comprised American vocalist/guitarist **Brian Molko**, Swedish bass player **Stefan Olsdal** and Swiss drummer **Robert Schultzberg**. The cosmopolitan trio formed after Olsdal met Molko at school in Luxembourg when both were just over 10 years old. Their next meeting would be several years later at London's South Kensington tube station.

This momentous second rendezvous, they decided, should be marked by the formation of a band. As a result, Molko abandoned his ambitions to become an actor (he had attended Goldsmiths College to study drama in the interim – an influence which still pervades their live shows). The trio's initial slipshod art-rock sound stiffened through confidence and experience to a more basic pop base with hints of glam-rock and punk – with Bowie devotee Molko's androgynous looks and foetal whine the most distinctive element. At this time they were joined by Schultzberg, then studying percussion in London, who had previously played in a Swedish band with Olsdal.

The group's first single came at the end of 1995 with "Bruise Pristine" for Simon Williams' acclaimed Fierce Panda indie. A major-label bidding war ensued, with Placebo eventually opting to establish their own label, Elevator Music, via Hut Records. In the meantime they released a second single,

"Come Home", on Deceptive in February 1996, and toured Europe in support of David Bowie.

The next single, "36 Degrees" – which alluded to the body's temperature when brinking on overdose – arrived early in the summer, but this, however, was more of a water-treading exercise for Placebo whilst the band's debut LP was in its final preparation. Oddly, PLACEBO (1996) proved something of a 'sleeper', coinciding as it did with the first moment of turmoil in the band's development. Following Placebo's first, triumphant live TV appearance in Britain on Channel Four's *The White Room*, Molko dramatically sacked Robert Schultzberg, claiming that he wasn't dedicated to the group cause.

The television appearance paid off in that the third Hut single – the infectious "Teenage Angst" – finally saw Placebo in the British Top 30 in October. A replacement percussionist, former Boo Radleys and K-Klass drummer, **Steve Hewitt** – who had played on the band's original demos – was duly sought. After this pit stop, the Placebo F1 set off again with a pre-Christmas tour of the UK. Now, interest was at a premium – a mood exploited by Hut, who tactically withdrew the LP from the shops until the next single was released.

In January 1997, the fabulously abrasive and totally infectious "Nancy Boy" entered the UK singles chart

J. D. MONDINO

Molko's (centre) Placebo in pieces

at #4, following relentless (but deserved) airplay, not to mention a frenetic live performance on *Top Of The Pops*. Placebo looked and sounded like the next big thing waiting to happen, whilst young girls and boys began to doll themselves up in smudged Molko-style face paint. No one was more shocked by this sudden fame than the singer himself. With almost childlike enthusiasm, he began introducing live performances with the camply drawled, 'Hey, we're Placebo! Welcome to our dream come true!'

PLACEBO was duly reissued in February, taking an immediate Top 5 slot, and finally gaining the broader accolades it had deserved first time around. The LP – produced by Brad Wood of experimental US noodlers Tortoise – had taken just two months to complete, but despite the obvious strength of many of its tracks it perhaps lacked the lustre of that single. However, versions of all five singles were present, which made it essential for all new converts. The press had been generous in their appraisal of the debut: 'It is dangerous, mysterious and utterly addictive,' said the *NME*. As the album's sales eventually began to wane, a new version of "Bruise Pristine" saw the band hurtle back into the singles Top 20, although the new mix clearly lacked the urgency of the Fierce Panda original.

At this stage, the only real criticism of Placebo was that they perhaps needed to explore a world wider than that which they so clearly inhabited. Brian Molko's universe appeared so completely contained within the parameters of sleaze that many found an entire album of low-rent characters a little hard to cope with, and the inevitable detractors quickly began to manifest themselves in the press.

A year away – which found the irrepressible Molko cropping up on television (his appearance on music quiz *Never Mind The Buzzcocks* was particularly memorable) and in the movie *The Velvet Goldmine* – refreshed Placebo, the group returning strongly in July 1998 with the excellent single "Pure Morning". An instant airplay smash, this record indicated a more considered direction for the band, although lyrics such as 'a friend with breasts and all the rest, a friend who's dressed in leather' suggested that Brian's subject area would not be compromised. Now a major singles act in the UK, Placebo followed this Top 5 hit with another, the less substantial but equally well-received "You Don't Care About Us" featuring a promo in which the band was fed to sharks!

The latter two singles had been culled from Placebo's much-vaunted second album, WITHOUT YOU I'M NOTHING. While boasting further intriguing lyrics and progression, this set largely lacked the powerful immediacy of "Nancy Boy" et al. However, the inclusion of chord-driven numbers like its dynamic third hit, "Every You, Every Me", gave the record potential long-term sales expectations.

After another spell out of the limelight, Placebo returned in September 2000 with a third album, BLACK MARKET MUSIC. Although its hastily released

singles "Taste In Men" and "Slave to the Wage" represented the band's lowest chart entries in four years, expectations were still high for the collection, in which Molko overall delivered the goods in familiar style.

In May 2002, the singer's unmistakeable tones could once again be heard, this time on UK dance act **Alpinestars**' single, "Carbon Kids", but it was with 2003's SLEEPING WITH GHOSTS that Placebo once again found their footing. The set was spiky and driven, and fitted in well with the alternative chart's prevailing punky pop sound. The album reminded many that the music scene is that much more colourful a place when Brian Molko's star is shining.

Placebo (1996; Elevator).
Comprising unlikely additional elements such as toy instruments (on "Hang On To Your IQ" and "I Know") and a didgeridoo, this generally pleasing (though occasionally irritating) collection serves notice of Molko's ability to articulate mood and feeling – best represented here on "Nancy Boy" and a reprised "Bruise Pristine".

Sleeping With Ghosts (2003; Elevator).
Placebo once again open the sordid casebook of their psychosexual misadventures. Stand-out cut "Protect Me From What I Want" even sees dirty little Brian looking for some head space and a way to escape his grubby temptations. Perhaps a cold shower would do the trick?

Alex Ogg & Jeremy Simmonds

THE POGUES

Formed London, 1983.

Scan the fuzzy stills of late-70s punk gigs and you'll come across the unmistakeable figure of **SHANE MACGOWAN**, sporting a lurid Union Jack T-shirt, a half-empty beer glass, and an inane and toothless grin. By the time of the formation of **The Pogues** a few years later, the T-shirt had gone, the glass had most definitely remained, and the unbridled energy and enthusiasm of punk's heyday was being channelled into a raucous folk/rock hybrid which would produce some of the most innovative and captivating music of the 80s.

To the musical anarchy of punk The Pogues (originally Pogue Mahone – "Kiss My Arse" in Gaelic) added a tradition of working-class and Irish folk music reaching back to the last century and beyond. Traditional instruments mixed with electric guitars, and traditional themes with modern concerns – an unlikely brew, but it worked perfectly. There was a nostalgia, certainly, but a nostalgia tempered by a clear sense of history. MacGowan's lyrics, carefully structured and at best beautifully evocative, told of death, love, war and foreign lands, and the drunken old soaks who have experienced it all.

It was after the demise of his punk band The Nipple Erectors that MacGowan surrounded himself with the musicians who would realize The Pogues' sound. MacGowan (vocals/guitar), **Jimmy Fearnley** (accordion), **Jem Finer** (banjo), **Kate O'Riordan** (bass/vocals), **Spider Stacy** (whistle) and **Andy Ranken** (drums) comprised The Pogues' line-up for

THE POGUES
If I Should Fall From Grace With God

the debut album, RED ROSES FOR ME (1984). The set was more a powerful confirmation of potential than a finished article, but however chaotic the sound might sometimes have become, The Pogues always retained a strong sense of infectious melody – a trend that would continue. Significantly, six of the album's thirteen songs were covers or, rather, dazzling arrangements of traditional folk songs.

The next two albums constituted The Pogues' most fertile period. RUM, SODOMY AND THE LASH (1985) and IF I SHOULD FALL FROM GRACE WITH GOD (1988) were powerful, haunting, wonderfully accomplished testaments to the writing talent of MacGowan, and to a lesser extent Jem Finer. "The Sick Bed Of Cuchulainn", "A Pair Of Brown Eyes" and "Sally MacLennane" from RUM, and "Turkish Song Of The Damned", "Fairytale Of New York" and "Birmingham Six" (MacGowan at his most openly political) from IF I SHOULD FALL..., stood out among a wealth of gorgeous tunes, adept playing, and lyrics that conjured the most graphic images and gritty tales with effortless grace. Once again, the covers and traditional arrangements, from "I'm A Man You Don't Meet Every Day" to "Medley", displayed an uncanny sense of the appropriate – in fact "Medley", a haphazard amalgamation of old folk arrangements, displayed the full spectrum of Poguetry. It was far from normal chart fodder (and from The Pogues' 'alternative' contemporaries as well), and yet "Fairytale Of New York", a song of drunken, bitter realization and fading dreams, was the UK's Christmas #2 in 1988.

The Pogues were never to repeat the success of these two records. Though they were easily filling big venues by now, their shows were revealing the problems that PEACE AND LOVE, released in 1989, would make painfully evident. Shane MacGowan's AWOL lifestyle was betraying his talent. PEACE AND LOVE was not a bad album, but was rarely inspired and, of MacGowan's six contributions, only two – "White City" and "Down All The Days" – came close to his own high standards. His vocal performance, too, was badly affected. The rest of the band

tried hard, but not even the accomplished Finer could fill the gap left by MacGowan. The Pogues were nearing the end.

To make things worse, the PEACE AND LOVE tour was shambolic. MacGowan lurched off stage at regular intervals, usually to return with a refilled glass; he forgot the words he himself had written; he fell over. In the end Spider Stacy had to take over much of the vocal work. Still, MacGowan did get it together enough to release one more album with The Pogues – 1990's HELL'S DITCH. Surprisingly competent, it represented at least a partial return to form. "Summer In Siam", in particular, proved one more time and with simple style just how adept The Pogues were at producing the most delicate and moving of ballads.

MacGowan and The Pogues went their separate ways, inevitably, after HELL'S DITCH, though they reunited again briefly in 1994. The Pogues have subsequently collaborated, quite successfully, with **Joe Strummer**, and with guitarist-producer **Michael Brook** have recorded WAITING FOR HERB (1993) and POGUE MAHONE (1995), creditable and enjoyable outings, if not quite the inspirational fare of old. Shane MacGowan, meanwhile, has a new band, **The Popes**, and a new style to boot. Those are different stories. For many, the verve and the genius of The Pogues, especially from 1985 to 1988, will remain the abiding memory.

⊙ **Rum, Sodomy And The Lash** (1985; Stiff).
Perhaps The Pogues' finest moment. Style ranges from "A Pair Of Brown Eyes" and "The Band Played Waltzing Matilda", two of the most haunting of the band's many ballads, to the raucous "Sally MacLennane" and "Billy's Bones", the cause of a thousand minor altercations on dance floors across the nation.

⊙ **If I Should Fall From Grace With God** (1988; Stiff).
Less spontaneous than its predecessor, but nonetheless the work of a band at the peak of creativity and confidence. "Turkish Song Of The Damned", "Fiesta", "Bottle Of Smoke", "South Australia" – all different, all palpably The Pogues, and all a joy.

Hugh Wilson

THE POISON GIRLS

Formed Brighton, England, 1977; disbanded 1989.

In 1977 **Vi Subversa** was 42 years old. Yet she had the resolve, spirit and energy to put thousands of kids to shame, as over the following thirteen years she fronted **The Poison Girls** – one of the most uncompromising bands in rock history, challenging racism, sexism, the nuclear industry and all manner of abuses at every step. Her partners in crime, as the group made the transition from hippiedom to punk, were Welsh anarchist **Lance D'Boyle** (drums) and **Richard Famous** (guitar). Bassists were always a problem – the band employed thirteen different ones over the years.

Early gigs at Brighton's Vault club built up a local following for The Poison Girls, then in late 1978 the band linked up with fellow anarcho-punksters Crass, in what was to prove a fruitful partnership. They released their first single, the jerky "Piano Lessons", the following year as a joint release with Fatal Microbes – a band which featured Vi's kids along with a 14-year-old girl vocalist, Honey Bane, who was on the run from a detention centre. *Sounds* made it *Single of the Week* and the group followed with HEX, an album of threatening intensity and with a humour often lacking in their contemporaries. "Old Tart's Song" was laden with irony and "Jump Mama Jump" was another thought-provoker, fixing the plight of women in the minds of many a young punk.

By this stage **Bernhardt Rebours** was installed on bass – he was to prove their most stable player, with three years' service. The group were based at an Epping commune from which sprang the fanzines, posters and sloganeering that were to be the hallmark of the band's career. But they attracted the attention of English fascists, too, and a clash with the British Movement at Stratford Theatre Royal left D'Boyle in hospital.

1980 saw the "Persons Unknown" single, with Crass, and the band's own CHAPPAQUIDDICK BRIDGE LP, but they were beginning to feel that they had exhausted punk's larder. The live album TOTAL EXPOSURE marked the end of the association with Crass, and the next studio work, WHERE'S THE PLEASURE (1982), explored more tender areas of human behaviour. This was Greenham Common anti-nuclear demonstration time, and "Take The Toys", a lilting shanty-style song, was adopted as an anthem by those dauntless campaigners. At last the music press began to take The Poison Girls more seriously.

By late 1984 and early 1985 the band were as near to the limelight as they ever would be. The single "Real Women" was released as a prelude to the SONGS OF PRAISE album, while Subversa and co were supporting benefits for the miners' strike, amongst many other causes. But 1985 was the year of Live Aid, and, for a band that for eight years had played for nothing in support of every worthwhile crusade, it was galling to see fading superstars kick-starting their careers with a show of conspicuous concern. The big names won the press campaign, few sharing The Poison Girls' viewpoint as expressed on their poster of a crowned Bob Geldof uttering the words 'Let Them Eat Vinyl'.

The band now had a keyboard player in **Cynth Ethics** and D'Boyle left, to be replaced by **Agent Orange**. The 1986 EP THE PRICE OF GRAIN AND THE PRICE OF BLOOD seemed to signify greater things. But The Poison Girls would never issue another release, although they gigged until 1989 when they played for the final time, in Zagreb, conflict never far from view.

◉ **Statement** (1995; Vital/Cooking Vinyl).
Four-CD box set covering the group's complete career, from earliest recordings to post-1986 unreleased material. An invaluable document, complete with lyric book and group manifesto.

Pip Southall

POLE

Emerged Düsseldorf, Germany, 1997.

As an employee at Dubplates & Mastering, the renowned minimal techno label Basic Channel's record-cutting plant in Berlin, it's not surprising that **Stefan Betke** came to find fascination in the depths of bass. Using a damaged Waldorf 4 Pole-Filter as both the basis of his scratchy sound and as inspiration for his recording identity, **Pole**, Betke set about producing warmly glitched, bass-heavy recordings of analogue electronics.

First came the groundbreaking POLE EP, followed closely by the POLE 1 album in 1998. Taking the blueprint of Basic Channel's sparse grooves and the CD-skips of Oval as starting points, Betke rendered his own particular brand of filtered interference onto the mix, almost dispensing with conventional beats entirely. Instead, the Pole sound rode on an enveloping wash of dub bass and layered filter clicks and pops, creating shifting patterns of hypnotic electronic convolutions and faint hints of melody. In interviews Betke has been unwilling to reveal his methods and influences, and asserts that his exposure to the classic dub productions of the likes of King Tubby and Augustus Pablo have been minimal, yet to the listener, their methodology is most definitely in there, somewhere.

Whatever the connection, his debut releases were deservedly lauded by the music press, mainstream and otherwise. Accompanied by extensive live touring schedules, which took in Barcelona's Sonar Festival and Labradford's Festival Of Drifting in London, Betke developed his Pole sound with even deeper bass rhythms, evidence of which is on his second album, logically titled POLE 2 (1999). His second album, along with a series of remixes for the likes of Appliance and Laub, firmly established Pole as one of the mainstays of ultra-reduced electronica in a relatively short time. He launched his own label for him and kindred spirits alike called **Scape** (along with an associated Berlin club night) in August 1999. Scape released material by San Franciscan **Kit Clayton** and Cologne dubster **Burnt Friedman**.

On a bizarre note, Pole was the subject of what seemed to have been a practical joke, when his contribution to a Fat Cat split single turned out to have not been his work at all; the DAT having been posted by person(s) unknown to the label as if from Betke, causing some confusion and ultimately, the repressing of the record. The adulterated version of it will no doubt become a collector's oddity.

His own, entirely genuine 12", "Rondell", arrived in Spring 2000 and received rave reviews, in advance of the unsurprisingly titled POLE 3 in May (and an extremely limited triple CD of POLES 1-2-3). Pole's recent work has included the R album (2001), a collection of versions and reconstructions of the track "Raum"; a 'remix war' with **Kieran Hebden** called the POLE VS FOUR TET EP, released through Leaf;

and the funkier POLE album (2003). This collection was the most expansive of Betke's career: the pulses and thuds had been fleshed out with dub-heavy grooves, while hip-hop rhyming, saxophone and upright bass added humanizing elements to the sound.

Betke has also branched out with his own mastering studio and publishing company, and seems well on his way to becoming a veritable independent music production tycoon.

● **Pole 1** (1998; PIAS/Kiff SM).
A minimalist swarm of changing rhythms, echoes and filtered electronic glitches, elegantly packaged in a simple dark blue sleeve. Reflective and amorphous, capable of being ambient or booming.

● **Pole 2** (1999; PIAS/Kiff SM).
A mini-album, presented in vibrant red this time round, of more smoothly vibrating electronic dub pulses, expanded into comparatively upbeat drumless rhythms and drop-out skanks.

● **Pole 3** (2000; PIAS/Kiff SM).
From its minimal yellow cover to the stately bass rhythms of the eight tracks inside, Stefan Betke's third album expands his roots from a dub blueprint into more complex territories. Mesmerizing.

Richard Fontenoy

THE POLICE

Formed London, 1977; disbanded 1986.

"I want to say that the truth about The Police – me and Stewart and Andy – is that we loved each other ... too much." Sting

The Police were giants of the early 80s, providing a steady flow of hit singles and albums that showcased a tightly knit rhythmic unit and the expressive vocals of frontman/bassist Gordon Sumner (**STING**). Though some of their music now sounds dated, the group's best songs have taken on the aura of modern classics, and with a recent 'best of' compilation selling impressively, they have remained in the public imagination longer than many of their contemporaries.

The group came together in London from diverse musical backgrounds. Ex-teacher Sting had played jazz bass with Newcastle combo Last Exit, American **Stewart Copeland** was the drummer with prog-rockers Curved Air, while the hugely accomplished guitarist **Andy Summers** had played with artists as diverse as Kevin Coyne, Kevin Ayers and Eric Burdon. An early single release ("Fall Out"), with Summers' predecessor Henri Padovani, was a mediocre stab at punk rock but sold well enough. But it was with Sting in place, and a new all-blond hair image adding visual appeal, that the group began to make waves. They did so on the punk circuit, although they differed from most of the other punks in possessing well-seasoned instrumental talents, enabling them to experiment – notably with reggae – while other groups had difficulty just playing in time.

Signed to A&M, the group released their debut album, OUTLANDOS D'AMOUR, in late 1978. Though occasionally sounding duty-bound to punk ("Born In The 50s", "Peanuts"), the album also introduced the group's capacity for catchy pop music. "Can't Stand Losing You" was the first of The Police's big hits, followed into the charts by "So Lonely" and "Roxanne". They all featured novel 'white reggae' rhythms, which were to become the

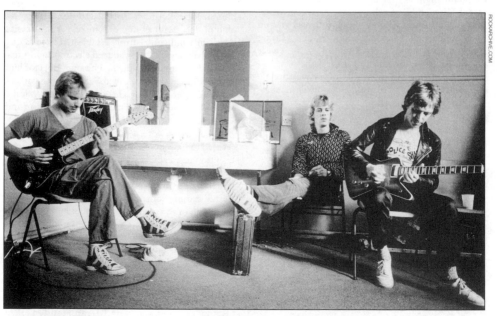

Don't sit so close to me: Sting, Stewart Copeland and Andy Summers backstage in Scotland, 1979

trademark Police sound, although they still sounded strained when attempting to extend the groove on a track like "Masoko Tanga".

The follow-up, REGATTA DE BLANC (1979), quickly ironed out any rough edges, and reeled off the hits "Walking On The Moon" and "Message In A Bottle", along with one of Sting's best songs, "The Bed's Too Big Without You" and the intense "Bring On The Night". Sting's voice had lost some of the harshness it had shown on the first album and developed a husky, jazzy feel, while his lyrics were both clever and witty. More impressive still was the group's ability to work its way around a catchy tune, with Copeland's drums and Sting's bass leading the song and Summers' distorted guitar adding details, a refreshing alternative to the norm of guitar-driven bands.

Breaking America proved an effortless step for The Police with the student–teacher drama of "Don't Stand So Close To Me", although critics of Sting's pretensions found ammunition in such rhymes as 'shake and cough'/'Nabokov'. There was a hint of self-congratulation about the band, too, and both tendencies surfaced in the title of the group's next album, ZENYATTA MONDATTA (1980), Sanskrit for 'top of the world'. The album itself was a little muted as the group fell back on an effortless rhythmic groove with few melodic highlights.

Much more effective was GHOST IN THE MACHINE (1981), which saw The Police moving towards a funkier sound on "Too Much Information" and "Demolition Man", and produced its quota of hits with the jaunty "Every Little Thing She Does Is Magic" and the politically inclined "Invisible Sun" (about the Irish troubles). The music sounded denser with the addition of extra instrumentation, although the trademark rhythmic interplay still provided the solid base.

Sting had long since become the focal point of the group, a position strengthened by his acting roles in, among other projects, the film *Quadrophenia* in 1979. The fact that he contributed the majority of the Police songs (and all their hit singles) added to the well-documented tension within the group, a state of affairs that sometimes flared into punch-ups. Nonetheless, SYNCHRONICITY (1983) turned out to be the group's strongest album as well as their last, and the group's cohesion had never seemed tighter. The masterful rhythms of "Tea In The Sahara" and "Walking In Your Footsteps" were matched by the driving rock of "Synchronicity 2" and the more complex arrangement of "King Of Pain". Best of all was "Every Breath You Take", as powerful a distillation of obsession as has ever been recorded. Copeland's lightweight "Miss Gradenko" and Summers' grating "Mother" demonstrated why Sting ended up with the lion's share of the writing.

The individual members of The Police then went their own ways with differing levels of success – Sting's predictably stratospheric – reuniting only for a weird remake of "Don't Stand So Close To Me" for a greatest hits package in 1986. The release of a first ever live album in 1995 also rekindled some media interest, but it is those original studio albums which showcase this inventive and popular group to greatest effect.

⊙ **Synchronicity** (1983; A&M).
The group's best album in terms of sheer songwriting consistency, and in the variety of musical styles mastered over the course of 45 minutes. Contains the unimpeachable "Every Breath You Take".

⊙ **Greatest Hits** (1992; A&M).
The best of three compilations available, demonstrating that The Police were one hell of a singles outfit.

⊙ **The Very Best Of Sting/The Police** (1998; A&M).
Having spent the best part of fifteen years establishing a separate identity as a solo performer, Sting and his greatest hits ruin everything by appearing alongside the best of the classic pop he created as a Policeman. A great album: half the mellow reflections of the solo act; and half the mad, bounce-inducing blend of pop, reggae and punk patented by the Police.

Nicholas Oliver

THE POLYPHONIC SPREE

Formed Texas, 2000.

If you've ever had the pleasure of attending a **Polyphonic Spree** gig, you are by now either residing in some far-flung religious retreat having been enlightened by the combo's ecstatic sun-loving chants, or you will have drastically altered your opinion of what qualifies as alternative rock in these strange times. For starters, The Polyphonic Spree boast an abnormally impressive head count (a choir of ten accompany a thirteen-strong band of musicians), which coupled with the fact that they're all dressed in monastic white robes, means that the average Spree concert feels more like the warm-up act for a TV evangelist than a bunch of Generation-X-ers rockin' out.

Sonically, The Polyphonic Spree are even more surprising. Though they've been compared to the likes of The Flaming Lips and Mercury Rev, their sound is far more blissful, their songs invariably consisting of little more than a seemingly endless euphoric chorus of gospel vocals and hand-claps backed by a melange of hypnotizing, vaguely twisted instrumentation.

At the head of this grinning, cultish clan is the outfit's spiritual leader **Tim DeLaughter**, one-time member of **Tripping Daisy** – a band that came to an untimely end when guitarist Wes Berggren died of an overdose. Tim lost both a group and a good friend.

For a long while Tim had voiced his wish to form a large-scale choral band, but it wasn't until 2000 that his dream became a reality. A close friend, Chris Penn (now the collective's manager), took the initiative and informed Tim that he had booked the as-yet-unformed band a gig and he had only a couple of weeks to get the show on the road.

The Polyphonic Spree came into existence as a fifteen-strong combo, playing as support to Grandaddy at Dallas's Gypsy Tea Room in July 2000. Soon after

Monastic mayhem at a Polyphonic Spree gig

they spent an intensive three days in the studio and laid down the tracks that would become their debut album, THE BEGINNING STAGES OF...

By 2002 the group had a head count of 23. They took their joyful noise to the South by South West Music conference in Austin, and made a big impression – particularly with the British delegation. Before long the group's name and tales of their exhilarated antics were being bandied around on both sides of the Atlantic. In June the group made their UK debut at David Bowie's Meltdown festival in London.

The summer was theirs: Fierce Panda released the "Soldier Girl" single to rapturous reviews, the troupe played more gigs and graced the festival circuit. By September, the album was released.

Though The Polyphonic Spree have yet to show whether they have the staying power to wow the press and their fans a second time, their music is undeniably compulsive, uplifting and refreshingly peculiar in this age of sonic mediocrity.

⊙ **The Beginning Stages Of...** (2002; Good Records). This collection's lilting melodies tickle the hairs on your neck, backed up by some spine-tingling brass and flute arrangements, but every now and again the guitars and percussion let fly with a winding blow to the stomach. Full of surprises, emotion and quirk, this debut is a delight.

Peter Buckley

THE POOH STICKS

Formed Swansea, Wales, 1987.

Perpetual teenagers and perennial losers, **The Pooh Sticks** are the best-kept secret of the British indie scene. This is a band that swears eternal allegiance to the unholy trinity of the MC5 ("Back In The USA" era), 60s bubblegum music and mid-70s big pop. Girls are 'groovy' and, for the men, slouching and smoking in the boys' room are compulsory, as the sweet dreams of sussed but cute adolescence burn long and deep.

Formed by **Huw Williams** (vocals) in late 1987, the line-up was completed by **Trudi Tangerine** (tambourine/piano), **Paul** (guitar), **Alison** (bass) and **Stephanie** (drums) – they are loath to reveal their surnames. The early sound was a bizarre genre-hopping hybrid of two-minute jangle pop, 'enthusiastic' harmonizing, three-chord punk, girl-group cuteness and, beneath it all, a sharp wit aimed squarely at the po-faced indie scene of the time.

The band's first crudely produced single, "On Tape" (1988), parodied the indie trainspotter with such lines as: 'I've got Falling and Laughing – the original Postcard version/I've got all the Sky Saxon solo albums on tape!' Tracks such as "Indie Pop Ain't Noise Pollution" and "I Know Someone Who Knows Someone Who Knows Alan McGee Quite Well" kept up the parodic energy.

In the best spirit of marketing disasters (à la Moby Grape), early Pooh Sticks singles were released in a box set, prior to being transferred onto the debut album, POOH STICKS (1988). Japery occasionally lapsed into tweeness ('Goody goody gumdrops, my heart is doing flip flops'), but generally The Pooh Sticks sidestepped smugness in favour of genuine charm and enthusiasm. Though undeniably derivative, the band owed no more or less debts to illustrious predecessors than did, say, The Jesus & Mary Chain. The difference was that The Pooh Sticks were somewhat less hip – The Archies' "Sugar, Sugar" rather than Lou Reed's "Heroin". The group maintained their obscurity with more low-key releases: TRADE MARK OF QUALITY (1998), FORMULA ONE GENERATION (1990) and a retrospective compilation, MULTIPLE ORGASM (1991).

The band toured the States in 1990, and their next studio album emerged in 1991. THE GREAT WHITE WONDER souped up the sound and reflected an ever-growing embrace of kitsch Americana, previous sleeve notes having praised *The Partridge Family* and the *Banana Splits*. Amongst the usual teen call-to-arms ("Young People") and pretty ballads ("Who Loves You"), the LP also featured more expansive guitar soloing, particularly on the fourteen-minute "I'm In You" – paying dues to 70s-styled AOR. Notwithstanding, success in the States eluded them and, with a UK scene in transit between Manchester and Seattle, things proved no better at home.

Undeterred, The Pooh Sticks managed to secure major backing for their next (and best) album, MILLION SELLER (1993). A winning amalgam of Rundgren-styled 70s power pop ("I Saw The Light") and 60s light psychedelia ("Riding The Rainbow"), it should have been massive, but wasn't. Neither was 1995's follow-up, OPTIMISTIC FOOL, leaving the distinct impression that the band possessed an acute ability to be in the wrong place at the wrong time. As Britpop evolved into a distinctly English proposition, The Pooh Sticks, enthralled by American music, found it hard to strike a chord. Their eccentricities and sweet wit never quite saw them through; though The Pooh Sticks have now been silent for many years, perhaps their time will come.

⊙ **Formula One Generation** (1990; Fierce).
Now available again through Sympathy in the States, this long-lost classic features the marvellous "Radio Ready" and "Soft Bed, Hard Battles".

⊙ **Million Seller** (1993; BMG).
Unabashedly melodious, pure pop released while grunge still held sway over the world's youth. To be reassessed as an 'overlooked gem' sometime in the 21st century.

Nig Hodgkins

IGGY POP

Born Muskegan, Michigan, 1947.

"There are things I don't remember ... I'd wake up with bumps on the head, blood on my shirt and something green coming out of my penis."

The life of **Iggy Pop**, as reported in the press, as stated on record and as amplified by gossip, is a classic rock'n'roll myth of ventures on the brink of the abyss, of madness, repentance and renewal. Iggy's gods, and the demons he has struggled with, belong to the essential culture of rock'n'roll.

James Jewel Osterburg was born just west of Detroit (British dad, American ma) and made his first appearances in local high-school bands – including drumming for and getting his name from **The Iguanas** – in the mid 60s. None of the early bands featuring Iggy were ever going to be more than neighbourhood successes and he left the Prime Movers, the University of Michigan and the city of Detroit in 1966, moving to Chicago to hang out with Sam Lay (ex Howlin' Wolf and Paul Butterfield Blues Band drummer). An early legend has him drumming for Phil Spector on "To Know Him Is To Love Him".

He returned to Detroit as Iggy Stooge, guitar player and singer, where with **Ron Asheton**, his pal from the Prime Movers, he unleashed the nastiness of **THE STOOGES** upon the world. Originally The Psychedelic Stooges, Iggy (guitar/vocals) and Ron (bass), with drums provided by Ron's brother **Scott**, made their debut on Halloween night, 1967. Having picked up a lot of showmanship tips from seeing The Doors play, Iggy gave The Stooges his own personal stamp, the inspiration coming from a mix of consciousness-twisting drugs. They started off as fun-loving, drug-taking youth-gone-wrong outfit; by 1973, though, the band were at one another's throats, with heroin and apathy producing the final break-up.

Iggy demonstrating characteristic lust for life

Iggy, by now under the wing of David Bowie, producer of a fairly crappy mix of The Stooges' final album, extricated himself from the wreckage with a heroin habit and a fair degree of mental confusion. He went to Florida and played golf for a while, did some time as a voluntary patient in a Detroit mental hospital, recorded here and there, and – in between periods of staying clean of most drugs – continued to create his own legend as a live performer with a phenomenal capacity for physical and chemical self-abuse.

The mid-70s were Iggy's period in the wilderness. He was wasting away through a lousy diet and other rock'n'roll habits, and burning up what little flesh remained with the intensity of his live appearances. This was the period of Iggy slicing his chest open on stage with a razor or broken bottle, and breaking his teeth by ramming the microphone through them. This was the period when he was rumoured to have shown up at a post-gig party, consumed an entire packet of speed, blacked out on the spot, remained motionless for twenty minutes and then leapt up, said 'thanks man, great speed, great party' and left.

He finally cleared the heroin fog-bank in 1977 – sometime between his two albums of the year (indeed of the decade): the narcotic lowlife drawlings of THE IDIOT album, and the miraculous conversion of LUST FOR LIFE, which was still sleazy but with a generally positive outlook. The track "Here Comes Success" encapsulates the moment: it's a fun song, with its ragged call-and-response routines, but listen to Iggy's style of delivering these upbeat lyrics and you know this is a man who'd rather exercise by taking a handful of pills and twitching for six hours than by going for a jog with Mick Jagger.

Iggy looked healthy, he was touring and selling loads of records. The punks had adopted him as the 'Godfather' of the movement – every band you went to see in London at the time seemed to have either a Stooges number, a Velvet Underground cover or a New York Dolls rarity in the set-list (on a bad night, they'd have all three). He'd been dragged away from the brink, to some extent, by the intervention

of **David Bowie**, who'd produced both THE IDIOT and LUST FOR LIFE, and Iggy had in turn appeared on one of Bowie's albums, LOW.

Musically, both records saw Bowie very much in the forefront, helping Iggy reinvent himself away from The Stooges' punk-metal tendencies, moving on THE IDIOT to a kind of electro-sleaze. LUST FOR LIFE saw a more confident Iggy rocking through a set of ironic Bowie R&B. Needless to say, both are essential items, as is Iggy's Bowie-enhanced live album of the period, TV EYE (1978), recorded with **Fred 'Sonic' Smith** (ex-MC5) on guitar.

Despite the Bowie connection, and despite working with a number of other 'big names', Iggy didn't do much of any quality over the next few years, although he continued to record – NEW VALUES (1979), SOLDIER (1980), PARTY (1981), ZOMBIE BIRDHOUSE (1982) – and tour. He didn't finally clean up his act, either, until the mid-80s, when he joined up again with Bowie to record BLAH, BLAH, BLAH (1986). On the album Iggy did a blistering cover of a 50s rock'n'roller "Real Wild Child", strong enough to be released as a single, which took him into the charts, and to #10 in the UK.

Subsequent recordings – INSTINCT (1988, with **Steve Jones** from Sex Pistols) BRICK BY BRICK (1990, with **Slash** and **Duff McKagan** of Guns N' Roses), AMERICAN CAESAR (1993), NAUGHTY LITTLE DOGGIE (1996) – were patchy, with only one or two tracks per album being real cursing-in-the-teeth-of-a-gale Iggy. A swift cash-in of a compilation, BEST OF … LIVE (1996), was recorded at various shows on a US tour and was released just in time to spoil Virgin's damn-good-by-comparison NUDE AND RUDE compilation (1997). Though the Virgin collection peters out towards the end, the MCA live set was badly recorded and no amount of amplifier-tweaking could restore the guts to it.

However, the man then branched out from being just your everyday rock'n'roll hero into acting, appearing as various amoral good guys in *Cry Baby* with Johnny Depp (would you lie on the roof of a speeding car with Iggy at the wheel?), *The Color Of Money*, the atrocious *Sid And Nancy*, and *Dead Man*, again alongside Depp. Iggy was actually in danger of growing into some kind of counterculture elder statesman: he charted with "Did You Evah", recorded with Debbie Harry for the AIDS benefit album RED HOT AND BLUE, and he even contributed a literate and elegant foreword to Nick Kent's book, *The Dark Stuff*. A new album in 2001, BEAT 'EM UP, lacked the charisma of his finest work, but few could accuse him of mellowing his style.

Iggy, live and in the right mood, is an unbeatable, bad-behaviour night out. The best of his live albums include the splendid LIVE AT THE HIPPODROME PARIS 1977 set, which captured the master on tour in full-confessional, birth-of-punk-rock style, and LIVE ON THE KING BISCUIT FLOWER HOUR – a recording from 1988 in which he promises 'We're just gonna rock it straight, no bullshit'.

The Idiot (1977; RCA).
Crisp Bowie production and a collection of vintage, death's-door Iggy. Classics include "Nightclubbing", "China Girl" and that Saturday-night songs-to-get-ready-to favourite, "Fun Time".

Lust For Life (1977; RCA).
Is this the same man? Every song is a winner on this album. There's a good level of sleaze and menace ("Turn Blue" deals with the thoughts running through the mind of a junkie who's just taken a serious overdose), but overall it's a happy album, and probably his best non-Stooge work.

TV Eye (1978; RCA).
Most recordings of Iggy live are fairly low-quality. This, however, is a magnificently exciting celebration of a rock-'n'roll legend, truly fucked-up on drugs. Aided by the keyboards and wailing of Bowie, this is a must-have recording.

Kill City (1992; Bomp!).
Bomp! are keepers of the flame and publishers of a series of recordings called 'The Iguana Chronicles'. This album, recorded in the aftermath of the Stooges 'Raw Power' sessions, is wildman Iggy at his uncaring best. A mix of then-unreleased Stooges numbers performed by Iggy and fellow Stooge, James Williamson, friends Tony and Hunt Sales, together with Gayna from the Count Dracula Society on backing vocals.

American Caesar (1993; Virgin).
Certainly not his hardest collection, but possibly one of Iggy's most eclectic and, even, experimental.

Beat 'Em Up (2001; Virgin).
Not since RAW POWER has Iggy sounded as aggressive and on fire than on his first release of the 21st century. While not as consistent as his 'classic' albums, the set's first three dense rockers are worth the price of admission alone – "Mask", "L.O.S.T.", and "Howl".

Al Spicer

THE POP GROUP

Formed Bristol, England, 1977; disbanded 1981.

"Nothing is impossible when you're living on the brink – show the world... " From Y

The Pop Group were formed, like hundreds of other acts, after the first Sex Pistols gigs. Being based in Bristol rather than London, however, and spending as much time talking conspiracy theory at the local weird bookshop as Iggy Pop with other punk boys, they were from the start a rather unusual proposition. As much funk as punk, and employing a dub-like sound that anticipated trip-hop by the best part of two decades, they have become, in muso circles at least, a bit of a legend.

The band were formed by **Mark Stewart** (vocals), **Gareth Sager** (ancient Burns guitar) and **Bruce Smith** (drums), later supplemented by **Simon Underwood** (bass) and **Jon Waddington** (guitar). All were in their teens, and Stewart still at school, when they played their first gig, running through easy-chord numbers such as Marc Bolan's "Solid Gold, Easy Action" and the Modern Lovers' "Pablo Picasso". Group influences ranged far more freely than on the London punk scene: all of the band loved Miles Davis, and members were into Can, free jazz and reggae (Bristol's West Indian

community had its own scene). It was quite a boiling pot.

Unlike most of their contemporaries, The Pop Group resisted knocking out a DIY single, or gigging very often, preferring to build up an original set, which they unveiled at 'events'. Their best-known song, for example, "(She Is) Beyond Good And Evil" was played, over and over one evening in an old church to invited guests, before being issued as a single in early 1979. It was a stunning debut: an anti-Thatcher rant (in the year in which she took power), lyrics nodding at Nietzsche, recorded with a 'live' reggae sound.

It preceded by a couple of months the band's first album, Y (1979). After a false start with John Cale, this was recorded by Dennis Bovell (then leading reggae band Matumbi), and turned out a maelstrom of noise and ideas. Stewart's vocals – spoken or screamed rather than sung – cut across savage guitars, saxes and echoing pianos, while empty spaces were penetrated by biting noise. It was free rock, in a free-jazz kind of way, and it was angry and political, with Stewart shrieking like some disregarded prophet in a Greek drama ('Words That Make The Air Bleed' promised the adverts). The lyric sheet, too, was collaged with images of violent injustice, and the cover depicted New Guinea ceremonials. All good primal stuff, and if there wasn't too much to hum along to, songs like "Time" ('You – We – Are Time... ') got across the excitement and dub feel of the group live, and amid the frantic sounds were odd patches of beauty.

Still, it almost certainly wasn't what Warners, who had underwritten the album with Jake Rivera's label Radar, were expecting, and if The Pop Group had any visions of ambivalence rather than irony in their name, then they weren't making the moves. The next year's album, FOR HOW MUCH LONGER DO WE TOLERATE MASS MURDER (1980), for more simpatico Rough Trade, wore its heart even more openly on its sleeve, with Stewart's polemics buried beneath yet heavier sheets of noise, and a collaboration with The Last Poets on "One Among Many".

It was on the fascinating side of unlistenable, and reflected a group veering off in diverse musical (and political) directions.

After a last London appearance, on the back of a truck at a Campaign against Nuclear Disarmament rally in Trafalgar Square, Stewart directed the troops down Whitehall towards the Ministry of Defence. The band was seen no more.

Stewart continued merging politics and reggae with Adrian Sherwood's **On-U Sound**, a great dub version of "Jerusalem" (Blake's proto-socialist anthem) presaging a series of paranoiac albums: AS THE VENEER OF DEMOCRACY STARTS TO FADE, SURVIVAL and, most recently, CONTROL DATA (1996). Sager went off to form **RIP, RIG & PANIC**, with rather more tuneful vocalist Neneh Cherry. Underwood, who had left after Y, found an outlet for his love of James Brown with **Pigbag**, best remembered for the joyous horns-and-bass funk of their UK #3 single, "Papa"s Got A Brand New Pigbag"; these days he works in film. Smith, who was already doubling up on drums for The Slits, went on to work with, among others, Björk, Soul II Soul, and Public Image Ltd. (on HAPPY? and NINE). Waddington formed soul-funk outfit **Maximum Joy**, and is now back in Bristol with punk-funk trio **Normal 2000**.

Needless to say, it was the germs of all these diverse experiments that had made The Pop Group, at their best, hugely original and compelling.

⊙ **Y** (1979; Radar).
Rereleased on CD in 1996, this got the plaudits second time round for its seminal dub-funk-punk, echoed in the 90s on Bristol output from Tricky (an old flatmate of Stewart's) and Massive Attack. The CD reissue includes the single, "(She Is) Beyond Good And Evil".

⊙ **We Are All Prostitutes** (1998; Radar).
Absolutely essential compilation of album tracks and singles.

Mark Ellingham

POP WILL EAT ITSELF

Formed Stourbridge, England, 1986; split 1996.

Named after an *NME* article on the crew that would spawn Carter USM, **Pop Will Eat Itself** began gigging around the Black Country in 1986. **Clint Mansell** (vocals/guitar), **Adam Mole** (guitar/keyboards), **Graham Crabb** (drums) and **Richard March** (bass) soon released a self-produced EP entitled POPPIES SAY GRRR! (1986), which they packaged in brown paper bags and sold for a quid. In keeping with the independent ethic, they signed a deal with Birmingham-based indie label Chapter 22, who put out several PWEI singles and their debut album BOX FRENZY (1987), featuring the glorious "There Is No Love Between Us Anymore".

These early releases were jingly-jangly indie music similar to that of the band's Stourbridge contemporaries The Wonder Stuff, whose frontman Miles Hunt started out in the same outfit as Clint Mansell.

But while The Wonder Stuff adhered closely to the same formula throughout their career, the Poppies swiftly ventured into unknown territory. Firstly, they discovered sampling, taking chunks from sources such as James Brown and Iggy Pop. Then drummer Graham Crabb abandoned his kit to meet up with Clint centre stage, and for the next five years a machine did all the stick work. Coining the term 'grebo', they became known as something of a rock–rap–pop crossover.

The band soon waved goodbye to the indie charts by joining the major world of RCA, with whom they were to have a less than beautiful relationship for the following three years. Hits came in the form of "Def Con One" (1988), which has left many a student singing about a popular *McDonald's* meal choice, and "Can U Dig It?" (1989). They got kicked off a Public Enemy tour for not satisfying the hardcore rap contingent; they hooked up with Italian porn-star-turned-MP La Cicciolina to record an alternative World Cup anthem; and they kept the music-press gossip columns busy with sordid tales of groupiedom.

On top of all that, PWEI managed to make three groundbreaking albums during their time at RCA: THIS IS THE DAY, THIS IS THE HOUR, THIS IS THIS (1989); THE PWEI CURE FOR SANITY (1990), moving into dance terrain with vocals from one **Sylvia Tella**; and THE LOOKS OR THE LIFESTYLE (1992), for which the band traded in their drum machine in favour of **Fuzz**, a real drummer.

In 1993 the band had their biggest ever hit (a UK #9) with "Get The Girl Kill The Baddies" and were simultaneously dropped by RCA. They returned to the indie fraternity when a deal was struck with the Infectious label run by Korda Marshall, who as an A&R man had originally signed them to RCA. This seemed like a good time for the Poppies to change track again, jumping on the political bandwagon of the likes of Rage Against The Machine. In 1994 they released a collaboration with Fun-Da-Mental, the antifascist anthem "Ich Bin Ein Ausländer" ('I Am A Foreigner'), and headlined a Lollapalooza-style event featuring such diverse talents as Trans-Global Underground and Credit To The Nation.

Perhaps due to the influence of Nine Inch Nails, with whom PWEI toured stateside in 1994 (NIN frontman Trent Reznor also signed the band to his Nothing label in the US), their fifth studio album, DOS DEDOS MIS AMIGOS (1994), had something of an industrial sound, a far cry from the days of "Sweet Sweet Pie". A remix album, TWO FINGERS MY FRIEND, was released the following year.

But that was to be the end; though Pop Will Eat Itself had weathered the changes in pop culture, often with dignity, sometimes without, they finally hung up their grebo hats in 1996.

⊙ **Box Frenzy** (1987; Chapter 22).
This debut album is a glorious grebo-fest, nostalgia trip into the Poppies' meaningful past – from the decidedly non-PC "Beaver Patrol" to the anthemic "Grebo Guru".

- **The PWEI Cure For Sanity** (1990; RCA).
  Gems such as "92°F (The 3rd Degree)", "Dance Of The Mad" and the notorious "Cicciolina" see the Poppies delving into dance.

- **16 Different Flavours Of Hell** (1993; RCA).
  A cream-of-the-crop compilation from the RCA years, including "Def Con One", "Can U Dig It" and "Get The Girl Kill The Baddies".

- **PWEI Product 1986-1994: The Pop Will Eat Itself Anthology** (2002; Castle).
  A mammoth double-CD collection that clearly shows how PWEI managed to become torchbearers for the grebo movement.

Lara Kilner

POPOL VUH

Formed Munich, Germany, 1969; largely inactive since 1983.

"It is truly unexpected and magical music." Julian Cope

The late-60s interest in alternative lifestyles and religions was reflected in the almost simultaneous appearance, in two different European countries, of two bands with the name of **Popol Vuh**, the Mayan sacred book. The Norwegian variant lasted only a couple of years and albums, but the German band, with whom we concern ourselves here, rolled through more than thirty albums – compilations included. Although a (Kraut)rock band, performing and recording, they are best known for their soundtrack work for the remarkable Werner Herzog, for whom they have scored the films *Heart of Glass*, *Aguirre (Wrath Of God)* and *Fitzcarraldo*.

Popol Vuh was founded in 1969 by **Florian Fricke** (Moog/keyboards), with a personnel fluctuating to suit specific projects. On their first outing, AFFENSTUNDE (1970), with **Frank Fiedler** (synthesizer) and **Holger Trülzsch** (ex-Embryo; percussion), Fricke gave rein to his interest in Mayan religion, though the record gained most attention for his pioneering use of the Moog, which he used to generate the rhythms. It was, however, as Julian Cope observes in *Krautrocksampler*, 'merely a shadow compared to the impending' IN DEN GARTEN PHARADS (1972), an amazing mix of ambient electronics and natural percussion that sounded not unlike Brian Eno's or Harold Budd's work fifteen years on. 'One of the great meditational holy works', Cope concludes.

In 1972, Fricke converted to Christianity and Hinduism, and rejected electronics in favour of ethnic and acoustic instrumentation, employing guitars, oboe, tamboura and a Japanese soprano vocalist, **Djong Yun**, on the gorgeous meditative HOSIANNA MANTRA (1973). He then struck up a partnership with former **AMON DÜÜL II** drummer **Daniel Fichelscher**, which was to last through the decade. They debuted with SELIGPREISUNG (1973), on which Fricke sung the Song Of Solomon, against a guitar and percussion backdrop from Fichelscher. They then created their masterpiece in EINJAGER UND SIEBENJAGER (1975), a unique album of airy guitar, ethereal piano and Dyong Yun's melancholic voice.

As the 70s progressed, Popol Vuh developed their interest in ethnic instruments, employing Al Groer (sitar) and a variety of tabla and tamboura percussionists, on what was dubbed 'raga rock'. Among a string of albums, HERZ AUS GLAS (an elaboration of the *Heart of Glass* soundtrack; 1977) and DIE NACHT DER SEELE – TANTRIC SONGS (1979) stand out. On the latter, choral music was fused with Indian tantras, with Fricke's keyboards an almost inaudible backdrop. It featured vocals from Djong Yun and from **Renate Knaup** of Amon Düül II.

Popol Vuh wound down in the early 80s, after AGAPE AGAPE (1983), an astonishing variety of sound and styles, ranging through ritualistic chanting to Eno/Cluster-style ambient meditations. The group reunited for SPIRIT OF PEACE (1985) and again for SHEPHERD'S SYMPHONY (1997), but both these seemed almost afterthoughts.

Still, Popol Vuh's legacy is as individual, eclectic and hypnotic as any in the Krautrock canon, and they were early pioneers in the fusion of world music and rock.

- **In Den Garten Pharads/Aguirre** (1972; Celestial Harmonies).
  A double-CD remix of two early albums, highlighted by the (on vinyl, side-long) introspective piano piece "Spirit Of Peace'.

- **Einjager Und Siebenjager** (1975; Spalax).
  This is a classic, reissued on CD by French label Spalax. Infinitely evocative.

- **Agape Agape** (1983; Spalax).
  This was Popol Vuh's last great album – and probably their most accessible.

Paul O'Brien

PORNO FOR PYROS

Formed Los Angeles, 1992; split 1997.

When **Perry Farrell** split his group, **JANE'S ADDICTION**, in 1991, it seemed to be reaching its commercial and creative peak, after a hugely successful American tour. It gained him exalted status in the rock'n'roll pantheon, but also bemusement from critics and fans alike. As he pooled his energies into the acclaimed Lollapalooza festival tour, a lot of eyes were on his formation of a new group. This turned out to be **Porno For Pyros**, for which he retained Jane's Addiction drummer **Stephen Perkins**, and enlisted guitarist **Peter DiStefano** and bassist **Martyn Le Noble** (the latter had previously played in Thelonious Monster).

If many anticipated that Farrell's obtuse songs would miss the input of Jane's guitarist David Navarro, the new band's debut album, PORNO FOR PYROS (1993), blew such doubts away. The songs rocked in the way that Jane's Addiction had – and with a renewed creative urgency and experimentation. The terrain was similar – blues, molten metal, hypnotic and unpredictable rhythms, jagged guitar lines, and high-pitched vocal improvisations – but the delivery was more in-your-face, ploughing a primal furrow. 'I've got the devil in me', proclaimed Farrell at the start, before turning his attention to carnal knowledge ("Orgasm"), spirituality ("Sadness"), and sex and politics ("Black Girlfriend").

Although the album received plaudits and high chart placings (#3 in the US, #13 in the UK), Farrell's involvement with Lollapalooza – and certain recreational substances – hindered further Pyro projects. It was not until summer 1996 that the band's second album, GOOD GOD'S URGE, emerged. This saw Farrell reunited with **David Navarro** (by now with the **RED HOT CHILI PEPPERS**) on "Freeway", and, overall, returning to the brooding, dark, drugged atmospherics of Jane's Addiction days – throwing into the cocktail lashings of funk, metal, punk rock and folksy hippie-isms. The tone, however, was calmer, sweeter, mellower, throwing in exotic down-tempo psychedelia ("100 Ways") while introducing tender lyrics and acoustic harmonies on the love song "Kimberly Austin".

Soon after that Porno For Pyros was put on hold indefinitely as Farrell decided to concentrate on his solo career; REV (1999) pulled together rarities from both the Jane's Addiction and Porno For Pyros vaults, while including some new solo songs. SONG YET TO BE SUNG (2001) indicated that, if anything, Farrell was not about to compromise his own artistic values for the sake of commercialism. And then, of course, we have the Jane's Addiction reunion to keep the fires of hope burning.

⊙ **Porno For Pyros** (1993; Warners).
An indication of where Jane's Addiction might have gone next. Jane's fans won't feel let down, but many new converts will be drawn in by the back-to-basics primitivism that lies at its bleeding heart.

Perry Farrell – calmer, sweeter, mellower . . .

⊙ **Good God's Urge** (1996; Warners).
Farrell steers his way out of the downward spiral of drugs and grunge, crafting a swirl of guitar rock and funk-metal that seems positively serene by comparison with his earlier outings.

Michael Sumsion

PORTISHEAD

Formed Bristol, England, 1991.

If anyone ever writes a history of auspicious first albums, **Portishead**'s DUMMY will deserve prime billing. One of the most breathtaking debuts of the 90s, DUMMY managed to combine impeccable avant-garde credentials with populist appeal, effortlessly taking its innovation to the top of the UK charts and, without so much as a tour, making inroads in the US.

Portishead are based around the core partnership of **Geoff Barrow** (programmer) and **Beth Gibbons** (singer/lyricist), who got together after meeting on a local training scheme in 1991. Barrow had been working as a studio tape-op in Bristol with the likes of Massive Attack and Neneh Cherry, and was looking to set up his own music production company, while Gibbons had been singing with various pub bands in the area. They took the name Portishead from Geoff's home town, a small port on the Bristol Channel – the down-at-heel tone of the seaside resort being very appropriate to the sounds they were to produce.

After a period of writing and recording, the band first came to public notice in June 1994 when they released a short film called *To Kill A Dead Man*, a pastiche of 60s spy movies. This was followed over the next two months with two singles, "Numb" and "Sour Times", both taken from the album that appeared in August.

The singles and album blended a range of disparate musical ingredients in the creation of a singularly atmospheric soundscape. DUMMY combined loping hip-hop beats, old-school scratching of a type not fashionable since the mid 80s, lush swaths of ambient sound, the retro-cheese of outdated instruments like the Hammond organ, **Adrian Utley**'s reverb-drenched guitar twang, and distorted and manipulated samples from old soul records. Somehow Barrow managed to make these elements fit together, and provide the eerie accompaniment to Beth Gibbons' deliciously melancholic torch-song vocals. Film soundtracks were a key reference, with many critics comparing them to film noir, though, as *To Kill A Dead Man* had indicated, the sleazy allure of 60s thrillers like *The Ipcress File* was more appropriate.

Portishead's combination of ambient and hip-hop aesthetics led them, along with fellow Bristolians Massive Attack and Tricky, to be categorized by the press under the term 'trip-hop'. Despite half-hearted protests by the artists, there were some obvious affinities between these acts, who had all worked with each other at various times.

Portishead's Beth Gibbons keeping half an eye on the time

DUMMY topped numerous 1994 polls, and in August 1995 the album's achievement was rounded off when it was awarded the UK Mercury Music Prize for *Album of the Year*, holding off competition from the Britpop mafia. Following this, the peak of their success, Barrow and Gibbons went into hibernation, while a host of lesser acts sprung up in their wake, happy to ape the style without challenging their innovation.

The ironic result of Portishead's massive impact was that their once startling sound, now subject to lazy dilution by others, began to seem distinctly clichéd. The problem this presented for the band was that producing the 'difficult second album' was made even harder by the need to avoid coming across like one of their own imitators. By all accounts the delivery of this album was an extremely torturous one, and at one point a whole set's worth of work was scrapped by Barrow in a fit of self-doubt.

The eventual solution to the problem, as heard on PORTISHEAD (1997), came not through branching out into new directions, but rather in producing something the same but more so, a bleaker-than-thou extra-strength concentration of their essential elements. Some critics complained that PORTISHEAD sounded too much like its predecessor, but for many it constituted a very successful reminder of their original brilliance. There was no touring and little promotion for the album, but it was launched with a one-off live show in New York, complete with orchestral accompaniment, which was recorded and later released as a well-received live album, PNYC (1998).

There has been no real news from the Portishead camp since then, though Gibbons did pop up in 2002 with **Paul 'Rustin' Man' Webb** (formally of **TALK TALK**) for the album OUT OF SEASON. Beth's voice was, as ever, beautiful and tragic, though the musical accompaniment was a little too weak to offer anything to make up for the lack of a new Portishead product. Hopefully soon Barrow, Gibbons, et al will figure out how to follow that difficult second album with an even more difficult third album.

⊙ **Dummy** (1994; Go! Beat).
Melancholia has rarely sounded so sweet, emotional desolation rarely so blissful. A spellbinding blues for the post-modern age.

⊙ **Portishead** (1997; Polygram).
Gibbons' voice much improved by a few years of angst on the road, dealing with fame and what sounds like a serious interest in Scotch and cigars. The music, as ever, cinematic and magnificent.

⊙ **PNYC** (1998; Polygram).
A disc that brilliantly captures Portishead's live vibe. Gibbons sings her heart out, the scratches fly, and the whole thing is drenched in some serious string arrangements.

Ian Canadine

PREFAB SPROUT

Formed Newcastle-upon-Tyne, England, 1982.

S inger and songwriter **Paddy MacAloon** spent much of the 70s daydreaming of pop stardom, and invented imaginary band names to perform imaginary concept albums. One such name was

Prefab Sprout, and it was this identity that he adopted for the band formed with his brother **Martin** (guitar) and vocalist **Wendy Smith**. Signing in 1983 to Newcastle indie label Kitchenware Records, their early singles "Lions In My Own Garden" and "Don't Sing", and their debut album, SWOON (1984), found them compared to the likes of Aztec Camera – tuneful, wistful pop described by some critics as 'too good for the charts'.

If music journos were impressed by SWOON, their reactions to album number two were even more eulogistic, and STEVE MCQUEEN (1985 – retitled TWO WHEELS GOOD on its US release, after a complaint from the late actor's family) remains one of the best-ever LPs dealing with unrequited love. By now, the trio had been augmented to a quartet with the appointment of **Neil Conti** (drums). The album marked the beginning of a long-running working relationship between the band and its producer **Thomas Dolby**, who applied a glossy 80s veneer to a sterling set of songs, notably "When Love Breaks Down", which finally reached the UK Top 30 on its second reissue, in the autumn of 1985.

MacAloon was a hugely prolific songwriter at this time, with entire albums apparently ready in the vaults. The Sprouts were planning to release another album, mere months after STEVE MCQUEEN, which had been made in a matter of a few weeks. They aimed to sell copies at the venues on a rare British tour in Autumn 1985, but at the last minute, these plans were thwarted; CBS, their new record distributors, felt there would be too much new Prefab Sprout product on the market at once. The album was eventually titled PROTEST SONGS, but it was 1989 before it was released, amid minimal publicity.

By then, the band had reached #5 in the UK album charts (they never made it in the US) with FROM LANGLEY PARK TO MEMPHIS (1988), an affectionate swipe at American culture, the myth of celebrity and being down-and-out. While some of the musical content verged on MOR, the lyrics were as sharp as ever – 'Some things hurt more, much more, than cars and girls', wrote MacAloon of Springsteen. The album's opening track, "The King Of Rock'N'Roll", even gave them a proper UK hit single: #7 in the summer of 1988, thanks largely to a deliberately nonsensical refrain ('Hot dog/Jumping frog/Alberquerque'). Co-produced by Dolby and Jon Kelly, the album also featured cameos from The Who's Pete Townshend on "The Golden Calf", gospel group The Andrae Crouch Singers on "Venus Of The Soup Kitchen", and even Stevie Wonder, with a distinctive harmonica solo on "Nightingales".

MacAloon's interest in Americana continued unabated on JORDAN: THE COMEBACK (1990), notably with a quartet of songs about the life, career and demise of Elvis Presley. Other subjects ranged from loss of innocence to acid house, and from doo-wop to God. A little too long for one sitting, it nevertheless contained some of MacAloon's most addictive songs to date.

As a group, save for a 'best of' compilation, A LIFE OF SURPRISES (1992), Prefab Sprout remained silent for a time, with no new product scheduled. However, MacAloon's songwriting was said to be as prolific as ever. In an interview with the *NME* in March 1995, he spoke of a concept album about Earth as just one of many projects he was preparing. In the event, it was 1997 before the next Sprout product appeared in the stores.

ANDROMEDA HEIGHTS (1997) contained further exquisite pop gems from McAloon's reportedly huge collection of unreleased songs. It returned Prefab Sprout to the upper end of the LP chart, although long-term fans began to wonder if the much-rumoured concept albums were merely legend – for them, ANDROMEDA HEIGHTS served merely to stimulate rather than sate the appetite for more. McAloon's songwriting credentials cannot be questioned, and Jimmy Nail's best-selling 1994 album CROCODILE SHOES contained no less than three of his compositions, including the hit "Cowboy Dreams". The song cropped up again on the Prefab Sprout album THE GUNMAN AND OTHER STORIES (2001), a gorgeous collection of country-tinged ballads and meandering nods to Americana.

(•) **Steve McQueen/Two Wheels Good** (1985; Kitchenware/ Columbia).
It takes a few hearings, but once you get the hooks, you're hooked. From the surprisingly aggressive countrified opener, "Faron Young", to "When The Angels", one of the few Marvin Gaye tributes worth saving, STEVE MCQUEEN is quite simply one of the best albums of the 80s.

(•) **Jordan: The Comeback** (1990; Kitchenware/Columbia).
Nineteen tracks provide the broadest sweep of MacAloon's pop vision yet. It failed to yield any hits, and was a bigger critical than commercial attraction, but it still suggested an incredible potential for MacAloon in the 90s.

(•) **A Life Of Surprises** (1992; Kitchenware/Columbia).
A useful 'best of' as opposed to 'greatest hits' (that would have been a very short album indeed). Despite just one track from SWOON ("Cruel"), it otherwise features all the album cuts you'd expect, plus the hit singles "The Sound Of Crying" and "If You Don't Love Me".

Justin Lewis

THE PRESIDENTS OF THE USA

Formed Seattle, 1993; split December 1997.

They may come from the home town of grunge, but **The Presidents Of The United States Of America** stand at a distant remove from its spirit. Their trademarks are total daftness, riff-heavy rock with a strong punk influence, and extremely short songs: their debut single "Lump", for instance, was just over two minutes, while "Kick Out The Jams" (not one of their own) clocked in at a concise one minute twenty-four seconds.

Chris Ballew (two-string 'basitar') and **Dave Dederer** (three-string 'guitbass') went to the same junior high and high school, but only started writing songs together after leaving college in 1985. Dederer and **Jason Finn** (drums) first met in the toilets at a rock concert in 1984. The band's name was suggested by Ballew: they had previously been known as The Dynamic Duo, then Pure Frosting, and then The Low-Fi's, before settling for The Presidents Of The USA.

The Presidents recorded a ten-song demo in 1994, to sell at gigs. The limited run of 500 copies sold out after five shows, and in the autumn of 1994 they released their debut album THE PRESIDENTS OF THE UNITED STATES OF AMERICA on the Pop Llama label. Turning down Madonna's advances (she had wanted to sign them to her Maverick label), they then signed to Columbia, who remastered the disc before giving it a mainstream release.

It sold two million copies in the US – adding a touch of irony to one of the tracks, "We Are Not Going To Make It", and before long Weird Al Yankovic was paying them the respect of a lampoon – turning their US and UK hit "Lump" into a condensed history of Forrest Gump.

In the two years that passed before THE PRESIDENTS OF THE UNITED STATES OF AMERICA II (1997) hit the shops, the enthusiasm of both the music press and the public cooled, and the album suffered from weak reviews and poor sales. Bellew's lyrics were just as flaky, the music was just as quirky but the joke seemed to have fallen flat. In an admirable, though rare, case of rock band reading the writing on the wall, they went back to their day jobs at the end of 1997. A posthumous compilation of sweepings from the cutting-room floor, PURE FROSTING (1998), was their epitaph.

⊙ **The Presidents Of The United States Of America** (1995; Columbia).
The origins of tinned fruit; bizarre forms of animal communication; little cars ... Is this what The Joker meant when he said 'I don't suffer from mental illness, I enjoy it'? Judge for yourself – just don't try to make sense out of The Presidents' inspired silliness.

George Luke

ELVIS PRESLEY

Born Tupelo, Mississippi, January 8, 1935; died August 16, 1977.

"Without Elvis, none of us could have made it." Buddy Holly

Medieval theologians used to debate how many angels could dance on the head of a pin; equally profitably, musicologists have argued about the first rock'n'roll record. Most would agree that for all but the hippest of rednecks, rock started when **Elvis Presley** released "Heartbreak Hotel" in 1956. No record before or since has had comparable impact. In the eyes of the world, Elvis appeared fully formed with that record, a supremely self-confident, sexually charged kid who somehow embodied a spirit of change that was sweeping America. The only precedent was provided by the recently deceased James Dean, but *he* had been forced to play

Hollywood's game – Elvis had the advantage of writing his own rules.

And his rules in the early days were basically to do nothing: he was aware he had a unique voice, but he didn't play concerts, he didn't try to form or join a band, he just registered his existence with a local label, and waited for the revolution to come calling. Fortunately for everyone, that label was Sun, whose 31-year-old owner, Sam Phillips, was obsessed with finding new music. Under his direction, Elvis was put in touch with guitarist **Scotty Moore** and bassist **Bill Black**, both of whom had been kicking their heels on routine sessions for some time. Elvis already knew he was a star (Moore recalled that at their first meeting he was 'wearing a pink suit and white shoes and a ducktail') and, given the time to mess around in the studio, his inspiration pushed Moore and Black to new heights of experimentation.

Five singles were issued on Sun, mutating hillbilly into rock'n'roll, a wild alchemical mix of the disparate strands of American popular music. Elvis loved country, blues, gospel, doo-wop and Vegas crooning in equal measure, and threw it all together with reckless abandon. Even today the excitement of "That's All Right", the stuttering hiccups of "Baby Let's Play House", the sheer power of "Mystery Train" and, particularly, the unearthly weird wailing of "Blue Moon" have a raw beauty that is beyond compare.

The last single on Sun, "I Forgot To Remember To Forget", was his first national hit, making #1 in the country charts in 1955. By the end of that year Presley's new manager, **Colonel Tom Parker**, had signed his boy to RCA for $35,000, the biggest advance then known.

Parker's involvement has always been controversial. A fairground hustler with little discernible interest in music, whose previous career high point had been to exhibit dancing chickens (they danced on electric mesh), he seemed to see Elvis as another sideshow property. His business acumen, however, was beyond question: he knew that Elvis could hit a mass audience, and he did everything he could to ensure that it happened, even down to paying girls to scream during the early concerts.

In January 1956 Elvis recorded "Heartbreak Hotel", an angst-racked tale rendered more painful by Elvis's slurred delivery and the eerie, sparse backing. Smashing every category, it made the pop, country and R&B charts (#1 in the first two, #2 in the third) and inaugurated the rock age. The previous year had seen hits by Bill Haley, Little Richard, Chuck Berry and Fats Domino, but "Heartbreak Hotel" was different: Elvis was the first white man to approach a microphone with such an explicit fuck-me attitude, and the first to present rock'n'roll not as a dance party but as the soundtrack of alienated youth. The sound quality – appalling even at the time – has dated the record, but it still smoulders with the frustration of teen sexuality.

The first sessions for RCA – which produced another massive hit in his bellicose version of "Blue

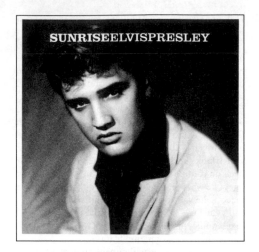

SUNRISEELVISPRESLEY

Suede Shoes" – were a joyous affirmation of everything Elvis had promised at Sun. With the line-up augmented by **D. J. Fontana** (drums) and **Shorty Long** (piano), this was probably the greatest rock-'n'roll band ever.

It wasn't to last. By the end of 1956 Elvis had effectively given up genuine rock'n'roll: with a few exceptions (particularly Leiber and Stoller's compositions such as "Jailhouse Rock" and "King Creole"), very little of the next decade was of value. There were some strong pop songs amidst the easy-listening ballads, but the increasingly bland instrumentation and the irritating male backing vocals by **The Jordanaires** made Elvis lazy. His potential was seldom realized, because Elvis – who never wrote a song in his life – had very little idea what to do with his talent. He liked so many different styles that he copied whomever he heard; successful beyond his wildest dreams, he didn't have to try. So he didn't.

And though Presley's 1957–67 era was one of unrelenting hits over the whole world, it was of little musical significance compared to what else was happenning at the time – the likes of Buddy Holly, The Beatles and Bob Dylan soon made him seem redundant. The most famous records date from this period – "Hound Dog", "Love Me Tender", "Can't Help Falling In Love" and the other stalwarts of oldie radio programming – but nowadays they are unlikely to excite anyone who wasn't there at the time.

The same is even more true of his thirty-odd movies, not a single one of which justifies its existence. The best were (again) *Jailhouse Rock* and *King Creole*, but only for their music, not as cinema: next to Elvis, Madonna looks like a method actor.

The definitive break came in March 1958 when he was drafted into the US Army, to spend two years on a PR promotion for Uncle Sam. John Lennon used to claim that his appearance in army uniform, shorn of his sideburns, marked the death of rock-'n'roll, but in reality Elvis had abandoned the rebelliousness of his youth much earlier. He returned as a sergeant two years later, made a single TV appearance and decamped seemingly forever for

Hollywood and irrelevance. After the momentary glory of the ELVIS IS BACK sessions of 1960, Presley became an irrelevance. There were to be no more live performances until 1968.

In that year, having long since been dismissed as an embarrassment to his legend, he made the most spectacular comeback in pop. A TV special on NBC presented him dressed in black leather, looking every inch the moody rocker he used to be, and delivering devastating versions of the old songs. Now 33, he seemed comfortable with his status as the most successful recording artist in history, and confident enough to play with his role as the king of rock-'n'roll. There had always been a sense of humour in his best work, and its reappearance after years of conveyor-belt movies was more than welcome at a time when rock was getting too serious for its own good.

Concerts followed and, though they were in Las Vegas hotels rather than rock venues, he found a new lease of life. At the beginning of 1969 he released "If I Can Dream", a record that confirmed the rebirth of Elvis. That song missed the Top 10 in both America and Britain, but it was a towering achievement: the voice had matured into a hugely powerful instrument that resonated with authority and conviction, and he easily swamped a full orchestral arrangement with the passion of his delivery. It may not have been full-blown rock'n'roll, but it was an awesome reinvention of himself. The year ended with ELVIS IN MEMPHIS and, suddenly, the king was back.

The following year he stormed the international charts with two of his best ever records, "In The Ghetto" and "Suspicious Minds". By now he was treating middle-of-road balladeering as though he were a gospel singer, fired up with the spirit of optimistic forbearance. Admittedly most of the other records, and particularly the albums, were well below par, and his live audience consisted mainly of blue-rinsed matrons reliving their youth, but he was still a stunning performer who could work a crowd like no other, as the movie *Elvis On Tour* (1972) demonstrated.

And there were still the occasional flashes of genius, in particular the 1972 hit "An American Trilogy", on which he medleyed a Southern rebel anthem, a Yankee marching song and a spiritual. Apparently under the impression that he was capable on his own of uniting a nation torn by generation, race and war, Elvis spoke on this record as the voice of all America in a way that no one else would have dared. Possibly his most powerful post-Sun recording, "An American Trilogy", was a Top 10 hit in Britain but significantly failed to climb beyond #66 in the US; the man whose first major-label recording had coincided with the birth of the civil rights struggle no longer seemed powerful enough to straddle the boundaries as he once had.

In personal terms, the 70s were difficult for Elvis. His renaissance in 1968 had followed his marriage to Priscilla; when she left him in 1973, his life collapsed.

His drug and cheeseburger intake spiralled out of control, and the omnisexual, untamed youth ballooned into the obese, rhinestone-clad figure of fun that prompted The Clash to bracket him with other has-beens: 'No Elvis, Beatles or Rolling Stones in 1977'.

It was an impressive prophecy. Elvis died in August 1977, and was promptly canonized as a saint of the American century. Since his death, his image has been reproduced so often and his life retold so many times that he has effectively ceased to exist as a human being. Posthumous merchandizing has generated more money than he ever did during his lifetime.

The fact that Elvis achieved so much, and that his best work was so damned good, inevitably leaves regrets for the wasted years. Colonel Parker has long been cast as the villain of the piece, responsible for forcing his client into appalling career decisions – an argument that ignores Parker's contribution to giving the world Elvis in the first place. A more likely explanation for the abandonment of rock'n'roll is simply that no other option presented itself: Elvis's career was so unprecedented that no one quite knew what he should do next. Even in 1956 he was talking of rock as being possibly a passing fad, comparable to the Charleston craze of the 20s. And, anyway, his level of success was such that there must have seemed little point in taking any greater risks – a TV special, *Aloha From Hawaii*, pulled an audience of one billion in 1973, and with those kind of ratings you don't worry too much about pleasing critics.

The twentieth anniversary of his death prompted a music-business feeding frenzy of unprecedented proportions, culminating in a two-week Elvis Festival in Memphis. RCA cashed in with a PLATINUM – A LIFE IN MUSIC – an enthusiasts-only collection of 100 tracks, some 77 of them previously only available on bootlegs – and ELVIS AARON PRESLEY (1998), a CD reissue of a bloated eight-album set from 1980. Then in 2002 Elvis's "A Little Less Conversation" was back in the charts, brutally remixed for a new generation by **Junkie XL**.

Elvis – the corporation – has sold over a hundred million dollars' worth of product since his death, and Elvis – the icon – is still regularly being seen in fish'n'chip shops, liquor stores and burger joints around the world. As Warren Zevon stated, 'Elvis is Everywhere'. Ultimately his legacy is the entire phenomenon of rock music. Possibly if he hadn't popularized it, someone else would have, but with (say) Bill Haley at the helm, it would have been an entirely different and less exciting proposition.

⊙ **The Legend Begins** (1992; Magnum Force).
Early live recordings that show his rapid progress. In 1954 he was a nervous youth, unsure how an audience was going to react to his innovations; in 1955 he was confident enough to cover black hits like Chuck Berry's "Maybelline" to an all-white audience on the country show *Louisiana Hayride*; by 1956 he sounded invincible, fronting an awesome wall of noise with the assurance of an old hand.

⊙ **The Sun Sessions** (1987; RCA).
Rock'n'roll's year zero. In the space of 24 songs Elvis,

Scotty and Bill start from scratch and invent the most popular art form of the century. A couple of tracks are dispensable, but most are startlingly fresh.

⊙ **The All Time Greatest Hits** (1987; RCA).
A 45-track double-CD compilation from "Heartbreak Hotel" through to "Way Down", his posthumous #1. From rock to ballads to pop to tear jerkers to kitsch, it demonstrates just how extraordinarily versatile his music was. Some of the records are dreadful ("Return To Sender"), but none of them are dull, or even repetitive. There are literally hundreds of other releases, but this and the Sun sessions cover the ground thoroughly enough for all but the besotted.

Alwyn W. Turner

THE PRETENDERS

Formed London, 1976.

Akron, Ohio-born **Chrissie Hynde** was in at the birth of British punk. She had moved to London in the mid 70s and found work at the *NME*, and at the King's Road clothes shop, SEX, run by Malcolm McLaren and Vivienne Westwood. Thus positioned, she began a personal odyssey through various non-starting groups, including embryonic formations of The Clash, The Damned and Johnny Moped, as well as the tackily named Moors Murderers. However, the punk explosion detonated without her and Hynde's main claim to fame in year zero – 1977 – was a friendship with Sid Vicious, who would offer to marry her when she hit visa problems over her stay. (Needless to say, he got wasted on the proposed day of their nuptials.)

Hynde was already writing songs, however, and early in 1978 she demoed them for the first time, with Fred Berk of the Moped Band on bass and Nigel Pegrum of Steeleye Span on drums. The recordings impressed Dave Hill at Anchor Records, who was in the process of setting up a new label, Real, and Hynde was invited to sort out a proper band. Her first recruit was **Pete Farndon** (bass), who became her lover, and he brought along a friend from Hereford, **James Honeyman-Scott** (guitar), who, legend has it, was initially paid session fees in amphetamines. With **Gary Mackleduff** on drums, the still-unnamed group entered Regent's Park Studio in July 1978 to record five tracks. One of these, a cover of The Kinks' "Stop Your Sobbing", drew the attention of Nick Lowe, who agreed to produce it as their first single. Mackleduff was then ousted in favour of another Hereford native, **Martin Chambers**, and the group fixed on a name – **The Pretenders** – a simple but evocative title which perfectly fitted Hynde's 60s influences.

"Stop Your Sobbing" was released in January 1979 and created an instant furore in the music press, who were all too happy to have songs back again, especially when so unimpeachably cool. The band set off on a tour of small venues and colleges and the press loved them still more; as well they might, for Hynde was proving one of the best new vocalists around, and with impressive self-penned material, to boot. Propulsion towards the big time was furthered when

The Pretenders on the Kenny Everett Show (really), 1979, from left: Chambers, Farndon, Honeyman-Scott and Hynde

the Real label was swallowed up by EMI, and a second single, the resonant ballad "Kid", brokered further positive reviews. It was backed by "Tattooed Love Boys", and Hynde was never more lascivious than when delivering the line 'And you showed me what that hole was for' to her band's rockabilly rush.

The group scaled the top of the UK charts with their next single, "Brass In Pocket", a song Hynde loathed, but bowed to record company pressure to release; it went on to chart at #14 in the US. A few months later came the debut album, PRETENDERS (1980), produced by Chris Thomas, and this too went to #1 in the UK charts, and sold millions of copies worldwide. A major American tour followed – during which Hynde began a relationship with Ray Davies of The Kinks – and on the band's return, sessions were booked for a follow-up album.

The much-delayed PRETENDERS II (1981) emerged to a less rapturous reception, having broken no new ground from the debut, and problems were bubbling under the surface. Farndon was becoming increasingly isolated from the rest of the band through his hard-drug dependency and in June 1982, after the completion of American and Far East dates, he was fired. Just two days later, James Honeyman-Scott was found dead in his London flat, victim of a drug overdose.

Hynde and Chambers returned to the studio to fulfil their obligations, recording "Back On The Chain Gang", with the assistance of guitarist **Billy Bremner** and Big Country bass player **Tony Butler**. Released in October 1982, it was their first

record to break the US Top 10. After it Hynde retired to give birth to a daughter, conceived with Davies, but further black news lay ahead: departed bassist Farndon died from a cocaine and heroin cocktail in April 1983. The first chapter of The Pretenders' existence closed with the double tragedy.

In 1983 a new line-up was inaugurated with **Robbie McIntosh** (guitar) and his friend **Malcolm Foster** (bass). US dates followed, with Hynde accompanied by her baby daughter. Motherhood was also reflected in the title of The Pretenders' third album, LEARNING TO CRAWL (1984). At the end of the tour to promote it – it reached #5 in the US, #11 in the UK – Hynde met and married the next of her famous consorts, Jim Kerr of Simple Minds. Another daughter was born shortly after.

Chrissie's only record release of 1985 was a duet with **UB40**, a hugely successful revision of Sonny And Cher's hippie classic, "I Got You Babe", premiered at Live Aid. The first Pretenders single for two years, "Don't Get Me Wrong", released in September 1986, was later revealed to be a song written for friend John McEnroe. It pushed the band back into the UK Top 10 after an absence of nearly five years.

The advent of the fourth studio album, GET CLOSE (1984), saw Hynde sever most of her remaining links with the past. Long-standing drummer Chambers was out, much to his chagrin, with Haircut 100 drummer **Blair Cunningham** and former James Brown bassist **T. M. Stevens** providing a new rhythm section (though Foster returned for live dates). For the first time, too, producer Chris Thomas was sidestepped – in favour of Bob Clearmountain and Jimmy Iovine. A far stronger album than its predecessor, GET CLOSE announced Hynde's ongoing politicization with the acidic "How Much Did You Get For Your Soul", an attack on artists who associate themselves with multinational products. Its antithesis arrived a few months later when Hynde penned the theme to the new James Bond movie, "If There Was A Man", the final contribution from McIntosh, who wanted to pursue his own career. Hynde managed to recruit **Johnny Marr**, recently departed from The Smiths, for live engagements with U2, which coincided with the release of a highly effective singles retrospective.

In 1988 Hynde's activities were principally political. She led the all-star vegetarian pressure group Reprieve, helped form Ark as an alternative fast-food chain to McDonald's, and lent support to campaigns including the Rain Forest Appeal, the Lynx anti-fur action, and various children's charities. With The Pretenders seemingly on hold, there was also time for a second UB40 collaboration, "Breakfast In Bed".

However, the band was back in the 90s. PACKED! (1990) saw Billy Bremner return as substitute for Marr, who co-wrote one of the stronger tracks, "When Will I See You?" Hynde's vocals, by turns imploring and triumphant, were again superb, but this time stretched over lyrics which lacked the guile of old. 1994's LAST OF THE INDEPENDENTS, which brought Chambers back into the fold, suffered from the same problems but had a little more zest. Both, however, charted respectably in the UK and US, if not with the mega-sales of old.

If The Pretenders seemed to be getting formulaic, ISLE OF VIEW, released at the end of 1995, showed that Hynde could still take risks, and still possessed one of the great voices in rock. The album was essentially 'Hynde – Unplugged', a thrilling acoustic rendezvous with the best of her material, performed with a string quartet in front of an invited audience. Likewise, VIVA EL AMOR (1999) and LOOSE SCREW (2003) proved to be a critical success, and Hynde continued to tour with The Pretenders.

- **Pretenders** (1980; Real).
  In which Honeyman-Scott proves what a superb guitarist he was, dovetailing with Hynde's gripping delivery of material like "Tattooed Love Boys", a witty hard-life rejoinder to the more melancholy "Kid" and "Stop Your Sobbing".

- **Pretenders II** (1981; Real).
  The singles here – "Messages Of Love" and "Talk Of The Town" – are weaker, but "The Adulteress" and "Bad Boys Get Spanked" ooze sexual brinkmanship.

- **The Singles** (1987; Real).
  The Pretenders were a great singles band, and this retrospective collection puts their biggest hit, "Brass In Pocket", in its proper context (ie way down the list). Despite the duff packaging, this is unquestionably The Pretenders album to own.

- **Isle Of View** (1995; WEA).
  Highlights abound on this acoustic set ("Lovers Of Today" is sublimely rendered), revisiting the best of Hynde's songbook. And there's even some pub piano from Damon Albarn on "I Go To Sleep".

Alex Ogg

THE PRETTY THINGS

Formed Kent, England, 1963; disbanded 1976; reformed sporadically.

One of the great hard-luck stories in British rock, **The Pretty Things** were formed at Sidcup Art College in 1963 by vocalist **Phil May** and guitarist **Dick Taylor**. Taylor had been the original bassist with The Rolling Stones, but chose to complete his art-school course before pursuing music, thus giving Bill Wyman a job.

The Pretty Things were cast in the same mould as the early Stones, and worked hard to catch up with Jagger and Jones's growing reputation for outrage: they had longer hair and a trashier name, drank heavier and played harder, dirtier versions of R&B standards, concentrating particularly on Bo Diddley's back catalogue. For a while, it looked as though it was all going to work: signed almost immediately to Fontana, they hit the Top 10 in 1964 with "Don't Bring Me Down", and the following year did the same with their eponymous debut album. This was to be as good as it got.

Subsequent singles and the second album brought diminishing returns and, as the tide of British music began to turn away from R&B, the band struggled against being washed away. The third album, EMOTIONS (1967), saw the group augmented by strings and brass; long overdue for rediscovery, it was a superb example of the mellowing of British beat, and showed the band keeping pace artistically with their old rivals, The Stones. But where the latter's BETWEEN THE BUTTONS spent six months in the charts, EMOTIONS made no impact at all.

Dropped by Fontana, and with a new line-up behind May and Taylor – most notably the addition of **Twink** (later of **THE PINK FAIRIES**) on drums and, uhh, mime – The Pretty Things were reborn in the 'Summer Of Love' as one of the crucial London psychedelic bands. A new contract with Columbia was inaugurated by their finest single, "Defecting Grey", in 1967. Constructed from several fragmentary tunes, with abrupt switches back and forth, "Defecting Grey" blended acid rock with English art-school whimsy in a way that only Syd Barrett's Pink Floyd were capable of matching. Needless to say, it had to settle for the status of cult legend.

A similar fate overtook the 1968 album, SF SORROW. Now acknowledged as the first 'rock opera', the album followed its eponymous hero from birth to death, through love, war, insanity and sickness. Regrettably, it provided an inspiration for Pete Townshend to write TOMMY, but it far excelled that work and remains one of the few concept albums worth hearing.

Taylor left during the recording of SF SORROW, which he had co-written, and Twink moved on soon after. Without Taylor the band got heavier but continued to display a sense of adventure and flexibility that was matched only by the profound indifference of the British and American public. By 1969 the group were reduced to appearing in the Norman Wisdom movie *What's Good For The Goose*. The following year the hard rock PARACHUTE (album of the year in *Rolling Stone*) edged into the UK Top 50, the first hit since the debut, and their last.

The band struggled on for a while, but not even the endorsement of Led Zeppelin (on whose Swansong label a couple of mid-70s albums appeared), and of Bowie (who covered their hits "Rosalyn" and "Don't Bring Me Down" on PIN-UPS) was sufficient to give them a break. In 1976 May finally left his own group, and The Pretty Things effectively came to an end, though members continued to work with each other, and over recent years there have been repeated reunions. 1998 saw three early albums (THE PRETTY THINGS, GET THE PICTURE? and EMOTIONS) reissued on Snapper Records having been remastered for CD, and spruced up with classy sleeve notes. But what the old geezers make of the CD-ROM films tacked on to the music is anyone's guess.

⊙ **SF Sorrow** (1968; Edsel).
Produced by the legendary Norman Smith, this is the first 'rock opera' and still the most convincing. Lacking the bombast and the absurdities of TOMMY, it's actually quite affecting as an account of the trials and tragedy of human life.

⊙ **Singles 1967–1971** (1989; See For Miles).
Listen to this immaculate collection of rock masterpieces and marvel at how not a single one of them troubled the charts.

⊙ **Unrepentant – The Anthology 1964–1995** (1996; Fragile/ Vital).
A two-disc compilation with, conveniently, everything you might want to listen to on disc one. This includes all the hits, plus selections from the albums up to Parachute: the loudest, wildest pieces of British R&B, demonstrating that – despite Dick Taylor's beard – The Pretty Things were undeniably punk.

Alwyn W. Turner

PRIMAL SCREAM

Formed London, 1984.

Primal Scream were formed in 1984 by their vocalist, **Bobby Gillespie**, who at the time was also drummer for **THE JESUS & MARY CHAIN**. The initial blueprint was an indie revisiting of 60s rock, but by the onset of the 90s Primal Scream had moved this on to the dance scene, producing a mix that commanded a huge British following, appealing to everyone from MOR rock fans to hardcore dance fanatics, and pretty much every student in the country.

The band has had a shifting line-up, with Gillespie the only constant. After a couple of uncertain singles for Creation, "All Fall Down" (1985) and "Crystal Crescent" (1986), and a track on the *NME*'s celebrated C86 indie compilation, the key figures were Gillespie and guitarists **Andrew Innes** and **Robert Young**. It was this trio and guests who recorded the debut album SONIC FLOWER GROOVE for Elevation,

a label run, like Creation, by the band's manager Alan McGee.

That album and its follow-up, PRIMAL SCREAM (1989), were interesting indie fare, with core influences The Stooges, Johnny Thunders, MC5 and, above all, The Stones. However, as the 90s neared, the band became involved with the dance and club scene, and added a whole new dimension. This was the time of acid-house exuberance, and Primal Scream's "Loaded" (1990) was the anthem the punters had been crying out for.

"Loaded" was actually a remix of a 1989 track, "I'm Losing More Than I'll Ever Have", radically reworked by soon-to-be famous producer **Andrew Weatherall**. The guitar was sunk back into the mix, the song structure taken apart, and a funk-dub backing was crossed with samples of *Easy Rider* and additional funk piano and horns to create something entirely new. It wasn't a straightforward dance track, it was far too lazy to be rave, but it was no longer rock'n'roll.

Further dance-rock singles followed over the next eighteen months: first "Come Together" (in mixes by both Weatherall and Terry Farley), then The Orb-mixed "Higher Than The Sun" (accurately described by Creation as 'Hallucinogenic space blues'), and finally "Don't Fight It, Feel It". The 1991 album SCREAMADELICA compiled them and added another host of gems, showcasing Primal Scream as a rock band going somewhere different, harnessing technology with a sense of unbridled possibility. As Creation readily admitted, the Scream wore their influences on their sleeve. "Movin' On Up", the album's opener, and "Damaged" were pure Stones, and deliberately so, produced by Jimmy Milner, who had been involved in LET IT BLEED and STICKY FINGERS. It was plagiarism turned inside out: write a song like The Stones, then see what the man who mixed The Stones would do with it twenty years on. Not many people complained about the results, and in 1992 the album received the first ever Mercury Music Prize.

The band's reputation was done no harm by its live incarnation, which headlined Glastonbury in 1992 and appeared with The Orb at the Miners' Benefit in Sheffield the same year. Looking for new ideas, Primal Scream then took off to Memphis and recorded with soul producer Tom Dowd in the Ardent Studios. The Memphis Horns were enlisted to help out; George Drakoulias, mixer for The Black Crowes, remixed three tracks; and George Clinton, the godfather of P-Funk (see **FUNKADELIC** and **PARLIAMENT**) took three more and sang on two of them.

The result was GIVE OUT BUT DON'T GIVE UP (1994), an album that, inevitably, disappointed those who wanted another SCREAMADELICA – and found themselves witnessing a return to R&B. Judged on its own merits, though, it was a superb album, filled with uncluttered, soulful rock songs. Gillespie's trademark wailing vocals lifted the material and the huge

cast of musicians never put a foot wrong, playing as if their lives depended on it. "Rocks" sounded more like The Stones than The Stones do these days, and the band had clearly stopped paying any attention to criticism of their approach to other people's ideas.

Two of the best tracks on VANISHING POINT (1997), their fifth album, were full-on speed-tributes: stand-out track "Kowalski" (a homage to the protagonist of the film *Vanishing Point*) ran on little white pills just as much as the character in the film did, losing focus here and there but getting it together again just in time to keep the car on the asphalt, while their cover of "Motörhead" – Lemmy's ode to the joys of amphetamines – trundled along like a bad-tempered cranked-up juggernaut. The rest of the album wandered between the dreaminess of "Long Life" and the joyful optimism of "Star".

Released only three months later, ECHO DEK (1997) offered up remixed versions of VANISHING POINT tracks courtesy of dub veteran Adrian Sherwood. Sherwood ripped the originals back to their bare bones, allowing the bass to dominate in sparse and disturbing landscapes.

Both the release of the single "Swastika Eyes" and their involvement with the campaign to free the jailed Satpal Ram seemed part of an increasingly politicized Primal Scream, brought to a head by the release of the bruising XTRMNTR (2000). The last ever album to be released on Creation (the label was then wound down by Alan McGee), XTRMNTR attempted to make a statement in the face of an 'indie' scene that had become increasingly apolitical and apathetic. It didn't always work, but Gillespie et al captured enough righteous indignation to show that they really meant it. The presence of My Bloody Valentine's **Kevin Shields** also ensured that the band's sound was at times cacophonous and experimental.

A prophetic new track, "Bomb The Pentagon", was premiered live just before the attacks of 9/11 and despite its controversial stance looked set to make an appearance on their next album, but in a dramatic u-turn, the band rerecorded the cut, and when EVIL HEAT (2002) finally appeared, the song, complete with new lyrics, appeared as "Rise". The remainder of the set had a retro-electro-punk-krautrock-ish style; Weatherall was back in the fold, and Shields remained, again forcing number after number through his distortion mincer.

Far from becoming elder statesman of an earlier era of indie rock, Primal Scream continue to maintain their position at the head of the pack and are today producing some of the most relevant music of their career.

⦿ **Sonic Flower Groove** (1987; Elevation).
This album documents The Scream's early incarnation as indie-janglers. Though most definitely of its time, cuts such as "Gentle Tuesday" and "Imperial" still sound glorious.

⦿ **Screamadelica** (1991; Creation).
The most important dance-rock record of the 90s. Gloriously original and still perfect enchantment more than half a decade on.

⦿ **Give Out But Don't Give Up** (1994; Creation).
The Scream get soul. A major shift from its predecessor but just as heartfelt and defiantly funky.

⦿ **Vanishing Point** (1997; Creation).
Stands head and shoulders above the universally panned GIVE OUT BUT DON'T GIVE UP and at times reaches the heights of SCREAMADELICA.

⦿ **Xtrmntr** (2000; Creation).
Considering the production duties were assigned to a diverse crew – including David Holmes, the Chemical Brothers, The Automator and Kevin Shields – the album's sound is triumphantly coherent, the high point being Shields' wah-wah-horned cacophony "MBV Orchestra" (previously released as the single "If They Move Kill 'em").

Chris Wright

THE PRIMITIVES

Formed Coventry, England, 1985; disbanded 1991.

T**he Primitives** were perhaps the most frenetic band of the 80s, making a name for themselves with their live sets in which they might run through six songs in ten minutes. They were fronted, by the time they got into their stride, by startling peroxide-blonde singer **Tracy Tracy**, with high-energy support from **Paul Court** (guitar/vocals), **Steve Dullahan** (bass) and **Pete Tweedie** (drums).

The band's first single, "Thru The Flowers" (1986), was a concoction of feedback-fed bubblegum pop, and brought rewards in the shape of four different Radio 1 sessions. The follow-up, "Really Stupid", released later in the year, was a student dance-floor stomper and saw The Primitives firmly established in the indie charts. Its buzz-saw guitar epitomized the band's live performance, and was brought to the fore on the next single, "Stop Killing Me", a UK indie #1 which established the band in the vanguard of an explosion of guitar groups.

Everyone seemed to want to jump on the bandwagon, and even Morrissey was photographed wearing a "Stop Killing Me" T-shirt. The major record companies now came calling and The Primitives signed to RCA in 1987, stopping only to rerecord "Thru The Flowers" as a goodbye gesture to their indie label, Lazy. Their RCA debut, "Crash", was released in February 1988 and soared to #5 in the UK after a memorable live appearance on *Top Of The Pops*. By now Tracy's face was shining out from a plethora of magazine covers and it was no surprise when The Primitives' debut album, LOVELY, stormed into the UK Top 10 on the week of its release in April 1988.

With new drummer **Tig Williams**, the band set off on their first major tour. Although a sellout, the gigs exposed their limitations, as songs which had glowed in the studio were left flat and faltering in the live arena. Still, they got better as they went along, and set off to try and break into the US market. They did so with some success, with LOVELY selling in excess of 150,000 copies and "Crash" remaining in the college chart for six months.

The band then returned to England and set to work on a second album, eventually re-emerging from the studio in July 1989 with Tracy having become a brunette and the band trimmed down to a three-piece, Steve Dullahan having left. The first fruit of their labours was the single "Sick Of It", a fine song reminiscent of "Really Stupid", though it failed to catch the imagination of the record-buying public and faltered at #24.

RCA alarm bells started to ring when the next single, "Secrets", failed even to reach the UK Top 40, and the fall from grace was confirmed when the album PURE was released to generally lacklustre reviews in October 1989, peaked at #33 in the UK and spent just two weeks in the chart. A compilation album of all the early singles, released by Lazy a month before PURE, highlighted the band's lack of progression.

The Primitives returned to release "You Are The Way" in August 1991, but they were seen as a spent force, and split up not long afterwards.

⊙ **Lovely** (1988; RCA).
An album that freeze-frames a precise moment in rock history. Girl-fronted English guitar bands were all the rage and after the success of "Crash" – naturally track one, side one – LOVELY was held up as the album from which all others should take their lead. A collection of classic pop melodies alongside psychedelic-tinged offerings.

Andy Lowe

PRIMUS

Formed San Francisco, 1984.

Thrash rock, psychedelia, funk and weird Zappa-esque humour are among elements combined – often to inspired effect – in West Coast band **Primus**. The group was formed in 1984 by **Les Claypool** (bass/vocals), **Todd Huth** (guitar – later replaced by **Larry Lalonde**) and **Tim 'Herb' Alexander** (drums – later replaced by **Brian 'Brain' Mantia**), and from their inception have been dominated by Claypool's cough-linctus bass and bemused vocals.

The band began as an underground phenomenon, and took the best part of five years to release their debut, SUCK ON THIS (1989), an album recorded live at a local club date and issued on their own Prawn Song (a joke on Led Zep's Swansong) label. Its material showcased their offbeat lyrics (concerned with, among other things, the group's favourite pastime of deep-sea angling) and dense, repetitive rhythms.

Many of the same songs were subsequently reprised for FRIZZLE FRY (1991), their first studio outing, which preceded a move to a bigger recording budget with Interscope Records. Having toured widely with such acts as Faith No More and Jane's Addiction, the Primus career upswing continued with their Interscope debut, SAILING THE SEAS OF CHEESE (1991). Guests included Tom Waits, who contributed vocals to a version of "Tommy The Cat" – another song rescued from the group's now unobtainable debut album. It also featured prominently in the film *Bill & Ted's Bogus Journey*.

An EP, MISCELLANEOUS DEBRIS, followed in 1992, and featured covers of material by XTC, Peter Gabriel, The Residents, Pink Floyd and The Meters – a roster of inspirational reference points. Then came the breakthrough album, PORK SODA (1993), which sailed into the mainstream US charts, peaking at a mighty #7. Characteristically, it was still recycling material from the debut album – in this case, "The Pressman".

Claypool then renewed relations with Huth and Jay Lane (one of Primus's many former drummers) to record RIDDLES ARE ABOUND TONIGHT (1993) – an extracurricular venture credited to Sausage. Judged on the results of TALES FROM THE PUNCHBOWL (1995), however, another major American success, such activities had not dulled Claypool's ambitions for Primus. The new outing was funky, irreverent and wilfully absurd as ever. They followed it with THE BROWN ALBUM (1997), seventeen tracks of classy mayhem guaranteed to please the fans and drive the rest of the world screaming from the room.

Stopping only to fling out RHINOPLASTY (1998), a covers EP, Primus were now on a mission to stretch themselves artistically as far as possible. Pulling in a frankly bizarre set of collaborators – including the likes of Limp Bizkit's **Fred Durst**, ex-Faith No More guitarist **Jim Martin**, former Police drummer **Stewart Copeland** and Rage Against The Machine's **Tom Morello** – they spewed forth ANTIPOP (1999), which sounded strange even by Primus's standards. It was a brave move and just what Claypool needed, seemingly, to purge himself creatively before putting the band on hold and concentrating on releases from his various side projects, including **Frog Brigade** and **Oyster Head**.

⊙ **Pork Soda** (1993; Interscope).
Primus are hardly an original concept, but you can forgive a band a great deal if they take themselves so (un)seriously and deliver songs as catchy and immediate as these.

Alex Ogg

PRINCE

Born Minneapolis, Minnesota, 1958.

"Prince is bad. It's like seeing Sly, James Brown and Jimi Hendrix all at once." Johnny Guitar Watson

In the late 70s, just three percent of the population of Minneapolis were black, and, although the city held relatively liberal values, black culture had to cross over to the whites if it was going to do any real business. So, any talented individual from the city had to have a hefty additional streak of drive, ambition and confidence. One such, from the moment he emerged, was a man who started life as **Prince Rogers Nelson** – a musician whom many rate as the greatest of his generation.

A precociously talented guitarist, drummer and pianist, Prince formed his first band, **Grand Central**, at high school around 1972–73. The boy wonder (guitar/vocals) was joined by Andre Anderson (later **Andre Cymone**; bass) and **Morris Day** (drums) for a work-out heavily influenced by Sly Stone, Jimi Hendrix and The Rolling Stones. Over the next few years, Prince attempted several further prequels of The Revolution, the most interesting of which was the short-lived **94 East**, formed by Linster Willie (aka **Pepe Willie**) and recorded for posterity on an album of instrumental recordings entitled MINNEAPOLIS GENIUS – THE HISTORIC 1977 RECORDINGS (belatedly issued in 1985).

By the time of 94 East, interest in Prince's prodigious talents had reached several minor labels, although it was Warners who eventually signed him, for a six-figure advance, in early 1978. The corporation were uneasy about their charge being given the full artistic control he demanded but relented – wisely – and permitted him to write, arrange, produce and perform albums from the outset. It was a breakthrough, not so much on account of the artist's age (he was still not yet 20), but his colour. Amongst black solo artists, only Stevie Wonder had been allowed such artistic and creative freedom so young – and that was when he'd already been a Motown recording artist for nearly ten years.

Prince's debut album, FOR YOU, was issued in June 1978. Its sweet soul and unusually risqué lyrics were aimed largely at a black audience, although its closing track, "I'm Yours", was a noisy rock crossover which anticipated PURPLE RAIN. It didn't chart, but by the end of 1979 Prince had chalked up a hit single, "I Wanna Be Your Lover" (a US #11 and Top 50 UK), the opener of his second album, PRINCE (1979), which went to #22 in the US. The album's closing number was notable, too: "I Feel For You" was a song that, like much of Prince's output, would chart as a later cover version (in this case, five years on, for Chaka Khan).

By 1979, Prince had also formed his first tour band, which he had deliberately chosen to include black and white, male and female, musicians – an ideology which has survived various line-up changes through his career. This first line-up comprised old associate Andre Cymone (bass), **Gayle Chapman** (keyboards), **Dr. (Matt) Fink** (keyboards), **Dez Dickerson** (guitar) and **Bobby Z (né Rifkin)** on drums.

The sexually explicit content of Prince's 1980 release, DIRTY MIND, lost it any radio exposure and, in any case, its (white) New Wave influence appeared to confuse white radio programmers. All the same, it created a great deal of press interest. But the follow-up, CONTROVERSY (1981), seemed to be entrenched more firmly in shock value than good songwriting, including a bizarre pro-Republican track, "Ronnie Talk To Russia". The same year, the band also played the two most disastrous shows of its career – supporting The Rolling Stones in San Francisco, where a sizable minority of the crowd chose to hurl anything from shoes to a bag of chicken's innards. Mainstream acceptance, it appeared, was still some way off.

That was before the release of 1999 (1982), a stunning double album right from the apocalyptic excitement of its title track, and equipped with a song, "Little Red Corvette", which outSpringsteened The Boss and soared into the American Top 10. It owed its ascent, in large part, to heavy MTV rotation, a triumph for Prince and for black music; along with Michael Jackson's "Billie Jean" single, "Corvette" was the first black crossover video on MTV, and it spearheaded a steady broadening of the cable channel's playlist.

Worldwide success followed with PURPLE RAIN (1984), which tied in with a semi-autobiographical movie of the same name, starring Prince himself, Morris Day (now of funk band The Time) and 'love interest' Apollonia. The film itself was absurd (as indeed have been all of Prince's celluloid productions), but saved by its marvellous soundtrack. By now, the touring band had metamorphosed into **The Revolution**, who also accompanied Prince on record. The line-up at this point was Bobby Z, Dr. Fink, **Brown Mark** (bass), **Wendy Melvoin** (vocals/guitar) and **Lisa Coleman** (vocals/keyboards).

PURPLE RAIN's success was accompanied by controversy and eccentricity in equal measures. Having written and produced songs for The Time, Jill Jones and Apollonia, Prince's ditty for Sheena Easton, "Sugar Walls" (about female masturbation), ran into trouble with the newly formed pro-censorship lobby, the PMRC (Parents' Music Resource Centre). Other Prince recordings "Darling Nikki" (from PURPLE RAIN) and "Let's Pretend We're Married" (from 1999) attracted complaints, too, owing to sexually explicit material. During 1985, Prince's eccentric lifestyle was also under scrutiny by the world's press, as he refused interviews, accepted awards with the briefest of speeches, and ended his world tour by announcing that he was retiring from live performances, as he was going to 'look for the ladder'.

The Genius Once Upon A Time Known As Prince Rogers Nelson

Revolution disbanded. **Wendy And Lisa** went on to the most prominent level of solo success, signing to Virgin, and only Matt Fink would work with Prince on a regular basis again.

Meanwhile, Prince, seemingly in the most prolific period of his career, issued a solo double LP. SIGN O'THE TIMES (1987) ranked as perhaps his most consistent set of songs, while maintaining his enthusiasm for diversity, and his most convincing union of love, sex and God. It even spawned a decent movie – Prince, shrewdly for once, sticking to film footage of the live show.

His new band comprised Fink, sax player **Eric Leeds**, drummer **Sheila E**, guitarist **Mico Weaver**, bassist **Levi Seacer, Boni Boyer** (keyboards) and dancer/singer **Cat Glover**. This was likely also the line-up for the legendary BLACK album, withdrawn at the last minute from Warners' release schedule at Christmas 1987 and issued, legally at least, only in 1994. Its tracks included libidinous funk marathons like "Le Grind" and "Rock Hard In A Funky Place", a sprawl of free-jazz called "2 Nigs United 4 West Compton", and even an unsettling rap pastiche called "Bob George". Despite Prince's (reported) reservations, it was diverting, and its hollow hedonism is still more effective than much of his more recent funk output.

One track from BLACK, the melt-on-the-tongue ballad "When 2 R In Love", actually made it onto Prince's next official album, LOVESEXY, in May 1988. This also contained an excellent single in "Alphabet St.", but although a massive selling LP in Britain and Europe sold very poorly in America, causing Prince to cancel a US tour over the summer of 1988 and close off his Paisley Park label for the time being.

What saved his commercial skin was a superhero whose signature tune was an early favourite of the young pianist. Director Tim Burton was making the first *Batman* movie (1989), with Michael Keaton, Jack Nicholson and Kim Basinger, and needed a few songs to complement Danny Elfman's score. Prince obliged by making an entire album, including a wild spontaneous track consisting of cut-ups, snatches of dialogue, and even samples from the rest of his own album. Admittedly, the hype surrounding the movie helped it along but, even so, "Batdance" had to be one of the strangest #1 singles in American chart his-

Prince's seventh album, and his second with The Revolution, was AROUND THE WORLD IN A DAY, released in April 1985 on his own newly formed Paisley Park record label. Criticized mainly for its abandonment of PURPLE RAIN's funk-rock in favour of psychedelia and gospel, it has aged better than expected, especially the witty anti-drug song "Pop Life", and hit single "Raspberry Beret". Although the finale, "Temptation", was a preposterous overindulgence of the spiritual, the sexual and the religious, The Revolution was a tight, economical and exciting band, and they made these middle-period albums some of the most diverse and innovative projects that Prince has been involved with. No one appears to know exactly what went wrong, but Prince And The Revolution were to work together on just one more LP, PARADE (1986), the soundtrack to Prince's second movie, *Under The Cherry Moon*, a critical and commercial dud, again redeemed only by its music. After a world tour, The

tory. Meanwhile, the BATMAN album sold seven million copies in America, and the same number again worldwide.

Yet, as he entered the 90s, there was something about Prince's artistic output that seemed to be on autopilot. Yet another film, *Graffiti Bridge* (1990), some kind of sequel to *Purple Rain*, barely made it to the cinemas, while its soundtrack of undistinguished funk sounded unusually dated. DIAMONDS AND PEARLS (1991) was a triumphant return to form, with the reformed New Power Generation producing awesome contemporary funk and lush balladry, enhanced by Rosie Gaines' gospel-influenced vocals. However, the touch disappeared just as swiftly, with SYMBOL (1992) and COME (1994), which offered little beyond their sex talk.

Most alarmingly, more seemed to be written about Prince's image and 'weirdness' than about his music, especially after the 1993 announcement that he was to be renamed as an icon ❤ – then 'Victor' – and finally 'The Artist Formerly Known As Prince' (TAFKAP). Then, just two years after signing another multimillion-dollar contract with Time Warner, it was revealed that there were internal wranglings between artist and label, leading to the release of his hit single, "The Most Beautiful Girl In The World" (1994), and its parent album of remixes, THE BEAUTIFUL EXPERIENCE (1994), on independent labels worldwide. ❤ tried to escape his Warners contract by finally issuing the BLACK album, as well as a couple of greatest hits sets (boxed together, for devotees, with their B-sides as THE HITS: THE B-SIDES).

Meantime, the creative juices seemed a bit dry. THE GOLD EXPERIENCE (1995), material that had dominated the year's tour set, featured ever-more-desperate attempts to shock and arouse ("Endomorphinemachine", "P-Control"), with irksome interval tracks. Only the belated reappearance of "The Most Beautiful Girl In The World" and the jazzy "I Hate U" were up to standard. CHAOS AND DISORDER (1996), fulfilling contractual obligations to Warner Bros, had even less going for it: a P-Funk jam recorded in short order in Florida, with a lot of Princely guitar soloing and just the one stand-out song, "Dinner With Dolores". It was accompanied by the news that this would be the last outing for The Power Generation.

EMANCIPATION, released in 1997, gave Prince another vanity label – **New Power Generation** – and the opportunity to dig out some of the better new tunes from his legendarily prodigious output – he is said to have hundreds of songs in the vault, even a full orchestral symphony. It was a wild and joyously rambling album, coming in at around the three-hour mark on three discs, self-indulgent here, shamelessly romantic there, preoccupied with lust and dancing throughout. The first disc of the three is strong enough to have been released as an album in its own right, with outstanding tracks like "Somebody's Somebody" and "In This Bed I Scream" strutting the Artist's funky stuff for him just like in the old days. Disc two was the weakest, being little more than a Valentine to the dancer formerly known as Mayte (and then known as Mrs Prince), but it was redeemed by the magnificent, pure beauty of "The Holy River". The third disc had highlights in the B-boy posing of "Face Down" and the dance-floor-wrecking "The Human Body".

CRYSTAL BALL (1998) was another marathon, this time spread over four CDs. The package of thirty new tracks, on the whole unheard anywhere before, plus a dozen acoustic tracks recorded during 1997, was previously only available to the Internet-capable, credit-card-owning sections of the community. They received an extra disc of ballet music, "Kamasutra", written by Prince for Mrs Prince.

Despite these welcome improvements, the highlights of CRYSTAL BALL dated back several years to a period when his creative powers were at a peak. Contrastingly, newly recorded material continued to sound aimless and grey in comparison, and – as one critic remarked on its release – it was difficult to muster up disappointment for most of NEW POWER SOUL (1998). Perhaps if the Purple One was persuaded to employ an editor to help sift through his work, we might yet hear albums of consistent excellence as those he produced during the 1980s, which were mined once more for the enjoyable, but inevitably reductive 2001 VERY BEST OF collection.

Prince

⊙ **Dirty Mind** (1980; Warner Brothers).
With its songs about oral sex ("Head"), incest ("Sister") and a ménage à trois ("When You Were Mine"), this shocked the States on its release. The melodies ensure that, even at barely half an hour long, it remains the most essential early outing.

Prince and the Revolution

⊙ **Purple Rain** (1984; Warners).
Melodramatic and bombastic, this catapulted Prince into the big league. At least six Prince classics feature, including the pulsating hit single "When Doves Cry", the narcissistic anguish of "The Beautiful Ones", and an anthemic title track. Deservedly one of the world's biggest-selling records in the mid-80s, although it set a commercial peak which Prince would be hard-pushed to reach again.

Parade (1986; Paisley Park/Warners).
Unjustly dismissed by Prince soon afterwards as a 'disaster', this kaleidoscopic display of pop, funk and psychedelia occasionally sounds a little crowded, and a couple of the ballads now seem half-written. However, inimitable pop flirtations like "Girls & Boys", "New Position" and the extraordinary "Kiss" single result in a delightfully addictive record.

Prince

Sign O'The Times (1987; Paisley Park/Warner Brothers).
Prince's deepest foray into black music since his earliest work produced this stunning double set. While the title track was a sincere (if naive) view of the world's social decline, other tracks embraced rock, soul, gospel and exhilarating dance music. "It's Gonna Be A Beautiful Night", recorded live in Paris, marks the end of The Revolution on record, while three tracks boast lead vocals by a mysterious 'female' singer called 'Camille' (guess who).

Prince and the New Power Generation

Diamonds And Pearls (1991; Warners).
An impressive return to form, this concentrates on libidinous funk and lush balladry, enhanced by Rosie Gaines' gospel-influenced vocals. Highlights include the audacious "Gett Off" and "Cream", plus the perceptive social commentary of "Money Don't Matter 2 Nite".

The Hits (1993: Warner Brothers; available as two individual albums, or as a three-CD set, with a third album of B-sides and rarities).
It was most likely planned as a contractual obligation, but THE HITS 1 & 2 were truly long-awaited greatest hits sets. As for what's included, it is perhaps easier to list what's missing – there's nothing from PARADE, bar "Kiss", or from BATMAN. Suffice it to say that even on Prince's weaker albums, there were always two or three songs worth saving. Most can be found here, as can an otherwise unavailable live version of his own "Nothing Compares 2U", first recorded by Paisley Park group The Family, and famously covered by Sinéad O'Connor.

Justin Lewis

JOHN PRINE

Born Maywood, Illinois, October 10, 1946.

Songwriters have always appreciated **John Prine**; audiences, only intermittently. His songs are musically loose-limbed and pleasant, but it's his words that stick in the mind – his favourite images are everyday things in which you can only see the magic when the light hits them right.

Prine grew up in a Chicago suburb, in a supportive musical environment: his brothers Dave and Billy played fiddle and guitar, and the whole family enjoyed playing and singing together. After working as a mailman and a hitch in the army, Prine started playing showcase gigs in Chicago, attracting the notice of rising folkie Steve Goodman, who introduced his songs to risen folkie Kris Kristofferson, who helped get the young songwriter a contract with Atlantic.

The songs most people know Prine for, including "Your Flag Decal Won't Get You Into Heaven Anymore", "Sam Stone", and the pseudo-morose "Illegal Smile" ('A bowl of oatmeal tried to stare me down/and won'), stamped his distinctive kind-hearted drollery on the debut album, JOHN PRINE (1971). He could not only sing with feeling about a junkie veteran, he could be inventive about him without sounding supercilious. His voice also had an appealingly backwoodsy sound that was inherited from his Kentucky-born parents. Prine was immediately established in the second tier of 70s folkies from whom big things were expected.

Prine felt nervous and unsure in his vocalizing on his first album; his voice on DIAMONDS IN THE ROUGH (1972), which included his classic love elegy "The Great Compromise", was much looser and in some ways more expressive, but also hoarser, perhaps showing the effects of barleycorn nerve medicine. Though his writing continued to improve on SWEET REVENGE (1973) and COMMON SENSE (1975), his attitude was more pessimistic ('that common sense don't make no sense no more') and his voice more unreliable.

The folk boomlet passed, but Prine hung in. Off Atlantic and on Asylum, he passed a relatively unheralded middle period, producing great tunes and having fun (most evidently on the eccentric folk-rockabilly PINK CADILLACS, which had a very odd version of "Ubangi Stomp"), but no hits. In 1984 he joined small label Oh Boy, and immediately could hear a sigh of relief in his music. The songs showed all their previous values, but also a calm sureness of purpose that made them soothing to listen to.

His fourth Oh Boy release, the appropriately titled THE MISSING YEARS (1991), won a Grammy and more attention than anything Prine had done since his debut. The whimsical-cum-rueful songs – notably "Jesus: The Missing Years" – were among his best ever, his voice was warm and relaxed, and the production by Howie Epstein (of Tom Petty And The Heartbreakers) gave Prine's music a comfortable sound that found him a new audience in the newly folk-friendly country radio market. LOST DOGS AND MIXED BLESSINGS (1995) continued to work this groove, not only demonstrating warmth but generating income.

Next came an interesting live album LIVE ON TOUR (1997), recorded on his home turf in Chicago and in Nashville, that picked up some of his greatest hits and boasts an impressive cut of "Jesus: The Missing Years". This was followed by another Grammy-nominated set, IN SPITE OF OURSELVES (1999), which largely comprised covers, and saw Prine singing with the likes of Lucinda Williams and Emmylou Harris. More good stuff turned up the following year on SOUVENIRS (2000), a package of rerecorded Prine classics. John Prine appears to have slid into middle age with his sense of humour intact and most of his other creative faculties at their height – as pleasing a development as a folkie can expect these days.

John Prine (1971; Atlantic; reissued by Rhino).
"Paradise", "Sam Stone", "Angel From Montgomery" – this is one of those debuts that sounds like a greatest hits.

- **The Missing Years** (1991; Oh Boy/Ryko).
  The comeback, in which the minstrel finds time beginning to heal all wounds.
- **Lost Dogs And Mixed Blessings** (1995; Oh Boy/Ryko).
Sharp lyrics, a warm sound, and Marianne Faithfull on backing vocals. What more could you ask for at this stage of a career?
- **Great Days** (1993; Rhino).
  A superb two-CD retro from top to bottom.

Roy Edroso

THE PROCLAIMERS

Formed Edinburgh, Scotland, 1985.

Twins **Craig** (vocals/percussion/harmonica/lyrics) and **Charlie Reid** (guitar/vocals/lyrics) formed the acoustic band **The Proclaimers** in 1985 and set about making a name for themselves on the Scottish folk circuit. Sell-out concert tours of their homeland, together with victories in talent contests, brought the boys to the attention of Chrysalis. On the strength of a demo tape and a sizeable cult following, the brothers were offered a deal.

With their thick accents and *Revenge Of The Nerds* appearance, The Proclaimers did not seem cut out for mainstream success: 'We're not your average pin-up', Charlie once told *Smash Hits*. No one was more surprised than the brothers, then, when the guitar version of "Letter To America" made the UK Top 5 in 1987. Some attributed the boys' success to gimmickry: Craig and Charlie were twins, they looked like geeks, they pronounced back 'barrrrrrk' – with so many quirks, how could they fail to have a hit?

The failure of the follow-up single, "Make My Heart Fly", suggested the band might be a one-off novelty for the pop charts. Those who had actually seen the band, though, were aware that there was more to the Reids than geeky spectacles and impenetrable accents, and prior to the release of their debut album, THIS IS THE STORY (1987), the brothers embarked on an extensive British tour. It paid dividends, and by the end of the year they had such a big fan base that the album went gold.

THIS IS THE STORY captured The Proclaimers at a stage in their career when they were basically two lads with a guitar and a good grounding in country/folk. For their second album, the boys put aside the harmonica and picked up electric guitars. Thematically, the songs on SUNSHINE ON LEITH (1988) had much in common with the earlier recordings – lots of stuff about women and drinking. What the new electric edge did was make the sound more accessible. Released as a single in August 1988, the jazzed-up folk number "I'm Gonna Be (500 Miles)" provided the brothers with their second UK Top 20 single. Another tour, complete with electric backing band, and two more singles followed. By adding to their sound, the Reids had graduated to the mainstream.

Subsequent to their tour, The Proclaimers decided to take a two-year break from recording. Two years became four when, with the third album half-written, the boys left the studios to assist with the campaign to save their beloved local football team, Hibernian. Such was the band's dedication to the cause that they released just one record in the UK between 1989 and 1994, a cover of "King Of The Road" (1990).

Meantime, however, they broke through in America, on the back of the opening scene of the movie *Benny And Joon*, in which two misfits find one another to the tune of "I'm Gonna Be (500 Miles)". A minor hit at the US box office, *Benny And Joon* transformed The Proclaimers into major recording artists in the US. While the single climbed the Hot 100, the album, SUNSHINE ON LEITH, released five years earlier in the UK, went double platinum.

Cracking America without lifting a finger left Craig and Charlie in a position of rare power with their record company. It was this new-found influence that allowed the twins to record HIT THE HIGHWAY (1995), on which, perhaps smitten with their American triumph, the boys set out to become a fully fledged country outfit. Even their accents began to take on a distinct mid-Atlantic twang. After what seemed like an eternity they issued PERSEVERE (2001), which was just as distinct and querky. For all their success, The Proclaimers remain a charmingly idiosyncratic outfit, retaining their own, staunchly loyal constituency.

- **Sunshine On Leith** (1988; Chrysalis).
  The Proclaimers discover the electric guitar. The band's new-found musical maturity is shown on stomping anthems ("I'm Gonna Be", "I'm On My Way") and touching ballads (the title track and "My Old Friend The Blues").

Richard Luck

PROCOL HARUM

Formed London, 1966; disbanded 1977; re-formed 1991.

The statistics aren't very impressive: in a decade of existence **Procol Harum** managed a mere 56 weeks in the British singles charts, half of them with their first release, while the albums did even worse – just eleven weeks and nothing in the Top 20. They did a little better, late in their career, in the States. But even these tallies are deceiving: few people can name more than the group's one hit – "A Whiter Shade Of Pale". Nonetheless, the group have an assured place in any rock book – and rightly so.

The band's origins lie in the decision of Southend R&B band, The Paramounts, to call it a day in 1966. Looking for a new outlet, singer **Gary Brooker** was introduced by the legendary Guy Stevens, then an Island A&R man, to an as-yet-untried lyricist, **Keith Reid**. Quickly knocking out four songs for a Stevens-produced demo, the duo recruited some musicians (Reid never performed with the band) and signed to Decca's new 'progressive' label, Deram.

One of those songs was "A Whiter Shade Of Pale", which was released as a single in May 1967.

Perfectly encapsulating the nascent 'Summer Of Love', it featured a melody stolen from Bach, some beautiful Hammond organ from new boy **Matthew Fisher** and a set of wonderfully incomprehensible lyrics that sounded like Dylan without discipline. Within two weeks it was at #1 in the UK, where it stayed for six weeks, and on its way to selling four million copies worldwide.

Unfortunately, after thirty years of constant radio and jukebox play, paint-advert and dreadful cover versions (stand up Annie Lennox), "A Whiter Shade Of Pale" now sounds annoying rather than classic, and not even period footage of the kaftan-clad minstrels miming on *Top Of The Pops* can restore to the song the charm it once had.

At the time the main worry was the overnight stardom, which almost destroyed the newly formed band. The addition, however, of guitarist Robin Trower, also formerly of The Paramounts, and the release of a follow-up hit, "Homburg", did much to stabilize matters. Over the next two years the group released three excellent albums: PROCOL HARUM (1967), SHINE ON BRIGHTLY (1968) and A SALTY DOG (1969). Though the group were irredeemably tagged as flower-power prog-rockers, these albums showed a surprisingly tough sound, dominated by Trower's metal-blues riffs and Fisher's soulful Hammond, all unmistakeably derived from R&B. Reid's lyrics, especially on the yearning, string-laden "A Salty Dog", were way beyond those of most of his contemporaries. The only weak spot was the interminable suite, "Held 'Twas In I", on the second album.

At this stage Fisher and bassist **David Knights** left, to be replaced by ex-Paramount **Chris Copping**. Completed by drummer **B. J. Wilson**, the quartet was now effectively The Paramounts in all but name, and the next two albums, HOME (1970) and BROKEN BARRICADES (1971), were heavier and bluesier, with Trower particularly making his presence felt. Then Robin Trower, too, left, just as the band were making inroads into the American market.

The self-explanatory 1972 release, LIVE IN CONCERT WITH THE EDMONTON SYMPHONY ORCHESTRA AND THE DE CAMERA SINGERS, went gold in America and produced a hit single in "Conquistador", a reworking of a song from the first album. The follow-up, GRAND HOTEL (1973), was also a US success, but didn't do enough to launch the group into the real big league.

As the 70s dragged on, Procol took the bold step of drafting in rock'n'roll veterans Leiber and Stoller (writers of "Poison Ivy", the first and best-selling Paramounts single) to produce PROCOL'S NINTH in 1975, and managed their biggest British hit of the decade with "Pandora's Box". But time was against them, and 1977, the year of punk, was graced by their worst album, SOMETHING MAGIC, after which retirement was the only option.

In 1991 Brooker decided to re-form the band, having in the interim become a champion fly-fisher, and enjoyed some success in America with PRODIGAL

STRANGER, featuring once again both Fisher and Trower.

⦿ **30th Anniversary Anthology** (1998; Westside).
The first four albums and the single A- and B-sides, with a selection of alternate mixes and outtakes bolted on for good measure.

Alwyn W. Turner

THE PRODIGY

Formed Braintree, England, 1991.

"If people say we killed rave, then it was worth killing, because we're having a great time!" Keith Flint

The **Prodigy**, led by boy genius and sole musical force **Liam Howlett**, exploded out of Britain's rave scene at the start of 1991, just as it reached its zenith. The WHAT EVIL LURKS EP (their first release) made its way around the country's raves and enabled the band to tour Europe. Basically a bunch of like-minded mates, The Prodigy also included **Maxim Reality** (MC) and two dancers – the elastic **Leeroy Thornhill** and the electric **Keith Flint**. This fizzing phenomenon got an ecstatic welcome from ravers across the continent.

Their second release later that year was the storming "Charly", which marked the arrival of rave into mainstream consciousness – and thus heralded its diffusion into chart-pap imitations. A brilliant take on an old government safety cartoon (this was the year that government clampdowns on raves began), "Charly" was a great hard-dance record, reaching #1 in the UK dance chart and #3 in the pop chart. None of the imitations which followed came close either to its harnessing of rave's wild hedonism or to its wit.

Two more singles, "Everybody In The Place" and "Fire", made The Prodigy's name synonymous with manic dance-floor abandon. The LP which followed – THE PRODIGY EXPERIENCE (1992) – was a smashing album, clocking up 100,000 sales on the back of touring throughout the world, where the non-musical aspects of The Prodigy really came into their own in the scary mania of their live set.

Strange things were going on in Liam's mind after this success, and the next few tracks veered off in diverse directions. The techno of 1993's "One Love" bounced oddly off the manic, helium-voiced pop of "No Good Start The Dance" released in the summer of 1994, and this in turn was a strange prelude to their second album, the hard-driving and superlative MUSIC FOR THE JILTED GENERATION. Far from pandering to the white-gloved warehouse whistlers of summers long past, this tangled with jungle, hard-beat and hip-hop, and gave them a damned good hiding. The result was met enthusiastically by the critics and punters, entering the UK charts at #1 and gaining a nomination from the Brit Awards, unprecedented for a dance act. In essence it was still hard dance, but tracks like "Voodoo People", the manic "Full Throttle" and the buzz-saw grumble of "Their Law" (a collaboration with **Pop Will Eat Itself**) fused pop and hardcore inextricably to produce mainstream art.

THE FAT OF THE LAND (1997) turned a peculiar by-product of Brit rave into a World-Straddling Phenomenon. The opener, "Smack My Bitch Up", sampled a dopey track from years ago ("Give The Drummer Some" by Ultramagnetic MCs) dressed up with a gut-punching lower register that was likely to turn your speakers inside out. If you'd suspected that Liam and the guys were misogynistic lads from the redneck heartlands of Essex, then this was all the ammunition you needed. Though, in reality, media manipulation was the order of the day. And, with the scary videos for "Firestarter" and "Breathe" sending kids scurrying for cover behind reassuring bits of furniture, The Prodge demonstrated their supreme ability to walk it like they talk it. With the improbably monikered **Gizz Butt** providing purple-haired rock-dance crossover guitar and enough keyboards to sonically stun a herd of charging bison, they could afford to let lyrics as inane as 'Serial Thrilla, Serial Killa' slip through. Best of all, though, were the minimally worded total wig-outs such as "Funky Shit".

And with that world-changing release behind them the band effectively put things on hold for almost two years until Howlett decided to prove what a great DJ he was by releasing THE DIRTCHAMBER SESSIONS VOL. 1 (1999). And for anyone who has experienced the Prodigy's live set, there is no doubt that they bridge the divide between the cutting edge and mass entertainment. You can dance to them as well – a fact that was borne out by the "Baby's Got A Temper" single in 2002. Meanwhile, the various members of the group were all dabbling in their own interests, not least Thornhill who left to pursue his solo project **Flightcrank** in 2000, and Keith, who is now working with his own band, **Flint**, alongside Howlett, **Jim Davies** (Pitchshifter) and **Kieran Pepper**.

⊙ **The Prodigy Experience** (1992; XL).
While the house piano motifs and mechanistic beats can sound a bit dated, it's a frenetic, funny and danceable first album. Features an interesting drum'n'bass version of "Charly" and the loony tune antics of "Out Of Space".

⊙ **Music For The Jilted Generation** (1994; XL).
Classy interpretation of the hydra-headed British dance scene, served up in a wickedly accessible way. Moving into darker shadows, and all the more thrilling for it.

⊙ **The Fat Of The Land** (1997; XL).
In which Liam and the lads clear the traditionally 'difficult' third-album hurdle, landing on their feet in the US.

Andrew Stone

PROPAGANDA

Formed Düsseldorf, Germany, 1982; disbanded 1986; re-formed 1989.

Propaganda was the discovery/creation of British record producer **Trevor Horn** (ex-Buggles, late-period Yes, and other crimes), who signed them up for his embryonic ZTT label in late 1983. The band comprised **Ralf Dorper** (keyboards), who had been working in a bank in Düsseldorf and playing in post-punk groups with **Andreas Thein** (keyboards), plus **Susanne Freytag** and **Claudia Brücken** (vocals) from Los Topolinos (The Mickey Mouses), and **Michael Mertens** (percussion) from the Düsseldorf Symphony Orchestra. After Horn had signed them, he produced their first single, "Dr. Mabuse", which hit the British Top 30 in April 1984, on the coat-tails of label-mates Frankie Goes To Hollywood's "Relax", and then went massive in Europe. An eerie but addictive single, "Mabuse" was complemented by a memorable monochromatic promo video, directed by rock lensman Anton Corbijn.

Very little was heard from Propaganda over the next twelve months, beyond Claudia's marriage to ZTT's propagandist, Paul Morley, as the label concentrated on Frankie and their in-house hip-hop pioneers Art Of Noise. However, in spring 1985, Propaganda returned, minus Thein, with a classic pop single, "Duel", described in a few (complimentary) reviews as 'Abba from hell'. It was subtitled 'bittersweet' on the sleeve, appropriate for a song which examined the inherent violence of loyalty and betrayal in love (the flip side, subtitled 'cut rough', stomped the point home with an industrial mix).

Critical acclaim and night-time radio play created interest for the band's debut album, A SECRET WISH (1985), a pinnacle of mid-80s pop. Its sumptuous production – by Steve Lipson – was said to have influenced Quincy Jones, and you can perhaps hear echoes in his production of Michael Jackson's BAD album two years later. It had certainly cost ZTT a packet, soaring way over budget (beyond half a million pounds), and a #16 UK chart appearance was less than ZTT had hoped for. Internal wranglings between the label and group became apparent when Dorper did not take part in the British shows of late 1985, and the band were unhappy with a hastily issued remix album, WISHFUL THINKING (1985).

A premature and acrimonious split followed in the summer of 1986. Brücken continued to record for husband Morley's label, and had already recorded a duet with Heaven 17's **Glenn Gregory**, "When Your Heart Runs Out Of Time" in 1985, taken from Nicolas Roeg's movie *Insignificance*. She then joined forces with Thomas Leer under the name of Act, who made one terrific single, "Snobbery And Decay" (1987), which took over from where Propaganda left off, and an LP, LAUGHTER, TEARS AND RAGE (1988), that was more uneven fare, even if it did contain a bizarre melodramatic cover of The Smiths' "Heaven Knows I'm Miserable Now". Most recently, Brücken resurfaced on the Island label with the solo album, LOVE AND A MILLION OTHER THINGS (1991).

Meanwhile, Michael Mertens decided to resurrect the name of Propaganda in 1989, joining forces with

American vocalist **Betsi Miller**, and two ex-members of **SIMPLE MINDS** – **Derek Forbes** (bass) and **Brian McGee** (drums) – both of whom had played on the original line-up's 1985 tour. An album, 1234, released on Virgin Records in 1990, contained some attractive, filmic instrumentals, but many of the songs had more in common with American AOR than A SECRET WISH. A somewhat underwhelming conclusion for a group who in the mid-80s had promised so much...

○ **A Secret Wish** (1985; ZTT).
A stunning, hypnotic set of cerebral and danceable Europop, embracing influences as diverse as Ennio Morricone, Richard Wagner and punk rock. You can certainly hear where the budget went, with guest musicians like David Sylvian, The Police's Stewart Copeland, and Yes's Steve Howe. Contains both "Duel" and "Jewel", "Dr. Mabuse", and "Dream Within A Dream", featuring a poem by Edgar Allan Poe. Exhilarating stuff.

○ **Outside World** (2001; ZTT).
An essential collection of remixes and oddities from the archives; it also includes both "Dual" and its alter ego, "Jewel".

Justin Lewis

PSYCHEDELIC FURS

Formed London, 1977; disbanded 1993.

Though **Richard Butler** (vocals), **Roger Morris** (guitar), **John Ashton** (guitar), **Duncan Kilburn** (saxophone/keyboards) and **Tim Butler** (bass) formed the **Psychedelic Furs** back in 1977, it was not until 1979, by which time they had recruited drummer **Vince Ely**, that they began to receive significant press. Following a session for John Peel they were offered a contract with CBS, for whom they made their debut in February 1980 with "Sister Europe", an intoxicating song that announced the group's distinctive style: an update of The Velvet Underground spiced with LOW-era Bowie.

"Sister Europe" was included on THE PSYCHEDELIC FURS (1979), a chaotic, savage and compelling debut. However, the group's greatest achievement came with TALK TALK TALK (1981). Rick Butler's croaking monotone still didn't bother to make too many concessions, but the songs emerged complete and unerringly direct. While "Pretty In Pink" was the hit single most remember (it later inspired a sickly film of the same title), it was just one among many stand-outs, alongside "Into You Like A Train" and "I Just Wanna Sleep With You" – testosterone pop-rock at its best – and "All Of This And Nothing", Butler's rasping career highlight.

Ely went off to drum for Robyn Hitchcock's band and was replaced by **Phil Calvert** (of **THE BIRTHDAY PARTY**) for the third album, FOREVER NOW (1982). This was a Todd Rundgren production – and, polished as that implies, Rundgren evidently persuaded Butler to work on his vocal technique. Apart from "Love My Way" and "President Gas", however, there was a notable absence of the lustre (or sheer lust) of its predecessor. So, too, with MIRROR MOVES (1984), made after Kilburn, Morris and Calvert had left, to be replaced by former Waitresses saxophonist **Mars Williams** and drummer **Keith Forsey**. Though strong in parts, once again the project lacked the grit of old. **Phil Garisto** (later of **THE CURE**) then became the group's fourth drummer (Ely eventually returned to that position in 1987), but MIDNIGHT TO MIDNIGHT (1987) again encouraged frustration with a once-great band. Butler himself admitted to hating it.

Several compilations followed before the release of BOOK OF DAYS in 1989. Escaping the prettiness of previous productions, this utilized a carpet of down-at-heel guitar on which Butler arrayed his always interesting but increasingly irrelevant lyrics. WORLD OUTSIDE (1991), with another new drummer, **Don Yallitch**, provoked even less critical interest or sales.

Wisely, the group sensed the end of their natural life span and broke up in 1993, with Butler joining **Love Spit Love** for some revitalized work.

○ **Talk Talk Talk** (1981; CBS).
A gold mine of superior songwriting, from the discordant sax of "Dumb Waiters" to the plangent "Pretty In Pink" and the marvellously insulting "I Just Wanna Sleep With You". Elsewhere the Furs said it with flowers, but on TALK TALK TALK they just said it.

○ **All Of This And Nothing** (1988; CBS).
The compilation to go for, by dint of the fact that it was released before the Furs' career went into free fall.

○ **Should God Forget – A Retrospective** (1998; Columbia Legacy).
A glorious two-CD collection of pure, proto-goth misery.

Alex Ogg

PSYCHIC TV

Formed London, 1981.

Neil Megson – aka **Genesis P-Orridge** – formed **Psychic TV** (PTV) after the demise of **THROBBING GRISTLE**. Its first incarnation also featured Throbbing Gristle's **Peter Christopherson** but he was soon to leave (founding **COIL**). The band has always been primarily P-Orridge's show. Even by the standards of his old band, it's been a bizarre career, and one shadowed by a fierce following from the Temple Of Psychick Youth (TOPY), a loosely based cult who adopted the group as gurus in a pantheon headed by Aleister Crowley. Over the years they have run graffiti campaigns, pestered the media and proselytized on behalf of PTV, though the music press has shown minimal interest.

Psychic TV's debut LP, FORCE THE HAND OF CHANCE (1982), featured P-Orridge and Christopherson on the back cover, shaven-headed and garbed as sinister-looking priests, like cult leaders in search of a following. Roping in **Alex Ferguson** (ex-**ALTERNATIVE TV**) to add to the all-round menace, the music on this and subsequent early-80s albums – DREAMS LESS SWEET (1983), A PAGAN DAY (1985), THEMES (a trilogy, 1985–87) – was a mix of minimalism and noise, opaquely ritualistic, and laden with unsettling samples: human bone instruments, wolf howls, orgasmic sighs or the ranting of a Jim Jones or Charles Manson. And the group was even weirder live, as was only to be expected from ex-situationist, ex-performance artist, Genesis.

Since then the public persona of Psychic TV has undergone a series of chameleon-like changes, reflecting the interests and often misinterpreted humour of its guru-like leader. In 1986, tiring of the shamanism, PTV declared itself 'hyperdelic', and warned ticketholders at gigs that they would be refused entry unless they wore multicoloured clothes. Black-clad industrial music miserables turned their backs on the band, but others turned on and tuned in to hypnotic, lengthy and often erotically charged performances.

In the same year, PTV were to deliver their most accessible record to date – "Godstar", a sublime bubblegum pop song about Rolling Stone Brian Jones, which cheekily recycled the riff from "Brown Sugar" and charted in the UK. (Genesis met Brian Jones once, and in interviews claimed supernatural contact with the dead singer through the mixing desk.)

In 1986 PTV also commenced a sequence of 23 live albums, each recorded in a different city, and each released on the 23rd of the month (the number's magic qualities were revealed to Genesis by William Burroughs, another figure in the Psychic TV pantheon). The following year saw release of the EP, MAGICKAL MYSTERY D TOUR, an aptly hyperdelic cover of The Beach Boys' "Good Vibrations", and a record about Roman Polanski containing references to Charles Manson – one of P-Orridge's more dubious obsessions.

PTV's interest in psychedelics, and a trip to Chicago by P-Orridge, led to their embrace of the burgeoning acid-house scene in the late 80s. Adopting the guise of DJ Doctor Megatrip, Genesis explored the tribal aspects of raves and the transcendent possibilities of 120bpm dance records well before trance was born. With the SUPERMAN 12" (1987), PTV proudly claimed to have released the first ever UK-recorded acid-house record. The band's excursions into house were gathered, with numerous remixes, on 1990's HIGH JACK: THE POLITICS OF ECSTASY album. More trippy experiments followed, along with the sampler-ridden BEYOND THEE INFINITE BEAT (1990), which included a recording of the birth of Genesis and wife Paula's child, Genesee.

The weirdest incident in the tale of PTV came in early 1992, when police raided the Temple's Hackney HQ while Genesis and Paula were away in Nepal. This was triggered by a TV programme about child abuse that had featured footage from a P-Orridge performance video. Officers snatched PTV's huge archive, including writing, tapes, videos and artwork from William Burroughs and Brion Gysin. None was ever returned, and the duo were advised that they risked arrest, or imposed custody of their daughters, should they ever return to the UK.

In the wake of the raid Genesis and Paula moved to California, where they collaborated with **Tim Leary** and others, as well getting into some memorable scrapes – such as a studio fire in April 1995, which put Genesis in hospital and for which he received a million-dollar insurance payout in 1998. PTV remains based in California, heavily involved in the dance-ambient scene.

In May 1999 Psychic TV reassembled for a grand extravaganza at London's Festival Hall that included guest appearances from The Master Musicians Of Jajouka and Quentin Crisp (via videolink). Their music continues to filter through: 2002 saw the release of a compilation, ORIGIN OF THE SPECIES VOL.3.

(•) **Dreams Less Sweet** (1983; Some Bizarre).
A spooky outing recorded in Zuccarelli holophonic surround-sound, this is a mixed bag of metal-bashing and sweetness, recorded in a church, a cave, PTV's adult nursery, and Caxton Hall (used in the past by Aleistair Crowley).

(•) **High Jack: The Politics Of Ecstasy** (1990; Wax Trax!).
A compilation of PTV's pioneering acid-house records. Includes the memorable "Tune In (Turn On Thee Acid House)".

(•) **Hex Sex: The Singles** (1994; Cleopatra!).
Perhaps the best place to start an exploration of PTV, including such accessible highlights as "Godstar" and "Good Vibrations".

Simon Whittaker

PUBLIC ENEMY

Formed Hempstead, New York, 1982.

"Rap is teaching white kids what it means to be black, and that causes a problem for the infrastructure." Chuck D

The collective that would become **Public Enemy** – the most influential and controversial rap group to date – began in 1982 at Adelphi University in Long Island, New York. Carlton Ridenhour was a graphic arts student who rapped under the name **Chuck D**, as well as co-managing Spectrum City, a DJ and concert promotion company, with fellow student **Hank Shocklee**. At the invitation of **Bill Stephney**, another Adelphi student, Shocklee and Chuck D began hosting their own rap show on the college radio station, which provided a platform for Chuck D to develop his lyrical skills and for him and Shocklee to experiment musically. One of their most avid fans was William Drayton, aka **Flavor Flav**, who joined the show as a co-host in 1983.

Chuck D's first outing on vinyl was a track called "Lies", produced with Spectrum City on the Vanguard label in 1985. It was very far from a hit, but a demo of "Public Enemy No. 1"– one of several tunes he and Shocklee had produced for their radio show – caught the attention of Def Jam Records' Rick Rubin. Rubin spent the next six months telephoning Chuck D with the offer of a record deal. Two years passed before Chuck D agreed, by which time he and his associates had already made a name for themselves as managers of Long Island's first hip-hop venue, the Entourage.

As a team, they worked out a strategy: Shocklee and Stephney would co-manage the outfit, which would be a rap cross between Run-D.M.C. and The Clash; Entourage DJ Norman Rogers, aka **Terminator X**, would handle turntable duties; Flavor Flav would play clown to Chuck D's straight man; while Richard Griffin (aka **Professor Griff**) was appointed the group's 'Minister Of Information'. The stage line-up was completed with the Entourage's bouncers – **Roderick Chillous**, **James Allen** and **James Norman** – who were dubbed the S1Ws (Security of the First World). Their records would be produced by a production team called **The Bomb Squad** (Chuck D, Eric 'Vietnam' Sadler, Hank Shocklee and his brother Keith).

Public Enemy's debut album, YO! BUM RUSH THE SHOW, was released in May 1987, on the back of their support slot on The Beastie Boys' US tour. The Bomb Squad sound was a collage of noises and sound bites, with samples flowing thick and fast. Sometimes they would have two or more drum machines play different rhythm patterns simultaneously – anarchic music that complemented the upfront lyrics perfectly. It hardly needs saying that all of this broke brand-new ground.

The group's uncompromising politics came to the fore with IT TAKES A NATION OF MILLIONS TO HOLD US BACK (1988). Including "Rebels Without A Pause", "Bring The Noise", "Don't Believe The Hype" and "Black Steel In The Hour Of Chaos", the album was the most confrontational record ever made, and one of the most audacious. On "She Watch Channel Zero?!" the group used disembodied James Brown loops and swiped a snarling guitar line from Slayer. The disc was as funky as hell, and – charting Top 50 in both the US and UK – was embraced by an audience across the entire spectrum of pop music. That, however, would soon disintegrate.

In May 1989, Griff was interviewed by David Mills from the *Washington Post*. In the interview, Griff was quoted as saying, 'Jews are responsible for the majority of wickedness that goes on across the globe.' The media scrutiny was intense, and grew more so after Spike Lee's *Do The Right Thing* was released, with Public Enemy's awesome "Fight The Power" (1989) as its theme song.

Public Enemy's response to the controversy was an uncompromising single, "Welcome To The Terrordome" (1990), an amelodic soundscape constructed almost entirely from James Brown splices and remaking funk in its own image. A menacing, brooding scowl, far removed from party music, it portraying Public Enemy as the real victims of the furore, and ignited renewed accusations of anti-Semitism. There was more controversy to come:

violence at their gigs led to at least two deaths, and it was later discovered that the group featured prominently in an FBI report on the effects of rap music on national security.

Despite their group defence, Griff and the rest of Public Enemy clearly did not see eye to eye any more, and after a UK tour in March 1990 he left the group. Signing to the Luke Skywalker label, his solo debut, PAWNS IN THE GAME, was released to coincide with his former colleagues' new offering, FEAR OF A BLACK PLANET (1990). With the exception of "Terrordome", FEAR lacked the reckless invention of its predecessor, though songs like "Burn Hollywood Burn" effectively fused political sloganeering to galvanizing grooves. It charted Top 10 in both the US and Britain.

In 1991, after Griff's replacement, Lisa Williamson, aka **Sister Souljah**, had been criticized by Bill Clinton for remarks she made about the LA riots, the band's future was thrown into doubt once more when Stephney fell out with Shocklee. However, things were straightened out in time for the release of what would be their third platinum album, APOCALYPSE 91 ... THE ENEMY STRIKES BLACK, in September. Featuring a new production team, the Imperial Grand Ministers Of Funk, and a collaboration with thrash-metal outfit, **ANTHRAX**, this was a retreat from the confrontational experimentalism of their previous albums, evincing a more straight-ahead, albeit heavy, take on funk. The American market went crazy for it, and it enjoyed an all-time high #4 place.

In the meantime, Flav was getting into trouble. After a jail sentence in early 1991 for assaulting his girlfriend, 1992 started with his arrest for driving without a licence and for nonpayment of child support. Then in November 1993, he was arrested and charged for attempted murder, after a row with a neighbour ended with shots being fired. It was only then that the full extent of his drug addiction became known.

Flav checked into the Betty Ford Clinic, and was back on form for MUSE SICK-N-HOUR MESS AGE (1994), an album that provided a much-needed alternative to gangsta tunes: tracks like "Watcha Gonna Do Now?" struck a chord with many who loved rap but were fed up of hearing about guns, bitches and 'ho's. But, despite the positivity of its raps, the album's music was out of sorts – Public Enemy were trying to keep up, rather than setting the agenda.

MUSE SICK... also signalled a temporary end to Public Enemy's relationship with Def Jam. After a dispute between Chuck D and label-head Bob Simmonds, the band left the label, signing directly to Island. In keeping with his role as communicator, Chuck D (already in demand on the US lecture circuit) branched out into television, devising and hosting two shows: an entertainment news magazine called *Inside The Rhyme* and a talk show, *Rap Live With Chuck D*. By 1998, however, he was back with the old firm, recording the soundtrack to Spike Lee's film *He Got Game* (1998), the original line-up augmented by the awesome **KRS-One** and the anachronistic **Stephen Stills**.

During the band's post-album hiatus, Chuck D released a solo album, THE AUTOBIOGRAPHY OF MISTACHUCK, and joined the Fox News Channel as a reporter. In 1997, he was given the *Patrick Lippert Humanitarian Award* for his work with the Rock The Vote campaign. The band briefly reunited with Professor Griff for a special 'History of Hip-Hop' concert in New York, on a bill that also featured KRS-One and Run-D.M.C.

1997 also saw Chuck D acting alongside Sly Stallone and Whoopi Goldberg in the film *Burn, Hollywood, Burn*. His first book, *Fight The Power* – co-written with Yusuf Jah – was published later that year, accompanied by a lecture tour in which he advised young black people on how to avoid ending up 'picking electronic cotton' in the new millennium.

In 1999 they released THERE'S A POISON GOIN' ON..., which may not have had the millennial fervour of old, but like Christopher Hitchens, Chuck D was naming names and it wasn't pretty. Everyone from Puffy to Funkmaster Flex to Def Jam came under the gaze of Chuck's rhetorical cross hairs and no one survived intact. No wonder it was released almost exclusively on the Internet. Yet being pissed off at the industry could never produce music as great as being pissed off with the world, but, then again, there is no more awesome sound in the world than a pissed off Chuck D, no matter the reason.

2002's REVOLVERLUTION offered more rabid class, but was dragged down by several uninspiring remixes that just made you wanna hear the power of originals, such as the unmatched "Shut Em Down" and "Public Enemy No.1". As Chuck said, quoting fifteen-times world heavyweight champion Ric Flair, 'If you want to be the man, you got to beat the man.' No one has yet.

It Takes A Nation Of Millions To Hold Us Back (1988; Def Jam).
The Bomb Squad's layered collages of James Brown and white noise is a startling synthesis. Absolutely essential.

Fear Of A Black Planet (1990; Def Jam).
Another brilliant work, since labelled 'prophetic', thanks to a spot-on prediction of the Rodney King assault and subsequent LA riots in "Burn Hollywood Burn". "Welcome To The Terrordrome" is one of hip-hop's crowning achievements.

Apocalypse '91...The Enemy Strikes Black (1991; Def Jam).
The pairing up with Anthrax might have upset a few purists, but the revamped "Bring The Noise" is one of PE's most memorable recordings. It also helped open whatever doors had remained shut.

Singles 'N' Remixes 1987–1992 (1992; Def Jam).
No one could argue with the choice of tracks on this compilation. After NATION OF MILLIONS, this has to be the next best starting point for the PE novice.

Muse Sick-N-Hour Mess Age (1994; Island).
As upfront and frank as any of its predecessors, with grooves to match. Its worthy anti-gangsta stance was much needed; unfortunately, they were mainly preaching to the converted.

George Luke and Peter Shapiro

PUBLIC IMAGE LTD.

Formed London, 1978; disbanded 1991.

Forming **Public Image Ltd.** was **John Lydon**'s get-out clause from the increasingly restrictive pantomime of the **SEX PISTOLS**. Completed by fellow punk rejects **Keith Levene** (guitar) and **JAH WOBBLE** (bass) – plus a revolving team of drummers – PiL began with gigs that usually resulted in aggressive standoffs between the band and their hardcore punk audience, which the ever-confrontational Lydon doubtless relished.

The debut album, PUBLIC IMAGE (1978), was split between tracks like "Low Life" and "Public Image", which took their lead from Pistols-style, chainsaw pop, and more interesting material like "Theme" – all oppressive low-end sludge – and "Annalisa", which harked back to The Stooges while anticipating The Birthday Party's most unbalanced demolitions.

Any assumptions that PiL were simply going to replay the punk wars were laid to rest on their next album, METAL BOX (1979). Heralded by a remarkable single, "Death Disco", and originally released in a metal film canister (and retitled SECOND EDITION when rereleased in a more sensible format), this remains an unearthly collection of songs. Lydon's vocal was no longer the cocky punk sneer but a tormented moan amid a distressed landscape of bass detonations, bursts of manic keyboard and, most compellingly, clusters of fractured guitar which were like a cross between the action-painting splatter of Richard Hell And The Voidoids and the cut-and-fold improvisation of jazz guitarist James 'Blood' Ulmer.

A sense of unlocatable disquiet permeated the whole album. On "Careering", a dub bass line struggled for life under an almost unbearable pile-up of electronic screams. "Radio 4" was like muzak from beyond the grave and "Bad Baby" dangled a strange, suspended narrative in a heavy limbo of drums, bass and Casio synthesizer drone. Most unsettling of all was the appalling drama of "Poptones", with its unending, cyclic guitar pattern creating an effect of nightmarish, looped *déjà vu*.

METAL BOX was never to be bettered. The next album was the live PARIS AU PRINTEMPS (1980) which, though scrappy and pointless, contained some amusing bouts of typical Lydon audience-baiting. After this, Wobble left in acrimonious circumstances to pursue a variety of eccentric projects with ex-members of Can.

Lydon and Levene continued with the album FLOWERS OF ROMANCE (1981), a more self-consciously experimental set than METAL BOX. It slid occasionally into mere studio-doodling, but contained moments of greatness like the lumbering funk of "Go Back", the Einstürzende Neubauten-on-amphetamines rush of "Francis Massacre", the arid mantras of "Four Enclosed Walls", and the title track, which was one of the most freakish hit singles since Laurie Anderson's "O Superman".

Pil pals John Lydon (left) and the manual-grasping Jah Wobble

When Levene left in 1984, it was less to do with the riot fiasco at a New York show than with a near-homicidal bust-up with Lydon. Anxious to show that he was the true personality behind PiL, Lydon rushed out THIS IS WHAT YOU WANT ... THIS IS WHAT YOU GET (1984). Despite its reputation, this was at least fifty percent good stuff, suggesting ways that some of the more awkward moments of FLOWERS could be tethered to more coherent (more commercial, even) structures.

For 1986's ALBUM, Lydon hooked up with New York's guru of tasteful experimentalism, **BILL LASWELL**, and produced an enjoyable record full of thunderous drumming, unreconstructed axe-god histrionics, and epic sneering. It looked as though this new PiL-not-PiL could be fun. But it wasn't to be. Lydon formed a regular band and the subsequent releases – HAPPY? (1987), 9 (1989) and THAT WHAT IS NOT (1991) – were inoffensive pop-funk, almost as lightweight as INXS.

Of the three originals, Wobble has been the most successful, with New Age fusion musos **Invaders Of The Heart**. Levene remains underexposed and undervalued, releasing only one rather weak album

under the banner **Violent Opposition**. Meanwhile, Lydon – who, fairly or not, will always be seen as the guiding spirit behind PiL – seemed content to release records whenever he felt like flexing his ageing Johnny Rotten persona in public, before in 1996 going the whole hog and re-forming Sex Pistols for the nostalgia circuit. PLASTIC BOX (1999) a four-CD compilation, sees Lydon cashing in for the second time in a decade.

⦿ **Public Image** (1978; Virgin).
This was one of the earliest albums to indicate an escape route from the punk rut without losing the raw energy of the scene that produced it.

⦿ **Metal Box/Second Edition** (1979; Virgin).
An hour-long journey through very troubled inner space. Accompanied by great sound-bite slogans ('death disco' and 'anti-rock'n'roll'), this was a model for subsequent deconstructions of rock.

⦿ **Plastic Box** (1999; Virgin).
More beautiful packaging, this compilation squeezes virtually every track from the band's first four albums onto four CDs and finds ample room to cover the highlights of HAPPY?, 9 and THAT WHAT IS NOT. With splendid sleeve notes by Lydon, BBC sessions dating back to "Poptones" and 12" disco-mixes to boot, this is the ideal introduction to the band and the ideal replacement for all those scratched vinyl METAL BOX singles.

Ben Smith

PUBLIC IMAGE LTD.

PULP

Formed Sheffield, England, 1981.

Do you remember the first time you heard **Pulp**? Perhaps it was during the autumn of 1993 when the British backlash against grunge began. Overnight, bands like Blur became fervent patriots; kitted out in Fred Perrys and armed with cockney accents, they led the Britpop nostalgia war against everything American. Pulp, whose marriage of disco and art-rock was far removed from laddishness, suddenly found itself centre stage. The band's quintessential Englishness was the reason: **Jarvis Cocker**'s vignettes about the everyday desperation of provincial life, coupled with his eccentric live performances ('an erotic coat hanger' quipped one critic), are as British as the Queen Mum.

Pulp (or Arabacus Pulp, as it was first known) formed in Sheffield in 1981. Vocalist, lyricist and unlikely latter-day heart-throb Cocker was still at school – the band's live debut was in the school canteen during lunch hour. Cocker formed the group for the typical reason: 'So that girls would like me, because I had glasses and bad teeth, and wasn't any good at sports.' That said, the group's first release – IT (1983) – was a remarkably strong effort, reminiscent of early Smiths and Lloyd Cole And The Commotions. Lush arrangements, dominated by acoustic guitar and strings, served as background for Cocker's sunny crooning. The album, buttressed by a successful John Peel radio session, convinced Cocker 'that [I] was going to be a child prodigy'. Little did he know how long it would take.

By the time the respectable but mediocre FREAKS (1986) and its cash-in companion piece, MASTERS OF THE UNIVERSE (recorded 1985–86, released 1994) were made, Pulp's sound had changed radically. Three of the group's final personnel – Cocker, **Candida Doyle** (piano/organ) and **Russell Senior** (guitar/violin) – were in place, and Cocker had begun to write his trademark tales of bungled relationships and stewed emotions. Cocker also began cultivating his cult of personality when, forced to spend a year in a wheelchair after he jumped out of a window to impress a woman, he incorporated the chair into the band's live shows. He continued to use the seat as a prop long after his legs had healed.

With the addition of **Nick Banks** on drums and **Steve Mackey** on bass, Pulp's line-up coalesced, recording SEPARATIONS in 1989. Although the album wasn't released until 1992, the band was in fine form, with synthesizers churning, drums steady, strings moaning, and Cocker caught up in a sexual frenzy, sometimes singing with the breathy, dramatic swagger of Scott Walker and sometimes pattering on about lying in bed with a woman 'and waiting for the ceiling to cave in/But it never did'. As the record company dallied about with the album, the group independently released "My Legendary Girlfriend" (1990), a tale with a bass line out of "Shaft". The single was a significant breakthrough, and served as impetus for the group to start its own label, Gift.

In 1993, Island signed Pulp and kicked off with INTRO: THE GIFT RECORDINGS (1993), which collected these hits with a half-dozen other songs charting the band's streamline sound, and found Cocker serving as a physical manifestation of sexual tension. HIS'N'HERS (1994) was released shortly afterwards, and Pulpmania erupted. The album crystallized Cocker's tactic of examining details for broader truths in highly narrative lyrical scenarios: taking a girl to the reservoir for a romp; hiding in a wardrobe to watch an older sister's sexual encounters; drinking tea while fantasizing about frolicking with his hostess. The sexual heat was made more intense when, in lieu of a traditional video for "Do You Remember The First Time?", Cocker and bassist/film MFA Mackey directed a 26-minute short that posed the question to various celebrities, including John Peel and Justine Frischmann (from Elastica). Tastefully done, the film proved there was just as much elation and pain in the stars' experiences as in ordinary people's.

Continuing to focus on everyday details and experiences, Pulp released the brilliant DIFFERENT CLASS in 1995. Stripping away the glamour from Britpop's idealization of the working class, Cocker sang about the sobering reality of those who have no money, who 'dance, and drink and screw/Because there's nothing else to do'. With their Bowie-esque backing tunes (circa ZIGGY STARDUST) heightening the interplay between artifice and reality, Pulp mashed the rest of the Britpop pack by moving forward while the others stayed rooted in the past.

The success of DIFFERENT CLASS resulted in one of the great pieces of rock cabaret: invited to a music-business back-slapping awards show in London, Jarvis felt compelled to invade the stage during Michael Jackson's nauseating performance and to make certain gestures which won him the heart of every non-Jackson fan repulsed by the messianic posturing of the now-married father of two. Jarvis was arrested and detained for a short while (presumably on the charge of 'Being rude to a famous American', as no real laws were apparently broken). The story turned Pulp into a household name and won Jarvis much recognition on the streets.

After so long in the shadows waiting for their big break to come, Pulp deserved some time off and, apart from hectic touring and acres of press coverage, nothing was heard from the band until 1998's THIS IS HARDCORE. The title suggests that Jarvis still lurked in the sweatier recesses of an adolescent mind, but this image was shattered as soon as the album was heard for the first time. There was a claustrophobic, darker feel to a lot of the music, reflecting the gold-fish-bowl effect of instant fame. The title track, though, was the stand-out piece – cinematic, lounge-style arrangement and a sensitively structured

Pulp at Glastonbury, 1995, from the left: Steve Mackey, Jarvis Cocker, Russell Senior, Nick Banks and Candida Doyle

lyric. The band's most accomplished piece of work to date.

For 2001's WE LOVE LIFE the group managed to tempt Scott Walker out of his hermitage to take up the production reins. There was a pastoral trend running throughout, reflected in "Wickerman" and "The Trees", though they hadn't got all Fairport on us quite yet; Walker's strings and the Left Bank trendiness fell well inside the taste threshold while lyrically Jarvis's obsessions took a more outward view. Far friendlier than THIS IS HARDCORE, it lacked an obvious single, or even a defining moment, yet remained definitively – and marvellously - them.

At this point the band split with Island records and Pulp was, basically, put on ice. Most recently, Jarvis was to be found performing with a new band, **Relaxed Muscle**.

● **His'N'Hers** (1994; Island).
Pulp's conceptual coup was the framing of working-class banality in the synth-glitz of Roxy Music. The result is some of the funniest, smartest, savviest British pop of the decade.

● **Different Class** (1995; Island).
At times heartbreaking, at times hilarious, occasionally both at once, Cocker's songs show the touch of a master pop craftsman. The centrepiece, "Common People", is one of the singles of the 90s. The rest of the album, meanwhile, is inclusive enough to steal from both Bowie and 80s schlock-diva Laura Brannigan.

● **This Is Hardcore** (1998; Island).
A more grown-up album, reflecting the vastly changed circumstances that million-sellers can bring about, Jarvis is no longer hiding behind shabby furniture to get his kicks; these days, he's having expensive furniture shipped in specially.

Julie Taraska

PUSSY GALORE

Formed Washington DC, 1985; disbanded 1990.

"That's the real legacy of Pussy Galore: losing your friends." Jon Spencer

Guitarists **Jon Spencer** and **Julie Cafritz** met while the former was studying semiotics and history of art in quaint, secular Provincetown, Rhode Island. Without much anguish they jointly decided to drop out of college and head for DC. 'I hated the people, the course, everything,' Jon said. 'I just wanted to play rock'n'roll.' Once in DC they hooked up with a drummer, **John Hammill**, and recorded FEEL GOOD ABOUT YOUR BODY, an EP released in 1985, as **Pussy Galore**, on their own Shove label. Four songs – "Die Bitch", "HC Rebellion", "Constant Pain" and "Car Fantasy" – laid down a benchmark of vice-grip garage, industrial, hardcore, punk.

Alienated by the nation's capital (then murder capital of the US), the duo rode out of town to their logical destination: New York. The move embraced third guitarist **Neil Hagerty**, while drummer John was replaced by former Sonic Youther **Bob Birt**, who introduced a different kind of drum kit, incorporating 'street signs, the gas tank from a large American car ... and Steve Albini's cock ring'. By 1986, **Cristina Martinez**, formerly group photographer, had become fourth guitarist, and she stayed in Pussy Galore all the way until September of that year, just after the release of the band's 550-copies-only letter-perfect version of EXILE ON MAIN STREET. Martinez quit acrimoniously, however, having tired of being Spencer's 'whipping girl'. Today she and Spencer are husband and wife.

A further album, RIGHT NOW! (1987), kept the wolf from the door as acclaim and outrage gathered over Pussy Galore like polarized clouds. In early 1988 the group came to England where they played at London's Mean Fiddler, and then, back at their home base in NYC, they recorded SUGARSHIT SHARP with Steve Albini, for Caroline Records. Their triumphant return to the Mean Fiddler could have been phoned in: the band left the stage after thirty seconds. And they said The Jesus & Mary Chain played short sets.

Then it was Julie's turn to leave, just before the release of DIAL M FOR MOTHERFUCKER (1988), which is widely regarded as the band's consummate moment. The album LA HISTORIA DE LA MUSICA ROCK (1990) was a case of Exile on Mainline Street – it was recorded in two days in what would seem to have been a Nissen hut during an air raid, by a producer who must have stepped on a land mine on the way to the session. Covers of "Little Red Rooster" and "Crawfish" were sublime; the rest was not.

"SuGarShit SharP"

After that, the main players deconstructed into various permutations – Free Kitten, Action Swingers, **BOSS HOG**, **ROYAL TRUX** and the **JON SPENCER BLUES EXPLOSION**.

⊙ **Corpse Love** (1992; Hut).
'I find it surprising that people are now looking back and saying we were a great band,' said Cristina Martinez, 'because they should have realized it then.' As compilation legacies go, this one's like a slap from beyond the grave.

Susan Compo

SUZI QUATRO

Born Detroit, Michigan, 1950.

Suzi Quatro was well on her way to becoming a rock'n'roll rebel by the time she'd reached 15. She played bongos for her dad, Art's, jazz band at age 8, dropped out of school at 14, and started a rock group, **The Pleasure Seekers**, with her sisters a year later. The band developed a reputation for young, loud snottiness on the Michigan club circuit and went on to record a garage-band classic "What A Way To Die" – later featured on the garage-band collection of the same name. Having mutated into the harder-rockin' Cradle, Quatro and the band gigged across the United States, and even played a US military base in Vietnam.

While performing at a Detroit dance hall, Cradle were spotted by British producer Mickie Most. Best known for his work with Donovan, Lulu and Herman's Hermits, Most saw Suzi's star potential and signed her as a solo act. Her first single, "Rolling Stone," was released in 1972. With **Len Tuckey** (guitar), **Dave Neal** (drums), and **Alistair McKenzie** (keyboards; soon to be replaced by **Mike Deacon**), Quatro hit the road with Slade later that year.

The debut single failed to make an impression, so Most sought help from The Sweet's zero-cred but incredibly successful songwriting team Nicky Chinn and Mike Chapman – responsible for some of the most dire UK pop of the 70s, Chapman would later produce hits for the Knack and Blondie.

The Chinnichap machine provided Quatro with a stream of a dozen hits, starting with "Can The Can" in 1973 and followed by "48 Crash", "Devil Gate Drive", and others. Her image, having been spooned into a leather catsuit and kitted out with the biggest, longest bass guitar in the UK, helped make Suzi a UK and European sensation, but she saw little chart action in the US, where she is remembered more as a TV personality than as a singer. She played the predictably leather-clad Leather Tuscadero (pretty much her on-stage persona) in *Happy Days* and often performed on the show. To Quatro's credit, she never appeared as anything less than a proud, raunchy totally-in-control woman.

With the arrival of more convincing black leather stars in the punk explosion, Quatro and her glam-pop peers were headed for the shelf. Although she continues to record and perform (most notably in a British revival of *Annie Get Your Gun*), Suzi Quatro's

heyday came and went with the end of the 1970s; she finally made the American Top Five in 1979 via an MOR duet with, ahem, Chris Norman (the lead singer of Smokie), "Stumblin' In". Her guitar-driven songs and aggressive on-stage manner paved the way for female guitar-rock acts from Joan Jett and the Runaways right up to the 'riot grrrl' movement. She was most recently heard on BBC Radio 2 presenting a rock'n'roll nostalgia show. Never renowned as an album act, Quatro fans will be best served by one of the many singles compilations cluttering up the bargain bins.

⊙ **The Wild One – Classic Quatro** (1996; Razor & Tie). The best of the current crop, with all the hits and a smattering of album tracks.

Charlotte Robinson

FINLEY QUAYE

Born Edinburgh, Scotland, 1974.

It may have been claimed that because he is the uncle of Tricky – even though he is seven years his junior – **Finley Quaye** is a somewhat dubious talent. However, his work stands on its own.

Musical proficiency extends across the Quaye family: Finley's father Cab was a jazz composer, while brother Caleb was a much-touted session guitarist. From this background, Finley assimilated a wide range of influences and, in 1993, he moved to college in Manchester, where he enrolled on a music and sound engineering course. The following year, he embarked on some sessions with A Guy Called Gerald's mainman **Gerald Simpson**. The sessions were short-lived, but Quaye returned from a tour abroad with eco-anarchists Rainbow Tribe to find that Simpson had reworked some of the material into an irresistible blend of breakbeat and ambience called "Finley's Rainbow". A three-track demo, which included an embryonic rendition of what became his first hit, "Sunday Shining", was circulated around the major labels, and he finally signed to Sony subsidiary Epic Records in September 1996.

Teaming up with Sheffield-based producers Kevin Bacon and Jonathan Quarmby, he began work on what emerged a year later as the languid, life-affirming debut album, MAVERICK A STRIKE. Although a great deal was initially made of Quaye's bloodline in relation to Tricky, the warm and sensuous rerecording of "Sunday Shining" appeared and dispelled any doubts. Not even Britain's coldest, wettest early summer in years could prevent this delight climbing to #16 in the charts. "Even After

All" and "It's Great When We're Together" maintained the hit momentum – the latter was remixed for its single release by Fun Lovin' Criminals – and the uplifting charms of MAVERICK A STRIKE helped Quaye to win the *Best British Male Artist* at the Brit Awards in February 1998.

After a period of silence Quaye re-emerged in 2000 with a new single "Spiritualized" and a second album, VANGUARD. Though not as consistent as his debut, it was a confident and eclectic collection that embraced everything from reggae to soul to drum'n'bass.

Sometimes portrayed as difficult, he is simply an artist who is keen to test his audience and unwilling to stick with designated musical genres. Whatever his next move, after the eclecticism of his first two albums it should be fascinating.

⊙ **Maverick A Strike** (1997; Epic/Sony).
The first half of this debut is extraordinarily addictive – a simple but effective mix of reggae, funk and acid-rock. The second half cannot help but flag slightly, but even here "Sweet And Loving Man" is superior lovers' rock, and "The Way Of The Explorer" is a nifty slice of roots reggae.

Justin Lewis

QUEEN

Formed London, 1971; disbanded 1991.

**"We're the Cecil B. de Mille of rock'n'roll, always wanting to do things bigger and better."
Freddie Mercury**

Nobody has done stadium rock like **Queen** – and nobody's likely to surpass them, either. This was a band with a unique sense of theatricality, camp but ever-rocking, and one whose songs, even solos, seem at their best rendered by a crowd of 50,000-plus, arms aloft and swaying. Witness the fact that they stole the show at the London Live Aid concert, or that British football crowds love nothing better than to sing along (word perfect, of course) to "We Will Rock You" – or, on those special occasions, "We Are The Champions", and, if offered the choice, would doubtless exchange pretty much any Queen song for their national anthem. It's some legacy.

Oddly, the band were slow off the starting blocks. **Brian May** (guitar) and **Roger Taylor** (drums) enjoyed little success in the late 60s with their first group Smile, and when they teamed up as Queen with **Freddie Mercury** (vocals) and **John Deacon** (bass) in 1971, they initially struggled to make much impression with their glam-tinged heavy rock.

The man who helped them break was producer Roy Thomas Baker, who developed with the band a brilliant studio sound – an all-encompassing affair, based around multitracked guitars and huge choruses of layered vocal parts, and anchored by a dynamic rhythm section. Refusing to use synthesizers, Queen relied on the manipulation of May's self-constructed guitar to achieve whatever special effects were required. They were exceptional in that all the members were capable songwriters (although the bulk of the material was written by Mercury and May), and that first album, QUEEN (1973), showed huge promise, featuring the early stage favourite "Liar" and the first single, "Keep Yourself Alive".

For all that, it got virtually no airplay, even in Britain, and the band were nowhere until an appearance on BBC TV's *Top Of The Pops* in early 1974 changed their profile overnight. The rush-released single "Seven Seas Of Rhye" entered the UK Top 10, and QUEEN II (1974), released on the back of a riotously received headlining tour, was also a resounding chart success, reaching #5 in the UK and an encouraging #43 in the US. Even at this early stage, Queen were a superb visual act, with stage outfits designed by Zandra Rhodes and Mercury's confident posturing established as trademark.

By the end of 1974 Queen were sitting pretty, having well and truly arrived with their next single, "Killer Queen", and the strongest album so far, SHEER HEART ATTACK (1974), both of which charted #2 in the UK and #12 in the US. The album was immaculate, showcasing everything from power rock to ballads, beautifully segued together, while the final song, "In The Lap Of The Gods", was a prototype of the singalong anthem Queen would soon be taking from the city hall to the stadium.

Queen's ascendance would doubtless have taken place in any circumstances, but it happened at a time when some of Britain's biggest 'heavy' groups were inactive or in tax-imposed exile, and 'glam' artists were struggling to convince with more mature material. Queen's combination of hard-rock riffs and intelligently constructed albums, their commercial melodies and a strong visual presence, thus appealed to both markets. Not that the British were the only takers. In 1975 Queen captured Japan and the US, with consummate stage shows.

Shortly after returning to Britain, the group spent months working on what was at the time the most expensive rock record ever made, A NIGHT AT THE OPERA (1975). The album was recorded and mixed in six different studios, and carried some breathtakingly ambitious vocal arrangements, which stretched the recording technology of the time to its limits. The mock-operatic "Bohemian Rhapsody" took three weeks to record and was a watershed in popular music history – it was accompanied by what is widely recognized as being the first promotional video. The single spent nine weeks at #1 in Britain over the Christmas period of 1975 and went Top 10 in the US.

The following year Queen staged a free concert in Hyde Park, London, which broke all attendance records. Another epic single, "Somebody To Love", was closely followed by the self-produced album, A DAY AT THE RACES (1976), which again contained a wide range of material and charted #1 in the UK

Queen's Roger Taylor, Freddie Mercury and Brian May share an intimate moment

and #5 in the US. The advent of punk rock in Britain had little effect on Queen's popularity, although the band were unwittingly responsible for making the infamous Sex Pistols and Bill Grundy television debacle possible; Queen had originally been scheduled to appear on the programme but pulled out at the last minute, thus paving the way for their EMI stable-mates to swear their way into television history.

1977 saw release of the double-sided anthems "We Are The Champions"/"We Will Rock You", hits in all areas. These previewed NEWS OF THE WORLD (1977), which had a more direct production, and saw the band heading in a more straightforward rock direction. The return of producer Roy Thomas Baker for JAZZ (1978) suggested a lack of confidence and the album was patchy. The promotional campaign for its first single, "Fat Bottomed Girls"/"Bicycle Race" featuring 65 naked girls on racing bikes, was universally panned as being in dubious taste even for a band of Queen's outré tendencies.

An indifferent live album, LIVE KILLERS (1979), marked time the following year, before the band reaffirmed their staying power with the eclectic singles, "Crazy Little Thing Called Love" and "Another One Bites The Dust", both taken from THE GAME (1980), which saw the band using synthesizers for the first time and was the group's first

American #1 album. FLASH GORDON (1980) was a brief foray into soundtrack work, which was hurriedly recorded and poorly received, although it married well to the film itself.

Ten years after their humble beginnings, the band celebrated their anniversary by releasing a greatest hits album, a video compilation and a pictorial history simultaneously in October 1981. It was again a ground-breaking move and would help to set the trend for how rock and pop would be marketed in future. The album was also one of the first titles by any band to be available on compact disc. A month later, Queen returned to #1 in Britain for the first time in six years with "Under Pressure" (1981), a collaboration with fellow superstar **DAVID BOWIE**. HOT SPACE (1982), the album it came from, was, however, a generally weak attempt at white funk.

Refreshed after time apart, the band reconvened with the anthemic "Radio Ga Ga" and the attendant album, THE WORKS (1984). Then in July 1985 Queen's show-stealing appearance at the Live Aid concert confirmed that they were the consummate stadium band and set the whole back catalogue off into orbit again.

Since the early 80s, Queen had made a point of staging enormous concerts in territories that were not used to seeing rock music at all and, on releasing A

QUEEN

836

KIND OF MAGIC (1986), the band embarked on a series of large-scale events, which included the first concert in Hungary by a Western act since 1964. The tour culminated in an appearance in front of a 120,000-strong crowd in England's Knebworth Park.

After a three-year break from group-related activity, they returned with THE MIRACLE (1989), evidence that by now they were quite happy to stick to a formula. Any pretences towards subtlety had long since been ditched in favour of bombastic productions, with Mercury's histrionic vocals and May's patent guitar to the fore.

It was at this time that rumours began to circulate concerning Mercury's illness, and the group's uncharacteristic reluctance to perform live provided fuel for the fire. INNUENDO (1991), a #1 album with a title track that became a #1 single, was a remarkable achievement considering that Mercury was by this time seriously ill – "The Show Must Go On" seemed to refer directly to the singer's battle against failing health. Following a last-minute statement that he was suffering from AIDS, Mercury died on November 24, 1991.

In the spring of 1992, some of the biggest names in the entertainment world, ranging from Liza Minnelli and Elizabeth Taylor to Def Leppard and Guns N' Roses, took part in an exuberant celebration of Queen's music at Wembley Stadium, with the band in support. The concert raised millions for the Mercury Phoenix Trust for AIDS awareness. The last chapter in the Queen phenomenon came with the release of the material that Mercury had been working on with the band in his last months. MADE IN HEAVEN (1995) wasn't a masterpiece, but bravely banished any trace of self-pity, finishing on as high a note as possible.

⊙ **A Night At The Opera** (1975; EMI).
Queen's SERGEANT PEPPER. Besides the legendary single "Bohemian Rhapsody", the album calls at all stops from menacing heavy rock ("Death On Two Legs") to pop ("You're My Best Friend") to music-hall pastiche ("Seaside Rendezvous"). The often overlooked epic, "Prophet's Song", manages to outdo even "Rhapsody" for multi-layered vocals, and segues beautifully into one of Mercury's finest ballads, "Love Of My Life".

⊙ **The Works** (1984; EMI).
A return to form after some mixed experimentation, this is definitive Queen, 80s-style. The accent is firmly on straight-ahead big production rock. Taylor's "Radio Ga Ga" and Deacon's "I Want To Break Free" became stadium-stompers the world over, and, although some of the lesser tracks display a lyrical naivety, the album works brilliantly as loud music for boy racers.

⊙ **Greatest Hits Volumes I & II** (1981 & 1991; EMI).
In truth, most of Queen's albums were patchy, but their choice of singles was usually impeccable. These two seventeen-track sets represent a remarkably varied, yet consistently successful singles career.

⊙ **Rocks** (1998; Parlophone).
When the fancy took them, Queen could rock it out with the best of them. This eighteen-track collection sets out its stall with track one "We Will Rock You" and, with the exception of the tear-jerking final song, "No One But You (Only The Good Die Young)", this is a headbanging festival of riffing, screaming fun, with a hefty dose of aspirin recommended prior to usage.

Steve Dinsdale

QUEENS OF THE STONE AGE

Formed California, 1997.

Some bands achieve a legendary status only after they've been consigned to the great outdoor festival in the sky, and so it was with proto-stoner outfit **KYUSS**, who blazed a trail of sludged-out riffs and gargantuan rhythms during the 90s, disintegrated and then mutated into the mighty stoner rock outfit **Queens Of The Stone Age.**

After Kyuss imploded, founding guitarist **Josh Homme** headed for Seattle to tour with the Screaming Trees, while also recording a number of 7" singles with the likes of Soundgarden's **Matt Cameron** and Dinosaur Jr's **Mike Johnson** under the name **Gamma Ray**, which, unfortunately, also proved to be the name of a dodgy German metal band stuck in an 80s time warp. Next Homme recruited former Kyuss drummer **Alfredo Hernandez**, along with a bunch of helpful mates and adopted Queens Of The Stone Age as the project name. They set about creating QUEENS OF THE STONE AGE (1998), which eventually emerged on the cool indie label Loosegroove. By Homme's own admission the task was to concentrate on songwriting rather than free-form jamming. The results were tight, almost surgical in places, but the focus on melody and power brought a welcome punch and groove to the elements inher-

TONY MOTT/SIN

Queens Josh Homme and Nick Oliveri

ited from the fluid Kyuss style. The album was hailed as an underground triumph.

At this point former Kyuss bassist **Nick Oliveri** left The Dwarves, where he had played under the moniker **Rex Everything**, and joined Homme in Queens. He had also spent some of the interim messing about with his own **Mondo Generator** project, which eventually yielded an album, COCAINE RODEO (2000), oddly enough featuring both Homme and former Kyuss drummer **Brant Bjork**. Needless to say, Kyuss fans were getting very excited, but Homme chose to maintain his artistically philandering approach to music-making and continued to take part in projects such as the various DESERT SESSIONS albums released on Man's Ruin. Meanwhile, the Queens' momentum grew.

Heavy touring ensured that the band's next album was highly anticipated. When R (2000) appeared on Interscope it was instantly dubbed a masterpiece. **Dave Catching** (keyboards) filled the band's sound out and **Nicky Lucerno** and **Gene Trautmann** appeared on drums and percussion. R was towering, angular, and seriously groovy, its name taken from the 'R' indicating 'Restricted' in the American film classification system. All of which made perfect sense when lead track "Feel Good Hit Of The Summer" consisted basically of the line 'Nicotine, valium, vicodin, marijuana, ecstasy and alcohol … c-c-c-c-cocaine!!!!' screamed over and over. There was no need to guess what Homme and his buddies got up to when they indulged in a spot of r&r.

SONGS FOR THE DEAF arrived in 2002 and featured a line-up that included **Dave Grohl** (**FOO FIGHTERS**) and **Mark Lanegan**; it easily managed to exceed the high expectations created by its predecessor, thanks to its complex and intoxicating cocktail of speed-rock and generally devastating guitar pyrotechnics.

(•) **Queens Of The Stone Age** (1998; Loosegroove/Roadrunner).
A more song-orientated approach to the raw riffery of the 70s. Homme's vocals provide an eerily silky counterpoint to the groovy heaviness.

(•) **R** (2000; Interscope).
Working with long-time production collaborator Chris Goss obviously suits the Queens because this is the album that truly kicked them into the limelight. Weirdly experimental at times, this is, nevertheless, a *tour de force* of style and content.

(•) **Songs For The Deaf** (2002; Interscope).
Once again the Queens redefine rock with their tight, blistering assault on your ears. Cuts such as "The Sky Is Falling" and "No One Knows" are both impenetrable and all enveloping. Listening to SONGS… will leave you feeling like you've been digested by a shark.

Essi Berelian

QUEENSRŸCHE

Formed Seattle, 1981.

Despite having several excellent albums under their belts, **Queensrÿche** have never quite lodged in the mainstream consciousness – a strange state of affairs for a high-class, thoughtful metal outfit with both gold and platinum discs to their credit.

In 1981, vocalist **Geoff Tate** was hanging out in Easy Street Records, an independent record shop in Bellevue, Washington, when he bumped into a group of friends who were in a band called The Mob. **Chris De Garmo** (guitar), **Michael Wilton** (guitar), **Eddie Jackson** (bass) and **Scott Rockenfield** (drums) persuaded Tate to join them, playing covers in the clubs of Seattle. After a while getting nowhere, the band decided to start writing their own material and break away from the club circuit. The outlook changed, and so did the name.

Queensrÿche's first break came in June 1982, when they recorded a four-track demo, which included "Queen Of The Ryche", a track still played live today. The demo was played to Easy Street owners Kim and Diana Harris, who liked it so much they set up their own independent label, 206 Records, to get the demo released. Preceded by plays on several rock stations, the eponymously titled EP emerged in May 1983, in an edition of 3500 copies.

EMI got wind of the band, and in August signed them up to a seven-album deal. The first was THE WARNING (1984), produced by James Guthrie, who had worked on Pink Floyd's THE WALL. However, Guthrie and the band were pulling in opposite directions, and Queensrÿche weren't happy with the result, claiming that it wasn't heavy enough. July 1986 saw the release of the RAGE FOR ORDER, beginning the drift away from all-out metal. The stage image advertised an increasing element of art-rock futurism, with flowing overcoats studded with sequins and stuffed with shoulder pads, plus lashings of face make-up. The album was OK, but the look was naff, and the outfits were ditched.

With producer Peter Collins (Rush, Gary Moore) on board, they made the breakthrough album, OPERATION: MINDCRIME, in May 1988. A tale of media manipulation, mental domination and revolution, it was described by *Metal Hammer* magazine as 'an extraordinary, prophetic, revolutionary concept', and went gold in the States. Whereas this concept album was precision-made and meticulously planned, the follow-up, EMPIRE (1990), was a more spontaneous creation, and went down even better with the public, going platinum accompanied by MTV's repeated playings of the videos for "Silent Lucidity" and "Resistance".

The band laid low until the release of their fifth album, PROMISED LAND (1994), a set described by Tate as a kind of self-analysis, a look back at all the things that had changed within the lives of the band since the success of EMPIRE. It went gold within a few months, confirming the band's status as masters of the progressive-metal scene.

Another lengthy silence ensued, broken in 1997 with HEAR IN THE NOW FRONTIER. The band had once again revised their sound to match the tastes of the market, opting for a less orchestral, rockier sound. There was no escaping their musical craft and influences, however, and some of the tracks still veered closer to the classic prog-rock sounds of the 70s than to the 'stripped for the new millennium' metal of the late 90s.

Nothing could prepare anyone for what was to happen next, however. Founding member and lead guitarist Chris DeGarmo jumped ship just as the band were putting together their next opus. His replacement was **Kelly Gray**, originally the project's producer. Sadly, Q2K (1999) accurately reflected Queensrÿche's confused state at this time and one couldn't help but feel that the band were still reeling from losing such a key musician. While DeGarmo dabbled in a side project, which included various members of Alice In Chains, his former band-mates had embarked on a supporting slot with the newly revitalized Iron Maiden on the BRAVE NEW WORLD reunion tour. Also sharing the stage was **Rob Halford**, who was enjoying something of a resurgence after some years in the metal wilderness after leaving Judas Priest. As a result an idea was hatched for **Dickinson**, Tate and Halford to form a sort of metal supergroup. Though the notion was intriguing it never really amounted to much, and in the aftermath one wonders whether Queensrÿche will scale the same gloriously bombastic heights of progressive metaldom ever again.

⊙ **Operation:Mindcrime** (1988; EMI).
Arguably the best of Queensrÿche, this is a very rare item – a successful, heavy concept album. The production is spot-on and meticulous.

⊙ **Empire** (1990; EMI).
A more emotive and wide-ranging album – "Empire" is about gun control, "Della Brown" tackles homelessness, "Jet City Woman" treats long-distance relationships. Metal comes no more brilliant.

Richard Allan

QUICKSILVER MESSENGER SERVICE

Formed San Francisco, 1964; disbanded 1975.

The career of the **Quicksilver Messenger Service**, like their music, is firmly rooted in the San Francisco scene of the late 60s, where inspired music went hand in hand with drug busts and spontaneous decision-making. All played their part in the Quicksilver story.

The band's initial strength lay in the fact that it had recruited members from two traditions, as coffee-house folkies traded licks with members of former garage bands inspired by the British invasion of the early 60s. The San Francisco scene gave the band a platform for their musical skills, and the explosive twin lead-guitar interplay of **John Cipollina** and **Gary Duncan** was soon a feature of the local club scene. Equally happy stretching out a basic blues to include time changes and searing guitar battles, or delivering their own well-crafted interpretations of songs from the emerging counterculture, the band were the very essence of San Francisco.

Most of the band's status as prime exponents of late-60s rock rests on the first two albums, QUICKSILVER MESSENGER SERVICE (1968) and HAPPY TRAILS (1969). Both albums were cut by the quartet of Cipollina, Duncan, **Greg Elmore** (drums) and **David Freiberg** (bass), following founding member **Dino Valenti**'s (guitar/vocals) jailing for a drugs offence. Quicksilver were one of the few Bay Area bands to successfully transfer the power and invention of their live performance to vinyl. A mixture of live and studio work, HAPPY TRAILS in particular gives a real insight into the period, and includes a side-long suite based on Bo Diddley's "Who Do You Love".

By 1969 Valenti was a free man again and his first serious move was to relocate to New York with Duncan in the hope of making something happen musically. It didn't, and in the meantime Quicksilver replaced Duncan with English session pianist **Nicky Hopkins**. Hopkins had stints with **JEFF BECK** and **STEVE MILLER** behind him, and a notable period with **THE ROLLING STONES** to come. His melodic piano changed the sound of Quicksilver, and the patchy SHADY GROVE (1969) was an altogether more mainstream effort. On ballads like "Flashing Lonesome" the spontaneity was replaced by a considered approach to creating atmosphere. Valenti and Duncan were soon back from New York and it was inevitable that they would seek out their old pals.

Quicksilver were now a six-piece, but the results of so much collected talent palled in comparison with the early magic. Valenti was a prolific folk-based songwriter, but his material stifled the skills of Cipollina, Duncan and Hopkins, who were all at their best embellishing basic rock with moments of improvised brilliance. Like many bands from the same scene, the future for Quicksilver would be one of shifting line-ups, disappointing new starts and occasional flashes of brilliance.

Of the stuff that really matters, "Fresh Air" hit the US singles charts in 1970 and "What About Me" was an anthem for die-hard hippies still into dope and antiwar protests. Both tracks used solid rhythmic chops behind powerful vocals and provided killer hook lines that worked up the live crowds. If only every track had been as good.

Too much of a hippie band to fit easily into the radio-based rock scene of the 70s, Quicksilver carried on through albums and a major line-up change to ever-diminishing returns. They effectively disappeared for three years from 1972 until 1975, when Valenti, Cipollina, Freiberg, Duncan and Elmore reformed. SOLID SILVER (1975) had the expected high-quality playing but little musical focus. The name continued and albums like PEACE BY PEACE threw in synthesizers and rap sounds in a desperate attempt to remain relevant, but Cipollina's death in 1989 put paid to any reunion with the word 'defini-

tive' attached. The name continues in line-ups fronted by Gary Duncan, which retain the extended jamming style.

⊙ **Happy Trails** (1969; Beat Goes On).
Exceptional stuff. A late-60s album that captures the kind of magic old hippies still discuss. Great guitar work, real presence and that massive version of "Who Do You Love".

⊙ **The Ultimate Journey** (1993; See For Miles).
The best thing about inconsistent bands is that the compilation albums really do cook and don't come over-priced. The only notable absence is the storming suite built around "Who Do You Love", although this does open with the single version of the same track. Otherwise the collection is definitive. An obscure B-side, "Stand By Me", is one of the band's best ever cuts; "Gold And Silver" gives you some idea of the twin lead power of Cipollina and Duncan; and "Fresh Air" and "What About Me" are both included.

Neil Nixon

R

RADIO BIRDMAN

Formed Sydney, Australia, 1974;
disbanded 1978; re-formed 1996.

Radio Birdman was one of the more influential, but largely unrecognized, Australian bands
of the 1970s – a band which embraced the ethos of
punk but always refused to be classified as such,
wishing to avoid the negative connotations of musical
incompetence that it implied.

Formed from the remains of Sydney bands The
Rats and TV Jones, which were already playing high-
energy Stooges-type rock in 1972–73 (a style adopted
keenly by the class of 1977), Radio Birdman comprised US-born **Deniz Tek** (guitar, most of the
lyrics), **Rob Younger** (vocals), **Carl Rourke** (bass),
Ron Keeley (drums) and **Pip Hoyle** (keyboards).

The band started playing live in 1975 at some of
the more basic pubs in Sydney's Darlinghurst/Surry
Hills areas. It wasn't long before Carl Rourke was
replaced on bass by **Warwick Gilbert** and later that
same year **Chris Masuak** joined as guitarist when
Pip Hoyle took a sabbatical to concentrate on his
medical studies. Initially, the set was mainly made up
of covers of The Stooges/New York Dolls/MC5
numbers, and although more self-written material
was gradually introduced, they never lost sight of
their influences and cover versions always formed an
important part of their set.

Radio Birdman's performances at times caused a
violent reaction, especially when the crowd included
narrow-minded rednecks, unwilling to accept their
original interpretations and style. In an early attempt
to break into the circuit of large suburban pubs where
AC/DC or Sherbert were more acceptable, a disastrous gig took place at Millers, in the Sydney suburb
of Brighton, when the plug was pulled and the band
were attacked by the bouncers as they loaded their
equipment into their van.

Things started to look up when they sneaked a gig
at the Oxford Tavern (later The Oxford Funhouse)
in Darlinghurst. They convinced the manager to let
them play with the story that Lou Reed was in town
that day and had agreed to attend. In the end Lou
didn't show but the band went down so well that
they won themselves a residency. The crowds started
to build up and enjoyed drink-fuelled and adrenaline-
soaked performances which ranked as some of the
band's best.

Their recorded work demonstrated more of their
uncompromising attitude. Although a couple of
major labels had shown interest, Trafalgar was the
only label to tolerate the band's attitude – in particular, their insistence on 'total artistic control' – and
allow them to record their EP BURN MY EYE (1977)
featuring "Smith And Wesson Blues", "Snake",
"I–94", and "Burned My Eye" – all classy, high-
energy rockers.

Radio Birdman continued to elicit violent reactions from the punters, particularly when they started
to wear their 'uniform' – black shirts with arm-
patches – and to display the Radio Birdman symbol.
Understandably, there were accusations of fascism,
not helped by the title of one of their tracks, "New
Race" (also adopted as the name of the band which
succeeded Radio Birdman), although the band has
always vehemently denied these accusations.

RADIOS APPEAR (1977) contained a set of fine
songs, displaying more subtlety and variety while
maintaining the energy of their live work.
Outstanding tracks included "Man With Golden
Helmet", featuring Pip Hoyle's offbeat, at times
atonal piano and Deniz Tek's incisive guitar licks, and
"Descent Into The Maelstrom". The album received
rave reviews, and a distribution deal was set up
through WEA. An overseas version of the LP was
issued in 1978 with a different tracklisting, including
the single "Aloha Steve And Danno", a fast rocker
extolling the delights of watching *Hawaii 5-0*!

Radio Birdman's last Australian gig was at
Paddington Town Hall in December 1977 – it once
again mutated into violence in a hint of the discord
that was soon to split the band.

Their English debut did not get off to an auspicious
start – there was little interest from the mainstream
music press and the only review was scathing. The
gigs in fact varied between superb and dire, with frequent arguments within the band. Having booked
into Rockfield Studios in Wales to record their
second album, LIVING EYES (released posthumously
in 1981), divisive forces began to take over, with pressures increasing during the continental leg of their
tour and the band's final disintegration after an apparently problem-free gig back in England. Rob
Younger went on to form **New Race**, and then the
longer-lasting **New Christs**. Chris Masuak reappeared in **Klondyke**, a rather uninspired soft
rock/country outfit, while Deniz Tek has produced
four powerful solo albums as well as working with
Deep Reduction, formed with the **Stump
Wizards**, resulting in one eponymous album in 2000.

Radio Birdman's enduring influence on the
Australian alternative music scene revealed itself
when they re-formed and played ten well-received
gigs in January 1996, followed by a studio perfor-

R

mance before an invited audience, broadcast on Triple R's *Caught In The Act* show and released as RITUALISM (1996).

⊙ **Radios Appear** (1977; Trafalgar; reissued on Citadel).
The debut album displays the band's high standard of songwriting, although production standards are variable.

⊙ **Living Eyes** (1981; WEA).
Contains some of the most accomplished music ever written by the band, including "Hanging On" and the sadly prophetic "Time To Fall".

Steve Thompson

RADIOHEAD

Formed Oxford, England, 1988.

Conceived in an Oxford private school in the late 80s, **Radiohead** have always been defiant and difficult. Yet, it's the group's stubbornness, coupled with their powerful and unquashable talent that has propelled them to the top. No longer just another grouchy indie band, Radiohead are arguably the twenty-first century's most important group. They've achieved phenomenal sales worldwide; with albums such as OK COMPUTER and KID A they rewrote the compositional rulebook and, even now that fame courts the group so forcefully, paranoia and self-deprivation are still the primary concerns of their music.

Early on, their big hang-up about being undervalued and misunderstood – shared by **Jonny Greenwood** (guitar), **Colin Greenwood** (bass), **Ed O'Brien** (guitar/backing vocals), **Phil Selway** (drums) and the particularly bolshie **Thom Yorke** (vocals/guitar) – manifested itself in aggressively self-pitying lyrics about such problems as the elitist attitudes of Oxford students ("Prove Yourself") and the bitterness of unrequited love ("Creep"). It was their fierce 'if you can't join them, beat them' outlook that led a then nominally 'indie' band to sign with EMI and in turn amplify the commercial clout of their melodic sound, eventually becoming so huge that even the most esoteric twists in their muse would result in platinum sales.

Their first EP, DRILL (1992) – a tinny collection of demos recorded when the band was still known as On A Friday – mixed antisocial moaning with R.E.M.-ish strums and vocals, interspersed with Nirvana-ish walls of guitar; it was not greatly welcomed. "Creep" (1992), however, was different. Not realizing the tape was running, the band recorded the song in one spontaneous take, and so captured something of the abrasive excitement of their three-guitar live sound. The band's stock rose with critics and punters alike after the release of the next two EPs – ANYONE CAN PLAY GUITAR and POP IS DEAD – and their debut album, PABLO HONEY (1993), which surged into the UK Top 30.

Thom Yorke snoozes mid-song

Despite this taste of success, however, the lads weren't happy. Thom told his public, 'if you're not interested, fuck you', and the band insisted they were perfectly happy to develop their skills without the help of the national papers (who still weren't interested in them). The group also had mixed feelings about the release of the uneven, poorly sequenced and overly familiar – featuring six previously heard tracks – PABLO HONEY. So it was under a cloud that they departed on a headlining tour of Europe in May 1993, only to hear some weeks later that, as if by magic, "Creep" had become the most requested alternative track on US radio, with heavy MTV rotation to match. Quickly changing their plans, Radiohead shot off to America for the first of several sell-out tours that would eventually have them co-headlining with Belly, and supporting Tears For Fears.

PABLO HONEY soon went gold in the States, paving the way for a UK Top 10 hit with the re-released "Creep", a world tour in the summer of 1994, and a big-selling follow-up album, THE BENDS (1995). Produced by John Leckie (Pink Floyd, Magazine, The Stone Roses) THE BENDS earned widespread acclaim even in the major journals, and the five young men from Oxfordshire seemed in danger of losing their angsty inspiration: a lack of critical and popular acceptance. Fortunately for them, all that time in the US offered up a whole new set of subjects to feel irked by – artificial lifestyles ("Nice Dream" and the lovely "Fake Plastic Trees"), drug dependency ("Bones"), and the horrors of retro 60s fashion ("The Bends"). All of which, combined with a new willingness to experiment with strings and synthesizers, was kindling enough to make THE BENDS a far more assured and full-sounding record than its predecessor. The set subsequently won the kind of approval that they had previously only dreamt of: their heroes R.E.M. asked Radiohead to support them on their 1995 European and US tours.

However, it was with their next release, OK COMPUTER (1997), that Radiohead truly made their mark. Though older voices opined from the sidelines that Pink Floyd had done this sort of thing to death, and better, Thom's self-loathing and patent disgust with the world around him struck a chord with the punters. Everyone from bedroom rebels and misunderstood adolescents to disgruntled housewives and stock market traders embraced the group and their music. The collection featured twelve tracks (including "Lucky", previously heard on the WAR CHILD charity compilation); Thom's bitter vocals were honed razor-sharp by the glancing blade of Johnny Greenwood's glittering raw-edged guitar, while meticulously programmed beats and synthesized chords rippled through the set. OK COMPUTER was more than a DARK SIDE OF THE MOON for the 90s: Yorke's piercing, yet tired lyrics outdid the Floyd for jaded world-weariness and the gentle progression of their theme ('the world's a mess, I'm a mess, I wish I could go play with the aliens') had a

subtlety that Roger Waters lost way back. The first single taken from the album, "Paranoid Android", clocked in at something over six minutes and was the breathtaking high point of their headlining appearance at the Glastonbury Festival in 1997. Undervalued no longer, Radiohead were everywhere, ranking highly across the board in the press's end-of-year charts; Q magazine's readers' poll even went so far as to vote OK COMPUTER as 'The Greatest Album Of All Time'.

Three years later Radiohead returned with the more difficult KID A (2000). The set sported no obvious singles, and yet gorgeous melodies were everywhere. For Yorke it was the perfect tool to disperse both the media hurricane of its predecessor's glory, and his own internal demons. Though often chaotic and experimental, the cathartic KID A presented a matured, purposeful Radiohead, making music on their own terms, with – as the album's opening number declared – "Everything In Its Right Place". The release was accompanied by more sellout tours – defiantly devoid of Radiohead branding, the shows were promoted by a demonic teddy-bear logo – and, particularly in the US, sales of the album were astoundingly large.

The group promised the swift release of another, more radio-friendly album, which surfaced in June 2001 in the form of AMNESIAC. The set was another masterpiece that bristled with sparkling innovation and blindingly perfect pop. The collection's release was preceded by a single – "Pyramid Song", a haunting, almost dirge-like, piano-led number that saw the band bewildering a somewhat numbed *Top Of The Pops* audience on British TV. Toward the end of the year Radiohead surfaced again with a live album, I MIGHT BE WRONG: LIVE RECORDINGS. The set featured a smattering of the newer material, and though well received by fans, lacked the studio magic of KID A and AMNESIAC.

2003 brought the group's next studio album, HAIL TO THE THIEF. Where KID A and AMNESIAC had twisted Radiohead's sound into unexpected improvisational contortions and OK COMPUTER had offered a utopian glimpse of perfect art rock, this set had the feel of a culminating, glorious compromise. Radiohead had tempered their more outlandish excursions and shoehorned them into a far more accessible template. But Yorke and co. had not lost their angry edge: if anything, they had found a means of expression that transcended the screams and wails of their earlier lyrical catalogue, replacing them with complex metaphor and multifaceted language.

It seems likely that Radiohead's tsunami is going to get much larger before its momentum shows any signs of faltering.

⊙ **Pablo Honey** (1993; Parlophone/Capitol).
The debut album features "Creep", the entertainingly laid-back "Coke Babies" and, perhaps the best cut, "Anyone Can Play Guitar" – a weirdly structured track which revels in off-key, staccato Sonic Youth-style guitars.

⊙ **The Bends** (1995; Parlophone/Capitol).
Even though the lyrics aren't always as impressively consistent as the tunes, this is a fine second collection.

⊙ **OK Computer** (1997; Parlophone/Capitol).
OK Computer is an incredible album that documents Radiohead at the height of their powers. With an extraordinary eye for both emotional and technical detail, the set draws on everything from rock, pop and techno to seminal jazz-fusion albums like Miles Davis's Bitches Brew. Essential.

⊙ **Kid A** (2000; Parlophone/Capitol).
The majority of the tracks disregard conventional song structures, while extended free-form brass work-outs and layers of sound recall both the off-kilter mellow moods of the Impulse jazz imprint and a thousand forgotten exponents of krautrock. But far from offering a derivative mess Kid A is a sumptuous feast of cyclical melodies and textures.

⊙ **Hail To The Thief** (2003; Parlophone/Capitol).
Musically, the album's sound is dense, with acoustic and digital sources blanketed together like a well-made bed. Though it may take you a while to get comfortable with this most recent Radiohead offering, the songs are blinders – well worth persevering with.

Piers Clifton and Peter Buckley

RAGE AGAINST THE MACHINE

Formed Los Angeles, 1992.

A perfect example of rap's influence on worldwide rock culture, **Rage Against The Machine** were formed from the ruins of several LA bands: **Zack de la Rocha** (vocals) had been with Headstance and Inside Out; guitarist **Tom Morello** joined from Lock Up; while drummer **Brad Wilk** had played for a time with Pearl Jam's Eddie Vedder. Bassist **Timmy C** became the fourth and final member. Armed with one of the most powerful amalgams of rap, rock and funk yet created, they first made an impact in early 1993, with "Killing In The Name", a howling, expletive-driven tirade against the ills of American society.

The song trailed an equally polemical album, Rage Against The Machine (1993), which soon went Top 50 in the US and UK, and spawned further hit singles in "Bullet In The Head" and

"Bombtrack", but it was the band's live performances which really gained their reputation. As with all the best hardcore gigs, they were no place for the faint-hearted.

Critics suggested that the band's polemical force was focused (or rather unfocused) on vague targets, and pointed to their position on the roster of Columbia subsidiary Epic – a place seemingly at odds with lyrics given to railing against the 'machine' of the 'overall corporate capitalist bureaucracy which we are trained to obey from birth'. The band answered that some kind of alliance with the 'machine' was necessary in order to connect with the widest possible audience.

Some were convinced by the defence, and there was after all a personal conviction to some of the rage. Morello's father was part of the Mau Mau uprising against British rule in Kenya during the 50s, his uncle Jomo Kenyatta was the first Kenyan president, and his mother became a leading light in Parents For Rock And Rap, an organization which seeks to defend rock and rap musicians against censorship. La Rocha's father, too, is a well-known political artist and activist in LA.

All interesting matter for articles, but the band took an alarmingly long time to consolidate on disc the success of their opening tirades. Indeed, there were reports that recordings had been fraught with tension between band members prior to the release of the second album, Evil Empire, in the spring of 1996. It marked no great progression, but sales held up well, and it confirmed that the band's following had kept faith. An extensive tour of the US in summer 1997 proved a success and a video compilation was released in the US later the same year.

Never ones to push themselves when it came to writing fresh material, it took two years for the band to come up with The Battle Of Los Angeles (1999), a record which dispensed with Evil Empire's creakier moments and found the band riffing on all the usual political targets with renewed vigour – a fact which made their subsequent split all the harder to fathom. Reportedly, Zack felt that the band's political ideals were being undermined somehow by the machinery surrounding them. He departed to record a hip-hop album, leaving his former band-mates with the unenviable task of promoting covers album Renegades (2000). What should have been a diversionary instalment from the studio, intended to merely showcase the band's formative influences, thus became the main focus of attention.

Since then rumour has been rife about who would step into the fold as vocalist and at one stage even **Chris Cornell** of Soundgarden was named as likely successor – apparently he and the band had spent some time writing songs together. In the meantime, Live & Rare (2002) emerged as a stopgap release and the band continue to fight the power in true Rage campaigning style – quite where they will go with their future music remains to be seen, however.

Andy Lewis

RAIN PARADE

Formed Los Angeles, 1981; disbanded 1988.

"We wanted to play very soft music." David Roback

One of the pivotal sounds of the 'Paisley Underground' scene of the mid 80s, the **Rain Parade**'s inspired modern psychedelia has earned them a position as one of the great lost US underground bands. They were formed in 1981 by Minneapolis college friends **Matt Piucci** and **David Roback** (guitars), initially trading under the name The Sidewalks, whose garage punk also featured David's younger brother **Steven** (bass/vocals). But the band tired of the volume, welcomed in keyboardist **Will Glenn**, and set to work upon a new softer direction as The Rain Parade.

Despite the trauma of trying to secure a drummer who wouldn't batter his kit too loudly, the band managed a single on the tiny Llama label in 1982, "What She's Done To Your Mind", a fantastic folk-rocker in Byrds/Hollies style. The Rain Parade became cult LA faves and, beginning work on an album in spring 1983, found themselves in pole position in the Paisley Underground, an invented scene of 60s-influenced US popsters. Though at pains to deny allegations of scenester-ship, David Roback nevertheless worked on the all-star RAINY DAY album of mellow 60s and 70s covers. Featuring The Bangles' Susannah Hoffs, The Dream Syndicate's Kendra Smith and The Three O'Clock's Michael Quercio, it was pleasant but inconsequential stuff.

Thankfully, The Rain Parade's own EMERGENCY THIRD RAIL POWER TRIP (1983), recorded with permanent drummer **Eddie Kalwa**, showed they were furlongs ahead of the pack. Named after a sign on a San Francisco subway wall, it was powerful in spite of its laid-back, Baroque sound, while its lyrics of post-punk alienation rooted it firmly in the 1980s. Now ascendant stars, the band braved a lengthy tour but succumbed to sibling ego-clash. In January 1984 a shocked David Roback was given his marching orders.

Determined not to be crippled, Rain Parade dropped the definite article from their name, cut off their long hair and threw themselves into EXPLOSIONS IN THE GLASS PALACE (1984), an EP that showed that the band's majesty was undiminished. They then signed to Island, who rush-released BEYOND THE SUNSET (1985), a weedy and uninspired live album recorded in Japan. With only a couple of decent new songs to recommend it, there was an all-too-obvious odour of hasty cash-in. Things didn't improve. 1986's CRASHING DREAM studio set, on which Piucci and Steven Roback took the helm of a line-up that included John Thoman on guitar and Mark Marcum on drums, was packed with worthwhile songs but sounded watered down. The band weren't impressed with it, either: their original demos (available on the ultra-scarce mail-order DEMOLITION CD) reveal plans for a much denser, Television-influenced album. The Paisley Underground had fragmented, CRASHING DREAM sank and so did Rain Parade. As they began work on a reputation-salvaging double album, Island ditched them.

It would be another two years before Steven Roback and Matt Piucci reconvened the band. Live shows were reputedly earthshaking, but this line-up couldn't capture its new-found dark and bitter power in the studio (only demos remain), and in 1988 Rain Parade's dream finally crashed for good.

Steven Roback almost immediately resurfaced and roped most of the final Rain Parade line-up into his new band **Viva Saturn** (Piucci was notably absent, having been unexpectedly recruited by **Crazy Horse**). Their SOUNDMIND and BRIGHTSIDE albums continued the parent band's journey, rediscovering the plaintive melodicism mislaid in their 1988 comeback.

Alumnus David Roback, meanwhile, had moved ahead of the pack, working on a folky solo project, CLAY ALLISON, with girlfriend Kendra Smith, then shifting to a heavier, bluesy sound with Opal, before forming **MAZZY STAR**.

Chris Tighe

RAINBOW/RITCHIE BLACKMORE

Rainbow formed 1975; disbanded 1984.

After **Ritchie Blackmore**'s feud with David Coverdale drove the guitarist out of Deep Purple in 1975, he muscled in on the New York metal band Elf who had previously recorded the hard-rock semi-classic CAROLINA COUNTY BALL (1974) under the auspices of Purple's Roger Glover. Ditching Elf's guitarist Steve Edwards, Blackmore commandeered the rest of the band – vocalist **Ronnie James Dio**, keyboardist **Mickey Lee Soule**, bassist **Craig Gruber** and drummer **Gary Driscoll** – for his first solo project, RITCHIE BLACKMORE'S RAINBOW (1975). While the album largely replayed Deep Purple's power-chord-plus-

Steppenwolf-organ-hooks formula with less pop savvy, RITCHIE BLACKMORE'S RAINBOW marked the emergence of Ronnie James Dio as metal's schlockiest mystic this side of Robert Plant on tracks like "Catch The Rainbow" and "Man On The Silver Mountain".

Realizing that Dio was quickly becoming one of metal's definitive vocalists and the rest of the band was nothing but dead weight, Blackmore ditched Soule, Driscoll and Gruber in favour of **Cozy Powell** (drums), **Tony Carby** (keyboards) and **Jimmy Bain** (bass) on RAINBOW RISING (1976). Less obviously Deep Purple redux than the first album, RAINBOW RISING would come to define the future of heavy metal with its production values, cod-symphonic pretensions, Dio's castrato octave flights, Blackmore's furthering distance from the blues, and deeply lame up-tempo numbers.

Blackmore continued to be the air guitarist's wet dream on the live album, RAINBOW ON STAGE (1977), which was the band's first real commercial success. A British Top 10 album, RAINBOW ON STAGE considerably upped the balls quotient on both up-tempo tracks like "Kill The King" and tales of chivalry like "16th Century Greensleeves". Tiring of his musicians yet again, Blackmore hired bassist **Bob Daisley** and keyboardist **David Stone**, moved the band to California and recorded LONG LIVE ROCK 'N' ROLL (1978). "Gates Of Babylon" was a disgraceful rip-off of late-period Led Zeppelin and "Lady Of The Lake" took Dio's knight-errantry as far as it could, but the album managed to dent the British Top 10 again largely on the strength of the stomping title track.

By this point, though, Dio and Blackmore couldn't stand each other and Dio left to take the hardest job in rock – replacing Ozzy in Black Sabbath. As usual, Blackmore fired everyone except for Powell and called in old pal **Roger Glover** (bass), **Don Airey** (keyboards) and **Graham Bonnet** (vocals) for DOWN TO EARTH (1979). Bonnet sang in a voice about three octaves lower than Dio and his resemblance to Kiss's Paul Stanley was emphasized in the Sunset Strip hedonism that Glover brought to the group. The album spawned two British Top 10 singles in the definitive lust/loss tales, "All Night Long" and "Since You've Been Gone", and the filler wasn't half-bad, either.

Typically, though, the line-up couldn't survive the recording period and **Joe Lynn Turner** (vocals) replaced Bonnet, while **Bob Rondinelli** replaced Powell. DIFFICULT TO CURE (1981) replicated its predecessor's success, however, with the same blend of power chords and synth hooks on the UK #3 single, "I Surrender", and the duplicate of "All Night Long", "Can't Happen Here". With **Dave Rosenthal** taking over for Airey, Rainbow followed the same path on STRAIGHT BETWEEN THE EYES (1982) and BENT OUT OF SHAPE (1983), but the band was obviously in a rut and Blackmore and Glover jumped ship to re-form Deep Purple in 1984.

⊙ **The Best Of Rainbow** (1981; Polydor).
The definitive overview of one of the definitive metal bands.

Peter Shapiro

THE RAINCOATS

Formed London, 1977; disbanded 1984; re-formed 1993.

"They showed post-punk music to have another face – one that could be defiant in its spirituality without being corny." Kim Gordon, Sonic Youth

In 1977, punk's year of glory, DIY philosophy and cheek changed the rules. Music was enfranchising the silenced, and suddenly you could hear new voices, disparate sounds, conflicting viewpoints. A guitar or a drum could change minds, or so believed the proto-political bands – the Gang Of Four, The Pop Group, Delta 5 – that formed during punk's second wave. Among their number were **The Raincoats**, an all-women band, seen as marginal in most accounts, but namechecked repeatedly by Kurt Cobain and Courtney Love, and a host of others in the grunge years to come.

That's moving ahead, however. The band was formed by **Ana da Silva** (vocals/guitar/keyboards) and **Gina Birch** (vocals/bass) and, after several personnel changes, enlisted **Palmolive**, a founding member of **THE SLITS**, as drummer. Meanwhile, violinist **Vicky Aspinall** answered the group's advert for a woman who played an unusual instrument. With encouragement from friend and manager Shirley O'Loughlin, the quartet recorded "Fairytale In A Supermarket" (1979), a track which Paul Morley named *NME Single of the Week*, and characterized as 'some of the tenderest and harshest music since Nico sang with electric guitars'.

In November 1979 the band followed with their debut album, THE RAINCOATS. It was an astonishing work: despite little musical training, the four women created songs so singular and emotional that they did not fit under any conventional rubric. Their fragile cacophonies challenged 'girl group' and female stereotypes alike, proving that indeed a woman's place was on stage.

The title of the second album, ODYSHAPE (1981), was, as Birch explained, 'a play on body shape and people's expectations'. Before the album was recorded, **Ingrid Weiss** had replaced Palmolive, who had moved to India in search of enlightenment. The majority of the album's songs were written when the band was drummerless, and so bass and percussion – rather than a steady backbeat – formed the songs' rhythmic structures. Supporter Robert Wyatt helped out.

Sonically disjointed, MOVING (1984) was recorded as the band was breaking up. The separation seemed inevitable: the group's emotive lyrics had been replaced by quotes from Blake and Brecht, and the addition of a sax player – that New Wave mistake – merely seemed precious. The band's experimentation with effects added sonic depth but increased the distance between them and the listener. To The Raincoats' credit, though, they were attempting to unite influences as disparate as disco, funk, Cajun and rock – different foci which, as they themselves admitted, eventually pulled them apart. The fiercer, more physical versions of MOVING's songs that were recorded during the band's gig at NY club The Kitchen and released on THE KITCHEN TAPES (1983) amended the surface of the problem but ignored its crux.

As a result of their influence being revitalized by Riot Grrrl and Cobain/Love's trumpeting of the group, The Raincoats re-formed in 1993. Their three Rough Trade releases were reissued with extra tracks and extensive sleeve notes by the band. In addition, da Silva and Birch teamed up with drummer **Steve Shelley** (of Sonic Youth) and violinist **Anne Wood** to record EXTENDED PLAY (1994), an EP containing two new songs – "Don't Be Mean" and "We Smile" – along with reworked versions of "No One's Little Girl" and "Shouting Out Loud", and the following year released an album, LOOKING IN THE SHADOWS (1995). The records, along with a short tour, showed The Raincoats in fine form, and their music was as relevant as ever. Birch later contributed to recordings by Hefner and The Hangovers.

⊙ **The Raincoats** (1979; Geffen).
Perhaps the ultimate statement of the Utopian possibilities opened up by punk. Although the album is an attempt to create a new musical language, it never dissolves into self-indulgent doggerel or formless experimentalism.

Julie Taraska

BONNIE RAITT

Born Burbank, California, 1949.

Bonnie Raitt is not only blessed with an exceptionally powerful and emotive voice, but is just about the only woman in mainstream rock to be recognized as a guitar virtuoso. But for all her talent for blues interpretations and her songwriting skills, international success was a long time in coming.

The daughter of Broadway star John Raitt, Bonnie was already playing on the Boston and Philadelphia folk and blues scenes in her teens, and sometimes shared the stage with her idols Mississippi John Hurt, Howlin' Wolf and Sippie Wallace. Aged 22, she made her Warner Brothers debut, BONNIE RAITT (1971), setting the tone for all her later work – an eclectic mixture of country-blues, R&B, and well-chosen covers of West Coast songwriters like Jackson Browne and Randy Newman. She followed with GIVE IT UP (1972), a great set, which alternated pain and downright dirt with equal intensity – highlighted by the desperation of "Love Has No Pride" and the lust-fuelled blues of "Love Me Like A Man".

For TAKIN' MY TIME (1973), Raitt was joined by session players like Taj Mahal, Jim Keltner and Little Feat's Lowell George. It also featured some particularly fine bottleneck slide guitar on "Kokomo Blues". Over the next decade, Raitt moved to a more out-and-out rockier style, best heard on SWEET FORGIVENESS (1977), which provided Raitt with her first US hit with a raunchy rework of Del Shannon's "Runaway", and on 1982's GREEN LIGHT, recorded with a band featuring ex-Faces keyboard player Ian McLagan.

Following this record, however, Raitt dropped out of the business for a while, undergoing drugs and alcohol rehabilitation. She was nine albums into her career, and it seemed she had reached an impasse, her disdain for musical fashion doing little to expand her audience.

But anyone tempted to write Raitt off under 'minor cult following' had reckoned without the unlikely auspices of Walt Disney and Don **WAS (NOT WAS)**, with whom she recorded a stunningly soulful rendition of "Baby Of Mine" for Disney covers project STAY AWAKE (1988). Released as a single, it led to a new record deal with Capitol, and Don Was in the producer's chair for NICK OF TIME (1989), whose title track revealed Bonnie's ruminations on age, love and the biological clock. To everyone's surprise, the album won three Grammys and shot to the top of the US charts, while she earned a fourth Grammy for "In The Mood", a duet recorded with John Lee Hooker for his 1989 album, THE HEALER.

Suddenly Bonnie Raitt was a superstar, but although LUCK OF THE DRAW (1991) was an even bigger seller, and winner of three more Grammys, it was in many ways a disappointment, with weaker songs and less guitar work than its predecessor. Even so, her circle of musical aficionados had expanded even more widely: Bruce Hornsby and Richard Thompson both played on LUCK OF THE DRAW, and duets followed with B. B. King, Elton John, Willie Nelson, Aretha Franklin and Gloria Estefan. Meanwhile she became a founder member and vice-chair of the Rhythm & Blues Foundation, dedicated to sponsoring R&B artists who had paid their dues but had received little money in return.

1994 saw a return to form with LONGING IN THEIR HEARTS, with yet more Grammys and multiplatinum sales in its wake. Especially noteworthy was a cover version of Richard Thompson's "Dimming Of The Day", and "Feelin' Of Fallin'", a smouldering piece of slow funk about desire, drugs and redemption. The following year saw the even greater treat of a live album – her first, despite a legendary live status. ROAD TESTED contained duets with Bruce Hornsby, Jackson Browne and blues veterans Ruth and Charles Brown. Let down by a rather plodding rock work-out with Bryan Adams, the album nonetheless caught fire on a cover of Talking Heads' "Burning Down The House" and the all-star finale of John Prine's "Angel From Montgomery".

All went quiet for four years until FUNDAMENTAL (1998), a typically good-quality album of strong material, arranged and recorded excellently but lacking any major excitement. Nevertheless, she spent the summer following its release winning hordes of new fans as a mainstay of the mega-successful 1998 *Lillith* tour across America. Riatt most recently rewarded her fans with SILVER LINING (2002), another competent set, with backing from her regular road crew. There were few surprises, though the set does feature "Gnawin' It", a grizzly slide guitar battle with Roy Rogers.

Few rock artists have compromised their art so little as Bonnie Raitt in thirty years of recording; even fewer have had such success so late in their careers. As the *L.A. Times* observed, 'Bonnie Raitt may be our foremost singer of the secular gospel. Someone whose songs of hopes dashed, deferred and realized at last encompass the broad lead from mid-life crisis to mid-life catharsis.'

⊙ **Nick Of Time** (1989; Capitol).
The great comeback album, with a superb Don Was production, and every track a tune to remember. Bonnie's two songs – the title track and "The Road's My Middle Name" – are the best on the album; John Hiatt's "Thing Called Love" also stands out, a veritable riot of bottleneck rock'n'roll. A little too polished for folk or blues purists, but sufficiently heartfelt to impress anyone else who likes their R&B smooth but authentic.

⊙ **The Bonnie Raitt Collection** (1990; Warners).
A great twenty-track introduction covering 1971–86, although the high standard dips towards the end. At one extreme there is the straight rock'n'roll of "Runaway", while at the other there is the slow and painful "I Feel The Same", a song of bitter recrimination. There is plenty of blues, too, and a previously unreleased live duet with blues veteran Sippie Wallace on "Women Be Wise".

Chris Coe

RAMONES

Formed New York, 1974; disbanded 1996.

"We wanted to kind of save rock'n'roll, keep it exciting and fun and the whole bit." Joey Ramone

Johnny (Cummings; guitar), **Joey** (Jeff Hyman; vocals), **Dee Dee** (Douglas Colvin; bass) and **Tommy** (Erdelyi; drums) forged the **Ramones** in 1974. Adopting the common surname – Ramone was a pseudonym used by Paul McCartney – these four misfits from Queens, New York, were the advance troops of a revolution: their purpose was to bring the primal energy back to rock'n'roll, to recapture the spirit of early Elvis and Little Richard and, above all, to make it fun again. They shouted out a call to arms, and the rallying cry – 'Hey ho, let's go' – started a movement that changed the course of rock.

In the early 70s the Ramones were key figures among the emergent punk scene at the now-legendary CBGB's club on on New York's Lower East

Side. Their debut album, RAMONES (1976), together with a seminal gig at London's Roundhouse on bicentennial day, July 4, 1976, gave the punk movement a kick-start, and spurred dozens of aspiring young bands to take up the banner. English bands like The Clash, Buzzcocks and the Sex Pistols subsequently went on to eclipse the New Yorkers in terms of chart success and notoriety, but punk heroes like Joe Strummer readily admitted their debt to the American 'fab four' who had created it all.

The Ramones were nihilists with a sense of humour, and their ground-breaking debut album defined punk: the perfect black-and-white cover shot, fourteen tracks inside just over thirty minutes, driving bass lines, vocals that smacked you in the face with their yobbishness. Uncompromising, and ultra-cool, RAMONES returned the compliment The Beatles had paid to the US in 1964.

The mainstream music business and radio programmers ignored the Ramones, pilloried them, misunderstood them, and hoped they'd go away. The second LP, however, LEAVE HOME (1977), continued the aural assault: passionate, blistering, no-frills, 1-2-3-4 fun, it also introduced Carbona, pinheads, headbangers, and the chant of 'Gabba Gabba Hey'. In Britain, if not yet in the States, the band was beginning to find an audience, and the album made a first inroad into the UK Top 50.

ROCKET TO RUSSIA (1977), arguably the definitive Ramones album, underlined their ability to combine the punk approach with catchy melodies. In slightly over two minutes, "Teenage Lobotomy" encapsulated everything there is to say about teenage alienation. The album also contained the song which became the band's first UK Top 30 hit, "Sheena Is A Punk Rocker", as well as the pure pop genius of "Rockaway Beach". It found its way into every punk collection – and that's both fans and musicians. 'Seminal', for once, is the *only* word.

In May 1978 Tommy Ramone quit the drum seat for a career in production, to be replaced by **Marky** (Marc Bell, formerly of Richard Hell's Voidoids). Marky brought with him a heavier drum sound for the 1978 album ROAD TO RUIN. Another classic, its shock tactics included acoustic guitars, songs lasting longer than two minutes, and guitar solos, albeit short ones. The stripped-down style was embellished but not compromised; the integrity remained. "I Wanna Be Sedated" became an anthem.

The double album IT'S ALIVE (1979), recorded at London's Rainbow Theatre on New Year's Eve 1977, captured the band at the peak of their powers. Containing an entire Ramones set, it showed that few bands could match the fury and passion of the twice-the-speed-of-sound shows for which they are so revered.

As the punk movement fizzled out and evolved into the safety of New Wave, the Ramones' wall of sound collided with another, as the band collaborated with legendary producer Phil Spector for the 1980 album END OF THE CENTURY. The Ramones had

"Gabba Gabba Hey!" Ramones Dee Dee (bass), Tommy (drums), Joey (vocals) and Johnny (guitar)

encountered Spector through their involvement in the classic B-movie *Rock'N'Roll High School*. Although Spector provided them with a UK Top 10 hit, "Baby I Love You", working with the famously unpredictable producer was a chastening experience, and the meeting of spiritual opposites resulted in an album that pleased nobody very much.

Despite much internal wrangling and disillusionment with the music business in general, the Ramones continued into the 80s. Hardcore, the bastard child of punk, arrived on the scene, and another wave of bands who owed their existence to the Ramones proceeded to eclipse them in fame and fortune. TOO TOUGH TO DIE (1984) found the Ramones back at their hard-hitting best. Marky Ramone had been replaced on drums by **Richie** (Richard Beau), and Tommy produced. Their first overtly political song, "Bonzo Goes To Bitberg" (1985), a hilarious dig at Ronald Reagan following his much-criticized visit to a cemetery containing SS graves, confirmed that the quasi-Nazi imagery of early Ramones songs and symbols had been outrageously ironic jokes. In the same year, Joey Ramone contributed to the anti-apartheid single "Sun City", finally nailing the myth of the band as a bunch of right-wing rednecks.

As the decade closed, the Ramones were still around, and they still meant business, even though mainstream success continued to elude them. They contributed the title track to the Stephen King film *Pet Semetary*, Joey appeared as himself in the cult film *Roadkill*, and then founder member and songwriting mainstay Dee Dee left the band suddenly.

Undaunted, the Ramones gave themselves a shot in the arm with the recruitment of **CJ** (Chris Ward). A former fan, he stepped neatly into Dee Dee's shoes, and gave the band a new sense of purpose. MONDO BIZARRO (1992), although too perfectly produced for some punk die-hards, surprised many critics who had written the Ramones off as an anachronism, while an album of covers, ACID EATERS (1993), provided an odyssey through the band's own influences, including covers of songs by artists as diverse as The Who, Jefferson Airplane, Love and Bob Dylan. This eclectic collection underlined the secret of the Ramones' craftsmanship twenty years on, and they were still stripping rock down to its underwear.

The rediscovery of punk in America in the early 90s, and the success of heavily Ramones-influenced bands like Offspring, Green Day and Rancid, has caused a major rethink. These bands have brought punk rock into the realm of platinum-selling albums and Grammy awards. The philosophical spirit of punk and the corporate music business may make strange bedfellows, but at long last the Ramones are receiving some credit. The band's latest and last studio release, ADIOS AMIGOS (1995), showed them going back to their roots, with all the attack, vision, humour and punch of their early work.

After finally calling it a day twenty long hard years later (imagine playing "Blitzkrieg Bop" every night for twenty years – can you conceive of the horror?), we've seen two live albums, MCA's GREATEST HITS LIVE (1996) and Radioactive's WE'RE OUTTA HERE! (1996; re-released Eagle; 1998). Neither should really have seen the light of day.

RAMONES

Since the band split, individual Ramones have remained musically active. Apart from Johnny Ramone, that is, who swore never to pick up a guitar again (but who recently made a guest appearance at a Pearl Jam show nevertheless). The youngblood CJ Ramone has been touring and recording with his new band, Los Gusanos. Drummer Marky has a new band, The Intruders, and recently released his home-video collection of life on the road (*Ramones Around The World*, Rhino Home Video) a kind of *Spinal Tap* but, of course, Ramones-style. Original drummer Tommy is set to unleash some new material. Dee Dee Ramone has released a solo album (AIN'T IT FUN; Blackout Records) as well as an autobiography, *Poison Heart, Surviving The Ramones* (Firefly/Helter Skelter), which makes harrowing yet hilarious reading. Forget the bystanders' views in Legs McNeill's *Please Kill Me*; Dee Dee's account is the real thing, smashing the 'bruddas' myth once and for all. Singer Joey Ramone produced a record for Ronnie Spector and still managed to perform regularly – until he finally succumbed to lymphatic cancer in April 2001, aged 49. Right up to his death he had been working on DON'T WORRY ABOUT ME (2002), which featured guest appearances from the likes of Captain Sensible and Marky Ramone. Shortly after this release the Ramones were inducted into the Rock and Roll Hall of Fame.

One might have thought that the passing of their lead singer would scotch any possibility of a Ramones reunion, but it seems that the remaining members of the various line-ups have been working on a tribute single called "The Bowery Electric", a tune penned by New York songwriter Jed Davis.

In this light will there ever be a Ramones reunion of sorts? Most unlikely, and for that we should be grateful. Let's remember the Ramones as they were, and, as Lemmy said, 'don't forget them'.

⊙ **Rocket To Russia** (1977; Sire).
The peak of punk perfection. Brash and tuneful, every track is a miniature masterpiece.

⊙ **It's Alive** (1979; Sire).
This is the live album to beat all live albums.

⊙ **Ramonesmania** (1989; Sire).
Utterly wondrous compilation of the Ramones at their dizzying peak.

Veronica Kofman

RANCID

Formed Albany, California, 1990.

Bondage trousers, mohawks and platinum records – **Rancid** seemed too much of an anachronism, too obvious a Clash throwback, to make the transition to the mainstream in the mid 90s. That they did so was due largely to a solid, if not entirely original, punk-pop songwriting platform.

Rancid's roots lay in the cult American ska/punk band, **Operation Ivy**. Formed in 1987, this featured **Tim 'Lint' Armstrong** (guitar/vocals), **Matt Freeman**, aka Matt McCall (bass), **Dave Mello**

(drums) and **Jesse Michaels** (vocals), and drew inspiration in equal measure from the Ruts/Clash axis and the UK's two-tone movement. They made their debut with the HECTIC EP for Lookout Records in January 1988, followed by a full-length album, ENERGY (1989). However, the group collapsed in May 1989 as months of unbroken touring took their toll. Jesse Michaels became a Buddhist monk. Freeman and Armstrong elected to form a new band, recruited drummer **Brett Reed**, and became Rancid.

They made their debut in 1992 with the I'M NOT THE ONLY ONE EP, and released an album, RANCID, in April 1993, at which time they were joined by second guitarist (and ex UK Sub) **Lars Frederiksen**. Their connections with emerging punks **GREEN DAY** – whose Billy Joe Armstrong had almost joined Rancid before Frederiksen became a fixture – were cemented when Armstrong co-authored their "Radio, Radio, Radio" single.

A second album, LET'S GO (1994), comprised no fewer than 23 strident songs. Buoyed by the international acclaim greeting Green Day's transition to stadium-rock status, it achieved platinum sales, and led to much courting by major labels. Rancid elected to remain instead with their 'ethical indie', Epitaph, for ...AND OUT COME THE WOLVES (1995), a strong album that revisited the group's ska punk roots, bashing out the songs in as punchy, rowdy and unaffected a way as ever.

LIFE WON'T WAIT, (1998) ropes in homophobic-misogynist-turned-righteous-rasta **Buju Banton** on the ska-ed-up title track and elsewhere calls on members of The Specials, showing there is more to the band than a desperate desire to be The Clash after all. This claim is backed up by possibly their most raucous and consistent record to date, RANCID (2000), an album that clocks in at well under 40 minutes and boasts a cracking 22 tracks.

⊙ **Let's Go** (1994; Epitaph).
If you can get your head around the logistical absurdity of punk rock being a mid-90s phenomenon, LET'S GO, with its sloppy rhythms, choppy riffs and regular-guy lyrics, is a wholly enjoyable record.

⊙ **...And Out Come The Wolves** (1995; Epitaph).
More madcap fun with California's unreconstructed punk rockers. Although they're not doing anything here that fans of The Clash or Specials haven't heard before, the playing is both strong and supple.

Alex Ogg

RARE BIRD

Formed UK, 1968/69; disbanded 1975.

"And sympathy is what you need my friend 'cos there's not enough love to go round..." Graham Field

In 1969, Tony Stratton-Smith, heavyweight band manager and concert promoter, founded the famous Charisma label, fed up with the constant hassle his bands – such as the Bonzos, the Nice and Creation – seemed to be having with record companies. His own bands were still tied up with other labels (although both the Nice and Creation later had records released on Charisma) so the hunt was on for new talent.

The first signing was **Rare Bird**, and more significantly their single, "Sympathy", the first release on the new label, which was a massive hit all over continental Europe, although only reaching #27 in the UK. "Sympathy" was a fine paean to universal peace and understanding, but it wasn't truly representative of the band's more blues-based raw organ pop sound, and the first album, RARE BIRD (1969), failed to capitalize on the single's success. In retrospect, this album, although containing one or two very fine songs, most notably "Beautiful Scarlet", was very much of its time and the band took on a more progressive hue for the second album, AS YOUR MIND FLIES BY (1970). The line-up was eminently suited to a more progressive sound and was considered quite bizarre at the time, comprising **Graham Field** (organ), **Dave Kaffinetti** (electric piano), **Steve Gould** (bass) and **Mark Ashton** (drums).

Unfortunately, this second album failed to produce a hit single and its release went largely unnoticed in the UK. A shame, since it represented a quantum leap from the first and held some breathtaking moments as well as a much stronger set of songs. Curiously, when reissued in Germany in the early 1980s, AS YOUR MIND FLIES BY topped the UK import charts for the best part of two months (from charts compiled for *Melody Maker*)!

Although going down a storm at clubs like Mothers and prestige gigs at the Lyceum (where they supported Kevin Ayers and the Whole World), the band, without any further success, quietly fell apart. Graham Field, who was generally regarded as the main songwriter, formed the imaginatively named **Fields**, who sounded so similar to Rare Bird as to earn him forgiveness for writing off the other members as no-hopers. Fields didn't last very long, however, and the drummer, Andy McCulloch, defected to new band Greenslade. Gould and Kaffinetti, meanwhile, joined the London session scene, Gould playing on Colin Scot's first (and best) album, whilst Kaffinetti added some wonderful electric piano to Gordon Haskell's magnificent IT IS AND IT ISN'T album. Mark Ashton later resurfaced as vocalist and guitarist in Headstone and later as a solo artist with a pleasant album on Ariola cunningly entitled SOLO.

You just can't keep a good band down, and 1972 saw a new line-up, a new label and a new sound. Kaffinetti and Gould (the latter having switched to guitar) were complemented by **Ced Curtis** and **Dave Holland** on guitars, **Paul Karas** (later of Stackridge fame) on bass and **Fred Kelly** on drums. Gone was the dominating organ, to be replaced by a triple-guitar frontal assault. The first album on

Polydor was EPIC FOREST, which included an extra side's worth of music on a free EP to the delight of the fans. In the UK, however, Rare Bird still meant "Sympathy" to the majority of the rock fraternity and the album was largely ignored at home whilst the LP and a single nutted from it charted in the States – where "Sympathy" had hardly caused a ripple. Suddenly, the band found themselves in that curious pigeonhole, along with such fine bands as Tranquility and Bush, of being extremely well received in the States but virtual unknowns in their homeland.

SOMEBODY'S WATCHING (1973) saw a slimmed-down line-up and included **Nic Potter** from **VAN DER GRAAF GENERATOR**, an old mate from the Charisma days, on bass and **Kevin Lamb** on backing vocals. Two stand-outs from the quieter songs were "High In The Morning" and Lamb's "Who Is The Hero", where Gould proved that his bluesy rasping vocals could also caress, whilst on the heavy side, "Dollars" (a treatment of Morricone's "A Fistful Of Dollars" theme) saw the band jamming a treat, John Wetton's guest bass ensuring the track packed some heat.

Suddenly, the band were down to a trio of Gould, Kaffinetti and Kelly, and the final album, BORN AGAIN (1974), marked another change in direction. Although **Andy Rea** added some bass and Kevin Lamb again appeared on backing vocals, Gould decided to play the rest of the guitar and bass parts himself (even adding some electric piano) and Kaffinetti tried to fill out the sound by dabbling with the new Korg synthesizer. Although not very well received, BORN AGAIN stands up well today, tracks such as "Redman" and "Lonely Street" being particularly worth the entrance fee.

After a couple of low-key, but charming, singles, Rare Bird finally threw in the towel, due, perhaps, to the fact that most fans sadly ignored BORN AGAIN for the Charisma retrospective album nostalgically named SYMPATHY (or might it have been due to the scantily clad, airbrushed lady on the sleeve?). A Polydor retrospective did them even less justice, opting either for the more commercial songs or editing classic songs, such as "Epic Forest", down to half-length and losing all grandeur in the process.

Steve Gould went on to play with Alvin Lee, Runner, Kevin Lamb, Mark Ashton and Clair Hamill, whilst Dave Kaffinetti changed his name to David Kaff and moved to Canada where he finally achieved stardom of sorts as Vic Savage, keyboard player with **SPINAL TAP** and utterer of the immortal words, 'Have a good time, all of the time'. See if you can spot the bit in the film where David St Hubbins accidentally calls him Dave!

◉ **Rare Bird** (1969; Charisma).
Strong organ-dominated debut – a shame it didn't include "Devil's High Concern", the B-side of "Sympathy".

◉ **As Your Mind Flies By** (1970; Charisma).
In the progressive vein, but with a strong set of songs to keep the interest up. Twin keyboard attack plus choir and gutsy vocals – in places they give Van Der Graaf Generator a run for their money.

● **Epic Forest** (1972; Polydor).
Re-formation albums don't come finer. A more guitar-orientated sound – including some lovely countryish songs and building up to an apocalyptic climax. Make sure, if you track a vinyl copy down that it comes complete with EP – the three bonus tracks are excellent.

● **Born Again** (1974; Polydor).
A different year, a different sound – poppier and funkier. A cleaner production job adds to the beauty of the gentler songs – "Lonely Street" in particular shines – whilst harmony vocals lift, especially on "All That I Need", a perfect pop song.

Mark Jones

THE RASCALS

Formed New York, 1965; disbanded 1972.

The Rascals were the best blue-eyed soul group of the 1960s – and one of the few white rock bands of any era to fuse R&B and rock with the finesse and fierce energy of genuine African-American soul stars. **Felix Cavaliere**'s Hammond organ dominated a string of classic hit singles in the late 1960s, paced by the gritty vocals of Felix and his songwriting partner, singer **Eddie Brigati**. Writing most of their own material, they adapted their sound to the psychedelic era without compromising their soulful qualities, although they proved unable to produce the strong album-length statements that would have put them up with the very top groups.

When The Rascals formed in the mid 60s, they were already weathered veterans of New York R&B and dance-club bands. Cavaliere met Brigati and Canadian guitarist **Gene Cornish** when he joined them in the Starlighters, the backup outfit for "Peppermint Twist" singer Joey Dee. The musicians found the fading Dee's commercial sound too confining, but the gig gave them invaluable tutoring in the art of working up a sweat on the dance floor. Spurred by the success of The Beatles into doing their own thing, they began jamming and writing together, with the addition of Cavaliere's friend **Dino Danelli**, who had drummed for jazz and R&B stars like Lionel Hampton and Little Willie John. They never did find a bass player, and all of the group's recordings featured session players on the instrument.

After establishing themselves as a hot attraction on the New York club circuit, the group hooked up with manager Sid Bernstein, who had been responsible for promoting The Beatles' Carnegie Hall and Shea Stadium shows. After having them change their name to the Young Rascals (to the group's annoyance), Bernstein got them a deal with Atlantic. The slow-burning "I Ain't Gonna Eat My Heart Anymore" was a promising debut, but the frenetic follow-up "Good Lovin'" (first performed by the R&B group the Olympics), went to #1 in 1966, immediately putting them into the top echelon of American rock bands. Such was their soulful cry that some listeners thought the musicians were black, and throughout their heyday The Rascals would pick up some airplay and sales in the R&B/soul market as well as the pop charts.

The group's first recordings were heavily dominated by cover material, and although these were executed very well indeed, they were inspired by the British Invasion to start generating their own material. At first these originals were heavily coated in R&B sounds, and modest hit singles like "You Better Run" and "Love Is A Beautiful Thing" were quite convincing fusions of soul and rock energy. The psychedelic era was dawning, however, and it's an enormous credit to the band that they were able to move into more introspective, personal material and increasingly eclectic arrangements, reflecting Latin, gospel and mild experimental influences. The keyboard-guitar-drums combo was embellished by tasteful (on the singles, at least) strings, harps, horns and harmonicas. And the Young Rascals were finally able to drop the unwanted prefix and become the plain Rascals.

This transition started in 1967 with "I've Been Lonely Too Long" and "A Girl Like You", and peaked with "Groovin'", "How Can I Be Sure" and "Beautiful Morning". All had a light, beautifully serene grace, perhaps reflecting Cavaliere's increasing infatuation with Eastern mysticism in general, and guru Swami Satchinanda in particular. This was soul music of a new sort, equal parts white and black, driven as much by soul-searching concerns as by romantic ones. Almost as if to prove they could still shake it down with the best of them, in 1968 they delivered one of their most rabble-rousing dance tunes, the horn-driven "People Got To Be Free", a moving plea for racial unity that was inspired by an incident at a Florida concert. The group put their sentiments into deeds as well, announcing that they would not play concerts unless the bill was fifty percent integrated.

"People Got To Be Free" was a monster hit, topping the charts for five weeks, but would prove to be their last Top 20 entry. The group were never able to deliver consistent albums, and 1969's double LP FREEDOM SUITE found them succumbing to the excesses of the era, delving into jazz and filling up an entire disc with three experimental instrumentals. Jazz notables like Ron Carter, Alice Coltrane and David Newman popped up on The Rascals' albums in the late 60s and early 70s and, although the ambition was laudable, the results seemed to emphasize that their experiments worked best within the constraints imposed by the 45 rpm single.

Although in the late 60s they managed a few small hits with a pronounced gospel feel, the death knell for the group sounded when Brigati, who was chiefly responsible for penning the lyrics for Cavaliere's music, left in 1970. Cornish followed a year later, and although Cavaliere and Danelli recruited other musicians and struggled on for a couple more albums in the early 1970s, The Rascals' force was spent when they broke up in 1972. None of the members went on to do anything notable outside of the band: Cavaliere has been the most active, releasing several lukewarm solo albums.

◉ **The Very Best Of The Rascals** (1993; Rhino).
Although missing a few topnotch tracks, this sixteen-track retrospective is a good single-disc distillation, including all of their major hits.

◉ **Anthology** (1965–1972) (1992; Rhino).
This double-CD, 44-track set may be too extensive for most fans, but it does have goodies ("Baby Let's Wait", "Silly Girl", "Sueno") that aren't found on the shorter compilation, plus R&B covers from the early days and lesser tracks from their later albums.

Richie Unterberger

THE RASPBERRIES

Formed Cleveland, Ohio, 1970; disbanded 1975.

Formed in an era of progressive rock and stadium boogie, **The Raspberries** blew fearlessly in the face of fashion. Their sound was a synthesis of primary influences the Beatles, Who, Small Faces and Beach Boys – tight, purposeful rock'n'roll with wondrous hooks and harmonies. Leader **Eric Carmen** (guitar/bass/keyboards/vocals) wrote songs that almost rivalled those of his idols, and which were too often and too easily dismissed by critics as imitation or pastiche.

The band formed in 1970 out of Carmen's group, Cyrus Eyrie, although all of the group, save Carmen, had also been members of Cleveland's Choir, whose "It's Cold Outside" was a modest American hit in 1967. In addition to Carmen, the line-up was **Jim Bonfanti** (drums/vocals), **Wally Bryson** (guitar/vocals) and **Dave Smalley** (bass/guitar/vocals). They started out playing the clubs around Cleveland, were an immediate success, and in 1972 signed to Capitol.

RASPBERRIES (1972), the band's debut album, suffered from austere production, stiff playing and patchy material, but was saved by the instant classic "Go All The Way", a schizophrenic assemblage of metallic riff and smooth, sweetly sung verse and chorus. Carmen's delivery of the bluntly sexual lyric in a tone of sheer innocence avoided a radio ban, and

it charted Top 10 in the US in the summer of 1972. Encouraged, the band headed back into the studio for FRESH (1972), a much stronger effort, but one on which a prevailing early Beatles feel was extended to the sleeve's confrontationally dated image of a smiling band in matching white suits. Sadly, The Raspberries' pitch for a return to the innocent excitement of Beatles-era rock'n'roll was widely misinterpreted, not least by Capitol, whose marketing strategies effectively alienated much of their potential audience; the cover of "Let's Pretend", a beautiful ballad released as the second single, offered fans the opportunity to win a customized Volkswagen by voting for the 'foxiest Raspberry'.

The dispirited Raspberries, by now squabbling over singles and group direction, ditched the suits and turned out the tougher-sounding LP, SIDE 3 (1973). Carmen's contributions included three glorious tracks – "Ecstasy" was a powerhouse rocker, "On The Beach" a dazzling Shadow Morton update, and "Tonight" was a contender for their finest single ever. However, its flawless combination of power and melody failed to translate to sales, and by early 1974 the band had splintered, as Smalley's dismissal prompted the resignation of Bonfanti.

Michael McBride (drums/vocals) and the highly talented **Scott McCarl** (bass/guitar/vocals) filled the gaps, and the revamped Raspberries came up with STARTING OVER (1974), a brilliant album that was overshadowed only by its hit single. "Overnight Sensation (Hit Record)" was a reaffirmation of faith, a production masterpiece during which Carmen's jaded narrative welled up into the world through a transistor radio. Although the single was a success, fulfilling its own fantasy, STARTING OVER was not, and The Raspberries broke up in 1975.

After his first fine solo record spawned a huge international hit in the much-covered tear-jerker "All By Myself" (1976), Eric Carmen headed for MOR territory. The other members' projects made little impact.

◉ **The Raspberries – Capitol Collectors Series** (1991; Capitol).
"On The Beach" and "Play On" are both missing, but otherwise this is a fine compilation. There's even the bonus of entertaining radio ads for FRESH and STARTING OVER.

Robert Coyne

RAVEN

Formed Newcastle, England, 1975.

Amongst metal fans, who really care about such things, the debate about who invented speed metal more often than not includes this bunch of Geordie (Newcastle) headcases. Formed back in the mid 70s by brothers **Mark** (guitar/vox) and **John Gallagher** (bass/vox), the initial line-up went through the usual formative shake-ups whilst they developed their sound – a none-too-inspiring heavy metal racket. It wasn't until 1977 that they started to make some headway with a more stable line-up fea-

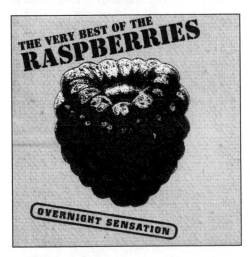
THE VERY BEST OF THE RASPBERRIES
OVERNIGHT SENSATION

turing **Paul Bowden** (guitar/vox) and **Mick Kenworthy** (drums). At this point the band would play any time, any place, anywhere, and one infamous occasion involved playing at a Hell's Angels outdoor rally. The band ended up playing "Born To Be Wild" five times in torrentially heavy rainfall before one of them had the bright idea of faking an electric shock so they could make their escape. So far they had gained a reputation for some inspired stage insanity and a lot of gear-trashing.

By 1979 they had became a three-piece, with **Rob Hunter** joining them on drums. It was at this point that the true **Raven** identity was forged. John's lead high-pitched vocal style was undeniably unique whilst their adoption of extreme speed made them a stand-out act on the burgeoning 'New Wave Of British Heavy Metal' scene. Getting a deal to record the single "Don't Need Your Money" for Neat Records in 1980 heralded the four-year period of their greatest success, during which they released ROCK UNTIL YOU DROP (1981), WIPED OUT (1982), ALL FOR ONE (1983) and LIVE AT THE INFERNO (1984), and a handful of well-received EPs. They described themselves as 'athletic rock' – even though they were arguably well ahead of their time as one of the earliest progenitors of the thrash movement.

Fed up with waiting for the rest of the music world to catch up with them, they made what was, in hindsight, a very bad move. They relocated to the US and secured a deal with Atlantic in an effort to crack bigger markets. In order to achieve this they adopted a more melodic sound and released STAY HARD (1985), which did relatively well in the States but which had fans at home feeling somewhat bewildered at the change in direction. At a time when some of the biggest names in metal, such as Judas Priest, were experimenting with the possibilities of guitar synths and studio technology, THE PACK IS BACK (1986) reflected a similar modern approach.

After LIFE'S A BITCH (1987), possibly one of their heaviest albums, problems with Atlantic came to a head, Rob Hunter left, to be replaced by **Joe Hasselvander**, and they moved label to Combat/Relativity. NOTHING EXCEEDS LIKE EXCESS (1989) was a return to their more abrasive signature sound but further problems and arguments with their label seriously hampered their progress, a situation from which they never really recovered.

A series of albums followed – ARCHITECT OF FEAR (1991), HEADS UP! (1992), GLOW (1994), DESTROY ALL MONSTERS – LIVE IN JAPAN (1995), EVERYTHING LOUDER (1997), ONE FOR ALL (1999) and RAW TRACKS (1999) – which failed to set the world alight but were well received by die-hard fans the world over, particularly in Japan.

Despite what many believe about this band's demise, they seem determined never to give in. A new album is apparently on the way.

⊙ **Rock Until You Drop** (1981; Neat Records).
This sounds pretty rough due to a distinct lack of production polish. Highly innovative for the period, this is a basic thrash blueprint.

⊙ **All For One** (1983; Neat Records).
Much like the first, only with a more dynamic production job from Michael Wagener and Accept's Udo Dirkschneider.

Essi Berelian

THE RED CRAYOLA

Formed Houston, Texas, 1966; disbanded and re-formed many times since.

The history of **The Red Crayola** is complex, to say the least, but is clarified by tracing the path of singer and guitarist **Mayo Thompson**, who formed the band in 1966 with bassist **Steve Cunningham** and drummer **Rick Barthelme**, later to find fame as a writer of 'dirty realist' fiction. (Also briefly involved was **Guy Clark**, later one of the stalwarts of the 'new country' scene.)

Initial covers of material like "Hey Joe" seemed straightforward enough, but then it became clear that the group was starting to veer off into deeper psychedelic waters, with more unstructured and perplexing music. Moreover, a group of friends, later dubbed The Familiar Ugly, had started to participate in the band's live shows, also appearing on the "Free-Form Freak-Out" intermissions that separated The Crayola's offerings on their first album, 1967's PARABLE OF ARABLE LAND. There were up to one hundred participants on some of the album's 'Ugly' segments, while **Roky Ericson**, then of The 13th Floor Elevators, appeared on two of the Crayola tracks, adding harmonica to "Transparent Radiation" and organ to "Hurricane Fighter Plane".

Public apathy drove the band apart for a time, but a determined Thompson and Cunningham reunited within a year and, with the help of drummer **Tommy Smith**, cut GOD BLESS THE RED KRAYOLA AND ALL WHO SAIL WITH IT (1968), under the name **The Red Krayola**. In complete contrast to the weird lengths of the debut, this was a series of short, even fragmentary, songs, some of which were acoustic. Although more accessible, it was no more successful.

Thompson went on to produce a startling and under-appreciated solo album, CORKY'S DEBT TO HIS FATHER, and to found **Saddlesore** (a band that eventually popped up again in the mid 90s on Drag City). Then, in the winter of 1974–75, he encountered the drummer **Jesse Chamberlain** in New York, formed a new Red Crayola, and teamed up with the avant-garde arts partnership **Art & Language** on their 1976 album, CORRECTED SLOGANS. Art & Language returned the favour by working on a few Red Crayola albums during the late 70s, notably on SOLDIER TALK (1978), which also featured cameos by Lora Logic and members of Pere Ubu. By now based in London, Thompson found that, although his music was more in tune with the culture, it still failed to sell, and he proceeded to join Pere Ubu until their collapse.

He reappeared as Crayola with KANGAROO? (1981), an album credited to The Red Crayola With Art & Language and also featuring Logic, Pere Ubu's Allen Ravenstine (synthesizer), The Swell Maps' Epic Soundtracks, and Gina Birch of The Raincoats. Quirky, ramshackle songs dealt with such everyday rock'n'roll topics as "A Portrait Of V. I. Lenin In The Style Of Jackson Pollock", "The Principles Of Party Organization" and "The Mistakes Of Trotsky". Ravenstine, plus Art & Language, rejoined for BLACK SNAKES (1983), before Thompson embarked on production work, notably for The Chills.

Following a further relocation – to Düsseldorf – Thompson recruited a German rhythm section for the next Red Crayola album, MALEFACTOR ADE (1989), along with free-jazz saxophonist **Rudiger Carl**. Thompson has also recorded with Carl's COWWS Quintet, with Epic Soundtracks, Slovenly, and also Chicago experimental guitarist **Jim O'Rourke** (GASTR DEL SOL).

These outings notwithstanding, a new Crayola album, spelt and entitled, this time, THE RED KRAYOLA, showed up in 1994, its seventeen short, textural songs boasted the characteristic Thompson mark. It was produced by a seven-piece line-up, with O'Rourke on lo-fi Moog, alongside **John McEntire** of Tortoise. The confusingly titled THREE SONGS ON A TRIP TO THE UNITED STATES (1993) – which in fact comprised eight songs on a 12" vinyl disc – included five live tracks and is highly recommended. As is LUDWIG'S LAW (1998), a collaboration between Mayo and **Moebius & Plank**, of **CLUSTER** fame.

⊙ **Parable Of Arable Land and God Bless The Red Crayola And All Who Sail With It** (1967 & 1968; Charly; currently unavailable).
It's worth hunting around for this reissue of The Crayola's first two 60s albums, which remain diverting. They have also been issued, separately, by Collectables.

⊙ **The Red Krayola** (1994; Drag City).
Thompson's latest Red C/Krayola outing keys remarkably with the output of 90s bands like Tortoise.

Gerard F. Tierney

RED HOT CHILI PEPPERS

Formed Hollywood, California, 1983.

Funky punksters the **Red Hot Chili Peppers** were formed from the remains of the garage band Anthem. Led by **Anthony Kiedis** (vocals) and featuring **Hillel Slovak** (guitar), Michael Balzary aka **Flea** (bass) and **Jack Irons** (drums), they set about changing the face of rock in the only way they knew how: by blending thrashing punk with the sublime smooth funk sounds of the 70s – and taking their clothes off.

The creation of their first release, THE RED HOT CHILI PEPPERS (1984), was a traumatic affair. Contractual obligations meant that **Jack Sherman** (guitars) and **Cliff Martinez** (drums) of Captain Beefheart fame were used for the recording sessions, while production was handled by Gang of Four's

Andy Gill. The result failed to capture their brash pumping live sound, but it laid down the band's manifesto: sex, good times, a smattering of social conscience, and more sex. Live, they built their reputation through outrageous excess: the lithe Kiedis would indulge in acrobatics, whilst Flea and Slovak would hip-grind their way through the set wearing nothing but sweat-soaked underpants.

Their second studio effort, FREAKY STYLEY (1985), was produced by none other than the Funk-meister General himself, George Clinton. The full line-up played and were augmented by a horn section featuring, amongst others, Maceo Parker and Fred Wesley, both veterans of James Brown's band. This time round the group did themselves greater justice: Kiedis was developing his own rapping style while the arrangements were far catchier than their debut. Occasionally the funk-punk polarity grated but the overall standard was higher and showed their musical influences quite clearly.

The next stage of the band's career saw them shamelessly hype their own notoriety. The ABBEY ROAD EP (1987) heralded the infamous 'socks on cocks' era: the cover art was a pastiche of The Beatles' ABBEY ROAD sleeve, the important fact being that the group were stark naked save for socks covering their genitals. Images of the band were plastered everywhere. Pushing the boat out even further was the UPLIFT MOFO PARTY PLAN (1987), which went one step beyond the smoothness of FREAKY STYLEY by throwing in a major dose of psychedelia aided by producer Michael Beinhorn. Not being a band to shy away from controversy, the album contained the "Special Secret Song Inside". The need for a cryptic title became clear when the band all joined in on the chorus of 'I want to party on your pussy, baby'. Such lyrics posed a question that has dogged the band since their conception: are the Chili Peppers sexy or sexist? Whatever the answer, it did no harm to their profile.

Just as the hype machine began to roll, the partying and mayhem were cut short when Slovak overdosed on heroin in June 1988. His death threw the band into turmoil; extremely upset, Irons left and two new members were found: **Chad Smith** (drums) and **John Frusciante** (guitar).

Pulled back from the edge of self-destruction, the funky monks put all their energy into MOTHER'S MILK (1989), which they dedicated to the memory of Slovak. Perhaps reflecting the chaos of the preceding year, the album sounded distinctly half-baked in places. Acknowledging their formative influences once more, they included covers of Hendrix's "Fire" and Stevie Wonder's "Higher Ground".

Despite their growing international profile, MOTHER'S MILK proved to be their last outing with EMI. Snapped up by Warners, they next came out with the wonderfully titled BLOOD SUGAR SEX MAGIK (1991), produced by Rick Rubin. Usually associated with the heavier end of the metal spectrum (Slayer, Danzig), Rubin helped to shape a more cohesive sound for the group, accentuating their ballad-writing. The result was the sublime "Breaking The Girl" and the tear-jerking nostalgia of "Under The Bridge".

Although the band seemed to have finally hit their stride, personnel problems began to loom again, as touring pressures began to push Frusciante to the edge. His replacement, in June 1992, was **Arik Marshall** (guitar), who stayed with the band during the subsequent bout of summer festivals. However, after personality clashes, Marshall departed, leaving a significant vacuum. They finally settled on **Dave Navarro** (formerly of **JANE'S ADDICTION**), whose talent for melody and shuddering power enhanced the hard-edged funk-punk recipe.

The strength of the songwriting on ONE HOT MINUTE (1995) was a testament to a band at the peak of their creativity, boasting everything from the soulful mellowness of "Walkabout" to the chaos of "Warped". Despite the obvious strengths of the record, Navarro's role in the band had always seemed just a little too strained to last and, having ironed out his personal problems, Frusciante was reinstated. With the guitarist back on a relatively even keel the Chilis created the marvellous CALIFORNICATION (1999) album, a record simply dripping with succulent funk riffs and the requisite lewd'n'crude attitude that had made the band a byword for risqué rock entertainment.

Remarkably the band managed to keep its act together while touring at a cracking pace and, as if the point needed proving, they released the expansive live document OFF THE MAP (2002) as a DVD. A new album, BY THE WAY, followed later in the year, heralded by the single of the same name. The band were once again back on top, and had produced one of their finest moments and reaffirmed their position as one of the world's stand-out rock/funk outfits.

○ **Blood Sugar Sex Magik** (1991; Warners).
Integrated, polished and accomplished; at last they sound truly together. Rick Rubin's crisp production and the inclusion of emotive ballads and sexy choruses make this a vital release.

○ **One Hot Minute** (1995; Warners).
Produced by Rick Rubin again, the songwriting is tight, while then new boy Dave Navarro shines. Assured, mature and a logical progression from their previous album.

○ **By The Way** (2002; Warners).
More bold, funky compositions; while the single "By The Way" became the set's radio anthem, many of the other cuts surpass it: check out "Don't Forget Me" and "Tear".

Essi Berelian

RED HOUSE PAINTERS

Formed San Francisco, 1990.

One of the smaller movements in 90s rock was 'new miserablism'. Invented by journalists, it didn't catch the public's imagination in the same way as the later 'new acoustic movement', but this was scarcely surprising as it included just two bands: American Music Club and **Red House Painters**.

After a couple of years' apprenticeship playing the coffee houses and clubs of San Francisco, **Mark Kozelek**'s Red House Painters recorded their first album, DOWN COLOURFUL HILL (1992), for British label 4AD. The eight stripped-down acoustic numbers fitted in well with the label's characteristic melancholia, with Kozelek's aching voice giving them a disarmingly honest feel, though the set didn't share the ethereal grandeur of many 4AD acts (Cocteau Twins, This Mortal Coil, etc). The songs were deceptively simple, with numbers such as "Japanese To English" revealing an alliance of sensitive lyrics and memorable melody.

DOWN COLOURFUL HILL gained a great deal of music press acclaim, and was followed up by two records both called RED HOUSE PAINTERS. The first was a fourteen-track double set that contained the lovely "Grace Cathedral Park", and the almost catchy "New Jersey", on which Kozelek lamented that 'New Jersey ain't the whole world'. The second version (also 1993) contained a passionate version of Simon & Garfunkel's "I Am A Rock", where the melody of the song fitted Kozelek's yearning voice and bare instrumentation perfectly. A second, rockier interpretation of "New Jersey" confirmed it as his finest song to date.

A tour of Britain, with label mate Heidi Berry as support, revealed just how different Red House Painters were from the rest of 4AD's roster, as Berry's minimal stage presence was outweighed by Kozelek's equally downbeat but tougher material. Beginning the set with the unaccompanied "Michael", the sparseness of the records was emphasized, although the full band – with guitarist **Gorden Mack** and bassist **Jerry Vessel** – brought the set to an end, showing they could rock out with the best.

After a prolific early career, Red House Painters took a two-year sabbatical, returning in 1995 with OCEAN BEACH. Again showcasing Kozelek's songwriting talents, it gave more space to the rockier side of the band and garnered further excellent reviews.

In its wake, Kozelek recorded an album of typically gloomy songs and bleak melodies, and insisted that 4AD release it under his own name. Alarmed by the band's previous lack of sales, and predicting that Kozelek's solo effort would not improve financial matters, the label refused.

Kozelek and his band felt they had no choice but to leave the label and in 1996 signed to Island, releasing their first album for the label, SONGS FOR A BLUE GUITAR, in the summer. Virtually a Kozelek solo recording, it was released under the RHP moniker in the hope of stirring up public interest. Due to a flurry of record company mergers and acquisitions, there followed a period of silence and frustration for the band who had recorded material ready for the push. But the final release by Island was the 2CD RETROSPECTIVE (1999) collection, not the freshly recorded cuts. The first CD featured 13 tracks culled from the band's five albums and the second was a completists-only amalgam of demos and outtakes.

OLD RAMON, recorded in 1997, was eventually released on Sub Pop in 2001. This Kozelek production was another strong set of songs firmly in the RHP style. Meanwhile Kozelek signed to San Francisco's Badman label, releasing a solo album entitled ROCK'N'ROLL SINGER. It comprised three originals, three AC/DC covers and a John Denver tune.

Following the warm reception of his previous covers Kozelek's next outing was an album full of them: WHAT'S NEXT TO THE MOON. All were originally by AC/DC, and though perhaps not the most obvious choice of material it leant itself surprisingly well to his vocal talents. The connections between Kozelek and AC/DC's Bon Scott as rock'n'roll singers eventually seemed more powerful than their differences.

(•) **Down Colourful Hill** (1992; 4AD).
Red House Painters' first album is actually a demo tape that Mark Kozelek handed to supremo Ivo Watts-Russell. The sound is spartan and minor-key, but full of atmosphere and gorgeous melodies. Everything is dominated by Kozelek's voice and emotional charge, yet Meck's electric guitar work is notable, too, especially on the haunting "Medicine Bottle".

Mike Martin

RED LORRY YELLOW LORRY

Formed Leeds, England, 1982; disbanded 1992.

The surly, burly **Red Lorry Yellow Lorry** emerged from the incestuous post-punk Leeds and Bradford scene of the early 80s, alongside bands such as The Cult, Sisters Of Mercy and The Mission. They shared with these outfits a penchant for black clothing and blistering guitar work-outs, but with their workmanlike directness and the absence of fanciful imagery in their lyrics they managed to be remarkably un-goth.

The original line-up was singer and guitarist **Chris Reed** (vocals/guitar), **Dave Wolfenden** (guitar), **Steve Smith** (bass) and **Mick Brown** (drums). Reed was a notoriously sullen frontman, with a

bowel-opening, glass-gargle of a voice. With the fretmen thrashing instruments slung at knee level, the emphasis was on a full-blooded, four-pronged assault capable of leaving an audience reeling. There eventually came to be more than a hint of the industrial antics of Test Department in their approach, but on the whole jagged guitar lines and thunderous momentum was their forte. In the early days, they ended their sets, memorably, with "Happy", one of the most miserable songs ever written, and often accompanied by the trashing of equipment and tantrums.

Three singles were released on the Red Rhino label between 1982 and 1983 – "Beating My Head", "Take It All" and "He's Read" – before bassist Smith left to join Sisters Of Mercy refugee Gary Marx in Ghostdance, and later Fiat Lux. He was replaced by **Paul Sothern** and the band embarked on a low-key US tour, releasing further singles, "Monkeys On Juice", "Hollow Eyes", "Chance", "Spinning Round", "Walking On Your Hands", "Cut Down" and "Crawling Mantra" (as The Lorries). Red Rhino also released the LPs TALK ABOUT THE WEATHER (1985) and PAINT YOUR WAGON (1986), before the band signed to the Situation 2 label for the release of NOTHING WRONG (1988), and BLOW (1989), arguably their best album. The band fell apart soon afterwards, but regrouped with Reed and Gary Weight for one more album, BLASTING OFF (1991) – essentially a mediocre bookend for a band that once promised (and often delivered) great things.

It is perhaps fair to say the Lorries never quite established a unique enough voice to get themselves up into the premier division, and when Sothern left the band it was never to find a stable line-up again. Mick Brown eventually ran off with **THE MISSION**, for whom Wolfenden also played guitar on a couple of tours.

Cherry Red Records obtained the rights to the Red Rhino back catalogue a few years ago and reissued TALK ABOUT THE WEATHER, PAINT YOUR WAGON and a mastered-from-crackly-vinyl collection, 1982–1987 THE SINGLES. Most recently the catalogue has been rehashed further with a VERY BEST OF collection and a double whammy reissue of NOTHING WRONG and BLOW.

(•) **The Very Best Of Red Lorry Yellow Lorry** (2000; Cherry Red).
Seek it out for a potted history lesson in pounding West Yorkshire miserablism.

(•) **The Singles 1982-1987** (2000; Cherry Red).
This twenty-six strong collection offers an alternative introduction to the group as well as being an essential purchase for fans.

Ada Wilson and Mark Turrell

REDD KROSS

Formed Los Angeles, 1980.

Few bands just out of their teens command respect from the US underground indie scene, but **Redd Kross** managed to overcome an appallingly wacky choice of name to influence the likes of Sonic Youth and Faith No More. The band's good-natured enthusiasm and ear for a top tune has ensured that this respect has been maintained, although the band's consistency level has been dangerously threatened at times by a failure to keep their lead guitarists on a leash.

Early Redd Kross material was often hilarious, ranging from songs about Linda Blair in *The Exorcist* to the self-explanatory "Notes & Chords Mean Nothing To Me". 'I wanna break my guitar ... it won't get me nowhere!' yelped the teenage **Jeffrey McDonald**, supported by his even younger brother **Steven** (bass/vocals) and a cast of whoever their mates at school were at the time. Two-chord, sixty-second bursts of prepubescent tantrums made up the debut Redd Kross album, BORN INNOCENT (1981), which was cute and chaotic, and helped to establish their underground credibility – the band always saw themselves as a kind of punk Partridge Family.

The band paid tribute to their influences with typical youthful gusto on the TEEN BABES FROM MONSANTO mini-album, released on Reckless in 1984, giving the full Redd Kross garage treatment to, among others, David Bowie ("Saviour Machine"), The Stooges ("Ann") and The Rolling Stones ("Citadel"), with a rerecording of "Linda Blair" thrown in for good measure. Surprisingly, for a band so keen on The Beatles, no Beatles material was attempted, although Redd Kross have been known to play live sets consisting entirely of Beatles covers.

Following one more indie album, NEUROTICA (1987), which veered wildly between the inspired and the overly cheesy, the band's crossover potential was spotted by Atlantic, who put out THIRD EYE in 1990. The timing of the release was unfortunate, however. The rough edges had been smoothed away, and Redd Kross now sounded far too pop to appeal to the hardcore 'alternative' underground, and yet fell uncomfortably close to the hard-rock market, mainly due to lead guitarist Robert Hecker's fretboard noodlings. "Annie's Gone" was a hit single to anyone with a pair of ears, but the band's campy, androgynous image probably confused much of their potential audience, and Atlantic decided that one bite of the cherry was all Redd Kross were getting. To add insult to injury, the debut album by Jellyfish (who were heavily influenced by Redd Kross, and even featured Steven McDonald on one track) was doing the business around this time.

However, dejection would never have suited the happy-go-lucky Kross, and a new line-up – **Eddie Kurdziel** replaced Robert Hecker on guitar, **Gere Fennelly** was brought in on keyboards and **Brian Reitzell** on drums – was followed by an indie deal with This Way Up Records, and a higher profile in the UK due to regular tours and appearances at festivals. A couple of singles ("Trance" and "Switchblade Sister") were followed by the confident PHASESHIFTER (1993). Although "Jimmy's

Fantasy" was standard riffola, the follow-up "Lady In The Front Row" single was a deserved Single of the Week in *Melody Maker*, drawing comparisons to "Paperback Writer" and The Stone Roses.

Never the most prolific of bands, they managed to get their sixth album, SHOW WORLD (1997), out during their seventeenth year together. Gorgeous song titles such as "One Chord progression" and "Mess Around" indicated that there was no fear of this band growing up anytime soon.

With the need to issue a Redd Kross LP out of their systems the band set to work having about as much fun as they could with their various side projects, most notably the **Steven McDonald Group** and **Ze Malibu Kids**, who released SOUND IT OUT in 2002. Quite when they'll get around to being Redd Kross again is anyone's guess.

⊙ **Third Eye** (1990; Atlantic).
Unluckily released prior to the alternative-rock explosion, this disappeared without trace. If only it had been promoted properly, "Annie's Gone" would have surely been the smash it deserved to be.

Mauro Venegas

OTIS REDDING

Born Dawson, Georgia, September 9, 1941; died December 10, 1967.

More than any other performer, **Otis Redding** exemplified Stax Records, the Memphis-based label whose laconic, rougher-edged, grits'n'cornbread records competed with Motown's slicker, more orchestrated 'Sound of Young America' for 60s soul supremacy. As producer, songwriter, arranger and talent scout, Redding helped to create the Stax sound, which was defined by the tight, deep-in-the-pocket rhythm section of drummer Al Jackson and bassist Duck Dunn, Steve Cropper's tautly strummed guitar, plus the interventions of The Bar Kays' horns and Booker T. Jones's organ. Topping it off was Redding's passionately gruff voice, which combined Sam Cooke's phrasing with a brawnier delivery, and could testify like a hell-bent preacher, croon like a tender lover, or get down and dirty with a bluesy yawp. He was a major star on the R&B charts, and you can only wonder what Redding could have accomplished in the pop field, if it were not for his death in a plane crash in December 1967.

Redding first came to the attention of Macon producer Phil Walden (later Capricorn Records founder) as a member of The Pinetoppers, but did not make any impression until recording the heavily Little Richard-influenced "Shout Bamalama" for Confederate Records in 1960. He soon signed with Stax and hit the charts with his first release, "These Arms Of Mine" (1962). All the elements of the classic Stax sound were in place on Redding's debut album, PAIN IN MY HEART (1964), but it was essentially a collection of singles padded with covers of soul hits. It's worth hearing, if only for Redding's range.

Starting with THE GREAT OTIS SINGS SOUL BALLADS (1965), Redding began to take greater control of his albums. While SOUL BALLADS was a step forward from the debut, with two of Redding's signature songs "Mr. Pitiful" and "That's How Strong My Love Is", it still lacked cohesion, even if the filler material was filler of a high order. Redding hit his stride with a series of albums that are the foundation of his legacy: OTIS BLUE (1966), THE SOUL ALBUM (1966) and THE DICTIONARY OF SOUL (1966).

OTIS BLUE showed Redding expanding his repertoire. While it contained the expected Sam Cooke cover, a volcanic version of "Shake", there was also a propulsive version of The Rolling Stones' "Satisfaction" (Jagger's favourite cover of a Stones song), and his original version of "Respect" – a hit for Aretha Franklin, but Redding's scorching version resonated with a personal and racial pride that stung in the civil rights era of the 60s.

THE SOUL ALBUM was a more personal affair, from the morning-after languor of "Cigarettes And Coffee" and the new-love euphoria of "It's Growing", to the glorious covers of Sam Cooke's "Chain Gang", Slim Harpo's "Scratch My Back" and Roy Head's "Treat Her Right". DICTIONARY OF SOUL was just that: a compendium that proved Redding's mastery of the form from the swinging "Fa-Fa-Fa-Fa-Fa (Sad Song)" to a breathless "Day Tripper" and the dirty gutbucket blues of "Hawg For You".

By this time, Redding had had more than twenty US Top 10 R&B hits, but the rock world would soon find out about Redding, via his stunning performance at 1967's Monterey Festival. Unfortunately, this performance, paired by Warners with Jimi Hendrix's Monterey breakthrough, is now out of print, and due to contractual problems will probably never see the light of day. And Redding was never able to savour his success, dying less than six months later in a plane crash outside of Madison, Wisconsin. His death was made only more tragic by the #1 American pop success of "(Sittin' On) The Dock Of The Bay" in 1968.

⊙ **The Very Best of Otis Redding** (1993; Rhino).
The perfect single-disc collection of Redding's output.

⊙ **Otis! The Definitive Otis Redding** (1993; Rhino).
One of the few box sets that is not just for completists. No other soul singer, with the exception of Aretha Franklin, had a broader emotional or musical range. From the excruciatingly moving "Cigarettes And Coffee" to the introspective "(Sittin' On) The Dock Of The Bay" and the funk classic "Tramp", Redding epitomized the grace, dignity, sweat, horniness and tenderness of Southern soul.

Steven Mirkin

THE REDSKINS

Formed York, England, 1981; disbanded 1986.

If there is one neglected field of English pop it is surely the protesting, social realism of the mid 80s, when Thatcherism reached its alarming peak against the backdrop of the year-long miners' strike. **The Redskins** were purveyors of some of that era's finest political pop records, offering a powerfully defiant groove and brilliant live performances.

Redskins frontman was **Chris Dean** (aka *NME* journalist Chris Moore), a passionate socialist with a knack for fashioning his ideals into natty tunes. Dean chose not the path of indie rock or anarcho-thrash to drive home his message but soulful, danceable tunes with attitude that appealed to the alternative crowd. Some dubbed it New Wave soul, while Dean cited his musical ambition as wanting to 'sound like The Supremes and dance like The Clash'.

In October 1982 Dean, **Nick King** (drums) and **Martin Hewes** (bass) recorded their first John Peel session for the BBC. One song from this superb session, "The Peasant Army", made their position abundantly clear, but the artillery was only just beginning to emerge. Having released the double A-sided single, "Lev Bronstein"/"The Peasant Army" in July 1982, The Redskins returned in 1983 with "Lean On Me"/"Unionize!". In 1984, they left ENT Records for Decca, where their next single, "Keep On Keepin' On", made the UK Top 50. A rushing, brassy beat tune with more than a nod to Paul Weller, its encouragement of working-class solidarity still sounds fresh and exciting, even if its message is largely forgotten by all major political parties.

During the miners' strike of 1984–85, The Redskins gigged relentlessly at benefit concerts, combining terrific entertainment with genuine outrage and compassion. With Style Council drummer **Steve White** briefly joining the fold, The Redskins reached the UK Top 40 with their 1985 single, "Bring It Down (This Insane Thing)", but by the release of a much-delayed album, NEITHER WASHINGTON... NOR MOSCOW... (1986), the strike was long broken, the unions seemed crushed and the camaraderie of those spirited times had evaporated. Nonetheless, the record was a cracker, with Dean and Hewes joined by **Paul Hookham** (drums), a powerful horn section, and various members of the Socialist Workers Party.

Unfortunately, The Redskins' devotion to far-left socialism left them out of step with the broad-based Red Wedge movement, which garnered plenty of support on the UK rock scene. As Red Wedge united and alienated the socialist youth vote in one sweep, The Redskins became marginalized and disintegrated after one last single, "It Can Be Done", unleashed in May 1986. The Redskins may have received little ultimate reward for all their efforts, but during a brief career they undoubtedly gave it their best shot.

⊙ **Live** (1994; Dojo).
Perhaps the best representation available of this great live band, this is an exhilarating ride through numbers like "Don't Talk To Me About Whether", "Reds Strike The Blues", "Plateful Of Hateful" and "The Power Is Yours", with Dean peppering the set with scathing social comment.

Pip Southall

LOU REED

Born Freeport, New York, 1942.

"One chord is fine. Two chords are pushing it. Three chords and you're into jazz." Lou defines rock'n'roll

Just as it's possible to be very big in rock without having any lasting influence, it is also possible to have tremendous influence without being terribly big. Even at his commercial peak, **Lou Reed** never sold as well as, say, Chicago, but his music, lyrics and persona have infiltrated popular culture to such an extent that he would remain a major figure even if all his records from here on tanked.

Part of the reason is Reed's integrity. His approach of treating extremes of human emotion and behaviour with a cool air of poetic detachment was virtually unseen in rock'n'roll songwriting before he introduced it; now it's ubiquitous. And through sheer force of talent and perseverance, he forced his image as a street-hardened, sexually ambiguous poet *maudit* into the iconography of rock. That he achieved this without ever pandering to his audience – frequently, in fact, challenging and even showing hostility toward it – makes him even more remarkable.

Reared in the suburbs of Long Island, Reed was intellectually precocious, devoting his energies to writing poems, stories and songs, playing guitar, and listening to rock'n'roll and R&B. He became severely rebellious in his teens, exhibiting mood swings and hints of sexual precocity which caused his parents to submit the 17-year-old to electroshock therapy. Far from the result his parents hoped for, Reed emerged from his zappings even more committed to rebellion. (Contempt for middle-class life and aspirations became a prominent secondary theme in his work – except for a late period, when he was pursuing it himself.) At Syracuse University, while exploring sex, drugs and rock-'n'roll, Reed also studied with the poet Delmore Schwartz, who inspired him and encouraged his creativity, and met Sterling

Morrison, later the second guitarist in the **THE VELVET UNDERGROUND**.

After college Reed worked briefly as a songwriter/performer/producer for a low-rent song factory called Pickwick International. A Welsh classical musician named John Cale came to Pickwick to do a session for some fast money, and the two established a rapport. Reed joined Cale in New York's Lower East Side, and the two started to work on some of Reed's college tunes, including "I Found A Reason" and "Heroin", as well as new tunes and songs of Cale's. Reed then contacted Morrison and hired Maureen Tucker to play drums, and The Velvet Underground was born.

Many of Reed's songs from The Velvets period (1965–70) featured subject matter that was, to say the least, unusual for pop music in the late 60s. "Heroin" and the numb yet orgiastic "Sister Ray" are only the

Transformer man Lou Reed

most obvious examples. More significant was the subtle tension in love songs like "Pale Blue Eyes" and "I'll Be Your Mirror", which, however sweetly arranged, also contained acknowledgements of despair and hopelessness that brought the crying-time sentiments of most sad rock songs up to a new, challenging level of expressiveness. While Reed's plangent guitar style and his voice (which has always tended toward the underside of the appropriate pitches) helped raise the songs' discomfort level, Reed's ear for melody was so strong, and his enthusiasm for rock and R&B formats so genuine, that his Velvets material could conceivably have been accepted as pop, albeit of a new kind. Cale's classical/experimental leanings, however, tended to go the other way, and the resulting strangeness of the band's music confused many listeners, even after Andy Warhol famously turned the spotlight on them and the band got big record deals.

After Reed left The Velvets in 1970, he tried to crack the singer/songwriter market. In his early solo efforts, he tried to balance his deeper, darker concerns with prettier music than The Velvets' format generally allowed. Lou Reed (1972) had a big, lush sound, soul backing vocals, and some strangely stock pop-song sentiments, but Reed's New York slyness usually muscled its way to the front, as in "Wild Child": 'Then we spoke of some kids from the coast ... and how suicides don't leave notes'. Sharper still was the follow-up, Transformer (1972), which was produced by David Bowie. There were baroque flourishes such as the tuba obbligato on "Make Up", but they were used as accents, not wallpaper. The songs were pretty in an almost conventional way, but the lyrical twists redeemed them ('You made me feel like I was someone else/Someone good'). With Transformer, Reed was still feeding the public with images to which it was unaccustomed, but now the public was buying them. Young men who had never thought of gay men without contempt smiled when "Walk On The Wild Side", the album's polysexual hit, came on the stereo.

Typical of Reed's self-destructiveness, he followed the modest success of Transformer with Berlin (1973), a difficult album that produced such divided responses that *Rolling Stone* was compelled to answer its own negative review of it with a countervailing essay. Conceived as a 'film for the ear' about an unhappy *ménage à trois* in the divided city of Berlin, the album featured morose songs about speed-induced anxiety and sexual rage, and Weill-flavoured ballads about suicide and a mother separated from her children. Whereas Transformer's dark undertones were made palatable to general audiences by its buoyant energy, Berlin challenged Reed's new wider audience to accept the bleakness without the buoyancy – a challenge that audience didn't accept.

After this, Reed seemed to retreat a bit, producing some of his most commercially viable material. On Rock 'N' Roll Animal (1974), a live album chronicling his Transformer-era stage-show, a slightly fussy band supported a guitarless Reed as he performed his 'hits' rock-cabaret-style in dead-white make-up and black lipstick. Reed had a minor hit with this – perhaps because it highlighted his image over his imagery – and RCA later followed with Lou Reed Live (1975) from the same tour. Sally Can't Dance (1974) and Coney Island Baby (1976) contained palatable tunes with crisp arrangements (including their title tracks), and they performed well in the marketplace. But even these chart-ready LPs contained harsh eccentricities like the electroshock-inspired "Kill Your Sons" and "Kicks" ('And when the blood came down his neck/You know it was much better than sex'). In between these two albums, Reed unleashed Metal Machine Music (1975), a double record of annoying feedback that still remains the ultimate statement of rock misanthropy.

His first release on Arista, Rock And Roll Heart (1976), broke no new ground, but around this time punk rock was launching and Lou was showing up at CBGB's to catch the new acts (including The Voidoids, whose guitarist, Bob Quine, would later play with Reed). Though Reed did not absorb the punk sound (he didn't need to – with The Velvets, he had helped invent it), the new, acerbic musical environment seemed to invigorate him. On Street Hassle (1978), Reed offered the sharp "Dirt", the sour jokes of "I Wanna Be Black", and the epic title tune. In Street Hassle, all of Reed's hallmarks coalesced: life in the demimonde, contempt for standard solutions, unhappy love, and the poeticism of street talk.

Reed was having problems with Arista by now, publicly criticizing label head Clive Davis and releasing the double-live oddity, Live – Take No Prisoners (1978), in which his epic rants overshadowed the music. The Bells (1979) was mostly grooves and riffs built around slabs of inchoate feeling (sometimes effectively, as with the ruined reunion of "Families"). At decade's end, Reed appeared to be in a mood as bad as his Metal Machine Music era.

After Reed got married to Sylvia Morales, settled in New Jersey, and started playing with **Robert Quine** and bassist **Fernando Saunders**, his attitude changed. His return to RCA, THE BLUE MASK (1982; reissued 1998; BMG), was an explosion of creative power, with the Quine/Saunders nexus (abetted here by Doane Perry's drums) providing much of the juice as Reed swung breathtakingly between examinations of pain ("The Gun", "Waves Of Fear") and promise ("Heavenly Arms" and the exultant "My House"). LEGENDARY HEARTS (1983) followed with similar themes, leaning heavily on renunciations of past excesses ("Bottoming Out", "The Last Shot").

In the mid 80s Reed released Quine and much of his recently acquired musical bite, attempting to put over his concerns now with lush, radio-friendly arrangements. The results were mixed: NEW SENSATIONS (1984) and MISTRIAL (1986) were enjoyable but puzzling hybrids of 80s AOR and Lou Reed, but 1989's NEW YORK benefited from the unifying theme of civic life and from a new adventurousness in his lyrics.

The 90s found Reed branching out again, first by reuniting with Cale for the Warhol elegy, SONGS FOR DRELLA (1990), and then with the mortality-inspired MAGIC AND LOSS (1992). There was also a brief, rather abortive Velvet Underground reunion. A new Reed album, SET THE TWILIGHT REELING, was released in 1996, Lou declaiming dark blank verse over hard-rock noise workouts – abetted by Saunders and drummer **Tony Smith** – and writing fierce satire on tracks such as "Sex With Your Parents (Motherfucker)".

Sadly, it was the altogether more mundane "Perfect Day" that the BBC chose as its inflated self-advertisement in 1997, though the cloying nature of the video (featuring dozens of performers from the rock and other musical spheres) couldn't completely disguise the 'This song promotes the use of heroin' aftertaste; it was easily Reed's most subversive hit since "Walk On The Wild Side".

PERFECT NIGHT; LIVE IN LONDON (1998), was a far from inspiring run-through of old favourites and less successful newer songs. Lou himself seemed subdued throughout, despite the adulation he has invariably received in the UK; it was as if he'd convinced himself the Brits hated him as much as he hated them.

ECSTASY (2000), found him back on form, growling his way through stripped down rockers like "Paranoia Key Of E" and the epic, eighteen-minute-long "Like A Possum". 2000 also saw the release of a book, *Pass Thru Fire*, which collected all of Reed's lyrics in a sumptuous hardback package. This was followed in 2003 by the indulgent, but interesting, horror-concept-album, THE RAVEN.

Ultimately, Reed's lasting significance may prove to be his devotion to what Reed himself calls 'adult rock records' – music that appeals to both a popular desire for instant gratification (as with all good rock)

and a universal desire for meaning and understanding (as with all good art). This goal is apparent even in his failures; with his successes, he may well be twentieth-century rock music's most powerful transformer.

⊙ **Transformer** (1972; RCA).
One of the most uncompromising pop records ever made. The only glam-rock record ever to explore the contradictions of glamour.

⊙ **Coney Island Baby** (1976; RCA).
The most pleasing of Reed's soft-rock albums. His sense of humour has never been better than on "A Gift", and the title track reminds you why Jonathan Richman idolized Reed: who else would have had the nerve to try to find 'the glory of love' in the reveries of a troubled would-be high-school football player (in doo-wop style, no less)?

⊙ **Street Hassle** (1978; Arista).
Lou Reed slides into the Scorsese/Sex Pistols late-70s tip with no problem. A triumphal homecoming for the godfather of punk. Also boasts the lovely Vibralux version of "Real Good Time Together".

⊙ **The Blue Mask** (1982; RCA).
Songs of married life, side by side with songs of rape and torture. Gradually you figure out the connection: there is fear behind love, and love behind fear. This is Reed at the height of his artistry, with a very hot band and a clear sense of purpose.

⊙ **Between Thought And Expression** (1992; MCA).
Excellent three-CD summation of pre-NEW YORK Reed. Includes the rarities "Little Sister" and "Here Comes The Bride", a live version of "Heroin" with jazz trumpeter Don Cherry, and, for joy-poppers, a three-minute clip from METAL MACHINE MUSIC.

⊙ **The Raven** (2003; Sire).
Inspired by the Edgar Allan Poe story of the same name, THE RAVEN is one of the more adventurous projects to have been unleashed by this ageing Velvet in recent years. The CD is awash with pompous production, overly indulgent Shakespearian acting (from, among others, Willem Dafoe), improvised clatter, and the kind of grating noise that has not been heard from Reed since METAL MACHINE MUSIC. And yet, as a whole, it works.

Roy Edroso

REEF

Formed Bath, England, 1993.

Reef are a curious commodity on the modern rock scene as they combine blatantly free-style, vintage blues rock with an attitude that sits well with current laddish trends.

They first made their way into the public eye as a result of a TV ad for the Sony Minidisc in which they played a young metal band trying to impress an implacable A&R man with a demo tune. Prior to this, **Gary Stringer** (vocals), **Kenwyn House** (guitar), **Jack Bessant** (bass) and **Dominic Greensmith** (drums) recorded their door-opening PURPLE demo tape in the autumn of 1993 whilst sharing a house in west London. Sony S2 saw the potential and sent the band out on the road. The demo found its way into the hands of Paul Weller, who invited them to support him for three nights at the Royal Albert Hall. Such high-profile endorsement could hardly fail to add to the media interest whipped up by their early advertising foray.

Autumn 1994 saw them in the studio recording REPLENISH (1995), a shamelessly blues-based hard rock album in the lengthy tradition of Jimi Hendrix and Led Zeppelin. Fearing an early burnout (in the grand style of Stiltskin and other long-forgotten bands briefly illuminated by the ad world), they declined to release "Naked", the Minidisc song, and instead opted for "Good Feeling", a tune which entered the charts at #24. When the former song was finally released it gained the group instant TV exposure on BBC TV's *Top Of The Pops*, as it entered the charts at #11. The summer brought a rash of prestigious UK festival slots at Glastonbury, Reading, Phoenix and T in the Park.

Work on 1997's GLOW album began in Sydney, Australia, during a world tour. Production duties fell to George Drakoulias, whose past credits include The Beastie Boys, but more importantly the rockier-sounding Primal Scream and Black Crowes. Drakoulias took Reef's retro-rock habit and presented it as a positive virtue. House's guitar work was brought to the fore, as were Stringer's rasping vocals. First single "Place Your Hands" entered the charts at #6 and saw the band embraced by both the mature rock press as well as the trendier male-lifestyle magazines which were in the grip of rampant 'laddism'; Reef with their love of nostalgic heavy rock fitted in nicely alongside favourites like Ocean Colour Scene and Oasis. Although their success has not been in the same stratospheric league as the latter's, they remain talented exponents of a style of music which has long been out of favour with the trendier music press.

By the end of 1998 the band had recorded their third album but were dithering on the name. During the winter tour, however, a number of new tracks – "Sweetie", "New Bird" and new single "I've Got Something To Say" – were aired and revealed a band quite comfortable with the blues-rock niche they had created for themselves. In fact the only real experimentation was on new track "Locked Inside", which featured the vocal talents of bassist Jack Bessant rather than laddish foghorn Gary Stringer.

Likewise with album number four – rather mundanely titled GETAWAY (2000) – the band were even more dependent on their established template. In fact the only real change came with the slightly sprightlier production, courtesy of Al Clay, who had worked similar miracles for the Stereophonics. The subsequent tour did well enough, with the new material sounding a great deal punchier in a live context. The band's next effort was Together (2003), which was, disappointingly, largely comprised of older 'hits', with only five fresh songs to show for itself. It is now hard to imagine what tricks they will have to pull from the bag to prevent themselves sliding down the slippery slope of self parody.

⊙ **Replenish** (1995; Sony S2).
A hard-rocking debut of style and substance. All the hallmarks of an excellent rock education are present. Contains the infamous "Naked" as well as a number of other well-crafted tunes.

⊙ **Glow** (1997; Sony S2).
Stringer's vocal style is almost unbearably annoying for the first few spins, particularly on hit single "Place Your Hands". If you can get your head past this production flaw, there are a number of brilliant songs on offer, including the single "Come Back Brighter".

⊙ **Getaway** (2000; Sony S2).
Basically, this is Reef confirming their belief that if it ain't broke don't fix it. Again, the only thing that occasionally grates is singer Gary Stringer's annoyingly rasped delivery – when he let's himself off the leash it can become just a little too sandpapery to tolerate.

Essi Berelian

R.E.M.

Formed Athens, Georgia, 1980.

"I probably embody that whole idealism/cynicism conundrum that my generation and people younger than me carry." Michael Stipe

It's just possible that **R.E.M.** have turned accepted rock industry wisdom on its head. For over a decade, they've drawn 'Greatest Rock'n'Roll Band in the World?' headlines in the mainstream press, and their best two albums have sold, respectively, seven and ten million copies. They should be crap, shouldn't they? They should be Hootie & The Blowfish, or Phil Collins, or Bryan Adams? Yet they are wonderful: a band endowed with melodic and lyrical brilliance, and possessed of an uncompromising spirit that has provided a voice for a frustrated generation.

The foil to all the success is the band's aw-shucks attitude. R.E.M. released albums throughout the 80s to reviews that fell all over themselves in their rush to praise; they garnered an increasingly hard-core fan base, and toured almost constantly; but only in the 90s did they reach fully fledged stardom. Unlike Nirvana, a gradual evolution from college parties to football stadiums gave them time to adapt – or, as **Michael Stipe** says, Kurt Cobain's fate could easily have been his if such expectations had been thrust upon him so early.

That success did not come immediately to R.E.M. is no big surprise. Their music is not stadium rock and the fact that stadiums are where they now ply their trade remains as puzzling to them as it must be pleasing to the suits at Warner Brothers. **Bill Berry** (drums), **Peter Buck** (guitar), **Mike Mills** (bass) and Michael Stipe (vocals), four undergraduates at the University of Georgia in Athens, formed the band to play a few parties, became increasingly competent, if not spectacular, and were signed by the tiny Hib-Tone label to record a single, a moment duly celebrated in the annals of indie rock.

That song was "Radio Free Europe" (1981), now a major collector's item in its original pressing, despite the fact that the 'Hib-Tone version', as it's sometimes

R.E.M.'s Michael Stipe

the heights of "Radio Free Europe" on "Gardening At Night", its delicate melody shrouding Stipe's fragile, high delivery of lyrics, alluding, darkly, to unhappy times.

An R.E.M. classic, the aptly titled MURMUR album, was released in 1983 to major applause from the critics. This album was the perfection of the R.E.M. sound. Shared songwriting contributed a diversity of styles, from the lilting "We Walk" to the more sinister rock of "Moral Kiosk", while, throughout, an intrinsic sense of melody offset Stipe's mumbling and the stop-start structuring of songs like "Pilgrimage" and "9-9". More straightforward were "Sitting Still", "Catapult" and "Talk About The Passion", which build from the most basic of hooks, and "Radio Free Europe" surfaced again in a more polished form. Listening to MURMUR is akin to overhearing secrets – eminently alluring and nearly indecipherable. Its accomplishment is uncanny and it stands as one of the greatest and most listenable albums of the 80s.

Many fine American bands – Hüsker Dü and The Minutemen, to name two – were emerging around this time, but for those bands' speed and power, R.E.M. substituted invention. Few have ever wrenched so much out of the simple four-piece format as R.E.M. did on MURMUR, their lack of technical accomplishment notwithstanding. Mills's bass was an instrument of melody rather than rhythm; Buck often chose to pick rather than strum his chords; and the harmonies of Mills and Stipe were everywhere, yet never out of place. But it was Stipe's lead vocals, at times sounding almost like a worded yawn, which more than anything came to define the band.

All these traits were revisited on RECKONING (1984). The album lacked the impact of its predecessor, perhaps due to the more polished production of songs like "Southern Central Rain" and "(Don't Go Back to) Rockville", though both were standout tracks. Overall, however, RECKONING felt like more a collection of good songs – very good songs indeed – than an accomplished whole. A rare sense of musical and lyrical imagination was nonetheless in place: "Harbour Coat" managed to sound urgent without an ounce of strain, and "Second Guessing" like a happy accusation. Journalists could see a hint of The Byrds, Big Star, even British punk, while, lyrically, Dylan and Patti Smith were more obvious influences. R.E.M., however, sounded like none of

known (a different version appears on the band's full-length debut), can be found on subsequent 'best of' albums. Strange and melodic at the same time, "Radio Free Europe" perfectly captures R.E.M.'s early style and musically delivers on the band's name – as if the song were seeping out of the unconscious, just out of tangible reach. Snatches of beguiling lyrics made out from murmured vocals lent the song, and the band, an air of mystery that remains to this day.

"Radio Free Europe" hit the right mark. Soon after its release R.E.M. were signed to the burgeoning IRS label, and in 1981 the mini-album CHRONIC TOWN was released. Much of this five-song collection may seem average fare in comparison to subsequent albums, but the elements could be seen clicking into place. The same obscure vocals covered innovative if simple playing, and they almost reached their predecessors – by the time more exact replicas were emerging, it was because R.E.M. were the imitated, not the other way around.

If RECKONING gave a nod towards the market, albeit a subtle one, then FABLES OF THE RECONSTRUCTION (1985) took a step back. A difficult, less accessible album, it was recorded far from home in England, and found band members in seemingly pensive mood. Strange, haunting and oblique, filled with erratic mixes and an almost haphazard production, FABLES was about storytelling, the Deep South and, in "Wendell Gee" and "Old Man Kensey", the simple souls that merge the two. Its highlight was "Driver 8", an elliptical, foreboding tale set to a pulsing beat, and a song few R.E.M. fans would leave off a list of all-time favourites.

After the release of FABLES, R.E.M. began their most gruelling tour to date, starting in Britain. Just quite how eccentric and compellingly watchable Stipe had become was soon evident. In Glasgow he ambled menacingly around the stage with the word 'dog' written in felt tip across his forehead. On other occasions his between-song banter would verge on the surreal. 'Chicken is a chicken' he growled on one occasion – tossing aside the conventional 'Are you feeling all right?' absurdity – 'except for his bill. Little salt and pepper, chicken still'. When he went on to recite, a cappella, "What's New Pussycat", there was no more doubting that here, quite simply, was a star. The world, outside of college radio, was just taking a little longer to recognize the fact.

The three albums that followed, LIFE'S RICH PAGEANT (1986), DOCUMENT (1987) and GREEN (1989), marked a new era in R.E.M.'s development. With each album, the sound became brasher and louder, the lyrics more open and confident, something hard to fathom for longtime devotees who had prided themselves on their ability to decode the lyrics. LIFE'S RICH PAGEANT featured more obvious rock production, punchier guitars and feedback. If FABLES was an introspective Southern album, PAGEANT was an outgoing American one. Between

the bold notes that opened the album – "Begin The Begin" – and the roar of the closer "Superman", the band's first recorded cover, came songs of decay and renewal, change and hope. 'This land is the land of ours', sang Stipe during "Cuyahoga", recalling an old Woody Guthrie line, and setting the tone and scope of his concerns on this environmental eulogy. Both "Fall On Me" (a minor single) and "I Believe" continued in a similar, if more upbeat, vein, and boasted two of the most poignant melodies R.E.M. have yet produced.

DOCUMENT rocked even harder, and lyrically verged on discernible. Released in the midst of the Reagan era, the album is R.E.M.'s most openly political to date. 'Sharpening stones, walking on coals, to improve your business acumen', snarled Stipe on "Exhuming McCarthy". Rather than allowing others to explain the difference between want and need, as he asked on "I Believe", Stipe took it upon himself, during the rallying cry, "Finest Worksong", to declare, 'What we want and what we need has been confused.' R.E.M. emerged from the closet not only as social spokesmen but as rockers (a testament repeated a decade on with MONSTER); drums were pushed well up in the mix and Mills's bass, for the first time, took backstage to Buck's increasingly confident riffing. DOCUMENT also spawned R.E.M.'s first true hit, "The One I Love", which, with its subtle kiss-off of a lyric, peaked at #9 in the US. Meanwhile, the fervent, legendary rave-up "It's The End Of The World As We Know It (And I Feel Fine)" was very nearly a party song and did more to spread the gospel.

R.E.M. had somehow snuck up on the big time and with GREEN they became an institution. Signed for a small fortune to Warners, they were still able to satisfy all factions of fans, producing hits without relinquishing their vision. Sometimes deeply personal, sometimes bleak and uncomfortable, and sometimes just pure pop for today's people, GREEN was a sprawling statement of a band given the 'green' light. "Turn You Inside Out" inverted the riff of "Finest Worksong", but as a threatening innuendo rather than a call to arms. There was the intense, confidential "World Leader Pretend", where Stipe assumed that mantle, sounding almost comfortable with the position. "Stand", the major hit single (#6 in the US), was an inane piece of singsong, while the not-quite-hit "Orange Crush" was more biting, though equally catchy. As a counter to all the pop, rock and guitars, GREEN also featured three acoustic tracks, two of which – "You Are The Everything" and "Hairshirt" – were important harbingers of the simplicity that beckoned on future works.

The tour that accompanied GREEN was enormous; R.E.M. hit the world, suddenly finding themselves arena-size, and in those arenas Stipe was still attempting various theatrics. Adorned in a white suit and inch-thick black eyeliner, he would wail into megaphones, dance like a child, play the anti-sex symbol. The dates all sold out instantly – R.E.M. had definitely hit the big time – and the fans, though they did not know it, were doubly fortunate, as the band would not tour again until 1995. Little filtered through to the outside world until later, but the scale of the GREEN operation clearly took its toll.

The egregious Miles Copeland and his label got their retaliation for the label change in early, with EPONYMOUS (1988; IRS; reissued 1998) appearing in the stores a month before GREEN. An exercise in squeezing the last few cents from a band's back catalogue, this is at least easily available and helps complete the collection. A fine collection, with stand-out track the original Hib-Tone label recording of "Radio Free Europe". In the meantime, implausibly, R.E.M. became a major singles band, and the next two albums happily promoted themselves. OUT OF TIME (1991) was R.E.M. at their most bankable and Stipe at his most openly personal. "Losing My Religion" and "Shiny Happy People" were huge hits on both sides of the Atlantic, while "Radio Song", "Near Wild Heaven" and "Texarkana" all received generous airplay. The album again contained a largely acoustic element. "Losing My Religion", "Half A World Away"and "Country Feedback" all emphasized just what accomplished musicians R.E.M., and Buck in particular, had become. Looking to add texture and new possibilities to the sound, they were now experimenting, successfully, with keyboards, horns and woodwind, and Buck with mandolin and slide guitar. "Losing My Religion" was the album's centrepiece, a confessional piece of disarming intimacy ('That's me in the corner, that's me in the spotlight'), beautifully simple and surprisingly infectious, and one of the band's three or four defining moments on record.

The acoustic sound reached its zenith on AUTOMATIC FOR THE PEOPLE (1992), the second absolutely essential R.E.M. album. From "Try Not To Breathe" to "Find The River", it captivated and provoked with gorgeous tunes and uncomfortable words. On the single "Man On The Moon", R.E.M. showed themselves as warm and intimate as they had ever been, and whether on the slow-motion opener "Drive", the plaintive "Everybody Hurts" or the wistful "Nightswimming", every song enticed with a simplicity of structure, a sturdy tunefulness and the quality of Stipe's voice. Fully in command of his range and talents, Stipe delivered probably his best singing to date on the album, almost leaping off the record on the exuberant "Sidewinder Sleeps Tonight", nearly puncturing with sorrow on "Sweetness Follows".

AUTOMATIC spawned hits and a plethora of rumours. The mood of the lyrics – downbeat, filled with references to death – coupled with Stipe's gaunt appearance, led some commentators to conclude that the singer had AIDS. But all Stipe had was a need to write the proper requiem for the Reagan/Bush years, to lay to rest the losses he and the rest of America had suffered.

MONSTER (1994) was a return to the loud, guitar-driven rock of DOCUMENT, but with a snarling, grungey edge that was not entirely successful. The best tracks (which were also the hits) – "Crush With Eyeliner", "What's The Frequency, Kenneth?", "Bang And Blame" and "Star 69" – found the right balance between noise and melody, while "Tongue" confirmed once more that R.E.M. know a good ballad when they hear one. Stipe, moreover, seemed to have ditched his obsession with death for a healthy interest in sex: playful come-ons and brighter images dominated, and the band was defiantly (perhaps too much so) re-energized. A few tracks, though, seemed extraneous and overplayed, and perhaps only on "Crush With Eyeliner" did the band really reach the dizzy heights of which they are so palpably capable. Still, maybe MONSTER had to react against the sublime and quiet inventions that had preceded it, and, more practically, R.E.M. wanted to tour again and needed songs easily adapted to live performance.

Despite Bill Berry's serious illness, which suspended operations for a couple of months, the tour was a vast success, playing to rave reviews and big ticket sales. The band worked on unrecorded material which went over well, some of which later appeared on the NEW ADVENTURES IN HI-FI album in September 1996, only four months after the band came off the road. Despite the bandquake of Berry's departure in July 1998 (the first line-up alteration in almost two decades) their next album, UP (1998), was open, conversational and a welcome step back from their more recent stadium-pleasing sound. With their rediscovered vigour, they were in no mood to do what they had intended for many years and break up the band on New Year's Eve 1999.

As the trio entered their third decade in the music business, Stipe took to being a film producer (*Being John Malkovich*), while the band recorded several new songs (and revisited some old favourites) for the Andy Kaufman tribute movie *Man On The Moon*. The soundtrack was to spawn a single, "The Great Beyond", which in the early months of 2000 became their biggest ever UK hit, peaking at #3. The year 2001 wasn't all plain sailing however: Buck found himself in court accused of disorderly behaviour on a London-bound flight, but was later cleared. REVEAL (2001) turned out to be their most consistent and intriguing since AUTOMATIC FOR THE PEOPLE, and proved that the trio were anything but a spent force in rock music.

2003 saw the group hit the road once again, this time in support of a new greatest hits package: IN TIME: THE BEST OF R.E.M. 1988-2003.

Murmur (1983; IRS).
The perfect incarnation of R.E.M.'s early style. Tuneful, innovative and lyrically elusive, MURMUR has taken on increasingly legendary status.

Reckoning (1984; IRS).
R.E.M.'s second album continues the trend MURMUR set with guitars and vocals that chime, rebound, hover and hide. If not as effective, it does contain some killer tunes, including "(Don't Go Back to) Rockville" and "Harbour Coat".

Document (1987; IRS).
The album that hit for the band offers a strong rock sense, with healthy doses of politics. Includes the breakthrough single "The One I Love".

R.E.M.

Out Of Time (1991; Warners).
New fans should start here, marvelling at the melodies, lyrics and musicianship of "Losing My Religion," "Shiny Happy People," "Radio Song" and "Half A World Away." Essential – really.

Automatic For The People (1992; Warners).
Peter Buck had said a few years earlier that R.E.M. had not made their BIG STAR 3, their HIGHWAY 61 REVISITED, their REVOLVER. Arguably, now they had – a meditative, nearly perfect album.

Up (1998; Warners).
Some tracks – one suspects they are those closest to Stipe's heart – are touchingly ordinary, confessional, even naked: the sound is stripped of the slightly glam, brash, androgynous rock'n'roll swagger and adopts an altogether more confessional, less oblique tone. UP wasn't instantly acclaimed but it will eventually be seen as a great R.E.M album.

Reveal (2001; Warners).
It Is Stipe's hazy sunny-day vocals that really steal the show, particularly on the dreamy "I've Been High" and "Saturn Return". REVEAL is another stunning album full, as ever, with richlyrical images.

Hugh Wilson

THE REPLACEMENTS

Formed Minneapolis, Minnesota, 1980; disbanded 1992.

"I kinda like the idea of us being a bunch of losers. Not in the sense of the guy who has nothing, but as the guy who has nothing to lose." Paul Westerberg

The Replacements were formed in late 1980 when a young **Paul Westerberg** (guitar) was drawn to a racket blasting from a basement window in downtown Minneapolis. The guys creating this sound-from-hell were 14-year-old **Chris Mars** (drums), **Tommy** (bass), and **Bob Stinson** (lead guitar). Taking Westerberg on board, they kicked off their career as one of the most celebrated American bands of the post-punk era – a blend of Ramones-style guitar and ragged vocals.

Their early albums, on Twin/Tone, captured perfectly the frustrations of being a teenager in the wasteland of the Reagan years. When the cover of SORRY MA, FORGOT TO TAKE OUT THE TRASH (1981) suggested 'file under power trash' it was not an idle boast, more a threat. This eighteen-track debut clocked in at just under 35 minutes of wounded attitude and raw emotion, from the searing "Rattlesnake" to the beautiful, sparse melody of "Johnny's Gonna Die". Mini-album STINK (1982) delivered more of the same – a swift kick in the teeth to authority in "Kids Don't Follow" and "Fuck School". The songs were all bullet-hard punk nuggets.

HOOTENANNY (1983) and LET IT BE (1984) followed the blueprint, with the latter featuring some of their most stupidly brilliant songs in "Tommy Gets His Tonsils Out" and "Gary's Got A Boner". These excesses of deliberate dumbness were balanced by some of their most vulnerable creations in "Sixteen Blue" and "I Will Dare", which featured Pete Buck of R.E.M. on guitar. Most of the songs were written by Westerberg, who had a genius for hooky melodies and lyrics inspired by teenage experience.

However, great albums did not guarantee great gigs: even die-hard fans admit that they were one of the sloppiest live bands around. Stories abound of them taking the stage blind drunk, attempting to play, hurling abuse at the audience and then shambling off only to be beaten up in the car park by irate bar-goers. These accounts of wilful laziness complement tales of their electric brilliance on stage. The semi-official release, THE SHIT HITS THE FANS (1984), was a testament to their live efforts. The band lurched gloriously from their own material to hilarious attempts at "Misty Mountain Hop" (Led Zeppelin) and "Iron Man" (Black Sabbath).

After signing to Sire, the albums TIM (1985) and PLEASED TO MEET ME (1987) marked a growth in maturity and stature. TIM featured none other than seminal influence Alex Chilton, on "Left Of The Dial". Thrashier numbers sat alongside more minimal personal sketches such as "Here Comes A Regular", a laid-back slice of drink-fuelled melancholia. **Slim Dunlap** replaced Bob Stinson after the recording of PLEASED TO MEET ME, and their sound diversified with smatterings of strings and a horn section used liberally throughout. One moment they were a smoky, sleazy bar band ("Night-Club Jitters"), the next Westerberg would deliver an acoustic vignette on unrequited love ("Skyway").

Despite the critical acclaim, major success eluded them, and by the time of DON'T TELL A SOUL (1989) they were prepared to create a more radio-friendly release with producer Matt Wallace. The result lacked the kick of their previous efforts – only on "Anywhere Is Better Than Here" did they sound like they were firing on all cylinders. Worse, the album failed to secure the airplay hoped for by the record company.

Coupled with this, the band were scheduled to support Tom Petty later in the year. Every night for three months they tried to win over several thousand indifferent Tom Petty fans. Being rejected on such a huge scale, along with self-doubt and confusion on Westerberg's part, left the band floundering, and when Westerberg recorded ALL SHOOK DOWN (1990) without much help from the others, the crisis deepened. After an apparently successful European tour, they finally split in 1992 to pursue solo careers.

Since then, Mars has concentrated on his painting and sculpting and has recorded four fine albums, HORSESHOES AND HANDGRENADES (1992), 75% LESS FAT (1993), TENTERHOOKS (1995) and ANONYMOUS BOTCH (1996); Tommy Stinson's **Bash And Pop** released FRIDAY NIGHT IS KILLING ME (before he bizarrely went on to record with Guns 'N Roses for a while) and Westerberg embarked on a critically acclaimed solo career recording 14 SONGS (1993) and EVENTUALLY (1996), as well as contributing songs to the soundtrack of grunge-inspired slacker comedy *Singles*. His most recent albums – SUICAINE GRATIFACTION (1999) and STEREO (2002) – saw him mellow somewhat, although STEREO did include a second MONO album recorded under Westerberg's altogether more raucous rock'n'roll alias of **Grandpa Boy**. Excellent songwriting was still in evidence in these solo efforts, but the sheer energy of their earlier material was not matched; fans had to wait for the double-album ALL FOR NOTHING (1997) to get a taste of unreleased material from the group's glory days. Bringing The Replacements' story to a final close, Bob Stinson died from a drug overdose in early 1995.

⦿ **Sorry Ma, Forgot To Take Out The Trash** (1981; Twin/Tone).
This is definitive Replacements: they were too drunk to be vicious, but it is a raucous recording all the same.

⦿ **Let It Be** (1984; Twin/Tone).
The whole thing sounds like it was recorded in a week (as it probably was), but they prove here that they were capable of greater things than two-minute fits of fury.

⦿ **Pleased To Meet Me** (1987; Sire).
Their last great album before the slide toward adulthood. Buy it just to hear "Can't Hardly Wait", a damn-near-perfect pop song. Indispensable.

Essi Berelian

THE RESIDENTS

Formed Shreveport, Louisiana, 1970 – allegedly.

"The two things [The Residents] really enjoy doing are creating music that nobody has ever heard before and then taking other people's music and making it sound like music that nobody has ever heard before". Jay Clem

When **The Residents** formed in the early 70s, they took the (highly visible) step of never publicly revealing their names, faces or giving interviews, maintaining a studious anonymity in tuxedos and giant-eyeball masks. All contact with the group was channelled through The Cryptic Corporation, members of which have included the not-terribly-authentic-sounding Homer Flynn, John Kennedy, Jay Clem and the redoubtable Hardy Fox. Influenced by the R&B of their Southern roots, as well as by Sun Ra's sci-fi jazz, Captain Beefheart, Frank Zappa, and avant-garde composers such as Harry Partch, The Residents have always had a humorous edge to their desire to challenge musical boundaries, over what is now a thirty-year career.

The group moved to San Francisco in the late 60s and, in 1972 set up Ralph Records for their first release – a 300-disc printing of "Santa Dog", mailed out free to radio stations and to a privileged group encompassing Frank Zappa and Richard Nixon. This presaged the group's first album, MEET THE RESIDENTS (1973; reissued 1998), which apparently notched up sales of just forty copies in its first year (the band, still holding down day jobs at the time, had themselves sold most of these to local record stores) and would perhaps have disappeared without trace had Capitol not considered it worth making legal threats when it was rereleased in 1977, on account of its Beatles-parody cover and title. (The Fab Four, it is said, enjoyed the joke.)

The 1974 recording, NOT AVAILABLE, was another wheeze; placed in storage, it was supposedly never to be released (although it emerged in 1978 to fulfil contractual obligations). Meanwhile, the next 'official' outing was THIRD REICH'N'ROLL (1976), whose cover again courted controversy, bedecked with swastikas and depicting US TV presenter Dick Clark as Hitler clutching a large orange carrot. Weird and discordant, it featured twisted covers of pop songs from the 50s and 60s, rounding off with "Hey Jude". A small cult following was set in motion.

It was The Residents' cover of "Satisfaction" (a very limited-edition single in 1976, given a more widespread release in 1978), that unleashed the band to a wider audience, both in the US and Britain, where its jagged thrash suited the newborn punk ethos. The record was used to announce The Cryptic Corporation, which replaced the band's previous public face, The Residents Unincorporated. It sold out, as did two further singles, "Aphids In The Hall" (recorded with Schwump) and the neatly entitled "The Beatles Play The Residents And The Residents Play The Beatles".

Ralph expanded its operations to include bands such as the industrial MX-80 Sound, and Tuxedomoon, putting out the Subterranean Modern compilation, which naturally also included The Residents. A trio of EPs, BUY OR DIE, featuring the three bands – plus guitarist **Philip 'Snakefinger' Lithman**, who later collaborated extensively with The Residents – surfaced free with Ralph's catalogues around this time. Further releases on the label included Yello's debut SOLID PLEASURE, and albums by Renaldo & The Loaf, Half Japanese, Fred Frith, The Art Bears and Negativland.

Through the mid 70s, The Residents rolled out a stack of albums: FINGERPRINCE (1976), DUCK STAB/BUSTER & GLEN (1978), ESKIMO (1979) and THE COMMERCIAL ALBUM (1980), each increasing the band's popularity in an era of post-punk acceptance of the bizarre, particularly in the UK music press. DUCK STAB is regarded by many as The Residents' finest moment; it featured "Birthday Boy", a disturbing take on the party favourite. ESKIMO envisioned life among those people before state housing arrived in the 60s. COMMERCIAL was a collection of forty one-minute pieces, designed for use as eccentric jingles, or (on its CD rerelease) for programming as instant three-minute pop songs.

In 1981, THE MOLE TRILOGY commenced (currently at the, unusual-for-a-trilogy, sixth part of the story), with a costly touring *Mole Show*, and the albums, THE MARK OF THE MOLE (1981), THE TUNES OF

The Residents Play The Residents

TWO CITIES (1982) and THE BIG BUBBLE (1985). This operatic creation told of an epic struggle between the Moles and the Chubs, describing their war, music and eventual reconciliation. Avoiding prog-rock pomp, the tale is told through sheer strangeness. The bizarre live Residents experience is documented on the *Mole Show* video (1984) with a bonus of salvaged footage from the hyper-surreal *Whatever Happened To Vileness Fats* film, abandoned in 1976.

The third album was delayed due to the departure of Clem and Kennedy from Cryptic (having had enough of the Mole story and the interminable, loss-making tour), taking Yello and the Corporation offices with them, just as Ralph was celebrating its tenth anniversary. The label returned as New Ralph, selling off stock, rare releases and Residents memorabilia to raise cash. Various compilations emerged (some Residents-only), along with a Residents/Renaldo & The Loaf collaboration, TITLE IN LIMBO (1983).

Despite all the activity, control of Ralph passed out of the Cryptic's hands in 1986, and, preoccupied with business concerns, The Residents released only two titles in their projected American Composers Series – GEORGE & JAMES (1984) and STARS & HANK FOREVER (1986) – reinterpreting, respectively, Gershwin, James Brown, Sousa and Hank Williams. Further work on Dylan and Sun Ra, and Harry Nilsson and Harry Partch, was shelved in favour of a return to one-off albums: GOD IN THREE PERSONS (1988), a wild exercise in talking blues (remastered in 2000 with, bizarrely, an instrumental bonus album), and THE KING & EYE (1989), a disappointing Elvis reworking.

A return to form came with 1991's release of FREAK SHOW, a concept album on the theme of circus sideshow attractions. It coincided with the band regaining control of its back catalogue – albeit as two separate Ralphs (Euro and America) – and an extensive CD rerelease programme was undertaken by East Side Digital. The Ralphs also combined for a twentieth-anniversary CD compilation, OUR FINEST FLOWERS (1992).

Meanwhile, multimedia was beckoning; The Residents responded with a groundbreaking laserdisc TWENTY TWISTED QUESTIONS in 1992. The same year FREAK SHOW was rereleased as a CD-ROM – the first of several new titles, along with THE RESIDENTS HAVE A BAD DAY, the soundtrack to a CD-ROM game *Bad Day On The Midway*.

The Residents have been on the scene for over a quarter of a century – an anniversary marked by OUR TIRED, OUR POOR, OUR HUDDLED MASSES (1997) 'weirdest hits' retrospective – and, more than many of their less hard-working contemporaries, have wholeheartedly embraced the digital era, releasing exclusive MP3s through their website. For nigh on 30 years their pioneering use and abuse of electronics, film and theatre, have made The Residents a force to be reckoned with. The WORMWOOD: CURIOUS STORIES FROM THE BIBLE (1998) album saw them firmly back on track musically, with their accompanying best-ever live tour (1999) spawning the ROADWORMS (2000) live-studio interpretation. Onward to the half-century!

Third Reich'N'Roll (1976; Euro Ralph).
Merciless reinterpretation of The Residents' musical roots, as if performed by Adolf Hitler. Demented vocal harmonies over a blitzed version of rock'n'roll. The Euro Ralph CD reissue is 100 percent swastika-free.

Duck Stab/Buster & Glen (1978; Euro Ralph).
With tracks such as "Krafty Cheese" and "Semolina", The Residents present their surreal poetry. Mysterious, sinister and hilarious songs of life on the strange side. Reissued as a double 3" CD.

- **The Mole Trilogy: The Mark Of The Mole/The Tunes Of Two Cities/The Big Bubble** (1981, 1982 & 1985; Ralph).

The band's wacko opera is punctuated by moments of genius, most notably the tracks "Marching To The Sea", "Smack Your Lips (Clap Your Teeth)" and "Sorry".

- **Our Tired, Our Poor, Our Huddled Masses** (1997; Ralph).

Massive 4CD box set celebrating 25 years of obscure innovation and deranged creativity. The American Dream has never sounded so nightmarish.

- **Wormwood: Curious Stories From The Bible** (1998; Ralph).

A distinctly monocular delve into the curious stories of the Bible, from Genesis to Apocalypse, interpreted Residents-style. The tour album ROADWORMS (2000) gives an even greater buzz to the songs; it was recorded in-studio while on the road.

Richard Fontenoy

PAUL REVERE AND THE RAIDERS

Formed Caldwell, Idaho, US, 1959;
disbanded 1962;
re-formed 1963; disbanded 1977; re-formed 1983.

If **Paul Revere Dick** (keyboards) and **Mark Lindsay** (vocals/saxophone) had stuck with their original name, The Downbeats, the world would have been deprived of rock'n'roll's finest set of novelty costumes. But with Dick's genuine middle name as inspiration, the duo and assorted backing musicians donned tricorn hats, ruffled shirts and other remnants of colonial haberdashery to become one of the better American bands of the mid 60s.

After a couple of going-nowhere singles, the original incarnation of Paul Revere And The Raiders just about dented the American Top 40 with the instrumental "Like, Long Hair" (1961). The group had to disband, however, as Revere was drafted, but they re-formed in Portland, Oregon, in 1963. With **Drake Levin** (guitar/vocals), **Phil Volk** (bass) and **Mike Smith** (drums) in tow, Revere and Lindsay crafted the band into one of the best on the crowded Northwest frat-rock circuit and their version of "Louie, Louie" caught the attention of Columbia, who made the Revolution-era revivalists their first rock signing.

In 1965, the group became the house band on Dick Clark's *Where The Action Is* TV show and the exposure turned Lindsay into a heart-throb. Despite their teenybop status, however, Paul Revere And The Raiders' sound was as tough as any of their contemporaries on the American garage rock scene. With a monolithic Vox organ riff, a droning two-note bass line and stinging guitar runs, "Steppin' Out" (1965) scraped the US Top 50. Stealing the intro from "In The Midnight Hour", their follow-up, "Just Like Me" (1965), was one of the definitive pre-Summer of Love American rock tracks. The proto-power-chord riffs were somewhere between The Kinks and the Kingsmen, and the Vox riff was

a classic, but it was the slightly off-time, primitive handclaps that propelled the record to #11 in the American charts. Their second album, PAUL REVERE AND THE RAIDERS, which featured both of their great singles, did even better and reached #5 in the album chart.

Lindsay might have sung, 'Kicks just seem harder to get', on their next single, but the hits just seemed easier to get: "Kicks", "Hungry" (both 1966), "Good Thing" and "Him Or Me – What's It Gonna Be?" (both 1967) all reached the American Top 10, while "The Great Airplane Strike" – one of the best airplane songs ever – reached #20. After "Hungry", Levin and Volk left to form their own band, The Brotherhood, and they were replaced by **Freddy Weller** (guitar) and **Charlie Coe** (bass), while **Jim Valley** replaced Smith on the sticks. All of their albums of the period went Top 10 as well, but by the time they released REVOLUTION! in late 1967 it was clear that the real musical revolution was happening elsewhere.

Even though they continued to chart with singles like "Too Much Talk" (1968) and "Mr. Sun, Mr. Moon" (1969), the long-hairs they once praised largely ignored their straightforward three-chords-and-a-cloud-of-dust rock in favour of the lysergic emissions emanating from San Francisco and London. With the tide of fashion against them, the band streamlined their name to The Raiders in 1970 and scored an unlikely #1 with "Indian Reservation (The Lament Of The Cherokee Reservation Indian)" (1971). By this time, Lindsay was focusing his energies on a solo career as an adult contemporary balladeer and had a moderate hit with the vaguely anti-hippie "Arizona" (1970).

The Raiders stumbled through the 70s as a lounge act, relying more on their eighteenth-century slapstick schtick than music, and predictably re-emerged briefly with the godawful Bicentennial misfire, "The British Are Coming" (1976). More impressively, Sundazed have recently reissued many Raiders titles, complete with extra cuts.

- **Greatest Hits** (1997, Eclipse).
An excellent retrospective of one of the more underappreciated bands of the 60s.

Peter Shapiro

REVOLTING COCKS/ PIGFACE

Formed RevCo, 1987; Pigface, 1991.

"Remember – RevCo is making this world a better place for you and your hog bitch girlfriend." Sleeve note to *You Goddamned Son Of A Bitch*

Revolting Cocks came about in 1987 as a side-project for Alain (later just shortened to Al) Jourgensen outside of the increasingly guitar-oriented and politicized Ministry. Initially consisting of

Jourgensen, Front 242's Richard 23 and Belgian new beat hero Luc Van Acker, the Cocks' first album, Big Sexy Land (1987), was a more minimalist, electro take on Ministry's Twitch album, containing large amounts of what was fast becoming Jourgensen's trademark – bouncing electronic bass lines and vocals that sounded (no matter which of the assembled musicians provided them) like the little kid in The Exorcist cursing the priest. Lines plucked from sci-fi movies – 'Attack Ships On Fire' – and unpleasant news items – 'Union Carbide (Bhopal Version)', anyone? – topped off the mix and provided what was, for a while at least, the recognizable RevCo (as polite music journalists and people easily bored by too many syllables renamed them) sound, later made louder and more shouty on the live album, You Goddamned Son Of A Bitch (1988).

All this was soon to change, however, with the release of what was to become the definitive RevCo offering, BEERS, STEERS, AND QUEERS (1990), which saw the departure of Richard 23, but the addition of **William Rieflin**, **Paul Barker** and, of course, a white Scots dread (from Finitribe) by the name of **Chris Connelly**. BEERS... took the Cocks in a louder, chunkier, more industrial direction, and also saw the point where Jourgensen decided to 'get funny', as the remix single of the title track, complete with samples from *Deliverance* proved, becoming a regular floor-filler at, oh, just about any industrial club you care to mention. Anywhere. The legendary accompanying tour saw them dogged by controversy, police involvement, allegations of cruelty to animals and misogyny, and finally touched down in England where quality newspaper *The Sport* kindly provided Jourgensen and crew with (allegedly unrequested) strippers to add to the ambience of sleaze that had come to surround this wholesome young troupe.

At roughly the same time as the Chicago-based Cocks were (allegedly) torching live cattle with flame-throwers (although now all the smoke's cleared, so to speak, this seems highly improbable), **Martin Atkins** of **KILLING JOKE** fame was also toying with the idea of reviving the 70s 'supergroup' concept for the industrial age, and thus **Pigface** were born. Their debut album, GUB (1991), was a very minimalist and experimental affair, with tape loops and shouting augmented by Atkins' relentless drum patterns, soon to become one of the defining characteristics of the Pigface sound. From Revolting Cocks Atkins took Connelly, Barker and Rieflin, along with members of The Jesus Lizard, KMFDM, Skinny Puppy, and a certain **Trent Reznor**, who as **NINE INCH NAILS** had just stolen the show at Lollapalooza. GUB is notable mostly for Reznor's contribution to the track "Suck", a stripped-down, earlier version of the song that would later appear as a bonus track on NIN's own BROKEN mini-album. Skinny Puppy's **Ogre** would later vocalize a more funk-metal-orientated version of the song on the live album WELCOME TO MEXICO, ASSHOLE (1991), and for a while became Pigface's main vocalist, at least

until they reached England, when seminal grebo band **GAYE BYKERS ON ACID**'s **Mary Byker** became something akin to a frontman.

1993 saw the return of RevCo, who, with new member, rapper **Dwayne Buford**, released LINGER FICKEN GOOD (1993). This saw a return to the stripped-down style of yore, though with the sleazy redneck vibe still firmly in place. Coming as it did on the heels of the apocalyptic PSALM 69, Ministry's biggest success to date LINGER FICKEN GOOD was not so well received as earlier Cocks output, although the accompanying single, an ironic reading of Rod Stewart's "Do Ya Think I'm Sexy" joined BEERS... as one of the first choices of the discerning industrial DJ. LINGER FICKEN GOOD's most memorable track, however, is the opener, "Gila Copter", a BIG SEXY LAND-era beat and bass line spoken over by **Dr. Timothy Leary**. Accompanied by a much-hyped second UK tour, which never actually took place, LINGER FICKEN GOOD ironically saw RevCo losing ground to Ministry, at this stage a hard-edged rock band holed up in a studio somewhere recording their follow-up to PSALM 69.

By now Pigface had quietly built up what amounts to a huge extended musical family, with their original brief expanded to take in such diverse elements as Silverfish's **Leslie Rankine** (now better known as trip-hop artist Ruby), Swans' **Michael Gira**, and entire Japanese bubblegum-pop girl-band Shonen Knife, as well as the increasingly central figure of **Genesis P-Orridge**, who with **THROBBING GRISTLE** is widely held to have invented modern industrial music.

Interestingly, a glance at Pigface's recent discography shows many similarities with P-Orridge's Psychic TV project – a series of live albums by ever-changing personnel, varying in theme as much as style. The latest addition to Pigface's oeuvre, EAT SHIT YOU FUCKING REDNECK (1998), came out on Devotion Records; then again the ardent disciple of noise might want to sample the band on THE BEST OF PIGFACE: PREACHING TO THE PERVERTED (2001).

Revolting Cocks

(●) **Big Sexy Land** (1987; Wax Trax).
Like a more fluid Nitzer Ebb, BIG SEXY LAND ably demonstrates where the whole New Beat/Electronic Body Music scene was at the time.

(●) **You Goddamned Son Of A Bitch** (1988; Wax Trax).
BIG SEXY LAND, basically, but louder. And with people clapping.

(●) **Beers, Steers, And Queers** (1990; Wax Trax).
Essential cyberfunk for hillbillies, this album more than any came to define the more danceable end of that much-misused term 'industrial'.

(●) **Linger Ficken Good** (1994; Devotion).
Drug paranoia, industrial-strength sleaze-funk, Timothy Leary and (probably) sex with farm animals. A bit of a decline, though.

Pigface

(●) **Gub** (1991; Invisible/Devotion).
Lots of drums. Loads of interesting noises. Steve Albini producing. Plenty more drums. Great.

Welcome to Mexico, Asshole (1991; Invisible/Devotion).
Patchy but largely impressive live set featuring Ogre reworking "Suck" for the Rollins/Chili Peppers crowd.

Notes From Thee Underground (1994; Invisible/Devotion).
Great. Shouting, swearing, solid steel grooves, and a lunatic sense of humour. Rhythmic punk rock from space. Yeah!

Eat Shit You Fucking Redneck (1998; Invisible/Devotion).
Another live album. Get back in the studio! Now!

Justin Farrington

THE REZILLOS/REVILLOS

Formed Edinburgh, Scotland, 1976; disbanded 1985; re-formed early 1990s.

As punk spread across Britain, **The Rezillos** became a good-time component of the New Wave with their fast, jerky tunes. They were formed by art-school friends **Eugene Reynolds** (guitar/vocals) and **Luke Warm** (Jo Callis; guitar/vocals), along with **Hi-Fi Harris** (guitar), **Dr. D. K. Smythe** (bass) and **Angel Paterson** (drums), and they soon gained a reputation as eccentrics.

With **Fay Fyfe** installed on vocals, the band debuted with "I Can't Stand My Baby" in August 1977. It soon became unavailable and highly collectable. The next month, Smythe and Harris both left, and the band signed to Sire, who issued a further single, "(My Baby Does) Good Sculptures", with **William Mysterious** (bass), at the end of the year. By the following summer, their debut album, CAN'T STAND THE REZILLOS, was unleashed, showcasing the group's sci-fi punk, heavily influenced by fanzines and comics. It reached #16 in the UK charts, and from it came the single "Top Of The Pops", which became their best-remembered song and their biggest hit. The band found themselves on the TV show that the song had attacked, with Fay resplendent in her customary multicoloured metallic minidress, delivering the line 'Do I look up to date?' to a bemused audience.

Mysterious left the band to be replaced by **Simon Templar** as the group recorded "Destination Venus", which never appeared on the album but was regarded as their finest moment. It came complete with a luridly coloured 'flying saucer' picture sleeve, but sadly and surprisingly failed to chart. Commercially, The Rezillos were past their peak, and by the end of 1978 they had split, with Callis, Paterson and Templar forming Shake and later Boots For Dancing. Callis later joined **THE HUMAN LEAGUE** for much of their 80s heyday.

Meanwhile, after a contractual live LP, MISSION ACCOMPLISHED BUT THE BEAT GOES ON (1979), Fyfe and Reynolds formed **The Revillos**, an outfit completed by the return of Harris and the addition of drummer **Rocky Rhythm**. Female backing vocalists came and went, but the style remained much the same, save for a slight shift towards 50s American popsicle tunes, beat bands and surfing. They released three fairly good singles – "Where's The Boy For Me?", "Motorbike Beat" and "Hungry For Love" – during 1979–80, but even TV exposure couldn't boost their appeal, and only "Motorbike Beat" scraped into the charts.

Throughout the early 80s, line-ups continued to shift, as Mysterious returned and **Kid Krupa** was added on guitar. THE REV UP album was released in 1980 and six more singles emerged with three different record companies. Despite such great titles as "(She's Fallen In Love With A) Monster Man", their moment had gone.

Fay Fyfe went into TV acting, but returned to a re-formed Rezillos in the 90s, touring mainly in Japan. Following the Japanese success the band released a video of live footage, *Re Animated*, together with an album, TOTALLY LIVE. WIRELESS RECORDINGS (1998) collected all the remaining BBC radio sessions – previously unavailable elsewhere – on one glorious CD and, with sleeve notes by Rocky Rhythm, it was an essential addition to any space-age collection.

The Rezillos

Can't Stand The Rezillos/Mission Accomplished But The Beat Goes On (1978 & 1979; Sire).
A joint CD reissue of the band's studio and live albums, including some ill-advised covers ("Glad All Over") but plenty of rewards with the likes of "Cold Wars", the infectious "2000 RD", and "It Gets Me".

The Revillos

Motorbike (1978/1979; Sire).
This compilation packages together the best of the Revillo years.

Pip Southall

THE RICH KIDS

Formed London, 1977; disbanded 1978.

After being sacked from the **SEX PISTOLS** in February 1977, **Glen Matlock** (bass/vocals) recruited ex-teenybop rocker **Midge Ure** (guitar/vocals), **Rusty Egan** (drums) and **Steve New** (guitar) in an effort to create a sound that mixed a pop sensibility with punk energy and would stand some chance of chart success. From the start, expectations were high: Matlock was seen as 'the Pistol who could play', and was known to have written some of that band's best songs. Punk seemed to be losing its direction, but anything to do with the Pistols was still big news – so **The Rich Kids** were bound to generate enormous interest.

For a few short months at the end of 1977 and the start of 1978, they were the hottest band around, their gigs packed with press and fellow musicians. The band was musically tight: Ure was a surprisingly effective frontman, while New's aggressively inventive guitar was anchored by Matlock's dependable bass. The songs were a mix of old Small Faces numbers and two-minute punk-pop anthems: they even played the Pistols' classic "Pretty Vacant" for an encore, Matlock telling anyone who would listen 'I wrote it, so I'll bloody well play it'. In response, Rotten took to wearing a T-shirt on stage with the legend 'Never Mind the Rich Kids, Here's the Sex Pistols'. It was a rare compliment.

The band's first single, "Rich Kids" (1978), was two minutes of controlled adrenaline, and greeted ecstatically in the music press. Although tuneful, it was very much a punk single – indeed, Matlock had written it originally as a Pistols song. It was a knockout debut, but credibility problems were there from the start. Matlock, for all his ability, had always been 'the straight one' in the Pistols, and never shared their penchant for wildness, while Ure had previously fronted the execrable Slik, once hyped as 'the new Bay City Rollers', although he had once been offered the job of Pistols frontman by Malcolm McLaren. The other two suffered from alarming haircuts: New had a punk pedigree (he'd briefly been a member of the legendary London SS) but a floppy fringe; Egan, meanwhile, had a reputation as a wideboy, and had what can only be described as a leonine cut.

Inevitably, the media attention, so useful at first, began to be a hindrance. To their horror, the band were hailed as leaders of 'a new wave of new wave' – dubbed 'power pop' – and were categorized with anodyne bands like The Pleasers and The Boyfriends. As if in response, band members started mucking around on other projects. Matlock and New joined with Rat Scabies and Sid Vicious to form 'punk supergroup' The Vicious White Kids, who played a one-off gig at London's Electric Ballroom. The idea was to prove that Matlock and Vicious were friends, though musically it was a disaster, as a bootleg of the event testifies.

Meantime, the band cut a second single, the anti-fascist anthem "Marching Men" (1978), which was released to a less than rapturous response. It was better than the press implied, but the band's hipness rating had gone through the floor. A third single, "Ghosts Of Princes In Towers" (1978), was a contrastingly catchy piece of pure pop, but was critically hammered and did not sell.

The writing was on the wall. The band grew their hair in an effort to distance themselves from punk (now in its death throes) and from the dreaded power pop, but their one and only album, GHOSTS OF PRINCES IN TOWERS, released in October 1978, was a lacklustre affair, and the intensive gigging undertaken to promote it ensured their end. The inevitable split came when Ure suggested that the band should add synthesizers.

In the years since, Matlock continued to play poprock with, among others, The Spectors and, for a short while, Iggy Pop, and in 1996 was allowed back into the Pistols fold for their summer get-together. New joined **Johnny Thunders**, but reportedly battled with heroin addiction. Ure went on to join **ULTRAVOX** and write the Band Aid single with Bob Geldof. Egan joined Steve Strange (another old Pistols fan) in **Visage**, and became his partner in the London nightclub business.

⦿ **Ghosts Of Princes In Towers** (1978; Dojo/BMG).
CD release of the solitary album, with all the singles plus their B-sides, including a scorching version of The Small Faces' hit "Here Come The Nice", recorded live in 1977.

Roger Sabin

JONATHAN RICHMAN AND THE MODERN LOVERS

Formed Boston, Massachusetts, 1969.

"To me sophistication and gaol have a lot in common."

The early story of **Jonathan Richman And The Modern Lovers** is well-known: the lonely suburban New England kid who grew up obsessed with The Velvet Underground, followed the band to New York and eventually formed a group that sounded as much like his heroes as he could manage. It seems a world apart from where Richman has ended up – as lovable, acoustic eccentric, doo-wop songsmith – but it was a damn fine beginning in any musician's life story.

Richman's first Modern Lovers line-up lasted a couple of years before, in 1971, he assembled the classic team of keyboardist **Jerry Harrison** (later of **TALKING HEADS**), drummer **David Robinson** (later of **THE CARS**) plus bassist **Ernie Brooks**. It was this squad who, in 1973, with The Velvets' John Cale as producer, made the seminal debut album THE MODERN LOVERS, which included the breakthrough single, "Roadrunner". This offbeat, geekish album would later forge the band's reputation as punk forerunners, but Warners did not want it and they dropped the band without releasing a song.

THE MODERN LOVERS was finally bought by West Coast indie label Beserkley, who released it in 1976, getting a chart hit in "Roadrunner" and a burgeoning cult following for the album, which in some respects was a proto-punk release. Certainly, its easy-

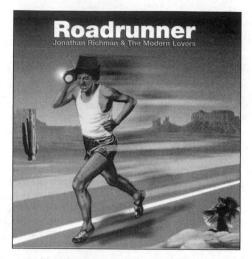

Roadrunner
Jonathan Richman & The Modern Lovers

chord songs were covered by dozens of punk bands in Britain in 1977.

However, Richman's band, by this time, bore little relation to the group of three years ago, and nor did much of his new material. The 'follow-up albums', JONATHAN RICHMAN AND THE MODERN LOVERS (1976) and ROCK'N'ROLL WITH THE MODERN LOVERS (1977), were largely acoustic, based on 50s and early 60s rock, doo-wop and pop, with some ethnic influences thrown in on songs characterized by a faux-childlike vision. The Modern Lovers, meantime, retained only Robinson, along with **Leroy Radcliffe** (guitar) and **Greg 'Curly' Keranen** (bass). After ROCK'N'ROLL, Robinson also left, along with Keranen, being replaced, respectively, by **D. Sharpe** and **Asa Bremner**.

This new line-up toured Britain in 1978, surprising and delighting punk and student audiences with their life-affirming weirdness. They had further chart success in the UK, too, in the wake of "Roadrunner", with "Egyptian Reggae" (1977) and a live version of "Morning Of Our Lives" (1978) – both deserved hits. Richman never went much further commercially, however, retiring from the scene after the solo-credited 1979 album BACK IN YOUR LIFE, another set of whimsy- and doo-wop-styled songs.

When Richman re-emerged in 1982, it was as a cult artist, resolutely out of time with the rock world's new obsessions, and with a fluid set of musicians. The approach, however, was consistent, with an underlying nostalgia or melancholy customarily mixed in with the playfulness, and Richman's guitar sound (crisp, percussive and expressive) and voice, now mellowing from its flat, adolescent-nasal tones, giving the sound a distinctive character. Cast changes occasionally altered the emphasis: singer Ellie Marshall added a sweet sound to JONATHAN SINGS! (1983), ROCKIN' AND ROMANCE (1985) and the (disappointing) IT'S TIME FOR JONATHAN RICHMAN AND THE MODERN LOVERS (1986), while the stripped-down trio of Richman, **Brennan Totten**

and **Johnny Avila** gave MODERN LOVERS 88 (1988) a slightly harder rock'n'roll sound, aided by Jonathan's usually underused saxophone.

Each of these albums saw Richman returning to his lyrical obsessions with nature, outer space, buildings, food and relationships. At times, the subject and style could wear a bit thin and Richman seemed to be floundering with the solo JONATHAN RICHMAN (1989). However, he turned to new inspirations, to fine effect, with JONATHAN GOES COUNTRY (1990) and a Spanish-language album, I JONATHAN TE VAS A EMOCIONAR (1994). Both were delightful if uncommercial outings, issued on the American folk/roots label, Rounder. The same label issued another of Jonathan's most recent solo outings, YOU MUST ASK THE HEART, his strongest collection of new songs for many years, and with keyboards unusually to the fore. In 1996, a swift change of label (to Vapor – an offshoot of WEA) prompted SURRENDER TO JONATHAN, another fine set of songs from the heart, built on a rock-solid brass section.

These days numerous young bands acknowledge the influence of Jonathan Richman – The Rockingbirds wrote a tribute song, "Jonathan Jonathan", in 1990, and the BMX Bandits covered Richman's "That Summer Feeling" in 1995. His cameo appearance in the 1998 film *There's Something About Mary* – an otherwise totally forgettable movie vehicle for the limber bodies of Cameron Diaz and Matt Dillon – was both hilarious and subversive. Jonathan stole the show, delivering commentary from deep in the background at the end of a street or, with accompaniment from his unfortunate drummer, stuck up in a tree. Movie career aside, you can still catch him touring with his (usually, these days) one-man shows. To see him live is an utterly original and compelling experience.

I'M SO CONFUSED (1999), produced by Ric Ocasek (ex-The Cars), saw Richman in an uncharacteristic state of deep sadness - even the smile on the cover photo looked forced. The twelve tracks, however, were all classic Richman: the stand-out "Nineteen In Naples", "I Can Hear Her Fighting With Herself" and "True Love Is Not Nice" (this last also featured in *There's Something About Mary*) were all grown-up, considered and thoughtful songs. HER MYSTERY NOT OF HIGH HEELS AND EYE SHADOW (2001), was every bit as uncompromising, if less rounded.

⊙ **The Modern Lovers** (1976; Beserkley/Rhino).
The must-have debut album that anticipated punk rock. The sound is urgent, driving and garagey, the songs of loneliness and insecurity have a real emotional depth. Includes classic tracks like "Hospital", "Roadrunner" and "Pablo Picasso".

⊙ **Jonathan Sings!** (1983; Sire).
This has a smoother, sweeter sound and includes some of his strongest songs from the 80s. "Give Paris One More Chance" is still a live favourite, and the nostalgic, celebratory "That Summer Feeling" sums up the Richman spirit as much as any single track can.

⊙ **23 Great Recordings** (1990; Essential/Castle).
A great compilation of tracks from the Beserkley years,

bracketed by the two versions of "Roadrunner". Material ranges from the punk of the first Modern Lovers through to the more whimsical later songs, and there is a good cross-section of tracks from each album.

(•) **Having A Party** (1991; Cheree/Rounder). Recorded live at various venues, this is a selection of typical 1990s Richman songs – funny, touching and almost innocent, even when the themes are not ("My Career As A Homewrecker", "When I Say Wife"). "Monologue About Bermuda", a seven-minute reworking of "Down In Bermuda", sees the 40-year-old Jonathan impersonating his 20-year-old self to the delight of his audience.

Penny Kiley

RIDE

Formed Oxford, England, 1988; disbanded 1996.

"We try to make the music the personality and keep ourselves quite anonymous." Andy Bell

Often held responsible for the derided 'shoe-gazing' movement of the early 90s, **Ride** have suffered through the changes in musical fashion. However, their eight-year life span showed that they could stay the course beyond the dozens of sounda-likes who followed them.

As art-college students, **Mark Gardener** (vocals/guitar), **Laurence Colbert** (drums) and **Andy Bell** (guitar/vocals) rehearsed in Colbert's parents' garage, before recruiting **Steve Queralt** (bass). Bored and frustrated with college but united by their love of My Bloody Valentine, The House Of Love and The Jesus & Mary Chain, they began by jamming a set of covers, including a rowdy version of The Stooges' "I Wanna Be Your Dog".

Small gigs attracted the attention of local promoter and journalist Dave Newton, who became their manager in 1989, and by the year's end Ride's multi-layered racket had begun to excite London's media circus. Lyrics and vocals were indecipherable amidst the distorted guitar shapes, but this was perhaps just as well, given that Gardener and Bell were still developing their songwriting talents. Despite this, the band was a perfect antidote to Manchester's early 90s 'indie dance' explosion.

Snapped up by innovative label Creation, Ride did not disappoint on the eagerly awaited RIDE EP. Released in early 1990, this four-track guitar maelstrom featured the white-noise excursion "Drive Blind" and the poppy "Chelsea Girl". It quickly sold out its initial pressing of 5000 copies, and went on to top the 20,000 mark, even scraping the lower reaches of the UK charts.

Steady touring built up a following, confirmed when a second EP, PLAY, shot into the UK Top 40. Featuring the thrilling start-stop pop of "Like A Daydream", the EP further consolidated their reputation as hot young guns, and they spent the summer of 1990 in the studio preparing their debut album. The first fruits of these sessions arrived in October with yet another EP, called FALL, which contained airplay favourite "Taste" and the startling "Dreams Burn Down".

They seemed unable to do any wrong, and the release of NOWHERE (1990) amazingly lived up to the fevered expectations of it: from the effects-swamped "Seagull" to the dreamy "Vapour Trail", it suggested that Ride would be around for some time to come. A fourth EP in March 1991, TODAY FOREVER, showed a more mature and reflective side to their sound, and became their first Top 20 record.

After a prolific first year of recording, Ride had a quiet 1991, apart from the occasional festival date, but their return to the scene in February 1992 gave them the only Top 10 hit of their career – an eight-minute prog-rock epic called "Leave Them All Behind". A second album, GOING BLANK AGAIN (1992), was also a UK chart success, despite luke-warm reviews. By this stage, however, band members (especially Bell) were beginning to resent the press's perception of them as a backing group for Gardener, and Ride now took a two-year sabbatical.

Gardener and Bell developed their individual writing talents (Bell contributed to the debut album by Swedish label-mate Idha Ovelius – his wife), then in April 1994 Ride came back with Bell's epic, psychedelic "Birdman", the first Ride song credited to a single member. The band found their thunder had been stolen by the emergence of Britpop press darlings like Suede and Blur, who were suddenly making Ride appear lumpen and pretentious. As a result, 1994's CARNIVAL OF LIGHT, while by no means a bad LP, was overlooked by many, and dismissed as unadventurous by others. The backlash had arrived, but worse was to follow: Gardener moved to New York in early 1995, and by the middle of that year he had announced his departure from the band.

Ride's swansong, TARANTULA, released in March 1996, was regarded by some critics as their finest album, but it was deleted after just one week in the shops. Gardener announced that he was now working with dance producer **Paul Oakenfold** and **Gary Stonedage** (ex-Big Audio Dynamite); Bell went on to form **Hurricane #1**.

With Hurricane #1 failing to make any real headway, 1999 found Bell recruited into the Gallagher brothers' ranks, though whether he can help to suppress **OASIS**'s self-destructive tendencies remains to be seen. In 2000 Gardener and Colbert reappeared on the Boilerhouse imprint with a new band, **Animalhouse**, and an album, READY TO RECEIVE. Despite one or two good tunes, the set was unremarkable and was poorly received.

(•) **Smile** (1990; Creation/Sire). This compilation mini-LP of Ride's first two EPs is the sound of a band exploring the boundaries of their burgeoning talent. A noisy and tender trip through the heady days of youth.

(•) **Nowhere** (1990; Creation/Sire). Lush, noisy tunes full of power.

Gavin Stoker

Formed Bristol, England, 1980; disbanded 1983.

Rip, Rig & Panic took their name from a wild avant-jazz album by Rahsaan Roland Kirk – a pointer to one of the group's many influences, which also ranged through punk, funk, dub-reggae, African music, and odd bits of the classical canon. They were formed by ex-**POP GROUP** founders **Gareth Sager** (sax/guitar/keyboards) and **Bruce Smith** (drums), with **Mark Springer** (keyboards), **Sean Oliver** (bass) and vocalist **NENEH CHERRY** – the (then) very youthful stepdaughter of jazz trumpeter Don Cherry. Oliver's sister, **Andrea**, was also drafted into the line-up, giving the band a very powerful dual vocal presence. Essentially improvisational – and often joined by additional percussionists, horn players and vocalists – they could be shambolic and wonderful in the space of a concert or, for that matter, on record.

The group gigged around Bristol and London, pulling in an avant-rock audience for what could be an all-embracing experience, with music of great spirit mixed with exuberant singing, dancing and chanting. Smith and Sean Oliver were a hugely powerful engine room, driving the music on in all directions, yet capable of playing with great subtlety. Springer added a virtuoso touch, his piano echoing a love of African influences, in particular Dollar Brand's form of township jazz, then veering off into wild experimentation, while his horn battles with Sager (and others) were an on-stage highlight. Sager himself was simply irrepressible, a great showman whether hollering out vocals, tearing it up on sax or bass clarinet, or launching into wild guitar explorations. And then there was Neneh Cherry, just beginning to explore her enormous potential.

The band produced three records, GOD (1981), I AM COLD (1982) and ATTITUDE (1983), the first two each comprising a pair of 12" singles. The studio pieces were endowed with bizarre titles, which must have been a giggle for Sager and Smith after the political seriousness of The Pop Group: "Wilhelm Show Me The Diagram (Function Of The Orgasm)", "Those Eskimo Women Speak Frankly", "It Don't Mean A Thing If It Ain't Got That Brrod", give the flavour. Not that the silly titles were all. This was wild avant-jazz-rock, which at moments was inventive, expansive and great – I AM COLD especially, with Don Cherry lending an extra dimension.

It was a fun, boho group, but the records sold next to nothing, the gigs had many mouths to pay, and constant improvisation was demanding. Little surprise, then, that after a couple of years the band members headed off in different directions. Sager formed **Float Up CP** (who made just one album, KILL ME IN THE MORNING), and then, back in Bristol, **Head**, more of a rock band, though one with a typically anarchic approach; they lasted three albums, best of which was the first, A SNOG ON THE ROCKS. He currently plays in Bristol group

Pregnant. Springer worked a great deal with viola player Sarah Sarhandi, exploring a variety of sounds and textures without falling into the New Age traps. Oliver died tragically young from sickle cell anaemia. Smith's qualities had long been recognized, and he was not long short of employment behind the traps, moving on to **PUBLIC IMAGE LTD**, among others. Andrea continued to work with a number of different music projects and then branched out into both radio and television work. Neneh Cherry, of course, had a whole new career ahead of her.

⊙ Knee Deep In Hits (1990; Virgin).
The title is as ironic as that of Sager and Smith's old band, The Pop Group, and a (last word) anagram of a Rip, Rig & Panic standby. Enjoy.

Gerard F. Tierney

Born Toronto, 1944.

Guitarist and main songwriter with **THE BAND** until their first demise in 1977, **Robbie Robertson** went on to achieve great success as a solo artist in the sophisticated AOR field. It was a big shift from the rootsy Americana of The Band's best work, and the move found a mixed response with both public and critics alike.

After the movie of The Band's farewell concert, *The Last Waltz* (1976), Robertson continued to work with its director Martin Scorsese, providing soundtracks for some of his subsequent movies. He also wrote and directed *Carney*, an evocative look at the world of the American freak show, and produced artists such as Neil Diamond and Jesse Winchester.

He was not tempted to join The Band's mid-80s reunion; instead he set about recording a solo LP, which was eventually released in 1987. Featuring the talents of U2, Peter Gabriel, Daniel Lanois – as well as The Band's Rick Danko and Garth Hudson – ROBBIE ROBERTSON was a big seller, thanks mainly to an unexpected hit with "Somewhere Down The Crazy River", an atmospherically mumbled depiction of the Deep South. The impressive ballads "Broken Arrow" and "Fallen Angel" were similarly suited to Robertson's hoarse, half-spoken vocal delivery, the former exploring his native American heritage, while the latter remembered ex-Band member, the late Richard Manuel. Elsewhere, though, the album was often forced and formulaic, while Robertson lacked the vocal distinction and grace to overcome the plodding MOR of songs like "American Roulette" and "Hell's Half-Acre".

If his first solo effort ultimately failed to rival his work with The Band, Robertson came closer with STORYVILLE (1991), an album based thematically and musically on the sounds of New Orleans. Aided by Louisiana musicians like **THE NEVILLE BROTHERS**, it skilfully weaved R&B and gospel into its musical fabric on effective ballads such as "What About Now" and "Breaking The Rules", yet Robertson's lyrics continued to let him down, relying on empty symbolism and chest-thumping declamations. With no obvious hit single, it sold poorly and Robertson disappeared from the music scene once more.

In 1994, he re-emerged with the soundtrack to an American TV documentary called *The Native Americans*. The soundtrack album, issued on Capitol, mixed traditional native songs and chants with Robertson originals that again featured his characteristic mumble and discreet guitar work. The tasteful synthesized backing to "Golden Feather" and "Ghost Dance" reprised moments from the earlier albums without breaking any new musical ground, although on the closing "Twisted Hair" Robertson created a genuinely magical mood piece. He followed up with an ambient-tinged electronic album, CONTACT FROM THE UNDERWORLD OF RED BOY (1998), a collaboration with flavour-of-the-month DJ/producer **Howie B**. Whether he will learn any lessons from this musical experiment is debatable, though, as he seems happy to continue pursuing a career in tasteful adult MOR.

⊙ **Storyville** (1991; Geffen).
Despite the awful "Go Back To Your Woods", this is much more effective and affecting than the solo debut; Robertson even holds his own on "What About Now", a gorgeous duet with the magical voice of Aaron Neville.

Nicholas Oliver

TOM ROBINSON

Born Cambridge, England, 1950.

The **Tom Robinson** Band arrived as a musical force in 1977, representing the more overtly political wing of the New Wave, and producing some of the most forthright and infectious radical anthems of the day. Then, as quickly as they'd hit the limelight, they were gone and Tom was left to carve out his career carrying the weight of a not-altogether-accurate image as a sloganeering gay punk.

Like fellow New Wave icons Joe Strummer and Elvis Costello, Robinson had a struggling pre-punk past. Between the ages of 16 and 22 he lived in a 'therapeutic community for disturbed adolescents' in Kent, where he met **Danny Kustow** and formed **Davanq** in 1971. By 1973 Robinson had moved to London and joined folk-rock ensemble **Café Society**, who attracted the attention of Ray Davies's Konk label. An album, CAFE SOCIETY, appeared in 1974, but the band soon fell out with Davies.

By 1975, Tom Robinson had formed a new group, firmly establishing his leadership by calling it The Tom Robinson Band. Picking up an EMI contract, Robinson (bass/vocals) and Kustow (guitar) were joined by **Mark Ambler** (keyboards) and **Dolphin Taylor** (drums). Their timely no-nonsense rock set was to go down well on the London circuit, especially with Robinson's rousing didactics at the heart of the shows.

The first single, trucker's anthem "2-4-6-8 Motorway", was a huge hit, reaching #5 in the UK

charts in October 1977. Having grabbed the attention, Robinson introduced his political agenda on the follow-up EP, RISING FREE, which contained the strident "Don't Take No For An Answer", but will be best remembered for its inclusion of the unambiguous and stirring "(Sing If You're) Glad To Be Gay". It led to TRB showing their commitment to a variety of causes, including Rock Against Racism rallies.

The political content was maintained on the 1978 debut album, POWER IN THE DARKNESS, complete with its clenched-fist band logo on the cover. The predominance of power-guitar riffing under Robinson's slightly hoarse vocal delivery on "Up Against The Wall" and "Long Hot Summer" made this an essential New Wave album, and it duly reached the UK Top 5. Doubts arose about TRB's punk credentials, but the mainstream media adopted him as the lefty, thinking man's punk.

Things started going downhill when Ambler and Dolphin quit and Robinson found it hard to find settled replacements. Despite being produced by Todd Rundgren, their second album, TRB 2, was little more imaginative than its title, and subsequent singles saw a free fall in sales. By the end of 1979, finances had dwindled, and TRB folded.

Robinson formed **Sector 27**, but a self-titled album, released in 1980 on his newly formed Panic label, received scant attention, and he moved to East Germany to record solo. The resulting NORTH BY NORTH-WEST (1982) demonstrated a mellowing of his style, but the strength and range of his songwriting reached well beyond the confines of TRB material.

On returning to Britain, he notched up some unexpected chart success in 1983 with the candid beauty of "War Baby" and with "Listen To The Radio: Atmospherics", the latter co-written by Peter Gabriel. He tried his hand at covering Steely Dan's "Rikki Don't Lose That Number" in 1984 but it failed to chart. These and other treasures were included on the well-rounded HOPE AND GLORY (1984), and there was a further softening of touch on STILL LOVING YOU (1986).

Since then, Robinson has remained a tireless performer, doing solo cabaret appearances as well as a series of TRB reunion gigs that were mostly an excuse for thrashing out the old favourites. He also remains a prolific songwriter with an appreciative audience; LOVE OVER RAGE (1994) showed his eye for detail and ear for a catchy chorus were still sharp. Indeed, "Days" was an honest appraisal of the days when Tom Robinson took on the world as the punk with politics. His next album, HAVING IT BOTH WAYS (1996), referenced his 'outing' in British tabloid newspapers for living with a woman and fathering a child – he created his own ironic tag in 'The Artist Formerly Known as Gay' – and again showed his songwriting as good as ever, with a standout tribute to Dan Hartman in "Connecticut".

In 1997 he formed the Castaway Northwest record label, rereleasing and remixing some of the back catalogue, including BLOOD BROTHER (1997), a collaboration with virtuoso guitarist **Jakko Jakszyk** (first put out in 1990 as WE NEVER HAD IT SO GOOD), and the definitive version of a 1983 set, LAST TANGO: MIDNIGHT AT THE FRINGE (1997), recorded at the Edinburgh Festival. A series of CDs has also been released for the most dedicated fans through his Castaway Club. The intriguing spoken-word set SMELLING DOGS appeared in 2001.

⊙ **Power In The Darkness** (1978; Cooking Vinyl).
Definitive TRB, containing many a three-chord classic voicing some strident rhetoric on the issues of the day. "2-4-6-8 Motorway" is an obvious highlight.

⊙ **The Collection 77–87** (1987; EMI).
The best of a number of compilation releases.

Nick Dale

THE ROCHES

Formed New York, late 60s.

When the world could be changed just by wielding a guitar in a crowded coffee shop, **Margaret Roche** (vocals/guitar/synthesizer) and her sister **Terre** (vocals/guitar) left school to dabble in doo-wop and barbershop. This caught the attention of Village vulture Paul Simon, and the duo sang backing vocals on 1970's THERE GOES RHYMIN' SIMON. Simon's enthusiasm for **The Roches** led to a CBS contract and SEDUCTIVE REASONING (1975). Alas, the world was not starved for singer–songwriter product, even if The Roches were more kooky than most and, frustrated, the group moved to Louisiana, pursuing amour fous, and announced their retirement at the 1976 Women's Music Festival.

Then little **Suzzy Roche** (vocals/guitar) turned up, having finished her education in upstate New York. They decided to give The Roches another go as a trio. It was back to the Village to sing quirky tales of life in Louisiana and life on the road. Their eclecticism and deft lyrics led rock's own Dr Frankenstein, Robert Fripp, to take an interest and produce THE ROCHES (1979) for Warner Brothers. The album featured "Married Men", which was covered by Phoebe Snow, and "Mr Sellak", on which they begged their boss for their old waitressing jobs back. 'Let the other 40,000,307 people who want to get famous,' sang Terre.

The Roches would never be famous, but they never stopped trying to stay commercial. NURDS (1980), another Fripp job, boasted "One Season", with The Roches showing off their trick of harmonizing perfectly out of tune. The gimcrackery continued on KEEP ON DOING (1982), where the sisters went Swingle, covering Handel's "Hallelujah chorus".

Disappointed at the lack of commercial success, The Roches made sure their next two albums were more radio-friendly. ANOTHER WORLD (1985) did away with Fripp's absent-minded hums for a rock-band backing. SPEAK (1989) had an airplay hit in the

hook-filled "Big Nuthin'", while comic tunes like "The Anti Sex Backlash Of The 80s" competed with more obtuse offerings like "Cloud Dancing", based on a sixteenth-century Chinese lyric.

The Roches have never lacked a following, and will never lack a deal, as every label needs its equivalent of the McGarrigles, similarly feted folkies incapable of selling records. THREE KINGS (1990) was a Noo Yawk-accented collection of Christmas songs. A DOVE (1992) showed that in their feminist sexual frankness, The Roches hid Riot Grrrl sentiments in a velvet glove. As essential as they are unfashionable, The Roches moved to the punky Rykodisc label (which released their Doc Martened offering, CAN WE GO HOME? in 1995), but, two years later, announced a split. Terre Roche And Her Moodswings made an appearance soon afterwards (THE SOUND OF A TREE FALLING was released in 1998), and Suzzy released her solo debut, HOLY SMOKES, in 1997 and three years later followed it with the snappily titled SONGS FROM AN UNMARRIED HOUSEWIFE AND MOTHER, GREENWICH VILLAGE, USA. Suzzy and Maggie reunited for a guest appearance on BLEECKER STREET (1999), a collection of 60s US folk songs, and managed an entire album in ZERO CHURCH (2002), but it appears that the Roches act is no more, even though the bond is still there.

The Roches

⊙ **The Roches** (1979; Warners).
A bold, accessible debut which sucks in the listener with cutesy rock'n'roll tales, only to become a darker affair with the brooding "Runs In The Family" and the blue-collar lament of "Quitting Time".

⊙ **Speak** (1989; MCA).
The AOR sheen is twisted into complex and unexpected arrangements in an odyssey that incorporates more emotions than Harry Chapin managed in his entire career. The anthem "Big Nuthin'" will have you singing along before the ladies open their mouths.

Suzzy Roche & Maggie

⊙ **Zero Church** (2002; Red House).
Stemming from the duo's involvement in a seminar at *Harvard University's Institute On The Arts And Civic Dialogue,* this collection offers a set of beautiful prayers augmented by some angelic music.

Charles Bottomley

ROCKET FROM THE CRYPT

Formed San Diego, California, 1990.

There is a brutality about **Rocket From The Crypt** which makes them remarkable. Their most obvious influence is The Misfits – a comparison that can be stretched from their shared wrong-side-of-the-tracks 50s imagery (Elvis shirts/tattoos/sideburns) through to the sustained intensity of the records.

The group shrouds itself in snappy pseudonyms: **Speedo** (John Reis; vocals/guitar) fronting, supported by **Atom** (drums), **Apollo 9** (saxophone),

Petey X (bass) and **N.D.** (guitar) and, recently, **JC 2000** (trumpet). 'Yes, these are their real names', claims their record company biography, before going on to claim that they have played shows supporting not only The Misfits, but also James Brown and Sun Ra. Hmmm.

The band have enjoyed a cult following from the outset, reaching alternative-rock sections in the groovier US stores with their first album, PAINT AS A FRAGRANCE (1991), released by Headhunter a year after the band's formation. They then embarked on a succession of singles for cult American labels, the first three of which – "Yum Kippered" for Helter Skelter, "Boychucker" for Sympathy For The Record Industry, and "Normal Carpet Ride" for Sub Pop – were all excellent. Along with further releases for Drunken Fish and Pusmort, these were compiled on ALL SYSTEMS GO! (1993).

In the meantime the group had released their second studio album, CIRCA: NOW! (1992). As with the singles, huge riffs and Speedo's sneering delivery (though he can actually sing when he puts his mind to it) were the central musical planks. The production was slightly less crude and the musicianship more considered than their debut, but those differences were marginal.

1995 was the year that Rocket's Olympian bid for world supremacy began. THE STATE OF ART IS ON FIRE was a six-track vinyl release for old friends Sympathy For The Record Industry, promoted by a tour of America where they played to fans for free (as 'Ambassadors Of Very Good Will', according to Speedo). Their largesse cost them their transport, when they were forced to sell their van to make ends meet, but another mini-album, HOT CHARITY, this time nine songs long, was released in October by Elemental, their new British label. That left them with just enough time to complete the recording of their showcase, SCREAM, DRACULA, SCREAM!, which followed in January 1996.

Earlier records had revealed a band largely content to blow away audiences by force of will and presence alone. There was certainly no lack of power playing on SCREAM!, but Rocket From The Crypt also man-

aged to divine nuances from their established preoccupation with Americana. The rude sax of Apollo 9 proved a key ingredient on tracks such as "Misbeaten", a song that came perilously close to punk doo-wop. Nothing more was seen in the record stores until 1998 – though the band followed a punishing schedule of gigs in the meantime. Their time on the road pulled the already-tight band into a clenched-fist unit. Preceded by the single and stand-out track "When in Rome", RFTC (1998; Interscope) proved to be one of the top R.O.C.K. albums of the year, with new producer Kevin Shirley keeping all the band's rough edges intact, just shining them up and making them into a feature.

After this relative triumph came the obligatory record label troubles and RFTC found themselves locked in a messy battle with Interscope from whose clutches they finally escaped to create GROUP SOUNDS (2001), which emerged on the far more punk-friendly Vagrant Records. Superchunk drummer **Jon Wurster** thrashed the skins for most of the recording sessions after founding drummer Atom decided the way of the Rocket was no longer for him, but the position behind the kit was eventually filled by scene vet **Mario Rubalcaba**, aka **Ruby Mars**.

Appreciative reviews and an ever-growing fan base (cultivated via a string of loyalty-inducing freebies) still augur well for the future.

⊙ **Scream, Dracula, Scream!** (1996; Elemental). Employing period microphones and antiquated studio equipment at Gold Star Studios, RFTC overcome nostalgia for the ghosts of Presley and Spector (who also recorded there) by tapping into their spirit and playing some of the most ferocious American rock'n'roll of the modern age.

Alex Ogg

THE ROLLING STONES

Formed London, 1962.

"Getting old is a fascinating thing. The older you get, the older you want to get... " Keith Richards

More than anybody else, **The Rolling Stones** have defined the parameters of rock'n'roll. Of course, without Robert Johnson, Chuck Berry, Bo Diddley and Buddy Holly, **Keith Richards** (guitar) and **Bill Wyman** (bass) would probably be lowlifes propping up the bar at their local pub and **Charlie Watts** (drums) might be nothing but an unfulfilled jazz aficionado. If there had been no **Mick Jagger** (vocals), however, hard rock, heavy metal, glam, punk and grunge would have been unthinkable. While that may be unfair to the talents of Richards and **Brian Jones**, who both hot-wired blues guitar riffs into something else entirely, and may sell short the ability of Watts, who is surely the swingingest drummer in rock, Jagger has unquestionably developed much of rock's lyrical terrain and, more importantly, created the rock'n'roll persona.

The Rolling Stones clear the hall, even without an amp in sight

Single-handedly, Jagger invented that peculiarly British notion of part-brat, part-camp, self-conscious stardom that has been picked up by everyone from David Bowie to Jarvis Cocker. For Americans, who have never been very attuned to irony and posturing, Jagger's macho, don't-give-a-fuck attitude and threatening snarl became the obligatory rock-star stance and played a large part in launching The Standells, The Stooges, Aerosmith and Pussy Galore.

Aside from forging rock's iconography and subject matter and reaffirming its blues-based foundations, The Rolling Stones have defined its basic sound: its gritty textures and overloaded highs and lows. By fortuitous mistakes and clever experimentation, they have pioneered the use of the studio as a musical instrument. And, as the concept of The Stones began to fizzle out, they shamelessly jumped onto passing bandwagons and changed with the times to re-create rock as the noise of commerce. Essentially, from its adolescence as a bona fide youth movement to its present middle age of bloated, corporate product, the history of rock'n'roll is the history of The Rolling Stones.

Although The Stones mythology started to take shape when the future 'Glimmer Twins', Mick Jagger and Keith Richards, met as schoolboys in

Kent, The Rolling Stones as such began their thirty-year-plus career in the nether regions of southwest London during Britain's beat boom. Richmond was one of the centres of England's burgeoning blues-club scene and The Stones got a gig as the house band at its most famous venue, The Crawdaddy. After being spotted by 'producer' Andrew Loog-Oldham, they recorded their first single, a cover of Chuck Berry's "Come On", for Decca in 1963. Loog-Oldham knew next to nothing about music: his talent was as an *agent provocateur*. In the early years, it was perhaps his gift for publicity that was chiefly responsible for their bad-boy image. This media manipulation reached its culmination when he convinced *Melody Maker* to run the headline, 'Would You Let Your Daughter Go With A Rolling Stone?'

Under the leadership of Brian Jones, the music on The Stones' first few albums – THE ROLLING STONES (aka ENGLAND'S NEWEST HITMAKERS) (1964), 12x5 (1964) and THE ROLLING STONES, NOW! (1965) – was R&B stripped down to the street-fighting basics of Jones's stinging slide guitar, the bumptious rhythm section and Jagger's smart-ass vocals. The Stones, and all of the blues-based bands that followed in their wake, figured that the only way for them to reproduce the abandon of guitarists like Hubert Sumlin or the darkly sexual yelp of Howlin' Wolf was to turn the blues into energy music exuding a casual violence. This conflation of sex and power would become The Stones' great, but often troubling, theme. At this stage Jagger-Richards originals like "Heart Of Stone" (1965) did little more than reflect the careless misogyny of Swinging London.

The key moment from this period was their cover of Slim Harpo's "I'm A King Bee" (1964). Aside from expanding on the usual bar-band repertoire of Muddy Waters, Howlin' Wolf and Chuck Berry covers, their version of "King Bee" signalled their affinity for the make-do-with-what-you-got inventiveness of Harpo's producer Jay Miller. Miller owned a tiny studio in the Louisiana bayou and compensated for his lack of technology by experimenting with echo and encouraging his artists to play around with novel instrumentation. Throughout their career The Stones have compressed their sound to achieve a dirty edginess and Miller's necessity-is-the-mother-of-invention spirit would pay handsome dividends during the next period of their career.

"(I Can't Get No) Satisfaction" (1965) was The Stones' breakthrough record and remains one of pop music's breathtaking moments. While the lyric was a hilarious deconstruction of consumerism and desire that got the song banned from radio play in the States, it was the guitar riff that made history. Legend has it that the monumental riff was the result of a blown amp, which produced its buzzing distortion; others have suggested that the guitar sound was The Stones' way of compensating for their lack of a horn section. Whichever way it came about, the fuzz-guitar line has become as elemental as the "Johnny B. Goode" lick which kick-started their career and has given Richards the nickname of 'the human riff'.

The song shot straight to #1 on both sides of the Atlantic and laid the foundation for The Stones' complete mastery of the American rock'n'roll market. With the increasing record sales came growing clout, and while on tour in the States they were able to arrange one of pop music's transcendent moments. In order for them to appear for an awards ceremony, *The TAMI Show* (available on videotape), the Stones insisted that black musicians be invited to take part as well. Among the hand-picked guests were Howlin' Wolf and Ray Charles. The Stones played well but were, along with everyone else, blown off the stage by James Brown at the height of his powers. As a display of musical virtuosity, *The TAMI Show* was magnificent; as a victory over de facto segregation, it is still unsurpassed.

"Satisfaction" signalled the growth of the Jagger-Richards songwriting partnership and a gradual move away from R&B covers as the basis of The Stones' material. Over the next couple of years, Jagger and Richards would expand their repertoire from gyno-phobic outlaw anthems ("Under My Thumb" and "Let's Spend The Night Together"; 1966) to break-up ballads ("As Tears Go By"; 1965 and "Ruby Tuesday"; 1966) and *Zeitgeist* criticism ("Get Off of

My Cloud"; 1965 and "Mother's Little Helper"; 1966). While the singalong nonchalance of "Under My Thumb" somehow undercut its gender hatred in the popular imagination, there was no mistaking the vitriol of "Have You Seen Your Mother, Baby, Standing In The Shadow?" (1966). This was The Stones at their most punk: lyrically baiting their audience while Jones, Richards and Wyman overloaded their amps, creating a tightly packed distortion that strained to the technological brink.

On the other hand, "Paint It Black" (1966), with its dopey, surreal lyrics and sitar obbligato, seemed to presage the acid fallout of the end of the 60s. During this time, Brian Jones was fascinated with Moroccan music and obsessed with keeping up with The Beatles, of which there is ample evidence on "Paint It Black". This reached its peak with The Stones' response to SGT. PEPPER, the appalling THEIR SATANIC MAJESTIES REQUEST (1967), which trawled the depths of 60s drug culture with its awful sci-fi concept and misguided space music.

BEGGAR'S BANQUET (1968), on the other hand, was the response that SGT. PEPPER demanded. Every inch the concept album, BEGGAR'S BANQUET applied The Beatles' logic to an imagined return to roots – the album is their fantasy of how a Mississippi Fred McDowell record would have sounded like, given proper equipment and money. Reacting against the hippie bullshit around them, Jagger and Richards realigned themselves towards the often acoustic music of rural America in search of a sense of certainty amongst growing social, political and pharmacological chaos. As opposed to the complex tape-edits and orchestral grandeur of SGT. PEPPER, The Stones and producer Jimmy Miller (they ditched Loog-Oldham in 1967) used improving studio technology to achieve precise instrumental definition. Its clarity of sound and purpose made BEGGAR'S BANQUET a powerful plea for sanity, just as darkness was beginning to surround the band.

The Rolling Stones' erstwhile leader, Brian Jones, was found dead in July 1969. In typically morbid fashion, The Stones released their last British #1 on

the day after his funeral. "Honky Tonk Woman" was perhaps the quintessential Stones song. With its monolithic Keith Richards riff and almost claustrophobic sound – achieved by recording the guitar and drums next to each other in the studio – it defined mainstream rock for the next decade, but the thoughtless misogyny of its lyric was a thumbnail sketch of rock'n'roll decadence. The single's B-side was the remarkably bleak "You Can't Always Get What You Want", whose mutation of rhythm into a kind of existential fog anchored their next album, LET IT BLEED (1969).

From the nastiness of its title to a song sequence which worked from "Gimme Shelter" to "You Can't Always Get What You Want", it was apparent that LET IT BLEED was no celebration of the Woodstock Nation. Always the most rhythmic rock-'n'roll band, on LET IT BLEED The Stones became an apocalyptic juggernaut: Richards' guitar riffs fused with the bass and drums to achieve an edginess that went beyond functional propulsion. The music's savagery perfectly echoed the brutality of Jagger's lyrics, which ranged from the chilling sex/death equations of "Gimme Shelter" and "Midnight Rambler" to the unbearably caustic title track. Keith Richards made his vocal debut, sounding as ravaged as he looked, on "You Got The Silver". Their reading of Robert Johnson's "Love In Vain", meanwhile, proved that The Stones had succeeded in remaking the blues in their own image.

As evidenced on GET YER YA-YAS OUT (1970), the music that The Stones played on their 1969 American tour was uncompromising and undiluted. Ex-Bluesbreaker **Mick Taylor** replaced Brian Jones and his gnarled guitar lines on "Stray Cat Blues" and "Love In Vain" added a feral bite to the already fearsome music of Richards, Wyman and Watts. Although better played on other documents of this tour, "Sympathy For The Devil" had shed its overblown pomp and circumstance and gained an intensity that was almost punk. The final date of their tour was supposed to be a free concert at Golden Gate Park in San Francisco, but the city council pulled out and, at the last moment, the concert was moved to the northern California wasteland of Altamont. The organization was a disaster. The venue change and numerous delays tested the limits of the peace and love vibe. Fights broke out amongst the crowd, but the real violence was monopolized by the security staff. In a move that summed up the naivety of the 60s, The Grateful Dead suggested that the Hell's Angels provide the security at the concert. During Jefferson Airplane's set, singer Marty Balin was punched in the face by one of the Angels; as The Stones played in the face of rising tension, a member of the audience was stabbed to death by a member of the 'security force'. The 60s were over.

Their first response to Altamont was a retreat into the self-generated mythology which has always been their safety blanket. STICKY FINGERS (1971) was the first release on their own imprint and featured the now-famous cartoon rendition of Mick Jagger's mouth inspired by a poster for a porn flick. The album's single, "Brown Sugar", was an ironic but cheap joke about interracial sex aimed at restoring the band's reputation for bad-boy antics. "Wild Horses" and "I Got The Blues" were the kind of mannered, insincere ballads that Jagger would specialize in during the 70s, and the jazzy outro of "Can't You Hear Me Knockin'" was lazy and out of place. The rest of the album, however, picked up where LET IT BLEED left off: the one overt Altamont reference was the gallows humour of "Dead Flowers", while their cover of Fred McDowell's "You Got To Move" was nearly as good as "Love In Vain". The highlight, though, was Marianne Faithfull's "Sister Morphine", with its raw, acoustic guitar and aching lyric.

EXILE ON MAIN STREET (1972) was the summation of everything that The Rolling Stones were working towards. This double album was the only Stones album where the music didn't declare its intention with Keith's first riff. EXILE showed The Stones using the studio as an instrument that was as fundamental to its blues sound as a harmonica or guitar: the album was shrouded in a bleary, narcotic haze that was sometimes so thick that it sounded like Charlie Watts was recorded under water. Jagger's voice was so blurred and slurred that it frequently faded into the horn charts, while the guitars of Richards and Taylor sounded hoarse, stale and hungover. The lyrics that do call attention to themselves, like 'Don't want to walk and talk about Jesus/Just want to see his face' or 'Can't say yes and I can't say no' were desolate and directionless. The songs were dialogues between Jagger and his image, his lifestyle, his age.

After EXILE ON MAIN STREET, The Stones would begin to run out of ideas. GOAT'S HEAD SOUP (1973) was a lazy, infinitely less convincing exploration of the same territory, while IT'S ONLY ROCK 'N' ROLL (1974) was indeed just that and marked the beginning of the band coasting on the clichés that they invented. With Mick Taylor's replacement by ex-Faces guitarist **Ron Wood** in 1975, The Stones started to carve out their niche as caricatures of the worst rock'n'roll excesses. On BLACK AND BLUE (1976), they tried to answer LeRoi Jones's comment that white people were 'the keepers of last year's blues' by appropriating contemporary funk and reggae stylings, with mixed results. SOME GIRLS (1978) was probably their strongest album since EXILE, but that's not saying much. But SOME GIRLS also represented the ultimate indignity, as they went disco on "Miss You" in a blatant attempt to move product.

The 80s began with The Stones reprising their disco journey with a dull thud on EMOTIONAL RESCUE (1980). As disco went back underground to its real constituency in the face of hip-hop, The Stones could go safely back to straight-ahead rock on TATTOO YOU (1981). There was nothing particularly 'Rolling Stones' about the record, but formulaic anthems like "Start Me Up" had their pleasures. By this point, The Stones were essentially a stadium-rock band, and, pumping out old favourites for the faithful in shows, they continued to be masters. But their records went from bad to worse. With its unspeakably lame political theme, 1984's UNDERCOVER was a career low, but it would be surpassed by the disgraceful STEEL WHEELS (1989), VOODOO LOUNGE (1994), by which point they'd lost Bill Wyman – replaced by **Darryl Jones** – and STRIPPED (1995), where they finally stripped themselves of the band's only remaining glory by bogging down Charlie Watts' irrepressible swing in the digital murk of modern production values.

Staggering on towards the new millennium like some marathon runner on his last legs, the band recorded and toured the world with BRIDGES TO BABYLON (1997), making more millions they'll never have time to spend, and followed that up with yet another freshly culled live set called NO SECURITY. As if one gargantuan millennial world tour wasn't enough, the band announced yet another global trek for 2002/3 with the intention of embracing China this time round.

The faithful continue to turn out en masse to see the self-titled 'world's greatest rock'n'roll band' go through its paces. But perhaps 'the world's most professional rock'n'roll band' would be a more appropriate moniker, as they shamelessly plumb the depths of corporate sponsorship. In recent times Jagger has twice returned to a band he obviously no longer wants any part of, to put out careless, cynical albums and undertake mega-million-dollar, megalomaniacal tours with ticket prices that exclude all but wealthy middle-aged fans.

 ⊙ **The Rolling Stones** (1964; London).
As the beginning of one of rock's most enduring formulas – snotty white boys messing around with the blues – this is much more than the sum of its parts. It's still fascinating to listen to Jagger take first steps towards the nasty poses he based his career on.

 ⊙ **Beggar's Banquet** (1968; London).
Half classic Stones swagger ("Street Fightin' Man" and "Stray Cat Blues"), half urban pastoral ("Factory Girl" and "Salt Of The Earth"), this is probably the least formulaic Stones album. They are already beginning to feel the end of the 60s close in around them.

 ⊙ **Let It Bleed** (1969; London).
"Gimme Shelter", an impossibly dark reinterpretation of popular music's greatest subject – release – gets their most frightening album off to a chilling start. Rock's clichés start to signify something beyond resistance to work and adulthood.

 ⊙ **Exile On Main Street** (1972; Rolling Stones).
One of the five or six greatest albums ever made. It's thoroughly alienating on the first several listenings, but its murky gravity exerts an undeniable force, imploding every contradictory aspect of The Stones' mythology.

 ⊙ **The Singles Collection** (1989; London).
The only worthwhile retrospective. This three-disc set compiles all of their singles (including B-sides) for London in more or less chronological order.

Peter Shapiro

HENRY ROLLINS

Born Washington, DC, February 13, 1961.

"I don't enjoy playing unless I see blood or get hurt."

One of rock's most ferocious singers, **Henry Rollins** (Henry Garfield) gives performances of a unique combination of insanity and discipline. He was the fourth and longest-lasting singer with the legendary punk band **BLACK FLAG**, where he made a name for himself with his hardcore attitude and one of the most intense vocals ever put on vinyl – the title track of DAMAGED (1981). During his tenure with Black Flag, Rollins covered his body with an awesome array of tattoos (including a sun emblazoned across his back beneath the motto 'Search & Destroy'), developed his distinctive vocal attack and, perhaps most importantly, refined his writing talent.

Rollins' solo career started before he left Black Flag. In 1984 he started giving spoken-word performances, published the first of his books, and established his own publishing company (even though he was living in a tool shed). By the mid 80s most of the themes and obsessions that were to dominate his solo career were well rehearsed.

In August 1986 Gregg Ginn, the founding member of Black Flag, quit. Henry decided to go solo and by October 1986 was in the studio with a new band and new material. The initial line-up of **The Rollins Band** – **Chris Haskett** (guitar), **Mick Green** (drums) and **Bernie Wandell** (bass) – produced HOT ANIMAL MACHINE (1987). In terms of musical complexity and production quality, this was quite a large step backwards from Black Flag. It did, however, have a rawness and a freshness that the later Black Flag material lacked, taking very simple rhythms and overlaying brash guitar. From the same recording session came the DRIVE BY SHOOTING EP, released under the name Henrietta Collins And The Wife-Beating Child Haters. This featured a title track that parodied The Beach Boys, and a cover version of Queen's "We Will Rock You" entitled "I Have Come To Kill You", with a sermon by the Reverend Henry Rollins Of The Church Of The Annihilation.

Early in 1987 Rollins revamped the band to include **Simeon Cain** on drums and **Andrew Weiss** on bass, the rhythm section of Gregg Ginn's instrumental side-project, Gone. The first recordings from the new line-up appeared as LIFE TIME and DO IT (both 1988), both produced by Ian MacKaye of Minor Threat and Fugazi. With these two albums, The Rollins Band established their musical territory. LIFE TIME was bursting with energy and attitude as Rollins explored isolation, self-loathing, desolation and self-destructiveness. DO IT, a lighter album, opened with Rollins screaming the title track, which became one of the staples of the band's set, then moved on to a massive revision of "Move Right In" from HOT ANIMAL MACHINE – a track that showed exactly why Andrew

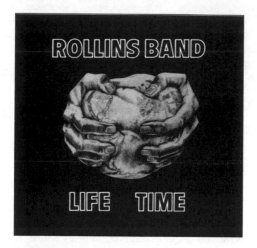

and Sim were so essential to the band.

At the end of 1988 the band were back in the studio recording HARD VOLUME, on which a more expensive production overcame the rawness that made the earlier albums such intense experiences. Yet Rollins delved further and further into himself to dredge up material for the lyrics, with the result that the album was unremittingly oppressive. Next off was the 1990 collaboration between Rollins and Andrew Weiss that produced FAST FOOD FOR THOUGHT, released under the name Wartime. Musically, it diverged quite severely from the direction The Rollins Band had been pushing, being a lot fuzzier and more experimental, albeit with the intense dynamism of all Rollins' best work.

1991 was a breakthrough year for The Rollins Band, as they got the opening slot on the massive Lollapalooza tour, and for the first time were exposed to a mass audience across America. Rollins resumed his career in underground movies, starring alongside Lydia Lunch in *Kiss Napoleon Goodbye*, but the only record release was a collaboration between Rollins and **The Hard-Ons**, a manic cover of AC/DC's "Let There Be Rock". Then on December 19, things nearly came to an abrupt end: Rollins and Joe Cole were mugged, and Joe was shot dead in the ensuing fight.

Most people would probably take some time out if they witnessed their best friend's death. Rollins, however, took the experience on tour with him. After the release of THE END OF SILENCE (1992), he played 162 concerts with the band and twenty spoken-word concerts, delivering some of his heaviest performances. **Melvin Gibbs** (bass) replaced Andrew Weiss in 1993, but the intensity showed no signs of flagging on WEIGHT (1994), in which Rollins analysed the bull-shit of being a rock star while taking the band into stadium-rock territory, which is now their chosen arena. Meanwhile Henry had become a regular feature on MTV, appearing as the angriest man in the world, and expanded from underground films to Hollywood with a role alongside Charlie Sheen in the lame comedy *The Chase* (1994), and a more creditable cameo in the much-praised *Heat* (1996).

The Rollins Band were whipped back into the studio and not allowed out until they'd delivered COME IN AND BURN (1997) – Henry's first musical outing since WEIGHT. It was another lyrical feast washed down with the purest industrial grunge noises.

Following COME IN AND BURN it almost seemed as if Henry might turn his back on music entirely as the man concentrated on his many other artistic endeavours. Apparently the experience of working with LA band **Mother Superior**, however, persuaded Rollins to ditch his group's former incarnation and recruit the guys from Mother Superior to create an all-new line-up. That's not to say that GET SOME GO AGAIN (2000) deviated far from the original bone-crushing noise, merely that it sounded so much pacier and more tightly focused. And, as if things couldn't get much heavier, NICE (2001) merely reaffirmed Rollins' funking, hard-as-hell rock direction, while anyone who hankered for the earlier incarnation of the Rollins Band was well catered for with INSERT BAND HERE: LIVE IN AUSTRALIA 1990 (2002). Despite this spate of quality output, Rollins continues to stick his fingers into some unlikely pies: he has most recently been spied on British TV co-hosting a ludicrous show entitled *Full Metal Challenge*, in which customized trucks … erm … wrestle.

Henry Rollins deserves the fame and success he is now realizing: he has worked harder and longer than most to get where he is. The trouble is that what he is doing now does not live up to his potential. With luck he will remember that he can do much better than swim in the mainstream. At the end of the day, nobody does it like the Rollins boy.

⦿ **Hot Animal Machine** (1987; Fundamental).
Rollins' superb solo debut – a fresh, raw, intelligent record.

⦿ **Life Time** (1988; Fundamental).
Arguably Rollins' best work: Ian MacKaye's production is great, the music is superb, the lyrics are brilliant. Every song on the album destroys.

⦿ **Rollins: The Boxed Life** (1993; Imago).
The most engaging of Rollins' numerous spoken-word records, showing a humour that sometimes cuts through his problematic world-view.

⦿ **Get Some Go Again** (2000; Imago).
This album burns with the incandescent rage of a star going nova, Highpoints include the fourteen-minute album closer "LA Money Train", which crosses Rollins' hallmark spoken-word style with a hard-as-nails funk work-out that features ex-MC5 guitarist Wayne Kramer.

Glenn Gossling

MICK RONSON

Born Hull, England, 1946; died 1993.

"I don't think he had the respect he deserved – and of course it's too late now." Morrissey

Yorkshireman **Mick Ronson** has often been portrayed as the bluff northern lad nonplussed by the bisexuality paraded in the Bowie camp through the glory years 1971 to 1974. However, he had always dreamt of becoming a rock star like his hero Jeff Beck, and vowed to escape Hull at the earliest opportunity. Leaving school with only his piano lessons and his skill at playing a violin in the manner of a guitar, he headed for London and through several dead-end 60s bands, before returning to Hull to brush success with a group called **The Rats**. After their demise Ronson turned his back on music and spent some years as a municipal gardener, but when The Rats drummer, John Cambridge, was recruited by **DAVID BOWIE**, he suggested Ronson as lead guitarist.

Still paying off previous rock'n'roll debts, Ronson reluctantly returned to London and joined Bowie's concept – then called **Hype**, a rock band of comic book heroes. The 25-year-old Ronson played his first concert with Hype at the London Roundhouse in February 1970, dressed in Bowie's silver 'Space Oddity' suit and taking the role of Gangsterman. Glam-rock was born. The name Hype was dropped during the recording of THE MAN WHO SOLD THE WORLD (1970) and they became Bowie's band. Aside from a brief hiatus when he recorded a single under the name **Ronno**, Ronson's star was hitched thereafter to Bowie and MainMan management.

The vibrant duo of Bowie and Ronson are for ever encapsulated in an iconic image of Bowie fellating Ronson's guitar on stage in 1972. More than a convenient phallic symbol, Ronson's guitar, at turns stinging and haunting, became a crucial element in the success of the next three Bowie albums – including his first #1, ALADDIN SANE (1973). Like his hair, Ronson was increasingly highlighted until finally, when Bowie dramatically announced his retirement from the stage, MainMan turned to Ronson to maintain the fervour. An overkill MainMan campaign, including a six-storey billboard over NY's Times Square for weeks on end, created an insurmountable shortfall between expectation and product.

Ronson's first solo album, SLAUGHTER ON 10TH AVENUE (1974; reissued with bonus tracks 1998; Snapper), reached the UK Top 10 but he was ill-prepared for the slings and arrows accompanying his new-found stardom and gladly stepped out of the limelight to fill **MOTT THE HOOPLE**'s need for a guitarist and a publicity jolt for their autumn tour. Unfortunately, before the tour got under way, RCA released a new Ronson solo single, "Billy Porter", which was mauled in the music press. With the new Mott single floundering and the press waiting to pounce once more, Ronson slipped away with singer Ian Hunter and announced a new venture – **The Hunter/Ronson Band**. RCA decided this was the right time to release a second Mick Ronson solo album, PLAY DON'T WORRY (1975; reissued with bonus tracks 1998; Snapper), which was held up to national ridicule. It slunk in and out of the Top 30 in three weeks.

Hunter remembers Ronson in the recording studio reading a music paper review and turning red

with rage before recording a particularly blistering guitar section for their first album. The resultant material was a startling return to form for both of them, but due to contractual obligations the album was released on CBS as a solo Ian Hunter album and called, just to make it clear, IAN HUNTER (1975). It was a chart success in both the UK and US, and its follow-up, ALL AMERICAN ALIEN BOY (1976), again credited to Hunter, sold pretty well, too.

While performing late-night sessions with Hunter in New York's Other End club, Ronson started hanging out with **BOB DYLAN**. This resulted in his next unlikely berth, touring with Dylan's Rolling Thunder Revue, musically perhaps the most innovative stage of Dylan's career, as captured on the album HARD RAIN (1976). Eventually, perhaps due to glowing reports of Ronson's stage presence, Dylan took over lead guitar duties. From this time Ronson settled in the US and spent a long period either producing or supporting artists more for pleasure than expectation of acclaim.

In 1991 Ronson was diagnosed as suffering from liver cancer, but carried on working when possible, playing again with Bowie on BLACK TIE WHITE NOISE (1993), and planning a belated third solo album. This final project grew into a collaborative venture as stars such as Chrissie Hynde queued up to pay tribute to his talents and to return past favours. He finally succumbed to cancer in April 1993 and the long-awaited album, HEAVEN AND HULL (1994), was released posthumously. This time the critics too paid their respects.

In 1996 there was a star-studded MICK RONSON MEMORIAL CONCERT at the Hammersmith Apollo, which is now available on double CD (1997; Citadel). The long defunct The Rats reformed for the event, and subsequently recorded a few old Ronson-authored songs. These have now been released on a Rats compilation CD with the unfortunate title THE RISE AND FALL OF BERNIE GRIPPLESTONE AND THE RATS FROM HULL (1998). The most pertinent facet of this release was perhaps the lengthy booklet focusing on Mick Ronson's time with The Rats.

⊙ **Only After Dark** (1994; Golden Years). SLAUGHTER ON 10TH AVENUE and PLAY DON'T WORRY merged and bolstered with bonus tracks.

Tony Drayton

ROSETTA STONE

Formed Liverpool, England, 1988.

"It isn't an insult for us to be called goth. It's one type of music, music that we like." Porl King

Porl King (vocals/guitars) and **Karl North** (bass) had been working together for some time when they launched **Rosetta Stone** in 1988.

Touring extensively, they soon defined their moody, haunting sound and by late 1989 had built up a strong following, released a series of now highly collectable cassettes and had been invited to open for The Mission. Their first vinyl release, the DARKNESS AND LIGHT EP, was produced by Colin Richardson, who had previously worked with The Mission, and was released in May 1990. By the end of the year the band had been signed up by the Expression label.

The first album, AN EYE FOR THE MAIN CHANCE, followed in 1991. The music, dark and brooding, but delivered with undeniable force, took charge of the more traditional elements of goth and directed them into music with a distinct pop hook; at last, goth you could dance to! Their first single, "Leave Me For Dead", broke into the indie charts and gave the band some well-deserved acknowledgement from the music press. A second guitarist, **Porl Young**, was added to the line-up for a time and the band toured widely. They were offering their audiences a classic goth sound in the tradition of the Sisters Of Mercy, The Mission and The March Violets, but with an incisive danced-up edge. Audiences loved it.

By 1992 this dance element was being explored more deeply and exploited in the highly successful single "Adrenaline", an indication of how the band were going to develop. Another single, "The Witch", carried them towards the release of their second album in 1993: ON THE SIDE OF ANGELS, a compilation of remixes and unavailable material spanning their career. The band continued to move forward, developing their sound and augmenting it with an infusion of the industrial scene's power and rhythm. At the same time interest in the band spread to America and they signed to Cleopatra Records for American distribution (this has resulted in several US releases including the FOUNDATION STONES compilation).

1994 saw them touring in America and working towards the next album. The single "Nothing", an angry, strident track, prefigured the release of THE TYRANNY OF INACTION (1995). This album marked a new phase in the musical career of the band and was, at first, slow to establish itself amongst the older fans. In time, though, the album not only took hold with the fans, but also attracted a new following from those interested in the heavier Industrial sound. TYRANNY is a powerful musical statement, filled with energy and aggression, conveyed through a more extensively developed synthesized sound and pared-down lyrics. Where their earlier material favoured imagery and illusion, King's lyrics were now cynical, critical statements about contemporary life.

During 1995, disillusioned with the UK music industry, the band took control and released GENDER CONFUSION independently, distributing it through the Internet. This album proved Rosetta's talent for remixing and their ability to take synthesized sound and reinvent it continually. HIDING IN WAITING was released by Cleopatra in 1996 and featured new material together with remixes and covers, expanding and extending their musical applications, proving themselves yet again.

1998 saw the release of a live studio tracks album, CHEMICAL EMISSIONS, while a 1999 Madonna tribute album, also on Cleopatra, includes their cover of "Rain". They also produced and mixed for other bands, including goth outfits such as Gene Loves Jezebel and The Wake, as well as more mainstream bands, such as Mulu. The start of 1999 found Rosetta Stone stepping back from the scene to rethink their position, the result being a split, with North joining the **Dream Disciples** and King taking on the Rosetta Stone identity for a solo crusade. So far he has issued an album of 80s cover versions, Unerotica (2000), and persists in exploring the creative boundaries of the genre.

Rosetta Stone's name continues to stand as a symbol of gothdom and its metamorphosis as a genre.

⊙ **An Eye For The Main Chance** (1991; Expression). This is a classic goth album, filled with moody elements and delivered with style and clarity. From the racing beats of tracks like "Deeper" to the wickedly atmospheric cover of Led Zeppelin's "When The Levee Breaks", this album investigates and exhibits the dark side of sound.

⊙ **The Tyranny Of Inaction** (1995; Minority One). With a highly developed and harder-edged synth sound, the industrial influence is clearly apparent across the album. The music is ferocious; the rhythms, unrelenting. The dance element has been punched up into the forefront – tracks like "Side Effect" and "Friends And Executioners" positively exude vitality and energy.

⊙ **Hiding In Waiting** (1996; Cleopatra). A diverse collection of tracks, exhibiting all the band's interests and skills. From the steady passion of the title track, to covers of Blancmange's 1980s hit single "Living On The Ceiling" and the decadence of The Velvet Underground's "Venus In Furs", this is full of aural surprises. Discover.

Valerie Palmer

DAVID LEE ROTH

Born Bloomington, Indiana, 1955.

In the summer of 1985 **David Lee Roth** ruled the American airwaves and charts with weirdo covers of The Beach Boys' "California Girls" and Louis Prima's "Just A Gigolo". Dave's been wondering what went wrong ever since.

Roth made his name as the mouth of **VAN HALEN**, having formed the band with the brothers at Pasadena City College, where he was studying theatre. Roth was the American spiv, a 'Ziggy Stardust' junkie armed with a leer. His allure was that of a blow-dried stud, a carbon copy of Steve Tyler with the gift of the gab ('The guy who said money can't buy you happiness didn't know where to go shopping!'). His hollers were like a cocaine rush, and his trademark 'Whooo!' made putting bug powder up your nose seem almost worthwhile. Worldwide recognition came with the Philip-Glass-gone-metal hit "Jump", from the album 1984.

Disappointed at the delay in following up this epochal moment, he recorded the solo CRAZY FROM

THE HEAT EP (1985), casting himself as an 80s Sinatra crooning Brian Wilson and Marlene Dietrich. No swimming pool was complete without it, and it peaked at #6 in the US. CBS even gave him $10 million to produce a film based on the record, but pulled out following a well-publicized audition featuring Dave cavorting with hundreds of jiggling babes. Roth blamed the subsequent Van Halen split on drug problems, and released EAT 'EM AND SMILE (1986). SMILE's extravagant techno-metal, provided by ex-Zappa band guitarist Steve Vai, swaggered into the UK Top 30 and the US Top 10.

Van Halen had become shadows of their former selves. But at least they were successful shadows. Roth released "Just Like Paradise" (1988), a synth-polished ode to decadence, with a chorus you would be unashamed to punch the air to. It effortlessly went to #8 in America, but became a brilliant anachronism as the poodle-rockers that Roth inspired threw away the Max Factor, dusted off their copies of LED ZEPPELIN I and refused to bathe. Dave's burlesque SKYSCRAPER tour in 1988 was a financial disaster, complete with a giant skateboard, a boxing ring, and an audience who stayed at home. Desperate for ideas, he listened to some Mick Ronson records and released A LITTLE AIN'T ENOUGH – a wretched, rootsier record which somehow went Top 5 in the UK in 1991 – and YOUR FILTHY LITTLE MOUTH (1994).

Dave thought reggae was the future, but he might as well have put a gun to his head. The man who introduced "California Girls" to the phrase 'Hot diggum yo' was a joke he no longer got, known as 'David Weave Roth' because of mane problems. Then there was a pathetic drug bust in New York for possession of $15 of dope.

A best-selling poster for the 1984 album captures the quintessential Roth: clad in a necklace of raccoon tails and bottomless strides, gazing into a mirror, aghast at his own mascara-ed beauty, Bolivian boo sparkling on his gums. You can hear the teenyboppers hammering on the hotel-room door. It might have been best to remember him this way, but there was no chance this party animal would lay down and die. First there was his rollicking tell-all autobiography *Crazy From The Heat* in 1997, and then, despite a career that was languishing in the doldrums, he bounced back with the no-frills DLR BAND (1998) and at last the genius spark of glam vaudeville and roots and roll seemed to be flickering again behind his baby blues.

And then there were the constant rumours of a reunion with his former band-mates that had begun all the way back in 1996 when Roth and Van Halen had appeared together to present an MTV Music Award. A reunion of sorts resulted in two Roth/Van Halen tunes gracing Van Halen's BEST OF VOLUME I. Unfortunately, it became clear afterwards that things had nose-dived from there when ex-Extreme singer Gary Cherone turned up on the frankly appalling VAN HALEN III. Whether the two parties

will ever get together again without the whiff of potential homicide in the air is open to debate, but a single bizarre twist may have put paid to that angle already: Roth and ex-Van Halen singer Sammy Hagar toured the States together in 2002, with the whole affair ending on a very sour note.

More recently, Roth bounced back with a new album of his own, DIAMOND DAVE (2003), on which our hero tackled cuts by the likes of Hendrix, Savoy Brown and The Doors.

⊙ **Skyscraper** (1988; Warners).
Some bright spark has added the unlikely, prancing covers of "California Girls" and "Just A Gigolo" to the CD reissue of Dave's second album. Nestled alongside "Just Like Paradise", these hits are the perfect soundtrack to shove cucumbers down your trousers to. Vai's guitar conflagrations are where metal meets the avant-garde.

⊙ **The Best** (1998; Rhino).
Twenty tracks (including one new song); all you're ever likely to need by the ultimate wannabe California bimbo.

Charles Bottomley

MICHAEL ROTHER

Born Hamburg, Germany, 1950.

Multi-instrumentalist **Michael Rother**'s closest counterpart is perhaps Mike Oldfield, but the German guitar and synth wizard's overall output has been far more satisfying. He's been a major star in his home country, and deserves to be a lot better known elsewhere.

Rother started out in a proto-version of **KRAFTWERK**, before leaving to found the equally seminal **NEU!** with Klaus Dinger. When Neu! split, Rother joined forces with **CLUSTER**'s Moebius and Roedelius, as **HARMONIA**, but in 1975 he went solo and started out on a sequence of meditative instrumental albums, playing all the instruments himself, except for drums, which were supplied on his first four albums by **CAN**'s brilliant and ubiquitous **Jaki Liebezeit**.

The first of these suites was FLAMMENDE HERZEN (1976), which with its yearning guitar lines and melodic electronics garnered sales of over 100,000 copies in Germany and became a movie soundtrack, too. Yet almost nobody bought it in Britain or the US, where Krautrock was fast plummeting from such fashion as it had ever achieved. STERNTALER (1977) continued in similar vein, again selling well in Germany and Europe, being voted album of the year in the main Berlin newspaper and establishing Rother as a major artist in prog-rock-loving Italy.

The British press began to catch up with KATZENMUSIK (1979) and the following year's FERNWARME (1982), which the *NME* considered to be 'getting close to perfection'. The latter was Rother's last collaboration with Liebezeit; in future he played all instruments, as he moved towards simpler arrangements than the multi-instrumental overlays of his earlier work. His next two albums – LUST (1983) and SUSSHERZ UND TIEFENSCHARFE

(1987) – depended on electronics to a greater degree, the former introducing a Fairlight to create many of the instrumental sounds. In 1987, Rother also released his first entirely electronic album, TRAUMREISEN.

This has been followed by a long silence on the album front, although dance-floor interest in Rother's past work has kept him busy remixing tracks. At the same time, he has been producing new songs as bonus tracks for CD reissues of his albums on his own Random Records label. A 1993 singles compilation, RADIO, underlined his status as one of European music's most important figures, and in 1996 he finally issued a new album, ESPERANZA, his first for nine years, revisiting older technology and on "Spirit Of 72" revisiting the sounds of Neu!

1998 saw him playing live in Gemany and the US – his first live performances for 22 years – with Moebius, recording a new track for a Neu! tribute album, HOMAGE TO NEU, and completing a new album, with a female singer.

And now that his earlier Neu! is finally readily available, Rother is a man who threatens to give New Age music a good name.

⊙ **Sterntaler** (1977; Random).
With every listen revealing another nuance, this is a fresh, spacious album with tunes that seem to have been in your dreams for ever.

⊙ **Katzenmusik** (1979; Random).
A suite of twelve 'songs' on a single, simple theme, climaxing together. New Age music, and ahead of its time.

⊙ **Traumreisen** (1987; Random).
Rother's first all-electronic album, packed full of wonderful tunes.

Paul O'Brien

JOSH ROUSE

Born Nebraska, 1972.

"I'm just a guy who sits on his couch and makes stuff up ... I've never really considered myself a songwriter."

Josh **Rouse** has always been given an alt-country hat to wear, but it doesn't sit neatly on the head of this Nashville resident singer-songwriter. Though he possesses a smokey, bruised voice and a penchant for heart-sick ballads, his three albums to date also contain jangly guitars, jaunty melodies and brisk drums that make his music fall un-neatly between alt-country, pop and out-and-out rock.

Rouse's childhood was a nomadic one, rolling through the mid-western and southern states with his mother and stepfather. While his classmates were headbanging to Megadeath, the young Josh was listening to soft rock radio and soaking up sounds from across the Atlantic: The Cure, The Psychedelic Furs, The Smiths.

After learning to play Neil Young songs on the guitar, Rouse began writing his own. Hungry for a

happening music scene and itching to be a part of it, he headed down to Nashville, the capital of country music. It was here that he met **David Henry**, a cello player fresh off a Cowboy Junkies tour. Together they played a few gigs and recorded a demo tape; soon Rouse had landed a deal with Rykodisc's Slow River subsidiary.

Recorded for less than $5000 and with Henry as co-producer, Rouse's first album, DRESSED UP LIKE NEBRASKA (1998), much to his surprise, was met with critical acclaim. Blending acoustic guitar and subtle arrangements, including haunting cello and the occasional lonely trumpet, as well as up-tempo melodies and brisk beats, this was music for gazing mournfully at the stars or for singing along to on the open highway – feet up on the dashboard, not-so-cold beer in a box on the back seat. With the album fresh on the shelves Rouse toured the US, supporting the likes of Son Volt, Golden Smog and Joe Henry, and later Aimee Mann and Wilco.

A collaboration with fellow Nashvillian **Kurt Wagner** (**LAMPCHOP**) ensued and received similar praise. Recorded on an 8-track in just four nights, the mini-album CHESTER, wrapped Rouse's plaintive vocals and easy melodies around Wagner's brooding tales of small-town America, and did much to cement the idea that Rouse was a member of the alt-country scene.

By the time HOME was released in 2000, Rouse was able to give up his day job as a parking valet and concentrate on his music. But HOME was a mixed bag. While DRESSED UP LIKE NEBRASKA had a certain raw quality, the follow-up sporadically suffered from 'production overkill' and pop blandness. Nevertheless, the set offered enough of the same yearning and hope woven through insidious melody and toe-tapping beats that marked Rouses's debut. With the Wild West dustiness of "Afraid To Fall", the oozing slide of "And Around" and the radio-friendly "Directions" (which also appeared on the Vanilla Sky soundtrack), HOME, while failing to break new ground, placed Rouse firmly on the musical map.

UNDER COLD BLUE STARS (2002), saw Rouse expanding on a sound that was already hard to pigeonhole. There were echoes of Prefab Sprout, Big Star, The Cowboy Junkies and even British New Wave of the 80s. Produced by **Roger Moutenot**, who had worked with Yo La Tengo and Freedy Johnston, this was a set of songs steeped in pathos – an eclectic mix of gently driving pop with horns, loops, keyboards and percussion. Following a loose narrative thread (a couple's life from marriage to eventual separation), tracks such as "Feeling No Pain" were deviously catchy while "Christmas With Jesus", with its fuzzbox hooks, simmered with understated brooding.

With the success of UNDER COLD BLUE STARS, an ever-growing fan base and a new album due in late 2003 (entitled 1972 – reflecting the music of the year he was born), the self-deprecating Rouse is making waves that reach far beyond the confines of his couch and the brim of his ill-fitting alt-country hat.

⊙ **Dressed Up Like Nebraska** (1998; Slow River).
This fine debut features a collection of songs that convey both wistful longing and youthful exuberance.

⊙ **Under Cold Blue Stars** (2002; Slow River).
Though again varied in style, this set is a far more stark, haunting affair. The rock-tinged "Feeling No Pain" stands out (a cut allegedly written in an airplane toilet).

Michelle Bhatia

ROXY MUSIC

Formed London, 1971; disbanded 1976; re-formed 1978; disbanded 1983.

"We had everything in there from King Curtis to The Velvet Underground to systems music to 50s rock'n'roll." Phil Manzanera

When **Roxy Music** arrived in 1972 they signalled a new genre as much as a rock group. They were a brilliantly warped hybrid: far too intellectual and stylish to fit in glam-rock's cod futurism, and too strange, kitsch and sequined to represent any continuum with post-hippie prog-rock. Roxy Music, rather, was a fetishized projection of cinematic, rock-'n'roll and pop-art romanticism. The vision of singer and novice songwriter **BRYAN FERRY**, it was filtered and mutated by kindred conceptualists **Andy Mackay** (oboe/sax) and **BRIAN ENO** (synthesizer/tapes).

Ferry had studied in Newcastle under pop art innovator Richard Hamilton, a man arguably as important to the Roxy blueprint as Warhol had been to The Velvets. When Ferry moved to London to form a group around himself and bass player **Graham Simpson** (they'd played together in The Gas Board, a Newcastle R&B band), he began to evolve a style of cosmopolitan postmodernism shot through with an avant-garde sleaze-pop that could be danced to.

Andy Mackay was a trained classical player, whose interest in experimental musical performance had led to a friendship with the enigmatic Brian Eno, who had hired him to lecture at Winchester College Of Art. Eno was known for taking tape recorders apart and this random technical knowledge led to him being invited to operate Mackay's synth and become general technical supervisor. By then Ferry had made quite a coup by recruiting ex-Nice guitarist **David O'List**. This embryonic line-up was made even odder by the addition of classical avant-garde percussionist **Dexter Lloyd**.

Demo tapes were made, but there were personality clashes and O'List was swiftly replaced by **Phil Manzanera**, formerly of intricate avant-prog band Quiet Sun, while Lloyd gave way to **Paul Thompson** – a straight-ahead 4/4 drummer whose style became the band's rock-steady base.

Still with no bite from labels, 'Roxy Music' (the name was originally in ironic quotation marks) began playing gigs towards the end of 1971, revealing a bizarre aesthetic stew garnished with turbo-glam allure. Dressed like a sex-changed mermaid, Eno would electronically feed the instruments (including Ferry's already mannered voice) through his synths, while Ferry prowled the stage, orchestrating a sexy-tense, sneering vibrato. The band was a visual cacophony of satin and silver PVC, platform shoes, bejewelled shades and leather cladding. Eno, Manzanera and Thompson had long hair – which was just about the only thing that located them in 1971.

It was a link with prog-rock icons King Crimson that led to Roxy finally getting a deal. Ferry had auditioned as Crimson's singer after Greg Lake left in 1970; Crimson were on E. G. Management, who liked Ferry's songs and hyped them to an initially sceptical Island Records. The debut album ROXY MUSIC was released in June 1972, adorned with a sleeve that encapsulated a concept that was a red rag to arbiters of rock cred: Kari-Ann, a model introduced to Ferry by fashion designer Anthony Price, reclined in copious effusions of pastel pink and blue, sharing her silk sheet

with a gold record. Inside, modelled portraits of the band displayed 'clothes, make-up & hair by Anthony Price'. The sleeve notes, written by publicist Simon Puxley, simultaneously confused and clarified: 'musicians lie rigid-&-fluid in a mannerist canvas of hard-edged blackleather glintings, red-satin slashes, smokey surrounding gloom', he explained.

It was a smart, stunning debut, but it was their first single, "Virginia Plain" – perversely not included on the album – that blasted them into a star's orbit. A two-and-a-half-minute roller-coaster ride, it was based on a painting of Ferry's that explored the ambiguity of Virginia Plain as a girl, a locale and a cigarette. A real motorbike revving up in the studio ('You're so sheer/you're so chic/teenage rebel of the week'), a strange synth riff coaxed from Eno's VCS3, and a trick ending to catch out the DJs, all added to the charm. It reached #4 in the UK and was by far the best song of a truly awful chart era.

Bassist Simpson had been replaced by **Rik Kenton** by this time; he in turn soon left, heralding a succession of bassists called John: **John Porter**, **John Wetton** (ex-King Crimson) and **John Gustafson** were all involved for the next few years.

A less than satisfactory tour of America supporting old lags like Edgar Winter and Jethro Tull didn't dampen their zest, and in early 1973 Roxy were back with another strange hit single, "Pyjamarama", which again featured on no album and allowed Mackay a left-field roam on the B-side. Next up was FOR YOUR PLEASURE (1973), on the cover of which Amanda Lear tottered against a neon cityscape, leading a panther towards Ferry in chauffeur attire. Things had got weirder, more honed, and altogether more decadent. Even the hyper-sardonic dance cuts like "Do The Strand" and the manic "Editions Of You" couldn't prepare you for the bleak ethereality of the second side. "In Every Dream Home A Heartache" was an insidious, stretched-out elegy to a reclusive, twilight world of 'plain wrapper baby' auto-sex, but it was the closing title track that saw all the elements of Roxy Music coalesce into a startling evocation of melancholia, loneliness and dislocation. It was also Eno's finest hour with the band: using primitive tape loops and found sounds, he created an awesome sonic landscape for Ferry's strangest prose to linger.

Ferry was becoming increasingly prolific. In 1973 he created his first solo album of covers, THESE FOOLISH THINGS, and hit the singles charts with a brazenly commercial rendition of Dylan's "Hard Rain's Gonna Fall". He was also moving from exotic rock star to household name – a guest spot on the CILLA BLACK TV show, and the emergence of the white-tuxedo-and-bow-tie-lounge-lizard image confirmed his interest in some sort of crossover.

'What it lacks for me is insanity', claimed Eno as he left the band in July of that year, his fervent experimentalism having become incompatible with Ferry's smoother aspirations – to say nothing of the threat Eno's cross-dressing presented to Ferry's standing as visual focus. As Eno set off on his extraordinary solo career, Ferry drafted in **Eddie Jobson** on neon violin and keyboards, a precocious talent who had played with **CURVED AIR** before joining Ferry during his solo work.

STRANDED, released at the end of 1973, continued Roxy's ascendance, reaching #1 in the UK chart. With Eno gone, the ensemble collisions of Roxy's original formation might have been shed, but Ferry's ability to create a widescreen *tour de force* was undimmed. "Song For Europe" had a haunting, even ridiculous, sense of elegance ('And the bridge ... it sighs') and co-writer Mackay's oboe and sax embellishments found a new sublimity. The single from the album, "Street Life", hurled its existential trash-aesthetic ('education is an important key/but the good life's never won by degrees... ') into the chart, too, with Jobson's violin providing a different icing on a different cake.

Incredibly, given all the side-projects that were on the go – Ferry solo at the Albert Hall; Manzanera dropping in on sessions with Eno, John Cale, Robert Wyatt and reactivating Quiet Sun; Mackay tooting with Mott and recording as Eddie Riff – the fourth Roxy album, COUNTRY LIFE (1974), was strange and hyperbolic enough to represent a last blast of the real Roxy Music. It reached #4 in the UK and made a first inroad into the US Top 40. Had they stopped

here, Roxy would have been a legend for ever.

There was no intention of that, however, as Ferry led the band off on tour with a Price-designed 'GI look' and host of babe backup singers. It increasingly looked like a camp circus spinning around someone whose ego had begun to transcend all irony. The proof came with the sterile SIREN (1975) and its languid big hit single "Love Is The Drug". Yes, you could dance to it, but nothing seemed to happen in the song. Motown-inspired bass lines and lyrics about cruising singles bars were a glimpse of the obsessions Ferry would consolidate when he rather desperately re-formed the band two years after they'd sensibly split in 1976.

The comeback, though, was understandable. Punk had rendered Ferry's solo projects less than crucial listening, and a revived Roxy seemed to offer a chance to realign his creative powers. However, despite the involvement of Mackay, Manzanera and Thompson, the project was Ferry's from now on, as he reinvented himself as godfather of elevator smooch music. MANIFESTO, delivered in 1979, was full of fragile pop vignettes concerning the bittersweet follies of love ("Dance Away", "Angel Eyes"). FLESH & BLOOD (1980) and AVALON (1982) were arch, highly polished, formulaic winners, each with their moments of pop-craft brilliance, but what was left of Roxy Music was little more than a meticulously resprayed and unthreatening pop; soundtracks for a fantasy uptown paradise.

- **Roxy Music** (1972; EG).
  From the muted buzz of collective cocktail chatter to a finale with Ferry crooning 'and that should make the cognoscenti think', this was an arrogant, knowing, wonderful debut.

- **For Your Pleasure** (1973; EG).
  Roxy Music crystallizing their own genre on the album Ferry refers to as 'The one that captured what I wanted to do most clearly'.

- **Stranded** (1973; EG).
  With Eno gone, this is slicker than the previous albums, but it's still an iconoclastic record, with touches of delicious kitsch.

- **Country Life** (1974; EG).
  Shorter songs and a much heavier unfrilled rock dynamic at work – notably Manzanera's guitar on perhaps their best single, "All I Want Is You". Ferry's lyrics and intonations on the warped "Casanova" make it his last great moment with Roxy.

- **The Thrill Of It All** (1996; Virgin).
  This four-CD set is perfect for fans who never replaced the vinyl, or newcomers, picking from the nine studio albums and the 1976 live farewell, VIVA. The first two discs are devoted to Roxy I, the third highlights the second coming, while a fourth gathers the non-album singles along with various extended remixes.

Chris Brook

ROYAL TRUX

Formed Chicago, 1989; split 2001.

Royal Trux were conceived via the strange, pulpish imaginations of **Jennifer Herrema** and **Neil Hagerty**, once the guitarist with

PUSSY GALORE. Based in Chicago, the duo started out performing as a singularly odd lo-fi 'art' project, intent on producing an unholy marriage of free-form discordance and garbled, scuzzy, sci-fi imagery.

The fruits of this bad trip to the pharmacy can be found on their first album ROYAL TRUX (1988), and even more so on the follow-up, the self-produced TWIN INFINITIVES (1990), both released on the Drag City label. With titles such as the fifteen-minute "(Edge Of The) Ape Oven" and "Yin Jim Versus The Vomit Creature", the record inevitably drew comparisons with other uncompromising avant-garde art terrorists – particularly Captain Beefheart's TROUT MASK REPLICA and the parodic dissonance of early Frank Zappa. However, if Zappa's dissection and reassembly of musical textures was a playful experiment, Royal Trux's often unlistenable mess of sound (howls, feedback, rants and sound effects) seemed more an inability to do anything else.

The follow-up, also called ROYAL TRUX (1992), was a more disciplined attempt to produce fully realized 'songs'. The music followed more traditional patterns, but almost invariably journeyed along a trail towards the furthest outposts of narcotic-drenched blues – a scary journey best avoided by the faint-hearted.

With 1993's CATS AND DOGS (made with session musicians) the band reined in their excesses a lot further in favour of a sinewy rock sound, hinting that a great rock'n'roll band was waiting in the wings.

Signing to Virgin in 1994, Royal Trux became a quintet for THANK YOU (1995). Likened to The Stones' STICKY FINGERS, it also drew inspiration from the unfashionable heads-down 70s boogie of Black Oak Arkansas and Grand Funk Railroad. Produced by David Briggs (of Neil Young fame), THANK YOU recalled a time when hard rock retained the hip-shaking residues of its small club origins, before heavy metal brutalized those traces away. Briggs allowed space behind the beats, leaving the bass and rhythm guitar to propel the 70s-styled grooves, as the band started to shoot from the hip, rather than the vein. Not that this was a traditional 'straight rock' album: atonally growled vocals and the bizarre lyrics of "The Sewers Of Mars" and "Shadow Of The Wasp" kept their edge of cool outsiderdom, an image maintained on a 1995 tour with Teenage Fanclub and kept up even through the recording of SWEET 16 (1997).

In this second full-length recording, a lot of the relatively tight control seen in the production of THANK YOU had been allowed to loosen – one of the tracks, "Don't Try Too Hard", has valuable advice for the duo in its title – and this lack of focus undeniably detracts from the album. SWEET 16 polarized opinions with its feral brew of dubbed-up glam-rock and conspiracy-theory-fuelled noise terrorism. Virgin/Hut hated it and dispensed with the band's services, slipping them a cool $1.3 million as a golden handshake. The money from Virgin was allegedly invested in Wall Street and the pair have become astute fiscal operators.

Herrema and Hagerty went to live wild in the woods, built their own studio and unleashed the trashy, dumb, catchy pop classic that is ACCELERATOR (1998). Of course, the phrase 'catchy pop classic' means something completely different once you enter Truxworld, the set retaining that familiar toxic noise on "White Light/White Heat" and vicious power-riffing on "Achilles Last Stand". Hard to believe, ACCELERATOR also drew on the bubblegum pop ethos of *The Banana Splits*, with the band running through inane slogans and sing-along tunes – though artfully bludgeoning them with effects pedals and strangled vocals.

Now freed from any major label restrictions and well established at Domino, the group following the well-received five-track AUDIO/VIDEO EP with POUND FOR POUND (both 2000), their fifth album in five years. It was a triumphant and sporadically radio-friendly set, yet again was quietly received.

As **Adam & Eve**, Hagerty and Herrema were also busy producing such American indie rock luminaries as Palace, The Make Up, Edith Frost, Delta 72 and Brother JT. Yet in early 2001 it seemed that American-indie's John Travolta and Olivia Newton-John had split. Though it may just have been a ruse to garner more publicity for Hagerty's solo debut, NEIL MICHAEL HAGERTY (2001), there has been no sign of Herrema since.

As for Neil's solo debut, it sounding like Clinic raised on Budgie and Blue Öyster Cult instead of the Velvet Underground, NEIL MICHAEL HAGERTY was the sound of a classic rock casualty, sitting alone in his well-kitted-out studio vamping on his toy keyboards and wigging out on his guitars to the heavenly sound he conjured in his head. It was followed by a second solo collection, ...PLAYS THAT GOOD OLD ROCK AND ROLL (2002). The same year also saw Neil playing in a new Drag City band, **Weird War**, and the emergence of a Royal Trux offering from the vaults: HAND OF GLORY was a long-lost album from the same era as TWIN INFINITIES and featured a difficult mass of crazed funk, guitar and gruelling looped tape arrangements. Though interesting, it by no means made up for the lack of fresh Trux material.

In 2003 Hagerty released a third solo record, THE HOWLING HEX, a sprawling concept album of hard rock and noise experiments. His best yet, it further hinted that Royal Trux had once and for all been laid to rest.

Royal Trux

⦿ **Thank You** (1995; Hut/Virgin).
In which Royal Trux distil their wasted, narcotic ramblings into tight, swaggering rock'n'roll music – the 'shake your hips' groove of EXILE ON MAIN STREET reinvented for a more fractured era.

⦿ **Singles, Live, Unreleased** (1997; Domino).
An uneven, occasionally startling selection of radio sessions and uncompromising live recordings. The current taste for US 'lo-fi' bands such as Guided By Voices and Yo La Tengo has resulted in some belated recognition for the Trux, although this remains a million miles from the lo-fi mainstream. Handle with care.

⦿ **Pound For Pound** (2000; Domino).
Easing off the distortion and the artsy indulgence that has sometimes marked them out as noise-core ghetto dwellers, Royal Trux here concocted their best album to date, which will appeal to a mainstream rock crowd as well as their regular devotees. Supercool maximum rock 'n' roll at its best.

Neil Michael Hagerty

⦿ **The Howling Hex** (2003; Drag City).
This outstanding double-album bursts with fine rockin' songs. That said, the set seems to last an eternity and would have benefited from a little pruning – keep your finger near the 'Skip' button on your CD player.

Nig Hodgkins

THE RUNAWAYS

Formed Los Angeles, 1975; disbanded 1979.

The Runaways have seldom received their due. They are significant not just because they were the first all-female guitars-and-drums band to achieve prominence, but because their music was a unique hard-rock variant charged with teenage energy and conviction.

By the time 16-year-old guitarist/vocalist **JOAN JETT** suggested forming an all-female band to her acquaintance **Kari Krome** (aged 14), Krome was already signed as a lyricist to music-business maverick **KIM FOWLEY**, whom she had impressed with a sample of her writing at a Hollywood party for Alice Cooper. Krome wasn't interested in performing, but felt her material should be sung and played by girls her own age. Fowley made an exploratory call to Jett, and within a few days drummer **Sandy West** (16) was drafted in for a jam session. They jelled immediately, Fowley was installed as manager, and bassist/vocalist **Micki Steele** (19) joined soon after.

These Runaways played their first professional engagement in late August 1975, less than a month

Runaways Jackie Fox, Micki Steele, the ever-fetching Joan Jett, and Lita Ford

after forming. Crude demos recorded even earlier (released in 1991 as BORN TO BE BAD) reveal that Jett's distinctive muted rhythm guitar style, the biggest determining element of The Runaways sound, was already well developed. Steele, however, failed to generate the required excitement on stage, and was replaced by vocalist **Cherie Currie**; with the addition of flashy lead guitarist **Lita Ford** and bassist **Jackie Fox** all changes were completed. Median age of the final line-up was 16.

Appearances in the Los Angeles area made an enormous impact, and in February 1976 The Runaways signed to Mercury, who released their first album, produced by Fowley, in May. THE RUNAWAYS was compressed heavy metal: short, incisively catchy high-energy songs, dense sound and arrangements, no rambling, no boring guitar solos – the only other debut of comparable force and intent released that year was THE RAMONES.

Heavy press coverage, however, failed to translate into sales, and soon The Runaways had problems. There was a suspicion that the band were a manufactured novelty (an idea Fowley encouraged); their unabashedly sexual act attracted leering attention; and the extra attention accorded to Currie, who had been pictured alone on the album's front cover, was contributing to internal friction. Still, after a European tour, the band returned to California to record a second album. QUEENS OF NOISE (1977) was a concept LP of sorts, the diary of a band caught on the roller coaster of decadent Hollywood. Effectively synthetic production by Fowley and ex-Sparks guitarist Earle Mankey raised the glitter factor, while supporting the queasy mood.

During a June tour of Japan, where The Runaways were genuine superstars, Jackie Fox quit, and when

bad feeling among the remaining members finally came to a head – soon after the arrival of replacement bassist **Vicki Blue** – Currie left too. The capable Jett was sole lead singer on WAITIN' FOR THE NIGHT (1977), a more metallic, less distinctive album, but including a few great songs – "School Days", "Wait For Me", "Waitin' For The Night", the last a co-credit for Kari Krome, long withdrawn from the team.

Though LIVE IN JAPAN (1977) was terrific, the band was now in terminal decline. They split from Fowley in early 1978, and released AND NOW ... THE RUNAWAYS – an album thin on material, low on chemistry and poorly produced – in Japan and a few other territories late that year, but didn't even try it in the US or UK until the band was over. That happened on New Year's Eve 1978, when they played a final gig in San Francisco.

Currie subsequently released two slick, enjoyable solo LPs in 1978 and 1980, the first with Fowley producing, the second a team-up with sister Marie, and has had some success as an actress. Sandy continues to play and sing with her own band, while Jackie Fox is a Harvard-trained lawyer. Micki Steele became a **BANGLE**; Lita Ford and Joan Jett became solo stars.

◉ **The Runaways** (1976; Polygram, Japan).
Features evergreen teenage anthem "Cherry Bomb" and the strange and wonderful "American Nights".

◉ **Queens Of Noise** (1977; Polygram, Japan).
A pop-metal pinnacle, encompassing driven rockers ("I Love Playin' With Fire", "Take It Or Leave it") and doleful ballads ("Midnight Music", "Heartbeat").

◉ **Live In Japan** (1977; Mercury, Japan).
Perhaps the very best from an era of classic hard-rock live albums (Cheap Trick's LIVE AT BUDOKAN is the challenger). Includes essential tracks "I Wanna Be Where The Boys Are" and "All Right You Guys", not on the studio LPs.

Robert Coyne

RUN-D.M.C.

Formed New York City, 1982; disbanded 2002.

Run-D.M.C. was the hip-hop group that took rap music back to a tougher 'street' level. Formed by **Joseph Simmons** (Run), **Daryl McDaniel** (D.M.C.) and **Jason Mizell** (Jam Master Jay) in 1982, their songs weren't marathon party-orientated funk anthems, they wore their street clothes on stage and their voices were far rougher than those of The Furious Five, The Sugarhill Gang and other contemporary competitors. Their first single, "Sucker M.C.'s", gave them the jump on the competition and started a new street music revolution.

On their first album, RUN-D.M.C. (1983), the music was pared down to two voices, with occasional record scratches from Jam Master Jay laid thick over a heavy drum-machine backbeat. When a little extra was needed in the mix it was kept to a minimum – an occasional synth blast or funk bass line here ("It's Like That") and some Hendrix-style metal guitar there ("Rock Box"); nothing much to get in the way of their new bragging rhyme style and socially conscious messages. The album blazed the trail for many a rapper to come and the preaching style foretold Run's subsequent career as a reverend.

Their next album, KING OF ROCK (1985), was a temporary letdown. In their frenzy to 'keep it real' they almost drove their trademark sound into the ground with dull, formulaic beats replacing fresh ideas. Yet they managed to return to strength with RAISING HELL (1986), which went on to become the first African-American double-platinum-selling hip-hop album. An improvement on their 'huge beats with a minimal arrangement' formula, the album featured the first metal/hip-hop collaboration ("Walk This Way" with **AEROSMITH**) and won back the attention of the growing hip-hop audience. The single was a crossover success on the pop charts and, combined with their triumphant role in the Raising Hell tour of 1986–87 (appearing alongside Public Enemy, The Beastie Boys, and L. L. Cool J), brought them back in style and saw them featured in 1986 as the first African-American rap act to make the cover of Rolling Stone magazine.

RAISING HELL's producers Russell Simmons and Rick Rubin financed a flick in 1988 – *Tougher Than Leather* – with Rubin directing, which, whilst not exactly the second coming of *The Harder They Come* or *Shaft* (or even *Wild Style*, for that matter), had a Run-D.M.C. soundtrack that did steady business and would've made a good double album with the best of RAISING HELL. Run and D.M.C. remained lyrically sharp – even on an odd cover of The Monkees' "Mary Mary" (with thankfully no members of The Monkees in sight).

The hip-hop revolution was still going on. But revolutions, once they get started, sometimes see the mob outpacing the leaders. A brand new wave of rappers would leave Run-D.M.C. in the dust both artistically and financially. By late 1989, young guns were aiming for the hip-hop throne from all over. Rhyme-style-wise, Run and D.M.C. were beginning to sound old when compared to the flows of the Cold Chillin Records posse (Big Daddy Kane, Biz Markie, Kool G. Rap) and the Native Tongues crew (De La Soul, A Tribe Called Quest). Music-wise, even their sparse arrangements looked weak next to the sounds of Boogie Down Productions and Raising Hell tour mates Public Enemy. Finance-wise, Tone Loc's WILD THING matched RAISING HELL's double-platinum sales in a few months. Even street-wise, the authenticity they had pioneered was being redefined by Ice-T and NWA.

Their next couple of albums looked to new trends and guest appearances to spark renewed interest. BACK FROM HELL (1990) was their attempt at New Jack Swing-style R&B and is the weakest album they've ever made. The 'guest appearance mania' of DOWN WITH THE KING (1993) – which featured Pete Rock, C. L. Smooth and a number of other talented rappers – was incidental to the much-improved music, and the album proved they could hold their own with anybody from the new-skool rap crews.

After the early 90s the camp was pretty quiet. Jam Master Jay signed and produced Onyx and worked in A&R for Profile Records. Run, true to his socially conscious lyrics and tone, became a minister, started a Christian church and hip-hop label, Rev Run Records. Then, techno dance act Jason Nevins remixed "It's Like That" back to life for the speed-garage generation, selling millions worldwide to a new generation of break-dancing, Adidas-stomping, Saturday-night kids.

A new collection, CROWN ROYAL (1999), was much delayed and when it finally appeared, you could see why. With all the nu metal schlock, it seemed as if Fred Durst was more prominent on the album than DMC. But then again, maybe this was the inevitable outcome of calling themselves the kings of rock.

Tragically, the story of Run-D.M.C. came to a close in October 2002 when Jam Master Jay was shot and killed in a Queens recording studio, an incident that both shocked and appalled all quarters of the music industry, especially considering the group's longtime reputation as being the gentle giants of the hip-hop scene.

It was a sad end to a story of three true pioneers.

Run-D.M.C. (1983; Profile).
Huge beats, huge rhymes. One of the best hip-hop albums ever and an undeniable classic. Topnotch bragging and 'conscious' lyrics mixing well with amazing minimal production.

Greatest Hits 1983–1991 (1991; Profile).
The first hip-hop 'greatest hits' CD. This collection stands out for its inclusion of the hard-to-find "Together Forever" and oft-sampled "Here We Go" (who would have thought that one of the most popular samples ever would be D.M.C. simply saying 'Aw Yeah'?) The singles hold up even more than when they were originally released.

Chris Lark

TODD RUNDGREN

Born Philadelphia, 1948.

Todd **Rundgren** has achieved moments of pure genius in his recorded output, but has also released more unadulterated bombast than any other comparable artist. Ever the workaholic, he has balanced his own releases with a career as a respected producer and, as a techno whizzkid, moved into the 90s at the forefront of the CD-ROM experiment.

Rundgren emerged from his native Philadelphia in the late 60s as a member of **THE NAZZ**, whose musical licks were markedly Beatles-ish. Having gained valuable recording lessons with the band, Rundgren became in-house producer/engineer at Bearsville studios, and in the next few years built up a reputation working on albums by groups such as The Band, Badfinger and The New York Dolls.

Rundgren's first solo album, RUNT (1970), took its title from a nickname given him by Patti Smith, the pseudonym under which his first two sets were released. Echoing The Nazz's mix of hard-rocking songs and ballads, the stand-out track was "We Gotta Get You A Woman", whose infectious hook-line helped to create Rundgren's first hit. THE BALLAD OF TODD RUNDGREN (1971) followed and showed his skill as a melodic balladeer: "A Long Way And A Long Time To Go", "Wailing Wall" and "Boat On The Charles" featured Todd at his piano with just a gorgeous tune for company.

Recording under his own name, Rundgren then released his masterpiece, SOMETHING/ANYTHING? (1972), a double album, on three sides of which he played everything himself, recording the fourth with a studio group. This was Todd at the top of his game, taking on straight pop ("I Saw The Light", "It Wouldn't Have Made Any Difference"), psychedelic pop ("Couldn't I Just Tell You"), pop parody ("Wolfman Jack"), oddball whimsy ("Song Of The Viking"), hard rock ("Little Red Lights") and balladry ("Torch Song", "Cold Morning Light") with equal aplomb.

As the critics enthused about the new Brian Wilson, Rundgren proceeded to demonstrate the eccentricity that has dogged as well as enlivened his career. With a busy producing schedule still on the side, his own musical vision started to go off the rails. A WIZARD, A TRUE STAR (1973) was an attempt at reproducing a whole psychedelic trip on record, a triumph of concept over content with its synth-noodlings, the sound of dogs getting off, and tracks where the title was better than the song ("Just Another Onionhead"). Yet there were some superb songs on WIZARD. The Philly soul of "Sometimes I Don't Know What To Feel" and the medley of soul covers on side two, plus the shimmering synthesized beauty of "Just One Victory" and "Zen Archer", showed how focused Rundgren could be when he wanted.

TODD (1974) produced less evidence. One of the dullest double albums ever made, it covered a Gilbert And Sullivan song alongside a 3000-strong chorus for "Sons Of 1984", and suggested our hero was taking himself far too seriously. Rundgren then decided to launch a new prog-rock group on the world – **Utopia** – which saw him heading down the road of synthesized jazz-rock fusion complete with overblown lyrical conceits. Two albums of such stuff (no highlights) bracketed the solo album INITIATION (1975), which wasn't much better itself, with its weighty metaphysical concerns and a thirty-minute instrumental bogging down the excellent "Real Man".

Thankfully Rundgren rediscovered some of his old touch with FAITHFUL (1976), though one side was devoted to letter-perfect covers of classic 60s songs. But, with original material like the catchy "Love Of The Common Man", "Cliché" and the gorgeous eight minutes of "The Verb – To Love", Rundgren showed his pop sensibility had not been killed by all the art-rock fixations. A new-look Utopia even began moving towards more commercial grounds with OOPS WRONG PLANET (1977), and then Rundgren returned to his one-man act with HERMIT OF MINK HOLLOW (1978), his best for a long while. Despite the clunker of "Onomatopeia", Rundgren reconfirmed his hit-making potential (the awesome hooks of "Can We Still Be Friends?") and reeled off a string of typically great ballads, capping it all with the sublime chorus of "You Cried Wolf".

Nothing Rundgren has done since has matched this late-70s peak. A desultory live LP, BACK TO THE BARS (1979), and various forgettable Utopia outings, were followed by the solo HEALING (1981) and THE EVER POPULAR TORTURED ARTIST EFFECT (1983), which at least had the wonderfully moronic single "Bang The Drum All Day". A CAPPELLA (1985) was Rundgren alone with his multitracked voice, but was more strange than good.

The disbanding of Utopia in 1986 was followed by Rundgren's most coherent album for a while, NEARLY HUMAN (1989), which revisited the Philly soul style on tracks like "Parallel Lines" and "Fidelity". Ever the master of overstatement, Rundgren employed a full gospel choir on the final track. Unfortunately, the belated follow-up, SECOND WIND (1991), was a blast of hot air, and Rundgren returned once again to his old tricks.

More recently, there's been Rundgren's CD-ROM, NO WORLD ORDER (1993), on which he urged the listener to programme a personal running order. Whatever the merits of that, it contained a feast of worthwhile music – even Todd's attempts at rapping were surprisingly good. Indeed this album, and the interactive live shows to promote it, showed that this is one pop legend who's not content to trade on old glories into middle age.

By 1999 a superb series of digitally remastered classic albums had been prepared on the Castle label, including RUNT (1971), THE BALLAD OF TODD RUNDGREN (1971), SOMETHING/ANYTHING (1972), A WIZARD, A TRUE STAR (1973), TODD (1974) and, lastly, GO AHEAD, IGNORE ME, a 41-

track anthology. With the back catalogue given new impetus, Rundgren continued to capitalize on his archival trip and began issuing various live and rarities packages while also concentrating on his Internet activities. Sections of his autobiography appeared on his official website as well as various recordings that were available through subscription – a compilation of these songs was eventually issued as ONE LONG YEAR (2000). Despite all this studio and online activity Rundgren also found time to continue producing records for other artists and embark on several tours, making him possibly one of the busiest contemporary rock musicians in the world.

⦿ **The Ballad Of Todd Rundgren** (1971; Bearsville). The cover picture of Rundgren sitting at the piano with a rope around his neck neatly sends up the singer-songwriter movement, while the contents affirm his ability as a balladeer of the highest order.

⦿ **Something/Anything?** (1972; Bearsville). Not only the starting point for anyone interested in investigating Rundgren's music, but one of the greatest distillations of popular music ever recorded. A masterpiece.

⦿ **Hermit Of Mink Hollow** (1978; Bearsville). A welcome antidote to the prog-rock horrors of Rundgren's mid-70s Utopia work, this is an album that demonstrates the merits of a great tune.

⦿ **Anthology** (1993; Rhino). The best Rundgren compilation available, taking in his work with Nazz, and cherry-picking songs from albums that might otherwise be overlooked. If you can't track the Rhino disc down, Castle's ANTHOLOGY offers a satisfactory alternative.

Nicholas Oliver

RUSH

Formed Toronto, 1968.

It's astonishing to think that **Rush** have had more than a thirty-year career, since convening in Toronto in September 1968. It's a long time in hard rock, even with sci-fi concept albums to keep the albums flowing.

The band was formed by **Alex Lifeson** (guitar) and **Geddy Lee** (vocals/bass) with drummer **John Rutsey**, who left after six years – a mere transient in Rush terms – to be replaced by **Neil Peart**. It was a crucial change, for it's been Peart's lyrics and percussion that have set Rush apart from their hard-rock rivals over the years, along, of course, with Lee's high-pitched singing – an immediately identifiable element of their sound, with the power to alienate or entrance in seconds.

With Peart in place, Rush signed to Mercury, and proceeded to record four albums in under two years – RUSH (1973), FLY BY NIGHT (1975), CARESS OF STEEL and 2112 (both 1976). The first three sold poorly, and the band landed some incongruous support slots – including a 1975 tour with Aerosmith and Kiss. 2112, based on a work by the hyper-right-wing novelist Ayn Rand, wasn't a big seller either, but it won them a loyal fan base, which helped the live ALL THE WORLD'S A STAGE (1976) become the first Rush album to reach the US Top 40.

A FAREWELL TO KINGS (1977) repeated the trick on both sides of the Atlantic, as did 1978's HEMISPHERES, and PERMANENT WAVES (1980), which not only hit the British and American Top 5 but even spawned a major hit single in "The Spirit Of Radio". Rush were throwing off the shackles of prog-rock and heavy metal, although many critics simply accused them of plagiarizing The Police, whereas previously they had been dismissed as Led Zeppelin clones.

The 80s were a period dominated by sell-out tours and an annual album of unwavering quality: from MOVING PICTURES and the double live LP EXIT ... STAGE LEFT (both 1981), to HOLD YOUR FIRE (1987). But by the decade's end even Rush enthusiasts were worried that the band had fallen into a rut, where only the cover art and the fall-off in Lifeson's playing distinguished one release from another. A career low came with yet another live album, the lacklustre A SHOW OF HANDS (1989).

Happily, a change of label from Mercury to Atlantic resulted in a new lease of life for Rush. Coming after the triple-LP compilation of CHRONICLES (1990), ROLL THE BONES (1991) and COUNTERPARTS (1993) were their freshest offerings in a decade, and both made the US Top 3. They returned to the well-worn prog-rock they know so well for TEST FOR ECHO (1996), a wise move for a band whose major strengths lie in skilled playing rather than in perceptive lyrics. Another live album – this time three CDs' worth, DIFFERENT STAGES – followed a couple of years later, and proved to be something of a departure from the usual Rush gig format with the first two discs concentrating on material recorded during the *Test For Echo* tour, and the third disc showcasing an old 1978 radio recording from London's Hammersmith Odeon (as it was then). A veritable treasure trove of vintage classics was up for grabs. More recently, Lee dabbled in the world of solo projects with MY FAVORITE HEADACHE (2000), before the band decamped to the studio to work on VAPOR TRAILS, which was released in early 2002, leading to the promise that their first tour in five years would include a whole host of older and neglected material.

To the irritation of critics and the delight of fans, they can now do whatever they like, whenever they like.

⦿ **2112** (1976; Mercury). Highly entertaining prog-rock, with an influence on countless subsequent concept albums like Queensrÿche's OPERATION: MINDCRIME.

⦿ **Moving Pictures** (1981; Mercury). A favourite among fans, this includes the single "Tom Sawyer", later sampled by rap act Young Black Teenagers on the grounds that 'It's the phattest shit and it deserves to be rekindled'.

⦿ **Counterparts** (1993; Atlantic). Ferocious but tuneful, with Lifeson back to the fore.

⦿ **Retrospective Vol I and Vol II** (1997; Atlantic). Volume I covers 1974–80, the second covers the years 1980–87. Both outclassing and replacing CHRONICLES, these two albums give the perfect summary of a long and respectable career.

Bruno MacDonald

THE RUTS

Formed London, 1978; disbanded 1983.

Hard-punk outfit **The Ruts**, noted for their love of reggae and solid musicianship, were formed by **Malcolm Owen** (vocals), **Dave Ruffy** (drums), **Vince Segs** (aka John Jennings; bass) and **Paul Fox** (guitar). Their early years were characterized by relentless gigging, honing a set of breakneck stormers like "Criminal Mind" and "Human Punk", which were interspersed by slower, reggae-influenced numbers. They played numerous Rock Against Racism benefits, often appearing on the same bill as London reggae artists Misty.

January 1979 saw a first wave of national recognition. A debut single, "In A Rut", financed by Misty's People Unite label, was an excellent mix of heavy power chords and a barked chorus of 'You're in a rut, and you gotta get out of it!' Although it missed Britain's Top 40, the band were rewarded with three sessions for BBC Radio, and a contract with Virgin.

The second single, "Babylon's Burning", was even better: opening with emergency sirens, it featured an irresistible escalating punk riff and lyrics decrying the pressure cooker of Britain's inner cities. A commercial breakthrough, it reached the UK Top 10 in May 1979, but live appearances were beginning to attract the unwelcome attentions of skinheads, some of whom did not share the band's anti-racist stance.

The consequent violence became a source of great depression, especially for Owen, whose heroin habit was also causing problems. Nevertheless, The Ruts' debut LP, THE CRACK (1979), demonstrated that musically they were one of the most accomplished products of the punk rock era. Numbers like "Something That I Said" (the third single) and "Savage Circle" were tuneful power-punk anthems, and "Jah War", an account of an anti-National Front riot, underlined their mastery of dub rhythms, while "SUS", a song about excessive police powers, showed their political commitment hadn't cooled.

"Staring At The Rude Boys", their first single of the 80s, was the band's most accessible, and charted Top 30 in the UK. Tragically, though, it was to be their epitaph: in July 1980, Malcolm Owen's heroin-related death brought everything to a halt.

Virgin cashed in with a compilation of old material, GRIN AND BEAR IT (1980). Meanwhile, the remaining Ruts regrouped with **Gary Barnacle** (saxophone/keyboards), and with Fox taking over as lead vocalist, as **Ruts DC** (from the Latin da capo, meaning 'from the beginning'). But the creative chemistry had gone, and two further albums – ANIMAL NOW (1981) and RHYTHM COLLISION DUB VOL. 1 (1982) – were a disappointing mix of pop-punk, funk and reggae.

By 1983 the band had disintegrated. Ruffy joined **AZTEC CAMERA** and Barnacle became a busy session musician. Nevertheless, the original band's influence lived on: bands as diverse as New Model Army and Nirvana cited them as an inspiration, and posthumous releases such as THE RUTS LIVE (1987) and THE BEST OF THE RUTS (1995) have testified to their continuing appeal.

⦿ **The Crack** (1979; Virgin).
The Ruts' only complete album, this features "Babylon's Burning" and the proto-hardcore "Criminal Mind", a close contender for the LP's best track.

⦿ **The Peel Sessions** (1990; Strange Fruit).
A wonderfully raw historical document, this features one-take recordings of the early singles.

Roger Sabin

THE SABRES OF PARADISE

Formed London, 1990; disbanded 1995.

It is hard to believe that **Andy Weatherall** had never set foot inside a recording studio before the day he transformed **PRIMAL SCREAM** from under-achieving guitar rockers into innovative dance-floor groovers. It was his radical reconstruction of the group's ballad, "I'm Losing More Than I'll Ever Have" (1990), into the club landmark "Loaded" that pointed the way forward for British dance music as well as prompting a slew of white-boy guitar groups to seek studio wizards like Weatherall and Paul Oakenfold in order to gain credibility in the clubs. With "Loaded", 'indie-dance' (or 'dance-rock') was born, and its force was confirmed in 1991 with Weatherall's ground-breaking production of Primal Scream's SCREAMADELICA, and by his remix work for the likes of Saint Etienne, Galliano and Happy Mondays.

Weatherall had emerged from an eclectic background of Ibiza club culture (and Shoom!, the London club that brought the Balearic vibe to British shores), the soulboy scene, dub, *Boys Own* (the dance music fanzine and record label), punk rock, and the DIY sampler aesthetic of the late 80s. At the end of the Balearic boom, he formed the three-piece **Sabres Of Paradise** group with producers **Jagz Kooner** and **Gary Burns**, as well as setting up his own Sabres Of Paradise label, with its distinctive packaging and underground direction. Other activities included the label offshoot Sabrettes (bossed by Weatherall's one-time girlfriend, Nina Walsh), the Sabresonic club in London and nomadic DJing slots across Britain.

SABRESONIC (1993), the Sabres' debut album for the influential Sheffield label Warp, was a characteristic mishmash of influences both contemporary and historical, drawing upon the spirit of electro, Brian Eno, Lee Perry, film soundtracks, Detroit techno and even Alan Vega's Suicide. The LP was preceded by the atmospheric single "Smokebelch", which gained favour in DJ sets the length and breadth of the UK.

While working with Weatherall as Sabres Of Paradise, Kooner and Burns branched out into side-projects with the urban collective **The Aloof**, producing a fine album, COVER THE CRIME (1994). Weatherall continued to put out quality material like Secret Knowledge's "Sugar Daddy", Musical Science's "Musical Science" and Jack Of Swords' "Vegagod" – all featured on the Sabres Of Paradise compilation SEPTIC CUTS (1994).

The second Sabres Of Paradise album, HAUNTED DANCEHALL (1995), was a trawl through the underbelly of a nightmarish London of blades, gangs and alleyways. With its fictional narrative, the set was more focused than SABRESONIC, without abandoning the freestyle pluralism of the band's musical palette. Tracks such as "Planet D" and "Tow Truck" picked up on and assimilated the innovations of Bristol triumvirate Massive Attack, Portishead and Tricky. The album produced a flurry of remixes from The Chemical (nés Dust) Brothers, Depth Charge, LFO, Nightmares On Wax, and In The Nursery, which were all collected on the SABRES OF PARADISE VERSUS collaboration.

At the end of 1995, Warp stated that Weatherall was no longer working with the others and that no further Sabres Of Paradise releases were planned. Since they split, Weatherall has taken a further left turn with a diverse body of work released under the **2 Lone Swordsmen** moniker in collaboration with **Keith Tenniswood**. Currently the duo are ploughing much of their time into a new label, The Rotters' Golf Club.

Weatherall remains an admirable rarity in that, just when he might have been expected to cash in on his Screamadelica reputation, he deliberately took his thing back underground and instead concentrated on his craft. The Sabres' sound was so innovative and prescient, however, that "Smokebelch" was adorning mobile phone ads on television five years after release of the group's last record.

The Sabres Of Paradise

⊙ **Sabresonic** (1993; Warp).
Featuring "Smokebelch", this is a definitive portrait of British industrial techno.

⊙ **Haunted Dancehall** (1995; Warp).
"Wilmott" shows that Weatherall has a sense of groove rather than a puritan allegiance to the clipped sparseness of techno minimalism.

2 Lone Swordsmen

⊙ **Stay Down** (1998; Warp).
A breathtaking collection of murky rhythmic oddness.

⊙ **Tiny Reminders** (2000; Warp).
A vast eclectic mass of dark electronics and chunky beats. Essential.

Michael Sumsion

SAINT ETIENNE

Formed London, 1989.

Named after legendary French football team, **Saint Etienne** was the creation of **Bob Stanley** and **Pete Wiggs**, childhood friends who dreamt of appearing on TV with their name emblazoned on the front of the bass drum. By their late teens, the pair's ambitions had extended to compiling party tapes, where diverse music jostled with snatches of film dialogue, writing fanzines and, in Stanley's case, work for music press weekly *Melody Maker*. It was a small step to starting a band, and in 1990 they did just that, recording Neil Young's "Only Love Can Break Your Heart" with Faith Over Reason's **Moira Lambert** on vocals. It became a British dance-floor anthem, edged into the US Top 100, and prompted the boys to a second single, this time reshaping The Field Mice's C86 classic "Kiss And Make Up" with vocalist **Donna Savage**.

With their third single, the self-penned "Nothing Can Stop Us" (1991), Saint Etienne's line-up expanded to include full-time vocalist **Sarah Cracknell**, although they have continued to use guest vocalists – rapper Q-Tee, Tim Burgess of The Charlatans, Stephen Duffy, Shara Nelson (formerly of Massive Attack), and French pop singer Etienne Daho. The regular band line-up was completed by engineer and guitarist **Ian Catt**.

The introduction of Cracknell as regular singer helped develop a sound as sweet as it was unsettling. This polarity of styles (matching the kitsch of pure pop with an 'indie-dance' leaning and an occasional sense of the avant-garde) was hardly surprising – the band have claimed Glen Campbell, George McCrae and The Fall as equally important influences. Armed with an instinctive and playful love for the pop single, the only drawback to Saint Etienne's masterplan has been a relative lack of consistent chart success: after the Spector-esque single "You're In A Bad Way" in early 1993, subsequent releases did not repeat its Top 20 success.

Their albums have generally sold more consistently, and their debut, FOXBASE ALPHA (1991), was nominated for Britain's inaugural Mercury Music Prize the following year. SO TOUGH (1993) was a more polished and focused affair, a brilliant and evocative tribute to London, complete with the eight-minute "Macarthur Park" pastiche "Avenue", which had scraped into the singles charts in the autumn of 1992. Meanwhile, there were darker treats to be found on their single B-sides, the pick of which were later highlighted on the compilation, YOU NEED A MESS OF HELP TO STAND ALONE (1993), named in homage to an early-70s release by The Beach Boys.

After a stab at the seasonal market with the exuberant "I Was Born On Christmas Day" at the end of 1993 (a duet with Tim Burgess which sadly underperformed in the UK charts), the trio's sound matured and warmed considerably on TIGER BAY (1994), which dared to be downbeat and melancholy, and introduced a folksy element on songs like "Former Lover". But even toe-tapping epics like "Pale Movie" failed to find a home in the Top 10, and Saint Etienne announced a temporary retirement at the end of that year.

This came as little surprise to those who had closely followed the band's outside projects: in 1991, Stanley and Wiggs founded the Ice Rink record label, home to Oval, Earl Brutus, Golden and (briefly) Shampoo. They also wrote and produced Cola Boy's 1991 hit single "7 Ways To Love", remixed tracks by Flowered Up, World Of Twist and The Boo Radleys, and masterminded Shara Nelson's exquisite Motown pastiche "One Goodbye In Ten" (1993). Sarah Cracknell, meanwhile, took time out to guest on **DAVID HOLMES**' 1995 album THIS FILM'S CRAP LET'S SLASH THE SEATS – "Gone" is a wondrous exercise in desolation – and released a solo LP in 1997 called LIPSIDE, which partly due to distribution problems by the ailing Total label was scarcely noticed by press or public.

In spite of these extracurricular activities Saint Etienne's life span was not timed out; a new song, "He's On The Phone", hit #11 in the UK charts at the end of 1995, their biggest hit so far. Its simultaneous inclusion on a singles retrospective compilation, TOO YOUNG TO DIE (1995), and an equally impressive remix package called CASINO CLASSICS (1996) kept the rumours of their demise alive.

Thankfully, their sporadic but welcome returns to the charts with the poppy GOOD HUMOR (1998), the more adventurous SOUND OF WATER (2000), and FINISTERRE (2002) have helped underline how firmly entrenched in British pop they have become. In May 2000, they even finally cracked the UK top ten when they teamed up with **Paul Van Dyk** on the trance anthem "The Riddle", a timely reminder of their dance-floor roots from some ten years earlier. A double-CD anthology, SMASH THE SYSTEM, also appeared in 2001, while Cracknell has also now firmly established herself as a solo artist.

⊙ **Foxbase Alpha** (1991; Heavenly/Warners).
The cut-and-paste 'party-tape' sound of Stanley and Wiggs lives on. Side one is a succession of three-minute pop gems; side two is less immediate but ultimately more rewarding, culminating in the chilling "Like The Swallow".

You Need A Mess Of Help To Stand Alone (1993; Heavenly/Warners).
Whether you want their dance-floor moments, their tear-jerking ballads or their genius for hummable melodies, it's all here. But if it's the singles you want, TOO YOUNG TO DIE is better.

Tiger Bay (1994; Heavenly/Warners).
Gone are the samples and gimmickry, replaced by a much more sophisticated veneer in the songwriting department. Sarah Cracknell's vocals have vastly improved – check out the exquisite ballad "Former Lover". Woefully overlooked on its release, this is still well worth investigating.

Too Young To Die – The Singles (1995; Heavenly/Warners).
One of the great singles bands of the 90s has their complete set of 45s collected on one album for the first time, and the result is a development of style and content.

Sound Of Water (2000; Mantra).
This ambitious but affecting album finds the group employing the pop/dance/avant-garde template of their earliest releases, but the content and songwriting is warmer and less detached than before.

Smash The System (2001; Heavenly).
A fine introduction to their varied output.

Justin Lewis

THE SAINTS

Formed Brisbane, Australia, 1975; disbanded 1992; re-formed 1997.

Brisbane's **Saints** predated the emergence of punk in Europe by more than a year, being formed in 1975 by seminal guitar stylist **Ed Kuepper**, along with his friends **Kim Bradshaw** (bass), **Ivor Hay** (drums) and **Chris Bailey** (vocals/guitars). With a high-energy, R&B-fuelled rock style, they set to, playing the Sydney circuit and recording a pulsating debut single, "(I'm) Stranded". The record was picked up by the New Wave vigilantes at London-based *Sounds* magazine, and suddenly the band found themselves as (sole) antipodean representatives on Britain's punk scene.

The subsequent first album, for old prog-rock label Harvest, was again called I'M STRANDED (1977), and much heralded by reviewers and a growing body of fans. From it came a second single, the fabulous "This Perfect Day" – which, thanks to considerable radio play from (naturally) John Peel and, unusually, Radio Luxembourg, became a UK Top 40 hit. With these records under their belts, The Saints seemed poised for, at the very least, 'alternative' stardom, especially as – like British contemporaries Eddie And The Hot Rods – they were able to straddle several styles and gained a following on London's R&B/pub-rock circuit as well as among the punks.

Sadly, personality clashes were to screw further development of what was a potentially great band, and The Saints' refusal to pander to punk fads made their demise rapid. First off, Ed Kuepper decided he had had enough, leaving the group in early 1978, just before the release of the second album, ETERNALLY YOURS. The album was still well received but sales were down.

On returning to Australia, the estranged guitarist formed the **Laughing Clowns**, who released the popular Kuepper-penned Saints' title cut "Eternally Yours" as their own single in 1984. The remainder of The Saints, meanwhile, continued gigging, and issued the album PREHISTORIC SOUNDS at the end of 1978. The indifferent reaction to this latest release prompted the line-up to disintegrate later in the year.

Disappointed with the break-up, Chris Bailey set about finding members for a new band, and eventually opted to keep the name Saints. His line-ups recorded a couple of unexceptional albums, MONKEY PUZZLE (1981) and CASABLANCA (1982), and, more interestingly, appeared as themselves in a movie version of TV's *The Saint*, as a resident club band.

In 1984 Bailey persuaded Hay to re-form the original Saints (without Kuepper), and they remained a prolific outfit through the decade. Their albums included A LITTLE MADNESS TO BE FREE (1984), the live IN A MUD HUT (1985) and, most impressive, ALL SAINTS' DAY (1986), which were picked up by old loyal followers and a new cult audience. The sales never looked hugely promising, however, and after a rushed-sounding studio set, PRODIGAL SON, and PERMANENT REVOLUTION (1992), The Saints went to ground.

They surfaced again in 1997 with HOWLING, another album of Stooges-style rock growled and bellowed in Bailey's best gargling-gravel voice. Sheer bliss to the committed, but just more of the same to the undecided. Since then Bailey has released numerous albums as a solo artist.

(I'm) Stranded (1977; Harvest/Sire).
Pure full-on early punk rock, stoked up with speed and attitude.

The Most Primitive Band In The World (1988; Mushroom).
Featuring one of the earliest live Saints performances recorded in Ed's mother's garage, this includes early classics such as "This Perfect Day", and also concert favourites "Lies", "Wild About You" and "Do The Robot". Awful sound and an (at best) approximate execution of the songs, a must-have for the more committed.

Jeremy Simmonds

RYUICHI SAKAMOTO

Born Nakano, Japan, January 17, 1952.

Probably doomed for eternity to be held up by the West as the epitome of Japanese pristine precision, **Ryuichi Sakamoto** actually started his career poking fun at such Asian stereotypes. After dabbling with academic music, a stint as a studio musician and 1978's strange solo album, 1000 KNIVES OF RYUICHI SAKAMOTO, Sakamoto (keyboards, percussion) formed the world's first 'techno-pop group', **YELLOW MAGIC ORCHESTRA**, in 1978, with **Haruomi Hosono** (bass/keyboards) and **Yukihiro Takahashi** (drums/vocals).

Their self-titled debut album (1979) was a collection of highly stylized synth-heavy pop pastiches that was largely ironic, but taken at face value by a Western audience that was still addicted to authenticity.

Typically, it was the nascent hip-hop community that appreciated their electro-scapes, and a maxi-single taken from the album featuring "Computer Game" and their cover of Martin Denny's "Firecracker" became a minor hit in the US largely on the back of "Firecracker"'s success in the Bronx. ("Firecracker" can be heard being cut to bits by Afrika Bambaataa on his legendary DEATH MIX EP.)

Yellow Magic Orchestra's skewering of Western Orientalism was taken to its extreme in their live appearances where the band would dress either as stereotypical Japanese businessmen with prim suits and cameras or in the uniforms of Communist China (causing some commentators to actually think they were Chinese). This idea reached its logical conclusion on the sleeve of X INFINITY MULTIPLIES (1980) which played on Occidental fears of the 'yellow devil' replicating like rabbits into an invasion force. With heretical covers of Archie Bell & The Drells' "Tighten Up" and The Beatles' "Day Tripper", the music inside didn't do much to assuage any anxieties created by the album cover.

Despite, or perhaps because of, their confidence games with identity, YMO became enormous pop stars in Japan and their pastiches quickly became suburban muzak. BGM (1981) suffered from a severe sense-of-humour failure, while albums like TECHNODELIC (1981) and NAUGHTY BOYS (1983) didn't make it out of Japan.

By this time, though, Sakamoto had his eyes on a solo career and in 1981 he released B-2 UNIT, which featured the electronic classic "Riot In Lagos". The following year found Sakamoto moving to London and collaborating with **DAVID SYLVIAN** and Robin Scott (aka M of "Pop Muzik" fame). YMO officially split in 1983 and Sakamoto reunited with Sylvian for the gamelan-influenced soundtrack to *Merry Christmas Mr. Lawrence*, in which Sakamoto also co-starred with David Bowie.

Working with **DAVID BYRNE**, Sakamoto's score for Bernardo Bertolucci's *The Last Emperor* (1987) won an Academy Award. Focusing on his concept of 'outernationalism' in which the world's boundaries dissolve, NEO GEO (1988) was produced by Bill Laswell and featured **Bootsy Collins**, the legendary drummer **Tony Williams** and **Iggy Pop**. More outernational still was "Calling From Tokyo" from BEAUTY (1990), which featured Senegalese vocalist **Youssou N'Dour** duetting with **Brian Wilson** on top of a rhythm provided by Indian tablas and reggae drummer extraordinaire **Sly Dunbar**, while Okinawan vocalists chanted in the background.

Sakamoto did more soundtrack work for Bertolucci on *The Sheltering Sky*, Pedro Almodovar (*High Heels*) and for Oliver Stone's *Wild Palms* TV series in the early 90s, while his own SWEET REVENGE (1994) moved his post-Tangerine Dream electro-chamber music into the corporate soul realm inhabited by Soul II Soul and M People.

As well as recording a post-ambient album for the British Ninja Tune label, Sakamoto went on to compose the soundtrack for Brian DePalma's *Snake Eyes*. Most recently he has found himself in a troop alongside **Jacques Morelenbaum**, playing romantic, bossa nova selections by the likes of Antonio Carlos Jobim. Two albums have been released under the moniker **Morelenbaum²/Sakamoto**, CASA (2002) and A DAY IN NEW YORK (2003).

- ⊙ **Ryuichi Sakamoto – B-2 Unit** (1981; Island). Featuring Sakamoto's weirdest recording, "Riot In Lagos", this is his edgiest, and best, record.

- ⊙ **Yellow Magic Orchestra – Techno Bible** (1992; Alfa).
You might have to go to Japan to find it, but this is probably the best of the available greatest hits packages of this very under-appreciated band.

Peter Shapiro

SALARYMAN

Formed Champaign, Illinois, 1996.

Salaryman, a corruption of the Japanese term for a devoted worker, is the alter ego of **The Poster Children** – a North American band which personified the die-hard indie work ethic – comprising married couple **Rose Marshack** and **Rick Valentin** (bass/vocals and guitar/vocals), Rick's brother **Jim** (guitar) and **Howie Kantoff** (drums). The four have threaded their post-Creation, melody-infected pop tunes for more than ten years, touring extensively and retaining complete artistic control over all their artwork and material, despite finally signing to the major label, Reprise.

In 1996, having been offered a support slot at a friend's forthcoming shows – on condition that they forwent their traditional instruments – the four Poster kids set about rediscovering their extensive collection of keyboards and electronic equipment before spending two days writing and recording songs. Rose's determination not to miss a favourite TV show led to the television being incorporated into their practice sessions, adding a random, improvised element to their sound – carried across into their live shows by having TV sets on stage (they prefer shopping channels).

Their debut album, SALARYMAN (1997), was recorded live over two days in Studio Tedium, located in their basement. A pleasing mix of simple, steady beats, underpinned by snatches of manipulated TV dialogue, thrumming keyboards and deft samples, all tinged with the warm glow of analogue electronics (including a theremin), the album demonstrates a firm grasp of the post-rock aesthetic. To complement the faceless, corporate spirit of the album, the various members became HDK, RGM, JEV and RNV.

Ironically, Salaryman found greater favour in Europe than in their native US, which has proved resilient to much electronic music, so they split themselves between indie-rock and electronic-rock identities on each side of the Atlantic. In 1997 the band toured Europe with Tortoise and Mouse On Mars as part of

City Slang's 'Wow! and Flutter' package, wowing audiences with their campy stage show, enhanced by flickering screens and the Salaryman 'uniform' of shirt and tie. Salaryman's success amongst the loosely grouped bands of the post-rock scene may be a one-off. The band members agree that Salaryman is a very different animal from The Poster Children, although the response has been overwhelmingly positive.

Post-rock, whether pushing the boundaries of instrumental music, fusing jazz, post-punk, electro and techno influences, has arisen from a maturing US (and to a lesser extent, UK) post-punk scene. As musicianship and songwriting abilities have improved, the trend towards the middle-aged spread that soured the tail end of punk has been eschewed for a more innovative, experimental approach. The support of an enthusiastic fan network and sympathetic record labels (and critics) has ensured the genre's success. To the categorizer, Salaryman belong to the offshoot of post-rock known as space rock. Salaryman's success among the loosely grouped bands of the post-rock scene has been steady, with the excellent VOIDS + SUPERCLUSTERS remix EP (1998) and their second album KAROSHI (1999) – appropriately, a Japanese term meaning death through over-work. As well as some fine music the latter featured extensive multimedia content including screensavers and a game, which is just as well because fans found themselves waiting a relatively long time for news of a third Salaryman album. In the meantime The Poster Children issued DDD (2000).

⊙ **Salaryman** (1997; City Slang).
Stand-out tracks include "Voids & Superclusters", with its stabbing sample and sawing bass, and the eerie closer, "Hummous", threaded with mysterious Eastern vocals.

⊙ **Karoshi** (1999; City Slang).
Thanks to the tight rhythmic interaction of live and drumpad percussion, oscillator tones, and scrawled guitars, Karoshi exudes a distinct electronic grooviness. From the intensely phased swoons of "Thomas Jefferson Airplane" via the scratches and barks of the mellow, organ-led "My Dog Has Fleas" to the almost choral title track, it's a mesmerizing ride.

Jonathan Bell

SAM & DAVE

Formed Miami, Florida, 1961; split 1970; reformed sporadically until 1981.

If the heyday of soul music has an anthem, **Sam & Dave**'s "Soul Man" would be as good a candidate as any. While the back-and-forth passion of gospel was at the centre of the duo's performances, their vocals were complemented by punchy, horn-driven arrangements and sophisticated songwriting that were thoroughly contemporary. Along with Otis Redding, they were the primary exponents of the sound of Stax, a label which stands for the best in Southern soul. Unlike Redding, their career was not short-circuited by tragedy but by incompatibility and unfortunate record company politics that cut off their access to Stax/Volt's support.

The gospel flavour of Sam & Dave is unsurprising, given their extensive roots in the music. **Sam Moore** sang with the Miami gospel groups the Gales and the Melionaires in the 1950s, and was even offered a spot in one of gospel's top acts, the Soul Stirrers (which he turned down). **Dave Prater** had also done time on the gospel circuit with the Sensational Hummingbirds. But by the time they hooked up at Miami's King Of Hearts nightclub in 1961, each was determined to enter the pop market.

Sam & Dave did some recording for the Marlin and Roulette labels before being signed by Atlantic A&R legend Jerry Wexler in the mid 60s. It was at Stax, an Atlantic affiliate, that they truly found their voice, with records that were really a collaboration between the singers, the great Stax house band of Booker T And The MGs, and the songwriting team of David Porter and Isaac Hayes. It's even been suggested that Porter and Hayes primarily adopted Sam & Dave as their chief vehicles because the staff songwriters were in need of somebody to sing their material.

Porter and Hayes couldn't have found better mouthpieces. The chemistry was already apparent on Sam & Dave's initial pair of flop singles for Stax, "A Place Nobody Can Find" and the chugging "I Take What I Want", both of which were as taut and fully developed as their hits. In late 1965, "You Don't Know Like I Know" made the R&B Top 10. But the follow-up, "Hold On! I'm A Comin'", was a much more important release, topping the R&B charts and becoming a pop hit as well. Driven by a compelling horn riff and impassioned, pleading chorus, "Hold On!" was, along with Wilson Pickett's "In The Midnight Hour", the song most responsible for spreading the gospel of the Stax sound.

Dave Prater would take the lead on most of Sam & Dave's Stax material, and over the next few years they were the most popular duo act in soul, equally capable of handling up-tempo dance tunes and emotional ballads. They spread their popularity to Europe in early 1967, when they toured with the Stax-Volt Revue, along with Otis Redding, Arthur Conley, and The MGs, winning raves (as they did everywhere) for their mesmerizing live act. They didn't make their true breakthrough to the pop audience, though, until late 1967, when "Soul Man" made #2 in the US. The record was a manifesto for soul music without being at all self-conscious; Steve Cropper's economic, biting guitar licks are some of the greatest decorative flourishes in all of rock and soul.

"I Thank You" gave the duo another US Top 10 hit in early 1968, but Sam & Dave would pass their peak by the middle of that year. When Stax's distribution deal with Atlantic ended, Sam & Dave – who had really been signed to Atlantic all along, rather than Stax – became exclusive to the Atlantic label. This meant that Booker T and his crew would no longer be backing them on record. It also meant that much of their work in the late 60s was not produced by Porter and Hayes, who had eventually assumed the production, as well as the songwriting, duties for Sam & Dave at Stax.

In Peter Guralnick's book *Sweet Soul Music*, Steve Cropper went as far as to claim that Jerry Wexler killed Sam & Dave's career after they were reclaimed for Atlantic. Their work actually didn't suffer that much – Atlantic was hardly the worst label for a soul act at the time. In truth, Sam & Dave probably wouldn't have lasted much longer, no matter which label issued their records: even at their commercial peak, it was rumoured that they barely spoke to each other off stage.

Still an extremely popular live attraction when they broke up in 1970, they reunited off and on for the next dozen years, but nothing could rekindle their commercial flames, or stop their descent into the nostalgia circuit. The Blues Brothers helped revive interest in Sam & Dave's work with their lame cover of "Soul Man" in 1979, but Sam Moore and Dave Prater would never perform together after 1981. Prater died in a car accident in 1988. Moore was last heard lending harmonies to Bruce Springsteen's 1992 album, HUMAN TOUCH.

⊙ **The Very Best Of Sam & Dave** (1995; Rhino).
Sixteen-track collection with all of the big hits, including "Soul Man", "Hold On! I'm A Comin'", "I Thank You", and lesser-known singles that were big items with R&B listeners.

⊙ **Sweat'N'Soul** (1993; Rhino).
Most listeners will be satisfied by THE VERY BEST OF, but this two-CD, fifty-track set is pretty consistent, and much more extensive, covering the Stax/Atlantic period 1965–71. It has all of their chart hits, some worthy B-sides and album tracks, and a couple of Sam Moore solo singles.

Richie Unterberger

SANDII & THE SUNSETZ

Formed Japan, 1977.

D espite heavyweight endorsements from the likes of David Bowie and the Eurythmics during the early 80s, **Sandii & The Sunsetz** never broke through to a truly worldwide audience from their Japanese base. What stymied their progress outside the country was Sandii's lack of a foreign deal, the consequently patchy availability of her records, and the strength of the yen, which put the price of Japanese imports up to as much as quadruple that of a domestic British or American disc.

Sandii (born Sandy O'Neale) and **Makoto Kubota** formed **Makoto Kubota And The Sunset Orchestra** – the proto-Sandii & The Sunsetz – in 1977. Sandii's striking looks were an advantage, and the cover of the debut album, EATING PLEASURE (1980), was an exploitative bid to feed male fantasies – an approach accentuated by songs such as "Sticky Love" (a Top 10 hit in Australia) and the wistful version of "Jimmy Mack". EATING PLEASURE's "Alive" was one of the finest Western-slanted Japanese pop songs of the 1980s, its Okinawan-tinged chorus stamping the track with pan-Asian promise, something that Sandii would explore and develop more assiduously in the 1990s. Haruomi Hosono of the Yellow Magic Orchestra produced the album and Sandii reciprocated by singing on YMO's XOO MULTIPLES (1980).

Hosono was invited back to produce the Sunsetz' HEAT SCALE (1981), by which point the Sunsetz line-up had settled down as Sandii (vocals), Makoto Kubota (vocals/guitars/piano/percussion), **Keni Inoue** (guitar/vocals), **King Champ Onzo** (bass/vocals) and **Hideo Inoura** (drums). HEAT SCALE was the first to bring Sandii & The Sunsetz to wider attention in Europe and the US. IMMIGRANTS (1982), one of the great Japanese pop artefacts of the 1980s, fed that interest by adroitly blending Western and Eastern technology and pop sensibilities. Nevertheless, The Sunsetz languished in the shadows, despite the release of Alfa/Sire's excellent anthology VIVA LAVA LIVA (1984).

By the late 1980s, Sandii was all but cast into the wilderness in the West, and exchange rates further ensured that BANZAI BABY (1986) made only a fleeting visit to the import racks. Back in Japan, Sandii and Makoto Kubota switched to making albums under Sandii's name, and with MERCY (1990) they returned to the fray. PACIFICA (1992) was another station in the evolution of Sandii's world-view, looking to Polynesia and Hawaii, while with AIRMATA (1993) Sandii turned her attention to Indonesian *dangdut* and other styles.

This re-creation of Asian music within a highly produced pop format came to fruition in DREAM CATCHER (1994), adorned with a sleeve by the French artist duo Pierre et Gilles depicting Sandii in screamingly over-the-top iconic madonna pose. The album incorporated influences from Indonesia, Malaysia, Singapore and Japan, mixed in with **Mamadou Doumbia**'s West African electric guitar. Its stand-out, however, was "Sunset-Million Years", a shooby-dooby-dooby pop-Brazilian ambience set against a muscular bass and drum groove.

It showed that Sandii had developed into a gripping and mature singer – and it's just a pity she didn't have the chance to prove it on a wider stage.

Sandii & The Sunsetz

⊙ **Viva Lava Liva** (1984; Alfa/Sire).
A fine retrospective of the Sunsetz' work from the early 1980s. Volcanically remixed or revamped material from EATING PLEASURE, HEAT SCALE and IMMIGRANTS make the lava flow.

Sandii

⊙ **Dream Catcher** (1994; Sushi).
Sandii's most recent pan-Asian excursions, brilliantly produced by Makoto Kubota.

Ken Hunt

SANTANA

Formed San Francisco, 1966.

"For pure spirituality and emotion, Carlos Santana is number one."
Eric Clapton

F ormed by Mexican-born guitarist **Carlos Santana** in October 1966, **Santana** introduced

American and European rock audiences to Latin influences – salsa and samba in particular – which they incorporated with blues and hard-rock influences to extraordinary effects of great immediacy. They're perhaps best remembered for their show-stealing appearance at Woodstock, featuring dazzling 16-year-old drummer **Mike Shrieve** and the subtle dynamics of Carlos's guitar work, but it's been a long career, with blinding highlights.

Santana's rhythm section – **Mike Carabello** and **Jose 'Chepito' Areas** (percussion), **Shrieve** (drums) and **Dave Brown** (bass) – were an astonishing driving force, way out front in the 60s, and a dream backdrop for the virtuosity of Carlos Santana and keyboard player **Gregg Rolie**. Santana, who had developed his skills in the red-light district of Tijuana, was one of the outstanding guitarists of the era, possessing a lyrical style and an ability to sustain a single note longer than anyone, and with limitless intensity.

Their first album, SANTANA (1969), was released on the back of the band's brilliant performance at Woodstock, and kicked off with the show-stealer, "Soul Sacrifice". Its appearance on the live album and film of the event helped push the album to #4 in the American charts and consolidate the band's position as one of the brightest new hopes of American music. ABRAXAS (1970), their second album, exceeded all expectations, spending weeks at #1 in the US and reaching #7 in the UK, fired up by single stand-out tracks – a cover of Fleetwood Mac's blues "Black Magic Woman" and a version of Tito Puente's salsa classic, "Oye Como Va" backed by "Samba Pa Ti", a paean to the guitar on which Carlos squeezed the last drops of spirituality.

Prior to the release of SANTANA III (1971), a second guitarist, future **JOURNEY** axeman **Neil Schon**, and an additional percussionist, **Coke Escovedo**, were added to the band. The sound was fleshed out and the playing ever more sophisticated, as the group incorporated additional percussive influences – notably from Brazil. It spent five weeks atop the US album charts.

Teaming up with drummer-vocalist **Buddy Miles** for a tour, they jammed their way through numbers by Miles and Santana hits like "Evil Ways". A live album from the tour, credited as CARLOS SANTANA AND BUDDY MILES LIVE (1972) was less than thrilling, but charted nonetheless, and if fans were disappointed then they had a dazzling new Santana album to make up for it, CARAVANSERAI (1972). This was a more reflective, less bluesy, effort, and saw line-up changes, with Brown, Carabello and Escovedo ousted by session men, and individual line-ups listed for each of the tracks. It was gorgeous stuff, but it was clearly the end of the original Santana.

The following year Carlos Santana teamed up with fellow guitarist **JOHN MCLAUGHLIN**, the duo declaring themselves followers of the Indian guru Sri Chimnoy and unveiling an album of John Coltrane and McLaughlin material, LOVE DEVOTION SURRENDER (1973). Credited to Carlos Devadip Santana and Mahavishnu John McLaughlin, it featured jazz-rock fusioneers Larry Young, Jan Hammer and Billy Cobham. It had something of a companion piece in WELCOME (1973), which Santana's record label promoted as the first fruit of **The New Santana Band**. Of the eight musicians, only Carlos, Chepito and Shrieve remained from the original line-up.

After another meditative jazz outing, ILLUMINATIONS (1974), pairing Carlos Santana and jazz harpist **Alice Coltrane** (John's widow), the Santana band's popularity was falling off. BORBOLETTA (1974) did little to revive it, but AMIGOS (1976) returned to an earthier sound and Columbia were allegedly so pleased with the result that they signed Carlos (it was, by now, clearly his group, Shrieve having left) to their biggest ever contract. They were given patchy rewards in the Santana albums and Carlos solo outings of the late 70s and early 80s, although there were occasional single hits, noably "Winning" (a US #17) from ZEBOP! (1981), probably the best album of the period.

During the late 80s and early 90s, Santana albums only just broke into the US Top 100 and failed to make any impact at all in the UK. However, live, the group remained formidable, and in 1982 they performed in front of their biggest audience since Woodstock: 400,000 turned up to a festival sponsored by Apple Computers' Steve Wozniak in San Bernadino. Three years later their twentieth-anniversary concert featured everyone who had ever played in the band. It was a good period for Carlos, providing music for the movie *La Bamba* in 1986 and receiving a Grammy for his album, BLUES FOR SALVADOR in 1989. A small cloud hovered when he was arrested in 1991 at Houston Airport for alleged possession of cannabis, but the sentence was a sensible one – to perform an anti-drug, fund-raising concert. He followed that with a trip back to Mexico, playing two concerts in his home town, Autlan de Navarro, during the course of which he joined his father Jose in a mariachi band.

Even with new backing from Polydor (who took

over Carlos Santana's label Guts And Grace in 1992), it seemed unlikely that Santana would ever regain anything like the following and position that they held in the early 70s. However, his guest appearance on the Grammy-nominated MISEDUCATION OF LAURYN HILL, playing on "To Zion", apparently tuned in a new generation's ears to his sublime skills and something quite unexpected happened in 1999's SUPERNATURAL. Largely due to the hit single "Smooth" and perhaps guest appearances from the likes of **Lauryn Hill**, SUPERNATURAL turned into a twenty-four carat success, netting Santana a record eight Grammys in 2000, a feat equalling Michael Jackson's similar award-storming success with THRILLER back in 1983. Now all Carlos had to do was ensure that it wasn't a fluke.

For his next outing, 2002's SHAMAN, he again tried the old trick of filling the ranks with 'worthy' guests, this time the likes of **Dido** and **Macy Gray**. Though it pleased some, for many the set saw Carlos trying a little too hard to please the masses rather than displaying his own true colours.

⦿ **Santana** (1969; CBS; reissued 1998; Legacy).
A remarkably assured debut album with a sound that would remain constant over the next three years. The outstanding track is "Soul Sacrifice", but "Jin-Go-Lo-Ba" provides the first opportunity to hear the length and clarity of Santana's guitar as he sustains notes for unbelievable periods.

⦿ **Abraxas** (1970; CBS; reissued 1998; Legacy).
Arguably the band's finest album, every track remains listenable nearly thirty years after its release. From the gentle and evocative sound effects of the opening "Singing Winds, Crying Beasts", to the powerful "Incident At Neshabur", the musicianship is faultless, with a mix that allows every member to shine.

⦿ **Caravanserai** (1972; CBS).
Like ABRAXAS, this opens with an evocative and eerie instrumental, "Eternal Caravan Of Reincarnation", which then flows into "Waves Within". An album with more of a single sound than the other early albums, this is viewed by many as their best, but the use of effects pedals makes it sound dated.

⦿ **Viva!** (1995; Columbia).
This two-CD compilation is the best Santana anthology, a coherent retrospective sensibly biased towards the early 70s albums, and including several live and unreleased tracks.

⦿ **Supernatural** (1999; Arista).
A remarkable collection of hallmark solos, rhythms and some cohesive collaborations that catapulted Santana back into the limelight.

Paul O'Brien

SAVAGE REPUBLIC

Formed Los Angeles, 1980; disbanded 1989.

"It's like taking your record collection, putting it in a blender and watching it come out." Ethan Port

If ever there were a surf-psychedelic band for the post-punk era, **Savage Republic** was it. Recorded with an ever-changing line-up throughout

the 1980s, their albums were hardly concerned with song structures in the conventional pop sense. Lyrics, choruses, messages – none of that mattered nearly as much as the mood, which more often than not evoked desolate landscapes with haunting guitar riffs and hypnotic rhythms, though they often lumbered their material with harsh, half-baked chanted vocals and clanging industrial percussion. It makes for a most erratic recorded legacy, but one which is comparable to little else of the period, with highlights of shimmering beauty compensating for the grating noise-rock exercises.

The one constant in Savage Republic was guitarist **Bruce Licher**, who also ran their label, Independent Project. Savage Republic took root in the utility tunnels under UCLA, where Licher and drummer **Mark Erskine** would bang together whatever metal they could find to get a cool echo. With new members, they evolved into **Africa Corps**, changing their name to Savage Republic just before the release of their first recordings in 1982.

Their first releases emphasized their droning, industrial-percussive bent with instruments like oil cans, 55-gallon drums, metal pipes, and guitars that sometimes featured six identically tuned strings. After a few singles and an album (TRAGIC FIGURES), the group went into limbo for a while in late 1983, when **Robert Loveless** and **Phil Drucker** left to form 17 Pygmies. A much more guitar-orientated and melodically inclined line-up released the TRUDGE EP and CEREMONIAL album in 1985: these were the outings on which the band concentrated most on their strengths – vaguely Arabic-Middle Eastern instrumentals tinged by an elegant melancholy, anchored by ringing, circular guitar riffs. Unexpected touches like mournful trombone add a sense of grandeur, and **Louise Bailik** adds quasi-siren vocals to "Andalusia".

Yet Savage Republic, more than most bands, were best experienced live, as their odd guitar tunings and percussive instruments often gained an acoustic resonance that was impossible to capture in the studio. The band did release a few documents of their live work, the best of which is LIVE TREK (1985–86). They were also determined to make almost every show a singular event: thus you could find the band playing in California's Mojave Desert, at a Great Peace March benefit, at a Kansas City factory (where guitarist-bassist-percussionist **Ethan Port** destroyed a huge bookshelf he was using for percussion), New York's trendy Danceteria club (where they were filmed for a Chinese TV documentary on American music), or for an audience of junkies, bums and prostitutes on Skid Row in downtown Los Angeles. Port would also set fire to dustbins of pampas leaves during gigs to add that special touch of danger and excitement, which sometimes came close to causing real danger.

With further personnel changes, there were two more studio albums, JAMAHIRIYA (1988) and CUSTOMS (1989), featuring future **Medicine** founder **Brad Laner** on percussion. Both were patchy affairs that saw the band occasionally return (unwisely) to their industrial roots. Savage Republic quietly dissolved by the end of the 80s, after which Licher left LA for the desert in Sedona, Arizona.

Probably more popular in Europe than their native US, Savage Republic were not the sort of band which was easily imitated. Licher remains most renowned for the distinctive hand-letterpressed designs of Independent Project Records releases (the first Camper Van Beethoven LP being the most famous). His story is far from over – he continues to run IPR from Arizona, remaining an acclaimed sleeve designer (he did R.E.M.'s Christmas fan-club package), and formed a new band, **Scenic**.

Their debut release, INCIDENT AT CIMA (1995), was a wholly instrumental effort that expanded the moods and textures of Savage Republic into more melodic, exotic, cinematic territory. ACQUATICA (1996) built solidly on this approach and was a well-received follow-up. After what seemed like an age, Scenic followed on with THE ACID GOSPEL EXPERIENCE (2003). As well as his concerns with scenic, Licher now runs an award-winning design company; they produce all of Scenic's exquisite lithographically printed packaging, and also worked on the recently reissued Savage Republic catalogue, available through Mobilization Records.

It may have taken a while for Licher to finally dispense with the industrialisms, but Scenic's initial releases indicate that his best music may be yet to come. And with the rise of acts such as Godspeed You Black Emperor and Set Fire To Flames, Licher's earlier work seems more relevant than ever.

⊙ **Ceremonial** (1985; Independent Project).
It falters sometimes, but this is the best recorded reflection of the shimmering instrumental majesty that Savage Republic were capable of producing.

⊙ **Trudge** (1985; Play It Again Sam).
Although only four songs in length, this EP, with about half an hour of music, is more than just a collection of stray tracks. Similar in mood to CEREMONIAL, they would by no means have been filler if they had been included on that recording; in fact, they would have rated as some of the album's better pieces.

Richie Unterberger

SAXON

Formed Barnsley, England, 1979.

Rejoicing under their original name of Son Of A Bitch, **Saxon** started out as an amalgamation of two bands doing the rounds in South Yorkshire during the mid- to late 70s, Sob and Coast. Not surprisingly they had little success until they changed their name, and the line-up featured **Biff Byford** (vocals), **Paul Quinn** (guitar), **Graham Oliver** (guitar) **Steve Dawson** (bass) and **Pete Gill** (drums). They may have been a little late to spearhead the growing new wave of British heavy metal but they would soon come to embody some of its quintessential qualities.

After all the usual battles getting a record deal they were picked up by Carrere Records, and their debut

SAXON (1979) was unleashed on a metal scene that had hitherto experienced them only as a support act to the likes of the Ian Gillan Band and the Heavy Metal Kids, amongst a whole host of other rock acts. Several things made their debut hard to ignore: it featured some of the worst, most embarrassing cover art ever to grace a chunk of vinyl (a Saxon warrior wielding a bloodstained weapon) and some of the dumbest song titles and lyrics you could wish for in tunes such as "Stallions Of The Highway" and "Big Teaser".

They were definitely not subtle, but they possessed an ability to pen melodic metal anthems with great ease. And at a time when Iron Maiden had their mascot Eddie, and Motörhead were showing off their Bomber, Saxon had a lighting gantry shaped like a giant eagle, dubbed 'Biff's Budgie' by the road crew. Soon to follow was the classic metal album WHEELS OF STEEL (1980) and its rapid follow-up STRONG ARM OF THE LAW (1980). These two efforts gave the band some of their most enduring stage favourites in the title tracks, as well as the hits "Dallas 1pm" and "747 (Strangers In The Night)". The following year brought the cheesy but indispensable DENIM AND LEATHER, the title of which requires no explanation. It was at this point that Pete Gill injured his hand and was replaced two days before a major European tour by **Nigel Glockler**, who remains in the band to this day.

With 1982 came plans to crack the good ol' US of A, resulting in a series of insane dashes around the world culminating in the band touring America, flying back to the UK to play the Donington Monsters of Rock festival, returning to America for another show then scooting back to Europe for a festival date in Germany. It was at this point that THE EAGLE HAS LANDED (1982) live album was released to consolidate their status as one of the most prolific and hard-working bands on the scene.

Subsequent albums POWER AND THE GLORY (1983) and CRUSADER (1984) were part of a concerted effort to build on their established profile in the US, but whilst the albums were relatively strong the band appeared to be smoothing their sound somewhat to appeal more to the mainstream. The mid- to late 80s brought a string of increasingly wimpy albums – INNOCENCE IS NO EXCUSE (1985), ROCK THE NATIONS (1986), DESTINY (1988) and the live ROCK AND ROLL GYPSIES (1989) – and some line-up changes, as new bassist **Paul Johnson** stepped in only to be eventually replaced by **Tim 'Nibbs' Carter**. Meanwhile, Nigel Glockler went off to play for GTR, was replaced briefly by **Nigel Durham**, and then returned after GTR bit the dust.

The 1990s saw the advent of grunge and a purging wave of anti-metal sentiment. If Saxon had been viewed as a cliché before then, they were now considered deadwood to all but the hardiest of rock fans. Somehow they weathered the nosedive in popularity with a continuing stream of releases: GREATEST HITS LIVE (1990), SOLID BALL OF ROCK (1990), FOREVER

FREE (1992), DOGS OF WAR (1995) and THE EAGLE HAS LANDED PART II (1996) all emerged to little excitement in the UK but were presumably welcomed in the European bastions of metal such as Germany, where irony-free titles are still embraced with enthusiasm.

Metal bands never die – they just end up touring on the continent. During this period Graham Oliver inexplicably decided it would be a good idea to leave and re-form Son Of A Bitch with Steve Dawson and Pete Gill. He was replaced by **Doug Scarrat**.

The next studio album, UNLEASH THE BEAST (1997), and subsequent tour went a long way to re-establishing the band in people's consciousness and was helped, no doubt, by a general resurgence of interest in all things metallic. It was a real pleasure once again to experience a shamelessly unreconstructed rock band plying their trade, a feeling that extended to the band's two subsequent efforts, METALHEAD (1999) and KILLING GROUND (2001), both of which found Biff and his hoary cohorts resolutely firing on all cylinders.

⊙ **Wheels Of Steel/Strong Arm Of The Law** (1997; EMI).
A stonking double-CD package of two classic metal albums, replete with eleven (count 'em), eleven bonus live tracks. You can't go wrong with this one.

Essi Berelian

SKY SAXON

Born Salt Lake City, Utah, 1945.

The 60s punk/garage-band scene never faded away: it dissolved in acid. The psychedelic revolution had opened many minds and changed many more but it also turned some of the leading lights among the three-chord tricksters truly mad. **Sky Saxon** (**Richard Marsh**) fell into this category. When his classic garage-meisters **THE SEEDS** split following their incarnation as **Sky Saxon's Blues Band**, Sky still needed to be with the flowers. So he moved to Hawaii.

There he became Sky Sunlight the guru. His solution to Watergate was preaching the petal power. 'Our message is', he explained, 'love, man, get back and grow what you need, whether it's fruits or sacred herbs. Dress and live as you need. The earth will take care of you.'

Meantime, he was gathering disciples – groups like The Neon Boys, who heard the Seeds gospel on Lenny Kaye's seminal NUGGETS compilation. The cool and the crazy, ranging from Alex Chilton to Andy Taylor, lined up to pay tribute to Sunlight in his Oahu exile.

In 1984, however, Sky Sunlight Saxon resurfaced in Los Angeles, and formed the **Stars New Seeds Band** out of a band of acid refugees. From Fraternity Of Man came **Elliot Englebar** (guitar). From **STEPPENWOLF** came **Mars Bonfire** (bass), the author of "Born To Be Wild". **IRON BUTTERFLY**'s **Ron Bushy** sat ominously on drums and **Rainbow**

Starburst, a longtime adherent, appeared on rhythm guitar. After an album, DESTINY'S CHILDREN (1986), Sunlight Saxon dropped out of sight for a while, reappearing in Los Angeles with The Dragonslayers – starring Mars Bonfire on bass again and **Mitch Mitchell** (ex Jimi Hendrix) on drums – with a recording titled JUST IMAGINE (1989).

In 1995 Sky formed **Fast Planet** featuring **Sam Andrews** (ex-Janis Joplin) on guitar, and **George Michalski** (ex-Blue Cheer) on keyboards. The band recorded DOWN THE NILE in 1995, and a live CD ROCKIN THE CROC/WEST COAST, which included two bonus tracks; "Dying Butterfly" – an all-time classic antiwar song – and "Summer Of Love" – recorded in 1997 for the thirtieth anniversary of the Summer of Love – featuring **Pete Sears** (ex-**JEFFERSON STARSHIP**) on bass.

1997 found Sky recording with his 'old Beethoven mystical friend' **Daryl Hooper** of The Seeds. The Seeds were revived in 1998 and a new album, A FADED PICTURE, released for the occasion. Legendary rather than obscure, Sky keeps his message for those prepared to seek it out – and 2001 found him plundering the past and issuing GOLDEN VAULTS VOL.1: TIMELESS as well as EARLY SKY SAXON, under the name of **Richard Marsh and the Hoodwinks**, both on Radio V Records. His recorded output has become rock's Ark of the Covenant – hard to find and intense enough to melt your face off.

⊙ **Golden Vaults Vol.1: Timeless** (2001; Radio V).
Saxon invites you on a trip around the Milky Way. This is punk as it was meant to be – hard and dirty, with desperate men playing fuzz guitars not heard since "Psychotic Reaction".

Charles Bottomley
Thanks to Sky himself for updates

THE SCIENTISTS

Formed Perth, Australia, 1978; split 1981; re-formed 1982; finally disbanded 1987.

Perth is the most isolated city in the world – 2000 miles of desert separate it from its closest neighbour, and as that's Adelaide the drive is hardly worth it. Emerging from a music scene as barren as its environs, **The Scientists – James Baker** (drums), **Kim Salmon** (guitar/vocals), **Boris Sujdovic** (bass) and **Rod Radalj** (guitar) – drew on the power and attitude of the New York Dolls, Heartbreakers and early Flamin' Groovies, and the earthy R&B melodies of the Troggs, Kinks and Stones. Their songs were Larry Page-esque "Kinda Girl", "Pretty Girl", "That Girl", "Girl", and the two-chord epic, "Baby, You're Not For Sale".

Squabbles about clothing led to Sujdovic's departure during the recording of "Frantic Romantic" (1979), the debut single. Radalj left out of loyalty to Sujdovic and probably, judging by Salmon's penchant for pink Peter Noone shirts, sympathy for his cause. **Denis Byrne** filled in on bass and the record received glowing reviews in the UK and US. Greg

Shaw bought a few hundred for his fledgling BOMP label.

A revamped line-up of Salmon, Baker, **Ian Sharples** (bass) and **Ben Juniper** (guitar) subsequently billed themselves as 'The Legendary Scientists: BOMP Recording Artists'. Juniper brought tough, Kinky, Beatle-ish harmonies to such tunes as "She Said She Loves Me" and "We'll Get Back Together Again" and augmented them with neat guitar pieces on the group's EP LAST NIGHT, particularly the title track, which the group performed on *Countdown* (Australia's chart show).

When Juniper departed in 1980, The Scientists continued as a three-piece with Salmon amply filling the guitar gap on the feedback-teetering rousers: "Teenage Dreamer", "It'll Never Happen Again" and "High Noon". However, the band finally split later that year and issued THE SCIENTISTS (the 'Pink' album) posthumously. Baker joined Rod Radalj in **THE HOODOO GURUS**, and Salmon formed **Louie Louie** with drummer Brett Rixon.

In 1982 the Scientists Mark 2 appeared in Sydney, comprising Salmon, Sujdovic, Brett Rixon and **Tony Thewlis** (guitar). They began again playing raucous pop – "The Land That Time Forgot", "Swampland" and "Teenage Dreamer" – but this soon mutated into a truly wild, pop-tinged raucousness. Giving these guys songs like "When Worlds Collide" and "Rev Head" was like giving The Stooges arc-welders for Christmas. With a fashion sense plummeting into the crater left by the music (they had the longest hair, lowest-slung trousers and tackiest shirts in town), they were difficult to ignore.

Although live shows teetered on the brink of chaotic implosion, the new band's first single, "This Is My Happy Hour"/"Swampland" (1982), harked back to the R&B/pop roots they seemed to be abandoning. On their EP, BLOOD RED RIVER, and single, "We Had Love" (1983), they hinted at their erratic best: Salmon whispered and howled like some schizoid scanner with the jitters; Sujdovic got monomaniacally fixed on a two-note riff; Rixon, once described as 'an assembly line misfit blankly contemplating murder', sounded like he was punching the holes in Monaro head-gaskets; and Thewlis seemed to be test-driving a nuclear Hoover to clear up the mess.

Moving to London, the band recorded YOU GET WHAT YOU DESERVE (1985), an organized, crystallized, pure record. Each song had the unique Scientists imprint: mountains of fuzz guitar, John Fogerty-inspired twang, and inventive, deceptively simple rhythms. Success loomed and Rixon, with impeccable timing, quit. With drummer **Leanne Chock**, the band released an LP of rerecordings, WEIRD LOVE (1986), with one 'new' song, a version of Nancy Sinatra's "You Only Live Twice". Then, when Sujdovic also quit, Salmon, Thewlis and drummer **Nick Combe** recorded a final LP, THE HUMAN JUKEBOX (1987), toured Australia with Rixon playing bass, and called it a day.

Salmon formed **Kim Salmon & The Surrealists**; Boris Sujdovic formed the **Dubrovniks** with James Baker and Rod Radalj; Tony Thewlis formed **The Interstellar Villains**; and Brett Rixon died of a heroin overdose on Christmas Eve 1993.

⦿ **Absolute** (1991; Sub Pop).
A comprehensive selection of The Scientists (Mk 2) from "Swampland" to THE HUMAN JUKEBOX, including the magnificent, sprawling "Backwards Man". At some desert crossroad, the weedy, high-speed drill bit of "Rev Head" screams towards collision with the Mack truck roo-bar of "Demolition Derby". Who would argue with these guys?

Danella Taylor

SCORN

Formed Birmingham, England, 1991.

"We are stripped-down and minimal; when we play live we still use traditional instrumentation, so in that sense we are still a rock'n'roll band."
Nic Bullen

Following their split from **NAPALM DEATH** in 1991, **Justin Broadrick** founded **GODFLESH**, while **N. J. Bullen** and **Mick Harris** formed **Scorn** (with occasional guitar from Broadrick) as a slower, densely dub-influenced project. Emphasizing rhythm over melody, the music they produced was effectively Napalm Death slowed down, occasionally to a crawl. Their first recorded releases were the "Lick Forever Dog" single, a crushing, primeval metal-dub collision, and the lengthy VAE SOLIS (1992) album, both on the Earache label.

Well received in grindcore circles, Scorn's first European tour (with **Pat McCahan** replacing Broadrick) and a Peel session won many converts to their bass-heavy, misanthropic metal sound. Built on claustrophobic rhythms, overlaid with macabre atmospherics and drawing on images of bondage, religion and decay, Scorn's sound was uncomfortable, cathartic listening. The single, "Deliverance", a forty-minute epic of apocalyptic dread, was followed by a 10" mini album, WHITE IRISES BLIND in April 1993.

The more varied COLOSSUS (1993) album reflected the isolationist mood of related post-metal groups such as Main and Godflesh at that time, with extended ambient abstractions mixed with song-based structures. Using increasing amounts of electronics and effects, it wasn't long before Bullen and Harris produced the complex EVANESCENCE double LP (1994).

Critically acclaimed in underground rock, dance and experimental circles, EVANESCENCE relied heavily on sample programming (though some guitar was provided by **James Plotkin** of Old/Flux and Death Ambient) along with didgeridoo and bass. Scorn were now on European festival bills with The Orb and Moby, as well as more industrial-rock-based groups, and the electronic connection was made complete in 1995 with the ELLIPSIS remix CD.

Developed from a Meat Beat Manifesto 12" mix of "Silver Rain Fell," the album's remixers included Coil, Scanner, Autechre, Germ and the New York dub meister himself, Bill Laswell, who joined with Harris and avant-jazz/thrash saxophonist John Zorn as **Painkiller** for several releases, and with Harris and Eraldo Bernocchi (SIMM) as the ritualistic **Equations Of Eternity** in 1996.

Harris was by now engaged in a slew of solo projects and collaborations. Since 1992 his ambient project **Lull** has released several hard-to-find CDs, while he also records under his own name with Martyn Bates, and as **Matera** with Mauro Teho Tearo (of Meathead). The acrimonious departure of Bullen in 1995 has also effectively made Scorn another Harris solo project, and as if that wasn't enough, he also records drum'n'bass as **Quoit**, while running Possible Records and doing extensive production and remix work.

As Scorn, Harris then produced four further albums' worth of heavyweight instrumentals influenced by hip-hop, dub and drum'n'bass. GYRAL (1995) and LOGGHI BAROGGHI (1996) were his last for Earache before his move to Belgian label KK (and Invisible in America) for ZANDER (1997) and the live CD WHINE (1997). Progressively more abstract and resembling hyper-complex drum solos on occasion, these albums allowed Harris to indulge fully in the exploration of rhythm and deep, deep bass, along with the "Beat vols. 1 & 2" and "Leave It Out" singles in 1996.

Harris then decided to concentrate on his other projects until he could resist the lure of Scorn no more. The name which Harris said was effectively dead after WHINE suddenly became the source of yet more wildly experimental adventures in bass. ANAMNESIS: RARITIES 1994-97 (1999), pulled together a host of odds and ends, with some early Peel session tracks being of particular interest. This was followed by IMAGINARIA AWARD, a five-track EP that served as a precursor to GREETINGS FROM BIRMINGHAM (2000), which found Harris yet again carving a fresh direction for the ever-flexible Scorn sound.

With all this frenetic activity, Scorn progressed well past the days when they redefined grindcore metal as well as ambient dub; the obsession with rhythm and atmospherics may not always justify Harris's lengthy explorations, but future presentations – whether as Scorn, Lull or any of the other names under which Harris operates – will no doubt be prolific and heavy on the low end.

- **Vae Solis** (1992; Earache).
  Metal and dub collide in a horror-show atmosphere of dread and misanthropy.

- **Evanescence** (1994; Earache).
  Let down by unconvincing vocals from Bullen, this is nevertheless a triumphantly controlled combination of dub, hip-hop, techno and isolationist rock.

- **Ellipsis** (1995; Scorn Recordings/Earache).
  Phenomenal remixes extend Scorn's already highly atmospheric EVANESCENCE in diverse directions. Also released as a five-12" box set with a bonus Coil remix.

- **Gyral** (1995; Scorn Recordings/Earache).
  Fantastic use of hypnotic machine rhythms and bass textures to redirect the bleak atmosphere into abstraction. Thankfully, it is entirely vocal-free.

- **Whine** (1997; KK/Invisible).
  The live sound of scorn captured on CD.

- **Anamnesis: Rarities 1994-1997** (1999; KK/Invisible).
  A bass-heavy collection of some Scorn cuts that slipped through the cracks.

Richard Fontenoy

SCORPIONS

Formed Hanover, Germany, 1969.

It's a little strange to think that a country where heavy metal seems to be perennially popular has produced only one truly world-class rock act. The early **Scorpions** consisted of **Rudi Schenker** (guitar/vocals), **Karl Heinz Follmer** (guitar), **Lothar Heimberg** (bass) and **Wolfgang Dziony** (drums) and went about trying to blend Pink Floyd's weird psychedelic dabblings into their own peculiarly Germanic notion of hard rock. It wasn't until Schenker passed singing duties on to **Klaus Meine** and recruited his own brother **Michael** as lead guitarist that the band began to vaguely resemble the Teutonic outfit that would one day ask the world 'Do yew vahnt to rawk?'

Their first unremarkable album, ACTION (1972), formed the soundtrack to the movie *Das Kalte Paradies* and was later issued overseas as LONESOME CROW. Michael's six-string expertise couldn't fail to go unnoticed, however, and he was pinched by Brit rockers **UFO**, who had recently lost Bernie Marsden. **Uli Jon Roth** stepped into the fold and a string of mid-70s albums – FLY TO THE RAINBOW (1974), IN TRANCE (1975), VIRGIN KILLER (1976) and TAKEN BY FORCE (1977) – charted the development of their sound from psychedelia to a more straightforward hard rock. Despite courting controversy, not least by their growing taste for outrageous sleeve art – VIRGIN KILLER, for instance, originally featured a naked pre-pubescent girl and a sheet of fortuitously positioned glass – they toured to only mediocre success. They were big in Japan, however, hence the double live effort TOKYO TAPES (1978), which was the last long-player to feature Roth, who departed with new group Electric Sun.

At this point UFO decided to part company with Michael Schenker and kicked him straight back into the welcoming arms of his brother's band. He didn't stay for long but did manage to help the Scorpions pen their breakthrough album, LOVEDRIVE (1979). The bizarre artwork, featuring a woman on the back seat of a car with bubblegum over her breast, resulted in the cover being banned in the US. The band survived America's inability to comprehend the German sense of humour and lived to rhyme 'fire' with 'desire' another day. The line-up now included Michael Schenker's replacement **Matthias Jabs**, **Francis Buchholz** (bass) and **Herman 'The German' Rarebell** (drums).

Suddenly the band's trademark – flying V guitars and stripy spandex strides – were everywhere and heralded a lengthy period of major worldwide success with ANIMAL MAGNETISM (1980), featuring yet another weird cover with strange sexual connotations, and BLACKOUT (1982). By now even the Americans were succumbing to Scorpions' peculiar charms, but it was LOVE AT FIRST STING (1984) that made them into superstars as "Rock You Like A Hurricane" stormed onto MTV. The album also contained the worldwide hit ballad "Still Loving You". WORLDWIDE LIVE (1985) was a testament to their huge popularity, with the cover featuring their show-stopping feat of daring – the human pyramid!

When a band becomes truly successful the periods between albums usually become increasingly protracted, and in this case SAVAGE AMUSEMENT emerged a full three years later, yet still continued to spawn hits. But it wasn't until 1990 that CRAZY WORLD made them one of the biggest bands in the world. The album included the major hit single "Wind Of Change", and saw possibly the only example of whistling in a heavy metal song.

Ralph Riekermann (bass) and **James Kottak** (drums) were recruited after the release of CRAZY WORLD, and a steady stream of albums – FACE THE HEAT (1993), LIVE BITES (1995), PURE INSTINCT (1996) and EYE TO EYE (1999) – kept things ticking over. But the band became one of the many rock acts to fall victim to the winds of grunge sweeping through the music scene during the 90s. This state of affairs was not helped by their somewhat odd decision to record first a symphonic album and then an acoustic effort – MOMENT OF GLORY (2000) and ACOUSTICA (2001) respectively – at a time when such moves were surely passé. Only a return to driving hard rock can prevent what seems to be a gradual decline.

⊙ **Animal Magnetism** (1980; EMI)
Yet another strange cover, but that doesn't detract from the intrinsic quality of the songs.

⊙ **Love At First Sting** (1984; EMI)
A monster hit album, once again featuring a hard-rocking and extremely commercial selection of tunes.

Essi Berelian

GIL SCOTT-HERON

Born Chicago, April 1, 1949.

The career trajectory of **Gil Scott-Heron** has taken him from radical, avant-garde poet to the status of jazz-funk's singer-songwriter with a conscience. The transformation began when he recorded a reading of his volume of poetry, *Small Talk At 125th And Lenox*, to a Last Poets-style background of congas and bells for jazz producer Bob Thiele's Flying Dutchman label. Released in 1972, SMALL TALK AT 125TH AND LENOX documented the uncompromising world-view of the Black Arts Movement with songs such as "Whitey On The Moon", a very funny attack on American economic priorities, and a skeletal version of what would become his most famous song, "The Revolution Will Not Be Televised". The latter was rerecorded the following year on PIECES OF A MAN, with a hard-funk bass line that enhanced the moody menace of the lyrics.

As he added more instrumentation, Scott-Heron began to sing his poem-songs, allowing a more empathetic conception of politics to enter into his music. The first fully formed and successful work of the more musical Gil Scott-Heron was "The Bottle" (from WINTER IN AMERICA; 1974; reissued 1998; Charly), a tough and danceable anti-alcohol song that featured **Brian Jackson**'s flute. The partnership between Scott-Heron and Jackson began when they were both students at Lincoln College in Pennsylvania and continued until the 1980 album. Another key factor in Scott-Heron's artistic (if not commercial) success was his underrated bassist **Robert Gordon** ('The Secretary of Entertainment'), who was equally comfortable with virtuosic solos and fluid grooves.

Following in the footsteps of the dance-floor success of "The Bottle" and a switch to Arista, "Johannesburg" (from the 1975 album FROM SOUTH AFRICA TO SOUTH CAROLINA) proved that disco could celebrate something aside from hedonism (the anti-apartheid struggle) and yet still move bodies. The mid 70s saw Scott-Heron become the most eloquent, if least famous, of music's antinuclear campaigners in songs like "South Carolina (Barnwell)" (1975), "We Almost Lost Detroit" (1977) and "Shut 'Um Down" (1979). Just as his music was slipping into a soft-jazz formula, he brought back a harsh, deep funk for his substantial American black radio hit, "Angel Dust" (1978). Along with "Third World Revolution", "Angel Dust" anchored his strong SECRETS album with its spacey but direct groove-based attack on the latest scourge to hit America's inner cities.

In the early 80s Scott-Heron furthered his brooding minimalism on the excellent albums REFLECTIONS (1981) and MOVING TARGET (1982). "B Movie" (1981) was perhaps the most bitter and explicitly political song ever to be a hit on radio. With its smart setting (a second-rate western) and savage characterizations of Reagan and his cronies, "B Movie" perfectly captured the Left's mood at the time. Despite his misgivings, Scott-Heron's collaboration with Bill Laswell, "Re-Ron" (1984), made explicit the underlying political slant of the mechanistic, urban funk of the 1980s.

In spite of almost constant touring, and probably because of personal problems, Scott-Heron released no new material until SPIRITS (1993), a lacklustre album which suffered from weak material and the departure of Robert Gordon. 1998, however, saw Scott-Heron back with a vengeance. Via a linkup with TVT Records, he set up his own label, Rumal-Gia, which rereleased eleven of his albums from the 70s bulked up with previously unreleased live tracks that featured his often hilarious rap sermon-lectures on 'bluesology'.

- ● **The Revolution Will Not Be Televised** (1974; BMG).
  An excellent compilation of his first three Flying Dutchman albums, testifying to the breadth of his growing musical vision.

- ● **The Best Of Gil Scott-Heron** (1984; Arista).
  A nearly faultless greatest hits package. It surveys his singles from "The Revolution Will Not be Televised" to "Re-Ron" in revelatory chronological order.

- ● **Ghetto Style** (1998; Camden/BMG).
  Yet another excellent compilation of the artist's 1970–72 work. A fine introduction.

Peter Shapiro

SCREAMING TREES

Formed Ellensburg, Washington, 1985;
disbanded 2000.

Even on first appearance, **Screaming Trees** had more sense of history, and a load more talent, than the welter of grunge-styled bands formed in the Seattle/Washington area in the mid 80s. And it was a promise they fulfilled with their 1996 masterpiece, DUST.

The group was the creation of heavyweight brothers **Gary Lee** (guitar) and **Van Conner** (bass), who found splendid accompaniment in **Mark Lanegan** (vocals) and **Mark Pickerell** (drums). At the outset their songs were bar-room travelogues on life and love in the slow lane of rural Ellensburg, redolent of both 70s rock and 60s psychedelia, though their initial musical platform was pure punk rock.

After an inconclusive debut album, CLAIRVOYANCE (1986), Screaming Trees switched to SST Records for a trio of albums beginning with EVEN IF AND ESPECIALLY WHEN (1987). Unafraid of introspection, this set the scene for the rest of their 80s output, with vivid scenarios conveyed menacingly by Lanegan's taut, emphatic delivery. INVISIBLE LANTERN (1988) and BUZZ FACTORY (1989) saw a growing fan base, without ever breaking out of the domestic alternative-

rock ghetto. It was followed by TIME SPEAKS HER GOLDEN TONGUE EP (1989) for Sub Pop – but in truth the Screaming Trees were never a 'Seattle band', only playing that city once or twice a year.

UNCLE ANESTHESIA (1991), the Trees' first effort for a major label – Epic – was produced by Terry Date and Soundgarden singer Chris Cornell, but the results never really meshed. The incohesion was perhaps in part due to the impending departure of Mark Pickerell, who was replaced by **Barrett Martin** from Skin Yard. However, the lack of creative impetus might also have had something to do with numerous extracurricular activities during this period. Lanegan, having relocated to Seattle while his band-mates stayed 'up in the mountains in Ellensburg', released an intense solo album for Sub Pop, THE WINDING SHEET. It included a cover of Leadbelly's "Where Did You Sleep Last Night?", which Kurt Cobain (who had contributed to the album) would later reprise on Nirvana's UNPLUGGED session. WINDING SHEET somewhat overshadowed the Conner brothers' outings: Gary Lee with **Purple Outside** (MYSTERY LANE) and Van with **Solomon Grundy** (SOLOMON GRUNDY).

Back together as a band, and with the time out seeming to have revitalized the creative juices, Screaming Trees recorded SWEET OBLIVION (1992), a much more distinctive set – subdued, less eager to please, yet far more accessible than anything preceding it. CHANGE HAS COME (1993) continued in this vein, if with less verve.

With DUST (1996), however, everything seemed to have come together. Recorded after two years of abortive sessions, this was the record fans feared the Trees would never make: a perfect synthesis of their many influences, with splashes of Byrds and Hendrix-style guitar, and use of sitars and tablas, produced with unerring clarity by George Drakoulias. Lanegan was on top vocal form, the lyrics (sin, redemption, cold turkey) perfect in their restraint, and the guitars and instrumentation wild.

It was, simply, the best thing out of Washington state in years – since IN UTERO, to be precise. Not that anyone could continue to tag the Trees as grunge: they ploughed far too wide a furrow. Ironically, however, the band's most brilliant work was to be their last. In 2000 they played their last gig together at the opening of Seattle's Experience Music Project interactive rock museum. Lanegan continues to pursue his solo recording career and has produced a number of albums displaying his love of America's rich musical history.

Though the Trees' future seemed rather tentative from time to time, they always managed to continue – only time will tell if this particular parting of the ways is permanent.

- ● **Anthology** (1991; SST).
  This compilation neatly dissects the Screaming Trees' three-album stint with SST, including the mighty "Transfiguration". Music to drink, crawl home and get bawled out to.

⊙ **Sweet Oblivion** (1992; Epic).
With its distinctive artwork shot by famed New York photographer Michael Levine, SWEET OBLIVION includes the deftly vulnerable single, "Nearly Lost You". 'No woman no cry' is the cornerstone of the Screaming Trees' philosophy, and here it hits home.

⊙ **Dust** (1996; Epic).
A stunner, which takes the whole grunge legacy and repositions it amid the Trees. If you've not heard the band before, get yourself to a listening station and check out "Sworn And Broken", then reach for your wallet.

Alex Ogg

SCRITTI POLITTI

Formed Leeds, England, 1977.

The first indication that **Scritti Politti** were going to amount to something more than another bunch of scratchy punk also-rans – whose interviews were more interesting than their music – was the release of C81, the *NME*/Rough Trade compilation of 1981. This opened with their "The Sweetest Girl" – an achingly beautiful ballad with a gentle rock-steady lilt, and a meandering middle eight. It ushered in the voice of **Green Garside** in all its splendour, and stood head and shoulders in terms of production and structure above the contributions from the rest of the Rough Trade stable in 1981.

Former Young Communist Green Gartside put a proto-version of Scritti together with bass player **Nial Jinks** and drummer **Tom Morley** at Leeds Art College in early 1977, inspired by the Sex Pistols. The trio moved to London a year later and began playing low-key punk venues, releasing "Skank Bloc Bologna" on their own St Pancras label. Hard to believe, given Green's later career path, it was a pretty regular punk outing, and it was followed by a tour as support to Joy Division and the Gang Of Four.

During the tour, however, Green collapsed and was diagnosed as suffering from a heart complaint. He spent 1980 at home with his parents in Wales recuperating and writing the songs that would comprise the meat of the revamped – if not downright unrecognizable – band. Morley was held over from the first incarnation, but the group was clearly controlled from the Green helm from now on. "The Sweetest Girl" was issued as a single and followed by "Faithless" and "Asylums In Jerusalem", both of which topped the UK's indie chart and hovered on the outskirts of the regular Top 40. **ROBERT WYATT** guested on keyboards on "Sweetest Girl" and there was more than a touch of his voice discernible in the plaintive, mid-register of Green and his diversionary methods of song construction.

All three tracks graced the debut album, SONGS TO REMEMBER (1982), which was released to wide acclaim and charted in the UK at #12. Its mix'n'-match styles triumphantly illustrated the breadth of Green's vision, the music ranging through free-blowing sax and gospel backing vocals, and featuring perhaps the longest double-bass solo to appear on a rock album, on "Rock-A-Boy-Blue". More intelligent and better read than the average rock hero, Green became the darling of the music press, his references to French philosophers ("Jacques Derrida"), Italian terrorists and violent art theorists holding journalists in thrall.

Inevitably, the group got too big for Rough Trade and Green signed to Virgin, moving to New York where he began work with super-slick producer Arif Mardin and top session musicians, Morley having departed. Ex-Miles Davis bassist **Marcus Miller** helped out on "Wood Beez (Pray Like Aretha Franklin)" (1984), a song Green would revisit through the 80s, while **David Gamson** (keyboards) and **Fred Maher** (drums) were enlisted for Scritti's second album, CUPID AND PSYCHE '85 (1985). With its lush, soul, dance sensitivity, this was an almost total break from SONGS, and signalled Green's growing quest for perfect production and song craft. Bemusing old fans, but gaining many more, it charted at #5 in the UK, and edged into the US Top 50, on a wave of gorgeous singles – "Absolute", "The Word Girl", "Perfect Way" – each released in 7" and extended 12" versions.

Green became something of a recluse, ever perfecting his work in the studio, experimenting with drum and keyboard programming, and casting his net for musicians to realize his vision. In 1988 he struck gold, with **MILES DAVIS** contributing one of his all-time great trumpet solos to "Oh Patti (Don't Feel Sorry For Loverboy)". (Davis had earlier paid Green the compliment of recording "Perfect Way" on his 1986 album TUTU.) The song, however, was just one stand-out on PROVISION (1988), an album that took Green's white-boy soul-funk-pop to a glorious conclusion. Here was an album of three years' work in the studio – and which sounded like it. With "Overnite", Green had produced a ballad more sublime even than "The Sweetest Girl", each chord change squeezing out the emotion. And he showed himself ahead of the times, producing an impeccable dub reprise of "Boom! There She Was".

SCRITTI POLITTI
with RANKING ANN
THE WORD GIRL
(Flesh & Blood)
1985

During the 90s, Green was furthering his obsessions, so fans had to make do with covers of Green songs elsewhere (the title track of Al Jarreau's L Is FOR LOVER album; appearances on Madonna's *Who's That Girl* soundtrack; and records by Chaka Khan and Madness), and a couple of 1991 experiments with reggae. These were impressive and enjoyable – a ragga cover of Lennon and McCartney's "She's A Woman" with **Shabba Ranks**, and a dance-hall version of the Gladys Knight song "Take Me In Your Arms" with **Sweetie Irie**.

The silence was broken in 1999 by ANOMIE & BONHOMIE. Written mainly by Green, again produced by David Gamson, it featured contributions from New York rapper **Mos' Def** and **Me'Shell N'degeocello**. Green has been a unique talent in pop music, and it's perhaps not stretching it too far to see him as a kind of English equivalent of Prince.

⊙ **Songs To Remember**
(1982; Rough Trade; reissued 2001; Virgin).
Unavailable for many years, its reissue served as a reminder of its power in deconstructing emotive pop-soul cliches but without ever reducing its own beauty in the process.

⊙ **Cupid And Psyche** (1985; Virgin).
Mardin-produced, sharp-as-a-diamond collection of the dance-floor hits "Wood Beez", "Absolute" and "Perfect Girl".

⊙ **Provision** (1988; Virgin).
Perfect pop programmed by Green and David Gamson – and with that Miles solo (twice) on the 7" and 12" versions of "Oh Patti".

Ada Wilson

THE SEA AND CAKE

Formed Chicago, 1993.

An alternative-rock supergroup that makes remarkably intimate music, **The Sea And Cake** craft flowing sonics that call to mind bossa nova, German prog, and even the 70s post-hippie act Steely Dan. Along with label-mates Tortoise, The Sea And Cake honed a post-rock sound that challenged a Chicago underground scene traditionally dominated by hard rock (Big Black had provided the most frequently copied musical blueprint), and quickly became the city's definitive musical style

Lead singer and founding member **Sam Prekop** had been prominent on the Chicago scene since 1986, when he had formed Shrimp Boat, a quartet whose jazzy pop had earned a cult following and provided the foundation for the groovier sound of The Sea And Cake, in which Prekop joined forces with guitarist **Archer Prewitt** (The Coctails), drummer **John McEntire** (**TORTOISE**) and bassist **Eric Claridge**. Jazzy guitars characterized the band's first album, THE SEA AND CAKE (1994), and sophomore album THE BIZ (1995), but by the time of NASSAU (1995) a growing interest in electronic music was becoming clear. Over the next year or so, band members were increasingly occupied by side projects (McEntire in particular as producer, working with

the sea and cake
one bedroom

Stereolab on DOTS AND LOOPS and remixing for, among others, Blur), leading to rumours of a break-up, but THE FAWN (1997) proved that the band had only benefited from McEntire's experience as a producer and engineer. Traditional rock hooks and riffs were now abandoned in favour of tone and ambience, with drum machines and synthesizers adding looped backgrounds to Prekop's quiet croons.

The band was put on hold following the release of THE FAWN, and Prewitt went on to release two solo efforts, IN THE SUN (1997) and WHITE SKY (1999), while Prekop delivered his own self-titled solo debut, also in 1999. None of these collections deviated greatly from the band's sound, even though Prekop's effort emphasized the bossa nova elements of his songwriting, substituting string instruments, cornet, and Latin-flavoured percussion for electronic effects. Recorded with McEntire, and with Prewitt playing guitar and piano, SAM PREKOP was to all intents and purposes a sixth Sea And Cake release.

The Sea and Cake regrouped towards the end of 1999 to record OUI, which was followed in 2003 by the even poppier ONE BEDROOM. With prominent vibes and horn from McEntire and string arrangements from **Paul Mertens** (who held a similar post on a Brian Wilson comeback tour), OUI saw the quartet seamlessly blending strings and synthesizers to take their polished pop vision even further.

⊙ **The Biz** (1995; Thrill Jockey).
Quietly epic songs, filled with rolling melodies, subdued vocals and abstract lyrics.

⊙ **Oui** (2000; Thrill Jockey).
This collection finds the group in a comfortable and breezy groove that evokes late period Talking Heads.

Ken Miller

SEAHORSES

Formed England, 1996; disbanded 1999.

The Seahorses' short career was based upon a totally 'retro' approach to rock music, involving hard work, radio-friendly songwriting and traditional pop values such as optimism and romance.

By contrast to the bitterness and bitching seen when guitarist **John Squire**'s previous band – the ego-ridden **STONE ROSES** – fell to pieces (Squire denies any significance in 'The Seahorses' being an anagram of 'He hates Roses'), the Seahorses story has all the haphazard, low-budget charm of the great 60s acts.

Squire, who played the glorious riffs that typified The Stone Roses' best work, saw the end was in sight and jumped ship without even bothering to arrange passage to another band as a lifeboat. Given his pedigree, however, Squire had many options and a huge number of well-placed contacts in the industry. Indeed, one song which later surfaced on the Seahorses' debut album, LOVE ME AND LEAVE ME, started life when Squire followed the 1996 English soccer Cup Final with a visit to his friend Liam Gallagher of Oasis.

Keen to get on with his music, but wary of falling into another nest of thorny personalities, Squire picked up a band of younger, less-experienced musicians in a series of chance encounters: **Stuart Fletcher** was filling in for another bassist suffering an attack of repetitive strain injury when a well-lubricated Squire chanced on his pub gig one night in York; **Chris Helme** was busking with his guitar in the same city; and **Andy Watts** was recruited, on Helme's recommendation, when the new songs obliged the band to find a drummer who could help out with vocals. The usual round of intense rehearsals and gigs ensued, soon leading to a deal with major label Geffen.

Squire had always shown more traditional rock leanings than his erstwhile colleagues in The Roses, and talked of his tacit intention to keep the new songs down to the three- to four-minute range. The hiring of an established producer with a track record of honing radio-friendly hit sounds – Tony Visconti, best known for his work with glam idols Bowie and Bolan in the 70s – completed the groundwork necessary, and DO IT YOURSELF (1997) burst out of the studios, sounding good and selling well.

Visconti had taken the band's own distinctive sound and combined it with classic rock/pop strengths – the resulting blend couldn't fail in a British market that was devoted to straightforward rock from acts such as Cast and Ocean Colour Scene. Both the album and first single, "Love Is The Law", reached high chart positions. The early gigs showed the band working hard to build an audience and successfully keeping egos in check.

Despite the general approval which greeted their live work and recordings, their emergence from the ruins of a band with such a strong following as The Roses' did draw some cynical comments, and despite the individual band members' obvious strengths they were bound to be overshadowed by Squire and his reputation to some extent, yet other indicators – like the full-length version of "Love Is The Law" (seven and a half minutes long, and to hell with the tacit intentions!), and the melodic "Blinded By The Sun" (composed by Helme) on the album – suggested the

Seahorses would continue to build on their promising start.

By late 1997, when "Love Me And Leave Me" – the chance-inspired co-composition with Liam Gallagher – was released as a single, the band had started a serious attempt to 'crack the US' and other territories using live performances as their weapon of choice. Andy Watts departed at this crucial point, leaving the band up the creek without a drummer. After struggling on for a while without him, the Seahorses finally split, whilst recording their second album early in 1999. Another good idea which never really got off the ground.

⊙ **Do It Yourself** (1997; Geffen).
Not perfect by any means, but an album rich in riffs, stunning-quality guitar work and classic rock/pop elements. Many other bands in this guide opened their account with far less accomplished records.

Neil Nixon

SEBADOH

Formed Northampton, Massachusetts, 1989.

Prior to forming **Sebadoh**, bassist **Lou Barlow** was with **DINOSAUR JR.**, whom he left in 1989, none too enamoured of their growing commercial success and media attention. His most conspicuous presence in Dinosaur's recorded output had been the segment of cut-up noise and melody that was "Poledo", the track which closed the second Dinosaur album, YOU'RE LIVING ALL OVER ME, and its credits, stating that it was 'recorded on two crappy tape recorders in Lou's bedroom'. These were to be the new band's working practices as they led the so-called lo-fi 90s avant-garde.

Lo-fi did not, however, mean slacking. Barlow is one of the most prolific workers around, and through the early 90s he created vast numbers of songs, both solo and in collaboration with **Eric Gaffney**, a multi-instrumentalist who had been a drummer in the Massachusetts hardcore scene in the 1980s. These largely acoustic snippets of song ideas were released on a couple of mini-albums – FREEDMAN and WEED FORESTIN – which were compiled, of course, on FREED WEED (1990).

In 1991, Barlow and Gaffney were joined by **Jason Lowenstein**, a one-time drummer, who contributed bass, guitar and vocals to a new electric and punky Sebadoh sound – previewed on the single "Gimme Indie Rock". This was followed by the wonderful SEBADOH III (1991), an anarchic wedge of everything that interested the trio – R.E.M.-like acoustic songs, lo-fi guitar noise and hard rock-pop. More of the same emerged on the UK release, ROCKING THE FOREST, and SEBADOH VS. HELMET (both 1992), on which they covered songs by The Byrds and Nick Drake. These sessions were collected on their first Sub Pop release, SMASH YOUR HEAD ON THE PUNK ROCK (1992).

BUBBLE AND SCRAPE (1993), Sebadoh's first entirely studio-recorded release, saw an apparent bid for more than just the cult college lo-fi audience that had been following the band. It was a more conventional outing, upping the group sound and melodic content. Barlow, meanwhile, was giving vent to his determined lo-fi, home-grown material on side excursions released as **Sentridoh** and (with guitarist **John Davis**) as **FOLK IMPLOSION**.

In 1994, Gaffney left the band, replaced by drummer Bob Fay, and almost in spite of themselves Sebadoh broke through into mainstream sales with a new album, BAKESALE. This showed the group could do alternative rock as well as anyone around, and was followed by impressive tour dates which yielded a live IN TOKYO album (1995), on which they added covers of such bands as Flipper and Hüsker Dü. Then in 1996 songs by Barlow's Folk Implosion, also, came to the fore with a US hit single, "Natural One", their contribution to the soundtrack of *Kids*; meanwhile, Sebadoh ended the year with HARMACY (1996), coming dangerously close to public attention.

For all this success, however, Sebadoh represent an axis of US alternative rock that remains defiantly outside the main sphere of the music industry. With a new drummer, **Russ Pollard**, replacing Fay, and THE SEBADOH (1999), the time seemed to be ripe for the group to straddle this divide. "Flame", released as a single, crosses white-boy soul with a doomy techno vision; elsewhere, the album verged on slowed-down-to-the-max post-rock wanderings. All great, depressive stuff. Sebadoh then went quiet.

But it was clear that Lou had never stopped writing, and that his primary concerns were his countless lo-fi sketches and home-recorded meanderings. Throughout Sebadoh's career Lou's solo offerings have emerged on 7"s, cassettes and CDs released on countless minor labels, each offering a minute gem of inspiration for 4-track troubadours everywhere.

Ironically as the end of the millennium neared, it was the Folk Implosion that were starting to become better known than his original band. Since then Barlow has branched out, recording under his own

name as part of a 'collaboration' with **Deus' Rudy Trouvé** on SUBSONIC 6 (2000). The two effectively split the album down the middle, so collaboration is probably the wrong word; nevertheless there's a surprising coherence to it: noisy, lo-fi, quirky, slightly deranged – all the things we love about Lou Barlow.

And for fans of acoustic hiss and rumble, 2002 brought a new Sentridoh collection, FREE SENTRIDOH FROM LOOBIECORE, as ever full of heart-felt ballads and lo-fi oddness. A worthwhile filler while we wait for Sebadoh, the band, to return.

Sebadoh

- **Sebadoh III** (1991; Homestead).
  A stunning, sprawling collection of near-whispered ballads and screaming, eccentric hardcore.

- **Rocking The Forest** (1992; Sub Pop).
  Contains the classic "Gimme Indie Rock", as well as typically eccentric songs punctuated by bursts of noise.

- **Bakesale** (1994; Sub Pop)
  From lo-fi to mid-fi, this is solid but highly individual alternative power-rocking.

- **Harmacy** (1996; Domino)
  A new maturity. "The Beauty Of The Ride" (the first single from the album) was an elegiac lament, backed with a Palace Brothers cover, "Riding", and a self-explanatory "Slintstrumental".

Sentridoh

- **Winning Losers – A Collection Of Home Recordings** (1994; Smells Like Records).
  A great collection of Lou's early home recordings.

- **Losing Losers '82-'91** (1995; Shrimper).
  Another great collection of Lou's early home recordings.

Jonathan Bell

THE SEEDS

Formed Los Angeles, 1965; disbanded 1972.

During the 60s, suburban garages across America rocked to the fuzz-drenched frenzy created by kids hoping to emulate the success of 'British Invasion' groups, The Rolling Stones, The Kinks and The Yardbirds. **The Seeds** were one of the biggest and best to emerge from this garage-band phenomenon. Their style was undeniably simple but nonetheless brilliantly original.

They were the creation of the charismatic **SKY SAXON** (vocals), who in the early 60s had recorded an obscure clutch of singles. He recruited **Jan Savage** (guitar), **Daryl Hooper** (keyboards) and **Rick Andridge** (drums), and trucked a deal with local LA label GNP, home to several other legendary garage punksters, for a debut 45, "Can't Seem To Make You Mine" (1965). This was a slow, angry piece which highlighted Saxon's unique vocal style – an inspired nasal snarl punctuated by howls, wails and yelps. The single flopped, but its successor, "Pushin' Too Hard" (1965), the ultimate Seeds song, reached #36 in the *Billboard* chart. It was based around a simple driving riff, over which Saxon vented his teen angst, and was characterized by a

sebadoh

masterful minimalism that would make the band a source of inspiration for the CBGB bands of the mid 70s.

The Seeds' debut album arrived in April 1966. Saxon's lyrics were infected by a naive charm, while the blend of British, C&W and blues influences served notice that The Seeds were developing a sound quite distinct from that of their "Louie Louie"-based rivals. The centrepiece was "Evil Hoodoo", a piece of high-octane freak-beat that was as much a genuine slice of punk as anything the 70s threw up.

A second, more adventurous LP, A WEB OF SOUND, appeared in October 1966, with **Harvey Sharpe** added on bass. The album brimmed with scratchy mid-60s classics, including the fourteen-minute "Up In Her Room" and the tight groover "Mr. Farmer", which provided The Seeds with another foray into the lower reaches of the American charts.

The band then ditched their punky style and threw their lot in with the emergent flower-power movement. The result was FUTURE (1967). Saxon's compositions now contained a strong element of acid-tinged horticultural whimsy ("Flower Lady And Her Assistant" and "March Of The Flower Children"), while the band dabbled with Eastern-style instrumentation. Commercial success seemed just around the corner, especially when the group cameoed in Jack Nicholson's *Psych Out* movie, but the follow-up 45, "The Wind Blows Your Hair" (1967), flopped, as fellow Californians Love and The Doors experienced a meteoric rise to fame.

Subsequent disputes with GNP led to the dreadful contract-fulfilling album, A SPOONFUL OF SEEDY BLUES (1967), released under the moniker **Sky Saxon Blues Band** and featuring sleeve notes by Muddy Waters. The Seeds were back, however, for the 1968 album RAW AND ALIVE, which featured powerful versions of the band's classic material as well as a new stormer, "Satisfy You". Nevertheless, it was probably testimony to the band's increasing unpopularity that the frantic audience reaction sounds strangely overdubbed. Following a failed project with legendary producer Kim Fowley and several deranged singles for MGM, Saxon folded The Seeds.

During the 70s, Saxon, like fellow cult-rockers Roky Erickson and Syd Barrett, seemed to drift off into permanent interstellar overdrive, but he has more recently released albums under a variety of names (Sky Sunlight Saxon; Sky Sunlight). The Seeds' achievements, meanwhile, were revived through the plethora of 60s garage compilation albums that appeared during the 80s.

Evil Hoodoo (1988; Bam Caruso).
Contains many of the best tracks from the first two albums, as well as highlights of later years. It also features the previously unreleased C&W/ funker "Falling Off The Edge Of My Mind" and fuzzy groover "Chocolate River". Proves that anyone who thinks that punk started in 1976 is wrong.

Malcolm Russell

THE SELECTER

Formed Birmingham, England, 1979;
disbanded 1981; re-formed 1992.

There was a period of about twelve months, right at the end of the 70s, when every British party seemed to play **The Selecter**. While The Selecter's stuff was jumping out of the speakers, you couldn't get to the kitchen for a beer because there were too many people trying to dance. Next time you give a party, stock up on their second-generation ska before you send out the invites. The Selecter effect still fills the dance-floor.

The band had an unusual beginning. The Selecter was initially nothing more than the instrumental B-side to The Specials' single "Gangsters". **Noel Davis** (guitar) and **THE SPECIALS'** John Bradbury (drums) formed a band with **Desmond Brown** on keyboards, **Kevin Harrison** on guitar and an alleged **Steve** on bass to record it. By the time "Gangsters" took off, John was back full-time with The Specials, Noel had moved on elsewhere, leaving Des and Kevin to cobble together a completely new group to take on the road.

Pauline Black's inspired vocals put the humour and optimism into British ska, and with the new band behind her – **Charley Anderson** on bass and **Charles Bembridge** on drums giving the rock-steady backing to Des'n'Kevin, with extra vocals from **Arthur Hendrickson** and extra guitar from **Compton Amanour** – The Selecter were set for their three minutes of heroics.

Like all the great pop bands, they came to represent the time during which they flourished. Their music carried some fairly heavy lyrics and summed up the foreboding that many felt at the change of government in 1979. Having said that, their first hit single, "On My Radio", was a bouncy, catchy, hummable girl-meets-boy-then-loses-him piece of chart fodder that zoomed into the Top 10. It was followed by the equally delicious sing-along ambition of "Three Minute Hero" and a Top 5 album, TOO MUCH PRESSURE, in 1980.

Subsequent releases were more downbeat as the two-tone/ska revival began to fade and as the 80s depression began to kick in: the next single, "Missing Words", was a tale of pure heartbreak. Before the follow-up, "The Whisper", had made it to the shops, the often-fatal process of line-up changes had begun – Charley's bass was now **Adam Williams'** bass and Desmond Brown, founder member from when there wasn't even a band at all, had been replaced by **James Mackie**.

With a title like CELEBRATE THE BULLET, we knew we were in for a serious sit-down talking-to from the 1981 album. Sure, it was still pop music, it was still Britska (a term that, thankfully, was never widely used), it was still Pauline and the lads dancing around with lots of brass and a beat you could lean against, but it wasn't happy, not at all. Titles like

THE SEEDS ■ THE SELECTER

"Washed Up And Left For Dead", "Bombscare" and "Selling Out Your Future" gave away the prevailing mood of gloom (it came out at a time of widespread fear that even if you hadn't yet been arrested by the police it would only be a matter of time before nuclear war destroyed the whole planet).

The pressure was certainly too much for The Selecter. They split up in 1981 and didn't re-form until 1992. Since then, especially when there's a flurry of interest in The Specials, The Beat or Madness, the singles get dusted off at the radio stations and there may be a series of gigs up and down the country. Keep an eye out for them and go and see them if you can, but first off get a copy of TOO MUCH PRESSURE and throw a party.

- **Too Much Pressure** (1980; Two-Tone).
  Gorgeous, Saturday-night, throw-open-the-doors party music. Classic songs include "On My Radio", "Thee Minute Hero", "Missing Words" and, of course, "Too Much Pressure" plus "Carry Go Bring Come", a ska-ed up James Bond theme and their tribute to dope-smokery, "My Collie (Not A Dog)".

- **Out On The Streets** (1992; Receiver).
  The Selecter's greatest hits. All thirteen of them.

Al Spicer

THE SENSATIONAL ALEX HARVEY BAND

Formed London, 1972; disbanded 1977.

The pre-punk 70s were kind to old rockers: however long you'd been struggling to get nowhere, a lick of paint could turn you into Gary Glitter or Alvin Stardust. Even so, **Alex Harvey**'s success was unexpected.

Born in Glasgow in 1935, Harvey had been heralded as the Scottish Tommy Steele back in the 50s, before moving into R&B in the early 60s and then on to the house band for the London production of *Hair*, finally linking up with also-ran progressive-rock band, Tear Gas, to form **The Sensational Alex Harvey Band** (SAHB) in 1972. From there on, it was a straightforward matter of cod-theatrics, endless touring and sheer hard graft.

The band cast Harvey as an ageing street punk, dressed down in jeans and rugby shirt, while guitarist **Zal Cleminson** wore make-up derived from the Joker in *Batman* and some lovely glitter catsuits. It was a *tour de force*. Harvey looked both hard and wise: he'd done his drinking and fighting a long way back, and alongside the trash-glam follies of Cleminson he seemed even more menacing and yet somehow reassuringly stable. And the band had a sense of gleeful fun to balance out the aggression.

They specialized in eccentric cover versions: Jacques Brel's "Next", Irving Berlin's "Cheek To Cheek" and the fascist anthem "Tomorrow Belongs To Me" from *Cabaret*. They added crushingly powerful originals like "Faith Healer" and "Swampsnake", in which they'd set up a simple mutation of an R&B riff that didn't develop at any stage, but just spent seven or eight minutes getting heavier and heavier. More than any other group between The Velvet Underground and Suicide, SAHB understood the beauty of repetition. Frequently they would leave the riff cycling for several minutes before any singing came in; when it did, it was to reveal the greatness of Harvey's voice. Soaked in whisky, aggro and melodrama, he could handle deranged shouting, truculent growls and a sarcastic sneer that pre-empted Rotten.

After a couple of years working through the live circuit, they broke through from cult status to mainstream success when THE IMPOSSIBLE DREAM (1974) hit the album charts. The next year they scored a British Top 10 hit with a cover of Tom Jones's "Delilah", on which Harvey alternated between psychopathic boasting and pub sing-along – unlike Jones, he sounded unhinged enough to have committed the murder. The follow-up was an equally lurid tale of violence, "Gamblin' Bar Room Blues".

More importantly, they had three albums in the charts in 1975 – TOMORROW BELONGS TO ME, NEXT and LIVE – and another two in 1976, with PENTHOUSE TAPES and SAHB STORIES. In 1976 they had a final hit single with "The Boston Tea Party", calculated to exploit the American Bicentennial.

They were still going strong at this point: the music was exuberant and the covers were as eclectic as ever, Leadbelly's "Goodnight Irene" nestling alongside The Osmonds' "Crazy Horses" on PENTHOUSE TAPES. But things were slipping away from them. SAHB had been too punk to make it really big in the early 70s, and lacked sufficient support to survive the arrival of fully fledged punk in 1976.

Curiously, although he was awarded due credit by other musicians such as Bon Scott of AC/DC and Nick Cave, Harvey was uncited by the punks, and he reciprocated the disinterest, initially refusing to acknowledge the new era, though he later (and too late to be funny) recorded an orchestral version of "Anarchy In The UK". Neither an album by SAHBWA (that's 'Without Alex'), nor releases by Harvey alone did much business, and both faded from sight. Harvey's death – from a heart attack on February 4, 1982 – revived memories for the faithful.

- **Best Of The Sensational Alex Harvey Band** (1991; Music Club).
  The usual flaws of 70s hard rock – indulgent solos, undisciplined jams, formless structures – are all conspicuous by their absence; instead you get humour, honesty and power. SAHB have been shamefully neglected over the years, and this compilation effortlessly stakes their claim to greatness.

Alwyn W. Turner

SEPULTURA

Formed Belo Horizonte, Brazil; 1984; disbanded 1996; re-formed 1997.

From their roots in Belo Horizonte, Brazil's third largest city, **Sepultura** have developed from an enthusiastic, if generic, thrash band to a genuinely inventive and versatile international act. Influenced by styles ranging from British punk to extreme heavy metal, the original line-up came together in 1984, naming themselves after the Portuguese word for 'grave'.

The band – **Jairo T** (lead guitar), brothers **Igor** (drums) and **Max Cavalera** (vocals/rhythm guitars), and **Paulo Jr** (bass) – wasted little time in emulating the conventions of the burgeoning thrash scene of the mid 80s. Their first great adventure in a recording studio was a project shared with another Brazilian band, Overdose. The BESTIAL DEVASTATION EP (1985) was the result, featuring every cliché of heavy metal, from the church-crushing devil on the cover to titles such as "Antichrist" and "Necromancer".

The following year brought more thrash-by-numbers in MORBID VISIONS (1986), showing the band still firmly caught up in the bullet-belted, spikes and leather image. Soon after, Jairo T was replaced by **Andreas Kisser** (guitars) and the solid line-up that exists today was formed. Although the production values of the recordings improved in terms of clarity and overall ferocity, SCHIZOPHRENIA (1987) still suffered from howling heavy-metal clichés. However, it was mixed by veteran thrash producer Scott Burns, whose involvement in future recordings would see the creation of some of the band's finest moments.

It was not until BENEATH THE REMAINS (1989), their first album for Roadrunner, that the band's true potential was tapped. The increasingly powerful production accentuated the brutal speed of the twin guitar interplay, while Max Cavalera's roaring vocals sounded truly bloodcurdling. Gone was the cheesy artwork and the overindulgence in typical heavy metal lyrics, as their political undertones came to the fore on tracks such as "Mass Hypnosis" and "Primitive Culture".

Sepultura had survived the wave of thrash metal they had surfed in on, and it was a measure of their growing international stature that the band played before huge audiences at the Dynamo and Rock In Rio festivals of 1990. On ARISE (1991), their first album recorded outside South America, they continued to experiment within the genre, constantly redefining their position – the music had grown in depth while the terse lyrics reflected feelings of hate, injustice and righteous anger.

By the time CHAOS AD (1993) was released, the band's sound and direction had taken them towards greatness. With Andy Wallace at the production helm, they largely reduced their reliance on speed to wield their sense of outrage like a deadly weapon. The songs about demons had finally been replaced by militant political aggression – from "Refuse/ Resist" to "Clenched Fist", the album was a guttural scream of rage. Infamous punk agitator Jello Biafra provided lyrics for "Biotech Is Godzilla", while the instrumental "Kaiowas" (inspired by a Brazilian Indian tribe who committed mass suicide in protest against the government) pointed towards the experimentation of their next album.

The following year brought further acclaim and a continued rise in their fortunes as they put in a performance of hair-raising intensity at the Donington Monsters Of Rock festival. The next stage of their development, ROOTS (1996), was their most adventurous recording to date. Gathering acclaim from a wide variety of critics, the band included more personal songs alongside the polemics, with the overall theme being a return to cultural and musical roots. Featuring a roster of guest musicians – including famed Brazilian percussionist **Carlinhos Brown**, members of Brazil's Xavantes tribe, **DJ Lethal** (House Of Pain) and **Mike Patton** (Faith No More) – the album was a landmark release and was brought out in a number of successive formats, featuring additional rare material to entice fans and completists alike.

Success, however, was a short-lived luxury for the band, as a tragic turn of events turned their future literally upside down. Just prior to the band's appearance at the Donington Monsters Of Rock Festival, Max Cavalera and his wife Gloria (also their manager) returned to the US after receiving news of the death of Gloria's son. The devastating news had a profound effect on the band's future and led to a rift between Max and the rest of the band. He was unhappy with their desire to continue touring while he and Gloria were still coming to terms with their loss. To add to the confusion, the other three members suddenly fired Gloria, a few days before Christmas, and Max resigned, outraged at the band's treatment of someone who had been with them for seven years.

From the ashes of Sepultura Mark 1 rose Sepultura Mark 2. After what seemed like an interminable period of flux, the remaining three members recruited the imposing figure of Derrick Green as the band's vocal roar. Standing at six feet plus, the dreadlocked Green lives up to his nickname 'The Predator' in both stature, stage presence and vocal abilities. With a new member installed they set about creating AGAINST (1998), an album which took their previous ethno-metal dabblings and focused them in hitherto unexplored directions. Max on the other hand began a relatively successful new career with his new outfit Soulfly, which sounded remarkably like the first incarnation of Sepultura.

Sadly, the initial rush of excitement that greeted Sepultura's triumphant emergence from the ashes gradually turned to indifference with NATION (2001). All the requisite stylings were in place, as was the band's healthy disrespect for power and authority, but they had lost a great deal of momentum with the departure of Max. As a result they parted company with Roadrunner Records and are rumoured to be writing a new album without a record deal.

● **Beneath The Remains** (1989; Roadrunner).
Reissued in 1998, this is a steamrolling collection of fierce time-changes and blitzing guitar speed. The conventions of thrash metal are very much in evidence, but the intensity of the music makes it a fine example of what could be done within the genre.

● **Chaos AD** (1993; Roadrunner).
The beginning of a hugely successful and experimental phase, abandoning the heavy metal standards for a more

political approach. The repeated chant of "We Who Are Not As Others" says it all. Also contains a stunning cover of New Model Army's "The Hunt".

⊙ **Roots** (1996; Roadrunner).
A sonic experience of monumental proportions. Check out the rattling Portuguese of "Ratamahatta", the instrumental interlude "Jasco", and the mantric chants of "Itsári", for examples of innovation and diversity. Sheer brilliance.

⊙ **Against** (1998; Roadrunner).
Everyone thought they were finished until they came up with this. Every bit as intense and diverse as their previous efforts, and then some. A highly impressive return to form.

Essi Berelian

SEX GANG CHILDREN

Formed London, 1982; disbanded 1985;
re-formed Los Angeles, 1991.

The name 'Sex Gang Children' was a dynamic tag dreamt up and discarded by Malcolm McLaren in favour of 'Bow Wow Wow'. It then passed to Boy George, who used it until he signed to Virgin and came over all consumer-friendly as Culture Club. Aware of its pedigree, a fledgling band called Panic Button grabbed the baton and decked themselves out in appropriate fetish-punk garb. Decadent and furious, the Sex Gang Children proceeded to revitalize punk in the early 80s.

It was Panic Button vocalist **Andi Sex Gang** and bass player **Dave Roberts** who formed the new group, enlisting **Terry McLeay** (guitar) and **Rob Stroud** (drums). Their timing was immaculate: punk-pop bands such as Theatre Of Hate and Wasted Youth were beginning to falter, and the post-Adam And The Ants audience starting to fracture. Sex Gang Children stepped into the void and became big on the scene very quickly, releasing NAKED (1982), an acclaimed, cassette-only live album.

A prestigious Futurama festival appearance coincided with the Sex Gang Children's first vinyl record, BEASTS!, an EP consisting of four reworked tracks from NAKED and the macabre title track. This and the follow-up single, "Into The Abyss" (1982), both hovered in the higher echelons of the UK indie charts for months.

1983 saw release of a debut album, SONG & LEGEND, which shot to the top of the indie charts along with its accompanying single, "Sebastianne". At the same time, Dave Roberts put together THE WHIP, a compilation album including a fine duet between Andi and Marc Almond entitled "The Hungry Years". The accumulated pressure of this workload came to a head when, on the first date of a tour to promote SONG & LEGEND, Stroud failed to appear.

The difficulties of Stroud's untimely departure were exacerbated when the band's label, Illuminated, declined to extend their deal and a major label withdrew an offer after Sex Gang Children refused to abbreviate their name. Ex-Theatre Of Hate drummer **Nigel Preston** filled in for a one-off single with Clay Records – the captivating "Mauritia Mayer" – before joining Death Cult. For their first American tour, Sex Gang engaged Death Cult's former drummer, **Ray Mondo**, who culminated an eventful affair by getting himself deported to his native Sierra Leone upon their return to England.

The turbulent year of 1983 ended with Dave Roberts leaving to form another (you'll never make it with that name) band, **Car Crash International**. This signalled the end of the Sex Gang group, though a cassette of their final US concert was released under the title ECSTASY AND VENDETTA OVER NEW YORK on the back of favourable notices they'd attracted in the States.

Andi and Terry carried on a while with new bassist **Cam Campbell** and drummer **Kevin Matthews**, before Andi also went solo, releasing two albums under the name **Andi Sex Gang**. Dave Roberts responded by forming a group called **The Children**, while Terry lent his guitar virtuosity to all manner of unsuccessful projects. However, in 1991 Receiver Records put out a compilation CD, THE HUNGRY YEARS: THE BEST OF SEX GANG CHILDREN, and it caused enough of a stir for Andi and Dave to reconcile and reconvene the group in Los Angeles.

The Sex Gang Children Mark 2 toured the West Coast in 1991, playing to a hybrid breed of goths. A new album was recorded in Los Angeles with a variety of musicians and released on Cleopatra in 1993 under the title MEDEA. The same label issued a compilation album, DIECHE, and reissued the ECSTASY AND VENDETTA OVER NEW YORK cassette on CD.

ECSTASY AND VENDETTA would have been the title of their unreleased follow-up to SONG & LEGEND – and bits of it crop up on various SGC compilations that sporadically appear, such as WELCOME TO MY WORLD (1998). The most significant of these recent compilations was SHOUT & SCREAM (1997). Sex Gang's most recent studio offering was BASTARD ART (2002); the group is still on the road, and shows no signs of slowing down.

⊙ **The Hungry Years: The Best Of Sex Gang Children** (1991; Receiver).
A compilation prepared with loving care. Here is the whole SONG & LEGEND album in all its pouting and scratchy glamour, all the singles, and even an unreleased track.

⊙ **Welcome To My World** (1998; Receiver).
Another compilation, prepared with loving care.

⊙ **Shout & Scream** (1999; Age of Panik).
This double CD was compiled by Andi Sex Gang himself, includes tracks off his own solo releases, and should satisfy all but the most insatiable enthusiast.

Tony Drayton

SEX PISTOLS

Formed London, 1975; disbanded 1978.

"Ever get the feeling you've been cheated?" Johnny Rotten, ending the last gig in San Francisco, 1978

Now and again, a band comes along and takes a sledgehammer to the definition of rock music:

The Pistols rehearse (yep – they really did): Vicious, Cook and Rotten

billy revival (broad London accents coming from pasty white guys dressed up like New Orleans pimps), and a back-to-basics pub-rock scene that was mainly R&B cover versions (more white boys wishing they were black). Not a promising scene.

Nevertheless, bunches of kids with guitars still met up for 'jams' and still dreamt of stardom. Some bought guitars, some borrowed. **Steve Jones**, a good rock'n'roll tearaway, went out and stole his, and with his old schoolmate, drummer **Paul Cook**, who had been 'in a band' since 1972, acquired enough equipment to stage a medium-sized rock festival. They still had little idea of what (or how) they were going to play, but veered towards bands they admired, the glam-rock idols (Bowie, The New York Dolls, The Stooges) and the 'Lads' Bands' (The Faces, Mott The Hoople, The Who), and with a couple of mates worked up a passable set – as **The Strand** – in rehearsal at the end of the King's Road.

Jones had already become a regular visitor to McLaren's shop; his band needed a manager and Malcolm had worked with The New York Dolls. A deal was done. They recruited a bass player, **Glen Matlock**, who'd previously worked in the shop, and he was slotted into the group alongside **Wally Nightingale** (the Pete Best character in this story).

They were at this stage a four-piece standard rock band, albeit with a Svengali manager who made them work in his shop. McLaren saw himself as a bit of a rebel, flogging situationist T-shirts and dodgy bondage wear designed in collaboration with Vivienne Westwood and Bernie Rhodes (later to manage The Clash), and hoped to combine a touch of rock'n'roll with a sprinkling of teenage anarchy and to sell a lot of trousers as a result. He dreamt up a neat name – Sex Pistols – but needed something more in his band, something to bring up the tension. Wally, nice guy though he was, had to go.

John Lydon wandered into McLaren's boutique. Legend has it he arrived wearing a Pink Floyd T-shirt with the words 'I HATE' scrawled above the logo. Whatever the truth, he was cajoled into singing along with Alice Cooper's "Eighteen" on the Sex jukebox,

the **Sex Pistols** were one of those bands. To a large extent, they were the creation of their manager, **MALCOLM MCLAREN**, owner of Sex, a clothes shop in London's King's Road, but, like Frankenstein's monster, the band escaped its creator and went on to raise havoc before being hounded to destruction by villagers with flaming torches.

It's necessary to have a little context. Music in the UK during the mid 70s was in a terrible state. 'Progressive' rock had become a bloated parody of itself: Emerson, Lake And Palmer toured with three forty-foot trailers of equipment, while Led Zeppelin fuelled rumours of goldfish bowls full of cocaine, fearsome personal greed and rock-overlord behaviour. Away from the stadium circuit, live rock comprised long-haired trench-coat-wearing student gigs, a 50s-style teddy-boy 'trad' rock'n'roll/rocka-

survived the laughter that followed, and ended up as Johnny Rotten, Sex Pistol.

For their first gig, the Pistols played support to a band called Bazooka Joe, whose singer immediately left the band and went off to transform himself into Adam Ant. Playing more support gigs on the art-school and pub-rock circuits, Sex Pistols picked up a following of arty weirdos and disenchanted speed freaks like Siouxsie and her pals. A scene – 'the cult with no name', in the words of one memorable headline – was beginning to start.

The Pistols achieved fame with one British TV show on December 1, 1976. By this time, they'd signed with EMI and were making a name for themselves with gigs in and around London. The cosy local news programme (on a station part-owned by EMI) had been ready to do a nice little interview with Queen (EMI recording artists). When Queen decided not to show up, an EMI man suggested that the Pistols fill in. It was a bad move to pull in the Pistols and their fans from a rehearsal, a worse move to fill them with booze, and really dumb to leave them for hours, to get bored and mischievous. Bill Grundy, the show's presenter, also partial to a drink, started provoking the boys, and during the course of the interview managed to elicit a few swear words from the band and to make a sweaty, lecherous old fool of himself over Siouxsie. The magnificent disaster began when he challenged Steve to 'Say something outrageous'. Steve did so, several times, and thus ended the career of Mr Grundy. The Pistols, however, were an instant household name throughout Britain, where almost nobody before had said 'fuck' on telly.

The Pistols went on tour with The Clash and The Damned, only to have most of the dates cancelled at the last moment. McLaren retreated to the rag trade, devoting himself more to his shop, now renamed Seditionaries, than to the Pistols. By early January 1977, the original punk band couldn't play in front of an audience and couldn't get their records out. Rotten was picked up in possession of a wrap of speed and the press had another story. This was the final straw for EMI, who dropped their contract, waved goodbye to the £40,000 advance and wished them 'every success with their next recording contract'. Great publicity again, stoking the scene, encouraging fans to rush out to buy French imports of the Pistols' debut single, "Anarchy In The UK".

Although "Anarchy In The UK" wasn't the first punk single – that honour goes to The Damned's "New Rose", released some weeks earlier by Stiff – it was the record people had been waiting for. The majority of Sex Pistols fans had never seen them play live and had existed on the limited amount of live footage being shown in 'Save our kids from this filth' reports on TV. Searingly relevant in the political doldrums of the 70s, the song had a snotty-nosed arrogance of the finest rock-'n'roll kind: Steve Jones's guitar kicked in the windows and Johnny Rotten's sneering, venomous

vocal took no prisoners. It was everything that punk was supposed to be about.

In early 1977, the Pistols parted company with Glen Matlock (he formed **THE RICH KIDS** soon after) and **Sid Vicious** took his place. Sid had been a friend of Johnny Rotten for years. He'd worked in McLaren's shop; he'd bashed the journalist Nick Kent at a Pistols gig; it was he, allegedly, who threw a glass during The Damned's set at the punk all-dayer at the 100 Club, blinding a girl in one eye; he'd played in one of the proto-punk bands, Flowers of Romance, as a drummer; he couldn't play bass but he had the look. He was in.

Soon after joining the Pistols, Sid hooked up with Nancy Spungeon, who had been banned from even seeing Jerry Nolan of the Heartbreakers by their manager, for fear of how badly she could mess him up with drugs. Sid concentrated on learning the bass, unaware of the black clouds gathering around his head, while Malcolm went ahead and did the deals, getting the band a recording contract, floating the idea of a film.

A&M were the next label to take on the Pistols. They lasted about a week before the group's behaviour at company HQ after the signing ceremony lost them another contract – though, as was becoming traditional, they kept the advance (£75,000). This time, however, the single that was lost was their magnificent "God Save The Queen", a track guaranteed to cause outrage in a country being wound up into a jingoistic fervour for the Queen's silver jubilee year. Richard Branson's Virgin Records took the Pistols when almost no other company was prepared to (signing them for a miserly £15,000 advance), and released "God Save The Queen" in time for 'Stuff the Jubilee' celebrations. The single never officially made it to #1 in the charts, which somehow showed Rod Stewart's latest miraculously reverse its declining sales to remain at the top – but everybody knew the Pistols had really been the best seller that week.

To promote the record, Virgin and McLaren, working together for once, dragged the reluctant

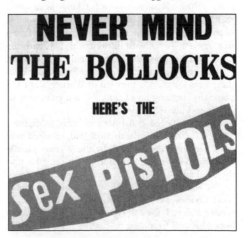

Pistols onto a river boat, the well-named *Queen Elizabeth*. The boat powered up and down the Thames, past the Houses of Parliament, blaring out "Anarchy", "God Save The Queen" and the rest of the Pistols' limited set. Things on board got a little bit lively when the booze and the speed kicked in and the captain radioed for assistance. A police boat escorted them to the shore. In the ensuing fracas, a lot of fans and the Pistols management team were arrested and given a right good kicking in the back of the van on the way to the police station. Allegedly.

After this, and the blasphemy of "God Save The Queen", it was open season on punk rockers. Members of the band were attacked, with Johnny Rotten being knifed in the leg and Paul Cook being beaten up by teddy boys. A mini-tour of Scandinavia was organized to keep the boys busy and away from the thugs on the streets (although there was a heavy Scando-ted presence that broke up the Stockholm gig), and a couple more singles were released to keep everybody on the edge of their seats. There was even a secret tour of the UK (under various assumed names), but it wasn't until November 1977 that the album NEVER MIND THE BOLLOCKS, HERE'S THE SEX PISTOLS was released.

Once again there was trouble with Britain's moral minority. The word 'bollocks' was enough to trigger harassment under the 1899 Indecent Advertisements Act. Window displays were removed, chain stores refused to stock it, they weren't permitted to advertise it on TV – and it still went straight to #1. (Branson called in a major-league lawyer to defend the title in court, won his case and kept his 'bollocks' in the public eye.) It was a great album, and each of the tracks became instant hits at the punk clubs, where audiences were word-perfect when it came to singing along with the PA.

Sid Vicious, in the meantime, was fast becoming a junkie. McLaren's response was to send in the office staff to kidnap Nancy, put her on a plane to New York and smooth over the cracks with Sid later. The 'rescue' was a fiasco and served only to alienate the lovers, pushing them deeper into their own company. Johnny Rotten, who was taking more speed than was probably good for him, had started to distance himself from the rest of the group. McLaren was more involved with his film deal than with the band, and Steve and Paul just wanted to get out and play. As the year came to an end, a final furore over their visas for the US tour led to Warner, their US company, putting up $1,000,000 as a guarantee of their good behaviour on US soil.

The tour started in Atlanta and ended in disaster. The first date was fairly abysmal; Sid, in a bad way with heroin, was beaten up by the Warner people hired to ensure that the million dollars came back to the company at the end of the tour. San Antonio, Texas, was the venue for the next gig and the trouble started as soon as the boys came on stage. With necks redder than red, the audience pelted the Pistols with beer cans and food. Sid reacted by suggesting that

'You cowboys are all a bunch of fucking faggots' and was obliged to defend his point of view by administering a tap on the head with his bass guitar to a member of the audience. End of gig.

Baton Rouge followed, then Dallas (Sid on stage with 'GIMME A FIX' scrawled on his chest), then Tulsa – which passed pretty much without incident. But irreparable cracks had appeared. Steve Jones wouldn't travel on the bus any more and, together with his old pal Paul, was taking planes to the gigs. Johnny Rotten hated everybody, especially Malcolm, and Sid was barely making it from one city to another before getting serious withdrawal.

Rotten had had enough of the Pistols by the time he arrived in San Francisco for the lousy final gig. Malcolm suggested going to Rio de Janeiro to hook up with Ronnie Biggs (British train robber and folk hero to some), after the tour. Rotten wasn't impressed, Sid didn't care really, but the Jones–Cook axis were keen enough. After the performance, Johnny Rotten went to a different hotel from the rest of the band and the party was over.

The aftermath was messy. Sid went first to New York, where he promptly overdosed, then he stayed with McLaren for a while, recording his immaculate "My Way" and a couple of Eddie Cochran tracks, "Somethin' Else" and "C'mon Everybody". Eventually he went back to New York, got even more messed up on heroin, became involved in the death of Nancy and killed himself. He was 21 when he died.

Johnny Rotten disappeared, although John Lydon was back on the scene soon afterwards with **PUBLIC IMAGE LTD**. Jones and Cook went to Rio and made their novelty record with Ronnie Biggs. Later on, they bolted on a couple of off-the-shelf musicians and toured as **Professionals**. A head-on road smash, somewhere in the middle of the US, caused serious injuries and stopped their new venture in its tracks. McLaren finally finished his film, released as *The Great Rock'N'Roll Swindle*. It was a mess, with Rotten present only in archive footage, Matlock airbrushed from the picture, and shreds of three story lines hammered together, but it's still the best record of the Pistols' life and times, and even has elements of truth.

The Pistols were a distillation of all the best of what had gone before in teenage rebellion. They were loud and noisy and they didn't care what you thought. They came from nowhere to generate a legend and then exploded before they could turn into what they'd once despised. They challenged the monolithic music industry, broke into it and changed the way that bands looked at it. There was no 'do-it-yourself' scene before the Pistols and no destroying it after they'd gone. They only recorded one album, didn't sell phenomenal quantities of records but, in the history of rock'n'roll, they are as important as The Rolling Stones.

In 1996 four fattish, middle-aged white Londoners – Lydon, Jones, Cook and Matlock – got together to play a few outdoor concerts and record a live album.

A tight, well-rehearsed rock band, they played their greatest hits while the audience went wild. A marvellous time was had by all and the filthy lucre rolled in. The whole tour was a celebration and thousands of fans managed to see the band for the first time. But it wasn't punk any more. That had died in San Francisco, eighteen years before. Julian Temple, the man who'd first filmed the band, added his own viewpoint to the Pistols mythology with the 2000 film release of *The Filth And The Fury*, a title lifted from the bands' best-ever tabloid headline. Essentially, the film was yet another documentary, charting the nasty, brutish and short life of the band, and filling in a few previously deep holes in their story. It was nostalgia time for the old punks who made the pilgrimage to the cinema, and an eye-opener for thousands of younger followers around the world.

⊙ **Never Mind The Bollocks Here's The Sex Pistols** (1977; Virgin).
The most important punk album of all. Even given a listen now, the music has all the urgency and swagger it had when it was released.

⊙ **Indecent Exposure** (various labels).
Nearly all the Pistols' bootleg live albums seem to have been recorded on cheap cassette players at gigs where the band weren't playing well. This is an exception, recorded off the mixing desk at a gig in Burton on Trent on September 24, 1976.

⊙ **This Is Crap** (1996; Virgin).
If you're thinking of investing in Sex Pistols product, might we recommend this little gem? A double-CD package including NEVER MIND THE BOLLOCKS, the legendary Spunk bootleg, and the band's earliest Chris Spedding-produced demos.

Al Spicer

RON SEXSMITH

Born St Catherine's, Ontario, Canada, 1964.

"The best record I've heard all year." Elvis Costello on Sexsmith's debut

The alarmingly young-looking **Ron Sexsmith** stands firmly in the Canadian tradition of deep, sensitive singer-songwriters. His songs work on the 'less is more' principle: the melodies are bittersweet and deceptively simple and every word is carefully chosen and just right.

Sexsmith started forming bands in high school, then waited for the big break while pounding the streets of Toronto for a courier firm. He claims that to write songs he has to be doing something else requiring no concentration, and this no-brainer job enabled him to write hundreds. The first fruits of this tedium-enhanced creativity appeared on the independently released GRAND OPERA LANE cassette.

Demos led to a deal with Interscope, who recognized quality when they heard it. Top producer Mitchell Froom (Crowded House, Elvis Costello) offered to produce his first album, RON SEXSMITH (1995). Before recording started, Sexsmith sent

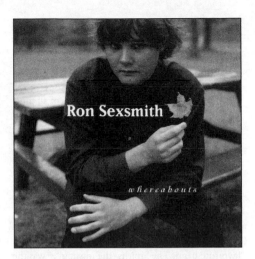

Ron Sexsmith
whereabouts

Froom a load of records he liked, notably Tim Hardin and some early Kinks stuff. These influences showed up very subtly on the album, in instrumental textures and nuances of mood rather than in the wholesale lifting of melodies that lesser artists get away with nowadays. Harry Nilsson was another presence (Sexsmith contributed a cover of "Good Ol' Desk" to a Nilsson tribute album), while his voice sometimes had the sombre melancholy that characterizes Jackson Browne's best work or Warren Zevon's ballads – though Sexsmith's lyrics are far less flip and more direct than Zevon's.

The follow-up recording, OTHER SONGS (1997), was, despite its self-deprecatory title, again a collection of beautifully observed short stories, delivered in Sexsmith's unadorned voice and guitar. WHEREABOUTS (1999) was even more ambitious and confident. BLUE BOY (2001) was a more cumbersome affair and saw Sexsmith trying too hard to embrace too many styles.

2002's COBBLESTONE RUNWAY, however, witnessed a successful shift in direction to embrace beats and synth ornamentations. The collection's profile was boosted by the presence of Coldplay's **Chris Martin** on the song "Gold In Them Hills"; the number was later released as a single, marketed under both singers' names.

Having earned the respect of top fellow songwriters like John Hiatt and Elvis Costello, his biggest concern now might be finding a continuing supply of mind-numbing tasks to aid his writing. Perhaps endless interviews with journalists and radio shows on the promotional circuit will fit the bill.

⊙ **Ron Sexsmith** (1995; Interscope).
An album that gradually makes itself a permanent resident in the listener's psyche. The deceptive simplicity of songs like "Secret Heart", "There's A Rhythm" (a brooding extra version, produced by Daniel Lanois, is tacked onto the end of the album), and "Lebanon, Tennessee", continue to haunt long after the final track.

⊙ **Cobblestone Runway** (2002; Parlophone).
Folk meets pop meets dance-floor beats – but still, unmistakeably, Sexsmith.

Andy Smith

SHAKESPEARS SISTER

Formed London, 1988; disbanded 1993.

At the start of 1988, **Siobhan Fahey** (vocals) was one third of **Bananarama**, one of the most successful British female pop bands of all time, but she was far from happy. Increasingly weary of Bananarama's likeable but lightweight ditties, and frustrated by the conveyor-belt approach of producers Stock Aitken Waterman, she finally decided to leave the group to form a partnership with New Yorker **Marcella Detroit** (vocals/guitar). Although not well known in her own right, Detroit had previously worked with Eric Clapton, Philip Bailey and Aretha Franklin, and had co-written Clapton's classic "Lay Down Sally". The pair decided on the name Shakespears Sister after a song by Fahey's favourite band, The Smiths (the missing 'e' was the result of a graphic designer's spelling mistake) and signed with London Records in the summer of 1988.

The new beginning turned into a false start when their debut single, "Break My Heart", failed to chart, but after a lengthy gap its follow-up, "You're History", created considerable interest. A cool and slinky pop gem, its appeal lay in the contrast in style between the two vocalists, with Detroit's soaring falsetto perfectly complementing Fahey's sardonic, almost menacing drawl. It had hit written all over it and eventually reached #7 in the UK, creating a strong base for their debut album, SACRED HEART (1989). Although both members regarded the band as an equal partnership, Fahey was very much the focal point of this album: it was her face on the cover, with Detroit appearing only as a blurred background figure on the inner sleeve. The record enjoyed favourable reviews and made the British Top 10, but its content was something of a disappointment, with nothing to match the stylish charm of "You're History". Despite several attempts, there were to be no further hits from this set.

The duo re-emerged with HORMONALLY YOURS (1992), so called because both Fahey and Detroit had been pregnant during its recording. The first single, "Goodbye Cruel World", made little impression, and once again it was the second release that took off. "Stay" was a tender and inventive postmodern love song whose plaintive 'stay with me' refrain struck an immediate chord with the British public. It took only a month to reach #1 and stayed there for eight weeks, one of the longest chart-topping runs in recent years. (Only Whitney Houston's "I Will Always Love You" was a bigger UK seller in 1992.) The album, which was a more confident development of the goth/glam sound of their debut, was also an immediate hit. Although its overall mood was upbeat, the highlight was the closing "Hello (Turn Your Radio On)", a thoughtful and reflective piano/electric guitar lament which revealed a new maturity to their songwriting. It was one of four fur-

ther UK hit singles, including a return to the Top 10 with the jaunty "I Don't Care".

When "Stay" repeated its Top 5 success in the States, it seemed that Shakespears Sister had the world at their feet, but there were growing rumours of tension between the two (fuelled when Fahey failed to turn up to collect a Brit Award for "Stay") and tabloid speculation about the health of both Fahey and her husband, ex-Eurythmic Dave Stewart. Although reports of a split were denied, Detroit eventually began working on a solo album, Fahey withdrew from the spotlight to spend more time with her family, and there was a gradual realization that the pair had drifted apart.

Detroit was quick to establish herself as a solo artist, enjoying two hit singles and reaching the UK Top 20 with JEWEL (1994). Fahey, meanwhile, dusted down the Shakespears Sister banner in 1996 to launch her own solo career; the response was a muted one, with critics lamenting the end of the old partnership. For the moment, the closing line of their last album together serves as a fitting epitaph: 'Life is a strange thing/Just when you think you've learnt how to use it, it's gone.'

Sacred Heart (1989; London).
Very much promoted and perceived at the time as Siobhan Fahey's solo album, this shows great promise despite the unfinished feel of some of the material. High point is the shimmering, sneering "You're History", low point is a half-hearted stab at Bob Marley's "Could You Be Loved".

Hormonally Yours (1992; London).
An edgy and entertaining collection in which the now firmly established Fahey/Detroit partnership creates a mood of brooding tension and weary cynicism, offset by the occasional moment of serenity. Its energy and wit (plus a global megahit with "Stay") made this a considerable success.

Jonathan Kennaugh

SHAM 69

Formed Hersham, England, 1976; disbanded 1980; re-formed 1987.

Sham 69 are typical of the kind of band unleashed by the **SEX PISTOLS'** do-it-yourself ethic. Loud, raw and aggressively working-class, they made their name through **Jimmy Pursey** bellowing his political broadsides over a sparse, trebly buzz-saw guitar sound.

The band's first single, "I Don't Wanna"/"Red London"/"Ulster Boy", earned massive street credibility right away. With its photo cover of six police officers 'arresting' a protester at an anti-Nazi demo, it was released on the ferociously indie Step Forward label with production by John Cale (ex-Velvet Underground) and beers provided by Mark Perry (of the seminal *Sniffin Glue* fanzine and later of punk band Alternative TV).

Sham tended to produce good, sing-along anthems, full of broad-brush generalizations and crude, laddish humour: at some of their early gigs they gave away a live recording, entitled "Song Of The Streets", which revolved around a call-and-

Sham 69's Jimmy Pursey having a run-in with the old bill outside The Vortex, 1979

response of 'What've we got? Fuck All!' Trouble was, their music tended to attract the more yobbish punks, and attending a Sham 69 gig was perceived as a risk by the more sensitive, art-school liberal wing of the punk movement. They always had hard-drinking fans who enjoyed a fight, but as time passed, neo-Nazi skinheads were seen more frequently at their gigs. Eventually they lost their original punk following to a gang of right-wing headcases, much to Jimmy's disgust. Although he was slow to come out and declare his position, he appeared on stage with the avowedly non-racist **CLASH** on several occasions, most notably at the Rock Against Racism event in Hackney, London in 1978.

Before all this foolishness, however, Jimmy and the boys – **Albie Slider** on bass, **Mark Cain** replacing Billy Bostik on drums, and **Dave Parsons** replacing Neil Harris (who'd replaced the implausibly named Johnny Goodfornothing) on guitar – put together a set of fine punk tunes dealing with all your favourite punk themes. After the magnificent "I Don't Wanna", the band signed to Polydor before producing "Borstal Breakout", a combination of Eddie Cochran and Alex from *A Clockwork Orange*. The album Tell Us The Truth (1978) contained few musical surprises: Jimmy and the boys were getting good at the cockney anthem business, and track titles like "Hey Little Rich Boy" and "We Gotta Fight" tell you as much as you need to know. (For the trivia-minded, Jimmy's mum's voice at the beginning of "Family Life" – 'You bloody get upstairs and have a wash!' – was provided by actress Wendy Richard,

who plays an almost identical character in the British soap opera *EastEnders*.) The album also showcased the band's cause célèbre, their masterpiece of agit-pop "George Davis Is Innocent (OK)". The said Davis eventually returned to prison under circumstances that left his lack of innocence in no doubt and the song was recycled as "The Cockney Kids Are Innocent".

After three UK top 20 singles – "Angels With Dirty Faces", "If The Kids Are United" and the self-parodying "Hurry Up Harry" – their second album, THAT'S LIFE, was released in November 1978. Again it contained little to challenge their fans. The idea of using snippets of dialogue to introduce some of the tracks was extended, but the social horror stories and tales of laddish behaviour remained essentially the same.

Though Sham were always touring (and their gigs almost always descending into fights), they kept at it in the studio, knocking out another couple of chart singles and introducing more complex lyrical ideas and more considered music on their third album, THE ADVENTURES OF THE HERSHAM BOYS (1979). But by the time they recorded the fourth album, THE GAME, there was nothing more to be said and Jimmy was sick of the mindless fans. By November 1980 there was a posthumous compilation available, THE FIRST, THE BEST AND THE LAST.

Jimmy had a solo career of sorts, bringing out two LPs – IMAGINATION CAMOUFLAGE and ALIEN ORPHAN – before re-forming Sham 69 in 1987 with his old crony Dave Parsons. In 1988 the new Sham put out an album, VOLUNTEER, which didn't do particularly well, and the project went on hold till 1992, when a trickle of singles releases started. Sham 69 still exist today, playing greatest hits sets to old punks and mellowed skinheads but still doing it with the swagger that made them a great band to see back in the old days. They also returned unexpectedly to the review pages in 1995 with SOAPY WATER & MR MARMALADE, a (ahem) concept album, themed on British soap operas and marijuana. This having been justly skipped over, 1996's rerelease (on Dojo) of the four albums gave the record-buying public a chance to sample what they'd missed.

The last we heard from Jimmy and the boys was a couple of 1997 releases on Scratch Records: CODE BLACK, a Pursey solo effort (ageing punk does drum'n'bass, anyone?) was not terribly well received; THE A FILES, a 'proper' Sham album, was much more like it – a glorious ramshackle mix of politics, injustice and 'goin' daaaahn the pub'. Stand-out track "Swampy" – a Sham praise-song in the tradition of their own "George Davis Is Innocent" – celebrates the unlikely hero of anti-road protest in the UK.

⊙ **Tell Us The Truth** (1978; Revenge).
A wonderful bit of late-70s memorabilia, this is whiny teenage rock'n'roll at its best. Jimmy and the boys are really angry about a lot of things and don't mind telling us about it.

⊙ **The First, The Best And The Last** (1980; Polydor).
All the greatest singles and album tracks – pretty much the ideal Sham 69 sampler.

Al Spicer

THE SHAMEN

Formed Aberdeen, Scotland, 1984.

The Shamen have embraced the culture of psychedelic drugs more wholeheartedly than any other rock band since The Grateful Dead. Originally a four-piece centred on **Colin Angus** (keyboards), with **Derek McKenzie** (guitar/vocals), **Keith McKenzie** (drums) and **Alison Morrison** (bass), the band in its early incarnation played LSD-influenced indie rock. Their first release as the Shamen was a flexidisc given away with *Skipping Kitten* fanzine "Four Letter Girl"/"Stay in Bed"; though their first 'real' single, "They May Be Right", was released in April 1986 on the One Big Guitar label, and was followed by "Something About You" (1986) and the album DROP (1987). The music was based on a 60s guitar sound reminiscent of bands like Love.

The Shamen's next single, "Christopher Mayhew Says" (1987), had a rather more abrasive sound and sampled a 1955 interview with a Labour MP who took a dose of mescaline for a TV documentary when the drug was still legal. By this time, **Will Sinott** (bass) had replaced Derek McKenzie, and after two further singles and the *Jesus Is A Lie* tour (which led to excommunication from the Bishop of Aberdeen), Colin and Will, eager to move in the direction of sampling, raps and breakbeats, left the rest of the band behind and moved down to London, where they got involved in the London rave scene.

Angus and Sinott demonstrated the result of the band's metamorphosis, releasing the "Shamen Vs. Bam Bam" single (1988) with acid-houser Bam Bam. It was followed by IN GORBACHEV WE TRUST (1989), an album which captured the dance/indie crossover experimentation typical of the period. Now established on the indie circuit, they began to make a name for themselves as dance musicians too. Their last release on Moksha, the 10" PHORWARD (1989), went even further from rock, being faster and less bumpy than GOBRBACHEV, with a lot more reliance on drum machines, samplers and synthesizers.

The band moved to a new label, One Little Indian, for "Omega Amigo" (1989), some mixes of which remained unreleased because the frequencies used were too extreme to be cut onto vinyl. It was, however, their next release, "Progen (Move Any Mountain)" (1990) that really brought The Shamen to the notice of the now rapidly diversifying dance scene. Attracting little attention at first, "Progen" was suddenly discovered by DJs on the rave scene, and became a major club hit. It was eventually rereleased and remixed almost endlessly, and the theme remains one of their staples. That year's album, EN-TACT, sold over 100,000 copies.

Meanwhile The Shamen had opened a club night, Synergy, at London's T&C2, something between a rave and a gig, with records and live music both on the bill. DJs included Mixmaster Morris of the Irresistible Force, considered by many to be the world's #1 ambient DJ, and underground acid-house disc spinner Mr. C from the legendary Rip Club. Singer Plavka was another member of the Synergy crew and hallucinogenic visual stimuli complemented the sounds. As far as other stimuli went, some said the club had more dealers than punters.

But then, in May 1991, tragedy struck. Out in the Canary Islands to film a video for the "Progen" re-release, Will Sinott was drowned. After a lot of soul-searching, Colin decided to carry on, recruiting **Mr. C** and a changing cast, including the likes of vocalist **Jhelisa Anderson** from Soul Family Sensation. A single, "LSI" (1992), followed, and then the British #1, "Ebeneezer Goode" (1992), with a cockney rap and a chorus that sounded suspiciously like 'E's are good! E's are good!'

The Shamen followed up "Ebeneezer Goode" with a string of further hits and an LP, BOSS DRUM (1992), and extended their audience to an enthusiastic following on the US West Coast. San Francisco became their second home, and the band's travels in that part of the world brought them into contact with cult writer Terence McKenna, 'a Timothy Leary for the 90s'. McKenna outlined some favourite Shamen themes on their joint single "Re-Evolution" (1993), tying traditional shamanism in with modern Western psychedelia.

The AXIS MUTATIS album (1995) – with **Victoria Wilson James**, formerly of Soul II Soul, replacing Anderson on vocals – featured political raps and ambient, atmospheric dubs as well as a track called "S2 Translation", which was claimed to have been generated by a program for turning DNA sequences into music. It was released in tandem with an ambient album, ARBOR BONA ARBOR MALA. They followed this in 1996 with the distinctly herbalized flavour of HEMPTON MANOR, an album of rootsier drum'n'bass mixed in with moments of trance; a similar offering came as UV in 1999.

The Shamen have come a long, long way since their beginnings – if indeed they can even be considered the same band – but they still retain a deep commitment to the psychedelic movement. They became commercial, as Colin Angus put it, to 'continue the process of insinuating the shamanic' into the mainstream; but today they are back where they belong, well and truly underground (assuming they still exist at all!). According to their website, all future Shamen activity will be strictly online, though Mr. C did release his own solo album, CHANGE, in 2002.

⊙ **In Gorbachev We Trust** (1989; Demon).
The Shamen's best indie-rock album, developing their interest in electronics without abandoning their rock'n'roll past.

⊙ **En-Tact** (1990; One Little Indian).
The Shamen's definitive album, and Will Sinott's last record, featuring the original versions of "Progen", "Omega Amigo" and "Make It Mine", and a version of "Hyperreal" too. A fine album, capturing the band at their most creative.

⊙ **Boss Drum** (1992; One Little Indian).
Purists said that this album was too commercial, but less elitist fans made this The Shamen's best-selling album (it sold over a million and was in the UK chart for 27 weeks). It certainly features their best-known hits, including "Ebeneezer Goode", "LSI", "Phorever People" and, of course, the title track.

Daniel Jacobs & David Wren

SHAPES

Formed Leamington Spa, England, 1976;
disbanded 1981.

A kind of Midlands Rezillos, the **Shapes** were a band that at first tried to copy the punk image coming out of London's Roxy Club in 1976, but found that, left to their own devices, they quickly moved towards and then through a Gerry Anderson-fuelled Buzzcocks-like sound.

Seymour Bybuss (vocals), **Tim Jee** and **Steve Richards** (guitars), **Brian Helicopter** (bass), with **Dave Gee** (drums), played their first gig with The Models, The Killjoys and Spizz at the tail end of the first punk explosion. The self-financed EP PART OF THE FURNITURE (1979) won the attention of John Peel with tracks such as "I Saw Batman In The Launderette", and "What's For Lunch Mum, Not Beans Again?" A Peel session followed and much touring supporting the likes of the Cure, Fall and the Photos.

After signing a deal with

Northern Ireland's Good Vibrations Records in May 1979 they released their second single "Blast Off"/"Airline Disaster". By this time, Steve Richards had left, and the Shapes trimmed down to a four-piece for their last single, "Jennifer The Connifer"/"Let's Go To Planet Skaro"/"My House Is A Satellite" (1980).

Never a band with a single clue of what to do with themselves other than just play live and make quirky independent pop singles, they were swallowed whole by the Two Tone craze from Coventry – just ten miles away from sleepy ol' Leamington Spa. Finding themselves the only band in the Midlands unable to play ska, and having nothing in common with the more negative direction punk was taking, they called it a day, leaving behind a brief legacy of rather snappy and witty singles, and some blisteringly anarchic stage shows. Later bands such as the Not Sensibles and Piranhas paid tribute to the Shapes and, in 1996, a Scottish band called The Muck recorded three of their songs as a tribute.

These days Seymour Bybuss is writing and playing with punk/art/folk/music collective **The Ambassadors Of Plush**; Brian Helicopter is a medal-winning skydiver living in California; Dave Gee took up with a nude all-in wrestling show that toured Scandinavia; while Tim Jee played briefly with **The Captain Black Solution**, but now runs a shop selling cravats.

Happily, after years of searching for obscure compilations on long-forgotten labels, the glorious release of SONGS FOR SENSIBLE PEOPLE (1998) means that all the Shapes' music is now available for us to love.

⊙ **Songs For Sensible People** (1998; Overground).
At last, the complete career retrospective: demos, previously unreleased material and all the single/EP tracks. Form an orderly queue outside the record store right now.

Gareth Holder

The Shapes relax in the only Leamington Spa pub that let them in

SHED SEVEN

Formed York, England, 1991.

Fronted by snake-hipped, prepubescent mini-sex god **Rick Witter** (vocals), **Shed Seven** swaggered from the cobbled confines of provincial York. Having started out as a band called Brockley New Haven in their teens, Witter, childhood friend **Alan Leach** (drums), **Paul Banks** (guitar) and **Tom Gladwin** (bass) slogged their way through gigs and supermarket shelf-stacking before signing, as Shed Seven, to Polydor in 1994.

Their first single, "Mark"/"Casino Girl", failed to dent the charts, but the heavy dose of northern swagger, with Rick sounding like a young Pete Shelley without the self-doubt, was enough to get them cited as the 'next big thing'. "Dolphin", the second single, hit the UK Top 30, and *Top Of The Pops* beckoned. Another guitar-based song, "Dolphin", offered nothing extraordinary but was simply a good tune that was more than reminiscent of The Stone Roses. The sight of young Rick and company cavorting like a mini-pops Rolling Stones caused many a teen heart to flutter. "Speakeasy", another swagger of a song with a pouting chorus and a sleazy underbelly, was released in August 1994 and gave Shed Seven their second hit. CHANGE GIVER (1994) was a collection of workmanlike rock/pop tunes delivered with a cocksure grin. Nothing seminal, but likeable nonetheless.

1995 saw the band floundering slightly. "Where Have You Been Lately?" and "Ocean Pie" both reached the UK Top 30, but the songs were seen by some, and later by the band themselves, as 'more of the same'. Yet the band were huge in Europe and gigantic in Thailand: such was the passion of Southeast Asia for the skinny northerners that "Ocean Pie" knocked "Sure" by Take That off the #1 spot.

With its brass section and fat, cheeky chorus, "Getting Better" (1996) continued the success by entering the UK charts at #14. Armed with new tunes, obstinate self-belief and those skinny hips, the band proved with A MAXIMUM HIGH (1996) that they were the band they had always boasted of being. Never before had their arrogance seemed so well founded.

A couple of years' hard labour, measuring the length of Britain's motorways in a seemingly endless tour, finally led to LET IT RIDE (1998). Sharpened by publc exposure and probably a little stung by some of the more barbed comments in the music press, the band give it their all from start to finish. Stand-out track is "She Left Me On Friday", where Shaun Ryder meets The Rolling Stones. A further single, "Devil In Your Shoes", again failed to set the charts alight. Increasingly, the band seemed pigeonholed as a solid yet rather dull rock combo, destined to tour more and chart less in the future.

In 1998, Shed Seven were suddenly dropped by Polydor, victims of a wave of cost-cutting that swept the music industry. After a lengthy silence, they re-emerged in 2001 without guitarist Paul Banks, but with the return of **Joe Johnson**, who had been guitarist in very early incarnations of the band. Also a new full-time member was **Fraser Smith** (keyboards), who joined Witter and Johnson as the songwriting team for a fourth album, TRUTH BE TOLD, released on the Artful label. No longer hitting the top 20, Shed Seven retained a loyal fan base, and their tour schedule for 2001 was almost as busy as that of 1996. A live album, WHERE HAVE YOU BEEN TONIGHT? (2003), documented their on-stage busyness.

⦿ **Change Giver** (1994; Polydor).
Owing more than a little to The Stone Roses, The Smiths, and particularly Inspiral Carpets, this album has some very good songs, the odd bad one and several mediocre efforts.

⦿ **Going For Gold** (1999; Polydor).
This is their best of collection; it does contain some fine moments but there's a lot of padding here as well.

⦿ **Truth Be Told** (2001; Artful).
The eleven songs are short, sharp, and unpretentious. On the minus side, the group's approach is just a little too samey, and a sense of distinctiveness is often missing.

Maxine McCaghy

SHEEP ON DRUGS

Formed London, 1991.

Formed in response to the so-called 'Second Summer Of Love' by **Duncan X**, aka King Duncan (vocals) and Dead Lee, later **Lee 303** (electronics/guitar), the splendidly named **Sheep On Drugs** set out to simultaneously mock and revel in the excesses of pop culture. Blending a mixture of sleazy rock, hard techno and punk nihilism into their own peculiar cabaret act of a rock'n'roll band, they set out on tour with buckets of fake blood, syringes and a pulpit from which Duncan could rant at Punter (as they termed the audience), who lapped it up with a knowing postmodern acceptance of their own commodification.

SOD (as they are appropriately referred to) released their first single, "Catch 22"/"Drug Music", in 1991. Two sides of sardonic observation of the world of work and the rave scene respectively established them as favourites on the electronic body music/industrial scene, though ravers were not amused at being the butt of the jokes.

Keeping up an unhealthy live schedule, Sheep On Drugs perfected a live show which extended to *Grand Guignol* theatrics – bloody dummies suspended over the stage, blank rounds fired above the audience, and the ever-scathing Duncan acting out the dark side of club culture. "Motorbike"/"Mary Jane" (1992) took the sleazy disco out on the road of a Saturday night, proving that as far as anthemic nihilism went, SOD could deliver the goods. The remixes and ironic sloganeering of the TV USA and

Sheep On Drugs' Duncan X (right) and friend

TRACK X EPs followed later in the year, leading to a deal with Island that December.

Not allowing their major-label contract to restrict their invective, SOD released what may be the closest they will ever have to a mainstream hit single, "15 Minutes Of Fame", in the spring of 1993, closely followed by what was only semi-ironically entitled GREATEST HITS.

With major-label backing, the venues and stageshows became bigger and more sophisticated, with slides and neon slogans projecting Sheep On Drugs' message: sex is death, drugs are for sheep, buy the product. The proliferation of product available included two new EPs, FROM A TO H AND BACK AGAIN (1993) and LET THE GOOD TIMES ROLL (1994), and the tasteful Rubber Johnnies range of SOD condoms. But, as their own slogan, 'flavour of the month', warned, their flirtation with Island lasted no longer than one further outing ON DRUGS (1994). Despite several excellent tracks, this failed to work as a coherent album; the attempted subtlety and seriousness of some of the tracks fell short of their own previous stands, and Island soon dropped the band.

Following the return to independence with their own Drug Squad label, the duo released the jungle-influenced SUCK EP, and the uneven STRAPPED FOR CASH EP in 1995, before signing to Martin Atkins' Invisible in 1996. The first product of this alliance was the DOUBLE TROUBLE (1996) CD, repackaging the Drug Squad singles for American release, followed in 1997 by the energetic ONE FOR THE MONEY. Updating Sheep On Drugs' populist trash aesthetics with booming drum'n'bass, the album capitalized on their increasing popularity in America and Japan, mercilessly encouraging attempts to ban their live film shows and proudly upholding their boast of being 'the most decadent band of all time!'

But the band's relationship with Invisible was beginning to deteriorate, and little material appeared for several years. A rejuvenated SOD are expected to release a fresh set late in 2003.

Greatest Hits (1993; Island).
Not only the remixed greatest hits, but a few new tracks to boot, of which "Überman" is the most invective-laden and self-mocking. Buy this: you'll definitely impress your friends.

On Drugs (1994; Island).
Some of the tracks on this album are just too clever for their own good, but "Slim Jim" makes up for it, mocking and celebrating amphetamine abuse in the way that is Sheep On Drugs' speciality.

One For The Money (1997; Invisible).
Tracks like "Joyrider", "Crime Time" and "The Money Machine" revel in nihilistic baiting of Middle America, but the highlight has to be the junglist interpretation of The Velvets' "Waiting For The Man". There's even a tabloid newspaper, The Daily Grind, denouncing Lee and Duncan, included in the packaging.

Richard Fontenoy

SHELLAC

Formed Chicago, 1991.

"I don't know why there aren't more songs about three-cushion billiards, which I think is the most beautiful and graceful thing a human being can do." Steve Albini

S tarted as a low-profile side-project by former **BIG BLACK** and Rapeman member **Steve Albini** (guitar/vocals), ex-Breaking Circus drummer **Todd Trainer** and **Robert Spur Weston** (bass) from Volcano Suns, **Shellac** went public around May 1993, playing a few gigs in Chicago bars. They then released a debut 7" single, "The Rude Gesture (A Pictorial History)" (1993), refused to do any publicity, and found themselves atop the indie charts.

It was followed shortly by another 7", "Uranus", which, like its predecessor, showed that the combination of Albini's production experience and the Velcro-tight contributions of Trainer and Weston could create guitar-bass-drums music that sounded fresh in the mid 90s. Live, Todd Trainer opened each show as his alter ego Brick Layer Cake, initially as an almost execrably bad solo singer/guitarist, and on later dates with a full band to somewhat better effect. Shellac showed themselves to be one of the most entertaining and energetic live acts around, their sets often featuring the dance of the aeroplanes during "Wingwalker" and surreal audience banter. In one show a large amount of bottled water was thrown liberally over Todd Trainer while he drummed his way through a solo encore.

The band's debut album, AT ACTION PARK, was released in September 1994, with the typically pro-vinyl step of releasing the CD some six weeks later. Topping the indie charts for several months without benefit of advertising or promotion, the album received critical praise as a finely crafted and exciting debut.

Fans waited three and a half years for the follow-up, TERRAFORM, but when it arrived many were disappointed by its excessive cleverness; it was considered a sad letdown.

Their most recent opus, 1000 HURTS (2000), fell more favourably on fans' ears with its return to blistering form as the trio pounded out refreshingly skewed guitar-based music in an era that seemed to lack any really independent major rock bands. Shellac remain the last truly great exponents of an overwhelmingly tired genre, and the very infrequency of their record releases and energetic tours makes each an eagerly anticipated event.

🔘 **The Rude Gesture: A Pictorial History** and **Uranus** (both 1993; Touch & Go).
These two singles are a matched pair of choppy guitars and earthquaking rhythms, with the drums lovingly recorded to sound like a real kit (which makes a change). The packaging is a treat too: thick card envelopes hand-printed with simple designs. Not a B-side between them. And still only available on vinyl.

🔘 **At Action Park** (1994; Touch & Go).
Albini snarls and skings [sic], while Trainer and Weston shake the floor through a great album, highlights of which are the metronomic "Crow", the sardonic "Song Of The Minerals", and the Nietzschean "Il Porno Star" – not forgetting "The Dog And Pony Show" either. All in another slab of thick brown card, courtesy of Chicago's excellent Fireproof Press.

🔘 **1000 Hurts** (2000; Touch & Go).
Another sonically triumphant and visually sumptuous product from Shellac, this time packaged in a 70s-style reel-to-reel tape box. The album features songs about revenge, songs about hate and even a cut on the benefits of harnessing squirrel-power! Albini's acerbic story-telling persona hasn't sounded so good in ages, and the trio's music snarls, scrapes and runs its economical course in fits and precise starts.

Richard Fontenoy

SHINEHEAD

Shinehead conceived New York, 1986.

When New-York-raised Edmund Carl Aitken, aka **Shinehead**, broke onto the scene in 1986 with his first album, ROUGH AND RUGGED, no one was too surprised to learn that the album featured a couple of cover versions among its tracks. After all, reggae versions of current underground soul favourites are a familiar phenomenon in Jamaica, where Shinehead's roots lay. What was surprising, however, was that one of the covers was a Whitney Houston song, while the other was Michael Jackson's "Billie Jean". Clearly here was an artist with no time for musical purism.

Elsewhere on the record was the single "Who The Cap Fits", a mournful tale of divine retribution which fused reggae and rap with unprecedented ease. There had been attempts at combining the two genres before, but these had mostly consisted either of American rappers making poor attempts at imitating Jamaican DJs, or of genuine Jamaican DJs guesting on rap songs (such as Run-D.M.C.'s 1985 collaboration with Yellowman, "Roots Rap Reggae"). Neither of these approaches had reaped convincing results. Shinehead, on the other hand, had grown up in Jamaica but was resident in New York, and lived both cultures on a daily basis. He was able to switch from one to the other seamlessly and the end product was something unique.

Shinehead was to draw on influences from further afield on his next outing, UNITY (1988). The title track, a plea to the rap scene to stop its infighting, borrowed its chorus melody from The Beatles' "Come Together". Then there was his tribute to the New York subway system, "Chain Gang Rap", whose glorious appropriation of Sam Cooke's "Chain Gang" was only upstaged by a video in which Shinehead hurtled on and off trains, at one point rapping while hanging upside down from a pole. Natural enough behaviour for a man who once stated his preferred listening as being 'Pat Boone, Bing Crosby, Bob Hope, Tom Jones, Dean Martin, Bruce Springsteen and Bob Marley'.

Next came THE REAL ROCK (1990). A continuation of the mix'n'match formula, this album featured a version of Sly And The Family Stone's "Family Affair", as well as a "Love And Marriage Rap". But there was plenty of originality on display too, with "World Of The Video Game", a tongue-in-cheek study of Nintendo addiction set to a backing of arcade-style tunes, and "Cigarette Breath", a pure reggae track describing some of the less publicized drawbacks of smoking.

Shinehead's long-overdue commercial breakthrough album came in August 1992, with the release of SIDEWALK UNIVERSITY. Produced in part by Norman Cook, there was a definite UK flavour at work here, particularly on the bizarre "Rainbow", a house/reggae version of the British children's TV show theme. It was Sting, however, who provided the inspiration and melody for the album's big pop hit, "Jamaican In New York", a skilfully adapted cover of "Englishman In New York". After this moment of brilliance you could forgive Shinehead anything, even his cover version of "I Just Called To Say I Love You".

TRODDIN' (1994) and PRAISES (1999) have put Shinehead into a unique category of survivors in the rap and reggae fields, where packs of young pretenders are constantly snapping at the heels of established artists. Without a doubt, the qualities that have kept him active in the business are his unpredictability and his rare reluctance to stick within the boundaries of any genre. Most recently he was spotted in 2001 providing vocals for Trevor Jackson's **Playgroup** project.

⊙ **Unity** (1988; Elektra).
A joyous, effortless blend of rap, reggae and balladry: its themes and cosmopolitanism make this a gleeful celebration of the possibilities of the Big Apple.

⊙ **Sidewalk University** (1992; Elektra).
Fourteen tracks long and featuring almost as many different musical permutations. His constantly strengthening voice makes straight soul songs like "Should I" more convincing than ever.

Robin Morley

Rock animals Atsuko, Naoko and Michie

SHONEN KNIFE

Formed Osaka, Japan, 1981.

One of the few Japanese rock groups to make an international impact, **Shonen Knife** seem, at first glance and listen, like kewpie dolls come to life, wearing matching dresses and singing cute, perky tunes in heavily accented English about Barbie dolls, toy animals and ice cream. Shonen Knife (the name means 'boy's knife') are no mere novelty act, however. They may have done little to stretch rock's horizons, but their infectiously melodic pop-punk recordings include some of the most enjoyable and uplifting rock of the post-punk era.

Shonen Knife's constituency lies very much within the indie underground. The band were formed in 1981 in Osaka by bored office workers and college friends **Naoko Yamano** (guitar/vocals), **Michie Nakatani** (bass/vocals) and Naoko's younger sister **Atsuko Yamano** (drums). In the best punk tradition, none of them had played their instruments before, but their spectrum of influences was not limited to the Sex Pistols and The Jam: Naoko cited 60s pop, psychedelic music, 'before and after 80s punk', Southeast Asian pop, reggae and Motown as wellsprings of inspiration.

The band were also fans of the Ramones, Buzzcocks and XTC, and that's the sort of pop/punk thrust which dominated their early recordings, which were dotted by wiry fuzz guitars, fast, nervous rhythms, crashing drums, and simple catchy riffs and vocal hooks. Not many women formed punkish bands in Japan – then or now – and in the early days Nakatani had to hide her bass from her parents; when the band started to get some press attention, they told their parents that Shonen Knife were in fact three other musicians, and when they left for their first US tour, they told their families it was for a holiday.

The band got a deal with Japanese indie Zero Records in 1982, singing in both English and Japanese on their debut EP, BURNING FARM (on subsequent efforts, they stuck to English almost exclusively). Their rawest effort, this introduced Shonen Knife's most charming trademarks: exuberant vocals, preoccupations with (and celebrations of) pop culture kitsch like jellybeans and fast food, odd touches of anvil-like percussion and blasts of dissonant harmonica, and unpredictable ensemble choruses that bring to mind nothing so much as a mutant variation of the early Beatles' moptop-shaking 'woo!'s. Their second EP, YAMANO ATTCHAN, was in the same vein, if a bit more subdued and ornately produced.

Calvin Johnson, of the Washington state indie band Beat Happening, heard Shonen Knife during an extended stay in Japan in the early 80s, and arranged to release BURNING FARM with a few other tracks on cassette through his K label. Starting to accumulate a greater following in the States than in their native Japan, the band made their stateside debut with PRETTY LITTLE BAKA GUY in 1986; the first two EPs, as well as a few other stray tracks, were assembled on one album, SHONEN KNIFE, for US release in 1990.

One could argue that all but hard-bitten fans could stop there and get the basic idea. The group have improved their instrumental proficiency since the early days, but in some respects they're a little like fellow pop primitive Jonathan Richman: while you can always count on Shonen Knife to make you hum and smile, you're not going to get any noticeable progression or deviation from album to album. And, like Richman, the band's continued obsession with cute but lightweight lyrical fodder betrays a degree of arrested development.

It's a bit peevish, though, to carp about a band that's never aspired to do much beyond deliver high-spirited, pleasantly raw rock of the catchiest sort. Some of Shonen Knife's biggest fans are fellow indie rock notables, who actually banded together to produce a tribute album of Shonen Knife covers, EVERY BAND HAS A SHONEN KNIFE WHO LOVES THEM (1989); it included renditions by Redd Kross and Sonic Youth, among others.

Sonic Youth guitarist Thurston Moore also appeared on ROCK ANIMALS (1993), which featured slightly more eclectic material and somewhat more accomplished production values than has been the band's habit. BRAND NEW KNIFE (1997) and HAPPY HOUR (1998) saw them return to the irresistible blend of punk and pop that had first attracted their audience. And no less a star than Kurt Cobain once said that, after watching Shonen Knife play live, he knew exactly how all those screaming teenage girls felt when they saw The Beatles in the mid-60s. Not that Shonen Knife are much like Nirvana, or The Beatles; they're a law unto themselves.

Michie retired from the group in 1999 and since then interest in the Knife has unfortunately waned; STRAWBERRY SOUND (2000) and HEAVY SONGS (2002) were only released in Japan.

⊙ **Pretty Little Baka Guy** (1986; Rockville).
Their first internationally available album doesn't measure up to their early recordings in imagination or energy, but still delivers enough punch to satisfy listeners hungry for female pop/punk that's similar to, but much rawer than, Blondie or The Go-Go's. The CD has eight bonus tracks recorded live in Japan.

⊙ **Shonen Knife** (1990; Giant).
Over twenty tracks, including their first two EPs and a few other early cuts. Their rawest and, in most essential respects, best material.

Richie Unterberger

SHRIEKBACK

Formed London, 1981; disbanded 1989; re-formed 1993.

The uncompromising and challenging **Shriekback** were formed by **Barry Andrews** (keyboards), formerly of **XTC** and **ROBERT FRIPP**'s League Of Gentlemen, bass player **Dave Allen**, who had quit **GANG OF FOUR** in July 1981, and guitarist **Carl Marsh**, who had his own band, Out On Blue Six. Developing Allen's work in Gang Of Four, Shriekback endeavoured to combine elements of rock and funk in a way that avoided the dilettantism of consciously formal 'fusion' music.

This effort was primarily channelled through complex and singular rhythmic experimentation: the percussion was often seemingly at right angles to Allen's bass line at the outset, then Allen or Marsh, or both, would slowly turn the beat around until the two met and meshed. It was a disorientating and intoxicating dialogue over which Andrews laid slivers and stabs of sound, sometimes virtually inaudible, sometimes building up to great, white-hot slabs of overdriven keyboard. With chanted vocals to top it all, this potentially disastrous approach somehow produced songs which combined hypnotic inductions with a genuine pop sensibility. This was clearly heard on two of their earliest singles, "My Spine (Is The Bassline)" and "Lined Up", on the Y label, for whom they also recorded an EP, TENCH, and an album, CARE (1983), which remains their most focused work.

In 1984 Shriekback moved to Arista and achieved some success with JAM SCIENCE, which developed their knotty rhythmic tensions to near-telepathic levels. The best tracks were the singles "Hand On My Heart" and "Mercy Dash", the former flirting with the UK Top 40 in the summer of Frankie Goes To Hollywood. Live, the band's characteristic chanted vocals became more widely spread through the material, aiming for and partly attaining, a near-mantric effect. The downside to all this was that even audiences who knew what to expect felt somewhat marginalized, as if they had accidentally stumbled upon some secret ceremony. One suspects that this was reflected in their record sales, always lower than the stock of their reputation.

Perhaps addressing this, subsequent albums lightened up a little, with OIL & GOLD (1985) and their first album for Island, BIG NIGHT MUSIC (1987), both accentuating the poppier elements of their sound, most successfully on the former's "Fish Below The Ice" and the latter's "Gunning For The Buddha".

By now, Allen and Marsh had jumped ship, leaving Andrews to recruit new members. The 1988 album, GO BANG, was again a mix of the commercial and the abrasively indulgent, but the feeling among the public, and the press, was that Shriekback's time had passed. The group dissolved in 1989.

The advent of the 1990s dance scene, with its eclectic mix of rhythms, samples and stylings, appealed to Barry Andrews, who, having done little of consequence since the split, re-formed Shriekback as a looser unit in 1993, releasing SACRED CITY on their own Shriek label in February 1994. Many of the features which characterized the band in the mid 80s showed up here – the disorientating cross-rhythmic stew, the snatches of exotic and mysterious sampled voices – yet, in something of a vindication of their early hunches, it sounded startlingly contemporary. Although silent since then, the band may yet continue to make a distinctive contribution at rock's rhythmic frontiers.

Other than a couple of retrospectives, nothing was then heard until 2000, when NAKED APES AND

POND LIFE rekindled the band's flame. The following year another collection was issued, ABERRATIONS 1981-1984; it was packaged with a free copy of NAKED APES... for those who hadn't already picked up a copy.

⊙ **Priests And Kannibalists** (1994; Arista).
The latest of three such compilations, this contains a representative selection of the Y, Arista and Island material from "Sexthinkone" to "Get Down Tonight" via the sinuous formulations of their best singles, notably the defining "My Spine (Is The Bassline)".

⊙ **The Best Of...** (2000; Essential).
This double-CD set is as good a place as any to start.

Peter Mills

SHUT UP AND DANCE

Formed London, 1988.

It is relatively easy to become a dance/clubland hero. One anthemic 12", one well-placed sample and you've joined the elite. In a scene where artists come and go almost on a daily basis, **Shut Up And Dance**, the band and label, have consistently produced innovative material that takes no prisoners.

Smiley and **PJ** from Stoke Newington, London, formed the SUAD label in 1989, the year after they began recording as artists in their own right as acid-house swept Britain. The duo's tastes, however, ranged wider than the Detroit-Chicago-derived rhythms packing the warehouse raves. Their first single, "5678" (1988), was a massive club hit and the two follow-ups, "£10 To Get In" and its remix "£20 To Get In", both grazed the regular UK Top 60 and featured rough-hewn hip-hop beats and samples (notably Suzanne Vega).

This success was consolidated by "Lamborghini" (1989), a hard-hitting track based around the Eurythmics "Sweet Dreams". SUAD had the knack of appropriating other artists' work but making it entirely their own through injecting a high dose of street-tough dub and further imaginative sampling.

The duo's debut album, DANCE BEFORE THE POLICE COME (1990) stormed the UK dance charts and remained at #1 for two weeks. Highlights included the sinister "Derek Went Mad", on which ambient strings and a melancholy vocal simmered over a brutal techno drum pattern, and "This Town Needs A Sheriff", where the duo showed off their rhyming skills, telling it like it is on the front line in multicultural Britain.

Around this time the SUAD label went from strength to strength with the signing of the Ragga Twins, who fused hardened dub, Detroit house and Jamaican toasting. They had success, too, with the PJ and Smiley-produced Nicolette, a singer who passed too briefly through the Massive Attack orbit, and with Rum And Black, who spat out the controversial "Fuck The Legal Stations".

SUAD the band were back firing on all cylinders in 1991 with DEATH IS NOT THE END, which included the duo's biggest hit, the scene classic

"Raving I'm Raving". The LP was a typically diverse affair, including the disturbing hip-hop tale, "Runaways", and the simple, streetwise, acoustic poetry of "Autobiography Of A Crack Head". This was SUAD at their best, but, just as the UK dance scene was about to bow down before them, royalty and contractual problems forced them out of business.

While these problems were being sorted out, a new force emerged in British black music – jungle, an inspired mix of breakbeat, ragga, dub and techno. Many have laid claim to being among the originators of this sound, but, alongside DJs Mickey Finn and Grooverider, few would deny that SUAD, with their roughneck beats, sinister ambience and industrial-strength dub, were a major influence. (Although SUAD themselves denounce the term 'jungle' as racist.)

1995 brought better tidings for the duo and PJ and Smiley re-emerged on Pulse8 records with "Save It", a single in the style of "Lamborghini". Based around a Duran Duran track, it was a stylish return, but the album, BLACK MEN UNITED (1995), was disappointing. Instead of capitalizing on their junglist tendencies, SUAD took on a more polished sound and made some rather lame forays into cheesy pop and swingbeat.

The duo's re-emergence three years later, however, saw a definite return to form with the release of the single "Got 'Em Locked" (1998) to much critical acclaim. With breakbeat reigning supreme on clubland's dance floors, the track's skanking rhythm, blazing drum pattern and sheer attitude meant SUAD sounded as utterly contemporary as they had a decade earlier. The duo also relaunched the SUAD label and began releasing their own material once again, as well as producing for other artists.

A live mix compilation, THE MAGNOLIA COLLECTION (2002), released on Shut Up And Dance subsidiary New Deal Recordings, keeps SUAD users bang up to date with the duo, still right on the mettle blending their own remixes of tracks from No Doubt, Red Snapper and Freddy Fresh (among others) as well as recordings under their Hackney Soldiers production nom de guerre.

⊙ **Dance Before The Police Come** (1990; SUAD).
As the title suggests, this is SUAD at their most uncompromising.

⊙ **Fuck Off And Die – Compilation** (1990; SUAD).
Contains most of the label's classic material from the likes of SUAD, Ragga Twins, Rum And Black, and Soulman Ade.

Malcolm Russell

JANE SIBERRY

Born Toronto, Canada, October 12, 1955.

One of the most original talents working within the rock idiom, **Jane Siberry** began composing before her feet could reach the floor as she sat on the piano stool. Her words and music reflect the classical and operatic influences she absorbed when young, with characteristically swift mood changes, eccentric rhythmic juxtapositions and often shared narrative viewpoints, delivered in an elegant, delicately pitched voice.

As a student, Siberry took a job as a waitress and, so legend has it, used her tips to finance her 1981 debut album JANE SIBERRY, on which she wrote, played and produced. The rolling, piano-based simplicity was sometimes suggestive of early, pre-kitsch Elton John, but the material was primarily self-reflective, suggesting a quirky and unusual lyrical world-view, notably on the Angela Carter-style fairy-tale of "Above The Treeline". Her second album, NO BORDERS HERE (1984), showed this talent growing, particularly on "Mimi On The Beach", a vivid flurry of flashing images, edited to suggest the randomness of an experienced sequence. This cinematic style was to become a key element in Siberry's work.

The attention garnered by "Mimi On The Beach" stepped up interest for 1985's THE SPECKLESS SKY. Co-produced with John Switzer, it combined joyous evocations of the Canadian big country with exquisite close focus upon minute detail. Siberry's inventiveness reached new levels on her first album for Warner/Reprise, THE WALKING (1988). Few major-label debuts have been so radical in scope: no track is much below five minutes, and two are over ten. The album opens daringly with one such, "The White Tent The Raft", and concludes with the similarly bold "The Bird In The Gravel". Both were effectively soundtracks to invisible films, featuring non-musical sound effects and images which fly past, seemingly undeveloped yet having sustained effect. The album's shorter, more conventional numbers such as "Red High Heels" and "The Walking (And Constantly)" remain among her best work, their apparently slick AOR surfaces being shifted and bent out of shape by the emotional force of Siberry's performances.

Though lauded by critics and devotees, the album sold only modestly and Siberry attempted a more commercial direction with her next album, 1989's BOUND BY THE BEAUTY. Where the previous outing had been epic and open, this was concise and exhilarating – a delight throughout – with stand-outs in the title track, the childhood memoir "Hockey", and the supreme "Everything Reminds Me Of My Dog".

Although receiving attention and praise – alongside fellow Canadians k. d. lang and Mary Margaret O'Hara – the record did not make the splash it deserved. However, sales improved enough to warrant Reprise issuing a compilation drawn from the first five albums, SUMMER IN THE YUKON (1992). This also featured "Calling All Angels", an incandescent duet with k. d. lang (featured in the Wim Wenders film Until The End Of The World) and a remix of "The Life Is The Red Wagon" from BOUND BY THE BEAUTY. The concessions to dance

culture made in this remix pointed the way forward for Siberry; she said she was concerned that most of her records were 'undanceable'. Coincidentally, Siberry had received a fan letter from Brian Eno in which he offered his production services for her next album; eager for change, she hired him.

Eno's influence was clear on 1993's WHEN I WAS A BOY, on which the awesomely lusty "Temple" and the fragmented scope of "An Angel Stepped Down" established new areas for Siberry. The centrepiece was "The Vigil", a rambling, gorgeous piece dedicated to her recently deceased father, which includes cathedral bells and a minute's silence at the track's end – a characteristic mix of unforced emotion and creative invention.

Apart from another contribution for Wim Wenders – for the movie Faraway So Close – and a collaboration with ambient composer Hector Zazou on his wonderful album SONGS FROM COLD SEAS (1994) – little else was heard from Siberry until summer 1995 when the album MARIA was released. Recorded more or less live in the studio with a jazz quintet, this was a much more jazz-inflected affair, with the musicians well attuned to her improvisational flair. The sassy "Lovin' Cup" and the deliciously piano-rich, heel-kicking full-pelt of "Begat Begat" were highlights of the album, which concluded with the twenty-minute "Oh My My", incorporating excerpts from "Puff The Magic Dragon".

TEENAGER (1996) was an album of material from her sophomore year, dragged out from under the bed, dusted off and made ready for a new decade, while CHILD: MUSIC FOR THE CHRISTMAS SEASON (1997) was a double live CD collection of music for Yuletide enjoyment. It was recorded in New York, and was part of a live trilogy, the other two parts, TREE (MUSIC FOR FILMS AND FORESTS) and LIPS (MUSIC FOR SAYING IT), being available only from Siberry's own company, Sheeba. By now Siberry had freed herself from contractual obligations and all her work henceforth has emerged via Sheeba: the imprint has also made available her back catalogue, fan-interest projects such as the 29-minute sound-collage A DAY IN THE LIFE, poetry and art publications, and typically eclectic Siberry memorabilia – a Sheeba lamb, anyone?

Early 2001 saw the website-only release of the lush, understated yet gorgeous HUSH, an album of traditional American and Celtic songs such as "Streets Of Laredo" and "Old Man River", which subsequently enjoyed a richly deserved wider release. For latecomers to her career, MAP OF THE WORLD (2002) was an excellent résumé of an artist whose versatility has often been sorely underrated. She remains an adventurous presence in the contemporary songwriting world.

The Walking (1988; Reprise).
To be filed next to Captain Beefheart's TROUT MASK REPLICA and Tim Buckley's STARSAILOR in rock's Difficult Beauty file. As with those, persistence is rewarded n-fold. This is deep Siberry.

Bound By The Beauty (1989; Reprise).
A stunning album, the first half (vinyl side) of which is a near-perfect sequence, from the title track – a metaphysical speculation on beauty and reincarnation, set to a folk-country ditty – to "The Valley", which lifts the guitar intro from "Purple Rain" and ends up like something somehow omitted from PET SOUNDS.

When I Was A Boy (1993; Reprise).
Although Eno's ambience doesn't always suit Siberry's voice, he gives it all kinds of new dimensions and a rockier treatment. Her most powerful album to date.

Maria (1995; Reprise).
A rich, sensuous collection; the jazz sensibility suits Siberry's style well, allowing her to wing her lyrics and vocals up and over and around the funky, mellow, brandy-warm grooves.

Peter Mills

SIGUR RØS

Formed Reykjavik, Iceland, 1994.

If a natural history documentary was ever to require music to accompany footage of vast sea creatures moving silently through icy North Atlantic waters, then perhaps the atmospheric melancholia crafted by Iceland's **Sigur Røs** would present a stirring option.

At a time when Björk was giving Iceland's profile a massive international lift, Sigur Røs emerged quietly from their home town of Reykjavik; within five years they would add their own not insignificant chapter to that nation's musical heritage. Founder member **Jøn 'Jønsi' Por Birgisson** had fronted Icelandic grunge bands **Stoned** and **Bee Spiders** (a Smashing Pumpkins-style act that once picked up a talent show award for *Most Interesting Band*). Suffice to say Sigur Røs was a slight departure. Jønsi named the new group in honour of his baby sister (apparently born the day of the band's conception), her name, Sigurrøs, meaning 'Victory Rose'. His strange asexual vocal style became the first trademark of the band's sound, the full spatial composition completed by his guitars and effects, alongside the bass of **Georg 'Goggi' Holm** – known as 'White Fang' for his supposed ability to catch live trout with his teeth – and **Agúst**'s percussion.

Sigur Røs's first recording, the 1996 album VON ('Hope'), saw the light of day on the Reykjavik label Smekkleysa and times were such that Jønsi and his cohorts had to offer to paint the studio in return for recording time. Despite not being especially rated by the band, the results of the sessions attracted a small amount of press that likened them to AR Kane and My Bloody Valentine. Although Sigur Røs were hasty in claiming that they hadn't heard either band, they have always been in agreement about one major influence: their homeland. 'It is a wonderful place,' explains Birgisson, 'The sky is so big in this country – and we have all these big empty places where no one lives, with glaciers and lava.' As though emphasizing the importance of the country to his band's work, he adds that leaving Iceland would be like 'cutting the umbilical chord'.

At this early stage in the band's development, support was being harnessed from leading Icelandic luminaries such as Gus Gus and Múm, who were to restyle tracks from the Sigur Røs debut for a remix collection entitled VON BRIGĐL ('Recycle Bin').

The real milestone was, however, ÁGAETIS BYRJUN ('A Good Beginning' – after the understated opinion of a friend), a vast canvas of textures and tints, recorded by Sigur Røs in Iceland late in 1998, by which time they had added the keyboard skills of **Kjartan 'Kjarri' Sveinsson**. Although this epic-sounding CD was an immediate hit at home, it wasn't until August 2000 that ÁGAETIS BYRJUN found a release on the forward-thinking UK imprint Fat Cat. The collection then made an impact in the USA, where the band walked off with the $10,000 *Virgin Shortlist* prize (the artistic equivalent of the UK's *Mercury Award*) in California. The achievement was made all the more impressive by the fact that Sigur Røs had opted to sing not only in Icelandic, but also in their own invented language of 'Hopelandish', adding to the set's mystique and mythology.

The record's standout cut was undoubtedly the extraordinary, ten-minute "Svefn-g-Englar" ('Sleepwalkers'), a dreamlike piece, full of subaquatic sonic illusion; it featured heavily in 2000's year-end

REDFERNS

Sigur Røs – 'bow selecta'

polls. Another single, "Ny Batteri" ('New Batteries'), was a further departure, Sigur Røs disclosing an astute recognition of the power of acoustic instruments in atmospheric music. These sonic weapons apparently included a road-kill cymbal found in the street by the band.

Following the recording of the album, Agúst left the group to pursue a career in graphic design; he was replaced on drums by **Orri Páll Dyrason**. Although a third album proper was not to appear until the end of 2002, Sigur Røs were far from idle, working with Icelandic composer **Hilmar Hilmarsson** (on the soundtrack to the film *Angels Of The Universe*), underground poet **Didda** and singing fisherman **Steindor Andersson**.

Recorded in a converted swimming pool, the group's bizarrely entitled third collection, **( )**, was distinctly rawer than ÁGÆTIS BYRJUN; the melodies were not so easy to pin down, while the song structures teasingly fell somewhere between the concrete and the abstract. Though at times the glacial expanses of guitar texture suggested that a little pruning would have yielded more approachable results, overall the band had managed to craft another truly beautiful album, filled with inexplicable lyrics and the promise of more to come.

⊙ **Ágætis Byrjun** (1999/Fat Cat).
A delirious, restless collection that both evokes and provokes, lulling one minute, swamping the next.

⊙ **( )** (2002/Fat Cat).
A musical avalanche of whiteout texture propels this set in seemingly contradictory directions, sounding aimlessly lethargic yet ultimately satisfying. And as for the title, it has been translated to mean everything from 'the void between brackets album' to 'the kissing sausages album'.

Jeremy Simmonds

SILVER APPLES

Formed New York, 1967; disbanded 1969; re-formed 1996.

The mysterious **Silver Apples** appeared at the furthest reaches of rock'n'roll with a self-titled, electronics and drums LP in 1968, and vanished without apparent trace after an even wilder second LP, CONTACT (1969). Their music, which still sounds shocking and exciting, has left its mark here and there: Alan Vega, singer with New York near-contemporaries Suicide, was a fan; Australia's Scientists featured "A Pox On You" (from CONTACT) as part of their set; and ELECTRONIC EVOCATIONS – A TRIBUTE TO THE SILVER APPLES, a various-artists mini-LP of covers, was issued in late 1995.

Chief among Silver Apples' mysteries is that their records were ever released in the first place. CONTACT's inner bag proudly displayed the Kapp Records catalogue – Jack Jones, Eartha Kitt, Burt Bacharach, The Waikikis, The Latin Souls, and so on – with the SILVER APPLES LP lodged incongruously, black-sheep-like, in a corner.

Neither group name nor photo appeared on the first LP's front cover (stencilled apples on flashy silver card), but a glossy poster introduced the players. Pictured performing, relaxing and hauling equipment on a New York rooftop in the shadow of the Empire State Building, **Dan Taylor** (drums/vocals) and **Simeon** (lead vocals/'Simeon') sported an undistinguished hippie look (paisley trousers, pudding-bowl haircuts). More impressive was Simeon's self-named instrument, a primitive array of heavy-duty knobs, dials, meters and buttons on chunky grey cabinets, with conventional keyboards entirely absent. According to the accompanying notes, 'The Simeon presently consists of nine audio oscillators and eighty-six manual controls, enabling Simeon to express his musical ideas. The lead and rhythm oscillators are played with the hands, elbows and knees and the bass oscillators are played with the feet.'

The sound of SILVER APPLES was amazing: sci-fi warbling, whistling and whizzing, fruity bass pulses and chattering, back-to-front drums. On the downside, chirping flutes, bad poetry (provided by non-performing **Stanley Warren** – 'Smoldering charades of smoky verity/Things are what they seem to players of the pipe... ', etc), and polite singing added a tone-lowering air of whacked-out hippie mysticism. Yet, despite all the strangeness, the songs were tight and usually melodic, if also so alien-sounding as to be completely uncommercial. "Oscillations" was adjudged most likely to hit by a hopelessly optimistic/sympathetic record company, and released as a single paired with "Whirly-Bird" – which featured a recurring "Jingle Bells" rhythm and some of the album's most extravagantly silly lyrics: 'Whirly-Bird unzip my mind/So nuts and bolts spill out... ' Unsurprisingly, neither album nor single sold well – if at all.

Tones were richer on CONTACT and brutally treated, while Simeon's abandoned playing was more powerful. Wailing, wandering leads featured heavily along with a high-pitched, theremin-type sound (on "You And I"). Lyrics were also much improved by crazed unintelligibility and the exchange of the first LP's love and peace poetry for convincing tales of mixed-up menace and paranoia, most from the pen of Simeon. With "A Pox On You", Silver Apples delivered their most enduring song. The jumbled language (taking in witchcraft, Seeds-style teenage snot and emotional blackmail) combined with an incredible electronic rendering of sexual frustration for a fantastic, off-kilter punk rocker. Sadly, after the closing "Fantasies" (sung, puzzlingly, in the manner of W. C. Fields), Silver Apples went silent for three decades.

The unexpected 1996 resurrection comprised Simeon and a new partner **Xian Hawkins**; "Fractal Flow" resulted as a single. Since then, Silver Apples – these days essentially 'Simeon plus one' – have recorded (BEACON and DECATUR, both 1998) and toured extensively, even reaching the UK to be feted as part of John Peel's prestigious Meltdown Festival on London's South Bank. More recently, Simeon and Taylor have resumed contact and, together, they've assembled THE GARDEN (1998) from vintage 1969 tracks, fleshed out with freshly added noodling from Simeon. In 1999 Simeon teamed up with the ever-droning **Sonic Boom** for the album A LAKE OF TEARDROPS, released under the moniker of **Spectrum Vs Silver Apples**.

⊙ **Silver Apples/Contact** (1968 & 1969; TRC).
The raw, emotionally expressive quality of the music compiled on this two-for-one CD suggests that the potential of electronic rock'n'roll may have been partially squandered. These records are unique, and ought to be heard, if only to be believed. Sampling opportunities abound.

Robert Coyne

SIMON & GARFUNKEL

Both born New York, 1941.

Inspired by the rock'n'roll of his youth – doo-wop vocal groups, The Everly Brothers, Atlantic R&B – **Paul Simon** started out performing effervescent, harmony-led pop. His first hit, made when he and **Art Garfunkel** were known as Tom And Jerry, was a sugary pop song called "Hey Schoolgirl" (1957). But by 1963 he had begun to move to folk, and in 1964, with Garfunkel again, he produced his first folk album, WEDNESDAY MORNING 3AM. It was a generally insipid effort, and much bettered by the solo PAUL SIMON SONGBOOK (1965), where he wrote lucidly about alienation and fatalism, themes that were to recur throughout his work. Alongside this characteristically reflective work, he included a few obligatory folkie political songs, but Simon could never sustain the anger for protest.

Taking a cue from Dylan and The Byrds – and despite protests from the duo – producer Tom Wilson overlaid "The Sound Of Silence" (from WEDNESDAY MORNING 3AM) with electric guitars and drums and released it as a single. It became a US #1 hit at the beginning of 1966. Encouraged by this taste of stardom, **Simon & Garfunkel** hastily rehashed a selection of old songs to make a new album in this 'folk-rock' mould, entitled the SOUNDS OF SILENCE (1966). It charted on both sides of the Atlantic and for a few years the duo rode a wave of rising fortune.

They immediately set to work on PARSLEY, SAGE, ROSEMARY AND THYME

(1966), a more carefully structured set than its predecessor. Simon produced the album, with engineer Roy Halee, his foil in the studio for much of his subsequent career. Then, in 1967, the duo recorded the soundtrack for the Mike Nichols film *The Graduate*, on the back of which they burst into international superstardom. With the release in 1968 of the masterful BOOKENDS they reached the artistic apogee of their career together.

In commercial terms, however, the best was just around the corner – BRIDGE OVER TROUBLED WATER (1970), which went to #1 in the US and UK, spent an amazing 300 weeks in the latter chart, and spawned four hit singles. It was an unashamedly commercial album, of course, with Simon controlling both the songwriting and recording, and Art Garfunkel hated it. The duo split without further recording, Simon announcing, in coded form, "So Long, Frank Lloyd Wright".

Simon made four studio albums in the 70s – PAUL SIMON (1972), THERE GOES RHYMIN' SIMON (1973), STILL CRAZY AFTER ALL THESE YEARS (1975) and ONE TRICK PONY (1979). The first stayed very much in the vein of BRIDGE OVER TROUBLED WATER, producing catchy, rhythmic hits in songs such as "Mother And Child Reunion" and "Me And Julio Down By The Schoolyard". However, the output became blander and less memorable as the decade progressed, and although he could write well

"How about parsley, sage, rosemary and a little basil?": Simon (left) and Garfunkel

on, say, the disarray of collapsing love affairs, too often the songs were inconsequential or, at worst, inane. With ONE TRICK PONY, the soundtrack of a disastrous film of the same name, written and directed by Simon, he seemed to have overreached himself.

At an impasse, Simon reunited with Garfunkel, and for a while it seemed it might work. The pair gave a massive free concert in Central Park in 1981, leading to a popular live album. Encouraged by this success, in 1982 they began a money-spinning world tour and set out plans to do a new album together, but the project fell apart through Garfunkel's refusal to play second fiddle. As this partnership collapsed again, Simon's marriage to actress Carrie Fisher acrimoniously broke up. Midlife crisis beckoned.

In the midst of it all, Simon managed to pull together HEARTS AND BONES (1983), which significantly marked the return of Roy Halee. Like those preceding it, this album contained some lifeless attempts at glitzy pop, but it also had some of Simon's most elegant music, both beautiful and forlorn. HEARTS AND BONES succeeded because, for the first time in years, the songs were stripped of heavy instrumentation in favour of Simon's serene vocals and a gently wandering guitar line. Solitude is a recurring concern of his music, and this set proved he explored it most effectively when the sound was uncluttered and private.

And yet, with GRACELAND (1986) and THE RHYTHM OF THE SAINTS (1990), Simon set off on a new path, developing a looser approach to composition and instrumentation with enormous success. In contrast to his habitual method of painstakingly building a song from a tightly wrought lyric, with GRACELAND he began with tapes he'd made of South African groups, then built up the tracks in New York, adding his own ideas in conjunction with those of other American and African musicians. The result was far more diverse and musically inventive than any preceding Simon album, but it brought accusations of cultural imperialism, and apartheid-boycott breaking, and even some of his admirers had to admit that tales of middle–class angst didn't sit particularly well with the sublimely spiritual music of black South Africans. In defence Simon would say, and with justice, that he did much to develop a market in the West for this (and other world) music. And "Homeless" was a remarkable song – his best for many years.

THE RHYTHM OF THE SAINTS fared better, largely because the music was less centred on Simon's voice. In fact, melody and lyrics were the last elements to evolve, as the album was developed around a tape of intricate Brazilian drumming which drifted in and out of the mix throughout. A sense of interiority remained, but, rather than the customary self-absorption, there was an expansive spirituality at work. The search for peace and fulfilment has never been far from Simon's work, but it was only fully explored here, on an album in which the music rolled as a shifting pattern, propelled by rhythms that were

mecurial, intricate and powerfully hypnotic. It stands as his finest creation to date.

SONGS FROM 'THE CAPEMAN' (1998) saw Simon wearing his snappiest Latin American threads on the album of the show of the life of Salvador Agron, a Puerto Rican emigrant who ended up, via street gangs in New York, as a murderer. An album with some heart-stoppingly beautiful moments – "Born In Puerto Rico" is the stand-out track – the New York setting gives him the opportunity to work on his home turf in a piece that compares very well against that classic tale of New York Gang warfare, *West Side Story*. In 2000 Simon returned again with YOU'RE THE ONE, a pleasantly restrained batch of ethnologically tinged compositions and lyrical meanderings.

Simon & Garfunkel

(•) **Bookends** (1968; CBS).
The best Simon & Garfunkel album by far, sketching a journey from youth to old age with a delicacy rare in concept albums of any era.

Paul Simon

(•) **Graceland** (1986; Warners).
A musical milestone, and the lyrics are as good as Simon's have ever been. "Homeless", "The Boy In The Bubble" and "All Around The World" are the stand-outs on a consistently strong set.

(•) **The Rhythm Of The Saints** (1990; Warners).
Simon's best, a gorgeous album that communicates as much through the sublime sway of its music as through its lyrics.

David Castle

SIMPLE MINDS

Formed Glasgow, Scotland, 1978.

"A lot of people have asked us if we still think we're relevant." Jim Kerr

Issuing a solitary single on the independent Chiswick label, Glaswegian punk band Johnny And The Self Abusers splintered into two factions on the very day of its release. The nucleus of the band, which included **Jim Kerr** (vocals), **Charlie Burchill** (guitar) and drummer **Brian McGee**, evolved into **Simple Minds**, leaving the opposing camp to languish in relative obscurity as the Cuban Heels.

Augmented by **Duncan Barnwell** (guitar), **Mick McNeil** (keyboards) and **Derek Forbes** (bass), the new six-piece began grabbing favourable attention with a stark and powerful stage-show which exhibited the influence of Bowie, Roxy Music and contemporaries Magazine. Signing with the small Edinburgh-based Zoom label, and having parted company with Barnwell, Simple Minds released a debut album, LIFE IN A DAY (1979), which charted at #30 in the UK. It wasn't a classic, and suffered from lifeless production, but it showed they could pen a tune and Kerr could sing it. The band was on its way.

After a defiant bout of touring, which included their first London shows, Simple Minds returned to the studio. The resultant REAL TO REAL CACOPHONY (1979) was a major improvement, as they actively engaged with the recording process to produce an uncompromising mix of oblique experimentation and ambient atmospherics. It sold a whole lot less, but the group were getting tighter, and becoming an impressive stage act, touring extensively in Europe. Then came an odd avenue, as the band pursued a European electro sound for EMPIRES AND DANCE (1980). "I Travel" became a dance-floor favourite in London's clubs, and for a short time Simple Minds became chief exponents of the early 80s futurist movement.

It really wasn't them, and when in early 1981 the band were freed from their contract with Arista, and taken on board by Virgin, they set about redefining their sound. After minor hit singles with "The American" and "Love Song", their first album for the label, the double set SONS AND FASCINATION/SISTER FEELINGS CALL (1981), peaked at a healthy #11 in the UK. It was an oddity – released initially as a two-for-the-price-of-one package and then as two separate entities – and its sprawling set highlighted a great versatility, which encompassed both radio-friendly songs and panoramic soundscapes. However, it was not until the band learned to fuse these two strands together in the form of NEW GOLD DREAM 81, 82, 83, 84 (1982) that they truly made their breakthrough.

With Brian McGee departing, no fewer than three drummers, including eventual permanent replacement **Mel Gaynor**, were used in the recording of NEW GOLD DREAM. Gone was the quirky angularity of old in favour of a series of lush, breezy, multi-layered melodies. Providing the band with their first UK Top 10 single, "Promised You A Miracle", the album initiated a period of innovation and heralded the arrival of the expansive Simple Minds sound, which would for a time see the band vying for stadium supremacy with U2.

On SPARKLE IN THE RAIN (1984) the band's previously deft melodies were buried beneath a barrage of drums, clumsy song structures and Steve Lillywhite's overblown production. Yet it was difficult to resist the bass-heavy power of the single "Waterfront", which helped pave the way for the album's entry at the top of the chart. The album also provided Simple Minds with the all-important American breakthrough, courtesy of a modest #64 in the album charts, though it was to take the single "Don't You Forget About Me" to truly establish them as an international force. Written for the soundtrack for the 1985 bratpack movie *The Breakfast Club*, the song had a distinctive sing-along refrain which, coupled with heavy MTV airplay and the film's box office success, conspired to give the band their only US #1.

As if to capitalize on their stateside success, ONCE UPON A TIME (1985) was recorded in America with

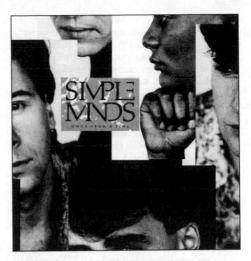

producers Jimmy Iovine and Bob Clearmountain. Less cluttered than SPARKLE IN THE RAIN, the new album seemed tailor-made to meet the requirements of America's powerful rock FM stations, and confirmed that the band were no longer prepared to sacrifice commercial success for artistic adventurism. And the record had its own merits, succeeding in employing big rock hooks and anthemic choruses to effect, particularly on the title track and the singles "Sanctify Yourself" and "All The Things She Said".

With all proceeds from the third single, "Ghostdancing", going to Amnesty International, the album also provided evidence of a developing political consciousness, which came to the fore in 1989 with STREET FIGHTING YEARS. Home to the UK #1 hit single, "Belfast Child", STREET FIGHTING YEARS also included a moving rendition of Peter Gabriel's hauntingly evocative "Biko".

Unfortunately, the lengthy gap between the two albums resulted in the band's failure to consolidate their standing in the USA, though an expedient live album LIVE IN THE CITY OF LIGHT (1987) maintained their profile at home with another #1. Despite this success, the period was one of internal turmoil, with both Derek Forbes and Mick McNeil leaving the band.

With the further departure of Forbes's replacement **John Gibling**, Kerr, Burchill and Gaynor returned to the studio with sundry session players for the recording of REAL LIFE (1991). Undertaking keyboard duties and writing all of the music, Burchill alluded to the album as a new dawn for Simple Minds. Nevertheless, Kerr and Burchill seemed content to replicate a successful formula, and, despite a UK #2 chart position, REAL LIFE gave notice that the band had reached a plateau.

The following year saw the release of GLITTERING PRIZE (1992), a 'best of' compilation which topped the UK album chart and proved that, in Britain at least, the band's popularity remained undiminished. It was not until 1995, however, that we were to see any further product from Kerr and Burchill. GOOD

NEWS FROM THE NEXT WORLD offered little that was new, but constituted Simple Minds' strongest set for some time. Yet the album's poor chart showing suggested that the band had failed to break the public's perception of them as an 80s phenomenon. The sense that the band had reached the end of the line was compounded when, after a fruitful fifteen years, they were released from their contract with Virgin.

1998 opened with a new single, "Glitterball", and a new album, NEAPOLIS, which compares well with the Minds' strongest work from the early 80s and has deflated much of their trademark unnecessary pomp. By no means a stripped-down, raw album, this is recognizably the work of the stadium masters; they're just a bit older and more world-weary.

As Duran Duran proved in 1995 with THANK YOU, paying tribute to your heroes and influences can be a terrible idea. Simple Minds obviously didn't listen to it as with NEON LIGHTS they ride roughshod over Patti Smith, Neil Young and, most bizarrely, a thoroughly inadvisable version of Joy Division's "Love Will Tear Us Apart". A bad move, not really compensated by 2002's CRY − their first album of new material since NEAPOLIS. A far better bet was Virgin's BEST OF (2002), which recalled their stadium-filling glory days.

- **New Gold Dream 81, 82, 83, 84** (1982; Virgin).
  An early masterpiece that marked the closure of one chapter in the band's career and the opening of another.
- **Once Upon A Time** (1985; Virgin).
  An album where the themes are big and the songs are anthems.
- **The Best Of Simple Minds** (2002; Virgin).
  An excellent overview of the band's 80s hits and more.

Ian Lowey

SIMPLE RED

Formed Manchester, England, 1985.

Inspired by a 1976 Sex Pistols gig in Manchester, art student **Mick Hucknall** (vocals) decided at the age of 15 on a career as a performer, and within a year he was fronting a chaotic punk outfit called The Frantic Elevators. Hucknall managed to persuade several local labels to release Elevators material, but by the time the group wearily split in 1984, their only success had been limited critical acclaim for their final single, "Holding Back The Years".

Realizing that his powerful voice could yet be his fortune, Hucknall next linked up with polytechnic social-secretary-turned-manager Elliot Rashman, whose enthusiasm for Hucknall's potential knew no bounds. By early 1985 they had assembled a group of highly proficient musicians and enough decent songs to interest several major record companies, and having adopted the name **Simply Red** (after Hucknall's nickname, which denoted hair colour, football allegiance − Manchester United − and political affiliation), they signed to Elektra and began recording and rehearsing. This was a volatile period in which several musicians who had made contribu-

tions to Simply Red's development were dispensed with as success loomed, creating bitterness which in some cases endures to this day and establishing Hucknall's reputation as a ruthless operator.

The first single was "Money's Too Tight (To Mention)" (1985), a cover of a Valentine Brothers soul track championed by Hucknall in his days as a DJ. Its obvious message (opening line: 'I've been laid off from work, my rent is due') struck a chord with enough people to make it a Top 20 hit, while its energy and Hucknall's blistering vocal established Simply Red as a name to watch.

A run of flops was halted a year later when "Holding Back The Years", a smoky reworking of the old Frantic Elevators song, soared to #2 in Britain, and later #1 in America. Suddenly Simply Red were stars, and their debut album, PICTURE BOOK (1985), an underachiever when first released, began to fly off shelves the world over. Hucknall's image as a latter-day Oliver Twist, with walking cane, woolly jumper and cloth cap covering an unruly mop of red curls was distinctive enough, but soon seemed inappropriate as the platinum discs poured in.

For the second album, MEN & WOMEN (1987), a more sober style was adopted, with bowler hats and colourful suits replacing the ragamuffin look. The music had changed too, with the introspection and social comment of their debut replaced by a bold, funky soul groove. It was at this point that Hucknall became a target for the tabloid press, who pounced on the suggestive lyrics to the hit single, "The Right Thing", threw in a few lurid tales of his womanizing, and began to portray the singer as a lecherous loudmouth. Despite the bad press, and a roasting from the critics − one of whom, to Hucknall's disgust, memorably labelled it 'designer soul' − MEN & WOMEN performed well enough to keep the band's momentum going.

Before starting work on the third album, Hucknall made a decision to put together an album of quality music aimed at a mass audience rather than continue the fruitless pursuit of credibility. On A NEW FLAME (1989), the Simply Red sound became smoother and classier, perfectly illustrated by the cover of Harold Melvin's "If You Don't Know Me By Now", which became their second US #1 and one of the biggest worldwide singles of the year. After that kind of success, there was no turning back: Hucknall began to be photographed with some of the world's most beautiful women and courted by Hollywood celebrities (Jack Nicholson and Diana Ross were among those to declare themselves fans), and Simply Red found themselves firmly in the superstar bracket.

By 1991, Hucknall was declaring himself a European citizen and finally admitting that Simply Red was essentially a solo project. He also produced the sharpest, most articulate songs of his career on STARS (1991), an album on which Hucknall perfected the art of dressing political lyrics in such a way as to avoid alienating his huge, mainly apolitical, audience. (The smoochy ballad "Wonderland", for example, disguised a bitter attack on Margaret Thatcher.) STARS was Britain's bestselling album for both 1991 and 1992, but (perversely) was their least popular in the US.

Two more arduous years of touring and promotion followed STARS, but Simply Red returned stronger than ever in 1995. The comeback single, "Fairground", became the band's first ever British #1. Its popularity gave LIFE (1995) a welcome kick-start, and by the end of the year it had sold more than a million copies in the UK alone, making it the fourth-biggest seller of the year after just ten weeks in the shops – a remix album, FAIRGROUND, followed soon afterwards. BLUE (1998) was essentially a covers album, with worthy versions of Greg Isaac's "Night Nurse" and two disastrous attempts to inject life into "The Air That I Breathe" – originally a dire Hollies single.

Though Simply Red fans continue to buy Hucknall's products in droves, both 1999's LOVE AND THE RUSSIAN WINTER and 2003's HOME were weak, bloated affairs. Despite the absence of anything resembling the group's finest moments, it seems that Hucknall's public will continue to empty their pockets for him and, as such, his story is likely to run and run.

◉ **Picture Book** (1985; Elektra).
An arresting debut, which turned Hucknall's long slog towards acceptance into a diary of vigorous, uncompromising songs. The full-on howl at the end of "Holding Back The Years" remains the single most memorable moment in the Simply Red repertoire.

◉ **Stars** (1991; East West).
Hucknall's globetrotting provided the impetus for this diverse and confident record, which benefited from a more relaxed vocal style and some lush, fluent arrangements. The title track is a soaring delight, and the radiant "For Your Babies" is Hucknall's best song to date.

◉ **Greatest Hits** (1996; East West).
All the Simply Red you could ask for, neatly collected in the one package.

Jonathan Kennaugh

SIOUXSIE AND THE BANSHEES

Formed London, 1976; split 1996.

"My earliest memory is pretending to be dead. My mum used to step over me while I was laying on the kitchen floor."

Through all the mutations of her image – from Sex-Pistols-fan-cum-go-go-dancer, via 80s icon to relaxed 90s rock veteran – **Siouxsie Sioux** has defined **The Banshees**. Members have come and gone – transients **ADAM ANT** and **THE CURE**'s Robert Smith among them – but she has always been the pivot of the band.

Born Susan Dallion in 1957, Siouxsie was one of a gang of bored suburban teenagers known as the

Bromley Contingent, a crew who embodied the decadent end of early British punk, and had a fondness for Nazi regalia. A proto-Banshees (featuring Sid Vicious on drums) debuted at the almost-mythical 'Punk Festival' held at London's 100 Club in 1976 with a twenty-minute bludgeoning of the Lord's Prayer that ensured them a place in punk lore. A few weeks later, Siouxsie was part of the group of fans that helped destroy Bill Grundy's TV career when the Pistols came onto his show.

Two years, dozens of gigs and a forest of press coverage later, The Banshees – Siouxsie Sioux (vocals), **Steven Severin** (bass), **John McKay** (guitar) and **Kenny Morris** (drums) – were at the cutting edge of the New Wave, beloved of John Peel and scaring the pants off new arrivals on the scene. After the pop-punk effervescence of their first UK Top 10 hit, "Hong Kong Garden", their sound was captured perfectly on the splendid THE SCREAM (1978), which chewed up bleak visions of urban collapse in brilliantly attitudinous, brooding music. The Banshees' total rewiring of The Beatles' "Helter Skelter" – which closed the album – was a classic piece of punk subversion. Acclaim and sales followed.

A shame, then, that their follow-up, JOIN HANDS (1979), should be a half-finished chart and critical failure, though it did include a rather fetching "Lord's Prayer", in the spirit of the glorious 100 Club version. The band then split acrimoniously mid-tour. Sioux and Steve Severin persevered, bringing in ex-Slits' drummer **Budgie** and guitarist **John McGeogh**.

The atmospheric, synth-fuelled KALEIDOSCOPE (1980) featured the skewed pop genius of "Happy House" (a UK Top 20 hit) and the LP made the UK Top 5. As they moved gradually away from their hardcore punk roots, Siouxsie And The Banshees began to build a wider audience and it was the vastly influential JUJU (1981) that propelled them to the very front of the alternative-rock scene. This brilliant album created more templates for 80s psychedelia, goth and shoe-gazing than their more press-friendly copyists even knew existed.

Siouxsie and Budgie embarked on a parallel project at this point, forming an on-off splinter group called **THE CREATURES**, while keeping The Banshees' momentum going. The Banshees' mesmerizing A KISS IN THE DREAMHOUSE (1982) pushed forward experimentally, throwing tape loops, strings, recorders and dance rhythms into an intoxicating brew and, as the year closed, The Banshees' old claim to be 'the best band in the world' seemed more and more reasonable. Their claim to be the only major British band to play a benefit gig for the Italian Communist Party stands unchallenged.

Typically, they threw it all away. October 1983 brought a UK Top 3 hit with another Beatles cover, "Dear Prudence", with **Robert Smith** handling guitar duties in the wake of McGeogh. But, with no new material, the rush-released live double LP NOCTURNE was an unconvincing cash-in.

Still, in the eyes of their solid fan base, The Banshees could do little wrong. They'd changed into something approaching goth and spent the mid 80s noodling around with moods and atmospheres in the studio, and still the faithful were happily trotting off to the record stores. It mattered little to them that HYAENA (1984) was written off as an overproduced and uninspired set by the music press, which had just fallen in love with guitar pop again. Nor that TINDERBOX (1986), with John Carruthers replacing Smith, was seen as slightly better, if flawed. And after that, a cover version of Dylan's "This Wheel's On Fire" – which owed far more to Julie Driscoll's version than it did to Bob's – took the band back into the UK singles chart and prompted an entire LP of covers, THROUGH THE LOOKING GLASS (1987), which brought the band into even wider public view.

Following a long break, the band recruited the cellist/keyboardist **Martin McCarrick** and guitarist **Jon Klein** (replacing Carruthers), and stormed back again with one of their best singles and LPs. "Peek-A-Boo" soared up the UK and US charts, carried on house rhythms and waltzing accordions, and the masterful, menacing PEEPSHOW (1988) took them once more into unfamiliar stylistic terrain. SUPERSTITION (1991) followed and proved their most accessible set, distinguished by perfect dance-pop like "Kiss Them For Me", which broke the US Top 30. Another long break preceded the elegant and critically acclaimed THE RAPTURE (1995), which again stands among The Banshees' finest work, adding another remarkable stage in their remarkable career.

Siouxsie and Budgie (who married in 1991) split the band in 1996, partly as a response to the Sex Pistols reunion. Yet The Banshees themselves reformed for a string of gigs in 2002 to promote a new 'best of' album. The collection featured the hits, a bunch of remixes and a couple of exclusive new cuts, though no plans for more new material have been revealed.

⊙ **The Scream** (1978; Polydor/ Geffen).
Suburban life collapses to a soundtrack of Siouxsie wailing, blistering guitars and industrial rhythms.

⊙ **Juju** (1981; Polydor/Geffen).
The Cure, Psychedelic Furs, Cocteau Twins, and numerous others, owe their careers to this goth classic.

⊙ **Peepshow** (1988; Polydor/Geffen).
The Banshees kick back into life with this brilliantly diverse record. "Last Beat Of My Heart" features Siouxsie's best singing ever.

⊙ **Once Upon A Time / Twice Upon A Time** (1981 and 1992; Polydor/Geffen).
These compilation sets stand as a reminder of what a great singles band The Banshees are, and of their colossal influence on countless 'alternative' bands. This is the history of 80s art-pop.

Neil Blackmore

SIR DOUGLAS QUINTET

Formed Texas, 1964; disbanded 1973; re-formed 1976.

Although they made their reputation in late-60s San Francisco, the main men of **Sir Douglas Quintet** were from Texas. However, following a drugs bust in 1965, the band hightailed it to California, where, like fellow émigrés Janis Joplin and Steve Miller, they brought a blues toughness to the folk-rock of early psychedelia.

The original quintet had formed in 1964, comprising vocalist **Doug Sahm** (who had cut his first rock'n'roll single at the tender age of 12), horn player **Francisco Morin**, and a rhythm section of **Harvey Kagan** on bass and **John Perez** on drums. The distinctively cheesy electronic organ sound, with block chords close to the beat, was provided by **Augie Meyer**.

Initially the band's manager, Houston-based producer Huey P. Meaux, established the pretence that they were part of the British Invasion, though Sahm's strong accent soon gave the game away. Their name, first used on a 1964 single, "Sugar Bee", honoured their frontman, and certainly sounded English, as did their music. Their smash hit single "She's About A Mover" owed much to first-generation Britpop, with the kind of organ patented by The Animals, and the up-and-down beat of Paul McCartney's "She's A Woman". Its success saw them touring as opening attraction for bands of the calibre of The Beatles and The Beach Boys.

Sahm did not tour for many years after, and the path that he and the band have pursued since that early hit has been both weird and wonderful, as confusing for the would-be rock historian as it has been fascinating for the fan. The band's first LP, a ragbag of singles and Merseybeat copies, was boldly titled THE BEST OF THE SIR DOUGLAS QUINTET (1966). Two years later, a new line-up – lacking Meyer, and featuring three more SF Texan exiles, including **Wayne Talbert** on piano – released the bizarre PLUS 2: HONKY BLUES. A collision course of avant-garde jazz, country, and wigged-out rock, it was an experiment in democracy: the title referred to two members of blues band Mother Earth, who formed a kind of musicians' pool for the recording.

Far more satisfying was 1969's MENDOCINO,

SIOUXSIE AND THE BANSHEES • SIR DOUGLAS QUINTET

which resurrected the essential sloppiness of the band, and indeed its original line-up. The music anticipated the direction taken by the likes of The Flying Burrito Brothers and Commander Cody – that tasty hybrid, country-rock. It was about now that Sahm adopted his trademark stetson hat, a Texas boy you wouldn't want to mess with. The title track became the band's sole million-seller when released as a single.

They were never to hit such commercial heights again, but artistically the band was on a roll. The 1970 album, 1+1+1 = 4 was back to blues basics. One track, "Be Real", had been originally issued as a single under the pseudonym Wayne Douglas, and this kind of mystification has continued to be part of the Sahm style ever since. The same year, TOGETHER AFTER FIVE featured two medleys recorded live in the studio, which displayed the band's almost telepathic unity.

1971's RETURN OF DOUG SALDANA saw the band return to Texas. One track, "The Railpak Dun Done In The El Monte", was apparently recorded in an extreme state of inebriation, or something. The swan song of the original Sir Douglas Quintet was 1973's ROUGH EDGES, in which rough 1969 live tapes were moulded into a coherent album that provided a fascinating document of a band in full control of its material and audience.

The lead-singer-cum-fiddle-player's first solo effort, DOUG SAHM AND BAND, also appeared in 1973. Despite cameo appearances by Dr. John and Bob Dylan, and Flaco Jimenez's accordion flourishes, it was a leaden record. TEXAS TORNADO, credited to the Sir Douglas Band and released the same year, was a return to form, with the singer backed by a big band containing both Dr. John and Augie Meyer on keyboards.

The band re-formed in 1976, and has been recording and gigging ever since, without ever quite recapturing past glories. Pick of subsequent releases were 1981's BORDER WAVE and 1988's SIR DOUG'S RECORDING TRIP, but Sahm and Meyers have been bashing out their relaxed brand of 60s rock for so long now that they could do it on their deathbeds, and probably will. Rights to their back catalogue have passed on to Demon, who are in the process of resurrecting this primal Tex-Mex stew.

⊙ **Mendocino** (1969; Smash).
This collection is somehow more than the sum of its parts, and helps encapsulate a time long lost. There is a delicacy and a lack of hurry which no one else has recaptured. Highlights are "At The Crossroads" (later covered with a heavier backbeat by Mott The Hoople), a remake of "She's About A Mover" and the rolling title track.

⊙ **Sir Doug's Recording Trip** (1988; Edsel).
A great collection of good-time Tex-Mex by the band that practically invented the genre. Contains most of the hits plus some choice rarities.

Brian Hinton

SISTERS OF MERCY

Formed Leeds, England, 1980.

Formed above a chemist's shop in Leeds during 1980, the **Sisters Of Mercy** – the name was taken from a Leonard Cohen song – are the group most associated with the 'goth' tag. A topnotch rock-'n'roll band, at their peak in the mid-80s they stimulated sales of black hair dye and crimpers like no band before or since.

The original band was a duo: drummer/guitarist **Andrew Eldritch**, armed with a Joey Ramone mop haircut and a working knowledge of the poetry of T. S. Eliot, and his mate **Gary Marx**, singer and guitarist who owned a primitive drum machine they dubbed Doktor Avalancher. They recorded a single, "Damage Done" (1980), and put it out on their own Merciful Release label to minimal reaction.

For the second single, "Body Electric" (1982), the pair recruited bassist **Craig Adams**, a big fan of Motörhead and Hawkwind, and guitarist **Ben Gunn**, who would later be replaced by the flamboyant ex-Dead Or Alive guitarist, **Wayne Hussey**.

Early Sisters singles and an EP, THE REPTILE HOUSE (1983), saw a steady improvement in the musicianship behind their anthemic songs, but the breakthrough came with the storming dance-floor EP, ALICE/FLOORSHOW/PHANTOM/1969. This signalled the emergence of the full Sisters sound – dark rock'n'roll psychedelia with a punk edge – and earned them a major deal with Warners. They toured relentlessly, mastering the art of looking pale and skinny, and almost making the British charts with "Temple Of Love" (1983).

FIRST AND LAST AND ALWAYS (1985), the debut LP, was a slightly patchy affair but not without its highlights: "Nine While Nine" and "Amphetamine Logic", a hymn to their infamous intake of speed at that time. Its unevenness, though, reflected the splits already appearing in the band, and when the Sisters played a farewell gig at London's Royal Albert Hall, Gary Marx had already departed. Soon afterwards Wayne and Craig left to form **THE MISSION**, while Eldritch rush-released a single, "Giving Ground" (1986), as **The Sisterhood**, in order to stop Wayne and Craig using the name. With vocal duties handled not by Eldritch but by similarly ultra-deep-voiced **James Ray**, the Sisterhood released an LP titled THE GIFT (1986).

Ex-Gun Club bassist **Patricia Morrison** debuted with The Sisterhood before partnering Eldritch in the next incarnation of the Sisters of Mercy. In 1988 they achieved their first fully fledged hit single, "This Corrosion", an overblown production by Jim 'Meat Loaf' Steinman, replete with Mozart rip-off chord intro. The album that followed, FLOODLAND (1987), replaced the Zeppelin medievalisms of Hussey's guitar with a more synth-driven sound.

By the time of the third Sisters album, VISION THING (1990), Patricia Morrison had gone: the new line-up featured guitarists **Andreas Bruhn** and ex-All About Eve man **Tim Bricheno**, and **Tony James**, survivor of Generation X and Sigue Sigue Sputnik, on bass. It was an altogether rockier sound than before, but Eldritch's lyrics remained dark and mysterious, and not without a sense of humour.

Sisters off on a picnic (from left): Ben Gunn, Craig Adams, Wayne Hussey and Andrew Eldritch

After a co-headlining tour of America with Public Enemy was aborted due to poor attendances, Eldritch seems to have gone to ground somewhat. One new track,"Under The Gun", appeared on a compilation and reached #3 in the indie charts as a single. The band still tours sporadically, but what happens next is anybody's guess.

⊙ **Some Girls Wander By Mistake** (1992; East West). All their releases up to the first album collected together. If you only buy one Sisters record, this is the one to get.

⊙ **A Slight Case Of Over Bombing** (1993; East West). A collection of all their major-label singles. Highlights include "Lucretia My Reflection" (wherein Eldritch betrays his classical education) and "Doctor Jeep".

Ross Holloway

SIX BY SEVEN

Formed Nottingham, England, 1991.

Six By Seven began back in 1991 as a three-piece, comprising university friends **Chris Olley** (vocals/guitars) and **Sam Hempton** (guitar), with percussion provided by **Chris Davies** – a line-up soon augmented by **Paul Douglas** (bass) and **James Flower** (sax and Hammond organ). It wasn't until December 1996, however, that the break-through began, when Ed Horrox, A&R man for Mantra Records (a subsidiary of Beggar's Banquet), attended a gig in the band's home town. The man from Mantra was impressed, and by the time of

1997's Phoenix Festival, he wasn't alone. Six By Seven played the festival as an unsigned quantity and left with several offers, plumping eventually for Mantra.

The first release, however, was issued on vinyl on their own MFS label in September 1997. The seven-minute-plus "European Me" was such a staggering piece of work that music journalists were left grasping for superlatives: the *NME* made it *Single Of The Week* and was moved to describe it as 'one of the all-time great debut singles', while *Melody Maker* went on to make it their number two single of 1997, behind Embrace's "All You Good, Good People". After two more singles – "88-92-96" and "Candlelight" – all was set for the debut album, THE THINGS WE MAKE (1998), a set whose brooding demeanour and spartan grandeur drew comparisons with Radiohead and Joy Division, though Chris Olley's lyrics tended to speak of a dedication to the nicer things in life. One track from the album, "For You", was released as a single and came within an ace of Top 40 success, and was followed by "Two And A Half Days In Love With You", which failed to trouble the charts.

The second Mantra collection, THE CLOSER YOU GET (2000), was an altogether darker set, its powerful opener (and the most striking single since "European Me") "Eat Junk, Become Junk" firing a strong broadside at consumerism. Despair of a more personal nature featured in other stand-outs such as "Ten Places To Die" and "Another Love Song", the singer's delivery wavering between the delicate and the savage. For guitarist Sam Hempton, though, this set was to prove the swan song: following disagreements with the band, the founder member bowed out after Six By Seven's appearance at Glastonbury.

Following Hempton's departure, a more melodic sound was notable on the third album, THE WAY I FEEL TODAY (2002), though the set contained many uncompromising moments ("Flypaper For Freaks", "Bad Man"), and Olley's vocal performance retained a rough-hewn honesty befitting the personal integrity of his lyrics. Sadly, however, neither of the singles from the album – "So Close" and "IOU Love" – made much of an impact, and Six By Seven remain one of the UK's best-kept secrets.

⊙ **The Things We Make** (1998; Mantra).
All the singles to the end of 1998, plus six other superb statements of wellbeing.

⊙ **The Closer You Get** (2000; Mantra).
Less compromising but more fully realized than its predecessor, this album emphasizes the group's tenacity and singularity of vision. This time, influences are worn more readily on the sleeve: "England & A Broken Radio" could be a Sparklehorse demo.

⊙ **The Way I Feel Today** (2002; Mantra).
The stubborn insistence remains, but with a broader appeal.

Jeremy Simmonds and Susan Compo

60FT DOLLS

Formed Newport, Wales, 1993; split 1999.

There was something undeniably endearing about the musical and philosophical honesty of the **60ft Dolls**. Critics rightly pointed to the limitations of their sound – Hüsker Dü meets The Jam, with some detectable vocal Wellerisms from singer and guitarist **Richard Parfitt** – but there are far worse historical antecedents to borrow from.

The band was built around the long-standing friendship of Parfitt and **Mike Cole** (vocals/bass), two Gwent social security cases who nurtured musical ambitions. After starting the band in 1993 they bought a four-track and recruited **Carl Bevan** (drums). Their first vinyl appearance came on the I WAS A TEENAGE GWENT BOY compilation. With interest in Welsh rock reviving, thanks primarily to The Manic Street Preachers, they released their debut single on their manager's own Townhill Records label. "Happy Shopper" was a perfect introduction – all blazing guitars and self-deprecating valley angst.

In the meantime, the trio's capacity for alcohol was witnessed at first hand by headline acts such as Oasis, Elastica and Dinosaur Jr. Following a typically frantic appearance at 1994's In The City Festival they were snapped up by Rough Trade. 1995 brought the BratBus tour, sponsored by the *NME* (and several breweries), preceding their second single, "White Knuckle Ride"/"No. 1 Pure Alcohol". However, Rough Trade was soon on the ropes, not for the first time in its history, and the band subsequently moved on to Indolent.

Their new label debut, "Stay", featured some impressively operatic backing vocals buried among the usual clatter. By this time they had completed a nationwide tour with label-mates Sleeper and they were beginning to take umbrage at journalists more interested in their drinking stories than their music. They certainly didn't enjoy universal support from the inkies – 'All I can hear is punk bluster and half-assed attitude, but the animated moshing going off around me tells a different story,' noted Neil Kulkarini in a *Melody Maker* live review. "Talk To Me" finally became their debut Top 40 single and preceded the release of THE BIG 3, an Al Clay (Boo Radleys/Pixies) production with some nice moments and more subtlety than 60ft Dolls' hard-men image might have suggested.

But all went horribly wrong: after another single, "Alison's Room" (1998), the group were dropped by Indolent – they split soon after. A second album, JOYA MAGICA, was released post-disintegration, though nobody seemed to notice.

⊙ **The Big 3** (1996; Indolent).
An engaging collection of songs with strong hints that 60ft Dolls could have been massive.

Alex Ogg

THE SKIDS

Formed Dunfermline, Scotland, 1977; disbanded 1982.

The Skids, it seemed, picked their moment well. Comprising the songwriting axis of **Richard Jobson** (vocals) and **Stuart Adamson** (guitar), together with the rhythm section of **William Simpson** (bass) and **Tom Kellichan** (drums), they rode into British consciousness on the New Wave backwash to the ebbing tide of punk. The release of their self-financed, attention-grabbing CHARLES EP came at the time Richard Branson's Virgin label were busy accruing an eclectic roster of post-punk hopefuls. Consequently, with almost indecent haste, the band were tethered to what was to prove an optimistic eight-album deal.

On the flip side of their first Virgin single, "Sweet Suburbia" (1978), the band proclaimed themselves to be 'Open Sound', which was essentially a description of the soaring histrionics of Adamson's guitar style. When married to the martial rhythms of the drumming and the bellowing, chant-like vocals of Jobson, this sound conspired to lend their repertoire a rousing, anthemic quality. It was heroic music which at its best, as on the first album, SCARED TO DANCE (1979), seemed to capture the drama and turbulence of battle. Unfortunately, the sound was an all-too-graphic reflection of the band's own stormy relationships, a turbulence which was to settle only with the departure of Adamson in the summer of 1981.

The Skids' decline was in large part due to the portentous designs of Richard Jobson, who sought to mould the band into a vehicle for his ever-more-convoluted lyrics. This became most evident in the recording of the second album, DAYS IN EUROPA (1979). Following the departure of original drummer Tom Kellichan in the traditional rock'n'roll style (ie after the first album), The Skids recruited a temporary replacement in the form of ex-Rich Kids drummer and Jobson cohort, **Rusty Egan**, and a producer in the form of ex Be-Bop Deluxe man Bill Nelson. Together, both Nelson and Egan contrived to free the band from the strictures of punk-pop in favour of a more polished, almost danceable sound. Ultimately it was a case of too many cooks, and the resultant album proved to be a misguided attempt at redefining The Skids' sound. This in turn alienated a great many fans, and also cost them the services of bassist Simpson during the troubled tour that ensued.

For Jobson and Adamson it was back to the drawing board, and 1980 saw a rejuvenated Skids with a new rhythm section in the form of **Russell Webb** (bass) and **Mike Baillie** (drums). The resultant album, THE ABSOLUTE GAME (1980), produced this time by Mick Glossop, was a commercial success, giving the band their first and only British Top 10 album. Artistically, too, it heralded a return to form, dispensing with the excess baggage of the previous outing and playing to the dual strengths of Adamson's guitar stylings and Jobson's lyrical bombast. Unfortunately, this rejuvenation coincided with Jobson's increasing commitment to a burgeoning London scene. Adamson's departure had as much to do with geographical differences as to musical and personal ones; a point evinced by Adamson's eventual return to Dunfermline, where he formed the internationally successful **BIG COUNTRY**.

Following Adamson's departure, the final dissolution of the band was soon to follow. Unfortunately, however, not before Jobson and Webb issued a dour and ill-conceived concept album, JOY (1981), which served only to illustrate that, when Adamson left, he took all of the best tunes with him. Not surprisingly the album failed to chart, and proved a sorry end to a short career which had begun with so much spark and promise.

(•) **Scared To Dance** (1979; Virgin).
Ebullient cod heroics for a less than heroic age. Containing three of the first four singles, this is The Skids as we most fondly remember them.

(•) **Dunfermline** (1987; Virgin).
A 'best of' compilation, and a reminder of The Skids' strength as a sparkling singles band.

Ian Lowey

SKINNY PUPPY

Formed Canada, 1983; disbanded 1995.

Formed around the core of **Nivek Ogre** (alter ego of Kevin Ogilvie), **Cevin Key** and **Dwayne Rudolph Goettel**, the early **Skinny Puppy** created a highly experimental brew of raw bleeps and beats, though they gradually became characterized by a dense interaction of textures. Obscure and disparate samples, from snatches of B-movie themes to menacing dialogue from news broadcasts and documentaries, were coupled with sounds representative of every era of electronic music, as cheap Euro-synths collided with early acid-house technology to unnerving, alienating effect. Another innovative and influential Puppy trick was to sample heavy metal guitar riffs, and use the resulting noise as a dense, repeating rhythm, pre-empting the more obvious work of bands like The Young Gods.

Preoccupied with the environmental destruction, disease and dark side of the human psyche (they sampled Charles Manson long before Nine Inch Nails did), Skinny Puppy put on a traumatic live show, often including film footage of vivisection experiments, combined with fake blood and pyrotechnics. But the impossibility of reducing the sprawling chaos of the Skinny Puppy sound into an MTV-friendly slice of dance music condemned the band to the fringes, despite major-label support (from Capitol) and a growing cult following. Long-term drug addiction didn't help either – it finally took its toll on Dwayne Goettel in August 1995, when he died of a suspected heroin overdose.

The band released their final album, THE PROCESS, in February 1996, its production marred by Goettel's death. Ironically, it was their most commercial outing, with a polished sheen of guitar and drum samples. Their influence had also been heard in Nine Inch Nails' 1995 contribution to the soundtrack of the film *Seven* – which exemplified how much a genre once deemed irreversibly alienated from the mainstream has become another facet of 'alternative' music culture.

Skinny Puppy members had already been involved in a side-project, **Download**, before Goettel's death, and they continued to record and perform under the name. Members also featured in **Pigface**, a sprawling, experimental and largely unsuccessful industrial supergroup, which produced several albums in the early 90s, (see **REVOLTING COCKS**).

The band's influence lives on, and Key continues to release multimedia discs compiling the band's extensive history. These include archive footage, discographies and rare remixes, as well as a sample CD-ROM stuffed with 'hand-picked' Skinny Puppy-esque samples for aspiring sonic terrorists.

(•) **Cleanse, Fold & Manipulate** (1987; Nettwerk).
Contains the chilling "The Mourn" and the even spookier "Epilogue", which finishes the album with a statement about the Turin Shroud. Uneasy listening in the extreme.

(•) **Too Dark Park** (1990; Capitol).
A truly chaotic album. The stand-out track is "Shore Lined Poison", with its off-kilter drumbeat, punctuated with stabbing samples.

Jonathan Bell

SKUNK ANANSIE

Formed London, 1994; disbanded 2000.

Skunk Anansie were named after a combination of the endearing black-haired, white-striped creature and a spider that features in Jamaican folk tales. Offering a venomous, corrosive antidote to the plodding clichés of traditional metal, they were formed by **Skin** (vocals), **Ace** (guitars), **Cass** (bass) and **Robbie** (drums), and snapped up by the One Little Indian label after only their second gig. While their early sound was akin to aural terrorism (a hybrid of soulful vocals and very heavy metal), the visuals complemented their confrontational attitude with variations on army-surplus chic. Skin could safely say that she was the only black female singer to ever shave her head and paint on a white stripe from back to front, and the group as a whole sported combat fatigues and Doc Martens.

Their initial foray into the world of recording came in the shape of a BBC radio session. So impressive was their appearance that Radio 1 took the unprecedented step of releasing a track from the session as a limited-edition 7" single. "Little Baby Swastikkka" came out on mail order only and sold out very quickly. The song was typical of what would become the Skunk Anansie trademark, with taut and angry lyrics based on Skin's personal experiences of racism.

Already making a name for themselves as a passionate live band, they set about touring with Killing Joke and Senser. With a considerable buzz growing about them, 1995 saw the band go into overdrive. The release of "Selling Jesus" was their first official record company outing; a nightmare pyrotechnic assault on the hypocrisies of religion, it was backed with three similarly charged shards of fury.

September brought the long-awaited release of SUNBURNT AND PARANOID (1995), an album firmly rooted in heavy metal, but with influences that clearly ranged through to soul and funk. The arrangements were inventive, Skin's vocals shimmered with emotion, and the songs covered everything from relationships ("Charity", "Pity") to racism ("Intellectualise My Blackness") with lyrical finesse. Clearly the caustic politics and no-holds-barred delivery appealed across the musical spectrum; not only was the album well received, but the group were voted best new band of 1995 by *Kerrang!* readers.

After an appearance in the film *Strange Days*, **Mark** was brought in on drums. The release of STOOSH (street slang for 'wickedly cool') in late 1996 merely underlined the fact that, although the band were always keen to root the music in some kind of political context (witness opening track "Yes, It's Fucking Political") it didn't detract from the fact that they basically write songs with an almost unerring sense of melody.

A third album, POST ORGASMIC CHILL (1999) produced further hit singles in "Charlie Big Potato", "Secretly" and "Lately", before the announcement came that the band were to split. Skin released her first solo collection, FLESHWOUNDS, in 2003. Produced by David Kosten (**FAULTLINE**), the set was sparse and clinical, but boasted some strong, chart-pleasing material.

⊙ **Sunburnt And Paranoid** (1995; One Little Indian).
A confident first release from a band that treats its listeners like intelligent people: the lyrics are honest expressions of emotion, while the musicianship is second to none.

⊙ **Stoosh** (1996; One Little Indian)
Despite the somewhat overplayed political correctness this is yet another savage set of tunes about love, lies and politics.

Essi Berelian

SLADE

Formed Wolverhampton, England, 1966.

"I judge a good rock and roll encyclopaedia by whether or not Slade is included." – Robert Christau, music critic *Rolling Stone* and *Village Voice*

Hailing from the Black Country, **Slade** created some of the most raucous pop tunes ever to storm the charts and after outliving the glam era have become affectionately regarded as something of a national institution. The band began in 1966 as The 'N' Betweens, consisting of **Noddy Holder** (vocals/guitar), **Jim Lea** (bass/violin), **Dave Hill** (guitar) and **Don Powell** (drums). After auditioning several vocalists, including Robert Plant, Holder assumed vocal duties and his rasping, soulful tones would become a trademark of the Slade sound.

A meeting with legendary producer Kim Fowley resulted in a single on Columbia Records, "You Better Run" (1966), which enjoyed little success. After two years gigging around the Midlands, the band moved to London, changed their name to Ambrose Slade and released a debut album BEGINNINGS (1969), consisting mainly of R&B covers.

The album failed to set the charts alight, but the band were spotted by former Animals bassist and then-manager of Jimi Hendrix, Chas Chandler who shortened their name to Slade and encouraged their new direction as a skinhead group complete with suede-heads, Doc Martens and braces. This phase resulted in the excellent singles "Wild Winds Are Blowing" (1969) and "Shapes Of Things To Come" (1970), and the hard-hitting PLAY IT LOUD (1970) album.

Mainstream success still proved elusive, however, and in 1970 the band cultivated an even more outrageous glam-rock image and released live favourite "Get Down And Get With It", which took them into the UK Top 20 for the first time. On BBC TV's *Top Of The Pops* they were now donning tartan, top hats, stack heels and in Holder's case outrageous sideburns. Holder and Lea began to write all the band's material, relying on crunching riffs, stomping beats, simple yet memorable lyrics and deliberately misspelt song titles. The result was the #1 single "Coz I Luv You" (1971), which was the first of an incredible six chart-toppers over the next three years. These included "Take Me Back 'Ome", "Mamma Weer All Crazee Now", "Come On Feel The Noise" and the rather dubious "Skweeze Me Pleeze Me". The band's finest album from this era, SLAYED (1973), is now regarded as a classic.

During their glam phase Slade also produced arguably the best Christmas single ever, "Merry Christmas Everybody" (1973), which has recharted most Christmases since. Slade have always enjoyed a reputation as legendary live performers, and there is no better illustration of this than the 1972 album SLADE ALIVE, on which Holder punctuates a quieter moment with a loud belch!

After the surprisingly gritty and well-received 1974 movie *Slade In Flame*, and its mature, rather world-weary soundtrack, the band's fortunes began to wane. A run of unsuccessful albums followed, including the aptly titled WHATEVER HAPPENED TO SLADE (1977). Although punk had much in common with Slade's raucous approach, there was no place for the Black Country boys in the emerging scene.

The 1980s, however, saw a revival of interest in the group. After a crowd-pleasing performance at the 1980 Reading Festival, Slade were embraced by the heavy-metal fraternity and this was reflected in the rockin' albums WE'LL BRING THE HOUSE DOWN (1980) and TILL DEAF DO US PART (1981). In 1983 Slade finally found success on both sides of the Atlantic with the anthemic singles "My Oh My" and "Run Run Away" and AMAZING KAMIKAZE SYNDROME album. However, the cancellation of their planned American tour meant that this spark of interest was soon extinguished.

Ever the working-class professionals, Slade continued to enjoy sporadic chart success into the early 90s when Holder and Lea left the band. Hill and Powell continue to gig and record under the name **Slade II**, Holder is a successful radio presenter (and frequent guest on TV shows), while the band's classic material has received much critical acclaim and accolades from artists as diverse as Kurt Cobain and Oasis.

Slade Alive (1972; Polydor).
One of the all-time great live rock albums. Noddy and the boys provide the perfect pre-punk antidote to early-70s rock pomposity.

Slayed (1973, Polydor)
The cover makes the band look like petty criminals with bad hangovers, but the tunes epitomize Slade's no-nonsense, good-time approach. Never mind The Beatles, this is the more likely blueprint for 90s lad-rock.

Malcolm Russell

SLAPP HAPPY

Formed Hamburg, Germany, 1972; merged with Henry Cow 1975; re-formed for one-off projects in 1982, 1990 and 1998.

"Our ambivalence towards pop music expresses itself in a sinister kind of whimsy." Peter Blegvad

There are music fans – one of this book's editors among them – who find themselves musing how finer by far the pop world could have been had it only paid more attention to **Slapp Happy**. The group, in its brief lives, was the wittiest of combos, the most charming and tuneful of cults – and pleasingly eccentric. Witness the fact that they played live just once, seven years after splitting up, wearing luminous fish masks and singing a ditty about slimming: 'Listen my children and you will hear/You can shed weight and still drink beer/It's better with a friend but you can do it alone/Just slapp a happy platter on the gramaphone [sic]'.

The Slapp Happy story began, a tad unpromisingly, in 1970s Hamburg, where **Dagmar Krause** (vocals) had been singing in clubs on the Reeperbahn and with a German folk-protest group, The City Preachers, before meeting Englishman **Anthony Moore** (guitars/keyboards/vocals). Moore was working in experimental film and music, and had released a couple of frankly tedious avant-garde solo LPs, PIECES OF THE CLOUDLAND BALLROOM (1971) and SECRETS OF THE BLUE BAG (1972). After his record label, Polydor Germany, turned down a third such project, he floated a 'pop album' with Dagmar, his then-partner, and an American-born friend, **PETER BLEGVAD** (guitar/vocals). Blegvad was an associate of the Hamburg-based **FAUST**, and the trio set to work in the band's studio, using their musicians and their producer, Uwe Nettelbeck, to record a delightful, utterly original waxing, SORT OF ... SLAPP HAPPY (1972). The disc 'championed' – as Blegvad put it on the sleeve – 'Naive Rock, the Douanier Rousseau sound'.

SORT OF was a captivating debut, Blegvad and Moore combining to create songs of playful wit and melody which were the perfect outlet for Dagmar's German-inflected vocals. It was avant-garde only in the sense of doing something distinct from the currents of the day, and its cool romanticism was both accessible and fun. It sold lamentably few copies, handicapped as a German product (and not even Krautrock), and perhaps as much by Moore and Blegvad's decisions not to do concerts 'like a real pop group'. Still, Polydor financed the trio for a follow-up, which they again recorded with the Faust crew. (Blegvad was to further the association by touring with Faust in 1973.)

That second recording was CASABLANCA MOON – eleven songs of whimsy, romance and wit, which saw the Slapp Happy songwriting team reach maturity. From the opening line of the title track ('He used to wear fedoras/Now he sports a fez/There's cabalistic innuendos in everything he sez'), sung to a tango lilt, through "Mr Rainbow" (a Rimbaud poem, sung in French), to the instant romantic hook of "A Little Something", it was a record of perfect enchantment, and again stood quite apart from its time. In 1973, rock was in the midst of its 'progressive' phase, with which Slapp Happy – with their crafted, cabaret-like songs – had absolutely nothing in common.

However, Virgin Records, in the throes of their first post-TUBULAR BELLS expansion, were picking

groups almost on account of their eccentricity, and before Polydor could (or would) issue CASABLANCA MOON, Slapp Happy found themselves at Virgin's Manor studios, rerecording the album with a virtual chamber orchestra of session musicians. The results, issued as SLAPP HAPPY (1974), created a small cult following, including goodly sections of the music press, and other Virgin musicians – notably Robert Wyatt and avant-rockers, **HENRY COW**.

The Cow talked good politics, and the Slapp Happy trio, attracted by a group who stood as far outside the rock mainstream as themselves, agreed to an alliance. The idea was to produce two records together, one created largely by Slapp Happy, the other by Cow. The first of these, DESPERATE STRAIGHTS (1974), appeared to positive and heavyweight reviews in the British music press. It was fascinating: a series of dark-to-apocalyptic songs, nodding to Blake in the lyrics, but welded musically with Cow's trademark discordance. Dagmar's singing had turned into an art-voice; songs to compositions. The Cow-dominated album that followed, IN PRAISE OF LEARNING (1975), took the process still further, and resulted in a split. Moore left before the album's release; Blegvad was fired ('for whimsy'); Dagmar remained with Henry Cow, for further tours and records.

Post-Slapp Happy, each of the trio has recorded solo, and with various collaborators. Blegvad's and Krause's careers are covered elsewhere in this book. Anthony Mo(o)re's has been less successful, at least as a solo artist. Following Virgin's failed attempt to launch him as a pop star, with a couple of singles and an album, OUT (1976), he found himself sidelined in the hunt for post-punk stars, having to self-finance and distribute a rather splendid disc called FLYING DOESN'T HELP (1978). Two further and less memorable albums, WORLD SERVICE (1981) and ONLY CHOICE (1984), followed, before Moore found more lucrative work writing lyrics for the Watersless Pink Floyd and lecturing on music back in Germany.

The Slapp Happy story, meanwhile, was not quite over. The trio stayed in touch, and in 1982 recorded a single, the afore-quoted "Everybody's Slimmin'", released on their own Half-Cat label, and, seemingly for the hell of it, did their first ever gig at London's ICA, playing all the old songs from those first two albums. Then, in 1990, Blegvad and Moore were commissioned to create an opera – one of a series of 'TV Opera Works' – for Britain's Channel Four. *Camera* was finally shown in 1993 (more recently released as a CD in 2000), featuring Dagmar as a waif-like figure in a kind of magical reality, threatened by bureaucratic intruders. It fell between poles – with a score a little too self-consciously operatic – but reopened the idea of a future Slapp Happy collaboration.

This at last came about in 1997, when Geoff Travis, ex-boss of Rough Trade and now of V2, offered Slapp Happy recording time. The result was ÇA VA (1998), a tuneful, surprisingly textured, surprisingly rhythmic album. It lacked the sparse charm of earlier waxings – ironically, it might have done rather well back in the 70s – but it delighted the following, and, of course, vanished without a trace.

Slapp Happy

(•) **Acnalbasac Moon** (1980; ReR).
The 'original' CASABLANCA MOON album, recorded with Faust in 1973, together with four extra songs, including the single "Everybody's Slimmin'", from the 1982 get-together. Needless to say, it's utterly delightful, and the rockier treatments suggest the pre-Virgin MOON could have won more fans at the time.

(•) **Casablanca Moon/Desperate Straights** (1973 & 1974; Virgin).
A 1993 CD reissue of the Virgin SLAPP HAPPY and DESPERATE STRAIGHTS albums, with notes on the group's history from Blegvad. You travel quite a way from one album to the next, but highlights abound, and no collection can have too many versions of Blegvad's "A Little Something".

(•) **Ça Va** (1998; V2).
The end-of-millennium incarnation, with programmed drums as well as the wit of old.

Anthony Moore

(•) **Flying Doesn't Help** (1978; Voiceprint).
More (he dropped an 'o' here) was at his best on this quirky disc, with its strange lyrics of love and war, oddly memorable tunes, and segues that give a feeling of feverish disconnection.

Mark Ellingham

SLAYER

Formed Huntington Beach, LA, 1982.

In the dark and gloomy world of heavy metal music, the name **Slayer** is synonymous with thrash of the most intense and disturbing variety. No other first-division outfit has ever managed to consistently produce records as compellingly unpleasant and brutally fast. The writing nucleus of **Tom Araya** (bass/vocals), **Kerry King** (guitar) and **Jeff Hanneman** (guitar) was completed with **Dave Lombardo** (drums), to form the classic line-up, debuting in 1983 with its contribution to the METAL MASSACRE III compilation.

Already making a name for themselves locally as one of the fastest bands in the burgeoning thrash scene, the Metal Blade label signed them and unleashed SHOW NO MERCY (1984) and HELL AWAITS (1985). These two genre-bending releases demonstrated clearly that subtlety was not to be the band's watchword; each was a scorching blast of satanic speed metal, dished out with numbing technical precision and an obvious delight in shock-tactic lyrics. Although the merit of these recordings was lost in the abysmal production, they did prepare the world for their finest hour or, more precisely, 28 minutes. Teaming up with hip producer Rick Rubin, Slayer came up with REIGN IN BLOOD (1986), one of the most vicious and caustic metal releases ever. This time production came in crisp and clear, allowing the listener to appreciate the precise care with which each tuneless guitar solo was delivered and the loving manner in which each tasteless line was growled. The opening track, "Angel Of Death", insensitively detailed the atrocities perpetrated by Nazi doctor Josef Mengele, opening the gates to a torrent of criticism, whilst the remainder of the album merely refined their previous agenda of satanic torture, death and carnage. LIVE UNDEAD (1987), a minor addition to their catalogue, showed that they could reproduce their deadly noisefest live without missing a beat.

Follow-up studio outings SOUTH OF HEAVEN (1988) and SEASONS IN THE ABYSS (1990) had more than a whiff of sulphur about them and saw Rubin reprise his powerful production job whilst the band experimented by slowing down occasionally to a mere brisk sprint. LIVE – DECADE OF AGGRESSION (1991), an intense double album, boasted no overdubs but instead put studio favourites through the live shredder in a brutal and definitive manner.

Throughout their apparently effortless ascent, Slayer have always suffered from self-destructive personality clashes. With Dave Lombardo's departure the band were left looking for a permanent replacement who could replicate his power and proficiency – Lombardo himself has yet to achieve any major success with his new outfit **Grip Inc. Paul Bostaph** took over for the notable period during which DIVINE INTERVENTION (1994) was recorded and which also saw the bulk of the material coming from King. In the same year the band also worked alongside Ice-T on a cover of The Exploited's "Disorder" for the *Judgment Night* soundtrack.

In a move that most other groups would deem to be commercial suicide, their next effort, UNDISPUTED ATTITUDE (1996), was an all-out covers album re-creating the punk and hardcore music that had influenced them along the way. No sooner was this album complete than Bostaph left, claiming that the band's style was too limiting, to be replaced by **John Dette**. It took another two years before a major return to form for the band, in the shape of the mighty and brutal DIABOLUS IN MUSICA (1998). Bostaph was back in tow by this time and with 2001's GOD HATES US ALL once again the focus was on tried-and-tested thrash, the band's re-energized intent evident throughout.

Whether one regards them as talentless, blistering white-noise merchants or the last true thrash band to produce commercially viable metal music for the new millennium, there can be no denying that Slayer are a singularly influential, unchanging and uncompromising unit.

⊙ **Reign In Blood** (1986; Def Jam).
An offensive and extreme thrash album which went on to become one of the most influential heavy-metal albums of the 80s. Sheer, unadulterated speed predominates from start to finish.

⊙ **Diabolus In Musica** (1998; American/Columbia).
Yet more songs about death, torment, war and, of course, the horned geezer downstairs (the Latin title means 'The Devil In Music'). If twisted rhythms, vicious twin lead guitars, and some of the fastest, nastiest riffing in metal is what you want, then look no further.

Essi Berelian

SLEATER-KINNEY

Formed Olympia, Washington, 1994.

The fledgling **Sleater-Kinney** emerged out of the riot grrrl scene in Olympia, Washington, taking their name from an intersection close to their rehearsal space. They shared riot grrrl street politics – based around feminist, HIV and gay issues – and the band's founders, **Corin Tucker** (guitar/vocals) and **Carrie Brownstein** (guitar/vocals), were themselves an item around the time of their first album on the Queercore label.

Like much riot grrrl material, Sleater-Kinney's defining sound was garage punk (inspired by the likes of Pavement and Sonic Youth), which they crossed with a trebled-up surf guitar on their debut EP, YOU AIN'T IT/SURF SONG (1994). The band's nervy subject matter was to gain them comparisons with the Throwing Muses, early PJ Harvey and Alanis

Morissette, though they were working out their own ideas and had an obvious individuality. The impressive album CALL THE DOCTOR (1996) was a taut affair, benefiting from a cleaner production than the riot grrrl norm. It was a disc that really established the band's identity, with its focus on sexual and feminist politics.

A change of US label to Kill Rock Stars heralded the band's big push forward. With **Janet Weiss** replacing **Lora MacFarlane** on drums, the new album DIG ME OUT (1997) wedded righteous anger to the power chord; the track "Little Babies" was like a meeting between the Ronettes and the Ramones in some parallel universe.

1999's THE HOT ROCK was strongly anticipated by all parties (*Spin* magazine described the band as being among 'the most important musicians in the world today'). Named after a Robert Redford film, its thirteen songs blast off with an uncompromising intro, "Start Together", and fuse the dynamics of earlier albums with that of girl-band harmonies. In an attempt to sidestep critics who anticipated a sellout in the wake of beckoning commercial success, it was, in many ways, a return to old ideals.

The following year saw the trio contributing backing-group support to Robert Forster and Grant McLennan on their triumphant **GO-BETWEENS** comeback album, THE FRIENDS OF RACHEL WORTH (2000); the new millennium also hailed the arrival of another fine Sleater-Kinney collection, ALL HANDS ON THE BAD ONE (2000). This, their fifth album, built proudly on the queer-core foundations of their earliest releases and the alternative-mainstream success of THE HOT ROCK and DIG ME OUT. On this outing their garage-punk drive and power-chord chug was accompanied by more confident lyrics and even more accomplished musical arrangements.

2002's ONE BEAT was another stormer, boosted by refreshingly intelligent lyrics and strong riffage. The group again confirmed their position as one of the most important bands to have survived, and lived beyond, Olympia's riot grrrl scene.

The story of Sleater-Kinney to date has been of a bunch of kids, juiced up on the radicalism of youth, managing to traverse the span between indie ghetto and mainstream. Compare them to The Slits – in certain ways quite a similar band of twenty years before – and one realizes how far Tucker et al have come. Great things for the future are currently predicted and, given their combination of political nous and intensity, it would be a pleasure to see it happen.

⊙ **Call The Doctor** (1996; Matador/Chainsaw).
Banshee guitars, vibrating vibratos and great songs like "Stay Where You Are". An early shot across the bows to those who doubted S-K's staying power.

⊙ **Dig Me Out** (1997; Matador/Kill Rock Stars).
Indie big time starts now. Direct, sharpened post-riot, surf-punked fem-rock.

⊙ **The Hot Rock** (1999; Matador/Kill Rock Stars).
Going from strength to strength, everything came together here on the fast, three-minute songs. All recorded in a massive three and a half weeks.

⊙ **All Hands On The Bad One**
(2000; Matador/Kill Rock Stars).
Corin and Carrie's guitars beautifully bounce over each other to construct delicate surf-twang backdrops to the group's intelligent and powerful lyrics of feminism, stardom and love. The set's highpoints include the majestically spat "Male Model" and the ambling, yet funky "Milkshake 'n' Honey".

Louise Gray

PERCY SLEDGE

Born Leighton, Alabama, November 25, 1941.

Along with his contemporary, Otis Redding (born a couple of months apart), the sly agony uncle Joe Tex, and the up-tempo rasper Wilson Pickett, **Percy Sledge** defined the mid-60s sound of Southern deep soul. Sledge's particular strength was a type of secular sermon, delivered in a rich baritone both impassioned and beautifully modulated. As with Tex and Solomon Burke, one of the features of Sledge's work was that it carried traces of the country-music ballad style filtered through a rich bed of Southern blues – indeed, many of his songs have come from country writers like Kris Kristofferson and Charlie Rich.

Sledge served the familiar apprenticeship in church choirs, and after leaving school he became a hospital nurse while also singing in a local group called The Esquires Combo. He took the basic idea of "When A Man Loves A Woman" to local disc jockey and aspiring record producer Quin Ivy, who hired Spooner Oldham to add the distinctive organ phrasing to a rich but rudimentary soul backing. Ivy leased the record to the hugely successful independent label Atlantic, which was adding to its reputation in R&B and jazz by virtually cornering the market in Southern soul. The result was a church-drenched testament to love that went to #1 in the US and #4 in the UK in 1966, and became one of the most distinctive sounds of the decade. Echoes of the song could be heard thousands of miles away in another of the decade's biggest hits, Procol Harum's "A Whiter Shade Of Pale", which for many years has been featured in Sledge's live set – such is his intensity as a performer that he sings the words as if they mean something.

The follow-up, "Warm And Tender Love", was similar enough to be instantly identifiable as Sledge but was no pale copy, and it confirmed that soul music had a substantial new talent. For several years Sledge remained a force in the US charts, never matching the impact of his debut, but amassing a rich catalogue. Oldham and his songwriting partner Dan Penn provided such towering love songs as "It Tears Me Up", Sledge's third hit of 1966, and "Out Of Left Field", while Steve Davis's "Take Time To Know Her", with Sledge narrating a cautionary tale, was one of the most moving of all 'cheating songs'.

In 1969 the hits faded and Sledge moved on to the cabaret circuit, but in 1974 a switch to Capricorn (owned by Ivy's early Alabama partner Phil Walden) revived his career with the up-to-scratch "I'll Be Your Everything". By 1980 Sledge was rerecording his hits for Stan Shulman, a producer who specialized in contracting former hit-makers to reproduce carbon copies of their big moments. Occasional forays away from the circuit of Southern clubs and US air bases confirmed to a wider public that the spine-chilling voice remained in good working order.

The next career boost came in 1987, when Levis, pursuing their policy of raiding rock's heritage for use in jeans commercials, picked "When A Man Loves A Woman" and the song became a UK hit all over again. In 1994 Sledge was back with a new album, BLUE NIGHT.

Such fellow giants as Redding and Tex are long dead, but Sledge remains an active link with the golden age of soul. He still works all over the world, and though economics dictate that when he travels abroad he must take a chance on the quality of his pick-up band, the voice remains fine. On stage he mixes a selection of his own hits with those of other soul greats, notably Otis Redding, and since the release of BLUE NIGHT he's also had some new Sledge tracks to spice up the set. His live show can be heard on the surprisingly decent PERCY SLEDGE LIVE IN LOUISIANA (2002) CD, released on his own label.

⊙ **It Tears Me Up** (1992; Rhino).
Another flawless compilation by the Rhino archivists. Proves definitively that Sledge was more than just "When A Man Loves A Woman".

⊙ **The Very Best Of** (1998; Rhino).
And another flawless compilation from the Rhino folk.

⊙ **Blue Night** (1994; Sky Ranch/Virgin).
Sledge's first proper album in two decades is no disappointment, building towards its climax in Otis Redding's beautiful "I've Got Dreams To Remember". Lead guitar duties are shared between soul legends Steve Cropper, Bobby Womack and ex-Rolling Stone Mick Taylor.

John Collis

SLEEPER

Formed London, 1992; disbanded 1998.

After meeting at Manchester University in the early 90s, **Louise Wener** (vocals/guitar) and her then-boyfriend **Jon Stewart** (guitar) slogged their way through various college bands, including the interestingly named Surrender Dorothy, before emerging as **Sleeper** in 1992 with **Andy Maclure** on drums and **Diid Osman** on bass.

A brief spate of gigging followed before signing to Indolent Records in 1993. Then, more swiftly than a flick of Louise's ever-mobile eyelashes, the band began bottling their fizzy guitar pop, quickly becoming the darlings of every college disco in Britain. Their debut single, "Alice In Vain" – a look at female bullying – combined scratchy guitars with Louise's breathy, wayward vocals. Several EPs followed, each assailing the indie charts, while their live single, "Bucket and Spade", sold 3000 copies in less than three days.

"Delicious" followed in May 1994. A lusty female howl to the delights of sex, the song insisted we do it 'till we make each other raw'. A thousand student pimples burst in fright, Joe Public began to take note and Louise negotiated a year out from her studies to concentrate on the pop biz. In January 1995 "Inbetweener" became the band's first UK Top 20 hit. A wry look at suburban reality coupled with a pneumatic gurgling guitar riff, the song stamped the band on pop's consciousness and made Louise a medium-sized star. Girls clamoured for A-line skirts like Louise's, while male fans and journalists began to focus unhealthily on this babe with the sharp tongue.

The debut album, SMART, followed in February. A collection of catchy pop tunes with rough-edged guitars and knowing lyrics, SMART made Top 5 in the UK album charts, but some critics were muttering that this band was musically quite ordinary. With barely time to breathe, "Vegas" came out in March. Although it was another UK chart success, and fully established Sleeper in the court of Britpop, the band were still fighting against being seen as just 'another female-fronted band', as Louise's T-shirt exclaimed. What with Elastica, Echobelly and Salad, women in bands were ten-a-penny. The *NME*, rather cruelly, invented the term 'Sleeperbloke' to describe the ranks of anonymous indie guys in bands around the UK, paying their dues behind more charismatic frontwomen.

Armed with an almost obsessive desire to have an opinion on everything, Louise set about upsetting every right-minded person in the Western world, attacking feminists and vegetarians, ripping apart the banner of political correctness with her bare teeth. Press attention soared, depicting Louise as a reactionary skinhead. Journalist Lucy O'Brien urged women to demonstrate at Sleeper gigs in protest at Louise's anti-feminist stance, whilst anti-Nazi protesters verbally attacked Louise for stating that the British National Party should be allowed to express their views in public. Louise noted that men such as Morrissey were not hounded for voicing similarly provocative ideas – even though it was blatantly untrue (see Morrissey's slating in the *NME* after he decided to wrap himself in the Union Jack, for example).

In October, preceding a UK tour, "What Do I Do Now?" became the band's third UK Top 20 hit. A look at the breakdown of a relationship amidst the weekend routine of pubs and clubs, it displayed a sensitivity to the 'ordinary' that rivalled that of Jarvis Cocker, and had the musical nous of Blondie.

Despite mutterings of bandwagon-jumping – and a change of partners (Louise splitting with Jon in favour of drummer Andy) – Sleeper go from strength to strength. "Sale Of The Century" previewed the second album, THE IT GIRL (1996), which kept on with the band's winning formula and crashed into the UK Top 10.

In 1997 "She's A Good Girl" revealed a more

mature, orchestral sound for Sleeper, but their third album PLEASED TO MEET YOU failed to match their earlier success. The Britpop bubble had finally burst. A national tour saw the band cancelling or downsizing venues due to poor ticket sales. At some venues, a bitter Louise would verbally attack those members of the music press who had been less than kind to the band.

Dissatisfied with their record label, Sleeper negotiated a release in December 1998. A month later they announced that they had split. The band had actually split at the end of their tour in March 1998.

Though Sleeper may yet reappear, phoenix-like from the ashes, Louise has now made a name for herself as a novelist, having published two paperbacks, *Goodnight Steve McQueen* and *The Big Blind*.

⊙ **Smart** (1995; Indolent).
With bursts of indie pop, indie rock, and smatterings of Britpop, this is like walking into a student's record collection. It contains all the early singles, and hints at darker depths.

⊙ **The It Girl** (1996; Indolent).
A follow-up too soon, perhaps: the songwriting hasn't moved on a lot, while tunes often elude them. But the singles, "What Do I Do Now?" and "Sale Of The Century" show they could do it.

Maxine McCaghy

SLINT

Formed Louisville, Kentucky, 1987;
disbanded 1991.

Guitarist/vocalist **Brian McMahan** began playing in bands aged 12, drummer **Britt Walford** at 11, hooking up a while later to play gigs at the Café Dog in Louisville. In the mid 80s, they formed a band called **SQUIRREL BAIT**, which mutated into the now legendary **Slint** in 1987, retaining **Ethan Buckler** (bass) and **David Pajo** (guitar).

That same year Slint recorded their first album, TWEEZ, which was released in 1988 on their own Jennifer Hartman label. Reflecting the bizarre nature of the music, its two vinyl sides were entitled 'Bemis' and 'Gerber', after the brand name of a toilet, while the tracks were named after the members' parents and the drummer's dog. Production was carried out by former Big Black and Rapeman head honcho Steve Albini – David Pajo has cited Big Black as an obvious inspiration.

By the summer of 1990 Ethan Buckler had been replaced on bass by **Todd Brasher** for the recording of SPIDERLAND (1991). A record that could be placed in no genre, it later spawned a subset of 'Slint bands' and homages – Huggy Bear, for instance, dedicated to Slint a song called "Cakecrumb Trail", as a nod to "Breadcrumb Trail". The album was recorded over three weekends, while all four band members were trying to hold down day jobs, and rumour has it that the band committed themselves to mental asylums after recording, such was the intensity of the situation.

Whatever the truth of the matter, Slint split up soon after SPIDERLAND's release. David Pajo went on to attend art college and later joined post-art rockers **TORTOISE** before embarking upon his own solo career as **PAPA M**; more recently he was to be found hanging out with ex-Smashing Pumpkins members in **Zwan**. Britt Walford played with **THE BREEDERS** under the name Shannon Doughton, but rejoined McMahan and Brasher in **WILL OLDHAM**'s Palace Brothers, in which all four Slint members have appeared. The Oldham association went way back – he was credited for the cover photo of SPIDERLAND.

Slint themselves released a two-song single in 1994 – featuring "Glenn", recorded in 1989, and "Rhoda", recorded in 1994 – and rumours, alas unfounded, abound regarding their re-formation.

⊙ **Tweez** (1988; Touch & Go).
TWEEZ was like nothing else that had come before it. Darkly brooding in places ("Kent"), playful ("Ron"), lighthearted and almost poppy in others, it is idiosyncratic and inspirational. Though the tracks are largely instrumental, the vocals range from consequentially and inconsequentially detailed to crazed, screaming intensity.

⊙ **Spiderland** (1991; Touch & Go).
This is a work of greater sophistication than TWEEZ, but still capable of swinging from one extreme to another. Again it is largely instrumental, but its vocals instil a feeling of internal travel.

Helen Waddell

SLIPKNOT

Formed Des Moines, Iowa, 1995.

Call it thrash metal, call it rap or, more fashionably, nu-metal, for one of the main embodiments of the latest rock mutation look no further than these nine masked and numbered men who took a few elements prevalent on the metal scene and bolted together a genuinely scary Frankenstein's monster. Out in the vast conservative emptiness of middle America there's precious little to stimulate the mind, but in the heart of mid-90s Iowa some like-

The charming Corey Taylor

in 1997 and producer Ross Robinson got his evil-genius hands on them in the studio.

When the band finally erupted into the metal consciousness they caused a sensation with both their music and image, grabbing headlines and media attention as they exploited the twisted circus-sideshow facet of their stage show. Each band member took a number instead of a name and they hid their identities further by each donning identical boiler suits and adopting a stage persona reflected in a unique mask. Most readily identifiable were bassist Paul Gray in his pig mask and Shawn Crahan who was dubbed 'Clown' for obvious reasons.

It was as though a bunch of lunatics had escaped an asylum via a Halloween jumble sale and somehow found their way into a studio. When SLIPKNOT (1999) crashed into the charts it proved to be an accurate encapsulation of youthful frustration and alienation. The music took the basic thrash metal sound of Sepultura, all tribal rhythms and harsh guttural roars, and amplified it to a terrifyingly intense and dense level, not least by having Joey Jordison's thundering drums augmented by two sets of custom percussion kits. Of course, Chris Fehn and Shawn 'Clown' Crahan didn't just pummel seven shades of shit out of their oil-drums/drum kits while playing live; the two of them acted as weird cheerleaders throwing mocking and menacing shapes at the crowd, as well as raising the level of percussive violence.

It was heavy, it was ugly, it was utterly beguiling to teenagers who wanted something with which to shock their parents and teachers. The debut album went to #1 on *Billboard*'s Heatseekers chart purely through the hysteria generated by their unhinged live show. A year and a half later they had toured the world and picked up accolades around the globe; in the UK, *Kerrang!* magazine voted them *Best International Live Act*. They had taken the nu-metal phenomenon into the mainstream alongside other breakthrough acts such as Korn and Limp Bizkit.

Consolidation came in the form of IOWA (2001). The anticipation surrounding the launch of the new album was even more intense than for their debut; how would they top the aural insanity of SLIPKNOT? What would these sickos from the middle of nowhere do next? Could they be even more offensive? Fans needn't have worried because IOWA was so grotesquely extreme it eclipsed pretty much every other heavy release when it hit the shelves, the band having opting to go for an almost death'n'black metal intensity. It was harsh, brutal, and ridiculously over the top, being once again produced by Ross Robinson. Not surprisingly it rocketed to the top of most album charts around the world and teenagers out shopping with their mums on a Saturday morning could be seen wearing 'People = Shit' hoodies and T-shirts.

Such high levels of excitement are tough for even the most experienced performers to maintain and so it proved for Slipknot. IOWA may well have been

minded musicians were indulging their passion for metal, the more extreme the better – hardly surprising really; Des Moines was the town where Ozzy Osbourne's infamous bat-munching episode occurred back in 1982.

Slipknot comprises **Sid Wilson, #0** (DJ), **Joey Jordison, #1** (drums), **Paul Gray, #2** (bass), **Chris Fehn, #3** (custom percussion), **James Root, #4** (guitars), **Craig Jones, #5** (samples), **Shawn 'Clown' Crahan, #6** (custom percussion), **Mick Thomson, #7** (guitar) and **Corey Taylor, #8** (vocals). Prior to their skull-caving, nine-man incarnation the band enjoyed a shifting line-up and produced one self-financed album, charmingly titled MATE, FEED, KILL, REPEAT (1996), which currently changes hands on the Internet for silly money. Apparently no one in the band owns a copy. They tried in vain to get a proper deal; one executive at Epic records was heard to comment that if Slipknot were the future of music then he didn't want to live. There's no indication of what the person in question did when the band signed to Roadrunner Records

more accomplished than their first album, but with the general feeling that nu-metal was running out of steam, it has been hard to predict where the gang of nine will head next. Joey Jordison recently revealed another project; glam-tastic trash punkers the **Murderdolls**, while lead singer Corey Taylor has been concentrating on his **Stone Sour** project. Could this spell the end for one of the most viscerally exciting metal bands on the planet? Or will they return sicker than ever?

● **Slipknot** (1999; Roadrunner).
Take a generous helping of Sepultura, down tune even more, throw in a helluva lot of drumming and let a bloke wearing a rubber mask shot through with devil's dreads scream over the top about his miserable childhood. Ah, bliss.

● **Iowa** (2001; Roadrunner).
More of the same only heavier. And with a black (presumably) satanic goat on the front. This album features one of the band's nihilistic slogans, 'People = Shit', turned into a song. Nice.

Essi Berelian

THE SLITS

Formed London, 1976; disbanded 1981.

O f all the British punk groups, **The Slits** were prime exponents of the principle that put enthusiasm above musical professionalism. None of the original line-up – **Kate Kaos** (guitar), **Suzy Gutz** (bass), Spanish exile **Palmolive** (drums) and 14-year-old singer **Arianna Forster**, daughter of a German newspaper heiress – could play to save their lives. However, all were members of punk's inner circle around The Clash and Sex Pistols, and after some months of dissolute rehearsals, they made their debut supporting The Clash in Harlesden, London, in March 1977.

Almost immediately the band reshaped themselves. Kaos (who went off to form pop-punkettes The Modettes) and Gutz were replaced by **Viv Albertine**, who played guitar with Sid Vicious in the short-lived Flowers Of Romance, and **Tessa Pollitt** who, appropriately, had never learned to play the

bass. Forster, meanwhile, changed her name to **Ari Up** and the group became a fixture on the punk circuit, playing exuberant songs like "A Boring Life" and "Let's Do The Split".

After a nationwide tour with The Clash, The Slits set to work on their sound and emerged as an almost cohesive unit – Albertine's scratchy guitar and Pollitt's thumping bass giving the group a more rhythmic approach, which was driven by Palmolive's powerful drum style and harmonized by Ari's yelping, Germanic vocal phrasings. New songs such as "New Town" and "Shoplifting" suggested that the rhythm was more crucial than the melody. In common with many New Wave musicians, The Slits were great fans of reggae, particularly dub, and they incorporated the sparsity of this sound into their work.

Despite recording two acclaimed sessions for John Peel, The Slits were the last of the major first wave of punk groups to get a recording contract. After rumours that they were going to become protégées of Malcolm McLaren, they finally signed to Island in mid 1979 and started work on an album for the label with reggae producer Dennis 'Blackbeard' Bovell, who was also working with other bands from the post-punk period, notably The Pop Group.

During recordings, Palmolive left to join **THE RAINCOATS**, apparently unable to keep up with the more intricate rhythms of the new and rearranged material. She was replaced by Budgie (Peter Clark), who had been in legendary Liverpool group Big In Japan, and eventually the album, CUT (1979), emerged. It was well received and grabbed attention with its cover shot of the three naked and mud-covered Slits, making a 'back-to-nature' statement. Musically, though, it was just as remarkable, creating a unique reggae-infected style of punk. The Slits even had a minor UK chart hit, soon after, with their radically reconstructed version of the Marvin Gaye classic, "I Heard It Through The Grapevine".

The band returned to the stage, collaborating with avant-garde jazz trumpeter Don Cherry and reggae toaster Prince Hammer, but these all too often indulged in aimless jams. However, after **Budgie** (who joined **SIOUXSIE AND THE BANSHEES**) was replaced by **THE POP GROUP** sticksman **Bruce Smith** (doubling duties for both bands at first), The Slits regained their focus on singles released on the indie Human and Y labels, including a great cover of John Holt's reggae classic "The Man Next Door".

Surprisingly, the band were signed by another major, CBS, but their second and final album, THE RETURN OF THE GIANT SLITS (1981), didn't compare to their first. More disappointing, however, was their subsequent disappearance from the music scene.

● **Cut** (1979; Island).
Produced by the undersung Dennis Bovell, this stands as one of post-punk's greatest moments. An album of oblique but compelling rhythms and atonal but playful vocals.

● **Peel Sessions** (1998; Strange Fruit).
Excellent compilation and companion volume to your well-thumbed copies of CUT.

Robert E. Murray

SLOWDIVE

Formed Reading, England, 1990; disbanded 1995.

"A lot of bands are so precious about influences, thinking they're massively original. We're not."

Slowdive 'fell together' after schoolfriends **Rachel Goswell** (vocals/guitar) and **Neil Halstead** (vocals/guitar) had drifted through several dodgy covers bands. They recruited **Nick Chaplin** (bass) at college, and took up the offer of **Christian Saville** (guitar), who penned a begging letter to join. As drummers came and went, Slowdive struck gold after a handful of gigs, when their demo tape attracted notice from Creation supremo Alan McGee. With an average age of just 19 they found themselves signed to the hippest UK indie label, and their first EP, the eponymous SLOWDIVE, was released in November 1990 to rapturous applause from the press.

Another EP, MORNINGRISE, followed in 1991, with **Simon Scott** now a permanent fixture on drums, and the Slowdive sound was established: gorgeous washes of distorted guitar and quiet harmonies forming a wall of sound. Comparisons with My Bloody Valentine and The Jesus & Mary Chain were drawn and Slowdive didn't initially dispute them, as, with the likes of Ride, Moose and Chapterhouse, they gained the tag of 'shoe-gazers' – 'the scene that celebrates itself', as the music press characterized their socializing at each others' gigs. Although hailed at first as pioneers of the British indie scene, these bands were to become targets of derision.

Nonetheless, Slowdive's third EP, HOLDING OUR BREATH (1991), almost broke the Top 40, and was greeted by near-hyperbolic reviews, with *Melody Maker* exclaiming 'Slowdive are impossible, immaculate and serene'. This was the last great praise the band were to receive from the British music press. They played the festival scene that summer with other 'shoe-gazing' bands and found themselves compared to emerging grunge acts, such as Nirvana, who took Reading Festival by storm. The words 'fey' and 'apathetic' made the first of many appearances, just in time for the release of their debut album, JUST FOR A DAY (1991), which was dismissed as dreary and lacking in ideas (not entirely untrue). The backlash worsened with the return to the scene of My Bloody Valentine, whose stunning LOVELESS forced a critical reappraisal of the bands they'd spawned.

It was spring 1993 before Slowdive returned to the public eye in Britain, releasing an EP, OUTSIDE YOUR ROOM, and a second album, SOUVLAKI. Though *Melody Maker* trashed the latter as 'a soulless void', it was a progression from their first album, presenting songs that were no longer cloaked in layers of distortion, and it reached the upper echelons of the indie charts.

Slowdive toured Britain for the first time in eighteen months, and later in the year released a fifth EP, originally titled 5EP (1993), which marked a change in direction. Building on SOUVLAKI's more ambient tracks, 5EP embraced technology with open arms, toning down the plodding drums and bass in favour of synthesized chords and whispered vocal refrains. Slowdive's new openness towards studio trickery led to respected techno acts Reload and Bandulu remixing "In Mind" with stunning results. The press simply didn't know how to respond, coining the unfortunate phrase 'shoe techno'. Old prejudices were proving hard to overcome.

The band's 1995 album, PYGMALION, was a gorgeous follow-on, employing drum'n'bass to create a stunning swirl of sound. It should have been heralded, in the same way as (say) Everything But The Girl were revived, but it was received with indifference by press and public alike and, in mid-year, Creation dropped the band to concentrate on such first-division acts as Oasis. With no label or popular support, Nick and Christian quit the band, and Slowdive effectively ceased to exist.

The songwriting nucleus, Neil and Rachel, plus drummer Ian, formed a new band called **Mojave 3** and signed to 4AD. Their first two albums, ASK ME TOMORROW (1995) and OUT OF TUNE (1999), were released to good reviews but disappointing sales, suggesting that, despite their new-found country sound, they remained stymied by the 'shoe-gazing' tag that had so dogged Slowdive's progress. In early 2000 they released another critically acclaimed set, EXCUSES FOR TRAVELLERS, though it wasn't until 2002 that Halstead received the kind of attention he deserved. His debut solo album, SLEEPING ON ROADS, was a glorious evocation of great tunes and unashamedly obvious Nick Drakeisms. Meanwhile, Goswell turned up on The Zephyrs' 2001 debut album, strumming and singing in true Slowdive style.

Slowdive

(•) **Slowdive** (1990; Creation).
Bathed in guitar effects, these songs are beautifully haunting. Grown men used to cry during "Avalyn" at early Slowdive gigs.

(•) **5EP** (1993; Creation).
Gorgeous synthesized shimmering sounds and haunting vocals.

(•) **Pygmalion** (1995; Creation).
Quiet drums and dubby bass hide behind repeating guitars and vocals, which are barely recognizable at times. Cruelly ignored on release, tracks like "Crazy For You" are mesmerizing.

Mojave 3

(•) **Excuses For Travellers** (2000; 4AD).
A polished gem of alternative-country twangs and memorable songs. The confidence of Neil Hallstead's writing and singing slots in nicely with both the shimmering desert ballads – "My Life In Art" – and the more up-tempo numbers, like the banjo jaunt "Return To Sender" and the opening cut, "In Love With A View".

Neil Halstead

(●) **Sleeping On Roads** (2002; 4AD).
These songs are beautiful, brightly constructed and softly sung, dealing throughout with relationships and, as the title hints, travelling.

Joanna Severs

SLY AND THE FAMILY STONE

Formed San Francisco, 1966; disbanded 1979.

I f there were ever a band that lived up to the cliché of 'defining the times' it was **Sly And The Family Stone**. For three brief years in the late 60s Sly Stone's happy-faced vision of integration and his charming synthesis of psychedelic pop and innovative funk rhythms dominated the American music scene. Of course, as The Undisputed Truth sang, 'smiling faces sometimes tell lies', and beneath the music's blissful surface was a coded, sardonic humour that mocked everything, especially Sly himself.

Sly Stone began his adult career in music as a radio DJ in the San Francisco Bay Area under his given name **Sylvester Stewart**. He was hired by Autumn Records as an A&R rep and producer and worked with Bobby Freeman, The Beau Brummels, The Mojo Men and The Great Society (Grace Slick's first band). Getting fed up with The Great Society, he decided to change his name and make his own music. After a couple of false starts, Sly recruited trumpeter **Cynthia Robinson**, sax player **Jerry Martini**, pianist **Rosie Stone**, guitarist **Freddie Stone**, drummer **Greg Errico** and, most importantly, bassist **Larry Graham**.

The Family Stone's diverse racial make-up unwrapped the hidden fact that soul music was often a synthesis created by both black and white musicians. Perhaps even more radical was the crucial role women played as instrumentalists, rather than just vocal wallpaper to round out the band's sound. The band's early arrangements, which perfectly mirrored the lyrical platitudes, emphasized the variety of individual voices, both instrumental and vocal. Stone used his band as the embodiment of his exploration of the political implications of pop's great subject: 'everybody is a star'. It was a philosophy that would particularly influence Miles Davis and Ornette Coleman, as they reconceived the jazz ensemble as a democratic unit.

As the title of their first album says, Sly And The Family Stone were indeed A WHOLE NEW THING (1967). Their fusion of the head-trip effects of psychedelic rock with the pulse of dance music had an audacity that seems commonplace now. Their first great moment was the 1968 single "Dance To The Music". As a piece of craftsmanship, it can't be beaten – every element is unforgettable, from Greg Errico's stadium-rock drumming to Cynthia and Jerry shouting 'All the squares go home'. While its irresistibility pushed it into the American Top 10, the message of their next single made it #1 for a month.

The catchphrase from "Everyday People" – 'different strokes for different folks' – applied the libertarian axioms of Haight-Ashbury's privileged white bohemia to the struggle for civil rights and turned hippiedom's spoiled-brat consumerism into a fully fledged political statement. Meanwhile, the B-side, "Sing A Simple Song", practically invented the wah-wah pedal as a funk instrument and its main riff would appear wholesale on Miles Davis's JACK JOHNSON.

"Everyday People" was the highlight of the band's first album masterpiece, STAND! (1969). Full of rousing horn charts, Graham's thundering bass propulsion and acid-rock guitar sounds, welded to Memphis soul phrasing and ecstatic vocal revelry, STAND! was the joyful noise of the American Dream realized – a fully integrated micro-society that harmonized into bottom-heavy metal. "Don't Call Me Nigger, Whitey", however, was the first evidence of Sly's dark humour as the title phrase was endlessly repeated over a gloomy funk vamp. Their following single, "Hot Fun In The Summertime", while superficially breezier, was an ironic commentary on America's long, hot summer of racial unrest.

"Hot Fun" reached #2 in the American charts as almost nobody got the joke. Even fewer people seemed to understand their next single, "Thank You (Fallettin Me Be Mice Elf Agin)" (1970), as it stayed at #1 for two weeks. Perhaps the most savage chart-topper ever, "Thank You" downplayed the 'gorgeous mosaic' of voices that marked their early records in favour of a snarling, popping bass line in which Larry Graham invented the slap-bass technique. The music was mean, but the lyrics were as caustic as anything the Sex Pistols ever conjured up. 'Dying young is hard to take, but selling out is harder,' sung Sly, before proceeding to mock nearly all of his hit singles.

During this period, Sly was feeling intense pressure from his record company to put out a new album, getting muscled by black nationalist leaders to make his music more radical, receiving death threats, failing to show up for concerts and wrestling with cocaine addiction. THERE'S A RIOT GOIN' ON finally came out in 1971, preceded by the wonderful cool funk of "Family Affair", and it sounded like nothing else before or since. It began with a song called "Luv'N'Haight" and its opening line was, 'Feels so good inside myself don't wanna move'. The album was ravaged by fallout: from cocaine, from the 60s, from the failure of black nationalism, from the bloatedness of the counterculture, from being a superstar. It was shrouded in a veil of cynicism: Sly's contribution to the 'smiling faces' trope of 70s soul was called "You Caught Me Smiling" and then there was the sardonic nastiness of calling attention to the nonexistent title track.

FRESH (1973) tackled similar themes but was more engaged with the outside world. It was also a return to the buoyancy of their 60s tunes, but this didn't reflect the situation within the band. Larry Graham left in 1972 to form Graham Central Station (replaced by Rusty Allen) and Greg Errico swiftly followed suit (replaced by Andy Newmark). With the exception of his appearance on Funkadelic's THE ELECTRIC SPANKING OF WAR BABIES (1981), the rest of Sly's career has been a series of half-hearted releases and idiotic marketing schemes (1979's TEN YEARS TOO SOON was a disco remix album of his 60s hits).

Stand! (1969; Epic).
One of the most influential albums ever made. Its hits ("Everyday People", "I Want to Take You Higher" and the title track) made crossover appeal seem like a political Utopia, while its extended funk jams ("Don't Call Me Nigger, Whitey" and "Sex Machine") permanently altered the face and structure of black music.

There's A Riot Goin' On (1971; Epic).
The only good album ever made about the pitfalls of fame. Sly avoids the star-as-ingrate trap by linking his pain with wider social issues. He might have pissed off his fans, but his 'betrayal' was the retribution for the betrayal of both the civil rights movement and the sellout of the counterculture. Oh, and the album has the sublime "Family Affair".

Fresh (1973; Epic).
Less brutal than its predecessor, FRESH aligns post-civil-rights politics with easier grooves. "Skin I'm In" and "Babies Making Babies" are as effective, clever and galvanizing as anything Sly produced.

Takin' You Higher – The Best Of Sly And The Family Stone (1992; Sony).
This collects a body of music so brilliantly conceived that the seriousness of its politics never drags down the joy of the simple act of making music. As intelligent as Dylan, as fun as Motown, with innumerable highlights, including "I Want To Take You Higher", "Dance To The Music", "Family Affair" and "Thank You... ".

Peter Shapiro

THE SMALL FACES

Formed London, 1964; disbanded 1969.

"I can't see what all the fuss is about. I mean if I saw a five-foot-three spotty degenerate I wouldn't flip much." Steve Marriott

In 1964 **Ronnie Lane** (bass) and **Kenny Jones** (drums) played together in a band called The Outcasts. While buying a new guitar, Lane invited the shop assistant to attend one of their gigs. **Steve Marriott** (guitar) appeared that evening and wrecked the piano belonging to the pub the band were playing at. They were barred, and Lane invited Marriott to form a new band with himself and Jones. Marriott then invited **Jimmy Langwith** (keyboards) to join. While playing in Langwith's parents' pub, they were spotted by the owner of The Cavern in Leicester Square, who offered them a gig. They needed a name. A girlfriend of Marriott suggested **The Small Faces** because they were small (under 5' 4" in their socks) and Faces (ie top mods).

The band proved so successful at The Cavern that they were booked for a five-week residency. Relying mainly on feedback and volume, they would play four or five soul and R&B covers and make them last an hour and a half. The fledgling Small Faces were soon attracting larger audiences of young mods who identified the band as one of their own. This gave them an advantage over their main rivals, The Who, currently packing them in at The Marquee. Kit Lambert, manager of The Who at the time, recognized this and tried to sign The Small Faces, but the band decided instead to go with Don Arden and the Decca label.

Within weeks they had recorded their debut single, "Whatcha Gonna Do About It" (1965), which reached #14 in the charts by focusing on Marriott's gruff vocals and including one of the first uses of feedback on record. During TV appearances, Langwith (or Winston as he now called himself) would attempt to hog the limelight. This annoyed the band, particularly Marriott, and he was sacked. **Ian McLagan** (keyboards) was his replacement.

The next single was a Marriott-Lane composition, "I've Got Mine" (1965), which flopped in the chart but gained critical acclaim. The lack of success, however, meant the next single was left to professional songwriters; they delivered "Sha La La La Lee", which reached the UK Top 3 in January 1966. Suddenly The Small Faces were appearing in every magazine and newspaper, on all the TV pop programmes, and even had a cameo in the film *Dateline Diamonds*. The next single, a Marriott-Lane number called "Hey Girl", went Top 10 and in May their eponymous debut album was released. Recorded in roughly three hours, it was basically the band's live set and it won rave reviews. The Small Faces were being touted as the best band in the country and their fifth single, "All Or Nothing", reflected their popularity by becoming their first and only #1.

At this time the band were constantly touring and the pressure was beginning to manifest itself in arguments with Arden. Eventually the band left Decca and signed with Andrew Loog-Oldham's Immediate label early in 1967. Immediate offered Marriott and Lane more scope and the result was "Here Comes The Nice", a wistful tune with ambiguous lyrics hinting at drug use – a taste of what was to come with "Itchycoo Park", released in August. Banned by some radio stations because of its drug references and the way it encouraged children to play truant, it became the band's first American hit. Although basically an acoustic pop song, it was revolutionary in its use of phasing on the cymbals, the first time this effect had been heard, and again showed The Small Faces as creative and imaginative songwriters.

The second album followed quickly, also called SMALL FACES (1967), and it saw the band augmenting their line-up with brass, woodwind, percussion and anything else that was lying around the studio that day. From these chaotic sessions came their third hit in six months. "Tin Soldier" began with a lone Hammond organ and built to a raging cacophony of noise, and would prove to be one of The Small Faces' most enduring creations. While promoting the

Marriott threw his guitar to the floor, stormed off stage, and that was that.

Marriott would later form **HUMBLE PIE** and win the respect he had longed for, while Lane, Jones and McLagan, along with Ronnie Wood, became **THE FACES** and backed Rod Stewart to international stardom. It was a brief but spectacular career for The Small Faces. In four years they had progressed from teen idols to respected songwriters and, along the way, had created innovative studio techniques. It is only relatively recently, due to the crop of young Britpop bands citing them as influences, that The Small Faces have finally been accorded the status they always deserved.

⊙ **Ogden's Nut Gone Flake** (1968; Sony). Side one contains some of the strongest tunes Marriott and Lane wrote together, in "Afterglow" and "Song Of A Baker". Side two sees them out of their collective tree as psychedelia, hippiedom and acid collide, leaving in its trail a modern fairy-tale with a happy ending.

⊙ **The Singles As And Bs** (1990; See For Miles). As good a compilation as any, containing all the singles, and some excellent flip sides not available elsewhere.

Small Faces (from left): Ronnie Lane, Steve Marriott, Ian McLagan and Kenny Jones

single the band had already begun work on their third and final studio album, OGDEN'S NUT GONE FLAKE (1968), which took a year to record and went straight to #1, winning countless awards on its way.

The second side of the album took everyone by surprise. It was the story of Happiness Stan and his attempt to find the missing half of the moon, each song being linked by a narrative spoken by the master of gobbledegook, Stanley Unwin. The idea proved so successful that an entire TV programme, *Colour Me Pop*, was devoted to it with the band playing the songs in the studio, joined by Unwin, who provided the links.

Paradoxically, it was this album that proved the group's undoing. The audiences at their gigs stopped screaming and began to listen. This also meant the band could hear themselves play, and they were not happy with what they heard. Immediate released two more singles, "Lazy Sunday" and "The Universal" (both 1968), against the band's wishes, and when the latter failed critically and commercially it became too much. At the end of a gig on New Year's Eve 1968,

Andrew Jeffries

SMASHING PUMPKINS

Formed Chicago, 1988; disbanded 2000.

"Have you heard the words/I'm singing in these songs?" From *Mellon Collie And The Infinite Sadness*

More than any other rock genre, heavy metal appears to be in a perpetual state of reinvention and no band epitomizes its 90s mutation better than Chicago group **Smashing Pumpkins**. They were formed by guitarist, singer and songwriter **Billy Corgan** and guitarist **James Iha** (guitar), who ran into bassist **D'Arcy** in an argument outside a nightclub, decided she looked just right for the band, and completed their recruiting operations with **Jimmy**

Corgan in his Pumpkin days

Chamberlin (drums). The band made an early impact in the American Midwest, securing a record deal with Caroline Records and generally being lumped in with the grunge crew. But, for all their new connections with Nirvana, Soundgarden and Alice In Chains, the Pumpkins were part of a musical heritage that dated back to Black Sabbath rather than the Sex Pistols.

Nevertheless, the band teamed up with Nirvana producer and later Garbage drummer Butch Vig to record their debut LP, GISH (1991). Together with extensive touring, this built up a sizeable underground following – enough to allow minor chart success in late 1992 for a rerelease of the single "I Am One", and with the release of the seminal album SIAMESE DREAM (1993), interest turned into full-blown commercial success – or, to be precise, sales of five million plus. Slewing from out-and-out heavy rock to gentle ballads, the album marked the Pumpkins out at the vanguard of US alternative rock. Following its release, further frantic bursts of touring ensued, and in early 1994 a selection of outtakes and B-sides was compiled for PISCES ISCARIOT, which displayed more of Corgan's songwriting versatility.

The next album proper was 1995's MELLON COLLIE AND THE INFINITE SADNESS – two astonishing hour-long CDs subtitled 'Dawn To Dusk' and

'Twilight To Starlight'. Some accused Corgan of self-indulgence, but, while the album could well have benefited from some judicious editing, it featured a startling breadth of style and sound texture, and its high points became the benchmarks by which the band would be judged in future. It was preceded by a headlining set at the 1995 Reading Festival, which confirmed their standing to the British audience.

But the Smashing Pumpkins' longevity seems more dependent on the members' ability to stay together without killing each other than on the public's continuing approval. As ever, the lengthy touring after MELLON COLLIE stretched the band to breaking point. In July 1996 Chamberlin was found alive but overdosed next to the dead body of touring keyboard player Jonothon Melvoin (brother of Wendy, of Prince and Wendy & Lisa fame). Five days later Chamberlin was sacked, to be replaced for touring by **Matt Walker**.

Touring continued into 1997, including a support slot with The Rolling Stones, with the band barely pausing to scoop up armfuls of awards. A five-CD set of all five singles from MELLON COLLIE, with all B-sides and some unreleased material, hit the shops at the end of 1996 under the title THE AEROPLANE FLIES HIGH. New material was restricted to two soundtrack songs, "The End Is The Beginning Is The End" and "Eye".

In the autumn of 1997 work began on a new album, reportedly an acoustic (or at least less heavy) set, rather than the electronic album hinted at by the singles, with Brad Wood (who produced Liz Phair's EXILE IN GUYVILLE) at the controls. **Matt Cameron** (ex-Soundgarden) did some of the drumming, but announced in January 1998 that he would not be joining permanently. Corgan had said that the lack of a drummer would be a profound influence on the next record, and ADORE (1998) certainly suffered from the rotation of drummers – human and electronic. The music didn't lend itself to live presentation either, and the band was already drained by the exertion and tragedy of the mammoth MELLON COLLIE tour. When the Pumpkins clambered back onto the live stage, most of the ADORE material was missing and the group was already testing out some much harder material for the next album. 'Sometimes you've got to go backwards to go forwards,' Corgan told audiences and, as if to prove the point, finally revealed Chamberlin's permanent replacement on drums: Jimmy Chamberlin.

But the reunion of the original quartet lasted only seven months. D'Arcy Wretzky bailed out in September 1999, reportedly to start a movie career, and Corgan drafted in **Melissa Auf de Maur** from **HOLE**. Maur was credited with playing on the new album, MACHINA / THE MACHINES OF GOD (2000), although it had already been recorded before D'Arcy's departure. Probably Corgan had repeated his SIAMESE DREAM trick of playing bass himself.

Whoever actually played on the album, MACHINA proved a vibrant and vigorous comeback: crisp and clear, yet brash and heavy. All the more surprising, then, that Corgan announced in May 2000 that the end of the year would also see the end of the Smashing Pumpkins. 'It's hard to keep trying to fight the good fight against the Britneys,' he admitted, adding that the Pumpkins had been at the start of one alternative revolution, and another was beginning.

But Corgan was not to vanish. Before long rumours of a new band, **Zwan**, started to circulate. At the start of 2003 Corgan's Zwan – featuring the likes of **David Pajo** (SLINT/PAPA M), **Jimmy Chamberlin**, **Matt Sweeney** (Bonnie 'Prince' Billy) and **Paz Lenchantin** (A Perfect Circle) – released MARY STAR OF THE SEA. The set was a rich, dense triumph of stadium-styled rock that saw Corgan managing to strip away much of the pomp and nonsense associated with The Pumpkins at their worst.

⊙ **Siamese Dream** (1993; Hut/Virgin).
This album retains its coherence over a bewildering array of styles. Savage riffing and delicate, gentle playing betray a range of influences from heavy metal to indie and pop. "Cherub Rock" hits where it hurts, while "Soya" helps repair the damage.

⊙ **Mellon Collie And The Infinite Sadness** (1995; Hut/Virgin).
SIAMESE DREAM was mainly Corgan's work; this is more of a band effort with Corgan and Iha taking a broad canvas and throwing potfuls of guitar over it. The result could have been a mess, and there are certainly some superfluous slow numbers, but the insistent metal of "Zero" and the intensity of "Tonight Tonight" are offset by the delicacy of "By Starlight" and "Thru The Eyes Of Ruby". Essential listening.

⊙ **Adore** (1998; Hut/Virgin).
Even the human drummers sound like machines, showing how much the Pumpkins miss Jimmy. Some of the musical spark is submerged under the gorgeous production: where it works, it carries enormous power; where it doesn't, one pines for the raw power of, say, "Zero" – but it's still distinctive.

⊙ **Rotten Apples** (2001; Hut/Virgin).
Their greatest hits package is a reasonable introduction to the band, though, as a whole, it lacks the compositional cohesion of, say, SIAMESE DREAM.

Patrick Neylan-Francis & Guy Davies

Born Nebraska, August 6, 1969 (probably).

"There are two big enemies: bitterness and style. If I can escape them both, then I'll be happy."

In 1993, while still a member of Oregonian punk quartet **Heatmiser**, **Elliott Smith** started branching out on his own, playing solo shows in the Portland area and recording material in friends' basements. The songs were a stylistic departure: strictly acoustic, far removed from Heatmiser's abrasive thrash. Local independent label Cavity Search showed an immediate interest, and the eight tracks emerged as the ROMAN CANDLE mini-album in 1994. Employing the old Scott Walker trick of leaving half the album's tracks untitled, it was a formative set – thirty minutes of stripped-down guitar and vocals with the title track and the naggingly catchy "No Name #1" as stand-outs.

1995 brought a change of label – to Kill Rock Stars, based in Olympia, Washington – and a second album, simply entitled ELLIOTT SMITH. By this point, he was still recording in local basements, but had graduated to eight-track. More importantly, the elements of the man's style were falling into place. Since it was acoustic, early commentators placed his music in a folk bracket, but this proved a lazy and inaccurate label. Rather, Smith's songs resonate across a broad rock/pop canon, with echoes of The Clash, The Beatles (c. 1968), The Saints and, perhaps most of all, another maverick American pop genius, Alex Chilton. The eponymous second album was a dark, disquieting work, by turns furious ("Southern Belle"), and desperate ("The Biggest Lie").

By now, Heatmiser were in the process of dissolving. Smith stayed in his living room, honing his songwriting craft by playing guitar through endless TV reruns of *General Hospital*. After disentangling himself from a contract with Virgin Records, he set about his third album, once again spurning recording studios in favour of 'Joanna's house, my house, the shop'. When this collection finally emerged in February 1997, as EITHER/OR, it was a quantum leap. Here was a brilliant sequence of snapshots: some were glimpses of urban lowlife, identifiable as Portland ("Alameda", "Rose Parade"), others were emotional vignettes, intense and telling. Above all, Smith married his wired, oblique lyrics and quavering vocals with the prettiest, most delicate melodies. The sour words and sweet tunes reflected his tongue-in-cheek ambition to be 'both John Lennon and Paul McCartney at once'.

EITHER/OR received favourable critical notices, but little attention outside the Pacific Northwest. However, for Elliott Smith, matters were about to take an unexpected turn. An old Portland friend of his, Gus Van Sant, was gathering music for his film

Good Will Hunting. When the soundtrack appeared, it featured four gems from EITHER/OR, an oldie from ROMAN CANDLE, and one brand new track, "Miss Misery", which plays over the film's closing credits. To the amazement of all concerned, it picked up an Academy Award nomination for Best Original Song, up against the likes of Celine Dion and Trisha Yearwood. Overnight, Smith was (reasonably) hot property. He accepted his invitation to perform at the 1998 Awards telecast, swapping the black Hank Williams T-shirt he'd worn for the previous two years for an ill-fitting white suit. The reflective two minutes of "Miss Misery" provided a stark contrast to the grandiose productions of the other four nominees. For reasons best known to the gala's producers, though, the song's first line ('I'll fake it through the day/With some help from Johnny Walker Red') was completely inaudible. He didn't win the Oscar, of course, but it was a victory of sorts.

By this time, Smith had signed with a major label, DreamWorks, and was recording in the more salubrious surroundings of Sunset Sound studios, LA. Fears that his songs would be swamped by a lush, bigger-budget production were soon allayed. New instruments were used judiciously: a horn section to punctuate the bold retro of "A Question Mark", discreet strings for the resignation of "Oh Well, Okay", and a rolling piano for the gorgeous 3/4 lilt of the single cut, "Waltz #2". At the last minute, Smith switched the new album's title from GRAND MAL (a form of epileptic fit) to the rather punchier XO (as in 'hugs and kisses'; 1998). Retaining his indie sensibilities, Smith opted to put out the record as a vinyl LP on the obscure Bong Load imprint, a full two weeks before the rest of the world could pick it up on CD. XO met with a warm critical reception, and no wonder.

Almost simultaneously, in August 1998, the first three albums finally gained a European release on the Domino label, after registering healthy sales on import. Smith moved to New York, toured the US extensively, and even found time for a couple of brief jaunts around Europe.

In 2000, FIGURE 8 was released, Smith's fifth solo album, and second for DreamWorks (as before, a vinyl release appeared on Bong Load). Picking up where XO left off, the set glistens with the sparingly utilized gilt of big-budget production, which overlays the simple, folky voice/guitar blueprint. Many of the tracks – like "Can't Make A Sound", one of his career's best – begin acoustically, gradually allowing strings, organs, guitars and multitracked backing harmonies to thumb a lift, building toward cacophonous crescendos of sweetness and warmth. The album was well received and sold strongly; Smith toured extensively to support the release, taking in several festivals and playing a blinding set at Glastonbury 2000.

A sixth album, FROM THE BASEMENT ON THE HILL, is recorded but as yet unreleased. It is not expected to be issued by DreamWorks, but instead an independent. Tellingly, Smith often closes his gigs with an impassioned reading of Big Star's "Thirteen". Alex Chilton never sold as many records as he deserved to, but for Elliott Smith the future looks bright and interesting.

⊙ **Either/Or** (1997; Kill Rock Stars/Domino).
A true underground classic for the late 90s. Flawless, from the breathy urgency of "Speed Trials" to the guarded optimism of "Say Yes". Make room for it in your record collection.

⊙ **XO** (1998; DreamWorks).
Another *tour de force*. Smith's irritation and weary solipsism are bathed in a whole clutch of perfect tunes. An unlikely but brilliantly realized combination.

⊙ **Figure 8** (2000; DreamWorks).
The Beatles and Big Star influences shine through, particularly on the Lennon & McCartney-ish "Stupidity Tries" and "Color Bars". Thanks to this fine album Elliott Smith's prevailing underground adulation has spilled over into mainstream critical acclaim.

Duncan Cooper

PATTI SMITH

Born Chicago, 1946.

"Three chord rock merged with the power of the word." Patti Smith defining her music

Brought up in suburban New Jersey by a Jehovah's Witness mother and an atheist father, **Patti Smith** endured a childhood that was further complicated by a severe case of scarlet fever that resulted in recurring hallucinations. When she became involved in the narcissistic, narcotic high life of the New York art scene in the late 60s, her early experiences became the basis of her examinations of redemption and guilt – speed-freak assemblages of mystical raptures inhabited by the ghosts of her heroes: Rimbaud and Baudelaire, Jimi Hendrix and Jim Morrison.

Smith gave her first concert on February 10, 1971. It was ostensibly a poetry reading, augmented by amateurish, and sometimes demented, guitar backing from local rock journalist Lenny Kaye. Performing "Oath", she spoke the words which, nearly five years later, would introduce her first album, HORSES: 'Jesus died for somebody's sins ... but not mine.' She published three volumes of poetry – *Seventh Heaven* (1971), *Kodak* (1972) and *Witt* (1973) – which, when performed live, developed a high-octane mix of stream-of-consciousness babble and volatile jazz improvisation.

Gradually she moved into the territory of rock-'n'roll, contributing a poem for Todd Rundgren's A WIZARD, A TRUE STAR, and a Morrison-fixated ode for ex-Doors man Ray Manzarek's second solo album. Meantime, **Richard Sohl** (piano) joined Kaye and Smith for her first single, "Piss Factory"/"Hey Joe" (1974), a 2000-copy pressing funded by photographer (and Patti's then-boyfriend) Robert Mapplethorpe. It was an amazing debut. Smith turned "Hey Joe" into the story of Patty Hearst's kidnap, while "Piss Factory" set out the bleakness of life in a New Jersey factory with a heartfelt social realism.

Drawn to CBGB's, where her friends Richard Hell and Tom Verlaine were performing as **TELEVISION**, Smith was galvanized into recruiting **Ivan Kraal** (bass) and **Jay Daugherty** (drums) to her crew and, finding herself in possession of a band, the **Patti Smith Group**, signed to Arista and commenced work on HORSES (1975), with producer John Cale.

Cale imposed a driving force on Smith's less-focused ramblings and HORSES turned out a brilliant, obsessive and cathartic set. "Kimberley" (the name of Smith's sister) challenged the narrowness of a religious upbringing; "Break It Up" had Smith seeking inspiration at Jim Morrison's grave, and finding none; extended pieces such as "Land" channelled her outpourings into a 'sea of possibilities'; and, by contrast, "Gloria" revisited the ferocious energy of garage rock, and cloaked it in enigma. HORSES was the first 'new underground' rock album to break through into the mainstream, entering the *Billboard* Top 50, despite the lack of a single to promote it, and it has remained a genuine classic.

In early 1976 Smith released live versions of "Gloria" and "My Generation", her respect for 60s idols contrasting with the deep loathing affected by punks – or at least the British punks – towards rock 'tradition'. Some found this

a strange contradiction – the high priestess of the alternative scene praising the rock deities others thought she had come to bury. This feeling was compounded by her band's second release, RADIO ETHIOPIA (1976), which *NME* punk champion Charles Shaar Murray described as 'just another well-produced, competently played mid 1970s rock'n'roll record'. Certainly Smith seemed, at times, to be swamped by straight guitar dynamics, but "Radio Ethiopia: Abyssinia" was anything but conventional – a bizarre, cacophonous free-jazz exploration that would replace "Land" as the centrepiece of the band's live shows.

Reaction to the album was cool, and a backlash was developing to Smith's perceived arrogance and self-indulgence. As the band tightened as a performing outfit, Smith's own performance sometimes confused intensity with extravagant incoherence. Then, at a concert in Tampa, Florida, in January 1977, Smith broke her neck in a fall from the stage. As she described it: 'I was doing my most intense number, "Ain't It Strange", a song where I challenge God to talk to me in some way ... spin like a dervish and say "Hand of God I feel

Patti Smith – waiting for the muse with Lenny Kaye (left)

the finger, Hand of God I start to whirl, Hand of God, I don't get dizzy. Hand of God I do not fall now." But I fell... ' She saw this as a warning to retreat from the maelstrom she had created.

Work on the third album was in any case delayed while Smith recuperated, in traction, and published a fourth poetry collection entitled *Babel*. Comeback shows at CBGB's – by now a punk location, with Smith installed as high priestess – were seen as a kind of resurrection by Smith and, in this spirit, the third album was titled EASTER (1978). This was the Patti Smith Group's most commercial effort, with some tight, well-crafted rock'n'roll songs stridently produced by Jimmy Iovine. "Because The Night' (co-written with Bruce Springsteen) provided a Top 10 hit in the UK and ensured that EASTER was the first Patti Smith LP to chart in Britain, eventually reaching #16.

Smith's next album, the Todd Rundgren-(over)produced WAVE (1979), was her most overtly religious, but because she had seemingly stopped questioning and started believing, it lacked the compelling disharmony of her best music, and seemed a little arch in its joyous exaltations. Yet the final performance of the Patti Smith Group was a benefit in Detroit in June 1980, in which she came full circle by returning to the experimentation of her early-70s shows. An improvised melange of saxophone and feedback provided a soundtrack to a backdrop film featuring Jackson Pollock.

Over the following decade Smith retired to a private life in Detroit with husband Fred 'Sonic' Smith (MC5's guitarist), raising their children and preparing two poetry collections, *Early Work* and *Woolgathering*, for publication. Her only recording work was DREAM OF LIFE (1988), with Fred, which appeared way out of time and sank without trace.

Patti Smith's life was shattered in November 1994 with the death of Fred Smith, from heart failure – a personal tragedy compounded by the loss of her brother Todd, and of Robert Mapplethorpe, who had remained a close friend. In the year previously, Patti had been working with Fred on some new songs, and in 1995 she turned back to the rock world, with recording work, and her first live shows since 1980. She was, by her own admission, amazed to find she 'still had any significant impact', but she had been championed at intervals during her absence, and, most recently by Kurt Cobain (whose music she admired) and by R.E.M.'s Michael Stipe (who became a friend).

It was an old rocker, however, who brought Patti Smith back onto the main stage – Bob Dylan, who invited her to do a support slot on his winter East Coast dates. Reuniting Lenny Kaye, Jay Dee Daugherty and, on lead guitar, Tom Verlaine, Smith tore through old and new material, including challenging feedback excursions on "About A Boy", her tribute to Cobain. She and the band received rapturous applause. Meantime, Smith was back on disc, with her first recordings since 1988: the haunting

ballad "Walkin' Blind" for the movie *Dead Man Walking*, and an exquisite rendition of Nina Simone's "Don't Smoke In Bed" for feminist-covers album, AIN'T NUTHIN BUT A SHE THING.

Patti then returned to New York's Electric Ladyland studios – where HORSES had been recorded twenty years before – and emerged with the album GONE AGAIN (1996), dedicated to the memory of Fred. It was unashamedly elegiac, resonating with downbeat acoustic musings: the organ and mandolin of "Ravens" and the dulcimer on the dustbowl country ballad "Dead To The World" created a sombre tone. But elsewhere the songs had the stormy abandon and rough edges of HORSES or EASTER, with a raging version of Dylan's "Wicked Messenger" and "Alone Again", on which guests included Cale and Jeff Buckley. It was an album, clearly, about the wilderness, and about finding some kind of peace. It was also an enormously welcome and timely return for one of the greatest rock poet-artists of a generation.

PEACE AND NOISE (1997) followed close on the heels of GONE AGAIN as Smith continued to grieve on disc. Cathartic yet less intensely pained than on the previous recording, Smith explored her own situation as rocker-turned-parent. There was less instrumental angst and more concentration on the lyrics as she returned to her poetic roots.

2000's GUNG HO had a far broader vision, and saw Smith revisiting the sound of New Wave under the watchful eye of producer Gil Norton.

Horses (1975; Arista).
Everything that mid-70s American rock wasn't – it's challenging, discordant, and crammed with the dense imagery of Smith's fevered imagination.

Easter (1978; Arista).
As Smith edged towards a more becalmed persona, EASTER was her last gasp as a genuinely innovative voice 'outside of society'.

Gone Again (1996; Arista).
Smith's moving elegy to husband Fred is a dark, restless album that rates with the very best of her 70s work.

Masters Boxset (1996; Arista).
A fine investment if you're planning to go digital and need to convert your complete collection in one go. But despite the remastering and repackaging, it contains nothing new for the more casual fan.

Nig Hodgkins

THE SMITHS

Formed Manchester, England, 1982;
disbanded 1987.

"When the Smiths came on *Top Of The Pops* for the first time, that was it for me. From that day on I wanted to be Johnny Marr." Noel Gallagher

T he phenomenon of **The Smiths** is a strange one: four years of incessant critical adoration and some of the most ardent fan worship in rock history, yet hardly a Top 10 hit to show for it on either side of the Atlantic. Yet, without ever coming close to the commercial impact of a Beatles or Nirvana, the Morrissey/Marr partnership couched a generation with some of rock's most original and stubbornly unclassifiable music.

The first meeting between **Steven MORRISSEY** (vocals) and **Johnny Marr** (guitars), like those of so many great songwriting partnerships, has been the subject of much embellishment over the years, not least by Morrissey himself: 'Johnny came up and pressed his nose against my window, quite literally. It left a terrible smudge.' The reality may have been less messy, but the boundlessly enthusiastic Marr was immediately struck by Morrissey's bookish intelligence and deep knowledge of pop history, while Morrissey was quick to recognize a kindred spirit with the vigour to shake him from his self-imposed isolation. Galvanized by this meeting of minds, and by the successful trial marriage of Morrissey's lyrics and Marr's music, the pair forged an intense, full-time partnership and set about creating a band.

Marr and Morrissey had settled on the name The Smiths long before the final line-up had been established: it was gritty and very obviously English (much like their music), as well as being a reaction

Steven Morrissey reflecting

against the lengthy, pretentious or just plain daft band names of the time, such as Orchestral Manoeuvres In The Dark and Haysi Fantayzee. With local musicians **Mike Joyce** (drums) and **Andy Rourke** (bass) now completing a sturdy team, The Smiths played their first gig at Manchester's Ritz club on October 4, 1982, and embarked on six months of sporadic gigging, during which time they excited the interest of Rough Trade supremo Geoff Travis.

It was during this period that Morrissey's legendary early stage props made their first appearances, too – the back pocket stuffed with gladioli (later evolving into small thickets), the hearing aid and NHS specs, all of which garnered The Smiths plenty of press attention as they prepared to launch their first single, "Hand In Glove", in May 1983. Released on Rough Trade, it was an instant success in the indie chart, but mainstream radio and the public at large found its retro imagery and Morrissey's disconsolate drone decidedly resistible. (A more colourful 1984 interpretation by Morrissey heroine Sandie Shaw fared

better, restoring her to the Top 30 for the first time in fifteen years.)

The months after "Hand In Glove" passed in a flurry of music press hyperbole, Radio 1 sessions (later preserved on the HATFUL OF HOLLOW collection) and major-label interest. Keen to keep their independent flag flying, however, Morrissey and Marr opted to stay with Rough Trade and signed a long-term deal whose financial rewards were potentially substantial, but which ultimately proved inadequate as the group's success and ambition mushroomed.

By the end of 1983, their reputation had grown sufficiently to send the winsome "This Charming Man" into the Top 30, earning The Smiths an unforgettable UK TV debut on *Top Of The Pops*. Although they steadfastly refused to make videos until 1986, Morrissey in particular lapped up live TV performances, and was in fine form on the show he had watched since childhood. His arm-flinging, hip-swivelling stage persona was always in sharp contrast to the tortured loneliness and self-doubt which his lyrics expressed, and which he discussed at length in interviews: 'I can't converse politely with the man next door. But situations that are considered quite surreal I find intensely natural – appearing on TV, touring – they're nice things to do, glamorous.'

When the group's first album, THE SMITHS, emerged in February 1984 it was to a buzz of real excitement. Their third single, "What Difference Does It Make?", had teased the UK Top 10, and the album stormed to #2 on a wave of critical euphoria, although its muddy production and rough edges suggested a rush job. (In fact, early sessions had been rejected by the band, and John Porter was drafted in to take over at the eleventh hour.) Technical grumbles aside, the record was a breath of fresh northern air, a collection of vivid finger paintings that, even at this early stage, confirmed the depth of songwriting talent in the group.

Even the British tabloid press took notice, although their interpretation of Morrissey's recurring 'innocence corrupted' theme as a glorification of paedophilia drew stern denials. There was further controversy over "Suffer Little Children", a haunting and heartfelt elegy to the Moors murder victims which caused a press backlash and led to some retailers refusing to stock Smiths product. The row was defused when Ann West, mother of one of the Moors victims, described the song as 'very touching' and even struck up a correspondence and friendship with the group. The episode caused Morrissey to develop a deep mistrust of the press that sometimes bordered on the paranoiac.

It was typical of The Smiths that their greatest moment should be hidden away as the 12" B-side of "William It Was Really Nothing", a 1984 single. For Marr in particular, "How Soon Is Now?" was a triumph, his searing guitar drone hovering over Morrissey's desolate yet defiant lyric: 'You shut your mouth, how can you say/I go about things the wrong way/I am human and I need to be loved/Just like everybody else does'. This was Marr and Morrissey in perfect, passionate harmony and it became the ultimate Smiths anthem, although an underachiever when belatedly issued as a single in its own right at the beginning of 1985.

Amid a blitzkrieg of Smiths activity at this time came their second album MEAT IS MURDER (1985), which saw Morrissey sitting jauntily astride a new hobby horse, vegetarianism. Lyrically, the album was more direct, less world-weary, while Marr's multi-layered guitar backdrops and some disciplined performances from Rourke and Joyce took The Smiths to new artistic heights and gave them a richly deserved first UK #1 album.

The first cracks in The Smiths' armoury appeared in 1986, when Rourke was fired, as his heroin habit began to take its toll on his performances. **Craig Gannon** was drafted in to replace him, and he continued for a brief spell as the 'fifth Smith' when Rourke was reinstated later in the year. At the same

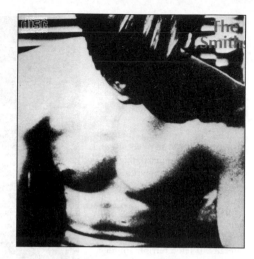

time, a dispute with Rough Trade meant that the group's third – and finest – album, THE QUEEN IS DEAD (1986), was delayed for six months as relations between band and label reached an impasse. When the record finally emerged, it was quickly hailed as a classic, breathtaking in its scale and variety, musically thrilling and lyrically inspired, from the sprightly slapstick of "Frankly Mr. Shankly" to the bleak power of "I Know It's Over". Just as the world was digesting its brilliance, The Smiths launched "Panic", a feisty new song which implored its audience to 'burn down the disco'. It became another Smiths classic, but, like so many before, it somehow managed to avoid the Top 10.

Morrissey and Marr's consternation at this continuing lack of chart glory both at home and in America, where they were regularly playing to packed houses, led to a parting of the ways with Rough Trade at the end of 1986. The Smiths then signed to EMI in a move which Marr described as 'a merging of two great institutions', but which had indie purists screaming 'sellout'. The new deal seemed to drive a wedge between the two songwriters as Marr came to feel increasingly pressurized and constrained by the intensity of being an eight-days-a-week Smith. Over a period of months, the close relationship between the two became strained and ultimately broke down as a burned-out Marr jetted off to LA amid rumours of a permanent Smiths split. Morrissey later reflected on how gossip had fanned the flames of what was initially no more than a communication breakdown: 'Suddenly we were overtaken by events, and the rumour became reality. But if everybody had remained quiet, the problems could have been resolved in private.' When Marr quit the band for good, Morrissey, Rourke and Joyce attempted to soldier on (very briefly) as a trio, but it became clear that Marr, rather than Morrissey, had been The Smiths' secret ingredient all these years.

Although their final, posthumously issued album STRANGEWAYS HERE WE COME (1987) had been completed before the rot set in, its foreboding atmosphere suggested otherwise, as the vigorous self-belief of old was largely absent. The lengthy "Paint A Vulgar Picture", an attack on record company greed, took on a new irony when Warner Music bought the rights to the entire Smiths catalogue in 1992 and embarked on an energetic campaign of re-promotion which echoed the song's bitter 'Re-issue! Re-package! Re-evaluate the songs!' refrain. Highlight of the album was the incandescent "I Won't Share You", whose closing 'I'll see you somewhere/I'll see you sometime' provided an appropriately poignant epitaph.

So what of The Smiths' influence? Is it realistic to cite them as pioneers of Britpop, without whom Oasis, Blur and the rest would be languishing in obscurity? Probably not, but what they unquestionably did change was the public's perception of 'alternative' music. Pre-Smiths, the British indie community was populated by lank-haired shoegazers and hopeless goths, whose chances of reaching a wider audience were minimal at best. The Smiths' conviction, integrity and unfailing quality control opened the floodgates for bands such as The Stone Roses and Happy Mondays to reach the mainstream at the end of the decade, buoyed by the credibility which The Smiths had brought to the independent sector. And their music – seventy-plus songs in four astonishingly prolific years – remains as vibrant and intoxicating today as it was first time round, surely the most revealing test of all.

In a business where even Warhol's fifteen minutes of fame can sometimes seem optimistic, The Smiths stood tall, they made a difference, they truly mattered.

The Smiths (1984; WEA).
This intense, moving and utterly original album lit up the wasteland British rock had become in the mid-80s. With the benefit of hindsight, the music and lyrics often seem welded together rather than entwined as they were on later albums, and several songs have a tentative feel. But it rambles beautifully.

Hatful Of Hollow (1984; WEA).
Much more accomplished and self-assured is this sixteen-track assemblage of early singles, B-sides and Radio 1 sessions, which reveal just how much The Smiths achieved in their first eighteen months. The explosive "Handsome Devil" and the remarkable "How Soon Is Now?" are evidence of their burgeoning confidence and humour.

Meat Is Murder (1985; WEA).
Morrissey is in vitriolic form on this first great Smiths album, savaging sadistic schoolteachers on "The Headmaster Ritual", child abusers on "Barbarism Begins At Home" and meat eaters on the notorious title track. The music is similarly inspired, with Marr's jagged jangling at its multi-channelled best on "That Joke Isn't Funny Anymore".

The Queen Is Dead (1986; WEA).
Now widely acclaimed as the best album of the decade, this dizzying 'state of the nation' epic is the sound of rampant genius in full flow. Morrissey covers plagiarism ("Cemetery Gates"), ecclesiastical perversions ("Vicar In A Tutu") and stinging heartbreak ("I Know It's Over") with effortless brilliance, while Marr's musical vision is never more clearly defined. The passage of time has not withered the wit and power of this magnificent record.

Louder Than Bombs (1987; WEA).
A posthumous collection of singles and B-sides containing some of The Smiths' best work. More than twenty

tracks which were not on the studio albums, further exposing how classy the Morrissey-Marr songwriting duo was.

Rank (1988; WEA).
An ebullient live set, recorded in London in 1986, which at least partially captures the spirit of the group in the flesh. If Morrissey and Marr inevitably dominate the studio albums, the dynamism of RANK is a tribute to Rourke and Joyce, whose contributions to the group are often overlooked.

Singles (1994; WEA).
Essential listening. As the last bars of the glorious "There Is A Light That Never Goes Out" fade, you're left to ponder how these eighteen songs between them managed just three weeks in the UK Top 10. But statistics can go hang – The Smiths' place in rock history is assured.

Jonathan Kennaugh

SMOG

Conceived California, 1988.

S mog is the alias of **Bill Callahan**, a mysterious man who looks more like a mild-mannered librarian than a rock musician. While he began his career as an early proponent of the 'lo-fi' recording movement, once given broader options, this dedicated songsmith didn't hesitate in leaving his sonic bedroom for plusher studio quarters. Regardless of the amount of tape hiss accompanying his no-nonsense voice, what has remained constant in Callahan's work is his sad, poetic stance: his lyrics being melancholic, alienated, and regretful. Yet many of his songs have the habit of delivering a disturbing, often humorous punch line behind their frowns; it is this dry wit that has consistently helped Callahan to eschew the self-indulgent earnestness that burdens many of his contemporaries.

Smog was unveiled in 1988 with the sparse MACRAMÉ GUNPLAY, a self-released cassette. The next couple of years brought a handful of tapes that documented the one-man band's gestation, culminating with 1990's SEWN TO THE SKY LP (reissued on CD five years later). Smog's wheels really began to roll, however, when Callahan joined the fledgling roster of Drag City. Along with Royal Trux and Pavement, Smog helped establish the Chicago record label as a home for musical misfits proud of their bookish undertones. With an EP, FLOATING (1991), and a full-length album, FORGOTTEN FOUNDATION (1992), Callahan presented a vision of spare musical backdrops, with uncluttered lyrics, produced on inexpensive equipment.

Smog's next album, JULIUS CAESAR (1993), added strings, samples, and collaborators – **Cynthia Dall** (at the time Callahan's girlfriend; later a Drag City solo artist) and **Jim O'Rourke** (Gastr Del Sol/Sonic Youth) came along for the ride. Among the album's most memorable cuts were "I Am Star Wars!", and the beautifully tragic "Chosen One".

With JULIUS CAESAR, Smog became something of a name act, albeit in the American indie rock minor league. And Callahan didn't disappoint his new-found admirers: even now, rarely a year passes that doesn't see a significant Smog release. 1994 brought

Bill Callahan inspects the queue outside a Smog gig

BURNING KINGDOM, a six-song EP; the next year fans feasted on WILD LOVE, a bitter-tasting album that featured the surprisingly catchy "Bathysphere" – later covered by Cat Power's Chan Marshall, who was at the time romantically entwined with Callahan. In 1996 Smog released another full-lengther, THE DOCTOR CAME AT DAWN, as well as the short yet potent KICKING A COUPLE AROUND EP. With backings that often leaned towards a cappella, both works focused on the singer's careful and occasionally creepy lyrics ("And I hope you don't mind/If I grab your private life/Slap it on the table/And split it/With a knife" he offers in the track "You Moved In").

Smog's next couple of collections were produced with Jim O'Rourke, whose arrangements soaked the previously bare songs in instrumental gravy. RED APPLE FALLS (1997) added organs, piano, synthesizers, electronic drums, and hurdy-gurdy to Callahan's deadpan spiel, while KNOCK KNOCK (1999) – rumoured to have been written in the wake of Mr. Smog's affair with Ms. Cat Power – chronicled a romance's arc with backing that included, of all things, an amateur children's choir. Although patchier than many of his late-90s releases, KNOCK KNOCK featured some of Smog's sharpest three-minute moments.

Callahan eventually found himself in Chicago. He wasted no time soaking up the atmosphere of the city's fertile music scene, collaborating with mem-

bers of **Tortoise** to record DONGS OF SEVOTION (2000). Smog's best work to date, DONGS featured both delicate numbers that wouldn't feel out of place at a poetry reading and rock songs with thundering drums and gnawing electric guitars, while the opener, "Justice Aversion", carried faint dub flavours. But true to form, the best numbers doubled as the album's wittiest, particularly "Dress Sexy At My Funeral" ("Wink at the minister/Blow kisses to my grieving brothers") and "Bloodflow", a hypnotic groove-fest featuring tape effects, upright bass, and a trio of cheerleaders nicknamed **The Dongettes**.

After 2002's singles compilation ACCUMULATION: NONE and the addition of brackets to his name, (Smog) returned in 2003 with SUPPER, a far less emotionally mangled set that found Callahan and Dall in an almost chirpy mood whilst still serving up a platter of rich imagery and dark observation.

Long may his warped and tortured releases grace our ears.

⊙ **Julius Caesar** (Drag City, 1993).
The first Smog album to receive much attention, the decidedly lo-fi *Julius Caesar* focused predominantly on Callahan's songwriting but also introduced cello, violin, banjo, and a sample of "Honky Tonk Woman."

⊙ **The Doctor Came At Dawn** (Drag City, 1996).
Somber, cynical, and creepy as hell, Smog's mid-period gem finds Callahan bemoaning the current state of lies ("They Don't Make Lies Like They Used To"), searching through an ex-lover's clothing ("All Your Women Things"), and spitting bile into eyes ("Spread Your Bloody Wings").

Dongs Of Sevotion (Drag City, 2000).
The album that should convince any astute listener to sevote themselves to this band's dongs, Smog's millennium debut features dub-like synthesizers, contributions from members of Tortoise, and, on one song, a trio of female cheerleaders.

Supper (Drag City, 2003).
"Butterflies Drowned In Wine" (despite the title's mournful imagory) is a rousing rooker whore Bill barks like Lou Reed over heavy riffs, while the lovely "Morality" aches with love and hope. Thankfully, though, they aren't all ditties to skip through the daisies to: "Truth Serum" finds Callahan just as adrift on a raft of his own internal wrangling as he ever was.

Jay Ruttenberg

SNEAKER PIMPS

Formed London, England, 1993.

"Hopefully we don't fit in anywhere and a new hole will have to be made for us." Chris Corner

It's easy to see why both the dance and indie camps have tried to claim the **Sneaker Pimps** as their own; on the one hand, this British trio pushed the boundaries of post-trip-hop into an entirely new dimension, while on the other they sound just how a modern, state-of-the-art rock band ought to. The story of the band goes back to the dance music revolution days of 1992, when **Liam Howe** and **Chris Corner**, teenage friends from Hartlepool in northeast England, combined forces – first under the name F.R.I.S.K., later as Line Of Flight – and began releasing 12" acid-jazz and trip-hop tracks on the dance underground.

Their sights, however, were set on greater things and in 1993 the two spotted **Kelli Dayton** singing with indie rock band The Lumieres in a pub and asked her to join their project. Shortly after, the newly named Sneaker Pimps (name taken from a posse employed by The Beastie Boys to make trainer-buying runs to New York) released their first single "Tesko Suicide". The track's innovative fusion of spiky punk vocals and guitar over a tight, rolling kick drum attracted instant attention. Their second single, the slinkier, more down-tempo "Roll On", followed soon after, and helped establish the Pimps as a band who were forging a sound that was uniquely their own. While quick to acknowledge their debt to artists such as Tricky and Massive Attack, the group were equally keen to carve their own niche.

When the band's debut album, BECOMING X (1996) was released, it was hailed as one of the few albums to successfully cross dance with indie. The Pimps had cooked up an infectious, cutting-edge brew of trip-hop beats, girlie vocals, B-movie melodies and dirty production – and the moment was right for it. In October, the sultry, slow-beat sounds on "Six Underground", the first single off the album, shot straight into the UK Top 40 at #9 – the band's

biggest hit to date. Remixes by top names on the dance scene – Paul Oakenfold, DJ Sneak and Nellee Hooper – ensured the track stayed at the forefront of the dance as well as the indie scene.

"Spin Spin Sugar" came next, with beefy mixes by Armand Van Helden, and proved a big dance hit worldwide. The band toured heavily in the UK and North America to support the album, while the Van Helden mix of the track became a staple of that year's crop of 'speed garage' music compilations.

The Sneaker Pimps' next single "Post Modern Sleaze", a dark, rolling drum track with seedy vocals and a polished string section, entered the UK Top 40 briefly in late 1997. Meanwhile the band were finding themselves in demand as film-music writers, and contributed music to *The Saint* (starring Val Kilmer). While still involved in preparing material for their second album, SPLINTER (1999), a limited-edition remix album, BECOMING REMIXED (1998), kept their music in the clubs and their name in the minds of the record-buyers. But by the time SPLINTER was in the shops, Dayton had been asked to leave, as it was felt that Corner's vocals were far more suited to the newer material.

A third album, the harder-edged BLOODSPORT arrived in 2002, with Sneaker Pimps now comprising Corner, Howe, **David Westlake** and **Joe Wilson**. A new collection is expected in late 2003.

Becoming X (1996; Clean Up Records).
Random breakbeats with sub-bass hints, layered with teasing guitar and punk vocals. This album touches on many styles; glam-pop, drum'n'bass, punk rock and acoustic folk.

Gerard Grech & Sarah Dallas

JILL SOBULE

Born Denver, Colorado, 1961.

Jill Sobule writes songs that deal with secret lives and hidden identities, and does so with a lightness of touch that is genuinely subversive – she wraps serious points in humour and melodies that are almost bubblegum in their catchiness. "I Kissed A Girl", her first major single, featured a story in which the narrator and her girlfriend complain about boyfriends 'as dumb as a box of hammers' and obviously not really up to the job, and then find themselves drawn into a Sapphic snog. One Nashville radio station broadcast a public-service announcement along the lines of 'cover the kids' ears up and get them out of the room' each time they played the song – but they still played it. With a song this sweet they didn't have much choice – it had 'hit' written all the way through it.

Growing up in Denver, vet's daughter Sobule was the archetypal rock'n'roll loner kid who turned to music for solace during the long hours she had to spend by herself. Discouraged by the response she got (being a dirty-ass lead guitarist wasn't considered feminine in those days), she abandoned the guitar until her time at the University of Colorado, when she started busking with a friend during her junior year abroad in Spain. On her return, she dropped out to concentrate on music – the beginning of a dark period of some seven years, during which she suffered depression and a serious back injury, and battled with both anorexia and bulimia.

Her first album, THINGS HERE ARE DIFFERENT (1990), was produced by Todd Rundgren, whose presence seemed to intimidate her. The album did nothing, and the record company dropped her rather than release a second LP. Living in LA, she was working as assistant to a wedding photographer when her luck finally turned. Her lawyer played a demo tape to Atlantic's A&R man, who was so relieved by the contrast with the sub-Seattle grunge wannabes who infested the early 90s that he invited her to audition, and signed her the next day.

Sobule and her producers **Robin Eaton** (her songwriting partner) and **Brad Jones** (bass/keyboards/backing vocals) were determined to let the songs speak for themselves, so JILL SOBULE (1995) was recorded in a tiny Nashville studio. They succeeded triumphantly – the intelligence and sense of humour that saw her through the dark years shone through every track.

Her profile was further boosted when she sang "Supermodel" on the soundtrack to *Clueless*. She declared an ambition to collaborate with Burt Bacharach and to write a musical, something the strong narrative element of her songs eminently qualifies her to do. These perhaps lightweight statements balanced the more political content of her mid-90s material.

Sobule has avoided being slotted into a single musical pigeonhole (such as 'hippie-dippy songstress' or 'lesbian icon') by defying expectations. With both HAPPY TOWN (1997) and PINK PEARL (2000), she showed a maturity in both lyric and tune that won her an increased number of followers. Though her magic remains largely unknown, many carry one of her songs in their heart or head, having crossed its path on the radio or a movie soundtrack. A 'best of' collection, I NEVER LEARNED TO SWIM, quietly slipped out in 2001, and will hopefully gain her the wider acknowledgement she deserves.

⊙ **Jill Sobule** (1995; Lava/Atlantic).
Well-crafted tunes and sly wit – "Resistance Song" is a tale of gender reversal in wartime, "Karen By Night" presents a straight-laced shoe-store manageress who dresses up in leather, like the young Brando.

Andy Smith

SOCIAL DISTORTION

Formed Los Angeles, 1978.

Mike Ness (guitar), **Casey Royer** (drums), **Rikk Agnew** (vocals/guitar) and **Frank Agnew** (bass) provided **Social Distortion**'s initial formation, although by 1979 the Agnew brothers had left to form The Adolescents. Ness took over as vocalist, and **Dennis Dannell** (bass) and the sur-

name-less **Carrott** (drums) also joined, but line-up changes were to become a common procedure for the band – The Avengers' **Danny Furious** and DI's **Tim Mag** also passed through their ranks.

Following a brief stay with Posh Boy Records for one-off single "Mainliner", the group founded its own 13th Floor Records in 1981, as **Derek O'Brien** (also from DI) became their permanent drummer, and the arrival of **Brent Liles** (bass) allowed Dannell to move to rhythm guitar. This relatively stable line-up was to last three years, and was used to best effect on their 1983 album, MOMMY'S LITTLE MONSTER, which superbly mixed their lithe power-pop mechanics with more aggressive components from the embryonic US hardcore movement. In addition, traces of The Rolling Stones (a cover of "Under My Thumb" had been an early B-side) and even Creedence Clearwater Revival could be detected under a ferocious but always melodic twin-guitar assault.

They should have capitalized on this album, but by 1984 Ness's drug problems were devouring most of the band's income, and they practically vanished from view, with only the occasional Los Angeles or San Francisco date to keep any memories alive. Ness's behaviour saw off Liles, who joined the Agnew brothers in **Agent Orange**, and O'Brien, who briefly returned to DI, before signing up with Agent Orange himself and ultimately moving on once more to form **Extra Fancy**.

By the time Ness had recovered, replacements had been found in ex-Lewd drummer **Chris Reece**, and bass player **John Maurer**. PRISON BOUND (1988) comprised rock and country in roughly equal parts, with an obvious debt to Johnny Cash on cuts such as "Like An Outlaw" and "Indulgence". They were not a hardcore punk band any more, and their newfound maturity and musical sophistication was strangely becoming.

Yet 1990's SOCIAL DISTORTION, their first for major label Epic, returned them to the uncompromising rock sound of old, and suddenly they found themselves adopted by the heavy metal community. SOMEWHERE BETWEEN HEAVEN AND HELL (1992) found Ness exploring his alcohol and drug addiction on songs which were often autobiographically convincing. The album was generally recognized to have been their most significant, especially in light of the four-year pause that ensued.

When they did finally return, with WHITE LIGHT, WHITE HEAT, WHITE TRASH (1996), they'd revised their sound from stripped-back punk to the post-grunge, tidied-up metal that alt-rock fans looked for in the mid 90s and some of the allure of old was beginning to wear thin. Social Distortion had now pledged themselves fully to hoary old hard-rock motifs. Nevertheless, there was something deeply affecting about songs such as "I Was Wrong", where the performance values helped you to forget about some fairly middling arrangements and lyrics (although Ness did at least seem to be addressing some of his macho posturing of the past). And **Chuck Biscuits**, recently divorced from **DANZIG**, popped up to ensure his status as the most travelled (and best) drummer in hardcore history.

Ness still used his own life and problems as material, but the raw confessional style had been done to death (in some cases, literally) by more skilled and (unfortunately) more charismatic artists during the time the band had been away.

⊙ **Social Distortion** (1990; Epic).
Sympathetically produced by Dave Jerden, this collection adds quintessential cuts like "So Far Away" and "She's A Knockout" to their legacy. It's not perfect – the cover of Johnny Cash's "Ring Of Fire" is the main culprit – but it's pretty damned good.

⊙ **Somewhere Between Heaven And Hell** (1992; Sony).
Ness leads the band through a vainglorious exhumation of his past, thematically filtered through a twelve-step therapy programme. In short, Oprah on a grubby Harley Davidson.

⊙ **Mainliner: Wreckage Of The Past** (1995; Time Bomb).
The greatest hits collection for those not dedicated enough for the full back catalogue.

⊙ **Live At The Roxy** (1998; Time Bomb).
Explosive and raw, the live sound of Social Distortion at their best.

Alex Ogg

THE SOFT BOYS

Formed Cambridge, England, 1976; disbanded 1981; re-formed in 1994.

"When everyone else was throwing beer glasses at the stage and putting safety pins through their noses, all we wanted to do was eat cucumber sandwiches."
Robyn Hitchcock

Unlike most of their New Wave peers, **The Soft Boys** were unashamedly retro, taking their inspiration more from the melodic psychedelia of The Beatles than the nihilist punk rock of The Stooges. As a result, they found themselves out of step with the times, having great songs, stunning musicianship and an incendiary live act, but no audience. Yet, though they never enjoyed any commercial success at the time, their heady brew of Byrds guitars and lyrical surrealism left an enduring legacy, influencing many of the mid-80s Paisley Underground bands and, of course, R.E.M.

The prime mover behind the band was guitarist and singer, **ROBYN HITCHCOCK**. Born in London in 1953, he numbered Bob Dylan, John Lennon and Syd Barrett among his childhood heroes, though it was the last that seemed to dominate. In 1974 he arrived in Cambridge as a penniless art-school dropout. Already an accomplished live performer, he worked his way around the local folk circuit, finding his first stable line-up with Dennis & The Experts. They congealed into the embryonic Soft Boys

towards the end of 1976, with Hitchcock on guitar and vocals, **Alan Davies** on guitar, **Andy Metcalfe** on bass and **Morris Windsor** on drums.

After recording a demo tape in Hitchcock's front room, the band hit lucky with an offer from independent label, Raw Records. Their first session for them in March 1977 provided three strong tracks which were lifted for an EP, released in July. WADING THROUGH A VENTILATOR must rank as one of the most uncompromising debuts ever, with a wall of grinding guitars and thrashing drums backing Hitchcock's post-Beefheart howl. The lyrics, laying down a blueprint of crustacean, fish and dead-fly metaphors that would characterize much of their early output, conveyed extremes of comic invention and bitter alienation. Soon after the EP's release, **Kimberley Rew**, from rival Cambridge group The Waves, replaced Alan Davies on guitar, to establish the partnership with Hitchcock that would cement the band's rich harmonic guitar sound.

Thanks to their wild stage appearances, The Soft Boys were already attracting considerable interest, and by 1978 they were supporting such names as Elvis Costello and The Damned. In May they became one of the first groups to be signed to Radar Records, but after several disagreements and a single that bombed ("I Want To Be An Angle Poise Lamp", a marvellous track), they scrapped an entire album's worth of tracks recorded at Rockfield, and left the label.

Following this debacle, the band decided to go it alone. Between August and November, they were holed up in Spaceward Studios in Cambridge, recording fresh material for what was to be their first album, released on their own Two Crabs label. A CAN OF BEES turned out to be more of a curate's egg, and, judging by the number of different versions, the band weren't convinced by it either. Despite such pleasures as "Pigworker", "Human Music" and "Leppo & The Jooves", this too-long-player was too patchy a debut to register, and sold few copies.

But Hitchcock still had plenty more obsessions to explore, and recording continued until June 1979 on material which was never released at the time, but emerged in 1983 as INVISIBLE HITS on Midnight. Ironically, these outtakes formed a much stronger set: as well as the Bo Diddley rampage of "Wey-Wey-Hep-A-Hole", the album offered the bouncy "Have A Heart Betty (I'm Not Fireproof)" and the immortal "Rock'N'Roll Toilet".

With hindsight, this was the bridge between the fumblings of A CAN OF BEES and the excellent UNDERWATER MOONLIGHT, made after Andy Metcalfe had left to join Telephone Bill & The Smooth Operators and been replaced by **Matthew Seligman**, who'd previously worked with the legendary **ALEX CHILTON**. Recorded on four- and eight-track for only £600, UNDERWATER MOONLIGHT was released in 1980 on the Armageddon label, and has become acknowledged as a one-off psychedelic classic. Here was proof that

The Soft Boys, eating goldfish?

Metcalfe and Seligman's duelling basses, extra guitar splashes from **Sean Kilby** and the added delight of **Jim Melton**'s powerhouse harmonica. Their sellout at London's Astoria was a triumphant return after all those years in the wilderness.

In the wake of this success Hitchcock suggested that more reunions could well be in store and, after years of influential obscurity, The Soft Boys appeared to be back. A revamped version of UNDERWATER MOONLIGHT was released during 2001, complete with over two dozen extra tracks, and was soon followed by a brand new album, NEXTDOORLAND, which featured more than enough quintessential oddness and blinding melodies to keep the band's beacon alight.

The Soft Boys had established a refined and melodic identity of their own, while Hitchcock's songwriting was at its best on songs like "Kingdom Of Love", "Queen Of Eyes" and the title track, all of which showed sensitive arrangements that made full use of the band's dynamics.

Sadly, UNDERWATER MOONLIGHT sold little better than its predecessor. Without strong management or the backing of a big label, it seemed that The Soft Boys were doomed to the twilight world of cultdom. The album's release was followed by touring in the US and, even though they had a strong following there, they broke up in 1981, discouraged by the lack of wider recognition.

Hitchcock carried on in obscurity throughout the early 80s with a string of intriguing solo albums and singles. In 1984, he teamed up again with the original Soft Boys rhythm section of Metcalfe and Windsor, to form Robyn Hitchcock & The Egyptians. With the support of R.E.M., they went on to become a major draw on the US college circuit. Kimberley Rew rejoined his friends in The Waves and, with the addition of Kansas-born vocalist Katrina Leskanich, went on to achieve worldwide (if temporary) success as Katrina And The Waves.

Yet the ghost of The Soft Boys refused to go away. The three Soft Boys albums were given UK CD reissues in 1990, all with bonus tracks, and in 1993 came an excellent box set, THE SOFT BOYS 1976–81. One welcome side effect of all this CD reissue activity was the unexpected Soft Boys reunion tour in January 1994. Rew, Seligman, Metcalfe and Windsor had already played alongside Hitchcock at a benefit concert for Bosnia. This time round they played a clutch of dates as The Soft Boys, minus Rew, but with

⦿ **Underwater Moonlight** (1980; Ryko; reissued 2001; Matador).
Quintessential Soft Boys, containing their best tune, "Kingdom Of Love", and the superbly psychedelic title track.

⦿ **The Soft Boys 1976–81** (1993; Ryko).
Definitive Soft Boys overview, boasting a grand total of 38 tracks, many previously unreleased, plus a detailed history of the band.

Iain Smith

SOFT CELL

Formed Leeds, England, 1979; disbanded 1984; reformed 2001.

While Duran Duran sweated the union of the snake, **Soft Cell** minced through the early-80s pop scene knowing what evil lurked in the hearts of men, and seeking salvation in the stomp of northern soul.

The band began when **MARC ALMOND** (vocals) met **Dave Ball** (keyboards) at Leeds Polytechnic; Almond had been looking for a musician to accompany his cabaret seances for madames Garland and Piaf. Looking like an accident in a beautician's, Almond became known as Leeds' leading futurist, and Soft Cell were booked to play 1980's Futurama 2 festival. They released the MUTANT MOMENTS EP (1980) in the run-up to a performance that attracted the attention of Some Bizzare's teenage mogul. "The Girl With The Patent Leather Face" appeared on his SOME BIZZARE ALBUM (1980).

The band's own first single, "Memorabilia" (1981), was easily forgotten, but in July 1981 they released a studded jackboot at 45 rpm: a cover of Gloria Jones' northern soul classic, "Tainted Love".

Discos everywhere squirmed to the trilling hook, 'I love you though you hurt me so (Whoa-oh-oh-a-oh)', and "Love" handcuffed itself to the UK and US charts for the entire year. In December, Almond's wet dreams came true with NON-STOP EROTIC CABARET, a post-punk masterpiece. "Sex Dwarf" rubbed up against "Say Hello, Wave Goodbye", Almond wailing while Ball's machines simmered like a Tennessee Williams heroine.

The Cell mixed personality – the bow-tied Ball vs priapic whipping boy Almond – with music warm as mink, shiny as a diamond, and painful as a slap to the face. The band carried itself like a grand opera, and moved to the insomniac city of New York following their success there. Ball bashed out the lame remixes of the NON STOP ECSTATIC DANCING LP (1982), while Almond researched, watching the people come and go, talking of Traci Lords. Aping Jacques Brel, he traded the docks of Marseille for the dance floor on singles like "Torch" (1982). The press loathed his overly stylized mannerisms, and lambasted the band for their "Sex Dwarf" video, which lampooned video nasties.

The press, and a disastrous world tour that ended in a Spanish riot, fed the fatalism of 1983's THE ART OF FALLING APART. In the subsequent hiatus, Ball toyed with the dance novelty he would later revisit with **The Grid** on his IN STRICT TEMPO (1983) solo album. Marc played the diva with Marc And The Mambas, whose TORMENT AND TOREROS (1983) album showed the fear and loathing behind Almond's painted smile. When the critics sniffed, he announced his retirement from show business – a very brief retirement, it turned out. In 1984, Cell said goodbye with the industrial LAST NIGHT IN SODOM and an incendiary farewell tour.

Almond had claimed NON STOP ECSTATIC DANCING as the first MDMA album. The 1998 reissues of this, THE ART OF FALLING APART and LAST NIGHT IN SODOM gave us all the chance to troll down his darkened alleys once more, while setting the scene for 2001's nostalgia-fuelled reunion gigs.

But that was not all: the duo signed a brand new deal with Cooking Vinyl in early 2002 to release a stunning new studio collection, CRUELTY WITHOUT BEAUTY (2002). Their first album since 1984, CRUELTY WITHOUT BEAUTY was exactly what you might expect – a fusion of hefty synth pop and intelligent, dark, but exquisitely camp lyrical meanderings.

⊙ **Non-Stop Erotic Cabaret** (1981; Sire).
Sandwiched between the steamroller of "Tainted Love" and the used hanky of "Say Hello, Wave Goodbye" is every shag Marc ever had, every tear ever cried and every rose dropped in the gutter. Almond takes every song by force, while Ball's arrangements have a simplicity that belies their age.

⊙ **The Very Best Of Soft Cell** (2002; Universal).
A fine overview of Soft Cell's career to date.

Brian Connolly

SOFT MACHINE

Formed Canterbury, England 1966. Core line-up dissolved 1971; name used until early 80s.

"Eventually the name Soft Machine, the title of a book by William Burroughs was chosen. Having worked with him in 1961 it was my job to get permission, so I arranged to meet him on a street corner in Paddington. He appeared, hat over eyes, and said, 'Can't see whaa not!."
Daevid Allen

Soft Machine were Britain's first psychedelic band, switched on by the doyens of the mid-60s London underground. Alongside Pink Floyd, they were co-headliners of two seminal hippie happenings: the inauguration of alternative magazine International Times at Camden's Roundhouse and the '14-Hour Technicolour Dream' at Alexandra Palace.

Their germination followed an appropriate trail of absurd serendipity. A young **ROBERT WYATT**, dabbler in various instruments and would-be beatnik, fled Canterbury academic life for a reflective sojourn in Spain in early 1962. There he connected with one George Niedorf, a drummer who was to return with Wyatt to Canterbury a few months later, teaching Wyatt the drums in lieu of rent. Because of this, **Daevid Allen**, a globe-wandering Australian friend of Niedorf, was to permeate the embryo of the legendary 'Canterbury Scene', turning up to stay at Wyatt's mother's house. A fully fledged guitar and poetry-Beat freak, he bore benign artistic influence.

Wyatt and old schoolmates **Hugh Hopper** (bass) and **Mike Ratledge** (keyboards) had been hanging out together exploring the musics of radical jazzers Ornette Coleman, Charles Mingus and Thelonious Monk. For Allen, this too was the wailing Grail, and such shared perspectives suggested to him that the Canterbury boys might like to join him in London in early 1963 for some free-jazz and poetry 'happenings'. Blagging a

residency at Peter Cook's satirical Establishment Club (curtailed after four nights), and playing at the ICA with Brion Gysin and William Burroughs, the short-lived Daevid Allen Trio lark revealed a glimpse of the madness and beauty to come.

Allen moved to Paris, and Wyatt and Hopper found their way back to Canterbury, where they formed **The Wilde Flowers** (a template of both Soft Machine and **CARAVAN**) alongside the deep vocal langour of cherubic aesthete **KEVIN AYERS**, who was attracted to the recreational facets of the Wyatt gang. Significant, through this period, were trips to France to visit Allen for exposure to his experiments with tape loops, *musique concrète* and LSD. As yet The Beatles hadn't recorded "Love Me Do".

In 1966 Allen and Ayers met a kindred spirit, Wes Brunson, in Majorca. Here was a man from Tulsa, married with two kids, whom he'd 'turned on & tuned in' with and was now quickly dropping out with. And here was a man who would subsequently return to Oklahoma and sell his optometry business in order to subsidize a band that was at this point going to be known as Mister Head. He flew Allen, Ayers and American guitarist Larry Nolan to England and rented them a house in Canterbury where they could rehearse with the instruments and amplifiers he'd bought.

The fairy tale lurched towards substance with Wyatt joining on drums and vocals (he had developed an ability to sing, note for note, 40s Charlie Parker solos) and Mike Ratledge on organ. With the name Soft Machine sanctioned by Burroughs, the band were signed up by the same management as The Animals and began gigging, often to disbelief and hostility. It was only at those gigs run by and for the London freak clique where the Softs' warped and elongated R&B and strange attire made any kind of sense. Allen had by this time decided that he had to play electric guitar and Nolan disappeared.

Soft Machine's appearances at the underground club UFO were accompanied by psychedelic collaborations with Scottish sculptor-turned-liquid-light-show-alchemist, Mark Boyle. His visual sorcery was ground-breaking enough for him to project from within a tent – secreting techniques – and enhanced the band's curiosity value.

In 1967, the Soft Machine released their first – and indeed only – single, "Love Makes Sweet Music", produced by ex-Animals bassist Chas Chandler, who had produced "Hey Joe" for Jimi Hendrix (who was himself then living in London and had a reverence for the Softs). It was a deceptive little pop song with a far weirder B-side, "Feelin' Reelin' Squeelin'", sung by Ayers and produced by LA acid angel Kim Fowley.

This was to be the only official release from the original line-up. After a period in St Tropez compounding their modish repute by opening a production of Picasso's play *Desire Caught By The Tail*, and playing at a party thrown by Brigitte Bardot, Allen was refused re-entry into Britain on a visa technicality. His role in nascent Soft Machinery was over, and he went back to France to realize his **GONG** visions.

Soft Machine continued as a trio and spent months touring the States with the Jimi Hendrix Experience. Their first album SOFT MACHINE (1968) was recorded and mixed in around four days during their stay in New York. Here the character of the band was clarified: Ayers' gift for unorthodox, drifting pop structures framing his sinister but louche, ocean-deep vocal narrations; Ratledge's search for weird keyboard sonorities; and Wyatt's hoarse and perplexed vocal delivery. Of the songs – and they were very much songs – "We Did It Again" and "Why Are We Sleeping", Gurdjieff-inspired, dislocated epics of strangeness, were to surface again in Ayers' later work, while "A Certain Kind" was an early introduction to the charm of Wyatt's singing.

Ayers left after the album, disenchanted by life on the road, flogged his bass to Mitch Mitchell (drummer with Hendrix) and retreated to Ibiza. But disintegration was averted only when record company Probe demanded re-formation: the first album had been selling very well, and they wanted another. Wyatt and Ratledge invited old Canterbury cohort Hugh Hopper to play bass on SOFT MACHINE VOLUME TWO

(1969), and he stayed. The album was another treat of jazz-inflected pop, Hopper introducing his fuzz-bass to original effect (it was to tire in the years ahead), and Wyatt coming to the fore with conversational-style songs and voice on "Pataphysical Introduction" (reprised to thank everyone at the end) and a backwards delivery of the alphabet ("The Concise British Alphabet"). There was an innocence and magic to it all – nothing like this had been tried before.

Shortly after recording VOLUME TWO the new trio were approached by artist Peter Dockley to supply an original score for an experimental 'happening' at London's terminally hip, conically roofed Roundhouse theatre. *Spaced* was to involve ballet dancers and ex-army gymnasts stuck to and held within a three-dimensional geodesic dome of scaffolding. Wyatt, Hopper and Ratledge, aided at times by Hopper's brother Brian on sax, recorded chunks of instrumental mayhem to a brief requesting a suitably 'deranged and doomy' backing tape. These raw pieces were looped and stridently fucked around in collaboration with their recording engineer Bob Woolford; scissors, tape running through milk bottles on stairs, and the use of Stellavoxes and The Ferrograph (Britain's first domestically manufactured tape recorder) produced music colourfully radical enough to have boosted Soft Machine's avant-garde credibility still further. But it wasn't to be: after its week-long performance, *Spaced* came off stage and was forgotten, as were the band's tapes. They surfaced on US label Cuneiform as SPACED some 27 years later, digitally cleaned up and pruned by Woolford and a justified exhumation still in tune with the late 90s.

In 1970, the group annexed an entire front-line brass section for a brave experimental big-band tour. They were still, at this point, regarded as an underground 'rock' act, and effectively were the first to use instrumentation like this as more than a riff-strengthening device. However, it was a sign of things to come as Ratledge and Hopper championed jazz and instrumental directions. On THIRD (1970), sax player Elton Dean guested on a set that was entirely instrumental apart from Wyatt's enchanting side-long suite "The Moon In June".

The Soft Machine were midwifing that 1970s genre, jazz-rock fusion, with virtuoso soloing replacing song structures. The trend was confirmed by FOURTH (1971), after which Wyatt, voiceless on the album, was booted out, forming **Matching Mole** before embarking on his peculiar and wonderful solo career. Without him, the band was hugely diminished, the sense of anarchy and warmth entirely absent. Hopper stayed until SIX, Ratledge to SEVEN (both 1973), though nothing from this later series could be filed under rock. The band – in name only – continued until 1981.

An essential release for all late-period Softs fans was RUBBER RIFF (1997), a fourteen-track set on Blueprint, recorded in one day in London around August 1976. The line-up for the day was Karl Jenkins, John Etheridge, Roy Babbington, John

Marshall and Carol Barrat. The rooting around in the vaults has continued unabated with a seemingly unending flow of rare and unreleased recordings adding to the Soft Machine legacy. Most recently Cuneiform issued BACKWARDS (2002), featuring recordings spanning 1968-70, while Voiceprint unleashed FACELIFT: LIVE AT THE FAIRFIELD HALLS 1970 (2002). More archival gems are bound to follow.

⊙ **Soft Machine: The Peel Sessions** (1990; Strange Fruit).
BBC Radio recordings spanning 1969–71 on a fine double-CD pack. Contains the only recordings of the ambitious but short-lived seven-piece and a vocal improvisation by Wyatt of "The Moon In June" (to be treasured).

⊙ **Jet Propelled Photograph** (1987; Charly).
These are demo tapes from the original band – Allen, Ayers, Wyatt and Ratledge, and show why the Softs sounded comfortable alongside Syd Barrett-era Pink Floyd. A rough curio, but high on the list for Canterbury connoisseurs.

⊙ **Spaced** (1996; Cuneiform).
Seven pieces rescued from the 1969 theatrical soundtrack. Distended jams of bass, drums and Ratledge's Canterbury-copyright wild and windy organ solos combine with more laconic interludes, backwards loops and manipulation repetition to make an ambient success from this peculiar collage; fragments of "We Did It Again" peep through a loose Wyatt drum solo. Probably better as a document of Soft Machine's experimentation than it ever was as a soundtrack, this is a blueprint for many of Hopper's later recordings, notably "1984".

⊙ **Live At The Paradiso; 1969** (1995; Voiceprint).
Previously only available as a bootleg – and not one of the highest quality, with dodgy vocal levels and the bass and keyboards distorted and rough-sounding – this is essentially the raw, bleeding version of the VOLUME TWO set, glimpsed through the dry ice of 60s expressionism.

Chris Brook

SON VOLT

Formed Minnesota, 1994.

When **UNCLE TUPELO** broke up in early 1994, due to a breakdown in communications between the two chief singers and songwriters, critics and fans alike mourned the passing of a band considered the decade's great hope for country-rock. Disappointment was short-lived, though, as both figureheads quickly re-emerged at the helms of new groups, Jeff Tweedy firing the first salvo as **WILCO**, with a well-received debut album, A.M., in early 1995, and guitarist **Jay Farrar** countering a few months later with **Son Volt**'s TRACE, which, if anything, got more critical acclaim.

Farrar had begun assembling a band of his own the previous year, starting with bassist **Jim Boquist**, who had toured with Tupelo as a member of Joe Henry's band, and his multi-instrumentalist brother, **Dave Boquist** (guitar/banjo/fiddle/lap steel), and completing the line-up with former Tupelo drummer **Mike Heidorn**. At the outset, the members were based in three separate cities – New Orleans, St Louis and Minneapolis – but they came together in Minnesota for the recording of their debut in late 1994.

Travel featured high on that first album. Farrar had been spending a lot of time driving back and forth between New Orleans (where he had moved with his fiancée) and St Louis (where he eventually moved), and he claimed it was these drives along the Mississippi river that inspired TRACE. Not that the album exactly turned out rootsy. In fact, it alternates more or less evenly between mournful countryish numbers and straight-ahead rockers, the latter falling much closer to the alternative-rock norm than the more acoustic-orientated tunes.

Unsurprisingly, given the band's line-up, and the fact that all of the material is penned by Farrar, TRACE begged comparison with Uncle Tupelo, and with Wilco's A.M. On the whole, TRACE leans heavier on the moody, rural side of things, and if that's what you liked from Uncle Tupelo then this was your follow-up. It builds on the mother-band's country-indie-rock elements without ever sounding like a retread, and allows Farrar a far more individual voice. And it makes clear – as does Wilco's A.M. – that neither Farrar nor Tweedy need lean on each other to fashion worthwhile music.

This had obviously occured to Farrar by the time Son Volt's second album STRAIGHTAWAYS (1997) made it to the stores; the new album was more noticeably his own creation. Rather than simply stay in one place till he cheered up, he gave us an entire album of the depression that swirled around him as he drove from one lonesome town to the next.

WIDE SWING TREMELO (1998) was an altogether brighter affair, both in instrumental feel and lyrical pitch; at times it even verged on being 'groovy'. Little more was heard from Son Volt, although Farrar popped up again with more of the same on two solo albums, SEBASTOPOL (2001) and TERRIOR BLUES (2003). The latter was self-released and, as a result, was pleasingly self-indulgent. As well as the expected steel guitar misery, Farrar offered experimental noise pieces scattered amongst the twenty-plus cuts. Though Son Volt have never officially split, it would seem that Farrar has, at least for now, put the name behind him.

⊙ **Trace** (1995; Warners).
At its best when the material settles into a Neil Young-like acoustic mode, and Dave Boquist adds a country touch via his fiddle, lap steel or banjo. The more conventional rock tunes are less interesting.

Richie Unterberger

SONIC YOUTH

Formed New York, 1981.

"Crashing mashing intensified dense rhythms juxtaposed with filmic mood pieces. Evoking an atmosphere that could only be described as expressive fucked-up modernism. and so forth."
Thurston Moore

Sonic Youth formed amid the intensely creative and incestuous 'New York Noise' scene

of the early 80s, when **Thurston Moore** (guitars/vocals) got together with **Kim Gordon** (basses/vocals), a duo then joined by **Lee Ranaldo** (guitars/vocals) and **Richard Edson** (drums). An eponymous debut EP, released in 1982 on Glenn Branca's Neutral label, impressed the alternative scene with its uncharacteristically clean production, although "The Burning Spear" hinted at unusual things to come – it featured a power drill in the mix, recorded through a wah-wah pedal.

With new drummer **Bob Bert** joining in late 1982, Sonic Youth toured the East Coast with Swans and Lydia Lunch, but Bert was dropped at the end of the tour, reputedly for 'not being wild enough'. (His temporary replacement was **Jim Sclavunos**, who had previously played as part of Lunch's old band Teenage Jesus And The Jerks.)

Sonic Youth chose Wharton Tiers' eight-track studio to record their debut album, CONFUSION IS SEX (1983), which turned out to be a more lo-fi effort than the previous EP, even adding some rough cassette mixes to the final version. Barely noticed at the time, save for a couple of favourable reviews, it established the band as promising noise-makers without hardcore's self-important seriousness.

Bert returned to the line-up for a European tour, which introduced them to British audiences, while Paul Smith was so impressed by their radical sound that he set up the Blast First label specifically to release their second LP. BAD MOON RISING (1985) showed Sonic Youth at their most atmospheric and menacing, with its macabre references to Charles Manson on "Death Valley 69" and evocations of the underbelly of 60s West Coast counterculture. Although largely ignored in the US, it launched them as critical favourites in the UK.

As Bert quit to join **PUSSY GALORE** in mid 1985, his replacement **Steve Shelley** completed what remains Sonic Youth's core line-up, and they signed to Black Flag's label SST. However, 1986 saw them trashing their previous aura of studied cool, as their long-held passion for pop culture permeated both the LP, EVOL, and their sideline project **Ciccone Youth**. (The latter scored a dance-floor hit with a cover of Madonna's "Into The Groove(y)", recorded in collaboration with **The Minutemen** and fIRE-HOSE's **Mike Watt**.)

EVOL was Sonic Youth's politically aware and highly ironic version of pop music, a theme that continued on the follow-up, SISTER (1987). From its title's reference to late sci-fi writer Philip K. Dick, SISTER mixed science fiction with dream imagery, although the cyberpunk theme was expressed through the electric guitar rather than through the synthesizer.

Disagreements with SST over royalty payments, and their general attitude, led to Blast First obtaining a US distribution deal with Capitol subsidiary Enigma. Consequently, the more widely distributed double set, DAYDREAM NATION (1988), was their best-selling LP to date – and it was also their best.

During its recording, the Ciccone Youth alter ego was resurrected for THE WHITEY ALBUM (1988), a further attempt to recycle and subvert pop, highlighted by Kim Gordon's take on Robert Palmer's "Addicted To Love", which used a money-saving karaoke backing track of the original.

THE WHITEY ALBUM was regarded as a silly joke by most, but in 1990 Sonic Youth surprisingly leapt into the field of corporate rock, dumping Blast First in favour of Geffen/MCA. They responded to criticism by announcing that they saw embracing commercialism as a Warholian art-act. This led to GOO (1990), a more sophisticated expansion of their existing sounds. "Kool Thing", featuring Public Enemy's **Chuck D**, received extensive MTV airplay, and its video subverted the stereotypes of female images in contemporary rock and pop.

As well as shows with Public Enemy, Sonic Youth opened for Neil Young on his 1991 'Ragged Glory' tour, but then in turn brought less-established indie bands to support them – one of which was future Geffen signing Nirvana. DIRTY (1992) was comparatively overproduced, although Kim Gordon's politically abrasive songs like "Sugar Kane" and "Swimsuit Issue" masqueraded as pop to reach a wider youth audience. By contrast, EXPERIMENTAL JET SET, TRASH & NO STAR (1994) and WASHING MACHINE (1995) were like returns to old times, with sparse acoustic numbers alongside intense slices of psychedelia, along with (on WASHING MACHINE) a duet between Moore and The Breeders' **Kim Deal**.

Given the number and range of side-projects from band members – such as Moore's 1995 album PSYCHIC HEARTS; the short-lived, mysterious **Lucky Sperms** and **Mirror/Dash** outings; Kim Gordon's formation of **Free Kitten** with members of Pussy Galore, Pavement and The Boredoms; Lee Ranaldo's experimental LPs FROM HERE TO ETERNITY (1987) and EAST JESUS (1995); and Steve Shelley's alt.rock outfit **Two Dollar Guitar** – it's surprising that the band not only have time for diverse collaborations,

the release of three astounding improvised EPs on Moore's Sonic Youth Recordings label (1997), but also for frequent contributions to art exhibitions in New York, London and Europe. Following the birth of Coco Hayley Gordon-Moore, 1998 saw the release of what some critics touted as one of their best albums to date.

A THOUSAND LEAVES (1998) successfully combined the down'n'dirty noises that made them great in the first place with a new, mature vision. Guitar noise now came in delicate filigrees, replacing the Youth's earlier abrasiveness. The stand-out track, "Hits Of Sunshine", commemorated Allen Ginsberg, elder statesman of beat and the avant-garde. Elsewhere ("Sunday", "Hoarfrost" and "Wildflower Soul"), beautiful textures and feedback are coupled with more mature lyrics which seemed to reflect a quiet ecstasy and joy of life.

1998 also saw the release of SILVER SESSION (for Jason Knuth), 31 minutes of extraordinary art-noise released to commemorate the suicide of Jason Knuth – such a devoted Youth fan that he was sometimes called 'Sonic Knuth'. Try and imagine what a shimmering, vibrant swirling Jackson Pollock might sound like: that was the sound of the SILVER SESSION.

1999 found the band in experimental mood once again, recording GOODBYE 20TH CENTURY, a double CD of collaborations with the likes of renowned composer Pauline Oliveros, the ubiquitous **Jim O'Rourke** and turntablist Christian Marclay, the ensemble interpreting key works of the avant-garde, including pieces by John Cage, Steve Reich and Yoko Ono. Also that year disaster struck at their 4th July "This Ain't No Picnic" outdoor festival in Orange County, California, when a decade's worth of specially modified guitars and equipment was stolen. Despite a global appeal for information, they were never recovered. Making good their loss with a mix of new, borrowed and even older instruments, Sonic Youth returned to New York to work afresh on NYC GHOSTS AND FLOWERS (2000) at O'Rourke's studio, who had by then officially joined the group on bass and Powerbook, allowing Kim Gordon to concentrate on guitar.

Now having marked their twentieth anniversary, Sonic Youth have convincingly stated their case as possibly the most influential band on the US rock scene, and they still show no signs of slacking off, as proved by the release of 2002's brilliant MURRAY STREET.

⊙ **Bad Moon Rising** (1985; Blast First/Geffen).
Some of Sonic Youth's most skull-scraping moments appear here ("I'm Insane" and "Ghost Bitch"), but "I Love Her All The Time" is a simple, honest love song. The unavoidable highlight is the gory and theatrical "Death Valley 69".

⊙ **EVOL** (1986; Blast First/SST).
More accessible, but with a characteristic twist. "Star Power" and the Monroe-influenced "Marilyn Moore" are abrasive and iconoclastic, while the sardonic feedback fest of "Expressway To Yr Skull" (aka "The Crucifixion Of Sean Penn") has been described by Neil Young as the greatest guitar song ever written.

● **Daydream Nation** (1988; Blast First/DGC).
The classic Sonic Youth album for melody and ecstatic guitar noise – every song is excellent and varied, from the rebellious fuzz of "Teenage Riot" right through to "Trilogy", a brilliant evocation of urban horror and joy.

● **Goo** (1990; DGC).
"Dirty Boots" could have appeared on DAYDREAM NATION, but Goo diversifies from here on in – the Chuck D cameo on "Kool Thing", the lo-fi "Scooter + Jinx" and the Carpenters homage "Tunic (Song For Karen)". (Also released as a silly and scary video album.)

● **A Thousand Leaves** (1998; Geffen).
Picking up where WASHING MACHINE left off, this an older, wiser and less abrasive Youth. Beautiful lyrics, long subtle passages of guitar, gorgeous filigrees of sound. A must.

● **NYC Ghosts And Flowers** (2000; Geffen).
Drawing on the spoken word as much as soundscaping guitars and effects, this collection references the poetry and paintings of, amongst others, William Burroughs to craft a vibrant image of their adopted home town and inspiration.

Richard Fontenoy and Alun Severn

SOUL ASYLUM

Formed Minneapolis, Minnesota, 1981.

"I think it's all folk music, whether it's fast or slow. You've got three chords, an attitude, a story. I've always thought punk rock was folk music." Dave Pirner

Contrary to appearances, **Soul Asylum**'s turbulent history stretches much further back than their last couple of hit records. **Dave Pirner** (vocals/guitars) paid his dues in Minneapolis punk bands The Shits and then Loud Fast Rules, which featured **Dan Murphy** (guitars), **Karl Mueller** (bass) and finally **Pat Morley** (drums). They had no record deal but contributed songs to two Reflex cassette compilations, and gained a devoted following in their home city's underground clubs.

Changing name to Soul Asylum, the group recorded a nine-song EP, SAY WHAT YOU WILL ... EVERYTHING CAN HAPPEN (1984), showcasing a frantic cocktail of punk, country and trash rock. Produced by Bob Mould, its angst-fuelled and drunken sound had similarities to The Replacements' early output. Its rerelease as the album-length SAY WHAT YOU WILL, CLARENCE ... KARL SOLD THE TRUCK (1986) revealed further moments of brilliance, hinting that the band were capable of greater things.

After a brief split, Soul Asylum returned in 1985 with drummer **Grant Young** replacing Morley, and, with a string of furious live performances to their credit, they reunited with Bob Mould on MADE TO BE BROKEN (1986). Its more cohesive sound did not eliminate the stressed and frayed edges, and Pirner emerged as a talented lyricist, poignant and unsentimental. Further evidence of the band's prolific songwriting came later in the year with WHILE YOU WERE OUT, with the evocative "Closer To The Stars". It attracted attention from major label A&M, who signed the band in 1987 – although before any product was forthcoming, the band's Twin-Tone swansong, CLAM DIP AND OTHER DELIGHTS (1988), was released, featuring a pastiche of an album cover by A&M co-founder Herb Alpert.

Soul Asylum's three years at A&M saw the label's enthusiasm for HANGTIME (1988) turn first to wariness and then to monolithic indifference with SOUL ASYLUM AND THE HORSE THEY RODE IN ON (1990). Both albums were criminally ignored – HANGTIME featured the minor hit "Cartoon" and live favourite "A Little Too Clean", and Pirner was proven to be an expert storyteller on the follow-up's "Nice Guys Don't Get Paid" and "We Three".

It was too much for the band, and they drifted back into their day jobs – except for Pirner, who grew so depressed at the apparent end of his musical career that he became an outpatient at a psychiatric hospital. Furthermore, he believed that the band's loud rehearsals and performances had caused what he mistakenly took to be incipient deafness.

It was during this period that Pirner began writing more acoustic songs in order to preserve his hearing, and for Soul Asylum's first album on Columbia, 1992's GRAVE DANCERS UNION, he was the sole songwriter. Featuring the worldwide hit single "Runaway Train", the album's radio-friendly alternative rock rapidly broke them throughout and beyond America. Pirner, meanwhile, was rivalling Evan Dando as a tough, sensitive slacker teen idol, and the band's appeal extended to the White House, where Chelsea Clinton was apparently a big fan.

After another line-up change, which saw **Sterling Campbell** (drums) replace Young, the band began work on LET YOUR DIM LIGHT SHINE (1995), produced by Butch Vig, which trod an even more polished commercial path. There was nothing to match the success of "Runaway Train", but cracked, plaintive vocals and earthy songwriting saw Soul Asylum outlasting the short-lived popularity brought by a hit single. Next came CANDY FROM A STRANGER (1998), which contained the most powerful material the band had ever created. And, as if any proof were needed of the group's longstanding ability to produce quality rock music, select cuts of their most commercially satisfying songs were distilled into BLACK GOLD (2000), a 'best of' compilation concentrating mainly on their watershed Columbia years.

Inevitably, the album just provided a little breathing space for the various band members to indulge their own musical proclivities. Most noteworthy, Pirner created his first solo album, FACES AND NAMES (2002), a collection of songs influenced by the songwriter's move to New Orleans.

● **Hangtime** (1988; A&M).
A sadly ignored album, on which the band swing with ease between easy country-rock ("Ode") and the more aggressive "Cartoon", penned by Murphy. A fine collection of power-pop classics.

Soul Asylum And The Horse They Rode In On (1990; A&M).
Virtually buried by the label on its release, this excellent album is packed with superbly paced punk-influenced rock. Pirner's vocals are as emotional as ever, and the band seem incapable of writing a bad song.

Grave Dancers Union (1992; Columbia).
A glossy production and a larger proportion of mellow tunes. Despite losing their abrasive sound, this contains some excellent songs in "Black Gold", "Runaway Train", and the melancholy, lovelorn "Homesick". Reissued as a mid-price collection in 1999, with an additional half-dozen live tracks for good measure, this is an excellent introduction to their classic, laid-back rocking.

Essi Berelian

SOUNDGARDEN

Formed Seattle, 1986; split 1997.

Mastheads for the grunge generation, Soundgarden were initially dismissed by critics as mere metalheads: as vocalist/guitarist **Chris Cornell** put it, 'We never fitted. To the punk kids we were heavy metal and the heavy metal kids thought we were too punk rock'. Nevertheless, along with Nirvana and Green River, Soundgarden were the innovators, progenitors and paragons of everything grunge.

Soundgarden first started wielding the mighty tools of their trade when Cornell got together with mean-looking philosophy major **Kim Thayil** (guitar), **Hiro Yamamoto** (bass) and **Matt Cameron** (drums). Playing the Seattle circuit, they signed to local label Sub Pop, which they were partly responsible for forming, and released the two EPs, SCREAMING LIFE (1987) and FOPP (1988). A measure of the stature of these tracks is that, as among the earliest Sub Pop releases, they were a major factor in persuading Kurt Cobain to sign Nirvana to the label.

The Soundgarden approach was fundamentally inspired by heavy metal, although diverse influences like The Stooges, Led Zeppelin, the MC5 and Black

SOUNDGARDEN Screaming Life/Fopp

Sabbath pushed their music beyond the realms of cheesy riffs or exploding codpieces. The endemic darkness and moodiness of their sound and lyrics was distinctive and sincere, although much of their 1988 debut album, ULTRAMEGA OK, was sometimes too dense and tangled. The album was released on the SST label, whom they joined after Sub Pop had neglected to release their records in Europe.

Shifting to A&M, their second LP, LOUDER THAN LOVE (1989), was much more commercial, and boosted their sound with industrial-strength riffs, seismically grumbling bass, and Cornell's immense vocals. Yamamoto left the band shortly after its recording, and was replaced by **Jason Everman** and later **Ben Shepard**. Meanwhile, Cornell and Cameron embarked on a sideline project called **Temple Of The Dog** with former Mother Love Bone and future Pearl Jam members **Stone Gossard** and **Jeff Ament**. An eponymously titled album was released in the spring of 1991.

With the grunge movement firmly in the ascendant, BADMOTORFINGER (1991) provided Soundgarden with their breakthrough. They were now pared down to rocking beats, sparse and driving bass, sinuous guitar, colossal pop hooks and aggressive vocals. One highlight was the single "Jesus Christ Pose", a shimmering, cascading mass of stainless steel riffs and molten energy.

BADMOTORFINGER sold well, especially in the US, where it went Top 40, though it didn't quite manage to emulate the huge successes of Nirvana, Mudhoney or Pearl Jam. In the UK, heavy-metal magazine *Kerrang!* voted it Album of the Year, but tours with both Neil Young and Guns N' Roses broadened their appeal to the point where the media began to omit them from the list of definitive contemporary guitar bands.

Under the name **Hater**, Cameron and Shepard released a self-titled album in 1993, before Soundgarden returned the following year with the release of their finest and most diverse album, SUPERUNKNOWN (1994). Absorbing everything from blues through to The Beatles, the band stripped down and rebuilt their songwriting style on a base built from the best of 70s rock and psychedelia. A US #1 million-selling album of amazing virtuosity and elasticity, it finally gave them similar levels of critical and commercial standing.

Although their 1996 release, DOWN ON THE UPSIDE, met with a more muted response from critics, its more streamlined brand of pop-metal again soared up the US and UK charts, and led to headline appearances at the summer's *Lollapalooza* tour, with Metallica and the Ramones.

It all ended far too soon though, as, in 1997, touring and the rock'n'roll lifestyle in general led to the band collapsing under the pressure. The posthumous retrospective A-SIDES (1998) nicely sums up their decade of angst, gloom and rock'n'roll. Since then Cornell has released his first solo album, EUPHORIA MORNING (1999), and has been connected with Rage Against The Machine as a possible vocal replacement for the departed Zack de la Rocha. The other members continue to make low-key contributions to a variety of projects.

- ● **Louder Than Love** (1989; A&M).
  On which Soundgarden almost accidentally stumble onto the magic sound of grooving rhythms, great hooks and chunky guitars. This would have stamped them as the biggest and bestest Seattle band – had anyone noticed.

- ● **Badmotorfinger** (1991; A&M).
  A glorious reinvention of metal, featuring the classics "Jesus Christ Pose", "Outshined" and the abyss-like doom of "Room A Thousand Years Wide".

- ● **Superunknown** (1994; A&M).
  A seventy-minute masterpiece, and their best to date, with "Limo Wreck", "The Day I Tried To Live" and the suicidal depths of "Mailman", while "Fell On Black Days" features the most fuzzed-up piece of psychedelic guitar genius this side of Hendrix.

Andrew Stone

THE SOUNDTRACK OF OUR LIVES

Formed Gothenburg, Sweden, 1994.

Emerging in 1994 from the debris of cult Swedish rockers Union Carbide Productions, **Ebbot Lundberg** (vocals), **Ian Person** and **Bjorn Olsson** (both guitars) considered both "Jehovah Sunrise" and "Nobody Never" as band names before they stole a line of lyrics from their own song Firmament Vacation to become **The Soundtrack Of Our Lives** and set about creating the long overdue Viking Acid Rock scene.

Lundberg in particular had been moving away from UCP's brew of Beefheart-edged punk rock weirdness in search of something less frantic and, ganging up with **Karl Gustafsson**'s bass, **Martin Hederos**' keyboards and **Fredrik Sandsten**'s drums, he hammered out a modern take on the acid-tongued psychedelia of San Francisco's golden age. Their first outings, the "Four Ages" single on Dolores records and HOMO HABILIS BLUES EP on Telegram created a groundswell of local approval before the release of their debut album WELCOME TO THE INFANT FREEBASE in 1996, which picked up *Newcomer of the Year* at the Swedish Grammys.

Olsson walked out in 1997, depriving the band of a pivotal founder-member, a songwriter and an energetic guitarist in one blow. **Mattias Bärjed** came on board from the Nymphet Noodlers as a capable replacement in plenty of time to make his presence felt on the follow-up EXTENDED REVELATION FOR THE PSYCHIC WEAKLINGS OF WESTERN CIVILISATION, which stumbled, smiling blissfully, into the shops 1998. A child born of 70s space rock it was blessed with all the brain-caressing mystical meaninglessness that implies, from overlong titles through to the meandering marvellous music.

Dreamy and melancholic, the first two albums celebrate the band's interest in psychedelia, late-60s Stones, 70s rock and the chemical reactions that result in the mind's eye from their fusion. TSOOL's well-crafted music tips its hat towards almost every status

The Soundtrack Of Our Lives, whistling while they work

rock act of the last thirty years, confidently blending influences from the Beatles, Pink Floyd and The Who. The Soundtrack's skill and charm, however, lie in the translation: imitating the greats could easily sink into karaoke, but TSOOL are mature enough musicians to create a familiar but feel-good rock-out that evokes the nicer effects of nostalgia without seeming to wallow in the past.

The band spent much of 1998 and the next year on the road, building up a fan base in the UK and across Europe, adding skills and growing band unity on tour with Hurricane no.1 and The Cardigans. They played the 1998 Glastonbury festival (where Lundberg broke a leg after becoming stuck in that year's quite exceptional mudbath) and even managed to fulfil a dream by playing support to The Rolling Stones in Sweden.

2002's album BEHIND THE MUSIC saw the acid beginning to wear off slightly and the music orbiting a little closer to planet Earth. They cut the formula to a more accessible level, to feed a British market primed by fellow Swedes The Hives, and the rest of the new retro-rockers. With the album endorsed by the Gallagher brothers as 'the best to come out in the last six years', they needed do little except show up and play. Audiences went mad for the hard-driving sound and solid melodies of the newer tracks, whipped up by what had become a storming live act. Lundberg the showman – a bearded and kaftanned flashback from the 60s – commanded an unusual devotion from the black T-shirts and denim of his flock, rousing the indie rabble with the roughened and raucous stage versions of his satisfyingly round studio-crafted songs.

The band's ability to produce both convincing string-accompanied ballads and good old high-decibel amp-leaping antics is also seducing America. TSOOL may have taken a while to make their mark internationally, but it seems that now everyone wants a piece of the new Scando-rock action.

⊙ **Extended Revelation For The Psychic Weaklings Of Western Civilisation** (1998/WEA).
Take careful note of the title, turn off your mind, relax and float downstream on an hour-long trip through the ether.

Annebella Pollen

THE SOUP DRAGONS

Formed Glasgow, Scotland, 1985; disbanded 1992.

The **Soup Dragons** formed when **Sean Dickson** (vocals/guitars) and **Jim McCulloch** (guitar), both of whom had played in Scottish band **BMX BANDITS**, met up with **Ross A. Sinclair** (drums) and **Sushil K. Dade** (bass) and decided to name themselves after one of the characters from the classic spaced-out kids programme, *The Clangers*. Their first real exposure came with their contribution of "Pleasantly Surprised" to the *NME*'s C86 compilation tape, an attempt to band together many disparate independent groups into something approaching a scene. It also featured another Scottish

band, Primal Scream, comparisons to whom were to dog The Soup Dragons throughout their career.

In 1986 their first proper release, "Whole Wide World", got them the attention of ex-Wham! manager Jazz Summers, who set them up with their own label, Raw TV, in time for their next single "Hang Ten!" Both were blasts of Buzzcocks-style frantic guitars and youthful exuberance. "Can't Take No More" (1987) saw the same type of spiky pop freneticism, but was followed by the much gentler and summery jangle of "Soft As Your Face", both of which saw The Soup Dragons scrape into the UK Top 75.

Another single, the psychedelic "The Majestic Head" (1988), clinched them a deal with Sire. But the next release, "Kingdom Chairs" (1988), promptly disappeared without a trace. Their debut album, THIS IS OUR ART (1988), was subtitled with the preposterously pretentious shoutline 'Useless, Boring, Impotent, Elitist and Very, Very, Beautiful'. Although it rounded up the preceding three singles and added another batch of guitar-spiked tunes, it too vanished with barely a flutter.

Then the comparisons with that other band really took hold. Primal Scream's second, eponymously titled album saw them indulge in some raucous Stooges-influenced rock – a formula which The Dragons' next two singles, "Backwards Dog" and "Crotch Deep Trash" (1989), followed a little too closely for comfort. By 1990 the indie-dance/baggy scene had exploded, headed by the likes of The Stone Roses, Happy Mondays and The Charlatans, and Primal Scream had unleashed LOADED, a fusion of guitars and dance beats. The Soup Dragons remained in pursuit.

Drummer Sinclair departed and **Paul Quinn** was drafted in as replacement in time for "Mother Universe" (1990), which pinched a Marc Bolan riff and added a funky drummer backbeat. The second album, LOVEGOD (1990), was full of similar dance-inflected tunes and eventually proved to be the band's most successful album; a track from it, "I'm Free", a reworked Stones number with a dance beat and some toasting from reggae singer Junior Reid, shot into the UK Top 10, sold well worldwide, and was, at one point, the most-requested video on MTV. But by now they had been overshadowed by Primal Scream's epic SCREAMADELICA. The Soup Dragons' take on the indie-dance phenomenon had failed to convince and the accusations of bandwagon-jumping flew thick and fast.

There was to be one last change of direction, as they reverted to a more guitar-based sound for "Divine Thing" and HOTWIRED (1992). Neither made any impact and no one really noticed as The Soup Dragons were dropped, split up and drifted away to join various other bands.

⊙ **Lovegod** (1990; Raw TV).
It's all there: the funky backbeat, the spacey keyboards, the vague and vacuous lyrics – but it all sounds rather stilted, like someone had already written the tunes and grafted on the dancey bits later.

James Sutherland

SOUTHSIDE JOHNNY & THE ASBURY JUKES

Formed Asbury Park, New Jersey, 1972.

Back in the early 70s, when Bruce Springsteen was being touted as the new Bob Dylan, interest focused on his New Jersey upbringing and fellow musicians from Asbury Park, like Miami Steve Van Zandt and **Southside Johnny**. Although he got somewhat submerged through his association with Springsteen, unassuming Southside Johnny is a man who performs for the sheer love of it. Achieving world domination was never an item on his agenda.

Born Johnny Lyons, Southside Johnny was an R&B fanatic first and foremost, and emerged in the late 60s with The Blackberry Booze Band. Then, in 1972, he teamed up with schoolfriends **Billy Rush** (guitar), **Kevin Kavanaugh** (keyboards), **Allan 'Doc' Berger** (bass) and **Kenneth 'Mr Popeye' Pentifallo** (drums) to form **The Asbury Jukes**, a band supplemented by a horn section drawn from various sources.

Gigging constantly throughout New Jersey and its environs, the group cut LIVE AT THE BOTTOM LINE in 1976, and whetted the appetite of Epic Records. They were signed, and their major-label debut, I DON'T WANNA GO HOME (1976), was produced by Miami Steve (who also wrote the title track) and included the Springsteen composition "The Fever", with guest contributions from R&B vocalist Lee Dorsey and Ronnie Spector.

While this album convinced many that New Jersey was indeed a hotbed of untapped talent, the consensus was that Southside Johnny & The Asbury Jukes were best experienced live. The follow-up, THIS TIME IT'S FOR REAL (1977), only served to give weight to this conviction, as the group had toured in the meantime, showing European audiences their rollicking blend of R&B and soul. By now the group were distanced from Springsteen, but they still suffered from the backlash against him as punk took hold in the UK. Consequently, HEARTS OF STONE (1978) was not a big seller, and Epic decided against renewing their contract.

Unbowed by this setback, the group now boasted a full-time front-line brass section that comprised **Carlo Novi** and **Stan Harrison** (saxophones), **Ricki Gazda** and **Tony Palligrosi** (trumpets) and **Richard Rosenberg** (trombone), as well as additional guitarist **Joel Gramolini** and replacement drummer **Steve Becker**. After two albums – THE JUKES (1979) and LOVE IS A SACRIFICE (1980) – for new label Mercury, they released their defining moment, the live double LP, REACH OUT AND TOUCH THE SKY, in 1981. Complete with a ferocious Sam Cooke medley, here was a set that could not disappoint, but such was Southside Johnny's association with rock's old guard that it was only a moderate seller. Another live album followed, TRASH IT UP! LIVE (1983), but this was little more than an

extension of REACH OUT AND TOUCH THE SKY, offering little new.

After cutting IN THE HEAT (1984) for Polydor, Southside Johnny moved on to RCA for AT LEAST WE GOT SHOES in 1986, which featured a lyrical revival of The Left Banke's classic "Walk Away Renee", as well as "Hard To Find" and "You Can't Count On Me". The same year, Southside Johnny organized a charity single, "We Got The Love", under the collective umbrella of Jersey Artists For Mankind.

For the next five years or so, Southside Johnny concentrated on his forte of playing live, but in 1991 he returned with a new album, BETTER DAYS. Sounding relaxed and in full control, he covered Springsteen's "Walk You All The Way Home", while there were several contributions from Miami Steve. Further album releases have been scarce, although the band have continued to tour extensively – with a classic live performance captured on the double-CD release "SPITTIN' FIRE" (1997) – and a worthwhile studio set, ROAD TO JUKESVILLE, appeared in 2002. Joel Gramolini is working as Joel Cage these days, playing folk music.

⊙ **Reach Out And Touch The Sky** (1981; Mercury).
Hot and sweaty, here are the hits lovingly punched out with all the fervour that can be mustered.

⊙ **Better Days** (1991; RCA).
Sterling and stirring – if he had made this album twenty years ago his career might have been very different.

⊙ **All I Want Is Everything** (1993; Rhino).
A neat roundup that offers the salient moments in one perfectly formed package.

Hugh Gregory

SPACEMEN 3

Formed Rugby, England, 1982; disbanded 1990.

Guitarists **Sonic Boom** (real name Pete Kember) and **Jason Pierce** were the key players in **Spacemen 3**, a band whose enduring influence and fan base greatly exceeded the little commercial recognition they received during their real-time existence.

Spacemen 3 gained notoriety within the local Rugby scene for gigs which more often than not climaxed with twenty minutes of shimmering, narcotic guitar noise. Their music consisted largely of recycled guitar licks and lyrics, taken from the tail end of the psychedelic era, mixed liberally with howling feedback and walls of distorted guitar, aided by a battery of suitably vintage pedals and effects.

As well as Sonic and Pierce, the early line-up contained **Pete 'Bassman' Bain** (bass, naturally), and **Natty Brooker** on drums. An early demo tape, recorded in January 1986, was released as the bootleg TAKING DRUGS TO MAKE MUSIC TO TAKE DRUGS TO, summing up the group's philosophy and showcasing their hypnotic garage psychedelia. Their first album, SOUND OF CONFUSION, was released in July 1986, and the title track appeared as the first single in December, then reappeared again the next year on

THE PERFECT PRESCRIPTION, the second – and greatest – album, which also featured the band's classic preceding 12"s, "Walkin' With Jesus" and "Transparent Radiation". This pattern of recycling was to remain a feature: even cover versions, such as Bo Diddley's "It's Alright", were frequently re-recorded and rereleased as the band's fortunes, and hence recording quality, changed.

In 1989 the group released PLAYING WITH FIRE, a more mature but unsettlingly miscellaneous album, with "Lord Can You Hear Me", a plaintive cry for redemption, sitting next to "Suicide", a ten-minute squall of beats and heavy guitars. The stand-out track was "Revolution", a guitar-heavy but softly spoken call for drug legalization, which was covered by Seattle band Mudhoney, who altered the lyrics to parody the Spacemen's drug usage. Sonic, unsurprisingly, failed to see the funny side, and retaliated with a cover of Mudhoney's "When Tomorrow Hits", a song initially buried on a fanzine single before sneaking out on the next album, RECURRING.

RECURRING was released at the start of 1991, by which time Pierce had left to concentrate on what initially began as a solo project, SPIRITUALIZED. The use of Spacemen 3's name on the early releases and promotional material for Spiritualized incensed Sonic, who announced that he was breaking up the band. RECURRING was to be a testament to the perilous relationship between the two men. Sonic began his A-side with the epic "Big City" (also released as a single), a bubbling, disco-inspired trawl through a psychedelic suburbia. Subsequent tracks highlighted the group's predilection for recycling, with an 'orchestral mix' of "Just To See You Smile", previously released in 1989, at which point it had been a reworking of the even earlier "Honey". Pierce included "Hypnotized", a 1989 single which had highlighted his own songwriting talents, and had perhaps paved the way for his work in Spiritualized. Other songs on Pierce's B-side included "Feel So Sad", which eventually became a full-blown orchestral single for Spiritualized.

Sonic's post-Spacemen projects, including **Spectrum** (also the title of his first solo LP) and **Experimental Audio Research (E.A.R.)** with members of **MY BLOODY VALENTINE** and **God**, have been largely ignored, despite a high-profile commitment to unusual packaging. He continues to record to this day, and has even collaborated with such underground luminaries as the **SILVER APPLES**.

Ironically, Spiritualized themselves have been elevated to giddy heights, receiving increasingly rapturous praise for their majestic albums and live shows, effectively putting paid to speculation that each writing partner would flounder without the other's creative input. A reunion seems unlikely, although Spacemen 3's legacy lives on in a thriving bootleg and rerelease scene.

- **Sound Of Confusion** (1986; Fire).
  A collection of pulsating, primal rock sounds, hugely influential on the much-hyped 'shoe-gazing' scene.

- **The Perfect Prescription** (1987; Fire).
  The group's claim to classic status rests here, with "Take Me To The Other Side", "Walkin' With Jesus" and "Transparent Radiation". Guitar noise has rarely been so entrancing.

- **Playing With Fire** (1989; Fire).
  Another supreme outing; and, if not their finest moment, certainly their most diverse.

- **Recurring** (1991; Fire).
  This set documents the rift between Sonic and Jason. You basically get two albums for the price of one, with Jason presenting the template for Spiritualized and Sonic cementing the more electronic sound that he was to employ on subsequent solo releases.

- **Forged Prescriptions** (2003; Space Age).
  This double CD collects a whole bunch of outtakes and demos from the time of THE PERFECT PRESCRIPTION and stands as one of the better of numerous 'oddity' collections on the market.

Jonathan Bell

SPANDAU BALLET

Formed London, 1979; disbanded 1990.

"Like a lot of bands that have come up since the punk boom, we're conceptualists first and musicians second." Gary Kemp

With their kilts, frilly shirts and billowing scarves, **Spandau Ballet** were at the forefront of the New Romantic movement at the beginning of the 1980s, making a successful transition into the pop mainstream in later years. Formed from the ashes of failed school combo The Makers, the band comprised **Tony Hadley** (vocals), **Gary Kemp** (guitar), his brother **Martin Kemp** (bass), **Steve Norman** (guitar/saxophone) and **John Keeble** (drums), with ex-schoolmate Steve Dagger as their manager. Dagger was a pivotal figure in the band's early career, turning down a lucrative 1979 offer from Island Records and orchestrating an eye-catching campaign to promote his charges.

During 1980, the group performed live in London's Scala Cinema and on board the Thames-moored battleship HMS *Belfast* as part of an unconventional UK tour; and at the end of the year, after setting up their own label, Reformation, with backing from Chrysalis, they released their debut single "To Cut A Long Story Short". Already established as key figures in the glamorous Blitz clubbing scene, they had enough impetus to ensure it was a hit, and Spandau Ballet became the first of the New Romantics to break into the UK Top 40.

The band's debut album, JOURNEYS TO GLORY (1981), ushered in a period in which they became the hippest group in Britain. They teamed up with Britfunk outfit Beggar & Co. on the #3 smash, "Chant No. 1", pioneering the extended-mix 12" single, previously the preserve of disco music. The Spandau sound in this period was experimental electronic pop with leanings towards white funk, influenced by their love of the new London club culture. A shift to a more commercial style on DIAMOND (1982) was given the thumbs down by fans. They had their first failure when the ballad "She Loved Like Diamond" fell short of the Top 40, prompting them to bring in production maestro Trevor Horn to remix "Instinction". Horn's panoramic pyrotechnics restored them to the UK Top 10, and from that point on Spandau Ballet became an out-and-out pop band.

Ditching the already passé New Romantic look, they took to wearing Armani suits, and Gary Kemp's songwriting became less abstract as they began to look towards the lucrative American market. With Tony Swain and Steve Jolley – who also worked with Madness and Bananarama – taking over production duties, Spandau Ballet embarked on the most successful period of their career. They topped the UK album chart with TRUE (1983) and took its moody late-night title track to #1 across Europe, and later #4 in America. It was a personal triumph for Kemp, who admitted, 'I've always got a tingle up my spine listening to Marvin Gaye, or a song like "Easy" by the Commodores. My ambition was to make a record like that.'

Further success came with their fourth album, PARADE (1984), which continued the smooth, radio-friendly sound they had now perfected. It gave them four more Top 20 hits in the UK, but the lack of consistent success in the States caused concern, and ultimately led to a bitter legal dispute with Chrysalis that left the band sidelined for eighteen months, their only public activity in 1985 being a lacklustre set at Live Aid.

Retaining the Reformation banner after leaving Chrysalis, Spandau Ballet signed to Sony (then still known as CBS) and re-emerged in 1986. After a false start with the vacuous "Fight For Ourselves", they found themselves back in the Top 10 with the semi-acoustic "Through The Barricades" (Kemp's best song since "True") and its accompanying album, THROUGH THE BARRICADES (1986). This was to be their last major success. A ludicrous change of image

in 1988, when all five band members donned leather gear to promote their "Raw" single, proved a disaster, and the final album, HEART LIKE A SKY (1989), failed to reverse their declining fortunes.

Although the band has never officially split, each member has drifted into solo activity and, to date, no one has suggested a full reunion – though Hadley, Keeble and Norman have graced the nostalgia circuit as a trio. The Kemp brothers won acclaim for their lead roles in the 1989 movie *The Krays*, and both have continued to act to this day, with Martin having reacquainted himself with superstardom thanks to his role in the British soap opera *Eastenders*. Hadley signed a solo deal with EMI in 1992, releasing a clutch of uninspiring singles, and returned five years later with a high-profile album of cover versions (including, perversely, "Save A Prayer" by old rivals Duran Duran). Despite a generous record company promotional push, it achieved only modest success and confirmed that, like so many before them, Spandau Ballet will always struggle to live down their 80s excesses.

Journeys To Glory (1981; Chrysalis).
Now held up as a prime example of New Romantic naffness, this debut actually contains some cracking tunes, notably "To Cut A Long Story Short". Hadley's voice may be hideously bombastic in places, and of course the whole thing takes itself far too seriously, but it does have a youthful vigour which sets it apart from their later airbrushed epics.

The Best Of Spandau Ballet (1991; Chrysalis).
This inevitable retrospective is something of a mixed bag, but if you can ignore the dross ("Fight For Ourselves", "Highly Strung", etc), the highlights – "Instinction", "Chant No. 1", "True" – remain surprisingly enjoyable.

Jonathan Kennaugh

SPARKLEHORSE

Formed Richmond, Virginia, 1995.

If ever an ambitious friend leaves equipment at your home for any length of time, it might pay to heed the initiative of innovative musician **Mark Linkous**. The generosity of friend and ex-Camper Van Beethoven frontman, David Lowery – depositing his eight-track recorder with Linkous for two years while touring – enabled the maverick Linkous to galvanize his myriad ideas, and **Sparklehorse** was born.

Singer/guitarist Linkous was brought up in Virginia on a diet of country and bluegrass music, mainly Johnny Cash and George Jones records, but he became fascinated by rock'n'roll on hearing The Animals' "House Of The Rising Sun". Parading the homespun charm, Linkous fell for a sound that was 'louder than any dirt bike', and from this graduated to British punk and the heavier blues-influenced sound of Led Zeppelin. As a result, he formed his own first band, **Dancing Hoods** – an act at one point tipped to succeed the Minnesota legends, The Replacements. Recording a pair of independently issued albums, the group unsuccessfully pursed a major deal in LA and soon fizzled out. Mark then

Mark Linkous – sparkly and on a horse

returned to Virginia to beget a short-lived pop-based band, **The Johnson Family** (later **Salt Chunk Mary**).

Sparklehorse's early talents gave rise to a short-term deal with Slow River Records and the exquisite debut single "Spirit Ditch"; it wasn't long before this early incarnation of Sparklehorse – featuring more of Linkous's friends in support capacities, most notably **Bob Rupe** (bass, guitars), **David Charles** (bass, percussion, mixing), **Mike Lucas** (pedal steel) and **Johnny Hott** on drums – had signed a deal with Capitol. The album Vivadixiesubmarinetransmissionplot was recorded and produced mainly at Static King and Sound of Music studios in Virginia ('cow noise was often a problem') and emerged late in 1995.

Positive public response to the album was as immediate as it was deserved; during 1996 three of its more up-tempo tracks were pulled as singles and widely featured on radio playlists: "Hammering The Cramps", "Some Day I Will Treat You Good" and particularly "Rainmaker". This suggested that success for the supposedly quiet, retiring Mark Linkous now seemed a distinct possibility.

However, following a London concert, Linkous unwisely mixed prescription drugs and collapsed in his hotel room. When he was discovered some twelve hours later, having suffered a cardiac arrest, it appeared that he had befallen a fate similar to luminaries such as Nick Drake before him. Luckily Linkous pulled through this ordeal, but not without extensive surgery and rest in London.

The ordeal seemed to spur Mark Linkous and Sparklehorse forward. The group's second album, GOOD MORNING SPIDER (1998), featured material inspired by his 'stay' in Britain: the opening track, "Pig" documented his frustration at his predicament, while "Saint Mary" proffered public thanks to those that had helped. On the whole, the second album was a less absorbing affair than its predecessor, but was still spilling over with fine songs, notably splendid singles "Maria's Little Elbows" and "Sick Of Goodbyes". In the US the band had become a more than convincing live draw, an impressive touring band now consisting of guitarist **Paul Watson**, drummer **Scott Minor** and **Scott Fitzsimmons** on double bass.

For the majestic third Sparklehorse album, IT'S A WONDERFUL LIFE (2001), Linkous had added **Dave Fridmann**'s piano and bass, **Jane Scarpantoni**, **Joan Wasser** and **Margaret White** on cellos, with **Adrian Utley** on various unlikely instruments. On top of this, the not inconsiderable vocal talents of **Polly Harvey**, **Tom Waits** and The Cardigans' **Nina Persson** added to the record's uniqueness. Mark Linkous appeared to be experimenting with grades of light in Sparklehorse's mood, eccentric lyrics about livestock notwithstanding. Most recently Linkous was spotted supporting Will Oldham's band at London's Barbican Centre in 2003.

⊙ **Vivadixiesubmarinetransmissionplot** (1995; Capitol).
An unexpected marvel: the distorted melancholia of "Spirit Ditch" or "Homecoming Queen" and the tortured power of "Someday I Will Treat You Good" mesh to create a fascinating, poignant picture of the record's protagonist.

It's A Wonderful Life (2001; Parlophone).
Babies and birds replace horses and spiders: It's A
WONDERFUL LIFE is almost as fabulous as Linkous's first – but
not quite.

Jeremy Simmonds

SPARKS

Formed Los Angeles, 1968.

O riginally called Halfnelson, **Sparks** were
nobodies on their home turf who somehow
came to the British public consciousness with their
startling debut single, "This Town Ain't Big Enough
For Both Of Us" in 1974. Brothers **Ron** (keyboards)
and **Russell Mael** (bass/vocals) – who turned out to
be male models from LA – galvanized a placid *Top
Of The Pops*, one staring manically over tin-pot keyboards with a Chaplin moustache, the other prancing
his way through a vocal that was charming, if completely incomprehensible.

Under the guidance of Todd Rundgren associate
Muff Winwood, Sparks stripped and polished their act,
and Ron Mael composed a string of glittering, bub-
blegum-catchy lyrics and tunes. The resultant albums,
KIMONO MY HOUSE (1974) and PROPAGANDA
(1974), briefly hypnotized the British and European
pop audience. Their musical appeal fell somewhere
between Roxy Music and The Rubettes – a high-
speed, barely decipherable, falsetto vocal over a gutsy,
keyboard-driven backing.

The lyrics, thankfully printed on
the album sleeves, showed them to
be sharply satirical through dazzling
wordplay. However, after parting
with Muff Winwood, there was a
noticeable lack of bite on the Tony
Visconti-produced third album,
INDISCREET (1975). Despite being
voted 'Brightest Hope For 1975' in
Melody Maker, it was their final year
in the public eye. After a misconceived garage-rock album recorded
with expensive session musicians,
BIG BEAT (1976), they left Island
and returned to LA to lick their
wounds.

In 1979 Sparks returned out of
the blue in the new guise of electronic disco artists, having
dance-floor and chart success with
songs like the Giorgio Moroder-
produced "Number One Song In
Heaven" for Virgin. Since then
they have found a niche as a cult
band, especially in France, and
continue performing to sellout
crowds. Famous for flippant
frivolities, they continued to find
audiences, as fans of bands like
Depeche Mode and the Pet Shop
Boys discovered their roots.

In 1995 the Maels caused another minor ripple in
the pop mainstream when "When Do I Get To Sing
'My Way'?" reached the UK Top 40. An enduring,
if wearying, delight in wordplay was demonstrated
in the title of their most techno-embracing album,
GRATUITOUS SAX AND SENSELESS VIOLINS (1995).
Their European success continued unabated across
the continent with Virgin (Germany) issuing
PLAGIARISM (1997) to great acclaim. As befits the
Mael brothers' mentality, this album was no ordinary
affair, consisting of eighteen reworked Sparks
favourites, some orchestral, some as collaborative
ventures with the likes of Jimmy Somerville and
Faith No More. However, Virgin declined to release
it in the UK and the album eventually crept out there
on minor label Roadrunner. More Sparks oddness
followed with BALLS (1999) and LIL' BEETHOVEN
(2002), a collection of adventurous 'mini-operettas'.

Sparks show no signs of slowing down, and,
thankfully, no signs of diluting their vision for the
sake of the rest of the music industry.

● **Kimono My House** (1974; Island).
Although too much of the humour resides in the lyric
sheet rather than in the music, this is their best album, showcasing their tongue-in-chic bubblegum-pop concept.

● **Profile: The Ultimate Sparks Collection**
(1991; Rhino).
This is a major package covering twenty years and – incredibly – fifteen albums, pulling together the dance-mode Sparks
with the glam-gum stuff and all manner of US oddities.

Tony Drayton

Sparks Russ and Ron: mavericks to a man

SPEAR OF DESTINY

Formed London, 1982; disbanded and regrouped 1986–94 and 1996.

After post-punk band **THEATRE OF HATE** split up, **Kirk Brandon** (vocals/lyrics/guitar) and **Stan Stammers** (bass) formed **Spear Of Destiny** as the group's continuation. In fact, the run-off grooves of Theatre Of Hate's final single, "Eastworld", had foreshadowed this new incarnation with the message 'Welcome to the Spear of Destiny'.

Brandon, again the band's forthright spokesperson, recruited **Chris Bell** (drums) and **Lascelles James** (saxophone), and worked on new material, for the first Spear Of Destiny album, GRAPES OF WRATH (1983). Much anticipated, it disappointed critics, and Brandon himself, who admitted that its lacklustre production hadn't helped. James and Bell both left and were replaced by drummer **Dolphin Taylor** (ex-Tom Robinson Band and Stiff Little Fingers), **Neil Pyzer** (keyboards/organ/saxophone) and former Theatre Of Hate saxophonist **John 'Boy' Lennard**.

Lennard was soon replaced in turn by **Mickey Donnelly**, and **Alan St. Claire** was brought in as a second guitarist as Spear Of Destiny reached its creative peak with the critically acclaimed ONE EYED JACKS (1984). A mixture of poignant, soulful ballads and raucous rock'n'roll anthems, it racked up healthy sales, although its single releases – "Prisoner Of Love" and "Liberator" – fared less well.

Determined to prove any doubters wrong, the group undertook no fewer than three major tours during 1985 alone, on which they garnered a reputation as one of the finest live outfits around. The intensity of their shows was captured perfectly on their third studio LP, WORLD SERVICE (1985). It entered the UK charts at #11 but had been continually delayed by CBS, who had waited in vain for a Top 40 single to promote it. As a result, a bitter band and label parted company, and Spear Of Destiny disbanded.

Brandon re-emerged in late 1986 with a new line-up, devoid of all previous personnel. New recruits consisted of brothers **Pete** and **Steve Barnacle** (drums and bass respectively), ex-Sector 27 guitarist **Stevie Blanchard** and German keyboard player **Volker Janssen**. Signed to Virgin subsidiary 10 Records, they soon reaped dividends from Brandon's decision to go for a more guitar-orientated sound when, in March 1987, Spear of Destiny finally logged up their first UK Top 20 hit with "Never Take Me Alive".

ADAM AND THE ANTS' Marco Pirroni and then **Mick Proctor** took over on guitar before the release of the band's fourth LP, OUTLAND (1987). It was far from the uncomplicated and straightforward affair that Brandon had promised, but it quickly became their bestseller. Sellout shows followed this chart success, including a support slot to U2 at Wembley Stadium, but disaster struck on the eve of the band's appearance at that year's Reading Festival, as Brandon contracted an obscure blood disorder which forced the band to put all activity on hold for the best part of a year. His return coincided with the comeback of Alan St Claire, and the debut of ex-JoBoxers bassist **Chris Bostock**.

"So In Love" became the band's second UK Top 40 single, but its parent album, THE PRICE (1988), was released to largely negative reviews, and even another sellout tour could not halt the band's commercial decline. It came as little surprise when Brandon, still suffering from the effects of his illness, announced the split for what many believed would be the final time.

Yet in 1990, Brandon reunited with Stammers for a three-night sellout residency at London's Marquee venue, demonstrating that Spear Of Destiny had not been forgotten. The following summer saw Brandon, alongside Stammers, Janssen and Pete Barnacle, undertake a short tour under the Theatre Of Hate moniker. In addition, John Lennard returned on saxophone and **Marc Thwaite** was introduced on guitar.

The group reverted to the name Spear of Destiny for a sixth album, SOD'S LAW, released in 1992 but reissued with three extra tracks and remastered by Brandon (1998; Original Masters). It sold poorly, due in no small part to distribution problems, and a disillusioned and near-penniless Brandon threatened to quit the music business for good after moving briefly to America two years later. He decided instead to assemble **10:51**, an Anglo-American assembly of musicians including former **SIMPLE MINDS** bass-player **Derek Forbes**, releasing an album, STONE IN THE RAIN, in March 1995.

Brandon's new venture warranted barely a mention in the music press, but two years later the full glare of the national media was unexpectedly and dramatically centred on him. Now married with a young daughter, Brandon sued one-time friend Boy George for malicious falsehood over claims in George's autobiography that the two had enjoyed a brief homosexual relationship in the early 1980s. After a bitter war of words in and out of the High Court in London, Brandon lost the case and, despite declaring himself bankrupt, was left facing court costs of nearly £200,000. The decision, however, appeared to act as a catalyst and Brandon immediately set out on tour under the Theatre Of Hate banner.

Along with now long-term cohorts **Art Smith** (drums) and **John McNutt** (guitar), he recruited **Mark Celvallos** (bass), reverting back once again to the Spear Of Destiny name and releasing the album RELIGION (1997), his first new work for five years and arguably his best since the chart-success high point of OUTLAND.

Now very much a stripped-down guitar-based rock'n'roll outfit, Spear Of Destiny continue to tour and release fresh material, while Brandon has also been playing with the group **Dead Men Walking**.

Andy Lowe

THE SPECIALS

Formed Coventry, England, 1977; disbanded 1984; re-formed 1995.

The Specials spearheaded the two-tone movement which ska-ed up Britain in the late 70s and early 80s. Gerald Dankin, aka **Jerry Dammers** (keyboards), **Lynval Golding** (guitar) and **'Sir' Horace 'Gentleman' Panter** (bass) formed a punk/reggae fusion band, the Coventry Automatics, in the summer of 1977. After incorporating ska into their sound, they changed their name to the Coventry Specials, and then to the **Special AKA**. By now, the line-up had expanded, with **Roddy 'Radiation' Byers** (guitar), former roadie **Neville Staples** (percussion/vocals), **Silverton** (drums; later replaced by **John Bradbury**) and **Terry Hall** (vocals).

Dammers was the man with ideas in the early years. He set up the band's own label in 1979 to record a debut single, "Gangsters" (the £700 loan could only stretch to one song, so the B-side was given over to soon-to-be label mates The Selecter), and designed the 2-Tone logo – a reference to the band's multiracial line-up.

London-based indie pioneers Rough Trade pressed and distributed "Gangsters" and it made enough of an impression for several major labels to approach the band. They settled for Chrysalis, who took 2-Tone on as a subsidiary – their roster including The Selecter, The (English) Beat, the Bodysnatchers and, briefly, Madness. The re-released "Gangsters" (1979), now credited to The Specials, climbed to #6 in Britain. The follow-up, "A Message To You, Rudy" (1979), was another Top 10 hit, while their Elvis Costello-produced debut album, THE SPECIALS, got to #4. Jamaican-born trombonist **Rico Rodrigues** now became a permanent fixture in the band.

In February 1980, a live EP credited to the Special AKA gave them their first #1, with "Too Much Too Young" being the radio DJs' favourite track. More hit records followed: "Rat Race" (1980) and "Stereotypes" (1980) continued a run of Top 10 hits, and MORE SPECIALS (1980) got to #5. Having single-handedly started a ska revival the previous year, MORE SPECIALS saw the band venture into new territory – 'lounge music'.

The band and their label were the subject of *Dance Craze*, a film made in 1981, the year that brought the beginning of the end for The Specials, and ultimately for 2-Tone. Amidst the riots that flared in Brixton and Toxteth during the spring and summer, the lyrics of "Ghost Town" (1981) sounded eerily prophetic. It was their second #1, but their last hit together.

Hall, Golding and Staples left to form the **FUN BOY THREE**. Byers formed **Roddy Radiation & The**

The Specials party on (from left): adoring fan, Neville Staples, Lynval Golding, Sir Horace, Terry Hall and Roddy Radiation

Tearjerkers, while Panter left and later joined **General Public** before returning and quitting again. Dammers reverted to the old Special AKA name, and drafted in new members **Gary McManus** (bass), **John Shipley** (guitar), **Egidio Newton** (vocals), **Stan Campbell** (vocals) and **Rhoda Dakar** (vocals).

The Special AKA made a welcome return to the Top 10 with "Free Nelson Mandela" in April 1984, followed by the album IN THE STUDIO. The single marked an increase in the political side of Dammers' work, both on and off stage. In the years that followed, he took part in recording "Starvation" (one of several reggae equivalents of the Band Aid single), and in 1986 formed Artists Against Apartheid. Two years later, Wembley Stadium was the venue for one of the century's biggest birthday parties – the Nelson Mandela Seventieth Birthday Tribute, which Dammers helped organize, and for which "Free Nelson Mandela" was adopted as the theme song. The party returned to Wembley in 1990, this time with the freed Mandela as guest of honour.

Golding re-formed The Specials in 1995, in order to finance the home studio he had been building. Both Dammers and Hall declined to join, but Staples, Panter (who had become a teacher) and Byers accepted, and were joined by **Aitch Hyatt** (drums), **Mark Adams** (keyboards), **Adam Birch** (trumpet) and a brass section known simply as 'Four Bald Guys'. They signed to the Virgin-licensed Kuff label, owned by UB40's Ali Campbell, and in 1996 released "Today's Specials", a pleasing if not exactly earth-shattering covers album, taking ska and reggae classics as well as songs by The Clash, The Monkees ("Little Bit Me") and Ewan MacColl's "Dirty Old Town".

1998's GUILTY TIL PROVED INNOCENT was an album tailored to cash in on the late-90s US ska boom, with new material shown up as spineless and watery even when compared to the lacklustre versions of "Concrete Jungle", "Rat Race" and "Gangsters" presented alongside. In a letter to *Billboard* magazine in October 1997, Jerry Dammers dismissed the current Specials as 'a group of musicians masquerading as the originals' and intimated that he had been asked by Chrysalis to do a reworking of "Ghost Town" (Chrysalis have not yet confirmed whether this is ever likely to happen). Dammers has since been spotted unleashing his talents on the decks at various festivals, spinning a left-field mix of industrial scree and ska.

⊙ **The Specials Singles** (1991; Chrysalis).
The definitive hit collection. Features the moody "Ghost Town" and all those bounce-along ska tunes that never seem to age.

George Luke

PHIL SPECTOR

Born New York, December 26, 1940.

Phil Spector was inspired to write his first song – "To Know Him Is To Love Him" – by his father's epitaph, and recorded the song with school-

friend Annette Kleinbard singing lead. Released locally under the name the Teddy Bears, it was a US #1 smash in 1958. Promptly snapped up by a major label, Phil then had control of the recording sessions for an LP wrested from him. He vowed to become so adept in the studio that it could never happen again – and, right on cue, he met Lester Sill.

A&R man Sill hired Phil as understudy to his partner, **LEE HAZLEWOOD**, the man who used various echoes and tape speeds to create Duane Eddy's trademark guitar twang. Watching him, Phil realized that sounds didn't have to be 'real' at all. The monster sound he had in his head could be created in the studio.

Sill got Spector work in New York with Jerry Leiber and Mike Stoller, writers/producers for Elvis and The Drifters. Phil played guitar on Drifters sessions and wrote Ben E. King's "Spanish Harlem" with Leiber. His first production job was Ray Peterson's "Corrina, Corrina", a US Top 10 hit in 1960. After a few mediocre follow-ups, Sill and Hazlewood recalled him to LA to produce the Paris Sisters' "I Love How You Love Me", a Top 5 heart-wrencher in the vein of "To Know Him...", which oozed a dreamy sensuality achieved by close-miking the vocalist. Spine-tingling strings reinforced the tension.

Spector returned to New York a success. Attracting industry attention, not least for his black cape and pre-Beatles long hair, he was offered jobs with major labels but, to retain artistic freedom, he and Lester formed their own independent label. Philles Records went against the trend of releasing scores of records in the hope of a fluke hit: they only released hits. An impressive list of writers (Goffin/King, Greenwich/Barry, Mann/Weill) served up teen operas for their vehicle, The Crystals: "There's No Other (Like My Baby)" (1961), "Uptown" and the perverse "He Hit Me (And It Felt Like A Kiss)" (1962).

For The Crystals' "He's A Rebel" (1962) Spector worked with arranger Jack Nitzsche to build on his spiralling Wall Of Sound, and Darlene Love's awesome voice duly soared to #1. The sound, not the acts, sold Phil's records. Smashes by the interchangeable Crystals/Darlene Love/Bob B. Soxx proved it, culminating with "Da Doo Ron Ron" and "Then He Kissed Me".

In 1963, The Ronettes – fronted by Ronnie Bennett's knee-weakening vibrato – re-scaled Spector's wall. "Be My Baby" (1963) and "Walking In The Rain" (1964) wedded melodramatic sentimentality with heartfelt pain to create timeless odes to teenage desire. A CHRISTMAS GIFT TO YOU (1963), an album of Christmas faves by the whole Philles stable, rounded off the year. The best track, "Christmas (Baby, Please Come Home)", was given to Darlene Love; Ronnie, now married to Spector, began a forced retreat into Phil's shadow.

1964 saw Spector prove it wasn't just girls that sold his records. The Righteous Brothers' "You've Lost That Lovin' Feelin'" crashed to #1 worldwide and was followed by "Unchained Melody". By 1966, however, the US industry was tiring of his independence. After Spector hired Ike and Tina Turner, paid Ike $25,000 to stay home, and built "River Deep, Mountain High" (aka 'the biggest record of all time') around Tina alone, DJs declined to play the record, the press ignored it and it flopped. Phil retired in a huff.

It took John Lennon to coax Spector back into music. He produced "Instant Karma" (1969) and salvaged The Beatles' LET IT BE (1970). He went on to produce solo albums for Lennon and George Harrison, and later in the decade Leonard Cohen's DEATH OF A LADIES MAN (1977) and the Ramones' END OF THE CENTURY (1980).

Spector was inducted into the Rock And Roll Hall Of Fame in 1989, though the years since have not been pretty. In 2000 the litigation with The Ronettes came to a head, resulting in a massive royalty pay-out, and then in 2003 Spector was arrested and charged with murder after the body of a woman was found in his home.

⊙ **Back To Mono** (1991; ABKCO).
This comprehensive four-CD collection spans 1958 to 1969, when the records Phil produced were really his own rather than the work of the artists that sang them. All the masterpieces are here – including the whole Christmas album.

Tony Thewlis

JON SPENCER BLUES EXPLOSION

Formed New York, 1991.

It is one of the great ironies of 90s indie rock that the author of such calculated outrages as "You Look Like a Jew" and "Kill Yourself" has found success as an interpreter of Delta blues. Well, kind of.

Jon Spencer first came to punk rock prominence as the leader of DC- (later New York-) based **PUSSY GALORE** in the late 80s/early 90s. With a rotating cast of characters that sometimes included Spencer's girlfriend (later wife and Boss Hog frontwoman) **Cristina Martinez**, Pussy Galore was as clangorous as any Sonic Youth-inspired outfit, and had (witness the titles below) even worse attitude. Still, in Spencer they had a charismatic frontman and a musical talent that could take the group's oddly tuned guitars and rattling sheet-metal noises and arrange them into something resembling songs. By the end, Spencer and Pussy Galore were leaning toward something that presaged the Explosion: fractured pieces of lyrics sprinkled over odd, rock-based riffs and grooves.

In New York, post-Pussy Galore, Spencer worked with a number of other downtown musicians, including the Honeymoon Killers, from whom he inherited drummer **Russell Simins**, and **Judah Bauer**, who became his second guitarist. Under the **Jon Spencer Blues Explosion** rubric, the trio started putting out singles and occasionally playing shows around New York in 1992.

The overall JSBX flavour is sort of bluesy – blues scales, slurred words – but no one would mistake the band for Buddy Guy's. Like Pussy Galore, JSBX has no bass player – though bass (or rather, a guitar treated to sort of sound like one) may be added for audio bottom. The emphasis is on grooves, hooks, bits of melody and rhythm, stitched together so that they last long enough to suggest songs. While one element in each number is usually prominent enough to distinguish it, the multiplicity of other effects keeps it from coalescing as a rock tune; along with the various guitar sounds, a JSBX song might add a run of skronk sax, a Memphis-style organ line, handclaps, or a repeated scream to help carry it off. Lyrics are mostly used this way, too – single lines or snatches of words ("That's The Sweat Of The Blues Explosion!" "Awright!" and notably, "Take A Whiff Of My Panic/Pant Leg, Baby") coming in like instrumental cues. While most popular songs have metrically even and complementary verses and choruses, JSBX songs shift gears in unexpected places. The strangeness is JSBX's trump card: though they use the same basic parts as other bands, what they've built with them is unique.

The early singles helped compound Spencer's already-mighty indie-rock buzz, and with the release of Matador's JON SPENCER BLUES EXPLOSION, EXTRA WIDTH (1994) and ORANGE (1994) LPs the band became a big tour draw, with Spencer frenziedly conducting Simmins and Bauer, playing guitar and theremin (!), and howling his word-bits. Then they toured with The Beastie Boys and MTV grabbed them, and JSBX was suddenly in the big game.

True to their restless creativity, JSBX responded to their new success by issuing the EXPERIMENTAL REMIXES of their recent tunes, with diverse artists from Moby to Beck collaborating on the alternate versions. Following an album with Delta bluesman **R. L. Burnside**, released in 1996 as A ASS POCKET FULL O'WHISKEY, they released NOW I GOT WORRY (also 1996), ACME (1998) and XTRA-ACME USA (1999), all full to brimming with mean, sneaky, dirty, no-good, lowdown, rotten voodoo music.

1999 also saw the release of a JSBX collaboration with Calvin Johnson's **Dub Narcotic Sound System** entitled IN A DANCEHALL STYLE – a lovably loose collection of echoing bass and funky hollas. But by now the buzz had subsided; 2002's PLASTIC FANG was a spirited, but clichéd affair that seemed a little too out of step with a scene ruled by the likes of The White Stripes and The Strokes.

> ⊙ **Orange** (1994; Matador).
> "Take A Whiff Of My Panic, Baby!" There's not much to choose between this and the others, except that this has the hits "Bellbottoms" and "Flavor" and is at the moment what people think of when they think of Blues Explosion.

Roy Edroso

SPIN DOCTORS

Formed New York, 1988.

"We're the last of the quill before the keyboard and console take over." Chris Barron

The shape of 90s rock was pretty much defined by the end of 1991 – grunge was it, Seattle the place to be. But not everyone was enamoured with the melancholy and seemingly directionless anger of grunge. A few wanted to live a little, and the perfect soundtrack was provided by a quartet from New York. These guys remembered how good a live jam could sound, blended rock with funk, and wrote songs with a cheerful, sometimes bawdy, irreverence. The **Spin Doctors** exploded onto the scene around the same time as Nirvana and company, but had a completely different agenda.

New York's New School Of Jazz was where it all began, late in 1988. Music theory student **Chris Barron** (vocals) – a New Yorker raised in Australia – teamed up with fellow students **Eric Schenkman** (guitar) and **Aaron Comess** (drums). In his native Canada, Schenkman had been in a country-punk outfit called Dead Heroes. Comess, who hailed from Dallas, moonlighted in a punk/funk fusion band called Spade, from which he recruited Queens native **Mark White** (bass) to complete the line-up. They formed the band around the time the 1988 presidential election was taking place, and it was one of Schenkman's lecturers who suggested that they name themselves Spin Doctors.

Following their first gig at a Columbia University fraternity house, the band set about carving out a name for themselves on the NYC club circuit. The whole of 1989 was spent doing live gigs and recording tracks to sell at them. The Spin Doctors signed to Epic in 1990, and their first release, UP FOR GRABS, a live EP, was released the following year as a showcase to secure more live work for the band.

The debut album, POCKET FULL OF KRYPTONITE, was released in October 1992. An appearance on

Saturday Night Live and relentless plugging on college radio secured it a place in the US Top 30 by the end of the year. It eventually climbed to #3, selling over two million copies in the process, and spawning three hit singles: "Little Miss Can't Be Wrong", the MTV staple "Two Princes", and "Jimmy Olsen's Blues".

The Spin Doctors' runaway success annoyed almost as many people as it impressed – sharp-eared critics were quick to point out glaring similarities between their songs and the Steve Miller Band's mid-70s material, and cried 'rip-off'. Politically correct listeners complained about the sexist lyrics of songs such as "Little Miss Can't Be Wrong", "Yo' Mama's A Pajama" and "Big Fat Funky Booty". The band made some attempt to appease those who accused them of sexism with a little 'spin doctoring' of their own before performing the songs live. Eventually they gave up and Barron resorted to introducing "Big Fat Funky Booty" as 'a song about fat butts'.

The Doctors hit the road again in 1993, headlining the MTV-sponsored 'Alternative Nations' tour with Soul Asylum and Screaming Trees, as well as going on their own world tour. Between gigs, they recorded a cover of Creedence Clearwater Revival's "Have You Ever Seen The Rain?" for the *Philadelphia* soundtrack, and also released a live mini-album, HOMEBELLY GROOVE, which featured tracks first heard on UP FOR GRABS.

The following year saw the release of the band's third full album, TURN IT UPSIDE DOWN (1994), which stalled at #28 in the US charts, leaving the future of the band in some apparent doubt. However, early in 1995, Schenkman, who was tired of touring, was replaced by a new guitarist, **Anthony Krizan**, and the band returned to cracking funk-rock form with a new album, YOU'VE GOT TO BELIEVE IN SOMETHING (1996).

Sadly, good though it was, the album didn't relight any fires for the band. They teamed up with rapper **Biz Markie** and murdered the disco classic "That's The Way (I Like It)" for the *Space Jam* soundtrack. A song of theirs, "If Wishes Were Horse", was adopted as theme tune for the popular US sitcom *Spin City*, guaranteeing them a steady income during their fallow period.

But that fallow period turned into a disastrous period when the band was dropped by Epic. Re-emerging on Universal, the group released the messy HERE COMES THE BRIDE (1999), which only occasionally shone thanks to the addition of **Ivan Neville** (yes, a member of *that* Neville family) on keyboards. Epic recently cashed-in with a retrospective, JUST GO AHEAD (2003), but it seems that the Doctors have lost their spin.

> ⊙ **Pocket Full Of Kryptonite** (1992; Epic).
> The singles which made the band can all be found here, so if you intend to buy any of their albums, it might as well be this one.

> ⊙ **Homebelly Groove** (1993; Epic).
> There's nothing wrong with the studio albums, but this is how you really get to enjoy the Spin Doctors: live, loud and seriously blues-funky.

SPINAL TAP

Formed Wolverhampton, England, 1967.

**"I don't know how they managed it
but that film made us look like
buffoons. He filmed nights when
we had no problem finding the
stage but did he use them... ?"
Nigel Tufnell**

That **Spinal Tap** are still around after more than
thirty years in rock's premier league is surprising, but the fact that they've managed to retain a
freshness of approach, and more importantly their
dignity, when so many have fallen by the wayside, is
enough, surely, for a Rock And Roll Hall Of Fame
nomination.

Like so many classic songwriting teams, the
group's creative nucleus, **David St Hubbins** and
Nigel Tufnell, met and began writing songs
together while still at school in the late 1950s. Swept
along by the skiffle boom, they formed their first
group, The Lovely Lads, eventually metamorphosing
into the stylistically sharp and hard-edged R&B
outfit, The New Originals.

It was as The Thamesmen, however, that St
Hubbins and Tufnell, along with long-term bass
player, **Derek Smalls**, first achieved international
success in the mid 60s, enjoying a string of hits which
have subsequently become staples of retro-rock radio
the world over. Amongst them was the anthemic
"Listen To The Flower People", with Tufnell's distinctive harmonies and innovative treated guitars
providing the backdrop for St Hubbins' peerless
paean to youthful revolution.

The accidental death of drummer **Peter James
Bond** at the Isle of Lucy Jazz and Blues Festival in
1967 (the second sticksman lost in tragic circumstances) may in part have prompted the change of
name, but in becoming Spinal Tap the group were
also making a declaration of intention – shedding
provincial ties and asserting a desire for physical union
with the fans.

The need for contact is perhaps what has sustained
them over the relentless years of global touring, but
unlike lesser outfits, Tap thrive on the treadmill,
meeting its challenges head-on. They have never
stooped to churning out greatest hits shows to pander
to the whims of an audience. Having developed an
almost telepathic empathy, their unflagging creative
energy has resulted in over thirty albums in as many
years.

Their productivity and omnipresence, however,
may be the very reason they are taken so much for
granted. The St Hubbins-Tufnell songwriting team,
in particular, responsible for so many seamless gems,
remains undervalued. As a lyricist, St Hubbins manages to combine the authority of an old blues master
with a plaintive Englishness reminiscent at times of
Ray Davies, particularly when he's getting his teeth
into a traditional theme close to his heart, as in the
immortal "Stonehenge", or the bootleg-only Ripper
opera, "Saucy Jack".

Alas, the vaudevillian veneer which masks much
of St Hubbins' output has on occasions resulted in his
words being profoundly misinterpreted. The outcry
over "Sex Farm" – in fact a subdued howl of contempt for the subjugation of women, which conjures
up a mythical totalitarian regime of Orwellian proportions – was typical. SMELL THE GLOVE, Tap's
SERGEANT PEPPER or PET SOUNDS, was subject to
similar misunderstanding. It emerged with a defiantly
black sleeve and contained such timeless classics as
"Heavy Duty Rock'n'Roll", "Big Bottom", and the
orchestral mini-symphony, "Lick My Love Pump".
GLOVE's scope is, quite simply, staggering.

The melodic sensibility of Tufnell has also been
criminally neglected. A direct descendant of Bach and
Mozart in his virtuosity, Tufnell manages, with an
awesome array of hardware, to be louder than both of
them put together. On INTRAVENUS DE MILO,
Tufnell's subtle ecclesiastical fretwork, which is guaranteed to have your ears showing signs of the stigmata,
shows yet another side to this most multifaceted of
musicians. When he left the band briefly in the mid-
80s, along with legendary cricket-bat-wielding
Svengali-esque manager Ian Faith, Tap slumped to
their lowest ebb, becoming exceedingly reliant on the
experimental jazz compositions of Smalls.

Thankfully, both Tufnell and Faith finally returned
to the fold for a Japanese tour, and, with renewed
interest following Marti di Bergi's fly-on-the-wall
documentary of the band – that 'if you will rockumentary' as the band scathingly refer to it – Tap
emerged rejuvenated. The revival was all too cruelly
short-lived, however, as they split again amid

alimony, lawsuits and disputes over backstage catering. In the 'lost years' that followed, St Hubbins worked on a scat version of Bizet's *Carmen*, Smalls joined Christian rock band **Lambsblood**, and Tufnell became a Brian Wilson-like recluse. Then came the legendary chance meeting of the three at a 'Monsters of Jesus' festival in Orange County, California. Smalls 'decided to throw his lot in with the devil again' and the Tap headed back to the studio for 1990's acclaimed BREAK LIKE THE WIND.

After losing their sixth drummer, **Rick Shrimpton** (his current whereabouts unknown), while touring Wind, Tap hit lucky again, signing one of the 90s' most lucrative sponsorship contracts to date, with IBM, for a Third World Comeback Tour, 'bringing loud music to people who don't have food, basically', as Smalls explained it. With the new millennium well under way, it is surely time for a serious reassessment of this group's contribution to rock's tapestry. They've played everywhere, they've influenced bands and lifestyles from The Troggs to Black Sabbath. They are, quite simply, living legends. At long last, they at least have a website, which they're activating with a mass of merchandising ('We're not just a band – we're a brand'). Tap into the future – now!

⊙ **Break Like The Wind** (1990; MCA).
On its release, sources close to the band claimed this album was in fact recorded by a band of session musicians and that Tap, numbed by the rigours of touring, were artistically burned out. Even if this hadn't been denied emphatically by the band themselves, the question remains: If Tap's magic is so easily imitated, why isn't everyone doing it?

Ada Wilson

SPIRIT

Formed Los Angeles, 1967;
split and re-formed at intervals.

I t's early-60s California, you're 13 or 14 years old and you're practising your guitar in your bedroom when your stepfather bursts in. What does he say? Well, if your stepdad is **Ed Cassidy**, he says something like 'Hey groovy man, let's form a band! Where's my drum kit?'

Ed and stepson **Randy California** first teamed up in The Red Roosters in 1965, but **Spirit** weren't formed until 1967, when Randy returned from New York, where he had been playing in a band called The Blue Flames. That band had split when its other guitarist, one Jimi Hendrix, was lured away by Chas Chandler to England and stardom. Young Randy returned home with a few ideas learned from Hendrix, and rejoined his stepdad and his old high-school buddies from The Roosters – **Mark Andes** (bass), who had recently played on the novelty record "Monster Mash", **Jay Ferguson** (vocals) and **John Locke** (keyboards).

Spirit's debut album, SPIRIT, was released in 1968. Largely written by Ferguson, this delightful fusion of rock and jazz (Cassidy and Locke had both been jazz musicians) looked like the foundation of a hugely

successful career. Spirit had all the qualities to break big, with an inventive and highly polished sound, accessible songs and some marketable quirks in addition to the stepfather/stepson relationship – such as the contrast between Cassidy (who was 47 and bald) and his fresh-faced long-hair colleagues.

Two more albums followed – THE FAMILY THAT PLAYS TOGETHER (1968) and CLEAR SPIRIT (1969) – and a single, "I Got A Line On You", reached #25 in the US charts. Yet major success proved elusive – turning down the slot to play at Woodstock just before Hendrix didn't help matters. The band's last stab at the big time was TWELVE DREAMS OF DOCTOR SARDONICUS (1970), a set combining the full flowering of Randy California's writing talent with the last glow of Ferguson's creativity. There was the dreamy "Space Child", the heavy "Nothing To Hide", the gloriously exuberant "Morning Will Come", plus two classics – the acoustic "Nature's Way" and the gripping "Mr Skin" (written for Ed Cassidy). It was, in short, one of the finest rock albums ever recorded, and was highly influential among other artists. However, though it has seldom been out of catalogue, and its reputation has grown enormously over the years, it didn't really shift units at the time.

Ferguson, frustrated at the band's lack of progress and feeling increasingly sidelined as California did more of the vocal work, left with Andes to form **Jo Jo Gunne**. California was badly injured in a road accident shortly afterwards, and Spirit's next album FEEDBACK (1971) was recorded without him, with brothers **Chris** (guitar/vocals) and **Al Staehely** (bass/vocals) filling the breach. While Jo Jo Gunne made hay, Spirit looked finished.

Randy California bounced back in 1972, sporting a ridiculous handlebar moustache. He played on one of Deep Purple's US tours when Ritchie Blackmore fell ill, before recording a fine solo album, KAPTAIN KOPTER AND THE (FABULOUS) TWIRLYBIRDS. Here he showed what he had learned from Hendrix, with some breathtaking blues that positively dripped with electricity. Cassidy played drums under the pseudonym Cass Strange, and thus was Spirit reincarnated.

A clutch of albums followed over the next decade, notably SPIRIT OF '76 – which included some worthwhile covers of Jimi Hendrix material – and FUTURE GAMES (1977) – with its kooky *Star Trek* interludes – on the back of which they headlined a UK tour, with the fledgling Police as support. Locke and Andes drifted in and out, along with other musicians, and after a brief split in 1979, the Kaptain Kopter character was revived for Spirit's mock rock opera JOURNEY TO POTATOLAND (1981), a skit on George Orwell's *1984*.

Spirit split again in 1982, and California recorded two more solo albums before the original five members re-formed for 1984's THE THIRTEENTH DREAM, in which five very weak new songs were combined with five totally pointless rerecordings of Spirit classics. California's RESTLESS album the following year showed a lot more spunk, but the next Spirit album,

RAPTURE IN THE CHAMBERS (1988), with California, Locke and Cassidy, was again a rather drab affair.

Nonetheless, the band continued into the 90s (and Cassidy's seventies), still touring and playing with fervent enthusiasm, most recently with **Scott Monahan** on keyboards. But the story came to a sad end on January 2, 1997, when Randy was drowned while bodyboarding off the Hawaiian island of Molokai. He managed to haul his 12-year-old son Quinn out of the current before being swept out to sea himself. Incredibly, given the fact he was playing with Hendrix in 1966, Randy California was only 45 when he died. What turned out to be Spirit's last album, CALIFORNIA BLUES, had to be released posthumously. Sony rereleased SPIRIT, THE FAMILY THAT PLAYS TOGETHER, TWELVE DREAMS OF DOCTOR SARDONICUS and CLEAR SPIRIT as mid-price CDs at the end of 1996, each with a couple of previously unreleased bonus tracks bolted on, and Mercury fired back the following year with THE MERCURY YEARS – a compilation formed from the best parts of SPIRIT OF 76, SON OF SPIRIT, FARTHER ALONG and GREENBACK DOLLAR. 2002's SEA DREAM added to the legend with an archive selection of demos and instrumentals.

⦿ **Spirit** (1968; CBS).
A soft, melodic, jazzy record that's so laid-back it's almost stoned.

⦿ **Twelve Dreams Of Doctor Sardonicus** (1970; CBS).
A true masterpiece, neglected in its day, but so was van Gogh. Your music collection is incomplete without it.

⦿ **Journey To Potatoland** (1981; Beggars Banquet)
Two hippies, Kaptain Kopter and Commander Cassidy, stumble into the nightmare world of Potatoland. Here they find a hideously repressive dictatorship, where innocent potatoes are executed by public frying. However, there is some dynamite blues and R&B on offer, and the chocolate eclairs are quite superb.

⦿ **Spirit Live At La Paloma** (1996; CREW):
From 1993. Possibly the last live Spirit, as a more disciplined outfit, with jazzy passages, plus blues that demonstrate how California was the only guitarist who could come close to matching Hendrix.

⦿ **Mercury Years** (1996; Mercury).
A compilation of Spirit in the 70s, which gives a background for fans who don't want to shell out on all the albums of the period. Strongly biased towards the SPIRIT OF '76 album, it provides enough snatches of the others to give a useful summary to those who do not need the whole oeuvre.

Patrick Neylan-Francis

SPIRITUALIZED

Formed Rugby, England, 1990.

"It's soul music without using Otis Redding's dictionary of soul" - Jason Pierce

When cult trance-rockers **SPACEMEN 3** split in 1990, no one could have reasonably expected the new bands that rose from the ashes to be even farther out. But both Sonic Boom's Spectrum and E.A.R. projects and Jason Pierce's

Spiritualized have gone on to take the minimalist psychedelia-and-lethargy creed of the original 3 to new heights of droning intensity.

Centred on **Jason "Spaceman" Pierce** on guitar and vocals, Spiritualized featured **Mark Refoy** on guitars, **Kate Radley** on keyboards, **Willie B. Carruthers** on bass and **Jon Mattock** on drums for their ground-breaking LAZER GUIDED MELODIES album (1992). Their combination of Velvet Underground drones, orchestral arrangements and blissed-out production values attained a psychedelia that was not retro but 100 percent Nineties. "Run", also lifted as a single, was a knockout track, combining an early Velvets tune (for the chorus) with verses recycled from "They Call Me The Breeze" by bluesman J. J. Cale. It was one of the more up-tempo numbers on an album that portrayed drugged-up apathy and listlessness as rock'n'roll virtues. One track, "200 Bars", was even built around the idea of calling out each bar as it was played. By the 200th bar, you feel like you've had a pint in every one of them, and in some quarters, the album was jokingly retitled 'Lager-Guided Melodies'. A mail-order-only live album FUCKED UP INSIDE (1993) showed off the band's on-stage work to hallucinogenic effect, matched only by the eye-straining red/green sleeve art.

Two years later, the tirelessly lazy Spiritualized came up with PURE PHASE, using songs released as singles as far back as 1992. Refoy left to form **Slipstream**, and the new album was recorded by a stripped-down line-up of Radley and Pierce with **Sean Cook** on bass. This time round the sound was a little more 'live', reflecting more accurately the "Sister Ray" inclinations of their stage act. Opening with the hypnotic "Medication", it also boasted the soul-inflected "Good Times" and the uplifting "All Of My Tears", the latter propelled skywards by the surging strings of **The Balanescu Quartet**. There was also the majestic sound both of the single "Let It Flow", the flute-decorated space blues of "The Slide Song" and a nod to Jason's minimalist influences in the shape of Laurie Anderson's "Born, Never

Asked". A related oddity of the same era was the 12"-only instrumental drone EP "Pure Phase Test Tones For DJs" – very limited and very collectable.

LADIES AND GENTLEMEN, WE ARE FLOATING IN SPACE (1997) turned out to be one of the major British albums of the decade. The Balanescu Quartet's strings appeared again, this time augmented by the glorious voices of the London Community Gospel Choir and **Dr. John**'s inimitable swamp-blues piano, together producing a magnificent volume behind which Jason and his new band members **Damon Reece** (drums) and **John Coxon** (guitar) could hunker down and work on some serious drug music. This album, music aside, took junkie-chic to a new level: the packaging was directly based on the reassuring pastel-and-white design of prescription class A's ('for aural administration only' – there was even a limited edition version released as a set of mini-CDs in a blister pack), with the sleeve notes presented in the form of a dosage and side effects leaflet. The accompanying press promotional shot had the band, elegantly wasted and gaunt, posing in a pharmacist's stockroom looking like the ne'er-do-well scamps in the film *Drugstore Cowboy*.

Edging back towards the music, Jason was heard wailing about the 'hole in my arm where the money goes' ("Cop Shoot Cop"). This was an album to be taken in one dose, individual tracks being less important than the whole; and as the sleeve notes warned, it 'may cause drowsiness and hence avoid operating heavy machinery while under the influence'. Singles included "I Think I'm In Love", "Electricity" and "Come Together".

The only possible follow-up was a series of spectacular live shows at the top of some of the world's tallest buildings: Spiritualized achieved the official record-breaking 'Highest Show On Earth' at the CN Tower in Toronto, as well as the more down-to-mud Glastonbury appearances. The baroque surroundings of the ROYAL ALBERT HALL, OCTOBER 10 1997 provided the title and venue for a double live CD (1998) which captured the full-blown Spiritualized stage experience to rapturous heights of volume and bliss-out. By this time, Coxon had left to concentrate on **Spring Heel Jack** with Ashley Wales, his guitar duties taken over by **Michael Mooney**, while Radley was now split from both the band and Jason Spaceman. Her replacement at piano and Hammond organ was the extravagantly-Mohicaned and fake-fur clad **Thighpaulsandra**, friend of Julian Cope in pagan synth-duo Queen Elizabeth and sometime member of Coil. With saxophonist **Ray Dickaty** (Moonshake), this line-up recorded THE ABBEY ROAD EP in 1998 with expanded versions of "Cop Shoot Cop" and "Broken Heart" before Jason once again dispensed with most of the group, retaining only Thighpaulsandra and Dickaty's services. Mooney, Cook and Reece later emerged with Spacemen 3 and Spiritualized veteran John Mattock as sleazy psychedelic rock outfit **Lupine Howl**.

With an album widely acclaimed as a masterpiece behind him, Mr. Spaceman set out to explore a more orchestral live sound, initially at a benefit concert for legendary US minimalist La Monte Young in London and in collaboration with composer Steve Maitland in Edinburgh. Jason recruited a line-up of **Doggen** (guitar), **Martin Shellard** (bass), **Tom Edwards** (percussion) and **Kevin Bales** (drums), with Coxon back on guitar and keyboards and in the co-production seat. The new approach to composition resulted in the eagerly-awaited LET IT COME DOWN (2001), its ambient drones and introspective rock ecstasy swelling out as before with an extra-full sound on the heady mix of strings and brass to the forefront of a largely acoustic – though by no means quiet – album and its accompanying "Stop Your Crying" single. Perhaps the anticipation which preceded the set's eventual release could only have led to disappointment, but reactions from fans and critics ranged from bemusement to stunned rapture.

With Spiritualized, Jason Pierce has taken the drone-heavy euphoria/come-down music of his Spacemen 3 days into and beyond the mainstream of pop, the band's heartfelt sound truly justifying the term 'unique'.

- **Lazer Guided Melodies** (1992; Dedicated). Sublime, oceanic wash of sound. Follow the advice of some of the song titles and "Take Your Time" to "Step Into The Breeze" and enjoy the "Symphony Space".

- **Pure Phase** (1995; Dedicated). Rockier vibe but still out there with the fairies. Perfect listening for any connoisseur of repetition. For the full effect, seek out the special limited-edition version, presented in a sleek melamine case, styled like a make-up compact.

- **Ladies And Gentlemen, We Are Floating In Space** (1997; Dedicated). Music to turn blue to certainly, but what a way to go.

- **Let It Come Down** (2001; Spaceman/BMG) There's a fine line between the visionary and self-indulgent in music, and Spiritualized tread it carefully here. The vision remains both as epic and drowsy as the prescription before, but with the songs based firmly in live studio recordings. Jason and crew are on an apparently upbeat swing for the most part, and some moments stand out – "Stop Your Crying", "Out Of Sight".

- **The Complete Works Volume One** (2003; Spaceman/Arista). A well-thought-out compilation that has clearly been put together so as to both offer a good summation of the band's career and also unearth enough hard-to-find odds'n'ends to keep fans happy. The set opens with the group's stunning debut single, "Anyway That You Want Me" – which now sounds blissfully grainy and stoned compared to the hi-fi surround-sound ecstasy of Pierces more recent output – and then dives into a wealth of singles, B-sides and EP-cuts.

Iain Smith
updated by Richard Fontenoy

SPLIT ENZ

Formed Auckland, New Zealand 1972; disbanded 1984; brief comebacks 1989 and 1992.

I n the mid 70s **Split Enz** were best known for their striking image, which consisted of clownlike make-up, teased hairdos and brightly coloured suits.

Intially dismissed as post-art rockers, by the time of the early-80s New Wave era the Enz found themselves in the position of pioneers with a favourable cult following.

Starting off as a septet jug band, Split Ends were uniformed in white shirts and matching black ties. Soul songwriters **Tim Finn** (piano/vocals) and **Phil Judd** (mandolin/guitar/vocals) led **Eddie Rayner** (keyboard), **Jonathan Michael Chunn** (bass), **Emlyn Crowther** (drums) and **Noel Crombie** (percussion/spoons) through a series of early gigs to a national television appearance on a talent quest show, where the band won first prize. By the time the group left New Zealand for Australia, their image was pushed to extremes with eccentric colourful clothing and bizarre hairstyles. They signed to Mushroom records as Split Enz.

Their first album, MENTAL NOTES (1975), displayed the group's eclectic tastes in cabaret, epic ballads and zany pop, which included innovative song structures and oddball lyrics. In Australia the group's individuality was marred by comparisons with eccentric, local glam-rockers SkyHooks, and they were booed off the stage while playing as a support band to AC/DC. But a trip to London after catching the eye of Roxy Music's Phil Manzanera led to the production of SECOND THOUGHTS (1976), which featured rerecorded tracks of the debut along with new songs and saw the entry of short-term saxophonist **Robert Gillie**. Instantly the group received rave press in the UK. The *NME* labelled SECOND THOUGHTS 'Debut Album of the Year'.

After signing to Chrysalis Records for the release of their third album, DIZRYTHMIA (1977), problems began to occur. The group's position was ambiguous within the rising punk scene in Britain, and lack of interest in the buying public left the members struggling. Chunn, Crowther and Judd soon departed and a line-up change saw the entry of **Nigel Griggs** (bass), **Malcolm Green** (drums) and Tim's 17-year-old brother **Neil Finn** (guitar). Judd went on to form The Swingers with future **MIDNIGHT OIL** bassist Dwane 'Bones' Hillman and later to score a 1981 hit with "Counting The Beat". After a gruelling American tour the group released their fourth album, FRENZY (1979), with less than modest sales despite the impressive choice cuts – a plastic punk-pop single "I See Red" and the previous Tin Pan Alley ditty "My Mistake" (from DIZRYTHMIA).

Signing to A&M, the 80s shined on the Enz. With the release of TRUE COLOURS (1980), they scored a monster hit with "I Got You", which spent ten weeks on top of the Australian charts, as well as shooting up in the US Top 50 and UK Top 20. TRUE COLOURS was to be the group's most successful album, with instant hits "I Hope I Never" and "Poor Boy". These singles were followed by WAITA (1981) and TIME & TIDE (1982), which continued the group's recording tradition of epic ballads mixed with Neil's pop craft and Rayner's instrumentals. WAITA was modest compared to the previous album,

but did, however, supply the New Wave gem "History Never Repeats" as well as the tender classic "One Step Ahead".

As the 80s progressed, the Enz seemed to become more dependent on conventional pop structure and the group's eccentricity started to fade. New drummer **Paul Hester** joined for the two final albums, CONFLICTING EMOTIONS (1983) and SEE YA 'ROUND (1984). After the release of CONFLICTING EMOTIONS Tim quit the group for a solo career, which started with his first solo album, ESCAPADE (1983). Meanwhile Neil started to show strong songwriting talent with one of the Enz's last hits "Message To My Girl".

By 1985 the members had gone their separate ways. Neil Finn and Paul Hester formed **CROWDED HOUSE**, Eddie Rayner was working with Paul McCartney, while Nigel Griggs and Noel Crombie rejoined Phil Judd to form the quirky pop outfit **Schnell Fenster**, releasing THE SOUND OF TREES (1988) and OK ALRIGHT A HUH OH YEAH (1991). Rayner also reappeared in the early 90s with musician Brian Baker as **The Makers**, releasing two albums, THE MAKERS (1990) and HOKEY POKEY (1992). The Enz made some brief comeback tours during the late 80s and early 90s. The release of ENZO saw Tim and Neil Finn join Rayner in rerecording Enz material with the New Zealand Symphony Orchestra in 1996. Rayner followed this up two years later with the Finn-less ENZO 2, proving that Enz fever seemed to be lingering some fifteen years after the group's split.

◉ **True Colours** (1980; A&M).
This is the Enz's most successful album and was originally released in laser-etched vinyl in multicolours. As for the music, the Enz supplied some choice cuts, including "I Got You", "I Hope I Never", "Poor Boy" and "Shark Attack".

◉ **Spellbound** (1997; Mushroom).
Out of many compilation releases of the Enz work, this comes up being the best. Features 39 tracks of all the hit singles, some live recordings and odd album tracks.

Ryan Burger

BRUCE SPRINGSTEEN

Born Freehold, New Jersey, September 23, 1949.

"People deserve truth, they deserve honesty ... and the best music is there to provide you with something to face the world with."

For too many people **Bruce Springsteen** is equated with BORN IN THE USA (1984). Not that this was in any way a bad album, but so synonymous has its raucous bar-room rock and anthemic balladry become with its creator that an altogether darker and more subtle Springsteen has been all but eclipsed. The career of the man that they call 'The Boss' is one of wild contrasts, in both style and quality, but for all his faults, Springsteen's music has never been predictable – as the release of the sparse and despairing THE GHOST OF TOM JOAD, late in 1995, served to emphasize.

Springsteen's rise was less than meteoric. His first album was released in 1973 after all the usual trials and tribulations of an aspiring musician. GREETINGS FROM ASBURY PARK, N.J., along with THE WILD, THE INNOCENT AND THE E STREET SHUFFLE (1973), seemed to confirm Springsteen's early reputation as yet another 'new Bob Dylan'. GREETINGS... in particular was wordy and obscurantist, meandering in the Dylan style but lacking Dylan's insight. "Blinded By The Light" was the collection's best moment, while, on the second album, only "Rosalita (Come Out Tonight)" has endured – and this because of its more recent manifestation as a show stopper in his stupendous live sets. Neither album proved the commercial breakthrough that some critics had predicted.

That, instead, came in 1975, with the release of the now-legendary BORN TO RUN. The start of the circle that BORN IN THE USA would complete, BORN TO RUN caught the despairing characters of the later album in hopeful, dreamy youth. In "Born To Run", or "Thunder Road", the dreams had not yet been shackled. Escape was symbolized by the car and the highway, the girl and the guitar – in the eyes of its naive characters, physical and spiritual deliverance were merged into the long straight highway, the "Thunder Road". For Springsteen, the road and the journey, travelled in hope or despair, would become a recurring theme.

BORN TO RUN was a turning point in Springsteen's career. Suddenly he was bankable, with a US Top 5 album behind him and a highly successful American tour. Yet this would be the last release for three years (this was due, in part, to legal wrangling over contracts/managers, etc), and was followed, eventually, by the altogether more sombre but wonderfully evocative DARKNESS ON THE EDGE OF TOWN (1978), arguably Springsteen's best album. The characters in the small-town world of DARKNESS... struggled every step of the way against a harsh and unforgiving environment, and against despair. There was hope in the record, and some of the desire of youth remained, but it was a fragile hope that had to be fought for. The dreams of the girl in the haunting "Candy's Room" were a long way from the twilight highways of BORN TO RUN, because the dreams remained strictly within, and when the highway called again, in "Racing In The Street", it did so as a means of making money, not of escape. Musically, too, the album was an advance on its predecessor. Harder and more guitar-driven, the sound was starker and edgier, mirroring the psychic geography of small-town America.

Prior to the release of BORN IN THE USA, THE RIVER (1980) was perhaps Springsteen's best-known album, and it catapulted him towards international fame. Why it should have done so, however, remains a mystery. The title track aside, THE RIVER was two

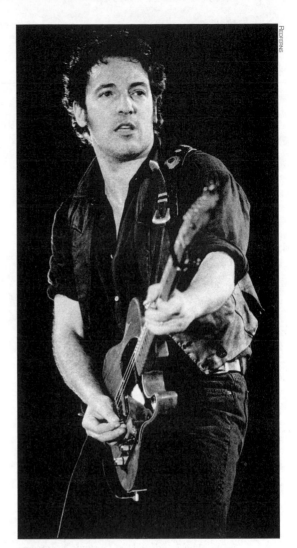
'The Boss'

records of weak ballads and banal attempts at a sort of feel-good rock'n'roll ("Out On The Street", "Cadillac Ranch"). It was as if Bruce had decided that he'd finished with the serious stuff, but when NEBRASKA (1982) came along it was as if the crass commercialization of THE RIVER had never happened.

NEBRASKA took us back to the style and concerns of DARKNESS ON THE EDGE OF TOWN, and then far beyond. The E Street Band were ditched, leaving Springsteen to rely on acoustic guitar, harmonica and an increasingly gravelly voice. To reinforce the raw, live sound, the whole album was recorded on simple four-track cassette at Springsteen's home in New Jersey. The sparseness of the sound emphasized the anger and futility of the tales of killers, gamblers and desperados, driven to their destiny by circumstance over which they have little control. Even on less

REDFERNS

intense tracks, like the single "Atlantic City", there was a sense of bitterness, of a breaking point soon to be breached.

BORN IN THE USA (1984) was the pinnacle of Springsteen's commercial success. Addressing blue-collar, post-Vietnam, post-Reaganomics small-town America, the album followed in the great tradition of white American protest music, stretching back through Dylan and Johnny Cash to Woody Guthrie. It did not take in-depth investigation to realize that this was no homage to the 'God Bless America' way of life, but Ronald Reagan assumed BORN IN THE USA was just that, until put right by Springsteen, live on stage. Few have described the downside of the American Dream as vividly as Springsteen did in the bitter resignation of the title track, the fading dreams of "No Surrender" and the hopeless nostalgia of "My Hometown". And few have had such success with so bleak a vision: this album made Spingsteen a global megastar, and within a year he was filling the largest venues with live shows that lasted up to four hours, each minute packed with boundless energy. The shows of 1985 were greatest hits packages interwoven with trademark storytelling and (perhaps less noted) a droll and earthy humour. The venues were too big, of course, but Springsteen live was a phenomenon.

NEBRASKA and BORN IN THE USA marked the end of an era for Bruce Springsteen. It was waved off with a solid and charismatic five-album set, LIVE 1977–1985 (1986), the footnotes of which hinted at the changes to come. The E Street Band, thanked for 'a thousand nights of good rocking' were soon to be dispensed with as a whole. Approaching 40 and in the midst of marriage, divorce, remarriage and fatherhood, Springsteen would become, for a while, more personal and intimate, less concerned with the problems of the world. 1987's TUNNEL OF LOVE was as despairing of romantic love as NEBRASKA had been of the American Dream, and it received excellent reviews. But in the other albums the passion was missing. The jointly released LUCKY TOWN and HUMAN TOUCH (1992) were, for the most part, bland and routine.

THE GHOST OF TOM JOAD (1995), then, came as another surprise, and one compounded by the lack of publicity that surrounded its release. Taking its title from the dustbowl hero of Steinbeck's *The Grapes Of Wrath*, this stripped-down set showed Springsteen staking his claim to the mantle of Woody Guthrie. Some saw TOM JOAD as a pale imitation of the Springsteen of old – an attempt to recapture the artistic high ground lost with the populism of BORN IN THE USA. To others, however, "Youngstown", "The Ghost Of Tom Joad" and "The Line" were a return to the sort of form that characterized the best of Springsteen's earlier work.

Following this apparent return to form Springsteen's output has been largely for the consumption of the already converted. TRACKS (1998) found him plundering the vaults for previously unreleased material, the kind of thing to have fans stroking their chins with delight. Meanwhile the more accessible LIVE IN NEW YORK CITY (2001) was a double-disc set and featured a reunited E Street Band recorded at a couple of Madison Square Gardens gigs at the end of Springsteen's 1999-2000 tour. Among the expected concert favourites the band unveiled a couple of new songs in the shape of "Land Of Hope And Dreams" and the controversial protest song "American Skin", a tune resulting from the shooting of an unarmed immigrant by New York cops in 1999. Needless to say, the song prompted calls from police organizations for the boycotting of the Boss's shows, but if anything it showed that Springsteen could still cut to the heart of an issue with remarkable and affecting clarity when his muse was so inspired.

In 2003 Springsteen maintained his form with THE RISING, his first E Street Band studio album in eighteen years. The lyrics were again strong and politically charged, while the music seemed to draw from all over the place. That said, the album's heart was still beating to the sound of epic rock'n'roll.

⊙ **Born To Run** (1975; CBS).
Considered a Springsteen classic by many, but some find its romanticism grates after a while, and it certainly lacks the anger that characterizes his best work.

⊙ **Darkness On The Edge Of Town** (1978; CBS).
The romance has gone on this, perhaps Springsteen's best album. Always overshadowed by more commercially successful records, DARKNESS remains a brilliant exploration of the dark side of town.

⊙ **Nebraska** (1982; CBS).
Springsteen goes unplugged well ahead of time on these stark, strident acoustic ballads.

⊙ **Born In The USA** (1984; CBS).
Neither as bleak nor as edgy as DARKNESS, BORN IN THE USA is, nevertheless, no commercial compromise. There is a hint of the 'feel-good' here, but it is offset by an anger and frustration bubbling just below the surface.

⊙ **Live 1977–1985** (1986; CBS).
Pretty much nobody rivals Springsteen live, and this massive box set revisits his work in utterly compelling fashion.

⊙ **The Ghost Of Tom Joad** (1995; CBS).
Bruce repudiates the doubters with this stunning return to roots and form.

⊙ **The Rising** (2003; CBS).
A charged album of joyously bruising riffs and some of Springsteen's best songs in years.

Hugh Wilson

SQUEEZE

Formed London, 1974; disbanded 1982; re-formed 1985.

I n 1974 a couple of south London likely lads, **Chris Difford** and **Glenn Tilbrook**, formed a songwriting partnership that was to provide a soundtrack for the lives of an adolescent generation. They recruited an irrepressible young keyboard player, **Jools Holland**, and a rhythm section of **Harry Kakoulli** (bass) and **Paul Gunn** (drums) to form **Squeeze**, and from the early days displayed an inspired grasp of the essentials of pop composition, marrying an engaging lyric to a compelling hook. After clocking up a string of hit singles, and surviving the 'new Lennon and McCartney' tag, Squeeze broke up just when international success was taking off.

After the early setback of having their first single, "Take Me I'm Yours" (1977), withdrawn by BTM, Gunn was replaced on drums by **Gilson Lavis** and the band put out the PACKET OF THREE EP on the Deptford Fun City label. Produced by John Cale, it helped secure a major deal with A&M, who finally released "Take Me I'm Yours" in 1978, whereupon it went into the UK Top 20. John Bentley joined as new bassist after the release of the eponymous debut album (1978), and from here on they hit a heady period of success, with the second album, COOL FOR CATS (1979) containing four UK hit singles. "Cool For Cats" and the classic tale of domestic woe, "Up The Junction", both reached #2 in the spring of 1979.

ARGY BARGY (1980) was taken by ebullient reviewers as confirmation of the arrival of a great songwriting team in the tradition of The Beatles and The Kinks. After two more pieces of pop mastery, "Another Nail In My Heart" and "Pulling Mussels (From The Shell)" (both 1980), Jools Holland left to seek his fortune as a boogie-woogie pianist, forming The Millionaires. **Paul Carrack**, the replacement, brought with him a wealth of experience as ex-Ace keyboardist and singer, and Elvis Costello was booked as co-producer for the well-received LP, EAST SIDE STORY (1981). In addition to the pop of "Is That Love?", the album showed a widening of horizons with Carrack's bluesy vocal on "Tempted" and the country-flavoured "Labelled With Love".

Carrack made a quick departure, to be replaced by **Don Snow** for SWEETS FROM A STRANGER (1982), but after five albums in five years the band were on the slide. The rigours of touring were taking their toll and, as Tilbrook later admitted, it was no fun any more. The decision to split came at the end of 1982.

But this was not the end of the story. Difford and Tilbrook stayed together to write a musical production, *Labelled With Love*, staged at their home venue, The Albany Empire, Deptford, and started recording again for a Difford and Tilbrook LP. And then Holland, who had become a music presenter on British TV show *The Tube*, returned for an impromptu reunion gig that led to the band reforming, with **Keith Wilkinson** on bass.

Over the last decade the faithful fan base has been treated to a catalogue of releases that have never moved too far from the tested formula. Having kicked off their second incarnation with the patchy COSI FAN TUTTI FRUTTI (1985), BABYLON AND ON (1987) gained better reviews and provided their biggest US hit with the breathless lyric of "Hourglass". After FRANK (1989) failed to consolidate this success, Jools left to play with his Big Band, and to pursue his TV career.

Squeeze were subsequently shocked out of their self-confessed complacency when dropped by A&M, and their next release, PLAY (1991), on Reprise, was widely regarded as a solid return. Returning to A&M, they showed no signs of flagging on SOME FANTASTIC PLACE (1993) and RIDICULOUS (1995). Songs like "Some Fantastic Place" and "Loving You Tonight" showed just how much the writing has grown in sensitivity and sophistication – though some of those who grew up with the straight-talking hits of old might lament the passing of the likely lads.

Late 1998 saw a major UK tour and the release of DOMINO (Quixotic) on which Difford and Tilbrook are joined by a whole new band of **Chris Holland** (keyboards), **Hilaire Pender** (bass) and **Ashley Soan** (drums). Despite the changes in personnel and lack of a major record label the craft of the songwriting was as strong as ever and lyrical concerns stayed in familiar kitchen sink territory. And with that Squeeze effectively went into hibernation again, allowing Glenn Tilbrook to work on his debut solo album THE INCOMPLETE GLENN TILBROOK (2001) and Chris Difford to concentrate on his own solo outing with the aid of **Francis Dunnery** of It Bites fame.

The Singles – 45 And Under (1982; A&M).
Released after the final single of Squeeze phase one, "Annie Get Your Gun", this collection is a reminder of just how many classics they'd delivered over the first five years.

Play (1991; Reprise).
Things looked grim after being dumped by A&M, but they regrouped with Matt Irving on keyboards, signed a new deal with Warners and put out this stunning collection of songwriting craft.

Some Fantastic Place (1993; A&M).
With ex-Attraction Pete Thomas on drums and the return of Paul Carrack, this became the most successful release since BABYLON AND ON, and for good reason. Highlights are the brilliant title track, "Cold Shoulder", and the use of an electric railway as emotional metaphor on "Third Rail".

Excess Moderation (1996; A&M).
Forty tracks spanning the A&M years and featuring album tracks, B-sides and alternative versions. This collection dovetails nicely with the singles compilation.

Nick Dale

SQUIRREL BAIT

Formed Louisville, Kentucky, 1983; split 1986.

Conceived at high school, when the members were all in their mid-teens, **Squirrel Bait** attained their legendary status more as a result of the subsequent careers of the various members than for their own extraordinary, angular music. In fact, their roster reads like a who's who of North American alt-rock, spawning musicians who went on to play in **SLINT**, Bastro, Palace Brothers, Evergreen, King Kong, Big Wheel, **GASTR DEL SOL** and others.

Their music has been described as 'emo-core' – hardcore with a sensitive side. **Peter Searcy** sang with a teenager's anguished howl, **David Grubbs** and **Brian McMahan** played guitar, **Clark Johnson** handled the bass and **Ben Daughtrey**, later to play for **THE LEMONHEADS**, drummed. **Britt Walford** and **Ethan Buckler**, later founder members of Slint, contributed to early releases.

Squirrel Bait received so much media attention, so quickly, that their break-up was inevitable and easy to foresee: 'These kids rock the fuck out', said Bob Mould at the time, when Hüsker Dü was the band to listen to, going on to say it was better than anything his band had ever done. An astonishing comment, given the age of the band (Searcy was just 16).

Their mini-LP, SQUIRREL BAIT (1985) was 'really just kind of coughed up like a hairball', according to Grubbs. However, the ensuing press and media attention encouraged the members to remain together despite the barely concealed antipathy and 'musical differences' (the record opens with the words 'I'm going to beat you up at the end of this', before slamming into the piledriving "Hammering So Hard"), that are common to all high-school bands. It was followed by SKAG HEAVEN (1986), a more focused, mature work, less of a thrashing hardcore workout than its predecessor, with experiments in tempos below 1,000,000 bpm.

It was Daughtrey's undeniable musical ability and his desire to experiment with jazzy frills and tempo changes – all of which helped define the Squirrel Bait sound – that finally drove wedges between the various members of the band. Grubbs, as a fan of the Necros and Minor Threat, for example, would have happily endured a drummer content to hammer out simple, fast rhythms. Other factions were less fundementalist, which, together with everybody's impending college commitments, ensured the final break-up. David Grubbs subsequently formed Bastro, Peter Searcy went on to join Big Wheel, and Brian McMahan emerged in Slint, perhaps one of the most influential American bands of recent years, before continuing his creepy, sleepy aesthetic in the **For Carnation**.

Slint's debut, TWEEZ (1987), owed a dynamic debt to the hardcore dues paid by Squirrel Bait. At a time when similarly precocious teens would be snapped up by trend-hopping record labels, it was refreshing to sit back and hear genuine, unaffected innovation.

(•) **Squirrel Bait** (1985; Homestead) and
Skag Heaven (1986; Homestead).
Both the above were rereleased on Dexter's Cigar Records in 1997. Clocking in at under 25 minutes each, go get them now and bathe in the fountain of youthful rage.

Jonathan Bell

STACKRIDGE

Formed Bristol, England, 1970; vanished 1976.

'**F**olk-rock' doesn't do justice to this eccentric British band that built up a fanatical, but never profitable, following in the early 70s following the release of a quirky first album STACKRIDGE (1971), featuring such unlikely characters as Dora (the

female 'explora') and Slark, the friendly monster who was played out in a fourteen-minute all-acoustic sound poem.

From the start **Stackridge** were best as a live band, playing clubs and pubs throughout the southern UK. Their starting line-up was **Andy Davis** (vocals/guitars/keyboards), **James Warren** (vocals/guitars), **Mike 'Mutter' Slater** (vocals/flute), **Billy Bent** (drums), **Jim 'Crun' Walter** (yet more vocals/guitars) and **Mike Evans** (violin). In the manner of The Grateful Dead, their gigs defined them better than the records. A loyal group of fans began to develop, who would bring bizarre accessories to the gigs (rhubarb and dustbin lids, for the crashing thereof). Their unusually clear live sound, plus a willingness on the part of the sound crew to swap a tape hook-up for a pint of beer led to a good trade in bootlegs that continues to this day.

The musical style blended Caravan, The Kinks, Jethro Tull and Fairport Convention with a jazzy attitude of 'never play it the same way twice'. The show combined eccentric theatricals and rambling song introductions from Mutter and Andy, all held together with superb musicianship. After their well-received second album FRIENDLINESS (1972), success seemed to loom, as their third album, MAN IN THE BOWLER HAT (PINAFORE DAYS in the US; 1974), was produced by Beatles' knob-twiddler George Martin. For some, this is their best work, with the upbeat "Galloping Gaucho" and wistful orchestrated "God Speed The Plough".

EXTRAVAGANZA (1975) revealed a harder, jazzier edge, and brought ex-Audience saxophonist **Keith Gemmell** into the band. Tracks include the playful angst saga "Highbury Incident", the sax-rich "Earthworm", and the lively instrumentals "Pocket Billiards" and "Who's That Up There With Bill Stokes".

But the albums didn't bring commercial success, and their next and final full-length recording, MR MICK (1976) – the long rambling story of an unloved tramp – was one eccentricity too far. In 1976, Stackridge disappeared. However, Warren and Davis reincarnated as the **Korgis** ("Everyone's Got To Learn Sometime") in 1979, and finally got a taste of the chart success that had eluded Stackridge.

(•) **Stackridge** (1971, MCA).
Introduced the world to Stackridge's bizarre characters, to a background of folky rock. Climaxes with the saga of the monstrous Slark.

(•) **The Man In The Bowler Hat** (1974; MCA).
Acoustic rock and whimsical English evocations, with orchestration by George Martin. For many, the band's best work.

(•) **Extravaganza** (1975, Rocket)
When you thought it couldn't get any better, Stackridge met jazz, mixing humour with tight sax.

(•) **Mr Mick** (1976, Rocket).
The last of the 'real' albums, it wasn't popular with the fans, nor opened Stackridge to a new audience.

Paul Reilly

THE STANDELLS

Formed Los Angeles, 1963; disbanded 1968.

The Standells were just one of an army of forgotten US garage punk bands that sprang up between 1965 and 1968, imitating the British Invasion of the Stones, Beatles and Kinks. Forgotten, that is, until 1972, when Lenny Kaye (bass player for Patti Smith) compiled NUGGETS, a double album that showcased the very best of the genre. Alongside more psychedelic outfits such as The Electric Prunes and The Chocolate Watch Band, The Standells, staring out from beneath their Brian Jones pageboy cuts, seemed to personify the ultimate in misunderstood teenage aggression. Their calling card was "Dirty Water", a stomping two and half minutes of pounding pleasure, served up with lashings of cheesy organ and tambourine.

But The Standells were a lot more than one-hit Rolling Stones clones, even if their image owed a lot more to commercial posturing than you might initially suspect. The original Standells were in fact a squeaky-clean frat-rock outfit, comprising frontman **Dick Dodd** on vocals and drums, **Larry Tamblyn** on keyboards, **Tony Valentino** on guitar and **Gary Lane** on bass. They had already released one album and a handful of nondescript singles before running into legendary writer/producer Ed Cobb, who saw them as a suitable vehicle for "Dirty Water", a little something he'd written about getting mugged by the waterfront in Boston. It seems the band hated it, but you'd never have guessed from their enthusiastic performance. Released on Tower, it was a surprise hit, reaching #11 in the US in the summer of 1966. THE DIRTY WATER album was also excellent, and their future seemed secure with the release of two more classic garage punk singles, "Sometimes Good Guys Don't Wear White" and "Why Pick On Me?".

Although the follow-up album, WHY PICK ON ME?, was another sound collection, THE HOT ONES, an exploitative set of ropey covers, stalled their momentum. It was a complete flop and discouraged punters from trying "Try It", a new single that was actually one of their best shots. Having the song banned for its risqué lyrics didn't help matters, nor releasing another single as The Sllednats – the backwards spelling fooled nobody.

The band experimented with new ideas, including psychedelia, but their last essential cut was "Riot On Sunset Strip", written for the soundtrack to the film of the same name, an exploitation flick based upon the 1966 teen riots in downtown Los Angeles. The Standells also played an excellent cameo in the film, along with The Chocolate Watch Band. Sadly, the group failed to achieve any more chart success and, following a parting of ways with Ed Cobb, they split up in 1968. Part of the problem was their desire to write and perform their own material, but since they owed both their image and success to the ideas of Ed Cobb, this was not a particularly bright idea. The

worst decision of all was rejecting "Tainted Love", a superb Ed Cobb tune that was to provide an international smash for Soft Cell in 1982.

The Standells reformed for a few one-off gigs during the 80s, and then, after a long silence, they had one last shot at glory before the beginning of the new millennium. November 1999 found The Standells stalking the stage for the first time in ten years: it was New York City's Cavestomp festival that gave these freakbeat fugitives a home. Dodd, Tamblyn, Valentino and replacement bassist Peter Stuart were faced with the unenviable task of following the Monks on stage; they more than rose to the occasion, delivering a punishing set. Luckily, the tape deck was rolling and captured every note. The resultant performance was issued a year later as BAN THIS!, strangely enough, the only live album The Standells ever issued.

The Standells could have been massive, but there again, their failure to make the big time has guaranteed them a place in the garage pantheon of glorious losers.

⊙ **The Best Of The Standells** (1987; Rhino).
All you really need to know of the band, from "Dirty Water" to "Try It".

⊙ **Hot Hits And Hot Ones – Is This The Way You Get Your High** (1993; Ace/BigBeat).
Another collection, with everything you need except a cheap moptop haircut for the full garage fuzztone experience.

Iain Smith

VIVIAN STANSHALL

Born Shillingford, England, 1943; died 1995.

The greatest radio comedian since Tony Hancock, and so much more, **Vivian Stanshall** was born in rural Oxfordshire but spent his formative years in urban Essex. Stanshall was a prodigy but was emotionally crippled by his father's inability to show him any affection – from this grew a lifetime's eccentricity and a refusal to conform, even with his own best instincts.

Fleeing suburbia for art school, Stanshall co-founded the **BONZO DOG DOO-DAH BAND** in 1965. After their demise in early 1970, he formed the **Sean Head Showband**, a combo that never gigged and produced just one (completely uncommercial) single, the tongue-twisting "Labio Dental Fricative", which was graced by Eric Clapton's presence. Viv now formed **Big Grunt**, and released the hilarious "Blind Date", coupled with a cover of "Suspicion" which nears paranoia – Elvis on LSD.

After a nervous breakdown and a job as the narrator for **MIKE OLDFIELD**'s TUBULAR BELLS, Stanshall was back on the music scene in 1974 with the album MEN OPENING UMBRELLAS AHEAD. **STEVE WINWOOD** guested on bass and organ, and Stanshall repaid the compliment by providing lyrics for some of Winwood's own solo projects, including "Vacant Chair", a sombre meditation on death which may well have been inspired by the premature demise of bass player Dennis Cowan.

The late lamented Sir Henry Rawlinson

saga, 1984's HENRY AT NDIDIS KRAAL, came over as one-dimensional and racist.

Stanshall had spent many years fighting an addiction to alcohol and tranquillizers, and a TV documentary of the time showed a pathetic figure, barely *compos mentis*. He had lost almost all of his possessions when his houseboat sank. After another stay in a mental hospital, he emerged to live in a small flat in Crouch End, from which he would sally forth in bedroom slippers to buy booze. It was here that he died in a fire on March 5, 1995, but not before his career and – more to the point – his wit had begun to revive. His play *Stinkfoot* was performed at London's Bloomsbury Theatre in 1988 and three years later he held a musical residency at the Angel, Islington. DOGENDS acted as a kind of premature wake, with former Bonzos like Neil Innes, Rodney Slater and Roger Ruskin Spear joining in the mayhem.

In a final irony, Vivian Stanshall died a century to the day after the demise of the real Sir Henry Rawlinson, a famed Victorian historian of the highest seriousness. There is as yet no sign of the album (on which Viv was working just before he died) being released. There is, though, a growing interest in Stanshall's eccentric lifestyle and the richness of his work, with a major biography being written on him by a philosophy don, no less.

SIR HENRY AT RAWLINSON END is now available on CD. During Christmas 1996, BBC Radio 4 re-broadcast five fifteen-minute segments, originally recorded for Radio l's John Peel programme, as short stories, taking the narrative even further into the surreal. As a primeval beast emerges from the egg, Sir Henry takes great delight in getting it in the sights of his twelve-bore. 'There's only room for one dinosaur at Rawlinson End', he chunters.

Around this time, Stanshall filled in for John Peel on Radio 1 and produced a month of verbal free association and outrageous scatology, while broadcasting a host of justly obscure records. He was often partnered by Who drummer Keith Moon, who assisted him in creating bizarre characters like the failed rocker, Johnny Wardrobe. Many of these were recycled in Stanshall's continuing Rawlinson End saga, broadcast sporadically by Peel. Some of the episodes were rerecorded for the 1978 album, SIR HENRY AT RAWLINSON END, and this in turn became a book and a film, in which Trevor Howard played his last major role, as Sir Henry.

Stanshall had long been a fan of Fairport Convention and its offshoots, so the presence of **RICHARD THOMPSON** on Stanshall's TEDDY BOYS DON'T KNIT (1981) was eagerly anticipated, but the record seemed half-baked, and the songs self-referential and either inconsequential or over-serious. Like many geniuses, Stanshall operated in fits and starts, and the second release in the Rawlinson End

⊙ **Men Opening Umbrellas Ahead** (1974; Warners)
His first solo LP reflects Stanshall's deep love and understanding of African music, allied to lyrics that are a mix of pure filth and bitterness. Stanshall tries on a series of roles and voices: in "Redeye", he comes on like an Old Testament prophet, and the result is both moving and scary.

⊙ **Sir Henry At Rawlinson End** (1978; Charisma).
Viv hot-wires his subconscious to bring us a weird take on English eccentricity and the last twitches of the English class system. Scrotum the wrinkled retainer, Sir Henry's private concentration camp, Hubert modelling a sundial with his own private parts ... it's best heard in a state of alcoholic excess.

Brian Hinton

THE STAPLE SINGERS

Formed Chicago, 1951.

Born in Winona, Mississippi, a few days after Christmas in 1915, **Roebuck 'Pops' Staples** grew up on the music of Delta bluesmen Robert Johnson and Charlie Patton, and started playing guitar at the age of 16. He sang with a gospel group called The Golden Trumpets until 1935, when he moved to Chicago with his wife Oceola, daughter **Cleotha** and son **Pervis**. Here he joined another gospel group, the Trumpet Jubilees, and continued with his guitar playing while holding down a day job in a steel mill. The family was soon joined by two new daughters when **Yvonne** was born in 1939, followed by **Mavis** in 1940.

Before long, it became evident that the children had inherited their father's musical talent, and they would sing with him accompanying on guitar. Back then, blues music was frowned upon by the black church, who considered it worldly or even sinful, and Pops' use of blues guitar in gospel songs was at the same time both innovative and alienating.

Pops first sang with his children as **The Staple Singers** in church in 1951. Their performances soon became a regular feature, but it was not until 1954, when Yvonne and Mavis had finished school, that they went into the studio for the first time. Signed to United Records (one of several small independent labels in Chicago), they recorded a traditional gospel song, "Sit Down Servant". The label's owner wanted them to sing rock'n'roll, which they refused to do, and they were contractually stuck with United for two years, recording nothing.

When their United contract expired, they signed to another independent, Vee Jay, and before long they were being hailed as 'the first family of gospel', with hit recordings such as "If I Can Get My Brother To Pray Again" and "Uncloudy Day". They stayed with Vee Jay for four years, recording around forty tracks. One of them, "This May Be The Last Time", provided the inspiration for a Rolling Stones hit, "The Last Time".

In 1961 the group moved to Columbia, following a brief stint at Riverside Records. Although Columbia struggled to find the right way to market a gospel group, the Staples started a very prolific recording career. Starting with GOSPEL PROGRAM in 1961, they released an album a year (sometimes two) until 1978, with only one or two breaks. However, it was not until they moved to Stax in July 1968 that the hits really started. A year earlier, Pops had deliberately moved away from strictly gospel-based material towards writing songs that contained positive messages and social comment without being overtly religious. With this new approach, they had scored two hit singles: "Why Am I Treated So Bad" (1967) and a cover of Buffalo Springfield's "For What It's Worth" (1967). They joined Stax on the invitation of producer Al Bell, who had intended to produce them himself, but had to wait two years before he got the chance. Pervis left the group in 1970 to work as a record producer, and Yvonne, who had taken a break, rejoined. Shortly after this reshuffle, they had their first major hit single, "Heavy Makes You Happy".

Their biggest hit came in 1972. "I'll Take You There" was their first US #1 and also made the Top 30 in the UK. The same year saw them grace the American R&B Top 10 with "Respect Yourself", while a remake of "I'll Take You There", "If You're Ready (Come Go With Me)", made it the following year. During their stay at Stax, Pops recorded a solo album, JAMMED TOGETHER (with Steve Cropper and Albert King), and Mavis recorded two: MAVIS STAPLES (1969) and ONLY FOR THE LONELY (1970).

In 1976 they signed to the Curtom label under the wing of Curtis Mayfield, and moved even further away from gospel music to more mainstream R&B. The alliance with Mayfield would give them their second US #1 single – the theme song from the Sidney Poitier/Bill Cosby film, *Let's Do It Again*. After this, though, the hits dried up as the black market was dominated by funk and disco.

The mid 80s saw a slight resurgence in their chart career, most notably with a cover of Talking Heads' "Slippery".

⊙ Respect Yourself: The Best Of The Staple Singers (1988; Stax).
A retrospective of the period in The Staples' career for which they are best remembered.

George Luke

STARSAILOR

Formed Wigan, England, 1999.

Starsailor don't bite the heads off chickens on stage, and they record the kind of music – rooted in the tradition of singer/songwriters such as Tim Buckley and Van Morrison – that prompts fathers to stumble into darkened teenage bedrooms to chirpily ask 'what's this?' But despite the group's seemingly universal appeal, their rise polarized the music press into two factions: those who saw Starsailor as the best new band around and those who saw the group as a bunch of wishy-washy indie no-hopers fronted by a singer with a voice that could curdle milk.

Starsailor's singer/guitarist **James Walsh** started to play the piano and write songs in the early 90s as a young teen, but his love of music led him beyond the confines of the indie-guitar Britpop scene of the time. It was the work of troubadours such as Nick Drake, Neil Young and Tim Buckley (whose 1970 album would provide Walsh with a name for his troop) that inspired this propitious songsmith to start a band.

Whilst studying music at college Walsh hooked up with **Ben Byrne** (drums) and **James "Stel" Stelfox** (bass): Starsailor was born. The band's sound was, for a while, augmented by the riffs of various

James Walsh (left) and his fellow Starsailors

electric guitarists – none of whom made the grade – before a permanent fourth member was enlisted, one **Barry Westhead** (keyboards), a classically trained musician with a jazz palette who frequently played the organ in a local church. With a permanent line-up and a solidified sound the band started to gig and demo their songs.

In April 2000 Starsailor played their first London show, at the Heavenly Social, and at around the same time a tape of "Fever", "Coming Down" and "Love Is Here" was circulating. By the middle of the year there were numerous record companies angling for the band, though it was EMI who landed the catch.

The group kicked off 2001 with an *NME*-sponsored tour alongside JJ72 and Amen, before unleashing their debut single, "Fever". Both "Fever" and its follow-up, "Good Souls", rocketed into the UK Top 20, while their third single, "Alcoholic" managed a Top 10 ranking.

Early in 2002 the group's debut album, LOVE IS HERE, hit the shelves. The set was critically praised and sold well, with many hailing a return of indie values that had not been witnessed since before the days of Britpop. But for others the band, and their sound, were stifled by the same terminal mediocrity that maintains MOR indie coasters such as Travis.

Starsailor have as yet not suffered the indignity of either a media backlash or a sales flop, but the signs are there and it is by no means certain that this band will continue to sail such calm seas as they have so far enjoyed.

Love Is Here (2002, EMI).
The whole set is defined by the overwrought vocals of James Walsh, whose stream of observations of love and human nature you will either despise or adore.

Peter Buckley

STATUS QUO

Formed London, 1962. Split briefly 1984; re-formed 1986.

Aspiring London band, The Spectre – **Francis Rossi** (guitar/vocals), **Alan Lancaster** (bass/vocals) and **John Coghlan** (drums) – recruited former Butlins camp entertainer **Rick Parfitt** (guitar/vocals) and changed their name to **Status Quo** to record the psychedelic hit single "Pictures Of Matchstick Men", in 1967. It was a prophetic name change for a band whose music has remained largely unchanged for the past 25 years.

After the similarly styled but unsuccessful album, PICTURESQUE MATCHSTICKABLE MESSAGES (1968), the band re-emerged with the British hit single "Down The Dustpipe" (1970), which signalled their move towards twelve-bar blues-rock. The album DOG OF TWO HEAD (1971) confirmed the appeal of their formulaic anglicized R&B. A dispute with Pye saw the band sign what would prove to be a mutually lucrative contract with Vertigo, for whom they delivered the more obstreperous PILEDRIVER (1973). Heavy enough to attract more discerning rock fans, it featured the pounding "Big Fat Mama", a version of The Doors' "Roadhouse Blues", plus the UK Top 10 hit, "Paper Plane".

HELLO (1973) entered the British album chart at #1 and spawned the hit single, "Caroline", sung by lead guitarist Rossi, whose cheery voice and waistcoats became identifying features of the band. QUO (1974) was another triumph, showcasing the band's professional interplay, customarily building a riff into a frenzied rock'n'roll jam. ON THE LEVEL (1975) saw the band reach their commercial peak, with "Down Down" providing a UK #1 single. Quo were now a national institution, indelibly associated with long hair and 'air guitar'. By the late 70s the band's recorded output had become shamelessly repetitious, though this mattered little to the dedicated fans, now fondly dubbed The Quo Army.

As Status Quo proceeded into the 80s, their music became tamer but the hits continued unabated. Drummer Coghlan was to leave in 1982 (being replaced by **Peter Kirchner**) while part-time keyboardist **Andy Bown** became a permanent member in 1984. Internal disagreements and drug problems caused the band to split briefly in 1984, although they provided a much-praised opening to the Live Aid concert at Wembley in 1985. Rossi and Parfitt reformed the group in 1986, much to the disdain of Lancaster, who began a successful career with **Australia's Party Boys**.

Eventually Rossi and Parfitt were complemented by the relatively solid line-up of Andy Bown (keyboards), **John 'Rhino' Edwards** (bass) and **Jeff Rich** (drums). Though their later albums, such as THIRSTY WORK (1994), plod along effortlessly, The Quo Army are still taking conscripts at their spirited and adequately heavy live shows.

Status Quo have now sold over 100 million records and amassed nearly fifty UK hits (they have never had much luck in the US), including "Whatever You Want" (1979), John Fogerty's "Rockin' All Over The World" (1977), the uncharacteristically sombre "In The Army Now" (1986), and, to celebrate 25 years in the business, the #2 hit "Anniversary Waltz" (1990). Meanwhile they chose to celebrate their thirtieth anniversary with DON'T STOP (1996), which consisted of stompalong covers of an eccentric choice of 'favourite songs', including "Fun Fun Fun", on which they persuaded The Beach Boys to guest.

Somewhat bizarrely, another covers set – FAMOUS IN THE LAST CENTURY (2000) – followed not long after, preceded by UNDER THE INFLUENCE (1999), which was hailed by some as one of the band's best latter-day recordings. Most recently, a three-CD anthology THE ESSENTIAL STATUS QUO (2001) was released, while **Matthew Letley** has taken over the drums after Rich left to spend more time with his family. A new album titled HEAVY TRAFFIC rolled out in 2002.

⦿ **Hello** (1973; Vertigo).
Twenty years on, Francis Rossi still cites this as his proudest work. Hits aside, the album includes a paean to laziness in "Softer Ride" and live favourite "Forty Five Hundred Times" (at nine minutes plus, a headbanger's stamina test).

⦿ **Quo** (1974; Vertigo).
Recorded at the band's peak, this is their rockiest album. A smoking set of twelve-bar bedlam.

⦿ **Twelve Gold Bars** (1980; Vertigo).
The obligatory collection of Quo hits, drawing material from the band's best years (1970–80).

Michael Andrews

Quo with uncharacteristic heads-up pose: Francis Rossi, Rick Parfitt and Alan Lancaster

Formed St. Alban's, England, 1969;
disbanded 1978; re-formed 1984.

With the single exception of Fairport
Convention, no band has created so successful a fusion of rock and traditional British folk
music as **Steeleye Span**. The group began when ex-
FAIRPORT CONVENTION bassist **Ashley Hutchings**
merged with two folk-club duos: **Maddy Prior**
(vocals) and **Tim Hart** (vocals/guitar/dulcimer), and
Terry (guitar/vocals) and **Gay Woods** (vocals/con-
certina). However, during sessions for their debut
album, HARK THE VILLAGE WAIT (1970), it transpired that the Woods were not in artistic accord
with the others. They were replaced by **Peter
Knight** (violin/mandolin) and renowned folk
revivalist singer **Martin Carthy**.

Thus the Steeleyes were born, recording, with this
line-up, the ground-breaking 1971 albums PLEASE
TO SEE THE KING and TEN MAN MOP (or MR.
RESERVOIR BUTLER RIDES AGAIN). As well as being
hugely original – in reworking traditional tunes in a
rock context – they were hugely popular, entering
the mainstream UK charts.

After Hutchings left to form the **Albion Country
Band** and Carthy to continue his solo career, the
group were signed to Chrysalis and enlisted **Rick
Kemp** (ex-bass player for Michael Chapman and,
briefly, **KING CRIMSON**) and guitarist **Bob Johnson**
who, prior to becoming an accountant, had served
P. J. Proby and Gary Glitter. After 1972's BELOW
THE SALT spawned a yuletide hit in the a cappella
Latin carol, "Gaudete", and the folk-pop treachery
of PARCEL OF ROGUES (1973), the group compounded their 'selling out' by augmenting their
sound with drummer (and flautist) **Nigel Pegrum**
for NOW WE ARE SIX (1974). The purist-defying
experimentation reached its limits when Peter Sellers
played ukelele on "New York Girls" from
COMMONERS' CROWN (1975).

Produced by Womble *Führer* Mike Batt, 1975's
ALL AROUND MY HAT and its title-track single
marked Steeleye Span's commercial apogee in both
Britain and the US, but they'd gone off the boil by
the release of the following year's ROCKET
COTTAGE. Individual members were less than com-
mitted to the group at this stage, as Prior formed the
Silly Sisters with June Tabor, and Knight and
Johnson departed before 1978's STORM FORCE
TEN.

Though they'd rallied by calling on Carthy and
accordionist John Kirkpatrick, this album was also
Steeleye Span's valediction, until the 1975 line-up,
minus Hart, reunited in 1984 for BACK IN LINE – on
which they sounded as if they'd never been away –
and, bar Kemp, for another album, 1989's TEMPTED
AND TRIED. In 1995, a charity concert – lasting eight
hours – at London's Forum united most past and present members of the outfit.

Since then the studio sets have come thick and fast,
with the most recent being 2000's BEDLAM BORN,
which featured Woods, Johnson and Knight, with
the addition of **Tim Harries** (bass/guitars) and **Dave
Mattacks** (drums). After its release Johnson departed
to be replaced by old-friend Kemp for the subsequent
tour.

⊙ **Please To See The King** (1971; Chrysalis).
This album defines their attitude towards musical and
historical context. Tracks like "Cold Rainy Windy Night",
"Bedlam Boys" and a radical overhaul of "The Blacksmith"
affirm the staying power.

⊙ **Now We Are Six** (1974; Chrysalis).
Produced by Jethro Tull's Ian Anderson, this display of
versatility embraces both mordant ballads and an arrangement of the Teddy Bears' "To Know You Is To Love You"
(with guest saxophonist David Bowie).

⊙ **Present – The Very Best Of...** (2002; Park Records).
This interesting 2CD document finds a classic line-up
rerecording their hits for the new millennium.

Alan Clayson

Formed Los Angeles, 1972; disbanded 1981;
re-formed 1993.

The most cynical and ferociously intelligent songwriting partnership in rock, **Walter Becker**
(bass/guitar) and **Donald Fagen** (vocals/keyboards)
met at Bard College, New York State, in 1967.
Discovering a shared interest in jazz and Dylan lyrics,
the geeky duo struggled for years, trying to sell their
early songwriting efforts to Brill Building publishers
and recording demos with jazzy guitarist **Denny
Dias**. After a stint in Jay and the Americans, they
were rescued by producer Gary Katz and whisked off
to LA as staff writers for ABC-Dunhill records.
Setting these two New York cynics loose on the laid-
back, ditzy Californian scene was a masterstroke.

With Katz they assembled a band to showcase
their compositions, including Dias, **Jeff 'Skunk'
Baxter** (guitars), **David Palmer** (vocals) and **Jim
Hodder** (drums), and named the outfit **Steely Dan**
after a piece of 'intimate hardware' in William
Burroughs' cult novel *The Naked Lunch*. Their first
single, "Dallas", aroused little interest, but in early
1973 the album CAN'T BUY A THRILL had the critics
falling over themselves with superlatives, as the sitar-
and-percussion-driven single "Do It Again" tore up
the US charts.

The songs on the album bore the Steely Dan hallmarks of bitter, world-weary or impenetrable lyrics,
jazz- and Latin-tinged melodies and immaculate
musicianship. Despite having a band that could play
the ass off most of their competition, Becker and
Fagen were already starting to bring in top-flight
session musicians to get the precise sound they
wanted, a trend that would intensify on future
albums. Palmer left after this album – Fagen's New
Jersey sneer was much better suited to the material
anyway.

The second album, COUNTDOWN TO ECSTASY

(1973), hit new heights of musicianship and textual obscurity, and consolidated their popularity with critics and album-buyers while mysteriously failing to produce any hit singles. And that despite the presence of "My Old School", with its gorgeous guitar break. Still, the situation was soon remedied by the more radio-friendly PRETZEL LOGIC (1974), which yielded the irresistibly pretty "Rikki Don't Lose That Number", their biggest hit single.

By this time Becker and Fagen, hating life on the road and afflicted by stage fright, were sick of touring – and happy to stay home writing and occasionally recording. This left the rest of the band without much to do. In 1974 Baxter left to join **THE DOOBIE BROTHERS**, and Hodder also departed. Dias left after the next album, KATY LIED (1974), a less focused set which nevertheless sold well in the US and the UK.

From now on Steely Dan was essentially Becker and Fagen. Their next two albums, THE ROYAL SCAM (1976), which spawned their white-reggae UK hit "Haitian Divorce", and AJA (1977), saw them refine the Dan formula of smooth, funky rock songs topped off with solos by top jazz players who were allowed no room for self-indulgence. Despite the duo's legendary studio perfectionism (often demanding as many as thirty takes), the music was so good that top-flight session musicians queued up to work with them. AJA was perhaps the best-produced and one of the best-written albums of the whole decade.

After a jazzy, slick but somewhat soulless follow-up, GAUCHO (1981), drugs, depression and boredom led the pair to call it a day. Becker retreated to Hawaii, occasionally producing albums for other artists, while Fagen released a dazzling solo album, THE NIGHTFLY (1982), and a rather over-refined follow-up, KAMAKIRIAD, a mere twelve years later.

In 1993, the Dan re-formed for a triumphant comeback tour of the US, raising hopes of a new album – although, if they continue to bring out 'solo' efforts as good as Becker's Fagen-produced world-weary masterpiece 11 TRACKS OF WHACK (1994), we could bear to wait indefinitely. Meantime, the duo put out a live record of their American dates, ALIVE IN AMERICA (1995), an album of sometimes-perverse arrangements that nonetheless allowed the old songs to breathe again.

Following another reunion tour in 1999 Steely Dan released TWO AGAINST NATURE – their first new studio album together in nearly twenty years. Sly and – given time to grow – engrossing, this wasn't quite the full-strength Dan of AJA but it was insidious and slick enough to be going on with. Similarly, 2003's EVERYTHING MUST GO wasn't quite as triumphant as earlier outings, but given the nature of 'come-back' recordings, it could have been a whole lot worse.

Steely Dan

⊙ Can't Buy A Thrill (1973; ABC).
Immaculately conceived, Latin-tinged pop perfection – and perhaps the best debut since ARE YOU EXPERIENCED?.

Check out Elliot Randall's incendiary lead guitar on "Reelin' In The Years".

⊙ Countdown To Ecstasy (1973; ABC).
Finds the band's regular guitarists at the height of their powers, from Dias' effortless fluidity on "Bodhisattva" to the icy kiss of the Skunk's pedal steel on "Razor Boy".

⊙ Pretzel Logic (1974; ABC).
In which they show off their versatility by covering Duke Ellington's "East St. Louis Toodle-oo" and dressing up the songs with increasingly sophisticated arrangements. Jazzy, tuneful and fresh.

⊙ Aja (1977; ABC).
The quintessential Dan album, with a pervading after-hours feel. Gorgeous jazz arrangements and impossibly difficult chord changes coax career-best performances from their sessioneers.

Donald Fagen

⊙ The Nightfly (1982; Warners).
Fagen's first solo album is just about perfect. From a party in his dad's fallout shelter to the glittering graphite Utopia of the future, he evokes the new-frontier optimism of the late 50s and early 60s. Buttoned-down and immaculate.

Walter Becker

⊙ 11 Tracks Of Whack (1994; Giant).
Musically simpler and tougher than the later-period group albums, Becker's solo album is the work of a man who's been through it and come out the other side. His lyrics make most other rock writers seem sophomoric, and his bruised vocals pack a genuine emotional whack.

Andy Smith

STEPPENWOLF

Formed Los Angeles, 1967.

"Get your motor running/Head out on the highway/Lookin' for adventure... " *Born To Be Wild*

Some are born great, some achieve greatness, and some are great for the three and a half minutes in which they tell us they are "Born To Be Wild" (1968). Whereas Ken Kesey and his tribe cultivated The Grateful Dead, the truly American subculture of the Hell's Angels had to make do with **Steppenwolf**'s elegy to heavy-metal thunder, and to having a quarter of a ton of chrome humming between your legs.

Like their heroes, the be-denimed Foreign Legion of beer-swilling, tattoo-sporting outlaws who got their motors running and headed out on the highway, Steppenwolf were men without a past or a future, staring out of album covers and facial hair like an out-of-time Wild Bunch. For the record, they were the cohorts of one **John Kay**, born Joachim Krauleday, who dominated the band with his raucous vocals and songwriting that dealt in off-the-peg mysticism. His cast of losers and dreamers were all seen through rose-tinted glasses that looked upon lines like 'He only had a dollar to live on to next Monday/But he spent it all on comfort for his mind' and didn't see anything wrong. Ripping off Hesse, Burroughs or Bergman was all in a day's work.

With **Jerry Edmonton** on drums, **Michael Monarch** on second guitar, **Nick St Nicholas** on bass, **Goldy McJohn** playing keyboards like he was just introduced to the instrument, and **Mars Bonfire** (really Jerry's brother Denny) beefing up the sound with a second guitar, the band plied their trade in the mid 60s as a Canadian blues band called Sparrow, before Kay whipped them into the gang of Steppenwolf. These grizzled stormtroopers were Kay's weapons against the music industry, which he plagued with at least two albums a year before Mars Bonfire handed him "Born To Be Wild".

When Dennis Hopper and Peter Fonda were looking for an anthem for their biker movie, Steppenwolf were the obvious choice to provide the soundtrack. "Born To Be Wild" and "The Pusher", the twin peaks of Steppenwolf's career, both featured in *Easy Rider*, and helped Kay foist six similar-sounding albums on the public over the next two years.

On the American highway, the Hell's Angels could still be seen chasing after their own definition. They always travel faster than the next man. They never stop. Steppenwolf could only limp on. In 1972 Kay split the band to go solo, but by 1974 they were back. Only the members changed: Mars Bonfire had bigger fish to fry with **SKY SAXON**, and **Bobby Cochran** joined on guitar. They continue to tour, leather-jacketed and tie-dyed, easy to ridicule as rockin' dinosaurs but, in their defence, still alive and kicking – unlike so many of their contemporaries who took on the rock'n'roll lifestyle and lost. The albums don't come as quickly nowadays – although the IRS label briefly flirted with Kay and set RISE AND SHINE (1998) on the world, while the latest in a string of solo outings, HERETICS AND PRIVATEERS, emerged in 2001– but they too are always rounding the next bend, chasing the white line to where the sun sets.

⊙ **16 Greatest Hits** (1973; MCA).
The cream of Steppenwolf's first eight albums skimmed into a barely digestible hour. It peaks early with "Born To Be Wild".

Charles Bottomley

THE STEREO MCS

Formed London, 1985.

Paradoxically, British hip-hop's resurgence in the early 90s coincided with **The Stereo MCs'** switch from the hip-hop staple of sampled beats to live instruments. If this increased the problem of how to categorize them, it also created a more coherent band that was finally able to stand clear of its influences. Britain's most credible rap act and one of the country's most impressive live bands, The Stereo MCs gained mainstream recognition in February 1994, when they won the Brit Awards for Best Group and Best Album (CONNECTED).

The band's creation was due in part to property developers. When rapper **Rob B** (aka Rob Birch) and DJ/producer **The Head** (aka Nick Hallam) were offered £7000 to leave a London flat, they used the money to form their own label, Gee Street. They quickly gained the support of New York's 4th & Broadway label, who helped distribute a succession of singles and, finally, a debut album, 33-45-78 (1989).

Original member **Cesare** left amicably after the album's release; **Owen If** (aka Owen Rossiter; drums) and backing vocalist **Cath Coffey** remained. A shrewd move on the latter's part, as the next single, "Elevate My Mind", became the first British rap record to enter the US *Billboard* chart in July 1990. Gearing up to the release of a second album, SUPERNATURAL (1990) a few months later, the band opened for Happy Mondays on a US tour, then returned to the UK to hit the road with EMF. The big breakthrough came with CONNECTED (1992), an album on which the band wrote and produced all the material themselves, and which spawned several hits – the title track, "Step It Up", "Creation" and "Ground Level", the last couple with Andy Weatherall's remixes of "Everything", a track that proved The Stereos could still appeal to clubbers even after their switch from samples to live sound.

A subsequent British and European tour sold out, and they supported U2 on some of their 1993 *Zooropa* tour, but The Stereos didn't take off in the US. But the band didn't seem too concerned: according to The Head, The Stereo MCs' philosophy is to mature and develop, without taking too much notice of trends or critical reception.

Perhaps this is just as well. After an eight-year absence, during which fans had little to ease their withdrawal symptoms, bar a few remixes and an admittedly excellent DJ KICKS mix compilation, the MCs returned with a barely evolved musical style that was frankly a little out of step. With dance music having undergone numerous schisms and a burgeoning UK hip-hop scene, DEEP, DOWN & DIRTY (2001) smelt decidedly anachronistic; despite a couple of reasonable grooves (the title track and the crudely amphetamine "Running") it was something of a disappointment after so long. 2003's RECONNECTED 'best of' was a pleasing reminder of past glories, but it seems that the Stereo MCs' time has now passed.

⊙ **Supernatural** (1990; 4th & Broadway).
A well-packed album, and lyrically superior to CONNECTED; though, as The Head says, 'it was easier to spot the influences'.

⊙ **Connected** (1992; 4th & Broadway).
A marked maturation in style and sound on their best seller to date.

⊙ **Deep, Down & Dirty** (2001; Island).
The scrubbed-up production of DEEP, DOWN & DIRTY lacks the live, primal feel of CONNECTED; it seems anything but dirty, and a little lightweight.

Matthew Grant

STEREOLAB

Formed London, 1990.

Avant-garde MOR, ambient boogie: these are a couple of self-suggested genres in which to slot **Stereolab** – a group formed from the embers of

The late Mary Hansen lost in the vibe with Tim Gane

indie band McCarthy by **Tim Gane** (guitars) and **Laetitia Sadier** (vocals/Moog), with the addition of **Martin Kean** (bass) and **Joe Dilworth** (drums). Their sound combines elements of such experimental stalwarts as The Velvet Underground and Neu!, with material drawn from outside the conventional areas of rock – ranging from French 60s girl pop groups to stereo-testing records (the name Stereolab was taken from Vanguard Records' hi-fi division). Laetitia Sadier's lyrics, meanwhile, contain a barbed array of situationist invective against orthodoxy, usually mixed low and/or sung in French, in subliminal counterpoint to the heady rush of the buzzing Moogs and one-note guitar solos.

The group's first single, "Super 45", was released through their own Duophonic Super 45s label in May 1991, and led to their second, "Super-Electric", appearing on the Too Pure label in the following autumn. A third single, "Stunning Debut Album" (Duophonic), completed a trio of records that sold out without publicity. After a brief tour with Moose, Stereolab recorded their first Too Pure album, PENG! (1992), which topped the UK indie charts, while their radio session was included on TOO PURE – THE PEEL SESSIONS. A singles compilation, SWITCHED ON, also appeared in 1992. These recordings were followed by a string of singles, often vinyl limited editions. As vinyl junkies themselves, Stereolab appreciate the aesthetics of the rare record, and have provided ample material for collectors and discographers.

During 1992 the group's line-up changed to include **Mary Hansen** (vocals/guitar/Moog), **Duncan Brown** (bass/vocals), **Andy Ramsay** (drums), and frequent collaborator **Sean O'Hagan** (keyboards), then fashioning **THE HIGH LLAMAS**. The band toured extensively, at times seeming to be playing every venue in Britain, small or large, both headlining and supporting.

In 1993, Stereolab were even more active, releasing no fewer than nine singles and one and a half LPs, and fitting in a first tour of the US. THE GROOP PLAYED SPACE AGE BACHELOR PAD MUSIC mini-LP appeared in March, a taster for the double-vinyl/CD TRANSIENT RANDOM NOISE BURSTS WITH ANNOUNCEMENTS, which marked their departure from Too Pure in favour of their own new subsidiary Duophonic Ultra-High Frequency Disks (with a licensing deal with Elektra in the US). The JENNY ONDIOLINE EP led to one track, "French Disko", in a shortened form, receiving widespread airplay. Stereolab continued determinedly to release experimental and vinyl-only records, including the Faust/Cluster-inspired Nurse With Wound collaborations "Crumb Duck" 10" (1993) and "Simple Headphone Mind" (1997) and the "Shimmies In Super 8" double 7" compilation with Huggy Bear and Colm (later to become Daft Punk following a *Melody Maker* review of the single).

With successful *Lollapalooza* and European tours completed in the spring and summer of 1994, Stereolab returned to the studio – with the addition

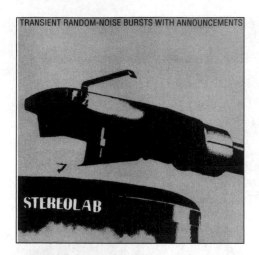
TRANSIENT RANDOM-NOISE BURSTS WITH ANNOUNCEMENTS

STEREOLAB

of **Katherine Gifford** on Moogs and Farfisas – to work on MARS AUDIAC QUINTET. This album launched them firmly into the higher stratum of indie pop, without quite tipping over into the mainstream. More accessible than previous releases, the album established them as an act able to sell out large venues, while maintaining their credibility as an experimental and eclectic group.

Katherine Gifford and Duncan Brown have since departed the group, replaced by **Morgane Lhote** and **Richard Harrison**. "Cybele's Reverie" and the album EMPEROR TOMATO KETCHUP (both 1996) were partly recorded in Chicago with John McEntire of **TORTOISE**, with whom Stereolab toured in early 1996. Further collaborations with McEntire and German electronic duo **MOUSE ON MARS** resulted in DOTS AND LOOPS (1997), a lateral leap into full-on melodic pop, which virtually abandoned the group's previous style, without losing the experimental edge. However, Gane and Sadier channelled their lo-fi energies into the **Turn On** and **Monade** side-projects respectively, as Stereolab proper stretched itself into unfamiliar shapes. They also initiated the CHINESE WHISPERS relay album for the Sprawl Imprint as a circular sample project, beginning and ending the ten remixes from various notables of UK electronica. Stereolab caught the remix bug, contributing to Microstoria's REPROVISERS (Mille Plateaux; 1997) and The Pastels' ILLUMINATI (Domino; 1998).

The SWITCHED ON series continued with REFRIED ECTOPLASM (SWITCHED ON VOLUME 2) (1996) and ALUMINUM TUNES (SWITCHED ON VOLUME 3) (1998). These excellent collections of singles and genuinely interesting rarities contrast nicely with the albums, providing periodic updates on the band's most recent musical directions and filling in the many gaps in fans' collections – caused by Stereolab's fascination with limited editions. Everything a collectors' series should be.

The group brought everybody's favourite experimentalist **Jim O'Rourke** in to co-produce COBRA AND PHASES GROUP PLAY VOLTAGE IN THE MILKY

NIGHT (1999) with McEntire, plus new bass player **Simon Johns**. This, THE FIRST OF THE MICROBE HUNTERS mini-album (2000) and SOUND-DUST (2001) took the DOTS & LOOPS future-pop template to new heights of studio production, and greater mass appeal than ever before.

A collection of Radio 1 sessions, ABC MUSIC, was released in the autumn of 2002. But tragedy was to strike the group in December when Mary Hansen, a core member of the troop for a decade, was killed in a cycling accident. Both the band and fans everywhere were shocked and saddened by this terrible and pointless loss. Since Hansen's death Laetitia has been working on Monade material, and Simon has been occupied with his other band, **Imitation Electric Piano**. Stereolab are now back in the studio, and new material is sure to follow soon.

◉ **Switched On** (1992; Too Pure).
This compilation of the first three singles is essential for "Super-Electric", Stereolab's first hit and still a live favourite. Two further collections of oddities, SWITCHED ON VOL. 2 (1995) and ALUMINUM TUNES - SWITCHED ON VOL. 3 (1998), complete the picture.

◉ **Transient Random Noise-Bursts With Announcements** (1993; Duophonic).
A tapestry of ephemeral self-reference from the cover via the sleeve notes to the music itself. Studio manipulations predominate in some of the group's most extreme recordings, including the epic 17-minute version of "Jenny Ondioline".

◉ **Mars Audiac Quintet** (1994; Duophonic).
Stereolab in situationist pop mode, with the lyrics getting the message over more blatantly to a wider audience. This is no bad thing, and the term Marxist Muzak seems to be a useful starting point.

◉ **Music For The Amorphous Body Study Center** (1995; Duophonic).
Accompanying Charles Long's sculptural installation in New York, the pieces on this mini-album apparently explore the relationship between the physical and the sonic through a collective listening environment.

◉ **Emperor Tomato Ketchup** (1996; Duophonic).
Avant-pop arrangements and the trademark noisy analogue synths in about equal proportions, with "Metronomic Underground" showing the funky influence of producer John McEntire.

◉ **Dots & Loops** (Duophonic; 1997).
The album that finally broke from the NEU! mould, inspired instead by Venezuelan psychedelic music and 60s Italian soundtracks.

◉ **Cobra And Phases Group Play Voltage In The Milky Night** (1999; Duophonic).
Here Jim O'Rourke injects Stereolab's sound with his unique taste for quirk and layers to produce the most satisfying of their more recent collections.

Richard Fontenoy

STEREOPHONICS

Formed Cwmaman, Wales, 1996.

The **Stereophonics** – comprising **Kelly Jones** (vocals/guitar), **Richard Jones** (bass) and **Stuart Cable** (drums) – are a power trio from a small town in South Wales, which, despite its apparently close-knit exterior, inspired Kelly Jones's lyrics to explore subject matters like infidelity, gossip, intrigue and murder – in other words topics equally applicable to those in the heart of the big city. This universality, as well as anthemic choruses, may explain how in only a short time they have become one of Britain's most highly touted rock bands.

The trio became well known in Wales after the screening of a BBC television documentary entitled *Alright Or What*, which combined film of their support slot on tour with the Manic Street Preachers with backstage footage. By the time the film scooped an award at the 1997 Welsh BAFTAs, the band had supported Skunk Anansie, Kenickie, and even The Who at a London show in December 1996.

Having already signed to V2 Records in the autumn of 1996, Stereophonics' first double A-sided single, "Looks Like Chaplin"/"More Life In A Tramp's Vest" quickly sold out its limited run. Follow-ups "A Thousand Trees" and "Traffic" charted healthily, and after a triumphant series of appearances at summer festivals across the UK, their debut LP, WORD GETS AROUND (1997) could conceivably have stormed the charts even without the support of the pop, rock and alternative music press. It shot to #6 in the LP charts and led to their nomination and subsequent victory as Best British Newcomer at the Brit Awards in February 1998. Public demand led to a rerelease of "The Local Boy In The Photograph", a minor hit in early 1997; this time round it reached #14.

Stereophonics' Kelly Jones

Even though most of 1998 passed without the release of much new material, they performed a spectacular show at Cardiff Castle (which was recorded for subsequent video release), embarked on a full-scale UK tour, and were reportedly invited round to dinner at the house of Kevin Spacey, Hollywood actor and Stereophonics fan. Constant touring meant that their name was not allowed to be forgotten, and their hard work was rewarded in November 1998 when their frenetic "The Bartender And The Thief" raced straight to #3 in the charts – their biggest hit to date. It rounded off an extraordinary twelve months, blighted only by the ugly news in July that Richard Jones had been assaulted outside a local pub, resulting in a broken nose and ribs.

The future looked undeniably rosy for Stereophonics: 1999 brought further Top 10 hits in "Just Looking" and "Pick A Part That's New", and an enormously successful second album in PERFORMANCE AND COCKTAILS (1999). They also became one of the biggest home-grown live draws of the year, including a sell-out show to 50,000 fans at Swansea's Morfa Stadium that same summer. Kelly Jones even found himself duetting with Tom Jones on a hit cover of Randy Newman's "Mama Told Me Not To Come". Unfortunately, the third Stereophonics album, JUST ENOUGH EDUCATION TO PERFORM (2001), suggested the formula was becoming exhausted, both in terms of content and form, but this did not stop it racing to the top of the charts and spawning equally well-received hit singles in "Mr Writer", "Have A Nice Day" and the monstrously successful "Handbags And Gladrags".

In 2003 they followed on with the confusing YOU GOTTA GET THERE TO COME BACK, which found the band ripping up rock's graveyard to present a collection of riff-heavy 70s rock sound-a-like numbers. Whether the group were just making the most of the freedom that success brings or simply reacting against it was unclear, but it certainly left many fans flummoxed.

Whatever their motivations, success has not spoiled them yet, and they have no plans to leave Cwmaman: they have all bought properties there.

⊙ **Word Gets Around** (1997; V2).
Stridently self-confident fare from a band unlikely to be one-album wonders, this boasts hard-edged rock music, shot through with Kelly Jones's sense of lyrical black comedy.

⊙ **Just Enough Education To Perform** (2001; V2).
The Stereophonics' third album, intended to be a low-key and intimate tour-bus travelogue, is not so much self-revealing as self-parodying. The difficulty is that the Stereophonics have, in recent times, had little to write about except the trappings of their own success. Hopefully, the next album will not feature cuts with titles like "Tuesday: Hilton Munich Room 119", "We Are The Stereophonics" and "Writer's Block" (which, if they were being playful, would have at least been an instrumental).

Justin Lewis

DAVE STEWART

Born Sunderland, England, 1952.

Dave Stewart was 15 when he attended his first rock concert. He was so knocked out by the experience that he left home immediately to travel with the group, folk-rockers The Amazing Blondel, as a roadie and sometime rhythm guitarist. He stayed for three years, leaving to form **Harrison & Stewart** (a duo with Brian Harrison), and then joining **Longdancer** on guitar for two albums on Elton John's Rocket record label. Little came of these ventures, and, by the mid 70s, drug abuse and a near-fatal car accident in Germany had left him uncertain about his future in music.

It began to turn around in the summer of 1976 when, in a London restaurant with fellow Geordie musician Peet Coombes, he met then-waitress, **ANNIE LENNOX**. The trio formed The Tourists, then Stewart and Lennox set up in 1981 as **EURYTHMICS**.

Before long, Stewart would become as well-known as a producer as a musician. In addition to his productions for Eurythmics, he was behind the desk for Tom Petty & The Heartbreakers' SOUTHERN ACCENTS album (1985), Daryl Hall's THREE HEARTS IN THE HAPPY ENDING MACHINE (1986), and for artists as diverse as Bob Dylan, Mick Jagger and Feargal Sharkey. Dylan, in particular, was drawn to the anonymity of Stewart's home studio, located in the north London suburb of Crouch End.

Stewart then teamed up with **Terry Hall** (formerly of, amongst others, **THE SPECIALS**), under the name **Vegas**. Their 1992 album of the same name was again palatable but somewhat nondescript, its stand-out track a cover of Charles Aznavour's standard "She" that, alas, emerged just too early for Britain's easy-listening revival fad.

Aside from a soundtrack to the film *Jute City* (1991), it was 1994 before Stewart's first official solo album, GREETINGS FROM THE GUTTER, emerged. The record, with a party list of guests that included Lou Reed, Laurie Anderson, Carly Simon and Bootsy Collins, was still, perhaps, not as immediate or persuasive as Stewart's finest Eurythmics work, but there were hints at future delights, notably on the single "Heart Of Stone". Since then Stewart has immersed himself in seemingly countless projects covering everything from film production to photography, and in 1999 he and Lennox were awarded the *Lifetime Achievement Award* at the Brits (the duo went on to release a new Eurythmics studio set, PEACE, in 2001). His most recent work has involved the setting up of the Artist Network, an alternative and anti-establishment entertainment company aiming to nurture talent in a manner the mainstream corporate industry seems incapable of.

⊙ **Greetings From The Gutter** (1994; Anxious/Warners).
The album that showed that, while Annie Lennox may have the higher profile, her longtime collaborator is still not to be underestimated.

Justin Lewis

ROD STEWART

Born London, January 10, 1945.

"Sometimes a woman can really persuade you to make an asshole of yourself."

Despite his latter-day slide into soft-rock mediocrity, **Rod Stewart** stands as one of popular music's greatest interpretative singers, and was once equally adept at writing songs full of the romantic bravado of his stage persona.

Stewart's roots go back to the London R&B scene of the mid 60s, where he developed his distinctive sub-Sam Cooke vocal technique in a variety of short-lived groups, including Steampacket (with Long John Baldry and Julie Driscoll) and Shotgun Express. At the same time, Stewart was desperately trying to start a solo career, but with little success. Greater recognition came with a two-year spell (1967–69) as lead vocalist in the **JEFF BECK** group, although his voice sometimes sounded at odds with the proto-hard rock that Beck favoured.

Stewart left Beck to join **THE FACES** in 1969, fronting the band for the next five years or so, his voice sounding perfectly at home against the backdrop of The Faces' good-time pub rock. Yet it was with his parallel solo career that Stewart really carved out his distinctive niche. The first of his solo albums, AN OLD RAINCOAT WILL NEVER LET YOU DOWN (released as THE ROD STEWART ALBUM in the US), introduced his blend of acoustic and electric music, drawing on folk, soul and R&B. Backed by an eclectic band – notably the slapdash rhythm section of **Ron Wood** and **Mick Waller**, and brilliant guitarist **Martin Quittenton** – Stewart mixed his own hard-bitten narratives ("Cindy's Lament" and "Blind Prayer") with covers of Ewan MacColl's "Dirty Old Town" and Mike D'Abo's superb "Handbags And Gladrags".

Though praised by the critics, Stewart was still struggling to make commercial headway at the time of the 1970 follow-up, GASOLINE ALLEY. Retaining the core of the musicians from the first album (as he would for the next two releases), Stewart again crafted a raw and heartfelt sound on a striking mix of covers and originals. He also produced his finest vocal performance yet on the album's title track, perfectly complementing Wood's distinctive slide guitar.

Still touring and recording with The Faces, Stewart got his payback for the hectic schedule when "Maggie May" became one of 1971's biggest singles (#1 in the UK and US), despite starting its chart life as a B-side (to a cover of Tim Hardin's "Reason To Believe"). The combination of Quittenton's catchy melody, Stewart's lusty vocal and a mandolin break courtesy of Lindisfarne's **Ray Jackson**, proved irresistible. This in turn propelled EVERY PICTURE TELLS A STORY (1971) to the top of the charts, and the album deserved every bit of its success. The well-chosen covers (particularly Bob Dylan's obscure "Tomorrow Is A Long Time" and a spot-on take of The Temptations' "I Know I'm Losing You") blended perfectly with Stewart's fine original material, the highlight of which was the lovely "Mandolin Wind".

Stewart had now made it into the big time, and his strategy from this point onward became one of consolidation. NEVER A DULL MOMENT (1972) was a fine album that reprised the stylistic unity of EVERY PICTURE with great success, and included "You Wear It Well", another huge hit. But the following two years saw only the compilation album, SING IT AGAIN ROD (1973), and the lacklustre SMILER (1974), on which he sounded close to a parody of both himself and his musical heroes. (The Faces had also fallen apart during this time, as Stewart's solo success caused friction among the others.)

By 1975, Stewart had headed to America and into the arms of glamour actress Britt Ekland – the first in his sequence of blondes. Living the life of Riley in the Hollywood hills, Stewart was a long way from the working-class life that he had characterized in his earlier songs, and this distance took its toll on his music. ATLANTIC CROSSING (1975) sold loads, sounded wonderful first time anyone listened to it, and contained the infuriatingly catchy "Sailing". But it was a shallow record, lacking any real heart, which was all the more sad considering Stewart had enlisted great soul musicians of the calibre of Steve Cropper and Donald 'Duck' Dunn, and had persuaded legendary Memphis producer Tom Dowd to handle the record.

Stewart's decline into stadium rock and empty posturing from this point onwards is one of rock's more dismal stories. There were odd surprises, particularly A NIGHT ON THE TOWN (1976), which contained a great take on Cat Stevens' "First Cut Is The Deepest", and one of Stewart's last genuine performances on "The Killing Of Georgie". But there were also the disco horrors of the late 70s ("Hot Legs", "Do Ya Think I'm Sexy?", "Passion"), and, by the time of 1983's BODY WISHES, even the album covers had reached an all-time nadir.

Of course, Stewart has continued to sell bucketloads of records. In the 90s he showed a glimmer of his old self on VAGABOND HEART (1991) and in the energetic reunion with Ron Wood on the live MTV special *Unplugged*, perhaps spurred by the accolades for the excellent retrospective STORYTELLER (1990). But it is only rarely these days (on record, at least) that Stewart puts that great white soul voice to work on a song that merits his attention. IF WE FALL IN LOVE TONIGHT (1996) is really the worst kind of slap in the face for his undeniable army of fans, being a collection of familiar last-song-at-the-school-disco smoochy numbers, topped off with a sprinkling of new stuff. It will sell thousands in the week prior to Valentine's Day for years.

WHEN WE WERE THE NEW BOYS (1998), on the other hand, was a different creature entirely: a collection of cover versions – recent hits by other, younger artists. Though it was easy to write off as the old mod listening once too often to his kids' CD collections, this was his first 'proper' album, and the first in which he got his voice into gear, in a good while. More covers followed in 2002 on IT HAD TO BE YOU, where Stewart tackled such classics as "Every Time We Say Goodbye" and "That Old Feeling".

⊙ **An Old Raincoat Will Never Let You Down** (1969; Mercury).
Stewart's debut was a hard-nosed beauty, investing songs like "Street Fighting Man" and "Dirty Old Town" with all the gritty toughness they deserved. His own material followed closely behind, but it was Mike D'Abo's "Handbags And Gladrags" that formed the emotional centre of the album.

- **Gasoline Alley** (1970; Mercury).
  Even better than his debut, GASOLINE ALLEY showed Stewart able to cover material by both Elton John ("Country Comfort") and Bob Dylan ("Only A Hobo"), with impressive results. And Stewart and Wood have never done anything better than the title track.

- **Every Picture Tells A Story** (1971; Mercury).
  Stewart broke commercially on an artistic high, a feat surprisingly few achieve. "Maggie May", "I Know I'm Losing You", "Reason To Believe" and the peerless "Mandolin Wind" all feature great performances from band and singer alike.

- **Storyteller** (1990; Warners).
  Excellent four-CD retrospective, concentrating on Stewart's finest periods and dragging plenty of worthy rarities out of the archives.

- **When We Were The New Boys** (1998; Warners).
  Don't judge it until you've heard Rodney take on Oasis's "Cigarettes And Alcohol".

Nicholas Oliver

STIFF LITTLE FINGERS

Formed Belfast, Northern Ireland, 1977;
disbanded 1982; re-formed 1987.

Stiff Little Fingers were formed by school-friends **Jake Burns** (vocals/guitars), **Henry Cluney** (vocals/guitar), **Ali McMordie** (bass/vocals) and **Brian Faloon** (drums), inspired by the punk rock explosion in London to the extent of taking their name from a Vibrators' lyric, 'if it wasn't for your stiff little fingers/nobody would know you were dead'. In November 1977, finding early gigs hard to come by in Belfast, they hired a room, and staged a gig under the guise of a 21st birthday party. Here they were seen by *Daily Express* journalist Gordon Ogilvie, who became their manager and co-lyricist (with Burns), staying with them until their first demise.

Burns' trademark growling vocal style was show-cased from their debut single release, "Suspect Device"/"Wasted Life" (1978), which was released on the band's own label, Rigid Digits. Night-time radio play led Rough Trade, the UK's largest independent record distributor at the time, to market the single. Further interest came with the follow-up, "Alternative Ulster" (1978), which was written to appear on a flexi-disc accompanying a Belfast fanzine of the same name, which never actually came to fruition.

However, it wasn't until late 1978, when they supported the Tom Robinson Band on a British tour, that Stiff Little Fingers really came to prominence. This led to their own sellout tour in spring 1979, promoting their much-acclaimed debut album, INFLAMMABLE MATERIAL, which immediately hit the UK Top 20. As the tour was completed, "Gotta Getaway" was recorded. An angst-ridden tale based on Jake Burns' uprooting from his home to London, it was a classic pop/punk single. It was also the debut of Sheffield window-cleaner **Jim Reilly**, who replaced the disenchanted Brian Faloon on drums.

The "Straw Dogs" single of late 1979 was the band's first for Chrysalis Records, and their first UK chart entry (#44). Its flip side, "You Can't Say Crap On The Radio", responded to Jake Burns' use of the offending word during a Newcastle radio interview. A second album, NOBODY'S HEROES (1979), featured loud, catchy guitar licks, and a maturing lyricism, but these progressions were at odds with sections of their most loyal fan base, who insisted on transforming gigs into aggression.

With the release of a stopgap live album, HANX! (1980), Stiff Little Fingers returned to the studio to record 1981's GO FOR IT, an album that retained the thunderous guitar hooks of old, especially on the underrated single "Just Fade Away". After further tours of the UK and France, Jim Reilly left the band, to be replaced by **Dolphin Taylor**, formerly with the **TOM ROBINSON** band.

1982 brought deserved further UK Top 40 success with the EP LISTEN! It was closely followed by the release of NOW THEN (1982), an album showing developments in instrumentation (notably the introduction of horn sections) and acoustically based songwriting, now with contributions from Cluney and Taylor. Despite music press support and the continuing popularity of their live shows, it sold indifferently, and was hindered by its inclusion of existing B-side tracks. Burns announced his departure from the group, who in turn decided to split up after a short farewell tour.

The band re-formed in 1987 and soon established a residency at the Brixton Academy, London, with **Bruce Foxton** (ex-**JAM**) on bass. New material appeared in the shape of FLAGS AND EMBLEMS (1991), and again on TINDERBOX (1997) – both full of raw rock energy, but by now a little stale. Better by far – but by no means classic – were HOPE STREET (1999), which featured a very fine 'best of' CD as part of the package, and the HANDHELD AND RIGIDLY DIGITAL (2000) live box set. Sadly, these are no longer the band's glory days, when they combined the confrontation of punk rock with infectious pop melodies, but over some of the younger punk bands they helped inspire these oldsters are infinitely more preferable.

- **Inflammable Material** (1979; EMI).
  Peerless political punk. "Alternative Ulster", "Suspect Device" and "White Noise" are still incendiary after all these years.

- **All The Best** (1983; EMI).
  After the original split came this sterling greatest hits compilation. This collects singles and other assorted highlights ranging from the raw excitement of the "Suspect Device" debut, through the chart success of "At The Edge", to the more subtle recordings of the last years.

Michael Hood

STEPHEN STILLS

Born Dallas, Texas, 1945.

It is **Stephen Stills'** misfortune to have been a rival and colleague of **NEIL YOUNG**, whose cult status and sporadic mass appeal has overshadowed Stills' respectable body of work. Although Stills has not

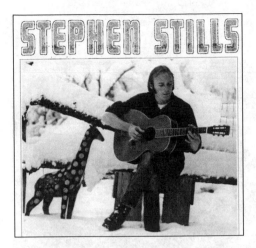

been fashionable for twenty years, it would be a shame if his songwriting, vocal and multi-instrumental skills (guitar/bass/keyboards/drums) were permanently overlooked. After all, bands as diverse as The Stone Roses and The Jayhawks wouldn't sound quite the same without his influence.

A graduate of New York's coffee-bar folk scene of the mid 60s, Stills moved to Los Angeles in 1966, where he failed an audition to join The Monkees (his friend Peter Tork was in luck), and instead formed **BUFFALO SPRINGFIELD** with **Richie Furay** and Neil Young. Stills' most famous composition for the band was "For What It's Worth", an anthemic US hit which perfectly caught the period's mood of unrest and vigilance. However, the band's life span was short-lived, and by 1968 they had split.

Stills went on to play sessions for the likes of Joni Mitchell and Judy Collins, and also had some 'guitar lessons' from Jimi Hendrix. (There are reputed to be stacks of unreleased tapes of Hendrix-Stills jams.) Other impromptu sessions with **David Crosby** (ex-Byrds) and **Graham Nash** (ex-Hollies) revealed that Stills' gruff voice blended supremely well with Crosby's tenor and Nash's high, saccharine tones. Between them, **Crosby, Stills and Nash** produced an astonishing three-part harmony, the like of which had never been heard in rock before. Later adding Neil Young on guitar, they took the world by storm, spawning a host of imitators. Stills' compositions and his acoustic playing (favouring unusual guitar tunings) were the mainstays of the group.

After the quartet finished a world tour at London's Royal Albert Hall, Stills stayed in England, recording a solo album, STEPHEN STILLS (1970), with an army of star guests, including Hendrix, Eric Clapton, Booker T. Jones, Lovin' Spoonful's John Sebastian, as well as Crosby and Nash. The album showcased his ability to pull the best out of his guests – notably Clapton – and create a unified group sound combining folk, soul and Latin influences to exhilarating effect. The critics and the US public loved it, and the much-covered hit song "Love The One You're With" has been a radio mainstay ever since.

STEPHEN STILLS II (1971) was recorded using a band formed around ex-CSNY sidemen, which soon evolved into the country-flavoured **Manassas**, as Stills recruited **Chris Hillman** (guitar/vocals) and **Al Perkins** (pedal steel) from The Flying Burrito Brothers. Manassas lasted two albums, and toured extensively.

By 1974, **CROSBY, STILLS, NASH & YOUNG** had reunited, but their drug problems were back, too, and Young left the following year. Stills' relationship with Young has been problematic, though he did interrupt a string of lacklustre solo albums to join the **Stills/Young Band** in 1976. The resulting album, LONG MAY YOU RUN, found neither artist at his best, and the same can be said of the eventual CSNY reunion LP, AMERICAN DREAM (1989).

After this, Stills, like Crosby, appeared to sharpened his act and during Crosby, Stills & Nash concerts in 1992 he still played rhythm guitar of astonishing power and subtlety, pulling out amazing harmonies, and unveiling fine new songs. From here on, however, new solo recordings were thin on the ground, to say the very least: even 2000's LIVE barely lasted half-an-hour.

⊙ **Stephen Stills** (1970; Atlantic).
Stills was at his best with Crosby, Nash and Young, but this is his finest solo work. Check out Stills' fluid keyboards and Hendrix's edgy solo on "Old Times, Good Times", and the exaltation of "Love The One You're With".

⊙ **Stephen Stills II** (1971; Atlantic).
More personal than the first album and with fewer walk-ons by star guests, though it does have Clapton's superb solo on "Fishes And Scorpions".

⊙ **Manassas** (1972; Atlantic).
Slightly marred by scrappy production, but excellent songs like "The Treasure" and "It Doesn't Matter", and the bluegrass-flavoured playing, make this double LP the better of the two Manassas albums.

Andy Smith

STING

Born Wallsend, England, 1951.

"Pretend I'm stupid? If that's the alternative, I'd rather be a pretentious wanker."

D issatisfied by the limitations of **THE POLICE**, and tired of the famous group's infamous infighting, **Sting** (Gordon Matthew Sumner), their principal songwriter, embarked on a solo career that was to epitomize the well-made, intelligent and tasteful superstar product.

His first album, DREAM OF THE BLUE TURTLES (1985), was recorded in Barbados with a jazz ensemble that included **Omar Hakim** (drums) and **Branford Marsalis** (saxophone), and although less of a departure than it appeared (his first group, **Last Exit**, had been a jazz band), it was a world away from The Police. Yet Sting's talent for writing tuneful pop songs was still well to the fore, even if singles like "Love Is The Seventh Wave" and "If You Love

The thoughtful Mr. Sting

Someone (Set Them Free)" failed to conquer the world.

Sting toured with many of the contributors to the BLUE TURTLES record, a trip documented in a rather self-indulgent documentary and album, BRING ON THE NIGHT (1986), the former being memorable mainly for showing his girlfriend giving birth and dad proudly cutting the umbilical cord. Sting the rock superstar had arrived.

His next studio outing, NOTHING LIKE THE SUN (1987), was one of the first albums conceived with the longer CD format in mind, and featured a line-up of superstar sidemen – among them Dire Straits' **Mark Knopfler**, **Eric Clapton** and legendary Miles Davis arranger **Gil Evans**. It was jazzy world music in style, characterized by tricksy time signatures (increasingly a Sting trademark) and unusual instrumentation. He'd also tired of the simple verse/chorus format and seemed more comfortable with more meandering structures: "We'll Be Together", a token attempt at a hit single, was a limp pastiche of Peter Gabriel's "Sledgehammer", conceived as earthy R&B. Despite the commercial failure of this and other singles, the album sold extremely well, and songs like "Fragile" and "They Dance Alone (Gueca Solo)" established Sting's profile as 'concerned' rock superstar. Indeed, his lyrics were increasingly becoming informed by his membership of Amnesty International, and he toured with Peter Gabriel, Tracy Chapman and Bruce Springsteen in support of their cause.

Sting's rather earnest brand of seriousness met with derision from some members of the music press, and even those who reviewed his records favourably were irked by what they took to be his pomposity and nar-

cissism. He didn't make things easy for himself by quoting Shakespeare's sonnets and Buckminster Fuller in his sleeve notes, next to a photograph portraying him with hand against furrowed brow – 'rock star as thinker', as Q magazine put it. On top of this, he got involved with rainforest charities: his Rainforest Foundation publicized the plight of the Brazilian Indians, and he went on a publicity tour with a tribal chief. All this po-faced do-gooding seemed a long way from rock'n'roll.

No new music was heard from Sting for four years (his side-career as a film actor, which began with *Quadrophenia*, claimed a lot of his time), and when he returned it was to revisit his past on the autobiographical THE SOUL CAGES (1991), which dealt with his childhood in Newcastle and his relationship with his recently deceased father. It was poorly received, although the single "All This Time" demonstrated that his gift for a strong melody and clever lyric hadn't deserted him.

TEN SUMMONER'S TALES (1993) was a much better record, demonstrating a wry sense of humour and containing some of his strongest material, while cuts lifted from the *Lethal Weapon 3* and *Demolition Man* soundtracks restored his standing as a singles artist. A greatest hits LP, FIELDS OF GOLD (1994), spawned further singles including "When We Dance", and a reworking of "This Cowboy Song", with reggae star **Pato Banton**, even moved Sting towards the contemporary dance-floor. MERCURY FALLING (1996) was a competent enough record, full of all the usual Sting motifs (weird time signatures, sharp-as-a-knife playing, etc) but it failed to advance his cause. Despite the big arrangements, many of the songs simply lacked the power of their predecessor.

Still, 1999's BRAND NEW DAY sold well enough, as did 2001's live offering ALL THIS TIME. What's more, recognized with a *Lifetime Achievement Award* at the 2002 Brits, the A&M compilation BEST OF STING AND THE POLICE finally topped the British album charts. Meantime, in a rather splendid development, A&M have digitally remastered Sting's albums and have reissued them with CD ROM video tracks as a bonus. It's just a shame he had to go and ruin it all in 2003 by hooking up with **Craig David** for the dreadful "Rise And Fall" single.

⊙ **Dream Of The Blue Turtles** (1985; A&M).
An enjoyable jazzy record, if a touch ponderous in places. Some great songs ("If You Love Somebody ..."), plus some real howlers.

⊙ **The Very Best Of Sting/The Police** (1998; A&M).
Having spent the best part of fifteen years establishing a separate identity as a solo performer, Sting and his greatest hits ruin everything by appearing alongside the best of the classic pop he created as a Policeman. A great album – half the mellow reflections of the solo act and half the mad, bounce-inducing blend of pop, reggae and punk patented by The Police.

Jonathan Holden

THE STONE ROSES

Formed Manchester, England, 1984;
disbanded 1996.

From the outset, **The Stone Roses** knew the importance of self-belief in setting themselves apart from the rest of the field. But until 1989, and the release of their eponymous debut album, the band were almost unknown outside of their home city. Inside Manchester, though, they had built up a following through appearances at a number of secret warehouse parties, and were soon able to fill thousand-capacity venues by word of mouth.

The group was formed around the songwriting nucleus of former schoolfriends **IAN BROWN** (vocals) and **John Squire** (guitar), and began life as a quintet, which included **Andy Couzens** (bass), **Reni** (drums) and an additional guitarist in the form of **Peter Garner**. It was this line-up that recorded the inauspicious first single, "So Young" (1985), a record the lads themselves later dismissed as 'angst-ridden rock'. Its follow-up, "Sally Cinnamon" (1987), showed the band's ability to craft a perfect three-minute pop song, but it was the robust Peter Hook-produced "Elephant Stone" (1988) that finally broke The Stone Roses to a wider audience.

With Peter Garner having departed after "So Young", and Gary 'Mani' Mountfield replacing Couzens on bass, "Elephant Stone" was the first recording to feature the familiar four-piece line-up. Fatefully, it was also the first Stone Roses recording to be issued on Andrew Lauder's Silvertone label, with whom the band had hastily signed an eight-album deal.

Decorated with John Squire's distinctive Jackson Pollock-inspired artwork, "Elephant Stone" drew upon the dual strengths of Squire's guitar work and Reni's dextrous drumming to produce a sound which was to come to full maturation on their first album, THE STONE ROSES (1989). Released after an attention-grabbing national tour, THE STONE ROSES drew effusive praise and was a fixture in the British album charts for 48 weeks. Remarkably confident and assured, it was a debut which more than lived up to the band's self aggrandizement and it featured prominently in the music press's Album of the Year reckonings.

Suitably impressed was one Mick Jagger, who offered The Roses a support slot on the North American leg of The Rolling Stones' world tour. Somewhat contemptuous of the offer, The Stone Roses opted instead for two high-profile shows in Blackpool and London, before leaving for tours of Europe and Japan.

Riding the crest of their popularity, as well as that of the Manchester-led 'baggy' movement, the band secured their first UK Top 10 placing with "Fools Gold". Clocking in at almost ten minutes on the 12" version, "Fools Gold" was a masterful rock/dance fusion highlighting Reni's talents in a mid-tempo 'funky drummer' workout, which served as a foundation for Squire's free-form guitar noodlings.

Just when it seemed that nothing could go wrong for The Stone Roses, the band, seduced by the notion of their own invincibility, ran aground on Spike Island, Widnes, in the summer of 1990. What was planned as an all-day rave-style party instead amounted to little more than a rockfest-style sit-in, as some 30,000 indie-kids sat in a field awaiting the arrival of The Roses, staying resolutely unmoved by the rhythms spun by a series of supporting club DJs. The Stone Roses' ambitious attempt at redefining the boundaries of the traditional rock concert lay in tatters, with the fireworks that followed the band's own lacklustre performance proving to be the only things that ignited on a disappointing day.

Sensing that the band had overreached themselves, the press closed in and a backlash began which became sustained with the release of "One Love"

(1990). A mammoth opus in its full 12" format, "One Love" saw the abandonment of conventional song structure in favour of an open-ended rhythmic jam in which John Squire's guitar playing appeared at times gratuitous.

Hitting #4 in the UK singles chart, the record became the last bona fide Stone Roses release for five years, due in part to a lengthy court battle in which the band eventually managed to extract themselves from their contract with Silvertone before signing with Geffen. In their absence, unsanctioned releases abounded as Silvertone attempted to recoup costs by issuing old material, while alleged sightings of the band became almost as fantastical as those of Elvis in provincial chip shops.

Finally, after a year in a North Wales studio, THE SECOND COMING (1994) emerged, laden with chugging, Led Zeppelin-style riffs. Suddenly, The Stone Roses seemed curiously out of step with the new generation of Britpop bands such as Blur and Oasis (who themselves owed much to the influence of the band's first album), not to mention the dance scene they once embraced.

Regardless, the album entered the UK chart at #4 and spawned a UK Top 5 single in the form of "Love Spreads". Nevertheless, the feeling remained that the band's heart was no longer in it. Certainly a full comeback was hampered by Reni's departure following a dispute over songwriting credits, and, despite the recruitment of the talented **Robbie Maddix** as a replacement, the further departure of John Squire in March 1996 signalled the end for a band that had teetered on the edge of greatness, only to succumb to its members' arrogance.

⊙ **The Stone Roses** (1989; Silvertone).
A stunning debut, which became a blueprint for a whole new generation of British guitar bands. The album succeeds in maintaining a stylistic unity, while it effortlessly touches base with a variety of moods, rhythms and tempos, from the offbeat charm of the chiming "Waterfall" to the driving funk-rock of "I Am The Resurrection". Essential.

⊙ **The Second Coming** (1994; Silvertone).
Though it failed to live up to expectations, this Zeppelinesque collection boasts some blinding moments.

⊙ **The Remixes** (2001; Silvertone).
On this CD you'll discover the likes of Soul Hooligan, Kinobe and Grooverider transforming Roses classics like "Fools Gold" into dance-floor-friendly samplathons. Perhaps the only way that a copy of this CD could offer a fitting tribute to Ian Brown et al, would be if it was spattered with paint and nailed to a wall.

Ian Lowey

STONE TEMPLE PILOTS

Formed San Diego, California, 1991.

"Did we turn into a butterfly, or from a maggot into a fly? It could have been either way." Scott Weiland

B ack in the early 80s **Scott Weiland** (vocals) and **Robert DeLeo** (bass) met at a Black Flag

concert in Long Beach. They were from diametrically opposed musical backgrounds – Weiland from punk, DeLeo from hard rock – but discovered that they were both seeing the same girl, and when she left town they moved into her empty apartment. Together they created a band called **Mighty Joe Young**, which eventually became known as **Stone Temple Pilots**. In addition to Weiland and Leo, it featured drummer **Eric Ketz** and – a while later – Robert's brother **Dean** on guitar.

The band made a decision to steer clear of the Los Angeles corporate music scene and build up their technique and following in the clubs of San Diego – a tactic that says much about their attitude and direction. But despite such honourable intentions it is hard to ignore the fact that they were ploughing the same musical furrow as Alice In Chains and Pearl Jam, which probably explained the rapid interest from Atlantic Records, with whom they signed in spring 1992.

The depth of the band's experience shone through on their masterly debut album CORE (1992). Years of practice, coupled with Brendan O'Brien's superb production, shot them to seemingly overnight success. "Sex Type Thing", "Plush" and "Creep" became firm video and radio favourites, but the album boasted a diversity of styles, with lyrics telling stories of twisted romance and alienation. What was more, Weiland's ability to dip into a variety of characters and styles added immeasurably to the album's emotional depth.

An inevitable touring schedule began with appearances on the *Lollapalooza* second stage, support slots with Megadeth, and an appearance at the MTV *Spring Festivities*. Eschewing the mainstream course briefly, they turned down a chance to tour with Aerosmith, and upheld their alternative credentials by co-headlining a national outing with the Butthole Surfers. The next year brought yet more live engagements and appearances at benefits for women's pro-choice causes.

In August 1993, still apparently keen to straddle both the alternative and mainstream camps, they played two sell-out shows at New York's Roseland Ballroom, where they sported full Kiss make-up in reverent emulation of their childhood heroes. Slipping easily from the wilfully bizarre to the prestigious, they also recorded an MTV Unplugged session, as their avalanche of success led to accolades from the music press and broadcast media.

With PURPLE (1994), Stone Temple Pilots opted for a more spontaneous live feel to the recording sessions, and the album was completed within a month. Like its predecessor, it bristled with a bewildering range of textures and emotions, ranging from the fluid melody of the hit "Interstate Love Song" to the ethereal "Big Empty", which appeared on the film soundtrack to *The Crow*. An instant #1 album in the US, it was followed by the usual prolonged bouts of touring, interrupted only by recording a version of "Dancing Days" for the compilation ENCOMIUM: A TRIBUTE TO LED ZEPPELIN (1995).

Things were confused for the band, however. Weiland had developed a drug addiction and had brushes with the law – he was arrested for possession of cocaine and heroin – and his continuing chemical dependency resulted in his being admitted to a rehab clinic, throwing touring and recording schedules into chaos. Nonetheless, the band's third album, TINY MUSIC ... SONGS FROM THE VATICAN GIFT SHOP (1996), was masterful, and combined cutting lyrics (often about the shallowness of corporate rock) with a fresh and open retro sound; tracks such as "Lady Picture Show" had a distinctly Beatles flavour. By the end of the year Weiland appeared to have his problems under some kind of control and the band set about recovering the time lost by embarking on a modest tour of the US. Despite their enforced period away, the fan reaction suggested that the Pilots hadn't lost much in the way of momentum.

Since then, luck has not been at the band's side. Whilst Weiland dealt with his addiction problems the remaining members worked on their side-project dubbed **Talk Show** and produced an album, TALK SHOW (1997). This, however, stiffed and though Weiland appeared to be in control of his vices he was yet again caught with narcotics. Throughout all this confusion he even managed to record and release a fairly well-received solo effort.

Amazingly, after all the turmoil, the Pilots managed to reconvene long enough to create NO.4 (1999), which at least proved that their desire to continue remained strong, even though it wasn't exactly their best work. In the meantime Weiland got his act together and sobered up, becoming a family man in the process, and was eventually diagnosed as suffering from bi-polar disorder, which results in bouts of depression, a possible partial reason for his behaviour. In interview, he also claimed not to be taking his medication, because it interfered with his creativity. Since then the band have been far more consistent and released a much better album in the form of SHANGRI-LA DEE DA (2001), once again trading off their love of the Beatles and bold, heavy arrangements.

Weiland is currently working in a new, nameless band alongside **Slash**, **Duff McKagan** and **Matt Sorum** (all ex-Guns N' Roses); so far, their output has consisted of two tracks donated to the soundtracks of *The Hulk* and the remake of *The Italian Job*.

⦿ **Core** (1992; Atlantic).
Leaving aside similarities with some of Seattle's finest, this boasts wicked riffs, unforgettable hooks, and a menacingly charismatic performance from Scott Weiland. An exceptional debut.

⦿ **Purple** (1994; Atlantic).
More songs of love and emptiness, by equal turns harsh and sweetly melodic. The live production sound gives the songs a furious urgency and a more haunting dimension, while the ironic 'easy-listening' epilogue is extremely funny.

⦿ **Tiny Music . . . Songs From The Vatican Gift Shop** (1996; Atlantic).
Another lurch through a whole menu of musical approaches, ranging from whimsical 60s pop through to scalding straight-ahead rock.

Essi Berelian

THE STOOGES

Formed Ann Arbor, Michigan, 1967; disbanded 1974.

"Oooh-ooh, I been dirt, and I don't care." Iggy Pop

The Stooges lurched into life when **James Jewel Osterburg** – aka **IGGY POP** – dragged **Ron** (guitar) and **Scott Asheton** (drums) into his garage-band mind. They recruited **Dave Alexander** to play the bass parts and launched a monstrous career as all-time bad influences, the drug-addled dark side of primitive glam-rock.

Iggy, who'd picked up his name when drumming for another Michigan band, The Iguanas, had previously worked with bassist Ron in the Prime Movers. Having Scott in to play drums added to the warm family atmosphere cultivated on the bus as the band gigged its way through 1968. Despite a promising early accusation of indecent exposure, it wasn't until the band were signed to Elektra in 1969 that they really began to make waves.

Their first album – THE STOOGES – opened with Iggy mumbling something about some girl who's "Not Right". As the song progressed, it transpired that Iggy was not right either, and that, pretty much, summed up The Stooges' appeal: they were a bunch of incoherent drug-related accidents with bad attitude. The album did well enough, helped in part by The Stooges' growing reputation as a wild live act. Rumours of backstage rituals of drug consumption were strengthened by Iggy's cowering and leaping around the stage, and rendered undeniable by the stoned immobility of the rest of the band, struggling to remember which song they were supposed to be playing and play an instrument at the same time.

The Stooges welcomed the 70s with FUN HOUSE, another collection of growling, scowling punk rock-'n'roll. There were a few personnel changes to organize before the next album was assembled. A combination of musical differences, personal antagonism and being too smashed to make it to the studio led to **James Williamson** being brought in on guitar; Ron Asheton, now playing bass, moving to the back of the stage to keep his brother company; and Dave Alexander leaving the band. The whole process took two years, with Iggy spending some time working as a greenkeeper on a Florida golf course. It could all have ended there, had it not been for David Bowie – then the rock star with the golden touch – who dug Iggy out of his bunker, cleaned him up a little and put him back into the studio with a re-formed band, now to be known as **Iggy And The Stooges**.

There's a lot of Stooges stuff in circulation on a number of French and American labels. Best by far are those issued by Bomp! in California as part of their 'Iguana Chronicles' project, a comprehensive

list of definitive versions of every Stooges recording (as an example of their dedication, one of their CD singles contains eight versions of "I Got A Right"). If you get a chance, track down ROUGH POWER, Bomp!'s 'Bowie-free' mixes of RAW POWER, and I'M SICK OF YOU (1996), a marvellous EP allegedly recorded in Iggy's basement. Most of their best material, however, made it onto their three studio albums.

All The Stooges' best songs deal with extremes, taking things to the limit in a way The Eagles could never imagine. Like bikes, blades and bombers, The Stooges are part of the teenage underworld, and usually you grow out of wanting them. But keep your Stooges albums, go and buy the ones you don't have, and have them ready for the next time a breeze blows through you and clears out those grown-up cobwebs.

⊙ **The Stooges** (1969; Elektra).
John Cale produced this album and was responsible for Ron's dentist's-drill guitar tone. Iggy's gloomy vampire vocals occasionally mutate into painful whoops, while Dave and Scott provide gang-fight rhythm-section support. High points include the sort-of-erotic "I Wanna Be Your Dog", the menacing offer of a "Real Cool Time" and the future Sex Pistols classic, "No Fun".

⊙ **Fun House** (1970; Elektra).
This is the album they should give away when you buy your first black leather jacket. Classic tracks include the snotty-nosed rebellion of "TV Eye", the gorgeous hymn to degradation, "Dirt", and the later cover by The Damned, "1970 (I Feel Alright)".

⊙ **Raw Power** (1973; Columbia).
James's guitar work sears through this recording, providing a solid lead guitar and quality co-authorship that had been missing from the first two albums. A strong, mean and nasty album, albeit less so than the original mixes (now available as a Bomp! CD) put together before Bowie got his hands on them. In a 1997 update to the apparently never-ending story of RAW POWER, Iggy himself has now remixed the album.

⊙ **Metallic KO** (1988; Skydog/Bomp!).
Recorded in Detroit in 1974 at one of their final appearances, this is the finest document of The Stooges' live performances. Iggy's provocation of the audience (particularly a biker gang whose induction ceremony required applicants to stop a Stooges performance) is extraordinarily courageous and really dumb.

Al Spicer

THE STRANGLERS

Formed Chiddingfold, England, 1974.

"It's very frightening that despite everything we are becoming a British institution, but all institutions deserve to be questioned and knocked down." **Jean-Jacques Burnel**

Institution though they were to become, as The Men In Black, **The Stranglers**' early years were none too successful. 'The only sense in which The Stranglers could be considered new wave is that no one has had the gall to palm off this rubbish before', commented *Melody Maker* in a 1975 review, and that wasn't untypical. Audience reactions were little better – early gigs sometimes provoked an audience walk-out or a fight. But then punk happened, and The Stranglers were on their way, hitching a ride on a bandwagon on which they never really belonged, even when they looked the part.

The group was made up of musicians **Hugh Cornwell** (guitar/vocals), **Jean-Jacques Burnel** (bass/vocals), **Dave Greenfield** (keyboards) and former ice-cream-van-fleet owner **Jet Black** (drums). Greenfield's keyboards, in conjunction with Burnel's heavy bass, created a meaty, dark, hard rock sound that characterized The Stranglers – together with sardonic wit, black clothing, a tough image and a hate-hate relationship with the media.

In 1976 The Stranglers received their first favourable reviews when they supported Patti Smith on tour. They signed to United Artists in December of that year and released a first, moderately successful, single "(Get A) Grip (On Yourself)" the following January. Next off was the provocatively sexual "Peaches", quickly banned from broadcast in the UK for use of the word 'clitoris', which helped sales of the single and the album from which it came, STRANGLERS IV (RATTUS NORVEGICUS) (1977). A "Peaches" radioplay version was then released with the word 'clitoris' replaced by 'bikini' and the single went Top 10 in the UK, as did the following "Straighten Out"/"Something Better Change" (the latter being The Stranglers' best shot at a punk anthem) and "No More Heroes". The last three tracks – arguably the most memorable The Stranglers were ever to achieve – all featured on the album NO MORE HEROES (1977), a set whose lyrics (on songs such as "Bring On The Nubiles") cemented their reputation as unreconstructed sexists. Still, it was one of the year's top ten punk albums and deservedly found its way into most record collections.

1978 began with the release of the dark and throbbing "Five Minutes", a full-force rock classic, quickly followed by the album BLACK AND WHITE, source of the single "Nice'N'Sleazy", the first Stranglers record to chart across Europe. Worldwide tours ensued, with the band whipping up controversy at each stop. A reworking of the Bacharach/David classic "Walk On By" failed to chart (possibly because 75,000 copies had already been given away on a free EP with BLACK AND WHITE), then came the LIVE X-CERTS (1979), featuring a notorious Battersea Park concert at which the band invited women to strip along to "Nice'N'Sleazy". Such scenes were to become something of a feature at gigs.

THE RAVEN, released later in 1979, brought the last UK Top 20 hit for two years, in "Duchess", which was accompanied by a fairly harmless video depicting the band dressed as choirboys – a combination the BBC felt obliged to ban. The year also saw solo albums from Burnel and Cornwell, the latter furthering his demonic image with NOSFERATU. Neither venture was a great success and 1980 was a bad year for The Stranglers: not only did they suffer their first downturn in sales, but Cornwell got busted for possession of narcotics. As he finished his two-month stint in Pentonville prison, the band split with their longtime manager Ian Grant and then found themselves arrested in France for 'inciting a riot' by cancelling a gig in Nice. The disastrous run of luck was rounded off in October by the theft of all the band's equipment during a US tour.

Meanwhile, they carried on recording THE MEN-IN-BLACK (1981), an album promoting The Stranglers' darkly humorous vision of FBI-type creeps who might possibly be in control of the universe. It was the first album that failed to produce a Top 40 single in the UK (the band have never charted in the US) and suggested their sell-by date might have arrived for a pop audience now moving on to Duran Duran and The Human League.

The band came back with LA FOLIE, a sardonic response to accusations that they 'never wrote love songs'. Highlight was "Golden Brown", which shot up to #2 in the UK and remained there for some weeks, even receiving regular airplay on middle-of-the-road BBC Radio 2 – who presumably hadn't twigged that it was a coded paean to drug use. The follow-up single, "La Folie",

only made #47, a fact not unrelated to its being six minutes long and sung in French.

The Stranglers' contractual obligations to EMI (who had taken control of United Artists two years earlier) came to an end with another hit, "Strange Little Girl" – the band's last laugh on the record company, who had rejected the song as a demo back in 1975. EMI hit back by releasing the inevitable COLLECTION album with the most non-Stranglers cover image imaginable – a 'keep fit' girl who looked like a refugee from tacky pop-dance troupe Pan's People.

So on to Epic in 1982, where the band continued to mellow and kept the hit singles coming at regular intervals for the next five years. Their first album for Epic, FELINE (1983), had a chart-worthy single in "The European Female", and AURAL SCULPTURE (1984) again brought singles chart success with "Skin

The Men in Black (from left): Burnel, Black, Greenfield and Cornwell

Deep". Moving ever further from the menacing rock of their earlier work, and introducing sax, trombone and trumpet on some tracks, The Stranglers were now shedding a lot of their fans-in-black, though sales suggested a new constituency had been won.

DREAMTIME (1986) spawned "Always The Sun", which performed well in the singles charts, and the band's reworking of The Kinks "All Day, And All Of The Night" (1987) helped shift their second live album, ALL LIVE, AND ALL OF THE NIGHT. The next studio album, TEN, had little to recommend it (though its single, "96 Tears", did go Top 20) and on tour the band looked distinctly bored. Hugh Cornwell quit for a low-key solo career following a final gig at London's Alexandra Palace in the summer of that year, and for most fans that was it.

The rest of the band decided to continue, however, replacing Cornwell first with **Paul Roberts** on vocals and **John Ellis**, ex-**VIBRATORS**, on guitar. The new line-up began touring in February 1991, playing later that year to a crowd of 100,000 in Estonia and supporting Simple Minds at Manchester's Maine Road football ground. IN THE NIGHT was released in 1992 on their own Psycho label, followed by three years of worldwide touring to maintain and extend the fan base. A twelfth studio album, ABOUT TIME, emerged in 1995, and a thirteenth, WRITTEN IN RED, hit the streets in 1997. Meanwhile COUP DE GRACE (1998) featured a good deal more songwriting input from J-J Burnel than was evident on the band's more recent efforts. Despite this, the album was not a patch on their glory days.

The future looks likely to see a continuation of the slow decline into mediocrity. Burnel's EUROMAN COMETH, which was filed under 'silly' on its original 1979 release, was reissued on Eastworld Records in 1998, not having matured a great deal in the intervening years. The band have been letting out sporadic bursts of archive material – for example, ACCESS ALL AREAS (1998), a rather good straight-from-the-mixing-desk live recording from the December 1995 tour, and 5 LIVE 01 (2001), at least proving that they could still cut it on the gigging front. Cornwell's solo career continues to potter along: GUILTY (1997), was a mature, even sensitive, recording, while HI FI (2000) and FOOTPRINTS IN THE DESERT (2002), were comprised of recordings spanning 1990-96. But The Stranglers are just not the same with the new line-up and, in any case, they are best remembered as they were in their leering, hard-rocking heyday at the back end of the 70s.

⊙ **Stranglers IV (Rattus Norvegicus)** (1977; United Artists).
There are no duffs on this punk year record and at least two tracks likely to rank in any fan's top ten: "Grip" and "Hanging Around".

⊙ **No More Heroes** (1977; United Artists).
More of the same, and worth buying if only for the title track, a rock'n'roll classic, and for "Something Better Change" (it didn't ...).

⊙ **Live X-Certs** (1979; United Artists).
The Stranglers at their peak, live. Particularly entertaining are clips of Cornwell's on-stage banter – 'Did someone say wanker?' and 'I know you like spitting, but we don't like being spat at.' Happy days.

⊙ **The Raven** (1979; United Artists).
A transitional album: the last great foot-stompers are here, while Burnel's lighter tones on some of the tracks reflect things to come. The title track, "Duchess" and "Nuclear Device" are among the band's best.

⊙ **Singles (The UA Years)** (1989; EMI).
Comprehensive collection of eighteen singles released between 1977 and 1982.

⊙ **Greatest Hits 1977–1990** (1990; Epic).
Contains fifteen tracks, most of them from the Epic era – best purchased with THE UA YEARS for a full 'greatest hits' collection. This was Epic's best-selling album of 1990, going triple platinum.

⊙ **The Hit Men** (1997; EMI Gold).
43 tracks telling the edited story of a twenty-year career. All the singles from Hugh Cornwell's time as front-man, plus a few tracks that had been planned as single releases. If you're planning on a first investment in The Stranglers' product, this walks all over the 1990 Epic collection.

⊙ **Access All Areas** (1998; Official Stranglers Fan Club – distributed by Voiceprint).
Tracks selected by the fan club provide the absolute cream of the fourteen-date tour the guys did at the end of 1995, and the track selection spans their career from the good old days of "No More Heroes" and "Goodbye Toulouse" through to the bitter 90s and "Genetix". Marvellous live (and still a bit dangerous) stuff!

Patrick Broomfield

THE STRAWBERRY ALARM CLOCK

Formed Los Angeles, 1966; continued to perform until 1971.

In the League Of Great Band Names, **The Strawberry Alarm Clock** must surely be up there with those other great exponents of psychedelic pop: The Electric Prunes, The Chocolate Watch Band and even Pittsburgh's fabulous Marshmallow Steamshovel. Tragically, they became associated in the public mind with the cynical exploitation of later bubblegum bands such as the Lemon Pipers and the Peppermint Trolley Company, leaving the band high and dry in their fading kaftans as rock returned to more down-to-earth sounds. Luckily, in their brief flash of fame, they had time to record the classic US #1 hit "Incense And Peppermints" and a couple of albums' worth of some of the best sweet-toothed psychedelia from the 60s.

Originally a garage-punk combo called The Sixpence, the band comprised **Mark Weitz** (vocals/organ), **Lee Freeman** (vocals/rhythm guitar), **Ed King** (lead guitar), **Gary Lovetro** (bass) and **Randy Seol** (drums). Inspired by "Strawberry Fields Forever", they changed their name in 67 and recorded the irresistible slice of psych-pop, "Incense And Peppermints", backed by the simply awesome "Birdman Of Alkatrash". At first a local hit, it took six months to climb to #1 in the national charts.

With the addition of second bassist **George Bunnell**, they recorded their debut album, unsurprisingly also called INCENSE AND PEPPERMINTS. For those who thought the band were merely one-hit wonders, here was a generous helping of beautifully crafted psychedelia, full of soaring harmonies and Doorsy organ melodrama. Stand-outs were the bongo-driven opener "Rainy Day Mushroom Pillow" and the brooding "The World's On Fire".

The band enjoyed four more minor chart hits, including "Tomorrow" and "Sit With The Guru" (presumably whilst enjoying your incense and peppermints), but it was the second album, WAKE UP IT'S TOMORROW, that was the band's real triumph. Who could resist "They Saw The Fat One Coming", "Black Butter-Present" or even "Pretty Song From Psych-Out", The Clock's contribution to the Jack Nicholson movie of the same name.

But despite their inventive flair and their live stage presence (Randy Seol was noted for playing bongos with his hands on fire), the scene had moved on and the third album, WORLD IN A SEASHELL, showed The Clock reverting to a more conventional pop format. The band struggled on into the 70s, until Ed King jumped ship for **LYNYRD SKYNYRD**. For The Strawberry Alarm Clock, time was up.

⊙ **Strawberries Mean Love** (1987; Big Beat).
The cream of the Strawberry crop, including "Incense And Peppermints", "Sit With The Guru" and the fabulous title track.

Iain Smith

THE STRAWBS

Formed London, 1967; disbanded 1978; re-formed 1983.

The Strawbs – originally The Strawberry Hill Boys – started out playing a kind of bluegrass music, which they gradually phased out and replaced by a more British folk approach. In this they were strengthened by the arrival of singer **Sandy Denny** and bassist **Ron Chesterman**, supplementing the original line-up of **Dave Cousins** (guitar/banjo), **Tony Hooper** (guitar) and **Arthur Phillips** (mandolin). It was this group who recorded the album, ALL OUR OWN WORK, in 1968, though it wasn't released until 1974, by which time Denny had long ago found fame with **FAIRPORT CONVENTION**.

Denny and Phillips in fact left in 1969 and it was as a trio that the band recorded their debut release, STRAWBS, a well-received album which previewed both the good and bad sides of Cousins' songwriting: "The Man Who Called Himself Jesus" showed his unsurpassed ability to write songs about religion, while "The Battle" demonstrated a tendency to long-winded pretentiousness.

The subsequent album, DRAGONFLY (1970), was an improvement, though the reviews were poor. Chesterman left soon after, replaced by **John Ford**, a bassist with an unusual, percussive style, while the line-up expanded to take in multi-instrumentalist **Richard Hudson** and a recent graduate from

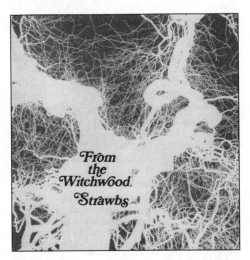

London's Royal Academy Of Music, **Rick Wakeman**, who had guested on DRAGONFLY. The live recording, JUST A COLLECTION OF ANTIQUES AND CURIOS (1970), showed their accomplishment, critics of the time raving about Wakeman's solo, though in hindsight it seems one of the shallower moments of a generally excellent album.

After another strong studio album, FROM THE WITCHWOOD (1971), Wakeman left to join **YES** and was replaced by **Blue Weaver** of **Amen Corner**. The Strawbs became a tighter band as a result and the change allowed Cousins to develop his input on electric guitar. This new sound was shown to good effect on GRAVE NEW WORLD (1972) and BURSTING AT THE SEAMS (1973), by which time Hooper had been replaced by **Dave Lambert**. The latter album also produced the band's only two hit singles, "Lay Down", and "Part Of The Union" (which was taken up by Britain's miners, impervious to satirical intent, as a rallying cry).

An unhappy tour of the US resulted in the departure of Hudson and Ford to go solo and later form **The Monks**, and **Blue Weaver**. The subsequent personnel – with **Rod Coombes**, **Chas Cronk** and **John Hawken** – were not to match earlier heights but the band struggled on, releasing a largely forgettable series of records, until 1978. They were back in 1983 for a one-off appearance at the Cambridge Folk Festival and toured sporadically over the following years. DON'T SAY GOODBYE (1988) was forgettable, however, and its weakness thrown into focus by UNCANNED PRESERVES, a collection of archive material, which came close to winning a Grammy in 1991.

At their peak, The Strawbs produced some of the most melodic and poetic songs in British folk-rock, but the reliance on Cousins' vocals, an acquired taste, and the later substandard line-ups, have dented what might have been quite a reputation.

In recent years, The Strawbs' recordings have been gradually rereleased on CD, many with extra tracks from the period and excellent notes, and the long-awaited HEARTBREAK HILL (recorded but never released fifteen years earlier) has finally made its appearance. In 1998, the line-up that recorded BURSTING AT THE SEAMS reunited for a 25th-birthday concert. This was so well received that they, with the addition of Cousins' school friend **Brian Willoughby**, have been touring like maniacs ever since. Releases have continued to flow too: as well as the expected archive collections, Willoughby, Cousins and Lambert produced the fine ACOUSTIC STRAWBS – BAROQUE & ROLL in 2001, and the following year Cousins was reunited with Wakeman for HUMMINGBIRD. 2003 then witnessed the release of BLUE ANGEL, the first Strawbs album in a decade to feature a full band. Talk about a second wind!

⊙ **Bursting At The Seams** (1973; Hannibal).
The Strawbs' most commercial album, featuring their hits "Lay Down" (a different cut from the chart version) and "Part Of The Union", and the excellent counterpoint guitars of "Down By The Sea" and "Tears And Pavan".

⊙ **Greatest Hits Live** (1995; Road Goes On Forever).
A compilation of recordings taken at various times throughout the band's career, providing a fair overview of their output.

⊙ **Halcyon Days** (1997; A&M).
A mammoth collection of album tracks, hits, B-sides, rare recordings and excellent notes. A must-have double CD, marred only by the lack of a chronological running order.

Paul O'Brien

REDFERNS

The Streets' Mike Skinner

THE STREETS

Mike Skinner, born London, 1980.

Inspiring preposterous epithets such as 'Britain's Eminem' and 'intelligent garage', **The Streets** (aka London-born/Brummie-reared **Mike Skinner**) was, for better or worse, 2002's critical favourite. The first wave of hype stated that Skinner was going to change the face of dance music, but in reality he was merely the latest in a long line of British groaners (John Cooper-Clarke, Ian Dury, Shaun Ryder) who loved dance music because that's where the drugs were, and didn't end up influencing anyone except the critics.

After an adolescence trying to sound like De La Soul, Skinner first gained attention with 2001's "Has It Come To This?", a singularly annoying tale about 'the life of a geezer' getting stoned and playing PlayStation over hollowed out garage beats. Sure, The Streets' tale of the UK's 'Barratt's class' (shorthand for the pre-fab homes that blight Britain's lower middle class suburbs) avoided the usual garage clichés, but garage and hip-hop have always been as much about how the lyrics are delivered as what the lyrics say, and Skinner is about as funky as cardboard.

His one cadence dragged even more over the course of ORIGINAL PIRATE MATERIAL (2002). Skinner may very well have been trying to capture the flatness of life in Blair's Britain, but his comic mugging (on tracks such as "The Irony Of It All", "Don't Mug Yourself" and "Too Much Brandy") gave the lie to this. In his effort to escape pop/garage

banality, Skinner only reinforced the original sin of late-90s/early-00s pop: hip-hop making everything overly declamatory. Everything on ORIGINAL PIRATE MATERIAL was forced, studied and awkward. Tracks like "Let's Push Things Forward" and "Geezers Need Excitement" found scribes reaching for comparisons to The Specials and Massive Attack, but that only brought the lack of subtlety and nuance into sharper relief.

⊙ **Original Pirate Material** (2002; Locked On).
The sound of Blair's Britain – no wonder this counrty's in such bad shape.

Peter Shapiro

THE STROKES

Formed New York City, 1998.

Though their sound is hardly original, **The Strokes**'s breakthrough was a refreshing event in the music world. It not only provided the new millennium with some much needed clout, but also reminded many of a bygone New Wave age when bands such as Television, also out of NYC, ruled the roost.

The band comprises five New York rich kids – singer/songwriter **Julian Casablancas**, guitarist **Albert Hammond Jr**, **Fabrizio Moretti** (drums), **Nick Valensi** (guitar) and **Nikolai Fraiture** (bass). They suffer from a perpetual collective bad-hair day of epic proportions and dress in a style that borrows from tailored Blondie and the drainpiped Ramones alike. Though the antithesis of blueprint bands like Take That and New Kids On The Block, much of The Strokes' success can be attributed to their boy-band-ish charm: in photo shoots they invariably look like startled bunnies; girls think they're dishy; boys think they're cool; and they display enough musical competence backed by the mythology of their rock'n'roll lifestyle to keep musos and the press happily bobbing along to the beat. Their music is far more accessible than punk, more precise than straight rock, and more 'pop' than many of their New Wave influences.

The Strokes came together in 1998, but Casablancas and Hammond had known each other for years, as they attended the same Swiss boarding school at the start of the decade (no, not very rock-'n'roll). Within a year The Strokes had gigged extensively in downtown NYC, gradually moving from fleapits to larger venues. At the Mercury Lounge they were spotted by Ryan Gentles, who later became their manager. With further support from producer Gordon Raphael and the group's mysterious, moustached 'guru' JP Bowersock,

Casablancas and his cohorts went into the studio and recorded a three-track demo, featuring "The Modern Age", "Last Nite" and "Barely Legal". Intercepted by Rough Trade Records in the UK, these recordings were impressive enough to be released as an EP in their raw state. The single was more than warmly received: the press were practically molten with excitement. A sell-out tour of the UK and stateside support slots with The Doves and Guided By Voices followed.

The band were soon signed to big-time label RCA, and after a further single – "Hard To Explain"/"New York City Cops", which peaked at #16 in the UK charts – their debut album, entitled Is This It (2001), was released. The set comprised eleven anthemic, tightly wound coils of punky pop – all with tunes to die for, condensed metronomic beats, and more punchy riffs than most bands would know what to do with. The album's vision of the rock'n'roll lifestyle led by the rich youth of NYC, however, often seemed far from genuine.

By the end of the year The Strokes had accrued a hefty stack of accolades, some impressive sales figures, and stardom. The world was their oyster.

Inevitably, though, the fickle British press began to chisel at the cracks in the band's veneer. Reports surfaced of record company disputes over TV appearances, and as the venues the group played became larger, doubts were posited as to the quintet's ability to adapt their gritty sound as required.

Whether they have the resilience and ability to cope with the pressures of becoming global property,

The Strokes' Casablancas (left) mastering his robotic moves

or the creative resources to match their debut next time around, remains to be seen. Whatever happens, they are sure to be remembered for producing a stunning debut album. The difficult second album is due in late 2003.

⦿ **Is This It** (RCA; 2001).
Borrowing from rock history like a speed-fuelled magpie, this album plunders The Stooges, the Velvet Undergroud, Television, and many more, distilling its loot into a sparkling collection of near-perfect punk-pop.

Peter Buckley

STUMP

Formed London, 1983; disbanded 1989.

When **Kev Hopper** (bass), **Rob McKahey** (drums) and **Chris Salmon** (guitar) formed **Stump** with singer **Nick Hobbs**, they did not have conventional rock'n'roll in mind. Their music largely consisted of a number of ludicrous noises stapled together: a fretless bass, a clean guitar sound with extensive use of the tremolo arm, and stumbling, tumbling drums, moving in and out of various time signatures at will.

Hobbs was kicked out of the band for 'excessive seriousness' at a fairly early stage, and replaced by **Mick Lynch**, who, like McKahey, had previously been with **MICRODISNEY**. Lynch's rich accent and gangling movements made him a superb frontman, and he somehow managed to make the music more palatable.

Their first EP, the breathtaking "Mud On A Colon", was released on Nottingham label Ron Johnson in early 1986. It was a critical success, and a John Peel session on BBC Radio was offered, before they contributed their best-known song, "Buffalo", to C86, the famed *NME* compilation cassette. The band's performance of the song on TV inspired numerous renditions of the unforgettable chorus, 'How much is the fish?/Does the fish have chips?' A video for "Buffalo", featuring Lynch supposedly eating live goldfish, ensured cult success for the six-track mini-LP QUIRK OUT (1986), and very soon the band signed to Ensign.

After a long spell in the studio with Holger Hiller producing, they returned with the single "Chaos" (1988). It saw the band in uncompromising mood – Hopper was now using samples as well as playing bass to create a wealth of strange sounds, influenced by The Residents, Renaldo & The Loaf, and (of course) Hiller himself.

But with the release of Stump's LP A FIERCE PANCAKE (1988), the backlash against C86 whimsy had set in. Few in the media were now prepared to champion them, with the notable exception of John Peel, and even the single "Charlton Heston", with additional dance remixes by The Irresistible Force, did little to endear them to the music press. As if to admit that the game was up, Stump released yet another version of "Buffalo" at the end of 1988, before going their separate ways. Lynch formed a

more traditional indie band by the name of Bernard, and Hopper released an excellent solo LP called STOLEN JEWELS (1990), which used samples much more extensively.

The originality of Stump's music should have transcended any accusations of wackiness, but when it came to the crunch they were labelled a joke band.

⦿ **Quirk Out** (1986: Stuff Records).
The record that catapulted Stump a bit higher than they were before, thanks to "Buffalo". Also present are an ode to hygiene ("Down On The Kitchen Table") and even a touch of the mellow and melodic on "Our Fathers".

⦿ **A Fierce Pancake** (1988: Ensign Records).
Beautiful production and songwriting, with Lynch's swooping voice fronting melodic tall stories. Rarely has such a fine LP been so completely ignored.

Rhodri Marsden

THE STYLE COUNCIL

Formed London, 1983; disbanded 1989.

"The more we seemed to annoy people, the more I liked it." Paul Weller

It took **PAUL WELLER** (vocals/guitar) just three months to return with a new band after he brought **THE JAM** to an end in 1982, and if the brevity of Weller's mourning raised a few eyebrows, that was nothing compared to the surprises sprung by **The Style Council**.

The Jam's live cover of Curtis Mayfield's "Move On Up" and the introduction of a brass section on their farewell tour hinted at Weller's plans, but The Style Council's first singles revealed a musical manifesto that some Jam fans found hard to swallow. Mayfield's influence extended beyond the music as Weller, and his new cohorts **Mick Talbot** (keyboards) and the gifted 18-year-old drummer **Steve White**, sought to mix social comment with sophisticated pop, packaging the end product with questionable fashions, pseudy sleeve notes (penned by the Cappuccino Kid), and some suspect French. Playing their first 'Council Meeting' at the Liverpool Empire in May 1983, Weller was forced to ask for quiet as choruses of 'We are the mods!' disturbed the presentation of his jazz- and soul-inspired material.

The Style Council's first single, "Speak Like A Child" (1983), was a brassy Motown mimic that reached #4 in the UK, probably off the back of The Jam's popularity. The funky "Money Go Round" (1983) was Weller's first, and not altogether unsuccessful, bass-heavy venture onto the dance floor. But it wasn't until "Long Hot Summer" that the new group hit the button with a languid, evocative, simple soul number that still ranks among Weller's finest work; the EP's accompanying homoerotic video helped give the band their biggest hit, a British #3 in August 1983.

Evidence of the extent of Weller's desire to reject his Beatles and Small Faces influences came the following year with The Style Council's smooth, cappuccino-fuelled debut album, CAFÉ BLEU (1984), on which continental jazz, soul and rap melded with surprising harmony. Talbot's keyboards dominated the A-side, whilst the now-classic "You're The Best Thing" and the chirpy "Headstart For Happiness" stood out on the B-side. A semi-acoustic guitar had ousted his Rickenbackers, but increasingly on stage Weller was discarding his guitar altogether.

CAFÉ BLEU gave The Style Council their only US hit, the poignant ballad "My Ever Changing Moods", but it was with the ambitious follow-up, OUR FAVOURITE SHOP (1985), that the band really began to assert their confidence. Claiming the album to be the best of the decade (it reached #1 in Britain in June), they were now introduced live as 'probably the best band in the world'. Weller's future wife **D. C. Lee** became a permanent member of the group on backing vocals and, with call-to-arms singles like "Shout To The Top" (1984) and "Walls Come Tumbling Down" (1985), The Style Council were on top of their game.

In 1984 The Style Council and friends (including Jimmy Ruffin and Junior Giscombe) had released a benefit single for the striking miners under the guise of **The Council Collective**, and in 1986 the band's political conscience led to involvement with Red Wedge, a tour of bands in support of the Labour Party. Perhaps it was disillusionment following the tour's failure that sapped Weller's creative appetite (he has since admitted it put him off any further political involvement), but whatever the reason the next two albums were anaemic.

A gaudy orange cover did little to lift the down-beat tone of THE COST OF LOVING, The Style Council's 1987 double album. The first, dreary single, "It Didn't Matter", failed to impress Prime Minister Thatcher, who reviewed it on BBC's *Saturday Superstore*, and for once her cognitive faculties were accurate. "Heavens Above", "Fairy Tales" (an attack on Thatcher) and the album's title track were worthy offerings, but they had little company. Worse was to come.

CONFESSIONS OF A POP GROUP (1988) reached only #15 in the UK chart (the band never cracked the States). Its cool pop/classical/jazz mix, lightened by flutes, harps and orchestral arrangements, contrived to make the album sound like dinner-party muzak. More thorough listening did reveal two choice tracks, however. "Changing The Guard" was worthy of Sinatra, whilst "How She Threw It All Away" was a driving, brassy return to the band's early days. It wasn't enough, though.

Thankfully these records weren't to be Paul Weller's pop epitaph. In 1989 Polydor rejected the band's next offering, a 'Chicago-style house album', and The Council called it a day. After a two-year sabbatical Weller returned with his guts restored, and took up where The Jam had left off, as though The Style Council had never happened. His solo career has confirmed him as one of the country's most powerful performers and songwriters.

⊙ **Café Bleu** (1984; Polydor).
Radical departure from the R&B of The Jam. Fuses continental jazz with chirpy pop in an innocent attempt at sophistication.

⊙ **Our Favourite Shop** (1985; Polydor).
A richer, more accomplished sound, as White's drumming energizes Weller's tripping melodies. A near masterpiece.

Michael Booth

SUBWAY SECT/VIC GODARD

Formed Mortlake, England, 1976; split 1981; name still used on some Godard 'solo' outings.

Subway Sect started out when Malcolm McLaren needed to make the Punk Festival at the 100 Club in London look like a bigger event. The band – **Vic Godard**, **Rob Symmons** (guitar), **Paul Myers** (bass) and **Paul Packham** (drums; sometimes substituted by **Mark Laff**, later of **GENERATION X**) – rehearsed for a few weeks and debuted at the Punk Festival supporting the Clash and the Pistols.

Early songs like "Out Of Touch" and "Don't Splitit" garnered a small loyal following for a sound that was more controlled than most punk bands, just as their on-stage image was monochromatic and motionless (The Velvet Underground and Television were major influences). They grabbed some media attention and toured with both The Clash and Buzzcocks, but no recording contract was forthcoming until 1978, by which time the Sect had drafted in new guitarist **Rob Miller** and drummer **Bob Ward**. They finally made their vinyl debut on Braik Records with "Nobody's Scared"/"Don't Splitit", a crashing piece of chaotic brilliance. Later in 1978, **John Britain** (guitar), **Colin Scott** (bass) and **Steve Atkinson** (keyboards) joined Godard and Ward for "Ambition"/"Different Story", another finely crafted single which built on the group's reputation.

But still there was no album, and the feeling grew that Subway Sect had been invited to the party but had not bothered to turn up. Godard became a key figure of the London punk scene and seemed to revel in the lack of success of the group, of which he was the only point of stability – indeed, it had mutated **into Vic Godard & The Subway Sect**. The line-up of Godard plus **Rob March** (guitar), **Dave Collard** (keyboards), **Sean McLusky** (drums) and **Chris Bostock** (bass) was the last before the band proper split in 1981.

In 1984 the Sect was commemorated with the album VIC GODARD & THE SUBWAY SECT: A RETROSPECTIVE 1977–1981. In the meantime, Godard had made some brassy and soulful solo recordings, while March, Collard, McLusky and Bostock had formed **The Jo Boxers**, who in 1983 reached the UK Top 10 with "Boxer Beat" and "Just

Got Lucky". Godard still recorded sporadically, while working as a postman, producing an album, END OF THE SURREY PEOPLE (1993), with Edwyn Collins and Paul Cook in 1993 and he re-formed the band for a one-off gig here and there.

He joined forces with The Bitter Springs and **EDWYN COLLINS** to record a session for Radio 1 in late 1996 and a single "George Blake Masterspy". In late 1998 Vic released his first studio album in five years, THE LONG TERM SIDE EFFECTS on Tugboat Records. Produced by Collins, who describes Godard as 'the finest songwriter of his generation', it features guest appearances from The Long Decline, **Roddy Frame** (ex-**AZTEC CAMERA**) and **Claire Kenny**.

As for the recurring gaps between recordings, as Vic says, 'I've got a lot of mail to deliver!'

⊙ **Vic Godard & The Subway Sect: A Retrospective** (1984; Rough Trade).
The band's main singles tied in with the two radio sessions, featuring hidden gems like "Parallel Lines", "Chain Smoking", "Head Held High" and "Stool Pigeon". Complete with some of Godard's later material, this is the best survey of Subway Sect's fragmented and spartan recording career.

⊙ **In T.R.O.U.B.L.E. Again** (1998; Tugboat).
A revamped reissue of his 1986 album (originally on Rough Trade) that goes some way to explaining the mysterious appeal of a gloomy postal worker.

Pip Southall

SUEDE

Formed London, 1989.

"People might think we're a bunch of fainting woofters who are going to release one album and then disappear. I desperately want to prove them wrong." Brett Anderson

S uede are certainly survivors: not many bands could say goodbye to members of the calibre of **Bernard Butler** (guitar) and **Justine Frischmann** (guitar) and carry on successfully.

Brett Anderson (vocals) grew up in the Sussex market town of Haywards Heath, where he went through the standard 80s teen-outsider phases of anarcho-punk, Bowie and Smiths obsessions. At the end of the 80s, he moved to London and decided to form a band with longtime friend **Mat Osman** (bass). Through ads in the *NME* in early 1990, they found an extraordinary young guitarist called **BERNARD BUTLER** and the band was under way, initially with a drum machine before it was replaced with the infinitely more interesting **Simon Gilbert**. Brett's then-girlfriend, Justine Frischmann, joined as second guitarist and came up with the name Suede. She soon left to pursue her own wiry pop vision with **ELASTICA**.

Although developing their own low-rent, bedsit style, Suede did not yet show signs of greatness. However, after a year spent gigging, building confi-

dence and a following, 1992 brought signs of success. A record deal with Nude was followed by music press pronouncements that they could be the next big thing – their profile was aided by Brett's tendency to say things like 'I'm a bisexual man who's never had a homosexual experience.' Hyperbole was in danger of becoming hype as *Melody Maker* put Suede on the cover before they'd released a record.

Then they did. Both the journos and the group were vindicated. "The Drowners" (1992) was a seething hot classic from the opening grindings of the guitar to the final fade-out. It was backed with "To The Birds" and "My Insatiable One", a stunning song that would have made a great single in its own right. Morrissey agreed and took to covering it in his live sets.

In September Suede released "Metal Mickey" (1992), another stormer, and found themselves at the head of a short-lived, *NME*-declared glam revival alongside Denim. The third single, "Animal Nitrate" (1993), was quickly followed by the SUEDE album in March 1993. It was a deserved critical and commercial success, heading to #1 in Britain and going gold almost instantly. Containing all the singles – including the fourth, "So Young" (1993) – along with half a dozen other could-have-been hits, it went on to win the 1993 *Mercury Music Prize*.

Once the album was released, Suede set out on a British tour, where they finally proved that they weren't big girl's blouses after all. They were sweaty rock pigs who just happened to wear big girl's blouses. Nine months had passed since their last release when "Stay Together" appeared in February 1994. At an epic eight minutes, it was their longest and their most ambitious song. But it worked, staying just the right side of ostentation and proving this was not a band content with running on the spot. "Stay Together" peaked at #3 in the UK charts and increased speculation as to what their second album would sound like.

DOG MAN STAR turned up in October and surpassed all expectations. The near-psychedelic first track, "Introducing The Band", showcased a mutating, more adventurous style very different from the simplicity of the first album. This experimentation continued throughout and climaxed with the addition of a forty-piece orchestra on the final track, "Still Life". Only "The Asphalt World" drifted into overlong indulgence.

However, DOG MAN STAR failed to sell in such large numbers as its predecessor. Suede were suffering from comparison with Blur and Oasis, both now in the ascendant, and Bernard Butler disappeared during the recording, leaving to form **McAlmont & Butler**. A replacement was found in the 17-year-old form of **Richard Oakes** through ads in the music press. Despite suspicions that he was taken on as an ingénue who'd do as Brett told him, Oakes rapidly proved himself in live performance and on "New Generation" (1995).

The band remained quiet for a year before re-emerging in 1996 with another new member, **Neil Codling**, playing keyboards and singing. A single, "Trash" (1996), showed the expanded band returning from the darkness of the previous album to a poppier sound. This was confirmed in September with the release of COMING UP, a bright, shining, fully-chromed dragster of an album packed with big, fat tunes. SCI-FI LULLABIES (1997) was a stopgap collection of B-sides, snapped up by the faithful, giving the band time to record their fourth album, HEAD MUSIC (1999). The thirteen tracks it contained included the stomping "Electricity", released as a single, and the equally impressive title track, but the album had a colder, darker edge than previously, as if the band had grown older, wiser and less directly engaged.

Things then went quiet until late 2002, when A NEW MORNING was released, offering more sociology essays dressed up as competent rock/pop. It'll be interesting to see what they throw at us next.

⦿ **Dog Man Star** (1994; Nude).
A quantum leap on from its predecessor. Not as immediate, maybe, but still superb.

⦿ **Coming Up** (1996; Nude).
Much more approachable than its predecessor, standouts being "Beautiful Ones", "She" (not the Charles Aznavour song, sadly) and the seven-minute contrepiece "The Chemistry Between Us", one of two songs co-written by new boy Neil Codling.

Glenn Law

SUGAR/BOB MOULD

Sugar formed Minneapolis, Minnesota, 1992; disbanded 1995.

After **HÜSKER DÜ** split up in 1987, **Bob Mould** surprised everyone with his debut solo album, the semi-acoustic WORKBOOK (1989). Produced at Paisley Park studios, the album was imbued with a dreamy melancholia into which Mould weaved Byrds-like harmonies and textured acoustics. When the album rocked, it did with an expansive guitar swagger reminiscent of Led Zeppelin at their most direct. The only track that echoed the feedback-drenched excesses of Hüsker Dü, "Whichever Way the Wind Blows", the album-closer, suggested an ironic coda to Mould's cacophonous past.

Despite being a wholly commercial proposition, WORKBOOK failed to sell, and Mould decamped to New York, where he teamed up again with WORKBOOK personnel **Anton Fier** (drums) and **Tony Maimone** (bass) to create an album that would serve as a catharsis for his anger and depression. BLACK SHEETS OF RAIN (1990) was a heavy album, both in musical style and lyrical content. "One Good Reason" and "Hanging Tree" recalled the abrasive sense of alienation of early Hüsker Dü, while the rest of the album veered between blistering power-chord thrash and epic, discordant soloing, via pretty pop songs ("It's Too Late", "Out Of Your Life") that were delivered full throttle, with the melody just about surviving intact amid the sonic brawling.

When this album also failed to connect, Virgin America released Mould from his contract in 1991, and he embarked on a solo acoustic tour, playing Hüsker Dü tracks to a loyal but small following. Resurrection was at hand, however, as the burgeoning grunge scene queued up to pay homage to Hüsker Dü as godfathers of frenetic guitar rock. Sensing a sea change in pop culture, Mould joined Alan McGee's Creation Records and formed **Sugar** with **David Barbe** (bass) and **Malcolm Travis** (percussion), resolving to create tight, muscular pop music that would be more commercially viable.

Sugar's debut album, COPPER BLUE (1992), exceeded expectations. Toning down the volume in favour of a sleek, charged production, the album managed to be melodic within a framework of dark textual edges and crunching, razor-sharp playing. It was a commercial and critical success, and Sugar wasted no time in following it up with the six-track EP BEASTER (1993), a more bruising affair comprising tracks from the COPPER BLUE sessions. An examination of organized religion ("Judas Cradle", "Jesus Christ Auto"), this set aimed for a concentrated sonic assault, sometimes built upon a Brian Wilson-style multi-layered production.

Belated recognition is better than no recognition at all, and Mould enjoyed a success that was dependent upon a movement for which he had sown the seeds a decade earlier. However, with Sugar's FILE UNDER EASY LISTENING (1994), Mould seemed to be acknowledging that grunge had become so assimilated into the mainstream that the style was now more straitjacketing than liberating. The album sounded 'typical' – a serious charge against a man who has consistently defied convention.

1995 saw a collection of Sugar B-sides and rarities and the band's demise was confirmed by the release of the solo album, BOB MOULD, in 1996. Self-played and self-produced, this lacked the bite or melody of Mould's first two solo albums – or of his work with Sugar – and, while he may think he's earned the right to be curmudgeonly, the po-faced spleen of "I Hate

Alternative Rock" was surely stretching the point, even for him. The record seemed out of time, again, too.

Much better was THE LAST DOG AND PONY SHOW (1998), with Mould proclaiming that it would be his last foray into electrified rock music; persistent tinnitus had affected his hearing to such an extent that a new less raucous direction seemed to be the only option left available. Sure enough, MODULATE (2002) documented Mould leaning more towards an electronic style of songwriting and seemingly using the album sessions to learn a new form of composition. From such a well-known creator of classic tunes, the release was one of his least successful, but it did show acutely just how determined and tenacious Mould was to push his creativity into hitherto unexplored sonic territories. To emphasize the new direction, Mould also released LONG PLAYING GROOVES (2002) under the name **LoudBomb**, as a recording available only on the Internet and at live shows. And while the latter found Mould pushing the electronic experiment even further, longtime fans were catered for by the **Bob Mould Band** and another Internet-and-show-only release, LIVE DOG 98 (2002).

Such fluctuations in fortune and direction have never dented Mould's talents or self-belief, and future releases will continue to be watched with much interest.

Sugar

⊙ **Copper Blue** (1992; Rykodisc).
Tight, controlled power pop with a vibrant, clean sound, just the right side of 'produced'. "If I Can't Change Your Mind" was Mould's most commercial song since "Flip Your Wig"-era Hüsker Dü, seven years previously. This time, however, the world was listening.

Bob Mould

⊙ **Workbook** (1989; Virgin).
Classy pop music with an edge, this introspective set dispenses with the 'guitar wars' sound of Hüsker Dü in favour of semi-acoustic folk music.

⊙ **The Last Dog And Pony Show** (1998; Rykodisc).
Excellent guitar pop, produced and written by a master craftsman.

Nig Hodgkins

THE SUGARCUBES

Formed Reykjavik, Iceland, 1986; disbanded 1992.

It's hard to date **The Sugarcubes'** formation – all had been friends for over a decade, and involved with each other in various musical and creative projects. However, it was 1986 when **BJÖRK Gudmundsdóttir** (vocals), **Einar Orn** (vocals/trumpet) and **Siggi Baldursson** (drums) decided to abandon the punk-ish KUKL, and join forces with **Bragi Olafsson** (bass), **Thor Eldon** (guitar) and **Magga Ornolfsdóttir** (keyboards).

The Sugarcubes' odd, spiky, avant-garde pop soon found an enthusiastic backer in British indie label One Little Indian, who released their debut single

"Birthday" in 1987. The first pop song anyone could remember coming out of Iceland, it made an unforgettable impact, with its low, vibrating bass and guitar tune, and Björk delivering prairie-dog yelps to introduce her distinctive vocal style to the world.

Björk always tended to be the public focus of the band, but she and all the others consistently asserted that the outfit was a democracy – their close-knit background determined that it couldn't be anything else. Einar, the 'other' singer and Björk's co-writer, would get his own share of the limelight, not least because his ranting and rapping vocal style contrasted dramatically with Björk's lead.

The Sugarcubes bombarded the public with more in the same vein – singles "Deus" and "Cold Sweat", and an album, LIFE'S TOO GOOD (1988). The LP was a critical and commercial success – enough to help the band fund a side-project, Bad Taste Ltd, to publish poetry and sign other bands. However, a second LP for One Little Indian, HERE, TODAY, TOMORROW, NEXT WEEK! (1989), had an underwhelming reception, and The Sugarcubes disappeared to pursue other interests, such as the creation of ad hoc jazz outfits. Only Björk stepped out in public much, collaborating with **Graham Massey** of 808 State, resulting in two contributions to their 1991 album, EX:EL, plus several gigs together.

This foray into techno and electronic music greatly affected The Sugarcubes' next album, especially as Siggi had started writing 'his own kind of acoustic dance music'. The single, "Hit", with its cartoon sperm on the cover, was an introduction to a brassy and infectious Sugarcubes, with comprehensible lyrics, while STICK AROUND FOR JOY (1992) provided further examples of their new-found eccentric danceability. This probably inspired the making of IT'S IT (1992), an album of Sugarcubes remixes that provided an interesting reinterpretation of some of their better moments.

By the end of the year, the band had decided to call it a day, maybe preferring to finish on a high note. Bragi remained involved with Bad Taste Ltd,

Einar continued to produce his surreal poetry, while Siggi occasionally joined Björk's backing band for her massively successful solo career.

⊙ **Life's Too Good** (1988; One Little Indian/Elektra). Perhaps the definitive Sugarcubes album, even if it is a little on the brief side. "Birthday" is an obvious highlight, although several other tracks approach its mix of the punky and the ethereal, especially "Deus" and "Mama". (The US edition is better value, with five bonus cuts.)

⊙ **Stick Around For Joy** (1992; One Little Indian/Elektra).
Loaded with trumpets, twiddly keyboards, wobbly bass and tambourines, there are twisted tunes galore on "Hit" and "Vitamin", while Björk also acts as agony aunt in "Leash Called Love" with the practical advice, 'He's a bastard, you should leave him.' All good stuff.

⊙ **The Great Crossover Potential** (1998; One Little Indian).
All the singles in one handy fourteen-track package.

Maria Lamle

SUICIDE

Formed New York, 1970; disbanded in 1980; re-formed briefly 1988 and 1998.

Formed by sometime sculptor **ALAN VEGA** (vocals) and free-jazz musician **Martin Rev** (keyboards), **Suicide** aimed to carry the flame ignited by The Velvet Underground. Their career was characterized by sporadic bursts of creativity and commercial failure, but with artists as diverse as Depeche Mode, Spiritualized and Sisters Of Mercy citing them as a major influence, could rock ever have been the same without them?

After the band's debut live performance in late 1970, which was roundly condemned by the few that had bothered to turn up, a guitarist was ditched and Suicide became a two-piece – effectively the first synth-pop duo. Further infamous performances showed that their aim was to be an all-encompassing 'art project', rather than a purely musical force. A sinister leather-clad Vega stalked the stage and audience, wielding a bicycle chain with which he habitually smashed chunks out of venue walls. Rev, meanwhile, pushed his primitive synthesizer to the limit to produce a grating two-note metallic drone. Such antics made it extremely difficult for the band to get gigs and, following the 1973 closure of one of the few venues that would tolerate them, Suicide went into a period of hibernation.

During this time the duo witnessed fellow New Yorkers the Ramones and Patti Smith begin their rise to fame and realized that, unless their sound became more commercial, they were destined for obscurity. The Suicide that re-emerged in 1976 arrived in the midst of the punk scene centred on the famed CBGB's club. They had transformed themselves from a performance-based project to a band capable of producing some of the most highly original avant-garde music of the decade. An eponymous album (1977) was released on the Red Star label run by Marty Thau (ex-manager of The New York Dolls). Vega had matured as a lyricist and vividly conjured up a motley array of characters, while his menacing vocal style had become a sort of sub-Elvis rockabilly croon to which copious amounts of echo were applied. The ballad "Cheree" was released as a single, but "Frankie Teardrop" epitomized the Suicide aural

Suicide's Alan Vega and Martin Rev

assault. A minimal, repetitive mantra-style keyboard riff pulsated as Vega told the sorry tale of Frankie, who one day snapped and murdered his wife and children before killing himself.

During the following year, Suicide attempted to capitalize on the European punk scene and supported The Clash and Elvis Costello on tour. They experienced a typically hostile reaction and Vega had his nose broken on stage in Crawley, while a full-scale riot was precipitated by a performance of "Frankie Teardrop" in Brussels. This gig can be heard on the flexi-disc album, 24 MINUTES OVER BRUSSELS (1980). The band were not discouraged, and Vega claimed it was the element of confrontation that made their performances so engaging.

A second album, ALAN VEGA/MARTIN REV – SUICIDE, appeared in 1980. The bastardized rockabilly style remained on tracks such as "Be-Bop Kid", but producer Ric Ocasek (of The Cars) injected a large dose of pop sensibility, most evident on "Shadazz" and "Sweetheart", and even featured them on his band's TV show.

Despite critical acclaim, the album sold badly and Suicide was put on hold while both members pursued solo careers. Vega was the more successful and his 1980 album, ALAN VEGA, included "Juke Box Babe", a Top 5 hit in France. The duo re-formed in 1988 and A WAY OF LIFE (1989) was released on Chapter 22, to be followed up by WHY BE BLUE (1992). Both records were proficient enough, but lacked the menace of earlier material.

In 1998, however, there was something of a resurgence in popularity. Vega and Rev once again re-formed Suicide to play a string of sell-out London gigs that coincided with the rerelease of their debut album and a wealth of favourable press. It seemed that their true originality and influence was finally being recognized. The duo released a new album, AMERICAN SUPREME, in 2002.

⊙ **Suicide**
(1977; RedStar/Demon; reissued 1998, Blast First). The duo in all their post-Velvets, electro, doom-laden, experimental glory. Vega swoons, croons, yelps and screams his way through some of the most frightening compositions ever committed to vinyl. Still fresh, exciting and dangerous twenty years on.

⊙ **Ghost Riders** (1998; ROIR).
A previously cassette-only rarity, this shows the guys playing live in Minneapolis in 1981. Vital.

Malcolm Russell

SUM 41

Formed Toronto, Canada, 1996.

They could so easily have formed in California. **Sum 41**'s ear-friendly brand of punk rock drips with such sunny harmonies it could have developed as a result of the West Coast climate. Next to Celine Dion and Rush, however, they could turn out to be one of Canada's biggest exports.

Forming a proto-Sum 41 in the suburbs of

Go ahead punk ... make our day

Toronto in the mid 90s, **Deryck 'Bizzy D' Whibley** (guitar/vocals) and **Steve 'Stevo32' Jocz** (drums) grew up with a soundtrack of metal and punk to their school days. So the jump to imitating their musical heroes was only natural. Several band names and line-ups later and **Jay 'Cone' McCaslin** (bass) and **Dave 'Brownsound' Baksh** (guitar/vocals) had joined their jolly pop-punk team. Almost as soon as the final band personnel pieces were falling into place they found themselves on the way to their first album.

HALF HOUR OF POWER (2000) was a fairly typical product of the times. Green Day, Blink 182, The Offspring, and innumerable other wannabes were peddling a formula of bright, hooky pop-influenced punk, and commercial channels such as MTV were more than willing to give time to a sound that attracted the kids with a mix of musical muscle and puerile humour – offering titles such as "Grab The Devil By The Horns And Fuck Him Up The Ass" and "Dave's Possessed Hair", it was neither cerebral, nor original but it was good enough to hike Sum 41 onto the same stages as The Mighty Mighty Bosstones, The Offspring and Blink 182.

With the kids loving their live show, they needed a record to display their studio abilities and find a wider audience. Enter producer Jerry Finn (knob-twiddler to Blink 182 and Green Day) for ALL KILLER NO FILLER (2001), who added a studio veneer that did justice to the band's knack with a catchy riff and sweet melody. The album was derivative, of course, following all the pop-punk signposts – tight playing, sugary harmonies, simple lyrics about home life, relationships, girls and having fun – but the delivery was effervescent and commercial enough to catapult them into the mainstream; the band would spend so much of their time on the road that they didn't even bother to find themselves permanent places to live; they just stepped out of their parents' homes and onto a tour bus. The album's prime cut, "Fat Lip", became the band's signature tune, appearing on computer games and the soundtrack to *American Pie 2*.

Living on the road, the band made sure they lived up to all the rock clichés – all good clean fun for four guys only just into their 20s who were playing in excess of 300 shows in a year. Their debauched lifestyle influenced them in more ways than one and DOES THIS LOOK INFECTED? (2002) was a title inspired, allegedly, by a 4-day bender at Singapore's most notorious brothel, 'Four Floors of Whores'. The new lyrics dealt with the same subjects as before but the music had grown into something tougher than their previous chipmunk punk. At the time of writing, nothing stands between Sum 41 and the hearts and minds of the planet's youth.

⊙ **All Killer No Filler** (2001; Mercury).
A slightly misleading title, seeing as much of this album has been trotted out by other bands in the same area. However, for a good-time blitz through memorable choruses you could do a whole lot worse.

⊙ **Does This Look Infected?** (2002; Mercury).
Better than their previous effort, this is party music for the kids, all choppy riffs and sparkling hooks. Heavier than the band's other material too, this could point the way forward for Sum 41 as they, er, mature.

Essi Berelian

THE SUN CITY GIRLS

Formed Phoenix, US, 1982.

Rising from the ashes of Paris 1942 – a short-lived collaboration with The Velvet Underground's 'Moe' Tucker – **The Sun City Girls** spread their wings in the smouldering Arizona punk scene of the early 80s. First emerging from Phoenix as a trio in 1982, brothers **Alan** and **Rick Bishop**, along with percussionist **Charles Gocher**, landed a deal with now-defunct skate-punk label Placebo in 1984 (most of the back catalogue is consequently out of print at time of writing). The SCG offered more than the three-cord squawk being slam-danced at the time; their free-form explorations favoured free jazz with a hint of world music. Their first two albums, SUN CITY GIRLS (1984) and GROTTO OF MIRACLES (1986) on Placebo were a blueprint for things to come, with hallucinatory, brain-tickling guitar work, beatnik banter and odes to Middle Eastern caravan brides. The next two albums, MIDNIGHT COWBOYS FROM IPANEMA (1986) and HORSE COCK PHEPNER (1987), venture into lewd political observations dealing with Nancy Reagan and other such luminaries. MIDNIGHT COWBOYS also has splendidly twisted covers of Rush's "Fly By Night" and Maria Muldaur's "Midnight At The Oasis".

Moving to the Majora record label, The SCG released their classic, TORCH OF THE MYSTICS (1990), which bore all the Girls', well-honed explorations of Third World mysticism, plus the expected gurgling vocals, searing guitar work and flashes of Andean folk interpreted in the unique SCG style. Following a storm of singles and EPs came the telepathic trio's most improvisational period, during which they increased the sonic level and developed a more intense improvisational cohesion on the albums DAWN OF THE DEVI, LIVE FROM THE PLANET BOOMERANG (1992), VALENTINES FROM MATAHARI (1993) and BRIGHT SURROUNDINGS AND DARK BEGINNINGS (1993).

In the early 90s, the Girls moved to Seattle and established their own record label, Abduction. The debut release was the LP KALIFLOWER (1994), another bout of Third World cosmic plundering. Their next two recordings were little more than soundtracks for unmade B-movies: JUGGERNAUT is best described as Ukrainian noir, while PIASA ... DEVOURER OF MEN, sounds like a film in which killer pterodactyls attack Moroccan villagers. After this jaunt, the Girls turned to the US's own musical lore with JACKS CREEK (1995); an exercise in America's own Third World, Appalachian and Wild West themes abound.

Having previously been staunch vinylists, The SCG launched two double CDs at once. The first, DANTE'S DISNEYLAND INFERNO (1996), a journey into what the band labelled 'the sexy graveyard' has percussionist Gocher take the listener into a mostly verbal foray as the satanic director, growling drunken shanties over a clamouring backdrop. Following DANTE'S ... came the return of the Girls' superpowers, with the marvellously titled 330,003 CROSSDRESSERS FROM BEYOND THE RIG VEDA (1996), one of the band's best.

Since then the group have remained prolific and obscure. Rick Bishop (aka Sir Richard Bishop) has also released several solo recordings, the most noteworthy being SALVADOR KALI on John Fahey's Revenant label.

⊙ **Midnight Cowboys From Ipanema** (1986; Breakfast Without Meat).
A studio jam session elevated to the status of a concept, this has all the hallmarks of a band's lost weekend without the disturbing smells. Golden Earring's "Radar Love" never sounded so urgent, so intense, so tongue-in-cheek.

Hisham Mayet

THE SUNDAYS

Formed London, 1988.

"You don't have to subscribe to the theory of following singles with albums with singles ... If people forget about you in the meantime, then too bad." David Gavurin

The bittersweet couplet 'If I can't be sure what I want anymore/It will come to me later', from their debut single "Can't Be Sure", perfectly defines the laid-back attitude of **The Sundays** – a band that have produced just three albums since their formation twelve years ago.

Harriet Wheeler (vocals) and **David Gavurin** (guitar) met at university, became lovers and then a musical unit. Gavurin was messing around with a guitar and four-track tape machine at home and enlisted Wheeler to sing on some demos. Moving to London and recruiting **Patrick Hannan** (drums) and **Paul Brindley** (bass), they became The Sundays, and played a handful of low-key gigs during the summer of 1988. Here, they were spotted by music press writers, who thrilled to the sound of Wheeler's angelic voice and Gavurin's guitar jangle, which owed a fair bit to The Smiths' Johnny Marr. Indeed, The Sundays' first batch of songs had much in common with the quintessentially English Morrissey-Marr school of introspective pop.

After a label bidding-frenzy, The Sundays plumped for indie stalwart Rough Trade, and released "Can't Be Sure" in January 1989, which gave the public at large the first opportunity to hear what the pundits had been shouting about. Few were disappointed by the song's shuffling, almost stuttering drumbeat and mournful guitar echo, combined with Wheeler's soaring vocals; indeed, it topped Britain's indie charts for two months, and was recognized as one of 1989's best singles.

A four-track John Peel radio session followed, showcasing tracks that were to form the backbone of the LP READING, WRITING AND ARITHMETIC, which finally appeared in early 1990, topping the UK indie chart and reaching #4 in the mainstream chart, too. The Sundays had been elevated to the status of indie heroes, but they were reluctant stars. Gigs were rare and when a national tour was organized to promote the album, Wheeler's voice suffered – a much-anticipated London finale had to be rescheduled. Similarly, although the LP reached the Top 40 in the US, the group were bemused by a back-slapping promotional touring schedule – a show in Dallas was advertised with the slogan 'See The Sundays on Sunday with ice-cream sundaes'.

Such extensive touring abroad meant that new product was slow to materialize. The creative process was further hampered by the band's decision to manage themselves, and the demise of Rough Trade in 1991.

Signed to EMI subsidiary Parlophone, The Sundays relaunched their career in the autumn of 1992, almost three years after their last British gig, with the single "Goodbye". It was only a minor hit, but it received healthy radio support, and revealed both a stronger vocal performance and a warmer multi-layered guitar sound. The B-side even featured a cover of The Rolling Stones' "Wild Horses", in an inimitable Sundays interpretation. The same year saw the band's second album, BLIND, which confirmed that The Sundays operated in their own world, untouched by musical trends, with its classic,

haunting guitar music. A short British tour followed in the winter of 1992, on which the group was rapturously received by fans starved of fresh product or gigs. Despite the obvious hunger, nothing more materialized for five years.

The Sundays returned with STATIC AND SILENCE (1997), a strong twelve-track collection of the classic, jingle-jangle guitar and beautiful vocals that were their trademark. Though it didn't win legions of new admirers, it at least kept the band's flame alive. Five years on there has been no news of a new album, but we do know that David and Harriet now have a young family and, as such, are probably way too busy to worry about their band…

⊙ **Reading, Writing And Arithmetic** (1990; Parlophone/ DGC).
Bright, breezy and full of the joys of spring, this is the sound of a band in the heady rush of youth.

⊙ **Blind** (1992; Parlophone/DGC).
A band slightly older, wiser, more moody and mournful. A perfect soundtrack for late nights lamenting lost loves, and well worth the wait.

Gavin Stoker

SUPER FURRY ANIMALS

Formed Cardiff, Wales, 1993.

"We want to be like the KLF – having number one hits, and still completely doing people's heads in." Gruff Rhys

British pop ate itself with such gluttony in 1995 that the taste-makers looked to more exotic climes for the Next Big Thing. They discovered Wales. As Gorky's Zygotic Mynci seemed content to cohabit in a caravan as creatures from *Dungeons and Dragons*, the crown once worn by Shirley Bassey, Tom Jones and John Cale passed to new glam-psychedelics **Super Furry Animals** – a band who had called their first (Welsh-language) EP LLANFAIRPWLLGWYNGYLLGOGERYCHWYRNDROBWL LLLANTSILIOGO-GOYOCYNY-GOFOD (IN SPACE).

The band first appeared as a techno unit, accompanying Welsh underground band Anhrefn on a tour of France and switching their drum machine to max 'to frighten the French hardcore punks'. But the techno background is really a red herring, for SFA – **Gruff Rhys** (vocals/guitar), **Huw Bunford** (guitar/vocals), **Guto Pryce** (bass), **Dafydd Ieuan** (drums) and **Cian Ciaran** (electronics) – play music steeped in classic pop values.

After a couple of EPs for Welsh-language rock label, Ankst, LLANFAIR PG (1995) and MOONDOG (both 1995), the band signed to Creation, agreeing to record no more than two Welsh-language tracks per album, on condition the label respected their right not to work on St David's Day. They debuted on Creation with "Hometown Unicorn", an indie smash in February 1996, whose stately pomp suggested that somebody had a copy of IN THE COURT

OF THE CRIMSON KING and a bunch of prog-rock and ELO records in their collection. (Rhys owned up to the latter.) "God! Show Me Magic", released a couple of months later, was more like it. Its guitars howled, there was nothing but chorus for miles, and it was over before anybody had a chance to breathe. The instrument-wrecking, Polish animation video was airplay-friendly, and SFA hit the UK Top 40 proper.

It prepared the way perfectly for the debut album, FUZZY LOGIC (1996), recorded with techno legend Gorwel Owen at Rockfield. This was four men and a Roxy-era Eno making one almighty racket, and twelve tunes going off in twelve directions at once. It was greeted by the British press – specialist and mainstream – with gushing enthusiasm, and it started selling in droves. It was prog-rock for a new age, and hugely fun, with songs about computer games, alien abduction and drugs smuggler Howard Marks – whose facial disguises were adopted for the cover art.

The band's subsequent tour with The Bluetones won them their place in the forefront of the British pop renaissance's second wave, and their second album RADIATOR (1997) confirmed their right to hold it. It was just as fizzy and fun as FUZZY LOGIC, but with a touch more skill and maturity in the songwriting.

Four singles were released from the set – "Hermann Loves Pauline", "International Language Of Screaming", "Play It Cool" and "Demons". In May 1998 the band released their finest moment to date, the "Ice Hockey Hair" EP, which took them to #12 in the UK charts. The rest of that year was spent touring and then recording self-produced material at the Real World Studios. An album of rarities and B-sides, OUT-SPACED, came late in 1998, and filled the gap before their next studio album proper.

In 1999 they completed two sold-out UK tours, visited the US and Europe and headlined the legendary 'Mash Up The CIA' gig at Cardiff's International Arena, complete with a mammoth surround-sound system transplanted especially for the band's set. Their third studio album GUERRILLA

(1999), preceded by the single "Northern Lites", was released in June and saw the band take another step forward, combining mind-blowing experimentation with their now distinctive and broadly appealing sound.

With the collapse of Creation Records, Super Furry Animals set up their own label, Placid Casual, and in 2000 – untethered from Creation's lingual restrictions – they released the entirely Welsh-language album MWNG. Though rougher, and not as instantly gratifying as previous releases, this was another wonderfully received collection of glam-rock anthems and psych-tinged oddities, which confirmed them as one of the most important independent bands of the moment. As well as their recognizable sound, their mutated creature artwork – supplied by illustrator **Pete Fowler** – has done much to define their image and cement their charms.

After MWNG, the band set about recording an album for Sony. Utilizing their new paymasters' extensive financial muscle, RINGS AROUND THE WORLD (2001) was a considerably more glossy affair than any of its predecessors. Apparently intended as a state-of-the-planet concept album, the slightly self-conscious grandeur of the set's themes and its lavish production occasionally threatened to overwhelm the Furries' essential wayward charm. However, its better moments were very good indeed. 2003's PHANTOM POWER was a brooding, darker follow-up that chilled as much as it thrilled.

They remain as unpredictable and invigorating as ever. Having transcended every media tag and fad – from Britpop to Welsh-rock – their future seems assured.

⊙ **Fuzzy Logic** (1996; Creation).
The sound of Britpop and music history collapsing in on itself, fooling around with some new instruments – and trying to play the national anthem of the fourth dimension.

⊙ **Radiator** (1997; Creation).
Catchy tunes and knowing lyrics – a splendid second album.

⊙ **Mwng** (2000; Placid Casual).
Another great chapter in Super Furry Animals' book, and it's one that's entirely written in Welsh. Recorded hastily, its rough rawness is refreshing and inviting on both the laid-back numbers – "Y Gwyneb Iau" (Liverface) – and the more up-tempo psych-garage stomps like "Ysbeidiau Heulog" ('Sunny Intervals'). Superb.

⊙ **Rings Around The World** (2000; Sony).
The joyous but deceptively subtle "Juxtaposed With U" is impossible to dislike but "Presidential Suite" seems trite and overcooked compared to much of the band's earlier work. For the most part, however, the band maintain a perfect balance between their experimental urges and melodic gifts. It's not an easy trick to pull off but SFA are no ordinary band.

Charles Bottomley

SUPERCHUNK

Formed Chapel Hill, North Carolina, 1989.

Superchunk – initially plain old Chunk – were formed by **Mac McCaughan** (guitar/vocals), **Laura Ballance** (bass) and **Chuck Garrison**

(drums), and built up an initial cult following with their brash melodic punk tunes, receiving rave reviews in the influential independent music magazine *Maximum Rock'N'Roll*. THE CHUNK EP, as with most of the band's subsequent American singles, was released on Merge Records, the company they set up themselves. As well as their anthemic "What Do I", the EP also included a cover of the Shangri Las' "Train From Kansas City", illustrating the band's love of pure pop, as well as revealing their obvious debt to the American hardcore and British punk scenes.

In 1990, by now trading as Superchunk, with **Jim Wilbur** handling guitar, they released the single "Slack Motherfucker" in May. With its catchy, expletive-driven chorus, the song became Superchunk's "Teen Spirit" or "Freak Scene", encapsulating the band's essence in three minutes of perfect punk for the 90s. The debut album, SUPERCHUNK, came out in 1990, but it was a second LP, NO POCKY FOR KITTY (1991), which really brought them to wide attention. A fine record, with Jon Wurster now on drums, cementing the band's reputation for getting the job done quickly, its twelve songs saw Superchunk trying to cram the maximum number of hooks into each three-minute track. From the masturbation-themed power pop of "Tossing Seeds" to the adrenaline-charged "Skip Steps 1 And 3", the album fulfilled all the promise of the early singles releases.

It was only a matter of time before the major labels started to become interested, but staunchly independent Superchunk stuck to their guns and turned their back on any lucrative deal. An excellent compilation, TOSSING SEEDS (SINGLES 89–91), was released in 1992, followed by two more studio albums in 1993 and 1994, ON THE MOUTH and FOOLISH. A further collection, INCIDENTAL MUSIC (1995), drove home how great a singles band they were. By now, though, the band's popularity was waning, despite attempts to expand their repertoire with longer and subtler songs. Later studio albums HERE'S WHERE THE STRINGS COME IN (1995) and INDOOR LIVING (1997) failed to redress the damage, with the band sounding ever more weary.

Perhaps as a result, McCaughan concentrated on his **Portastatic** side-project, whose debut I HOPE YOUR HEART IS NOT BRITTLE (1994) was a collection of ballads very far removed indeed from the pop-punk, postgrad disaffection of Superchunk. The same could be said of SLOW NOTE FROM A SINKING SHIP (1995), THE NATURE OF SAP (1997), and LOOKING FOR LEONARD (2001).

The unrealized developments of Superchunk's previous two albums finally came to fruition on COME PICK ME UP (1999), a fusion of horns and strings (courtesy of **Jim O'Rourke**, who handles production) and gleaming punk-pop, with an eye constantly attending to melody. If COME PICK ME UP was a welcome rebirth for the indie stalwarts, then 2001's HERE'S TO SHUTTING UP continued the

good work, developing the sound even further with McCaughan and Wilbur adding keyboards and acoustic guitars to the mix, their new, mature sound fleshed out by producer **Brian Paulson** (Son Volt, Wilco).

2002 spawned more material in the form of CLAMBAKE VOLUME 1 (a collection of in-store acoustic cuts) and CLAMBAKE VOLUME 2 (music recorded to accompany the classic silent Japanese movie by Kinugasa, *Page of Madness*). Both were interesting and far from the Superchunk sound of old.

⊙ **No Pocky For Kitty** (1991; Matador).
Mac's voice might not be the greatest in the world, but the band make up for the often grating vocals with tunes that are fast, furious and as catchy as they come. When they do slow the pace down, as on "Sidewalk", Superchunk also prove they are as talented songwriters as they are die-hard punk rockers.

⊙ **Tossing Seeds** (Singles 89–91) (1992; Merge).
Containing all of their early, now deleted, singles, this collection is a must for any latter-day Superchunk fans. "Slack Motherfucker" and "Fishing" are the pick of the bunch, for the obvious enthusiasm and energy that went into recording them.

Jonathan Swift

SUPERGRASS

Formed Oxford, England, 1992.

"It's a way out of washing dishes for the rest of my life." Gaz Coombes

Prior to forming **Supergrass**, **Gaz Coombes** (vocals/guitar) and **Danny Goffey** (drums) had already flirted with the music business – their band **The Jennifers** had released a single for Nude in 1990, when Coombes was just 14. When The Jennifers split, Coombes and Goffey vowed to play together again, and the arrival of **Mickey Quinn** (bass/vocals) gave them the ideal opportunity.

The trio's first single, "Caught By The Fuzz", was released in the summer of 1994 on the Backbeat label. A frenetic punk-pop tale of teenage drug-taking, it won them a deal with Parlophone and its rerelease in the autumn took them to the edge of the UK Top 40, winning widespread critical acclaim in the process.

Suddenly Supergrass were supporting Ride, Shed Seventeen and Blur around Britain – their set may have lasted just 25 minutes, but it was an exercise in thrilling, manic pop, topped off by the photogenic Gaz's wild facial hair. Those who tipped the band for huge success were not disappointed when "Mansize Rooster" charged into the UK Top 20 in early 1995. A lolloping cross between Madness and The Kinks, it showed them to be heirs-in-waiting to Blur's Britpop crown. Supergrass seemed to encapsulate pop music – they were young, good-looking, exuberant lads, and exhilarating live performers, too.

Spring 1995 saw a limited release of "Lose It" on Sub Pop, yet another perfect blast of noisy guitar pop.

Their third Parlophone single, "Lenny", might have been their weakest to date, but it became their first Top 10 single in the UK, and created enough interest for a US tour, even before they had released a record over there.

The debut album, I SHOULD COCO (1995), lived up to all expectations, but it also showed a different side to them. The knockabout singles were joined by slower tracks like the bluesy ballad "Time" and "Sofa (Of My Lethargy)". It spent several weeks at the top of the album charts, its success helped by a triumphant Glastonbury Festival performance, and a double-A-sided single "Alright"/"Time", which was very unlucky to miss the #1 spot on its release in July. "Alright", in particular, caught the summer mood perfectly, with its breezy lyrics and catchy melody, while its video summed up the band's irreverent sound and image.

From here on, Supergrass were to dominate press headlines. After an appearance in *Italian Vogue*, Gaz was offered, and turned down, a contract to advertise Calvin Klein underwear. I SHOULD COCO was nominated for the Mercury Music Prize Award, while American success was tempered by legal action, after they used a photograph of actor Hugh Grant in police custody for the stateside release of "Caught By The Fuzz".

Things continued to get better for the Oxford trio, with a return to the UK Top 10 with "Going Out" in early 1996, and 1997's IN IT FOR THE MONEY doing great business in the stores. Far from being a mere reprise of the cheerful chirpiness of I SHOULD COCO, this album was a critically approved, more mature work that showed Gaz and the boys to be serious artists. The album featured lots of good guitar work and excellent lyrics, with the band's sound filled out by a big brass section.

And if IN IT FOR THE MONEY showed the band were fully capable of material well beyond mere cheeky pop then SUPERGRASS (1999) found them pushing their sound even further, with lush string arrangements and forays into stomping glam – this was the sound of a band having real fun in the studio, which again led to solid-gold hits in the shape of "Moving" and "Pumping On Your Stereo".

2002's LIFE ON OTHER PLANETS was another trademark release, with rich arrangements, big guitars and its tongue firmly embedded in its cheek.

⦿ **I Should Coco** (1995; Parlophone).
It sounds exactly like it should: a whirl of silly voices and a fistful of great tunes, with stories of drugs, girls and small-town lunatics.

⦿ **In It For The Money** (1997; Parlophone).
At times psychedelic, at others deeply personal and inward-looking, this is a far more mature project than I SHOULD COCO. Still a lot of fun, though.

⦿ **Life On Other Planets** (2002; Parlophone).
Cuts such as "Za" and "Brecon Beacons" are classic Supergrass, while the set's closing numbers portray an almost prog-tinged side to the band's creativity.

James Sutherland

SUPERTRAMP

Formed London, 1969; disbanded 1971; re-formed 1973; disbanded 1988; re-formed again 1997.

Supertramp came into being through the 'Musicians wanted' sections of *Melody Maker*, that perennially fruitful source of British musical alliances. Thus **Richard Davies** (vocals/ keyboards) recruited **Roger Hodgson** (bass guitar/keyboards/vocals), **Richard Palmer** (guitar) and **Bob Miller** (drums).

With the financial assistance of Dutch millionaire Stanley Miesegaes, a deal was struck with A&M and an album, SUPERTRAMP (1970), issued. A rather anonymous slab of prog-pop, it disappeared without trace, and the line-up soon changed. **Frank Farrell** and **Kevin Currie** replaced Palmer and Miller and the sound of the band broadened with the addition of saxophonist **Dave Winthrop**. This flurry of personnel activity did little to improve the band's fortunes, however. INDELIBLY STAMPED (1971), with its tacky tattooed breasts sleeve, was as unprepossessing as its precursor.

Supertramp Mark I was laid to rest, lamented by few, but songwriters Davies and Hodgson persevered, with a new 1973 line-up: out went Farrell, Currie and Winthrop, in came wind player **John Anthony Helliwell** and a rhythm section of **Dougie Thompson** (bass) and **Bob Benberg** (drums). This kick-started a radical change in the band's fortunes. They entered Trident Studios with former David Bowie producer/engineer Ken Scott to record CRIME OF THE CENTURY (1974), the first and best of a string of million-selling albums. With its themes of loneliness, madness and paranoia, CRIME – a poppier, bastard son of DARK SIDE OF THE MOON – was prog-rock tempered with some storming melodies – "Hide In Your Shell", "If Everyone Was Listening" and, of course, "Dreamer", which rolled into the UK Top 20 as a single, bringing the album along with it. All the Supertramp trade-

SUPERGRASS
LIFE ON OTHER PLANETS

marks were present: distinctive acoustic and electric pianos, Benberg's drumming with its cannon-like tom fills, Helliwell's sax playing, Viv Stanshall-style backing vocals, hard-edged metal guitar riffs, and a pomp production turned up to eleven.

On the strength of this set, the team reassembled for CRISIS? WHAT CRISIS? (1975), which consolidated their success on both sides of the Atlantic. Although a much less consistent affair than CRIME, it had good moments, particularly "A Soapbox Opera", the best-realized example of the band's recurring 'who am I, where am I going?' songwriting.

In 1977, with punk's chill wind declaring death to the dinosaurs, Supertramp engaged famed Beatles engineer Geoff Emerick for EVEN IN THE QUIETEST MOMENTS (1977), their last half-decent album. It provided a US Top 20 hit with an uncharacteristically restrained acoustic song, "Give A Little Bit". Normal prog-rock service was resumed with "Babaji" (lost-little-boy spiritualism) and "Fool's Overture", in which Hodgson duetted with Winston Churchill.

By now the band had completely embraced AOR (Adult-Oriented Rock), and BREAKFAST IN AMERICA (1979), although their most successful album (US #1, UK #3; three hit singles) was real dross. Lacking any epic qualities, the songs accentuated the wishy-washy, hippie drippiness of the singing and the downright embarrassing lyrics – "The Logical Song" was a *tour de force* in the art of the forced rhyme. Punk obviously wasn't doing its job properly.

However, the formula was maintained, with slowly diminishing returns, on FAMOUS LAST WORDS (1982) (after which Hodgson jumped ship), BROTHER WHERE YOU BOUND (1985) and FREE AS A BIRD (1987). The last release was LIVE '88 (1988), which, in comparison with the hugely successful and much better PARIS (LIVE 29.11.79) (1980), seemed to sum up the band's decline. Indeed, Supertramp dissolved in 1988, staying out of the public gaze for almost a decade until resurfacing with SOME THINGS NEVER CHANGE (1997). A sell-out tour accompanied the album, which focused on the jazzier side of things whilst remaining instantly identifiable as Supertramp product. One for the dedicated fan only. The group followed on with more tours and SLOW MOTION in 2002.

You'd be hard pushed to portray Supertramp as being in any way influential; although they readily fused sound effects, nursery rhymes and out-of-context radio footage, it's forcing the point to hail them as precursors of the sampling age. But, alongside others, notably 10CC and Queen, they serve as a good example of that curious hybrid of melodic prog-rock that flourished between the genuine heavyweights of the 60s and late 70s. Their entire back catalogue was dusted down and reissued as part of A&M's mid-price list in 1997.

⊙ **Crime Of The Century** (1974; A&M).
The band's best album by some distance. Gloriously

preposterous production and arrangement, some irresistible choruses and – in the title track – the definitive prog-rock album-finisher.

⊙ **The Autobiography Of Supertramp** (1988; A&M).
For those emboldened to explore the Supertramp canon further, this includes excerpts from all the albums. Those from CRISIS? WHAT CRISIS? and EVEN IN THE QUIETEST MOMENTS are the most acceptable; the other stuff quite probably put the sneer on John Lydon's face.

Lance Phillips

THE SUPREMES

Formed Detroit, Michigan, 1959; disbanded 1978.

With twelve American #1s, sixteen records in the American Top 10 between 1964 and 1969, and some twenty million-selling records to their credit, **The Supremes** were by far the most successful female vocal group of the 60s, forming the launch pad for Berry Gordy's and Tamla Motown's assault on white America's listening habits, and later for the successful, high-profile solo career of **Diana Ross**. The Supremes were fortunate that their songwriters, Holland-Dozier-Holland, were among the most gifted pop stylists ever, and in Ross they possessed a lead vocalist with a unique and fresh sound, albeit with a restricted range.

Formed by Ross, **Florence Ballard**, **Mary Wilson** and **Betty Travis**, the group first traded under the name of **The Primettes**, regularly performing with The Primes, the nascent Temptations. With **Barbara Martin** replacing Travis, they recorded for the Lupine label in 1960 before being courted by Gordy, who sensed Ross's charisma and made her the focal point of the group. After "I Want A Guy" (1961), Martin left the quartet, whose initial releases, overseen by the production of Smokey Robinson and primarily featuring the grittier lead voice of Ballard, were just minor successes.

When Gordy handed the group over to the Holland-Dozier-Holland team, the torrent of pop gems began. In 1963 they achieved their first Top 40 success, "When The Lovelight Starts Shining Through His Eyes". However, it was their seventh release, the ground-breaking "Where Did Our Love Go?" (1964), that propelled them to the top of the charts, to be swiftly followed by "Baby Love" and "Come See About Me" (both 1964), on which Ross's upbeat, cooing vocals perfectly complemented the direct, on-the-fours pop productions. Their act was now as finely honed and precisely choreographed as their vinyl output, and the Supremes' hit singles continued unabated, pursuing much the same pop-soul terrain.

Their American #1s included the epochal "Stop In The Name Of Love", "Back In My Arms Again", "I Hear A Symphony" (all 1965), "You Can't Hurry Love" (1966), "You Keep Me Hangin' On" (1966), "Love Is Here And Now You're Gone" and the film theme "The Happening" (both 1967). At this point Ballard, who had become disenchanted with her sec-

The utterly wonderful Supremes (from left): Florence Ballard, Mary Wilson and Diana Ross

ondary role, left to be replaced by **Cindy Birdsong**, who remained until 1972. "Reflections" (1967) followed the first record billed as **Diana Ross And The Supremes**, a move that anticipated the eventual departure of Ross for a successful solo career. "Love Child" (1968) was their first major hit single after they renounced the alliance with Holland-Dozier-Holland, while Ross's split followed "Someday We'll Be Together" (1969).

Without her angular vocals The Supremes were little more than moderately talented backing singers. They began the 70s with **Jean Terrell** substituting Ross as the lead (she herself was to be ousted by **Scherrie Payne** in 1973). Like many on the Motown roster, The Supremes frequently cut sides with their label-mates. With **The Temptations** they had recorded "I'm Gonna Make You Love Me" (1968) and, with **The Four Tops**, a cover version of Ike and Tina Turner's "River Deep Mountain High" (1970). More Top 10 hits, including "Stoned Love" (1970), "Nathan Jones" (1971) and "Floy Joy" (1972), briefly revived their fortunes in Britain, but splits weakened the band. Eventually Wilson was the only original left, persevering with different line-ups – and scoring one more hit with "I'm Gonna Let My Heart Do The Walking" (1976) – before the group disbanded in 1978.

In 1989, Terrell, Payne and **Linda Lawrence** regrouped as The Supremes for recording and touring, but injunctions from Wilson followed. A sad end for a group so popular that they inspired a Broadway musical, Dreamgirls, which told the story of The Supremes from the perspective of Ballard (who had died destitute), portraying Gordy as a ruthless manipulator and Ross as his puppet. Wilson

published her own account of events, *Dreamgirl: My Life As A Supreme*, in 1984.

⊙ **Anthology** (1974; Motown).
Superior compilation of the hit singles, with the emphasis on the 60s material. About as infectious, upbeat and life-affirming as production-line Tamla, or indeed any pop music, got in that golden decade.

Michael Sumsion

SURF BANDS

The wave arrived 1961; surf was out by 1964.

Though **DICK DALE** created the surf sound, the public weren't buying it from him. Instead, they were purchasing the foam-flecked emissions of diverse high-school kids, session musicians, pop geniuses, DJs and even the spawn of Doris Day. While the glorious guitar reverb of Dale's "Miserlou" and "Let's Go Trippin'" collected dust at the bottom of the charts, the rest of the US in the early 60s hitched up their baggies, caught waves (even in Colorado and Minnesota), and grooved to the waxings of The Surfaris, The Chantelles, The Hondettes, The Trashmen, The Contours, the nobodies and the somebodies who would create a New Jerusalem of West Coast music, and influence the sound of an entire generation.

If JFK created Camelot, then the surfers were its knights without a cause. Like their leader, they were sandy-haired, well-built and impeccably tanned, but, where Jack had his hands full with Cuba and Marilyn Monroe, the surfers were only interested in the boom of the waves and the swell of the tide. They disdained the material success preached by the prophets of

Levittown in the 50s. They already had it, and frittered away their affluence on the latest fibreglass boards invented by Bob Simmons in 1948. Actor Cliff Robertson had set up his own surf shop in Los Angeles, shifting the centre of surf production from Hawaii (where the natives had pioneered the sport) to the West Coast. There, surfing found Zen, as elucidated in John Milius's movie *Big Wednesday*, and hanging ten became an existential act. The Outsider no longer walked the beach. He surfed it.

And when he (and it was always a he) wasn't surfing, he was soaking up the sounds at the Rendezvous Ballroom Balboa, dressed in his white Levis and Pendletons, and listening to Dick Dale. Although the earringed guitarist was ready to break big in the US market, he found himself scooped by **The Marketts**, who recorded his "Surfer Stomp" and had a #31 hit with Dale's own theme tune. Dale had outlined the philosophy of surf music, but as long as it was loud, fast, erred on the wrong side of sense and was recorded by someone familiar with sunshine, it was chart gold dust. Having a singing voice as flat as a surfboard helped. When **THE BEACH BOYS** recorded "Surfin'" (1961), LA became an open city for every musician who had seen a Jacques Cousteau film, trading staccato guitar riffs and **Bo Diddley** rhythms across the dunes. Bo even got in on the act himself on SURFIN' WITH BO DIDDLEY – not one for the faint-hearted.

If you couldn't get Bo, you got a session musician. **The Hondelles** were so corporate that the band photograph showed bank tellers who worked across the street from the studio. The thieving Marketts were sessioneers who had been given the "Stomp" by its author/producer, Joe Saraceno. They included **Leon Russell** and bassist **Ray Pohlman**, who shared his duties with the band and with Phil Spector's Wrecking Crew before going on to become the musical director of *Shindig*, a rival to Dick Clark's *American Bandstand*. The great drummer **Hal Blaine** had his own lo-fi hit with the Young Cougars called "Dance With The Surfin' Band", and appeared on countless other platters by bands long forgotten.

To make the music that bounced out of his fecund mind and off the concrete breeze blocks of his studio, **PHIL SPECTOR** would nab sessioneers who were making their crust peddling the surf beat. Spector was the lost wave in the surfing sound, paying attention to its attempts at capturing the pulse of the big blue, while putting his own talents into surrounding **CLASSIC GIRL GROUPS** with his take on the pipeline, the 'wall of sound'. **Carol Connors**, from his first group the **Teddy Bears**, went on to write several hot-rod classics: "Hey Little Cobra" by the Rip Chords, "Blond In The 406" by Dick Dale, and "Go Go GTO", which she recorded with her sister **Cheryl**. After the Teddy Bears' success with "To Know Him Is To Love Him", Spector served his apprenticeship with **LEE HAZLEWOOD**, the Debussy of the Desert, who contributed to the surfer bandwagon by writing "Batman" and "Baja" for the Astronauts, a rock'n'roll band from Colorado who could only get signed to a label provided they played surf music. Hazlewood, who would deliver to the world the Nancy Sinatra Frank never knew, also wrote "Your Baby's Gone Surfin'" with **Duane Eddy**, which the tyrant of twang recorded at the bottom of Hazlewood's water tank in Arizona.

Then there were the genuine bands, who just couldn't help being all wet. **The Pyramids** recorded the seminal "Penetration" and were briefly the new Beatles because they had shaved their heads. **The Trashmen** gave rock its most articulate moment with "Surfin' Bird" (1963), a shameless splice of The Rivingtons' incomprehensible "Papa-Oo-Mow-Mow" (1962) and "The Bird's The Word" (1963). They were sued by The Rivingtons, but had enough self-respect to support The Beach Boys, and then storm out of the concert in disgust at the headliners' performance. The Routers, who had a local hit with "Let's Go", were the first band of **Scott Walker**.

Best known were **The Surfaris** and **Jan & Dean**. The Surfaris were high-school kids who let their songs either come to them courtesy of their producers (1963's "Wipe Out") or in their dreams ("Surfer Joe", the drummer's nightmare). Jan & Dean penned their first hit "Jennie Lee", about a stripper, while another J & D classic was "Linda", inspired by Linda Eastman (later McCartney).

Jan & Dean proved to be the most durable of the surfing bands because of their association with **Brian Wilson**, who co-wrote much of their material. While The Surfaris went all folky on their public (yet retaining the terrible name), Jan Berry and Dean Torrence were surfing degree zero, hitting with "Surf City" (whose 'Two girls for every boy' intro was the most exciting Utopian promise since Marx), the original "Surfin'", and even "Sidewalk Surfin'", written for those surfers trapped in the inner cities. Jan loved his Corvette more than his board, and his passion inspired the prophetic "Deadman's Curve" (1964). Its pile-up finale came true when Jan crashed in 1966. Perhaps he was unhappy with J & D's latest album; JAN AND DEAN MEET BATMAN.

Wilson was constantly on the lookout for significant others to write songs with, and, on the Jan & Dean hits, **Roger Christian** and **Terry Melcher** were names that kept reappearing. Roger was a DJ turned lyricist, who co-wrote "Deadman's Curve" and seemed to have his name on every hot-rod song, from the Surf Super Stocks' "Surf Route 101" to The Knights' "Hot Rod High". Christian's reputation as a poet of the blacktop was so well established that when the police stopped him for speeding he was let off on the grounds of 'research'. "Curve" was inspired by the news that his hero Mel Blanc (the voice of Bugs Bunny) was in traction after wiping out on Westwood Avenue.

Melcher, the son of Doris Day, became a New York A&R man who hobnobbed with Sedaka, Goffin and King in the Brill Building, but went back to LA to become a surf producer: his first victim was Pat Boone. He had his own band with future Beach Boy **Bruce Johnson** as **Bruce & Terry**, he fine-tuned The Surfaris' "Boss Barracuda", and he was most of the members of The Rip Chords. As surf gave way to folk, he was reassigned to The Byrds. In true surfing fashion, he replaced everyone except Jim McGuinn, brought in some session players, and 'improved' upon Bob Dylan's "Mr. Tambourine Man" (1965). The record had surfing legs: the first ten seconds are clearly the most important (compare with "Wipe Out") and the massed harmonies owe as much to Brian Wilson as to Greenwich Village coffee bars. Melcher would later go on to promote the Monterey Festival.

Surf turned into a novelty that demanded continual repackaging, and no one did it better than **Gary Usher**. With teenage cohorts **P. F. Sloan** and **Steve Barri** (who would write Barry McGuire's gloomfest "Eve Of Destruction" while only 19), he created a myriad of bands rivalled only by Phil Spector for complete anonymity and sonic destructiveness. Their alias included the Fantastic Baggys, Gary Usher & The Usherettes, The Four Speeds, The Rally Packs (a Wilson/Jan & Dean supergroup!), The Lifeguards, Willie And The Wheels, The

Sunsets, The Devons and The Rincon Surfside Band. Subject matter rolled with the times: surfing, hot-rodding, skateboarding, horror songs, and eventually the electric folk pioneered by The Byrds, whose "So You Want To Be A Rock'n'Roll Star" (1967) Usher would produce, basing it on years of scamming experience.

Surf's end was Usher's beginning. He had written the lyrics for "In My Room" and encouraged the introspection that would lead Wilson away from the beach he hated and further into the maze of his own neuroses. Great music would come, but by 1964 it had nothing to do with surf. When The Rolling Stones learned of their Californian promotion man's fondness for the genre, they took the piss in "Under Assistant West Coast Promotion Man". As Brian Wilson's waistline expanded, the surf sound became more distant, until it had dropped into the dull roar at the bottom of a sea shell.

Various

⊙ **The History of Surf Music Volume 1** (Rhino).
This fine compilation is the obvious starting point, featuring many of the list discussed above. And if you're hooked, there are several further volumes.

The Surfaris

⊙ **Wipe Out! The Best of The Surfaris** (1963; Varese Sarabande).
A compelling group album, introduced by a board snapped over a microphone and a madcap's laugh.

The Trashmen

⊙ **Best Of The Trashmen** (1992; Sundazed).
Like the best surfing records, complete nonsense and completely stolen. Devotees claim the record is the impartation of wisdom by sacred shamen, including the answer to the question of where the 'g' went in 'surfing'. The Trashmen returned to their bins, never to be heard from again.

Charles Bottomley

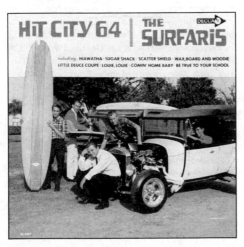

SWANS

Formed New York, 1982; disbanded 1996.

Swans were never a 'listener-friendly' venture, and could easily be criticized as oppressively negative, but at their peak they were one of the most radical bands in rock, and their single-minded experimentations dismantled the form at its very foundations.

The obsessive project of vocalist **Michael Gira**, the band featured numerous different personnel over the years, starting with a line-up completed by **Norman Westberg** (guitar), **Harry Crosby** (bass) and **Roli Mosiman** (percussion). Their first album, FILTH (1983), welded grating guitars onto crashing percussion, almost drowning out the tortured growl of Gira's vocals. It was unforgiving stuff, though still identifiable as rock music in some mutilated form.

Signing to British label K.422 in 1984, Swans released an EP, RAPING A SLAVE, and an album, COP. Both provided the first indications of their

SWANS

2CD

CHILDREN OF GOD · WORLD OF SKIN

deconstructive direction. This was rock slowed to an almost frozen standstill and reduced to its most basic component – the monolithic chord; barely recognizable as music any more, it was like newsprint magnified to the point of illegibility. In terms of lyrics, COP presented a nightmare trawl through a shadowy industrial wasteland, playing out endlessly brutal scenarios.

In 1986, the release of two albums – GREED and HOLY MONEY – and two singles called "Time Is Money (Bastard)" and "A Screw" conceptually represented a single project, with Gira's lyrics delineating a vision of all social existence as various forms of slavery. Introducing cavernous piano and the ghostly siren vocals of **Jarboe** to the band's sound, these recordings seemed to constitute some new and alien medium, constructed from the rubble of rock's collapse.

Swans' extreme world-view was matched in their punishingly loud live outings, captured on the album PUBLIC CASTRATION IS A GOOD IDEA (1987). Indeed, by then, their shows were surrounded by rumours that the sheer volume had caused audience members to throw up. Meantime, hints of beauty and delicacy had unexpectedly begun to appear on tracks like "Blackmail", Jarboe's fragile lullaby to the bliss of surrender. These elements were expanded upon in a Gira/Jarboe side-project under the name **Skin**. Recordings from late 1986 were released as two separate albums – BLOOD, WOMEN, ROSES (1987) and SHAME, HUMILITY, REVENGE (1988). Retaining the minimalism of Swans, but using acoustic instruments, Skin provided an exotic, other-worldly counterpoint to their brutality.

The lessons learned from Skin made themselves apparent on Swans' 1987 double LP, CHILDREN OF GOD, which combined the pounding heaviness of their earlier work with lighter, almost bluesy, sections. The album represented a broadening of their sound, although some of their force was inevitably lost in the process.

In 1988, Swans startled both fans and critics by releasing a folky acoustic cover version of Joy Division's "Love Will Tear Us Apart", on which

Gira renounced his previous avant-garde leanings in favour of the kind of totems (authenticity, soul, 'The Song') that Swans had always apparently opposed. Another move towards conventionality came in 1989, when they signed to major label MCA, and released the relatively traditional and linear THE BURNING WORLD. Sounding like a distant relative of a Leonard Cohen album, it was only partially successful, though when it shined the results were mesmerizing.

Their stint with MCA did not last long and, having parted company with final original Swans member Norman Westberg, Gira and Jarboe set up their own independent label, Young God Records. Their first release was TEN SONGS FOR ANOTHER WORLD (1990), released under the name **The World Of Skin**, as another act had already claimed legal ownership of their former name. A disappointing affair, the album lacked both the sophistication and discipline of the pair's earlier material, with lyrics increasingly straying into the realms of the gothic.

Unfortunately, this was to set the tone for subsequent Swans albums – WHITE LIGHT FROM THE MOUTH OF INFINITY (1991), LOVE OF LIFE (1992) and THE GREAT ANNIHILATOR (1994). A settled style had evolved, more conventionally musical than on former work, though still far from easy listening and ever preoccupied with the darker side of human existence. While containing some startling and compelling moments, these records had lost the stark power of the band's mid-80s period, and the group announced they were to split after a final tour and the release of SOUNDTRACKS FOR THE BLIND (1996). A two-CD document of their last ever gig, SWANS ARE DEAD (1998), however, captured their full sonic mastery.

Gira's post-Swans activities have already included several new musical projects, including **Bodylovers** and, more interestingly, **The Angels Of Light**, who formed in 1998 to release numerous albums on Young God Records. The label itself is well worth checking out as it continues to release powerful and often startlingly beautiful experimental music by a range of artists, as well as turning up the odd archive Swans release (CHILDREN OF GOD and WORLD OF SKIN were reissued together in 1997, while THE BURNING WORLD turned up as FOREVER BURNED in 2003). Gira has also penned a collection of writing, *The Consumer*, published by Henry Rollins' 2.13.61 imprint.

Swans

⊙ **Cop/Young God•Greed/Holy Money**
(1999; Some Bizarre). '
The contents of this double-CD document of early Swans material is the distorted soundtrack to the combined worst nightmares of Kafka and Burroughs, stalked by the shadowy figures of its song titles – such as "Butcher", "Cop" and "Thug". This is rock music at absolute zero: sparse reverberant piano, concussive drums and disembodied wails. This CD reissue also includes the RAPING A SLAVE EP.

SWANS

Swans Are Dead (1998; Young Gods Records).
A head-churning final statement, this double-CD collection of live material from 1995 and 1997 finds the Swans once again at ease with the unrepentant colossus of their earlier sound.

Feel Good Now (2002; Atavistic).
Another live reissue, this time from around the time of CHILDREN OF GOD. The CD features a classic Swans lineup and includes cuts such as "New Mind" and "Beautiful Child".

Forever Burned (2003; Young Gods Records).
A long-overdue reissue of the oft-misunderstood THE BURNING WORLD. The set also features several additional cuts lifted from the LOVE OF LIFE and WHITE HEAT albums.

Skin

Blood, Women, Roses (1987; Product Inc.).
The austerity of Swans is here marked out in the softer tones of swooning strings, crystalline piano and Jarboe's beautiful, yearning vocals. Set in some exotic mythical half-world, the album's heady atmosphere extends to its reinterpretations of old standards "Cry Me A River" and "The Man I Love".

The Angels Of Light

How I Loved You (1987; Young Gods Records).
Though Gira's post-Swans offerings have been largely melodic, and often acoustic, they are no less majestic or lyrically powerful than Swans at their height. This set features the stunning "Untitled Love Song" and an unforgettable closer, "New City In The Future".

Ian Canadine and Peter Buckley

THE SWEET

Formed 1968, disbanded 1979.

It all began back in 1966 when **Mick Tucker**, drummer with Middlesex club band, Wainwrights Gentleman, met Scottish-born vocalist **Brian Francis Connolly**. A year later the pair invited bassist **Steve Norman Priest** and guitarist **Frank Torpey**, an ex-schoolmate of Tucker, to join them in The Sweetshop. Shortened to **The Sweet**, they signed with Fontana, and recorded a single, "Slow Motion" – the only result of which was termination of their contract; replacing Torpey with Mick Stewart, almost a year passed before another label, Parlophone, could be convinced to sign them. After seven months, three forgotten singles and an equally depressing lack of success in concert (by this time they were performing covers of The Doors, The Byrds and Moby Grape – and not terribly well), The Sweet needed something fresh.

Mick Stewart decided to devote his life to marriage rather than teen-stardom and retired, opening a vacancy for Welshman **Andy Scott** and completing the legendary Connolly-Priest-Scott-Tucker line-up. The new team started by signing to RCA, then, on advice from producer Phil Wainman, teamed up with songwriters Nicky Chinn and Mike Chapman – responsible for the highest-selling, lowest-credibility British pop of the 1970s. "Funny, Funny" (1971) was the breakthrough the band had been looking for and went to #13 in the UK. Over the next four years they recorded a string of dire sing-along bubblegum kiddie-pop tunes ("Co Co", "Alexander Graham Bell", "Poppa Joe", "Little Willy", "Wig-Wam Bam", "Blockbuster", "Hell Raiser", "Ballroom Blitz" and "Teenage Rampage" – all of which charted respectably).

The technical side of the business was very simple. Chinn and Chapman did it the same way as Status Quo; they used few harmonies and a simple rhythm, saw to the melody, and kept it basic. In combination with powerful management, The Sweet emerged as the country's top singles band and a huge concert attraction.

In the grand glam tradition, the band paid much more attention to their image than to the music and their shows became a fusion of visual effects and sound. Tucker had starred in the film version of *The Man With The Golden Arm* and, apparently not content with Native American togs, feather headdresses, leather and glitter, had the film projected onto a screen behind the band while the drummer had a duel with his filmed self. There was nothing that couldn't be turned to the band's advantage: a controversial single "Turn It Down" was banned by BBC in 1974 and did not even go Top 40 in the UK, but, as if to compensate, it became the hottest track of the season in Europe. On the other side of the ocean "Little Willy" won the *Outstanding British Record* prize of 1973, having been nominated by the Professional Composers and Publishers of America. The hits rolled in, the gigs were all sellouts, sales surpassed 20 million, but the thrill of teen adulation was wearing off.

Having made their reputation as a bubblegum, glitter-pop band, they started looking for something fresh to do, went off to the studio and returned with SWEET FANNY ADAMS (1974). The guys had been known for giving their tracks schoolyard-risqué names but the similarity between "Sweet F.A." and previously written material ends with the title. Without assistance from Chinn and Chapman, the album charted at #27 and flopped after just two weeks, a seemingly poor debut as a no-jock hard-rock band. However, if nothing else, it helped to establish their new image and prepared the ground for future serious work. DESOLATION BOULEVARD (1974) followed SWEET F.A. by only eight months and brought back the confidence that kept them going through the 'pop' years. "Fox On The Run" from that album climbed to #2 in Britain.

The Sweet and their fans throughout Europe have pointed out the similarities between Deep Purple's heavier passages and the newborn Sweet, even down to the similar development of the two bands: both had replaced two musicians early on and both left the sunny side of the street ("Hush", Deep Purple's first single is not the kind of music one immediately associates with the band) for the gloomier, heavier side of the tracks.

Despite their success on the continent, after SWEET FANNY ADAMS and DESOLATION BOULEVARD the band lost momentum. They didn't crack the Top 10 again until 1978, when, back on Polydor, "Love Is Like Oxygen" got to #9.

As has happened to many other bands groaned at and loathed in the 70s, there are still fans who are eager to pay to see The Sweet live in concert. After Brian Connolly's departure from the band in 1979, **Steve Priest** became the singing bass guitarist in Andy Scott's Sweet, and Connolly became the frontman for the Brian Connolly's Sweet. Both bands toured – sometimes together, sometimes on their own – but neither was able to come up with a decent album, as significant as the earlier work. All hopes for reunions and studio work ceased when on Sunday February 9, 1997, the sad news of Brian's death (aged 52) was released to the public. The band's heyday was the early 70s as part of the ChinniChap stable and has been collected on innumerable 'best of's.

⊙ **Sweet Fanny Adams and Desolation Boulevard** (both 1974; RCA; reissued 1990; Castle).
SWEET F.A. is their biggest achievement. "AC-DC", "Peppermint Twist" and "Teenage Rampage" capture the essence of the band – from pop tunes to the powerful engine of rhythm section, emotional vocals and quite decent guitar solos. DESOLATION, if you get the original version of the album (not the edited version released in US), is their other full-length classic.

Pavel Gurevich

MATTHEW SWEET

Born Nebraska, 1964.

"Everybody has these stories –'My parents had all the great Muddy Waters records.' Well, mine had the *What's New Pussycat* soundtrack and stuff like that... "

Matthew Sweet should by rights be a pop icon, rather than holding what's little more than cult status. He's been around for nearly two decades and, though not heavy, he has a brilliant pop sensibility, soaked in such youthful influences as Elvis Costello, John Lennon, Brian Wilson and Gram Parsons, and obsessed with the quest for melody-mesmerizing choruses, crisp solos, Byrds-like harmonies and gorgeous ballads.

Sweet was something of a music prodigy and in 1985 signed to CBS, who released his debut album, INSIDE, the following year. Unfortunately, his pristine playing and sweetly crafted melodies were compromised, and the songs swamped by trappings of the age, like chiming synths and icily sequenced drums and keyboards. An array of producers, working on separate tracks in separate locations, exacerbated the music's lack of focus.

INSIDE taught Sweet the meaning of control, and this would be reflected in the rapid development of his own studio expertise, and in his urge to create a tight group of associates with whom he could form lasting allegiances. CBS had written him off, however, and he did not release an album again until

EARTH (1989). If the debut had shown the artist over-dressed, this one stripped back the excesses to reveal the taut edginess and airy melancholia that would characterize his best work. It also introduced relationships that have continued to blossom, in particular the raw, intense soloing of **Robert Quine** (ex-**LOU REED**) and the angular guitar lines of **Richard Lloyd** (ex-**TELEVISION**). They propelled the music into tight, knotty crescendos, only then to soften the sound and give space for moments of dreamy fragility.

Sweet's next effort, recorded in New York with a new label (BMG), was GIRLFRIEND (1991), and it proved to be the critical breakthrough on both sides of the Atlantic. Never allowing a stellar supporting cast – including Lloyd, Quine and **LLOYD COLE** – to mask his distinctive delivery, Sweet combined plaintive multitracked harmonies and urgent, pulsing guitar to great effect. While several tracks struck a loner's pose, it was mainly an album of love songs, epitomized by the gentle poise and balance of the country-tinged "Your Sweet Voice".

It would have been easy to go for a similar follow-up, but instead Sweet offered the weird ALTERED BEAST (1993). This pushed apart the twin extremes of hard-edged noise and languid balladry – beautifully aided by the piano work of the late **Nicky Hopkins** – leaving less middle ground for the uninitiated. The lyrics had taken a darker turn, with an unsettling dose of self-hate and psychosis bubbling below. It was at times brilliant, but its appeal was more readily apparent to the converted than to the curious, and it lost much of the commercial momentum Sweet had built up.

Sweet released a mini-album entitled SON OF ALTERED BEAST in 1994 in North America only. It has subsequently become a much-sought-after import. Mainly comprising live material, it features incendiary guitar work by Richard Lloyd and comes highly recommended.

Sweet's 1995 follow-up, 100% FUN – so titled both in recognition of Kurt Cobain's suicide note ('I can't pretend I'm having 100% fun every night') and as a personal reminder to lighten up. BLUE SKY ON MARS (1997) showed him taking his own advice – having headed for Los Angeles from his cold Nebraska base seemed to have worked. Easily his happiest recording and a direct exercise in clean, guitar dynamics, it should have provided Sweet with the sales his talent deserved. However, commercial success continued to elude him, for reasons that were hard to fathom.

Sweet was then embraced as something of an icon by the new power pop movement, as evidenced by the style of releases by groups such as Fountains Of Wayne and Silver Sun. Suddenly it was hip to boast of owning rare Raspberries singles and old Todd Rundgren albums. This sudden championing of American-styled power pop (big guitars, glistening hooks, crunching melodies, bold, multi-layered harmonizing) should've resulted in increased exposure for Sweet who, commercially at least, had struggled to step out of GIRLFRIEND's shadow.

It was disappointing to report, therefore, that BLUE SKY ON MARS failed to reignite Sweet's career. Jettisoning Quine and Lloyd in favour of a more straightforward, self-played sound, the album suffered primarily from a lack of ambition. Melodies were less distinctive than usual and one or two tracks had a 'Sweet by numbers' feel.

Sweet remained an in-demand influence, however, guesting on **The Jayhawks**' startling SOUND OF LIES album and featuring in Mike Myers backing band over the closing credits of the movie, *Austin Powers!* A useful compilation, TIME CAPSULE, and a new album, IN REVERSE, both appeared in 2000, and were followed by another collection, TO UNDERSTAND: THE EARLY RECORDINGS... (2002), and then KIMI GA SUKI (2003). Recorded and mixed at home, KIMI GA SUKI was a little less polished, but certainly wasn't lacking in the great tunes and hooks department.

Certainly he writes songs rather than singles, and his fear of flying has limited his touring, but these should not be hindrances to a talent of this sort.

⊙ **Girlfriend** (1991; Zoo/BMG).
The ghost of Gram Parsons hovers over the ballads, and Alex Chilton appears to offer his voice on the brash choruses, but GIRLFRIEND is undeniably Matthew Sweet's creation, and should have sold millions.

⊙ **100% Fun** (1995; Zoo/BMG).
Less personal than its predecessor, 100% FUN is Sweet's most direct appeal to the mainstream. Notwithstanding this broader appeal, the album retains the peculiar charms that make his work so beguiling.

⊙ **Kimi Ga Suki** (2003; Cutting Edge).
Dedicated to his Japanese fans, this most recent slice of Sweet pie is currently only available on import.

Nig Hodgkins

SWELL

Formed San Francisco, 1987.

"San Francisco screws you up, it seems." *NME*, April 16, 1994

Swell came out of the late-80s San Francisco scene which also gave the world Red House Painters and the wonderful American Music Club. But Swell's agenda was slightly different; yes they played apparently gloomy guitar-based rock, but unlike their counterparts their intention was clearly more subversive.

In August 1987 guitarist and singer **David Freel** and bassist **Tim Adams** met drummer **Sean Kirkpatrick**, and in true Generation X style started jamming with no particular plans for world domination. Their first record was recorded in the summer of 1989, and eventually saw the light on the band's own pSycho-sPecific [sic] label. Only 433 copies of SWELL (1990) were made, with the bands silkscreening the cover for every copy.

After numerous personnel changes and busking tours, the band began recording their first record proper in 1990, their masterpiece WELL?..., and opened for Mazzy Star. WELL?... was eventually

released in February 1992, and the band toured Europe, playing a John Peel session and sleeping on floors. The album caught the attention of *Melody Maker*, a review by Jim Arundel noting 'Swell don't grunge, they don't have a wall of sound. They have a shape, they curl like smoke in a subway tunnel.' The atmosphere is created with Freel's laconic, bassy delivery and acoustic strum producing a definitely spooky feel, before he unleashes a blistering shower of noise from his six-string. This claustrophobic classic cost just 900 dollars to produce.

Their next album, 41 (1994), opens with footsteps echoing up a bare wooden staircase, a clear sign that this is not going to be a joyous journey through life's lighter side. Instead, a dark moodiness prevails over the record, with an acoustic strum combining with David Freel's dry, spiky guitar sound and barely audible mumble recalling Joy Division and The Beloved. The *NME* observed, 'It's always been an organic, evocative eerie sound – more a soundtrack to a piss-stinking midnight street and characters than their own personal tribulations.'

With the first album reissued, November 1994 saw the band move from San Francisco to LA and begin work on their next LP. After many tortuous rethinks, reschedules and a move to New York, the band, now with **Monte Vallier** on bass, finally moved back to San Francisco, rerecorded all the songs, and the album emerged in February 1997 on Beggars Banquet. The band explained, 'We like all of our songs to be worth listening to, and fabulous, and marvellous. And that takes time ... Was it worth it? You tell us.'

The answer was definitely yes. TOO MANY DAYS WITHOUT THINKING marked no great shift in style, featuring the elements that made the first three albums so different. However, the production is much sharper and more polished, giving the space in the songs more chance to work, and the keyboard sound is fuller. Similarly, 1998's FOR ALL THE BEAUTIFUL PEOPLE boasted higher production values than either WELL?... or 41, but lacked the passion and rawness of those epics. EVERYBODY WANTS TO KNOW (2001) was a Freel solo album in all but name, but retained the band's hallmarks of musical invention and melancholy lyrics.

⊙ **WELL?...** (1990; pSycho-sPecific).
A classic slice of disturbing, disquieting rock. On "At Long Last", typical of the album, an acoustic guitar picks out the slenderest of tunes, with David Freel's voice barely a murmuring whisper over the top, before his coruscating guitar explodes all over the song, only to disappear just as quickly. With a weird backdrop of sound effects and mumbled talking, this is the American equivalent of Joy Division at their most unsettling.

Mike Martin

THE SWELL MAPS

Formed Leamington Spa, England, 1976; disbanded 1980.

In a low-key way, **The Swell Maps**' short and chaotic career epitomized the experimental vigour of the post-punk era. Early incarnations of the group, centred on brothers **Nikki Sudden** (guitar/vocals) and **Epic Soundtracks** (born Paul Godley; drums/piano), had existed as early as 1972, but it was punk's 'do-it-yourself' culture that prompted the duo to join forces with schoolfriends **Jowe Head** (bass/vocals) and **Richard Earl** (guitar).

With backing vocalists **Dikki Mint** and **Gordon Cockrill**, The Swell Maps released their first single, "Read About Seymour", in January 1978. Clocking in at a mere 1' 27", it was vaunted as the shortest New Wave single yet, and it was also one of the strangest; led by Sudden's wilfully tuneless vocals, the band battled gamely to hold the tune together for the first minute before the song descended into a gloriously shambolic racket.

Press and radio support led to a distribution deal with Rough Trade, but it was March 1979 before the appearance of the invigorating but discordant follow-up, "Dresden Style". Months later, an album, A TRIP TO MARINEVILLE, voiced the ideas of the whole band: though the punk spirit was much in evidence, so was the adventurous spirit of German avant-gardists like Can and Faust.

After the relatively restrained "Real Shocks" single, The Swell Maps' finest moment, "Let's Build A Car", was issued in early 1980. Distorted guitars splurged out of the speakers like black treacle, and Sudden's nasal monotone was topped off by the piano break from hell. However, a disastrous tour of Italy took the band to the brink of disintegration, and a second album, SWELL MAPS IN 'JANE FROM OCCUPIED EUROPE', was recorded and released almost as an afterthought. Curiously, the second album was perhaps the better of the two, with the addition of an organ into the mix, plus the sounds of concrete mixers, a typewriter and, perhaps strangest of all, an eiderdown.

Three further albums were released in the aftermath of the split: two outtakes collections, WHATEVER HAPPENS NEXT (1981) and TRAIN OUT OF IT (1987), plus a useful singles compilation, COLLISION TIME (1982). The individual Maps went on to various other bands, following different musical directions, and their pioneering spirit and interest in sci-fi and technology were later championed by the C86 generation, while their 'art-noise' tendencies have been cited as an influence by American racketeers such as Sonic Youth and Big Black. Epic Soundtracks worked stints with **THE RED CRAYOLA** and **CRIME AND THE CITY SOLUTION** until his untimely death in November 1997.

With most albums now being available on CD via Mute, future generations will also have the opportunity to sample the delights of a group who were an embodiment of punk's spirit of anarchy and empowerment.

A Trip To Marineville (1979; Mute).
A one-hour definition of the word 'eclectic', now packaged with bonus unreleased gems. The Maps veer from industrial chaos, through Can-ish nightmare music to gentle piano instrumentals. Much of it sounds on the verge of madness, but it's all the better for it.

Swell Maps In 'Jane From Occupied Europe' (1980; Mute).
More focused than their debut album, but still reassuringly odd, this is perhaps the purest distillation of The Maps' unique slant on rock'n'roll.

Collision Time (1982; Mute).
A marvellous singles compilation, this demonstrates how much more innovative The Maps were than their late-70s New Wave rivals.

James Wirth

SWERVEDRIVER

Formed London, 1990; dissolved 1999.

After listening to their first single, "Rave Down", you knew **Swervedriver** were on the right track. Where shoe-gazer bands like My Bloody Valentine had tempted the ears with swirling, looping, droney guitars, here at last was a band capable of packing it into the constraints of the pop song.

In 1990, Swervedriver – songwriting partners **Jimmy Hartridge** (guitar/vocals) and **Adam Franklin** (guitar), drummer **Graham Bonner** and bassist/spokesman **Adrian Vines** – put out their first two EPs, RAVE DOWN and SON OF MUSTANG FORD. These had the band being hailed the next big thing in UK heavy metal (of all things) but after releasing a third EP, SANDBLASTED, and supporting The Wonder Stuff, Swervedriver began to gain wider interest. Then it all started to happen.

RAISE, their first album, came out in 1991 and went straight into the UK Top 40, into the indie charts at #3, and into the metal charts (where it remained for over three months). It contained all the shoe-gazing fundamentals, but what made it so monumental were the traces of melody buried amid the multiple layers of guitar. In the US, where Swervedriver remained obscure, they went on tour with Soundgarden, which suited their style extremely well. Touring, however, didn't suit all the band; while in the US, drummer Bonner quit and headed home, and after British dates he was followed by Vines.

Jimmy and Adam played the bass parts themselves, and adopted a drunken drummer called **Jez** for the recording of their second album, MEZCAL HEAD (1993), a set that tended towards guitar-noise experimentation while tightening up the songs by bringing the melody to the fore. After this, Swervedriver were chosen as the opening band for the Smashing Pumpkins' 'Siamese Dream Tour', in which they were truly the band to watch. (Smashing Pumpkins' producer Alan Moulder also produced Swervedriver.)

Although many suspected that Swervedriver then fell off the face of the earth, in 1995 they returned with EJECTOR SEAT RESERVATION, the album they had been building up to. It took the shoe-gaziness of RAISE, the guitar exploits of MEZCAL HEAD, and put them into a classic pop-song structure. Here was the long-anticipated blending of guitar noise and tune-fulness; songs such as "The Other Jesus" and "I Am Superman" started off death-slow on their climb to guitar-walloping epiphanies. The album culminated with the wonderful track "Last Day On Earth", an eerily beautiful song that took the listener on a journey through the death of two lovers.

After the release of EJECTOR SEAT RESERVATION, problems began. They were dropped by Creation in the UK, and no tour followed. Independent label Zero Hour then came to the rescue and 99TH DREAM was released in 1997 – a mix of Brit indie rock and psychedelia.

Since 99TH DREAM all has been quiet, though Adam has since worked with a new band, **Toshack Highway**, who are well worth checking out. Though Swervedriver have never officially announced a split, it seems unlikely that they will ever 'rave down' again.

◉ **Raise** (1991; A&M).
The first three singles, plus a plethora of guitar-swirling, bass-thumping songs. A shoe-gazer classic.

◉ **Ejector Seat Reservation** (1995; Creation).
The band tones down a bit, for their best, poppiest songs to date, including "The Other Jesus" and "Last Day On Earth".

Jeffrey S. Kaye

DAVID SYLVIAN

Born London, 1958.

"If you think of the avant-garde as the bottom of the ladder and pop as the top, then I tend to work somewhere around the middle."

In 1982, unable to cope with the demands of stardom, **David Sylvian** (born David Batt) broke up **JAPAN** at the very height of their success. Over the next couple of years he collaborated with Ryuichi Sakamoto, formerly of Yellow Magic Orchestra, producing "Bamboo Music" (1982) and "Forbidden Colours" (1983). The latter, a heart-rending ballad written for the movie *Merry Christmas Mr Lawrence*, achieved a UK Top 20 placing, making it his most lucrative solo single.

Sylvian then found his feet on his solo debut album, BRILLIANT TREES (1984). Using respected musicians like Jon Hassell alongside former Japan companions Steve Jansen and Richard Barbieri, he wrote ballads with a somewhat jazzy and ambient feel. Critically acclaimed on release in 1984, it soared up the UK charts, as did the single "Red Guitar", although there was increasing evidence that Sylvian's new direction was alienating many Japan fans.

Sylvian began to experiment with the visual arts, and in June 1984 he held an exhibition of Polaroids in London. The following year, he made a twenty-minute ambient video called *Steel Cathedrals*, and returned to recording with WORDS WITH THE SHAMAN. Using sampled foreign voices and tribal rhythms, this EP was as far from Japan as Sylvian could possibly get, and his abandonment of bleached hair and make-up now eradicated the last traces of his former pop stardom.

The double album GONE TO EARTH (1986) divided press and public. Its gorgeous love songs and soaring guitar solos, courtesy of Bill Nelson and Robert Fripp, attracted accolades and the beginnings of a new cult following. SECRETS OF THE BEEHIVE (1987) mixed acoustic instrumentation with orchestral arrangements, reaching its peak with "Let The Happiness In", a song that showed Sylvian taking the ballad to new lengths.

Turning his back on songwriting, he then scored Gaby Agis's ballet *Kin*, which was staged at London's Almeida Theatre in 1987, before teaming up with ex-Can musician **HOLGER CZUKAY** on the instrumental album PLIGHT AND PREMONITION (1988) – twenty-minute assemblages of muttering voices floating over eerie sounds. Predictably, it missed the charts.

Despite an avowed hatred of playing live, Sylvian embarked upon a world tour in 1988 – some five years after Japan's final performance. He employed the talents of jazz musicians Mark Isham and David Torn to bring new life to old songs, and, despite the on-stage presence of Jansen and Barbieri, avoided any reference to his former band. 1984 had become his year zero.

A second Sylvian/Czukay album, FLUX AND MUTABILITY, emerged in 1989, the same year as a solo single called "Pop Song" and a CD box set, WEATHERBOX. But Sylvian's continuing work with Jansen and Barbieri, as well as appearances on Mick Karn's solo recordings, caused rumours about Japan's re-formation. When they did reunite in 1991, their frontman insisted – to the annoyance of all others concerned – on a new name, **Rain Tree Crow**. After one album, the band again came to an acrimonious end as Sylvian reverted to solo work with the book and CD EMBER GLANCE (1991), a lavish souvenir of a Tokyo exhibition set up by Sylvian with artist Russell Mills.

Sylvian also surfaced in 1992 on Ryuichi Sakamoto's single "Heartbeat", for which he duetted with his wife Ingrid Chavez, but his more recent work has been dominated by collaborations with **ROBERT FRIPP**, with whom he made the album THE FIRST DAY (1993), a noisy funk-rock shock to many Sylvian fans, which stormed into the album charts and gave him his highest chart placing since BRILLIANT TREES. This was followed by a world tour and live album, DAMAGE (1994), which featured several new ballads in more typical Sylvian style.

DEAD BEES ON A CAKE (1999) would have won prizes for best album title of the year but musically was no great leap forward.

In 2000 Virgin Records sought to mark Sylvian's 20 years of releases with a retrospective. The collection compiled by Sylvian himself was invitingly titled EVERYTHING AND NOTHING and steered clear of the regular 'best of' format, instead opting to preview undiscovered gems and new versions of familiar tracks. The set took in a vast array of material including some Japan nuggets and out-takes from the DEAD BEES... sessions.

⦿ Brilliant Trees (1984; Virgin).
A shock to Japan fans at the time, discarding Oriental tones for jazzy funk. Highlights include "Nostalgia", which sets the standard for later ballads, and the title track, on which Jon Hassell's beautiful trumpet playing is used to great effect.

⦿ Gone To Earth (1986; Virgin).
Boasting a cohesion that the first album lacked, Sylvian's songwriting comes on in leaps and bounds, with "Before The Bullfight" and "Wave" especially outstanding.

⦿ Secrets Of The Beehive (1987; Virgin).
Abandoning the atmospherics of GONE TO EARTH, this concentrates on simple folky material, while "Let The Happiness In" manages to convey a sense of unfailing hope in the face of despair. All in all, a masterpiece.

Joanna Severs

SYSTEM OF A DOWN

Formed Los Angeles, 1995.

Of all the bands to emerge from the mid-90s metal morass, **System Of A Down** are surely the most original and thought-provoking. While bands such as Korn may have set the level for what became known as nu-metal, and Slipknot pushed the genre to its theatrical limit, the four individuals at the heart of System Of A Down are powered by much more than personal angst, childhood issues and a desire to down-tune.

Way back in the early 90s, somewhere in the seedy netherworld of the Los Angeles music scene, two bands found themselves sharing a studio. **Daron Malakian** (guitar/vocals) was a member of one outfit and **Serj Tankian** (vocals/keyboards) was a member of the other. A mutual appreciation society formed and soon the two of them joined forces in a band known as Soil, with **Shavo Odadjian** (bass) managing them. A few line-up changes later, Odadjian, now appointed official bass player alongside drummer **John Dolmayan**, created a unique metal band with an overt Armenian heritage. And the name? Look no further than a Malakian-penned poem called "Victims Of A Down". System was thought to be a stronger word for a band name, and so named, they set about turning the post-grunge rock world upside down with a stunningly tight combination of disparate sounds, provocative political polemics and a stage show famed for its gymnastic intensity. Producer extraordinaire **Rick Rubin** witnessed one of their live meltdowns at the Viper Room in Hollywood and had the band signed to American Recordings in September 1997.

The first recorded result of Rubin's collaboration with the band, SYSTEM OF A DOWN (1998), left the metal scene reeling with its synthesis of grinding metal, jazzy weirdness, thrash, rap, Middle Eastern and Armenian influences. Tankian's bizarre vocal performance, captured on tape at Rubin's house, was chief in creating this paradigm-busting noise which veered between demon-possessed shriek and bowel-rupturing roar. The songs covered the personal and the political; "Soil" dealt with the suicide of a friend,

System Of A Down's Daron Malakian being tickled by fans

"D-Devil" merged four of Tankian's poems that covered subjects as diverse as cloning and plagiarism, "Cubert" was about limited and clichéd people, "P.L.U.C.K" (Politically. Lying. Unholy. Cowardly. Killers.) dealt with the Armenian genocide. Shot through with anger and artistic integrity the debut backed up the hype that surrounded the band. System had truly arrived in style.

TOXICITY (2001) demonstrated the band's musical growth and, once again, it mashed together a horde of different styles while staying true to their quirky and awesomely tight time changes. In terms of lyrics the subject matter veered from acerbic political satire ("Prison Song") to notorious killer Charles Manson's views on the environment ("Atwa"). The album also featured the multi-instrumental talents of **Art Tuncboyaciyan** (who has played with such jazz greats as Wayne Shorter and Chet Baker) playing everything from an empty Coke bottle to his bare chest.

The band's next full-length offering, STEAL THIS ALBUM (2002), however, was a collection of unheard songs from the TOXICITY sessions rush-released to stem the flow of poor-quality bootlegs. Properly mixed and mastered, but packaged to look exactly like a home-made compilation, it included material going back to the earliest stages of the band's career. The tracks clearly showed SOAD's development as among the metal scene's most inventive practitioners.

⦿ **System Of A Down** (1998; American).
Raw and brutal, the band's Armenian heritage shines through in the vocals while the metal provides a powerful and coruscating counterpoint. Includes the radio hit "Sugar".

⦿ **Toxicity** (2001; American).
A major leap in creativity. The band's previous tendency to bludgeon a musical idea to death during a song has been replaced with more polished songwriting and greater melody within the madness.

⦿ **Steal This Album** (2002; American).
A hotchpotch of unreleased tracks that rock righteously but were not included elsewhere because they didn't fit into a particular album's natural flow.

Essi Berelian

TAJ MAHAL

Born New York, May 17, 1942.

After a career of nearly thirty years as a multi-instrumentalist, singer, composer and arranger, a seeker of new musical forms and a guardian of old ones, **Taj Mahal** is the ultimate 'survivor'. His sales might be moderate, but his continuing ability to hold his audiences with a remarkable range of styles speaks volumes for his shrewd musical judgement and taste.

The young Henry Saint Clair Fredericks certainly took his music seriously, taking time to explore the origins of ethnic American music at a local folklore society, following the encouragement of his musical parents. He moved to Santa Monica from the East Coast in 1964 and formed **The Rising Sons** with new friend **RY COODER**, another brilliant instrumental stylist with similar interests in the exploration of familiar styles. The band landed a deal with Columbia, and although it had been rumoured that they never accomplished a recording session before breaking up, some tapes were eventually released by Legacy in 1993, as THE RISING SONS FEATURING TAJ MAHAL AND RY COODER. After the break-up, Taj remained with Columbia on a solo deal, which soon yielded TAJ MAHAL (1968) and THE NATCH'L BLUES (1969), fairly down-to-earth blues albums on which Cooder and Jesse Ed Davis contributed additional guitar.

It was typical of Taj Mahal that, having clearly defined his direction, he should change it by beginning to explore the bigger picture of black culture. Soon he was venturing towards Afro-Caribbean reggae and calypso, expanding his range by teaching himself to play numerous other instruments, including piano, harmonica, banjo, mandolin and electric bass.

It has been said that Taj Mahal was one of the first major artists, if not the very first one, to pursue the possibilities of world music. Even the blues he was playing for Columbia in the early 70s – RECYCLING THE BLUES AND OTHER RELATED STUFF (1972), MO' ROOTS (1974) – showed an aptitude for spicing the mix with flavours that always kept him a yard or so distant from being an out-and-out blues performer. For a brief period in 1974 he played exclusively on bass with the short-lived **The Great American Music Band**, later moving on to **The International Rhythm Band**, a fully fledged calypso orchestra, with whom he recorded two albums. In 1988, by way of another experiment, he released an album of children's songs, SHAKE

SUGAREE (the experiment was apparently a success, as it was followed in 1997 by a further collection in the same vein; SHAKIN' A TAILFEATHER).

Taj Mahal has always been something of a musician's musician. By the early 90s, returning to more blues-based material, he was accompanied on a number of new releases by an impressive array of guest performers. LIKE NEVER BEFORE (1991) featured Hall And Oates, Dr. John and The Pointer Sisters; DANCING THE BLUES (1993) featured powerhouse vocalist Etta James; PHANTOM BLUES (1996; reissued 1998; BMG) had Clapton and Bonnie Raitt guesting; and SEÑOR BLUES (1997) was a masterful collection of respectful and respectable covers. The follow-up albums SACRED ISLAND (1998), HULA BLUES (1998) and HANAPEPE DREAM (2003) had him experimenting once again, this time with the slack-key-guitar-driven sounds of the Hawaiian Islands – where he's lived for more than fifteen years.

It is to his credit that he has never sought to dilute his style or compromise his approach in the interests of gaining a bigger following. Taj Mahal continues to perform his personal, eclectic mix in small- to moderate-sized venues in both the US and Europe.

⊙ **Taj Mahal** (1968; Columbia).
Taj's debut solo album contains some good blues cuts, including a cover of Blind Willie McTell's "Statesboro Blues" and some contributions from Ry Cooder.

Phil Lynch,
with thanks to William for corrections

TALK TALK

Formed London, 1981; disbanded 1990; solo careers followed.

Britain's post-punk New Romantic movement is rarely remembered for any artistic worth, but it provided an unlikely platform for **Talk Talk**. Vocalist and multi-instrumentalist **Mark Hollis** (brother of Eddie And The Hot Rods' Ed) formed the band with drummer **Lee Harris**, bassist **Paul Webb** and keyboard player **Simon Brenner**. All save Brenner would stay for the duration, and the band would go on to be cited as influential by some of the most respected names in 1990s avant-garde, including Bark Psychosis and Spiritualized.

At the height of the New Romantic craze, Talk Talk launched themselves onto the London club circuit, and, having been championed by London's Capital Radio DJ David 'Kid' Jensen, were rapidly picked up by EMI, who proceeded to kit them out in white silken box-jackets and send them off on tour

TAJ MAHAL ■ TALK TALK

TALK TALK

LAUGHING STOCK

supporting label mates Duran Duran. Two singles, "Today" and "Talk Talk", both hit the UK charts in 1982, and remain well rated despite the early-80s synth-pop production. The hastily recorded first album, THE PARTY'S OVER (1982), though, was a different story; lacklustre save the singles, it showed a band uncomfortable with pop marketing.

Retiring from the year's exposure, Talk Talk returned, minus Brenner, with the single "My Foolish Friend" in March 1983. Gone, to EMI's chagrin, were the garish suits, replaced by donkey jackets, woolly hats and scruffy jeans. Still, Talk Talk were allowed to press ahead with a new album, this time helped by producer and musician Tim Friese-Greene, who would become Hollis's songwriting partner. The result, IT'S MY LIFE (1984), was a decided improvement, containing three classic singles, "Such A Shame", "Dum-Dum Girl" and the title track. Whilst retaining an undeniable commercial appeal, the band's sound had developed from New Romantic to latter-day Roxy Music. The LP was a huge success across Europe and America, if less warmly received in Britain.

Talk Talk had begun to experiment with a pool of guest musicians, all adding their styles to the unmistakeable sound of the three core members. The gamble paid off; despite a two-year break from the limelight, THE COLOUR OF SPRING (1986) became the band's most successful album release to date. Beautifully recorded and produced, with a supporting cast including Steve Winwood, bassist Danny Thompson, and Pretenders guitarist Robbie MacIntosh, this was one of the finest albums of the year. Its preceding single, "Life's What You Make It", remains perhaps their best-remembered track.

EMI were pleased and after a quiet 1987 Talk Talk returned to the studio armed with an unusually large budget. Recorded in a disused church, SPIRIT OF EDEN (1988) gathered together another host of musicians, but it was markedly different from their previous output, closer to Miles Davis than Roxy

Music, and, though the press were much taken by their achievements, EMI considered the exercise commercial suicide. Despite protests from the band and its management, an edited version of "I Believe In You" was released as a single, but, meaningless outside the context of the album, it flopped.

The episode caused an irrevocable rift between band and label, and Talk Talk parted company with EMI in 1989. A compilation LP, NATURAL HISTORY (1990), sold well, but an ill-conceived remix LP, HISTORY REVISITED (1990), provoked the band into legal action. At this point, the party really did seem to be over for Talk Talk but, although Paul Webb quit in 1990, Polydor signed them, and the following year, LAUGHING STOCK was released on its reactivated jazz subsidiary Verve. Moving still further into modern classical and free-form territory, it baffled Polydor and fans alike.

Since the split, EMI have issued a number of compilations of Talk Talk stuff, but there's a limit to the number of times any material can be recycled without degradation. Their latest venture is a 28-track collection of virtually every mix ever released of every single they did for the label. ASIDES & BESIDES (1998) had an excellent title but was really of interest only to the most devoted collector. Making it available for a limited six-month run at least gave it rarity value. LONDON 1986 (1999) recorded at the Hammersmith Odeon, captured the essence of the band's live performance and included most of their crowd-pleasers from the COLOUR OF SPRING period plus "Such A Shame" and "It's my Life".

Hollis retreated from the music scene for a time, concentrating on family matters and refining his techniques for constructing his music. Talk Talk disbanded, with Webb and Harris going on to form **O Rang** and Harris eventually surfacing in **Boymerang** – the drum'n'bass'n'experimental project which grew out of Bark Psychosis. Hollis himself re-emerged in 1998, blinking in the sudden glare of publicity, with a magnificent solo album, MARK HOLLIS, on Polydor. Purely acoustic, this was perhaps the quietest album of the decade – right down to the extended silences between tracks. It was warmly received by the British music press and keyed well with both the old Talk Talk following and a new audience familiar with the free-form 90s bands Hollis had influenced. Hopefully, the wait for MARK HOLLIS 2 won't be quite so long.

The Colour Of Spring (1986; EMI).
The band's final nod to commerciality or their first leap into experimentation? Either way, songwriting like "Happiness Is Easy" or "Living In Another World" can hardly be faulted on an album that could be described as an easy-listening version of Can.

Spirit Of Eden (1988; EMI).
From the opening plaintive strum of "The Rainbow", to the drifting solo organ that ends "Wealth", this is one of the mellowest albums ever, although be prepared for a rude awakening on "Desire". Melodies flow across soundscapes created by the oddest array of instruments seen this side of Tom Waits.

TALK TALK

TALKING HEADS

Formed Rhode Island, 1975; disbanded 1991.

"I think a certain note in a certain place is sensuous. To me that's a little deeper than rubbing your groin." David Byrne

The hippest band in the world in the late 70s and early 80s, **Talking Heads** were tailor-made for people who liked art-house movies and kept up with the best new writers. But, for all their ironic detachment, you could also dance to them, the 'whitest' of bands was also a state-of-the-art funk band, whose best work explored trance states and religious ecstasy. They were cool, they were intelligent and they were sassy.

DAVID BYRNE (vocals/guitar), **Chris Frantz** (drums) and **Tina Weymouth** (bass) met at the Rhode Island School Of Design in the early 70s. Byrne and Frantz formed a quintet called The Artistic (they sometimes appeared as The Autistic), playing mainly 60s covers but throwing in the occasional Byrne original, most notably "Psycho Killer" – its chorus based on a neat reworking of Otis Redding's "Fa Fa Fa Fa Fa (Sad Song)". Weymouth was a big fan.

After Tina and Chris graduated, the three of them moved to a loft on Chrystie Street in the Lower East Side of New York and decided to put together a new band. Tina learned to play bass, and they began to rehearse, mixing covers of bubblegum and 60s punk with further songs by Byrne. Working titles such as the Portable Crushers and the Vague Dots were rejected when a rummage through an old edition of *TV Guide* turned up the phrase 'Talking Heads'.

The group's live debut was in June 1975, supporting the Ramones at the legendary CBGB's. At this time New York was in the midst of the musical explosion which became known as the New Wave: artists such as Television and Patti Smith were reviving the legacy of The Velvet Underground to produce a scene with a decided art-school atmosphere, with the Ramones as cartoon street punks and Blondie as ironic bubblegum icons. Talking Heads fitted right in.

In October, Seymour Stein, the boss of Sire, was sufficiently impressed to offer them a deal, which they at first declined. In early 1976 they made their first demos for the Berserkley label, but they finally signed to Sire in November of that year. Their first single, "Love Goes To Building On Fire", was released in December.

Jerry Harrison (keyboards), formerly guitarist in the Modern Lovers, expressed an interest in joining as soon as he completed his architecture degree at Harvard. He gigged with Talking Heads occasionally through 1976 and became a permanent member in February 1977. In April the band began their first European tour, again in support of the Ramones. They arrived in the UK at just the right time: while they had nothing in common musically with most of the British punk bands, British audiences welcomed these leading lights in the American New Wave as part of the same movement. Headlining at London's Rock Garden, they were seen by Brian Eno, who was to form a lasting creative partnership with the band, and particularly with Byrne.

However, the band recorded TALKING HEADS '77, their first album, with pop producer Tony Bongiovi. Despite disagreements between band and producer, it was a critical success, introducing "Psycho Killer" and another enduring live song, "Don't Worry 'Bout The Government", and showcasing the band's edgy, punk-funk sound and off-kilter lyrical concerns.

It was utterly surpassed, though, by MORE SONGS ABOUT BUILDINGS AND FOOD (1978), which saw Brian Eno installed as house producer, providing room for the songs to unfold. The album also showed the Heads beginning to harden up their sound and realize their potential – few other artists could have tackled Al Green's awesome blend of sex and religion, "Take Me To The River", without the result being an embarrassment – in fact the song was a triumph and hit #26 in the US singles chart.

The following year's FEAR OF MUSIC, again produced by Eno, was their first masterpiece. The album caught the band in transition from a tight four-person unit to a looser ensemble, augmented by funk musicians, and incorporating elements of African and other world music. Byrne's singing was more expressive than before, and the music and lyrics were at once more assured and more experimental – the album opened with "I Zimbra", the nonsensical text of which came from a 'phonetic poem' by Dadaist Hugo Ball.

Critically, Talking Heads could now do no wrong, but from this point on individual members, particularly Byrne, began to feel the limitations of the band format, and the first signs of disagreement began to surface. Byrne established a parallel career in a number of areas outside the band, beginning with the

Talking Heads when the Big Suit was but a dream

hypnotic MY LIFE IN THE BUSH OF GHOSTS (1981), a collaboration with Eno using sampled world music and radio sounds. But Talking Heads survived as a band, transforming themselves into a nine-piece outfit with top-flight session musicians – including funksters Busta **Cherry Jones** (bass) and **Bernie Worrell** (keyboards), percussionist Steven Scales and guitar avant-noise merchant extraordinaire **Adrian Belew**. They had become a superlative live act.

The next band album, REMAIN IN LIGHT (1980), was again produced by Eno, who also helped compose the music. It spawned the single "Once In A Lifetime", which established the band firmly in the popular consciousness, in part thanks to the extraordinary video in which Byrne flailed and jerked about as if some invisible force were hitting him in the face again and again. Byrne had become interested in the ecstatic trance states that charismatic religion induces in its worshippers, and modelled both the lyrics and his movements on the ravings of televangelists.

After a hugely successful tour, recorded for posterity on a great double album THE NAME OF THIS BAND IS TALKING HEADS (1982), the band members worked on individual projects; Frantz and Weymouth started up their funk/novelty spin-off **TOM TOM CLUB**, who released the ludicrously catchy "Wordy Rappinghood" (a UK #7) and crucial "Genius Of Love" as a prelude to their excellent TOM TOM CLUB album (1981); Harrison released a solo album, THE RED AND THE BLACK (1981); while Byrne did the music for Twyla Tharp's ballet *The Catherine Wheel* and the following year produced the **B-52'S'** MESOPOTAMIA.

The next Heads studio album, SPEAKING IN TONGUES (1983), was the first to be produced by the band themselves, each of the members having grown confident in their abilities, and resenting Eno as too much of a unit with Byrne. "Slippery People" continued Byrne's interest in religious ecstasy, while other stand-outs included "Burning Down The House", which gave the band a US #9 hit single, and the beautiful "This Must Be The Place".

In December 1983 a Talking Heads concert at the Pantages Theater in Hollywood was filmed by Jonathan Demme. This became *Stop Making Sense* – arguably the best rock movie ever. The film opened with Byrne alone on stage, doing a mesmeric "Psycho Killer" with minimal rhythm accompaniment from a boom box, and in a meticulously staged show the other band members joined him one by one, number by number. The real visual coup came halfway through, when Byrne appeared wearing the 'Big Suit' – so big, in fact, that the suit stood still while he danced around inside it. A wonderful moment, it remains one of the iconic images of 80s rock. The STOP MAKING SENSE soundtrack (1984), though leaving out many tracks from the film, again demonstrated what a great live band Talking Heads had become.

The film and album caught Talking Heads at their peak, and from this point on the energies of the band members were increasingly poured into their spin-off projects. They still made great albums, still had hit singles, and made videos of unmatched originality, but without the focus of old. LITTLE CREATURES (1985), in fact, marked something of a return to the

TALKING HEADS

stripped-down sound of the early years, despite the choral feel of "Road To Nowhere" (a UK Top 10 single). Songs like "And She Was", however, another of the album's stand-outs, could have been Byrne solo, and the following year's TRUE STORIES consisted of Talking Heads versions of songs from David Byrne's film of the same name (a separate and utterly quirky soundtrack album was also released).

NAKED (1988), recorded in Paris and produced by Steve Lillywhite, sounded more like the group. The complex textures of tracks like "Nothing But Flowers" and the minor hit single "Blind" reflected the influence of African music, somewhat at the expense of the strong melodies of their middle period, but intriguingly so. It was followed, once again, by individual projects. These were again dominated by Byrne, who was also setting up a world music label, Luaka Bop, at this time. However, Harrison released THE CASUAL GODS in 1988 and WALK ON WATER in 1990, while Frantz and Weymouth continued to play and record as Tom Tom Club. The three of them finally reconvened – without Byrne – in August 1991 for a CBGB's revival tour, along with Deborah Harry and the Ramones. It turned out to be a farewell, and in December Byrne announced that the band had split.

After the split, it was inevitably Byrne who attracted most of the attention; and, while the others remained active musicians, they had diminishing success. In August 1995, the first-ever song by **The Heads**, comprising Weymouth, Frantz, Harrison, and new member **T. 'Blast' Murray** (plus vocals by Deborah Harry), came out on the soundtrack album VIRTUOSITY. It was a kind of re-formation, and a complete album from The Heads, NO TALKING JUST HEAD (1996), followed. David Byrne didn't appear and was rumoured to be peeved at the band's name, none of which diminished the quality of the album, vintage TH with just a different singer.

A reunion – of sorts – occurred in 2002 when all four members got together to perform at their inauguration into the US Rock And Roll Hall Of Fame. Whether this will lead to a full-scale reunion remains to be seen.

(•) **More Songs About Buildings And Food** (1978; Sire).
A beguiling mixture of acoustic and electronic space, created by Eno's masterful production, that lends weight to the arty lyrics.

(•) **Fear Of Music** (1979; Sire).
A strong candidate for album of the decade, bristling with hooks, riffs and killer lines. It's stuffed full of grade A off-centre songs: the edgy rush of "Life During Wartime", the spacey disorientation of "Drugs", the swoony perfection of "Heaven".

(•) **Remain In Light** (1980; Sire).
Perhaps the best monument to the spirit that dominated New York's music scene in the early 80s. The album is a unique blend of intellectualism, funk, atmospherics, polyrhythms and electronic noodlings. "Once In A Lifetime" was one of the band's best ever songs; "Houses In Motion" still bemuses foreign fans.

(•) **Popular Favourites 1976–1992: Sand In The Vaseline** (1992; EMI).
This double CD, excellent in itself, just isn't big enough to fit

in all the essential tracks. In addition to a sheath of highlights, it includes two early demos – "Sugar On My Tongue" and "I Want To Live" – plus "Love Goes To Building On Fire" and other rarities.

Andy Smith

TALL DWARFS/CHRIS KNOX

Formed Dunedin, New Zealand, 1981; disbanded 1994.

Tall Dwarfs comprised the duo **Chris Knox** and **Alec Bathgate**. Knox had been a central figure on New Zealand's Flying Nun label since the late 70s, when he formed his first band, The Enemy, and over the years has acquired quasi-legendary status in his native country, although success has been elusive elsewhere. In many ways, though, the band can be seen as pioneers, with their lo-fi home recordings.

Tall Dwarfs introduced this concept – accompanied by strong, richly melodic guitar-and-synth material – with the EP, THREE SONGS: A FUTURE (1981), the first of a succession of sporadic releases on the financially challenged Flying Nun. Early EP tracks were collected for the compilation HELLO CRUEL WORLD (1987), and with a grant from the New Zealand Arts Council they made their first proper album, WEEVILLE, in 1990. It showcased the band's sound and the sharp, political edge of Knox's satirical lyrics, and it was in retrospect their finest hour. The next – tenth anniversary – album, FORK SONGS (1991), was a more uneasy combination, with the alluring tunes at odds with Knox's increasingly bleak and morbid lyrics ('Thoughts of death inside us/Coil and eat the oatmeal of our brains').

By this point, Knox's solo career was beginning to overshadow Tall Dwarfs, who were put on hold after the release of THREE EPs (1994). Working solo, Knox produced a sequence of excellent albums – SEIZURE (1990), CROAKER (1991), DUCK-SHAPED PAIN (1993) and SONGS OF YOU AND ME (1995). Each of these showed his songwriting talent matched by a highly versatile voice – crooning, singing, sneering as the material demanded. Perhaps the best of the bunch was SEIZURE, which mixed pop and thrash with introspective songs, and in "Statement Of Intent" issued a splenetic tirade against New Zealand's music industry for failing to encourage and promote local talent. A strong stance on feminist issues has also characterized Knox's solo output, notably on tracks like "Woman Inside Of Me", "Rapist" and "Not A Victim".

The Dwarfs returned in 1997 with STUMPY (Flying Nun), a lo-fi gem featuring found sound, self-indulgence and two-minute songs stretched into twenty-minute noodle-fests.

In his recent work Knox has begun to assess himself and his career, self-deprecatingly but with some frustration, too, given his lack of recognition abroad. He most recently released BEAT (2000) on Flying Nun.

Tall Dwarfs

⊙ **Weeville** (1990; Flying Nun).
Tall Dwarfs' best record shines a fierce light on New Zealand and is none too pleased with what it finds on either a political or a personal level.

Chris Knox

⊙ **Meat** (1993; Flying Nun).
SEIZURE and CROAKER collected on one CD almost constitute a Knox 'best of', with such brilliant items as "Not Given Lightly" (a love song for people who don't like love songs), the weird but catchy "Meat", and the feminist morality tale, "Growth Spurt".

Chris Jenkins

TANGERINE DREAM

Formed in Berlin, Germany, 1967.

"From Dalí, I found that everything was possible. I thought I would do the same thing as he did in painting, in music." Edgar Froese

Krautrockers **Tangerine Dream** started life as a Pink Floyd-inspired psychedelic rock band, but soon lost interest in the rock aspect, pioneering instead ambient 'head' music, back in the days when it was played rather than programmed. Using the newly available Moog synthesizer and Mellotron, they launched into what is now a three-decade experiment with the melodic potential of electronics. Never purists, though, they have augmented their work with occasional guitar, flute, and even drums.

The original Dream was conceived by **Edgar Froese**, an artist and one-time guitarist who had hung out in Spain with Salvador Dalí. By the time of the group's first LP, ELECTRONIC MEDITATION (1970), he was partnered by **Klaus Schulze** and **Conrad Schnitzler**. This was a formidable trio (both Schulze and Schnitzler have produced a huge output of ambient material in years since), and quite some record: akin to Can and Faust in its 'free-rock' spirit, with lots of sound experiment through percussive noise and organ tapes, as well as 'rock' guitars (Froese) and drums (Schulze).

Schulze left soon after for **ASH RA TEMPEL**, to be replaced by a jazz-schooled drummer, **Chris Franke**, a move which alienated Schnitzler, who left to form the rhythmless experimental group, **CLUSTER**. With his replacement, **Peter Baumann**, the group took on its definitive form, recording a trio of albums, ALPHA CENTAURI (1971), ZEIT (1972) and ATEM (1973), for Polydor Germany. By the end of this process, they had stripped things down to the meditative electronics of Moog and organ. Ambient had arrived.

It was a new experiment in the rock world, and the label that loved such things in the first half of the 70s was Virgin, who signed the Dream for a new synths-only ambient album, PHAEDRA (1973). Recorded at Virgin's studios, with an ever-growing bank of sequencers and hardware, this was a quantum leap in quality that consolidated previous experiments and realized their surreal ambitions. It was also a reasonable commercial success, going Top 10 in the UK, such track titles as "Semblance At The Strand Of Nightmares", and bubbling cosmic soundscapes, appealing easily to the hippie head/student scene.

Like their contemporaries, Kraftwerk, the Tangs played live around this time. Early 70s audiences were prone to walking out, having turned up to hear rock music, but those into it all were happy enough. The band were largely improvisational live, and often performed rather more interestingly than in the studio. To make up your own mind, check out PHAEDRA's follow-up, RUBYCON (1975), and the live RICOCHET, issued the same year.

Tangerine Dream's atmospherics had the word 'soundtrack' writ large, and in 1977 they recorded the first of many film scores, SORCERER, for the William *Exorcist* Friedkin film of the same name. A dark, moody affair, it was Baumann's last record with the band. In his place came vocalist **Steve Jolliffe** (a member of the band in the earliest days, who left to front Steamhammer) and **Klaus Krieger**, from the unlikely quarter of Iggy Pop's band. If it was the challenge of new punk times that caused this departure for the Tangs, they couldn't have made a much worse response. CYCLONE (1978) was awful prog-rock excess. Mercifully, Joliffe departed and FORCE MAJEURE (1979) returned to unremitting psychedelia.

In 1980, the band played two concerts in communist East Berlin, the first major Western rock band to do so; the concerts were later documented on PERGAMON (1986). Joining Froese and Franke on this occasion was young sampling expert **Johannes Schmoelling**, and this trio settled into a fixed line-up. With Schmoelling, the Dream developed a sleeker sound that embraced the new digital technology, and their early-80s albums and soundtracks – notably EXIT (1981) and the live POLAND – THE WARSAW CONCERT (1984) – were something of an Indian summer. By the end of the decade, however,

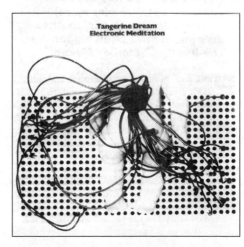

Tangerine Dream
Electronic Meditation

and especially after Schmoelling left in 1984, the Dream were sounding a bit tired alongside the new ambient innovators, and in the 90s they completely lost the plot. Fans of misplaced plots will no doubt thrill to the two live albums 220 VOLT and TOURNADO (1997; TDI) that they've released recently.

In addition to the thirty or so Dream albums, pretty much every member, and ex-member, of the band has recorded dozens of solo LPs. The most interesting is Edgar Froese's AQUA (1974), a classic 70s headphone experience recorded in super-quadrophonic sound. 1998 saw the issue of a couple of interesting compilations – THE PINK YEARS and THE BLUE YEARS (both Castle) highlighting the first five albums and the 1984–88 years respectively, while 2003's Mota Atma was a pleasing new recording that saw Tangerine Dream condensing their sound into shorter, sharper pieces. Castle has continued to reissue the group's catalogue, with some of their earliest sets being made available in 2002.

⦿ **Zeit** (1972; Castle).
The only problem with this, as Julian Cope observes on the sleeve notes, was that you had to turn it over. Now on CD, 'its unfolding, near static, vegetable organic-ness takes over the room and permeates the house'.

⦿ **Phaedra** (1973; Virgin).
The most important and influential of the Dream's Virgin records, reissued (like all their product for the label) on the mid-price "TD Definitive Editions" series.

⦿ **Ricochet** (Virgin; 1975).
A less ambient album, using guitar and drums, but one that fuses near-classical and rock idioms in exhilarating style.

⦿ **Exit** (1981; Virgin).
The band's best Schmoelling-era album, more rhythmically sophisticated and tighter structured. The sound is darker than before, too, soaring above Blade Runner soundscapes.

Ross Holloway

THE TEARDROP EXPLODES

Formed Liverpool, England, 1978; disbanded 1983.

"If The Teardrops had not been composed of three (or more) certified screwball sociopaths, they might have been bigger than The Beatles." *Melody Maker*

Punk rock came late to Liverpool, and when it did it created a scene that was unique. It was a scene that revolved around the legendary Eric's Club, and which had at its epicentre **The Teardrop Explodes**, a band of strident originality with their art-school poses, electronic dabblings and strong predilection for LSD (an unfashionable drug at the time).

The band's hub was **JULIAN COPE** (vocals/bass/lyrics), whose CV included a spell in A Shallow Madness with **Paul Simpson** (organ). Abetted by **Gary Dwyer** (drums) and **Mick Finkler** (guitar), they set out to change the punk soundscape

with swirling keyboards and three-chord bass backing Cope's mannered, often multi-layered vocals. Signing to Bill Drummond and **Dave Balfe**'s fledgling Zoo label, the band produced some engagingly off-centre quasi-psychedelia with their early singles, "Sleeping Gas" and "Bouncing Babies" (both 1979), the latter with Balfe replacing Paul Simpson on keyboards as well as handling production – a sure-fire way of making the keyboard sound central. The band, in any case, were resolutely anti-rock, even experimental. "Sleeping Gas" was clanging, hallucinatory electro-pop with a druggy, bizarre lyric. "Bouncing Babies" added a bit more force to the fog, but the organ bursts and choppy, abrasive guitar maintained the band's wacko status.

The Teardrops took to touring with Liverpool scene rivals, Echo And The Bunnymen, who were sometimes likened to The Doors, with their unsettling but thrilling pomposity. The Teardrops, for their part, had more in common with a group like Love, mixing the fractious, eccentric and melodic. Over the tour, they steadily streamlined their sound to concentrate on catchy, more accessible pop songs. The transition was complete with "When I Dream" in summer 1980, recorded with **Alan Gill** (ex-**DALEK I LOVE YOU**) replacing Finkler on guitar. A delightful, perfectly crafted song, it attracted the band's first serious airplay, edged into the UK Top 50, and even gained some attention in the US.

The group's debut album, KILIMANJARO, appeared in October 1980. It was a colourful record which, despite its debts to such lysergic misfits as The Seeds and The Electric Prunes, had an identity entirely its own, mainly through Cope's off-kilter lyrics, which added a surreal, childlike feel to a sinuous and mesmerizing backing. The album sold well, but the breakthrough came in early 1981 with The Teardrops' high-water mark – "Reward". Co-written by Cope and Gill, and augmented by a horn section and a classic Langer/Winstanley production, it hit the British Top 10, and was hotly pursued by a rerelease of "Treason (It's Just A Story)", which followed it into the Top 20.

Commercial success was marred by internal skirmishing, however. Cope was a natural figurehead, who was not really a leader, and Balfe (also their road manager) had a work ethic which antagonized Cope's lazier sensibilities. The sleeve notes on KILIMANJARO stated, 'Hop, Skip and Jump: Wait for the Bump' – words that would prove prophetic, as the band fell to earth.

Alan Gill was replaced by **Troy Tate** (guitar), as the group began work on their second album. Entirely written by Cope, WILDER (1981) was more ambitious and even more confused than KILIMANJARO. Cope seemed intent on distilling his record collection into 45 minutes, hence the Scott Walker-styled epic "The Great Dominions" and an over-precious Tim Buckley impersonation on "Falling Down Around Me". Still, WILDER had notable winning moments, and none greater than the

What do you mean you need to wear ties? The Teardrops model their neckwear range, Cope is in the middle

warm pop of "Passionate Friend" (the band's last major hit) and the haunting follow-up, "Tiny Children".

A disastrous US tour was the beginning of the end for The Teardrops. Troy Tate left, leaving Cope, Dwyer and Balfe to work on a third LP, which they had planned to project chartwards with the title EVERYBODY WANTS TO SHAG THE TEARDROP EXPLODES. In the end, only a five-track EP emerged –YOU DISAPPEAR FROM VIEW (1983) – and that was it for The Teardrops. The Teardrop Explodes' hard-to-find early singles were collected on the album, PIANO (Document Records) released in 1990, the only place to find original versions of "Bouncing Babies", "Sleeping Gas" et al without parting with serious cash. It's still seen occasionally in some discerning record stores on CD and tape.

Cope embarked on a solo career, compensating for The Teardrops' early demise, and documented his time in the band in a warts-and-all memoir, *Head On* (1994). Troy Tate joined **Fashion**. Balfe, meanwhile, re-emerged in the limelight at the end of the 80s running Food Records, home to Jesus Jones and Blur.

⊙ **Kilimanjaro** (1980; Mercury).
Despite containing inferior rerecordings of "Bouncing Babies" and "Sleeping Gas", and attempts at a psychedelic sound, this is still an excellent debut. Its reissues – vinyl and CD – include the wonderful "Reward".

⊙ **Wilder** (1981; Mercury).
Never short of audacity, Cope allows himself full rein on this ambitious follow-up. As such it embodies most of Cope's traits – it's colourful, exotic, catchy, and just a mite self-conscious. Brim full with too many ideas, its scattershot lunacy still hits more often than it misses.

⊙ **Everybody Wants To Shag The Teardrop Explodes** (1990; Fontana).
A posthumous compilation, including the You Disappear From View EP tracks and outtakes from the unfinished third album.

Nig Hodgkins

TEARS FOR FEARS

Formed Bath, England, 1981; disbanded 1989.

"I can put things together and make them happen, but I'm not a natural musician. People soon realize that when they ask me to play on their records." Roland Orzabal

The first musical collaboration between **Curt Smith** (vocals/bass) and **Roland Orzabal** (guitar/vocals) came in 1979, when as part of schoolboy 2-Tone wannabes Graduate they released a best-forgotten single entitled "Elvis Should Play Ska". When Graduate met a predictably sticky end in 1981, Smith and Orzabal formed **Tears For Fears**, taking their name from Arthur Janov's book on primal therapy, a favourite hobby horse of the earnest Orzabal.

The duo signed to Mercury and, after a couple of flops, achieved a major breakthrough when "Mad World", a typically melodic, brooding synth-pop number, reached the UK Top 3. It was swiftly followed by a #1 album, THE HURTING (1983), which yielded several more hit singles in a 65-week chart run. The combination of Orzabal's ear for a snappy tune and Chris Hughes' crisp production established Tears For Fears as a musical force, while the boyish looks of Smith put them alongside Duran Duran and Kajagoogoo in the teen-idol stakes.

While the gold discs began to pour in, Tears For Fears also acquired something of a reputation as gloomy bookworms whose interviews (and songs) often descended into sixth-form psychobabble. The case against them was strengthened by the often hilarious pretentiousness of their early videos: in "Mad World", for example, Smith gazed pensively from a window towards a small jetty, where Orzabal inexplicably writhed and cavorted as though fending off a swarm of killer bees. The later "Pale Shelter" depicted the duo walking in slow motion into the flight path of several hundred paper aeroplanes. Only in later years, with bigger budgets at their disposal, did they really get to grips with the visual medium.

A two-year gap between albums was bridged with a couple of uninspiring singles, but they firmly re-established themselves at the beginning of 1985 when the anthemic (if stodgy) "Shout" reached the UK Top 5. Thus began a year of amazing success: the next single, "Everybody Wants To Rule The World", was a worldwide monster hit, reaching #1 in the States and #2 in Britain, where it was outsold only by USA For Africa's Band Aid riposte, "We Are The World". Their second album, SONGS FROM THE BIG CHAIR (1985) – featuring a line-up now augmented by **Ian Stanley** (keyboards) and **Manny Elias** (drums) – sold eight million copies, its panoramic arrangements and layered melodies making it one of the earliest successes on the CD format. The plaudits and awards soon followed: Orzabal was named *Songwriter of the Year* at the 1986 Ivor Novello Awards, while "Everybody Wants To Rule The World" won the *Best British Single* category at the Brit Awards the same year. (The song was later rerecorded as "Everybody Wants To Run The World" and adopted as the theme to the 1986 Sport Aid/Race Against Time project for African famine relief.)

A successful world tour was followed by a lengthy period of inactivity. As work began on their third album and an assortment of producers were hired and fired, the strain on their partnership grew and rumours of a split gathered momentum. They struggled on, but by now it had become clear that Tears For Fears had effectively become a vehicle for Orzabal, with Smith's role reduced to little more than playing bass and looking pretty à la Andrew Ridgeley. After three years of recording and bickering, THE SEEDS OF LOVE (1989) finally emerged in a blaze of publicity and high expectations. The title track, an ambitious, episodic Beatles pastiche, had already been a Top 5 UK hit, and it set the tone for the band's most complex and sophisticated work to date. But, although the album shot to #1 in Britain,

its impact was short-lived and its eventual worldwide tally of four million sales was not nearly enough to balance out the astronomical recording and promotion costs. It was at this point that Smith finally decided to bail out.

Although the split was touted as being amicable, Orzabal's comments during an interview to promote the retrospective TEARS ROLL DOWN (1992) suggested otherwise: '[Smith] sang four songs on the first album, two on the second, one on the third – how many do you think he'd have sung on the fourth?' The simmering acrimony erupted into mudslinging with the release of the first post-Smith Tears For Fears album, ELEMENTAL (1993). Now working with Alan Griffiths, Orzabal echoed "How Do You Sleep?", John Lennon's mauling of Paul McCartney, with a savage attack on Smith entitled "Fish Out Of Water": 'The only thing you made was that tanned look on your face... '. It was the most interesting moment on a hollow, self-important record.

Smith launched his own solo career with SOUL ON BOARD (1993), an album of self-pitying slush that was panned by the critics and failed to chart in Britain or America. Little has been heard of him since. Orzabal has continued to fly the TFF flag alone, but with diminishing returns: RAOUL AND THE KINGS OF SPAIN (1995) failed to dent the Top 40 and the once-automatic hit singles have dried up. Apart, Orzabal's work may be pompous and Smith's vacuous, but in their years together they dampened each other's excesses and created a band that amounted to a great deal more than the sum of its parts.

⊙ **Tears Roll Down** (1992; Mercury).
The non-chronological track-listing here highlights just how consistently good a singles band Tears For Fears were over a surprisingly long period of time. The early material is simple, vulnerable and melodic, evolving into a more grandiose style (with varying degrees of success) as the years pass.

Jonathan Kennaugh

TEENAGE FANCLUB

Formed Glasgow, Scotland, 1989.

Throughout their career, **Teenage Fanclub** have managed to infuriate even their greatest devotees by their cavalier approach, especially to live work. Indeed the word 'career', in its secondary meaning of a headlong, impetuous hurtle, might have been coined for them.

The band was formed by refugees from Glasgow bands such as the seminal-but-crap **BMX BANDITS** and seem to have inherited the Bandits' quirky, often irritating sense of humour. The new group, however – **Norman Blake** (guitars/vocals), **Raymond McGinley** (guitars/vocals), **Gerard Love** (bass/vocals) and **Brendan O'Hare** (drums/vocals) – quickly proved to have ambitions beyond the insular Glasgow scene, and looked for inspiration in the limitless plains of the American Midwest, and in the crashing surf of the Pacific Ocean.

Teenage Fanclubbers (from left): Norman Blake, Brendan O'Hare, Gerard Love, and a bald guy after his pint

When audiences first heard Teenage Fanclub's sound, the most common comparison was with US proto-grunge outfit Dinosaur Jr., whose landmark BUG album had affected a marriage between the sludge and distortion of the Seattle sound and the melodic invention of an older American tradition. Between lengthy bouts of larking about, early gigs showcased a brilliant guitar-led sound, at the same time ragged and hard-edged. Their debut single, "Everything Flows" (1990) – which, like many of the best pop songs (and a good number of Fanclub songs), sounded like it was written in a minute – crashed over awestruck audiences like a wave of aural treacle. Along with lots of melodic noise, it was included on their debut album, A CATHOLIC EDUCATION (1990).

Their first record for Creation was a limited-edition instrumental album, THE KING (1991), a backhanded tribute to Elvis that failed to satisfy existing fans or to garner new ones. Their next album, however, the provocatively titled BANDWAGONESQUE (1991), saw the Fanclub hitting its stride with a gorgeously crafted set of songs that caught perfectly the mania for re-creating the sound of the late 60s, without retreating far from the dirtiness of their debut. At the same time, Primal Scream were exhuming the corpse of The Rolling Stones for their SCREAMADELICA album, and these two albums between them formed the high-water mark of this retro movement. But where Primal Scream had enlisted Andrew Weatherall to douse their necrophilia in dubscapes, Fanclub just cloaked themselves in the mantle of Beach Boy harmonies and Big Star-style guitars and 'meta-pop', which prompted a critical backlash.

This reaction intensified with THIRTEEN (1993). The pin-sharp melodies and West Coast sensibilities remained intact, but the rough edges that were such a part of the group's appeal were lost in a far more polished production. The songs were still pleasing, especially "Fear Of Flying" and the elegiac "Gene Clark", and the instinct for the killer hook had survived largely intact, but the set was shorn of much of the passion and energy of their earlier recordings.

The group nevertheless continued to consolidate its reputation for entertaining ever larger live audiences, in the States as well as closer to home. They also took time to collaborate with some kindred spirits, including Alex Chilton, who could thank Teenage Fanclub for a revival of interest in his Big Star, and former Pixies frontman Frank Black, another man with a scarcely concealed Beach Boys fixation. O'Hare left the group at this point, to be replaced on the drums by **Paul Quinn**. (O'Hare is now attracting critical plaudits with a new Glasgow band, **The Telstar Ponies**.)

The 1995 album, GRAND PRIX, was another joyously played collection, but the album still displayed the unhappy tendency to favour caress over uppercut, whereas SONGS FROM NORTHERN BRITAIN (1997) – their sixth full-length recording – was solidly built on a foundation of mellow, wry songwriting, incisive observation and damn good tunes, played well by competent musicians. With the demise of Creation records, the band found themselves signed to Columbia, a move that in no way diminished the group's desire to follow their own musical path. In 2000 they released HOWDY, a strong album with bright pop songs balanced by more introspective moments.

A collaboration with **Jad Fair** (of **HALF JAPANESE**) on WORDS OF WISDOM AND HOPE saw the group's trademark instrumental janglisms lend Fair a sense of gravitas that his winsome lyrics and whimsical voice desperately need. Leaving cynicism aside though, this was a joyous collection, particularly the acoustic, mellow "Love Will Conquer All".

Teenage Fanclub have always seemed to be oblivious to such modern music-biz imperatives as marketing strategies and long-term commercial planning. Consequently, it's difficult to predict whether the group will ever achieve the volume of sales that their talents deserve or their label demands.

⊙ Bandwagonesque (1991; Creation).
Soaring harmonies and liquid guitars make this a landmark release. Co-production by Don Fleming of Dinosaur Jr. helps ensure that the sound achieves a mixture of abrasiveness and charm to satisfy beach life and pond life alike.

⊙ Thirteen (1993; Creation).
The Fanclub's roots in Scottish noise give way to a fully fledged Californian sound. 'Add a new vibration/To the situation', the boys sang in clear homage to The Beach Boys; but those who persevered discovered that these songs were no mere carbon copies, but fine, original and articulate compositions.

Owen James

TELEVISION

Formed New York, 1973; disbanded 1978; re-formed 1993.

Television ignited New York's resurgence as the centre of cutting-edge rock in the 70s, leading a pack of punks and New Wavers to break new ground in the now-legendary CBGB's (Country, Bluegrass and Blues). The club eventually unveiled visionaries such as Talking Heads, the Ramones and Blondie, but not before **Tom Verlaine** and **Richard Lloyd**, Television's two guitarists, had persuaded the management into a gig on March 31, 1974, kicking off a new era in New York's music history.

In school, Tom Miller and Richard Meyer shared visions of escaping Delaware to live in New York City – Meyer to become a poet, Miller to become a musician. Meyer made it there first in 1967, restarting his life as **RICHARD HELL**, nihilist, punk poet and drug addict. Miller joined him in November, obsessed with John Coltrane and free-form jazz, but eventually traded in his sax for a guitar. Assuming the surname Verlaine, he turned his attention to rock music, captivated by The Velvet Underground and Rolling Stones.

In 1972 they formed the Neon Boys, an attempt to mix a garage sound with riff-happy British heavy guitar rock. Spiritual leader Hell, a prototype for Sid Vicious, knew no instruments and wound up, reluctantly, on bass. The line-up of Verlaine, Hell and **Billy Ficca** (drums) recorded just six songs during this phase. Verlaine wanted another guitarist to augment the sound, and though auditions – including sessions with Blondie's Chris Stein and the Ramones' Dee-Dee – proved fruitless, he eventually found his perfect foil, Richard Lloyd, on the club scene. Television was born, and the focus turned to interplay between Verlaine's free style and Lloyd's tight, riff-driven blues.

Early concerts were loud and frenzied, led by Hell's madcap pogoing antics, but Verlaine grew uneasy with the histrionics. He was also unhappy with Hell's lack of talent on bass, though Hell's songwriting couldn't be faulted, notably "Love Comes In Spurts" and "(I Belong To The) Blank Generation", an early punk anthem.

Island Records showed an interest in signing the band, and Brian Eno produced a six-track demo, but nothing happened, the sticking point being the song that was to make Television's name, the swirling epic "Marquee Moon". An eight-minute opus full of shifts and obtuse sequences, it grew longer and more complex by the end of the CBGB's residence, and Hell simply wasn't up to the task. Verlaine already knew whom he wanted to replace Hell – **Fred Smith** of Blondie, who ironically made the move because Television appeared to be the more commercially viable band. Hell left in March 1975, having never appeared on a Television record, to form Richard Hell And The Voidoids.

The first single Television released, on Ork Records, was the two-part "Little Johnny Jewel", a decision that so incensed Lloyd, who knew it would flop, that he quit. Verlaine quickly recruited **Peter Laughner** from Rocket From The Tombs, but Lloyd soon rejoined, and in 1976 they recorded the breathtaking debut MARQUEE MOON for Elektra. Nick Kent, writing for the *NME*, called it 'a 24-carat inspired work of genius', and the album is now commonly acknowledged as one of the most influential recordings of its decade. MARQUEE MOON reached #28 in the UK but failed to chart in the US. Two singles, "Marquee Moon" and "Prove It", made the UK Top 30.

After having spent many years perfecting the songs on MARQUEE MOON, the band members were hard-pressed to follow up their first effort. ADVENTURE (1978) had its moments, including the uplifting "Glory" and the superb single "Foxhole", prefaced by "The Star-Spangled Banner" when performed live. The album, however, was another commercial failure, and Verlaine and Lloyd again began to fall out. Their 1978 tour increasingly became the Tom Verlaine band, and one July day Lloyd finally snapped, closing the curtains on the band for some fifteen years.

After a lengthy solo career, Verlaine re-formed Television in the early 90s for one album,

Television at CBGB's (from left): Fred Smith, Billy Ficca, Tom Verlaine and Richard Lloyd

TELEVISION. It was solid enough to win Television the 1993 *Comeback of the Year* from *Rolling Stone*'s critics, and rekindled the hope that Verlaine and Lloyd would write some more. Sadly though, the egos clashed once again, solo projects seemed preferable and the band split a few months after their 1992 Glastonbury appearance. They seemed doomed to make no more rock'n'roll history, but have continued to influence it through their impact on artists such as Edwyn Collins, Lloyd Cole (whose vocal style is reminiscent of Verlaine) and Echo And The Bunnymen.

⊙ **Marquee Moon** (1976; Elektra).
The one essential Television purchase. The original vinyl release fades out "Marquee Moon" after about eight minutes, but the CD has restored the longer version, and not a single moment of the ten-plus minutes seems extraneous. The album offers a wealth of other gems, from the richly textured "See No Evil" to the rawer "Prove It".

Mike Martin

TELEVISION PERSONALITIES

Formed London, 1977.

The singer and songwriter of **Television Personalities**, **Dan Treacy**, is a maverick cult figure more influential than his one-hit-wonder status might suggest. Indie genre-definers like The Jesus & Mary Chain and The Pastels readily admit their debt to a man who's been described as a post-punk Syd Barrett.

Treacy claims an intimate introduction to punk: his mother ran the dry-cleaners opposite Malcolm McLaren's Sex boutique, and the Sex Pistols would wander in to get their spittle-drenched stage clothes refreshed. Whatever the truth of this story, Treacy was impressed enough to save up to record "14th Floor", a barely tuneful slice of lo-fi, high-rise angst, with members of his schoolfriends' band O Level. The Television Personalities' name was a last-minute afterthought. After John Peel raved over a test pressing, parental wallets were raided and a self-distributed 7" emerged, followed by 1978's classic WHERE'S BILL GRUNDY NOW? EP. All four of its songs tore into the increasing commercialization and dilution of the punk spirit, with the savagely funny sing-along "Part-Time Punks" standing proud atop the indie chart and thumbing its nose at all challengers. It was to be the TVPs' only genuine hit.

The first coherent line-up, involving organist/vocalist **Ed Ball** (of the Times) and guitarist **Joe Foster** (later to be instrumental in the founding of Creation Records), recorded two LPs, AND DON'T THE KIDS JUST LOVE IT (1981) and MUMMY, YOU'RE NOT WATCHING ME (1982). By now poles away from punk, the TVPs peddled pop art, mod thrash and echo-drenched folk-rock on a shoebox budget, while Treacy grew into a gifted songwriter able to handle potentially twee subjects with gauche grace, disarming honesty and a childlike voice that was sometimes plaintive and other times downright sinister. The TVPs became briefly fashionable once more in the psychedelic revival.

TELEVISION PERSONALITIES

PRIVILEGE

THEY COULD HAVE BEEN BIGGER THAN THE BEATLES (1983), an LP of quality outtakes and covers, appeared, as did MUMMY ... , on Treacy's own Whaam! label, eventually renamed Dreamworld after a hefty cash payoff from Wham!'s manager Simon Napier-Bell. This wad paid for THE PAINTED WORD (1985), a much darker collection packed with super-sad ballads and doom-laden social comment numbers. It couldn't settle the pressing plant's unpaid bills, though, and the album remained on the shelf for a year.

In the meantime, band upheavals had cemented a new line-up of Treacy (guitar/vocals), **Jeff Bloom** (drums) and **Jowe Head** (bass), which survives intact to this day. The TVPs should have been releasing influential records in the 1986 grassroots indie revival they helped inspire, but instead they entered their dark ages. Broke, cynical and label-less, Treacy wrote reams of three-chord beauties that fans could own only by taping their infrequent gigs, where Treacy would often introduce new songs unknown to his fellow band members, who improvised gamely but shambolically. A cult following was inevitable.

Finally rescued from obscurity by Fire Records in 1989, the TVPs proved their talents hadn't withered on the masterful PRIVILEGE (1990) album. There were the same 60s/mod styles as ever, but with greater confidence and songs that felt like standards waiting to be born. A follow-up double LP, CLOSER TO GOD (1992), sounded a little more contemporary, but by now the TVPs were a band out of time, critically ignored and unable to locate a new audience. Save the odd single and a retrospective live album, the TVPs eventually lapsed into stasis. An unexpected and low-key reappearance in 1995 with I WAS A MOD BEFORE YOU WAS A MOD showed Treacy's gifts for melody and sarcasm were still intact. The priceless compilation, YES DARLING, BUT IS IT ART? (1995; Early Singles & Rarities) was followed by DON'T CRY BABY IT'S ONLY A MOVIE (1998). Their final album, it had been recorded at around the same time as I WAS A MOD BEFORE YOU WAS A MOD – ten of Dan Treacy's favourites, including

Psychic TV's "Godstar" and Jonathan Richman's "Pablo Picasso".

A career overview of the band was completed with the combination of PART TIME PUNKS (1999) and a mop-up of oddities called THE BOY WHO COULDN'T STOP DREAMING (2000). However, these have been overshadowed by the disappearance of Dan Treacy. A diagnosed schizophrenic, Treacy's increasingly harrowing mood swings had inevitably affected the band's later recordings. With no sign of Treacy at the time of writing, his future is distressingly uncertain.

⦿ **Privilege** (1990; Fire).
If you don't fancy a compilation, this is the one to start with. The litany of unlikely guests at "Salvador Dali's Garden Party", the Kink-y anthem "Man Who Paints The Rainbows", and the exquisitely tear-drenched "Engine Driver Song", are all classics. Funny and moving.

⦿ **Yes Darling, But Is It Art?** (1995; Fire).
Invaluable gathering of singles and rarities from 1977 to recent times. "Part-Time Punks" is present and correct, as is the delirious "Smashing Time" and a hoard of other favourites-to-be.

⦿ **Part Time Punks** (1999; Cherry Red).
Priceless collection of all the very best single releases. Worth the price for "14th Floor", "Part-Time Punks" and "I Know Where Syd Barrett Lives" alone.

Chris Tighe

10CC

Formed Manchester, England, 1971;
disbanded 1983; re-formed 1992.

Named cheekily after the average emission of male sperm, 9cc, and then topping it, **10cc** were witty, if sometimes a bit too clever for their own good. All four members had long pedigrees in the Manchester beat scene of the 60s, and continued their penchant for approachable, bright music into the 70s. **Eric Stewart** had been a founding member of Wayne Fontana & The Mindbenders, and went on to lead the backing band when Fontana went solo. **Graham Gouldman** had been the lyricist of hit songs like Herman's Hermits' "No Milk Today" and The Hollies' "Bus Stop". **Kevin Godley** and **Lol Creme**'s background had been less memorable, although they experimented with psychedelia in the band Frabjoy & The Runcible Spoon. Meanwhile, Gouldman and Godley had played together in The Mockingbirds, and both had joined Creme in the Jewish Alliance Brigade (Stewart was to be the sole Gentile of 10cc).

The new band were originally formed to fulfil some live dates Gouldman had contracted. Then, checking into Eric Stewart's new Strawberry studios, Stewart, Godley and Creme formed **Hotlegs** and scored a surprise 1970 hit single with "Neanderthal Man" and, early the following year, released THINKS: SCHOOL TIMES, the sleeve of which was unwittingly pinched by Alice Cooper for his 1972 album SCHOOL'S OUT.

As 10cc, and signed to the UK label (owned by the impresario Jonathan King), the group began their

TELEVISION PERSONALITIES ▪ 10CC

career backing Neil Sedaka. Indeed, 10cc's first single, "Donna" (1972), parodied 50s doo-wop, and hit #2 in the British charts; its follow-up, "Rubber Bullets" (1973), went one better. Their first two LPs – 10CC (1973) and SHEET MUSIC (1974) – extended into all kinds of parody and spoof: "The Dean And I" was an update of "High School Confidential"; "Wall Street Shuffle" could have been The Beach Boys, if only Brian Wilson could have laughed at himself; and "Life Is A Minestrone" could have been Monty Python with a good tune.

In 1975 they reached their artistic and commercial zenith with "I'm Not In Love", a studio concoction of multitracked voices and instruments which denied emotion in the lyrics, while oozing it in the sound. It was one of the highlights of their third LP, THE ORIGINAL SOUNDTRACK (1975), a one-off success as intricate as its fold-out sleeve, with short tracks replaced by conceptual 'sound movies' like "Une Nuit A Paris".

In comparison, later singles like "Art For Art's Sake" (1975) and "I'm Mandy, Fly Me" (1976) seemed slight or juvenile. Then, after the release of HOW DARE YOU (1976), Godley and Creme left, to make the misconceived triple album CONSEQUENCES (1977), a laboured concept that introduced the world to the 'Gizmo guitar orchestrator'. They later became ace video directors.

Meanwhile Gouldman and Stewart recruited **Tony O'Malley** (keyboards), guitarist **Rick Fenn** and drummer **Stuart Tosh**. Despite further hits with "The Things We Do For Love" and the weak reggae pastiche "Dreadlock Holiday" (a third UK #1 in 1978), most of the zest had gone. The double live album LIVE AND LET LIVE (1977) was a good run through the band's repertoire, but albums like DECEPTIVE BENDS (1977) and BLOODY TOURISTS (1978) represented the kind of music that punk was put on earth to dismantle.

In the early 80s, the band was put on hold. **Godley & Creme** hit the singles charts with "Under Your Thumb" and "Wedding Bells" (both 1981). Stewart produced Mancunian flash-rockers Sad Café and worked on Paul McCartney's 1986 album PRESS

TO PLAY, while Gouldman joined crooner Andrew Gold in MOR combo Wax, and produced acts from Gilbert O'Sullivan to the Ramones.

In 1992 10cc reconvened for the album MEANWHILE, on which all the songs were written by Gouldman and Stewart. The following year saw MIRROR MIRROR, with its semi-acoustic retread of "I'm Not In Love", but Godley and Creme were notable by their absence.

⊙ **The Original Soundtrack** (1975; Mercury).
10cc's pop cynicism at its most palatable. "I'm Not In Love" suggests a vulnerability otherwise glossed over in the band's cleverness.

⊙ **Changing Faces: Best Of 10cc & Godley And Creme** (1987; Polydor).
The best overall compilation, which samples the band's whole career, and even rescues some snappy tunes from the Godley & Creme conceptual swamp.

Brian Hinton

10,000 MANIACS

Formed Jamestown, New York, 1981.

Has a band ever been more serious than **10,000 Maniacs** or tiptoed the line of self-importance more closely? Despite frequent avowals to the contrary, **Natalie Merchant**, the band's public face for thirteen years, always comes across as incurably solemn in her lyrics and interviews. What saves both the band's work and Merchant's solo output from folkie po-facedness are her fearlessly observant lyrics, the band's sweet melodies and Merchant's achingly sad voice.

The band began in 1981 as a shifting assemblage at Jamestown Community College, where Merchant studied and **Steven Gustafson** (bass) ran the campus radio station. Initially comprising up to twelve members, they covered English New Wave songs by the likes of Joy Division at local gigs. The name came from the misheard title of a B-movie horror film, *2,000 Maniacs*.

By 1982 they had slimmed down to a six-piece outfit, including **Robert Buck** and **John Lombardo** (guitars) and **Dennis Drew** (keyboards), and released a DIY five-track EP, HUMAN CONFLICT NUMBER FIVE. The following year, having acquired **Jerry Augustyniak** (drums), they released their album debut, SECRETS OF THE I CHING, which topped the UK indie chart (these two discs are collected on HOPE CHEST, released by Elektra in 1989). Thanks largely to Merchant's charismatic coupling of a plain-Jane thrift-store look with on-stage dervish-like abandon that belied an almost prim persona, they rapidly became darlings of the US college circuit.

Their second LP, THE WISHING CHAIR (1985), recorded in London with legendary folk-rock producer Joe Boyd, was a critical success on both sides of the Atlantic. In June 1987, Lombardo having departed, the band supported R.E.M. on a US tour, where the closeness between Merchant and the similarly tortured Michael Stipe sparked persistent questioning about their relationship. The next album,

IN MY TRIBE (1987), was a triumph – and the group's credibility soared when they removed their cover of Cat Stevens' "Peace Train" to protest against the former singer's support of the fatwa on Salman Rushdie. The album topped the US college chart and marked their US *Billboard* debut, peaking at #44.

After a successful UK tour, Merchant came down with meningitis, which reduced her appetite for performing, and in 1989, after a US tour to promote their well-received fourth album, BLIND MAN'S ZOO, she took a year off, surfacing the next April to perform with Stipe at an ecological benefit. Although the band had more commercial success with their next album, OUR TIME IN EDEN (1992), Merchant was growing increasingly frustrated with a lack of commitment from her band, most of whom still lived in Jamestown. She gave notice in 1991, hung on for another two years, and finally went solo in 1993 just as the band seemed on the brink of major commercial success, by virtue of an MTV 'Unplugged' show.

Merchant's subsequent solo releases, TIGERLILY (1995), OPHELIA (1998) and MOTHERLAND (2001), showed her becoming ever more introspective, melancholy and restrained, though singing better than ever. The Maniacs, meanwhile, continued without her, releasing LOVE AMONG THE RUINS (1997) and THE EARTH PRESSED FLAT (1999) with vocalist **Mary Ramsay**.

10,000 Maniacs

⊙ **In My Tribe** (1987; Elektra).
This is the pick of a fairly consistent bunch. Includes the almost-hit "What's The Matter Here?", among other catchy folk-rock swingers.

⊙ **MTV Unplugged** (1993; Elektra).
The slightly stripped-down format showcases the passion of Natalie's voice, covering much of their best material and their version of "Because The Night", a US chart hit.

Natalie Merchant

⊙ **Motherland** (2001; Elektra).
The best of Natalie's solo works, this set is heavy on ballads, and features some beautiful classical guitar work. Merchant's voice shines.

Andy Smith

TEN YEARS AFTER

Formed Nottingham, England, 1965;
disbanded 1975;
re-formed for one album in 1989.

"One more time, goin' home ..." *Goin' Home*

Prime movers in the 60s British blues boom, **Ten Years After** were fronted by **Alvin Lee**, the fastest guitar in the West. By the early 70s, they had become the kings of no-nonsense, heads-down boogie, but it was their ability to cover jazz (eg "Me And My Baby" from CRICKLEWOOD GREEN) and blues (eg Sonny Boy Williamson's "Help Me" on RECORDED LIVE) with conviction that set them apart from meat'n'potatoes contemporaries like Humble

Pie, Status Quo and Mountain. And, although never soulful, Lee seemed to have no trouble writing breezy pop tunes like "Two Time Momma" (from SSSSH) as well as killer riffs like that of "Love Like a Man", a hit single in 1970.

TYA formed in 1965 when Nottingham lads Alvin Lee and **Leo Lyons** (bass) got together with drummer **Ric Lee** (no relation) and **Chick Churchill** (keyboards), changed their name from The Jaybirds, and secured a residency at The Marquee. It was their electrifying performance of "Goin' Home" in the movie *Woodstock* that catapulted them to superstar status, and for a while Alvin Lee, with his trademark red Gibson, long blond hair, white clogs and loons, was the epitome of a certain kind of hippie cool. By 1975 the band had clocked up a record 28 tours of the US, and disbanded exhausted, Lee complaining that they had become little more than a 'travelling jukebox'. A brief re-formation in 1989 to record one album (ABOUT TIME) to try and steal some of ZZ Top's thunder, failed to make much impact.

Lee's solo career has never quite taken off, and too many of his solo efforts have been dominated by leaden rock'n'roll workouts. However, 1973's ON THE ROAD TO FREEDOM, made with gospel singer Mylon LeFevre and pals like George Harrison and Steve Winwood, was a fine country-tinged album. Despite a diminishing profile in the UK, he could attract large audiences in Europe well into the 80s, and still plays occasional low-key gigs as a solo artist. Meanwhile Ten Years After has been resurrected on a regular basis over the last few years to play various rock festival circuits around Europe, Scandinavia and the US; a reissued album or compilation every now and then has also kept the band's profile relatively buoyant, no doubt helped by the release of LIVE AT THE FILLMORE EAST 1970 (2001).

⊙ **Ssssh** (1970; Chrysalis).
A somewhat tongue-in-cheek romp through boogie, blues and country-pop served up with lashings of lightning guitar, groans, grunts and weird noises.

⊙ **Pure Blues** (1995; Chrysalis).
Good collection of Lee's bluesiest moments with TYA and solo, including the live "Help Me", "I Don't Want You Woman" from 1967, as well as later tracks like "The Bluest Blues". If you don't like extended guitar solos, do not buy this album.

Chris Coe

TERRELL

Charles Allen Terrell born Birmingham, Alabama,
March 15, 1961.

"On all the albums, songs I've written tie in together. The characters are repeating, and they're kind of going on their own journeys."

Hollywood-based singer-songwriter **Terrell** produced some exceptional albums during the 90s, but nonetheless has operated 'under the radar', barely registering on the music scene. Several qualities separate him from the pack: wildly literary, his songs frequently evoke the spirit of those writers he most admires – Faulkner, Henry Miller, Bukowski, Kerouac, et al. Not surprisingly then, his lyrics have an on-the-road feel and reflect a degree of beat obscurantism. Although his songs are not devoid of introspection and sensitivity, maudlin sincerity, cant and disappointment have no place in his work. Instead, rough-and-tumble honesty, taut irreverence and wry bemusement are the dominant emotions in his tales of dissipation, dereliction and occasional redemption. His naturally pleasing voice with its slight drawl is a perfect vehicle for his observations. Most importantly, Terrell's music rocks hard, incorporating electric guitar flash, smart Southern mannerisms, folk and blues roots, catchy melodicism, and an unpretentious yet close attention to musical detail, such as the use of bongos and ethereal female backup voice.

Raised in small-town Alabama, Terrell was drawn to music and other artistic pursuits, but constantly had to balance these interests against his double-whammy religious upbringing in Southern Baptist Fundamentalism and Episcopalian Protestantism. After high school, he headed for the Nashville area in order to attend a Baptist college, thinking that he was going to be a preacher. But the lure of music was too great, and he spent most of his time as a student in the college recording studio before dropping out a couple of years later. He stayed in the Nashville area for a few more years, eking out a meagre existence with his music, mostly playing as part of a guitar-harmonica duo before he eventually headed for Los Angeles (he financed the move with $600 earned by participating in a Vanderbilt Medical School experiment that involved a week-long implantation of a plastic tube through his nose to his intestine – though subjecting himself to the more lucrative experiment on radiation exposure was too big a sacrifice for art's sake, even for him).

Terrell put together a band, began playing clubs and, in short order, caught the attention of music-industry heavies, like Miles Copeland, who became his manager, and Irving Azoff, who signed him to his newly formed label, Giant Records. ON THE WINGS OF DIRTY ANGELS (1990), now virtually impossible to find, was a magnificent first album of straight-ahead melodic rock, one of the great lost albums of the decade. Featuring some wonderful electric guitar work from **Jim Phillips**, the album relentlessly presents one good song after another. Among its numerous highlights are the anti-censorship, freak-flag-waving "Shouting Ground", which reprises a verse from Dylan's "Subterranean Homesick Blues" to excellent effect; the scary slow blues-rocker "Right Outside"; the yin and yang sexual exploration "Women"; and the live-show favourite, the fantastical "Georgia O'Keefe" [sic].

Notwithstanding the album's excellence, not much good happened for Terrell after its release. The national tour had to be aborted when the band's van and equipment were stolen in Dallas. Worse, he had a bitter falling-out with Copeland ('I was young and cocky, he was old and arrogant' is Terrell's terse explanation). Then, his A&R rep died, leaving him without support at his record company. Under these pressures, the band fell apart. Terrell spent the next few years in limbo, under contract to a record company that didn't want to release his work. He got by painting portraits and selling his artwork, or working as a band roadie for a group called the Red Devils. With his personal life in shambles as well, he frequently was reduced to sleeping in his car, or pounding on doors at 3am, looking for a place to crash.

Terrell's fortunes eventually improved in 1995 when he caught the ear of John Wooler, head of Virgin Records' blues label, Pointblank (home to **JOHN LEE HOOKER**), which released ANGRY SOUTHERN GENTLEMAN, whose finely crafted songs elliptically detail Terrell's personal odyssey from the Deep South to the West Coast, via Music City.

Musically, the album explores blues, country and folk roots, incorporating acoustic bass, violin and dobro into the instrumental mix. It includes the wistful and gentle title track; the sly fantasy, "Dreamed I Was The Devil"; the jaunty organ romp, "Blacktop Runaways"; a cool and funny beatnik rap, "Toystore"; and the gospel tent revival closer, "Come On Down". It's hard to imagine that songs this good were once snubbed by his record company.

Terrell's next and, so far, most recent album, BEAUTIFUL SIDE OF MADNESS, was born of pain and anger. Terrell and his group, The Vibe Assassins, had just returned to LA from an extended tour, and, in his words, he and the band were 'broke and broken' and 'filled with road rage'. Though continuing to show his Southern roots, "Beautiful Side Of Madness" is Terrell's modern rock record, with keen observations about empty relationships ('Baby, pick up the phone, I don't want to see you but I don't want to be alone' from "Pour Our Souls Together"); alienation and isolation to an up-tempo beat ('I'm trapped in my head with nowhere to go' from "Whitley Flats"); and Hollywood drag queens ('Lipsticks and pantyhose, what you gonna do with those?' from "Hollywood Drag"). The album also updates "Georgia O'Keefe" and ends with the title track, a stunning duet with Joan Osborne.

Pointblank wasn't interested in Terrell's next project, *Taking the Jesus Pill*, a sort of Southern gothic morality play/anti-musical, featuring Terrell and band sharing the stage with non-singing actors. As of this writing, the music remains unreleased, but is being performed in LA clubs.

◉ **Angry Southern Gentleman** (1995; Pointblank/Virgin).
Both of Terrell's available albums are more than worthwhile, with this being the roots-rockier of the two.

◉ **Beautiful Side Of Madness** (1996; Pointblank/Virgin).
Equally compelling, but harder and edgier, with a 'parental advisory – explicit lyrics' sticker.

Michael Dixon

TERRORVISION

Formed Bradford, England, 1986; split 2001.

Terrorvision started life as The Spoilt Bratz in 1986, when Bradford boys **Tony Wright** (vocals), **Mark Yates** (guitar), **Leigh Marklew** (bass) and **Shutty** (drums) got together to play pubs and clubs. Their early shows were described by a local paper as 'a laugh, a joke and a crate of ale'.

After three demos, The Spoilt Bratz found the backing of a manager, Al Rhodes, who recommended an immediate name change. Copping the title from a cult 60s horror film, Terrorvision was born. The band continued plugging away, and their fourth demo, "Pump Action Sunshine", found its way to EMI, who signed them in late 1991.

The first collaboration between EMI and Total Vegas Recordings – the band's own label – resulted in the 1992 EP THRIVE, classified as a blend of Nirvana, Black Sabbath and the Red Hot Chili Peppers. At the end of the year, the band released a limited-edition pressing of their debut album, FORMALDEHYDE. Its reception was tremendous, and the rerecorded version of "My House" (originally featured on their demo) moved the band into the mainstream, gaining them a support slot for Def Leppard at the Don Valley Stadium in Sheffield – a far cry from their in-it-for-fun days of only a year before.

Terrorvision recorded their second album, HOW TO MAKE FRIENDS AND INFLUENCE PEOPLE (1994), under the aegis of producer Gil Norton. It contained the single "Oblivion", which was followed by two more tracks lifted as singles, "Pretend Best Friend" and "Alice, What's The Matter?" That summer they honed their act at a number of rock festivals, and took a turn on the main stage of the Reading Festival.

In 1995 the band were back on the festival circuit, keeping enthusiastic crowds on their toes at the Phoenix, with Tony Wright dancing away 'like a glove puppet' (as *Kerrang!* accurately summarized it). They then headed back to the studio, releasing REGULAR URBAN SURVIVORS (1996), which confirmed their standing as the fun guys of rock. The artwork parodied the 70s action-film genre, and the music was equally bouncy, with tongues kept firmly in cheek for songs like "Perseverance" and "Celebrity Hit List". SHAVING PEACHES (1998) yielded an unexpected chart single, "Tequila", which, with its drunken-party sing-along chorus helped truly establish the band as the Slade of the decade. Despite this, the band's label, EMI, decided there wasn't reason enough to keep them and they were summarily dropped. Proving themselves to be true regular urban survivors they regrouped and recorded the effervescent GOOD TO GO (2001). Everything seemed to be running smoothly for the band, but, suddenly, after all the positive vibes, they announced that they would split once their touring commitments had been fulfilled.

Needless to say, posthumous compilations were whipped out rather quickly with EMI's WHALES & DOLPHINS (2001) containing all the favourites and THE FIRST & THE LAST (2001) offering exactly what the title suggested, their first and last recordings as Terrorvision.

- **Formaldehyde** (1992; EMI/Total Vegas Recordings). This cheerful debut translates onto vinyl the lessons learned from playing pubs, highlighted by the single "My House".

- **How To Make Friends And Influence People** (1994; EMI/Total Vegas Recordings). "Oblivion" and "Pretend Best Friend" should be classics, while "Alice, What's The Matter?" displays a slightly sinister component in the mix.

- **Regular Urban Survivors** (1996; EMI/Total Vegas Recordings). Terrorvision further entrench themselves in rock history with more sparky melody and mania.

- **Good To Go** (2001; Papillon). This set finds Terrorvision back on familiar ground, with bags of energy and a clutch of catchy pop-rock choruses. The usual songs about girls and cars and generally acting irresponsibly abound, and it's pulled off with no small degree of aplomb.

Richard Allan

TEXAS

Formed Glasgow, Scotland, 1986

It was their reproduction of Ry Cooder's slide guitar style that originally defined **Texas**'s music, and so it's unsurprising that one of Scotland's finest rock-pop outfits should have taken their name from Wim Wender's cult movie *Paris, Texas,* which featured a stunning Cooder soundtrack. Together since the mid-Eighties, Texas were seldom far from the charts and, though the guitar twangs have, over the years, receded into the mix, the group's ability to incorporate new styles into their soulful blues/rock formula did, for a time, broaden their appeal.

The band was formed in Glasgow in 1986 by **Johnny McElhone** (bass), who had previously played with **Altered Images** and **Hipsway**. He was joined by ex-**Love And Money** member **Stuart Kerr** (drums), **Ally McErlaine** (guitar) and **Sharleen Spiteri** (vocals, guitar). After signing to Vertigo records and making their live debut at Dundee University in 1988 Texas were ready to take the next step and release a single – a single that was destined to become a radio classic: "I Don't Want A Lover" (1989). Though Texas was undoubtedly McElhone's baby, it was Ally and Sharleen who took centre stage, their combined moody looks and slide guitar licks playing a key role in the success of their chart smash. With its opening twangs and warbling harmonica, the song propelled Texas into the limelight and paved the way for their debut album SOUTHSIDE (1989). When it was finally released, after several abandoned recording sessions with heavy-handed producers, the Tim Palmer-produced debut peaked in the UK charts at #3. Much of the album dealt with the same theme as the single – a particularly ill-fated relationship of Sharleen's – and though an undoubtedly fine set, it failed to offer any more singles of equal calibre to their earlier hit.

Prior to Texas's next release Kerr was replaced on drums by **Richard Hynd** and the group's sound was distended by the keyboards of **Eddie Campbell**. The second collection, MOTHER'S HEAVEN (1991), was a rather drab affair, imbued with a sterile AOR sheen. Despite poor sales at home, Texas toured extensively in Europe and picked up many new fans along the way. It wasn't until 1992 that they managed to embrace the UK charts again with a soulful cover of Al Green's "Tired Of Being Alone". The single reached #19 in the UK and dropped a few hints as to their future R&B direction. The next album, RICK'S ROAD (1994), was recorded during 1993 at Bearsville Studios, Woodstock, the set taking its name from the dirt track that led to the studio building. The change of scene seemed to do wonders for the band. Recording in the wake of the studio's previous inhabitants – which had included Bob Dylan, The Band and Janis Joplin – Texas recorded their finest work to date. The collection featured backing vocals from Sly Stone's sister Rose, while "You Owe It All To Me" was imbued with a healthy dose of country and there was even a gospel element present on "So In Love With You"; the fans loved the set and it yielded several minor hits.

After another extended hiatus the group resurfaced with the landmark single "Say What You Want" (a version of which featured the **Wu Tang Clan**'s Method Man & **The RZA**), a stunning album WHITE ON BLONDE (1997), and a revamped image that saw the sultry Sharleen well and truly pushed to the fore. Where once there had been a group, there was now a pin-up pop siren with a backing band. The WHITE ON BLONDE material was recorded to four-track at Sharleen's house in Glasgow, then the individual cuts were built upon by various producers, among them **Grand Central**'s potent down-tempo duo **Rae & Christian**. The resultant set, an eclectic mix up hip-hop beats and lush orchestrations, sold

by the bucket load and redefined Texas for a new market. The press, however, was divided between those who loved them and those who saw them as tone-deaf plunderers of soul music.

In 1999 more polished R&B stylings came with THE HUSH and its Orientally tinged UK chart hit "In Our Lifetime". Again sales were good and, consequently, the following year saw the timely release of a GREATEST HITS package.

Since then Texas have been very quiet, largely due to the birth of Sharleen's daughter, though a new album is now under production. Considering that these days you are more likely to see Sharleen, with child, filling a gap in *Hello* magazine than draped across the cover of a style monthly, it will be interesting to see whether the group will manage to claw back their media presence next time around. One thing is clear, however, Texas have found a white-soul hat that fits, and they are unlikely to attempt another paradigmatic shift – but you never know.

⊙ **White On Blonde** (1997; Mercury).
This is the one that pulled Texas out of the doldrums. With catchy grooves, radio-friendly beats, and Sharleen's sultry whine at the fore, Texas never looked back.

Peter Buckley

THAT PETROL EMOTION

Formed Derry, Northern Ireland, 1984;
disbanded 1994.

Brothers **Damian** (bass) and **Sean** (guitar) O'Neill, newly politicized after their departure from the great **UNDERTONES**, proceeded to lay out a more direct Republican agenda through **That Petrol Emotion** – albeit an agenda underpinned by riveting, guitar-based pop music. They were partnered in this new venture by songwriting drummer **Ciaran McLaughlin**, guitarist **Reámann O'Gormáin** and, on athletic frontman vocals, US expat, **Steve Mack**.

The group's peripatetic relationship with record labels began with two singles, "Keen" and "V2", released in 1985 on Pink and Noise A Noise. John Peel was instantly hooked, so were the music press, and MANIC POP THRILL (1986) lived up to its billing – abrasive, contemporary punk pop/guitar rock without any of the affectations of prevailing trends. It earned them a contract with Polydor, whereupon "Big Decision" – with its centrepiece rap of 'activate, educate and organize' – became their closest flirtation with success, falling just short of the UK Top 40. "Big Decision" preceded BABBLE (1987) by two months. This was more of the same medicine, featuring climactic melodies with a heart of pure pop.

END OF THE MILLENNIUM PSYCHOSIS BLUES (1988), released for new label Virgin, was greeted with less than universal approval. The splintered funk of "Groove Check" was a bridge too far for some, although Sean O'Neill's political songwriting was never more effective than on "Cellophane". However, he was becoming disillusioned with the

music industry, his hostility compounded by family trouble and a long-standing dislike for touring. **John Marchini** became the group's new bass player, with the ever versatile Damian O'Neill reverting to guitar.

Many critics presumed the group's career would now enter its death throes – that it didn't was due in no small part to the emergence of McLaughlin as a writer. Two of the singles drawn from CHEMICRAZY (1990) – "Hey Venus" and "Sensitize" – were obvious shots at grabbing a wider audience, but never compromised their musicianship. The latter, in particular, featured a superb vocal performance from Mack in an almost religious execution of their emphatic pop-rock.

Yet still the records did not sell and Virgin dropped them in 1992. The writing was on the wall, though they persevered with another album, FIREPROOF (1993), for their own Koogat label. The group sundered shortly after its release.

⦿ **Manic Pop Thrill** (1986; Demon).
A vibrant pop squeal with backbeat overload and magnificent Celtic blues-pop guitar sludge.

⦿ **Chemicrazy** (1990; Virgin).
Here the Petrols' penchant for garage rock makes an easy fit with their declared ambition to write hit singles. If your hair doesn't stand on end when Mack hits the high notes on "Sensitize", you lack either a soul or the appropriate haircut.

Alex Ogg

THE THE

Formed London, 1979.

Conceived in the week of Margaret Thatcher's ascendancy to power, **The The** acquired cult status in the 80s for their startling musical portraits of an urban society atrophied by consumerism and despair. Essentially a brand name for **Matt Johnson**'s musical outings, the band started life on the experimental fringe of the post-punk New Wave, but eventually found artistic cohesion in his tortured, poetic lyrics rather than in the restless musical reinventions which have characterized the outfit's erratic progress.

Although originally released as a Matt Johnson record, 1981's BURNING BLUE SOUL was essentially The The's debut LP. A stunning collage of guitar effects, hypnotic drum loops, bedsit musings and psychedelic references, it gained a small but devoted audience. Further critical success met the subsequent "Uncertain Smile" and "Perfect", whose achingly subtle grooves displayed Johnson's instinctive pop sensibilities.

As Johnson became a more reluctant stage performer, The The developed their cult following through sporadic recordings, of which the remarkable SOUL MINING (1983) was a vastly influential milestone of 80s electronic music. Jools Holland's breathtaking piano solo at the close of "Uncertain Smile" provided just one highlight on an audaciously eclectic album whose blend of African, Cajun and pop still astonishes today.

MIND BOMB

Greater success, however, awaited 1986's INFECTED. Intense, brooding and brilliant, its grimly photogenic subject matter – urban decay, US militarism, sexual obsession – was underlined by the full-length video that Johnson produced to accompany the album's release. Tim Pope's stunning film noir reading of "Slow Train To Dawn" (Johnson's sweltering duet with **Neneh Cherry**) and Peter Christopherson's subtle documentary montage of "Heartland" worked in stunning counterpoint to the savagery of Johnson's lyrics and brutal insistency of his music. The guitar sound was straight from the crypt, and humour straight from the gallows, while a taut, muscular infrastructure of bass and drums kept the dance-floor crowd more than happy.

Johnson was not prepared, however, to trade upon the success of a winning formula. A radical rethink was in store for The The, and in 1988 he assembled a permanent group of musicians for the band. Securing the services of his old friend **Johnny Marr** represented a significant coup, and the ex-**SMITHS** guitarist determined much of the band's new sound. With **James Eller** on bass and ex-**ABC** drummer **David Palmer**, The The recorded MIND BOMB (1989), preceded by a UK Top 20 single, "The Beat(en) Generation". The album fared less well with critics, but an accompanying tour was well received, as Johnson's band found a greater cogency on stage than in the studio.

Aside from the 1991 EP, SHADES OF BLUE, Johnson and The The remained silent until the release of DUSK in early 1993. By then, the one-time champion of adolescent angst had refocused his muse upon more midlife concerns. DUSK was genuinely moving in places, but its sense of nostalgia was anathema to many of the faithful, and the honky-tonk waltz of "This Is The Night" and camped-up croon of "Bluer Than Midnight" sounded painfully anachronistic.

Without Johnny Marr, Johnson once again earned a reputation as an inconsistent live performer.

Meanwhile, as fans waited for new material, his mis-conceived tribute album to Hank Williams – wincingly titled HANKY PANKY (1995) – seemed to distance him still further from his indie following of the mid 80s.

It was a long wait for 2000's NAKED SELF, a fluid and well-produced collection that went some way to drag back those disillusioned by his work over the previous few years. Despite some flaky moments, there were several outstanding tracks – such as the slow-burning "December Sunlight" and the mes-merizing "Weather Belle". But like previous The The albums it took repeated immersions to really 'get' it; but, as ever, it was worth the effort.

- **Soul Mining** (1983; Some Bizarre/Epic).
  Repeated listening pays dividends on an album where dark shadows flit below the deceptively incandescent hooks, grooves and choruses. The sublime "This Is The Day" and "Uncertain Smile" remain Johnson's only outings into pure pop simplicity. This set was remastered and reissued in 2002 along with much of The The's catalogue.

- **Infected** (1986; Some Bizarre/Epic).
  Johnson embraces his demons in a tightly orchestrat-ed masterpiece of shifting surfaces and lurking menace.

- **Mind Bomb** (1989; Some Bizarre/Epic).
  Johnson's emotional washing is once again flapping in the wind, though this time around manic sweat-baths have been replaced by more spacious pieces and some serious global deconstructionism.

- **45 RPM: The Singles** (2002; Epic).
  A reasonable 'greatest hits' collection, though there are some criminal omissions. If you can, find the limited double with the additional CD of remixes.

Huw Bucknell

THEATRE OF HATE

Formed London, England, 1980; disbanded 1982.

"I realized our concerts were becoming a slaughter ground and I didn't want any part of it." Kirk Brandon

The short-lived **Theatre Of Hate** marked **Kirk Brandon**'s brief honeymoon with the press before he went on to front the much-maligned **SPEAR OF DESTINY**. With Brandon on guitar and vocals, **Luke Rendle** on drums, **Stan Stammers** on bass, **Steve Guthrie** on guitar and the classically trained **John Lennard** on sax, the group were lauded for their return to the raw energy of early punk at a time when the air in London was thick with the sound of clinking cocktail glasses. Brandon might once have played bass for the early Culture Club, but his line in apocalyptic visions set him apart from the preenings of his peers.

Following a showcase performance at the 2002 Review at the London Lyceum and an early John Peel session, Theatre Of Hate unleashed their debut single "Original Sin"/"Legion" (1980) to immediate UK indie success, though its issue on manager Terry Razor's SS label, not surprisingly, led to suspicions

that Brandon harboured 'dangerous sympathies'. Wisely, the label changed its name to Burning Rome Records, in anticipation, perhaps, of the band's third single, "Nero"/"Incinerator". In the meantime Theatre Of Hate had struck up an association with Clash guitarist Mick Jones, who was to produce the remainder of the band's output, beginning with their second single "Rebel Without A Brain"/"My Own Invention" (1981).

Jones's impact on the Theatre Of Hate sound was immediate, for, while the ragged, stripped-down "Original Sin" was little more than a continuation of Brandon's previous work with The Pack, "Rebel" was an altogether more measured affair, bringing to the fore the relentless rhythmic assaults of drummer Rendle in a performance which was infused with a sense of spaciousness through the use of echo and multitracking.

Nevertheless, Jones was an inexperienced pro-ducer and this, together with the untimely departure of guitarist Guthrie, took its toll on Theatre Of Hate's sole studio album DO YOU BELIEVE IN THE WESTWORLD? (1982). With sparse arrangements lent a curious unearthliness by John Lennard's plaintive sax contributions, the end result was a work that was heavy on atmospherics, but which ultimately failed to capture the live potency upon which the band's reputation had been built.

Still, the album went on to an impressive #17 in the British charts, preceded by a Top 40 singles-chart placing for the glorious title track. With its galloping drums, Morricone-style spaghetti western guitars and soaring vocal histrionics, this doom-laden tale of the aftermath of a neutron bomb was Theatre Of Hate's finest few minutes. Suddenly major labels were queuing up to sign them, but the band opted to stay with Burning Rome after having secured a licensing and distribution deal with the idiosyncratic Stiff label.

With a new guitarist in the form of **Billy Duffy**, and **Nigel Preston** replacing Rendle on drums, the future for a time looked rosy, yet the subsequent single, "The Hop" (1982), stalled in the UK charts at a lowly #70, and Brandon was fast becoming dis-illusioned. Theatre Of Hate concerts had degenerated into violence and macho posturing, and Brandon felt straitjacketed by an audience who showed no appetite for the quieter and more considered work that was to have made up the band's second LP, but which eventually saw the light of day on his Spear Of Destiny debut, THE GRAPES OF WRATH (1983). With the band having disintegrated upon its release, the last Theatre Of Hate single, "Eastworld" (1982), failed to chart and served as a fitting metaphor for the group's failed aspirations. Clumsy and contrived, the record bore testimony to its own deficiencies with its allusion by proxy to the far superior "Westworld".

Brandon was eventually to taste success with Spear Of Destiny, but he would never again be afforded the same degree of respect by a rock press who had perhaps invested too much in him the first time round. As for the rest of the band, Billy Duffy had jumped ship prior to "Eastworld" and teamed up again with Preston in Death Cult (later **THE CULT**). Bassist Stammers accompanied Brandon in his new incarnation until 1986, as did saxophonist John Lennard briefly, after a spell with The Diodes in his native Canada.

⊙ **Original Sin Live** (1985; Dojo).
A superlative live act, Theatre Of Hate for the most part failed to make a convincing transition to vinyl. This live set offers a truer reflection of their talents than the WESTWORLD album.

⊙ **Theatre Of Hate – Ten Years After**
(1993; Mau Mau).
Tenth-anniversary compilation which includes the band's singles plus the original recordings of a number of songs later to appear on THE GRAPES OF WRATH.

Ian Lowey

THEM

Formed Belfast, Northern Ireland, 1964; disbanded 1970.

As **VAN MORRISON**'s first major group, **Them** will always have a place in rock history. But, as well as being the launch pad for the portly bard's solo career, Them were one of the most exciting acts of the British R&B boom. Endless line-up changes killed the band, but not before they'd produced a clutch of classic 45s and album tracks, many featuring Van at his primal best.

George Ivan Morrison, the withdrawn, music-obsessed son of a Belfast Jehovah's Witness family, had been playing in bands since he was 12 and had first found success on the Irish show-band circuit with The Monarchs. After the band split, Morrison returned to Ireland and collected together a group of fellow blues, soul and R&B purists into the proto-Them. Like their contemporaries, the Animals, Stones and Pretty Things, Them specialized in covering obscure numbers by black American acts, but investing them with a garage-punk energy that would have horrified their creators.

With Van on vocals, the line-up was **Billy Harrison** (guitar), **Alan Henderson** (bass) and **Ronnie Millings** (drums), all from Belfast group The Gamblers, plus **Eric Wrixen** on keyboards. At first, they were greeted with showers of coins wherever they played, until a chance set secured them a residency at the Maritime Hotel. Here, the band found a blues-loving audience they could work into a sweat-drenched frenzy with wild extended versions of "Turn On Your Lovelight" and other R&B faves. Van has always mythologized this scene as being the 'real' Them, before they were ruined by the pressures of the music business. Yet, even before they'd left to try their luck in London, **Pat McCauley** had taken over on organ duties, the first of an endless succession of line-up changes.

Signing to Decca, Them debuted with a weak cover of Slim Harpo's "Don't Start Crying Now". However, they hit gold the second time around, with the double whammy of "Baby Please Don't Go" backed with "Gloria". The top side was an astonishingly powerful slice of souped-up R&B, crowned with Van's manic blues howl; in Britain it was a Top 10 smash and adopted as the theme tune for TV's *Ready Steady Go*. But it was the flip side that went on to inspire hundreds of cover versions from garage bands the world over, not to mention Jimi Hendrix, The Doors and Patti Smith. With its strutting EDA riff, Them's "Gloria" remains simple to play, but maddeningly impossible to better. It is the Zen koan of garage punk.

Them's next single, "Here Comes The Night", was an even bigger hit, reaching #2 in the UK and #24 in the US, and paved the way for a debut album, (ANGRY YOUNG) THEM (released as HERE COMES THE NIGHT in the US; 1965). Kicking off with the explosive "Mystic Eyes", one of the few occasions where the intensity of Them at the Maritime was captured in the studio, the record was a powerful collection of rowdy covers mixed up with interesting early Van compositions, most notably the bitter-tasting "You Just Can't Win".

But from here on it was strictly downhill for the group. None of the following singles had the immediacy of their earlier output, and line-up changes sapped morale. Worst of all, their 'Angry Young Them' image had started to backfire as the drunken exploits of the band alienated press and promoters alike. Still, sessions continued on a second album, THEM AGAIN, which emerged in 1966. An erratically inspired collection, it had a few treasures and an interesting attempt to develop the group's sound with the folk-rock flavoured "My Lonely Sad Eyes" and "Hey Girl"; the latter's dreamlike mood and swirling flutes pointed forward to Van's transcendent ASTRAL WEEKS album. A few more tracks were to surface on posthumous singles and compilations, including a lengthy spoken blues called "The Story Of Them", in which Van painted a nostalgic portrait of Them's outlaw status at the Maritime – the first of Van's many musical journeys into his past.

But the story doesn't quite stop here. Them did a final tour of America, climaxing with a legendary gig at the LA Whiskey A GoGo with The Doors and Captain Beefheart. Completely burned out, the band split and returned to Belfast.

Subsequently a Van-less Them (with only the bass player from the original Maritime line-up) decided to return to the US, where, trading under the notoriety of "Gloria", they carried on their career as garage rockers. After two albums, NOW AND THEM and TIME OUT TIME IN FOR THEM, this band split yet again. A further incarnation – one of several Them-styled groups kicking about formed by disgruntled former band members – released a couple more mediocre albums. All of these Thems, however, without Van, were doomed to failure.

⊙ **Them Featuring Van Morrison** (1970; Decca).
Workmanlike compilation that wraps up all the hits and most of the best album cuts.

⊙ **The Story Of Them Featuring Van Morrison** (1998; Decca).
With 49 tracks on two CDs, this is virtually everything they

ever did, complete with the talking-blues, seven-minute, "Story Of Them". Plotting their course from Kings of Irish R&B through to Psychedelic Jesters, this is a must for connoisseurs of Brit Beat.

Iain Smith

THERAPY?

Formed Belfast, Northern Ireland, 1987.

In 1988 **Andy Cairns** took a copy of the first self-financed single by his power trio, **Therapy?**, to a Revolting Cocks gig. He handed it over to the support band, Silverfish, and they helped him secure a deal with Wiiija Records – the start the band needed. (Years later, after Silverfish split, he returned the favour by having vocalist Lesley Rankine guest on the TROUBLEGUM album and various high-profile gigs.)

The Wiiija alliance spawned two mini-albums, BABYTEETH (1991) and PLEASURE DEATH (1992). Neither was easy listening, and Therapy? – Cairns (vocals/guitar), **Michael McKeegan** (bass), **Fyfe Ewing** (drums) – looked doomed to indie cultdom, with their obscure lyrics and vocals that sounded like they had been recorded from outside the studio. But PLEASURE DEATH took off unexpectedly, its brand of grunge-metal appealing to a post-Nirvana, post-Hüsker Dü market, who wanted it basic and real, and began hovering around the mainstream British Top 50. Therapy? was soon a very cool name to drop and the labels started buzzing, A&M eventually signing the band to their roster; it was quite a step from that debut on their own 'Multifuckingnational' label.

The group's A&M debut, NURSE (1992), preceded by the singles "Teethgrinder" and "Accelerator", showed a band maturing in their ability to match metal and melody. Greeted as 'postmodern metal', it ground its way into the mainstream UK charts at #38. However, this was as nothing to spring 1993, when Therapy? were catapulted into a new dimension courtesy of "Screamager", a song that captured a moment, and carried their SHORTSHARPSHOCK EP into the UK Top 10.

TROUBLEGUM (1994), the second album, went on to sell well over 100,000 copies in the UK, establishing Therapy? as perhaps the only band to successfully bridge the chasm between indie and metal. TROUBLEGUM was voted Album of the Year by the writers of the top metal mags of the day, *Raw* and *Kerrang!*, and was also one of the six nominees for the prestigious and right-on *Mercury Music Award*. Cairns' lyrical frankness on the album was something of a shock, coming from someone previously perceived as a happy-go-lucky sort with a love of the odd drink: the sprightly pop of "Screamager" only half masked the painful story of a loser's childhood, while "Femtex" raised eyebrows with the claim 'Masturbation saved my life/I was nervous as a child'.

End-of-year shows unveiled a plethora of new material that promised yet another departure, something borne out by INFERNAL LOVE (1995), which delivered the same emotional impact but in a more indirect manner. Cellist **Martin McCarrick** had been drafted in to play on the album, co-writing the frighteningly taut "Me Vs. You", and it was his contributions that gave an aching poignancy to Hüsker Dü's "Diane", where the cello is the sole musical instrument used. Elsewhere the trio still kicked up a furious noise and, when they did bite hard it hurt. Nevertheless INFERNAL LOVE was clearly more refined than TROUBLEGUM and promised great things to come.

The great things, however, were to be without Ewing, who departed at the beginning of 1996. The fact that he was rapidly replaced by **Graham Hopkin** suggested it was no great surprise to the band. McCarrick was also confirmed as a permanent member and the expanded line-up made its debut at the Irish Music Awards, Q magazine reporting the news everyone wanted to hear: 'New Therapy?? Same as old Therapy?'

After a surprising two-year hiatus (rumoured to be a result of Cairns' personal problems), SEMI DETACHED (1998) was a warm welcome back, previewed by the storming "Church Of Noise" single. Punkier than INFERNAL LOVE, it also carried a rich vein of pop, making it a damn sight more accessible – life was sweet once more. Or rather about as sweet as it could possibly be judging by the typically troubled lyrics and edgy poise displayed on the altogether harsher sounding SUICIDE PACT – YOU FIRST (1999), and the sarcastically titled 'best of' compilation SO MUCH FOR THE TEN YEAR PLAN: A RETROSPECTIVE 1990-2000 (2000).

With SHAMELESS (2001), Cairns and company roped in **Barrett Martin** (Screaming Trees) to play drums, whilst opting to spread their creative wings and collaborate with legendary producer Jack Endino, whose work shaped much of what became the classic Seattle grunge sound. The teaming produced what was possibly Therapy?'s most powerful work yet.

After two years they were back, with another new sticksman in the form of Neil Cooper. The resulting collection, HIGH ANXIETY (2003), found them heading resolutely down their own private rock highway while the rest of the world wallowed in the chart-hogging misery of nu-metal.

⊙ Troublegum (1994; A&M).
Fourteen magnificent tracks full of aggression, pain, sorrow and intelligence, from the infectiousness of "Screamager" and "Nowhere" to the agonizing noises of "Brainsaw" and "Unrequited". A key moment in the development of 90s music.

⊙ Infernal Love (1995; A&M).
An altogether new challenge that rewards Therapy?'s ambition and the listener's patience. This album sounds huge, whether unveiling the haunting "Diane" and "Me Vs. You", the pop of "Loose" and "Stories", or the closing jackhammer of "30 Seconds".

⊙ Shameless (2001; Ark 21).
Another album and another big sound. This is truly Therapy? at the height of their powers.

Hugh Hackett

THEY MIGHT BE GIANTS

Formed New York, 1985.

According to the sleeve notes to THEN (an anthology of old albums and B-sides), Boston-born duo **John Linnell** (vocals/accordion/keyboards) and **John Flansburgh** (vocals/guitar/bass drum) met in school while working on the school newspaper and later moved to Brooklyn to write songs together. Naming themselves after an early-70s movie starring George C. Scott, they created their own Dial-A-Song telephone service, on which callers would be treated to a new song every day. This innovation, along with sporadic live performances, led to the recording of their debut LP.

First issued on New York record label Bar None, THEY MIGHT BE GIANTS was picked up by Rough Trade for the British market, where it was released at the end of 1987. The vocal style immediately invited comparisons with R.E.M., while an offbeat lyrical view suggested Talking Heads. But perhaps **They Might Be Giants**' most significant influence was the eccentricity of The Residents; certainly song titles like "Put Your Hand Inside The Puppet Head" and "Youth Culture Killed My Dog" were one of the main talking points of this debut.

Linnell and Flansburgh's superior melodic gifts were also notable, and the catchy "Don't Let's Start" became a college radio favourite in America, as did 1989's LINCOLN, which reached the mainstream US charts and crossed over to the UK indie charts. By now, MTV had begun to take an interest in the duo's material, and their low-budget but imaginative promo videos gained heavy rotation on the cable channel.

At the end of 1989, They Might Be Giants made their major-label debut for Elektra with DON'T LET'S START, a gathering of lost singles, B-sides and general oddities. Then, in 1990, they achieved mass acceptance with FLOOD, a patchy nineteen-track journey through the weird and the wonderful. Charting on both sides of the Atlantic, it featured their one major UK hit, "Birdhouse In Your Soul", produced by British duo Langer and Winstanley, previously behind records by Madness, Elvis Costello and Dexys Midnight Runners. They followed that up with a frantic reworking of the standard "Istanbul (Not Constantinople)", which was a smaller hit.

APOLLO 18 (1992) was a little too esoteric for most tastes: one experiment was "Fingertips", a series of baffling musical excerpts designed to be programmed by CD listeners – a concept which was diverting but ultimately irksome. The duo recruited four extra band members for the undoubtedly superior JOHN HENRY (1994), which unexpectedly became their most successful release in America, and led to their involvement in a project which not even their surrealist vision could have predicted: they contributed a song, "Sensurround", for the 1995 movie, *Mighty Morphin Power Rangers*.

FACTORY SHOWROOM (1997) was their second full-length recording as a full band, and showed that they were still capable of marrying sardonic lyrics to infectious (and sometimes touching) melodies. Their appeal was unlikely to widen again, and most critics remained mystified by their following. For newcomers a 1998 compilation entitled SEVERE TIRE DAMAGE was an ideal place to start – as well as re-recordings of some old favourites, it featured a suite of songs in tribute to *Planet Of The Apes*. (A far better, broader anthology came in 2002, entitled DIAL-A-SONG.)

The Internet only LONG TALL WEEKEND filled a space while the group prepared to follow up FACTORY SHOWROOM, which they did competently with 2001's MINK CAR. Langer and Winstanley were back, presumably brought on board to rescue the group from the hit-free void of the preceding years. Incongruous guest appearances from **Cerys Matthews** and Soul Coughing's **M. Doughty** rounded out a pretty chaotic set held together by some great tunes, with the quirk quotient held just below irritation level.

2002's children's album NO! was perhaps the collection they were born to make – not necessarily meaning that it was their best, just that their playground style and sense of the ridiculous were well suited to kid's stuff (check "I Am Not A Grocery Bag"; "Bed Bed Bed"). Let's hope they never grow up.

⊙ **Lincoln** (1989; Elektra).
Lacks the self-indulgences of their debut, although this collection of short, sharp songs is perhaps best enjoyed in small doses. The approach ranges from the bright ("They'll Need A Crane") to the macabre ("You'll Miss Me"). Not everyone's idea of fun, but try it.

⊙ **Flood** (1990; Elektra).
In which our heroic duo are reincarnated as a bag of groceries ("Dead"), chair an evolutionary debate on "Particle Man" and, just for a change, indulge in a bit of straight talking on "Your Racist Friend". Another uneven set, although the melodies are delightful.

⊙ **Dial-A-Song** (2002; Elektra).
This double-CD collection features over fifty cuts, with the irksomely chirpie and catchy "Birdhouse In Your Soul" opening the show.

Justin Lewis

THIN LIZZY

Formed Dublin, Ireland, 1969; disbanded 1983.

Friends since their schooldays, **Phil Lynott** (vocals/bass) and **Brian Downey** (drums) had played together in Skid Row, Sugar Shack and Orphanage before they joined forces as **Thin Lizzy** with guitarist **Eric Bell**, previously with **THEM**. The band signed to Decca in 1970, and, though neither THIN LIZZY (1971) nor SHADES OF A BLUE ORPHANAGE (1972) achieved very much, a rock adaptation of the Irish folk song "Whiskey In The Jar", complete with a catchy guitar riff, shot out of nowhere into the UK Top 10.

The ensuing album, VAGABONDS OF THE WESTERN WORLD, released in September 1973,

foreshadowed Thin Lizzy's eventual power-chord style, but any success was temporarily offset by Bell's departure at the end of the year. Ex-Skid Row man **Gary Moore** made the first of several forays with the band in early 1974, leaving to join Colosseum after four months. He was replaced first by **Andy Gee** and **John Cann**, and then by **Scott Gorham** and **Brian Robertson**, who appeared with the band at the 1974 Reading Festival as well as on NIGHTLIFE (1974), Thin Lizzy's first album for Vertigo.

FIGHTING (1975) was their UK album chart debut, but its modest sales were quickly dwarfed by JAILBREAK (1976) which represented a turning point for Thin Lizzy. It reached the Top 20 in both the UK and US, and introduced their most famous song, "The Boys Are Back In Town", with Lynott's devil-may-care delivery and slamming twin-guitar chords. The singles "Jailbreak" and "Cowboy Song" followed, perpetuating Lynott's romanticism of the wronged outsider.

JOHNNY THE FOX (1976) consolidated the success but was overshadowed by Lynott's increasing drug dependency and a bout of hepatitis. Stardom seemed to take the band unawares – in March 1977, three months after severing the tendons in his hand in a fight, Robertson was replaced by Gary Moore for a US tour supporting Queen, but by May he had rejoined as Moore returned to Colosseum's ranks. In a brief period of stability, Thin Lizzy headlined Reading and put out BAD REPUTATION (1977), whose UK chart peak of #4 was their best yet.

This was itself bettered by the terrific LIVE AND DANGEROUS (1978), which captured Lynott's swaggering stage presence and the band's rare mix of energy and accuracy. Once more, Moore replaced Robertson in 1979, while Downey, who temporarily left to spend time with his son, was replaced by **Mark Nauseet**.

BLACK ROSE (A ROCK LEGEND) (1979) spawned two singles, "Waiting For An Alibi" and "Do Anything You Wanna Do", which probably constituted the band's finest hour. However, Moore was

now sacked and replaced by an old friend of Lynott's, **Midge Ure**, who reportedly learned the set-list on the flight out to the US to complete a tour. Ure stayed for two tours, and then left for ULTRAVOX and solo success; his replacement was **Snowy White**, formerly part of Pink Floyd's live band.

Despite the release of "Sarah" (1979), a wistful tribute to his baby daughter, and his marriage in early 1980 to Caroline Crowther (daughter of TV celebrity Leslie), Lynott's hell-raising days were far from over, and his music would never reach the peaks of BLACK ROSE again. Lynott's solo album, SOLO IN SOHO (1980), featuring his Elvis Presley tribute, "King's Call", and also remembered for "Yellow Pearl", a track co-written by Midge Ure that became the theme to BBC TV's *Top Of The Pops*, was followed by another Thin Lizzy LP – CHINATOWN (1980). A single, "Killer On The Loose", received restricted radio airplay in the UK, as it coincided with the serial murders committed by the so-called Yorkshire Ripper. RENEGADE (1981) was followed by THE PHIL LYNOTT ALBUM (1982).

THUNDER AND LIGHTNING (1983) was Thin Lizzy's last album, as Lynott formed the unproductive Grand Slam with Downey, although he later buried his differences with Gary Moore, and the two scored a hit with "Out In The Fields" (1985). That year, however, Lynott was charged with a drug offence and acquitted with the remark, 'as long as he is only using these drugs himself and not giving them to others, he is only destroying himself'. The words proved prophetic: on January 4, 1986, Lynott died, having been in a heroin-induced coma for eight days. He was 34.

(•) **Jailbreak** (1976; Vertigo).
'If the boys want to fight, you'd better let 'em' – Thin Lizzy's brimming self-confidence makes its presence felt on this wondrous collection of anthemic rock.

(•) **Live And Dangerous** (1978; Vertigo).
The album cover is pure Spinal Tap, but this is the definitive portrait of a wild but technically proficient rock band.

(•) **Black Rose (A Rock Legend)** (1979; Vertigo).
The best studio production, with at least three classic songs on side one alone. The album as a whole may be pretentious, especially with its twee Irish mysticism, but the band carry it off with untouchable panache.

(•) **Wild One** (1995; Vertigo).
The latest in a long line of repackaged compilations, and a fine place to start.

Chris Wright

THIN WHITE ROPE

Formed Davis, California, 1984; disbanded 1992.

In taking their name from William Burroughs' description of ejaculation, **Thin White Rope** demonstrated the perversity that would mark them out as one of the few worthwhile traditional American guitar rock bands of their era. While most of the essential groups of the time were pushing back the limits of the form, Thin White Rope had the distinction of managing to breathe new life into the genre from within.

Formed in a relatively isolated northern Californian town, away from the overheated environments of that state's major cities, the band initially comprised **Guy Kyser** (guitar/vocals), **Roger Kunkel** (guitar), **Jozef Becker** (drums) and **Stephen Tesluk** (bass). Their emergence coincided with the New Guitar movement (Long Ryders, Rain Parade, etc), which had revived country-rock/psychedelia in the wake of R.E.M.'s success, and they probably suffered from being tarred with the same brush as that essentially retrogressive trend. Certainly their first album, EXPLORING THE AXIS (1986), was largely overlooked, and, while it contained some traces of the twisted panoramas to come ("Dead Grammas On A Train"), it was not terribly remarkable.

However, a far more potent brew was to develop, their reference points including Crazy Horse at their most extreme, the weatherbeaten blues of Howlin' Wolf and Captain Beefheart, and contemporaries such as Hüsker Dü and the Butthole Surfers. Their second album, MOONHEAD (1987), brought this to the boil, and sounded like one of the most desperate rock albums since Neil Young's 1975 epic TONIGHT'S THE NIGHT. The two intertwining guitars of Kyser and Kunkel sounded more like two dozen, a dynamic of density and tension to reflect the mood of paranoia and despair in Kyser's lyrics. Subject matter included death ("Crawl Piss Freeze") and betrayal ("If Those Tears"), and Kyser later wrily admitted that the album 'barely had a grip on reality at all'.

A somewhat offhand mini-album, BOTTOM FEEDERS, followed, but the real successor to MOONHEAD came in the shape of IN THE SPANISH CAVE (1988). While retaining the intensity of MOONHEAD, the band had increased the emphasis on the dark humour of their music ("Mr. Limpet"'s tribute to cowboy ballad maestro Marty Robbins), and Kyser's lyrics had begun to move towards the documentation of an oblique interior landscape somewhere between Americana and surrealism. IN THE SPANISH CAVE, like MOONHEAD, was lauded by the British music press, and by the *Melody Maker* in particular, their popularity in Europe increasing considerably as a result.

Released after extensive touring and European festival appearances, Thin White Rope's next work was described as 'an album of songs that took shape on the road'. In fact, SACK FULL OF SILVER (1990) was more polished than any of their previous material and, as a result, not as engaging, though it still contained some classic Kyser writing in the enigmatic sketches of the title track and the poignant premonition of "The Ghost". It also included a surprising version of Can's "Yoo Doo Right", an example of the band's penchant for playing apparently incongruous covers, which they exercised further on the misguided 1991 collection, SQUATTER'S RIGHTS.

Compensation for this disappointing side-project soon arrived with what turned out to be Thin White Rope's final album, THE RUBY SEA (1991). More eclectic than any of their earlier work, the songs on this LP were like a collection of stories related by an assortment of loners and losers, climaxing in the haunting epiphany of "The Clown Song". In 1992, after eight years of recording and touring, they decided to call it a day and split amicably, the various members going on to pursue solo projects or to work with other California bands.

Though Thin White Rope had no direct lineage to country-rock, they were always a country band in the sense of belonging to the desert and to the broken-down places of America, just as the confrontational noise of groups like Sonic Youth and Big Black belonged to the city. In the end, perhaps, what their music portrayed was not just a physical desert, but the blighted hinterland of the American psyche.

⊙ **Moonhead** (1987; Frontier/Demon).
Thin White Rope's greatest album – taut, heavy, feedback-drenched. Its exorcism of personal demons is relieved only on the acoustic "Thing", a touching tale of friendship and consolation.

⊙ **In The Spanish Cave** (1988; Frontier/Demon).
From the alien blues of "Ahr-Skidar" to the epic majesty of "Red Sun", IN THE SPANISH CAVE opens out Thin White Rope's sound without sacrificing too much of its power.

Ian Canadine

THE THIRD EYE FOUNDATION

Emerged in Bristol, sometime in the early 1990s.

"Whenever I release an album I think someone might beat me to it, because what I want to do is so obvious. But it never happens." Matt Elliot

Matt **Elliot**, while playing guitar for Movietone and providing occasional percussion for **FLYING SAUCER ATTACK**, has also been active in his **Third Eye Foundation** guise for some years now.

The first recorded output of The Third Eye Foundation (apart from with FSA) was 1996's SEMTEX album, released by Elliot's own Linda's Strange Vacation label (through Domino), named after the band which preceded Flying Saucer Attack. SEMTEX is a remarkable record, taking the complex guitar feedback sculptures typical of Elliot's other projects, layered over cantankerous drum'n'bass skitterings to create dense, alienated soundscapes, sometimes blended with indiscernible vocals to create an almost spiritual sense of stasis. The atmosphere created can be both claustrophobic and cathartic, with stretches of contemplative dub displacing

THIN WHITE ROPE ■ THE THIRD EYE FOUNDATION

notions of genre in a manner reminiscent of some of the Aphex Twin's more challenging moments, or Main's rhythmic experiments.

The Third Eye Foundation's second release of the year was IN VERSION, a collection of remixes of various related bands' tracks. These include Amp's "Eternity" and "Short Wave Dub", pieces of unnerving noise backed by mechanical beats which are almost physically oppressive to the listener. Crescent's "Superconstellation" and Hood's "Eyes" receive subtler treatment, while Flying Saucer Attack bring the album to a close, stretched into trails of rumbling fragmented sound in "Way Out Like David Bowman".

A 7" single for Bristol's hip Planet Records, "Universal Cooler", several compilation appearances and the "Semtex"/"Science Fiction" single for Domino's Series 500 have kept the release schedule filled through the year, along with occasional live appearances. The latter record made the jungle influences more prominent than hitherto, and stands out as an excellent example of cross-genre fertilization. The Third Eye Foundation's prospects for expanding on its pioneering collision of guitars with drum'n'bass were consolidated with GHOST (1997), which also marked the departure of Parsons.

An intensely unsettling and frightening album, GHOST also dispensed gradually with guitars in favour of the sampler, moving into an area also under exploration by avant-garde guitar noise luminaries such as **Derek Bailey**. The guitars were finally dropped altogether on "The Sound Of Violence" EP (1997), a cathartic exploration of pain and death via abstracted drill'n'bass, while YOU GUYS KILL ME (1998) and the Latin-influenced "Fear Of A Wack Planet" showed off both Elliot's increasingly accomplished drum'n'bass skills and his warped sense of humour. Elliot saw out the 90s with his most refined album yet, LITTLE LOST SOUL (1999) and the accompanying "What Is It With You" EP, both of which refined The Third Eye Foundation's sound into unsettling break-beat soundscapes, some with operatic grandeur. It was followed by a collection of Elliot's remix work, I POO POO ON YOUR JUJU (2001), but since then all has been quiet.

The Third Eye Foundation has been a truly maverick concern providing a genuine alternative to neo-trad-rock and the often rather self-conscious crossover noodlings of post-rockers such as Tortoise. Hopefully Elliott will soon return to provide scene and trend-free provocation.

> **In Version** (1996; Linda's Strange Vacation).
> A drastic collection of remixes of other people's tracks, which starts with drum'n'bass intensity, and proceeds via dubby drones to abstracted atmospheric deconstructions.

> **Ghost** (1997; Domino).
> With track titles like "Corpses As Bedmates" and "What To Do But Cry?", this is not a happy record. Chilled like a morgue, and a paradigm of noisy electronica. This is another vital album. Less wilfully ugly than before, but in its strange way even more twisted and disturbing.

> **Little Lost Soul** (1999; Domino).
> With uplifting choral loops and breaks that effortlessly roll

and trill, this is Third Eye Foundation with a comparatively positive vibe. "What Is It With You", with its helium-treated operatic vocal swells, is the finest moment of an album that builds and demolishes walls of sampled sound and distended bass.

Richard Fontenoy & Ben Smith

THE 13TH FLOOR ELEVATORS

Formed Austin, Texas, 1965; disbanded 1968.

Most bands associated with the psychedelic period of American rock hailed from California, in particular the Bay Area. A few others were either one-hit wonders or descendants of New York's folk music scene. **The 13th Floor Elevators** were not only the main exception to this rule, but pacesetters for the entire counterculture.

The band was formed out of two Austin groups, The Lingsmen and The Spades, who between them contributed **ROKY ERICKSON** (rhythm guitar/lead vocals), **Stacey Sutherland** (lead guitar), **Ronnie Leatherman** (bass) and **John Ike Walton** (drums). They formed a pretty hot R&B-based combo, and adding **Tommy Hall**, a virtuoso of the electric jug, rounded out a unique sound and cemented a self-destructive course. Like many Texan bands they sought greater exposure on the West Coast, but when their version of Erickson's "You're Gonna Miss Me" – originally recorded by The Spades – became a local hit back home, they concentrated on creating a scene of their own far away from fashionable California.

They were aided by one Lelan Rogers, brother of Kenny 'The Gambler' Rogers, who came back from California to run the fledgling International Artists label. Rogers produced the first two Elevators albums and established International Artists as a short-lived but legendary outpost for psychedelic rock'n'roll. More significant was the emerging influence of Tommy Hall as the creator of the band's ethos of hallucinogenic indulgence. A psychology graduate from the University of Texas, Hall provided esoteric lyrics to most of The

Elevators' songs, as well as the proselytizing sleeve notes to their 1966 debut THE PSYCHEDELIC SOUNDS OF THE 13TH FLOOR ELEVATORS: 'The new system involves a major evolutionary step for man. The new man views the old man in much the same way as the old man views the ape.'

The pursuit of spiritual enlightenment lent the album a stylistic unity. Despite the obvious disparity between songs like the melodic "Splash 1" and the manic "Fire Engine", the album indeed sounded psychedelic, especially when compared to the work of contemporary bands still constrained by commercial considerations and mainly restricted to a blues- and folk-based repertoire.

However, the conspicuous consumption of drugs by the group's nucleus of Erickson, Hall and Sutherland attracted the attention of the police and alienated the rhythm section, who split in early 1967. After a period of laying low, The Elevators re- emerged in September 1967 with **Dan Galino** (bass) and **Danny Thomas** (drums). Although Erickson's increasingly erratic behaviour diminished their power as a live act, they did produce a second masterpiece in EASTER EVERYWHERE (1968). This was a more reflective work, a meditative retreat compared to the fire-and-brimstone sermonizing of the first album. "Slip Inside This House" and "Earthquake" were mantra-like, while "She Lives (In A Time Of Her Own)" and "Dust" displayed the fragile quality behind the maturing psychedelic sound.

By the time their final album, BULL OF THE WOODS, was completed in 1969, the group had disintegrated. Hall became a Christian, eventually disappearing from public view; Erickson and Sutherland were incarcerated for possession of marijuana; Sutherland was shot dead during a domestic quarrel in 1978. Only Erickson has continued to add anything to the band's legend, creating his own mythic status during an intermittently crazed and brilliant solo career.

⊙ **The Psychedelic Sounds Of The 13th Floor Elevators** (1966; Decal/ Charly).
Includes the classic "You're Gonna Miss Me" along with eleven other tracks that scale unimaginable heights of sonic ecstasy. Dig the crazy 'wobble' of the electric jug as well.

⊙ **Easter Everywhere** (1968; Decal/Charly).
A more mellow offering, though it kicks off with the rollicking "Slip Inside This House", a song recently covered by Primal Scream. It's a beautiful statement of musical enlightenment, despite the laborious cover of Dylan's "It's All Over Now, Baby Blue".

⊙ **The Best Of** (1998; Reactive).
Slip inside this house as you pass by on your search for the roots of psychedelia. A great collection.

⊙ **All Time Highs** (1998; Music Club).
Excellent-value compilation from the splendid Music Club label with twenty tracks – the cream of THE PSYCHEDELIC SOUNDS, EASTER EVERYWHERE and BULL OF THE WOODS in one convenient package.

⊙ **The Psychedelic World of the 13th Floor Elevators Box Set** (2002; Snapper).
If you really want to dive into this band's sound, try this collection that pulls together all four of their albums along with a whole bunch of live cuts and oddities.

Robert Murray

THIS HEAT

Formed London, 1975; disbanded 1982.

Experimental 'industrialists' **This Heat** consisted of **Charles Bullen** and **Charles Hayward**, who had performed free improvisations under the name Dolphin Logic, plus **Gareth Williams**. All three switched instruments and performed vocals as necessary, exploring a similar terrain to Can and Throbbing Gristle, with **Chris Blake** providing tape editing both live and in the studio. The use of tape loops and samples of their own playing, while not revolutionary – Holger Czukay and Lee Perry had pioneered these techniques – was taken in a new direction.

The group set up their own recording studio in a disused meat freezer in Brixton, South London, and, having attracted the attention of John Peel with a demo tape, broadcast the first of two sessions for his radio programme in January 1977. A publishing contract with Blackhill enabled them to record in a 24-track studio, where **David Cunningham** and **Anthony Moore** (ex-SLAPP HAPPY) co-produced their debut album, THIS HEAT (1979), released on Cunningham's Piano label.

In the interim, This Heat had performed extensively in London and other cities, working with film-makers, Indian dance groups, Ghanaian singer/percussionist Mario Boyer Diekuuroh, and Senegalese kora musicians – among others. This multicultural exchange was highly influential on the development of the group's ambitiously complex, and some might say unapproachable, sound mixes.

More highly regarded in Japan, Germany and America than at home, This Heat visited Europe during 1980, touring with a new PA developed by the group with **Jack Balchin** (ex-HENRY COW), while live tapes were operated by **Pete Bullen**. A 12" single, "Health And Efficiency", preceded their second LP, DECEIT (1981), which was mixed by reggae sound engineer Martin Frederick, later an On-U Sound collaborator. Frederick also took over live mixing, and This Heat played live between his dub sound systems, despite record label attempts to package them with acts like the then-unknown U2.

Gareth Williams left This Heat in late 1981 to study Indian dance. The group, with **Trevor Goronwy** (bass), **Ian Hill** (keyboards) and **Steve Rickard** (engineer), completed one last tour of Europe before folding. After the split came the release of REPEAT (1993), and the John Peel Sessions album MADE AVAILABLE. Gareth Williams died in 2001, a warm iconoclast, he will be deeply missed by London's free musicians.

⊙ **This Heat** (1979; These).
An unsettling mix of live and studio recordings. The approach is typified by "24 Track Loop", a piece based on a ten-second fragment, extended and warped into a flurry of rhythmic feedback.

⊙ **Deceit** (1981; These).
A more song-based album, influenced by dub-reggae techniques as well as Indian music. Veers towards energetic industrial folk music at times ("Cenotaph" and "S.P.Q.R."),

This Heat in the kitchen: Cunningham's hand, Bullen (juggling), Hayward and Williams

while "Independence" rereads the US Declaration in the light of rampant Thatcherism.

Made Available – John Peel Sessions (1996; These).
Long-awaited release for This Heat's legendary 1977 radio sessions. Features rawer versions of tracks from later albums, as well as lengthier tracks such as "Makeshift Swahili" (originally on the first album) and "Slither".

Richard Fontenoy

Thanks to Jeff Weiss for updates

THIS MORTAL COIL

Formed London, 1983; disbanded 1991.

Not so much a band as a collective, **This Mortal Coil** was a long-term project, which brought together a variety of musicians from top independent label 4AD and an assortment of guest artists, under the guidance of label supremo **Ivo Watts-Russell**. Although they released only three albums in their eight-year existence and never performed live, their inimitable sound helped them create their own niche in an ever-changing indie market. Their cover art was pretty ground-breaking, too.

The first This Mortal Coil release was a lengthy interpretation of an obscure Modern English song, "Sixteen Days – Gathering Dust", and featured the Cocteau Twins' **Elizabeth Fraser** on vocals. It was the B-side that got played, however – a wistful cover of Tim Buckley's "Song To The Siren", again featuring Fraser, whose vocals lent an eerie quality to the sparse atmosphere. The song quickly became a classic, staying in the indie chart for over a year and making two fleeting appearances in the UK Top 75 at the end of 1983.

Its (qualified) success encouraged Watts-Russell to organize an entire This Mortal Coil album, IT'LL END IN TEARS, which finally appeared in October 1984. The record assembled multitudes including **Howard Devoto**, violinist **Gini Ball**, and representatives from almost every other 4AD signing, from **Colourbox** to **Dead Can Dance** and Cocteau Twins, whose Elizabeth Fraser brought a poignant sorrow to Roy Harper's tale of a disintegrating relationship, "Another Day". Regrettably, this would be her last contribution to This Mortal Coil.

A demanding mixture of obscure cover versions and solemn instrumental pieces, IT'LL END IN TEARS surpassed modest sales predictions by reaching the UK Top 40, and the eagerly awaited follow-up album, FILIGREE & SHADOW (1986), used similar techniques on a much broader musical canvas. A double album of primarily atmospheric melancholy, it was a self-indulgent enterprise, but with enough moments of icy beauty to hold attention. Covers of songs by Tim Buckley, David Byrne and Van Morrison were carried off with varying degrees of success, but the achingly vulnerable vocals of new recruit **Dominic Appleton** (particularly on "The Jeweller" and "Tarantula"), and the haunting clarity of the little-known Rutkowski sisters, created spellbinding moments.

Inevitably, FILIGREE & SHADOW proved too bulky and inaccessible to reach the mainstream, with only a brief chart appearance, and some interest in the double-A-sided single, "Drugs"/"Come Here My Love". It would be another five years before the release of BLOOD (1991), which Watts-Russell had already decided would be This Mortal Coil's last LP. What had started as a pleasurable distraction was now putting the rest of 4AD's output in the shade, and the

only label-mates to collaborate on BLOOD were **Kim Deal** (Pixies/Breeders) and **Tanya Donelly** (Throwing Muses).

Nonetheless, the basic philosophy of This Mortal Coil remained unchanged. An abundance of song covers – Tim Buckley, Chris Bell, Syd Barrett and Randy California – all received suitably imaginative but reverential treatments. Watts-Russell's production continued to eschew conventional structure in favour of atmosphere and texture, but BLOOD demonstrated a keener ear for melody than either of its predecessors. The simple acoustic guitar on "You & Your Sister", for example, highlighted Deal and Donelly's yearning vocals to exquisite effect, while the tumultuous rock culture shock of "I Am The Cosmos" was balanced by Appleton's spaced-out interpretation of the despairing lyrics. BLOOD enjoyed positive reviews, and, despite the customary lack of promotion, went Top 30 in the UK, bringing a typically elegant conclusion to a long but hardly prolific career.

In 1993, a four-CD box set was issued in mainland Europe, containing all three This Mortal Coil albums, plus a bonus disc featuring the original songs that inspired their many cover versions. Copyright problems prevented its British release, but (for those not put off by the hefty import price tag), the set is a fascinating chronicle of an original and unclassifiable act.

⊙ **It'll End In Tears** (1984; 4AD).
A powerful and moving debut, occasionally difficult but more often exquisitely beautiful. The performances of Elizabeth Fraser and Gordon Sharp, in particular, are outstanding.

⊙ **Filigree & Shadow** (1986; 4AD).
More ambitious than its predecessor, this widens the pool of contributors, and at times suffers from a lack of focus. The best pieces – "Morning Glory", "The Jeweller", "Ivy & Neet" – have a Neoclassical quality, and a trimmed-down version would have made a stunning single album.

⊙ **Blood** (1991; 4AD).
Still stubbornly out of step with changing tastes and trends, this final album continues on the same stately path as before, but with several almost radio-friendly songs. A fitting farewell.

Jonathan Kennaugh

DAVID THOMAS

Formed London, 1981; disbanded 1985.

When **PERE UBU** came to an artistic halt in 1981, **David Thomas**, whose bulk and general air of wired intensity provided the visual focus of the band, took the usual frontman's leap into a solo career, but it was a peculiarly bizarre take on the whole process.

THE SOUND OF THE SAND AND OTHER SONGS OF THE PEDESTRIANS (1982) was an LP which played at 45 rpm 'for greater fidelity' and was sardonically dedicated to the Accounts Department. **The Pedestrians** – perhaps taking their name from the last Ubu LP, THE ART OF WALKING – took drummer **Anton Fier** and synthesizer genius **Allen Ravenstine** from the parent group, and added **Eddie Thornton** on trumpet, and bassist **Philip Moxham** from the quietly weird **YOUNG MARBLE GIANTS**. Joker in the pack was lead guitarist **RICHARD THOMPSON**, who belied his folk-rock past by playing free-form like a man possessed. Other tracks featured **Chris Cutler**, formerly the drummer in **HENRY COW**. The result was an album of distinctly off-kilter 'melodies' and arch lyrics.

A second Pedestrians album, VARIATIONS ON A THEME (1983), added two more musicians with a Cow past – **Lindsay Cooper** (bassoon) and **Jack Monck** (bass) – and continued exploring the rhythmless territory of English avant-rock. Then The Pedestrians made their final appearance on MORE PLACES FOREVER in 1985. This incorporated Ubu's **Tony Maimone** on bass, and its highlight was an eleven-minute title track, which brought Thomas back to earth after indulgent excursions inside his own head.

Thomas's next band, **The Wooden Birds**, released two LPs, MONSTER WALKS THE WINTER LAKE (1986) and BLAME THE MESSENGER (1987). Almost a Pere Ubu reunion, musicians included Ravenstine and Maimone. When **Scott Krauss** joined the band for a late 1987 concert in Cleveland, David Thomas declared 'it walked like a duck, looked like a duck, quacked like a duck, so it was a duck'. Thus, Pere Ubu was reborn.

More recently, Thomas has been working with **Two Pale Boys** (Andy Diagram and Keith Moline). Their joint releases EREHWON (1996) and SURF'S UP (2001) continued Thomas's lasting infatuation with the formless, unstructured outskirts of rock. One Pale Boys gig included a rare vocal appearance from **Linda Thompson**.

Thomas, dressed in a red plastic apron and playing bucolic accordion, and the Two Pale Boys – one of whom blew into his trumpet backwards – toured Britain in early 1997. In June of that year, Cooking Vinyl released the five-CD box set MONSTER, with an explanatory booklet. A complete history of Thomas's solo career, the box contained remasters, on CD for the first time, of THE SOUND OF THE SAND – Richard Thompson's guitar on "Man's Best

Friend" is even more startling in digital format – MONSTER WALKS THE WINTER LAKE and BLAME THE MESSENGER. Added to this are 'radical and definitive' remixes of VARIATIONS ON A THEME and MORE PLACES FOREVER, and a bonus CD called MEADVILLE. This was a live recording from a Two Pale Boys show in the French city of Rennes. With cuts like "Surfer Girl", "Beach Boys" and "Weird Cornfield", it is certainly Ubu. Thomas says of this concert that it is 'the best album I've ever made', with its songs sounding of a man fully inhabiting his own, strange world. During the tour, Thomas self-mockingly complained about the strain of totally improvising each night's set. When the author help-fully called out for the ancient Pere Ubu number, "On Alignment Pact", Thomas obliged by singing that song of terror and breakdown to a cheerful polka beat. A true original.

Since then Thomas has been true to his ever-eclectic muse and composed MIRROR MAN (1999), which was played by the Pale Orchestra. Dubbed 'musical the-atre', it was performed in 1998 at the Queen Elizabeth Hall in London with Thomas conducting a line-up which, apart from himself, featured, among others, Linda Thompson, Peter Hammill, and Chris Cutler. In 2000 the improvised album BAY CITY was released, recorded by 'David Thomas and foreigners' **P. O. Jørgens**, **Jørgen Teller** and **Per Buhl Acs**.

⊙ **The Sound Of The Sand** (1982; Rough Trade).
Sample verse (recited in a strangled yelp, like a man fighting for his last breath on the scaffold): 'Remember the birds, remember the shoes I wore/Remember the things I said before/I think 'em again'. On his version of The Beach Boys' "Sloop John B", Thomas sounds like a helplessly drunken sailor mumbling on his way back from the pub. The only comparison is the Bonzo Dog Band's deconstruction of "The Sound Of Music" on GORILLA, but this is presumably serious.

⊙ **Variations On A Theme** (1983; Rough Trade).
A little more mainstream, this includes the self-referen-tial "Pedestrian Walk" and, continuing the concept of the previous album, "The Egg And I" and "Bird Town". The cover features sketches of seagulls front and back.

⊙ **Monster** (1997; Cooking Vinyl/TimKerr).
The ultimate collection – a five-CD gathering with a six-teen-page booklet to boot – comprising the five studio albums he recorded between 1981 and 1987 in one little box.

Brian Hinton

RICHARD THOMPSON

Born London, 1949.

"Personally, being somewhat envious of Richard's songwriting and guitar playing, it's somewhat satisfying he's not yet achieved household-name status. It serves him right for being so good."
David Byrne

Though **Richard Thompson** has never enjoyed much in the way of sales, his reputation is awe-some. Over the past twenty years he has guested on guitar with everyone from **JOHN MARTYN** to **PERE UBU**, and he has forged his own body of work – twenty-five albums at last count – that is consistently listenable and often brilliant. His talents lie both as guitarist and songwriter. As a lyricist he can be as dark as anyone around, taking a story of blues-like horror and acting the devil's part, singing in that utterly dis-tinctive, deep English drawl.

Thompson first came to public attention with the original **FAIRPORT CONVENTION**, the finest of English folk-rock groups. He played on their first six albums, contributing heavily to the group's innova-tive mix of styles, and providing many of their best songs, most notably "Meet On The Ledge" on WHAT WE DID ON OUR HOLIDAYS and "Sloth" on FULL HOUSE. After working briefly as a sessionman, he made his solo debut with HENRY THE HUMAN FLY (1972), a continuation of Fairport's hybrid style. His backing singer on that album, Linda Peters, then became **Linda Thompson**, and the two recorded six albums over the next eight years, a period in which Thompson's songwriting voice came to the fore.

On the duo's I WANT TO SEE THE BRIGHT LIGHTS TONIGHT (1974), "Calvary Cross" intro-duced a favourite Thompson theme, the struggle between men and women, in an archaic narrative form. His guitar work also featured heavily, building on the sombre tone of the album, epitomized by "End Of The Rainbow" and "Withered And Died". The following album, HOKEY POKEY (1974), light-ened the tone with pseudo-traditional songs like the title track (about ice cream), "Smiffy's Glass Eye" and "Georgie's On A Spree". But it was noticeable that Thompson's melancholic side provided the best songs, with "I'll Regret It All In The Morning" and "A Heart Needs A Home", songs that foreshadowed POUR DOWN LIKE SILVER (1975). From that album, "For Shame Of Doing Wrong" remains one of his greatest songs, while "Dimming Of The Day" and "Night Comes In" are not far behind.

Both the Thompsons had converted to Sufi Islam by this point, and they spent the following three years building up their own Sufi community in Britain. Their comeback was FIRST LIGHT (1978), which oddly revealed a poppier side to their music ("Don't Let A Thief Steal Into Your Heart") along with the customary traditional-style material ("The Choice Wife" and "Died For Love"). SUNNYVISTA (1979) went further down the pop road, but for once the songs lacked focus. It was followed by STRICT TEMPO! (1981), a Richard Thompson all-instru-mental solo outing, recording traditional jigs and reels, and his own superbly moody "The Knife-Edge".

The razor-sharp SHOOT OUT THE LIGHTS (1982) was the Thompsons' final album as a duo before their marriage ended. There was an edginess throughout this set that was missing from their other records: Thompson's voice vividly conveyed the anger and

Hands of Greatness: Richard Thompson

the impressive lyrical styling of "Love In A Faithless Country". DARING ADVENTURES (1986) suffered from an overproduced feel, but Thompson was still capable of writing songs as beautiful as "How Will I Ever Be Simple Again?" and affecting as "Al Bowlly's In Heaven".

Moving label again (to Capitol), Thompson released AMNESIA (1988), which was perhaps too diverse for its own good. "Don't Tempt Me" revealed a slightly psychotic side to the Thompson songwriting persona, but "Waltzing's For Dreamers" and "You Can't Win" confirmed his penchant for regret and anger. RUMOR AND SIGH (1991) was Thompson's best album for a long time, achieving a perfect balance of a variety of styles: his narrative ability was shown on the superb "1952 Vincent Black Lightning", his lyrical wit on "Read About Love" and "Mother Knows Best", and his violent side on "I Feel So Good" and "Psycho Street". The music moved from balladry through straight rock, to polkas and blues.

SWEET TALKER (1992), a largely instrumental soundtrack, built on the solid musical groove of RUMOR AND SIGH, while MIRROR BLUE (1994) repeated the achievement of RUMOR with story-songs like "Shane And Dixie" and "Beeswing", and the savagely funny "I Can't Wake Up To Save My Life". With ex-Attraction **Pete Thomas** providing a satisfying clatter to the drum sound, Thompson's guitar work remained as impressive as ever. It was followed by the release of a tribute album featuring artists influenced by his fusion of folk and rock guitar styles.

YOU? ME? US? (1996), offered up separate acoustic and electric discs and introduced his son Teddy on backing vocals. While in part it seemed to be treading water – hardly surprising, given the career behind it – narrative songs like "Cold Kisses" and "Woods Of Darney" stand with the best of his work. INDUSTRY (1998) was a return to the good old-fashioned concept album, being a set of pieces centred on the Industrial Revolution and its continuing fallout. Thompson contributed six of the eleven pieces, the remainder comprising double-bass works by collaborator **Danny Thompson**. At was a dark, satanic mill of an album.

Next, MOCK TUDOR was released in 1999 and was rounded off with the live SEMI-DETACHED

nastiness of "Don't Renege On Our Love" and "Back Street Slide", whilst pleading the case for "A Man In Need". Equally, Linda's voice created a beautiful mood of regret on "Just A Motion" and "Walking On A Wire". (Linda went on to a solo career, sadly curtailed in 1988 by hysterical dysphonia – the vocal version of stage fright; her work has recently been anthologized as DREAMS FLY AWAY.)

HAND OF KINDNESS (1982), Richard Thompson's first proper solo album since 1972, sounded like a continuation of SHOOT OUT: "Tear Stained Letter" and "A Poisoned Heart And A Twisted Memory" were Thompson at his vitriolic best, dissecting a failed relationship, whilst "Two Left Feet" was a witty but scathing put-down. SMALL TOWN ROMANCE (1984; reissued 1998), a live solo recording, put those concerns on hold but offered the chance to hear Thompson record Richard and Linda songs as solos.

Introducing a more polished feel to his recordings, Thompson made two albums for Polydor. ACROSS A CROWDED ROOM (1985) returned to the emotional warfare of relationships ("She Twists The Knife Again", "When The Spell Is Broken") and featured

MOCK TUDOR (2002), which was followed in 2003 by THE OLD KIT BAG. Of course, Thompson spent the intervening time touring and contributing to a wide variety of projects, underlining his reputation as one of England's finest, if largely untrumpeted, guitarists and songwriters.

Richard and Linda Thompson

⊙ **Shoot Out The Lights** (1982; Hannibal).
The musical and lyrical high point of the Thompsons' duo career, even if the prevailing mood is one of anger and resignation.

Richard Thompson

⊙ **Rumor And Sigh** (1991; Capitol).
Not always on the mark, but when Thompson hits the right chord (as he does on "1952 Vincent Black Lightning" and "Read About Love"), his brutally incisive songwriting is hard to top.

⊙ **Watching The Dark** (1993; Hannibal).
Wonderful triple-CD overview of Thompson's career, featuring many unreleased live versions of favourite songs.

⊙ **The Old Kit Bag** (2003; Cooking Vinyl).
Coming three years after MOCK TUDOR, this stripped-down-band concoction displays some of Thompson's most confident and accomplished work of recent times. The acoustic cuts work just as well as the electric ones, but like so many of his sets, it takes a fair few listens to really get under your skin.

Nicholas Oliver

GEORGE THOROGOOD

Born Wilmington, Delaware, December 31, 1952.

A former semi-professional baseball player, guitarist and vocalist **George Thorogood** took up music after seeing a John Hammond show in 1970. Unlike many of his contemporaries, Thorogood has always kept the influence of the musicians who inspired him foremost in his writing, especially the R&B trinity of Chuck Berry, John Lee Hooker and Elmore James.

Forming his backing band, **The Destroyers**, in 1973, Thorogood persuaded **Ron Smith** (guitar), **Jeff Simon** (drums) and **Bill Blough** (bass) to relocate from their native Delaware to Boston, where they would regularly back visiting blues artists. After hooking up with the Rounder label, Thorogood and The Destroyers recorded their first, self-titled album, in 1975, although its release was initially delayed because of personnel changes. Always the blues purist, Thorogood has consistently mixed his own material with a considerable number of covers over the years, and it was with one of these covers, John Lee Hooker's "One Bourbon, One Scotch, One Beer", that catapulted Thorogood into the big time.

Thorogood's follow-up album, MOVE IT ON OVER (1978), went gold on its release, as have all his subsequent albums. Indeed, such was Thorogood's popularity that the MCA album, EVEN BETTER THAN THE REST (1979), a collection of demos which he publicly disowned, sold healthily. Shunning stadiums in favour of smaller clubs, he even took to

playing under pseudonyms in order to keep crowds smaller. He is ample proof that the blues are about feeling rather than technical excellence, and the release of LIVE (1986) forcefully proved the point, perfectly capturing the manic energy and enthusiasm of a Thorogood show – and more than half the album taken up with Thorogood playing his favourite artists' songs rather than his own compositions.

In the 1990s, Thorogood was less prolific, but his most recent releases, HAIRCUT (1993), LET'S WORK TOGETHER (1995), ROCKIN' MY LIFE AWAY (1997), LIVE IN '99 (1999), HALF A BOY HALF A MAN (1999) and ANTHOLOGY (2000), show no signs of mellowing.

⊙ **Live** (1986; EMI).
From Thorogood's opening yell of 'And away we go' on Bo Diddley's "Who Do You Love", through to his raucous version of Chuck Berry's "Reeling' And Rockin'", the audience is treated to over an hour of good-time R&B, played with the enthusiasm of a man who is blissfully unaware of all that modern musical technology has to offer.

⊙ **The Baddest Of** (1990; Demon).
All the crowd-pleasing hits you'd expect, such as "The Bottom Of The Sea" and "Bad To The Bone", and a whole lot more besides.

Paul Morris

3 COLOURS RED

Formed London, 1994; split 1999; re-formed 2000.

3 **Colours Red** first came to prominence by taking the chunky, punky rock traits of the Wildhearts as their blueprint, whilst touring with that band in 1995. Both the comparison and the choice of 3 Colours Red as support act were hardly surprising, as **Chris McCormack** (guitar) is the brother of the Wildhearts' Danny. **Pete Vuckovic** (vocals/bass), **Ben Harding** (guitar) and **Keith Baxter** (drums) comprise the rest of the group. Vuckovic had previously been a latter-day member of New Wave of British heavy metal stalwarts Diamond Head. Baxter and McCormack also worked together as backing musicians on Glen Matlock's 1996 solo album WHO'S HE THINK HE IS WHEN HE'S AT HOME.

Doubtless as a result, 3 Colours Red played first on the bill at the Sex Pistols' Finsbury Park reunion gig. Like many of the bands to break through in the mid 90s, the group's first single, "This Is My Hollywood", was released on Simon Williams' Fierce Panda independent. Afterwards Creation Records stepped in – perhaps seeing in the group a replacement for Bob Mould's much-lamented Sugar.

Others viewed 3 Colours Red as the ultimate homogenization of the punk/metal crossover. The singles "Nuclear Holiday" and "Sixty Mile Smile" won them plaudits in the music press and modest chart positions before the release of their 1997 debut album, PURE, produced by Terry Thomas. Although there was little stylistic variety in its contents, it proved that 3 Colours Red had become skilled purveyors of three-minute blast-furnace pop, the best tracks including "Love's Cradle" and "Copper Girl".

REVOLT (1999), preceded by the storming single "Beautiful Day", continued their intriguing blend of metal-tinted guitar fire, punkish brevity, angry attack and thoughtful lyrics. Stand-out tracks apart from the single include the opening track "Paralyse", "Back To The City" and "This Is My Time".

And then, just as the band seemed to be reaching some sort of creative peak, they dramatically disintegrated following the Leeds leg of the Carling Weekend Festival on 29 August 1999 – it proved to be their final gig. The cause of the split was put down to the usual clashes of egos and a desire to explore different musical terrain, especially in the case of Pete Vuckovic. The latter eventually formed the short-lived **Elevation** who managed an EP before being crushed by the monumental indifference of the music industry. McCormack's new outfit, **Grand Theft Audio**, fared a little better, managing to issue an album called BLAME EVERYONE. But it wasn't long before the band were back together.

The impetus for the re-formation came with the tentative offer of a summer festival slot if all concerned could kiss and make up. As a result, 3 Colours Red – bar guitarist Ben Harding, who couldn't commit to the arrangements – were officially back in the running. Whether this remains a permanent state of affairs, we shall have to wait and see, though 2003's "Repeat To Fade" single was a good start.

⊙ **Pure** (1997; Creation).
In some ways simplistic, but often compulsive pop/hard rock – popcore, as the Yanks used to call it. Includes the singles "This Is My Hollywood", "Nuclear Holiday" and "Sixty Mile Smile", the group's best song to date.

Alex Ogg

THE THREE JOHNS

Formed Leeds, England, 1981; split 1988.

"We're a mixture of everything, plus cajun."

Leeds art-college friends **John Hyatt** (vocals), **Jon Langford** (guitar) and **John Brennan** (bass) formed post-punk trio **The Three Johns** amid the Rock Against Racism movement, beginning their recording career with a cover of "English White Boy Engineer" (1982), a song by Langford's other band, **THE MEKONS**. Issued on the overtly political CNT label, it was a powerful, primitive two-chord rant against oppression in South Africa.

Gigs and singles, however, were to form just one part of The Johns' activities. Committed socialists, they helped run instrumental courses for the unemployed and produced a series for BBC Radio on the machinations of the music business. However, if that makes them sound earnest, forget it. The Three Johns

may have played countless benefits, but their political approach was relatively humorous – hence the recording of tracks like "Marx's Wife" and "The World Of The Workers Is Wild".

But back to the story. Following their debut, the band recorded "Men Like Monkeys" (1983), richer and more typical fare, with Langford and Brennan's guitar and bass throwing flesh over the skeleton of the drum machine, and Hyatt breaking through with alternate blues howls and falsetto yelps. They then shifted around the styles and made an album, ATOM DRUM BOP (1984). This was a distinctly experimental outing and, while the bubblegum punk of "Teenage Nightingales To Wax" and surreal pathos of "No Place" had immediate appeal, Langford's primitive blues riffs underscored by Brennan's industrial-strength bass seemed to lack the colour of earlier single releases.

Live shows, however, were a different story, as The Johns carved out an enviable reputation for wit, humour and drunken exuberance. Their LIVE IN CHICAGO album (1986) bore testament to a band at the peak of their performing powers, while showing their reaction to US culture, an even stronger strand on their second studio LP, THE WORLD BY STORM (1986). Tracks such as "Torches Of Liberty", "Atom Drum Bop" and "Death Of The European" were highly critical of America's nuclear policy, and the Reagan administration in general. Critically well received, STORM demonstrated Hyatt's powers of invective becoming ever more finely tuned.

More touring followed, expanding audiences at home and abroad, although regular day jobs ensured that they never strayed far from home for long. Then, in 1988, an ill-starred US tour saw the band fold and the release of their tellingly titled DEATH OF EVERYTHING AND MORE.... A real curiosity, it demonstrated the vast eclecticism of The Johns' influences; but, with the exception of the sublimely understated "Downhearted Blues", the album was a disappointment, replacing much of the old instrumental tension and interplay with guitar-driven bombast.

After the break-up, the multitalented Langford continued to work as a record producer for Cud and Gaye Bykers On Acid, as an artist and rock journalist, as well as playing with The Mekons. Hyatt became an art lecturer in Manchester.

⊙ **The World By Storm** (1986; Abstract; currently unavailable).
A glance at the lyric sheet gives a glimpse into the freakish cartoon world inhabited by the Three Super-Johns; their blokish, guitar-splashed musical surfaces give the nightmare its shape and form. Apocalyptic stuff, and their most cohesive album.

⊙ **Crime Pays ... Rock And Roll In The Demonocracy, Singles 1982–1986**
(1986; Abstract; currently unavailable).
Everything you ever wanted to know about The Three Johns but were too damned trendy to ask. Here are the CNT singles in all their lo-fi glory, the righteous bile of "Engineer" and the beery brilliance of "Brainbox".

Huw Bucknell

3 MUSTAPHAS 3

Formed Szegerely, Balkans/north London, 1982; currently on extended leave in their home town.

"I'm interested by how people do or don't accept music from the Balkans – it's part of our roots, yet people are more prepared to accept music from Africa." Hijaz Mustapha

The **3 Mustaphas 3** appeared, fully formed, amid a British 'roots music' scene revitalized by groups like The Pogues, The Men They Couldn't Hang and The Oyster Band, which was beginning to merge, in record racks, at festivals, and in pioneering magazines like *Folk Roots*, with that strange beast – world music. The Mustaphas were themselves a pretty worldly crew, having played in various punk, African, Latin, jazz and rock outfits, though the group's official line was that they had all been working for years in the Crazy Loquat Club in Szegerely, and that, as they modestly explained, was why they were so skilled, and so, uhh, Balkan.

The band had a floating cast, all bearing the Mustapha family name. The guiding spirits were **Uncle Patrel** (on saz, of course) and **Hijaz** (bouzouki/violin/Hawaiian guitar), while other founding Mustaphas included **Houzam** (drums), **Isfa'ani** (percussion), **Oussak** (cello) and **Niaveti Mustapha III** (accordion/flute/vocals). They made their live debut in London in August 1982, and in 1985 released a mini-album, BAM! MUSTAPHAS PLAY STEREO, on their own branch – Fez-o-phone – of the newly established Globestyle world music label.

BAM! promulgated a Balkan bad boy image and unleashed an eclectic mix of Greek songs alongside a version of the Kenyan classic "Singe Tema" (sung, like all their adapted material, in its original language) and an episode of the band's ongoing narrative, "A Chilling Tale", begun on their numerous sessions for the John Peel and Andy Kershaw shows on BBC Radio. It was recorded in an (empty) north London swimming pool – the first singing-in-the-baths album, Hijaz claims.

By the time of their first LP proper, SHOPPING (1987), the Mustaphas had lost Oussak, but gained an electric bassist and singer,

Sabah Habas – whose voice, oddly enough, resembled Bryan Ferry's – along with the prodigiously talented **Kemo** (accordion/keyboards). The band's Balkan beat remained intact on the album, but the musical range was extended to African and Indian styles, while later in the year the band sampled Algerian duo La'Azaz on a 12" single, "I'Shouffi Rhirou".

The Mustaphas were a very flexible (promiscuous, in their own words) unit and were occasionally joined by **Expensive Mustapha** (trumpet) and vocalist **Lavra Tima Daviz Mustapha**, who seemed equally at ease singing in Arabic, French, Greek, Hindi, Macedonian, Spanish and Swahili. The Mustapha projects ranged across cultures with superlative ease, with musicians confident in Latin and African, as well as Balkan, rhythms. In 1985 they surfaced in Berlin as **Orchestra BAM De Grand Mustapha International And Party**, a fifteen-piece ensemble, while in Britain, their musical eclecticism led to work backing visiting stars of the world music circuit, such as Israeli singer Ofra Haza, and West African kora players Dembo Konte and Kausu Kouyateh.

In their 'regular' incarnation, the Mustaphas recorded two further albums. HEART OF UNCLE

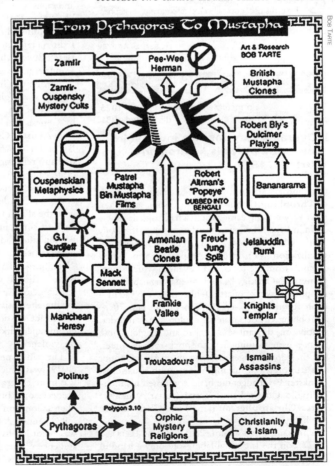

(1989) was a wild array of songs which may once have been Hindi *filmi* (film music) and Nigerian Hi-Life, but were transmuted into idiosyncratic Mustapha fare. SOUP OF THE CENTURY (1990) took the mix-and-match approach even further, with prominent woodwinds from new member **Daoudi Mustapha**, and material extending to the Japanese "Soba Song". Both discs showed the Mustaphas at the peak of their powers, the latter deservedly being voted #1 in that year's *Billboard* world music charts. These were followed by a compilation of B-sides, remixes and oddities, entitled FRIENDS, FIENDS & FRONDS (1991).

Unfortunately, the financial pressures of maintaining a big band, and one whose members worked in all kinds of other projects, and lived as far apart as Berlin and Jakarta, led to an extended sabbatical for the Mustaphas – back in Szegerely, of course. The silence has only been broken by 1997's mini-album BAM! MUSTAPHAS PLAY STEREO and PLAY MUSTY FOR ME (2001).

However, the Mustaphas are likely to re-emerge at intervals. Forward – as they say – In All Directions!

3 Mustaphas 3

⊙ **Heart Of Uncle** (1989; GlobeStyle).
This is the best possible introduction to the Mustaphas. Indeed, it's probably the best thing the Mustaphas have done to date.

Robert E. Murray

THROBBING GRISTLE

Formed Manchester, England, 1975;
disbanded 1981.

"Overall a very positive interest in our work prevails." Throbbing Gristle, 1977

Inventors of the term 'industrial music', **Throbbing Gristle** got off to a flying start when their very first gig earned them a half-page denunciation in Britain's vilest national newspaper, the *Daily Mail*, who labelled them 'The Wreckers Of Civilization'. For once, it was perhaps a measured reaction from the paper to an event in which singer **Genesis P-Orridge** had exhibited using nappies and tampons as works of art. Deliberately unpleasant – even for the punk-era Britain of the late 70s – Throbbing Gristle's material explored mass murder, mutilation, deviant sex, fascism and magic. These themes were nothing new to shock-rock devotees, but their low-budget incarnation of Alice Cooper was still pretty disturbing. Along with situationist prankster P-Orridge, the band comprised his then-girlfriend **Cosey Fanni Tutti** (guitar), **'Sleazy' Peter Christopherson** (tapes) and **Chris Carter** (keyboards).

The band's first album, 2ND ANNUAL REPORT (1977), on the Industrial label, sold only a handful of copies – partly because of its uncommerciality, but also because only 500 copies were pressed. The music, some of which had already surfaced on an EP, THE BEST OF THROBBING GRISTLE VOL 2 (yes, their *debut* release), was a dark messy swirl of mechanical noise, coupled with flat, buried vocals and tapes. One side featured live versions of works like "Slug Bait" and "Maggot Death", while the other consisted of the single piece "After Cease To Exist" (a reference to Charles Manson's song for The Beach Boys), which featured the taped confession of a murderer.

Throbbing Gristle's subsequent single, "United" (1977), was slightly more accessible, thanks to the presence of a rhythm but any charm was extinguished by Genesis's tuneless incantation of lyrics derived from **Aleister Crowley**, while the B-side, "Zyklon B Zombie", was a typically provocative (or dumb, perhaps) reference to the Zyklon B gas used in Nazi death camps.

The band received next to no music press coverage, but, undeterred, they re-emerged in 1978 with the album D.O.A. "United" made a reappearance of sorts, in a seventeen-second speeded-up version, alongside "Death Threats" compiled from hostile messages left on their answerphone, and "Hamburger Lady", inspired by an account of a burns victim. It was a blend of industrial music and self-conscious self-mythologizing too extreme even for the alternative-music industries, albeit that the darker side was accompanied by humour, with interests in supermarkets, muzak and Abba balancing out the violence.

The band's next outing, 20 JAZZ FUNK GREATS (1979), was something of a misnomer. Admittedly it was more electro-pop and easier to listen to than its predecessors, but it also contained the creepy "Persuasion", on which Genesis declared his love for soiled panties. A final LP, HEATHEN EARTH (1980), was recorded live in the studio before an invited audience of friends and admirers, and was perhaps a little more consistent.

In 1981 the group split in two: Genesis and Christopherson formed **PSYCHIC TV**, whilst the other two became **Chris & Cosey**, a relatively orthodox synth duo. Ironically, since their break-up, Throbbing Gristle's output has vastly increased, due to the appearance of numerous live recordings in cassette format. Collections of these tapes were issued first as 24 HOURS and then, for the committed, 36 HOURS, but most would be satisfied with their four original LPs, which formed a unique, uncompromising and uncomfortable statement of art terrorism.

⊙ **D.O.A.** (1978; Mute).
The best of the albums. The CD reissue comes with the addition of both sides of their finest single, "We Hate You Little Girls" and "Five Knuckle Shuffle".

⊙ **Greatest Hits: Entertainment Through Pain** (1981; Mute).
The first half of the title is ludicrous, the second is relatively accurate for a collection split between ugly distressing noise and early electro-pop rhythms. Though TG were never cited by anyone much as an influence, you can hear on this the seeds of much that was to come.

Alwyn W. Turner

THROWING MUSES

Formed Newport, Rhode Island, 1983.

In a medium where appearing 'mad' can be a career policy, **Kristin Hersh** (vocals/guitar) stands as an uncomfortable reminder of the trauma of genuine mental disorder. Subject to auditory hallucinations and incapacitating seizures, Hersh has been prey to a form of bipolarity since the age of 14. She has used the experience in her art, producing unself-conscious and unsettling songs ("Rabbits Dying", "Marriage Tree") that have won her group, **Throwing Muses**, critical plaudits and a cult following, if not the kind of mainstream audience they sometimes wistfully suggest they would like.

The group was launched in 1983 – as The Muses – by Hersh and **Tanya Donelly** (vocals/guitar), the half-sister with whom she had grown up on an LSD-sustained hippie commune. Three years later they were signed by 4AD boss Ivo Watts-Russell, who for the first time broke his 'embargo' on American acts. Backing Hersh and Donelly by that stage were **Leslie Langston** (bass) and **David Narcizo** (drums), both of whom managed, by dint of the former's tight bass patterns and the latter's cymbal-less military drumming, to provide some kind of anchorage for the baroque guitar work so beloved of Hersh, Donelly and Ivo Watts-Russell.

THROWING MUSES (1986), the debut album, may have had Hüsker Dü and the Meat Puppets as its credited influences, but it wasn't hard to see why the gothic 4AD had been so attracted to songs like Hersh's "Hate My Way" and "Soul Soldier". Dark, winding and frightening, these tracks were like nothing that had come out of the US before. It was an example of Kristin at work in her manic phase, her piercing, staccato voice cutting through songs characterized by violent mood swings and constantly shifting time signatures. Donelly also staked her presence as a songwriter with "Green", a beautiful and powerful love song.

The band's extremism was – perhaps inevitably – less pronounced on subsequent releases. HOUSE TORNADO (1988), the follow-up album, revealed a more melodic side to the band, even a poppier intent on such songs as Hersh's "Run Letter" or Donelly's "The River". The next album, however, HUNKPAPA (1989), showed little progression in any direction, and with a couple of notable exceptions – Hersh's "Bea", Donelly's "Angel" – the material was simply not as strong.

In 1989 Tanya Donelly, frustrated at the song-writing opportunities in a band dominated by Hersh, formed **THE BREEDERS**, initially with Narcizo, though she stayed with Throwing Muses through the recording of their next – and masterpiece – album, THE REAL RAMONA (1991). Whether charged or liberated by the impending split, this saw Hersh and Donelly moderating each other's material, creating brilliantly poppy, engaging and challenging songs. Hersh stand-outs included "Counting Backwards" and "Say Goodbye", while Donelly excelled on "Not Too Soon" and the cute/abrasive "Honeychain". Donelly then departed to form **BELLY**, taking Muses' then-bassist **Fred Abong** with her.

Hersh, defying expectations, quickly bounced back into the fray, with David Narcizo on drums and original bassist Langston forming a much rockier trio for RED HEAVEN (1992). This was as strong as anything that had come before, a great melodic noise-fest, replacing the giddying, double-guitar patterns with swaths of guitar distortion. Featuring some of her finest songs to date ("Summer St", in particular) and a duet with **Bob Mould** on "Dio", it loudly announced to the world that Hersh could get along very well without Donelly.

After taking time out for a solo album of dark, folky acoustic ballads, HIPS AND MAKERS (1994), Hersh reassembled the Muses with **Bernard Georges** on funky, lolloping bass, to record

UNIVERSITY (1995). This maintained the rocking out of RED HEAVEN, with an intense, almost punk edge to songs like "Start" and "Shimmer". LIMBO, the 1996 follow-up album, maintained this momentum with solid self-contained songwriting and a return to wicked lyricism. It augured well for an extended career but 1998 saw the band dissolved yet again, with Hersh releasing a second solo album soon after, and Narcizo forming a new band named **Lakuna**, who released the refreshingly percussive CASTLE OF CRIME in 1999.

STRANGE ANGELS, Hersh's 1998 project, picked up pretty much where her previous solo albums had left off. Still dark, folky and acoustic, Kirsten turned up the fader marked "Bleak" and reduced everything else to a whisper. Kirsten's solo recordings continue to roll out, her most recent releases being 2001's SUNNY BORDER BLUE and THE GROTTO (2003). Meanwhile, the Muses reconvened in 2003, complete with a returning Donelly, for the simply titled THROWING MUSES. It was the group's rawest offering in years and heralded something of a new beginning…

Throwing Muses

⦿ **Throwing Muses** (1986; 4AD).
Lyrics which might sound pretty cheesy coming from anyone else ('I slide your head across the ice') are given chilling authenticity by Hersh's banshee-like scream. An utterly absorbing debut.

⦿ **The Real Ramona** (1991; 4AD).
The Muses' poppiest, most accessible album, with Tanya Donelly's influence looming large in the Hersh compositions.

⦿ **Red Heaven** (1992; 4AD).
Hersh finally does what fellow Bostonians the Pixies had been suggesting she do for years – push down the distortion pedal, crank up the Marshalls, and let the world have it.

⦿ **In A Doghouse** (1998; 4AD).
This marvellous set pulls together THROWING MUSES, CHAINS CHANGED, the group's self-released DOGHOUSE demo tape, and several early Hersh recordings – a fine document of the younger Muses sound.

Kristin Hersh

⦿ **The Grotto** (2001; 4AD).
The bleakest of her solo efforts, THE GROTTO is an intriguing collection of folk meanderings and passionate, often desperate-sounding songs.

Piers Clifton

THUNDERCLAP NEWMAN

Formed London, 1969; disbanded 1970.

"The revolution's near and you know it's right … / We have got to get it together right now … "
Something In The Air

Thunderclap Newman were one of the oddest and most interesting one-shot groups of the 1960s. They were assembled, in 1968, by **Peter Townshend** of THE WHO, as a pop vehicle for two of his friends: jazz pianist **Andy Newman** and drummer **Speedy Keen**, a songwriter who had penned "Armenia, City In The Sky", the explosive slice of psychedelic pop that led off THE WHO SELL OUT. Keen would sing and write most of the material for the band, which was completed by 16-year-old guitar prodigy **Jimmy McCulloch**. Townshend himself functioned pretty much as a fourth member, playing bass under the alias of **Bijou Drains** and producing their sole LP.

Even before the album, Thunderclap Newman struck pay dirt with their anthemic debut single, "Something In The Air", which rose to #1 in Britain in the summer of 1969. Exemplifying the most Utopian aspects of late-60s rock, the song was distinguished by an unexpected piano boogie solo by Newman, and Keen's weird falsetto vocals, eccentric traits that would be amplified on the album, HOLLYWOOD DREAM (1970), a set of low-key, folkish rock with a pop bounce. Speedy's whiny vocals, pitched midway between Townshend's and the shrill tone employed by Canned Heat's Al Wilson on hits like "Going Up The Country", combined with Newman's ragtime-flavoured boogie detours and occasional bleats of soprano sax to make a record that had a whimsical, almost goofy, charm; Keen wrote all of the selections, with the exception of a McCulloch instrumental and a cover of the obscure Dylan composition, "Open The Door, Homer".

Thunderclap Newman was not built to last. They had met for the first time, after all, at the recording sessions for "Something In The Air", and couldn't count on undivided attention from Townshend at a time when TOMMY had launched him into international superstardom. They disbanded shortly after the release of HOLLYWOOD DREAM. Keen and Newman went on to record obscure, little-heard solo albums, while McCulloch played with **JOHN MAYALL**, Stone The Crows and Wings (see **PAUL McCARTNEY**) before his premature death in 1979.

⦿ **Hollywood Dream** (1970; Polygram).
Highlighted by "Something In The Air", "Hollywood #1" and "When I Think", this is recommended to those who enjoy Pete Townshend's early solo efforts – although it isn't quite in the same league. The CD reissue adds a few bonus tracks.

Richie Unterberger

JOHNNY THUNDERS

Born New York, 1952; died 1991.

"Rock'n'roll is about attitude. I couldn't care less about technique."

For a few years in the early 70s the thriftstore cowboys who called themselves the **THE NEW YORK DOLLS** were tipped as the next big thing. They were a gang of pan-stick icons in the making, and the biggest cult of them all was their lead guitar slinger, **Johnny Thunders**.

As a schoolboy, **Johnny Genzale** attended the World's Fair and witnessed legendary instrumental band The Ventures. From then on, plans to follow in the footsteps of his baseball idol Mickey Mantel were part of a forgotten dream. An investigation of his big sister's record collection revealed many more nuggets, and Johnny immersed himself in the sounds of the New York girl vocal groups, and then set out to merge elements of their pop sensibilities with the fast and furious sounds of the bands emerging from the US underground, notably the Detroit contingent – The Stooges and the MC5.

The ingredients for his early image were gathered on a trip to the psychedelic circus that was 1969 London. Here he rubbed shoulders with The Rolling Stones, and attended scores of concerts where he charted the rise of, amongst others, the proto-glam poet Marc Bolan. Most would agree that Johnny could walk it like Keith Richards talked it, but it is less widely acknowledged that his pouting and ego trips were borrowed from the Bolan Boogie.

The cocksure arrogance came to the fore when Johnny introduced himself to the founding members of **Actress** in Nobody's bar. Arthur Kane and his pals thought they had found a bassist who would rumble in their shadows – hence his new moniker 'Thunders' – but he had other plans and soon stepped into the spotlight as lead guitarist and singer. But even Thunders had to admit that he was not ready to hold centre stage and by Christmas 1971 the band had recruited a somebody from Nobody's: **David Johansen** filed his painted nails, tottered up to the microphone on his pink platforms and, letting rip with the clarion call of 'C'mon boys!', played Mick to Johnny's Keef at the birth of The New York Dolls.

The Dolls took their show to any cheap hotel that would have them, but it was their success as the number one draw at New York's Mercer Arts Center which provided the focal point for the city's emerging trash rock aesthetic. Second guitarist **Syl Sylvain**, with his tight corkscrew hair and even tighter licks, proved himself to be the epitome of a glam guitar god, but it was Thunders who captured the imagination. Johnny grew his hair into an improbable bush, sported the traditional symbols of rebellion – the skull and crossbones – and seesawed his way across the boards and along the frets. The accompanying sound, which was to become his trademark, was the drunken yowl of half-tuned strings, immortalized on stand-out tracks (such as "Subway Train") from the first Dolls' album, and repeated to full effect on solo classics like "You Can't Put Your Arms Around A Memory".

As with most Thunders vehicles, The Dolls were doomed from the start. They may have appeared to be mere caricatures, but they played out their exaggerated lifestyles with calamitous results. On their first visit to the UK they lost their drummer in a drink and drugs binge. A string of pointless deaths, such as that of his friend Sid Vicious, led Johnny to pen the poignant songs "Short Lives" and "Sad Vacation".

The Dolls' second drummer, **Jerry Nolan**, was to become a longtime Thunders sidekick – in fact it was Nolan who accompanied Johnny when he finally walked out of The Dolls in 1974. The **HEARTBREAKERS**, their new band, set out with the initial aim of aligning stomping rock with the clever-clever lyrics of Richard Hell. They began as a democratic trio but the fundamental rock sound favoured by Nolan and Thunders soon overshadowed Hell's artifice, and, with the recruitment of **Walter Lure** and **Billy Rath**, they became Johnny's band.

Following a couple of years' consistent hometown gigging, the Heartbreakers got the chance to bring their sound to a British audience. Malcom McLaren invited the band to join the Sex Pistols on their 'Anarchy Tour' of 1976 and, despite the fact that Thunders had been less than appreciative of McLaren's efforts as manager for the final incarnation of The Dolls, he wasn't about to turn down the price of a ticket to England and, with it, the opportunity to scan the emerging punk scene.

The tour lived up to its name and there was a certain prophetic truth to the title of the Heartbreakers' first single, "Born To Lose". Anyone who saw the band live knew this was a blistering anthem for the not-so-blank generation, but the mix of the track and of L.A.M.F. (1977), the album from which it originated, was as murky as a Hammer film fog. Each member of the band disowned the version which was finally released, and the arguments over who was to blame had not been resolved by the time Thunders went solo in 1978.

Through the 70s Thunders had gathered a network of devotees, including fledgling Clash guitarist Mick Jones and the young Morrissey, who would exchange gossip and opinions about their hero by post. Thunders also had many admirers who had already established themselves and, from the coterie of musicians at London's Speakeasy Club, he was able to cast SO ALONE (1978) with players from the Only Ones, Thin Lizzy and the Sex Pistols.

The early 80s saw a series of false starts resulting in the disintegration of numerous Thunders bands, such as the **Living Dead**. Back in the US Johnny got to work with Wayne Kramer in **Gang War** but, despite constructing a fine set of originals peppered with old gems, the two were to tire of the venture after recording just one album.

A major factor in the failure of all these projects was a growing dependence on drugs that made Thunders' gigs more like junkie sideshows than the high-octane performances of old. The audience were more interested in seeing whether he would survive the night than in the quality of his (increasingly rare) new material. Despite the problems, a series of comrades and hard-nosed managers pulled him back from the brink and, before the end of the decade, he had turned in some of his best ever recordings. Many of the releases were regurgitations of former glories, but when Johnny teamed up with New York songstress

Patti Palladin for COPY CATS (1988), it seemed that his voice had truly found its niche.

In one of his final interviews, Thunders confided that it was his intention to settle in New Orleans and form a band that could marry the jazz sounds of the region with his inimitable brand of buccaneer rock. No one will ever know how close he was to realizing this ambition when he finished touring with his last band, **The Oddballs**, and headed for the Delta City. He was found dead in his hotel room less than 24 hours later.

The coroner recorded the presence of cocaine and methadone in the body and, as the local police drew a veil over their investigations, many conspiracy theories began to arise. The true circumstances of Thunders' death may never be known but it has since come to light that he was suffering from lymphatic leukaemia, for which he refused treatment.

Director Lech Kowalski followed Thunders' career for many years and previewed his biopic *King Outlaw* at the Leeds Film Festival in 1998. This version of the Genzale boy's story is a dark and brooding affair, heavily dependent on the testament of the New York punk scene's walking wounded, and only redeemed by some tremendous live footage.

Since his passing, Thunders' influence has continued to grow and traces of his sound can be heard in a multitude of today's cult bands including the Sabrejets, New Bomb Turks and The Cramps. Syl Sylvain has recorded a tribute to all the dead Dolls, "Sleep Baby Doll", and it is a mark of the high esteem in which Thunders was held by his fellow musicians that Joey Ramone and Ronnie Spector chose "Memory" as one of the tracks to relaunch the latter's recording career on Creation Records. He's become another of those artists more prolific in death than when walking the boards, the best of his more recent posthumous releases being 1993's CHINESE ROCKS (ULTIMATE LIVE COLLECTION) and 1997's BELFAST ROCKS (both Anagram Records).

Johnny Thunders

● **So Alone** (1978; Real Records).
Thunders' flawed masterpiece. From the opening bars of surf standard "Pipeline" (the theme tune for live performances), to the final chords of the bum's lament "Downtown", the man gives us recurring glimpses of how good he was and how great he could have become. Steve Lillywhite proved himself to be the most sympathetic producer of the lipstick killer's career, and the inclusion of the single "Memory" justifies purchase in itself.

● **Copy Cats** (1988; Jungle).
Strictly speaking this is not a solo outing. Patti Palladin did most of the work, but her selection could have come from a disc-spinning session in the teenage Genzale's bedroom, and the resulting duets confirm this as one of the finest R&B covers albums on the market. Tracks range from the strip-joint weird ("Let Me Entertain You") to the wildly wonderful ("Treat Her Right").

The Screwballs (Thunders Tribute)

● **I Only Wrote This Song For You** (1994; Castle).
This tribute compilation is the album Johnny never made. Towards the end our Italian Stallion developed a heightened sense of social responsibility, which belied his image as chemical-imbibing, geetar-toting reprobate. Some of the better moments on this worthy disc, including "Society

Makes Me Sad", highlight this moral conscience and reveal just how touching (and touched) the old boy could be. A gang of JT's mates, working under the guise of The Screwballs, turn in a version of "Help The Homeless" which sounds like the Glitter Band on dodgy speed – something that would have appealed to Thunders' sense of camp. Thunders makes an appearance from beyond the grave on the uncredited title track, as if to prove that you can't keep a good man down.

Stephen Boyd

TIJUANA NO

Founded Tijuana, Mexico,1990.

Tijuana, thanks to its proximity to the United States, has always been a major pipeline for new music. In the 60s and early 70s, Tijuana groups like Ritual and Love And Peace, dominated the Mexican rock scene due in large part to their successful blending of the newest and best in Anglo rock with a truly Mexican heart and soul.

Though only three members of **Tijuana No** are Tijuanenses, this band best represents the *nortena* variant of Mexican rock, which found its own voice in the mid 80s with Caifanes, Maldita Vecindad, Café Tacuba and other bands in Mexico City. While earlier Mexican bands, particularly Maldita, had been known for their music of rebellion, which fused ska, rock, funk and jazz into a uniquely Latin rock blend with a clearly Mexican flavour, Tijuana No hit the scene harder with its punk and hardcore ska protests in Spanish and English and a clearly revolutionary character.

Singer and songwriter **Luis Guerena**'s connections with the Tijuana scene go back to the late 70s when, as a young punk, he organized music events with North American and British bands including the Dead Kennedys, The Damned and Black Flag, to raise money and consciousness about Central America. Guerena, after time away in Los Angeles hanging with John Doe of X and others, returned to Tijuana to muscle his way into music. He played first with local band Chantaje, then formed 'No' of Tijuana with some of those members. Guerena's lyrics, vocals and acrobatics are complemented by the impressive guitar work of **Jorge Jimenez** and the *nueva cançion*, rock and ska flair of **Teca García**, not to mention the haunting vocals and crafted keyboards of **Cecilia Bastida** (co-opting Edmundo Arroyo and Sax of Maldita as an impressive horn section when necessary). **Manu Chao** of France's multilingual, now defunct band, **MANO NEGRA**, added his touch of genius to the group, performing backup vocals on the first two albums.

Their hit single, "Pobre De Ti", won them the 1993 *Almohada de oro* (Golden Pillow Award) to the envy of the *chilango* (Mexico City bands) who had dominated the local rock scene up to that point. Their first album-length recording, INDEFINITION, was an experiment; ranging all over the rock map and setting out the band's direction in world beat/rock with a strong hardcore and ska edge.

Tijuana No's second album, TRANSGRESORES DE LA LEY took Mexican rock to a new level, from *rock rebelde* to *rock revolucionaria*. "Golpes Bajos" was a great ska piece along the lines of "Pobre De Tí" and guaranteed to get your feet moving. However, the title song, dedicated to so-called outlaws, the Zapatistas, was a more symphonic rock piece with a perfect harmony of lyrical power, a strong message, emphatic vocals and a raging chorus carried by ska rhythms. Follow up album CONTRA-REVOLUCION AVE (1998) continued their theme of 'up the rebels'.

Tijuana No has shared the stage with the top names in the international alternative underworld such as Rancid, Smashing Pumpkins, Rage Against The Machine, Negu Gorriak and Mano Negra (these latter two top bands from the Basque country of Spain and France, respectively). Further developments are awaited with interest...

⊙ **Transgresores De La Ley** (1994; RCA International). Revved up and ready to go, this is Mexican ska-punk at its fearsome finest.

Clifton Ross

TINDERSTICKS

Formed Nottingham, England, 1992.

When In-Tape Records, the small indie label run by ex-Fall player Marc Riley, went bust in 1991, it left a Nottingham band called the Asphalt Ribbons high and dry. **Stuart Staples** (vocals), **Dickon Hinchliffe** (violin), **Dave Boulter** (keyboards/glockenspiel), **Neil Fraser** (guitar), **Mark Colwill** (bass) and **Al Macaulay** (drums) decided to dump previous attempts at funk, and reinvent themselves as **Tindersticks**, a band inspired by Lee Hazlewood, the croaky 1960s singer and producer famous for his work with Nancy Sinatra. Staples did a mean impression of big Lee and his partners could play the music to match – a slow, brooding hybrid, mixing in bits of country with smoky urban laments, traces of Scott Walker and Tom Waits.

A first self-released single, "Patchwork", crept out in late 1992, to indifference, but the next one, "Marbles", a crackly spoken story narrated over sparse instrumentation and allegedly recorded on a Walkman, made *Single of the Week* in both the *NME* and *Melody Maker*. Suddenly, the Tindersticks were hip. They proceeded to put out a bewil-

dering number of singles, releasing records on six different labels during 1993, but these were just tasters for the main course.

By the summer the Tindersticks had signed to the new This Way Up label, and set about recording an under-budget, ahead-of-schedule double album. Rumours spread that they had bitten off more than they could chew, but TINDERSTICKS (1993) turned out to be a triumph, a long, dense piece of work, full of atmosphere and with some great arrangements and tunes. One of the stars of the piece was guest horn player **Terry Edwards**, a member of Tindersticks' closest contemporaries, Gallon Drunk. The album finished at or near the top of most of the annual critics' polls. And it sold pretty well, too.

After this whirlwind, 1994 was a quiet year for Tindersticks releases, with just one single, a version of Townes van Zandt's "Kathleen" – a song that might have been written for them – and a limited-edition live album, AMSTERDAM. They also made a surprise venture out of their dark haunts into the bright summer light of the Glastonbury Festival. But the guys were busy, working on a second album at Conny Plank's Cologne studio, and at Abbey Road, where Terry Edwards' increasingly sophisticated string arrangements were added.

The second album, TINDERSTICKS, emerged in May 1995 to justified acclaim. The songs were

Stuart Staples keeping the voice in trim

stronger, the orchestrations gorgeously lush, and the times had caught up. Britain was rediscovering easy-listening 60s songs, and Tindersticks, with their orchestrations and Hammond organ, were to some extent an update on this – albeit an intriguing one with their spoken narratives, and still-strong country influences.

The band set out to re-create and expand their music live – an expensive habit costing around £10,000 a gig for their chamber orchestra. Astonishingly, in view of rock's disasters in this area, they didn't lose the plot, and pulled it off with some zest, as showcased on the live album, THE BLOOMSBURY THEATRE 12.3.95 (1995), proving it to have been money well spent, particularly in view of their subsequent commission to provide the soundtrack to Claire Denis's film Nenette Et Boni, for which they reworked "Tiny Tears" and "My Sister" and conjured up a suitably swirling dark-edged atmosphere.

CURTAINS (1997) showed how beautiful lounge music could be if you hold the cheese. Staples' heart-breaking voice and tear-jerking lyrics managed to tread close to melodrama without ever straying across the line. Strings gushed, the brass section bubbled away, but it was Staples who grabbed the listener's attention and refused to let it go without imparting a little pain in the soul as a keepsake.

Although Staples felt that they had lost some creative freedom with 1999's SIMPLE PLEASURE it was an underrated album that elevated the soul, both literally and metaphorically. The instrumental "From The Inside" mixed Booker T, Nick Cave and The Doors in equal measures while both "Can We Start Again" and the closing "CF GF" had an almost spiritual quality.

Hinchcliffe's arrangements then conjured new levels of atmosphere on CAN OUR LOVE… ? (2001) as the group ventured into 70s soul territory, albeit tinged with a hint of contemporary darkness. They sounded refreshed after leaving major label pressures and returning to indie land – "People Keep Comin' Around" was a brooding epic while "Sweet Release" more than fulfilled the ambitions of its title by heading out into melancholy bliss. A second album followed later in the year: this time a masterful, haunting soundtrack to Claire Denis's cannibalistic art-house film Trouble Every Day. 2003's WAITING FOR THE MOON offered, well, more of the same: Staples' distinctive bass croon accompanying a tide of strings and some blissful melodies.

The Tindersticks now seem comfortably embedded in the UK's musical scenery, and are sure to be around for a while longer.

⊙ **TINDERSTICKS** (1993; This Way Up).
A moody, mighty debut, full of splendid things, from savage flamenco rockers ("Her") to delicate Burt Bacharach pop ("Patchwork"). Big, confusing and magnificent.

⊙ **tindersticks** (1995; This Way Up).
More late-night laments, wonderfully delivered, and refining the dark production and arrangements of the first

record. The rambling, surreal short story "My Sister", and the country duet "Travelling Light", are highlights.

⊙ **Donkeys 1992-1997** (1998; Island).
A great place to find some lost gems: "Patchwork", "City Sickness", "Travelling Light" and "Tiny Tears" are all among the group's finest pieces.

⊙ **Simple Pleasure** (1999; Island).
Soulful backing vocals and funky instrumentals lend this set an uncharacteristically uplifting feel. Some things never change though – Staples' sad baritone still chews on the gristle of tangled, doomed relationships.

Mark Elliot

TOM TOM CLUB

Formed Nassau, Bahamas, 1981.

It was during a **TALKING HEADS** recording session in Nassau that **Tom Tom Club** came into being, when founder members **Chris Frantz** (drums) and **Tina Weymouth** (bass/vocals) met up with studio engineer Steve Stanley and discovered a shared interest in dance music. The original three-some soon mushroomed into a twelve-piece collective, which included Weymouth's sisters **Laura**, **Lorie** and **Lani** on backing vocals and **Adrian Belew** on guitar. The first Club material came in June 1981 in the shape of "Wordy Rappinghood", a frothy funk concoction whose clattering typewriter rhythm and chattering chorus fitted in well with the early 80s' vogue for novelty hits, reaching #7 in the UK chart.

Beyond its surface frivolity, "Wordy Rappinghood" was a clever and inventive collage of sound which, along with Blondie's "Rapture", was one of the earliest white disco records to acknowledge rap music, but the band found the 'novelty' tag a difficult one to shake off. Their debut album TOM TOM CLUB followed in October 1981, but despite Island's high hopes it charted only briefly. From its childlike cover illustration on, the theme was fun and sun, set to an array of breezy, bass-heavy funk. Quality control did let them down in places but even the low points were infused with a *joie de vivre* which made them difficult to dislike.

The highlight of the album was undoubtedly "Genius Of Love", a track whose irresistibly lurching bass line, babbling synth effects and lazy handclaps, broke new ground in early-80s dance music. It topped the *Billboard* dance chart, and then crossed over to the pop chart where it reached # 31. In later years it was also reused by Rap pioneer Grandmaster Flash as the basis for his single "It's Nasty", and by pop diva Mariah Carey, who boosted her dance-floor credibility by welding the entire backing track, as well as sections of the lyric, onto "Fantasy", which topped dance charts on both sides of the Atlantic.

Island later reissued the album with an extra track, an insipid version of "Under The Boardwalk", which lacked the spontaneity of the rest of the album. Released as a single, it gave them a belated second hit, but artistically it was best forgotten. A second album, CLOSE TO THE BONE (1983) was an attempt to re-create the vibe of the first, but despite the promise of titles like "The Man With The 4-Way Hips" it was a pale imitation of past glories. It made little impression, and Frantz and Weymouth returned to the Talking Heads fold as their LITTLE CREATURES album began to take off.

An invitation to produce Ziggy Marley's CONSCIOUS PARTY in 1987 reawakened their enthusiasm for their own work, and Tom Tom Club signed a new deal with Phonogram. A three-week residency at New York's CBGB's venue heralded the band's third album BOOM BOOM CHI BOOM BOOM (1988). Five years had passed, and inevitably there had been changes, both in personnel (the group was now a slimline four-piece) and in musical direction. The new songs dispensed with the sunny innocence of old in favour of a harder sound with an undercurrent of tension – the cover of Lou Reed's "Femme Fatale", for instance, would have sounded out of place on either of the previous sets. Radio found it all too confusing, while club-goers, more interested in the euphoria of the new acid-house scene, found little to enthuse over in the album's polite white soul arrangements. The reborn Tom Tom Club found itself ignored, and the album sank without trace.

When the Talking Heads split was finally confirmed in December 1991, Tom Tom Club became a full-time concern for Frantz and Weymouth and, with new recruit **Bruce Martin** (keyboards), they unveiled a fourth album in October 1992. DARK SNEAK LOVE ACTION continued along the left-field funk-rock path of its predecessor, with much of its appeal centred on an intriguing cover of Hot Chocolate's "You Sexy Thing". The difference this time was that the band now found itself without a record deal in Britain and Europe, and with sales in the US sluggish, the Club was finding itself increasingly marginalized.

Around the central husband/wife nucleus of Frantz and Weymouth, the band has remained a popular live attraction, even if their recorded work has found fewer takers since the more frenetic, disposable 90s. For their ground-breaking early material at least, Tom Tom Club can justifiably claim to have made a contribution to the mainstream acceptance of experimental dance music.

⊙ **Tom Tom Club** (1981; Island).
On first hearing, you'd be forgiven for dismissing this as the ultimate lightweight summer pop album, but further listening reveals hidden depths of intricacy and experimentation. "Wordy Rappinghood" and "Genius Of Love" – both present in their extended glory here – rank among the most creative dance records of their time.

⊙ **Boom Boom Chi Boom Boom** (1988; Fontana).
A brave change of tack saw them adopt a more rugged sound on this third album, drawing on a wide range of musical styles and influences and adding a subtle trace of menace to the mix. Highlight is "Don't Say No", a tuneful, percussion-led pure pop anthem.

Jonathan Kennaugh

TOOL

Formed Los Angeles, 1991.

"I hope we can provide an alternative to all of the lowest common denominator shit going on right now." Danny Carey

Very few acts reject the music-business treadmill yet still successfully make a mark on the contemporary scene in the manner that **Tool** have. Formed in 1991 when **Maynard James Keenan** (vocals) convinced **Adam Jones** (guitars) to form a band based on the theories of Ronald Vincent's obscure text, *A Joyful Guide To Lachrymology*, Tool quickly scored support slots with Rage Against The Machine and Jane's Addiction and a record deal with Zoo Entertainment. Jones had previously been a member of Electric Sheep, a band featuring Tom Morello of Rage Against The Machine, while Keenan was in the army.

Paul D'Amour was enlisted to play bass while the group found a drummer in workaholic **Danny Carey**, who at the time was holding down a nine-to-five job whilst also playing with Carole King, Pygmy Love Circus and comedy metal-rockers Green Jelly. The first release on Zoo was the cement-mixer-heavy EP OPIATE, released in mid 1992, where the synergy of atmospheric metal and Keenan's idiosyncratic vocal style was welcomed by a public warming to the sounds of the new generation of hard-rock bands. The first release from OPIATE, "Hush", was a condemnation of censorship, something the band have repeatedly run into.

Included on UNDERTOW (1993) was a spoken-word collaboration with **HENRY ROLLINS** ("Bottom"), the out and out dirge of "Disgustipated" and the cathartic "Prison Sex", a depiction of child abuse. It was an unsettling affair, clocking in at just over an hour, but this didn't stop the public lapping it up and buying more than a million copies in the US alone. After continuous touring to push the album, D'Amour left to pursue a career in his own bands Lusk and The Replicants. His replacement was **Justin Chancellor** from British band Peach, with whom Tool had previously toured the UK. Meanwhile, Carey toured with industrial supergroup Pigface on their 1994 tour across western America.

The public had to wait another three and a half years for ÆNIMA. Produced by David Bottrill and 77 minutes long, it was a harrowing collection of atmospheres and experimentation that made the band harder to categorize, with some quarters even making comparisons to (gasp!) progressive rock. Offering the brooding energy of "Stinkfist", the epic "Third Eye" and the almost operatic "H", the album had substance, even if at times it seemed self-absorbed. Several of the tracks were segued together, with "Die Eier Von Satan" being an interesting attempt at Einstürzende Neubauten-type experimentation, and the lyrics being a recitation in German of a Mexican wedding cookie recipe.

Throughout it all, Tool have held close to their ideals, turning down slots on *Saturday Night Live*, refusing to edit singles for commercial airplay, even walking away from a contribution to the Led Zeppelin tribute album ENCOMIUM after the compilers of the album haggled with Tool over the length of their projected seven-minute version of Zep's "No Quarter".

The late 90s saw Keenan and sometime Tool collaborator **Billy Howerdel** (guitarist, songwriter, producer) furthering their musical ideals through the formation of the hard-rock outfit, **A Perfect Circle**, the name symbolizing the coming together of a group of people who complete one another. Their emotionally charged MER DE NOMS (2000) was an accomplished first album, with Keenan and Howerdel adamantly stating that the band was not simply a side-venture. Meanwhile, Tool split from their management company, and headed back into the studio to create possibly their finest work yet, LATERALUS (2001). It was a sprawling and multi-layered masterpiece pulling together all the artistic elements Tool had so far made their own, with the complexity and depth of the music reflected in the CD's dazzling artwork. Needless to say, the album topped many music critics' personal charts at the end of the year and the band's profile went stratospheric during the subsequent bout of touring. It's hard to guess how they will eventually top this one.

Tool

🔘 **ænima** (1996; Zoo).
The best album released in 1996, hands down. Rarely does an album this innovative make it to release, which meant the success it achieved was all the more peculiar. "H", "Forty Six & 2", "Eulogy" and "Stink Fist" are misted windows into the minds of one of the darkest bands on the planet, while the condemnation of LA in the title track is worth the price of entry alone.

A Perfect Circle

🔘 **Mer De Noms** (2000; Virgin).
The well-rounded MER DE NOMS proves there's more to A Perfect Circle's success than a perfect CV. From the towering inferno that is "Magdalena" to the softness of "Orestes", each beautifully crafted track demands your empathy. Indeed, as Keenan himself says, it is precisely these emotionally charged harmonies and layered vocals that distinguish this work from Tool's material.

Craig Joyce

TO ROCOCO ROT

Formed Berlin, 1995.

"Experiment has to be fun." Ronald Lippok

Following a stint in a free-form Berlin performance art and music collective, brothers **Robert** and **Ronald Lippok** teamed up with bassist **Stefan Schneider** to provide the music for an instal-

to rococo rot. the amateur view.

lation they were staging. In the best traditions of European contemporary art, the music was produced by a combination of electronic engineering and sampling, marrying theory and entertainment.

To demonstrate that their music wasn't just for the art-school leavers, the trio released an untitled vinyl-only picture disc, bizarrely featuring an injured Dangermouse figure on one side, and began playing as a live band under the palindromic name **To Rococo Rot**. The record was rereleased in 1996 with further tracks as the simply titled CD (Kitty Yo).

Mixing Schneider's dub-influenced bass playing with the Lippoks' turntable and sample manipulations, as well as environmental and random sounds, To Rococo Rot joined a burgeoning German electronic rock scene that harks back to the 70s experiments of Can, Neu! and Cluster, upgraded with a vengeance by innovations such as hard-disk recording, and the omnipresent digital sampler. Typically of such loose groupings, Ronald Lippok also has his own project – **Tarwater** – while Schneider continued playing bass in the highly regarded **KREIDLER** until he opted to join To Rococo Rot full time in 2000, as well as releasing two albums as Mapstation on the Staubgold and Domino labels, respectively, at the turn of the century.

To Rococo Rot have established themselves as one of the loosest, most organic groups in this ill-defined field, further consolidated by their first 'proper' studio album VEICULO (1997). Receiving much wider attention than the first full-length outing, it was warmly received in dance as well as rock circles – having a memorably strange name must have helped too. Successful live appearances at festivals such as Popkomm in Cologne preceded the release of the PARIS 25 EP, which was long enough to have once been called a mini-LP, with two remixed tracks and three newies to funk up the postmodern dance floor (or art gallery, even). An appearance at Mute Records' Mini-Meltdown festival in London with Kreidler and the legendary

Faust, and the pleasingly cyclic "Telema" 10" single preceded THE AMATEUR VIEW (1999), an album that sounded nothing but totally professional – dispassionate, calculating and shimmering with a glassy, precise beauty. Ambient meets Krautrock meets electronica to spellbinding effect.

To Rococo Rot then developed a collaborative bent, producing St Etienne's THE SOUND OF WATER in 2000, as well as remixing for, among others, Leftfield. Occasional live partner Darryl Moore put out a mini-LP as **torococorot+d** on his Soul Static Sound label (1998), while the group appeared on the LUME LUME CD (2000) which documented a 57-hour Ars Electronica installation on the banks of the Danube under the direction of **Alexander Balanescu**. The group also produced soundtracks for two radio plays and a documentary film, *No Ordinary Cowboy*. Robert in turn released a solo CD for Raster-Noton in 2001, and their paths crossed Balanescu's for a second time when he appeared on MUSIC IS A HUNGRY GHOST (2001), recorded with New Yorker Craig Willingham – aka **I-Sound**.

To Rococo Rot remain an important part of the proliferation of instrumental groups blending electronics with live instruments, from Germany's Kreidler and Mouse On Mars to US stalwarts such as Tortoise. At least as far as rock-derived music (as opposed to techno/drum'n'bass) is concerned, the futuristic present hasn't sounded this good for a very long time.

⊙ **cd** (1996; Kitty Yo).
Rough around the edges it may be, but that's a positive attribute in a bass, drums and sampler feast of shifting structures and hypnotic texturing.

⊙ **Veiculo** (1997; City Slang).
A selection of lo- and hi-tech devices blended into a groovy hybrid sound of music in transition, all bleeps, cycled samples, and heavy on the low end, too.

⊙ **The Amateur View** (1999; City Slang).
Slowly unfolding compositions characterize an album with a slightly lower density of dub, and greater emphasis on sparse arrangements of intricately mellow electronica, interspersed with moments of surging rhythmic intensity.

⊙ **Music Is A Hungry Ghost** (2001; City Slang).
The dreamlike drift continues much as before, strengthened seamlessly by Craig Willinham's contributions on sampler and turntables.

Richard Fontenoy

TORTOISE

Formed Chicago, 1990.

"We think of music in terms of how it fills up the spectrum ... and how it moves through time." John McEntire

In an attempt to find something new in a guitar-bass-drums formula that once seemed eternal but now seems repressive, lapsed academics doubling as indie kids have started to strip rock of its attitude, leaving only 'pure' sound. At the forefront of this early 90s post-rock movement were the elliptical abstractions of **Tortoise**. Like their fellow post-rockers Main, LaBradford and Ui, Tortoise are primarily concerned with the spatial organization of music and communicating through texture. To achieve this expansive effect, they have embraced the studio-as-instrument aesthetic promulgated by Jamaican dub and the cut'n'splice avant-garde.

An embryonic Tortoise began experimenting with a schematic rewiring of rock in 1990, when **Doug McCombs** (bass) and **John Herndon** (drums/synthesizers/vibraphone) began jamming together. They soon recruited **John McEntire** (synthesizers/drums/vibraphone) – a member of the fledgling **GASTR DEL SOL** – **Bundy K. Brown** (guitar/bass) and **Dan Bitney** (synthesizers/percussion) from Chicago's seemingly bottomless pool of underground rock weirdos. After a series of impossibly arcane singles and EPs, their debut album, TORTOISE, was recorded in a week in late 1993 and released the following year. The non-linear dynamics and stunted rhythms of their songs owed a debt to the oblique logic of the infamous Slint.

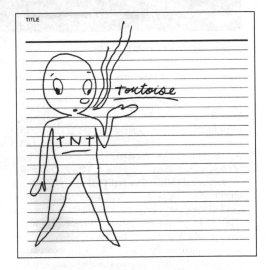

TITLE

The mesmerizing rush of the "Gamera" 12" for Stereolab's Duophonic label and RHYTHMS, RESOLUTIONS & CLUSTERS (1995) signalled the birth of something far more exciting. A collection of remixes of material from their debut album, the EP was immersed in the fog of a heavy bass pulse and decorated with all manner of found sounds and urban detritus. It was this dusty grit that transcended the occasionally scary echoes of prog-rock into which their rampantly intellectual approach inevitably sinks.

The band's debt to Slint was repaid when their former guitarist, **Dave Pajo** (now recording as **PAPA M** and as a member of **Zwan**), replaced Brown for the recording of the second Tortoise LP, MILLIONS NOW LIVING WILL NEVER DIE (1996). The highlight was the remarkable, 21-minute "Djed", whose

Tortoise – desperately trying to stay focused

stylistic twists and turns suggested the cut-and-mix mechanics of a club DJ working the crowd. This link was made evident in radical remixes of "Djed" by U.N.K.L.E and McEntire, and further reconstructions followed from experimentalists such as Oval, Jim O'Rourke, Luke Vibert, Springheel Jack, Autechre and techno producer Derrick Carter. Many of these were collected together as REMIXED (1996).

Occasional collaborator **Jeff Parker** replaced Pajo for the recording of the hit and miss complexities of TNT (1998) and the slightly more direct STANDARDS (2001). The band also joined forces with Dutch avant-punks **The Ex** for the "In The Fishtank" EP (1999) and curate the annual All Tomorrows Parties festival at a holiday camp in Camber Sands on the English south coast. Somehow or other, and largely by accident it seems, Tortoise have assumed the role of godfathers of post-rock, spawning a legion of imitators – for better or worse – along the way.

⦿ **Rhythms, Resolutions & Clusters** (1995; City Slang/Thrill Jockey).
Their best effort. Despite self-indulgent mixes by Steve Albini and Jim O'Rourke, the rest lives up to post-rock's theoretical foundation and reconfigures rock's instrumentation as something capable of exploring the expanses of space left unchartered by rock's nosedive into formula.

⦿ **Millions Now Living Will Never Die** (1996; City Slang/Thrill Jockey).
"Djed" and "Dear Grandma And Grandpa" are more than worth the price of admission. The remainder, however, is often cumbersome, as the music buckles under the weight of prog-rock's legacy, particularly the second half of "Glass Museum", which sounds alarmingly like a Yes bridge.

⦿ **Standards** (2001; Warp/Thrill Jockey).
STANDARDS shows that Tortoise can still run rings around a veritable confusion of prog-jazz-fusion motifs and get away with it – for the most part.

Peter Shapiro and Richard Fontenoy

ALLEN TOUSSAINT

Born New Orleans, January 14, 1938.

Songsmith, session player, producer, arranger and recording artist in his own right, **Allen Toussaint** forged a productive career in New Orleans R&B in the 60s and 70s. He spent the 60s writing and arranging for figures such as Dr. John, The Meters and Lee Dorsey, before recording his own material on albums that marked a shift away from his rollicking piano-led productions and sparse Southern funk towards a hazily evocative, laid-back, heart-warming sound still admired (and imitated) today.

In 1958, having sat in on sessions for Dave Bartholomew, Shirley & Lee, Lloyd Price and Fats Domino, Toussaint recorded an instrumental album, THE WILD SOUNDS OF NEW ORLEANS. While it owed an obvious stylistic debt to the piano style of Professor Longhair, enough promise was shown for trumpeter Al Hirt to record a million-selling cover version of one of its tracks, "Java".

He went on to record for the Minit label under the name of Allen Orange, and later with **The Stokes**. Among his successful productions were Irma

Thomas's impassioned soul ballad "Ruler Of My Heart" (1962), Jesse Hill's "Ooh Poo Pah Do" (1960), and the Showmen's "It Will Stand" (1962). Further success came with Lee Dorsey, whose "Ya Ya" (1961) became a major hit. The strutting dance classic, "Ride Your Pony" (1965), prompted a series of classic Toussaint-written and -produced successes, including "Working In A Coalmine", "Holy Cow" and "Get Out My Life Woman" (1966).

As the 60s closed, Toussaint enjoyed a successful period as producer for the New Orleans funk outfit, The Meters. On seminal records like "Cissy Strut" and "Sophisticated Cissy" (1969), he nudged the collective towards the lithe sound embodied by the acclaimed Dorsey album, YES WE CAN (1970). On the latter, each song bar one was penned by Toussaint.

TOUSSAINT (1971) included reconstructions of various old Lee Dorsey hits, a revival of the Joe Simon hit "The Chokin' Kind", the poignant and introspective "What Is Success", and the emotionally satisfying "From A Whisper To A Scream". This led to further production work for the likes of The Band and numerous mainstream rock and pop artists. One of his most successful and impressive enterprises was his collaboration with another giant of New Orleans music, **DR. JOHN**, on albums such as IN THE RIGHT PLACE (1973) and DESITIVELY BONNAROO (1974) – here Toussaint not only supplied backing vocals and percussion, but also keyboards, production, arrangements and organ.

Toussaint injected a tougher, rootsier feel to works by Labelle (notably on "Lady Marmalade"), Frankie Miller and Paul Simon throughout the early 70s, but he managed to engineer a heartier, smoother sound on records like "When The Party's Over", "Freedom For The Stallion", "What Do You Want The Girl To Do'" and, in particular "Southern Nights". These solo recordings formed the basis of his two acclaimed albums, LIFE, LOVE AND FAITH (1972) and SOUTHERN NIGHTS (1975). Neither album, nor the following MOTION (1978), were financially successful and Toussaint opted out of the music business for most of the 80s, though in 1987 he surprised many by appearing alongside Ruth Brown in the Broadway musical *Staggerlee*.

In the summer of 1994 Toussaint came out of exile to perform an accomplished, stripped-down set at the Southern Songwriters' Circle special event at London's Queen Elizabeth Hall, alongside such legends as Dan Penn, Joe South and Guy Clark. Leaving aside an album of Christmas songs, his most recent albums, CONNECTED (1996) and FROM A WHISPER TO A SCREAM (1997) have Toussaint recording some of his own material that was made famous by other performers. Toussaint's maverick talent remains in high esteem and he is currently ploughing his energies into a record label, NYNO Music.

(•) **The Minit Records Story** (1994; EMI).
A wonderful collection of Toussaint's work as A&R man, producer, arranger, songwriter and instrumentalist for New Orleans label Minit in the early 60s. Includes hits by Jesse Hill, Ernie K-Doe, Aaron Neville, The Showmen, Benny Spellman, Irma Thomas and Chris Kenner.

(•) **Southern Nights** (1975; Warners).
Toussaint's unique brand of heart-warming soul in excelsis. The stand-out title track provided Glen Campbell with a million-seller in the US.

(•) **The Allen Toussaint Collection** (1995; Warners).
As good an introduction to the man's oeuvre as you could expect, drawing upon the best of the clutch of obscure early 70s LPs, as well as the more sedate and shiny cocktail-lounge collection, MOTION.

Michael Sumsion

TRAFFIC

Formed Birmingham, England, 1967;
disbanded 1968;
re-formed 1970; disbanded 1974; re-formed 1994.

Technically adept and brimful of ideas, **Traffic** were one of the few really convincing progressive-rock acts of the late 60s and early 70s. Their main characteristics were **STEVE WINWOOD**'s keyboard dexterity and soul-inflected lead vocals, the imaginative use of wind instruments, and Jim Capaldi's articulate lyrics.

The original line-up was Winwood (keyboards/guitar/vocals), **Dave Mason** (guitar), **Chris Wood** (saxophone/flute) and **Capaldi** (drums). All of them were proven musicians already, but only Winwood was well known, having come to prominence as a youthful organist and second vocalist in **THE SPENCER DAVIS GROUP**. Their last hit, "I'm A Man", was still climbing the chart when Winwood left, announcing his intention to follow new directions in a group of his own.

Traffic's first release was the single "Paper Sun" (1967), which peaked at #5 in the British chart. Highly rhythmic and melodic, it demonstrated the group's instrumental virtuosity, particularly in Mason's pseudo-Indian guitar line and Winwood's electric harpsichord, two constituents at the cutting edge of musical fashion. Along with a handful of other songs, such as "Itchycoo Park" by The Small Faces and "I Can Hear The Grass Grow" by The Move, it managed to encapsulate the special mood of that summer, and their follow-up single, "Hole In My Shoe" (1967), was even more successful, reaching #2 in Britain and selling a million copies.

As anticipated by the singles, Traffic's first album, MR. FANTASY (1967), included some good psychedelia, particularly with "Heaven Is In Your Mind" and "House For Everyone", but it also passed through a range of other styles then in vogue – "Berkshire Poppies", for instance, with its knock-about inebriate humour, mimicked the quasi-vaudevillian work of The Kinks. The fact that none of the hit singles was featured emphasized that Traffic wished to be taken seriously as a progressive-rock band – they were happy enough to issue singles, but were principally concerned with albums.

Their next album, TRAFFIC (1968), demonstrated a considerable development in technical and com-

positional expertise. Winwood's "Don't Be Sad" established the yearning idealism of his best songwriting, while "Vagabond Virgin" featured one of Capaldi's finest lyrics, sympathetically portraying a teenage prostitute. Mason's "Feelin' Alright?" was later recorded by Joe Cocker, Grand Funk Railroad and Three Dog Night.

Traffic split up in December 1968 and, early the next year, LAST EXIT, an unsatisfactory set made up of studio and live recordings, was released and failed to chart. Wood joined Dr. John's backing group. Mason made a solo album, ALONE TOGETHER (1970), which featured Wood and Capaldi among the cast, and subsequently had a successful career collaborating with the likes of **Cass Elliott** (previously with The Mamas & The Papas). Meanwhile, Winwood formed **Blind Faith** with **ERIC CLAPTON**, **Ginger Baker** and **Rick Grech**. In just a few months this wrily named 'supergroup' made their eponymous album, performed to a crowd of 100,000 in London's Hyde Park, completed a traumatic US tour, and disbanded. Winwood was then briefly a member of Ginger Baker's similarly over-ambitious **Air Force**.

Chastened by these experiences, Winwood's next project was intended to be a solo album, but when Wood and Capaldi were called in for session work Traffic was re-formed. The resulting album, JOHN BARLEYCORN MUST DIE (1970), might be considered Traffic's masterwork. With the focus resting on Wood's flute and sax and Winwood's keyboards and vocals, the material showed Traffic at their most creative and included some of their finest instrumental performances. For the traditional ballad "John Barleycorn", for example, they employed acoustic guitar, flute, a little bit of piano and sparse percussion to back Winwood's vocal.

The band's distinctive format at this time probably placed too much pressure on Winwood, however, and at the end of 1970 Traffic became a quartet with the addition of bassist **Rick Grech**, previously a member of **FAMILY**, Blind Faith and Air Force. Early

the next year, the African percussionist **Reebop Kwaku Baah** also joined. For Traffic's UK tour during May and June, **Jim Gordon** from **Derek And The Dominoes** took over Capaldi's position at the drums and Mason temporarily rejoined the band. This line-up performed on the live album WELCOME TO THE CANTEEN (1971).

Comprising Winwood, Capaldi, Wood, Kwaku Baah, Grech and Gordon, Traffic then made THE LOW SPARK OF HIGH HEELED BOYS (1971). The desultory twelve-minute title track concerned the travails of rock musicians and the dreams of their fans. The similarly autobiographical "Rock'N'Roll Stew" was more melodic and concise, but arguably the best track was "Many A Mile To Freedom", on which Capaldi's lyric was tailor-made for the Winwood treatment.

Following a US tour early in 1972, Winwood fell seriously ill, making the band inactive for the rest of the year. Grech and Gordon had been replaced by American session musicians **David Hood** and **Roger Hawkins** before SHOOT OUT AT THE FANTASY FACTORY (1973), and this new rhythm section operated more effectively with the rest of Traffic than did their immediate forerunners. The album featured Kwaku Baah's best studio contributions for the band and also showed that Winwood was able at last to give a decent guitar solo. Meanwhile, Traffic made a successful world tour, from which came the excellent live album ON THE ROAD (1973), recorded in Germany.

The following studio album, WHEN THE EAGLE FLIES (1974), showed that Traffic's inspiration was nearly exhausted. Their virtuosity was still there in good measure, but Winwood appeared to be copying his earlier compositions instead of finding new forms of expression, and Capaldi's lyrics were becoming merely pretentious. Surprisingly, perhaps, this album reached #31 in the UK chart, making it Traffic's best-selling British release in the 70s. Traffic then made another US tour, shortly after which the band broke up. Their final appearance was at Reading Festival on August 31, 1974.

After the demise of the band, Capaldi enjoyed a couple of years' commercial success as a solo artist, including SHORT CUT DRAW BLOOD (1975) which featured **Paul Kossoff** (of Free), **Chris Spedding** (of Sharks) and Winwood. Steve Winwood's subsequent career began quietly but gained momentum, culminating with his slick 1980s albums, ARC OF A DIVER, TALKING BACK TO THE NIGHT, BACK IN THE HIGHLIFE and ROLL WITH IT.

Winwood and Capaldi re-formed Traffic as a duo in 1994 and made the album FAR FROM HOME. **Davy Spillane** contributed uillean pipes on "Holy Ground", and **Mick Dolan** rhythm guitar on "Nowhere Is Their Freedom", but otherwise all the instruments and vocals were handled by Winwood and Capaldi. The style of this album originated more from Winwood's solo activities in the 80s than from Traffic as it used to be, however, and it was a disappointing set, with Capaldi's lyrics well below par and the duo too much in the thrall of technology to produce much by way of soul.

⊙ **Traffic** (1968; Island).
The best album from the original band, and one showing Mason's songwriting at its peak – he contributed half of the material.

⊙ **John Barleycorn Must Die** (1970; Island).
Traffic's most eclectic and technically adventurous album. The band demonstrates an equal facility for jazz-rock, R&B and traditional folk music.

⊙ **On The Road** (1973; Island).
Marvellous live renditions of "Glad"/"Freedom Rider", "Tragic Muse", "Shoot Out At The Fantasy Factory", "Light Up Or Leave Me Alone" (and more) make this a more enduring outing than either Low Spark or Shoot Out.

Martin Haggerty

THE TRAGICALLY HIP

Formed Kingston, Ontario, Canada, 1986.

"Canadians and Americans are so intertwined, it's so hard to tell the difference." Bobby Baker

When discussing the past twenty or so years in rock music, Canada often gets a bad rap. And why not? This, after all, is the country that has produced Bryan Adams, Triumph and Loverboy, to name a few of the bigger acts. Often overlooked, however, is Canada's claim to hall-of-fame rockers such as Neil Young and The Band, perhaps because their music sounds so darn American. But, while both The Band and Young have largely been assimilated into US rock culture, writing songs straight from America's heartland, they have done so with a perspective only possible from growing up Canadian.

The Tragically Hip have spent the past fifteen years positioning themselves as Canada's top band, and they, too, are firmly planted in the same perspective. Though their straightforward brand of rock seems as if it could have come from Texas, California or Ohio, their songs have a strong sense of place, seemingly derived from Wallace Stegner's books and a deep love for their national sport, ice hockey.

Formed in 1986 by **Gordon Downie** (vocals), **Bobby Baker** (guitar), **Paul Langlois** (guitar), **Gord Sinclair** (bass) and **Johnny Fay** (drums), The Tragically Hip claim to have taken their name from an episode of Michael Nesmith's show *Elephant Parts* (though the phrase had been prominent earlier in Elvis Costello's song "Town Crier"). Signed to MCA, they released their self-titled debut the following year. Its tight, bluesy music belied their poseur name and established the blueprint for their guitar-driven amalgamation of styles ranging from British blues-rock to Southern country-rock – not too distant from The Black Crowes. Downie's growl, though not overly agile, was well suited to the tough melodies of the twin-guitar attack.

While sales were steadily increasing and the albums – Road Apples (1991) and Fully Completely

(1992) – were becoming more self-assured, the band failed to consolidate on their fanatical Canadian following with an international name for themselves. And that's despite touring with Young, The Rolling Stones, and Page And Plant, and organizing and headlining the 1995 Another Roadside Attraction music festival. The tuneful album, Trouble At The Henhouse (1996), which had wider distribution, and reviewers namechecking the band as 'a Canadian R.E.M.' attempted to turn things round. Phantom Power (1998) and In Violet Light (2002) managed to confirm their position as the best Canadian rock'n'roll band never to make it big in the US.

⊙ **Road Apples** (1991; MCA).
A good intro to their earthy rock, though strangely the highlight is the sleepy, acoustic "Fiddler's Green".

⊙ **Fully Completely** (1992; MCA).
The cream of The Hip's records, a solid collection from the opener "Courage", one of their best songs, to the charming album-ender "Eldorado".

Nomi Malone

TRANS AM

Formed Washington DC, 1992.

"I definitely like to play rock shows, but I also like the idea of anonymous performers sitting behind a bank of equipment... " Phil Manley

Drawing on influences from King Crimson, ZZ Top and Kraftwerk, **Phil Manley** (guitars/keyboards), **Nathan Means** (bass/keyboards) and **Sebastian Thompson** (drums/programming) formed at high school in Washington DC. They soon began incorporating overdriven Casio keyboards into the power-trio rock format, and gigging occasionally while finishing college and releasing a split 7" with Thigh Masterssen on the S.K.A.M. label

Thanks to the efforts of **TORTOISE**'s ubiquitous John McEntire, their first extended recording appeared as a self-titled debut on the home of American post-rock, Thrill Jockey, in 1995. Taken from a series of improvised instrumental jams produced by McEntire, the rock element was well to the fore, occasionally recalling the complexities of Shellac, and including the anthemic "American Kooter" (from the S.K.A.M. single) and the Van Halen arpeggios of "Orlando". Mixed in with the traditional rockisms were several moments of lo-fi keyboard noodling which occasionally filtered into the other songs, with even some Miles Davis influence apparent.

Trans Am began to hone their live sound on tour with Tortoise, but it was with the absorption of the avant-electronica of Autechre, Aphex Twin and Squarepusher that they began to push the envelope of so-called post-rock. The first recorded results were released as the "Illegal Ass" EP (1996), a stunning mix of rock with breakbeats and a hefty slice of disco to boot. With the addition of samplers, more keyboards and drum machines to their extensive equipment list, the group worked on perfecting their second album throughout 1996.

SURRENDER TO THE NIGHT (1997) was the result, opening with keyboard ambience and machine hum before kicking into the soaring guitar surge of "Motr" and the electro pulses of "Cologne" (reworked from "Illegal Ass"), followed by a complex construction of breakbeats, Kraftwerk bleeps, Michael Rother guitar melodies and not-quite drum'n'bass grooves. With the rock element toned down but never entirely absent – "Rough Justice" explodes with extreme distortion – SURRENDER TO THE NIGHT sounded almost like an eclectic and inventive compilation.

The follow-up, THE SURVEILLANCE (1998) was recorded live in their home-built studio – The Bridge – to dark and brooding effect. By stripping their sound down to match the energy of their live shows, the band produced an edgy work focused on paranoia and the constant fear of crime in American cities. After that, the almost breezy synthetic sounds of FUTUREWORLD (1999) were a welcome relief – cuts like the storming heads-down dystopian growler "City In Flames" shot through with blasts of comparative optimism. Then the "Who Do We Think You Are" EP (1999) skimmed along the future-rock out-groove with funky results. Album releases on Tokuma in Japan had up to ten extra tracks, and some of these versions and live cuts were compiled into YOU CAN ALWAYS GET WHAT YOU WANT (2000). Their most recent albums proper were RED LINE (2000), a more rock-heavy affair with strong doses of experimentalism stirred into the mix, and TA (2002), a broader-ranging set of electro guitar-fuelled sonic assaults.

With widespread critical acclaim (even getting a Dance Chart #1 in Singapore), Trans Am have produced at least a couple of classic records in a scene which abounds in innovative and cross-fertilized projects. Synth/guitar-based prog-rock has made some kind of a noisy comeback, in Trans Am's case in a shiny new digital guise with a knowing edge and sharp suits to boot.

⊙ **Trans Am** (1996; Thrill Jockey/City Slang).
Mini-album on 10" vinyl and CD, switching between prog-rock, boogie and Casio-keyboard workouts. "Firepoker" and "Prowler" mix the elements most successfully in a sketchy but promising debut.

⊙ **Surrender To The Night** (1997; Thrill Jockey/City Slang).
Another John McEntire/Trans Am co-production, ranging from the lo-fi drum'n'bass of "Tough Love" and "Night Dancing" to the Neu!-influenced "Carboforce", while still retaining the Casios for "Night Dreaming". Brimming with ideas, but with solid foundations in several decades of electronic and traditional rock music.

⊙ **The Surveillance** (1998; Thrill Jockey/City Slang).
A compact and energetic combination of the sinister electro-rock of "Access Control" and "Home Security" segues into the clean production values of rockouts like

"Shadow Boogie" and "Stereo Situation" like no one else on the planet.

⊙ **You Can Always Get What You Want** (2000; Thrill Jockey).
Essential collection of almost all the rare EP tracks, including a goofy cover of Kraftwerk's "Man-Machine". Not exactly a record for Trans Am beginners, expecting polished album continuity, but a vital release for all devotees.

Richard Fontenoy

TRAVELING WILBURYS

Formed Los Angeles, 1988.

The idea for the **Traveling Wilburys** was reputed to have been hatched at the home of **Dave Stewart**, producer and one-time Eurythmic. The participants in the project were big names: **BOB DYLAN, GEORGE HARRISON, ROY ORBISON, TOM PETTY** and **Jeff Lynne**. They had already worked together – Petty had played with Dylan and Orbison, Harrison had worked with Dylan, and Lynne had produced albums for Petty, Orbison and Harrison – so they got together, jammed, found they enjoyed each other's company, and wrote a batch of songs.

In the studio Harrison and Lynne turned their hands to production and the result was an album called TRAVELING WILBURYS VOLUME 1 (1988). A mythical band, the Wilbury Brothers, was devised as a cover: Dylan was Lucky Wilbury, Harrison was Nelson, Lynne Otis, Orbison Lefty and Petty Charlie. To complete the ruse, the famous five appeared on the album in disguise.

Such a project could easily have been a hugely embarrassing exercise in ego-massaging. Instead it turned out to be an unqualified success. "Handle With Care", a Harrison vocal with a tremulous Orbison refrain, provided the album with a hit single and set the tone for the rest of the tracks. Acoustic guitars dominated the mix, augmented by **Jim Keltner**'s big drum sound and a terrific, wraparound production job. The album featured lead vocals from all the participants and included a batch of what some critics regarded as Dylan's best songs for years. "Last Night", for instance, was infused with a humour that hadn't been apparent in his recent work, while the saga of "Tweeter And The Monkey Man" might have graced BLOOD ON THE TRACKS.

Most had expected that it would be the only outing for the Wilburys, especially after the death of Roy Orbison, just as his career was starting to take off again. But, in 1990, TRAVELING WILBURYS VOLUME 3 appeared. Once again Keltner hit the skins, and there were return appearances for **Ray Cooper** (percussion) and **Jim Horn** (saxophone). Special guest on the single, "She's My Baby", was **Gary Moore**, whose lead guitar dominated. This track apart, the songs picked up where the previous set left off. Dylan recounted the "7 Deadly Sins" as Petty described a "Cool Dry Place"; Harrison explained how some girl "Took My Breath Away" and Lynne led them through a jaunty "New Blue

TRANS AM ■ TRAVELING WILBURYS

Moon". Together they taught us all to do the "Wilbury Twist", complete with illustrated sleeve notes.

The joke was perhaps wearing a little thin – the names had changed this time out to Boo, Spike, Clayton and Muddy Wilbury – but it was still great to hear them in such fine form. What chance a third album with, say, Brian Wilson?

⊙ **Traveling Wilburys Volume 1** (1988; Warners).
The first and best, featuring the Big O (who gets to sing a typical up-tempo ballad, "Not Alone Any More") and Dylan very near to his best.

Simon Ives

TRAVIS

Formed Glasgow, Scotland, 1990.

The surname of an American country singer and the Christian name of the lead character in Scorsese's *Taxi Driver*, **Travis** is also the moniker of a Scottish quartet who emerged just as the Britpop bubble was bursting to remind people why they'd got so excited about UK music in the first place.

Three art-school lads from Glasgow, **Fran Healy** (singer, songwriter), **Andy Dunlop** (guitar), **Dougie Payne** (bass), and a bloke they met in a pub, **Neil Primrose** (drums), formed Travis back in 1990, but few had heard of the band until their signing to Andy 'Go! Discs' McDonald's new Independiente label in 1996 on the strength of their self-pressed ALL I WANNA DO IS ROCK EP of the same year. This deal, combined with hard gigging and the inevitable move south to London, saw that Travis's reputation was soon cemented. Tours with Oasis and Catatonia primed the indie masses for the debut album release, ensuring that 1997's GOOD FEELING went straight into the Top Ten. Tracks such as the barnstorming single "U16 Girls" showed that rock was the main focus of the band's intentions, and being cited as Noel Gallagher's favourite band at that time must have made the pigeon-holing clear, despite the presence of several soul-searching ballads.

Several years later, however, Travis made a very different record. THE MAN WHO (2000) was, the band claimed, 'an album for staying in rather than going out'. Banging in at #1 in the UK album charts, the set spawned endless accolades and numerous hit singles, including the tender "Writing To Reach You", "Driftwood" and the festival favourite, "Why Does It Always Rain On Me?". Reaching a more mature audience, the boys moved from the *NME* Brat Awards to the Brit Awards, winning *Best British Group* and *Best Album* in 2000. Credit could be, in part, attributed to the use of producer **Nigel Godrich** (Beck, Radiohead, The Divine Comedy), as well as the lyrical coming of age of Healy.

Travis's radio-friendly angst led to criticisms that they were little more than ambassadors for Blair's Britain: pleasant, yet dangerously devoid of substance. A little harsh, perhaps, but their next album, THE INVISIBLE BAND (2001), certainly lacked the strength to overpower its predecessor. Despite Healy's proclamation that 'these songs are so much bigger than us!', with the exception of the opening track, the single "Sing", it seemed that the band might have had some concerns about their stature. "Flowers In The Window", for example, was as lazy and spoon-fed as the worst of the band's oeuvre can be, while it was the gentle, swelling highpoints of THE MAN WHO that perfectly captured Travis's capacity and, one can only hope, their potential.

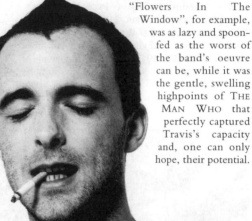

Fran Healy contemplating his next visit to the hairdresser

STEVE GULLICK

⊙ **Good Feeling** (1997; Independiente).
This set simply does what all good albums do: hits all the right notes and leaves no emotion untouched.

⊙ **The Man Who** (1999; Independiente).
This is the sort of poetically melancholic album Thom Yorke would love to write but is too self-involved to accomplish. Not only one of the records of 1999 but one of the better albums of the late 90s.

Annebella Pollen & Richard Luck

T REX

Formed 1968; extinction 1977.

"I'm relivin' my childhood at 18. I'm old, just too old." Marc Bolan, 1966

TRex started out as **Tyrannosaurus Rex** in 1968, back in the days when you could get away with album titles like MY PEOPLE WERE FAIR AND HAD SKY IN THEIR HAIR ... BUT NOW THEY'RE CONTENT TO WEAR STARS ON THEIR BROWS. Guitarist and vocalist **Marc Bolan** (born Mark Feld, London, 1947) had recorded a couple of singles earlier in the decade, but it wasn't until he hooked up with the improbably named **Steve Peregrine Took** (bongos/vocals) that he created any sort of ripples in the UK hippie ooze.

"Deborah", the first Tyrannosaurus Rex single, backed with the beautiful "Child Star", attracted the attention of DJ John Peel, who boosted the single and the band's subsequent four albums on his radio shows – as well as making a guest appearance on the debut album, reading a poem.

Bolan's cute looks (he'd previously worked as a model) and the unadulterated nonsense of his early lyrics were sufficient to make him an underground hero, and there were many concerts played to audiences of denim and afghan before Bolan cut the name down to pop size, ditched Steve Took (who slunk off to play with **THE PINK FAIRIES**), strapped on an electric guitar and made his bid for stardom. His new bongo-playing sidekick, the equally unlikely monikered **Micky Finn**, helped out on A BEARD OF STARS (1970), the album with which Bolan moved from acoustic LSD-tinged ramblings about prophets and magic to roaring rock'n'roll ramblings about prophets and magic. The stardom kicked in soon after with "Ride A White Swan", a bouncy, basic little rocker that encouraged Britain's pop kids to wear a tall hat and a tattooed gown. It went to #2 in the UK and with a puff of magic powder Bolan was the most gorgeous, pouting, corkscrew-haired pop star in town.

Drafting in **Steve Curry** as full-time bass player and **Bill Legend** as drummer, Bolan followed the hit single with a fairly uninspiring album, T REX

The Groover, grooving

(1970), that looked back to 'Summer Of Love' folderol. Never mind, the new band knocked out two smash singles "Hot Love" and "Get It On" (released as "Bang A Gong" in the US, where it charted at #10), both selling ridiculous quantities and hitting the top of the UK charts. ELECTRIC WARRIOR (1971), the first real T Rex album in most eyes, had loads of strutting guitar boogie, breath taking vocals and meaningless lyrics, and sold everywhere by the truckload. (A collection of alternative takes, B-sides and studio chat, ELECTRIC WARRIOR SESSIONS (Pilot) came out in 1997.)

During a period when bands were either serious 'album musicians' or were written off as singles-based chart fodder, Bolan managed to sell both. The early 70s albums – ELECTRIC WARRIOR, SLIDER, TANX and the thrill-has-gone-tinged ZINC ALLOY AND THE NEW RIDERS OF TOMORROW – were all proper albums, with themes and extended compositions, quite different from traditional pop industry cash-ins. That said, it was the singles that kids waited and saved their pocket money for. "Jeepster", "Telegram Sam", "Metal Guru", the sub-metal raunch of "Children Of The Revolution", the driving guitar exuberance of "Solid Gold Easy Action", the magnificent "20th Century Boy" and "The Groover" all went to the top end of the UK charts.

Pop groups, if they're very lucky, canny and well managed, can extend the mania that surrounds them to around three years. Bolan had three years as a pop idol. He had the whole range of rock-hero postures, he sang, he danced, he played guitar, and he slapped on the make-up and sparkle, thus virtually inventing 'glitter pop' and thereby being ultimately responsible for innumerable sins against taste. He starred in a film about the band, *Born To Boogie* (once again, a better-quality product than normally produced by pop bands), did interviews and photo-shoots, told countless teenagers his deepest secrets (like 'favourite colour', 'what do you look for in a girlfriend', 'what makes you sad') and generally played the Star.

It ended in mid 1973, as "The Groover" slid down the charts. It was around this time that he split with his wife, June Child, taking up instead with the powerfully voiced Gloria Jones, who had recorded the original version of "Tainted Love" (later to be covered by Marc Almond's Soft Cell) and had been working with the band as a backing vocalist for some months. T Rex's next single, "Truck On Tyke", did respectably but not well enough to prevent Marc and Gloria opting for exile in the US.

T Rex – or Marc Bolan & T Rex as they were often marketed – produced a few good songs in the mid 70s: "New York City" was fine, old-style raunch; "Dreamy Lady" had enough reverb to carry it along; and "I Love To Boogie" was no sillier than many of his other lyrics. But what really relaunched Bolan's career, alas, was his death in 1977. Gloria wrapped a yellow mini round an old oak tree on

September 16 and Marc attained instant pop immortality.

The cult of Marc shows no sign of dying out. Since 1977 there have been TV documentaries, innumerable compilations of 'greatest hits' and rarities (the most outlandish being a 92-track, three-CD monster called A WIZARD, A TRUE STAR released on Edsel in 1997) and a couple of peculiar 'tribute bands' featuring lookalike singers and ex-band members. He might not be selling in the millions these days, but play "Get It On" at a party even today and look for the grins of joy it sparks.

⊙ **Electric Warrior** (1971; Castle).
Teenage music at its best. Trashy, sleazy, drug-induced nonsense, screamed as if it were the meaning of life, all mixed up to perfection by Tony Visconti. Add clanging, power guitar, loads of hummable hooks and riffs and there you have it – instant boogie.

⊙ **Slider** (1972; Edsel).
More of the above. Glam-rock at its best, including "Metal Guru", "Buick McKane" and "Baby Boomerang".

⊙ **Bolan Boogie** (1989; Castle).
'Greatest hits' selection with the emphasis on the pre-electric stuff.

⊙ **The Ultimate Collection** (1991; Telstar).
A late-period 'greatest hits'. Pretty much all the singles worth having, plus a couple of tracks that aren't. If you can't get hold of this one, don't worry – there are plenty of rival anthologies.

⊙ **The BBC Recordings** (1998; NMC).
32 tracks of pure pop pleasure, this is the complete BBC stock of Marc in one convenient package. There's an accompanying EXTENDED PLAY (1998; NMC) containing seven tracks as a kind of postscript; more for the ardent completist than for the fan who actually listens to Bolan's stuff.

Al Spicer

TRICKY

Born Bristol, England, 1964.

Adrian Thawes was born and raised in Knowle West, Bristol, where from a very young age he was involved with a gang whose principal pursuits were chasing girls, fighting, burglary and stealing cars. Known as the weird one of his posse, **Tricky Kid** (his nickname) immersed himself in petty crime, soft drugs, psychedelics, his grandmother's Nina Simone records, The Specials and rap. After a short but traumatic time in youth custody, Tricky met **Miles Johnson**, and began hanging around with a group of Bristol musicians and various collaborators later to be known as the **Wild Bunch**, one of whom was **Nellee Hooper**, who was to achieve worldwide fame producing the likes of Soul II Soul, Björk and U2. Losing touch with his partners in petty crime, Tricky wrote ever more surreal raps and he became loosely involved with **MASSIVE ATTACK**, a collective of various members of the Wild Bunch.

His first recorded material – a claustrophobic dub-reggae piece called "Nothing's Clear" – appeared in 1991, on a compilation album entitled THE HARD SELL, which raised money for local charities. (The track was produced by Tricky and **Geoff Barrow**,

who would go on to form **PORTISHEAD** with Beth Gibbons.) Although he contributed to three tracks on Massive Attack's acclaimed debut album, BLUE LINES, and two more on the follow-up, PROTECTION, Tricky was never really part of the nucleus of the band, and felt somewhat isolated when Miles Johnson left the Wild Bunch.

As legend has it, one day, hanging around outside a local private school, Tricky began chatting to a girl called **Martina**, and invited her over to his flat. When she arrived, several days later, Tricky was out, so she got stoned with his flatmate, **Mark Stewart** (one-time **POP GROUP** singer), who discovered she had a great voice. Days later they recorded "Aftermath", which Tricky duly presented to Massive Attack. They were not impressed. He decided it was time to start working alone.

The fruits of this work surfaced in mid 1994. "Aftermath" was a slow, haunting, narcotic slab of hip-hop blues, while "Ponderosa", the drunken follow-up, contained the line 'I drink 'til I'm drunk, and smoke 'til I'm senseless', and climaxed with a rickety, rattling piano crescendo.

Tricky's debut album, MAXINQUAYE, was released at the beginning of 1995 when everybody involved with British music was talking about 'the Bristol scene' of Massive Attack and Portishead. But MAXINQUAYE blew them both away. Buried underneath a doped-out cloud of studio effects, eerie strings and blunted rhythms were Tricky's tales of paranoia, claustrophobia, fear and sexual dysfunction. Not since disco and punk reigned supreme had there been an album that took nothing for granted and rearranged stable reference points with such a brutal disregard. MAXINQUAYE was a stunning album and greeted as such by a fawning music press.

1996 saw Tricky's **Nearly God** project – a series of collaborations between Tricky, Martina, **Terry Hall**, **Alison Moyet**, **Neneh Cherry** and **Damon Albarn**. The resultant album, NEARLY GOD, with its crawling strings and sedated vocals, explored similar territory to MAXINQUAYE without quite the same brilliance.

Tricky's second album in his own name, PRE-MILLENNIUM TENSION (1996), pushed the hip-hop envelope still further, calling up the devil's own collection of muffled, dirty loops as the only suitable backing for the Tricky Kid's special brew of marijuana-stoked paranoia. With Martina's mysterioso vocals drifting in and out like a nosy landlady, the thoroughly angry street chat of disgruntled street yout' and Tricky's own wheezing words of miserable wisdom shaking trees and baiting the bourgeois, PMT may turn out to be an UNKNOWN PLEASURES for the new millennium.

ANGELS WITH DIRTY FACES (1998) is no less difficult, tense and unrelenting in its bleakness; while he continues to make edginess his trademark it's not surprising that with such a constant sense of threat inherent in the music that his audience is being scared off. Respite of sorts comes with Polly Harvey's vocal on "Broken Homes", but many wondered if he'd lost touch – I mean, how much does anyone really care about artists moaning about their record companies (on… er… "Record Companies").

The 1999 collaboration with Cypress Hill's DJ Muggs and DMX's Grease on JUXTAPOSE hinted at an attempt for broader appeal and in places (the formidable "She Said" and the essential opener "For Real") it really works. Too much of it sounds like off-cuts from previous efforts, however, and it doesn't grasp the hip-hop aesthetic as much as his collaborators would imply.

BLOWBACK (2001) was a collection of familiar stoned paranoia; the Tricky kid picked up a few rock co-stars in the shape of **Ed Kowalcyzk** (Live), **Anthony Kiedis** and **John Frusciante** of Red Hot Chili Peppers and – gasp – **Cyndi Lauper**. Had he lost his mind? Well, certainly not enough to go anywhere really interesting. Equally, 2003's VULNERABLE failed to hit the mark and found Tricky seemingly grasping at straws with a cover of The Cure's "The Love Cats".

Frightening, end-of-the-millennium psychosis might have been all the rage when Tricky exploded onto the scene, but, while his music is still interesting for the persistent few, Tricky is seemingly less and less able to tap into the minds of his punters.

Maxinquaye (1995; Island).
A brilliantly out-of-focus chaotic debut album: hip-hop blues, rolling skank-hop beats, sheets of sampled guitar, ghostly, androgynous vocals, shimmering keyboard textures, samples from Bladerunner and a cover of Public Enemy's "Black Steel In The Hour Of Chaos". A truly unique modern classic.

Andy Shields

THE TRIFFIDS

Formed Perth, Australia, 1980; disbanded 1989.

L ed by Velvet Underground fan **David McComb** (vocals/guitar/piano), Perth band **The Triffids** were completed by his brother **Robert** (violin/guitar/keyboards/vocals), **Martin Casey** (bass/vocals), **Phil Kakulas** (keyboards; replaced by **Jill Birt**, keyboards/vocals) and **Alsy McDonald** (drums/vocals).

A major influence on the group's sound was their geographical location. Isolated on the west coast of Australia, Perth backs onto a huge, empty desert that infused The Triffids' early work with a feeling of emptiness and loneliness. TREELESS PLAIN (1983) and RAINING PLEASURE (1984) were their first LPs, but it was their third album which brought them to the attention of record buyers. BORN SANDY DEVOTIONAL (1986) was an achingly beautiful, languid record, filled with McComb's epic sprawling songs and majestic raw vocals, along with the intimate slide guitar of new member **'Evil' Graham Lee**. Highlights included the monumental "Wide Open Road" and the mid-tempo ballad "Stolen Property".

Mere months after the release of this atmospheric masterpiece they came up with IN THE PINES (1986), which was recorded in a wool-shearing shed in the outback – and frankly sounded like it. CALENTURE (1987), with new guitarist **Adam Peters**, was a haunting, heart-rending return to form. Gil Norton's production emphasized McComb's vocals and songwriting, especially on the lamenting "A Trick Of The Light" and on the mournful "Jerdacuttup Man", for which McComb assumed the spirit of a skeleton found at an archeological dig.

CALENTURE may have been a classic, but its failure to trouble the charts prompted The Triffids to seek out Morrissey producer Stephen Street, who worked with them on 1989's THE BLACK SWAN. The production was certainly bright and sparkling, but an overabundance of gloss was applied to some fundamental cracks in the songwriting. The singles were poppy, particularly "Goodbye Little Boy", but the best songs were the country-tinged ballads evoking the Australian outback, specifically the gorgeous "Too Hot To Move, Too Hot To Sleep" and "New Year's Greetings".

By the end of 1989, The Triffids were bored by their lack of commercial success, and they disbanded, leaving behind a live recording, STOCKHOLM, which was finally issued in 1990. McComb eventually embarked on a solo career, and his excellent 1994 album LOVE OF WILL contained all The Triffids' best elements, from the expansive and majestic ballads to the country-rock meetings. Live with backing band **The Red Ponies**, he was more rock than on record, while his garage-rock roots were emphasized on some Velvet Underground covers.

On Saturday January 30, 1999, Dave McComb was involved in a car accident. He was not badly injured, spent the night in hospital, was released on the Sunday and went home to recuperate. A heart transplant recipient, he died suddenly in his Northcote home on February 2. In recent years McComb had been working with another group he formed, called Co-Star, which had been performing mainly in Melbourne. Another sad loss to the rock-'n'roll community worldwide...

⊙ **Australian Melodrama** (The Best Of The Triffids) (1994; Mushroom).
Complete with a live version of "In The Pines", and the lush "Bury Me Deep In Love", this essential purchase is a greatest hits package from a band who cruelly had no hits.

Mike Martin

THE TROGGS

Formed Andover, England, 1964.

"None of us were drug-mad; we had enough trouble with beer and Scotch." Chris Britton

Britain's most durable garage band, **The Troggs** were formed in 1964 in Andover, a charmless backwater of Hampshire. Of the original line-up – **Reg Presley** (vocals), **Chris Britton** (guitar), **Pete Staples** (bass) and **Ronnie Bond** (drums) – Presley and Britton remain in action, Staples having left when the hits ran out in 1968, and Bond in the late 80s.

In 1965 the band sent a demo to the London publisher/producer Larry Page, then riding high with The Kinks. Intrigued by a version of "You Really Got Me" that was more raucous than the original, he told them to come back in a year's time; exactly a year later, they returned and were signed to his label, Page One.

From the outset the band was primitive. While British music was getting mellow and expanding its horizons, The Troggs used the most elementary three-chord power riffs, with lyrics expressing little more than a need to get laid. When Reginald Maurice Ball changed his name to Reg Presley, he was aiming at the smouldering sensuality of his new namesake; instead he projected leering lasciviousness.

The second single shot the group to stardom. "Wild Thing" was an instant classic, a record that redefined the limits of just how wonderfully dumb rock could be. A chord sequence stolen from "Louie Louie" was topped with words that sounded like the scribblings on a beer mat after a frat party. A work of idiot genius, it went to #2 in the UK in 1966 and inspired hundreds of covers, including, most famously, Hendrix at Monterey and Tone-Loc's rap rework. With five minutes left at the end of the session, the band knocked out the follow-up, a Presley original "With A Girl Like You". Their only #1, it introduced their distinctive backing vocals, as basic as their musicianship. Two more Top 10 hits – "I Can't Control Myself" and "Any Way That You Want Me" – rounded off a spectacular year.

Thereafter, the going got tougher. 1967 yielded just one big hit, the mock-anthemic "Love Is All Around", which slowed down the "Wild Thing" chords and inadvertently caught the spirit of the 'Summer Of Love'. Subsequent releases saw a desperate lurch at every available bandwagon in a futile search for hits: acid ("Maybe The Madmen"), rock-'n'roll ("Surprise Surprise"), bubblegum ("Hip Hip Hooray"), heavy metal ("Feels Like A Woman") – all were filtered through a joyous cider-punk sensibility.

By keeping faith with three-chord three-minute thrashes, the band ensured that the tide of fashion would eventually restore them. A late-70s tour of the American punk circuit won them a new audience, and 'The Troggs Tape' – a bootleg of a protracted four-letter squabble – proved a key influence on Spinal Tap.

In the 90s the group had an unlikely collaboration with R.E.M., following their cover of "Love Is All Around", bringing new respectability, whilst Wet Wet Wet's 1994 version of the same song (used in the movie *Four Weddings And A Funeral*) brought Presley undreamt-of wealth; he promised to spend it on an investigation of crop circles. The Troggs' original remains the best. A series of trite clichés, the song only works when Reg's drooling makes it clear he doesn't mean a word of it; he's just trying to get some action: 'If you really love me, come on and let it show.'

An intriguing document of the band at their height was released in 1997. THE EP COLLECTION, released on the praiseworthy See For Miles label, assembles all the most enjoyable cuts from the English and French EPs they put out in the 60s – highly recommended. FROM NOWHERE and TROGGLODYNAMITE (1997) were released on a single CD at around the same time and serve as a reminder of why 'singles bands' didn't make albums in the 60s – not recommended.

⊙ **Live At Max's Kansas City** (1980; Max's Kansas City).
Recorded during their tour of American punk clubs, this gives a clue to the band's longevity. The songs are played exactly the same as they always were, and the sheer simplicity wows a generation raised on the Ramones. On a good night, they still sound this exuberant.

⊙ **Archeology** (1992; Fontana).
A double-CD retrospective of the first twenty years. 52

tracks featuring everything you need, plus a couple of disasters. A bonus CD has extracts from 'The Troggs Tape', including their recipe for chart success: 'Sprinkle some fucking fairydust on the bastard.'

⊙ **Greatest Hits** (1994; Polygram).
Released in the wake of Wet Wet Wet, a solid 25-track compilation, including the best of the R.E.M. collaborations.

Alwyn W. Turner

ROBIN TROWER

Born London, 1945.

"It's impossible to play a run with as much feeling as a single note."

One of the most distinctive guitarists to emerge from London, **Robin Trower** spent the early 60s in Southend-based R&B band The Paramounts, before forming an offshoot trio called The Jam, while his former allies created the rather more successful **PROCOL HARUM**. Although Trower did not actually play on their 1967 UK #1, "A Whiter Shade Of Pale", he joined them on five of their albums, where instrumentals like "Repent Walpurgis" allowed his stinging, confident guitar lines full prominence.

Leaving Procol in 1971, Trower formed power combo **Jude** with **Frankie Miller** (vocals), **Jim Dewar** (bass/vocals) and former Jethro Tull drummer **Clive Bunker**, but the results were jumbled and undistinguished. Trower retained Dewar and added **Reg Isadore** in **The Robin Trower Band**, a more laid-back, funky affair, strongly influenced by Hendrix, with lots of space for solos and for Dewar's soulful vocals. Trower lacked Hendrix's experimental edge, but he had already mapped out a unique territory, integrating loud blues guitar into what became known as classical rock. With Dewar's impressive range of vocal styles, Trower's first two records – TWICE REMOVED FROM YESTERDAY (1973) and BRIDGE OF SIGHS (1974) – were the band's best, with an intensity and freshness all of their own.

Almost as good were FOR EARTH BELOW (1975) and LONG MISTY DAYS (1976), for which Isadore was replaced by ex-Sly And The Family Stone drummer **Bill Lordan**. The same band's **Rustee Allen** (bass) joined for Trower's most personal album, IN CITY DREAMS (1977), as well as CARAVAN TO MIDNIGHT (1978), a funkier effort, with the additional help of session percussionist **Paulhino Dacosta**.

In the light of punk, Trower's image had become that of a has-been, which possibly inspired the angry but brilliant 1980 album VICTIMS OF THE FURY, a collaboration with old Procol Harum colleague **Keith Reid**. Soon afterwards, The Robin Trower Band broke up and, by 1981, Trower had formed **BLT** with Lordan and **Jack Bruce** (bass/vocals). The albums they produced, as compiled for 1989's NO STOPPING ANYTIME, rocked out righteously, with Bruce's thick bass tone spurring on Trower's lead lines. **Bruce & Trower** issued TRUCE (1982), but this, along with Trower's 1983 release BACK IT UP, was felt to be music well past its sell-by date, and so Chrysalis dropped the band from its roster.

After 1985's BEYOND THE MIST was issued on Music For Nations, Trower took a leaf from the New Wave and released the aptly named PASSION independently in 1987. Consequently, a fresh line-up of Trower, **David Bronze** (bass), **Davey Pattison** (vocals) and **Pete Thompson** (drums) was snapped up by Atlantic for TAKE WHAT YOU NEED (1988) and IN THE LINE OF FIRE (1990), which Trower himself described as being 'like making records by committee'.

Since then, he briefly rejoined Procol Harum for the stately yet bitter THE PRODIGAL STRANGER (1991) and a one-off live LP. He has produced two albums for Bryan Ferry, whom he claimed shared his affinity for 50s black music. Trower returned to solo work with 20TH CENTURY BLUES (1994), which climaxed with Lowell Fulson's "Reconsider Baby" – something which Trower has conspicuously never done, pursuing his love of the blues regardless of fashion. He's continued to tour, record and produce other artists throughout the 1990s, with his latest album SOMEDAY BLUES (1997) being the 'pure blues' session Trower had been promising for some time. It reunited the guitarist with drummer Reg Isadore, but Trower was now on lead vocals throughout for the first time.

Trower's back catalogue is being rereleased by BGO on CD as two for the price of one. TWICE REMOVED FROM YESTERDAY is paired with BRIDGE OF SIGHS, and FOR EARTH BELOW with LIVE, recorded in Stockholm and remixed by Trower himself and Geoff Emerick. The new CDs are remastered, with notes by Trower. An American import CD of an early performance recorded for King Biscuit Hour has recently hit the racks of larger British record stores (issued in Britain by Strange Fruit). Snap it up while it's there!

Robin Trower was notable by his absence at the recent Procol Harum reunion, which concluded with a live rendition of the magnum opus "In Held 'Twas I", surely inconceivable without Trower's stinging lead guitar. His early work with The Paramounts is collected on a new CD, THE PARAMOUNTS AT ABBEY ROAD 1963–1970, which also includes six previously unreleased rock'n'roll songs from a session recorded as **Liquorice John Death And The All Stars**.

- **Bridge Of Sighs** (1974; Chrysalis).
  Dewar shines as singer and co-writer on this string of hard-luck stories. The title track is a long, slow, hellish cry, ending with howling winds, but Trower is better on the more slow-burning offerings.

- **20th Century Blues** (1994; Demon).
  Livingstone Browne on vocals this time around, but fortunately for fans there's little change from Trower's basic formula, alternately riffing and providing lead lines.

- **Anthology** (1994; Connoisseur Collection).
  The pick of several compilations from Trower's Chrysalis output, because of its superior packaging, sleeve notes and modest price tag.

Brian Hinton

TRUE SOUNDS OF LIBERTY (TSOL)

Formed Los Angeles, 1980.

The True Sounds Of Liberty – TSOL – have had a messy and tangled career, even by the unruly standards of hardcore. Featuring **Ron Emory** (guitar), **Mike Roche** (bass), **Todd Barnes** (drums) and vocalist **Jack Greggors** (he changed his name on each album), they made their debut for Posh Boy Records with an eponymous EP, which provided pacy generic hardcore distinguished by strong musicianship and hearty vocals.

That style was partly abandoned for their debut album DANCE WITH ME (1981). Instead of sociopolitical analysis, the group now chose to zoom in on horror and pulp fiction themes, though the music's edgy but supple frame maintained some sense of continuity with the debut.

BENEATH THE SHADOWS (1981) provided further evidence of their volatility of approach. With the addition of keyboards from **Bob Kuehn** (later to work with Bob Dylan), this time TSOL occupied territory somewhere between mid-80s Damned (STRAWBERRIES) and Stranglers (THE RAVEN).

The multi-monikered lead singer departed in 1984 to join Cathedral Of Tears, then Tender Fury (naturally under another alias), and was replaced by **Joe Wood** (vocals/guitar), with **Mitch Dean** as the new drummer. The resultant CHANGE TODAY? (1984) lacked focus, and was the most dispensable of their early albums. From this point onwards, listeners could plot the decline of the band into tired glam-rock and heavy metal, though REVENGE (1986) did have some links with punk and hardcore stylings.

The remainder of TSOL's output in the late 80s and early 90s was crass and uninteresting. STRANGE LOVE (1990), in particular, was hideous. By this time all the group's original members had departed and re-formed as 'the original TSOL' to play revival shows, ensuring that competing line-ups were playing Los Angeles gigs on the same night under the same billing. As suitable an epitaph as any to a career thwarted by instability and personality clashes.

- **Thoughts Of Yesterday 1981–1982** (1987; Posh Boy).
  A welcome compilation of tracks from TSOL's hardcore days. It includes their best early composition, "Weathered Statues".

- **Beneath The Shadows** (1981; Alternative Tentacles).
  Though it confused their hardcore constituency, this is probably TSOL's most enduring record, combining punk rock gusto with more open-ended songwriting (the keyboard textures, in particular, give an impressive depth).

Alex Ogg

TRUMANS WATER

Formed San Diego, 1991.

"To our minds the only reason to make any structure at all is so you can destroy it – and maybe other people's in the process."

The extremists of **Trumans Water** emerged on the fringes of America's slacker fraternity with a clutch of singles and a self-released album – OF THICK TUM (1992) – which catapulted them to the forefront of the underground punk scene. Despite the deceptively orthodox line-up of **Ely Moyal** (drums), **Kevin Branstetter** (bass/vocals), **Glen Galloway** (guitar/vocals) and **Kirk Branstetter** (guitar/vocals), their songs were blasts of galvanizing hysteria. Crossing the art-experimental edge of slacker with the rough-and-ready recording techniques that were becoming known as 'lo-fi', Trumans Water caught the mood of the moment.

The resulting indie buzz, fed by an enthusiastic John Peel in the UK, led to a deal with Elemental Records. The much-anticipated fruits of their studio labour were released in early 1993 as a double album entitled SPASM SMASH XXXOXOX OX & ASS. They stuck to a defiant 'one-take' improvisation policy, describing their music as 'seeking to force tension out of sheer arbitrariness'. The resultant oblique and random chunkiness set the music industry alight, and the album became one of the most highly regarded releases of the year. The cuddly term 'squigglecore' was spawned to describe their particular brand of lo-fi No Wave and a follow-up, six-track EP, 10 X MY AGE (1994), was again generally well received. For the first time, however, some in the music press began to make 'emperor's new clothes' comments on their output.

A gritty, hardcore-punk-influenced album, GODSPEED THE PUNCHLINE (1994), did much to beat off a backlash by shunning the fashionable art aesthetic, but then Trumans Water withdrew to a positively subterranean position in the underground, issuing three vinyl-only albums. GODSPEED THE VORTEX, GODSPEED THE HEMORRHAGE and GODSPEED THE STATIC were described by one writer as 'masterpieces of plasm-pumping pulse-jazz', but few got the chance to hear them. To complicate matters further, all four GODSPEED albums were released on the same day, on different labels. Further down the road to wilful obscurity, Trumans Water complemented these albums with more experimental sessions released on scarcely distributed, lo-fi specialist, cassette-only labels.

In 1994 Glenn Galloway left the group, discovered Jesus and went on to found a new genre of Christian lo-fi with his group **Soul Junk**, whose catalogue of CDs and cassettes have covered everything from acoustic lo-fi to left-field hip-hop. After a slight hiatus in the Trumans camp, Kevin Branstetter transferred his skills to guitar and moved to France. Rehearsals with the other, US-based, band members wasn't a problem – the Trumans don't rehearse.

Despite the transatlantic inconvenience, Trumans Water played on, through a series of releases such as MILKTRAIN TO PAYDIRT (1995), FRAGMENTS OF A LUCKY BREAK (1998), TRUMANS WATER (2000) and YOU ARE STANDING IN THE LINE OF FIRE AND THEY ARE SHOOTING AT YOU (2002), and touring to a fervent following in continental Europe, more often than not alongside the UK's greatest undiscovered band, **I'm Being Good**.

Happily for fans of oblique and random chunkiness, the 'Godspeed... ' series has also slowly been reissued on CD (GODSPEED THE PUNCHLINE on Homestead, GODSPEED THE VORTEX on WayOut Sound; both 1997) and there was an excellent JOHN PEEL SESSIONS album on Strange Fruit (1995).

⊙ **Spasm Smash Xxxoxox Ox & Ass** (1993; Elemental).
Long, loud, sprawling example of the great collision between slacker, No Wave, art-punk and lo-fi.

⊙ **Milktrain To Paydirt** (1995; Elemental).
The story continued, with structures duly destroyed.

Tony Drayton

THE TUBES

Formed San Francisco, 1972; disbanded 1986.

The patented erotic outrage of **The Tubes** was always more high camp than sleaze. And, though ex-drama student **Fee Waybill** (vocals) was more famed for producing his pecker (or an unreasonable facsimile thereof) on stage, he also helped develop some of the quasi-punk genre's more endearing anthems.

The group were formed by Waybill (aka John Waldo) with guitarist **Bill Spooner**, **Vince Welnick** (keyboards), **Rick Anderson** (bass), **Roger Steen** (guitar), **Re Styles** (dancer) and art-school friends **Prairie Prince** (drums) and **Michael Cotten** (synthesizer), in the early 70s. Their music was hardly original, but the visual platform of stage characters such as Dr. Strangekiss ('a crippled Nazi') and Quay Lude was something different altogether. Imagine *Starlight Express* costumed by suppliers to peepshows.

Al Kooper produced THE TUBES (1975) after the group signed to A&M Records. It included the group's most renowned composition, "White Punks On Dope", a sort of anti-suburban mini-opera which became a Top 30 UK hit in November 1978; its B-side, "Don't Touch Me There", could easily have graced the soundtrack to *The Rocky Horror Show*. YOUNG AND RICH (1976) and THE TUBES NOW (1977) were entertaining, but no match for the stage-shows. You get an idea of what they were about from an incident in May 1978 when Waybill broke his leg falling off stage but carried on regardless – not even bothering to put his chainsaw down. WHAT DO YOU WANT FROM LIVE (1978) demonstrates the

The Tubes: white punks on dope, directed by Fee Waybill (with the mic)

delights of the Tubes' stage shows at the height of their powers – a feast of joyous excess.

The release of the Todd Rundgren-produced REMOTE CONTROL (1979) signalled a move away from punk and New Wave to lofty pop torch songs and music-hall ballads, a trait which had always been present but rarely given such prominence. The single "Prime Time" was the perfect example of this development. However, it failed to sell and their proposed 1980 album SUFFER FOR SOUND (also known as THE BLACK ALBUM) was dropped from A&M's schedules along with the band.

The group eventually gave up the ghost after three more albums for Capitol – THE COMPLETION BACKWARDS PRINCIPLE (1981), OUTSIDE INSIDE (1983) and LOVE BOMB (1986). All lacked sparkle, though The Tubes did achieve three major US successes with the ballad "Don't Want To Wait Anymore", "Talk To You Later" (1980) and "She's A Beauty" (1983). Waybill subsequently wrote songs for Richard Marx, of all people, and featured in films such as *Bill & Ted's Excellent Adventure*. Many of his former colleagues continued to tour under The Tubes' name. Welnick also joined up permanently, while Re Styles gave up see-through basques to become a landscape gardener.

◉ **T.R.A.S.H. (Tubes Rarities And Smash Hits)** (1981; A&M).
The best place to start, it includes all the best-known early work. "White Punks On Dope", "Don't Touch Me There" and "Prime Time" have a strange, nostalgic appeal.

Alex Ogg

'MOE' TUCKER

Born Jackson Heights, New York, 1944.

"In my mind, I wasn't trying to be a musician so it never occurred to me to look for someone else to play with. So I just went out and got a job."

We all know the story of **THE VELVET UNDERGROUND** and how the primitive, cymbal-less drumming of **Maureen 'Moe' Tucker** set the hypnotic backdrop for The Velvets' avant-garde angst. Growing up in Long Island, New York, Moe's brother was best friends with future Velvets guitarist **Sterling Morrison**. A fanatical admirer of both Bo Diddley and African drummer Babatunde Olatunji, she had been playing drums for quite a while when she was brought into The Velvets. After the band split in 1970, **LOU REED** and **JOHN CALE** made a number of fine, critically acclaimed albums but little was heard from Tucker. Busy raising her family in Phoenix, Arizona, she was so far out of the loop she was unaware that The Velvets had grown into one of the most influential bands in history. Who knows how long she would gone without this knowledge if a small record-label owner in Boston hadn't stumbled across a rare tape of her and **JONATHAN RICHMAN** duetting in 1974 on The Velvets' "I'm Sticking With You" and approached her to do a B-side for it.

Tucker had recently obtained a four-track recorder and started work. Things went so well that she decided to do a whole album of covers of her favourite rock'n'roll classics. This debut, PLAYIN' POSSUM (1981), on which she played all the instruments, was recorded in her living room and ranged through screeching covers of "Bo Diddley" and "I'll Be Your Baby Tonight" to "Louie, Louie" and Vivaldi's "Concerto in D Major". Moe even did a fine reverberating version of "Heroin". A loose, amateurish album made mostly for fun, it was very listenable. But there were still five young kids to raise and Moe was not even considering a return to the spotlight.

Tucker didn't resurface again until 1987. Over the years, she had found a kindred spirit of sorts in Jad Fair of the band **HALF JAPANESE** and she drummed and sang on 1987's raw MOE JAD KATE BARRY EP. She then joined **Penn Jillette**'s (of Penn & Teller fame) 50 Skidillion Watts label for LIFE IN EXILE AFTER ABDICATION (1989) – her first 'real' album, which also contained her first self-written lyrics. Songs such as "Spam Again" and "Work" venture into the rarely covered territory of making ends meet as a working single mother, and would become staples of her live show. Moe was starting to develop into a fine songwriter, as evidenced by her piano-driven tribute to Andy Warhol entitled "Andy" and the rave-up "Hey, Mersh!" The album also boasted a truly impressive group of volunteers from the alternative elite, including most of **Sonic Youth**, as well as friends Jad Fair (again), Don Fleming, Daniel Johnston, and Lou Reed, who gave his enthusiastic support. After the album's release, Moe continued to tour during her two-week vacations from her job at a Georgia Wal-Mart. After being convinced by Jad Fair that she could actually make more money by touring Europe (she was making less than $10,000 a year at the time), she quit her job to focus on her music.

In 1991, Tucker recorded I SPENT A WEEK THERE THE OTHER NIGHT with **Violent Femmes**' Victor DeLorenzo and Brian Ritchie, and reunited Lou Reed, John Cale and Sterling Morrison on the last song that the original four Velvets would ever work on together – the droning, synthesizer-driven "I'm Not". The highlights of the album, however, were the crashing pop-punk of "Fired Up", a beautiful reading of "Blue, All The Way To Canada", and a low-key cover of "Waiting For The Man". In 1993 The Velvet Underground re-formed for a brief tour of Europe that met with mixed reactions. After this, Sterling Morrison joined Moe's band as a more regular member, playing on the Phil Hadaway-produced DOGS UNDER STRESS (1993) and remaining until his death in 1995.

In 1996 Moe joined up with her friend and pen pal Mark Goodman and his Velvet-esque band, **Magnet**, returning to drumming on their well-received album DON'T BE A PENGUIN, and went out on the road for a brief tour. She also played bass drum with the oddly eclectic **Kropotkins**, and produced

Paul K And The Weathermen's LOVE IS A GAS. The following year she recorded the charming four-song GRL GRUP EP (1997) of her favourite 60s girl group covers and a single with new versions of "After Hours" and "I'm Sticking With You". More recently, she has appeared with various artists on the children's album NOT DOGS ... TOO SIMPLE (1998), and had a live album, MOE ROCKS TERRASTOCK (2002), released on the Captain Trip imprint.

⊙ **Playin' Possum** (1981; Trash).
Moe's first solo album of mostly covers is quite rough around the edges, but remains a very listenable and impressive debut.

⊙ **Life In Exile After Abdication** (1989; 50 Skidillion Watts).
An album of original material finds Moe supported by an all-star cast on gems like "Hey, Mersh!" and "Andy", as well as nicely done covers with the campfire folk of "Goodnite Irene", "Do It Right" and a beautiful version of "Pale Blue Eyes".

⊙ **I Spent A Week There The Other Night** (1991; Sky Records).
Probably her best work to date. Includes the quasi-Velvet reunion on "I'm Not", and her most catchy songwriting on "Fired Up", which should have been a college radio hit.

Matt Fink

TURIN BRAKES

Formed London, 1999.

Turin Brakes are just two earnest troubadours trying to make their way in the world, peddling a sound that harks back to the legacy of Buckley junior and senior, and even recalls the harmonies of the Everly Brothers. Having found their feet, despite being weighed down by the albatross of the New Acoustic Movement tag, the duo are now major players in the mainstream arena.

Friends since primary school, **Olly Knights** and **Gale Paridjanian** began playing music when they both received guitars for Christmas at the tender age of seven. At college Olly devised a score for a film as part of his studies; although the film never got made, the score became Turin Brakes' first release as THE DOOR EP on Anvil records in 1999.

The band signed to Source in 2000 and released THE STATE OF THINGS EP. That summer, Gale and Olly played the Reading and Leeds festivals with a full band in tow, and released the FIGHT OR FLIGHT EP soon after. "The Door" was reworked as a single for February 2001 release and the self-produced debut album THE OPTIMIST followed, breaking the Top 40.

Immediately bracketed as 'New Acoustic Movement' by the press, the album was critically applauded and the band was duly nominated for numerous 'Best New Band' awards. The punchy lyrics, complex harmonies and frenetic acoustic guitars of Turin Brakes' sound had arrived, fully formed and emotionally powerful. The songs married intense delivery to catchy choruses while sending out cryptic messages: 'With insects crawling in my hair/The trees are black and I don't care'.

The three singles from the album all penetrated the Top 40. The band spent much of 2002 writing material for the second album, ETHER SONG, which was recorded in Los Angeles with **Tony Hoffer**, (producer for Beck, Supergrass and Air). Olly and Gale went on an acoustic tour of Britain in the autumn and the album's first single, "Long Distance", entered the Top 20 in 2002. A second single, "Pain Killer", followed before the album's release at the start of 2003.

ETHER SONG frequently recalled Jeff Buckley's GRACE in its grand phrasing and emotional fragility, but also revealed a more ambitious, musically confident Turin Brakes. They had successfully expanded the atmosphere of their music with electric guitars, keyboards and samplers, presumably keen to distance themselves from the New Acoustic Movement, which was by then twitching its last. The arrangements demonstrated the versatility of Olly and Gale and the skills of new members **Justin Meldal-Johnson** (bass) and **Brian Reitzell** (Drums).

Turin Brakes are no longer the easily pigeonholed sing'n'tell acoustic harmonizers of their earliest recordings; their two albums and live performances document the maturity of a talented band that's worth watching.

⊙ **The Optimist** (2001; Source).
The heartbreak troubadours' debut album of earnest, insistent, skilful, acoustically driven songs is a remarkably consistent and mature first effort of big pop melodies and touching quiet times.

Turin Brakes live

⊙ **Ether Song** (2003; Source).
Adding spaceship sounds and studio trickery to the mix, the Brakes' songs are given a leg-up into epic territory to complement the euphoria and breadth of the lyrics, and sound fuller and more triumphant as a result.

Annebella Pollen

TINA TURNER

Born Nutbush, Tennessee, November 26, 1938.

"I look at what's there. What's there is legs and hair."

Perhaps it is not so remarkable that **Tina Turner**'s talent has proved to be so durable, nor that her appetite for hard work has sustained her as one of the most highly respected stars in the business. What is exceptional is that neither the greatest heights of wealth and public adulation, nor the depths of despair, abuse and failure, seemed to have affected her consistent good nature. Hers is an experience which would have defeated many others.

Annie Mae Bullock's home town of Nutbush was little more than the 'church house, gin house, schoolhouse, outhouse' she later sang about, but it was here that she learned to sing and dance at church talent shows. Her high-school yearbook confidently listed her future profession as 'entertainer', though it seems likely that she had little idea of how she could actually achieve it. When her parents separated, Annie Mae went with her mother to East St Louis, Missouri, where the downtown music clubs were an irresistible draw to the dance-crazy 17-year-old.

Many of the bands who frequented them were good, but she especially liked an act she caught one night at the Club Manhattan; so much so, in fact, that she pestered the band's leader for a chance to sing with him. **Izaear Luster 'Ike' Turner** was already something of a star; in addition to his considerable experience as a producer, talent scout, disc jockey and session player, he had also become a blues guitarist of some repute at the head of his band, The Kings Of Rhythm. Ike probably felt he had to humour her, but when she finally took her chance and proceeded to tear the place apart with her astonishingly mature voice he was quick to realize her crowd-drawing potential.

Ike decided to change her first name to something earthy, a 'jungle name', as he later described it. After their marriage, an impressive string of soul/R&B hits followed, beginning with "A Fool In Love" in 1960, but by and large the routine was the same – tough gig at a small roadside whistle stop, sleep in the car, long drive to next gig. Typical of the situation of most black artists, the duo often had to record on a shoestring budget in less than perfect circumstances – a condition that was ill-suited to the meticulous Ike Turner.

The Phil Spector-produced classic "River Deep, Mountain High" (1966) was a major hit in Britain, but barely scratched the surface in their homeland. It was a number of years before Ike and Tina would manage to create a specific identity for themselves. Fortunately, the recognition in England drew the attention of The Rolling Stones, who effectively relaunched Ike and Tina's careers by taking them as the support act on their 1969 tour. The flavour of the act became harder and produced some hot-and-greasy singles in the ensuing years, including the hit "Proud Mary" in 1971, and Tina's autobiographical "Nutbush City Limits" in 1973.

The touring was now international, and Tina was the major attention-grabber. She appeared without Ike in the film *Tommy*, turning in a riveting performance as The Acid Queen. Around this time, the true nature of Ike and Tina's stormy relationship began to manifest itself in the bruises on Tina's body. The end of the band and the end of the marriage came in the summer of 1975.

Ike was not the only thing that Tina left behind: she had left her job, her home, her money, her clothes; in fact everything but her self-respect. What was worse, her act of self-preservation was not seen too kindly by a large number of promoters, who felt she had wilfully disassembled an extremely potent financial concern. With no promoters, Tina Turner set about clawing her way back to the top by setting herself up with a few grassroots concert dates, starting with the hotel-convention circuit, then the cocktail lounges of Las Vegas.

Her talent was important, of course, and her star quality was unmistakeable, but ultimately it was her sheer determination that proved unstoppable. Rod Stewart showed up one night and asked her to take part in a number of shows he was staging, and in each one she dazzled. She opened again for The Stones and bowled over some significant brass from Capitol Records, who offered her a deal and in 1983 released her version of Al Green's "Let's Stay Together", which became a huge international hit. Its success – out of nowhere – was so unexpected that no plans had been laid for an accompanying album. PRIVATE DANCER (1984) was recorded hastily in two weeks and sold nearly fifteen million copies worldwide. Meantime, the follow-up single, "What's Love Got To Do With It", became Tina's first #1 and won a 1984 Grammy.

And the success continued. Turner made another highly acclaimed movie appearance in 1985 in *Mad Max 3 – Beyond Thunderdome* alongside Mel Gibson; there were two more Grammys; and there were a number of additional huge-selling albums, including BREAK EVERY RULE (1986) and FOREIGN AFFAIR (1989).

WILDEST DREAMS (1996) showed a superstar about to enter her sixties with the enthusiasm one would expect to see in someone a third her age. Supremely confident in her style and ability, Turner crooned her way through the naughty title track with the late, great, Barry White and got down with her funky self in "Something Beautiful Remains". This was fol-

lowed by TWENTY FOUR SEVEN (2000), another fine, assured album from a prime talent; it was testimony to her immense skill and determination that she's the only female artist to appear on the cover of *Rolling Stone* in three separate decades.

Ike And Tina Turner

⦿ **Live (The Ike And Tina Show)** (1965; Edsel). Classic soul revue includes Tina at her blistering best on "Finger Poppin'", "Twist And Shout" and "High Heeled Sneakers".

⦿ **River Deep, Mountain High** (1966; A&M). The classic title track sets the tone, but it doesn't overshadow the other high-quality singles included – "I Idolize You", "A Fool In Love".

Tina Turner

⦿ **Private Dancer** (1984; Capitol). Although this was not Tina's solo debut, it completely eclipsed her earlier efforts. The strength of the material alone (including "Better Be Good To Me", "Let's Stay Together", "What's Love Got To Do With It") would have been enough to make it special, and Tina sings as if there was no tomorrow.

Phil Lynch

THE TURTLES

Formed Los Angeles, 1961; disbanded 1970; re-formed 1982.

The Turtles bounced through the 60s juggling styles from surf-rock to Zappa-esque satire, and navigating numerous personnel changes, steadied only by the faith of founding vocalists **Mark Volman** and **Howard Kaylan**.

Volman, a New Yorker, and Kaylan, an LA native, had formed **The Nightriders** in 1961 with **Al Nichol** (guitar), **Chuck Portz** (bass) and **Don Murray** (drums). Originally a surf band, they changed their name to **The Crossfires** and recorded the unsuccessful singles "Fiberglass Jungle" and "Santa And The Sidewalk Surfer". Another name change (to the **Crosswind Singers**) and a new musical direction (folk-rock) again failed to turn the commercial trick. In 1965, the newly formed White Whale label gave them a last throw of the dice as The Tyrtles, quickly amended to The Turtles. Joined by second guitarist **Jim Tucker**, the group's version of Bob Dylan's "It Ain't Me Babe" combined folk-rock with surf harmonies, and became a hit. The band played on.

An association with writer P. F. Sloan, known for his work in the 'protest song' fad of the 60s, produced two more hits in 1966 – "Let Me Be" and the upbeat, slogan-free "You Baby". Reportedly, The Turtles passed on recording what was to become Sloan's biggest hit of the era, "Eve Of Destruction" (done by Barry McGuire), a melodramatic catalogue of nearly every issue worth protesting. However, songwriters **Gary Bonner** and **Alan Gordon** gave The Turtles their two biggest smashes the next year in "Happy Together" and "She'd Rather Be With Me", joyful sing-alongs representative of the archetypal Turtles sound. THE TURTLES PRESENT THE BATTLE OF THE HANDS appeared in 1968, an ambitious, self-produced album containing the hit "Elenore". That single, indeed the entire album, was a pastiche of popular contemporary styles, but such a convincing pastiche that it threatened to consume The Turtles' own voice.

Meanwhile, membership in the band had become a revolving door. Murray had left in favour of **John Barbara**, who was replaced by **John Seiter** when Barbara moved on to **CROSBY, STILLS, NASH & YOUNG**. **Jim Pons** succeeded **Chip Douglas**, who had succeeded original bassist Portz. In 1969 The Kinks' Ray Davies produced the album TURTLE SOUP; its cover of The Byrds' "You Showed Me" was their last successful single before the band broke up in 1970. In a strange twist, their final US chart appearance was a fortnight at #100 with a belated version of "Eve Of Destruction".

Kaylan and Volman joined **FRANK ZAPPA** as a vocal duo, **The Phlorescent Leech And Eddie** – aka **Flo & Eddie** – recording a mix of straight songs and parodies under that name through the 70s and into the 80s. They also acquired a decent reputation as backing vocalists for hire, most notably for Bruce Springsteen's "Hungry Heart". But The Turtles never really died, not as long as Volman and Kaylan were still kicking, and in 1982 they restarted the band as a nostalgia act, mirroring a trend started by The Monkees.

⊙ **Happy Together: The Very Best Of The Turtles** (1991; Music Club).
There is a lot of material in The Turtles' catalogue, but this collection covers the cream of the crop.

John Collis

THE DWIGHT TWILLEY BAND

Formed Tulsa, Oklahoma, 1973.

Students at the same Tulsa high school, **Dwight Twilley** (vocals/guitar/keyboards) and **Phil Seymour** (vocals/drums/bass) met, with characteristic style, at a matinee performance of *A Hard Day's Night* in the summer of 1967. The two teenagers struck up an instant rapport, and before very long they were performing locally as an acoustic duo called Oister.

In 1970 Oister set out for Nashville with a demo tape. Stopping off in Memphis en route, they blundered into Sun Records, and were sent by Jerry Philips (son of owner Sam) to see former Sun artist and Hi Records part-owner Ray Harris. A year later they were commuting from Tulsa every few months to record with Harris at his new studio. Nothing was issued from these sessions, but schooling in Sun rockabilly opened Twilley and Seymour's Beatles-dominated perspective, and vocal grit was added to their harmonizing. Eventually tapes of Twilley's new band, 1950, reached Denny Cordell in LA, and **The Dwight Twilley Band** – Twilley, Seymour and sideman **Bill Pitcock** – signed to his Shelter label, headquartered in Tulsa, in 1974.

The slinky, catchy rocker "I'm On Fire", released in April 1975, was a debut hit, peaking at #16 in the American charts. It should have been the first of a flood; instead the band were buried by delays and bad luck. Album tracks recorded in London with Robin Cable were judged to be overproduced and were rejected. The brilliant follow-up single, "Shark (In The Dark)", was performed on *American Bandstand* in July, but pulled before release because distributors MCA, who were handling the soundtrack to *Jaws*, felt the song could be construed as a cash-in, or the band as a novelty act. "You Were So Warm" was lost in the confusion of a distribution switch (MCA to ABC) and Shelter co-owner Leon Russell's lawsuit against the label blocked release of The Dwight Twilley Band's now completed LP. When the updated SINCERELY (1976) album – inventive, varied and totally accessible – finally limped into the shops, "I'm On Fire" was already a distant memory.

Returning to the studio after touring the US with an augmented line-up later in the year, Seymour and Twilley sang backup for label mates **Tom Petty & The Heartbreakers** (the harmonies on "American Girl" are Phil's); Petty repaid the favour with ringing guitar on "Looking For The Magic", emotional keynote of second-album masterpiece TWILLEY DON'T MIND (1977). Although sales were better than for SINCERELY, the new album was not a hit, and Seymour left in 1978.

The self-titled TWILLEY (1979) and SEYMOUR (1981) solo LPs were often great – Seymour's lovely "Precious To Me" was a US Top 40 hit – but lacked the intense chemistry of their partnership. Plagued by record company problems or crooked management, Dwight had a hit single with "Girls" in 1984, and released WILD DOGS in 1986; his talent had receded into anonymous production, but it still flashed on "Spider And The Fly", "Sexual" and "Shooting Stars". The inclusion of "Why You Wanna Break My Heart" on the *Wayne's World* soundtrack provided an unexpected windfall, however, and a greatest hits collection, XXI (1996), contained two new songs. His most recent release was 2001's THE LUCK. Phil Seymour, meanwhile, released one more solo album, in 1982, and appeared on another three with the Textones between 1984 and 1990; one of the most undervalued singers of the past twenty years, he died in 1993.

⊙ **Sincerely** (1976; DCC).
An album that presents The Dwight Twilley Band as a three-man wrecking crew capable of almost anything. "I'm Losing You" is a highlight, Twilley's lost, defeated vocal suspended above echoing double-picked guitar and washes of keyboard strings.

⊙ **Twilley Don't Mind** (1977; DCC).
"Looking For The Magic", emotionally dislocated but trying to recover lost feeling, defines the mood of this overlooked classic. Arrangements are pared down, and Twilley and Seymour's tremulous vocal harmonies reach a telepathic peak.

⊙ **The Great Lost Twilley Album** (1993; DCC).
Much of this music should be as commonplace as ABBEY ROAD, but instead remained unreleased for nearly twenty years.

Robert Coyne

TWISTED SISTER

Formed Long Island, New York, 1976;
disbanded 1988.

In the gutters of New York during the 70s, a bunch
of degenerates teamed up to pursue a common
goal: to be the loudest and brashest rock band ever.
Thus **Twisted Sister** was born, comprising **Dee
Snider** (vocals), **Eddie 'Fingers' Ojeda** and **Jay
Jay French** (guitars), **Mark 'The Animal'
Mendoza** (bass) and **Tony Petri** (drums).

After an independently released single, "I'll Never
Grow Up", Petri departed, to be replaced by **A. J.
Pero**. With the line-up stabilized, Twisted Sister
found that the UK was more welcoming than their
homeland, recording the RUFF CUTS (1982) EP for
British independent Secret. Shows at London's
Marquee had the press singing their praises, and the
public soon followed suit, although Pete Way's
shoddy production on their debut album, UNDER
THE BLADE (1982), only hinted at the awesome spectacle of the live show.

A larger-than-life appearance on UK TV show
The Tube sealed a deal with Atlantic, and triumphant
sets at the 1982 Reading Festival and the 1983
Monsters Of Rock ensued, by which time the band
were big news in Britain thanks to the success of
YOU CAN'T STOP ROCK 'N' ROLL (1983) and, in
particular, the hit single "I Am, I'm Me". Snider
became a major media celebrity, with a ready quote
and canny knack for publicity.

It was largely due to their UK popularity that
America finally caught on to the quintet, and STAY
HUNGRY (1984) confirmed their new status.
Combined with Snider's most consistent set of songs
were a pair of superb videos for "I Wanna Rock" and
"We're Not Gonna Take It". MTV, and hence
America, succumbed. This was to prove a brief love
affair though, for when COME OUT AND PLAY
(1985) was unleashed, the ticket sales for their headlining arena tour of the States were disastrously poor,
even though the album was highly worthwhile.

At the end of the tour Pero parted company with
the band, and there was a long silence before LOVE
IS FOR SUCKERS (1987) appeared to no fanfare,
unveiling a new drummer in **Joe Franco**. The
album was better than anyone expected, with
Snider's rabble-rousing anthems demonstrating a
new maturity, though sadly the parting shot "Yeah
Right!" was never aired live. However, relationships within the band had turned sour, and, when
Snider roped in Norwegian wizard **Ronni Le
Tekro** to beef up the guitar work, the camel's back
broke, and Twisted Sister disappeared without a
whimper.

Snider eventually reappeared, along with Franco,
in **Widowmaker**, but the other members largely
remained in the missing files, although Mendoza produced the long-overdue concert recording LIVE AT
HAMMERSMITH (1994), from a 1984 show. Ironically,

what should have been a suitable farewell prompted
suggestions of a reunion, although it soon appeared
that too much tension still existed to allow this to
happen. However, Snider and French, whose breakdown in communication was the principal reason for
the split, met in late 1998 and spoke for practically
the first time in ten years. This meeting, which
French later described as 'extraordinary', pushed the
rumour mill into overdrive. Meanwhile, 1999
brought a spate of bonus-track-laden reissues from
Spitfire Records and CLUB DAZE VOL. 1: THE
STUDIO SESSIONS, a bristling fistful of demos from the
band's early days, a packaging job which was repeated
a couple of years later with VOL.2: LIVE IN THE
BARS.

In 2000 Snider popped up again with the album
NEVER LET THE BASTARDS WEAR YOU DOWN.
With a band that featured, among others, Pero on
drums, this set showcased ten old Snider-penned
numbers that never made it onto the catalogue
albums. The following year brought TWISTED
FOREVER, a tribute album featuring the likes of
Motörhead, Anthrax and Vision Of Disorder
showing up in the studio to cut their favourite Sister
tunes. During this time Twisted Sister would reunite
on several occasions – but only for signing sessions at
various record stores.

Nevertheless, what everyone wanted was for the
band to actually pick up their instruments and play
together again, a wish that was eventually granted,
though under a very unusual set of circumstances.
Following the terrorist attacks on New York in
September 2001, a charity concert was organized at
the Hammerstein Ballroom on November 28 for the
families of the city's fallen police officers and fire-
fighters; for the first time in 14 years Twisted Sister
took to the stage as headliners. Whether this proves
to be the catalyst for a full-scale reunion, however,
remains unclear; Snider, for one, has already carved
himself too successful a niche in film and radio to
direct all his energies into a band project again. But
we shall see…

THE DWIGHT TWILLEY BAND • TWISTED SISTER

Stay Hungry (1984; Atlantic).
The peak of Twisted Sister's career, laden with bone-crunching work-outs. "We're Not Gonna Take It" and "I Wanna Rock" paved the way for sales of over three million.

Live At Hammersmith (1994; Music For Nations).
Anyone who laughs at Twisted Sister never saw them live. This shows them at the peak of their powers, with all the war cries, solos and Snider's gloriously overblown raps. A delight.

Hugh Hackett

TYPE O NEGATIVE

Formed Brooklyn, New York, 1989.

If **Type O Negative** were a film, it would be noir, complex, dangerously appealing, full of lush sensuality and earthy humour. The male lead would be the most beautiful man in rock, with a supporting cast of intense and talented players. The soundtrack would be fuelled by raging guitars, with a driving keyboard, multi-layered vocals reminiscent of the Righteous Brothers and sexy-as-hell drumming.

Back when the band first formed, lead singer/lyricist/bassist **Peter Steele**'s new project was expected to be more of the same kind of work he'd produced during his stint as singer for speed-metal, New York cult favourite, **Canivore**. It came close, but Steele and friends were already moulding their own hard-edged but beguiling style.

The original Type O line-up of Steele (bass/vocals), **Kenny Hickey** (vocals/guitar), **Josh Silver** (vocals/keyboards) and **Sal Abruscato** (drums) produced three albums. In 1993, their drum tech, **Johnny Kelly**, stepped in when Abruscato left. Kelly made his Type O recording debut on OCTOBER RUST, although he had toured with them for the three years prior to that.

SLOW, DEEP AND HARD (1991), was a nonstop tirade against life in general and unfaithful women in particular, earning them a reputation as right-wing misogynists. But the music – if you weren't afraid of threshing guitars, mile-a-minute drums plus a lot of screaming offset by liturgical interludes – was arresting, with its own brand of dark humour. When some of the 'instruments' listed on the label are hammers and axes, believe it, they're there. Yet even at its harshest, the music is melodic. Given his size and well-muscled physique, it could be pretty frightening when Steele growls out, 'Oh, you're dead now!', but if you listen carefully you'll hear that he's having far too much fun to be taken seriously.

THE ORIGIN OF THE FECES (1992) continued in a similar vein, starting off with a classic Type O flourish: an angry audience chanting, 'You suck! You suck!', to which Steele replies, ' ... You paid 15 dollars to be here ... We're getting paid ... Who's the real a**hole around here?' And it doesn't stop there: the thrash-metal anthem shortly trails off as Steele baits the crowd by crooning, 'I'm in the mood for love ... ', finishing off with a belly laugh at their obviously heightened fury. Intense.

But both albums display the band's musicality, softening their strident, driving sound with softer, more melodic passages. Then came their acid-goth phase, a move Steele quipped was made because he got tired of screaming. BLOODY KISSES (1993) and OCTOBER RUST (1996) are saturated with complex patterns of sound, none wasted and all right where it belongs; their lyrics are full of sexual symbolism and, again, humour. "Black No. 1", from BLOODY KISSES, is a send-up of 'professional goths', gently done, but amusing, with its musical tag from *The Munsters* television series.

The lyrics on the next two albums were almost an 180-degree turnaround from SLOW, DEEP AND HARD and THE ORIGIN OF THE FECES, whose overt, seeming hatred of women metamorphosed into a 'more in sorrow than in anger' approach on BLOODY KISSES, which progressed into an almost worshipful tone in OCTOBER RUST. This latter album had a mystical feel to it, both lyrically and musically, with songs such as "Druidess" and "Green Man", but it kicked off with the blatantly sexual "Love You To Death". One of the most popular and sensual songs, "Wolf Moon", had Steele's deep voice chanting lyrics of sex and werewolves to throbbing guitars and velvet-thick melodies that were wholly erotic. And then there's "My Girlfriend's Girlfriend". You figure it out.

Steele's lyrics on these later albums were visually evocative, with the music so densely layered you could almost touch it. Which was also true of WORLD COMING DOWN (1999), although if Steele's previous inspiration had come from sex and death it was arguably the other way round this time. Morbidly morose tunes such as "Everything Dies" and "Everyone I Love Is Dead" spoke volumes about Steele's state of mind following the loss of various family members during the period of the album's creation. Despite the anguished and bleak lyrical slant no one could accuse this lot of completely losing their black and perverse sense of humour, as the compilation THE LEAST WORST OF TYPE O NEGATIVE (2000) ably showed, giving the fans a few unreleased gems alongside the already familiar fare.

Late in 2001 Steele confirmed he was working on more songs for a new album, and hinted that a return to the sound of OCTOBER RUST combined with the fury of SLOW, DEEP AND HARD was in order. Unfortunately, when LIFE IS KILLING ME (2003) appeared, many were disappointed by the comically grotesque imagery and lighter musical mood.

The Origin Of The Feces (1992; Roadrunner Records).
Is it live or is it another Type O joke? Very similar to S, D and H, but with more spontaneous humour.

Bloody Kisses (1993; Roadrunner Records).
Goth, industrial, death metal – hard to label, but gloomy-sexy with lush music, and still those raging guitars.

October Rust (1996; Roadrunner Records).
More commercial, shorter songs, maybe a bit more poppy, but still darkly sensuous, with Steele's bass crooning and moaning to make you shiver.

Bibi L.

TYPE O NEGATIVE

U

UB40

Formed Birmingham, England, 1978.

Entering the national consciousness around the same time as Margaret Thatcher, **UB40** were initially considered a politically driven protest band. Associated with the 2-Tone label and ska revival of the late 70s, they named themselves after Britain's unemployment benefit cards. But, by the mid-80s, with no end to Conservative rule in sight, their 'agit-reggae' had softened into a pop-melodic 'reggae-lite' series of covers, culminating in the huge UK chart hits "Red Red Wine" (1983), "I Got You Babe" (1985 – with **Chrissie Hynde**) and "Can't Help Falling In Love With You" (1993).

UB40 were founded by brothers **Ali** (vocals/guitar) and **Robin Campbell** (guitar/ vocals), sons of Scottish singer Ian Campbell. They enlisted a gang of singers and musicians united by a love of reggae (in particular, singer Gregory Isaacs) and an active political commitment: **Nigerian Yomo Babayemi** (percussion), **Michael Virtue** (keyboards), **Earl Falconer** (bass), **Brian Travers** (saxophone), **Jim Brown** (drums) and **Norman Hassan** (percussion). After just two local gigs, how-ever, Babayemi was deported to Nigeria and replaced by toaster and singer **Astro** (aka Terry Wilson).

The early incarnation of UB40 set about creating something new by fusing reggae rhythms with UK rock and pop songwriting sensibilities. After a year of playing pubs and clubs, they got their big break,

when they recorded a BBC Radio session for John Peel and supported The Pretenders on a UK tour; within weeks, they had hit #4 in the UK charts with a debut single, "King"/"Food For Thought". A much-praised first album, SIGNING OFF, went straight to #2 in August, and was followed by the single "The Earth Dies Screaming" – perhaps the strongest song of their career, with its sax-led melody.

Shortly after the album, UB40 had left Graduate and set up their own label, DEP International Records, as well as a studio, known as The Abattoir. It was with this combination that they recorded and released PRESENT ARMS (1981), a #2 UK album, and later in the year its dubbed-up companion piece, PRESENT ARMS IN DUB. These, and the following year's album, UB44, were critical and commercial successes – breaking reggae in the UK charts in pretty much unprecedented fashion. Only Bob Marley had had previous Top 10 reggae albums.

In early 1993, however, they seemed to lose the magic formula with "I've Got Mine", and UB40 LIVE, recorded in Ireland, both of which hovered around the lower reaches of the Top 50. They rethought and came up with much more overtly commercial material, which kept a reggae framework whilst bringing to the fore the Campbells' back-ground in folk harmony singing. The process kicked off with a reworking of Neil Diamond's "Red Red Wine", and it was followed by a covers LP, LABOUR OF LOVE (1983), including an almost saccharine "Many Rivers To Cross". Both reached #1 in the US, edged into the UK Top 40, and thus began a second remarkably consistent run of hits.

Through the 80s and 90s, UB40 recruited a host of backing vocalists and musicians for live shows, and became known for their regular collaborations with other artists. They teamed up with old friend Chrissie Hynde on their addictive 1985 UK #1 "I Got You Babe" and 1988 hit "Breakfast In Bed"; helped on a 2-Tone single called "Starvation" to relieve famine in Ethiopia; and worked with **Herb Alpert** ("Rat In Mi Kitchen", 1987), Robert Palmer ("I'll Be Your Baby Tonight", 1990) and 808 State ("One In Ten", 1992). If the albums were none too memorable, the singles kept a-coming. 1989 also saw a second volume in the LABOUR OF LOVE covers series.

In 1993, UB40 hit bonanza with a #1 in both the UK and US, "Can't Help Falling In Love With You", on the strength of which its parent LP, PROMISES AND LIES (1993), became one of the year's biggest sellers (#1 in the UK, #6 in the US). The band then revisited their reggae roots backing **Pato Banton** on his chart-topping revival of The Equals' "Baby Come Back" (1994), before embarking on a sabbatical, while Ali Campbell issued the sentimental solo album BIG LOVE (1995). Meantime, the band's name was kept in the public eye with THE BEST OF UB40 VOLUME 2 (1995), a sequel to their 1987 compilation.

GUNS IN THE GHETTO (1997) then raised a storm of backbiting over their unfamiliarity these days with either guns or ghettoes, without making any other notable waves. Equally lacklustre were LABOUR OF LOVE III (1998) and COVER UP (2001).

⊙ **Present Arms** (1981; DEP/Virgin).
Fulfilling the promise of SIGNING OFF, this clarifies the band's distinctive early sound and turns it into a heavily disguised assault weapon. Listened to now, the harder dub tracks seem to foreshadow the subliminal force of Bristol's 'trip-hop' acts like Tricky and Massive Attack.

⊙ **Labour Of Love** (1983; DEP/Virgin).
Like its 1989 sequel, but unlike 1998's third installment, this covers LP is a meeting of strong arrangements and Ali Campbell's soulful voice. Basically it is pop music at its best: simple and catchy without being inane. All three sets were issued as a reasonably priced box-set in 2003.

⊙ **The Best Of UB40 Volume 1** (1987; Virgin).
Contains a fair smattering from the above two titles, plus pretty much the best of the rest, and an otherwise unavailable cover of The Jackson Five's "Maybe Tomorrow".

Matthew Grant

UFO

Formed London, 1969; disbanded 1983; re-formed 1985; disbanded 1988; re-formed 1991.

Initially Unbelievably Fucking 'Orrible – latterly Undistinguished, Forgotten and Ordinary – **UFO** were, in between, an Ultra Fine Outfit. Like Thin Lizzy, they stood a class apart from the sludge of British heavy metal in the 70s; their links with Uriah Heep ended at record-store racking.

Early UFO peddled a mixture of pedestrian boogie and excruciating 'space-rock'. Justly ignored at home, they won a cult following in the hard-rock outposts of Germany and Japan. A tour of the former in 1973

enabled singer **Phil Mogg**, bassist **Pete Way** and drummer **Andy Parker** to poach guitarist **Michael Schenker** from SCORPIONS and, armed with miraculously improved songwriting, they set off to conquer the world.

The aptly titled PHENOMENON (1974) provided two staples of 70s rock nights, "Doctor Doctor" and "Rock Bottom", but these were soon upstaged by UFO's increasingly sophisticated output. Their first peak was LIGHTS OUT (1977), which ranged from the breakneck title track to a reverential cover of Love's "Alone Again Or" and the slow-burning "Love To Love".

The UFO legend, however, was built not just on albums of escalating quality, but on rock'n'rolling of spiralling depravity. As gleefully detailed by UK music paper *Sounds* and its heavy metal heir *Kerrang!*, Mogg and Way set new standards for band-baiting, narcotic naughtiness, hotel horror and alcoholic abandon. An early victim was Schenker, who disappeared after a gig in June 1977. Variously rumoured to be dead or kidnapped, he popped up six months later, claiming he had just wanted to quit UFO, but hadn't known how to say so in English.

With stunt guitarist **Paul Chapman** promoted to lead (the fifth person to occupy that role), UFO made their 80s debut with the George Martin-produced NO PLACE TO RUN (1980). More impressive was 1981's THE WILD, THE WILLING AND THE INNOCENT, although (by this time) the group had been upstaged by a band who cited UFO as a pivotal influence: Iron Maiden.

The departure of Pete Way in 1982 almost dealt UFO a death blow. They issued the tragically underrated MAKING CONTACT (1983), then gracelessly fell apart on tour, finally calling it a day in April of that year. A comparatively cleaned-up Mogg revived the name, with an all-new band, in 1985, but this self-destructed within a couple of years. A reunion with Way produced the strong HIGH STAKES AND DANGEROUS MEN in 1992, but with even Iron Maiden now considered passé, a UFO re-formation was hardly likely to set punters' hearts and wallets alight. WALK ON WATER (1998), sprang from another reunion, six years down the line, of the classic – with added Schenker – line-up. It was a superior product to their 1992 effort, but still warmed-up leftovers rather than a freshly cooked gourmet delight when compared to some of their past glories. Nevertheless, with their ace guitarist back in tow the band now had the requisite firepower to at least pull in a few punters of old – sadly a complete inability to capitalize on the situation led to Schenker jumping ship to restart his Michael Schenker Group. Meanwhile Mogg and Way eventually released CHOCOLATE BOX (1999). And then, just to keep things interesting, Schenker decided that he really did want to be in UFO after all and the band managed to stay together long enough to record the rather fine COVENANT (2000) – until it all fell apart again.

In the end UFO are probably best regarded as having brought a touch of class to heavy metal, for having great tunes and a cool logo, and for being so out of it that even 'Mad Mickey' Schenker couldn't stand the heat.

⊙ **The Best Of UFO** (2000; EMI).
A stunning sixteen-track collection; one of several 'best of's on the market.

Bruno MacDonald

UI

Formed New York, 1991.

Ui (pronounced oo-ee) were a key group in the loosely defined category of post-rock; their music was centred on two intricately woven basses in collaboration with drums, samples, banjo and guitar. Funky and locked into a tight groove, influenced by jazz and modern classical as much as rock, hip-hop and drum'n'bass, their sparse instrumentals have occasionally been augmented by vocals.

Ui was formed by **Clem Waldmann** (drums/percussion) and **Sasha Frere-Jones** (bass/guitar/banjo/vocals), following on from the latter's previous group, Dolores. With **Alex Wright** (bass; also ex-Dolores) and **David Weeks** (DJ/tapes), they played together for a year before recording the Two-SIDED EP in 1993. By this time Weeks and Wright had left, with **David Linton** managing samples and live mixing for a brief stint, and third permanent member, **Wilbo Wright**, joining on bass, cello and synthesizer.

Another year passed before their debut album was released, allowing the band to perfect their rhythmic sound on tour, including a sojourn with Tortoise and LaBradford that led them to the Chicago arm of the transatlantic Southern label. However, their first actual album release was the UNLIKE remixes (1995), which preceded SIDELONG (1996) by nearly six months.

SIDELONG was warmly received, especially by certain sections of the British music press, who seemed to be searching for the next Tortoise. Regardless of the fashionable attention, the album itself was an instant classic, infusing Ui's skeletal motorik funk with hints of country and even disco to great effect. Ui soon hooked up with hip British label Soul Static Sound, who put out the epic SHARPIE EP, as well as two 7" singles "Match My Foot/D-Mix 1" and "D-Mix 2". The latter deconstructions (by Soul Static's Darryl Moore) fragmented the main track into unrecognizable shards of sound, a process which was repeated, with less ferocity, by Moore and **Ganger** on the follow-up single, "Dropplike" (1996).

The band's predilection for remixes and collaborations expanded in all directions, finally bearing fruit after lengthy post-production in 1998, with the FIRES EP of Brian Eno and Sun Ra covers recorded with Stereolab as **Uilab**, and their part in the cross-fertilized project TECHNO ANIMAL VERSUS REALITY, a transatlantic remix war also featuring Tortoise, Berlin's Porter Ricks and Alec Empire, and New York's Spectre. An album with Tortoise is still in the pipeline, while both the combined 2-SIDED/SHARPIE EP and LIFELIKE (1998) album showed that Ui remained the funkiest post-rockers around.

After another shift of personal – Waldmann, Frere-Jones and Wilbo Wright were now a trio – the group released ANSWERS (2003), a dynamic, shifting collection of bass-heavy experimentation and ESG-styled 'funk' (in the loosest sense of the word) that offered some compelling moments but, simultaneously, seemed a little behind the times.

⊙ **Sidelong** (1996; Southern).
Recorded and perfected over several years, this selection of tracks includes "Butterfly Who", with its memorable chorus of 'all you wanna do is fuck'n'rollerskate'. Catchy rhythms, sardonic attitude and finely tuned use of layered sound.

⊙ **Lifelike** (1998; Southern).
Never ones to hurry or follow fashions, slow-winding grooves and clever production are the hallmark of this fine, subtle recording.

Richard Fontenoy

U. K. SUBS

Formed London, 1976.

Although they entered the music scene tagged as second-wave, second-division punk rock, for many people the **U. K. Subs** were a way of life, with 1979 as their finest moment. They peaked early and, though they were not the best band to listen to for eternity, they captured many hearts with brilliant live performances and two excellent albums.

Charlie Harper, born David Charles Perez in 1944, was already something of a veteran when punk came along. He struggled to lose his 'old man' image, but he had the energy of a teenager on stage, and with **Nicky Garrett** (lead guitar) he made the U. K. Subs one of the most driving bands of the era. **Paul Slack** (bass) and **Lions** (drums) completed the quartet, who first appeared on vinyl on the 1978 compilation FAREWELL TO THE ROXY. The record featured some of the second wave of bands that played at the legendary short-lived club in London's Covent Garden. It was inferior to its predecessor (LIVE AT THE ROXY) and was rightly panned by pundit and punter alike. The Subs, however, produced two of the better tracks, "I Live In A Car" and "Telephone Numbers", and were to release the former on a double-A-sided single with "C.I.D" (a group anthem) in 1978 on City Records.

Late in 1978, **Pete Davis** replaced Lions on drums to form the essential Subs line-up. The summer of 1979 saw the release of "Stranglehold", which got into the UK Top 30, as did its follow-up, the superb "Tomorrow's Girls" with its choppy guitar and hook chorus. The much-awaited album, ANOTHER KIND OF BLUES (1979), remains the Subs' finest product. Without being overtly political, Harper/Garrett numbers were simple collections of catchphrases dealing with youth, mistrust of authority, amphetamine use and nuclear threat.

In November 1979 the band released an EP on green vinyl, which included the Zombies cover, "She's Not There", and the great "Kicks". Initially disappointing, BRAND NEW AGE (1980) was less immediate than its predecessor. "Warhead", however, remains their epic, with a stop-start radio-signal guitar and lyrics about Cold War angst. The live CRASH COURSE (1980) achieved their highest UK chart position of #18, but only two more singles were to nudge the Top 50 – "Party In Paris" (1980) and "Keep On Runnin' (Till You Burn)" (1981).

Slack and Davis had gone by now (replaced by **Alvin Gibbs** and **Steve Roberts**) and in 1982 the Subs were dealt a major blow when Garrett departed to form **Rebekka Frame**. Bland LPs – ENDANGERED SPECIES (1982), FLOOD OF LIES (1983) and others with equally hackneyed titles – ensued as Harper carried on rocking well into middle age. He even put out an awful solo album of covers, STOLEN PROPERTY (1981).

The Subs, with Davis back on drums, are still trekking round the circuit for beer money, gigging as keenly as ever in a form of punk rock cabaret. They surfaced briefly on the tail end of 1996's Twentieth Anniversary of Punk celebrations and squeezed out a couple of albums' worth of new, sharp material in 1997, QUINTESSENTIALS and RIOT, continuing their album titles' progress through the alphabet ('a' back in 77, with ANOTHER KIND … , 'b' in 80, with BRAND NEW AGE, 'c' for CRASH COURSE, etc). Charlie Harper joined forces with **Knox** (ex-**VIBRATORS**) to record as **Urban Dogs** and continues to tour with the Subs, playing material old and new ("Sub Versive") on the pub circuit.

⊙ **Another Kind Of Blues** (1979; Dojo).
Pill-popping, facile politics, lazy misogyny – no wonder they were the kids' favourites. That said, when the guitar rave-ups kick in, they work up an energy to satisfy the most insatiable speed freak.

⊙ **Crash Course** (1980; Dojo).
A valuable document of one of the era's best live bands in action.

Pip Southall

ULTRAMARINE

Formed Leamington Spa, England, 1988.

Emerging from the remains of 'avant-garde noise funksters' A Primary Industry, the **Ultramarine** duo – **Ian Cooper** (guitars/programming) and **Paul Hammond** (bass/programming) – turned out experimental material with an emphasis on beat and texture. But, while dance beats were the base of their experiment, the use of organ, accordion and Kevin Ayers lyrics has created something far removed from the disco.

Indeed, Ultramarine are more influenced by Robert Wyatt, Joni Mitchell and America than Chicago house artists. Too tight for the chill-out room and too complicated for the bigger dance floor, Ultramarine have found a market among those who enjoy their references to all kinds of cult music of the past, and those who like a band who refuse to join any clique.

Their first two EPs, WYNDHAM LEWIS (1989) and FOLK (1990), introduced their electronic pastoralism. Their work gradually became more focused around short melodic excursions until EVERY MAN AND WOMAN IS A STAR (1992) established an approach that they've maintained to the present day. EVERY MAN was packaged with a story in which Cooper and Hammond take a canoe trip with Dewey Bunnell from the band America. In interviews, the band have said that they admire the 'peculiar, organic, woody production' of early America recordings, and this album provided ample demonstration of this.

Ultramarine's fascination with the Canterbury scene of the 70s was writ large on their next release, UNITED KINGDOMS (1994). This homage to the

Ultramarine ÷ United Kingdoms

British experimental, jazzy scene was not only reminiscent of Soft Machine, but featured guest vocals from **ROBERT WYATT** as well. The next album, BEL AIR (1995), received a mixed reception on release, with some reviewers unenthusiastic about the celebration of US West Coast bland-out music. However, the album had re-created the sounds of a generation of terminally unfashionable musicians in a masterful way, and showed enough invention and experimentation to suggest that Ultramarine would continue happily on their own unique path, though sadly its volume of sales convinced the mighty WEA that the band would be better off elsewhere.

And so, A USER'S GUIDE (1998) sneaked out on a tiny indie label. An intriguing album, even jazzier than its predecessor, A USER'S GUIDE nodded towards techno with the odd lump of intensive beat madness but seemed happier hanging out in the atmospheric zone like the soundtrack to a psychological thriller.

In 2002 EVERY MAN AND WOMAN… received a timely reissue, and was followed by COMPANION (EVERY MAN AND WOMAN…) (2003), a collection of sensitive reworks by the duo as well as remixes from the likes of Spooky and Richard H Kirk.

⊙ **Every Man And Woman Is A Star** (1992; Rough Trade).
The best – simply because it is marginally less self-conscious, more joyous and more experimental than the recordings before or since.

Neil Nixon

ULTRASOUND

Formed London, 1995; disbanded 1999.

Despite all the media and music press hype, major success eluded **Ultrasound**. A larger-than-life band with sound and presence to match, they held court for four years before disappearing almost as mysteriously as they had arrived. The roots of the band go back to Wakefield College, in 1989, when **Andrew Wood** met up with classically trained cellist **Richard Green** (who at sixteen was some ten years his junior).

Completing the initial three-piece incarnation was ex-body-builder and motorcycle enthusiast, drummer **Andy Peace**. The trio all went on to qualify for a degree in music at Newcastle, where they recruited bassist and singer **Vanessa Best**, as well as local keyboard player **Matt Jones**. After short-lived periods with other bands, these five eventually coalesced as Ultrasound in 1995, and by 1997 had gained enough of a following to feature in the *NME's Unsigned Showcase* – an exposure they weren't about to waste. Fierce Panda, the label responsible for so many notable debuts of the 90s, put out an impressive single, "Same Band", which prompted the press to talk of "The Who's TOMMY squeezed into four and a half minutes", such was its epic quality. This panoramic sound was to become a notable feature of Ultrasound's work. Radio 1 loved them, playing "Same Band" and live

favourite "Kurt Russell" widely.

Ultrasound then moved to Nude records and released the limited edition single "Best Wishes" early in 1998. After touring as support to the more traditional Travis and Embrace (in both cases outperforming their hosts), Ultrasound made their television overture with the extraordinary third single "Stay Young" on the BBC's *Later With Jools Holland*. This track featured Wood at his theatrical best, and recalled his glam-rock leanings, boasting the lyric 'Gary Glitter's gone to seed, so who will lead us now… ?'. "Stay Young" became the *NME's Single Of The Week* and made the UK Top 30. The critics, not to mention the ever-growing legion of Ultrasound followers, anticipated a blistering album.

The debut collection, however, was a long time in coming. A flop single, "I'll Show You Mine", coincided with a public waning of interest: other new guitar acts – such as Idlewild – were much quicker to get their debut waxings to the shops. A wrist injury to drummer Peace delayed the album, as did the walkout – after just two sessions – of Radiohead producer **Nigel Godrich**. The group soldiered on, however, and even found time for some unlikely publicity stunts, including Jones and Peace's impromptu streak at the London Fashion Awards. After a return to the charts in the shape of "Floodlit World", EVERYTHING PICTURE, the calorific, sprawling set, finally arrived in 1999, and mystified as many as it charmed, alienating all but Ultrasound die-hards.

The final demise soon followed. Having played a wondrous set at Glastonbury, the band suddenly pulled all its remaining festival appearances throughout Europe. Despite a promising new single in "Aire And Calder", fears were confirmed when Ultrasound split in October 1999. So that was that. Wood spoke of a new project with Peace, hoping to be taken on by Nude – but this foundered when the label went into liquidation in 2002.

Indeed, the only Ultrasound member to stay in any way prominent was Matt Jones, whose new act **Minuteman** opened the year's *NME Carling shows* for The Charlatans, Doves and Cooper Temple Clause. An album, RESIGNED TO LIFE, followed; the band look set to keep the Ultrasound flame alive.

⊙ **Everything Picture** (1999; Nude).
A not-so-Tiny adventure into sound. In ten or fifteen years, Ultrasound's only album might just be revered as a classic of its era – or lost amid a sea of other late-90s hopefuls. Let's hope time is kind and that due is paid to this most generous, if short-lived, of bands.

Jeremy Simmonds

ULTRAVOX

Formed London, 1976; disbanded 1987; re-formed 1993.

Ultravox once had an exclamation mark after their name and a singer called **John Foxx** (real name Dennis Leigh), but once both of these were out of the way they were free to enjoy the chart success

which had previously eluded them, adding **Midge Ure** and his teen-idol sensibilities to the team and going on to create some classic pop. Their grandiose ballad "Vienna" (1981), complete with a heavily stylized video pastiche of *The Third Man*, epitomized Britain's late-70s New Romantic fad.

Nonetheless, the earlier incarnation, Ultravox! with Foxx, was a more interesting proposition by far. After a false start as Tiger Lily, Foxx, bassist **Chris St John** (who later became Chris Cross), Canadian drummer **Warren Cann**, **Billy Currie** (keyboards/violin) and **Steve Shears** (guitar) burst onto the New Wave scene of 1976. They were a little too arch and knowing to be accepted as anything other than gatecrashers at that year's private punk party, with their obvious Bowie and Roxy Music mannerisms, but they were a mesmerizing live experience. Foxx cut a heroic figure at the centre of a maelstrom whipped up by the slashing feedback of guitarist Shears and Currie's frenzied violin.

Live, they managed to retain both pace and melody, but even with the help of producer Brian Eno, ULTRAVOX! (1977) failed to recapture their on-stage energy. Even so, the scope of their intentions was confirmed by the contrast between its last two songs – the roaring "The Wild, The Beautiful And The Damned" and the wonderfully pretentious and narcissistic "My Sex".

Despite a considerable live following, single releases failed to connect with a wider public. But, if frustration and bitterness were detectable on the second album HA-HA-HA! (1977), it was all the more magnificent and animated for it. Melodies were often reduced to disdainful monotones and an embittered Foxx bickered in a voice stripped of any resonance, being particularly convincing on "Artificial Life". Backed for much of the time by banshee howls of disgust and shrill guitars, the only respite was offered by Currie's Satie-inspired keyboard intros, and the lush sax and layered building sound of the closer "Hiroshima Mon Amour".

HA-HA-HA! was Ultravox!'s finest hour, but it didn't chart and, with replacement guitarist **Robin Simon**, the band sulked off to Germany and the guidance of Conny Plank. The weary result, SYSTEMS OF ROMANCE (1978), was their final release for Island, and by 1979 Foxx had left for a solo career and further explorations of urban isolation. (Highlights were collected on the 1988 compilation, ASSEMBLY.)

Simon joined **MAGAZINE**, while the other band members decided to stick together and look for a new singer. Ure, who'd already made one quantum leap from the teenybop Slik to **THE RICH KIDS** with ex-Sex Pistol Glen Matlock, proved nothing if not versatile; while rehearsing with vox, he stood in as **THIN LIZZY**'s guitarist on a US tour.

Ure and Currie joined **Steve Strange** in **Visage**, and scored a Top 10 hit with "Fade To Grey" (1980), only weeks before "Vienna" became Ultravox's biggest hit and best-remembered track, beginning a string of hit singles which continued through the early 80s, compiled on the 1984 album, THE COLLECTION.

It was a kind of end. The same year Ure struck a partnership with Bob Geldof for Band Aid, and subsequently pursued a successful solo career, while Cann left the band in 1986, replaced by **BIG COUNTRY**'s **Mark Brzezicki**, for the LP, U-VOX. By 1987, Ultravox had folded, although Currie, Simon and vocalist **Marcus O'Higgins** carried on – forgettably – as U-Vox, eventually returning in 1993 as Ultravox with new vocalists and further synth-pop albums, most recently INGENUITY (1997). Since then Currie has released numerous solo efforts through Puzzle Records.

⊙ **Slow Motion** (1993; Spectrum).
A useful budget-priced compilation of the first three albums. Undeniably pretentious, but high on melody, attitude and enjoyment.

⊙ **The Collection** (1984; Chrysalis).
From "Vienna" and "Dancing With Tears In My Eyes" to "We Came To Dance", here's a race through Ultravox's early-80s pop incarnation. Doubtless currently available at a secondhand shop near you, testimony to the fickle nature of pop.

Thanks to Warren Cann for updates
Ada Wilson

UNCLE TUPELO

Formed Belleville, Illinois, 1982; disbanded 1993.

Uncle Tupelo were America's finest ever post-punk country band. In a four-album career spanning eleven years they represented all that is worthwhile and immortal in traditional American country music, while at the same time adding a caustic, sometimes savage dimension whose origins lay in punk and the repressed angst of small-town America.

Jay Farrar (guitar/vocals) formed the band with his high-school friend **Jeff Tweedy** (bass/vocals) when both were just 15. It would be eight years, though, before they released their first record, NO DEPRESSION (1990). A stunning debut, it was a statement of intent of everything that was to develop and emerge fully realized in subsequent releases: homespun, down-to-earth Guthrie-esque folk ballads, white country gospel and hard, often manic, unrelenting rock.

The band displayed a considerable gift for revitalizing and contemporizing the much-abused and largely homogenized genre of American country music, and this was much in evidence with the release of their follow-up, STILL FEEL GONE (1991). By this time Uncle Tupelo had begun to attract widespread critical acclaim and the enthusiastic endorsement of heavyweight contemporaries like R.E.M.'s Peter Buck, who stepped in to produce the glorious MARCH 16–20 1992 (1992), which was issued, like its predecessors, on Rockville, garnering the boys a reputation as 'America's best undiscovered band'. The album's title referred to the few days it took Buck and the band to record, and, although the results stripped away the rawness of sound that had made their previous work so exciting, it achieved near greatness for the quality of songs like "Grindstones"and "Shakyground".

It was only a matter of time before the major labels moved in, and in the event Sire beat off a flurry of rivals to sign the band. The ensuing album, ANODYNE (1993), however, turned out to be a swansong, with Farrar and Tweedy increasingly at odds, and nearing the end of what was already, in effect, a decade-plus partnership. Still, the record was a tribute to both parties, with the band's most perfect song (the heartbreaking "Slate") standing out amid as impeccable a contemporary-country set as the 90s ever produced.

Following the split, Farrar and Tweedy went on to front their own bands, respectively **SON VOLT** and **WILCO**, unleashing a fine pair of albums, A.M. and TRACE (both 1994), that showed they didn't need the partnership to maintain creative output. Though both outfits continue to release quality albums the Uncle Tupelo name still resonates with fans of the genre they helped to kick start. As a result UNCLE TUPELO 89/93: AN ANTHOLOGY was released in 2002 as a precursor to the reissue of the band's first three albums, complete with rarities and improved packaging.

○ **Still Feel Gone** (1991; Rockville).
A continuation of the themes of NO DEPRESSION, a year earlier, this album gnaws at the roots of American country music, from "Watch Me Fall", which draws on the sound of Phil Ochs, to the more traditional "Fall Down Easy". A good introduction to how good country music can be.

○ **March 16–20 1992** (1992; Rockville).
Less power, but the songs get better on this brilliant set.

○ **Anodyne** (1993; Sire).
Again, as perfect a set of American rural folk songs as can be found.

Shaun Goater

Formed Derry, Northern Ireland, 1975;
disbanded 1983.

The Undertones' story may ultimately have revolved around the concept of the perfect pop song (John Peel still proclaims their "Teenage Kicks" his all-time favourite), but the band's origins were somewhat less ambitious. Five friends – **Feargal Sharkey** (vocals), **John O'Neill** (guitar), **Damian O'Neill** (guitar), **Michael Bradley** (bass) and **Billy Doherty** (drums) – began by playing pop covers to sometimes hostile local audiences, until glam-rock then punk rock inspired them to concentrate on self-penned material.

Demos were rejected throughout England, but The Undertones consoled themselves with the idea of recording an EP for Terry Hooley's Good Vibrations label – at least they would be immortalized as the creators of Derry's first punk record. In an unexpected twist of fate, however, "True Confessions", the original choice to lead the EP, was rejected in favour of "Teenage Kicks", which gave the record a suitably summery aura.

As John Peel began playing the song incessantly on the radio, The Undertones accepted a deal with Seymour Stein's Sire Records, on the basis that they held Sire's Talking Heads in such high esteem. The EP was repackaged, and led to moderate chart success, British TV appearances, a rollicking second EP, GET OVER YOU, and a debut LP.

This, simply entitled THE UNDERTONES (1979), arrived in two formats – one with a black-and-white sleeve, the other in colour and boasting the two earlier releases as additional tracks. Alongside ready-made breakneck classic pop singles in "Jimmy Jimmy" and "Here Comes The Summer", it contained such unaffected gems as "Male Model", "Family Entertainment", "She's A Runaround" and a thirty-second tribute to "Casbah Rock", one of the few Irish venues that would harbour the group in their early days.

The second album, HYPNOTISED (1980), was preceded by what some esteem as the group's greatest single. "You've Got My Number (Why Don't You Use It)" featured a bracing, momentous riff, which was spliced by a guitar solo to rival The Only Ones' "Another Girl, Another Planet". Produced by Roger Bechirian, the album proved equally enduring, with songs addressing such topics as playground pecking order, gang membership and the group's complete lack of empathy with women. While many critics picked up on the agenda-setting opening, "More Songs About Chocolate And Girls", fewer noted a superbly perceptive view of reverence and alienation in relation to the opposite sex – although women were mentioned in nearly all early Undertones' songs, practically none were namechecked.

The staggering power of "My Perfect Cousin" and "Wednesday Week" gave The Undertones their

The Undertones on the road (front, from left): John, Mick and Billy, with Feargal behind

biggest chart successes during the summer of 1980, but the expectations of a voracious critical following were to prove their undoing. A third LP, POSITIVE TOUCH (1981), contained another UK Top 20 single, "It's Going To Happen!", but an increasingly sophisticated approach to both songwriting and performance didn't please all their fans. Still, it contained great songs, notably the emphatic "Tearproof", the shimmering "Julie Ocean" and The Rolling Stones pastiche "When Saturday Comes", which later inspired a soccer fanzine of the same name.

Critics were a little bewildered by POSITIVE TOUCH, but the band were not about to revert to the style of previous triumphs; in fact, the even more complex THE SIN OF PRIDE (1983) didn't merely divide audiences and critics, but also The Undertones themselves. John O'Neill requested a larger share of songwriting royalties to tie in with his greater input, but, when the ultimatum was ignored by Sharkey, the band had to split. There were even disagreements over the final track-listing of THE SIN OF PRIDE, released just before the break-up. "The Love Parade" was a classy slice of 60s melodrama, though, and the delicate "Soul Seven" was a latter-day reminder of John O'Neill's affinity for the pop ballad.

Sharkey preceded a solo career by collaborating with **Vince Clarke** (previously of **DEPECHE MODE** and Yazoo, later of Erasure); as **The Assembly** they hit the UK Top 3 with "Never Never" (1983). Two years on, he hit the very top of the charts with a cover of Maria McKee's "A Good Heart", and subsequently became an A&R executive. The O'Neill brothers, meanwhile, took their formidable twin-guitar abilities to **THAT PETROL EMOTION**. In 1993 there were signs that The Undertones were to re-form but Sharkey's refusal to join in put paid to a full reunion (and quite right, too). The remainder of the band, though, happily took to the stage in 2000 at the Fleadh Festival in London.

⊙ **The Best Of The Undertones: Teenage Kicks** (1993; Castle).
A mighty 25-track selection, and an ideal introduction to Northern Ireland's premier pop band. All the legendary singles are included, along with vital album cuts and even the occasional choice B-side, like "Mars Bars".

Alex Ogg

UNIVERS ZERO

Formed Brussels, Belgium, 1974; disbanded 1986; reformed 1997.

Belgium is not a country renowned for its cutting-edge traditions. Hard then to believe that one of the most credible prog-rock bands of all time should emerge from here. **Univers Zero** are undoubtedly prog: the unusual time signatures, frequency of pieces over seven minutes and odd instrumentation make that conclusion unavoidable. But you can play the Univers Zero records of your youth without cringing – their angular, dissonant music is frenzied, fresh, uncompromising and tough.

Their debut album release, 1313, seemed to spring fully formed out of nowhere with an eccentric line-up of bassoon, drums, violin, bass, viola, harmonium and guitar. More Bartók than Chuck Berry, it employed scraping strings, creepy winds, gothic keyboards and 13/8 time signatures. But it rocked with a frenzy through the superb drumming of **Daniel Denis** and angular guitar of **Roger Trigaux**, set against the keyboards of **Emmanuel Nicaise**.

By the next album, HERESIE (1979), the band had lost Nicaise (Trigaux played the keyboards) and recruited **Guy Segers** on bass; Segers was ideal for the band with his groaning, heaving sound. The album begins with low rumbles and whispered gothic vocals on the astonishing "La Faulx".

Looser than Magma, it seems as if it's going to fall apart at any moment, but crashes and stumbles its way forward until the familiar angular rhythms and woodwind start up again. The piece ends with dissonant violin and obsessive keyboard stabs. The rest of the album sustains this dark, introspective atmosphere.

Following these two records Roger Trigaux left the band to form **Present**, whose two early albums, TRISKAIDEKAPHOBIE and LE POISON QUI REND FOU, are now available on a single CD.

The third Univers Zero album, CEUX DU DEHORS (1981), was made without guitar. Though Daniel Denis was the primary writer, new full-time keyboard player **Andy Kirk** and Guy Segers each wrote a song, while Denis and Kirk also wrote a song together. It was a lighter album – the new keyboardist added fewer gothic textures – but still pretty harsh. The stand-out track was "Triomphe Des Mouches", five condensed minutes combining the best of older and newer Univers Zero: dark chords, mad harmonium and lunatic piano merged with faint suggestions of Stravinsky and Gypsy music.

With UZED (1984), only Daniel Denis remained of the previous line-up and synthesizers replaced the eccentric harmonium and harpsichord. There is a trace of twiddly jazz/rock fusion here and a more structured approach on offer. But the strong dissonant elements of East European folk music are still present. Particularly welcome is the beautiful writing for piano, cello and winds on "Celesta".

HEATWAVE (1986) had Andy Kirk back on keyboards – and writing most of the material. It was a more approachable disc, with the band tighter and more overtly disciplined, if also a little too electronic and amplified. However, the old spirit had a workout on the final track, "The Funeral Plain" – twenty minutes of staggering invention, odd electronic noises, piano, wind and strings.

No more was heard after that for quite a while. Daniel Denis released a couple of solo albums, interesting if not quite up to Univers Zero standard. Present have continued releasing more guitar-based albums with something of the original frenzy. And then, after an epic absence, Univers Zero returned with THE HARD QUEST (1999), which offered more adventurous, gothic-tinged concoctions. It was followed by more wild, classical hybrids on RHYTHMIX (2002).

⊙ **1313** (1977; Cuneiform).
The first album, perhaps the best, certainly the purest – it is almost acoustic for large amounts of time – and one of the scariest records in rock. Fans of King Crimson with strong nerves should check it out

⊙ **Heresie** (1979; Cuneiform).
More gloom, more darkness – scarier than ever.

⊙ **Heatwave** (1986; Cuneiform).
The last Univers Zero album is imperfect, but essential for the superb "Funeral Plain" alone.

Graham Taylor

URGE OVERKILL

Formed Chicago, 1986; split 1997.

Urge Overkill always split the critics. Fans of **National 'Nash' Kato** (Nathan Katruud; vocals/guitar), **Eddie 'King' Roeser** (bass) and latecomer **'Black Caesar' Onassis** (Johnny Rowan; vocals/drums) cited their observations on American trash culture as revelatory; others, less enamoured of the trio, thought they were simply trash.

Certainly subtlety was not part of the Urge Overkill equation, with overt early influences like Funkadelic (from whose song they took their name), Cheap Trick and AC/DC. The band's debut EP, STRANGE, I... (1986), released on Ruthless Records, established their agenda with a

psychedelic label, cartoon cover, and a mesh of 60s pop with metal riffs. The only downside was a neutered production, which also hindered their first album, JESUS URGE SUPERSTAR (1989), released on noted Chicago independent label Touch & Go. Its lacklustre mix buried a number of strong ideas, not least "Very Sad Trousers", Urge's tribute to Chicago's alternative rock sensations and serial substance abusers, Royal Trux.

It took the arrival of producer Butch Vig on AMERICRUISER (1990) to rectify the situation, but the songs had improved, too, perhaps because they seemed less desperate to impress as comic narratives. Even better was SUPERSONIC STORYBOOK (1991), produced by former flatmate and long-standing producer and mentor, Steve Albini. For once, the band's intention to satirize the whole rock firmament did not sacrifice cohesion and accessibility, and the introduction of Rowan on drums helped as well, adding rhythmic lustre to the group's formerly shambolic sound.

The STULL EP (1992), named after the ghost town situated at the exact midpoint of the US, included two of Urge Overkill's best-known recordings. Their cover of Neil Diamond's "Girl, You'll Be A Woman Soon" later became an MTV hit after its inclusion in the Quentin Tarantino movie *Pulp Fiction*, while "Goodbye To Guyville" influenced an enormously successful Liz Phair album. The broadening appeal of the band was confirmed by tours with both Pearl Jam and Nirvana.

By the advent of SATURATION (1993), Urge Overkill had left Touch & Go on fraught terms, and signed to major label Geffen. They had become notorious fixtures within Chicago's musical milieu, wilfully defying punk regulations with their flamboyant dress code and celebration of kitsch. (Albini publicly vilified their vaudevillian behaviour, which included touring the city in an open-top sports car or horse-drawn carriage, sipping martinis.) Produced by hip-hop team The Butcher Brothers, the album's homage to 70s rock reinforced comparisons to Cheap Trick, but yielded a number of catchy, if somewhat gaudy, singles.

In 1995 they were back again with a vengeance, on the strength of their *Pulp Fiction* appearance, releasing a new album, EXIT THE DRAGON, of marvellous, addictive, Big Star-like power pop. The promotion of the album, however, rapidly descended into disaster, with 'Blackie' Onassis busted for possession (though charges were later dropped) and support band Guided By Voices leaving mid-tour. The band kept their heads down for several months, with Roeser leaving at the end of 1996. **Nils St. Cyr** took his place and the band moved to 550 Records to record a new album, but when the label rejected their new material the band split. Onassis simply vanished but Roeser and Kato went on to work on various other projects, with the latter releasing DEBUTANTE (2000) on Pearl Jam guitarist Stone Gossard's Loosegroove Records.

- **Supersonic Storybook** (1991; Touch &Go).
  Their most powerful musical statement so far, with thundering songs such as "The Candidate" and "Bionic Revolution" marrying garage rock to almost every other existing style.
- **Saturation** (1993; Geffen).
  More self-consciously wacky than before, but with plenty of lugubrious pop melodies to sweeten the medicine, Urge Overkill become a subversive incarnation of the 'MTV generation' band.
- **Exit The Dragon** (1995; Geffen).
  The best yet, with its sparse rhythms, sublime chorus hooks and anthemic songs. Invest at once and tell your grandchildren.

Alex Ogg

URIAH HEEP

Formed London, 1968.

F ew bands have been as uncool as **Uriah Heep**, a crew so lacking in street cred they made Grand Funk Railroad look hip. If Led Zeppelin were the tasty curry of Britain's early-70s rock onslaught, then Uriah Heep were dismissed as the bad smell that follows in its wake. This was a band who almost defined the concept of a heavy-metal prog-rock cliché, who had lyrics about riding 'on a horse of crimson fire', and who had demons-and-wizards **Roger Dean** cover artwork to boot. It's hard not to feel a glimmer of nostalgia.

Formed in 1968 as **Spice** (the Dickensian name came the following year), the band featured three survivors from R&B/soul combo The Stalkers – guitarist **Mick Box**, singer **Dave Byron** and bassist **Tony Newton** – plus keyboard player **Ken Hensley** from The Gods and drummer **Nigel Olsson**. Rehearsals in the summer of 1969 in the Hanwell Community Centre in West London put them in a room adjacent to Deep Purple, who were exercising their new line-up in the rough-and-heavy rock sound that was to catapult them to stardom. Some of the noise permeated the thin walls, and, when Uriah Heep's first album, VERY 'EAVY, VERY 'UMBLE, appeared in 1970, there certainly seemed to have been some exchange of influences.

Even so, Heep's organ-dominated, bluesy sound had quite enough of its own character to mark the band out, and it wasn't long before the Heep influence was being displayed by European bands like Golden Earring, Scorpions and Titanic. Indeed, some would say it still lingers on the British metal scene.

Olsson was an early departure (he was to play on Elton John's GOODBYE YELLOW BRICK ROAD), to be replaced by **Ian Clarke** and then **Lee Kerslake**, while Tony Newton was replaced on bass by **Gary Thain**. Five albums were recorded in that hectic time between 1970 and 1972, with Hensley marking himself out as the band's leader by progressively taking more of the credits and writing the rather asinine sleeve notes. If the band's success was impressive, critical acclaim was distinctly lacking. The comment of one American journalist, 'If this band

makes it, I'll kill myself', was not untypical. But the public turned on to anthemic tracks like "Gypsy" (1970), "Bird Of Prey" (1971) and "July Morning" (1971).

The band's fourth and fifth albums – DEMONS AND WIZARDS and THE MAGICIAN'S BIRTHDAY (both 1972) – put Heep on the edge of the big time, each highlighted by a classic 70s metal track, respectively "Easy Livin'" and "Sweet Lorraine". These sets charted Top 40 in the UK and US, on the strength of some gruelling live work, as did URIAH HEEP LIVE (1973), WONDERWORLD (1974) and RETURN TO FANTASY (an all-time high UK #7).

Unfortunately, the band's Spinal Tap excesses caught up with them. In 1975 Gary Thain's drug and alcohol dependency led to his dismissal (and subsequent death), and the following year Dave Byron, too, was very publicly sacked. After a rather feeble solo career he vanished from the scene, eventually being found dead at his home in 1985.

Like most bands of their generation, Heep stagnated in the late 70s and seemed to disintegrate. After Ken Hensley left to join Blackfoot, and Lee Kerslake threw in his lot with **OZZY OSBOURNE**, Box disbanded Heep in 1981. Yet there was still some twitching in the corpse. In 1982 singer **Pete Goalby** (ex-Trapeze) was brought in along with bassist **Bob Daisley** (ex-**RAINBOW**). ABOMINOG (1982) brought unexpected returns as heavy metal was once again filling the venues, and Heep's funkier sound gave them a new lease of life that was consolidated by 1983's HEAD FIRST.

As metal moved on again with the appearance of thrash, Heep's 80s success began to wane, although appearances at festivals kept them in the public eye. While they remained popular in Europe (1990 saw the release of a live album recorded in Moscow), they were never going to strike gold again. By the mid 90s, Uriah Heep seemed to have become pretty much moribund, until the release of SEA OF LIGHT (1996). There was also a 25th-anniversary four-CD box set, A TIME OF REVELATION. By then, a line-up of Box, Kerslake, **Trevor Bolder** (bass; ex of Bowie's Spiders), **Bernie Shaw** (vocals) and the excellent **Phil Lanzon** (keyboards) had been in place for fully a decade. The 'corpse' was twitching vigorously enough to suggest life – a fact confirmed by the release of SONIC ORIGAMI in 1998 and an 8CD box-set in 2002, fittingly titled YOU CAN'T KEEP A GOOD BAND DOWN.

- **Demons And Wizards** (1972; Bronze).
  The situation in which this was recorded, during a quick break between tours, gives Heep's best album a sense of urgency. There's enough in a song like "Easy Livin'" to keep it going for five minutes, but the band tear through it in barely three. Some gentle guitar strumming gives longer tracks like "The Wizard" space to breathe, allowing Heep's more wistful side to show through.
- **Abominog** (1982; Castle).
  Heep hit back with a surprisingly good album just when they had been written off. A fuller, fruitier sound gave their music a weight it had always tended to lack, and for a time they were taken seriously again as a major force in heavy rock.

Sonic Origami (1998; Eagle).
Old man rock of the 80s, but done better than anyone has a right to expect. Nothing to convert the unconvinced, but enough to send the faithful into raptures. Includes a touching tribute to Thain and Byron. Top tracks: "Between Two Worlds" and "Everything In Life".

Patrick Neylan-Francis & Guy Davies

U2

Formed Dublin, Ireland, 1977.

"Most people think we got kicked out of the Garden of Eden. I'm not so sure. I think we kicked God out of it." Bono

Paradoxically, despite their status as 'biggest band in the universe bar none', **U2** have never inspired universal acclaim, for the passion of their army of fans is matched by the equally vocal contempt of a legion of detractors. It's perhaps a testament to the singularity of their vision that few bands have succeeded in polarizing opinion so completely. Unquestionably U2 have talent, energy and a total belief in everything they do and say. Such conviction, however, has provoked accusations of pretentiousness, bravado and egoism.

Their passion and their persuasions have been derided right from their post-punk beginnings, but in many ways the band have become a victim of their own achievement. The huge success of THE JOSHUA TREE (1987), for example, or their show-stopping Live Aid performance, meant that, by the late 1980s, it had become very difficult not to have an opinion about U2. It became a truism that U2 were 'important' – indeed, in 1985 *Rolling Stone* described the band as perhaps 'the only band that matters', a pretty hard tag to live up to. Yet, in spite of their success, U2 have often found themselves out of step with the prevailing *Zeitgeist* of pop. In the twilight of punk, for instance, U2's anger seemed too directed, too political. In the heyday of Britpop and grunge, their ambition seemed grandiose. Unlike, say, R.E.M., who have scaled similar heights of popularity with credibility intact, U2 have never inspired a legion of imitators. For the fashionable, U2 were always anathema: too big, too pretentious, too 'important'.

Only at the beginning, it might be argued, was the music the most important thing for U2. **Bono** (Paul Hewson) was always a charismatic figure, but the singularity of U2 was in their determination to do something different with the standard setup of bass, drums and guitar – duties performed, respectively, by **Adam Clayton**, **Larry Mullen** and **The Edge** (David Evans).

When BOY (1980), OCTOBER (1981) and WAR (1983) were released, against the often insipid backdrop of early-80s synth-pop, they sounded fresh indeed. And, if the sound was different, then so was

REDFERNS

U2: don't push me 'cos I'm close to The Edge...

the band's left-wing political commitment and religious ideals. Time and time again, U2 struggled against the grain of cynicism, insularity and political indifference. Compare the concerns of Bono with those of Morrissey, that other 80s figurehead, and the difference is stark.

For an Irish band to hold such concerns, however, was hardly surprising. While the lingering activists of English pop, the Wellers and Braggs of the patronizing and ill-fated Red Wedge movement, espoused party allegiance, no such answers were possible for Ireland. Responding to the impotence of pragmatic politics in the Irish situation, U2 went for a broader stroke, celebrating idealism in their songs, or lapsing into bleak pessimism. "I Will Follow" (1980), "Rejoice" (1981) and "Sunday Bloody Sunday" (1983) were songs with a passion and a focus unprecedented in pop music.

The band started to creep into popularity almost in spite of themselves. BOY had peaked at #52 in the UK; OCTOBER had reached #11; neither had charted in the US. Yet, in 1983, U2 went massive, with "New Year's Day" (1983) setting the ball rolling, before WAR propelled itself to #1 in the UK, #12 in the US. It was followed by UNDER A BLOOD RED SKY (also 1983), a record of just how raw and exhilarating U2's live performances could be, as well as how much they were prepared to experiment with sounds (and images).

The anthemic "Pride (In The Name Of Love)" ensured that THE UNFORGETTABLE FIRE (1984) maintained the chart success. This album was something of a departure for U2 – in hindsight, it was a dress rehearsal for the genius of THE JOSHUA TREE. The unabashedly political WAR had broken them on a world scale, but in a courageous move by the band, FIRE instead offered evidence of a trend towards the subtle, the complex and even the obscure. The excellent "Pride" seemed a throwback to the more openly political and unashamedly 'rock' leanings of earlier singles. Other tracks, notably "A Sort Of Homecoming" or "The Unforgettable Fire", were softer and richer, hinting at a new delicacy. In contrast to earlier albums, FIRE, created under the guidance of new producer Brian Eno, was very much a studio album, refined beyond anything the band had done before. And, again, it was a far cry from what anyone else was doing in 1984.

The tour that accompanied THE UNFORGETTABLE FIRE was, indeed, unforgettable at times, and it culminated, in 1985, with a Live Aid performance of such intensity that it marked U2 out in one of the greatest rock line-ups of all time. "Sunday Bloody Sunday" and "Bad", the latter in particular, were two of the most memorable moments of the whole show.

Two years later, in March 1987, U2 released THE JOSHUA TREE. The expectation that surrounded this release was immense: U2 had not made a record for three years, had done Live Aid and The Conspiracy Of Hope tour for Amnesty International, and found themselves arguably the biggest band in the world.

THE JOSHUA TREE more than lived up to its billing. A #1 album across the globe, it spawned a plethora of hit singles: "With Or Without You" was followed to the American top spot by two subsequent releases. In April U2 featured on the cover of *Time* magazine, an honour previously accorded to just two bands – The Beatles and The Who.

THE JOSHUA TREE represented U2 at their musical pinnacle. Mature and perceptive, it veered between the personal and the political, between the menace of "Bullet The Blue Sky" and the gentle anguish of "With Or Without You". Bono took most of the U2 acclaim, as the showman and the poet, but on many of these tracks the sound was as subtle as rock music had ever been. And it was a sound rather than just a tune, for few of these songs survived by a simple riff or a catchy hook. THE JOSHUA TREE marked the point when people started to talk of U2 as a phenomenon, not as a pop band. Fawning articles in serious magazines portrayed U2 as the saviours of rock'n'roll, the only band to have really done it 'their way', the yardstick by which all other musicians should be judged. It culminated the drive to superstardom, but for some it also marked the point at which the unrefined post-punk protest band transmuted into a carefully manipulated and manipulative organization, a triumph of style over content.

THE JOSHUA TREE was one of the best albums of the decade, and U2 would find it hard to regain its heights. A movie soundtrack out of control, RATTLE AND HUM (1988) was loud and brash and simple – perhaps a response to those who sought to consecrate every step on the path of U2. But then again, they sometimes seemed set on self-consecration: with *Zoo TV*, the tour that followed the release of ACHTUNG BABY (1991), it was as if U2 were claiming a special affinity with the momentous events of 1989. The Berlin Wall came down and U2 were the ones to put it into proper perspective, with Trabants hanging from the metalwork of huge American arenas. Still, if you fought through the blankets of sham, the overweening pretentiousness of Bono ringing celebrities from the stage, there was still some great music.

"One", in particular, seemed as heartfelt and honest as U2 had ever been, and "Who's Gonna Ride Your Wild Horses" confirmed the impression that ACHTUNG BABY, at its core, was – at last – an album about personal relationships. A much-needed injection of humour, a nod to the Madchester movement of 1990–91, even dance mixes: they all lent the album a sense of fun, and this despite some fairly pessimistic subject matter. Betrayal, sex, love and confusion: U2 had finally hit the small time. After the genius of THE JOSHUA TREE, and the confusion of RATTLE AND HUM, ACHTUNG BABY was contemporary, honest and straightforward.

Yet, with the self-importance of *Zoo TV*, U2 had again polarized opinion and found themselves even further out of kilter with the prevailing pop philosophy. ZOOROPA (1993), spawned from the ashes of *Zoo TV*, was less than remarkable but still went #1 on both sides of the Atlantic. Perhaps in reaction to the scale of these recent tours and epic albums, the four members of U2 set out with their producer Brian Eno to create a quite different project, ORIGINAL SOUNDTRACKS I (1995), released under the collective name Passengers. A pause from all stadium activity, all debate on U2's epic status, it caught most fans off guard. The album's fourteen tracks were written, supposedly, to accompany art films (although only four of the films were 'real'), and guests included **Howie B** and **Luciano Pavarotti**. It was as state-of-the-art avant-rock as U2 had ever been.

Now where the hell did they go from there? Suddenly it all got a lot more intriguing again. POP (1997) had the industry agog with talk of a projected ten million sales and a world tour that, if anything, actually succeeded in outdoing *Zoo TV* (at least in terms of pomp and pretension). Stadium audiences cowered from the forty-foot-high Bono who leered at the world from the screen backing the stage. Though far from being U2's 'dance' album, POP and the tour borrowed heavily from the various skeins of dance culture, calling in old pal Howie B to spin the discs before they appeared, and decking Bono out in an awful fake-muscleman T-shirt lifted straight from some dingy clubwear store. The music built on ACHTUNG BABY's foundations, but seemed a little unsure of which direction to take. They pulled out all the stops for "MoFo", a brooding beast of a track that wakes up as Bono seemingly descends into screaming madness. Old-time revival and salvation got their traditional U2 look-in on "Gone" but the star track had to be the 'lost-in-the-realm-of-the-senses' lust-fest "If You Wear That Velvet Dress".

In 1998 the group succumbed to a Greatest Hits collection with Bono referring to THE BEST OF 1980 – 1990 as "housekeeping". The timely double-CD set collected the hits from BOY to RATTLE AND HUM

on one disc alongside a disc of B-sides – it even spawned a hit of its own in the shape of a rerecorded "Sweetest Thing", written by Bono for his wife's birthday and originally the B-side to "Where The Streets Have No Name".

Meanwhile the group became more heavily involved with political pressure groups, with Bono lobbying the G8 leaders in Cologne (with, among others, Radiohead's Thom Yorke) and addressing both the United Nations and US Congress on behalf of the Jubilee 2000 debt campaign. All this was going on while the band worked on a new album, ALL THAT YOU CAN'T LEAVE BEHIND (2000). Produced once again by Brian Eno and Daniel Lanois it was the most straight-ahead guitar album that U2 had made since THE JOSHUA TREE. With the irony and shambolic experimentalism of recent efforts out of the way the foursome found themselves on more comfortable ground, particularly on the single "Beautiful Day" and the soaring "Walk On". Salman Rushdie even put in an appearance supplying lyrics for "The Ground Beneath Her Feet" (a cut taken from the soundtrack of the Wim Wenders movie *The Million Dollar Hotel*).

Amid a slew of international awards for ALL THAT YOU CAN'T LEAVE BEHIND (2000) the band headed out on tour, maybe not quite so spectacularly as in previous years, but with no one really challenging them for Greatest Band In The World status they probably don't need all the whiz-bang visuals and cringey gimmicks at the moment.

U2

⊙ **War** (1983; Island).
The album that broke U2, featuring "Sunday Bloody Sunday", "New Year's Day", "Two Hearts Beat As One". Introducing The Edge's trademark yearning guitar sound, WAR captures early U2 at their fiery best.

⊙ **The Unforgettable Fire** (1984; Island).
U2 meet their dream producer in Eno and you can hear the sound expanding. Songs include "Pride (In The Name Of Love)", "Bad" and "A Sort Of Homecoming" – all essential.

⊙ **The Joshua Tree** (1987; Island).
Simply the best U2 album, and one of the defining records of a decade.

⊙ **Achtung Baby** (1991; Island).
Most welcome after the unhappy RATTLE AND HUM, this is a deeply personal outing by Bono's standards and much the better for it. Bono finally gets a sense of irony, however small, and sheds his Messiah complex. And "One" remains U2's finest recent moment.

⊙ **All That You Can't Leave Behind** (2000; Island).
Daniel Lanois and Brian Eno are back on board trimming the edges of the group's trademark widescreen sound. It's not so much their music that makes this set great, it's more that the band carry off the idea of being U2 with such conviction that you can't help but be entranced.

Passengers

⊙ **Original Soundtracks I** (1995; Island).
U2 and Eno go ambient, creating futuristic soundtracks out of whispered poetry and unlikely liaisons.

Hugh Wilson

VAN DER GRAAF GENERATOR

Formed Manchester, England, 1967; disbanded 1971; re-formed 1975, disbanded 1978.

Van Der Graaf Generator seemed to emerge from nowhere, with music that combined cold beauty and a desperate romanticism. Although loosely tagged in the prog-rock bag, they were actually far closer to the kind of experimental rock being developed by German bands like Can than to British contemporaries; they were definitely not ELP or Barclay James Harvest. Nearly twenty years on from disbanding, they – and the group's singer and principal songwriter, **PETER HAMMILL** – retain a committed following.

The band formed in 1967, naming themselves after a machine that produces electrical static. The original line-up – Peter Hammill (vocals), **Chris 'Judge' Smith** (drums) and **Nick Pearne** (organ) met at Manchester University – produced one rare single ("The People You Were Going To"), before splitting the next year. Hammill, however, soon re-formed the band, recruiting **Hugh Banton** on organ and **Guy Evans** on drums, with Smith moving to vocals and sax before again leaving the group. (Smith's 1991 CD DEMOCRAZY contained demos of this line-up.) **Keith Ellis** was then added on bass for gigs and the recording sessions that produced the band's first album, AEROSOL GREY MACHINE (1969). Initially released in the US only, this was a fascinating beginning, with Hammill's intricate lyrics as poetic and engaging as anything produced in the prog arena, and his insistent, proto-punk delivery.

The band line-up remained fluid and Hammill rebuilt the Generator again, with **Nic Potter** on bass and **Dave Jackson** on saxophone, for THE LEAST WE CAN DO IS WAVE TO EACH OTHER (1970). This consolidated the band's distinctly off-kilter sound: a dense record, not exactly conceptual, but suggestive of occult happenings and some kind of apocalypse. What made it compelling was the mixture of Hammill's spooked vocals with a metallic music lacking the usual consolations of lead guitar. One review of the time described the lead singer as a 'male Nico', a reasonable summary of the album's glorious despair. The album introduced "Refugees", an anthemic cry of solidarity, which was to remain a live favourite for years to come. And it produced the band's only significant appearance in the charts, reaching a mighty #47 slot in the UK.

It was an active period with H TO HE WHO AM THE ONLY ONE (H = hydrogen, He = helium) released the same year. Nic Potter had left midway through recordings and Robert Fripp contributed guitar. The record was a mix of heavy balladry – "House With No Door" – and intense, organ- and sax-led riffing, such as the driving "Killer". At this point – hard to credit now –Van Der Graaf undertook a promotional tour for Charisma, headlining over Genesis, and they blossomed on stage, with Jackson – in black leather from hat to feet – as visually compelling as the spectrally thin Hammill.

Next off, still with Fripp guesting, was PAWN HEARTS (1971), a more prog-like album, with its epic work-outs. The fact that it was beaten to the shops by Hammill's first solo offering, FOOL'S MATE, suggested that the band were not really jelling, and within months they had broken up again.

Ironically, this was the time when prog-rock of a kind not wholly unlike Van Der Graaf was in the ascendant in Britain. Label mates Genesis were about to go Top 20 with FOXTROT, drawing others in their wake. Prog-rock, however, demanded bands, and for the next four years Hammill produced a series of albums – which were often pretty much Van Der Graaf in tone and personnel – as solo projects. The other members, meanwhile, issued an instrumental album, THE LONG HELLO, featuring loose jamming with not a tortured vocal in sight.

In 1975, Van Der Graaf re-formed and returned, with a French tour and the GODBLUFF LP. Musically, it was as if they'd never been away – which in a way was the case, as they'd continued rehearsing through the 'lost' years – and in tracks like "Arrow" they revisited the anthemic riffing of "Killer". As in the old days, sax and organ were to the fore, and, perhaps in deference to the fact that this was a band album, Hammill shared the limelight with instrumental soloing. The fans were more than satisfied and gigs saw a cult-like following.

They were never to transcend this status, however, as the times had moved away from Van Der Graaf. Gabriel had by now left Genesis to drift into AOR, and punk was on the horizon. Nonetheless, the next two albums, STILL LIFE and WORLD RECORD (1976), produced further classics in the tried-and-trusted vein, in particular the heavy ballad "La Rosa" and the title track off STILL LIFE.

By 1977's THE QUIET ZONE: THE PLEASURE DOME, two albums compacted into one, Jackson and Banton had left the band, and violinist **Graham**

Smith had joined. His brooding presence gave Van Der Graaf a softer focus, but the album was a swansong, and the double live album, VITAL (1978), was not the greatest testimony to what was at its best a superb live band. After its release, Hammill went solo again.

Still, Van Der Graaf continues in spirit through Hammill's solo career, even when he is performing alone. Along with John Cale and Richard Thompson, Hammill is a singer who can terrify an audience all by himself.

There has been a substantial rerelease programme on CD, with all the most important titles now available mid-price, along with two compilations, I PROPHESY DISASTER (1993) and NOW AND THEN. Even TIME VAULTS – provisional sessions never meant for release – is now available on silver disc. Oscar-winning director Anthony Minghella has recently declared his huge admiration for the band; indeed he once played keyboards with an Isle of Wight band who specialized in Peter Hammill-type epics. Judge Smith has meanwhile recorded a splendid 'song-story' called CURLY'S AIRSHIPS (2000), which reunites most of the original band.

⊙ **The Least We Can Do Is Wave To Each Other**
(1970; Virgin).
This is the clearest conceptual work the band produced. All succeeding Van Der Graaf albums follow on this version of apocalypse, with its dual references to the occult and nuclear science.

⊙ **Maida Vale** (1994; Band of Joy).
A CD resurrection of Radio 1 sessions recorded between 1971 and 1976; the versions of "Darkness" and "Man-Erg" demonstrate how effortlessly the band could perform their complex material live.

⊙ **I Prophesy Disaster** (1993; Virgin).
This compilation shows how targeted and intense the early Van Der Graaf material was. Most impressive of all is "W", previously available only as the flip side to their most bizarre single, a cover of George Martin's instrumental "Theme One".

Brian Hinton

VAN HALEN

Formed Pasadena, California, 1974.

"I just do everything the way I want to do it. Period. I mean, who is the God of Guitars who says it has to be held this way, if in the end result you get the same noises?" Eddie Van Halen

Of the many 70s acts heralded as 'the next Led Zeppelin', none staked so strong a claim to the title as **Van Halen**. They had a whizzkid on the six-string, a wailing, genre-defining frontman and a rough-and-tumble rhythm section hewn from the shit-hot strata. Mitigating the bass and drum solos with humour and harmony, they packed stadium after stadium and sold by the ton while the competition wilted.

David Lee Roth lets rip

Having hooked up in California in 1974, **Michael Anthony** (bass), **DAVID LEE ROTH** (vocals) and the **Van Halen** brothers – **Eddie** (guitar) and **Alex** (drums) – had several years to brush up their act, while A&R men spent time and money at discos instead of sweaty rock clubs. The handful who did pay attention included Kiss star Gene Simmons, who financed some early demos when the band was still known as Mammoth (they also toyed with the untenable Rat Salade). 'The guys still owe me a couple thousand bucks,' Simmons informed *Kerrang!* magazine in 1992.

Eventually signed to Warner Brothers, Van Halen released their debut in 1977. An exhilarating cocktail of metal and melody, VAN HALEN I provided the blueprint for the group's career and the course of American hard rock over the next decade. It remains among the few LPs of the 70s able to stand toe to toe with modern metal masterpieces such as Metallica's MASTER OF PUPPETS and Guns N' Roses' APPETITE FOR DESTRUCTION.

Four multi-platinum successors paved the way for Van Halen's headlining triumph at the 1983 US Festival in California. The 300,000-strong audience was another notch in the VH legend, one already embellished with Eddie's guitar solo on Michael Jackson's #1 single "Beat It" and the notorious contract rider that stipulated a bowl of colour-coded M&Ms for the band backstage.

Van Halen's stock rose further still with the album 1984 and its attendant smash "Jump" (not to mention the other rollicking hits, "Panama" and "Hot For Teacher"). This new stratosphere of success marked David Lee Roth's swan song; he enjoyed a quick spell of solo stardom with remakes of "California Girls" and "Just A Gigolo", then faded just as fast. His band-mates forged ahead with the older and wiser **Sammy Hagar** (a veteran of Montrose and a competent solo career), who – unlike Roth – could also play guitar, allowing Eddie further freedom to experiment with synth sounds.

With their new singer, the band managed a few classics – most notably "Why Can't This Be Love" (1986) – and maintained sales even during metal's lean years, eventually earning grudging respect from critics and fans who mourned Diamond Dave's departure. Laudably, they waited over a decade before padding their discography with a double live album (RIGHT HERE, RIGHT NOW in 1993) and even endured a European supporting slot with Bon Jovi. Emerging unscathed from such indignity, Van Halen endured, among the biggest and best in a much-maligned genre.

Finding themselves minus a singer with the departure of Sammy Hagar, the rumour machine got into full swing as people speculated that this might pave the way for David Lee Roth to return. All this proved to be complete fantasy in the end – although Diamond Dave did feature on two new tunes on the band's BEST OF VOL. 1 (1996) – as Eddie and the boys settled on ex-Extreme crooner **Garry Cherone**. The resulting album, VAN HALEN III (1998), was solid enough musically but failed to capture even the moderate levels of excitement generated when Hagar was in the band. Whilst Cherone was clearly a decent singer, the songs just didn't catch fire the way they should. The band also experienced a major setback when they had to cancel their entire European tour after drummer Alex Van Halen was injured by falling plaster during a pre-gig warm-up session in Hamburg.

Cherone was eventually dismissed in 1999, which again kicked off speculation as to whether Roth would rejoin the band. The rumours proved to be just that, however, as seemingly nothing could bridge the gap between Eddie and his former vocalist. To make matters worse Eddie was diagnosed with cancer – from which he has since recovered – and just a short time later the band left their long-time label Warners with a whole load of new material written, but no one to sing it. Quite where one of the world's biggest, and at one time best, rock bands will go now is anyone's guess – especially since Hagar and Roth toured the States together in summer 2002, and did not end on speaking terms.

⊙ **Van Halen I** (1977; Warners).
An essential hard-rock album, loaded with classics – "Jamie's Cryin", "Ain't Talkin' 'Bout Love", "Running With The Devil".

⊙ **1984** (1984; Warners).
Bookended by bubbling synths and rock-hard riffs, this is half as good as VH I, which is to say ten times better than the competition.

⊙ **5150** (1986; Warners).
The cream of the Van Hagar era. More big synth meets guitar, led by the hit "Why Can't This Be Love".

⊙ **Van Halen III** (1998; Warners).
The first album from the third incarnation of the band. New singer Garry Cherone is technically superb but what's the point when the songs are only moderately interesting? Overly radio-friendly and polished, there's a definite lack of energy here.

Bruno MacDonald

TOWNES VAN ZANDT

Born Fort Worth, Texas, March 7, 1944;
died January 1, 1997.

As such self-effacing album titles as THE LATE, GREAT TOWNES VAN ZANDT (1973) and LIVE AND OBSCURE (1985) indicate, the countrified singer-songwriter **Townes Van Zandt** does not take the record business entirely seriously. You sense that as long as big names continue to cover his songs, he's content to lie back and collect the money. If this is a false impression, and Townes is consumed with frustrated ambition, then he has fooled many with his wry drawl, delicate finger-picked guitar style, and reflective ballads that make J. J. Cale seem positively hyperactive. He also happens to be a member of one of Fort Worth's oil dynasties. Maybe royalties don't even matter.

But they do accrue, from songs such as "Pancho And Lefty", a tune tailor-made for Willie Nelson, also covered by Emmylou Harris and taken to the top of the country charts by Merle Haggard. "If I Needed You" was another smash recorded both by Harris and by Don Williams at the height of his fame. These two songs illustrate the contrasting strengths of Van Zandt's output – the sentimental rural narrative toughened by an ironic streak, and the deceptively straightforward love song.

Among Van Zandt's close friends during his early career was fellow Texan songwriter Guy Clark; between them, they helped define the 70s manifestation of 'new country'. The first such manifestation came, arguably, in the 50s, when Elvis Presley and Carl Perkins put a blues backbeat to hillbilly songs. A later wave – the Garth Brooks/George Strait generation, which was really the old wave in new hats – was also a raging success. But the Texans took a relaxed, anti-establishment route, which has led to cult status rather than superstardom.

Van Zandt began writing while in the Peace Corps and performed early on in the Delta Mama Boys, a tongue-in-cheek name more suggestive of an old-time gospel group than the brand of cough syrup it actually came from. His first album, FOR THE SAKE OF A SONG, was recorded in 1968; releases came fairly regularly over the next decade. THE LATE, GREAT TOWNES VAN ZANDT included the original version of "Pancho And Lefty" and was co-produced by Jack Clement, a legendary figure from Sun Records. No album really broke out, as all were released on small labels (eg Tomato) which had a bad habit of going out of business. Van Zandt, however, is not an artist who could flourish amid the corporate mentality of a major label, and he still affiliates himself with local setups whenever he's inspired to record.

More recent efforts include LIVE AND OBSCURE, recorded in Nashville and rereleased in the late 80s by Edsel as PANCHO AND LEFTY, and the 1987 album AT MY WINDOW, also co-produced by Clement. ROAD SONGS (1994) was an understated live album of cover versions he'd performed on tour in 1993/94, and NO DEEPER BLUE (1994) was to be his last studio recording.

Since his tragic and unexpected death, Van Zandt's reputation has grown and the reissue of his 1969 classic OUR MOTHER THE MOUNTAIN (1998) might go some way towards explaining the delicious appeal of this quintessentially maudlin balladeer.

⊙ **The Best Of Townes Van Zandt** (1996; Charly).
A recent compilation drawn from Van Zandt's 70s work on the deceased labels Poppy and Tomato. Includes such essentials as "Pancho And Lefty", "Kathleen" and "If I Needed You".

⊙ **Rear View Mirror** (1998; Normal).
A live set, which includes all Van Zandt's best-loved material. An excellent introduction to his work.

John Collis

STEVIE RAY VAUGHAN

Born Dallas, Texas, 1954; died 1990.

"Most of us play a 12-bar solo with two choruses, and the rest is repetition. With Stevie Ray, the longer he played, the better." B. B. King

Without a guitar in his hands, the unobtrusive skinny white kid **Stevie Ray Vaughan** may not have cut much of a figure alongside the physically gigantic blues singers he idolized – Albert King, Howlin' Wolf and Muddy Waters. But Vaughan's recording career, lasting little more than seven years, inspired a whole new generation of blues fans and artists.

Vaughan's thorough knowledge of the blues came early, through experiments on his older brother Jimmie's guitar and an attraction to the down-and-dirty blues dives in Dallas. He developed a distinctive sound, warm in tone but brutal in character, like the bars in which he showcased his prowess during his teens. Stevie Ray cut his teeth playing with hard-working bands in Austin and Dallas, finally forming his own outfit in 1976 – a five-piece named The Triple Threat Revue, the earliest incarnation of his backing group, **Double Trouble**.

A serious lack of money, as well as Vaughan's inclination for booze and, eventually, cocaine, led to changes within the band. They regrouped, with sax player **Johnny Reno** and bassist **Jackie Newhouse** joining Stevie Ray and the earlier band members

Fredde Pharoah (drums) and red-hot vocalist **Lou Ann Barton**. Soon **Chris 'Whipper' Layton** replaced Pharoah, and Reno and Barton also left; Vaughan was initially wrong-footed but the moves paid dividends, pushing him closer to centre stage. Double Trouble's line-up became finalized, with the addition of Austin crony **Tommy Shannon** and subtraction of Newhouse.

After securing a slot at the 1982 Montreux Jazz Festival, the band were witnessed by **DAVID BOWIE**, who offered Stevie Ray an appearance in his latest video. Jackson Browne also caught a Double Trouble show upon their return to the US, and, astonished that they were still unsigned, offered them free time in his Los Angeles studio. In the middle of a session, however, Bowie called to ask Vaughan to play on his upcoming album, LET'S DANCE, and the ensuing world tour.

Vaughan's performance on LET'S DANCE powered the album and its huge hit singles, but, whether due to loyalty to his band or Bowie's insistence on an exclusive contract, Vaughan quit before the monstrous 'Serious Moonlight' tour. His moment, however, had obviously come. Legendary talent scout and producer John Hammond had heard the tapes of the Montreux appearance and the rough mixes from Browne's studio; his recommendation alone was enough for Epic to offer Vaughan and Double Trouble a deal.

Hammond himself supervised the final remixes of the studio sessions that became TEXAS FLOOD (1983). A rude debut, full of the vitality and gutsy, no-nonsense blues which became Vaughan's hallmark, it deservedly won a Grammy as the year's *Best Traditional Blues* recording. Unfortunately, the more concerted effort which went into subsequent albums, COULDN'T STAND THE WEATHER (1984) and SOUL TO SOUL (1985), was not reflected in increased sales. Though the band was still getting tighter and Vaughan was stretching his wings further, notably on "Ain't Gone 'N' Give Up On Love", a languid blues off SOUL TO SOUL, the years of hard living were catching up. The combination of drugs, alcohol, tireless playing and the grief of his father's death put him into a rehab clinic. His marriage and his relationship with his manager came apart; but, after a slow recovery, Vaughan eventually emerged with his life and his talent reinvigorated.

The next studio album, IN STEP (1989), demonstrated greater variety and expanded technical limits; his rejuvenation showed through in the sheer passion of his playing. For the next twelve months, Stevie Ray seemed to exist on a different plane. He recorded an album with his brother, FAMILY STYLE, released in 1990; he had boundless energy, and a new love for his very first love – the blues. Invited to join Eric Clapton, Buddy Guy, brother Jimmie and Robert Cray at an outdoor concert in Alpine Valley, Wisconsin on August 26, 1990, Stevie Ray stole the show in a climactic head-to-head; Clapton grinned and stood back; Guy just shrugged.

Helicopters were to ferry the cast and crew out of the resort setting back to Chicago hotels; hurtling through the early-morning fog, the aircraft carrying Stevie Ray Vaughan and a number of Clapton's road crew slammed into the side of a hill, killing all aboard. Like other rock greats who have died prematurely, Vaughan has quickly been canonized, but there is no doubt that he died with his best days still ahead, his immense powers finally unsullied by addiction.

Stevie Ray Vaughan and Double Trouble

⊙ Texas Flood (1983; Epic).
Recorded before the band was signed, this album is shot full of high energy, and includes the stand-out "Pride And Joy".

⊙ Couldn't Stand The Weather (1984; Epic).
More polished than its predecessor, with such riffing as "Voodoo Chile", "The Things (That) I Used To Do" and "Tin Pan Alley".

⊙ In Step (1989; Epic).
Easily Stevie Ray's best recording, reflecting his growing sophistication and control.

⊙ Greatest Hits (1989; Epic).
OK, the title's a bit of a misnomer but the tracks here – "The House Is A Rockin'", above all – should by rights have been hits. This is basically a primer for newcomers, with just the one unreleased track – a cover of George Harrison's "Taxman".

Phil Lynch

ALAN VEGA

Born Brooklyn, New York, 1948.

In 1972, **Alan Vega** was involved in running an art space, exhibiting his 'light sculptures', and dabbling in music. The space, which he opened up for free, attracted the fifteen-piece jazz band Reverend B, featuring **Martin Rev** on electric piano. Vega teamed up with them, envisaging the 'group' – renamed **SUICIDE** – as a kind of sound sculpture. Needless to say, Suicide were perhaps the most unbookable group of all time, causing riots with support appearances for such as The Clash and Elvis Costello.

When Suicide called it a day in 1980, Vega stayed with music, releasing a solo album, ALAN VEGA (1980), that took everyone by surprise. Vega's endlessly echoed voice sounded eerily rockabillyish over Phil Hawk's minimal guitar work. The menacing drumbeats in "Bye Bye Bayou" dragged Creedence up to date, and threw them into the East Village jungle. "Ice Drummer" was the supposed euphoria that preceded hypothermia. "Speedway" was a nod at Elvis and made a rather shocking Top 5 appearance – albeit in the French charts.

Vega assembled an orthodox group for his next record, ready for the mainstream success that could have been just around the corner. COLLISION DRIVE (1981) emphasized the rockabilly edge, again distorted by a weird brain. "Be Bop A Lula" was sung over a Peter Gunn riff, while "Raver" pulled every possible nuance and variation out of its two chords.

The mammoth closer, "Viet Vet", was a one-chord nightmare that would have been their "Revolution #9" had it appeared on a Suicide record. The group toured Europe to ecstatic appreciation and Vega's sculptures were exhibited in a one-man show in New York.

In 1983 Vega signed to Elektra, who thought he'd give them a big disco hit. SATURN STRIP (1983) featured Hot Chocolate's "Every 1's A Winner", and the video to the single, "Wipeout Beat", had Vega kung-fu dancing on giant keyboards and targets before an interstellar backdrop. It wasn't a hit and Vega battled with Elektra for two years to produce JUST A MILLION DREAMS (1985), the company at one point trying to throw him out of his own sessions and take over themselves. Vega stuck to his guns, was dropped by the label, and toured the UK, again to critical acclaim. On the back of this, Suicide re-formed and did the same a year later.

Vega's next solo LP, DEUCE AVENUE (1990), was a while coming and saw him linked up with **Liz Lamere** ('machines'). Again light years ahead of anything else ever heard, the album was difficult to fathom until POWER ON TO ZERO HOUR (1991) appeared to provide the link for mere mortals. In 1993, Vega produced a new album, NEW RACEION, and a book, *Cripple Nation*, containing art, lyrics and other writings, which was published by fellow rock-'n'roll oddball Henry Rollins. All went quiet until 1997, when Vega let DUJANG PRANG out of the bag, an album that crept around the darker corners of rock'n'roll, scaring the children with weird mechanical noises, driving beats and the howling of a tortured soul on vocals.

The Suicide revival and an odd-job hook-up with Alex Chilton took up most of his time until mid 1998 when, in collaboration with **Messrs Vaisanen** and **Vainio** of Finland's Pan Sonic, he formed **VVV** and released ENDLESS (1998). A great swinging album of doom'n'drone in the old style, it would make a fine accompaniment to a descent into hell. A brilliant return to form from the patron saint of self-immolation.

In 1999 Vega was back with Lamere for the album 2007; since then his interests have largely revolved around Suicide's reunion and their AMERICAN SUPREME release.

⊙ Juke Box Baby/Collision Drive (1996; Infinite Zero).
Absolutely essential. Vega, imprisoned in a vacuum, creates antimatter music out of chunks of nothing.

Tony Thewlis

SUZANNE VEGA

Born Santa Monica, California, 1959.

While TV was pushing the kids from *Fame* as role models for aspiring artists, at the real-life New York High School for the Performing Arts **Suzanne Vega** was studying dance and practising her pout while getting lessons in Greenwich Village chic.

As a teenager she discovered Lou Reed and Leonard Cohen, which led to acoustic guitar lessons and the adoption of an understated style, which she showcased on the stone-dead folk scene of the early 80s. Her manager Steve Addabo received a mountain of rejection slips before A&M signed her in late 1984, commissioning ex-Patti Smith ally and Manhattan scenester Lenny Kaye to co-produce her debut album. The result, SUZANNE VEGA (1985), was a marvellously chilly modern take on the singer-songwriter, all moody atmosphere and whispered vocals. The critical response, revved up by memories of pre-jazz Joni Mitchell and early Cohen, was overwhelming. The LP made a dent in the US Top 100, and had significant UK chart success at #11, helped by radio play for the hit single "Marlene On The Wall".

Two singles followed – "Small Blue Thing" (from the first album) and "Luka", a brittle tale of child abuse that was an unlikely #3 chart success in the US and which appeared on SOLITUDE STANDING (1987) – a further commercial breakthrough, hitting #11 in the US, #2 in the UK, if not perhaps on the scale it deserved. By her third album, DAYS OF OPEN HAND (1990), all momentum from her brush with chart fame was gone, and Vega failed to deliver the goods. DAYS didn't know whether to aim for the head or the feet; in the end, it reached neither.

When, in 1990, UK hip-hop act DNA transformed Vega's a cappella song, "Tom's Diner", into a dance track, A&M threatened to sue. But a flattered and amused Vega lent her approval, and the song hit the top of the UK chart. So it was not altogether surprising that dance rhythms, synths and drum machines made an appearance on Vega's own 99.9F (1992), an album on which the songs set off in playful and perverse directions, with distortion accompanying funky melodies. The singles "Liverpool" and "Blood Makes Noise" exhibited, respectively, a delicate pop sweetness and threatening abrasiveness.

Her attempt to continue the upswing, NINE OBJECTS OF DESIRE (1997), her fifth album, was a collection of sharp-focus observations on various kinds of longing (love, sex, death, etc); lyrically intriguing, musically and vocally confident, it was a real pleasure from start to finish. TRIED AND TRUE, a timely 1999 compilation of highlights from her 15-year career, neatly bridged the gap prior to the release of SONGS IN RED AND GRAY (2001). Having split both personally and professionally from her husband, producer Mitchell Froom, Vega returned to the low-key sound and mood of her earlier discs. The same year also brought Vega's first book, a collection of writings, poems and lyrics entitled *The Passionate Eye*; another compilation, RETROSPECTIVE, followed in 2003.

⊙ **Suzanne Vega** (1985; A&M).
On this near-perfect folk album for the 1980s Vega displays her trademark restraint on stellar songs such as "Marlene On The Wall".

⊙ **99.9F** (1992; A&M).
After a dry stretch, 99.9F was a welcome return to form, tackling diverse material with style and intelligence.

⊙ **Songs In Red And Gray** (2001; A&M).
Filled with some of her most personal writing, this collection reconnected Vega with the restraint and vision of her earliest work.

Neil Blackmore

THE VELVET UNDERGROUND

Formed New York, 1965; disbanded 1971; re-formed 1992; disbanded 1995.

"The only reason we wore sunglasses onstage was because we couldn't stand the sight of the audience." John Cale

The Velvet Underground are unique in rock history. No other band ever achieved so little success during its life span and had such a vast influence on the generation that followed. And all **LOU REED** (guitar/vocals) ever wanted to be was to be a rock-'n'roll star.

Lou and **Sterling Morrison** (guitar) first met at Syracuse University, New York State. According to legend, Sterling stomped up to Reed's room, drawn by the sheer volume and general coolness of the music blaring from Lou's hi-fi. **JOHN CALE** (bass/viola/vocals), the 'serious' musician in the group, signed up later, when he and Lou were churning out songs-by-the-yard, working for a music publisher in New York. Lou was, even then, searching for a return to the most basic elements of music, and having roped Sterling and John into The Primitives had a measure of success with the ultra-basic "(Do) The Ostrich", a dumb dance tune apparently recorded while about thirty friends were having a party in the same room. They hooked up with **'MOE' TUCKER** (drums), culled the name The Velvet Underground from a pulp S&M novel, signed with MGM-Verve Records and set about rewriting the rock rule book.

The music they made was never comfortable, often dark and confrontational. Although full of experimentation (playing with the stereo channels, extending chords into drones) and chock-full of drug references, their music was miles away from the peace'n'love, acid-tinged visions emanating from the West Coast. And The Velvets were a uniquely cerebral rock band – smart enough to realize that an association with the darling of the NY art world could do them some good. Andy Warhol introduced a gloomy, vampire-junkie-style chanteuse in the form of **NICO**, produced the first album (in the financial sense) and gave them the banana logo that went on to be as much an icon as his Marilyn Monroes.

Some behind-the-scenes shenanigans held up The Velvets' first album, THE VELVET UNDERGROUND AND NICO (1967), until the week after the first Doors album hit the streets and grabbed the headlines for being the first 'Freak' album. But, despite poor initial sales, The Velvets' debut went on to be one of the biggest-selling 'alternative' albums of all time. The classic "Heroin" was the first rock song ever to try and explain the whys and the joys of taking smack (the band felt obliged to drop it from their live set for a while when a wave of deaths from overdose swamped the rock world). Other tracks dealt with the obscure pleasures of S&M ("Venus In Furs"), the 'everyday song of love between man and subway' ("Waiting For The Man") and the shabbier side of socializing in New York City ("All Tomorrow's Parties", "Femme Fatale"). To round it off were a couple of powerful, extended work-outs

with loads of feedback – "European Son" and "Black Angel's Death Song".

Nico left the band to pursue a solo career and drug habit, leaving the rest of the band to lock themselves in the studio, take a load of drugs, turn the amps up to '11' and release, in December 1967, their second album, WHITE LIGHT/WHITE HEAT. In case you'd been misled by the cheery banana motif on the first album cover, the new cover was all black on one side and had a glum group photo in stark, unsmiling monochrome on the other. Not a psychedelic album. Not so much LSD and marijuana as the sound of methedrine and heavy opiates. Take "Sister Ray", for example: it had a transsexual title, lyrics that dealt with murder, prostitution and intravenous drug abuse, and it quickly descended into a battle of the amps between Cale's organ riffs and Reed's chungalunga rhythm guitar, a duel resolved only when Reed and Cale agreed to give it up after 17 minutes and 39 seconds of a single take. Other tracks included "The Gift", a bizarre extended story of love gone wrong, and the completely wired "Heard Her Call My Name", in which the narrator hears the voice of his dead girlfriend calling him.

John Cale left after this album and had a successful solo career. The Velvets, meanwhile, turned toward Lou's vision for their future.

With Cale gone, there was a lot less tension within the band, reflected in a general mellowing-down of The Velvet Underground sound. Cale's replacement, the multi-talented 'plays anything with strings' **Doug Yule**, certainly filled any holes that may have been left in the mix, but lacked John's off-the-wall-and-

The Velvets' Doug Yule (with upside-down bass), Lou Reed, Sterling Morrison and 'Moe' Tucker

THE VELVET UNDERGROUND

Andy Warhol

out-the-window weirdness. When the third album, THE VELVET UNDERGROUND, sneaked out of the studio in 1969, only the loopiness of two completely different vocal tracks for extreme left and right channelling in "The Murder Mystery" really qualified as vintage Velvets experimental madness. The rest of the album was fine, thoughtful music, even melodic in places: there was the waif-like comedy of Moe Tucker's "After Hours", New York spiritual small talk in "Candy Says", vague hints of chemical epiphany in "Jesus" and "I'm Set Free" and, to crown it all, the heart-stoppingly beautiful "Pale Blue Eyes", one of the best love songs in the history of the world.

LOADED, The Velvets' last 'real' album – before the compilations, bootlegs and re-formations – came out in 1971 and turned out to be pretty much a standard rock album. The junkies and transvestites had been cleared out of the neighbourhood, and some of the tracks even verged on the insipid – "Who Loves The Sun", if listened to in the wrong state of mind, was enough to make your skin crawl. But it did contain two of Lou's greatest songs: the much-covered "Sweet Jane" and Chairman Reed's manifesto, "Rock And Roll". The reissue (1997) comprised the original album, bundled together with virtually a whole new album of previously unseen alternative versions.

By the time the album came out, though, Lou had left the band, heading off to stagger in an amphetamine blizzard through the 70s and 80s. Maureen Tucker went back home, bred five kids and had a solo career best explored on LIFE IN EXILE AFTER ABDICATION (1989). Sterling Morrison went back to Austin University, where he took a doctorate in English, then lectured for some time, before moving to the backwaters of ferryboat captaincy. Doug Yule and his brother Billy (who'd covered for Moe while she was having her first baby) roped in **Walter Powers** on bass and **Willie Alexander** as guitarist to knock out SQUEEZE, a Velvets album in name only (and a name later borrowed by southeast London's finest punk wannabes).

Although The Velvets had split up long before punk appeared, the punks' massed interest in the

band played a large part in their rediscovery in the late 70s. At one point in 1977–78, you could, by choosing carefully, work your way through The Velvet Underground's greatest hits, just by going to punk gigs. There were countless "White Light/White Heat" covers (even Bowie had a go at it), and even hopeful attempts at the more complicated workouts like "European Son". The renewed interest also prompted a couple of album-length collections of studio outtakes from recording sessions for a proposed fourth MGM/Verve release. VU – RARE RECORDINGS 68–69 and ANOTHER VIEW helped fill the gaps in the band's recorded history, and showed where Lou had originally cast some of his solo material.

A whole generation of guitar-noise kids had grown to love The Velvet Underground, and when Lou and John Cale could finally stand to be in the same room as one another again (coming together to record their tribute to – and exorcism of – Andy Warhol, SONGS FOR DRELLA), there was nothing to prevent them cashing in with the tour the world had been waiting for. They got back together in late 1992, rehearsed and headlined a European tour ('We're not going to be playing in the US', announced Reed; 'People always appreciated our music much more in Europe'), to rapturous audiences in stadiums all over the continent. Sure, the band had deeply etched wrinkles, but so did most of the audience. John Cale had to read the words to "The Gift" from an elegant little lectern, but the audience was word-perfect throughout.

The resulting album, LIVE MCMXCII, was a perfect farewell to The Velvet Underground, covering their whole back catalogue from "I'm Waiting For My Man" to "Rock And Roll". Some of the older songs were subjected to Lou's novelty vocal updates, but he'd been singing "White Light/White Heat" for a quarter of a century, and had earned the right to sing it as he wanted.

Nico died in 1988, after a fall from a bicycle in Mallorca. Sterling Morrison died suddenly in 1995. Lou Reed's immediate reaction was that, without Sterling, there could be no more Velvet Underground. After all this time, and with the rebellious myth dissolved by the pragmatism of Rock'N'Roll Incorporated, The Velvets are no more.

⊙ **The Velvet Underground And Nico** (1967; Polygram).
This is The Velvets making their first, and biggest, splash. The most essential purchase of them all.

⊙ **White Light/White Heat** (1967; Polygram).
The world's most telling drug album. For full effect, listen to it in a dark room, alone, when the rest of the world is asleep.

⊙ **The Velvet Underground** (1969; Polygram).
It's easy to forget how great Velvets love songs were. Here's the main evidence in "Pale Blue Eyes".

⊙ **1969 – The Velvet Underground Live, Vols. 1 & 2** (1979; Polygram).
Now only available in two instalments, this is the essential live album of The Velvets, working a couple of student audiences in Texas and San Francisco. The band are in excellent form and Lou is at his laconic best.

◉ **Velvet Underground – Peel Slowly And See**
(1995; Polygram).
A lovingly remastered boxed collection of the four studio
albums, plus demos, singles, live tracks and other stuff,
including an entire six-track CD of previously unreleased
recordings. The reason is soon apparent: the world never
needed to hear the fifteen-minute medieval troubadour version of "Venus In Furs", neither is there any real merit in the
Appalachian folk version of "I'm Waiting For The Man". That
said, if you're a Velvets fan moving from scratched-up vinyl to
the digital purity of CD, this is the obvious purchase. There's
a pretty picture book, too.

Al Spicer –

with thanks to Moe for getting in touch
and to Ken Macklin for corrections

VENOM

Formed Newcastle, England, 1980.

If you had to choose just one band as the main
driving force behind the black metal scene, then
Venom would have to figure pretty high on the
charge sheet. Claiming to be in league with the
horned one himself, Conrad Lant aka **Cronos**
(bass/vox), Jeff Dunn aka **Mantas** (guitar) and Tony
Bray aka **Abaddon** (drums) erupted onto the metal
scene with WELCOME TO HELL (1981), a poorly produced but brutal thrash album. Having originally
formed as a five-piece called Oberon in the late 70s,
these pioneering and overtly theatrical minions of hell
would go on to spawn a thousand imitators and
become one of the most influential thrash groups of
the early 80s.

Everything about this lot was exaggerated, from
the leather, studs and bullet belts, to the overt satanic
imagery – it was cartoon time, and Venom had their
very own prime-time show. No one had ever experienced anything quite so close to the bone; this lot
claimed not just to dabble in the black arts but to be
regular (blood) drinking buddies with the man
downstairs. So cocky and confident were they of
their success that they displayed a mocking disdain
for the usual routes to stardom. Not only was their
debut recorded in a mere three days, they allegedly
refused to support any other bands and so had never
actually played any live dates to speak of.

Their live debut – cunningly dubbed the 'Seventh
Date Of Hell' – was actually at the (then)
Hammersmith Odeon in June 1984. Very few bands
achieve such a remarkable cross-section in an audience, but Venom joined the ranks of acts such as
Motörhead in attracting a vastly diverse crowd
including metallers, bikers, punks and skinheads.
Pumped up on the hype, everybody wanted to see
whether these boys were as vicious live as their
recorded material promised. Precedents were set that
night for what would become Venom live-show staples: pyrotechnics of nuclear proportions threatened
to toast those unfortunate enough to have seats in the
stalls, the PA was one of the most powerful the band
could obtain, and every single piece of stage equip-

ment was reduced to piles of smoking splinters by the
end of the gig.

This level of intensity can be experienced across
their three follow-up albums, BLACK METAL (1982)
– apparently recorded in six days, this time – AT
WAR WITH SATAN (1984) and POSSESSED (1985),
which charted a band gradually learning how to play
their instruments and write decent rock. Inevitably
with the band's growing professionalism came a
honing of their trademark lunacy and aggression.
Whereas previously the band had deliberately cultivated stories about attacking people who got in their
way and drinking the blood of virgins, amongst many
other cuddly and colourful rock antics, it didn't help
that they eventually admitted to knowing very little
about the occult.

The following albums – EINE KLEINE
NACHTMUSIK (1986), CALM BEFORE THE STORM
(1987), PRIME EVIL (1989), TEMPLES OF ICE (1991)
and THE WASTE LANDS (1992) – recorded with various line-up changes, were of varying quality and
showed a competent band still trying to peddle a
satanic angle which was well past its expiry date.

At the start of this period Cronos broke ranks to
form a melodic rock outfit and to start a fitness-
training business – a move that appealed to die-hard
Venom fans not at all. A new vocalist, Tony Dolan
aka **Demolition Man**, was brought in, but no one
really cared any more and stories of extreme disharmony began to spread.

It appeared as though one of the black metal vanguard had really gone straight to hell until the THE
SECOND COMING (1996), a live video and CD box
set, showed that the old line-up could still muster
some of the former glory of their stage act. A studio
album, CAST IN STONE (1997), soon followed,
showing that the promise of cash could patch up all
manner of differences. While the latter proved that
Venom could still harness some of that ol' black
magic when they put their minds to it,
RESURRECTION (2000) was precisely the kind of
thing the band's ever faithful hellspawn were craving
after.

A spate of compilation albums have deluged the
market over the last couple of years, exploiting the
enduring appeal of these black metal progenitors.
Best of all, however, has been the rerelease of the
band's initial brace of albums originally recorded for
Neat Records, all of them repackaged with new
sleeve notes and a veritable horror feast of bonus
cuts.

◉ **Welcome To Hell** (1981; Neat Records).
An album so fast and heavy, it's almost hilarious. This
is the one to seek out if you fancy a spot of hell-raising.

◉ **Black Metal** (1982; Neat Records).
The definitive thrash blueprint spawned imitations the
world over. Fast, brutal, ugly – but again oddly amusing.

◉ **Cast In Stone** (1997; SPV).
Nasty stuff, only played with greater skill and precision.
The satanic theatrics are still in place and a bonus second
disc features ten rerecorded classics from the good old days.

Essi Berelian

TOM VERLAINE

Born Wilmington, Delaware, 1949.

It's a mystery to many that **Tom Verlaine**'s solo career, though quantitatively far more productive than his work with **TELEVISION**, has produced so few moments equal to those from the band's albums. Here was the New York guitarist of the moment; a major name you'd have tipped to have an enduring influence.

In 1979, the year after Television disbanded, both Verlaine and fellow Television guitarist Richard Lloyd released solo albums. TOM VERLAINE, on Elektra, the same label that had signed his band, received greater attention and better reviews, and the road ahead looked promising. A second solid album, DREAMTIME, appeared in 1981 on Warner Brothers, and it hit the US charts (albeit at #177), something MARQUEE MOON, Television's finest achievement,

failed to do. Verlaine's oblique, jagged guitar playing was drawing comparisons to Neil Young, and the lyrics were looking better than on Television outings, although some were turned off by his affectedly high voice.

Verlaine's next two albums were supported with live appearances on both sides of the Atlantic, and again both were glowingly reviewed without breaking through as major sellers. WORDS FROM THE FRONT (1982) and COVER (1984) did little to enlarge his fan base, but they did indicate slight departures. COVER, though full of now-dated drum technology (including the dreaded beatbox), was brightly produced, and used Verlaine's limited vocal range to great effect. He even had a go at a couple of ballads among his usual rhythms, including "O Foolish Heart", which bordered on the sentimental.

After a three-year hiatus, during which Verlaine lived in both New York and Europe, he released FLASHLIGHT (1987) on the Fontana label and did a great deal of promoting and touring in the UK. His live playing suddenly seemed disaffected, but FLASHLIGHT blistered, from the opening single "Cry Mercy, Judge", to the scintillating "A Town Called Walker", perhaps the best example of Verlaine's taut guitar patterns. "The Scientist Writes A Letter" was undoubtedly his best ballad to date, a delicate song in which Verlaine talk-sang to touching effect.

By 1990 Verlaine was talking about re-forming Television, and his old bass player, Fred 'Sonic' Smith, co-produced his next solo album, THE WONDER. It featured all the Verlaine trademarks, including the failure to chart, a factor in his re-forming Television for one more album, released in 1993. After a while out of the public gaze, which only saw the guitar-instrumental album WARM AND COOL (1992), Verlaine re-emerged in 1996 with a 'best of' anthology, A MILLER'S TALE, which suggested that, with a little more focus, things could have been different. Since then, he has worked with **Patti Smith** on her albums GONE AGAIN (1996) and GUNG HO (2000), and was producer on **Jeff Buckley**'s posthumously-released SKETCHES (FOR MY SWEETHEART THE DRUNK) (1998).

Tom Verlaine in Tom Waits-lookalike-contest triumph

Verlaine's sound has always been tricky to capture on record, but this snazzily produced album comes closest. His guitar work is peerless, and the tuneful "A Town Called Walker" and "Cry Mercy, Judge" shine, while the aching beauty of "The Scientist Writes A Letter" comes through in a rich vocal performance.

A Miller's Tale (1996; Virgin).
This is two discs: a 'best of', which isn't quite what it says, including uncollected singles for the fans; and a storming live CD recorded in London in 1982, which really is Verlaine at his best.

Mike Martin

American Thighs (1994; Minty Fresh).
A sweet-and-sour debut. Spunky, scrunchy guitars and wailing, waifish vocals combine to make this a poptastic treat for those missing the punch of the Pixies and the polished punk of The Go-Go's.

Resolver (2000; Velveteen).
Though sloppy at times, RESOLVER is a far better record than EIGHT ARMS… ; the guitars are bold and the arrangements raw, but lyrically Post misses the mark by miles.

Gavin Stoker

VERUCA SALT

Formed Chicago, 1993; split 1998; re-formed 2000.

Singer/guitarists **Louise Post** and **Nina Gordon** first teamed up following a New Year's Eve party in 1992, during which Post played a mutual friend some of the tapes she'd been making. A little musical matchmaking later, **Veruca Salt** were born, with **Steve Lack** on bass and **Jim Shapiro** on drums.

Named after the precocious rich kid in Roald Dahl's *Charlie And The Chocolate Factory*, the band grabbed attention with their debut single, "Seether" (1994), on tiny indie label Scared Hitless. Dealing with anger and the way that women feel obliged to suppress it, "Seether" had fuzzy guitar hooks and spirited vocals – that, as critics pointed out, were clearly inspired by The Breeders – and made an impressive dent on indie charts on both sides of the Atlantic. Their debut album on Minty Fresh, AMERICAN THIGHS (1994), silenced most doubters, containing more hits than misses among the Salt's fairly generic pop-punk sound. Stand-out songs included the stroppy "Get Back", the singalong "Number One Blind" (released as the second single in January 1995), and the delicious, slow-burn ballad "25".

After a long, quiet gap, the band released its third (and possibly weakest) single, "Victrola", in 1995. The band had clearly lost some of their initial momentum, and received lukewarm notices. Their signing to Geffen perhaps indicated that their sound was well calculated to gain simultaneous indie cred and major-label attention.

However, the next album EIGHT ARMS TO HOLD YOU (1997) was – compared to the power of AMERICAN THIGHS – a bland straight-vanilla rock album, blanded to perfection by Metallica's Bob Rock. It's a shame to see the anger smoothed away to the kind of pure professional harmony you can buy at any street-corner record store.

But all was soon to change. Gordon departed and Post ditched the remainder of the band, moved label and roughed up her sound a little. Veruca Salt was now well and truly her show, and with a new crew installed (**Jimmy Madla** on drums, **Suzanne Sokol** on bass, and **Stephen Fitzpatrick** on guitar) Post's Veruca Salt released RESOLVER (2000), a thundering return to form and a fine new beginning.

THE VERVE

Formed Wigan, England, 1990; split 1999.

You would never guess from their records that **The Verve** came from Wigan, a down-to-earth northern town famous more for its rugby, pier and pies. Yet without the frustrations of provincial boredom, their headlong flight into psychedelic intensity might never have been provoked.

At first, the band were part of the grand English tradition of cosmic escapism that runs from Pink Floyd to current heirs Spiritualized; but following a move to a more classic rock sound they hit the big time – only to throw it all away Stone Roses style.

The band got together at Wigan's Winstanley College, with **Richard Ashcroft** on vocals, **Nick McCabe** on guitars, **Simon Jones** on bass and **Peter Salisbury** on drums. At first they were just local heroes, yet they had a certain messianic quality that set them out from the pack. Early singles, "All In The Mind", "She's A Superstar" and "Gravity Grave", established their trademark swirling maelstrom of sound, but it was their first album, A STORM IN HEAVEN, that really showed their mettle. Recorded at an isolated studio in Cornwall, their debut comes from the same higher ground as say Van Morrison's ASTRAL WEEKS or Talk Talk's SPIRIT OF EDEN and sounds as if they simply decided to dispense with conventional verses and choruses altogether, to make an album of improvised middle-eights. Some of the pieces are almost completely ambient, lapping at your ears like a warm summer tide, but on others, such as "Slide Away" and "The Sun, The Sea", great waves of effects-laden guitar come crashing out of the mix.

For a band that gave the impression of being beautifully wasted, they proved to be no slackers in the self-promotion stakes and after touring the US with *Lollapalooza*, found a whole new audience - not to mention the threat of a legal action from US jazz label Verve. The dispute obliged a slight change of name to The Verve, but judging from their new harder sound on the second album, A NORTHERN SOUL, the definite article seemed suddenly appropriate. If the first album showed the ethereal, musically pretty side of the band, here was its hard rocking big brother. This time round the songs were more structured with the lyrics speaking from experience rather than pure escapism. "On Your Own", "History" and "This Is Music" are perhaps the stand-

The Verve's Richard Ashcroft

of the year. A second release, "The Drugs Don't Work", with its memorable drowning cat imagery gave the band their first #1, with their third long player, the majestic URBAN HYMNS, also topping the album charts. At last, the band had been able to turn their instinctive musicality into epic, chart-friendly songcraft; though on closer inspection, the album seemed strangely schizophrenic, with most of the songs originally written as solo compositions by Ashcroft and only "The Rolling People" – a storming mini-epic nearly seven minutes long – "Catching The Butterfly" and the scorching other-worldly "Come On" representing genuine fusions of the band's spirit. There was however one last big Verve statement still to be made before the inevitable divorce: a massive homecoming gig at Haigh Hall, just outside of Wigan.

The band fell apart again shortly afterwards and their demise was formally announced in May 1999. This time it looked pretty final, though from past experience, nothing is ever certain in the volatile world of The Verve. In the meantime, Richard Ashcroft finally pressed ahead with his postponed solo career and released the acclaimed ALONE WITH EVERYBODY in 2000. A relaxed, country-flavoured album, heavy with strings and slide guitar, it suggested that he had at last found some measure of personal happiness. After almost 10 years of rock'n'roll psychosis with The Verve, he'd earned it.

outs. Unfortunately, it seemed that the emotional intensity that was pushing them to new creative heights in the studio and ever more incendiary live shows on stage was also pulling them apart, and the exhausted band announced a surprise split in August 1995.

Tiring of rock'n'roll Valhalla, the newly-wed Richard Ashcroft decided to make the break into solo performing and was already well on his way, when a last minute change of heart prompted him to get back in touch with McCabe. Luckily for all concerned, they were able to patch up their differences and make a triumphant return in 1997 with "Bittersweet Symphony", perhaps the defining single

His currency as a performer undiminished by the lukewarm reactions that ALONE WITH EVERYBODY received, Ashcroft teamed up with the Chemical Brothers to record "The Test" for their album COME WITH US. A second solo album, HUMAN CONDITIONS (2002), was received with far more enthusiasm by fans. The collection contained many more Verve-isms and Ashcroft was again filling his songs with darkened corners.

Elsewhere band members Simon Tong and Simon Jones have worked together as **The Shining**, while McCabe has yet to resurface in the pop music world.

The Verve

- **A Storm In Heaven** (1993; Hut).
  Spacey, psychedelic jam-fest. The perfect platter for that late-night half-asleep state.

- **A Northern Soul** (1995; Hut).
  Harder, rock-edged psych-out, bearing the stamp of Oasis producer Owen Morris.

- **Urban Hymns** (1997; Hut).
  The Verve at their most accessible: a rich, thrilling collection of soaring melodies and dizzying acid-rock guitars. Unmissable.

Richard Ashcroft

- **Alone With Everybody** (2000; Hut).
  This is an assured solo debut, wrapped up in a luxurious kitchen sink production job. Slide guitar supremo BJ Cole and a host of session musicians ensure a sumptuous feast for the ears, from the gorgeous "A Song For The Lovers" to the epic closer, "Everybody" (this album's "The Drugs Don't Work"). Ashcroft's voice has never sounded better than it does here.

- **Human Conditions** (2002; Hut).
  Ashcroft makes light work of that difficult second album. The aching "Lord I've Been Trying" stands out as the set's confessional highpoint.

Iain Smith & Sarah Dallas

THE VIBRATORS

Formed London, 1976; disbanded 1978; re-formed 1982.

Pat **Collier** (bass/vocals) and **John Ellis** (guitar/vocals) met in the legendary pub-rock outfit Bazooka Joe, a band that underwent some 25 personnel changes (spawning Adam Ant en route) during the early to mid 70s. The pair left in early 1976 to form **The Vibrators** with another guitarist/vocalist, **Knox Ian Carnochan**, formerly of Lipstick, and a drummer known simply as **Eddie**.

They found a ready audience for their short, fast humour-laced songs, and threw a few Iggy Pop numbers into their shows to establish proper punk credentials. In fact, they bore more resemblance to the American punk scene than to the British safety-pin and spittle equivalent. Their break came at the infamous Punk Festival in September 1976, held at the 100 Club. Itinerant session guitarist and producer Chris Spedding noticed them, got them signed to Rak and produced a single, "We Vibrate", one of the first UK punk singles – and one of the worst.

With PURE MANIA in 1977, the band had a more fitting vinyl release. The album captured the band's raw edge, honed from countless shows, and showcased a surprising talent for writing catchy tunes. After the record failed to rocket them to superstardom, however, Collier jumped ship to front a power-pop band, **The Boyfriends**. **Gary Tibbs**, an avid Vibrators fan, was recruited in his stead, and the band subsequently developed a harder-rocking edge. A second album (with the title V2) was released in early 1978, but, after its singles "London Girls" and "Automatic Lover" failed to make much impact, the band relocated to Berlin. It was the beginning of the

end. Ellis left to join Peter Gabriel's band and, later, **THE STRANGLERS**. **David Birch** was brought in on guitar and **Don Snow** on keyboards, but after the failure of another single the band split.

Tibbs fortuitously joined **ROXY MUSIC**, while Eddie and Knox re-formed The Vibrators with **Ben Brierley** on bass and American guitarist **Greg Van Cook**. It was becoming Bazooka Joe all over again, and this incarnation lasted but a few months. Eddie went on to front The New Vibrators, and Knox embarked on a solo career. The New Vibrators toured intermittently, and a retrospective, BATTERIES INCLUDED, came out in 1980. Shamelessly, Eddie and Knox again revived The Vibrators in 1982, and they continue to record and gig extensively.

- **Pure Mania/V2** (2002; Track).
  For many their only essential recording is the punchy debut, PURE MANIA, which includes the hit they never had, "Whips And Furs", and other peaks "Baby, Baby" and "Into The Future (Sex Kick)". It's now available on a single disc with the group's second album and a bunch of extra tracks.

Simon Ives

GENE VINCENT

Born Norfolk, Virginia, 1935; died 1971.

After Elvis Presley's first pop hit in 1956, every American record company joined the race to sign their own rock singer/sex symbol; first off the blocks was Capitol in Hollywood, who landed an ex-sailor, Vincent Eugene Craddock, better known as **Gene Vincent**.

Vincent had taken up professional singing just a year earlier, recuperating from a motorcycle accident that broke his leg and ended his naval career. After seeing Elvis play, Vincent rapidly shed his country twang in an enthusiastic embrace of the new style; so convincing was he that, when Gladys Presley first heard "Be-Bop-A-Lula", she thought it was her son singing.

That record was Vincent's first and biggest song – a million-seller in the US and a huge chart hit in Britain, it trailed Elvis's non-country chart debut by two months. A definitive rock'n'roll recording, it positioned the breathy, barely controlled lechery of Vincent's vocals against the insidious rhythmic grind of his backing group, **The Blue Caps**, and the fluidity of its guitarist, **Cliff Gallup**. "Be-Bop-A-Lula" retains much of its excitement today, and the B-side, the raunchier "Woman Love", also stands up well.

By rights "Be-Bop-A-Lula" should have been the building block for a career; unfortunately Vincent was just one of the many singers to be short-changed by bad management and record company decisions. He had no one to guard him from exploitation, and later claimed he'd been talked into selling the songwriting rights to his big hit for just $25. More hits came, including "Lotta Lovin'" (another million-seller), "Race With The Devil" and "Bluejean Bop",

Gene Vincent (centre) and his Blue Caps – like the drum says

but they lacked the innovation shown by his contemporaries, and gradually the American public and even The Blue Caps lost interest. A new band was formed, but without Gallup they paled in comparison.

Vincent refocused his energies in Europe, where he retained a loyal fan base, especially in France and Britain. Though they didn't make the British Top 10, "Pistol Packin' Mama" and "She She Little Sheila" sold well; in 1960 alone he scored three hits on the heels of a double-header British tour with Eddie Cochran. The tour ended in tragedy, however, as Cochran died in a car crash that also saw Vincent damage his leg again.

His injuries only enhanced his image in the UK. He had already defined the look of the working-class rocker: dressed in black leather, encouraged by TV producer Jack Good to emphasize the bad leg ('Limp, you bugger, limp', Good used to shout from the wings), Vincent was both threatening and cool. Ultimately it was his image more than his music that was to influence artists from the sublime (Beatles, The Jesus & Mary Chain) to the ridiculous (Alvin Stardust, Billy Idol).

At the end of the 60s, Vincent had a minor comeback. Signed by John Peel's Dandelion label, he released I'M BACK AND I'M PROUD (1969) and found himself in demand on the rock'n'roll revival stadium circuit. Years of alcohol abuse, however, had taken their toll, and Vincent died of a bleeding ulcer in 1971.

Ian Dury, echoing the affection felt for Gene in Britain, gave him a fitting and beautiful epitaph, the poignant 1977 tribute, "Sweet Gene Vincent".

⊙ **The Best Of Gene Vincent And His Blue Caps** (1988; EMI).
A standard and limited compilation, but there was so little variety in Vincent's work that this covers most of the basics with some to spare.

⊙ **The Gene Vincent Box Set** (1990; EMI).
Six CDs is probably more than most people need, or want; but just in case, this is the complete works from 1956 to 1964, with some obscure gems among the handful of well-known songs.

Alwyn W. Turner

THE VINES

Formed Sydney, Australia, 1995.

The turn of the millennium rock scene was nothing if not volatile, what with nu-metal seemingly a spent force and the arbiters of cool looking for the next big sensation. Step up **The Vines**, a young band who happened to be in the right place at the right time to capitalize on the resurgence in garage rock ignited by the success of bands from the Detroit scene – not least The White Stripes.

Despite the appearance of overnight success, The Vines can be traced back to 1995 when **Craig Nicholls** (guitarist/vocalist), **Patrick Matthews** (bass player/backing vocalist) and drummer **David Olliffe** met at high school and shared the same kinds of dead-end casual jobs. Nicholls's dad just happened to have been guitarist/vocalist in an obscure Australian band from the 60s called The Vynes, so a tiny spelling alteration later and they had themselves a moniker with just the right vintage rock'n'roll resonance.

Instead of launching themselves into the fleapits of their home town and learning their art through good honest gigging they chose to concentrate on writing some half-decent tunes first and so toiled in relative obscurity until 2001 when their limited edition FACTORY EP was released to almost immediate acclaim from a press hungry for the spiritual healing power of trashy rock. In the UK the *NME* latched onto the band with a fervour bordering on the fanatical, making FACTORY *Single Of The Week* and putting The Vines top of their 35-bands-to-watch feature at the start of 2002. Things were going down well in the US too: they signed a worldwide deal with Capitol Records, and MTV2 latched onto the band, even though they had no video product with which to promote themselves.

At this point Olliffe left the band to be replaced by **Hamish Rosser**; a second guitarist, **Ryan Griffiths** (Nicholls' childhood best friend), completed the line-up. The pieces were in place for the band's first headline live appearance in February 2002 at the Vic on the Park, a small pub in Sydney. Despite the tiny size of the gig the press, especially *NME* in the UK, hailed it as some sort of second coming: somewhat bizarrely the press and the record label were keen to push the band as a kind of 'Nirvana Mark II', no doubt because Nicholl's skinny frame and ability to wig out on the guitar revived decade-old memories of Cobain.

The Vines – it's rude to stair

The album HIGHLY EVOLVED (2002) was very good but it was light years from NEVERMIND, being a synthesis of coruscating garage rock imbued with a sense of Beatlesy psychedelia and an acute pop sensibility. It was a potent and stylish enough brew to land them various prestigious TV slots, not least *Later With Jools Holland* in the UK, a programme which has become a showcase for what is deemed cool and of the moment. Despite, or perhaps because of, these swift successes the band found themselves under extreme pressure while gigging towards the end of 2002 and came to blows on stage, prompting rumours of early burnout. It's more likely that a spot of r'n'r will return them to their former glory.

⊙ **Highly Evolved** (2002; Capitol).
A bristling, snarling album shot through with attitude. The balance between trippiness and balls-out rock is keenly felt and the best track has to be the 93-second rolling mayhem of the title tune – short, sharp and straight to the point.

Essi Berelian

VIOLENT FEMMES

Formed Milwaukee, Wisconsin, 1981.

With their choppy guitar sound, pubescent lyrics and the kind of attitude that can only be cultured in a city devoid of attitude, **Violent Femmes** became one of the first big 80s alternative bands in the US. Though they remain active, their importance nowadays lies in their influence in the tight, fervent music of 'new punk' superstars such as Green Day.

Gordon Gano (guitar/vocals), **Brian Ritchie** (bass) and **Victor DeLorenzo** (percussion) initially presented themselves as all-American nerds straight out of a teen movie – the type who go dateless to the prom or have ketchup squirted on them in the lunch room. Ritchie, who named the band, claimed the words were 'just something that came out of my mouth'. But the passive-aggressive nature of their name perfectly reflected their style. Sarcastic put-downs and self-mocking lyrics were nervously stated or joyously shouted to tunes constructed around a simple bass line. At his best, Gano reduced complex, familiar emotions to simple, catchy choruses, elevating angst-rock to an art form.

'Why can't I get just one fuck?' demanded Gano on their 1982 landmark debut, VIOLENT FEMMES. The answer: 'Guess it's got something to do with luck.' This album, released on Slash Records, sold more than a million copies, although never charting and receiving little promotion. It took off on college radio and spilled down to American high-schoolers, who found a close friend in Gano's 'I'm uncool' persona. Without having a hit single ("Blister In The Sun", seemingly an ode to masturbation, was the closest), VIOLENT FEMMES made its name as an album on which every song was an anthem of rejection, where 'love is gone' and those who oppose have the open invitation to 'kiss off'.

Going against the grain, Femmes Victor, Gordon and Brian

What followed never lived up to the success of their debut. Gano, the son of a preacher man and a committed Christian, began to drift a bit, and what was once sexual frustration became odd righteousness on the Femmes' HALLOWED GROUND (1985). This album confused those who thrilled over the debut: "Country Death Song" was sort of cool, but the punchy riffs and vibrant lyrics were gone. Some fans were won back with THE BLIND LEADING THE NAKED (1986), if only due to its smart cover of T Rex's "Children Of The Revolution", but the band had little gas left in the tank. They split temporarily, a move some assumed was permanent – and might have been best if it had been, for the enduring fame of the Violent Femmes has little to do with any recordings of the past decade.

In 1989 the album 3 was released, then in 1991 WHY DO BIRDS SING?, after which De Lorenzo was replaced by **Guy Hoffman** of the BoDeans. After falling out with the Slash label, the Femmes were given more freedom and control in the studio by their new label Elektra. The results, NEW TIMES (1994) and ROCK (1995), were darker but irrelevant.

It took a good while for the Femmes to even get close to their former glory, but 2000's FREAK MAGNET went some way to proving that they still had a talent for classy, catchy folk'n'punk. The following year saw SOMETHING'S WRONG, an Internet-only album of rarities, emerge as a tempting little nugget for fans with computers. But even compilation albums, it seems, have been unable to capture the genius displayed when the Femmes truly blistered in the sun.

⊙ **Violent Femmes** (1982; Slash).
Angry and funny, this minimalist album contains most, if not all, of the band's classics. From "Gone Daddy Gone" to "Add It Up", this is the sarcastic heart of America's youth.

Matthew Grant

THE VIRGIN PRUNES

Formed Dublin, Ireland, 1978; disbanded 1987.

"Ireland never experienced Glam-Rock sexuality in a 70s ambiguous way, or the avant-garde, and The Virgin Prunes were all of that in one big explosion." Gavin Friday

The Virgin Prunes coalesced from a group of artistic and musical youths inspired by the first ripples of punk carried across the Irish Sea to Dublin. They formed a tightly knit community called Lypton Village, a private world of codes and cryptic pseudonyms. By 1978, The Prunes had become the 'official' band of the Village, and played their first gig in Ireland supporting The Clash. Their performance – offering simulated sexual intercourse between the two male frontmen, and unabashed full-frontal nudity from founding member **GAVIN FRIDAY** – gave them overnight cult-celebrity status.

Friday (born Fionnáin Hanvey) had been introduced to Lypton Village by one Paul Hewson, who was soon to become famous worldwide as Bono of U2. The two bands were initially very close – **Dik Prune** and U2's The Edge were brothers – but their careers followed wildly different trajectories. While U2 shrewdly ascended within the rock milieu, The Virgin Prunes interpreted the initial confrontational aesthetics of punk: performing savage, Dadaist events rather than rock gigs – to see them was to enter a grotesque theatre of psychosexual catharsis. Friday, **Guggi** and **Dave-Id Busarus** (all vocals/performance) might be screaming improvised profanities in dialogue, incompletely cross-dressed in a gothic chamber of thrones and candles. Meanwhile, musicians Dik (guitar), **Strongman** (bass), **Haa Lacka Binttii** (drums/keyboards) and the male **Mary O'Nellon** (drums) provided suitably disturbing and relentless sonic embroidery.

Rough Trade signed the group after a critically appraised, self-financed 1981 debut EP, TWENTY TENS. After the equally promising follow-up single, "In The Greylight", they decided to release a tie-in with a series of performances that had taken place at Dublin's Douglas Hyde gallery, collectively billed under the title A NEW FORM OF BEAUTY. Although promoted as an album, it befitted The Prunes' conceptual integrity by its appearance as separate 7", 10" and 12" singles; within this set lay some profoundly disturbing moments, notably "Come To Daddy" on the 10" format.

The singles "Baby Turns Blue" and "A Pagan Lovesong" (1982) captured The Prunes' passion and hinted at great things to come, before the band ventured on a vast European tour. Away from cloistered Dublin, however, they found their avant-garde nihilism seriously compromised. Their first 'proper' album, 1982's IF I DIE I DIE, compounded the problem – the music failed to sustain focus and interest without the visual accompaniment.

Musical differences was another factor in the slow disintegration of the group. In 1984, seminal members Guggi and Dik left, Mary switched to guitar, and original drummer Pod rejoined. But they were in danger of self-parody as they clung to the superficialities of what were once sublime shock aesthetics on the poorly received 1986 album THE MOON LOOKED DOWN AND LAUGHED.

Gavin Friday ended his involvement with The Virgin Prunes in 1987, and embarked on a multi-faceted solo career. Meanwhile, most of the remaining line-up soldiered on for a while as The Prunes, their shrunken name reflecting reduced expectations and achievements.

⊙ **The Hidden Lie (Live In Paris)** (1987; New Rose; currently unavailable).
The essential Virgin Prunes live experience – recorded in 1986, it captures their spirit better than anything else.

Chris Brook

VOICE OF THE BEEHIVE

Formed London, 1986.

The British indie scene of the mid-80s was a fairly dour affair. Goth was big, and the bedroom introspection of The Smiths was inspiring a legion of confused teenagers. Into its midst came California girl **Tracey Bryn** (guitar/vocals), so struck with London while on holiday there that she not only stayed, but persuaded her sister **Melissa Brooke Belland** (vocals) to join her. Soon the two siblings, whose father, Bruce Belland, had enjoyed Top 10 hits on both sides of the Atlantic with the Four Preps, were pumping fresh air into the London music game as **Voice Of The Beehive**.

An early demo accidentally came to the attention of Andy Ross and Dave Balfe from Food Records; it was discovered on the flip side of a tape sent in by Tracey's (then) boyfriend. The results were a fleshed-out band, featuring **Mike Jones** (guitar/vocals) and former Madness members **Daniel 'Woody' Woodgate** (drums) and **Mark 'Bedders' Bedford** (bass), and a single, "Just A City", released in early 1987.

Behind a media buzz, VOTB were signed to London Records; Bedford left, replaced by **Martin Brett**; the debut album LET IT BEE came out later that year, to public and critical acclaim. While Tracey and Melissa were engaging in an outlandish game of costume one-upwomanship, they were also putting the fun back into indie music. The pop gems "I Walk The Earth", "Don't Call Me Baby" and "I Say Nothing" smirked and bopped their way into the charts.

After a long break they re-emerged in 1991 with the single "Monsters And Angels", the three-day 'Orgy Under The Underworld' gigs in Camden and the album HONEY LINGERS. Though not as well received as the first album, it did lead to a successful carnival-atmosphere tour. Another recording hiatus followed, this one spurred by personal and business problems, before SEX & MISERY finally appeared in 1995. It showed Tracey and Melissa going it alone, and the rest of the band pretty much written out of the story. The UK music press and public showed virtually nil interest, though there was a new-found enthusiasm in the US alternative market.

The result was sadly predictable: the sisters returned to California where the closest they have come to making music has been Tracey's stint as a singing waitress. More fruitful forays into the world of art and writing followed, while Melissa started a successful clothing company. Mike, Woody, and Martin are still involved in the industry, after what was a rather unfortunate end to the brightest of beginnings.

⊙ **Let It Bee** (1987; London).
Swoonsome pop combined with lyrics about alcoholism, loneliness and barbarians in cars. The Wonder Stuff meets Lucille Ball in a dark alley, with The Go-Go's looking on.

⊙ **Sex & Misery** (1995; East West).
The boys are gone, replaced by Svengali producer and session musicians called 'Tufty'. Hints of the old spirit remain, nonetheless, on what is basically a damn fine grown-up pop album.

Phil Udell

THE VON BONDIES

Formed Detroit, Michigan, 2000.

There's no rush purer than that provided by primal rock'n'roll, and so it stands to reason that a band like **The Von Bondies** are one of the most exciting bands playing the devil's own music today.

Everything that goes around comes around, and while much of the mid- to late 90s was obsessed with nu-metal, rap-core, rap-metal or whatever you want to call it, it was inevitable that the pendulum of rock would swing back in favour of the hellish racket created in seedy garages the world over by teenagers playing guitar till their fingers bleed. And garages come no seedier than those in legendary Detroit.

Within its sprawl can be found the raw material, the million and one tales of love and survival that spawn great bluesy rock'n'roll. Think of the artists

the Von Bondies

Lack of Communication

shaped by the city: The Stooges, MC5, Alice Cooper, Ted Nugent And The Amboy Dukes. The Von Bondies have a strong heritage to live up to – even if their leader, **Jason Stollsteimer**, claims not to own any classic Detroit rock albums!

At the turn of the millennium the Detroit rock scene was dripping with bands trading on the city's name and former glories: The White Stripes, Electric 6, The Dirtbombs, The Detroit Cobras were all making waves. The Von Bondies were originally known as the Baby Killers but wisely opted for a name change, even if the music stayed the same. Jason Stollsteimer (guitar/vocals), **Marcie Bolen** (guitar), **Carrie Smith** (bass), **Don Blum** (drums) took the energy of punk and channelled it into the classic over-driven guitar template.

"It Came From Japan" (a tribute to rock'n'roll) and "Nite Train" (a tale about Stollsteimer getting loaded for the first time) were the first recordings to emerge in 2000. However, LACK OF COMMUNICATION (2001) was what first made ears prick up worldwide, being produced by White Stripes' **Jack White**, then seen as a man who could do no wrong. The White Stripes also took them as support act on their European tour, offering them the kind of exposure any young band would kill for. Not surprisingly the Bondies were headlining their own shows within six months and making a variety of prestigious appearances on various TV shows, such as *Later With Jools Holland*, and playing at the Leeds and Reading Festivals.

Where the rock will take them next is anyone's guess, but if you're willing to take a chance you're in for one hell of a great ride.

⊙ **Lack Of Communication** (2001; Sweet Nothing). Aggressive, impassioned and raw, this record takes the fury of punk and uses it to supercharge classic bluesy garage rock. No wonder Jack White wanted to produce them.

Essi Berelian

LOUDON WAINWRIGHT III

Born Chapel Hill, North Carolina, 1946.

"Our relationship, Is just a little ship, That's out on a stormy sea."

Loudon Wainwright III was one of several 'new Dylans' discovered during the American singer-songwriter boom of the late 60s and early 70s. The breeziest and least pretentious of that sullen bunch, Wainwright imposed his frankly suburban persona on a genre suffused with class guilt. But his sometimes overly clever lyrics and a brand of humour which can turn suddenly sour, like novelty-store garlic gum, have kept him from enjoying the success of more bombastic brethren.

Wainwright grew up comfortably middle-class – his father was a *Life* columnist and editor – and aspired to a theatre career, but after dropping out of Carnegie Mellon in 1967 he began to write and perform songs. Producer Milton Kramer saw his live act in New York in 1969 and brought him to Atlantic Records, the label that released his debut LOUDON WAINWRIGHT III (1970). That and the follow-up, ALBUM II, were mostly acoustic showcases on which Wainwright mixed a keen attention to craft with a sophomoric tendency to joke his way through serious subjects – like the one-minute "Suicide Song" ('When you get hung up, hang yourself up by the neck/what the hell, what the hell, what the heck'). He jumped to Columbia in 1972 and cut his best-received record, ALBUM III, which contained his one real hit, the *faux* bluegrass novelty, "Dead Skunk". Wainwright convincingly says it took fifteen minutes to write.

But the fad for folk-flavoured singer-songwriters faded in the mid 70s, and Wainwright's gentle virtues went begging in the Springsteen-suffused pop market (though Springsteen himself was hailed a 'new Dylan' as well). As a performer he remained gregarious, but as a songwriter he became withdrawn; his jokes often seemed insular or mean. ATTEMPTED MUSTACHE had some cheerful, accessible tunes (including the lively "Swimming Song"), but UNREQUITED was full of love-gone-wrong songs, which were bitter when not maudlin.

After a largely unsuccessful jump to Arista, Wainwright moved to London and spent five years on Demon/Rounder, where his public profile remained low, but his work, abetted and sometimes produced by kindred soul Richard Thompson, flourished. On these albums (FAME AND WEALTH,

I'M ALRIGHT and MORE LOVE SONGS), Wainwright was surlier than ever when talking about his career, as in "The Grammy Song" and "How Old Are You?" ('Are you bitter, have you grown lazy/Were you embarrassed about "Dead Skunk"?'), but surprisingly gentle and insightful about matters closer to the heart. MORE LOVE SONGS' "Your Mother And I", in which he explained divorce to his young child, was a particularly fine example. During this period Wainwright also logged some stage and screen time, acting in films (*Jacknife, The Slugger's Wife*), TV (*M*A*S*H*), and New York and London theatre.

Wainwright has continued to release mordantly humorous music, and his voice, once endearingly thin, has mellowed into a fine, expressive tenor. He may not ever have another "Dead Skunk", though he came close on GROWN MAN (1995), with "IWIWAL" (I Wish I Was A Lesbian), a catchy tune of minor notoriety which he claims took him only *eight* minutes to write. The album also featured a moving duet with his daughter Martha, "Father/Daughter Dialogue".

Recent releases show Wainwright happy to adopt an air of bemused domesticity. This theme certainly runs through LITTLE SHIP (1997) with tracks such as "Bein' A Dad" and "What Are Families For?" gently picking at the flakes on the surface of his relationships. And while SOCIAL STUDIES (1999) was a sharp-tongued battering of politicians and numerous other disagreeable public figures, 2001's LAST MAN ON EARTH was a far more sorrowful affair, being largely inspired by the death of his mother. Songs such as "Missing You" and "Out Of Reach" said it all.

⊙ **Album III** (1993; ZTT).
Mostly goofy stuff, Including a great tribute to sports fandom and a perfectly aimed, nice-white-boy version of Leiber and Stoller's "Smoky Joe's Café". And, of course, that one about the skunk.

⊙ **Therapy** (1989; Silvertone).
Musically this sounds a bit rushed, but the lyrics are some of his most acute. The gems include the one-night stand gone wrong "Aphrodisiac", and a wicked lady-killer's apologia "Nice Guys" ('I don't want to be the hero of my life/If I can be the villain of yours').

⊙ **Career Moves** (1993; Charisma/Virgin).
An excellent live snapshot alternating between some bouncy new songs and stripped-down versions of his classics.

⊙ **The BBC Sessions** (1998; Strange Fruit).
An excellent collection of 'live-in-the-studio' recordings spanning the period 1971–93. Stand-out tracks include the opening "Be Careful There's A Baby In The House" and "A Father And A Son".

Roy Edroso

Born Pomona, California, 1949.

"I've never met anyone who made it with a chick because they owned a Tom Waits album. I've got all three, and it's never helped me."

One of rock's most uncompromising individualists, **Tom Waits** (guitar/piano/vocals) has won an ever-increasing following for his distinctive, hoary rasp and his chronicles of the lowlifes and outsiders of urban America. His melancholy, bourbon-soaked world-view mixes the paintings of Edward Hopper and the writings of the Beat Generation with a soundtrack that encompasses everything from Broadway composers through Captain Beefheart to classic jazz and blues.

The instantly recognizable gravel of his voice was absent from his early club act – which attracted manager Herb Cohen, a collaborator with Frank Zappa and Tim Buckley – and his demos. In those days he sounded more like a bar-room country-blues singer, a trait that was still evident on his Asylum debut, the Jerry Yester-produced CLOSING TIME (1973), which contained songs later covered by Tim Buckley

REDFERNS

Tom Waits reaching for the extremes, as ever

("Martha") and label mates The Eagles ("Ø1' 55").

The drunken bohemian persona got its proper start on THE HEART OF SATURDAY NIGHT (1974) and the concert album NIGHTHAWKS AT THE DINER (1975), both of which captured a phlegmy growl on top of an understated orchestration that managed to sound heartfelt without falling into overblown sentimentality.

The jazzy flavour of those albums continued on SMALL CHANGE (1976) and FOREIGN AFFAIRS (1977). The first featured the self-explanatory "Invitation To The Blues" (namechecking James Cagney and Rita Hayworth) and the quintessential Waitsian titles "The Piano Has Been Drinking (Not Me)" and "Bad Liver And A Broken Heart". SMALL CHANGE also introduced his classic strategy of utilizing traditional songs as sources for his own material, with the chorus of "Waltzing Matilda" used as the central hook for "Tom Traubert's Blues" (later covered by Rod Stewart). On the latter album's "A Sight For Sore Eyes", he repeated that trick, subverting "Auld Lang Syne", and paid homage to his Beat progenitors on "Jack And Neal"/"California, Here I Come".

BLUE VALENTINE (1978) began inching towards a more guitar-orientated, more traditional rock sound, fleshed out on 1980's HEARTATTACK AND VINE. VALENTINE provided a haunting evocation of lost innocence in "Kentucky Avenue", full of emotions to be echoed on HEARTATTACK's "On The Nickel": 'So what becomes of all the little boys/Who run away from home/Well the world just keeps getting bigger/Once you get out on your own'. Complementing the R&B-flavoured rock was a foray back to the love ballad on "Saving All My Love For You", "Ruby's Arms" and "Jersey Girl" (which became a staple of Bruce Springsteen's live set). Following the release of the BOUNCED CHECKS compilation in 1981, Waits worked on the score for Francis Ford Coppola's film *One From The Heart* (1983), duetting with Crystal Gayle on various tracks. This format produced some of the most powerful imagery and melodies of his career.

After moving to Island Records, Waits produced the three most ambitious albums of his career. The first of these song cycles, SWORDFISHTROMBONES (1983), was a sprawling mix of seemingly disparate instrumentation and styles, drawing upon the services of brass bands and American avant-garde composer Harry Partch. RAIN DOGS (1985) was grounded in the same breadth of influence, encompassing raw blues, nursery rhymes, free-form jazz, tango and other styles. ("Downtown Train" was made a hit by Rod Stewart.) Acclaimed as two of the most important and visionary records of the decade, they were followed by the similarly innovative FRANK'S WILD YEARS (1987), initially a stage-show expanded from a brief song on SWORDFISHTROMBONES.

Another live album, BIG TIME (1988), brought together items from the three Island outings, underlining their unity of mood; then the albums dried up for a while, until the release of the score he composed

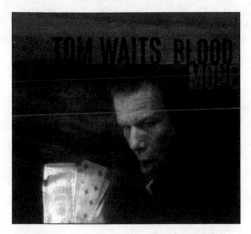

for Jim Jarmusch's *Night On Earth* in 1992. His full-fledged return to music came on BONE MACHINE (1992), a skeletal, lo-fi, fatalistic creation: 'Hell is boiling over/And Heaven is full/We're chained to the world/And we all gotta pull'. The music was bleak, croaky and sombre, with only the delicate "Who Are You" and "Whistle In The Wind" hinting at the piano auteur of old.

In 1993 Waits released BLACK RIDER, his own adaptation of the blackly comic opera on which he had collaborated with director Robert Wilson and Beat icon William Burroughs. As always, the music was quirky and wide-ranging, much like the films in which he has acted while pursuing that second career – *Rumblefish*, *The Cotton Club*, *Down By Law*, *Ironweed*, *Short Cuts* and *Dracula* to name a few. He always seems to be playing a bum or a crazy, solidifying his persona even more.

The latter part of the 90s found Waits lying relatively low on the album front while he concentrated on other projects and soundtrack work. MULE VARIATIONS (1999) was eventually followed, after a couple of compilation albums, by the double whammy of ALICE and BLOOD MONEY, both in 2002. The latter was inspired by the play *Woyzeck*, written by the German poet George Buchner in 1837 – the results were almost as scary as BONE MACHINE. ALICE, on the other hand, was the less shadowy of the two, with echoes of BLUE VALENTINE.

⊙ **Heartattack And Vine** (1980; Asylum).
Arguably Waits never bettered this accessible collection of gorgeous love letters and rootsy country-funk.

⊙ **Swordfishtrombones** (1983; Island).
Initially difficult and esoteric, but a very rewarding experience.

⊙ **Rain Dogs** (1985; Island).
A sprawling, catholic mix, underpinned by a keen sense of songwriterly craft.

⊙ **Asylum Years** (1985; Asylum) **and Beautiful Maladies: The Island Years** (1998; Island).
Near-definitive compilation albums of Waits' work. Stand-outs include "Martha", "Tom Traubert's Blues" and "Ruby's Arms".

⊙ **Mule Variations** (1999; Anti/Epitaph).
A sixteen-track *tour de force* introduced to the press

by Waits conducting interviews in a run-down Chinese diner. The equally quirky album oozes warmth, humanity and understanding, despite the presence of showcase ballads too bitter for Springsteen and lyrics as impenetrable as any he has produced. The work of an older and wiser Waits, formed by stability and marriage, raising kids rather than hell.

⊙ **Blood Money** (2002; Anti/Epitaph).
Written in collaboration with his wife Kathleen Brennan, this collection finds Waits torturing a menagerie of unrecognizable percussive beasts in a Brechtian vision of the best and worst of the human spirit.

Michael Sumsion

RICK WAKEMAN

Born London, 1949.

The only solo success of progressive rock's keyboard virtuosos, **Rick Wakeman** has proven to be an influential and tenacious survivor of this 1970s movement. After beginning as a dance-hall organist, Wakeman became a rather undedicated piano student at the Royal College of Music. Classes soon went to the wayside for studio sessions at the behest of David Bowie. Wakeman developed a Mellotron technique that overcame its eight-second note length, using it to create a crashing crescendo for the title track of SPACE ODDITY (1969). His gifts did not go unnoticed, and more session work followed. Finally ditching college in 1970, Wakeman cast his lot as a member of folk-rockers **THE STRAWBS**.

He never quite clicked with the band, though his "Temperament Of Mind" solo in JUST A COLLECTION OF ANTIQUES AND CURIOS (1970) garnered some attention. After his fine session work on HUNKY DORY (1971), Bowie offered him a lucrative spot in the upcoming Ziggy Stardust line-up. Meanwhile, prog-rockers **YES** also came courting for a replacement for the Hammond-handed Tony Kaye. As Wakeman notes in his 1995 autobiography, *Say Yes!*, he only knew that he was finally in Yes because guitarist Steve Howe kept showing up at his house to drive him to rehearsal. Wakeman was becoming a keyboard polymath, and Yes's FRAGILE (1971) was recorded in a rush just to pay for his huge bank of Mellotrons, pianos and synths. The single "Roundabout" brought stardom to the band and to Wakeman.

His playing dominated their next album, CLOSE TO THE EDGE (1972), a commercial and artistic peak for the band. Though he'd recorded an understandably rare album of Muzak-like covers titled PIANO VIBRATIONS (1971), Wakeman's real solo debut came with THE SIX WIVES OF HENRY VIII (1973), composed during the CLOSE TO THE EDGE sessions. It went gold and earned critical acclaim; with Yes now trapped in an unwieldy double album, TALES FROM TOPOGRAPHIC OCEANS (1974), Wakeman left to seek out solo fortune.

And a fortune it was. JOURNEY TO THE CENTER OF THE EARTH (1974) topped US and UK charts alike. An orchestra, choir, and rock band collabora-

TOM WAITS ▪ RICK WAKEMAN

tion built around the Jules Verne tale, it was followed by the similar studio album THE MYTHS AND LEGENDS OF KING ARTHUR AND THE KNIGHTS OF THE ROUND TABLE (1975). Despite tremendous sales, Wakeman's increasingly grand stage-shows took a toll on his finances and health alike, and he was struck by a heart attack at the age of 25. Perhaps as a result, NO EARTHLY CONNECTION (1976) eschewed orchestral music for an 'English Rock Ensemble.' A moody rock rumination on God, death and the musician's lot in life, it was a disppointment to fans and to his label, though in retrospect it represents an earnest stab at musical growth.

A bit humbled, Wakeman returned to Yes, first as a session player and finally as a member for GOING FOR THE ONE (1977). Bookended by the muscular Moog workouts of WHITE ROCK (1976) and the SIX WIVES-styled CRIMINAL RECORD (1977), it seemed that Wakeman's fortunes were on the rise again. But punk rock was nipping at Yes's heels; Wakeman lashed out at his label mates The Sex Pistols, finally driving them to Virgin Records. His musical response was a slide into cheesy synth-pop, evidenced by Yes's TORMATO (1978) and the limp RHAPSODIES (1979). Yes soon fell apart, and A&M Records dropped him from its roster.

The 80s saw him struggling to find steady work and a steady marriage, a task eased by his finding religion and quitting the bottle. Successful soundtracks like G'OLE (1982) were mixed with flat solo like SILENT NIGHTS (1985) and TIME MACHINE (1988). So Wakeman turned back to his original strengths: the piano and Yes. With ANDERSON BRUFORD WAKEMAN AND HOWE (1989) he scored a commercial if not an artistic hit, and some critical respect followed his piano trilogy of COUNTRY AIRS (1986), SEA AIRS (1989), and NIGHT AIRS (1990). He became a familiar and gregarious figure on Britain's Channel Four, making frequent appearances on Sunday religious shows. But the late 80s and 90s also brought a bewildering flood of one-offs by Wakeman on various labels, often hasty pastiches of his earlier and more popular work. Worthier entries include THE PIANO ALBUM (1995) and PRIVATE COLLECTION (1994), the latter being a fine array of JOURNEY outtakes and piano impromptus.

1996 saw a return to Yes yet again, with the mixed live and studio album KEYS TO ASCENSION. Though it was Yes's strongest work in years, on the eve of its follow-up Wakeman was out of the band again. His most recent collection was OUT THERE (2003), both by name and nature. More sub-Yes prog synth noodles filled the disc, and this time he was accompanied by The New English Rock Ensemble.

If history is any guide, it won't be long before he's back again – and with another string of solo albums in tow.

⊙ **The Six Wives of Henry VIII** (1973; A&M).
Ably backed by band-mates from Yes and The Strawbs, Wakeman's debut is a *tour de force* of keyboard bravado. From the driving piano of "Catherine Of Aragon" to the thundering organ prelude to "Jane Seymour", it's an ideal introduction to the Romantic borrowings and technical pyrotechnics of progressive rock.

⊙ **Journey To The Center Of The Earth** (1974; A&M).
Jules Verne's fantastic tale, recorded live at the Royal Festival Hall with a full choir and orchestra. It finishes what the Moody Blues started: a perfect mesh of rock, spoken-word and orchestral music. Moogs float over pensive cellos, clavinovas boogie, and ponderous underworld narration abounds ... What more could you want?

⊙ **The Piano Album** (1995; Castle).
Solo piano reworkings of originals and of his studio work with David Bowie, The Strawbs and Yes. Wakeman's originals, often not well served by studio production, particularly benefit from live solo performance.

⊙ **Voyage: The Very Best Of Rick Wakeman** (1996; A&M).
A remastered sampler of Wakeman's 70s heyday, including all of JOURNEY and most of SIX WIVES. Some tracks are from albums still unissued on CD. Wakeman had no input in this compilation, though, and NO EARTHLY CONNECTION is sorely missed.

Paul Collins

THE WALKABOUTS

Formed Seattle, 1984; still walking.

The Walkabouts' masterminds **Carla Torgerson** (vocals/guitars/cello/keyboards) and **Chris Eckman** (vocals/guitars/piano) met for the first time at a tinned-fish plant in Alaska. Luckily, though, their relationship developed into something a little more creative and, after college, the two put a band together with Chris's younger brothers **Grant** (drums/percussion) and **Curt** (bass). The Eckman brothers had already worked with a number of punk and pop groups, and Carla had experience singing in folk bands. The first full-length Walkabouts releases were SEE BEAUTIFUL RATTLESNAKE GARDENS (1988) and CATARACT (1989).

Shortly after, **Michael Wells** took over on bass and **Glen Slater**, with his unmistakeable organ, joined the band. While the rest of the Seattle guitar crowd – the Mudhoneys, Nirvanas and all the others – believed in grunge and the power of a loud guitar, The Walkabouts used a wider spectrum of instruments, experimenting with violin, cello and mandolin. The RAG AND BONE EP (1990) and the album SCAVENGER (1991) – with well-known guests Brian Eno and Natalie Merchant – are the results of these attempts.

The Walkabouts avoided the muddy sea of grunge and settled inside the triangle of electrified rock, subtle acoustics and storytelling in the country/folk tradition. Their compassionate and observant short stories of losers and the fading American dream – mostly written by Chris Eckman – earned them a wide European audience and a reputation as 'unembarrassed romantics, self-confident outsiders and melancholy hedonists'.

Terri Moeller took the drums for NEW WEST MOTEL (1993), a double album that was drenched in Neil Young-style guitar work and, indeed, featured a cover of his "Like A Hurricane". They swerved into smoother realms for the year's second release, SATISFIED MIND (1993). Containing thirteen covers of songs by Nick Cave, John Cale, Robert Forster and others, the album began to drag, despite being helped out by Peter Buck of R.E.M. and Mark Lanegan of Screaming Trees. SETTING THE WOODS ON FIRE (1994) led them back to more familiar territory, but was the last gasp of their intense, roaring guitars.

DEVIL'S ROAD (1996) was their first step down a fresh path. The band signed to a new company and recorded outside Seattle for the first time, landing in Cologne's famous Conny Plank studios, the home of early Kraftwerk and Can. With production by Victor Van Vugt (Nick Cave, Robert Forster) and string arrangements by the Warsaw Philharmonic Orchestra, The Walkabouts made the quantum jump into calm intensity with the vocals of Torgerson and Eckman floating above the precisely arranged carpet of instruments.

For NIGHTTOWN (1997), their most succesful effort to date, the band picked up a new bass player, **Baker Saunders**, and came into the city. An urban record with urban textures and the rediscovery of slowness, the album explored the dark sides of city life both lyrically and musically, employing drum loops, synthesizers and ambient noises.

Carla Torgerson and Chris Eckman were still the driving force behind the group despite having worked as a duo, **Chris & Carla**. First appearing on the live SHELTER FOR AN EVENING (1993), they have since released LIFE FULL OF HOLES (1995), NIGHTS BETWEEN STATIONS (1996) and SWINGER 500 (1998) – all three characterized by a rough charm and a sparing use of instruments.

The new millennium saw The Walkabouts release TRAIN LEAVES AT EIGHT – another covers album, which this time focused on Europe's musical heritage. The set included versions of songs by Jacques Brel, Scott Walker, Stina Nordenstam and, intriguingly, Neu!. Once again the nucleus of the band was augmented by fellow travellers Peter Buck, Robin Holcomb and a diverse supporting cast. Since then the albums have come thick and fast: ENDED UP A STRANGER (2001), DRUNKEN SOUNDTRACKS (2002's rarities collection) and WATERMARKS (2003; a retrospective) were all corking documents of a band that never seem to loose their stride.

The Walkabouts' Chris and Carla on stage, Germany, 1999

⦿ **Nighttown** (1997; Virgin).
Otherwise known as 'the rediscovery of slowness'. The Walkabouts' 'urban' record, dark and melancholic. Strings and other musical experiments catapult folk-rock into a new dimension. The right record for long autumn evenings.

⦿ **Train Leaves At Eight** (2000; Glitterhouse).
This is a well-crafted, intelligent album of covers; the interesting arrangements and Carla Torgerson's stunning voice combine and complement each other perfectly.

Christoph Heise

SCOTT WALKER

Born Hamilton, Ohio, 1944.

"In a song, I look for what I consider to be the truth. The people following me don't want sugar-coated rubbish."

Scott **Engel** sang on a handful of nowhere singles before a spell as bass player with The Routers, a Californian instrumental combo. Then in

1964 he teamed up with **John Maus** (guitar/vocals) and **Gary Leeds** (drums) as **The Walker Brothers**, a format in which the restyled **Scott Walker**'s formidable golden-brown baritone at first played a support role to Maus.

The trio decided to try their luck in Britain, and Scott came to the fore on their second 45, "Love Her", which climbed into the UK Top 20 in 1965. He remained the focus on the chart-topping "Make It Easy On Yourself" (UK #1, US #16) as well as on "My Ship Is Coming In" and "The Sun Ain't Gonna Shine Anymore", slowish outings framed in heavy-handed orchestration. Thus the Brothers became British pin-ups until a hat trick of poor-selling records and bickering between John and Scott caused the three to go their separate ways in 1967.

Maus made the UK Top 40 again before the year was out, but he and Leeds were no longer stars by the time Scott returned to solo prominence with "Jackie" (1967), "Joanna" (1968) and "Lights Of Cincinnati" (1969), and a trilogy of albums – SCOTT 1, SCOTT 2 and SCOTT 3. These established Walker as both the paramount interpreter of the great Belgian *chansonnier* Jacques Brel and as an intriguing writer in his own right. His voice proved capable of soaring above a Spectorish orchestral wall of sound, but those expecting the teen-hit songs must have become increasingly bemused by the melancholia of his output. While the songs on these albums included big romantic numbers, it was a jaded romance, matched by his oddball delivery, and the Brel numbers could be vicious and perplexing: "Next", for instance, on SCOTT 2, or "Funeral Tango" on SCOTT 3. Other covers included material by Weill/Mann, Bacharach-David and Tim Hardin, and it was immediately apparent that Walker's own songs – like "Plastic Palace People" (on SCOTT 2) – stood up among such exalted company.

Each of these albums charted high in Britain (SCOTT 2 went to #1), where Walker had his own TV series at the time, but the entirely self-penned SCOTT 4 (1969) could not be made to suit 1969's

charts any more than CLIMATE OF HUNTER could fifteen years later. Indeed, around this time, Scott moved abruptly from a mainstream to cult following. Although his voice was evidently a thing of wonder, his wider talents began to fall unnoticed until the advocacy of such luminaries as Julian Cope, Eno and David Bowie, a decade on, triggered a spasm of reissues, compilations and belated re-evaluations.

You could understand this neglect in view of Scott's stints in northern clubs and the easy-listening potboilers he churned out in the early 70s. Containing showbiz schmaltz, movie themes, country and western and the most conservative rock, albums like 'TIL THE BAND COMES IN (1970), THE MOVIEGOER (1972) and ANY DAY NOW (1973) seemed to be going through the motions. Then, after WE HAD IT ALL (1974), Walker suddenly dropped everything, and disappeared from view for two years.

He stuck his head above the parapet for a regrouping of The Walker Brothers, who proceeded to have a UK Top 10 smash with "No Regrets", and knock out two albums of MOR covers. Scott then redeemed himself by resisting tempting incentives for the Brothers to work the nostalgia ticket, instead forcing a complete reinvention of the group via 1978's startlingly morbid NITE FLIGHTS. The needle-time was divided in three on the disc, each 'Brother' taking an equal share of lead vocals and composing credits, but the two spin-off singles – the title song and "The Electrician" – were the work of Scott as singer and co-producer.

Both were pointers to the darkness of CLIMATE OF HUNTER (1984), an album that saw Scott cast off more of his old associations. Despite sporadic plaudits in the music press – part inspired by Julian Cope's great anthology, FIRE ESCAPE IN THE SKY: THE GODLIKE GENIUS OF SCOTT WALKER (1981) – its sales hardly registered, and Walker's new label, Virgin, didn't ask for more.

Contradictory and far-fetched rumours abounded about Walker in the years following, about the only one of substance being that he worked with Brian Eno, although nothing came of the collaboration. In fact, it turned out to be eleven years before Walker returned with new work. TILT (1995) was a most extraordinary return, an album of fractured lyrics and harsh beauty that sounded like nothing and nobody else, and fully confirmed the cult status. There was even a burst of interviews and a couple of performances on late-evening TV shows – just enough to re-establish himself on a contemporary footing, and assure the faithful (whether there from "Love Her" onwards or CLIMATE OF HUNTER latecomers) that the Scott Walker story still had a long way to go.

For one as reclusive as Walker the turn of the millennium saw a veritable frenzy of activity. His soundtrack to Leo Carax's acclaimed POLA X (1999) was predominantly instrumentals, Walker's compositions reflecting his more recent minimalist proclivities, taking their lead from the themes of TILT. Walker performs on half the album (the rest includes contributions from Smog and Sonic Youth) and while there are no vocals, this is delightful stuff.

Walker took on the curatorship of the South Bank's prestigious Meltdown festival in 2000, assembling a line-up that included Radiohead and Jarvis Cocker. The link to Pulp was made more explicit when Walker was persuaded to take up the production mantle for the band's 2001 album WE LOVE LIFE.

Scott Walker

● **Fire Escape In The Sky: The Godlike Genius Of Scott Walker** (1981; Zoo) and **Boy Child: The Best Of Scott Walker, 1967–70** (1981; Zoo).
These two compilations focus on Scotts 1–3, mixing the Brel and self-penned material.

● **Scott 4** (1969; Philips).
The projection and control of a coltish Sinatra imposed upon pieces that embrace fierce anger, ardent romanticism and world-weariness. Highlights are the sardonic gloom of "Hero Of The War", the spooky "Boy Child', and the Bergman tribute of "The Seventh Seal".

● **Climate Of Hunter** (1984; Virgin).
With less emphasis on melodic construction and verse-chorus arrangements, Scott concentrates on the development of a racked and menacing mood on what one reviewer described as 'the most terminal songs ever written'.

● **Tilt** (1995; Fontana).
Only the drums and electric bass put this in the realms of pop/rock. The music darts around and the melodies verge on the atonal as the artist picks the bones of a text that resembles the narrative of some wild dream.

The Walker Brothers

● **After The Lights Go Out** (1990; Fontana).
A trawl through The Walker Brothers' more enduring moments – "The Sun Ain't Gonna Shine Anymore", "Walking In The Rain", "Make It Easy On Yourself" – and with hints of the 'godlike genius' to come, with some of the Scott-penned B-sides and tracks from the three 60s albums.

Alan Clayson

JOE WALSH

Born in Wichita, Kansas, 1947.

"You know, Mozart and Beethoven never got royalty cheques." Joe Walsh on his commercial success

For a man who claims he looks for symmetry and patterns, guitarist **Joe Walsh** can be an awfully contrary bastard. Though classically trained, he writes rock anthems that are about as Baroque as a brick. Having extolled the virtues of the high life in "Life's Been Good", he then tries to convince us he mows his own lawn on "Ordinary Average Guy". He introduced The Eagles to the idea of the joke, while going so far up himself as to cover Ravel's Pavane on his SO WHAT album.

Walsh's mother, a pianist, taught him to love Mozart and Beethoven. He went to university in Cleveland to avoid the draft in 1965 and learned from professors Beck and Page by cutting class and playing his guitar along to the radio. He developed a

bludgeoning, ear-assaulting riffola style. Subtlety was not his strong point.

In 1969 he was invited to join **Jim Fox** (drums) and **Tom Kriss** (bass) in the **JAMES GANG**, a band he seized by the scruff of its neck, giving himself room to grandstand on lead and rhythm, and to indulge his strangulated singing. The Gang – a band so ugly they made The Mothers Of Invention look like Evan Dando – became a laboratory for Walsh, and, under the guidance of producer Bill Szymczyk (who would introduce Joe to The Eagles) they came up with a strong debut, YER ALBUM (1969). Two more albums followed until Joe left the band to follow his beloved 'textures' in 1971, claiming 'I didn't want to turn into a Blue Cheer.'

Turning down an offer to replace Peter Frampton in Humble Pie, Walsh formed **Barnstorm** with **Joe Vitale** (drums) and **Kenny Passarelli** (bass). Their second album, THE SMOKER YOU DRINK, THE PLAYER YOU GET, contained the Walsh signature track "Rocky Mountain Way"; expressing bitter resignation to riffing that was as weighty as a sumo wrestler, "Way" introduced the world to the 'talkbox', a gizmo that Frampton would make famous on "Show Me the Way". It hit the Top 40 on both sides of the Atlantic.

On 1974's SO WHAT, Joe was to be found fooling around with synths, backed by a band which included Glenn Frey, Don Henley and Randy Meisner. Walsh replaced Bernie Leadon in **THE EAGLES** after playing on ON THE BORDER, with the express intention of breaking the soft-rockers out of the 'sons of the desert ballad' stereotype. It was time to whip a band into shape again. The result was HOTEL CALIFORNIA (1976), featuring Joe's bruising guitar breaks, including the celebrated closing chords of the title track. "New Kid In Town" stated his predicament, where 'Everybody's been watching you'. Joe walked it like he talked it, and responded with "Life In The Fast Lane", one of the best riffs ever. The gold discs piled up.

After HOTEL's success, Walsh laid down his 1976 solo live album, YOU CAN'T ARGUE WITH A SICK MIND, for Anchor Records, including the cod-reggae "Life's Been Good", a twisted celebration of superstar hedonism: 'My Maserati goes 185/I lost my license, now I can't drive'. But Joe's sanity was also impounded, and he started packing a chainsaw in his tour suitcase. The interminable THE LONG RUN followed, and it was time to sack the band.

With The Eagles defunct, Walsh dedicated himself to making albums with great titles – the best being YOU BOUGHT IT: YOU NAME IT – and forgettable everything else. "Ordinary Average Guy" kept him in hot tubs, but it was his work for Wilson Phillips on their debut album that proved he still had the chops. Walsh threw his hat in the presidential ring for the 1984 and 1988 elections ('He has never lied to the American public', the voters were told), and recorded the overheated "Vote For Me" for his SONGS FOR A DYING PLANET album (1992).

With the re-formation of The Eagles, continuing tours and occasional recording commitments, life has been good to Joe again, even if it has made him old very quickly.

⊙ **Rocky Mountain Way** (1984; Polydor).
Joe works in two modes: the satirical rocker with a caveman's sophistication (the title track and "Welcome To The Club"); and the psychedelic workout ("Meadows"). On the apocalyptic "Turn To Stone", you can hear him come on like an Egyptian plague.

Charles Bottomley

THE WANNADIES

Formed Skellefteå, Sweden, 1987.

I f your idea of a pop act is a bunch of self-effacing Scandinavian hippies with smiles on their faces and tongues firmly in their cheeks, look no further than **The Wannadies**.

The small-town boredom of Skellefteå, northern Sweden was the initial catalyst for distinctively coiffured guitarist and singer **Pär Wiksten** to round up friends and musicians **Christina Bergmark** (vocals, keyboards), **Gunnar Karlsson** (drums), **Björn Malmquist** (violin) and brothers **Fredrik** (bass) and **Stefan Schönfeldt** (guitar). According to Wiksten, the band's name was inspired by frequent visits to his local video library's horror section; they came close to being named The Bleed-to-Deaths, but thankfully thought again.

The Wannadies impressed at early gigs, with the track "The Beast Cures The Lover" becoming a firm live favourite after the group selected it for their self-financed debut EP SMILE. Soon after they signed with independent label MNW, and moved one step closer to the limelight, or so they thought.

The first album proper, THE WANNADIES, emerged in 1990. It was a breezy affair, showcasing acute headline single "My Home Town" and its follow-up, "Heaven". Though the set was generally well received, The Wannadies were still pretty small fish, finding themselves used as little more than

THE WANNADIES
BAGSY ME

strategic pawns by MNW. The second album, AQUANAUTIC, emerged via the label's subsidiary imprint Snap in 1992, and while the group was undoubtedly pleased to have the follow-up on the market, their record company's general disregard was to prove a precursor to future record label miseries. There was sufficient interest, however, to lead to a speedy reissue of their debut, replete with a couple of added covers, The Go-Betweens' "Lee Remick" and T Rex's "Children Of The Revolution".

The recording of a third album, BE A GIRL, was plagued by setbacks as producer after producer came and went. And even after its completion, it took another year to capture the attention of a British label. Eventually Indolent issued the record in the UK in 1995, with one track standing head and shoulders above the rest: "You And Me Song". Already a hit in Sweden, the song was picked out by British radio programmers, receiving extensive airplay. Although the album was not an immediate hit, the success of the single paved the way for a couple of further singles ("Might Be Stars" and "How Does It Feel?"). "You And Me Song" was itself rereleased on the BAGSY ME (1997) and BE A GIRL albums after featuring on the soundtrack of the movie *Romeo + Juliet*.

All was not plain sailing, however: a fall-out with MNW led to BAGSY ME being released by BMG, and Karlsson then left the band, to be replaced by **Erik Dahlgren**. But despite this upheaval the album's best moment, "Hit" – a wickedly humorous précis of the group's recent woes – took the band back into the UK Top 20. By now, America was also getting hip to The Wannadies, thanks to *Romeo + Juliet*. WANNADIES, a compilation of tracks from their two most recent albums, also ensured that Sweden's best new pop band made good headway stateside.

Indeed, The Wannadies headed to New York to record the fourth album, YEAH (2000), with producer Rik Ocasek, late of US powerpop legends The Cars. YEAH was, perhaps rather unwisely, chock-a-block with further thinly veiled attacks on record companies but still boasted its good moments, particularly the title track and "Big Fan", both of which were 'up' in subject matter and subsequently picked as singles.

But record company problems persisted, leading Pär to describe his band at the 2000 Reading Festival as 'the best unsigned band in Europe'. 2002 saw the release of a double CD, BEFORE AND AFTER, though it has as yet not become widely available outside of Sweden. So, even though their music continues to flow well, The Wannadies could certainly do with some well-deserved consistency on the business side.

⊙ **Be A Girl** (1995; Indolent).
Full of cracking melody and ambiguous lyrical turn, their third album announced The Wannadies' arrival in style – and still sounds remarkably fresh today.

⊙ **Bagsy Me** (1997; Indolent).
Darker this time, but value-packed with sharp pop. Marvellous single "Hit" is here, effortlessly replacing the "You and Me Song" as the consummate Scandinavian 'tune'.

Jeremy Simmonds

WAR

Formed Long Beach, California, 1969.

In essence, **War** were Night Shift, a band formed to back former American football star Deacon Jones as he developed a soul singing career on the California club circuit. Into the frame wandered **EX-ANIMALS** singer **Eric Burdon**, who was looking for a blues-based band to back him on future recordings. To Burdon, Night Shift offered experience and the right background. To Night Shift, Burdon's musical pedigree offered more money and excitement than Deacon Jones. The name 'War' was chosen as a declaration of opposition to the love and peace vibe of the late 60s.

The first band – Burdon plus **Howard Scott** (guitar/vocals), **Harold Brown** (drums), **Lonnie Jordan** (keyboards/vocals), **Peter Rosen** (bass), **Charles Miller** (saxophone/clarinet) and **Lee Oskar** (harmonica) – had only lasted a few weeks when Rosen died of a drug overdose. He was replaced by **B. B. Dickerson**, who had been the bassist with The Creators, and **Papa Dee Allen** (keyboards/vocals) – a well-known musician in the Long Beach area with lengthy jazz experience – was also recruited to form a group that jammed, broke barriers and kicked against the musical grain.

With the exception of the bizarre "Spill The Wine", the band's debut album, ERIC BURDON DECLARES WAR (1970), was a turgid mishmash of distended, psychedelicized blues jams. Although it featured similar blues odysseys, War's second and final collaboration with Burdon, THE BLACK MAN'S BURDON (1971), began to map out the Latino LA funk terrain that became the basis of their career. The musicianship on these albums was beyond question, but Burdon's commitment was another matter. Having a little self-consciously bought himself the kind of rootsy cred to which The Animals had aspired, Burdon did the all-too-typical rock-star thing of declaring himself burned out mid-tour in February 1971. War finished the dates without him.

At the end of the tour the band laid their Burdon down for good, and manager Steve Gold secured a deal with United Artists. The UA deal lasted from 1971 to 1978 and saw War selling millions of records. The basic style – at its best on 1971's ALL DAY MUSIC – was a soulful sound underpinned by complex and solid percussion. Elements of blues, jazz, funk, Latin, gospel and almost anything else that seemed appropriate could be added to vary albums and live gigs. Vocally, the absence of Burdon's histrionics allowed the band to develop a close-harmony sound using the range of voices as an extra texture within the mix.

War were able to outlast other bands in the funk category because they didn't depend on one trend or audience group for their career. Brilliant singles like "Slippin' Into Darkness"/"Nappy Head" (1971), "Me And Baby Brother" (1973) and "Why Can't We Be Friends?" (1975) scrutinized the idea of racial separatism. On the other hand, "The Cisco Kid" (1973) and "Low Rider" (1976) celebrated the style of LA's Latino subculture.

Unfortunately, after the release of GREATEST HITS (1976), the usual scenario of self-importance and decline set in. As disco began to take over the world, the band's responses were either pompous or predictable: PLATINUM JAZZ (1977) was a collection of the instrumental jams from their previous albums; GALAXY (1977) could only manage routine disco production values; and MUSIC BAND 2 (1979) featured a sad cover of one of their best songs, "The World Is A Ghetto".

After a series of label changes and inactivity, the band's own Lax label was in charge and War enjoyed a revival in their fortunes on the back of extensive remixing of their catalogue in the late 80s. The band are still active today, although varying line-ups and outside interests have made it a loose collective rather than a fully functioning unit. War's sound, if not its message, remains a lingering influence on many forms of 'black music', especially hip-hop, whose producers admire the loose, chunky sound of Harold Brown.

Many of the younger hip-hop crowd have been spotted at recent War gigs, though these days Jordan is the only original regularly gigging with the band. Members – past and present – continue their own innovations. Oskar's virtuoso skills on the harmonica saw him leave the band in 1993. He now produces his own brand of harmonica, and in 1997 released the haunting SO MUCH IN LOVE.

⊙ **All Day Music** (1971; Rhino).
Featuring the staggering "Slippin' Into Darkness", this is perhaps War's best record. Part of a series of soul/funk records at the beginning of the 70s whose deep introspection still stands as some of the most original and disquieting music ever made.

⊙ **Grooves & Messages: The Greatest Hits Of War** (1999; Rhino).
If it only included the full album version of "Slippin' Into Darkness", this would be the definitive War album. This collection also includes a disc of remixes by the likes of Armand Van Helden and Ganja Kru.

Neil Nixon

WAS (NOT WAS)

Formed Detroit, Michigan, 1981; disbanded 1992.

"Oh, man. No ... I think there were different forms of punctuation though.' Don Was, asked whether they'd considered other band names

Childhood friends and multi-instrumentalists **Don Fagenson** and **David Weiss**, having become fascinated by jazz, soul and eventually pop, formed a group in early 1981. They hit on the **Was (Not Was)** name as 'living embodiment of Piaget's reversibility theory': Don's one-and-a-half year old 'was starting to grasp on to the concept of opposites and found it amusing to point to something blue and say 'red', and wait for a disapproving face and go 'not red'. It was only a short step from there for the duo to rename themselves Don and David Was, and sign to New York label Ze.

Preferring a low profile, Don and David recruited vocalists **'Sir' Harry Bobens** and **Sweet Pea Atkinson** as frontmen, and hired session players for recordings and live performances. Wayne Kramer (guitar) and David Murray were among those who appeared on WAS (NOT WAS) (1981), the first instalment of hummable melodies and danceable rhythms, offset by satirical and often puzzling lyrics. The album contained the original incarnation of "(Return To The Valley Of) Out Come The Freaks", a track which would reappear with a similar melody but different lyrics on most of their subsequent LPs, as well as the ballad "Where Did Your Heart Go?", later to be covered by Wham! in 1986.

After Sweet Pea released the solo LP, DON'T WALK AWAY (1982), Was (Not Was) signed to the Geffen label and released BORN TO LAUGH AT TORNADOES (1983). This time, featured musicians included guitarist Randy Jacobs, new vocalist Donny Ray Mitchell, and cameos from Knack singer Doug Fieger and Ozzy Osbourne, who featured on "Shake Your Head". (A pre-famous Madonna recorded on the session, although her contribution was eventually discarded.) Although "Out Come The Freaks" was almost a British hit in early 1984, Geffen were alarmed at low sales and their inability to market such an uncategorizable band, and dropped them soon afterwards.

Thankfully, by 1986 British label Fontana had signed them up, while they joined the Chrysalis Records roster in their homeland. The excellent single "Robot Girl" was misinterpreted as sexist and manipulative by some, when in fact it was satirizing such attitudes. Then, in 1987, they finally reached the UK singles charts with "Walk The Dinosaur", whose refrain of 'boom-boom-ackalackacka-boom' landed Was (Not Was) with a novelty tag for the rest of their career. The single would also reach the American Top 10 in 1989, by which time the eclectic WHAT'S UP, DOG? (1988) had impressed and bemused critics and public in equal measure. Though it predominantly featured radio-friendly pop-soul numbers, two brief oddities showed that Was (Not Was) hadn't lost their unsettling edge: the title track was a psychotic account of a trip to the garage armed with a pit bull terrier, while "Hello Dad I'm In Jail" was a riotous ninety-second anti-greeting.

Over the next few years, the two became highly regarded as backroom boys in American music. Don Was produced The B-52's' COSMIC THING (1989), Bonnie Raitt's Grammy-winning NICK OF TIME (1989), and even his idol Bob Dylan on his admittedly weak album UNDER THE RED SKY (1990). Nevertheless, another Was (Not Was) album appeared in 1990, ARE YOU OKAY?, which became their best-selling record. Best remembered for a reworking of The Temptations' "Papa Was A Rolling Stone", it also developed their mixture of the melodious and the dysfunctional. while some tracks, like "I Feel Better Than James Brown", were baffling but irresistible.

Outside projects for Don and David, especially with production duties, made this their final album of original material. They bade farewell to Was (Not Was) in 1992 with a cover of INXS's "Listen Like Thieves" and a new version of "Shake Your Head" featuring Ozzy Osbourne again, this time backed by actress Kim Basinger. Longtime fan Mark Knopfler of Dire Straits invited them to support his own band on the UK leg of their world tour of 1991–92, which marked Was (Not Was)'s final appearances as a live act. The saga closed with HELLO DAD I'M IN JAIL (1992), a compilation of all the singles, plus remixes and alternative versions.

Fagenson continued to work on the production side of the music industry for much of the 90s and was awarded a Grammy for Best Producer in 1994 after working with the likes of Willie Nelson and Paula Abdul. In 1998 he reconvened with Weiss to work on various scoring projects and, apparently, a new album is in development.

⊙ **Hello Dad I'm In Jail** (1992; Fontana).
This 'best of' album is the only title currently available on CD in both the US and Britain. It covers the full decade's offerings, includes a couple of new songs, and winds up with "Hello Dad I'm In Jail" to remind us of Was (Not Was)'s darker side.

Justin Lewis

THE WATERBOYS/MIKE SCOTT

Formed London, 1982; mutated into Mike Scott's solo career sometime around 1993–94; The Waterboys re-emerged in 2000.

A self-appointed maverick of the post-punk 80s scene, **Mike Scott** (guitar/vocals/piano) dropped out of university, because he was 'more interested in what Joe Strummer was saying than William Shakespeare', then finalized a group which built up a strong live reputation under the name **Another Pretty Face**. "All The Boys Love Carrie", their 1979 debut single for independent label New Pleasures, became *NME*'s *Single of the Week* and led to a record deal with Virgin.

APF's first and only release for Virgin was a single "Whatever Happened To The West" (1980), a confused record that paralleled the conflict between Scott and the label, who wanted them to be the new Skids. The band did record an album – with Only Ones bass player Alan Mair producing – but Virgin refused to release it and APF walked away; some of the material was released as singles on their own rapidly formed label, Chicken Jazz. On discovering another band had rights to the name APF, APF became **Funhouse**, under which tag they released an Only

Ones-influenced single, "Out Of Control" (1982), on the Ensign label.

After the demise of APF/Funhouse, Mike Scott performed in London with a new line-up under the name The Red And The Black, which also featured **Anthony Thistlewaite** (saxophone) from Holly And The Italians. Scott settled on the permanent name **The Waterboys** (taken from a desperately bitter Lou Reed song) and reinforced the point with an album, THE WATERBOYS, in 1983. Along with guitar and vocal duties, Scott played piano on the album, though for a first public performance they introduced keyboard virtuoso **Karl Wallinger**.

The trio of Scott, Thistlewaite and Wallinger became the backbone of a flexible Waterboys line-up, building a cult following through a series of powerful live performances, including three UK tours. Their second album, A PAGAN PLACE (1984), was generally a positive development, showing their distinctive, gutsy folk-punk growing in confidence and exuberance while staying just the right side of pomposity. Great things were being predicted for them, and they were widely tipped to be a critically cool, stadium-filling band superior to their pomp-punk contemporaries Simple Minds and U2.

THIS IS THE SEA (1985), The Waterboys' third album, was the fullest expression of their potential. Wallinger, an increasingly key element, proved an astute foil for Scott's pretensions, and together they produced a minor classic that spawned a surprise hit single, "The Whole Of The Moon". On the verge of major success, Wallinger departed, going on to make bouncy electric-folk under the name **WORLD PARTY** Both Thistlewaite and soon-to-be Waterboy, fiddler **Steve Wickham**, guested on Wallinger's debut album, PRIVATE REVOLUTION (1986).

Thistlewaite and Scott took up an invitation from Irish-born Wickham and retired from the pressures of the spotlight to the relaxing pastures of Galway. Thistlewaite expanded to electric mandolin in early 1986 and their tours of that year showed an increasing tendency towards, what they were to dub,

'raggle-taggle' music. The next album, FISHERMAN'S BLUES (1988), was the result of three years spent soaking up Celtic influences. Whittled down from a reputed forty finished tracks, the album was their masterpiece. Songs such as "Bang On The Ear" and the title track showcased Scott's passionate vocal in a delightfully rustic setting.

In 1989 Scott produced singles for support band Sawdoctors, and The Waterboys grew to become a seven-piece, drafting in noted Irish accordionist **Sharon Shannon**. The second album from this Irish era, ROOM TO ROAM (1990), was less focused though more lucrative, at last breaking the band into the UK album Top 10. By the time the album was released, Steve Wickham had left and a Thistlewaite/Scott-centred four-piece toured the UK as an all-out rock band. Having previously distanced their rock fans, they now perplexed their folk following. Ensign released a retrospective, BEST OF THE WATERBOYS, in 1991. Both this and the rereleased "Moon" narrowly missed the top spots in the charts, belatedly revealing a mass audience for The Waterboys.

Mike Scott moved to New York in September 1991, where he began formulating new Waterboys line-ups. However, his first album for new label Geffen, DREAM HARDER (1993), was solo in all but name. A hit single from the album, "Return Of Pan", was quality Waterboys material, and helped send the album to the Top 5 in the UK, but the music lacked the depth of earlier releases. This New York brand of The Waterboys was never a touring proposition and, with no further studio releases, Scott gradually drifted out of sight. Scott returned in 1995 with a solo album, BRING 'EM ALL IN (1995), for Chrysalis. The album's openness and folky sensibility found favour with an audience who still affectionately remembered The Waterboys, taking him back into the charts. STILL BURNING (1997), Scott's second solo album, saw the light undimmed, and the maverick untamed as he re-formed a touring version of circa-1985 Waterboys with Thistlewaite and Wickham. Hot on their heels came a magnificently

Mike Scott doing the Waterboy thing

gutsy, 'official bootleg' double CD, LIVE ADVENTURES OF THE WATERBOYS (1997).

In 2000 a sonically revamped Waterboys line-up appeared – which included an ex-member of Spiritualized – for the release of A ROCK IN THE WEARY LAND. The band's new sound was explosive and innovative, featuring hip-hop beats, electronics, gospel choirs and brass. This, the first Waterboys album proper in seven years, was hailed as a triumph and has opened many new doors for the tireless Mike Scott. It was followed by the sparser UNIVERSAL HALL (2003), released on the band's own Puck label.

⊙ **This Is The Sea** (1985; Ensign).
This early release is an unpolished nugget, Scott's angst-in-my-pants vocals beginning to mature into something very tasty indeed.

⊙ **Fisherman's Blues** (1988; Ensign).
One of the essential British albums of the late 80s, on which The Waterboys discover a rich and complementary musical vein in the Celtic traditions of Ireland. This album suggested that Mike Scott was about to become the new Van Morrison.

⊙ **Live Adventures Of The Waterboys** (1997; New Millennium).
It was always said The Waterboys never captured their live feeling, and here you can see why. In the mid 80s when they seemed to spend all their time on the road, the pomp fits the rough-and-ready circumstances. This double CD is a truly memorable document with more than its fair share of magic moments.

⊙ **Universal Hall** (2003; Puck).
A brave and quiet return after the bombastic A ROCK IN THE WEARY LAND. This soothing album offers a balm of melody, acoustic grace and Wickham's unsurpassed fiddling.

Tony Drayton

MUDDY WATERS

Born Rolling Fork, Mississippi, 1915; died 1983.

"I always felt like I could beat plowin' mules, choppin' cotton and drawin' water: I did all that and I never did like none of it."

It was the summer of 1941 when Stovall Plantation tractor driver McKinley Morganfield – later **Muddy Waters** – first cut a crude aluminium disc for Library Of Congress archivist Alan Lomax. The members of The Rolling Stones, who took their name from a Muddy Waters song, weren't even born yet.

Within the year Waters was in Chicago, where he came into contact with Big Bill Broonzy, the major musical influence of his life. Before the decade was out, he had mastered the electric guitar, signed to Aristocrat (forerunner of Chess) and released some fine R&B singles, including "Rollin' And Tumblin'" and "Rollin' Stone".

It was in the 1950s, however, that Muddy Waters transformed electric blues with music that was raw and invigorating in its freedom from hidebound convention. He had little sense of timing, he was always off the beat, yet it somehow worked. His sore-

They called him Muddy Waters

headed bear of a voice was full of surprising inflections and vibrato, and his steel-fingered strumming could be heart-stopping. Drawing on a pool of talented blues players including **Otis Spann**, **Jimmy Rogers**, **Walter Horton** and, perhaps most important, **Willie Dixon**, Waters produced a string of masterpieces for Chess, a label that actively marketed its output towards white audiences. The songs of this period, including "Got My Mojo Working", "Mannish Boy", "I'm Ready" and "Hoochie Coochie Man", have become staples, and it's debatable whether he ever bettered this work.

But he did come close. Waters made a strong comeback in the late 70s aided by the production of his protégé **JOHNNY WINTER**, a blues guitar hero in his own right. A trio of albums produced by Winter – HARD AGAIN (which Waters proclaimed got his pecker working, hence the title), I'M READY and MUDDY WATERS LIVE – took old material and breathed new life into some of his greatest compositions (and Dixon's as well). The rather patronizing *Best Traditional Recording* slot at the Grammy Awards seemed to have become more or less reserved for him (he claimed it in 1971, 1972, 1975, 1978 and 1979), and in 1978 he was clasped to the bosom of the American state when he picnicked at the White House with Jimmy Carter.

Waters died of a heart attack in 1983. His music has become a part of the collective consciousness, and occasionally re-emerges into the full light of day – as when the 1988 Levis ad campaign sold "Mannish Boy" to a fresh bunch of teens.

- **Muddy Waters At Newport** (1960; Chess).
  A testament to this great man's music and a master-
  piece by the classic line-up of Spann, Cotton, Francis Clay,
  Andrew Stevenson and Pat Hare.

- **Hard Again** (1978; Sony).
  Whoops of delight and encouragement from the musicians assembled by Johnny Winter introduce "Mannish Boy",
  the first cut on Muddy's finest post-Chess collection. Electric,
  raw and firing on all cylinders, the album pulses with renewed
  vigour.

- **They Call Me Muddy Waters** (1990; Instant).
  A fine anthology of Muddy's recordings from 1948 to
  1955. Not to be mistaken for the 1973 album of the same
  name.

- **Hoochie Coochie Man** (1993; Sony).
  A neat compilation of the meaty Winter-produced sessions.

- **The Complete Muddy Waters 1947–1967** (1983;
  Charly).
  A comprehensive nine-CD box set for the blues completist.

Ada Wilson

WEATHER REPORT

Formed New York, 1970; disbanded 1986.

Despite a variety of shifting line-ups, the nucleus of jazz-rock fusionists **Weather Report** was always **Joe Zawinul** (keyboards) and **Wayne Shorter** (saxophone). Both came from academic musical backgrounds. Zawinul arrived from Austria, having studied classical music in Vienna, to take up a scholarship at the Berklee School Of Music in Boston. Around the same time, Shorter was studying music at New York University by day and playing with Horace Silver by night.

Their paths crossed briefly in Maynard Ferguson's jazz ensemble in 1959, but they went their separate ways for much of the 60s. Zawinul spent nine years with Cannonball Adderley, and Shorter joined Horace Silver before graduating to **MILES DAVIS**'s celebrated 1960s quintet in 1964. This proved to be a crucial link in the chain that led Shorter and Zawinul to the birth of jazz-rock, a genre of which Weather Report became the embodiment.

Shorter and Zawinul both took writing and per-forming credits on Miles's epochal BITCHES BREW (1970), which experimented with electronics whilst utilizing rock rhythms to provide a tight structure against which jazz solos could explore the African roots of both musics. Shorter had already switched from tenor to soprano sax, establishing what would be the sound and style of much of his subsequent playing with Weather Report.

The founding line-up for the debut album WEATHER REPORT (1971) featured Zawinul and Shorter alongside celebrated Brazilian-born **Airto Moreira** (percussion), Czech musician **Miroslav Vitous** (bass) and **Alphonse Mouzon** (drums). From the start, Zawinul did the lion's share of the writing, and generally shared production duties with Shorter. For the follow-up, I SING THE BODY ELECTRIC (1972), the group were joined by the tal-ents of **Eric Gravatt** (drums) and **Um Ramao**

(bass). Both bestselling and critically acclaimed, they introduced the band's hallmark of tracks built around riffs, and minimal soloing – an innovation that left the jazz audience bemused.

SWEETNIGHTER (1972), MYSTERIOUS TRAVELLER (1973) and TALE SPINNIN' (1974) consolidated the band's burgeoning reputation with rock audiences, Zawinul coming increasingly to the fore along with the percussionists. However, it was with BLACK MARKET (1976), with **Jaco Pastorius** installed on bass, that Weather Report found their groove. Pastorius's arrival was accompanied by a switch to rock rhythms and gadgetry, with Zawinul utilizing the latest synth technology to effect, and **Chester Thompson** (drums) and **Alejandro Neciosup Acuna** (percussion) provided a tight structure for the band to let rip. Thompson then departed for the bigger bucks by touring with Genesis.

With HEAVY WEATHER (1977), Weather Report were established as jazz-rock fusionists *par excellence*. This was the record that introduced their best-known (and much-covered) theme, "Birdland", and, largely on the strength of this, the album sold in unprece-dented numbers for a jazz record, notching up some 400,000 units.

MR. GONE (1978) and the double live set, 8:30 (1979), raised their standing even higher, with **Pete Erskine** (drums) becoming part of a regular four-piece with Pastorius, Shorter and Zawinul. However, Pastorius left in 1980 to pursue his own project with **Word Of Mouth** (he later succumbed to alcoholism and died in a bar brawl in 1987) and the band lost some of its edge. PROCESSION (1983) saw Weather Report use vocals for the first time, in the form of **Janet Siegel** of Manhattan Transfer, and DOMINO THEORY (1984) suggested the fusion idea was wearing a little thin, with its bland vocals from soul singer **Carl Anderson** and suffocating synth from Zawinul. On this and other releases of the period, it was only Shorter's ability to retain a greater hold on the jazz part of the project that provided the musical highlights.

THIS IS THIS (1986) was the last Weather Report release. Zawinul – who, like Shorter, had already made solo albums – went on to form **Weather Update** with Pete Erskine and Steve Khan, and later continued his brand of eclecticism with the **Zawinul Syndicate**. In many ways Zawinul's latest outfit has kept the original project alive, not least as the excellent 1998 double live set "World Tour" features fellow ex-Weather Report members **Manolo Bandrena** on percussion and **Victor Bailey** on bass.

- **Black Market** (1976; CBS).
  The band's best outing, showcasing Zawinul, before technology swamped his jazz roots, and Shorter's devastat-ing soprano sax playing, against the impeccable rhythms of Pastorius and Thompson.

- **Weather Report – The Collection** (1981; Castle).
  Budget-price CD that covers the period 1976–80, when Weather Report were at their peak.

Neil Partrick

THE WEDDING PRESENT

Formed Leeds, England, 1985.

In rock's strange history there can have been few less likely candidates for cultdom than **David Gedge**. Lacking charisma and singing talent in equal measure, he nonetheless steered The Wedding Present from indie obscurity to a modest major-label success (showing an interest in Ukrainian folk along the way) while in his latter-day incarnation as frontman of **Cinerama** he reinvented himself as a millennial Serge Gainsbourg.

Gedge (vocals/guitar) formed The Weddoes – as they're known to the faithful – with **Peter Salowka** (guitar), **Keith Gregory** (bass) and **Shaun Charman** (drums), establishing a British student following, and long-term support from John Peel, with their blisteringly fast rhythm guitars and a refreshing disregard for the niceties of tuning. Briefly the darlings of the music press, they released their debut album, GEORGE BEST (1987), to considerable critical acclaim. Simultaneously touching and camply glum, Gedge's agonized vignettes of unrequited love and sexual frustration formed an irresistible counterpoint to the band's manically upbeat backing, and helped to crack The Smiths' mid-80s monopoly on bedsit angst.

After an uneven compilation of singles and sessions, TOMMY (1988), there were further sessions for John Peel, which resulted in the 1989 release of UKRAINSKI VISTUPI V JOHNA PEELA, a collection of Ukrainian folk songs with vocals by guest member Len Liggins – inspired by Salowka's father. Its arresting combination of traditional (balalaika, mandolin) and rock instruments made it an unusually credible rock and world music crossover. It also represented a crossover point for the band, with Charman playing drums on half of the tracks, and his eventual replacement **Simon Smith** playing on the remainder.

BIZARRO (1989) was a more conventional rock album and didn't please all the critics. The band self-deprecatingly stated that 'all the songs sound the same', yet the album indicated a growing musical maturity. "Bewitched" hinted at later dynamic contrasts, while "Brassneck" and "Kennedy" proved to be firm live favourites. Singles releases often showed a lighter side to the band, and an unhealthy obsession with 60s and 70s trash culture surfaced regularly. A chart entry with "Corduroy" in September 1990 was backed by a gloriously thrashy cover of Steve Harley & Cockney Rebel's "Make Me Smile (Come Up And See Me)", which was rendered all the more remarkable by the fact that its producer was ex-Big Black hardcore guru, Steve Albini.

Albini also produced The Wedding Present's next album, SEAMONSTERS (1991), where dense and expressionistic layers of guitar noise underpinned a sharper, more aggressive lyrical edge. The Sub Pop influence of SEAMONSTERS also accounted for some of The Wedding Present's growing stateside profile, where audiences knew nothing of their earlier reputation for poetic whimsy. The release of this LP saw the departure of Pete Salowka to explore rock-trad Ukrainian crossover further with **The Ukrainians**, and his replacement by **Paul Dorrington**.

This was also a period of astonishing and prolific success, with the band hitting the UK singles chart with new releases every month for the year 1992 – an experiment which gained them entry into the *Guinness Book Of Records*. Both sides of all twelve singles were included on two albums called HIT PARADE (both 1992), each consisting of six originals and six covers, including such reworkings as "Theme From Shaft", "Go Wild In The Country" and "Pleasant Valley Sunday".

After this period of frenzied activity, the band recuperated during 1993, but Keith Gregory left that year, to be replaced by **Darren Belk**. With Gedge the only original band member, they moved from RCA to Island for WATUSI (1994), a critically lauded (though desperately underexposed) album and moved again to Cooking Vinyl for their 1996 effort SATURNALIA, sadly an equally underexposed recording. However, The Wedding Present's diehard following remained, especially in the US, where WATUSI made highly respectable showings in the college radio charts.

Gedge re-emerged in 1998 along with Wedding Present associate **Sally Murrell** with a new group, **Cinerama**, making their debut for Cooking Vinyl with the album VA VA VOOM – a collection which won plaudits along with numerous cries of 'what took you so long?' As the name would suggest Cinerama marked a swerve toward the kind of soundtrack material that had been hinted at in Gedge's previous choice of cover versions (*Shaft, Twin Peaks*). Despite the seeming incongruity of the pairing, Cinerama hooked up with **Steve Albini** for their second offering, DISCO VOLANTE (2000), released on their own Scopitones label. Rejoined by SATURNALIA guitarist, **Simon Cleave**, Gedge's fractured tones were strangely affecting in a string-laden,

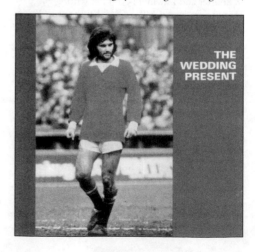

lounge-core environment: a worthy update of the kind of sleazy pop previously espoused by the Tindersticks and Pulp. CINERAMA HOLIDAY (2002) collected a bunch of the band's singles and was followed by a disc of Peel Session cuts in 2003.

While Cinerama may be foremost in Gedge's mind it doesn't necessarily mean that we've seen the last of the Wedding Present, though for the time being they remain firmly on hiatus.

The Wedding Present

⊙ **George Best** (1987; Reception).
A classic of the indie mid-80s: tracks like "You Can't Moan, Can You?" could not even have been ruined by Gedge's off-key grizzling.

⊙ **Seamonsters** (1991; RCA).
With Steve Albini lending some cult credibility, this features fewer memorable hooks than 1989's BIZARRO, but ultimately this is The Wedding Present at their most intense.

⊙ **Watusi** (1994; Island).
A distinct 60s feel lingers around WATUSI, but The Weddoes steal with such aplomb from so many sources that they can only be forgiven.

Cinerama

⊙ **Disco Volante** (2000; Scopitones).
With Albini at the mixing desk, Gedge combines the brass and strings of lounge music with his own unique brand of guitar indie.

Huw Bucknell

WEEN

Formed New Jersey, 1984.

"When Ween comes to your town, you are to bring us food. We're into it."

Legend has it that the warped 14-year-old minds of **Dean** and **Gene Ween** (aka Mickey Melchiondo and Aaron Freeman) were inspired to make music in homage to the demon Boognish. Either that, or they simply discovered the joys of manipulating four-track home recordings for psychedelic purposes and making strange sounds. The consequence of all this studio mucking around on the farm commune where they lived was a repertoire of more than a thousand tracks in wildly varying musical styles, some of which were collated onto Ween's debut double LP, GOD WEEN SATAN – THE ONENESS (1990).

The cult success of this first album led to Shimmy Disc/**BONGWATER** founder Kramer putting out yet another double LP's worth of material the next year as THE POD (named in homage to their home, from which they had recently been evicted). Accompanied by a backing tape, drum machine and the mysterious **Mean Ween** (who may or may not have been Kramer himself), the duo also played the occasional show, including a brief visit to Britain. A couple of tracks from their backlog were released on Sub Pop as "Skycruiser" (1992).

With enough material for a host of albums, it wasn't long before Ween attracted the attention of Creation Records, whose August division put out PURE GUAVA in 1993. Response in Britain was modest, but Ween found themselves playing stadiums in America (where they were on Elektra) and the single, "Push Th' Little Daisies" (1993) received frequent airplay on MTV. A white vinyl single, "I'm Fat" (1994), featured scatological guest vocals from Calvin Celsius, and showed that the pair had not lost their talent for gratuitous bad behaviour.

However, Dean and Gene soon found themselves dropped by Creation, and picked up by Flying Nun, for whom they produced the all-new CHOCOLATE AND CHEESE in late 1994. They also recorded two collections of warped Southern-fried rock tracks as The Moist Boyz for the Beastie Boys' Grand Royal label, while the "Freedom Of '76" was remixed by The Beasties' Mike D.

Now supported by a full band line-up on stage and in the studio, Ween have established themselves as an eccentric presence on the musical map, briefly heading well off its fringes with their 1996 album 12 GOLDEN COUNTRY GREATS, before a switch to the nautically themed The MOLLUSK (1997) and their most commercially viable album to date, WHITE PEPPER (2000). With album sales approaching the two million mark, and a contribution to the SOUTH PARK ALBUM (1998), the boys are now firmly wedged into the alt-pop scene, while a 1996 recording LIVE IN TORONTO CANADA, issued in 2001, continued to demonstrate their versatility and edge.

⊙ **God Ween Satan – The Oneness** (1990; Twin Tone).
This astonishingly eclectic album features traditional songs ("Up On Th' Hill"), a lascivious cover of Prince's "Shockadelica", the heart-wrenching "Birthday Boy", and full-on psychedelic work-outs worthy of Amon Düül II.

⊙ **The Pod** (1991; Flying Nun)
Further lunatic behaviour from Dean and Gene, with effects-drenched classics like "Captain Fantasy" and "Dr. Rock" revealing their close affiliation with chemical imbalance.

- **Pure Guava** (1993; August/Creation).
  Featuring a slightly more restrained and funkier selection of styles than hitherto, but Ween still retain their scatological humour. "Mourning Glory" is a lysergic fable of a baby pumpkin lost in a haze of feedback and noise, while "Don't Get 2 Close (2 My Fantasy)" is a real lighter-waver.

- **12 Golden Country Greats** (1996; Flying Nun).
  Sentimental, funny and weird by turns, this is a surprisingly good record of its genre, particularly the closing track, "Fluffy".

- **The Mollusk** (1997; Elektra/Mushroom).
  Much better than the last couple of offerings, tracks like "The Golden Eel" and "Buckingham Green" show Ween can still rock psychedelically – even if the arch humour is wearing a little thin.

- **White Pepper** (2000; Elektra/Mushroom).
  Trailed as being Ween's WHITE ALBUM and SERGEANT PEPPER all rolled into one, it's probably more fittingly described as a further step into the reaches of MTV-friendly weirdness.

Richard Fontenoy

WEEZER

Formed Los Angeles, 1993.

Having been drawn separately to Los Angeles with the dream of forming a band, guitarist/vocalist **Rivers Cuomo**, bassist **Matt Sharp** and drummer **Patrick Wilson** teamed up in the guise of **Weezer**. After over a year with no progression, the three-piece clinched a deal with Geffen, then recruited the final piece in the jigsaw, guitarist **Brian Bell**, just three days before entering the studio.

WEEZER (1994) was produced by former Cars singer Ric Ocasek, running a gamut of moods from top-of-the-world cheeriness to near-suicidal depression. Cuomo wore his emotions on his sleeve over a musical backdrop that was pop-punk at its purest. The album was loaded with hooks and irresistible melodies, especially on the first single, "Undone (The Sweater Song)". The apotheosis of this formula was The Beach Boys-meets-Ramones geek anthem, "Buddy Holly".

Despite the excellence of "Buddy Holly" as a single, it took one of the all-time great videos to get Weezer noticed, one which will probably become a millstone around their necks as it tends to dominate everyone's thoughts on the band. Directed by the incomparable pastiche master Spike Jones, the video took a scene from *Happy Days* and used the wonders of modern technology to replace the band performing at Arnold's drive-in with Weezer, who interacted with all of the characters until the Fonz himself arrived and freaked out on the dance floor to the quartet's tuneful mayhem.

On the back of the video, the single went into the UK Top 10, and helped propel WEEZER towards double-platinum status in the US. Inevitably, the 'nerd' tag was hauled out by the press and stuck like superglue. It was of little surprise when Weezer decided to take a lengthy break before setting about recording a second album. PINKERTON (1996) was greeted, however, with lack of interest by the record-buying public and, despite the limited success of "El Scorcho" – a track from the album – as a single, it soon sank from view.

At this time Sharp grew disillusioned with Weezer's apparent lack of progress and opted to concentrate on his **Rentals** side-project permanently, so the band recruited ex-Juliana Hatfield bassist **Mikey Welsh** in his place. Despite the initial reaction to PINKERTON the album went on to become a template for many a wannabe emo band in the late 90s; Cuomo's songwriting had hit all the requisite sensitive notes. It wasn't until 2001's WEEZER (helpfully dubbed 'The Green Album'), however, that the band really exceeded all expectations. The record was short – eleven songs in thirty minutes – and shimmered with pop-rock nuggets of such concise brilliance that fans and critics were bowled over at the consistent quality, helped no doubt by Ric Ocasek's punchy production.

By all accounts, as a songwriting natural, Cuomo could turn out memorable tunes in his sleep, but no one expected MALADROIT (2002) – the name chosen from fan suggestions on their website – to follow quite so quickly and to be so astonishingly complete in sound and direction. It didn't even matter that Weezer had to recruit yet another new bassist not long after: the rather imposing-looking **Scott Shriner**. Yet again Cuomo displayed the kind of nerdy lyrical preoccupations for which he had garnered a reputation; gradually he took to acting in an increasingly erratic and selfish fashion both on the road and off, as if he was having genuine trouble in dealing with the heightened levels of public exposure. But no one really seemed to care that much – just so long as the genius kept the hits flowing.

- **Weezer** (1994; Geffen).
  'Tuneful pop with balls' sums up this album, a likeable collection of typically American fare. "Buddy Holly" inevitably stands out as the prime moment, but there are other gems to be discovered in the shape of "Surf Wax America" and "My Name Is Jonas".

- **Weezer (The Green Album)** (2001; Geffen).
  The chugging metallic-sounding "Hash Pipe" stands out as one of the best cuts on this great collection that saw Weezer regaining their reputation.

- **Maladroit** (2002; Geffen).
  Following speedily in the wake of its predecessor, Weezer here prove that they're so much more than a bunch of geek rockers.

Hugh Hackett

PAUL WELLER

Born Woking, England, 1958.

When in 1989 **THE STYLE COUNCIL** suffered Polydor's ignominious rejection of their fifth album, **Paul Weller** split the group and sloped off to rethink. Bereft of a recording deal and a publishing contract, it seemed that the one-time uptight voice of a generation and mod god, had left the limelight for ever.

The next two years were spent with his young family, but then a couple of low-key tours as The

Paul Weller Movement in 1991–92 showed Weller shedding his cappuccino-jazz Style Council skin and picking up his guitar once more. In 1991 he released his first solo single, "Into Tomorrow", on his own label. It charted and, encouraged by this success and increasingly enthusiastic reviews for his live shows, he released "Uh Huh, Oh Yeh" (1992), as good a song as he had produced in years. Driven by an insistent metallic guitar above ex-Style Council drummer Steve White's percussion and psychedelic sound effects, the single confirmed a dramatic rebirth.

PAUL WELLER (1992) displayed an intensity comparable to the spiky raucousness of his first band, **THE JAM**. Though some of the soft funk and folky flutes of The Style Council persisted, the excellence of the two singles (both featured) and the soaring "Kosmos" served notice that the third phase of Weller's career could well be his finest. The lyrics, far removed from the political preaching that had typified his 80s output, spoke of the 'bitterness rising', 'self-doubt' and 'deep despair' of the previous two years. The album also turned out to be his biggest US success up to that point.

WILD WOOD (1993) consolidated this success as the critics and public, reconditioned by Britpop, drooled over his edgy yet melodic Small Faces-influenced R&B. The folky title-track ballad made the UK Top 10, and in "Sunflower" the album also produced possibly the finest single of his career. The disenchantment that had characterized his solo debut was replaced on WILD WOOD with thrilling optimism and a crackling 'live' sound. Weller's voice had matured almost beyond recognition, complemented by a vastly improved growling guitar style.

The spin-off, LIVE WOOD (1994), recorded between dates around Europe, couldn't quite capture Weller's vitality and passion on stage, while MORE WOOD (1994) offered the songs which deservedly hadn't made it onto WILD WOOD. But in October 1994 his new single, "Out Of The Sinking", provided his 45th Top 40 UK hit.

Named after the street in Woking he lived on as a child, STANLEY ROAD (1995) displayed the strong influences of Neil Young and Traffic in its soulful R&B ballads (Steve Winwood put in an appearance on one track). Although it fell short of WILD WOOD's perfection, STANLEY ROAD had its moments, chief among them the fierce and exhilarating "Changingman", the thumping "Out Of The Sinking" and the gospel hymn "Wings Of Speed". STANLEY ROAD entered the UK chart at #1 and went on to become a platinum seller.

In September 1995, Weller relished a career highlight when he was joined at Abbey Road Studios by **Paul McCartney** (and **Noel Gallagher**) to record a version of The Beatles' "Come Together" for the charity album HELP.

Interviewed while promoting HEAVY SOUL (1997), Weller reckoned that in another ten years

The magically revitalized Mr Paul Weller

he'd be playing the back rooms of pubs around his old home town of Woking. In the meantime, there was this little business of global adoration to get out of the way. Having totally rinsed off the grime and misdemeanours of his Style Council years, Weller once again rebuilt himself as a spokesman for his generation. Hailed by a host of younger guitar bands such as Ocean Colour Scene and Oasis, Weller dropped the jazzy noodlings of his previous couple of sets in favour of a raw, blokeish sound. Highlights of HEAVY SOUL proved to be "Peacock Suit", "Brushed" and the private world revealed in "Up In Suzie's Room".

Three years would pass before HELIOCENTRIC emerged and in that time Weller's stature as The Modfather had grown and grown. DAYS OF SPEED (2001) was a dazzling live acoustic document, but ILLUMINATION (2002) found Weller struggling to cram a host of 'worthy' guests into a set that would have been a whole lot more had it comprised a whole lot less. Despite the occasional flutter, Weller's musical pulse is steady, and as he and his audience mature – he has now been performing for thirty years – Weller may yet become the Van Morrison of his generation.

Wild Wood (1993; Go! Discs). Award-winning album that places Weller at the top of the songwriter/performer tree.

Stanley Road (1995; Go! Discs).
Highly personal R&B, and rougher-sounding than its predecessor, this has proved Weller's biggest commercial success to date.

Michael Booth

WHEAT

Formed Taunton, Massachusetts, 1996.

S ome bands have finally woken up to the fact that making music for adults doesn't necessarily mean you have to turn into Fleetwood Mac or Enya. While the angst and anger of teen rock has its place, it's something **Wheat** have clearly grown out of, opting instead to craft refreshingly ego-free music that manages to be grown-up without being patronizing or fuddy-duddy.

Hailing from Massachusetts, singer/guitarist **Scott Levesque**, drummer **Brendan Harney** and guitarist **Ricky Brennan** first got together in 1996 having all played with various other groups; the bass slot was originally filled by **Kenny Madaras**, later replaced by **Kevin Camara**.

The group now say that they never really courted label attention, making music instead that would 'cheer them up'. It took the kind attentions of a fan to land them a record deal – someone passed on a tape to Sugar Free Records after purchasing it at one of their shows.

Their first album, MEDEIROS (1998) was a low-key release and went largely unnoticed – until, that is, *NME* made the set's "Death Car" *Single Of The Week*. Ironically the attention they received in the UK caused folk back home to prick up their ears too.

The album was as elusive and mysterious as the sleeve artwork, which featured a series of eight-digit numbers that, presumably, mean something to Levesque et al. No explanation, no credits. The songs themselves were fragile. Gossamer-light pop tunes such as "Girl Singer" and "Death Car" floated amidst ambient collages. It was delightfully short too: Wheat

clearly didn't suffer from the 'quantity equals quality' disease of the CD generation. Reference points were slippery too, which is always a good sign – think early-90s UK indie (The House Of Love, Ride); Acetone and Spiritualized for the lazy, miasmic sound sketches; and then a dash of Pavement's studied low-fi elegance.

The Flaming Lips also entered the mix somewhere along the line, becoming a far more obvious influence on the next album, HOPE AND ADAMS (1999), perhaps because erstwhile Lips producer Dave Fridmann (he of Mercury Rev fame too) was manning the controls with Lips bass player Michael Ivins dropping in as assistant engineer. Don't be misled though – Wheat more than showed that they had a very different musical agenda, though no less unpredictable.

Released on City Slang, HOPE AND ADAMS was as stylistically varied as its predecessor. On first listen it had a half-finished feel, a lingering sense that there should be more – the instrumental "This Wheat", which hints at the post-rock sensibilities of Tortoise comes to an abrupt end, as does the following track. It takes a few listens for the band's genius to sink in – the songs have a cumulative effect - fourth, fifth time through and the rewards start springing on you. "And Someone With Strengths" had an understated grace; "Who's The One" was pure indie magnificence; the two-part "Body Talk" sandblasted Tom Petty's sound into a bare-boned beauty.

Everything was looking pretty rosy for our accidental heroes; signed to Nude they began work on their next album, PER SECOND, PER SECOND, PER SECOND, EVERY SECOND, which was duly completed and scheduled for release. Unfortunately Nude went under at the end of 2001 before the album saw the light of day, leaving the band in the lurch.

The trio withdrew, reconvened and returned to the studio to record new songs and recut some tracks destined originally for PER SECOND … EVERY SECOND. An Internet-only EP was then made available on the band's wheatmusic.com website; the long-awaited third album is promised soon. Fingers crossed…

Hope & Adams (City Slang; 1999).
This one is what you might call 'a grower'; it repays the attentive listener with gradually unfolding subtleties, thoughtful pop and unsettling sonic backdrops.

Derryck Strachan

THE WHITE STRIPES

Formed Detroit, Michigan, USA, 1997.

"The most exciting band since the Pistols or Jimi Hendrix… " John Peel, 2001

S o, the official word is 'brother and sister' – for the moment, at least. With the possible exception of The Strokes or The Darkness, no other

American band has received anything like the recent UK press attention afforded singer/guitarist **Jack White** and drummer **Meg White** – and not all of this pertains to their undoubtedly splendid music. The conjecture surrounding their relationship has proved something of a burden to the Detroit duo, **The White Stripes**. 'Are they really ex-husband and wife?' clamour tabloids, but White Stripes converts – and there are many – stopped caring some time ago. Whatever their relationship, this duo possesses more wit, artistic cunning, guile and pure energy than bands of three times their number.

Officially, Jack (born John Gillis) and Meg White are the youngest of ten children brought up by Catholic parents in a predominantly Mexican area of America's car capital. Schooldays were not the happiest for Jack: he and his sister fell into a minority among classrooms of '90% black kids', and, unfortunately, this was neither a time nor place where racial integration was a high priority. White found he had few friends and therefore missed the grounding in 80s US punk that's second nature to his current peers – as a result he had little use for the cheap Montgomery Ward Airline guitar given him as a boy in return for a favour.

On finishing education White chose a career in, of all métiers, upholstery, and it was an apprenticeship with a local tradesman that changed his musical vision. **Brian Muldoon** was also a drummer and taught Jack basic rockabilly percussion to his favoured garage acts, The Cramps and local heroes The Stooges and MC5, the pair even briefly forming a band, **The Upholsterers**. When this folded, Jack returned to the basic, beaten-up Airline having developed a passion for bluesmen Blind Willie McTell and Son House. Although the concerts he was now attending featured artists like Fugazi and the burgeoning Nirvana, White was sketching out House's "Death Letter" and "John The Revelator" on his guitar, while learning the a cappella "Grinnin' In Your Face". For Jack White, "Grinnin'" was the pivotal discovery in making his own music: 'It was the song I'd been waiting to hear all my life'.

The hammer that knocked the nail in, as it were, came in the unlikely form of Meg, whose clattering unrehearsed percussion accompaniment amused Jack so much that he just had to recruit his older sister, the occasional drummer of country outfit **Goober & The Peas**. Early gigs by The White Stripes (named after Meg's preferred candy) were fairly unhinged affairs, the pair dressed in matching red and white, and playing in a style described fondly by regular headliner and fan, Jim Diamond of The Dirtbombs, as 'stinky'. In 1997, local label Italy was moved to cut the duo's first two limited singles, "Let's Shake Hands" and "Lafayette Blues". In turn, the records were given to legendary cottage industry independent Sympathy For the Record Industry by Jason Stollsteimer, vocalist of Sympathy act The Detroit Cobras. The Long Beach label's 'guru' Long Gone John – a man with the conviction to have released a

record every week for well over a decade – had been taken with the notion of a female drummer; once he'd heard Jack's vocals, he needed little further convincing. Within weeks, THE WHITE STRIPES (1998) was recorded in Jim Diamond's Ghetto studio and Jack's front room. This collection consisted mainly of the band's live set, and flourished more than the odd reference to Son House (particularly "Cannon", which skipped into "John The Revelator" as much by accident as design). The opening track "Jimmy The Exploder", was, on the other hand, the tale of a monkey who blew up anything that wasn't the colour red.

As the broader impact of this great debut was slowly gathering momentum, The White Stripes hit again with DE STIJL, released early in 2000. Another blues-charged rock statement, the second album was named after a Dutch periodical co-founded by artist Piet Mondrian, whose 'back-to-basics' philosophy Jack White felt was appropriate to The White Stripes. Here, Jack's cover of "Death Letter" emerged as a centrepiece, its dark lyric compressed further by Meg's enclosed percussive thump. But, more importantly still, at this stage, Jack (now able to give up his upholstery day job) was nurturing his own songwriting and narrative style. Surreally, the duo was now talked about more than they were actually played, particularly in the UK.

The race to sign The White Stripes from Sympathy was won first by Richard Branson's V2 in the USA, and then by XL in Europe, who pitched out album number three, WHITE BLOOD CELLS (2001) to an eager public. The stand-out cut, "Fell In Love With A Girl", was a hugely played single during the summer of 2001. Live, The White Stripes were now London's hottest ticket, attracting 'beautiful people' such as Kate Moss and Winona Ryder to their London shows. The two-minute "Hotel Yorba" – written in homage to a Detroit retreat for elopers – became an unlikely #26 hit in the UK, and led to television appearances on the acclaimed BBC show, *Later With Jools Holland*. The reissued "Fell In Love With A Girl" quickly followed "Yorba" into the upper reaches of the charts and represented perhaps the first and only time an Airline guitar has ever been seen on *Top of the Pops*.

By the time of ELEPHANT (2003), the group had well and truly made their home in mainstream culture, but were still managing to produce defiantly magical music. The set had a slightly warmer sound than had been previously heard, but was still thrillingly sexy: a cover of Dusty Springfield's "I Just Don't Know What To Do With Myself", and a bizarre three-way love-in (Jack, Meg and **Holly Golightly**) entitled "It's True That We Love One Another" both standing out as cuts that shouldn't have worked, but did.

The pair's success has preceded a massive interest in other Detroit acts – such as The Von Bondies, the Soledad Brothers and, of course, The Dirtbombs – the city enjoying its biggest rock revival for decades. Despite becoming unwitting figureheads to this movement, Jack and Meg remain steadfast about their own band's image. The colour coordination prevails (despite a six-figure offer from clothing giants Gap to appear in commercials), as does the trademark stripped-down sound. But most interesting of all is the band's ability to play the media, building myth after myth about everything from their relationship to their recording techniques. The White Stripes are more than a great band, they are a brilliantly executed media work of art – and they know it, and love it.

⊙ **The White Stripes** (1999; XL).
Rattling through some seventeen tracks in a little over forty minutes, The White Stripes are best enjoyed on this great 'live-feel' debut.

⊙ **White Blood Cells** (2001; XL).
Jack White sets his stall as rock's new king of narrative on this, The Stripes' UK breakthrough. The ghost of Blind Willie McTell interfaces with the Top 40: where can it all go from here?

⊙ **Elephant** (2003; XL).
This set documents Meg and Jack at the height of their powers. Recorded in only two weeks in an East London studio, this velvet-smothered rock'n'roll masterpiece is destined to become a classic.

Jeremy Simmonds

WHITE ZOMBIE

Formed New York, 1985; disbanded 1998.

Hard rockers **White Zombie** found themselves an immensely successful niche as an almost cartoon concept band, an unholy metal act which helped revitalize the genre in the US after some lean years. Original members **Rob Zombie** (vocals), **J** (guitars), **Sean Yseult** (bass) and **Ivan de Prume** (drums) were drawn together by a mutual love of Sabbath-like metal and B-grade horror flicks. Early years of living in squats and half-starving eventually bore the rancid fruit of a mini-CD, PSYCHO-HEAD BLOWOUT (1987), and then their first full-length album, SOUL CRUSHER (1988), an indie release littered with such wickedly humorous titles as "Ratmouth", "Die Zombie Die" and "Shack Of Hate".

An outing for Caroline Records, MAKE THEM DIE SLOWLY (1989), was produced by rock veteran Bill Laswell, and, though more polished, it merely cemented the underground status of their funk-meets-death-metal vision of escapism. They didn't seem to be in it for the money. But it did come, by virtue of a move to Geffen, the production of Andy Wallace and an upgrade in song quality. A dazzling mix of horror and pure rock entertainment, LA SEXORCISTO: DEVIL MUSIC VOLUME I (1992) signalled White Zombie's arrival as cartoon merchants from hell. Rob Zombie's twisted lyrics and the cacophonic guitar grind on "Welcome To Planet Motherfucker (Psychoholic Slag)" and "Thunderkiss 65" were a technicolour tornado of irresistible bad taste.

The band toured for two years (during which de Prume left, replaced first by **Phil Buerstatte**, then by ex-Testament drummer **John Tempesta**); the album went platinum in the US and earned them a heavy-metal Grammy nomination. The true barometer of their cool, however, was the esteem granted by MTV's *Beavis And Butthead*.

The band's 1995 effort ASTROCREEP 2000: SONGS OF LOVE, DESTRUCTION, AND OTHER SYNTHETIC DELUSIONS OF THE ELECTRIC HEAD proved, if nothing else, that they hadn't lost their touch with freakish titles (witness "El Phantasmo And The Chicken Run Blast-o-rama"). Another excessive album of conceptualized dementia, this one featured fractured sampling, along with more of the Zombie growl and metal groove. But excess, not to mention dementia, was the point with White Zombie, whether in Rob's cover art and video direction, their live pyrotechnics or J's crunching guitar lines.

To any astute observers of the band it was pretty clear that the Zombie existed mainly as a vehicle for Rob Zombie and his own creative agenda. Having been involved with the band's video output and stage-show design for a long while, he embarked on a series of experiments involving movies but with no significant results. He even found time to launch his own Zombie A-Go-Go record label specializing in supercharged surf-rock. With the band on hold for a significant period a solo album was an inevitability and when HELLBILLY DELUXE (1998) proved to be a commercial hit, White Zombie were truly dead and buried.

With his former outfit finally laid to rest Zombie issued AMERICAN MADE MUSIC TO STRIP BY in 1999, featuring remixes of his solo material by a host of different artists; he then concentrated on a wildly eclectic series of projects ranging from soundtrack work to producing his own horror movie, catchily titled *House Of 1000 Corpses*. Most recently he took his unique B-movie-meets-metal formula to new heights with THE SINISTER URGE (2001), a cornucopia of sonic delights featuring contributions from the likes of Ozzy Osbourne, Slayer guitarist Kerry King, Limp Bizkit's DJ Lethal, and legendary drummer Tommy Lee.

● **La Sexorcisto: Devil Music Volume I** (1992; Geffen).
Brutal riffs and trash movie culture. A dazzling fusion of weird lyrics and cartoon satanism; guaranteed to upset those of a sensitive nature.

● **Astrocreep 2000: Songs Of Love, Destruction, And Other Synthetic Delusions Of The Electric Head** (1995; Geffen).
Another admirably sustained science-fiction horror experience full of frenetic sampling.

● **Supersexy Swingin' Sounds** (1996; Geffen).
Even better – the remix of ASTROCREEP 2000!

Essi Berelian

WHITESNAKE

Formed London, 1978; disintegrated 1997.

Following the acrimonious break-up of **DEEP PURPLE** in 1976, **David Coverdale**, the band's vocalist for the last three albums, was in no mood to return to the musical wilderness. After releasing two solo albums, he set about challenging for honours with a new band named, like his solo debut, **Whitesnake**.

Coverdale installed guitarists **Bernie Marsden** and **Micky Moody**, bassist **Neil Murray** and drummer **Dave 'Duck' Dowle** as the first of many Whitesnake line-ups. It was this crew that recorded SNAKEBITE (1978), an EP including an emotive cover of Bobby Bland's "Ain't No Love In The Heart Of The City", which remains an integral part of the Whitesnake live show. Soon after came TROUBLE (1978), the band's debut album, clearly defining what was to become a successful blues/rock crossover, dominated by Coverdale's voice.

Whitesnake included Deep Purple standards such as "Mistreated" in concerts, and the connection was bolstered by the arrival of ex-Purple keyboardist **Jon Lord** in time for TROUBLE and his staying on the team for LOVEHUNTER (1979), an impressive set graced by perhaps the most sexist album cover in history. The Deep Purple connection was further reinforced when Dowle was replaced behind the kit by **Ian Paice**. By the time READY AN' WILLING (1980) hit the shops, the band were established as a leading force in heavy rock, particularly on the live circuit where few matched their pulling power, and fewer still their excellence, a fact amply demonstrated on LIVE IN THE HEART OF THE CITY (1980), which caught them at the peak of their powers. The album features Dowle's drumming on the first half (taken from a gig in 1978) and Paice's pasting on the second (recorded in 1980).

It was then that the personnel merry-go-round started in earnest. Paice, Marsden and Murray were replaced by **Cozy Powell**, **Mel Galley** and **Colin 'Bomber' Hodgkinson** respectively for SLIDE IT IN (1984), a spanking return to form. By its release in the USA, though, Moody and Hodgkinson's parts

had disappeared, too, having been overdubbed by **John Sykes** and the returning Neil Murray (with Coverdale keeping his eye, as ever, on the US). Then, during the tour, Mel Galley injured his hand – in an altercation with Sykes, according to rumours. Despite encouraging talk from Coverdale, the guitarist never returned, and at the end of the tour Powell resigned, while Lord joined the re-formed Deep Purple.

A period of re-evaluation followed. To his obvious chagrin, Coverdale had yet to crack the American market, and a partnership with Sykes, the most overtly 'rock' guitarist to join Whitesnake, finally offered him the chance to do so. The pair wrote an album of polished, radio-friendly hard rock, and re-recorded "Here I Go Again" and "Crying In The Rain", a move that bore fruit when the former became a US #1. The album, WHITESNAKE 1987 (1987), had a mixed reception from old 'Snake fans, especially when Coverdale adopted an image tailored for MTV. But the ploy worked and it sold over ten million copies.

In typical Whitesnake fashion, Sykes, Murray and drummer **Aynsley Dunbar** all played on 1987 and departed before its release, and the all-new line-up fuelled fears that Coverdale was pandering to America. No one doubted the ability of **Rudy Sarzo** (bass), **Tommy Aldridge** (drums), plus guitarists **Adrian Vandenberg** and **Vivian Campbell**, but here was a classic British band now featuring just one Englishman, who himself was hellbent on looking every inch the Hollywood superstar.

This was bad enough, but when Campbell was ditched and an injury to Vandenberg put him temporarily out of the band, Coverdale hooked up with **Steve Vai**, an undoubted technical genius, but one lacking in all the qualities that Whitesnake traditionally espoused. SLIP OF THE TONGUE (1989) was a huge letdown, and sold only a tenth as much as its predecessor.

Having dabbled with Jimmy Page on the Coverdale/Page project, Coverdale re-emerged to promote Whitesnake's GREATEST HITS (1994) with a brief tour that left most critics wondering if there was a place for the band in the 1990s. RESTLESS HEART (1997) confirmed that there was not. A thoroughly uninspired affair featuring faceless session musos, with Coverdale sounding exactly what he was – a fading forty-something trying vainly to convince the world he remained a sex god. Accepting the inevitable, Coverdale hit the road one last time for a farewell tour, which only served to prove that the sands of time had long since run out on him. Along with the tour, an acoustic album, STARKERS IN TOKYO (1997), brought Whitesnake's career to a muted end. While Coverdale's natural hard rock vehicle appeared to have run out of momentum, the man himself still apparently had some juice left in him, so to speak. The result was INTO THE LIGHT (2000), a pleasantly rocking if thoroughly inconsequential solo effort.

Hugh Hackett

THE WHO

Formed London, 1964; disbanded 1983; re-formed for Live Aid in 1985 and sporadically since.

Somewhere between The Stones and The Beatles came **The Who**. Aggressive and energetic, defiantly London and working-class, they were threatening enough to frighten the 60s establishment while matching the Fabs for cheekiness, if not charm. Their penchant for loutish behaviour and violence both on and off stage made them notorious, and catapulted them to fame. Yet their slot in rock history rests not just on playing the finest British R&B of the era, but on the more dubious grounds of introducing that enduring turkey, the rock opera.

Originally known as The Detours, the band was formed by three pals from Acton County Grammar School: **John Entwistle** (bass), **Roger Daltrey** (lead guitar) and **Pete Townshend** (rhythm guitar), with the soon-to-be-eased-out **Dougie Sandon** (drums). In 1964 they traded as **The High Numbers**, with Daltrey swapping guitar for microphone and Townshend moving up to lead guitar. Gradually they built up a following on the London club circuit on the back of the mod movement. Their manager, Pete Meaden, bought 500 copies of their first single, "I'm The Face" (1964), in a vain effort to hype them into the charts, but the mods who watched them live were more interested in genuine American R&B product when it came to vinyl.

As long as they stayed as a mod band, they were doomed to remain doyens of a shrinking club scene. Daltrey, an ex-teddy boy, was always inclined towards the rock sound, but the band needed more energy than could be generated by just jumping about on stage. They got it in 1964 when, according to legend, a bloke in an orange suit jumped onto the stage at the Oldfield Hotel in Greenford and proceeded to demolish the band's drum kit. 'Your drummer's crap,' announced the stranger. 'I'm much better than him.' Exit Doug, enter **Keith Moon**.

During a gig at the Marquee, Townshend managed to snap the neck of his guitar on a low ceiling. When the audience failed to react, he went into a rage and smashed the ruined instrument to pieces on stage. Keith Moon joined in, kicking over his drum kit, and the audience went wild with delight. A new stage act was born. The High Numbers then reverted to a previous name that came from a conversation with a club manager at an early gig. 'We're The Detours,' said the band. 'The who?' asked the manager. Pause, then inspiration. 'Yeah, that's right. The Who.'

With a new name, a new drummer and an aggressive new management, The Who made a serious attempt in 1965 at getting into the charts. Their managers, Chris Stamp and Kit Lambert, got them kitted out in a style appropriate to the pop art of the time. Mod zoot suits were exchanged for target T-shirts and tailor-made suits made from Union Jack flags. The high-energy stage act remained, and the band toured under the catchphrase 'Maximum R&B', with black-and-white posters showing Townshend's windmill guitar style. The music began to display a stronger Beatles influence, essential for any group in the mid-60s English charts, and the single "I Can't Explain" (1965) gave the band its first chart action. The record sold slowly at first, and it was not until the public began to get a taste of the stage act on shows like *Ready Steady Go!* that the song made an impression. It then proceeded to reach #8 in the UK chart and edge its way into the lower reaches of the *Billboard* Top 100.

"Anyway Anyhow Anywhere" (1965) was an attempt to capture the band's stage energy on vinyl, but it was the third single that really made a mark. "My Generation" (1965) was an instant classic, full of sneer and rebellion, and with a line that gave rock-'n'-roll one of its first entries in the *Oxford Dictionary Of Quotations*: 'Hope I die before I get old'. It was John Entwistle's diving bass runs that provided the song's distinctive sound and they almost bankrupted him in the process. To get the sound he wanted, Entwistle had to buy an imported Danelectro bass for the unheard-of sum of £60. In the first recording session he broke all the strings. Back at the import shop he discovered that replacement strings were not available. Another guitar, another £60. Back to the studio, and soon another broken set of strings. Another guitar, another £60, until finally he got it right.

It was worth it. "My Generation" surged to #2 in the UK at the start of 1966, followed by the band's debut album, the hastily knocked-out MY GENERATION, and The Who were there. A string of British hit singles followed, with TV appearances that gave a glimpse of the energy of the stage show; "Substitute" (1966), "I'm A Boy" (1966) and "Pictures Of Lily" (1967) cemented their reputation as angst merchants for a generation.

By 1967 The Who felt ready to tackle America, the home of R&B, and their first visit saw them included on the bill of an event that was to become a landmark in rock history. The Monterey Pop Festival introduced America to Jimi Hendrix, Ravi

Shankar and The Who. It was designed as a showcase for the folk-based hippie bands of San Francisco, but California's flower children were given a shocking introduction to the vitriolic rock of England. D. A. Pennebaker's film of the festival shows the flower-painted gentle people watching in horror as The Who destroyed the stage at the end of their set, with the security men trying to restrain four young men who had clearly gone raving mad.

Hit singles and storming shows kept the momentum going on both sides of the Atlantic throughout 1968, but adrenaline is an ephemeral thing. The Who's songs had seldom been traditional intro-two-verses-chorus-verse-chorus affairs, and Townshend had already been experimenting with more extended musical ideas, most notably on the title track of the band's second album, A QUICK ONE (1966). When his ace-in-the-hole, "I Can See For Miles" (1967), and its brilliant concept album, THE WHO SELL OUT (1968), failed to have the desired impact in the UK (they were modest early successes for the band in the US, charting at #9 and #48 respectively), he decided it was time for something different if The Who were not to be swamped in the rush of new music.

Townsend careering past Moon in The Who's heyday

Much of the hippie movement's more mystical ideas had rubbed off on The Who during extensive US touring, as it had with The Beatles (in contrast with The Kinks, who were effectively banned from the States for most of the period). The result was that Townshend was having the first of many mid-life crises, and as he pondered The Meaning Of Life he came up with the idea of a rock opera that combined the themes of religion, stardom, perception of the world, perception of self and the quest for Truth. TOMMY was released in 1969, a few weeks before Woodstock, in a climate where experimentation was hip and the word 'pretentious' did not exist.

TOMMY was a milestone in rock history, and its tale of the deaf, dumb and blind boy has since acquired a life of its own. A version was recorded by the London Symphony Orchestra, it was filmed by

Ken Russell in 1974 (with Daltrey as the lead), and in 1995 it was made into a stage show for Broadway and the West End. It also had some good songs, of course: "Pinball Wizard", "See Me Feel Me", which The Who were rarely to equal.

TOMMY left Townshend drained, and its monumental success created the problem of making a follow-up that wouldn't be disappointing. The neat solution to both problems was LIVE AT LEEDS (1970), a glimpse of the band's stage show. While the live album fended off demands for new material, the band embarked on a film/music project called *Lifehouse*, which involved the band living with some of the fans, in the hope of creative feedback. 'It didn't work,' said Townshend later. 'All they wanted us to do was play "My Generation" and smash the equipment up.'

Retreating to the studio, The Who attempted to make something from the material they had got. Perversely, although *Lifehouse* was a major-league

REDFERNS

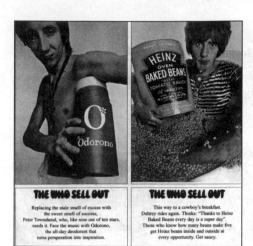

THE WHO SELL OUT

Replacing the stale smell of excess with the sweet smell of success, Peter Townshend, who, like nine out of ten stars, needs it. Face the music with Odorono, the all-day deodorant that turns perspiration into inspiration.

THE WHO SELL OUT

This way to a cowboy's breakfast. Daltrey rides again. Thinks: "Thanks to Heinz Baked Beans every day is a super day." Those who know how many beans make five get Heinz beans inside and outside at every opportunity. Get saucy.

failure, the resulting album, WHO'S NEXT (1971), was probably their best. A remarkable collection of crunching riffs, power chords and anthemic lyrics – most notably "Won't Get Fooled Again" – it virtually defined 70s hard rock.

An emboldened Townshend embarked on another rock opera, QUADROPHENIA (1973), which harked back to the band's mod roots with its theme of an adolescent mind pulled apart by peer pressure, hedonism and love in an existence with no future. Despite the mod theme and the heavy use of brass, QUADROPHENIA was the closest The Who came to heavy metal. It sold well enough, reaching #2 in both the UK and US, but by Who standards it was pretty ponderous stuff. Meanwhile, the other members were trying to peep out from Townshend's shadow with solo albums like Daltrey's RIDE A ROCK HORSE (1975), Moon's TWO SIDES OF THE MOON (1975) and Entwistle's MAD DOG (1975).

The Who's own next album, ODDS AND SODS (1974), a mishmash of outtakes and old recordings, was a poor effort to disguise a lack of cohesion and direction, and THE WHO BY NUMBERS (1975) was little better, despite "Slip Kid" and the hit single "Squeeze Box". Although still a hugely popular live act, it seemed that the band were foundering, outliving their rebellious youth as a new generation of punks showed up.

Still, WHO ARE YOU (1978) was an improvement, enjoyable rather than great, and two film projects suggested a resurgence of energy. *Quadrophenia* hit British cinemas on the back of a return to the violent beach fights of the mod/teddy-boy era (this time between skinheads and anyone else who happened to be around), while *The Kids Are Alright* was a kind of potted history of the past fifteen years in clips from TV shows and films of live shows. In the midst of it all, however, in September 1978, Keith Moon's dissolute lifestyle finally caught up with him. He died of an overdose of pills – ironically prescribed to curb his alcoholism – after a party commemorating Buddy Holly's birthday, and

was replaced by ex-Small Faces drummer **Kenny Jones**.

Frantic touring around the turn of the decade, as well as Daltrey's increasing film work (most notably *McVicar*) delayed the next album, FACE DANCES, until 1981, and it scarcely seemed worth the wait. Touring tailed off, too, a process hastened by the deaths of fifteen fans in a stampede in Cincinnati, and as Townshend took a job as an editor at literary publishers Faber and Faber, it seemed the band was finally defunct.

The Who came back together for Live Aid, on the back of which THE WHO COLLECTION charted. And they have re-formed at intervals since, burdened by Townshend's 'Hope I die before I get old' line, and looking an ever more ragged part-time outfit. At their best, of course, they had been up there in the stratosphere, with a stage set that was never going to lend itself with dignity to any middle-aged nostalgia revival. Townsend has occasionally made noises about issuing some new material, but in light of the tragic and unexpected death of John Entwistle in a Las Vegas hotel room in 2002, there are now serious questions to be asked about the future of the group. For now it's probably best to just pick up a copy of the remixed, remastered and now complete LIVE AT LEEDS (2001), and remember the Who for what they once were.

The Who Sell Out (1968; Polydor).
A real concept album, as The Who bring pirate radio onto record, adverts and all. Some ideas that were later to appear on TOMMY are here but, except for "I Can See For Miles", most songs are unfamiliar to non-fans.

Tommy (1969; MCA).
The beginning of the plot – the loss of a father in the war – is a key to the themes of personal loss and directionlessness that characterized so much British music of the time. The ideas may be outdated, but musically TOMMY still stands up to scrutiny, especially in "Pinball Wizard" and "Amazing Journey".

Who's Next (1971; MCA).
This album entered by that narrow window in a band's career when they maintained youthful creativeness and energy, and were able to get all their musical ideas down in the studio. "Baba O'Reilly", "Won't Get Fooled Again" and "Behind Blue Eyes" are enduring classics.

Meaty, Beaty, Big & Bouncy (1971; MCA).
This 1971 'best of' is still the best retrospective of The Who, when they were still basically a singles band, and when the songs – "My Generation', "Substitute", "I Can See For Miles", "Anyway, Anyhow, Anywhere" – really meant something to Townshend. The album includes a couple of the best moments of TOMMY too.

Quadrophenia (1973; Polydor).
After being seemingly forgotten, The Who's second concept album has gradually grown in popularity as TOMMY starts to look dated. Bold and brassy, and often heavy, this peers into the adolescent soul and captures the energy of the 70s Who better than any other studio album. Anger, violence and nihilism desperately try to smother the insecurity of a child growing up too fast.

Live At The Isle Of Wight Festival 1970 (1997; Castle).
Digital remastering has cleaned up the original, analogue tape that forms the basis of this two-CD set. This album captures the band at the height of their powers.

Patrick Neylan-Francis

WILCO

"Our old bus driver called us rock'n'roll with a steel guitar. I don't know, but I do know that Badfinger didn't have to call themselves country rock so why do we?"

In late spring 1997 **Wilco** played the Shepherd's Bush Empire in London. The set was marvellous, but the band seemed subdued, even belligerent: 'Where were you in 1995?', was one of the few comments from singer/guitarist **Jeff Tweedy**, a barbed remark about the band's overlooked support slot to The Jayhawks at the same venue two years previously. Why the bad feeling? A glance through the band members' CVs may offer a few clues.

Jeff Tweedy was co-leader of **UNCLE TUPELO**, a seminal country-rock band who cranked out a ripsnorting blend of country, bluegrass, rock and punk in the early 90s, inspiring masses of imitators. Their commercial failure may well account for Tweedy's occasional moments of chagrin towards the 'business'.

Jay Farrar, the other co-leader of Uncle Tupelo, went on to form **SON VOLT**, while Tweedy took remaining members **Ken Coomber** (percussion), **John Stirrat** (bass), and **Max Johnstone** (dobro/fiddle/mandolin/banjo etc) to create Wilco (as in radio shorthand for 'Will Comply'), signing for Sire/Reprise in 1994.

Whilst undeniably an individual proposition, Wilco also form part of the country-rock 'No Depression Movement', a loose amalgam of like-minded bands (such as The Bottle Rockets and Blue Mountain) bonded by a blue-collar rock'n'roll stance and a serious debt towards artists such as Lynyrd Skynyrd and Hank Williams. The 'No Depression' tag itself comes from Uncle Tupelo's debut album, reflecting the long shadow cast by that band.

Post-Uncle Tupelo, Tweedy and his cohorts guested on Steve Forbert's comeback album, ROCKING HORSE HEAD, prior to the release of their own debut album – A.M. (1995) – to a relatively warm critical reception but small sales. Wilco's take on country-rock is definitely not the pristine sub-Gram Parsons style favoured by early Jayhawks et al, and the songs sounded much like an extension of Tweedy's Tupelo contributions – loose, swinging country-rockers, their casual tone supplemented by Tweedy's homespun vocals. It all gave the impression of being recorded quickly, lazily, during late nights on back porches, but those porch sessions sure sounded fun.

Wilco took part in the 1995 H.O.R.D.E. Tour, which lumped together a number of 'rootsy' rock bands (headed by Blues Traveler) in a seeming effort to showcase prospects for the 'next Grateful Dead'. Certainly Tweedy's charming, sometimes slightly off-key vocals and the band's diverse instrumentation made them prime candidates. Tweedy also managed to find time to form and play with **Golden Smog**, an offshoot project featuring members of The Jayhawks and Soul Asylum. The band's DOWN BY THE OLD MAINSTREAM (1995) album is highly recommended.

Wilco's next offering was the double album BEING THERE (1996), an ambitious attempt to gain some distance from the past. Adding **Jay Bennett** on guitar/piano, plus horns, and a full – at times

STEVE GILLET

Wilco's Jeff Tweedy – once part of the 'No Depression' movement

Spectorish – production, it seemed like a leap from black and white to widescreen Americana. The album moved fairly easily from the glammy, sing-along stomp of "I Got You (At The End Of The Century)" through the earthy poignance of "Sunken Treasure" to a Turtles-esque high on "Why Would You Wanna Live?" As a double album, the project was viewed with suspicion by Sire/Reprise, and the band waived part of their royalties in order to keep the price down. In the end, it drew comparisons with classics of the genre such as EXILE ON MAIN STREET and, while it had some of the same sly swagger and chugging riffs, it occasionally lost its focus in patches of listless noodling. However it hit more often than it missed, impressed the critics and sold encouragingly. The title came from the film of the same name in which Peter Sellers played a kind of *idiot savant*. Tweedy explained the choice as follows: 'Rock bands in general are just kinda idiots, y'know, managing to say a few things that are truisms but have them all blown out of proportion into something mystical.'

1998 saw Wilco paying homage to one of their spiritual leaders, Woody Guthrie, on MERMAID AVENUE, in a co-production with British protest singer **BILLY BRAGG** A collection of fifteen of Woody's song lyrics, with music newly written by Wilco and Bragg, it boasted a vocal guest appearance by **Natalie Merchant**. In Bragg's words, 'This is NOT a tribute album, but a genuine collaboration between contemporary artists and the man who, in many respects, is the original singer/songwriter – Woody Guthrie.'

The upsurge of interest in Americana - New Country, alt-country, blue-collar country, etc. - propelled Wilco into the front rank of American rock bands. Jeff Tweedy featured strongly on the excellent 1998 Golden Smog album, WEIRD TALES, and produced The Handsome Family's THROUGH THE TREES album - many people's nomination for Album of the Year.

Wilco were now enjoying an exalted reputation stateside, particularly on the college circuit. But just as the 'No-Depression'-era movment shifted into mainstream focus and blended indistinguishably into the whole 'new country' boom, Wilco shrewdly moved on once more. SUMMER TEETH (1999) owed more to the spirit of The Beatles' WHITE ALBUM in the sprawling, casually offhand way it offered up moments of sparklingly brilliant pop, whilst managing to retain the inimitable flashes of trademark Wilco.

BEING THERE justified its tag as a great American rock album, but SUMMER TEETH sounded like a leap from monochrome to technicolour by comparison.

After a second volume of MERMAID AVENUE (2000), again with Billy Bragg, 2002's YANKEE HOTEL FOXTROT was to find Wilco expanding their range still further, but not without the difficulties that seemed to dog them. Not only did guitarist Jay Bennett leave the group during the recording ses-

sions, but Reprise were unwilling to release the finished product. Wilco refused to compromise their work, and so bought back the tapes, and left Reprise. A complex but rewarding set, YANKEE HOTEL FOXTROT maintained Wilco's considerable reputation through courageous and adventurous means, making them one of the few in contemporary rock still genuinely prepared to take risks when necessary.

⊙ **Being There** (1996; Reprise).
A breakthrough for Tweedy, flexing his muscles with this diverse, yet cohesive double CD. Opening with the desolate melancholy of "Misunderstood" (all fractured guitar noise and mournful echo), the album touches base with most of the key thrill points of 70s rock – Big Pop (the single, "Outta Mind/Outta Sight"), country picking ("Forget The Flowers"), slow-burn Memphis funk ("Kingpin"), and a range of other styles.

Nig Hodgkins & Andrew Rosenberg

THE WILDHEARTS

Formed London, 1989.

Born in South Shields, in the northeast of England, a singer known simply as **Ginger** (guitar/vocals) gloriously misspent his youth bouncing around various rock bands before finally creating a suitable outlet for his anger and energy, **The Wildhearts**. The first stable line-up – there was to be much shifting in personnel over the years – also included **CJ** (Chris Jadghar; guitars), **Danny McCormack** (bass) and **Stidi** (drums). Snapped up by East West, The Wildhearts have released some of the freshest rock music of the last decade – while being a major headache for their record company from day one at the office.

The band's first release, the brilliantly titled MONDO-AKIMBO-A-GO-GO EP (1992), showed signs of a rushed genesis and was whipped out to coincide with a special guest slot supporting the Manic Street Preachers, and was fuelled by Ginger's spiteful attacks on record companies. It was re-recorded, with production from Terry Date (Pantera, Soundgarden), along with four new cuts, later in the year as a mini-album, DON'T BE HAPPY ... JUST WORRY. This included the outstanding "Splattermania", a gore-movie lovefest, and the slacker song "Weekend (5 Days Long)", which displayed a previously unsuspected maturer side to their music.

The band continued to show disrespect for anyone within reach, whether being ditched after only one night on a tour with Izzy Stradlin (of Guns N' Roses fame) and then trashing him in the press, or releasing their first single, "Greetings From Shitsville", with artwork of their producer, Simon Efemy, defecating into a pitta bread pouch. That single, a limited release, came from The Wildhearts' first full album, EARTH VS THE WILDHEARTS (1993), which also featured their sensitive take on relationships, "My Baby Is A Headfuck". This album too was to be re-released, this time to include their second single,

"Caffeine Bomb", in March 1994. A cousin to Motörhead's "Ace Of Spades", the song skidded into the UK Top 30 with the help of an outrageous appearance on *Top Of The Pops*.

Behind the scenes, things had begun to fall apart: Stidi had left during 1993 (replaced by **Ritch Battersby**), CJ went off to form **HONEYCRACK**, McCormack battled drug demons, and Jadghar was sacked after much infighting. The group's 1994 Reading Festival slot, meanwhile, was marred by McCormack dislocating his knee during the opening number, and winding up the organizers by playing louder than the legal noise limit.

The fan-club-only FISHING FOR LUCKIES came later in 1994, a series of extended songs ranging from the Pogues-ish "Geordie In Wonderland" to the eleven-minute prog-metal piece "Sky Babies". But The Wildhearts were still making more press than their music. Following an erroneous report in metal magazine *Kerrang!* that McCormack was about to be booted out of the band, they marched into the magazine's offices and trashed the offending journalist's computer; the ensuing publicity only enhanced the myth. They had more trouble when guitarist **Mark Keds** (ex-Senseless Things), enlisted after Devin Townsend's interim tenure had ended, did not return from contractual obligations in Japan in time for the Phoenix Festival; the band was forced to cancel, and threatened to 'kick Keds' head in' if they got their hands on him. Unknown **Jeff Streatfield** replaced him.

The 1995 album P.H.U.Q. concentrated, despite its title, less on cartoon metal and more on a substantive rock sound. The critical acclaim it subsequently received, however, was not matched by record sales, and the band's relationship with East West – which Ginger described as 'hate-hate' – deteriorated further. The Wildhearts threatened to break up after their summer tour, and when East West wanted to release FISHING FOR LUCKIES with three new tracks through normal retail outlets, Ginger urged fans not to buy it. The album was finally re-released in 1996 with eight additional songs, by new label Round Records, who had distributed The Wildhearts' new single "Sick Of Drugs".

The remainder of the year brought further rumours of an imminent split, and the blatant East West cash-in release, THE BEST OF THE WILDHEARTS (1996), seemed to merely underline the possibility. The band, however, emerged from the studio having forged a new sound on ENDLESS NAMELESS (1997); the usual melodic trademarks were present but buried under a deliberately harsh industrial-style production job, making it frustratingly inaccessible at best, and at worst completely unlistenable.

Just to drive the 'we're here to irritate' philosophy home, the band split up in October 1997, only to re-form and announce a tour in June 1998. During the hiatus, however, ANARCHIC AIRWAVES (1998), a collection of live radio/concert tracks spanning three years, sneaked into the stores. The album – covering a number of differing line-ups and featuring material from several different concerts – was swiftly disowned by the band. However, the high count of stand-out tracks, which included a storming version of Elvis Costello's "Pump It Up", plus "Sick Of Drugs" and "Suckerpunch", made it an essential purchase for the true fan.

Since then the band's story has been on-off and rather volatile, only punctuated by the release of a patchy mini-album, RIFF AFTER RIFF AFTER MOTHERFUCKING RIFF (2003). More interesting were Ginger's attempts to recapture a taste of the old glory with his **Silver Ginger 5** project and solo material.

⊙ **Earth Vs The Wildhearts** (1993; East West).
An instant classic, packed with speedy ragged melodies, and containing such live favourites as "TV Tan" and "Suckerpunch".

⊙ **P.H.U.Q** (1995; East West).
Including their biggest hit, "I Wanna Go Where The People Go", this album is packed with classics. Ginger's lyrics are humorous and bitter, while the sound is heavier and more textured than previous releases.

⊙ **Fishing For Luckies** (1996; Round Records/Warners).
Initially a fan-club-only release, this shows a more esoteric side to the band's songwriting. The commercial version contains nearly double the original number of tracks.

⊙ **The Best Of The Wildhearts** (1996; East West).
The kind of collection that will have purists arguing over the relative merits of what is included and lamenting over the exclusion of particular favourites. A mere taste of what the band can do, but pretty good all the same.

Essi Berelian

HANK WILLIAMS

Born Georgiana, Alabama, September 17, 1923;
died January 1, 1953.

"A song ain't nuthin' in the world but a story just wrote with music to it."

A giant of popular music, **Hank Williams** provided the blueprint for modern country and western, but could just as easily be seen as a progenitor of rock'n'roll. Williams was possibly the first country performer to capitalize on sex appeal; he brought a stripped-down, no-nonsense sound and attitude to country; he lived hard and died young; and a good deal of his appeal was based on the fact that he lived what he sang about. Williams's songs charted a life that reached from inconsolable sadness to untrammelled joy. And he sang them with a voice that, while not blessed with great range, used an unerring sense of phrasing, tremolo effects and yodels that could break in heart-rending fashion to embody rather than merely represent the emotions of his songs.

Williams was born in 1923 into the Depression-era poverty of Alabama, and suffered from a congenital spinal problem that would trouble him throughout his life. Absorbing gospel at church and country music on the radio (Jimmy Rodgers was an early influence), Williams learned the blues from Rufus 'Tee-Tot' Payne, a black street singer. By 14, Williams had formed the first **Drifting Cowboys**, and by 16 was assured and talented enough to play the tough honky-tonk circuit, with his mother Lilly as his manager.

Williams then took two years out from music, moving to Mobile, where he worked in the shipyards and met his future wife, Audrey Sheppard Guy. They married, and in 1944 the couple returned to Montgomery, Lilly and the honky-tonks – only this time Audrey had joined the troupe. While Audrey had faith in her talents, she was probably the only one; later recordings confirmed the opinion of an unnamed member of Hank's band: 'the only way she could catch a tune was to sneak up on it ... and sometimes it got away.'

Although Hank and Audrey drifted ever deeper into discord and the bottle, Audrey immeasurably helped Hank's career by arranging his meeting with Fred Rose. Rose, partner with Roy Acuff in the Acuff-Rose country music powerhouse, became Williams's publisher, protector, mentor and collaborator. He helped Williams move from his turgid, mournful early songs ("When God Comes And Gathers His Jewels," "Six More Miles") to the craft and sophistication of "Mansion On The Hill" and "Your Cheatin' Heart". He was also responsible for Williams signing his contract with MGM in 1949.

These MGM recordings are the centrepiece of the Williams legacy. The classics are too numerous to list, but include the standards "Cold, Cold Heart", "(I Can't Help it) If I'm Still In Love With You", "Lovesick Blues", "I'm So Lonesome I Could Cry", "Kawliga", and the prophetically titled "I'll Never Get Out Of This World Alive", which was climbing the country charts when Williams died on New Year's Day 1953, in a limousine on his way to his next show. Legend has it he died with lyrics for a new song in his hand.

In his lifetime, Williams was strictly a singles artist, and the albums released after his death are, by their very nature, commercial constructs as opposed to unified artistic statements. Following in the footsteps of pop-hit cover versions of Williams's songs by Tony Bennett and Pat Boone, MGM (later Mercury, then Polygram) attempted to sell Williams as more of a pop artist, overdubbing his pithy, laconic recordings (the line-up of the Drifting Cowboys was usually acoustic and electric pedal-steel guitar, stand-up bass fiddle, and rudimentary drums) with strings, choruses and keyboards. This woeful state of affairs continued until the mid-80s, when Polygram, through their Chronicles reissue programme, released a series of eight double-LP sets (later reissued as single CDs) that assayed the complete Williams catalogue in chronological order, without overdubs. In 1995, these were also issued as a limited-edition package, known as 'The Cube'. It is to be hoped that Polygram keep the Chronicle editions in print, as essential documents of American music.

◉ **40 Greatest Hits** (1988; Polydor).
This is pretty much the perfect Hank introduction, presenting as generous a one-CD package of highlights as could be devised.

◉ **Volume 1: I Ain't Got Nothin But Time** (1991; Polydor).
Anyone developing a serious Hank interest should start here, with the first volume in Polygram's eight-CD series. Each of the volumes is a mix of singles, demos, outtakes and radio broadcasts. Volume 1 is a gem, including "Honky Tonkin'", "Move It Over" and "I Ain't Got Nothin' But Time". Other prime discs include VOLUME 4: I'M SO LONESOME I COULD CRY and the desolate VOLUME 8: I WON'T BE HOME NO MORE.

Steven Mirkin

LUCINDA WILLIAMS

Born Lake Charles, Louisiana, 1953.

"I would learn songs like 'Angel' by Jimi Hendrix, or a Cream song. I didn't ever think, 'Well, I'm a folk singer, and that's not a folk song – so I can't sing it.'"

Of the many singer-songwriters who successfully straddle the genres of folk and rock, none does it with the sweet abandon of **Lucinda Williams**. An ability to skip from ballsy blues to delicate ballads has marked a career that might be short on recordings but has always been unpredictable.

Williams's itinerant childhood – spent roaming from New Orleans to Mexico City to Santiago (her father was a visiting professor of literature) – brought her into contact with all sorts of musical influences. Taken particularly by country, Delta blues and jazz, she began performing at 16, soon gravitating to the clubs of New Orleans, Houston and Austin. She was signed to Moe Asch's legendary Folkways label and cut RAMBLIN' ON MY MIND (1979), a collection of traditional blues and country songs. The follow-up, HAPPY WOMAN BLUES (1980), consisted entirely of original material, illustrating the broad canvas of her influences, notably on the Cajun-tinged "Lafayette" and "Louisiana Man" and the Delta blues of the title

track. These albums were her stepping stones to an original style.

After briefly working the Greenwich Village folk-club circuit, Williams returned to the clubs of Houston and Austin, then moved to Los Angeles in 1984. For the next five years – despite lucrative inducements from various major companies – Lucinda worked on her material, played gigs and collaborated with a number of relative unknowns who were to become her permanent band. The eventual result, 1988's LUCINDA WILLIAMS, was worth the wait. A brilliant showcase for her emotional range, the album covered every base, hitting the pop-rock nail on the head with her best-known song, "Passionate Kisses", which was soon covered by country hit-maker Mary Chapin Carpenter. Williams also attracted the attention of Patti Loveless, who scored a US Top 10 country hit with a cover of "The Night's Too Long". The album sold well, due to Williams's relentless touring and a strong word of mouth, but her label, Rough Trade, could do little to help – it eventually closed up shop.

Four years passed before the release of SWEET OLD WORLD (1992), featuring guests such as fiddlers Byron Berline and Doug Atwell, as well as Benmont Tench of Tom Petty & The Heartbreakers. Songs like "Six Blocks Away", "Pineola" and "He Never Got Enough Love" were masterful vignettes, chronicling the vicissitudes of the human condition. The sly funk of "Hot Blood" and the slow waltz of "Little Angel, Little Brother" showed that she could reach into a big bag of tricks and pull out a winner, elevating the album above the customary introspective ramblings of the singer-songwriter genre.

Williams moved to Nashville to finish the CAR WHEELS ON A GRAVEL ROAD (1998) album, which finally saw the light of day six years after SWEET OLD WORLD. It was a set of powerful, gripping songs and added to her considerable reputation as a writer of 'quality' music. ESSENCE (2001) was subtler still, but continued to showcase Williams as an artist in control of her career. WORLD WITHOUT TEARS (2003) was another daring step forward and revealed Williams at her most raw and emotionally charged.

⊙ **Lucinda Williams** (1988; Rough Trade).
Featuring the horny "Passionate Kisses" and "I Just Want To See You So Bad", Williams's second set of original songs brilliantly merges a rock sensibility with her grounding in American roots music.

⊙ **Sweet Old World** (1992; Elektra/Chameleon).
Backed by a heavyweight crew of country-rockers, Williams comes close to the 'cosmic American music' espoused by Gram Parsons. Sound and lyrics cut deep on songs like "Pineola", "Sweet Old World" and "Little Angel, Little Brother".

⊙ **Car Wheels On A Gravel Road** (1998; Polygram).
Wonderful lyrics and great music – this is easily her best and most satisfying recording.

⊙ **Essence** (2001; Lost Highway).
The songs drip with love and pain with lust. The album's highpoint is "I Envy The Wind", a hopelessly romantic song that finds a lustful Williams caressing the arrangement with her lyric. This is a beautiful album from a woman with a voice you could collapse into.

Hugh Gregory

ROBBIE WILLIAMS

Born Newcastle-under-Lyme, England, 1974.

Following his departure from the boy band, **Take That**, in 1995 (and his subsequent removal from all their promotional material), it appeared that **Robbie Williams** was finished – in more ways than one. He astonished Take That fans by his drunken – and drugged – appearance at the Glastonbury Festival in June that year, hanging out backstage, playing soccer with the Gallagher brothers and appearing on stage with Oasis. This heralded the beginning of a wasteful year, culminating in rehab sessions and a step back from the limelight.

Having separated himself from his boy-band history and pulled himself out of the mire to a large extent, he signed to Chrysalis Records in June 1996. The following month, his first solo single – a celebratory, and appropriately titled, cover of George Michael's "Freedom" – reached #2 in the charts and sold 250,000 copies, despite Robbie's extracurricular activities at the time. Luckily, the tabloid press merely served to increase his popularity.

His debut album, LIFE THRU A LENS (1997), sold disappointingly until the Christmas-released single, "Angels", turned things round. With sales improving weekly, the album took 28 weeks to climb the charts but finally made it to #1. Its songs showed a wide mix of styles, from ballads such as "Angels" and "One Of God's Better People" to the rocking "Let Me Entertain You" (eventually released as a single in March 1998), most of them co-written by Robbie, and Guy Chambers (ex-Lemon Trees, World Party), who also co-produced the album. Despite the success, the Robster was not a happy bunny. Bitterly resentful towards his ex-management and old comrades, he took revenge with cathartic songs such as "Ego A Go-Go" (aimed at Gary Barlow).

In June 1998 Robbie was invited to perform at Glastonbury, and despite the dreadful weather made the festival his own with the audience singing along word for word to "Angels". This appearance signified the end of his 'booze'n'drugs hell', and saw him reinvent himself with a credibility that won him back the loyalty of pop kids whilst attracting new fans among the harder-to-please 'indie' audience.

He released his second album, I'VE BEEN EXPECTING YOU (1998), to great critical acclaim. It was another eclectic mix of songs and styles, with Robbie's no-nonsense lyrics to the fore in single releases "Strong" ('My breath smells of a thousand fags [British slang for 'cigarettes']/And when I'm drunk I dance like my Dad/I've started to dress a bit like him') and "No Regrets", which reached #4, featuring both Neil Tennant (Pet Shop Boys) and Neil Hannon (the Divine Comedy). Williams still had demons to exorcize, however, as seen in the lyrics to "Karma Killer" ('I hope you choke/On your Bacardi and Coke'); no bitterness there then! The strongest single, "Millennium", released in September 1998, went to #1 in the UK charts. Culling a distinctive sample from the Bond movie-theme song "You Only Live Twice", it offered another obliquely confessional lyric 'Live for lipo-suction/And detox for your rent/Overdose for Christmas/And give it up for Lent'.

By the turn of the millennium there could be no doubt in anybody's mind that Robbie was the UK's biggest star. 2000's SING WHEN YOU'RE WINNING closely followed the 'if it ain't broke don't fix it' maxim with typically sterling results. Williams, it seemed, could do no wrong with "Rock DJ" and "Kids" (a duet with his female counterpart **KYLIE MINOGUE**) soaring straight into the charts. Only an inadvisable cover of "Nutbush City Limits" soiled the album's solid selection.

At the top of his game – and poised (eternally it sometimes seems) on the brink of global stardom – Williams made the odd move of recording an album of Frank Sinatra songs, SWING WHEN YOU'RE WINNING, which included a duet with the man himself. Carried off – by a whisker – by Robbie's sheer charisma, the album was massively successful but came with the sound of warning bells. While his voice was well suited to his usual vibrant pop, he just couldn't croon like Frank can – he was nowhere near, in fact.

Next came ESCAPOLOGY (2002), which lived up to its title and found Robbie attempting to escape the shackles of novelty and pop by crafting a 'serious' collection of MOR rock.

Robbie Williams's main attraction, though – apart from his sex appeal (he's both guy and girly icon) – is his dynamic live stage performance: giving it his all, from appearances with his lifelong hero Tom Jones (at domestic pop-biz awards ceremony The Brits in 1998), to whizzing around the stage on a motorized toilet, to performing a punked-up version of the Take That song "Back For Good" (which charmed audiences during his tour of the UK and Ireland in 1999). Quite simply, Robbie is a great entertainer – and that is what he excels at. In his own words: 'Hell is gone and heaven's here/There's nothing left for you to fear/Shake your arse come over here/So come on let me entertain you.'

Now that his attentions have turned toward the US, where he remains largely undiscovered, one wonders how long he can sustain this level of popularity – after all it's been a while since "Angels" now.

- **Life Thru A Lens** (1997; Chrysalis).
  An assortment of songs and styles ranging from the bittersweet "Angels" to the stomping "Let Me Entertain You", via the Oasis-esque "Before I Die".

- **I've Been Expecting You** (1998; Chrysalis).
  Williams emanates a new-found confidence. The first three tracks – "Strong", "No Regrets" and "Millennium" – all reached the Top 10 in the UK singles charts.

- **Sing When You're Winning** (2000; Chrysalis).
  This time around our happy-go-lucky all-round top entertainer has spread his genre-ensnaring net wider than ever, to feature everything from his hallmark balladry to stadium rock, funk, disco, and even hip-hop. Yet, the set's best cut has to be the Kylie duet "Kids".

- **Swing When You're Winning** (2001; Chrysalis).
  However classic these hand-picked Rat-Pack covers might be, this album is an excessive indulgence. The only saving grace is the smooth and sexy duet of "Somethin' Stupid" with Nicole Kidman.

Jane Holly

VICTORIA WILLIAMS

Born Shreveport, Louisiana, 1959.

"Every day is poetry."

The first thing you notice about **Victoria Williams** is her voice – a shrill noise which could curdle cows, let alone milk. But what has won a following among alternative-rock fans – and glitterati – is the woman's startling songwriting, which is concerned, above all, with the tiny details of daily life.

The most-often quoted lyric on Williams' debut album, HAPPY COME HOME (1987), was one that advised listeners that 'every day is poetry'. Though several good songs were buried too deeply in the mix by Anton Fier and Stephen Soles, others such as the piquant, charming "TC" were redolent of frontier Americana in all its *Little House On The Prairie* innocence. Her observations on home, hearth and personal environment in an age of rock grandeur saw her venerated by a crop of peers including members of Soul Asylum, Pearl Jam, Lucinda Williams, Mike Scott and Lou Reed. As the one-time marital partner of Peter Case, she had always enjoyed friends in highish rock places.

SWING THE STATUE (1990) was comfortably her best album. Co-produced with Tom Waits (of whose unusual vocal range there are echoes in Williams' work) and Elvis Costello collaborator Michael Blair, it continued to flirt with some rather simplistic Christian imagery (the sleeve notes included 'Thank you for playing this record. May God bless you and your loved ones'). In "Summer Of Drugs", a beautiful exposition of a woman's coming of age, Williams wrote arguably the best song of her career (it was later covered by Soul Asylum). Yet the impression remained that Williams' celebrity fans were encouraging the line drawings of an enthusiastic little sister rather than the work of a new Rembrandt.

After the release of the album, Williams was diagnosed as suffering from multiple sclerosis. Several friends rallied round to record the tribute album SWEET RELIEF to pay her medical bills. The proceeds not only kept the wolf from the door, but made sure that LOOSE (1994) got a decent recording budget. A number of guests were again present, from session men Greg Cohen and Don Heffington to members of R.E.M. It also included a couple of rather average duets – one with new husband Mark Olson (of The Jayhawks) and another with Dave Pirner of Soul Asylum.

MUSINGS OF A CREEK DIPPER (1998) was another gentle album of reflections on life, love and death, which could be seen as either charmingly nostalgic or stomach-twistingly naive. WATER TO DRINK (2000), meanwhile, found particularly successful interpretations of "Until The Real Thing Comes Along" and "Young At Heart", and led to an all-covers album, SINGS SOME OL' SONGS, in 2002.

⊙ **Swing The Statue** (1990; Rough Trade/Mammoth). By turns deeply affecting and deeply irritating, SWING THE STATUE epitomizes both sides of Victoria Williams' art. When she's on form, she's enchanting. When she's not, she's the whining kid sister you want to lose at the fairground.

Danny Swann

JACKIE WILSON

Born Detroit, June 9, 1934; died January 21, 1984.

In 1953, an overconfident, brash kid with the voice of a streetwise angel, **Jackie Wilson**, landed his first plum role – as lead singer of **Billy Ward & The Dominoes** – by not only bragging that he was better than the recently departed singer, the legendary Clyde McPhatter, but, according to Ward himself, by proving it. By 1956, they'd had their first hit with Wilson on lead: "St. Therese Of The Roses", a surprising choice of religious material for a rock'n'rolling doo-wop act. The word got around that Wilson could walk the walk just as well as he talked the talk, and that even Elvis had been overheard commenting on his amazing vocal range and skills.

The ambitious Wilson soon became dissatisfied with sharing the adulation with a group, and left soon after "St. Therese" to start a solo career. 1957's "Reet Petite", written by the pre-Motown Berry Gordy, saw Jackie give a lustful vocal performance far exceeding the demands of the bouncy up-tempo tune. Gordy went on to provide Wilson with even better tunes, such as the timeless mid-tempo ballads "To Be Loved", and the magnificent "Lonely Teardrops", wherein Wilson's voice soars and glides dramatically in passion and frustation. Wilson then applied his gracious voice to the blues, gospel and even to traditional ballads like "Danny Boy". He was no slouch as a songwriter, either, responsible for the classic "Baby Workout" in 1963 and proved to be one of the premier live acts of the late 50s/early 60s. On stage he impressed both vocally and with astounding, sexy dance routines, earning the nickname 'Mr. Excitement' – though in 1961 he picked up a bullet from a woman fan and was seriously hurt, which curtailed the gymnastics to some extent.

He had six years at the top, but by the end of 1963 Wilson's career was in decline, the new British Invasion and change in direction for R&B having stolen his audience. Wilson had another two chart hits before retiring to the oldies circuit. "Whispers Getting Louder" and 1967's elegant, triumphant "Higher And Higher" – both of which equalled anything from his heyday but failed to put the fire back

into his career. Wilson wound up touring Vegas and other cities in oldies revues – a fate he shared with many other great acts of the 1950s.

Ironically, Wilson's collapse occured at the scene of his triumphs – on stage in 1975. He died in a coma nine years after suffering a heart attack at the Latin Casino in Cherry Hill, New Jersey, having spent his final years in hospital.

Wilson was complimented before his death in 1972 by Van Morrison, who named a song after him, "Jackie Wilson Said (I'm In Heaven When You Smile)" – later covered respectfully by Dexys Midnight Runners – and he had a posthumous UK hit with the rereleased "Reet Petite" in the mid 80s. The Commodores also tipped their hat to him on "Nightshift" (an elegy for Marvin Gaye and Jackie Wilson, who both died in 1984). But, more importantly, Wilson's influence continues to be seen in the work of the Isley Brothers, The Jackson Five, Michael Jackson and many others.

⊙ **The Jackie Wilson Story** (1983; Epic). The first CD compilation of his work and the best (until the box set from Rhino, that is). Most of his hits from 1957 to 1963, and lesser-known but still quality material (check out the amazing "I Just Can't Help It" and "She's Alright").

⊙ **The Very Best Of Jackie Wilson** (1997; Rhino). Not as good a compilation as the above, but probably easier to find. All his pop and R&B hits are here in chronological order and just as impressive.

⊙ **Mr. Excitement!** (1997; Rhino). The definitive look at the Wilson catalogue. This three-CD set starts with "St. Therese" and moves through a remarkable cavalcade of pop, soul, blues, ballads and duets. The best testament to his legendary status.

Chris Lark

EDGAR WINTER

Born Beaumont, Texas, December 28, 1946.

The younger brother of rock bluesman **JOHNNY WINTER**, **Edgar Winter** played in Johnny's bands through the late 60s, mastering a number of instruments, including alto sax and keyboards. It was a solid apprenticeship, and when Edgar cut out on his own in 1970 he was confident enough to play almost all the instruments on his debut album, ENTRANCE (1970). A lively and sometimes inspired effort, it put Edgar into the 'progressive rock' camp before the term was taken over by shameless British pomp-rockers. Edgar's stock in trade was collecting influences and recycling them against a basic rock background. His music, by turns jazzy, folky and heavy, was fashioned as much on the road as in the studio, and his policy of hiring the very best musicians gave his expansive imagination a vivid quality on record. Several Winter sidemen – Boz Scaggs, Dan Hartman, Rick Derringer and Ronnie Montrose – would later carve out their own solo careers in rock.

Winter's highest critical and commercial moments coincided with the confusion of rock's shift from the experimentalism of the late 60s to the more corporate and restrictive categories of the 70s. At this time Epic Records were fully behind a man whose ability to cover several musical styles, and appetite for ceaseless touring, made hits a distinct possibility. The solid showing of EDGAR WINTER'S WHITE TRASH (1971) and ROADWORK (1972) in the US charts paved the way for THEY ONLY COME OUT AT NIGHT (1973). The platinum success of this last album was achieved on the back of the eternal "Free Ride" and the grinding jazz/heavy rock instrumental "Frankenstein", which topped the singles chart in the US and gave Edgar his only Top 20 hit in the UK. The track was well titled, being both monstrous in its worldwide sales and freakish as a record.

Winter's mistake, if it can be called that, was to keep on aiming for musical merit, while others found a formula and honed it. Always something of a maverick, Winter collected masses of ideas for each album, and valued his independence. Although Winter could still pull and amaze a crowd, his parting with Epic after SHOCK TREATMENT (1974) signalled the end of his high-profile rock career. With the advent of the New Wave in America at the end of the decade, Winter found himself cut off from the younger college market who had always been a useful source of sales.

By this time, Edgar had rejoined Johnny, releasing TOGETHER in 1976, and started playing music that was truer to his jazz and blues roots. Subsequent releases – on Blue Sky Records and stacked as often as not in the jazz racks – have stuck closely to more traditional musical forms, but have still been notable for moments of invention and all-round musicianship. Against the odds, THE REAL DEAL (1996) united Edgar with Rick Derringer, Jermaine Jackson and Ronnie Montrose in a set that took on the mature rock market as if he'd never been away.

Winter has undoubtedly suffered from the fact that his best work resists pigeonholing. Dropping a needle at random on one of Edgar's Epic albums could give you a few bars that sound like The Beatles, John Coltrane or Vanilla Fudge. Winter was a few years ahead of the field: a maverick with such diverse talents would probably find more outlets and a more loyal audience today. Perversely, as the rock world became an easier place for wayward talents like Edgar, the man himself saw fit to make occasional, lucrative appearances on the US nostalgia circuit, pulling gigs with the likes of Steppenwolf. NOT A KID ANYMORE (1994) saw a brief return to rock sounds, though he has more recently chosen to work largely on film soundtracks.

⊙ **They Only Come Out At Night** (1973; Epic).
Arguably the best of the crop, containing the oddball "Frankenstein", the haunting Dan Hartman-penned ballad "Autumn", and the old standby, "Free Ride".

⊙ **Anthology** (1985; Back Track).
Covering the early 70s, this collects the best rock moments, but, given its reliance on the more commercial parts of the catalogue, it is unrepresentative of the experimental spirit of Edgar's work.

Neil Nixon

JOHNNY WINTER

Born Leland, Mississippi, 1944.

Born boss-eyed and albino, **Johnny Winter** (John Dawson Winter III) disregarded Mother Nature's unkindness to forge a career as one of the few great white blues-rockers. An early band, Johnny And The Jammers, issued the single "Schoolday Blues" in 1959, and Winter continued to play and record in Texan R&B outfits throughout the 60s, often with brother **EDGAR WINTER**. He gained a strong local reputation as a guitarist, commanding a good wage accompanying visiting black blues legends on stage and in the studio. His solo break came while hawking an album he'd recorded with **Red Turner** (drums) and **Tommy Shannon** (bass) for an obscure regional company. A *Rolling Stone* journalist caught wind of it and wrote a celebratory piece, catapulting Winter from local hero to headline status at New York's Scene club and the prestigious Fillmore East.

Coinciding with a compilation of old recordings called THE PROGRESSIVE BLUES EXPERIMENT, Johnny's 'official' debut album, JOHNNY WINTER (1969), was enthusiastically welcomed by the likes of John Lennon and The Rolling Stones, who opened their famous Hyde Park concert with Winter's "I'm Yours And I'm Hers". Each wrote songs for Johnny – "Rock'N'Roll People" and "Silver Train", respectively.

Buoyed by such big-time approbation and his own self-confidence ('In my own mind, I was the best white blues player around,' he said), Winter plunged into an exhausting, if lucrative, schedule on the hard rock circuit. With ex-McCoys **Rick Derringer** (guitar), **Randy Jo Hobbs** (bass) and **Randy Z** (drums), plus Edgar on sax and keyboards, he hit Woodstock and went down a storm. Edgar subsequently left to resume his solo career and Z was replaced by **Bobby Caldwell** for the live JOHNNY WINTER AND (1971), Johnny's biggest seller outside the US. Show stoppers such as "Rock 'N' Roll Hoochie Koo", "Stormy Monday" and Eddie Boyd's exquisite dirge, "Five Long Years", were drawn mostly from Johnny's Texas repertoire and the McCoys' bluesier stuff.

Johnny's increasing dependency on narcotics, and related bouts of suicidal depression, led to long layoffs and a fall in quality on the patchy STILL ALIVE AND WELL (1973) and JOHN DAWSON WINTER III (1974). Disgruntled, Derringer and the others offered their services to the steadier Edgar – who, nevertheless, teamed up with his brother for 1976's workmanlike TOGETHER (mostly soul and old-time rock'n'roll favourites).

This merger made commercial sense, as did Johnny's move to cut back on touring, moving to production duties for Muddy Waters' great comeback albums of the late 70s. Though the past twenty years have not seen much risk-taking by Winter, at least his

EDGAR WINTER ▪ JOHNNY WINTER

steady flow of albums – particularly 1987's Grammy-winning THIRD DEGREE (with Dr. John) and THE RETURN OF JOHNNY GUITAR (2002) – demonstrated that his fretboard dexterity had not deserted him.

⊙ **Second Winter** (1970; Columbia).
This was the lushest fruit of Johnny's liaison with the McCoys – the contrast with the recordings from his Texas apprenticeship and the lacklustre post-1972 efforts could not be more apparent.

⊙ **Johnny Winter And** (1971; Columbia).
Riven with the blistering intensity of Winter and Derringer's duelling guitar work, this atmospheric offering catches Johnny – who always functioned best on stage – at his peak.

⊙ **Live in NYC '97** (1998; Pointblank).
His singing never improved, but boy can he play that thing! Recently elected as the first white guitarist in the Blues Hall Of Fame, JW shows how he earned his place.

Alan Clayson

STEVE WINWOOD

Born Birmingham, England, 1948.

Raised on a diet of big-band and Dixieland jazz, the young **Steve Winwood** was introduced to the world of rock'n'roll by his uncle, before (with brother Muff) kicking off his career with his multi-instrumentalist father's band, The Muff Woody Jazz Band. In the early 60s, they gained a fanatical following in the Midlands, and broadened their repertoire to include R&B covers.

In 1963 the band shared a bill with guitarist Spencer Davis, and later that year the brothers helped him form **THE SPENCER DAVIS GROUP**, in which Stevie's precociously white soul vocals and keyboard prowess featured prominently. Before long, the success of Stevie's songs, notably "Gimme Some Lovin'" and "I'm A Man", encouraged him to extend his range beyond R&B. He did so by forming the ambitious **TRAFFIC** in 1967 and the short-lived 'supergroup' **Blind Faith**, with Eric Clapton and Ginger Baker, in 1969.

JOHN BARLEYCORN MUST DIE (1970) was originally conceived by Winwood as his first solo release, but was issued under the Traffic banner when Jim Capaldi and Chris Wood became involved. Two years on, though, an American Traffic tour was brought to a standstill when Winwood developed peritonitis. During his recovery, his interest in and capability for African percussion led to AIYE-KETA (1973), a collaboration with **Romi Kabaka** and **Abdul Lasisi Amao**, both of whom he had known since Ginger Baker's Air Force project.

After the final Traffic LP, WHEN THE EAGLE FLIES (1974), Winwood retreated to his studio in Gloucestershire, where he began making solo recordings. Meantime, he made session appearances on albums by Toots & The Maytals and Sandy Denny, and guested on GO (1976), an album by Japanese percussionist **Stomu Yamashta**. (By the 80s, Winwood had appeared on LPs by artists as diverse as Marianne Faithfull, John Martyn and Talk Talk.)

STEVE WINWOOD was released in 1977, just as punk was making its mark on Britain, and although the album's opening track, "Vacant Chair", boasted a memorably sparse arrangement, many felt he had tried too hard to re-create his late-60s triumphs. Winwood himself was disappointed with the final results, and insisted on full artistic control and sole instrumental input for ARC OF A DIVER, which was finally issued at the end of 1980. A critical and commercial success, especially in the US, it laid the groundwork for his increasingly high-profile 80s output. It also marked the beginnings of his association with lyricist Will Jennings.

Winwood and Jennings were to reunite on the rather pedestrian TALKING BACK TO THE NIGHT (1982) and the excellent BACK IN THE HIGH LIFE (1986). For the latter album, Winwood recruited top session stalwarts like Joe Walsh, Nile Rodgers, James Taylor and Chaka Khan, in a return to ensemble recording. The change in approach paid off – "Higher Love" topped the US charts in August 1986, and became his biggest British hit since Traffic's "Here We Go Round The Mulberry Bush" in 1967.

BACK IN THE HIGH LIFE was deservedly Winwood's biggest-selling solo album, and he found himself in the unexpected position of publicizing his work through promotional videos and TV appearances. He won two Grammy awards in 1987. The same year, an attractive offer from Virgin meant that a hastily compiled retrospective LP was his swan song for Island. With a solo catalogue of just four albums, CHRONICLES (1987) was a premature and incomplete compilation. Still, a rerecorded version of "Valerie" became a belated hit single, five years after its inclusion on TALKING BACK TO THE NIGHT.

Branson was delighted to have Steve Winwood on board at Virgin, and was doubtless even more so when ROLL WITH IT (1988) emerged. A reinvention of R&B glories from his Spencer Davis Group era, ROLL WITH IT also revisited psychedelic elements from Winwood's Traffic days. It repeated its predecessor's success, and its title track topped the American charts for a month.

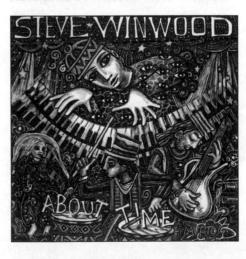

The subdued REFUGEES OF THE HEART (1990) was considerably less successful, but a collaboration with Jim Capaldi on one track – "One And Only Man" – encouraged the pair to resurface briefly as Traffic in 1994.

He returned to the record racks with JUNCTION SEVEN (1997) and trod the promotional trail – for example, appearing at a ghastly star-studded spectacular held at Wembley alongside Rod Stewart, Jon Bon Jovi and a stableful of other AOR dinosaurs. The album smouldered along in a gently psychedelic way without ever really bursting into flames. Winwood's voice showed him to be as startled by the world as ever, even when working through superficially unchallenging material such as the Latin-tinged "Got To Get Back To My Baby" or sweating his stuff to the funkier "Just Wanna Have Some Fun". Stand-out track, though, was his reappraisal of Sly And The Family Stone's "Family Affair", which he treated like a rare and fragile relic.

After a considerable absence, Winwood returned in 2003 with ABOUT TIME, a jazzier collection, released on his own new label, Wincraft Music.

⊙ **Arc Of A Diver** (1980; Island).
Winwood at last well and truly establishes his solo career. The US hit single, "While You See A Chance", is a fine blueprint for his later successes, and the title track's lyric is the unlikely work of Vivian Stanshall.

⊙ **Back In The High Life** (1986; Island).
The epitome of sophisticated mid-80s AOR, as Winwood adds Caribbean and gospel flavours to his pop, rock and R&B mix. The musicianship is as exemplary as ever, while tracks like "Higher Love", "Freedom Overspill" and the title song give the term 'radio-friendly' a good name.

⊙ **The Finer Things** (1993; Island).
This comprehensive four-disc survey traces Winwood's journey from the raw Spencer Davis Group sessions, through his Traffic and Blind Faith projects, to the long-overdue spell of solo stardom.

Justin Lewis

THE WIPERS

Formed Portland, Oregon 1978; still wiping, based in Arizona.

Bands such as Nirvana, Dinosaur Jr. and Sonic Youth have been credited with defining American indie guitar rock from the late 80s through to the early 90s, but they were all indebted in some way to **The Wipers**, one of the Pacific Northwest's all-time greatest bands.

Greg Sage, the band's main driving force (The Wipers comprise Sage plus a varying mix from a host of part-time and temporary members who play bass and drums) laid the foundations in 1978 with the BETTER OFF DEAD EP. The band's hard-edged, bluesy drone riffing and biting lyrical attack rapidly developed into a trademark sound that helped them stand out from the British and US punk packs. Two years after the foundations went down, Sage built the classic LP IS THIS REAL? (1979), a focused blast of late-70s angst.

The band continued to improve with the follow-up, the epic YOUTH OF AMERICA (1981). Six tracks of unbeatable psychedelia-tinged punk, the album showcased Sage's unrelenting grim and moody lyrical world-view (a punk/indie/alt-rock staple) and the disturbing sound he draped it in. OVER THE EDGE (1983) refined the attack of IS THIS REAL? with short, sharp songs that mixed the urgency of punk with the sharp details of the best pop writing. Sage's solo album STRAIGHT AHEAD (1985) was slower, more methodical and more personal, but it still retained an edgy fire.

Sage wandered a strange musical path through his next three records, stumbling upon a stimulating combination of his earlier 'in your face' thrash and more recent slower-paced solo work. This fresh formula was explored through LAND OF THE LOST (1986), FOLLOW BLIND (1987) and THE CIRCLE (1988). Jazzy distorted riffing hadn't sounded this invigorating since Hendrix or Robert Fripp had their heyday. Restless put out a BEST OF album in 1990, just as US indie rock was on the verge of a breakthrough in the shape of Nirvana – whose formula would owe as much to The Wipers' pioneering work as it did to 70s heavy-metal bruisers Black Sabbath. Grunge exploded and The Wipers were offered several top-dollar record contracts along with tour offers from Nirvana themselves.

Both tours and deals were turned down as Greg turned inward and released his most reflective solo work yet, SACRIFICE FOR LOVE (1991). Gently paced at times, it included his first cover ("For Your Love" by The Yardbirds) and seemed out of step with the rest of the scene. When the grunge hype was over in 1994 The Wipers returned with SILVER SAIL (1993), a return to THE CIRCLE's jazzy style of neo-psychedelic thrash.

Although it would be another three years before Sage would return with THE HERD (1996), his continued railing against complacency and constant clarity of vision gives the lie to those who believe indie rock is all tuneless noise and brainless slackerdom. Sage and co offered more evidence in the form of 1999's THE POWER IN ONE, another blazing album of six-string fire, while 2002's BOXSET pulled together remastered versions of IS THIS REAL?, YOUTH OF AMERICA and OVER THE EDGE along with 23 bonus tracks.

⊙ **Youth Of America** (1981; Restless).
Imagine an angrier version of MARQUEE MOON-era Television. Sage's lyrical concerns haven't changed (thank goodness), but the music now takes on a more psychedelic jazzy feel while retaining its fiery edge. An even more impressive classic.

⊙ **Best Of Wipers & Greg Sage** (1990; Restless).
Concise compilation of The Wipers' 80s work (although they should've added something from IS THIS REAL?). The best place to start for any newcomers.

⊙ **The Herd** (1996; Tim/Kerr).
A brilliant return to form for Greg Sage and co. Complacent 'slackerdom' – not just in the youth but in everyone – gets the full dose of his musical/lyrical invective.

Chris Lark

WIRE

Formed London, 1976; disbanded 1980; re-formed
1985; disbanded 1992; re-formed 1999.

"Punk was a confirmation for us of making music in a very simplified form."

In 1977, two of the worst insults you could level at aspiring punk stars were that they were old and that they were former art students. **Wire** were both – and unlike many of their contemporaries they never tried to pretend otherwise.

In early photographs, Wire resembled the kind of geography teachers who wear round-neck sweaters to avoid having to wear a tie – apart from bassist **Graham Lewis**, a glowering presence who appeared to have wandered in mistakenly from a nearby Sham 69 photo session. Original second guitarist **George Gill** left soon after they got going, in August 1976. Of the remaining quartet **Robert Gotobed** (drums) had played in R&B band The Snakes and **Bruce Gilbert** (guitar) had made recordings in 1974 using sound generators borrowed from the Watford College science lab, where he worked as a technician. **Colin Newman** (vocals) and Lewis may not have had any musical experience but they did have great punk aliases – Klive Nice and Hornsey Transfer.

More by luck than intention, their limited musicianship dovetailed neatly with the emergent punk scene. With the words, 'Pay attention, we're Wire', they debuted live at the fabled Roxy in April 1977. The event was recorded, and two tracks, "Lowdown" and "12XU", appeared on EMI's LIVE AT THE ROXY LP. EMI were so impressed (not to mention terrified of being left behind by punk after their recent Sex Pistols debacle) that they signed Wire to their Harvest subsidiary.

The band were teamed with producer Mike Thorne for their first LP, PINK FLAG (1977). From the minimalist sleeve to every one of its 21 concise songs, it was an unadulterated masterpiece. Songs were short because 'when the text ran out, they stopped'. "Mannequin" became their first single, although almost any track from the album would have been as good a choice.

A year and two excellent singles later, Wire released their second album, CHAIRS MISSING (1978). The cover was as stark as the first, but this time the songs were less frantic and more complex. Plus, horror of horrors, Mike Thorne added synthesizers to the mix. Years later, Graham Lewis defined the ethic of the group as being 'to move forward and be progressive'. 'Progressive' was a dangerous word in 1978, especially for a group signed to Pink Floyd's label. Indeed, reviews accused the album of having 'a case of the Floyds'. However, Wire believed that, like all the groups that survived beyond the initial noiseburst of punk, they had to evolve.

The next year was split between recording and touring. By the third LP, 154 (1979), the early aggression had largely been replaced by an almost psychedelic feel. It was followed by "Map Ref 41N93W" (1979), their last single for Harvest. The urge to experiment was strong (a Peel session in September 1979 consisted of one fifteen-minute song, "Crazy About Love") and began to pull band members in different directions. After recording "Our Swimmer" (1981) for Rough Trade and playing a final gig in February 1980, Wire split.

Colin Newman had already been working on his first solo LP, A–Z (1980), and followed with PROVISIONALLY ENTITLED THE SINGING FISH (1981). Gilbert and Lewis teamed up to make a series of, shall we say, unusual records, under such guises as Dome, Duet Emmo, Cupol, P'O, He Said and, remarkably enough, Gilbert And Lewis, over the next few years.

With the solo projects out of their system, Wire were ready to rejoin forces again in the mid 80s. A motive was provided by the Oxford Museum Of Modern Art, who asked the quartet to do a performance piece. They performed as Wire, with all new material, and a new deal was struck with Mute, the first fruits of which, the SNAKEDRILL EP (1986), hinted at the future by mixing pop with dissonance. The band's subsequent 80s output was marked by the combination of Colin Newman's melodic sensibility with Gilbert and Lewis's preference for repetition and 'structuring noise'. Their singles during this period often had a commercial edge and, in 1989, they came very close to a hit with "Eardrum Buzz".

In 1991, Robert Gotobed left to become an organic farmer. Being smartarses, the remaining trio redubbed themselves **Wir**, releasing an album and single (complete with Orb remix) under that name before calling it a day in 1992. After that, their influence on a new generation of British bands gradually become apparent, particularly in Elastica's sampling of their wares. Colin Newman was philosophical on the question of plagiarism, though – 'Every track on

WIRE

PINK FLAG is a recycled rock classic. Done at weird angles, maybe, but I can recognize them.'

Colin Newman then kept himself busy running a techno-ambient label, Swim, while Bruce Gilbert made a hell of a racket as **DJ Beekeeper** at the avant-noise Disobey club; and Graham Lewis began to record as **Halo**.

The original quartet were back together in 1999 for a series of gigs and by 2002 they had released a new mini-album, READ AND BURN VOL.1, and a sequel, READ AND BURN VOL.2; both demonstrated that they were still more than capable of producing abrasive, noisy, punky music. A full-length album, SEND, followed in 2003. Considering how long it had been since Wire were last a functioning unit, and how often such rebirths do little more than sweat nostalgia, it was refreshing to witness a reunion that spawned genuinely cutting-edge music.

⦿ **Pink Flag** (1977; Harvest).
By attempting to get rid of rock's extraneous impurities, Wire were far more punk than any of their contemporaries. Full of art-school humour and wilfully oblique textures, but utterly brilliant.

⦿ **Chairs Missing** (1978; Harvest).
Perhaps not as essential as PINK FLAG, but with songs like "I Am The Fly", "Outdoor Miner" and "French Film Blurred", it is a unique, uncompromising vision of music.

⦿ **154** (1979; Harvest).
This is where the Eno influence comes front and centre. There are some strangely beautiful songs, but there's some pretentious crap, too.

⦿ **Coatings** (1998; WMO).
A two-CD collection comprising John Peel sessions, rarities and a selection of album tracks from their second coming. One disc is entirely taken up with an eighteen-minute version of "Ambitious" – one for the hardcore fan.

⦿ **Send** (2003; Pink Flag).
Compiling cuts from the READ AND BURN releases along with several fresh tracks, SEND is a blistering excursion into a world of layered, distortion-drenched noise and sonic bustle. Mesmerizing.

Glenn Law

WISHBONE ASH

Formed London, 1969.

Wishbone Ash were formed in 1969 from the remnants of Tanglewood, a band managed in the early years by former CIA agent Miles Copeland, later to be manager of his brother Stewart's group, The Police. Their style was based around the twin guitars of **Andy Powell** and **Ted Turner**, who played heavy blues riffs over the rhythm section of **Martin Turner** (bass/vocals) and **Steve Upton** (drums). It was a format that at first restricted them to a well-performed but unmemorable boogie, similar to many British bands of the time, such as Humble Pie. In the musical world of the period, their lack of stage presence, beyond Powell's Flying V guitar, was irrelevant (although in later years it would count against them), and Wishbone Ash became popular throughout the UK club and college circuit, selling respectable numbers

of their first two albums, WISHBONE ASH (1970) and PILGRIMAGE (1971).

In 1973, the band produced their finest hour with their third album, ARGUS. Replete with medieval imagery and titles such as "The King Will Come", "Warrior" and "Throw Down The Sword", and with a cover which showed a knight watching a UFO flying over a Glastonbury-style landscape, it combined folk and hard rock in a fashion that – on a song like "Blowin' Free" – still sounds good today. Wishbone Ash found themselves riding near the top of the UK album charts.

Later the same year the Ash released their follow-up, WISHBONE 4. Extraordinarily, they had returned to their original basic style. Sales were down in the UK, though (oddly) they hit a chord in the US, reaching #12 from more or less nowhere. The record was followed by the then-obligatory live album, LIVE DATES (1974), a recording which appeared to have been made with the microphone hidden in a pillow. At this stage Ted Turner left, disillusioned by the band's lack of direction, and was replaced by **Laurie Wisefield**.

In 1974 the band recorded THERE'S THE RUB, another disappointing album, in Miami. It sold reasonably well, and the existence of a significant number of fans in the US led to the band's decision to become tax exiles. Thereafter they only returned occasionally to the UK, to play at events such as the Reading Festival.

In 1980, after a series of albums which sold adequately in the States but did little in the UK, Turner, the last remaining original member, left and was replaced by **John Wetton** of King Crimson and Roxy Music fame. Later additions were **Trevor Bolder** (bass) – ex-Bowie's Spiders From Mars – who replaced the Asia-bound Wetton, and **Claire Hamill**, formerly of Rick Grech's Square Dancing Machine, but the line-up split after one album.

Strangely, the split in the band and subsequent replacement of Bolder by **Mervyn Spence** gave Wishbone Ash a further lease of life, underlined when the original band reunited and recorded NOUVEAU CALLS (1988), their first all-instrumental album. The band continued to tour and record in the US, apparently content to rest on their laurels until ILLUMINATIONS (1996) appeared, a fine prog-rock album, livened up by the odd drop of funk. It may not have been 1972 any more, but this was a great album for anyone who wished it was. DISTILLATION (1997), the three-CD-box retrospective, was perhaps the ultimate Sword'n'Sorcery set. TRANCE VISIONARY (1998), on the other hand, was a crass attempt by the band to combine prog guitars and dance beats – it was anything but visionary. Thankfully, it was followed by the far more palatable BARE BONES (1999).

Their continued lack of success in the UK was underlined by an abortive tour that began and ended at the Camden Palace because of poor ticket sales. Nevertheless, with new members **Mark Birch** (guitar), **Bob Skeat** (bass and vocals) and **Ray Weston** (drums), their US audiences have yet to tire of them. Archive recordings are frequently released and Martin Turner is himself still on the scene. WALKING THE REEPERBAHN (1999) was one of his better melodic solo albums; it kept his bass playing hand in, just in time for the Thirtieth Anniversary tour.

In 2002 Wishbone Ash released BONA FIDE, having lost Mark Birch and recruited new guitarist **Ben Granfelt**. Though one of their best sets in years, the group again failed to make any ripples on the UK side of the pond.

⊙ **Pilgrimage** (1971; MCA).
If you want to hear what Wishbone Ash have sounded like for 99 percent of their career, this is the best option. It is also available as part of a double album in two different combinations – with their first album or with ARGUS. Don't go for the former.

⊙ **Argus** (1973; MCA).
Available as part of a double-header with PILGRIMAGE, or on its own. This album is not just streets ahead of anything the Ash have ever done; it's another five towns up the motorway. For once, the two guitars work: their harmonies and interplay are excellent, the differences in lead lines crucial to the songs. There isn't a dud track on the album, unless you include "No Easy Road", a bonus track not on the original LP.

Paul O'Brien

JAH WOBBLE

Born London, 1962.

The personality of **Jah Wobble** (aka John Wordle) is a strange mix of East End tough boy and transcendental mystic on a quest for the eternal. His superb musicianship reflects these polarities.

After learning to play on Sid Vicious's bass, Jah Wobble constituted part of the original line-up of John Lydon's **PUBLIC IMAGE LTD.** The music on the first two PiL albums – FIRST ISSUE (1978) and the great METAL BOX (1979) – rested on his raw, dubby bass playing. However, Lydon had him thrown out of PiL for using the latter's rhythm tracks as the basis for his debut solo LP, the punky dub of THE LEGEND LIVES ON... (1980). Lydon needn't have bothered – with Wobble's awful vocals, it sounded like a bid to stop his solo career in infancy.

However, Wobble knew better and went off to Germany, where he made the album FULL CIRCLE (1982) with ex-Can members Jaki Liebezeit and **HOLGER CZUKAY**. Seven tracks of cyclical groove, broken up with found sounds, it was a not-too-distant cousin of Brian Eno and David Byrne's MY LIFE IN THE BUSH OF GHOSTS. With the help of U2's The Edge, the trio also made the ethnically funky mini-album SNAKECHARMER (1983). Both albums previewed, in a more subdued sort of manner, the worldy-dance funk he would create in the 1990s.

Despite such high-profile collaborations, the 80s saw Wobble drift in and out of music, while doing time working on the London Underground. He kept his career more or less alive with sporadic 12" singles and albums, solo and with keyboard player **Ollie Marland**, before returning in earnest with fellow PiL originator Keith Levene and **Gary Clail** for Clail's On-U Sound track "Beef". Lifted from Clail's 1989 LP, END OF THE CENTURY PARTY, it became one of the club anthems of 1990.

In a similar vein, Wobble teamed up with **Justin Adams** and **Andrew Weatherall** (later of The Sabres Of Paradise) on a low-key single release called "Radio Morocco" (1989), on which ethnic sounds were fused with a ground-breaking dub-house groove. The duo came together again for the single "Bomba" (1990), which was released as **Jah Wobble's Invaders Of The Heart**, and featured vocals from Natacha Atlas (later of Trans-Global Underground). The track was a highlight on the Invaders' 1991 album, RISING ABOVE BEDLAM (1991), along with the beautiful (and near-hit) single, "Visions Of You", with lead vocals from Sinéad O'Connor.

For TAKE ME TO GOD (1994), Wobble put together a big touring group with a variety of guest vocalists, including Gavin Friday and British Asian singer **Najma Akhtar**, forging a kind of world-dance-funk along with groups like Trans-Global Underground and Loop Guru. TAKE ME TO GOD hit #13 in the UK charts, and spawned another fine near-hit single in "The Sun Does Rise" (1994), featuring The Cranberries' Dolores O'Riordan.

In addition to work with the Invaders, Wobble has also collaborated in the 90s with The Orb, Primal Scream and Brian Eno, reworking the cerebral one's soundtrack for Derek Jarman's home movies, a project issued as SPANNER (1995).

His 1996 release THE INSPIRATION OF WILLIAM BLAKE, featured Wobble reciting Blake's "Songs Of Innocence And Experience". Shortly after, the Invaders Of The Heart released THE CELTIC POETS (1997), which fed sitar, jazzy brass and synthesizers into the mix in addition to the expected bagpipes. The poets in question were, this time, of the twentieth century such as Shane McGowan and Brendan Kennelly, and the poetry featured worked more on the gut than the spirit. Vocals by **Ronnie Drew** (of Irish folkies The Dubliners) hammer home the words, resulting in a fine, bass-heavy worldy album that merits repeated listening.

For his next outings, JAH WOBBLE PRESENTS THE LIGHT PROGRAMME and REQUIEM (1997), Wobble left the bass at home and concentrated on synthesizer work. Either file under Emerson, Lake & Palmer and ignore, or chirrup with glee at the new prog-rock revival.

Wobble, once again, roped in the estimable voice of Natacha Atlas for UMBRA SUMUS (1998), but neither her presence and nor the soaring vocals of **Amila Sulejmanovic** could spark the excitement this album needed. Wobble devotees will bask in its ambient glory, while the rest of us will fail to understand.

With his own 30 Hertz imprint now well established Wobble went into another burst of creative overdrive, releasing THE FIVE TONE DRAGON (1998) with the harpist **Zi Lan Liao**. It was a peculiar convergence of Oriental instruments and Western orchestration. In 1999, followed the electronically tinged, deep trance amalgam DEEP SPACE, and shortly after came the more successful world-dub collage FULL MOON OVER THE SHOPPING MALL; both of these albums featured the input of long-time cohort **Jaki Leiberzeit**. More albums appeared in 2000 with a second Deep Space set BEACH FERVOUR SPARE – culled from improvised studio sessions reflecting his touring line-up of the time – and MOLAM DUB, Wobble's exploration into the ancient musical tradition of southern Laos. With his label still in its infancy and a whole world of music still waiting to receive the Wobble dub treatment, who's to know what will happen next.

⊙ **Rising Above Bedlam** (1991; Oval/West).
Wobble fuses a worldly funk, heavy on the bass, and featuring Arabic vocals from Natacha Atlas. More than worthwhile for "Bomba" and "Visions Of You" alone.

⊙ **Take Me To God** (1994; Island).
More of the same potent brew, this time featuring a rank of vocal collaborators, plus the tightest drummer in town – Jaki Liebezeit.

⊙ **Molam Dub** (2000; 30 Hertz).
This set finds Wobble filleting the traditional Molam music of southern Laos, with a bass-heavy mix of dancefloor friendly grooves and more ambient extended pieces.

Ross Holloway

THE WOLFGANG PRESS

Formed London, 1983; vanished late 90s.

The **Wolfgang Press**'s music developed from brooding soundscapes to funkier, more swaggering grooves, but while **Mark Cox** (keyboards) and **Andrew Gray** (guitar) allowed various influences to guide them, it was **Michael Allen**'s deadpan almost-spoken baritone that remained the unwavering factor, as did the stylish Alberto Ricci album covers.

The first Press album, THE BURDEN OF MULES (1983), gained some media interest with its doomy post-punk noise, though the band were to get more interesting with the ensuing trio of EPs, starting out with "Scarecrow" (1984), produced by the Cocteau Twins' Robin Guthrie, and followed by "Water" and "Sweatbox" (1985). "Cut The Tree" was also recorded around ths time and surfaced as one of the stand-outs on the 4AD compilation, LONELY IS AN EYESORE (1987).

By 1986 The Press were gaining quite a live following, consolidated by a strong second album, STANDING UP STRAIGHT (1986). This showed the band at their starkest: side one was particularly tormented, with the insistent "Dig A Hole" and the ice-cold drama of "My Life" and "Hammer The Halo".

With BIRDWOOD CAGE (1988), the mood changed somewhat, especially on the album's flag-ship single, "King Of Soul", which showed an absorption in dance/funk styles, and the follow-up, "Kansas", a record that gained much-overdue airplay for the group, partly owing to its memorable video. An unusual reworking of Three Dog Night's "Mama Told Me Not To Come" then preceded the release of QUEER (1991), an album inspired by De La Soul's THREE FEET HIGH AND RISING. Said Allen: 'It seemed such a joyous record. There was a freshness and ease about the way it was made that inspired us to reassess our working process.'

Although atmospheric, QUEER was but an incomplete blueprint for the band's strongest release, the engaging FUNKY LITTLE DEMONS (1995), in which they completed the transition from purveyors of austere commitment to proponents of a more positive musical ideal. This fine record's stand-out cuts included the single "Going South" – the closest the group ever came to a hit – the self-deprecating "Eleven Years" and the darkly syncopating "Blood Satisfaction". Shortly before the album was released, however, Cox went quiet and little more was heard from the band other than a retrospective EVERYTHING IS BEAUTIFUL (2001). Post Wolfgang Press, Gray has been working on a new project, **Limehouse Outlaw**.

As a bizarre footnote, one of The Press's fans was Welsh heart-throb Tom Jones, who covered their 1992 single, "A Girl Like You", commissioned the band to write the song "Show Me Some Devotion", and even joined them on stage at a gig in Los Angeles.

⊙ **Funky Little Demons** (1995; 4AD).
Not all 4AD bands sound the same. The Wolfgang Press manage to incorporate ideas fom hip-hop and dance into their glacial soundscapes.

Jeremy Simmonds

THE WOLFHOUNDS

Formed Essex, England, 1985; disbanded 1990.

The **Wolfhounds** evolved from garage band The Changelings, hitting the London trash scene with a frenzied live act and a socially conscious attitude. The original line-up of **David Callahan** (vocals), **Paul Clark** (guitar), **Andy Golding** (guitar), **Andy Bolton** (bass guitar) and **Frank Stebbing** (drums) was first picked up by the Pink label, which released the CUT THE CAKE EP in 1986. As confusing as it was thrilling, it contained two tracks of seering Birthday Party-ish intensity, the throwaway guitar pop of the title song, and the scratchy, atmospheric "Another Hazy Day On The Lazy 'A' ". On the strength of this outing, The Wolfhounds became involved in the *NME*'s C86 events – a cassette compilation and week of gigs promoting new British indie bands. The group's sneering, angular rock went against the grain of C86's hedonism and wackiness, but they still benefited from the exposure.

"The Anti-Midas Touch", a catchy thrash, helped cement The Wolfhounds' growing reputation, as did the follow-ups, "Cruelty" and "Me". But the debut LP, UNSEEN RIPPLES FROM A PEBBLE, was a disappointment. The songs were unable to survive the extended format, and the crackle of their live act was absent.

A year, a label change and a reshuffle (bassist **David Oliver** and guitarist **Matthew Deighton** replaced Bolton and Clark) later, The Wolfhounds re-emerged with their most-realized recording to date, "Son Of Nothing". The sound had become denser and darker, more in tune with Callahan's lyrics, but still melodically sharp. Two more singles, "Rent Act" and "Happy Shopper", ushered in a fresh period of creativity, and the LP which followed, BRIGHT AND GUILTY (1989), remains their crowning achievement. The Wolfhounds showed off the influences of 60s pop, punk and European avant-garde rock, while singing about homelessness, consumerism and apathy – an unfashionable approach in 1989. Later the same year, the mini-album BLOWN AWAY charted new territory, exploring a noisier sound, reminiscent of Sonic Youth. The highlight was the title track, a near-perfect collision of instinctive pop and roaring discord.

The Wolfhounds released ATTITUDE (1990) while on the verge of splitting up, and their disillusionment coloured the majority of the songs. Callahan's vocals seemed to be in direct competition with the aircraft howl of the music, which was increasingly uncompromising and uncomfortable. Callahan went on to form the experimental **Moonshake**, and Golding and Stebbing eventually joined forces in **Crawl**.

⊙ **The Essential Wolfhounds** (1988; September).
A compilation of the early Pink recordings, charting The Wolfhounds' development from garage band to skilled, world-weary pop combo.

⊙ **Bright And Guilty** (1989; Midnight Music).
Including "Son Of Nothing", "Rent Act" and "Happy Shopper", this was the album that should have catapulted the group to fame.

⊙ **Blown Away** (1989; Midnight Music).
The logical conclusion: a wall of noise whose mini-LP format ensures it never outstays its welcome.

James Robert

STEVIE WONDER

Born Saginaw, Michigan, May 13, 1950.

From the breathless, infectious pop of "Fingertips" and "Uptight (Everything's Alright)" through the funk militancy of "Superstition" and "Higher Ground" and on to the MOR of "I Just Called To Say I Love You", **Stevie Wonder**'s career encapsulates the rise and fall of the Motown aesthetic. It's a journey that parallels the hope, anger and resignation that followed in the wake of the civil rights movement.

Steveland Judkins Morris began his lengthy career when he joined his mother and siblings in the choir at Whitestone Baptist Church in their home town of Saginaw. At the age of 10, proficient on piano, harmonica and drums, Stevie teamed up with John Glover, who soon afterwards recommended him to his cousin, Ronnie White of The Miracles. In turn, White contacted label boss Berry Gordy and told him about this exceptional young talent. Thus, in early 1962, did Morris become known as 'Little Stevie Wonder' and release his debut single, "I Call It Pretty Music (But The Old People Call It The Blues)", featuring one Marvin Gaye on drums. The next year came "Fingertips" (1963), an upbeat harmonica instrumental that topped the Billboard charts, as did the full-length live LP THE 12 YEAR OLD GENIUS (1963).

By 1966, Stevie Wonder was no longer 'Little', but was caught in a difficult teenage phase where marketing and maintaining his early successes was problematic. However, "Uptight (Everything's Alright)" (1966), a driving up-tempo number said to have been inspired by The Stones' "Satisfaction", rapidly became an airplay favourite. The accompanying album of the same title displayed for the first time Wonder's growing social conscience with a cover of Dylan's "Blowin' In The Wind". For the rest of the 60s, Wonder continued along the same path, balancing an inspired pop sensibility with a liberal social vision.

When Holland-Dozier-Holland broke up their songwriting partnership, Wonder's compositional talent became vital to Motown's chart success. His writing partnership with producer Henry Cosby scored several hits, including "I Was Made To Love Her" (1967), "A Place In The Sun" (1966) and "My Cherie Amour" (1969). During this time Wonder also co-wrote "Tears Of A Clown" with Smokey Robinson and wrote "It's A Shame" for The Spinners.

In 1971, now aged 21, he received his childhood earnings – only to discover that he was entitled to just $1 million out of $30 million. Understandably keen to gain more control over his career, Wonder formed his own publishing companies, Taurus Productions and Black Bull. Marvin Gaye had already wrested artistic control from Gordy, and Wonder followed suit.

Clearly learning from Gaye and Sly And The Family Stone, Wonder produced an album that went far beyond the singles-with-filler formula. MUSIC OF MY MIND (1972), recorded with synthesizer specialists Robert Margouleff and Malcolm Cecil, marked his emergence as a serious album artist who wrote, arranged, performed and produced most of his work. A series of increasingly sophisticated LPs brought a broadening of his appeal – he supported The Stones on a fifty-date tour in the summer of 1972 and later that year joined John and Yoko in a benefit concert at Madison Square Garden.

Wonder's next single, the astonishing "Superstition" (originally written for rock guitarist

Jeff Beck), went straight to #1 in the States in 1972, a year marked by tense race relations, Watergate and the closing phase of the Vietnam War; its 'trust no one' message fitted the times perfectly. It was one of a feast of new compositions on TALKING BOOK (1972), which blended the tough funk of "Superstition" with ballads like "Blame It On The Sun" and "You Are The Sunshine Of My Life".

INNERVISIONS (1973) went one step further. Despite gorgeous songs like "Don't You Worry 'Bout A Thing" and "Golden Lady", and the anthemic "Higher Ground", the centrepiece was the awesome "Living For The City", a seven-minute epic about the perils of the ghetto. Days before its release in August 1973, Wonder was involved in a near-fatal car accident while on tour in North Carolina. He suffered multiple head injuries and spent several days in a coma, and cruelly added the loss of sense of smell to that of his sight.

INNERVISIONS won four Grammys in 1974, a feat repeated the following year with the release of FULFILLINGNESS' FIRST FINALE (1974) which featured the furious anti-Nixon diatribe, "You Haven't Done Nothin", on which he was backed by The Jackson Five. Now one of the most acclaimed and commercially successful songwriters and performers of the age, Wonder was honoured by the city of Los Angeles, who declared that November 22, 1974 would be 'Stevie Wonder Day'.

The double LP, SONGS IN THE KEY OF LIFE (1976), maintained Wonder's remarkable level of consistency, and even with a high retail price stormed to the top of the charts on both sides of the Atlantic. As well as soul-funk hits like "Another Star", "I Wish" and the jazz-inflected "Sir Duke", it featured "Pastime Paradise", a song covered almost twenty years on by rapper Coolio on his 1995 hit "Gangsta Paradise". However, "Isn't She Lovely", which opened the second half of the album, a song dedi-

cated to his newborn daughter, hinted that a shift to MOR wasn't far away.

Wonder's second consecutive double LP, JOURNEY THROUGH THE SECRET LIFE OF PLANTS (1979), was an aimless disappointment, dominated by meandering instrumentals, and peppered with a few pointless vocal breaks. HOTTER THAN JULY (1980) was a reasonable return to form and was especially popular in the UK, where it achieved Top 10 singles for the Bob Marley tribute, "Masterblaster (Jammin')", the ballad "Lately" and the eulogy to Martin Luther King, "Happy Birthday". Wonder for a long time refused to issue the last as a single in the US, but relented in 1986 when King's birthday was declared a holiday in the majority of US states.

However, Wonder's political activism couldn't mask the fact that his music was growing less appealing. THE ORIGINAL MUSIQUARIUM (1982) gathered together a second decade of hits plus three new tracks, but it coincided with the trite duet with Paul McCartney "Ebony And Ivory". Similar (admittedly highly effective) MOR fare was to follow in 1984 with "I Just Called To Say I Love You", extracted from the soundtrack to the dire Gene Wilder movie, *The Woman In Red*.

Wonder has only released four albums since then – IN SQUARE CIRCLE (1985), CHARACTERS (1987), JUNGLE FEVER (1991; the soundtrack from Spike Lee's movie) and CONVERSATION PEACE (1995) – which all hinted at the magic of old. Wonder remains a magnetic live performer, but it would appear that his most creative days are behind him. There would be few things better in music than if he proves us all wrong.

◉ **The Essential Stevie Wonder (**1987; Motown).
Even before he gained creative control, Stevie Wonder's first decade of recordings show an artist brimming with musical agility and stylistic innovation. This excellent two-disc retrospective contains just about all of his best-known 60s and 70s output, and sets the stage for subsequent delights.

◉ **Talking Book** (1972; Motown).
Wonder's first classic LP, this predominantly downbeat but dazzling set is packed full of top tunes including "You Are The Sunshine Of My Life", "I Believe (When I Fall In Love With You It Will Be Forever)" and, of course, "Superstition".

◉ **Innervisions** (1973; Motown).
A near-flawless mix of the personal and the political. "Higher Ground" and "Living For The City" are obvious standouts, but the exuberant "Don't You Worry 'Bout A Thing", "Golden Lady" and "He's Misstra Know It All" are first-rate examples of pop-soul.

◉ **Songs In The Key Of Life** (1976; Motown).
Wonder at his most inventive and melodic, ranging through the superior balladry of "Love's In Need Of Love Today" and "Knocks Me Off My Feet", through the punchy jazzy instrumentals of "Contusion" and "Sir Duke".

◉ **Original Musiquarium** (1982; Motown).
An indispensable, if expensive, singles collection spanning the peaks of the 70s and early 80s.

◉ **Song Review** (1996; Motown).
A more recent compilation available in two forms: a rather scrappy UK single-disc edition with the emphasis on the MOR end of the Wonder catalogue, or a US double set, which more accurately reflects his remarkably varied career.

Justin Lewis

THE WONDER STUFF

Formed Stourbridge, England, 1986; disbanded 1994; re-formed 2000.

Combining shagginess and funkiness like no one since War, **The Wonder Stuff** quickly became all the rage in the UK and almost as quickly flamed out after failing to conquer the rest of the world. **Miles Hunt** (guitar/vocals), **Malcolm Treece** (guitars), ex-Mighty Lemon Drop **Martin Gilks** (drums) and Rob Jones aka **The Bass Thing** (bass) joined forces after responding to an ad placed by wannabe drummer Hunt, vowing to become as big as local scene-setters Pop Will Eat Itself. The name came from Hunt, whose dad had been a friend of John Lennon: the infant Miles running around the house had prompted Lennon to utter the words 'Your boy sure has the wonder stuff'. The band spent time propping up Pop Will Eat Itself at the Stourbridge Irish Centre until The Bass Thing won some money on the horses in February 1987 and invested in recording a single, an unremarkable piece of sludge called "It's Not True". Six months later, another single, "Unbearable", was released on stomach-churning pink and green vinyl. *Record Mirror* spun it enough times to make it their 'indie' *Single of the Year*, though it was released by the major label Polygram.

Though they still found themselves supporting worthless bands in Britain's dives, The Wonder Stuff's sights were set on stadiums. Subsequent singles aimed for the anthemic jugular, and Hunt was always on the lookout for media attention, whether through his rabble-rousing on the road or his snarling lyrics. Both worked, and a devoted following began to jell, sending the band's thrashy 1988 debut album, THE EIGHT LEGGED GROOVE MACHINE, and its sardonic single, "It's Yer Money I'm After Baby", hurtling into the UK Top 40.

Hunt defined the band with catchy anti-industry rants such as "Astley In The Noose", available on the US CD pressing of GROOVE MACHINE, and "Radio Ass Kiss", a vicious rocker found on 1989's HUP, the second album. This featured new member **Martin Bell** (fiddle/mandolin/other stringed instruments), but was centred on a wah-wah guitar sound. HUP rode the hit "Don't Let Me Down Gently" into the UK Top 10 and allowed The Wonder Stuff to trade in nights of falling down in pubs for days of soaking in jacuzzis. The Bass Thing wasn't quite ready for such success, and he left in 1990 after the group's disco baptism on "Circlesquare". He formed a jazz combo in New York, but died in 1993. The Wonder Stuff replaced him with **Paul Clifford** in 1991.

That same year they recorded NEVER LOVED ELVIS, home of the disco-floor-filling hit "Size Of A Cow". The rest of the album disappointed, but they audaciously hit it big with the non-album single "Dizzy". A deconstruction of the 60s bubblegum pop song, it went #1 in the UK, fronted by the bellow of comedian **Vic Reeves**.

The band remained bolshy, abandoning a European tour and skipping the 1992 Brit Awards – they played Minthorpe High School instead. Tired of trying to break in America, they became even more discouraged after CONSTRUCTION FOR THE MODERN IDIOT (1993) failed to impinge on a Suede-fed British consciousness. A farewell gig at the 1994 Phoenix Festival and it was all over – at least for the rest of the 90s. Hunt went on to a brief stint as an MTV Europe VJ before forming the group **Vent**, while the others became **weknowwhereyoulive**, but this outfit eventually fizzled out without achieving anything of note. LIVE FROM MANCHESTER (1995) kept the Stuffies' memory alive for a while but Hunt put any possibility of re-forming firmly on the back burner while he pursued a solo career, of sorts. He wrote a brace of songs and started working with Treece again, the result being a successful American tour during the summer of 1998 and the albums MILES ACROSS AMERICA and BY THE TIME I GOT TO JERSEY (both 1998). His first solo album proper, HAIRY ON THE INSIDE, emerged in 1999.

By this point, it seemed that the band were ready to take the live plunge once again and they reunited to play five sold-out shows at *The Forum* in London, an immensely successful Christmas-time knees-up that coincided with Polydor's double-CD anthology, LOVE BITES AND BRUISES (2000). The double live album CURSED WITH INSINCERITY (2001) documented this monumental event in the Stuffies' universe.

Hunt released his second outing, THE MILES HUNT CLUB, in 2002, but whether a new Wonder Stuff album is in the pipeline remains to be seen.

⊙ If The Beatles Had Read Hunter ... The Singles (1994; Polygram).
Most of The Stuff's albums are incoherent affairs. Savour instead this splendid collection of hits and oddities, sung from a mountaintop with a pint in the hand and a tear in the eye.

Charles Bottomley

WORLD DOMINATION ENTERPRISES

Formed London, England, 1987.

In the early 80s, when punk was represented by Adam And The Ants and only the hardcore underground remained faithful to the original ideal, **Keith Dobson** was instrumental in setting up the Fuck Off cassette label, a provocatively titled outfit dedicated to releasing similarly provocative music, including Dobson's own outfit, **012**. From out of this scene, based in London's Ladbroke Grove, arose **World Domination Enterprises**, an unlikely band that appeared to be a disparate collection of conflicting parts. Dobson, playing a guitar allegedly strung with cheese wire and tuned by Satan himself, was joined by dub bassist **Steve Jameson** and drummer **Digger Metters**. From playing proto-raves organized by the original crusty-spawning squatting and arts collective, the Mutoid Waste Company, to headlining CND benefits and gracing the cover of *Melody Maker*, World Dom enjoyed a brief spell as the next big thing.

Mixing dub-influenced vocals, bass and drums with a scratching guitar, World Dom crossed and fused genres at a time when that 90s cliché – 'there's always been a dance element to our music' – had yet to be heard from the staunchly *guitarista* indie community. Their sonic assault was coupled with a heartfelt anti-corporate political message, as seen in their first single, the anti-pollution song, "Asbestos Lead Asbestos" (012's back catalogue anthem). A one-day busking tour of major corporate headquarters in London was captured for posterity by BBC2's *Snub* – and their first long player, LET'S PLAY DOMINATION (1988), spliced deep dub (U-Roy's "Jah Jah Call You") with more upbeat material ("Hotsy Girl" – a paean to their long-suffering Morris Minor van). Other covers included Lipps Inc.'s "Funkytown", complete with steel drums, and an inspired take on L.L. Cool J's "(I Can't Live Without My) Radio", which was remixed into something approximating genuine hip-hop. The whole album itself was dubbed, remixed, interfered with and released as DUB DOMINATION (1988) shortly afterwards.

Live on stage, World Dom were an altogether different prospect, allowing each instrument to let rip away from the confines of vinyl. The burgeoning noise scene at the tail end of the 80s offered tours with Loop and Godflesh as well as prestigious supports for Pussy Galore and a tour of the former Soviet Union. Fans were captivated by Dobson's haphazard, flailing approach to guitar playing – he claimed never to tune his guitar and his seemingly random slashings made Pussy Galore look like Wishbone Ash.

The band attempted to capture some of their live power with their second album, the haphazard LOVE FROM LEAD CITY (1989). With production from Dave Allen (who 'coaxed the performance of my life from me', according to Dobson), half the vinyl-only release, which was made to look like a bootleg, was dedicated to incendiary live takes of their best tunes.

In 1989, after the eastern bloc escapade, Digger quit, deciding that the band was incompatible with his Jehovah's Witness beliefs. Gamely, Dobson and Jameson struggled through a tour, but the replacement drummer was overawed by the challenge and performances were noticeably more muted. To the fans' horror, Dobson was even wielding a new guitar.

The end was inevitable but the final single, "Company News" (1989), with its grinding drum'n'bass and trademark guitar squalls was perhaps their finest moment, backed with a characteristically terse and jarring cover of Little Richard's rock'n'roll standard, "Tutti Frutti".

Coming too early to benefit from the widespread acceptance of remixes and new technology, World Domination Enterprises straddled the divide between indie and commercial in a way that seems almost unthinkable today. Influential, but never successfully imitated, they are fondly remembered by all who loved them.

⊙ **Let's Play Domination** (1988; Product Inc.).
Snap this gem up at any price. One guitar has never sounded quite so tortured and the dub bass is low down and perfectly synchronized with the pounding drums.

Jonathan Bell

WORLD PARTY

Formed London, 1986.

Prestatyn-born **Karl Wallinger** took the long and winding road to his virtual one-man band **World Party**. His musical career started in 1976 with Quasimodo, a group featuring eventual founding members of The Alarm, and Wallinger subsequently drifted in and out of go-nowhere acts until hooking up with **THE WATERBOYS** in 1983, making major contributions, songwriting and playing keyboards, to their critically acclaimed A PAGAN PLACE (1984) and breakthrough, THIS IS THE SEA (1985). However, he was edgy without creative control – and with Mike Scott as The Waterboys' definitive personality, this wasn't in the offing.

Wallinger eventually broke with the band in 1986, Scott commenting 'He was pregnant with World Party'. Gestation took a year, the single "Ship Of Fools" being released in February 1987, a memorable near-hit of a song, espousing an environmental tract to a strong pop melody. It eventually reached a wider audience by appearing on the GREENPEACE – RAINBOW WARRIORS (1989) benefit album.

On PRIVATE REVOLUTION (1987), the World Party debut album released a month after the single, Wallinger wrote, sang, produced and played almost every instrument (Sinéad O'Connor provided additional vocals). A mixed bag of early Prince (the title track), Lennon, Stones and Dylan (a cover of "All I Really Want To Do"), it had an underlying environmental theme, with the Party's all-in-it-together manifesto summed up in the chorus of "World

Party": 'World party – how can you say no? Go to the World party tonight'.

Wallinger then pretty well disappeared for a few years, though he returned O'Connor's favour with a guest turn on her album THE LION AND THE COBRA. He spent most of his time piecing together the stunning GOODBYE JUMBO (1990), on which he once again wore many hats, but this time surrounded himself with session musicians **Guy Chambers** (keyboards), **Jeff Trott** (guitar) and **Chris Whitten** (drums). Harder rocking, with a strange album cover of Wallinger in elephant ears and a gas mask, GOODBYE JUMBO captured the public's imagination far more than its predecessor had. It also caught some criticism for its liberal borrowings: the whoops on "Way Down Now" (a stand-out track) sounded a tad too much like "Sympathy For The Devil"; 'Hey Mr Postman, look and see if there's a letter in your bag for me', from "When The Rainbow Comes", was lifted straight from The Marvelettes. Nonetheless, it was potent pop stuff.

The Thank You World EP followed in 1991, combining remixes, a few new songs and a cover of The Beatles' "Happiness Is A Warm Gun", a filler until BANG! arrived in 1993. This new album was more of a team effort, co-produced by rock veteran Steve Lillywhite and listing **Chris Sharrock** and **Dave Caitlin-Birch** as fully fledged members of the band. It was also Wallinger's biggest commercial success, hitting #2 in the UK. Though containing more fodder for those critical of Wallinger's 'influences' ("Sunshine" drew on "Wild Horses"), the stylistic experimentalism, from power rock to minimalist pop, never infringed on Wallinger's convictions. 'And God said, "Look after the planet"' bellows an opera singer. 'But man said, "Fuck you!"'

EGYPTOLOGY (1997), the fourth WP album, trod the same familiar path; gorgeous Beatles-edged pop melodies wrapping up a touch of environmental concern here, a broken heart there. Stand-out track "She's The One" was pure unabashed sentimentalism and none the worse for that. A fifth Lennon-ish installment followed with DUMBING UP (2000), though Wallinger was by then probably more than happy to put his feet up, having provided Robbie Williams with the song "She's The One", with which he had a massive hit.

⊙ **Private Revolution** (1987; Ensign).
A sign of things to come, containing the excellent "Ship Of Fools" and "All Come True" amid much splendid retro fare.

⊙ **Goodbye Jumbo** (1990; Ensign).
Never did the apocalypse sound so melodic. The album that announced the 90s – or worse – while keeping the melodies flowing.

Chris Wright

LINK WRAY

Born Dunn, North Carolina, May 2, 1929.

There are those who claim that **Link Wray** invented heavy metal, an accusation based on

Guitarists' guitarist, Link Wray

his 1958 million-seller "Rumble", an intense, moody guitar instrumental. This brilliantly simple track has influenced everyone from The Kinks down to PJ Harvey, and it set the essential Link Wray style – rather than a lead line, Wray favoured a slow drag across distorted strings in an elementary chord progression. Though he was capable of more dextrous playing, Wray was a visionary who understood that, in rock, simplicity was best. Record company hype at the time pushed the story that the track was intended to capture the feel of a gang fight. In truth though, Wray, a rural Native American, had no intention to glorify such an urban pastime; the tune had been improvised at a 1956 sock hop and the title itself suggested by the young daughter of a local record store. In a fit of credulous righteousness, the song was banned, proving there is such a thing as bad publicity after all.

Following the success of "Rumble", Wray milked the formula for some years – notably on "Jack The Ripper" and "The Shadow Knows" – before the more melodic instrumental styles of Duane Eddy and The Ventures made him sound primitive and dated. He then abruptly shrank from the spotlight, publicly renouncing music in 1965 to become a farmer.

Fortunately Wray continued to record in the three-track he had built on his farm, and in 1971 he produced the glorious LINK WRAY. A blend of country, gospel and blues, it presented the kind of trans-American vision that critics have long claimed to be the property of The Band, but surpassed even their best work. The song titles occasionally sounded like old-time Link Wray – "Crowbar", "Black River Swamp" – but there was no other connection with his earlier incarnation. Though a lung condition had always precluded too much singing, here he let loose, revealing a hoarse, beautiful voice that creaked with authority. The effect was almost that of the land itself speaking.

A second album from the same sessions, BEANS AND FATBACK, was released by Virgin in 1973, though, like LINK WRAY, it was roundly ignored by the public. A couple of early-70s albums on Polydor also failed to connect, and Wray again faded from view.

In the late 70s, **Robert Gordon**, erstwhile singer for New York punks The Tuff Darts, brought Wray out of retirement for his new rock'n'roll revival project. Link played on two excellent albums and even toured with Gordon a bit, keeping his back to the audience in an effort to keep the focus on Gordon. Wray has also been rediscovered by The Cramps and their fellow psychobillies, though among knowledgeable musicians he has never needed any introduction.

He continues to record to this day, the latest offerings being SHADOWMAN (1997), a gloriously fiery live set WALKING DOWN A STREET CALLED LOVE (1997), and BARBED WIRE (2000), a varied album featuring both band material and Link playing solo. Being over 70 years of age obviously isn't going to stop him.

⊙ **Link Wray** (1971; Polydor).
The other side of Link Wray: from Willie Dixon's "Trail Dragger" to the earnest "Take Me Home Jesus", this album is absolutely faultless.

⊙ **Mr Guitar** (1995; Norton).
A double CD collecting the classic tracks that made his reputation. He sounds like a man with a Tarantino movie playing in his head.

Alwyn W. Turner

WRECKLESS ERIC

Born Newhaven, England, 1950.

In late 1976, **Eric Goulden** popped a cassette into an envelope and sent it to Stiff Records, the then-burgeoning independent label for all things maverick. The accompanying note began, with some honesty, 'I'm the sort of ★★★★ who sends tapes to record companies'. It was this commendable directness which, Stiff boss Dave Robinson later admitted, won him over to Goulden's cause. The former odd-job man came down to London, signed to Stiff and was given a new name that reflected both the spirit of the times and Goulden's own ramshackle demeanour; thus **Wreckless Eric** was born.

The original plan was to launch the careers of Wreckless and Stiff label-mate Elvis Costello in tandem by way of a shared album featuring seven songs by each artist, an idea abandoned due to Costello already having far more songs in the bag. Still, by the time Wreckless's debut single, "Whole Wide World" (1977), was released, anything on Stiff was guaranteed wide exposure in the music press, and the song, produced by Nick Lowe, deserved it – with its barbed-wire vocals atop a simple yet mesmeric arrangement somewhere between Dr. Feelgood and Duane Eddy. In the autumn of 1977, Wreckless toured for the first time as part of the legendary 'Stiff Live Stiffs' tour, alongside Costello, Lowe, Ian Dury and Larry Wallis. It was on this tour that his notorious fondness for drink was first noted.

His 1978 debut album, WRECKLESS ERIC, made a brief appearance in the UK Top 50. However, when the second Stiff package tour rolled around, Costello and Dury were bona fide stars and it felt as if Wreckless, though travelling between gigs on the train Stiff had hired for the tour, had somehow been left at the station. His second album, THE WONDERFUL WORLD OF WRECKLESS ERIC was, however, a more satisfying proposition than his debut, developing his patent hybrid of punk and pop with a 50s sensibility on tracks like "Walking On The Surface Of The Moon" and the lusty "I Wish It Would Rain".

Without the big breakthrough, Wreckless made a determined effort to write in a more commercial style, which resulted in out-and-out bubblegum like "Hit And Miss Judy" (1979), another heavily promoted but not-quite-hit single, and the forced "A Pop Song" (1980), a lament about the need to write a successful one. These songs appeared on the drily titled BIG SMASH (1980), which was issued as a double set, the second disc being a 'best of' collection. Despite these efforts of art and marketing, success refused to beckon and Eric dropped out of sight for five years. Apart from very occasional live sightings, the only action was, bizarrely, Cliff Richard covering "Broken Doll", from BIG SMASH.

In 1985, as Eric Goulden, our man signed to New Rose Records and released A ROOMFUL OF MONKEYS, aided by various members of The Blockheads, thus renewing the Stiff connection. This album was smartly followed by the formation of **The Len Bright Combo**, who recorded an eponymous album in 1986. Commercially the story was as before; this band dissolved and Wreckless decamped to France. Life there was much to his liking but he also found time to form **Le Beat Group Electrique**, with bassist **André Barreau** and drummer **Catfish Truton**. They continued to perform and record together, on and off, producing albums LE BEAT GROUP ELECTRIQUE (1989), AT THE SHOP (1990) and THE DONOVAN OF TRASH (1991). The latter albums were recognizably Wreckless products, now with a semi-acoustic whimsy sometimes suggestive of Jonathan Richman.

Though he is currently busy writing a book, Eric still occasionally tours, usually solo with his guitar. In a less pressurized (and more sober) context he has proved himself an unexpectedly fine raconteur and between-song storyteller, winning back part of his old audience but, as ever, never quite breaking through to a new one.

⊙ **Big Smash** (1980; Stiff).
Recommended primarily for the inclusion of a 'best of' selection, featuring tracks from the first two albums and a couple of rarities. The CD reissue strangely omits his best-loved song, "Whole Wide World".

Peter Mills

ROBERT WYATT

Born Bristol, England, January 28, 1945.

"You may notice some technical inadequacies in some of my performances – a hesitant beat here, a dodgy note there – these are of course entirely deliberate and reproduced as evidence of my almost painful sincerity."

It's hard to think of a rock musician who can interpret songs better than **Robert Wyatt** – a singer who so clearly thinks about the chords, the harmonies, the rhythms, the words, and who goes in there with such emotional energy. It's these qualities, and the man's transparent integrity and generosity of spirit, that instils such love among his followers and fellow musicians. All the more shame, then, that his is a talent so quietly expressed in rock's extrovert world. Not that he's shied away from recording. If you are yet to discover Wyatt, you have a thirty-year trove to explore. Start with some of the songs for which he's (relatively) best known, Elvis Costello's "Shipbuilding" or Peter Gabriel's "Biko", say, and listen to them alongside the writers' versions. And then try Wyatt's own stuff. The singing, with its conversational cadences, is something of an acquired taste, but it's addictive, and entirely original.

For the earliest Wyatt song, you need to go way back, prior to **SOFT MACHINE**, when Wyatt used to do James Brown medleys in The Wilde Flowers, the Canterbury group that set the whole Caravan/Softs scene in motion. Wyatt was also famed around this time for 'singing' note-perfect renditions of 1940s Charlie Parker solos, a voice-as-instrument technique that was to surface on the early Soft Machine albums, alongside much other pop-jazz quirkiness, and mature in his own later work.

Wyatt spent five years with Soft Machine, which he co-founded. He brought an avant-garde jazz sensibility to the group, for whom he drummed and – on the first three albums – composed songs and vocalized. By the time of the instrumental SOFTS 4 (1971), he was out of sympathy with the group's fusion style and, as he tells it, was kicked out. He had in fact already recorded his swan song in the side-long "Moon In June" suite on the Softs' THIRD

album, a tour de force of improvised drumming and singing, and had in 1970 recorded his first solo album, END OF AN EAR. This experimental jazz set was notable mainly for "To Caravan And Brother Jim", on which he set up a drone-like rhythm with his voice – something he'd return to often in his career. Wyatt also did the first of many guest sessions during this period, drumming for Syd Barrett (the early Softs often played with Pink Floyd) on THE MADCAP LAUGHS, and gigging with ex-Softs colleague **KEVIN AYERS'** band, The Whole World.

After the Softs' split, Wyatt set about forming a new band, retaining David Sinclair (ex-**CARAVAN**) from END OF AN EAR, alongside a to-be-frequent collaborator, **Bill MacCormick** (bass) and **Phil Miller** (guitar). The band was named **Matching Mole** – a pun on 'Soft Machine' in French – and produced two albums. MATCHING MOLE (1972) is remembered primarily for "O Caroline", still Wyatt's most affecting love song, co-written with David Sinclair. MATCHING MOLE'S LITTLE RED RECORD (1972), with **Dave McCrae** replacing Sinclair, Robert Fripp producing, and Eno guesting on VCS3, yielded two extraordinary voice pieces in "Gloria Gloom" and "God Song", immediate stand-outs amid rather prog-rockish instrumentals. Heralding future political directions, the band were depicted on the cover in Maoist garb and revolutionary pose.

Matching Mole disbanded shortly after the RED RECORD and Wyatt turned to composing a solo project, concentrating more on his voice. This was the basis of 1974's startling ROCK BOTTOM, but in the event the album's development was horrendously traumatic. In June 1973, drunk at a party, Wyatt fell from a fourth-floor window, breaking his back. He emerged permanently confined to a wheelchair.

By the end of the year, though, he was back at work, guesting on vocals with Hatfield and the North, formed by Phil Miller and other old Canterbury friends, while Pink Floyd and Soft Machine helped him out financially with a benefit at London's Rainbow. Then in early 1974 he began recording ROCK BOTTOM, with Floyd drummer Nick Mason producing. It was, simply, his masterpiece: a record of intense, yet almost abstract, emotions, odd nursery-rhyme lyrics, and even odder spoken words from the Scottish poet Ivor Cutler. Wyatt's vision – a sense of self, of loss, of suffering, and of love and spring – was realized with almost unbearable poignancy and stunning performances, from Wyatt himself on voice and keyboards, and from each of the guests – notably Mike Oldfield, who contributed sublimely delicate guitar runs.

ROCK BOTTOM was released on July 26, 1974 – the same day Wyatt married Alfreda Benge (who would provide the distinctive cover art – and inspiration – for many of his subsequent records) – and it was greeted by the British music press with all the praise it deserved. Indeed, it continues to find a place in most critics' Greatest Ever Record lists. It was a visionary disc, and especially so given the tedium of

The mighty Robert Wyatt and SWAPO singer comrades

short-wave radio broadcasts. He did a few guest spots in the late 70s (on Nick Mason's FICTITIOUS SPORTS and jazz composer Michael Mantler's THE HAPLESS CHILD, among other records), but found himself unable to 'write enough songs to sustain a recording career'. Then came a revelation: 'Elvis and Sinatra never wrote a song in their lives. What's the point in knocking yourself out for it?'

Wyatt signed up with Rough Trade, checked into the studio, and launched into a hugely creative period, covering songs he admired, often for both their musical and political content. These included, through 1980 and 1981, the Cuban songs "Arauco" and "Caimanera" (Guantanamera – the unofficial Cuban national anthem), Chic's haunting "At Last I Am Free", Billie Holiday's "Strange Fruit", "Stalin Wasn't Stallin'" (an a cappella American patriotic number from the last war), and a collaboration with London Bengali activists Dishari. All of these – plus a wonderful, defiant rendering of "The Red Flag" – were gathered on the album NOTHING CAN STOP US (1982). A rejuvenated Wyatt also found time in this period to guest with Scritti Politti (on SONGS TO REMEMBER), The Raincoats, with Ben Watt (pre-Everything But The Girl), and to record the soundtrack for Victor Schonfeld's animal rights THE ANIMALS FILM (released in 1984).

The song Wyatt is most associated with in this period, however, is "Shipbuilding" (1982), Elvis Costello's anti-Falklands War lament. Brilliantly understated in its narrative form, and perfectly rendered in Wyatt's aching and very English delivery, it was issued as a single, played constantly on Radio 1 by John Peel, and with a rare justice entered the UK charts.

Further political songs and collaborations followed. Wyatt contributed stirring vocals in Spanish (a language which suits his voice) to Working Week's Latin anthem "Venceremos – We Will Win" (1983), and recorded love songs by the murdered Chilean songwriter Victor Jara ("Te Recuerdo Amanda") and the Cuban Pablo Milanes ("Yolanda"), along with Peter Gabriel's "Biko" for a 1984 EP, WORK IN PROGRESS. He also contributed two songs to a Miners' Strike benefit album, THE LAST NIGHTINGALE (1984), and vocals for the Jerry Dammers-produced "The Wind Of Change" (1985), a song recorded with the SWAPO Singers to raise consciousness for the liberation struggle in Namibia.

Each of these ventures rank among the best political 'pop' ever recorded. They also punctuated an incredibly fertile period for Wyatt, which included

so much of the progressive rock around at the time.

It was also a hard act to follow. Wyatt, splendidly, pulled a rabbit from the bag with a playful cover of The Monkees' "I'm A Believer" – another triumph, and an unlikely UK chart single, which propelled the singer, in wheelchair, onto *Top Of The Pops*. Alas, Wyatt's pop career went no further, when Virgin declined to release his "Yesterday Man" cover, as originally projected.

1975 saw Wyatt touring with Henry Cow (he can be heard on the band's CONCERTS album) and recording RUTH IS STRANGER THAN RICHARD, a kind of coda to ROCK BOTTOM, revisiting his jazz roots, notably on Charlie Haden's "Song For Che" and on "Sonia", composed by and featuring South African trumpeter Mongezi Feza. Tragically, Feza died at the year's end in an English hospital from double pneumonia – a heavy blow for Wyatt, who had planned further collaboration with 'Mongs'. And, as he explained, he felt 'quite simply if he had been white he would not have died ... it gave me a strong push towards a sense of political urgency'.

There followed a period of reassessment as Robert and his wife Alfie involved themselves in Communist Party politics. Wyatt also developed a near-obsessive interest in world film, and world musics broadcast on

work on albums again for jazz composer Michael Mantler (MANY HAVE NO SPEECH; 1986) and Henry Cow-offshoot News From Babel (LETTERS HOME; 1986), as well as a new album of his own material, OLD ROTTENHAT (1985). This found Wyatt in uncompromising form, producing what he described as 'un-misusable music', songs that couldn't pop up on the Voice Of America representing the West. Indeed they couldn't. A bleak record, for the most part, it evoked the tone of British politics mid-80s: a beleaguered Left, in the wake of the Falklands War and the miners' defeat. It's not his most enduring work, but it has a stand-out in "East Timor", a three-line accusation of CIA misdeeds, and the drumming throughout is extraordinary – a reminder of just how imaginative a drummer Wyatt has always been.

The later 80s saw new Wyatt output restricted to guest appearances – with various Catalan groups (he had been spending time in Spain), with The Happy End big band ("Turn Things Upside Down" – another wonderful political song), and on Ryuichi Sakamoto's BEAUTY album (he sang The Rolling Stones' "We Love You" – 'I wanted the saddest voice in the world,' said Ryuichi).

Then, in 1991, Wyatt released DONDESTAN, a new album on Rough Trade, comprising arrangements of poems by Alfreda Benge (his wife). It was in many ways a return to the personal lyricism of ROCK BOTTOM: the music he 'hears in his head', created through multitracked vocals, keyboards and sparse percussion. Not that politics were absent. "Dondestan" was about lack of statehood, "Lisp Service" a rebuttal to Billy Joel's crass apologia for US interventions ("We Didn't Start The Fire"), while "Left On Man", the strongest track, had a soulful rhythm of Wyatt chorusing 'simplify-reduce-oversimplify' – the standard 'refutation' of Marxism. The music also showed just how much Wyatt had absorbed from his radio-dial tuning, working in snatches of world music rhythms in an utterly natural manner.

A quiet period followed – new solo work limited to just one mini-CD, 1992's A SHORT BREAK, 'five abstracted sketches' recorded at home on a four-track – until 1996 saw Wyatt back in a real studio, prompted (and provided) by Phil Manzanera (the ex-Roxy Music guitarist had worked with Wyatt back on RUTH IS STRANGER…). SCHLEEP, the resulting album (1998), was a collection of Robert's own songs, with help from a cast including Eno, Paul Weller and jazz guitarist Philip Catherine – the latter combining beautifully with Wyatt's vocals on the stand-out track, "Maryan". The album, rightly, drew plaudits from reviewers, and Wyatt found himself closing the century in a modest blaze of glory, amid remastered releases of all his back catalogue in Britain and the US, including a lavish five-CD box, EPS (1999), featuring all the mid-80s singles.

Wyatt joined a select group including Scott Walker and Jarvis Cocker when he curated the South Bank's Meltdown Festival in 2001 pulling together a bill that reflected his eclectic musical tastes. Pink Floyd's David Gilmour was one of the performers and Wyatt repaid him by guesting at Gilmour's solo gigs the following year. Fans, for the moment, will have to make do with that, as there is no sign of new material.

Robert Wyatt is a unique (and uniquely humane) talent – the kind of musician you feel his mate John Peel would have been on the other side of the vinyl. He is one of the very few artists who has brought (and brings) jazz and rock together to their mutual benefit, and his is a voice that can transport almost any material.

Rock Bottom (1974; Hannibal/Thirsty Ear).
Wyatt's unqualified masterpiece of 'drones and songs', recorded with support from old mates Richard Sinclair, Hugh Hopper, Mongezi Feza, Ivor Cutler and (at his all-time best) Mike Oldfield.

Nothing Can Stop Us (1982; Rough Trade/Thirsty Ear).
Another absolute essential, this takes in the early-80s singles for Rough Trade, including gorgeous renderings of "Caimanera", "Strange Fruit", Chic's "At Last I Am Free", "The Red Flag" and, on the CD reissue, Elvis Costello's "Shipbuilding".

mid-eighties (1993; Rough Trade).
The CD reissue includes the OLD ROTTENHAT album, but it's the aching, political mid-80s ballads that you need most here – above all "Yolanda" and Victor Jara's love song "Te Recuerdo Amanda". A further CD bonus is "Pigs", a quietly extraordinary take on the horrors of factory farming.

Schleep (1998; Hannibal/Thirsty Ear).
Robert's return to his own songs, with fruitful assistance from Eno (he and Wyatt duet splendidly on the opening track), Paul Weller, Phil Manzanera, and jazzers Annie Whitehead, Evan Parker and Philip Catherine.

Going Back A Bit: A Little History Of Robert (1994; Virgin).
This two-CD Wyatt-fest scores high on its highlights from the Softs ("Moon In June" from Three) and Matching Mole (including "O Caroline" and "God Song"), less well with out-of-sequence chunks from ROCK BOTTOM, but redeems itself with a scattering of Virgin one-offs ("I'm A Believer"), collaborative efforts and "The Internationale".

Flotsam &Jetsam (1994; Rough Trade).
Rarities, oddball delights and more collaborative efforts – for those already hooked, perhaps, though Wyatt is rarely

dondestan (revisited)   robert wyatt

better than on The Happy End's joyful "Turn Things Upside Down" or "The Wind Of Change" with Jerry Dammers and the SWAPO Singers. Plus he gets to sing with Slapp Happy.

⊙ **eps (1999; Hannibal/Thirsty Ear).**
A gorgeous five-CD package gets you the mid-80s treasures, an edited version of the *Animals* film, and a disc of Schleep remixes.

Note:several of the quotes in this article are taken from Michael King's book, Wrong Movements: A Robert Wyatt History (1994; SAF), heartily recommended to all Wyatt enthusiasts.

Mark Ellingham

PETE WYLIE/WAH!

Pete Wylie born Liverpool, England, 1958.

Pete **Wylie** (vocals/guitar), the might and mouth behind **Wah!**, first came to attention with the short-lived but semi-legendary **Crucial Three**, formed in the late 70s with Julian Cope and Echo and The Bunnymen's Ian McCulloch. After their dissolution, Wylie formed **Wah! Heat** with **Pete Younger** (bass) and **Rob Jones** (drums) in late 1979, making their debut for Inevitable Records with "Better Scream" (1980), a breakneck number which suggested Doors and Clash influences.

For "Seven Minutes To Midnight", Wah! Heat's second single, Younger and Jones were replaced by **Carl Washington** and **Joe Musker**, and the line-up was augmented by **King Bluff** (keyboards). The single missed the charts, but received plenty of radio play, and led to a label deal with WEA, whereupon the band changed their name to Wah!, and were joined by two former mainstays of It's Immaterial – **Paul Barlow** (drums) and **Henry Priestman** (keyboards).

Wah!'s debut album, NAH! POO! THE ART OF BLUFF (1981), was a disappointingly patchy affair; high points came only with "Seven Minutes To Midnight" and the follow-up singles "Forget The Down!" and "Somesay". The problem seemingly stemmed from Wylie's unstoppable but often aimless enthusiasm for pop's many forms, but a new, more focused, direction would develop during 1982, as a soul influence became prominent in their overall sound. Heralding the change in style, the band became **Shambeko! Say Wah!** for the three-minute pure pop fuzz of "Remember", and then waved goodbye to their thrashy guitar era with the compilation LP, WAH! THE MAVERICK YEARS 1981–1982.

Priestman went off to form **THE CHRISTIANS**, and Wylie and Washington unveiled a new Wah!, consisting of keyboard players **Charlie Griffiths** and **Jay Naughton**, plus drummer **Chris Joyce**. Wylie's pursuit of the epic finally reached fruition with "The Story Of The Blues", a remarkable song that cata-

pulted Wah! to a UK #3 chart hit. The follow-up, "Hope (I Wish You'd Believe Me)", unexpectedly stalled at #35, and contractual hitches with WEA meant it would be almost eighteen months before any new material appeared.

When Wah! returned as **The Mighty Wah!**, they had signed to WEA's Beggars Banquet subsidiary. A rockier sound on the brilliant "Come Back" rewarded them with a UK Top 20 entry in the summer of 1984, but despite the intensity and versatility of the album, A WORD TO THE WISE GUY (1984), it failed to yield any more hit singles – "Weekends", a well-aimed tirade about Duran Duran, stopped short of the Top 40.

By the end of 1984, a compilation LP, THE WAY WE WAH!, had signalled the end of the band. Chris Joyce joined Simply Red for a time. Wylie himself didn't reappear until mid-1986, when he signed to Virgin and, along with then-partner **Josie Jones**, took the infectious synth-pop of "Sinful" to #13 in the UK charts. Again, however, he had problems with follow-up material: both "Diamond Girl" and the delayed LP, SINFUL (1987), flopped.

It appeared that Wylie's chart career was over, but an unexpected experimental track, "Imperfect List", credited to **Big Hard Excellent Fish** (which had arisen from Josie Jones being asked by dancer/choreographer Michael Clark to produce a dance piece), and a cameo vocal on The Farm's hit "All Together Now", revitalized his profile in 1990. In 1991, he resurfaced with the same band under the moniker **Pete Wylie & Wah! the Mongrel!**. A remix of "Sinful" smacked of desperation, but it at least made the UK Top 40, unlike the uplifting "Don't Lose Your Dreams" single or the album INFAMY! OR I DIDN'T GET WHERE I AM TODAY (1991).

A bad fall in late 1991 left Wylie seriously injured, but after a lengthy period of convalescence, he re-emerged as a support act to another group on the comeback trail – Belinda Carlisle's reformed Go-Go's – before returning to the recording studio. In 2000, once again under the moniker of The Mighty Wah!, for the first time in sixteen years, Wylie released a new album, SONGS OF STRENGTH AND HEARTBREAK. Its contents were hardly innovative, but Wylie's characteristic triumphalism still packed quite a punch.

⊙ **A Word To The Wise Guy** (1984; Beggars Banquet).
Hard-hitting political pop, with extra helpings of rap, soul, rock and punk. Including the anthemic "Come Back", this is compulsive listening.

⊙ **Songs Of Strength And Heartbreak**
(2000; When!/Castle).
Pete Wylie's first album in almost a decade is reassuringly immodest. It's also unashamedly sentimental in places, but his heart-on-sleeve stance is ultimately an appealing one.

Andrew Mosley

X

LA art punks **X** spat out sacrilege with the best of them but knew their musical history far too well to succumb to three-chord nihilism. Led by married couple **Exene Cervenka** (vocals) and **John Doe** (vocals/bass), with **DJ Bonebrake** (drums) and **Bill Zoom** (guitar), they wrote songs that were hair-raising drag races through Californian pop culture.

LOS ANGELES (1981) was an impressive introduction, a righteous tilt at the living death of the city of angels in songs such as "Sex And Dying In High Society". The first of four albums to be produced by Ray Manzarek of The Doors, it included a version of that band's "Soul Kitchen", while the neurotic/narcotic vocals of John and Exene recalled a contemporary Jefferson Airplane. WILD GIFT (also 1981) was even better. On the menu was racial alienation, hateful landlords, adult books and the demise of Presley – "Back To Base" memorably coupled him with canines in a bizarre sex sleaze story. The two-minute songs flew by in an amphetamine rush that mirrored the emergent LA punk scene, but always maintained a pop edge, thanks principally to Zoom's somersaulting surf guitar. "We're Desperate", "White Girl" and "In This House That I Call Home" were peerless songs served up with a snotty indifference, which matched perfectly the doleful picture of modern California they evoked.

Several of the songs on UNDER THE BIG BLACK SUN (1982), the X debut for Elektra, were inspired by the death of Exene's sister Mary. But, while "Come Back To Me" was the most eloquent and moving song the group had written, elsewhere the lead duo returned to their hobby horses of glamorous sleaze and urban dysfunction. MORE FUN IN THE NEW WORLD (1983), the last X album to be produced by mentor Manzarek, revealed a group a little unsure as to their future direction. The dilemma was enshrined in "True Love Pt. 2", a deliberation on exactly that theme. In wondering out loud about commercial viability, X lost some of their original appeal.

Further problems followed. Doe and Cervenka divorced and, while other groups might have papered over the cracks, X titled their next album AIN'T LOVE GRAND (1985). A confused, disturbingly straight rock set, it featured production from Michael Wagener – an associate of Christian rockers Stryper. The results were unsurprisingly disappointing, and by the time the album came out, X – whose members also recorded a country album with **Dave Alvin** of The Blasters, credited to **The Knitters** – had lost their trump card with the departure of Zoom.

SEE HOW WE ARE (1987) featured **Tony Gilkyson** (ex-Lone Justice) as Zoom's replacement, but Alvin was responsible for the strongest track, alienation-homily "4th Of July". By 1988 the group had all but disbanded, though there were occasional regroupings from sundry solo activities. 1993's disappointing HEY ZEUS!, however, turned out to be their final studio album, the energy of old having dissipated in favour of a lukewarm shot at roots-rock.

⊙ **Wild Gift** (1981; Slash).
Wretched and self-loathing, this was X's finest hour. Doe and Cervenka's invocation of guilt, paranoia and grubby, stolen sex is exquisite; the muscle of Bonebrake's drumming and the climactic howl of Zoom's guitar the perfect counterpoint.

⊙ **Beyond And Back** (1997; Elektra).
All the X you could reasonably ask for, plus demos, live tracks and rehearsal recordings.

Alex Ogg

X-MAL DEUTSCHLAND

In the summer of 1982 4AD Records brought their new German signing over to support the Cocteau Twins in London. The band was **X-Mal Deutschland** and the crowd went wild over their Banshees/Joy Division/Killing Joke goth-punk mutant-disco, and the expressionless, half-sung vocals of lead singer **Anja Huwe**. "Schwarz Welt" and "Incubus Succubus", their two singles for the small German label Zick Zack, instantly became collector's items and FETISCH (1983) – their 4AD debut – became one of the label's bestselling albums that year. At a time when there was much attention on Germanic 'industrial' groups such as Einstürzende Neubauten, X-Mal Deutschland breezed into a slot as the most popular German band in Britain.

X-Mal Deutschland had formed in autumn 1980 as an all-girl five-piece, though by the time of the 4AD signing a couple of line-up shuffles had brought a 'token' male bassist, **Wolfgang Ellerbrock**, to join a line-up of Huwe, **Fiona Sangster** (keyboards), **Manuela Rickers** (guitar) and **Manuela Zwingmann** (drums). By 1984 and the release of the second album, TOCSIN, drummer **Peter Bellender** had become their second male member and first token Brit. TOCSIN groaned where FETISCH spat, and X-Mal Deutschland were beginning to look more like an ordinary rock band than the eccentric crew that had stood apart from the pack.

1982–84 were their salad days, after which they disappeared from 4AD and out of view until a single for Red Rhino Europe, "Sequenz", cropped up as evidence of their continued work. A career miscalculation in supporting The Stranglers followed a pruning of their name to **X-Mal** and their signing to major label Phonogram. Much of their initial UK following was alienated by these 'rock' moves, and the invigorating third album, VIVA, suffered from this sense of betrayal. A fourth album, DEVILS, was released in the late 80s on Phonogram Germany, but interest elsewhere was minimal.

Wolfgang Ellerbrock later rejoined Anja and assorted musicians, purportedly recording material in 1990 for a never-released comeback album for WEA. They are rumoured, however, to still play the occasional gig in the farthest outposts of Europe.

⊙ **Fetisch** (1983; 4AD).
Thunderous drums, a bass that for once is truly driving, snatches of synths and crescendo-guitar all conspire to clear a path for Anja's insistent, imperious vocals. The ponderousness that predominated in later work is here part of a rich texture, making one stumbling rush of a record. The 1985 reissue includes a remix of "Qual", one of 1983's best singles.

Tony Drayton

X-RAY SPEX

Formed London, 1977; disbanded 1979; re-formed 1995.

X-Ray Spex were a wonderful, shambling, musical mess of rebellion, fashion and fun. Main muse **Poly Styrene** danced, yelped, screamed and sang over the joyful noise belted out by her punchy buzzsaw'n'biscuit-tin band while fighting off **Laura Logic**'s sax honks from stage left – all with a smile of pure glee.

Poly was selling clothes from her stall in London's Beaufort Market when X-Ray Spex bumbled into the public eye – one of the earliest bands on the punk scene in the wake of the Sex Pistols. According to legend, after seeing a Pistols show in Hastings, our teen heroine placed an ad in the *Melody Maker* looking for 'Young Punx who want to stick it together'. **Jak Airport**, raw guitarist, answered the call, as did **Paul Dean**, able bassist, and **B. P. Hurding**, sturdy drummer. Laura, the mad sax-woman, was the final touch.

Poly's songwriting dealt in the sheer strangeness of everyday life and both the beauties and the horrors of the disposable society she observed. Her songs were full of witty, sometimes wry imagery, varying between full-on vintage punk thrash ("Obsessed With You" or "I Am A Poseur") and more gentle, helpless, teenage reflections on life ("I Can't Do Anything" or the sublime "Germ Free Adolescents"). When she got angry and really let rip, as in "The Day The World Turned Day-Glo", the images and music stormed round your head like an ancient fury with a severe hangover.

A group fronted by a couple of teenage girls who were bellowing something about bondage wasn't going to remain unnoticed for long. They were featured in a 'youth' programme on weekend TV and they made it punk big time with "Oh Bondage, Up Yours!", their contribution to the LIVE AT THE ROXY compilation, recorded during their second gig. The press reaction resulted in their first single, a fairly lacklustre studio version of "Oh Bondage" hitting the streets, on Virgin Records, within weeks.

Poly, herself of Anglo-Somali parentage, and the rest of the band (Laura had now left, replaced by **Rudi Thompson**), played for their largest live audience at the Rock Against Racism rally in London on April 30, 1978 – the gig that saved punk from being lumped in with boneheaded neo-fascists. Their next three singles charted and they finished the year with a storming album GERM FREE ADOLESCENCE. (Future rock academics will argue whether 'Adolescents' or 'Adolescence' is correct; the sleeve notes chop and change between them.)

The following year started well as X-Ray Spex's April single, "Age", sneaked in at the bottom end of the UK chart – and then nothing. **John Gun** was brought in on saxophone but didn't stop the band from splitting shortly afterwards. He went on to form **The Living Legend**, while B. P. Hurding ended up in **Classix Nouveau**, and Jak and Paul formed the splendidly named **Airport & Dean**. But what of Poly?

Poly, who was unable to land the kind of record deal she wanted, largely backed away from the music business and finally got religion. Never completely at home with the idea of being a pop star, she hooked up with the Hare Krishnas, reverted to her real name – Marion Elliot – and spent a few years bringing up her family before returning to the music scene with a beautiful and completely un-X-Ray Spex album TRANSLUCENCE (1980), an EP called GODS AND GODDESSES (1986), and a brief fling with **The Dream Academy** in 1990.

In 1995, however, Poly finally brought X-Ray Spex out of the cupboard, dusted them down and oiled their old bones, and they were rehearsing for a few 'one-off' gigs around the UK until she broke her hip early in 1996. The gigs never took place but the album that resulted, CONSCIOUS CONSUMER (1995), was almost enough to make up for the disappointment. Poly, together with Paul Dean and the welcome return of the prodigal Laura, put together a magnificent collection, flavoured with all the old concerns ("Junk Food Junkie" could have been taken from GERM FREE ADOLESCENCE) and spiced up with Poly's own spirituality and the greater maturity of all involved.

Whether or not any more gigs happen, she and the band will be remembered for one of the best albums and the most marvellous sound of the punk era.

⊙ **Germ Free Adolescence** (1978; Virgin).
A wonderful CD reissue that bundles in all the singles at no extra cost.

⊙ **X-Ray Spex: Live At The Roxy** (1991; Receiver).
Eight tracks of undiluted chaos and pleasure.

Al Spicer

XTC

Formed Swindon, England, 1975.

"The problem is that none of us have a streak of showbiz in us." Andy Partridge

by XTC

O ne of the most admired and frustrating British bands of the last twenty five years, **XTC** provoke a fervour which bands selling ten times as many albums would kill for. Drawing heavily on angular melody, pure pop psychedelia, rural folk, and straight-ahead 60s Beat, XTC combine a love of all things English – steam trains and fairgrounds, suburban gardens and village summers, West Country bitter and bungalows – with 50s Americana, the atom age, science fiction.

After ditching the name The Helium Kidz, XTC signed to Virgin in 1977, riding in on the coat-tails of punk. Chief songwriters **Andy Partridge** (vocals/guitar) and **Colin Moulding** (bass/vocals) were ably supported by **Terry Chambers** (drums) and frenzied keyboard player **Barry Andrews**. Their debut, the punchy WHITE MUSIC (1978), was welcomed warmly by the music press, and with the same year's follow-up, GO 2 (1978), it became clear that Partridge and Moulding were fine new writers, throwing conventional pop off-kilter with intricate melody lines and quirky lyrics.

Recruiting **Dave Gregory** (guitar/keyboards/vocals) to replace Andrews (whom Robert Fripp had persuaded to join The League of Gentlemen), XTC allied themselves with producer Steve Lillywhite and stepped up a gear, releasing a string of albums that would take them from also-rans to contenders. First up was DRUMS AND WIRES (1979), so named to describe the band's new sound, a subtle, imaginative, coherent album, which spawned a UK Top 20 hit, "Making Plans For Nigel".

Banged out remarkably quickly, BLACK SEA (1980) was stuffed with cracking songs ("Generals And Majors", "Sgt. Rock (Is Going To Help Me)", "Living Through Another Cuba"), all held together in a full but fuss-free production. Partridge imposed a strict discipline to the record: no overdubs unless they could be played live, keep the drums loud and the guitars 'cranked up'. Faced with their strongest album (and chart placings in both the UK and US), XTC did what all bands in that position do: embarked on a world tour of lunatic proportions, which was to have serious consequences.

After dispensing with Lillywhite's services, the band fashioned their masterpiece. ENGLISH SETTLEMENT (1982) showcased an impressive variety of styles: the folk-tinted "All Of A Sudden (It's Too Late)"; the rousing "Senses Working Overtime" (their highest chart placing); Moulding's warm, enveloping "Runaway"; and the bright and cheerful "Ball And Chain". Contemporarily, unashamedly English, it matched sales to reputation and further enhanced XTC's name in the US.

With a fearsome live reputation and a war chest of top-class material, XTC seemed to be merely a step away from the world stage. But the steps became a stumble, then a fall. Partridge, though happy with ENGLISH SETTLEMENT, viewed another world tour with fear and loathing, and his behaviour on the road was becoming ever more bizarre. He began to suffer from crippling stage fright: in Paris, in acute distress, he abruptly left the stage, causing the cancellation of the European and British dates. After just one performance in San Diego, he decided enough was enough. The whole US leg was abandoned and Partridge flew home. XTC would never recapture the high ground again. Released as singles, "Ball And Chain" and "No Thugs In Our House" flopped; Chambers, disillusioned with the tour debacle and the new direction, upped sticks and left.

XTC backstage with Talking Heads, from left: Harrison, Weymouth, Chambers, Byrne, Andrews, Frantz and Partridge

Once the dust had settled, XTC regrouped (drummer **Peter Phipps** came in for recordings), but successive producers were to struggle with Partridge over the interpretation of XTC's mercurial ideas. MUMMER (1983), an album with real charm and melodic grace ("Love On A Farm Boy's Wages"), was confused by the lack of continuity that three producers inevitably brought to it. THE BIG EXPRESS (1984) was little better – fussy, overproduced, underperformed.

With time and money in hand after an abortive Mary Margaret O'Hara production, Partridge set out on an all-out celebration of English psychedelia under the guise of band alter ego, **The Dukes Of Stratosphear**. Their 25 O'CLOCK (1985) outsold THE BIG EXPRESS and rekindled the band's appetite for the real thing. Virgin committed themselves, and XTC flew to America to work with Todd Rundgren (theoretically a marriage made in heaven) for SKYLARKING (1986). Out of the chaos brought about by rows between Rundgren and Partridge came a luscious pop album, richly textured, cinematically arranged, laced with a healthy dose of Brian Wilson. "Grass" unexpectedly began to pick up airplay in the US on the strength of its flip side, "Dear God", a track not on the album. Hastily re-pressed to include it, SKYLARKING sold 250,000 copies in the US, and it seemed as if a corner had been turned.

The Dukes reconvened, released PSONIC PSUNSPOT (1987), and the CD-only compilation CHIPS FROM THE CHOCOLATE FIREBALL, and then retired. Virgin wanted to consolidate on SKYLARKING'S success in America but Partridge

couldn't face another Rundgren run-in, so chose, by way of a Boy George remix, rookie producer Paul Fox. Recording, by and large trouble-free, though at times frustratingly slow, produced ORANGES AND LEMONS (1989), another wonderful album. Preceded by "The Major Of Simpleton", Partridge's lexicon wordplay set against a big twelve-string guitar sound, it was an inspiring set, and its reception encouraged XTC to embark tentatively on an acoustic 'tour' of US radio stations, setting foot outside the protective bubble of the studio at long last.

It's a recurring theme of XTC's career that, when it's all going right, it all goes wrong. ORANGES AND LEMONS finally ran out of steam (Partridge refusing any more live duties) and Virgin rejected two sets of songs that Partridge felt represented some of his best work. XTC ended a five-year lawsuit with one ex-manager and promptly lost the services of his replacement; dozens of producers auditioned for a new album, with veteran Gus Dudgeon winning selection. Once again, recording became a bruising affair: Partridge was aghast at what he felt was Dudgeon's blasé attitude to some of the more personal songs; Dudgeon felt it was high time XTC sold some records to reinforce their critical acclaim. Dudgeon was eventually fired, but NONSUCH (1992) was another splendid collection, a combination of the highly reflective ("Rook"), the soaringly melodic ("The Disappointed", "Dear Madam Barnum", "My Bird Performs"), and the downright menacing ("Books Are Burning"). At this point, the XTC story disintegrated for a while. NONSUCH faded fast, which was strange given the direction British music was about to take, with XTC and Virgin finally parting company amid some confusion.

Partridge and Gregory have indulged in several separate collaborative projects and productions with, amongst others, Harold Budd. Belatedly some appreciation for a band to whom the new generation of groups, whether they know it or not, clearly owe a debt has been forthcoming; 1995 saw the release (in the US only) of A TESTIMONIAL DINNER: THE SONGS OF XTC (Thirsty Ear Records), and Virgin themselves issued FOSSIL FUEL: THE XTC SINGLES COLLECTION (1996), by far the best of the various compilation efforts.

XTC, demos in hand, finally signed to Cooking Vinyl and proceeded with APPLE VENUS VOLUME 1 (1999). A stunning piece of work with magnificent orchestral arrangements, the album won lavish praise from the UK music press, with stand-out track "River Of Orchids" showing XTC at their heart-stopping best. Dave Gregory left the band during the recordings, though Andy Partridge and Colin Moulding pressed ahead with a four-CD set of BBC-recorded and live material, TRANSISTOR BLAST (1999).

A second set of the APPLE VENUS Volumes, WASP STAR (APPLE VENUS VOLUME 2) was released in Spring 2000. Forsaking the orchestrated and somewhat experimental nature of VOLUME 1 for more conventional sounding material, VOLUME 2 simply offered further proof that quality pop songwriting comes naturally to some people irrespective of age, major label status or chart position. Freed from an increasingly incompatible relationship with Virgin Records and with their future by and large in their own hands, these will be interesting times out West. Still love to see 'em live again, though.

- **Skylarking** (1986; Virgin).
A fabulous record – sensuous, summery and shimmering. Just be certain to make sure your copy has "Dear God" on it.

- **Oranges And Lemons** (1989; Virgin).
Not as retro as the cover would have you believe. It's breezy ("The Mayor Of Simpleton", "The Loving"), witty ("Pink Thing"), and earthy ("Garden Of Earthly Delights"). Messrs Partridge and Moulding are still there with the best of them.

- **Fossil Fuel: The XTC Singles Collection** (1996; Virgin).
Nobody else put out the kind of commercially suicidal singles that XTC dreamt up. So this may be a by-the-book vault-raider, but when that book is as beautifully diverse as this, who's complaining?

- **Apple Venus Volume 1** (1999; Cooking Vinyl).
Their first studio album in ages – clever, considered and cool. Work of this quality, created by a studio-bound duo, is bound to draw comparisons with Steely Dan. No bad thing, either.

- **Wasp Star (Apple Venus Volume 2)** (2000; Cooking Vinyl).
A companion piece rather than a sequel to Volume 1, this set sees the band put aside orchestration and dust down the old electrics to present a fine slice of guitar'n'drums pop. The best album to have been recorded in a garden shed for many a long year.

- **A Coat Of Many Cupboards** (2002; Virgin).
A four-CD box set of demos and band-picked favourites from down the years.

Lance Phillips

THE YARDBIRDS

Formed London, 1961; disbanded 1968; re-formed on the revival circuit in 1983 and from 1993.

"There were four rock bands in the world that really counted – and The Yardbirds was one of them."
Simon Napier-Bell

The original **Yardbirds** – **Anthony Topham** (lead guitar), **Chris Dreja** (rhythm guitar), **Paul Samwell-Smith** (bass), **Jim McCarty** (drums) and **Keith Relf** (vocals/harmonica) – delivered British R&B in bohemian haunts round the suburbs where London bleeds into Surrey. In 1962, Topham was replaced by **ERIC CLAPTON**, who, with Relf, was at the forefront of the open-ended instrumental 'rave-ups' that the group developed when they took over from The Rolling Stones as house band at Richmond's Crawdaddy club.

After The Stones pushed Home Counties R&B into the charts in 1963, The Yardbirds were well placed to do likewise. Signed to EMI, their second single, "Good Morning Little Schoolgirl", gained a toehold in the Top 50 in October 1964, and the in-concert FIVE LIVE YARDBIRDS album served as a holding operation before 1965's catchy "For Your Love", an international chartbuster that prompted dismayed blues purist Clapton to fly the nest and join **JOHN MAYALL**'s Bluesbreakers.

Enlisting the more adventurous **JEFF BECK**, The Yardbirds entered their golden age. Superimposing

symphonic tempo changes, Gregorian chant, Beck's mock-Oriental twang and other eruditions onto their musical grid, this most innovative of 60s rock groups kept the hits coming for two years with "Heart Full Of Soul", "Evil-Hearted You", "Still I'm Sad" (the first self-penned A-side), "Shapes Of Things" and "Over Under Sideways Down". The Beck-era classic album ROGER THE ENGINEER (Diablo) was reissued with otherwise impossible-to-find bonus tracks in 1998. Completists will be delighted – and the rest of us bemused – by the inclusion of mono *and* stereo mixes of the album. The reissued OVER UNDER SIDEWAYS DOWN (1998) has an equally confusing list of alternative versions to further impoverish the obsessive collector.

1966's best-selling YARDBIRDS album had the gifted Samwell-Smith at the console as well as the fretboard. With his departure a few weeks later, the outfit soldiered on with former session musician **Jimmy Page** on bass until Dreja was able to switch over. Page and Beck then functioned as joint lead guitarists, but, apart from a cameo in Antonioni's movie *Blow-Up*, the only recording credited to this edition was the psychedelic 45, "Happenings Ten Years' Time Ago" – the reason being that Beck was sacked during their penultimate and most harrowing US trek. The Yardbirds started to self-destruct with a US-only cover of Manfred Mann's "Ha! Ha! Said The Clown" and other substandard offerings that reflected a creative impasse. After a final show at Luton Technical College in 1968, Page formed the New Yardbirds, soon to be transformed into **LED ZEPPELIN**.

And that was it until the nostalgia circuit kicked in. Dreja amalgamated with McCarty and Samwell-Smith for two 1983 Yardbirds gigs with Beck among special guests, and this line-up recorded an LP as **A Box Of Frogs**. Then, a decade later, McCarty, Topham and Dreja played what was billed as another one-off Yardbirds reunion. In 1995, however, a more permanent regrouping (which by 1998 consisted of Jim McCarty, Chris Dreja on rhythm guitar, **'Detroit' John Idan** on bass, **Gypie Mayo** – ex-**DR. FEELGOOD** – lead guitar and **Alan Glen** on harmonica), attracted favourable reviews with a repertoire that included items from the Box Of Frogs episode as well as intriguing new compositions by McCarty, although what all the fans really wanted from these latter-day Yardbirds were the ambles down memory lane.

In 1999, the Yardbirds entered the Chiswick Reach Studios – which still used some analogue valve equipment – to record their first album in 32 years.

Birdland emerged in 2003 and featured guest slots from the likes of, among others, **Brian May** and **Slash**. Though far from being the group's greatest effort, the tunes were sweet and, overall, it was an astonishing achievement.

The Yardbirds continue to gig regularly, touring Europe, the United States and Australia. As a live unit, they still pack a potent punch. John Idan's bass work matches Samwell-Smith's melodic work, while his vocals better Relf's. Further, Gypie Mayo's fretwork certainly doesn't shame their guitarists' legacy. After all, it takes a certain amount of chutzpah to fill the shoes left vacant by Messrs. Clapton, Beck and Page. Some of the songs do come across as a tad threadbare, but their stunning new arrangement of "Still I'm Sad" that segues straight into "Dazed And Confused" shows that this unit has all the sound and fury of their predecessors. Long may they Yardmerize.

- **Five Live Yardbirds** (1964; Charly).
  Recorded in the Marquee in late 1964, The Yardbirds power through an atmospheric set.

- **The Yardbirds** (1966; Raven).
  Venturing into areas far removed from their R&B core, this combines Beck *tours de force* with instances of real lyricism.

- **Greatest Hits** (1968; Charly/Pulsar).
  All the hits, with rarities such as a studio version of "I'm A Man" to fill the remainder of the needle time.

Alan Clayson

THE YEAH YEAH YEAHS

Formed Brooklyn, New York, 2000.

Quiet New Jersey girl Karen Ohm buries her face in her hands, breathes deeply and swallows hard from a glass of chilled champagne, then pulls on a sleeveless red top decorated with white skulls, glitter and the legend 'Do You Wanna Go to Hell-Oh or Heaven-Oh?'. Now she is **Karen O** – formidable and fearless frontwoman of New York's latest, loudest shout, **The Yeah Yeah Yeahs**. Now she will spill beer and spit melodic venom.

Perhaps The Yeah Yeah Yeahs were really formed in Ohio – after all that is where freshman student and Jon Spencer-freak Karen met **Brian Chase** (drums) and in doing so, found someone who 'understood'. Oberlin College of Art may have seemed refreshingly liberal with its mixed-sex dorms, but Ohio itself held little for Karen. She dropped out early, leaving Brian behind, and headed to NYU to enrol in film school and let rip with songwriting and low-rent videos. The musical great leap forward came when she was introduced to photographer **Nicolas Zinner** (guitars), who loved the simplicity of the tracks Karen had committed to four-track. Nick rerecorded some of Karen's tunes with her – initially as the folksier **Unitard** – and went about telling anyone who would listen that they were 'the best band in New

The Yeah Yeah Yeahs' Karen O trying to remove a microphone from her nose

York'. This somehow got them onto the bottom of the bill at a White Stripes concert. For this now-legendary gig at the Mercury Lounge, Karen called upon Brian to sit at the drums, and the Yeah Yeah Yeahs were off the ground: Nick's method of playing guitar via two amps did away with the need for a bass player. But the *real* star in the making was, of course, the irrepressible Karen O herself – who even at this early stage showed all the requisite signs.

As well as her brash singing style and subtle-as-juggernaut stage presence, Karen's image was equally created by 'partner in crime' dress-designer **Christian Joy**, who puts together the singer's unique costumes. After an epochal night at the South By Southwest music festival in Austin, Texas, the rogue duo decided to trash British band Clinic's dressing room, stealing their surgical wear and sending Dame Courtney Love hurtling into a table of potato salad while making their escape.

The first evidence that YYY magic could work equally well in the studio came with 2001's five-track YEAH YEAH YEAHS EP – also known as the BANG! EP, after its incendiary lead track. "Bang!" not-so-quietly picked up airplay on both sides of the Atlantic, something of a surprise given the '... as a fuck, son, you suck!' refrain. The impressive follow-up, "Machine", cracked the UK charts late in 2002. Fans eager for the debut album, FEVER TO TELL, which finally arrived in April 2003, found it crammed with completely original material: only "Tick" and "Ten" have previously surfaced on BBC sessions, and the singles were nowhere to be seen.

Meanwhile, Karen O continues to wreak havoc both on and off stage. Mothers everywhere, please, lock up your sons for their own good.

⊙ **Fever To Tell** (2003; Polydor).
Live stand-out "A Date With the Night" heralds a raft of bitingly fresh songs that antagonize and endear in equal amounts – as the Yeah Yeah Yeahs *almost* justify the tag of 'NYC's Brightest New Thang'.

Jeremy Simmonds

YELLO

Formed Zurich, Switzerland, 1979.

The roots of techno, the beat-driven Euro-offspring of house, lie in the 70s, when, in the hands of outfits like Kraftwerk and Tangerine Dream, computer-generated music presented a serious exploration of the dilemmas presented by technology. Imitators like Gary Numan diluted this electronic innovation in the quest for mass appeal, but salvation arrived in its subversion for the purposes of dance. Prominent among the conspirators were the Swiss duo **Yello**, whose ironically glamorous sophistication has struck a chord with several other acts, notably the Pet Shop Boys.

The outfit's guiding spirit was the enigmatic **Dieter Meier**, by repute a millionaire who bolstered his fortune on the professional gambling circuit, while also finding time to turn out for the national golf team. Meier provided Yello's concept and lyrics, while the equally inscrutable Boris Blank wrote the music.

The early Yello albums SOLID PLEASURE (1980), CLARO QUE SI (1981) and YOU GOTTA SAY YES TO ANOTHER EXCESS (1983) proved popular with New Romantics and Pink Floyd fans, but wider commercial success proved elusive. The turning point came with the release of STELLA in 1985, following hard on the heels of the invention of the compact disc, a medium tailor-made for Meier's fusion of clinical beats, frantic sound and nonsensical lyrics. Tracks like "Domingo", "Desire" and "Vicious Games" raced into the realm of camp, sounding like Liberace revamped for the acid-dance revolution. Sales were helped too by the appearance of the driving innuendo of "Oh Yeah" on the soundtracks of *Ferris Bueller's Day Off* and *The Secret Of My Success*.

1986 saw the release of YELLO and an entertaining mix of their better tracks, THE NEW MIX IN ONE GO. The next year they collaborated with Billy Mackenzie and Shirley Bassey on ONE SECOND, which included the comparatively delicate "Call It Love". Meier was turning increasingly to film, and a vivid series of videos culminated in "The Race", taken from FLAG in 1988. The single was a massive dance hit across Europe and provided the duo with their only UK Top 10 hit. However, Meier's interest in music was waning by then, and the band have since released only BABY (1991), ZEBRA (1994), POCKET UNIVERSE (1997), ECCENTRIX and MOTION PICTURE (the latter two 1999). With the latest albums being of little interest to those on the cutting edge, and with a dwindling fan base, Yello should perhaps consider a full-time move away from music and into the film, golf, high-camp or whichever other world now holds an attraction for them.

⊙ **Stella** (1985; Mercury).
A sprightly, kitsch collection of soap operatics: whistles, strings and angel voices combine in a paean to fantasy and the potential of technology. Music to listen to while driving a Ferrari at night on a wet alpine road, clad solely in leather.

⊙ **The New Mix In One Go** (1986; Mercury).
Divine segue of Yello's finest moments up to 1986. A marvellous memorial to excess and desire, and an ample introduction to Meier's perturbing imagination.

⊙ **Flag** (1988; Mercury).
Takes their lapses of taste to even greater heights. The hustling beat now grates a little, even on "The Race", but Meier's tongue is stuck firmly in cheek as you might expect from titles like "Tied Up In Gear".

James Owen

YELLOW MAGIC ORCHESTRA

Formed Japan, 1977; disbanded 1983; re-formed 1992.

It may have been Kraftwerk who patented and popularized electronic music, particularly with their 1974 album AUTOBAHN, but over in Japan three individuals were preparing to combine their musical abilities and technological resources. **Yukihiro Takahashi** (drums/percussion) had contributed to three LPs by The Sadistic Mika Band, and **RYUICHI SAKAMOTO** (keyboards) had been a session stalwart, when they met **Haruomi Hosono** (bass/producer) who was working on a fourth solo album. With the Japanese technological boom in full swing for electronic equipment, their formation as **Yellow Magic Orchestra** was to be a fruitful decision.

Commercial success was certainly out of reach to begin with: a debut offering YELLOW MAGIC ORCHESTRA (1977) was undeniably innovative, but despite comparatively accessible singles such as "Cosmic Surfing", "La Femme Chinoise", "Computer Game" and a cover of "Bridge Over Troubled Water", the overall result was a brave but ultimately impenetrable album.

However, the follow-up, 1980's SOLID STATE SURVIVOR, not only established them in their home territory, but also helped break them internationally. Like Kraftwerk, there were signs of an emotional centre within their clinical framework, and they even scored an international hit single in 1980 when "Computer Game" was rereleased, reaching the British Top 20.

Any hit-making momentum was obliterated by X MULTIPLES (1980), which was a curious ragbag of the experimental, the melodic and the downright eccentric – the latter brought about by a series of comic skits. By BGM and TECHNODELIC (both 1981), their undeniable brilliance could not hide the fact that the next generation of electronic buffs were starting to catch up, and that their sound no longer seemed unique.

Yet even as the trio was set to part in 1983, they came up with NAUGHTY BOYS, a fine strong set which showcased a smoother, more streamlined but satisfying approach. Sakamoto and Takahashi subsequently returned to successful solo work, while Hosono resumed production duties, but YMO's cult influence became legendary down the years among a wide range of musicians: in 1992 an EP entitled RECONSTRUCTIONS featured reworkings of original material by dance icons such as Altern 8, The Orb and 808 State. This led to a brief re-formation of YMO's original line-up, which was marked by the release of a double live album FAKERHOLIC (1992) and then TECHNODON (1993).

◉ **Solid State Survivor** (1992; Restless).
The best of their original album releases, this is a sophisticated but accessible sequence of man and machine working together. Particularly worth hearing for "Behind The Mask", which was later blandly (but very successfully) adapted by Eric Clapton for a 1986 worldwide hit.

◉ **Characters – Kyoretsu Na Rhythm: The Best Of** (1992; Restless).
As many YMO albums are hard to find now, (even on CD), this compilation of highlights is a useful, consistent introduction to their work.

Justin Lewis

YES

Formed London, 1968; disbanded 1981; re-formed 1983 and on–off incarnations since then.

"Dawn of light lying between a silence and sold sources chased amid fusions of wonder in moments hardly seen forgotten."
Lyric from *Tales From Topographic Oceans*

Grandiose, full of noise, light and lasers, speaking portentous words and trailing clouds of dry ice – **Yes** were the ultimate prog-rockers. Since the dawn of punk it's been fashionable to vilify the band as pomp-rock hippies, and to airbrush them out of rock history. Yes were certainly guilty of many sins – self-indulgence, pretension and an emphasis on style over content – but these were the sins of enthusiasm and ambition, typical of an era when bands wanted more than just airplay and a slot on *Top Of The Pops*. In their prime, in the early 70s, this was one of the most imaginative, skilful and daring bands around – and the albums from that period stand up well enough.

The group were formed by **Jon Anderson** (vocals) and **Chris Squire** (bass/vocals), who recruited **Peter Banks** (guitar), **Tony Kaye** (keyboards) and **Bill Bruford** (drums). Their first releases, YES (1968) and TIME AND A WORD (1969), had a somewhat Led Zep hard-rock feel, though they hinted at the epic stylings and cosmic visions to come. The true Yes approach really began to take shape with THE YES ALBUM (1971), by which time Peter Banks had been replaced on guitars (and that's very definitely plural) by **Steve Howe**. Howe's arrival was a turning point for the band, as their music became denser and more elaborate (although THE YES ALBUM also contained an attractive slice of acoustic whimsy from Howe in "The Clap"). The real key to future directions, however, lay in extended 'suite-like' tracks such as "Yours Is No Disgrace" and "Starship Trooper", with their virtuoso instrumentation.

As Yes forged their reputation in Britain and in the US, another significant personnel change took place, Tony Kaye being ejected in favour of **EX-STRAWBS** man **Rick Wakeman** and his ever-growing battery of keyboards and synthesizers. Wakeman debuted on FRAGILE (1972), which featured "Roundabout" – a chart single in the US – and marked the beginning of the band's association with cover artist Roger Dean, whose artwork reflected the band's sci-fi bombast. The album, streets ahead musically of anything else on the British prog-rock scene, went Top 10 in both the UK and US.

The personnel remained the same for the next album, CLOSE TO THE EDGE (1972). An even more elaborate affair, it was acclaimed by reviewers for its 'classical' structure (this was a time when rock was

prone to staking a claim as a 'new' classical music), which consisted of just three 'songs', the opening title suite taking up the record's entire first side. A huge, long-standing success in the UK (#4) and US (#3) album charts, it set the prog-rock template with its expansive soundscapes, and did so with undoubted quality musicianship. Bruford's deft, jazz-tinged drumming and Squire's fluid but thunderous bass lines balanced out Anderson's high, clear voice, and, while Howe would never play one note where ten would do, he was a powerful guitarist, carving crystalline structures on electric and acoustic instruments. Wakeman's pseudo-classical stylings could, at times, be overly clever, but he also demonstrated a breathtaking versatility, playing with rock force or graceful beauty. Together, the band members forged startling settings for Anderson's obscure 'visionary' lyrics.

After CLOSE TO THE EDGE, Yes seemed unstoppable, and their concerts became juggernauts of light and sound, seen by the faithful as almost transcendental experience. The stage shows were captured on a triple live album, YESSONGS (1973), and an accompanying concert film, which in some ways is the best record of the period.

At this point, however, Bruford left, to be replaced by the less sensitive **Alan White**, and the band seriously overplayed their hand with their next release, TALES FROM TOPOGRAPHIC OCEANS (1973), an album that encapsulated all the flaws of prog-rock. Conceived and composed by Anderson and Howe, it was not just a concept album, but a double concept album of just four side-long pieces. Self-indulgent and overblown, with lyrics and sleeve notes that gave a new meaning to doggerel, it was in some ways the nadir of an era. Nonetheless, there were still moments of sublime musicianship, and the fans bought it by the truckload.

Wakeman, who had tasted huge solo success with THE SIX WIVES OF HENRY VIII (1973), decided to leave at this point. He was replaced by **Pat Moraz**, and the band came back with the more focused

RELAYER (1974), something of a return to the form of CLOSE TO THE EDGE, but with a colder feel and an underlying manic shrillness.

The next two years saw the individual members pursuing solo work and, by the time they came back together for GOING FOR THE ONE (1977), Wakeman had returned on keyboards. By now the musical world had changed: bands like Yes and Pink Floyd were the dinosaurs of rock. With GOING FOR THE ONE, Yes tried to update their act, sticking a sporty and populist title on a more accessible set of songs that veered from the downright rockist to the tweefully romantic. The change was accentuated in TORMATO (1978), which occasionally slipped into whimsy but presented the band as a down-to-earth bunch with a sense of humour and a social conscience.

For a while it looked as if Yes might be able to weather the punk era: sales were good, they were still playing stadiums in the US. But Wakeman split from the band again, and this time Anderson followed. Their replacements, **Trevor Horn** (vocals) and **Geoff Downes** (keyboards), both from the one-hit pop band The Buggles, didn't fit. The resultant album, DRAMA (1980), was a weak attempt to recycle old glories, and by the following year the band had dissolved.

Yes re-emerged, phoenix-like, in 1983, with Anderson, White and Squire all in place, Tony Kaye back from exile at keyboards and **Trevor Rabin** handling guitars. Displaying a renewed energy and a sharper, more contemporary sound, they released 90125 (1983), produced by Trevor Horn, and a single, "Owner Of A Lonely Heart". The single went to #1 in the US, the album to #5 in the US and #16 in the UK, and a whole new generation of fans climbed aboard. But, while BIG GENERATOR (1987) consolidated on the chart success, personality and legal problems once again caused a split. Anderson had got together with Bruford, Wakeman and Howe, and, unable to call themselves Yes (a name legally held by Squire), released an album as

ANDERSON, BRUFORD, WAKEMAN AND HOWE (1989), another Top 30 success.

The two opposing factions united for an album called, with a spark of genius, UNION (1991), but musically a somewhat uneven patchwork. By the time of their next release, TALK (1994), Yes were back to their 90125 line-up, and Rabin was not only producing but handling the majority of the song-writing as well. Despite the energy still present, the attempts to update and commercialize the band had resulted in a sort of Yes Lite, with jaunty choruses and guitar riffs taking the place of the long-ditched mysticism.

By 1996 Rabin and Kaye were out and Anderson, Howe and Wakeman were back in, bringing the group back round to its 'classic' 70s line-up. That spring, the group played three dates in San Luis Obispo in Southern California, and recordings from those dates were fashioned into KEYS TO ASCENSION (1996; Essential) a double-CD set which, although featuring a few middle-of-the-road 'adult-oriented rock' work-outs from the band's later years, provides definitive recordings of 'classic' Yes music – though many Yes-philes complain that the so-called 'live' tracks were substantially enhanced in post-production, with complete vocal lines added in. To promote the CD, the band dragged out its aged and creaky arrangement of Paul Simon's "America" in what some would say was a misguided attempt to get radio airplay. They took to playing this tune anywhere there were microphones or cameras, including the studio of shock jock Howard Stern and, for a live morning TV show, on the sidewalks of New York.

A follow-up to KTA called, poetically enough, KEYS TO ACENSION II (1997), used up all the left-over bits from the San Luis Obispo concerts and added a second CD of new studio work. On the verge of a promised summer tour, Wakeman once again walked out, with no explanation either from him or the remaining members. At summer's end, the band announced that former World Trade frontman and sometime Yes collaborator and producer **Billy Sherwood** was an official member of the band. In 1998 came yet another album, OPEN YOUR EYES (Eagle), a meandering mix of tweeness and neo-hippie philosophizing. 2001's MAGNIFICATION seemed to have a little more direction and, surprisingly, found the group plugging away without a keyboardist. YES REMIXES (2003), meanwhile, saw Steve's offspring, **Virgil Howe**, applying a techno/trance veneer to a selection of old Yes cuts

Yes still don't have the credibility or album sales of their fellow dinosaurs Pink Floyd (or even Genesis), but you have to admire their persistence.

⊙ **The Yes Album** (1971; Atlantic).
The pre-Wakeman Yes consolidate their sound, giving each member a chance to shine.

⊙ **Fragile** (1972; Atlantic).
The breakthrough album, containing "Roundabout" plus five pieces composed and arranged by individual members of the band – these are fairly hit-and-miss, but Squire's "The Fish" will change the way you look at the bass guitar forever.

⊙ **Close To The Edge** (1972; Atlantic).
'Progressive' music doesn't get much better than this: the sound is lush and multi-layered, and everything comes together perfectly. Go ahead – lose yourself.

Adam Kimmell

YO LA TENGO

Formed Hoboken, New Jersey, 1984.

Hailing from Frank Sinatra's birthplace gave **Yo La Tengo** a great deal to live up to, but their art-pop has managed to find a loyal audience, due partly to the enthusiasm of independent film director Hal Hartley (*Trust*, *Amateur*). Hartley has a habit of slipping Yo La Tengo songs and posters into his cool, arty films, which – like the band's songs – are always warm and sentimental at heart.

The band were formed by **Ira Kaplan** (guitar/vocals) and **Georgia Hubley** (drums/vocals), who searched for other members with an ad asking for musicians into The Soft Boys, Mission Of Burma and Love. Love was a key influence and a cover of Arthur Lee's "A House Is Not A Motel" was the B-side of their first single, "The River Of Water", in late 1985.

After a period of ever-changing bassists and second guitarists, Yo La Tengo's line-up seemed to stabilize with the arrivals of **Dave Schramm** (vocals/guitars) and **Mike Lewis** (bass). The resulting album, RIDE THE TIGER (1986), was dominated by a scrappy but endearing folk-rock sound and Schramm's countri-fied songs, marking Yo La Tengo as distant relatives of West Coast contemporaries Rain Parade and The Dream Syndicate.

However, Schramm and Lewis almost immediately left the band, and Kaplan assumed lead guitar and song-writing responsibilities for NEW WAVE HOT DOGS (1987), for which they were joined by bass player **Stephen Wichnewski**. A cover of The Velvet Underground's "It's Alright" was more in keeping with New York's bohemian rock tradition, although the best song was the country-flavoured "Did I Tell You?"

PRESIDENT YO LA TENGO (1989) saw the more traditionalist elements of the band's sound pushed aside by Kaplan's meandering, atonal guitar playing. The balance seemed in danger of being upset, but the next record, FAKEBOOK (1990), had hardly any electric guitars at all. The mix finally fell into place with the mini-album THAT IS YO LA TENGO (1991), on which producer Gene Holder took bass. It had slow, mysterious ballads whispered by Hubley, and Kaplan's contorted guitar was showcased on the latest version of one of their earliest and most epic songs, "Five Cornered Drone (Crispy Duck)".

By now Yo La Tengo were an indie-rock institution: reliable and high quality, but short on headline-grabbing drama. With **James McNew** taking over as bass player, albums such as MAY I SING WITH YOU (1992), the excellent PAINFUL (1993), ELECTR-O-PURA (1995), GENIUS+LOVE=YO LA

TENGO and I CAN HEAR THE HEART BEATING AS ONE (both 1997) were consistently fine, with an increasing tilt in the direction of My Bloody Valentine's dream-pop and Hubley doing more of the singing. High points remained the ballads, most notably "Pablo And Andrea" from ELECTR-O-PURA.

McNew's more idiosyncratic musical ideas were being funnelled into his side-project, **Dump**. A PLEA FOR TENDERNESS (1998), Dump's finest full-length outing, was an intriguing mix of camp cover versions (Jacques Dutronc's "Et Moi, Et Moi, Et Moi" and Love Affair's "Everlasting Love"), big-band samples and introspective despair. Home-recorded, but a tasty little morsel nonetheless.

Where most of their contemporaries have slid lazily into late-career complacency, Yo La Tengo continued to recognize the art inherent in pop music, most nobly demonstrated with the literate explorations of AND THEN NOTHING TURNED ITSELF INSIDE OUT (2000). Turning in a soundtrack to an undersea documentary by Jean Painleve on 2002's THE SOUNDS OF THE SOUNDS OF SCIENCE kept things interesting, possibly surreal, if it hadn't made such perfect, lovely sense. More delights came the following year with SUMMER SUN, where the group's cuts took in everything from electronica to 60s pop and bossa nova, and seemed to glide along like swans on a windless day.

After twenty years together, Yo La Tengo are still a slow-burning avant-rock force on the alternative scene.

⊙ **New Wave Hot Dogs and President Yo La Tengo** (1987 & 1989; City Slang).
Two top albums on one CD.

The Yo La Tengo surf team

⊙ **That Is Yo La Tengo** (1991; City Slang).
Pushing various aspects of The Velvets' legacy to the limits, this ranges from the unearthly stillness of "Swing For Life" to what might be the definitive version of their anthem, "Five Cornered Drone (Crispy Duck)".

⊙ **And Then Nothing Turned Itself Inside Out** (2000; City Slang).
A softer, Krautrock-influenced style sweeps through this set; the feedback freak-outs of old are few and far between – an exception being the guitar-driven "Cherry Chapstick", which sounds a lot like Sonic Youth circa SISTER.

⊙ **Summer Sun** (2003; Matador).
Despite all their experimental and jazz leanings, Yo La Tengo here prove that they are still at their best when peddling summery pop ("Season Of The Shark") and twanging melancholia, as they do on their take of Big Star's "Take Care".

Marc Elliot

NEIL YOUNG

Born Toronto, 1945.

"Rock'n'roll is like a drug. I don't take very much but when I do rock'n'roll, I fuckin' do it. But I don't want to do it all the time 'cause it'll kill me."

Neil Young appears to be two quite different musicians trapped in the same body. One is the mellow troubadour who has serenaded bedsits the world over; the other, an axe maniac who kicks out the jams with Crazy Horse. In fact, it's hard to believe that albums as different as HARVEST MOON and ARC are the work of the same person, to say nothing of the weird stuff he produced in the 80s, when he was sued by his label for making records that were not Neil Young enough. Ever ready to take a risk, and immensely prolific over a thirty-year recording career, he has, for someone with nothing left to prove, remained astonishingly keen to prove it. Indeed his creative fires seem to be burning as strongly now as they did in the 70s, and it's entirely possible that the best is yet to come.

Whether electric or acoustic, there is an engagingly ramshackle quality to Young's recordings – a shaky vocal here, a clumsy guitar solo there – that shows how close he remains to the original spirit of garage rock. No wonder Johnny Rotten named him as one of his faves back in 1977, or that he later became acknowledged as the founding father of grunge, the Seattle movement that copied his rawness, if little of his charm. For, whether he is playing with trusty disciples Crazy Horse or on his own, Neil Young always wears his heart on his sleeve.

Neil Young spent his formative years in Winnipeg, where he played in various 60s garage bands, including **The Squires**, an outfit notable for turning up for gigs in a 1948 Buick hearse. Tiring of life in provincial Canada, he jumped in his 1953 Pontiac hearse (the Buick had broken down) and headed across the border for the bright lights of Los Angeles.

There he met up with singer, guitarist and old friend Stephen Stills, with whom he formed **BUFFALO SPRINGFIELD** in 1966. The group had a national hit with Stills' "For What It's Worth", while Young's main contributions were "Mr. Soul" and the haunting "Broken Arrow". When the band split after two years and three albums, Young fitted his solo career around a commitment to the new supergroup **CROSBY, STILLS, NASH & YOUNG**, for whom he wrote "Ohio" and "Helpless". It was a lucrative gig that gave him the freedom to do more or less his own thing on solo records.

NEIL YOUNG (1969), his solo debut, was a rather lacklustre start, though redeemed somewhat by stand-out track "The Loner" – released a few months later as a single with the haunting "Sugar Mountain" (a song about his Canadian youth, which didn't make it onto a full-length recording until DECADE in 1977) on the B-side. EVERYBODY KNOWS THIS IS NOWHERE, however, released the same year, proved a much stronger collection – indeed one of Young's best and most enduring outings and signalled the first of many collaborations with **Crazy Horse**, an LA bar band comprising **Danny Whitten** on guitar, **Billy Talbot** on bass and **Ralph Molina** on drums. The album laid down a blueprint for their unique shambling rock, with the chunky riffing of "Cinnamon Girl" and the apocalyptic "Down By The River".

Neil Young heads for the feedback

Neil Young then saw in the 70s with the commercial breakthrough of AFTER THE GOLDRUSH (1970), a Top 10 album in both the US and UK. Its raw but mellow mood was encapsulated by the remarkable title track, a piece that evoked the dead dreams of the 60s in a weird mix of environmental consciousness, drugs and extraterrestrials. But the album was really a sequence of outstanding songs, including "Only Love Can Break Your Heart", "When You Dance I Can Really Love" and "Southern Man", which was to provide a springboard for some of Young's most intense and rocking guitar solos in the years to come.

Young then parted company with Crazy Horse for a while, recording what remains his bestselling album, HARVEST (1972), with backing from the Stray Gators, and guest appearances by Crosby, Stills and Nash, the London Symphony Orchestra and, notably, **Jack Nitzsche** on piano. The result – a #1 on both sides of the Atlantic – cemented his reputation as a singer-songwriter with such favourites as "Heart Of Gold", "The Needle And The Damage Done" and "Old Man".

While Young was achieving new heights of popularity, both solo and with CSN&Y, he was also developing serious rock-star habits to match. An intense and rather melancholic person by nature, he began drifting into heavily drugged-up states, as reflected on his two classic albums, ON THE BEACH (1974) and TONIGHT'S THE NIGHT (1975). The latter was actually recorded first, in August and September 1973, in the wake of the fatal overdoses of Danny Whitten and CSN&Y roadie Bruce Berry. Taped in a series of drunken all-night sessions, it lurched from depressed to suicidal over its forty minutes, and for cathartic intensity remains a career best. The accompanying 'Welcome To Miami Beach' tour, which exposed a dishevelled Young to an audience expecting to hear "Heart Of Gold", was a classic piece of confrontation theatre that cleared halls across the globe.

ON THE BEACH had a sharper focus and greater detachment, but was still a bleak trip. With its imagery of Charles Manson and his 'family' riding in on their dune buggies to slaughter the Laurel Canyon hippies on "Revolution Blues", it showed Young revelling in decadent, drugged-up alienation, though the mood varied with the wonderful "Walk On", "See The Sky About To Rain" and "For The Turnstiles".

Typically for Neil Young, though, smack chic was just another passing phase, and in 1975 he was back with Crazy Horse for the upbeat proto-grunge of ZUMA, best known for his discordant guitar duelling with new recruit **Frank 'Poncho' Sampedro** on the slow-burn "Cortez The Killer". It was another key album.

After a none-too-memorable outing with Steve Stills as the **Stills–Young Band**, LONG MAY YOU RUN (1976), Young issued AMERICAN STARS 'N BARS (1977), a more subdued outing than ZUMA, which introduced one of his best ever love songs, the sublime "Like A Hurricane". And then he went country-acoustic, for the insidiously charming COMES A TIME (1978), an outing so laid-back as to be virtually supine.

Though he had just released DECADE (1977), a thoughtfully compiled triple-disc career retrospective, Young could never be content to live in the past, and he was galvanized by punk rock into proving that the old guard could still cut it too. LIVE RUST (1979) was an excellent live set, documenting his mammoth world tour of 1978, when Crazy Horse played in front of giant Marshall stacks and roadies dressed as *Star Wars* aliens scuttled around the stage. Both sides of his muse were on display, with an achingly vulnerable acoustic set followed by an orgy of inspired Crazy Horse performances, most notably an industrial-strength "Like A Hurricane". RUST NEVER SLEEPS (1979) was a half-acoustic/half-electric counterpart that weighed in with "Powderfinger", "Sedan Delivery" and "My My, Hey Hey (Into The Black)", the last offering a skewed take on the 'hope I die before I get old' ethic.

Yet, just as Young's star seemed to be rising to new heights, he lapsed into a limbo of third-rate albums, obscurity and savagings from the critics – not least for his support for certain aspects of Ronald Reagan's world-view. The worst period was during his time at Geffen (1983–87), which saw him experimenting with AOR, synths and vocoders – badly. TRANS (1983) was inspired by Young's attempts to communicate with his disabled son, but despite such noble ambitions, the music, even on stand-out tracks such as "Sample And Hold", failed to catch fire. Sued for producing records that were 'unrepresentative' of himself, he quit Geffen amid much rancour.

Back on original label Reprise, credibility was restored with the single "This Note's For You", which was banned by MTV for its attack on corporate rock, and the superb FREEDOM album (1989), released just in time to end the decade on a high note. This was Neil Young back on white-hot form, particularly on the blistering "Rockin' In The Free World", a tirade against the results of Reaganomics that left no doubt about where he now stood politically. Astonishingly, this was just the start of a purple patch that lasted well into the 90s. Whilst most of the elder statesmen of rock were struggling to come up with even half-decent new albums, or endlessly retreading former glories, Neil Young was producing work every bit as good as in his 70s heyday.

FREEDOM was followed by the masterful RAGGED GLORY (1990), a manic outing that made even his rawest earlier efforts seem tame. To emphasize the point, he brought out the raucous WELD (1991), a live album of the accompanying 'Smell The Horse' tour that came accompanied by ARC, a mini-CD of collected feedback squalls that Young was encouraged to add by noise-merchants Sonic Youth, who had opened for him on the tour.

Yet he was able to switch effortlessly into mellow mode again for HARVEST MOON (1992), a thoughtful return to the territory of HARVEST. Remarkably, the new album turned out even better than its venerable precursor, with a serene air of calm reflection, particularly on the sublime title track. He capped this triumph with a superb UNPLUGGED (1993) set for MTV, one of the few such excursions to stand as an interesting work in its own right. Highlights were a harmonium-driven version of "Like A Hurricane" and a guitar version of the hitherto loathed "Transformer Man", which suddenly made it sound like one of his best compositions.

Tragically, Young's position as role model for the grunge generation was to be taken to a macabre conclusion when Kurt Cobain shot himself. Cobain left a lengthy suicide note that quoted Young's famous 'It's better to burn out... ' line from RUST NEVER

SLEEPS, an act which shook up its original author. Young reacted with the title track of SLEEPS WITH ANGELS (1994), a gloomy album that was surprisingly well received, unlike MIRROR BALL (1995), his dismal metallic collaboration with **Pearl Jam**. In 1996, Young returned with Crazy Horse for BROKEN ARROW, an album that suggested a need for stricter quality control. He followed it, however, with the brainstorming YEAR OF THE HORSE (1996) – a twelve-song live album of career highs, accompanied by a Jim Jarmusch film – and DEAD MAN (1996), a dark and atmospheric score of distorted guitar and organ overlaid by poetry readings from **Johnny Depp**, again, the soundtrack to a Jarmusch movie.

In 1999 Young was reunited with Crosby, Stills and Nash for the release of LOOKING FORWARD, of which some of the strongest moments were recorded, largely alone, by Young in his home studio. These cuts acted as a taster for Young's first offering of the new millennium. At the start of 2000 a refreshingly nostalgic studio album emerged, SILVER AND GOLD, a superb epilogue to the classic Harvest-era material. This release was swiftly followed by another live collection, the rather cumbersome ROAD ROCK VOL.1 (2000).

The air of nostalgia lingered into 2002's ARE YOU PASSIONATE? with **Booker T Jones** and cohorts helping the good ship Neil set sail in a southern soul direction. A reaction, at least in part, to the New York terrorist attacks, the album was surprisingly lacking in passion, only really kicking in when Crazy Horse cropped up for the raucous "Goin' Home".

Ups and downs are par for the course with Neil Young, and you have to admire the attitude of someone who isn't afraid to fall flat on his face from time to time. The guardian of the rock'n'roll flame, Young will no doubt be back next year with another record, either infuriating or blindingly brilliant – or both.

⊙ **After The Goldrush** (1970; Reprise).
The album that made his name.

⊙ **Harvest** (1972; Reprise).
A bedsit classic, showing Young in sensitive pastoralist mode. "Heart Of Gold", "Alabama" (later to rock out in style) and "The Needle And The Damage Done" have lasted rather better than some tracks, notably the non-PC ballad, "A Man Needs A Maid".

⊙ **On The Beach** (1974; Reprise).
The spectre of Charles Manson rides on "Revolution Blues", just one of eight bum trips on Neil Young's warped idea of a blues album. The autobiographical title track takes the confessional school of songwriting to new levels of voyeurism. Essential.

⊙ **Tonight's The Night** (1975; Reprise).
This anguished drugged-up nightmare platter is uneasy listening at its best. Virtually every track is outstanding, with Young and Crazy Horse rocking out on "Let's Go Downtown", Young slipping back into himself on "Mellow My Mind", unquiet blues on the reprised title track, and one of the world's greatest ever guitar breaks from Nils Lofgren on "Speakin' Out".

⊙ **Decade** (1977; Reprise).
This triple album/double CD is one of the best 'best of' compilations. Unlike many artists, Neil is a pretty fine judge of his own work, as this well demonstrates. The discs feature the cream of his solo work from 1968 to 1978, leavened with a few plum choices from Buffalo Springfield and CSN&Y.

⊙ **Live Rust** (1979; Reprise).
Raw as any punk album from the time, this live outing confirms Young's status as one of the few 60s folks who stayed on the bus. Amazingly, he makes the acoustic side sound as ragged as the stuff with Crazy Horse.

⊙ **Freedom** (1989; Reprise).
After years of indifferent musings in a variety of styles, this was a stunning return. Contains acoustic and band versions of "Rockin' In The Free World", plus "Too Far Gone" and "Hanging On A Limb".

⊙ **Ragged Glory** (1990; Reprise).
Psycho-country for the 90s. Perhaps his most intense outing with Crazy Horse, sporting a monstrous cover of the garage-band classic "Farmer John", "Country Home" and the supremely messy "F*!*in' Up".

⊙ **Harvest Moon** (1992; Reprise).
A 'Songs Of Experience' compared to Harvest's 'Songs Of Innocence', with reflective observations on the years between. Highlights are the magnificently eerie title track and "From Hank To Hendrix".

⊙ **Silver And Gold** (2000; Reprise).
For his first release of the new millennium, Young reawakens his slumbering countrified inclinations which were so sadly absent from many of his 90s studio outings. With its sumptuously simple production, this set stands out as a highpoint of this maverick musician's more recent catalogue.

Iain Smith

YOUNG FRESH FELLOWS

Formed Seattle, 1982; split 1993; reformed 2001.

While the early 90s saw everyone checking out Seattle as the epicentre of grunge, the durable **Young Fresh Fellows** continued to pursue their own idiosyncratic path, largely outside the glare of publicity.

The band – **Scott McCaughey** (vocals/bass), **Chuck Carroll** (guitar) and **Tad Hutchinson** (drums) – had launched themselves with THE FABULOUS SOUNDS OF THE PACIFIC NORTHWEST (1984), a typically frivolous selection of adolescent follies in which songs such as "Power Mowers' Theme" and "Rock And Roll Pest Control" declined to tackle big social issues in favour of highlighting the absurdity of modern consumerism and not getting girlfriends. By their second album, TOPSY TURVY (1985), **Jim Sangster** had been recruited on bass, allowing McCaughey to switch to guitar. The disc included more frippery – "You've Got Your Head On Backwards" reaffirmed a noble dedication to adolescent 'truth' – and was furnished with improved musicianship and production.

Staying in similar vein, THE MEN WHO LOVED MUSIC (1987) included a homage to dead rock stars in "Hank, Karen And Elvis", while "When The Girls Get Here" lovingly demonstrated the extraordinary lengths young men will be driven to in order to impress the opposite sex. The hormonal imperative was beautifully rendered, despite the fact that those concerned hardly qualified as kids any more. TOTALLY LOST (1988) addressed this dilemma by restraining the group's humour for a fuller rock-pop sound. Though still funny, it lacked some of the nerdish appeal of previous efforts.

Kurt Bloch was then recruited from local legends The Fastbacks to deputize for Carroll. His efforts helped shift THIS ONE'S FOR THE LADIES (1989) into new avenues, including a penchant for country/roots laments, which would become a characteristic of subsequent albums. ELECTRIC BIRD DIGEST (1991) was more unified and satisfying – "Once In A While" proved particularly effective in animating a sense of terminal disillusionment without dipping into mawkishness. IT'S LOW BEAT TIME (1993) was a decent outing, too, if not quite on a par with its predecessor. Their next full-length-ish release, the TEMPTATION ON SATURDAY EP (1993) took them back to their spiritual home at Pop Llama Records. The same year the group split. McCaughey was then spotted touring as backup guitarist with R.E.M., one of many bands to have publicly saluted the Young Fresh Fellows' achievements. He also chairs the ever-shifting line-up of Seattle supergroup, **Minus 5**; the band's members have included **Peter Buck**, **Ken Stringfellow** and **Jeff Tweedy**. DOWN WITH WILCO (2003) was their most recent offering – unsurprisingly, it featured all the members of **WILCO**.

As for the Young Fresh Fellows, they reconvened in 2001 for a split release with Minus 5 entitled BECAUSE WE HATE YOU/LET THE WAR AGAINST MUSIC BEGIN.

⊙ **The Men Who Loved Music** (1987; Frontier).
From the Amy Grant-baiting "Amy Grant" to "I Got My Mojo Working (And I Thought You'd Like To Know)", the band's bubblegum makes for great pop. Tellingly, the face of Henry Winkler (The Fonz) is printed on the CD.

⊙ **Electric Bird Digest** (1991; Frontier).
While they didn't exactly get serious, the Young Fresh Fellows did mellow a little on this, their most consistently entertaining record of the 90s.

Alex Ogg and Peter Buckley

THE YOUNG GODS

Formed Geneva, Switzerland, 1986.

"We try to go beyond language and comprehension. We aim straight for the feeling." Franz Treichler

The first band to really apply sampling technology to guitar-based rock, **The Young Gods** virtually reinvented Stooges-style punk metal as a sleek, futuristic expression of passion and fury. The band's linchpin and vocalist **Franz Treichler** was himself a guitarist, but a youth spent in the un-rock'n'roll environment of the provincial Swiss town of Fribourg persuaded him that tinkering with electronics was an easier way to make music than trying to form a band.

Whether recording his own guitar riffs or snatching samples of Jimi Hendrix, Treichler had assembled an intriguing library of sound before moving to Geneva and linking up with like-minded

experimentalists **Cesare Pizzi** and **Frank Bagnoud**. Their modus operandi was unique: Bagnoud would play the drums, keyboard wizard Pizzi would unleash a barrage of rock and orchestral samples, while Treichler's bloodcurdling rock howl would sail majestically over the resulting cacophony.

The trio's intensity was exemplified by Treichler's decision to carve the name of the band into his chest in order to supply the cover art for their 1987 debut single "Envoye", a self-financed release which won them a deal with respected Belgian indie label Play It Again Sam. An eponymously titled debut album was released the following year, and, although Treichler's darkly sensual lyrics were delivered in French, the record was an immediate critical success in the UK.

The album's stark power owed a lot to the production skills of former Swans member **Roli Mosimann**, who has remained an important studio collaborator ever since. Otherwise, The Young Gods were increasingly becoming Treichler's show: Bagnoud left in 1988 to be replaced by new drummer **Use**; Pizzi stayed for the recording of the group's second album, L'EAU ROUGE (1989), before giving way to **Al Comet** for the subsequent tour.

L'EAU ROUGE represented the high-water mark of The Gods' creativity, and subsequent output has often found the group moving sideways rather than forwards. An atmospheric cover of the Kurt Weill standard, "September Song", had long been a favourite in the group's live set, and the 1990 album, THE YOUNG GODS PLAY KURT WEILL, was an act of further homage enlivened by some startlingly original arrangements.

While hardly a critical success, the next album, TV SKY (1991), the first to be recorded wholly in the English language, won new fans in North America. A much more conventional rock record than its predecessors, it showcased the group's penchant for harsh guitar textures while containing little of the lyricism of L'EAU ROUGE. The subsequent live album, LIVE SKY TOUR (1993), was essentially a holding operation designed to keep the band in the public eye while they took a break from recording.

The Young Gods returned to rock's cutting edge in 1995 with ONLY HEAVEN, which confirmed their unique niche in rock, cherished equally by the heavy metal, indie, techno and industrial fraternities. With ONLY HEAVEN and HEAVEN DECONSTRUCTION (1997) Swiss dance-terrorism looked like it was in safe hands while they continued to dabble in a number of different side-projects. More recently SECOND NATURE (2000) and LIVE NOUMATROUFF 1997 (2001) found the band still at the forefront of extreme and artful noise, putting them in great demand with anyone looking for innovative music. But perhaps their strangest project of recent times was a commission to create a relaxing 30-minute piece of sound for the Swiss Health Bureau at the Swiss National Expo 2002.

⊙ **The Young Gods** (1988; Play It Again Sam).
An icy slab of rock leavened slightly by a curiously menacing version of Gary Glitter's "Hello Hello I'm Back Again".

- **L'Eau Rouge** (1989; Play It Again Sam).
  An ambitious collage of driving rock riffs, sweeping orchestral samples and accordion-driven *chanson*-type balladeering.
- **Only Heaven** (1995; Play It Again Sam).
  An other-worldly blend of grating guitars and ambient soundscapes best exemplified by the album's stand-out track, the fifteen-minute "Moon Revolutions".

Jonathan Bousfield

YOUNG MARBLE GIANTS

Formed Cardiff, Wales, 1978; disbanded 1981.

The career of Cardiff's fascinating, eclectic trio **Young Marble Giants** lasted just three years from 1978, when brothers **Stuart** (guitars/organ) and **Philip Moxham** (bass) invited singer **Alison Statton** to form the group. Comparisons have been made with The Au Pairs and Joy Division, amongst others, but to describe this band as anything other than original would be unjust. Stuart's talent for songwriting and minimalist musicianship blended with Philip's near-melodic bass and Alison's hauntingly uncomplicated voice to produce an extraordinary creation – and one, alas, that none of the band would ever match in their subsequent careers.

Having gained a following in their homeland in the immediate post-punk years, Young Marble Giants secured a deal with the vigilant Rough Trade in 1979. Their first and only LP, the wonderfully disquieting COLOSSAL YOUTH, surfaced in 1980. A triumph of understatement, its highlights included "Searching For Mr Right", the bass-hopping "Wurlitzer Jukebox", the matter-of-fact "Credit In The Straight World" (covered powerfully by Hole) and, especially, the accusingly insistent "Music For Evenings". Each of these were short, sparse tracks, almost dub-like in their recording, and utterly haunting and absorbing.

A cult following sprang up, and prospects seemed good for the band when their follow-up EP, TESTCARD (1981), made #3 in the British indie charts. Another impressive outing, this contained what the Moxhams described as 'instrumentals in praise and celebration of mid-morning television', though Stuart's organ tones suggested something rather closer to a David Lynch soundtrack.

At this point the group inexplicably, but amicably, decided to break up. The first of the three to resurface was Alison Statton, who moved to London following the Giants' demise. Picking up the bass, she teamed up with fellow Cardiff musician, **Spike** (guitars/viola), and jazz enthusiast **Simon Booth**, to form the bossa-nova-influenced **Weekend**, who released their first single, "A View From Her Room", in 1982. Featuring contributions from jazz veterans **Harry Beckett** (flugelhorn) and **Larry Stabbins** (tenor sax), it gave Alison's voice another foray into the indie chart. Further singles "Past Meets Present" and "Drumbeat For Baby" followed, but

the much-vaunted debut LP, LA VARIETÉ, was a lightweight affair. A rift set in when Booth and Stabbins attempted to lead towards a harder-edged jazz-dance. This led to their formation of the much-acclaimed Working Week; Statton played no part in this move, and returned to college in Cardiff.

During this period, Stuart Moxham formed **The Gist**, whose debut album, EMBRACE THE HERD, included the excellent single "Love At First Sight" – a British indie Top 20 hit in 1982. Unfortunately, however, that was the sum of their output, and little was heard of any YMG party until the French label Crepuscule reissued COLOSSAL YOUTH in 1990. Sometime later Alison Statton was involved in a brief collaboration with Ian Devine – notably an extraordinary reading of New Order's "Bizarre Love Triangle".

As for Stuart Moxham, he worked as an animator on *Who Framed Roger Rabbit?* and issued several solo releases, among them 1995's CARS IN THE GRASS, made with **The Original Artists** (a troop that included Spike, Philip Moxham and another brother, Andrew, on percussion). The overall sound was pleasing enough, but the CD fell well short of the Giants. Fans hungry for more material from the Giants would have to seek out SALAD DAYS (2000), which was released on Vinyl Japan and pulled together a collection of early band demos from 1979 that were originally only released on cassette.

- **Colossal Youth** (1980; Crepuscule).
  The CD reissue of this classic LP includes the TESTCARD EP, and is thus the essential YMG release.
- **Nipped In The Bud** (1984; Rough Trade).
  This rare LP ties together material from YMG, Weekend and The Gist.

Jeremy Simmonds

YOUNGBLOODS

Formed New York, 1965;
disbanded San Francisco, 1972.

The Youngbloods weren't quite ever a major band, but they produced a few good songs along the late-60s folk-rock way. They are usually identified with their cover version of Dino Valenti's "Get Together", which reached the US Top 10 (after it was used as a TV commercial for the National Council of Christians and Jews!) and is considered to be the definitive version despite also being recorded by Jefferson Airplane.

Members were **Jesse Colin Young** (guitars/lead vocals), who was the leader and main writer, **Jerry Corbitt** (guitar), **Lowell 'Banana' Levinger** (keyboards) and **Joe Bauer** (drums). Before forming the Youngbloods in 1966, Young had started as a Greenwich Village folk singer and had made a couple of albums, the second of which featured John Sebastian as one of the musicians.

The band's first two albums, THE YOUNGBLOODS

and EARTH MUSIC were produced by Felix Pappalardi, who later (and famously) worked with Cream, and were engaging but inconsistent. With their move to San Francisco their blues and jug-band influences were mellowed by Californian psychedelia, and in 1969 they produced their best album, ELEPHANT MOUNTAIN, produced by Charlie Daniels. The most impressive songs are short and neat and typical of the time, but it's doubtful whether Bauer or Banana had much creative input, apart (perhaps) from some jokey twiddly bits between Young's songs; Corbitt, the only other member who had tried to put pen to paper, departed during this project. As with the earlier albums, there's no overall style, but it's obvious where

the producer decided to make use of his session-musician budget with good deployment of strings and horns to complement the stronger tracks.

They turned out two live albums and another two studio albums, but despite the addition of **Michael Kane** on bass in 1971 the formula was by now growing weary and the band split into various solo projects in 1972. Jesse Colin Young had a long and moderately successful career as a singer-songwriter and is still musically active.

⊙ **Elephant Mountain** (1969; RCA).
Their finest moment., with some of Jesse Colin Young's best songs, including the impressive "Darkness, Darkness" and "Quicksand".

John Webber

FRANK ZAPPA

Born Baltimore, Maryland, 1940; died 1993.

"Historically, musicians have felt real hurt if the audience expressed displeasure ... We didn't do that. We told the audience to get fucked."

With his trademark moustache and goatee, **Frank Zappa** was one of the most distinctive-looking figures in modern music. He was also one of the most brilliant, original and provocative. Leader of The Mothers Of Invention, composer and guitar hero, perpetual irritant to radio stations and record companies, cultural adviser to Vaclav Havel's fledgling Czech Republic, Zappa was consistently controversial and unrepentant: 'My insensitivity is pretty evenly spread around,' he concluded in 1993.

His dazzling eclecticism was evident from the start. As a teenager Zappa was simultaneously enthralled by black R&B (Johnny 'Guitar' Watson, Guitar Slim), doo-wop (The Channels, The Velvets), the modernism of Igor Stravinsky and Anton Webern, and the dissonant sound experiments of Edgard Varèse. A fascination with chemistry (he knew how to make gunpowder at 6) led to suspension from high school after an ill-judged pyrotechnical display, but, despite not gaining sufficient units, he graduated from Antelope Valley High in June 1958 (Friday the 13th, to be precise). The school authorities were just happy that he wasn't coming back.

In 1960, after an unsuccessful year in Hollywood as a film-score writer, Zappa enrolled at Chaffey Junior College in Alto Loma, ostensibly to study music, but chiefly to meet girls. He met and married Kay Sherman, dropped out of college with her, then worked variously as an advertising copywriter, door-to-door encyclopedia salesman, and greetings-card designer. In 1962 he co-wrote and played on his first single, "Break Time" by The Masters, with one Paul Buff, who produced it at his Studio PAL in Cucamonga ("Wipeout" by The Surfaris had been made there). A succession of singles followed, each under a different name. "Tijuana Surf" by The Hollywood Persuaders was a #1 hit in Mexico for ten months. Zappa subsequently bought Buff's studio, renaming it 'Studio Z', and moved in whilst filing for divorce. The money for the studio had come from a score he'd written for the cowboy film *Run Home Slow* (released in 1965).

In 1963 Zappa appeared (minus moustache and goatee) on *The Steve Allen Show*, where he and Allen performed an improvisation on two bicycles, accompanied by a prerecorded tape and the TV studio band. Zappa also financed a concert of his own experimental music in 1963 at a private Catholic college in Los Angeles. It was recorded and broadcast on local radio, and included such delights as "Piece No. 2 Of Visual Music For Jazz Ensemble And 16mm Projector".

By 1964 he'd joined The Soul Giants, a bar band playing in Pomona, Los Angeles. Zappa was keen to try original material and on Mother's Day 1964, after minor personnel changes, they were renamed The Mothers, finally securing their first recording deal with producer Tom Wilson. Out of necessity their name was amended to **The Mothers Of Invention**.

Their 1966 debut, FREAK OUT (pipped only by BLONDE ON BLONDE as rock's first double album), was a mix of sneering songs ("Who Are The Brain Police?"), sharp social comment ("Trouble Comin' Every Day") and wild experimentalism ("The Return Of The Son Of Monster Magnet"). The line-up ran: Zappa (guitar/vocals), **Ray Collins** (lead vocals), **Jimmy Carl Black** (drums), **Roy Estrada** (bass/vocals) and **Elliot Ingber** (guitar). This was later augmented by the talents of, amongst others, **Ian Underwood**, **Bunk Gardner**, **Arthur Tripp**, **Don Preston** and **Jim 'Motorhead' Sherwood**.

1967 found The Mothers in New York with a six-month residency at The Garrick Theater, where their freakish style – the show included rotting vegetables and a giraffe that sprayed whipped cream at the audience – was better received than on the West Coast. Subsequent albums included ABSOLUTELY FREE (1967) and UNCLE MEAT (1969), the latter arguably their most subversive and compendious LP, including some of Zappa's most enduring tunes ("Uncle Meat", "Dog Breath" and "King Kong"). With WE'RE ONLY IN IT FOR THE MONEY (1968) Zappa took aim at The Beatles' SGT PEPPER and at 'Flower Power' conformity. On the LP sleeve (a perfect parody of PEPPER's) he urged listeners to read Franz Kafka's short story *In The Penal Colony* prior to sampling "The Chrome Plated Megaphone Of Destiny", the sinister flip side to The Beatles' "Day In The Life". One factor behind Zappa's mistrust of hippie counterculture was his enduring anti-drugs stance, an attitude unprecedented during the era of 'peace and love'. His preference was for cigarettes and black coffee, rather than substances that made you stumble into the furniture.

Believe it or not, there's a statue of this man in Riga

By October 1969, Zappa had disbanded the original Mothers and released HOT RATS. Essentially an instrumental affair, its only song was "Willie The Pimp", sung by old high-school friend Don Van Vliet (aka **CAPTAIN BEEFHEART**), whose seminal TROUT MASK REPLICA album Zappa had produced that year. Though later at odds with one another, Beefheart toured with Zappa in 1975, with performances captured on BONGO FURY (1975).

In 1970, fostering a more vaudevillian style for the reformed Mothers, Zappa brought in two members of teen band The Turtles, **Mark Volman** and **Howard Kaylan** ('Flo & Eddie') on lead vocals. Zappa's simultaneously stunning and throwaway film, *200 Motels* (1971), encapsulated this period and the vagaries of life on the road. It featured Ringo Starr as Zappa-lookalike 'Larry the Dwarf' and Keith Moon as a nun, with animation designed by Cal Schenkel (Zappa's long-standing cover artist) and bemused contributions from London's Royal Philharmonic Orchestra. The project produced a soundtrack album ("The Pleated Gazelle", a suite of five orchestral/choral pieces, was one of the highlights of Zappa's career) and a touring show, banned from the Royal Albert Hall in London on the grounds of obscenity.

Throughout the 1970s Zappa released a wealth of material, from the quirky big-band 'jazz' of THE GRAND WAZOO (1972) and the cartoonish virtuosity

on STUDIO TAN's "The Adventures Of Greggery Peccary" (1978), to the raucous rock and studied sarcasm of SHEIK YERBOUTI (1979) – Zappa's best-selling album. ONE SIZE FITS ALL (1975), held in high regard by many fans, brought slick jazz-rock mythologizing of flying saucers, poverty, pyjamas, in-flight snacks, incarceration, cowboy actors, sofas – and, on "Evelyn, A Modified Dog", the echidna that Zappa and his family adopted at the Los Angeles zoo.

As ever, Zappa's work was full-to-overflowing with cross-references, musical quotes, band in-jokes/folklore, and a host of 'low-rent Americana'. Who else would, or could, write a song about growing dental floss on the prairie, the subject of OVER-NITE SENSATION's "Montana" (1973) – a track all the more bizarre for the uncredited Tina Turner and the Ikettes on backing vocals (uncredited at Ike Turner's insistence). Whilst many dismissed Zappa's songs as mere smut and nonsense, he contended that they were his form of social anthropology. Targets ranged from politicians, evangelists and yuppies to Jewish princesses, truck drivers, groupies, and (in 1982) the "Valley Girl" – a rare 'hit' for Zappa featuring daughter Moon Unit's arresting monologue as an airheaded LA teenager.

Such unexpected chart success did little to assuage Zappa's bitterness at 'basically, being shut-off at every turn when I tried to do something original and creative'. Indeed, 1977 should have seen the release of

LîTHER (pronounced 'leather'). Planned as a quadruple box set, it encompassed every genre in which he was working – live rock performances, orchestra, chamber jazz, guitar improvisations – propelling the listener into uncharted realms. Warner Brothers, his label at the time, refused to release LîTHER and pulled strings to ensure he couldn't do so elsewhere. Incensed, Zappa took to the airwaves. Sounding uncharacteristically tipsy, he played the entire set on KROQ radio in Pasadena, urging listeners to tape it – an inevitable bootleg went into circulation. LîTHER achieved quasi-mythic status as the great 'lost' Zappa album, but in 1996 it was resurrected by Rykodisc as a three-CD set, thanks to a little forward motion from Gail Zappa (Frank and Gail had married in 1967) and complete with a cover concept by 'heir-guitarist' son Dweezil.

Zappa regularly toured, pushing the technical skills of band members to the limit. A twelve-CD series of live recordings from 1965 to 1988, YOU CAN'T DO THAT ON STAGE ANYMORE (1988–92), displays Zappa's disciplinarian traits – auditions were notoriously gruelling and merciless. At various times band members included **Steve Vai**, **Terry Bozzio**, **George Duke**, **Jean-Luc Ponty**, **Warren Cucurullo** (Duran Duran) and **Adrian Belew** (Bowie, Talking Heads, King Crimson).

During the 1980s, working from a state-of-the-art home studio (The Utility Muffin Research Kitchen), Zappa gained critical acclaim as a 'serious' composer with concerts and recordings of his work by the London Symphony Orchestra – LSO VOLS. 1 & 2 (1983/1987) – and The Ensemble Intercontemporain, conducted by Pierre Boulez – THE PERFECT STRANGER (1984) – as well as commissions from the Kronos Quartet and the Aspen Wind Quintet. These projects were dogged by his dissatisfaction with orchestras used to 'snoozing their way through Handel or Mozart', and by the mid-80s he was realizing many of his ideas on a Synclavier computer, which provided the freedom and control he was after.

In 1984, Zappa, posing as his real-life eighteenth-century namesake, FRANCESCO ZAPPA, issued an eponymous album of 'digital baroque dinner party music'. The humour of this album and of the Synclavier's instrumentation, sending up classical music's growing obsession with authentic performance and the (big) business of 'hit' composers, seemed lost on critics and fans alike. Back in 1968, CRUISING WITH RUBEN & THE JETS had created a similarly bamboozling effect, as Zappa and The Mothers delivered their leering tribute to doo-wop subculture and cheesy teenage love songs.

Zappa's contrary activities were never more acute than in 1984. Alongside FRANCESCO ZAPPA and THE PERFECT STRANGER appeared the vertiginous rock of THEM OR US, amidst a June-to-December world tour of some 112 dates. Then there was *Them Or Us (The Book)*, a 300-page story and screenplay of delirious magnitude available through Zappa's mail-order outlet Barfko-Swill. And then there was THING-FISH. Often cited as Zappa's most offensive and incomprehensible release, this was originally conceived as an off-Broadway musical, an avenging parable of an America choking on racial, sexual, religious and political oppression. A plot extract was published with colour photos in the American porno mag *Hustler* just to add to the contention.

In 1985 Zappa testified to the US Congress, fighting music censorship proposals initiated by the Parents' Music Resource Center. Excerpts from the congressional proceedings appeared, suitably mutilated, on the cannily titled FRANK ZAPPA MEETS THE MOTHERS OF PREVENTION (1985). When, in 1987, the title track of JAZZ FROM HELL (1986) earned a Grammy for *Best Rock Instrumental*, Zappa recognized a music industry titbit designed to shut him up – 'The Grammys are all fake', he declared, an extension of his contempt for MTV, corporate rock, and the increasing trend towards stylistic regurgitation (he termed it 'Death By Nostalgia'). Once again turning his back on the industry, he put together a twelve-piece band (the biggest combo he'd used since 1972) and was on tour throughout 1988.

After a visit to post-revolutionary Czechoslovakia in 1990 (President Havel was a fan), Zappa was briefly made an overseas trade representative, an appointment soon thwarted by US governmental pressure. A year later, Zappa announced that he was considering standing as a non-partisan presidential candidate, having summarized his political outlook as 'practical conservatism'. Confirmation of prostate cancer in late 1991 sidelined these ambitions; but, despite worsening health, Zappa continued to work right up to the end. September 1992 saw concerts with Germany's Ensemble Modern in Frankfurt, Berlin and Vienna, with specially commissioned pieces premiered alongside older works. Zappa was thrilled: 'I've never had such an accurate performance at any time for the kind of music that I do.'

Frank Zappa died, aged 52, on December 4, 1993 at his home in Los Angeles. Since his death, the music industry has been making what it can from his remains. STRICTLY GENTEEL (1997) was a compilation of great dollops of music for films and other neo-orchestral stuff; CUCAMONGA (1998) was a collection of juvenilia, doo-wop and greasy kids' stuff; and HAVE I OFFENDED SOMEONE? (1997) was a compilation of tracks chosen by the man himself the year before he died, selected for their power to get beneath the skins of minority lobby group members.

⦿ **Lump Gravy** (1967; Rykodisc).
Zappa at his most original. A cut-up of orchestra, R&B, jazz, *musique concrète* and mumblings from inside a grand piano. A masterpiece that anticipated sampling technology.

⦿ **Uncle Meat** (1969; Rykodisc).
Freakish songs ("Sleeping In A Jar") amidst electric chamber works ("King Kong"), with Zappa presiding as the Fu Manchu of absurd musical theatre. The reissue includes dialogue from the movie Uncle Meat (1987/93).

⦿ **Roxy & Elsewhere** (1974; Rykodisc).
A sumptuous Zappa/Mothers live outing. Enter the broom-cupboard universe of drug psychosis ("Pygmy Twylyte"), roller-coaster through monster-movie clichés ("Cheepnis"), and exit via the "Be-Bop Tango" dance contest.

⦿ **Sleep Dirt** (1979; Rykodisc).
An overlooked gem. "Filthy Habits" and "Regyptian Strut" are two of Zappa's best tunes. The title track sparkles around an irritated acoustic guitar solo. The CD reissue adds dynamic vocals by Thana Harris.

⦿ **Joe's Garage, Acts I, II & III** (1979; Rykodisc).
A kaleidoscopic vision of censorship run amok and music-biz excesses ("Dong Work For Yuda"). Outrageous entertainment, with unparalleled 'xenochronous' guitar playing on "Keep It Greasy".

⦿ **Shut Up 'N Play Yer Guitar** (1981; Rykodisc).
A three-CD collection of Zappa's guitar playing at its creative peak. Vinnie Colaiuta (drums) is equally exceptional.

⦿ **London Symphony Orchestra Vols 1 & 2** (1983/1987; Rykodisc).
A dazzling programmatic burlesque ("Bogus Pomp", "Bob In Dacron"). The antidote to 'cottage cheese' minimalism, cheerfully outside the ballpark of academia. Complete with spiky Zappa sleeve notes.

⦿ **The Yellow Shark** (1993; Rykodisc).
Premier live performances by the Ensemble Modern of Zappa's most demanding compositions, notably "The Girl In The Magnesium Dress", "Get Whitey", "None Of The Above" and "G-Spot Tornado".

Ian Stonehouse

WARREN ZEVON

Born Chicago, 1947.

"Going to a 7-Eleven in the middle of the night and hearing the clerk whistling one of my songs – that's my idea of a great cover version."

It is no coincidence that **Warren Zevon**'s fan base includes several of America's hippest crime fiction writers. His idiosyncratic and highly literate songs, shot through with violence and black humour, are strewn with edgy, marginal misfits, mercenaries of the gun and of the heart, seedy chancers and downright villains. Though he's often compared with Randy Newman, Zevon's dark output and uncom-

promising style have never translated to long-term commercial acceptance. Once again, the words 'cult' and 'maverick' spring to mind.

A classical music prodigy, born to Russian immigrant parents, Zevon was introduced to the composer Igor Stravinsky in his early teens. Discovering Bob Dylan a few years later steered him towards rock, and Zevon spent the mid-60s as an aspiring songwriter, before recording an album called WANTED DEAD OR ALIVE (1969) with arch-scamster **KIM FOWLEY**. The record disappeared without trace, though Zevon's career in music had rather more success – and substantial royalties – in a song he contributed to the *Midnight Cowboy* soundtrack, "He Quit Me Man", performed by Leslie Miller.

In the early 70s, Zevon became The Everly Brothers' musical director, shortly before their split, and by 1975 associations with David Geffen and Jackson Browne had resulted in a solo deal with Asylum Records. WARREN ZEVON (1976), his debut solo album, contained everyday tales of sadomasochism on "Poor Poor Pitiful Me", while "I'll Sleep When I'm Dead" sketched the antithesis of the golden LA lifestyle, with vocals from The Eagles, Fleetwood Mac's Lindsay Buckingham and Stevie Nicks, and Phil Everly.

After Linda Ronstadt had covered three Zevon numbers and named her big-selling HASTEN DOWN THE WIND after one of them, more of a spotlight fell on Zevon's EXCITABLE BOY (1978), which combined his trademarks of punchy, piano-led rock and rich, growling voice in his customary macabre tales. The title track, a doo-wop number about a psychopathic killer, both thrilled and repelled, as did the mercenary ghost story, "Roland The Headless Thompson Gunner", and the infamous "Werewolves Of London", his one hit single. This haunted imagination also informed the almost unbearable tenderness of "Accidentally Like A Martyr" and "Veracruz". The album was a deserved cult and commercial success, reaching the US Top 10.

Zevon proceeded to hit the bottle, and produced a largely pessimistic and bloody-minded follow-up, BAD LUCK STREAK IN DANCING SCHOOL (1980). Including "Play It All Night Long" (a prod at the redneck sensibility), the melancholic "Bill Lee" and a collaboration with Bruce Springsteen on the ballad "Jeannie Needs A Shooter", it nevertheless made the US Top 20. It was followed by a live album, STAND IN THE FIRE (1981), a thunderous and gloriously demented performance, and by the brief calm of THE ENVOY (1982), on which "Ain't That Pretty At All" satirized Zevon's own lifestyle and Elvis Presley was remembered on "Jesus Mentioned".

Neither of these records charted, though, and over the next four years Zevon spent time checking in and out of detoxification centres. Then, in 1986, he recorded a single with fans Peter Buck, Bill Berry and Mike Mills of R.E.M. Released under the name of **Hindu Love Gods**, "Gonna Have A Real Good Time" marked the beginning of Zevon's resurrec-

Warren Zevon in his dancing school streak of bad luck

headlong version of Prince's "Raspberry Beret" – but attempts at Muddy Waters or Robert Johnson standards were somewhat ill-advised.

Happily, Zevon's devious sense of invention was back with a vengeance on the splendid Mr. BAD EXAMPLE (1991), which confirmed him as the very epitome of the cult artist. The following year came an acoustic live album, LEARNING TO FLINCH (1993), which covered the length and breadth of his career, including a few new songs that reappeared in studio versions on the relatively mellow MUTINEER (1995).

In 1996, a 44-track anthology, I'LL SLEEP WHEN I'M DEAD emerged via Elektra/Rhino, covering the period 1975–1995. It included unreleased cuts and rarities; two of them were written-for-TV numbers, perfect miniatures coming in under the 100-second mark. Thereafter, semi-retirement beckoned until Jackson Browne intervened, introducing Zevon to former Nirvana manager and rock-legend-of-a-kind Danny Goldberg. Zevon was duly signed to Goldberg's new Artemis imprint and in early 2000 they issued LIFE'LL KILL YA, which extended Zevon's template of bleak irony to new lengths – see "I Was In The House When The House Burnt Down" and the cautionary tale for bright-young-things everywhere, "My Shit's Fucked Up". Zevon's first ever UK tour in spring 2000 delighted his secret fan base, all gigs selling out in days. Another album, MY RIDE'S HERE followed in 2002.

Sadly, later that year it was announced that Zevon was suffering with terminal lung cancer. In typical Zevon style he quipped 'I'm OK with it, but it'll be a drag if I don't make it till the next James Bond movie comes out.'

⊙ **Stand In The Fire** (1981; Asylum).
A stunning, bone-crunching live set, featuring predominantly material from Excitable Boy.

⊙ **Sentimental Hygiene** (1987; Virgin America).
Zevon's best latter-period recording, backed by a host of luminaries. The acoustic textures and sitar on "Bad Karma" and the righteously outraged tone of "Even A Dog Can Shake Hands" are particular thrills.

Peter Mills

tion. Meanwhile, after "Werewolves Of London" was featured in the movie *The Color Of Money*, Asylum duly issued a Zevon compilation album, sardonically titled A QUIET NORMAL LIFE (1986).

This renewal of interest landed Zevon a deal with Virgin America for SENTIMENTAL HYGIENE (1987), where he was assisted by members of R.E.M., plus guests including Neil Young, Bob Dylan and George Clinton. More guitar-led than much of his work, the album was a critical hit, but, despite its stellar cast, failed to sell. The rather laboured TRANSVERSE CITY (1989) fared no better, although "Splendid Isolation" was an excellent opener.

Thereafter, the Virgin contract ended, and Zevon, now with WEA subsidiary Giant, reunited Hindu Love Gods on an eponymously titled 1990 album of covers. Some remakes were successful – notably a

THE ZOMBIES

Formed England, 1962; disbanded 1967; briefly re-formed 1969.

The Zombies were formed, just as the UK Beat boom was gathering speed, by sixth-form grammar schoolboys **Colin Blunstone** (vocals), **Rod Argent** (piano), **Paul Atkinson** (guitar) and **Hugh Grundy** (drums), soon joined by **Chris White** on bass. Having won a newspaper competition organized by the *London Evening News*, they made a cover of "Summertime" that attracted Decca, who were trying to compensate for their recent blunder in turning down The Beatles.

The first single was an Argent original, "She's Not There", an easy beat ballad dominated by jazz-tinged piano and Blunstone's gorgeous high tenor. Released in July 1964, the week the band turned professional, it missed the UK Top 10 but reached #2 in the US, where it sold a million. It was a similar story with their next 45, "Tell Her No", which missed the UK charts altogether. Marketed as the thinking kids' beat group, much play was made of The Zombies' academic background, but it was their musical subtlety and creativity that stood out. Indeed, after The Beatles, they became the first British band to strike gold in the States with self-penned material. The first album, BEGIN HERE (1965), featured not only Argent's work but also that of White, who was rapidly emerging as a fine writer.

Why such an exemplary start led to nothing is an enduring mystery: the band had pre-empted rock's mid-60s development into more reflective and adventurous areas, but the band failed to take off in Britain, and in America sales began to slip alarmingly. The deal with Decca lapsed in 1967, the option wasn't renewed and The Zombies signed to CBS. A few months later, they released their second and final album ODESSEY AND ORACLE, its title misspelt by an careless sleeve designer (though Rod and the rest of the band tried to cover this up at the time, claiming the misspelling was intentional). Recorded at Abbey Road Studios just after the SERGEANT PEPPER sessions, it was produced by Argent and White, who also financed much of the studio time themselves. In spite of a restricted budget – a Mellotron had to substitute for an orchestra – it was a gem, cherished by many as one of the finest flowerings of Britpop. Indeed a 1995 critics' poll in *Mojo* magazine named it one of the hundred best albums ever made. But such subtle experimentation was not brash enough to survive the climate of the late 60s, and anyway, according to Blunstone, 'when the last track was recorded, the band was within two weeks of breaking up'.

Belatedly released in the US, the album made the Top 100, and its single, "Time Of The Season", eventually hit the Top 3 in 1969 and was a million-seller in the States and in Japan. The Zombies re-formed without Blunstone, but within three months disillusionment set in, and Rod Argent formed **ARGENT** with songwriter Russ Ballard, achieving a few 70s hits. Blunstone enjoyed a more lucrative solo career in the 70s.

◉ **Odessey And Oracle** (1968; Repertoire).
One of the great lost albums of the 60s. File it alongside REVOLVER and PET SOUNDS, for its blend of inspired hooks, classy jazz-pop arrangements and vocal harmonies.

◉ **Best Of The Zombies** (1991; MCI).
A respectable collection of the finest moments. The limited amount of recording they undertook ensures that any compilation is worth having.

Alwyn W. Turner

ZZ TOP

Formed Houston, Texas, 1970.

The cunningly rack-end-named **ZZ Top** have spent over three decades grinding out boogie based on the rolling blues riffs of Elmore James. They added synthesizers and electronic percussion in the 80s and have gradually cleaned up of some of their rougher edges, but the basic formula has stayed the same. The reward has been a career that has spanned the roughest Texas roadhouses and the rarefied world of 80s megastardom.

Billy Gibbons, guitarist with seminal Texas garage punks The Moving Sidewalks, was noted as one of the most promising young players of his generation by Jimi Hendrix. In 1970, Gibbons and manager Bill Ham recruited **Dusty Hill** (bass/vocals) and **Frank Beard** (drums), the rhythm section of American Blues, who had recorded two unsuccessful albums. Thus was created the unchanging ZZ Top line-up.

The stark simplicity of their sound gained its power from the band's love of the basic blues and boogie, and from seven years spent almost continuously on the road between the start of 1970 and the end of 1976. The luxury of long recording sessions didn't figure in a strategy that saw the group supporting acts like Ten Years After and Janis Joplin at the start of the decade and outselling them within a few years. It was all part of the masterplan of Bill Ham, one of the great rock bosses: ceaseless touring gave ZZ Top a presence that demanded radio play, and record sales soon followed.

The breakthrough came with their third album, TRES HOMBRES (1973), and its monster single, "La Grange". By this stage ZZ Top were headlining festivals over acts like Joe Cocker, Bad Company and Santana, and in 1976 they took one of the decade's biggest shows on the road. The *World-Wide Texas Tour* took in a hundred US dates as well as gigs in Europe, Japan and Australia, with a Texas-shaped stage playing host to the band plus a buffalo, steer and assorted Texan snakes. Breaking all house records for ticket sales, the tour propelled ZZ Top into the financial big league.

In the early 80s the band began to crack the world market on the back of a series of videos accompanying the ELIMINATOR album (1983). ZZ Top were the first of the old guard to capitalize on MTV's potential by turning rock's adolescent sexual fantasy world into something resembling flesh. The videos for "Gimme All Your Lovin'", "Sharp Dressed Man" and "Legs" lifted the images of come-hither sex kittens from fashion magazines and projected them on to screens the world over. The same ploy was used for the multi-platinum follow-up, AFTERBURNER (1985), and its "Velcro Fly" video.

The structure of ZZ Top's music never strayed from the slow blues base, and their world-view often embraced cars and women, ensuring an overlap with the preoccupations of the core mainstream rock audience. But, at the same time, their oddball observations have provided moments of real character like "Jesus Just Left Chicago" from TRES HOMBRES or the sublime "Cheap Sunglasses" from DEGUELLO (1979). And, for all the self-mytholo-

ZZ Top's Billy Gibson (left) and Dusty Hill in Spinal Tap 'lost drummer' episode

gizing sexism of the videos, there is a real comic-book charm about ZZ Top – encapsulated in the famous beards sported by Gibbons and Hill (but not Beard), which haven't seen a pair of scissors since 1979, and their wilfully regionalist image as Texan good ol' boys. The group also, incidentally, claim to hold advance bookings for the first passenger flight to the moon.

In 1996 ZZ Top threw commercial wisdom aside to record RHYTHMEEN, an album that rekindled the rootsy blues spirit that had first inspired the band, and moved away from previous AOR elements. At the same time, Frank Beard's lower jaw began to sprout some ominous foliage.

As Bill Clinton's presidency teetered on the edge in 1998 one website displayed a picture of the boys presenting the Comeback Kid with the keys to the Tushmobile – a route to magic transformation in ZZ Top videos. Clinton's poll ratings recovered. The site also claimed that discussions were in hand concerning government funds for the building of ZZ Top's own space shuttle. Only a fool would have bet against it.

Despite all these indications that ZZ apparently enjoy solid levels of popularity stateside, the band's fortunes have doubtless dwindled elsewhere, a fact underlined by XXX (1999), an album which found the band ploughing the same self-styled modern boogie formula to little effect beyond their own domestic market. Their fourteenth album, MESCALERO, arrived in 2003, again receiving a warm welcome stateside. At the time of writing the boys are yet to receive delivery of their shuttle.

Deguello (1979; WEA).
Including "Fool For Your Stockings" and "Cheap Sunglasses", this is quintessential Top, with storming blues riffs and expressive playing on the slower numbers.

Greatest Hits (1992; WEA).
All the big sellers from the 80s, plus a few of the rugged 70s stage favourites.

Neil Nixon

DIRECTORY OF BANDS AND ARTISTS

Names in plain type have an individual entry; those in italics are covered within a major entry – for example, the index entry for Donald Fagen takes you to the Steely Dan piece, where Fagen's solo career is covered. The word 'The' has been ignored in alphabetizing the entries, but not 'A': thus 'The Fall' appear under 'F', whereas 'A House' appear under 'A'.